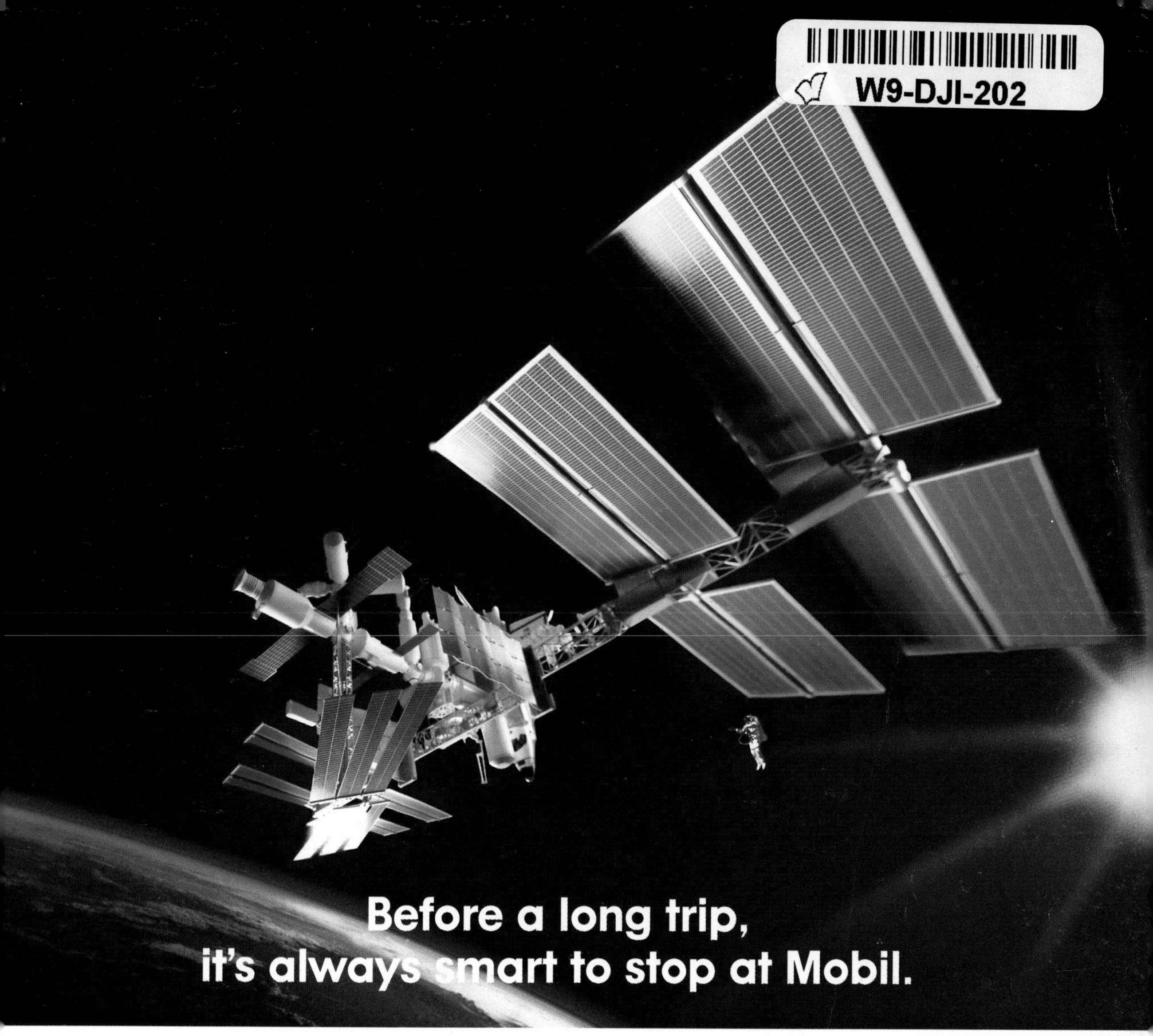
Before a long trip,
it's always smart to stop at Mobil.

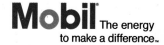

1.00

Mobil 1998 TRAVEL GUIDE®

Major Cities

NORTH AMERICA'S 45 MOST VISITED CITIES

Fodor's Travel Publications, Inc.

Guide Staff

General Manager: Diane E. Connolly
Editorial/Inspection Coordinators: Sara D. Hauber, Doug Weinstein
Inspection Assistant: Brenda Piszczek
Editorial Assistants: Korrie Klier, Julie Raio, Kathleen Rose, Kristin Schiller, Elizabeth Schwar
Creative Director: Fabrizio La Rocca
Cover Design: John Olenyik
Cover Photograph: H. Mark Weidman

Acknowledgments

We gratefully acknowledge the help of our more than 100 field representatives for their efficient and perceptive inspection of every lodging and dining establishment listed; the establishments' proprietors for their cooperation in showing their facilities and providing information about them; the many users of previous editions of the *Mobil Travel Guide* who have taken the time to share their experiences; and, for their time and information, the thousands of chambers of commerce, convention and visitors' bureaus, city, state, and provincial tourism offices, and government agencies who assisted in our research.

Mobil 

Published in 1998 by Fodor's Travel Publications, Inc.
201 E. 50th St.
New York, NY 10022

Major Cities
ISBN 0-679-03499-4
ISSN 0076-9789

Printed in the United States of America
10 9 8 7 6 5 4 3 2 1

Contents

Cities

A Word to Our Readers

Whether you're going on an extended family vacation, a weekend getaway, or a business trip, you need good, solid information on where to stay and eat and what to see and do. It would be nice if you could take a corps of well-seasoned travelers with you to suggest lodgings and activities, or ask a local restaurant critic for advice on dining spots, but since these options are rarely practical, the *Mobil Travel Guide* is the next best thing. It puts a huge database of information at your disposal and provides the value judgments and advice you need to use that information to its fullest.

Published by Fodor's Travel Publications, Inc., in collaboration with Mobil Corporation, the sponsor since 1958, these books contain the most comprehensive, up-to-date information possible. In fact, listings are revised and ratings reviewed annually, based on inspection reports from our field representatives, evaluation by senior staff, and comments from more than 100,000 readers. These incredible data are then used to develop the *Mobil Travel Guide*'s impartial quality ratings, indicated by stars, which Americans have trusted for decades.

Space limitations make it impossible for us to include every fine hotel and restaurant in the country, so we have picked a representative group, all above-average for their type. There's no charge to any establishment for inclusion, and only places that meet our standards are chosen. Because travelers' needs differ, we make every effort to select a variety of establishments and provide the information to decide what's right for you. If you're looking for a lodging at a certain price or location, or even one that offers 24-hour room service, you'll find the answers you need at your fingertips. Take a minute to read the next section, How to Use This Book; it'll make finding the information you want a breeze.

Also look at Making the Most of Your Trip, the section that follows. It's full of tips from savvy travelers that can help you save money, stay safe, and just get around more easily—the keys to making any trip a success.

Of course, the passage of time means that some establishments will close, change hands, remodel, improve, or go downhill. Though every effort has been made to ensure the accuracy of all information when it was printed, change is inevitable. Always call and confirm that a place is open and that it has the features you want. Whatever your experiences at any of the establishments we list—and we hope they're terrific—or if you have general comments about our guide, we'd love to hear from you. Use the convenient postage-paid card near the end of this book, or drop us a line at the *Mobil Travel Guide,* Fodor's Travel Publications, Inc., 4709 W. Golf Road, Suite 803, Skokie, IL 60076.

So pack this book in your suitcase or toss it next to you on the front seat. If it gets dog-eared, so much the better. We here at the *Mobil Travel Guide* wish you a safe and successful trip.

Bon voyage and happy travels.

THE EDITORS

Welcome

For 40 years, the *Mobil Travel Guide* has provided travelers in North America with reliable advice on finding good value, quality service, and the attractions that give a destination its special character. During this time, our teams of culinary and hospitality experts have worked hard to develop objective and exacting standards. In so doing, they seek to fully meet the desires and expectations of a broad range of customers.

At Mobil, we demonstrate the energy to make a difference through a commitment to excellence that allows us to bring the best service and products to the people we serve. We believe that the ability to respond to and anticipate customers' needs is what distinguishes good companies from truly great ones.

It is our hope, whether your travels are for business or leisure, over a long distance or a short one, that this book will be your companion, dependably guiding you to quality and value in lodging and dining.

Finally, I ask that you help us improve the guides. Please take the time to fill out the customer feedback form at the back of this book or contact us on the Internet at www.mobil.com/travel.

Lucio A. Noto
Chairman and
Chief Executive Officer
Mobil Corporation

How to Use This Book

More than 4,000 lodgings and restaurants in over 40 major U.S. cities are profiled in the *Mobil Travel Guide: Major Cities.* Each city section, listed alphabetically, starts with vital statistics, an overview of the city, and general references and phone numbers for information sources, points of interest, attractions, events, neighborhoods, and more. Street/neighborhood maps are provided as well.

The bulk of each city section is devoted to quality-rated lodging and dining choices, and in most cities, a list of restaurants by neighborhood is included. What follows is an explanation of the wealth of information you'll find in the listings.

Lodging and Restaurant Listings

LODGING CLASSIFICATIONS

Each property is classified by type according to the characteristics below. Because the following features and services are found at most motels, lodges, motor hotels, and hotels, they are not shown in those listings:

- Year-round operation with a single rate structure unless otherwise quoted
- European plan (meals not included in room rate)
- Bathroom with tub and/or shower in each room
- Air-conditioned/heated, often with individual room control
- Cots
- Daily maid service
- Phones in rooms
- Elevators

Motels and Lodges. Accommodations are in low-rise structures with rooms easily accessible to parking (usually free). Properties have outdoor room entry and small, functional lobbies. Service is often limited, and dining may not be offered in lower-rated motels and lodges. Shops and businesses are found only in higher-rated properties, as are bellhops, room service, and restaurants serving three meals daily.

Lodges differ from motels primarily in their emphasis on outdoor recreational activities and in location. They are often found in resort and rural areas rather than in major cities or along highways.

Motor Hotels. Offering the convenience of motels along with many of the features of hotels, motor hotels range from low-rise structures offering limited services to multistory buildings with a wide range of services and facilities. Multiple building entrances, elevators, inside hallways, and parking areas (generally free) near access doors are some of the features of a motor hotel. Lobbies offer sitting areas and 24-hour desk and switchboard services. Often bellhop and valet services as well as restaurants serving three meals a day are found. Expanded recreational facilities and more than one restaurant are available in higher-rated properties.

The distinction between motor hotels and hotels in metropolitan areas is minor.

Hotels. To be categorized as a hotel, an establishment must have most of the following facilities and services: multiple floors, a restaurant and/or coffee shop, elevators, room service, bellhops, a spacious lobby, and recreational facilities. In addition, the following features and services not shown in listings are also found:

- Valet service (one-day laundry/cleaning service)
- Room service during hours restaurant is open
- Bellhops
- Some oversize beds

Resorts. These specialize in stays of three days or more and usually offer American Plan and/or housekeeping accommodations. Their emphasis is on recreational facilities, and a social director is often available. Food services are of primary importance, and guests must be able to eat three meals a day on the premises, either in restaurants or by having access to an on-site grocery store and preparing their own meals.

Inns. Frequently thought of as a small hotel, an inn is a place of homelike comfort and warm hospitality. It is often a structure of historic significance, with an equally interesting setting. Meals are a special occasion, and refreshments are frequently served in late afternoon. Rooms are usually individually decorated, often with antiques or furnishings representative of the locale. Phones, bathrooms, and TVs may not be available in every room.

DINING CLASSIFICATIONS

Restaurants. Most dining establishments fall into this category. All have a full kitchen and offer table service and a complete menu. Parking on or near the premises, in a lot or garage, is assumed. When a property offers special parking features, or when only street parking is available, it is noted in the listing.

Unrated Dining Spots. These places, listed after Restaurants in many cities, are chosen for their unique atmosphere, specialized menu, or local flavor. They include delis, ice-cream parlors, cafeterias, tearooms, and pizzerias. Because they may not have a full kitchen or table service, they are not given a *Mobil Travel Guide* rating. Often they offer extraordinary value and quick service.

QUALITY RATINGS

The *Mobil Travel Guide* has been rating lodgings and restaurants on a national basis since the first edition was published in 1958. For years the guide was the only source of such ratings, and it remains among the few guidebooks to rate restaurants across the country.

All listed establishments were inspected by experienced field representatives or evaluated by a senior staff member. Ratings are based upon their detailed inspection reports of the individual properties, on written evaluations of staff members who stay and dine anonymously, and on an extensive review of comments from our readers.

You'll find a key to the rating categories, ★ through ★★★★★, on the inside front cover. All establishments in the book are recommended. Even a ★ place is above average, usually providing a basic, informal experience. Rating categories reflect both the features the property offers and its quality in relation to similar establishments.

For example, lodging ratings take into account the number and quality of facilities and services, the luxury of appointments, and the attitude and professionalism of staff and management. A ★ establishment provides a comfortable night's lodging. A ★★ property offers more than a facility that rates one star, and the decor is well planned and integrated. Establishments that rate ★★★ are professionally managed and staffed and often beautifully appointed; the lodging experience is truly excellent, and the range of facilities is extensive. Properties that have been given ★★★★ not only offer many services but also have their own style and personality; they are luxurious, creatively decorated, and superbly maintained. The ★★★★★ properties are among the best in the United States, superb in every respect and entirely memorable, year in and year out.

Restaurant evaluations reflect the quality of the food and the ingredients, preparation, and presentation as well as service levels and the property's decor and ambience. A restaurant that has fairly simple goals for menu and decor but that achieves those goals superbly might receive the same number of stars as a restaurant with somewhat loftier ambitions but whose execution falls somewhat short of the mark. In general, ★ indicates a restaurant that's a good choice in its area, usually fairly simple and perhaps catering to a clientele of locals and families; ★★ denotes restaurants that are more highly recommended in their area; ★★★ restaurants are of national caliber, with professional and attentive service and a skilled chef in the kitchen; ★★★★ reflects superb dining choices, where remarkable food is served in equally remarkable surroundings; and ★★★★★ represents that rarefied group of the best restaurants in the country, where in addition to near perfection in every detail, there's that special something extra that makes for an unforgettable dining experience.

Each rating is reviewed annually and each establishment must work to maintain its rating (or improve it). Every effort is made to assure that ratings are fair and accurate; the designated ratings are published purely as an aid to travelers.

In general, properties that are very new or have recently undergone major management changes are considered difficult to assess fairly and are often listed without ratings.

Good Value Check Mark. In all locales, you'll find a wide range of lodging and dining establishments with a ✔ in front of a star rating. This indicates an unusually good value at economical prices as follows:

Lodging: average \$105–\$125 per night for singles; average \$115–\$140 per night for doubles

Restaurants: average \$25 for a complete lunch; average \$40 for a complete dinner, exclusive of beverages and gratuities

LODGINGS

Each listing gives the name, address, directions (when there is no street address), neighborhood and/or directions from downtown, phone number (local and 800), fax number, number and type of rooms available, room rates, and seasons open (if not year-round). Also included are details on recreational and dining facilities on property or nearby, the presence of a luxury level, and credit-card information. Terms and abbreviations used in the listings are described below. A key to the symbols at the end of each listing is on the inside front cover. (Note that Mobil Corporation credit cards cannot be used for payment of meals and room charges.)

All prices quoted in the *Mobil Travel Guide* publications are expected to be in effect at the time of publication and during the entire year; however, prices cannot be guaranteed. In some localities there may be short-term price variations because of special events or holidays. Whenever possible, these price changes are noted. Certain resorts have complicated rate structures that vary with the time of year; always confirm listed rates when you make your plans.

RESTAURANTS

Listings give the name, address, directions (when there is no street address), neighborhood and/or directions from downtown, phone number, hours and days of operation (if not open daily year-round), reservation policy, cuisine (if other than American), price range for each meal served, children's meals (if offered), specialties, and credit card information. Additionally, special features such as chef ownership, ambience, and entertainment are noted. By carefully reading the detailed restaurant information and comparing prices, you can easily determine whether the restaurant is formal and elegant or informal and comfortable for families.

TERMS AND ABBREVIATIONS IN LISTINGS

A la carte entrees With a price, refers to the cost of entrees/main dishes only that are not accompanied by side dishes.
AP American plan (lodging plus all meals).
Bar Liquor, wine, and beer are served in a bar or cocktail lounge and usually with meals unless otherwise indicated (e.g., "wine, beer").
Business center The property has a designated area accessible to all guests with business services.
Business servs avail The property can perform/arrange at least two of the following services for a guest: audiovisual equipment rental, binding, computer rental, faxing, messenger services, modem availability, notary service, obtaining office supplies, photocopying, shipping, and typing.
Cable Standard cable service; "premium" indicates that HBO, Disney, Showtime, or similar services are available.
Ck-in, ck-out Check-in time; check-out time.
Coin lndry Self-service laundry.
Complete meal Soup and/or salad, entree, and dessert, plus nonalcoholic beverage.
Continental bkfst Usually coffee and a roll or doughnut.
Cr cds: A, American Express; C, Carte Blanche; D, Diners Club; DS, Discover; ER, enRoute; JCB, Japanese Credit Bureau; MC, MasterCard; V, Visa.
D Followed by a price, indicates room rate for a "double"—two people in one room one or two beds (the charge may be higher for two double beds).
Downhill/x-country ski Downhill and/or cross-country skiing within 20 miles of property.
Each addl Extra charge for each additional person beyond the stated number of persons at a reduced price.
Early-bird dinner A meal served at specified hours, typically around 4:30–6:30 pm.
Exc Except.
Exercise equipt Two or more pieces of exercise equipment on the premises.
Exercise rm Both exercise equipment and room, with an instructor on the premises.
Fax Facsimile machines available to all guests.
Golf privileges Privileges at a course within 10 miles
Hols Holidays
In-rm modem link Every guest room has a connection for a modem that's separate from the phone line.
Kit. or kits. A kitchen or kitchenette that contains stove or microwave, sink, and refrigerator and that is either part of the room or a separate room. If the kitchen is not fully equipped, the listing will indicate "no equipt" or "some equipt".
Luxury level A special section of a hotel, covering at least an entire floor, that offers increased luxury accommodations. Management must provide no less than three of these four services: separate check-in and check-out, concierge, private lounge, and private elevator service (key access). Complimentary breakfast and snacks are commonly offered.
MAP Modified American plan (lodging plus two meals).
Movies Prerecorded videos are available for rental.
No cr cds accepted No credit cards are accepted.
No elvtr In hotels with more than two stories, it's assumed there are elevators; only their absence is noted.
No phones Phones, too, are assumed; only their absence is noted.
Parking There is a parking lot on the premises.
Private club A cocktail lounge or bar available to members and their guests. In motels and hotels where these clubs exist, registered guests can usually use the club as guests of the management; the same is frequently true of restaurants.
Prix fixe A full meal for a stated price; usually one price is quoted.
Res Reservations.
S Followed by a price, indicates room rate for a "single," i.e., one person.
Semi-a la carte Meals include vegetable, salad, soup, appetizer, or other accompaniments to the main dish.
Serv bar A service bar, where drinks are prepared for dining patrons only.
Serv charge Service charge is the amount added to the restaurant check in lieu of a tip.
Table d'hôte A full meal for a stated price, dependent upon entree selection; no a la carte options are available.
Tennis privileges Privileges at tennis courts within 5 miles.
TV Indicates color television; B/W indicates black-and-white television.
Under certain age free Children under that age are not charged for if staying in room with a parent.
Valet parking An attendant is available to park and retrieve a car.
VCR VCRs in all guest rooms.
VCR avail VCRs are available for hookup in guest rooms.

Special Information for Travelers with Disabilities

The *Mobil Travel Guide* symbol **D** shown in accommodation and restaurant listings indicates establishments that are at least partially accessible to people with mobility problems.

The *Mobil Travel Guide* criteria for accessibility are unique to our publication. Please do not confuse them with the universal symbol for wheelchair accessibility. When the **D** symbol appears following a listing, the establishment is equipped with facilities to accommodate people using wheelchairs or crutches or otherwise needing easy access to doorways and rest rooms. Travelers with severe mobility problems or with hearing or visual impairments may or may not find facilities they need. Always phone ahead to make sure that an establishment can meet your needs.

All lodgings bearing our D symbol have the following facilities:

- ISA-designated parking near access ramps
- Level or ramped entryways to building
- Swinging building entryway doors minimum 3′0″
- Public rest rooms on main level with space to operate a wheelchair; handrails at commode areas
- Elevators equipped with grab bars and lowered control buttons
- Restaurants with accessible doorways; rest rooms with space to operate wheelchair; handrails at commode areas
- Minimum 3′0″ width entryway to guest rooms
- Low-pile carpet in rooms
- Telephone at bedside and in bathroom
- Bed placed at wheelchair height
- Minimum 3′0″ width doorway to bathroom
- Bath with open sink—no cabinet; room to operate wheelchair
- Handrails at commode areas; tub handrails
- Wheelchair accessible peephole in room entry door
- Wheelchair accessible closet rods and shelves

All restaurants bearing our D symbol offer the following facilities:

- ISA-designated parking beside access ramps
- Level or ramped front entryways to building
- Tables to accommodate wheelchairs
- Main-floor rest rooms; minimum 3′0″ width entryway
- Rest rooms with space to operate wheelchair; handrails at commode areas

In general, the newest properties are apt to impose the fewest barriers.

To get the kind of service you need and have a right to expect, do not hesitate when making a reservation to question the management in detail about the availability of accessible rooms, parking, entrances, restaurants, lounges, or any other facilities that are important to you, and confirm what is meant by "accessible." Some guests with mobility impairments report that lodging establishments' housekeeping and maintenance departments are most helpful in describing barriers. Also inquire about any special equipment, transportation, or services you may need.

Making the Most of Your Trip

A few diehard souls might fondly remember the trip where the car broke down and they were stranded for a week, or the vacation that cost twice what it was supposed to. For most travelers, though, the best trips are those that are safe, smooth, and within their budget. To help you make your trip the best it can be, we've assembled a few tips and resources.

Saving Money

ON LODGING

After you've seen the published rates, it's time to look for discounts. Many hotels and motels offer them—for senior citizens, business travelers, families, you name it. It never hurts to ask—politely, that is. Sometimes, especially in the late afternoon, desk clerks are instructed to fill beds, and you might be offered a lower rate, or a nicer room, to entice you to stay. Look for bargains on stays over multiple nights, in the off-season, and on weekdays or weekends (depending on location). Many hotels in major metropolitan areas, for example, have special weekend package plans, which offer considerable savings on rooms and may include breakfast, cocktails, and meal discounts. Prices change frequently throughout the year, so phone ahead.

Another way to save money is to choose accommodations that give you more than just a standard room. Rooms with kitchen facilities enable you to cook some meals for yourself, reducing restaurant costs. A suite might save money for two couples traveling together. Even hotel luxury levels can provide good value, as many include breakfast or cocktails in the price of the room.

State and city sales taxes as well as special room taxes can increase your room rates as much as 25% per day. We are unable to bring this specific information into the listings, but we strongly urge that you ask about these taxes when placing reservations in order to understand the total price to you.

Watch out for telephone-usage charges that hotels frequently impose on long-distance calls, credit-card calls, and other phone calls—even those that go unanswered. Before phoning from your room, read the information given to you at check-in, and then be sure to read your bill carefully before checking out. You won't be expected to pay for charges that weren't spelled out. (On the other hand, it's not unusual for a hotel to bill you for your calls after you return home.) Consider using public telephones in hotel lobbies; the savings may outweigh the inconvenience.

ON DINING

There are several ways to get a less-expensive meal at a more-expensive restaurant. Early-bird dinners are popular in many parts of the country and offer considerable savings. If you're interested in sampling a ★★★★ or ★★★★★ establishment, consider going at lunchtime. While the prices are probably relatively high, they may be half of those at dinner and come with the same ambience, service, and cuisine.

FOR SENIOR CITIZENS

Look for the senior-citizen discount symbol in the lodging and restaurant listings. Always call ahead to confirm that the discount is being offered, and be sure to carry proof of age. At places not listed in the book, it never hurts to ask if a senior-citizen discount is offered. Two organizations provide additional information for mature travelers: the American Association of Retired Persons (AARP), 601 E St NW, Washington, DC 20049, phone 202/434-2277, and National Council of Senior Citizens, 8403 Cosville, Suite 1200, Silver Springs, MD 20910, phone 301/528-8800.

Tipping

Tipping is an expression of appreciation for good service, and often service workers rely on tips as a significant part of their income. However, you never need to tip if service is poor.

AT LODGINGS

Doormen in major city hotels are usually given $1 for getting you a cab. Bellhops expect $1 per bag, usually $2 if you have only one bag. Concierges are tipped according to the service they perform. It's not mandatory to tip when you've asked for suggestions on sightseeing or restaurants, or help making reservations for dining. However, when a concierge books you a table at a restaurant known to be difficult to get into, a gratuity of $5 is appropriate. For obtaining theater or sporting event tickets, $5–$10 is expected. Maids, often overlooked by guests, may be tipped $1–$2 per day of stay.

AT RESTAURANTS

Coffee shop and counter service wait staff are usually given 8%–10% of the bill. In full-service restaurants, tip 15% of the bill, before sales tax. In fine restaurants, where the staff is large and shares the gratuity, 18%–20% for the waiter is appropriate. In most cases, tip the maitre d' only if service has been extraordinary and only on the way out; $20 is the minimum in upscale properties in major metropolitan areas. If there is a wine steward, tip him or her at least $5 a bottle, more if the wine was decanted or if the bottle was very expensive. If your busboy has been unusually attentive, $2 pressed into his hand on departure is a nice gesture. An increasing number of restaurants automatically add a service charge to the bill in lieu of a gratuity. Before tipping, carefully review your check.

AT AIRPORTS

Curbside luggage handlers expect $1 per bag. Car-rental shuttle drivers who help with your luggage appreciate a $1 or $2 tip.

Staying Safe

The best way to deal with emergencies is to be prepared enough to avoid them. However, unforeseen situations do happen, and you can prepare for them.

IN YOUR CAR

Before your trip, make sure your car has been serviced and is in good working order. Change the oil, check the battery and belts, and make sure tires are inflated properly (this can also improve gas mileage). Other inspections recommended by the car's manufacturer should be made, too.

Next, be sure you have the tools and equipment to deal with a routine breakdown: jack, spare tire, lug wrench, repair kit, emergency tools, jumper cables, spare fan belt, auto fuses, flares and/or reflectors, flashlights, first-aid kit, and, in winter, a windshield scraper and shovel.

Bring all appropriate and up-to-date documentation—licenses, registration, and insurance cards—and know what's covered by your insurance. Also bring an extra set of keys, just in case.

En route, always buckle up!

If your car does break down, get out of traffic as soon as possible—pull well off the road. Raise the hood and turn on your emergency flashers or tie a white cloth to the roadside door handle or antenna. Stay near your car. Use flares or reflectors to keep your car from being hit.

IN YOUR LODGING

Chances are slim that you will encounter a hotel or motel fire. The ◙ in a listing indicates that there were smoke detectors and/or sprinkler systems in the rooms we inspected. Once you've checked in, make sure that any smoke detector in your room is working properly. Ascertain the locations of fire extinguishers and at least two fire exits. Never use an elevator in a fire.

For personal security, use the peephole in your room's door.

PROTECTING AGAINST THEFT

To guard against theft wherever you go, don't bring any more of value than you need. If you do bring valuables, leave them at your hotel rather than in your car, and if you have something very expensive, lock it in a safe. Many hotels have one in each room; others will store your valuables in the hotel's safe. And of course, don't carry more money than you need; use traveler's checks and credit cards, or visit cash machines.

For Travelers with Disabilities

A number of publications can provide assistance. Fodor's *Great American Vacations for Travelers with Disabilities* ($19.50) covers 38 top U.S. travel destinations, including parks, cities, and popular tourist regions. It's available from bookstores or by calling 800/533–6478. The most complete listing of published material for travelers with disabilities is available from *The Disability Bookshop,* Twin Peaks Press, Box 129, Vancouver, WA 98666, phone 360/694–2462. A comprehensive guidebook to the national parks is *Easy Access to National Parks: The Sierra Club Guide for People with Disabilities* ($16), distributed by Random House.

The Reference Section of the National Library Service for the Blind and Physically Handicapped (Library of Congress, Washington, DC 20542, phone 202/707–9275 or 202/707–5100) provides information and resources for persons with mobility problems and hearing and vision impairments, as well as information about the NLS talking-book program (or visit your local library).

Important Toll-Free Numbers

and On-Line Information

HOTELS AND MOTELS

Adam's Mark 800/444–2326
Web www.adamsmark.com
Best Western .... 800/528–1234, TDD 800/528–2222
Web www.bestwestern.com
Budgetel Inns 800/428–3438
Web www.budgetel.com
Budget Host 800/283–4678
Clarion 800/252–7466
Web www.clarioninn.com
Comfort 800/228–5150
Web www.comfortinn.com
Courtyard by Marriott 800/321–2211
Web www.courtyard.com
Days Inn 800/325–2525
Web www.travelweb.com/daysinn.html
Doubletree 800/528–0444
Web www.doubletreehotels.com
Drury Inns 800/325–8300
Web www.drury-inn.com
Econo Lodge 800/446–6900
Web www.hotelchoice.com
Embassy Suites 800/362–2779
Web www.embassy-suites.com
Exel Inns of America 800/356–8013
Fairfield Inn by Marriott 800/228–2800
Web www.marriott.com
Fairmont Hotels 800/527–4727
Forte 800/225–5843
Four Seasons 800/332–3442
Web www.fourseasons.com
Friendship Inns 800/453–4511
Web www.hotelchoice.com
Hampton Inn 800/426–7866
Web www.hampton-inn.com
Hilton .... 800/445–8667, TDD 800/368–1133
Web www.hilton.com
Holiday Inn .... 800/465–4329, TDD 800/238–5544
Web www.holiday-inn.com
Howard Johnson .... 800/654–4656, TDD 800/654–8442
Web www.hojo.com
Hyatt & Resorts 800/233–1234
Web www.hyatt.com
Inns of America 800/826–0778
Inter-Continental 800/327–0200
Web www.interconti.com
La Quinta .... 800/531–5900, TDD 800/426–3101
Web www.laquinta.com
Loews 800/235-6397
Web www.loewshotels.com
Marriott 800/228–9290
Web www.marriott.com
Master Hosts Inns 800/251–1962
Meridien 800/225–5843
Motel 6 .... 800/466–8356
Nikko International 800/645–5687
Web www.hotelnikko.com
Omni 800/843–6664
Web www.omnirosen.com
Park Inn 800/437–7275
Web www.p-inns.com/parkinn.html
Quality Inn 800/228–5151
Web www.qualityinn.com
Radisson 800/333–3333
Web www.radisson.com
Ramada .... 800/228–2828, TDD 800/228–3232
Web www.ramada.com/ramada.html
Red Carpet/Scottish Inns 800/251–1962
Red Lion 800/547–8010
Web www.travelweb.com/travelweb/rl/common/redlion.html
Red Roof Inn 800/843–7663
Web www.redroof.com
Renaissance 800/468–3571
Web www.niagara.com/nf.renaissance
Residence Inn by Marriott 800/331–3131
Web www.marriott.com
Ritz-Carlton 800/241–3333
Web www.ritzcarlton.com
Rodeway 800/228–2000
Web www.rodeway.com
Sheraton 800/325–3535
Web www.sheraton.com
Shilo Inn 800/222–2244
Signature Inns 800/822–5252
Web www.signature-inns.com
Sleep Inn 800/221–2222
Web www.sleepinn.com
Super 8 .... 800/848–8888
Web www.super8motels.com/super8.html
Susse Chalet 800/258–1980
Web www.sussechalet.com
Travelodge/Viscount 800/255–3050
Web www.travelodge.com
Vagabond 800/522–1555
Westin Hotels & Resorts 800/937-8461
Web www.westin.com
Wyndham Hotels & Resorts 800/822–4200
Web www.travelweb.com

AIRLINES

Air Canada 800/776–3000
Web www.aircanada.ca
Alaska 800/426–0333
Web www.alaska-air.com/home.html
Aloha 800/367–5250
American 800/433–7300
Web www.americanair.com/aahome/aahome.html

America West 800/235–9292
Web www.americawest.com
British Airways 800/247–9297
Web www.british-airways.com
Canadian 800/426–7000
Web www.cdair.ca
Continental 800/525–0280
Web www.flycontinental.com
Delta 800/221–1212
Web www.delta-air.com
Hawaiian 800/367–5320
IslandAir 800/323–3345
Mesa 800/637–2247
Northwest 800/225–2525
Web www.nwa.com
SkyWest 800/453–9417
Southwest 800/435–9792
Web www.iflyswa.com
TWA 800/221–2000
Web www.twa.com
United 800/241–6522
Web www.ual.com
USAir 800/428–4322
Web www.usair.com

TRAINS

Amtrak 800/872–7245
Web www.amtrak.com

BUSES

Greyhound 800/231–2222
Web www.greyhound.com

CAR RENTALS

Advantage 800/777–5500
Alamo 800/327–9633
Web www.goalamo.com
Allstate 800/634–6186
Avis 800/331–1212
Web www.avis.com
Budget 800/527–0700
Web www.budgetrentacar.com
Dollar 800/800–4000
Web www.dollarcar.com
Enterprise 800/325–8007
Web www.pickenterprise.com
Hertz 800/654–3131
Web www.hertz.com
National 800/328–4567
Web www.nationalcar.com
Payless 800/237–2804
Rent-A-Wreck 800/535–1391
Web www.rent-a-wreck.com
Sears 800/527–0770
Thrifty 800/367–2277
Web www.thrifty.com
Ugly Duckling 800/843–3825
U-Save 800/272–8728
Value 800/327–2501
Web www.go-value.com

Albuquerque

Founded: 1706
Pop: 331,767
Elev: 5,311 feet
Time zone: Mountain
Area code: 505
Web: www.abqcvb.org

Santa Fe

Settled: 1607
Pop: 48,953
Elev: 7,000 feet
Time zone: Mountain
Area code: 505
Web: www.santafe.org

Dominated by forested mountains, high plains, dramatic mesas, dry air and plentiful sunshine, Albuquerque and Santa Fe are situated in the most visited part of this Land of Enchantment. The area's variety of terrain is matched only by the diversity of its inhabitants who have endowed New Mexico with a unique history.

Named after the Duke of Alburquerque, Viceroy of New Spain in 1706, Albuquerque (the first "r" was dropped later) is the state's largest city. Sister city Santa Fe was founded nearly a century earlier (1609) and is the oldest continually used capital in the nation.

Albuquerque's original magnetism was its location near the Rio Grande and its possibilities for better irrigation. By 1790, the population was 5,959, a very large city for its time. Except for one brief period, Albuquerque has continued to be the largest city in New Mexico.

Santa Fe was founded by Don Pedro de Peralta. He laid out the Plaza and built the Palace of the Governors in 1607. By 1617 the Franciscan friars claimed to have converted 14,000 Indians to Catholicism. But in 1680, the Pueblo people revolted against the Spanish invaders and drove them out. The city remained in Pueblo hands until 1692, when 300 Spaniards led by General Don Diego de Vargas made a peaceful reentry. The city has been an important Catholic center ever since.

Trade played an important role in the development of Santa Fe. Goods were carried to and from New Mexico over old horse and mule trails that were first developed to accommodate the missions. Toward the middle of the 19th century, the Santa Fe Trail connected this part of the country to towns in Colorado, Kansas and western Missouri. Not surprisingly, Santa Fe became the headquarters of the wave of new settlement in the Southwest.

As Easterners came to Santa Fe, they found a strange culture shaped by Native Americans, Spaniards, soldiers and early pioneers. Huge caravans of wagons began to carry people and goods to and through the town. Although trade between Mexico and eastern cities flourished with the coming of the railroads in the 1860s and 1870s, the railroads also ended use of the trail as a major artery.

Business

World War II ushered in the atomic age, and New Mexico became a center for research and development. More than 60 firms are engaged in electronics manufacturing here. Albuquerque's largest business is Sandia National Laboratories, a laboratory with more than 6,000 employees engaged in solar and nuclear research. The communications industry employs another 4,000 people. For several years there has been expansion in contract construction and in manufacturing, particularly of durable goods.

In Santa Fe, the capital city, government jobs are common. Santa Fe is also attentive to the arts, boasting a number of unique museums and more than 150 art galleries.

Convention Facilities

Albuquerque can accommodate major conventions in a Convention Center that provides general session and banquet seating for up to 2,500 people. There are 20 meeting rooms with built-in screen and sound systems, seating 16 to 3,000. Total exhibit space is 90,000 square feet, and 2,500 cars can be parked within close walking distance of the center. An addition in the fall of 1990 increased the exhibit space by 275,000 square feet, including a 106,000 square-foot free-span exhibit hall and 14 additional conference rooms. Hotels and motels in the city have a total of more than 7,000 rooms. Santa Fe's Sweeney Convention Center on Marcy Street has conference seating for 1,600 and banquet facilities for 800. Hotel accommodations for about 3,000 are available within 10 minutes of the Center.

Sports & Recreation

The University of New Mexico in Albuquerque has an outstanding athletic program. The University Arena seats 17,000; the football stadium holds 30,000. The New Mexico State Fair is held here annually, featuring a major rodeo. A race meet at the State Fair grounds permits parimutuel betting.

New Mexico's sunny climate makes golf and tennis very popular. Many tennis courts are open to the public.

Both Santa Fe and Albuquerque have major skiing areas nearby. The Sandia Mountain area is reached by the Sandia Peak Aerial Tramway, a 2.7-mile cableway reaching to more than 10,300 feet.

Sandia Peak's 7,500-foot double chairlift operates both winter and summer, carrying passengers through beautiful stands of pine and aspen to a lodge and cafe. At the base terminal are riding stables, curio shops and a restaurant.

Numerous lakes for boating, fishing and waterskiing are within a few hours' drive. New Mexico's forests abound with deer, elk, bighorn sheep and other game. Santa Fe is the headquarters for Santa Fe National Forest, which covers more than a million acres.

Entertainment

Albuquerque is home to the New Mexico Symphony Orchestra. Twelve performing arts facilities present amateur and professional music, dance and drama. Santa Fe has an excellent opera company which performs traditional and modern works outdoors from late June to August. Backstage tours are available in season. Flamenco and country and western music are heard in many of the hotel bars in the area. Be sure to catch the year-round Native American art shows and ceremonial feasts.

Historical Areas

Albuquerque's Old Town is the part of the city established in 1706. A romantic city within a city, it has a gaslit plaza, bandstand and shops selling piñatas, handmade jewelry, pottery, wrought iron, and fiesta and Native American dresses.

Santa Fe's Plaza is dominated by the Palace of the Governors, which is more than 360 years old. The palace has been the seat for six distinct governments: the Spanish Empire from 1609 to 1680 and from 1692 to 1821; the Pueblo from 1680 to 1692; the Mexican Empire during 1821-1822; the Republic of Mexico from 1822 to 1846; the United States Territory of New Mexico from 1846 to 1907; and the Confederacy for nearly a month in 1862.

Today the building houses the Museum of New Mexico, whose exhibits and displays recount more than two millennia of the area's events from Stone Age to modern times.

Sightseeing

Few areas in the United States have as much to offer sightseers as the area surrounding Albuquerque and Santa Fe. This part of the Southwest is a varied landscape of rugged mountains, volcanic peaks, lush forests, lakes and streams, and the fertile valley of the Rio Grande. The Native American pueblos here give visitors an unforgettable look at their culture.

North of Santa Fe are the three adjacent towns that make up Taos. Taos proper, an adobe town built around a colorful plaza, was a Spanish-American settlement that is now an artists' colony and popular headquarters for skiers. Ranchos de Taos, four miles south, is a farming and ranching center and the location of one of the most beautiful churches in the Southwest, St. Francis of Assisi Mission Church. It was built in 1732 by the Franciscans and rebuilt in 1772.

Taos Pueblo, two and a half miles north of Taos, is one of the oldest, most picturesque and most famous of all the Native American pueblos. There are two ancient apartment-like houses, one four stories tall and the other five stories.

In addition to Taos Pueblo, 16 other pueblos are located in the immediate vicinity of Albuquerque and Santa Fe, with three more lying farther to the west in New Mexico. The total population of the pueblos in New Mexico is about 31,900.

There are Native American dances and ceremonies nearly every month of the year at the pueblos. Tourists are welcome at many villages on most feast days; Pueblo officials do enforce certain restrictions, limiting photography, sketching and painting. Certain areas are closed to the public. All visitors to the pueblos are asked to contact the individual Pueblo governor or his/her representatives to pay necessary fees and inquire about local regulations.

Pueblo is a Spanish word meaning "community" or "village." The 19 Native American pueblos in New Mexico occupy a fraction of the land that the Native Americans held during the early Spanish occupation. The Pueblo people fall into three distinct language groups: the Keresan, Tanoan and Zuñian. The Keres located their pueblos, for the most part, on rocky knolls, buttes and mesas, while the Tanos preferred the more fertile valley floors.

The three western pueblos—Ácoma, Laguna and Zuni—are quite large in area and population, numbering several thousand inhabitants. Ácoma and Laguna people are Keresan. Their pueblos are just off I-40, west of Albuquerque. The residents of Ácoma are famous for their fine pottery and for their ancient mesa-top Sky City; those of Zuni (which is reached by NM 32, south from Gallup), for beautiful jewelry made of turquoise, silver, shell and jet.

Between Albuquerque and Santa Fe, clustered along the Rio Grande and NM 44, are five pueblos of the eastern Keresan group: Cochiti, Santo Domingo, San Felipe, Santa Ana and Zia. The Cochiteños are descended from the cliff dwellers who once lived in what is now Bandelier National Monument. Soft leather goods, beaded ornaments, pottery, jewelry and drums are made at Cochiti for sale to tourists.

Santo Domingo residents produce pottery as well as shell, turquoise and silver jewelry. Their Corn Dance in early August, featuring about 500 dancers, is the largest of the pueblo dances. San Felipe is renowned for a magnificent drama, the Green Corn Dance, which is held on May 1 of each year. Santa Ana's feast day is July 26; the rest of the year this tiny pueblo is a quiet place.

The ancient sun symbol that appears on the state flag of New Mexico came from the Zia. Zia women are makers of excellent pottery, and many Zia men have become well-known artists, working primarily in watercolors. A number of colorful dance ceremonies are held during the year.

Tanoan Indians reside in 10 pueblos, of which Taos is one. Isleta, 13 miles south of Albuquerque, and Sandia, 14 miles north of the city, belong to a subgroup known as the southern Tiwa, which also includes a very small number who live at Las Cruces. The southern Tiwa are primarily farmers, and a few of the women of Isleta produce a red, black and white "tourist style" pottery. The northern Tiwa pueblos of Picuris (also known as San Lorenzo) and Taos are both north of Santa Fe. At Picuris one can buy well-fired pottery.

Another subgroup, the Tewa, occupy six pueblos north of Santa Fe—San Juan, Santa Clara, San Ildefonso, Nambe, Tesuque and Pojoaque. The original Pueblo structures have disappeared at Pojoaque. Those at Tesuque are well-preserved and date back to about 1250 A.D.

Exceptionally fine artistic pottery is made at San Juan, Santa Clara and San Ildefonso, and a number of potters and painters have achieved distinction and fame. Dances and festivals are held throughout the year, and arts and crafts are exhibited and sold.

Only one pueblo, Jemez, represents the subgroup of Towa. These people include descendants of the original inhabitants of what is now Pecos National Monument. Jemez is located on NM 4, almost 50 miles north and west of Albuquerque. A number of colorful ceremonies are held during the year, and the residents make baskets, pottery, fine woven objects and watercolor paintings.

At Bandelier National Monument, off NM 4 west of Santa Fe, are ruins of dwellings built near the cliff walls at the edge of Rio de los Frijoles (Spanish for "Bean Creek"). Trails lead to other fascinating areas. At Jemez State Monument, a few miles from Jemez Pueblo, are ruins of a very large settlement. Pecos National Monument, off US 85 southeast of Santa Fe, was an even larger community and a great trading center.

Los Alamos, 35 miles west of Santa Fe on NM 502, is where the atomic bomb was developed. Here you will find the Bradbury Scientific Museum and the Los Alamos Historical Museum.

Coronado State Monument, off NM 44 north of Albuquerque, has a number of underground chambers, or kivas, with a wealth of mural paintings of ceremonial activities. Within the metropolitan area is Petroglyph National Monument, where rock paintings of kachinas, birds, animals and flute players can be seen.

General References Albuquerque

Area code: 505

Phone Numbers

POLICE & FIRE: 911

POISON CONTROL CENTER: 911 or 843-2551

TIME & WEATHER: 247-1611

Information Source

Albuquerque Convention & Visitors Bureau, 20 First Plaza NW, 87102; 842-9918 or 800/284-2282.

Transportation

AIRLINES: American; America West; Continental; Delta; Southwest; TWA; United; USAir; and other commuter and regional airlines.

AIRPORT: Albuquerque International Sunport, 842-4366.

CAR RENTAL AGENCIES: (See IMPORTANT TOLL-FREE NUMBERS) Avis 842-4080; Budget 884-2600; Hertz 842-4235; National 842-4222; Thrifty 842-8733.

PUBLIC TRANSPORTATION: Suntran, 601 Yale SE, 843-9200.

RAILROAD PASSENGER SERVICE: Amtrak 800/872-7245.

Newspapers

Albuquerque Journal; Albuquerque Tribune

Convention Facility

Albuquerque Convention Center, 2nd & Marquette, 768-4575.

Sports & Recreation

(For information contact the Albuquerque Convention & Visitors Bureau.)

Cultural Facilities

Theaters

Albuquerque Little Theatre, 224 Pasquale SW, 242-4750.

Rodey Theatre, Fine Arts Center, University of New Mexico, 277-4569.

Vortex Theatre, 2004 Central Ave SE, 247-8600.

Concert Halls

KiMo Theatre, 423 Central NW, 848-1374.

Popejoy Hall, University of New Mexico, 277-3121.

Museums

Albuquerque Museum, 2000 Mountain Rd NW, 242-4600.

Fine Arts Center, University of New Mexico campus, 277-4569.

Maxwell Museum of Anthropology, Redondo Dr, University of New Mexico campus, 277-4405.

Museum of Geology and Meteoritics, University of New Mexico campus, 277-4204.

National Atomic Museum, Kirtland AFB (east), Bldg 20358, 2 1/2 mi S of I-40 on Wyoming Blvd, 284-3243.

New Mexico Museum of Natural History, 1801 Mountain Rd NM, 841-2800.

Telephone Pioneer Museum, 201 3rd NW, Ste 710, 245-5883.

Points of Interest

Historical

Coronado State Monument, 15 mi N on I-25, then 2 mi on W on NM 44, crossing bridge over Rio Grande, 867-5351.

Indian Pueblo Cultural Center, 2401 12th St NW, 843-7270.

Isleta Pueblo, 13 mi S, off US 85, 877-0370.

Old Town, 1 blk N of Central Ave at Rio Grande Blvd.

Petroglyph National Monument, 9 mi W on Unser Blvd.

San Felipe de Neri Church, on Santa Fe Chihuahua Trail.

Zia Pueblo, 24 mi beyond Santa Ana off NM 44.

Other Attractions

Albuquerque Civic Light Opera. Popejoy Hall, 345-6577.

New Mexico Symphony Orchestra, Popejoy Hall, 842-8565.

Rio Grande Nature Center, E bank of Rio Grande at 2901 Candelaria Rd NW, 344-7240.

Rio Grande Zoological Park, 903 10th St SW, 843-7413.

Sandia Crest, 17 mi E on I-40, then 6 1/2 mi N on NM 14, follow signs & scenic road for 14 mi.

Sandia Peak Aerial Tramway, 5 mi NE via I-25 & Tramway Rd, 856-7325.

Sandia Peak Tramway Ski Area, 16 mi E on I- 40, 7 mi N on NM 14, then 6 mi NW on NM 44, 242-9052 or -9133.

Sightseeing Tour

Gray Line bus tours, 800 Rio Grande Blvd NW, Ste 22, 87104; 242-3880.

Annual Events

King's Day, all pueblos. Early Jan.

Corn and Turtle Dances, Isleta Pueblo. Feb, Sept.

Gathering of Nations Pow-wow. Mid- Apr.

Old Town Fiesta. 1st wkend June.

New Mexico Arts & Crafts Fair, Fairgrounds. Last wkend June.

Feria Artesana. Late Aug.

New Mexico State Fair. Sept 4-27.

Kodak Albuquerque International Balloon Fiesta. 1st 2 wkends Oct.

Luminaria Tour. Dec 24.

Dances, at all pueblos. Late Dec.

Santa Fe

Area code: 505

Phone Numbers

POLICE & FIRE: 911

POISON CONTROL CENTER: 911 or 843-2551

TIME: 473-2211

Information Sources

Santa Fe Convention & Visitors Bureau, PO Box 909, 87504; 800/777-CITY.

Eight Northern Indian Pueblos Council, PO Box 969, San Juan Pueblo 87566; 852-4265.

Transportation

AIRPORT: See Albuquerque. Santa Fe Municipal, 473-7243.

CAR RENTAL AGENCIES: (See IMPORTANT TOLL-FREE NUMBERS) Avis 982-4361; Budget 984-8028; Hertz 982-1844.

RAILROAD PASSENGER SERVICE: Amtrak 800/872-7245.

Newspapers

The New Mexican; Santa Fe Reporter.

Convention Facility

Sweeney Convention Center, Box 909, 201 W Marcy St, 984-6760.

Sports & Recreation

(For further information contact the Convention & Visitors Bureau.)

Cultural Facilities

Theaters

Greer Garson Theatre, College of Santa Fe, 473-6511.

Santa Fe Community Theatre, 142 E De Vargas St, 988-4262.

Concert Hall

Santa Fe Opera House (summer only), 7 mi N on US 84/285; Box 2408, 986-5955.

Museums

Laboratory of Anthropology, 710 Camino Lejo, 827-6344.

Old Cienega Village Museum, 10 mi S off I-25, 471-2261.

Palace of the Governors, Palace Ave, 827-6474.

Art Museums

Institute of American Indian Arts Museum, 108 Cathedral Pl, 988-6281 or -6211.

Museum of Fine Arts, 107 W Palace, at Lincoln, 827-4455.

Museum of Indian Arts & Culture, Camino Lejo, 827-6344.

Museum of International Folk Art, Camino Lejo, 827-6350.

Wheelwright Museum, 704 Camino Lejo, 982-4636.

Points of Interest

Historical

Cathedral of St Francis, Cathedral Pl near Palace Ave, 982-5619.

Cristo Rey Church, Canyon Rd.

Federal Court House, Federal Pl.

Glorieta Pass, approx 19 mi E on I-25, US 84/285.

La Fonda Hotel, 100 E San Francisco St at Plaza, 982-5511.

Loretto Chapel, 219 Old Santa Fe Trail.

National Park Service, Southwest Regional Office, 1100 Old Santa Fe Trail, 988-6011.

Oldest House, Old Santa Fe Trail & De Vargas St.

Pecos National Monument, 25 mi E via US 25, 757-2616 or -6414.

The Plaza, Palace Ave.

San Miguel Mission, Old Santa Fe Trail & De Vargas St, 983-3974.

Santuario de Guadalupe, 100 Guadalupe St, 988-2027.

Scottish Rite Temple, NE of Federal Court House, Federal Pl.

Other Attractions

Bandelier National Monument, N on US 84/285 about 16 mi, then W on NM 4 about 26 mi to turnoff, 672-3861.

Camino Del Monte Sol, off Canyon Rd.

Hyde Memorial State Park, 8 mi NE via NM 475.

Los Alamos, N on US 84/285 approx 16 mi, then W on NM 4 about 13 mi, beyond turnoff to Bandelier National Monument.

San Ildefonso Pueblo, N on US 84/285 about 16 mi, then W on NM 502, 455-2273.

Santa Fe Pro Musica, Box 2091, 988-4640.

Santa Fe Ski Area, 16 mi NE on NM 475, 982-4429.

Sena Plaza and Prince Plaza, Palace Ave.

State Capitol, Old Santa Fe Trail & De Vargas St, 986-4589.

Taos and Taos Pueblo, 25 mi N via US 84/285, then 45 mi NE on NM 68. Taos Pueblo, 758-9593.

Sightseeing Tours

Discover Santa Fe, Box 2847, 87504; 474-6552.

Gray Line, 1330 Hickox St, 87501; 983-9491.

Annual Events

Feast Day at San Ildefonso Pueblo. Late Jan.

Candelaria Day Celebration, Cochiti, San Felipe, Santo Domingo pueblos. Early Feb.

Fiesta & Green Corn Dance, San Felipe Pueblo. Early May.

Riverman Day, Cochiti Pueblo. Early May.

Spring Corn Dances, Cochiti, San Felipe, Santo Domingo and other pueblos. Late May-early June.

St Anthony's Feast-Comanche Dance. San Juan pueblo. Late June.

Santa Fe Opera. Late June-late Aug.

Santa Fe Rodeo. 4 days mid-July.

Fiesta at Cochiti Pueblo. Mid-July.

Spanish Market, Santa Fe Plaza, 983-4038. Last wkend July.

Fiesta at Santo Domingo Pueblo. Early Aug.

Invitational Antique Indian Art Show. 2 days mid-Aug.

Indian Market, Plaza, 983-5220. 2 days mid-Aug.

Santa Fe Fiesta. 2nd wkend Sept.

Christmas Eve Celebrations, Santa Fe & nearby villages.

Lodging and Food Albuquerque

Motels

(Rates may be higher during the Balloon Fiesta, the State Fair and other special events)

★ ★ ★ **BEST WESTERN INN AT RIO RANCHO.** *(1465 Rio Rancho Dr, Rio Rancho 87124) 3 mi W on I-40 exit 155, then 8 mi N on NM 45. 505/892-1700; FAX 505/892-4628.* 121 rms, 10 kits. S $55-$73; D $61-$73; each addl $6; kit. units $61-$67; under 12 free. Crib $6. Pet accepted, some restrictions; $3/day. TV; cable (premium), VCR avail. Pool; whirlpool, poolside serv. Coffee in rms. Restaurant 6:30 am-10 pm. Rm serv. Bar 11-2 am; entertainment Fri, Sat. Ck-out 11 am. Coin Indry. Meeting rms. Business servs avail. In-rm modem link. Valet serv. Sundries. Gift shop. Free airport, RR station, bus depot transportation. Golf privileges, greens fee, pro, putting green, driving range. Downhill/x-country ski 20 mi. Exercise equipt: weights, stair machine. Lawn games. Microwaves avail. Picnic tables, grills. Cr cds: A, C, D, DS, JCB, MC, V.

D SC

★ ★ **CLUBHOUSE INN.** *1315 Menaul Blvd NE (87107), at I-25. 505/345-0010; FAX 505/344-3911.* Web www.clubhouseinn.com. 137 units, 2 story, 17 kit. suites. S $74, D $84; each addl $10; kit. suites $85-$105; under 16 free; wkly, wkend rates. Crib free. TV; cable (premium). Heated pool; whirlpool. Complimentary bkfst buffet. Ck-out noon. Meeting rms. Business servs avail. Health club privileges. Private patios, balconies. Picnic tables, grills. Cr cds: A, C, D, DS, MC, V.

D SC

✔★ ★ **COMFORT INN EAST.** *13031 Central NE (87123), I-40 at Tramway exit 167. 505/294-1800; FAX 505/293-1088.* 122 rms, 2 story. May-mid-Sept: S $52-$55; D $58-$67; each addl $6; under 17 free; lower rates rest of yr. Crib free. Pet accepted; $6/day. TV; cable (premium). Pool; whirlpools. Complimentary full bkfst. Restaurant 6-10 am, 5-8:30 pm. Ck-out noon. Coin Indry. Meeting rms. Business servs avail. Downhill ski 9 mi. Cr cds: A, C, D, DS, JCB, MC, V.

D SC

★ ★ ★ **COURTYARD BY MARRIOTT.** *1920 Yale SE (87106), near Intl Airport. 505/843-6600; FAX 505/843-8740.* Web www.marriott.com. 150 rms, 4 story. S $89; D $99; suites $109-$119; under 12 free; wkend rates. Crib free. TV; cable (premium). Indoor pool; whirlpool. Complimentary coffee in rms. Restaurant 6 am-10 am, 5-10 pm; Sat, Sun 7 am-11 am. Rm serv. Bar 4-11 pm. Ck-out 1 pm. Meeting rms. Business servs avail. Valet serv. Free airport transportation. Downhill/x-country ski 15 mi. Exercise equipt; weights, bicycles. Refrigerator in suites. Balconies. Picnic tables. Cr cds: A, C, D, DS, MC, V.

D SC

✔★ ★ **DAYS INN.** *6031 Iliff Rd NW (87121), I-40 exit 155. 505/836-3297; FAX 505/836-1214.* 81 rms, 2 story. June-Oct: S $55-$75; D $60-$80; each addl $5; under 12 free. Pet accepted; $5/day. TV; cable (premium). Indoor pool; whirlpool, sauna. Complimentary continental bkfst. Restaurant nearby. Ck-out 11 am. Guest Indry. Business servs avail. Downhill/x-country ski 10 mi. Cr cds: A, D, DS, JCB, MC, V.

D SC

✔★ **DAYS INN.** *13317 Central Ave NE (87123). 505/294-3297; FAX 505/293-3973.* 72 rms, 2 story. S $52-$60; D $55-$65; each addl $5; under 12 free. Crib free. TV; cable (premium). Indoor pool; whirlpool, sauna. Complimentary full bkfst. Restaurant adj open 24 hrs. Ck-out 11 am. Business servs avail. Cr cds: A, C, D, DS, MC, V.

SC

★ **HAMPTON INN.** *5101 Ellison NE (87109), I-25 exit 231. 505/344-1555; FAX 505/345-2216.* 125 rms, 3 story. May-Aug: S $57-62; D $63-$67; under 18 free; lower rates rest of yr. Crib free. Pet accepted, some restrictions. TV; cable (premium), VCR avail. Heated pool. Complimentary continental bkfst. Restaurant nearby. Ck-out noon. Health club privileges. Cr cds: A, C, D, DS, MC, V.

D SC

★ **HOWARD JOHNSON.** *15 Hotel Circle (87123), 6 mi E on I-40, exit 165. 505/296-4852; FAX 505/293-9072.* 150 rms, 2 story. S, D $48-$88; each addl $5; under 18 free. Crib free. TV; cable (premium). Heated pool; whirlpool. Restaurant 6 am-10 pm. Rm serv. Ck-out noon. Coin Indry. Business servs avail. In-rm modem link. Bellhops. Valet serv. Free airport, RR station, bus depot transportation. Exercise equipt; weight machine, bicycle. Some refrigerators. Cr cds: A, C, D, DS, MC, V.

D SC

★ ★ **LA QUINTA-AIRPORT.** *2116 Yale Blvd SE (87106), 1 mi E of I-25 Gibson Airport exit, near Intl Airport. 505/243-5500; FAX 505/247-8288.* 105 rms, 3 story. S $69; D $75; each addl $8; suites $105; under 18 free. Crib free. Pet accepted, some restrictions. TV; cable (premium). Pool. Continental bkfst. Restaurant adj 6 am-10 pm. Ck-out noon. Coin Indry. Business servs avail. Valet serv. Free airport transportation. Downhill ski 20 mi. Microwave in suites. Cr cds: A, C, D, DS, MC, V.

D SC

★ ★ **LE BARON INN.** *2120 Menaul Blvd NE (87107), at jct I-25 Menaul exit, I-40. 505/884-0250; FAX 505/883-0594; res: 800/444-7378.* 200 units, 2 story, 33 suites. S, D $55-$64; suites $76-$135; under 12 free. Crib free. TV; cable (premium). Heated pool. Complimentary continental bkfst. Restaurant adj open 24 hrs. Ck-out noon. Coin Indry. Meeting rms. Business servs avail. Valet serv. Free airport transportation. Downhill ski 15 mi. Bathrm phones; some refrigerators. Cr cds: A, C, D, DS, MC, V.

D SC

★ **TRAVELERS INN.** *411 McKnight Ave NW (87102), I-40 at 4th St. 505/242-5228; FAX 505/766-9218; res: 800/633-8300.* 96 rms, 4 story. S $42.99; D $49.99; each addl $4; suites $57.59-$63.89; under 18 free. Crib free. TV; cable (premium). Heated pool; whirlpool. Complimentary continental bkfst. Restaurant adj open 24 hrs; Sun to 11 pm. Ck-out 11 am. Meeting rm. Business servs avail. Some minibars. Cr cds: A, C, D, DS, MC, V.

D SC

✔★ **TRAVELODGE.** *13139 Central Ave NE (87123). 505/292-4878; FAX 505/299-1822.* 41 rms, 2 story. May-Oct: S, D $40-$100; each addl $5; under 17 free; lower rates rest of yr. Crib free. Pet accepted, some restrictions; $5. TV; cable (premium). Complimentary continental bkfst. Complimentary coffee in rms. Restaurant nearby. Ck-out 11 am. Business servs avail. Downhill/x-country ski 8 mi. Cr cds: A, C, D, DS, JCB, MC, V.

D SC

Motor Hotels

★ ★ **AMBERLY SUITE HOTEL.** *7620 Pan American Frwy NE (87109), I-25 & San Antonio Rd N. 505/823-1300; FAX 505/823-2896; res: 800/333-9806.* Web www.calav.com/amberly. 170 suites, 3 story. S, D $99-$118; each addl $10; under 16 free; monthly rates. Crib free. Pet accepted; $5. TV; cable (premium). Heated pool; whirlpool. Complimentary full bkfst; afternoon refreshments. Restaurant 6 am-9 pm. Bar 4-11 pm. Ck-out noon. Coin Indry. Meeting rms. Business servs avail. In-rm modem link. Free airport, RR station, bus depot transportation. Downhill ski 5 mi. Exercise equipt; weights, bicycles, sauna. Refrigerators, microwaves. Courtyard; fountain. Cr cds: A, C, D, DS, MC, V.

D SC

★ **BEST WESTERN WINROCK INN.** *18 Winrock Center NE (87110), in Winrock Shopping Center. 505/883-5252; FAX 505/889-3206.* 173 rms, 2 story. S, D $69-$82; each addl $10; suites $110; under 18 free. Crib free. TV; cable. Heated pool. Complimentary bkfst buffet. Restaurant nearby. Ck-out noon. Coin lndry. Meeting rms. Business servs avail. Bellhops. Health club privileges. Some refrigerators. Cr cds: A, C, D, DS, MC, V.

D SC

★ ★ ★ **HOLIDAY INN-MOUNTAIN VIEW.** *2020 Menaul Blvd NE (87107), 1 blk E of I-25, I-40, Menaul Blvd exit. 505/884-2511; FAX 505/884-5720.* 363 rms, 4-5 story. S, D $99-$109; each addl $10; under 18 free. Crib free. TV; cable (premium). Heated pool; whirlpool, poolside serv. Restaurant 6:30 am-2 pm, 5-10 pm. Rm serv. Bar 11-1 am; Sun noon-midnight. Ck-out noon. Coin lndry. Meeting rms. Business servs avail. Bellhops. Valet serv. Sundries. Downhill ski 15 mi. Exercise equipt; bicycles, sauna. Some private patios, balconies. Cr cds: A, C, D, DS, JCB, MC, V.

D SC

✔★ ★ **PLAZA INN.** *900 Medical Arts Ave NE (87102), I-25 Lomas Blvd exit. 505/243-5693; FAX 505/843-6229; res: 800/237-1307.* 120 rms, 5 story. S, D $70-$90; each addl $5; under 17 free. Pet accepted. TV. Heated pool; whirlpool. Restaurant 6 am-midnight. Bar 11-2 am; Sun noon-midnight. Ck-out noon. Coin lndry. Meeting rms. Business servs avail. Valet serv. Free airport, RR station, bus depot transportation. Downhill ski 14 mi. Exercise equipt; weight machine, stair machine. Some refrigerators. Private patios, balconies. Cr cds: A, C, D, DS, ER, JCB, MC, V.

D SC

★ ★ ★ **RADISSON INN-AIRPORT.** *1901 University SE (87106), I-25 exit 222, near Intl Airport. 505/247-0512; FAX 505/843-7148.* 150 rms, 2-3 story. S $75-$95; D $85-$105; each addl $10; suite $95-$110; under 18 free; wkly, wkend rates. Crib free. TV; cable (premium), VCR avail (movies). Heated pool; whirlpool, poolside serv. Restaurant 6 am-10 pm. Rm serv. Bar 2 pm-midnight. Ck-out noon. Meeting rms. In-rm modem link. Bellhops. Free airport, RR station, bus depot transportation. Downhill ski 20 mi. Health club privileges. Cr cds: A, C, D, DS, ER, MC, V.

D SC

★ ★ **RAMADA INN.** *25 Hotel Circle NE (87123), I-40 Eubank Blvd exit E 165. 505/271-1000; FAX 505/291-9028.* 205 rms, 2 story. S $63-$83; D $73-$93; each addl $10; suites $89-$150; under 18 free; wkend rates. Crib free. TV; cable (premium). Heated pool. Restaurant 6 am-2 pm, 5-10 pm. Rm serv. Bar 2 pm-midnight; Sun from 1 pm. Ck-out noon. Coin lndry. Meeting rms. Business servs avail. Valet serv. Free airport transportation. Downhill ski 10 mi. Cr cds: A, C, D, DS, MC, V.

D SC

✔★ ★ **SUMNER SUITES.** *2500 Menaul Blvd NE (87107). 505/881-0544; FAX 505/881-0380; res: 800/747-8483.* 125 kit. suites, 6 story. S $69-$82; D $69-$87; each addl $5; under 12 free; higher rates: special events, hols. Crib free. TV; cable (premium). Pool. Complimentary continental bkfst. Complimentary coffee in rms. Restaurant nearby. Ck-out noon. Coin lndry. Meeting rms. Business servs avail. Valet serv. Downhill/x-country ski 17 mi. Exercise equipt; weights, bicycle. Cr cds: A, C, D, DS, MC, V.

D SC

Hotels

★ ★ ★ **CROWNE PLAZA PYRAMID.** *5151 San Francisco Rd NE (87109), I-25 at Paso Del Norte exit 232. 505/821-3333; FAX 505/828-0230.* E-mail lypyrd@aol.com. 311 units, 10 story. S, D $111-$126; each addl $15; suites $126-$275; under 19 free. Crib free. TV; cable (premium). Indoor/outdoor pool; whirlpool, poolside serv. Restaurant 6 am-10 pm. Bar 11-2 am. Ck-out noon. Convention facilities. Business center. In-rm modem link. Concierge. Shopping arcade. Downhill ski 8 mi. Exercise equipt; weights, bicycles, sauna. Health club privileges. Some refrigerators. Private patios. Atrium lobby; waterfall. Luxury level. Cr cds: A, C, D, DS, JCB, MC, V.

D SC

★ ★ ★ **DOUBLETREE.** *201 Marquette Ave NW (87102). 505/247-3344; FAX 505/247-7025.* 294 rms, 15 story. S, D $125-$145; each addl $10; suites $140-$475; under 18 free. Crib free. TV; cable (premium). Pool. Restaurant 6 am-10 pm. Bar 11:30-2 am; Sun from noon. Ck-out noon. Convention facilities. Business servs avail. Gift shop. Downhill ski 15 mi. Exercise equipt; weights, bicycles. Health club privileges. Cr cds: A, C, D, DS, ER, JCB, MC, V.

D SC

★ ★ ★ **HILTON INN.** *1901 University Blvd (87125), 1 blk E of I-25 Menaul Blvd exit. 505/884-2500; FAX 505/889-9118.* Web www.hilton.com. 262 rms, 12 story. S $89-139; D $99-$149; each addl $10; suites $395-$495; under 18 free. Crib free. TV; cable (premium). 2 pools, 1 indoor; whirlpool, poolside serv. Coffee in rms. Restaurants 6 am-11 pm. Bar 11-1 am; Sun from noon; entertainment. Ck-out noon. Convention facilities. Business center. In-rm modem link. Tennis. Downhill ski 15 mi. Exercise equipt; weights, stair machine, sauna. Health club privileges. Some bathrm phones, refrigerators. Balconies. Luxury level. Cr cds: A, C, D, DS, ER, JCB, MC, V.

D SC

★ ★ ★ **HYATT REGENCY.** *330 Tijeras NW (87102). 505/842-1234; FAX 505/766-6710.* Web www.hyatt.com.go:hyatt(compuserv). 395 rms, 20 story. S $150; D $175; each addl $25; suites $375-$750; under 15 free. Crib free. Garage parking $8; valet $11. TV; cable (premium), VCR avail. Heated pool; poolside serv. Restaurant 6 am-10:30 pm. Bar 11 am-midnight; entertainment. Ck-out noon. Convention facilities. Business servs avail. Concierge. Shopping arcade. Beauty shop. Downhill/x-country ski 18 mi. Exercise equipt; weights, bicycles, sauna. Health club privileges. Refrigerator, wet bar in suites. Microwaves avail. Convention center adj. Cr cds: A, C, D, DS, ER, JCB, MC, V.

D SC

★ ★ **LA POSADA DE ALBUQUERQUE.** *125 2nd St NW (87102), at Copper. 505/242-9090; FAX 505/242-8664; res: 800/777-5732.* 114 rms, 10 story. S, D $99-$115; each addl $15; suites $195-$275; under 17 free; wkend rates. Crib free. TV; cable (premium). Restaurant (see CONRAD'S DOWNTOWN). Bar 11 am-midnight. Ck-out 1 pm. Meeting rms. Business servs avail. Shopping arcade. Health club privileges. Downhill ski 15 mi. Refrigerator in suites. Cr cds: A, C, D, DS, MC, V.

D SC

★ ★ ★ **MARRIOTT.** *2101 Louisiana Blvd NE (87110). 505/881-6800; FAX 505/888-2982.* 411 rms, 17 story. S, D $155; suites $250-$500; under 18 free; seasonal rates. Crib free. TV; cable (premium). Indoor/outdoor pool; whirlpool, poolside serv. Restaurant 6:30 am-11 pm. Bar 11 am-midnight; Sun from noon. Ck-out noon. Coin lndry. Convention facilities. In-rm modem link. Gift shop. Downhill ski 10 mi. Exercise equipt; weights, bicycles, sauna. Rec rm. Luxury level. Cr cds: A, C, D, DS, ER, JCB, MC, V.

D SC

★ ★ **SHERATON UPTOWN ALBUQUERQUE.** *2600 Louisiana NE (87110), I-40 Louisiana Blvd exit N. 505/881-0000; FAX 505/881-3736.* E-mail 105561.1633@compuserve.com; web ittsheraton.com. 296 rms, 8 story. S $129; D $139; each addl $10; suites $150-$300; under 18 free; wkend rates. Crib free. TV; cable (premium). Indoor pool; whirlpool. Restaurant 6 am-11 pm. Bar 11-2 am. Ck-out noon. Coin lndry. Convention facilities. Business servs avail. Gift shop. Downhill ski 7 mi. Exercise equipt; weight machines, bicycles, sauna. Refrigerators. Tennis, golf nearby. Cr cds: A, D, DS, MC, V.

D SC

★ ★ ★ **SHERATON-OLD TOWN.** *800 Rio Grande Blvd NW (87104), 2 blks S of I-40 Rio Grande exit. 505/843-6300; FAX 505/842-9863.* 188 rms, 11 story. S $105-$120; D $115-$130; each addl $10; suites $150; under 18 free; wkend rates. Crib free. TV; cable (premium). Heated pool; whirlpool, poolside serv. Coffee in rms. Restaurant 6-11 am; dining rm 11 am-10:30 pm. Bar 4-11 pm. Ck-out noon. Meeting rms. Business servs avail. In-rm modem link. Shopping arcade. Barber, beauty shop. Downhill ski 20 mi. Exercise equipt; weight machine, bicycles, steam rm.

Some refrigerators. Some balconies. In historic Old Town. Cr cds: A, C, D, DS, MC, V.

D SC

★ ★ ★ **WYNDHAM.** *2910 Yale Blvd SE (87106), 2 blks E of I-25 Gibson Blvd exit, at Intl Airport. 505/843-7000; FAX 505/843-6307.* 276 rms, 14 story. S $89-$180; D $99-$130; each addl $10; suites $150-$300; under 12 free; wkend rates. Crib free. TV; cable (premium). Heated pool; poolside serv. Restaurant 6 am-11 pm. Bar 11-1:30 am; Sun to midnight. Ck-out noon. Meeting rms. Business center. In-rm modem link. Gift shop. Free airport transportation. Tennis. Downhill ski 15 mi. Exercise equipt; bicycles, stair machine. Some refrigerators. Balconies. Cr cds: A, C, D, DS, JCB, MC, V.

D SC

★ ★ ★ **WYNDHAM GARDEN.** *6000 Pan American Frwy NE (87109). 505/821-9451; FAX 505/858-0329.* 150 rms, 5 story. S $99; D $104; each addl $10; under 18 free. Crib free. TV; cable. Indoor/outdoor pool; whirlpool. Restaurant 6:30 am-2 pm, 5-10 pm. Bar 4 pm-midnight. Ck-out noon. Meeting rms. Business servs avail. Coin Indry. Free airport transportation. Exercise equipt; bicycle, treadmill, sauna. Some balconies. Cr cds: A, D, DS, MC, V.

D SC

Inns

★ ★ ★ **APACHE CANYON RANCH.** *(4 Canyon Dr, Cañoncito 87026) 26 mi W on I-40, N at exit 131. 505/836-7220; res: 800/808-8310; FAX 505/836-2922.* E-mail apacabnb@thuntek.net. 5 rms, 2 share bath, guest house. June-Oct, MAP: S $75-$225; D $90-$225; each addl $25; guest house $225; golf, package plans; lower rates rest of yr. Children over 12 yrs only. TV; VCR avail (movies). Complimentary coffee in rms. Rm serv. Ck-out 11 am, ck-in 3 pm. Business servs avail. Luggage handling. Concierge serv. Gift shop. Putting green. Massage. Many in-rm whirlpools; some fireplaces; microwaves avail. Picnic tables, grills. View of mountains. Totally nonsmoking. Cr cds: A, MC, V.

D

★ ★ ★ **CASA DEL GRANJERO.** *414 C de Baca Ln NW (87114). 505/897-4144; FAX 505/897-9788; res: 800/701-4144.* E-mail granjero @RT66.com; web www.virtualcities.com/. 7 rms, 2 with shower only, 5 suites, 1 kit. unit. No rm phones. S $79-$149; D, suites, kit. unit $79-$159; each addl $10; wkly, wkend, hol rates; ski plans. Children over 3 yrs only. Crib $10. TV in common rm; cable, VCR (movies). Whirlpool. Complimentary full bkfst; afternoon refreshments. Ck-out 11 am, ck-in 11 am-2 pm. Luggage handling. Concierge serv. Business center. Downhill/x-country ski 10 mi. Lawn games. Some refrigerators; microwaves avail. Hacienda built in 1880; kiva fireplaces, carved Mexican furniture. Totally nonsmoking. Cr cds: A, MC, V.

D SC

★ ★ ★ **CASAS DE SUEÑOS.** *310 Rio Grande SW (87104). 505/247-4560; FAX 505/842-8493; res: 800/242-8987.* 19 units, 5 suites, 8 with kit. S, D $85-$250; each addl $15; suites, kit. units $110-$250; 3-day min Balloon Fiesta. Children over 12 yrs only. TV; cable (premium). Complimentary full bkfst. Restaurant nearby. Ck-out 11 am, ck-in 3-7 pm. Business servs avail. In-rm modem link. Separate adobe units surround courtyard; European antiques. Totally nonsmoking. Cr cds: A, C, D, DS, MC, V.

✔★ ★ **CHOCOLATE TURTLE.** *(1098 W Meadowlark Ln, Corrales 87048) 15 mi N on I-25 exit Alameda, E to Corrales Rd, N to Meadowlark. 505/898-1800; res: 800/898-1842.* E-mail turtlebb@aol.com; web www.collectorsguide.com/chocturtle. 4 air-cooled rms, 3 with shower only, 1 suite. No rm phones. S $55-$70; D $70-$75; each addl $10; suite $85-$95; package plans; wkends (2-day min). Children over 6 yrs only. TV in common rm; cable (premium), VCR avail (movies). Complimentary full bkfst. Restaurant nearby. Ck-out 11 am, ck-in 4-6 pm. Business servs avail. Concierge serv. Downhill ski 15 mi. Whirlpool. Totally nonsmoking. Cr cds: A, DS, MC, V.

★ ★ ★ **HACIENDA ANTIGUA.** *6708 Tierra Dr NW (87107). 505/345-5399; FAX 505/345-3855.* 5 air-cooled rms. No rm phones. S $85-$110; D $95-$125; each addl $25; 3-day min Balloon Fiesta. Children over 6 yrs only. TV in common rm. Pool; whirlpool. Complimentary full bkfst; afternoon refreshments. Ck-out 11 am, ck-in 4-6 pm. Business servs avail. Downhill/x-country ski 12 mi. Refrigerators. Picnic tables. Spanish colonial house built 1790 that once served as stagecoach stop; many antiques. Cr cds: A, DS, MC, V.

D

★ ★ ★ **HACIENDA VARGAS.** *(1431 El Camino Real (US 66), Algodones 87001) N on I-25, exit 248, W to El Camino Real, turn left. 505/867-9115; FAX 505/867-1902; res: 800/261-0006.* E-mail hacvar @swcp.com; web www.swcp.com/hacvar/. 3 rms, 5 suites. No rm phones. S, D $79-$149; each addl $15; suites $109-$149. Complimentary full bkfst; afternoon refreshments. Ck-out 11 am, ck-in 4 pm. Business servs avail. Site has been a stagecoach stop, train depot, and a trading post. Totally nonsmoking. Cr cds: MC, V.

★ ★ ★ **JEMEZ RIVER BED & BREAKFAST.** *(16445 Scenic Hwy 4, Jemez Springs 87025) N on I-25 to NM 44, exit 242, W 23 mi, N on Scenic Hwy 4 approx 16 mi. 505/829-3262; res: 800/809-3262.* E-mail jemezriverbb@jemez.com; web www.jemez.com/jemezriverbb. 7 rms, 1 casita. Apr-Oct: S $79-$99; D $99-$119; each addl $15; casita $129-$189; package plans; lower rates rest of yr. Children under 12 yrs in casita only. Crib free. TV; cable (premium), VCR avail (movies). Complimentary full bkfst. Restaurant nearby. Ck-out 11 am, ck-in 2-8 pm. Concierge serv. X-country ski on site. Sauna. Massage. In-rm whirlpool, refrigerator, microwave in casita. Picnic tables, grills. On river. Adobe casita built in 1902. Totally nonsmoking. Cr cds: A, DS, MC, V.

SC

★ ★ ★ **LA HACIENDA GRANDE.** *(21 Baros Lane, Bernalillo 87004) approx 20 mi N on I-25, exit 242, W on NM 44, right on Camino del Pueblo, left on Baros Lane. 505/867-1887; FAX 505/867-4621; res: 800/353-1887.* E-mail lhg@swcp.com; web www.viva.com/nm/lahaci.html. 6 rms. S $95-$119; D $99-$119; each addl $15; ski, golf plans; higher rates hols (2-day min). Children over 12 yrs only. TV; cable (premium), VCR avail (movies). Complimentary full bkfst. Complimentary coffee in rms. Ck-out 11 am, ck-in 4-6 pm. Luggage handling. Concierge serv. Business servs avail. 18-hole golf privileges, greens fee $32. Downhill/x-country ski 15 mi. Spanish hacienda built in 1750s. Rms surround courtyard with covered portico. Totally nonsmoking. Cr cds: A, D, DS, MC, V.

SC

✔★ ★ **W.E. MAUGER ESTATE.** *701 Roma Ave NW (87102). 505/242-8755; FAX 505/842-8835.* Web www.thuntele.net/tcart/mare ger. 8 air-cooled rms, shower only, 3 story. S, D $79-$149; each addl $15. Crib free. Pet accepted. TV; cable (premium), VCR avail. Complimentary full bkfst; afternoon refreshments. Complimentary coffee in rms. Restaurant nearby. Ck-out 11 am, ck-in 4-6 pm. Business servs avail. In-rm modem link. Downhill/x-country ski 12 mi. Health club privileges. Sun porch. Restored Queen Anne house (1897). Cr cds: A, C, D, DS, MC, V.

SC

Restaurants

★ ★ **ANTIQUITY.** *112 Romero St NW (87104). 505/247-3545.* Hrs: 5-9 pm; Fri, Sat to 9:30 pm. Closed most major hols. Res accepted. Continental menu. Wine, beer. Semi-a la carte: dinner $14.75-$21.95. Specializes in seafood, steaks, salmon. Romantic hacienda atmosphere. Antiques. Cr cds: A, C, D, DS, MC, V.

★ ★ **THE ARTICHOKE.** *424 Central St (87102). 505/243-0200.* Hrs: 11 am-2:30 pm, 5:30-10 pm; Sat from 5:30 pm. Closed Sun; Jan 1, Thanksgiving, Dec 25. Res accepted. Continental menu. Wine, beer.

Semi-a la carte: lunch $4.95-$10.95, dinner $11.95-$24.95. Child's meals. Specializes in pasta, fresh seafood, lamb. Own bread. Outdoor dining. Contemporary decor. Cr cds: A, DS, MC, V.

★★ **CAFE DE LAS PLACITA.** *(664 NM 165, Placitas 87043) 505/867-1610.* Hrs: 11:30 am-2:30 pm, 6-9 pm; Fri, Sat 6-9:30 pm. Closed Sun; Jan 1, Thanksgiving, Dec 25. Res accepted. Continental menu. Wine, beer. Semi-a la carte: lunch $7-$10, dinner $13-$22. Specializes in tandoori shrimp, beef, lamb. Outdoor dining. Adobe brick walls, high ceilings, plants. Cr cds: A, DS, MC, V.

D

★★ **CAFE OCEANA.** *1414 Central SE. 505/247-2233.* Hrs: 11 am-11 pm; Fri to 11:30 pm; Sat 5-11:30 pm. Closed Sun; most major hols. Bar. Semi-a la carte: lunch $5-$10, dinner $6.95-$18.95. Child's meals. Specializes in fresh seafood. Patio dining. Cr cds: A, D, DS, MC, V.

D

✔★★ **CAFE SPOLETO.** *2813 San Mateo NE (87110). 505/880-0897.* Hrs: 5:30-9:30 pm. Closed Sun, Mon; also major hols. Res accepted. Mediterranean menu. Wine, beer. Semi-a la carte: dinner $12.25-$16.50. Specialties: chicken under a brick, grilled salmon, braised lamb. Three different dining rms. Totally nonsmoking. Cr cds: A, DS, MC, V.

✔★★ **CHEF DU JOUR.** *119 San Pasquale SW (87104), 1 3/4 mi W on Central to San Pasquale. 505/247-8998.* Hrs: 11 am-2 pm. Closed Sat, Sun; major hols. Res accepted. Eclectic menu. Semi-a la carte: lunch $2.50-$7.50. Specializes in fresh seasonal foods. Own baking. Menu changes wkly. Outdoor dining. Intimate atmosphere; open kitchen. Totally nonsmoking. No cr cds accepted.

D ♥

✔★ **CHRISTY MAE'S.** *1400 San Pedro NE (87110). 505/255-4740.* Hrs: 11 am-8 pm. Closed Sun; hols. Semi-a la carte: lunch $4.50-$7.50, dinner $5.50-$9.50. Child's meals. Specializes in grilled sandwiches, chicken pot pie, homemade soup. Cr cds: A, D, DS, MC, V.

D SC

★★ **CONRAD'S DOWNTOWN.** *(See La Posada De Albuquerque Hotel) 505/242-9090.* Hrs: 6:30 am-10 pm. Res accepted (dinner). Spanish, Amer menu. Bar. Semi-a la carte: bkfst $3.95-$7.50, lunch $3.95-$8, dinner $14.50-$22. Specializes in veal, paella, salmon. Guitarist Fri, Sat eves. Valet parking. Cr cds: A, C, D, DS, MC, V.

D ♥

★ **THE COOPERAGE.** *7220 Lomas Blvd NE, 1 mi S of I-40 Louisiana Blvd exit. 505/255-1657.* Hrs: 11 am-2:30 pm, 5-10 pm; Fri to 11 pm; Sat noon-2:30 pm, 5-11 pm; Sun noon-9 pm; early-bird dinner 5-7 pm. Closed Dec 25. Res accepted. Bar to 2 am; Sun to 10 pm. Semi-a la carte: lunch $4.50-$7.50, dinner $12.95-$27.95. Child's meals. Specializes in prime rib, lobster. Salad bar. Entertainment Fri, Sat. Built like an enormous barrel; circular rms with many intimate corners, booths; atrium dining rm. Cr cds: A, DS, MC, V.

D SC

★★ **COUNTY LINE BBQ.** *9600 Tramway Blvd NE. 505/856-7477.* Hrs: 5-9 pm; Fri, Sat to 10 pm; Sun 4-9 pm. Closed some major hols. Bar. Semi-a la carte: dinner $8.95-$16.95. Child's meals. Specializes in barbecue ribs, steak, fish. View of mountains, valley, city. Cr cds: A, C, D, DS, MC, V.

D

✔★ **EL NORTEÑO.** *6416 Zuni SE (87108), 4 mi E of downtown. 505/255-2057.* Hrs: 11 am-9 pm. Closed most major hols. Res accepted. Mexican menu. Wine, beer. Semi-a la carte: lunch $3.95-$6.95, dinner $5.95-$12.95. Child's meals. Specialties: chile rellenos, cabrito al horno, lengua. Old Mexico decor. Cr cds: A, DS, MC, V.

D

✔★ **EL PINTO.** *10500 4th St NW, off I-25, Tramway Rd exit 234W. 505/898-1771.* Hrs: 11 am-9 pm; Fri, Sat to 10 pm. Closed Jan 1, Thanksgiving, Dec 25. Contemporary Mexican, Amer menu. Bar. Semi-a la carte: lunch $4.15-$10.95, dinner $5.95-$13.55. Child's meals. Specialties: chicken adobada, carne adobada ribs. Patio dining with waterfall. Hacienda decor. Cr cds: A, DS, MC, V.

D

✔★ **GARDUÑO'S.** *10551 Montgomery NE. 505/298-5000.* Hrs: 11 am-10 pm; Fri to 10:30 pm; Sun from 10:30 am; Sun brunch to 3 pm. Closed Thanksgiving, Dec 25. Contemporary Mexican menu. Bar. Semi-a la carte: lunch $4.95-$11.95, dinner $7.25-$12.95. Sun brunch $9.95. Child's meals. Specializes in enchiladas, fajitas. Entertainment Thurs-Sun. Outdoor dining. Festive atmosphere; Mexican decor. Family-owned. Cr cds: A, C, D, DS, MC, V.

D

★★ **HIGH NOON.** *425 San Felipe St NW, in Old Town Plaza. 505/765-1455.* Hrs: 11 am-9 pm; Fri, Sat to 10:30 pm; Sun from noon. Closed Jan 1, Dec 25. Res accepted. Southwestern menu. Bar. Semi-a la carte: lunch $4.95-$8.95, dinner $8.75-24.95. Specializes in pepper steak, seafood, game. Guitarist Thurs-Sat. Original 2 rooms built in 1785. Colonial Mexican, Western, and Native American decor; kiva fireplaces. Cr cds: A, C, D, DS, MC, V.

D

★ **LA HACIENDA DINING ROOM.** *302 San Felipe NW, Old Town Plaza, 3 blks S of I-40 Rio Grande exit S. 505/243-3131.* Hrs: 11 am-9 pm; summer to 10 pm. Closed Thanksgiving, Dec 25. Res accepted. Mexican, Amer menu. Serv bar. Semi-a la carte: lunch $4.25-$9.95, dinner $7.95-$13.95. Child's meals. Specialties: enchiladas New Mexican, sopaipillas. Entertainment Wed-Sun. Patio dining. Mexican decor in old hacienda; antiques, Native American art. Cr cds: A, C, D, MC, V.

✔★★★ **LE CAFE MICHE.** *1431 Wyoming NE, in shopping center. 505/299-6088.* Hrs: 11:30 am-1:30 pm, 5:30-9 pm; Sat from 5:30 pm. Closed Sun, Mon; major hols. Res accepted. French country menu. A la carte entrees: lunch $5.50-$8, dinner $10-15. Specialties: veal piccata, chow-chow. French cafe atmosphere. Totally nonsmoking. Cr cds: C, D, DS, MC, V.

D

★★ **LE MARMITON.** *5415B Academy Blvd NE. 505/821-6279.* Hrs: 5-9 pm; Fri, Sat to 9:30 pm. Closed Thanksgiving, Dec 25. Res accepted. French menu. Wine, beer. Semi-a la carte: dinner $15.95-$19.95. Specialties: fantaisie aux fruits de mer, canard aux framboises. French art; hand-painted plate display. Cr cds: A, D, DS, MC, V.

D

✔★ **M & J.** *403 2nd St SW (87102). 505/242-4890.* Hrs: 9 am-4 pm. Closed Sun; major hols. Mexican menu. Semi-a la carte: lunch, dinner $5-$8.50. Child's meals. Specialties: tamales, carne adovada, blue corn enchilada plate. No cr cds accepted.

D SC

★★ **MAINE-LY LOBSTER & STEAKHOUSE.** *300 San Pedro NE (87109), at Candelaria. 505/878-0070.* Hrs: 5-10 pm. Closed Mon. Res accepted. Wine, beer. Semi-a la carte: dinner $10.95-$32.95. Child's meals. Specializes in fresh seafood, steak. Nautical decor. Cr cds: A, C, D, MC, V.

D

★★ **MARIA TERESA.** *618 Rio Grande Blvd NW (87104), 1/4 mi S of I-40, Rio Grande Blvd exit in Old Town Albuquerque. 505/242-3900.* Hrs: 11 am-2:30 pm, 5-9 pm; Sun brunch to 2:30 pm. Res accepted. Continental, Mexican menu. Bar 11 am-10 pm. Semi-a la carte: lunch $6.50-$10.95, dinner $12.95-$23. Sun brunch $10.95-$16.95. Child's meals. Specializes in Mexican cuisine. Fountain Courtyard for lunch, cocktails. Restored adobe hacienda (1840); antique decor; art, fireplaces, walled gardens. Cr cds: A, C, D, MC, V.

D

★★ **MONTE VISTA FIRE STATION.** *3201 Central NE. 505/255-2424.* Hrs: 11 am-2:30 pm, 5-10:30 pm; Fri to 11 pm; Sat 5-11 pm;

Sun 5-10:30 pm. Closed Thanksgiving, Dec 25. Res accepted. Southwestern nouvelle menu. Bar 11-2 am; Sat from noon; Sun to midnight. Semi-a la carte: lunch $4.95-$13.95, dinner $13.95-$19.95. Specializes in seafood, game, pasta. Own baking. Outdoor dining. In old fire station (1936); brass fire pole; bar upstairs in former sleeping quarters. Cr cds: A, D, DS, MC, V.

D

✔★ **NEW CHINATOWN.** *5001 Central Ave NE (US 66) (87108). 505/265-8859.* Hrs: 11 am-9:30 pm; Fri, Sat to 10:30 pm. Closed Thanksgiving. Res accepted. Chinese menu. Bar to midnight. Semi-a la carte: lunch $3.25-$5.75, dinner $6.50-$14.95. Lunch buffet $5.45. Child's meals. Specializes in Cantonese, Szechwan dishes. Piano bar. Unusual modern Chinese decor; artwork; Chinese garden. Family-owned. Cr cds: A, C, D, DS, MC, V.

D

★ **OASIS.** *5400 San Mateo NE, Sun West Center. 505/884-2324.* Hrs: 11 am-3 pm, 5-9 pm; Fri to 10 pm; Sat noon-10 pm; Sun 5-9 pm. Closed Thanksgiving, Dec 25. Res accepted. Mediterranean, Greek menu. Bar. Semi-a la carte: lunch $4-$6, dinner $8-$19.95. Child's meals. Specialties: lamb marsala, Athenian chicken, vegetarian combination plate. Belly dancer Wed-Sat. Enclosed garden dining. Cr cds: C, D, DS, MC, V.

D

★ ★ ★ **PRAIRIE STAR.** *(255 Prairie Star Rd, Bernalillo) 17 mi N on I-25 exit 242, W on NM 44 to Jemez Dam Rd. 505/867-3327.* Hrs: 5-10 pm; Fri, Sat to 11 pm. Closed Dec 25-Jan 1. Continental menu. Bar. Wine cellar. Semi-a la carte: dinner $15-$20. Specialties: chateaubriand, venison. Own baking. Adobe building; art. View of river valley, mountains. Cr cds: A, C, D, DS, MC, V.

D

★ ★ **RIO BRAVO.** *515 Central Ave (87102). 505/242-6800.* Hrs: 11:30 am-10 pm. Closed Sun; some major hols. Res accepted. Southwestern menu. Semi-a la carte: lunch $3.95-$8.95, dinner $7.95-$18.95. Child's meals. Specialties: wild mushroom enchiladas, New Mexico fettucine Alfredo. Entertainment Fri, Sat. Microbrewery on site. Cr cds: A, DS, MC, V.

D

★ ★ ★ **ROSA!.** *1100 San Mateo NE (87110), at Lomas. 505/255-7672.* Hrs: 11 am-2:30 pm, 5-10 pm; Fri to 11 pm; Sat 5-11 pm. Closed some major hols. Res accepted. Southwestern, Mediterranean menu. Semi-a la carte: lunch $5.95-$9.95, dinner $9.95-$19.95. Child's meals. Specializes in grilled meat, pasta. Outdoor dining. Contemporary Southwestern decor. Cr cds: A, C, D, DS, MC, V.

D

★ ★ ★ **SCALO.** *3500 Central Ave SE (87106), near Carlisle. 505/255-8782.* Hrs: 11:30 am-2:30 pm, 5-11 pm; Sun 5-9 pm. Closed most major hols. Res accepted. Italian menu. Bar. Semi-a la carte: lunch $4.95-$9.95, dinner $7.95-$17.75. Specialties: salmon padellata, bianchire herring, grilled fish. Own pasta. Patio dining. Dining areas on several levels. Cr cds: A, D, DS, MC, V.

D

★ ★ ★ **STEPHENS.** *1311 Tijeras Ave NW, at 14th & Central NW. 505/842-1773.* Hrs: 5:30-9:30 pm; Fri to 10:30 pm; Sat to 10 pm; Sun to 9 pm. Closed Jan 1, Dec 25. Res accepted. Contemporary Amer menu. Bar. Wine cellar. A la carte entrees: dinner $16-$25. Specializes in pasta, fresh seafood, prime beef. Elegant dining. Cr cds: A, D, MC, V.

D

★ ★ **TRATTORIA TROMBINO.** *5415 Academy Blvd NE. 505/821-5974.* Hrs: 11 am-2:30 pm, 5-10 pm; Fri, Sat to 10:30 pm; Sun 4-9 pm. Closed Thanksgiving, Dec 25. Italian menu. Bar. Semi-a la carte: lunch $5.50-$9.95, dinner $7.95-$16.95. Child's meals. Specializes in pasta, seafood, steak. Cr cds: A, C, D, DS, MC, V.

D

✔★ **YESTER-DAVE'S GRILL, BAR & BAKERY.** *10601 Montgomery NE. 505/293-0033.* Hrs: 11 am-10 pm; Fri, Sat to 10:30 pm; Sun 10 am-9:30 pm; Sun brunch to 3 pm. Closed Thanksgiving, Dec 25. Bar. Semi-a la carte: lunch $5.25-$12.95, dinner $5.25-$12.95. Complete meals: dinner $9.50-$12.50. Sun brunch $8.95. Specializes in hamburgers & shakes, chicken-fried steak, barbecued ribs & chicken. Entertainment. Outdoor dining. Vintage car on display; soda fountain and soda jerk; decor and atmosphere reminiscent of rock 'n roll era. DJ takes requests. Cr cds: A, C, D, DS, MC, V.

D

✔★ ★ **ZIA DINER.** *6601 Uptown Blvd NE. 505/884-8383.* Hrs: 11 am-10 pm. Closed Dec 25. Southwestern, Amer menu. Bar. Semi-a la carte: lunch $5.95-$8.95, dinner $5.95-$11.95. Child's meals $3.25. Specializes in pasta, fajitas. Outdoor dining. Festive diner. Cr cds: A, MC, V.

D

Unrated Dining Spots

66 DINER. *1405 Central Ave NE. 505/247-1421.* Hrs: 11 am-11 pm; Fri to midnight; Sat 8 am-midnight; Sun 8 am-10 pm. Closed major hols. Wine, beer. Semi-a la carte: bkfst $1.95-$4.25, lunch, dinner $3-$6.95. Child's meals. Specialty: green chile cheeseburger. Outdoor dining. Roadside diner; photographs, music of the '40s, '50s and '60s. Cr cds: A, DS, MC, V.

D

SOUPER SALAD. *4411 San Mateo NE, on grounds of Montgomery Plaza Ctr. 505/883-9534.* Hrs: 11 am-9 pm; Sun noon-8 pm. Closed Jan 1, Thanksgiving, Dec 25. Semi-a la carte: lunch, dinner $2.65-$5.95. Specializes in homemade soup, baked potatoes. Salad bar. No cr cds accepted.

D

Santa Fe

Motels

(Rates may be higher during the Balloon Fiesta, the State Fair and other special events)

★ ★ **BEST WESTERN LAMPLIGHTER.** *2405 Cerrillos Rd (87505). 505/471-8000; FAX 505/471-1397.* 80 rms, 2 story, 16 kits. May-Oct: S $69-$77; D $75-$85; suites $95-$100; kit. units $95-$100; under 18 free; lower rates rest of yr. Crib free. TV; cable (premium). Indoor pool; sauna. Complimentary coffee in rms. Restaurant 7 am-10 pm. Bar. Ck-out 11 am. Guest Indry. Business servs avail. Refrigerators. Picnic tables. Cr cds: A, C, D, DS, ER, JCB, MC, V.

SC

★ **DAYS INN.** *3650 Cerrillos Rd (87505). 505/438-3822; FAX 505/438-3795.* 97 rms, 2 story. Memorial Day-Labor Day: S $65-$105; D $66-$120; each addl $10; suites $95-$195; under 12 free; higher rates special events; lower rates rest of yr. Crib free. Pet accepted, some restrictions. TV; cable (premium). Indoor pool; whirlpool. Complimentary continental bkfst. Ck-out 11 am. Coin Indry. Business servs avail. Downhill/x-country ski 20 mi. Some refrigerators. Balconies. Cr cds: A, C, D, DS, MC, V.

D SC

★ ★ ★ **DOUBLE TREE.** *3347 Cerrillos Rd (87505). 505/473-2800; FAX 505/473-4905.* E-mail dtreesf@rt66.com. 213 rms, 3 story. May-Oct: S, D $89-$139; each addl $10; under 12 free; ski rates; higher rates: Dec 25, Indian Market; lower rates rest of yr. Crib free. Pet accepted. TV; cable (premium). Indoor pool; whirlpools. Restaurant 7 am-1:30 pm, 5-9:30 pm.

Bar. Ck-out 11 am. Coin Indry. Meeting rms. Business center. In-rm modem link. Gift shop. Free airport transportation. Downhill/x-country ski 17 mi. Exercise equipt; weights, bicycles. Refrigerators; microwaves avail. Some private patios, balconies. Cr cds: A, C, D, DS, MC, V.

D SC

✔★ ★ **EL REY INN.** *1862 Cerrillos Rd (87502), I-25 Business Loop. 505/982-1931; FAX 505/989-9249.* 86 rms, 1-2 story, 7 kits. May-Oct: S, D $56-$130; each addl $12; kit. suites $98-$207. Crib free. TV; cable (premium). Pool; whirlpool. Playground. Complimentary continental bkfst. Restaurant nearby. Ck-out noon. Coin Indry. Business servs avail. Downhill/x-country ski 17 mi. Some fireplaces. Picnic tables. Cr cds: A, C, D, DS, MC, V.

D

★ **GARRETT'S DESERT INN.** *311 Old Santa Fe Trail (87501). 505/982-1851; FAX 505/989-1657; res: 800/888-2145.* 82 rms, 2 story. July & Aug: S, D $89-$99; suites $109; lower rates rest of yr. TV; cable. Heated pool. Restaurant 7 am-8 pm. Bar. Ck-out noon. Meeting rms. Business servs avail. Cr cds: A, C, D, DS, MC, V.

D

★ ★ **HOMEWOOD SUITES.** *400 Griffin St (87501). 505/988-3000; FAX 505/988-4700.* 105 kit. suites, 4 story. Mid-June-Oct: 1-bedrm $150-$170; 2-bedrm $255-$310; wkly, monthly rates; higher rates: Indian Market, hols; lower rates rest of yr. Crib free. Pet accepted; $150 deposit & $10/day. TV; cable, VCR (movies $5). Heated pool; whirlpools. Complimentary bkfst buffet. Complimentary coffee in rms. Restaurant nearby. Ck-out noon. Coin Indry. Meeting rms. Business center. In-rm modem link. Bellhops. Concierge. Exercise equipt; weights, bicycles. Microwaves. Many balconies. Picnic tables. Cr cds: A, C, D, DS, MC, V.

D SC

★ **HOWARD JOHNSON.** *4044 Cerrillos Rd (87505), 1 mi N of I-25 exit 278. 505/438-8950.* 47 rms, 2 story. Mid-May-Aug: S $54-$98; D $65-$120; each addl $6; under 18 free; lower rates rest of yr. Crib avail. TV; cable (premium). Complimentary continental bkfst. Restaurant adj 6:30 am-10 pm. Ck-out 11 am. Business servs avail. Downhill/x-country ski 20 mi. Near airport. Cr cds: A, D, DS, MC, V.

D SC

★ ★ ★ **INN ON THE ALAMEDA.** *303 E Alameda (87501), 2 blks from Plaza. 505/984-2121; FAX 505/986-8325; res: 800/289-2122.* 67 rms, 2-3 story. July-Oct: S, D $170-$350; each addl $15; suites $240-$350; lower rates rest of yr. Pet accepted. TV; cable (premium), VCR avail. Complimentary continental bkfst. Restaurant nearby. Bar 2:30-11 pm. Ck-out noon. Meeting rm. Business servs avail. In-rm modem link. Valet serv. Downhill/x-country ski 15 mi. Exercise equipt; weights, stair machine. Whirlpools. Massage. Health club privileges. Private patios, balconies. Library. Kiva fireplaces. Cr cds: A, C, D, DS, MC, V.

D

★ ★ **LA QUINTA.** *4298 Cerrillos Rd (Business Loop I-25) (87505). 505/471-1142; FAX 505/438-7219.* 130 rms, 3 story. Mid-May-late Oct: S, D $80-$90; each addl $8; suites $121; under 18 free; lower rates rest of yr. Crib free. Pet accepted. TV; cable (premium). Pool. Complimentary continental bkfst. Restaurant adj open 24 hrs. Ck-out noon. Coin Indry. Downhill/x-country ski 14 mi. Microwaves avail. Cr cds: A, C, D, DS, MC, V.

D SC

★ **LUXURY INN.** *3752 Cerrillos Rd (87505), 3 mi N of I-25 exit 278. 505/473-0567; res: 800/647-1346; FAX 505/471-9139.* E-mail luxury inn@travelbase.com. 51 rms, 2 story. May-Oct: S $35-$55; D $70-$90; under 10 free; wkly rates; ski plan; higher rates special events; lower rates rest of yr. Crib free. TV; cable (premium). Pool; whirlpool. Complimentary continental bkfst. Restaurant adj 11 am-9 pm. Ck-out 11 am. Cr cds: A, C, D, DS, JCB, MC, V.

D SC

✔★ **QUALITY INN.** *3011 Cerrillos Rd (I-25 Business Loop) (87501). 505/471-1211; FAX 505/438-9535.* 99 rms, 2 story. May-Oct: S $63-$90; D $70-$90; each addl $10; under 18 free; lower rates rest of yr. Crib free. Pet accepted, some restrictions. TV; cable (premium). Pool. Restaurant 7 am-9 pm. Rm serv. Ck-out noon. Meeting rm. Business servs avail. Airport transportation. Downhill/x-country ski 17 mi. Some refrigerators. Balconies. Cr cds: A, C, D, DS, ER, JCB, MC, V.

D SC

★ **RAMADA INN.** *2907 Cerrillos Rd (87505), 3 mi N of I-25 exit 278. 505/471-3000.* 101 rms, 2 story. Mid-June-Oct: S $80; D $90; each addl $5; under 17 free; ski plan; lower rates rest of yr. Crib free. Pet accepted. TV; cable (premium). Pool. Restaurant 7-10:30 am, 11 am-2 pm, 6-9 pm. Bar. Meeting rms. Business servs avail. Downhill/x-country ski 20 mi. Health club privileges. Game rm. Cr cds: A, C, D, DS, ER, JCB, MC, V.

D SC

★ ★ **RESIDENCE INN BY MARRIOTT.** *1698 Galisteo St (87501). 505/988-7300; FAX 505/988-3243.* Web www.marriott.com. 120 kit. suites, 2 story. June-late Oct: kit. suites $169; under 12 free; wkly, ski rates; lower rates rest of yr. Crib free. Pet accepted, some restrictions; $150 deposit & $10/day. TV; cable (premium). Heated pool; whirlpools. Complimentary continental bkfst. Ck-out noon. Coin Indry. Meeting rms. Business servs avail. In-rm modem link. Valet serv. Airport transportation. Downhill ski 16 mi. Some private patios, balconies. Picnic tables, grills. Cr cds: A, C, D, DS, JCB, MC, V.

D SC

✔★ **STAGE COACH.** *3360 Cerrillos Rd (I-25 Business Loop) (87505). 505/471-0707; FAX 505/473-1090.* 15 rms, 1-2 story. Mid-May-mid-Oct: S, D $49-$80; each addl $5; lower rates rest of yr. TV; cable (premium). Restaurant nearby. Ck-out 10 am. Downhill/x-country ski 20 mi. Picnic tables, grills. Cr cds: A, MC, V.

SC

Motor Hotels

★ ★ ★ **HILTON OF SANTA FE.** *100 Sandoval St (87501), just off Plaza, downtown. 505/988-2811; FAX 505/986-6439.* 158 rms, 3 story. Mid-June-Oct: S $139-$229; D $159-$249; each addl $20; suites $275-$675; family rates; ski packages; lower rates rest of yr. Crib free. TV; cable (premium), VCR avail (movies). Heated pool; whirlpool. Restaurants 6:30 am-midnight (also see PIÑON GRILL). Rm serv. Bar from 11 am. Ck-out noon. Meeting rms. Business servs avail. In-rm modem link. Bellhops. Concierge. Exercise equipt; weight machine, treadmill. Gift shop. Airport transportation. Downhill ski 15 mi. Minibars. Cr cds: A, C, D, DS, JCB, MC, V.

D SC

★ ★ **HOLIDAY INN.** *4048 Cerrillos Rd (I-25 Business Loop) (87501). 505/473-4646; FAX 505/473-2186.* 130 rms, 4 story. Mid-June-Sept: S $75-$135; D $85-$145; each addl $10; under 18 free; lower rates rest of yr. Crib free. Pet accepted, some restrictions. TV; cable (premium). Heated indoor/outdoor pool; whirlpool, poolside serv. Complimentary coffee in rms. Restaurant 6:30 am-10 pm. Rm serv. Bar from noon. Ck-out noon. Meeting rms. Business servs avail. In-rm modem link. Bellhops. Sundries. Airport, bus depot transportation. Downhill/x-country ski 20 mi. Exercise equipt; treadmill, weight machines, sauna. Refrigerator. Private patios, balconies. Cr cds: A, D, DS, JCB, MC, V.

D SC

★ ★ ★ **HOTEL LORETTO.** *211 Old Santa Fe Trail (87504), just off the plaza. 505/988-5531; FAX 505/984-7988.* 140 rms, 4 story. July-Aug: S $180-$210; D $195-$225; each addl $15; under 12 free; lower rates rest of yr. Crib free. TV; cable (premium), VCR avail. Coffee in rms. Heated pool; whirlpool, poolside serv. Restaurant 6:30 am-9 pm; dining rm from 5:30 pm. Rm serv. Bar 11-1 am; Sun noon-midnight. Ck-out noon. Guest Indry. Meeting rms. Business servs avail. Bellhops. Concierge. Shopping arcade. Barber, beauty shop. Massage. Downhill/x-country ski 15 mi.

Refrigerators. Private patios, balconies. Adobe building. Cr cds: A, C, D, DS, MC, V.

D SC

★ ★ **HOTEL PLAZA REAL.** *125 Washington Ave (87501), 1 blk north of plaza. 505/988-4900; FAX 505/983-9322; res: 800/279-REAL.* Web plazareal 6 rms, 3 story, 44 suites. June-Oct: S, D $159-$249; each addl $15; suites $249-$475; under 12 free; ski plans; lower rates rest of yr. Garage parking $10. TV; cable (premium). Complimentary continental bkfst. Restaurant adj 9 am-6 pm. Bar 3-11 pm. Ck-out noon. Meeting rms. Business servs avail. In-rm modem link. Bellhops. Concierge. Health club privileges. Downhill/x-country ski 15 mi. Wet bar in suites. Refrigerators. Some balconies. Territorial-style architecture; fireplaces, handcrafted Southwestern furniture. Cr cds: A, D, DS, MC, V.

D SC

★ ★ ★ **HOTEL SANTA FE.** *1501 Paseo de Peralta (87501), at Cerrillos Rd. 505/982-1200; FAX 505/984-2211; res: 800/825-9876.* E-mail hotelsf@newmexico.com; web www.hotelsf.com/guest. 131 rms, 3 story, 91 suites. Late June-Aug: S, D $109-$139; suites $149-$199; under 17 free; ski plans; lower rates rest of yr. Crib free. TV; cable (premium). Pool; whirlpool. Restaurant (see CORN DANCE CAFE). Bar 4 pm-midnight; entertainment Fri, Sat. Ck-out noon. Coin Indry. Meeting rms. Business servs avail. Bellhops. Valet serv. Concierge. Gift shop. Airport transportation. Downhill/x-country ski 10 mi. Health club privileges. Minibars. Balconies. Pueblo-revival architecture; original art by Native Americans. A Native American enterprise. Cr cds: A, C, D, DS, MC, V.

D SC

★ ★ ★ **INN OF THE GOVERNORS.** *234 Don Gaspar Ave (87501). 505/982-4333; FAX 505/989-9149; res: 800/234-4534.* Web www.inn-gov.com. 100 rms, 2-3 story. S, D $109-$257; each addl $10; under 18 free. Crib free. TV; cable. Pool. Restaurant (see MAÑANA). Rm serv. Bar 11:30 am-midnight; Sun from noon; entertainment. Ck-out noon. Meeting rm. Business servs avail. In-rm modem link. Bellhops. Concierge. Downhill/x-country ski 14 mi. Some minibars, fireplaces. Balconies. Cr cds: A, C, D, DS, MC, V.

D SC

★ ★ ★ **LA POSADA DE SANTA FE.** *330 E Palace Ave (87501), 2 blks from Plaza. 505/986-0000; FAX 505/982-6850; res: 800/727-5276.* E-mail zinalapo@roadrunner.com; web www.travelbase.com/destinations/santa-fe/la-posada. 119 rms, 1-2 story. May-Oct & hols: S, D $115-$330; suites $195-$395; under 12 free; package plans; lower rates rest of yr. Crib $5. TV; cable (premium). Pool; poolside serv. Restaurant (see STAAB HOUSE). Rm serv. Bar 11 am-midnight; Sun noon-11 pm. Ck-out noon. Meeting rms. Business servs avail. Concierge. Bellhops. Beauty shop. Downhill/x-country ski 15 mi. Many fireplaces. Adobe casitas surround Victorian/Second Empire Staab Mansion (1882); guest rms either pueblo revival or Victorian in style. On 6 acres; gardens. Cr cds: A, C, D, DS, MC, V.

D SC

★ ★ ★ **RADISSON.** *750 N St Francis Dr (87501), US 84, 285. 505/982-5591; FAX 505/988-2821.* Web www.radisson.com. 161 rms, 2 story. May-Dec: S, D, studio rms $139; each addl $20; suites $169-$434; ski packages; lower rates rest of yr. TV; cable (premium). Heated pool; poolside serv. Restaurant 6:30 am-10 am, 11:30 am-2 pm, 6-10 pm. Rm serv. Bar noon-midnight; entertainment. Ck-out noon. Meeting rms. Business servs avail. Bellhops. Free RR station, bus depot transportation. Downhill/x-country ski 18 mi. Health club privileges. Cr cds: A, C, D, DS, JCB, MC, V.

D SC

★ ★ ★ **ST FRANCIS.** *210 Don Gaspar Ave (87501). 505/983-5700; FAX 505/989-7690; res: 800/529-5700.* E-mail hst@ix.netcom.com. 83 rms, 3 story. May-Oct: S, D $98-$188; each addl $15; suites $228-$353; under 12 free; lower rates rest of yr. Crib free. TV; cable. Tea 3-5:30 pm. Restaurant 7-10 am, 11:30 am-2 pm, 5:30-10 pm; wkends 7 am-2 pm. Rm serv. Bar noon-midnight. Ck-out 11 am. Meeting rms. Business servs avail. In-rm modem link. Concierge. Downhill ski 15 mi. Refrigerators. European ambience; antiques, original artwork. Cr cds: A, C, D, DS, MC, V.

D SC

Hotels

★ ★ ★ ★ **ELDORADO.** *309 W San Francisco (87501), 2 blks from the Plaza. 505/988-4455; FAX 505/988-5376; res: 800/955-4455.* E-mail res@eldoradohotel.com; web www.eldoradohotel.com. In this Pueblo revival-style hotel in the town's historic district, all the chic Southwestern guest rooms have views of the Santa Fe mountains. 219 rms, 5 story. S, D $169-$309; suites $280-$750; under 18 free. Crib free. Garage parking $9. Pet accepted. TV; cable (premium), VCR avail (movies). Rooftop pool; whirlpool, poolside serv. Restaurant 7 am-9:30 pm (also see THE OLD HOUSE). Bar 11:30-2 am; entertainment. Ck-out 11:30 am. Convention facilities. Business center. In-rm modem link. Concierge. Shopping arcade. Barber, beauty shop. Downhill ski 12 mi; x-country ski 7 mi. Exercise rm; instructor, weight machine, treadmill, sauna. Massage. Refrigerators, minibars. Balconies. Cr cds: A, C, D, DS, MC, V.

D SC

★ ★ ★ ★ **INN OF THE ANASAZI.** *113 Washington Ave (87501), just off the Plaza, in the historic Plaza District. 505/988-3030; FAX 505/988-3277; res: 800/688-8100.* Web www.innoftheanasazi.com. This sophisticated adobe hotel one block from the Plaza embodies Santa Fe style. Contained within are native and Southwestern art and artifacts, four-poster beds and kiva fireplaces in the guest rooms. 59 units, 3 story. Apr-Oct: S, D $235-$395; each addl $20; under 12 free; lower rates rest of yr. Crib free. Valet parking $10/day. Pet accepted, some restrictions; $30. TV; cable (premium), VCR (movies $5). Complimentary coffee in rms. Restaurant (see THE ANASAZI). Ck-out noon. Business servs avail. Concierge. Tennis privileges. 18-hole golf privileges, putting green, driving range. Downhill ski 13 mi; x-country ski 7 mi. Exercise equipt; treadmill, bicycle. Massage. Health club privileges. Microwaves avail. Cr cds: A, C, D, DS, ER, JCB, MC, V.

D SC

Inns

★ ★ **ADOBE ABODE.** *202 Chapelle (87501). 505/983-3133; FAX 505/986-0972.* E-mail adobe@sprynet.com. 6 rms, 3 with shower only. S $100-$140; D $110-$150; each addl $15; suite $140-$150. TV; cable (premium). Complimentary full bkfst. Ck-out 11 am, ck-in 2 pm. Luggage handling. Individually decorated rms with antiques from all over the world. Cr cds: DS, MC, V.

D

★ ★ ★ **ALEXANDER'S INN.** *529 E Palace Ave (87501). 505/986-1431.* E-mail alexander@aol.com; web www.collectorsguide.com/alexandinn. 9 rms, 2 share bath, 2 with shower only, 2 story. Mid-Mar-mid-Nov: S, D $85-$160; each addl $20; higher rates: Indian Market, Dec 25; lower rates rest of yr. Pet accepted, some restrictions. TV; cable, VCR avail. Whirlpool. Complimentary continental bkfst; afternoon refreshments. Ck-out 11 am, ck-in by arrangement. Business servs avail. Luggage handling. Concierge serv. Downhill ski 17 mi; x-country ski 10 mi. Health club privileges. Five rms in renovated house built 1903. Totally nonsmoking. Cr cds: MC, V.

★ ★ **DANCING GROUND OF THE SUN.** *711 Paseo de Peralta (87501). 505/986-9797; FAX 505/986-8082; res: 800/645-5673.* 5 casitas, 5 kit. units, 2 story. May-Oct: S, D $95-$160; each addl $20; lower rates rest of yr. TV; cable. Complimentary continental bkfst. Complimentary coffee in rms. Restaurant nearby. Ck-out 11 am, ck-in 3-6 pm. Business servs avail. Concierge serv. Microwaves. Balconies.

Most rms with Native American theme. Totally nonsmoking. Cr cds: MC, V.

D

★ ★ ★ **DOS CASAS VIEJAS.** *610 Agua Fria St (87501), 2 blks SW off Guadalupe. 505/983-1636; FAX 505/983-1749.* 7 rms, 1 suite. No A/C. D $165-$235; suite $165-$245. TV; cable (premium). Heated pool. Complimentary continental bkfst. Coffee in rms. Restaurant nearby. Ck-out noon, ck-in 3-6 pm. Business servs avail. Refrigerators. Two historical buildings in a 1/2-acre walled compound; renovated to restore 1860s architecture. Mexican tiled floors and wood-burning kiva fireplaces. Totally nonsmoking. Cr cds: MC, V.

D

✔★ ★ **EL PARADERO.** *220 W Manhattan (87501), near Capitol. 505/988-1177.* Web www.nets.com/santafe/elparadero/index.html. 12 rms, 2 kit. suites. Apr-Oct: S $60-$130; D $70-$130; each addl $15; kit. suites $130; lower rates rest of yr. Children over 4 yrs only. Pet accepted. TV in sitting rm; cable in suites. Complimentary full bkfst. Restaurant nearby. Ck-out 11 am, ck-in 2 pm. Downhill ski 18 mi; x-country ski 9 mi. Balconies. Renovated Spanish adobe house (ca 1820) with details from 1880 & 1912 remodelings. Library/sitting rm; skylights, fireplaces, antiques. Cr cds: MC, V.

★ ★ ★ **GALISTEO INN.** *(9 La Vega, Galisteo 87540) approx 23 mi S; S on US 285, then S on NM 41. 505/466-4000; FAX 505/466-4008.* E-mail Galisteoin@aol.com. 12 rms, 4 share bath. No A/C. No rm phones. S $65-$185; D $110-$185; each addl $20. Closed 5 wks Jan-Feb. Children over 6 yrs only. 4 TVs. Pool; whirlpool. Sauna. Complimentary full bkfst. Complimentary coffee. Restaurant Wed-Sun 6-8:30 pm. Ck-out noon, ck-in 4 pm. Business servs avail. Hacienda on 8 acres built in 1750s. Totally nonsmoking. Cr cds: DS, MC, V.

D SC

★ ★ ★ **GRANT CORNER.** *122 Grant Ave (87501). 505/983-6678; FAX 505/984-9003.* 12 rms, 2 share bath, 3 story. June-Oct: S, D $80-$155; each addl $20. Children over 8 yrs only. TV; cable. Complimentary full bkfst; afternoon refreshments. Restaurant nearby. Rm serv. Ck-out noon, ck-in 2-6 pm. Business servs avail. Downhill/x-country ski 15 mi. Colonial manor house built 1905; antiques. Massage. Totally nonsmoking. Cr cds: MC, V.

D

★ ★ ★ **GUADALUPE.** *604 Agua Fria (87501), near La Tertuliana. 505/989-7422.* Web www.guadalupeinn.com. 12 rms, 2 story. Mid-Apr-mid-Jan: S, D $125-$175; each addl $15; wkend rates; 4-day min Indian Market; lower rates rest of yr. Crib. TV; cable (premium). Whirlpool. Complimentary full bkfst. Restaurant adj. Ck-out 11 am, ck-in 3-6 pm. Concierge. Business servs avail. Downhill ski 15 mi; x-country ski 10 mi. Balconies. Picnic tables. Individually decorated rms. Totally nonsmoking. Cr cds: A, DS, MC, V.

D

★ ★ **INN OF THE ANIMAL TRACKS.** *707 Paseo de Peralta (87501), east of the plaza. 505/988-1546.* 5 rms. S, D $90-$130; each addl $20. TV; cable (premium). Complimentary full bkfst. Restaurant nearby. Ck-out noon, ck-in 4 pm. Business servs avail. Downhill/x-country ski 15 mi. Picnic tables. In 1890 adobe house; fireplaces. Guest rms overlook tree-shaded lawn, garden. Totally nonsmoking. Cr cds: A, MC, V.

D

★ ★ ★ **INN ON THE PASEO.** *630 Paseo de Peralto (87501). 505/984-8200; FAX 505/989-3979; res: 800/457-9045.* 18 rms, 2-3 story. July-Oct: S, D $75-$155; suite $155; 2-day min summer wkends, Indian market. TV; cable (premium). Complimentary bkfst buffet; afternoon refreshments. Restaurant nearby. Ck-out 11 am, ck-in 3 pm. Business servs avail. Sun decks. Totally nonsmoking. Cr cds: A, D, MC, V.

D

★ ★ ★ **LA TIENDA INN.** *445-447 W San Francisco St (87501). 505/989-8259; res: 800/8897611; FAX 505/820-6931.* Web www.latiend abb. com/inn/. 7 rms. S, D $90-$160. Adults only. TV; cable (premium). Complimentary continental bkfst. Restaurant nearby. Ck-out 11 am, ck-in 3-6 pm. Luggage handling. Concierge serv. Downhill/x-country ski 17 mi. Territorial house built ca 1900 has 3 rms; 4 rms in Old Store adobe wing. Totally nonsmoking. Cr cds: MC, V.

D

★ ★ ★ **PRESTON HOUSE.** *106 Faithway St (87501), 4 blks E of the plaza. 505/982-3465; FAX 505/982-3465.* 15 rms, 2 with shower only, 3 story, 2 suites. Some A/C. Mar-Oct, hols: S, D $75-$160; each addl $20; suites $165-$167; lower rates rest of yr. Pet accepted, some restrictions. TV. Complimentary continental bkfst; afternoon refreshments. Restaurant nearby. Ck-out 11 am, ck-in 3 pm. Business servs avail. Downhill/x-country ski 17 mi. Some fireplaces. Queen Anne house (1886) with antique furnishings and sitting rm. Totally nonsmoking. Cr cds: A, MC, V.

✔★ ★ **PUEBLO BONITO.** *138 W Manhattan (87501), near Capitol. 505/984-8001; FAX 505/984-3155.* Web www.travelbase.com/destinations/santafe/pueblo. 18 rms, 1-2 story, 7 suites, 6 kits. No A/C. May-Oct: S $90; D $95-$140; each addl $10; suites, kit. units $140; lower rates rest of yr. TV; cable. Whirlpool. Complimentary continental bkfst. Restaurant nearby. Ck-out noon, ck-in 2 pm. Downhill/x-country ski 18 mi. Fireplaces. Some balconies. Renovated adobe casitas on 1880s estate; private courtyards, gardens, mature trees. Antique furnishings, baskets. Cr cds: MC, V.

D

★ ★ **SPENCER HOUSE.** *222 McKenzie (87501). 505/988-3024; res: 800/647-0530.* 5 air-cooled rms. May-Oct: S, D $100-$150; lower rates rest of yr. Children over 12 yrs only. TV; cable (premium). Complimentary full bkfst. Restaurant nearby. Ck-out 10:30 am, ck-in 4-6 pm. Luggage handling. Downhill/x-country ski 15 mi. Country cottage atmosphere with antiques from England, Ireland and Wales. Cr cds: A, MC, V.

★ ★ ★ **TERRITORIAL INN.** *215 Washington Ave (87501), 1 blk from plaza. 505/989-7737; FAX 505/986-9212.* E-mail smalwood@santafehotels.com. 10 rms, 2 with shower only, 2 story. S, D $80-$160; each addl $20. Children over 10 yrs only. TV; cable (premium). Complimentary continental bkfst; evening refreshments. Restaurant nearby. Ck-out 11 am, ck-in 3 pm. Business servs avail. Downhill/x-country ski 15 mi. Health club privileges. Whirlpool. Some fireplaces. House (ca 1895) blends New Mexico's stone & adobe architecture with pitched roof, Victorian-style interior; sitting rm, antiques; garden and tree-shaded lawns more typical of buildings in the East. Cr cds: A, D, MC, V.

★ ★ ★ **WATER STREET INN.** *427 W Water St (87501), downtown. 505/984-1193.* 11 rms. S, D $125-$195; each addl $15. TV; cable, VCR (movies $3). Whirlpool. Complimentary continental bkfst in rms. Restaurant nearby. Ck-out 11 am, ck-in 2-6 pm. Business servs avail. In-rm modem links. Downhill/x-country ski 17 mi. Restored adobe building; fireplaces, antique stoves. Totally nonsmoking. Cr cds: A, DS, MC, V.

D

Guest Ranches

★ ★ ★ ★ **BISHOP'S LODGE.** *Bishop's Lodge Rd (87504), 3 mi N of the Plaza. 505/983-6377; FAX 505/989-8739; res: 800/732-2240.* E-mail bishopslodge@nets.com; web www.bishopslodge.com. Nestled in a secluded valley in the foothills of the Sangre de Cristo Mountains, this all-season lodge offers 1,000 acres of amenities, including riding stables, tennis courts and hiking trails. Rooms are individually decorated, some with kiva fireplaces and private patios. 88 rms in 1-3-story lodges. No elvtr. June-early Sept: S, D $165-$431; each addl $15-$53; lower rates rest of yr. TV; cable (premium), VCR avail. Heated pool; whirlpool, poolside serv, lifeguard. Playground. Supervised child's activities (June-Sept); ages 4-12. Dining rm 7:30 am-9 pm. Child's dining rm. Rm serv. Box lunches, picnics. Bar 11:30 am-midnight; Sun from noon. Ck-out noon, ck-in mid-late afternoon. Business servs avail. In-rm modem link. Concierge. Sports dir. Tennis, pro. 18-hole golf privileges. Stocked pond. Fishing pond for children. Downhill/x-country ski 18 mi. Skeet, trap shooting; pro. Riding instruction; bkfst & lunch rides; children's rides. Lawn games. Exercise equipt; stair machine, bicycles, sauna. Soc dir; entertainment. Rec rm. Many refrigerators; some fireplaces. Some private patios. Cr cds: A, D, DS, MC, V.

D

★ ★ ★ **RANCHO ENCANTADO.** *(87501). N on US 285 to North Tesuque exit, SE on NM 592 to ranch. 505/982-3537; FAX 505/983-8269; res: 800/722-9339.* Web www.nmhotels.com/html/sfranchencantado.html. 87 units, 16 cottages. Late June-mid-Oct: S, D $175-$375; each addl $10; cottages $210-$250; ski plan; lower rates rest of yr. Crib avail. TV. Pool; whirlpool. Complimentary coffee in rms. Dining rm 7:30-10:30 am, 11:30 am-2 pm, 5:30-10 pm. Box lunches. Picnics. Bar 4-10 pm. Ck-out 11 am, ck-in 3 pm. Gift shop. Grocery 3 mi. Coin Indry 8 mi. Bellhops. Meeting rm. Business servs avail. Tennis; pro. X-country ski 12 mi. Hiking trails. Minibars. Picnic tables. Cr cds: A, C, D, DS, MC, V.

D SC

Restaurants

★ ★ ★ ★ **THE ANASAZI.** *(See Inn of the Anasazi Hotel) 505/988-3236.* Web innoftheanasazi.com. Stone walls, a beamed ceiling, artwork and antiques set the scene for innovative takes on local and regional cuisine. Southwestern menu. Specialties: tortilla soup, fresh fish, cinnamon chile with mango salsa. Menu changes seasonally. Hrs: 7-10:30 am, 11:30 am-2:30 pm, 5:30-10 pm; Sun brunch 7 am-2:30 pm. Res accepted. Bar 11 am-midnight. Wine cellar. A la carte entrees: bkfst $5.25-$9.50, lunch $4-$12.75, dinner $6.50-$29. Sun brunch $6-$12.75. Child's meals. Classical guitarist (brunch). Cr cds: A, C, D, DS, ER, JCB, MC, V.

D

★ ★ **ANDIAMO.** *322 Garfield (87501). 505/995-9595.* Hrs: 5:30-9 pm. Closed Tues. Res accepted. Italian menu. Wine, beer. Semi-a la carte: dinner $12.50-$16.50. Child's meals. Specializes in pasta. Outdoor dining. Three dining areas. Contemporary decor. Totally nonsmoking. Cr cds: DS, MC, V.

D

★ ★ **BABBO GANZO.** *130 Lincoln Ave, in Lincoln Place shopping mall. 505/986-3835.* Hrs: 11:30 am-2 pm, 5:30-10 pm; Sun from 5:30 pm. Res accepted. Northern Italian menu. Bar. A la carte entrees: lunch $5.25-$9.75, dinner $9.25-$24. Complete meals: lunch, dinner $12-$35. Specializes in classic Tuscan dishes, fresh fish, free range veal. Own pasta. Tuscan trattoria decor; murals. Located on upper level of building. Cr cds: A, MC, V.

D

★ ★ ★ **BISTRO 315.** *315 Old Santa Fe Trail (87501). 505/986-9190.* Hrs: 11:30 am-2 pm, 5:30-9:30 pm. Closed major hols. Res accepted. French, Amer menu. Wine, beer. Semi-a la carte: lunch $5-$12, dinner $6-$23. Specialties: steak frites, pâte. Outdoor dining. Contemporary decor. Cr cds: A, MC, V.

D

✔★ **BLUE CORN CAFE.** *133 Water St, on 2nd floor. 505/984-1800.* Hrs: 11 am-11 pm. Closed Jan 1, Thanksgiving, Dec 25. Mexican menu. Bar to 12:30 am. Semi-a la carte: lunch, dinner $5.95-$8.95. Child's meals. Specialties: chile rellenos, fajitas, enchiladas. Southwestern decor; fireplace. Cr cds: A, C, D, DS, MC, V.

D

★ ★ **CAFE PASQUAL'S.** *121 Don Gaspar, just off the plaza. 505/983-9340.* E-mail pasquals@nets.com. Hrs: 7 am-3 pm, 6-10:30 pm; Sun brunch 8 am-2 pm. Closed Thanksgiving, Dec 25. Res accepted. New Mexican, Amer menu. Wine, beer. Semi-a la carte: bkfst $4.75-$13.10, lunch $7.95-$10.75, dinner $14.75-$26. Sun brunch $7.95-$10.75. Specialties: grilled salmon burrito, char-grilled chicken quesadillas, char-grilled rack of lamb. Hand-painted murals; festive Old Santa Fe decor. Totally nonsmoking. Cr cds: A, MC, V.

✔★ ★ **CELEBRATIONS.** *618 Canyon Rd (87501). 505/989-8904.* Hrs: 7:30 am-2:30 pm, 5:30-9:30 pm; Wed, Thurs to 9 pm; Sun brunch 11 am-2:30 pm. Closed Jan 1, Thanksgiving, Dec 25. Res accepted. Continental menu. Bar. Semi-a la carte: bkfst $3.95-$7.95, lunch $4.75-$7.95, dinner $6.95-$13.95. Sun brunch $5.95-$9.95. Specializes in American bistro dishes, New Orleans dishes, rack of lamb. Outdoor dining. 3 dining areas; fireplaces. Cr cds: MC, V.

D

★ **CHOW'S.** *720 St Michaels Dr (87501). 505/471-7120.* Hrs: 11:30 am-2 pm, 5-9 pm; Sat noon-3 pm, 5-9 pm. Closed Sun. Res accepted. Chinese menu. Wine, beer. A la carte entrees: lunch, dinner $2.95-$15.95. Specialty: green bean chicken. Outdoor dining. Contemporary Chinese decor. Cr cds: MC, V.

★ **CORN DANCE CAFE.** *(See Hotel Santa Fe Motor Hotel) 505/982-1200.* Hrs: 11:30 am-2 pm, 5:30-9 pm. Closed Sun, Mon. Res accepted. Native Amer menu. Bar to 10 pm; Sun, Mon from 4 pm; Fri, Sat to 11 pm. Semi-a la carte: lunch, dinner $6.25-$21.95. Specialties: little big pies, buffalo rib eye steak, Potawatomi prairie chicken. Own baking. Outdoor dining. Southwestern decor; large fireplace; Native American art and artifacts. Totally nonsmoking. Cr cds: A, D, DS, MC, V.

D

★ ★ ★ **COYOTE CAFE.** *132 W Water St, off the plaza. 505/983-1615.* Hrs: 5:30-9:45 pm; Sat, Sun 11 am-1:45 pm, 5:30-9:45 pm. Southwestern menu. Bar/cantina (May-Oct) 11:30 am-9:45 pm. A la carte entrees: lunch $7-$13, dinner $39.50. Specialties: cowboy rib chop, caesar salad, griddled corn cakes with shrimp. Outdoor dining on rooftop cantina. Adobe structure; Southwestern decor; fireplace. View of mountains. Cr cds: A, C, D, DS, MC, V.

D

★ ★ **EL NIDO.** *(Bishop's Lodge Rd, Tesuque 87574) 6 mi N on 285 to NM 591. 505/988-4340.* Hrs: 5:30-9:30 pm; Fri, Sat to 10 pm; Sun from 6 pm. Closed Mon; Jan 1, Thanksgiving, Dec 25; also Super Bowl Sun. Res accepted. Bar. Semi-a la carte: dinner $8.95-$24.95. Specializes in fresh seafood, beef, lamb. 1920 adobe building; fireplaces. Folk art of Tesuque Village. Cr cds: A, MC, V.

✔★ ★ **GABRIEL'S.** *Rte 11, Box 5 (87501), 20 mi NW on I-285. 505/455-7000.* Hrs: 11:30 am-9 pm; Fri, Sat to 10 pm; Sun brunch to 3 pm. Closed Thanksgiving, Dec 25. Res accepted. Southwestern, Mexican menu. Bar. Semi-a la carte: lunch $5.25-$10.25, dinner $6.95-$15.50. Sun brunch $8.50-$9.95. Child's meals. Specialties: guacamole, pato carnitas, rellenos de Santa Fe. Outdoor dining. Adobe bldg has four dining areas, two large fireplaces; Southwestern decor. Cr cds: A, D, MC, V.

D

✔★ **GARDUÑO'S.** *130 Lincoln Ave, 2nd fl. 505/983-9797.* Hrs: 11 am-10 pm; Fri, Sat to 10:30 pm; Sun 10:30 am-10 pm; Sun brunch to 3 pm. Closed Thanksgiving, Dec 25. Mexican menu. Bar. Semi-a la carte: lunch $5.50-$12.95, dinner $6.50-$13.95. Sun brunch $10.95. Child's meals. Specializes in chimichangas, fajitas, seafood. Entertainment. Southwestern decor. Family-owned. Cr cds: A, C, D, DS, MC, V.

D SC

★ ★ ★ **GERONIMO.** *724 Canyon Rd (87501). 505/982-1500.* Hrs: 11:30 am-2:30 pm, 6-10 pm; Mon from 6 pm. Res accepted. Bar to midnight. Semi-a la carte: lunch $8-$15.50, dinner $17.50-$30. Specializes in Southwestern fare. Outdoor dining. Historic adobe house (1753). Cr cds: A, MC, V.

D

★ ★ **IL PIATTO.** *95 W Marcy (87501). 505/984-1091.* Hrs: 11:30 am-2 pm, 5:30-9:30 pm. Closed Jan 1, Thanksgiving, Dec 25; also Super

Bowl Sun. Res accepted. Italian menu. Semi-a la carte: lunch $4-$15, dinner $5-$15. Specializes in fresh pasta. Country Italian kitchen theme. Cr cds: A, MC, V.

D

★ ★ **INDIA PALACE.** *227 Don Gaspar (87501). 505/986-5859.* E-mail indiapalace@dsrt.com. Hrs: 11:30 am-2:30 pm, 5-10 pm. Closed Super Bowl Sun. East Indian menu. Wine, beer. Lunch buffet $6.95. A la carte entrees: lunch, dinner $6.95-$24.95. Specializes in Tandoori dishes. Outdoor dining. Indian decor. Cr cds: A, D, DS, MC, V.

D

★ ★ ★ **JULIAN'S.** *221 Shelby St, just off the plaza. 505/988-2355.* E-mail julians221@aol.com. Hrs: 5:30-10 pm. Closed Thanksgiving. Res accepted. Italian menu. Bar. Semi-a la carte: dinner $12-$24. Specialties: pollo al agro dolci, gamberi alla marinara, piccata di vitello. Outdoor dining. Fine art; etched-glass windows; 2 fireplaces. Elegant Italian ambience. Cr cds: A, C, D, DS, MC, V.

★ ★ ★ **LA CASA SENA.** *125 E Palace Ave (87501), at Sena Plaza. 505/988-9232.* Hrs: 11:30 am-3 pm, 5:30-10 pm. Closed Thanksgiving, Dec 25. Res accepted. No A/C. Southwestern menu. Bar. Wine cellar. Semi-a la carte: lunch $7.75-$10, dinner $18-$23. Own baking. Singing waitstaff. Outdoor dining. Hacienda-style adobe built 1831; Southwestern art; large courtyard with fountain, greenery. Cr cds: A, D, DS, MC, V.

★ ★ ★ **LA TERTULIA DE SANTA FE.** *416 Agua Fria St. 505/988-2769.* Hrs: 11:30 am-2 pm, 5-9:30 pm; Sept-May to 9 pm. Closed Mon; major hols; also 1st wk Dec. Res accepted. New Mexican, Amer menu. Serv bar. Semi-a la carte: lunch $6-$9, dinner $8-$22. Child's meals. Specialties: chiles rellenos, carne adovada, pollo adovo. Elegant Spanish decor; Spanish-colonial art collection. Garden rm & outdoor garden area. Located in restored area of 18th-century convent. Cr cds: A, C, D, DS, MC, V.

D

★ ★ **LITTLE ANITA'S.** *2811 Cerrillos (87501). 505/473-4505.* Hrs: 6:30 am-9 pm. Closed Thanksgiving, Dec 24, 25. Mexican menu. Wine, beer. Semi-a la carte: bkfst $2.75-$5.95, lunch, dinner $5.25-$8. Child's meals. Specialties: chimichanga, fajitas. Southwestern decor. Cr cds: A, MC, V.

D

★ ★ **MAÑANA.** *(See Inn of the Governors Motor Hotel) 505/982-4333.* E-mail www.inn-gov.com. Hrs: 6:30 am-10 pm. Res accepted. Southwestern menu. Bar. A la carte entrees: bkfst $3.75-$6.75, lunch $4.75-$15.25, dinner $4.75-$15.25. Child's meals. Specializes in woodfired pizza, woodroasted salmon, blue corn pancakes. Pianist, vocalist. Patio dining. Two dining rms. Cr cds: A, C, D, DS, MC, V.

D

★ ★ **MARIA'S KITCHEN.** *555 W Cordova Rd (87501). 505/983-7929.* Hrs: 11 am-10 pm; Sat, Sun from noon. Closed Thanksgiving, Dec 25. Res accepted. Bar. Semi-a la carte: lunch $4.95-$8.95, dinner $7.25-$15.75. Child's meals. Specialties: tortillas, magaritas. Extensive Mexican beer selection. Patio dining. Original art. Cr cds: A, C, D, DS, MC, V.

★ **MONROE'S.** *727 Cerrillos Rd (87501). 505/989-7575.* Hrs: 9 am-9 pm. Closed July 4, Thanksgiving, Dec 25. Mexican menu. Wine, beer. Semi-a la carte: bkfst $2.10-$7.75, lunch $4.75-$9.50, dinner $7.15-$9.50. Child's meals. Specializes in blue corn enchiladas. Patio dining. Family-owned. Cr cds: A, D, DS, MC, V.

D

★ **NATURAL CAFE.** *1494 Cerrillos Rd (87505). 505/983-1411.* Hrs: 11:30 am-2:30 pm, 5-9:30 pm; Sat, Sun from 5 pm. Closed Mon; Dec 25. Res accepted. Southwestern menu. Semi-a la carte: lunch $4.75-$8.50, dinner $8.50-$16. Child's meals. Specialties: New Mexican polenta, Szechuan chicken, grilled salmon. Entertainment. Patio dining. Totally nonsmoking. Cr cds: DS, MC, V.

D

★ ★ ★ **THE OLD HOUSE.** *(See Eldorado Hotel) 505/988-4455.* Hrs: 5:30-10 pm. Closed Mon. Res accepted. Southwestern menu. Bar. Wine list. Semi-a la carte: dinner $16.95-$26.95. Specializes in Southwestern cuisine. Valet parking. Intimate dining in elegant surroundings. Contemporary Southwestern decor. Cr cds: A, C, D, DS, MC, V.

D

★ **OLD MEXICO GRILL.** *2434 Cerrillos Rd (87501). 505/473-0338.* Hrs: 11:30 am-2:30 pm, 5:30-9 pm; Fri to 9:30 pm; Sat, Sun 5:30-9 pm. Closed major hols; also Super Bowl Sun. Mexican menu. Bar. A la carte entrees: lunch $6.95-$10.75, dinner $9.50-$17.95. Specializes in fajitas, taco al carbon, steaks. Cr cds: DS, MC, V.

D

★ ★ **ORE HOUSE.** *50 Lincoln Ave, on the plaza. 505/983-8687.* Hrs: 5:30-10 pm; Sun noon-2:30 pm; hrs may vary mid-May-Oct. Closed Thanksgiving, Dec 25. Res accepted. Bar to 1 am; entertainment Fri-Sun. Semi-a la carte: dinner $14-$22. Child's meals. Specializes in steak, seafood, rack of lamb. Outdoor dining (lunch). Plaza view. Cr cds: A, MC, V.

✔★ ★ **OSTERIA D'ASSISI.** *58 S Federal Place (87501). 505/986-5858.* Hrs: 11 am-9 pm; Fri, Sat to 10 pm. Closed Sun; Jan 1, Dec 25. Res accepted. Italian menu. Wine, beer. Semi-a la carte: lunch $3.95-$9.75, dinner $6-$16. Specializes in pasta, pizza, panini. Outdoor dining. Country decor. Totally nonsmoking. Cr cds: A, D, MC, V.

★ ★ ★ **PALACE.** *142 W Palace Ave, just off the plaza. 505/982-9891.* Hrs: 11:30 am-4 pm, 5:45-10 pm; Sun from 5:45 pm. Closed Dec 25. Res accepted. Continental, Italian menu. Bar from 11:30 am. Semi-a la carte: lunch $4.50-$12, dinner $10.50-$24. Specializes in New Mexican lamb, seafood, pasta. Pianist. Patio dining. Turn-of-the-century Victorian decor. Cr cds: A, C, D, DS, MC, V.

D

★ ★ ★ **PAUL'S.** *72 W Marcy St (87501). 505/892-8738.* Hrs: 11:30 am-2 pm, 5:30-9 pm. Closed July 4, Dec 25. Res accepted. Wine, beer. Semi-a la carte: lunch $4.95-$8.95, dinner $13.95-$19.95. Specializes in duck, seafood, lamb. Contemporary decor. Totally nonsmoking. Cr cds: A, DS, MC, V.

D

★ ★ **PIÑON GRILL.** *(See Hilton of Santa Fe Motor Hotel) 505/986-6400.* Hrs: 5-10 pm. Res accepted. Bar. A la carte entrees: dinner $12-$19. Child's meals. Specializes in grilled steaks, fish, free range poultry. High-beamed, mission-style ceilings; Native American artifacts. Cr cds: A, C, D, DS, MC, V.

D

★ ★ **PINK ADOBE.** *406 Old Santa Fe Trail (US 84, 85, 285), just off the plaza. 505/983-7712.* Hrs: 11:30 am-2:30 pm, 5:30-10 pm; Sat, Sun from 5:30 pm. Closed major hols. Res accepted. Some A/C. Bar. New Mexican, continental menu. Semi-a la carte: lunch $6.50-$8.50, dinner $10.25-$22.25. Specialties: porc Napoleone, poulet Marengo, steak Dunigan. Entertainment Tues-Thurs, Sat. Fireplace in dining rms. Historic pink adobe building ca 1700. Family-owned. Cr cds: A, C, D, DS, MC, V.

D

★ ★ **PRANZO GRILL.** *540 Montezuma. 505/984-2645.* E-mail ravioli@roadrunner.com. Hrs: 11:30 am-3 pm, 5 pm-midnight; Sun from 5 pm. Closed July 4, Thanksgiving, Dec 25. Res accepted. Italian menu. Bar noon-midnight. Semi-a la carte: lunch $5.95-$9.35, dinner $5.95-$19.95. Specialties: cioppino, pizza, osso bucco Milanese. Outdoor dining. Contemporary decor. Cr cds: A, C, D, DS, MC, V.

D

★ ★ **RISTRA.** *548 Agua Fria (87501). 505/982-8608.* Hrs: 5:30-9:30 pm; Fri, Sat to 10 pm. Res accepted. French, Southwestern menu. Wine, beer. Semi-a la carte: dinner $12-$19. Specialties: rack of lamb, filet mignon, Alaskan halibut. Outdoor dining. Three intimate dining rms in house of former congressman. Cr cds: A, MC, V.

D

★ ★ ★ **SANTACAFE.** *231 Washington Ave, just off the plaza. 505/984-1788.* Web www.interart.net/restaurants/santacafe. Hrs: 11:30 am-2 pm, 5:30-10:30 pm; Sat, Sun from 5:30 pm. Res accepted. Bar. A la carte entrees: lunch $6-$12, dinner $17-$24. Specializes in modern American cuisine with regional touches. Own baking. Patio dining. Historic adobe house (1850); landscaped courtyard. Cr cds: A, MC, V.

D

✔★ **THE SHED.** *Prince Patio, 113 1/2 E Palace Ave, 1/2 blk E of plaza. 505/982-9030.* Hrs: 11 am-2:30 pm, 5:30-9 pm; Mon, Tues to 2:30 pm. Closed Sun. New Mexican, Amer menu. Wine, beer. Semi-a la carte: lunch $3.75-$8, dinner $6.50-$13.95. Specializes in blue corn enchiladas, mocha cake. Patio dining. Distinct restaurant in oldest part of town. Artwork, wall hangings. Family-owned. Totally nonsmoking. Cr cds: DS, MC, V.

D

★ ★ **SHOHKO-CAFE.** *321 Johnson St, downtown, off the Plaza. 505/983-7288.* Hrs: 11:30 am-2 pm, 6-9:30 pm; Fri, Sat to 10 pm. Closed Sun; hols. Res accepted. Chinese, Japanese menu. Wine, beer. Semi-a la carte: lunch $6-$12, dinner $9-$18. Specializes in tempura, sushi, seafood. Cr cds: A, MC, V.

D ♥

★ ★ ★ **STAAB HOUSE.** *(See La Posada De Santa Fe Motor Hotel) 505/986-0000.* Hrs: 7 am-10 pm. Res accepted. Continental menu. Bar 11-2 am; Sun from noon. Semi-a la carte: bkfst $5.95-$9.95, lunch $5.95-$8.95, dinner $9.95-$19.95. Child's meals. Specializes in creative Southwestern, Mediterranean cuisine. Entertainment (seasonal). Outdoor dining. In historic Staab mansion (1882); hand-crafted furniture; fireplace. On 6 acres. Cr cds: A, C, D, MC, V.

D

★ ★ **STEAKSMITH AT EL GANCHO.** *Old Las Vegas Hwy, approx 5 mi S of plaza, at El Gancho Tennis Club. 505/988-3333.* Hrs: 5:30-10 pm; Sun 5-9 pm. Closed most major hols. Res accepted. Continental menu. Bar from 4 pm. Complete meals: dinner $8.95-$26.95. Specializes in prime rib, fresh seafood, tapas. Southwestern decor. Cr cds: A, D, DS, MC, V.

D

✔★ **TECOLOTE CAFE.** *1203 Cerrillos Rd (87501). 505/988-1362.* Hrs: 7 am-2 pm. Closed Mon; Dec 24, 25, Thanksgiving; also Fri after Thanksgiving. Southwestern, Mexican menu. Semi-a la carte: bkfst, lunch $3.25-$10. Child's meals. Specializes in bkfst dishes. Original Southwestern art. Cr cds: A, C, D, DS, MC, V.

D

✔★ ★ **TOMASITA'S.** *500 S Guadalupe. 505/983-5721.* Hrs: 11 am-10 pm. Closed Sun; Jan 1, Thanksgiving, Dec 25. Northern New Mexican, Amer menu. Bar. Semi-a la carte: lunch $4.50-$9.50, dinner $4.95-$9.95. Child's meals. Specializes in quesadillas, burritos, enchiladas. Outdoor dining. Located in a historic train station (1904). Cr cds: MC, V.

D

★ ★ **VANESSIE OF SANTA FE.** *434 W San Francisco St (87501). 505/982-9966.* Hrs: 5:30-10 pm. Closed Easter, Thanksgiving, Dec 25. Bar to 2 am. A la carte entrees: dinner $12.95-$42.95. Specializes in rack of lamb, lobster, steak. Pianist evenings. Patio dining. Cr cds: A, C, D, DS, MC, V.

D

★ **WHISTLING MOON CAFE.** *402 N Guadalupe St. 505/983-3093.* Hrs: 11 am-9:30 pm; Sat, Sun from 9 am. Closed July 4. Mediterranean menu. Wine, beer. Semi-a la carte: lunch $8-$10, dinner $10-$15. Child's meals. Specializes in lamb, salads, pasta. Southwestern decor. Cr cds: MC, V.

D

Unrated Dining Spots

THE BURRITO COMPANY. *111 Washington Ave (87501). 505/982-4453.* Hrs: 7:30 am-7 pm; Sun 10 am-5 pm. Closed Dec 25. Mexican menu. A la carte entrees: bkfst $2-$3.50, lunch, dinner $1.65-$4.75. Child's meals. Specializes in burritos, enchiladas. Fast-food style restaurant famous for bkfst burritos. No cr cds accepted.

GRANT CORNER INN. *122 Grant Ave (87501). 505/983-6678.* Hrs: 8-9:30 am; Sat to 11 am; Sun to 1 pm. Res accepted. Brunch menu: $8.50-$10.50; Sun $10.50. Child's meals. Specialties: hearts of palm eggs Benedict, chile rellenos souffle, pumpkin raisin pancakes. Guitarist Sun. Outdoor dining. Colonial-style house built 1905. Cr cds: MC, V.

PLAZA. *54 Lincoln Ave, on the plaza. 505/982-1664.* Hrs: 7 am-9 pm; wkends 8 am-10 pm. Closed Thanksgiving, Dec 25. Continental menu. Wine, beer. Semi-a la carte: bkfst $2.50-$6.50, lunch $4.50-$8, dinner $6-$15. Child's meals. Specialties: blue corn enchiladas, sopaipillas, New Mexico meatloaf. Century-old building with many original fixtures; stamped-tin ceiling; photos of early Santa Fe. Art deco lunch-counter design. Family-owned since 1947. Cr cds: DS, MC, V.

Atlanta

Founded: 1837
Pop: 394,017
Elev: 1,050 feet
Time zone: Eastern
Area code: 404

Peachtree Plaza, 73 stories of iron and glass dominating the city skyline, symbolizes one side of this nerve center of the New South. Atlanta is a booming city. Strikingly modern skyscrapers, busy streets and varied entertainments give a sense of boundless energy. Yet Atlanta, rebuilt on the ashes left by General Sherman's march to the sea, holds to its Southern traditions.

After Georgia's secession from the Union on January 19, 1861, the city became a manufacturing, storage, supply and transportation center for the Confederate forces. This made Atlanta the target and last real barrier on General Sherman's march. Atlanta finally surrendered after four months of seige. Although the terms promised protection of life and property, all but 400 of the 3,600 houses and commercial buildings were destroyed in the subsequent burning. Many citizens had returned to the city by January of 1865; by June, steps had been taken to reorganize business and repair wrecked railroad facilities. Atlanta was made the federal headquarters for Reconstruction in the area in 1866. It became the state capital two years later. Atlanta's recovery and expansion received a large boost in 1872, when two more railroads met here.

Business

Conventions and tourism are foremost in the business of Atlanta. The city is also a retail/wholesale trade and distribution center and has one of the world's busiest airports, Hartsfield Atlanta International. Service jobs, manufacturing and government service also rank high. Many Fortune 500 corporations have offices here. The city is a financial center as well, with dozens of banking and investment firms.

Peachtree Center, in downtown Atlanta, has proven to be a model of urban development. Designed by architect John Portman, the center contains office towers, hotels and a variety of shops and stores. It features open garden plazas punctuated with contemporary sculpture and glass-enclosed skyways connecting the buildings—a beautiful, modern city within a city. The center was expanded to include more shopping, entertainment and the 1,674-room Marriott Marquis.

Other imaginative complexes following the lead of Peachtree Center include Colony Square, at Peachtree and 14th streets, and CNN Center, across International Boulevard from the Georgia World Congress Center. The building boom in Atlanta during the last quarter of this century has made this one of the most dynamic and prosperous cities in the nation and a center of activity for the entire Southeast.

Convention Facilities

The Georgia World Congress Center provides 640,000 square feet of exhibit space. It has 70 meeting rooms of various sizes, a 33,000-square-foot ballroom and a 2,000-seat auditorium. Permanent simultaneous interpretation equipment in six languages is available. The Atlanta Market Center, designed by John Portman, contains the Atlanta Merchandise and Apparel Mart, the Atlanta Decorative Arts Center, and Inforum, a high-technology showcase area. There are 280,000 square feet of exhibit space. Skywalks connect the facility to Peachtree Center across the street.

The Georgia International Convention and Trade Center provides 112,000 square feet of exhibit space with 35 meeting rooms of various sizes. There are 51,000 guest rooms in the metropolitan Atlanta area, 11,000 located in the center of the city.

Sports & Recreation

Crowds flock to Turner Field in spring and summer to watch the national baseball league Atlanta Braves; and in fall and winter, crowds fill the Georgia Dome for Falcons football and Hawks basketball.

South of the city is the Atlanta Motor Speedway, where the NASCAR Winston Cup and Busch Grand National draw racing enthusiasts from all over the country.

Golfers enjoy the BellSouth Golf Classic in early May and the many public courses throughout the city. Tennis facilities are numerous.

For those interested in outdoor recreation, the Appalachian Trail is only about a two-hour drive from the city. There is camping, backpacking and hiking throughout the area. There is boating on lakes Lanier and Allatoona, just north of the city. The Chattahoochee River is a major attraction for summer activities. Water excitement can also be found at White Water theme park, located north of Atlanta in Marietta.

Entertainment

Music, drama and visual arts provide cultural enrichment for residents and visitors. The Robert W. Woodruff Arts Center is home to the Atlanta Symphony Orchestra and the Alliance Theater Company. The symphony season runs from September to May and mid-June-mid-August. Theater of the Stars presents a summer play season. Other repertory groups offer year-round productions.

Nightclubs, jazz clubs, pubs, dancing spots, cabarets, comedy clubs and the like are scattered throughout the city. Like any metropolitan area, Atlanta is constantly changing. Consult local arts and entertainment magazines for current information.

Historical Areas

Contrary to the impression many strangers have about Atlanta, it is not an old city. However, it does have a past, the details of which can be

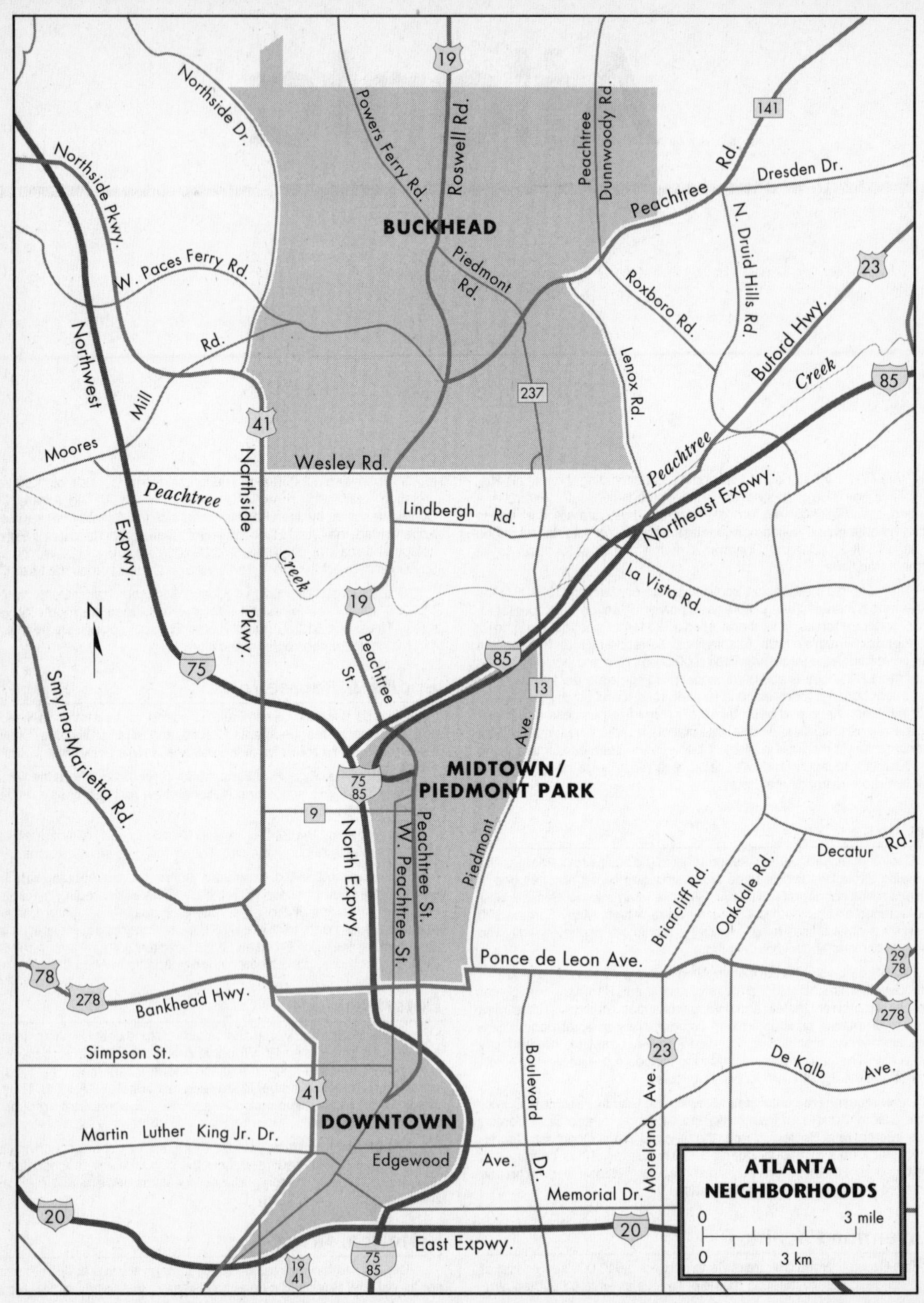

ATLANTA NEIGHBORHOODS
BUCKHEAD
MIDTOWN/ PIEDMONT PARK
DOWNTOWN
Northside Dr.
Northside Pkwy.
Powers Ferry Rd.
Roswell Rd.
Peachtree Dunnwoody Rd.
Peachtree Rd.
Dresden Dr.
N. Druid Hills Rd.
W. Paces Ferry Rd.
Piedmont Rd.
Roxboro Rd.
Buford Hwy.
Northwest Expwy.
Moores Mill Rd.
Lenox Rd.
Peachtree Creek
Wesley Rd.
Northside Pkwy.
Lindbergh Rd.
Northeast Expwy.
La Vista Rd.
Peachtree St.
Piedmont Ave.
Smyrna-Marietta Rd.
North Expwy.
Peachtree St.
W. Peachtree St.
Briarcliff Rd.
Oakdale Rd.
Decatur Rd.
Ponce de Leon Ave.
Bankhead Hwy.
Simpson St.
Boulevard Dr.
Moreland Ave.
De Kalb Ave.
Martin Luther King Jr. Dr.
Edgewood Ave.
Memorial Dr.
East Expwy.
N
19
141
23
85
237
41
13
75
9
75 85
78
278
29 78
20
19 41
0
3 mile
3 km

found in the exhibits at the Georgia Department of Archives and History and at the headquarters of the Atlanta Historical Center. On the grounds of the Historical Center are the beautiful neoclassical Swan house and a restored 1840s farmhouse, as well as outbuildings where exhibits are displayed and traditional craft demonstrations are held.

Historic Roswell is a small community founded in 1830. Located in the north Atlanta metro area, it contains numerous antebellum houses, including Bulloch Hall, the childhood home of President Theodore Roosevelt's mother.

The Martin Luther King, Jr National Historic Site is a two-block area that serves as a memorial to the famed leader of the civil rights movement. The gravesite with the eternal flame is here, as are King's birthplace and the church at which he was co-pastor from 1960 to 1968.

Twenty miles northwest of the city is Kennesaw Mountain National Battlefield Park, site of a crucial encounter in General Sherman's Atlanta campaign.

The city boasts many venerable educational institutions: Oglethorpe University was founded in 1835, Emory University in 1836, Atlanta University in 1865, Morehouse in 1867, Clark in 1869, both Spelman and Morris Brown in 1881, Georgia Institute of Technology in 1885 and Georgia State University in 1913.

Sightseeing

Areas in and around Atlanta offer a wide variety of sightseeing. For many tourists, a walk through the ultramodern downtown complexes can be an interesting experience. The Cyclorama in Grant Park gives visitors a multimedia history of the Battle of Atlanta. (One word of caution: Atlanta is notorious for its rush-hour traffic congestion. Sightseeing should, therefore, be planned accordingly.)

Major shopping areas include Lenox Square and Phipps Plaza, both north of town. There is also shopping in Peachtree Center.

A six-block area known as Underground Atlanta provides a "festival marketplace" of shops, restaurants, nightclubs and attractions in the heart of downtown. Abandoned in the 1920s, when the street level was raised, the district's below-ground storefronts have been rescued and refurbished; its Victorian-era cobblestone streets are now linked to above-ground plazas, promenades and fountains.

Within one to three hours' drive are many points of interest. Visitors to Dahlonega, a boomtown in 1828 when gold was discovered, may pan for gold and visit the Dahlonega Courthouse Gold Museum. New Echota is a restoration of the last eastern capital of the Cherokee nation. The Little White House, at Warm Springs, was the favorite refuge of Franklin Delano Roosevelt during his presidency, and the modest house in which he died is open to the public. Callaway Gardens, at Pine Mountain, combines a botanical preserve with a family resort.

Several tourist attractions near Atlanta are nationally famous. Stone Mountain Park, with 3,200 acres, surrounds a huge granite monolith on which a deep relief carving memorializing the leaders of the Confederacy has been created. It is a beautiful place for picnicking and exploring nature trails. Six Flags Over Georgia, just beyond the city limits, is a 331-acre family entertainment center where Georgia's history under the flags of England, France, Spain, the Confederacy, Georgia and the United States is featured.

General References

Area code: 404

Phone Numbers

POLICE & FIRE: 911

POISON CONTROL CENTER: 616-9000

TIME: 770/455-7141 **WEATHER:** 770/486-8535

Information Sources

Atlanta Convention & Visitors Bureau, Peachtree Center/Harris Tower, 233 Peachtree St NE, Suite 2000, 30303; 222-6688.

Lenox Square Mall Visitors Center, 3393 Peachtree Rd.

Peachtree Center Mall Visitors Center, 231 Peachtree St.

Underground Atlanta Visitors Center, 65 Upper Alabama St.

Department of Parks & Recreation, 817-6788.

Transportation

AIRLINES: Aeromexico; Air Canada; Air Jamaica; Air South; ALM; American; America West; British Airways; Canadian Airlines Intl; Cayman Airways; Continental; Delta; Japan Airlines; Kiwi International; Korean Air; Lufthansa (Germany); Midwest Express; Northwest; Sabena (Belgium); Swissair; TWA; United; USAir; Vanguard; Varig; Western Pacific; and other commuter and regional airlines.

AIRPORT: Hartsfield Atlanta International, 530-6600.

CAR RENTAL AGENCIES: (See IMPORTANT TOLL-FREE NUMBERS) Avis 530-2700; Budget 530-3000; Dollar 766-0244; Hertz 530-2900; National 530-2800.

PUBLIC TRANSPORTATION: Metropolitan Atlanta Rapid Transit Authority (MARTA), 848-4711.

RAILROAD PASSENGER SERVICE: Amtrak 800/872-7245.

Newspapers

Atlanta Constitution; Atlanta Daily World; Atlanta Journal.

Convention Facilities

Atlanta Market Center, 240 Peachtree St NW, 220-3000.

Georgia International Convention & Trade Center, 1902 Sullivan Rd, 770/997-3566.

Georgia World Congress Center, 285 International Blvd NW, 223-4000.

Sports & Recreation

Atlanta Motor Speedway, 27 mi S on I-75, 770/946-4211 (auto racing).

Georgia Dome, 1 Georgia Dome Dr (Falcons, football, 223-8000; Hawks, basketball, 827-3800).

Turner Field, Capitol Ave SE (Braves, baseball, 522-7630).

Cultural Facilities

Theaters

Alliance Theater (Robert W. Woodruff Arts Center), 1280 Peachtree St NE, 733-5000.

Civic Center, 395 Piedmont Ave NE, 523-6275.

Onstage Atlanta, 420 Courtland St, 897-1802.

Theater of the Stars, Fox Theater, 660 Peachtree St NE, 252-8960.

Concert Halls

Civic Center, 395 Piedmont Ave NE, 523-6275.

Fox Theatre, 660 Peachtree St NE, 881-2100.

Symphony Hall, Robert W. Woodruff Arts Center, 1280 Peachtree St NE (Atlanta Symphony Orchestra, 733-5000).

Museums

Georgia Capitol Museum, State Capitol (fourth floor), 656-2844.

High Museum of Art (Robert W. Woodruff Arts Center), 1280 Peachtree St NE, 733-4400.

Museum of the Jimmy Carter Library, 1 Copenhill Ave, 331-0296.

SciTrek—the Science and Technology Museum of Atlanta, 395 Piedmont Ave, 522-5500.

World of Coca-Cola, Underground Atlanta, 55 Martin Luther King Jr Dr SW, 676-5151.

Points of Interest

Historical

Atlanta History Center: Swan House & Tullie Smith Farm, 130 W Paces Ferry Rd NW, 814-4000.

Fort McPherson, main gate on Lee St, US 29, about 3 mi SW via I-75 & Lakewood Frwy, 464-3556.

Kennesaw Mt Natl Battlefield Park, 25 mi NW off US 41, 427-4686.

Little White House Historic Site, approx 70 mi SW in Warm Springs, 706/655-5870.

Martin Luther King, Jr National Historic Site, 450 Auburn Ave NE, 331-5190.

New Echota State Historic Site, approx 60 mi NW on I-75 near Calhoun, 706/629-8151.

State Capitol, Capitol Sq, 656-2844.

Stone Mountain Park, 19 mi E on US 78, 770/498-5600.

Wren's Nest, 1050 Ralph D. Abernathy Blvd SW, 753-7735.

Other Attractions

Atlanta State Farmers' Market, 10 mi S on I-75 in Forest Park, 366-6910.

Atlanta Zoo, Grant Park, Cherokee Ave SE, 624-5600.

Callaway Gardens, approx 65 mi SW on US 27 in Pine Mountain, 706/663-2281 or 800/282-8181.

Chastain Memorial Park, between Powers Ferry Rd & Lake Forest Dr.

Fernbank Science Center, 156 Heaton Park Dr NE, 378-4311.

Lake Lanier Islands, 35 mi NE off I-85, 770/932-7200.

Piedmont Park, off Monroe Dr at Park Dr, 875-7275.

Six Flags Over Georgia, 12 mi W via I-20, 770/948-9290.

Underground Atlanta, bounded by Wall, Central, Peachtree Sts & Martin Luther King Jr Dr, 523-2311.

Sightseeing Tours

Atlanta Preservation Center, (Feb-Nov) 156 7th St NE, Suite 3, 30308; 876-2040.

Gray Line bus tours, 2541 Camp Creek Pkwy, College Park 30337; 767-0594.

Annual Events

Atlanta Steeplechase, Seven Branches Farm in Cumming, 237-7436. 1st Sat Apr.

Atlanta Dogwood Festival, 329-0501. Mid-Apr.

Georgia Renaissance Festival, 770/964-8575. 7 wkends late Apr-June.

BellSouth Golf Classic, Marietta, 770/951-8777. Early May.

City Neighborhoods

Many of the restaurants, unrated dining establishments and some lodgings listed under Atlanta include neighborhoods as well as exact street addresses. Geographic descriptions of these areas are given, followed by a table of restaurants arranged by neighborhood.

Buckhead: South of the northern city limits, west of Lenox and Peachtree Rds, north of Wesley Rd and east of Northside Dr.

Downtown: South of North Ave, west of I-75/85, north of I-20 and east of Northside Dr. **North of Downtown:** North of North Ave. **East of Downtown:** East of I-75/I-85.

Midtown/Piedmont Park: South of I-85, west of Piedmont Park, north of North Ave and east of I-75/85.

Lodgings and Food

ATLANTA RESTAURANTS BY NEIGHBORHOOD AREAS
(For full description, see alphabetical listings under Restaurants)

BUCKHEAD
103 West. 103 W Paces Ferry Rd
Abruzzi Ristorante. 2355 Peachtree Rd NE
Anis. 2974 Grandview Ave
Anthony's. 109 Piedmont Rd NE
Arugula. 3639 Piedmont Rd NE
Atlanta Fish Market. 265 Pharr Rd
Bacchanalia. 3125 Piedmont Rd
Basil's Mediterranean Cafe. 2985 Grandview Ave
The Bistro. 56 E Andrews Dr NW
Blue Ridge Grill. 1261 W Paces Ferry Rd
Bone's. 3130 Piedmont Rd NE
Brasserie Le Coze. 3393 Peachtree Rd
Buckhead Diner. 3073 Piedmont Rd
The Cabin. 2678 Buford Hwy NE
The Cafe (The Ritz-Carlton, Buckhead Hotel). 3434 Peachtree Rd NE
Cafe Tu Tu Tango. 220 Pharr Rd
Carbo's Cafe. 3717 Roswell Rd
Cassis (Grand Hyatt Hotel). 3300 Peachtree Rd
Chops. 70 W Paces Ferry Rd
The Colonnade. 1879 Cheshire Bridge Rd
Dante's Down The Hatch. 3380 Peachtree Rd NE
The Dining Room (The Ritz-Carlton, Buckhead Hotel). 3434 Peachtree Rd NE
Fratelli Di Napoli. 2101-B Bennett St
Georgia Grille. 2290 Peachtree Rd
Imperial Fez. 2285 Peachtree Rd NE
Jim White's Half Shell. 2349 Peachtree Rd NE
Kudzu Cafe. 3215 Peachtree Rd NE
La Grotta. 2637 Peachtree Rd NE
Luna Si. 1931 Peachtree Rd
Maggiano's Little Italy. 3368 Peachtree Road NE
McKinnon's Louisiane. 3209 Maple Dr
Nakato. 1776 Cheshire Bridge Rd NE
Nava. 3060 Peachtree Rd
Nino's. 1931 Cheshire Bridge Rd
Ok Cafe. 1284 W Paces Ferry Rd
Palisades. 1829 Peachtree Rd NE
Pano's And Paul's. 1232 W Paces Ferry Rd
Pekaso. 3167 Peachtree Rd NE
Phoenix Brewing Co. 5600 Roswell Road NE
Pricci. 500 Pharr Rd
Prime. 3393 Peachtree Rd NE
Rib Ranch. 25 Irby Ave
Riviera. 519 E Paces Ferry Rd NE
South Of France. 2345 Cheshire Bridge Rd
Sundown Cafe. 2165 Cheshire Bridge Rd
Tomtom. 3393 Peachtree Rd
Toulouse. 2293-B Peachtree Rd NE
The Varsity Jr. 1085 Lindbergh Dr NE

DOWNTOWN
City Grill. 50 Hurt Plaza
Dailey's. 17 International Blvd
Haveli. 225 Spring St
Hsu's Gourmet Chinese. 192 Peachtree Center Ave
Lombardi's. 94 Upper Pryor St
Mick's Underground. 75 Upper Alabama St
Mumbo Jumbo Bar And Grill. 89 Park Pl NE
Nikolai's Roof (Hilton & Towers Hotel). 255 Courtland St NE
Pittypat's Porch. 25 International Blvd
The Restaurant (The Ritz-Carlton Hotel). 181 Peachtree St NE
Rio Bravo Grill. 240 Peachtree St

NORTH OF DOWNTOWN
Cafe Chanterelle. 4200 Paces Ferry Rd NE
Canoe. 4199 Paces Ferry Rd NW
Food Studio. 887 W Marietta St
Horseradish Grill. 4320 Powers Ferry Rd
La Grotta Ravinia (Crowne Plaza Ravinia Hotel). 4355 Ashford Dunwoody Rd
La Paz. 6410 Roswell Rd
McKendrick's. 4505 Ashford Dunwoody Rd
Mi Spia. 4505 Ashford Dunwoody Rd
Ray's On The River. 6700 Powers Ferry Rd
Ruth's Chris Steak House. 5788 Roswell Rd
Villa Christina. 45 Perimeter Summit Blvd
The Vinings Inn. 3011 Paces Mill Rd

EAST OF DOWNTOWN
Babette's Cafe. 471 N Highland Ave NE
Cafe La Glace. 562 Boulevard St SE
Dusty's Barbecue. 1815 Briarcliff Rd
Harvest. 853 N Highland Ave NE
Petite Auberge. 2935 N Druid Hill Rd
Rj's Uptown Kitchen And Wine Bar. 870 N Highland Ave NE
Thai Chili. 2169 Briarcliff Rd NE

MIDTOWN/PIEDMONT PARK
The Abbey. 163 Ponce de Leon Ave NE
Agnes & Muriel's. 1514 Monroe Dr
Bistango. 1100 Peachtree St NE
Camille's. 1186 N Highland Ave
Ciboulette. 1529 Piedmont Ave
Country Place. 1197 Peachtree St NE
Fat Matt's. 1811 Piedmont
Indigo Coastal Grill. 1397 N Highland Ave
The Mansion. 179 Ponce de Leon Ave
Mary Mac's Tearoom. 224 Ponce de Leon Ave
Pirozki's. 1447 Peachtree Rd NE
Pleasant Peasant. 555 Peachtree St
The Restaurant (Four Seasons Hotel). 75 Fourteenth St
South City Kitchen. 1144 Crescent Ave
Terra Cotta. 1044 Greenwood Ave
Varsity. 61 North Ave
Veni Vidi Vici. 41 14th St
Zocalo. 187 10th St

Note: When a listing is located in a town that does not have its own city heading, it will appear under the city nearest to its location. In these cases, the address and town appear in parenthesis immediately following the name of the establishment.

Motels

✓★★ **COMFORT INN BUCKHEAD.** *2115 Piedmont Rd NE (30324), in Buckhead. 404/876-4365; FAX 404/873-1007.* 186 rms, 3 story. Jan-Sept: S, D $59-$95; each addl $6; suites $99-$149; under 18 free; higher rates special events; lower rates rest of yr. Crib $6. TV; cable (premium). Pool. Complimentary continental bkfst. Bar 6-11 pm. Ck-out noon. Coin lndry. Meeting rms. Business servs avail. Some refrigerators. Cr cds: A, D, DS, MC, V.

D SC

✓★ **COMFORT INN-FOREST PARK.** *3701 Jonesboro Rd SE (30354), south of downtown. 404/361-1111; FAX 404/366-0294.* 73 rms, 2 story. S $45-$150; D $50-$150; each addl $5; suites $75-$90; under 18 free. Crib $5. TV; cable (premium). Pool. Complimentary continental bkfst. Restaurant nearby. Ck-out 11 am. Coin lndry. Meeting rms. Business servs avail. In-rm modem link. Sundries. Cr cds: A, C, D, DS, ER, MC, V.

D SC

★★ **COUNTRY HEARTH INN.** *5793 Roswell Rd NE (30328), in Sandy Springs, north of downtown. 404/252-6400; FAX 404/851-9306.* 82 rms, 5 story. S, D $65-$100; each addl $6; under 18 free; higher rates hols. Crib $7. TV; cable (premium). Pool. Complimentary continental bkfst.

Complimentary coffee in rms. Restaurant adj 11:30 am-2 pm, 6-10:30 pm. Ck-out noon. Meeting rm. Business servs avail. Health club privileges. In-rm modem link. Cr cds: A, C, D, DS, MC, V.

D SC

★ ★ **COURTYARD BY MARRIOTT-NORTHLAKE.** *(4083 La Vista Rd, Tucker 30084) I-285 exit 28, adj to Northlake Festival Mall, east of downtown. 770/938-1200; FAX 770/934-6497.* 128 units, 2 story, 20 suites. S $99; D $109; suites $105-$115; under 18 free; wkly, wkend rates. Crib free. TV; cable (premium). Pool. Complimentary coffee in rms. Restaurant 6:30-10 am; Sat, Sun from 7 am-noon. Bar 4-11 pm. Ck-out noon. Coin Indry. Meeting rms. Business servs avail. In-rm modem link. Valet serv. Exercise equipt; weights, bicycles, whirlpool. Some refrigerators. Private patios, balconies. Cr cds: A, C, D, DS, MC, V.

D SC

★ ★ ★ **EMORY INN.** *1641 Clifton Rd NE (30329), north of downtown. 404/712-6700; FAX 404/712-6701; res: 800/933-6679.* E-mail sales@ecch.emory.edu. 305 rms, 2 story. S, D $89-$175; under 12 free. Crib free. TV; cable (premium). Indoor pool; whirlpool, poolside serv. Coffee in rms. Restaurant 7 am-2 pm, 5-10 pm; Sat 7-10 am, 5-10 pm. Ck-out noon. Coin Indry. Convention facilities. Business center. In-rm modem link. Bellhops. Valet serv. Tennis. Exercise equipt; bicycles, stair machines. Microwaves avail. Antiques. Library/sitting rm. Cr cds: A, C, D, DS, ER, MC, V.

D SC

★ ★ **FAIRFIELD INN BY MARRIOTT.** *1470 Spring St NW (30309), in Midtown/Piedmont Park. 404/872-5821; FAX 404/874-3602.* 182 rms, 4 story. S $74; D $84; each addl $10; under 18 free; higher rates conventions. Crib free. TV; cable (premium). Pool. Complimentary continental bkfst. Ck-out noon. Meeting rms. Business servs avail. Exercise equipt; weights, bicycle. Some refrigerators. Cr cds: A, C, D, DS, MC, V.

D SC

✓★ ★ **HAMPTON INN-BUCKHEAD.** *3398 Piedmont Rd NE (30305), in Buckhead. 404/233-5656; FAX 404/237-4688.* 154 rms, 6 story. S $82-$90; D $92-$115; higher rates: wkends, special events; under 18 free. Crib free. TV; cable (premium). Pool. Complimentary continental bkfst. Restaurant adj 11 am-11 pm. Ck-out noon. Meeting rms. Business servs avail. In-rm modem link. Valet serv. Health club privileges. Cr cds: A, C, D, DS, MC, V.

D SC

✓★ **RED ROOF INN-DRUID HILLS.** *1960 N Druid Hills Rd (30329), I-85 exit 31, north of downtown. 404/321-1653; FAX 404/248-9774.* 115 rms, 3 story. S, D $48-$65; under 18 free. Crib free. Pet accepted, some restrictions. TV; cable (premium). Complimentary coffee in lobby. Restaurant nearby. Ck-out noon. In-rm modem link. Health club privileges. Cr cds: A, C, D, DS, MC, V.

D

★ ★ **RESIDENCE INN BY MARRIOTT-DUNWOODY.** *1901 Savoy Dr (30341), I-285 at Chamblee-Dunwoody exit, north of downtown. 770/455-4446; FAX 770/451-5183.* 144 kit. suites, 2 story. S, D $99-$119; wkend rates. Crib free. Pet accepted, some restrictions; $82.50-$125. TV; cable (premium), VCR avail. Heated pool; whirlpools. Complimentary continental bkfst. Ck-out noon. Coin Indry. Meeting rm. Business servs avail. In-rm modem link. Valet serv. Health club privileges. Many fireplaces; microwaves avail. Private patios, balconies. Picnic tables, grills. Cr cds: A, D, DS, MC, V.

D SC

★ ★ ★ **STONE MOUNTAIN INN.** *(Robert E Lee Blvd, Stone Mountain 30086) 16 mi E on US 78, Stone Mountain Park exit, in Stone Mountain Park. 770/469-3311; FAX 770/498-5691; res: 800/277-0007.* 92 rms, 2 story. $6 parking fee (required to reach motel). Mid-May-early Sept: S, D $79-$99; each addl $10; under 12 free; lower rates rest of yr. Crib free. TV; cable (premium). Pool. Restaurant 7 am-9 pm (hrs vary off-season). Ck-out 11 am. Coin Indry. Meeting rms. Business servs avail. In-rm modem link. Bellhops. Gift shop. Lighted tennis. 36-hole golf, pro. Balconies; private patios for poolside rms. Cr cds: A, C, D, DS, JCB, MC, V.

D SC

★ ★ **SUMMERFIELD SUITES.** *760 Mt Vernon Hwy (30328), north of downtown. 404/250-0110; FAX 404/250-9335; res: 800/833-4353.* 122 kit. suites, 2-3 story. 1-bedrm $159; 2-bedrm $199; wkend rates. Crib free. Pet accepted; some restrictions. TV; cable (premium), VCR (movies $6). Heated pool. Complimentary continental bkfst. Complimentary coffee in rms. Ck-out 11 am. Coin Indry. Meeting rms. Business servs avail. In-rm modem link. Sundries. Exercise equipt; treadmill, bicycles, whirlpool. Microwaves avail. Picnic tables, grills. Cr cds: A, C, D, DS, JCB, MC, V.

D SC

★ ★ **SUMMERFIELD SUITES.** *505 Pharr Rd NE (30305), in Buckhead. 404/262-7880; FAX 404/262-3734.* 88 suites, 3 story. No elvtr. S, D $179-$219; wkend rates. Crib free. Pet accepted, some restrictions. TV; cable (premium), VCR (movies $6). Heated pool. Complimentary continental bkfst. Complimentary coffee in rms. Restaurant opp 11 am-midnight. Ck-out 11 am. Coin Indry. Meeting rms. In-rm modem link. Valet serv. Sundries. Exercise equipt; bicycle, treadmill, whirlpool. Refrigerators, microwaves. Balconies. Picnic tables, grills. Cr cds: A, C, D, DS, JCB, MC, V.

D SC

★ ★ **TRAVELODGE-DOWNTOWN.** *311 Courtland St NE (30303), downtown. 404/659-4545; FAX 404/659-5934.* 71 rms, 3 story. S $69-$87; D $84-$104; each addl $8; under 18 free; wkend rates. Crib free. TV; cable (premium), VCR avail (movies). Pool. Complimentary continental bkfst. Coffee in rms. Ck-out noon. Valet serv. Health club privileges. Some balconies. Cr cds: A, C, D, DS, ER, JCB, MC, V.

D SC

Motor Hotels

★ ★ ★ **COURTYARD BY MARRIOTT-CUMBERLAND CENTER.** *3000 Cumberland Circle (30339), I-285 Cobb Pkwy exit, north of downtown. 770/952-2555; FAX 770/952-2409.* 182 rms, 8 story. S $99; D $109; under 12 free. Crib free. TV; cable (premium). Indoor pool. Complimentary coffee in rms. Restaurant 6:30-10 am, 5-10:30 pm; wkends 7 am-11 am. Bar 5-11 pm. Ck-out noon. Meeting rms. Business servs avail. In-rm modem link. Valet serv. Sundries. Exercise rm; instructor, weights, bicycles, whirlpool, sauna. Some refrigerators. Balconies. Cr cds: A, C, D, DS, MC, V.

D SC

✓★ ★ **LENOX INN.** *3387 Lenox Rd NE (30326), in Buckhead. 404/261-5500; FAX 404/261-6140; res: 800/241-0200.* 180 rms, 2-3 story. S $78; D $82; each addl $10; suites $99-$260; under 18 free. Crib free. TV. 2 pools. Complimentary continental bkfst. Restaurant 6:30-9:30 am; Sat, Sun 7-11 am. Bar 5:30-8 pm. Ck-out noon. Meeting rms. Business servs avail. Valet serv. Health club privileges. Some refrigerators. Cr cds: A, C, D, DS, MC, V.

SC

✓★ ★ **QUALITY INN-NORTHEAST.** *2960 NE Expy (I-85) (30341), I-85 exit 33, at Shallowford Rd, north of downtown. 770/451-5231; FAX 770/454-8704.* 153 rms, 2 story. S, D $42-$51; family rates. Crib free. TV; cable (premium). Pool. Continental bkfst 6-10 am. Ck-out noon. Coin Indry. Meeting rms. Business servs avail. In-rm modem link. Bellhops. Microwaves avail. Cr cds: A, C, D, DS, MC, V.

D SC

✓★ ★ **RAMADA INN-SIX FLAGS.** *4225 Fulton Industrial Blvd (30336), I-20W exit 14, west of downtown. 404/691-4100; FAX 404/691-2117.* 229 rms, 4-5 story. Apr-mid-Sept: S, D $58-$78; each addl $10; lower rates rest of yr. Crib $10. TV; cable (premium). Pool. Bar 3 pm-2:30 am; entertainment. Ck-out 11 am. Coin Indry. Meeting rms. Business servs avail. In-rm modem link. Game rm. Some refrigerators. Grill. Cr cds: A, D, DS, MC, V.

D SC

★ ★ ★ **WYNDHAM GARDEN.** *2857 Paces Ferry Rd (30339), I-285 exit 12, north of downtown. 770/432-5555; FAX 770/436-5558.* Web www.travelweb.com. 159 rms, 4 story. S, D $119-$129; suites $130-$140; under 18 free; wkend rates. Crib free. TV; cable (premium). Heated pool; whirlpool, poolside serv. Restaurant 6:30 am-2 pm, 5-10 pm. Rm serv from 10 pm. Bar 4 pm-midnight. Ck-out noon. Meeting rms. Business servs avail. In-rm modem link. Valet serv. Tennis privileges. Health club privileges. Private patios, balconies. Cr cds: A, C, D, DS, ER, JCB, MC, V.

D SC

Hotels

★ ★ **BEST WESTERN INN AT THE PEACHTREES.** *330 W Peachtree St NW (30308), downtown. 404/577-6970; FAX 404/659-3244.* 110 rms, 4 story. S $145; D $165; each addl $10; under 18 free. TV; cable (premium). Complimentary full bkfst. Ck-out noon. Coin Indry. Meeting rm. Business center. Covered parking. Airport transportation avail. Exercise equipt; bicycle, weight machine. Health club privileges. Some refrigerators, microwaves. Near Merchandise Mart & Apparel Mart. Cr cds: A, C, D, DS, JCB, MC, V.

D SC

★ ★ **THE BILTMORE SUITES.** *30 5th St NE (30308), at W Peachtree St, in Midtown/Piedmont Park. 404/874-0824; FAX 404/872-0067; res: 800/822-0824.* 60 kit. suites, 10 story. Kit. suites $59-$249. TV; cable, VCR avail (movies). Complimentary continental bkfst. Restaurant nearby. Ck-out noon. Free covered parking. Microwaves. Some balconies. Built 1924; Georgian design with vaulted ceilings, skylights and limestone detailing. Cr cds: A, C, D, DS, MC, V.

★ ★ **COMFORT INN-DOWNTOWN.** *101 International Blvd (30303), downtown. 404/524-5555; FAX 404/221-0702.* 260 rms, 11 story. S, D $79-$229; each addl $10; under 18 free; wkend rates. Crib free. Garage in/out $10. TV; cable (premium). Pool; whirlpool. Restaurant 6:30-10:30 am, 11:30 am-1:30 pm, 5:30-10 pm. Bar 4 pm-12:30 am. Ck-out noon. Meeting rms. Business servs avail. In-rm modem link. Gift shop. Exercise equipt; bicycle, stair machine. Health club privileges. Adj to Atlanta Market Center and World Congress Center. Cr cds: A, C, D, DS, ER, JCB, MC, V.

D SC

★ ★ ★ **CROWNE PLAZA RAVINIA.** *4355 Ashford-Dunwoody Rd (30346), 1 blk N I-285 exit 21, adj Perimeter Mall, north of downtown. 770/395-7700; FAX 770/392-9503.* 495 rms, 15 story. S $149-$189; D $159-$199; each addl $10; suites $350-$1,150; under 18 free; wkend rates. Crib free. Valet parking $9. TV; cable (premium), VCR avail. Indoor pool; whirlpool. Restaurants 6 am-10:30 pm (also see LA GROTTA RAVINIA). Rm serv to 1 am. Bar; entertainment exc Sun. Ck-out noon. Convention facilities. Business center. In-rm modem link. Concierge. Gift shop. Lighted tennis. Exercise equipt; weights, bicycles, sauna. Microwaves avail; refrigerator in suites. Luxury level. Cr cds: A, C, D, DS, JCB, MC, V.

D SC

★ ★ **DAYS INN-DOWNTOWN.** *300 Spring St (30308), downtown. 404/523-1144; FAX 404/577-8495.* 263 rms, 10 story. S $89-$199; D $99-$209; each addl $10; under 18 free. Crib free. Garage $7/day. TV; cable (premium). Pool. Coffee in rms. Restaurant 6:30 am-10 pm. Bar 5 pm-midnight. Ck-out 11 am. Meeting rms. Business servs avail. In-rm modem link. Gift shop. Airport, RR station, bus depot transportation. Some refrigerators. Balconies. Cr cds: A, C, D, DS, JCB, MC, V.

D SC

★ ★ ★ **DOUBLETREE GUEST SUITES HOTEL-ATLANTA PERIMETER.** *6120 Peachtree-Dunwoody Rd (30328), north of downtown. 779/668-0808; FAX 770/668-0008.* Web www.doubletreehotels.com. 224 suites, 6 story. Suites $89-$140; under 18 free; wkend rates. Crib free. TV; cable (premium), VCR avail. Indoor/outdoor pool; whirlpool. Restaurant 6:30 am-10:30 pm. Bar 4:30 pm-2 am. Ck-out noon. Coin Indry. Meeting rms. Business center. In-rm modem link. Exercise equipt; weight machine, bicycles, sauna. Health club privileges. Refrigerators; microwaves avail. Cr cds: A, C, D, DS, ER, JCB, MC, V.

D SC

★ ★ ★ **DOUBLETREE GUEST SUITES-ATLANTA GALLERIA.** *2780 Whitley Rd (30339), I-285 Cobb Pkwy exit, north of downtown. 770/980-1900; FAX 770/980-1528; res: 800/843-5858.* 155 suites, 8 story. Suites $145-$165; under 12 free; wkly, wkend rates. Crib free. TV; cable (premium), VCR avail. Pool. Complimentary full bkfst. Complimentary coffee in rms. Restaurant 5 am-10 pm. Rm serv. Bar 11-2 am, Sun to 12:30 am; entertainment Fri-Sat. Ck-out noon. Meeting rms. Business servs avail. In-rm modem link. Exercise equipt; weights, bicycles, sauna. Bathrm phones, in-rm whirlpools, refrigerators. Some private patios, balconies. Cr cds: A, C, D, DS, MC, V.

D SC

★ ★ ★ **EMBASSY SUITES.** *3285 Peachtree Rd NE (30305), GA 400, Buckhead exit. 404/261-7733; FAX 404/261-6857.* 317 suites, 16 story. Suites $159-$225; under 18 free; wkend rates; higher rates special events. Crib free. TV; cable (premium). 2 pools, 1 indoor; whirlpool. Complimentary full bkfst. Complimentary coffee in rms. Restaurant 11 am-2 pm, 5-10 pm. Bar 11-1 am. Ck-out noon. Coin Indry. Meeting rms. Business servs avail. In-rm modem link. Gift shop. Airport transportation. Exercise equipt; bicycles, treadmill, sauna. Health club privileges. Refrigerators, wet bars. Cr cds: A, C, D, DS, JCB, MC, V.

D SC

★ ★ ★ **EMBASSY SUITES-GALLERIA.** *2815 Akers Mill Rd (30339), I-285 exit 13, north of downtown. 770/984-9300; FAX 770/955-4183.* Web www.embassy-suites.com. 261 suites, 9 story. S $159-$199; D $189-$219; each addl $20; under 16 free; wkend rates. Crib free. TV; cable (premium). Indoor pool; whirlpool, sauna. Complimentary full bkfst. Restaurant 11 am-10 pm. Bar to midnight. Ck-out noon. Meeting rms. Business servs avail. In-rm modem link. Gift shop. Health club privileges. Game rm. Refrigerators; microwaves avail. Garden atrium, glass elvtrs. Cr cds: A, C, D, DS, MC, V.

D SC

★ ★ ★ ★ **FOUR SEASONS.** *75 Fourteenth St (30309), Grand Bldg, in Midtown/Piedmont Park. 404/881-9898; FAX 404/873-4692.* Occupying the first 20 floors of the Grand Building, this luxury hotel combines Old World traditions with New South hospitality. A fifth-floor terrace provides skyline views, while the fourth floor boasts a grand ballroom. 244 rms, 19 story. S, D $195-$225; each addl $25; suites $450-$1,500; under 16 free; wkend rates. Crib free. Pet accepted. Garage parking, valet $15. TV; cable (premium), VCR avail. Indoor pool; whirlpool, poolside serv. Restaurant 6 am-11 pm (also see THE RESTAURANT). Rm serv 24 hrs. Bar 11:30-1 am; entertainment. Ck-out noon. Meeting rms. Business center. In-rm modem link. Concierge. Gift shop. Barber, beauty shop. Exercise rm; instructor, weight machine, bicycles, sauna, steam rm. Spa. Refrigerators, minibars. Cr cds: A, C, D, ER, JCB, MC, V.

D

★ ★ ★ ★ **GRAND HYATT.** *3300 Peachtree Rd (30305), in Buckhead. 404/365-8100; FAX 404/233-5686.* The focus of the dual-height lobby is the adjacent tri-level Japanese garden and 35-foot cascading waterfall. The spacious, comfortable and understated rooms feature marble baths. 439 rms, 25 story. S $184-$245, D $209-$270; each addl $25; suites $450-$2,500; wkend rates. TV; cable (premium), VCR avail. Pool. Restaurants (see CASSIS). Rm serv 24 hrs. Bars 11-1 am; entertainment, pianist. Ck-out noon. Convention facilities. Business center. In-rm modem link. Concierge. Gift shop. Garage, valet parking. Tennis privileges. Golf privileges. Exercise equipt; bicycles, treadmill, sauna. Massage. Bathrm phones, minibars. Luxury level. Cr cds: A, C, D, DS, ER, JCB, MC, V.

D

★★★ **HILTON & TOWERS.** *255 Courtland St NE (30303), at Harris St, downtown. 404/659-2000; FAX 404/222-2868.* Web www.hil ton .com. 1,224 rms, 30 story. S $145-$225; D $165-$245; each addl $20; suites from $350; family, wkend rates. Crib free. Valet parking $12, garage avail. TV; cable (premium), VCR avail. Pool; whirlpool, poolside serv. Restaurant open 24 hrs; dining rm (see NIKOLAI'S ROOF). Bars 11:30-2 am; Sun 12:30 pm-midnight; entertainment. Ck-out 11 am. Convention facilities. Business center. In-rm modem link. Shopping arcade. Lighted tennis, pro. Exercise rm; instructor, weights, bicycles, sauna. Massage. Health club privileges. Some bathrm phones. Balconies. Luxury level. Cr cds: A, C, D, DS, ER, JCB, MC, V.

D SC

★★★ **HOLIDAY INN SELECT.** *4386 Chamblee Dunwoody Rd (30341), I-285, exit 22, north of downtown. 770/457-6363; FAX 770/936-9592.* 250 rms, 5 story. S $129; D $139; each addl $10; suites $225-$400; under 18 free; wkend rates. Crib free. Pet accepted; some restrictions. TV; cable (premium). Heated pool. Complimentary coffee in rms. Restaurant 6 am-2 pm, 5-10 pm; wkends 7 am-2 pm. Bar 4 pm-midnight. Ck-out noon. Coin Indry. Meeting rms. Business servs avail. In-rm modem link. Exercise equipt; treadmill, bicycle. Microwaves avail. Cr cds: A, C, D, DS, ER, JCB, MC, V.

D SC

★★ **HOLIDAY INN-ATLANTA CENTRAL.** *418 Armour Dr NE (30324), in Midtown/Piedmont Park. 404/873-4661; FAX 404/872-1292.* 331 units, 5 story. S, D $79-$110; suites $150-$300; under 19 free; wkend rates. Crib free. TV; cable (premium). Pool; poolside serv. Coffee in rms. Restaurant 6:30 am-2 pm, 5-10 pm. Bar 5-11 pm. Ck-out noon. Coin Indry. Convention facilities. In-rm modem link. Concierge. Gift shop. Barber, beauty shop. Exercise equipt; weight machine, bicycles. Refrigerators, microwaves avail. In-rm whirlpool, refrigerator, wet bar, fireplace in suites. Balconies. Cr cds: A, C, D, DS, ER, JCB, MC, V.

D SC

★★ **HOLIDAY INN-BUCKHEAD.** *3377 Peachtree Rd NE (30326), GA 400, Buckhead exit. 404/264-1111; FAX 404/233-7061.* 297 rms, 11 story. S, D $119-$149; each addl $10; suites $150-$250; under 18 free; wkend, hol rates; higher rates special events. Crib free. TV; cable (premium), VCR avail. Pool. Complimentary coffee in rms. Restaurant 6 am-2 pm, 5-11 pm. Bar from 5 pm. Ck-out 11 am. Coin Indry. Meeting rms. Business servs avail. In-rm modem link. Concierge. Health club privileges. Many refrigerators. Cr cds: A, C, D, DS, JCB, MC, V.

D SC

★★★ **HYATT REGENCY.** *265 Peachtree St NE (30303), in Peachtree Center, downtown. 404/577-1234; FAX 404/588-4137.* 1,264 rms, 23 story. S, D $185-$240; each addl $25; suites from $450; under 18 free; wkend rates. Crib free. Garage $17-$20. TV; cable (premium). Pool; poolside serv. Restaurant 6:30-1 am. Bar noon-2 am. Ck-out noon. Convention facilities. Business center. In-rm modem link. Concierge. Gift shop. Exercise equipt; weights, bicycles. Health club privileges. Minibars; many refrigerators in suites. Many balconies. Luxury level. Cr cds: A, C, D, DS, JCB, MC, V.

D SC

★★★ **J W MARRIOTT.** *3300 Lenox Rd NE (30326), at Peachtree Rd, in Buckhead. 404/262-3344; FAX 404/262-8689.* 371 units, 25 story. S, D $240; suites $300-$1,000; under 18 free. Crib free. Garage $8, valet $14. TV; cable (premium), VCR avail. Indoor pool; whirlpool. Restaurant 6:30 am-11 pm. Rm serv 24 hrs. Bar noon-1 am; Fri, Sat to 2 am. Ck-out noon. Convention facilities. Business center. In-rm modem link. Concierge. Valet serv. Shopping arcade. Exercise equipt; weight machine, bicycles, sauna. Massage. Bathrm phones, minibars. Luxury level. Cr cds: A, C, D, DS, JCB, MC, V.

D SC

★★★ **THE MARQUE OF ATLANTA.** *111 Perimeter Center West (30346), north of downtown. 770/396-6800; FAX 770/394-4805; res: 800/683-6100.* 274 rms, 12 story, 154 kit. suites. S $99-$165; D $109-$179; each addl $15; kit. suites $99-$165; under 16 free; wkend rates. Crib free. TV; cable (premium). Pool; whirlpool, poolside serv. Complimentary coffee in lobby. Restaurant 6-10 am, noon-2 pm, 6-10 pm. Rm serv 6 am-11 pm. Bar 5:30 pm-midnight. Ck-out noon. Coin Indry. Meeting rms. Business servs avail. Exercise equipt; weight machine, bicycles, sauna. Microwaves avail. Balconies. Situated in park-like setting. Cr cds: A, C, D, DS, JCB, MC, V.

D SC

★★★ **MARRIOTT MARQUIS.** *265 Peachtree Center Ave (30303), downtown. 404/521-0000; FAX 404/586-6299.* 1,674 rms, 47 story. S, D $220-$240; each addl $20; suites $350-$1,500; under 18 free; wkend rates. Crib free. Garage $17. TV; cable (premium), VCR avail. Indoor/outdoor pool; whirlpool, poolside serv. Restaurants 6 am-10:30 pm. Rm serv 24 hrs. Bar 11-2 am, Sun from 12:30 pm. Ck-out noon. Convention facilities. Business center. In-rm modem link. Shopping arcade. Barber, beauty shop. Exercise equipt; weight machines, bicycles, sauna. Massage. Health club privileges. Refrigerators. Bathrm phone in suites. Luxury level. Cr cds: A, C, D, DS, ER, JCB, MC, V.

D SC

★★★ **MARRIOTT NORTH CENTRAL.** *2000 Century Blvd NE (30345), in Century Center Park, north of downtown. 404/325-0000; FAX 404/325-4920.* 287 rms, 15 story. S, D $169; suites from $275; wkend rates. Crib free. TV; cable (premium). Heated pool; poolside serv. Complimentary coffee in lobby. Restaurant 6:30 am-2 pm, 5-11 pm. Bar 2 pm-midnight. Ck-out noon. Convention facilities. Business servs avail. In-rm modem link. Gift shop. Barber. Lighted tennis. Exercise equipt; weights, bicycles. Some refrigerators. Luxury level. Cr cds: A, C, D, DS, ER, JCB, MC, V.

D SC

★★★ **OMNI HOTEL AT CNN CENTER.** *100 CNN Center (30335), downtown. 404/659-0000; FAX 404/525-5050.* 458 rms, 15 story. S $220; D $240; each addl from $20; suites $250-$1,200; under 18 free; wkend rates. Crib free. Garage in/out $15-$18. TV; cable (premium), VCR avail. Restaurant 7 am-11 pm. Rm serv 6:30-2 am. Bars 11-1 am. Ck-out noon. Convention facilities. Business center. In-rm modem link. Concierge. Shopping arcade. Barber, beauty shop. Valet parking. Airport transportation. Health club privileges. Bathrm phones, minibars, wet bars. Balconies. Omni Sports Coliseum, Georgia World Congress Center adj. Cr cds: A, C, D, DS, ER, JCB, MC, V.

D SC

★★★ **RADISSON HOTEL.** *165 Courtland St (30303), downtown. 404/659-6500; FAX 404/524-1259.* E-mail radinfo@radisson.atl.com; web www.radisson.atl.com. 747 rms, 12 story. S $170; D $180; each addl $10; suites $275-$675; under 18 free; wkend rates. Crib free. Covered parking $12. TV; cable (premium). Indoor/outdoor pool; whirlpool, poolside serv. Restaurant 6:30 am-11 pm. Bar 11-2 am, Sun to 12:30 am. Ck-out noon. Convention facilities. Business center. In-rm modem link. Concierge. Shopping arcade. Barber, beauty shop. Exercise equipt; weights, bicycles, sauna. Health club privileges. Game rm. Some bathrm phones. Some private patios, balconies. Cr cds: A, C, D, DS, ER, JCB, MC, V.

D SC

✔★★★ **RADISSON INN-EXECUTIVE PARK.** *2061 N Druid Hills Rd NE (30329), at I-85 exit 31, in Buckhead. 404/321-4174; FAX 404/636-7264.* 208 rms, 9 story. S, D $104-$114; each addl $10; under 18 free; wkend rates. Crib free. TV; cable (premium), VCR avail. Pool. Complimentary continental bkfst. Complimentary coffee in rms. Ck-out noon. Meeting rms. Business servs avail. In-rm modem link. Near Lenox Square. Luxury level. Cr cds: A, C, D, DS, ER, JCB, MC, V.

D SC

★★ **REGENCY SUITES.** *975 W Peachtree St NE (30309), at 10th St, in Midtown/Piedmont Park. 404/876-5003; FAX 404/817-7511; res: 800/642-3629.* E-mail sales@regencysuites.com. 96 kit. suites, 9 story. Suites $144-$244; under 18 free; wkend, monthly rates. Crib free. Garage, covered parking $7.50. TV; cable (premium). Complimentary continental bkfst. Complimentary coffee in rms. Ck-out 11 am. Coin Indry. Meeting rms. Business servs avail. Exercise equipt; weight machines, bicycles. Microwaves. Adj MARTA station. Cr cds: A, C, D, DS, MC, V.

D SC

★ ★ ★ ★ **RENAISSANCE WAVERLY.** *2450 Galleria Pkwy (30339), north of downtown. 770/953-4500; FAX 770/953-0740.* Web www.renaissancehotels.com. One of northwest Atlanta's most luxurious hotels is especially good for conventioneers and shoppers: The Galleria Specialty Mall makes up the building's west half. The ample rooms are appealingly decorated in earth tones and pastels and have 19th-century English reproductions. 521 rms, 14 story. S $169-$234; D $189-$254; each addl $20; suites $700-$1,400; under 18 free; wkend rates. Crib free. TV; cable (premium), VCR avail. 2 pools, 1 indoor; whirlpool. Complimentary coffee in rms. Restaurant 6 am-10 pm. Rm serv 24 hrs. 3 bars 11:30-1 am. Ck-out noon. Convention facilities. Business center. In-rm modem link. Concierge. Shopping arcade. Exercise rm; instructor, weight machines, bicycles, sauna, steam rm. Massage. Racquetball. Bathrm phones; refrigerator in suites. Luxury level. Cr cds: A, C, D, DS, ER, JCB, MC, V.

D SC

★ ★ ★ **RENAISSANCE-DOWNTOWN.** *590 W Peachtree St NW (30308), at North Ave, in Midtown/Piedmont Park. 404/881-6000; FAX 404/815-5010.* 504 rms, 25 story. S $165-$215; D $180-$240; suites $370-$750; under 18 free; wkend rates. Crib free. TV; cable (premium). Pool; poolside serv. Coffee in rms. Restaurant 6:30 am-midnight. Bar from 11 am. Ck-out noon. Meeting rms. Business center. Concierge. Gift shop. Free garage, valet parking. Exercise equipt; weights, bicycles. Health club privileges. Bathrm phones, minibars; some refrigerators, wet bars. Balconies. Luxurious rms; European-style personal service. Luxury level. Cr cds: A, C, D, DS, ER, JCB, MC, V.

D SC

★ ★ ★ ★ **THE RITZ-CARLTON.** *181 Peachtree St NE (30303), downtown. 404/659-0400; FAX 404/688-0400.* E-mail zrca@mindspring.com. This quiet retreat in downtown Atlanta has all the important facilities for business travelers and vacationers. The mood at this luxuriously decorated hotel is set by traditional afternoon tea served in an intimate sunken lobby beneath an 18th-century chandelier. 447 rms, 25 story. S, D $186-$265; suites $450-$1,165; under 12 free; wkend, hol rates. Crib free. Valet parking $17, in/out $10. TV; cable (premium), VCR avail. Restaurant (see THE RESTAURANT). Rm serv 24 hrs. Bar 11:30-2 am; entertainment. Ck-out noon. Convention facilities. Business center. In-rm modem link. Concierge. Gift shop. Exercise equipt; weight machine, treadmill, steam rm. Massage. Health club privileges. Refrigerators, minibars. Luxury level. Cr cds: A, C, D, DS, ER, JCB, MC, V.

D SC

★ ★ ★ ★ **THE RITZ-CARLTON, BUCKHEAD.** *3434 Peachtree Rd NE (30326), in Buckhead. 404/237-2700; FAX 404/239-0078.* Here is a busy but elegant and eminently comfortable place where you can unwind after a busy day or even spend a busy day. Decorated with the Ritz's signature 18th- and 19th-century antiques, this elegant gem bids a discreet welcome both to visitors and to locals who come to enjoy its many bars and restaurants, including the Dining Room, which serves haute cuisine. 553 rms, 22 story. S, D $170-$295; suites $365-$1,200; under 12 free; wkend rates. Crib free. Valet parking $14; self-park in/out $8. TV; cable (premium), VCR avail. Indoor pool; whirlpool, poolside serv. Restaurants 6:30 am-midnight (also see THE CAFE and THE DINING ROOM). Rm serv 24 hrs. Bar 11-2 am; entertainment. Ck-out noon. Convention facilities. Business center. In-rm modem link. Concierge. Shopping arcade. Airport transportation. Tennis privileges, pro. Golf privileges, greens fee $75-$150. Exercise rm; instructor, weight machines, bicycles, sauna, steam rm. Massage. Bathrm phones, minibars. Luxury level. Cr cds: A, C, D, DS, ER, JCB, MC, V.

D SC

★ ★ ★ **SHERATON COLONY SQUARE.** *188 14th St NE (30361), in Midtown/Piedmont Park. 404/892-6000; FAX 404/872-9192.* 467 rms, 27 story. S, D $185-$195; suites $350-$800; under 18 free; wkend rates. Crib free. Valet parking $10. TV; cable (premium), VCR avail. Pool; poolside serv. Restaurant 6:30 am-midnight. Bars 11-1 am, Sun to midnight. Ck-out noon. Convention facilities. Business center. In-rm modem link. Concierge. Shopping arcade. Tennis privileges. Golf privileges. Exercise equipt; weight machine, bicycles. Massage. Luxury level. Cr cds: A, C, D, DS, ER, JCB, MC, V.

D SC

★ ★ ★ **SHERATON SUITES-GALLERIA.** *2844 Cobb Pkwy SE (30339), I-285 exit 13, north of downtown. 770/955-3900; FAX 770/916-3165.* 278 suites, 17 story. S, D $199; each addl $20; under 18 free; wkend rates. Crib free. TV; cable (premium), VCR avail. 2 pools, 1 indoor; whirlpool, poolside serv. Complimentary coffee in rms. Restaurant 6:30 am-10:30 pm. Bar 11 am-midnight. Ck-out noon. Convention facilities. Business center. In-rm modem link. Gift shop. Free garage parking. Exercise equipt; weights, bicycles. Refrigerators, microwaves, minibars. Cr cds: A, C, D, DS, ER, MC, V.

D

✔ ★ ★ **SIERRA SUITES.** *2010 Powers Ferry Rd (30339), NW on I-285 to I-75 exit 110, north of downtown. 770/933-8010; res: 800/474-3772; FAX 770/933-8181.* Web www.sierrasuites.com. 89 kit. suites, 3 story. S $49.95-$89.95; D $59.95-$89.95; each addl $20; family rates; wkly, wkend; higher rates hols. Crib free. TV; cable (premium), VCR (movies avail). Complimentary coffee in rms. Restaurant nearby. Business servs avail. In-rm modem link. Coin Indry. Exercise equipt; bicycle, stair machine. Health club privileges. Pool. Refrigerators, microwaves. Grills. Cr cds: A, C, D, DS, JCB, MC, V.

D SC

★ ★ ★ **SUITE HOTEL-UNDERGROUND.** *54 Peachtree St (30303), at Underground Atlanta, downtown. 404/223-5555; FAX 404/223-0467; res: 800/477-5549.* 156 suites, 16 story. S $135-$210; D $145-$220; each addl $10; under 16 free; wkend rates. Crib free. Valet parking $12. TV; cable (premium). Coffee in rms. Restaurant 7-10 am, 5-11 pm. Ck-out noon. Meeting rms. Business servs avail. In-rm modem link. Health club privileges. Bathrm phones, minibars. Cr cds: A, C, D, DS, ER, JCB, MC, V.

D

★ ★ ★ **SWISSÔTEL ATLANTA.** *3391 Peachtree Rd NE (30326), in Buckhead. 404/365-0065; FAX 404/365-8787; res: 800/253-1397.* E-mail atl!slatl!ebabur@swissatl.mail.att.net; web www.travelweb.com/thisco/swiss/common/swiss.html. 365 rms, 22 story. S $165-$260; D $185-$285; suites $380-$1,500; under 16 free; wkend rates. Crib free. Garage parking $11, valet $15. TV; cable (premium), VCR avail. Indoor pool; poolside serv. Restaurant 6:30 am-11 pm. Rm serv 24 hrs. Bar 11 am-midnight, Fri, Sat to 1 am. Ck-out noon. Convention facilities. Business center. In-rm modem link. Concierge. Gift shop. Beauty shop. Exercise equipt; stair machine, weight machine, steam rm. Bathrm phones, minibars. Art and photo collection. Luxury level. Cr cds: A, C, D, DS, ER, JCB, MC, V.

D SC

★ ★ ★ **TERRACE GARDEN INN.** *3405 Lenox Rd NE (30326), in Buckhead. 404/261-9250; FAX 404/848-7391; res: 800/241-8260.* 361 rms, 10 story. S $135-$175; D $150-$190; suites $275-$495; under 14 free; wkend rates. Crib free. Covered parking $8. Pet accepted, some restrictions. TV; cable (premium), VCR avail. 2 pools, 1 indoor; whirlpool, wading pool, poolside serv. Restaurant 6:30 am-2 pm, 5-10 pm. Bars noon-2 am. Ck-out noon. Convention facilities. Business center. In-rm modem link. Concierge. Gift shop. Exercise equipt; weight machines, bicycles, sauna. Raquetball courts. Some refrigerators, wet bars; bathrm phone in suites. Some balconies. Luxury level. Cr cds: A, C, D, DS, MC, V.

D SC

★ ★ ★ **WESTIN ATLANTA NORTH.** *7 Concourse Pkwy (30328), north of downtown. 770/395-3900; FAX 770/395-3935.* 370 rms, 20 story. S $152; D $162; each addl $20; suites $275-$850; under 17 free; wkend rates. Crib free. TV; cable (premium), VCR avail. Heated pool; whirlpool, sauna, poolside serv. Restaurant 6:30 am-11 pm. Rm serv 24 hrs. Bar 4:30 pm-1 am, Sun to 12:30 am; entertainment Tues-Sat. Ck-out noon. Convention facilities. Business servs avail. In-rm modem link. Free parking.

Tennis privileges. 18-hole golf privileges, pro. Health club privileges. Some refrigerators. Luxury level. Cr cds: A, C, D, DS, ER, JCB, MC, V.

D SC

★ ★ ★ **THE WESTIN PEACHTREE PLAZA.** *210 Peachtree St (30303), at International Blvd, downtown. 404/659-1400; FAX 404/589-7424.* Web www.westin.com. 1,068 rms, 73 story. S $185-$205; D $235-$255; each addl $25; suites $385-$1,450; under 18 free; wkend rates. Crib free. Pet accepted, some restrictions. Garage $16; valet, in/out $15. TV; cable (premium), VCR avail. Indoor pool; poolside serv. Restaurants 6 am-11 pm. Rm serv 24 hrs. Bars (1 revolving rooftop) 11-2 am; entertainment. Ck-out 1 pm. Convention facilities. Business center. In-rm modem link. Concierge. Shopping arcade. Exercise equipt; weights, bicycles, sauna. Massage. Health club privileges. Many bathrm phones; refrigerators avail. 73-story circular tower built around 8-story atrium. Luxury level. Cr cds: A, C, D, DS, ER, JCB, MC, V.

D

★ ★ ★ **THE WYNDHAM GARDEN HOTEL-BUCKHEAD.** *3340 Peachtree Rd NE (30326), , in Buckhead. 404/231-1234; FAX 404/231-5236.* 221 rms, 6 story. S, D $119-$129; each addl $10; suites from $159; under 18 free; wkend rates. Crib $10. TV; cable (premium). Complimentary coffee in rms. Restaurant 6:30 am-10 pm, Sat & Sun from 7 am. Bar 4 pm-midnight, Sun from noon. Ck-out noon. Meeting rms. Business servs avail. In-rm modem link. Sundries. Health club privileges. Cr cds: A, C, D, DS, JCB, MC, V.

D SC

★ ★ ★ **WYNDHAM MIDTOWN.** *125 10th St (30309), at Peachtree St, in Midtown/Piedmont Park. 404/873-4800; FAX 404/870-1530.* 191 rms, 11 story. S $258; D $278; each addl $10; suites $250-$500; under 18 free; wkly, wkend rates. Crib free. Covered in/out parking $5; valet parking $12. TV; cable (premium), VCR avail. Indoor pool; whirlpool. Complimentary coffee in rms. Restaurant 6:30 am-10 pm; Sat, Sun from 7 am. Bar 4:30 pm-11 pm, Fri, Sat to 1 am. Ck-out noon. Meeting rms. Business servs avail. In-rm modem link. Exercise equipt; bicycles, weight machines, sauna, steam rm. Massage. Many refrigerators. Cr cds: A, C, D, DS, MC, V.

D

Inns

★ ★ **ANSLEY INN.** *253 15th St NE (30309), north of downtown. 404/872-9000; FAX 404/892-2318; res: 800/446-5416.* 23 rms, 3 story. S, D $100-$450; wkly, monthly rates. TV; cable (premium). Complimentary continental bkfst. Restaurant nearby. Ck-out noon, ck-in 3 pm. Business servs avail. In-rm modem link. Luggage handling. Valet serv. Concierge serv. In-rm whirlpools. Turn-of-the-century English Tudor house; art gallery. Cr cds: C, D, DS, ER, MC, V.

D

✔★ ★ **BEVERLY HILLS INN.** *65 Sheridan Dr (30305), in Buckhead. 404/233-8520; FAX 404/233-8659; res: 800/331-8520.* Web www.beverlyhillsinn.com. 18 kit. suites, 3 story. S, D $90-$120; each addl $10-$15; wkly, monthly rates. Crib avail. Pet accepted, some restrictions. TV; cable. Pool privileges. Complimentary continental bkfst. Restaurant nearby. Ck-out noon, ck-in 2 pm. Valet serv. Business servs avail. In-rm modem link. Health club privileges. Microwaves avail. Balconies. European-style hotel restored to 1929 ambience. Cr cds: A, C, D, DS, JCB, MC, V.

★ ★ ★ **GASLIGHT INN.** *1001 St Charles Ave NE (30306), 3 mi NE on I-75 to I-85 exit 96; in Midtown/Piedmont Park. 404/875-1001; FAX 404/876-1001.* E-mail innkeeper@gaslightinn.com; web www.gaslightinn.com. 6 rms, 2 story, 3 suites. S, D $85-$125; each addl $12; suites $149-$195; under 12 free; wkly rates; wkend rates (2-day min). TV; cable (premium), VCR (avail). Complimentary continental bkfst. Restaurant nearby. Ck-out noon, ck-in 3 pm. Business servs avail. In-rm modem link. Luggage handling. Street parking. Many refrigerators; some in-rm whirlpools, microwaves, minibars, wet bars, fireplaces. Balconies. Grills avail. Built in 1903. Totally nonsmoking. Cr cds: A, C, D, MC, V.

D

★ ★ **KING-KEITH HOUSE.** *889 Edgewood Ave NE (30307), downtown. 404/688-7330; FAX 404/584-0730.* Web travelbase.com. 5 rms, 2 share bath, 3 story. S $50-$100; D $60-$125; each addl $10; under 12 free. Cable TV in common rm. Complimentary full bkfst. Restaurant nearby. Ck-out noon, ck-in 2 pm. Luggage handling. Valet serv. Concierge. Gift shop. Guest lndry. Street parking. Some refrigerators. Picnic tables, grills. Antiques. Totally nonsmoking. Cr cds: MC, V.

✔★ ★ ★ **SHELLMONT.** *821 Piedmont Ave NE (30308), in Midtown/Piedmont Park. 404/872-9290; FAX 404/872-5379.* Web www.innbrook.comgaatl.shellmont. 4 rms, 2 story, carriage house. S, D $85-$115; each addl $20; carriage house $115-$150. Children under 12 in carriage house only. Crib free. TV; cable (premium). Complimentary full bkfst. Restaurant nearby. Ck-out 11 am, ck-in 3 pm. Some patios, balconies. Restored Victorian house (1891); Tiffany windows, antiques, artwork. Totally nonsmoking. Cr cds: A, D, JCB, MC, V.

★ ★ ★ **SUGAR MAGNOLIA.** *804 Edgewood Ave NE (30307), east of downtown. 404/222-0226; FAX 404/681-1067.* E-mail dstar 37866@aol.com. 4 rms, 2 story. S, D $65-$100. Crib free. TV. Complimentary continental bkfst; coffee in library. Ck-out 11 am, ck-in 2 pm. Luggage handling. Concierge serv. Business center. Street parking. Refrigerators; some fireplaces. Balcony. Victorian house (1892) in historic Inman Park district; period furnishings. Totally nonsmoking. Cr cds: MC, V.

Resort

★ ★ ★ **EVERGREEN CONFERENCE CENTER.** *(1 Lakeview Dr, Stone Mountain 30086) W on US 78, in Stone Mountain State Park. 770/879-9900; FAX 770/464-9013; res: 800/722-1000.* Web www.stonemountainpark.org. 238 rms, 5 story. $6 park entrance fee (required to reach resort). Apr-Oct: S $129; D $149; each addl $20; suites $200-$300; family, wkend, wkly, hol rates; golf plans; lower rates rest of yr. Crib $8. TV; cable (premium). 2 pools, 1 indoor; whirlpool, wading pool, poolside serv. Coffee in rms. Restaurant 6:30 am-10 pm. Box lunches, snacks, picnics. Rm serv 24 hrs. Bar. Ck-out noon, ck-in 4 pm. Business center. In-rm modem link. Gift shop. Grocery 1 mi. Bellhops. Concierge. Valet serv. Sports dir. Lighted tennis. 36-hole golf, greens fee $42-$45, pro, putting green, driving range. Swimming beach; boats. Hiking. Bicycles (rentals). Social dir. Game rm. Exercise equipt; weight machine, bicycles. Massage. Health club privileges. Refrigerators. Balconies. Picnic tables. Situated on lake within Stone Mountain State Park. Cr cds: A, C, D, DS, ER, JCB, MC, V.

D SC

Restaurants

★ ★ ★ **103 WEST.** *103 W Paces Ferry Rd (30305), in Buckhead. 404/233-5993.* Web www.buckheadrestaurants.com. Hrs: 6-11 pm; Fri, Sat from 5:30. Closed Sun; major hols. Res accepted. Contintenal, French menu. Bar. Wine cellar. A la carte entrees: dinner $15.50-$32.50. Specialties: smoked Cascade Mountain trout, sauteed medallions of venison from the loin, broiled noisettes of lamb. Own baking, desserts. Pianist. Valet parking. Chef-owned. Cr cds: A, C, D, DS, MC, V.

D

★ ★ ★ **THE ABBEY.** *163 Ponce de Leon Ave NE, at Piedmont Rd & North Ave, in Midtown/Piedmont Park. 404/876-8831.* E-mail abbey33@aol.com. Hrs: 6-10 pm. Closed major hols. Res accepted. Continental menu. Bar from 5 pm. Wine cellar. A la carte entrees: dinner $19-$25. Specializes in seafood, chicken, veal. Own baking, desserts.

Harpist. Valet parking. Former church; 50-ft arched and vaulted ceiling. Costumed servers. Cr cds: A, C, D, DS, MC, V.

★ ★ ★ **ABRUZZI RISTORANTE.** *2355 Peachtree Rd NE, at Peachtree Battle Shopping Center, in Buckhead. 404/261-8186.* Hrs: 11:30 am-2:30 pm, 5:30-10:30 pm; Fri, Sat 5:30-11 pm. Closed Sun; some major hols. Res required. Italian menu. Bar. Semi-a la carte: lunch $15, dinner $25. Specialties: Capellini alla Nico, homemade spinach ravioli, osso buco. Parking. Florentine decor. Jacket. Cr cds: A, D, MC, V.

D

✔★ **AGNES & MURIEL'S.** *1514 Monroe Dr (30324), in Midtown/Piedmont Park. 404/885-1000.* Hrs: 11 am-11 pm; Fri to midnight; Sat 10 am-midnight; Sun 10 am-11 pm; Sat, Sun brunch 10 am-3 pm. Closed Thanksgiving, Dec 25. Bar. A la carte entrees: lunch $3.95-$10.95, dinner $3.95-$14.95. Sat, Sun brunch $3.95-$10.95. Specializes in turkey meatloaf, grilled salmon pot pie. 1950s decor. Totally nonsmoking. Cr cds: A, C, D, DS, JCB, MC, V.

D

✔★ ★ **ANIS.** *2974 Grandview Ave (30305), in Buckhead. 404/233-9889.* Hrs: 11:30 am-2:30 pm, 6-10 pm; Fri, Sat to 10:30 pm; Sun brunch to 2:30 pm. Closed some major hols. Southern French menu. Bar. Semi-a la carte: lunch, dinner $7-$15. Sun brunch $6-$12. Specialties: grilled tuna with aioli, bouillabaise. Entertainment Thurs. Parking. Outdoor dining. European decor. Cr cds: A, D, MC, V.

★ ★ ★ **ANTHONY'S.** *3109 Piedmont Rd NE (30305), in Buckhead. 404/262-7379.* E-mail cwik@atlanta.com. Hrs: 6-11 pm. Closed major hols. Res accepted. Continental menu. Bar. Wine cellar. A la carte entrees: dinner $18.95-$29.95. Specialties: mixed grill of wild game, yellow fin tuna, fried green tomato Napolean. Own baking. Valet parking. Plantation house (1797); antiques, fireplaces. Cr cds: A, C, D, DS, JCB, MC, V.

D

✔★ ★ **ARUGULA.** *3639 Piedmont Rd NE (30305), in Buckhead. 404/814-0959.* Hrs: 11:30 am-2:30 pm, 5-10 pm; Fri to 11 pm; Sat 5-11 pm; Sun from 5 pm. Closed some major hols. Res accepted. Contemporary Amer menu. Bar. Semi-a la carte: lunch $7-$10.50, dinner $10.50-$19.50. Specialties: Mahi Mahi, roasted garlic soup, upside down apple "Gabby." Valet parking wkends. Outdoor dining. Modern decor. Cr cds: A, MC, V.

D

★ ★ **ATLANTA FISH MARKET.** *265 Pharr Rd (30305), in Buckhead. 404/262-3165.* Hrs: 11 am-11 pm; Fri, Sat to midnight; Sun 4:30-10 pm. Closed Thanksgiving, Dec 25. Bar. Semi-a la carte: lunch $7.50-$25, dinner $12.50-$26.50 Child's meals. Specializes in seafood. Parking. Cr cds: A, C, D, DS, MC, V.

D

✔★ ★ **BABETTE'S CAFE.** *471 N Highland Ave NE (30307), 3½ mi E on Freedom Pkwy, exit 96, S on N Highland Ave, east of downtown. 404/523-9121.* Hrs: 6-10 pm; Fri, Sat to 11 pm; Sun 5-9 pm; Sun brunch 10:30 am-2:30 pm. Closed Mon; some major hols. Bar. Semi-a la carte: dinner $9.50-$17.50. Sun brunch $4.75-$8.50. Child's meals. Specialties: cassoulet, artichoke ravioli, steamed mussels with strawberries and serrano peppers. Romantic dining. Cr cds: A, D, DS, MC, V.

D

★ ★ ★ ★ **BACCHANALIA.** *3125 Piedmont Rd (30305), in Buckhead. 404/365-0410.* Angels highlight the walls and tables of this small restaurant, one of Atlanta's most charming. Austrian crystal chandeliers, Oriental rugs and original art and antiques add to the ambience. Baking is done on the premises. Specializes in seafood, game. Hrs: 6-9:30 pm; Fri, Sat to 10 pm. Closed Sun, Mon; some major hols. Res required. Wine, beer. Prix fixe: dinner $40. Parking. Totally nonsmoking. Cr cds: A, D, MC, V.

D

✔★ ★ **BASIL'S MEDITERRANEAN CAFE.** *2985 Grandview Ave (30305), in Buckhead. 404/233-9755.* Hrs: 11:30 am-2:30 pm, 6-10 pm; Fri, Sat to 11 pm. Closed Sun; some major hols. Res accepted. Mediterranean menu. Bar. A la carte entrees: lunch $4.50-$8.25, dinner $8.25-$16.95. Parking. Outdoor dining. Mediterranean decor. Cr cds: A, D, DS, MC, V.

D ♥

✔★ **THE BEEHIVE.** *(1090 Alpharetta St, Roswell 30075) Approx 5 mi NW on Holcomb Bridge Rd (US 140). 770/594-8765.* Hrs: 5-10 pm; Fri-Sat to 11 pm; Sun 5-9 pm. Closed Mon, Tues; most major hols. Bar. Semi-a la carte: dinner $4.95-$13.95. Specializes in sandwiches, fresh pasta. Parking. Converted house. Cr cds: MC, V.

★ ★ ★ **BISTANGO.** *1100 Peachtree St NE (30309), in Midtown/Piedmont Park. 404/724-0901.* Hrs: 11:30 am-2:30 pm, 5:30-9 pm; Fri, Sat to 10 pm. Closed Sun; most major hols. Res accepted. Continental menu. Bar. Wine list. Semi-a la carte: lunch $8.95-$15.95, dinner $14.95-$23.95. Specialties: stuffed veal chop, rack of lamb, seared salmon on purple rice. Parking. Outdoor dining. Modern decor. Cr cds: A, C, D, DS, MC, V.

D

★ ★ **THE BISTRO.** *56 E Andrews Dr NW (30305), in Buckhead. 404/231-5733.* Hrs: 6-11 pm. Closed Sun, Mon; Jan 1, Thanksgiving, Dec 25. Res accepted. French menu. Bar. Semi-a la carte: dinner $18-$28. Specialties: lamb chops, grilled salmon steak, braised filet of Chilean sea bass. Parking. Outdoor dining. Many paintings; antique German mirrors. Cr cds: C, D, DS, JCB, MC, V.

D

★ ★ **BLUE RIDGE GRILL.** *1261 W Paces Ferry Rd (30327), in Buckhead. 404/233-5030.* Hrs: 11:30 am-2:30 pm, 5:30-11 pm; Sat, Sun brunch to 2:30 pm. Closed most major hols. Res accepted. Bar. Semi-a la carte: lunch $7.95-$14.95, dinner $14.95-$37.95. Sat, Sun brunch $7.95-$13.95. Specializes in fish, duck, grilled vegetables. Alpine mountain lodge. Cr cds: A, D, DS, MC, V.

D

★ ★ ★ **BONE'S.** *3130 Piedmont Rd NE (30305), in Buckhead. 404/237-2663.* Hrs: 11:30 am-2:30 pm, 6-11 pm; Sat, Sun from 6 pm. Closed major hols. Res accepted. Bar. Wine cellar. Semi-a la carte: lunch $8.95-$16.95. A la carte entrees: dinner $21.95-$36. Specializes in aged prime beef, seafood, live Maine lobster. Own desserts. Valet parking. Club atmosphere; wood paneling, fireplace. Cr cds: A, C, D, DS, MC, V.

D

✔★ ★ ★ **BRASSERIE LE COZE.** *3393 Peachtree Rd (30326), in Lenox Square Mall, in Buckhead. 404/266-1440.* Hrs: 11:30 am-2:30 pm, 5:30-10 pm; Fri 11:30 am-3 pm, 5:30-11 pm; Sat 11:30 am-3:30 pm, 5:30-11 pm. Closed Sun; Thanksgiving, Dec 25. Res accepted. Country French menu. Bar. Wine list. Semi-a la carte: lunch $7.50-$16, dinner $13-$19.50. Specializes in roast chicken, shepherd's pie, desserts. Outdoor dining. Stylish decor. Cr cds: A, D, MC, V.

D ♥

★ ★ **BUCKHEAD DINER.** *3073 Piedmont Rd (30305), in Buckhead. 404/262-3336.* Web www.buckheadrestaurants.com. Hrs: 11 am-midnight; Sun 10:30 am-10 pm. Closed Thanksgiving, Dec 25. Bar. A la carte entrees: lunch $5.95-$14.95, dinner $5.95-$15.95. Specialties: sautéed grouper, veal and wild mushroom meat loaf, white chocolate banana cream pie. Valet parking. Update of classic, stainless steel-wrapped diner. Cr cds: A, C, D, DS, MC, V.

D

★ ★ **THE CABIN.** *2678 Buford Hwy NE (30324), in Buckhead. 404/315-7676.* Hrs: 11:30 am-2:30 pm, 5:30-10 pm; Fri to 11 pm; Sat 5:30-11 pm. Closed Sun; some major hols. Res accepted. Bar. Semi-a la carte: lunch $4.95-$9.95, dinner $16.95-$27.95. Child's meals. Valet parking (dinner). Specializes in steak, seafood. Log cabin built in 1931. Cr cds: A, C, D, DS, MC, V.

D

★★★ **THE CAFE.** *(See The Ritz-Carlton, Buckhead Hotel) 404/237-2700.* Hrs: 6:30 am-midnight; Sun brunch 11:30 am-2:30 pm. Bar. A la carte entrees: bkfst $7-$15, lunch $10-$22, dinner $20-$30. Sun brunch $38. Child's meals. Specializes in regional cuisine. Own pastries. Pianist. Valet parking. Antiques, original art. Totally nonsmoking. Cr cds: A, C, D, DS, ER, JCB, MC, V.

D

✔★★ **CAFE CHANTERELLE.** *4200 Paces Ferry Rd NE (30039), north of downtown. 770/433-9775.* Hrs: 11:30 am-2:30 pm, 6-10 pm; Fri, Sat to 11 pm. Closed some major hols. Res accepted. Continental menu. Bar. A la carte entrees: lunch $5.95-$9.95, dinner $8.95-$19.95. Specializes in fresh seafood, pasta, desserts. Parking. Cr cds: A, D, DS, MC, V.

D

✔★★ **CAFE LA GLACE.** *562 Boulevard St SE (30312), east of downtown. 404/622-3114.* Hrs: 11 am-2 pm; Thurs, Fri also 6-10 pm; Sat from 6 pm. Res accepted. French menu. Wine, beer. Semi-a la carte: lunch $4.50-$8, dinner $13-$20. Specialties: sautéed duck foie gras, chateaubriand of beef tenderloin, sautéed lump crab cakes. Own desserts. Outdoor dining. French bistro atmosphere. Totally nonsmoking. Cr cds: A, DS, MC, V.

D

✔★★ **CAFE TU TU TANGO.** *220 Pharr Rd (30305), in Buckhead. 404/841-6222.* Hrs: 11:30 am-11 pm; Wed to midnight; Thurs to 1 am; Fri, Sat to 2 am. Eclectic menu. Bar. A la carte entrees: lunch, dinner $3.95-$7.95. Specialties: Cajun chicken egg rolls, Barcelona stir-fry, Hurricane shrimp. Valet parking. Outdoor dining. Artist's studio decor; painters at work. Cr cds: A, D, MC, V.

D

★★ **CAMEAUX LOUISIANA BAR & GRILL.** *(9925 Haynes Bridge Rd, Alpharetta 30202) 25 mi N on GA 400, exit 9. 770/442-2524.* Hrs: 11 am-10 pm; Fri, Sat to 11 pm; Sun brunch to 3 pm. Closed Jan 1, Dec 25. Res accepted. Cajun menu. Bar. Semi-a la carte: lunch $3.95-$9.95, dinner $8.95-$21.95. Sun brunch $14.95. Child's meals. Specialties: boiled crawfish, crab cakes, crawfish etouffee. Jazz and blues Tues, Thurs-Sat. Cajun ambience. Cr cds: A, DS, MC, V.

✔★ **CAMILLE'S.** *1186 N Highland Ave (30306), in Midtown/Piedmont Park. 404/872-7203.* Web www.camilles.com. Hrs: 5:30-11 pm. Bar. Semi-a la carte: dinner $10.25-$14.95. Specialties: calamari, linguini with clams, rice balls. Parking. Outdoor dining. Cr cds: A, D, MC, V.

D

★★★★ **CANOE.** *4199 Paces Ferry Rd NW (30339), north of downtown. 770/432-2663.* E-mail canoe@bellsouth.net. Wonderfully landscaped grounds dotted with walkways and benches add to the outdoor dining experience here. Inside, brick walls, wrought iron and splashes of Southwestern upholstery accent the dining areas. Specialties: slow-roasted pork with gorgonzola polenta and spicy escarole, Florida grouper with roasted sweet corn and lobster succotash, chocolate hazelnut praline cake. Hrs: 10:30 am-2:30 pm, 5:30-10:30 pm; Fri to 11:30 pm; Sat 5:30-11:30 pm; Sun 10 am-2:30 pm (brunch), 5:30-9 pm. Closed Jan 1, Thanksgiving, Dec 25. Res accepted. Bar. Wine list. Semi-a la carte: lunch $5.95-$13.95, dinner $12.95-$19.95. Sun brunch $7.95-$13.50. Valet parking. Outdoor dining. Cr cds: A, C, D, MC, V.

D

★★★ **CARBO'S CAFE.** *3717 Roswell Rd (30342), in Buckhead. 404/231-4433.* Hrs: 5:30-10:30 pm; Fri, Sat to 11:30 pm. Closed major hols. Res accepted. Continental menu. Bar 5 pm-3 am. Wine cellar. Complete meals: dinner $13.25-$28.95. Specializes in seafood, veal, steak. Own baking. Piano bar. Valet parking. European decor; antiques, fireplaces, fountain. Cr cds: A, C, D, MC, V.

D

★★★ **CASSIS.** *(See Grand Hyatt Hotel) 404/365-8100.* Hrs: 6:30 am-10:30 pm; Fri, Sat to 11 pm; Sun brunch 11:30 am-3 pm. Res accepted. Continental menu. Bar. Wine list. A la carte entrees: bkfst $8.25-$13, lunch $8.50-$16.50, dinner $8.50-$26. Buffet: bkfst $13. Sun brunch $34. Child's meals. Specializes in grilled meats, fish, bistro items. Valet parking. Outdoor dining. View of waterfall and gardens. Cr cds: A, C, D, DS, ER, JCB, MC, V.

D

★★★ **CHOPS.** *70 W Paces Ferry Rd (30305), in Buckhead. 404/262-2675.* Web www.buckheadrestaurants.com. Hrs: 11:30 am-2:30 pm, 5:30-11 pm; Fri to midnight; Sat 5:30-midnight; Sun 5-10 pm. Closed some major hols. Res accepted. Bar. A la carte entrees: lunch $7.95-$15.95, dinner $14.75-$34.50. Specializes in steak, fresh seafood. Own pastries. Valet parking. Art deco motif. Cr cds: A, C, D, DS, MC, V.

D

★★★ **CIBOULETTE.** *1529 Piedmont Ave (30324), in Midtown/Piedmont Park. 404/874-7600.* Hrs: 6-10 pm; Fri, Sat 5:30-11 pm. Closed Sun; major hols. French menu. Bar. Semi-a la carte: dinner $16.95-$27.95. Specialties: nage of fish, duck liver pâté, game. Own desserts. Valet parking (wkends). Open kitchen. Elegant atmosphere. Cr cds: A, C, D, DS, MC, V.

D

★★★ **CITY GRILL.** *50 Hurt Plaza (30303), in the Hurt Bldg, downtown. 404/524-2489.* Hrs: 11:30 am-2:30 pm, 5:30-10 pm; Sat from 5:30 pm. Closed Sun; most major hols. Res accepted. Contemporary Amer menu. Bar. Wine cellar. A la carte entrees: lunch $7-$15, dinner $17-$25. Specialties: blue crab cakes with lemon linguine, mustard-crusted aged New York strip, chocolate pecan soufflé. Own pastries. Valet parking (dinner). Rotunda entrance, bronze chandeliers, marble columns, wall murals. Cr cds: A, C, D, DS, MC, V.

D

✔★ **THE COLONNADE.** *1879 Cheshire Bridge Rd (30324), in Buckhead. 404/874-5642.* Hrs: 11 am-2:30 pm, 5-9 pm; Fri, Sat to 10 pm; Sun 11 am-9 pm. Closed Dec 24-25. Southwestern menu. Bar. Semi-a la carte: lunch $4.50-$14, dinner $5.95-$16. Specializes in fried chicken, turkey, seafood. Parking. Casual dining. Family-owned. No cr cds accepted.

D

★★★ **COUNTRY PLACE.** *1197 Peachtree St NE (30361), Colony Square Complex, in Midtown/Piedmont Park. 404/881-0144.* Hrs: 11:30 am-2:30 pm, 5:30-11 pm; Sat from 5:30 pm; Sun 11 am-3 pm (brunch), 5:30-10 pm. Closed Thanksgiving, Dec 25. Bar. Semi-a la carte: lunch $8.95-$12.95, dinner $14.95-$21.00. Sun brunch $6.95-$13.95. Pianist Thur-Sat. Parking. Cr cds: A, C, D, DS, MC, V.

D

★★ **DAILEY'S.** *17 International Blvd (30303), downtown. 404/681-3303.* Hrs: 11 am-3:30 pm, 5:30-11 pm; Fri, Sat to midnight. Closed major hols. Res accepted. Bar. Semi-a la carte: lunch $4.95-$12.95, dinner $16-$25. Specializes in pepper-crusted swordfish, desserts. Pianist. Converted warehouse; vaulted ceiling. Cr cds: A, C, D, DS, MC, V.

D

★★ **DANTE'S DOWN THE HATCH.** *3380 Peachtree Rd NE (30326), across from Lenox Square, in Buckhead. 404/266-1600.* Hrs: 4-11:30 pm; Fri, Sat to 12:30 am; Sun 5-11 pm. Closed Jan 1, Dec 25. Res accepted. Bar. Semi-a la carte: dinner $12.50-$26. Specializes in mixed fondue dinners. Own desserts. Classical guitarist; jazz trio. Parking. Nautical decor. Antique English, Polish ship figureheads. Ship-board dining within multilevel vessel. Family-owned. Cr cds: A, C, D, DS, MC, V.

D

★ ★ **DICK & HARRY'S.** *(1570 Holcomb Bridge Rd, Roswell 30076) in Holcomb Woods Village shopping center. 770/641-8757.* Hrs: 11:30 am-2 pm, 5:30-10 pm; Fri to 11:30 pm; Sat 5:30-11:30 pm. Closed Sun; major hols. Res accepted. Contemporary Amer menu. Bar. Semi-a la carte: lunch $5-$14, dinner $12-$28. Child's meals. Specialties: crab cakes, barbecued salmon, emu. Valet parking Fri, Sat. Outdoor dining. Casual dining. Cr cds: A, C, D, DS, MC, V.

D

★ ★ ★ ★ ★ **THE DINING ROOM.** *(See The Ritz-Carlton, Buckhead Hotel) 404/237-2700.* Chef Joel Antunes's daily menu is limited, but it embraces the best that the season offers in elegant surroundings. Traditional European menu with Asian influences. Specializes in light contemporary cuisine. Own baking, pasta, ice cream. Menu changes daily. Hrs: 6-9:30 pm. Closed Sun; major hols. Res accepted. Bar. Wine cellar. Prix fixe: dinner $65-$78. Valet parking. Jacket. Cr cds: A, C, D, DS, ER, JCB, MC, V.

D

✔★ **DUSTY'S BARBECUE.** *1815 Briarcliff Rd (30306), east of downtown. 404/320-6264.* Web www.dustys.com. Hrs: 11 am-9 pm; Fri, Sat to 10 pm. Closed Jan 1, Thanksgiving, Dec. 25. Semi-a la carte: lunch, dinner $3.70-$12.25. Child's meals. Specializes in chicken, beef, baby back ribs. Parking. Casual dining. Cr cds: A, D, DS, MC, V.

✔ ★ ★ **EBBET'S FIELD GRILL.** *(875 Mansell Rd, Roswell 30076) in Mansell Square Shopping Center. 770/645-1299.* Hrs: 11:30 am-2:30 pm, 5:30-10 pm; Fri to 11 pm; Sat 5:30-11 pm; Sun from 5:30 pm. Closed Easter, Memorial Day, Dec 25. Res accepted Tues-Thurs dinner. Continental menu. Bar. Semi-a la carte: lunch $5.25-$8.95, dinner $7.95-$18.95. Child's meals. Specialties: sweet and sour calamari, pistachio-crusted grouper, New York strip. Baseball memorabilia. Cr cds: A, C, D, DS, MC, V.

D

✔★ ★ **EMBERS SEAFOOD GRILLE.** *(234 Hilderbrand Dr, Sandy Springs 30328) N on GA 9. 404/256-0977.* Hrs: 11:30 am-2:30 pm, 6-10:30 pm. Res accepted. Bar. Semi-a la carte: lunch $5.95-$7.95, dinner $10.95-$16.95. Child's meals. Specializes in seafood, steak. Parking. Modern wall hangings. Cr cds: A, C, D, DS, MC, V.

D

★ ★ **FOOD STUDIO.** *887 W Marietta St (30318), north of downtown. 404/815-6677.* Web www.boldamerican.com. Hrs: 5:30-11 pm; Fri, Sat to midnight. Closed most major hols. Res accepted. Bar. Semi-a la carte: dinner $15.95-$22.95. Specialties: tuna taretare, rabbit enchilada, mushroom-encrusted tilapia. Valet parking. Outdoor dining. Contemporary decor in refurbished 1904 plow factory bldg. Totally nonsmoking. Cr cds: A, D, MC, V.

D

✔★ ★ **FRATELLI DI NAPOLI.** *2101-B Bennett St (30309), in Buckhead. 404/351-1533.* Hrs: 5-11 pm; Fri, Sat to midnight; Sun 4-10 pm. Closed Thanksgiving, Dec 25. Italian menu. Bar. Semi-a la carte: dinner $12-$18. Child's meals. Specializes in pasta, veal. Valet parking. Italian decor. Totally nonsmoking. Cr cds: A, D, DS, MC, V.

D

✔★ **GEORGIA GRILLE.** *2290 Peachtree Rd (30309), in Buckhead. 404/352-3517.* E-mail Richard@menus.atlanta.com; web menus .atlanta.com. Hrs: 6-10 pm; Fri, Sat to 11 pm. Closed Dec 25, Thanksgiving. Southwestern menu. Bar. Semi-a la carte: dinner $3.95-$18.95. Specializes in pork, chicken, seafood. Parking. Outdoor dining. Southwestern decor. Totally nonsmoking. Cr cds: A, MC, V.

D

✔ ★ ★ **HARVEST.** *853 N Highland Ave NE (30306), 5 mi NE on Ponce de Leon to N Highland Ave, east of downtown. 404/876-8244.* Hrs: 5:30-10 pm; Fri, Sat to 11 pm; Sun brunch 11 am-2:30 pm. Closed Labor Day, Thanksgiving, Dec 25. Contemporary Amer menu. Bar. Semi-a la carte: dinner $10.95-$17.95. Sun brunch $6.95-$10.95. Specialties: seared Chilean sea bass, open-faced vegetable ravioli, chili-rubbed pork tenderloin. Valet parking. Outdoor dining. Paintings, antiques; 3 fireplaces. Totally nonsmoking. Cr cds: A, D, MC, V.

D

✔★ ★ **HAVELI.** *225 Spring St (30303), in Gift Mart, downtown. 404/522-4545.* Hrs: 11:30 am-2:30 pm, 5:30-10 pm; Sun from 5:30 pm. Closed Dec 25. Res accepted. Indian menu. Bar. A la carte entrees: dinner $11.95-$15.95. Specialties: fish tikka, daal maharani, baingan bharta. Parking. Indian decor. Cr cds: A, D, DS, MC, V.

D

★ ★ **HORSERADISH GRILL.** *4320 Powers Ferry Rd (30342), north of downtown. 404/255-7277.* Web www.horseradishgrill.com. Hrs: 11:30 am-10 pm; Fri, Sat to 11:30 pm; Sun to 9 pm. Closed Jan 1, Thanksgiving, Dec 25. Bar. Semi-a la carte: lunch $6.95-$15.95, dinner $14.50-$23.95. Child's meals. Specialties: skillet fried chicken, grilled prime veal chops, lemon chess pie. Parking. Outdoor dining. Modern art, stone fireplace; garden area with stone walk. Totally nonsmoking. Cr cds: A, C, D, DS, MC, V.

D

★ ★ ★ **HSU'S GOURMET CHINESE.** *192 Peachtree Center Ave (30303), downtown. 404/659-2788.* Hrs: 11:30 am-10:30 pm; Sun 5-10 pm. Closed July 4, Thanksgiving, Dec 25. Res accepted. Chinese menu. Bar. Wine list. A la carte entrees: lunch $5.95-$11.95, dinner $10.95-$18.95. Specialties: Peking Duck, asparagus shrimp in black bean sauce, steamed salmon with ginger sauce. Validated parking (dinner). Chinese decor. Cr cds: A, C, D, DS, MC, V.

D

★ ★ ★ **IMPERIAL FEZ.** *2285 Peachtree Rd NE (30309), in Buckhead. 404/351-0870.* E-mail rafih@mindspring.com; web www.imperial fez.com. Hrs: 6-11 pm. Res accepted. Moroccan menu. Serv bar. A la carte entrees: dinner $13.50-$18. Complete meal: dinner $35-$45. Child's meals. Specialties: lamb couscous, shish kebab, fish tagine. Moroccan dancers. Valet parking. Tented ceilings, low tables with silk cushioned seating. Cr cds: A, C, D, DS, JCB, MC, V.

D

★ **INDIGO COASTAL GRILL.** *1397 N Highland Ave (30306), in Midtown/Piedmont Park. 404/876-0676.* Hrs: 5:30-10 pm; Fri, Sat to 11:30 pm; Sun brunch 10 am-3 pm. Closed July 4, Dec 25. Res accepted. Bar. Semi-a la carte: dinner $12.75-$18.95. Sun brunch $6.95-$10.95. Specializes in seafood, organically grown vegetables, Key lime pie. Outdoor dining. Nautical decor. Vintage 1950s jukebox. Cr cds: A, D, MC, V.

D

★ ★ **JIM WHITE'S HALF SHELL.** *2349 Peachtree Rd NE (30305), in Peachtree Battle Shopping Center, in Buckhead. 404/237-9924.* Hrs: 5-10 pm; Fri, Sat to 11 pm. Closed Sun; most major hols. Bar. Semi-a la carte: dinner $13.95-$29. Child's meals. Specializes in seafood. Parking. Nautical decor. Family-owned. Cr cds: A, D, MC, V.

D

★ ★ **KUDZU CAFE.** *3215 Peachtree Rd NE (30305), in Buckhead. 404/262-0661.* Hrs: 11 am-11 pm; Fri, Sat to midnight; Sat, Sun brunch to 2:30 pm. Closed some major hols. Southern contemporary menu. Bar. Semi-a la carte: lunch $5.50-$16.95, dinner $9.95-$21.95. Sat, Sun brunch $7.95-$16.95. Specializes in grilled chicken, fish, pork chops. Parking. Casual dining. Cr cds: A, D, DS, MC, V.

D

★ ★ ★ **LA GROTTA.** *2637 Peachtree Rd NE (30305), in Buckhead. 404/231-1368.* Hrs: 6-10:30 pm. Closed Sun; major hols; also last wk June-1st wk July. Res accepted. Northern, regional Italian menu. Bar. Wine list. Semi-a la carte: dinner $15-$25.50. Specializes in veal, seafood, steak. Own pasta, sauces, desserts. Valet parking. Seasonal outdoor dining. Jacket. Totally nonsmoking. Cr cds: A, C, D, DS, MC, V.

★ ★ ★ **LA GROTTA RAVINIA.** *(See Crowne Plaza Ravinia Hotel) 770/395-9925.* Hrs: 11:30 am-2 pm, 5:45-10 pm. Closed Sun; major hols. Res accepted. Northern Italian menu. Serv bar. Wine list. A la carte entrees: lunch $7.95-$13.95, dinner $12.95-$22.95. Specialties: grilled veal chops, portabello mushrooms, black and white linguine. Valet parking. Outdoor dining. Windows overlook gardens and patio. Cr cds: A, C, D, DS, JCB, MC, V.

D

★ ★ **LA PAZ.** *6410 Roswell Rd (30328), in Sandy Springs, north of downtown. 404/256-3555.* Hrs: 11 am-10 pm; Fri, Sat to 11 pm. Mexican menu. Bar. A la carte entrees: dinner $5.95-$16.95. Child's meals. Own desserts. Parking. Outdoor dining. Cr cds: A, C, D, DS, MC, V.

D

★ ★ **LOMBARDI'S.** *94 Upper Pryor St (30303), downtown. 404/522-6568.* Hrs: 11 am-10 pm; Fri to 11 pm; Sat 5-11 pm; Sun 5-10 pm. Closed some major hols. Res accepted. Italian menu. Bar. A la carte entrees: lunch $7.50-$11.50, dinner $8.95-$15.95. Specializes in pasta, pizza, veal. Parking. Cr cds: A, C, D, DS, MC, V.

D

✔★ ★ **LUNA SI.** *1931 Peachtree Rd (30309), in Brookwood Village Shopping Center, in Buckhead. 404/355-5993.* Hrs: 5:30-10:30 pm; Fri, Sat to 11 pm. Closed July 4, Thanksgiving, Dec 25. Res accepted. Seafood menu. Bar. Semi-a la carte: dinner $15-$19. Menu changes monthly. Works by local artists. Totally nonsmoking. Cr cds: A, C, D, DS, JCB, MC, V.

D

★ ★ **MAGGIANO'S LITTLE ITALY.** *3368 Peachtree Road NE (30326), 8 mi N on Peachtree Rd, in Buckhead. 404/816-9650.* Hrs: 11:30 am-2:30 pm, 5-10 pm; Fri to 11 pm; Sat 11:30 am-11 pm; Sun noon-10 pm. Closed Thanksgiving, Dec 25. Res accepted. Italian menu. Bar. A la carte entrees: lunch $3.95-$13.95, dinner $5.95-$29.95. Specialties: calamari fritte, mostaccioli eggplant marinara, New York steak Contadina-style. Valet parking. Outdoor dining. Cr cds: A, C, D, DS, MC, V.

D

★ ★ ★ **THE MANSION.** *179 Ponce de Leon Ave, in Midtown/Piedmont Park. 404/876-0727.* Hrs: 11 am-2 pm, 6-10 pm; Sat, Sun brunch to 2 pm. Closed Dec 25. Res accepted. Continental menu. Bar 11 am-11 pm. Wine list. Semi-a la carte: lunch $7-$16, dinner $16-$25. Sat, Sun brunch $9-$15. Specializes in fresh seafood, aged beef, lamb. Own baking. Parking. Shingle-style Victorian mansion (1885) with garden, gazebo. Cr cds: A, C, D, DS, ER, JCB, MC, V.

D

✔★ **MARY MAC'S TEAROOM.** *224 Ponce de Leon Ave (30308), in Midtown/Piedmont Park. 404/876-1800.* Hrs: 11 am-9 pm; Sun to 3 pm. Closed major hols. Serv bar. Complete meals: $6-$10. Child's meals. Specializes in baked and fried chicken, fresh vegetables. Own desserts. Parking. Informal neighborhood cafe. Family-owned. Totally nonsmoking. No cr cds accepted.

D

★ ★ **McKENDRICK'S.** *4505 Ashford Dunwoody Rd (30346), 10 mi NE on I-285, exit 21, north of downtown. 770/512-8888.* Hrs: 11:30 am-2:30 pm, 5:30-10:30 pm; Fri to 11 pm; Sat 5:30-11 pm; Sun 5:30-10 pm. Closed most major hols. Res accepted. Bar. Semi-a la carte: lunch $7.95-$14.95, dinner $15.95-$49. Valet parking. Globe lighting. Cr cds: A, C, D, DS, MC, V.

D

★ ★ **McKINNON'S LOUISIANE.** *3209 Maple Dr (30305), in Buckhead. 404/237-1313.* Hrs: 6-10 pm; Fri, Sat to 10:30 pm. Closed Sun; major hols. Res accepted. Cajun, Creole menu. Bar. Semi-a la carte: dinner $13.95-$18.95. Specializes in fresh seafood. Parking. Pianist (wkends). Country French decor. Family-owned. Cr cds: A, C, D, DS, MC, V.

D

★ ★ ★ **MI SPIA.** *4505 Ashford Dunwoody Rd (30346), in Park Place Shopping Center, north of downtown. 770/393-1333.* Hrs: 11:30 am-2:30 pm, 5-10 pm; Fri to 11 pm; Sat 5-11 pm; Sun 5-10 pm. Closed most major hols. Res accepted. Northern Italian menu. Bar. Semi-a la carte: lunch $7.95-$10.95, dinner $11.95-$21.95. Specialties: honey-glazed salmon, grain mustard marinated pork chops, saffron fettuccine. Outdoor dining. Contemporary decor. Totally nonsmoking. Cr cds: A, C, D, DS, MC, V.

D

✔★ **MICK'S UNDERGROUND.** *75 Upper Alabama St (30303), downtown. 404/525-2825.* Hrs: 11 am-11 pm; Fri, Sat to 1 am; Sun noon-10:30 pm. Closed Thanksgiving, Dec 25. Bar. Semi-a la carte: lunch, dinner $3.50-$12.95. Child's meals. Specializes in hamburgers, chicken, pasta. Own desserts. Cr cds: A, D, DS, MC, V.

D ♥

★ ★ **MUMBO JUMBO BAR AND GRILL.** *89 Park Pl NE (30303), downtown. 404/523-0330.* E-mail mj89park@aol.com. Hrs: 11:30 am-2:30 pm, 5:30-11:30 pm; Sat, Sun from 5:30 pm. Closed most major hols. Res accepted. Eclectic menu. Bar. Semi-a la carte: lunch $4.95-$14.95, dinner $7.95-$28.50. Specialties: mumbo jumbo gumbo, sesame-crusted salmon, black Angus filet. Entertainment Thurs. Valet parking (dinner). Spanish decor. Cr cds: A, C, D, DS, JCB, MC, V.

D

★ ★ ★ **NAKATO.** *1776 Cheshire Bridge Rd NE (30324), in Buckhead. 404/873-6582.* Hrs: 5:30-10 pm; Fri & Sat to 11 pm; Sun 5-10 pm. Res accepted. Japanese menu. Bar. Semi-a la carte: dinner $11-$35. Child's meals. Specializes in sushi, teppan, sashimi. Valet parking. Japanese garden. Cr cds: A, C, D, DS, JCB, MC, V.

D

★ ★ ★ **NAVA.** *3060 Peachtree Rd (30305), in Buckhead. 404/240-1984.* Hrs: 11 am-2:30 pm, 5:30-11 pm; Fri to midnight; Sat 5 pm-midnight; Sun 5:30-10 pm. Closed most major hols. Res accepted. Southwestern menu. Bar. Wine cellar. Semi-a la carte: lunch $4.95-$11.95, dinner $5.50-$24.95. Specialties: red chile-seared giant scallops, wood-roasted pork tenderloin, sun corn-crusted snapper. Valet parking. Outdoor dining. Genuine New Mexican plaster, sculpture and artwork. Totally nonsmoking. Cr cds: A, C, D, DS, MC, V.

D

★ ★ ★ **NIKOLAI'S ROOF.** *(See Hilton & Towers Hotel) 404/659-2000.* Web www.hilton.com. Sittings: 6:30 & 9:30 pm. Res accepted. Classic French menu with Russian flair. Wine list. Prix fixe: six-course dinner $62.50. Specialties: turbot à la vapeur sur un lit de chanterelles, la coupe royale de gibier aux airells et poivres, piroshkis. Own baking, desserts. Menu recited. Valet parking. Jacket. Elegant decor with views from 30th floor. Cr cds: A, C, D, DS, ER, JCB, MC, V.

✔★ **NINO'S.** *1931 Cheshire Bridge Rd (30324), in Buckhead. 404/874-6505.* Hrs: 5:30-11 pm. Closed Jan 1, Dec 25. Res accepted. Italian menu. Bar. Semi-a la carte: dinner $8.95-$18.95. Specializes in veal, pasta. Parking. Outdoor dining. Oil paintings, Italian sculpture. Cr cds: A, C, D, DS, MC, V.

✔★ **OK CAFE.** *1284 W Paces Ferry Rd (30327), in Buckhead. 404/233-2888.* Open 24 hrs. Closed Mon 11 pm-Tues 6 am; some major hols. Wine, beer. Semi-a la carte: bkfst $4-$8, lunch $4-$10, dinner $4.95-$12. Parking. Diner atmosphere. Totally nonsmoking. Cr cds: A, D, DS, MC, V.

D

★ ★ **PALISADES.** *1829 Peachtree Rd NE (30309), in Buckhead. 404/350-6755.* Hrs: 5-10 pm. Closed Dec 25. Res accepted. Continental, Amer menu. Bar. Semi-a la carte: dinner $12.95-$24.95. Complete meal (Sun-Thurs): dinner $17.95-$29.95. Specializes in fresh fish, steak, crab cakes. Parking. Cr cds: A, C, D, DS, MC, V.

D

★★★ **PANO'S AND PAUL'S.** *1232 W Paces Ferry Rd (30327), in Buckhead. 404/261-3662.* Web www.buckheadsrestaurants.com. Hrs: 6-10:30 pm; Fri, Sat 5:30-11 pm. Closed Sun; major hols. Res accepted. Continental menu. Bar from 5 pm. Wine cellar. Semi-a la carte: dinner $15.95-$28.50. Specialties: cold water lobster tail, broiled prime veal sirloin steak with morel mushrooms, white and dark chocolate mousse. Own baking. Pianist Fri, Sat. Parking. Chef-owned. Cr cds: A, C, D, DS, MC, V.

D

★★ **PEKASO.** *3167 Peachtree Rd NE, in Buckhead. 404/467-0400.* E-mail pekaso@menus.atlanta.com; web menus.atlanta.com /pekaso. Hrs: 6-10 pm; Fri, Sat to 10:30 pm; Sun brunch 11 am-2 pm. Closed Mon; also July 4, Thanksgiving, Dec 25. Continental menu. Serv bar. A la carte entrees: dinner $9-$22. Brunch $6.95-$12.50. Specializes in Hawaiian seafood, pasta, veal chops. Valet parking. Cigar martini bar. Cr cds: A, D, DS, MC, V.

D

★★★ **PETITE AUBERGE.** *2935 N Druid Hill Rd (30329), Toco Hills Center, east of downtown. 404/634-6268.* Hrs: 11:30 am-2:15 pm, 6-10 pm; Sat from 6 pm. Closed Sun; most major hols. Res accepted. Continental menu. Bar. Wine list. Semi-a la carte: lunch $5.95-$9.95, dinner $9.95-$18.95. Specializes in beef Wellington, rack of lamb, fresh seafood. European decor. Family-owned. Cr cds: A, C, D, DS, MC, V.

D

✔★★ **PHOENIX BREWING CO.** *5600 Roswell Road NE (30342), in Buckhead. 404/843-2739.* Hrs: 11 am-3 pm, 5:30-10 pm; Fri to midnight; Sat noon-midnight; Sun from 5:30 pm. Closed Jan 1, Thanksgiving, Dec 25. Res accepted. Bar 11-2 am; Sat, Sun noon-2 am. Semi-a la carte: lunch $5.95-$9.95, dinner $6.95-$22.95. Child's meals. Specializes in buffalo, venison. Own desserts. Outdoor dining. Windows overlook brewing house. Cr cds: A, C, D, DS, MC, V.

D

★★★ **PIROZKI'S.** *1447 Peachtree Rd NE (30309), in Midtown/Piedmont Park. 404/607-0809.* Hrs: 11:30 am-3 pm, 5:30-11 pm; Sat 5:30 to midnight. Closed Sun; most major hols. Res accepted. Russian menu. Bar. Wine list. Semi-a la carte: lunch $6.95-$9.95, dinner $15.95-$24.95. Specializes in rack of lamb, lobster Alexander, chicken Kiev. Pianist. Valet parking. Outdoor dining. Paintings with Russian theme. Cr cds: A, C, D, DS, MC, V.

D

★★ **PITTYPAT'S PORCH.** *25 International Blvd (30303), downtown. 404/525-8228.* Hrs: 5-9 pm; Fri, Sat to 10 pm. Closed Labor Day, Dec 25; also 1 wk in Dec. Res accepted. Southern menu. Bar. Semi-a la carte: dinner $17.95-$23.95. Child's meals. Specialties: fresh coastal fish, Savannah crab cakes, coastal venison pie. Salad bar. Own desserts. Pianist. Parking. Collection of rocking chairs in lounge. Cr cds: A, C, D, DS, MC, V.

★★ **PLEASANT PEASANT.** *555 Peachtree St (30308), in Midtown/Piedmont Park. 404/874-3223.* Hrs: 11:30 am-2:30 pm, 5:30-11 pm; Fri to midnight; Sat 5:30 pm-midnight. Closed Thanksgiving, Dec 25. Res accepted. Bar. Semi-a la carte: lunch $7.50-$12.95, dinner $12.95-$22.95. Child's meals. Specialties: peppercorn steak, pecan-crusted salmon, lemon caper chicken. Parking. New York-style bistro. Cr cds: A, C, D, DS, MC, V.

★★★ **PRICCI.** *500 Pharr Rd (30305), in Buckhead. 404/237-2941.* Web www.buckheadrestaurants.com. Hrs: 11 am-11 pm; Fri to midnight; Sat 5 pm-midnight; Sun 5-10 pm. Closed Jan 1, Dec 25. Res accepted. Italian menu. Bar. Semi-a la carte: lunch $5.50-$12.75, dinner $9-$22.50. Own breads. Parking. Cr cds: A, C, D, DS, MC, V.

D

★★ **PRIME.** *3393 Peachtree Rd NE (30326), in Buckhead. 404/812-0555.* Web www.prime-atlanta.com. Hrs: 11:30 am-2:30 pm, 5-10 pm; Fri to 11 pm; Sat 11:30 am-3 pm, 5-11 pm; Sun noon-9 pm; Sun brunch to 4 pm. Closed some major hols. Res accepted. Japanese, Amer menu. Bar. A la carte entrees: lunch $8.95-$14, dinner $14.95-$32.50. Sun brunch $8.95-$14. Specializes in steak, seafood, sushi. Pianist Fri, Sat. Valet parking. Japanese-American atmosphere. Cr cds: A, C, D, DS, JCB, MC, V.

D

★★ **RAY'S ON THE RIVER.** *6700 Powers Ferry Rd (30339), I-285, exit 15; north of downtown. 770/955-1187.* Hrs: 11 am-3 pm, 5:30-10:30 pm; Fri, Sat to midnight; Sun 9:30 am-3 pm, 5-10 pm. Closed Dec 25. Bar 11 am-midnight; Fri, Sat to 1 am; Sun 12:30-10 pm. Semi-a la carte: lunch $4.95-$9.50, dinner $10.95-$17.95. Sunday brunch $17.95. Child's meals. Specializes in hickory-grilled seafood, steaks. Jazz eves Tues-Sat. Valet parking. Outdoor dining. View of Chattahoochee River. Cr cds: A, C, D, DS, MC, V.

D

★★★★ **THE RESTAURANT.** *(See The Ritz-Carlton Hotel) 404/659-0400.* A private club atmosphere reigns at this hotel restaurant decorated with objets d'art. French, continental menu. Specialties: grilled fresh duck foie gras, seared baby red snapper, grilled Sonoma lamb rack. Own baking, ice cream, pasta. Hrs: 6-10 pm. Closed Sun. Res accepted. Wine cellar. A la carte entrees: dinner $28-$40. Prix fixe: dinner $55 & $85. Valet parking. Jacket. Cr cds: A, C, D, DS, JCB, MC, V.

D

★★★ **THE RESTAURANT.** *(See Four Seasons Hotel) 404/881-9898.* Hrs: 6-10:30 pm; Fri, Sat to 11 pm. Closed Sun, Mon. Res accepted. Continental menu. Bar. Wine cellar. Semi-a la carte: dinner $17-$27. Complete meals: 3-course dinner $38. Specialties: rack of lamb, foie gras and smoked duck fricasse, spicy carrots consommé. Pianist. Valet parking. Elegant dining. Cr cds: A, C, D, ER, JCB, MC, V.

D

★ **RIB RANCH.** *25 Irby Ave (30305), in Buckhead. 404/233-7644.* Hrs: 11 am-11 pm; Sun noon-10 pm. Closed Easter, Thanksgiving, Dec 25. Semi-a la carte: lunch, dinner $3.75-$25.95. Child's meals. Specializes in chicken, ribs. Validated parking. Outdoor dining. Casual dining with unique decor. Totally nonsmoking. Cr cds: MC, V.

★ **RIO BRAVO GRILL.** *240 Peachtree St (30303), lobby level of Merchandise Mart, downtown. 404/524-9224.* Hrs: 11 am-11 pm; Fri to midnight; Sat noon-midnight; Sun 5-10 pm. Closed Thanksgiving, Dec 25. Tex-Mex menu. Bar. Semi-a la carte: lunch $5.95-$7.95, dinner $6.49-$14.99. Child's meals. Specialties: camarones diablo, fajitas. Southwestern decor. Cr cds: A, C, D, DS, MC, V.

D

★★★ **RIVIERA.** *519 E Paces Ferry Rd NE (30305), in Buckhead. 404/262-7112.* Hrs: 6-10 pm; Fri, Sat 5:30-10:30 pm. Closed Sun; most major hols. Res accepted. French, Mediterranean menu. Bar. Wine list. A la carte entrees: dinner $21-$32. Specialties: sautéed pompano, roast duckling, grilled lamb chops. Valet parking. Outdoor dining. Cozy dining in house with fireplace. Totally nonsmoking. Cr cds: A, D, DS, MC, V.

D

✔★ **RJ'S UPTOWN KITCHEN AND WINE BAR.** *870 N Highland Ave NE (30306), east of downtown. 404/875-7775.* Hrs: 5 pm-midnight. Closed most major hols. Res accepted. Contemporary Amer menu. Bar. Semi-a la carte: dinner $14-$19. Specialties: grilled lamb loin, sea scallops, green chile crab cake. Outdoor dining. Former filling station (1939); wine shop adj. Cr cds: A, C, D, DS, MC, V.

D

★ ★ ★ **RUTH'S CHRIS STEAK HOUSE.** *5788 Roswell Rd, north of downtown, in Sandy Springs. 404/255-0035.* E-mail rcshss@aol.com. Hrs: 5-11 pm. Closed July 4, Dec 25. Res accepted. Bar. Wine list. A la carte entrees: dinner $16.95-$29.95. Specializes in prime beef, fresh seafood. Valet parking. Cr cds: A, C, D, DS, MC, V.

D

★ ★ **SOUTH CITY KITCHEN.** *1144 Crescent Ave (30309), in Midtown/Piedmont Park. 404/873-7358.* Web www.boldamerican.com. Hrs: 11 am-11 pm; Fri, Sat to midnight; Sun brunch to 3 pm. Closed Memorial Day, Thanksgiving, Dec. 25. Res accepted. Bar. Semi-a la carte: lunch $6.95-$11.50, dinner $9.95-$21.95. Sun brunch $6.95-$16. Specialty: grilled barbecue swordfish. Parking. Outdoor dining. Contemporary decor. Cr cds: A, MC, V.

★ ★ **SOUTH OF FRANCE.** *2345 Cheshire Bridge Rd (30324), in Buckhead. 404/325-6963.* Hrs: 11:30 am-2 pm, 6-10:30 pm; Fri to 11:30 pm; Sat 6-11:30 pm. Closed Sun; major hols. Res accepted. Country French menu. Bar. A la carte entrees: lunch $7.95-$12.95, dinner $12.95-$24.95. Specialties: bouillabaise a la Marseillaise, rack of lamb, duck with orange sauce. Parking. Entertainment Wed-Sat. Country French decor. Cr cds: A, C, D, DS, MC, V.

D

✔★ **SUNDOWN CAFE.** *2165 Cheshire Bridge Rd (30324), in Buckhead. 404/321-1118.* Hrs: 11 am-2 pm, 5:30-10 pm; Fri, Sat to 11 pm. Closed Sun; most major hols. Southwestern menu. Bar. Semi-a la carte: lunch $5.95-$6.95, dinner $8.95-$14.95. Specializes in burritos, enchiladas, fajitas. Parking. Outdoor dining. Southwestern decor. Cr cds: A, C, D, MC, V.

D

✔★ ★ **TERRA COTTA.** *1044 Greenwood Ave (30306), 2 mi NE on Ponce de Leon, in Midtown/Piedmont Park. 404/853-7888.* Hrs: 6-10 pm; Fri, Sat 5:30-10:30 pm; Sun 5:30-9:30 pm. Closed Mon; some major hols. Res accepted. Eclectic menu. Bar. Semi-a la carte: dinner $13.50-$19.75. Specialties: Thai crab cake, grilled pork tenderloin, Maine salmon. Contemporary artwork; casual dining. Totally nonsmoking. Cr cds: A, C, D, DS, MC, V.

D

✔★ ★ **THAI CHILI.** *2169 Briarcliff Rd NE (30329), in Briar Vista Shopping Center, east of downtown. 404/315-6750.* Hrs: 11 am-2:30 pm, 5-10 pm; Fri to 11 pm; Sat, Sun 5-11 pm. Closed Dec 25. Res accepted. Thai menu. Wine, beer. Semi-a la carte: lunch $5.25-$8.95, dinner $6.95-$15.95. Child's meals. Specialties: salmon curry, veggie and tofu delight, spicy pork. Elegant decor. Totally nonsmoking. Cr cds: A, DS, MC, V.

D

★ ★ **TOMTOM.** *3393 Peachtree Rd (30326), in Lenox Square Mall, in Buckhead. 404/264-1163.* Web menus.atanta.com/home/tomtom .html. Hrs: 11:30 am-10 pm; wkends to 11 pm. Closed Easter, Thanksgiving, Dec 25. Res accepted. Bar. Semi-a la carte: lunch $7-$11, dinner $8-$16. Specializes in fresh fish, pasta, chicken. Pianist evenings. Valet parking. Outdoor dining. Cr cds: A, C, D, DS, JCB, MC, V.

D

★ ★ **TOULOUSE.** *2293-B Peachtree Rd NE (30309), in Buckhead. 404/351-9533.* Hrs: 6-10 pm; Fri, Sat to 11 pm. Closed Jan 1, Dec 25. Res accepted. Bar. Semi-a la carte: dinner $10-$15. Specializes in fish, oven-roasted cuisine. Own baking. Valet parking wkends. Outdoor dining. Paintings by local artists. Totally nonsmoking. Cr cds: A, D, MC, V.

D

★ ★ **VENI VIDI VICI.** *41 14th St (30309), at W Peachtree, in Midtown/Piedmont Park. 404/875-8424.* Web www.buckheadrestaurants.com. Hrs: 11 am-11 pm; Fri to midnight; Sat 5 pm-midnight; Sun 5-10 pm. Closed Jan 1, Thanksgiving, Dec 25. Res accepted. Regional Italian menu. Bar 11 am-midnight. A la carte entrees: lunch $4.95-$12.95, dinner $10.95-$22.50. Specializes in homemade pasta, antipasta, wood burning rotisserie meats. Valet parking. Outdoor dining. Vaulted ceilings. Open kitchen. Cr cds: A, C, D, DS, MC, V.

D

★ ★ ★ **VILLA CHRISTINA.** *45 Perimeter Summit Blvd (30319), north of downtown. 404/303-0133.* Hrs: 11:30 am-2 pm, 6-9 pm. Closed Sun; most major hols. Res accepted. Italian menu. Bar. Wine list. Semi-a la carte: lunch $7.25-$16.95, dinner $12.95-$28.95. Specializes in prime steak, fresh seafood, desserts. Valet parking. Outdoor dining. Contemporary decor. Windows overlook 8 acres of gardens, walks and waterfalls. Totally nonsmoking. Cr cds: A, C, D, DS, MC, V.

D

✔★ ★ **THE VININGS INN.** *3011 Paces Mill Rd (30339), north of downtown. 770/438-2282.* Hrs: 11:30 am-2:30 pm, 5:30-10 pm. Bar from 5 pm. Semi-a la carte: lunch $6.50-$9.95, dinner $14.95-$25.95. Specializes in crab cakes, lamb, pasta. Free valet parking. Outdoor dining. In 1840s house. Original fireplace. Oil paintings. Cr cds: A, DS, MC, V.

D

★ ★ **VINNY'S WINDWARD.** *(5355 Windward Pkwy, Alpharetta 30201) 770/772-4644.* Hrs: 11:30 am-3 pm, 5 pm-midnight; Sun 5-10 pm. Closed July 4, Thanksgiving, Dec 25. Res accepted. Italian menu. Bar. Semi-a la carte: lunch $3.75-$13.25, dinner $9.75-$25.95. Specialties: rack of lamb with raspberry demi-glaze, shrimp and scallops with pumpkinseed pesto, spinach and ricotta-stuffed veal chop. Valet parking. Outdoor dining. Cr cds: A, C, D, DS, MC, V.

D

✔★ **ZOCALO.** *187 10th St (30309), in Midtown/Piedmont Park. 404/249-7576.* Hrs: 11:30 am-2:30 pm, 5:30-10 pm; Fri, Sat 11:30 am-11 pm. Closed some major hols. Mexican menu. Semi-a la carte: lunch $3.50-$7.75, dinner $5.95-$12.50. Specialties: chiles rellenos, carnos asada, taco bar. Parking. Outdoor dining. Mexican decor. Cr cds: A, C, D, DS, MC, V.

D

Unrated Dining Spots

FAT MATT'S. *1811 Piedmont (30324), in Midtown/Piedmont Park. 404/607-1622.* Hrs: 11:30 am-11:30 pm; Fri, Sat to 12:30 am; Sun 2-11:30 pm. Closed Easter, Dec 25. Semi-a la carte: lunch, dinner $3.25-$14. Child's meals. Specializes in fried fish and chicken, barbecue pork. Entertainment nightly. Parking. Outdoor dining. Casual dining; colorful decor. No cr cds accepted.

VARSITY. *61 North Ave, in Midtown/Piedmont Park. 404/881-1706.* Hrs: 7-12:30 am; Fri, Sat to 2 am. Specializes in hot dogs, hamburgers, fried peach pie. Avg ck: $4-$4.50. Parking. One of world's largest drive-ins. Graffitiesque decor; tiered seating. Adj Georgia Tech campus. No cr cds accepted.

THE VARSITY JR. *1085 Lindbergh Dr NE (30324), in Buckhead. 404/261-8843.* Hrs: 10 am-11 pm; Fri & Sat to midnight; Sun from 11 am. Closed Thanksgiving, Dec 25. Semi-a la carte: lunch, dinner $1-$3. Specializes in hot dogs. Parking. Outdoor dining. 1950s drive-in. Family-owned. No cr cds accepted.

D

Atlanta Hartsfield Airport Area

Motels

✔★ ★ **COMFORT INN-ATLANTA AIRPORT.** *(1808 Phoenix Blvd, College Park 30349) S on I-85 to I-285, E on I-285, exit 43 (Riverdale Rd S), then W on Phoenix Blvd. 770/991-1099; FAX 770/991-1076.* 194 rms, 4 story. S $69-$89; D $69-$74; each addl $5; under 17 free; wkend rates; higher rates special events. Crib free. TV; cable (premium). Heated pool. Continental bkfst. Complimentary coffee in lobby. Restaurant 6-11:30 am, 6-11 pm; Sat, Sun 7 am-noon, 6-11 pm. Bar 6-11 pm. Ck-out 11 am. Coin Indry. Meeting rms. Business servs avail. Valet serv. Sundries. Balconies. Cr cds: A, C, D, DS, ER, JCB, MC, V.

D SC

★ ★ **COURTYARD BY MARRIOTT.** *(2050 Sullivan Rd, College Park 30337) S on I-85 to Riverdale Rd, E to Best Rd, S to Sullivan Rd. 770/997-2220; FAX 770/994-9743.* 144 rms, 3 story. S $99; D $109; each addl $10; suites $125-$135; under 12 free; wkly, wkend rates. Crib free. TV; cable (premium). Indoor pool; whirlpool. Coffee in rms. Restaurant 6:30-10 am. Bar 4-11 pm. Ck-out noon. Coin Indry. Meeting rms. Business servs avail. In-rm modem link. Valet serv. Sundries. Exercise equipt; weights, bicycles. Some private patios, balconies. Cr cds: A, C, D, DS, MC, V.

D SC

✔★ ★ **HAMPTON INN ATLANTA AIRPORT.** *(1888 Sullivan Rd, College Park 30337) S via I-85 exit 18, E on Riverdale Rd to Sullivan Rd. 770/996-2220; FAX 770/996-2488.* 130 units, 4 story. S, D $62-$74; under 18 free. Crib free. TV; cable (premium). Pool. Complimentary continental bkfst. Restaurant adj 11-2 am. Ck-out noon. Meeting rm. Business servs avail. In-rm modem link. Free airport transportation. Health club privileges. Public park adj. Cr cds: A, C, D, DS, MC, V.

D SC

Motor Hotels

★ ★ **DAYS INN.** *(4601 Best Rd, College Park 30337) S on I-85, exit Riverdale Rd W, then N on Best Rd. 404/761-6500; FAX 404/763-3267.* 162 rms, 6 story. S, D $62-$89; each addl (after 4th person) $10; higher rates special events. Crib free. TV; cable (premium). Pool. Playground. Coffee in rms. Restaurant 6 am-10 pm. Rm serv. Bar 5 pm-midnight. Ck-out noon. Meeting rms. Business center. Valet serv. Exercise equipt; weights, bicycle. Many refrigerators. Cr cds: A, C, D, DS, MC, V.

D SC

★ ★ ★ **RADISSON HOTEL-ATLANTA AIRPORT.** *(1419 Virginia Ave, Atlanta 30337) N on I-85, exit Virginia Ave W. 404/768-7800; FAX 404/767-5451.* Web www.radisson.com. 245 rms, 6 story. S, D $75-$275; each addl $10; suites $95-$295; under 12 free. Crib free. TV; cable (premium). Pool. Restaurant 6 am-10 pm. Rm serv. Bar 5 pm-1 am. Ck-out noon. Coin Indry. Meeting rms. Business servs avail. In-rm modem link. Bellhops. Valet serv. Free airport transportation. Exercise equipt; weight machines, bicycles, sauna. Some in-room whirlpools; microwaves avail. Cr cds: A, C, D, DS, JCB, MC, V.

D SC

Hotels

★ ★ ★ ★ **HILTON & TOWERS.** *(1031 Virginia Ave, Atlanta 30354) N on I-85, exit 19 Virginia Ave E. 404/767-9000; FAX 404/559-6828.* This sleek high-rise comes with an incredible array of facilities and services unusual in airport hotels. 503 rms, 17 story. S $127-$186; D $142-$206; each addl $15; suites $350-$450; family, wkend rates. Crib free. TV; cable (premium), VCR avail. 2 pools, 1 indoor; whirlpool, poolside serv. Coffee in rms. Restaurant 6 am-midnight. Rm serv 24 hrs. Bar 11:30-1 am; entertainment. Ck-out noon. Convention facilities. Business center. In-rm modem link. Concierge. Gift shop. Barber, beauty shop. Valet parking. Free airport, RR station, bus depot transportation. Lighted tennis. Exercise rm; instructor, weight machines, bicycles, sauna. Massage. Minibars; some bathrm phones, wet bars; refrigerators avail. Luxury level. Cr cds: A, C, D, DS, ER, JCB, MC, V.

D SC

★ ★ **HOWARD JOHNSON-ATLANTA AIRPORT.** *(1377 Virginia Ave, Atlanta 30344) 404/762-5111; FAX 404/762-1277.* 189 rms, 6 story. S $99; D $109; each addl $10; under 18 free; wkend rates; higher rates special events. Crib free. TV; cable (premium). Pool. Complimentary coffee in lobby. Restaurant 6:30 am-midnight. Bar noon-2 am. Ck-out noon. Coin Indry. Meeting rms. Business servs avail. In-rm modem link. No bellhops. Free airport transportation. Health club privileges. Cr cds: A, C, D, DS, MC, V.

D SC

★ ★ ★ **MARRIOTT-ATLANTA AIRPORT.** *(4711 Best Rd, College Park 30337) S on I-85, exit Riverdale Rd W. 404/766-7900; FAX 404/209-6808.* 638 rms, 15 story. S $142-$165; suites $200-$650; under 18 free; wkly, wkend, hol rates. Crib free. TV; cable (premium), VCR avail. Indoor/outdoor pool; whirlpool, poolside serv. Restaurant 6:30 am-midnight. Bar 5 pm-2 am, Sun 12:30 pm-midnight; entertainment. Ck-out noon. Convention facilities. Business center. In-rm modem link. Concierge. Gift shop. Barber, beauty shop. Free airport transportation. Lighted tennis. Exercise equipt; weight machines, bicycles, sauna. Game rm. Refrigerators avail. Some balconies. Luxury level. Cr cds: A, C, D, DS, JCB, MC, V.

D SC

★ ★ ★ ★ **RENAISSANCE.** *(One Hartsfield Centre Pkwy, Atlanta 30354) I-85 exit 20, at Hartsfield Centre. 404/209-9999; FAX 404/209-7031.* Web renaissancehotels.com. Conveniently located, this is the only hotel that has been built on the airport's property. Each room opens up to a dramatic 11-story interior atrium that serves as the hotel's center of activity. 387 rms, 11 story. S $165-$205; D $185-$225; each addl $20; suites $225-$1,450; family, wkend rates. Crib free. Valet parking $6. TV; cable (premium), VCR avail. 2 pools, 1 indoor; whirlpool, poolside serv. Complimentary coffee in rms. Restaurant 6 am-11 pm. Rm serv 24 hrs. Bar 11-1 am; entertainment exc Sun. Ck-out 1 pm. Convention facilities. Business center. In-rm modem link. Concierge. Gift shop. Exercise equipt; weight machine, bicycles, sauna. Massage. Refrigerators, minibars; microwaves avail. Balconies. Luxury level. Cr cds: A, C, D, DS, ER, JCB, MC, V.

D SC

★ ★ ★ **SHERATON GATEWAY.** *(1900 Sullivan Rd, College Park 30337) S on I-85, exit 18. 770/997-1100; FAX 770/991-5906.* Web www.ittsheraton.com-access. 395 rms, 12 story. S $159; D $169; each addl $10; suites $350; under 17 free; wkend rates. Crib $10. Pet accepted, some restrictions. TV; cable (premium). 2 pools, 1 indoor; whirlpool, poolside serv. Complimentary coffee in rms. Restaurant 6 am-10 pm. Rm serv 24 hrs. Bar 11-2 am; entertainment. Ck-out noon. Convention facilities. Business center. In-rm modem link. Concierge. Gift shop. Free airport transportation. 18-hole golf privileges, pro, putting green, driving range. Exercise equipt; weights, bicycle. Microwaves avail; refrigerator in suites. Cr cds: A, C, D, DS, ER, JCB, MC, V.

D SC

★ ★ ★ **WESTIN.** *(4736 Best Rd, Atlanta 30337) S on I-85, exit Riverdale Rd W. 404/762-7676; FAX 404/763-4199.* 495 units, 10 story. S $170; D $185; each addl $15; suites $175-$600; wkend plans. Crib free. Pet accepted, some restrictions. TV; cable (premium), VCR avail. Indoor/outdoor pool; whirlpool, poolside serv. Complimentary coffee in rms. Restaurant 6:30 am-2:30 pm, 5:30-11 pm. Rm serv 24 hrs. Bar 11-2 am. Ck-out noon. Convention facilities. Business center. In-rm modem link. Gift shop. Exercise equipt; weights, bicycles, sauna. Minibars; some bathrm phones; microwave in suites. Luxury level. Cr cds: A, C, D, DS, ER, JCB, MC, V.

D SC

Baltimore

Settled: 1661
Pop: 736,014
Elev: 32 feet
Time zone: Eastern
Area code: 410
Web: www.baltimore.com

Baltimore, a major East Coast manufacturing center and world seaport, is one of the nation's oldest cities. It began to expand rapidly in the early 19th century, first as a result of the opening of the National Road, which encouraged trade with Midwestern cities, and later as the terminus of the nation's first railroad, the Baltimore & Ohio (incorporated 1827). In 1904, a disastrous fire destroyed 140 acres of the business district and waterfront area, causing losses of more than $50 million. But the city revived rapidly, and during World Wars I and II it was a major shipbuilding and repair center.

The economic health of Baltimore was threatened again during the 1950s and 1960s; buildings decayed and were not replaced, and both people and businesses left for the suburbs. In an effort to revitalize the city, area businessmen, aided by local government and bold city planners, launched a major redevelopment program. Hundreds of acres of slums were cleared to make way for new apartment, office and public buildings; rotting wharves and warehouses were removed to turn Inner Harbor over to public use for the first time in 200 years. Today, festivals, museums, shops and restaurants bring millions of tourists and residents downtown.

Business

Baltimore is the largest city in Maryland and one of the most populous in the nation; it is the heart of a five-county metropolitan area. The city thrives, as it has for two centuries, because of its world seaport. In the 1960s, Baltimore's marine terminals pioneered the use of container shipping. The Port Authority continues to expand in this direction today.

Baltimore has traditionally been one of the East Coast's major industrial and manufacturing centers; virtually all major manufacturing groups are represented. It is best known for its steel mills, automotive assembly plants, can companies, electronics firms and clothing, tool, spice and cosmetic factories. Baltimore is also a financial, retail and transportation hub, with overland shipping of port cargo by rail and truck.

The city's urban renaissance has been applauded and emulated by city planners around the world. The most important business development is the 33-acre Charles Center project, which consists of major office buildings, apartment towers, restaurants, boutiques, theaters, European-style plazas and an elevated walkway system that allows pedestrians to walk 14 blocks without crossing a street.

Convention Facilities

The expanded Baltimore Convention Center opened in April 1997 with 300,000 square feet of exhibit space, 50 meeting rooms, and a 37,000 square-foot ballroom, the largest in Maryland.

The Baltimore Arena, a 14,000-seat entertainment arena, hosts concerts, circuses, ice and horse shows, meetings and sporting events. The arena is equipped with a permanent stage, modern concessions, dressing room facilities and a sophisticated sound system.

Sports & Recreation

The Pimlico Race Course conducts its annual meet in spring, highlighted on the third Saturday in May by the Preakness Stakes, middle jewel in racing's Triple Crown for three-year-old Thoroughbreds. Between Baltimore and Washington, DC, is Laurel Race Track, with racing in the fall and winter. Timonium's half-mile track in Baltimore County operates during the Maryland State Fair in the late summer.

Oriole Park at Camden Yards hosts Orioles' baseball from April through September. The Baltimore Arena hosts the Major Indoor Soccer League's Baltimore Spirit and the Thunder, a world championship box lacrosse team. The Baltimore Ravens, one of the NFL's newest teams, rip up the turf in Memorial Stadium.

Facilities for boating, jogging, swimming, biking and many other activities can be found throughout the city.

Entertainment

The Baltimore Symphony Orchestra season runs from October through May at Meyerhoff Symphony Hall, and the Baltimore Opera Company performs at the Lyric Opera House. Nightclub entertainment is provided at major hotels and clubs. Broadway shows come to the Morris Mechanic Theatre, and repertory plays are performed at Center Stage.

Baltimore hosts many annual festivals, including more than a dozen ethnic festivals and the Preakness Celebration. In June, the Harbor Expo celebrates the city's salty roots with seafood, rowing regattas and visits by antique and modern ships. From June to September, the Inner Harbor's Pier 6 Concert Pavilion presents entertainment several nights a week.

Some major department stores are located in suburban malls, such as Security Square and Golden Ring. Chic shopping is found around Harborplace and the Gallery at the Inner Harbor, as well as such neighborhood developments as Cross Keys, Old Town Mall and the Rotunda. Seven city markets, including historic Lexington Market, abound with fresh meats, seafood and produce.

Historical Areas

Many of Baltimore's historically and architecturally significant neighborhoods are undergoing extensive private restoration. Fell's Point, the

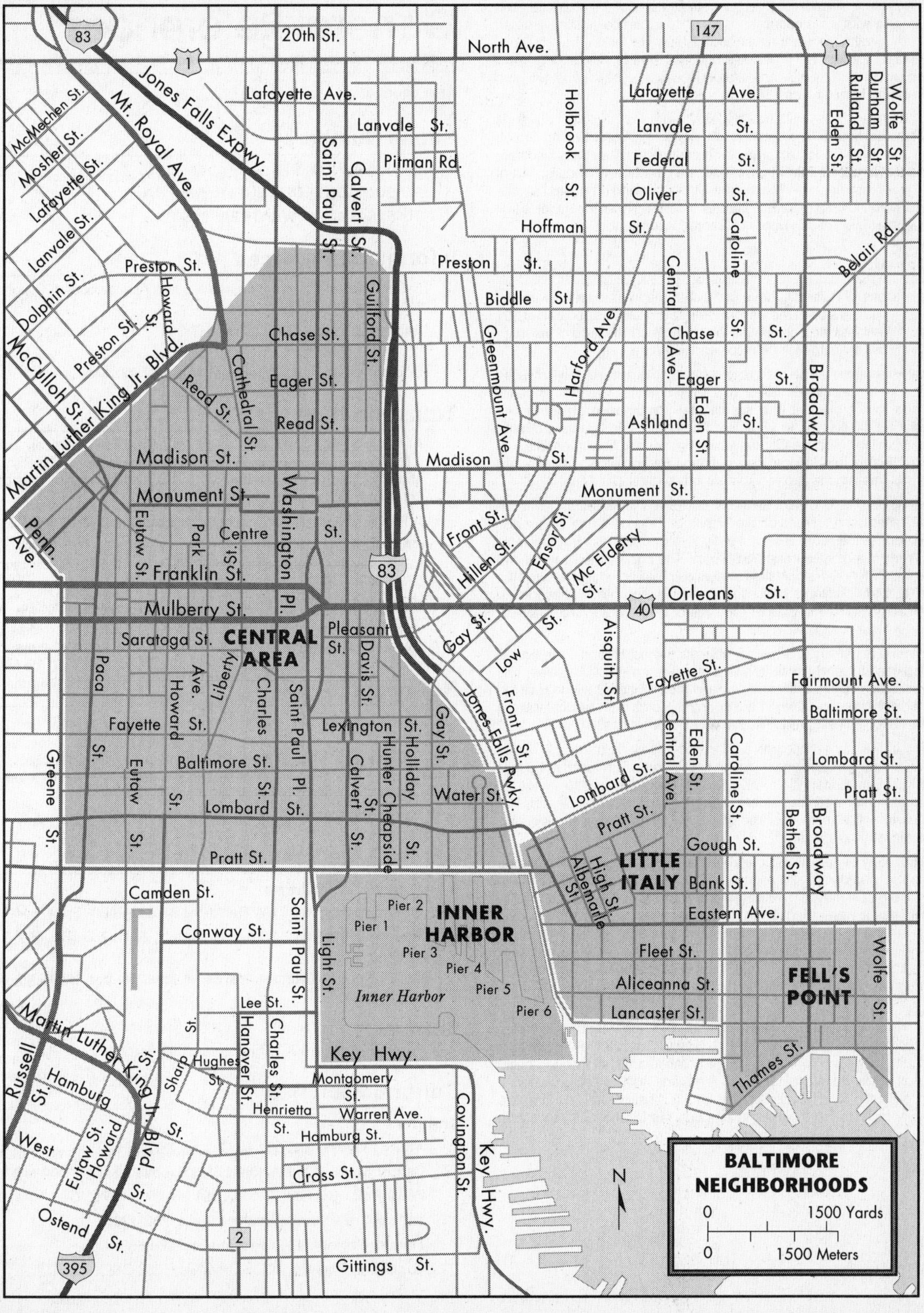

BALTIMORE NEIGHBORHOODS

0 1500 Yards

0 1500 Meters

N

CENTRAL AREA

INNER HARBOR

LITTLE ITALY

FELL'S POINT

Inner Harbor

Pier 1

Pier 2

Pier 3

Pier 4

Pier 5

Pier 6

83

1

147

40

2

395

20th St.

North Ave.

Jones Falls Expwy.

Mt. Royal Ave.

Lafayette Ave.

Lanvale St.

Pitman Rd.

Saint Paul St.

Calvert St.

Holbrook St.

Federal St.

Oliver St.

Hoffman St.

Caroline St.

Central Ave.

Rutland St.

Durham St.

Wolfe St.

Eden St.

Belair Rd.

McMechen St.

Mosher St.

Lafayette St.

Lanvale St.

Dolphin St.

Preston St.

Howard St.

McCulloh St.

Martin Luther King Jr. Blvd.

Guilford St.

Preston St.

Biddle St.

Chase St.

Eager St.

Read St.

Cathedral St.

Greenmount Ave.

Harford Ave.

Ashland St.

Eden St.

Broadway

Madison St.

Monument St.

Penn. Ave.

Eutaw St.

Park St.

Centre St.

Washington Pl.

Franklin St.

Mulberry St.

Front St.

Hillen St.

Ensor St.

Mc Elderry St.

Orleans St.

Saratoga St.

Pleasant St.

Gay St.

Low St.

Aisquith St.

Fayette St.

Fairmount Ave.

Paca St.

Liberty St.

Howard Ave.

Charles St.

Saint Paul Pl.

Davis St.

Jones Falls Pkwy.

Front St.

Baltimore St.

Lexington St.

Holliday St.

Hunter Cheapside St.

Calvert St.

Water St.

Lombard St.

Greene St.

Eutaw St.

Pratt St.

High St.

Albemarle St.

Gough St.

Bank St.

Bethel St.

Caroline St.

Eastern Ave.

Camden St.

Conway St.

Light St.

Fleet St.

Aliceanna St.

Lancaster St.

Thames St.

Lee St.

Hanover St.

Sharp St.

Hughes St.

Key Hwy.

Montgomery St.

Russell St.

Hamburg St.

Henrietta St.

Warren Ave.

Covington St.

West St.

Eutaw St.

Howard St.

Cross St.

Ostend St.

Gittings St.

city's 18th-century shipbuilding center, retains its nautical character and colonial charm with picturesque houses, shops, bistros and new urban inns. Nearby in Little Italy, churches and restaurants reflect the residents' ethnic heritage. Federal Hill provides a beautiful skyline view of downtown Baltimore; while Bolton Hill has stately town houses, mansions and churches dating from the late 1860s.

Tyson Street, Seton Hill and Charles Village, with Victorian buildings and student residences, are areas worth exploring. Along Stirling Street, Otterbein and Barre Circle are former tenements that were purchased from the city for $1 in a lottery and then renovated by the new owners. Mount Vernon Place, downtown on Monument St, has splendid houses, institutions and a hotel built along formal squares extending from the nation's first major monument, erected in honor of George Washington.

Sightseeing

Many areas of Baltimore have great charm and interest for walkers. Visitors are invited to stop at the visitors information centers, located at 301 West Pratt Street and the kiosk on the West Shore promenade of the Inner Harbor (summer only), to pick up maps and literature.

Inner Harbor, just south of the city center on the basin of the Patapsco River, is one of Baltimore's major accomplishments. Cleared of warehouses and rotting piers, it is a spectacular combination of public and commercial facilities covering 95 acres. The harborside boasts a promenade, the Maryland Science Center, which houses the Davis Planetarium and IMAX Theater, the National Aquarium and Harborplace, a unique mall housing 140 small shops and restaurants in two glass pavilions.

The World Trade Center extends out over the water and has an observation deck and exhibits on the 27th floor. Docked along the promenade and open to the public are the *Minnie V.,* a Chesapeake Bay skipjack, and the World War II submarine USS *Torsk.* Throughout the summer and early fall, the *Baltimore Patriot* takes visitors on narrated cruises around the harbor. The *Lady Baltimore* cruises to Annapolis and other Chesapeake Bay destinations, while the *Clipper City*, one of the harbor's largest sailing crafts, offers luxurious excursions.

Baltimore is famous for its many educational institutions. Foremost is Johns Hopkins University, with its world-renowned medical facilities. The downtown campus of the University of Maryland includes Davidge Hall, the oldest medical school building in the country. Morgan State University is one of the nation's finest predominantly black universities.

Many of the city's museums are located in historic buildings. Mount Clare Station, the first passenger station built in the US, houses the B & O Railroad Museum. Edgar Allan Poe's house and grave remind visitors of the poet's life and mysterious death. The Maryland Science Center, National Aquarium, Baltimore Zoo and city parks and gardens provide journeys into the world of nature.

A full history of early Baltimore is gathered into an outstanding group of lithographs, photographs, paintings, artifacts and furniture in the Peale Museum, the oldest museum building in the country. The Maryland Historical Society has a vast collection of American art and literature, including the original manuscript of "The Star-Spangled Banner." Outstanding examples of archaeological art are found at the Walters Art Gallery, and many fine 19th- and 20th-century paintings, including an extensive collection of French Impressionist works, are on display at the Baltimore Museum of Art.

Baltimore is a prime gateway to many of the attractions in the mid-Atlantic region. To the north are Gettysburg and the Pennsylvania Dutch region; to the west are Harper's Ferry, Antietam National Battlefield and the Appalachians. Washington, DC (see) and historic Annapolis are a short drive south; to the east lies the great Chesapeake Bay and the Eastern Shore, with its poultry and produce farms and bustling ocean resorts.

General References

Area code: 410

Phone Numbers

POLICE & FIRE: 911

POISON CONTROL CENTER: 528-7701

TIME: 844-1212 **WEATHER:** 936-1212

Information Sources

Baltimore Area Convention and Visitors Association, 100 Light St, 12th Floor, 659-7300.

Baltimore Area Visitor's Center, 301 E Pratt St, Constellation Pier.

Department of Parks & Recreation, 396-7900.

Transportation

AIRLINES: Air Aruba; Air Canada; Air Jamaica; American; America West; British Airways; Continental; Delta; El Al; Icelandair; Midway; Northwest; Southwest; TWA; United; USAir; and other commuter and regional airlines.

AIRPORT: Baltimore/Washington International, 859-7100.

CAR RENTAL AGENCIES: (See IMPORTANT TOLL-FREE NUMBERS) Avis 859-1680; Budget 859-0850; Hertz 850-7400; National 859-8860.

PUBLIC TRANSPORTATION: Mass Transit Administration, 539-5000; Metro Rail Subway, 539-5000.

RAILROAD PASSENGER SERVICE: Amtrak 800/872-7245.

Newspapers

Afro-American; City Paper; The Sun.

Convention Facilities

Convention Center, 1 W Pratt St, 659-7000.

Baltimore Arena, 201 W Baltimore St, 347-2020.

Sports & Recreation

Major Sports Facilities

Baltimore Arena, 201 W Baltimore St, 347-2020 (Spirit, soccer).

Memorial Stadium, 33rd & Greenmill, 654-6200 (Ravens, football).

Oriole Park at Camden Yards, at Inner Harbor, 685-9800 (Orioles, baseball).

Racetrack

Pimlico, Hayward & Winner Aves, 542-9400.

Cultural Facilities

Theaters

Arena Players, Inc, 801 McCulloh St, 728-6500.

Center Stage, 700 N Calvert St, 332-0033.

Fell's Point Corner Theatre, 251 S Ann, 276-7837.

Morris A. Mechanic, Hopkins Plaza, 752-1200.

Theatre Project, 45 W Preston St, 752-8558.

Vagabond Players, 806 S Broadway, 563-9135.

Concert Halls

Lyric Opera House, 140 W Mt Royal Ave, 685-5086.

Meyerhoff Symphony Hall, 1212 Cathedral St, 783-8100.

Peabody Institute of the Johns Hopkins University, Friedberg Hall, 1 E Mt Vernon Pl, 659-8124.

Pier 6 Concert Pavilion, Pier 6, 625-1400.

Museums

Baltimore & Ohio Railroad Museum, Pratt & Poppleton Sts, 752-2490.

Baltimore Maritime Museum (USS *Torsk,* Coast guard cutter *Taney* and lightship *Chesapeake*), Pier 3, Pratt St, 396-5528.

Baltimore Museum of Industry, 1415 Key Hwy, 727-4808.

Baltimore Streetcar Museum, 1901 Falls Rd, 547-0264.

Lovely Lane Museum, 2200 St Paul St, 889-4458.

Maryland Historical Society, 201 W Monument St, 685-3750.

Mount Clare Mansion, Carroll Park at Monroe St & Washington Blvd, 837-3262.

Public Works Museum & Streetscape Sculpture, 751 Eastern Ave, 396-5565.

Star-Spangled Banner Flag House and 1812 Museum, 844 E Pratt St, 837-1793.

Art Museums & Galleries

Baltimore Museum of Art, Art Museum Dr near N Charles & 31st Sts, 396-7100 or 396-7101.

Maryland Institute, College of Art, 1300 W Mt Royal Ave at W Lanvale St, 669-9200.

Peale Museum, 225 Holliday St, 396-3523.

Walters Art Gallery, 600 N Charles St at Centre St, 547-9000.

Points of Interest

Historical

Babe Ruth Birthplace/Baseball Center, 216 Emory St, 727-1539.

Basilica of the National Shrine of the Assumption, Cathedral & Mulberry Sts, 727-3565.

Battle Monument, Calvert & Fayette Sts.

Carroll Mansion, 800 E Lombard St, 396-3523.

City Courthouse, St Paul & Fayette Sts.

City Hall, 100 N Holliday St, 396-3100.

Edgar Allan Poe Grave, Westminster Burying Ground, Fayette & Greene Sts, 706-7228.

Edgar Allan Poe House, 203 N Amity St, 396-7932.

Eubie Blake Cultural Center, 34 Market Pl, 625-3113.

First Unitarian Church, Charles & Franklin Sts, 685-2330.

Fort McHenry National Monument and Historic Shrine, E end of Fort Ave, 962-4299.

Hampton National Historic Site, 535 Hampton Ln, Towson, 962-0688.

H.L. Mencken House, 1524 Hollins St, 396-7997.

Jewish Historical Society of Maryland, 15 Lloyd St, 732-6400.

***Minnie V.* Skipjack,** near Pier 1, Pratt St, 522-4214.

Mother Seton House, 600 N Paca St, 523-3443.

Old Otterbein United Methodist Church, Conway & Sharp Sts, 685-4703.

Patterson Park, Baltimore St, Eastern & Patterson Park Aves.

Shot Tower, Fayette & Front Sts.

Washington Monument, Charles & Monument Sts, 396-7939.

Other Attractions

Baltimore Zoo, Druid Hill Park, 366-5466.

Charles Center, bounded by Lombard, Saratoga, Charles & Liberty Sts.

Cylburn Arboretum, 4915 Greenspring Ave, 396-0180.

Enoch Pratt Free Library, 400 Cathedral St, 396-5430.

Federal Hill Park, Warren St & Battery Ave.

Fell's Point, E of Inner Harbor, S of Fleet St, W of Wolfe St & E of Caroline St.

Harborplace, 200 E Pratt St at Inner Harbor, 332-4191.

Holocaust Memorial, Water & Gay Sts.

Inner Harbor, just S of city center, bordered by Light & Pratt Sts.

Johns Hopkins Medical Institutions, Broadway & Monument Sts.

Lacrosse Hall of Fame, 113 W University Pkwy, 235-6882.

Lexington Market, 400 W Lexington St between Eutaw & Paca Sts, 685-6169.

Maryland Science Center & Davis Planetarium, 601 Light St at Key Hwy, 685-5225.

Morgan State University, Cold Spring Ln & Hillen Rd, 319-3333.

National Aquarium, Pier 3, Pratt St, 576-3800.

Sherwood Gardens, Stratford Rd & Greenway, 366-2572.

World Trade Center Top of the World Observation Deck, Pratt St at the harbor, 837-4515.

Sightseeing Tours

Baltimore Patriot, Inner Harbor, 685-4288.

Clipper City, Inner Harbor, 575-7930.

Spirit of Baltimore, Inner Harbor, 752-7447.

Annual Events

Atlantic Crafts Council Crafts Fair, Convention Center. Late Feb.

Maryland House and Garden Pilgrimage, 1105-A Providence Rd, 21286; 821-6933. Late Apr-early May.

Flower Mart, Mt Vernon Pl. Early May.

Preakness Celebration, 837-3030. Ten days preceding 3rd Sat May.

Showcase of Nations Ethnic Festivals, downtown, 837-4636. June-Sept.

Baltimore International Jumping Classic, Baltimore Arena, 347-2020. Early Oct.

New Year's Eve Extravaganza, Convention Center/Festival Hall and Inner Harbor.

City Neighborhoods

Many of the restaurants, unrated dining establishments and some lodgings listed under Baltimore include neighborhoods as well as exact street addresses. Geographic descriptions of these areas are given, followed by a table of restaurants arranged by neighborhood.

Central Area: South of Mt Royal Ave, west of I-83, north of the Inner Harbor and Pratt St and east of Martin Luther King Jr Blvd and Greene St. **North of Central Area:** North of Chase. **East of Central Area:** East of I-83.

Fell's Point: Waterfront area east of Inner Harbor; south of Fleet St, west of Wolfe St and east of Caroline St.

Inner Harbor: Waterfront area south of Central Baltimore at Pratt St, west of E Falls Ave and east of Light St.

Little Italy: East of Inner Harbor; south of Lombard St, west of Caroline St, north of Lancaster St and the waterfront and east of E Falls Ave.

Lodgings and Food

BALTIMORE RESTAURANTS BY NEIGHBORHOOD AREAS
(For full description, see alphabetical listings under Restaurants)

CENTRAL AREA
Kawasaki. 413 N Charles St
Louie's The Bookstore Cafe. 518 N Charles St
Prime Rib. 1101 N Calvert St
Ruby Lounge. 802 N Charles St
Ruth's Chris Steak House. 600 Water St
Tio Pepe. 10 E Franklin St
Water Street Exchange. 110 Water St
The Wild Mushroom. 641 S Montford Ave

NORTH OF CENTRAL AREA
Angelina's. 7135 Harford Rd
Cafe Hon. 1002 W 36th St
Jeannier's. 105 W 39th St
Morgan Millard. 4800 Roland Ave
Mt Washington Tavern. 5700 Newbury St
Polo Grill (Doubletree Inn at The Colonnade Hotel). 4 W University Pkwy
Spike & Charlie's. 1225 Cathedral St

EAST OF CENTRAL AREA
Haussner's. 3244 Eastern Ave
Ikaros. 4805 Eastern Ave
Karson's Inn. 5100 Holabird Ave

FELL'S POINT
Bertha's. 734 S Broadway
Captain Louie's. 606 S Broadway
Henninger's Tavern. 1812 Bank St
John Steven Ltd. 1800 Thames St
Obrycki's. 1727 E Pratt St
Pierpoint. 1822 Aliceanna St
Savannah (Admiral Fell Inn). 888 S Broadway
Waterfront Hotel. 1710 Thames St

INNER HARBOR
City Lights. 301 Light St
Hampton's (Harbor Court Hotel). 550 Light St
Joy America Cafe. 800 Key Hwy
Wayne's Bar-B-Que. 201 Pratt St

LITTLE ITALY
Boccaccio. 925 Eastern Ave
Chiapparelli's. 237 S High St
Dalesio's. 829 Eastern Ave
Germano's Trattoria. 300 S High St
La Scala. 411 S High St
Rocco Capriccio. 846 Fawn St
Velleggia's. 829 E Pratt St

Note: When a listing is located in a town that does not have its own city heading, it will appear under the city nearest to its location. In these cases, the address and town appear in parenthesis immediately following the name of the establishment.

Motels

(In this area I-95 is Kennedy Memorial Hwy; I-695 is the Beltway)

(Rates may be much higher Preakness wkend, mid-May)

✔★ **CHRISTLEN.** *8733 Pulaski Hwy (US 40) (21237), I-695 exit 35B, east of Central Area. 410/687-1740.* 28 rms. S $32-$38; D $38-$42; each addl $5. Crib $5. TV; cable (premium). Restaurant adj open 24 hrs. Ck-out 11 am. Some refrigerators; microwaves avail. Picnic tables. Cr cds: A, D, DS, MC, V.

D

★ **DAYS INN-WEST.** *5801 Baltimore Natl Pike (21228), on US 40, just E of I-695 exit 15A, west of Central Area. 410/744-5000; FAX 410/788-5197.* 98 rms, 3 story. S, D $55-$75; under 12 free. Crib free. TV; cable (premium). Pool; lifeguard. Complimentary continental bkfst. Restaurant 7 am-1 pm, 5-10 pm. Ck-out noon. Coin Indry. Meeting rms. Business servs avail. Cr cds: A, C, D, DS, MC, V.

D SC

★ ★ **HAMPTON INN.** *8225 Town Center Dr (21236), east of Central Area. 410/931-2200; FAX 410/931-2215.* 127 rms, 4 story, 16 suites. S $75; D $80; suites $95; under 18 free. Crib $10. TV; cable (premium). Complimentary continental bkfst. Restaurant nearby. Ck-out noon. Meeting rms. Business center. In-rm modem link. Bellhops. Free airport transportation. Exercise equipt; bicycle, stair machine. Health club privileges. Heated pool; lifeguard. Wet bar in suites. Refrigerators, microwaves avail. Picnic tables. Cr cds: A, D, DS, MC, V.

D SC

★ ★ **HOLIDAY INN SECURITY/BELMONT.** *1800 Belmont Ave (21224), I-695 exit 17, north of Central Area. 410/265-1400; FAX 410/281-9569.* 135 units, 2 story. S, D $59-$83. Crib free. Pet accepted. TV; cable (premium). Pool; lifeguard. Restaurant 6 am-2 pm, 5-10 pm; Sat, Sun from 7 am. Rm serv. Bar 5 pm-midnight. Ck-out noon. Meeting rms. Business servs avail. In-rm modem link. Valet serv. Sundries. Health club privileges. Some refrigerators; microwaves avail. Cr cds: A, C, D, DS, ER, JCB, MC, V.

D SC

✔★ **SUSSE CHALET.** *4 Philadelphia Court (21237), I-695 exit 34, north of Central Area. 410/574-8100; FAX 410/574-8204.* 132 rms, 5 story. S $56.70; D $61.70; each addl $3. Crib free. TV; cable (premium). Pool; lifeguard. Complimentary continental bkfst. Restaurant nearby. Ck-out 11 am. Coin Indry. Business servs avail. Sundries. Microwaves avail. Cr cds: A, C, D, DS, MC, V.

D SC

Motor Hotels

★ ★ **BEST WESTERN-EAST.** *5625 O'Donnell St (21224), I-95 exit 57, east of Central Area. 410/633-9500; FAX 410/633-2812.* 175 rms, 12 story. S, D $89-$94; each addl $10; suites $129-$229. Crib avail. TV; cable (premium). Indoor pool; lifeguard. Restaurant 6:30 am-10 pm. Rm serv. Bar. Ck-out noon. Coin Indry. Meeting rms. Business servs avail. In-rm modem link. Gift shop. Bus depot transportation. Exercise equipt; weight machines, bicycles, sauna. Game rm. Microwaves avail. Cr cds: A, D, DS, JCB, MC, V.

D SC

★ ★ ★ **CROSS KEYS INN.** *5100 Falls Rd (21210), north of Central Area. 410/532-6900; FAX 410/532-2403; res: 800/532-5397.* 148 rms, 4 story. S $105-$175; D $115-$185; each addl $15; suites $195-$425; under 16 free; wkend rates. Crib free. TV; cable (premium). Pool; poolside serv, lifeguard. Complimentary coffee in rms. Restaurant 6:30 am-11 pm. Rm serv. Bar 11 am-midnight. Ck-out noon. Meeting rms. Business servs avail. In-rm modem link. Shopping arcade. Barber, beauty shop. Tennis privileges. Health club privileges. Bathrm phones; microwaves avail. Some private balconies. Cr cds: A, C, D, DS, MC, V.

D SC

★ **DAYS INN INNER HARBOR.** *100 Hopkins Pl (21201), in Central Area. 410/576-1000; FAX 410/576-9437.* 250 rms, 9 story. S $90-$120; D $100-$130; each addl $10; suites $140-$180; under 12 free; higher rates special events. Crib free. Garage $8.50. TV; cable (premium). Pool; poolside serv, lifeguard. Restaurant 6:30 am-10 pm. Rm serv. Bar. Ck-out 11 am. Meeting rms. Business center. Bellhops. Concierge. Sundries. Health club privileges. Some refrigerators, microwaves avail. Cr cds: A, D, DS, MC, V.

D SC

✔★ **HOWARD JOHNSON.** *5701 Baltimore Natl Pike (21228), 1/2 mi E of I-695 exit 15A, west of Central Area. 410/747-8900; FAX 410/744-3522.* 145 rms, 7 story. S $40-$70; D $48-$75; each addl $8; under 18 free. Crib free. TV; cable (premium), VCR avail (movies). Pool; whirlpool, lifeguard. Ck-out 11 am. Coin Indry. Meeting rms. Business servs avail. Sundries. Some refrigerators. Balconies. Cr cds: A, C, D, DS, ER, JCB, MC, V.

D SC

Hotels

★ ★ ★ **BROOKSHIRE INNER HARBOR SUITE HOTEL.** *120 E Lombard St (21202), Inner Harbor. 410/625-1300; FAX 410/625-0912; res: 800/647-0013 (exc MD).* 90 suites, 12 story. S $170-$305; D $190-$325; each addl $20; children free; wkend rates. Crib free. TV; cable. Coffee in rms. Restaurant 6:30-10 am, 5-9 pm. Bar 5-10 pm. Ck-out noon. Meeting rms. Concierge. Health club privileges. Bathrm phones, refrigerators, minibars; microwaves avail. Cr cds: A, C, D, DS, MC, V.

D SC

★ ★ ★ **CLARION.** *612 Cathedral St (21201), at Mt Vernon Place, north of Central Area. 410/727-7101; FAX 410/789-3312; res: 800/292-5580.* 103 rms, 14 story. S, D $114-$154; each addl $10; suites $189-$350; under 18 free; wkend rates; package plans. Crib free. Valet parking $12. TV; cable (premium), VCR avail (movies). Pool privileges. Restaurants 6:30 am-11 pm. Bar. Ck-out 11 am. Meeting rms. In-rm modem link. Concierge. Health club privileges. Some in-rm whirlpools. Restored hotel built in 1927. Marble floors, stairs in lobby. Period furnishings, artwork, crystal chandeliers. Cr cds: A, C, D, DS, ER, JCB, MC, V.

D SC

★ ★ ★ **DOUBLETREE INN AT THE COLONNADE.** *4 West University Pkwy (21218), Charles St N to University Pkwy, north of Central area. 410/235-5400; FAX 410/235-5572.* Web www.doubletreehotel.com. 125 units, 3 story, 31 suites. S, D $124-$169; each addl $15; suites $149-$475; family rates; wkend plans. Crib free. Pet accepted. TV; cable (premium). Indoor pool; whirlpool, poolside serv, lifeguard. Coffee in rms. Restaurant 6 am-11 pm (also see POLO GRILL). Rm serv to 10 pm. Ck-out noon. Meeting rm. Business center. In-rm modem link. Gift shop. Barber, beauty shop. Exercise equipt; bicycles, treadmill. Some wet bars; microwaves avail. Balconies. Biedermeier-inspired furnishings; extensive collection of 18th-century European masters. Adj to Johns Hopkins University. Cr cds: A, C, D, DS, ER, JCB, MC, V.

D SC

★ ★ ★ **HARBOR COURT.** *550 Light St (21202), Inner Harbor. 410/234-0550; FAX 410/659-5925; res: 800/824-0076.* Web www.harbor.com. 203 rms, 8 story, 25 suites. S $205-$245; D $220-$260; suites $375-$2,000; under 18 free; wkend rates; some package plans. Crib free. Covered parking: self-park $15; valet $18. TV; cable (premium), VCR avail. Heated pool; whirlpool, poolside serv, lifeguard. Restaurant 7 am-11 pm (also see HAMPTON'S). Rm serv 24 hrs. Bar 11-2 am; entertainment exc Sun. Ck-out noon. Meeting rms. Business center. In-rm modem link. Concierge. Airport transportation. Tennis. Exercise rm; instructor, weight machines, bicycles, sauna. Massage. Racquetball. Lawn games. Bathrm phones, refrigerators. Elegant retreat located on Inner Harbor; panoramic view of city. Cr cds: A, C, D, DS, ER, JCB, MC, V.

D SC

★ ★ ★ **HILTON AND TOWERS.** *20 W Baltimore St (21201), in Central Area. 410/539-8400; FAX 410/625-1060.* 419 rms, 23 story. S $189; D $209; each addl $15; suites $275-$400; kit. units $600-$800; under 17 free; wkend rates. Crib free. Valet parking $15. TV; cable. Restaurants 6:30 am-10 pm. Bar 11-2 am. Ck-out noon. Meeting rms. In-rm modem link. Exercise equipt; weight machines, bicycles, whirlpool, sauna. Health club privileges. Microwaves avail. Historic landmark; near harbor. Cr cds: A, C, D, DS, ER, MC, V.

D SC

★ ★ **HOLIDAY INN BALTIMORE-INNER HARBOR.** *301 W Lombard St (21201), in Central Area. 410/685-3500; FAX 410/727-6169.* 375 rms; 10, 13 story. Apr-Sept: S $139; D $149; each addl $10; suites $275; under 13 free; lower rates rest of yr. Crib free. Pet accepted, some restrictions. Garage parking $6. TV; cable (premium). Indoor pool; lifeguard. Complimentary coffee in rms. Restaurant 6:30 am-11 pm. Bar 11-1 am. Ck-out noon. Convention facilities. Business center. Gift shop. Exercise equipt; weight machine, bicycles, sauna. Some balconies. Cr cds: A, C, D, DS, ER, JCB, MC, V.

D SC

★ ★ ★ **HYATT REGENCY.** *300 Light St (21202), Inner Harbor. 410/528-1234; FAX 410/685-3362.* Web www.travelweb.com/hyatt.html. 486 rms, 14 story. S $185; D $210; each addl $25; suites $350-$900; under 18 free; wkend plan. Crib free. Valet parking $14. TV; cable (premium). Pool; whirlpool, lifeguard. Restaurant 6:30-1 am. Bar 11:30-2 am; entertainment Fri, Sat. Ck-out noon. Convention facilities. Business center. In-rm modem link. Concierge. Gift shop. Tennis. Exercise rm; instructor, weight machine, bicycles. Putting green. Basketball 1/2 court. Minibars; refrigerators avail. Luxury level. Cr cds: A, C, D, DS, ER, JCB, MC, V.

D SC

★ ★ ★ **MARRIOTT INNER HARBOR.** *110 S Eutaw St (21201), Inner Harbor. 410/962-0202.* Web www.marriott.com. 525 units, 10 story. S, D $209; suites $195-$650; under 18 free; wkend rates. Crib free. Covered parking $8. TV; cable (premium), VCR avail. Indoor pool; whirlpool, lifeguard. Restaurant 6 am-10 pm. Bar noon-2 am; entertainment. Ck-out noon. Convention facilities. Business center. In-rm modem link. Concierge. Exercise equipt; weights, bicycles, sauna. Opp baseball stadium at Camden Yards. Luxury level. Cr cds: A, C, D, DS, ER, JCB, MC, V.

D SC

★ ★ ★ **OMNI INNER HARBOR.** *101 W Fayette St (21201), Inner Harbor. 410/752-1100; FAX 410/625-3805.* 707 rms in 2 bldgs, 23, 27 story. S, D $149-$179; each addl $20; suites $200-$750; under 17 free; wkend rates. Crib free. Garage $9; valet parking $14. TV; cable (premium). Pool; poolside serv, lifeguard. Coffee in rms. Restaurant 6:30 am-midnight. Bars noon-2 am. Ck-out noon. Convention facilities. Business center. In-rm modem link. Exercise equipt; weights, bicycles. Health club privileges. Minibars; some refrigerators; microwaves avail. Cr cds: A, C, D, DS, ER, MC, V.

D SC

★ ★ ★ **RENAISSANCE HARBORPLACE.** *202 E Pratt St (21202), Inner Harbor. 410/547-1200; FAX 410/539-5780.* Web www.renaissancehotels.com. 622 rms, 12 story. S $215-$285; D $235-$305; each addl $20; suites $450-$1,500; under 18 free; wkend rates. Covered parking $10; valet $14. Crib free. TV; cable (premium), VCR avail. Indoor pool; whirlpool, poolside serv, lifeguard. Coffee in rms. Restaurant 6:30 am-11 pm. Rm serv 24 hrs. Bar 11-1:30 am; entertainment. Ck-out noon. Convention facilities. Business center. In-rm modem link. Concierge. Shopping arcade. Exercise equipt; weight machines, bicycles, sauna. Minibars; bathrm phones. Luxury level. Cr cds: A, C, D, DS, ER, JCB, MC, V.

D SC

★ ★ ★ **SHERATON INNER HARBOR.** *300 S Charles St (21201), in Inner Harbor. 410/962-8300; FAX 410/962-8211.* E-mail resdept@erols.com; web www.ittsheraton.com. 337 rms, 15 story. Mar-June, Sept-Dec: S, D $170-$230; each addl $15; suites $425-$1,400; under 17 free; wkly, wkend rates; lower rates rest of yr. Crib free. Covered parking $12, valet parking $19. TV; cable (premium), VCR avail (movies). Indoor pool; lifeguard. Restaurant 6:30 am-11 pm. Bar 11:30-2 am. Ck-out noon. Convention facilities. Business center. In-rm modem link. Concierge. Gift shop. Exercise equipt; bicycles, treadmill, sauna. Health club privileges.

Minibars; some bathrm phones, refrigerators. Cr cds: A, C, D, DS, ER, JCB, MC, V.

D SC

✔★★ **TREMONT.** *8 E Pleasant St (21202), in Central Area. 410/576-1200; FAX 410/244-1154; res: 800/873-6668.* 58 kit. suites, 13 story. S $89-$119; D $109-$139; each addl $20; under 16 free; wkend rates. Crib free. Pet accepted; $5. Valet parking $11. Pool privileges. TV; cable, VCR avail (free movies). Complimentary continental bkfst. Restaurant 5-9 pm. Bar to 10 pm. Ck-out noon. Meeting rms. Business servs avail. Health club privileges. Microwaves. Cr cds: A, C, D, DS, MC, V.

D SC

Inns

✔★★★ **ABACROMBIE BADGER.** *58 W Biddle St (21201), west of Central Area. 410/244-7227; FAX 410/244-8415.* 12 rms, 4 story. S $79; D $105-$135. TV; cable. Complimentary continental bkfst. Restaurant 11 am-10 pm; Fri, Sat to midnight; closed Mon. Bar to midnight; Fri, Sat to 2 am. Ck-out 11 am, ck-in 4 pm. Business servs avail. Turn-of-the-century building; many antique furnishings. Cr cds: A, C, D, DS, MC, V.

★★★ **ADMIRAL FELL.** *888 S Broadway (21231), in Fell's Point. 410/522-7377; FAX 410/522-0707; res: 800/292-4667 (exc MD).* E-mail admiral1@erols.com; web www.admiralfell.com. 80 rms, 5 story. S, D $105-$195; each addl $20; suites $225-$355; wkly rates. TV; cable (premium). Complimentary continental bkfst. Dining rm 11:30 am-10 pm. Bar 11-2 am. Ck-out noon, ck-in 4 pm. Meeting rms. Business servs avail. In-rm modem link. Concierge. Health club privileges. Some in-rm whirlpools; microwaves avail. Cr cds: A, D, MC, V.

D SC

★★★ **CELIE'S WATERFRONT BED & BREAKFAST.** *1714 Thames St (21231), in Fell's Point. 410/522-2323; FAX 410/522-2324; res: 800/432-0184.* E-mail celies@aol.com. 7 rms, 1 with shower only, 3 story. S $95-$175; D $115-$200; hol, wkend rates. Children over 9 yrs only. TV; cable. Complimentary continental bkfst. Complimentary coffee in rm. Restaurant nearby. Ck-out 11 am, ck-in 3-6 pm. Business servs avail. In-rm modem link. Health club privileges. Refrigerators; some in-rm whirlpools, fireplaces. On harbor; many antiques. Roof deck. Totally nonsmoking. Cr cds: A, DS, MC, V.

D

★★★ **HOPKINS INN.** *3404 St Paul St (21218), north of Central Area. 410/235-8600; FAX 410/235-7051.* 25 rms, 4 story. S, D $100-$140; wkly, monthly rates. Covered parking $6. TV. Complimentary continental bkfst. Restaurant nearby. Ck-out 11 am, ck-in 3 pm. Meeting rms. Business servs avail. 1920's Spanish-revival building. Rms individually furnished in variety of styles. Totally nonsmoking. Cr cds: A, C, D, DS, MC, V.

★★★ **INN AT GOVERNMENT HOUSE.** *1125 N Calvert St (21202), north of Central Area. 410/539-0566; FAX 410/539-0567.* 18 rms, 4 story. S, D $125-$150; wkly rates; Preakness (2-day min). TV. Complimentary continental bkfst; afternoon refreshments. Restaurant nearby. Ck-out noon, ck-in 3-8 pm. Business servs avail. Part of complex of several Federal and Victorian mansions and town houses (1888). Totally nonsmoking. Cr cds: A, C, D, DS, MC, V.

D SC

★★ **THE INN AT HENDERSON'S WHARF.** *1000 Fell St (21231), in Fell's Point. 410/522-7777; FAX 410/522-7087; res: 800/522-2088.* E-mail sales@hendersonswharf.com; web www.hendersonswharf.com. 38 rms. Apr-Nov: S, D $120-$160; kit. suites $400; under 18 free; higher rates special events; lower rates rest of yr. TV; cable (premium). Complimentary continental bkfst. Restaurant nearby. Ck-out noon, ck-in 3 pm. Coin lndry. Meeting rms. Business servs avail. In-rm modem link. Valet serv. Exercise equipt; weight machine, bicycles. Some refrigerators. On waterfront; dockage avail. 19th-century tobacco warehouse. Cr cds: A, C, D, MC, V.

D SC

★★★★ **MR MOLE BED & BREAKFAST.** *1601 Bolton St (21217), north of Central Area. 410/728-1179; FAX 410/728-3379.* This restored 1870 red brick row house with oriel windows still possesses many original details, including 14-foot ceilings, plaster moldings, marble fireplaces and gilt mirrors and cornices. The large guest rooms are furnished with 18th- and 19th-century antiques and stocked with vintage books. 5 rms, 5 story, 2 suites. S $87; D $97-$125; each addl $15; suites $100-$145; 2-day min wkends Mar-Dec. Children over 12 yrs only. Complimentary bkfst. Restaurant nearby. Ck-out 11 am, ck-in 4-6 pm. Business servs avail. In-rm modem link. Health club privileges. Totally nonsmoking. Cr cds: A, C, D, DS, MC, V.

Restaurants

★★ **ANGELINA'S.** *7135 Harford Rd (21214), north of Central Area. 410/444-5545.* Hrs: 11:30 am-10 pm; Fri, Sat to 11:30 pm. Closed Mon; Thanksgiving, Dec 25. Italian, seafood menu. Bar. Semi-a la carte: lunch $5-$16.95, dinner $9-$29. Child's meals. Specializes in crab cakes, seafood. Entertainment Fri. Cr cds: A, DS, MC, V.

★ **BERTHA'S.** *734 S Broadway (21231), in Fell's Point. 410/327-0426.* E-mail berthas@ix.netcom.com. Hrs: 11:30 am-11 pm; Fri, Sat to midnight; Sun brunch to 2 pm. Closed major hols. Res required for Scottish afternoon tea (Mon-Sat). Bar. Semi-a la carte: lunch, dinner $4.95-$19.25. Sun brunch $7.95-$8.50. Specializes in mussels, seafood. Eclectic decor. Historic 19th-century building. Cr cds: MC, V.

SC

★★★ **BOCCACCIO.** *925 Eastern Ave (21231), Little Italy. 410/234-1322.* Hrs: 11:30 am-2:30 pm, 5-11 pm; Sat from 5 pm; Sun 3-10 pm. Closed Thanksgiving, Dec 25. Res required eves. Italian menu. Bar. Semi-a la carte: lunch $9.75-$15.75, dinner $13.50-$28.50. Specializes in veal, seafood, pasta. Formal decor. Cr cds: A, C, D, MC, V.

D

✔★ **CAFE HON.** *1002 W 36th St (21211), north of Central Area. 410/243-1230.* Hrs: 7 am-10 pm; Sat from 9 am; Sun 9 am-3 pm (brunch). Closed most major hols. Bar. Semi-a la carte: bkfst $1.25-$5.95, lunch, dinner $4.25-$13.95. Sun brunch $1.50-$6.50. Child's meals. Specialties: crab cakes, meatloaf. Eclectic cafe reminiscent of 1930s Baltimore soda fountain. Totally nonsmoking. Cr cds: A, MC, V.

D

✔★★ **CAPTAIN LOUIE'S.** *606 S Broadway (21231), in Fell's Point. 410/558-3600.* Hrs: 11-2 am. Res accepted. Bar. A la carte entrees: lunch $6.75-$11, dinner $12-$18. Specializes in seafood, sushi bar. Cr cds: A, MC, V.

★★ **CHIAPPARELLI'S.** *237 S High St (21202), Little Italy. 410/837-0309.* Hrs: 11 am-10 pm; Fri, Sat to midnight. Closed Thanksgiving, Dec 25. Res accepted. Italian menu. Semi-a la carte: lunch $7-$14, dinner $10-$25. Child's meals. Specialty: Piatto Napolitano. Valet parking after 5 pm. Built 1870; original brick walls, oak paneling. 7 dining rms on 2 levels. Family-owned. Cr cds: A, C, D, DS, MC, V.

D

★★ **CITY LIGHTS.** *301 Light St (21202), Light St Pavilion, Inner Harbor. 410/244-8811.* Hrs: 11:30 am-10 pm; Fri to 11 pm; Sat to midnight; Sun to 9 pm. Closed Thanksgiving, Dec 24, 25. Res accepted. Bar. A la carte entrees: lunch, dinner $5-$18. Child's meals. Specializes in Chesapeake Bay seafood. Own desserts. Outdoor dining. Cr cds: A, C, D, DS, JCB, MC, V.

★ ★ ★ **DALESIO'S.** *829 Eastern Ave (21202), Little Italy. 410/539-1965.* Hrs: 11:30 am-3 pm, 5-10 pm; Sun 4-9 pm. Closed Thanksgiving. Res accepted. Northern Italian menu. Bar. A la carte entrees: lunch $5.95-$9.95, dinner $10.95-$21.95. Specializes in Northern Italian spa cuisine. Own cakes, pasta. Outdoor dining. Cr cds: A, D, MC, V.

D ♥

★ ★ **GERMANO'S TRATTORIA.** *300 S High St (21202), Little Italy. 410/752-4515.* Hrs: 11:30 am-11 pm; Fri, Sat to midnight. Closed Thanksgiving, Dec 25. Res accepted. Italian menu. Bar. Semi-a la carte: lunch $5.95-$9.95, dinner $7.50-$22. Child's meals. Specializes in Tuscan cuisine and seafood. Cr cds: A, C, D, DS, MC, V.

D ♥

★ ★ ★ ★ **HAMPTON'S.** *(See Harbor Court Hotel) 410/234-0550.* This hotel dining room's setting is similar to an 18th-century mansion. Specializes in seafood, regional dishes. Own pastries. Hrs: 5:30-11 pm; Sun to 10 pm; Sun brunch 10:30 am-3 pm. Closed Mon. Res required. Serv bar. Extensive wine list. A la carte entrees: dinner $23-$36. Vegetarian prix fixe dinner: $36-$49. Sun brunch $19.95-$27.95. Valet parking. Jacket. Totally nonsmoking. Cr cds: A, C, D, DS, ER, JCB, MC, V.

D

★ ★ ★ **HAUSSNER'S.** *3244 Eastern Ave (21224), east of Central Area. 410/327-8365.* Hrs: 11 am-10 pm. Closed Sun, Mon; Dec 25. German, Amer menu. Bar. Semi-a la carte: lunch, dinner $8-$24.50. Specializes in seafood. Own baking. Braille menu. Extensive dining room display of original 19th century artwork. Old-world atmosphere. Family-owned. Cr cds: A, C, D, DS, MC, V.

D

★ **HENNINGER'S TAVERN.** *1812 Bank St (21231), in Fell's Point. 410/342-2172.* Hrs: 5-10 pm; Fri, Sat to 11 pm. Closed Sun, Mon; Jan 1, Dec 25. Bar to 1 am. A la carte entrees: dinner $12.75-$17.95. Specializes in seafood. Late 1800s atmosphere. Cr cds: A, D, JCB, MC, V.

✔★ ★ **IKAROS.** *4805 Eastern Ave (21224), east of Central Area. 410/633-3750.* Hrs: 11 am-10 pm; Fri, Sat to 11 pm. Closed Tues; Thanksgiving, Dec 25. Greek, Amer menu. Serv bar. Semi-a la carte: lunch $4-$9, dinner $8-$15. Specializes in lamb, squid, fresh whole fish. Cr cds: A, C, D, DS, MC, V.

★ ★ **JEANNIER'S.** *105 W 39th St (21211), north of Central Area. 410/889-3303.* E-mail tr_ jeannier@juno.com. Hrs: noon-2:30 pm, 5:30-9:30 pm; Fri to 10 pm; Sat 5:30-10 pm; early-bird dinner 5:30-7 pm. Closed Sun; most major hols. French, continental menu. Bar noon-11 pm. A la carte entrees: lunch $6-$11, dinner $13.95-$25. Complete meals: dinner $14-$25. Specializes in seafood, country-French cuisine. Own desserts. Country chateau decor. Cr cds: A, C, D, MC, V.

★ ★ **JOHN STEVEN LTD.** *1800 Thames St (21231), in Fell's Point. 410/327-5561.* Hrs: 11 am-11 pm; Fri, Sat to midnight. Res accepted. Bar to 2 am. A la carte entrees: lunch $6-$11, dinner $7-$21. Specializes in seafood, sushi. Outdoor dining. Located in building built 1838. Cr cds: A, C, D, DS, MC, V.

D

★ ★ ★ **JOY AMERICA CAFE.** *800 Key Hwy (21230), in American Visionary Art Museum, Inner Harbor. 410/244-6500.* Hrs: 11:30 am-3:30 pm, 5:30-10 pm; Sun brunch 11 am-4 pm. Closed Mon; Labor Day, Thanksgiving, Dec 25. Res accepted. Contemporary Amer menu. Bar. Semi-a la carte: lunch $9-$15, dinner $19-$28.50. Sun brunch $11.50-$14. Child's meals. Specialties: chicken and dried cherry dim sum, Thai-grilled rack of lamb. Outdoor dining. View of city and Inner Harbor. Totally nonsmoking. Cr cds: A, D, MC, V.

D

★ ★ **KARSON'S INN.** *5100 Holabird Ave (21224), east of Central Area. 410/631-5400.* Hrs: 11 am-9:15 pm; Sat from 4 pm; Sun 11 am-8:15 pm. Closed Mon; Thanksgiving, Dec 25. Res accepted; required hols. Bar. Semi-a la carte: lunch $6.95-$11.50, dinner $10.95-$32. Child's meals. Specializes in steak, seafood. Parking. Family-owned. Cr cds: A, DS, MC, V.

D

★ ★ **KAWASAKI.** *413 N Charles St (21201), in Central Area. 410/659-7600.* Hrs: 11:30-2:30 pm, 5-11 pm; Fri to midnight; Sat 5-midnight. Closed Sun; most major hols. Japanese menu. Bar. A la carte entrees: lunch, dinner $2.50-$9. Semi-a la carte: lunch $5.95-$9.50, dinner $9.50-$18. Specializes in Japanese seafood, sushi rolls. In townhouse; Japanese decor. Cr cds: A, C, D, JCB, MC, V.

★ ★ **LA SCALA.** *411 S High St (21231), in Little Italy. 410/783-9209.* Hrs: 4:30-10 pm; Fri, Sat to 11 pm; Sun 2-10 pm. Closed Jan 1, Thanksgiving, Dec 25. Res accepted. Italian menu. Bar. Semi-a la carte: dinner $9.95-$29.95. Specializes in veal, pasta. Contemporary decor. Cr cds: A, C, D, DS, MC, V.

★ ★ **MORGAN MILLARD.** *4800 Roland Ave (21210), north of Central Area. 410/889-0030.* Hrs: 11:30 am-9:30 pm; Fri, Sat to 10:30 pm; Sun 11 am-8:30 pm; Sun brunch to 3 pm. Closed most major hols. Res accepted (dinner). Regional Amer menu. Bar. Semi-a la carte: lunch $5.95-$11.50, dinner $5.95-$22. Sun brunch $6.95-$12.95. Child's meals. Specialties: pan-fried catfish, barbecued duck breast. Own baking. In historic Roland Park area; local artwork and music featured. Totally nonsmoking. Cr cds: A, MC, V.

D

★ ★ **MT WASHINGTON TAVERN.** *5700 Newbury St (21209), I-83 N, exit Northern Pkwy E, W at Falls Rd, W onto Kelly Ave Bridge, E on Sungrave, 1 blk to Newbury, north of Central Area. 410/367-6903.* Hrs: 11:30 am-10 pm; Sat to 11 pm; Sun brunch to 3 pm. Closed Dec 25. Res accepted. Bar. Semi-a la carte: lunch $5.95-$12.95, dinner $12.95-$22.95. Sun brunch $5.95-$12.95. Child's meals. Specializes in Angus beef, veal chops, steamed shrimp. Entertainment Wed, Sat. Outdoor dining. Tavern atmosphere has varied dining areas. Cr cds: A, D, MC, V.

D ♥

★ ★ **OBRYCKI'S.** *1727 E Pratt St (21231), in Fell's Point. 410/732-6399.* Web www.obrycks.com. Hrs: noon-11 pm; Sun to 9:30 pm. Closed mid-Dec-Mar. Bar. Semi-a la carte: lunch $5.50-$17.95, dinner $13.25-$27.95. Child's meals. Specializes in crab. Family-owned. Cr cds: A, C, D, DS, MC, V.

D

★ ★ **PIERPOINT.** *1822 Aliceanna St (21231), in Fell's Point. 410/675-2080.* Hrs: 11:30 am-2:30 pm, 5:30-9:30 pm; Fri to 10:30 pm; Sat 5:30-11 pm; Sun 4-9:30 pm. Closed Mon; Jan 1, July 4, Dec 25. Res accepted. Bar. A la carte entrees: lunch $5.95-$8.95, dinner $5.95-$24. Specializes in Maryland cuisine. Contemporary decor. Cr cds: A, MC, V.

D

★ ★ ★ **POLO GRILL.** *(See Doubletree Inn at The Colonnade Hotel) 410/235-8200.* Hrs: 6:30-10 am, 11:30 am-4 pm, 5:30-11 pm; Fri to midnight; Sat 7-10:30 am, 11:30 am-4 pm, 5:30 pm-midnight; Sun 7-10:30 am, 11 am-2:30 pm, 5:30-10 pm. Res accepted. Bar. A la carte entrees: lunch $5.95-$19.50, dinner $10.95-$36.95. Complete meals: bkfst $7.50-$7.95. Specializes in seafood, pasta. Valet parking. English hunt decor. Cr cds: A, C, D, DS, ER, JCB, MC, V.

D

★ ★ ★ **PRIME RIB.** *1101 N Calvert St (21202), in Central Area. 410/539-1804.* Hrs: 5 pm-midnight; Sun 4-11 pm. Closed Thanksgiving. Res accepted. Bar. Wine list. A la carte entrees: dinner $20-$25. Specializes in steak, seafood, lamb. Pianist. Parking. Black laquered walls. Paintings and prints displayed. Jacket. Family-owned. Cr cds: A, C, D, MC, V.

D

★ ★ **ROCCO CAPRICCIO.** *846 Fawn St (21202), Little Italy. 410/685-2710.* Hrs: 11:30 am-10:30 pm; Fri, Sat to 11:30 pm. Closed

Thanksgiving, Dec 25. Res accepted. Northern Italian menu. Bar. Semi-a la carte: lunch $6.25-$12, dinner $9.95-$28. Child's meals. Specialties: fettucine frutta de mare (white or red), veal Capriccio. Own pasta. Cr cds: A, C, D, DS, MC, V.

★ ★ ★ **RUBY LOUNGE.** *802 N Charles St (21201), in Central Area. 410/539-8051.* Hrs: 5:30-11 pm; Fri, Sat to midnight. Closed Sun, Mon; also most major hols. Res accepted. Bar. A la carte entrees: dinner $9.95-$15.95. Specializes in duck, pork, seafood. Valet parking. Casual decor. Cr cds: A, MC.

★ ★ ★ **RUTH'S CHRIS STEAK HOUSE.** *600 Water St (21202), in Central Area. 410/783-0033.* E-mail serioussteaks.com. Hrs: 5-10 pm; Fri, Sat to 11 pm. Closed Thanksgiving, Dec 25. Res accepted. Bar. A la carte entrees: dinner $15.95-$28.95. Specializes in steaks, seafood. Free valet parking. Upscale furnishing. Cr cds: A, C, D, DS, ER, JCB, MC, V.

D

★ ★ ★ **SAVANNAH.** *(See Admiral Fell Inn) 410/522-2195.* E-mail admiral1@erols.com; web www.admiralfell.com. Hrs: 11:30 am-2 pm, 5:30-10 pm; Fri, Sat to 11 pm; Sun brunch 11 am-3 pm. Res accepted. Bar. A la carte entrees: lunch $8-$12, dinner $13-$21. Sun brunch $8-$12. Child's meals. Specializes in southern cuisine. Free valet parking. Outdoor dining. Contemporary decor. Cr cds: A, D, MC, V.

D

★ ★ ★ **SPIKE & CHARLIE'S.** *1225 Cathedral St (21201), north of Central Area. 410/752-8144.* Hrs: 5:30-10 pm; Fri, Sat to midnight. Closed Mon; most major hols. Res accepted. Bar. Semi-a la carte: dinner $8-$26. Specializes in seafood. Own baking. Contemporary decor. Cr cds: A, MC, V.

D

★ ★ ★ **TIO PEPE.** *10 E Franklin St (21202), in Central Area. 410/539-4675.* Hrs: 11:30 am-2:30 pm, 5-10:30 pm; Fri to 11:30 pm; Sat 5-11:30 pm; Sun 4-10:30 pm. Closed most major hols. Res required. Spanish, continental menu. Bar. Wine cellar. Semi-a la carte: lunch $9-$14, dinner $13.75-$24. Specialties: shrimp in garlic sauce, suckling pig. Spanish casa atmosphere. Jacket. Cr cds: A, C, D, DS, MC, V.

D

★ ★ **VELLEGGIA'S.** *829 E Pratt St (21202), Little Italy. 410/685-2620.* Hrs: 11 am-11 pm; Fri to midnight; Sat to 1 am. Closed Dec 24, 25. Res accepted. Italian menu. Bar. A la carte entrees: lunch $4.95-$9.95, dinner $9.25-$19.95. Child's meals. Specializes in veal, seafood. Own pasta. Family-owned. Cr cds: A, D, MC, V.

D

✔★ **WATER STREET EXCHANGE.** *110 Water St, in Central Area. 410/332-4060.* Hrs: 11:30 am-8 pm; Mon to 3 pm; Tues to 6 pm; Sat from 5:30. Closed Sun; major hols. Res accepted. Bar to 2 am. Semi-a la carte: lunch $5.95-$13, dinner $13-$26. Specializes in pasta, seafood. Outdoor dining. Victorian decor. Cr cds: A, C, D, DS, MC, V.

★ **WATERFRONT HOTEL.** *1710 Thames St (21231), in Fell's Point. 410/327-4886.* Hrs: 11 am-10 pm; Fri, Sat to 11 pm. Closed Dec 25. Res accepted. Continental menu. Bar 10-2 am. Semi-a la carte: lunch $4.50-$9.95, dinner $11.95-$20. Child's meals. Specializes in seafood, beef. Restored building (1771) located on waterfront; 3-story brick fireplace, stained-glass windows. Cr cds: A, C, D, MC, V.

✔★ **WAYNE'S BAR-B-QUE.** *201 Pratt St (21202), Inner Harbor. 410/539-3810.* Hrs: 8 am-11 pm; Fri, Sat to midnight. Closed Thanksgiving. Res accepted. Bar to 2 am. A la carte entrees: bkfst $4.50-$7.95, lunch, dinner $5-$12.95. Child's meals. Specializes in barbecue dishes, desserts. Outdoor dining. View of harbor. Cr cds: A, C, DS, MC, V.

D SC

★ ★ **THE WILD MUSHROOM.** *641 S Montford Ave (21231), in Central Area. 410/675-4225.* Hrs: 11:30-1 am. Closed Sun; Jan 1, Thanksgiving, Dec 25. Bar. A la carte entrees: lunch $4.95-$12.95, dinner $6.95-$25. Specializes in mushroom-driven dishes. Contemporary decor. Cr cds: A, C, D, DS, JCB, MC, V.

Unrated Dining Spot

LOUIE'S THE BOOKSTORE CAFE. *518 N Charles St, in Central Area. 410/962-1224.* Hrs: 11:30-1 am; Mon to midnight; Fri, Sat to 2 am; Sun 10:30 am-midnight; Sun brunch to 3 pm. Closed major hols. Bar. A la carte: lunch $3.50-$10.95, dinner $3.95-$16.95. Sun brunch $3.25-$9.95. Specializes in international bistro fare. Outdoor dining. Chamber music. Original artwork. Cr cds: A, MC, V.

D

Baltimore/Washington Intl Airport Area

Motels

★ ★ **COURTYARD BY MARRIOTT.** *(1671 W Nursery Rd, Linthicum 21090) Approx 1 mi N on Nursery Rd. 410/859-8855.* Web www.courtyard.com. 149 rms, 3 story. Apr-Nov: S, D $104-$114; suites $123-$134; under 10 free; lower rates rest of yr. TV; cable (premium). Indoor pool; whirlpool, lifeguard. Complimentary coffee in rms. Restaurant 6:30-10:30 am, 5-10 pm; Sat, Sun 7 am-noon. Bar 4-10 pm. Ck-out noon. Meeting rms. Business servs avail. Coin lndry. Free airport transportation. Exercise equipt; bicycles, weight machine. Some refrigerators. Cr cds: A, C, D, DS, MC, V.

D SC

★ ★ **HAMPTON INN.** *(6617 Governor Ritchie Hwy, Glen Burnie 21061) I-695, exit 3B, in Governor Plaza Shopping Ctr. 410/761-7666; FAX 410/761-0253.* 116 rms, 5 story. S $92; D $99; suites $110; under 18 free; higher rates special events. Crib free. TV; cable (premium). Complimentary continental bkfst. Restaurant adj open 24 hrs. Ck-out noon. Meeting rms. Business servs avail. In-rm modem links. Valet serv. Sundries. Health club privileges. Microwaves avail. Cr cds: A, C, D, DS, MC, V.

D SC

✔★ **HOLIDAY INN-GLEN BURNIE SOUTH.** *(6600 Ritchie Hwy, Glen Burnie 21061) I-195 to I-695, E to MD 2 (Ritchie Hwy). 410/761-8300; FAX 410/760-4966.* 100 rms, 3 story. S, D $75; each addl $10; under 18 free. Crib free. Pet accepted, some restrictions. TV; cable (premium). Pool; lifeguard. Restaurant 6 am-2 pm, 5-10 pm; Sat, Sun from 7 am. Rm serv. Bar 4 pm-midnight. Ck-out noon. Meeting rms. In-rm modem link. Valet serv. Health club privileges. Microwaves avail. Mall opp. Cr cds: A, C, D, DS, ER, JCB, MC, V.

D SC

Motor Hotels

✔★ ★ **BEST WESTERN AT BWI AIRPORT.** *(6755 Dorsey Rd, Dorsey 21227) I-295 S to MD 176. 410/796-3300; FAX 410/379-0471.* 134 rms, 4 story. S $69; D $74; each addl $5; under 18 free. Crib free. TV; cable (premium), VCR avail. Indoor pool; whirlpool. Complimentary coffee in lobby. Restaurant adj 7 am-11 pm; Sat, Sun 8 am-10 pm. Ck-out noon. Meeting rms. In-rm modem link. Valet serv. Airport transportation. Exercise equipt; weight machines, bicycles, sauna. Cr cds: A, C, D, DS, ER, MC, V.

D SC

★ ★ **COMFORT INN-AIRPORT.** *(6921 Baltimore Annapolis Blvd (MD 648), Baltimore 21225) N on MD 170 to Baltimore Annapolis Blvd. 410/789-9100; FAX 410/355-2854.* 188 rms, 6 story. S $79; D $89; each addl $8; suites $125-$225; studio rms $79-$89; under 12 free; wkend rates. Crib free. Pet accepted. TV; cable (premium), VCR avail. Complimentary bkfst buffet. Restaurant 7 am-11 pm. Bar 11 am-midnight. Ck-out 11 am. Meeting rms. Business servs avail. In-rm modem link. Bellhops. Valet serv. Airport transportation. Exercise equipt; weights, bicycles, sauna. Whirlpool. Game rm. Microwaves avail. Cr cds: A, C, D, DS, ER, JCB, MC, V.

D SC

✔★ **HAMPTON INN.** *(829 Elkridge Landing Rd, Linthicum 21090) From I-95 or I-295 take I-195E to exit 1A (MD 170N). 410/850-0600; FAX 410/691-2119.* 139 rms, 5 story. S $79; D $85; under 18 free. Crib free. Pet accepted. TV; cable (premium). Complimentary continental bkfst. Restaurant nearby. Ck-out noon. Meeting rms. In-rm modem link. Valet serv. Free airport transportation. Microwaves avail. Cr cds: A, C, D, DS, ER, JCB, MC, V.

D SC

★ ★ ★ **SHERATON INTERNATIONAL AT BWI AIRPORT.** *(7032 Elm Rd, Baltimore 21240) N of terminal. 410/859-3300; FAX 410/859-0565.* Web www.sheraton.com. 196 rms, 2 story. S $129-$139; D $129-$149; each addl $10; suites $145-$175; under 16 free; wkend rates. Crib free. TV; cable (premium). Pool; poolside serv, lifeguard. Complimentary continental bkfst. Coffee in rms. Restaurant 6:30 am-10:30 pm. Rm serv 24 hrs. Bar 11-2 am; entertainment. Ck-out noon. Meeting rms. Business servs avail. In-rm modem link. Bellhops. Sundries. Gift shop. Airport transportation. Exercise equipt; weights, bicycles. Cr cds: A, C, D, DS, MC, V.

D SC

★ **SUSSE CHALET.** *(1734 W Nursery Rd, Linthicum 21090) 410/859-2333; FAX 410/859-2357.* 130 rms, 5 story. S, D $68.70-$75.70; each addl $7; suites $89.70-$99.70; under 18 free. Crib free. TV; cable (premium). Pool; lifeguard. Complimentary continental bkfst. Restaurant nearby. Ck-out 11 am. Coin Indry. Business servs avail. In-rm modem link. Airport, RR station transportation. Microwaves avail. Cr cds: A, C, D, DS, MC, V.

D SC

Hotels

★ ★ ★ **DOUBLETREE GUEST SUITES.** *(1300 Concourse Dr, Linthicum 21090) N on MD 170 to Elkridge Landing Rd, NW 1½ mi to Winterson Rd, W to Concourse Dr; or I-295 to W Nursery Rd exit, then to Winterson Rd. 410/850-0747; FAX 410/859-0816.* Web www.doubletreehotels.com. 251 suites, 8 story. S $99-$160; D $109-$170; each addl $10; under 18 free; wkend rates. Crib free. TV; cable (premium). Indoor pool; whirlpool, lifeguard. Complimentary coffee in rms. Restaurant 6:30 am-10 pm; wkends to 11 pm. Bar 11-1 am. Ck-out noon. Convention facilities. Business servs avail. In-rm modem link. Gift shop. Airport transportation. Exercise equipt; weights, bicycles, sauna. Bathrm phones, refrigerators, wet bars; microwaves avail. Cr cds: A, C, D, DS, MC, V.

D SC

★ ★ ★ **MARRIOTT.** *(1743 W Nursery Rd, Linthicum 21240) Approx 1 mi N on Nursery Rd. 410/859-8300; FAX 410/691-4515.* 310 rms, 10 story. S, D $149-$159; each addl $15; suites $143-$350; under 18 free. Crib free. TV; cable (premium). Indoor pool; whirlpool. Complimentary coffee in lobby. Restaurant 6:30 am-10 pm. Bar 4 pm-1:30 am. Ck-out noon. Convention facilities. Business servs avail. Free airport transportation. Exercise equipt; bicycles, weight machine. Cr cds: A, C, D, DS, ER, JCB, MC, V.

D SC

Pikesville

Motels

✔★ **COMFORT INN-NORTHWEST.** *10 Wooded Way, at I-695 exit 20. 410/484-7700; FAX 410/653-1516.* 103 rms, 2-3 story. No elvtr. S, D $59-$89; under 18 free; wkly, monthly rates. Crib free. TV; cable (premium). Pool; wading pool, lifeguard. Complimentary continental bkfst. Coffee in rms. Restaurant adj 6:30 am-11:30 pm. Ck-out 11 am. Coin Indry. Meeting rms. Business servs avail. In-rm modem link. Valet serv Mon-Fri. Health club privileges. Microwaves avail. Cr cds: A, C, D, DS, ER, JCB, MC, V.

D SC

★ **HOLIDAY INN.** *1721 Reisterstown Rd, at I-695 exit 20S. 410/486-5600; FAX 410/484-9377.* Web www.holiday-inn.com. 108 rms, 2 story. S, D $69; under 18 free; higher rates Preakness. Crib free. Pet accepted. TV; cable (premium). Pool; poolside serv, lifeguard. Restaurant 6 am-1 pm, 5-10 pm; Sat, Sun from 7 am. Rm serv. Bar 5 pm-midnight. Ck-out noon. Meeting rms. Business servs avail. Valet serv. Health club privileges. Some refrigerators; microwaves avail. Cr cds: A, C, D, DS, ER, JCB, MC, V.

D SC

Motor Hotel

★ ★ ★ **HILTON.** *1726 Reisterstown Rd, at I-695 exit 20S. 410/653-1100; FAX 410/484-4138.* E-mail pikhi_ds@hilton.com; web www.hilton.com. 171 rms, 5 story. S $97-$150; D $97-$160; each addl $10; suites $300-$390; wkend plans; family rates. Crib $10. TV; cable (premium), VCR avail (movies). Pool; lifeguard. Coffee in rms. Restaurant 7 am-11 pm. Rm serv. Bar 11-1 am. Ck-out noon. Meeting rms. Business servs avail. Bellhops. Valet serv. Gift shop. Barber, beauty shop. Airport transportation. Tennis privileges. Exercise equipt; weight machines, stair machines. Bathrm phones; microwaves avail. Cr cds: A, C, D, DS, ER, MC, V.

D SC

Inn

★ ★ ★ **GRAMERCY.** *(1400 Greenspring Valley Rd, Stevenson 21153) I-695 exit 23N, Falls Rd to 2nd light, left on Greenspring Valley Rd. 410/486-2405.* 8 rms, 3 story, 2 suites. S, D $145-$250; each addl $25; suites $250. Crib $10. TV; VCR (movies). Pool. Complimentary full bkfst. Ck-out noon, ck-in after 3-6 pm. Business servs avail. In-rm modem link. Tennis. Lawn games. Picnic tables. Mansion (1902) on 45-acre wooded estate. Flower, herb gardens. Totally nonsmoking. Cr cds: A, DS, MC, V.

Restaurants

★ ★ **DUE.** *(25 Crossroads Dr, Owings Mills 21117) I-695, exit 20. 410/356-4147.* Hrs: 5:30-10 pm; Fri, Sat to 11 pm; Sun 5-9 pm. Closed most major hols. Res accepted. Italian menu. Bar. A la carte entrees: dinner $9.95-$24.95. Specializes in pasta, veal, chicken. Contemporary decor. Cr cds: A, D, MC, V.

D

★ ★ ★ **LINWOOD'S CAFE.** *(25 Crossroads Dr, Owings Mills 21117) I-695, exit 20. 410/356-3030.* Hrs: 11:30 am-3 pm, 5:30-10 pm; Fri, Sat to 11 pm; Sun 5-9 pm. Closed most major hols. Res accepted; required Fri, Sat. Bar. A la carte entrees: lunch $4.95-$14.95, dinner $9.95-$27.95. Specializes in chicken, seafood, steak. Formal decor. Cr cds: A, D, MC, V.

D

★ ★ **PUFFINS.** *1000 Reisterstown Rd, at Sherwood Ave. 410/486-8811.* Hrs: noon-2:30 pm, 5:30-close; Sun 5-8:30 pm. Closed most major hols. Res accepted Fri, Sat dinner. Bar. Semi-a la carte: lunch $6-$9.75, dinner $13-$21. Specializes in vegetarian, chicken, seafood dishes. Own breads. Modern decor; artwork. Totally nonsmoking. Cr cds: A, D, MC, V.

D

★ ★ **STIXX CAFE.** *1500 Reisterstown Rd, at Club Center. 410/484-7787.* Hrs: 11:30 am-2:30 pm, 5-10 pm; Fri to 11 pm; Sat 5-11 pm; Sun 4-9:30 pm. Closed Thanksgiving. Res accepted Fri, Sat dinner. Continental menu. Bar. A la carte entrees: lunch, dinner $5.50-$17. Specializes in sushi. Own baking. Outdoor dining. Contemporary atmosphere. Totally nonsmoking. Cr cds: A, C, D, DS, MC, V.

D

Boston

Founded: 1630
Pop: 574,283
Elev: 0-330 feet
Time zone: Eastern
Area code: 617
Web: bweb.com/bostonweb

No city in the United States attracts more historically interested visitors than venerable, picturesque, dynamic Boston. Named the capital of Massachusetts Bay Colony in 1630, the Boston settlement soon grew to be the largest town in New England. By the middle of the 18th century, Boston was a thriving cultural and political center.

The American Revolution began in Boston in 1770, when British troops fired on an angry mob, killing six citizens. The "Boston Massacre," as it came to be known, was followed by the Boston Tea Party in 1773 and the midnight ride of Paul Revere in 1775.

In the years following the Revolution, Boston's prominence continued to grow as many fortunes were made in shipbuilding and international trade. Greater Boston has been a leader in education since 1636, when Harvard College was founded in Newtowne. Today, this area has a tremendous concentration of institutions of higher learning, including Massachusetts Institute of Technology, Tufts, Boston University and Northeastern University.

The Boston metropolitan area, populated by more than 3 million people, is an interesting combination of old and new. It continues to be regarded by many of its natives as the "hub of the universe."

Business

Investment in construction of commercial structures, medical, educational and cultural facilities and housing has increased in Boston during the last few years. The economy of the city is heavily diversified, with a base of finance and insurance, business services, higher education, medical services, recreation and tourism, retail trade and industry.

Boston's harbor, which covers more than 30,000 acres, is one of the world's largest and busiest, and millions of tons of cargo are handled at this port. The harbor has been a major economic asset to the city since its founding.

Hundreds of manufacturing firms make Boston a major industrial center as well.

Convention Facilities

Boston is a favorite city for conventions because it has so much to offer visitors. Its many educational, medical and scientific institutions are a magnet for scholars, researchers and scientists, and the city's varied industrial and commercial activities draw in the business community. In addition, Boston's historical heritage, sightseeing, cultural activities and entertainment make up an urban package that is difficult to match.

The John B. Hynes Veterans Memorial Convention Center has more than 193,000 square feet of exhibit space; a 5,000-seat auditorium with complete stage facilities and dressing rooms; 38 permanent meeting rooms, the largest of which seats up to 1,200, several modular rooms with seating capacities ranging from 125 to 375, and smaller rooms for groups of 25 to 50. There is direct access on the first floor to the Prudential Plaza and on the second to an adjacent hotel.

The 865,000-square-foot World Trade Center on Commonwealth Pier houses meetings, conferences and exhibitions.

Sports & Recreation

Boston has something for everyone in the recreation category. There are the Red Sox for baseball, the Celtics for basketball, the New England Patriots for football and the Bruins for hockey. Visitors can choose among greyhound, Thoroughbred and harness racing. Within a few miles are many lovely Atlantic beaches and several amusement parks.

For the very energetic, a 15-mile jogging trail offers runners not only an opportunity to train for the famed Boston Marathon in April, but also spectacular scenery and attractive sights along its course. It stretches westward from the city along the Charles River, past sailboats and sculling crews, past Massachusetts Institute of Technology, Boston University and Harvard.

Entertainment

Boston has many museums, a planetarium and an aquarium. Symphony concerts, opera and theater are also here to enjoy.

The Boston Symphony season extends from October through April with performances at Symphony Hall. The Boston Ballet season is October to December and February through May. The Boston Pops perform at Symphony Hall from May to mid-July and give free outdoor concerts at the Edward Hatch Memorial Shell on and in the week of July 4th. The Opera Company of Boston season is fall to early spring.

Boston is home to restaurants of every imaginable type, including some of the country's best seafood places, which keep alive the city's heritage as a fishing port.

Many entertainment spots are available throughout Greater Boston, but one of the charms of the city is that a great many of them are within walking distance of the major hotels. Boston is a pedestrian's city, and to enjoy it fully visitors must do some exploring on foot.

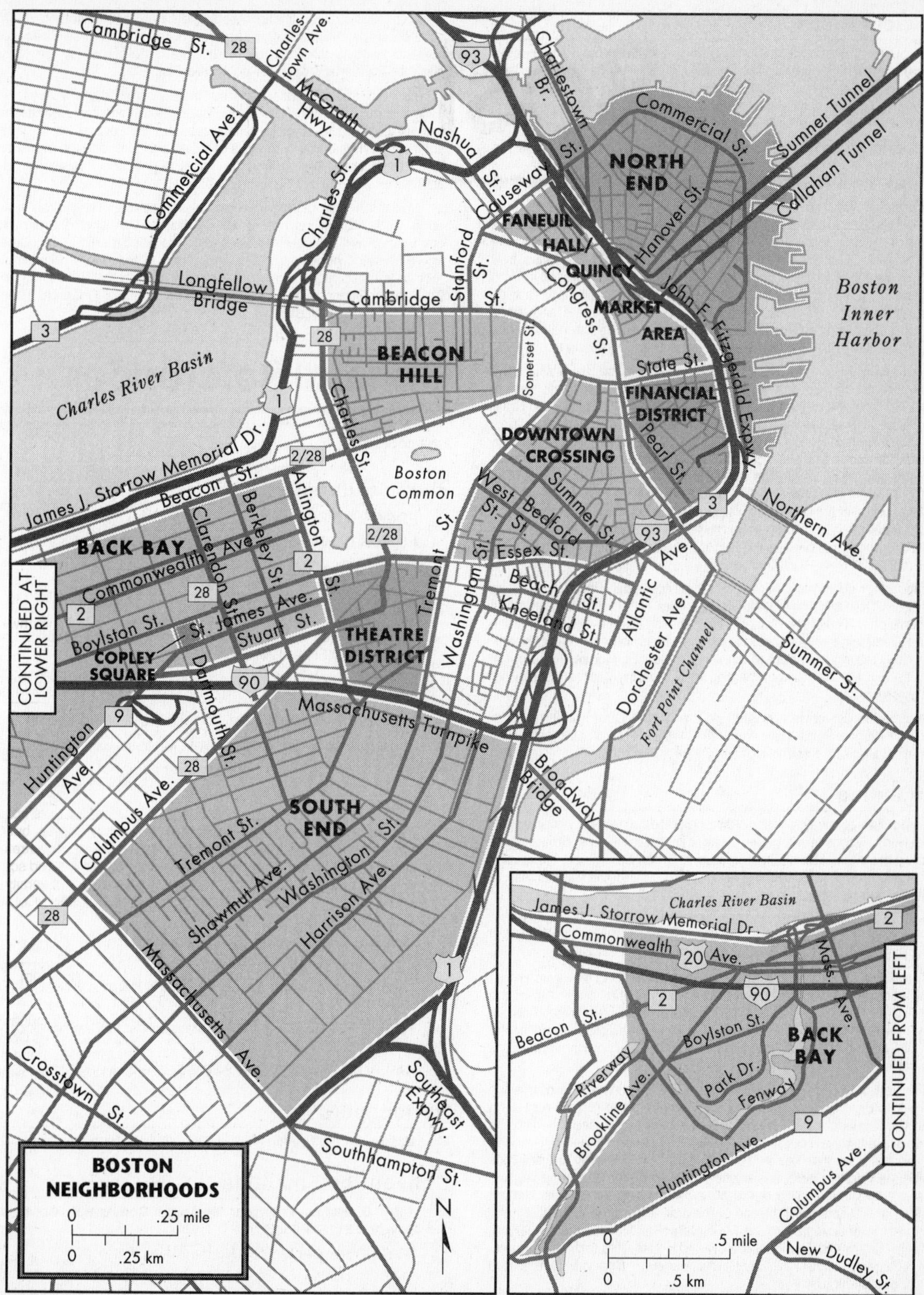
BOSTON
NEIGHBORHOODS
NORTH END
FANEUIL HALL/ QUINCY MARKET AREA
BEACON HILL
FINANCIAL DISTRICT
DOWNTOWN CROSSING
BACK BAY
THEATRE DISTRICT
COPLEY SQUARE
SOUTH END
Boston Common
Charles River Basin
Boston Inner Harbor
Fort Point Channel
Cambridge St.
Charlestown Ave.
McGrath Hwy.
Nashua St.
Charlestown Br.
Commercial St.
Sumner Tunnel
Callahan Tunnel
Commercial Ave.
Charles St.
Causeway St.
Stanford St.
Hanover St.
Congress St.
John F. Fitzgerald Expwy.
Longfellow Bridge
Somerset St.
State St.
Pearl St.
James J. Storrow Memorial Dr.
Beacon St.
Arlington St.
Berkeley St.
Clarendon St.
Commonwealth Ave.
St. James Ave.
Boylston St.
Stuart St.
Dartmouth St.
Tremont St.
Washington St.
West St.
Bedford St.
Summer St.
Essex St.
Beach St.
Kneeland St.
Atlantic Ave.
Dorchester Ave.
Northern Ave.
Summer St.
Massachusetts Turnpike
Broadway Bridge
Huntington Ave.
Columbus Ave.
Shawmut Ave.
Harrison Ave.
Massachusetts Ave.
Crosstown St.
Southeast Expwy.
Southhampton St.
CONTINUED AT LOWER RIGHT
0 .25 mile
0 .25 km
N
Charles River Basin
James J. Storrow Memorial Dr.
Commonwealth Ave.
Mass. Ave.
Beacon St.
Boylston St.
BACK BAY
Riverway
Brookline Ave.
Park Dr.
Fenway
Huntington Ave.
Columbus Ave.
New Dudley St.
CONTINUED FROM LEFT
0 .5 mile
0 .5 km
1
2
2/28
3
9
20
28
90
93

Historical Areas

Almost all of Boston could be classified as a "historical area," but the most famous and interesting of its many sights have been marked for walking and bus tours as the Freedom Trail. A map and the official guidebook to Boston are available at Boston information centers and at the Greater Boston Convention and Visitors Bureau.

Before taking the trail, visit the Custom House Observation Tower to scan downtown Boston and the harbor and locate points of interest found on the maps and brochures. The ornate stone tower is 500 feet tall; for many years it was the highest vantage point in Boston.

The Freedom Trail begins at Boston Common, an area used by the residents of the town since 1634, originally for the grazing of cattle and the training of militia. The following spots are designated: the State House, built in 1795 by architect Charles Bulfinch; Park Street Church, where William Lloyd Garrison gave his first antislavery speech in 1829; Granary Burying Ground, where John Hancock, Samuel Adams, Paul Revere and many others are buried; King's Chapel, built in 1749; the site of the nation's first public school, built in 1635; a statue of Benjamin Franklin, dating from 1856.

Also along the Trail are Old South Meeting House, from which the group of patriots left to launch the Boston Tea Party; the Old State House, built in 1713; the site of the Boston Massacre, just outside the Old State House; Faneuil Hall, public marketplace, meeting place and "cradle of liberty"; Paul Revere House, built ca 1680, the oldest building in the city; Old North Church, 1723, an architectural gem, oldest standing church in Boston and the place where the two lanterns were hung on the night of April 18, 1775; the USS *Constitution*, "Old Ironsides," a 44-gun frigate built in 1797; a replica of the brig *Beaver*, scene of the Boston Tea Party on the night of December 16, 1773; and finally, the Bunker Hill Monument in Charlestown, commemorating the first major battle of the Revolution on June 17, 1775.

Although a good many of the city's historical sites are situated along the Freedom Trail, the entire Boston area is filled with places that preserve the nation's past. The Black Heritage Trail walking tour covers much of the Beacon Hill section that relates to the history of 19th-century black Boston. To take this walking tour, start at the African Meeting House. An informal walking tour of the Back Bay area can lead to many interesting sites of early Boston.

Information centers are located on the Boston Common, the Visitor Center in Prudential Plaza West and at the National Park Visitor Hospitality Center at 15 State St. For information, phone 536-4100.

Sightseeing

Boston is a gateway to many New England destinations. Among them are the north woods and rugged seacoast of Maine, the breathtaking scenery of the White Mountains, the serene Green Mountains, ski resorts in all directions and the charming and scenic old Rhode Island cities of Providence and Newport.

But close enough for Boston to serve as your headquarters are four major regions: the North Shore, the South Shore, Cape Cod and the suburbs of Boston.

The North Shore includes Rockport, a seacoast art colony with more than 60 shops, galleries and craft studios; Gloucester, once one of the nation's largest fishing ports and still one of the finest places for seafood; and the "bewitched" city of Salem, now a quiet sea town, home of the House of Seven Gables and interesting mansions built by captains of the clipper ships.

On the South Shore, which runs from Boston to Cape Cod, are two places not to be missed. One is Quincy, home of John Adams and John Quincy Adams, where three 17th- and 18th-century houses in which the two presidents lived are open to the public. The second town is Plymouth, where there is enough to see and do for at least one full day. The tiny rock on which the Pilgrims landed is enshrined in an observation cupola, and nearby is a full-scale replica of the *Mayflower.* South of town is Plimoth Plantation, a 100-acre reproduction of the first settlement. Other points of interest are the Antiquarian House, Major John Bradford House, Burial Hill, Cole's Hill, Harlow Old Fort House, Howland House, Pilgrim Hall Museum, Pilgrim Village, Plymouth National Wax Museum, Spooner House and Richard Sparrow House.

Cape Cod is a mecca for artists and sailing enthusiasts. Swimmers, scuba divers, sunbathers and sand-lovers have more than 300 miles of shoreline to enjoy. Most of the outer cape is preserved by the National Seashore Park and is open for public recreation.

The suburbs of Boston are as interesting as the city itself. Cambridge—home of Harvard University, Radcliffe College and the Massachusetts Institute of Technology—has been an intellectual community for centuries. Homes of many famous scholars are here, and the museums of Harvard University are among the most varied and interesting on the continent.

Lexington and Concord, where the American Revolution actually began, have numerous memorials to the past. A stroll through these communities will take the visitor past dozens of markers, monuments, restored historic houses and buildings open to the public. Guides stand ready to tell fascinating stories of the early days of the Revolution and of 19th-century Concord, when the city was the home of Emerson, Thoreau, Hawthorne and the Alcotts.

General References

Area code: 617

Phone Numbers

POLICE & FIRE: 911

POISON CONTROL CENTER: 800/682-9211 or 232-2120.

TIME: 637-1234 **WEATHER:** 936-1234

Information Sources

Greater Boston Convention & Visitors Bureau, Prudential Tower, PO Box 990468, 02199; 536-4100.

Boston Common Information Center, Boston Common, Tremont St, 536-4100.

National Park Visitor Center, 15 State St, 02109; 242-5642.

Parks & Recreation Department, 10 Massachusetts Ave, 635-4505.

Transportation

AIRLINES: Aer Lingus (Ireland); Air Canada; Air France; Alitalia; American; America West; British Airways; Cape Air; Continental; Delta; El Al (Israel); Lufthansa (Germany); Midwest Express; Mohawk; Northwest; QANTAS (Australia); SABENA (Belgium); Skymaster; TWA; United; USAir; and other commuter and regional airlines.

AIRPORT: Logan International, 800/235-6426.

CAR RENTAL AGENCIES: (See IMPORTANT TOLL-FREE NUMBERS) Avis 561-3500; Budget 497-1800; Hertz 569-7272; National 569-6700.

PUBLIC TRANSPORTATION: Massachusetts Bay Transportation Authority, 722-3200.

RAILROAD PASSENGER SERVICE: Amtrak 800/872-7245.

Newspapers

Boston Globe; Boston Herald; Christian Science Monitor.

Convention Facilities

John B. Hynes Veterans Memorial Convention Center, 900 Boylston St, 424-8585.

World Trade Center, 164 Northern Ave, 439-5000.

Sports & Recreation

Major Sports Facilities

Fleet Center, 1 Fleet Center Pl (Bruins, hockey, 624-1050; Celtics, basketball, 523-6050).

Fenway Park, Jersey St at Brookline Ave, 267-9440 (Red Sox, baseball).

Foxboro Stadium. US 1, Foxboro, 508/543-1776 (New England Patriots, football).

Racetracks

Suffolk Downs, US 1A, East Boston, 567-3900 (horse racing).

Wonderland, US 1A, Revere, 284-1300 (greyhound racing).

Cultural Facilities

Theaters

(Bostix, Faneuil Hall Marketplace, 723-5181, offers half-price tickets for same-day theater, music and dance performances)

American Repertory Theater, 64 Brattle St, Cambridge, 547-8300.

Boston Ballet Co, 19 Clarendon St, 695-6950.

Boston Center for the Arts, 539 Tremont St, 426-5000.

Charles Playhouse Theatre, 74 Warrenton St, 426-5225.

Colonial Theatre, 106 Boylston St, 426-9366.

Opera Laboratory Theatre, 162 Boylston St, 426-4943.

Shubert Theatre, 265 Tremont St, 426-4520.

Concert Halls

Berklee Performance Center, 136 Massachussetts Ave, 266-7455.

Boston Center for the Arts, 539 Tremont St, 426-5000.

Symphony Hall, 301 Massachusetts Ave, 266-1492.

Museums

African Meeting House, Museum of Afro-American History, 46 Joy St, on Beacon Hill, 742-5415.

Bell's Laboratory, New England Telephone Bldg, 185 Franklin St, in lobby, 743-9800.

Blue Hills Trailside Museum, 1904 Canton Ave, Milton, 333-0690.

Boston Tea Party Ship and Museum, Congress St Bridge on Harborwalk, 338-1773.

Cape Ann Historical Museum, 27 Pleasant St, Gloucester, 508/283-0455.

Children's Museum, Museum Wharf, 300 Congress St, 426-8855.

Computer Museum, Museum Wharf, 300 Congress St, 423-6758.

Concord Museum, 200 Lexington Rd, Concord, 508/369-9609.

DeCordova Museum, 51 Sandy Pond Rd, Lincoln, 259-8355.

Gibson House Museum, 137 Beacon St, 267-6338.

Harvard University Museums of Cultural and Natural History, 24 Oxford St, Cambridge, 495-2341.

Museum at the John Fitzgerald Kennedy Library, University of Massachusetts Columbia Point campus, 929-4523.

Museum of Our National Heritage, 33 Marrett Rd, Lexington, 861-6559.

Museum of Science and Charles Hayden Planetarium, Science Park, Charles River Dam Bridge, 723-2500 or 523-6664.

Museum of Transport, 15 Newton St, Lars Anderson Park, 522-6547.

New England Aquarium, Central Wharf, 973-5200.

Nichols House Museum, 55 Mt Vernon St, 227-6993.

Peabody Museum, East India Sq, Salem, 508/745-9500 or 745-1876.

Salem Witch Museum, 19 1/2 Washington Sq N, Salem, 508/744-1692.

USS *Constitution*, Boston National Historical Park, 426-1812 or 242-5670.

Art Museums

Boston Center for the Arts, 539 Tremont St, 426-5000.

Concord Art Association, 37 Lexington Rd, Concord, 508/369-2578.

Fogg Art Museum, 32 Quincy St, Harvard University, Cambridge, 495-9400.

Guild of Boston Artists, 162 Newbury St, 536-7660.

Institute of Contemporary Art, 955 Boylston St, 266-5152.

Isabella Stewart Gardner Museum, 280 The Fenway, 566-1401 or 734-1359.

Museum of Fine Arts, 465 Huntington Ave, 267-9300.

Sackler Art Museum, 485 Broadway, Harvard University, Cambridge, 495-9400.

Points of Interest

Historical

Battle Green, center of town, Lexington.

Beauport, 75 Eastern Point Blvd, Gloucester, 508/283-0800.

Black Heritage Trail, start at African Meeting House, Smith Ct, 742-1854 or 742-5415.

Boston Common, Beacon & Tremont Sts.

Boston Massacre Monument, Boston Common.

Boston Massacre Site, 30 State St.

Boston National Historical Park, visitor center located at 15 State St, 242-5642.

Boston Public Library, 666 Boylston St, 536-5400.

Buckman Tavern, 1 Bedford St, Lexington, 862-5598.

Bunker Hill Monument, Monument Sq, Lexington & High Sts, Charlestown, 242-5641.

Central Burying Ground, Boston Common.

Copley Square, Boylston St, W of Trinity Cathedral (Trinity St), N of St James Ave and E of the Public Library.

Copp's Hill Burying Ground, Hull & Snow Hill Sts.

Faneuil Hall, Merchants Row & Faneuil Hall Sq, 523-1300 or 227-1638.

Frederick Law Olmstead National Historic Site, 99 Warren St, Brookline, 566-1689.

The Freedom Trail, starts at Visitor Information Center on Boston Common. Follow signs and redbrick sidewalk line.

Gloucester Fisherman, off Western Ave on the harbor, Gloucester.

Granary Burying Ground, Tremont St, opp Bromfield St.

Hammond Castle Museum, 80 Hesperus Ave, Gloucester, 508/283-7673.

Hancock-Clarke House, 36 Hancock St, Lexington, 861-0928.

Harrison Gray Otis House, 141 Cambridge St, 227-3956.

House of Seven Gables, 54 Turner St, at Derby St, Salem, 508/744-0991.

Isaac Royall House, 15 George St, Medford, 396-9032.

John F. Kennedy National Historic Site, 83 Beals St, Brookline, 566-7937.

King's Chapel, Tremont & School Sts.

Longfellow National Historic Site, 105 Brattle St, Cambridge, 876-4491.

Louisburg Square, Mt Vernon St.

Minute Man National Historical Park, North Bridge Unit, 174 Liberty St, Concord, 508/369-6993.

Munroe Tavern, 1332 Massachusetts Ave, Lexington, 862-1703.

The Old Manse, Monument St at the North Bridge, Concord, 508/369-3909.

Old North Church, 193 Salem St, 523-6676.

Old South Meeting House, 310 Washington St, 482-6439.

Old State House, 206 Washington St, at State St, 720-3290.

Orchard House and School of Philosophy, 399 Lexington Rd, Concord, 508/369-4118.

Park Street Church, 1 Park St, 523-3383.

Paul Revere House, 19 North Sq, 523-2338.

Peabody Essex Museum, East India Sq, Salem, 508/744-3390

Plimoth Plantation, MA 3A (Warren Ave), Plymouth, 508/746-1622.

Plymouth Rock, Water St, Plymouth.

Ralph Waldo Emerson House, 28 Cambridge Tpke, at Lexington Rd, Concord, 508/369-2236.

Sargent House Museum, 49 Middle St, Gloucester, 508/281-2432.

Site of the First Public School, School St, opp Old City Hall.

Sleepy Hollow Cemetery, Bedford St, Concord.

State House, Beacon St at head of Park St, 727-3676.

Statue of Benjamin Franklin, School St, near Old City Hall.

Trinity Church, Copley Sq, 536-0944.

USS *Constitution*, Boston National Historical Park, 426-1812.

Walden Pond State Reservation, 915 Walden St, Concord, 508/369-3254.

The Wayside, Lexington Rd, Concord, 508/369-6975.

Other Attractions

Back Bay Area, Commonwealth Ave.

Cape Cod, SE of Boston.

Copley Place, 100 Huntington Ave, Copley Sq, 375-4477.

Franklin Park Zoo, S on Jamaicaway, then E on MA 203, in Dorchester area, 442-2002.

Harvard University, Harvard Sq, Cambridge, 495-1573.

John Hancock Observatory, 200 Clarendon St, at Copley Sq, 572-6429.

Market District, Haymarket Sq.

The Mother Church, The First Church of Christ, Scientist, Christian Science Center, Huntington & Massachusetts Aves, 450-3790.

Prudential Center, 800 Boylston St, 236-3318.

Public Garden, Charles St.

The Skywalk, Prudential Tower.

"Whites of their Eyes," Bunker Hill Pavilion, 55 Constitution Rd, Charlestown, 241-7575.

Sightseeing Tours

Bay State Cruise Company, Commonwealth Pier, 457-1428.

Boston by Foot, 77 N Washington St, 367-2345.

Boston Tours, 56 William St, Waltham, 899-1454.

Brush Hill Tours, Prudential Center, 236-2148.

Massachusetts Bay Lines, 60 Rowes Wharf, 542-8000.

Old Town Trolley Tours, 329 W 2nd St, 269-7010.

Annual Events

Chinese New Year. Feb.

St Patrick's Day and Evacuation Day. Mid-Mar.

Patriots Day. 3rd Mon Apr.

Boston Marathon. 3rd Mon Apr.

Bunker Hill Day. Mid-June.

Harborfest, Hatch Shell on the Esplanade. Early July.

Esplanade Concerts. Late June-early July.

Charles River Regatta. 3rd Sun Oct.

First Night Celebration. New Year's Eve.

City Neighborhoods

Many of the restaurants, unrated dining establishments and some lodgings listed under Boston include neighborhoods as well as exact street addresses. Geographic descriptions of these areas are given, followed by a table of restaurants arranged by neighborhood.

Back Bay: South of Memorial Dr along the Charles River Basin, west of Arlington St, north of Stuart St and Huntington Ave and east of Boston University campus and Brookline.

Beacon Hill: South of Cambridge St, west of Somerset St, north of Beacon St and east of St Charles St.

Copley Square: South of Boylston St, west of Trinity Cathedral (Trinity St), north of St James Ave and east of the Public Library (Dartmouth St).

Downtown Crossing: At intersection of Washington St and Winter and Summer Sts; area south of State St, north of Essex St, east of Tremont St and west of Congress St.

Faneuil Hall/Quincy Market Area: South and west of the John F. Fitzgerald Expy (I-93), north of State St and east of Congress St.

Financial District: South of State St, west and north of the John F. Fitzgerald Expy (I-93) and east of Congress St.

North End: Bounded by Boston Harbor and the John F. Fitzgerald Expy (I-93).

South End: South of I-90, west of John F. Fitzgerald Expy (I-93), north of Massachusetts Ave and east of Columbia Ave.

Theatre District: South of Boylston St, west of Tremont St, north of I-90 and east of Arlington St.

Lodgings and Food

BOSTON RESTAURANTS BY NEIGHBORHOOD AREAS

(For full description, see alphabetical listings under Restaurants)

BACK BAY
Biba. 272 Boylston St
Bristol Lounge (Four Seasons Hotel). 200 Boylston St
Cafe Louis. 234 Berkley St
Casa Romero. 30 Gloucester St
Charley's. 284 Newbury St
Ciao Bella. 240A Newbury St
Davio's. 269 Newbury St
The Dining Room (The Ritz-Carlton, Boston Hotel). 15 Arlington St
Dubarry Restaurant Francais. 159 Newbury St
Grill 23. 161 Berkeley St
Kashmir. 279 Newbury St
L'espalier. 30 Gloucester St
Mercury. 116 Boylston St
Morton's Of Chicago. One Exeter Plaza
Pignoli. 79 Park Plaza
Small Planet Bar & Grill. 565 Boylston St
Spasso. 160 Commonwealth Ave
Top Of The Hub. 800 Boylston St
Zinc. 35 Stanhope St

BEACON HILL
Cafe Marliave. 10 Bosworth St
Hungry I. 71½ Charles St
Lala Rokh. 97 Mt Vernon St
Library Grill At The Hampshire House. 84 Beacon St
Ristorante Toscano. 47 Charles St

COPLEY SQUARE
Ambrosia. 116 Huntington Ave
Cafe Budapest (Copley Square Hotel). 90 Exeter St
The Oak Room (Fairmont Copley Plaza Hotel). 138 St James Ave
Palm. 200 Dartmouth St
Turner Fisheries (The Westin Hotel, Copley Place). 10 Huntington Ave

DOWNTOWN CROSSING AREA
Aujourd'hui (Four Seasons Hotel). 200 Boylston St
Locke Ober. 3 Winter Place
Maison Robert. 45 School St

EAST OF DOWNTOWN CROSSING AREA
Anthony's Pier 4. 140 Northern Ave

SOUTH OF DOWNTOWN CROSSING AREA
Ginza. 16 Hudson St

FANEUIL HALL/QUINCY MARKET AREA
Bay Tower. 60 State St
Durgin Park. 30 N Market St
Plaza Iii. 101 S Faneuil Hall Marketplace
Seasons (The Regal Bostonian). Faneuil Hall Marketplace
Ye Olde Union Oyster House. 41 Union St
Zuma's Tex Mex Cafe. 7 N Market St

FINANCIAL DISTRICT
Jimmy's Harborside. 242 Northern Ave
Julien (Meridien Hotel). 250 Franklin St
Rowes Wharf (Boston Harbor Hotel). 70 Rowes Wharf

NORTH END
Davide. 326 Commercial St
Felicia's. 145A Richmond St
Filippo. 283 Causeway St
Mamma Maria. 3 North Square
Michael's Waterfront. 85 Atlantic Ave
Ristorante Lucia. 415 Hanover St

SOUTH END
Bob The Chef's. 604 Columbus Ave
Claremont Cafe. 535 Columbus Ave
Hamersley's Bistro. 553 Tremont St
Icarus. 3 Appleton St
Metropolis Cafe. 584 Tremont St

THEATRE DISTRICT
Kyoto. 201 Stuart St

Note: When a listing is located in a town that does not have its own city heading, it will appear under the city nearest to its location. In these cases, the address and town appear in parenthesis immediately following the name of the establishment.

Motel

✔★ ★ **SUSSE CHALET.** *800 Morrissey Blvd (02122), I-93 exit 12, 3 mi S of Downtown Crossing Area. 617/287-9100; FAX 617/265-9287.* 250 rms, 2-3 story. S $62.70-$69.70; D $76.70-$86.70; each addl $3-$7; under 18 free. Crib $3. TV; cable (premium). Pool; lifeguard. Restaurant adj 6:30 am-10:30 pm. Ck-out 11 am. Coin lndry. Meeting rms. Business servs avail. In-rm modem link. Gift shop. Health club privileges. Game rm. Refrigerators, microwaves avail. Cr cds: A, C, D, DS, MC, V.

D SC

Hotels

★ ★ **BEST WESTERN BOSTON-THE INN AT CHILDREN'S.** *342 Longwood Ave (02115), in Back Bay. 617/731-4700; FAX 617/731-6273.* 155 rms, 8 story. S $129-$250; D $139-$275; each addl $15; kits. $179; under 18 free. Crib free. Covered parking $14. TV; cable (premium). Restaurant 7 am-10 pm, dining rm 11:30 am-2:30 pm, 5-10 pm. Bar; entertainment. Ck-out noon. Meeting rms. In-rm modem link. Shopping arcade. Health club privileges. Cr cds: A, C, D, DS, ER, MC, V.

D SC

★ ★ ★ ★ **BOSTON HARBOR.** *70 Rowes Wharf (02110), on the waterfront, in Financial District. 617/439-7000; FAX 617/330-9450; res: 800/752-7077.* Located on Boston's waterfront within walking distance of major sights, this property has a copper-domed observatory with views of Boston. Numerous objets d'art embellish the public areas. 230 rms, 16 story, 26 suites. S $195-$450; D $225-$485; each addl $50; suites $435; under 18 free; wkend rates. Crib free. Pet accepted, some restrictions. Garage parking, valet $26; self-park. TV; cable (premium), VCR avail. Indoor pool; whirlpool, poolside serv. Restaurant 6 am-11 pm (also see ROWES WHARF). Rm serv 24 hrs. Bar 11:30-1 am; entertainment. Ck-out 1 pm. Meeting rms. Business center. In-rm modem link. Concierge. Airport transportation. Exercise rm; instructor, weight machines, bicycles, sauna, steam rm. Extensive spa. Bathrm phones, minibars; microwaves avail. Balconies. Cr cds: A, C, D, DS, JCB, MC, V.

D

★ ★ **BOSTON PARK PLAZA HOTEL & TOWERS.** *64 Arlington St (02116), in Back Bay, opp Boston Public Garden. 617/426-2000; FAX 617/426-5545; res: 800/225-2008.* Web www.bostonplaza.com. 960 rms, 15 story. S $225; D $245; each addl $20; suites $375-$1,500. Garage $20; valet. TV; cable (premium). Pool privileges. Restaurant 6:30 am-midnight. Rm serv. Bar 11-1:30 am. Ck-out noon. Convention facilities. Business center. In-rm modem link. Concierge. Shopping arcade. Barber, beauty shop. Exercise equipt; stair machine, bicycles. Health club privileges. Game rm. Refrigerators. Cr cds: A, C, D, DS, ER, JCB, MC, V.

D SC

★ ★ ★ **THE COLONNADE.** *120 Huntington Ave (02116), in Back Bay, opp Hynes Convention Ctr, adj to Copley Plaza Shopping Ctr.*

617/424-7000; FAX 617/424-1717; res: 800/962-3030. 288 rms, 11 story. Apr-June, Sept-Nov: S $205-$265; D $230-$290; suites $435-$1,400; under 12 free; wkly, wkend & hol rates; higher rates: marathon, graduation; lower rates rest of yr. Crib free. Pet accepted, some restrictions. Parking $20. TV; cable (premium), VCR avail. Pool (in season); poolside serv. Supervised child's activities (May-Sept); ages 8-13. Restaurant 7 am-11 pm. Rm serv 24 hrs. Bar; entertainment Fri, Sat. Ck-out noon. Meeting rms. Business center. In-rm modem link. Concierge. Exercise equipt; weights, bicycles. Minibars; refrigerators avail. Cr cds: A, C, D, DS, ER, JCB, MC, V.

D SC

★ ★ **COPLEY SQUARE HOTEL.** *47 Huntington Ave (02116), exit 22 off MA Turnpike, in Copley Square. 617/536-9000; FAX 617/267-3547; res: 800/225-7062.* Web www.copleysquarehotel.com. 143 rms, 7 story. S, D $165-$195; each addl $10; suites $299-$325; under 17 free. Crib free. Garage $18. TV; cable (premium). Complimentary coffee in rms. Restaurants 7 am-11 pm (also see CAFE BUDAPEST). Bar 11:30-2 am. Ck-out noon. Meeting rms. Business servs avail. In-rm modem link. Concierge. Health club privileges. Family-owned hotel; established 1891. Cr cds: A, C, D, DS, ER, JCB, MC, V.

D SC

★ ★ ★ **DOUBLETREE GUEST SUITES.** *400 Soldiers Field Rd (02134), west of Back Bay, north of Brookline, I-90 exit Storrow Dr. 617/783-0090; FAX 617/783-0897.* 310 suites, 16 story. S, D $159-$249; each addl $20; under 18 free; wkend packages. Crib free. TV; cable (premium). Indoor pool; whirlpool. Complimentary coffee in rms. Restaurant 6:30 am-10 pm. Bar 11:30-12:45 am; entertainment Wed-Sat. Ck-out noon. Coin Indry. Meeting rms. Business servs avail. In-rm modem link. Concierge. Downtown Boston, Cambridge transportation. Exercise equipt; bicycles, stair machine, whirlpool, sauna. Game rm. Bathrm phones, refrigerators, minibars; some microwaves. Some private patios, balconies. On river. Cr cds: A, C, D, DS, ER, JCB, MC, V.

D SC

★ ★ ★ ★ **THE ELIOT.** *370 Commonwealth Ave (02215), at Massachusetts Ave, in Back Bay. 617/267-1607; FAX 617/536-9114; res: 800/44-ELIOT.* E-mail bostbest@aol.com; web www.hoteleliot.com. The Eliot exudes the atmosphere of an elegant European hotel. Suites have marble baths and period furnishings. 95 kit. suites, 9 story. S $205-$245; D $245-$265. Crib free. Pet accepted, some restrictions. Valet parking $20. TV; cable (premium), VCR avail (movies). Restaurant 6:30-10:30 am, 5:30-10 pm; Sat, Sun 7-11 am, 5:30-10 pm. Ck-out noon. Meeting rms. Business center. In-rm modem link. Concierge. Health club privileges. Minibars; microwaves avail. Some balconies. Cr cds: A, D, MC, V.

D

★ ★ ★ **FAIRMONT COPLEY PLAZA.** *138 St James Ave (02116), in Copley Square. 617/267-5300; FAX 617/247-6681.* 373 rms, 7 story. S $159-$349; D $179-$379; each addl $30; suites $379-$1,500; under 17 free; special wkend rates. Crib free. Pet accepted, some restrictions. Valet parking $24. TV; cable (premium), VCR avail. Pool privileges. Restaurants (also see THE OAK ROOM). Rm serv 24 hrs. Bars 11:30-2 am; pianist. Ck-out 1 pm. Meeting rms. Business center. In-rm modem link. Concierge. Shopping arcade. Barber, beauty shop. Exercise equipt; bicycles, weights. Cr cds: A, C, D, DS, ER, JCB, MC, V.

D SC

★ ★ ★ ★ **FOUR SEASONS.** *200 Boylston St (02116), in Boston Common, in Downtown Crossing Area. 617/338-4400; FAX 617/423-0154.* Web www.fshr.com. The Four Seasons hotel is elegant, has a highly attentive staff and is eminently comfortable for leisure or work. Rooms are large and tastefully furnished, and most face the Boston Public Garden or an attactively landscaped business area behind it. 288 rms, 15 story. S $295-$455; D $350-$490; each addl $40; suites $455-$3,000; under 18 free; wkend rates. Crib free. Pet accepted, some restrictions. Valet, garage parking $28. TV; cable (premium), VCR avail (movies). Indoor pool; whirlpool, poolside serv. Complimentary continental bkfst. Restaurants 7-12:30 am (also see AUJOURD'HUI and BRISTOL LOUNGE). Rm serv 24 hrs. Bar 11-2 am; entertainment. Ck-out 1 pm. Convention facilities. Business center. In-rm modem link. Concierge. Gift shop. Exercise rm; instructor, weights, bicycles, sauna. Massage. Bathrm phones, refrigerators. Cr cds: A, C, D, ER, JCB, MC, V.

D

★ ★ ★ **HARBORSIDE HYATT CONFERENCE CENTER & HOTEL.** *101 Harborside Dr (02128), at Logan Intl Airport, on Boston Harbor. 617/568-1234; FAX 617/568-6080.* 270 rms, 14 story. S $200-$250; D $250-$270; suites $475. Crib free. TV; cable, VCR avail. Indoor pool; whirlpool. Coffee in rms. Restaurant 6 am-11 pm. Bar. Ck-out noon. Conference facilities. Business center. In-rm modem link. Free airport transportation. Exercise equipt; weights, bicycles, sauna. Refrigerator in suites. Adj to water shuttle. Cr cds: A, C, D, DS, ER, JCB, MC, V.

D SC

★ ★ **HILTON-BACK BAY.** *40 Dalton St (02115), in Back Bay adj to Hynes Convention Ctr. 617/236-1100; FAX 617/267-8893.* 335 rms, 26 story. S $170-$250; D $190-$270; each addl $20; suites $400-$900; family, wkend rates. Pet accepted, some restrictions. Garage $15. TV; cable (premium), VCR avail (movies). Indoor pool. Restaurant 7 am-midnight. Bar 5:30 pm-12:30 am. Ck-out noon. Convention facilities. Business center. In-rm modem link. Concierge. Gift shop. Exercise equipt; weight machine, bicycles. Some balconies, sundeck. Cr cds: A, C, D, DS, ER, JCB, MC, V.

D SC

✓★ ★ **HOLIDAY INN AIRPORT.** *225 McClellan Hwy (02128), 1 mi N of Logan Intl Airport on Rte 1A. 617/569-5250; FAX 617/569-5159.* 350 rms, 12 story. S $99-$179; D $109-$189; each addl $10; under 18 free; higher rates fall season. Crib free. TV; cable (premium). Pool. Coffee in rms. Restaurant 6 am-10 pm. Bar 11-2 am. Ck-out noon. Meeting rms. Business servs avail. In-rm modem link. Gift shop. Free airport transportation. Exercise equipt; weight machine, bicycle. Microwaves avail. Cr cds: A, C, D, DS, JCB, MC, V.

D SC

★ ★ ★ **HOLIDAY INN-SELECT.** *5 Blossom St (02114), at Cambridge St at Govt Ctr. 617/742-7630; FAX 617/742-4192.* 303 rms, 15 story. Apr-Nov: S, D $199-$259; each addl $20; under 18 free; wkend rates; higher rates graduation wkends; lower rates rest of yr. Crib free. Garage $20. TV; cable (premium). Pool. Restaurant 6 am-11 pm. Bar. Ck-out noon. Coin Indry. Business servs avail. In-rm modem link. Exercise equipt; weights, bicycles. Overlooks Charles River. Luxury level. Cr cds: A, C, D, DS, JCB, MC, V.

D SC

★ ★ ★ **LE MERIDIEN.** *250 Franklin St (02110), in Financial District. 617/451-1900; FAX 617/423-2844.* Web www.lemeridien.com. 326 rms, 9 story. S, D $275-$295; each addl $25; suites $400-$790; under 12 free; wkend rates. Crib free. Pet accepted, some restrictions. Valet parking $29. TV; cable (premium), VCR avail. Pool. Restaurants 7 am-10 pm (also see JULIEN). Rm serv 24 hrs. Bar 5 pm-1 am; pianist. Ck-out 1 pm. Meeting rms. Business center. In-rm modem link. Concierge. Exercise rm; instructor, weights, treadmill, sauna. Massage. Bathrm phones, minibars, refrigerators; microwaves avail. Renaissance Revival bldg. Cr cds: A, C, D, DS, ER, JCB, MC, V.

D

★ ★ ★ **THE LENOX HOTEL.** *710 Boylston St (02116), at Exeter St; Prudential Center, in Back Bay. 617/536-5300; FAX 617/267-1237; res: 800/225-7676.* Web www.lenoxhotel.com. 212 rms, 11 story. S, D $200-$295; each addl $20; suites $450; under 18 free. TV; cable, VCR avail. Restaurants 6:30-1 am. Bars 11:30-1:30 am. Ck-out noon. Meeting rms. Business servs avail. In-rm modem link. Barber. Airport transportation avail. Exercise equipt; rower, treadmill. Microwaves avail. Many decorative and wood-burning fireplaces. Cr cds: A, C, D, DS, ER, JCB, MC, V.

D SC

★ ★ ★ **MARRIOTT-COPLEY PLACE.** *110 Huntington Ave (02116), in Copley Square. 617/236-5800; FAX 617/236-5885.* 1,147 rms, 38 story. S, D $245; suites $400-$1,200; under 18 free; wkend rates. Crib free. Valet parking $24. TV; cable (premium), VCR avail (movies). Pool;

whirlpool. Restaurant 6:30-1 am. Rm serv 24 hrs. Bar 11-2 am; entertainment. Ck-out noon. Convention facilities. Business center. In-rm modem link. Concierge. Shopping arcade. Exercise rm; instructor, weights, bicycles, sauna. Massage therapy. Game rm. Luxury level. Cr cds: A, C, D, DS, ER, JCB, MC, V.

D SC

★★ **MARRIOTT-LONG WHARF.** *296 State St (02109), on waterfront, in Faneuil Hall/Quincy Market Area. 617/227-0800; FAX 617/227-2867.* 400 rms, 7 story. S, D $189-$309; suites $300-$1,200; under 18 free; wkend rates. Crib free. Valet parking $25. TV; cable (premium), VCR avail (movies). Indoor pool; whirlpool; poolside serv. Restaurant 6:30-2 am. Bar. Ck-out noon. Coin Indry. Convention facilities. Business center. In-rm modem link. Gift shop. Exercise equipt; weights, bicycles; sauna. Luxury level. Cr cds: A, C, D, DS, ER, JCB, MC, V.

D SC

★★ **OMNI PARKER HOUSE.** *60 School St (02108), 1 blk N of Boston Common, Downtown Crossing Area. 617/227-8600; FAX 617/742-5729.* 535 rms, 14 story. June, early Sept-mid-Nov: S, D $109-$205; suites $199-$225; under 17 free; wkend rates; lower rates rest of yr. Crib free. Garage $24. TV; cable (premium), VCR avail. Restaurant (see PARKER'S). Bar 6:30 am-midnight; entertainment exc Sun. Ck-out noon. Convention facilities. Business servs avail. In-rm modem link. Concierge. Gift shop. Health club privileges. Oldest continuously operating hotel in the US. Cr cds: A, C, D, DS, JCB, MC, V.

D SC

✓★★ **RADISSON.** *200 Stuart St (02116), in Theatre District. 617/482-1800; FAX 617/451-2750.* 356 rms, 24 story. S, D $115-$269; each addl $20; suites $230-$350; under 18 free. Crib free. Valet parking $12. TV; cable (premium). Indoor pool. Restaurant 6:30 am-10 pm; dining rm 11:30 am-11 pm, Sun noon-10 pm. Bar. Ck-out noon. Business servs avail. In-rm modem link. Gift shop. Exercise equipt; weight machine, treadmills. Cr cds: A, C, D, DS, ER, JCB, MC, V.

D SC

★★ **RAMADA-LOGAN AIRPORT.** *Logan Intl Airport (02128), on grounds of Logan Intl Airport. 617/569-9300; FAX 617/569-3981.* 516 rms, 14 story. S $129-$195; D $149-$245; each addl $20; suites $400; family, wkend rates. Crib free. Pet accepted, some restrictions. TV; cable (premium). Pool; poolside serv, lifeguard. Restaurant 5:30 am-10:30 pm. Bar 11-2 am. Ck-out 11 am. Convention facilities. Business center. In-rm modem link. Concierge. Free airport transportation. Exercise equipt; treadmill, stair machine. Many minibars. Cr cds: A, C, D, DS, ER, JCB, MC, V.

D SC

★★★ **REGAL BOSTONIAN.** *9 Blackstone St N (02109), near Logan Intl Airport, in Faneuil Hall/Quincy Market Area. 617/523-3600; FAX 617/523-2454.* Web www.regal-hotels.com/boston. 152 rms, 7 story. S, D $245-$345; each addl $20; suites $450-$625; under 18 free; wkend rates. Valet parking $24. TV; cable (premium), VCR (movies). Complimentary coffee in lobby. Restaurant (see SEASONS). Rm serv 24 hrs. Bar 2 pm-1 am; entertainment Tues-Sat. Ck-out 3 pm. Meeting rms. Business servs avail. In-rm modem link. Concierge. Tennis privileges. Exercise equipt delivered to rm. Bathrm phones, minibars; some in-rm whirlpools, fireplaces. Many balconies. 1 blk to harbor. Cr cds: A, C, D, DS, JCB, MC, V.

D SC

★★★ **THE RITZ-CARLTON, BOSTON.** *15 Arlington St (02117), at Newbury St, in Back Bay. 617/536-5700; FAX 617/536-1335.* 278 rms, 17 story. S $260-$375; D $300-$415; each addl $20; 1-2 bedrm suites $345-$1,495; under 12 free; wkend rates. Crib free. Pet accepted, some restrictions. Garage $22. TV; cable (premium), VCR avail (movies). Restaurants 6:30 am-midnight (also see THE DINING ROOM). Rm serv 24 hrs. Bar 11:30-1 am. Ck-out noon. Convention facilities. Business servs avail. In-rm modem link. Concierge. Barber. Airport transportation. Exercise equipt; weights, bicycles, sauna. Massage. Health club privileges. Bathrm phones, refrigerators. Fireplace in suites. Overlooks Public Garden. Luxury level. Cr cds: A, C, D, DS, ER, JCB, MC, V.

D

★★★ **SHERATON BOSTON HOTEL & TOWERS.** *39 Dalton St (02199), at Prudential Ctr, in Back Bay. 617/236-2000; FAX 617/236-6061.* 1,181 rms, 29 story. S $189-$240; D $209-$260; each addl $20; suites from $260; under 18 free; wkend rates. Crib free. Pet accepted. Garage $23. TV; cable (premium). Indoor/outdoor pool; whirlpool; poolside serv. Coffee in rms. Restaurant 6:30-1:30 am. Bars 11:30-2 am; entertainment. Ck-out noon. Convention facilities. Business center. In-rm modem link. Gift shop. Exercise equipt; weights, bicycles. Luxury level. Cr cds: A, C, D, DS, ER, JCB, MC, V.

D SC

★★★ **SWISSÔTEL.** *1 Avenue de Lafayette (02111), in Financial District. 617/451-2600; FAX 617/451-2198; res: 800/621-9200.* 500 rms, 22 story. S, D $235-$260; each addl $25; under 16 free; wkend rates. Crib free. Pet accepted, some restrictions. Garage $22, valet parking $26. TV; cable (premium), VCR avail (movies). Indoor pool. Restaurant 7 am-11 pm. Rm serv 24 hrs. Bar 4 pm-1 am; entertainment. Ck-out noon. Convention facilities. Business center. In-rm modem link. Concierge. Gift shop. Exercise equipt; bicycles, rowers, sauna. Luxury level. Cr cds: A, C, D, DS, ER, JCB, MC, V.

D SC

★★ **TREMONT HOUSE.** *275 Tremont St (02116), in Theatre District, 2 blks from Boston Common. 617/426-1400; FAX 617/482-6730; res: 800/331-9998.* 322 rms, 15 story. S, D $144-$250; each addl $10; under 17 free. Crib free. Valet parking $20. TV; cable (premium), VCR avail (movies). Restaurant 6:30 am-11:30 pm. Bar 4-11 pm; entertainment Thurs-Sat. Ck-out noon. Meeting rms. Business center. In-rm modem link. Gift shop. Cr cds: A, C, D, DS, ER, JCB, MC, V.

D SC

★★★ **THE WESTIN HOTEL, COPLEY PLACE.** *10 Huntington Ave (02116), in Copley Square, I-90 Copley Sq exit. 617/262-9600; FAX 617/424-7483.* Web www.westin.com. 800 rms, 36 story. S $189-$280; D $219-$310; each addl $25; suites $400-$1,500; under 18 free. Crib free. TV; cable (premium). Indoor pool; whirlpool. Coffee in rm. Restaurants (also see TURNER FISHERIES). Rm serv 24 hrs. Entertainment. Ck-out noon. Business center. In-rm modem link. Concierge. Exercise equipt; weights, bicycles, sauna. Massage. Minibars. Copley Place shopping gallery across skybridge. Luxury level. Cr cds: A, C, D, DS, ER, JCB, MC, V.

D SC

Inns

★★ **COPLEY INN.** *19 Garrison St (02116), in Back Bay. 617/236-0300; FAX 617/536-0816; res: 800/232-0306.* 21 kit. units, 6 with shower only, 4 story. May-Dec: S, D $95-$115; wkly rates; lower rates rest of yr. Crib free. TV; cable. Restaurant nearby. Ck-out 11 am, ck-in 9 am-5 pm. Brownstone built in 1880s. Cr cds: A, MC, V.

★★ **NEWBURY GUEST HOUSE.** *261 Newbury St (02116), in Back Bay, between Gloucester & Fairfield. 617/437-7666; FAX 617/262-4243; res: 800/437-7668.* 32 rms, 4 story. Mar-Dec: S $85-$130; D $95-$140; each addl $10; under 3 free; higher rates: marathon, graduations. Parking $10. TV; cable. Complimentary continental bkfst. Ck-out noon, ck-in 3 pm. In-rm modem link. Sitting rm. Built 1882. Cr cds: A, C, D, DS, MC, V.

D

Restaurants

★★★ **AMBROSIA.** *116 Huntington Ave (02116), in Copley Square. 617/247-2400.* Specialty: St Pierre fish imported from France. Hrs: 11:30 am-2 pm, 5:30-10 pm; Fri to 11 pm; Sat 5-11 pm; Sun 5-9 pm.

Closed some major hols. Semi-a la carte: lunch $5-$12, dinner $16-$29. Valet parking (dinner). Spacious and elegant atmosphere. Cr cds: A, D, MC, V.

D

★ ★ ★ **ANTHONY'S PIER 4.** *140 Northern Ave (02210), adj to World Trade Center, east of Downtown Crossing Area. 617/482-6262.* Specializes in smoked salmon, lobster, bouillabaisse. Hrs: 11:30 am-11 pm; Sat from noon; Sun noon-10 pm. Closed Dec 25. Res accepted. Bar. Semi-a la carte: lunch $9.95-$26.95, dinner $13.95-$26.95. Parking. Outdoor dining. Nautical decor; view of city and Boston Harbor. Jacket in main dining rm. Family-owned. Cr cds: A, C, D, DS, ER, JCB, MC, V.

D

★ ★ ★ ★ **AUJOURD'HUI.** *(See Four Seasons Hotel) 617/338-4400.* If you're lucky enough to get a table near the broad windows, you can dine on regional specialties while gazing out on the Boston Public Garden. Menu changes seasonally. Own baking. Hrs: 6:30 am-2:30 pm, 5:30-10:30 pm; Sat 7 am-noon, 5:30-10:30 pm; Sun 7-11 am, 6-10:30 pm; Sun brunch 11:30 am-2:30 pm. Res accepted. Bar. Wine cellar. A la carte entrees: bkfst $15-$18.50, lunch $18-$22.50, dinner $34-$42. Degustation menu: dinner $78. Sun brunch $44. Child's meals. Valet parking. Jacket (dinner). Cr cds: A, C, D, ER, JCB, MC, V.

D

★ ★ **BAY TOWER.** *60 State St (02109), 33rd floor, in Faneuil Hall/Quincy Market Area. 617/723-1666; FAX 617/723-7887.* Hrs: 5:30-10 pm; Fri, Sat to 11 pm. Closed Sun; Dec 25. Res accepted. Bar 4:30 pm-1 am; Fri, Sat to 2 am. Semi-a la carte: dinner $18-$36. Pianist Mon-Thurs 6-11 pm; wkends to 9 pm; band wkends from 9 pm. Valet parking Fri, Sat. Harbor view. Parking. Jacket. Cr cds: A, C, D, DS, MC, V.

D

★ ★ ★ ★ **BIBA.** *272 Boylston St (02116), in Back Bay. 617/426-7878.* This is a popular people-watching spot—both inside and out—from the huge windows in the downstairs bar. Striking art and vivid murals deck the dining room. The seasonal menu showcases fresh and innovative meals for affordable prices. Hrs: 11:30 am-2:30 pm, 5:30-10 pm; Fri to 11 pm; Sat 5:30-11 pm; Sun 11:30 am-3 pm, 5:30-10 pm. Closed some major hols. Res accepted. Bar. A la carte entrees: lunch $8-$16, dinner $16-$36. Valet parking. Cr cds: A, C, D, DS, MC, V.

D

✔★ ★ **BOB THE CHEF'S.** *604 Columbus Ave (02118), in the South End. 617/536-6204.* Creole/Cajun menu. Specialties: chicken & ribs combo, Creole jambalaya, mustard-fried catfish. Hrs: 11:30 am-2:30 pm, 5-10 pm; Thurs, Fri to midnight; Sat 11 am-midnight; Sun 11 am-10 pm; Sun brunch to 3:30 pm. Closed Mon; some major hols. Bar. Semi-a la carte: lunch $6-$10, dinner $8.95-$13.95. Sun brunch $15.95. Jazz Thurs, Fri evening, Sun brunch. Bistro decor; intimate dining. Totally nonsmoking. Cr cds: A, MC, V.

★ ★ **BRISTOL LOUNGE.** *(See Four Seasons Hotel) 617/338-4400.* Contemporary Amer menu. Specializes in tapas, seasonal dishes. Own baking. Hrs: 11 am-11:30 pm; Fri, Sat to 12:30 am; Sun 10 am-11 pm; Sun brunch to 2 pm. Res accepted. Bar. Semi-a la carte: lunch, dinner $14-$26. Sun brunch $32. Pianist, jazz duo. Valet parking. Art-deco decor with large windows overlooking Boston Gardens and flowered terrace. Cr cds: A, C, D, DS, ER, JCB, MC, V.

D

★ ★ **CAFE BUDAPEST.** *(See Copley Square Hotel) 617/266-1979.* Hungarian, continental menu. Specialties: veal goulash, cherry soup, chicken paprikash. Own baking. Hrs: noon-3 pm, 5-10:30 pm; Fri, Sat to midnight; Sun 1-10:30 pm. Closed Jan 1, Dec 25; also wk of July 4. Res accepted. Bar. Semi-a la carte: lunch $14.50-$16.50, dinner $20-$33. Violin & piano Tues-Sat nights. Original paintings. Old World atmosphere. Family-owned. Jacket. Cr cds: A, C, D, DS, MC, V.

D

★ ★ ★ **CAFE LOUIS.** *234 Berkley St (02116), in Back Bay. 617/266-4680.* Contemporary French menu. Specializes in game, local seafood. Hrs: 11:30 am-3 pm, 5:30-10 pm; Fri, Sat to 11 pm. Closed Sun; most major hols. Res accepted. Beer. Wine cellar. A la carte entrees: lunch $9-$17, dinner $16-$32. Complete meal: dinner $59. Jazz in summer. Free valet parking. Outdoor dining. Contemporary, intimate cafe. Totally nonsmoking. Cr cds: A, MC, V.

D

✔★ **CAFE MARLIAVE.** *10 Bosworth St (02108), in Beacon Hill. 617/542-1133.* Italian menu. Specializes in fresh seafood, beef. Hrs: 11 am-10 pm. Closed some major hols. Res accepted. Bar. Semi-a la carte: lunch $5-$10.50, dinner $9-$22. Parking. Original artwork. Cr cds: A, D, MC, V.

✔★ ★ **CASA ROMERO.** *30 Gloucester St (02115), in Back Bay, enter on alley off Glouchester St. 617/536-4341.* Mexican menu. Specialties: marinated tenderloin of pork, giant shrimp in cilantro and tomatillos. Hrs: 6-10 pm; Fri, Sat to 11 pm. Closed Jan 1, July 4, Dec 25. Res accepted. Serv bar. Semi-a la carte: dinner $12-$17.50. Outdoor dining. Authentic Mexican decor. Family-owned. Totally nonsmoking. Cr cds: C, D, DS, MC, V.

★ ★ **CHARLEY'S.** *284 Newbury St (02115), at Gloucester & Newbury, in Back Bay. 617/266-3000.* Specializes in fresh seafood, baby-back ribs, steaks. Hrs: 11:30 am-midnight; Sat, Sun from 11 am. Res accepted. Bar 11:30-2 am. Semi-a la carte: lunch $5.99-$10.99, dinner $8.99-$22.95. Child's meals. Outdoor dining. Renovated Victorian school. Cr cds: A, D, DS, MC, V.

D

★ ★ **CIAO BELLA.** *240A Newbury St (02116), at Newbury & Fairfield, in Back Bay. 617/536-2626.* E-mail ciaobella@concierge.org; web www.concierge.org/ciaobella. Italian menu. Specializes in veal chops, swordfish chops, seafood. Hrs: 11:30 am-11 pm; Thurs-Sat to 11:45 pm; Sun brunch to 3:30 pm. Closed Thanksgiving, Dec 25. Res accepted. Bar. A la carte entrees: lunch $6.50-$14.95, dinner $8.95-$30. Sun brunch $4.95-$11.50. Valet parking (Tues-Sat evening). Outdoor dining. European decor. Cr cds: A, C, D, DS, MC, V.

★ **CLAREMONT CAFE.** *535 Columbus Ave (02118), in the South End. 617/247-9001.* Continental menu. Specializes in herb-roasted chicken, seafood, tapas. Hrs: 7:30 am-3 pm, 5:30-10 pm; Fri to 10:30 pm; Sat 8 am-10:30 pm; Sun 9 am-3 pm (brunch). Closed Mon; major hols. Bar. Semi-a la carte: bkfst $3.50-$9.95, lunch $4.95-$9.95, dinner $12.95-$21.95. Sun brunch $6.50-$10.95. Valet parking. Outdoor dining. Corner cafe with artwork by local artists. Totally nonsmoking. Cr cds: MC, V.

★ ★ ★ **DAVIDE.** *326 Commercial St (02109), in the North End. 617/227-5745.* Northern Italian menu. Specializes in potato gnocchi, veal chop with fontina and prosciutto. Own pasta, ice cream. Hrs: 5-10 pm; Fri, Sat to 11 pm. Closed Sun. Bar. A la carte entrees: dinner $12-$22. Valet parking. Cr cds: A, C, D, DS, MC, V.

★ ★ **DAVIO'S.** *269 Newbury St (02116), in Back Bay. 617/262-4810.* Northern Italian menu. Specializes in veal chops, homemade sausage, pizza. Hrs: 11:30 am-10:30 pm; Fri, Sat to 11 pm; Sun to 10 pm. Closed Thanksgiving, Dec 25. Res accepted. Bar. Semi-a la carte: lunch $3.95-$12.95, dinner $3.95-$26.95. Child's meals. Valet parking dinner. Outdoor dining. Cr cds: A, C, D, DS, MC, V.

★ ★ ★ **THE DINING ROOM.** *(See The Ritz-Carlton, Boston Hotel) 617/536-5700.* Continental, regional menu. Hrs: 5:30-10 pm; Fri, Sat to 11 pm; Sat hrs vary in fall & winter; Sun brunch 10:45 am-2:30 pm. Closed Mon. Res accepted; required wkends. Bar. Wine cellar. A la carte entrees: dinner $29-$43. Complete meals: lunch $29-$38, dinner $42-$55. Sun brunch $47. Child's meals. Pianist. Valet parking. Jacket. Cr cds: A, C, D, DS, ER, JCB, MC, V.

D

★ ★ **DUBARRY RESTAURANT FRANCAIS.** *159 Newbury St (02116), in Back Bay. 617/262-2445.* French menu. Specialties: canard à l'orange, lapin dijonaise. Hrs: noon-2:30 pm, 5:30-10 pm; Sat 12:30-3 pm, 5:30-10 pm; Sun 5:30-9:30 pm. Closed Sun (summer); major hols. Res accepted. Wine. A la carte entrees: lunch $3.75-$17, dinner $12-$22. Child's meals. Outdoor dining. Casual dining. Original art. Family-owned. Cr cds: A, C, D, DS, MC, V.

D

✔★ ★ **DURGIN PARK.** *30 N Market St (02109), in Faneuil Hall/Quincy Market Place. 617/227-2038.* Specializes in prime rib, Indian pudding, strawberry shortcake. Hrs: 11:30 am-10 pm; Sun 11:30 am-9 pm. Closed Dec 25. Some A/C. Bar to 2 am; entertainment. A la carte entrees: lunch $4.95-$16.95, dinner $5.95-$16.95. Own soups. Near Faneuil Hall. Established 1826. Cr cds: A, D, DS, MC, V.

D

✔★ ★ **FELICIA'S.** *145A Richmond St (02109), on 2nd floor, in the North End. 617/523-9885.* Italian menu. Specializes in shrimp scampi, chicken verdicchio. Own pasta. Hrs: 4-9:30 pm; Fri, Sat to 10:30 pm; Sun 2-9:30 pm. Closed Easter, Thanksgiving, Dec 24, 25. Wine, beer. Semi-a la carte: dinner $7.95-$14.95. Italian antique furnishings; paintings. Cr cds: A, C, D, DS, MC, V.

D

★ ★ ★ **FILIPPO.** *283 Causeway St (02109), in North End. 617/742-4143.* Italian menu. Specialty: cappello del Contadino. Hrs: 11:30 am-10:30 pm; Sun from noon. Closed Thanksgiving, Dec 25. Res accepted. Bar. Wine list. Semi-a la carte: lunch $5.50-$8.50, dinner $11.95-$18.50. Valet parking (dinner). Italian decor with large murals. Cr cds: A, MC, V.

D

★ ★ ★ **GINZA.** *16 Hudson St (02111), South of Downtown Crossing Area. 617/338-2261.* Japanese menu. Specializes in maki special, sushi. Hrs: 11:30 am-2:30 pm; 5 pm-4 am; Sat 11:30 am-4 pm, 5 pm-4 am; Mon, Sun 11:30 am-4 pm, 5 pm-2 am. Res accepted. Wine, beer. Semi-a la carte: lunch $7.50-$11.75, dinner $12.50-$38.50. Upscale Japanese dining with sushi bar. Cr cds: A, MC, V.

D

★ ★ ★ **GRILL 23.** *161 Berkeley St (02116), in Back Bay at Stuart. 617/542-2255.* Web www.grill23.com. Specializes in aged beef, New England seafood. Open kitchen; menu changes wkly. Hrs: 5:30-10:30 pm; Fri, Sat to 11 pm. Closed major hols. Res accepted. Bar from 4:30 pm. A la carte entrees: $18.75-$26.75. Valet parking. 1920s decor. Former Salada Tea Bldg. Cr cds: A, C, D, DS, MC, V.

D

★ ★ ★ ★ **HAMERSLEY'S BISTRO.** *553 Tremont St (02116), in South End. 617/423-2700.* Hamersley's includes a full bar and cafe area as well as a large dining room that's a bit more formal. The menu changes daily; the wine list is replete with offerings from France, Spain, Italy and California. French, Amer menu. Specialties: mushroom sandwich, roast chicken, lemon custard. Hrs: 6-10 pm; Sat, Sun from 5:30 pm. Closed major hols. Bar. A la carte entrees: dinner $21-$30. Valet parking. Outdoor dining. Totally nonsmoking. Cr cds: A, D, DS, MC, V.

D

★ ★ ★ **HUNGRY I.** *71 1/2 Charles St (02114), on Beacon Hill. 617/227-3524.* French country menu. Specialties: maison paté, venison au poivre. Hrs: 6-9:30 pm; Fri, Sat to 10 pm; Sat, Sun brunch 11 am-2 pm. Closed July 4, Thanksgiving, Dec 25. Res accepted. Wine, beer. A la carte entrees: dinner $20-$30. Sun brunch $9-$15. Patio dining Sun brunch only. 1840s house in historic district. Fireplace. Cr cds: A, C, D, MC, V.

★ ★ ★ **ICARUS.** *3 Appleton St (02116), in the South End. 617/426-1790.* Specialties: grilled shrimp with mango and jalepeno sorbet, seared duck breast, game. Hrs: 6-10 pm; Fri, Sat to 11 pm; Sun brunch 11 am-3 pm (exc June-Aug). Closed most major hols. Res accepted; required wkends. Bar from 5:30 pm. Semi-a la carte: dinner $19-$29. Sun brunch $7-$12. Valet parking. Jazz Fri evening. Converted 1860s building. Cr cds: A, C, D, DS, MC, V.

★ ★ **JIMMY'S HARBORSIDE.** *242 Northern Ave (02210), adj to Financial District, E of World Trade Center. 617/423-1000.* Specializes in shrimp, lobster, broiled fish. Hrs: noon-9:30 pm; Sun 4-9 pm. Closed Dec 25. Res accepted. Bar. A la carte entrees: lunch $9-$22, dinner $10-$32. Child's meals. Valet parking. Nautical decor. Family-owned. Cr cds: A, C, D, MC, V.

D

★ ★ ★ **JULIEN.** *(See Meridien Hotel) 617/451-1900.* French, English menu. Specializes in seafood, lamb, breast of duck. Own baking. Hrs: noon-2 pm, 6-10 pm; Sat 6-10:30 pm; hrs vary July-Aug. Closed Sun; wk of July 4. Res accepted. Bar 5 pm-midnight, closed Sun. Wine list. A la carte entrees: lunch $14.50-$18.50, dinner $27-$34. Complete meals: lunch $25, 5-course dinner $65. Pianist. Valet parking. Elegant surroundings; high carved-wood ceilings, crystal chandeliers. Former Federal Reserve Bank Bldg. Jacket. Cr cds: A, C, D, DS, JCB, MC, V.

D

★ ★ **KASHMIR.** *279 Newbury St (02116), in Back Bay. 617/536-1695.* Indian menu. Specialties: tandoori tikki dal, tandoori duck kadahi, tandoori seafood masala. Hrs: 11 am-11 pm; Sun to 3 pm. Res accepted. Beer, wine. Buffet: lunch $7.95. A la carte entrees: dinner $8.95-$19.95. Complete meals: dinner $14.95-$39.95. Child's meals. Valet parking. Outdoor dining. Indian artifacts and decor. Jacket evenings. Cr cds: A, D, JCB, MC, V.

★ ★ **KYOTO.** *201 Stuart St (02116), in Theatre District. 617/542-1166.* Japanese menu. Specializes in hibachi swordfish. Hrs: 11:30 am-2 pm, 5-10 pm; Fri to 11 pm; Sat 4-11 pm; Sun 4-9 pm. Closed some major hols. Res accepted. Bar. Complete meals: lunch $5.75-$10, dinner $12.50-$21.95. Child's meals. Parking. Japanese decor. Teppanyaki grill. Cr cds: A, C, D, DS, JCB, MC, V.

D

★ ★ ★ ★ **L'ESPALIER.** *30 Gloucester St (02115), in Back Bay. 617/262-3023.* Elegance prevails in the three small dining rooms of this 19th-century Back Bay townhouse. Contemporary French menu. Specialties: grilled beef short ribs with black bean mango salsa, ragout of dayboat wolffish, pan-roasted free-range chicken in tamarind orange glaze with radishes. Own baking. Hrs: 6-10 pm. Closed Sun; most major hols. Res accepted. Bar. Wine cellar. Prix fixe: dinner $62. Menu dégustation (Mon-Fri): dinner $78/person. Valet parking. Daily menu. Totally nonsmoking. Cr cds: A, C, D, DS, MC, V.

★ ★ **LALA ROKH.** *97 Mt Vernon St (02114), on Beacon Hill. 617/720-5511.* Persian menu. Specializes in authentic Persian dishes. Own baking. Hrs: 5:30-10 pm. Closed some major hols. Res accepted. Wine. Semi-a la carte: dinner $14-$17. Several dining areas with authentic decor; Iranian art. Cr cds: A, D, MC, V.

D

★ ★ ★ **LIBRARY GRILL AT THE HAMPSHIRE HOUSE.** *84 Beacon St (02108), on Beacon Hill. 617/227-9600.* Continental menu. Hrs: 5-10:30 pm; July-Aug from 6 pm; Sun brunch 10:30 am-2:30 pm. Res accepted. Bar. A la carte entrees: dinner $19-$28. Sun brunch $8-$16. Pianist Thurs-Sat evenings; jazz Fri, Sat evenings, Sun brunch. Valet parking. In 1910 townhouse. Cr cds: A, C, D, MC, V.

D ♥

★ ★ **LOCKE OBER.** *3 Winter Place (02108), Downtown Crossing Area. 617/542-1340.* Continental menu. Specializes in wienerschnitzel, baked lobster Savannah. Hrs: 11:30 am-10 pm; Sat from 5:30 pm. Closed Sun; major hols. Bar. Semi-a la carte: lunch $11.50-$20, dinner $18.75-$29.50. Built in 1875. Old World atmosphere. Jacket. Cr cds: A, C, D, DS, MC, V.

D

★ ★ ★ **MAISON ROBERT.** *45 School St (02108), Downtown Crossing Area. 617/227-3370.* French menu. Specializes in rack of lamb, fresh seafood. Hrs: 11:30 am-2:30 pm, 5:30-10 pm; wkend hrs vary.

Closed some major hols. Res accepted. Bar. Semi-a la carte: lunch $9-$22, dinner $17-$32. Valet parking. Outdoor dining in courtyard of former city hall. Jacket. Cr cds: A, C, D, MC, V.

D ⊐ ♥

★ ★ ★ **MAMMA MARIA.** *3 North Square (02113), in the North End. 617/523-0077.* Italian menu. Menu changes seasonally. Hrs: 5-10 pm; Fri, Sat to 11 pm. Closed most major hols. Res accepted. Bar. A la carte entrees: dinner $18-$24. Valet parking. Private dining rms. Overlooks historic area; Paul Revere house across square. Cr cds: A, C, D, DS, MC, V.

D

★ ★ **MERCURY.** *116 Boylston St (02116), in Back Bay. 617/482-7799.* Mediterranean menu. Specializes in seasonal Mediterranean dishes. Own baking. Hrs: 5:30-10 pm; Thurs-Sat to 11 pm. Closed Sun, Mon; some major hols. Res accepted. Bar 5 pm-2 am. Semi-a la carte: dinner $15-$19. Entertainment Wed-Sat. Valet parking. Chic bar atmosphere with ornate wood paneling, open kitchen. Cr cds: A, D, DS, MC, V.

D ⊐

★ ★ ★ **METROPOLIS CAFE.** *584 Tremont St (02118), in the South End. 617/247-2931.* Contemporary Amer menu. Specialties: garlic-roasted chicken with grilled ramps, skillet-roasted Maine salmon, warm chocolate pudding cake with vanilla ice cream. Own pasta. Hrs: 5:30-10 pm; Thurs-Sat to 11 pm; Sat, Sun brunch 9 am-3 pm. Closed Jan 1, Thanksgiving, Dec 25. Res accepted. Bar. Wine list. Semi-a la carte: dinner $12.95-$18.95. Sat, Sun brunch $3.95-$6.95. Valet parking. Bistro decor with high ceilings, brass tables. Totally nonsmoking. Cr cds: A, D, MC, V.

★ ★ **MICHAEL'S WATERFRONT.** *85 Atlantic Ave (02110), on Commercial Wharf, in the North End. 617/367-6425.* Specializes in rack of lamb, swordfish, lobster. Hrs: noon-4 pm; 5:30-10 pm; Mon from 5:30 pm; Fri, Sat to 10:30 pm. Closed July 4. Res accepted. Bar from 4 pm. A la carte entrees: lunch $2-$13, dinner $12.95-$25.95. Valet parking. Outdoor dining. Several dining areas on 2 floors of historic Commercial Wharf. Cr cds: A, C, D, MC, V.

⊐

★ ★ **MORTON'S OF CHICAGO.** *One Exeter Plaza (02116), at Boylston & Exeter, in Back Bay. 617/266-5858; FAX 617/266-9521.* Specializes in prime dry-aged beef, fresh seafood. Hrs: 5:30-11 pm; Sun 5-10 pm. Closed major hols. Res accepted. Bar. A la carte entrees: dinner $16.95-$29.95. Valet parking. Menu recited. Cr cds: A, C, D, JCB, MC, V.

D ⊐

★ ★ ★ **THE OAK ROOM.** *(See Fairmont Copley Plaza Hotel) 617/267-5300.* Specializes in steak, seafood. Own baking, pasta. Hrs: 5:30-10 pm; Fri, Sat to 11 pm. Res accepted. Bar. A la carte entrees: dinner $18.95-$39.95. Complete meal: dinner $38 or $68. Valet parking. Turn-of-the-century decor with carved moldings, crystal chandeliers. Cr cds: A, C, D, DS, ER, JCB, MC, V.

★ ★ ★ **OLIVES.** *(10 City Square, Charlestown 02129) 617/242-1999.* Country Mediterranean menu. Specialty: spit-roasted herb and garlic chicken. Own baking, pasta. Hrs: 5:30-10:15 pm; Sat 5-10:30 pm. Closed Sun, Mon; major hols. Bar. Wine list. Semi-a la carte: dinner $15.95-$28.95. Valet parking. Rustic European decor; large windows overlook square. Cr cds: MC, V.

D

★ ★ **PALM.** *200 Dartmouth St (02116), in Copley Square. 617/867-9292.* Specializes in steak, lobster, Italian dishes. Own baking. Hrs: 11:30 am-10:30 pm; Sat 5-11 pm; Sun 5-9:30 pm. Closed some major hols. Res accepted. Bar. A la carte entrees: lunch $8-$16, dinner $14-$36. Complete meal: lunch $10-$30, dinner $30-$50. Valet parking. Caricatures of regular clientele on walls. Family-owned since 1926. Cr cds: A, C, D, MC, V.

★ ★ ★ **PIGNOLI.** *79 Park Plaza (02116), in Back Bay. 617/338-7500.* Italian menu. Hrs: 11:30 am-2:30 pm, 5:30-10 pm; Fri, Sat to 11 pm; Sun from 5:30 pm. Late night menu Wed-Sat to 2 am. Bar. Semi-a la carte: lunch $8-$15, dinner $11-$25. Patio dining. Cr cds: A, C, D, DS, MC, V.

D

★ ★ **PLAZA III.** *101 S Faneuil Hall Marketplace (02109), in Faneuil Hall/Quincy Market Area. 617/720-5570.* Specializes in steaks, prime rib, fresh seafood. Hrs: 11 am-10 pm; Sun from 4 pm; Thurs-Sat to 11 pm. Res accepted. Serv bar. A la carte entrees: lunch, dinner $7.50-$28.50. Outdoor dining. Cr cds: A, D, DS, MC, V.

D ⊐

★ ★ ★ **PROVIDENCE.** *(1223 Beacon St, Brookline 02146) W on Commonwealth Ave to Beacon St. 617/232-0300.* Specialties: grilled pork chop, bibb salad. Hrs: 5:30-10 pm; Fri, Sat to 11 pm; Sun to 9:30 pm; Sun brunch 11 am-2 pm. Closed Mon; Thanksgiving, Dec 25. Res accepted. Bar. A la carte entrees: dinner $16-$25. Sun brunch $17-$23. Child's meals. Valet parking. Ornate decor; marble pillars, decorated walls. Cr cds: A, C, D, MC, V.

D SC

★ ★ ★ **RISTORANTE LUCIA.** *415 Hanover St (02113), in North End. 617/367-2353.* Regional Italian menu. Specializes in linguini with seafood, homemade pasta, grilled veal chops. Hrs: 4-11 pm; Fri-Sun from 11:30 am. Closed Thanksgiving, Dec 25. Res accepted. Bar. Semi-a la carte: lunch $4-$10, dinner $8.95-$17. Child's meals. Valet parking (dinner). Painted frescoes on walls and ceilings. Cr cds: A, MC, V.

D ⊐

★ ★ **RISTORANTE TOSCANO.** *47 Charles St (02114), on Beacon Hill. 617/723-4090.* Northern Italian menu. Specializes in veal, fish, pasta. Hrs: 11:30 am-2:30 pm, 5:30-10 pm; Fri, Sat to 10:30 pm; Sun 5:30-10 pm. Closed some major hols. Res accepted. Bar. A la carte entrees: lunch $9-$20, dinner $18-$30. Valet parking (dinner). Authentic Italian decor. Cr cds: A.

D ⊐

★ ★ ★ **ROWES WHARF.** *(See Boston Harbor Hotel) 617/439-3995.* Specialties: roast rack of Vermont lamb, Maine lobster sausage over lemon pasta, seared yellowfin tuna. Own baking. Hrs: 6:30 am-10 pm; Sun brunch 10:30 am-2:30 pm. Res accepted. Bar 11:30-2 am. Wine cellar. A la carte entrees: bkfst $6-$11, lunch $11-$19, dinner $18-$30. Complete meals: dinner $30-$45. Sun brunch $42. Child's meals. Valet parking. View of Boston Harbor. Jacket. Cr cds: A, C, D, DS, JCB, MC, V.

D ⊐ ♥

★ ★ ★ **SEASONS.** *(See The Regal Bostonian) 617/523-3600.* Contemporary Amer menu. Specializes in roast duckling, seasonal dishes. Own baking, pasta. Hrs: 6:30-10:30 am, 11:30 am-2 pm, 6-10 pm; Sat 7 am-noon, 6-11 pm; Sun 7 am-noon. Res accepted. Bar. Extensive wine list. Semi-a la carte: bkfst $8-$16, lunch $10-$24, dinner $21-$39. Child's meals. Valet parking. Rooftop restaurant overlooks Faneuil Hall and city. Cr cds: A, C, D, JCB, MC, V.

D ⊐

✔★ ★ **SMALL PLANET BAR & GRILL.** *565 Boylston St (02116), in Back Bay, opp Hancock Bldg. 617/536-4477.* Specializes in fresh seafood. Hrs: 11:30 am-midnight; Sun from 5 pm; Sun brunch 11-3 pm. Closed Thanksgiving, Dec 25. Bar. A la carte entrees: lunch $3.95-$7.95, dinner $7.95-$15.95. Colorful interior. Outdoor dining on Copley Square. Cr cds: A, C, D, DS, MC, V.

D ⊐

✔★ ★ **SPASSO.** *160 Commonwealth Ave (02116), in Back Bay at Dartmouth Ave. 617/536-8656.* Italian menu. Specialty: veal chops. Hrs: 11:30 am-10 pm; wkends to 11 pm; Sun brunch noon-3 pm. Closed Thanksgiving, Dec 25. Bar 11:30-1 am. A la carte entrees: dinner $9.95-$15.95. Buffet: lunch $7.95. Sun brunch $12.95. Valet parking. Outdoor dining. Colorful Italian atmosphere. Cr cds: A, D, DS, MC, V.

D ⊐

★ ★ ★ **TOP OF THE HUB.** *800 Boylston St (02199), at top of Prudential Bldg, in Back Bay. 617/536-1775.* Web www.topofthehub.com. Hrs: 11:30 am-2:30 pm, 5:30-10 pm; Fri, Sat to 11 pm; Sun brunch 10 am-2:30 pm. Closed Dec 25. Res accepted. Bar. Wine list. A la carte entrees: lunch $6-$15, dinner $18-$30. Various jazz groups daily. Panoramic view of Charles River and downtown Boston. Cr cds: A, C, D, DS, MC, V.

D

★ ★ **TURNER FISHERIES.** *(See The Westin Hotel, Copley Place) 617/424-7425.* Seafood menu. Specialties: pan-seared sea scallops, untraditional bouillabaisse, tuna carpaccio. Hrs: 11-12:30 am; Sun 10:30 am-midnight; Sun brunch to 2:30 pm. Res accepted. Bar. Semi-a la carte: lunch $9-$15, dinner $17-$27. Sun brunch $28.50. Child's meals. Jazz Tues-Sat. Valet parking. Cr cds: A, D, MC, V.

D SC

★ ★ **YE OLDE UNION OYSTER HOUSE.** *41 Union St (02108), in Faneuil Hall/Quincy Market Area. 617/227-2750.* Specializes in shore dinner, seafood platter. Hrs: 11 am-9:30 pm; Fri, Sat to 10 pm; Sun brunch 11 am-3 pm. Closed Thanksgiving, Dec 25. Res accepted. Bar. Semi-a la carte: lunch $7-$12, dinner $11.50-$20. Sun brunch $9.95. Child's meals. Valet parking (dinner). Historic oyster bar established 1826; originally a silk & dry goods shop (1742). Family-owned. Cr cds: A, C, D, DS, JCB, MC, V.

D

★ ★ ★ **ZINC.** *35 Stanhope St (02116), in Back Bay. 617/262-2323.* French menu. Specializes in fresh seafood. Hrs: 5:30 pm-1:30 am; Sun to 11:30 pm. Closed Mon. Res accepted. Bar to 2 am; Sun to midnight. Wine list. Semi-a la carte: dinner $16.50-$22.95. Valet parking. Inimate atmosphere; European bistro decor; menu changes daily. Cr cds: A, D, MC, V.

D

✓★ **ZUMA'S TEX MEX CAFE.** *7 N Market St (02109), in Faneuil Hall/Quincy Market Area. 617/367-9114.* Tex-Mex menu. Specializes in fajitas, enchiladas, neon margaritas. Hrs: 11:30 am-11 pm; Fri, Sat to midnight; Sun noon-10 pm. Closed Dec 25. Bar. Semi-a la carte: lunch, dinner $5-$12. Cr cds: A, C, D, DS, MC, V.

D

Unrated Dining Spot

RUBIN'S KOSHER DELICATESSEN. *(500 Harvard St, Brookline) W on Beacon St. 617/731-8787.* Kosher deli menu. Hrs: 10 am-8 pm; Fri 9 am-3 pm; Sun 9 am-8 pm. Closed Sat; Jewish hols. Semi-a la carte: lunch $3.50-$12, dinner $6.50-$15. Parking. Family-owned. Totally nonsmoking. No cr cds accepted.

D

Chicago

Settled: 1803
Pop: 2,783,726
Elev: 596 feet
Time zone: Central
Area codes: 312 & 773 (city); 630, 708 & 847 (suburbs)
Web: www.ci.chi.il.us

Chicago was incorporated as a city in 1837. Only four years later, in 1841, grain destined for world ports began to pour into the city. Almost immediately, Chicago became the largest grain market in the world. In the wake of the grain came herds of hogs and cattle for the Chicago slaughterhouses. Tanneries, packing plants, mills and factories soon sprang up. The completion of the Illinois and Michigan Canal in 1848 quadrupled imports and exports, and the railroads fanned out from the city, transporting merchandise throughout the nation and bringing new produce to Chicago. By the 1850s the city included 18 square miles of boom town and quagmire—its streets more bog than thoroughfare. The Civil War doubled grain shipments from Chicago, and in 1865 the square-mile Union Stock Yards were established.

Chicago was riotously prosperous, and its population had skyrocketed when, on October 8, 1871, fire erupted in a West Side barn. It roared through the city, destroying 15,768 buildings, killing approximately 300 people and leaving a third of the population homeless. But rebuilding started at once, and Chicago emerged from the ashes to take advantage of the rise of industrialization. The labor unrest of the period produced the Haymarket Square Riot as well as the Pullman and other strikes. In the 1880s and 1890s, Chicago witnessed the development of a new urban architectural form for which the term "skyscraper" was coined. The World's Columbian Exposition of 1893, a magnificent success, was followed by a depression and municipal corruption. Nevertheless, Chicago's fantastic rate of growth continued into the 20th century, while Al Capone, the prohibition gangster, and Samuel Insull, the financial finagler whose stock manipulations left thousands penniless, were the symbols of the times. The stock market crash of 1929 brought down the shakier financial pyramids; the repeal of prohibition quieted the rackets; and a soberer Chicago produced the Century of Progress Exposition in 1933-1934. The city's granaries and steel mills helped carry the country through World War II. Today the city is still booming as of old, with the world's largest inland port and the largest concentration of rail, truck and air transportation.

Business

Metropolitan Chicago has more than 10,000 factories with a sales volume of $98 billion. Chicago ranks as one of the top cities in the United States in the marketing of furniture and in the production of candy, canned and frozen foods, metal products, machinery, tool and die making, petroleum products, railroad equipment, printing and office equipment, musical instruments, telephones, housewares and lampshades. It has the world's busiest airport, largest commodity futures exchange and biggest mail-order business. It is a great educational center (58 institutions of higher learning, 800 technical schools); the world's largest convention and tradeshow city; and a marketplace, shopping and financial center. Wholesale trade volume is over $90 billion annually, retail trade about $15 billion. Tourism is a significant industry in Chicago, which attracts more than 8 million visitors annually.

Convention Facilities

Chicago's McCormick Place, overlooking Lake Michigan, is one of the largest convention complexes in the world. Its statistics are staggering: its three distinct areas—McCormick Place North, McCormick Place South and Lakeside Center—have a combined total of more than 2.2 million square feet of exhibit space. The center also features seating for 40,000 people at one time in the Don Maxwell Hall; parking for 12,000 cars (2,200 of them under roof); 9 restaurants that can feed a total of 20,000 people; banquet capacity of 25,000; over 65 meeting rooms holding from 50 to more than 4,000 people; and the Arie Crown theater, with a seating capacity of 4,319.

Some of the annual exhibitions and trade shows draw more than a million people over a short period of time. Waiting in line for any type of service is seldom necessary, even when more than 100,000 people are on the premises.

Chicago's Apparel Center and Expocenter/Chicago are located downtown on the Chicago River. The Apparel Center marks Chicago's emergence as a major fashion design center. Expocenter/Chicago contains 140,000 square feet of exhibition space; parking and many amenities are available on the premises.

Rosemont Convention Center, near O'Hare International Airport, has 450,000 square feet of exhibition space on one level, 48,000 square feet of meeting space and 25 meeting rooms; parking is available for 5,000 cars.

In addition, there are many hotels in the Chicago area that provide extensive meeting facilities.

Sports & Recreation

For baseball, there are the Cubs (National League), who play at Wrigley Field, and the White Sox (American League), whose home field is Comiskey Park. The city's professional football team, the Bears, play at Soldier Field. The Blackhawks play hockey and the Bulls play basketball at the United Center.

College sports include the DePaul Blue Demons, the Loyola Ramblers and the Northwestern Wildcats.

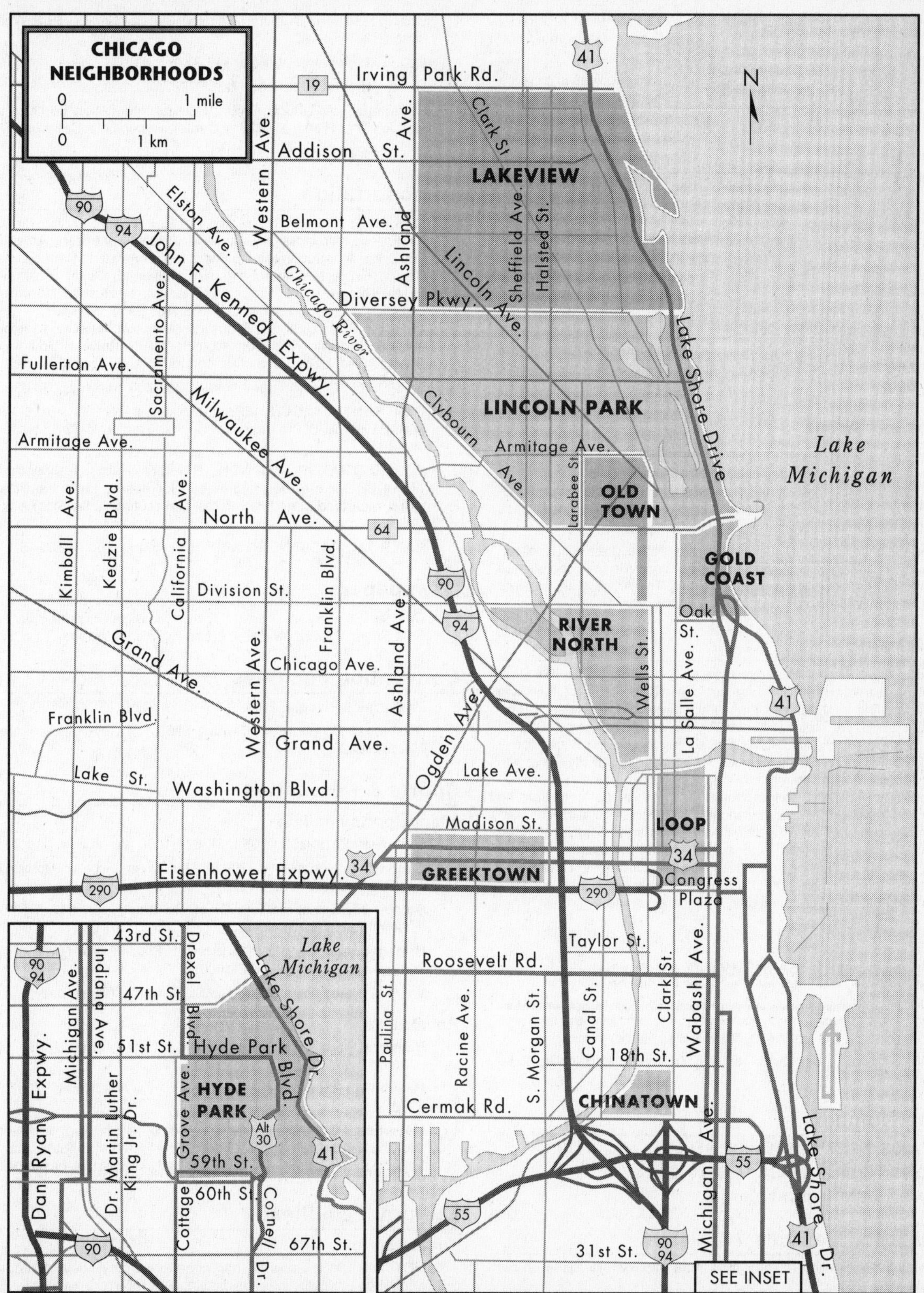
CHICAGO NEIGHBORHOODS
0 1 mile
0 1 km
N
Irving Park Rd.
Addison St.
Belmont Ave.
Diversey Pkwy.
Fullerton Ave.
Armitage Ave.
North Ave.
Division St.
Chicago Ave.
Grand Ave.
Franklin Blvd.
Lake St.
Washington Blvd.
Lake Ave.
Madison St.
Eisenhower Expwy.
Congress Plaza
Taylor St.
Roosevelt Rd.
18th St.
Cermak Rd.
31st St.
Western Ave.
Ashland Ave.
Clark St.
Sheffield Ave.
Halsted St.
Lincoln Ave.
Elston Ave.
Chicago River
John F. Kennedy Expwy.
Sacramento Ave.
Milwaukee Ave.
Clybourn Ave.
Larabee St.
Kimball Ave.
Kedzie Blvd.
California Ave.
Franklin Blvd.
Grand Ave.
Ogden Ave.
Wells St.
La Salle Ave.
Oak St.
Lake Shore Drive
Paulina St.
Racine Ave.
S. Morgan St.
Canal St.
Clark St.
Wabash Ave.
Michigan Ave.
Lake Shore Dr.
LAKEVIEW
LINCOLN PARK
OLD TOWN
GOLD COAST
RIVER NORTH
LOOP
GREEKTOWN
CHINATOWN
Lake Michigan
SEE INSET
43rd St.
47th St.
51st St.
59th St.
60th St.
67th St.
Hyde Park Blvd.
HYDE PARK
Drexel Blvd.
Grove Ave.
Cottage Grove Ave.
Cornell Dr.
Lake Shore Dr.
Dan Ryan Expwy.
Michigan Ave.
Indiana Ave.
Dr. Martin Luther King Jr. Dr.
Lake Michigan
19
41
90
94
64
34
290
55
Alt 30

Horse racing is another popular spectator sport; local racetracks around the city include Balmoral Park Race Track, Hawthorne Race Course, Maywood Park Race Track and Sportsman's Park.

For those athletes who wish to participate, Lake Michigan is a mecca for all water sports during warm months, and the city's enormous park areas can be enjoyed year-round.

Entertainment

This is a city known for its excellence in the arts of all types. Especially noteworthy are the Chicago Symphony and the Lyric Opera. Theater companies in Chicago and surrounding areas are too numerous to list; however, major theaters within the city proper are the Goodman, Royal George and the Auditorium. Theater companies are thriving, offering productions ranging from Second City's satirical reviews to Steppenwolf's award-winning dramas.

Chicago is teeming with night spots of every style imaginable. The city, though, is probably best known for jazz and blues. Step into almost any lounge or nightclub on the Near North Side, Lincoln Avenue in the Lincoln Park area or on Halsted Street in New Town for superb live entertainment.

Historical Areas

Old Prairie Avenue, once known as "Millionaires' Row," caught the attention of preservation-minded citizens. This area, known as the Prairie Avenue Historic District, has undergone some renovation. On the far South Side, most of the original buildings still stand in the Pullman House District, the famous industrialist's visionary model company town.

The Chicago school of architecture has had a great influence on international building design. World famous landmarks in the Loop, as well as many neighborhoods, are well worth visiting. The ArchiCenter features exhibits and tours of the city's architectural highlights.

Sightseeing

A one-week vacation does not allow sufficient time to see this great city, but for a start, either head for the observation floors of the John Hancock Building (100 stories), the world's tallest office-residential skyscraper, or the Sears Tower (110 stories), the world's tallest building, for an unforgettable experience. *Here's Chicago*, located in the Water Tower Pumping Station, presents a multimedia introduction to the city along with cultural exhibits. During summer months, boat cruises on the river provide a different view of the city. Visitors should also not miss the Art Institute on Michigan Avenue, which includes world-renowned collections of American and European art; the Field Museum of Natural History on Roosevelt Road at Lake Shore Drive; the John G. Shedd Aquarium on Lake Shore Drive; and the Museum of Science and Industry on 57th Street and Lake Shore Drive, featuring more than 2,000 displays, many hands-on, showing how science and industry have contributed to modern-day life.

General References

Area codes: 312 & 773 (city); 630, 708 & 847 (suburbs)

Note: When no area code is listed next to a phone number below, assume 312.

Phone Numbers

POLICE, FIRE & AMBULANCE: 911

POISON CONTROL CENTER: 800/942-5969

TIME & WEATHER: 976-1616

Information Sources

Chicago Convention & Tourism Bureau, McCormick Place on the Lake, 567-8500.

Chicago Office of Tourism, Chicago Cultural Center, 78 E Washington St, 744-2400.

Cultural Information Hotline, 346-3278.

Hot Tix, theater information line, 977-1755.

Department of Cultural Affairs, Cultural Information Booth in the east lobby of Richard J. Daley Center, Randolph & Dearborn Sts.

Chicago Park District, 294-2200.

Transportation

AIRLINES: *O'Hare International:* Aer Lingus; Aeroflot; Air Canada; Air France; Air India; Air Jamaica; Alitalia; American; American Trans Air; America West; Austrian; British Airways; Canadian Intl; Casino Express; China Eastern; Continental; Delta; El Al; JAL; KLM; Korean; LOT Polish; Lufthansa; Mexicana; Northwest; RenoAir; Royal Jordanian; SABENA; SAS; Swissair; Taesa; TAROM; TWA; United; USAir; and other commuter and regional airlines. *Midway:* American; Continental; Northwest; Southwest; TWA; United; USAir; and other commuter and regional airlines.

AIRPORTS: O'Hare International, 686-2200; Midway, 767-0500.

CAR RENTAL AGENCIES: (See IMPORTANT TOLL-FREE NUMBERS) Avis 694-5600; Budget 686-4950; Hertz 686-7272; National 694-4640.

PUBLIC TRANSPORTATION: RTA/CTA Public Transportation Travel Center provides information for buses, rapid transit and trains regarding schedules, fares and routing; CTA & RTA 836-7000.

RAILROAD PASSENGER SERVICE: Amtrak 800/872-7245.

Newspapers

Chicago Sun-Times; Chicago Tribune; Crain's Chicago Business; Wall Street Journal (Midwest Edition); Chicago Reader.

Convention Facilities

McCormick Place, E 23rd St & S Lake Shore Dr, 791-7000.

Rosemont Convention Center, 5555 N River Rd, Rosemont, 708/692-2220.

Sports & Recreation

Major Sports Facilities

Comiskey Park, 333 W 35th St, 674-1000 (White Sox, baseball).

Rosemont Horizon, 6920 N Mannheim Rd, in Rosemont, 708/390-0404 (Wolves, hockey).

Soldier Field, Lake Shore Dr at McFetridge Dr, 847/295-6600 (Bears, football).

United Center, 1901 W Madison St (Blackhawks, hockey, 455-7000; Bulls, basketball, 455-4000).

Wrigley Field, 1060 W Addison St, 404-2827 (Cubs, baseball).

Racetracks

Balmoral Park Race Track, IL 394 & Elmscourt Ln, Crete, 568-5700 or 708/672-7544.

Hawthorne Race Course, 3501 S Laramie Ave, Cicero, 708/780-3700.

Maywood Park Race Track, 8600 W North Ave, Maywood, 708/343-4800.

Sportsman's Park, 3301 S Laramie Ave, Cicero, 242-1121.

Cultural Facilities

Theaters

HOT TIX, 108 N State St, half-price (cash only), day-of-performance theater tickets when available, 977-1755.

Apollo, 2540 N Lincoln Ave, 773/935-6100.

Arie Crown, McCormick Place, 791-6000.

Auditorium Theater, 50 E Congress Pkwy, 902-1500.

Briar Street, 3133 N Halsted St, 773/348-4000.

Goodman, 200 S Columbus Dr, at the Art Institute, 443-3800.

Mayfair, *Shear Madness,* 636 S Michigan Ave, 786-9120.

North Shore Center for the Performing Arts, 9550 Skokie Blvd, Skokie, 847/679-9501.

Royal George, 1641 N Halsted, 988-9000.

Second City, 1616 N Wells, in Old Town, 337-3992.

Shubert, 22 W Monroe St, 902-1500.

Steppenwolf, 1650 N Halsted, 335-1650.

Victory Garden, 2257 N Lincoln Ave, 773/871-3000.

Concert Halls

Lyric Opera of Chicago, 20 N Wacker Dr, 332-2244.

Orchestra Hall, 220 S Michigan Ave, 435-6666.

Ravinia, Green Bay Rd at Lake Cook Rd, Highland Park, 847/728-4642.

Rosemont Horizon, 6920 N Mannheim Rd, Rosemont, 708/635-6600.

Museums

Adler Planetarium, 1300 S Lake Shore Dr, 322-0300 or 322-0304.

Balzekas Museum of Lithuanian Culture, 6500 S Pulaski Rd, 773/582-6500.

Cernan Earth and Space Center, 20 mi W, 2000 N 5th Ave, River Grove, 708/456-5815.

Chicago Academy of Sciences, 2001 N Clark St, in Lincoln Park, 871-2668.

Chicago Children's Museum, 435 E Illinois St, 527-1000.

Chicago Fire Academy, 558 W DeKoven St, 747-8151.

Chicago Historical Society, Clark St at North Ave, 642-4600.

DuSable Museum of African-American History, 740 E 56th Pl, 773/947-0600.

Field Museum of Natural History, Roosevelt Rd at Lake Shore Dr, 922-9410

Morton B. Weiss Museum of Judaica, 1100 E Hyde Park Blvd, 773/924-1234.

Museum of Broadcast Communications, 78 E Washington St, at Michigan Ave, 629-6000.

Museum of Holography/Chicago, 1134 W Washington Blvd, 226-1007.

Museum of Science and Industry and Crown Space Center, E 57th St & S Lake Shore Dr, 773/684-1414.

Oriental Institute Museum, 1155 E 58th St, 773/702-9521.

Peace Museum, 350 W Ontario St, 440-1860.

Polish Museum of America, 984 N Milwaukee Ave, 773/384-3352.

Spertus Museum, 618 S Michigan Ave, 322-1747.

Art Museums

Art Institute of Chicago, 111 S Michigan Ave at Adams St, 443-3600.

Museum of Contemporary Art, 220 E Chicago Ave, 280-2660 or 280-5161.

Terra Museum of American Art, 666 N Michigan Ave, 664-3939.

Points of Interest

Historical

Glessner House, 1800 S Prairie Ave, headquarters of Chicago Architecture Foundation, 922-3432.

Jane Addams' Hull House, 800 S Halsted St, on University of Illinois at Chicago campus, 413-5353.

Monadnock Building, 53 W Jackson Blvd, 922-1890.

Prairie Ave Historic District, Prairie Ave between 18th & Cullerton Sts, 922-3432.

Pullman Historic District, Visitor Center, 11141 S Cottage Grove, 773/785-8181.

Robie House, 5757 S Woodlawn Ave, 702-8374.

The Rookery, 209 S LaSalle St, 553-6150.

Water Tower, Michigan Ave at Chicago Ave, 440-3160.

Other Attractions

Brookfield Zoo, 14 mi SW at 31st St & 1st Ave, Brookfield, 242-2630 or 708/485-0263.

Buckingham Fountain, foot of Congress St in Grant Park.

Chicago Botanic Garden, 21 mi N off I-94 in Glencoe, 847/835-5440.

Chicago Cultural Center, 78 E Washington St, at Michigan Ave, 346-3278.

Chicago Mercantile Exchange, 30 S Wacker Dr, 930-8249.

Garfield Park and Conservatory, 300 N Central Park Blvd, 746-5100.

Greektown, Halsted St from Madison St S to Van Buren.

Here's Chicago, Water Tower Pumping Station, Michigan & Chicago Aves, 467-7114.

John Hancock Center Observatory, 875 N Michigan Ave, 751-3681.

Lincoln Park stretches along almost entire N end of the city on the lake.

Lincoln Park Zoo, Farm and Conservatory, west entrance Lincoln Park, Webster Ave & Stockton Dr, 742-2000 or 742-7736.

Magnificent Mile, Michigan Ave, Chicago River N to Oak St.

Marshall Field & Co, 111 N State St, 781-4882.

Navy Pier, E end of Grand Ave at the lake.

Newberry Library, 60 W Walton St, 255-3510.

New Town, area of Lakeview S of Addison St, W of the lake, N of Diversey Pkwy & E of Clark St.

Old Town, area of Wells St between Division St on the S & North Ave on the N; also area of Lincoln Park S of Armitage Ave, W of Clark St, N of North Ave & E of Larrabee St.

Richard J. Daley Center and Plaza, Washington, Randolph, Clark & Dearborn Sts.

River North, area N of the Merchandise Mart & Chicago River, W of LaSalle St, S of Division St & E of the river's North Branch.

Rockefeller Memorial Chapel, 5850 S Woodlawn Ave, on University of Chicago campus, 702-8374.

John G. Shedd Aquarium, 1200 S Lake Shore Dr, 939-2438.

Sears Tower, 233 S Wacker Dr, 875-9696.

Tribune Tower, 435 N Michigan Ave, 222-3994.

University of Chicago, 5801 S Ellis Ave, 702-8374.

Water Tower Place, 835 N Michigan Ave, 440-3165.

Wrigley Building, 400 N Michigan Ave.

Sightseeing Tours

American Sightseeing, 251-3100.

Chicago Architecture Foundation, 224 S Michigan Ave, 922-3424.

Gray Line bus tours, 427-3107.

Mercury, the Skyline Cruiseline, Wacker Dr & Michigan Ave, S side of Chicago River at Michigan Ave bridge, 332-1353.

Wendella Sightseeing Boats, 400 N Michigan Ave, at Wrigley Building, N side of Chicago River at Michigan Ave bridge, 337-1446.

Annual Events

Chicago Auto Show, McCormick Place. Early Feb.

St Patrick's Day Parade. Mar 17.

Blues Festival, Grant Park. Early or mid-June.

Old Town Art Fair, N Lincoln Park W. Usually 2nd wkend June.

Concert & Fireworks, Grant Park. July 3.

Taste of Chicago, Grant Park. Late June-early July.

Chicago to Mackinac Race, on Lake Michigan. 3rd wkend July.

Air & Water Show, North Ave Beach. Aug.

Venetian Night, Monroe St harbor and along lakefront. Aug.

Jazz Festival, Grant Park. Late Aug-early Sept.

Chicago International Film Festival. 3 wks Oct.

City Neighborhoods

Many of the restaurants, unrated dining establishments and some lodgings listed under Chicago include neighborhoods as well as exact street addresses. Geographic descriptions of these areas are given, followed by a table of restaurants arranged by neighborhood.

Chinatown: South of the Loop on Wentworth St at Cermak Rd.

Gold Coast: South of North Ave, west of the lake, north of Oak St and east of LaSalle St.

Greektown: West of the Loop on Halsted St between Van Buren St on the south and Madison St on the north.

Hyde Park: South of the Loop; south of 47th St, west of the lake, north of the Midway Plaisance (60th St) and east of Cottage Grove Ave.

Lakeview: Includes New Town and Wrigleyville, south of Irving Park Rd, west of the lake, north of Diversey Pkwy and east of Ashland Ave.

Lincoln Park: Old Town and DePaul, south of Diversey Pkwy, west of the lake, north of North Ave and east of Clybourn Ave.

Loop: Area within the "loop" of the elevated train tracks; south of Lake St, west of Wabash Ave, north of Congress Pkwy and east of Wells St. **North of the Loop:** North of Lake St. **South of the Loop:** South of Congress Pkwy.

Old Town: Wells St between Division St on the south and North Ave on the north; also area of Lincoln Park south of Armitage Ave, west of Clark St, north of North Ave and east of Larrabee St.

River North: Area north of the Merchandise Mart and Chicago River, west of LaSalle St, south of Division St and east of the river's North Branch.

Lodgings and Food

CHICAGO RESTAURANTS BY NEIGHBORHOOD AREAS

(For full description, see alphabetical listings under Restaurants)

CHINATOWN
Emperor's Choice. 2238 S Wentworth Ave

GOLD COAST
Biggs. 1150 N Dearborn St
Brasserie Bellevue (Sutton Place Hotel). 21 E Bellevue Place
Pump Room (Omni Ambassador East Hotel). 1301 N State Parkway
Salpicón. 1252 N Wells St

GREEKTOWN
Greek Islands. 200 S Halsted St
Parthenon. 314 S Halsted St
Santorini. 800 W Adams St

LAKEVIEW
Ann Sather. 929 W Belmont Ave
Arco De Cuchilleros. 3445 N Halsted St
Bella Vista. 1001 W Belmont Ave
Erwin. 2995 N Halsted St
Mia Francesca. 3311 N Clark St
N.N. Smokehouse. 1465 W Irving Park
Schulien's. 2100 W Irving Park Rd

LINCOLN PARK
Ambria (Belden-Stratford Hotel). 2300 N Lincoln Park West
Blue Mesa. 1729 N Halsted St
Café Ba Ba Reeba. 2024 N Halsted St
Chapulin. 1962 N Halsted St
Charlie Trotter's. 816 W Armitage Ave
Emilio's Tapas. 444 W Fullerton St
Geja's. 340 W Armitage Ave
Pockets. 2618 N Clark St
Relish. 2044 N Halsted St
Sole Mio. 917 W Armitage Ave
Un Grand Cafe (Belden-Stratford Hotel). 2300 Lincoln Park West
Vinci. 1732 N Halsted St

THE LOOP
Berghoff. 17 W Adams St
The Big Downtown (Palmer House Hilton Hotel). 124 Wabash Ave
Everest. 440 S La Salle St
La Strada. 155 N Michigan Ave
Nick's Fishmarket. 1 First National Plaza
Russian Tea Cafe. 63 E Adams St
Trattoria No. 10. 10 N Dearborn St
Vivere. 71 W Monroe St

NORTH OF THE LOOP
Arun's. 4156 N Kedzie Ave
Avanzare. 161 E Huron St
Bice. 158 E Ontario St
Bistro 110. 110 E Pearson St
Blackhawk Lodge. 41 E Superior St
Boulevard (Inter-Continental Hotel). 505 N Michigan Ave
Cape Cod Room (The Drake Hotel). 140 E Walton Place
Cielo (Omni Chicago Hotel). 676 N Michigan Ave
Como Inn. 546 N Milwaukee Ave
Con Fusion. 1616 N Damen Ave
Cuisines (Renaissance Hotel). 1 W Wacker Dr
Eli's The Place For Steak. 215 E Chicago Ave
Entre Nous (Fairmont Hotel). 200 N Columbus Dr
Gibsons Steakhouse. 1028 N Rush St
Grappa. 200 E Chestnut St
Hatsuhana. 160 E Ontario St
House Of Hunan. 535 N Michigan Ave
Il Toscanaccio. 636 N St Clair St
Iron Mike's Grille (Tremont Hotel). 100 E Chestnut St
Lawry's The Prime Rib. 100 E Ontario St
Le Bouchon. 1958 N Damen Ave
Les Nomades. 222 E Ontario St
Lutz's Continental Cafe & Pastry Shop. 2458 W Montrose Ave
Marché. 833 W Randolph St
Morton's. 1050 N State St
Nix (Regal Knickerbocker Hotel). 163 E Walton Pl
Palm (Swissôtel Hotel). 323 E Wacker Dr
Papagus (Embassy Suites Hotel). 620 N State St
Park Avenue Cafe (Doubletree Guest Suites Hotel). 198 E Delaware Pl
Pizzeria Uno. 29 E Ohio St
Ritz-Carlton Dining Room (The Ritz-Carlton Hotel). 160 E Pearson St
Riva. 700 E Grand Ave
The Saloon. 200 E Chestnut
Sayat Nova. 157 E Ohio St
Seasons (Four Seasons Hotel). 120 E Delaware Place
Shaw's Crab House. 21 E Hubbard St
Signature Room At The 95th. 875 N Michigan Ave
Spiaggia. 980 N Michigan Ave
Spruce. 238 E Ontario St
Streeterville Grille & Bar. 301 E North Water St
Su Casa. 49 E Ontario St
Szechwan East. 340 E Ohio St
Tucci Benucch. 900 N Michigan Ave
Tucci Milan. 6 W Hubbard St
Vivo. 838 W Randolph
Zinfandel. 59 W Grand Ave

SOUTH OF THE LOOP
Buckingham's (Hilton & Towers Hotel). 720 S Michigan Ave
Prairie (Hyatt On Printers Row Hotel). 500 S Dearborn St
Printer's Row. 550 S Dearborn St
Tuscany. 1014 W Taylor St

RIVER NORTH
Ben Pao. 52 W Illinois St
Big Bowl Cafe. 159½ W Erie St
Brasserie Jo. 59 W Hubbard St
Celebrity Cafe (Westin River North Chicago Hotel). 320 N Dearborn St
Centro. 710 N Wells St
Chicago Chop House. 60 W Ontario St
Club Gene & Georgetti. 500 N Franklin St
Coco Pazzo. 300 W Hubbard St
Ed Debevic's. 640 N Wells St
Frontera Grill. 445 N Clark St
Gordon. 500 N Clark St
Hard Rock Cafe. 63 W Ontario St
Harry Caray's. 33 W Kinzie St
Hat Dance. 325 W Huron St
Kiki's Bistro. 900 N Franklin
Klay Oven. 414 N Orleans St
Maggiano's. 516 N Clark St
Mango. 712 N Clark St
Michael Jordan's. 500 N La Salle St
Planet Hollywood. 633 N Wells St
Redfish. 400 N State St
Scoozi. 410 W Huron
Spago. 520 N Dearborn St
Topolobampo. 445 N Clark St
Trattoria Parma. 400 N Clark St

Note: When a listing is located in a town that does not have its own city heading, it will appear under the city nearest to its location. In these cases, the address and town appear in parenthesis immediately following the name of the establishment.

Motels

★ ★ **HAMPTON INN.** *(6540 S Cicero Ave, Bedford Park 60638) 2 blk S of Midway Airport. 708/496-1900; FAX 708/496-1997.* Web www.hamptoninn.com. 171 rms, 5 story. S $89; D $99; under 18 free. Crib free. TV; cable (premium). Complimentary continental bkfst. Restaurant nearby. Rm serv. Ck-out noon. Meeting rms. Business servs avail. In-rm modem link. Valet serv. Free airport transportation. Exercise equipt; treadmill, stair machine. Cr cds: A, C, D, DS, MC, V.

D SC

★ ★ **SLEEP INN.** *(6650 S Cicero Ave, Bedford Park 60638) W on I-55, S on Cicero Ave, near Midway Airport. 708/594-0001; FAX 708/594-0058.* 120 rms, 118 with shower only, 3 story. S $79-$85; D $85; each addl $6; under 18 free. Crib free. TV; cable (premium). Complimentary continental bkfst. Ck-out noon. Meeting rms. Business servs avail. In-rm modem link. Free airport transportation. Exercise equipt; bicycle, treadmill. Whirlpool. Cr cds: A, C, D, DS, JCB, MC, V.

D SC

Motor Hotels

★ **BEST WESTERN RIVER NORTH.** *125 W Ohio St (60610), west of N Michigan Ave, River North. 312/467-0800; FAX 312/467-1665.* 148 rms, 7 story. S $105-$129; D $117-$141; each addl $8; suites $150-$170; under 18 free; wkend rates; higher rates special events. Crib free. TV; cable (premium), VCR avail. Indoor pool. Complimentary coffee in rms. Restaurant 6:30 am-11 pm; Sat, Sun to 1 am. Rm serv. Ck-out noon. Meeting rm. Business servs avail. In-rm modem link. Bellhops. Free parking. Exercise equipt; weights, bicycles, sauna. Some refrigerators. Cr cds: A, C, D, DS, MC, V.

SC

✔★ **COMFORT INN.** *601 W Diversey Pkwy (60614), Lincoln Park. 773/348-2810; FAX 773/348-1912.* 74 rms, 5 story. S $78-$115; D $88-$125; each addl $10; suites $205-$215; under 18 free. TV; cable (premium). Complimentary continental bkfst. Ck-out noon. Meeting rm. Business servs avail. Saunas. Health club privileges. Some in-rm whirlpools, saunas. Cr cds: A, C, D, DS, ER, JCB, MC, V.

SC

★ ★ **HOLIDAY INN-MIDWAY AIRPORT.** *7353 S Cicero Ave (IL 50) (60629), near Midway Airport, south of the Loop. 773/581-5300; FAX 773/581-8421.* 161 rms, 5 story. S $84; D $94; each addl $10; under 18 free; wkend rates. Crib free. TV; cable (premium). Pool. Complimentary full bkfst. Restaurant 6 am-10 pm. Rm serv. Bar 5 pm-1 am; entertainment wkends. Ck-out noon. Meeting rms. Business servs avail. Bellhops. Free airport transportation. Exercise equipt; treadmill, weight machine. Cr cds: A, C, D, DS, JCB, MC, V.

D SC

★ **RAMADA INN LAKE SHORE.** *4900 S Lake Shore Dr (60615), Hyde Park. 773/288-5800; FAX 773/288-5745.* 182 rms, 2-4 story. S $89; D $94; each addl $10; suites $155; under 19 free; wkend rates. Crib free. Pet accepted, some restrictions. TV; cable (premium). Pool; poolside serv. Restaurant 6:30 am-10 pm. Rm serv. Bar 11-1 am. Ck-out 11 am. Meeting rms. Business center. Bellhops. Valet serv. Many rms with view of Lake Michigan. Cr cds: A, C, D, DS, MC, V.

D SC

Hotels

★ ★ **AMBASSADOR WEST.** *1300 N State Pkwy (60610), at Goethe St, Gold Coast. 312/787-3700; FAX 312/640-2967.* 219 rms, 12 story. S, D $199-$229; each addl $20; suites $239-$1,200; under 18 free; wkend rates; package plans. Crib free. Valet parking $23.50. TV; cable (premium), VCR avail. Restaurant 6:30 am-10:30 pm. Rm serv. Bar from 4:30 pm. Ck-out noon. Meeting rms. Business servs avail. Barber, beauty shop. Exercise equipt; weight machine, bicycles. Minibars; wet bars in suites; microwaves avail. Cr cds: A, C, D, DS, JCB, MC, V.

D SC

★ ★ **BELDEN-STRATFORD.** *2300 Lincoln Park West (60614), Lincoln Park. 773/281-2900; FAX 773/880-2039; res: 800/800-8301.* 50 kit. units in 16 story landmark bldg. S, D $125-$205; wkly, wkend rates. Crib $10. Valet parking $18. TV; cable, VCR avail. Complimentary coffee in rms. Restaurants (see AMBRIA and UN GRAND CAFE). Bar 6-11 pm. Ck-out noon. Coin Indry. Business servs avail. In-rm modem link. Barber, beauty shop. Exercise equipt; weight machines, treadmill. Microwaves. Views of park, Lake Michigan and skyline. Cr cds: A, C, D, DS, MC, V.

D SC

★ ★ **BEST WESTERN INN.** *162 E Ohio St (60611), north of the Loop. 312/787-3100; FAX 312/573-3140.* 358 rms, 22 story. S, D $129-$169; suites $235-$425; under 17 free; package plans. Valet parking $16. TV; cable. Restaurant 6:30 am-10:30 pm; Fri, Sat to midnight. Bar 11-2 am. Ck-out noon. Guest Indry. Meeting rms. Gift shop. Airport transportation. Indoor tennis privileges. Health club privileges. Sun deck on top floor. Cr cds: A, C, D, DS, JCB, MC, V.

D SC

✔★ **CITY SUITES.** *933 W Belmont Ave (60657), Lakeview. 773/404-3400; res: 800/248-9108; FAX 773/404-3405.* Web www.cityinns.com. 45 rms, 4 story, 29 suites. S $85; D $95; each addl $10; suites $99; under 12 free; wkly rates. Crib free. Pet accepted, some restrictions; $200 deposit. Garage parking $7. TV; cable (premium), VCR avail. Complimentary continental bkfst. Restaurant adj 7 am-10 pm. Ck-out noon. Coin Indry. Health club privileges. Refrigerator in suites. Microwaves avail. Cr cds: A, C, D, DS, ER, MC, V.

SC

★ ★ **CLARIDGE.** *1244 N Dearborn Pkwy (60610), Gold Coast. 312/787-4980; FAX 312/266-0978; res: 800/245-1258.* E-mail claridge-hotel@att.net; web www.claridge.com. 168 rms, 14 story. S $119-$175; D $135-$190; each addl $15; suites $250-$450; under 18 free; wkend packages. Crib free. Pet accepted, some restrictions. Valet parking $20.25. TV. Complimentary continental bkfst. Restaurant 6:30 am-10:30 pm. Bar noon-2 am. Ck-out noon. Meeting rms. Business servs avail. Concierge. Airport transportation. Health club privileges. Minibars. Fireplace in some suites. Library. In historic residential area. Cr cds: A, C, D, DS, JCB, MC, V.

D SC

★ ★ ★ **COURTYARD BY MARRIOTT.** *30 E Hubbard St (60611), north of the Loop. 312/329-2500; FAX 312/329-0293.* 334 rms, 15 story. S, D $115-$209; suites $199-$249; under 18 free; wkly, wkend rates. Crib free. Garage parking, in/out $22. TV; cable (premium). Indoor pool; whirlpool. Complimentary coffee in rms. Restaurant 6:30 am-11 pm. Bar 4 pm-midnight. Ck-out 1 pm. Coin Indry. Meeting rms. Business servs avail. In-rm modem link. Gift shop. Exercise equipt; weight machine, bicycles. Health club privileges. Refrigerators; microwaves avail. Cr cds: A, C, D, DS, MC, V.

D SC

✔★ ★ **DAYS INN LAKE SHORE DRIVE.** *644 N Lake Shore Dr (60611), at Ontario St, opp Lake Michigan, north of the Loop. 312/943-9200; FAX 312/255-4411.* 578 rms, 33 story. S $89-$189; D $99-$199; each addl $15; suites $275-$800; under 17 free; wkend rates. Crib free. Garage, in/out $18. TV; cable. Pool. Restaurant 6:30 am-10 pm; Fri, Sat to 11 pm. Bar 11 am-midnight. Ck-out noon. Coin Indry. Meeting rms. Business center. In-rm modem link. Gift shop. Airport transportation. Exercise equipt; weight machine, bicycle. Some refrigerators. Panoramic view. Overlooks lake. Cr cds: A, C, D, DS, ER, JCB, MC, V.

D SC

★ ★ ★ **DOUBLETREE GUEST SUITES.** *198 E Delaware Place (60611), north of the Loop. 312/664-1100; FAX 312/664-9881.* Web www.doubletreehotels.com/chicago. 345 suites, 30 story. S, D $129-$265; each addl $25; under 18 free; wkend rates. Crib free. Valet parking, in/out $23.50. TV; cable (premium), VCR avail. Indoor pool; whirlpool. Coffee in rms. Restaurants 6:30-2 am. Rm serv 24 hrs. Bar 11-2 am. Ck-out noon. Coin Indry. Meeting rms. Business center. In-rm modem link. Concierge.

Gift shop. Exercise equipt; weight machine, stair machine, sauna. Game rm. Refrigerators, microwaves, minibars. Cr cds: A, C, D, DS, MC, V.

D SC

★ ★ ★ **THE DRAKE.** *140 E Walton Place (60611), at Lake Shore Dr & N Michigan Ave, north of the Loop. 312/787-2200; FAX 312/787-1431; res: 800/553-7253.* Web www.hilton.com. 535 rms, 10 story. S, D $265-$335; suites $365-$2,150; family, wkend rates. Crib free. Valet parking $23.25/night; in/out privileges. TV; cable (premium), VCR avail. Restaurant 6:30 am-11 pm (also see CAPE COD ROOM). Rm serv 24 hrs. Bar 11-2 am; piano bar. Ck-out noon. Convention facilities. Business center. In-rm modem link. Concierge. Shopping arcade. Barber. Exercise equipt; rower, stair machine. Health club privileges. Minibars; microwaves avail; wet bar in some suites. Overlooks Lake Michigan. Luxury level. Cr cds: A, C, D, DS, ER, JCB, MC, V.

D

★ ★ ★ **EMBASSY SUITES.** *600 N State St (60610), north of the Loop. 312/943-3800; FAX 312/943-7629.* 358 suites, 11 story. S, D $249-$279; under 12 free. Crib free. Garage, in/out $22. TV; cable (premium), VCR avail. Indoor pool; whirlpool. Complimentary full bkfst. Complimentary coffee in rms. Restaurant (see PAPAGUS). Bar. Ck-out noon. Meeting rms. Business center. In-rm modem link. Concierge. Gift shop. Exercise equipt; weights, bicycles, sauna. Health club privileges. Refrigerators, microwaves, minibars, wet bars. Cr cds: A, C, D, DS, JCB, MC, V.

D SC

★ ★ **EXECUTIVE PLAZA.** *71 E Wacker Dr (60601), on the south bank of the Chicago River, north of the Loop. 312/346-7100; FAX 312/346-1721.* 417 rms, 39 story. S $159-$199; D $179-$219; each addl $20; suites $295-$850; under 18 free; wkend rates; package plans. Garage, in/out $20. TV; cable. Coffee in rms. Restaurant 6:30 am-11 pm. Bar to 2 am. Ck-out noon. Meeting rms. Business center. Concierge. Gift shop. Exercise equipt; weight machine, treadmill. Health club privileges. Bathrm phones, minibars. Some wet bars in suites. Cr cds: A, C, D, DS, MC, V.

D SC

★ ★ ★ ★ **FAIRMONT.** *200 N Columbus Dr (60601), north of the Loop. 312/565-8000; FAX 312/856-1032; res: 800/527-4727.* E-mail chifairmont@aol.com; web www.fairmont.com. An international collection of art and antiques grace the interior of this neo-classical pink granite tower. Guest rooms are exceptionally spacious with windows that open on dramatic lake and city views. 692 rms, 42 story. S, D $199-$329; each addl $35; suites $500-$3,600; under 18 free. Crib free. Valet parking, in/out $26. TV; cable (premium), VCR avail. Pool privileges. Restaurants (see ENTRE NOUS). Rm serv 24 hrs. Bar 11-2 am; entertainment Tues-Sat. Ck-out 1 pm. Convention facilities. Business center. In-rm modem link. Concierge. Health club privileges. Bathrm phones, minibars. Cr cds: A, C, D, DS, ER, JCB, MC, V.

D

★ ★ ★ ★ **FOUR SEASONS.** *120 E Delaware Place (60611), at 900 N Michigan Ave complex, north of the Loop. 312/280-8800; FAX 312/280-1748.* E-mail fourtiff@aol.com; web www.fourseasonsregent.com. From the spacious English country manor-style lobby of this sparkling hotel, it's easy to forget that you're on the seventh floor of a 66-story skycraper, just above a chic shopping mall on Chicago's fashionable North Michigan Avenue. Many of the guest rooms, which begin on floor 30, have spectacular views of the city and/or Lake Michigan and all the necessities and comforts for work or relaxation. 343 rms, 66 story bldg, guest rms on floors 30-46, 157 suites. S $325-$445; D $365-$485; each addl $30; suites $690-$995; wkend rates; special packages. Crib free. Pet accepted. Self-park adj, in/out $15.25. TV; cable (premium), VCR avail (movies). Indoor pool; whirlpool. Restaurant (see SEASONS). Rm serv 24 hrs. Bar 11:30-1 am; entertainment. Ck-out noon. Convention facilities. Business center. In-rm modem link. Concierge. Shopping access to 900 North Michigan Mall. Barber, beauty shop. Extensive exercise rm; instructor, weight machine, stair machine, sauna, steam rm. Massage. Bathrm phones, minibars; some wet bars. Lake 3 blks. Cr cds: A, C, D, DS, ER, JCB, MC, V.

D

★ ★ ★ **HILTON & TOWERS.** *720 S Michigan Ave (60605), opp Grant Park, south of the Loop. 312/922-4400; FAX 312/922-5240.* Web www.hilton.com. 1,543 rms, 25 story. S $165-$185; D $190-$210; each addl $25; suites from $250; wkend rates. Crib free. Garage $19; valet parking $21. TV; cable (premium). Indoor pool; whirlpools. Complimentary coffee in rms. Restaurants 5:30-1:30 am (also see BUCKINGHAM'S). Rm serv 24 hrs. Bars to 2 am; entertainment. Ck-out 11 am. Convention facilities. Business center. Concierge. Shopping arcade. Barber, beauty shop. Exercise rm; instructor, weights, bicycles, sauna. Massage. Minibars. Luxury level. Cr cds: A, C, D, DS, ER, JCB, MC, V.

D SC

★ ★ ★ **HOLIDAY INN-CITY CENTRE.** *300 E Ohio St (60611), north of the Loop. 312/787-6100; FAX 312/787-6238.* 500 rms, 26 story. S, D $165-$240; each addl $20; suites $400-$700; under 18 free; wkend plan. Crib free. Garage adj $17.50. TV; cable (premium), VCR avail. Pool; whirlpools, lifeguard. Restaurant 6:30 am-11 pm. Bars 11:30-2 am. Ck-out noon. Coin lndry. Meeting rms. Business center. In-rm modem link. Tennis privileges. Exercise rm; instructor, weights, bicycles, sauna, steam rm. Massage. Sauna in suites. Cr cds: A, C, D, DS, JCB, MC, V.

D SC

★ ★ **HOLIDAY INN-MART PLAZA.** *350 N Orleans St (60654), atop Apparel Center, adj Merchandise Mart, River North. 312/836-5000; FAX 312/222-9508.* 526 rms, 23 story; guest rms on floors 16-23. S $119-$219; D $134-$244; each addl $16; suites $325-$525; under 18 free; wkend rates; package plans. Crib free. Pet accepted, some restrictions. Garage $13/day. TV. Indoor pool. Restaurant 6:30 am-2 pm, 5-10:30 pm. Bars noon-2 am. Ck-out noon. Coin lndry. Convention facilities. Shopping arcade. Barber, beauty shop. Airport transportation. Exercise equipt; bicycles, treadmill. Refrigerator in suites. Cr cds: A, C, D, DS, JCB, MC, V.

D SC

★ ★ **HYATT AT UNIVERSITY VILLAGE.** *625 S Ashland Ave (60607), at Rush-Presbyterian-St Luke's Medical Center, west of the Loop. 312/243-7200; FAX 312/243-1289.* Web www.hyatt.com. 114 rms, 4 story. S $120-$195; D $120-$220; each addl $25; suites $185-$560; under 18 free; wkend, wkly, monthly rates. Crib free. TV; cable (premium), VCR avail. Pool privileges. Restaurant 6:30 am-10 pm. Rm serv. Bar 11 am-midnight. Ck-out noon. Meeting rms. Business center. Valet serv. Valet parking. Tennis privileges. Exercise equipt; weight machine, bicycles. Health club privileges. Some refrigerators; microwaves avail. Near University of Illinois Chicago campus. Cr cds: A, C, D, DS, MC, V.

D SC

★ ★ **HYATT ON PRINTERS ROW.** *500 S Dearborn St (60605), Printer's Row, south of the Loop. 312/986-1234; FAX 312/939-2468.* Web www.hyatt.com. 161 rms, 7-12 story. S $165-$205; D $185-$230; each addl $25; suites $450-$1,000; wkend rates. Crib free. Valet parking $24; self-park $16. TV; cable (premium), VCR avail. Restaurant 6:30 am-11 pm (also see PRAIRIE). Bar 11-1 am. Ck-out noon. Meeting rms. Business servs avail. Airport transportation. Exercise equipt; bicycles, treadmill. Massage. Health club privileges. Bathrm phones, minibars. Financial district nearby. Cr cds: A, C, D, DS, ER, JCB, MC, V.

D SC

★ ★ ★ **HYATT REGENCY.** *151 E Wacker Dr (60601), opp Chicago River, north of the Loop. 312/565-1234; FAX 312/565-2966.* 2,019 rms, 34 story (East Tower), 36 story (West Tower). S $119-$289; D $119-$309; each addl $25; suites $565-$3,500; under 18 free; package plans. Crib free. Garage, in/out $24. TV; cable (premium), VCR avail (movies). Restaurant open 6 am-midnight. Rm serv 24 hrs. Bar 11-2 am; entertainment. Ck-out noon. Convention facilities. Business center. In-rm modem link. Concierge. Shopping arcade. Barber, beauty shop. Health club privileges. Minibars; some in-rm steam baths, whirlpools. Bathrm phone, refrigerator in suites. Luxury level. Cr cds: A, C, D, DS, ER, JCB, MC, V.

D SC

★ ★ ★ **INTER-CONTINENTAL.** *505 N Michigan Ave (60611), just north of the Chicago River, at Grand Ave, north of the Loop. 312/944-4100; FAX 312/944-1320; res: 800/327-0200.* 845 rms, 2 bldgs, 26 & 42 story, 42 suites. S, D $179-$319; each addl $25; suites from $375; under 14 free. Crib free. Covered parking $25/day. TV; cable, VCR avail. Indoor pool; poolside serv. Coffee in rms. Restaurants 6:30 am-11 pm. Rm serv 24 hrs.

Afternoon tea 2-5 pm. Bar 11-1 am; entertainment Thurs-Sun. Ck-out noon. Convention facilities. Business center. In-rm modem link. Concierge. Gift shop. Exercise rm; instructor, weight machines, bicycles, sauna. Massage. Minibars, bathrm phones; microwaves avail. Two buildings, one of which was originally constructed (1929) as the Medinah Athletic Club. Cr cds: A, C, D, DS, ER, JCB, MC, V.

D SC

★★ **LENOX SUITES.** *616 N Rush St (60611), north of the Loop. 312/337-1000; FAX 312/337-7217; res: 800/445-3669.* 324 kit. units, 17 story. S $149-$209; D $159-$219; each addl $10; under 16 free; wkend, monthly rates. Crib free. Valet parking $17.50. TV; cable (premium), VCR avail. Complimentary continental bkfst. Restaurants 6 am-11 pm. Rm serv. Bar 11-2 am. Ck-out 11 am. Coin lndry. Meeting rms. Business servs avail. In-rm modem link. Concierge. Exercise equipt; treadmill, bicycle. Health club privileges. Microwaves. Cr cds: A, C, D, DS, JCB, MC, V.

D SC

★★★ **MARRIOTT.** *540 N Michigan Ave (60611), at Ohio St, north of the Loop. 312/836-0100; FAX 312/836-6139.* 1,172 rms, 46 story. S $159-$249; D $189-$299; suites $590-$1,150; under 18 free; wkend rates. Crib free. Pet accepted. Valet parking $23.25. TV; cable (premium), VCR avail. Indoor pool; whirlpool, poolside serv. Coffee in rms. Restaurant 6:30 am-midnight. Bar 11-2 am. Ck-out noon. Convention facilities. Business center. In-rm modem link. Concierge. Shopping arcade. Barber, beauty shop. Exercise rm; instructor, weight machines, bicycles, sauna. Massage. Basketball courts. Game rm. Bathrm phone in suites; microwaves avail. Luxury level. Cr cds: A, C, D, DS, ER, JCB, MC, V.

D SC

★★ **MIDLAND.** *172 W Adams St (60603), the Loop. 312/332-1200; FAX 312/332-5909; res: 800/621-2360.* 257 rms, 10 story. S, D $175-$225; each addl $20; suites from $450; under 18 free; wkend rates. Crib free. TV; cable (premium). Complimentary full bkfst. Restaurant 6:30 am-11 pm. Bar 11 am-midnight. Ck-out noon. Convention facilities. Business servs avail. Gift shop. Airport transportation. Exercise equipt; weight machine, bicycles. Massage. Health club privileges. Some refrigerators, microwaves. Cr cds: A, C, D, DS, JCB, MC, V.

D SC

★ **MOTEL 6.** *162 E Ontario St (60611), north of the Loop. 312/787-3580; FAX 312/787-1299.* 191 rms, 15 story. June-Aug: S $89; D $99; each addl $10; suites $99-$109; under 17 free; wkend rates; higher rates: New Years Eve, special events; lower rates rest of yr. Crib free. Valet parking $16. TV; cable. Restaurant 11:30 am-9:30 pm. No rm serv. Ck-out noon. Meeting rms. Health club privileges. Cr cds: A, C, D, DS, MC, V.

SC

★★ **OMNI AMBASSADOR EAST.** *1301 N State Parkway (60610), at Goethe St, Gold Coast. 312/787-7200; FAX 312/787-4760.* 275 rms, 17 story. S $170-$180; D $200-$210; each addl $20; suites $200-$400; under 17 free; wkend rates. Crib free. Valet parking $23.50. TV; cable (premium). Restaurant (see PUMP ROOM). Rm serv 24 hrs. Bar 11-1 am. Ck-out noon. Meeting rms. Business servs avail. Concierge. Barber, beauty shop. Airport transportation. Health club privileges. Minibars; microwaves avail. Cr cds: A, C, D, DS, JCB, MC, V.

D SC

★★★★ **OMNI CHICAGO HOTEL.** *676 N Michigan Ave (60611), north of the Loop. 312/944-6664; FAX 312/266-3015; res: 800/THE-OMNI.* Web ww.omnihotels.com. This hotel, with its marble floors, vaulted ceilings and art-deco touches of dark wood, occupies the first 25 floors of the 40-story City Place building, an office and retail complex. 347 rms, 25 story. S $275; D $295; suites $320-$2,000; under 12 free. Crib free. Parking in/out $24. TV; cable (premium), VCR avail. Indoor pool; whirlpool. Coffee in rms. Restaurant (see CIELO). Rm serv 24 hrs. Bar 11 am-midnight; entertainment. Ck-out noon. Meeting rms. Business center. In-rm modem link. Concierge. Exercise equipt; weight machine, bicycles, sauna. Minibars, wet bars; microwaves avail. Sun deck. Cr cds: A, C, D, DS, JCB, MC, V.

D SC

★★★ **PALMER HOUSE HILTON.** *17 E Monroe St (60603), at State St, the Loop. 312/726-7500; FAX 312/263-2556.* 1,639 rms, 23 story. S $175-$300; D $200-$325; each addl $25; suites from $650; family, wkend rates. Crib free. Pet accepted. Garage $15, valet $21.25. TV; cable (premium), VCR avail. Indoor pool; whirlpool. Complimentary coffee in rms. Restaurants 6:30-2 am. Bars 11:30-2 am; entertainment. Ck-out noon. Convention facilities. Business center. In-rm modem link. Concierge. Shopping arcade. Barber, beauty shop. Airport transportation. Exercise rm; instructor, weights, bicycles, sauna, steam rm. Massage. Minibars. Refrigerator in suites. Luxury level. Cr cds: A, C, D, DS, ER, JCB, MC, V.

D SC

✔★ **PARK BROMPTON INN.** *528 W Brompton Ave (60657), in Lakeview. 773/404-3499; res: 800/727-5108; FAX 773/404-3495.* Web www.cityinns.com. 52 rms, 4 story, 22 kit. suites. S $85; D $95; each addl $10; suites $99; under 12 free; wkend rates (2-day min). Crib free. Pet accepted, some restrictions; $200 deposit. Garage parking $7. TV; cable (premium). Complimentary continental bkfst. Restaurant nearby. Ck-out noon. No bellhops. Coin lndry. Health club privileges. Refrigerator, microwave, wet bar in suites. Cr cds: A, C, D, DS, ER, MC, V.

SC

★★★ **RADISSON.** *160 E Huron (60611), north of the Loop. 312/787-2900; FAX 312/787-5158.* E-mail radchgo@ix.netcom.com. 341 rms, 40 story, 96 suites. Apr-Dec: S $139-$199; D $134-$209; each addl $15; suites $179-$259; under 17 free; wkend rates; lower rates rest of yr. Crib free. Pet accepted, some restrictions. Valet parking $21. TV; cable (premium), VCR avail. Pool; poolside serv. Complimentary coffee in rms. Restaurant 6 am-11 pm. Rm serv 24 hrs. Bar noon-midnight. Ck-out noon. Convention facilities. Business center. In-rm modem link. Concierge. Gift shop. Barber. Exercise equipt; weight machine, bicycle. Minibars; some refrigerators; microwaves avail. Cr cds: A, C, D, DS, ER, JCB, MC, V.

D SC

★★ **RAMADA CONGRESS.** *520 S Michigan Ave (60605), south of the Loop. 312/427-3800; FAX 312/427-7264.* 840 rms, 8-14 story. S $75-$135; D $85-$155; each addl $20; suites $300-$700; under 17 free; higher rates Taste of Chicago. Crib free. Valet parking $17; garage $17. TV; cable, VCR avail. Complimentary coffee in rms. Restaurant 6:30 am-10:30 pm. Bar 5 pm-1 am. Ck-out noon. Convention facilities. Business servs avail. Concierge. Shopping arcade. Barber. Coin lndry. Exercise equipt; treadmill, stair machine. Cr cds: A, C, D, DS, ER, JCB, MC, V.

SC

★★ **RAPHAEL.** *201 E Delaware Place (60611), north of the Loop. 312/943-5000; FAX 312/943-9483; res: 800/821-5343.* 172 rms, 17 story, 72 suites. S, D $150-$200; each addl $20; under 12 free; suites $170-$250; wkend rates. Crib free. Valet parking, in/out $22.50. TV; cable (premium), VCR avail. Restaurant 6:30-11 am, 11:30 am-2 pm, 5-10 pm; Sun 5-9 pm. Rm serv. Bar 11-1:30 am; entertainment Fri, Sat. Ck-out 1 pm. Meeting rms. Health club privileges. Minibars. Cr cds: A, C, D, DS, MC, V.

D SC

★★★ **REGAL KNICKERBOCKER.** *163 E Walton Place (60611), north of the Loop. 312/751-8100; FAX 312/751-9205; res: 800/621-8140.* Web www.regalhotels.com/chicago. 305 rms, 14 story. S $145-$225, D $165-$245; each addl $20; suites $250-$1,000; under 18 free; wkend rates. Crib free. Valet parking, in/out $23.50. TV; cable (premium) VCR avail. Pool privileges. Restaurant (see NIX). Rm serv 24 hrs. Bar 11-2 am. Ck-out noon. Meeting rms. Business servs avail. In-rm modem link. Concierge. Indoor tennis privileges. Exercise equipt; weights, treadmill. Health club privileges. Minibars; some refrigerators. Luxury level. Cr cds: A, C, D, DS, JCB, MC, V.

D SC

★★★★ **RENAISSANCE.** *1 W Wacker Dr (60601), on the Chicago River, north of the Loop. 312/372-7200; FAX 312/372-0093.* Web www.renaissancehotels.com. The interior of this white-stone-and-glass lodging evokes a grand 19th-century hotel with its multiple fountains, crystal chandeliers, marble accents and grand staircase. All guest rooms have sitting areas and many offer dramatic river views. 553 units, 27 story. S $270-$350; D $290-$370; each addl $20; suites $500-$900; under 18 free; wkend plans. Crib free. Pet accepted, some restrictions. Garage; valet parking in/out $26. TV; cable (premium), VCR avail. Indoor pool; whirlpool, poolside serv. Restaurants 6 am-midnight (also see CUISINES). Rm serv 24 hrs. Bar 11-2 am; pianist, jazz trio. Ck-out 1 pm. Convention facilities. Business center. In-rm modem link. Concierge. Shopping arcade. Tennis privileges. Exercise rm; instructor, weight machine, bicycles, sauna. Massage. Minibars; bathrm phone in suites. Luxury level. Cr cds: A, C, D, DS, ER, JCB, MC, V.

D SC

★ ★ **RESIDENCE INN BY MARRIOTT.** *201 E Walton Place (60611), north of the Loop. 312/943-9800; FAX 312/943-8579.* 221 kit. suites, 19 story. Suites $169-$325; wkend, wkly, monthly rates. Crib free. Pet accepted, some restrictions; $5. Valet parking, in/out $22. TV; cable (premium). Pool privileges. Complimentary continental bkfst; afternoon refreshments. Complimentary coffee in rms. Restaurant adj 6:30 am-10 pm. Ck-out noon. Coin Indry. Meeting rms. Business servs avail. In-rm modem link. Exercise equipt; weight machine, bicycles. Health club privileges. Microwaves. One blk from Oak St beach. Cr cds: A, C, D, DS, JCB, MC, V.

D SC

★ ★ ★ ★ **THE RITZ-CARLTON.** *160 E Pearson St (60611), at Water Tower Place, north of the Loop. 312/266-1000; FAX 312/266-1194; res: 800/621-6906 (exc IL).* Magnificent flower arrangements, a fountain, wicker and palms set the tone in the two-story greenhouse lobby here. The guest rooms upstairs are spacious with mahagony furniture, cherry-wood armoires and wingback chairs. 429 rms, 31 story, 84 suites. S, D $315-$395; each addl $30; suites $415-$1,050; under 12 free; wkend rates, special packages. Crib free. Pet accepted. Parking in/out $25.50/day. TV; cable (premium), VCR avail. Heated pool $10; whirlpool. Restaurant 6:30-1 am (also see RITZ-CARLTON DINING ROOM). Rm serv 24 hrs. Bar from 11 am; Fri, Sat to 2 am. Ck-out 1 pm. Convention facilities. Business center. In-rm modem link. Concierge. Tennis privileges. Exercise rm; instructor, weights, bicycles, sauna, steam rm. Massage. Bathrm phones, minibars; refrigerators avail. Kennels avail. Cr cds: A, C, D, DS, ER, JCB, MC, V.

D

★ ★ **THE SENECA.** *200 E Chestnut St (60611), north of the Loop. 312/787-8900; FAX 312/988-4438; res: 800/800-6261.* 122 rms, 17 story, 85 kit. suites. S $149-$245; D $169-$265; each addl $20; under 12 free; wkend, hol rates. Crib $10. Valet parking $22. TV; cable (premium), VCR avail. Complimentary coffee in rms. Restaurants 7:30 am-10:30 pm. Bar from 11:30 am. Ck-out noon. Coin Indry. Meeting rms. Business servs avail. In-rm modem link. Concierge. Beauty shop. Exercise equipt; weights, bicycle. Refrigerators. Cr cds: A, C, D, DS, MC, V.

D SC

★ ★ ★ **SHERATON CHICAGO HOTEL & TOWERS.** *301 E North Water St (60611), Columbus Dr at Chicago River, north of the Loop. 312/464-1000; FAX 312/464-9140.* Web www.sheraton.com. 1,204 rms, 34 story, 54 suites. S $199-$269; D $219-$289; each addl $25; suites $350-$3500; under 17 free. Pet accepted, some restrictions. Garage, in/out $24. TV; cable (premium), VCR avail. Indoor pool. Complimentary coffee in rms. Restaurant 6-1 am. Rm serv 24 hrs. Bar 11-1:30 am; pianist. Ck-out noon. Convention facilities. Business center. In-rm modem link. Concierge. Gift shop. Tennis privileges. Exercise equipt; weight machines, bicycles, sauna. Massage. Minibars. On Chicago River, near Navy Pier. Views of Lake Michigan and skyline. Luxury level. Cr cds: A, C, D, DS, ER, JCB, MC, V.

D SC

★ ★ ★ **SUMMERFIELD SUITES.** *166 E Superior St (60611), north of the Loop. 312/787-6000; FAX 312/787-4331.* 120 suites, 29 story, 100 kit. suites. Mar-Dec: S, D $149-$259; each addl $25; under 16 free; wkend, hol rates; lower rates rest of yr. Crib free. Garage parking $17; valet $27. TV; cable (premium), VCR (movies). Heated pool. Complimentary full bkfst. Complimentary coffee in rms. Restaurant 11 am-10 pm. No rm serv. Bar from 5 pm. Ck-out noon. Coin Indry. Meeting rms. Business servs avail. In-rm modem link. Concierge. Barber. Exercise equipt; weights, bicycle. Health club privileges. Refrigerators, microwaves. Cr cds: A, C, D, DS, JCB, MC, V.

D SC

✔★ **SURF.** *555 W Surf St (60657), Lakeview. 773/528-8400; res: 800/787-3108; FAX 773/528-8483.* Web www.cityinns.com. 55 rms, 4 story. S $79-$89; D $99-$129; each addl $10; suites $99-$129; under 12 free; wkends (2-day min). Crib free. Pet accepted; $200 deposit. Garage parking $8. TV; cable. Complimentary continental bkfst. Restaurant nearby. No rm serv. Ck-out 11 am. In-rm modem link. No bellhops. Concierge. Health club privileges. Cr cds: A, C, D, DS, ER, JCB, MC, V.

SC

★ ★ ★ **SUTTON PLACE.** *21 E Bellevue Place (60611), Gold Coast. 312/266-2100; FAX 312/266-2103; res: 800/606-8188.* E-mail info@chi.suttonplace.com; web www.travelweb.com/sutton.html. 246 rms, 22 story, 40 suites. S $245-$270; D $260-$285; each addl $25; suites $315-$725; under 16 free; wkend rates. Crib free. Pet accepted, some restrictions; $200 refundable. Valet parking $24. TV; cable (premium), VCR (movies). Restaurant (see BRASSERIE BELLEVUE). Rm serv 24 hrs. Bar 11:30-1 am; Fri, Sat to 2 am. Ck-out noon. Meeting rms. Business center. In-rm modem link. Concierge. Airport transportation. Exercise equipt; stair machine, treadmill. Health club privileges. Bathrm phones, minibars. Penthouse suites with garden terrace. Cr cds: A, C, D, DS, JCB, MC, V.

D SC

★ ★ ★ **SWISSÔTEL.** *323 E Wacker Dr (60601), off Chicago River East, at Michigan Ave, south of the Loop. 312/565-0565; FAX 312/565-0540; res: 800/644-7263.* 630 rms, 43 story. S $309-$349; D $329-$369; each addl $20; suites $395-$2,500; under 14 free. Covered parking, in/out $26. TV; cable (premium), VCR avail. Indoor pool; whirlpool. Restaurant 6 am-10:30 pm. Rm serv 24 hrs. Bar 11-2 am. Ck-out 1 pm. Convention facilities. Business center. In-rm modem link. Concierge. Gift shop. Exercise rm; instructor, weight machines, bicycles, sauna. Massage. Bathrm phones, minibars. Panoramic views of city and Lake Michigan. Cr cds: A, C, D, DS, ER, JCB, MC, V.

★ ★ ★ **TREMONT.** *100 E Chestnut St (60611), north of the Loop. 312/751-1900; FAX 312/751-8691; res: 800/621-8133.* 129 rms, 16 story. S, D $225-$245; suites $345-$925; under 18 free; wkend rates. Crib free. Pet accepted, some restrictions. Parking $23. TV; cable (premium), VCR (movies). Coffee in rms. Restaurant 6:30 am-11 pm. Rm serv 24 hrs. Bar 11-midnight. Ck-out noon. Meeting rms. Business servs avail. In-rm modem link. Concierge. Bathrm phones, minibars; microwaves avail. Cr cds: A, C, D, DS, JCB, MC, V.

D

★ ★ ★ **WESTIN.** *909 N Michigan Ave (60611), at Delaware Place, north of the Loop. 312/943-7200; FAX 312/649-7447.* Web www.westin.com. 740 rms, 27 story. S, D $269-$329; each addl $20; suites $350-$1,500; under 18 free; package plans. Crib free. Pet accepted, some restrictions. Valet parking, in/out $25. TV; cable (premium). Restaurant 6:30 am-10 pm. Rm serv 24 hrs. Bar 11-1:30 am. Ck-out noon. Convention facilities. Business center. In-rm modem link. Concierge. Gift shop. Exercise equipt; weights, bicycles, sauna. Massage. Minibars; many bathrm phones; microwaves avail. Luxury level. Cr cds: A, C, D, DS, ER, JCB, MC, V.

D SC

★ ★ ★ ★ **WESTIN RIVER NORTH CHICAGO.** *320 N Dearborn St (60610), River North. 312/744-1900; FAX 312/527-2650.* The polished granite, black lacquer and mahogany interior of this hotel has an understated elegance. Floor-to-ceiling windows look out on a rock garden. Guest rooms are furnished in either contemporary or traditional style. 422 rms, 20 story. S $275-$315; D $270-$310; each addl $25; suites $450-$2,500 under 18 free; special packages. Crib free. Pet accepted, some restrictions. Valet parking $26 in/out. TV; cable (premium), VCR avail. Coffee in rms. Restaurant 6:30 am-11 pm (also see CELEBRITY CAFE). Rm serv 24 hrs. Bar 11-1:30 am; pianist 6 days. Ck-out noon. Convention facilities. Business center. In-rm modem link. Concierge. Exercise rm; instructor, weights, bicycles, sauna. Massage. Bathrm phones, minibars. Cr cds: A, C, D, DS, ER, JCB, MC, V.

D SC

★ ★ ★ **WHITEHALL.** *105 E Delaware (60611), north of the Loop. 312/944-6300; FAX 312/944-8552; res: 800/948-4255.* E-mail chiwhitehall@worldnet.att.net; web www.preferredhotels.com/preferred.html. 221 rms, 21 story. S, D $285-$385; each addl $25; suites $550-$2,000; under 12 free; wkly, wkend rates. Crib free. Valet parking $24.50. Restaurant 6:30 am-10 pm. Rm serv 24 hrs. Bar from 11 am. Ck-out noon. Meeting rms. Business servs avail. In-rm modem link. Concierge. Exercise equipt; weight machines, treadmills. Health club privileges. Minibars. Luxury level. Cr cds: A, C, D, DS, JCB, MC, V.

D SC

Inn

★ ★ **GOLD COAST GUEST HOUSE.** *113 W Elm St (60610), Gold Coast. 312/337-0361; FAX 312/337-0362.* Web www.bbchicago.com. 4 rms, 2 with shower only, 3 story. Apr-Dec: S, D $119-$165; wkly rates; lower rates rest of yr. TV; VCR avail. Complimentary continental bkfst. Restaurant nearby. Ck-out noon. Business servs avail. Indoor tennis privileges. Health club privileges. Renovated brick townhome built in 1873. Cr cds: A, DS, MC, V.

Restaurants

★ ★ ★ ★ **AMBRIA.** *(See Belden-Stratford Hotel) 773/472-5959.* The mood is retro-elegance at this restaurant housed in a turn-of-the-century hotel and decorated with dark wood and Art Nouveau fixtures. French, continental menu. Specializes in fresh seafood, seasonal offerings. Menu changes seasonally; daily specialties. Own baking. Hrs: 6-9:30 pm; Fri, Sat to 10:30 pm. Closed Sun; major hols. Res accepted. Bar. Wine list. A la carte entrees: dinner $22-$30. Prix fixe: dinner $48 & $64. Valet parking. Chef-owned. Cr cds: A, C, D, DS, JCB, MC, V.

D

✔★ **ANN SATHER.** *929 W Belmont Ave, Lakeview. 312/348-2378.* Web www.gwebb.com/a/ann.html. Hrs: 7 am-10 pm; Fri, Sat to 11 pm. Swedish, Amer menu. Bar. A la carte entrees: bkfst $3.75-$6.75, lunch & dinner $4.25-$6.95. Complete meals: lunch, dinner $6.95-$10.95. Specializes in Swedish pancakes, beefsteak, fresh fish. Bkfst menu avail all day. Opened 1945. Cr cds: A, MC, V.

D SC

★ ★ ★ ★ **ARUN'S.** *4156 N Kedzie Ave, north of the Loop. 773/539-1909.* This bi-level dining room has lots of natural wood, complemented by Thai art and a small art gallery—world's apart from the typical storefront ethnic restaurant. Seafood is a must; daily specials supplement the extensive basic menu. Thai menu; special "chef-designed" menus. Specialties: phad Thai, three-flavored red snapper, spicy roast eggplant. Hrs: 5-10 pm; Sun to 9 pm. Closed Mon; major hols. Res accepted. Bar. A la carte entrees: dinner $11.95-$24.95. Cr cds: A, C, D, DS, MC, V.

★ ★ ★ **AVANZARE.** *161 E Huron St, north of the Loop. 312/337-8056.* Hrs: 11:30 am-2 pm, 5:30-9:30 pm; Fri to 10:30 pm; Sat 5-10:30 pm; Sun 5-9 pm. Closed major hols. Res accepted. Italian menu. Bar. A la carte entrees: lunch $11-$17, dinner $13-$26. Specialties: grilled prime veal chop with wild mushroom lasagna, seared salmon with artichokes & tomatoes, pappardelle with shrimp & calamari. Own pasta. Outdoor dining. Contemporary decor with Frank Lloyd Wright accents; Virginio Ferrari sculptures. Cr cds: A, C, D, DS, JCB, MC, V.

D

★ ★ **BELLA VISTA.** *1001 W Belmont Ave, Lakeview. 773/404-0111.* Hrs: 11:30 am-2:30 pm, 5-11 pm; Fri to midnight; Sat 5 pm-midnight; Sun 5-9 pm. Closed Thanksgiving, Dec 25. Res accepted. Contemporary Italian menu. Bar. A la carte entrees: lunch $6-$10.50, dinner $9-$17.95. Specialties: fire-roasted calamari with lemon rosemary sauce, grilled salmon with angel hair pasta. Valet parking (dinner). Contemporary, eclectic decor. In renovated bank building (1929). Cr cds: A, D, DS, MC, V.

D

✔★ ★ **BEN PAO.** *52 W Illinois St (60610), River North. 312/222-1888.* Hrs: 11:30 am-2 pm, 5-10 pm; Fri to 11 pm; Sat 5-11 pm; Sun 4-9 pm. Closed most major hols. Res accepted. Chinese menu. Bar. A la carte entrees: lunch $7.95-$10.95, dinner $8.95-$16.95. Child's meals. Specializes in grilled satays, black peppered scallops, seven-flavored chicken. Own desserts. Valet parking. Outdoor dining. Dramatic Chinese decor with waterfall columns. Cr cds: A, C, D, DS, JCB, MC, V.

D

★ **BERGHOFF.** *17 W Adams St, the Loop. 312/427-3170.* Web www.Berghoff.chicago.com. Hrs: 11 am-9 pm; Fri to 9:30 pm; Sat to 10 pm. Closed Sun; major hols. Res accepted. German, Amer menu. Semi-a la carte: lunch $6.50-$11, dinner $9-$17. Child's meals. Specialties: Wienerschnitzel, chicken Dijon, sauerbraten. In 1881 building. Family-owned since 1898. Cr cds: A, MC, V.

D

★ ★ **BICE.** *158 E Ontario St, north of the Loop. 312/664-1474.* Hrs: 11:30 am-10:30 pm; Fri, Sat to 11:30 pm. Closed Jan 1, Dec 25. Res accepted. Northern Italian menu. Bar. A la carte entrees: lunch $11-$20, dinner $14-$25. Own pastries, desserts, pasta. Valet parking (dinner). Outdoor dining. Contemporary Italian decor. Cr cds: A, C, D, MC, V.

★ ★ **THE BIG DOWNTOWN.** *(See Palmer House Hilton Hotel) 312/917-7399.* Hrs: 11-2 am. Res accepted (dinner). Bar. Semi-a la carte: lunch $8-$16, dinner $10-$22. Specialties: barbecue ribs, rotisserie chicken, banana tiramisu. Own baking. Blues & jazz Fri, Sat. 1940s-style diner with jazz memorabilia, miniature replica of the Chicago El. Cr cds: A, C, D, DS, ER, JCB, MC, V.

D

★ ★ ★ **BIGGS.** *1150 N Dearborn St (60610), Gold Coast. 312/787-0900.* Hrs: 5-10 pm. Closed some major hols. Res accepted. Continental menu. Bar. Wine cellar. A la carte entrees: dinner $17.95-$32.95. Specialties: beef Wellington, rack of lamb, caviar. Valet parking. Outdoor dining. Formal dining in mansion built 1874. Original oil paintings. Cr cds: A, C, D, DS, MC, V.

★ ★ **BISTRO 110.** *110 E Pearson St, north of the Loop. 312/266-3110.* Hrs: 11:30 am-11 pm; Fri, Sat to midnight; Sun brunch 11 am-4 pm. Closed some major hols. Res accepted. French, Amer menu. Bar. A la carte entrees: lunch $7.95-$15.95, dinner $10.95-$24.95. Sun Jazz brunch $6.95-$14.95. Specializes in chicken prepared in wood-burning oven, fish. Valet parking. Outdoor dining. French bistro atmosphere. Cr cds: A, C, D, DS, MC, V.

D

★ ★ **BLACKHAWK LODGE.** *41 E Superior St, north of the Loop. 312/280-4080.* Hrs: 11:30 am-3 pm, 5-10 pm; Fri, Sat to 11 pm; Bluegrass Sun brunch 11 am-3 pm. Closed some major hols. Res accepted. Bar. Semi-a la carte: lunch $7.95-$15.95, dinner $12.95-$22.95. Sun brunch $7.95-$14.95. Specializes in fresh fish, smoked tenderloin of beef, seasonal game. Valet parking. Outdoor dining on screened porch. Lodge atmosphere; eclectic artifacts. Cr cds: A, C, D, DS, MC, V.

D

✔★ **BLUE MESA.** *1729 N Halsted St (60614), Lincoln Park. 312/944-5990.* Hrs: 11:30 am-2:30 pm, 5-10:30 pm; Fri to 11:30 pm; Sat 11:30 am-midnight; Sun 4-10 pm; Sun brunch 11 am-2:30 pm. Closed Thanksgiving, Dec 25. Res accepted. Southwestern menu. Bar. Semi-a la carte: lunch, dinner $6.95-$13.95. Sun brunch $6.95-$12.95. Child's meals. Specialties: blue corn chicken enchilada, stuffed sopaipilla, fajitas. Valet parking. Outdoor dining. Cr cds: A, C, D, DS, MC, V.

D

★ ★ ★ **BOULEVARD.** *(See Inter-Continental Hotel) 312/321-8888.* Hrs: 6:30-10:30 am, 11:30 am-2 pm, 6-10 pm; Sat from 6 pm. Closed Sun; some major hols. Res accepted (lunch, dinner). Mediterranean menu. Bar. Wine cellar. Complete meal: bkfst $10-$15. A la carte entrees: lunch $8-$18, dinner $11-$30. Child's meals. Specialties: cornmeal-crust pizza, paella Valencia, tapas. Own baking, pasta. Jazz Wed-Sat. Formal dining in elegant atmosphere with ornate ceiling, artwork. Cr cds: A, C, D, DS, JCB, MC, V.

D ♥

★ ★ **BRASSERIE BELLEVUE.** *(See Sutton Place Hotel) 312/266-9212.* E-mail info@chi.suttonplace.com; web www.travelweb.com/sut ton.html. Hrs: 7 am-11 pm; Sun brunch 11 am-2:30 pm. Res accepted. Contemporary American, Bistro menu. Bar. Semi-a la carte: bkfst $7.95-$10.95, lunch $7.95-$15.95, dinner $9-$26.95. Sun brunch $13.95. Valet parking. Outdoor dining. Modern decor with Art Deco accent. Cr cds: A, C, D, DS, JCB, MC, V.

D

★ ★ ★ **BRASSERIE JO.** *59 W Hubbard St (60610), River North. 312/595-0800.* Hrs: 11:30 am-midnight; Fri to 1 am; Sat 5 pm-1 am; Sun from 4 pm. Closed Thanksgiving, Dec 24, 25. Res accepted. French menu. Bar. Wine cellar. Semi-a la carte: lunch $7.95-$15.95, dinner $9.50-$19.95. Specialties: smoked salmon, onion tart Uncle Hansi, Brasserie steak pomme frites. Own baking, pasta. Valet parking. Outdoor dining. Authentic French brasserie decor; casual European elegance. Cr cds: A, C, D, DS, JCB, MC, V.

D

★ ★ ★ **BUCKINGHAM'S.** *(See Hilton & Towers Hotel) 312/294-6600.* Web www.hilton.com. Hrs: 5:30-10 pm; Sun brunch 10 am-2 pm. Res accepted. Bar. Wine list. A la carte entrees: dinner $16.50-$26.95. Sun brunch $37.95. Prix fixe: dinner $33.95. Child's meals. Specialties: Australian lamb chops, Buckingham's porterhouse, Maryland crab cakes. Own baking. Valet parking. Elegant decor; cherrywood pillars, Italian marble; artwork. Cr cds: A, C, D, DS, ER, JCB, MC, V.

D

★ ★ **CAPE COD ROOM.** *(See The Drake Hotel) 312/787-2200.* Web www.hilton.com. Hrs: noon-11 pm. Closed Dec 25. Res accepted. International seafood menu. Bar. Semi-a la carte: lunch, dinner $19-$37. Specialties: Maryland crab cakes, turbot, bookbinder's soup. Own baking. Valet parking. Nautical decor. View of Lake Michigan. Cr cds: A, C, D, DS, ER, JCB, MC, V.

D

★ ★ ★ **CELEBRITY CAFE.** *(See Westin River North Chicago Hotel) 312/836-5499.* Hrs: 6:30-11 am, 11:30 am-10:30 pm; Fri, Sat to 11 pm; Sun brunch 10 am-2 pm. Res accepted. Bar from 11 am. A la carte entrees: bkfst $7-$13, lunch $6-$14, dinner $14-$25. Sun brunch $39. Child's meals. Specialties: sea bass wrapped in crispy potato, grilled 16-oz prime sirloin steak, grilled salmon with honey-mustard glaze. Menu changes seasonally. Own pastries. Valet parking. Overlooks Chicago River. Cr cds: A, C, D, DS, ER, JCB, MC, V.

D

★ **CENTRO.** *710 N Wells St, River North. 312/988-7775.* Hrs: 11 am-11 pm; Fri, Sat to 11:30 pm; Sun 4-10 pm. Closed Easter, Dec 25. Res accepted. Italian menu. Bar. A la carte entrees: lunch $6-$12, dinner $7.50-$25. Specialties: pappardelle, chicken Vesuvio, baked cavatelli. Valet parking. Outdoor dining. Bistro atmosphere. Cr cds: A, C, D, DS, MC, V.

D

✔★ ★ **CHAPULIN.** *1962 N Halsted St (60614), Lincoln Park. 773/665-8677.* Hrs: 5-10:30 pm; Fri, Sat to 11:30 pm. Closed Mon; major hols. Res accepted. Mexican menu. Bar. Semi-a la carte: dinner $10-$19. Specialties: molcajete with grilled chicken, grilled pork loin in anchiote, red snapper Vera Cruz. Valet parking. Mexican decor with vibrant colors, original artwork by local artist Oscar Romero. Cr cds: A, C, D, DS, MC, V.

D

★ ★ ★ ★ ★ **CHARLIE TROTTER'S.** *816 W Armitage Ave, Lincoln Park. 773/248-6228.* A young culinary wizard named Charlie Trotter puts his magic to work in a contemporary restaurant offering two six-course dinner menus, one of them a vegetable tasting menu. There are three dining rooms, plus a chic table for four set up in the busy kitchen. American menu with French and Asian influences. Specialties: hand-harvested sea scallop, organic beef strip loin, artichoke & goat cheese terrine. Two dégustation menus available nightly. Own baking. Hrs: 5:30-10 pm. Closed Sun, Mon; major hols. Res required. Bar. Wine cellars. A la carte entrees: dinner $32-$40. Table d'hôte (dégustation menu): dinner $70-$90. Valet parking. Chef-owned. Jacket. Totally nonsmoking. Cr cds: A, C, D, JCB, MC, V.

D

★ ★ **CHICAGO CHOP HOUSE.** *60 W Ontario St (60610), River North. 312/787-7100.* Hrs: 11:30 am-11 pm; Fri to 11:30 pm; Sat 4-11:30 pm; Sun 4-11 pm. Closed some major hols. Res accepted. Bar. Semi-a la carte: lunch $5.95-$18.95, dinner $15.95-$28.95. Specializes in prime rib, NY strip steak, lamb chops. Valet parking. Entertainment. Turn-of-the-century Chicago decor. Cr cds: A, C, D, DS, JCB, MC, V.

★ ★ ★ **CIELO.** *(See Omni Chicago Hotel) 312/944-7676.* Hrs: 6:30 am-10 pm; Fri, Sat to 11 pm; Sun brunch 10:30 am-2 pm. Res accepted. Mediterranean menu. Bar to midnight. Wine list. A la carte entrees: bkfst $4.95-$11.95, lunch $8.25-$12.50, dinner $8.50-$30. Sun brunch $24.95. Specialties: soft shell crabs, wood-burned pizza. Pianist, vocalist Tues-Sat. Valet parking. Elegant, stylish dining with view of city. Original art. Cr cds: A, C, D, DS, JCB, MC, V.

D

★ ★ **CLUB GENE & GEORGETTI.** *500 N Franklin St (60610), River North. 312/527-3718.* Hrs: 11:30 am-midnight. Closed Sun; major hols; also 1st wk July. Res accepted. Italian, Amer menu. Bar. Semi-a la carte: lunch $7-$18, dinner $12.50-$23.50. Specialties: prime strip steak, filet mignon, chicken Vesuvio. Valet parking. Chicago saloon atmosphere. Family-owned. Cr cds: A, C, D, MC, V.

D

★ ★ ★ **COCO PAZZO.** *300 W Hubbard St, River North. 312/836-0900.* Hrs: 11:30 am-2:30 pm, 5:30-10:30 pm; Fri to 11 pm; Sat 5:30-11 pm; Sun 5-10 pm. Closed major hols. Res accepted. Italian menu. Serv bar. Semi-a la carte: lunch $10.95-$16, dinner $12-$27. Specializes in Tuscan dishes, cacciucco, bistecca alla Florentina. Own baking. Valet parking. Outdoor dining. Contemporary decor. Cr cds: A, C, D, MC, V.

D

★ ★ **COMO INN.** *546 N Milwaukee Ave, north of the Loop. 312/421-5222.* Hrs: 11:30 am-11 pm; Fri, Sat to midnight; Sun noon-11 pm. Closed some major hols. Res accepted. Northern Italian menu. Bar. A la carte entrees: lunch $5.95-$12.95, dinner $12.95-$22.95. Child's meals. Specialties: chicken Vesuvio, veal al limone, veal Marsala. Pianist (dinner). Valet parking. Italian decor; antiques. Family-owned. Cr cds: A, C, D, DS, MC, V.

D

★ ★ **CON FUSION.** *1616 N Damen Ave (60647), in Bucktown, north of the Loop. 773/772-7100.* Hrs: 11:30 am-2 pm, 5:30-10 pm; Fri to 11 pm; Sat 5:30-11 pm; Sun 5:30-9 pm. Closed major hols. Res accepted. Fusion menu. Bar. A la carte entrees: lunch $8-$9, dinner $14-$23. Specialties: tuna tartar with ginger wasabi dressing, sautéed breast of duck in black peppercorn sauce, roasted loin of ostrich. Own baking. Valet parking. Outdoor dining. Minimalist decor with black and white furnishings. Cr cds: A, D, MC, V.

D

★ ★ ★ **CUISINES.** *(See Renaissance Hotel) 312/372-4459.* Hrs: 11:30 am-2 pm, 5:30-10:30 pm. Closed major hols. Res accepted. Mediterranean menu. Bar. Wine cellar. Semi-a la carte: lunch $6.95-$16.95, dinner $6.95-$24.95. Specialities: veal medallions with wild mushrooms, crabmeat & Shiitake mushrooms in phyllo with smoked tomato coulis, seared snapper with artichokes. Valet parking. Intimate dining in Mediterranean atmosphere. Cr cds: A, C, D, DS, ER, JCB, MC, V.

D

★ ★ **ELI'S THE PLACE FOR STEAK.** *215 E Chicago Ave, north of the Loop. 312/642-1393.* Hrs: 11 am-3 pm, 5-10:30 pm; Fri to 11 pm; Sat, Sun from 5 pm. Closed major hols. Res accepted. Bar to midnight. Semi-a la carte: lunch $8.95-$12.95, dinner $19.95-$32.95. Specializes in steak, liver. Own cheesecake. Piano bar. Valet parking. Club-like atmosphere; original artwork of Chicago scenes. Cr cds: A, C, D, DS, MC, V.

D

★ **EMILIO'S TAPAS.** *444 W Fullerton St (60614), Lincoln Park. 773/327-5100.* Hrs: 11:30 am-10 pm; Fri, Sat to 11 pm. Closed major hols. Res accepted. Spanish tapas menu. Bar. A la carte entrees: lunch $3.50-$7.95, dinner $3.50-$16.95. Specialties: garlic potato salad, baked goat cheese, paella de mariscos. Own pastries. Valet parking. Outdoor dining. Casual Spanish garden atmosphere; overlooks courtyard. Cr cds: A, D, MC, V.

D

★ **EMPEROR'S CHOICE.** *2238 S Wentworth Ave, Chinatown. 312/225-8800.* Hrs: 11:45-12:30 am; Sun to 11:30 pm. Cantonese seafood menu. Serv bar. A la carte entrees: lunch, dinner $6.95-$19.95. Semi-a la carte (Mon-Fri): lunch $5.95-$9.95. Prix fixe: dinner for two $38-$58. Specialties: whole steamed oysters with black bean sauce, lobster, poached shrimp in shell with soy dip. Chinese artifacts including Ching dynasty emperor's robe; ink drawings of emperors from each dynasty. Cr cds: A, DS, MC, V.

D

★ ★ ★ **ENTRE NOUS.** *(See Fairmont Hotel) 312/565-7997.* Hrs: 5:30-10:30 pm; Sat to 11 pm. Closed Sun. Res accepted. Continental menu. Bar. Extensive wine list. Semi-a la carte: dinner $18-$27. Prix fixe: dinner $29. Specializes in regional Amer cuisine, seasonal dishes. Pianist. Valet parking. Elegant dining. Cr cds: A, C, D, DS, ER, JCB, MC, V.

D

✔★ ★ **ERWIN.** *2995 N Halsted St (60657), Lakeview. 773/528-7200.* Hrs: 5:30-10 pm; Fri, Sat to 11 pm; Sun 5-9:30 pm; Sun brunch 10:30 am-2:30 pm. Closed Mon; most major hols. Res accepted. Bar. Semi-a la carte: dinner $12.95-$16.95. Sun brunch $3.95-$9.95. Specializes in smoked trout appetizers, wood-grilled pork tenderloin, fresh seafood. Valet parking. Casual bistro atmosphere. Cr cds: A, C, D, DS, MC, V.

D

★ ★ ★ ★ ★ **EVEREST.** *440 S La Salle St, 40th floor of Midwest Stock Exchange, the Loop. 312/663-8920.* Chef/owner Jean Joho has brought fine Alsatian cuisine and a broad array of appropriate wines to this 40th-floor, art deco-ish aerie with African safari murals in a downtown Chicago financial skycraper. Creative French menu with Alsatian influence. Specialties: marbre of cold bouillabaisse, seafood and shellfish; Maine lobster with Alsace gewurztraminer and ginger; poached tenderloin of beef, pot au feu style, with horseradish cream. Hrs: 5:30-9:30 pm (last sitting); Fri, Sat to 10 pm (last sitting). Closed Sun, Mon; major hols. Res required. Serv bar. Extensive wine list; specializes in wines from Alsace. A la carte entrees: dinner $23-$35. Prix fixe: 8-course dinner $79. Free valet parking. Chef-owned. Jacket. Cr cds: A, C, D, DS, JCB, MC, V.

D

★ ★ ★ **FRONTERA GRILL.** *445 N Clark St, River North. 312/661-1434.* Hrs: 11:30 am-2:30 pm, 5-10 pm; Fri to 11 pm; Sat 5-11 pm; Sat brunch 10:30 am-2:30 pm. Closed Sun, Mon. Mexican menu. Bar. A la carte entrees: lunch $8-$12, dinner $9-$18.95. Sat brunch $5.95-$9.50. Specialties: grilled fresh fish, duck breast adobo, carne asada. Valet parking. Outdoor dining. Regional Mexican cuisine; casual dining. Cr cds: A, C, D, DS, MC, V.

D

★ **GEJA'S.** *340 W Armitage Ave, Lincoln Park. 773/281-9101.* Hrs: 5-10:30 pm; Fri to midnight; Sat to 12:30 am; Sun 4:30-10 pm. Closed some major hols. Res accepted Sun-Thurs. Fondue menu. Bar. Complete meals: dinner $18.50-$29.95. Specializes in cheese, meat, seafood & dessert fondues. Flamenco and classical guitarist nightly. Variety of wines, sold by the glass. Cr cds: A, C, D, DS, MC, V.

★ ★ ★ **GIBSONS STEAKHOUSE.** *1028 N Rush St (60611), north of the Loop. 312/266-8999.* Hrs: 3 pm-1 am; Sun 4 pm-midnight. Closed major hols. Bar 3 pm-2 am. Wine list. Semi-a la carte: dinner $10-$32. Specializes in prime-aged steak, Chicago-cut steak, fresh seafood. Pianist in bar nightly. Valet parking. Art deco decor. Cr cds: A, C, D, DS, MC, V.

D

★ ★ ★ **GORDON.** *500 N Clark St, River North. 312/467-9780.* Hrs: noon-2 pm, 5:30-9:30 pm; Mon from 5:30 pm; Fri to 11:30 pm; Sat 5:30 pm-midnight; Sun 5-9:30 pm. Closed major hols. Res accepted. Bar. Wine list. A la carte entrees: lunch $8-$15, dinner $14-$29. Pre-theatre menu (3 courses): $29. Specialties: original artichoke fritter, flourless chocolate cake. Menu changes seasonally. Own pastries, ice cream. Pianist nightly, jazz trio Sat (winter). Valet parking. Jacket (dinner). Cr cds: A, C, D, DS, JCB, MC, V.

D

★ ★ **GRAPPA.** *200 E Chestnut St (60611), north of the Loop. 312/337-4500.* Hrs: 11:30 am-2:30 pm, 5-10 pm; Fri, Sat to 11 pm. Closed most major hols. Res accepted. Italian menu. Bar. Semi-a la carte: lunch $7.95-$12.95, dinner $11.95-$24.95. Specialties: grilled tuna, rabbit, seafood stew. Valet parking. Sophisticated trattoria-style decor; open cooking area. Cr cds: A, C, D, DS, JCB, MC, V.

D

✔★ ★ **GREEK ISLANDS.** *200 S Halsted St, Greektown. 312/782-9855.* Hrs: 11 am-midnight; Fri, Sat to 1 am. Closed Thanksgiving, Dec 25. Res accepted Sun-Thurs. Greek, Amer menu. Bar. A la carte entrees: lunch $5-$8.50, dinner $5.95-$15.95. Complete meals: lunch, dinner $9.95-$16.95. Specialties: lamb with artichoke, broiled red snapper, saganaki. Valet parking. Greek decor; 5 dining areas. Family-owned. Cr cds: A, C, D, DS, MC, V.

D

★ ★ **HARRY CARAY'S.** *33 W Kinzie St, at Dearborn St, River North. 312/828-0966.* Web www.harrycarays.com. Hrs: 11:30 am-3 pm, 5-10:30 pm; Fri to 11 pm; Sat 5-11 pm; Sun 4-10 pm. Closed Dec 25. Res accepted. Italian, Amer menu. Bar. A la carte entrees: lunch, dinner $8.95-$39.95. Specializes in chicken Vesuvio, lamb chop oreganato, steak. Valet parking. Baseball memorabilia. Cr cds: A, C, D, DS, MC, V.

D

✔★ ★ **HAT DANCE.** *325 W Huron St, River North. 312/649-0066.* Hrs: 11:30 am-2 pm, 5:30-10 pm; Fri to 11:30 pm; Sat 11:30 am-3:30 pm, 5-11:30 pm; Sun 5-9 pm. Closed most major hols. Res accepted. Nouvelle Mexican menu. Bar. A la carte entrees: lunch $6-$10.95, dinner $7.95-$15.95. Specialties: corn pudding, marinated pork chops, wood-roasted chicken. Valet parking evenings. Outdoor snack bar. Unique decor with Aztec accents. Cr cds: A, C, D, DS, MC, V.

D

★ ★ **HATSUHANA.** *160 E Ontario St, north of the Loop. 312/280-8808.* Hrs: 11:45 am-2 pm, 5:30-10 pm; Sat from 5 pm. Closed Sun; some major hols. Res accepted. Japanese menu. Serv bar. A la carte entrees: lunch $9-$19, dinner $10-$24. Complete meals: dinner $14-$26. Specialties: tempura, Hatsuhana and sushi specials. Sushi bar. Traditional Japanese decor. Cr cds: A, C, D, JCB, MC, V.

D

★ **HOUSE OF HUNAN.** *535 N Michigan Ave, north of the Loop. 312/329-9494.* Hrs: 11:30 am-10:30 pm. Closed Thanksgiving. Res accepted. Chinese menu. Bar. Semi-a la carte: lunch $6.95-$9.50, dinner $8.95-$19.95. Specialties: spicy beef & scallops, Neptune delight, empress chicken. Chinese decor. Cr cds: A, C, D, DS, JCB, MC, V.

D

★ ★ **IL TOSCANACCIO.** *636 N St Clair St (60611), north of the Loop. 312/664-2777.* Hrs: 7:30-10 am, 11:30 am-2:30 pm; 5:30-10:30 pm; Fri to 11 pm; Sat 5:30-11 pm; Sun 5-10 pm; Sat, Sun brunch 11:30 am-3 pm. Res accepted. Italian menu. Bar. A la carte entrees: bkfst $1.50-$2.50, lunch $11.50-$15, dinner $11-$17. Sat, Sun brunch $8-$12. Specialties:

rigatoni Toscanaccio, grilled portabello mushroom with roasted peppers, salmon filet sautéed with shrimp. Own pasta. Valet parking (dinner). Outdoor dining. Casual, rustic Italian atmosphere with murals, wrought-iron fixtures. Cr cds: A, D, MC, V.

D

★ ★ **IRON MIKE'S GRILLE.** *(See Tremont Hotel) 312/587-8989.* Hrs: 7 am-11 pm; Sun brunch 11 am-3 pm. Res accepted. Bar. Buffet: bkfst $8.95. A la carte entrees: lunch $10-$15, dinner $30-$45. Sun brunch $10-$15. Specialties: duck cigar, Iron Mike's 20-oz pork chop, paddle steak. Own baking. Pianist exc Mon. Valet parking. Outdoor dining. Sports club atmosphere; tribute to former Chicago Bears coach. Cr cds: A, C, D, DS, ER, JCB, MC, V.

D

✔★ ★ **KIKI'S BISTRO.** *900 N Franklin (60610), River North. 312/335-5454.* Hrs: 11:30 am-10 pm; Fri to 11 pm; Sat 5-11 pm. Closed Sun; major hols. Res accepted. French Provençale menu. Bar. Semi-a la carte: lunch $7-$14.50, dinner $12-$17. Specialties: roasted chicken, sautéed duck breast with leg confit, sautéed calves liver with pearl onions. Own desserts, ice cream. Rustic, country-French decor with unfinished woodwork, brick walls. Cr cds: A, C, D, DS, MC, V.

D

★ ★ **KLAY OVEN.** *414 N Orleans St, River North. 312/527-3999.* Hrs: 11:30 am-2:30 pm, 5:30-10:30 pm. Closed major hols. Res accepted. Indian menu. Bar. A la carte entrees: lunch buffet $7.95, dinner $6.95-$25.95. Specialties: sikandari champa, tandoori batera, jheenga bemisaal. Tableside preparation in elegant surroundings. Modern Indian art display. Cr cds: A, D, MC, V.

D

★ ★ ★ **LA STRADA.** *155 N Michigan Ave, opp Grant Park, at Randolph St, the Loop. 312/565-2200.* Hrs: 11:30 am-10 pm; Fri to 11 pm, Sat 5-11 pm; early-bird dinner 5-6:30 pm. Closed Sun; some major hols. Res accepted. Northern Italian menu. Bar. Wine cellar. A la carte entrees: lunch $11-$15, dinner $11-$29. Specialties: zuppe de pesce, red snapper, veal scaloppini. Own baking, desserts. Pianist from 5 pm. Valet parking. Tableside cooking. Cr cds: A, C, D, DS, MC, V.

D

★ ★ ★ **LAWRY'S THE PRIME RIB.** *100 E Ontario St, north of the Loop. 312/787-5000.* Hrs: 11:30 am-2 pm, 5-11 pm; Fri, Sat to midnight; Sun 3-10 pm. Closed July 4, Dec 25. Res accepted. Bar. Wine list. Semi-a la carte: lunch $5.75-$10.95, dinner $19.95-$29.95. Child's meals. Specializes in prime rib, English trifle. Own baking. Valet parking (dinner). In 1896 McCormick mansion. Chicago counterpart of famous California restaurant. Cr cds: A, C, D, DS, JCB, MC, V.

SC

✔★ **LE BOUCHON.** *1958 N Damen Ave (60647), in Bucktown, north of the Loop. 773/862-6600.* Hrs: 5:30-11 pm; Fri, Sat 5 pm-midnight. Closed Sun; major hols. Res accepted. French menu. Bar. Semi-a la carte: dinner $11-$14.95. Specialties: roast duck for two, Jean Claude onion tart, maravis au choclat. Own pastries, desserts. French bistro decor with lace curtains, pressed-tin ceiling. Cr cds: A, C, D, DS, MC, V.

★ ★ ★ **LES NOMADES.** *222 E Ontario St (60611), north of the Loop. 312/649-9010.* Hrs: 5-9:30 pm; Fri, Sat to 10:30 pm. Closed Sun, Mon; most major hols. Res accepted. French menu. Bar. Wine list. A la carte entrees: dinner $18-$26. Specialties: grilled razor clams, cochon de lait braised in white wine and Dijon mustard. Own baking, pasta. Valet parking. Contemporary French decor; polished woods, tile murals, zinc bar. Jacket. Totally nonsmoking. Cr cds: A, C, D, MC, V.

★ ★ **MAGGIANO'S.** *516 N Clark St (60610), River North. 312/644-7700.* Hrs: 11:30 am-2 pm, 5-10 pm; Fri to 11 pm; Sat 11:30 am-11 pm; Sun noon-10 pm. Closed Thanksgiving, Dec 25. Res accepted. Southern Italian menu. Bar. A la carte entrees: lunch $7.95-$14.95, dinner $9.95-$29.95. Specialties: Maggiano's salad, country-style rigatoni, roasted chicken with rosemary. Own baking. Valet parking. Outdoor dining. 1940s, family-style decor with wood columns and bistro-style seating. Cr cds: A, C, D, DS, MC, V.

D

★ ★ **MANGO.** *712 N Clark St (60610), River North. 312/337-5440.* Hrs: 11:30 am-2 pm, 5-11 pm; Fri to midnight; Sat 5 pm-midnight; Sun 4-9 pm. Closed most major hols. Res accepted. Contemporary Amer menu. Bar. A la carte entrees: lunch $8-$13, dinner $9-$17. Specialties: duck mango with proscuitto, Mediterranean fish soup, Wright's flourless chocolate cake. Own baking. Lively atmosphere with vibrant colors, artwork. Cr cds: A, C, D, DS, MC, V.

D

✔★ ★ ★ **MARCHÉ.** *833 Randolph St, north of the Loop. 312/226-8399.* Hrs: 11:30 am-2 pm, 5:30-10 pm; Thurs to 11 pm; Fri to midnight; Sat 5:30 pm-midnight; Sun from 5:30 pm. Closed major hols. Res accepted. French menu. Bar. Wine list. A la carte entrees: lunch $8-$15, dinner $13-$29. Specialties: spit-roasted chicken with pommes frites, spit-roasted rabbit with lavender sauce, yellowfin tuna. Own baking, desserts. Valet parking, Contemporary decor with custom-crafted furnishings, open kitchens. Cr cds: A, C, D, MC, V.

D

✔★ ★ **MIA FRANCESCA.** *3311 N Clark St, in Lakeview. 773/281-3310.* Hrs: 5-10:30 pm; Fri, Sat to 11 pm; Sun to 10:30 pm. Closed major hols. Italian menu. Bar. A la carte entrees: dinner $7.95-$18.95. Child's meals. Specialities: linguine Sugo di scampi, skatewing al Balsamic, penne Siciliana. Valet parking. Marble colonnades; photographs of Rome. Cr cds: A, MC, V.

D

★ ★ ★ **MORTON'S.** *1050 N State St, north of the Loop. 312/266-4820.* Hrs: 5:30-11 pm; Sun 5-10 pm. Closed major hols. Res accepted. Bar. Wine cellar. A la carte entrees: dinner $17-$30. Specialties: Maine lobster, prime dry-aged porterhouse steak, Sicilian veal chops. Valet parking. Menu on blackboard. English club atmosphere, decor. Cr cds: A, C, D, DS, JCB, MC, V.

D

✔★ **N.N. SMOKEHOUSE.** *1465 W Irving Park (60613), Lakeview. 773/868-4700.* Hrs: 11:30 am-10 pm; Fri to 11 pm; Sat noon-11 pm; Sun noon-9 pm. Closed Mon; most major hols. Wine, beer. Semi-a la carte: lunch $4.75-$9.50, dinner $5.85-$14.75. Child's meals. Specialties: spare ribs, Memphis pulled pork, Mississippi fried catfish. Own baking. Casual southern smokehouse atmosphere. Cr cds: C, D, DS, MC, V.

D ♥

★ ★ ★ **NICK'S FISHMARKET.** *1 First National Plaza, Dearborn & Monroe Sts, the Loop. 312/621-0200.* E-mail nicks@earthlink.net; web www.harmonnickolas.com. Hrs: 11:30 am-3 pm, 5:30-11 pm; Fri to midnight; Sat 5:30 pm-midnight. Closed Sun; major hols. Res accepted. Bar 11-2 am. A la carte entrees: lunch $8.50-$55, dinner $14-$55. Specializes in fresh seafood, live Maine lobster, veal. Pianist exc Mon (dinner). Valet parking. Braille menu. Cr cds: A, C, D, DS, JCB, MC, V.

D

★ ★ **NIX.** *(See Regal Knickerbocker Hotel) 312/751-8100.* Hrs: 6 am-10:30 pm; Sun brunch 9 am-2 pm. Res accepted. Bar. A la carte entrees: bkfst $6-$10.50, lunch $8-$9, dinner $14-$26. Sun brunch $15.95. Child's meals. Specialties: fajita egg rolls, southwestern Peking duck, grilled lamb chop in wonton shell. Own desserts. Valet parking. Outdoor dining. Crisp, contemporary decor; casual dining. Cr cds: A, C, D, DS, JCB, MC, V.

D

★ ★ **PALM.** *(See Swissôtel Hotel) 312/616-1000.* Hrs: 11:30 am-11 pm. Res accepted. Bar. A la carte entrees: lunch $8-$15, dinner $14-$32. Specializes in prime aged beef, jumbo Nova Scotia lobsters, fresh seafood. Own desserts. Valet parking. Outdoor dining. Casual, energetic atmosphere; caricatures of celebrities and regular customers line walls. Family-owned. Cr cds: A, C, D, MC, V.

D

✔★ ★ **PAPAGUS.** *(See Embassy Suites Hotel) 312/642-8450.* Hrs: 11:30 am-10 pm; Fri to midnight; Sat noon-midnight; Sun noon-10 pm. Res accepted. Greek menu. Bar. A la carte entrees: lunch $3.95-$14, dinner $7.75-$24.95. Specializes in braised lamb with orzo, Greek chicken, seafood. Valet parking. Outdoor dining. Rustic, country taverna atmosphere. Cr cds: A, C, D, DS, JCB, MC, V.

D

★ ★ ★ **PARK AVENUE CAFE.** *(See Doubletree Guest Suites Hotel) 312/944-4414.* Hrs: 5-11 pm; Sun to 10 pm; Sun brunch 10:30 am-2 pm. Closed Jan 1, Dec 25. Res accepted. Contemporary Amer menu. Bar. Wine list. A la carte entrees: dinner $18.50-$29.75. Tasting menu: dinner $52. Sun brunch $30. Specialties: brioche-crusted cod with wild mushrooms, pot au feu of squab, hot and cold foie gras. Own baking, pasta. Valet parking. Warm atmosphere with antique barber poles and American folk art. Cr cds: A, C, D, DS, JCB, MC, V.

D

✔★ **PARTHENON.** *314 S Halsted St (60661), Greektown. 312/726-2407.* Hrs: 11-1 am; Sat to 2 am. Closed Thanksgiving, Dec 25. Greek, Amer menu. Bar. A la carte entrees: lunch $4.95-$9.95, dinner $5.95-$10. Child's meals. Specializes in broiled whole fresh fish, saganaki, lamb. Free valet parking. Ancient Greek decor. Family-owned. Cr cds: A, C, D, DS, MC, V.

D

★ ★ ★ **PRAIRIE.** *(See Hyatt On Printers Row Hotel) 312/663-1143.* Hrs: 6:30-10 am, 11:30 am-2 pm, 5:30-10 pm; Fri to 11 pm; Sat 7 am-2 pm, 5:30-11 pm; Sun 7-10:30 am, 5:30-10 pm; Sun brunch (winter) 10 am-2 pm. Res accepted. Bar. A la carte entrees: bkfst $5-$7, lunch, dinner $14-$26. Sun brunch $9-$16. Specialties: grilled baby Coho salmon with bacon, leeks and black walnuts; grilled sturgeon with vegetables and wild rice; grilled buffalo steak. Own pastries. Seasonal menu. Valet parking. Decor in the style of Frank Lloyd Wright; oak trim, architectural photographs and drawings. Cr cds: A, C, D, DS, ER, JCB, MC, V.

D

★ ★ ★ **PRINTER'S ROW.** *550 S Dearborn St, south of the Loop. 312/461-0780.* Hrs: 11:30 am-2:30 pm, 5-10 pm; Fri to 11 pm; Sat 5-11 pm. Closed Sun; major hols. Res accepted. Continental menu. Bar. Wine list. A la carte entrees: lunch $8.75-$12.95, dinner $14.95-$21.95. Specializes in fresh seafood, duck, seasonal game. Own pastries, desserts. In old printing building (1897). Cr cds: A, C, D, DS, MC, V.

D

★ ★ ★ **PUMP ROOM.** *(See Omni Ambassador East Hotel) 312/266-0360.* Hrs: 7 am-2:30 pm, 6-11:45 pm; Sun 7-11 am, 5-9:45 pm; Sun brunch 11 am-2:30 pm. Res accepted. Bar. Wine list. Semi-a la carte: bkfst $6-$10.50. A la carte entrees: lunch $10.50-$15.95, dinner $17.50-$30.50. Sun brunch $25.95. Specializes in seared salmon, prime rib, lamb chops. Own pastries, sorbet. Pianist. Valet parking. Famous dining rm; was once haunt of stars, celebrities; celebrity photographs. Cr cds: A, C, D, DS, MC, V.

✔★ **REDFISH.** *400 N State St (60610), River North. 312/467-0325.* Hrs: 11:30 am-10 pm; Fri to 11 pm; Sat noon-11 pm; Sun noon-10 pm. Closed most major hols. Res accepted. Cajun/Creole menu. Bar to midnight. Semi-a la carte: lunch $10-$18, dinner $15-$18. Child's meals. Specialties: redfish, jambalaya. Jazz & blues Thurs-Sat. Valet parking. Outdoor dining. Louisiana roadhouse with Mardi Gras decor; masks, voodoo doll displays. Cr cds: A, C, D, DS, JCB, MC, V.

D

★ ★ **RELISH.** *2044 N Halsted St, Lincoln Park. 312/868-9034.* Hrs: 5:15-10 pm; Fri, Sat to 11 pm; Sun to 9 pm. Res accepted. Continental menu. Bar. A la carte entrees: dinner $9.50-$16.75. Specialties: shrimp-stuffed brook trout, wild mushroom and goat cheese picnic, herb-stuffed chicken. Valet parking. Outdoor dining. California atmosphere. Original paintings by local artists. Chef-owned. Cr cds: A, C, D, MC, V.

D

★ ★ ★ ★ **RITZ-CARLTON DINING ROOM.** *(See The Ritz-Carlton Hotel) 312/227-5866.* Burled wood paneling, crystal chandeliers and forest-green banquettes lend elegance to this split-level dining room classic. French-inspired menu. Specialties: lobster with couscous, New Zealand venison steak in pepper crust, Colorado rack of lamb glazed with thyme and honey. Own pastries. Hrs: 6-11 pm; Sun to 10:30 pm; Sun brunch 10:30 am-2:30 pm. Res accepted. Bar. A la carte entrees: dinner $26-$37. Sun brunch $42. Pianist. Valet parking. Menu changes daily. Cr cds: A, C, D, DS, ER, JCB, MC, V.

D

★ ★ ★ **RIVA.** *700 E Grand Ave (60611), at Navy Pier, north of the Loop. 312/644-7482.* Hrs: 11:30 am-3 pm, 5-11 pm; Fri, Sat to midnight; Sun noon-9 pm. Res accepted. Continental menu. Bar. Wine list. A la carte entrees: lunch $12.95-$26.95, dinner $14.95-$31.95. Specialties: filet of tuna, cedar plank fish, Chilean sea bass. Own baking, pasta. Valet parking. Semi-formal atmosphere with striking views of Lake Michigan and Chicago skyline. Cr cds: A, DS, MC, V.

D

★ ★ **RUSSIAN TEA CAFE.** *63 E Adams St (60604), the Loop. 312/360-0000.* Hrs: 11 am-11 pm; Mon to 4 pm; Fri to midnight; Sat noon-midnight; Sun 1-9 pm. Closed Jan 1, Memorial Day. Res accepted. Russian, Ukrainian menu. Bar. Semi-a la carte: lunch $7-$13, dinner $18-$27. Specializes in borscht, shashlik, wild game. Traditional caviar service. Russian dolls on display. Cr cds: A, C, D, DS, JCB, MC, V.

D

★ ★ **THE SALOON.** *200 E Chestnut (60611), north of the Loop. 312/280-5454.* Hrs: 11 am-11 pm. Closed some major hols. Res accepted. Bar. Semi-a la carte: lunch $5.95-$11.95, dinner $14.95-$27.95. Specializes in steak, prime rib, fresh seafood. Modern steakhouse atmosphere. Cr cds: A, C, D, DS, MC, V.

D

★ ★ **SALPICÓN.** *1252 N Wells St (60610), Gold Coast. 312/988-7811.* E-mail seviche@msn.com; web www.salpicon.com. Hrs: 5-10 pm; Fri, Sat to 11 pm; early-bird dinner to 6:30 pm; Sun brunch 11 am-2:30 pm. Closed Tues; Jan 1, Thanksgiving, Dec 25. Res accepted. Mexican menu. Bar. Semi-a la carte: dinner $12.95-$21.95. Complete meal: dinner $19.95. Tasting menu: $37. Sun brunch $8.95-$15.95. Specialties: shrimp with garlic sauce, beef tenderloin with wild mushrooms, lamb loin chops with garlic pasilla chile sauce. Own desserts. Valet parking. Outdoor dining. Casual yet elegant atmosphere with vibrant colors, original artwork. Totally nonsmoking. Cr cds: A, C, D, DS, MC, V.

D

★ ★ **SANTORINI.** *800 W Adams St, Greektown. 312/829-8820.* Hrs: 11 am-midnight; Fri, Sat to 1 am. Closed Thanksgiving, Dec 25. Res accepted. Greek menu. Bar. A la carte entrees: lunch $6.50-$13.95, dinner $9.95-$22.95. Specializes in fresh seafood, grilled lamb chops, Greek-style chicken. Valet parking. Simulated Greek town. Cr cds: A, D, MC, V.

D

★ **SAYAT NOVA.** *157 E Ohio St (60611), north of the Loop. 312/644-9159.* Hrs: 11:30 am-10:30 pm; Sat noon-11 pm; Sun 3-10 pm. Closed major hols. Res accepted. Armenian menu. Bar. Semi-a la carte: lunch $6.95-$11.95, dinner $9.90-$16.95. Specializes in lamb chops, charbroiled kebab, cous cous. Family-owned. Cr cds: A, C, D, DS, MC, V.

★ **SCHULIEN'S.** *2100 W Irving Park Rd, Lakeview. 773/478-2100.* Hrs: 11:30 am-midnight; Fri to 1 am; Sat 4 pm-1 am; Sun 4-10 pm. Closed Mon. German, Amer menu. Bar. Semi-a la carte: lunch $5.95-$11, dinner $10.95-$21.95. Specialties: barbecued ribs, Wienerschnitzel, planked whitefish. Magician (dinner). Parking. Authentic Chicago saloon decor. Established 1886. Family-owned. Cr cds: A, C, D, DS, MC, V.

★ ★ **SCOOZI.** *410 W Huron (60610), River North. 312/943-5900.* Hrs: 11:30 am-2 pm, 5-9:30 pm; Fri to 10:30 pm; Sat 5-10:30 pm; Sun 4-9 pm. Closed Thanksgiving, Dec 25. Res accepted. Italian menu. Bar. A la carte entrees: lunch $7-$15, dinner $7-$21. Specializes in wood-burning-oven pizza, antipasti, homemade pasta. Own pasta, desserts. Valet parking. Outdoor dining. Casual atmosphere with loft-style ceilings, woodburning oven and antipasti bar. Cr cds: A, C, D, DS, JCB, MC, V.

D

★ ★ ★ ★ **SEASONS.** *(See Four Seasons Hotel) 312/649-2349.* Walnut paneling and old porcelains grace this refined dining room. Specialties: potato-crusted Atlantic salmon with dill-mustard gnocchi, rack of lamb with garlic-roasted artichoke, Nantucket stew of lobster, crab & sunchokes. Menu changes seasonally. Own baking. Hrs: 6:30-9:30 am, 11:30 am-2 pm, 6-10 pm; Sun brunch 10:30 am-1:30 pm. Res accepted. Bar 11:30-1 am. A la carte entrees: bkfst $9.50-$15, lunch $12-$22, dinner $24-$36. Prix fixe: 3-course lunch $21.50, 5-course dinner $62. Sun brunch $45. Child's meals. Pianist, jazz trio Sat. Valet parking $15; validated self-parking $5. Jacket. Cr cds: A, C, D, DS, ER, JCB, MC, V.

D ♥

★ ★ **SHAW'S CRAB HOUSE.** *21 E Hubbard St, north of the Loop. 312/527-2722.* Hrs: 11:30 am-10 pm; Fri, Sat to 11 pm; Sun from 5 pm. Closed Thanksgiving, Dec 25. Res accepted. A la carte entrees: lunch $7.95-$14.95, dinner $13.95-$23.95. Specializes in grilled fish, crab cakes, oysters. Entertainment Tues, Thurs 7-10 pm. Valet parking. Decor re-creates look and atmosphere of 1940s seafood house. Cr cds: A, C, D, DS, MC, V.

D

★ ★ **SIGNATURE ROOM AT THE 95th.** *875 N Michigan Ave (60611), in John Hancock Center, north of the Loop. 312/787-9596.* Hrs: 11 am-2 pm, 5-11 pm; Sat 11 am-2:30 pm, 5:30-11 pm; Sun brunch 10:30 am-2 pm. Closed Jan 1, Dec 25. Res accepted. Bar 11-12:30 am; Fri, Sat to 1:30 am. Semi-a la carte: lunch $5.95-$7.25. Buffet: lunch $8.75. A la carte entrees: dinner $21-$29.95. Specializes in seafood, lamb, beef. Pianist Fri, Sun; jazz trio Sat. Magnificent views of city and lake from 95th floor. Cr cds: A, C, D, DS, JCB, MC, V.

D

✔★ **SOLE MIO.** *917 W Armitage Ave, Lincoln Park. 773/477-5858.* Hrs: 11:30 am-2 pm, 5:30-10 pm; Fri, Sat 5:30-11 pm; Sun from 5:30 pm. Closed major hols. Res accepted. Italian, French menu. Bar. A la carte entrees: lunch, dinner $8.95-$16.95. Specialties: pappardelle verdi al prosciutto, grilled beef tenderloin, mushroom ravioli in gargonzola sauce. Valet parking (dinner). Cr cds: A, D, MC, V.

★ ★ **SPAGO.** *520 N Dearborn St (60610), River North. 312/527-3700.* Hrs: 11:30 am-2:30 pm, 5:30-10 pm; Fri 11:30 am-2:30 pm, 5 pm-midnight; Sat 5 pm-midnight. Closed some major hols. Res accepted. Bar. A la carte entrees: lunch $11.50-$16.75, dinner $18.75-$28.50. Specializes in pasta, seafood, pizza with duck sausage. Own baking. Valet parking. Contemporary decor with light woods, vibrant colors. Cr cds: A, D, DS, MC, V.

D

★ ★ ★ ★ **SPIAGGIA.** *980 N Michigan Ave, on 2nd level of One Magnificent Mile building, north of the Loop. 312/280-2750.* Elegant, modern decor—complete with two-story atrium, arches and Italian marble colonnades—adds to the luxurious dining experience at Spiaggia. There are breathtaking views of Lake Michigan through 34-foot-high windows. Elaborate filled pasta dishes, delightful desserts and remarkable wines add adventure. Italian menu. Specialties: wood-roasted veal chops, skewered boneless quail, scallops with porcini mushrooms. Own pastries, pasta. Hrs: 11:30 am-2 pm, 5:30-9:30 pm; Fri, Sat to 10:30 pm; Sun 5:30-9 pm. Closed major hols. Res accepted. Bar to 11 pm; Fri, Sat to midnight; Sun to 10 pm. Extensive wine list. A la carte entrees: lunch $8.95-$17.95, dinner $16.95-$32.95. Pianist (dinner). Seasonal menu. Parking. Jacket (dinner). Cr cds: A, C, D, DS, JCB, MC, V.

D

★ ★ ★ **SPRUCE.** *238 E Ontario St (60611), north of the Loop. 312/642-3757.* Hrs: 11:30 am-2 pm, 5:30-10 pm; Fri to 11 pm; Sat 5:30-11 pm. Closed Sun; major hols. Res accepted. Contemporary Amer menu. Bar 11:30 am-10 pm; Fri, Sat to 11 pm. Wine cellar. A la carte entrees: lunch $9-$19, dinner $17-$24. Tasting menu: lunch $15-$17, dinner $45. Specializes in seasonal dishes, chef's tasting menu. Own baking. Valet parking. Contemporary decor with light woods, large floral arrangements; below street level with windows looking out to sidewalk. Cr cds: A, D, DS, MC, V.

★ ★ **STREETERVILLE GRILLE & BAR.** *301 E North Water St (60611), north of the Loop. 312/670-0788.* Hrs: 11:30 am-10 pm; Fri to 10:30 pm; Sat 5-10:30 pm; Sun brunch 10 am-2 pm. Closed Jan 1, Dec 25. Res accepted. Serv bar. Semi-a la carte: lunch $8-$17. A la carte entrees: dinner $18-$30. Specializes in steak, prime rib, pasta. Valet parking. Outdoor dining. Cr cds: A, C, D, DS, ER, JCB, MC, V.

D

✔★ **SU CASA.** *49 E Ontario St, north of the Loop. 312/943-4041.* Hrs: 11:30 am-11 pm; Fri, Sat to midnight. Closed Thanksgiving, Dec 25. Res accepted. Mexican menu. Bar. Semi-a la carte: lunch, dinner $4.95-$12.95. Specialties: chicken poblano, shrimp a la Veracruzana, pan-fried red snapper. Valet parking. Outdoor dining. 16th-century Mexican decor; Mexican artifacts. Cr cds: A, C, D, DS, MC, V.

D

★ ★ **SZECHWAN EAST.** *340 E Ohio St (60611), north of the Loop. 312/255-9200.* Hrs: 11:30 am-2 pm, 5-10 pm; Sun brunch to 2 pm. Closed Thanksgiving. Res accepted. Chinese menu. Bar to 1 am. Buffet: lunch $8.95. A la carte entrees: dinner $7.95-$23.95. Sun brunch $15.95. Specialties: Governor's chicken, steamed black sea bass with ginger and scallions, orange beef. Valet parking. Outdoor dining. Chinese decor with large golden Buddha, etched glass. Cr cds: A, C, D, DS, JCB, MC, V.

D

★ ★ ★ **TOPOLOBAMPO.** *445 N Clark St, River North. 312/661-1434.* Regional Mexican menu. Specializes in gourmet cuisine featuring complex sauces, exotic wild game. Own pastries. Hrs: 11:30 am-2 pm, 5:30-9:30 pm; Fri, Sat 5:30-10:30 pm. Closed Sun, Mon. Res accepted. Bar. Wine list. A la carte entrees: lunch $8-$14, dinner $15.50-$22. Valet parking. Outdoor dining. Intimate dining. Cr cds: A, C, D, DS, MC, V.

D

★ ★ ★ **TRATTORIA NO. 10.** *10 N Dearborn St, the Loop. 312/984-1718.* Hrs: 11:30 am-2 pm, 5:30-9 pm; Fri to 10 pm; Sat 5:30-10 pm. Closed Sun; major hols. Res accepted. Italian menu. Bar. Wine list. A la carte entrees: lunch, dinner $10.95-$22.95. Specialties: ravioli, rack of lamb, veal chop. Own pastries. Valet parking. Dining in grotto-style trattoria. Cr cds: A, C, D, DS, MC, V.

D

★ ★ **TRATTORIA PARMA.** *400 N Clark St (60610), River North. 312/245-9933.* E-mail parma@vinci-group.com. Hrs: 11:30 am-2 pm, 5:30-10:30 pm; Sat 5:30-11 pm; Sun 4-9:30 pm. Closed some major hols. Res accepted. Italian menu. Bar. A la carte entrees: lunch $5.95-$11.95, dinner $9.95-$15.95. Specialties: stuffed rigatoni with tomato cream sauce, grilled pork chop with ricotto whipped potatoes. Valet parking (dinner). Outdoor dining. Murals of Venice, artwork. Cr cds: A, D, MC, V.

D

✔★ **TUCCI BENUCCH.** *900 N Michigan Ave, 5th floor, north of the Loop. 312/266-2500.* Hrs: 11:30 am-10 pm; Fri, Sat to 11 pm; Sun noon-9 pm. Closed Thanksgiving, Dec 25. Northern Italian menu. Bar. A la carte entrees: lunch, dinner $8.95-$13.95. Child's meals. Specializes in pasta, thin-crust pizza, salads. Own desserts. Replica of Italian country villa. Totally nonsmoking. Cr cds: A, C, D, DS, MC, V.

D

✔★ **TUCCI MILAN.** *6 W Hubbard St, north of the Loop. 312/222-0044.* Hrs: 11:30 am-10 pm; Fri to 11 pm; Sat noon-11 pm; Sun 5-9 pm. Res accepted. Northern Italian menu. Bar. A la carte entrees: lunch, dinner $6.95-$19. Specializes in fresh pastas, rotisserie items, organic vegetable dishes. Valet parking (dinner). Original art. Cr cds: A, C, D, DS, MC, V.

D

★★ **TUSCANY.** *1014 W Taylor St (60607), south of the Loop. 312/829-1990.* Hrs: 11 am-3:30 pm, 5-11 pm; Fri to midnight; Sat 5 pm-midnight; Sun 2-9:30 pm. Closed most major hols. Res accepted. Northern Italian menu. Bar. Semi-a la carte: lunch $8.95-$15, dinner $8.75-$30. Specialties: grilled baby octopus, ravioli pera, New Zealand lamb. Valet parking. Storefront windows, wood-burning pizza oven. Cr cds: A, C, D, DS, MC, V.

D

★★ **UN GRAND CAFE.** *(See Belden-Stratford Hotel) 773/348-8886.* Hrs: 6-10:30 pm; Fri, Sat to 11:30 pm; Sun 5-9:30 pm. Closed major hols. Res accepted. Serv bar. A la carte entrees: dinner $14-$19. Specializes in fresh grilled seafood, steak frites, salads. Valet parking. Outdoor dining. French bistro decor. Cr cds: A, C, D, DS, JCB, MC, V.

✔★★ **VINCI.** *1732 N Halsted St (60614), Lincoln Park. 312/266-1199.* Web www.vinci-group.com. Hrs: 5:30-10:30 pm; Fri, Sat to 11:30 pm; Sun 3:30-9:30 pm; Sun brunch 10:30 am-2:30 pm. Closed most major hols. Res accepted. Italian menu. Bar. A la carte entrees: dinner $6.95-$17.95. Child's meals. Specialties: polenta con funghi, grilled duck breast, linguine della Nonna. Valet parking (dinner). Warm, rustic atmosphere. Cr cds: A, C, D, MC, V.

D

★★★ **VIVERE.** *71 W Monroe St, main floor of the Italian Village complex, the Loop. 312/332-4040.* Hrs: 11:30 am-2:30 pm, 5-10 pm; Fri to 11 pm; Sat 5-11 pm. Closed Sun; major hols. Res accepted. Regional Italian menu. Bar. Extensive wine list. A la carte entrees: lunch $11-$21, dinner $16-$31. Specialties: tortelli di pecorino dolce, pesce del giorno come volete, medaglione di vitello, petto d'anatra con balsamico dolce. Valet parking. One of 3 restaurants in the Italian Village complex. Elegant dining in a contemporary Baroque setting; marble mosaic flooring. Family-owned. Cr cds: A, C, D, DS, JCB, MC, V.

D

★★ **VIVO.** *838 W Randolph, north of the Loop. 312/733-3379.* Hrs: 11:30 am-2:30 pm, 5:30-10 pm; Thurs to 11 pm; Fri to midnight; Sat, Sun 5:30 pm-midnight. Closed some major hols. Res accepted. Southern Italian menu. Bar. A la carte entrees: lunch $6-$14, dinner $10-$26. Specialties: black linguine with crabmeat, baked whole snapper, risotto with white asparagus. Own baking, pasta. Valet parking. Outdoor dining. Dramatic, contemporary decor with unique artwork and lighting. Cr cds: A, C, D, MC, V.

D

★★★ **ZINFANDEL.** *59 W Grand Ave (60610), north of the Loop. 312/527-1818.* Hrs: 11:30 am-2:30 pm, 5:30-10 pm; Fri, Sat to 11 pm. Sat brunch from 10:30 am. Closed Sun, Mon; major hols. Res accepted. Bar. Wine list. Semi-a la carte: lunch $7-$11, dinner $16-$18.95. Sat brunch $4.75-$10.50. Specializes in regional American cuisine. Menu changes monthly with emphasis on different regions. Valet parking. Eclectic art. Cr cds: A, C, D, MC, V.

D

Unrated Dining Spots

ARCO DE CUCHILLEROS. *3445 N Halsted St, Lakeview. 773/296-6046.* Hrs: 4 pm-11 pm; Fri, Sat to midnight; Sun noon-10 pm; Sun brunch to 3 pm. Closed Mon; most major hols. Spanish tapas menu. Bar. A la carte entrees: lunch, dinner $1.95-$5.95. Specialties: fish cheeks sauteed with garlic & white wine, mussels in white wine & cream sauce, boiled potatoes in fresh garlic mayonnaise. Patio dining. Casual atmosphere. Cr cds: A, C, D, MC, V.

BIG BOWL CAFE. *159½ W Erie St, River North. 312/787-8297.* Hrs: 11:30 am-10 pm; Fri, Sat to 11 pm. Closed Sun; Thanksgiving, Dec 25. Wine, beer. Semi-a la carte: lunch, dinner $1.95-$6.95. Specializes in Asian cuisine. Casual, informal atmosphere. Cr cds: A, C, D, DS, MC, V.

D

CAFÉ BA BA REEBA. *2024 N Halsted St, Lincoln Park. 773/935-5000.* Hrs: 11:30 am-2:30 pm, 5:30-11 pm; Mon from 5:30 pm; Fri, Sat to midnight; Sun noon-10 pm. Closed some major hols. Spanish tapas menu. Bar. A la carte entrees: lunch, dinner $1.95-$7.95. Specialties: baked goat cheese, grilled squid with lemon, garlic and olive oil. Valet parking. Authentic Spanish tapas bar. Cr cds: A, C, D, DS, MC, V.

D

ED DEBEVIC'S. *640 N Wells St, River North. 312/664-1707.* Hrs: 11 am-10 pm; Fri & Sat to midnight. Closed Thanksgiving, Dec 24-25. Bar. Semi-a la carte: lunch, dinner $1.50-$6.95. Specializes in chili, hamburgers, meat loaf, salads. Own desserts. Valet parking. Replica of 1950s diner. No cr cds accepted.

D

HARD ROCK CAFE. *63 W Ontario St, River North. 312/943-2252.* Hrs: 11:30 am-11 pm; Fri to midnight; Sat 11 am-midnight; Sun to 10 pm. Closed Thanksgiving, Dec 25. Bar to 12:30 am; Fri, Sat to 1:30 am; Sun to midnight. Semi-a la carte: lunch, dinner $5.95-$11.95. Specializes in lime barbecue chicken, watermelon ribs, hamburgers. Valet parking. Rock memorabilia. Cr cds: A, D, MC, V.

D

LUTZ'S CONTINENTAL CAFE & PASTRY SHOP. *2458 W Montrose Ave, north of the Loop. 773/478-7785.* Hrs: 11 am-10 pm. Closed Mon; major hols. Wine, beer. A la carte entrees: lunch, dinner $5.50-$10.50. Specializes in light lunches, whipped cream tortes, hand-dipped truffles. Own candy, ice cream. Outdoor dining. Bakeshop. Continental café atmosphere. Family-owned. Cr cds: MC, V.

D

MICHAEL JORDAN'S. *500 N La Salle St, River North. 312/644-3865.* Hrs: 11 am-10 pm; Fri, Sat to 11:30 pm. Res accepted (lunch). Bar. Semi-a la carte: lunch $4.95-$12.95, dinner $11.95-$26.95. Specialties: Michael's "Nothin But Net" burger, Juanita's macaroni & cheese, steak. Valet parking. High-ceilinged bar (1st floor) featuring large video wall. Dining rm (2nd floor), Michael Jordan memorabilia displayed; artwork; casual dining. Cr cds: A, C, D, DS, JCB, MC, V.

D

PIZZERIA UNO. *29 E Ohio St, north of the Loop. 312/321-1000.* Hrs: 11:30-1 am; Sat to 2 am; Sun to midnight. Closed Thanksgiving, Dec 25. Bar. Limited menu. Lunch, dinner $2.95-$8. Specialty: deep-dish pizza. Cr cds: A, D, DS, MC, V.

PLANET HOLLYWOOD. *633 N Wells St, River North. 312/266-7827.* Hrs: 11 am-midnight; Fri, Sat to 1 am. Italian, Mexican, Amer menu. Bar to 1:45 am. Semi-a la carte: lunch, dinner $6.95-$17.95. Specialties: turkey burgers, vegetable pizza, pasta. Faux palm trees and searchlights evoke the glamour of Hollywood. Authentic Hollywood memorabilia displayed. Gift shop. Cr cds: A, D, DS, MC, V.

D

POCKETS. *2618 N Clark St, Lincoln Park. 773/404-7587.* Hrs: 11 am-11 pm; Fri, Sat to midnight; Sun to 10 pm. Closed Thanksgiving, Dec 24-25. A la carte entrees: lunch, dinner $3.50-$6.25. Specialties: chipati sandwiches, calzone, pizza. No cr cds accepted.

Chicago O'Hare Airport Area

Motels

★ ★ **COURTYARD BY MARRIOTT.** *(2950 S River Rd, Des Plaines 60018) 2 mi N of I-90 exit River Rd. 847/824-7000; FAX 847/824-4574.* 180 rms, 5 story. S, D $149; suites from $159; under 12 free; wkend rates. Crib free. TV; cable (premium). Indoor pool; whirlpool. Complimentary coffee in rms. Restaurant 6:30 am-2 pm, 5-10 pm. Rm serv from 5 pm. Bar 4 pm-midnight. Ck-out 1 pm. Coin Indry. Meeting rms. Business servs avail. In-rm modem link. Valet serv. Sundries. Gift shop. Free airport transportation. Exercise equipt; weights, bicycles. Refrigerator in suites. Some balconies. Cr cds: A, C, D, DS, MC, V.

D SC

★ ★ **EXEL INN.** *(2881 Touhy Ave (IL 72), Elk Grove Village 60007) 847/803-9400; FAX 847/803-9771.* 123 rms, 3 story. S $52.99-$60.99; D $62.99-$64.99; under 18 free. Crib avail. Pet accepted, some restrictions. TV; cable. Complimentary continental bkfst. Coffee in rms. Restaurant nearby. Ck-out noon. Coin Indry. Business servs avail. In-rm modem link. Free airport transportation. Exercise equipt; bicycle, treadmill. Refrigerators avail. Cr cds: A, C, D, DS, MC, V.

D SC

★ ★ **HAMPTON INN.** *(100 Busse Rd, Elk Grove Village 60007) 1½ mi N on US 12/45 to Higgins Rd (IL 72), then 4 mi W to jct Busse Rd (IL 83). 847/593-8600; FAX 847/593-8607.* 125 rms, 4 story. S $79-$85; D $89; under 18 free; wkend rates. Crib free. TV; cable (premium). Complimentary continental bkfst. Restaurant nearby. Ck-out noon. Meeting rm. Business servs avail. In-rm modem link. Free airport transportation. Health club privileges. Cr cds: A, C, D, DS, JCB, MC, V.

D SC

★ **HOWARD JOHNSON LODGE.** *(8201 W Higgins Rd, Chicago 60631) 773/693-2323; FAX 773/693-3771.* 110 rms, 2 story. May-Aug: S, D $99-$109; under 12 free; lower rates rest of yr. Crib free. TV; cable (premium). Ck-out noon. Coin Indry. Business servs avail. Free airport transportation. Cr cds: A, C, D, DS, ER, JCB, MC, V.

D SC

✔★ ★ **LA QUINTA.** *(1900 Oakton St, Elk Grove Village 60007) 2 mi NW on I-90 to Elmhurst Rd, then N to Oakton St. 847/439-6767; FAX 847/439-5464.* 142 rms, 4 story. S $79-$84; D $84-$91; each addl $7; under 18 free. Crib free. Pet accepted, some restrictions. TV; cable (premium). Heated pool. Complimentary continental bkfst. Restaurant opp 7 am-11 pm. Ck-out noon. Meeting rms. Business servs avail. In-rm modem link. Valet serv. Free airport transportation. Health club privileges. Some refrigerators. Cr cds: A, C, D, DS, MC, V.

D SC

★ ★ **RESIDENCE INN BY MARRIOTT.** *(9450 W Lawrence, Schiller Park 60176) 847/725-2210; FAX 847/725-2211.* 169 kit. suites, 3-6 story. 1-bedrm $129-$179; 2-bedrm $149-$179; 3-bedrm $450; monthly rates. Crib free. Pet accepted; $100. TV; cable (premium). Pool, whirlpool. Complimentary continental bkfst. Coffee in rms. Restaurant adj. Ck-out noon. Coin Indry. Meeting rms. Business center. In-rm modem link. Valet serv. Free airport transportation. Health club privileges. Refrigerators, microwaves. Balconies. Picnic tables, grills. Cr cds: A, C, D, DS, JCB, MC, V.

D SC

Motor Hotels

✔★ ★ **BEST WESTERN MIDWAY.** *(1600 Oakton St, Elk Grove Village 60007) 2 mi NW on I-90 to Elmhurst Rd, then N to Oakton St, then W. 847/981-0010; FAX 847/364-7365.* 165 rms, 3 story. S $75-$95; D $88-$105; each addl $10; suites from $150; under 12 free. Crib free. TV; cable (premium). Pool; whirlpool. Complimentary continental bkfst. Complimentary coffee in rms. Restaurant 6 am-2 pm, 5-10 pm. Rm serv. Bar 4 pm-midnight. Ck-out noon. Meeting rms. Business servs avail. In-rm modem link. Symposium theater. Bellhops. Free airport transportation. Sauna. Game rm. Some refrigerators. Cr cds: A, C, D, DS, JCB, MC, V.

D SC

★ ★ **COMFORT INN.** *(2175 E Touhy Ave, Des Plaines 60018) Touhy Ave & River Rd. 847/635-1300; FAX 847/635-7572.* 148 rms, 3 story. S $94-$104; D $104-$114; each addl $10; suites $120-$130; under 18 free. Crib free. TV; cable (premium). Complimentary continental bkfst. Coffee in rms. Restaurant adj 5:30-2 am. Bar 11-1 am. Ck-out 1 pm. Meeting rms. Business servs avail. Valet serv. Free airport transportation. Exercise equipt; weight machine, bicycle. Whirlpool. Cr cds: A, C, D, DS, ER, JCB, MC, V.

D SC

Hotels

★ ★ **HOLIDAY INN.** *(5440 N River Rd, Rosemont 60018) on US 45, 1 mi E of O'Hare Intl Airport. 847/671-6350; FAX 847/671-5406.* 507 rms, 14 story. S $159; D $169; each addl $10; suites $175-$200; under 18 free; wkend package. Crib free. Pet accepted. TV; cable (premium). 2 pools, 1 indoor; whirlpool. Restaurant 6:30 am-midnight. Bars 11-2 am; wkends to 4 am; entertainment exc Sun. Ck-out noon. Coin Indry. Meeting rms. Business center. In-rm modem link. Free airport transportation. Exercise equipt; weight machine, stair machine, sauna. Game rm. Refrigerators avail. Minibars. Cr cds: A, C, D, DS, MC, V.

D SC

★ ★ ★ **HOTEL SOFITEL.** *(5550 N River Rd, Rosemont 60018) 2 blks S of I-90 exit River Rd S. 847/678-4488; FAX 847/678-4244.* 304 rms, 10 story. S $205-$215; D $225-$235; each addl $10; suites $305-$325; under 18 free. Crib free. Pet accepted, some restrictions. Valet parking $12. TV; cable (premium). Indoor pool. Restaurants 6:30-12:30 am. Rm serv 24 hrs. Bar 11-1 am. Ck-out noon. Convention facilities. Business center. In-rm modem link. Concierge. Gift shop. Free airport transportation. Exercise equipt; weights, bicycles, sauna. Bathrm phones, minibars; refrigerators avail. Traditional European-style hotel. Cr cds: A, C, D, DS, ER, JCB, MC, V.

D SC

★ ★ ★ **HYATT REGENCY.** *(9300 W Bryn Mawr Ave, Rosemont 60018) River Rd (US 45) at Kennedy Expy exit River Rd S. 847/696-1234; FAX 847/698-0139.* 1,100 rms, 10 story. S $189-$225; D $194-$250; each addl $25; suites $300-$800. Crib free. Parking $13. TV; cable (premium). Indoor pool. Restaurants 6 am-midnight. Rm serv 24 hrs. Bars noon-2 am. Ck-out noon. Convention facilities. Business center. In-rm modem link. Free airport transportation. Exercise equipt; weights, bicycles, sauna, steam rm. Massage. Wet bar in suites. Many balconies. 12-story atrium lobby. Luxury level. Cr cds: A, C, D, DS, ER, JCB, MC, V.

D SC

★ ★ ★ **MARRIOTT.** *(8535 W Higgins Rd, Chicago 60631) on IL 72, 1½ mi E of O'Hare Intl Airport at Kennedy Expy, Cumberland Ave N exit. 773/693-4444; FAX 773/714-4297.* 681 rms, 12 story. S, D $149-$204; suites $179-$450; under 18 free; wkend plans. Crib free. Pet accepted. TV; cable (premium). 2 pools, 1 indoor/outdoor; wading pool, whirlpool, poolside serv. Restaurants 6:30 am-10 pm. Rm serv to midnight. Bars 11:30-1:30 am. Ck-out noon. Coin Indry. Convention facilities. Business center. In-rm modem link. Concierge. Gift shop. Valet parking. Free airport transportation. Exercise equipt; weights, bicycles. Refrigerators, microwaves avail. Private patios, balconies. Luxury level. Cr cds: A, C, D, DS, ER, JCB, MC, V.

D SC

★ ★ ★ **MARRIOTT SUITES.** *(6155 N River Rd, Rosemont 60018) I-190E exit River Rd N. 847/696-4400; FAX 847/696-2122.* 256 suites, 11 story. S $189; D $199; wkend rates. Crib free. Pet accepted. TV; cable (premium), VCR avail. Indoor pool; whirlpool. Coffee in rms. Restaurant 6:30 am-10:30 pm. Bar 11:30 am-midnight. Ck-out 1 pm. Meeting rms. Business servs avail. In-rm modem link. Gift shop. Free airport transportation. Exercise equipt; bicycles, stair machine, sauna. Health club privileges. Refrigerators, wet bars; microwaves avail. Cr cds: A, C, D, DS, ER, JCB, MC, V.

D SC

★ ★ **RAMADA PLAZA HOTEL O'HARE.** *(6600 N Mannheim Rd, Rosemont 60018) 2 mi N of O'Hare Intl Airport, just N of jct US 12/45, IL 72, N of Kennedy Expy (I-90) Mannheim Rd exit. 847/827-5131; FAX 847/827-5659.* 723 rms, 2-9 story. S, D $119-$151; each addl $10; suites $175-$485; studio rms $145; under 18 free; wkend rates. Crib free. Parking. TV; cable (premium). Indoor/outdoor pool; whirlpool, poolside serv. Restaurants 6 am-11 pm. Bars 11-2 am. Ck-out noon. Convention facilities. Business center. In-rm modem link. Gift shop. Free airport transportation. Tennis. Lighted 9-hole par-3 golf, putting green. Exercise equipt; weight machine, stair machine, sauna. Game rm. Lawn games. Refrigerator in some suites. Many private patios, balconies. Cr cds: A, C, D, DS, ER, JCB, MC, V.

D SC

★ ★ ★ **ROSEMONT SUITES O'HARE.** *(5500 N River Rd, Rosemont 60018) 2 blks S of Kennedy Expy (I-90). 847/678-4000; FAX 847/928-7659; 800 888/476-7366.* 294 suites, 8 story. S, D $177-$215; under 17 free; wkend rates. Crib free. TV; cable (premium). Indoor pool; whirlpool. Complimentary full bkfst. Restaurant 11 am-11 pm. Rm serv 6-1 am. Bar to 1 am. Ck-out noon. Meeting rms. Business center. In-rm modem link. Gift shop. Free airport, RR station transportation. Exercise equipt; weight machine, bicycles, sauna. Health club privileges. Refrigerators, microwaves, minibars, wet bars. Opp Rosemont Convention Center. Cr cds: A, C, D, DS, ER, JCB, MC, V.

D SC

★ ★ ★ **SHERATON GATEWAY SUITES.** *(6501 N Mannheim Rd, Rosemont 60018) 1/2 mi N of I-190 exit Mannheim Rd N. 847/699-6300; FAX 847/699-0391.* Web www.sheraton.com/sheraton/html/properties/hotel_and_resorts/040.html. 297 suites, 11 story. Sept-Dec: S, D $200-$245; each addl $10; under 18 free; wkend rates; lower rates rest of yr. Crib free. Pet accepted. TV; cable (premium), VCR avail. Indoor pool; whirlpool. Complimentary coffee in rms. Restaurant 11 am-2 pm, 5-10 pm. Rm serv 24 hrs. Bar 11-2 am. Ck-out noon. Convention facilities. Business center. In-rm modem link. Gift shop. Free airport transportation. Exercise equipt; treadmills, stair machine, sauna. Health club privileges. Refrigerators; some microwaves. Cr cds: A, C, D, DS, ER, JCB, MC, V.

D SC

★ ★ **SHERATON SUITES.** *(121 NW Point Blvd, Elk Grove Village 60007) 847/290-1600; FAX 847/290-1129.* 255 rms, 7 story. Apr-June & mid-Sept-mid-Nov: S, D $159-$169; under 18 free; wkend rates; lower rates rest of yr. Crib free. Pet accepted, some restrictions; $50. TV; cable (premium), VCR avail. 2 pools, 1 indoor; whirlpool. Complimentary coffee in rms. Restaurant 6:30 am-10 pm. Bar 11:30 am-midnight. Ck-out 1 pm. Coin lndry. Meeting rms. Business servs avail. In-rm modem link. Gift shop. Free airport transportation. Exercise equipt; treadmills, rower, sauna. Game rm. Refrigerators; some microwaves. Cr cds: A, C, D, DS, ER, JCB, MC, V.

D SC

★ ★ ★ **THE WESTIN-O'HARE.** *(6100 River Rd, Rosemont 60018) I-90E exit River Rd N. 847/698-6000; FAX 847/698-4591.* 525 rms, 12 story. S $189-$245; D $209-$265; each addl $20; suites $220-$1,000; under 18 free; wkend rates. Valet parking $10. TV; cable (premium). Indoor pool; whirlpool, poolside serv. Restaurant 6 am-11 pm. Rm serv 24 hrs. Bar 2 pm to midnight. Ck-out 1 pm. Convention facilities. Business center. Gift shop. Free airport transportation. Exercise rm; instructor, weights, bicycles, sauna. Minibars; some bathrm phones. Luxury level. Cr cds: A, C, D, DS, ER, JCB, MC, V.

D SC

Restaurants

★ ★ **BLACK RAM.** *(1414 Oakton St, Des Plaines 60018) 1 mi N of I-90 (Kennedy Expy) River Rd (US 45) exit N. 847/824-1227.* Hrs: 11 am-11 pm; Sat from 4 pm; Sun 1-10 pm. Closed most major hols. Res accepted. Bar. Semi-a la carte: lunch $8-$15, dinner $15-$25. Specializes in steak, veal, fresh seafood. Own pastries. Entertainment Fri, Sat. Parking. Family-owned. Cr cds: A, C, D, DS, MC, V.

D

★ ★ ★ **CAFE LA CAVE.** *(2777 Mannheim Rd, Des Plaines 60018) 1 mi N on Mannheim Rd, N of jct US 12/45, 1 blk N of jct IL 72. 847/827-7818.* Hrs: 11:30 am-11:30 pm; Sat from 5 pm; Sun 5-9:30 pm. Closed some major hols. Res accepted. French, continental menu. Bar. Wine list. Semi-a la carte: lunch $6-$14.95, dinner $18.95-$33.95. Specialties: steak Diane prepared tableside, Dover sole, medallions of lobster. Valet parking. Cr cds: A, C, D, DS, JCB, MC, V.

D

★ ★ **CARLUCCI RIVERWAY.** *(6111 N River Rd, Rosemont 60018) 2 1/2 mi E off I-90 River Rd exit. 847/518-0990.* E-mail carlucci@enteract.com; web www.enteract.com/~carlucci. Hrs: 11 am-2:30 pm, 5-10 pm; Fri to 11 pm; Sat 5-11 pm; Sun 4:30-9 pm. Closed major hols. Res accepted. Tuscan, Italian menu. Bar to 1 am. A la carte entrees: lunch $7.95-$12.95, dinner $10.95-$22.95. Specializes in fresh pasta, seafood, rotisserie items. Own pastries. Valet parking. Outdoor dining. Tuscan decor; traditional trattoria setting; frescos. Cr cds: A, C, D, DS, MC, V.

D

★ ★ ★ **NICK'S FISHMARKET.** *(10275 W Higgins Rd, Rosemont 60018) jct Mannheim & Higgins Rds. 847/298-8200.* E-mail nicksfish@earthlink.net. Hrs: 6-10 pm; Fri, Sat to 11 pm. Closed most major hols. Res accepted. Continental menu. Bar to 2 am. Wine list. A la carte entrees: dinner $14-$55. Specializes in fresh seafood, steak, veal. Own pastries. Jazz combo Fri, Sat. Valet parking. Braille, Japanese menu. 3 large saltwater aquariums. Cr cds: A, C, D, DS, JCB, MC, V.

D

★ ★ **ROSEWOOD.** *(9421 W Higgins Rd, Rosemont 60018) E of airport, at River Rd. 847/696-9494.* Hrs: 11 am-11 pm; Sat from 4 pm; Sun 4-9 pm. Closed most major hols. Res accepted. Bar. Semi-a la carte: lunch $10-$14, dinner $25-$30. Specializes in steak, fresh seafood, pasta. Pianist Wed-Sat. Valet parking. Intimate atmosphere. Rosewood millwork throughout. Cr cds: A, C, D, DS, MC, V.

D

★ ★ **SAYAT NOVA.** *(20 W Golf Rd, Des Plaines 60016) On IL 58. 847/296-1776.* Hrs: 11:30 am-2 pm, 4-10:30 pm; Sat 4-11:30 pm; Sun 4-10 pm. Closed Mon; most major hols. Res accepted. Middle Eastern menu. Serv bar. Semi-a la carte: lunch $6-$10, dinner $10-$15. Specializes in shish kebab, sautéed chicken, lamb chops. Own desserts. Parking. Middle Eastern decor. Cr cds: A, C, D, DS, MC, V.

D

★ ★ ★ **WALTER'S.** *(28 Main, Park Ridge 60068) 3 1/2 mi NE of O'Hare Airport; 1 1/2 mi N of Kennedy Expy Cumberland exit N. 847/825-2240.* Hrs: 11:30 am-2 pm, 5:30-9 pm; Sat from 5:30 pm. Closed Sun, Mon; major hols. Res accepted. Serv bar. Wine list. A la carte entrees: lunch, dinner $4.95-$26.95. Specializes in grilled seafood, rack of lamb, steak. Own baking, pasta. Parking. In 1890s building; atrium dining; 30-ft skylight. Seasonal menu. Cr cds: A, C, D, DS, JCB, MC, V.

D

Cincinnati

Settled: 1788
Pop: 364,040
Elev: 683 feet
Time zone: Eastern
Area code: 513
Web: www.cincyusa.com

The site of Cincinnati was chosen by the early settlers because it was an important river crossroads long used by Native Americans. The Miami Canal, completed in 1827, and the coming of the railroad in 1846 spurred the development of transportation and commerce.

During the 1840s and 1850s, Cincinnati prospered as a supplier of produce and goods to the cotton-rich South. Great fortunes were accumulated. It was an important station on the Underground Railroad and was generally loyal to the Union during the Civil War. Cincinnati's location on the Mason-Dixon line and its loss of trade with the South, however, caused many citizens to have mixed emotions about the outcome of the war.

After the war, continued prosperity brought art, music, a new library and a professional baseball team. A period of municipal corruption in the late 19th century was ended by a victory for reform elements and the establishment of a city-manager form of government.

Business

Business people have coined the term "blue chip city" to describe business in Cincinnati; like blue chip stocks, the city has performed reliably and grown tremendously.

The economy is diverse, a factor that has helped the city weather economic downturns better than many of its neighbors. No single company employs more than three percent of the population.

Cincinnati is home to a number of national and international companies, including Procter and Gamble, G.E. Aircraft Engine Business Group, Kroger, Federated Department Stores, Cincinnati Milacron, American Financial Corp, and Western-Southern Life Insurance.

Convention Facilities

The Dr. Albert B. Sabin Cincinnati Convention Center is a first-class meeting and exposition complex, offering a 161,000-square-foot exhibit hall, which can be divided into three sections. There are 43 meeting rooms seating from 50 to 4,000 people.

A banquet kitchen is adjacent to the center's 30,000-square-foot ballroom, which seats 4,000 for meetings and 2,500 for food functions. Other features include a 30,000-square-foot lobby, enclosed loading docks with drive-in access, individual show offices, indoor landscaping, numerous lounge areas and two outdoor terraces.

Sports & Recreation

The Cincinnati Reds baseball team, the Cincinnati Bengals football team and the University of Cincinnati and Xavier University basketball teams have a devoted following among sports fans.

Cincinnati is home port of the only remaining overnight paddle-wheel boats traveling the nation's riverways. Riverboat excursions on the *Delta Queen* and the *Mississippi Queen* vary from three to 20 days, stopping at the ports of Pittsburgh, St Louis, Memphis, New Orleans and Minneapolis. In 1995, the *American Queen,* a tribute to the boats of the 19th century, was introduced. For information and bookings, write to the Delta Queen Steamboat Co, 30 Robin Street Wharf, New Orleans, LA 70130, 800-543-1949.

The Cincinnati Zoo has one of the nation's outstanding exhibits of exotic cats, including the rare white Bengal tiger. The world's first insectarium is here, along with many gorillas, a fresh and saltwater aquarium and an exhibit on birds of prey.

Within the 1,476 acres of Mt Airy Forest, there is the Mt Airy Arboretum, which contains an extensive collection of trees and woody plants. Garden of the States contains a tree, flower or shrub from each of the 50 states.

Entertainment

Cincinnati is justly proud of its symphony orchestra, which was founded in 1895. The orchestra's season is September through May, with performances at the Cincinnati Music Hall. It also offers a pop series, summer concerts in the park, young people's concerts and summer opera with Metropolitan Opera stars. The Music Hall is also home for the Cincinnati Ballet Company.

The *Majestic,* built in 1923 as a showboat, is the last of the original floating theaters still in operation today. The showboat runs a full season of drama, comedy and musical shows.

While the Cincinnati Art Museum prides itself on a world-famous collection of paintings, sculpture, prints and decorative art collectibles, the Contemporary Arts Center takes pride in being a forum for artistic ideas, rather than a museum of collected objects.

Historical Areas

The birthplace and boyhood home of William Howard Taft, maintained by the National Park Service, is now a national historic site.

The John Hauck House, an example of Italianate architecture, was once the home of a prominent brewer. It is furnished with appropriate 19th-century furniture.

In Sharon Woods County Park is Sharon Woods Village, an outdoor museum of restored 19th-century buildings transported from various parts of southwestern Ohio. It includes the Old Kemper House, a log house built in 1804 that has displays of 18th- and 19th-century utensils and furnishings.

Sightseeing

This city is an ideal headquarters from which to see much of a three-state area. It is an hour and a half away from the beautiful bluegrass country around Lexington, Kentucky. Not much farther away, directly west in Indiana, is scenic Brown County, a center for arts and crafts. Along the Ohio River are fascinating examples of old residences known by the descriptive architectural name "Steamboat Gothic."

A few minutes north of the city is the popular family theme park, Paramount's Kings Island. Another large amusement park, Americana, is located northwest of the city.

Shopping

Major hotels, stores, office complexes, restaurants, entertainment centers and the Convention Center are connected by an extensive skywalk system, making the city easily accessible to pedestrians. The second-level pedestrian Skywalk virtually turns the downtown area into a mall, with clothing, jewelry, home furnishing stores and art galleries. Many of the suburbs offer a change of pace from the usual suburban mall with the town square concept of neighborhood shopping. Among these cities are Hyde Park, Glendale, Mt Lookout, Montgomery and O'Bryonville.

General References

Area code: 513

Phone Numbers

POLICE & FIRE: 911

POISON CONTROL CENTER: 558-5111

TIME: 721-1700 **WEATHER:** 241-1010

Information Sources

Greater Cincinnati Convention and Visitors Bureau, 300 W 6th St, 45202; 800/CINCY-USA.

Greater Cincinnati Chamber of Commerce, 300 Carew Tower, 441 Vine St, 45202; 579-3100.

Transportation

AIRLINES: American; Continental; Delta; Northwest; TWA; United; USAir; and other commuter and regional airlines.

AIRPORT: Cincinnati/Northern Kentucky International, 606/283-3151.

CAR RENTAL AGENCIES: (See IMPORTANT TOLL-FREE NUMBERS) Avis 621-1479; Budget 606/283-1166; Hertz 606/767-3535.

PUBLIC TRANSPORTATION: Queen City Metro 621-4455.

RAILROAD PASSENGER SERVICE: Amtrak 800/872-7245.

Newspapers

Cincinnati Enquirer; Cincinnati Post.

Convention Facilities

Dr. Albert B. Sabin Cincinnati Convention Center, 525 Elm St, 352-3750.

Sharonville Convention Center, 11355 Chester Rd, Sharonville, 771-7744.

Sports & Recreation

Major Sports Facilities

Cinergy Field, Pete Rose Way & Broadway, 352-5400 (Reds, baseball, 421-4510; Bengals, football, 621-3550).

Riverfront Coliseum, 100 Broadway, adj to Cinergy Field, 241-1818.

Racetracks

River Downs, 6301 Kellogg Ave, 10 mi E on US 52, 232-8000.

Turfway Park Race Course, 7500 Turfway Rd, 10 mi SW off I-75 exit 184, in Florence, KY, 606/371-0200.

Cultural Facilities

Theaters

Aronoff Center for the Arts, Walnut & 7th Sts.

Cincinnati Playhouse In the Park, 962 Mt Adams Circle, 421-3888 or 800/582-3208 (OH).

Showboat *Majestic,* Public Landing, at foot of Broadway, 241-6550.

Concert Halls

Conservatory of Music, University of Cincinnati, 556-4183.

Music Hall, 1241 Elm St, 621-1919.

Riverfront Coliseum, 100 Broadway, 241-1818.

Museums

Cincinnati Art Museum, Art Museum Dr in Eden Park, 721-5204.

Cincinnati Fire Museum, 315 W Court St, 621-5553.

Contemporary Arts Center, 115 E 5th St, 721-0390.

Museum of Natural History & Science, 1301 Western Ave, in Cincinnati Union Terminal, 287-7020.

Taft Museum, 316 Pike St, at 4th St, 241-0343.

Vent Haven (ventriloquism museum), 33 W Maple Ave, Fort Mitchell, KY, 606/341-0461.

Points of Interest

Historical

Sharon Woods Village, N on I-75, E on I-275 exit at US 42, then 1 mi S, Sharon Woods County Park, 563-9484.

Museum Center at Union Terminal, 1301 Western Ave, 287-7000.

William Henry Harrison Memorial, US 50, North Bend.

William Howard Taft National Historic Site, 2038 Auburn Ave, 684-3262.

Other Attractions

Americana Amusement Park, 20 mi N off I-75, Middletown, 539-7339.

Ault Park, 8 mi E, at E end of Observatory Rd in Hyde Park.

Carew Tower Observatory, 5th & Vine Sts, 241-3888.

Cincinnati Zoo and Botanical Garden, 3400 Vine St, 281-4700.

Civic Garden Center, 2715 Reading Rd, 221-0981.

Eden Park & Krohn Conservatory, Eden Park Dr, 352-4086.

Harriet Beecher Stowe Memorial, 2950 Gilbert Ave, 632-5120.

Paramount's Kings Island Theme Park, 20 mi N, I-71 & Kings Mills exit, Kings Mills, 398-5600.

Meier's Wine Cellars, 6955 Plainfield Pike, Silverton, 891-2900.

Mt Airy Forest & Arboretum, 5080 Colerain Ave, 352-4080.

Sightseeing Tours

Cities on Tour, 5658 Locust Dr, 531-1411.

Accent on Cincinnati, 105 W 4th St, 721-8687.

Annual Events

American Negro Spiritual Festival, Music Hall. Mid-Mar.

May Festival, Music Hall. Late May.

Taste of Cincinnati, downtown. Late May.

Riverfest USA, riverfront. Labor Day wkend.

Celtic Music and Cultural Fest, Ault Park. Mid-Sept.

City Neighborhoods

Many of the restaurants, unrated dining establishments and some lodgings listed under Cincinnati include neighborhoods as well as exact street addresses. Geographic descriptions of the Downtown and Mt Adams are given, followed by a table of restaurants arranged by neighborhood.

Downtown: South of Central Pkwy, west of I-71, north of the Ohio River and east of I-75. **North of Downtown:** North of Central Pkwy. **East of Downtown:** East of I-71. **West of Downtown:** West of I-71/I-75.

Mt Adams: South of Eden Park, west of Columbia Pkwy, north of I-471 and east of I-71.

Lodgings and Food

CINCINNATI RESTAURANTS BY NEIGHBORHOOD AREAS

(For full description, see alphabetical listings under Restaurants)

DOWNTOWN
La Normandie Tavern and Chophouse. 118 E Sixth St
Leboxx Cafe. 819 Vine St
Maisonette. 114 E 6th St
Mecklenburg Gardens. 302 E University
Nicola's. 1420 Sycamore St
Orchid's (Omni Netherland Plaza Hotel). 35 W 5th St
The Palace (Cincinnatian Hotel). 601 Vine St
The Phoenix. 812 Race St
Pigalls Cafe. 127 W 4th St
Primavista. 810 Matson Place
Seafood 32 (Regal Cincinnati Hotel). 150 W Fifth St

NORTH OF DOWNTOWN
Aglamesis Bros. 3046 Madison Rd
Chateau Pomije. 2019 Madison Rd
Cheng-1 Cuisine. 203 W McMillan St
Chester's Road House. 9678 Montgomery Rd
China Gourmet. 3340 Erie Ave
Darci's. 7328 Kenwood Rd
DeSha's. 11320 Montgomery Rd
The Diner on Sycamore. 1203 Sycamore St
Forest View Gardens. 4508 North Bend Rd
Germano's. 9415 Montgomery Rd
Grand Finale. 3 East Sharon Ave
House of Tam. 889 W Galbraith Rd
Lenhardt's. 151 W McMillan St
Montgomery Inn. 9440 Montgomery Rd
Pacific Moon. 8300 Market Place Ln
Tandoor. 8702 Market Place Ln
Window Garden. 3077 Harrison Ave

EAST OF DOWNTOWN
The Blackstone. 455 Delta Ave
Heritage. 7664 Wooster Pike (OH 50)
National Exemplar (Best Western Mariemont Inn Motel). 6880 Wooster Pike
The Precinct. 311 Delta Ave

WEST OF DOWNTOWN
Fore & Aft. 7449 Forbes Rd

MT ADAMS
Adrica's. 934 Hatch St
Celestial. 1071 Celestial St
Cherrington's. 950 Pavilion St
Montgomery Inn Boathouse. 925 Eastern Ave
Petersen's. 1111 St Gregory
Rookwood Pottery. 1077 Celestial St
Teak. 1049 St Gregory

Note: When a listing is located in a town that does not have its own city heading, it will appear under the city nearest to its location. In these cases, the address and town appear in parenthesis immediately following the name of the establishment.

Motels

(Rates may be higher during Kool Jazz Festival)

★ ★ **AMERISUITES.** *11435 Reed Hartman Hwy (45241). 513/489-3666; FAX 513/489-4187.* 127 suites, 6 story. May-Sept: S, D $99-$149; each addl $10; under 18 free; lower rates rest of yr. Crib avail. Pet accepted. TV; cable (premium), VCR (movies). Heated pool. Complimentary continental bkfst. Restaurant nearby. Ck-out noon. Meeting rms. Business center. Valet serv. Coin lndry. Exercise equipt; treadmill, stair machine. Health club privileges. Microwaves. Cr cds: A, C, D, DS, MC, V.

D SC

★ ★ ★ **BEST WESTERN MARIEMONT INN.** *6880 Wooster Pike (45227), east of downtown. 513/271-2100; FAX 513/271-1057.* 60 rms, 3 story. S $59-$62; D $64-$71; each addl $5; suites $79-$89; under 12 free. Crib free. TV; cable (premium). Complimentary coffee in lobby. Restaurant (see NATIONAL EXEMPLAR). Rm serv. Bar 11 am-midnight. Ck-out noon. Coin lndry. Business servs avail. In-rm modem link. Valet serv. Cr cds: A, C, D, DS, JCB, MC, V.

SC

★ ★ **COMFORT INN.** *9011 Fields Ertel Rd (45249), I-71 exit 19, north of downtown. 513/683-9700; FAX 513/683-1284.* 115 rms, 3 story. May-Sept: S, D $89-$115; each addl $10; under 18 free; lower rates rest of yr. Crib free. TV; cable (premium). Pool. Complimentary continental bkfst. Restaurant adj open 24 hrs. Ck-out 11 am. Meeting rms. Business servs avail. Valet serv. Health club privileges. Cr cds: A, C, D, DS, MC, V.

D SC

★ ★ **COMFORT SUITES.** *(11349 Reed Hartman Hwy, Blue Ash 45241) N on I-71, W on OH 126 to Reed Hartman Hwy. 513/530-5999; FAX 513/530-0179.* 50 suites, 3 story. Mid-June-late Aug: S, D $150; each addl $6; under 17 free; lower rates rest of yr. Crib free. TV; cable (premium), VCR avail (movies). Pool. Complimentary continental bkfst. Coffee in rms. Bar 4:30-11 pm; closed Sat, Sun. Ck-out 11 am. Meeting rms. Business servs avail. Valet serv. Sundries. Exercise equipt; weight machine, bicycles, sauna. Health club privileges. Refrigerators. Cr cds: A, C, D, DS, MC, V.

D SC

★ ★ **COURTYARD BY MARRIOTT.** *(4625 Lake Forest Dr, Blue Ash 45242) I-275 exit 47. 513/733-4334; FAX 513/733-5711.* Web www.courtyard.com. 149 rms, 2-3 story. May-Aug: S, D $94-$109; under 12 free; suites $109-$119; wkend rates; lower rates rest of yr. Crib free. TV; cable (premium). Indoor pool; whirlpool. Complimentary coffee in lobby. Restaurant 6:30-10:30 am; wkends 7-11:30 am. Bar 5-11 pm. Ck-out 1 pm. Coin lndry. Meeting rms. Business servs avail. Exercise equipt; weight machines, stair machine. Health club privileges. Microwaves in suites. Sun deck. Cr cds: A, C, D, DS, MC, V.

D SC

✔★ ★ **CROSS COUNTRY INN.** *(330 Glensprings Dr, Springdale 45246) N on I-75 to I-275W, exit at OH 4 (exit 41). 513/671-0556; FAX 513/671-4953; res: 800/621-1429.* 120 rms, 2 story. S $37.99-$44.99; D $49.99-$56.99; each addl $8; under 18 free. Crib free. TV; cable (premium). Heated pool. Complimentary coffee in lobby. Restaurant adj 11 am-midnight. Ck-out noon. Meeting rm. Business servs avail. Cr cds: A, C, D, DS, MC, V.

D SC

✔★ ★ **CROSS COUNTRY INN.** *4004 Williams Dr (45255), off I-275 exit 65 at OH 125, south of downtown. 513/528-7702; FAX 513/528-1246.* 128 rms, 2 story. S, D $35.99-$54.99; under 18 free. Crib free. TV; cable (premium). Pool. Complimentary coffee in lobby. Restaurant adj 6 am-11 pm. Ck-out noon. Business servs avail. Health club privileges. Cr cds: A, DS, MC, V.

D SC

★ ★ **FAIRFIELD INN BY MARRIOTT.** *(11171 Dowlin Rd, Sharonville 45241) I-75 exit 15, then 1 blk E. 513/772-4114.* 135 rms, 3 story. Mat-Oct: S, D $45-$83; each addl $7; under 18 free; higher rates special events; lower rates rest of yr. Crib free. TV; cable (premium). Pool. Complimentary continental bkfst. Restaurant adj 6 am-midnight. Ck-out noon. Meeting rms. Business servs avail. In-rm modem link. Valet serv. Health club privileges. Cr cds: A, C, D, DS, MC, V.

D SC

★★ **HAMPTON INN.** *10900 Crowne Point Dr (45241), off I-75 exit 15, north of downtown. 513/771-6888; FAX 513/771-5768.* Web www.hampton-inn.com. 130 rms, 4 story. June-Aug: S, D $79-$89; under 18 free; higher rates special events; lower rates rest of yr. Crib free. TV; cable (premium). Pool. Complimentary continental bkfst. Restaurant nearby. Ck-out noon. Meeting rm. Business servs avail. Health club privileges. Cr cds: A, C, D, DS, MC, V.

D SC

✔★ **RED ROOF INN.** *11345 Chester Rd (45246), I-75 Sharon Rd exit 15, north of downtown. 513/771-5141; FAX 513/771-0812.* 108 rms, 2 story. S $45.99-$55.99; D $50.99-$69.99; each addl $7; under 18 free; higher rates special events. Crib $5. Pet accepted. TV; cable (premium). Restaurant adj 11-2 am. Ck-out noon. Business servs avail. Valet serv. Health club privileges. Cr cds: A, C, D, DS, MC, V.

★★ **RESIDENCE INN BY MARRIOTT.** *11689 Chester Rd (45246), north of downtown. 513/771-2525; FAX 513/771-3444.* 144 kit. suites, 1-2 story. 1 bedrm $89-$129; 2 bedrm $109-$159; higher rates July. Pet accepted; $75-$95. TV; cable (premium). Pool; whirlpool. Complimentary continental bkfst. Ck-out noon. Coin Indry. Business servs avail. Valet serv. Health club privileges. Microwaves. Picnic tables, grills. Cr cds: A, C, D, DS, JCB, MC, V.

D SC

★★ **SIGNATURE INN.** *8870 Governor's Hill Dr (45249), off I-71 & Mason-Montgomery Rd, exit 19, north of downtown. 513/683-3086; FAX 513/683-3086, ext. 500.* 99 rms, 2 story. Memorial Day-Labor Day: S, D $99-$115; under 17 free; lower rates rest of yr. Crib free. TV; cable (premium), VCR avail. Pool. Complimentary continental bkfst. Ck-out noon. Meeting rms. Business center. In-rm modem link. Health club privileges. Game rm. Cr cds: A, C, D, DS, MC, V.

D SC

★ **SUPER 8.** *11335 Chester Rd (45246), I-75 Sharon Rd exit 15, north of downtown. 513/772-3140; FAX 513/772-1931.* 144 rms, 2 story. S $46-$73; D $53-$80; each addl $7; under 18 free; higher rates: wkends, special events. Crib free. Pet accepted, some restrictions. TV; cable (premium). Pool. Complimentary continental bkfst. Restaurant adj 11 am-11 pm. Ck-out noon. Coin Indry. Meeting rms. Business servs avail. Valet serv. Cr cds: A, C, D, DS, MC, V.

D SC

Motor Hotels

★★ **HARLEY.** *8020 Montgomery Rd (45236), I-71 exit 12, north of downtown. 513/793-4300; FAX 513/793-1413.* Web www.harleyhotels.com. 152 rms, 2 story. S, D $110-$120; each addl $10; under 18 free. Crib free. TV; cable (premium). 2 pools, 1 indoor; whirlpool. Restaurant 6:30 am-10 pm; Fri, Sat to 11 pm; Sun 7 am-9 pm. Rm serv. Bar; entertainment Fri, Sat. Ck-out 11 am. Meeting rms. Business center. Bellhops. Lighted tennis. Putting green. Exercise equipt; bicycles, stair machine, sauna. Rec rm. Private patios, balconies. Cr cds: A, C, D, DS, JCB, MC, V.

D SC

★★ **IMPERIAL HOUSE.** *5510 Rybolt Rd (45248), I-74 exit 11, north of downtown. 513/574-6000; FAX 513/574-6566; res: 800/543-3018.* 196 rms, 2-5 story, 27 kits. S $49-$76; D $58-$76; each addl $5; suites $130-$150; family rates. Crib free. TV; cable (premium). Pool. Restaurant 6:30 am-10 pm. Bar 11-2:30 am; Sun 1 pm-1 am; entertainment Thur-Sat. Ck-out noon. Coin Indry. Meeting rms. Business servs avail. In-rm modem link. Sundries. Sauna, steam rm. Cr cds: A, C, D, DS, MC, V.

D SC

★★ **QUALITY HOTEL & SUITES CENTRAL.** *4747 Montgomery Rd (45212), north of downtown, OH 42 at Norwood Lateral. 513/351-6000; FAX 513/351-0215.* 146 rms, 8 story. S, D $76-$99; each addl $5; under 18 free; wkend rates. Pet accepted. TV; cable (premium), VCR avail. Pool; poolside serv. Complimentary continental bkfst. Restaurant 11 am-2:30 pm, 5-10:30 pm; Sat 7-10 am, 5-11:30 pm; Sun 7-10 am, 4-9 pm. Rm serv. Bar 11-2 am, Sat from 1 pm, Sun 4-11 pm. Ck-out noon. Meeting rms. Business center. In-rm modem link. Bellhops. Free airport transportation. Health club privileges. Some bathrm phones; refrigerators, microwaves in suites. Some private patios, balconies. Picnic tables, grills. Cr cds: A, C, D, DS, ER, JCB, MC, V.

D SC

★★ **WOODFIELD SUITES.** *(11029 Dowlin Dr, Sharonville 45241) 12 mi N on I-75 exit 15. 513/771-0300; res: 800/338-0008; FAX 513/771-6411.* 151 suites, 7 story. May-Oct: S, D $89-$189; each addl $10; under 17 free; lower rates rest of yr. Crib free. Pet accepted, some restrictions; $10. TV; cable (premium), VCR avail. Complimentary continental bkfst. Coffee in rms. Restaurant nearby. Ck-out noon. Meeting rms. Business servs avail. In-rm modem link. Bellhops. Valet serv (Mon-Fri). Coin Indry. Exercise equipt; treadmills, stair machines. Indoor pool; whirlpool. Rec rm. Refrigerators, microwaves; some wet bars, in-rm whirlpools. Cr cds: A, C, D, DS, MC, V.

D SC

Hotels

★★★ **CINCINNATIAN.** *601 Vine St (45202), downtown. 513/381-3000; FAX 513/651-0256; res: 800/942-9000.* E-mail info@cincinnatianhotel.com; web www.cincinnatianhotel.com. 147 rms, 8 story. S, D $205-$270; suites $450-$1,500; under 12 free; wkend rates. Crib free. Covered parking $14. TV; cable (premium), VCR avail. Restaurant 6:30 am-11 pm (also see THE PALACE). Rm serv 24 hrs. Bar 11:30 am-11 pm; entertainment. Ck-out noon. Meeting rms. Business servs avail. Concierge. Exercise equipt; weight machine, bicycles, sauna. Bathrm phones, minibars; microwave avail. Landmark hotel (1882); restored. Cr cds: A, C, D, DS, JCB, MC, V.

D

★★ **CROWNE PLAZA.** *15 W Sixth St (45202), at Vine St, downtown. 513/381-4000; FAX 513/381-5158.* Web www.crowneplaza.com. 326 rms, 11 story. S, D $139-$159; suites $200-$350; family rates. Crib free. Valet parking (fee). TV; cable (premium). Coffee in rms. Restaurant 6 am-11 pm; Sun to 10 pm. Bar 11-2 am. Ck-out 1 pm. Convention facilities. Business center. Concierge. Barber, beauty shop. Exercise equipt; weights, bicycles, sauna. Whirlpool. Refrigerators, minibars. Cr cds: A, C, D, DS, ER, JCB, MC, V.

D SC

★★★ **EMBASSY SUITES BLUE ASH.** *4554 Lake Forest Dr (45242), north of downtown at Reed Hartman Hwy. 513/733-8900; FAX 513/733-3720.* E-mail cybga@aol.com. 235 suites, 5 story. S, D $89-$179; each addl $10; under 12 free; higher rates special events. Crib free. TV; cable (premium). Indoor pool; whirlpool. Complimentary full bkfst. Complimentary coffee in rms. Restaurant 11:30 am-10 pm. Bar 5 pm-1 am; closed Sun. Ck-out 1 pm. Coin Indry. Meeting rms. Business servs avail. Gift shop. 18-hole golf privileges. Exercise equipt; weight machine, bicycles, sauna. Health club privileges. Refrigerators, microwaves, wet bars. Balconies. Cr cds: A, C, D, DS, JCB, MC, V.

D SC

★★ **GARFIELD HOUSE.** *2 Garfield Place (45202), 2 blks W of Fountain Square, downtown. 513/421-3355; FAX 513/421-3729; res: 800/367-2155.* 133 kit. suites, 16 story. 1-bedrm $165-$185; 2-bedrm $175-$200; penthouse suites $425-$1,200; monthly rates. Crib free. Pet accepted; $75. Garage parking $4-$8. TV; cable (premium), VCR avail. Complimentary continental bkfst. Complimentary coffee in rms. Restaurant 11 am-9 pm; wkends from 5 pm. Rm serv 5-10 pm. Bar. Ck-out noon. Coin Indry. Meeting rms. Business servs avail. Exercise equipt; weight machine, stair machine. Health club privileges. Microwaves. Some balconies. Cr cds: A, C, D, DS, MC, V.

D SC

★★★ **HOLIDAY INN.** *4501 Eastgate Blvd (45245), east of downtown. 513/752-4400; FAX 513/753-3178.* 247 rms, 6 story. S, D $94-$99; each addl $10; suites $200-$275; under 18 free; wkend rates; higher rates special events. Crib free. TV; cable (premium). Complimentary coffee in rms. Restaurant 6:30 am-11 pm; Sun to 10 pm. Bar 11 am-midnight; Sun to 10 pm. Ck-out 11 am. Meeting rms. Business center. Gift shop. Exercise equipt; bicycle, treadmill. Health club privileges. Indoor pool; whirlpool. Bathrm phone, in-rm whirlpool, refrigerator, microwave, wet bar in suites. Cr cds: A, C, D, DS, JCB, MC, V.

D SC

★ ★ **HOLIDAY INN-QUEENSGATE.** *800 W Eighth St (45203), I-75 at Linn, west of downtown. 513/241-8660; FAX 513/241-9057.* 246 rms, 11 story. S, D $99-$119; suites $189-$210; under 18 free. Crib free. Pet accepted. TV; cable (premium). Pool. Coffee in rms. Restaurant 6:30 am-2 pm, 5-9 pm. Bar 4 pm-2 am; closed Sun. Ck-out noon. Coin Indry. Meeting rms. Business servs avail. In-rm modem link. Exercise equipt; stair machine, bicycle. Health club privileges. Refrigerators avail. Cr cds: A, C, D, DS, ER, JCB, MC, V.

D SC

★ ★ **HYATT REGENCY.** *151 W Fifth St (45202), downtown. 513/579-1234; FAX 513/579-0107.* Web www.hyatt.com. 485 rms, 22 story. S, D $187-$214; each addl $25; suites $400-$750; under 18 free; wkend rates; higher rates special events. Crib free. TV; cable (premium). Indoor pool; whirlpool, poolside serv. Restaurant 6:30 am-midnight. Bar 11-2:30 am. Ck-out noon. Convention facilities. Business center. Concierge. Shopping arcade. Barber. Exercise equipt; weight machines, bicycles, sauna. Some bathrm phones; refrigerator in suites. Luxury level. Cr cds: A, C, D, DS, JCB, MC, V.

D SC

★ ★ ★ **MARRIOTT-NORTHEAST.** *9664 Mason-Montgomery Rd (45040), NE on I-71 exit 19, north of downtown. 513/459-9800; FAX 513/459-9808.* 303 rms, 6 story. S, D $119-$139; each addl $10; suites $225; under 12 free; higher rates special events. Crib avail. TV; cable (premium). Complimentary coffee in rms. Restaurant 6:30 am-2 pm, 5-10:30 pm. Bar 11:30-1 am. Ck-out noon. Convention facilities. Business center. In-rm modem link. Gift shop. Exercise equipt; bicycle, weight machine. 2 pools, 1 indoor; poolside serv. Bathrm phone, refrigerator in suites. Luxury level. Cr cds: A, C, D, DS, JCB, MC, V.

D SC

★ ★ ★ **OMNI NETHERLAND PLAZA.** *35 W Fifth St (45202), off I-75, downtown. 513/421-9100; FAX 513/421-4291.* 607 rms, 29 story. S $175-$210; D $205-$235; each addl $30; suites $250-$1,680; under 18 free; wkly, wkend rates. Crib free. Valet parking. TV; cable (premium), VCR avail. Indoor pool. Restaurant (see ORCHID'S). Bar 11-2 am; entertainment. Ck-out noon. Business center. Concierge. Shopping arcade. Health club privileges. Some private patios. Cr cds: A, C, D, DS, ER, JCB, MC, V.

D SC

★ ★ **REGAL CINCINNATI.** *150 W Fifth St (45202), I-75 exit 5th St, downtown. 513/352-2100; FAX 513/352-2148.* 882 rms, 21-32 story. S, D $94-$179; each addl $10; suites $250-$1,100; under 18 free. Crib free. Garage $13. TV; cable (premium). Heated pool. Restaurant 6:30 am-11 pm; Sun to 10 pm (also see SEAFOOD 32). Bars 11-2:30 am; Sun from 1 pm. Ck-out 11 am. Convention facilities. Business center. In-rm modem link. Concierge. Shopping arcade. Barber. Health club privileges. Luxury level. Cr cds: A, C, D, DS, JCB, MC, V.

D SC

★ ★ **SHERATON-SPRINGDALE.** *(11911 Sheraton Lane, Springdale 45246) N on OH 4, at I-275 exit 41. 513/671-6600; FAX 513/671-0507.* 267 rms, 10 story. May-Aug: S $99-$109; D $109-$119; each addl $10; suites $130-$150; under 18 free; package plans; lower rates rest of yr. Crib free. TV; cable (premium), VCR avail. Indoor pool; whirlpool. Coffee in rms. Restaurant 6:30 am-10 pm; Fri, Sat to 11 pm. Bar 11-2 am; entertainment. Ck-out noon. Coin Indry. Meeting rms. Business servs avail. In-rm modem link. Gift shop. Exercise equipt; weight machine, bicycle. Game rm. Some bathrm phones. Cr cds: A, C, D, DS, MC, V.

D SC

★ ★ **VERNON MANOR.** *400 Oak St (45219), north of downtown. 513/281-3300; FAX 513/281-8933; res: 800/543-3999.* Web ver non/manor.com. 173 rms, 7 story. S, D $150-$165; each addl $15; suites $235-$450; studio rms $175-$195; under 16 free. Crib free. TV; cable (premium). Complimentary coffee in lobby. Restaurant 6:30 am-10 pm; Sun brunch 10:30 am-2:30 pm. Bar 11-2 am; Sun 1 pm-midnight. Ck-out noon. Coin Indry. Meeting rms. Business center. In-rm modem link. Barber. Valet parking. Exercise equipt; weights, treadmill. Some refrigerators. Cr cds: A, C, D, DS, MC, V.

D SC

★ ★ ★ **WESTIN.** *Fountain Sq (45202), 5th & Vine Sts, downtown. 513/621-7700; FAX 513/852-5670.* 448 rms, 17 story. S $195-$205; D $215-$235; each addl $20; suites $300-$1,200; under 18 free; wkend packages. Crib free. Garage $13.95. TV; cable (premium), VCR avail. Indoor pool; whirlpool, poolside serv. Complimentary coffee in rms. Restaurant 6:30 am-10 pm; Fri, Sat to midnight. Rm serv 24 hrs. Bar 11:30-2:30 am; Sun from 1 pm. Ck-out 1 pm. Convention facilities. Business center. In-rm modem link. Shopping arcade. Valet parking. Exercise equipt; weights, bicycles, sauna, steam rm. Massage. Some bathrm phones, refrigerators. Sun deck. Luxury level. Cr cds: A, C, D, DS, ER, JCB, MC, V.

D SC

Restaurants

✔★ **ADRICA'S.** *934 Hatch St (45202), in Mt Adams. 513/721-5329.* Hrs: 5-11 pm; Fri, Sat to midnight. Closed Jan 1, Dec 25. Res accepted. Italian menu. Bar. A la carte entrees: dinner $7.95-$12.95. Specialties: hand-tossed fresh pizza, lasagne, eggplant Parmesan. Outdoor patio dining. Cr cds: A, C, D, DS, MC, V.

★ ★ **BLACK FOREST.** *(8675 Cincinnati-Columbus Rd, Pisgah 45069) 3 1/2 mi N of I-275, exit 46, on OH 42. 513/777-7600.* Hrs: 11:30 am-2 pm, 4:30-10 pm; Fri to 11 pm; Sat 4:30-11 pm; Sun 4:30-10 pm. Closed some major hols. Res accepted. German menu. Bar. Semi-a la carte: lunch $4.25-$9, dinner $6.95-$17. Buffet: lunch $5.95. Child's meals. Specialties: Wienerschnitzel, Oktoberfest chicken, sauerbraten. German band Fri, Sat. Parking. Old World German decor. Family-owned. Cr cds: A, C, D, DS, MC, V.

D

★ ★ **THE BLACKSTONE.** *455 Delta Ave, east of downtown. 513/321-0010.* Hrs: 5-11 pm; Fri, Sat to midnight; Sun 11 am-3 pm, 4:30-8:30 pm. Closed major hols. Res accepted. Bar. Semi-a la carte: dinner $11.95-$22.95. Child's meals. Specializes in fresh fish, pasta. Parking. Patio dining. Cr cds: A, C, D, DS, MC, V.

D

★ ★ ★ **CELESTIAL.** *1071 Celestial St (45202), in Highland Tower Apts, in Mt Adams. 513/241-4455.* Hrs: 11:30 am-2:30 pm, 5:30-10 pm; Fri, Sat to 11 pm. Closed Sun; some major hols. Res accepted. Continental menu. Bar. Wine list. Semi-a la carte: lunch $6.50-$13.50, dinner $18.95-$24.50. Specializes in game, fresh seafood. Own baking. Jazz Tues-Sat. Free valet parking. Panoramic view of city. Jacket. Cr cds: A, C, D, MC, V.

D

✔★ ★ **CHATEAU POMIJE.** *2019 Madison Rd (45208), north of downtown. 513/871-8788.* Hrs: 11 am-2:30 pm, 5:30-9:30 pm; Fri to 10:30 pm; Sat 5:30-10:30 pm. Closed Sun; major hols. Continental menu. Wine, beer. Semi-a la carte: lunch $6-$10, dinner $10-$18. Specialties: cioppino, Chateau chicken, fresh salmon. Own desserts. Street parking. Outdoor dining. Casual, cafe dining; adj wine shop. Cr cds: DS, MC, V.

D

★ **CHENG-1 CUISINE.** *203 W McMillan St (45219), north of downtown. 513/723-1999.* Hrs: 11 am-10 pm; Fri to 10:30 pm; Sat noon-10:30 pm; Sun 4:30-10 pm. Closed Thanksgiving, Dec 25. Chinese menu. Serv bar. Semi-a la carte: lunch $4.25-$5.75, dinner $5.50-$12.95. Specialties: cashew chicken, pan-fried moo-shu, sizzling shrimp & scallops. Cr cds: A, DS, MC, V.

D 

★★ **CHERRINGTON'S.** *950 Pavilion St (45202), in Mt Adams. 513/579-0131.* Hrs: 7-10 am, 11 am-3 pm, 5-9 pm; Fri, Sat to 11 pm; Sat 8-11:30 am, 5-11 pm; Sun 11 am-3 pm, 4-9 pm. Closed Mon; some major hols. Res accepted. Bar. Semi-a la carte: bkfst $2.95-$6.95, lunch $4.95-$8.95, dinner $8.95-$22.95. Specializes in fresh seafood. Outdoor dining. Blackboard menu. Guitarist Fri, Sat. Renovated residence (1880). Cr cds: A, C, D, MC, V.

★★ **CHESTER'S ROAD HOUSE.** *9678 Montgomery Rd (45242), north of downtown. 513/793-8700.* Hrs: 11:30 am-2:30 pm, 5-10 pm; Fri to 10:30 pm; Sat to 11 pm; Sun 5-9 pm. Closed Jan 1, July 4, Dec 25; also Super Bowl Sun. Res accepted. Bar. Semi-a la carte: lunch $6.50-$9.50, dinner $9.50-$22.95. Specializes in fresh seafood, rack of baby lamb, steak. Salad bar. Parking. Garden atmosphere; in converted brick farmhouse (1900). Family-owned. Cr cds: A, C, D, DS, MC, V.

D

★★ **CHINA GOURMET.** *3340 Erie Ave (45208), Hyde Park East, north of downtown. 513/871-6612.* Hrs: 11:30 am-10:30 pm; Fri to 11 pm; Sat noon-11 pm. Closed Sun; major hols. Res accepted. Chinese menu. Bar. A la carte entrees: lunch $6-$9.95, dinner $9.95-$27.50. Specializes in fresh seafood. Parking. Cr cds: C, D, MC, V.

D

★★ **DeSHA'S.** *11320 Montgomery Rd (45249), north of downtown, 1 mi N of I-275. 513/247-9933.* Hrs: 11 am-2:30 pm, 5-10 pm; Fri to 11 pm; Sat 5-11 pm; Sun brunch 10 am-2 pm. Closed Jan 1, Dec 25. Res accepted. Bar. Semi-a la carte: lunch $8-$10, dinner $12-$20. Sun brunch $11.95. Child's meals. Specializes in steak, prime rib, seafood. Parking. Outdoor dining on patio. Casually elegant dining. Cr cds: A, C, D, DS, MC, V.

D

✔★ **THE DINER ON SYCAMORE.** *1203 Sycamore St, north of downtown. 513/721-1212.* Hrs: 11 am-midnight; Fri, Sat to 1 am; Sun brunch 11 am-2:30 pm. Closed Dec 25. Bar. Semi-a la carte: lunch, dinner $4.95-$15.95. Sun brunch $4.95-$7.25. Child's meals. Specialties: Caribbean white crab chili, seafood Diablo, crab cakes. Parking. Outdoor dining. Nostalgic diner atmosphere. Cr cds: A, C, D, DS, MC, V.

D

★ **FORE & AFT.** *7449 Forbes Rd, off US 50 (River Rd), 12 mi west of downtown,. 513/941-8400.* Hrs: 11 am-10 pm; Fri to 11 pm; Sat 4 pm-11 pm. Closed Jan 1, Dec 24, 25. Res accepted. Bar. Semi-a la carte: lunch $5.75-$14.95, dinner $8.75-$17.95. Child's meals. Specializes in hand-cut steak, prime rib, seafood. Parking. Outdoor dining. Floating barge on Ohio River; nautical memorabilia. Cr cds: A, MC, V.

SC

★ **FOREST VIEW GARDENS.** *4508 North Bend Rd (45211), S of I-74 exit 14, north of downtown. 513/661-6434.* Hrs: Edelweiss Rm: 11 am-2 pm, 5-7:30 pm; Sat from 5 pm; Show Rm: Broadway music shows (sittings): Thurs 6 pm, Fri 7 pm, Sat 5 & 8 pm, Sun 5 pm. Closed Mon; Dec 24, 25; also 1st wk Jan. Res accepted; required for shows. German, Amer menu. Bar. Semi-a la carte: lunch $3.95-$7.50, dinner $11.95-$18.95. Child's meals. Specializes in Wienerschnitzel, sauerbraten, prime rib. Parking. Outdoor dining in beer garden. Bavarian Fest atmosphere. Banquet-style seating. Family-owned. Cr cds: A, C, D, DS, MC, V.

D

★★ **GERMANO'S.** *9415 Montgomery Rd (45242), north of downtown. 513/794-1155.* Web www.cincy.com/dining/germano. Hrs: 11:30 am-2:30 pm, 5:30-10 pm; Fri to 11 pm; Sat 5-11 pm. Closed Sun; Easter, Thanksgiving, Dec 25. Res accepted (dinner). Italian menu. Serv bar. Semi-a la carte: lunch $5.95-$8.95, dinner $10.95-$21.95. Specializes in pasta, seafood, veal. Own desserts. Tuscan decor with framed art, tapestries. Totally nonsmoking. Cr cds: A, DS, MC, V.

D

★★★ **GRAND FINALE.** *3 East Sharon Ave, north of downtown. 513/771-5925.* Hrs: 11:30 am-10:30 pm; Fri, Sat to 11 pm; Sun 5-10 pm; Sun brunch 10:30 am-3 pm. Closed Mon; Dec 25. Continental menu. Bar. Semi-a la carte: lunch $4.95-$11.95, dinner $14.95-$19.95. Sun brunch $10.95. Child's meals. Specialties: steak salad Annie, chicken Ginger, rack of lamb. Own baking. Parking. Outdoor dining. Remodeled turn-of-the-century saloon. Cr cds: A, C, D, DS, MC, V.

D

★★★ **HERITAGE.** *7664 Wooster Pike (OH 50) (45227), east of downtown. 513/561-9300.* Web www.theheritage.com. Hrs: 11:30 am-2:30 pm, 5-9 pm; Sat 5-10 pm; Sun 10:30 am-2 pm, 5-9 pm. Closed some major hols. Res accepted. Bar. Wine list. Semi-a la carte: lunch $5.95-$8.95, dinner $13.95-$20.95. Sun brunch $12.95. Child's meals. Specializes in regional American cuisine. Own baking. Valet parking. Outdoor dining. Restored 1827 farmhouse. Own herb garden. Family-owned. Cr cds: A, C, D, DS, MC, V.

✔★★ **HOUSE OF TAM.** *889 W Galbraith Rd, Finneytown at Winton, north of downtown. 513/729-5566.* Hrs: 11 am-9:30 pm; Fri to 10 pm; Sat 5-10:30 pm. Closed Sun; some major hols. Res accepted. Chinese menu. Bar. Semi-a la carte: lunch $4.50-$6.50, dinner $5.95-$15.95. Specialties: pine nuts chicken, sea emperor's feast, strawberry chicken. Parking. Totally nonsmoking. Cr cds: A, DS, MC, V.

D

★★ **LA NORMANDIE TAVERN AND CHOPHOUSE.** *118 E Sixth St, downtown. 513/721-2761.* Web www.maisonette.com. Hrs: 11:30 am-2:30 pm, 5-11 pm; Sat from 5 pm. Closed Sun; major hols. Res accepted. Bar. Semi-a la carte: lunch $6.99-$12.50, dinner $15.50-$24.50. Specializes in aged beef, fresh fish. Valet parking. Four-sided fireplace. Family-owned. Cr cds: A, C, D, DS, MC, V.

✔★ **LEBOXX CAFE.** *819 Vine St (45202), downtown. 513/721-5638.* Hrs: 11:30 am-8 pm. Closed Sat, Sun; major hols. Contemporary Amer menu. Semi-a la carte: lunch $2-$5, dinner $4-$6. Child's meals. Specializes in meatloaf, ribs, burgers. Casual decor. Cr cds: A, DS, MC, V.

D

★ **LENHARDT'S.** *151 W McMillan St (45219), I-71 exit 4, north of downtown. 513/281-3600.* Hrs: 11 am-9:30 pm; Sat from 4 pm. Closed Sun, Mon; July 4; also 1st 2 wks Aug, 2 wks at Christmas. Res accepted. German, Hungarian menu. Bar 7 pm-2 am; closed Sun. Semi-a la carte: lunch $3.75-$9.50, dinner $7.95-$15.95. Specialties: Wienerschnitzel, sauerbraten, Hungarian goulash. Free parking. Former Moerlin brewery mansion. Cr cds: A, DS, MC, V.

★★★★★ **MAISONETTE.** *114 E 6th St, downtown. 513/721-2260.* Web www.maisonette.com. Exceptionally attentive service puts guests at ease to enjoy Chef Jean-Robert de Cavel's blend of classical and modern cuisine. The three salmon-colored dining rooms are adorned with paintings by famous Cincinnati artists, including Frank Duvanek, whose self-portrait hangs over the bar. French cuisine. Specialties: escalopes de foie gras, fresh, imported French fish dishes, seasonal offerings. Own pastries. Hrs: 11:30 am-2:30 pm, 6-10:30 pm; Mon from 6 pm; Sat 5:30-11 pm. Closed Sun; major hols. Res accepted. Bar. Wine cellar. A la carte entrees: lunch $13.75-$17.75, dinner $25-$36. Valet parking (dinner). Jacket. Cr cds: A, C, D, DS, MC, V.

D

✔★★ **MECKLENBURG GARDENS.** *302 E University (45219), downtown. 513/221-5353.* Hrs: 11 am-10 pm; Fri to 11 pm; Sat, Sun 5-10 pm. Closed major hols. Res accepted. German menu. Bar to 1 am. Semi-a la carte: lunch $5-$9, dinner $7-$17. Specialties: sauerbraten, potato pancakes, Mecklenburg pies. Own desserts. Entertainment Wed, Fri, Sat. Valet parking Fri, Sat. Outdoor dining. Casual dining; grapevine motif. Cr cds: A, C, D, DS, MC, V.

D

★★ **MONTGOMERY INN.** *9440 Montgomery Rd, north of downtown. 513/791-3482.* Web www.montgomeryinn.com. Hrs: 11 am-10:30 pm; Fri to midnight; Sat 3 pm-midnight; Sun 3-9:30 pm. Closed major hols. Res accepted. Bar. A la carte entrees: lunch $4.50-$8.50, dinner $12.50-$20.95. Child's meals. Specializes in barbecued ribs, chicken. Parking. Family-owned. Cr cds: A, C, D, DS, MC, V.

D

★★ **MONTGOMERY INN BOATHOUSE.** *925 Eastern Ave, 1 mi E of Riverfront Stadium, on OH 50/52, Mt Adams. 513/721-7427.* Web www.montgomeryinn.com. Hrs: 11 am-10:30 pm; Fri to 11 pm; Sat 3-11 pm; Sun 3-10 pm. Closed major hols. Res accepted Sun-Fri. Bar. A la carte entrees: lunch $4.95-$17.95, dinner $9.95-$22.95. Child's meals. Specializes in barbecued ribs, seafood, chicken. Valet parking. Outdoor dining (in season). Unique circular building, located at the river; scenic view. Cr cds: A, DS, MC, V.

D

✔★ **NATIONAL EXEMPLAR.** *(See Best Western Mariemont Inn Motel) 513/271-2103.* Hrs: 7 am-2 pm, 5:30-10 pm; Fri, Sat to 10:30 pm; Sun 5-9 pm. Closed Dec 25. Res accepted. Bar. Semi-a la carte: bkfst $3.25-$6.95, lunch $4.50-$6.95, dinner $9.95-$16.95. Child's meals. Specializes in omelettes, steak, seafood. Casual early American decor. Cr cds: A, DS, MC, V.

D

★★ **NICOLA'S.** *1420 Sycamore St (45210), downtown. 513/721-6200.* Hrs: 11:30 am-2 pm, 5:30-10 pm; Fri to 11 pm; Sat 5:30-11 pm. Closed Sun; major hols. Res accepted. Northern Italian menu. Bar. Semi-a la carte: lunch $5.50-$9.95, dinner $9.95-$28. Specializes in regional Italian dishes, fresh fish. Own pasta, desserts. Valet parking. Outdoor dining. Contemporary decor; casual dining. Cr cds: A, C, D, DS, MC, V.

D

★★★★ **ORCHID'S.** *(See Omni Netherland Plaza Hotel) 513/421-1772.* Located in the Carew Tower's grand Omni Netherland Plaza, this restaurant in the Palm Court echoes the elegant, art-deco atmosphere of the hotel. The menu features creative American cuisine. Specializes in fresh seafood, veal, beef. Hrs: 11 am-2 pm, 6-10 pm; Sat 6-11 pm; Sun from 6 pm; Sun brunch 10 am-2 pm. Res accepted. Bar to 2 am; Sun 1 pm-midnight. Wine list. Semi-a la carte: lunch $13.25-$18.95. A la carte entrees: dinner $24.95-$54. Sun brunch $21.95. Pianist; jazz Fri, Sat evenings. Valet parking. Cr cds: A, C, D, DS, ER, JCB, MC, V.

D

★ **PACIFIC MOON.** *8300 Market Place Ln (45242), north of downtown. 513/891-0091.* Hrs: 11 am-10 pm; Fri, Sat to 11 pm. Closed Thanksgiving. Res accepted. Asian menu. Bar. Semi a-la carte: lunch $5.50-$9.50, dinner $12-$22. Specializes in pork, seafood, chicken. Entertainment Sat. Outdoor dining. Contemporary decor. Cr cds: A, C, D, DS, JCB, MC, V.

D

★★★ **THE PALACE.** *(See Cincinnatian Hotel) 513/381-6006.* E-mail info@concinnatianhotel.com; web www.cincinnatianhotel.com. Hrs: 6:30 am-2:30 pm, 6-10:30 pm; Sun to 9:30 pm; Sun brunch (Labor Day-Mother's Day) 10:30 am-2 pm. Res accepted. Bar 11-1 am; Fri, Sat to 2 am. Wine list. A la carte entrees: bkfst $5.75-$14.95, lunch $6.50-$17, dinner $22-$32. Specializes in seafood, rack of lamb, steak. Own baking. Pianist, jazz trio, harpist (dinner). Valet parking. Jacket. Cherrywood paneling, decorative columns, and tables with silver table lamps create an elegant neoclassical setting. Cr cds: A, C, D, DS, JCB, MC, V.

D

★ **PETERSEN'S.** *1111 St Gregory, in Mt Adams. 513/651-4777.* Hrs: 11:30 am-10 pm; Fri, Sat to 11 pm. Closed Sun; major hols. Wine. A la carte entrees: lunch $4.75-$9.75, dinner $6.75-$13.75. Specializes in black bean burrito, pasta, desserts. Jazz Mon-Sat. Cr cds: A, C, D, DS, MC, V.

D

★★★ **THE PHOENIX.** *812 Race St (45202), downtown. 513/721-2255.* Hrs: 5-9 pm; Sat 5:30-10 pm. Closed Sun, Mon; major hols. Res accepted. Wine cellar. A la carte entrees: dinner $11.95-$24.95. Specializes in seafood, pasta, lamb chops. Pianist Sat. Valet parking. Formal dining. Built in 1893; white marble staircase, 12 German stained-glass windows from the 1880s, hand-carved library breakfront built on site in 1905. Totally nonsmoking. Cr cds: A, C, D, DS, MC, V.

D

★★ **PIGALLS CAFE.** *127 W 4th St, downtown. 513/651-2233.* Hrs: 11 am-2:30 pm, 5-10 pm; Fri to 11 pm; Sat 5-11 pm. Closed Sun; major hols. Italian, Amer menu. Bar. Semi-a la carte: lunch $6.99-$9.99, dinner $8.99-$18.99. Specialties: calypso coconut shrimp, Pigalls cafe salad, fresh seafood. Valet parking Fri, Sat. Bistro-style cafe with murals of Paris. Cr cds: A, C, D, DS, MC, V.

D

★★★ **THE PRECINCT.** *311 Delta Ave (45226), east of downtown. 513/321-5454.* Hrs: 5-10 pm; Fri, Sat to 11:30 pm. Closed some major hols. Res accepted. Bar 5 pm-2:30 am. Wine list. Semi-a la carte: dinner $16.95-$28.50. Specializes in steak, veal, fresh seafood. Own pastries. Entertainment. Valet parking. In 1890s police station. Cr cds: A, C, D, DS, MC, V.

D

★★ **PRIMAVISTA.** *810 Matson Place (45204), Price Hill, downtown. 513/251-6467.* Hrs: 5:30-10 pm; Fri from 5 pm; Sat 5-11 pm; Sun 5-9 pm. Closed major hols. Res accepted. Italian menu. Bar. Semi-a la carte: dinner $13.95-$28.95. Specialties: Branzino con Aragosta, Costolette di Vitello. Contemporary Italian decor, view of river. Cr cds: A, D, DS, MC, V.

D

★ **ROOKWOOD POTTERY.** *1077 Celestial St (45202), in Mt Adams. 513/721-5456.* Hrs: 11 am-10 pm; Fri, Sat to 11:30 pm. Closed Memorial Day, Thanksgiving, Dec 25. Bar. Semi-a la carte: lunch $5-$10, dinner $9-$17. Child's meals. Specializes in gourmet burgers, seafood, salads. Free parking. Originally housed production of Rookwood Pottery; some seating in former pottery kilns. Collection of Rookwood Pottery. Cr cds: A, C, D, MC, V.

SC

★★ **SEAFOOD 32.** *(See Regal Cincinatti Hotel) 513/352-2160.* Hrs: 5-10 pm; Fri, Sat to 11 pm. Closed Sun; Thanksgiving, Dec 25. Res accepted. Bar. Semi-a la carte: dinner $17.50-$24.95. Specialties: wild mushroom-crusted salmon, cioppino Thirty-2. Entertainment. Revolving restaurant overlooks the city. Cr cds: A, D, DS, MC, V.

D

✔★ **TANDOOR.** *8702 Market Place Ln (45242), north of downtown. 513/793-7484.* Hrs: 11:30 am-2 pm, 5:30-9:30 pm; Fri, Sat to 10:30 pm. Closed Sun; Dec 25. Res accepted. Northern India menu. Bar. Buffet: lunch $6.50. Complete meal: lunch, dinner $4.95-$18.95. Specializes in tandoori cooking. Outdoor dining. Indian decor. Cr cds: A, C, D, MC, V.

D

✔★ **TEAK.** *1049 St Gregory (45202), in Mt Adams. 513/665-9800.* Hrs: noon-3 pm, 5-9 pm; Fri to 10 pm; Sat 3-11 pm; Sun 5-9 pm. Closed major hols. Res accepted. Thai menu. Bar. Complete meals: lunch, dinner $6.50-$14.95. Specializes in noodle dishes, curry dishes. Outdoor dining. Contemporary decor with Thai art. Cr cds: A, C, D, DS, MC, V.

★ **WINDOW GARDEN.** *3077 Harrison Ave, I-75 Harrison Ave exit, north of downtown. 513/481-2743.* Hrs: 11 am-8 pm; Sun brunch to 2 pm. Closed Dec 25. Res accepted; required hols. Bar. Semi-a la carte: lunch $5-$7.75, dinner $7.95-$14.95. Sun brunch buffet $9.50. Child's meals. Parking. Cr cds: A, C, D, DS, MC, V.

SC

Unrated Dining Spots

AGLAMESIS BROS. *3046 Madison Rd, north of downtown. 513/531-5196.* Hrs: 10 am-10 pm; Fri, Sat to 11 pm; Sun noon-10 pm. Closed Jan 1, Easter, Dec 25. Avg ck: $5.50. Specializes in homemade ice cream & candy. Old-time ice cream parlor; established 1908. Family-owned. Cr cds: MC, V.

DARCI'S. *7328 Kenwood Rd, north of downtown. 513/793-2020.* Hrs: 7 am-10 pm; Fri, Sat to 11 pm. Closed Thanksgiving, Dec 25. French menu. Wine, beer. A la carte entrees: bkfst 89¢-$6.89, lunch, dinner $1.49-$12.99. Specializes in croissants, French delicatessen foods. Own baking. Cr cds: A, MC, V.

D

Cleveland

Founded: 1796
Pop: 505,616
Elev: 680 feet
Time zone: Eastern
Area code: 216

When the Ohio Canal opened in 1832, it linked Cleveland with the Ohio and Mississippi rivers and initiated the growth of the frontier settlement into an industrial and commercial center for northern Ohio. The town prospered after becoming a thriving center for shipping and later railroads; by the mid-1800s, the new city had a population of 43,000.

By the time of the Civil War, Cleveland was in a position to take advantage of the accessibility of iron ore from the Lake Superior region and coal from Ohio and Pennsylvania. Its steel industry grew to meet the nation's needs for machinery, railroad equipment, farm implements, ships, stoves and hardware.

Just after the Civil War, Cleveland became the center of the oil industry in the United States. In 1870, Standard Oil began here, under the stewardship of John D. Rockefeller, Samuel Andrews and Henry Flagler. Corporate giants, such as industrialist Marcus Hanna, Jeptha H. Wade and the Van Sweringen brothers, also helped foster the industrial expansion and cultural growth of the city.

In the last decade, Cleveland has gone through an economic transformation after almost falling apart in the 1970s. The heavy industries slowed down after World War II, and total manufacturing in greater Cleveland declined by more than one-third between 1970 and 1985. The turnaround was led by Cleveland Tomorrow, a group of CEOs from the city's top 50 companies, who concentrated on improving such problems of the city as politics, labor relations and modernization of manufacturing technology.

The new economic progress led the way to a rebuilding of the "north coast city" centered around the $279-million Tower City Center project, an enormous retail and office complex created behind the Terminal Tower at Public Square. The once-industrial Flats in the Cuyahoga River Valley is now known as a main entertainment area, with restaurants and bars lining the river. The $65-million Nautica development on the river's west bank consists of restaurants, clubs, a boardwalk and amphitheater. North Coast Harbor is the site of an ambitious, $900-million project that is developing several museums, including the Rock-and-Roll Hall of Fame.

Business

Cleveland enjoys a strategic location for transportation and commerce. Its excellent harbors make it one of the busiest ports along the St Lawrence Seaway-Great Lakes system. It handles a significant volume of iron ore receipts for the entire Great Lakes region.

Greater Cleveland occupies less than nine percent of Ohio's land area but has roughly one-sixth of the state's population. The Cleveland consolidated statistical area is one of the nation's largest consumer and industrial markets.

New technological advances in manufacturing durable goods, defense hardware and aerospace and medical equipment are responsible for the new employment expansion and diversity here. The service sector is also growing, especially in the financial, legal and health care areas. The health care industry has become the number one employer in Cleveland, providing jobs for thousands of people.

People come from all over the US and many foreign countries to Cleveland Clinic, a pioneer and leader in kidney transplants and open-heart surgery. Cleveland's Case Western Reserve University School of Medicine boasts an innovative medical curriculum, and the University Hospitals complex is a world leader in medical research through direct application.

The Greater Cleveland area is one of the foremost in the country in the number and quality of educational institutions. It includes Cleveland State University, Case Western Reserve University, the Cleveland Institute of Art, Cleveland Institute of Music, Dyke, Cuyahoga Community College and Notre Dame and Ursuline colleges.

John Carroll University in University Heights (1890) and Baldwin-Wallace College in Berea (1845) are located within the county. Other nearby schools are Kent State University (1910) and Oberlin College (1833), the first coeducational institution of higher learning in the United States.

Convention Facilities

The Cleveland Convention Center is located in the heart of downtown Cleveland, within walking distance of major hotels, which have a combined room capacity of 2,300.

There are 379,000 square feet of exhibit space. The main arena can seat 10,000; the Music Hall 3,000; the Little Theater 605. There are 33 meeting rooms, each able to accommodate 100 persons or more, and a ballroom for 4,000.

The International Exposition Center (I-X Center), located next to Cleveland Hopkins International Airport, is the largest single-building exposition facility in the world. It offers 2.5 million square feet of indoor space with more than 70,000 square feet of conference area available.

In addition, Cleveland has four hotels capable of handling meetings of 1,000 or more: Sheraton-City Center, Holiday Inn-Lakeside, Stouffer Tower City Plaza and Marriott Society Center.

Sports & Recreation

Sports fans enjoy living in Cleveland, home of the Cleveland Indians baseball team, Cleveland Cavaliers basketball team and the Cleveland Crunch soccer team.

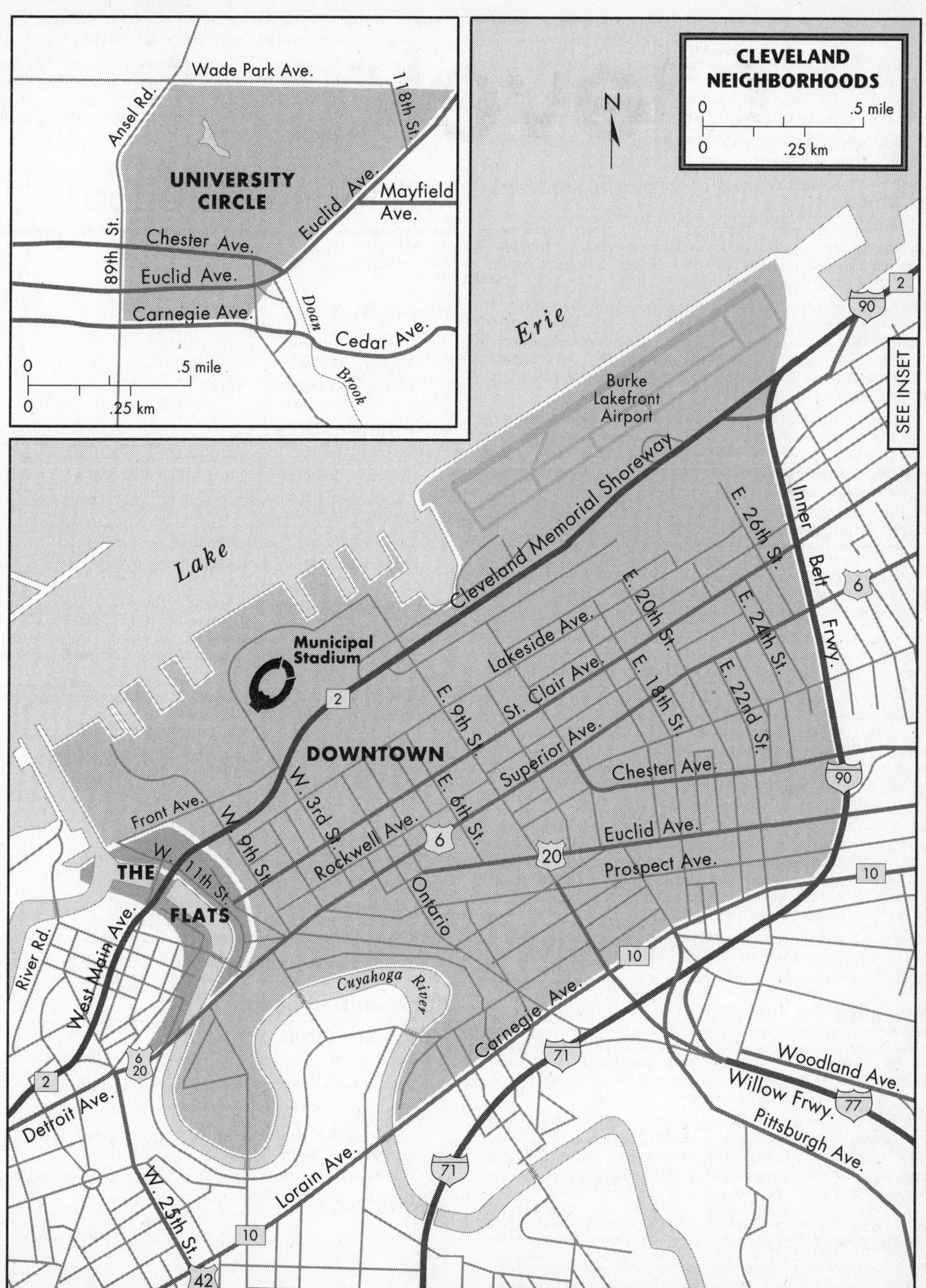
CLEVELAND
NEIGHBORHOODS
0
.5 mile
0
.25 km
N
Wade Park Ave.
Ansel Rd.
118th St.
UNIVERSITY
CIRCLE
Euclid Ave.
Mayfield
Ave.
89th St.
Chester Ave.
Euclid Ave.
Carnegie Ave.
Doan
Brook
Cedar Ave.
0
.5 mile
0
.25 km
Lake
Erie
Burke
Lakefront
Airport
SEE INSET
Cleveland Memorial Shoreway
Municipal
Stadium
DOWNTOWN
E. 26th St.
Inner Belt Frwy.
E. 20th St.
E. 24th St.
Lakeside Ave.
St. Clair Ave.
E. 18th St.
E. 22nd St.
E. 9th St.
Superior Ave.
Chester Ave.
W. 3rd St.
E. 6th St.
Front Ave.
W. 9th St.
Rockwell Ave.
Euclid Ave.
Prospect Ave.
W. 11th St.
THE
FLATS
Ontario
River Rd.
West Main Ave.
Cuyahoga River
Carnegie Ave.
Woodland Ave.
Willow Frwy.
Pittsburgh Ave.
Detroit Ave.
Lorain Ave.
W. 25th St.
2
90
6
90
20
10
10
71
77
71
10
42
2
6
20
6

Within 45 minutes driving time of the city are 188 golf courses. There are two horse-racing tracks and two auto-racing tracks nearby.

Tennis is popular, and facilities are easily found. The Northeast Ohio Tennis Association has 40 member clubs. In addition, nearly every municipality in the greater Cleveland area has public courts. The Harold T. Clark Tennis Stadium, where major tournaments are held annually, is downtown.

Skiing is close at hand at Alpine Valley Ski Area in Chesterland. Other winter sports include tobogganing, skating and snowmobiling.

Entertainment

The Cleveland Orchestra, organized in 1918, brings outstanding guest soloists and conductors to perform at Severance Hall from mid-September to mid-May and presents summer concerts at Blossom Music Center, about 28 miles south of town.

Several theaters present varied programs of classical and contemporary drama, music and dance. One of the best-known of these is Karamu House and Theatre, also a center for arts and interracial communication. The Cleveland Play House is one of the oldest professional resident theaters in the country. The Front Row Theatre offers top-name Las Vegas-style performers year round.

Nightlife in Cleveland centers around Playhouse Square Center, three renovated motion picture palaces with a combined capacity larger than New York City's Lincoln Center. The Flats, along both sides of the Cuyahoga River, is also a favorite area for nightlife, with a variety of nightclubs and restaurants.

Historical Areas

Ohio City, west of downtown Cleveland and across the Cuyahoga River, is undergoing redevelopment. Settled shortly after Cleveland was founded, its homes are being renovated, and new shops and restaurants add to the charm of the "just like old" neighborhood.

The Dunham Tavern Museum (1830) has been preserved and houses period furnishings as well as other items from the 19th century. The tavern was originally a rest stop for the stagecoach that ran from Detroit to Buffalo.

A unique phase of history is preserved in the Dittrick Museum of Medical History, where thousands of objects relating to the history of medicine, dentistry, pharmacy and nursing are on display. There are exhibits on the development of medical concepts from ancient times to the 19th century and on the history of the X ray and microscopes; an 1880 doctor's office and a pre-Civil War pharmacy are re-created.

The Western Reserve Historical Society Museum and Library has pioneer, Native American and Shaker exhibits; it also includes the Crawford Auto-Aviation Museum, which has more than 175 classic and antique automobiles and historical exhibits. The museum also has original manuscripts dating back to the founding of Cleveland, including some of the records of the Connecticut Land Company.

Lawnfield, President John A. Garfield's house, is northeast in Mentor; his impressive tomb is in Lakeview Cemetery, along with John D. Rockefeller's monument.

Sightseeing

A good way to view the port of Cleveland and the Cuyahoga River is on a cruise aboard the *Goodtime III,* which operates from mid-June through September. Trolley Tours of Cleveland offers a 20-mile ride (one or two hours) covering 70 points of interest.

There are beautiful parks in Cleveland: Wade Park, with 88 acres, a lagoon, rose and herb gardens; Rockefeller Park with cultural gardens combining landscaping and sculpture of 22 nationalities; Gordon Park with 119 acres on the shore of Lake Erie; Brookside Park, which includes the Cleveland Metroparks Zoo; Sea World, the largest inland marine life park in the Midwest. Next door is Geauga Lake Park, with more than 50 amusement rides. Another amusement park, Cedar Point, is situated 55 miles west on the shores of Lake Erie.

For a change of pace, go back in time nearly 200 years to Hale Farm and Western Reserve Village in the heart of the beautiful Cuyahoga Valley National Recreation Area. The 19th-century village can be reached on weekends by a train pulled by an old-fashioned locomotive.

Located in University Circle are the Cleveland Museum of Art and the Cleveland Museum of Natural History. Nationally acclaimed, the Museum of Art houses extensive collections of medieval, Oriental and Renaissance art. The Museum of Natural History features exhibits of dinosaurs, mammals, birds and geological specimens.

General References

Area code: 216

Phone Numbers

POLICE & FIRE: 911

POISON CONTROL CENTER: 231-4455

TIME & WEATHER: 931-1212

Information Sources

Convention and Visitors Bureau of Greater Cleveland, 3100 Terminal Tower, 50 Public Square, 44113; 800/321-1001.

Greater Cleveland Growth Association, 200 Tower City, 44113; 621-3300.

Visitor Information Center, 621-8860.

Department of Parks & Recreation, 664-3552.

Transportation

AIRLINES: Air Canada; American; Continental; Delta; Northwest; Southwest; TWA; United; USAir; and other commuter and regional airlines.

AIRPORTS: Cleveland Hopkins International, Cuyahoga County, 265-6000; Burke Lakefront, 781-6411.

CAR RENTAL AGENCIES: (See IMPORTANT TOLL-FREE NUMBERS) Avis 265-3700; Budget 433-4433; Dollar 267-3133; Hertz 267-8900; National 267-0060; Thrifty 267-6811.

PUBLIC TRANSPORTATION: RTA 621-9500.

Newspaper

Cleveland Plain Dealer.

Convention Facilities

Cleveland Convention Center, 500 Lakeside Ave, 348-2200.

International Exposition Center, 6200 Riverside Dr, 676-6000.

Sports & Recreation

Major Sports Facilities

Gund Arena, Ontario & Huron (Cavaliers, basketball, 420-2000).

Jacobs Field, Carnegie & Ontario (Indians, baseball, 420-4200).

Racetracks

Northfield Park Harness, 15 mi S, 10705 Northfield Rd (OH 8), Northfield, 467-4101.

Thistledown, 11 mi SE on Northfield Rd (OH 8), at Emery Rd in North Randall, 662-8600.

Cultural Facilities

Theaters

Beck Center for the Cultural Arts, 17801 Detroit Ave, Lakewood, 521-2540.

Cleveland Play House, 8500 Euclid Ave, 795-7000.

Karamu House and Theatre, 2355 E 89th St, 795-7070.

Ohio Theater, State Theater and Palace Theater, Playhouse Square Center, 1501 Euclid Ave, 241-6000.

Concert Halls

Convention Center, 500 Lakeside Ave, 348-2200.

Severance Hall, 11001 Euclid Ave, at East Blvd, 231-7300.

Museums

Cleveland Children's Museum, 10730 Euclid Ave, 791-KIDS.

Cleveland Health Education Museum, 8911 Euclid Ave, 231-5010.

Cleveland Museum of Natural History, Wade Oval Dr, at University Circle, 231-4600.

Crawford Auto-Aviation Museum, 10825 East Blvd, at University Circle, 721-5722.

Dittrick Museum of Medical History, 11000 Euclid Ave, 368-3648.

Dunham Tavern Museum, 6709 Euclid Ave, 431-1060.

NASA Lewis Visitor Center, 21000 Brookpark Rd, 433-2001.

Rock & Roll Hall of Fame, North Coast Harbor, E 9th St Pier, 781-ROCK.

Shaker Historical Museum, 16740 S Park Blvd, Shaker Heights, 921-1201.

Western Reserve Historical Society Museum and Library, 10825 East Blvd, at University Circle, 721-5722.

Art Museums

Cleveland Museum of Art, 11150 East Blvd, at University Circle, 421-7340.

Temple Museum of Religious Art, 1855 Ansel Rd, 831-3233.

Points of Interest

Historical

Hale Farm and Western Reserve Village, 2686 Oak Hill, S on I-77 to Wheatley Rd in Bath, 330/666-3711.

Lake View Cemetery, 12316 Euclid Ave, 421-2665.

Lawnfield, 8095 Mentor Ave, 27 mi NE in Mentor, 255-8722.

Other Attractions

Alpine Valley Ski Area, 10620 Mayfield Rd, 30 mi E on US 322 in Chesterland, 285-2211.

The Arcade, 401 Euclid Ave, 621-8500.

Blossom Music Center, 1145 W Steels Corners Rd, about 28 mi S via US 422, OH 8 in Cuyahoga Falls, 330/920-8040.

Cleveland Metroparks Zoo, 3900 Brookside Park Dr, 661-6500.

Cultural Gardens, Rockefeller Park, along East & Martin Luther King, Jr Blvds.

Cuyahoga Valley National Recreation Area, along the Cuyahoga River between Cleveland & Akron, 650-4636 or 524-1497.

Edgewater Park, West Blvd & Cleveland Memorial Shoreway, 881-8141.

Galleria, E 9th & St Clair, 621-9999.

Garden Center of Greater Cleveland, 11030 East Blvd, 721-1600.

Geauga Lake Park, 1060 Aurora Rd, in Aurora, 562-7131.

Gordon Park, E 72nd St & Cleveland Memorial Shoreway, 881-8141.

Lake Erie Nature and Science Center, 28728 Wolf Rd, 14 mi W on US 6 or I-90 to Bay Village, Metropark Huntington, 871-2900.

Public Square, Ontario St & Superior Ave.

Sea World, 1100 Sea World Dr, 23 mi SE on OH 43 in Aurora, 562-8101.

Shaker Lakes Regional Nature Center, 2600 S Park Blvd, 6 mi E on OH 87 in Shaker Heights, 321-5935.

USS *COD* (submarine), foot of E 9th St, 566-8770.

Wade Park, Euclid Ave near 107th St, at University Circle, 721-1600.

Sightseeing Tours

Goodtime III, pier at E 9th St, 861-5110.

North Coast Tours, 601 Rockwell Ave, 579-6160.

Lolly the Trolley Tours of Cleveland, Burke Lakefront Airport, 771-4484.

Annual Events

Home and Flower Show, Cleveland Convention Center, 529-1300. Late Feb.

Greater Cleveland Auto Show, International Exposition Center. Late Feb-early Mar.

St Patrick's Day Parade, downtown. Mar 17.

Great American Rib Cook-Off, North Coast Harbor, 247-2722. May.

Boston Mills Art Festival, 467-2242. Late June-early July.

Riverfest, The Flats, 696-7700. Late July.

Cuyahoga County Fair, fairgrounds in Berea, 243-0090. Early or mid-Aug.

Cleveland Grand Prix, Burke Lakefront Airport, 781-3500. July.

Slavic Village Harvest Festival, Slavic Village (Fleet Ave at E 55th St), 271-5591. Mid-Aug.

Cleveland National Air Show, Burke Lakefront Airport, 781-0747. Labor Day wkend.

Johnny Appleseed Festival, Mapleside Farms, in Brunswick, 225-5577. Sept.

Medieval Feasts & Spectacles, Trinity Cathedral, 579-9745. Dec.

City Neighborhoods

Many of the restaurants, unrated dining establishments and some lodgings listed under Cleveland include neighborhoods as well as exact street addresses. Geographic descriptions of these areas are given, followed by a table of restaurants arranged by neighborhoods.

Downtown: South of Lake Erie, west of I-90, north of Carnegie Ave and east of the Cuyahoga River. **South of Downtown:** South of OH 10. **West of Downtown:** West of Cuyahoga River.

The Flats: Area along both sides of the Cuyahoga River south of Front Ave and north of Superior Ave.

University Circle: East of Downtown; south of Wade Park Ave, west of Euclid Ave, north of Cedar Ave and east of E 89th St.

Lodgings and Food

CLEVELAND RESTAURANTS BY NEIGHBORHOOD AREAS
(For full description, see alphabetical listings under Restaurants)

DOWNTOWN
Alvie's. 2033 Ontario St
Diamondback Brewing Company. 724 Prospect Ave
John Q's Steakhouse. 55 Public Sq
Marlin. 1952 E 6th St
Morton's of Chicago. 1600 W Second St
New York Spaghetti House. 2173 E 9th St
Piccolo Mondo. 1352 W 6th St
Riverview Room (The Ritz-Carlton, Cleveland). 1515 W Third St
Sammy's. 1400 W 10th St
Sans Souci (Renaissance Hotel). 24 Public Square
Sweetwater's Cafe Sausalito. 1301 E 9th St

SOUTH OF DOWNTOWN
Johnny's Bar. 3164 Fulton Rd

WEST OF DOWNTOWN
Don's Lighthouse Grille. 8905 Lake Ave
Great Lakes Brewing Co. 2516 Market St
Heck's Cafe. 2927 Bridge Ave
Keka. 2523 Market Ave
Miracles'. 2391 W 11th St
Parker's. 2801 Bridge Ave

THE FLATS
Watermark. 1250 Old River Rd

UNIVERSITY CIRCLE
Baricelli Inn (Baricelli Inn). 2203 Cornell Rd
Classics (Omni International Hotel). 2065 E 96th St
Club Isabella. 2025 University Hospital Dr
Guarino's. 12309 Mayfield Rd
That Place on Bellflower. 11401 Bellflower Rd

Note: When a listing is located in a town that does not have its own city heading, it will appear under the city nearest to its location. In these cases, the address and town appear in parenthesis immediately following the name of the establishment.

Motels

★ ★ **COMFORT INN.** *(17550 Rosbough Dr, Middleburg Heights 44130) approx 13 mi S on I-71 exit 235. 216/234-3131; FAX 216/234-6111.* 136 rms, 3 story. S, D $79-$99; each addl $5; under 18 free; wkend rates. Crib free. Pet accepted, some restrictions. TV; cable (premium). Pool. Complimentary continental bkfst. Coffee in rms. Restaurant nearby. Ck-out noon. Meeting rms. Business center. Valet serv. Sundries. Free airport transportation. Microwaves avail. Cr cds: A, C, D, DS, ER, JCB, MC, V.

D SC

✔★ **CROSS COUNTRY INN.** *(7233 Engle Rd, Middleburg Heights 44130) 13 mi S on I-71 exit 235. 216/243-2277; FAX 216/243-9852.* 112 rms, 2 story. S $44.99-$51.99; D $47.99-$54.99; each addl $7; under 18 free. Crib free. TV; cable (premium). Heated pool. Complimentary coffee in lobby. Restaurant adj open 24 hrs. Ck-out noon. Meeting rm. Downhill ski 18 mi; x-country ski 5 mi. Cr cds: A, D, DS, MC, V.

D SC

★ ★ **FAIRFIELD INN BY MARRIOTT.** *(16644 Snow Rd, Brook Park 44142) S on I-90, W then S on I-71, near Intl Airport. 216/676-5200; FAX 216/676-5200, ext. 709.* 135 rms, 3 story. May-Aug: S, D $67.95; each addl $7; under 18 free; lower rates rest of yr. Crib free. TV; cable (premium). Pool. Complimentary continental bkfst. Ck-out noon. Business servs avail. Cr cds: A, D, DS, MC, V.

D SC

✔★ **RED ROOF INN.** *(17555 Bagley Rd, Middleburg Heights 44130) 13 mi SW via I-71 exit 235. 216/243-2441; FAX 216/243-2474.* 117 rms, 3 story. S $42.99-$54.99; D $47.99-$56.99; each addl $10; under 18 free. Crib free. Pet accepted. TV; cable (premium). Complimentary coffee. Restaurant nearby. Ck-out noon. Cr cds: A, C, D, DS, MC, V.

D

★ ★ ★ **RESIDENCE INN BY MARRIOTT.** *(17525 Rosbough Dr, Middleburg Heights 44130) 16 mi S on I-71 exit 235. 216/234-6688; FAX 216/234-3459.* 158 kit. suites, 2 story. S, D $109-$169; wkend, wkly, monthly rates. Crib free. Pet accepted, some restrictions. TV; cable (premium), VCR avail (movies). Heated pool; whirlpool. Complimentary continental bkfst. Complimentary coffee in rms. Restaurant adj 6 am-midnight. Ck-out noon. Coin Indry. Business servs avail. Valet serv. Sundries. Airport transportation. Downhill ski 15 mi; x-country ski 5 mi. Lawn games. Exercise equipt; bicycles, treadmill. Microwaves; many fireplaces. Picnic tables, grills. Cr cds: A, C, D, DS, JCB, MC, V.

D SC

Motor Hotel

★ ★ **HARLEY HOTEL-WEST.** *(17000 Bagley Rd, Middleburg Heights 44130) I-71 Bagley Rd exit. 216/243-5200; FAX 216/243-5240.* Web www.harleyhotels.com. 253 rms, 2 story. S $86-$96; D $96-$112; each addl $10; suites $125-$195; under 18 free; wkend rates. Crib free. TV; cable (premium). 2 pools, 1 indoor; wading pool, lifeguard. Restaurant 6:30 am-10 pm; Fri, Sat to 11 pm. Rm serv. Bar; entertainment Fri, Sat. Ck-out 11 am. Coin Indry. Meeting rms. In-rm modem link. Bellhops. Valet serv. Sundries. Free airport transportation. Sauna. Cr cds: A, C, D, DS, MC, V.

D SC

Hotels

★ ★ ★ **EMBASSY SUITES.** *1701 E 12th St (44114), downtown. 216/523-8000; FAX 216/523-1698.* Web www.embassy-suites.com. 268 suites, 10 story. S, D $119-$169; under 18 free; kit. units $119-$169; wkend rates. Crib free. Pet accepted. Valet parking $12. TV; cable. Indoor pool. Complimentary coffee in rms. Restaurant 6:30 am-10:30 pm. Bar 11-1 am. Ck-out noon. Coin Indry. Meeting rms. In-rm modem link. Concierge. Lighted tennis. Exercise equipt; weights, bicycles, sauna. Minibars, microwaves. Balconies. Cr cds: A, C, D, DS, ER, JCB, MC, V.

D SC

★ ★ ★ **MARRIOTT AIRPORT.** *4277 W 150th St (44135), west of downtown. 216/252-5333; FAX 216/251-1508.* Web www.marriott.com. 371 rms, 4-9 story. S $139; D $159; suites $175-$350; under 18 free; wkend package. Crib free. Pet accepted; $50. TV; cable (premium), VCR avail. Indoor pool; whirlpool, poolside serv. Restaurant 6 am-11 pm. Bar 11:30-2 am. Ck-out noon. Coin Indry. Convention facilities. Business servs avail. In-rm modem link. Gift shop. Free airport transportation. Exercise equipt; weights, bicycles, sauna. Cr cds: A, C, D, DS, ER, JCB, MC, V.

D SC

★ ★ ★ **MARRIOTT DOWNTOWN AT KEY CENTER.** *127 Public Sq (44114), downtown. 216/696-9200; FAX 216/696-0966.* 400 rms, 25 story. S, D $159-$169; suites $250-$750; under 18 free. Crib free. Garage $13. TV; cable (premium), VCR avail. Indoor pool; whirlpool. Restaurant 6 am-11 pm. Bar 11-2 am. Ck-out noon. Coin Indry. Convention facilities. Business center. In-rm modem link. Concierge. Gift shop. Exercise equipt; weight machine, treadmill, sauna. Minibars. Luxury level. Cr cds: A, C, D, DS, ER, JCB, MC, V.

D SC

★ ★ ★ **OMNI INTERNATIONAL.** *2065 E 96th St (44106), at Carnegie, in University Circle area. 216/791-1900; FAX 216/231-3329.* 302

rms, 17 story. S, D $209; each addl $10; suites $225-$1,300; under 18 free. Crib free. Garage parking $8. TV; cable (premium), VCR avail. Restaurant (see CLASSICS). Bar 11-1 am; Sat, Sun from noon. Ck-out noon. Convention facilities. Business servs avail. In-rm modem link. Gift shop. Entertainment in lobby. Exercise equipt; weights, bicycle. Minibars. Luxury level. Cr cds: A, C, D, DS, MC, V.

D SC

★ ★ ★ **RADISSON INN-CLEVELAND AIRPORT.** *(25070 Country Club Blvd, North Olmsted 44070) 12 mi W on I-480, exit 6B, then N adj Great Northern Mall. 216/734-5060; FAX 216/734-5471.* 140 rms, 6 story. May-Oct: S, D $139-$149; each addl $10; suites $160; under 18 free; wkend, hol rates; higher rates conventions; lower rates rest of yr. Crib free. TV; cable (premium), VCR avail. Indoor pool; whirlpool. Complimentary coffee in rms. Restaurant 6:30 am-2 pm, 5-10 pm; Sat, Sun from 7 am. Bar 11 am-11 pm. Ck-out noon. Meeting rms. Business servs avail. In-rm modem link. Free airport transportation. Downhill ski 15 mi; x-country ski 10 mi. Exercise equipt; stair machine, bicycle, sauna. Some refrigerators; microwaves avail. Some balconies. Cr cds: A, C, D, DS, ER, JCB, MC, V.

D SC

★ ★ ★ **RENAISSANCE.** *24 Public Square (44113), downtown. 216/696-5600; FAX 216/696-0432.* 491 rms, 14 story. S $125-$204; D $125-$224; each addl $20; suites $250-$1,500; under 18 free; wkend rates. Crib free. TV; cable (premium), VCR avail (movies). Indoor pool. Complimentary coffee. Restaurant (see SANS SOUCI). Bar 11-2 am; entertainment. Ck-out noon. Convention facilities. Business center. In-rm modem link. Concierge. Gift shop. Garage parking. Exercise rm; instructor, weights, bicycles, sauna. Health club privileges. Bathrm phones, refrigerators, minibars. 10-story indoor atrium. Luxury level. Cr cds: A, C, D, DS, ER, JCB, MC, V.

D SC

★ ★ ★ ★ **THE RITZ-CARLTON, CLEVELAND.** *1515 W Third St (44113), at Tower City Center, downtown. 216/623-1300; FAX 216/623-0515.* Web www.ritzcarlton.com. China cabinets in the halls and guest rooms with easy chairs add Victorian flourish to the modern elegance of this hotel. 208 rms, 7 story, 21 suites. S, D $149-$209; suites $259-$359; under 12 free; wkend rates. Pet accepted. Valet parking (fee). TV; cable, VCR avail (movies). Indoor pool; whirlpool, poolside serv. Restaurant 6:30 am-11 pm (see RIVERVIEW ROOM). Afternoon tea. Rm serv 24 hrs. Bar 11:30-1 am; pianist. Ck-out noon. Meeting rms. Business center. In-rm modem link. Concierge. Exercise equipt; weight machine, bicycles, sauna. Massage. Health club privileges. Bathrm phones, minibars. Luxury level. Cr cds: A, C, D, DS, ER, JCB, MC, V.

D

★ ★ ★ **SHERATON-CITY CENTER.** *777 St Clair Ave (44114), downtown. 216/771-7600; FAX 216/566-0736.* 470 rms, 22 story. S, D $154; each addl $15; suites $179-$850; under 18 free. Crib free. Garage $13. TV; cable (premium). Restaurant 6:30 am-11 pm. Bar from 11 am, Sun from 1 pm. Ck-out noon. Convention facilities. Business center. In-rm modem link. Gift shop. Airport transportation. Exercise equipt; weight machine, bicycle. Health club privileges. Many rms with view of lake. Luxury level. Cr cds: A, C, D, DS, MC, V.

D SC

★ ★ ★ **WYNDHAM.** *1260 Euclid Ave (44115). 216/615-7500; FAX 216/615-3355.* 205 rms, 14 story. S $149-$189; D $169-$209; each addl $20; suites $249; under 16 free. Crib avail. Valet parking $15. TV; cable. Indoor pool; whirlpool. Complimentary coffee in rms. Restaurant 6 am-10:30 pm. Bar to 2 am. Ck-out noon. Meeting rms. Business servs avail. Sundries. Valet serv. Exercise equipt; bicycle, treadmill. Sauna. Health club privileges. Cr cds: A, C, D, DS, MC, V.

D SC

Inn

★ ★ ★ **BARICELLI.** *2203 Cornell Rd (44106), at Cornell & Murray Hill, in University Circle area. 216/791-6500; FAX 216/791-9131.* 7 rms, 3 story. S, D $125-150. TV; cable. Complimentary continental bkfst. Dining rm (see BARICELLI INN). Ck-out 11 am, ck-in 2 pm. Business servs avail. Antiques, stained glass. Brownstone (1896) with individually decorated rms. Cr cds: A, C, D, MC, V.

Restaurants

★ ★ ★ **BARICELLI INN.** *(See Baricelli Inn) 216/791-6500.* Hrs: 5:30-11 pm. Closed Sun; most major hols. Res accepted. Continental menu. Wine, beer. Semi-a la carte: dinner $19.50-$39. Specialties: lobster & crab ravioli, beef tenderloin. Outdoor dining. Fireplaces, stained glass and paintings throughout room. Cr cds: A, C, D, MC, V.

★ **CABIN CLUB.** *(30651 Detroit Rd, Westlake 44145) 216/899-7111.* Hrs: 11 am-10:30 pm; Fri, Sat to 11:30 pm; Sun 4-10:30 pm. Closed most major hols. Res accepted. Bar to 1 am. Semi-a la carte: lunch $8-$16, dinner $15-$30. Child's meals. Specializes in steak, seafood, chicken. Log cabin decor. Cr cds: A, D, MC, V.

★ ★ **CENA COPA.** *(2206 Lee Rd, Cleveland Heights 44118) 8 mi E on US 322. 216/932-6995.* Hrs: 5:30-10 pm; Fri, Sat to 11 pm. Closed Sun; major hols. Res accepted; required Fri, Sat. Continental menu. Bar to 11 pm; Fri, Sat to midnight. Semi-a la carte: dinner $15.95-$24.95. Specializes in seafood. Own baking. Jazz Thurs. Valet parking. Outdoor dining. Contemporary, black-and-white decor. Cr cds: A, MC, V.

D

★ ★ ★ **CLASSICS.** *(See Omni International Hotel) 216/791-1300.* Hrs: 11:30 am-2:30 pm, 5:30-9:30 pm; Sat 5-10 pm. Closed Sun; major hols. Res accepted. Continental menu. Bar to 11 pm. Wine list. Semi-a la carte: lunch $15-$20, dinner $19-$29. Specialties: rack of lamb, steak Diane. Entertainment. Elegant decor. Jacket. Cr cds: A, C, D, DS, MC, V.

D

★ **CLUB ISABELLA.** *2025 University Hospital Dr (44106), in University Circle area. 216/229-1177.* Hrs: 11:30 am-11 pm; Fri to 1 am; Sat 5:30 pm-1 am. Res accepted; required wkends. Bar. Semi-a la carte: lunch $4.95-$7.95, dinner $8.95-$17.95. Live jazz nightly. Valet parking (dinner). Outdoor dining. Former stagecoach house. Cr cds: A, C, D, MC, V.

★ ★ **DIAMONDBACK BREWING COMPANY.** *724 Prospect Ave (44103), downtown. 216/771-1988.* Hrs: 11:30 am-10 pm; Fri to midnight; Sat 5 pm-midnight; Sun hrs vary. Closed most major hols. Res accepted. Continental menu. Bar. Semi-a la carte: lunch $6-$12, dinner $12-$24. Specializes in tapas. Own baking. Latino music Fri, Sat. Valet parking. Multi-level restaurant with brewery and champagne bar. Cr cds: A, C, D, DS, MC, V.

D

★ ★ **DON'S LIGHTHOUSE GRILLE.** *8905 Lake Ave (44102), west of downtown. 216/961-6700.* Hrs: 11:30 am-10 pm; Fri to 11 pm; Sat 5 pm-11 pm; Sun 4:30-9 pm. Closed some major hols. Res accepted. Continental menu. Bar. Semi-a la carte: lunch $6.95-$9.95, dinner $10-$20. Specializes in fresh seafood, steaks. Valet parking. Contemporary decor. Cr cds: A, C, D, DS, MC, V.

D

★ ★ **GREAT LAKES BREWING CO.** *2516 Market St (44113), opp West Side Market, west of downtown. 216/771-4404.* Hrs: 11:30 am-midnight; Fri, Sat to 1 am; Sun 3-10 pm. Closed major hols. Res accepted. Bar. Semi-a la carte: lunch, dinner $6-$16. Child's meals. Specializes in crab cakes, fresh pasta, seafood, brew master's pie. Own beer. Outdoor dining. Microbrewery. Located in historic 1860s brewery; turn-of-the-century pub atmosphere. Cr cds: A, C, D, MC, V.

✔★ ★ **GUARINO'S.** *12309 Mayfield Rd (44106), in University Circle area. 216/231-3100.* Hrs: 11:30 am-10:30 pm; Thurs to 11 pm; Fri, Sat to 11:30 pm; Sun 1-8 pm. Closed major hols. Res accepted; required

Fri, Sat. Italian, Amer menu. Bar. A la carte entrees: lunch $7-$9.25, dinner $12-$16.75. Child's meals. Specializes in Southern Italian cuisine. Valet parking. Outdoor dining. Oldest restaurant in Cleveland. In heart of Little Italy; antiques. Cr cds: A, C, D, DS, MC, V.

★ ★ **HECK'S CAFE.** *2927 Bridge Ave (44113), west of downtown. 216/861-5464.* Hrs: 11:30 am-9:30 pm; Tues, Wed to 10:30 pm; Thurs to 11:30 pm; Fri, Sat to midnight; Sun brunch 11 am-3 pm. Closed major hols. Res accepted. Semi-a la carte: lunch $4.15-$8.95, dinner $4.15-$18.95. Sun brunch $6.95-$9.95. Specializes in bouillabaisse, hamburgers. Outdoor dining. In historic 19th-century building. Cr cds: A, MC, V.

D

★ ★ **JOHN Q'S STEAKHOUSE.** *55 Public Sq (44113), downtown. 216/861-0900.* Hrs: 11:30 am-10 pm; Fri to 11 pm; Sat 4-11 pm; Sun from 4 pm. Closed major hols. Res accepted. Bar. Semi-a la carte: lunch $7.95-$18.95, dinner $15.95-$24.95. Child's meals. Specialty: 16-oz pepper steak. Vocalist Fri. Valet parking Sat. Outdoor dining. Traditional decor with dark wood floors and walls. Cr cds: A, C, D, DS, MC, V.

D SC

★ ★ **JOHNNY'S BAR.** *3164 Fulton Rd (44109), south of downtown. 216/281-0055.* Hrs: 11:30 am-3 pm, 5-10 pm; Fri to 11 pm; Sat 5-11 pm. Closed Sun; most major hols. Res accepted; required Fri, Sat. Italian menu. Bar. Semi-a la carte: lunch $6-$13.95, dinner $14.50-$29.95. Specialties: "Italian Feast," veal chops. Former neighborhood grocery. Family-owned. Cr cds: A, D, MC, V.

★ ★ **KEKA.** *2523 Market Ave (44113), west of downtown. 216/241-5352.* Hrs: 11:30 am-11 pm; Fri to 1 am; Sat 4 pm-1 am; Sun 5-10 pm. Closed Mon; major hols. Res accepted. Spanish menu. Bar. Semi-a la carte: lunch $4-$10, dinner $14-$20. Specializes in tapas, paella, seafood. Own baking. Jazz Wed-Fri. Valet parking. Outdoor dining. Spanish decor; high ceilings, artwork. Cr cds: A, MC, V.

D

✔★ ★ **LEMON GRASS.** *(2179 Lee Rd, Cleveland Heights 44118) 8 mi E on US 322. 216/321-0210.* Hrs: 11:30 am-2:30 pm, 5-10 pm; Fri to 11 pm; Sat 5-11 pm. Closed Sun; some major hols. Res accepted (dinner). Thai menu. Bar. Semi-a la carte: lunch $7-$10, dinner $11-$21. Specializes in seafood, curry dishes. Blues, jazz Fri. Outdoor dining. Thai decor with two distinct dining areas—one formal, one informal. Cr cds: A, MC, V.

D

★ ★ **MARLIN.** *1952 E 6th St (44114), downtown. 216/589-0051.* Hrs: 11:30 am-10 pm; Sat from 5:30 pm. Closed Sun; most major hols. Res accepted. Contemporary Amer menu. Bar. Semi-a la carte: lunch $8.25-$14, dinner $17-$29. Specializes in seafood. Bistro decor. Cr cds: A, D, DS, MC, V.

D

✔★ **MIRACLES'.** *2391 W 11th St (44113), 2 mi W on I-90, west of downtown. 216/623-1800.* Hrs: 11:30 am-9 pm; Mon to 2:30 pm; Fri, Sat to 10 pm; Sun 10:30 am-2:30 pm (brunch). Closed most major hols. Res accepted Fri-Sun. Bar. Semi-a la carte: lunch $5-$10, dinner $8-$17. Sun brunch $4.50-$6.95. Specializes in potato pancakes, homemade soups, fresh fish. Own baking. Outdoor dining. Casual dining in 1860 bldg. Cr cds: C, D, DS, MC, V.

★ ★ ★ **MORTON'S OF CHICAGO.** *1600 W Second St (44113), downtown. 216/621-6200.* Hrs: 11:30 am-2:30 pm, 5-11 pm; Sat from 5 pm; Sun 5-10 pm. Closed most major hols. Res accepted. Bar. Wine list. A la carte entrees: lunch $14-$23, dinner $21-$36. Specializes in steak, prime beef. Club atmosphere. Cr cds: A, C, D, JCB, MC, V.

D

★ **NEW YORK SPAGHETTI HOUSE.** *2173 E 9th St (44115), downtown. 216/696-6624.* Hrs: 11 am-9:30 pm; Fri, Sat to 10:30 pm; Sun 3-7 pm. Closed major hols. Res accepted. Italian, Amer menu. Bar. Semi-a la carte: lunch $6-$7, dinner $8-$24. Specializes in veal. Mural scenes of Italy. In former parsonage. Family-owned. Cr cds: A, DS, MC, V.

★ ★ ★ **PARKER'S.** *2801 Bridge Ave (44113), west of downtown. 216/771-7130.* French, Amer menu. Hrs: 11:30 am-2:30 pm; 5:30-9:15 pm. Closed Sun; major hols. Res accepted. Bar. Wine cellar. A la carte entrees: lunch $8-$14. Complete meals: dinner $41. Valet parking. Country French atmosphere. Jacket. Totally nonsmoking. Cr cds: A, DS, MC, V.

★ ★ **PICCOLO MONDO.** *1352 W 6th St (44113), downtown. 216/241-1300.* Hrs: 11:30 am-11 pm; Fri, Sat to midnight. Closed Sun; most major hols. Res accepted. Italian menu. Bar. Semi-a la carte: lunch $9-$20, dinner $11-$32. Specialties: veal scallopine, brick oven pizza. Italian villa decor. Cr cds: A, C, D, DS, MC, V.

D

★ ★ **PIER W.** *(12700 Lake Ave, Lakewood 44107) Shoreway via Rte 2 to Lake Ave. 216/228-2250.* Hrs: 11:30 am-3 pm, 5:30-10 pm; Fri, Sat 5 pm-midnight; Sun 9:30 am-2:30 pm, 4:30-10 pm; Sun brunch to 2:30 pm. Closed Dec 25. Res accepted. Bar. Semi-a la carte: lunch $5.95-$12.95, dinner $14.95-$47.95. Sun brunch $17.95. Specializes in seafood. Own pastries. Entertainment Fri, Sat. Valet parking. Nautical decor. On water with view of Lake Erie, Cleveland skyline. Cr cds: A, C, D, DS, MC, V.

D

✔★ **PLAYERS ON MADISON.** *(14523 Madison Ave, Lakewood 44107) 216/521-2600.* Hrs: 5-10 pm; Fri, Sat to 11 pm. Closed major hols. Italian menu. Bar. Semi-a la carte: dinner $14-$20. Specializes in pizza, pasta. Italian bistro decor. Cr cds: A, D, DS, MC, V.

D

★ ★ ★ **RIVERVIEW ROOM.** *(See The Ritz-Carlton, Cleveland Hotel) 216/623-1300.* Hrs: 6:30 am-10 pm; Fri, Sat to 11 pm; Sun brunch 10:30 am-2:30 pm. Res accepted; required brunch. Contemporary Amer menu. Bar. Wine cellar. Complete meal: bkfst $10.50-$15, lunch $15-$25, dinner $30-$40. Semi-a la carte: bkfst $8.50-$12, lunch $12.50-$17.50, dinner $24-$35. Bkfst buffet $8.50-$10.50. Sun brunch $32. Child's meals. Specialty: mushroom mystic. Own baking, pasta. Valet parking. Elegant restaurant with antiques and artwork throughout; large windows offer view of river and downtown. Cr cds: A, C, D, DS, ER, JCB, MC, V.

D

★ ★ **SAMMY'S.** *1400 W 10th St (44113), downtown. 216/523-5560.* Web www.dinersource.com/sammys/sammmain.html. Hrs: 5:30-10 pm; Fri, Sat to midnight. Closed Sun; major hols. Res accepted. Bar. Wine list. Semi-a la carte: dinner $19.95-$28.95. Specialties: boule de neige, fresh fish. Raw bar. Own baking. Entertainment. Valet parking. In restored 1850 warehouse; view of Cuyahoga River and bridges. Cr cds: A, C, D, DS, JCB, MC, V.

D

★ ★ ★ **SANS SOUCI.** *(See Renaissance Hotel) 216/696-5600.* Hrs: 11:30 am-2:30 pm, 5:30-10 pm; Fri, Sat to 11 pm; Sun from 5:30 pm. Closed most major hols. Res accepted. Mediterranean menu. Bar to 2 am. Wine list. Semi-a la carte: lunch $5.75-$15, dinner $11.95-$19.50. Specializes in seafood. Mediterranean decor. Cr cds: A, C, D, DS, JCB, MC, V.

D

★ ★ **SWEETWATER'S CAFE SAUSALITO.** *1301 E 9th St (44114), in the Galleria at Erieview, downtown. 216/696-2233.* Hrs: 11:30 am-9 pm; Fri, Sat to 10 pm. Closed Sun; Thanksgiving, Dec 25. Res accepted. Bar to midnight. Semi-a la carte: lunch $5.50-$10.95, dinner $6.95-$16.95. Specialties: seafood, pasta, black bean soup. Pianist Fri, Sat (dinner). Valet parking. Dinner theater package. Cr cds: A, D, DS, MC, V.

D 

★ ★ **THAT PLACE ON BELLFLOWER.** *11401 Bellflower Rd (44106), in University Circle area. 216/231-4469.* Hrs: 11:30 am-3 pm, 5:30-10 pm; Fri, Sat to 11 pm; Sun 5-8:30 pm; Mon to 3 pm. Closed major hols. Res accepted. Varied menu. Bar. Semi-a la carte: lunch $4.95-$6.95, dinner $9.95-$16.95. Child's meals. Specializes in beef Wellington, fresh salmon. Valet parking. Outdoor dining. Converted turn-of-the-century carriage house. Cr cds: A, D, MC, V.

D

✓★ ★ **WATERMARK.** *1250 Old River Rd (44113), in The Flats. 216/241-1600.* Hrs: 11:30 am-10 pm; Fri, Sat to 11 pm; Sun brunch 11 am-2:30 pm. Res accepted. Bar. Semi-a la carte: lunch, dinner $7.95-$17.95. Sun brunch $15.95. Child's meals. Specializes in marinated and grilled seafood. Free valet parking. Outdoor dining. Former ship provision warehouse on Cuyahoga River. Cr cds: A, C, D, DS, JCB, MC, V.

D

Unrated Dining Spot

ALVIE'S. *2033 Ontario St, downtown. 216/771-5322.* Hrs: 6:30 am-7 pm; Sat 9 am-3 pm. Closed Sun; major hols. Beer. Semi-a la carte: bkfst $2-$4, lunch $2-$5. Specializes in deli foods, salads. Own soups. Family-owned. No cr cds accepted.

Columbus

Founded: 1812
Pop: 632,910
Elev: 780 feet
Time zone: Eastern
Area code: 614
Web: www.columbuscvb.org

Ohio's capital and largest city, Columbus offers a balance of commerce, culture and recreation. Downtown, modern buildings overlook the Scioto River, while German Village, an historic district south of downtown, draws visitors with its Old World atmosphere. The city prospers from banking, insurance, computer and research facilities, and its educational institutions include Ohio State University.

In 1812, seeking a central location for the state capital, the Ohio legislature selected a site on the eastern shore of the Scioto River, laying the area out as a capital city and naming it after Christopher Columbus. Four years later the state government moved to Columbus from the temporary capital of Chillicothe, and in 1834 the city was incorporated. In 1871, Columbus annexed Franklinton, a town founded in 1797 on the western shore of the Scioto.

With improved transportation as a catalyst, Columbus grew to become a center of trade and commerce. In the early 1830s, a new canal linking the city with the Ohio and Erie Canal expedited trade with the East Coast. During the same period, Columbus became a stop for pioneers traveling to the West on the National Road. In the mid-1800s, the railroad came to Columbus, further increasing commercial activity.

After a 1913 flood, Columbus's worst natural disaster, the city widened the Scioto River, built flood walls and bridges and began construction on the Civic Center, a group of buildings covering several blocks on both shores of the Scioto.

Columbus continued to grow in the latter 20th century, both in area—the result of a program to annex several square miles of unincorporated land yearly—and in facilities, with the Columbus City Center and Greater Columbus Convention Center drawing thousands of visitors each year.

Business

Transportation equipment, machinery, fabricated and primary metals, food, printing and publishing are among the principal industries, but education and government are Columbus' most important functions. Its people are civic-minded, sports-minded and cultured. The city has more than 900 churches and 13 colleges and universities.

Convention Facilities

The Greater Columbus Convention Center has a total exhibition floor space of 1.2 million square feet, which includes 54 meeting rooms, an exhibition hall and ballroom.

The Ohio Expositions Center has a total of 56 buildings and accommodates sporting events, business seminars, custom car shows, exhibitions and concerts.

Veterans Memorial has a total exhibition floor space of 110,000 square feet in three interconnected, ground-level-access exhibition halls, eight meetings rooms and a 3,940-seat auditorium.

Sports & Recreation

College-sports fans follow the Ohio State Buckeyes, Big 10 competitors in football, basketball, baseball and other collegiate sports. The Ohio Stadium is the site of many Ohio State sports events.

Other sports teams include the Columbus Chill, a minor-league hockey team that plays at the Ohio Expo Center; the Crew, a major-league soccer team that plays at the Ohio Stadium; and the Clippers, a AAA baseball team that plays at Cooper Stadium.

Auto racing is found at the National Trail Raceway and the Columbus Motor Speedway; harness racing at Scioto Downs; Thoroughbred racing at Beulah Park.

Opportunities for participant sports are available throughout Columbus at public tennis courts, public swimming pools and municipal and daily-fee golf courses. Across the street from the O'Shaughnessy Reservoir, about 19 miles northwest of Columbus, is the Wyandot Lake Water Park.

The Hoover Reservoir area offers fishing, boating, nature trails and picnic sites, as does the O'Shaughnessy Reservoir, which has waterskiing as well. The Chadwick Arboretum, run by Ohio State University, has display gardens and a park dedicated to cancer survivors, in addition to the arboretum.

Entertainment

Columbus provides many opportunities to attend live performances. BalletMet and the Columbus Symphony Orchestra perform at the Ohio Theatre, which dates from the 1920s, and the Palace Theater hosts Opera/Columbus. These two theaters, plus the Capitol Theater, are also venues for CAPA (Columbus Association of Performing Arts) performances, such as Broadway shows. In the Park of Roses, with its more than 10,000 rosebushes and picnic facilities, music is performed on summer Sundays.

The Brewery District, near German Village south of downtown, and the Short North, on High Street just above Goodall Park, are full of lively bars and other nightspots, and comedy clubs are found throughout Columbus.

Historical Areas

In the 1800s, many German immigrants made Columbus their home, settling in the area south of downtown. Known today as German Village, this historic district contains restored homes, shops, gardens and Old World foods.

During the Civil War, the largest Northern prison for Confederate soldiers was in Columbus, and the soldiers that died in the prison are buried in the Camp Chase Confederate Cemetery.

The exhibits in the Ohio Historical Center portray the archaeological and natural history of the area and include background that will enlighten a tour of Ohio's prehistoric Native American mounds. On the Historical Center grounds is Ohio Village, a reconstructed town of the 1860s, complete with buildings and costumed craftspeople.

A tribute to the city's namesake, the *Santa Maria* is a full-scale replica of Columbus's flagship.

Sightseeing

Spanning both shores of the Scioto River are the buildings that make up the Columbus Civic Center. Most government buildings are on the eastern shore, among them the State Office Tower Building, with an observation window on its 40th floor, and City Hall, a Greco-Roman structure. In City Hall Plaza stands a bronze statue of Christopher Columbus, a 1955 gift from the people of Genoa, Italy. Heading south from City Hall Plaza, on Civic Center Drive, are two blocks lined with the flags of the 50 states. The Martha Kinney Cooper Ohioana Library, housed in the Ohio Departments Building, contains reference books by and on Ohioans.

The Ohio Statehouse, which took 22 years to build and was completed in the 1860s, is a Greek-revival limestone building that recently underwent a $100-million restoration. On the northwest corner of the 10-acre Capitol Square are bronze statues by Levi T. Scofield, depicting soldiers and statesmen. At the west end of the entrance to the capitol gardens is the McKinley Memorial, a statue of President McKinley.

Of interest to families is the COSI (pronounced "co-sigh"), the Center of Science and Industry, a hands-on museum with exhibits, programs and demonstrations. The Columbus Zoo, at the dam in the O'Shaughnessy Reservoir, has birds, mammals, fish, reptiles and a children's zoo.

Art museums include the Wexner Center for the Arts, on the Ohio State campus, which focuses on contemporary art, film and performing arts; and the Columbus Museum of Art, exhibiting 19th- and 20th-century works by Europeans and Americans and 16th- and 17th-century works by Dutch and Flemish masters.

Tours are offered of Ohio State University, founded in 1870 and one of the nation's largest universities, with 19 colleges, a graduate school, a medical center and more than 4 million volumes in its library collections.

General References

Area code: 614

Phone Numbers

POLICE & FIRE: 911

POISON CONTROL CENTER: 228-2272

TIME & WEATHER: 469-1010

Information Sources

Tourist brochures and a quarterly calendar of events may be obtained at the Greater Columbus Convention & Visitor Bureau, 2nd Level of Columbus City Center Shopping Mall, 90 N High St, phone 800/345-4FUN. A visitor information center is located at the Columbus International Airport, I-670E, I-270. For public transportation information phone 228-1776.

Transportation

AIRLINES: America West, American, Continental, Delta, Northwest, Southwest, TWA, United, and USAir; and other commuter and regional airlines.

AIRPORT: Port Columbus International Airport, 239-4083.

CAR RENTAL AGENCIES: (See IMPORTANT TOLL-FREE NUMBERS) Alamo; Avis; Budget; Dollar; Hertz; National; Payless; Thrifty.

PUBLIC TRANSPORTATION: Central Ohio Transit Authority (COTA), 228-1776.

RAILROAD PASSENGER SERVICE: Amtrak 800/872-7245.

Newspaper

Columbus Dispatch.

Convention Facilities

Greater Columbus Convention Center, 400 N High St, 645-5000.

Ohio Expositions Center, 171 E 17th St, 644-3247.

Veterans Memorial, 300 W Broad St, 221-4341.

Sports & Recreation

Major Sports Facilities

Columbus Motor Speedway, 1845 Williams Rd, 491-1047.

Cooper Stadium, 1155 W Mound St, 462-5250.

National Trail Raceway, 2650 National Rd SW, Hebron, 928-5706.

Ohio Expo Center, 717 E 17th Ave, 644-4014.

Ohio Stadium, 410 Woody Hayes Dr, 292-6861.

Racetracks

Beulah Park Jockey Club, Southwest Blvd, in Grove Park, 871-9600.

Scioto Downs, 9 mi S on US 23 (High St), 3 mi S of I-270, 491-2515.

Cultural Facilities

Theater

Capitol Theater, 77 S High St, in the Riffe Center, 469-0939.

Ohio Theatre, 55 E State St, 229-4848.

Palace Theatre, 34 W Broad St, 461-0022.

Museums

COSI, Ohio's Center of Science & Industry, 280 E Broad St, 228-2674.

Ohio Historical Center, 17th Ave at I-71, 297-2300.

Art Museums

Columbus Museum of Art, 480 E Broad St, 221-6801.

Wexner Center for the Arts, 15th Ave at High St, 292-0330.

Points of Interest

Historical

Camp Chase Confederate Cemetery, Sullivant Ave between Powell Ave & Binns Blvd.

German Village, Livingston Ave, Blackberry Alley, Nursery Ln & Pearl Alley, 221-8888.

McKinley Memorial, W entrance to capitol grounds.

Ohio Village, on Historical Center grounds, 297-2680.

Santa Maria **Replica,** Battelle Riverfront Park, Marconi Blvd & Broad St, 645-8760.

Other Attractions

City Hall, N Front, W Gay, W Broad Sts & Marconi Blvd.

Columbus Zoo, 9990 Riverside Dr, 645-3550.

Federal Building, 200 N High St.

Hoover Reservoir Area, 12 mi NE on Sunbury Rd, 645-3350.

Martha Kinney Cooper Ohioana Library, 65 S Front St, 466-3831.

Ohio Prehistoric Native American Mounds, begin at 17th Ave at I-71.

Ohio Statehouse, High, Broad, State & 3rd Sts, 466-2125.

Ohio State University, N High St & 15th Ave, 292-3980 (tour) or 292-4070.

O'Shaughnessy Reservoir, 16 mi N on Riverside Dr.

State Office Tower Building, Civic Center Dr.

Park of Roses, Acton & High Sts, 6 mi N in Whetstone Park.

Wyandot Lake Water Park, 10101 Riverside Dr, 19 mi NW in Powell.

Sightseeing Tours

Columbus City Center, 111 S 3rd St, 221-4900.

Annual Events

Actors Theater, Schiller Park. June-Aug.

Greater Columbus Arts Festival, Downtown riverfront area. Early June.

Ohio State Fair, Expositions Center, 800/BUCKEYE. Early-mid-Aug.

Columbus Day Celebration. Early Oct.

Lodgings and Food

Motels

★ ★ **AMERISUITES.** *7490 Vantage Dr (43235). 614/846-4355; FAX 614/846-4493.* 126 suites, 6 story. S, D $98-$118; under 12 free. Crib free. TV; cable (premium), VCR avail (movies). Heated pool. Complimentary continental bkfst. Restaurant adj 6 am-11 pm. Ck-out noon. Meeting rms. Business center. Valet serv. Coin lndry. Free airport transportation. Exercise equipt; weight machine, bicycle. Microwaves. Cr cds: A, C, D, DS, MC, V.

D SC

★ **BEST WESTERN-EAST.** *(2100 Brice Rd, Reynoldsburg 43068) E on I-70, exit 110. 614/864-1280; FAX 614/864-1280, ext. 388.* 143 rms, 2 story. S $60-$72; D $69-$79; under 18 free; higher rates special events. Crib free. Pet accepted. TV; cable (premium). Pool; poolside serv. Restaurant 6 am-11 pm. Rm serv. Bar 11 am-midnight. Ck-out noon. Meeting rms. Businesss servs avail. Free airport transportation. Cr cds: A, C, D, DS, MC, V.

D SC

★ ★ **COURTYARD BY MARRIOTT.** *7411 Vantage Dr (43085). 614/436-7070; FAX 614/436-4970.* 145 rms, 4 story. S, D $95-$99; each addl $10; suites $105-$125; under 18 free; wkend rates. Crib free. TV; cable (premium). Indoor pool; whirlpool. Complimentary coffee in rms. Restaurant 6:30-10 am. Bar 4:30-11 pm. Ck-out 1 pm. Coin lndry. Meeting rms. Business servs avail. In-rm modem link. Valet serv (Mon-Fri). Exercise equipt; weights, bicycles. Game rm. Refrigerator in suites. Balconies. Cr cds: A, C, D, DS, MC, V.

D SC

✔★ ★ **CROSS COUNTRY INN-NORTH.** *4875 Sinclair Rd (43229). 614/431-3670; FAX 614/431-7261.* 136 rms, 2 story. S $39.99-$41.99; D $46.99-$49.99; family rates. Crib free. TV; cable (premium). Heated pool. Restaurant adj 6 am-11 pm. Ck-out noon. Business servs avail. Cr cds: A, DS, MC, V.

D SC

★ ★ **FAIRFIELD INN BY MARRIOTT.** *887 Morse Rd (43229). 614/262-4000.* 135 rms, 3 story. Apr-Oct: S, D $49-$66; each addl $6; under 18 free; lower rates rest of yr. Crib free. TV; cable (premium). Pool. Complimentary continental bkfst. Restaurant nearby. Ck-out noon. Meeting rm. Business servs avail. In-rm modem link. Cr cds: A, C, D, DS, MC, V.

D SC

★ ★ **HAMPTON INN.** *4280 International Gateway (43219), near Port Columbus Airport. 614/235-0717; FAX 614/231-0886.* 129 rms, 4 story. S, D $65-$70; each addl $5; suites $90; under 18 free. Crib free. TV; cable (premium). Complimentary continental bkfst. Restaurant adj 6 am-midnight. Ck-out noon. Meeting rms. Business servs avail. In-rm modem link. Bellhops. Valet serv (Mon-Fri). Free airport transportation. Health club privileges. Heated pool. In-rm whirlpool in suites. Cr cds: A, C, D, DS, MC, V.

D

★ ★ **HOMEWOOD SUITES.** *115 Hutchinson Ave (43235), jct I-270 & US 23N. 614/785-0001; FAX 614/785-0143; res: 800/225-5466.* 99 kit. units, 3 story, 99 suites. S, D $99-$115; wkend rates. Crib free. Pet accepted; from $10/day. TV; cable (premium), VCR (movies $5). Heated pool; whirlpool. Complimentary bkfst. Complimentary coffee in rms. Restaurant adj 6 am-midnight. Ck-out noon. Coin lndry. Meeting rms. Business center. In-rm modem link. Sundries. Tennis privileges. Exercise equipt; weight machine, stair machine. Lawn games. Microwaves. Grills. Cr cds: A, C, D, DS, JCB, MC, V.

D SC

✔★ **RED ROOF INN-MORSE ROAD.** *750 Morse Rd (43229), I-71 Morse-Sinclair exit 16. 614/846-8520; FAX 614/846-8526.* 107 rms, 2 story. S $42.99-$52.99; D $49.99-$59.99; under 18 free. Crib free. Pet accepted. TV. Complimentary coffee in lobby. Restaurant adj 7 am-11 pm. Ck-out noon. Business servs avail. Cr cds: A, C, D, DS, MC, V.

D SC

★ ★ **SIGNATURE INN.** *6767 Schrock Hill Ct (43229), N of I-270, Cleveland Ave exit. 614/890-8111.* 125 rms, 2 story. S, D $67-$77; under 17 free. Crib free. TV; cable (premium), VCR avail (movies). Pool. Complimentary continental bkfst. Restaurant adj 8 am-midnight. Ck-out noon. Meeting rms. Business center. Health club privileges. Cr cds: A, C, D, DS, MC, V.

D SC

★ ★ **TRUEMAN CLUB HOTEL.** *900 E Dublin-Granville Rd (43229), just W of I-71 exit 117 (OH 161). 614/888-7440; FAX 614/888-7879; res: 800/477-7888.* 182 rms, 5 story, 22 suites. S, D $124-$134; each addl $10; suites $145-$155. Crib free. TV; cable (premium). Indoor pool; whirlpool. Complimentary continental bkfst. Restaurant adj 6 am-11 pm. Bar 4 pm-1 am. Ck-out noon. Coin lndry. Meeting rms. Business servs avail. Free airport transportation. Exercise equipt; bicycles, stair machines. Health club privileges. Some refrigerators, wet bars. Cr cds: A, C, D, DS, MC, V.

D SC

Motor Hotels

✔★ **BEST WESTERN-NORTH.** *888 E Dublin-Granville Rd (43229). 614/888-8230; FAX 614/888-8223.* 180 rms, 2 story. S, D $69-$74; each addl $5; suites $95; under 18 free; wkend rates. Crib free. TV; cable (premium). 2 pools, 1 indoor. Restaurant 6:30 am-10 pm. Rm serv. Bar 5 pm-2 am. Ck-out noon. Coin lndry. Business servs avail. Valet serv. Health club privileges. Cr cds: A, C, D, DS, MC, V.

SC

★ ★ **COURTYARD BY MARRIOTT.** *35 W Spring St (43215). 614/228-3200; FAX 614/228-6752.* 149 rms, 5 story. S, D $100-$107; each addl $10; suites $130-$140; under 18 free. Crib free. Valet parking $12.50. TV; cable, VCR avail. Indoor pool; whirlpool. Complimentary coffee in rms. Restaurant 6:30-10 am, 5-10 pm; Sat, Sun 7 am-noon. Bar 5-11 pm. Ck-out noon. Meeting rms. Business servs avail. In-rm modem link. Bellhops. Sundries. Valet serv. Coin lndry. Exercise equipt; bicycles, weight machine. Health club privileges. Some refrigerators. Cr cds: A, C, D, DS, MC, V.

D SC

★ ★ **HARLEY.** *1000 E Dublin-Granville Rd (43229), at I-71 exit 117. 614/888-4300; FAX 614/888-3477.* Web www.harleyhotels.com. 150 rms, 2 story. S, D $102-$112; each addl $10; suites $130; under 18 free. Crib free. TV; cable (premium). Sauna. 2 pools, 1 indoor; whirlpool. Restaurant 6:30 am-10 pm. Rm serv. Bar 4:30 pm-1 am, Sun to 10 pm; entertainment wkends. Ck-out 11 am. Meeting rms. Business servs avail. Parking. Free airport transportation. Lighted tennis. Putting green. Health club privileges. Game rm. Lawn games. Private patios, balconies. Cr cds: A, C, D, DS, MC, V.

D SC

★ ★ ★ **HOLIDAY INN.** *175 Hutchinson Ave (43235), I-270 exit 23. 614/885-3334; FAX 614/846-4353.* 316 rms, 6 story. S, D $99-$115; suites $205-$220; under 17 free. Crib free. Pet accepted. TV; cable (premium), VCR avail. Indoor pool. Complimentary coffee in rms. Restaurant 6 am-11 pm. Rm serv. Bar. Ck-out noon. Coin lndry. Convention facilities. Business servs avail. In-rm modem link. Bellhops. Gift shop. Free airport transportation. Exercise equipt; weight machine, stair machine. Refrigerator in suites. Cr cds: A, C, D, DS, MC, V.

D SC

★ **HOLIDAY INN-AIRPORT.** *750 Stelzer Rd (43219), near Port Columbus Airport. 614/237-6360; FAX 614/237-2978.* 236 rms, 3 story. S $89.95-$109.95; D $108.95-$119.95; each addl $10; suites $135-

$175; under 18 free; wkend rates. Crib free. Pet accepted. TV; cable. Indoor pool; whirlpool. Complimentary coffee in rms. Restaurant 6:30 am-2 pm, 5:30-10 pm. Rm serv. Bar 1 pm-midnight. Ck-out noon. Coin lndry. Meeting rms. Business servs avail. In-rm modem link. Sundries. Gift shop. Airport transportation. Exercise equipt; weights, bicycles, sauna. Cr cds: A, C, D, DS, JCB, MC, V.

D SC

✔★ ★ **LENOX INN.** *(I-70E at OH 256, Reynoldsburg 43086) exit 112B. 614/861-7800; FAX 614/759-9059; res: 800/821-0007.* 151 rms, 2 story. S, D $49-$77; each addl $6; suites $109-$134; under 18 free. Crib free. Pet accepted; $10. TV; cable (premium). Pool. Restaurant 6:30 am-10 pm. Rm serv. Bar. Ck-out 11 am. Meeting rms. Business servs avail. In-rm modem link. Valet serv. Sundries. Free airport transportation. Health club privileges. Cr cds: A, C, D, DS, MC, V.

D SC

★ ★ ★ **WOODFIN SUITES.** *(4130 Tuller Rd, Dublin 43017) N on OH 315, W on I-270 to exit 20, S to Dublin Center Dr, right 1 blk to Tuller Rd. 614/766-7762; FAX 614/761-1906; res: 800/237-8811.* 88 kit. suites, 2 story. 1 bedrm $140-$150; 2 bedrm $189; each addl $10; under 12 free; wkend rates. Crib free. TV; cable (premium), VCR (free movies). Heated pool; whirlpool. Complimentary bkfst buffet. Complimentary coffee in rms. Restaurant nearby. Ck-out noon. Coin lndry. Meeting rms. Business center. In-rm modem link. Valet serv. Microwaves. Cr cds: A, D, DS, MC, V.

D SC

Hotels

★ ★ ★ **ADAM'S MARK.** *50 N Third St (43215), downtown. 614/228-5050; FAX 614/228-2525.* 415 rms, 21 story. S, D $175-$195; each addl $20; suites $700; under 18 free; higher rates special events. Crib free. Valet parking $13; garage parking $10. TV; cable (premium), VCR avail. Restaurant 6:30 am-11 pm. Rm serv 24 hrs. Bar 11-2 am; Sun to 11 pm. Ck-out noon. Convention facilities. Business servs avail. In-rm modem link. Gift shop. Coin lndry. Exercise equipt; treadmill, stair machine, sauna. Heated pool; whirlpool. Cr cds: A, C, D, DS, JCB, MC, V.

D SC

★ ★ ★ **CONCOURSE.** *4300 International Gateway (43219), at Port Columbus Airport. 614/237-2515; FAX 614/237-6134.* 147 rms, 2 story. S, D $113-$125; each addl $10. Crib free. TV; cable (premium), VCR avail (movies). 2 pools, 1 indoor; whirlpool, poolside serv. Restaurants 6 am-11 pm. Bar 11-1 am. Ck-out noon. Meeting rms. Business servs avail. In-rm modem link. Free airport transportation. Valet serv. Exercise equipt; weights, treadmills, sauna, steam rm. Cr cds: A, C, D, DS, MC, V.

SC

★ ★ ★ **CROWNE PLAZA.** *33 Nationwide Blvd (43215), downtown. 614/461-4100; FAX 614/461-5828.* Web www.crowneplaza.com. 384 rms, 12 story. S, D $150-$190; suites $350-$500; under 12 free; wkend rates. Crib free. Garage $13. TV; cable. Indoor pool. Coffee in rms. Restaurant 6:30 am-11 pm. Bar from 11 am. Ck-out noon. Coin lndry. Convention facilities. Business servs avail. In-rm modem link. Gift shop. Exercise equipt; weight machines, bicycles, sauna. Connected to Convention Center. Luxury level. Cr cds: A, C, D, DS, JCB, MC, V.

D SC

★ ★ ★ **DOUBLETREE GUEST SUITES.** *50 S Front St (43215). 614/228-4600; FAX 614/228-0297.* 194 suites, 16 story. S, D $179-$219; each addl $20; under 18 free; wkend rates; higher rates special events. Crib free. TV; cable (premium). Coffee in rms. Restaurant 6:30 am-10 pm; Sat from 7 am-11 pm; Sun 7 am-10 pm. Bar 11 am-midnight, Sun from 1 pm. Ck-out noon. Business center. In-rm modem link. Covered parking. Health club privileges. Refrigerators; microwaves avail. Opp river. Cr cds: A, C, D, DS, MC, V.

D SC

★ ★ ★ **EMBASSY SUITES.** *2700 Corporate Exchange Dr (43231), off I-270 exit 27. 614/890-8600; FAX 614/890-8626.* 217 kit. suites, 8 story. S $109-$139; D $119-$149; each addl $10; suites $200-$300; under 18 free; wkend rates. Crib free. TV; cable (premium), VCR avail. Indoor/outdoor pool; whirlpool, poolside serv. Complimentary full bkfst. Restaurant 11 am-10 pm; wkends to 11 pm. Bar 11-1 am. Ck-out noon. Meeting rms. Business servs avail. Concierge. Gift shop. Free airport transportation. Exercise equipt; stair machine, treadmill, sauna. Game rm. Refrigerators, microwaves. Cr cds: A, C, D, DS, MC, V.

D SC

★ ★ **HOLIDAY INN-CITY CENTER.** *175 E Town St (43215). 614/221-3281; FAX 614/221-2667.* 240 rms, 12 story. S, D $119-$150; under 18 free. Crib free. Pet accepted. TV; cable (premium). Pool. Complimentary coffee in rms. Restaurant 6:30 am-2 pm, 5-10 pm; Sat, Sun from 7 am. Bar 4 pm-midnight. Ck-out noon. Meeting rms. Business servs avail. Free airport transportation. Health club privileges. Cr cds: A, C, D, DS, ER, JCB, MC, V.

D SC

★ ★ **HOLIDAY INN-EAST.** *4560 Hilton Corporate Dr (43232), I-70 Hamilton Rd exit 107. 614/868-1380; FAX 614/863-3210.* E-mail 102175,426@compuserve.com. 278 rms, 21 story. S, D $109-$130; each addl $10; wkend plan. Crib free. TV; cable (premium). Indoor pool; wading pool, poolside serv. Playground. Coffee in rms. Restaurant 6 am-midnight. Bar 11-2 am. Ck-out noon. Convention facilities. Business center. In-rm modem link. Free airport transportation. Exercise equipt; bicycle, stair machine, sauna. Health club privileges. Cr cds: A, C, D, DS, JCB, MC, V.

D SC

★ ★ ★ **HYATT ON CAPITOL SQUARE.** *75 E State St (43215), at Columbus City Center. 614/228-1234; FAX 614/469-9664.* Web www.hyatt.com. 400 rms, 21 story. S, D $203-$228; each addl $25; suites $250-$400; under 18 free; wkend packages. TV; cable (premium). Restaurant 6:30 am-10 pm; wkends to 11 pm. Bar 11 am-midnight; wkends to 1 am; entertainment. Ck-out noon. Meeting rms. Business center. In-rm modem link. Concierge. Shopping arcade. Exercise equipt; weights, bicycles, sauna. Massage. Some private patios, balconies. Luxury level. Cr cds: A, C, D, DS, JCB, MC, V.

D SC

★ ★ ★ **HYATT REGENCY.** *350 N High St (43215), at Greater Columbus Convention Ctr. 614/463-1234; FAX 614/280-3046.* Web www.hyatt.com. 631 rms, 20 story. S, D $180-$205; each addl $25; suites $625-$1,000; under 18 free. Crib free. Valet parking $14.50. TV; cable (premium). Indoor pool. Restaurant 6:30 am-2:30 pm, 5-11 pm; Thurs-Sat 5 pm-midnight; Sun 6:30 am-11 pm. Bar 11-1:30 am; entertainment. Ck-out noon. Business center. In-rm modem link. Concierge. Shopping arcade. Exercise equipt; stair machine, treadmill. Luxury level. Cr cds: A, C, D, DS, JCB, MC, V.

D SC

★ ★ ★ **MARRIOTT-NORTH.** *6500 Doubletree Ave (43229), I-71 exit 117. 614/885-1885; FAX 614/885-7222.* 300 rms, 9 story. S, D $175-$190; suites $395-$450; wkend rates. Crib free. TV; cable (premium). Indoor/outdoor pool; whirlpool, poolside serv. Restaurant 6:30 am-10 pm. Bar 11:30 am-midnight. Ck-out noon. Coin lndry. Convention facilities. Business center. In-rm modem link. Gift shop. Free airport transportation. Tennis privileges. Exercise equipt; weight machine, stair machine, sauna. Health club privileges. Game rm. Refrigerator avail. Microwaves in suites. Cr cds: A, C, D, DS, MC, V.

D SC

★ ★ ★ **RADISSON-AIRPORT.** *1375 N Cassady Ave (43219), I-670 exit 9. 614/475-7551; FAX 614/476-1476.* Web www.radisson.com. 247 units, 6 story. S, D $109-$129; each addl $10; suites $175-$250; under 18 free; wkend, hol rates. TV; cable, VCR avail. Indoor pool; whirlpool. Coffee in rms. Restaurant 6 am-midnight. Bar 10-1 am, Sun noon-midnight. Ck-out noon. Coin lndry. Meeting rms. Business servs avail. In-rm modem link. Gift shop. Free airport transportation. Exercise equipt; weights, bicycles, sauna. Some bathrm phones, refrigerators, in-rm whirlpools. Cr cds: A, C, D, DS, JCB, MC, V.

D SC

★ ★ **RADISSON-NORTH.** *4900 Sinclair Rd (43229), near jct I-71 & Morse Rd. 614/846-0300; FAX 614/847-1022.* 268 rms, 5-6 story. S, D $138; each addl $10; suites $125-$175; under 18 free; wkend rates. Pet accepted, some restrictions. TV; cable (premium), VCR avail. 2 pools, 1 indoor; wading pool, whirlpool, poolside serv. Restaurant 6:30 am-2 pm, 5-11 pm. Bar 11-2 am; entertainment Thurs-Sat. Ck-out noon. Convention facilities. Business center. In-rm modem link. Gift shop. Free airport transportation. Exercise equipt; weight machines, bicycles. Game rm. Cr cds: A, C, D, DS, JCB, MC, V.

D SC

✔★ ★ **RAMADA UNIVERSITY.** *3110 Olentangy River Rd (43202). 614/267-7461; FAX 614/263-5299.* 239 rms, 5 story. S, D $89-$99; each addl $10; suites $175-$195; under 18 free. Crib free. TV; cable (premium), VCR avail. Pool; poolside serv. Complimentary coffee in rms. Restaurant 6 am-10 pm. Ck-out noon. Meeting rms. Business servs avail. Free airport transportation. Health club privileges. Refrigerator, minibar in suites. Cr cds: A, C, D, DS, JCB, MC, V.

D SC

★ ★ ★ **SHERATON SUITES.** *201 Hutchinson Ave (43235), just NE of jct I-270 & OH 23N. 614/436-0004; FAX 614/436-0926.* 261 suites, 9 story. S, D $140-$150; each addl $10; under 18 free; wkend, extended rates. Crib avail. TV; cable (premium), VCR avail. 2 pools, 1 indoor; whirlpool, poolside serv. Complimentary coffee in rms. Restaurant 6 am-10:30 pm; Sat from 7 am. Bar. Ck-out 1 pm. Coin lndry. Meeting rms. Business servs avail. In-rm modem link. Gift shop. Free airport transportation. Exercise equipt; stair machine, treadmill. Health club privileges. Refrigerators; microwaves avail. Cr cds: A, C, D, DS, ER, JCB, MC, V.

D

★ ★ ★ **WESTIN.** *310 S High St (43215). 614/228-3800; FAX 614/228-7666.* 196 rms, 6 story. S, D $155-$195; each addl $15; suites $175-$500; family rates; wkend rates; higher rates special events. TV; cable (premium). Coffee in rms. Restaurant 6 am-11 pm. Rm serv 24 hrs. Bar 3 pm-2 am. Ck-out noon. Meeting rms. Business servs avail. Health club privileges. Luxury level. Cr cds: A, C, D, DS, JCB, MC, V.

D SC

★ ★ ★ **WYNDHAM DUBLIN.** *(600 Metro Place North, Dublin 43017) I-270 exit 17A. 614/764-2200; FAX 614/764-1213.* 217 rms, 3 story. S, D $140-$160; suites $280-$400; under 18 free; wkend rates. Crib free. TV; cable (premium), VCR avail. Indoor pool. Coffee in rms. Restaurant 6:30 am-10 pm. Rm serv 24 hrs. Bar 11-1 am; Sat to 2 am; closed Sun. Ck-out 1 pm. Meeting rms. Business servs avail. In-rm modem link. Gift shop. Sauna. Health club privileges. Balconies. Cr cds: A, C, D, DS, ER, JCB, MC, V.

D SC

Inn

★ ★ ★ **WORTHINGTON.** *(649 High St, Worthington 43085) 8 mi N on High St (US 23). 614/885-2600; FAX 614/885-1283.* 26 rms, 3 story. S, D $140-$175; suites $175-$275. TV; cable. Complimentary full bkfst. Dining rm (see SEVEN STARS DINING ROOM). Rm serv. Bar 5 pm-midnight. Ck-out noon, ck-in 3 pm. Business servs avail. Concierge. Bellhops. Tennis privileges. Renovated Victorian inn. Cr cds: A, C, D, DS, MC, V.

Restaurants

✔★ **A LA CARTE.** *2333 N High St. 614/294-6783.* Hrs: 5-9:30 pm; Fri, Sat to 10:30 pm. Closed Sun, most major hols. Res accepted. Mediterranean menu. Serv bar. Wine cellar. A la carte entrees: dinner $6.95-$10.95. Specializes in fresh seafood, lamb, veal. Parking. Outdoor dining. Menu changes wkly. Cr cds: A, C, D, DS, MC, V.

★ ★ ★ **ALEX'S BISTRO.** *4681 Reed Rd, in Arlington Square Center. 614/457-8887.* Hrs: 11:30 am-2 pm, 5:30-10 pm. Closed Sun; major hols. Res accepted. French, Italian menu. Bar. Wine list. A la carte entrees: lunch $5.50-$8.95, dinner $9.50-18.50. Specializes in fresh seafood, wild game, pastas. Parking. Menu changes seasonally. French brasserie atmosphere. Cr cds: A, D, MC, V.

D

★ ★ **BEXLEY'S MONK.** *2232 East Main St (43209). 614/239-6665.* Hrs: 11:30 am-2:30 pm, 5-10 pm; Fri, Sat to 11 pm; Sun from 5 pm. Closed major hols. Res accepted. Eclectic menu. Bar. A la carte entrees: lunch $6-$11, dinner $10-$20. Specializes in seafood, pasta. Entertainment. Contemporary decor. Cr cds: A, C, D, DS, MC, V.

D

✔★ **BISTRO ROTI.** *1693 W Lane Ave (43221). 614/481-7684; FAX 614/481-7814.* Hrs: 11:30 am-2 pm, 5:30-10 pm; Fri, Sat to 11 pm. Closed Sun; major hols. Res accepted. Eclectic menu. Bar. Semi-a la carte: lunch $5-$10, dinner $11-$17. Specializes in seafood, pastas, chicken. Contemporary decor. Cr cds: A, C, D, DS, MC, V.

D

★ ★ **BRAVO! ITALIAN KITCHEN.** *3000 Hayden Rd (43235). 614/791-1245.* Hrs: 11 am-10 pm; Fri to midnight; Sat 5 pm-midnight; Sun 5-9:30 pm. Closed major hols. Res accepted. Italian menu. Bar. A la carte entrees: lunch $8-$10, dinner $8-$17. Specializes in northern Italian cuisine. Valet parking. Outdoor dining. Upscale bistro atmosphere. Cr cds: A, C, D, DS, MC, V.

D

✔★ ★ **CAMERON'S.** *(2894 E Main St, Bexley 43209) E on OH 40. 614/235-3662.* Hrs: 5-10 pm; Fri, Sat to 11 pm; Sun to 9 pm. Closed most major hols. Res accepted. Contemporary Amer menu. Bar to 11 pm; Fri, Sat to midnight; Sun to 10 pm. Semi-a la carte: dinner $7.50-$17.95. Child's meals. Specializes in walleye, crab cakes, rack of lamb. Jazz Mon. Valet parking. Bright, contemporary decor. Cr cds: A, C, D, DS, MC, V.

D

✔★ **CAP CITY DINER.** *1299 Olentangy River Rd (43212). 614/291-3663.* Hrs: 11 am-10 pm; Fri, Sat to midnight; Sun from 4 pm. Closed major hols. Contemporary Amer menu. Bar. Semi-a la carte: lunch $4.95-$8.95, dinner $5.95-$16.95. Child's meals. Specializes in veal & mushroom meatloaf, desserts. Entertainment Sun, Tues. Outdoor dining. Upscale diner. Cr cds: A, C, D, DS, MC, V.

D

✔★ **CHINA DYNASTY.** *1677 W Lane Ave (43221). 614/486-7126.* Hrs: 11 am-10 pm; Fri, Sat to 11 pm; Sun 11 am-9 pm. Closed July 4, Thanksgiving. Res accepted. Chinese menu. Bar. Semi-a la carte: lunch $4.50-$7.25, dinner $6.50-$12.95. Specializes in Hunan, Szechwan, Mandarin dishes. Casual Chinese decor. Cr cds: A, DS, MC, V.

D

★ **CLARMONT.** *684 S High St, in German Village. 614/443-1125.* Hrs: 7 am-2:30 pm, 5-10 pm; Fri, Sat 7-11 pm; Sun 4-9 pm. Closed some major hols. Res accepted. Bar to 10 pm; Fri, Sat to midnight. Semi-a la carte: bkfst $2.95-$7.50, lunch $5.95-$7.25, dinner $12.95-$21.95. Specializes in steak, fresh seafood, jumbo shrimp cocktail. Parking. Cr cds: A, C, D, MC, V.

D SC

✔★ **COOKER BAR & GRILLE.** *6193 Cleveland Ave (43229). 614/899-7000.* Hrs: 11 am-10:30 pm; Fri, Sat to 11:30 pm; Sun to 10 pm; Sun brunch 11 am-3 pm. Closed Thanksgiving, Dec 25. Bar. Semi-a la carte: lunch, dinner $6-$14.95. Sun brunch $6-$9.75. Child's meals. Specializes in prime rib, fresh fish, meatloaf. Own biscuits. Parking. Patio dining. Casual family-style dining. Cr cds: A, C, D, DS, MC, V.

D

★ ★ **ENGINE HOUSE NO. 5.** *121 Thurman Ave. 614/443-4877.* Hrs: 11:30 am-10 pm; Fri, Sat 4-11 pm; Sun 4-9 pm; early-bird dinner

Mon-Sat 4-6 pm. Closed some major hols. Res accepted. Bar. Semi-a la carte: lunch $6-$16, dinner $14-$30. Child's meals. Specializes in fresh seafood, homemade pastas. Pianist Fri, Sat. Old firehouse; firefighting equipment displayed. Parking. Cr cds: A, C, D, DS, MC, V.

D

★★ **FIFTY-FIVE AT CROSSWOODS.** *55 Hutchinson Ave (43235). 614/846-5555.* Hrs: 11 am-2:30 pm, 5-10 pm; Fri to 11 pm; Sat 5-11 pm; Sun 5-9 pm; Sun brunch 10 am-2:30 pm. Closed major hols. Res accepted. Bar 11-1 am; Sat from 5 pm; Sun 5-10 pm. A la carte entrees: lunch $5.95-$8.95, dinner $12.95-$19.95. Sun brunch $15.95. Child's meals. Specialties: hand-cut steak, linguine fruit de mer, Maryland crab cakes. Own pasta. Parking. Cr cds: A, C, D, DS, MC, V.

D

★★ **FIFTY-FIVE ON THE BOULEVARD.** *55 Nationwide Blvd, opp Convention Center. 614/228-5555.* Hrs: 11 am-2:30 pm, 5-10 pm; Fri to 11 pm; Sat 5-11 pm; Sun 5-9 pm. Closed some major hols. Res accepted. Bar to 1 am. Semi-a la carte: lunch $5.95-$9.95, dinner $12.95-$19.95. Child's meals. Specializes in fresh fish, pasta, Norwegian salmon. Valet parking. Cr cds: A, C, D, DS, MC, V.

D

✔★ **GALAXY CAFE.** *(33 Beech Ridge Dr, Powell 43065) 614/846-7776.* Hrs: 11 am-3 pm, 5-9 pm; Fri to 10 pm; Sat 8 am-3 pm, 5-10 pm; Sun 8 am-2 pm. Closed Mon; major hols. Eclectic menu. Semi-a la carte: bkfst $2.50-$5, lunch $3-$8, dinner $3.50-$9.50. Child's meals. Specializes in salads, pasta, chicken. Casual decor. Totally nonsmoking. Cr cds: MC, V.

D

★★★ **HANDKE'S CUISINE.** *520 S Front St, downtown, near German Village in Brewery district. 614/621-2500.* Hrs: 5:30-10 pm. Closed Sun; Dec 25. Res accepted. International menu. Bar. Extensive wine list. A la carte entrees: dinner $9.75-$23.75. Specializes in veal chop, duck, fresh seafood. Valet parking. Located in historic brewery building, the former Schlee Brewery; main dining rm on lower level. Cr cds: A, DS, MC, V.

★★ **HUNAN HOUSE.** *2350 E Dublin-Granville Rd (43229). 614/895-3330.* Hrs: 11:30 am-10 pm; Fri, Sat to 10:30 pm. Closed Thanksgiving. Res accepted. Chinese menu. Bar. A la carte entrees: lunch $5-$8, dinner $8-$18. Specialties: Szechwan, Hunan and Mandarin delicacies. Parking. Cr cds: A, C, D, MC, V.

★★ **HUNAN LION.** *2000 Bethel Rd (43220), in Crown Point. 614/459-3933.* Hrs: 11:30 am-10 pm; Fri, Sat to 10:30 pm. Res accepted. Chinese, Thai menu. Bar. Semi-a la carte: lunch $5.95-$8.95, dinner $8.95-$18. Specializes in Szechwan dishes, basil seafood, black pepper steak. Parking. Modern decor with Oriental touches. Cr cds: A, C, D, MC, V.

D

✔★ **K2U.** *641 N High St (43215). 614/461-4766.* Hrs: 11 am-midnight; Sat from 5 pm. Closed Sun; Memorial Day, Thanksgiving, Dec 25. Res accepted. Eclectic menu. Bar. Semi-a la carte: lunch $3-$11, dinner $3-$16. Specializes in soups, pasta, sandwiches. Entertainment Mon, Thur, Fri. Outdoor dining. Casual European-style bistro. Cr cds: A, C, D, DS, MC, V.

D

★ **KAHIKI.** *3583 E Broad St. 614/237-5425.* Hrs: 11:30 am-10:15 pm; Fri to 11:15 pm; Sat 4:30-11:15 pm; Sun brunch 11:30 am-3 pm. Closed major hols. Res accepted. Chinese, Polynesian menu. Serv bar. Semi-a la carte: lunch $5.95-$9.95, dinner $13.95-$24.95. Child's meals. Parking. Sea village decor; thatched-roof huts. Tropical rain forest, birds; aquariums; display of native objets d'art. Cr cds: A, C, D, DS, MC, V.

★★★ **L'ANTIBES.** *772 N High St #106 (43215). 614/291-1666.* E-mail lantibe@aol.com; web users.aol.com/lantibes. Hrs: 5-9 pm; Fri, Sat to 11 pm. Closed Sun, Mon; Thanksgiving, Dec 25. Res accepted. French menu. A la carte entrees: dinner $14-$24. Specializes in fresh fish, veal, lamb. Parking. Modern decor. Art collection of owners displayed. Cr cds: A, MC, V.

D

★★ **LINDEY'S.** *169 E Beck St (43206). 614/228-4343.* Hrs: 11:30 am-2:30 pm, 5:30-10 pm; Thurs-Sat to midnight. Closed most major hols. Res accepted. Bar. Semi-a la carte: lunch $5.95-$8.95, dinner $7.95-$19.95. Sun jazz brunch 11:30 am-2:30 pm. Specialties: angel hair pasta, grilled tournedos with Bearnaise sauce, gourmet pizza. Entertainment Thurs, Sun. Valet parking. Outdoor dining. Restored building (1888) in German Village. Cr cds: A, C, D, MC, V.

✔★ **MARBLE GANG.** *1052 Mt Vernon Ave, Mt Vernon Plaza shopping ctr. 614/253-7396.* Hrs: 10 am-midnight; Fri, Sat to 3:30 am. Closed Sun. Res accepted. Bar. Semi-a la carte: lunch, dinner $5.50-$12.95. Child's meals. Specialties: barbecued ribs, chicken. Jazz Thurs evenings. Cr cds: A, C, D, MC, V.

D

★★★ **MERLOT.** *(5252 Norwich St, Hilliard 43026) 614/529-1995.* Hrs: 5-10 pm. Closed Sun; major hols. Res accepted. Wine list. A la carte entrees: dinner $15-$32. Specialties: cedar-roasted salmon, honey curry roasted duckling, lobster bisque. Outdoor dining. Elegant decor. Cr cds: A, C, D, DS, MC, V.

D

★★★ **MORTON'S OF CHICAGO.** *2 Nationwide Plaza. 614/464-4442; FAX 614/464-2940.* Hrs: 5-11 pm; Sun to 10 pm. Closed major hols. Res accepted. Bar. A la carte entrees: dinner $18.95-$29.95. Specializes in prime aged beef, fresh seafood, dessert soufflés. Valet parking. Contemporary decor; in downtown office complex. Cr cds: A, C, D, DS, MC, V.

D

✔★ **OLD MOHAWK.** *821 Mohawk St (43206), in German Village. 614/444-7204.* Hrs: 11 am-midnight; Tues, Wed to 1 am; Thur, Fri to 2:30 am; Sat 9-2:30 am; Sun from 9 am. Closed some major hols. Bar. Semi-a la carte: lunch, dinner $4.95-$9.95. Specialties: turtle soup, quesadillas. Building from 1800s was once a grocery and tavern; exposed brick walls. Cr cds: A, D, MC, V.

D

★★★ **REFECTORY.** *1092 Bethel Rd. 614/451-9774.* Web www.columbuspages.com/restaurants/refectory. Hrs: 5-10:30 pm. Closed Sun; major hols. French menu. Bar 4:30 pm-midnight; Fri, Sat to 1 am. Res accepted. Wine cellar. A la carte entrees: dinner $19.95-$26.95. Specialties: cotelette de salmon, rosage d'agneau aux olives, filet de beouf à l'estragon. Own pastries. Parking. Outdoor dining. Former schoolhouse and sanctuary. Cr cds: A, C, D, DS, MC, V.

★★ **RIGSBY'S CUISINE VOLATILE.** *698 N High St (43215). 614/461-7888.* Hrs: 11 am-11 pm. Closed Sun. Res accepted. Mediterranean menu. Bar. A la carte entrees: lunch $8-$14, dinner $12-$24. Specializes in pasta, rack of lamb, seafood. Entertainment Wed, Thurs. Valet parking. Outdoor dining. Ultramodern decor. Cr cds: A, D, DS, MC, V.

D

✔★ **SCHMIDT'S SAUSAGE HAUS.** *240 Kossuth St. 614/444-6808.* Hrs: 11 am-10 pm; Fri to 11 pm; Sat to midnight. Closed Easter, Thanksgiving, Dec 25. German, Amer menu. Bar. Semi-a la carte: lunch $5.15-$6.95, dinner $7.15-$18.95. Child's meals. Specializes in homemade sausage, desserts. German music Thurs-Sat. Parking. Family-owned. Cr cds: A, C, D, DS, MC, V.

D

★★★ **SEVEN STARS DINING ROOM.** *(See Worthington Inn) 614/885-2600.* Hrs: 7-10 am, 11 am-3 pm, 5:30-10 pm; Fri, Sat to 11 pm; Sun 5-9 pm; Sat brunch 11 am-3 pm. Closed some major hols. Res accepted. Regional Amer menu. Bar. Wine list. Semi-a la carte: bkfst $5-$10, lunch $6.50-$12, dinner $14.95-$29.95. Sat brunch $6.50-$12, Sun buffet 11 am-2:30 pm, $14.95. Specializes in rack of lamb, fresh seafood, beef. Own baking. Entertainment Fri, Sat. Parking. Outdoor dining. Cr cds: A, C, D, DS, MC, V.

★ ★ **TAPATIO.** *491 N Park St (43215). 614/221-1085.* Hrs: 11:30 am-3:30 pm, 5-10 pm; Fri, Sat to 11 pm; Sun 5-10 pm. Closed Thanksgiving, Dec 25. Res accepted. Eclectic menu. Bar. Semi-a la carte: lunch $4-$9, dinner $6-$22. Specializes in seafood, beef tenderloin. Outdoor dining. Modern contemporary bistro. Cr cds: A, C, D, DS, MC, V.

★ **TONY'S.** *16 W Beck St, at High St. 614/224-8669.* Hrs: 11:30 am-10 pm; Fri to 11 pm; Sat 5:30-11 pm. Closed Sun; major hols. Res accepted. Italian menu. Bar. A la carte entrees: lunch $4-$8, dinner $8-$17. Specialties: linguine, spinach & cheese canneloni, classic Italian dishes. Pianist Sat evenings. Parking. Outdoor dining. Cr cds: A, D, MC, V.

★ **THE TOP.** *2891 E Main St. 614/231-8238.* Hrs: 4 pm-midnight. Closed Jan 1, Dec 24, 25. Bar. Semi-a la carte: dinner $14.95-$24.95. Specializes in steak, seafood, barbecued ribs. Parking. Family-owned. Cr cds: A, C, D, DS, MC, V.

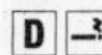

Unrated Dining Spots

KATZINGER'S. *475 S 3rd St. 614/228-3354.* Hrs: 8:30 am-8:30 pm; Sat, Sun from 9 am. Closed Easter, Thanksgiving, Dec 25. Continental menu. Beer. A la carte entrees: lunch, dinner $2.35-$9. Child's meals. Specializes in deli, ethnic foods. Outdoor dining. Delicatessen in German Village. Totally nonsmoking. Cr cds: MC, V.

UMBERTO'S CAFFÈ DOLCE CAFE. *3145 Kingsdale Center. 614/451-2722.* Hrs: 9 am-10 pm; Fri, Sat to 11:30 pm; Sun 11:30 am-5 pm. Closed major hols. Italian, Amer menu. Bar. Avg ck: lunch $5.45, dinner $6.95. Specializes in soup, salad, pasta. Cr cds: A, C, D, DS, MC, V.

Dallas

Founded: 1841
Pop: 1,006,887
Elev: 450-750 feet
Time zone: Central
Area codes: 214, 972
Web: www.dallas.com

Fort Worth

Founded: 1849
Pop: 447,619
Elev: 670 feet
Time zone: Central
Area code: 817
Web: www.fortworth.com

While Texas is still often associated with oil, cities like Dallas and Fort Worth encourage their visitors to discover all aspects of these modern metropolises. With skyscrapers of glass and steel rising alongside aristocratic old houses, it is difficult to maintain an image of a Texas "cow town."

Dallas has become one of the Southwest's largest business and cultural centers. While the city houses the main offices of major oil companies, it is also one of the nation's top fashion centers and has emerged as an important location for the production of commercials and feature-length films. Dallas began as John Neely Bryan's trading post on the upper Trinity River in 1841. Two years later it acquired the name of Dallas. Bryan's customers were, for the most part, the Caddo. By 1890, however, Dallas was the largest city in Texas. It was eventually surpassed by Houston. In 1930 the discovery of a huge oil field southeast of the city brought great prosperity to the area.

While Dallas is sophisticated and fashionable, Fort Worth takes pride in being a warm and friendly progressive Western metropolis—a blending of cattle, oil, finance and manufacturing. Contrary to its name, Fort Worth was never a fort. Originally, it was a camp with a garrison to protect settlers from marauding Native Americans. After the Civil War, great herds of longhorn cattle were driven through the area en route to the Kansas railheads. Camping outside of town, cowboys came into Fort Worth at night to carouse. The citizens of the town desperately wanted a peaceful, prosperous city, which they believed could be achieved by the building of a railroad that would link the town to the East. In July of 1876, this was finally accomplished, and Fort Worth became a shipping point. It would, however, remain a part of the "wild West" for decades to come.

During World War II both Dallas and Fort Worth grew in population and wealth from defense and aircraft industries. The area also became a leading producer of electronic equipment. There has always been a friendly rivalry between the two cities, but economic and planning cooperation has resulted in benefits to both.

Business

Dallas ranks high as a business and industrial center. There are 200 planned industrial districts in Dallas. It is the home office for 250 insurance companies and many major oil companies. It is one of the major fashion markets in the United States and one of the nation's leading exporters in the cotton market.

In Fort Worth the largest segment of employment is in the defense and transportation industries, with American Airlines and Lockheed Martin

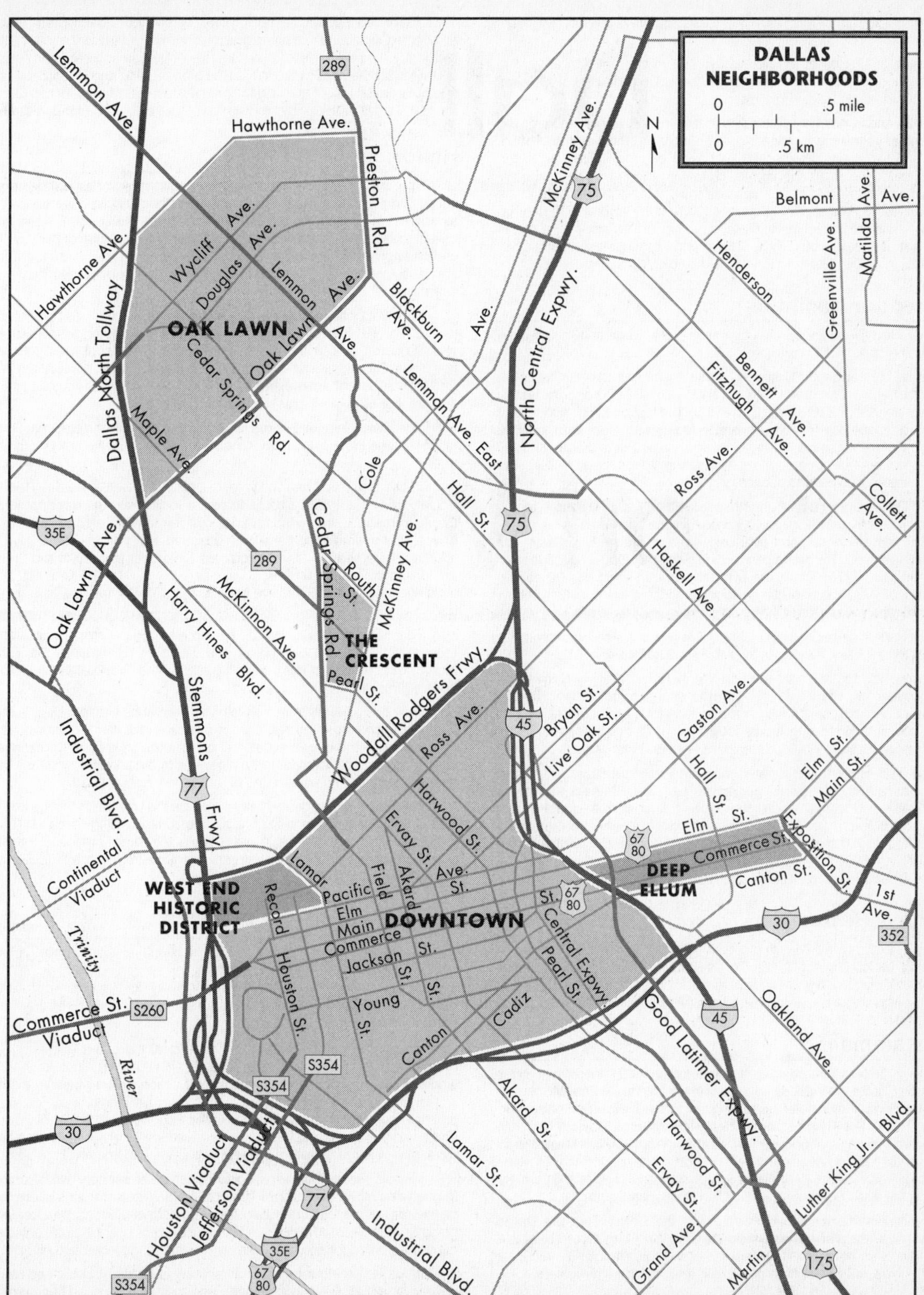

DALLAS NEIGHBORHOODS
0
.5 mile
0
.5 km
N
OAK LAWN
THE CRESCENT
WEST END HISTORIC DISTRICT
DOWNTOWN
DEEP ELLUM
Lemmon Ave.
Hawthorne Ave.
Preston Rd.
McKinney Ave.
Belmont Ave.
Greenville Ave.
Matilda Ave.
Henderson
Wycliff Ave.
Douglas Ave.
Lemmon Ave.
Oak Lawn Ave.
Blackburn Ave.
Cedar Springs Rd.
Dallas North Tollway
Maple Ave.
Lemmon Ave. East
North Central Expwy.
Bennett Ave.
Fitzhugh Ave.
Ross Ave.
Collett Ave.
Cole
Hall St.
Haskell Ave.
Routh St.
McKinney Ave.
McKinnon Ave.
Harry Hines Blvd.
Oak Lawn Ave.
Pearl St.
Woodall Rodgers Frwy.
Stemmons Frwy.
Industrial Blvd.
Bryan St.
Live Oak St.
Gaston Ave.
Ross Ave.
Harwood St.
Ervay St.
Akard St.
Field St.
Pacific Ave.
Lamar
Elm St.
Main St.
Exposition St.
Commerce St.
Canton St.
1st Ave.
Continental Viaduct
Record
Elm
Main
Commerce
Jackson St.
Houston St.
Young St.
Central Expwy.
Pearl St.
Cadiz
Canton
Good Latimer Expwy.
Oakland Ave.
Trinity River
Commerce St. Viaduct
Akard St.
Lamar St.
Harwood St.
Ervay St.
Martin Luther King Jr. Blvd.
Grand Ave.
Houston Viaduct
Jefferson Viaduct
Industrial Blvd.
289
75
35E
77
45
67 80
30
352
S260
S354
175

heading the list. More than 1,500 manufacturing firms are located within the city limits.

Nearly one-fourth of all Texans live in this metropolitan area, and more than one-sixth of all nonfarm jobs are here. Thirty percent of all Texas bank deposits are in Dallas/Fort Worth.

Dallas and Fort Worth are easily accessible—with more than a dozen major highways leading to each city, a transcontinental bus line, Amtrak service and two major airports—Dallas Love Field and Dallas/Fort Worth International. DFW International has 13 major airlines and several commuter airlines, with flights connecting with most of the principal cities in the United States, Mexico and most major airports of the world. DFW International Airport is the largest in the world, covering 18,000 acres, and one of the busiest. It is bigger than JFK, O'Hare and Los Angeles airports combined; it is, in fact, bigger than the whole island of Manhattan.

Convention Facilities

There are five major centers for conventions, trade shows and exhibitions in the Dallas/Fort Worth area.

Dallas Market Center Complex, within minutes of downtown Dallas, comprises three major areas: Market Hall, with 202,000 square feet of exhibit space; Apparel Mart, with 111,000 square feet of exhibit space; and Infomart, a unique, full-service convention facility with more than 165,000 square feet of exhibit space, 35 meeting rooms, a 510-seat theater and two 500-seat conference rooms. Flexible meeting space is available. The complex has 10,000 parking spaces.

The Dallas Convention Center has more than 800,000 square feet of exhibit space total, with 525,000 square feet in one open area. A heliport—the largest elevated urban port ever built—was recently added. There are 105 meeting rooms. The arena can hold more than 25,000, and the theater has seating for 1,770. There are two ballrooms totalling 46,000 square feet. A 1,000-seat cafeteria-dining room is located off the main lobby. Inside parking is available for 1,107 cars.

Fair Park in Dallas has 330,000 square feet of exhibit space among its seven exhibit halls. Parking is available for 9,000 cars.

In downtown Fort Worth, the Fort Worth/Tarrant County Convention Center covers ten city blocks. The center contains more than 200,000 square feet of exhibit space with arena seating for 14,000. There are two exhibit halls and 25 meeting rooms for groups of 22 to 1,100 people. The theater offers seating for 3,000, and there is an 800-car garage.

The Will Rogers Memorial Center in Fort Worth's Amon Carter Square has a 100,000-square-foot exhibit hall, a 2,964-seat auditorium and a 9,467-seat arena, where the "world's largest and oldest indoor rodeo" is held each year. The center has added a ten-acre equestrian center with a 2,000-seat arena and 10,000 square feet of exhibit space along with an 800-car garage. Also near the center is Casa Mañana Theatre, America's first permanent musical-arena theater.

Sports & Recreation

Dallas covers the field with professional sporting events. The season begins with baseball in April for the Texas Rangers in Arlington. The Dallas Cowboys supply the fun and excitement of football for the Texas fans, and the Dallas Mavericks take the crowds to court with basketball.

Entertainment

The countless opportunities for entertainment in these two cities range from ballet and opera to amusement parks. At the Morton H. Meyerson Symphony Center patrons listen to the Dallas Symphony Orchestra. The Dallas Theater Center, designed by Frank Lloyd Wright, is a magnificent building that houses two theaters. Works by Shakespeare as well as modern plays are enjoyed here. In Fort Worth, performances of the Fort Worth Dallas Ballet, Fort Worth Symphony and Fort Worth Opera are staged at the Bass Performing Arts Hall in Sundance Square.

Family entertainment can be found at the Dallas Zoo, the Dallas Aquarium or at the many museums in the area. Six Flags Over Texas is a theme park with more than 100 rides, shows and attractions, including musical shows, a 300-foot-high oil derrick, and strolling entertainers.

There are numerous music clubs, large and small, where visitors enjoy the quiet sound of a piano or a small combo. Many of these are along McKinney Avenue, Lovers Lane, Greenville Avenue and Lemmon Avenue in Dallas. Dallas Alley in the West End MarketPlace and Deep Ellum also offer an eclectic mix of music in their nightclubs. Entertainment can also be found in Fort Worth's 14-block downtown area called Sundance Square.

Historical Areas

The once-elegant streets—still lined with huge trees—of two areas called Old East Dallas and the Oak Cliff Historic District have undergone extensive restoration. Between 1890 and 1930, many fine houses were built in these areas for the cultural, social and political elite of the city. The craftsmanship was excellent, and the architectural styles were individualistic and interesting. They have returned to the showplaces they were years ago.

The west end of downtown Dallas has been declared a historical district. The 1916 Union Station has been restored to its original beaux-arts style. Located at 400 South Houston Street in the southwest sector of downtown Dallas, the station offers Amtrak passenger service. At the West End MarketPlace there are more than 100 merchants in a renovated candy and cracker factory—Texas's first festival market.

The Swiss Avenue Historic District, now listed in the National Register of Historic Places, is another "museum" of early 20th-century architecture.

In Old City Park, near downtown Dallas, the Dallas County Heritage Society has established a heritage center to illustrate the development of Dallas from the 1840s to modern days. Millermore, an elegant antebellum house, has been placed there and furnished with period pieces. Two log structures are nearby. Other structures have been moved to the area to demonstrate visually how early pioneers lived. The 37 Old City Park buildings contain an impressive collection of 19th-century crafts and furniture.

The Fort Worth Stockyards National Historic District is an area of renovated buildings housing retail and dining establishments; the Tarantula, a restored steam train, travels between the Stockyards District and nearby Grapevine.

Only five minutes from Fort Worth's central business district is Ryan Place. Here too are wide, tree-shaded streets and stately Victorian houses. The residents of the area squelched plans a few years ago to raze these structures to make room for more highways to the suburbs, and they have worked together to preserve and beautify the neighborhood.

Adjacent to Forest and Trinity parks are the Log Cabin Village and the Van Zandt Cottage. This area consists of original dwellings circa 1850. Van Zandt Cottage, once used as a stopping place by both stagecoach passengers and cattlemen, is now restored and furnished with antiques in the same period.

Sightseeing

There are more than 100 lakes in the countryside surrounding metropolitan Dallas/Fort Worth with facilities for swimming, boating, fishing, camping and picnicking. An exceptionally lovely drive in Fort Worth can be taken through Trinity and Forest parks on the Clear Fork of the Trinity River.

Unusual for a city the size of Fort Worth, there is a unique cultural district within a four-square-block area. The Kimbell Art Museum features works of art from all periods in history; the Amon Carter Museum exhibits works of Remington and Russell; the Modern Art Museum of Fort Worth presents contemporary artworks; and the Fort Worth Museum of Science and History is the largest educational museum for children in the southwest, offering natural history displays, a planetarium and an Omni Theater.

Visitors are treated to a unique change of scenery while strolling through downtown Fort Worth. The Fort Worth Water Gardens offers three distinct areas comprised of waterfalls and sprays blended with beautiful, grassy areas. Also downtown is Sundance Square, a 14-block entertainment area noted for shopping, dining, museums, galleries and nightlife.

In Dallas, another group of attractions is located three miles east of downtown at Fair Park, including the Age of Steam Railroad Museum, the

African American Museum, Cotton Bowl, Hall of State, The Science Place and the Dallas Museum of Natural History. A Shakespeare festival is held in the bandstand. The Dallas Horticultural Center features beautiful gardens, and the midway is open four weeks during the state fair in October.

General References Dallas

Area codes: 214, 972

Phone Numbers

POLICE & FIRE: 911

POISON CONTROL CENTER: 800/764-7661 (TX)

TIME: 844-6611 **WEATHER:** 787-1111

Information Sources

Dallas Convention and Visitors Bureau, 1201 Elm St, Ste 2000, 75270; 746-6679 (hotline).

Dallas Convention Center, 650 S Griffin, 75202; 939-2700.

Park & Recreation Department, 670-4100.

Transportation

AIRLINES: American; British Airways; Continental; Delta; Lufthansa; Midwest Express; Northwest; Southwest; TWA; United; USAir; and other commuter and regional airlines.

AIRPORTS: Dallas-Fort Worth International, 972/574-3197; Love Field, 670-6080.

CAR RENTAL AGENCIES: (See IMPORTANT TOLL-FREE NUMBERS) Avis 574-4130; Budget 574-2121; Hertz 453-0370; National 574-3400.

PUBLIC TRANSPORTATION: Dallas Area Rapid Transit (DART), 979-1111.

RAILROAD PASSENGER SERVICE: Amtrak 800/872-7245.

Newspapers

Dallas Morning News; Dallas Business Journal.

Convention Facilities

Dallas Convention Center, 650 S Griffin St, 939-2700.

Dallas Market Center, 2100 Stemmons Frwy, 655-6100.

Fair Park, 2 mi E of downtown via I-30, 670-8400.

Sports & Recreation

The Ballpark at Arlington, W of jct TX 360, Dallas-Ft Worth Tpke (Texas Rangers, baseball, 817/273-5222).

Cotton Bowl, Fair Park Dallas, 638-BOWL.

Fair Park, Parry & 2nd Ave, 670-8400.

Reunion Arena, 777 Sports St (Mavericks, basketball, 748-1808; Stars, hockey, 868-2890).

Texas Stadium, TX 183 & Loop 12, Irving, 972/438-7676 (Cowboys, football, 556-9900).

Cultural Facilities

Theaters

Bob Hope Theatre, Southern Methodist University, 768-ARTS.

Convention Center Theater, 650 S Griffin, 939-2700.

Kalita Humphry Theatre, 3636 Turtle Creek Blvd, 526-8857.

Margo Jones Theatre, Southern Methodist University, 768-ARTS.

Morton H. Meyerson Symphony Center (Dallas Symphony), Pearl & Flora Sts, 670-3600.

Music Hall, Fair Park, 565-1116.

Theatre Three, 2800 Routh St, 871-3300.

Museums

African American Museum, Fair Park, 565-9026.

Age of Steam Railroad Museum, Fair Park, 428-0101.

Conspiracy Museum, 110 Market St, 741-3040.

Dallas Memorial Center for Holocaust Studies, 7900 Northaven, 750-4654.

Dallas Museum of Natural History, 3535 Grand Ave at Robert L. Cullum Blvd, Fair Park, 421-3466.

Hall of State, Fair Park, 421-4500.

The Science Place, 1318 2nd Ave, Fair Park, 428-5555.

The Sixth Floor Museum, 411 Elm St, 653-6666.

Art Museums

Biblical Arts Center, 7500 Park Ln at Boedeker, 691-4661.

Dallas Museum of Art, 1717 Harwood St, 922-1200.

Meadows Museum, Southern Methodist University, 768-2516.

Points of Interest

Historical

Hall of State, Fair Park, 421-4500.

John Neely Bryan Cabin, Main, Elm & Market Sts.

Old City Park (Dallas County Heritage Society), Gano & Harwood Sts, 421-5141.

West End Historical District, downtown, 665-9559.

Other Attractions

Dallas Aquarium, 1st Ave & M.L. King Jr Blvd, Fair Park, 670-8453.

Dallas Arboretum and Botanical Gardens, 8525 Garland Rd, 327-8263.

Dallas Horticulture Center, 2nd Ave & M.L. King Jr Blvd, Fair Park, 428-7476.

Dallas Market Center Complex, 2100 Stemmons Frwy, 655-6100.

Dallas Zoo, 650 S R.L. Thorton Frwy, 670-5656.

Fair Park, 2 mi E of downtown via I-30, 670-8400.

J.F. Kennedy Memorial Plaza, Main, Commerce & Market Sts.

Kennedy Historical Exhibit, The Sixth Floor, 411 Elm St, 653-6666.

Mesquite Rodeo, 6 1/2 mi E at jct I-635 & Military Pkwy, in Mesquite, 972/285-8777.

Observation Deck, Hyatt Regency Reunion Tower, 300 Reunion Blvd, 741-3663.

Six Flags Over Texas, 16 mi W, at jct TX 360 & I-30 in Arlington, 817/640-8900.

Sightseeing Tour

Gray Line bus tours, 4411 Leston Ave, 824-2424.

Annual Events

Cotton Bowl Festival. New Year's Day & preceding wk.

Byron Nelson Golf Classic, Four Seasons Club Resort. May.

State Fair of Texas, Fair Park, 565-9931. Sept 25-Oct 18.

Fort Worth

Area code: 817

Phone Numbers

POLICE & FIRE: 911

POISON CONTROL CENTER: 800/764-7661 (TX)

TIME: 844-6611 **WEATHER:** 429-2631

Information Sources

Fort Worth Convention & Visitors Bureau, 415 Throckmorton, 76102; 336-8791 or 800/433-5747.

Dept of Parks & Recreation, 871-5700.

Transportation

AIRPORTS: Dallas Fort Worth International, 972/574-8888; Meacham International, 871-5400.

CAR RENTAL AGENCIES: (See IMPORTANT TOLL-FREE NUMBERS) Avis 214/574-4110; Budget 329-2277; Hertz 214/453-0370; National 214/574-3400.

PUBLIC TRANSPORTATION: Transportation Authority of Fort Worth, 871-6200.

RAILROAD PASSENGER SERVICE: Amtrak 800/872-7245.

Newspaper

Fort Worth Star-Telegram.

Convention Facilities

Fort Worth/Tarrant County Convention Center, 1111 Houston St, 884-2222.

Will Rogers Memorial Center, 3401 W Lancaster St, 871-8150.

Sports & Recreation

The Ballpark at Arlington, I-30, near jct TX 360, Dallas-Ft Worth Tpke, Arlington (Texas Rangers, baseball, 273-5222).

Racetracks

Texas Motor Speedway, I-35W & TX114, 215-8500 (NASCAR and Indy car raceway).

Texas Raceway, S New Hope Rd, Kennedale, 483-0356 (car racing).

Cultural Facilities

Theaters

Casa Mañana, 3101 W Lancaster Ave, 332-CASA.

Circle Theatre, 230 W 4th St, 877-3040.

Hip Pocket Theatre, 1620 Las Vegas Trail N, 927-2833.

Jubilee Theatre, 506 Main St, 338-4411.

Omni Theater, Ft Worth Museum of Science & History, 732-1631.

Stage West Theater, 3055 S University, 784-9378.

Fort Worth Theatre at the Scott, 3505 W Lancaster Ave, 738-7491.

Concert Halls

Fort Worth/Tarrant County Convention Center Theatre, 1111 Houston St, 884-2222.

Will Rogers Auditorium, 3401 W Lancaster, 871-8150.

Museums

Cattlemen's Museum, 1301 W 7th St, 332-7064.

Fort Worth Museum of Science and History, 1501 Montgomery St, 732-1631.

Palace of Wax/Ripley's Believe It or Not, 601 E Safari Pkwy, off I-30, in Grand Prairie, 972/263-2391.

Stockyards Museum, 131 E Exchange Ave, 625-5087.

Art Museums

Amon Carter Museum, 3501 Camp Bowie Blvd, 738-1933.

Kimbell Art Museum, 3333 Camp Bowie Blvd, 332-8451.

Modern Art Museum of Fort Worth, 1309 Montgomery St, at Camp Bowie Blvd, 738-9215.

Sid Richardson Collection of Western Art, 309 Main St, 332-6554.

Points of Interest

Historical

Fort Worth Stockyards National Historic District, E Exchange & N Main Sts, 624-4741.

Log Cabin Village, Log Cabin Village Ln at South University Dr, 926-5881.

Sundance Square Downtown Entertainment District, between Throckmorton & Calhoun from 2nd to 5th Sts, 390-8711.

Thistle Hill, 1509 Pennsylvania Ave, 336-1212.

Other Attractions

Billy Bob's Texas (country & western bar), 2520 Rodeo Plaza, Fort Worth Stockyards, 624-7117.

Botanic Garden, 3220 Botanic Garden Blvd, 871-7686.

Caravan of Dreams (music club), 312 Houston St, 877-3000.

Fort Worth Japanese Garden, Botanic Gardens.

Fort Worth Nature Center & Refuge, 9 mi NW via TX 199 to Buffalo Rd, 237-1112.

Fort Worth Zoo, 1989 Colonial Pkwy, in Forest Park, 871-7050.

Omni Theater, at the Fort Worth Museum of Science & History, 732-1631.

Six Flags Over Texas, 16 mi E on I-30, just W of jct TX 360, I-30, 640-8900.

Water Gardens, downtown Fort Worth.

Will Rogers Memorial Center, 3401 W Lancaster St, 871-8150.

Annual Events

Southwestern Exposition and Livestock Show. Mid-Jan-early Feb.

Mayfest. 1st wkend May.

Chisholm Trail Roundup, Fort Worth Stockyards. Mid-June.

Pioneer Days. Labor Day wkend.

Fort Worth Airshow. Oct.

Red Steagall Cowboy Gathering. 4th wkend Oct.

City Neighborhoods

Many of the restaurants, unrated dining establishments and some lodgings listed under Dallas and Fort Worth include neighborhoods as well as exact street addresses. Geographic descriptions of neighborhoods in both cities are given, followed by a table of restaurants, arranged by neighborhood.

Dallas

The Crescent: North of Downtown; bounded by Cedar Springs Rd, Maple Ave, McKinney Ave and Pearl St; also Routh St between Cedar Springs Rd and McKinney Ave.

Deep Ellum: East of Downtown; south of Elm St, west of Exposition St, north of Canton St and east of I-45.

Downtown: South of Woodall Rodgers Frwy, west of I-45, north of I-30 and east of I-35E (US 77). **North of Downtown:** North of Woodall Rodgers Frwy.

Oak Lawn: North of Downtown; along Oak Lawn Ave between Hawthorne and Maple Aves; also along Lemon Ave between Oak Lawn Ave and Dallas North Tollway.

West End Historic District: Area of Downtown south of McKinney Ave, west of Lamar St, north of Pacific Ave and east of Record St and railroad tracks.

Fort Worth

Downtown: South of Heritage Park, west of I-35W and the railroad yards, north of Lancaster Ave and east of Henderson Ave (TX 199). **North of Downtown:** North of TX 199 and US 377. **South of Downtown:** South of I-30. **West of Downtown:** West of Trinity River.

Museum/Cultural District: South of Camp Bowie Blvd, west of University Dr, north of Crestline St and east of Montgomery St; particularly along Lancaster Ave.

Lodgings and Food Dallas

DALLAS RESTAURANTS BY NEIGHBORHOOD AREAS

(For full description, see alphabetical listings under Restaurants)

DOWNTOWN
Dakota's. 600 N Akard St
French Room (The Adolphus Hotel). 1321 Commerce St
Lombardi's. 311 N Market
Pyramid Room (Fairmont Hotel). 1717 N Akard St
Seventeen Seventeen. 1717 N Harwood

NORTH OF DOWNTOWN
Adelmo's. 4537 Cole Ave
Alessio's. 4117 Lomo Alto
Arthur's. 8350 N Central Expy
Athenee Cafe. 5365 Spring Valley #150
Barclays. 2917 Fairmount St
The Bistro. 5405 W Lovers Lane
Blue Mesa Grill. 5100 Belt Line Rd
Bread Winners Cafe & Bakery. 3301 McKinney Ave
Cafe Pacific. 24 Highland Park Village
Celebration. 4503 W Lovers Lane
Chez Gerard. 4444 McKinney Ave
City Cafe. 5757 W Lovers Ln
The Enclave. 8325 Walnut Hill
Fog City Diner. 2401 McKinney Ave
Gershwin's. 8442 Walnut Hill Ln
Javier's. 4912 Cole Ave
Jennivine. 3605 McKinney Ave
L'Ancestral. 4514 Travis #124
La Trattoria Lombardi. 2916 N Hall St
Laurel's (Sheraton Park Central Hotel). 12720 Merit Dr
Lavendou. 19009 Preston Rd
Lawry's The Prime Rib. 3008 Maple Ave
Mediterraneo. 18111 Preston Rd, Suite 120
Mi Piaci. 14854 Montfort
Nana Grill (Wyndham Anatole Hotel). 2201 Stemmons Frwy
Patrizio. 25 Highland Park Village
Restaurant At The Mansion On Turtle Creek (Mansion On Turtle Creek Hotel). 2821 Turtle Creek Blvd
Riviera. 7709 Inwood Rd
Rooster. 3521 Oak Grove
Royal Tokyo. 7525 Greenville Ave
Ruggeri's. 2911 Routh St
Ruth's Chris Steak House. 5922 Cedar Springs Rd
Savino. 2929 N Henderson
Star Canyon. 3102 Oak Lawn Ave, suite 144
Sushi (Stoneleigh Hotel). 2927 Maple Ave
Thai Taste. 3101 N Fitzhugh Ave
Toscana. 4900 McKinney Ave
Uncle Tai's. 13350 Dallas Pkwy
York Street. 6047 Lewis St
Ziziki's. 4514 Travis St, Suite 122

OAK LAWN
Joey's. 4217 Oak Lawn Ave
The Landmark (Melrose Hotel). 3015 Oak Lawn Ave
Old Warsaw. 2610 Maple Ave

WEST END HISTORIC DISTRICT
Morton's Of Chicago. 501 Elm St
Newport's Seafood. 703 McKinney Ave
Palm. 701 Ross Ave
Sonny Bryan's. 302 N Market St

Note: When a listing is located in a town that does not have its own city heading, it will appear under the city nearest to its location. In these cases, the address and town appear in parenthesis immediately following the name of the establishment.

Motels

(Rates may be higher State Fair, Cotton Bowl, Texas/OU wkend and city-wide conventions. Most accommodations near Six Flags Over Texas have higher rates when the park is open daily.)

★ ★ **BEST WESTERN PARK SUITES.** *(640 E Park Blvd, Plano 75074) 10 mi N on US 75. 972/578-2243; FAX 972/578-0563.* 84 suites, 3 story. Suites $88-$95; family rates. Crib free. Pet accepted, some restrictions. TV; cable (premium). Complimentary continental bkfst. Complimentary coffee in rms. Restaurant nearby. Bar. Ck-out noon. Meeting rms. Business servs avail. In-rm modem link. Valet serv. Sundries. Coin Indry. Exercise equipt; weight machines, treadmill. Pool; whirlpool. Refrigerators, microwaves; some in-rm whirlpools. Cr cds: A, C, D, DS, JCB, MC, V.

D SC

✔★ ★ **BEST WESTERN-NORTH.** *13333 N Stemmons Frwy (75234), I-35E, exit at Valwood, north of downtown. 972/241-8521; FAX 972/243-4103.* 186 rms, 2 story. S $65-$69, D $75; each addl $6; suites $125; under 12 free; wkend rates. Pet accepted; $20 deposit. TV; cable (premium). Pool; whirlpool, sauna. Coffee in rms. Restaurant 6:30 am-10 pm; hrs vary Sat, Sun. Rm serv. Bar 5 pm-midnight. Ck-out 11 am. Coin Indry. Meeting rms. Business servs avail. In-rm modem link. Valet serv. Airport transportation. Health club privileges. Microwaves avail. Cr cds: A, C, D, DS, MC, V.

D SC

★ ★ **CLARION SUITES.** *2363 Stemmons Tr (75220), I-35E exit 436, north of downtown. 214/350-2300; FAX 214/350-5144.* 96 suites, 3 story. S $85-$110; D $85-$125; each addl $5; under 18 free; wkend rates. Crib free. TV; cable (premium). Pool; whirlpool. Complimentary continental bkfst. Restaurant adj open 24 hrs. Ck-out noon. Coin Indry. Meeting rms. Business servs avail. In-rm modem link. Valet serv. Gift shop. Free airport transportation. Exercise equipt; weight machine, bicycle. Refrigerators, microwaves. Cr cds: A, C, D, DS, ER, JCB, MC, V.

D SC

✔★ ★ **CLASSIC MOTOR INN.** *9229 Carpenter Frwy (75247), north of downtown. 214/631-6633; FAX 214/631-6616; res: 800/662-7437.* 134 rms, 2 story. S $42-$50; D $52-$59; each addl $5; suite $65. Crib free. TV; cable (premium), VCR avail. Pool. Complimentary continental bkfst. Restaurant adj. Ck-out noon. Coin Indry. Meeting rms. Business servs avail. In-rm modem link. Valet serv. Free airport transportation. Exercise equipt; weights, bicycles, sauna. Bathrm phones; some refrigerators; microwaves avail. Cr cds: A, C, D, DS, MC, V.

D SC

✔ ★ **COMFORT INN.** *(14040 Stemmons Frwy, Farmers Branch 75234) I-35 at Valwood Pkwy. 972/406-3030; FAX 972/406-2929.* 50 rms, 2 story. May-Sept: S $62-$75; D $62-$80; each addl $5; family, wkend, wkly rates; higher rates special events; lower rates rest of yr. Crib free. TV; cable (premium). Complimentary continental bkfst. Restaurant adj open 24 hrs. Bar; entertainment. Ck-out noon. Meeting rms. Business servs avail. In-rm modem link. Sundries. Coin Indry. Pool; whirlpool. Microwaves avail. Cr cds: A, C, D, DS, JCB, MC, V.

SC

★ ★ ★ **COURTYARD BY MARRIOTT.** *2383 Stemmons Trail (75220), 8 mi N on I-35 E, Northwest Hwy exit 436, north of downtown. 214/352-7676; FAX 214/352-4914.* 146 rms, 3 story. S $97; D $107; suites $109-$119; under 12 free; wkly rates. Crib free. TV; cable (premium). Pool; whirlpool. Complimentary coffee in rms. Bar 5-11 pm. Ck-out 1 pm. Coin Indry. Meeting rms. Business servs avail. In-rm modem link. Valet serv. Sundries. Exercise equipt; weight machine, stair machines. Refrigerators, microwaves avail. Balconies. Cr cds: A, D, DS, JCB, MC, V.

D SC

★ ★ **DRURY INN-NORTH.** *2421 Walnut Hill (75229), I-35E Walnut Hill exit, north of downtown. 972/484-3330; FAX 972/484-3330.* 130 rms, 4 story. S $68-$74; D $78-$84; each addl $10; under 18 free. TV; cable (premium). Pool. Complimentary continental bkfst. Restaurant adj open 24 hrs. Ck-out noon. Meeting rms. Business servs avail. In-rm modem link. Valet serv. Sundries. Some refrigerators; microwaves avail. Cr cds: A, C, D, DS, MC, V.

D SC

✔★ **FAIRFIELD INN BY MARRIOTT.** *2210 Market Center Blvd, north of downtown. 214/760-8800; FAX 214/760-1659.* 117 rms, 3 story. S $69-$79; D $74-$84; each addl $5; under 12 free. Crib free. TV; cable (premium). Indoor pool; whirlpool. Complimentary continental bkfst. Restaurant adj 6:30 am-10 pm. Ck-out noon. Valet serv. Health club privileges. Cr cds: A, C, D, DS, MC, V.

D SC

✔★ ★ **HAMPTON INN-GARLAND.** *12670 E Northwest Hwy (75228), I-635 exit 11B, east of downtown. 972/613-5000; FAX 972/613-4535.* 125 rms, 3 story. S $64; D $71; under 18 free. Crib free. TV; cable (premium). Pool. Complimentary continental bkfst. Restaurant opp 11-2 am. Ck-out noon. Meeting rm. Business servs avail. In-rm modem link. Valet serv. Cr cds: A, C, D, DS, ER, MC, V.

D SC

★ ★ **HAMPTON INN-SOUTHWEST.** *4154 Preferred Place (75237), I-20 exit 463, south of downtown. 972/298-4747; FAX 972/283-1305.* Web www.hamptoninn/duncanville.com. 119 rms, 2 story. S, D $59; family, wkly, wkend, hol rates; higher rates auto races. Crib free. TV; cable (premium). Pool. Complimentary continental bkfst. Restaurant nearby. Ck-out noon. Coin Indry. Meeting rms. Business servs avail. In-rm modem link. Valet serv. Sundries. Microwaves avail. Adj to shopping mall. Cr cds: A, C, D, DS, MC, V.

D SC

★ **HAWTHORN SUITES.** *7900 Brookriver Dr (75247), north of downtown. 214/688-1010; FAX 214/638-5215; res: 800/527-1133.* Web www.hawthorn.com. 97 kit. suites, 2 story. S $130; D $168; wkend, wkly, hol rates. Crib free. Pet accepted, some restrictions; $25. TV; cable (premium). Pool. Complimentary full bkfst. Complimentary coffee in rms. Ck-out noon. Coin Indry. Meeting rms. Business servs avail. In-rm modem link. Valet serv Mon-Fri. Sundries. Free airport transportation. Health club privileges. Lawn games. Microwaves avail. Balconies, patios. Cr cds: A, C, D, DS, MC, V.

D

★ ★ **LA QUINTA INN-EAST.** *8303 E RL Thornton Frwy (I-30) (75228), I-30 exit Jim Miller, east of downtown. 214/324-3731; FAX 214/324-1652.* 102 rms, 2 story. Mar-Oct: S $59-$65; D $66-$73; suites $135; each addl $10; under 18 free; higher rates wkends; lower rates rest of yr. Crib free. Pet accepted, some restrictions. TV; cable (premium). Pool. Complimentary continental bkfst. Restaurant adj 6 am-midnight. Ck-out noon. Business servs avail. In-rm modem link. Sundries. Valet serv Mon-Fri. Microwaves avail. Cr cds: A, C, D, DS, MC, V.

D SC

✔★ ★ **LA QUINTA NORTHWEST-FARMERS BRANCH.** *13235 Stemmons Frwy N (75234), I-35E exit Valleyview, north of downtown. 972/620-7333; FAX 972/484-6533.* 121 rms, 2 story. S, D $64; each addl $6; under 18 free. Crib free. Pet accepted, some restrictions. TV; cable (premium). Pool. Complimentary continental bkfst. Coffee in rms. Restaurant adj 6 am-11 pm. Ck-out noon. Meeting rms. Business servs avail. In-rm modem link. Free airport transportation. Some refrigerators; microwaves avail. Cr cds: A, C, D, DS, MC, V.

D SC

★ ★ **RESIDENCE INN BY MARRIOTT.** *13636 Goldmark Dr (75240), US 75 exit Midpark, W to Goldmark, north of downtown. 972/669-0478; FAX 972/644-2632.* 70 kit. suites, 1-2 story. Suites $129-$149; wkend rates. Crib free. Pet accepted, some restrictions; $60. TV; cable (premium). Pool; whirlpool. Complimentary continental bkfst. Ck-out noon. Coin Indry. Business servs avail. In-rm modem link. Valet serv. Health club privileges. Refrigerators, microwaves, fireplaces. Private patios, balconies. Grill. Cr cds: A, C, D, DS, MC, V.

D SC

★ ★ **RESIDENCE INN BY MARRIOTT.** *6950 N Stemmons (75247), north of downtown. 214/631-2472; FAX 214/634-9645.* 142 kit. suites, 3 story. S $120; D $160; wkend rates. Crib free. Pet accepted; $50. TV; cable (premium). Pool; whirlpool. Complimentary continental bkfst. Complimentary coffee in rms. Ck-out noon. Coin Indry. Meeting rms. Business servs avail. Valet serv. Exercise equipt; weight machine, treadmill. Health club privileges. Microwaves avail. Picnic tables. Cr cds: A, D, DS, JCB, MC, V.

D SC

★ **SLEEP INN.** *(4801 W Plano Pkwy, Plano 75093) 20 mi N on North Dallas Tollway, Plano Pkwy exit. 972/867-1111; FAX 972/612-6753.* 104 rms, 2 story. S $65-$80; D $70-$80; each addl $6; under 19 free; wkend rates. Crib free. Pet accepted. TV; cable. Heated pool. Complimentary continental bkfst. Restaurant nearby. Ck-out noon. Meeting rms. Business servs avail. In-rm modem link. Valet serv. Cr cds: A, C, D, DS, ER, JCB, MC, V.

D SC

Motor Hotels

★ ★ ★ **COURTYARD BY MARRIOTT.** *2150 Market Center Blvd (75207), north of downtown. 214/653-1166; FAX 214/653-1892.* 184 rms, 5 story. S, D $99-$124; each addl $10; under 12 free. Crib free. TV; cable (premium), VCR avail. Pool; whirlpool. Complimentary coffee in rms. Restaurant 6:30 am-2 pm, 4:30-10:30 pm. Bar. Ck-out 1 pm. Coin Indry. Meeting rms. Business servs avail. In-rm modem link. Sundries. Valet serv. Exercise equipt; treadmills, bicycles. Health club privileges. Some refrigerators; microwaves avail. Balconies. Cr cds: A, C, D, DS, MC, V.

D SC

★ ★ **HARVEY HOTEL-ADDISON.** *14315 Midway Rd (75244), I-635 exit Midway Rd, north of downtown. 972/980-8877; FAX 972/788-2758.* 429 rms, 3 story. Feb-May: S $99-$120; D $109-$135; each addl $10; under 12 free; wkly, wkend, hol rates. Crib free. Pet accepted, some restrictions; $125 ($100 refundable). TV; cable (premium), VCR avail. Pool; whirlpool. Restaurant 10:30 am-10 pm. Rm serv. Coin Indry. Business center. In-rm modem link. Garage parking. Airport transportation. Exercise equipt; weight machine, treadmill. Health club privileges. Some refrigerators. Microwaves. Cr cds: A, C, D, DS, ER, MC, V.

D SC

★ ★ **HARVEY HOTEL.** *7815 LBJ Frwy (75240), I-635 exit 19A Coit Rd, north of downtown. 214/960-7000; FAX 214/788-4227; res: 800/922-9222.* 313 rms, 3 story. S $99-$129; D $109-$139; each addl $10; suites $125-$250; under 17 free. Crib free. Pet accepted; $125 ($100 refundable). TV; cable. Pool. Restaurant 6:30 am-11 pm. Rm serv 24 hours. Bar 11 am-midnight. Ck-out 1 pm. Meeting rms. Business servs avail. In-rm modem link. Health club privileges. Valet serv. Gift shop. Covered parking. Microwaves avail. Cr cds: A, C, D, DS, JCB, MC, V.

D SC

★ ★ **HARVEY HOTEL-PLANO.** *(1600 N Central Expy, Plano 75074) 12 mi N on Central Expy (US 75), 15th St exit. 972/578-8555; FAX 972/578-9720.* 279 rms, 3 story. S $109-$159; D $119-$169; each addl $10; suites $159; under 16 free. Crib free. Pet accepted; $125 ($100 refundable). TV; cable, VCR avail. Pool; whirlpool, poolside serv. Restaurants 6:30 am-11 pm. Rm serv. Bar 10 am-midnight; Sat to 1 am. Ck-out 1 pm. Coin Indry. Meeting rms. Business servs avail. In-rm modem link. Bellhops. Valet serv. Sundries. Gift shop. Game rm. Exerise equipt; weight machine, treadmill. Microwaves avail; refrigerator, wet bar in suites. Cr cds: A, C, D, DS, MC, V.

D SC

★ ★ **HOLIDAY INN SELECT-LBJ NORTHEAST.** *11350 LBJ Frwy (75238), at Jupiter Rd exit, downtown. 214/341-5400; FAX 214/553-9349.* 243 rms, 3-5 story. S, D $89-$105; under 18 free. Crib $10. TV; cable (premium). Pool. Restaurant 6 am-2 pm, 5-11 pm. Rm serv. Bar 5 pm-1 am; entertainment. Ck-out noon. Coin Indry. Meeting rms. Business servs avail. In-rm modem link. Bellhops. Valet serv. Gift shop. Exercise equipt; weight machine, treadmill, sauna. Microwaves avail. Luxury level. Cr cds: A, C, D, DS, JCB, MC, V.

D SC

Hotels

★ ★ ★ ★ **THE ADOLPHUS.** *1321 Commerce St (75202), downtown. 214/742-8200; FAX 214/651-3588; res: 800/221-9083.* 17th-century Flemish tapestries grace the lobby of this Beaux Arts hotel created by beer baron Adolphus Busch in 1912. Guest rooms, unusually soundproof, are furnished in Queen Anne and Chippendale styles. 426 rms, 22 story. S, D $200-$300; each addl $25; suites $400-$2,000; under 12 free; wkend rates. Crib free. Valet parking $10. TV; cable (premium), VCR avail. Restaurants 6 am-10 pm (also see FRENCH ROOM). Rm serv 24 hrs. Bar 11-2 am. Ck-out 1 pm. Convention facilities. Business servs avail. In-rm modem link. Concierge. Gift shop. Barber, beauty shop. Tennis privileges. Golf privileges. Exercise equipt; weight machine, bicycles. Health club privileges. Massage. Bathrm phones, refrigerators, minibars; microwaves avail. Some private patios. Cr cds: A, C, D, DS, MC, V.

D

★ ★ ★ **BRISTOL SUITES.** *7800 Alpha Rd (75240), I-635 exit 19A to Coit Rd, north of downtown. 972/233-7600; FAX 972/701-8618; res: 800/922-9222.* 295 suites, 10 story. Suites $149-$239; each addl $15; under 17 free; some lower rates summer. Crib free. Pet accepted; $125 ($100 refundable). TV; cable. Indoor/outdoor pool; whirlpool, poolside serv. Complimentary full bkfst. Restaurant 6:30 am-10 pm. Bar 11 am-midnight. Ck-out 1 pm. Coin Indry. Convention facilities. Business center. In-rm modem link. Gift shop. Exercise equipt; weights, bicycle. Refrigerators, microwaves; some bathrm phones. Cr cds: A, D, DS, MC, V.

D SC

★ ★ ★ ★ **CRESCENT COURT.** *400 Crescent Court (75201), at Maple & McKinney Ave, in the Crescent area, north of downtown. 214/871-3200; FAX 214/871-3272; res: 800/654-6541.* Web www.rosewood-hotels.com. Modeled after the Royal Crescent spa in Bath, England, this hotel is part of a castle-like complex that includes a posh retail gallery. Furnishings are reminiscent of those in an English manor house; all the suites have hardwood floors and some have lofts. 216 rms, 7 story. S $270-$360; D $300-$390; each addl $30; suites $580-$1,600; under 12 free; wkend rates. Crib free. Pet accepted, some restrictions; $25. Garage $5.50; valet $12. TV; cable (premium), VCR avail. Pool; whirlpool, poolside serv. Restaurant 6:30 am-midnight. Afternoon tea 3-5 pm. Rm serv 24 hrs. Bar 11:30-2 am. Ck-out 1 pm. Meeting rms. Business center. In-rm modem link. Concierge. Shopping arcade. Free airport transportation. Exercise rm; instructor, weights, bicycles, sauna, steam rm. Spa. Bathrm phones, refrigerators. Cr cds: A, C, D, DS, ER, JCB, MC, V.

D

★ ★ **DALLAS GRAND.** *1914 Commerce St (75201), downtown. 214/747-7000; FAX 214/749-0231; res: 800/421-0011.* 709 rms, 20 story. S $129-$149; D $139-$169; each addl $10; suites $250-$550; under 17 free; wkend rates. Crib free. TV; cable (premium), VCR avail. Restaurant 6:30 am-11 pm. Bar 2 pm-2 am. Ck-out noon. Coin Indry. Convention facilities. Business servs avail. In-rm modem link. Gift shop. Valet parking. Exercise equipt; weights, rower, rooftop whirlpools. Some refrigerators; microwaves avail. Sun deck. Cr cds: A, C, D, DS, ER, JCB, MC, V.

D SC

★ ★ ★ **EMBASSY SUITES-LOVE FIELD.** *3880 W Northwest Hwy (75220), near Love Field Airport, north of downtown. 214/357-4500; FAX 214/357-0683.* 248 suites, 9 story. S $145-$165; D $155-$175; each addl $10; wkend rates. TV; cable (premium). Indoor pool; wading pool, whirlpool. Complimentary full bkfst. Coffee in rms. Restaurant 11 am-2 pm, 5-10 pm. Bar 4 pm-midnight; Sat, Sun to 10 pm. Ck-out noon. Guest Indry. Meeting rms. Business servs avail. In-rm modem link. Covered parking. Free airport transportation. Exercise equipt; weight machines, treadmill, sauna. Refrigerators; some bathrm phones; microwaves avail. Cr cds: A, C, D, DS, MC, V.

D SC

★ ★ ★ **FAIRMONT.** *1717 N Akard St (75201), at Ross, in Dallas arts district, downtown. 214/720-2020; FAX 214/720-5269.* E-mail fdallas1@aol.com. 550 rms, 25 story. S, D $135-$215; salon suites $325; under 17 free; wkend rates. Crib free. Garage parking $12. TV; cable (premium), VCR avail. Pool; wading pool, poolside serv. Restaurant 6 am-midnight (also see PYRAMID ROOM). Rm serv 24 hrs. Bar 11-2 am; entertainment. Ck-out 1 pm. Convention facilities. Business center. In-rm modem link. Shopping arcade. Tennis privileges. Golf privileges. Health club privileges. Bathrm phones. Cr cds: A, C, D, DS, ER, JCB, MC, V.

D SC

★ ★ **HAMPTON INN-WEST END.** *1015 Elm St (75202), in West End Historic District. 214/742-5678; FAX 214/744-6167.* 311 rms, 23 story. S $86; D $93; under 16 free; wkend rates; higher rates special events. Crib free. Pet accepted; $125 ($100 refundable). In/out parking $5. TV; cable (premium). Complimentary continental bkfst. Restaurant nearby. No rm serv. Ck-out noon. Business servs avail. In-rm modem link. Concierge. Barber. Coin Indry. Exercise equipt; treadmill, stair machine. Pool. Cr cds: A, C, D, DS, MC, V.

D SC

★ ★ ★ **HARVEY HOTEL-BROOKHOLLOW.** *7050 N Stemmons Frwy (75247), near Market Center, north of downtown. 214/630-8500; FAX 214/630-9486.* 356 rms, 21 story. S $99-$129; D $109-$139; each addl $10; under 18 free; wkend rates. Crib $10. TV; cable (premium). Indoor pool; whirlpool. Restaurant 6 am-2 pm, 5-11 pm. Bar 2 pm-midnight. Ck-out 1 pm. Coin Indry. Convention facilities. Business center. In-rm modem link. Gift shop. Exercise equipt; weight machines, bicycles, sauna. Cr cds: A, C, D, DS, MC, V.

D SC

★ ★ ★ **HILTON-DALLAS PARKWAY.** *4801 LBJ Frwy (75244), jct Dallas N Tollway, north of downtown. 972/661-3600; FAX 972/661-1060.* 310 rms, 15 story. S $99-$165; D $109-$175; each addl $10; suites $250-$375; under 18 free; wkend, special rates. Crib free. TV; cable (premium). Indoor/outdoor pool, whirlpool. Restaurant 6:30 am-11 pm. Bar 11 am-midnight. Ck-out 1 pm. Convention facilities. Business center. In-rm modem link. Gift shop. Exercise equipt: treadmill, weight machine, sauna. Health club privileges. Cr cds: A, C, D, DS, ER, JCB, MC, V.

D SC

★ ★ ★ **HOLIDAY INN-ARISTOCRAT.** *1933 Main St (75201), at Harwood, downtown. 214/741-7700; FAX 214/939-3639.* 172 rms, 15 story. S $135-$179; D $145-$189; under 12 free; wkend rates. Crib $10. TV; cable (premium), VCR avail. Complimentary coffee in lobby. Restaurant 6:30 am-10:30 pm. Bar 11-1 am. Ck-out noon. Meeting rms. Business servs avail. In-rm modem link. Concierge. Exercise equipt; weights, bicycles. Health club privileges. Bathrm phones, refrigerators, minibars; microwaves avail. Historic landmark, built in 1925 by Conrad Hilton and the first to bear his name; restored to its original Sullivanesque style. Cr cds: A, C, D, DS, ER, JCB, MC, V.

D SC

★ ★ **HOLIDAY INN SELECT.** *1241 W Mockingbird Lane (75247), near Love Field Airport, north of downtown. 214/630-7000; FAX 214/638-6943.* 348 rms, 13 story. S $139; D $149; each addl $10; suites $225-$550; under 18 free; wkend, hol rates. Crib free. Pet accepted, some restrictions; $50. TV; cable (premium). Pool; wading pool, poolside serv. Coffee in rms. Restaurant 6:30 am-2 pm, 5-10 pm. Bar 11-2 am. Rm serv 6 am-11 pm. Ck-out noon. Coin Indry. Convention facilities. Business servs avail. In-rm modem link. Gift shop. Free airport transportation. Exercise equipt; weight machine, stair machine. Health club privileges. Cr cds: A, C, D, DS, ER, JCB, MC, V.

D SC

★ ★ **HOLIDAY INN SELECT-NORTH.** *2645 LBJ Frwy (75234), north of downtown. 972/243-3363; FAX 972/484-7082.* 374 rms, 6 story. S, D $139; each addl $10; suites $149-$600; under 19 free; wkend rates. Crib free. TV; cable (premium). Indoor/outdoor pool; whirlpool, poolside serv. Coffee in rms. Restaurants 6:30 am-midnight. Bar 11-1 am; Fri, Sat to 2 am; entertainment. Ck-out 1 pm. Convention facilities. In-rm modem link. Concierge. Gift shop. Exercise equipt; weight machine, bicycle. Some refrigerators. Some balconies. Cr cds: A, C, D, DS, MC, V.

D SC

★ ★ ★ **HYATT REGENCY.** *300 Reunion Blvd (75207), downtown. 214/651-1234; FAX 214/742-8126.* Web www.hyatt.com.dallas. 939 rms, 28 story. S $195; D $220; each addl $25; suites $350-$3,000; under 18 free; wkend rates. Valet parking $12. TV; cable (premium), VCR avail (movies $5). Pool; whirlpool, poolside serv. Restaurant 6 am-midnight. Bar noon-1:30 am. Ck-out noon. Convention facilities. Business center. In-rm modem link. Gift shop. Airport transportation. Lighted tennis. Exercise equipt; weights, bicycles, sauna. Health club privileges. Minibars; some refrigerators. Luxury level. Cr cds: A, C, D, DS, ER, JCB, MC, V.

D SC

★ ★ ★ **INTER-CONTINENTAL.** *15201 Dallas Pkwy (75248), Dallas N Tollway exit Arapahoe, north of downtown. 972/386-6000; FAX 972/991-6937; res: 800/426-3135.* 529 rms, 15 story. S $175; D $195; each addl $20; suites $325-$1,250; under 17 free. Crib free. Valet parking $9 overnight. TV; cable (premium), VCR avail. Indoor/outdoor pool; whirlpool, poolside serv. 2 restaurants 6 am-10:30 pm. Rm serv 24 hrs. Bars 11-2 am. Ck-out noon. Convention facilities. Business center. In-rm modem link. Concierge. Shopping arcade. Barber, beauty shop. Covered parking. Lighted tennis. Golf privileges. Exercise rm; instructor, weight machine, bicycles, sauna, steam rm. Bathrm phones; some refrigerators. Private patios. Luxury level. Cr cds: A, C, D, DS, MC, V.

D SC

★ ★ ★ ★ ★ **MANSION ON TURTLE CREEK.** *2821 Turtle Creek Blvd (75219), north of downtown. 214/559-2100; FAX 214/528-4187; res: 800/527-5432 (exc TX), 800/442-3408 (TX).* This well-known hotel was converted from the 1926 home of a cotton baron. It retains an atmosphere of privilege and calm, thanks to a turret-shaped white-marble lobby with European antiques and a glass-domed roof, and deep-carpeted guest rooms with French windows. 140 rms, 9 story. S $290-$370; D $320-$400; each addl $40; suites, kit. units $495-$1,500; wkend rates. Crib free. Valet parking $10. TV; cable (premium), VCR. Heated pool; poolside serv. Restaurants 7 am-10:30 pm (also see RESTAURANT AT THE MANSION ON TURTLE CREEK). Rm serv 24 hrs. Bar 11-2 am; entertainment. Ck-out 2 pm. Meeting rms. Business center. In-rm modem link. Concierge. Beauty shop. Airport transportation. Lighted tennis privileges. Golf privileges. Exercise rm; instructor, weights, treadmills, sauna, steam rm. Health club privileges. Massage. Bathrm phones, minibars; microwaves avail; wet bar in suites. Private patios, balconies. Cr cds: A, C, D, DS, ER, JCB, MC, V.

D

★ ★ ★ **MARRIOTT HOTEL QUORUM.** *14901 Dallas Pkwy (75240), N Dallas Tollway, exit Beltline, north of downtown. 972/661-2800; FAX 972/934-1731.* 548 rms, 12 story. S, D $129-$149; suites $250-$450; under 12 free; wkend rates. Crib free. TV; cable (premium), VCR avail. Heated indoor/outdoor pool; whirlpool, poolside serv. Restaurants 6:30 am-midnight. Bar 11 am-midnight. Ck-out 1 pm. Lndry serv. Convention facilities. Business center. In-rm modem link. Concierge. Gift shop. Free covered parking. Tennis. Exercise equipt; weights, bicycles, sauna. Health club privileges. Refrigerators avail. Luxury level. Cr cds: A, C, D, DS, ER, JCB, MC, V.

D SC

★ ★ **MEDALLION.** *4099 Valley View Ln (75244), north of downtown. 972/385-9000; res: 800/808-1011; FAX 972/458-8260.* 300 rms, 10 story. S, D $130-$165; each addl $10; suites $145-$390; under 12 free; wkend rates (2-day min). Crib avail. TV; cable, VCR avail. Restaurant 6:30 am-10 pm. Bar noon-midnight. Ck-out noon. Convention facilities. Business center. In-rm modem link. Concierge. Tennis privileges. Golf privileges. Exercise rm; instructor, bicycles, stair machines. Massage. Pool; poolside serv. Luxury level. Cr cds: A, C, D, DS, MC, V.

D

★ ★ ★ **MELROSE.** *3015 Oak Lawn Ave (75219), in Oak Lawn. 214/521-5151; FAX 214/521-2470; res: 800/MEL-ROSE.* E-mail melrose @dusit.com. 184 rms, 8 story. S $155-$185; D $165-$195; suites $250-$1,200; wkend rates. Crib free. TV; cable (premium), VCR avail. Pool privileges. Restaurant (see THE LANDMARK). Rm serv 24 hrs. Bar 11-2 am; entertainment. Ck-out noon. Meeting rms. Business servs avail. In-rm modem link. Concierge. Gift shop. Valet parking. Free airport transportation. Health club privileges. Some refrigerators; microwaves avail. Restored 1924 hotel; library. Luxury level. Cr cds: A, C, D, DS, JCB, MC, V.

D

★ ★ ★ ★ **OMNI MANDALAY AT LAS COLINAS.** *(221 E Las Colinas Blvd, Irving 75039) W on I-35E to TX 114, O'Connor exit, E to Las Colinas Blvd. 972/556-0800; FAX 972/556-0729.* Located on five elaborately landscaped acres, this luxury property is conveniently located on the Mandalay Canal and Lake Carolyn. An extensive art collection gives the public areas a special touch. 410 rms, 28 story. S, D $195-$220; each addl $10; suites $210-$260; under 18 free; wkend rates. Crib free. Valet parking $8/day. TV; cable (premium), VCR avail. Heated pool; whirlpool, poolside serv (seasonal). Supervised child's activities (Memorial Day-Labor Day). Restaurant (see ENJOLIE). Rm serv 24 hrs. Bar 11:30-1:30 am. Ck-out noon. Convention facilities. Business center. In-rm modem link. Concierge. Gift shop. Tennis privileges. Golf privileges. Exercise rm; instructor, weights, bicycles, sauna. Massage. Bathrm phones. Some private patios, balconies. Cr cds: A, C, D, DS, ER, JCB, MC, V.

D SC

★ ★ ★ **OMNI PARK WEST.** *1590 LBJ Frwy (75234), off I-635 Luna Rd exit, north of downtown. 972/869-4300; FAX 972/869-3295.* Web www.omnihotel.com. 337 rms, 12 story. S, D $149-$169; suites $195-$1,200; under 17 free; wkend rates. Crib free. TV; cable (premium). Heated pool; whirlpool, poolside serv. Restaurant 6 am-10 pm. Bar 11-1 am. Ck-out noon. Convention facilities. Business center. In-rm modem link. Concierge. Gift shop. Free airport transportation. Exercise equipt; weight machine, bicycles, sauna. Massage. Health club privileges. Luxury level. Cr cds: A, C, D, DS, ER, JCB, MC, V.

D SC

★ ★ **RADISSON.** *2330 W Northwest Hwy (75220), north of downtown. 214/351-4477; FAX 214/351-4499.* 198 rms, 8 story. S $119-$139; D $129-$159; each addl $10; suites $129-$149; under 18 free; wkly, wkend, hol rates. Crib free. Pet accepted, some restrictions; $25 deposit. TV; cable (premium), VCR avail. Pool; whirlpool, poolside serv. Coffee in rms. Restaurant 6:30 am-10 pm. Bar 11-1 am. Ck-out noon. Coin lndry. Meeting rms. Business servs avail. In-rm modem link. Concierge. Gift shop. Free airport transportation. Exercise equipt; weight machine, treadmill. Health club privileges. Microwaves avail. Some balconies. Cr cds: A, C, D, DS, ER, JCB, MC, V.

D SC

★ ★ **RADISSON CENTRAL.** *6060 N Central Expy (75206), US 75 at Mockingbird Blvd exit, north of downtown. 214/750-6060; FAX 214/750-5959.* 288 rms, 9 story. S, D $89-$119; each addl $10; suites $140-$400; under 18 free; wkend rates. Crib free. TV; cable (premium), VCR avail. Indoor/outdoor pool; whirlpool, sauna, poolside serv. Restaurant 6:30 am-2 pm, 5-10 pm. Bar noon-1 am. Ck-out noon. Meeting rms. Business servs avail. Gift shop. Free airport transportation. Health club privileges. Some refrigerators; microwaves avail. Cr cds: A, C, D, DS, ER, JCB, MC, V.

D SC

✔★ ★ **RAMADA PLAZA CONVENTION CENTER.** *1011 S Akard (75215), downtown. 214/421-1083; FAX 214/428-6827.* 236 rms, 12 story. S $69-$140; D $79-$150; each addl $10; suites $350-$450; under 18 free; wkend rates. Crib free. Pet accepted. TV; cable (premium). Indoor pool; whirlpool. Restaurant 6 am-11 pm. Bar 4 pm-2 am. Ck-out noon. Meeting rms. Business center. In-rm modem link. Free garage parking. Airport transportation. Exercise equipt; weights, bicycles. Health club privileges. Balconies. Cr cds: A, C, D, DS, ER, JCB, MC, V.

D SC

✔★ **RAMADA-MARKET CENTER.** *1055 Regal Row (75247), north of downtown. 214/634-8550; FAX 214/634-8418.* 322 units, 12 story. S, D $89-$109; each addl $10; suites $125-$350; under 16 free. Pet accepted, some restrictions. TV; cable, VCR avail. Pool; poolside serv. Restaurant 6:30 am-2 pm, 5-10 pm. Bar 4 pm-1 am. Ck-out noon. Convention facilities. Business servs avail. Valet serv. Gift shop. Free covered parking. Free airport transportation. Game rm. Tennis. Exercise equipt; bicycle, treadmill. Some refrigerators. Cr cds: A, C, D, DS, JCB, MC, V.

D SC

★ ★ ★ **RENAISSANCE.** *2222 Stemmons Frwy (I-35E) (75207), near Market Center, I-35E exit 430C, north of downtown. 214/631-2222; FAX 214/634-9319.* 538 rms, 30 story. S $174-$194; D $194-$214; each addl $20; suites $214-$1,000; under 18 free; wkend rates. Crib free. Pet accepted, some restrictions. TV; cable (premium), VCR avail. Heated pool; whirlpool. Complimentary coffee. Restaurant 6:30 am-10 pm. Bar 3 pm-2 am; entertainment. Ck-out 1 pm. Convention facilities. Business center. In-rm modem link. Gift shop. Exercise equipt; weights, bicycles, sauna, steam rm. Some refrigerators. Three-story chandelier; art objects. Luxury level. Cr cds: A, C, D, DS, ER, JCB, MC, V.

D

★ ★ ★ **SHERATON PARK CENTRAL.** *12720 Merit Dr (75251), I-635 N at Coit Rd, north of downtown. 972/385-3000; FAX 972/991-4557.* 545 rms, 20 story. S $175; D $195; each addl $10; suites $250-$950; under 18 free; wkend rates. Crib avail. Valet parking $12. TV; cable (premium), VCR avail. Pool; poolside serv. Restaurant (see LAUREL'S). Rm serv 24 hrs. Ck-out 1 pm. Convention facilities. Business center. In-rm modem link. Gift shop. Concierge. Tennis. Exercise equipt; weight machine, treadmill. Health club privileges. Bathrm phones. Luxury level. Cr cds: A, C, D, DS, ER, JCB, MC, V.

D SC

★ ★ ★ **SHERATON SUITES-MARKET CENTER.** *2101 Stemmons Frwy (75207), I-35E at Market Center exit, northwest of downtown. 214/747-3000; FAX 214/742-5713.* Web www.sheraton.com/sheraton/html/properties/hotels_and_resorts/096.html. 251 suites, 11 story. S $185; D $200; each addl $15; under 18 free; wkend rates. TV; cable (premium). Indoor/outdoor pool; whirlpool, poolside serv. Complimentary coffee in rms. Restaurant 6 am-11 pm. Bar 11 am-midnight. Ck-out noon. Guest Indry. Business servs avail. In-rm modem link. Sundries. Exercise equipt; weight machine, treadmill. Refrigerators, wet bars; microwaves avail. Some balconies. Cr cds: A, C, D, DS, ER, JCB, MC, V.

D SC

★ ★ ★ **STONELEIGH.** *2927 Maple Ave (75201), in turtle creek district, north of downtown. 214/871-7111; FAX 214/871-9379; res: 800/255-9299.* Web www.netpp.com/stoneleigh. 153 units, 11 story. S, D $160-$195; each addl $15; suites $225-$455; kit. units from $160; family, wkend rates. Crib free. TV; cable (premium), VCR avail. Pool. Playground. Restaurants 6:30 am-11 pm (also see SUSHI). Bar 11-1 am. Ck-out noon. Business servs avail. In-rm modem link. Concierge. Valet parking. Free airport transportation. Health club privileges. Refrigerator in some suites. Microwaves avail. Restored 1924 hotel. Cr cds: A, C, D, DS, MC, V.

D SC

★ ★ ★ **THE WESTIN.** *13340 Dallas Pkwy (75240), north of downtown. 972/934-9494; FAX 972/851-2869.* 431 rms, 21 story. S $194-$230; D $209-$245; each addl $25; suites $385-$1,260; under 18 free; wkend rates. Crib free. Garage parking, valet $12. TV; cable (premium), VCR avail. Heated pool; poolside serv. Restaurants 6:30 am-10 pm. Rm serv 24 hrs. Bar 11-2 am. Ck-out 1 pm. Convention facilities. Business center. Concierge. Barber, beauty shop. Health club privileges. Refrigerators. Balconies. Adj Galleria Mall complex. Luxury level. Cr cds: A, C, D, DS, ER, JCB, MC, V.

D SC

★ ★ ★ **WYNDHAM ANATOLE.** *2201 Stemmons Frwy (75207), opp Dallas Market Center, north of downtown. 214/748-1200; FAX 214/761-7520.* 1,620 rms, 27 story. S, D $185-$250; each addl $15; suites $300-$1,400; under 18 free; wkend rates. TV; cable (premium), VCR avail. 3 pools, 2 indoor; whirlpool, poolside serv. Coffee in rms. Restaurants (see NANA GRILL). Bar 11-2 am; entertainment. Ck-out noon. Convention facilities. Business center. In-rm modem link. Concierge. Shopping arcade. Barber, beauty shop. Garage parking; valet. Lighted tennis. Exercise rm; instructor, weights, bicycles, steam rm, sauna. Bathrm phones, refrigerators, minibars. Luxury level. Cr cds: A, C, D, DS, JCB, MC, V.

D SC

✔★ ★ **WYNDHAM GARDEN.** *2015 Market Center Blvd (75207), north of downtown. 214/741-7481; FAX 214/747-6191.* 254 rms, 11 story. S, D $119-$129; under 18 free. Crib free. TV; cable (premium). Pool. Restaurant 6:30-2 pm, 5-10 pm. Ck-out noon. Coin Indry. Meeting rms. Business servs avail. In-rm modem link. Exercise equipt; weights, bicycles. Health club privileges. Some private patios, balconies. Cr cds: A, C, D, DS, JCB, MC, V.

D

Inn

★ ★ ★ ★ **HOTEL ST GERMAIN.** *2516 Maple Ave (75201), in Oak Lawn. 214/871-2516; FAX 214/871-0740; res: 800/683-2516.* Combining old-world character with modern amenities, this restored 1906 Victorian house features elegant French antiques and wood-burning fireplaces. The dining room opens onto a New Orleans-style walled courtyard. 7 suites, 3 story. S, D $245-$600. TV; cable (premium), VCR (free movies). Complimentary refreshments. Dining rm: bkfst hrs flexible for inn guests; dinner res required; public by res (wkends only, dinner). Rm serv 24 hrs. Ck-out noon, ck-in 4 pm. Business servs avail. Luggage handling. Valet serv. Concierge serv. Health club privileges. Minibars. Wraparound balcony; library/sitting rm. Cr cds: A, MC, V.

D

Restaurants

★ ★ **ADDISON CAFE.** *(5290 Belt Line Rd #108, Addison 75240) 15 mi N on N Dallas Toll Rd, exit Belt Line Rd, at jct Montfort. 972/991-8824.* Hrs: 11:30 am-2 pm, 5:30-10 pm. Closed Dec 25. Res accepted. French menu. Bar. Semi-a la carte: lunch $8-$12, dinner $13-$22. Complete meal: dinner $45. Specializes in seafood, duck, rabbit. Elegant, romantic atmosphere. Cr cds: A, C, D, DS, MC, V.

D

★ ★ **ADELMO'S.** *4537 Cole Ave (75205), north of downtown. 214/559-0325.* Hrs: 11:30 am-2 pm, 6-10:30 pm; Sat from 6 pm. Closed Sun; major hols. Res accepted. Mediterranean menu. Bar. Semi-a la carte: lunch $8.50-$14.50, dinner $12-$29. Specialties: 20 oz veal chop, duck with strawberry brandy sauce, lobster. Parking. Cr cds: A, C, D, DS, MC, V.

★ ★ **ALESSIO'S.** *4117 Lomo Alto (75219), north of downtown. 214/521-3585.* Hrs: 11:30 am-2 pm, 6-10:30 pm; Sun, Mon to 10 pm. Closed some major hols. Res accepted. Northern Italian menu. Bar. Semi-a la carte: lunch $9-$17, dinner $16-$30. Specialties: jumbo scallops Madagascar, fettuccine Genovese, scaloppine al Marsala. Pianist Fri & Sat. Valet parking. Wood paneling. Original paintings. Cr cds: A, C, D, DS, MC, V.

D

★ **ARC-EN-CIEL.** *(3555 W Walnut, Garland 75042) 17 mi E on I-635, exit Greenville, N to Village Plaza Shopping area. 972/272-2188.* Hrs: 11 am-10 pm; Fri to 11 pm; Sat 10 am-11 pm; Sun from 10 am. Res accepted. Vietnamese menu. Setups. Semi-a la carte: lunch $3.75-$4.50, dinner $7.95-$18.95. Specialties: Vietnamese egg rolls, lobster baked with cheese, charcoal-broiled pork. Own baking. Casual dining; curtained dining areas. Cr cds: A, D, DS, MC, V.

D

★ ★ ★ **ARTHUR'S.** *8350 N Central Expy (75206), 100 Campbell Centre, north of downtown. 214/361-8833.* Hrs: 11:30 am-2:30 pm, 6-

10:30 pm; Fri, Sat 6-11 pm. Closed Sun; major hols. Res accepted. Bar to 2 am; Sat from 6 pm. Semi-a la carte: lunch $7.25-$13, dinner $12.90-$25. Specializes in steak, seafood, veal. Entertainment. Valet parking. Cr cds: A, C, D, DS, MC, V.

D

✔★★ **ATHENEE CAFE.** *5365 Spring Valley #150 (75240), north of downtown. 972/239-8060.* Hrs: 11 am-2 pm, 5:30-11 pm; Sat from 5:30 pm. Closed Sun; Thanksgiving, Dec 25. Res accepted; required Fri, Sat. European menu. Serv bar. A la carte entrees: lunch $6.95-$8.95, dinner $11.95-$14.95. Specialties: stuffed cabbage, eggplant moussaka, gypsy sausage. Library paneling. Fountain. Cr cds: A, D, DS, MC, V.

D

★★★ **BARCLAYS.** *2917 Fairmount St (75201), north of downtown. 214/855-0700.* Web web2.airmail.net/barclays/. Hrs: 5-11 pm. Closed Tues-Wed; some major hols. Res accepted. French menu. Bar. A la carte entrees: dinner $25-$35. Specialties: oven-roasted chicken Grand mére, crab cakes, rack of lamb. Own desserts. Valet parking. Outdoor dining. French country decor in converted house. Cr cds: A, C, D, DS, MC, V.

D

★★★ **THE BISTRO.** *5405 W Lovers Lane (75209), north of downtown. 214/352-1997.* Hrs: 11:30 am-2 pm, 5:30-10 pm; Fri-Sat to 11 pm. Closed Sun; some major hols. Res accepted. French, Mediterranean menu. Bar. Wine list. A la carte: lunch $5.95-$9.95, dinner $12.50-$18. Specializes in tapas, lamb chop, Dover sole. Antique furnishings, original art and several tapestries add a touch of elegance. Family-owned. Cr cds: A, C, D, DS, MC, V.

D

✔★ **BLUE MESA GRILL.** *5100 Belt Line Rd (75240), 12 mi N on N Dallas Toll Rd, exit Belt Line Rd, north of downtown. 972/934-0165.* Hrs: 11 am-10 pm; Fri, Sat to 11 pm; Sun 10 am-9:30 pm; Sun brunch to 2:30 pm. Closed Thanksgiving, Dec 24, 25. Res accepted. Southwestern menu. Bar. Semi-a la carte: lunch $6-$8, dinner $8-$12. Sun brunch $12.50. Child's meals. Specialties: Adobe pie, tequila-roasted duck, smoked chicken enchiladas. Own baking. Outdoor dining. Southwestern atmosphere; casual dining. Cr cds: A, MC, V.

D

✔★ **BREAD WINNERS CAFE & BAKERY.** *3301 McKinney Ave (75204), north of downtown. 214/754-4940.* Hrs: 7 am-10 pm; Mon, Tues to 4:30 pm; Fri, Sat to 11 pm; Sun brunch 9 am-3 pm. Closed Dec 25. Res accepted. Semi-a la carte: bkfst $2.95-$6.95, lunch $4.95-$7.35, dinner $7.50-$16.95. Specialty: grilled tenderloin. Parking. New Orleans-style courtyard. Cr cds: A, C, D, DS, MC, V.

D

★★★ **CAFE PACIFIC.** *24 Highland Park Village (75205), at Mockingbird & Preston Rd, north of downtown. 214/526-1170.* Hrs: 11:30 am-2 pm, 5:30-10 pm; Fri to 11 pm; Sat 11:30 am-2:30 pm, 5:30-11 pm. Closed Sun; some major hols. Res accepted. Bar 11 am-midnight. Wine cellar. A la carte entrees: lunch $6.90-$11.90, dinner $12.90-$24.90. Specializes in seafood. Valet parking. Outdoor terrace dining. View of kitchen behind glass. Cr cds: A, C, D, DS, MC, V.

✔★ **CELEBRATION.** *4503 W Lovers Lane (75209), north of downtown. 214/351-5681.* Hrs: 11 am-2:30 pm, 5:30-10 pm; Fri, Sat to 10:30 pm; Sun 11 am-10 pm. Closed Thanksgiving, Dec 24-25. Bar. Semi-a la carte: lunch $4-$9, dinner $5.95-$13.95. Child's meals. Specializes in fresh vegetables, fish, pot roast. Own breads and desserts. Parking. Rustic decor; copper tables. Cr cds: A, C, D, DS, MC, V.

D SC

★★ **CHAMBERLAIN'S.** *(5330 Belt Line Rd, Addison 75240) 10 mi N on Toll Rd, exit Belt Line Rd, in Addison Town Hall Sq. 972/934-2467.* Hrs: 5:30-10:30 pm; Sat to 11 pm; Sun to 9 pm. Closed most major hols. Res accepted. Bar from 5 pm. Semi-a la carte: dinner $14.95-$28.95. Child's meals. Specializes in lamb, aged prime beef, wild game. Valet parking. Club atmosphere with multiple dining areas; European posters. Cr cds: A, C, D, DS, MC, V.

D

★★★ **CHEZ GERARD.** *4444 McKinney Ave (75205), north of downtown. 214/522-6865.* Web www.chezgerard.com. Hrs: 11:30 am-2 pm, 6-10:30 pm; Sat from 6 pm. Closed Sun; major hols. Res accepted. French menu. Bar. A la carte entrees: lunch $6.50-$9.50, dinner $13.50-$16.50. Specializes in fish, rack of lamb. Outdoor dining. Cr cds: A, C, D, DS, MC, V.

D

★★ **CITY CAFE.** *5757 W Lovers Ln (75209), north of downtown. 214/351-2233.* Hrs: 11:30 am-2:30 pm, 5:30-10 pm; Sun brunch 11 am-2:30 pm. Closed most major hols. Res accepted. Bar. Wine list. Semi-a la carte: lunch $7-$11, dinner $14-$21. Sun brunch $6-$12. Specializes in fresh tomato soup, fresh seafood. Valet parking. Outdoor dining. Cr cds: A, C, D, DS, MC, V.

D

★★★ **DAKOTA'S.** *600 N Akard St (75201), downtown. 214/740-4001.* Hrs: 11 am-2:30 pm, 5-10 pm; Fri to 10:30 pm; Sat 5-10:30 pm; Sun 5:30-9 pm. Closed some major hols. Res accepted. A la carte entrees: lunch $6.50-$12, dinner $9.95-$24.95. Specializes in fresh seafood, steaks. Own breads, pasta. Pianist Fri, Sat. Free valet parking. Patio dining with unusual 5-tiered waterfall. Cr cds: A, D, DS, MC, V.

D

★★★ **THE ENCLAVE.** *8325 Walnut Hill (75231), north of downtown. 214/363-7487.* Hrs: 11 am-2:30 pm, 5:30-10:30 pm; Sat 5:30-11 pm. Closed Sun; major hols. Res accepted. Continental menu. Bar to 2 am. Semi-a la carte: lunch $6-$16.50, dinner $18-$26. Specializes in French cuisine, steak, veal. Pianist. Big-band music Tues-Sat evenings. Valet parking. Elegant dinner club atmosphere. Family-owned. Cr cds: A, C, D, MC, V.

D

★★★ **ENJOLIE.** *(See Omni Mandalay at Las Colinas Hotel) 972/556-0800.* Hrs: 6:30-10 pm. Closed Sun, Mon. Res accepted. Bar. Wine list. Semi-a la carte: dinner $25-$32. Prix fixe: dinner $57. Child's meals. Specializes in grilled fish, roast game. Own baking, smoked meats and seafood. Valet parking. Outstanding view of grounds. Cr cds: A, C, D, DS, ER, JCB, MC, V.

D SC

✔★★ **FERRARI'S ITALIAN VILLA.** *(14831 Midway Rd, Addison 75244) 13 mi N on N Dallas Toll Rd, exit Belt Line Rd, W to Midway Rd, then S. 972/980-9898.* Hrs: 11 am-2 pm, 5-10 pm; Fri to 11 pm; Sat 5-11 pm. Closed Sun; some major hols. Res accepted. Italian menu. Bar. A la carte entrees: lunch $8.95-$11.95, dinner $11.95-$17.95. Child's meals. Specialties: linguini pescatore, veal chop, veal piccata al limone. Own pasta. Valet parking. Country Italian decor; masonry oven in dining area. Cr cds: A, C, D, DS, MC, V.

D

★★ **FOG CITY DINER.** *2401 McKinney Ave (75201), north of downtown. 214/220-2401.* Hrs: 11 am-10:30 pm, Fri, Sat to midnight. Closed Thanksgiving, Dec 25. Res accepted. Bar. Semi-a la carte: lunch, dinner $6.95-$22.95. Child's meals. Specialties: pork chops, flatiron pot roast. Diner atmosphere. Cr cds: A, C, D, DS, MC, V.

D

★★★★ **FRENCH ROOM.** *(See The Adolphus Hotel) 214/742-8200.* Exceptionally detailed presentations—such as veal that arrives looking like a delicately wrought hummingbird—match the ornate Louis XIV style and service of this gorgeous restaurant. Neo-classic cuisine. Specialties: Dover sole, roast rack of lamb, sautéed Norwegian salmon. Menu changes with season. Hrs: 6-10 pm. Closed Sun. Res accepted. Bar 5 pm-1:30 am. Wine list. A la carte entrees: dinner $28.50-$41. Valet parking. Jacket. Cr cds: A, C, D, DS, MC, V.

D

★ ★ **GERSHWIN'S.** *8442 Walnut Hill Ln (75231), at Greenville Ave, north of downtown. 214/373-7171.* Hrs: 11 am-10 pm; Fri to 11 pm; Sat 5-11 pm; Sun from 5 pm. Closed major hols. Res accepted. Bar. Semi-a la carte: lunch $3.95-$12.95, dinner $9.50-$26.50. Child's meals. Specialties: seared tuna, wild game trio, chocolate stack dessert. Own baking. Pianist. Valet parking. Outdoor dining. Contemporary decor; copper-framed windows, marble-top bar. Cr cds: A, D, DS, MC, V.

D

★ ★ **JAVIER'S.** *4912 Cole Ave (75205), north of downtown. 214/521-4211.* Hrs: 5:30-10:30 pm; Fri, Sat to 11 pm; Sun to 10 pm. Closed major hols. Res accepted. Continental, Mexican menu. Bar. Semi-a la carte: dinner $12.95-$19.95. Specialties: filete Cantinflas, red snapper mojo de ajo. Complimentary valet parking. Eclectic decor; antiques from Mexico. Cr cds: A, C, D, DS, MC, V.

D

★ ★ **JENNIVINE.** *3605 McKinney Ave (75204), north of downtown. 214/528-6010.* Hrs: 11:30 am-2:30 pm, 6-10 pm. Closed Sun; most major hols. Res accepted. Bar. Semi-a la carte: lunch $7-$8, dinner $12-$18. Specializes in rack of lamb, beef tenderloin, duck. Parking. Outdoor dining. British pub atmosphere. Cr cds: A, C, D, DS, MC, V.

D

★ ★ **JOEY'S.** *4217 Oak Lawn Ave (75219), at Herschel, in Oak Lawn. 214/526-0074.* Hrs: 11:30 am-2 pm, 5-11 pm; Fri to midnight; Sat 5 pm-midnight; Sun 5-9 pm. Closed Thanksgiving, Dec 24, 25. Res accepted. Italian menu. Bar. Semi-a la carte: lunch $6.95-$12.95, dinner $8.95-$24.95. Specialties: stuffed baby Coho salmon, pan-seared red snapper. Own baking, pasta. Valet parking. Outdoor dining. Modern, lighthearted decor with pop-art wall coverings, live lobster tank, display kitchen. Cr cds: A, D, DS, MC, V.

D ♥

★ ★ **L'ANCESTRAL.** *4514 Travis #124 (75205), north of downtown. 214/528-1081.* Hrs: 11:30 am-2 pm, 6-10 pm; Fri, Sat to 11 pm. Closed Sun; some major hols. Res accepted. Country French menu. Bar. A la carte entrees: lunch $6.50-$13.50, dinner $12.50-$19.50. Complete meals: dinner $22.50. Specializes in pepper steak, lamb tenderloin, grilled salmon. Outdoor dining. Cr cds: A, C, D, DS, MC, V.

D

★ ★ ★ **LA TRATTORIA LOMBARDI.** *2916 N Hall St (75204), north of downtown. 214/954-0803.* Hrs: 11 am-2 pm, 5:30-10:30 pm; Fri, Sat to 11 pm. Closed some major hols. Res accepted. Italian menu. Bar. Wine cellar. A la carte entrees: lunch $6.95-$16.95, dinner $10.95-$25. Specializes in pasta, seafood, veal. Valet parking. Outdoor dining. Italian decor. Cr cds: A, C, D, MC, V.

D

★ ★ ★ **THE LANDMARK.** *(See Melrose Hotel) 214/521-5151.* Hrs: 6 am-2 pm, 6-10 pm; Sat 6 am-11 am, 6-11 pm; Sun 6 am-2 pm, brunch from 11 am. Res accepted. Bar. Wine cellar. Semi-a la carte: bkfst $8-$12, lunch $9-$14, dinner $20-$28. Sun brunch $29.50. Valet parking. Specialties: Thai BBQ duck, pumpkin seed-crusted beef filet. Attractive decor in same 1920s style as hotel. Cr cds: A, C, D, DS, JCB, MC, V.

D

★ ★ ★ **LAUREL'S.** *(See Sheraton Park Central Hotel) 972/851-2021.* Hrs: 5:30-10 pm. Closed Sun; some major hols. Res accepted. Bar. Wine list. A la carte entrees: dinner $18-$42. Complete meals: dinner $48. Specializes in fresh seafood, beef. Pianist Mon-Sat. Valet parking. View of city. Cr cds: A, C, D, DS, ER, JCB, MC, V.

D

✔ ★ ★ **LAVENDOU.** *19009 Preston Rd (75252), 15 mi N on N Dallas Toll Rd, exit Frankfort Rd, E to Preston Rd, north of downtown. 972/248-1911.* Hrs: 11:30 am-2 pm, 6-10 pm; Fri, Sat to 11 pm. Closed Sun; major hols. Res accepted. French menu. Bar. Semi-a la carte: lunch $3.50-$13.95, dinner $4.95-$18.50. Specializes in rotisserie, Southern French dishes, French pastries. Own baking. Outdoor dining. Country French atmosphere with pottery, art. Totally nonsmoking. Cr cds: A, MC, V.

D

★ ★ ★ **LAWRY'S THE PRIME RIB.** *3008 Maple Ave (75201), north of downtown. 214/521-7777.* Hrs: 11:30 am-2 pm, 5:30-10 pm; Fri to 11 pm; Sat 5:30-11 pm; Sun 11:30 am-2 pm (brunch), 5-10 pm. Closed July 4, Dec 25. Res accepted. Bar. Wine cellar. Semi-a la carte: lunch $8.95-$12.95, dinner $19.95-$29.95. Sun brunch $8.95-$13.95. Child's meals. Specializes in prime rib, lobster tails, fresh fish. Free valet parking. Tableside preparation of meat chosen by patrons from silver cart; formal, Old English atmosphere. Cr cds: A, D, DS, MC, V.

D SC

✔ ★ ★ **LOMBARDI'S.** *311 N Market (75202), downtown. 214/747-0322.* Hrs: 11 am-11 pm; Fri to midnight; Sat 5 pm-midnight; Sun 5-10 pm. Italian menu. Bar. A la carte entrees: lunch, dinner $9.95-$23.95. Specializes in pasta, pizza. Outdoor dining. Valet parking. Cr cds: A, C, D, MC, V.

D

★ ★ ★ **MEDITERRANEO.** *18111 Preston Rd, Suite 120 (75252), N on N Dallas Tollway, Frankford exit, 3 mi E, north of downtown. 972/447-0066.* Hrs: 11:30 am-2 pm, 6-11 pm; Sat from 6 pm. Closed Sun, major hols. Res accepted. French, Italian menu. Bar. Wine list. Semi-a la carte: lunch $7.50-$13, dinner $11.50-28.50. Speicalizes in fresh seafood. Entertainment Mon-Sat. Valet parking. Outdoor dining. Mediterranean villa setting. Cr cds: A, C, D, MC, V.

D

★ ★ **MI PIACI.** *14854 Montfort (75240), N on Toll Rd to Belt Line Rd, north of downtown. 972/934-8424.* Hrs: 11:30 am-10:30 pm; Fri to 11 pm; Sat 5-11 pm; Sun 5-7 pm. Closed some major hols. Res accepted. Northern Italian menu. Bar. A la carte entrees: lunch $8.95-$15.95, dinner $10.95-$22.95. Specialties: Dover sole, osso bucco, linguine pirata. Own baking. Valet parking. Outdoor dining. Overlooks pond. Cr cds: A, C, D, DS, MC, V.

D

★ ★ ★ **MORTON'S OF CHICAGO.** *501 Elm St (75202), in West End Historic District. 214/741-2277.* Hrs: 5:30-11 pm; Sun 5-10 pm. Closed major hols. Res accepted. Bar. A la carte entrees: dinner $17.95-$29.95. Specializes in steak, seafood, lamb. Valet parking. Open grill; meat displayed at table for patrons to select. Cr cds: A, C, D, DS, JCB, MC, V.

D

★ ★ ★ **NANA GRILL.** *(See Wyndham Anatole Hotel) 214/761-7479.* Hrs: 11:30 am-2 pm, 6-10 pm; Fri, Sat to 10:30 pm. Res accepted. Bar from noon; Sat from 5:30 pm. Wine list. A la carte entrees: lunch $12-$18, dinner $18-$33. Specializes in ostrich, rack of lamb, buffalo. Entertainment. Valet parking. Located on 27th floor; view of city. Cr cds: A, C, D, DS, JCB, MC, V.

D

★ ★ **NEWPORT'S SEAFOOD.** *703 McKinney Ave (75202), in the Brewery, in West End Historic District. 214/954-0220.* E-mail kaed@postoffice.swbell.net; web www.dallasdineso.com. Hrs: 11:30 am-2:30 pm, 5:30-10:30 pm; Sat, Sun from 5:30 pm. Closed major hols. Bar. A la carte entrees: lunch $8.95-$10.95, dinner $12.95-$26.95. Specializes in mesquite-grilled seafood, steak, chicken. Extensive seafood selection. Parking. Tri-level dining in turn-of-the-century brewery; 50-ft-deep freshwater well in dining area. Cr cds: A, C, D, DS, MC, V.

D

★ ★ ★ **OLD WARSAW.** *2610 Maple Ave (75201), in Oak Lawn. 214/528-0032.* Hrs: 5:30-10:30 pm. Res required. French, continental menu. Bar. Wine cellar. A la carte entrees: dinner $21-$28. Specializes in lobster, steak au poivre, Dover sole. Own baking. Violinist, pianist. Valet parking. Lobster tank. Family-owned. Jacket. Cr cds: A, C, D, DS, MC, V.

★ ★ **PALM.** *701 Ross Ave (75202), in West End Historic District. 214/698-0470.* Hrs 11:30 am-10:30 pm; Sat from 5 pm; Sun 5:30-9:30 pm. Closed some major hols. Res accepted. Bar. Semi-a la carte: lunch $6.50-$18, dinner $14-$28. Specializes in prime aged beef, veal, lobster. Valet parking. Cr cds: A, C, D, MC, V.

D

✔★ ★ **PATRIZIO.** *25 Highland Park Village (75205), north of downtown. 214/522-7878.* Hrs: 11 am-11 pm; Sun, Mon to 10 pm; Tues-Thurs to 11 pm; Fri-Sat to midnight. Closed Jan 1, Thanksgiving, Dec 25. Italian menu. Bar. A la carte entrees: lunch $5.20-$7.30, dinner $6-$13.95. Specialties: angel hair pasta with artichokes, sautéed crab claws, grilled chicken portabella salad. Valet parking. Outdoor dining. Oriental rugs, original oil paintings. Cr cds: A, D, DS, MC, V.

D

★ ★ ★ **PYRAMID ROOM.** *(See Fairmont Hotel) 214/720-5249.* Hrs: 6-10:30 pm. Closed Sun. Res accepted. Continental menu. Bar 6 pm-1:30 am. Wine list. A la carte entrees: dinner $18.50-$35. Specializes in beef, veal, seafood. Own baking. Entertainment. Valet parking. Jacket. Cr cds: A, C, D, DS, MC, V.

D

★ ★ ★ ★ ★ **RESTAURANT AT THE MANSION ON TURTLE CREEK.** *(See Mansion On Turtle Creek Hotel) 214/559-2100.* Dean Fearing's exuberant cuisine is a perfect match for this famous hotel's famous dining room, entered through a fantastical circular black-and-white marble-floored lobby. A capacious living room with an intricately carved ceiling, an oak-paneled library, and the sweeping veranda of a former cotton baron's mansion have been transformed into this nationally known restaurant. Amer Southwest menu. Specialties: tortilla soup, lobster taco, crème brulée. Own baking. Hrs: noon-2:30 pm, 6-10:30 pm; Fri, Sat to 11 pm; Sun brunch 11 am-2:30 pm. Res accepted; required Fri, Sat. Bar 11-2 am. Wine cellar. A la carte entrees: lunch from $15, dinner from $30. Sun brunch $29.50. Valet parking. Jacket, tie. Cr cds: A, C, D, DS, ER, JCB, MC, V.

D

★ ★ ★ **RIVIERA.** *7709 Inwood Rd, north of downtown. 214/351-0094.* Hrs: 6:30-10:30 pm; Sat to 11 pm. Closed most major hols. Res accepted. Continental menu. Bar. Wine list. A la carte entrees: dinner $26-$34. Complete meals: dinner $45-$65. Specialties: escargots and tortilloni, rack of lamb, gulf shrimp pancake with scallops. Valet parking. Country French decor. Jacket. Cr cds: A, C, D, MC, V.

D

★ ★ ★ **ROOSTER.** *3521 Oak Grove (75204), north of downtown. 214/521-1234.* Hrs: 11:30 am-2:30 pm, 5:30-10 pm; Sun 11 am-2:30 pm (brunch). Closed most major hols. Res accepted. Contemporary, regional Amer menu. Bar. Wine list. Semi-a la carte: lunch $7-$15, dinner $15-$24. Sun brunch $7-$15. Specialties: roasted Vadalia onion soup, molasses pecan-encrusted catfish, herb-grilled lamb loin. Own baking. Gospel music Sun. Valet parking. Outdoor dining. Relaxed atmosphere has rooster theme. Cr cds: A, C, D, DS, MC, V.

D

★ ★ **ROYAL TOKYO.** *7525 Greenville Ave (75231), 2 mi S of LBJ Frwy; 3/4 mi E of US 75, Walnut Hill exit, north of downtown. 214/368-3304.* Hrs: 11:30 am-2 pm, 5:30-11 pm; Fri to 11:30 pm; Sat noon-2:30 pm, 5:30-11:30 pm; Sun 5:30-10:30 pm; Sun brunch 11:30 am-2:30 pm. Closed Jan 1, Thanksgiving, Dec 25. Res accepted. Japanese menu. Bar. Semi-a la carte: lunch $4-$15, dinner $14.25-$35. Sun brunch $18.95. Child's meals. Hibachi chefs. Specialties: tempura, shabu-shabu, hibachi steak. Sushi bar. Pianist. Parking. Traditional seating avail. Japanese motif; outdoor water gardens. Cr cds: A, C, D, DS, JCB, MC, V.

D

★ ★ **RUGGERI'S.** *2911 Routh St (75201), north of downtown. 214/871-7377.* Hrs: 11:30 am-2 pm, 6-11 pm; Sat, Sun from 6 pm. Closed some major hols. Res accepted. Northern Italian menu. Bar. Semi-a la carte: lunch $6.95-$12.95, dinner $10.95-$28. Specializes in fresh seafood, veal chops. Pianist. Valet parking. Cr cds: A, C, D, DS, MC, V.

D

★ ★ ★ **RUTH'S CHRIS STEAK HOUSE.** *5922 Cedar Springs Rd, I-35 N to Mockingbird, north of downtown. 214/902-8080.* Web ruthchris .com. Hrs: 5-11 pm, Sun to 10 pm. Closed Thanksgiving, Dec 25. Res accepted. Bar. Wine list. A la carte entrees: $17.95-$33.95. Specializes in steak, fresh seafood. Valet parking. Cr cds: A, C, D, DS, MC, V.

D

★ ★ **SAVINO.** *2929 N Henderson (75206), north of downtown. 214/826-7804.* Hrs: 6-10:30 pm; Fri, Sat 5:30-11 pm. Closed Sun; major hols. Res accepted. Italian menu. Bar. Semi-a la carte: dinner $9.75-$16.50. Child's meals. Specialties: escargot with cognac and shallots, carpaccio, arugula salad with cheese and olives. Own baking, pasta. Valet parking. Outdoor dining. Intimate dining; contemporary Italian murals. Cr cds: A, MC, V.

D

★ ★ **SEVENTEEN SEVENTEEN.** *1717 N Harwood (75201), on 2nd floor of Dallas Art Museum, downtown. 214/880-0158.* E-mail chef@dani1717.com; web www.dani1717.com. Hrs: 11 am-2 pm, 6-10 pm; Sat to 11 pm; Sun brunch 11 am-2 pm. Closed Mon; Jan 1, July 4, Dec 25. Res accepted. Continental menu. Bar. Semi-a la carte: lunch $10-$14, dinner $16-$40. Sun brunch $27.50. Child's meals. Seasonal specialties. Classical pianist Fri, Sat. Valet parking. Outdoor dining. Contemporary decor; windows overlook garden, artwork. Cr cds: A, DS, MC, V.

D SC

✔★ **SONNY BRYAN'S.** *302 N Market St (75202), at Pacific, in West End Historic District. 214/744-1610.* Hrs: 11 am-10 pm; Fri, Sat to 11 pm; Sun noon-9 pm. Closed Easter, Thanksgiving, Dec 25. Barbecue menu. Bar. Semi-a la carte: lunch $3.50-$10.99, dinner $3.50-$14.99. Child's meals. Specialties: beef brisket, pork ribs, beef-stuffed baked potato. Outdoor dining. Old West atmosphere; meats smoked on premises. Cr cds: A, C, D, DS, JCB, MC, V.

D

★ ★ ★ **STAR CANYON.** *3102 Oak Lawn Ave, suite 144 (75219), in Centrum Bldg, north of downtown. 214/520-7827.* Hrs: 11:30 am-2 pm, 6-10:30 pm; Fri to 11 pm; Sat 6-11 pm; Sun 6-10 pm. Closed some major hols. Res required. Wine list. A la carte entrees: lunch $6.50-$13, dinner $15-$23. Specialties: tamale tart with roast garlic custard and Gulf crabmeat, bone-in cowboy ribeye with red chile onion rings. Valet parking. Outdoor dining. Stylish yet unpretentious dining experience among award winning Texan decor. Cr cds: A, D, DS, MC, V.

D

★ **SUSHI.** *(See Stoneleigh Hotel) 214/871-7111.* Hrs: 11 am-2 pm, 5:30-11 pm; Fri, Sat to midnight. Closed Sun; most major hols. Res accepted. Japanese menu. Bar. Semi-a la carte: lunch, dinner $7.25-$18. Specialties: spider roll, granoff roll, Stoneleigh roll. Valet parking. Outdoor dining. Unique decor; kimonos and scrolls decorate walls. Totally non-smoking. Cr cds: A, C, D, DS, MC, V.

D

✔★ ★ **THAI TASTE.** *3101 N Fitzhugh Ave (75204), at McKinney, north of downtown. 214/521-3515.* Hrs: 11 am-2:30 pm, 5-10 pm; Fri, Sat to 11 pm; Sun from 5 pm. Closed Thanksgiving. Res accepted. Thai menu. Bar. Semi-a la carte: lunch $4.95-$6.50, dinner $6.95-$14. Specialties: panang curry chicken, mint leaf spicy beef, pad Thai shrimp. Cr cds: A, C, D, DS, MC, V.

D

★ ★ ★ **TOSCANA.** *4900 McKinney Ave (75205), at Monticello, north of downtown. 214/521-2244.* Hrs: 11:30 am-2 pm, 6-10 pm; Fri to 11 pm; Sat 6-11 pm; Sun from 6 pm. Closed Jan 1, Thanksgiving, Dec 25. Res accepted. Italian menu. Bar 5-11 pm. Wine cellar. Semi-a la carte: lunch $6.50-$14.50, dinner $12-$29. Child's meals. Specializes in foods from Italy's Tuscany region. Own pasta. Jazz Tues-Thurs. Valet parking. Outdoor dining. Contemporary, casual dining in Tuscan village setting. Cr cds: A, C, D, MC, V.

D

★ ★ **UNCLE TAI'S.** *13350 Dallas Pkwy (75240), in the Galleria Shopping Plaza, north of downtown. 972/934-9998.* Hrs: 11 am-10 pm; Fri, Sat to 10:30 pm; Sun noon-9:30 pm. Closed some major hols. Res accepted. Chinese menu. Serv bar. A la carte entrees: lunch $7.50-$10.50, dinner $11-$17. Specializes in beef, chicken, seafood. Totally nonsmoking. Cr cds: A, C, D, MC, V.

D

★ ★ **YORK STREET.** *6047 Lewis St (75206), north of downtown. 214/826-0968.* Hrs: 6-10 pm; Fri, Sat to 11 pm. Closed Sun, Mon; most major hols. Res accepted. Semi-a la carte: $16-$26. Specialties: sautéed soft-shelled crab, pepper steak with cognac sauce, rack of lamb provencal. Totally nonsmoking. Cr cds: MC, V.

D

★ ★ ★ **YVETTE.** *(14775 Midway Rd, Addison 75244) 13 mi N on I-635, exit Midway Rd. 972/503-9777.* Hrs: 11 am-2:30 pm, 5-11 pm; Fri to midnight; Sat 5 pm-midnight. Closed Sun; Jan 1, Thanksgiving, Dec 25. Res accepted. Continental menu. Bar; Fri, Sat to 1 am. Wine cellar. A la carte entrees: lunch $6-$15, dinner $15-$35. Specialties: Dover sole, chateaubriand, Australian lobster tails. Musicians exc Sun. Valet parking. Elegant atmosphere; ballroom, murals, wine racks. Cr cds: A, C, D, DS, MC, V.

D

✔★ ★ **ZIZIKI'S.** *4514 Travis St, Suite 122 (75205), north of downtown. 214/521-2233.* Hrs: 11 am-11 pm; Fri, Sat to midnight. Closed Sun; major hols. Mediterranean menu. Bar. Semi-a la carte: lunch $6.95-$8.95, dinner $10.95-$19.95. Specialties: grilled rack of lamb, spanakopita. Parking. Outdoor dining. Intimate bistro setting. Cr cds: A, D, MC, V.

D

Fort Worth

FORT WORTH RESTAURANTS BY NEIGHBORHOOD AREAS

(For full description, see alphabetical listings under Restaurants)

DOWNTOWN
Reflections (Worthington Hotel). 200 Main St

NORTH OF DOWNTOWN
Joe T. Garcia's. 2201 N Commerce

WEST OF DOWNTOWN
Balcony. 6100 Camp Bowie Blvd
Cafe Aspen. 6103 Camp Bowie Blvd
Celebration. 4600 Dexter
Edelweiss. 3801-A Southwest Blvd
Lucile's. 4700 Camp Bowie

MUSEUM/CULTURAL DISTRICT
Saint-Emilion. 3617 W 7th St

Note: When a listing is located in a town that does not have its own city heading, it will appear under the city nearest to its location. In these cases, the address and town appear in parenthesis immediately following the name of the establishment.

Motels

✔★ **BEST WESTERN-WEST BRANCH INN.** *7301 W Frwy (76116), I-30 at TX 183, west of downtown. 817/244-7444; FAX 817/244-7902.* 118 rms, 2 story. S $46-$76; D $59.95-$89.95; each addl $5; suites $69.95-$109.95; under 12 free. Crib free. Pet accepted, some restrictions. TV; cable (premium), VCR avail. Pool. Complimentary continental bkfst. Restaurant adj 4 pm-2 am; closed Sun-Tues. Ck-out noon. Coin Indry. Meeting rms. Business servs avail. In-rm modem link. Some refrigerators; microwaves avail. Cr cds: A, C, D, DS, JCB, MC, V.

SC

★ **COMFORT INN.** *4850 N Frwy (76137), north of downtown. 817/834-8001; FAX 817/834-3159.* 60 rms, 2 story. Apr-Oct: S $60; D $65; under 18 free; lower rates rest of yr. Crib free. TV; cable (premium). Pool. Complimentary continental bkfst. Ck-out noon. Coin Indry. Business servs avail. Sundries. Microwaves avail. Cr cds: A, D, DS, MC, V.

D SC

★ ★ ★ **COURTYARD BY MARRIOTT.** *(2201 Airport Frwy, Bedford 76021) 11 mi E on TX 121 from I-35, Central Dr N exit. 817/545-2202; FAX 817/545-2319.* 145 rms, 3 story, 14 suites. S $98; D $108; suites $118-$128; under 12 free; wkend rates. Crib free. TV; cable (premium). Pool; whirlpool. Complimentary coffee in rms. Restaurant 6:30-10:30 am; wkends 7 am-noon. Bar 4-11 pm. Ck-out noon. Coin Indry. Meeting rms. In-rm modem link. Valet serv Mon-Fri. Sundries. Exercise equipt; weight machine, bicycles. Refrigerator in suites. Patios, balconies. Cr cds: A, D, DS, MC, V.

D SC

★ ★ **HAMPTON INN.** *4681 Gemini Place (76106), I-35, exit Meacham Blvd, north of downtown. 817/625-5327.* 65 rms, 3 story. S $74; D $84; under 18 free; higher rates NASCAR races. TV; cable (premium). Complimentary continental bkfst. Complimentary coffee in rms. Restaurant adj 6 am-10 pm. Ck-out noon. Meeting rms. Business servs avail. In-rm modem link. Coin Indry. Pool. Cr cds: A, C, D, DS, MC, V.

D SC

✔★ ★ **LA QUINTA-WEST.** *7888 I-30W (76108), west of downtown. 817/246-5511; FAX 817/246-8870.* 106 rms, 3 story. S $65; D $72; each addl $8; under 18 free. Crib $5. Pet accepted. TV; cable (premium). Pool. Complimentary continental bkfst. Restaurant adj open 24 hrs. Meeting rms. In-rm modem link. Microwaves avail. Cr cds: A, C, D, DS, MC, V.

D SC

★ ★ **RESIDENCE INN BY MARRIOTT.** *1701 S University Dr (76107), west of downtown. 817/870-1011; FAX 817/877-5500.* 120 kit. suites, 2 story. Suites: $112-$155; wkend rates. Crib free. Pet accepted; $5/day. TV; cable (premium). Heated pool; whirlpool. Complimentary continental bkfst. Restaurant nearby. Ck-out noon. Coin Indry. Meeting rm. Business servs avail. In-rm modem link. Valet serv. Microwaves. Private patios, balconies. Picnic tables, grills. Cr cds: A, C, D, DS, ER, JCB, MC, V.

D

Motor Hotels

★ ★ ★ **GREEN OAKS PARK HOTEL.** *6901 W Frwy (76116), I-30 at TX 183, west of downtown. 817/738-7311; FAX 817/377-1308; res: 800/433-2174 (exc TX), 800-772-2341 (TX).* E-mail greenoak@onramp .net. 284 rms, 2-3 story. S $86-$99; D $96-$114; suites $96-$135; each addl $10; under 18 free; wkend rates; package plans. Crib free. Pet accepted. TV; cable (premium). 2 pools; poolside serv. Restaurant 6 am-2 pm, 5-10 pm. Rm serv. Bars 4 pm-2 am; entertainment exc Sun. Ck-out noon. Convention facilities. Business servs avail. In-rm modem link. Sundries. Lighted tennis. Exercise equipt; weights, bicycles, sauna. Adj Naval Air Station, Carswell Joint Reserve Base, 18-hole golf course. Cr cds: A, D, DS, MC, V.

D SC

★ ★ **HOLIDAY INN-CENTRAL.** *2000 Beach St (76103), I-30E, exit 16C, east of downtown. 817/534-4801; FAX 817/534-3761.* 192 rms, 2-3 story. S, D $69-$99; each addl $10; suites $99-$200; under 18 free; some wkend rates. Crib free. TV; cable (premium). Pool; whirlpool. Restaurant 6:30 am-2 pm, 5:30-10 pm. Rm serv. Bar 4 pm-midnight. Ck-out noon. Meeting rms. Business servs avail. In-rm modem link. Tennis. Exercise equipt; weight machine, bicycles. Cr cds: A, C, D, DS, MC, V.

D SC

★ ★ **HOLIDAY INN-NORTH.** *2540 Meacham Blvd (76106), I-35W at Meacham Blvd exit, north of downtown. 817/625-9911; FAX 817/625-5132.* 247 rms, 6 story. S, D $97; suites $185; under 18 free; some wkend rates. Crib free. TV; cable (premium), VCR avail. Indoor pool; whirlpool. Restaurant 6 am-2 pm, 5-11 pm; Sat, Sun from 7 am. Rm serv. Bar 2 pm-2 am; Sat from noon; Sun to midnight; entertainment. Ck-out noon. Coin Indry. Meeting rms. Business servs avail. In-rm modem link. Airport transportation. Bellhops. Sundries. Gift shop. Exercise equipt; bicycles, sauna. Bathrm phone, wet bar, whirlpool in suites. Cr cds: A, C, D, DS, ER, JCB, MC, V.

D SC

Hotels

★ ★ ★ **RADISSON PLAZA.** *815 Main St (76102), downtown. 817/870-2100; FAX 817/882-1300.* 517 rms, 15 story. S $138-$148; D $148-$158; each addl $10; suites $250-$1,000; under 18 free; wkend, hol rates. Crib free. Valet parking $8; garage parking $6. TV; cable (premium). Pool; poolside serv. Complimentary coffee in rms. Restaurant 6 am-11 pm. Bar 11 am-4 am. Ck-out noon. Convention facilities. Business center. In-rm modem link. Concierge. Gift shop. Barber, beauty shop. Tennis privileges. Golf privileges. Exercise equipt; bicycle, treadmill, sauna. Some refrigerators. Cr cds: A, C, D, DS, JCB, MC, V.

D SC

★ ★ ★ **STOCKYARDS.** *109 E Exchange St (76106), north of downtown. 817/625-6427; FAX 817/624-2571; res: 800/423-8471 (exc TX).* Web www.stockyardshotel.com. 52 rms, 3 story. S $125, D $135; each addl $10; suites $160-$350; higher rates: Chisholm Trail Round-up, Pioneer Days, Dec 31. Valet parking $5. TV, cable. Restaurant 7 am-10 pm; Fri, Sat to 11 pm. Bar; Fri, Sat to 2 am. Ck-out noon. Business servs avail. In-rm modem link. Restored turn-of-the-century hotel. Western decor. Cr cds: A, C, D, DS, MC, V.

★ ★ ★ ★ **WORTHINGTON.** *200 Main St (76102), downtown. 817/870-1000; FAX 817/335-3847; res: 800/433-5677.* This ultra-modern high-rise stretches along two city blocks, forming a dramatic glassed-in bridge over Houston Street. Fresh flowers in every room are among the many luxurious touches. 504 rms, 12 story. S $195-$215; D $205-$225; each addl $10; suites $400-$1,000; under 18 free; wkend rates; package plans. Crib free. Covered parking $7; valet parking $10. TV; cable (premium), VCR avail. Indoor pool; whirlpool, poolside serv. Restaurant 6 am-11 pm (also see REFLECTIONS). Rm serv 24 hrs. Bar 11-2 am; Sun from noon. Ck-out noon. Convention facilities. Business center. In-rm modem link. Concierge. Shopping arcade. Tennis. Golf privileges. Exercise rm; instructor, weights, bicycles, sauna. Massage. Some refrigerators. Private patios, balconies. Cr cds: A, C, D, DS, MC, V.

D SC

Restaurants

★ ★ **BALCONY.** *6100 Camp Bowie Blvd (76116), in Ridglea Village, west of downtown. 817/731-3719.* Hrs: 11:30 am-2 pm, 6-10 pm; Fri to 10:30 pm; Sat 6-10:30 pm. Closed Sun; major hols. Res accepted. Continental menu. Bar. Semi-a la carte: lunch $5.25-$14.95, dinner $12-$25. Specialties: chateaubriand, rack of lamb, baked red snapper. Pianist wkends. Parking. Glassed-in balcony. Cr cds: A, C, D, DS, MC, V.

D

✔★ ★ **CAFE ASPEN.** *6103 Camp Bowie Blvd (76116), W on I-30, exit Bryant Irvin, west of downtown. 817/738-0838.* Hrs: 11 am-2:30 pm, 6-10 pm. Closed Sun; most major hols. Res accepted. Bar; wkends to 1 am. Semi-a la carte: lunch $5-$10, dinner $12-$17. Specializes in fresh fish. Entertainment Fri, Sat. Cr cds: A, MC, V.

D

✔★ **CELEBRATION.** *4600 Dexter (76107), west of downtown at Camp Bowie & Hulen. 817/731-6272.* Hrs: 11 am-2:30 pm, 5-9 pm; Fri, Sat 11 am-10 pm; Sun 11 am-9 pm. Res accepted. Bar. Semi-a la carte: lunch $3.50-$8.95, dinner $6.95-$13.95. Child's meals. Specializes in fresh vegetables, fish, pot roast. Own desserts. Outdoor dining. Converted ice house. Cr cds: A, C, D, DS, MC, V.

D SC

★ **EDELWEISS.** *3801-A Southwest Blvd (76116), west of downtown. 817/738-5934.* Hrs: 5-10:30 pm; Fri, Sat to 11 pm. Closed Sun, Mon; some major hols. German, Amer menu. Bar. Semi-a la carte: dinner $9.95-$18.95. Specializes in wienerschnitzel, sauerbraten, red cabbage. Entertainment. Beer garden atmosphere. Family-owned. Cr cds: A, C, D, DS, MC, V.

D

★ **JOE T. GARCIA'S.** *2201 N Commerce (76106), north of downtown. 817/626-8571.* Hrs: 11 am-11 pm. Closed Thanksgiving, Dec 25. Mexican menu. Bar. Semi-a la carte: lunch $5.25-$9, dinner $9-$11. Child's meals. Specialties: chicken and beef fajitas, family-style dinners. Mariachi band Fri-Sun. Outdoor dining; courtyard with fountain, garden. Family-owned more than 50 yrs. No cr cds accepted.

D

★ ★ **LUCILE'S.** *4700 Camp Bowie (76107), west of downtown. 817/738-4761.* Hrs: 11:30 am-10 pm; Fri to 11 pm; Sat 9 am-11 pm; Sun from 9 am. Closed Dec 25. Res accepted. Bar. Semi-a la carte: bkfst $3.95-$9.95, lunch, dinner $5.25-$25.95. Specializes in pasta, wood-roasted entrees. Outdoor dining. Bldg used as a restaurant since 1930s; original pressed-tin ceiling. Cr cds: A, D, DS, MC, V.

D

★ ★ ★ **REFLECTIONS.** *(See Worthington Hotel) 817/870-1000.* Web www.worthingtonhotel.com. Hrs: 5:30-10 pm; Sun brunch 10 am-2:30 pm. Res accepted. Continental menu. Bar 11:30-2 am; Sun noon-1 am. Wine cellar. A la carte entrees: dinner $19.95-$40. Sun brunch $25.95. Child's meal. Specializes in beef, seafood, veal. Own baking. Pianist. Valet parking. Multi-level elegant dining. Cr cds: A, C, D, DS, JCB, MC, V.

D

★ ★ ★ **SAINT-EMILION.** *3617 W 7th St (76107), near Museum/Cultural District. 817/737-2781.* E-mail stemiltonfw@aol.com. Hrs: 6-10 pm; Sun 5:30-9 pm. Closed Mon; some major hols. Res accepted. French menu. Prix fixe: dinner $19.75-$28.75. Specializes in roast duck, imported fresh fish. Comfortable country French atmosphere. Cr cds: A, C, D, DS, JCB, MC, V.

D

Dallas/Fort Worth Airport Area

Motels

★ ★ **AMERISUITES.** *(4235 W Airport Frwy, Irving 75062) on TX 183, exit Esters Rd. 972/659-1272; res: 800/833-1516; FAX 972/570-0676.* 128 suites, 6 story. S, D $104; under 18 free; wkend rates. Crib free. TV; cable (premium). Pool. Complimentary continental bkfst. Ck-out 11 am. Meeting rms. Business servs avail. Coin Indry. Free airport transportation. Exercise equipt; weights, bicycle. Refrigerators, microwaves. Cr cds: A, C, D, DS, MC, V.

D SC

★ ★ **COMFORT SUITES.** *(1223 Greenway Circle, Irving 75083) TX 114, exit McArthur Blvd. 972/518-0606; FAX 972/518-0722.* 54 suites, 3 story. S, D $99-$109; each addl $5; under 18 free. Crib free. TV; cable (premium). Complimentary continental bkfst. Ck-out 11 am. Meeting rm. Business servs avail. Valet serv. Exercise equipt; bicycles, treadmill. Microwaves avail. Cr cds: A, C, D, DS, JCB, MC, V.

D SC

✔★ ★ **COUNTRY SUITES BY CARLSON.** *(4100 W John Carpenter Frwy, Irving 75063) TX 114 exit Esters Blvd. 972/929-4008; FAX 972/929-4224.* 72 kit. suites, 18 kit. units, 3 story. S $59-$119; D $69-$129; each addl $10; under 16 free. Crib free. TV; cable (premium). Heated pool; wading pool, whirlpool. Complimentary continental bkfst. Ck-out noon. Meeting rms. Business servs avail. In-rm modem link. Coin Indry. Free airport transportation. Refrigerators; microwaves avail. Cr cds: A, C, D, DS, JCB, MC, V.

D SC

★ ★ **DRURY INN.** *(4210 W Airport Frwy, Irving 75062) TX 183 & Esters Rd. 972/986-1200.* Web www.DruryInn.org. 129 rms, 4 story. S $71-$81; D $81-$91; each addl $10; under 18 free. Crib free. Pet accepted, some restrictions. TV; cable (premium). Pool. Complimentary continental bkfst. Restaurant adj 11-2 am. Ck-out noon. Meeting rms. Business servs avail. In-rm modem link. Sundries. Free airport transportation. Cr cds: A, C, D, DS, MC, V.

D SC

✔★ **FAIRFIELD INN BY MARRIOTT.** *(4800 John Carpenter Frwy, Irving 75063) TX 114 exit Esters Blvd. 972/929-7257; FAX 972/929-7257.* 109 rms, 3 story. Mar-Oct: S $69.95; D $77; each addl $10; under 16 free; lower rates rest of yr. Crib free. TV; cable (premium). Pool; whirlpool. Complimentary continental bkfst. Ck-out noon. Business servs avail. Valet serv. Cr cds: A, C, D, DS, JCB, MC, V.

D SC

★ ★ **HAMPTON INN.** *(4340 W Airport Frwy, Irving 75062) on TX 183, exit Esters Rd. 972/986-3606; FAX 972/986-6852.* 81 rms, 4 story. S $75; D $85; suites $87; under 18 free. Crib free. Pet accepted. TV; cable (premium). Pool. Complimentary continental bkfst. Restaurant adj 11-2 am. Ck-out noon. Sundries. Valet serv. Free airport transportation. Some refrigerators; microwaves avail. Cr cds: A, C, D, DS, MC, V.

D SC

✔★ ★ **LA QUINTA-DFW.** *(4105 W Airport Frwy, Irving 75062) TX 183 & Esters Rd. 972/252-6546; FAX 972/570-4225.* 169 rms, 2 story. S $68-$78; D $78-$88; each addl $10; suites $87-$108; under 18 free. Crib free. Pet accepted. TV; cable (premium). Pool. Complimentary continental bkfst. Restaurant adj open 24 hrs. Ck-out noon. Meeting rm. Business servs avail. In-rm modem link. Free airport transportation. Health club privileges. Cr cds: A, C, D, DS, MC, V.

D SC

Motor Hotels

★ ★ ★ **HARVEY SUITES.** *(4550 W John Carpenter Frwy, Irving 75063) TX 114 off Esters Blvd exit. 972/929-4499; FAX 972/929-0774; res: 800/922-9222.* 164 suites, 3 story. S, D $129-$139; under 18 free; wkend rates. Crib free. Pet accepted; $25 deposit. TV; cable, VCR avail (movies). Pool; whirlpool, poolside serv. Complimentary continental bkfst. Complimentary coffee in rms. Restaurant 6:30-11 am; Sat, Sun from 7 am. Bar 4 pm-midnight. Ck-out 1 pm. Coin Indry. Meeting rms. Business servs avail. In-rm modem link. Valet serv. Sundries. Gift shop. Free airport transportation. Exercise equipt; treadmill, bicycles. Health club privileges. Refrigerators, wet bars; microwaves avail. Picnic tables, grills. Cr cds: A, C, D, DS, JCB, MC, V.

D SC

★ ★ ★ **HOLIDAY INN SELECT-DFW AIRPORT NORTH.** *(4441 TX 114, Irving 75063) TX 114 exit Esters Rd. 972/929-8181; FAX 972/929-8233.* 282 rms, 8 story. S $129-$134; D $139-$149; each addl $10; suites $150-$250; under 12 free; wkend, hol rates. Crib free. TV; cable (premium). Pool; poolside serv. Coffee in rms. Restaurant 6:30 am-11 pm. Rm serv. Bar 11-1 am. Ck-out noon. Coin Indry. Meeting rms. Business servs avail. In-rm modem link. Gift shop. Valet serv. Free airport transportation. Exercise equipt; weight machine, bicycles. Some refrigerators; microwaves avail. Cr cds: A, C, D, DS, ER, JCB, MC, V.

D SC

★ ★ ★ **HOLIDAY INN SELECT-DFW SOUTH.** *(4440 W Airport Frwy, Irving 75062) TX-183, exit Valley view. 972/399-1010; FAX 972/790-8545.* 409 rms, 4 story. S $99-$139; D $109-$149; each addl $10; suites $150-$350; under 18 free; wkend rates. TV; cable (premium). Indoor/outdoor pool; wading pool, whirlpool. Restaurant 6 am-midnight. Rm serv. Bar 3 pm-2 am. Ck-out noon. Coin Indry. Meeting rms. Business servs avail. In-rm modem link. Bellhops. Valet serv. Sundries. Gift shop. Free airport transportation. Exercise equipt; stair machine, treadmill, sauna. Health club privileges. Game rm. Rec rm. Microwaves avail. Cr cds: A, C, D, DS, ER, JCB, MC, V.

D SC

★ **WILSON WORLD.** *(4600 W Airport Frwy, Irving 75062) 972/513-0800; FAX 972/513-0106.* 200 rms, 5 story, 96 suites. S, D $79-$119; suites $89-$129; under 18 free; wkend rates. Crib free. Pet accepted, some restrictions. TV; cable (premium). Indoor pool; whirlpool. Restaurant 6 am-1:30 pm, 5:30-10 pm. Bar 5 pm-midnight. Ck-out noon. Meeting rms. Business center. In-rm modem link. Gift shop. Free airport transportation. Exercise equipt; weight machine, stair machine. Refrigerators; microwaves avail. Cr cds: A, C, D, DS, MC, V.

D SC

Hotels

★ ★ ★ **DFW LAKES HILTON EXECUTIVE CONFERENCE CENTER.** *(1800 TX 26E, Grapevine 76051) TX 121N, Bethel Rd exit. 817/481-8444; FAX 817/481-3160.* E-mail 74161.547@compuserve.com; web www.dolce.com. 395 rms, 9 story. S, D $89-$159; each addl $15; suites $225-$950; under 18 free; wkend rates. Crib free. TV; cable (premium), VCR avail. 2 pools, 1 indoor; whirlpool, poolside serv. Coffee in rms. Restaurant 6:30 am-midnight (also see MERITAGE GRILLE). Bars 11-2 am; entertainment. Ck-out noon. Convention facilities. Business center. In-rm modem link. Concierge. Gift shop. Free airport transportation. 8 tennis courts, 2 indoor. Golf privileges, driving range. Exercise rm; instructor, weights, bicycles, steam rm. Minibars; some bathrm phones, refrigerators. Wooded grounds with lake. Luxury level. Cr cds: A, C, D, DS, JCB, MC, V.

D SC

★ ★ ★ **DOUBLETREE GUEST SUITES.** *(4650 W Airport Frwy, Irving 75062) TX 183 & Valley View Ln. 972/790-0093; FAX 972/790-4768.* 308 suites, 10 story. S, D $159; each addl $10; under 18 free; wkend rates. Crib free. TV; cable (premium), VCR avail. Indoor pool; whirlpool, sauna. Restaurant 6 am-2 pm, 5-10 pm; Fri, Sat to 11 pm. Bar to midnight; Fri, Sat to 2 am. Ck-out noon. Coin Indry. Meeting rms. Business servs avail. In-rm modem link. Gift shop. Free airport transportation. Health club privileges. Microwaves. Balconies. Atrium lobby with tropical plants. Cr cds: A, C, D, DS, ER, MC, V.

D SC

★ ★ ★ ★ **FOUR SEASONS RESORT & CLUB.** *(4150 N MacArthur Blvd, Irving 75038) NW via TX 114, exit MacArthur Blvd, S 2 mi. 972/717-0700; FAX 972/717-2550.* This property combines top-notch resort amenities—including a superb health center and spa—and state-of-the-art conference facilities with the comforts of an elegant hotel. 357 rms, 9 story. S, D $290-$340; suites $500-$1,100; under 18 free; golf, spa, wkend plans. Pet accepted, some restrictions. Valet parking $5. TV; cable (premium), VCR avail. 4 pools, 2 heated, 1 indoor & 1 child's; whirlpool, poolside serv, lifeguard (wkends in season). Supervised child's activities; ages 6 months-8 yrs. Restaurant (see CAFE ON THE GREEN). Rm serv

24 hrs. Bar 11-2 am. Ck-out noon. Convention facilities. Business center. In-rm modem link. Concierge. Gift shop. Barber, beauty shop. 12 tennis courts, 4 indoor, pro. 18-hole golf, greens fee $130 (incl cart), pro, 2 putting greens, driving range. Exercise rm; instructor, weight machines, bicycles, sauna, steam rm. Massage. Lawn games. Minibars; microwaves avail. Private patios, balconies. Cr cds: A, C, D, JCB, MC, V.

D

★ ★ ★ **HYATT REGENCY-DFW.** *(E & W towers on Intl Pkwy, DFW Airport 75261) At airport. 972/453-1234; FAX 972/456-8668.* 1,367 rms, 12 story. S $175; D $200; each addl $25; suites $275-$1,200; under 18 free; wkend rates. TV; cable (premium), VCR avail. Heated pool; poolside serv. Restaurant open 24 hrs. Rm serv. Bar 11-2 am; entertainment. Ck-out noon. Convention facilities. Business center. In-rm modem link. Concierge. Shopping arcade. Free airport transportation. Indoor, outdoor tennis, pro. 36-hole golf, greens fee $60-$75, pro, putting green, driving range. Exercise equipt; weights, bicycles, steam rm, sauna. Many refrigerators; some bathrm phones; microwaves avail. Balconies. Luxury level. Cr cds: A, C, D, DS, ER, JCB, MC, V.

D SC

★ ★ ★ **MARRIOTT-DFW AIRPORT.** *(8440 Freeport Pkwy, Irving 75063) TX 114 at N entrance to airport. 972/929-8800; FAX 972/929-6501.* Web www.marriott.com/marriott/dfwap. 491 rms, 20 story. S, D $159-$189; suites $200-$425; under 12 free; wkend rates. Crib free. Pet accepted, some restrictions. TV; cable (premium). Indoor/outdoor pool; whirlpool, poolside serv. Restaurants 6 am-11 pm. Bar 11-2 am. Ck-out 1 pm. Coin lndry. Convention facilities. Business center. In-rm modem link. Sundries. Gift shop. Free airport transportation. Tennis privileges. Golf privileges. Exercise equipt; weights, bicycles, sauna. Some refrigerators. Luxury level. Cr cds: A, C, D, DS, ER, JCB, MC, V.

D

Restaurants

✔★ ★ ★ **CAFE ON THE GREEN.** *(See Four Seasons Resort & Club Hotel) 972/717-0700.* Hrs: 6:30 am-11 pm; Sat, Sun from 7 am; Sun brunch 11 am-2:30 pm. Res accepted. Bar. Wine cellar. A la carte entrees: bkfst $5-$12, lunch $9-$15, dinner $33. Buffet: bkfst $13.50, lunch $18.50, dinner $30. Sun brunch $28.50. Serv charge 16%. Specialties: rack of lamb with lentil, cedar planked salmon filet, open ravioli with scallops & shrimp. Own baking. Valet parking. Garden-like setting; overlooks villas, pool. Cr cds: A, C, D, JCB, MC, V.

D

★ ★ ★ **DORRIS HOUSE CAFE.** *(224 E College St, Grapevine 76051) 817/421-1181.* Hrs: 11:30 am-2 pm, 5:30-10 pm; Sat from 5:30 pm. Closed Sun, Mon; Thanksgiving, Dec 25. Res accepted. Contemporary Amer menu. Wine list. A la carte entrees: lunch $5.95-$13.95, dinner $13.95-$24.95. Child's meals. Specialties: filet mignon with wine sauce, pan-seared salmon. Fine dining in Victorian house filled with antiques. Cr cds: A, C, D, DS, MC, V.

D

★ ★ ★ **MERITAGE GRILLE.** *(See DFW Lakes Hilton Executive Conference Center Hotel) 817/481-8444.* Hrs: 6:30 am-11 pm. Res accepted. Southwestern menu. Wine list. A la carte entrees: bkfst $5-$9, lunch $7-$15, dinner $12-$20. Specializes in fresh seafood, beef. Valet parking. Patio dining. Dark wood paneling gives this hotel dining rm an Old World club atmosphere; view of gardens. Cr cds: A, C, D, DS, JCB, MC, V.

D

★ ★ ★ **MONET'S.** *(5005 Colleyville Blvd, Colleyville 76034) 817/498-5525.* Hrs: 6-10 pm; Fri, Sat 5:30-11 pm. Closed Sun; Thanksgiving. Res accepted. Continental menu. Bar to midnight. Wine list. Semi-a la carte: dinner $12-$26. Specialties: beef tenderloin, venison tenderloin with blackberry port, crayfish cakes. Jazz trio Fri, Sat. Outdoor dining. Elegant dining among Claude Monet prints; some menu items selected from his journals. Totally nonsmoking. Cr cds: A, D, DS, MC, V.

Denver

Settled: 1858
Pop: 467,610
Elev: 5,280 feet
Time zone: Mountain
Area code: 303
Web: www.denver.org

The state capital of Colorado had its beginnings as a small community of adventurers searching for gold. Today, Denver still attracts those with a sense of adventure, but nowadays they come in search of opportunity, excitement and recreation. The abundant scenic beauty throughout the area helps make Denver one of the most appealing cities in the US.

As a growing community rich in mineral resources, natural beauty and wild game, Denver quickly realized the need for a transportation link with the rest of the country. For several years the people of Denver actively promoted the idea of a railroad link with the Union Pacific, and a line finally was opened between Denver and Cheyenne in 1870. The ensuing rush of immigration boosted both property values and economic development, furthering the effects of the gold and silver booms of the late 1800s. Already the capital of the Colorado Territory, Denver in 1876 became the capital of the 38th state.

In the wake of its "boom town" days, Denver continues to thrive, attracting many people with its dry, mild climate and proximity to recreational activities—most notably skiing in the Rockies. A new airport 17 miles from downtown Denver is an indication of the city's vitality. Denver International Airport encompasses 53 square miles (more than Dallas/Fort Worth and Chicago's O'Hare airports combined), and was planned to be a virtual city unto itself, with hotels, shops and dining and entertainment spots. It is expected to become one of the world's busiest airports, apparently anticipating continuing prosperity for Denver in the future.

Business

Manufacturing has made great strides in Colorado due to the state's central location, diverse transportation facilities and abundant natural resources. The state is still a storehouse of mineral wealth, producing much of the nation's supply of metallic and nonmetallic minerals. Denver is an important energy center, with half of its downtown office space rented by energy-related firms.

In the Denver area there are approximately 180 major businesses, each with more than 250 employees. The range of industry is great—construction; electrical machinery; metal products; food, hospital and dental equipment; leather; lumber; paper; petroleum; and glass. There are also finance, insurance and real estate companies and other service industries, such as health care, education, recreation and government. Printing, publishing and allied industries add to the picture, and wholesale and retail trade areas are thriving.

Convention Facilities

There are three major convention buildings in Denver: the Denver Convention Complex, the Denver Merchandise Mart and the Colorado Convention Center. Up to 16,000 hotel rooms can be guaranteed for a convention.

The Colorado Convention Center, part of the Denver Convention Complex, contains 300,000 square feet of exhibit space and 100,000 square feet of meeting space, including a 35,000-square-foot ballroom, 46 meeting rooms and theater-style seating for 7,500.

In the Convention Complex, the Currigan Exhibition Hall has 100,000 square feet of unobstructed space. Banquets can be served here for 9,000 people, or 14,000 can be seated theater-style. The theater seats 2,240; five to 20 rooms can be set up in the conference area for a total capacity of 3,470 people.

At the Merchandise Mart, the Exposition Building has 100,000 square feet of space, which can hold 4,000 people; 200 individual showrooms can seat an additional 4,000 people at peak capacity. The main building has 400 permanent showrooms, plus a 65,000-square-foot hall.

Sports & Recreation

With the Rockies nearly hovering over the city, Denver has long been a mecca for skiers, climbers and hikers. Fishing, camping and snowmobiling are also popular mountain activities. Spreading out over the Rocky Mountain foothills, the Denver Mountain Park System is a spectacular recreation area. The system covers 13,448 acres in a chain beginning 15 miles west of the city and extending to Summit Lake, 60 miles west. The city parks provide picnic and playground areas, golf courses, tennis courts, lakes and swimming pools.

For sports fans, the Denver Broncos football team plays at Mile High Stadium, the Nuggets basketball team and the Colorado Avalanche hockey team play at McNichols Arena, and the Colorado Rockies baseball team plays at Coors Field. In addition, universities in and near Denver have active sports programs.

There is dog racing at the Mile High Kennel Club and auto racing at Bandimere and Lakeside speedways.

The National Western Livestock Show, Horse Show and Rodeo is held in Denver each January, attracting many of the nation's finest rodeo performers, as well as buyers and sellers of livestock from all over the world.

Entertainment

The Colorado Symphony Orchestra plays in Boettcher Hall, the first "surround" orchestra hall in the US, from September through early June. During the fall, winter and spring, the Denver Center Theatre Company performs in the Helen Bonfils Theater Complex at the Denver Performing Arts Complex. The complex is known as one of the most innovative and comprehensive performing arts facilities in the country, offering a variety of entertainment, including musicals, classics and new plays. The addition of the 2,800-seat Temple Hoyne Buell Theatre in late 1991 made the Denver Performing Arts Complex one of the largest in the nation.

Historical Areas

Railroading was very important to the development of this part of the country, and much of its history has been preserved in such places as the Forney Transportation Museum and the Colorado Railroad Museum at Golden.

Some of the feeling of the Old West can be recaptured at the Buffalo Bill Memorial Museum on Lookout Mountain. Exhibits are centered around Buffalo Bill's Wild West Show, as well as other aspects of his exciting life.

The Molly Brown House pays homage to one of Denver's earlier and more flamboyant citizens, Margaret Tobin. A survivor of the *Titanic* disaster, she was known as the "unsinkable" Molly Brown. Molly came west to Leadville to make her fortune—and she did. Her extravagant house in Denver was built during the Victorian period, and Molly decorated the interior accordingly, particularly with purchases made during her numerous trips to Europe.

Sightseeing

The State Capitol dome, which is covered with gold leaf from Colorado mines, offers visitors a panoramic view of the city. Also downtown is the US Mint, where guided tours are conducted and a display of gold may be seen on the mezzanine. In the Civic Center complex are the Denver Public Library, the largest public library in the Rocky Mountain region, the outdoor Greek Theatre and the Denver Art Museum, with a fine collection of Native American arts.

The Denver Zoo and the Denver Museum of Natural History are located in City Park. The museum has mammals and birds from four continents displayed against natural backgrounds, geology and dinosaur exhibits, and a collection of Native American artifacts. Also in the museum is the Charles C. Gates Planetarium, which presents a variety of space science programs including star and laser light shows. The Denver Botanic Gardens and the Boettcher Memorial Conservatory have plants representative of the various climatic zones of the world.

Lakeside and Heritage Square in Golden are amusement parks in the Denver area. Fitch Gardens amusement park is in the downtown area. Larimer Square is a restoration of Denver's oldest—and at one time wildest—streets. Where outlaws and desperados once walked, today musicians, artists and craftsmen work, and visitors enjoy restaurants, galleries and shops housed in Victorian buildings.

More than half of Colorado's land west of Denver lies within the boundaries of national forests, and two of the most popular areas of the National Park system are within the state: Rocky Mountain National Park and Mesa Verde National Park.

General References

Area code: 303

Phone Numbers

POLICE & FIRE: 911

POISON CONTROL CENTER: 629-1123

TIME & WEATHER: 850-7050

Information Sources

Denver Metro Convention and Visitors Bureau, 1555 California St, Ste 300, 80202; 892-1505.

Denver Chamber of Commerce, 1445 Market St, 80202; 534-8500.

Dept of Parks and Recreation, 964-2500.

Transportation

AIRLINES: Air Canada; American; America West; Continental; Delta; Frontier; Lone Star; Lufthansa; Martinair Holland; Mexicana; Midwest Express; Northwest; Reno Air; TWA; United; USAir; Vanguard and other commuter and regional airlines.

AIRPORT: Denver International, 342-2300 or 800/AIR-2-DEN.

CAR RENTAL AGENCIES: (See IMPORTANT TOLL-FREE NUMBERS) Avis 398-3725; Budget 341-2277; Hertz 342-3800; National 321-7990.

PUBLIC TRANSPORTATION: Regional Transportation District 299-6000.

RAILROAD PASSENGER SERVICE: Amtrak 800/872-7245.

Newspapers

Denver Post; Rocky Mountain News.

Convention Facilities

Colorado Convention Center, 14th & California Sts, 640-8050.

Denver Convention Complex, 14th & Welton Sts, 640-8000.

Merchandise Mart, 451 E 58th Ave, 292-6278.

Sports & Recreation

Major Sports Facilities

Coors Field, 20th & Blake Sts (Rockies, baseball, 762-5437).

McNichols Arena, W 17th Ave & Clay St (Nuggets, basketball, 893-6700; Avalanche, hockey, 893-6700).

Mile High Stadium, W 19th & Eliot Sts (Broncos, football, 433-7466).

Racetracks

Bandimere Speedway, 3051 S Rooney Rd, in Morrison, 697-6001 (auto racing).

Mile High Kennel Club, 7 mi NE at jct I-270 & Vasquez Blvd, at 6200 Dahlia St, 288-1591 (greyhound racing).

Cultural Facilities

Theaters

Arvada Center for the Arts & Humanities, 6901 Wadsworth Blvd, Arvada, 431-3939.

Auditorium Theater, Denver Performing Arts Complex, 14th & Curtis Sts, 640-2862.

The Changing Scene, 1527½ Champa St, 893-5775.

Country Dinner Playhouse, 6875 S Clinton St, 799-1410.

The Helen Bonfils Theatre Complex, Denver Performing Arts Complex, 14th & Curtis Sts, 893-4100.

Temple Hoyne Buell Theatre, Denver Performing Arts Complex, 14th & Curtis Sts, 640-2862.

Concert Hall

Boettcher Concert Hall, Denver Performing Arts Complex, 14th & Curtis Sts, 640-2862.

Museums

Buffalo Bill Memorial Museum, Lookout Mountain, I-70W exit 256, 526-0747.

Children's Museum of Denver, 2121 Children's Museum Dr, 433-7433.

Colorado History Museum, 1300 Broadway, 866-3682.

Colorado Railroad Museum, 17155 W 44th Ave, Golden, 279-4591.

Denver Firefighters Museum, 1326 Tremont Place, 892-1436.

Denver Museum of Natural History, 2001 Colorado Blvd, City Park, 322-7009.

Forney Transportation Museum, 1416 Platte St, near I-25 exit 211, 433-3643.

Molly Brown House Museum, 1340 Pennsylvania St, 832-4092.

Art Museums

Denver Art Museum, 100 W 14th Ave Pkwy, in Civic Center, 640-2793.

Museum of Western Art, 1727 Tremont Place, 296-1880.

Turner Museum, 773 Downing St, 832-0924.

Points of Interest

Denver Botanic Gardens, Boettcher Memorial Conservatory, 1005 York St, entrance off Cheesman Park, 331-4000.

Denver Public Library, 1357 Broadway, 640-6200.

Denver Zoo, E 23rd Ave, between Colorado Blvd & York St in City Park, 331-4110.

Elitch Gardens Amusement Park, downtown, 595-4386.

Heritage Square, jct CO 40, 93, in Golden, 279-2789 or 277-0040.

Lakeside Amusement Park, W 44th Ave & Sheridan Blvd, 477-1621.

Larimer Square, Larimer St between 14th & 15th Sts.

Outdoor Greek Theater, S side of Civic Center.

Red Rocks Park, 12 mi SW, off CO 26 between I-70 & US 285.

Sakura Square, Lawrence to Larimer Sts on 19th St, 295-0305.

State Capitol, E Colfax Ave & Sherman St, 866-2604.

United States Mint, 320 W Colfax Ave, 844-5588.

Sightseeing Tours

Gray Line bus tours, PO Box 17527, 80217-0527; 289-2841.

Historic Colorado Tours, Education Dept, 1300 Broadway, 80203; 866-4686.

Annual Events

National Western Livestock Show, Horse Show & Rodeo, National Western Complex and Coliseum. Jan.

Cherry Blossom Festival, Sakura Square. 2nd wkend June.

City Neighborhoods

Many of the restaurants, unrated dining establishments and some lodgings listed under Denver include neighborhoods as well as exact street addresses. Geographic descriptions of the Downtown and 16th St Mall are given, followed by a table of restaurants arranged by neighborhood.

Downtown: Southeast of Wynkoop St, west of Grant St, north of 14th St and east of Speer Blvd. **North of Downtown:** North of Wynkoop St. **South of Downtown:** South of 14th Ave. **East of Downtown:** East of Grant St. **West of Downtown:** West of Cherry Creek.

16th St Mall: 16th St from Market St on the NW to Broadway on the SE.

Lodgings and Food

DENVER RESTAURANTS BY NEIGHBORHOOD AREAS
(For full description, see alphabetical listings under Restaurants)

DOWNTOWN
Al Fresco. 1040 15th St
Aubergine Cafe. 225 E 7th Ave
Augusta (Westin Hotel Tabor Center). 1672 Lawrence St
Bella Ristorante. 1920 Market St
Brasserie Z. 815 17th St
The Broker. 821 17th St
City Spirit Cafe. 1434 Blake
Denver Chophouse & Brewery. 1735 19th St
European Cafe. 1060 15th St
Le Central. 112 E 8th Ave
McCormick's Fish House. 1659 Wazee St
Old Spaghetti Factory. 1215 18th St
Palace Arms (Brown Palace Hotel). 321 17th St
Rocky Mountain Diner. 800 18th St
Tommy Tsunami's. 1432 Market St
Trinity Grille. 1801 Broadway
Wynkoop Brewing Company. 1634 18th St
Z-Teca. 550A Grant

NORTH OF DOWNTOWN
Brittany Hill. 9350 Grant
Morton's Of Chicago. 1710 Wynkoop

SOUTH OF DOWNTOWN
Barolo Grill. 3030 E 6th Ave
Bistro Adde Brewster. 250 Steele St
Buckhorn Exchange. 1000 Osage St
Chives American Bistro. 1120 E 6th Ave
Coos Bay Bistro. 2076 S University Blvd
Fourth Story. 2955 E 1st Ave
Fresh Fish Co. 7800 E Hampden Ave
India's. 3333 S Tamarac
Japon. 1028 S Gaylord St
Papillon. 250 Josephine
Pour La France. 730 S University Blvd
Tuscany (Loews Giorgio Hotel). 4150 E Mississippi Ave
Wellshire Inn. 3333 S Colorado Blvd

EAST OF DOWNTOWN
Annie's Cafe. 4012 E 8th St
Chipotle Grill. 745 Colorado
Cliff Young. 700 E 17th Ave
Hugh's New American Bistro. 1469 S Pearl St
Mel's Bar And Grill. 235 Fillmore
Normandy French Restaurant. 1515 Madison
Starfish. 300 Fillmore St
Strings. 1700 Humbolt St
Tante Louise. 4900 E Colfax Ave
Zaidy's Deli. 121 Adams St

WEST OF DOWNTOWN
Baby Doe's Matchless Mine. 2520 W 23rd Ave
Empress. 2825 W Alameda Ave
Imperial Chinese. 431 S Broadway
Today's Gourmet-Highland's Garden Cafe. 3927 W 32nd Ave

Note: When a listing is located in a town that does not have its own city heading, it will appear under the city nearest to its location. In these cases, the address and town appear in parenthesis immediately following the name of the establishment.

Motels

★★ **COURTYARD BY MARRIOTT.** *7415 E 41st Ave (80216), I-70 exit 278, east of downtown. 303/333-3303; FAX 303/399-7356.* 146 rms, 3 story. S, D $69-$92; each addl $10; suites $80-$115; under 18 free; wkend rates. Crib free. TV; cable (premium). Indoor pool; whirlpool. Complimentary coffee in rms. Restaurant 6-10 am, 5-10 pm; Sat, Sun 7-11 am. Bar 4-10 pm. Ck-out 1 pm. Coin Indry. Meeting rms. Business servs avail. In-rm modem link. Valet serv. Exercise equipt; weight machine, bicycles. Microwaves avail; refrigerator in suites. Balconies. Cr cds: A, D, DS, MC, V.

D SC

★★ **LA QUINTA AIRPORT.** *3975 Peoria St (80239), I-70 exit 281, east of downtown. 303/371-5640; FAX 303/371-7015.* Web www.laquinta.com. 112 rms, 2 story. S, D $69-$89; each addl $10; under 18 free. Crib free. Pet accepted, some restrictions. TV; cable (premium). Heated pool. Complimentary continental bkfst in lobby. Restaurant adj open 24 hrs. Ck-out noon. Coin Indry. Business servs avail. In-rm modem link. Valet serv. Free airport transportation. Health club privileges. Refrigerators, microwaves avail. Cr cds: A, D, DS, MC, V.

D SC

✔★★ **LA QUINTA DOWNTOWN.** *3500 Park Ave W (80216), I-25 exit 213, west of downtown. 303/458-1222; FAX 303/433-2246.* Web www.laquinta.com. 105 rms, 3 story. S, D $70-$80; each addl $10; under 18 free. Crib free. Pet accepted. TV; cable (premium), VCR avail. Pool. Complimentary bkfst. Complimentary coffee in lobby. Restaurant adj open 24 hrs. Ck-out noon. Business servs avail. In-rm modem link. Valet serv. Cr cds: A, C, D, DS, MC, V.

D SC

★★ **QUALITY INN SOUTH.** *6300 E Hampden Ave (80222), I-25 exit 201, east of downtown. 303/758-2211; FAX 303/753-0156.* 185 rms, 1-2 story. S, D $75-$120; each addl $10; under 18 free. Crib free. Pet accepted; $5/day. TV; cable (premium). Pool; whirlpool, sauna, poolside serv. Complimentary coffee in rms. Restaurant 6 am-11 pm. Rm serv. Bar from 4 pm. Ck-out 11 am. Coin Indry. Meeting rms. Business servs avail. In-rm modem link. Health club privileges. Lawn games. Some refrigerators. Private patios, balconies. Picnic tables. Cr cds: A, C, D, DS, ER, JCB, MC, V.

D SC

✔★ **QUALITY INN WEST.** *(12100 W 44th Ave, Wheat Ridge 80033) off I-70 to 44th Avenue. 303/467-2400; FAX 303/467-0198.* 107 rms, 5 story. May-Aug: S $54-$59; D $64-$79; under 18 free; lower rates rest of yr. Crib free. Pet accepted, some restrictions; $25 deposit. TV; cable (premium). Complimentary coffee in lobby. Restaurant 6 am-10 pm. Rm serv. Bar. Ck-out 11 am. Meeting rms. Business center. Exercise equipt; bicycles, weight machine. On lake. Cr cds: A, D, DS, MC, V.

D SC

★★ **RESIDENCE INN BY MARRIOTT-DOWNTOWN.** *2777 Zuni (80211), jct Speer Blvd N, I-25 exit 212B, west of downtown. 303/458-5318.* 156 kit. suites, 2 story. S $89-$119; D $109-$145. Crib free. Pet accepted; $10. TV; cable, VCR avail. Heated pool; whirlpool. Complimentary continental bkfst. Restaurant nearby. Ck-out 11 am. Meeting rms. Business servs avail. Valet serv. Free grocery shopping serv. RR station, bus depot transportation. Exercise equipt; weights, bicycles. Refrigerators, microwaves; many fireplaces. Private patios, balconies. Cr cds: A, D, DS, JCB, MC, V.

D SC

Motor Hotels

★★ **FOUR POINTS BY SHERATON.** *3535 Quebec St (80207). 303/333-7711; FAX 303/322-2262.* 195 rms, 8 story. S $85-$105; D $95-$115; each addl $15; under 17 free; wkend plans. Crib free. TV; cable (premium), VCR avail. Indoor pool; whirlpool. Restaurant 6 am-midnight; Sun from 7 am. Rm serv. Bar 11-2 am, Sun to midnight. Ck-out noon. Coin lndry. Meeting rms. Business center. Bellhops. Valet serv. Gift shop. Free airport transportation. Exercise equipt; weight machine, stair machine. Lawn games. Microwaves avail. Some private patios, balconies. Cr cds: A, C, D, DS, MC, V.

D SC

✔★ **QUALITY INN AND SUITES.** *4590 Quebec St (80216), just N of I-70 exit 278, east of downtown. 303/320-0260; FAX 303/320-7595.* 182 rms, 5 story. May-Sept: S $65-$75; D $70-$75; each addl $7; suites $115-$135; under 17 free; lower rates rest of year. Crib free. Pet accepted; $25. TV; cable (premium). Pool; whirlpool. Complimentary coffee in rms. Restaurant 6-9:30 am, 5:30-10 pm; Sat-Sun 6-11 am, 5:30-10 pm. Rm serv. Bar 4 pm-midnight, Sat & Sun from 5 pm. Ck-out noon. Coin lndry. Meeting rms. Business servs avail. In-rm modem link. Valet serv. Gift shop. Free airport transportation. Exercise equipt; weight machine, bicycles. Cr cds: A, C, D, DS, MC, V.

D SC

★ ★ **RAMADA INN-AIRPORT.** *3737 Quebec St (80207), east of downtown. 303/388-6161; FAX 303/388-0426.* 148 rms, 4 story. S, D $74-$99; each addl $10; under 18 free; wkend rates. Crib free. Pet accepted. TV; cable. Heated pool. Complimentary coffee in rms. Restaurant 6 am-10 pm. Rm serv. Bar 2 pm-2 am, Sun to midnight. Ck-out noon. Meeting rms. Business servs avail. In-rm modem link. Bellhops. Valet serv. Gift shop. Free airport transportation. Exercise equipt; weight machine, bicycle. Health club privileges. Some refrigerators. Cr cds: A, C, D, DS, ER, MC, V.

D SC

Hotels

★ ★ ★ **ADAM'S MARK.** *1550 Court Place (80202), on 16th St Mall. 303/893-3333; FAX 303/623-0303.* E-mail sales@denver.adamsmark.com. 1,225 rms, 2 bldgs, 8 & 22 story. S, D $150-$190; each addl $15; suites $375-$1,000; under 18 free; wkend rates. Crib free. Garage $14; in/out privileges. Pet accepted, some restrictions; $100 deposit. TV; cable (premium). Pool; poolside serv (seasonal). Restaurants 6:30 am-11 pm. Rm serv 24 hrs. Bar 11-2 am; entertainment. Ck-out noon. Coin lndry. Convention facilities. Business center. In-rm modem link. Concierge. Barber, beauty shop. Airport transportation. Exercise equipt; stair machine, bicycles, steam rm, sauna. Health club privileges. Microwaves avail. Luxury level. Cr cds: A, C, D, DS, ER, JCB, MC, V.

D SC

★ ★ ★ ★ **BROWN PALACE.** *321 17th St (80202), downtown. 303/297-3111; FAX 303/293-9204; res: 800/321-2599 (exc CO), 800/228-2917 (CO).* Web www.brownpalace.com. Opened in 1892, this grand dame of Colorado hotels has lodged luminaries from President Eisenhower to the Beatles. A dramatic stained-glass window tops the nine-story lobby; rooms are decorated with Victorian flair. 237 rms, 9 story. S, D $195-$245; each addl $15; suites $255-$775; under 12 free; wkend rates. Garage in/out $15. Crib free. TV; cable (premium), VCR avail. Restaurants (also see PALACE ARMS). Afternoon tea noon-4:30 pm. Rm serv 24 hrs. Bar 10:30 am-midnight; entertainment exc Sun. Ck-out noon. Meeting rms. Business center. In-rm modem link. Concierge. Shopping arcade. Barber. Valet parking. Exercise equipt; bicycles, treadmills. Health club privileges. Some refrigerators. Cr cds: A, C, D, DS, JCB, MC, V.

D SC

★ ★ ★ **BURNSLEY.** *1000 Grant St (80203), downtown. 303/830-1000; FAX 303/830-7676; res: 800/231-3915 (exc CO).* 82 kit. suites, 16 story. Suites $159-$180; each addl $15. Pet accepted, some restrictions; $50. TV; cable (premium). Pool. Complimentary bkfst. Complimentary coffee in rms. Restaurant 6:30 am-2 pm, 6-9 pm. Rm serv to 11 pm. Bar from 11 am. Ck-out noon. Meeting rms. Business center. Garage parking. Health club privileges. Microwaves. Balconies. Converted apartment building in residential area, near State Capitol. Cr cds: A, C, D, MC, V.

SC

✔★ ★ **COMFORT INN.** *401 17th St (80202), downtown. 303/296-0400; FAX 303/297-0774.* 229 rms, 22 story. S, D $85-$130; each addl $10; suites $150-$300; under 18 free; wkend rates. Covered valet parking $10. TV; cable (premium), VCR avail. Complimentary continental bkfst. Restaurant adj 6:30 am-9 pm. Rm serv 24 hrs. Bar 10:30 am-midnight. Ck-out noon. Meeting rms. Business center. In-rm modem link. Barber, beauty shop. Health club privileges. Cr cds: A, C, D, DS, JCB, MC, V.

D SC

★ ★ ★ **EMBASSY SUITES.** *7525 E Hampden Ave (80231), off I-25E exit 201, south of downtown. 303/696-6644; FAX 303/337-6202.* Web www.embassyden.com. 206 suites, 7 story. S $180; D $200; each addl $10; under 12 free; wkend rates. Crib free. TV; cable (premium), VCR avail. Indoor pool; whirlpool. Complimentary full bkfst. Coffee in rms. Restaurant 11:30 am-2 pm, 5-10 pm. Bar to 2 am; Sun to midnight. Ck-out 1 pm. Coin lndry. Meeting rms. Business center. In-rm modem link. Gift shop. Exercise equipt; bicycles, stair machine, sauna, steam rm. Refrigerators, microwaves, minibars. Balconies. Cr cds: A, C, D, DS, MC, V.

D SC

★ ★ ★ **EMBASSY SUITES-AIRPORT.** *4444 N Havana St (80239), N of I-70 at exit 280, east of downtown. 303/375-0400; FAX 303/371-4634.* 212 suites, 7 story. Suites $124-$145; each addl $12; under 12 free; ski plans, wkend package. Crib free. Pet accepted, some restrictions; $150 deposit. TV; cable (premium), VCR avail. Indoor pool; whirlpool, poolside serv. Complimentary full bkfst. Coffee in rms. Restaurant 6 am-11 pm. Bar to 1 am. Ck-out 1 pm. Coin lndry. Meeting rms. Business servs avail. In-rm modem link. Valet serv. Gift shop. Free airport transportation. Exercise equipt; weights, bicycles, steam rm, sauna. Refrigerators, microwaves, wetbars; some minibars. Cr cds: A, C, D, DS, MC, V.

D SC

★ ★ **EXECUTIVE TOWER.** *1405 Curtis St (80202), downtown. 303/571-0300; FAX 303/825-4301; res: 800/525-6651.* E-mail sales@exectowerhotel.com; web www.exectowerhotel.com. 337 rms, 16 story. S $147-$174; D $157-$182; each addl $10; suites $180-$340; under 16 free; wkend rates. Crib free. Pet accepted, some restrictions. TV; cable (premium), VCR avail. Indoor pool; whirlpool. Restaurants 6:30 am-9 pm, wkends to 10 pm. Bar 4 pm-midnight. Ck-out noon. Coin lndry. Meeting rms. Business servs avail. In-rm modem link. Garage. Valet serv. Tennis. Exercise equipt; weights, stair machine, sauna, steam rm. Rec rm. Cr cds: A, C, D, DS, MC, V.

D SC

★ ★ **HOLIDAY INN.** *(10 E 120th Ave, Northglenn 80233) 6 mi N on I-25, exit 223. 303/452-4100; FAX 303/457-1741.* 235 rms, 6 story. Apr-Sept: S, D $89-$125; each addl $10; suites $150-$175; under 17 free; wkend rates; lower rates rest of yr. Crib avail. Pet accepted. TV; cable. Indoor pool; whirlpool, poolside serv. Restaurant 6 am-11 pm. Bar 11 am-11 pm. Ck-out noon. Convention facilities. Business center. In-rm modem link. Gift shop. Airport transportation. Exercise equipt; bicycle, treadmill. Health club privileges. Cr cds: A, C, D, DS, JCB, MC, V.

D SC

★ ★ ★ **HYATT REGENCY DENVER.** *1750 Welton St (80202), downtown. 303/295-1234; FAX 303/292-2472.* 511 rms, 26 story. S $99-$195; D $99-$200; each addl $25; suites $350-$1,000; wkend rates. Crib free. Garage, valet parking $15. TV; cable (premium), VCR avail. Indoor pool; poolside serv. Complimentary coffee in rms. Restaurant 6 am-11 pm. Bar 10:30-2 am. Ck-out noon. Meeting rms. Business center. In-rm modem link. Concierge. Airport transportation. Tennis. Exercise equipt; weight machines, treadmills. Health club privileges. Bathrm phones, minibars; some refrigerators. Luxury level. Cr cds: A, C, D, DS, ER, JCB, MC, V.

D SC

★ ★ ★ **HYATT REGENCY TECH CENTER.** *7800 Tufts Ave (80237), SE of jct I-25, I-225, south of downtown. 303/779-1234; FAX 303/850-7164.* 448 rms, 11 story. S $175-$189; D $200-$214; each addl $25; suites $350-$900; under 18 free; wkend plans. Crib free. TV; cable (premium), VCR avail (movies). Indoor pool; whirlpool, poolside serv. Complimentary coffee in rms. Restaurant 6:30 am-11 pm. Bar 3 pm-1 am; Sun to midnight. Ck-out noon. Convention facilities. Business center. In-rm modem link. Concierge. Gift shop. Valet parking. Airport transportation. Lighted tennis. Exercise equipt; weights, bicycles, sauna. Refrigerators;

some bathrm phones; microwaves avail. Luxury level. Cr cds: A, C, D, DS, ER, JCB, MC, V.

D SC

★ ★ ★ **LOEWS GIORGIO.** *4150 E Mississippi Ave (80222), N of I-25, south of downtown. 303/782-9300; FAX 303/758-6542.* E-mail elarson@loewshotels.com; web www.loewshotels.com. A modern steel-and-glass facade conceals an Italian Renaissance-style interior distinguished by magnificent frescoes. Guest rooms are spacious and elegant. 183 rms, 11 story. S $199-$229; D $219-$249; each addl $20; suites $259-$900; under 18 free; wkend rates. Crib free. Pet accepted, some restrictions. TV; cable (premium), VCR avail (movies). Complimentary coffee in lounge. Restaurant (see TUSCANY). Bar noon-1 am. Ck-out 11 am. Meeting rms. Business center. Concierge. Gift shop. Valet parking. Exercise equipt; treadmills, stair machines. Health club privileges. Bathrm phones, minibars; some refrigerators; microwaves avail. Library. Cr cds: A, C, D, DS, JCB, MC, V.

D SC

✔★ ★ **MARRIOTT DENVER TECH CENTER.** *4900 South Syracuse (80237), off I-25 exit 199, south of downtown. 303/779-1100; FAX 303/740-2523.* 626 rms, 2-10 story. S, D $87-$149; suites $260-$500; under 17 free; wkend plans. Crib free. Pet accepted. TV; cable (premium), VCR avail. 2 pools, 1 indoor; whirlpool. Restaurant open 24 hrs. Bar 11 am-midnight. Ck-out noon. Convention facilities. Business center. In-rm modem link. Shopping arcade. Valet parking. Exercise equipt; weights, bicycles, steam rm, sauna. Health club privileges. Rec rm. Refrigerators. Some balconies. Cr cds: A, C, D, DS, JCB, MC, V.

D

★ ★ ★ **MARRIOTT-CITY CENTER.** *1701 California St (80202), downtown. 303/297-1300; FAX 303/298-7474.* 615 rms, 19 story. S $164-$174; D $180-$195; each addl $10; suites $225-$825; under 12 free; wkend plans. Crib free. Valet parking; fee. Pet accepted, some restrictions. TV; cable (premium), VCR avail. Indoor pool; whirlpool. Restaurant 6:30 am-10 pm. Rm serv to midnight. Bar 11-2 am. Ck-out noon. Convention facilities. Business center. In-rm modem link. Concierge. Shopping arcade. Exercise equipt; weight machine, stair machine, sauna. Health club privileges. Game rm. Some bathrm phones, refrigerators; microwaves avail. Luxury level. Cr cds: A, C, D, DS, ER, JCB, MC, V.

D SC

★ ★ ★ **MARRIOTT-SOUTHEAST.** *6363 E Hampden Ave (80222), I-25 exit 201, south of downtown. 303/758-7000; FAX 303/691-3418.* 595 rms, 11 story. S, D $82-$154; suites $150-$350; under 18 free; wkend package plan. Crib free. Pet accepted, some restrictions. TV; cable (premium), VCR avail. 2 pools, 1 indoor; whirlpool, poolside serv. Complimentary coffee. Restaurant 6 am-11 pm. Bar 11 am-midnight. Ck-out 1 pm. Coin lndry. Convention facilities. Business center. In-rm modem link. Concierge. Shopping arcade. Barber, beauty shop. Covered parking. Airport transportation. Exercise equipt; weight machine, bicycles. Game rm. Some bathrm phones, refrigerators. Balconies; some private patios. Luxury level. Cr cds: A, C, D, DS, ER, JCB, MC, V.

D SC

★ ★ ★ **OXFORD.** *1600 17th St (80202), downtown. 303/628-5400; FAX 303/628-5413; res: 800/228-5838 (exc CO).* 81 rms, 5 story. S $125-$169; D $145-$179; each addl $10; suites from $275; under 12 free. Crib free. Valet parking $12. TV; cable (premium), VCR avail. Restaurant 6:30-10 am, 11 am-2 pm, 5-10 pm; Fri, Sat to 11 pm; Sun 7 am-10 pm. Rm serv 24 hrs. Bar. Ck-out 1 pm. Meeting rms. Business servs avail. In-rm modem link. Concierge. Barber, beauty shop. Exercise rm; instructor, weight machine, stair machine, steam rm. Whirlpool. Minibars. Elegant, European-style; many antiques. First luxury hotel built in Denver (1891). Cr cds: A, D, DS, MC, V.

D SC

★ ★ ★ **RENAISSANCE.** *3801 Quebec St (80207), I-70, S on Quebec St exit, east of downtown. 303/399-7500; FAX 303/321-1783.* Web www.renaissancehotels.com. 400 rms, 12 story. S $159-$169; D $160-$170; each addl $10; suites $250; under 18 free; wkend ski plans. Covered parking $4; valet $6. TV; cable (premium), VCR avail. 2 heated pools, 1 indoor, whirlpool. Complimentary coffee in rms. Restaurant 6:30 am-10 pm. Rm serv 24 hrs. Bar 11-1 am; entertainment. Ck-out 1 pm. Convention facilities. Business center. In-rm modem link. Concierge. Gift shop. Free airport transportation. Exercise equipt; weight machines, bicycles, steam rm. Minibar, some bathrm phones. Balconies. 10-story central atrium. Luxury level. Cr cds: A, C, D, DS, ER, JCB, MC, V.

D SC

★ ★ **STAPLETON PLAZA HOTEL AND FITNESS CENTER.** *3333 Quebec St (80207), east of downtown. 303/321-3500; FAX 303/322-7343; res: 800/950-6070.* E-mail stapletonplaza@juno.com web www.stapletonplaza.com. 300 rms, 11 story. S, D $125-$135; each addl $10; suites $205-$395; under 12 free; wkly, wkend package plans. Crib free. TV; cable (premium). Pool; whirlpool. Complimentary coffee. Restaurant 6 am-11 pm. Bars 11-2 am; Sun to midnight. Ck-out noon. Convention facilities. Business center. In-rm modem link. Shopping arcade. Free garage parking. Free airport transportation. Exercise rm; instructor, weight machines, stair machine, sauna, steam rm. Balconies. Built around 11-story atrium; glass-enclosed elvtrs. Cr cds: A, C, D, DS, MC, V.

D SC

★ ★ ★ **THE WARWICK.** *1776 Grant St (80203), downtown. 303/861-2000; FAX 303/839-8504; res: 800/525-2888.* 194 rms, 15 story. S, D $165-$175; each addl $20; suites $200-$800; under 18 free; wkend package plan. Crib free. Garage $10. Pet accepted. TV; cable (premium). Rooftop pool (in season); poolside serv. Complimentary continental bkfst. Restaurant 6:30 am-2 pm, 6-10 pm; Fri, Sat 7-11 am, 6-10 pm. Rm serv 24 hrs. Bar 11 am-midnight. Ck-out 1 pm. Meeting rms. Business servs avail. In-rm modem link. Concierge. Valet serv. Airport transportation. Free RR station, bus depot transportation. Health club privileges. Bathrm phones, refrigerators; many wet bars; microwaves avail. Many balconies. Cr cds: A, C, D, DS, JCB, MC, V.

D SC

★ ★ ★ **WESTIN HOTEL TABOR CENTER.** *1672 Lawrence St (80202), in Tabor Center, downtown. 303/572-9100; FAX 303/572-7288.* 420 rms, 19 story. S $222; D $237; each addl $15; suites $350-$900; under 18 free. Crib free. Pet accepted, some restrictions. Garage $8-$14. TV; cable (premium), VCR avail. Indoor/outdoor pool; whirlpool, poolside serv. Restaurant (see AUGUSTA). Rm serv 24 hrs. Bar 5 pm-1:30 am; pianist Tues-Sat. Ck-out 1 pm. Convention facilities. Business center. In-rm modem link. Shopping arcade. Exercise equipt; bicycles, stair machine, sauna, steam rm. Health club privileges. Refrigerators, minibars; some bathrm phones. Some balconies. Luxury level. Cr cds: A, C, D, DS, ER, JCB, MC, V.

D SC

Inns

★ **THE CAMBRIDGE.** *1560 Sherman St (80203), downtown. 303/831-1252; FAX 303/831-4724; res: 800/877-1252.* 31 suites, 3 story. S, D $129-$139; under 12 free. Crib $10. Valet parking $10. TV; cable (premium). Complimentary continental bkfst. Complimentary coffee in rms. Restaurant 11 am-10 pm, Sat 5-11 pm, closed Sun. Rm serv. Ck-out noon, ck-in after 3 pm. Business servs avail. In-rm modem link. Bellhops. Valet serv. Concierge. Health club privileges. Wet bars, refrigerators. Microwaves avail. Antique furnishings, oil paintings, original prints; no two suites alike. Cr cds: A, D, DS, MC, V.

SC

★ ★ ★ **CAPITAL HILL MANSION.** *1207 Pennsylvania St (80203), near State Capitol, in Historic District. 303/839-5221; res: 800/839-9329; FAX 303/839-9046.* 8 rms, many with A/C, 3 story, 3 suites. Apr-mid-Nov: S $80-$150; D $90-$165; each addl $10; suites $105-$165; lower rates rest of yr. TV; cable (premium). Complimentary full bkfst. Complimentary coffee in rooms. Restaurant nearby. Ck-out 11 am, ck-in 4:30-8 pm. Business servs avail. Concierge serv. Some in-rm whirlpools, fireplaces. Some balconies. Built in 1891; Romanesque style with turrets, chimneys and curved porch. Totally nonsmoking. Cr cds: A, DS, MC, V.

D

✔★ ★ ★ **CASTLE MARNE.** *1572 Race St (80206), east of downtown. 303/331-0621; FAX 303/331-0623; res: 800/926-2763.* E-mail the marne@ix.netcom.com. 9 rms, 3 story. S $70-$220; D $85-$220. Children over 10 yrs only. Complimentary full bkfst; afternoon refreshments. Restaurant nearby. Ck-out 11 am, ck-in 4 pm. Business center. In-rm modem link. Luggage handling. Valet serv. Concierge serv. Gift shop. Some street parking. Game rm. Health club privileges. In-rm whirlpools. Some balconies. Antiques. Library/sitting rm. Built 1889; Romanesque mansion was residence of museum curator. Whirlpools. Cheesman Park 3 blks. Totally nonsmoking. Cr cds: A, C, D, DS, MC, V.

SC

★ ★ ★ **HAUS BERLIN.** *1651 Emerson St (80218), downtown. 303/837-9527; res: 800/659-0253.* E-mail haus.berlin@worldnet.att.net; web www.virtualcities.com. 4 rms, 3 story, 1 suite. S, D $90-$115; suite $140. TV (in 3 rms); cable (premium). Complimentary full bkfst. Restaurant nearby. Ck-out 11 am, ck-in 4-8 pm. Built in 1892 for Rev Thomas N Haskell, founder of Colorado College. Totally nonsmoking. Cr cds: A, C, D, DS, MC, V.

✔★ ★ **HOLIDAY CHALET.** *1820 E Colfax Ave (80218), east of downtown. 303/321-9975; FAX 303/377-6556; res: 800/626-4497.* 10 kit. suites, 3 story. S, D $72.50-$104; each addl $5; under 12 free; wkly rates. Crib free. Pet accepted; $50 deposit. TV; VCR avail. Garage parking $5/day. Complimentary bkfst. Complimentary coffee in rms. Restaurant nearby. Ck-out noon. Concierge. Microwaves avail. Restored brownstone built in 1896. Library; 1880 salt water fish prints. Totally nonsmoking. Cr cds: A, D, DS, MC, V.

SC

★ ★ **LUMBER BARON.** *2555 W 37th Ave (80211), in Historic District. 303/477-8205; res: 800/697-6552; FAX 303/477-0269.* 5 rms, 3 story. S, D $125-$195; wkend rates. TV; VCR avail (movies). Complimentary full bkfst. Complimentary coffee in rms. Restaurant nearby. Ck-out 11 am, ck-in 4 pm. Business servs avail. Luggage handling. Street parking. Lawn games. Some fireplaces. Built in 1890. Totally nonsmoking. Cr cds: A, DS, MC, V.

SC

★ ★ ★ **QUEEN ANNE.** *2147 Tremont Place (80205), downtown. 303/296-6666; FAX 303/296-2151; res: 800/432-4667.* E-mail queen anne@worldnet.att.net web www.bedandbreakfastinns.org/queenanne. 14 rms, 3 story. S, D $75-$145; each addl $15; suites $145-$175. Complimentary full bkfst. Ck-out noon, ck-in 3 pm. Business servs avail. In-rm modem link. Health club privileges. Some in-rm whirlpools. Built in 1879; antiques; garden. In the Clement Historic District. Totally nonsmoking. Cr cds: A, D, DS, MC, V.

D

★ ★ **TREE HOUSE.** *(6650 Simms St, Arvada 80004) west on I-70 exit Kipling St, 3 mi N. 303/431-6352; FAX 303/456-1414.* E-mail thetreehouse@aol.com. 5 rms, 1 with shower only, 2 story. No rm phones. S, D $69-$109; each addl $15; under 10 free. Crib free. TV; cable. Complimentary full bkfst; afternoon refreshments. Restaurant nearby. Ck-out 11 am, ck-out noon. Guest Indry. Health club privileges. Whirlpool. Some fireplaces. 10 acres of forest with over 100 kinds of trees, plants, and wildlife. Totally nonsmoking. Cr cds: A, MC, V.

SC

✔★ ★ **VICTORIA OAKS.** *1575 Race St (80206), east of downtown. 303/355-1818; res: 800/662-6257.* E-mail vicoaksinn@aol.com. 9 rms, 2 share bath, 3 story. S $50-$75; D $60-$85. TV in sitting rm. Complimentary continental bkfst; refreshments. Ck-out noon, ck-in 3 pm. In-rm modem link. Kitchen, Indry privileges. 1896 mansion, Victorian antiques. Cr cds: A, C, D, DS, MC, V.

SC

Restaurants

★ **AL FRESCO.** *1040 15th St (80202), downtown. 303/534-0404.* Hrs: 11 am-2 pm, 5-10 pm; Fri, Sat to 11 pm. Res accepted. Northern Italian menu. A la carte entrees: lunch $6.95-$11.95, dinner $13.95-$24.95. Specializes in pizza. Outdoor dining. Cr cds: A, C, D, DS, MC, V.

D

★ ★ **AUBERGINE CAFE.** *225 E 7th Ave (80203), downtown. 303/832-4778.* Hrs: 11:30 am-10 pm; Fri to 11 pm; Sat 4-11 pm; Sun 4-9 pm. Closed Mon; major hols. Res accepted. Mediterranean menu. Serv bar. A la carte entrees: lunch $6-$9, dinner $13-$17. Child's meals. Specialties: roasted eggplant, stewed mussels, roast tuscan chicken. Outdoor dining. Cr cds: A, C, D, DS, MC, V.

D

★ ★ ★ **AUGUSTA.** *(See Westin Hotel Tabor Center) 303/572-7222.* Hrs: 6 am-11 pm; Sun brunch 10 am-2 pm. Res accepted. Mediterranean menu. Bar. Wine list. Semi-a la carte: bkfst $10-$13, lunch $13-$20, dinner $28-$40. Sun brunch $24.95. Specialties: swordfish Provençale, ginger breast of duck. Pianist. Valet parking. Elegant, private club atmosphere. Totally nonsmoking. Cr cds: A, C, D, DS, MC, V.

D

★ ★ **BABY DOE'S MATCHLESS MINE.** *2520 W 23rd Ave (80211), west of downtown. 303/433-3386.* Hrs: 11 am-2:30 pm, 4:30-10 pm; Fri, Sat to 11 pm; Sun 4-10 pm; Sun brunch 9 am-2 pm. Res accepted. Semi-a la carte: lunch $4.95-$12.95, dinner $7.95-$32. Sun brunch $15.95. Specializes in seafood, steak. Parking. Replica of Matchless Mine in Leadville; memorabilia of era. Panoramic view of city. Cr cds: A, C, D, DS, MC, V.

D SC

★ ★ **BAROLO GRILL.** *3030 E 6th Ave (80206), east 6th Avenue in Cherry Creek, N at Milwaukee St, south of downtown. 303/393-1040.* Hrs: 5-10:30 pm. Closed Sun, Mon; major hols. Res accepted. Northern Italian menu. Bar. A la carte entrees: dinner $15-$25. Complete meal: dinner $38.95. Child's meals. Specialties: wine-marinated duck, tuna puttanesca, lamb chops. Free valet parking. Outdoor dining. Paintings. Cr cds: A, C, D, DS, MC, V.

D

✔★ ★ **BELLA RISTORANTE.** *1920 Market St (80202), downtown. 303/297-8400.* Hrs: 11 am-11 pm; Mon to 9 pm; Tues, Wed to 10 pm; Sun 10 am-2 pm (brunch), 4-9 pm. Closed Dec 25. Res accepted. Italian menu. Bar. A la carte entrees: lunch $3.95-$9.95. Semi-a la carte: dinner $7.95-$17.95. Sun brunch $7.95-$13.95. Specialties: lasagna, chicken marsala, gnocchi. Own breads. Valet parking Thurs-Sat. Outdoor dining. In warehouse converted to restaurant. Cr cds: A, C, D, DS, MC, V.

D

★ ★ **BISTRO ADDE BREWSTER.** *250 Steele St (80206), south of downtown. 303/388-1900.* Hrs: 11:30 am-10 pm; Fri, Sat to 11 pm. Closed Sun; major hols. Res accepted. Continental menu. Bar. Wine list. Semi-a la carte: lunch $8-$20, dinner $8-$30. Specialties: salmon salad, bistro burger, gravlax. Bistro atmosphere. Cr cds: A, C, D, MC, V.

D

★ ★ **BRASSERIE Z.** *815 17th St (80202), downtown. 303/293-2322.* Hrs: 11 am-11 pm; Sat from 5 pm; Sun 5-10 pm. Closed some major hols. Res accepted. Contemporary Amer menu. Bar. Semi-a la carte: lunch $6-$9.50, dinner $7.75-$19.50. Child's meals. Specializes in roasted sea bass, steak frites, vegetarian entrees. Own baking. Valet parking (dinner). Mediterranean atmosphere; palm trees, atrium ceiling, murals. Bldg was bank lobby in 1920s. Cr cds: A, D, MC, V.

D

★ **BRITTANY HILL.** *9350 Grant (80229), I-25 exit 220, north of downtown. 303/451-5151.* Hrs: 11 am-2 pm, 4-9 pm; Fri, Sat to 11 pm; Sun 4-10 pm; Sun brunch 9 am-2:30 pm. Res accepted. Continental menu.

Bar to 11 pm. Semi-a la carte: lunch $6.95-$8.95, dinner $13.95-$25.95. Sun brunch $17.95. Specializes in prime rib, fresh seafood. Patio deck. Scenic view of city, mountains. Cr cds: A, D, DS, MC, V.

D

★ ★ ★ **THE BROKER.** *821 17th St (80202), downtown. 303/292-5065.* Hrs: 11 am-2:30 pm, 5-11 pm; Sat, Sun from 5 pm. Closed Dec 25. Res accepted. Continental menu. Bar. Semi-a la carte: lunch $6-$12, dinner $21-$35. Specialties: prime rib, filet Wellington. In vault & board rms of converted bank (1903). Cr cds: A, C, D, DS, JCB, MC, V.

★ **BUCKHORN EXCHANGE.** *1000 Osage St (80204), south of downtown. 303/534-9505.* Web www.buckhorn.com. Hrs: 11 am-2 pm, 5:30-9:30 pm; Fri, Sat 5-10 pm; Sun 4-9 pm. Closed major hols. Res accepted. Bar. Semi-a la carte: lunch $6.95-$14, dinner $17-$39. Specializes in steak, buffalo, elk. Entertainment Wed-Sat. Roof garden dining. Historical landmark & museum, built 1893. Cr cds: A, C, D, DS, MC, V.

D

✔★ ★ **CHIVES AMERICAN BISTRO.** *1120 E 6th Ave (80218), south of downtown. 303/722-3800.* Hrs: 5 pm-midnight; Fri & Sat 4 pm-1 am. Closed Thanksgiving, Dec 25. Res accepted. Varied menu. Bar. Semi-a la carte: dinner $6.95-$17.95. Specializes in grilled fresh seafood, pasta. Parking. Cr cds: A, MC, V.

D

✔★ **CITY SPIRIT CAFE.** *1434 Blake (80202), downtown. 303/575-0022.* Hrs: 11 am-midnight; Tues, Fri, Sat to 2 am. Closed Sun; major hols. Continental menu. Bar. Semi-a la carte: lunch, dinner $5.95-$8.95. Specializes in house-made dressings, lasagna. Entertainment Tues, Fri, Sat. Outdoor dining. Eclectic decor. Cr cds: A, C, DS, MC, V.

D

★ ★ **CLIFF YOUNG.** *700 E 17th Ave (80203), east of downtown. 303/831-8900.* E-mail cliffyngs@aol.com. Hrs: 6-11 pm; Sun to 10 pm. Closed major hols. Bar. Wine list. Semi-a la carte: dinner $18-$38. Specialty: herb-crusted Colorado rack of lamb. Own baking. Entertainment. Valet parking. In renovated Victorian storefront and office building (1890). Cr cds: A, C, D, DS, JCB, MC, V.

D

★ ★ **COOS BAY BISTRO.** *2076 S University Blvd (80210), south of downtown. 303/744-3591.* Hrs: 11:30-2:30 pm, 5:30-10 pm; Fri, Sat 5-11 pm. Closed major hols. Res accepted. Italian, French menu. Bar. Wine list. Semi-a la carte: lunch $4.50-$10, dinner $7-$16. Specialties: Thai pasta, marinated duck breast with blackberry sauce, seared ahi tuna. Outdoor dining. Totally nonsmoking. Cr cds: A, D, MC, V.

D

★ ★ **DENVER CHOPHOUSE & BREWERY.** *1735 19th St (80202), downtown. 303/296-0800.* Hrs: 11 am-2:30 pm, 4:30 pm-midnight; Fri-Sun 4:30-10 pm. Res accepted. Bar. Semi-a la carte: lunch $7.25-$13.95, dinner $9-$24.95. Specializes in steaks, seafood. Outdoor dining. Historic warehouse converted into restaurant; microbrewery. Cr cds: A, C, D, MC, V.

D

★ ★ **EMPRESS.** *2825 W Alameda Ave (80219), west of downtown. 303/922-2822.* Hrs: 11 am-9 pm; Sat, Sun from 10:30 am. Chinese menu. Bar. A la carte entrees: lunch $4.25-$13, dinner $6-$13. Specializes in seafood. Oriental artwork. Cr cds: A, DS, MC, V.

D

★ ★ **EUROPEAN CAFE.** *1060 15th St (80202), downtown. 303/825-6555.* Hrs: 11 am-2 pm, 5-10 pm; Fri, Sat to 11 pm. Res accepted. Continental menu. Bar. A la carte entrees: lunch $5.95-$12.95, dinner $8.95-$26.95. Specialties: rack of lamb, spicy tuna. Valet parking. Intimate dining. Victorian decor. Cr cds: A, C, D, DS, MC, V.

D

★ ★ **FOURTH STORY.** *2955 E 1st Ave (80206), south of downtown. 303/322-1824.* E-mail books@tatteredcover.com; web www.tatteredcover.com. Hrs: 11 am-4 pm, 5-10 pm; Sun 11 am-3 pm (brunch). Closed some major hols. Res accepted. Contemporary Amer menu. Bar. Semi-a la carte: lunch $6-$14, dinner $11-$24. Sun brunch $7-$12. Child's meals. Specializes in fresh seafood. Own baking. Entertainment. Casual dining above bookstore. View of mountains. Cr cds: A, MC, V.

D

★ ★ **FRESH FISH CO.** *7800 E Hampden Ave (80237), south of downtown. 303/740-9556.* Hrs: 11:30 am-2:30 pm, 5-11 pm; Sat from 5 pm; Sun 10 am-2 pm (brunch), 5-10 pm. Closed Dec 25. Res accepted. Bar. Semi-a la carte: lunch $6.25-$12.95, dinner $13.95-$38.95. Sun brunch $16.95. Child's meals. Specializes in calamari, salmon, sushi. Many large aquariums throughout restaurant. Cr cds: A, C, D, DS, MC, V.

D

★ ★ **HUGH'S NEW AMERICAN BISTRO.** *1469 S Pearl St (80210), east of downtown. 303/744-1940.* Hrs: 11 am-2 pm; Sat 5-10 pm; Sun 5-9 pm. Closed Mon; most major hols. Res accepted. Eclectic menu. Bar. Semi a la carte: lunch $7-$10. A la carte entrees: dinner $9-$20. Child's meals. Specialties: enchiladas, butternut squash with goat cheese, grilled pomegranate duck, grilled pork tenderloin with whiskey molasses sauce. Decorated by local artist. Cr cds: A, D, MC, V.

D

★ ★ ★ **IMPERIAL CHINESE.** *431 S Broadway (80209), west of downtown. 303/698-2800.* Hrs: 11 am-10 pm; wkends to 10:30 pm. Closed July 4, Thanksgiving, Dec 25. Chinese menu. Bar. Extensive wine list. Semi-a la carte: lunch $5.95-$8.95, dinner $7.95-$15.95. Specialties: sesame chicken, whole steamed bass. Parking. Contemporary Chinese decor with many artifacts. Cr cds: A, D, MC, V.

D ♥

★ ★ **INDIA'S.** *3333 S Tamarac (80231), south of downtown. 303/755-4284.* Hrs: 11:30 am-2:15 pm, 5:30-9:30 pm; Fri to 10 pm; Sat noon-2:15 pm, 5:30-10 pm; Sun 5:30-9 pm. Res accepted. Northern Indian menu. Bar. Semi-a la carte: lunch $6.95-$10.95, dinner $7.95-$15.95. Complete meal: dinner $16.95-$34.95. Specialties: vaishnav thali, akbar boti, ticca jehangir. Indian decor. Cr cds: A, C, D, DS, MC, V.

D

★ **JAPON.** *1028 S Gaylord St (80209), south of downtown. 303/744-0330.* Hrs: 11:30 am-2 pm, 5-10 pm; Fri, Sat to midnight; Sun from 5 pm. Closed July 4, Thanksgiving. Res accepted. Japanese menu. Serv bar. Semi-a la carte: lunch $5-$10, dinner $10-$25. Specializes in sushi. Industrial decor. Totally nonsmoking. Cr cds: A, DS, MC, V.

D

✔★ ★ **LE CENTRAL.** *112 E 8th Ave, at Lincoln St, downtown. 303/863-8094.* Hrs: 11:30 am-2 pm, 5:30-10 pm; Sun 5-9 pm; Sat, Sun brunch 11 am-2 pm. Closed most major hols. Res accepted. French menu. Serv bar. Semi-a la carte: lunch $5.95-$7.95, dinner $8.50-$14.95. Sat, Sun brunch $5-$8. Specializes in country French dishes. Cr cds: MC, V.

★ ★ **McCORMICK'S FISH HOUSE.** *1659 Wazee St (80202), downtown. 303/825-1107.* Hrs: 6:30-10 am, 11 am-2 pm, 5-10 pm; Fri to 11 pm; Sat 7 am-2 pm, 5-11 pm; Sun 7 am-2 pm, 5-10 pm; Sun brunch 7 am-2 pm. Closed Dec 25. Res accepted. Bar. Semi-a la carte: bkfst $4-$8, lunch, dinner $5-$20. Sun brunch $4-$10. Sterling silver chandeliers. Cr cds: A, C, D, DS, MC, V.

D

★ ★ **MEL'S BAR AND GRILL.** *235 Fillmore (80206), east of downtown. 303/333-3979.* Hrs: 10:30 am-2:30 pm, 5-9:30 pm; Sun from 5 pm. Closed major hols. Res accepted. Contemporary continental menu. Bar. Wine list. A la carte entrees: lunch $8-$15, dinner $12.75-$21.95. Specializes in seafood, pasta, lamb. Entertainment. Outdoor dining. Cr cds: A, D, DS, MC, V.

★ ★ ★ **MORTON'S OF CHICAGO.** *1710 Wynkoop (80202), north of downtown. 303/825-3353.* Hrs: 5:30-11 pm; Sun 5-10 pm. Closed major hols. Bar from 5 pm. Wine list. A la carte entrees: dinner $16.95-$29.95. Specializes in steak, lobster. Valet parking. Menu recited. Cr cds: A, C, D, JCB, MC, V.

D ⇌

★ ★ ★ **NORMANDY FRENCH RESTAURANT.** *1515 Madison, at E Colfax Ave, east of downtown. 303/321-3311.* Hrs: 11:30 am-2 pm, 5-10 pm; Sat from 5 pm; Sun 5-9 pm. Closed Mon. Res accepted; required hols. French menu. Bar. Wine cellar. A la carte entrees: lunch $7.25-$15.50, dinner $9.95-$28. Child's meals. Specializes in osso bucco, rack of lamb, châteaubriand. Family-owned. European decor. Cr cds: A, C, D, DS, MC, V.

⇌

✔★ **OLD SPAGHETTI FACTORY.** *1215 18th St (80202), at Lawrence St, downtown. 303/295-1864.* Hrs: 11:30 am-2 pm, 5-9:30 pm; Fri to 10:30 pm; Sat 4:45-10:30 pm; Sun 4-9:30 pm. Closed Thanksgiving, Dec 24, 25. Italian menu. Bar. Semi-a la carte: lunch $3.25-$5.55, dinner $5.75-$10. Specialties: homemade lasagne, chicken Parmesan. Located on ground floor of Tramway Cable Bldg (1889). Trolley car, antique display. Cr cds: D, DS, MC, V.

D ⇌

★ ★ ★ ★ **PALACE ARMS.** *(See Brown Palace Hotel) 303/297-3111.* Artifacts from the Napoleonic era—among them dueling pistols believed to have belonged to Bonaparte and Josephine—are displayed near the red leather booths of this intimate dining room, which also features a mirrored ceiling and huge chandelier. Continental, regional Amer menu. Specializes in rack of lamb, buffalo, fresh seafood. Own baking. Hrs: 11:30 am-2 pm, 6-10 pm; Sat from 5:30 pm; Sun from 6 pm. Res accepted. Bar to 1 am. Extensive wine list. A la carte entrees: lunch $8.50-$16, dinner $22-$38. Valet parking. Jacket, tie. Cr cds: A, C, D, DS, JCB, MC, V.

D ♥

★ ★ ★ **PAPILLON.** *250 Josephine (80206), south of downtown. 303/333-7166.* Hrs: 11 am-3 pm, 5-10 pm; Fri, Sat to 11 pm. Closed Jan 1, Memorial Day, July 4. Res accepted. French, Asian menu. Bar. Wine list. A la carte entrees: lunch $8-$12, dinner $12.95-$24.95. Child's meals. Specialties: Bangkok scallops, Louisiana crab cakes, shrimp fritters. Contemporary decor. Chef owned. Totally nonsmoking. Cr cds: A, D, MC, V.

D

✔★ **POUR LA FRANCE.** *730 S University Blvd (80209), south of downtown. 303/744-1888.* Hrs: 7 am-10 pm; Fri, Sat to 11 pm. Closed Thanksgiving, Dec 25. French, Amer menu. Bar. Semi-a la carte: bkfst $2-$6.95, lunch $2.95-$7.95, dinner $6.95-$13.95. Child's meals. Specializes in desserts, pastries. Outdoor dining. Near Univ of Denver. Cr cds: A, DS, MC, V.

D SC ⇌

✔★ **ROCKY MOUNTAIN DINER.** *800 18th St (80202), at Stout, downtown. 303/293-8383.* Hrs: 11 am-11 pm; Sun 10 am-9 pm. Closed most major hols. Res accepted (dinner). Bar. Semi-a la carte: lunch, dinner $4.95-$16.95. Child's meals. Specialties: buffalo meatloaf, duck enchiladas. Outdoor dining. Saloon-style decor, western motif. Cr cds: A, D, DS, MC, V.

D

★ ★ **STARFISH.** *300 Fillmore St (80206), east of downtown. 303/333-1133.* Hrs: 11:30 am-2:30 pm, 5:30-10 pm. Closed Sun; major hols. Res accepted. Seafood menu. Bar. Semi-a la carte: lunch $5.95-$9, dinner $11.50-$25.95. Specializes in calamari, crab cakes, fresh fish. Own desserts. Pianist. Outdoor dining. Contemporary decor with ocean theme; framed posters, original artwork. Cr cds: A, D, DS, MC, V.

D

★ ★ ★ **STRINGS.** *1700 Humbolt St (80218), east of downtown. 303/831-7310.* Hrs: 11 am-10 pm; Fri, Sat to 11 pm; Sun 5-10 pm. Closed some major hols. Res accepted. Bar. Extensive wine list. Semi-a la carte: lunch $10-$17, dinner $18-$30. Child's meals. Specializes in pastas, daily menu. Valet parking. Outdoor dining. Six dining areas, each with its own decor and ambience. Chef-owned. Cr cds: A, C, D, DS, MC, V.

D ⇌

★ ★ ★ **TANTE LOUISE.** *4900 E Colfax Ave (80220), east of downtown. 303/355-4488.* Web www.tantelouise.com. Hrs: 5:30-10 pm. Closed Sun. Res accepted. Continental menu. Bar. Wine cellar. Semi-a la carte: dinner $17-$32.95. Child's meals. Specializes in duck, roast rack of lamb. Own pastries, dressings. Valet parking. Outdoor dining. French decor. Cr cds: A, C, D, DS, MC, V.

D ⇌ ♥

★ ★ ★ **TODAY'S GOURMET-HIGHLAND'S GARDEN CAFE.** *3927 W 32nd Ave (80212), west of downtown. 303/458-5920.* Hrs: 11 am-2 pm, 5-9 pm; Sat, Sun 10 am-2 pm (brunch), 5-9 pm. Closed Mon; major hols. Res accepted. Wine, beer. Wine list. Semi-a la carte: lunch $7-$12, dinner $15-$25. Sun brunch $6.50-$12. Specialties: lamb loin chops, bouillabaisse, salmon in poblano pepper. House (1892) converted into restaurant. Cr cds: A, MC, V.

D

★ ★ **TOMMY TSUNAMI'S.** *1432 Market St (80202), downtown. 303/534-5050.* Hrs: 11 am-10 pm; Thurs to 11 pm; Fri to midnight; Sat noon-midnight; Sun from noon. Closed Thanksgiving, Dec 25. Res accepted. Pacific Rim menu. Bar. Semi-a la carte: lunch $6.75-$17.95, dinner $13.95-$23.95. Specializes in sushi, teriyaki, noodles. Outdoor dining. Modern decor with Japanese influence; sushi bar. Totally nonsmoking. Cr cds: A, D, DS, MC, V.

D

★ **TRINITY GRILLE.** *1801 Broadway (80202), downtown. 303/293-2288.* Hrs: 11 am-2:30 pm, 5:30-10 pm; Sat from 5:30 pm. Closed Sun; most major hols. Res accepted. Bar. Semi-a la carte: lunch $4.50-$12.95, dinner $8.95-$29.95. Specializes in Maryland crab cakes, fresh seafood. Casual dining. Cr cds: A, D, DS, MC, V.

D ⇌

★ ★ ★ **TUSCANY.** *(See Loews Giorgio Hotel) 303/782-9300.* Hrs: 6 am-10 pm; Sat, Sun from 7 am. Res accepted; required Sun, hols. Northern Italian menu. Bar noon-midnight. Wine cellar. Semi-a la carte: bkfst $2.50-$12.50, lunch $8.25-$16, dinner $12.50-$25. Sun brunch $27.95. Child's meals. Specializes in pasta, seafood. Pianist Fri-Sun. Harpist Sun brunch. Valet parking. Quiet, elegant dining rm; fireplace, frescoes. Outdoor dining. Cr cds: A, C, D, DS, JCB, MC, V.

D ⇌

★ ★ ★ **WELLSHIRE INN.** *3333 S Colorado Blvd (80222), south of downtown. 303/759-3333.* Hrs: 7-10 am, 11:30 am-2:30 pm, 5-10 pm; Fri to 11 pm; Sat 11:30 am-2:30 pm, 5-11 pm; Sun 10 am-2 pm (brunch), 5-9 pm. Closed Jan 1, Memorial Day, Labor Day. Res accepted. Bar. Semi-a la carte: bkfst $4.75-$9.75, lunch $8.25-$12.95, dinner $14.95-$28. Sun brunch $6.95-$12.95. Specializes in salmon, rack of lamb, steak. Parking. Outdoor dining. Tudor-style inn. Totally nonsmoking. Cr cds: A, C, D, DS, MC, V.

D

✔★ **WYNKOOP BREWING COMPANY.** *1634 18th St (80202), downtown. 303/297-2700.* E-mail wynkoopmkt@aol.com; web www.wynkoop.com. Hrs: 11-2 am; Sun 10 am-midnight; Sun brunch 10 am-2 pm. Closed Thanksgiving, Dec 25. Bar. Semi-a la carte: lunch $4.95-$7.50, dinner $4.95-$15.95. Sun brunch $8.95. Specialties: shepherd's pie, bangers & mash. Entertainment Thurs-Sat. Outdoor dining. In J.S. Brown Mercantile Bldg (1899). Brewery kettles displayed; beer brewed on premises. Cr cds: A, C, D, DS, JCB, MC, V.

D ⇌

★ **Z-TECA.** *550A Grant (80203), jct 6th, Grant, downtown. 303/765-5878.* Hrs: 11 am-10 pm. Closed Easter, Thanksgiving, Dec 25. Mexican menu. Beer. Semi-a la carte: lunch, dinner $4-$9. Specialties:

poblano pesto, papa roja, fajita ranchera. Mexican photographs. Cr cds: MC, V.

D ♥

✔★ **ZAIDY'S DELI.** *121 Adams St (80206), east of downtown. 303/333-5336.* Hrs: 7 am-8 pm; Mon, Tues to 3 pm; Sat, Sun 8 am-7 pm. Closed Thanksgiving, Rosh Hashanah, Yom Kippur. Res accepted. Bar. Semi-a la carte: bkfst $3.25-$8.50, lunch $4.50-$8, dinner $5.95-$9. Child's meals. Specializes in blintzes, deli sandwiches. Own baking, soups. Outdoor dining. Totally nonsmoking. Cr cds: MC, V.

D SC

Unrated Dining Spots

ANNIE'S CAFE. *4012 E 8th St (80220), east of downtown. 303/355-8197.* Hrs: 6:30 am-9 pm; Sat 8 am-9 pm; Sun 8 am-3 pm. Closed major hols. Bar. A la carte entrees: bkfst $3.50-$5.50, lunch $3.50-$5.95, dinner $4-$7.95. Child's meals. Specializes in chili, hamburgers. Setting of old fashioned drug store. Totally nonsmoking. Cr cds: D, MC, V.

D

CHIPOTLE GRILL. *745 Colorado (80206), east of downtown. 303/333-2121.* Hrs: 11 am-10 pm. Closed Thanksgiving, Dec 25. Mexican menu. Beer. A la carte entrees: $3.95-$4.75. Specializes in chicken fajitas, barbacoa, vegetable burritos. Outdoor dining. Cr cds: MC, V.

Denver International Airport Area

Motel

★ ★ **HAMPTON INN AURORA.** *(1500 S Abilene St, Aurora 80012) I-70 W to I-225, S to exit 7. 303/369-8400; FAX 303/369-0324.* 132 rms, 4 story. S $69-$77; D $77-$83; under 18 free. Crib free. TV; cable (premium). Heated pool. Coffee in rms. Complimentary buffet bkfst. Ck-out noon. Coin Indry. Meeting rms. Business servs avail. In-rm modem link. Valet serv. Health club privileges. Some refrigerators; microwaves avail. Cr cds: A, C, D, DS, JCB, MC, V.

D SC

Motor Hotel

★ ★ **BEST WESTERN EXECUTIVE.** *(4411 Peoria St, Denver 80239) N of I-70. 303/373-5730; FAX 303/375-1157.* 199 rms, 2-3 story. Apr-Sept: S, D $85-$89; each addl $10; suites $129; under 18 free; lower rates rest of yr. Crib avail. Pet accepted; $10. TV; cable (premium), VCR avail. Heated pool. Complimentary coffee in rms. Restaurant 6 am-midnight. Rm serv. Bar. Ck-out noon. Coin Indry. Meeting rms. Business servs avail. In-rm modem link. Valet serv. Bellhops. Concierge. Free airport transportation. Exercise equipt; bicycles, treadmill. Balconies. Cr cds: A, D, DS, MC, V.

D SC

Hotels

★ ★ **DOUBLETREE.** *(3203 Quebec St, Denver 80207) 303/321-3333; FAX 303/329-5233.* 571 rms, 9 story. S, D $159; suites $300-$500; each addl $10; under 18 free; wkend rates. Crib free. Pet accepted. TV; cable, VCR avail. Indoor pool; whirlpool. Coffee in rms. Restaurant 6 am-11 pm. Rm serv 24 hrs. Bar 5 pm-2 am, Sun to midnight. Ck-out noon. Convention facilities. Business center. In-rm modem link. Free airport transportation. Exercise equipt; weight machine, stair machine, sauna. Refrigerators avail. Some balconies. Sun deck. Cr cds: A, C, D, DS, ER, MC, V.

D SC

★ ★ ★ **DOUBLETREE.** *(13696 East Iliff Place, Aurora 80014) I-70 W to I-225, S to exit 5. 303/337-2800; FAX 303/752-0296.* 254 rms, 6 story. S $130; D $150; each addl $10; suites $150; under 18 free; wkend rates. Crib free. TV; cable (premium), VCR avail (movies). Indoor pool; poolside serv. Restaurant 6:30 am-10 pm. Bar 11-2 am. Ck-out noon. Business center. In-rm modem link. Gift shop. Tennis privileges. Golf privileges. Exercise equipt; bicycles, stair machine. Health club privileges. Some bathrm phones, in-rm whirlpools. Cr cds: A, C, D, DS, JCB, MC, V.

D SC

Detroit

Founded: 1701
Pop: 1,027,974
Elev: 600 feet
Time zone: Eastern
Area code: 313
Web: www.visitdetroit.com

The city that put the US on wheels and gave birth to Motown music is an American symbol of elbow grease and productive might; its name is synonymous with automobiles.

When the Stars and Stripes first flew over Detroit on July 11, 1796, the settlement was already nearly a century old. It was, however, little more than a trading post and remained so until the opening of the Erie Canal and the introduction of steam navigation on the Great Lakes. With the development of better transportation, the city became a hub of industry and shipping. Population doubled every decade between 1830 and 1860.

In the 1890s, the first automobile frames were made in Detroit. By the turn of the century, the auto industry dominated the city, and it changed from a quiet town that brewed beer and produced carriages and stoves to a city bursting with such industrial might that it profoundly influenced not only the rest of the nation, but the world. A century from now, historians may judge that the man who most influenced the tide of world economy in the 20th century was Henry Ford, who revolutionized industry with his production line, his understanding of mass marketing and his astonishing decision to raise wages to $5 a day when the going salary was half that amount.

Business

It's surprising that in a city built on the automobile industry (nearly 25 percent of the nation's automobiles are produced here) less than 10 percent of Detroit's labor force is actually employed in the industry. Detroit is a manufacturing town; it outranks many other US cities by producing a large percentage of the country's machine-tool accessories, dies, tools and jigs, internal combustion engines and metal-cutting tools. Detroit is also a major manufacturer of airplane parts, automation and military equipment, machine tools and plastics.

In addition to manufacturing, Detroit is a major world port; exports from the Michigan Customs District rank among the country's five highest in value. The Detroit River's total tonnage in an eight-month shipping season averages more than 125 million tons. Detroit is also among the largest financial centers in the United States. The city's Renaissance Center is a $430-million complex that includes 5 million square feet of office space in six high-rise towers, 80 retail stores and lounges, and a magnificent lobby alive with greenery. In the middle of the complex is Michigan's tallest building, the Westin Hotel, rising 73 stories.

Convention Facilities

Cobo Conference/Exhibition Center and Arena is an innovative, modern convention center. The arena can seat 12,191 for sporting events. A movable stage can be set up for concerts, and the main ballroom can seat up to 2,000 people for banquets. If more space is needed, there are five exhibition areas of up to 250,000 square feet each, which can seat 10,000. Three of the exhibition areas, totaling 620,000 square feet, are interconnecting.

The facility has exhibit space totaling 720,000 square feet. In addition, 84 more meeting rooms are available with seating capacities from 50 to 5,000 people. Parking for Cobo Conference/Exhibition Center is located on the roof; public transportation is easily accessible.

Next door to Cobo is the Joe Louis Arena, which seats 21,000.

Sports & Recreation

All major professional sports are played in and around Detroit. The Tigers play baseball at the 53,000-seat Tiger Stadium; the Lions play football at the Silverdome in Pontiac; the Pistons play basketball nearby at the Palace of Auburn Hills; and the Red Wings play hockey at the Joe Louis Arena.

Belle Isle in the Detroit River offers many outdoor recreational activities, including golf, guided nature walks, swimming, fishing, boating with rentals, picnicking, baseball, softball and tennis.

More than 400 lakes and streams are within an hour's drive of the city, and the surrounding Huron-Clinton Metroparks provide numerous beaches, picnicking areas, golf courses, hiking and biking trails and winter activities.

There is horse racing in the outlying suburban areas as well as in Detroit proper; downhill skiing is available northwest near Pontiac.

Entertainment

The Detroit Symphony, one of America's major orchestras, gives concerts in Orchestra Hall. The orchestra also performs at the Meadow Brook Pavilion during the summer. The Michigan Opera Theatre performs at the renovated Detroit Opera House.

The University of Detroit Performing Arts Center and Wayne State University offer theatrical entertainment in the university theaters from October to mid-April. Numerous professional, repertory and neighborhood theaters, offering a wide variety of drama and comedy, can be found in the metropolitan area.

Historical Areas

The most famous of Michigan's historical areas is the Henry Ford Museum and Greenfield Village complex, located just west of Detroit's city

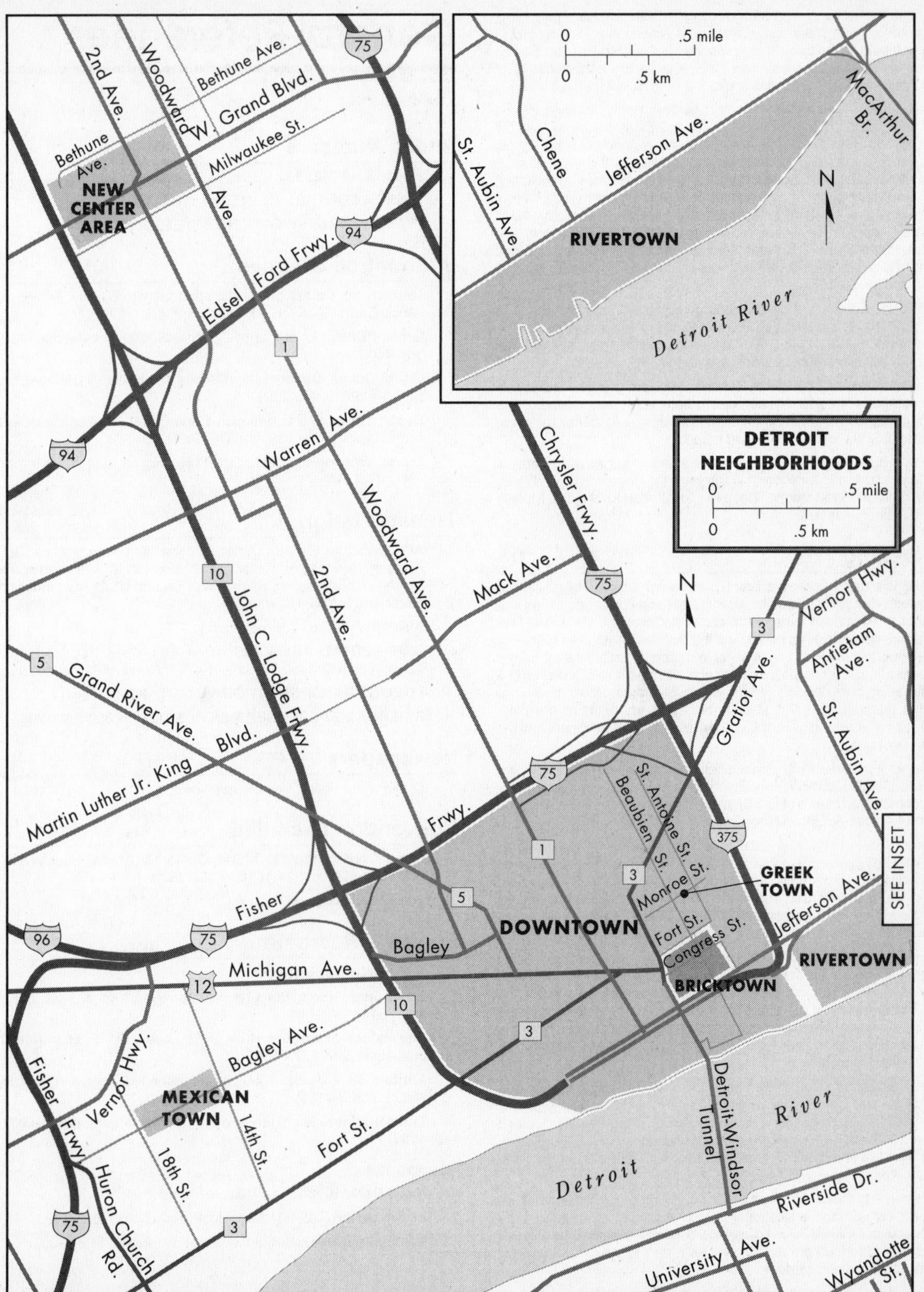
DETROIT NEIGHBORHOODS
0 .5 mile
0 .5 km
N
RIVERTOWN
Detroit River
St. Aubin Ave.
Chene
Jefferson Ave.
MacArthur Br.
NEW CENTER AREA
Bethune Ave.
W. Grand Blvd.
Milwaukee St.
2nd Ave.
Woodward Ave.
Edsel Ford Frwy.
Warren Ave.
Chrysler Frwy.
Woodward Ave.
2nd Ave.
Mack Ave.
John C. Lodge Frwy.
Grand River Ave.
Martin Luther Jr. King Blvd.
Fisher Frwy.
Vernor Hwy.
Antietam Ave.
St. Aubin Ave.
Gratiot Ave.
St. Antoine St.
Beaubien St.
Monroe St.
GREEK TOWN
Fort St.
Congress St.
Jefferson Ave.
SEE INSET
DOWNTOWN
Bagley
Michigan Ave.
BRICKTOWN
RIVERTOWN
Bagley Ave.
Vernor Hwy.
MEXICAN TOWN
14th St.
18th St.
Fort St.
Huron Church Rd.
Detroit-Windsor Tunnel
Detroit River
Riverside Dr.
University Ave.
Wyandotte St.

limits in Dearborn. In a 93-acre setting is a re-created, full-scale panorama of American life—an unequaled collection of Americana. Built by Henry Ford as a tribute to the culture and resourcefulness of the United States, the museum and village stand as monuments to the achievements of famous Americans. The area was dedicated in 1929 to Thomas Edison.

Greenfield Village includes more than 80 historic buildings moved from all sections of the country and restored to appear exactly as they did during the 18th and 19th centuries. Here are historic houses, shops, schools, mills, stores and laboratories that figured in the lives of such creative Americans as Lincoln, Webster, Foster, Burbank, McGuffey, Carver, the Wright brothers, Edison and Ford. Among the buildings are a courthouse where Abraham Lincoln practiced law, the Wright brothers' cycle shop, Henry Ford's birthplace, Edison's Menlo Park laboratory and the residences of H.J. Heinz, Noah Webster and Luther Burbank. Guided tours and rides are offered on horse-drawn carriages, a steam train, a riverboat and Model T Fords.

Mariners' Church, the oldest stone church building in the city, was completed in 1848. It was moved 800 feet to its present site as part of the Civic Center complex. At the time of the move, extensive restoration was done, and a bell tower with a carillon was added.

Major urban renewal projects and restoration are going on in Detroit's metropolitan area. Eastern Market, dating from 1891, was restored. It is now a farmers' market offering customers a chance to barter for fruits, vegetables, flowers and freshly baked bread.

Detroit has many fine old residential areas designated as national historic districts. Particularly worth visiting are the Boston/Edison district, Indian Village and Woodbridge. Detroit's oldest brick house, the Moross House, has been restored.

Sightseeing

Belle Isle is a 1,000-acre island-park in the Detroit River. On the island is the Whitcomb Conservatory, with seasonal flower shows, as well as continuing exhibits of ferns, cacti, palms and orchids; the Safari-Trail Zoo; a nature center; the Aquarium; and the Dossin Great Lakes Museum, with scale models of Great Lakes ships, a restored "Gothic salon" from a Great Lakes liner, marine paintings, a reconstructed ship's bridge and a full-scale racing boat, the *Miss Pepsi*. Boblo Steamers cruise down river during the summer from Detroit to Boblo Park, where there are playgrounds, picnic areas, an historic blockhouse, an amusement park and the 314-foot Sky Tower.

The century-old Detroit Institute of Arts is the fifth-largest in the nation. The Detroit Historical Museum offers visitors a walk through history along reconstructed streets of Old Detroit. In Detroit's Cultural Center is the Museum of African-American History.

Wayne State University, established in 1868, has 13 professional schools and colleges and a graduate division. Among notable buildings on campus are the De Roy Auditorium, the ultramodern McGregor Memorial Community Conference Center and the Prentis Building, all designed by Minoru Yamasaki. Also on campus is the Walter P. Reuther Library of Labor and Urban Affairs, the nation's largest labor library.

The 11-acre Hart Plaza overlooks the river and connects the Cobo Conference/Exhibition Center, the Veterans Memorial Building, Ford Auditorium and Mariners' Church. The plaza also features a park and amphitheater. In the middle of the plaza is a $2-million computerized fountain capable of sending more than a million gallons of water per hour into the air through 300-plus nozzles and jets. The fountain was designed by sculptor Isamu Noguchi.

The Renaissance Center is probably the most concentrated shopping area in downtown Detroit. The revolving restaurant on the top floor is a comfortable place to relax after a day of shopping. Trappers Alley, located on Monroe in Detroit's Greektown area, is housed in a restored historic building. This five-level center features gift shops, restaurants, exhibits and entertainment.

Northwest of Detroit, in Bloomfield Hills, is Cranbrook, an internationally known cultural and educational center. An array of sculptures by Swedish sculptor Carl Milles and various buildings designed by Finnish architect Eliel Saarinen grace the complex's 300 acres. Also here are museums, galleries and gardens.

General References

Area code: 313

Phone Numbers

POLICE & FIRE: 911

POISON CONTROL CENTER: 745-5711

TIME: 472-1212 **WEATHER:** 810-356-3982

Information Sources

Metropolitan Detroit Convention and Visitors Bureau, 100 Renaissance Center, Suite 1900, 48243; 800/DETROIT.

Greater Detroit Chamber of Commerce, 600 W Lafayette, 48226; 964-4000.

City of Detroit, Department of Public Information, 608 City-County Bldg, 48226; 224-3755.

Detroit Visitor and Information Center, 100 Renaissance Center, Street Level, Suite 126, 800/DETROIT.

Detroit Recreation Dept, 224-1180; Huron-Clinton Metroparks, 810-227-2757.

Transportation

AIRLINES: Air Canada; America West; American; Asiana; British Airways; Continental; Delta; Great Lakes; KLM; Midwest Express; Northwest; Southwest; Spirit; TWA; United; USAir; and other commuter and regional airlines.

AIRPORT: Detroit Wayne County, 942-3550.

CAR RENTAL AGENCIES: (See IMPORTANT TOLL-FREE NUMBERS) Avis 942-3450; Hertz 941-4747; National 941-7000.

PUBLIC TRANSPORTATION: SMART, 962-5515.

RAILROAD PASSENGER SERVICE: Amtrak 800/872-7245.

Newspapers

Detroit Free Press; The Detroit News.

Convention Facilities

Cobo Conference/Exhibition Center & Arena, E Jefferson & Washington Blvd, 224-1010 or 396-7600.

Joe Louis Arena, 600 Civic Center, 396-7600.

Sports & Recreation

Major Sports Facilities

Joe Louis Arena, the Civic Center (Red Wings, NHL hockey, 396-7544).

The Palace of Auburn Hills, 3777 Lapeer Rd, Pontiac (Pistons, basketball, 248/377-0100).

Pontiac Silverdome, 1200 Featherstone Rd, Pontiac (Lions, football, 248/335-4151).

Tiger Stadium, Michigan Ave at Trumbull (Tigers, baseball, 962-4000).

Racetracks

Hazel Park, 1650 E Ten Mile Rd, 398-1000.

Ladbroke-DRC, 28001 Schoolcraft Rd, Livonia, 525-7300.

Northville Downs, 301 S Center St, Northville, 349-1000.

Cultural Facilities

Theaters

Bonstelle Theater, 3424 Woodward Ave, Wayne State University, 577-2960.

Detroit Institute of Arts Auditorium, 5200 Woodward Ave, 833-7900.

Detroit Opera House, 1526 Broadway, 874-7464.

Fisher Theater, W Grand & Second Blvds, 872-1000.

Hilberry Theatre, 4743 Cass Ave, Wayne State University, 577-2972.

Music Hall Center for the Performing Arts, 350 Madison Ave, 963-7680.

The Theatre Company-University of Detroit, 4001 W McNichols Rd, 993-1130.

Concert Halls

Masonic Temple Theatre, 500 Temple Ave, 832-2232.

Symphony Orchestra Hall, 3711 Woodward Ave, 833-3700.

Museums

Children's Museum, 67 E Kirby Ave, 494-1210.

Detroit Fire Department Historical Museum, 2737 Gratiot, 596-2957.

Detroit Historical Museum, 5401 Woodward Ave, 833-1805.

Dossin Great Lakes Museum, Belle Isle, 267-6440.

Motown Museum, 2648 W Grand Blvd, 875-2264.

Museum of African-American History, 315 E Warren Ave, 833-9800.

Art Galleries

Detroit Institute of Arts, 5200 Woodward Ave, between Warren Ave & Kirby St, 833-7900.

International Institute, 111 E Kirby Ave, 871-8600.

Points of Interest

Historical

Henry Ford Museum and Greenfield Village, 1/2 mi S of US 12, 1 1/2 mi N of Southfield Rd, on Oakwood Blvd, Dearborn, 271-1620 or 271-1976.

Mariners' Church, 170 E Jefferson Ave, 259-2206.

Other Attractions

Aquarium, Belle Isle, 267-7159.

Belle Isle, Island Park, reached by MacArthur Bridge, 267-7115.

Belle Isle Zoo, Belle Isle, 852-4083.

Christ Church Cranbrook, Bloomfield Hills, 644-5210.

City-County Building, 2 Woodward Ave, 224-5585.

Cranbrook Academy of Art and Museum, 500 Lone Pine Rd, between MI 1 & US 24, Bloomfield Hills, 645-3312.

Cranbrook Gardens, Bloomfield Hills, 645-3149.

Cranbrook House, Bloomfield Hills, 645-3149.

Cranbrook Institute of Science, between MI 1 & US 24, Bloomfield Hills, 645-3200 or 645-3142.

Detroit Public Library, 5201 Woodward Ave, 833-1000.

Detroit Zoo, 8450 W Ten Mile Rd, at Woodward Ave, Royal Oak, 398-0903.

Eastern Market, 2934 Russell, via I-75 at Gratiot, 833-1560.

Fisher Building, W Grand & Second Blvds, 874-4444.

Hart Plaza & Dodge Fountain, Jefferson Ave.

Michigan Consolidated Gas Company Building, 1 Woodward Ave.

New Center One, 3031 W Grand Blvd, 874-4444.

Renaissance Center, Jefferson Ave at Beaubien, 568-5600.

Trappers Alley, 508 Monroe Ave at Beaubien, in Greektown, 963-5445.

Washington Boulevard Trolley Car, downtown, 933-1300.

Whitcomb Conservatory, Belle Isle, 267-7134.

Sightseeing Tours

Diamond Jack's River Tours, Hart Plaza, 843-9376.

Gray Line bus tours, 1301 E Warren Ave, 48207; 935-3808.

Annual Events

North American International Auto Show, Cobo Conference/Exhibition Center, 810/673-0250. Mid-Jan.

Grand Prix, 259-7749. Mid-June.

International Freedom Festival, 887-8200. Late June-early July.

Michigan State Fair, Michigan Exposition & Fairgrounds, 369-8250. Late Aug-early Sept.

Montreux-Detroit Jazz Festival, Hart Plaza, 259-5400. Early Sept.

Christmas Carnival, Cobo Conference/Exhibition Center, 887-8200. Early Dec.

City Neighborhoods

Many of the restaurants, unrated dining establishments and some lodgings listed under Detroit include neighborhoods as well as exact street addresses. Geographic descriptions of these areas are given, followed by a table of restaurants arranged by neighborhood.

Bricktown: Area of downtown south of Fort St, west of St Antoine St, north of the Renaissance Center (Jefferson St) and east of Randolph St.

Downtown: South of Fisher Frwy (I-75), west of Walter P Chrysler Frwy (I-375), north of the Detroit River and east of John C Lodge Expy (MI 10). **East of Downtown:** East of I-375.

Greektown: Area of downtown on Monroe St between Beaubien St on the west and St Antoine St on the east.

Mexican Town: West of downtown along Bagley Ave between 14th and 18th Sts.

New Center Area: North of downtown; south of Bethune Ave, west of Woodward, north of Milwaukee and east of MI 10.

Rivertown: East of downtown; south of Jefferson Ave, west of Belle Isle Bridge and north of the Detroit River.

Lodgings and Food

DETROIT RESTAURANTS
BY NEIGHBORHOOD AREAS
(For full description, see alphabetical listings under Restaurants)

DOWNTOWN
Caucus Club. 150 W Congress St
Opus One. 565 E Larned
Traffic Jam & Snug. 511 W Canfield St
Tres Vite. 2203 Woodward Ave
The Whitney. 4421 Woodward Ave

EAST OF DOWNTOWN
Joe Muer's. 2000 Gratiot Ave
Van Dyke Place. 649 Van Dyke Ave

GREEKTOWN
Fishbone's Rhythm Kitchen Cafe. 400 Monroe St
Pegasus Taverna. 558 Monroe St

MEXICAN TOWN
El Zocalo. 3400 Bagley

NEW CENTER AREA
Pegasus In The Fisher. 3011 W Grand Blvd

RIVERTOWN
Baron's Steakhouse (The River Place Hotel). 1000 River Place
Rattlesnake Club. 300 Stroh River Place

Note: When a listing is located in a town that does not have its own city heading, it will appear under the city nearest to its location. In these cases, the address and town appear in parenthesis immediately following the name of the establishment.

Motels

★ ★ **BEST WESTERN LIVONIA PARK SUITES.** *(16999 S Laurel Park Dr, Livonia 48154) 30 mi W on I-96 to I-275, N on I-275 to jct Six Mile Rd. 313/464-0050; FAX 313/464-5869.* 123 rms, 2 story. S $59-$79; D $59-$129; each addl $8. Crib free. TV; cable (premium). Heated pool. Complimentary continental bkfst. Ck-out noon. Meeting rms. Business servs avail. In-rm modem link. X-country ski 5 mi. Exercise equipt; weight machine, rower. Refrigerators; some in-rm whirlpools, minibars. Cr cds: A, C, D, DS, ER, JCB, MC, V.

D SC

★ ★ ★ **COURTYARD BY MARRIOTT.** *(17200 N Laurel Park Dr, Livonia 48152) W via I-96 to I-275, N to Six Mile Rd. 313/462-2000; FAX 313/462-5907.* 149 rms, 3 story. S, D $96-$106; suites $125-$135; wkend rates. Crib free. TV; cable (premium). Indoor pool; whirlpool. Restaurant 6:30-10 am; Sat 7-11 am; Sun 7 am-1 pm. Bar 4-11 pm; closed Sat, Sun. Ck-out noon. Coin Indry. Meeting rms. Business servs avail. In-rm modem link. Valet serv. Downhill/x-country ski 20 mi. Exercise equipt; weights, bicycles. Refrigerator in suites. Private patios, balconies. Cr cds: A, D, DS, MC, V.

D SC

★ ★ **PARKCREST INN.** *(20000 Harper Ave, Harper Woods 48225) NE on I-94, exit 224B. 313/884-8800; FAX 313/884-7087.* 49 rms, 2 story. S $59; D $67-$72; kit. units $84; family rates. Crib free. Pet accepted. TV; cable (premium). Heated pool. Restaurant 6:30-2:30 am; Sun 7:30 am-10 pm. Rm serv. Bar to 2 am. Ck-out 11 am. Valet serv. X-country ski 15 mi. Cr cds: A, C, D, DS, MC, V.

SC

✔★ **SHORECREST MOTOR INN.** *1316 E Jefferson Ave (48207), downtown. 313/568-3000; FAX 313/568-3002; res: 800/992-9616.* 54 rms, 2 story. S $49-$63; D $55-$79; family, wkly, wkend rates. Crib free. Pet accepted, some restrictions. TV; cable (premium). Restaurant 6 am-10 pm; wkends from 7 am. Rm serv. Ck-out noon. Business servs avail. Valet serv. Refrigerators. Cr cds: A, C, D, DS, MC, V.

D SC

Motor Hotel

★ ★ ★ **HOLIDAY INN.** *5801 Southfield Service Dr (48228), west of downtown. 313/336-3340; FAX 313/336-7037.* 347 rms, 6 story. S, D $99; suites $250; under 18 free; wkend rates. Crib free. TV; cable (premium). 2 pools, 1 indoor; whirlpool. Coffee in rms. Restaurant 6 am-2 pm, 5-10 pm; Sat, Sun from 7 am. Rm serv. Bar 11 am-midnight. Ck-out noon. Convention facilities. Business center. Bellhops. Gift shop. Exercise equipt; bicycles, stair machine, sauna. Game rm. Cr cds: A, C, D, DS, JCB, MC, V.

D SC

Hotels

★ ★ ★ **ATHENEUM.** *1000 Brush Ave (48226), in Greektown. 313/962-2323; FAX 313/962-2424; res: 800/772-2323.* 174 suites, 10 story. Suites $125-$600; each addl $20; family, wkly rates. Crib free. Valet parking $8. TV; cable (premium), VCR avail. Restaurant adj 8 am-midnight. Rm serv 24 hrs. Bar. Ck-out noon. Meeting rms. Business servs avail. In-rm modem link. Concierge. Gift shop. Exercise equipt; bicycle, stair machine. Minibars; some bathrm phones. Neoclassical structure adj International Center. Cr cds: A, C, D, DS, ER, JCB, MC, V.

D SC

★ ★ ★ **DOUBLETREE-DOWNTOWN.** *333 E Jefferson Ave (48226), downtown. 313/222-7700; FAX 313/222-6509.* 255 rms, 21 story. S $180-$250; D $190-$250; each addl $20; suites $250-$1,000; under 18 free; wkend rates. Valet parking $9. Crib free. TV; cable. Indoor pool; whirlpool, poolside serv. Coffee in rms. Restaurant 6:30 am-10 pm; Fri, Sat to 11 pm. Bar 11-2 am. Meeting rms. Business center. In-rm modem link. Shopping arcade. Barber, beauty shop. Tennis. Racquetball. Exercise rm; instructor, weights, bicycles, sauna. Bathrm phone & TV, refrigerator in suites. Opp river. Cr cds: A, C, D, DS, MC, V.

D SC

★ ★ **EMBASSY SUITES.** *(19525 Victor Pkwy, Livonia 48152) W on I-96 to I-275N, exit Seven Mile Rd E. 313/462-6000; FAX 313/462-6003.* 239 suites, 5 story. S $129-$149; D $139-$159; each addl $10; under 12 free (max 2); wkend rates; higher rates special events. Crib free. TV; cable (premium), VCR avail. Indoor pool; whirlpool. Complimentary full bkfst. Complimentary coffee in rms. Restaurant 6-9 am, 11 am-4 pm, 5-10 pm; hrs vary Fri-Sun. Bar 5 pm-midnight; closed Sun. Ck-out noon. Coin Indry. Meeting rms. Business servs avail. In-rm modem link. Gift shop. Exercise equipt; weight machine, rowers, sauna. Refrigerators. Balconies. Five-story atrium. Cr cds: A, C, D, DS, JCB, MC, V.

D SC

★ ★ ★ **MARRIOTT.** *(17100 Laurel Park Dr N, Livonia 48152) 30 mi W on I-96 to I-275, N on I-275 to Six Mile Rd. 313/462-3100; FAX 313/462-2815.* 224 rms, 6 story. S, D $124-$139; suites $225; family, wkend rates. Crib free. TV; cable (premium), VCR avail. Indoor pool; whirlpool, poolside serv. Restaurant 6:30 am-10 pm. Bar noon-midnight. Ck-out noon. Meeting rms. Business center. In-rm modem link. Gift shop. Free garage parking. Downhill/x-country ski 20 mi. Exercise equipt; weights, bicycles, sauna. Health club privileges. Connected to Laurel Park Mall. Luxury level. Cr cds: A, C, D, DS, ER, JCB, MC, V.

D SC

★ ★ **THE RIVER PLACE.** *1000 River Place (48207), in Rivertown. 313/259-9500; FAX 313/259-3744; res: 800/890-9505.* 108 rms, 5 story, 18 suites. S $115-$185; D $135-$205; each addl $20; suites $165-$500; under 12 free; hol rates; higher rates some special events. Crib free. Valet parking $6. Pet accepted. TV; cable (premium), VCR avail. Indoor pool; whirlpool. Restaurant (see BARON'S STEAKHOUSE). Bar 11 am-11 pm; Fri, Sat to 1 am. Ck-out noon. Meeting rms. Business servs avail. In-rm modem link. Tennis privileges. Exercise rm; instructor, weight machine, treadmill, sauna. Massage. Croquet court. On Detroit River. Cr cds: A, C, D, DS, JCB, MC, V.

D SC

★ ★ ★ **WESTIN-RENAISSANCE CENTER.** *Renaissance Center (48243), Jefferson Ave at Brush, downtown. 313/568-8000; FAX 313/568-8146.* 1,400 rms, 73 story. S $105-$165; D $130-$180; each addl $20; suites $330-$1,200; under 18 free; wkend rates. Crib free. Pet accepted. TV; cable, VCR avail (movies). Indoor pool. Restaurants 6 am-11 pm. Rm serv 24 hrs. Bar 11:30-1:30 am. Ck-out 1 pm. Convention facilities. Business center. In-rm modem link. Shopping arcade. Barber, beauty shop. Exercise rm; instructor, weights, bicycles, sauna. Many minibars. Luxury level. Cr cds: A, C, D, DS, ER, JCB, MC, V.

D SC

Restaurants

★ ★ ★ **BARON'S STEAKHOUSE.** *(See The River Place Hotel) 313/259-4855.* Hrs: 7 am-10 pm; Fri, Sat to 11 pm; Sun 7 am-2 pm. Closed Dec 25. Res accepted. Bar to 11 pm. Semi-a la carte: bkfst $4.95-$11.95, lunch $4.95-$16.95, dinner $13.95-$28.95. Sun brunch $12.95. Child's meals. Specializes in beef, chicken, seafood. Entertainment Fri, Sat. Outdoor dining. Overlooks Detroit River. Cr cds: A, C, D, DS, JCB, MC, V.

D

★ ★ ★ **CAUCUS CLUB.** *150 W Congress St (48226), in Penobscot Bldg, downtown. 313/965-4970.* Hrs: 11:30 am-8:30 pm; Fri to 10 pm; summer hrs vary. Closed Sat, Sun; major hols. Res accepted. Continental menu. Semi-a la carte: lunch $7.75-$17.25; dinner $15-$24. Child's meals. Specializes in fresh Dover sole, steak tartare, baby back ribs. Entertainment Mon-Fri. Cr cds: A, C, D, DS, MC, V.

✔★ **EL ZOCALO.** *3400 Bagley (48216), in Mexican Town. 313/841-3700.* Hrs: 11-1 am; Fri, Sat to 2:30 am. Closed some major hols. Res accepted Sun-Thurs. Mexican menu. Bar. Semi-a la carte: lunch $5.95-$8.95, dinner $6.35-$9.95. Specialties: chiles rellenos, queso flameado, chimichangas. Parking. Mayan and Aztec art. Cr cds: A, C, D, DS, MC, V.

D

★ ★ **FISHBONE'S RHYTHM KITCHEN CAFE.** *400 Monroe St (48226), at Brush Ave, in Greektown. 313/965-4600.* Hrs: 6:30 am-midnight; Fri, Sat to 1:45 am; Sun brunch 10:30 am-2:30 pm; dinner 2 pm-midnight. Closed Dec 25. Southern Louisiana, Creole, Cajun menu. Bar. Semi-a la carte: lunch $5.95-$12.95, dinner $5.95-$19.95. Sun brunch $13.95. Specialties: smoked whiskey ribs, jambalaya, crawfish etoufee. Valet parking. Bourbon Street bistro atmosphere; tin ceilings, antique lamps. Cr cds: A, C, D, DS, MC, V.

D SC

★ ★ ★ **INTERMEZZO.** *1435 Randolph St (48226), downtown. 313/961-0707.* Hrs: 11 am-10 pm; Fri, Sat to 11 pm. Closed Sun, Mon; major hols. Res accepted. Italian menu. Bar. Semi-a la carte: lunch $6-$12, dinner $12-$24. Specializes in veal, pasta. Entertainment Fri, Sat. Outdoor dining. Contemporary decor. Cr cds: A, D, DS, MC, V.

D

★ ★ ★ **JOE MUER'S.** *2000 Gratiot Ave (48207), east of downtown. 313/567-1088.* Hrs: 11:15 am-2:30 pm, 4:30-10 pm; Sat 5-11 pm. Closed Sun; major hols. Bar. Semi-a la carte: lunch $9-$16, dinner $19.25-$26. Child's meals. Specializes in seafood. Tudor-style with beamed ceilings. Jacket. Cr cds: A, C, D, DS, MC, V.

D

★ ★ ★ **OPUS ONE.** *565 E Larned (48226), downtown. 313/961-7766.* Hrs: 11:30 am-10 pm; Fri to 11 pm; Sat 5-11 pm. Closed Sun; major hols. Res accepted. Bar. Wine cellar. French, Amer menu. Semi-a la carte: lunch $8.95-$16.95, dinner $19.50-$34.50. Child's meals. Specializes in seafood, aged beef. Own baking, ice cream. Pianist Tues-Sat (dinner). Valet parking. In building designed by Albert Kahn; etched glass, original artwork. Jacket. Cr cds: A, C, D, DS, MC, V.

D

✔★ **PEGASUS IN THE FISHER.** *3011 W Grand Blvd (48202), in New Center Area. 313/875-7400.* Hrs: 11 am-11 pm; Mon to 9 pm; Fri to midnight; Sat 4 pm-midnight. Closed Sun; most major hols. Res accepted. Continental menu. Bar. Semi-a la carte: lunch $5-$7, dinner $7-$16. Specializes in steak, pasta, fresh seafood. Entertainment Fri & Sat evenings. Valet parking. Art-deco decor; hand-painted ceilings. Cr cds: A, C, D, DS, MC, V.

D

★ ★ **PEGASUS TAVERNA.** *558 Monroe St (48226), in Greektown. 313/964-6800.* Hrs: 11-1 am; Fri, Sat to 2 am; Sun to midnight. Greek, Amer menu. Bar. A la carte entrees: lunch $4.95-$7.95, dinner $5.95-$17.95. Child's meals. Specializes in lamb chops, seafood, spinach cheese pie. Parking. Lattice-worked ceiling; hanging grape vines. Cr cds: A, D, DS, MC, V.

D

★ ★ ★ **RATTLESNAKE CLUB.** *300 Stroh River Place (48207), in Rivertown. 313/567-4400.* Hrs: 11:30 am-10 pm; Fri to midnight; Sat 5:30-midnight. Closed Sun; most major hols. Res accepted. Bar. Semi-a la carte: lunch $7-$18, dinner $14.95-$29.95. Specializes in seasonal dishes. Entertainment Fri, Sat. Valet parking. Outdoor dining. Modern decor; two dining areas overlook Detroit River. Cr cds: A, C, D, DS, MC, V.

D

✔★ ★ **TRES VITE.** *2203 Woodward Ave (48201), downtown. 313/964-4144.* Hrs: 11:30 am-8 pm; Fri to 11 pm; Sat 5-11 pm. Closed Sun (exc special events) & Mon; major hols. Res accepted. Mediterranean menu. Bar. A la carte entrees: lunch $5.95-$12.95, dinner $6.95-$17.95. Specializes in pizza, pasta, steak. Valet parking. In historic Fox Theatre building. Cr cds: A, DS, MC, V.

D

★ ★ ★ **VAN DYKE PLACE.** *649 Van Dyke Ave (48214), east of downtown. 313/821-2620.* Hrs: 6-9:30 pm; Fri, Sat from 5 pm. Closed Sun, Mon; major hols. Res accepted. Serv bar. Wine list. A la carte entrees: dinner $23-$28. Specializes in contemporary American fare with French accents. Own baking. Valet parking. Turn-of-the-century Louis XVI town house. Cr cds: A, D, MC, V.

★ ★ ★ **THE WHITNEY.** *4421 Woodward Ave (48201), downtown. 313/832-5700.* Hrs: 11 am-2 pm, 6-9:30 pm; Wed, Thurs 5-10 pm; Fri, Sat 5-11 pm; Sun 5-8 pm; Sun brunch 11 am-2:30 pm. Closed major hols. Res recommended. Bar 5 pm-2 am; closed Sun. Wine cellar. A la carte entrees: lunch $6.95-$16.95, dinner $16-$30. Prix fixe: dinner $44-$55. Sun brunch $21.95. Specializes in veal, beef, seafood. Own baking. Entertainment. Valet parking. Cr cds: A, D, MC, V.

D

Unrated Dining Spot

TRAFFIC JAM & SNUG. *511 W Canfield St (48201), at Second St, downtown. 313/831-9470.* Hrs: 11 am-9 pm; Mon to 3 pm; Thurs to 10:30 pm; Fri to midnight; Sat 5 pm-midnight. Closed Sun; most major hols. Serv bar. Semi-a la carte: lunch $6-$10, dinner $9-$13. Child's meals. Own pastries, desserts, ice cream, cheese. Micro brewery and dairy on premises. Parking. Rustic decor, many antiques. Cr cds: DS, MC, V.

D

Detroit Wayne County Airport Area

Motels

★ ★ ★ **COURTYARD BY MARRIOTT.** *(30653 Flynn Dr, Romulus 48174) N on Merriman Rd to Flynn Dr. 313/721-3200; FAX 313/721-1304.* 146 rms, 3 story. S, D $93; each addl $10; suites $110; under 16 free; wkend rates. Crib free. TV; cable (premium). Indoor pool; whirlpool. Complimentary coffee in rms. Restaurant 6:30 am-2 pm, 5-10 pm; Sat 7 am-1 pm, 5-10 pm; Sun 7 am-1 pm. Bar. Ck-out noon. Coin Indry. Meeting rms. Business servs avail. In-rm modem link. Valet serv. Free airport transportation. Exercise equipt; weight machine, treadmill. Refrigerator in suites. Balconies. Cr cds: A, C, D, DS, MC, V.

D SC

★ ★ **HAMPTON INN.** *(30847 Flynn Dr, Romulus 48174) N on Merriman Rd to Flynn Dr. 313/721-1100; FAX 313/721-9915.* 136 rms, 3 story. S, D $69.95-$89.95; under 17 free. Crib $5. TV; cable (premium). Pool. Complimentary continental bkfst. Restaurant adj 6 am-10 pm; Fri, Sat to 11:30 pm. Ck-out noon. Meeting rms. Business center. In-rm modem link. Valet serv. Free airport transportation. Cr cds: A, C, D, DS, MC, V.

D SC

★ ★ **QUALITY INN.** *(7600 Merriman Rd, Romulus 48174) 1/2 mi N on Merriman Rd. 313/728-2430; FAX 313/728-3756.* 140 rms. S, D $54-$89; each addl $5; under 12 free; wkly rates. Crib free. TV; cable (premium). Complimentary continental bkfst. Restaurant adj 11-1 am. Bar. Ck-out noon. Coin Indry. Meeting rms. Business servs avail. In-rm modem link. Free airport transportation. Cr cds: A, D, DS, MC, V.

D SC

Motor Hotels

★ ★ ★ **HILTON SUITES.** *(8600 Wickham Rd, Romulus 48174) N on Merriman Rd to Wickham Rd. 313/728-9200; FAX 313/728-9278.* 151 suites, 3 story. S $129; D $139; each addl $10; family rates. Crib free. TV; cable (premium), VCR (movies $6). Indoor/outdoor pool; whirlpool, poolside serv. Complimentary full bkfst. Complimentary coffee in rms. Restaurant 6 am-11 pm. Bar. Ck-out noon. Coin Indry. Meeting rms. Business center. In-rm modem link. Bellhops. Valet serv. Sundries. Free airport transportation. Downhill ski 10 mi. Exercise equipt; weight machine, bicycles. Game rm. Refrigerators. Some balconies. Cr cds: A, C, D, DS, MC, V.

D SC

★ ★ **RAMADA INN.** *(8270 Wickham Rd, Romulus 48174) N on Merriman Rd to Wickham Rd. 313/729-6300; FAX 313/722-8740.* 243 rms, 4 story. S, D $79-$89; each addl $10; suites from $150; family, wkend rates; package plans. Crib free. TV; cable (premium). Indoor pool. Playground. Restaurant 6 am-10 pm. Rm serv. Bar 11-2 am; Sun from noon; entertainment. Ck-out noon. Meeting rms. Business servs avail. Bellhops. Valet serv. Sundries. Free airport transportation. X-country ski 4 mi. Exercise equipt; weight machine, bicycle, sauna. Cr cds: A, C, D, DS, ER, JCB, MC, V.

D SC

Hotels

★ ★ ★ **CROWNE PLAZA.** *(8000 Merriman Rd, Romulus 48174) 1 mi N on Merriman Rd. 313/729-2600; FAX 313/729-9414.* 365 rms, 11 story. S, D $104-$132; each addl $10; suites $179-$229; family, wkend rates. Crib free. Pet accepted, some restrictions. TV; cable (premium), VCR avail. Indoor pool; whirlpool. Coffee in rms. Restaurant 6 am-10 pm. Bar noon-1 am. Ck-out noon. Convention facilities. Business center. In-rm modem link. Gift shop. Free airport transportation. Exercise equipt; weights, bicycles. Game rm. Some balconies. Luxury level. Cr cds: A, C, D, DS, JCB, MC, V.

D SC

★ ★ ★ **MARRIOTT.** *(30559 Flynn Dr, Romulus 48174) N on Merriman Rd to Flynn Dr. 313/729-7555; FAX 313/729-8634.* 245 rms, 4 story. S, D $119; suites $350; family, wkend rates. Crib free. TV; cable (premium). Indoor pool; whirlpool. Restaurant 6:30 am-10 pm. Bar from 11 am. Ck-out noon. Meeting rms. Business servs avail. In-rm modem link. Gift shop. Free airport transportation. Downhill ski 15 mi. Exercise equipt; weight machine, bicycles. Some bathrm phones. Refrigerator, minibar in suites. Luxury level. Cr cds: A, C, D, DS, ER, JCB, MC, V.

D SC

Southfield

Motels

★ ★ ★ **COURTYARD BY MARRIOTT.** *27027 Northwestern Hwy (MI 10) (48034). 810/358-1222; FAX 810/354-3820.* 147 rms, 2-3 story. S $89; D $99; suites $99-$109; wkend rates; higher rates special events. Crib free. TV; cable (premium). Indoor pool; whirlpool. Restaurant 6:30-10 am. Serv bar. Ck-out noon. Coin Indry. Meeting rms. Business servs avail. In-rm modem link. Valet serv. Exercise equipt; weights, bicycles. Balconies. Cr cds: A, C, D, DS, MC, V.

D SC

★ ★ **HAMPTON INN.** *27500 Northwestern Hwy (MI 10) (48034). 810/356-5500; FAX 810/356-2083.* 153 rms, 2 story. S $65-$75; D $75-$85; under 18 free; some wkly, wkend rates. Crib free. TV; cable. Indoor pool; whirlpool. Complimentary continental bkfst. Restaurant nearby. Ck-out noon. Coin Indry. Meeting rms. Business servs avail. In-rm modem link. Valet serv. Downhill/x-country ski 20 mi. Exercise equipt; weights, bicycles. Picnic tables. Cr cds: A, C, D, DS, MC, V.

D SC

✓★ **MARVINS GARDEN INN.** *27650 Northwestern Hwy (48034). 810/353-6777; FAX 810/353-2944.* 110 rms, 2 story. S, D $40-$45; family rates. Crib $6. TV; cable (premium). Complimentary continental bkfst. Complimentary coffee in rms. Restaurant nearby. Ck-out noon. Meeting rms. Some refrigerators. Cr cds: A, C, D, DS, MC, V.

D SC

Motor Hotel

★ ★ ★ **HOLIDAY INN.** *26555 Telegraph Rd (48034). 810/353-7700; FAX 810/353-8377.* 417 rms, 2-16 story. S, D $75-$81; each addl $8; suites $175-$249; under 19 free; wkend rates. Crib free. Pet accepted, some restrictions. TV; cable (premium). Indoor pool; whirlpool. Restaurant 6:30 am-2 pm, 5-10 pm; Sat, Sun from 7 am. Rm serv. Bar 11-1 am. Ck-out noon. Coin Indry. Convention facilities. Bellhops. Sundries. Gift shop. Barber, beauty shop. Downhill/x-country ski 20 mi. Game rm. Rec rm. Many rms in circular tower. Cr cds: A, C, D, DS, JCB, MC, V.

D SC

Hotels

★ ★ **HILTON GARDEN INN.** *26000 American Dr (48034). 810/357-1100; FAX 810/799-7030.* 195 rms, 7 story. S, D $89; each addl $10; suites $175; under 12 free; wkend rates. Crib free. Pet accepted, some restrictions. TV; cable (premium). Indoor pool; whirlpool. Restaurant 6-10 am, 11 am-2 pm, 5-10 pm; wkend hrs vary. Bar 5 pm-midnight. Ck-out 1 pm. Meeting rms. Business center. In-rm modem link. Exercise equipt;

weight machine, stair machine, sauna. Cr cds: A, C, D, DS, ER, JCB, MC, V.

D SC

★ ★ ★ **MARRIOTT.** *27033 Northwestern Hwy (MI 10) (48034). 810/356-7400; FAX 810/356-5501.* 222 rms, 6 story. S, D $109-$129; suites $250; under 16 free; wkend rates. Crib free. TV; cable, VCR avail. Indoor pool; whirlpool. Restaurant 6:30 am-11 pm. Bar 11-1 am. Ck-out noon. Meeting rms. In-rm modem link. Concierge. Gift shop. Exercise equipt; weights, bicycles, sauna. Health club privileges. Refrigerator. Luxury level. Cr cds: A, C, D, DS, ER, JCB, MC, V.

D

★ ★ ★ **RADISSON PLAZA AT TOWN CENTER.** *1500 Town Center (48075). 810/827-4000; FAX 810/827-1364.* 385 rms, 12 story. S $123-$163; D $135-$175; each addl $15; suites $180-$425; under 17 free. Crib free. Valet parking $6. TV; cable (premium), VCR avail. Indoor pool; whirlpool, poolside serv. Restaurant 6:30 am-10:30 pm. Rm serv 24 hrs. Bar 11-2 am; Sun noon-midnight; entertainment Tues-Sat. Ck-out noon. Convention facilities. Business servs avail. In-rm modem link. Concierge. Downhill/x-country ski 20 mi. Exercise equipt; weights, bicycles, sauna. Refrigerators avail. Luxury level. Cr cds: A, C, D, DS, JCB, MC, V.

D SC

Restaurants

✔★ ★ ★ **CHIANTI VILLA ITALIA.** *28565 Northwestern Hwy (48034). 810/350-0055.* Hrs: 11:30 am-10 pm; Fri to 11 pm; Sat 4-11 pm; Sun 4-8:30 pm. Closed Memorial Day, Dec 25. Res accepted. Italian menu. Bar. A la carte entrees: lunch $5.95-$9.95, dinner $8.95-$15.95. Child's meals. Specializes in pasta. Italian villa decor. Cr cds: A, D, DS, MC, V.

D

★ ★ ★ **GOLDEN MUSHROOM.** *18100 W Ten Mile Rd (48075). 810/559-4230.* Hrs: 11:30 am-4 pm, 5-11 pm; Fri to midnight; Sat 5:30 pm-midnight. Closed Sun; major hols. Res accepted. Continental menu. Bar 11:30 am-midnight. A la carte entrees: lunch $9-$15, dinner $20.50-$32.50. Specializes in wild game dishes. Own baking. Valet parking. Cr cds: A, C, D, DS, JCB, MC, V.

★ ★ **LE METRO.** *29855 Northwestern Hwy (MI 10) (48034), in Applegate Square. 810/353-2757.* Hrs: 11:30 am-10 pm; Fri, Sat to 11 pm; early-bird dinner Mon-Fri 4:30-6:30 pm; Sun 4:30-5:30. Closed major hols. Res accepted. Bar. Semi-a la carte: lunch $5.95-$12.95, dinner $7.25-$18. Specialties: Norwegian salmon, stuffed medallions of provimi veal, pasta. Entertainment Wed, Thurs. Parking. Lively atmosphere. Cr cds: A, C, D, DS, MC, V.

D

★ ★ ★ **MORTON'S OF CHICAGO.** *One Town Square (48076), between Civic Center Dr & Lahser. 810/354-6006.* Hrs: 5:30-11 pm; Sun 5-10 pm. Closed major hols. Res accepted. Bar. A la carte entrees: dinner $16.95-$59.90. Specializes in fresh seafood, beef. Valet parking (dinner). Menu recited. Semi-formal steak house atmosphere. Cr cds: A, C, D, MC, V.

D

★ ★ **SWEET LORRAINE'S CAFE.** *29101 Greenfield Rd (48076). 810/559-5985.* Hrs: 11 am-10:30 pm; Fri, Sat to midnight; Sun to 9 pm. Closed some hols. Bar. A la carte entrees: lunch $4.95-$9.95, dinner $9.45-$16.95. Specialties: pecan chicken, Jamaican "Jerk" chicken & shrimp Creole, vegetarian entrees. Modern-style bistro. Cr cds: A, C, D, DS, MC, V.

D

✔★ ★ ★ **TOM'S OYSTER BAR.** *29106 Franklin Rd (48034). 810/356-8881.* Hrs: 11 am-midnight. Closed Jan 1, Dec 25. Res accepted. Bar. Semi-a la carte: lunch $5-$10, dinner $10-$18. Child's meals. Specializes in seafood. Entertainment. Outdoor dining. Contemporary decor. Cr cds: A, C, D, DS, MC, V.

D

Warren

Motels

★ ★ ★ **BEST WESTERN STERLING INN.** *(34911 Van Dyke Ave, Sterling Heights 48312) N on MI 53 (Van Dyke Ave), at 15 Mile Rd. 810/979-1400; FAX 810/979-0430.* 160 rms, 2-3 story. S $69-$85; D $69-$90; each addl $5; suites $135-$275; under 12 free; wkend rates. Crib free. TV; cable. Indoor pool; whirlpool. Restaurant 6-11 pm; Fri to midnight; Sat 7 am-midnight; Sun 7 am-10 pm. Rm serv. Bar from 11 am; Sat to midnight; Sun noon-10 pm. Ck-out noon. Meeting rms. Business servs avail. In-rm modem link. Valet serv. Downhill/x-country ski 18 mi. Exercise equipt; weight machine, bicycles, sauna. Refrigerators; some in-rm whirlpools, bathrm phones. Cr cds: A, C, D, DS, MC, V.

D SC

★ ★ ★ **COURTYARD BY MARRIOTT.** *30190 Van Dyke Ave (48093). 810/751-5777; FAX 810/751-4463.* 147 rms, 3 story, 14 suites, 113 kit. units. S $85; D $95; each addl $10; suites $95-$105; under 5 free; wkend rates. Crib free. TV; cable (premium), VCR avail. Indoor pool; whirlpool. Complimentary coffee in rms. Bkfst avail. Restaurant adj open 24 hrs. Ck-out 1 pm. Coin Indry. Meeting rms. In-rm modem link. Valet serv. Exercise equipt; weights, bicycle. Refrigerators in suites. Balconies. Cr cds: A, C, D, DS, MC, V.

D SC

✔★ ★ **FAIRFIELD INN BY MARRIOTT.** *7454 Convention Blvd (48092). 810/939-1700; FAX 810/939-1700, ext. 709.* 132 rms, 3 story. S, D $45-$59; each addl $7; under 18 free. Crib free. TV; cable (premium). Heated pool. Complimentary continental bkfst. Restaurant nearby. Ck-out noon. In-rm modem link. Valet serv. Cr cds: A, C, D, DS, MC, V.

D SC

★ ★ **GEORGIAN INN.** *(31327 Gratiot Ave, Roseville 48066) 13 Mile Rd at I-94. 810/294-0400; FAX 810/294-1020; res: 800/477-1466.* 111 rms, 2 story. Mid-May-mid-Sept: S, D $60-$73; each addl $5; suites $135; kit. units $81; under 12 free; lower rates rest of yr. Crib free. Pet accepted, some restrictions. TV; cable. Heated pool; poolside serv. Restaurant 6 am-11 pm. Rm serv. Bar. Ck-out noon. Coin Indry. Meeting rms. Business servs avail. In-rm modem link. Valet serv. Exercise equipt; weights, bicycle. Game rm. Cr cds: A, C, D, DS, MC, V.

SC

★ ★ **HAMPTON INN.** *7447 Convention Blvd (48092). 810/977-7270; FAX 810/977-3889.* 124 rms, 3 story. S $52-$57; D $58-$63; suites $75-$81; under 18 free; wkend rates. Crib $6. TV; cable (premium). Complimentary continental bkfst. Restaurant nearby. Ck-out noon. Meeting rms. In-rm modem link. Valet serv. X-country ski 20 mi. Refrigerator, wet bar in suites. Cr cds: A, D, DS, MC, V.

D SC

★ ★ **HOLIDAY INN EXPRESS.** *11500 Eleven Mile Rd (48089), I-696 exit Hoover Rd. 810/754-9700; FAX 810/754-0376.* 125 rms, 2 story. S, D $62; under 17 free; wkend rates. Crib free. TV; cable (premium). Pool. Complimentary continental bkfst. Restaurant adj 11 am-midnight. Ck-out noon. Meeting rms. In-rm modem link. Valet serv. Cr cds: A, C, D, DS, ER, JCB, MC, V.

D SC

★ ★ **HOMEWOOD SUITES.** *30180 N Civic Center Dr (48093). 810/558-7870; FAX 810/558-8072; res: 800/225-5466.* 76 kit. suites, 3 story. Suites $64-$139. Crib avail. Pet accepted, some restrictions; $100 refundable. TV; cable (premium), VCR. Pool; whirlpool. Complimentary continental bkfst. Complimentary coffee in rms. Restaurant nearby. Ck-out noon. Coin Indry. Meeting rms. Business center. In-rm modem link. Valet serv. Sundries. Gift shop. Downhill/x-country ski 20 mi. Exercise equipt; weight machine, bicycles. Grills. Cr cds: A, C, D, DS, MC, V.

D

✔★ **RED ROOF INN.** *26300 Dequindre Rd (48091). 810/573-4300; FAX 810/573-6157.* 136 rms, 2 story. S $32.99-$42.99; D $46.99-$53.99; 3 or more $44.99-$60.99; under 18 free; higher rates special events. Crib free. Pet accepted, some restrictions. TV; cable (premium). Complimentary coffee. Restaurant nearby. Ck-out noon. Business servs avail. In-rm modem link. Cr cds: A, C, D, DS, MC, V.

D SC

★ ★ **RESIDENCE INN BY MARRIOTT.** *30120 Civic Center Dr (48093). 810/558-8050; FAX 810/558-8214.* 133 kit. suites, 3 story. Mid-May-mid-Sept: S, D $104; under 18 free; wkly, wkend rates; lower rates rest of yr. Crib free. Pet accepted; $50 deposit & $8/day. TV; cable (premium), VCR. Pool; whirlpool. Complimentary continental bkfst. Complimentary coffee in rms. Restaurant nearby. Ck-out noon. Coin Indry. In-rm modem link. Valet serv. Exercise equipt; weight machine, bicycle. Health club privileges. Some balconies. Picnic tables. Cr cds: A, C, D, DS, ER, JCB, MC, V.

D SC

Restaurant

★ ★ **ANDIAMO ITALIA.** *7096 Fourteen Mile Rd (48092). 810/268-3200.* Hrs: 11 am-11 pm; Fri to midnight; Sat 4 pm-midnight; Sun 4-9 pm. Closed some major hols. Italian menu. Bar. Semi-a la carte: lunch $8-$14, dinner $9-$22. Specializes in pasta, gnocchi, bocconcini di vitello. Valet parking. Player piano. Cr cds: A, MC, V.

D

District of Columbia

Founded: 1790
Pop: 606,900
Elev: 1-410 feet
Time zone: Eastern
Area codes: 202 (DC); 703 (Virginia); 301 & 410 (Maryland)
Web: www.washington.org

Washington, DC, the first American city planned for a specific purpose, is perhaps the world's largest company town. The town's early history, like the government of the time, was inconspicuous. Washington was muddy or dusty, depending upon the season, insect-ridden and the object of savage jokes. There were few houses, still fewer public buildings, and the residents' social lives centered around the few saloons.

Not many people visited Washington prior to the Civil War. But in late May 1865, more than 100,000 people flocked to the capital city to witness the Grand Review of the victorious Union Army. For two days the throng watched 150,000 Union soldiers parade up Pennsylvania Avenue. Both tourists and soldiers stayed over the weekend to see the sights, doubling the city's normal population of 100,000. It was the beginning of Washington's biggest industry—tourism.

Washington underwent great expansion periods during the two World Wars, when new industry, new buildings and many thousands of new residents appeared almost overnight. When the wars ended, few of the migrants ever returned home.

Today, Washington is the center of a vast metropolitan area that encompasses the District of Columbia and areas of two states—Maryland and Virginia. Nearly 20 million tourists come to the city every year. George Washington's Federal City, once the butt of endless jokes, is indeed a thriving, vital metropolis.

Business

Washington has two major industries—government and tourism. Because government business rarely slackens, the city does not suffer from the economic fluctuations that plague many other cities. More than half a million Washingtonians work for the government. Tourism contributes approximately $4 billion in direct revenues to the local economy and accounts for nearly 60,000 jobs in the area.

Convention Facilities

The city of Washington and its immediate surroundings have a total of about 64,000 hotel and motel rooms. Conventions meet here often, and as many as 30,000 delegates have been hosted at one time. The Washington, DC Convention Center at 9th St and New York Ave NW has 3 exhibition halls, 40 meeting rooms and 381,000 square feet of exhibition space.

Sports & Entertainment

Washington has three professional sports teams—the Capitals (hockey), Wizards (basketball) and Redskins (football). The new $170-million MCI Center boasts 20,000 seats and is home to the Capitals and the newly-renamed Wizards.

The city boasts many good restaurants and nightclubs, as well as several dinner theaters. In the summer there are frequent outdoor concerts in various parts of town. First-class entertainment is presented at the John F. Kennedy Center for the Performing Arts, which contains a concert hall, opera house, movie theater, the Eisenhower Theatre for Drama and the innovative Terrace Theatre; the Grand Foyer has free performances nightly. The Arena Stage is popular among theatergoers, and the National Theater attracts numerous Broadway plays.

A concentration of jazz, blues and rock bars are located in Georgetown, near Georgetown University; Blues Alley is renowned for attracting the biggest names in jazz. Also in the college area is Georgetown Park, a three-level entertainment and shopping mall surrounding a Victorian garden.

On Pennsylvania Avenue on Capitol Hill are casual restaurants and many jazz bars and lounges. The restored beaux-arts Union Station on Massachusetts Avenue has a collection of shops, restaurants and movie theaters.

Sightseeing

Helpful information for tourists is easily available in Washington. The National Park Service maintains two information kiosks on the Mall: at the Washington Monument and at the Vietnam Veterans Memorial.

One of the best things about vacationing here is that the most interesting places usually have no admission charge. Following is a list of some of the more popular attractions.

—The Capitol, seat of Congress since 1800, where visitors watch the US government in action.

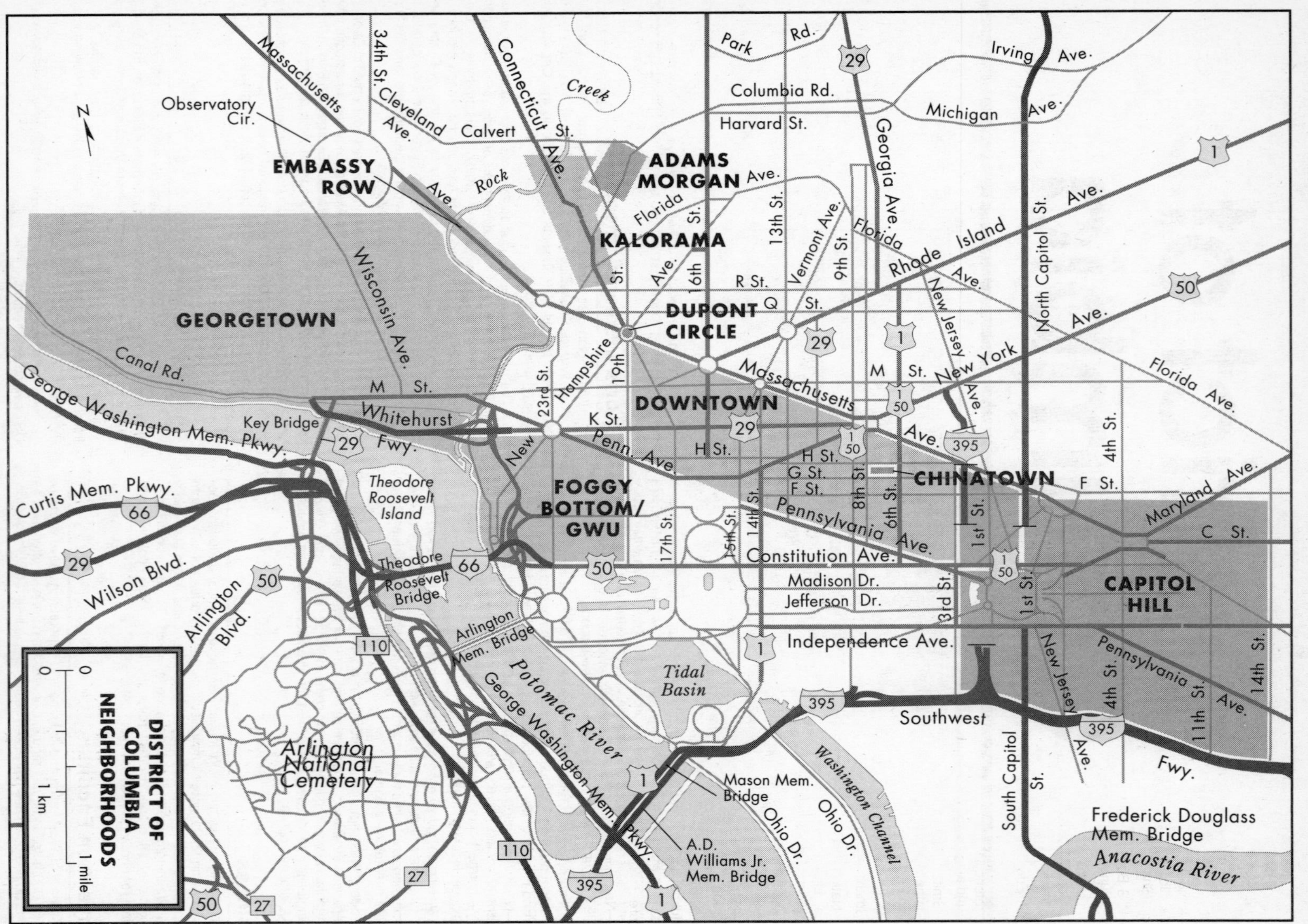
DISTRICT OF COLUMBIA NEIGHBORHOODS
0
1 mile
0
1 km
EMBASSY ROW
ADAMS MORGAN
KALORAMA
DUPONT CIRCLE
GEORGETOWN
DOWNTOWN
CHINATOWN
FOGGY BOTTOM/ GWU
CAPITOL HILL
Arlington National Cemetery
Theodore Roosevelt Island
Theodore Roosevelt Bridge
Arlington Mem. Bridge
Tidal Basin
Potomac River
Washington Channel
Anacostia River
Frederick Douglass Mem. Bridge
Mason Mem. Bridge
A.D. Williams Jr. Mem. Bridge
George Washington Mem. Pkwy.
Southwest Fwy.
Whitehurst Fwy.
Key Bridge
Canal Rd.
Curtis Mem. Pkwy.
Wilson Blvd.
Arlington Blvd.
Rock Creek
Observatory Cir.
Massachusetts Ave.
Wisconsin Ave.
Connecticut Ave.
Cleveland Ave.
Calvert St.
34th St.
Park Rd.
Columbia Rd.
Harvard St.
Irving Ave.
Michigan Ave.
Georgia Ave.
Florida Ave.
Rhode Island Ave.
New Jersey Ave.
New York Ave.
North Capitol St.
South Capitol St.
Maryland Ave.
Pennsylvania Ave.
Penn. Ave.
Constitution Ave.
Independence Ave.
Madison Dr.
Jefferson Dr.
Vermont Ave.
New Hampshire
Ohio Dr.
M St.
K St.
H St.
G St.
F St.
C St.
Q St.
R St.
1st St.
3rd St.
4th St.
6th St.
8th St.
9th St.
11th St.
13th St.
14th St.
15th St.
16th St.
17th St.
19th St.
23rd St.
1
29
50
66
110
27
395

—The Library of Congress, ornately designed, with numerous changing exhibits.

—The Supreme Court, where court cases are open to the public and often provide an exciting show. Lectures are given when court is not in session.

—Folger Shakespeare Library, North America's foremost Shakespearean library, with an Elizabethan theater, a model of the Globe Theatre and a Shakespeare first folio edition of 1623.

—US Botanic Gardens, a huge greenhouse with a waterfall and a miniature jungle.

—National Archives, where the Declaration of Independence, Bill of Rights, Constitution and other historical documents, maps and photographs are displayed.

—J. Edgar Hoover Building, FBI, fingerprint rooms and crime-detection labs.

—Interior Department, displays exhibits and dioramas depicting the history and activities of the department and its bureau.

—Smithsonian Institution Building, the "castle," an 1855 building housing the administrative offices of the institution, James Smithson's tomb and a visitors' information center.

—Arts and Industries Building, "150 Years of Collecting," also a part of the Smithsonian.

—National Air and Space Museum, houses the Wright brothers' airplane, Lindbergh's *Spirit of St Louis*, a special effects theater and Spacearium, plus hundreds of other exhibits.

—National Museum of Natural History, exhibiting the world's largest stuffed elephant, the Hope diamond and more.

—National Museum of American History, with many types of exhibits, period rooms.

—National Gallery of Art, an extensive collection of masterpieces in beautiful buildings.

—Hirshhorn Museum and Sculpture Garden, displays modern art and sculpture.

—National Museum of African Art, a branch of the Smithsonian, features traditional African sculpture and textiles.

—National Portrait Gallery, a fine building housing portraits and statues of people who have made significant contributions to the history, development and culture of the US.

—National Museum of American Art, features American art since the 18th century.

—Freer Gallery of Art, displays art of the Far East, Mid-Orient and Near East.

—Renwick Gallery, features American crafts and design.

—Anacostia Museum, a capsule museum with changing exhibits, designed to serve the neighborhood community.

—US Holocaust Memorial Museum, architecturally significant building houses exhibits depicting the many aspects of the Holocaust using genuine oral testimonies, photographs, documentary films and artifacts.

—Bureau of Engraving and Printing, where new money is made and old money is burned.

—Explorers Hall, at the headquarters of the National Geographic Society, exhibits show the society's explorations of land, sea and space.

—National Museum of Women in the Arts, displays of paintings, sculpture, and pottery by women from the Renaissance to the present.

—B'nai B'rith Klutznick Museum, houses Jewish ceremonial objects, history and art exhibits.

—Art Museum of the Americas, dedicated exclusively to Latin American and Caribbean contemporary art.

—US National Arboretum, exhibits floral displays year round. Also here is a Japanese garden and the National Bonsai Collection.

—Treasury Building, with a collection of rare money.

—White House, with free guided tours Tuesday-Saturday.

—Washington Monument, a 555-foot obelisk, finished in 1884. (Elevator ride free.)

—Lincoln Memorial, probably the nation's most impressive and inspirational shrine.

—Jefferson Memorial, an exquisite white marble building on the Tidal Basin. Japanese cherry trees surround the basin.

—Vietnam Veteran's Memorial, currently the capital's most popular attraction, includes the names of all who gave their lives in or are missing from the Vietnam War.

—Arlington National Cemetery, location of the Tomb of the Unknown Soldier and the grave of John F. Kennedy.

—Iwo Jima Statue, Marine Corps War Memorial.

—The Pentagon, the largest office building in the world, houses offices of the US Department of Defense.

—Emancipation Statue, bronze work by Thomas Ball, paid for by voluntary subscriptions from emancipated slaves.

—John F. Kennedy Center for the Performing Arts, a magnificent building filled with art treasures; tours.

—Theodore Roosevelt Island, a quiet wilderness area with a statuary garden including a likeness of Teddy, nature trails and guided hikes.

—Georgetown, a section of the city built a century before the capital was located here, lovely houses, good restaurants and many shops.

—Washington National Cathedral, begun in 1907 and completed in 1990, Gothic in style, was built completely by hand and in the manner of medieval cathedrals. The tomb of Woodrow Wilson and many memorials are here.

—Rock Creek Park, 1,754 acres within the city; trails, riding, biking, picnic groves, nature center, playing fields.

—National Zoological Park, with the only pandas in this hemisphere. (The zoo parking area requires a fee.)

—Ford's Theatre, restored to its 1865 appearance. Lincoln Museum is in the basement. Across the street is the house where Lincoln died (Petersen House).

—National Building Museum, exhibiting advances in architecture.

—National Shrine of the Immaculate Conception, largest Roman Catholic church in America and one of the largest in the world. Nearby is the Franciscan Monastery, with catacombs and gardens (some bloom at Christmastime).

—United States Navy Memorial, featuring *At Sea,* a high-tech, large-format film.

—Navy Museum, with models, documents, weapons, displays about naval history.

—Marine Corps Museum, weapons, uniforms and artifacts describe the history of the US Marine Corps, including a display on military music.

—Organization of American States, permanent secretariat of the organization is located here. The OAS was established to maintain international peace and security and to raise the social, economic, educational and cultural standards of the people of the Americas.

—Anderson House Museum, a museum of the American Revolution, with portraits by Early American artists. Books, medals, swords, silver, glass and china on display.

—Phillips Collection, one of the finest private art collections in the world.

—Frederick Douglass Home, Cedar Hill, the house where the renowned black leader lived from 1877 until his death. Another of his residences now houses the Museum of African Art.

—Old Post Office Pavilion, featuring Romanesque architecture and a 315-foot clock tower; now houses federal offices and the Pavilion, which consists of restaurants and shops around a courtyard.

—Great Falls of the Potomac, a popular attraction since Native Americans lived here.

—C & O Canal, a pleasant place for biking, hiking, canoeing, picnicking and winter ice-skating.

During the summer there are free concerts at the Capitol and at the Jefferson Memorial; during the rest of the year, concerts are performed at the National Gallery of Art and at the East Garden Court.

No visit to the Washington area would be complete without a pilgrimage to Mount Vernon and to the Alexandria landmarks that relate to George Washington's life—Gadsby's Tavern, the Stabler-Leadbeater Apothecary Shop, George Washington National Masonic Memorial and historic Christ Church.

Today's interest in restoration and preservation of historic buildings and districts would warm the heart of Ann Pamela Cunningham of South Carolina, who founded the Mount Vernon Ladies' Association in 1853. Her struggle to preserve this beautiful plantation consumed all her energies, but she won a place in history as the grandmother of the preservation movement. Mount Vernon remains for all to enjoy thanks to the dedicated efforts of Miss Cunningham, her colleagues and those who followed. It is still one of the most impressive of all historic sites.

In Georgetown, the National Park Service maintains the Old Stone House, a pre-Revolutionary landmark. Craftsmen and women in colonial dress make pomander balls and bake cookies in the kitchen fireplace and demonstrate cabinet-making, quilting and candle-dipping.

Several houses of historic and architectural interest in the city charge a nominal admission fee or request donations. Among the most interesting are the 1818 Decatur House on Lafayette Square, operated by the National Trust for Historic Preservation; Octagon House, 1798-1800, the house into which James and Dollie Madison moved after the British burned the White House in the War of 1812; the Woodrow Wilson House, former residence of the 28th president; the Christian Heurich House, an ornate Victorian mansion housing the Columbia Historical Society; Hillwood Museum, former house of Marjorie Merriweather Post, heiress to the Post Toasties fortune and collector of Russian art and antiquities; the Yellow House, one of Georgetown's oldest houses; Tudor Place, residence of one of Washington's oldest families (descendants of Martha Custis Washington) and designed by Dr. William Thornton, architect of the Capitol; and Dumbarton Oaks, a Georgetown estate with Federal-style, early 19th-century mansion, elegant collections of silver and china and spectacular terraced gardens.

Four outlying attractions operated by the National Park Service are well worth special excursions. Claude Moore Colonial Farm at Turkey Run, next to the CIA complex on the outskirts of the city near McLean, Virginia, is a working farm of the revolutionary era. Oxon Hill Farm, south of the city on the Maryland shore of the Potomac, exhibits farm animals and machinery; demonstrations of farm work are given. Fort Washington National Park in Maryland is a reconstructed outpost of the earliest defense for the city. At Wolf Trap Farm Park for the Performing Arts, in Vienna, Virginia, just 15 miles from Washington, performances of all sorts are held throughout the year. This 100-acre park of lovely rolling woodland has walking paths and picnic areas.

General References

Area codes: 202 (DC); 703 (Virginia); 301 & 410 (Maryland)

Phone Numbers

POLICE & FIRE: 911

POISON CONTROL CENTER: 625-3333

TIME: 844-1111 **WEATHER:** 936-1212

Information Sources

Washington DC Convention and Visitors Association, 1212 New York Ave NW, Suite 600, 20005; 789-7000.

Office of Recreation Info, 673-7660.

Transportation

AIRLINES: Aeroflot; Air France; American; British Airways; Continental; Delta; Lufthansa; Northwest; TWA; United; USAir; Virgin Atlantic Airways; and other commuter and regional airlines.

AIRPORTS: National, 703/419-8000; Dulles, 703/419-8000; Baltimore-Washington Intl (BWI), 410/859-7100.

CAR RENTAL AGENCIES: (See IMPORTANT TOLL-FREE NUMBERS) *National (703):* Avis 800/331-1212, Budget 920-3360, Hertz 800-654-3131; *Dulles (703):* Avis 661-3500, Budget 661-6639, Dollar 661-6630, Hertz 471-6020; *BWI (410):* Avis 859-1680, Budget 859-0850, Dollar 684-3315, Hertz 850-7400.

PUBLIC TRANSPORTATION: Metro Transit System 637-7000 or 962-1234.

RAILROAD PASSENGER SERVICE: Amtrak 800/872-7245.

Newspapers

Washington Post; Washington Times.

Convention Facility

Washington, DC Convention Center, 900 9th St NW, 789-1600.

Sports & Recreation

Major Sports Facilities

Jack Kent Cooke Stadium, in Landover, MD (Redskins, football, 703/478-8900).

MCI Center, 601 F St NW, 301/773-2255 (Wizards, basketball; Capitals, hockey).

RFK Stadium, E Capitol St & 22nd St NE (DC United, soccer, 546-2222).

Racetrack

Rosecroft Raceway, 6336 Rosecroft Dr, 8 mi SE in Oxon Hill, MD, 301/567-4000 (harness racing).

Cultural Facilities

Theaters

Arena Stage, 6th St & Maine Ave SW, 488-3300.

Carter Barron Amphitheatre, 16th St & Colorado Ave NW, 426-6837.

Ford's Theatre, 511 10th St NW, 347-4833.

John F. Kennedy Center for the Performing Arts, New Hampshire Ave at F St NW, 467-4600.

National Theatre, 1321 Pennsylvania Ave NW, 628-6161.

Concert Halls

John F. Kennedy Center for the Performing Arts, New Hampshire Ave at F St NW, 467-4600.

Wolf Trap Farm Park for the Performing Arts, 14 mi NW via Washington Memorial Pkwy, VA 123, US 7, then S on Towlston Rd (Trap Rd) (VA 676) in Vienna, VA, 703/255-1900.

Museums

Anacostia Museum (Smithsonian), 1901 Fort Place SE, 357-2700.

Anderson House, 2118 Massachusetts Ave NW, 785-2040.

Arts and Industries Building (Smithsonian), 900 Jefferson Dr SW, 357-2700.

B'nai B'rith Klutznick Museum, B'nai B'rith International Center, 1640 Rhode Island Ave NW, 857-6583.

Capital Children's Museum, 800 3rd St NE, 675-4120.

Dumbarton Oaks, 1703 32nd St NW, 339-6400.

Fondo del Sol, 2112 R St NW, 483-2777.

Hillwood Museum, 4155 Linnean Ave NW, 686-8500.

Lincoln Museum, Ford's Theatre (see Theaters).

Marine Corps Museum, Bldg 58, Navy Yard, 433-3840.

National Air and Space Museum (Smithsonian), Independence Ave & 7th St SW, 357-1686.

National Building Museum, Judiciary Square NW, 272-2448.

National Museum of American History (Smithsonian), Constitution Ave & 14th St NW, 357-2700.

National Museum of Health and Medicine, Building #54, Walter Reed Army Medical Center, Alaska Ave & 16th St NW, 782-2200.

National Museum of Natural History (Smithsonian), Constitution Ave & 10th St NW, 357-2700.

Navy Museum, Bldg 76, Navy Yard, 9th & M Sts SE, 433-4882.

Textile Museum, 2320 S St NW, 667-0441.

US Holocaust Memorial Museum, 100 Raoul Wallenberg Pl (15th St SW), 488-0400.

Washington Dolls' House and Toy Museum, 5236 44th St NW, 363-6400.

Art Museums & Galleries

Art Museum of the Americas, 201 18th St NW, 458-6016.

Corcoran Gallery of Art, 17th St & New York Ave NW, 639-1700.

Freer Gallery of Art (Smithsonian), 12th St & Jefferson Dr SW, 357-2700.

Hirshhorn Museum and Sculpture Garden (Smithsonian), Independence Ave at 8th St SW, 357-2700.

National Gallery of Art, 4th St & Constitution Ave NW, 737-4215.

National Museum of African Art (Smithsonian), 950 Independence Ave SW, 357-2700.

National Museum of American Art (Smithsonian), 8th & G Sts NW, 357-2700.

National Museum of Women in the Arts, 1250 New York Ave NW, 783-5000.

National Portrait Gallery (Smithsonian), 8th & F Sts NW, 357-2700.

Phillips Collection, 1600 & 1612 21st St NW, 387-2151.

Renwick Gallery (Smithsonian), 17th St & Pennsylvania Ave NW, 357-2700.

Points of Interest

Historical

Antietam National Battlefield Site and Cemetery, 1 mi N of Sharpsburg on MD 65.

Arlington National Cemetery, Arlington, VA, 703/979-0690.

Blair House, 1651 Pennsylvania Ave NW.

Christ Church, 118 N Washington St, Alexandria, VA, 703/549-1450.

Christian Heurich Mansion, 1307 New Hampshire Ave NW, 785-2068.

Clara Barton National Historic Site, 5801 Oxford Rd, Glen Echo, MD, 301/492-6245.

DAR Buildings, 1776 D St NW, 628-1776.

Decatur House, 748 Jackson Pl NW, 842-0920.

Emancipation Statue, Lincoln Park, E Capitol St between 11th & 13th Sts NE.

Executive Offices, Pennsylvania Ave & 17th St NW, on White House grounds.

Fort Stevens Park, Piney Branch Rd & Quackenbos St NW, 282-1063.

Frederick Douglass National Historic Site, "Cedar Hill," 1411 W St SE, 426-5961.

Gadsby's Tavern, 134 N Royal St, Alexandria, VA, 703/838-4242.

Georgetown, W of Rock Creek Park, N of K St NW.

House where Lincoln died (Petersen House), 516 10th St NW, 426-6830.

Interior Department, C & D Sts NW, between 18th & 19th Sts NW, 208-4743.

Iwo Jima Statue, Turkey Run Park, 703/285-2598.

Judiciary Square, 2 blks bounded by F, 4th & 5th Sts NW & Indiana Ave.

Manassas (Bull Run) National Battlefield Park, 26 mi SW of Washington, at jct US 211, VA 234.

Mount Vernon, 18 mi S via George Washington Memorial Pkwy.

National Archives, Constitution Ave between 7th & 9th Sts NW, 501-5000.

National Presbyterian Church & Center, 4101 Nebraska Ave NW, 537-0800.

The Octagon, 1799 New York Ave at 18th & E Sts NW, 638-3105.

Old Stone House, 3051 M St NW, 426-6851.

Pavilion at the Old Post Office, Pennsylvania Ave & 12th St NW, 289-4224.

St John's Church, 3240 O St NW, 338-1796.

Sewall-Belmont House, 144 Constitution Ave NE, 546-3989.

Stabler-Leadbeater Apothecary Shop, 105-107 S Fairfax St, Alexandria, VA, 703/836-3713.

Treasury Building, Pennsylvania Ave & 15th St NW, 622-0896.

Tudor Place, 1644 31st St NW, in Georgetown, 965-0400.

US Court of Appeals, 5th & E Sts NW.

US District Court, Indiana Ave, between 4th & 5th Sts NW, 273-0555.

Washington Monument, Mall at 15th St NW, 426-6839.

White House, 1600 Pennsylvania Ave NW, 456-7041.

Woodrow Wilson House, 2340 S St NW, 387-4062.

Yellow House, 1430 33rd St NW.

Other Attractions

American Red Cross, 3 buildings bounded by 17th, 18th, D & E Sts NW, 737-8300.

American University, 4400 Massachusetts Ave NW, 885-1000.

At Sea, US Navy Memorial (see).

Bureau of Engraving and Printing, 14th & C Sts SW, 847-3019.

C & O Canal, W of 30th St & S of M St.

Catholic University of America, 620 Michigan Ave NE, 319-5000.

Chinatown, G & H Sts, between 6th & 8th Sts NW.

Claude Moore Colonial Farm at Turkey Run, McLean, VA, 703/442-7557.

Department of Commerce, Pennsylvania Ave between 14th & 15th Sts NW.

Department of Justice, Pennsylvania Ave, between 9th & 10th Sts NW.

Explorers Hall, 17th & M Sts NW, 857-7588.

Federal Reserve Building, C St between 20th & 21st Sts NW.

Federal Trade Commission, 6th St & Pennsylvania Ave NW, 326-2222.

Folger Shakespeare Library, 201 E Capitol St SE, 544-4600.

Fort Dupont Park, Randle Circle & Minnesota Ave S, 426-7723.

Fort Washington National Park, 4 mi S on MD 210, 3½ mi on Fort Washington Rd, in Fort Washington, MD, 301/763-4600.

Georgetown University, 37th & O Sts NW, 687-3600.

George Washington Masonic National Memorial, 101 Callahan Dr, Alexandria, VA, 703/683-2007.

George Washington University, 19th-24th Sts NW, F St-Pennsylvania Ave, 994-6460.

Government Printing Office, N Capitol between G & H Sts.

House Office Buildings, along Independence Ave, S side of Capitol grounds at Independence & New Jersey Aves.

Howard University, 2400 6th St NW between W & Harvard Sts NW, 806-0970.

Internal Revenue Building, Constitution Ave between 10th & 12th Sts NW.

Interstate Commerce Commission, Constitution Ave & 12th St NW.

Islamic Center, 2551 Massachusetts Ave NW, 332-8343.

J. Edgar Hoover Building, Pennslyvannia Ave between 9th & 10th Sts NW, 324-3447.

Jefferson Memorial, S edge of Tidal Basin.

Labor Department, 200 Constitution Ave NW, at 3rd St, 219-5000.

Lafayette Square, Pennsylvania Ave opp White House.

Library of Congress, 10 1st St SE, 707-8000.

Lincoln Memorial, W Potomac Park at 23rd St NW.

National Academy of Sciences, 2101 Constitution Ave between 21st & 22nd Sts NW, 334-2436.

National Aquarium, US Department of Commerce Building, 14th St & Constitution Ave NW, 482-2826.

National Colonial Farm, 20 mi S via I-495 exit 3A to MD 210, 10 mi right on Bryan Point Rd, 4 mi on Potomac River, 301/283-2113.

National Shrine of the Immaculate Conception, 4th St & Michigan Ave NE, 526-8300.

National Zoological Park (Smithsonian), in Rock Creek Park, 3000 blk of Connecticut Ave NW, 673-4800.

New York Ave Presbyterian Church, 1313 New York Ave at H St NW, 393-3700.

Organization of American States, Constitution Ave & 17th St NW, 458-3000.

Oxon Hill Farm, just W of jct MD 210 & I-95 in Oxon Hill, MD, 301/839-1177.

Potomac Park, N & S of Jefferson Memorial & Tidal Basin.

Rock Creek Park, NW on Beach Dr.

Senate Office Buildings, Constitution Ave, on both sides of 1st St NE.

Smithsonian Institution, The Mall & nearby, 357-2700.

Smithsonian Institution Building (the "Castle"), 900 Jefferson Dr SW, 357-2700.

State Department Building, 21st, 22nd, C & D Sts NW.

Supreme Court Building, Maryland Ave & 1st St NE, 479-3211.

Theodore Roosevelt Memorial, N end of Theodore Roosevelt Island, 703/285-2598.

US Botanic Gardens, Maryland Ave & 1st St SW, SW corner of Capitol grounds, 225-8333.

US Capitol, 1st & East Capitol Sts, 225-6827.

US National Arboretum, 3501 New York Ave NE, 544-8733.

US Naval Observatory, 3450 Massachusetts Ave NW, 653-1507.

US Navy Memorial, Pennsylvania Ave at 7th & 9th Sts NW, 737-2300.

US Postal Service, 475 L'Enfant Plaza West SW.

Vietnam Veterans Memorial, Constitution Ave between Henry Bacon Dr & 21st St NW, 634-1568.

Voice of America, 330 Independence Ave SW, between 3rd & 4th Sts SW, 619-3919.

Washington National Cathedral, Massachusetts & Wisconsin Aves NW, 537-6200.

Sightseeing Tours

Gray Line bus tours, 5500 Tuxedo Rd, Tuxedo, MD 20781; 301/386-8300.

Spirit of Washington* and *Mt Vernon, Pier 4, 554-8000.

Tourmobile Sightseeing, 1000 Ohio Dr SW, 20024; 554-7950.

Annual Events

Cherry Blossom Festival, The Mall. Late Mar-early Apr.

Georgetown House Tour, 338-1796. Late Apr.

Georgetown Garden Tour, 333-4953. Late Apr-early May.

Goodwill Industries Embassy Tour, 636-4225. 2nd Sat May.

Memorial Day Ceremony at Tomb of the Unknown Soldier, Arlington National Cemetery, VA.

July 4 Celebration, Washington Monument & Capitol W steps.

Pageant of Peace, Ellipse, S of White House. Dec.

City Neighborhoods

Many of the restaurants, unrated dining establishments, and some lodgings listed under Washington include neighborhoods as well as exact street addresses. Geographic descriptions of these areas are given, followed by a table of restaurants arranged by neighborhood.

Adams Morgan: North of Dupont Circle; along Columbia Rd between 18th St NW and Kalorama, NW/Kalorama Park.

Capitol Hill: Both the Hill upon which the Capitol is built (south of Constitution Ave, west of 1st St NE & SE, north of Independence Ave and east of 1st St NW & SW) and the surrounding historic neighborhood south of F St NW & NE, west of 14th St NE & SE, north of the Southwest Frwy (I-395) and east of 3rd St NW & SW.

Chinatown: Area of Downtown along G and H Sts NW between 6th and 8th Sts NW.

Downtown: South of Massachusetts Ave, west of N Capitol St, north of Pennsylvania Ave and east of 19th St. **North of Downtown:** North of Massachusetts Ave. **South of Downtown:** South of Independence Ave. **West of Downtown:** West of 19th St.

Dupont Circle: On and around the circle where Massachusetts, New Hampshire, Connecticut Aves and 19th and P Sts NW intersect.

Embassy Row: Area north of Dupont Circle; along Massachusetts Ave between Observatory Circle on the north and Sheridan Circle on the south.

Foggy Bottom: Area along the Potomac River south of K St NW (US 29), west of 19th St NW and north of Constitution Ave and I-66 interchange.

Georgetown: Northwest of Downtown; south of the Naval Observatory and W St NW, west of Rock Creek Park and north and east of the Potomac River; area around intersection of Wisconsin Ave and M St NW.

Kalorama: East and west of Connecticut Ave NW, south of Rock Creek Park and Calvert St, west of Columbia Rd and north of R St.

Lodgings and Food

DISTRICT OF COLUMBIA RESTAURANTS BY NEIGHBORHOOD AREAS

(For full description, see alphabetical listings under Restaurants)

ADAMS MORGAN

Cities. 2424 18th St NW
The Grill From Ipanema. 1858 Columbia Rd NW
I Matti Trattoria. 2436 18th St NW
La Fourchette. 2429 18th St NW
Meskerem. 2434 18th St NW
Miss Saigon. 1847 Columbia Rd NW
Saigonnais. 2307 18th St NW

CAPITOL HILL

The Capitol Grill. 601 Pennsylvania Ave
La Colline. 400 N Capitol St NW
Monocle On Capitol Hill. 107 D Street NE
Two Quail. 320 Massachusetts Ave NE

CHINATOWN

Burma. 740 6th St NW
Hunan Chinatown. 624 H Street NW
Mr. Yung's. 740 6th St NW
Tony Cheng's Mongolian Barbecue. 619 H Street NW

DOWNTOWN

701. 701 Pennsylvania Ave NW
Bice. 601 Pennsylvania Ave NW (entrance on Indiana Ave)
Bombay Club. 815 Connecticut Ave NW
Bombay Palace. 2020 K St NW
Cafe Mozart. 1331 H Street NW
Coco Loco. 810 7th St NW
Georgia Brown's. 950 15th St NW
Gerard's Place. 915 15th St NW
Haad Thai. 1100 New York Ave NW
Jaleo. 480 7th St NW
The Jefferson (Jefferson Hotel). 16th & M Sts
La Fonda. 1639 R Street NW
Lafayette (Hay-Adams Hotel). 800 16th St NW
Les Halles. 1201 Pennsylvania Ave NW
Luigino. 1100 New York Ave NW
Maison Blanche/Rive Gauche. 1725 F Street NW
Notte Luna. 809 15th St NW
Occidental Grill. 1475 Pennsylvania Ave NW
Old Ebbitt Grill. 675 15th St NW
The Oval Room. 800 Connecticut Ave
Prime Rib. 2020 K Street NW
Primi Piatti. 2013 I Street NW
Red Sage. 605 14th St NW
Sichuan Pavilion. 1820 K Street NW
Star Of Siam. 1136 19th St NW
Taberna Del Alabardero. 1776 I Street NW
Thai Kingdom. 2021 K Street NW
Willard Room (Willard Inter-Continental Hotel). 1401 Pennsylvania Ave NW

NORTH OF DOWNTOWN

Armand's Chicago Pizzeria. 4231 Wisconsin Ave NW
Fio's. 3636 16th St
Guapo's. 4515 Wisconsin Ave NW
Krupin's. 4620 Wisconsin Ave NW
Lavandou. 3321 Connecticut Ave NW
Le Caprice. 2348 Wisconsin Ave NW
Lebanese Taverna. 2641 Connecticut Ave NW
Murphy's Of D.C. 2609 24th St NW,
New Heights. 2317 Calvert St NW
Old Europe Restaurant & Rathskeller. 2434 Wisconsin Ave NW
Petitto's Ristorante D'italia. 2653 Connecticut Ave NW
Saigon Gourmet. 2635 Connecticut Ave NW
Sushi Ko. 2309 Wisconsin Ave NW
Thai Taste. 2606 Connecticut Ave NW

SOUTH OF DOWNTOWN

Hogate's. 9th St & Maine Ave SW
Market Inn. 200 E Street SW
Phillips Flagship. 900 Water St SW

WEST OF DOWNTOWN

Melrose (Park Hyatt Hotel). 24th & M Street NW
Provence. 2401 Pennsylvania Ave NW

DUPONT CIRCLE

Alekos. 1732 Connecticut Ave NW
Anna Maria's. 1737 Connecticut Ave
Bacchus. 1827 Jefferson Place NW
Be Du Ci. 2100 P St NW
Bua. 1635 P Street NW
C.F. Folks. 1225 19th St NW
Cafe Petitto. 1724 Connecticut Ave NW
Gabriel (Radisson Barcelo Hotel). 2121 P St NW
Il Radicchio. 1509 17th St NW
Kramerbooks & Afterwords. 1517 Connecticut Ave
Lauriol Plaza. 1801 18th St NW
Nora. 2132 Florida Ave NW
Obelisk. 2029 P Street NW
Palm. 1225 19th St NW
Pesce. 2016 P St NW
Pizzeria Paradiso. 2029 P Street NW
Sam & Harry's. 1200 19th St NW
Vidalia. 1990 M St NW
Vincenzo Al Sole. 1606 20th St NW

EMBASSY ROW

Jockey Club (The Ritz-Carlton Hotel). 2100 Massachusetts Ave NW

FOGGY BOTTOM

Galileo. 1110 21st St NW
Kinkead's. 2000 Pennsylvania Ave NW
Roof Terrace. 2700 F Street NW
Sholl's Colonial Cafeteria. 1990 K Street NW

GEORGETOWN

1789. 1226 36th St NW
Aditi. 3299 M Street NW
Austin Grill. 2404 Wisconsin Ave NW
Billy Martin's Tavern. 1264 Wisconsin Ave NW
Bistro Francais. 3128 M Street NW
Bistrot Lepic. 1736 Wisconsin Ave NW
Busara. 2340 Wisconsin Ave NW
Cafe Milano. 3251 Prospect St NW
Citronelle (The Latham Hotel). 3000 M St NW
Clyde's. 3236 M St NW
El Caribe. 3288 M Street
Filomena Ristorante. 1063 Wisconsin Ave NW
Garrett's. 3003 M Street NW
Germaine's. 2400 Wisconsin Ave NW
Guards. 2915 M Street NW
J Paul's. 3218 M Street NW
La Chaumière. 2813 M Street NW
Las Pampas. 3291 M Street NW
Morton's Of Chicago. 3251 Prospect St NW
Mr. Smith's. 3104 M Street NW
Music City Roadhouse. 1050 30th St NW
Nathans. 3150 M Street NW
Paolo's. 1303 Wisconsin Ave NW
Patisserie-Cafe Didier. 3206 Grace St NW
River Club. 3223 K Street NW
Sarinah Satay House. 1338 Wisconsin Ave NW
Sea Catch. 1054 31st St NW
Seasons (Four Seasons Hotel). 2800 Pennsylvania Ave NW

Sequoia. 3000 K Street NW
The Tombs. 1226 36th St NW
Tony And Joe's. 3000 K Street NW
Zed's Ethiopian. 3318 M St NW

Note: *When a listing is located in a town that does not have its own city heading, it will appear under the city nearest to its location. In these cases, the address and town appear in parentheses immediately following the name of the establishment.*

Motor Hotels

★ ★ **CHANNEL INN.** *650 Water St SW (20024) on waterfront, south of downtown. 202/554-2400; FAX 202/863-1164; res: 800/368-5668.* Web www.channelinn.com. 100 rms, 3 story. S, D $115-$145; each addl $10; suites $145-$175; under 13 free; wkend rates. Crib free. TV; cable (premium). Pool; lifeguard. Restaurant 7 am-11 pm; Sun to 9 pm. Rm serv. Bar 11:30-1 am; Fri, Sat to 2 am; Sun to 10 pm; entertainment. Ck-out noon. Meeting rms. In-rm modem link. Bellhops. Garage parking. Health club privileges. Balconies. Near piers. Cr cds: A, C, D, DS, JCB, MC, V.

D SC

✔★ ★ **HOWARD JOHNSON PREMIER HOTEL.** *2601 Virginia Ave NW (20037) in Foggy Bottom. 202/965-2700; FAX 202/337-5417.* 192 rms, 8 story. Mid-Mar-Oct: S, D $89-$159; each addl $10; under 18 free; lower rates rest of yr. Crib free. TV; cable (premium). Rooftop pool; lifeguard (Memorial Day-Labor Day). Restaurant 6 am-11 pm. Fri, Sat 24 hrs. Ck-out noon. Coin Indry. Meeting rm. Business servs avail. In-rm modem link. Gift shop. Exercise equipt; rower, treadmill. Refrigerators. Some balconies. Cr cds: A, C, D, DS, JCB, MC, V.

D SC

★ **WINDSOR PARK.** *2116 Kalorama Rd NW (20008) off Connecticut Ave & 21st St, in Kalorama. 202/483-7700; FAX 202/332-4547; res: 800/247-3064.* 43 rms, 5 story, 6 suites. S $88-$98; D $98-$108; each addl $10; suites $125-$155; under 16 free; wkend rates (2-day min). TV; cable (premium). Complimentary continental bkfst. Restaurant nearby. Ck-out noon. Business servs avail. Refrigerators. Cr cds: A, C, D, DS, MC, V.

SC

Hotels

★ ★ ★ **ANA.** *2401 M St NW (20037), west of downtown. 202/429-2400; FAX 202/457-5010; res: 800/262-4683.* 415 rms, 10 story. S, D $280-$310; each addl $30; suites $695-$1,650; under 18 free; wkend, summer rates. Crib free. Covered parking; valet $19. Pet accepted, some restrictions. TV; cable (premium), VCR avail. Indoor pool; whirlpool. Restaurant 6:30 am-11 pm. Rm serv 24 hrs. Bar 4 pm-midnight; entertainment. Ck-out 1 pm. Convention facilities. Business center. In-rm modem link. Concierge. Gift shop. Local shopping transportation. Exercise rm; instructor, weight machines, bicycles, sauna, steam rm. Massage. Squash, racquetball courts. Bathrm phones, refrigerators, minibars. Some balconies. Luxury level. Cr cds: A, C, D, DS, JCB, MC, V.

D SC

★ ★ **THE CANTERBURY.** *1733 N St NW (20036), downtown, off Dupont Circle. 202/393-3000; FAX 202/785-9581; res: 800/424-2950.* 99 kit. units, 10 story. S $140-$195; D $160-$215; each addl $20; under 12 free; wkend plans. Crib free. Garage $13. TV; cable (premium), VCR avail. Complimentary continental bkfst. Complimentary coffee in rms. Restaurant 7 am-2:30 pm, 5-10 pm. wkend hrs vary. Bar 5-10 pm. Ck-out noon. Meeting rms. Business servs avail. In-rm modem link. Health club privileges. Refrigerators, microwaves. On site of "Little White House," where Theodore Roosevelt lived during his vice-presidency and first weeks of his presidency. Cr cds: A, C, D, DS, JCB, MC, V.

SC

★ ★ ★ **THE CAPITAL HILTON.** *16th & K St NW (20036), downtown. 202/393-1000; FAX 202/639-5784.* Web www.hilton.com. 544 rms, 15 story. S $195-$275; D $220-$300; each addl $25; suites $495-$1,100; family, wkend rates; package plans. Crib free. TV; cable (premium). Restaurants 6:30 am-midnight (also see FRAN O'BRIEN'S). Rm serv 24 hrs. Bar 11-2 am; entertainment Tues-Sat. Ck-out noon. Convention facilities. Business center. In-rm modem link. Concierge. Shopping arcade. Barber, beauty shop. Valet parking 24 hrs. Exercise equipt; weights, bicycles, sauna. Minibars; many wet bars; some refrigerators. Luxury level. Cr cds: A, C, D, DS, JCB, MC, V.

D SC

★ **CAPITOL HILL SUITES.** *200 C St SE (20003), on Capitol Hill. 202/543-6000; FAX 202/547-2608; res: 800/424-9165.* 152 kit rms, 5 story. Feb-June: S $139; D $149; each addl $20; suites $169; under 18 free; lower rates rest of yr. Crib free. Valet parking $12. TV; cable (premium), VCR avail. Complimentary continental bkfst. Coffee in rms. Restaurant nearby. Ck-out noon. Meeting rms. Business servs avail. Valet serv. Health club privileges. Refrigerators. Cr cds: A, D, DS, MC, V.

SC

★ ★ ★ **THE CARLTON.** *923 16th St NW (20006), downtown. 202/638-2626; FAX 202/638-4231.* Web www.sheraton.com. 192 rms, 8 story. S $260-$310; D $285-$350; each addl $25; suites $550-$2,100; under 18 free; wkend rates. Crib free. Pet accepted, some restrictions. Covered valet parking $22. TV; cable (premium), VCR avail. Pool privileges. Restaurant (see LESPINASSE). Afternoon tea 3-5:30 pm. Rm serv 24 hrs. Bar. Ck-out 1 pm. Meeting rms. Business servs avail. In-rm modem link. Concierge. Gift shop. Tennis privileges. Exercise equipt; bicycles, treadmill. Health club privileges. Bathrm phones, refrigerators, minibars; microwaves avail. Italian Renaissance mansion with courtyard terrace. Cr cds: A, C, D, DS, ER, JCB, MC, V.

D SC

★ ★ ★ **COURTYARD BY MARRIOTT.** *1900 Connecticut Ave NW (20009), in Kalorama. 202/332-9300; FAX 202/328-7039; res: 800/842-4211.* 147 rms, 9 story. S $69-$170; D $69-$200; each addl $15; under 18 free; wkend rates (2-day min). Crib free. Garage parking, valet $10. TV; cable (premium), VCR avail. Pool; lifeguard. Coffee in rms. Restaurant 7-10:30 am, 5-10 pm. Bar 5-11 pm. Ck-out noon. Coin Indry. Meeting rms. Business servs avail. In-rm modem link. Exercise equipt; treadmill, stair machine. Some minibars. Cr cds: A, C, D, DS, MC, V.

D SC

✔★ **DAYS PREMIER-CONVENTION CENTER.** *1201 K St NW (20005), downtown. 202/842-1020; FAX 202/289-0336.* E-mail 10545. 2452@compuserve.com. 219 rms, 9 story. Mar-May, Aug-Oct: S, D $75-$175; each addl $10; family, wkend rates; higher rates Cherry Blossom Festival; lower rates rest of yr. Crib free. Garage $12. Pet accepted, some restrictions. TV; cable (premium). Pool; lifeguard. Restaurant 7 am-10 pm; Sat, Sun 7-10:30 am, 5-10 pm. Bar. Ck-out noon. Coin Indry. Meeting rms. Business servs avail. In-rm modem link. Sundries. Exercise equipt; weight machines, treadmill. Microwaves avail. Cr cds: A, C, D, DS, JCB, MC, V.

D SC

★ **DOUBLETREE GUEST SUITES.** *2500 Pennsylvania Ave NW (20037), in Foggy Bottom. 202/333-8060; FAX 202/338-3818.* Web www.doubletree.com. 123 kit. suites, 10 story. S $109-$169; D $109-$184; each addl $15; under 18 free. Crib free. Pet accepted; $12/day. Garage $15. TV; cable (premium). Coffee in rms. Restaurant adj 11 am-midnight. Ck-out noon. Business servs avail. In-rm modem link. Health club privileges. Microwaves. Cr cds: A, C, D, DS, MC, V.

SC

★ ★ ★ **DOUBLETREE PARK TERRACE.** *1515 Rhode Island Ave NW (20005), in Embassy Row area. 202/232-7000; FAX 202/332-7152.* Web www.doubletreehotels.com. 220 rms, 8 story, 40 suites. S $155-$175; D $175-$195; each addl $20; suites $185-$225; higher rates Apr-June, Sept-mid Nov; under 16 free. Crib free. Valet parking $12.50. TV; cable (premium). Pool privileges. Complimentary coffee in rms. Restaurant 6 am-11 pm. Rm serv 24 hrs. Bar from 4 pm. Ck-out noon. Coin Indry. Meeting rms. Business servs avail. In-rm modem link. Gift shop. Exercise equipt; weight machine, treadmill. Health club privileges. Minibars; microwaves avail. Cr cds: A, C, D, DS, JCB, MC, V.

D SC

★ **DUPONT PLAZA.** *1500 New Hampshire Ave NW (20036), in Dupont Circle area. 202/483-6000; FAX 202/328-3265; res: 800/841-0003.* 314 rms, 8 story. S $155-$205; D $175-$215; each addl $20; suites $205-$385; under 18 free; wkend rates. Crib free. Garage $15; valet parking. TV; cable (premium). Coffee in rms. Restaurant 6:30 am-11 pm; Fri, Sat to midnight. Bar 11-1 am. Ck-out 1 pm. Meeting rms. Business servs avail. In-rm modem link. Health club privileges. Bathrm phones, refrigerators, wet bars. Cr cds: A, C, D, DS, MC, V.

D SC

★ ★ ★ **EMBASSY SQUARE SUITES.** *2000 N St NW (20036), in Dupont Circle area. 202/659-9000; FAX 202/429-9546; res: 800/424-2999.* E-mail emsgreserv@staydc.com; web www.staydc.com. 265 units, 10 story, 127 suites. Mar-mid-June, mid-Sept-mid-Nov: S $139-$250; D $159-$279; each addl $20; under 18 free; wkly, wkend rates; lower rates rest of yr. Crib free. Garage $12. TV; cable (premium). Pool; lifeguard. Complimentary continental bkfst; afternoon refreshments. Ck-out noon. Coin Indry. Meeting rms. Business servs avail. In-rm modem link. Exercise equipt; bicycles, stair machine. Health club privileges. Microwaves. Some balconies. Cr cds: A, C, D, DS, ER, JCB, MC, V.

D SC

★ ★ **EMBASSY SUITES.** *1250 22nd St NW (20037), west of downtown. 202/857-3388; FAX 202/293-3173.* Web www.embassydc.com. 318 suites, 9 story. S $159-$219; D $179-$239; each addl $20; 2-bedrm suites $500-$900; under 16 free; wkend rates. Crib free. Parking avail. TV; cable (premium). Indoor pool; whirlpool, lifeguard. Complimentary full bkfst. Complimentary coffee in rms. Restaurant 11 am-11 pm. Bar. Ck-out noon. Meeting rms. Business center. In-rm modem link. Concierge. Exercise equipt; weight machine, bicycles, sauna. Health club privileges. Game rm. Refrigerators, microwaves, wet bars. Cr cds: A, C, D, DS, JCB, MC, V.

D SC

★ ★ **EMBASSY SUITES CHEVY CHASE PAVILION.** *4300 Military Rd NW (20015), north of downtown. 202/362-9300; FAX 202/686-3405.* Web www.embassy-suites.com. 198 suites, 8 story. Mar-Oct: S, D $160-$200; each addl $15; wkend rates; lower rates rest of yr. Crib avail. Garage $10. TV; cable (premium). Indoor pool. Complimentary full bkfst. Complimentary coffee in rms. Rm serv 11:30 am-10 pm. Ck-out noon. Coin Indry. Meeting rms. Business servs avail. Exercise rm; instructor, weights, stair machines. Refrigerators, microwaves, wet bars. Atrium. Connected to shopping center. Cr cds: A, C, D, DS, MC, V.

D SC

★ ★ ★ ★ **FOUR SEASONS.** *2800 Pennsylvania Ave NW (20007), in Georgetown. 202/342-0444; FAX 202/944-2076.* E-mail seasons@erols.com; web www.fshr.com. This highly efficient, midsize hotel on the edge of Georgetown has a strong dedication to guest service. Rooms, some of which have park views, are comfortably furnished and well-lighted. 196 rms, 6 story. S $320-$365; D $350-$395; each addl $30; suites $750-$2,400; under 18 free; wkend rates. Crib free. Pet accepted. Valet parking $22. TV; cable (premium), VCR avail (movies). Indoor pool. Restaurant 7-2 am (also see SEASONS). Rm serv 24 hrs. Afternoon tea. Bar from 11 am. Ck-out noon. Meeting rms. Business center. In-rm modem link. Concierge. Exercise rm; instructor, weight machine, bicycles, steam rm. Spa. Bathrm phones, minibars; microwaves avail. Some balconies. Cr cds: A, C, D, ER, JCB, MC, V.

D

★ **GEORGETOWN DUTCH INN.** *1075 Thomas Jefferson St NW (20007), in Georgetown. 202/337-0900; FAX 202/333-6526; res: 800/388-2410.* 47 kit. suites, 7 story. Feb-mid-June, Sept-mid-Nov: S $135-$165; D $145-$180; each addl $20; suites $250-$350; under 16 free; wkly, monthly rates; higher rates Cherry Blossom season; lower rates rest of yr. Crib free. TV; cable (premium). Complimentary continental bkfst. Ck-out noon. Business servs avail. In-rm modem link. Limited free covered parking. Health club privileges. Bathrm phones. Cr cds: A, C, D, MC, V.

SC

★ ★ **GEORGETOWN INN.** *1310 Wisconsin Ave NW (20007), in Georgetown. 202/333-8900; FAX 202/625-1744; res: 800/424-2979.* 96 rms, 6 story, 10 suites. S, D $195-$225; each addl $20; suites $275-$325; under 13 free; wkend, hol rates. Crib free. Valet parking $15. TV; cable (premium), VCR avail. Restaurant 6:30 am-2 pm, 5-11 pm. Bar 11-1 am. Ck-out noon. Meeting rms. Business servs avail. In-rm modem link. Exercise equipt; treadmill, stair machine. Refrigerators avail. Cr cds: A, C, D, DS, JCB, MC, V.

D SC

★ **GOVERNOR'S HOUSE.** *1615 Rhode Island Ave (20036), at 17th Street NW & Scott Circle, downtown. 202/296-2100; FAX 202/331-0227; res: 800/821-4367.* 149 units, 9 story, 24 kits. Mar-June, Sept-Oct: S $125-$195; D $140-$210; each addl $15; suites $175-$225; kit. units $145-$155; under 16 free; wkend, monthly rates; higher rates Cherry Blossom Festival; lower rates rest of yr. Crib free. Valet parking $14. TV; cable (premium). Pool; lifeguard. Restaurant 7 am-midnight. Bar from 11:30 am. Ck-out noon. Meeting rms. Business servs avail. In-rm modem link. Exercise equipt; weight machine, treadmill. Health club privileges. Microwaves avail. On original site of Governor of Pennsylvania's house. Cr cds: A, C, D, DS, JCB, MC, V.

D SC

★ ★ ★ **GRAND HYATT WASHINGTON.** *1000 H St NW (20001), opp Washington Convention Center, downtown. 202/582-1234; FAX 202/637-4781.* Web www.travelweb.com/hyatt.html. 888 rms, 12 story. S $199-$239, D $224-$264; each addl $25; suites $425-$1,500; under 18 free; wkend rates. Crib free. Garage in/out $12. TV; cable (premium), VCR avail. Indoor pool; whirlpool. Restaurant 6:30-1 am. Bar; entertainment. Ck-out noon. Convention facilities. Business center. In-rm modem link. Gift shop. Exercise rm; instructor, weights, bicycles, steam rm, sauna. Minibars. 12-story atrium lobby; 3-story cascading waterfall. Luxury level. Cr cds: A, C, D, DS, JCB, MC, V.

D SC

★ ★ **HAMPSHIRE.** *1310 New Hampshire Ave NW (20036), at N & 20th St, in Dupont Circle area. 202/296-7600; FAX 202/293-2476; res: 800/368-5691.* Web www.expedia.msn.com. 82 rms, 10 story. Mid-Mar-June, early Sept-mid-Nov: S $189; D $209; each addl $20; under 12 free; wkend, monthly rates; lower rates rest of yr. Crib free. Valet parking $12. TV; cable (premium). Complimentary coffee in rms. Restaurant 7 am-10 pm. Bar. Ck-out noon. Meeting rms. Business center. In-rm modem link. Health club privileges. Refrigerators, microwaves, minibars. Some balconies. Cr cds: A, C, D, DS, JCB, MC, V.

SC

★ ★ ★ **HAY-ADAMS.** *800 16th St NW (20006), opp White House, downtown. 202/638-6600; FAX 202/638-2716; res: 800/424-5054.* 143 rms, 8 story. S, D $275-$475; each addl $30; suites $550-$2,250; under 13 free; wkend rates. Pet accepted, some restrictions. TV; cable (premium). Restaurant (see LAFAYETTE). Rm serv 24 hrs. Bar 4:30 pm-midnight; Fri, Sat to 1 am. Ck-out noon. Business servs avail. In-rm modem link. Meeting rms. Concierge. Valet parking $20. Health club privileges. Bathrm phones; some refrigerators, minibars, fireplaces; microwaves avail. Some balconies. Cr cds: A, C, D, ER, JCB, MC, V.

★ ★ ★ **HENLEY PARK.** *926 Massachusetts Ave NW (20001), 1 blk from Washington Convention Center, downtown. 202/638-5200; FAX 202/638-6740; res: 800/222-8474.* 96 rms, 8 story. Mar-May, Oct-Nov: S $165-$235; D $185-$255; each addl $20; suites $295-$875; under 16 free; wkend rates; lower rates rest of yr. Crib free. Valet parking $16. TV; cable (premium). Restaurant 7-10:30 am, 11:30 am-2 pm, 6-10 pm. Rm serv 24 hrs. Bar 11-12:30 am; entertainment. Ck-out noon. Meeting rms. Business servs avail. In-rm modem link. Health club privileges. Bathrm phones, refrigerators, minibars. Wet bar in suites. Tudor detailing; 1918 structure. Cr cds: A, C, D, DS, MC, V.

SC

★ ★ **HILTON-EMBASSY ROW.** *2015 Massachusetts Ave (20036), in Embassy Row. 202/265-1600.* 195 rms, 9 story. Mar-mid-June, Sept-mid-Nov: S $195-$235; D $215-$255; each addl $20; suites $350-$500; under 17 free; family, wkend, wkly, hol rates; higher rates special events; lower rates rest of yr. Crib free. Valet parking $14. TV; cable (premium), VCR avail. Complimentary coffee in rms. Restaurant 6:30 am-11 pm. Rm serv 24 hrs. Bar 11:30-1 am; entertainment. Ck-out noon. Meeting rms. Business center. In-rm modem link. Concierge. Free guest Indry. Exercise equipt; bicycles, treadmills. Pool; poolside serv, lifeguard. Many bathrm phones; some refrigerators, microwaves, wet bars. Cr cds: A, C, D, DS, MC, V.

D SC

★ **HOLIDAY INN GEORGETOWN.** *2101 Wisconsin Ave NW (20007), in Georgetown. 202/338-4600; FAX 202/333-6113.* 296 rms, 7 story. S $110-$140; D $120-$149; each addl $10; suites $175; under 18 free. Crib free. Parking in/out $10. TV; cable (premium). Pool; lifeguard. Restaurant 6:30 am-2 pm; 5-10 pm. Bar 4-11 pm. Ck-out noon. Coin Indry. Meeting rms. Business servs avail. In-rm modem link. Gift shop. Exercise equipt; weight machine, treadmill. Refrigerators avail. Cr cds: A, C, D, DS, JCB, MC, V.

D SC

✔★ ★ **HOLIDAY INN ON THE HILL.** *415 New Jersey Ave NW (20001), on Capitol Hill. 202/638-1616; FAX 202/638-0707.* 342 rms, 10 story. Feb-May, Sept-Nov: S, D $99-$169; each addl $10; suites $198-$475; under 18 free; wkend rates; lower rates rest of yr. Crib free. Pet accepted, some restrictions. TV; cable (premium). Rooftop pool; poolside serv, lifeguard. Supervised evening child's activities (Memorial Day-Labor Day); ages 4-14. Restaurant 6:30 am-midnight. Bar 11-2 am. Ck-out noon. Business servs avail. In-rm modem link. Sundries. Covered parking. Exercise equipt; bicycles, stair machine. Cr cds: A, C, D, DS, JCB, MC, V.

D SC

★ ★ **HOLIDAY INN-CAPITOL.** *550 C St SW (20024), 2 blks from Mall museums, south of downtown. 202/479-4000; FAX 202/479-4353.* 529 rms, 9 story. S, D $160; suites $209-$289; under 18 free; wkend packages. Crib free. Garage $10. TV; cable (premium), Pool; lifeguard. Restaurant 6 am-10 pm. Bar 11-1 am. Ck-out noon. Coin Indry. Convention facilities. Business servs avail. In-rm modem link. Exercise equipt; bicycles, treadmill. Microwaves avail. Cr cds: A, C, D, DS, JCB, MC, V.

D SC

✔★ ★ **HOLIDAY INN-CENTRAL.** *1501 Rhode Island Ave NW (20005), north of downtown. 202/483-2000; FAX 202/797-1078.* E-mail holiday@inn-dc.com; web www.inn-dc.com. 213 rms, 10 story. Apr-May & Oct: S, D $89-$149; family, wkly, wkend rates; lower rates rest of yr. Crib free. Covered parking $10. TV; cable (premium). Pool; lifeguard. Coffee in lobby. Restaurant 6:30 am-5 pm. Rm serv to 10 pm. Bar to 10 pm. Ck-out noon. Free guest Indry. Meeting rms. Business servs avail. In-rm modem link. Gift shop. Exercise equipt; weight machine, stair machine. Game rm. Some refrigerators. Balconies. Cr cds: A, C, D, DS, JCB, MC, V.

D SC

✔★ **HOTEL HARRINGTON.** *11th & E Sts NW (20004), downtown. 202/628-8140; res: 800/424-8532; FAX 202/343-3924.* E-mail reservations@hotel-harrington.com; web www.hotel-harrington.com. 260 rms, 11 story, 29 suites. Mar-Oct: S $72-$78; D $78-$88; each addl $5; suites $109; under 16 free; family, wkend, wkly, hol rates; lower rates rest of yr. Crib free. Pet accepted, some restrictions. Garage $6.50/day. TV; cable (premium). Restaurants 7 am-midnight. Bar from 11 am. Ck-out noon. Meeting rm. Business servs avail. Gift shop. Barber. Coin Indry. Refrigerators avail. Cr cds: A, D, DS, JCB, MC, V.

D SC

★ ★ ★ **HOTEL SOFITEL.** *1914 Connecticut Ave NW (20009), in Kalorama area. 202/797-2000; FAX 202/462-0944; res: 800/424-2464.* 144 units, 9 story, 40 suites. S $225-$245; D $245-$265; each addl $20; suites $275; under 12 free; wkend rates. Crib free. Pet accepted; $50 deposit. Garage parking; valet $15. TV; cable (premium). Restaurant 6:30 am-10:30 pm. Rm serv 24 hrs. Bar noon-11:30 pm; Fri, Sat to 1 am; pianist. Meeting rms. Business servs avail. In-rm modem link. Concierge. Exercise equipt; rower, treadmill. Bathrm phones, minibars; microwaves avail. Refurbished apartment building; built 1904. Cr cds: A, C, D, JCB, MC, V.

SC

★ ★ **HOWARD JOHNSON.** *1430 Rhode Island Ave NW (20005), downtown. 202/462-7777; FAX 202/332-3519.* 184 units, 10 story, 158 kit. units. S $109-$129; D $119-$139; each addl $10; under 18 free; wkend rates. Crib free. Garage parking; valet $10. TV; cable (premium). Pool; lifeguard. Restaurant 7 am-2:30 pm, 5-10:30 pm. Bar 5-11 pm. Ck-out noon. Coin Indry. Business servs avail. In-rm modem link. Health club privileges. Exercise equipt; weight machine, bicycle. Game rm. Microwaves avail. Cr cds: A, C, D, DS, JCB, MC, V.

D SC

★ ★ ★ **HYATT REGENCY WASHINGTON ON CAPITOL HILL.** *400 New Jersey Ave NW (20001), 2 blks N of Capitol. 202/737-1234; FAX 202/737-5773.* E-mail pr@hyattdc.com; web www.hyatt.com. 834 rms, 11 story. S $210; D $235; each addl $25; under 18 free. Crib free. Garage $16. TV; cable (premium). Indoor pool. Restaurants 6:30 am-11 pm. Bar 11-2 am. Ck-out noon. Meeting rms. Business center. In-rm modem link. Concierge. Gift shop. Barber, beauty shop. Exercise rm; instructor, weight machines, bicycles, sauna. Minibars; some refrigerators; microwaves avail. Luxury level. Cr cds: A, C, D, DS, JCB, MC, V.

D SC

★ ★ ★ **J.W. MARRIOTT.** *1331 Pennsylvania Ave NW (20004), at National Place, 2 blks E of White House, downtown. 202/393-2000; FAX 202/626-6991.* Web www.marriott.com/marriott/dc-042.htm. 772 rms, 12 story. S, D $214-$239; each addl $20; suites $275-$1,550; Mar-June, Sept-Nov higher rates; lower rates rest of year; family, wkend rates. Crib free. Limited valet parking $16. TV; cable (premium). Indoor pool; whirlpool. Restaurant 7 am-11 pm. Rm serv 24 hrs. Bars; entertainment. Ck-out noon. Convention facilities. Business center. In-rm modem link. Concierge. Shopping arcade. Exercise rm; instructor, weights, bicycles, sauna. Massage. Game area. Bathrm phones in suites. Refrigerator in suites. Private patios on 7th, 12th floors. Luxurious hotel with elegant interior detail; extensive use of marble, mirrors; a large collection of artwork is displayed throughout the lobby. Luxury level. Cr cds: A, C, D, DS, JCB, MC, V.

D SC

★ ★ ★ **JEFFERSON.** *16th & M Sts NW (20036), downtown. 202/347-2200; FAX 202/331-7982; res: 800/368-5966.* E-mail jeffersonres@compuserve.com; web www.slh.com/slh/jefferson. 100 rms, 8 story, 32 suites. Jan-June, Sept-Nov: S $270-$305; D $285-$320; each addl $25; suites $350-$1,000; under 12 free; wkend rates; lower rates rest of yr. Crib free. Garage, valet parking $20. TV; cable (premium), VCR (movies avail). Pool privileges. Restaurant 6:30 am-10:30 pm (also see THE JEFFERSON). Rm serv 24 hrs. Afternoon tea 3-5 pm. Bar 11-1 am. Ck-out 1 pm. Business servs avail. In-rm modem link. Concierge. Health club privileges. Microwaves avail. Opened in 1923; individually decorated rms have four-poster beds, antiques. Cr cds: A, C, D, DS, JCB, MC, V.

D

★ ★ **THE LATHAM.** *3000 M St NW (20007), in Georgetown. 202/726-5000; FAX 202/337-4250; res: 800/368-5922 (exc DC), 800/LATHAM-1.* 143 rms, 10 story. S $135-$190; D $165-$210; each addl $20; suites $225-$390; under 18 free; wkend rates. Valet parking $14. TV; cable (premium). Pool. Restaurant (see CITRONELLE). Bar 11-1 am; Fri, Sat to 2 am. Ck-out noon. Meeting rms. Business servs avail. In-rm modem link. Concierge. Health club privileges. Some minibars. Refrigerators avail. Sun deck. Overlooks historic Chesapeake & Ohio Canal. Cr cds: A, C, D, DS, MC, V.

D SC

★ **LINCOLN SUITES.** *1823 L St NW (20036), downtown. 202/223-4320; FAX 202/223-8546; res: 800/424-2970.* 99 rms, 10 story,

24 kit. units. S, D, kit. units $175; each addl $15; under 17 free. Crib free. Garage parking $13. TV; cable (premium). Complimentary coffee in rms. Restaurant 7-10 am, 11:30 am-1:30 pm, 5-10 pm. Bar. Ck-out noon. Meeting rms. Business servs avail. Health club privileges. Refrigerators, microwaves. Cr cds: A, C, D, DS, MC, V.

D SC

★ ★ ★ ★ **LOEWS L'ENFANT PLAZA.** *480 L'Enfant Plaza SW (20024), south of downtown. 202/484-1000; FAX 202/646-4456.* Web www.loewshotels.com/lenfanthome.html. The center piece of L'Enfant Plaza, this is an upscale hotel with a pretty lobby and pleasant rooms. The hotel is popular with travelers doing business with nearby government agencies. 370 rms on floors 11-15. S, D $190-$250; each addl $20; suites $370-$1,200; under 18 free; wkend rates. Crib free. Pet accepted. Valet parking $18. TV; cable (premium), VCR (movies avail). Pool; poolside serv, lifeguard. Restaurant 6:30 am-midnight. Bar from 11:30 am. Ck-out 1 pm. Convention facilities. Business center. In-rm modem link. Concierge. Underground shopping arcade with Metro subway stop. Gift shop. Extensive exercise rm; instructor, weights, bicycles. Refrigerators, minibars; microwaves avail. Many balconies. Cr cds: A, C, D, DS, MC, V.

D SC

★ ★ **LOMBARDY.** *2019 Pennsylvania Ave (20006), Foggy Bottom, west of downtown. 202/828-2600; FAX 202/872-0503; res: 800/424-5486.* 125 units, 11 story. Mar-May, Sept-Oct: S $130-$150; D $150-$170; each addl $20; suites $170-$200; under 16 free; wkend rates; lower rates rest of yr. Crib free. TV; cable. Restaurant 7 am-2:30 pm, 5:30-9:30 pm; Sat, Sun 8 am-1 pm, 5-9:30 pm. Ck-out noon. Meeting rms. Business servs avail. In-rm modem link. Health club privileges. Refrigerators, minibars. Cr cds: A, C, D, DS, MC, V.

SC

LUXURY COLLECTION. *(New management, therefore not rated) 2100 Massachusetts Ave NW (20008), 1 blk NW of Dupont Circle, in Embassy Row Area. 202/293-2100; FAX 202/293-0641; res: 800/241-3333.* 206 rms, 8 story. S, D $215-$235; suites $295-$2,100; under 18 free; wkend rates. Crib free. Valet parking $22. TV; cable (premium), VCR avail. Restaurant 6:30 am-10:30 pm (also see JOCKEY CLUB). Bar 11:30-1 am; entertainment. Ck-out noon. Meeting rms. Business center. In-rm modem link. Concierge. Tennis privileges. Golf privileges. Exercise rm; instructor, weights, stair machines, sauna. Massage. Health club privileges. Bathrm phones, minibars. Elegant ballroom. Luxury level. Cr cds: A, C, D, DS, JCB, MC, V.

D SC

★ ★ ★ **THE MADISON.** *15th & M Sts NW (20005), downtown. 202/862-1600; FAX 202/785-1255; res: 800/424-8577.* 353 rms, 14 story. S, D $230-$395; each addl $30; suites $395-$3,000; wkend packages. Crib $25. Valet, garage $14. TV; cable (premium). Restaurant 6:30 am-11 pm. Rm serv 24 hrs. Bar 11-2 am. Ck-out 1 pm. Meeting rms. Business center. In-rm modem link. Concierge. Exercise rm; instructor, weight machine, bicycles. Bathrm phones, refrigerators, minibars. Original paintings, antiques, Oriental rugs. Cr cds: A, C, D, JCB, MC, V.

D

★ ★ **MARRIOTT.** *1221 22nd St NW (20037), at M St, west of downtown. 202/872-1500; FAX 202/872-1424.* 418 rms, 9 story. S, D $179-$199; suites $250-$500; under 18 free; wkend rates. Crib free. Garage $15. TV; cable (premium). Heated pool; whirlpool, poolside serv, lifeguard. Complimentary coffee in lobby. Restaurant 6:30 am-10 pm; Fri, Sat to 11 pm. Bars 11:30 am-midnight. Ck-out noon. Meeting rms. Business center. In-rm modem link. Concierge. Gift shop. Exercise equipt; weight machines, bicycles, sauna. Refrigerators avail. Luxury level. Cr cds: A, C, D, DS, JCB, MC, V.

D SC

★ ★ **MARRIOTT AT METRO CENTER.** *775 12th St NW (20005), downtown. 202/737-2200; FAX 202/347-5886.* 456 rms, 15 story. Late Feb-June, mid-Sept-mid-Nov: S, D $179-$219; wkend rates; higher rates Cherry Blossom; lower rates rest of yr. Crib free. Valet parking $16. TV; cable (premium). Indoor pool; whirlpool. Restaurant 6:30 am-2:30 pm, 5:30-10 pm; Sat, Sun 6:30 am-noon, 5:30-10 pm. Rm serv to midnight. Bar 11 am-midnight. Ck-out noon. Meeting rms. Business center. In-rm modem link. Concierge. Gift shop. Exercise rm; instructor, weight machine, treadmill, sauna. Minibars; microwaves avail. Luxury level. Cr cds: A, C, D, DS, JCB, MC, V.

D SC

✔★ ★ **NORMANDY INN.** *2118 Wyoming Ave NW (20008), in Kalorama. 202/483-1350; FAX 202/387-8241; res: 800/424-3729.* 75 rms, 6 story. S $103-$133; D $113-$143; each addl $10; under 12 free. Crib free. Garage $10. TV; cable (premium). Complimentary coffee in rms. Restaurant nearby. Ck-out noon. Coin Indry. In-rm modem link. Health club privileges. Refrigerators. In residential neighborhood. Cr cds: A, C, D, DS, MC, V.

D SC

★ ★ **OMNI SHOREHAM.** *2500 Calvert St NW (20008), north of downtown. 202/234-0700; FAX 202/332-1373.* 771 rms, 8 story. S $215, D $245; each addl $30; suites $400-$1,600; under 18 free; wkend, hol rates. Crib free. Pet accepted, some restrictions. Garage $14. TV; cable (premium), VCR avail. Pool; wading pool, poolside serv, lifeguard. Restaurant 6:30 am-11 pm. Rm serv. Bar 11-2 am; entertainment. Ck-out noon. Meeting rms. Business center. Shopping arcade. Lighted tennis, pro. Exercise equipt; weight machines, bicycles, sauna. Lawn games. Microwave avail in suites. Cr cds: A, C, D, DS, JCB, MC, V.

D SC

★ ★ **ONE WASHINGTON CIRCLE.** *One Washington Circle NW (20037), at New Hampshire Ave, in Foggy Bottom. 202/872-1680; FAX 202/887-4989; res: 800/424-9671.* E-mail sales@onewashcirclehotel.com; web www.onewashcirclehotel.com. 151 kit. suites, 9 story. S, D $125-$275; each addl $15; under 18 free; wkend rates. Garage $15. TV; cable (premium), VCR avail. Pool. Coffee in rms. Restaurant 7 am-11:30 pm; Fri, Sat to midnight. Bar; entertainment. Ck-out noon. Meeting rms. Business servs avail. In-rm modem link. Concierge. Health club privileges. Some bathrm phones; microwaves avail. Balconies. Elegant furnishings; landscaped grounds. Cr cds: A, C, D, MC, V.

SC

★ ★ ★ ★ **PARK HYATT.** *24th & M St NW (20037), west of downtown. 202/789-1234; FAX 202/457-8823.* Web www.hyatt.com. An impressive collection of modern art distinguishes the interiors of this hotel, softened by touches of bronze and chinoiserie. Guest rooms are furnished with a mix of contemporary and antique pieces as well as museum reproductions of Oriental antiques. 224 units, 10 story, 133 suites. S $244-$299; D $269-$325; each addl $25; suites $270-$1,975; under 18 free; wkend rates; lower rates July, Aug. Crib free. TV; cable (premium), VCR avail. Indoor pool; whirlpool, poolside serv. Restaurant (see MELROSE). Afternoon tea 3-5 pm, Thurs-Sun. Rm serv 24 hrs. Bar 11:30-1 am; Fri, Sat to 2 am; pianist. Ck-out noon. Meeting rms. Business servs avail. In-rm modem link. Concierge. Gift shop. Barber, beauty shop. Underground valet parking. Golf privileges. Exercise rm; instructor, weight machines, bicycles, steam rm, sauna. Massage. Bathrm phones, refrigerators; microwaves avail. Cr cds: A, C, D, DS, JCB, MC, V.

D SC

★ ★ **PHOENIX PARK.** *520 N Capitol St NW (20001), opp Union Station, on Capitol Hill. 202/638-6900; FAX 202/393-3236; res: 800/824-5419.* E-mail phoenixpark@worldnet.att.net. 148 rms, 9 story. S $169-$209; D $189-$229; each addl $20; suites $338-$750; under 16 free; wkend plans. Crib free. Valet parking $15. TV; cable (premium). Coffee in rms. Restaurant 7-2 am. Bar from 11 am; Fri, Sat to 3 am; entertainment. Ck-out 1 pm. Meeting rms. Business center. In-rm modem link. Exercise equipt; weight machines, bicycles. Minibars; some refrigerators. Near Capitol; traditional European decor. Cr cds: A, C, D, DS, MC, V.

D SC

★ ★ **QUALITY HOTEL DOWNTOWN.** *1315 16th St NW (20036), downtown. 202/232-8000; FAX 202/667-9827.* E-mail qualityht@erols.com; web www.quality-suite.com/online/quality .html. 135 kit. units, 10 story. S $140; D $160; each addl $12; under 16 free; wkend rates. Crib free. Garage $10. TV; cable (premium), VCR avail. Pool privileges. Restaurant 7 am-10 pm. Rm serv 7 am-2 pm, 5-9:30 pm. Bar 5-11 pm. Ck-out noon. Guest lndry. Meeting rms. Business center. In-rm modem link. Gift shop. Exercise equipt; weight machine, bicycles. Health club privileges. Microwaves avail. Cr cds: A, C, D, DS, JCB, MC, V.

D SC

★ ★ **RADISSON BARCELO.** *2121 P St NW (20037), in Dupont Circle area. 202/293-3100; FAX 202/857-0134.* 301 rms, 10 story. S, D $160-$180; each addl $20; suites $210-$550; under 17 free; wkend rates. Crib free. Valet parking $15. TV; cable (premium). Pool; lifeguard. Restaurant (see GABRIEL). Bar 11 am-midnight. Ck-out noon. Meeting rms. Business servs avail. In-rm modem link. Concierge. Gift shop. Exercise equipt; weights, bicycles, sauna. Bathrm phones, minibars. Cr cds: A, C, D, DS, JCB, MC, V.

D SC

★ ★ ★ **RENAISSANCE MAYFLOWER.** *1127 Connecticut Ave NW (20036), 4 blks NW of White House, downtown. 202/347-3000; FAX 202/466-9082.* Web www.renaissancehotels.com. 660 rms, 10 story, 78 suites. S, D $250-$360; each addl $30; suites $450-$3,500; under 19 free; wkend rates. Crib free. Garage adj $11.50. TV; cable (premium), VCR avail. Complimentary coffee in rms. Restaurant 6:30 am-11:30 pm. Rm serv 24 hrs. Bar 11-1:30 am; entertainment. Ck-out 1 pm. Convention facilities. Business center. In-rm modem link. Concierge. Exercise equipt; weight machines, bicycles. Health club privileges. Bathrm phones; refrigerators, microwaves avail. Foreign currency exchange. Opened in 1925 for Calvin Coolidge's inauguration; ornate gilded interior, stained-glass skylights. Cr cds: A, C, D, DS, ER, JCB, MC, V.

D SC

★ ★ ★ **RENAISSANCE WASHINGTON.** *999 9th St NW (20001), near Convention Center & MCI Arena, downtown. 202/898-9000; FAX 202/289-0947.* E-mail sales@renhotels.com; web www.renaissance.com. 801 rms, 16 story. Apr-June, Sept-Nov: S, D $219-$260; each addl $25; suites $500-$2,000; under 18 free; wkend rates; lower rates rest of yr. Crib free. Pet accepted, some restrictions. Garage $15. TV; cable (premium), VCR avail. Indoor pool; whirlpool. Complimentary coffee in rms. Restaurant 6:30 am-11 pm. Rm serv 24 hrs. Bar 11-1 am. Ck-out 1 pm. Convention facilities. Business center. In-rm modem link. Concierge. Shopping arcade. Exercise rm; instructor, weight machines, bicycles, sauna. Minibars; some bathrm phones; microwaves avail. Luxury level. Cr cds: A, C, D, DS, ER, JCB, MC, V.

D SC

★ ★ **RIVER INN.** *924 25th St NW (20037), 2 blks from Kennedy Center, in Foggy Bottom. 202/337-7600; FAX 202/337-6520; res: 800/424-2741.* E-mail Riverinn@erols.com. 126 kit. suites. S $125-$175; D $140-$190; each addl $15; under 18 free; wkend rates; higher rates Apr-May, Sept-Oct. Crib free. Pet accepted, some restrictions; $100. Parking $15. TV; cable (premium). Restaurant 7-10 am, 11:30 am-2 pm, 5-10 pm; Sat 8-10 am, 11 am-2 pm, 5:30-11:30 pm; Sun 8-10 am, 11 am-2 pm, 5-10 pm. Bar. Ck-out noon. Meeting rm. Business servs avail. In-rm modem link. Health club privileges. Microwaves. Cr cds: A, C, D, MC, V.

D SC

★ ★ ★ **SHERATON.** *2660 Woodley Rd NW (20008), north of downtown. 202/328-2000; FAX 202/234-0015.* Web www.ittsheraton.com. 1,505 rms, 10 story. Mar-June: S, D $167-$220; each addl $30; suites $250-$2,250; under 12 free; lower rates rest of yr. Crib free. Pet accepted. Valet parking $17; garage $15. TV; cable (premium), VCR avail. Heated pool. Complimentary coffee in rms. Restaurants 6:30 am-11 pm. Bar 11-2 am. Ck-out noon. Convention facilities. Business center. Valet serv. Concierge. Gift shop. Barber. Exercise equipt; weight machines, bicycles, sauna. Some refrigerators. Balconies. Cr cds: A, D, DS, JCB, MC, V.

D

★ ★ **SHERATON CITY CENTRE.** *1143 New Hampshire Ave NW (20037), at 21st & M Sts, west of downtown. 202/775-0800; FAX 202/331-9491.* 353 rms, 9 story. March-May, Aug-Oct: S $195-$220; D $210-$245; each addl $15; suites $250-$600; under 18 free; lower rates rest of yr. Crib free. Parking $14. TV; cable (premium). Coffee in rms. Restaurant 6 am-10 pm. Bar noon-1 am; entertainment Mon-Fri. Ck-out noon. Meeting rms. Business center. In-rm modem link. Concierge. Gift shop. Exercise equipt: stair machine, weights. Some refrigerators. Luxury level. Cr cds: A, C, D, DS, JCB, MC, V.

D SC

★ ★ **ST JAMES.** *950 24th St NW (20037), in Foggy Bottom. 202/457-0500; FAX 202/659-4492; res: 800/852-8512.* Web www.weborgs.com. 195 kit. suites, 12 story. Feb-June, Sept-Oct: suites $139-$169; under 16 free; wkend rates; higher rates: Cherry Blossom Festival; lower rates rest of yr. Crib free. Garage parking $16; valet. TV; cable, VCR avail. Pool; lifeguard. Complimentary continental bkfst. Coffee in rms. Restaurant nearby. Ck-out noon. Coin lndry. Meeting rms. Business servs avail. In-rm modem link. Concierge. Exercise equipt; weights, treadmill. Cr cds: A, D, DS, MC, V.

D SC

★ ★ **STATE PLAZA.** *2117 E St NW (20037), in Foggy Bottom. 202/861-8200; FAX 202/659-8601; res: 800/424-2859.* 223 kit. suites, 8 story. S $95-$145; D $115-$165; each addl $20; under 16 free; wkend rates; higher rates Mar-June, Sept-Nov. Crib free. Garage $12. TV; cable (premium). Complimentary continental bkfst. Restaurant 7 am-11 pm. Bar from 11 am. Ck-out noon. Coin lndry. Meeting rms. Business servs avail. In-rm modem link. Exercise equipt; bicycle, treadmills. Minibars, microwaves. Two rooftop sun decks. Cr cds: A, C, D, DS, JCB, MC, V.

D SC

✔★ **TRAVELODGE-CENTER CITY.** *1201 13th St NW (20005), north of downtown. 202/682-5300; FAX 202/371-9624.* 100 rms, 8 story. Apr-Sept: S $85-$115; D $95-$125; each addl $10; under 16 free; wkend rates; lower rates rest of yr. Parking $10 in/out. TV; cable (premium). Complimentary continental bkfst. Coffee in rms. Restaurant. Ck-out 11 am. Coin lndry. Meeting rm. Business servs avail. In-rm modem link. Cr cds: A, C, D, DS, MC, V.

D SC

★ ★ **WASHINGTON.** *515 15th St NW (20004), at Pennsylvania Ave, 1 blk from White House, downtown. 202/638-5900; FAX 202/638-4275; res: 800/424-9540.* 344 rms, 11 story. S $170-$235; D $185-$235; each addl $18; suites $430-$668; under 14 free; wkend rates. Crib free. Pet accepted, some restrictions. TV; cable (premium). Restaurant 7 am-10 pm. Bar 11-1 am. Ck-out 1 pm. Meeting rms. Business center. In-rm modem link. Gift shop. Exercise equipt; weight machine, bicycles, sauna. Bathrm phones. Original Jardin D'Armide tapestry (1854). One of the oldest continuously-operated hotels in the city. Cr cds: A, C, D, DS, JCB, MC, V.

D SC

★ ★ ★ **THE WASHINGTON COURT ON CAPITOL HILL.** *525 New Jersey Ave NW (20001), on Capitol Hill. 202/628-2100; FAX 202/879-7918; res: 800/321-3010.* 264 rms, 15 story. S, D $175-$250; each addl $25; suites $360-$1,500; under 16 free; wkend rates. Crib free. Pet accepted, some restrictions. Valet parking $15. TV; cable (premium), VCR avail. Restaurant 6:30 am-11 pm. Bar; pianist. Ck-out noon. Meeting rooms. Business servs avail. In-rm modem link. Concierge. Exercise equipt; weight machines, bicycles, sauna. Gift shop. Bathrm phones, refrigerators. Large atrium lobby. Cr cds: A, C, D, DS, MC, V.

D SC

★ ★ ★ **WASHINGTON HILTON AND TOWERS.** *1919 Connecticut Ave NW (20009), in Kalorama. 202/483-3000; FAX 202/265-8221.* Web www.hilton.com. 1,123 rms, 10 story. S $200-$265; D $225-$285; each addl $20; suites $444-$1,400; wkend rates. Crib free. Pet accepted, some restrictions. Garage $12. TV; cable (premium), VCR avail (movies). Heated pool; poolside serv, lifeguard (in season). Supervised child's activities (May-Sept). Restaurants 6:30 am-11 pm. Bar 11:30-2 am; entertainment. Ck-out noon. Convention facilities. Business center. In-rm modem link. Gift shop. Lighted tennis, pro. Exercise rm; instructor, weight machines, bicycles, steam rm. Minibars. Resort atmosphere; on 7 landscaped acres. Luxury level. Cr cds: A, C, D, DS, JCB, MC, V.

D SC

★ ★ ★ **THE WATERGATE.** *2650 Virginia Ave NW (20037), adj Kennedy Center, in Foggy Bottom. 202/965-2300; FAX 202/337-7915; res:*

800/424-2736. 231 rms, 13 story. S $275-$410; D $300-$435; each addl $25; suites $400-$1,885; under 18 free; wkend, hol rates. Crib free. Pet accepted, some restrictions. Valet parking $25. TV; cable (premium), VCR avail (movies). Indoor pool; whirlpool, lifeguard. Restaurant (see AQUARELLE). Rm serv 24 hrs. Bar 11:30-1 am; pianist. Ck-out noon. Meeting rms. Business center. In-rm modem link. Concierge. Shopping arcade. Barber, beauty shop. Complimentary downtown & Capitol transportation. Exercise rm; instructor, weight machines, bicycles, sauna, steam rm. Massage. Health club privileges. Bathrm phones, minibars; microwaves avail. Many balconies. Kennedy Center adj. Overlooks Potomac River. Cr cds: A, C, D, DS, JCB, MC, V.

D

★ ★ ★ **WESTIN HOTEL WASHINGTON.** *2350 M St NW (20037), east of Georgetown. 202/429-0100; FAX 202/429-9759.* 262 rms. Sept-June: S $219-$279; D $249-$309; each addl $30; suites $450-$3,000; under 18 free; wkend packages; lower rates rest of yr. Crib free. Covered valet parking $18/day. TV; cable (premium), VCR avail. Heated pool; poolside serv. Restaurant 6:30 am-10:30 pm. Rm serv 24 hrs. Bar. Ck-out 1 pm. Meeting rms. Business center. In-rm modem link. Concierge. Gift shop. Exercise equipt; weight machines, bicycles. Minibars. Bathrm phones; some fireplaces; whirlpool in suites. Some balconies. Many rms with view of landscaped interior courtyard. Luxury level. Cr cds: A, C, D, DS, JCB, MC, V.

D SC

★ ★ ★ ★ **WILLARD INTER-CONTINENTAL.** *1401 Pennsylvania Ave NW (20004), 2 blks E of White House, downtown. 202/628-9100; FAX 202/637-7326.* This opulent Beaux Arts hotel was host to every president from Franklin Pierce to Dwight D. Eisenhower on the eve of their inaugurations. A faithful renovation has returned elegance to the stately columns, mosaic floors and turn-of-the-century decor. Guest rooms are furnished with mahogany Queen Anne-style reproductions. 341 units, 12 story, 35 suites. S $335-$450; D $365-$480; each addl $30; suites $800-$3,600; under 14 free; wkend rates. Crib free. Pet accepted, some restrictions. Covered parking, valet $20. TV; cable (premium), VCR avail. Restaurant 6:30 am-11 pm (also see WILLARD ROOM). Rm serv 24 hrs. Bar 11-1 am; Sun 11:30 am-midnight; entertainment. Ck-out noon. Convention facilities. Business center. In-rm modem link. Concierge. Shopping arcade. Exercise equipt; weight machine, treadmill. Bathrm phones, minibars; some microwaves avail. Cr cds: A, C, D, DS, JCB, MC, V.

D SC

★ ★ ★ **WYNDHAM BRISTOL.** *2430 Pennsylvania Ave NW (20037), west of downtown. 202/955-6400; FAX 202/955-5765.* 240 kit. units, 8 story, 37 suites. S $179-$219; D $199-$229; each addl $20; suites $285-$850; under 17 free; monthly rates; wkend plans. Crib free. Valet garage parking $16. TV; cable, VCR avail. Complimentary coffee in rms. Restaurant 7 am-11 pm. Rm serv 24 hrs. Bar 11-2 am. Ck-out noon. Meeting rms. Business servs avail. In-rm modem link. Concierge. Exercise equipt; stair machine, treadmills. Bathrm phones; microwaves avail. Classic English furnishings, art. Cr cds: A, C, D, DS, JCB, MC, V.

D SC

Inns

✔★ **KALORAMA GUEST HOUSE AT KALORAMA PARK.** *1854 Mintwood Place NW (20009), in Kalorama Triangle. 202/667-6369; FAX 202/319-1262.* 31 rms, some share bath, 3 story. S $45-$95; D $50-$105; each addl $5; suites $75-$125; wkly rates. TV in common rm. Complimentary continental bkfst; afternoon refreshments. Ck-out 11 am, ck-in noon. Limited parking avail. Business servs avail. Created from 4 Victorian town houses (1890s); rms individually decorated, antiques. Garden. Cr cds: A, D, DS, MC, V.

SC

✔★ **KALORAMA GUEST HOUSE AT WOODLEY PARK.** *2700 Cathedral Ave NW (20008), north of downtown. 202/328-0860; FAX 202/328-8730.* 19 rms, 7 share baths, 4 story, 2 suites. No rm phones. Mar-mid-June, Sept-Nov: S $45-$95; D $55-$105; each addl $5; wkly rates; lower rates rest of yr. Children over 5 yrs only. TV in sitting rm. Complimentary continental bkfst; afternoon refreshments. Restaurant nearby. Ck-out 11 am, ck-in noon. Free Indry facilities. Limited off-street parking. Sitting rm; antiques. Two early 20th-century town houses (1910). Cr cds: A, D, DS, MC, V.

SC

★ ★ ★ **MORRISON-CLARK.** *1101 11th St NW (20001), at Massachusetts Ave, downtown. 202/898-1200; FAX 202/289-8576; res: 800/332-7898.* 54 units, 4 story, 14 suites. Mar-June, Sept-Nov: S $135-$220; D $155-$240; each addl $20; suites $160-$220; under 12 free; wkend rates; lower rates rest of yr. Crib free. TV; cable (premium), VCR avail. Complimentary continental bkfst. Dining rm (MORRISON-CLARK). Rm serv. Ck-out noon, ck-in 3 pm. Bellhops. Valet serv. Business servs avail. In-rm modem link. Exercise equipt; weight machine, treadmills. Health club privileges. Underground parking. Minibars; microwaves avail. Restored Victorian mansion (1864); period furnishings. Cr cds: A, D, DS, MC, V.

SC

✔★ **TAFT BRIDGE INN.** *2007 Wyoming Ave (20009), in Kalorama. 202/387-2007; FAX 202/387-5019.* 12 rms, 7 share bath, 3 with shower only, 3 story. Mar-June, Sept-Nov: S $49-$99; D $69-$109; each addl $10; kit. unit $109-$119; wkly, hol rates; lower rates rest of yr. TV in some rms; cable, VCR avail. Complimentary continental bkfst. Restaurant nearby. Ck-out 11 am, ck-in 2 pm. In-rm modem link. Valet serv. Guest Indry. Some balconies. Georgian-style house built in 1905; eclectic antique, art collection. Totally nonsmoking. Cr cds: MC, V.

✔★ **WINDSOR.** *1842 16th St NW (20009), north of downtown. 202/667-0300; FAX 202/667-4503; res: 800/423-9111.* 45 rms, 4 story, 9 suites. No elvtr. S $79-$110; D $89-$125; suites $105-$175; under 14 free; wkend rates. Crib free. TV; cable (premium). Complimentary continental bkfst; afternoon refreshments. Restaurant nearby. Ck-out noon, ck-in 2 pm. Business servs avail. Refrigerator in suites. Originally a boarding house (1922); bed & breakfast atmosphere. Cr cds: A, C, D, MC, V.

SC

Restaurants

★ ★ ★ **1789.** *1226 36th St NW (20007), in Georgetown. 202/965-1789.* Hrs: 6-10 pm; Fri, Sat to 11 pm. Closed Dec 25. Res accepted. Bar. Wine list. Semi-a la carte: dinner $18-$32. Prix fixe: pre-theater dinner $25. Specializes in seafood, rack of lamb. Own baking. Valet parking. In restored mansion; 5 dining rms on 3 levels. Federal-period decor. Fireplace. Jacket. Cr cds: A, D, DS, MC, V.

★ ★ ★ **701.** *701 Pennsylvania Ave NW (20004), across from the National Archives, downtown. 202/393-0701.* Hrs: 11:30 am-3 pm, 5:30-10:30 pm; Wed, Thurs to 11 pm; Fri to 11:30 pm; Sat 5:30-11:30 pm; Sun 5-9:30 pm. Closed major hols. Res accepted. Continental menu. Bar. Wine list. Semi-a la carte: lunch $8.50-$19.50, dinner $13.50-$23.50. Specializes in seafood, lamb chops, New York strip steak. Pianist Sun-Thurs, Jazz combo Fri, Sat. Free valet parking (dinner). Outdoor dining. Overlooks fountain at Navy Memorial. Cr cds: A, C, D, MC, V.

D

✔★ ★ **ADITI.** *3299 M St NW (20007), in Georgetown. 202/625-6825.* Hrs: 11:30 am-2:30 pm, 5:30-10 pm; Fri, Sat to 10:30 pm. Closed Thanksgiving. Res accepted. Indian menu. Serv bar. Semi-a la carte: lunch $4.95-$9.95, dinner $4.95-$13.95. Specializes in tandoori charbroiled meats, vegetarian dishes, seafood. Cr cds: A, C, D, DS, MC, V.

★ ★ **ANNA MARIA'S.** *1737 Connecticut Ave (20009), on Dupont Circle. 202/667-1444.* Hrs: 11-1 am; Fri to 3 am; Sat 5 pm-3 am; Sun 5 pm-1 am. Closed most major hols. Res accepted. Italian menu. Bar. Semi-a la carte: lunch $7.95-$10.95, dinner $12.95-$19.95. Specializes in homemade pasta, veal. Atrium rm; fireplace. Cr cds: A, C, D, MC, V.

★ ★ ★ **AQUARELLE.** *(See The Watergate Hotel) 202/298-4455.* Hrs: 7-10:30 am, 11:30 am-2:30 pm, 5:30-10:30 pm; Sun brunch 11:30

am-2:30 pm; early-bird dinner 5:30-7 pm. Res accepted. Continental menu. Bar 11:30-1 am. Wine cellar. A la carte entrees: bkfst $7-$16, lunch $12-$20, dinner $14-$25. Complete meal: dinner $35-$65. Sun brunch $38. Specialties: quail stuffed with wild game bird mousseline, filet of sea bass in pesto broth, warm plumb tart. Own pasta. Valet parking. Panoramic view of the Potomac River. Cr cds: A, C, D, DS, JCB, MC, V.

D

✔★ ★ **BACCHUS.** *1827 Jefferson Place NW (20036), in Dupont Circle area. 202/785-0734.* Hrs: noon-2:30 pm, 6-10 pm; Fri to 10:30 pm; Sat 6-10:30 pm. Closed Sun; most major hols. Res accepted. Lebanese menu. A la carte entrees: lunch $6.50-$10.75, dinner $11.75-$16.25. Specializes in authentic Lebanese cuisine. Valet parking (dinner). Cr cds: A, MC, V.

★ ★ **BE DU CI.** *2100 P St NW (20037), in Dupont Circle. 202/223-3824.* Hrs: 11:30 am-2:30 pm, 5:30-10 pm; Fri to 10:30 pm; Sat 5:30-10:30 pm; Sun 5:30-9:30 pm. Closed late Aug; major hols. Res accepted. Mediterranean menu. Bar. Semi-a la carte: lunch $9.50-$23, dinner $10.50-$25. Specializes in game, seafood. Three dining areas. Contemporary decor. Cr cds: A, C, D, DS, MC, V.

★ ★ **BICE.** *Indiana between 6th & 7th Aves (20004), downtown. 202/638-2423.* E-mail bice@dcnet.com; web www.bice.washington.com. Hrs: 11:30 am-2:30 pm, 5:30-10:30 pm; Fri to 11:30 pm; Sat 5:30-11:30 pm. Closed Sun; Jan 1, Thanksgiving, Dec 25. Res accepted. Northern Italian menu. Bar. Semi-a la carte: lunch $11-$20, dinner $12-$30. Specializes in pasta, risotto, veal. Valet parking (dinner). Outdoor dining. Bright, modern Italian decor; windows on 3 sides of dining rm. Cr cds: A, C, D, MC, V.

D

★ **BILLY MARTIN'S TAVERN.** *1264 Wisconsin Ave NW (20007), in Georgetown. 202/333-7370.* Hrs: 8-1 am; Fri, Sat to 2:30 am; Sat, Sun brunch to 5 pm. Closed Dec 25. Res accepted. Bar. Semi-a la carte: bkfst $3.95-$7.95, lunch $5.95-$8.95, dinner $6.50-$18.95. Sat, Sun brunch $5.95-$12.95. Specializes in steak, seafood, chops, pasta. Parking. Outdoor dining. Established 1933. Family-owned. Cr cds: A, D, DS, MC, V.

♥

★ ★ **BISTRO FRANCAIS.** *3128 M St NW (20007), in Georgetown. 202/338-3830.* Hrs: 11-3 am; Fri, Sat to 4 am; early-bird dinner 5-7 pm, 10:30 pm-1 am; Sat, Sun brunch 11 am-4 pm. Closed Dec 24 eve, 25. Res accepted. Country French menu. Semi-a la carte: lunch $6.95-$11.95, dinner $12.95-$19.95. Wkday brunch: $11.95. Sat, Sun brunch $13.95. Specializes in rotisserie chicken, fresh seafood. Cr cds: A, C, D, JCB, MC, V.

✔★ ★ **BISTROT LEPIC.** *1736 Wisconsin Ave NW (20007), in upper Georgetown. 202/333-0111.* Hrs: 11:30 am-2:30 pm, 5:30-10 pm; Fri, Sat to 10:30 pm; Sun to 9:30 pm. Closed Mon; major hols. Res accepted. French menu. Semi-a la carte: lunch $9.75-$12.95, dinner $13.95-17.95. Specialties: roasted rack of lamb, beef tenderloin, preserved rabbit leg. Storefront restaurant. Cr cds: A, DS, MC, V.

✔★ **BLUE PLATE.** *2002 P St NW (20036), in Dupont Circle. 202/293-2248.* Hrs: 11:30 am-11 pm; Fri, Sat to midnight; Sun noon-10 pm. Closed most major hols. Serv bar. Semi-a la carte: lunch, dinner $8.25-$11.95. Specializes in grilled fish, steak. Own baking. Casual cafe atmosphere. Totally nonsmoking. Cr cds: MC, V.

★ ★ ★ **BOMBAY CLUB.** *815 Connecticut Ave NW (20006), across from White House, downtown. 202/659-3727.* Hrs: 11:30 am-2:30 pm, 6-10:30 pm; Sat 6-11 pm; Sun 5:30-9 pm; Sun brunch 11:30 am-2:30 pm. Closed some major hols. Res accepted. Indian menu. Bar 11:30 am-3 pm, 5-11 pm. Semi-a la carte: lunch, dinner $7-$18.50. Sun brunch $16.50. Specialties: tandoori salmon, thali, lamb Roganjosh, chicken Tikka Makhani. Pianist evenings, Sun brunch. Valet parking (dinner). Outdoor dining. Extensive vegetarian menu. Elegant club-like atmosphere reminiscent of British colonial India. Cr cds: A, C, D, MC, V.

D

✔★ ★ **BOMBAY PALACE.** *2020 K St NW (20006), downtown. 202/331-4200.* Hrs: 11:30 am-2:30 pm, 5:30-10 pm; Fri, Sat to 10:30 pm. Res accepted. Northern Indian menu. Bar. A la carte entrees: lunch, dinner $8.50-$19.95. Complete meals: lunch, dinner $16.95-$19.95. Specialties: butter chicken, gosht patiala, jumbo prawns tandoori. Indian decor and original art; 350-gallon fish tank. Totally nonsmoking. Cr cds: A, D, MC, V.

D

✔★ **BUA.** *1635 P St NW (20036), in Dupont Circle. 202/265-0828.* Hrs: 11:30 am-2:30 pm, 5-10:30 pm; Fri to 11 pm; Sat noon-4 pm, 5-11 pm; Sun noon-4 pm. Closed Thanksgiving, Dec 25. Res accepted. Thai menu. Bar. A la carte entrees: lunch $5.85-$7.75, dinner $7.50-$12.95. Specializes in seafood. Outdoor dining on 2nd-floor balcony. In townhouse on side street; fireplace. Cr cds: A, D, DS, MC, V.

★ **BURMA.** *740 6th St NW (20001), in Chinatown. 202/638-1280.* Hrs: 11 am-3 pm, 6-10 pm; Sat, Sun from 6 pm. Closed major hols. Res accepted. Burmese menu. Serv bar. Semi-a la carte: lunch, dinner $5.95-$7.95. Specialties: green tea leaf salad, tamarind fish, mohingar. Burmese decor. Cr cds: A, C, D, DS, MC, V.

★ ★ **BUSARA.** *2340 Wisconsin Ave NW (20007), in Upper Georgetown, near the Naval Observatory. 202/337-2340.* Hrs: 11:30 am-3 pm, 5-11 pm; Fri to midnight; Sat 5 pm-midnight; Sun 5-11 pm. Closed most major hols. Res required Fri, Sat. Thai menu. Bar. Semi-a la carte: lunch $5.95-$8.50, dinner $7.25-$15.95. Specialties: panang gai, crispy whole flounder, pad Thai. Outdoor dining in a Japanese garden. New wave decor. Cr cds: A, C, D, DS, MC, V.

D

✔★ ★ ★ **CAFE ATLÁNTICO.** *405 8th St NW (20004), in Penn Quarter, downtown. 202/393-0812.* Hrs: 11:30 am-10 pm; Fri, Sat to 11 pm; Sun 5:30-10 pm. Closed most major hols. Res accepted. Latin Amer menu. Bar to midnight. Wine cellar. Semi-a la carte: lunch $7.95-$13.95, dinner $13.95-$16.50. Complete meal (Sun-Wed): dinner $19.95-$21.95. Specialties: Cordero a la Boliviana, Jamaican jerk chicken, quail tamal fingido. Valet parking. Outdoor dining. Contemporary decor with modern artwork; central circular stairway leads to second dining level. Cr cds: A, D, MC, V.

D

★ ★ **CAFE MILANO.** *3251 Prospect St NW (20007), in Georgetown. 202/333-6183.* Hrs: 11-1 am; Sun noon-11 pm. Closed Thanksgiving, Dec 25. Res accepted. Italian menu. Bar. Semi-a la carte: lunch $9-$26, dinner $13-$28. Specialties: strozzapreti moschino, costoletta di vitello. Outdoor dining. Large tie/scarf collection hanging on walls. Cr cds: A, D, MC, V.

D

★ **CAFE MOZART.** *1331 H St NW (20005), behind deli, downtown. 202/347-5732.* Hrs: 7:30 am-10 pm; Sat from 9 am; Sun from 11 am. Closed Jan 1, Thanksgiving, Dec 25. Res accepted. German, Austrian menu. Bar. Semi-a la carte: bkfst $3.10-$6.95, lunch $4.85-$21.50, dinner $8.95-$22.50. Child's meals. Specialties: Wienerschnitzel, pork roast, Kasseler rippchen. Entertainment Thurs-Sat. German deli on premises. Cr cds: A, C, D, DS, JCB, MC, V.

D

★ ★ ★ **THE CAPITOL GRILL.** *601 Pennsylvania Ave NW (20004), on Capitol Hill. 202/737-6200.* Hrs: 11:30 am-3 pm, 5-10 pm; Fri to 11 pm; Sat 5-11 pm; Sun 5-10 pm. Closed Thanksgiving, Dec 25. Res accepted. Bar. A la carte entrees: lunch $9.95-$19.95, dinner $15.95-$27.95. Specializes in steak. Club atmosphere. Cr cds: A, C, D, DS, MC, V.

D

★ ★ **CASHION'S EAT PLACE.** *1819 Columbia Rd NW (20009), in Adams Morgan area. 202/797-1819.* Hrs: 5:30-11 pm; Sun, Tues to 10 pm; Sun brunch 11:30 am-2:30 pm. Closed Mon; most major hols. Res accepted. Bar. Semi-a la carte: dinner $10.95-$17.95. Complete meal: dinner $25-$40. Sun brunch $3.95-$8.95. Specializes in lamb, duck, seafood. Own desserts. Valet parking. Outdoor dining. Contemporary decor; skylights. Cr cds: MC, V.

★ ★ ★ **CITRONELLE.** *(See The Latham Hotel) 202/625-2150.* Hrs: 6:30-10:30 am, 11:30 am-2 pm, 6-10 pm; Fri, Sat 5:30-10:30 pm; Sun brunch 11:30 am-2:30 pm. Res accepted. French menu. Bar. Semi-a la carte: bkfst $7.50-$12.50, lunch $15-$25, dinner $28-$45. Sun brunch $10-$18. Specialties: terrine of smoked salmon, shiitake mushroom Napoleon, shrimp wrapped in kataifi. Multi-level dining rm. Contemporary decor with modern art. Cr cds: A, C, D, DS, MC, V.

D

✔★ ★ **CLYDE'S.** *3236 M St NW (20007), at Wisconsin Ave, in Georgetown. 202/333-9180.* Hrs: 11:30-2 am; Fri to 3 am; Sat 10-3 am; Sun from 9 am. Closed Dec 25. Res accepted. Bars. Semi-a la carte: lunch $6.95-$10.95, dinner $9.95-$14.95. Sun brunch $4.25-$9.95. Child's meals. Specializes in seafood, crab cakes, ribs. Parking. Atrium dining. Cr cds: A, C, D, DS, MC, V.

D

★ ★ **COCO LOCO.** *810 7th St NW (20001), downtown, in Chinatown. 202/289-2626.* Hrs: 11:30 am-2:30 pm, 5:30-10:30 pm; Sat 5:30-11 pm. Closed Sun. Res accepted. Spanish menu. Bar. A la carte entrees: lunch $4.50-$11, dinner $5-$12. Prix fixe: $29.95. Specialties: stuffed ravioles, grilled chicken, stuffed shrimp. Salad bar. Entertainment. Outdoor dining. Modern tropical decor. Cr cds: A, D, MC, V.

D

✔★ ★ **COPPI'S VIGORELLI.** *3421 Connecticut Ave NW (20008), in Cleveland Park area, north of downtown. 202/244-6437.* Hrs: noon-11 pm; Fri to midnight; Sat noon-3 pm, 5 pm-midnight; Sun 5-11 pm. Closed Thanksgiving, Dec 24, 25. Northern Italian menu. Bar. Semi-a la carte: lunch, dinner $7.95-$15.95. Child's meals. Specialties: wood-oven broiled fish, baked ligurian risotto. Own pasta. Decor celebrates Italian bicycle racing. Cr cds: A, D, DS, MC, V.

D

★ **EL CARIBE.** *3288 M St (20007), in Georgetown. 202/338-3121.* E-mail cfearless@aol.com; web www.digitalcity.com/caribe. Hrs: 11:30 am-11 pm; Fri, Sat to 11:30 pm; Sun to 10 pm. Res accepted. South Amer, Spanish menu. Bar. Semi-a la carte: lunch $6.95-$12.95, dinner $9.95-$19.50. Specialties: fritadas con Llapingachos, paella. Spanish decor. Family-owned. Cr cds: A, C, D, DS, MC, V.

★ ★ **FILOMENA RISTORANTE.** *1063 Wisconsin Ave NW (20007), off M St on the canal, in Georgetown. 202/338-8800.* E-mail Filorest@erols.com; web www.erols.com/eire/filomena.html. Hrs: 11:30 am-11 pm; Sat, Sun brunch to 3 pm. Closed Jan 1, Thanksgiving, Dec 25. Res accepted. Italian menu. Bar. A la carte entrees: lunch $5.95-$12.95, dinner $11.95-$29.95. Lunch buffet $7.95. Sat, Sun brunch $9.95. Specializes in pasta, seafood, regional Italian dishes. Own baking, pasta. Italian garden-like atmosphere; antiques. Overlooks Chesapeake & Ohio Canal. Cr cds: A, D, DS, JCB, MC, V.

✔★ **FIO'S.** *3636 16th St (20010), in Woodner Apts, Mt Pleasant, north of downtown. 202/667-3040.* Hrs: 5-10:45 pm. Closed Mon; some major hols; last 2 wks Aug. Italian menu. Bar. Semi-a la carte: dinner $5.50-$12.50. Specializes in seafood, veal, pasta. Own bread, pasta. Free garage parking. Informal atmosphere; building overlooks Rock Creek Park. Cr cds: A, C, D, DS, MC, V.

D

★ ★ ★ **FRAN O'BRIEN'S.** *(See The Capital Hilton Hotel) 202/783-2599.* Hrs: 11:30 am-11 pm; Sat, Sun from 5 pm; Sun brunch 10:30 am-3 pm (football season). Closed most major hols. Res accepted. Bar to midnight. Wine cellar. Semi-a la carte: lunch $8.25-$19.95, dinner $17.95-$29.95. Sun brunch $22-$24. Child's meals. Specialties: rib-eye steak, filet mignon, Maryland crab cakes with lobster cream sauce. Own desserts. Pianist evenings exc Sun. Valet parking (dinner). Club-like atmosphere with sport themes; large collection of football memorabilia. Cr cds: A, D, MC, V.

D

✔★ **FRATELLI ITALIAN.** *(5820 Landover Rd, Cheverly MD 20784) jct Baltimore Washington Pkwy & MD 202. 301/209-9006.* Hrs: 11 am-10 pm; Fri, Sat to 11 pm; Sun 2-9 pm. Italian menu. Bar. Semi-a la carte: lunch $5.95-$11.25, dinner $9.95-$13.95. Specializes in pasta, chicken, seafood. Contemporary decor. Cr cds: A, MC, V.

★ ★ **GABRIEL.** *(See Radisson Barcelo Hotel) 202/956-6690.* Hrs: 6:30 am-10 pm; Sat 7 am-11 pm; Sun to 9 pm; Sun brunch 11 am-3 pm. Closed Dec 25. Res accepted. Spanish/Latin Amer menu. Bar 11 am-midnight. Semi-a la carte: bkfst $3.50-$9.50, lunch $7.25-$15, dinner $8-$24. Sun brunch $16.75. Specialties: grilled sea scallops, grilled lamb chops, smoked black bean soup. Outdoor dining. Mediterranean decor. Cr cds: A, C, D, DS, JCB, MC, V.

D

★ ★ ★ **GALILEO.** *1110 21st St NW (20036), in Foggy Bottom. 202/293-7191.* E-mail roberto@robertodonna.com; web www.robertodonna.com. Hrs: 7:30-9:30 am, 11:30 am-2 pm, 5:30-10 pm; Fri to 10:30 pm; Sat from 5:30 pm; Sun 5:30-8:30 pm. Closed some major hols. Res accepted. Northern Italian menu. Bar. Wine cellar. A la carte entrees: bkfst $3.95-$9.95, lunch $10.95-$17.95, dinner $16.95-$29.95. Specializes in game, seasonal dishes, pasta. Free valet parking (dinner) exc Sun. Outdoor dining. Mediterranean decor. Cr cds: A, C, D, DS, MC, V.

D

✔★ **GARRETT'S.** *3003 M St NW (20007), in Georgetown. 202/333-1033.* E-mail rhinorest@aol.com. Hrs: 11:30 am-10:30 pm; Fri, Sat to 11 pm. Res accepted. Bars 11:30-2 am; Fri, Sat to 3 am. Semi-a la carte: lunch $3.95-$8.50, dinner $4.75-$13.95. Specializes in steaks, pasta, seafood. 1794 landmark bldg; originally house of MD governor T.S. Lee. Cr cds: A, C, D, DS, MC, V.

★ ★ ★ **GEORGIA BROWN'S.** *950 15th St NW (20005), at McPherson Square, downtown. 202/393-4499.* Hrs: 11:30 am-11 pm; Fri to midnight; Sat 5:30 pm-midnight; Sun brunch 11:30 am-3 pm, 5:30-11 pm. Closed Dec 25. Res accepted. South Carolina Low Country menu. Bar. Semi-a la carte: lunch, dinner $10.95-$19.95. Specialties: head-on Carolina shrimp with spicy sausage, frogmore stew, Southern fried chicken. Jazz & blues Sun afternoons. Valet parking (dinner). View of McPherson's Square. Cr cds: A, C, D, DS, MC, V.

D

★ ★ ★ **GERARD'S PLACE.** *915 15th St NW (20005), at McPherson Square, downtown. 202/737-4445.* Hrs: 11:30 am-2:30 pm, 5:30-10 pm; Fri to 10:30 pm; Sat 5:30-10:30 pm. Closed Sun; most major hols. Res accepted. French menu. Wine list. A la carte entrees: lunch $15.50-$19.50, dinner $16.50-$32.50. Prix fixe: dinner $58. Specializes in contemporary French cooking. Outdoor dining. Casual bistro atmosphere. Some modern art. Cr cds: A, C, D, MC, V.

★ ★ **GERMAINE'S.** *2400 Wisconsin Ave NW (20007), in Upper Georgetown. 202/965-1185.* Hrs: 11:30 am-2:30 pm, 5:30-10 pm; Fri to 11 pm; Sat 5:30-11 pm; Sun 5:30-10 pm. Closed Jan 1, Dec 25. Res accepted. Pan-Asian menu. Bar. A la carte entrees: lunch $7.25-$12.95, dinner $12.25-$28. Specializes in grilled Asian dishes, seafood. Skylighted atrium dining rm. Cr cds: A, C, D, MC, V.

★ ★ ★ **GOLDONI.** *1113 23rd St NW (20037), west of downtown. 202/293-1511.* Hrs: 11:30 am-2 pm, 5:30-10 pm; Fri 11:30 am-2 pm, 5-10:30 pm; Sat 5-10:30 pm; Sun 5-9:30 pm. Closed most major hols. Res accepted. Italian menu. Bar. Wine list. Semi-a la carte: lunch $11.95-$18.95, dinner $14.95-$26.95. Complete meal: dinner $35.95-$48.95. Specialties: grilled wild rockfish with polenta, mushrooms and cherry tomatoes; cappellacci with lobster and foie gras with white truffles. Own pasta, desserts. Validated parking nearby. Gallery setting has look and feel of Italian villa; skylights. Cr cds: A, C, D, DS, MC, V.

★ **THE GRILL FROM IPANEMA.** *1858 Columbia Rd NW (20009), in Adams Morgan area. 202/986-0757.* Hrs: 5-11 pm; Fri to midnight; Sat noon-midnight; Sun noon to 11 pm; Sat, Sun brunch to 4 pm. Closed Jan 1, Dec 25. Res accepted. Brazilian menu. Bar. Semi-a la carte: dinner $8.95-$15.95. Sat, Sun brunch $11.95. Specialties: feijoada, moqueca, bobo de camarao. Cr cds: A, C, D, DS, MC, V.

D

✔★ **GUAPO'S.** *4515 Wisconsin Ave NW (20016), north of downtown. 202/686-3588.* Hrs: 11:30 am-11:30 pm; Fri, Sat to midnight. Res accepted. Latin Amer, Mexican menu. Bar. Semi-a la carte: lunch $3.95-$10.25, dinner $4.95-$13.95. Specializes in fajitas. Outdoor dining. Colorful dining rms with Mexican decor. Cr cds: A, DS, MC, V.

D

★ **GUARDS.** *2915 M St NW (20007), E end of Georgetown. 202/965-2350.* Hrs: 11:30 am-11 pm; Fri, Sat to midnight; Sun brunch 11:30 am-5 pm. Res accepted. Continental menu. Bar. Semi-a la carte: lunch $5.50-$12.95, dinner $13.95-$22.95. Sun brunch $5.95-$12.95. Specializes in veal, Angus beef, fresh seafood. Valet parking $4. Atrium dining rm; country-English decor. Cr cds: A, C, D, DS, MC, V.

SC

✔★ **HAAD THAI.** *1100 New York Ave NW (20005), downtown. 202/682-1111.* Hrs: 11:30 am-2:30 pm, 5-10:30 pm; Sun from 5 pm. Closed most major hols. Res accepted. Thai menu. Bar. Semi-a la carte: lunch $5.95-$7.95, dinner $8.95-$13.95. Specialties: pad Thai, pla yang, surf-n-turf. Tropical atmosphere. Cr cds: A, D, MC, V.

D

★ ★ **HOGATE'S.** *9th St & Maine Ave SW (20024), on the waterfront, south of downtown. 202/484-6300.* Hrs: Mon-Thurs 11 am-10 pm; Fri to 11 pm, Sat noon-11 pm; Sun 10:30 am-10 pm; Sun brunch to 2:30 pm. Closed Dec 25. Res accepted. Bar. Semi-a la carte: lunch $6-$13, dinner $13-$35. Lunch buffet $12.95. Sun brunch $18.95. Child's meals. Specialties: mariner's platter, wood grilled fish, rum buns. Brunch entertainment. Indoor parking $1.50/hr. Outdoor dining. Overlooks Potomac River. Cr cds: A, C, D, DS, MC, V.

D

★ ★ **HUNAN CHINATOWN.** *624 H St NW (20001), in Chinatown. 202/783-5858.* Hrs: 11 am-10 pm; Fri, Sat to 11 pm. Hunan, Szechwan menu. Serv bar. Semi-a la carte: lunch $6.50-$12, dinner $8-$23. Specialties: General Tso's chicken, tea-smoked half-duck, crispy prawns with walnuts. Parking (dinner). Modern, bi-level dining room. Cr cds: A, C, D, DS, MC, V.

♥

✔★ ★ **I MATTI TRATTORIA.** *2436 18th St NW (20009), in Adams Morgan area. 202/462-8844.* E-mail imatti@robertodonna.com; web www.robertodonna.com. Hrs: noon-2:30 pm, 5:30-10:30 pm; Fri to 11 pm; Sat noon-2:30 pm, 5:30-10:30 pm; Sun 5:30-10 pm. Closed Jan 1, Thanksgiving, Dec 25. Res accepted. Northern Italian menu. Bar to 11 pm Fri, Sat. A la carte entrees: lunch, dinner $10-$17. Specializes in traditional Tuscan cooking. Valet parking Tues-Sat. Upscale dining; lower dining area less formal. Cr cds: A, D, MC, V.

D

★ ★ ★ **ISABELLA.** *809 15th St NW (20005), at McPherson Square, downtown. 202/408-9500.* Hrs: 11:30 am-3 pm, 5:30-10:30 pm; Fri to 11 pm; Sat 5:30-11 pm; Sun from 5:30 pm. Closed most major hols. Res accepted. Mediterranean menu. Bar. Wine list. Semi-a la carte: lunch $9.95-$17.95, dinner $14.25-$21.50. Child's meals. Specializes in seafood, pastas, grilled meats. Own baking. Free valet parking (dinner). Outdoor dining. Contemporary Mediterranean decor; fabric wall hangings; palm trees. Cr cds: A, DS, MC, V.

D

★ **J PAUL'S.** *3218 M St NW (20007), in Georgetown. 202/333-3450.* Hrs: 11:30-1 am; Sun 10:30 am-11:30 pm; Sun brunch to 4 pm. Bar to 1:30 am. Semi-a la carte: lunch, dinner $5.25-$20.95. Sun brunch $7.95-$12.95. Child's meals. Specializes in ribs, crab cakes, burgers. Turn-of-the-century saloon decor; antique bar from Chicago's old Stockyard Inn. Cr cds: A, D, DS, MC, V.

★ ★ **JALEO.** *480 7th St NW (20004), downtown. 202/628-7949.* E-mail tapasymas@msn.com; web dc.diningweb.com/restaurants/jaleo. Hrs: 11:30 am-11:30 pm; Sun, Mon to 10 pm; Fri, Sat to midnight. Closed Thanksgiving, Dec 24, 25. Spanish menu. Bar. Semi-a la carte: lunch $7.75-$9.95, dinner $10.50-$18. Specializes in hot & cold tapas, Spanish-style fish. Sevillanas dancers Wed nights. Valet parking $5. Murals of flamenco dancers cover the walls of this lively restaurant. Cr cds: A, D, DS, MC, V.

D

★ ★ ★ **THE JEFFERSON.** *(See Jefferson Hotel) 202/833-6206.* Hrs: 6:30-11 am, 11:30 am-2:30 pm, tea 3-5 pm, 6-10:30 pm. Sun brunch 10:30 am-2:30 pm. Res accepted. Bar 11-1 am. Wine list. Semi-a la carte: bkfst $4.50-$14.50, lunch $13-$22, dinner $22-$27. Sun brunch $19.50-$25.75. Specializes in natural American cuisine. Valet parking. Jeffersonian-era cuisine and decor. Cr cds: A, C, D, DS, JCB, MC, V.

D

JOCKEY CLUB. *(New management, therefore not rated) (See Luxury Collection Hotel) 202/659-8000.* Hrs: 6:30-11 am, noon-2:30 pm, 6-10:30 pm; Sat, Sun 7-11:30 am, noon-2:30 pm, 6-10:30 pm. Res accepted. Classic French, international menu. Bar. A la carte entrees: bkfst $3.75-$16.50, lunch $11.50-$23, dinner $24.50-$34. Specializes in veal, fresh seafood, crab cakes. Own baking. Complimentary valet parking. Tableside cooking. Club-like atmosphere in 1928 landmark building. Jacket. Cr cds: A, C, D, DS, JCB, MC, V.

D

★ ★ ★ ★ **KINKEAD'S.** *2000 Pennsylvania Ave NW (20006), at I St, in Foggy Bottom. 202/296-7700.* Chef Bob Kinkead has created two distinct but delicious dining options in this multichambered restaurant. Downstairs is a more informal and inexpensive pub-style eatery, while upstairs you can watch Kinkead and company turn out grilled dishes with an emphasis on seafood. Specialties: pepita-crusted salmon, pepper-seared tuna, grilled squid. Hrs: 11:30 am-10 pm; Fri, Sat to 10:30 pm; Sun brunch to 2:30 pm. Closed Jan 1, Thanksgiving, Dec 25. Res accepted. Bar to midnight. Semi-a la carte: lunch $12-$16, dinner $18-$22. Sun brunch $8-$12. Free valet parking (dinner). Outdoor dining. Jazz pianist Mon-Sat. Cr cds: A, C, D, DS, MC, V.

D

✔★ ★ **KRUPIN'S.** *4620 Wisconsin Ave NW (20016), north of downtown. 202/686-1989.* Hrs: 8 am-10 pm. Closed Dec 25. Semi-a la carte: bkfst $3.50-$15.95, lunch, dinner $5.25-$15.95. Child's meals. Specializes in smoked fish, meatloaf, beef stew. Old fashioned decor. Cr cds: A, C, D, MC, V.

D

★ ★ **LA CHAUMIÈRE.** *2813 M St NW (20007), E end of Georgetown. 202/338-1784.* Hrs: 11:30 am-2:30 pm, 5:30-10:30 pm; Sat from 5:30 pm. Closed Sun; major hols. Res accepted. Country French menu. Semi-a la carte entrees: lunch $10.95-$15.95, dinner $14.95-$24.95. Specializes in seafood, veal, game. Intimate room with beamed ceiling, open-hearth fireplace. Family-owned. Cr cds: A, C, D, MC, V.

★ ★ **LA COLLINE.** *400 N Capitol St NW (20001), on Capitol Hill. 202/737-0400.* Hrs: 7-10 am, 11:30 am-3 pm, 6-10 pm; Sat from 6 pm. Closed Sun; major hols. Res accepted. French menu. Bar. Semi-a la carte: bkfst $3.50-$8.75, lunch $9-$17, dinner $15-$22. Prix fixe: dinner $22-$27.

Specializes in seasonal foods, fowl, seafood. Outdoor dining. Across from Union Station. Cr cds: A, C, D, MC, V.

D

★★ **LA FOURCHETTE.** *2429 18th St NW (20009), in Adams Morgan area. 202/332-3077.* Hrs: 11:30 am-10:30 pm; Sat 4-11 pm; Sun 4-10 pm. Closed major hols. Res accepted. French menu. Semi-a la carte: lunch $8.95-$19.95, dinner $10.95-$21.95. Specialties: bouillabaisse, rack of lamb, poitrine de poulet farcie au crabe. Outdoor dining. Former townhouse; painted murals on walls. Cr cds: A, C, D, MC, V.

★★★ **LAFAYETTE.** *(See Hay-Adams Hotel) 202/638-2570.* Hrs: 6:30 am-2 pm, 5-10 pm; Sat, Sun from 7 am; Sun brunch 11:30 am-2 pm. Res accepted. Wine list. Semi-a la carte: bkfst $5.50-$15.25, lunch $14-$24, dinner $18-$29. Sun brunch $37.50. Specialties: grilled Dover sole in lobster pesto sauce, veal stuffed with asparagus and crab, sauteed big eye tuna in rice paper crust. Pianist. Overlooking Lafayette Park and the White House. Cr cds: A, D, DS, MC, V.

D

★★ **LAURIOL PLAZA.** *1801 18th St NW (20009), in Dupont Circle. 202/387-0035.* Hrs: 11:30 am-11 pm; Fri, Sat to midnight; Sun brunch 11 am-3 pm. Res accepted wkdays. Latin Amer menu. Bar. A la carte entrees: lunch, dinner $5.95-$15. Sun brunch $5.95-$7.95. Specialties: paella, pollo asado, lomo saltado. Outdoor dining. Oil paintings and exotic flower arrangements. Cr cds: A, C, D, DS, MC, V.

✔★★ **LAVANDOU.** *3321 Connecticut Ave NW (20008), north of downtown. 202/966-3002.* E-mail FD3321@aol.com; web www.dinenet.com. Hrs: 11:30 am-2:30 pm, 5-10 pm; Fri to 11 pm; Sat 5-11 pm; Sun 5-10 pm. Closed most major hols. Res accepted, required on wkends. Southern French menu. Serv bar. Semi-a la carte: lunch $9.95-$13.50, dinner $12.95-$17.95. Complete meals: dinner (to 6:30 pm) $14.95. Specialties: clam á l'ail, truite saumnonée, daube Provençale. French bistro atmosphere features country artifacts. Free parking. Cr cds: A, D, MC, V.

✔★★ **LEBANESE TAVERNA.** *2641 Connecticut Ave NW (20008), north of downtown. 202/265-8681.* Hrs: 11:30 am-2:30 pm, 5:30-10:30 pm; Fri, Sat to 11 pm; Sun 5-10 pm. Closed major hols. Lebanese menu. Bar. Semi-a la carte: lunch $8-$12, dinner $10-$16. Specializes in falafel, shish kabob. Contemporary decor. Cr cds: A, D, DS, MC, V.

D

★ **LES HALLES.** *1201 Pennsylvania Ave NW (20004), downtown. 202/347-6848.* Hrs: 11:30 am-midnight; Sun brunch to 4 pm. Res accepted. French, Amer menu. Bar. Semi-a la carte: lunch $12.50-$19.95, dinner $15-$22.50. Sun brunch $14.95. Child's meals. Specialties: onglet, cassoulet. Outdoor dining. Three-level dining area. Cr cds: A, D, DS, JCB, MC, V.

★★★★ **LESPINASSE.** *(See The Carlton Hotel) 202/879-6900.* Ornate chandeliers, French provincial furnishings and an elaborately detailed wood-beam ceiling make this elegant dining room unforgettable. Chef Troy Dupuy's entrees, featuring complex seasonings and lustrous flavors, are equally memorable. French menu. Specialties: shellfish bouillon with quinoa, sorrel and fenugreek; cauliflower-sweet pea papadum croustade with tamarind; squab breast with laratte potatoes and périgord truffles. Hrs: 7-10:30 am, noon-2 pm, 6-10 pm; Sat 7-11 am, 6-10 pm; Sun to 11 am. Closed most major hols; also Aug. Res accepted. Bar noon-midnight. Semi-a la carte: bkfst $6-$19, lunch $22-$27, dinner $27-$39. Prix fixe: lunch $36, dinner $75 or $95. Valet parking. Jacket. Cr cds: A, C, D, DS, ER, JCB, MC, V.

D

★★ **LUIGINO.** *1100 New York Ave NW (20005), downtown. 202/371-0595.* E-mail luigino@erols.com; web www.erols.com/luigino. Hrs: 11:30 am-2:30 pm, 5:30-10:30 pm; Fri to 11:30 pm; Sat 5:30-11:30 pm; Sun 5-10 pm. Closed major hols. Res accepted. Italian menu. Bar. Semi-a la carte: lunch $8.25-$15.50, dinner $12.50-$22.50. Child's meals. Specializes in pasta, seafood, game. Outdoor dining. Trattoria with contemporary atmosphere. Cr cds: A, D, MC, V.

D

★★★ **MAISON BLANCHE/RIVE GAUCHE.** *1725 F St NW (20006) near the White House, downtown. 202/842-0070.* Hrs: 11:45 am-2 pm, 6-9:30 pm; Sat from 6 pm. Closed Sun; major hols. Res accepted. French menu. Bar. Semi-a la carte: lunch $15-$27, dinner $26.50-$36. Prix fixe: lunch $21.95, dinner $32. Specialties: dessert souffles, Dover sole, lobster fricasée. Own pastries. Free valet parking from 5 pm. Jacket. Cr cds: A, C, D, DS, MC, V.

D

★ **MARKET INN.** *200 E St SW (20024), south of downtown. 202/554-2100.* E-mail seafrest@aol.com. Hrs: 11 am-11 pm; Fri to midnight; Sat 4:30 pm-midnight; major hols from 5 pm. Closed Thanksgiving, Dec 25. Res accepted. Bar. Semi-a la carte: lunch $6-$13.50, dinner $12.95-$24.95. Sun brunch $18.95. Child's meals. Specializes in Maine lobster, beef. Entertainment; jazz Sun brunch. Free valet parking. Outdoor dining. English pub ambience. Family-owned. Cr cds: A, C, D, DS, JCB, MC, V.

✔★★ **McCORMICK & SCHMICK'S.** *1652 K St NW (20006), downtown. 202/861-2233.* Hrs: 11 am-11 pm; Fri to midnight; Sat 5 pm-midnight; Sun 5-10 pm. Closed Dec 25. Res accepted. Seafood menu. Bar to midnight; Fri, Sat to 1 am; Sun to 11 pm. Semi-a la carte: lunch, dinner $5.95-$19.95. Child's meals. Specialties: Alaskan halibut stuffed with dungeness crab, bay shrimp and brie; cedar plank salmon with berry sauce; seared yellowfin tuna with wasabe and soy sauce. Own pastries. Valet parking (dinner). Old fashioned decor with large open grill. Cr cds: A, C, D, DS, JCB, MC, V.

D

★★★ **MELROSE.** *(See Park Hyatt Hotel) 202/955-3899.* Hrs: 6:30 am-2:30 pm, 5:30-10:30 pm; Fri, Sat to 11 pm; Sun brunch 10:30 am-2:30 pm. Res accepted. Contemporary Amer menu. Bar 11-1 am; Fri, Sat to 2 am. Wine cellar. Semi-a la carte: bkfst $8.50-$15, lunch $14-$22, dinner $19-$28. 7-course tasting dinner $55. Sun brunch $33-$36. Child's meals. Specializes in fresh fish, seafood, veal. Own baking. Pianist. Valet parking. Outdoor dining. Sunlit atrium. Italian fountain. Cr cds: A, C, D, DS, JCB, MC, V.

D

✔★★ **MESKEREM.** *2434 18th St NW (20009), in Adams Morgan area. 202/462-4100.* Hrs: noon-midnight; Fri, Sat to 1 am. Closed Thanksgiving, Dec 25. Res accepted. Ethiopian menu. Bar. Semi-a la carte: lunch, dinner $8.50-$11.95. Specializes in lamb, beef, chicken. Own Ethiopian breads. Ethiopian band Fri-Sun. Tri-level dining rm; traditional Ethiopian decor, sunny and bright. Cr cds: A, C, D, MC, V.

✔★ **MISS SAIGON.** *1847 Columbia Rd NW (20009), in Adams Morgan area. 202/667-1900.* Hrs: noon-10:30 pm; Fri to 11 pm; Sat, Sun 5-11 pm. Closed July 4, Thanksgiving, Dec 25. Res accepted. Vietnamese menu. Bar. Semi-a la carte: lunch $5.95-$8.95, dinner $7.95-$10.95. Specialties: caramel salmon, Vietnamese steak, roast quails. Outdoor dining. Garden setting. Cr cds: A, D, MC, V.

★★ **MONOCLE ON CAPITOL HILL.** *107 D St NE (20002), adj to US Senate Office Bldg, on Capitol Hill. 202/546-4488.* Hrs: 11:30 am-midnight. Closed Sat, Sun; major hols. Res accepted. Bar. A la carte entrees: lunch $7-$16, dinner $12-$25. Child's meals. Specializes in seafood, aged beef. Valet parking. Located in 1865 Jenkens Hill building; fireplace. Close to Capitol; frequented by members of Congress and other politicians. Family-owned. Cr cds: A, C, D, MC, V.

★★★ **MORRISON-CLARK.** *(See Morrison-Clark Inn) 202/898-1200.* Hrs: 11:30 am-2 pm, 6-9:30 pm; Fri to 10 pm; Sat 6-10 pm; Sun brunch 11 am-2 pm. Closed some hols. Res accepted. Bar. Wine cellar. Semi-a la carte: lunch $13-$16, dinner $18-$24. Sun brunch $25-$27.50.

Specialties: sautéed chicken breast with country ham and sage, marinated wild rockfish in citrus with fava beans and fennel, grilled rabbit with rabbit sausage and shelled beans. Own desserts. Free valet parking. Outdoor dining. Elegant Victorian dining rm; antiques; elaborately dressed floor-to-ceiling windows. Jacket. Cr cds: A, D, DS, MC, V.

★★★ **MORTON'S OF CHICAGO.** *3251 Prospect St NW (20007), in Georgetown. 202/342-6258.* Hrs: 5-11 pm; Sun 5-10 pm. Closed some major hols. Res accepted. Bar. Wine list. A la carte entrees: dinner $17.95-$29.95. Specializes in steak, lobster, seafood. Valet parking. Collection of Leroy Neiman paintings. Cr cds: A, C, D, JCB, MC, V.

D

✔★ **MR. SMITH'S.** *3104 M St NW (20007), in Georgetown. 202/333-3104.* E-mail mrsmith@aol.com. Hrs: 11:30-2 am; Fri, Sat to 3 am; Sat, Sun brunch 11 am-4:30 pm. Bar. Semi-a la carte: lunch, dinner $4.95-$14.95. Sat, Sun brunch $4.50-$8. Specializes in seafood, pasta, hamburgers. Pianist 9 pm-1:30 am. Old tavern atmosphere. Outdoor dining. Family-owned. Cr cds: A, C, D, MC, V.

★ **MR. YUNG'S.** *740 6th St NW (20001), in Chinatown. 202/628-1098.* Web www.menusonline.com/cities/ wash_dc/ desc/mryungs.shtml. Hrs: 11 am-10:30 pm. Chinese, Cantonese menu. Serv bar. Semi-a la carte: lunch $5.95-$7.95, dinner $6.95-$25.95. Specialties: sauteed shrimp with snow pea leaves, steamed lobster in garlic sauce. Enclosed outdoor dining. Modern Asian decor. Cr cds: A, DS, MC, V.

D

✔★ **MURPHY'S OF D.C.** *2609 24th St NW (20008), at Calvert St, north of downtown. 202/462-7171.* Hrs: 11-2 am. Irish, Amer menu. Beer. Semi-a la carte: lunch $5.95-$7.95, dinner $5.95-$11.95. Child's meals. Specializes in steaks, burgers, seafood. Traditional Irish music. Patio dining. Wood-burning fireplace. Cr cds: A, D, MC, V.

✔★ **MUSIC CITY ROADHOUSE.** *1050 30th St NW (20007), between M & K in the Foundry Building, in Georgetown. 202/337-4444.* E-mail mergm@aol.com. Hrs: 4:30 pm-2 am; Fri, Sat to 3 am; Sun 11 am-midnight; Sun brunch to 2 pm. Closed Mon; also most major hols. Res accepted. Bar. Semi-a la carte: dinner $10.95-$13.95. Sun brunch $12.95. Child's meals. Specializes in fried chicken, BBQ ribs, country fried steak. Old fashioned roadhouse with pictures of country singers. Cr cds: A, C, D, DS, MC, V.

D

★★ **NATHANS.** *3150 M St NW (20007), in Georgetown. 202/338-2000.* Hrs: 11 am-3 pm, 6-11 pm; Thurs-Sat to midnight; Sat, Sun brunch 10 am-3 pm. Res accepted. Northern Italian, Amer menu. Bar 11-2 am; Fri, Sat to 3 am. Semi-a la carte: lunch $5.25-$12.50, dinner $14.50-$30.50. Sat, Sun brunch $5.25-$12.50. Specializes in pasta, grilled fish. Entertainment Fri, Sat. Antiques. Family-owned. Cr cds: A, C, D, MC, V.

★★★ **NEW HEIGHTS.** *2317 Calvert St NW (20008), north of downtown. 202/234-4110.* Hrs: 5:30-10 pm; Fri, Sat to 11 pm; Sun brunch 11 am-2:30 pm. Closed major hols. Res accepted. New Amer cuisine. Bar from 5 pm. Semi-a la carte: dinner $15-$25. Sun brunch $8-$15. Specializes in calamari fritti, grilled salmon, fresh trout. Menu changes seasonally; some entrees offered in half-portions. Outdoor dining. Main dining rm on 2nd floor overlooks Rock Creek Park. Cr cds: A, C, D, DS, MC, V.

★★★ **NORA.** *2132 Florida Ave NW (20008), in Dupont Circle. 202/462-5143.* E-mail tthyme@erols.com; web www.noras .com. Hrs: 6-10 pm; Fri, Sat to 10:30 pm. Closed Sun; major hols; also last 2 wks Aug. Res accepted. Bar. Semi-a la carte: dinner $17.95-$24.95. Specializes in American organic cuisine with continental and Mediterranean influence. Menu changes daily. Own desserts. Atrium dining. In 1890 building with American folk art, Amish quilts on walls. Totally nonsmoking. Cr cds: MC, V.

★★ **OBELISK.** *2029 P St NW (20036), in Dupont Circle. 202/872-1180.* Hrs: 6-10 pm. Closed Sun; major hols. Res accepted. Italian menu. Serv bar. Complete meals: dinner $40-$42. Specializes in seasonal dishes. Menu changes daily. Intimate dining rm on 2nd floor of town house. Totally nonsmoking. Cr cds: D, MC, V.

★★ **OCCIDENTAL GRILL.** *1475 Pennsylvania Ave NW (20004), downtown. 202/783-1475.* Hrs: 11:30 am-11 pm; Sun noon-9:30 pm. Closed Thanksgiving, Dec 25. Res accepted. Regional Amer menu. Bar. A la carte entrees: lunch $8-$20, dinner $13-$27. Specializes in grilled seafood, beef, lamb. Own desserts. Turn-of-the-century Victorian decor with autographed photos of celebrities; originally opened 1906. Cr cds: A, C, D, MC, V.

D

✔★★ **OLD EBBITT GRILL.** *675 15th St NW (20005), downtown. 202/347-4801.* Hrs: 7:30-1 am; Sat from 8 am; Sun from 9:30 am; Sun brunch to 4 pm. Res accepted. Bar to 2 am; Fri, Sat to 3 am. Semi-a la carte: bkfst $5.95-$9.95; lunch, dinner $7.95-$16.95. Sun brunch $6.95-$16.95. Specializes in fresh oysters, seafood, hamburgers. Own pasta. Valet parking (dinner, Sun brunch). In old vaudeville theater built in early 1900s. Victorian decor, gaslights; atrium dining. Cr cds: A, C, D, DS, MC, V.

D

★★ **OLD EUROPE RESTAURANT & RATHSKELLER.** *2434 Wisconsin Ave NW (20007), north of downtown. 202/333-7600.* Hrs: 11:30 am-3 pm, 5-10 pm; Sun 4-9 pm. Closed July 4, Dec 24, 25. Res accepted. German menu. Serv bar. Semi-a la carte: lunch $5-$9, dinner $10-$20. Child's meals. Specialties: schnitzel Old Europe, Wienerschnitzel, sauerbraten. Pianist Thurs-Sun. Cr cds: A, C, D, MC, V.

★★ **THE OVAL ROOM.** *800 Connecticut Ave (20006), 1 1/2 blocks from White House, downtown. 202/463-8700.* Hrs: 11:30 am-3:00 pm, 5:30-10:30 pm; Fri to 11 pm; Sat 5:30-11 pm. Closed Sun; some major hols. Res accepted. Bar. A la carte entrees: lunch $10.50-$22.50, dinner $13.50-$22.50. Specializes in New American cuisine. Menu changes seasonally. Pianist. Valet parking after 5:30 pm. Outdoor dining. Oval office theme is prevalent throughout this restaurant, from chandeliers to bar area. The decor and cooking style are strictly American. Cr cds: A, D, MC, V.

D

★★ **PALM.** *1225 19th St NW (20036), in Dupont Circle. 202/293-9091.* Hrs: 11:30 am-10:30 pm; Sat from 6 pm; Sun 5:30-9:30 pm. Closed major hols. Res accepted. Bar. A la carte entrees: lunch $8.50-$17, dinner $14-$30. Specializes in steak, lobster. Valet parking (dinner). 1920s New York-style steak house. Family-owned. Cr cds: A, D, MC, V.

D

★★ **PAOLO'S.** *1303 Wisconsin Ave NW (20007), in Georgetown. 202/333-7353.* Hrs: 11:30-2 am; Fri, Sat to 3 am; Sun 11 am-2 am; Sat, Sun brunch to 4 pm. Italian menu. Bar. Semi-a la carte: lunch, dinner $7.95-$18.95. Sun brunch $6.95. Specializes in pizza, pasta, seafood. Jazz combo Sun afternoons. Patio dining; wood-burning pizza oven. Cr cds: A, C, D, DS, MC, V.

★★ **PESCE.** *2016 P St NW (20036), on Dupont Circle. 202/466-3474.* Web www.robertodonna.com. Hrs: 11:30 am-2:30 pm, 5:30-10 pm; Fri, Sat to 10:30 pm; Sun 5-9:30 pm. Closed Labor Day, Dec 25. Semi-a la carte: lunch, dinner $13.50-$22.95. Specializes in seafood. Valet parking Thurs-Sat. Modern decor. Cr cds: A, D, MC, V.

SC

★★ **PETITTO'S RISTORANTE D'ITALIA.** *2653 Connecticut Ave NW (20008), north of downtown. 202/667-5350.* Hrs: 5:30-10:30 pm;

Sun to 9:30 pm. Closed major hols. Res accepted. Italian menu. Bar. A la carte entrees: dinner $11-$18. Specializes in pasta, fish, veal. Valet parking. Outdoor dining. Dessert, cappuccino rm downstairs. Turn-of-the century Victorian townhouse overlooking Connecticut Ave; fireplaces. Cr cds: A, C, D, DS, MC, V.

✔★ **PIZZERIA PARADISO.** *2029 P St NW (20036), in Dupont Circle. 202/223-1245.* Hrs: 11 am-11 pm; Fri, Sat to midnight; Sun noon-10 pm. Closed some major hols. Italian menu. Wine, beer. A la carte entrees: lunch, dinner $5.50-$15.95. Specializes in pizza, salads, sandwiches. Lively, colorful atmosphere; pizza-makers visible from dining area. Totally nonsmoking. Cr cds: D, MC, V.

★ ★ ★ **PRIME RIB.** *2020 K St NW (20006), downtown. 202/466-8811.* Hrs: 11:30 am-3 pm, 5-11 pm; Fri to 11:30 pm; Sat 5-11:30 pm. Closed Sun; major hols. Res accepted. Bar. Semi-a la carte: lunch $8-$17. A la carte entrees: dinner $15-$27. Specializes in roast prime rib, Chesapeake seafood, aged thick-cut steak. Pianist. Free valet parking (dinner). Art deco decor; 1920s lithographs. 1940s New York supper club atmosphere. Jacket. Cr cds: A, D, MC, V.

D

✔★ ★ **PRIMI PIATTI.** *2013 I St NW (20006), downtown. 202/223-3600.* Hrs: 11:30 am-2:30 pm, 5:30-10:30 pm; Fri, Sat 5:30-11:30 pm. Closed Sun; most major hols. Res accepted. Italian menu. Bar. Semi-a la carte: lunch $10-$15.50, dinner $11-$20. Specializes in grilled fish, meat. Own pasta. Outdoor dining. Cr cds: A, C, D, MC, V.

D

★ ★ ★ **PROVENCE.** *2401 Pennsylvania Ave NW (20037), west of downtown. 202/296-1166.* Hrs: noon-2 pm, 6-10 pm; Fri to 11 pm; Sat 6-11 pm; Sun 6-9:30 pm. Res accepted. French menu. Bar. Semi-a la carte: lunch $12-$20, dinner $17.50-$29. Specializes in French Provencal cooking. Mediterranean setting. Cr cds: A, C, D, MC, V.

D

✔★ **RAKU.** *1900 Q St NW (20009), in Dupont Circle. 202/265-7258.* Web www.dinersgrapevine.com/raku. Hrs: 11:30 am-midnight; Fri, Sat to 1 am; winter to 11 pm; Fri, Sat to midnight. Closed Thanksgiving, Dec 25. Pan-Asian menu. Bar. Semi-a la carte: lunch, dinner $4-$18. Specializes in noodle dishes, dumplings, satays. Street parking. Outdoor dining. Casual teahouse decor with varied Asian accents. Cr cds: MC, V.

D

★ ★ **RED SAGE.** *605 14th St NW (20005), in Westory Bldg, downtown. 202/638-4444.* Web www.dinersgrapevine.com/redsage. Hrs: 11:30 am-2 pm, 5:30-10 pm; Sun from 5 pm. Closed Dec 25. Res accepted. Eclectic menu. Bar. A la carte entrees: lunch $8.50-$15.50, dinner $18.50-$31. Specializes in Western dishes with Native American influences. Validated parking. Designed as a contemporary interpretation of the American West; each of dining level's four major areas exhibits a particular style and mood. Cr cds: A, C, D, DS, MC, V.

D

★ ★ **ROOF TERRACE.** *2700 F St NW (20566), within Kennedy Center, in Foggy Bottom. 202/416-8555.* Hrs: 11:30 am-3 pm only on matinee days, 5:30-9 pm on performance eves. Sun brunch 11:30 am-2:30 pm. Res accepted. Semi-a la carte: lunch $12-$16, dinner $20-$29. Sun brunch $25.95. Child's meals. Specializes in regional American cuisine. Garage parking. Summer outdoor dining. Contemporary decor; floor-to-ceiling windows offer views of Lincoln Memorial, Washington Monument, Potomac River and Virginia. Totally nonsmoking. Cr cds: A, C, D, JCB, MC, V.

D

★ ★ **SAIGON GOURMET.** *2635 Connecticut Ave NW (20008), north of downtown. 202/265-1360.* Hrs: 11 am-3 pm, 5-10:30 pm. Closed Thanksgiving. Res accepted. Vietnamese menu. Serv bar. Semi-a la carte: lunch $5.95-$7.95, dinner $8.95-$13.95. Specialties: Saigon roasted noodles, roasted quail, caramel chicken. Valet parking. Patio dining overlooking upper Connecticut Ave. Cr cds: A, D, DS, MC, V.

D

✔★ **SAIGONNAIS.** *2307 18th St NW (20009), in Adams Morgan area. 202/232-5300.* Hrs: 11:30 am-3 pm, 5-11 pm; Sun 5-10:30 pm. Closed Jan 1, Thanksgiving, Dec 25. Res accepted. Serv bar. Vietnamese menu. Semi-a la carte: lunch, dinner $7.95-$14.50. Specialties: lemon-grass beef, shrimp on sugar cane stick. Outdoor dining. Vietnamese artwork. Cr cds: A, MC, V.

★ ★ ★ **SAM & HARRY'S.** *1200 19th St NW (20036), in Dupont Circle. 202/296-4333.* Hrs: 11:30 am-2:30 pm, 5:30-10:30 pm; Sat from 5:30 pm. Closed Sun; major hols. Res accepted. Bar. A la carte entrees: lunch $8.95-$22.95, dinner $17.95-$32.95. Specializes in prime-aged beef, Maine lobster, fresh seafood. Valet parking (dinner). Club-like atmosphere with mahogany paneling, paintings of jazz legends. Cr cds: A, C, D, DS, MC, V.

D

★ **SARINAH SATAY HOUSE.** *1338 Wisconsin Ave NW (20007), in Georgetown. 202/337-2955.* Hrs: noon-3 pm, 6-10:30 pm; Sun from 6 pm. Closed Mon; Dec 25. Res accepted. Indonesian menu. Bar. A la carte entrees: lunch $5.95, dinner $7.90-$14.95. Specialties: gado gado, satays, rijsttafel. Two levels of dining in a lush, tropical atmosphere; Indonesian artifacts. Cr cds: A, C, D, DS, MC, V.

★ ★ **SEA CATCH.** *1054 31st St NW (20007), at M St, in Georgetown. 202/337-8855.* Hrs: noon-3 pm, 5:30-10 pm. Closed Sun. Res accepted. Bar. Semi-a la carte: lunch $4.75-$12, dinner $16-$24. Specializes in fresh seafood, lobster, crab cakes. Own pastries. Valet parking. Outdoor dining on deck overlooking historic Chesapeake & Ohio Canal. Cr cds: A, D, DS, MC, V.

D

★ ★ ★ **SEASONS.** *(See Four Seasons Hotel) 202/342-0444.* Hrs: 7-11 am, noon-2:30 pm, 6:30-10:30 pm; Sun brunch 10 am-2:30 pm. Res accepted. Bar 11-2 am. Wine list. Semi-a la carte: bkfst $9-$21, lunch $14-$23, dinner $23-$35. Child's meals. Specializes in regional and seasonal dishes. Own baking. Pianist. Valet parking. Overlooks Rock Creek Park. Cr cds: A, C, D, ER, JCB, MC, V.

D

★ ★ **SEQUOIA.** *3000 K St NW (20007), Washington Harbour complex, in Georgetown. 202/944-4200.* Hrs: 11:30 am-midnight; Fri, Sat to 1 am; Sat, Sun brunch 10:30 am-4 pm. Res accepted. Bar. Semi-a la carte: lunch, dinner $7.95-$28.95. Sun brunch $14.95. Outdoor dining. Terrace and multi-story dining rm windows overlook Kennedy Center, Potomac River and Roosevelt Bridge, Island. Cr cds: A, D, DS, MC, V.

D

★ **SUSHI KO.** *2309 Wisconsin Ave NW (20007), north of downtown. 202/333-4187.* E-mail sushiko@vni.net; web www.sushiko.com. Hrs: noon-2:30 pm, 6-10:30 pm; Mon from 6 pm; Sat 5-10:30 pm; Sun 5-10 pm. Closed July 4, Thanksgiving, Dec 25. Res accepted. Japanese menu. Semi-a la carte: lunch $6.50-$10.50, dinner $7.50-$18.50. Specializes in traditional and modern Japanese dishes. Casual decor. Cr cds: A, MC, V.

★ ★ ★ **TABERNA DEL ALABARDERO.** *1776 I St NW (20006), entrance on 18th St, downtown. 202/429-2200.* Hrs: 11:30 am-2:30 pm, 6-10 pm; Fri to 11 pm; Sat 6-11 pm. Closed Sun; major hols. Res accepted. Basque, Spanish menu. Bar. Semi-a la carte: lunch $14-$20, dinner $16-$28. Complete meals: lunch $17.50, dinner $35. Specializes in beef, fish, paella. Tapas bar. Own baking. Flamenco dancers Mar, Oct. Garage parking (dinner). Outdoor dining. Ornate, 19th-century Spanish decor. Jacket. Cr cds: A, D, DS, MC, V.

✔★ **THAI KINGDOM.** *2021 K St NW (20006), downtown. 202/835-1700.* Hrs: 11:30 am-2:30 pm, 5-10:30 pm; Sat noon-11 pm; Sun noon-10 pm. Closed some major hols. Res accepted. Thai menu. Bar. A la carte entrees: lunch $6.50-$8.95, dinner $7.25-$9.95. Specialties: crispy chili fish, scallops wrapped in minced chicken, Thai Kingdom grilled chicken. Outdoor dining. Bi-level dining rm with full windows overlooking K St; authentic Thai decor. Cr cds: A, C, D, MC, V.

D

★ **THAI TASTE.** *2606 Connecticut Ave NW (20008), north of downtown. 202/387-8876.* Hrs: 11:30 am-10:30 pm; Fri, Sat to 11 pm. Closed some major hols. Res accepted. Thai menu. A la carte entrees: lunch, dinner $6.95-$10.95. Specializes in fish, chicken, seafood combinations. Outdoor dining. Cr cds: A, D, MC, V.

✔★ **THE TOMBS.** *1226 36th St NW (20007), in Georgetown. 202/337-6668.* Hrs: 11:30 am-midnight; Sat from 11 am; Sun brunch 9:30 am-3 pm. Closed Thanksgiving, Dec 24, 25. Bar. Semi-a la carte: lunch, dinner $4.95-$10.95. Sun brunch $5.25-$7.95. Specializes in chicken, pasta, burgers. Vintage crew gear and prints on walls. Cr cds: A, C, D, DS, MC, V.

★ ★ **TONY AND JOE'S.** *3000 K St NW (20007), at Washington Harbour complex, in Georgetown. 202/944-4545.* Web www.diningweb.com/restaurants/tonyandjoe's. Hrs: 11 am-11 pm; Fri, Sat to midnight; Sun brunch to 3 pm. Closed Dec 25. Res accepted. Bar Fri, Sat to 2 am. Semi-a la carte: lunch $6.95-$22.95, dinner $14.95-$27.95. Sun brunch $17.95. Specializes in seafood. Own desserts. Entertainment Tues-Sat. Outdoor dining. Overlooks Potomac River. Cr cds: A, C, D, DS, JCB, MC, V.

D

★ ★ **TONY CHENG'S MONGOLIAN BARBECUE.** *619 H St NW (20001), in Chinatown. 202/842-8669.* Hrs: 11 am-11 pm; Fri, Sat to midnight. Res accepted. Mongolian barbecue menu. Prix fixe: lunch $8.50, dinner $13.95 (serv charge 15%). Food bar encircles Mongolian grill. Diners may select own ingredients to be stir fried, grilled or steeped tableside. Asian decor. Cr cds: A, MC, V.

★ ★ **TWO QUAIL.** *320 Massachusetts Ave NE (20002), on Capitol Hill. 202/543-8030.* Hrs: 11:30 am-2:30 pm, 5-10:30 pm; Sat, Sun from 5 pm. Closed Dec 25. Res accepted. Semi-a la carte: lunch $7-$14, dinner $11-$19. Specializes in New American cuisine, baked pork chops, seafood. Country inn atmosphere in Victorian townhouse; eclectic furnishings. Cr cds: A, C, D, DS, MC, V.

★ ★ ★ **VIDALIA.** *1990 M St NW (20036), in Dupont Circle. 202/659-1990.* Hrs: 11:30 am-2:30 pm, 5:30-10 pm; Fri to 10:30 pm; Sat 5:30-10:30 pm; Sun 5-9:30 pm. Closed most major hols. Res accepted. Bar. Semi-a la carte: lunch $11-$19, dinner $18-$25. Specialties: sauteed shrimp with creamed grits, pan roasted sweetbreads. Country manor house decor. Cr cds: A, DS, MC, V.

D

★ ★ **VINCENZO AL SOLE.** *1606 20th St NW (20009), in Dupont Circle. 202/667-0047.* Hrs: 6-10 pm. Closed Sun; major hols. Res accepted. Italian menu. Bar. Semi-a la carte: dinner $15.75-$24.75. Specializes in fresh seafood. Valet parking (dinner). Four dining rms, including atrium. Outdoor dining. Cr cds: A, C, D, MC, V.

D

★ ★ ★ **WILLARD ROOM.** *(See Willard Inter-Continental Hotel) 202/637-7440.* Hrs: 7:30-10 am, 11:30 am-2 pm, 6-10 pm; Sat, Sun from 6 pm. Res accepted. Bar 11-1 am. Wine list. European, regional Amer menu. A la carte entrees: bkfst $7.50-$12.75, lunch $10.50-$17.50, dinner $18.50-$29.50. Complete meals: breakfast $12-$17.50, lunch $24-$28, dinner $36-$65. Specializes in regional seafood, lamb, beef. Seasonal specialties. Own pastries. Pianist. Valet parking (dinner). Cr cds: A, C, D, DS, JCB, MC, V.

D

✔★ **ZED'S ETHIOPIAN.** *3318 M St NW (20007), in Georgetown. 202/333-4710.* Hrs: 11 am-11 pm. Closed most major hols. Ethiopian menu. Serv bar. Semi-a la carte: lunch $6.95-$10.75, dinner $7.75-$12.95. Specializes in seafood, beef, vegetarian dishes. No silverware is used at the restaurant; communal dining from trays. Cr cds: A, D, DS, MC, V.

✔★ ★ **ZUKI MOON.** *824 New Hampshire Ave NW (20037), 2 blks NE of Kennedy Center, in Foggy Bottom. 202/333-3312.* Hrs: 7-10 am, 11:30-2:30 pm, 5-11 pm; Sat 8-11 am, 5-11 pm; Sun 8-11 am, 5-10 pm. Closed some major hols. Res accepted. Japanese menu. Bar. A la carte entrees: bkfst $2-$4.50. Semi-a la carte: lunch, dinner $7.95-$15.50. Specializes in meal-in-a-bowl noodle soups, grilled meats and fish. Valet parking (lunch & dinner). Outdoor dining. Modern Japanese garden decor. Totally nonsmoking. Cr cds: A, D, MC, V.

D

Unrated Dining Spots

ARMAND'S CHICAGO PIZZERIA. *4231 Wisconsin Ave NW, north of downtown. 202/686-9450.* Hrs: 11:30 am-11 pm; Fri, Sat to 1 am. Closed Thanksgiving, Dec 25. Bar. A la carte entrees: lunch, dinner $4-$7. Buffet: lunch (pizza & salad) $4.99. Specializes in Chicago-style deep-dish pizza, sandwiches, salads. Outdoor dining. Cr cds: A, DS, MC, V.

AUSTIN GRILL. *2404 Wisconsin Ave NW, in Georgetown. 202/337-8080.* Hrs: 11:30 am-11 pm; Fri, Sat to midnight; Sat brunch to 3 pm; Sun brunch 11 am-3 pm. Closed Thanksgiving, Dec 25. Tex-Mex menu. Bar. Semi-a la carte: lunch, dinner $4.95-$12.95. Sat, Sun brunch $4.95-$6.95. Specializes in enchiladas, fajitas. Southwestern decor. Cr cds: A, D, DS, MC, V.

C.F. FOLKS. *1225 19th St NW, in Dupont Circle. 202/293-0162.* Hrs: 11:45 am-3 pm. Closed Sat, Sun; major hols. Semi-a la carte: lunch $4.95-$8.95. Complete meals: lunch $7-$10. Specializes in daily & seasonally changing cuisines. Outdoor dining. Old-fashioned lunch counter. No cr cds accepted.

CAFE PARMA. *1724 Connecticut Ave NW, in Dupont Circle. 202/462-8771.* Hrs: 11:30 am-11:30 pm; Fri, Sat to midnight; Sun to 10 pm; Sat, Sun brunch to 3 pm. Italian menu. Bar. A la carte entrees: lunch, dinner $6-$13. Sat, Sun brunch $10.75. Specializes in pizza, pasta, hoagies. Cr cds: A, C, D, MC, V.

KRAMERBOOKS & AFTERWORDS. *1517 Connecticut Ave, in Dupont Circle. 202/387-1462.* Hrs: 7:30-1 am; Fri, Sat open 24 hrs; Sun brunch 9:30 am-3 pm. Closed Thanksgiving, Dec 25. Bar. Semi-a la carte: bkfst $3.95-$7.50, lunch, dinner $6.75-$12.75. Sun brunch $8.25-$13.25. Specialties: Thai jambalaya, grilled portobello mushroom sandwich. Entertainment Thurs-Sun. Outdoor dining. In 2-story greenhouse & terrace behind Kramerbooks bookshop. Cr cds: A, DS, MC, V.

PATISSERIE-CAFE DIDIER. *3206 Grace St NW (20007), in Georgetown. 202/342-9083.* Hrs: 8 am-7 pm; Sun to 5 pm. Closed Mon; Jan 1, Dec 25. Semi-a la carte: bkfst $1.10-$7.95, lunch $5.99-$8.99. Specializes in European desserts, quiche, pizza. European-style cafe and pastry house. Cr cds: C, D, DS, MC, V.

PHILLIPS FLAGSHIP. *900 Water St SW, on waterfront, south of downtown. 202/488-8515.* Hrs: 11 am-2 pm, 5-10 pm; Fri to 11 pm; Sat, Sun 11 am-11 pm. Closed Dec 25. Bar. Buffet: lunch $14.95, dinner $24.95; Sun $19.95. A la carte bar menu: $3.50-$9.95. Specializes in seafood. Sushi bar. Garage parking. Outdoor dining. Antiques; Tiffany lamps, stained glass. Cr cds: A, C, D, DS, MC, V.

D SC

SHOLL'S COLONIAL CAFETERIA. *1990 K St NW, in Esplanade Mall, in Foggy Bottom. 202/296-3065.* Hrs: 7 am-2:30 pm, 4-8 pm. Closed Sun; major hols. Avg ck: bkfst $3, lunch, dinner $5. Specialties: spaghetti, liver & onions, homemade pie. Family-owned. No cr cds accepted.

D

Arlington County (National Airport Area), VA

Motels

✔★ ★ **COMFORT INN BALLSTON.** *1211 N Glebe Rd (22201), at Washington Blvd. 703/247-3399; FAX 703/524-8739.* 126 rms, 3 story. Mar-Oct: S $90-$110; D $95-$125; each addl $10; suites $135; under 18 free; wkend rates; lower rates rest of yr. Crib free. TV; cable (premium). Pool privileges. Complimentary continental bkfst. Restaurant 6:30 am-10:30 pm. Rm serv. Bar 4-11 pm. Ck-out 11 am. Meeting rms. Business servs avail. In-rm modem link. Valet serv (Mon-Fri). Sundries. Gift shop. Garage parking. Refrigerators avail. Cr cds: A, C, D, DS, ER, JCB, MC, V.

D SC

★ ★ **EXECUTIVE CLUB SUITES.** *108 S Courthouse Rd (22204). 703/522-2582; FAX 703/486-2694.* 74 kit. suites, 2-3 story. Mar-Sept: kit. suites: $159-$179; wkend, wkly, hol rates; higher rates Cherry Blossom Festival; lower rates rest of yr. Crib free. Pet accepted, some restrictions; $250 deposit ($25 nonrefundable). TV; cable (premium), VCR avail. Complimentary continental bkfst. Complimentary coffee in rms. Ck-out noon. Meeting rms. Business servs avail. Valet serv. Sundries. Coin Indry. Free airport transportation. Exercise equipt; weights, weight machine, sauna. Health club privileges. Pool; whirlpool, lifeguard. Refrigerators, microwaves. Picnic tables, grills. Cr cds: A, C, D, DS, MC, V.

SC

✔★ ★ ★ **TRAVELODGE-WASHINGTON/ARLINGTON CHERRY BLOSSOM.** *3030 Columbia Pike (22204). 703/521-5570; FAX 703/271-0081.* E-mail cherryblossom.travelodge@jung.com. 76 rms, 3 story, 12 kit. units. Mid-Mar-Nov: S, D $59-$70; each addl $7; kit. units $76; under 18 free; lower rates rest of yr. Crib free. TV; cable (premium), VCR avail. Pool privileges. Complimentary continental bkfst. Complimentary coffee in rms. Restaurant 11 am-11 pm. Ck-out noon. Coin Indry. Business servs avail. Valet serv. Exercise equipt; weight machine, stair machines. Refrigerators; microwaves avail. Cr cds: A, C, D, DS, ER, JCB, MC, V.

D SC

Motor Hotels

★ ★ ★ **COURTYARD BY MARRIOTT.** *1533 Clarendon Blvd (22209). 703/528-2222; FAX 703/528-1027.* 162 rms, 10 story, 18 suites. Apr-June, Aug-Oct: S $134; D $144; each addl $10; suites $154-$164; under 12 free; wkend rates; lower rates rest of yr. Crib free. Garage parking $6 Mon-Fri; wkends free. TV; cable (premium), VCR avail. Complimentary coffee in rms. Restaurant 6-11 am, 5-10 pm. Rm serv from 5 pm. Bar from 5 pm. Ck-out noon. Meeting rms. Business servs avail. Bellhops. Valet serv. Sundries. Coin Indry. Exercise equipt; bicycle, stair machine. Health club privileges. Indoor pool; whirlpool, lifeguard. Some refrigerators; microwaves avail. Many balconies. Cr cds: A, C, D, DS, MC, V.

D SC

★ ★ **DAYS INN CRYSTAL CITY.** *2000 Jefferson Davis Hwy (22202). 703/920-8600; FAX 703/920-2840.* 247 rms, 8 story. Mar-June, Sept-Nov: S $120-$150; D $130-$160; each addl $10; under 16 free; wkend, hol rates; lower rates rest of yr. Crib free. TV; cable (premium). Pool; lifeguard. Complimentary coffee in rms. Restaurant 6 am-2 pm, 5-10 pm; wkends 7 am-noon, 5-10 pm. Rm serv. Bar 4:30-10 pm. Ck-out 11 am. Meeting rms. Business servs avail. In-rm modem link. Bellhops. Gift shop. Valet serv. Garage parking. Free airport transportation. Exercise equipt; weight machine, treadmills. Cr cds: A, C, D, DS, ER, MC, V.

D SC

★ ★ ★ **QUALITY INN-IWO JIMA.** *1501 Arlington Blvd (Fairfax Dr) (22209), 1/2 mi W of Iwo Jima Memorial. 703/524-5000; FAX 703/522-5484.* 141 rms, 1-3 story. Mar-Nov: S, D $85-$110; each addl $7; wkend, family rates; higher rates special events; lower rates rest of yr. Crib free. TV; cable (premium), VCR avail. Indoor pool; poolside serv, lifeguard. Restaurant (in season) 6:30 am-10 pm; Sat, Sun from 7 am. Rm serv. Bar. Ck-out noon. Coin Indry. Meeting rms. Business servs avail. In-rm modem link. Bellhops. Sundries. Exercise equipt; bicycle, stair machine. Health club privileges. Refrigerators, microwaves avail. Some balconies. Cr cds: A, C, D, DS, ER, JCB, MC, V.

D SC

Hotels

★ ★ **BEST WESTERN KEY BRIDGE.** *1850 N Fort Myer Dr (22209). 703/522-0400; FAX 703/524-5275.* 178 rms, 11 story. S $113; D $123; suites $125-$155; under 12 free. Crib free. Pet accepted. TV; cable (premium). Pool. Restaurant 6:30 am-2 pm, 5-10 pm. Ck-out noon. Meeting rms. Business servs avail. Exercise equipt; bicycles, treadmill. Some refrigerators; microwaves avail. Cr cds: A, C, D, DS, MC, V.

D SC

★ ★ ★ **COURTYARD BY MARRIOTT.** *2899 Jefferson Davis Hwy (22202), near National Airport. 703/549-3434; FAX 703/549-7440.* 272 rms, 14 story. S, D $139-$154; each addl $15; suites $200-$250; under 12 free. Crib free. Garage parking $8. TV; cable (premium), VCR avail. Indoor pool; whirlpool, lifeguard. Complimentary coffee in rms. Restaurant 6-10 am, 5-10 pm. Rm serv from 5 pm. Bar 4 pm-midnight. Ck-out 1 pm. Coin Indry. Meeting rms. Business servs avail. In-rm modem link. Valet serv. Sundries. Free airport transportation. Exercise equipt; weights, bicycles, treadmill. Health club privileges. Some refrigerators, wet bars; microwaves avail. Cr cds: A, C, D, DS, ER, JCB, MC, V.

D SC

★ ★ **DOUBLETREE.** *300 Army/Navy Dr (22202). 703/416-4100; FAX 703/416-4126.* Web www.doubletreehotels.com. 632 rms, 15 story, 265 suites. S, D $190; suites $200-$400; under 18 free; wkend rates. Crib free. Pet accepted. Garage $10; valet $12. TV; cable (premium). Indoor pool; sauna, lifeguard. Restaurant 6:30 am-11 pm. Bar 11-2 am; entertainment. Ck-out noon. Convention facilities. Business servs avail. In-rm modem link. Gift shop. Free airport transportation. Health club privileges. Bathrm phones; some refrigerators; microwaves avail. Some balconies. Luxury level. Cr cds: A, C, D, DS, ER, JCB, MC, V.

D SC

★ ★ ★ **EMBASSY SUITES-CRYSTAL CITY.** *1300 Jefferson Davis Hwy (22202), entrance at 1402 S Eads St, near National Airport. 703/979-9799; FAX 703/920-5947.* 267 suites, 11 story. Feb-June, Sept-Nov: S $179-$209; D $189-$219; each addl $10; under 12 free; wkend rates; lower rates rest of yr. Crib free. TV; cable (premium). Heated pool; lifeguard. Complimentary full bkfst. Complimentary coffee in rms. Restaurant 11:30 am-10 pm; Fri, Sat to 11 pm. Bar to 11 pm. Ck-out noon. Meeting rms. Business servs avail. In-rm modem link. Gift shop. Free covered parking. Free airport transportation. Exercise equipt; weight machine, bicycles. Refrigerators. Atrium lobby. Cr cds: A, C, D, DS, JCB, MC, V.

D SC

★ ★ ★ **HILTON.** *950 N Stafford St (22203), at Fairfax Dr. 703/528-6000; FAX 703/528-4386.* 209 rms, 7 story. S $165-$185; D $185-$205;

suites $225; under 18 free; wkend rates. Crib free. TV; cable (premium). Indoor pool; whirlpool, lifeguard. Restaurant 6:30 am-11 pm. Bar 11 am-midnight. Ck-out noon. Coin Indry. Meeting rms. Business servs avail. In-rm modem link. Concierge. Gift shop. Health club privileges. Metro stop in building. Luxury level. Cr cds: A, C, D, DS, ER, JCB, MC, V.

D SC

★ ★ ★ **HOLIDAY INN NATIONAL AIRPORT.** *1489 Jefferson Davis Hwy (22202). 703/416-1600; FAX 703/416-1615.* 306 rms, 11 story. S, D $145; each addl $10; suites $159-$165; under 20 free; wkend, hol rates. Crib free. Pet accepted, some restrictions. Garage $6. TV; cable (premium), VCR avail. Pool; lifeguard. Restaurant 6 am-10 pm; Sat, Sun from 7 am. Bar 11 am-midnight. Ck-out noon. Meeting rms. Business servs avail. In-rm modem link. Gift shop. Free airport transportation. Health club privileges. Game rm. Refrigerators avail. Cr cds: A, C, D, DS, JCB, MC, V.

D SC

★ ★ ★ **HOLIDAY INN ROSSLYN WESTPARK.** *1900 N Ft Myer Dr (22209). 703/807-2000; FAX 703/522-8864.* 306 rms, 20 story. S, D $109-$119; suites $135-$150; under 18 free; wkly, wkend, hol rates. Crib free. Pet accepted. TV; cable (premium). Indoor pool, lifeguard. Restaurant 6:30 am-11 pm. Bar 11:30 am-midnight. Ck-out noon. Coin Indry. Convention facilities. Business center. In-rm modem link. Garage parking. Exercise equipt: stair machine, treadmill. Health club privileges. Some refrigerators. Balconies. Overlooking Potomac River. Cr cds: A, C, D, DS, ER, JCB, MC, V.

D SC

★ ★ ★ **HYATT ARLINGTON.** *1325 Wilson Blvd (22209), near Key Bridge at Nash St & Wilson. 703/525-1234; FAX 703/875-3393.* 302 rms, 16 story. S $185; D $210; each addl $25; suites $275-$575; under 12 free; wkend rates. Crib free. Pet accepted, some restrictions. Garage $10 (Sun-Thurs). TV; cable (premium), VCR avail. Restaurant 6:30 am-midnight. Bars 11 am-midnight. Ck-out noon. Free guest Indry. Meeting rms. Business center. In-rm modem link. Gift shop. Exercise equipt; bicycles, treadmill. Health club privileges. Metro adj. Cr cds: A, C, D, DS, ER, JCB, MC, V.

D SC

★ ★ ★ **HYATT REGENCY-CRYSTAL CITY.** *2799 Jefferson Davis Hwy (22202), near National Airport. 703/418-1234; FAX 703/418-1289.* E-mail wasrc1@erols.com. 685 rms, 20 story. S $185; D $210; each addl $25; suites $350-$725; under 18 free; wkend rates. Crib free. Garage; valet $9. TV; cable (premium), VCR avail. Heated pool; whirlpool, poolside serv, lifeguard. Complimentary coffee in rms. Restaurant 6-2 am. Bar 3 pm-1 am. Ck-out noon. Convention facilities. Business center. In-rm modem link. Concierge. Gift shop. Free airport transportation. Exercise equipt; weight machine, stair machine, saunas. Health club privileges. Some refrigerators, wet bars; microwaves avail. Some balconies. Cr cds: A, C, D, DS, ER, JCB, MC, V.

D SC

★ ★ ★ **MARRIOTT CRYSTAL GATEWAY.** *1700 Jefferson Davis Hwy (US 1) (22202), entrance on S Eads St, between 15th & 17th Sts, near National Airport. 703/920-3230; FAX 703/271-5212.* 700 units, 16 story. S, D $192-$220; suites $199-$700; under 18 free; wkend rates. Crib free. Pet accepted, some restrictions. Garage $12. TV; cable (premium). Indoor/outdoor pool; whirlpool, lifeguard. Restaurant 6:30-2 am. Bar 11-2 am. Ck-out 1 pm. Convention facilities. Business center. In-rm modem link. Concierge. Free airport transportation. Tennis privileges. Exercise equipt; weights, bicycles, sauna. Health club privileges. Original artwork. Luxury level. Cr cds: A, C, D, DS, ER, JCB, MC, V.

D SC

★ ★ ★ **MARRIOTT KEY BRIDGE.** *1401 Lee Hwy (22209). 703/524-6400; FAX 703/524-8964.* 584 rms, 2-14 story. S, D $159; suites $225-$500; wkend rates. Crib free. Garage $8. TV; cable (premium), VCR avail. Indoor/outdoor pool; whirlpool, poolside serv, lifeguard. Restaurant (see JW'S STEAKHOUSE). Bar 11-2 am; entertainment exc Sun. Ck-out 1 pm. Convention facilities. Business center. In-rm modem link. Concierge. Gift shop. Barber, beauty shop. Exercise equipt; weights, bicycles, sauna. Health club privileges. Refrigerators, microwaves avail. Some balconies. Overlooks Washington across Potomac River. Luxury level. Cr cds: A, C, D, DS, ER, JCB, MC, V.

D SC

★ ★ ★ **MARRIOTT-CRYSTAL CITY.** *1999 Jefferson Davis Hwy (22202). 703/413-5500; FAX 703/413-0192.* 345 rms, 12 story. S $189; D $209; suites $250-$400; under 18 free; wkend rates. Crib free. Valet parking $15. TV; cable (premium), VCR avail. Indoor pool; whirlpool, lifeguard. Complimentary coffee in rms. Restaurant 6:30 am-10:30 pm; Sat, Sun from 7 am. Bar 11:30 am-midnight. Ck-out 1 pm. Coin Indry. Convention facilities. Business center. In-rm modem link. Concierge. Gift shop. Free airport transportation. Exercise equipt; weight machine, stair machines, sauna. Health club privileges. Luxury level. Cr cds: A, C, D, DS, ER, JCB, MC, V.

D SC

✔★ ★ **QUALITY HOTEL COURTHOUSE PLAZA.** *1200 N Courthouse Rd (22201). 703/524-4000; FAX 703/522-6814.* Web www.qualityhotelarlington.com. 391 rms, 1-10 story. S $59.95-$125.95; D $65.95-$135.95; each addl $10; suites $109.95-$169.95; under 18 free; wkend, wkly rates. Crib free. Pet accepted, some restrictions. TV; cable (premium). Pool; lifeguard. Coffee in rms. Restaurant 6:30 am-2 pm, 5-9:30 pm. Bar 4-10 pm. Ck-out noon. Coin Indry. Convention facilities. Business servs avail. In-rm modem link. Concierge. Gift shop. Exercise equipt; weight machine, rowers, sauna. Microwaves avail. Balconies. Luxury level. Cr cds: A, C, D, DS, ER, JCB, MC, V.

D SC

★ ★ ★ **RESIDENCE INN BY MARRIOTT.** *550 Army Navy Dr (22202). 703/413-6630; FAX 703/418-1751.* 299 kit. suites, 17 story. Kit. suites $170-$235; wkend, wkly rates. Crib free. Garage parking $10/day. TV; cable (premium). Complimentary continental bkfst. Complimentary coffee in rms. Restaurant nearby. No rm serv. Ck-out noon. Meeting rms. Business servs avail. No bellhops. Concierge. Coin Indry. Free airport transportation. Exercise equipt; treadmill, stair machine. Indoor pool; whirlpool, lifeguard. Refrigerators, microwaves. Picnic tables. Cr cds: A, C, D, DS, MC, V.

D SC

★ ★ ★ ★ **THE RITZ-CARLTON, PENTAGON CITY.** *1250 S Hayes St (22202), in Pentagon City Fashion Centre Mall, near National Airport. 703/415-5000; FAX 703/415-5061.* The Persian carpets, fine art and 18th-century antiques of this quiet hotel contrast with its surroundings. Guest rooms are lavishly appointed with silk drapes and Federal-style furnishings and have panoramic views of the Capitol and the Potomac River. 345 rms, 18 story, 41 suites. S, D $184-$239; each addl $30; suites $299-$1,600; under 19 free; wkend rates. Crib free. Garage, valet parking $20. TV; cable (premium), VCR avail (movies). Indoor pool; whirlpool, lifeguard. Supervised child's activities (hols). Restaurant (see THE GRILL). Bar; entertainment. Ck-out noon. Convention facilities. Business center. In-rm modem link. Concierge. Shopping arcade. Free airport transportation. Tennis privileges. Golf privileges. Exercise rm; instructor, weight machine, bicycles, sauna, steam rm. Massage. Bathrm phones, minibars; microwaves avail. Luxury level. Cr cds: A, C, D, DS, ER, JCB, MC, V.

D

★ ★ ★ **SHERATON CRYSTAL CITY.** *1800 Jefferson Davis Hwy (22202), entrance on S Eads St; 1/2 mi S of I-395 on US 1, near National Airport. 703/486-1111; FAX 703/769-3970.* E-mail perrya@ix.netcom.com. 197 rms, 15 story. S $155-$180; D $175-$200; each addl $20; under 18 free; wkend packages. Crib $20. TV; cable (premium), VCR avail. Rooftop pool; lifeguard, sauna. Coffee in rms. Restaurant 6:30 am-10 pm; Sat, Sun from 7 am. Bar 11 am-midnight; entertainment, pianist. Ck-out 1 pm. Meeting rms. Business center. In-rm modem link. Gift shop. Free airport transportation. Exercise equipt; bicycle, rowing machine. Minibars, refrigerators; some bathrm phones. Luxury level. Cr cds: A, C, D, DS, MC, V.

D SC

Restaurants

★★ **ALPINE.** *4770 Lee Hwy (22207). 703/528-7600.* Hrs: 11:30 am-11 pm; Sun noon-10 pm. Closed most major hols. Res accepted. Italian, continental menu. Bar. Semi-a la carte: lunch $5.95-$10.75, dinner $10.95-$17.95. Specializes in veal, pasta dishes, seafood. Own pasta. Parking. Family-owned. Cr cds: A, C, D, MC, V.

D ♿

✔★★ **BISTRO BISTRO.** *4021 S 28th St (22206). 703/379-0300.* Hrs: 11 am-10 pm; Fri, Sat to 11 pm; early-bird dinner Mon-Thurs 5-6:30 pm; Sun brunch 10:30 am-3 pm. Closed Thanksgiving, Dec 25. Res accepted. Bar to 1:30 am. A la carte entrees: lunch $5.75-$10.95, dinner $6.95-$16.95. Sun brunch $6-$12. Specializes in pasta, seafood, oyster stew. Outdoor dining. Bistro atmosphere, eclectic decor. Cr cds: A, MC, V.

D ♿

★ **CAFÉ DALAT.** *3143 Wilson Blvd (22201), at N Highland St. 703/276-0935.* Hrs: 11 am-9:30 pm; Fri, Sat to 10:30 pm. Closed Chinese New Year, July 4, Thanksgiving, Dec 25. Vietnamese menu. Serv bar. Complete meals: lunch $4.25. Semi-a la carte: dinner $7.50-$8.95. Lunch buffet $4.95. Specialties: sugar cane shrimp, grilled lemon chicken. Own desserts. Totally nonsmoking. Cr cds: MC, V.

✔★★ **CARLYLE GRAND CAFE.** *4000 S 28th St (22206), S on I-395, Shirlington exit. 703/931-0777.* Hrs: 11:30 am-11 pm; Fri, Sat to midnight; Sun brunch 10:30 am-2 pm. Closed Thanksgiving, Dec 25. Bar. Semi-a la carte: lunch $5.95-$11.65, dinner $8.95-$18.95. Sun brunch $4.95-$11.95. Specialties: Virginia trout, baby back ribs, smoked salmon filet. Outdoor dining. Totally nonsmoking. Cr cds: A, MC, V.

D

✔★ **COWBOY CAFE.** *4792 Lee Hwy (22207). 703/243-8010.* Hrs: 11 am-11 pm; Fri to midnight; Sat 9 am-midnight; Sun 9 am-9 pm. Bar to 11:30 pm; Fri, Sat to 12:30 am; Sun 11 am-8:30 pm. Semi-a la carte: bkfst $2.99-$5.95, lunch, dinner $2.75-$7.95. Specializes in hamburgers, bkfst dishes. Musicians Thurs-Sat. Casual, Western decor. Cr cds: A, C, D, DS, MC, V.

♿

★ **FACCIA LUNA.** *2909 Wilson Blvd (22201). 703/276-3099.* Hrs: 11 am-11 pm; Fri, Sat to midnight; Sun noon-11 pm. Closed Thanksgiving, Dec 24, 25. Italian menu. Bar. Semi-a la carte: lunch $4.95-$5.95, dinner $7.75-$11.75. Child's meals. Specializes in pasta, pizza. Upscale pizzeria. No cr cds accepted.

D ♿

★★★ **THE GRILL.** *(See The Ritz-Carlton, Pentagon City Hotel) 703/412-2760.* Hrs: 6:30 am-10:30 pm; Sat, Sun 7 am-11 pm; Sun brunch 11 am-2:30 pm. Res accepted. Bar. Wine list. Semi-a la carte: bkfst $5-$15, lunch $6.50-$25, dinner $20-$32. Buffet: bkfst $8.75-$12.50. Sun brunch $45. Child's meals. Seasonal, Mid-Atlantic specialties including macrobiotic daily specials and cuisine vitale. Pianist Fri, Sat evenings. Valet parking. English club-like decor and atmosphere. Fireplace. Cr cds: A, C, D, DS, ER, JCB, MC, V.

D ♿ ♥

★★★ **JW'S STEAKHOUSE.** *(See Marriott Key Bridge Hotel) 703/284-1407.* Hrs: 5-10 pm; Fri to 11 pm; Sat 6-11 pm; Sun 5:30-9:30 pm; Sun brunch 10 am-2:30 pm. Closed Jan 1. Res accepted; required July 4. Bar. Wine list. A la carte entrees: dinner $15.95-$24.95. Sun brunch $23.95-$25.95. Specializes in seafood, steak. Parking. View of Washington across Potomac. Cr cds: A, C, D, DS, ER, JCB, MC, V.

D SC ♿

★★ **KABUL CARAVAN.** *1725 Wilson Blvd (22209), in Colonial Village Shopping Ctr. 703/522-8394.* Hrs: 11:30 am-2:30 pm, 5:30-11 pm; Sat, Sun from 5:30 pm. Closed Thanksgiving, Dec 25. Res accepted. Afghan menu. Serv bar. Prix fixe dinners for 2-4: $55.95-$115.95. Semi-a la carte: lunch $7.95-$11.95, dinner $10.95-$16.95. Specialties: sautéed pumpkin with yogurt & meat sauce, orange pallow, eggplant & shish kabob. Outdoor dining. Walls covered with Afghan clothing, pictures, rugs, artifacts, jewelry. Cr cds: A, MC, V.

D ♿

★★ **L'ALOUETTE.** *2045 Wilson Blvd (22201). 703/525-1750.* Hrs: 11:30 am-2:30 pm, 6-10 pm; Fri to 10:30 pm; Sat 6-10:30 pm. Closed Sun; major hols. Res accepted. French menu. Serv bar. Semi-a la carte: lunch $7.50-$11.95. A la carte entrees: dinner $14.95-$19.25. Prix fixe: dinner $18.95. Specializes in seasonal dishes. Cr cds: A, C, D, DS, MC, V.

♿

★★ **LA COTE D'OR CAFE.** *6876 Lee Hwy (22213). 703/538-3033.* Hrs: 11:30 am-3 pm, 5:30-11 pm; Sun brunch 11 am-3 pm. Closed Jan 1, Dec 25. Res accepted. French menu. Bar. Semi-a la carte: lunch $5.95-$12.75, dinner $18.25-$22.95. Sun brunch $7.50-$7.95. Specializes in seafood, veal. Pianist Wed. Outdoor dining. French decor. Cr cds: A, MC, V.

D

✔★★ **LEBANESE TAVERNA.** *5900 Washington Blvd (22205), in Westover Shopping Center. 703/241-8681.* Hrs: 11:30 am-2:30 pm, 5-10 pm; Sun 4-9 pm. Closed major hols. Res accepted Mon-Thurs. Lebanese menu. Bar. Semi-a la carte: lunch, dinner $4.50-$14. Specialties: chicken shawarma, lamb kabob, sharhat ghanam. Own baking. Lebanese decor; large windows. Family-owned. Totally nonsmoking. Cr cds: A, C, D, MC, V.

D

✔★★ **LITTLE VIET GARDEN.** *3012 Wilson Blvd (22201). 703/522-9686.* Hrs: 11 am-2:30 pm, 5-10 pm; Sat, Sun 11 am-10 pm. Closed Thanksgiving, Dec 25. Res accepted. Vietnamese menu. Bar. Semi-a la carte: lunch $4.95-$6.95, dinner $5.95-$11.95. Specialties: Viet Garden steak, grilled jumbo shrimp. Parking. Outdoor dining. Cr cds: A, C, D, DS, MC, V.

♿

★ **MATUBA.** *2915 Columbia Pike (22204). 703/521-2811.* Hrs: 11:30 am-2 pm, 5:30-10 pm; Fri, Sat 5:30-10:30 pm; Sun 5:30-10 pm. Res accepted. Japanese menu. Semi-a la carte: lunch $4.95-$8.50, dinner $5.50-$11.50. Specializes in seafood, poultry. Japanese decor. Cr cds: A, MC, V.

✔★★ **QUEEN BEE.** *3181 Wilson Blvd (22201). 703/527-3444.* Hrs: 11 am-10 pm. Vietnamese menu. Serv bar. Semi-a la carte: lunch $3.95-$7.50, dinner $6.50-$7.95. Specialties: spring roll, Hanoi beef noodle soup, Hanoi-style grilled pork. Totally nonsmoking. Cr cds: A, MC, V.

D

★ **RED HOT & BLUE.** *1600 Wilson Blvd (22209). 703/276-7427.* Hrs: 11 am-10 pm; Fri, Sat to 11 pm. Closed Thanksgiving, Dec 25. Bar. Semi-a la carte: lunch, dinner $4.69-$11.99. Specializes in Memphis pit barbecue dishes. Parking. Memphis blues memorabilia. Cr cds: A, DS, MC, V.

D ♿

★ **RT'S SEAFOOD KITCHEN.** *2300 Clarendon Blvd (22201). 703/841-0100.* Hrs: 11 am-10:30 pm; Fri, Sat to 11 pm; Sun 4-9:30 pm. Closed Jan 1, Thanksgiving, Dec 25. Cajun menu. Bar to midnight. Semi-a la carte: lunch $7.95-$10.95, dinner $11.95-$17.95. Child's meals. Specializes in Cajun-style seafood. Outdoor dining. Contemporary decor. Cr cds: A, C, D, DS, MC, V.

D

✔★ **SILVER DINER.** *3200 Wilson Blvd (22201). 703/812-8600.* Hrs: 7 am-midnight; Thurs to 1 am; Fri, Sat to 3 am; early-bird dinner Mon-Fri 4-6 pm; Sat, Sun brunch 11 am-3 pm. Closed Dec 25. Wine, beer. Semi-a la carte: bkfst $2.99-$7.99, lunch $4.99-$7.99, dinner $4.99-$11.99. Sat, Sun brunch $5.99-$7.99. Child's meals. Specializes in meatloaf, chicken, pasta. Own desserts. Reminiscent of 1950s-style aluminum-sided diner. Cr cds: A, C, D, DS, MC, V.

D SC ♿

★ ★ ★ **TIVOLI.** *1700 N Moore St (22209). 703/524-8900.* Hrs: 11:30 am-2:30 pm, 5:30-10 pm; Sat from 5:30 pm. Closed Sun; major hols. Res accepted; required Fri, Sat. Italian menu. Bar 11:30 am-midnight. Semi-a la carte: lunch $8.50-$11.50; dinner $12.50-$23.50. Prix fixe: dinner $60-$65. Specializes in pasta, seafood, veal. Contemporary decor. Cr cds: A, C, D, DS, MC, V.

D

★ ★ **TOM SARRIS' ORLEANS HOUSE.** *1213 Wilson Blvd (22209). 703/524-2929.* Hrs: 11 am-11 pm; Sat from 4 pm; Sun 4-10 pm. Res accepted. Bar. Semi-a la carte: lunch $4.25-$7.95, dinner $7.95-$14.95. Child's meals. Specializes in prime rib, NY steak, seafood. Salad bar. Parking. New Orleans atmosphere; fountains, iron railings, Tiffany lampshades. Family-owned. Cr cds: A, C, D, DS, MC, V.

★ **VILLAGE BISTRO.** *1723 Wilson Blvd (22209). 703/522-0284.* Hrs: 11:30 am-2:30 pm, 5-10:30 pm; Fri, Sat to 11 pm; Sun 5-10 pm; early-bird dinner 5-7 pm. Closed Thanksgiving, Dec 25. Res accepted; required Fri, Sat. Continental menu. Bar. Semi-a la carte: lunch $5.50-$12.95, dinner $7.95-$17.95. Specializes in seafood, pasta. Parking. Outdoor dining. Monet prints on walls. Cr cds: A, C, D, DS, MC, V.

D

★ ★ **WOO LAE OAK.** *1500 S Joyce St (22202), on grounds of River House complex. 703/521-3706.* Hrs: 11:30 am-10:30 pm. Closed Jan 1. Res accepted. Korean menu. Semi-a la carte: lunch, dinner $8-$20. Specializes in barbecued dishes prepared tableside. Parking. Large, open dining rm; Korean decor. Cr cds: A, C, D, MC, V.

Dulles Intl Airport Area, VA

Motels

★ ★ **COMFORT INN.** *(200 Elden St, Herndon 20170) Dulles Toll Rd exit 12, then left on Baron Cameron Ave (VA 606). 703/437-7555; FAX 703/437-7572.* 103 rms, 3 story. S, D $79-$229; under 19 free; wkend plans. TV; cable (premium), VCR avail. Complimentary continental bkfst. Complimentary coffee in rms. Restaurant adj 11 am-10 pm. Rm serv. Ck-out noon. Meeting rms. Business servs avail. Valet serv. Free airport transportation. Exercise equipt; weights, bicycles. Refrigerators; microwaves avail. Cr cds: A, C, D, DS, ER, JCB, MC, V.

D SC

★ ★ ★ **COURTYARD BY MARRIOTT.** *(3935 Centerview Dr, Chantilly 20151) in Dulles Business Park. 703/709-7100; FAX 703/709-8672.* 149 rms, 3 story. S $95; D $110; suites $119; under 12 free; wkly rates; higher rates special events. Crib free. TV; cable (premium). Indoor pool; whirlpool, lifeguard. Complimentary coffee in rms. Restaurant opp 11 am-midnight. Ck-out noon. Coin Indry. Meeting rms. Business servs avail. In-rm modem link. Valet serv. Sundries. Free airport transportation. Exercise equipt; treadmill, bicycle. Microwaves avail. Balconies. Picnic tables. Cr cds: A, C, D, DS, MC, V.

D SC

★ ★ ★ **COURTYARD BY MARRIOTT.** *(533 Herndon Pkwy, Herndon 20170) Dulles Toll Rd exit 11. 703/478-9400; FAX 703/478-3628.* Web www.courtyard.com/iadhc. 146 rms, 3 story. S $110; D $120; each addl $10; suites $129-$139; under 16 free; wkend rates. Crib free. TV; cable (premium). Indoor pool; whirlpool, lifeguard. Complimentary coffee in rms. Restaurant 6-10 am, 5-10 pm; wkends 7-11 am, 5-10 pm. Bar 5-10 pm. Ck-out noon. Coin Indry. Meeting rms. Business servs avail. In-rm modem link. Sundries. Valet serv. Free airport transportation. Exercise equipt; weight machine, stair machine. Cr cds: A, C, D, DS, MC, V.

D SC

★ ★ **HOLIDAY INN EXPRESS.** *(485 Elden St, Herndon 20170) Dulles Toll Rd exit 10, then E on Elden St. 703/478-9777; FAX 703/471-4624.* E-mail disales@bfsaulco.com. 115 rms, 4 story. S, D $84-$99; each addl $6; under 19 free. Crib free. Pet accepted, some restrictions. TV; cable (premium). Complimentary continental bkfst. Complimentary coffee in rms. Restaurant nearby. Ck-out 11 am. Meeting rm. Business servs avail. Valet serv. Free airport transportation. Exercise equipt; weights, bicycles. Refrigerators, microwaves avail. Cr cds: A, C, D, DS, JCB, MC, V.

D SC

★ ★ ★ **RESIDENCE INN BY MARRIOTT.** *(315 Elden St, Herndon 20170) Dulles Toll Rd exit 12, then left on Baron Cameron Rd (VA 606). 703/435-0044; FAX 703/437-4007.* Web www.marriott.com. 168 kit. units, 2 story. S, D $135-$169; wkend rates. Crib free. Pet accepted; $100 nonrefundable, $6/day. TV; cable (premium), VCR avail (movies). Pool; whirlpool, lifeguard. Playground. Complimentary continental bkfst. Complimentary coffee in rms. Restaurant opp 6:30 am-10 pm. Ck-out noon. Coin Indry. Business servs avail. In-rm modem link. Valet serv. Sundries. Lighted tennis. Health club privileges. Microwaves. Picnic tables. Cr cds: A, C, D, DS, JCB, MC, V.

D SC

Motor Hotels

✔★ **DAYS INN.** *(2200 Centreville Rd, Herndon 20170) 2 mi E on Dulles Toll Rd, exit 10. 703/471-6700; FAX 703/742-8965.* E-mail dullesdaysinn@daysinn.com; web www.shirenet .com\daysinn. 205 rms, 4 story. Apr-June, Sept-Oct: S, D $64-$139; each addl $10; under 18 free; wkend, monthly rates; lower rates rest of yr. Crib free. TV; cable (premium). Pool; whirlpool, lifeguard. Complimentary continental bkfst. Complimentary coffee in rms. Restaurant 6-1 am. Bar. Ck-out noon. Business servs avail. In-rm modem link. Bellhops. Sundries. Gift shop. Free airport transportation. Exercise equipt; weight machines, bicycles. Cr cds: A, C, D, DS, JCB, MC, V.

D SC

★ ★ ★ **HOLIDAY INN.** *(1000 Sully Rd, Sterling 20166) Dulles Toll Rd exit 9B (US 28/Sully Rd), then 1 mi N. 703/471-7411.* 296 rms, 2 story. S, D $125; suites $130-$160; each addl $10; under 18 free; wkend rates. Crib free. Pet accepted, some restrictions. TV; cable (premium). Indoor pool; whirlpool, lifeguard. Restaurant 6:30 am-10:30 pm. Rm serv to midnight. Bars 11-1:30 am, Sun to midnight; entertainment. Ck-out noon. Coin Indry. Meeting rms. Business center. In-rm modem link. Bellhops. Gift shop. Valet serv. Free airport transportation. Exercise equipt; weights, bicycles, sauna. Refrigerators avail. Rec rm. Cr cds: A, C, D, DS, JCB, MC, V.

D SC

Hotels

✔★ ★ ★ **HILTON.** *(13869 Park Center Rd, Herndon 22171) On Sully Rd (VA 28), Dulles Toll Rd exit 9A, then 1 mi S to McLearen Rd. 703/478-2900; FAX 703/834-1996.* Web www.alma.net/hilton-wda. 301 rms, 5 story. S, D $110-$165; suites $360-$690; under 18 free; wkend rates. Crib free. Pet accepted, some restrictions. TV; cable (premium), VCR avail. 2 pools, 1 indoor; poolside serv, lifeguard. Coffee in rms. Restaurant 6 am-11 pm; Sat, Sun from 6:30 am. Rm serv 24 hrs. Bars 11:30 am-midnight; entertainment. Ck-out noon. Convention facilities. Business center. In-rm modem link. Gift shop. Barber, beauty shop. Free airport transportation. Tennis. Exercise equipt; weight machines, bicycles. Some bathrm phones, refrigerators. Luxury level. Cr cds: A, C, D, DS, ER, JCB, MC, V.

D SC

★ ★ ★ **HYATT.** *(2300 Dulles Corner Blvd, Herndon 20171) Dulles Toll Rd exit 9A (VA 28/Sully Rd), then S, left on Frying Pan Rd, left on*

Horsepen Rd, then left on Dulles Corner Blvd. 703/713-1234; FAX 703/713-3410. Web www.hyatt.com. 317 rms, 14 story. S $179; D $204, suites $300-$700; wkly, wkend rates. Crib free. TV; cable (premium), VCR avail. Indoor pool; whirlpool, lifeguard. Restaurant 6 am-midnight. Bar from noon; pianist. Ck-out noon. Business center. In-rm modem link. Gift shop. Free airport transportation. Exercise equipt; weights, bicycles, sauna. Refrigerators, microwaves avail. Cr cds: A, C, D, DS, ER, JCB, MC, V.

D SC

★ ★ ★ **HYATT REGENCY-RESTON TOWN CENTER.** *(1800 President's St, Reston 22190) Dulles Toll Rd Reston Pkwy exit 12, at Reston Town Center. 703/709-1234; FAX 703/709-2291.* Web www.hyatt.com. 514 rms, 12 story. S $199; D $224; each addl $25; suites $275-$550; under 18 free; wkend packages. Crib free. Garage parking; valet (fee). TV; cable (premium), VCR avail. Indoor pool; whirlpool, poolside serv, lifeguard. Restaurant (see MARKET STREET BAR & GRILL). Bar 11:30-2 am; entertainment Fri-Sun. Ck-out noon. Convention facilities. Business center. In-rm modem link. Concierge. Shopping arcade. Free airport transportation. Tennis privileges. Golf privileges. Exercise rm; instructor, weights, bicycles, sauna. Luxury level. Cr cds: A, C, D, DS, ER, JCB, MC, V.

D SC

★ ★ ★ **MARRIOTT SUITES.** *(13101 Worldgate Dr, Herndon 20170) Dulles Toll Rd exit 10, in Worldgate Center. 703/709-0400; FAX 703/709-0434.* Web www.marriott.com. 254 suites, 11 story. S $175; D $190; under 18 free; wkend rates. Crib free. TV; cable (premium), VCR avail. Indoor/outdoor pool; whirlpool, lifeguard. Complimentary coffee in lobby. Restaurant 6:30 am-10:30 pm. Bar to 11 pm. Ck-out 1 pm. Free guest Indry. Meeting rms. Business servs avail. In-rm modem link. Free garage parking. Free airport transportation. Exercise equipt; weight machine, rowers, sauna. Health club privileges. Refrigerators, wet bars; microwaves avail. Cr cds: A, C, D, DS, ER, JCB, MC, V.

D SC

★ ★ ★ **MARRIOTT WASHINGTON.** *(333 W Service Rd, Chantilly 20221) Dulles Access Rd, at airport. 703/471-9500; FAX 703/661-8714.* Web www.marriott.com. 367 rms, 3 story. S $135; D $150; each addl $15; suites $275-$300; under 18 free; wkend plans. Crib free. TV; cable (premium), VCR avail. 2 pools, 1 indoor; whirlpool, poolside serv. Restaurant 6 am-midnight; Sat, Sun from 6:30 am. Bar 11:30-1 am. Ck-out noon. Coin Indry. Convention facilities. Business center. In-rm modem link. Concierge. Gift shop. Free airport transportation. Lighted tennis. Exercise equipt; weights, bicycles. Lawn games. Microwaves avail. Picnic area. On 21 acres with small lake; attractive landscaping. Luxury level. Cr cds: A, C, D, DS, ER, JCB, MC, V.

D SC

Resort

★ ★ ★ **WESTFIELDS MARRIOTT.** *(14750 Conference Center Dr, Chantilly 20151) 8 mi S on VA 28. 703/818-0300; FAX 703/818-3655.* Web www.marriott.com. 340 rms, 4 story. S $195; D $215; each addl $20; suites $295-$695; under 12 free; MAP avail; wkend rates. Crib free. Pet accepted, some restrictions. TV; cable (premium), VCR avail (movies). 2 pools, 1 indoor; whirlpool, poolside serv, lifeguard. Complimentary coffee in lobby. Restaurant (see PALM COURT). Rm serv 6-1 am. Box lunches, picnics. Bar 11-1 am; entertainment. Ck-out 1 pm, ck-in 3 pm. Bellhops. Valet serv. Concierge. Gift shop. Convention facilities. Business center. In-rm modem link. Valet parking. Free airport transportation. Sports dir. Lighted tennis, pro. 18-hole golf, greens fee $75. Hiking. Bicycles. Lawn games. Basketball. Exercise rm; instructor, weights, bicycles, sauna, steam rm. Massage. Health club privileges. Minibars. Balconies. Picnic tables. Cr cds: A, C, D, DS, JCB, MC, V.

D SC

Restaurants

★ ★ **CLYDE'S.** *(11905 Market St, Reston 20190) 4 mi E on Dulles Toll Rd, exit 12. 703/787-6601.* Hrs: 11 am-10 pm; Fri, Sat to 1 am; Sun from 10 am; early-bird dinner Mon-Fri 4:30-6 pm; Sun brunch to 4 pm. Closed Dec 25. Contemporary Amer menu. Bar to 2 am. Semi-a la carte: lunch $4.95-$10.95, dinner $4.95-$18.50. Sun brunch $4.95-$10.95. Specializes in aged beef, fresh seafood, hamburgers. Own baking, ice cream. Outdoor dining. Contemporary pub decor; toys, art and artifacts reminiscent of youth. Cr cds: A, C, D, DS, MC, V.

D

★ ★ **FORTUNE.** *(1428 N Point Village Ctr, Reston 22094) on VA 602 (Reston Pkwy). 703/318-8898.* Hrs: 11 am-10:30 pm; Fri, Sat to 11:30 pm. Res accepted; required Fri, Sat dinner. Chinese menu. Serv bar. A la carte entrees: lunch $1.95-$5.50, dinner $6.25-$20. Specializes in dim sum, seafood, traditional Hong Kong dishes. Chinese decor. Cr cds: A, DS, MC, V.

D

★ ★ **IL CIGNO.** *(1617 Washington Plaza, Reston 20190) in Lake Anne Shopping Center, off VA 606. 703/471-0121.* Hrs: 11:30 am-2:30 pm, 5:30-10 pm. Closed Sun (exc summer); most major hols. Res accepted; required Fri, Sat. Northern Italian menu. Bar. Semi-a la carte: lunch $7.95-$12.95, dinner $9.95-$18.95. Specializes in fish, veal, pasta. Outdoor dining overlooking Lake Anne. Split-level dining rm with original art. Cr cds: A, C, D, MC, V.

D

✔★ ★ **A LITTLE PLACE CALLED SIAM.** *(328 Elden St, Herndon 22070) Dulles Toll Rd exit 11N. 703/742-8881.* Hrs: 11:30 am-10 pm; Fri to 10:30 pm; Sat noon-10:30 pm; Sun noon-9:30 pm; early-bird dinner Sun-Thurs 4:30-6:30 pm. Closed Dec 25. Res accepted; required Fri, Sat dinner. Thai menu. Bar. Semi-a la carte: lunch $6.95-$12.95, dinner $9.95-$15.95. Specializes in pad Thai, Thai curry, seafood. Own desserts. Outdoor dining. Contemporary Thai decor with light woods, etched glass. Cr cds: A, C, D, MC, V.

★ ★ ★ **MARKET STREET BAR & GRILL.** *(See Hyatt Regency Reston Town Center Hotel) 703/709-6262.* Hrs: 11:30 am-2:30 pm, 5:30-10 pm; Fri, Sat to 11 pm; Sun 10:30 am-2:30 pm, 5-9 pm. Closed Memorial Day, July 4, Labor Day. Res accepted; required Fri, Sat. Contemporary Amer, Asian menu. Bar. A la carte entrees: lunch $6.95-$12.95, dinner $10.75-$22.75. Sun brunch $15.95. Seasonal specialties. Entertainment Fri-Sun. Valet parking. Outdoor dining. Bistro decor. Cr cds: A, C, D, DS, ER, JCB, MC, V.

D

★ ★ ★ **PALM COURT.** *(See Westfields Marriott Resort) 703/818-3520.* Hrs: 7 am-2 pm, 6-10 pm; Sun brunch 10 am-2 pm. Res accepted; required Fri, Sat, Sun brunch. Continental menu. Bar 11-1 am. Semi-a la carte: bkfst $4.75-$9.95, lunch $6.95-$14.95. A la carte entrees: dinner $21-$29.95. Sun brunch $30. Child's meals. Specializes in fresh seafood, game. Pianist. Valet parking. Formal decor. Cr cds: A, C, D, DS, JCB, MC, V.

D

★ ★ ★ **RUSSIA HOUSE.** *(790 Station St, Herndon 20170) Dulles Toll Rd exit 10. 703/787-8880.* Hrs: 11:30 am-2:30 pm, 5:30-10 pm; Sat 5:30-10:30 pm; Sun 5-9 pm. Closed most major hols. Res accepted; required Fri, Sat. Continental, Russian menu. Bar. Wine list. Semi-a la carte: lunch $8-$12.95, dinner $14-$21.95. Complete meals (wkends): dinner $25-$45. Specializes in fresh seafood, beef, veal. Pianist, violinist Fri, Sat. Parking. Modern decor highlighted by Russian artwork. Cr cds: A, C, D, DS, MC, V.

D

★ ★ **SWEETWATER TAVERN.** *(14250 Sweetwater Ln, Centreville 22020) 9 mi S on VA 28. 703/449-1100.* Hrs: 4:30-11 pm; Fri, Sat noon-1 am; Sun noon-10 pm; early-bird dinner Mon-Thurs to 6 pm. Closed Thanksgiving, Dec 25. Res accepted Sun-Thurs dinner. Bar. Semi-a la carte: lunch $4.95-$9.95, dinner $4.95-$16.95. Child's meals. Specializes in hickory-fired Angus beef, fresh seafood, chops. Own baking, desserts. Outdoor dining. Totally nonsmoking. Cr cds: A, MC, V.

D

✔★ **TORTILLA FACTORY.** *(648 Elden St, Herndon 20172) Off Dulles Toll Rd exit 10, Pines Shopping Center. 703/471-1156.* E-mail tortfact@aol.com. Hrs: 11 am-10 pm; Mon to 9 pm; Fri, Sat to 10:30 pm; Sun noon-9 pm. Closed most major hols. Res accepted. Mexican menu. Serv bar. Semi-a la carte: lunch $4.75-$6.50, dinner $5-$11.25. Child's meals. Specialties: carne machaca, chimichangas. Own tortillas. Folk music Tues. Cr cds: A, C, D, DS, MC, V.

D SC

★ **WINFIELD'S.** *(5127 Westfield Blvd, Centreville 20120) 7 mi S on VA 28, in Sully Station Shopping Center. 703/803-1040.* Hrs: 11 am-midnight; Fri, Sat to 1:30 am; Sun to 9 pm, brunch to 2 pm. Closed major hols. Res accepted; required Fri, Sat dinner. Bar. Semi-a la carte: lunch $5.25-$8.50, dinner $7.95-$14.95; Sat buffet $18.95. Sun brunch $14.95. Child's meals. Specializes in red salmon, seafood buffet (Sat). Outdoor dining. Sports bar; informal dining. Cr cds: A, C, D, MC, V.

D

Bethesda, MD

Motor Hotel

★★ **AMERICAN INN OF BETHESDA.** *8130 Wisconsin Ave (20814). 301/656-9300; FAX 301/656-2907; res: 800/323-7081.* E-mail innkeeper@american-inn.com; web www.american-inn.com. 76 rms, 5 story. S $120; D $130; each addl $5; under 18 free; wkend, wkly, monthly rates. Crib free. TV; cable (premium), VCR avail. Pool; lifeguard. Complimentary continental bkfst. Restaurant 11:30 am-10 pm; Fri, Sat to midnight; Sun to 10 pm. Ck-out 12:30 pm. Coin Indry. Meeting rms. Business center. Sundries. Valet serv. Some refrigerators. Cr cds: A, C, D, DS, MC, V.

SC

Hotels

✔★★ **HOLIDAY INN-CHEVY CHASE.** *(5520 Wisconsin Ave, Chevy Chase 20815) S on Wisconsin Ave. 301/656-1500; FAX 301/656-5045.* E-mail cornel@pop.net; web www.holidayinn.com. 215 rms, 12 story. S, D $79-$139; each addl $10; suites $115-$169; under 18 free. Crib free. Pet accepted, some restrictions; $50 deposit. TV; cable (premium), VCR avail. Pool. Complimentary coffee in rms. Restaurant 6:30 am-11 pm. Bar. Ck-out noon. Free Indry facilities. Meeting rms. Business center. In-rm modem link. Gift shop. Health club privileges. Bathrm phones; microwaves avail. Cr cds: A, C, D, DS, ER, JCB, MC, V.

D SC

★★★ **HYATT REGENCY.** *One Bethesda Metro Center (20814). 301/657-1234; FAX 301/657-6453.* Web www.hyatt.com. 381 rms, 12 story. S $195; D $220; each addl $25; suites $200-$600; under 18 free; wkend rates. Crib free. Covered parking $10; valet $12. TV; cable (premium), VCR avail. Indoor pool; lifeguard. Restaurant 6:30 am-11:30 pm. Bar 11:30-12:30 am. Ck-out noon. Convention facilities. Business center. In-rm modem link. Exercise equipt; bicycles, rower, sauna. Bathrm phones. Private patios, balconies. 12-story atrium lobby; extensive collection of artwork. Luxury level. Cr cds: A, C, D, DS, ER, JCB, MC, V.

D SC

★★★ **MARRIOTT.** *5151 Pooks Hill Rd (20814), 1 blk S of I-495 exit 34. 301/897-9400; FAX 301/897-0192.* 407 rms, 4-16 story. S $175; D $195; suites $300-$750; under 18 free; wkend plan. Crib free. TV; cable (premium), VCR avail. Indoor/outdoor pool; whirlpool, poolside serv, lifeguard. Restaurants 6:30 am-10 pm. Rm serv to 1 am. Bar 11:30 am-midnight; entertainment. Ck-out noon. Convention facilities. Business center. In-rm modem link. Gift shops. Lighted tennis. Exercise equipt: weight machines, bicycles, sauna. Game rm. Microwaves avail. Some balconies. On 18 landscaped acres. Luxury level. Cr cds: A, C, D, DS, ER, JCB, MC, V.

D SC

★★★ **MARRIOTT SUITES.** *6711 Democracy Blvd (20817). 301/897-5600; FAX 301/530-1427.* Web www.marriott.com. 274 suites, 11 story. Suites $155-$220; family rates. Crib free. TV; cable (premium), VCR avail. Indoor/outdoor pool; whirlpool, poolside serv, lifeguard. Complimentary coffee in rms. Restaurant 6:30 am-10:30 pm. Bar noon-midnight. Ck-out 11 am. Meeting rms. Business center. In-rm modem link. Metro station transportation. Exercise rm; instructor, weights, bicycles. Wet bars; microwaves avail. Balconies. Cr cds: A, C, D, DS, ER, JCB, MC, V.

D SC

★★★ **RESIDENCE INN BY MARRIOTT.** *7335 Wisconsin Ave (20814). 301/718-0200; FAX 301/718-0679.* 187 kit suites, 13 story. S, D $179-$275; under 16 free; wkend, wkly, monthly rates. Crib free. Pet accepted; $100 and $5/day. Valet parking $12. TV; cable (premium), VCR avail (movies). Pool; lifeguard. Complimentary continental bkfst. Complimentary coffee in rms. Restaurant adj 6:30 am-midnight. Ck-out noon. Coin Indry. Meeting rms. Business servs avail. Exercise equipt; weight machine, bicycles, sauna. Rec rm. Microwaves. Cr cds: A, C, D, DS, JCB, MC, V.

D SC

Restaurants

★★★ **ANDALUCIA DE BETHESDA.** *4931 Elm St (20814). 301/907-0052.* Hrs: 11:30 am-2:30 pm, 5:30-10 pm; Fri, Sat to 10:30 pm; Sun 5-9:30 pm. Closed some major hols. Res accepted; required Fri, Sat dinner. Spanish menu. Bar. Wine list. Semi-a la carte: lunch $7.25-$10.95, dinner $13.95-$22.95. Specialties: zarzuela Mediterraneo, mero en salsa verde. Own desserts. Classical guitar Sun-Thurs. Cr cds: A, C, D, DS, MC, V.

D

✔★ **AUSTIN GRILL.** *7278 Woodmont Ave (20814), at Elm St. 301/656-1366.* E-mail austingrill@aol.com; web www.austingrill.com. Hrs: 11:30 am-11 pm; Mon to 10:30 pm; Fri to midnight; Sat 11 am-midnight; Sun 11 am-10:30 pm; Sun brunch to 3 pm. Closed Thanksgiving, Dec 24, 25. Tex-Mex menu. Bar. Semi-a la carte: lunch $6-$9, dinner $6-$14. Sun brunch $5-$7. Child's meals. Specializes in chicken, fresh seafood, vegetarian dishes. Outdoor dining. Contemporary Southwestern motif. Totally nonsmoking. Cr cds: A, C, D, DS, MC, V.

D

★★ **BACCHUS.** *7945 Norfolk Ave (20814). 301/657-1722.* Hrs: noon-2 pm, 6-10 pm; Fri to 10:30 pm; Sat 6-10:30 pm; Sun 6-10 pm. Closed Thanksgiving. Res accepted; required Fri, Sat. Lebanese menu. Serv bar. Complete meals: lunch $8. Semi-a la carte: dinner $12.25-$16.25. Specialties: falafel, shish kebab. Valet parking. Outdoor dining. Cr cds: A, MC, V.

D

✔★★ **BOMBAY DINING.** *4931 Cordell Ave (20814). 301/656-3373.* Hrs: 11:30 am-2:30 pm, 5:30-10 pm; Sat, Sun noon-3 pm, 5:30-10:30 pm. Res accepted. Indian menu. Bar. Semi-a la carte: lunch, dinner $7.95-$14.95. Sat, Sun brunch $8.95. Specializes in tandoori, curries, vegetables. Salad bar. Free valet parking (dinner). Elegant decor. Cr cds: A, D, DS, MC, V.

D

★★ **BUON GIORNO.** *8003 Norfolk Ave (20814). 301/652-1400.* Hrs: 11:30 am-2:30 pm, 5:30-10 pm; Fri to 10:30 pm; Sat 5:30-10:30 pm; Sun 5:30-10 pm. Closed Mon; Jan 1, Thanksgiving, Dec 25; also mid-Aug-mid-Sept. Res accepted; required Fri, Sat. Italian menu. Serv bar. Semi-a la carte: lunch $8.95-$10.95, dinner $12.95-$19.95. Specialties:

trenette alla Genovese, pappardelle alla contadina, fresh fish. Own pasta. Valet parking (dinner). Cr cds: A, C, D, MC, V.

D

★ ★ ★ **CAFE BETHESDA.** *5027 Wilson Lane (20814), at Cordell Ave. 301/657-3383.* Hrs: 11:30 am-2 pm, 5-10 pm; Sat, Sun from 5 pm. Closed most major hols. Res accepted; required Fri, Sat. French menu. Wine, beer. Semi-a la carte: lunch $8-$12, dinner $14-$25. Complete meal (5-6 pm, Mon-Fri): dinner $17.50. Specializes in rack of lamb, seafood, veal. Valet parking. Outdoor dining. Atmosphere of French country inn. Totally nonsmoking. Cr cds: A, C, D, MC, V.

✔★ **CAPITAL WRAPPS.** *4733 Bethesda Ave (20814). 301/654-0262.* Hrs: 11:30 am-8 pm; Fri, Sat to 9 pm. Closed Sun; major hols. Southwestern menu. Bar. A la carte entrees: lunch, dinner $4.95-$5.95. Child's meals. Specializes in international foods wrapped in tortillas. Outdoor dining. Mediterranean open market atmosphere. Totally nonsmoking. No cr cds accepted.

D

★ ★ ★ **CESCO TRATTORIA.** *4871 Cordell Ave (20814). 301/654-8333.* Web www.robertdona/cesco.com. Hrs: 11:30 am-2 pm, 5:30-10 pm; Fri to 11 pm; Sat 5:30-11 pm; Sun 5:30-9 pm. Closed major hols. Res accepted; required Fri, Sat dinner. Italian menu. Bar. Wine list. A la carte entrees: lunch, dinner $12.95-$19.95. Specializes in fresh seafood, Tuscan cuisine, pasta. Own pasta. Valet parking. Outdoor dining. Contemporary Italian trattoria atmosphere. Cr cds: A, MC, V.

★ ★ **COTTONWOOD CAFE.** *4844 Cordell Ave (20814). 301/656-4844.* Web www.cottonwood-cafe.com. Hrs: 11:30 am-10 pm; Fri, Sat to 11 pm; Sun from 5:30 pm. Closed most major hols. Res accepted. Southwestern menu. Bar. Semi-a la carte: lunch $5.95-$7, dinner $12.65-$20.95. Specializes in grilled meats, seafood. Valet parking (dinner). Outdoor dining. Southwestern atmosphere. Mural of adobe village. Cr cds: A, MC, V.

D ♥

✔★ ★ **FOONG LIN.** *7710 Norfolk Ave (20814). 301/656-3427.* Hrs: 11 am-10:30 pm; Fri, Sat to 11 pm. Closed Thanksgiving. Res accepted. Chinese menu. Bar. Semi-a la carte: lunch $4.50-$7.50, dinner $7.25-$19.95. Specializes in fresh fish, Peking duckling, crispy beef. Cr cds: A, MC, V.

D ♥

★ ★ **FRASCATI RISTORANTE ITALIANO.** *4806 Rugby Ave (20814). 301/652-9514.* Hrs: 11 am-2:30 pm, 4-10:30 pm; Sat from 5 pm; Sun 4-9:30 pm; early-bird dinner Tues-Fri, Sun 4-6:30 pm. Closed Mon; Jan 1, Easter, Dec 25. Res accepted; required Fri, Sat. Italian menu. Semi-a la carte: lunch $4.75-$6.95, dinner $9.75-$15.95. Child's meals. Specializes in fresh fish, veal, pasta. Outdoor dining. Totally nonsmoking. Cr cds: A, C, D, DS, MC, V.

D

★ ★ **HAANDI.** *4904 Fairmont Ave (20814). 301/718-0121.* Hrs: 11:30 am-2:30 pm, 5-10 pm; Fri, Sat to 10:30 pm; Sun from 5 pm. Res accepted. Indian menu. Bar. Semi-a la carte: lunch $4.95-$10.95, dinner $7.95-$14.95. Buffet lunch: $6.95. Specialties: tandoori dishes, vegetarian dishes, murg makhini. Totally nonsmoking. Cr cds: A, C, D, MC, V.

D

★ ★ **IL RITROVO.** *4838 Rugby Ave (20814). 301/986-1447.* Hrs: 11:30 am-2:30 pm, 5:30-11 pm; Sat, Sun from 5:30 pm. Closed most major hols; also Sun July-Aug. Res accepted Sat, Sun. Mediterranean menu. Bar. Semi-a la carte: lunch $2.95-$11.95, dinner $8.95-$16.95. Specializes in fresh seafood. Own baking, pasta. Outdoor dining. Mediterranean decor. Cr cds: A, C, D, DS, MC, V.

D

★ ★ **JEAN-MICHEL.** *10223 Old Georgetown Rd (20814). 301/564-4910.* Hrs: 11:30 am-2:30 pm, 5:30-10 pm; Sat from 5:30 pm; Sun 5:30-8:30 pm. Closed Sun (July-Aug); also most major hols. Res accepted. French menu. Serv bar. Semi-a la carte: lunch $9.50-$13.25, dinner $12.95-$21.75. Specialties: mussels marinieres, venison with chestnut puree & cranberry jelly. French decor. Cr cds: A, C, D, MC, V.

D

★ ★ ★ **LA FERME.** *(7101 Brookville Rd, Chevy Chase 20815) E on MD 186. 301/986-5255.* Hrs: noon-2 pm, 6-10 pm; Sat from 6 pm; Sun 5-9 pm. Closed Mon; Dec 25. Res accepted; required Fri, Sat dinner. French menu. Serv bar. Wine cellar. Semi-a la carte: lunch $7.25-$10.75, dinner $15.75-$22.75. Specialties: duck with turnips & apple cider; lobster, shrimp, scallops and grouper in saffron broth; boneless breast of chicken. Pianist. Outdoor dining. Country inn decor. Cr cds: A, C, D, MC, V.

D

★ ★ **LA MICHE.** *7905 Norfolk Ave (20814). 301/986-0707.* Hrs: 11:30 am-2 pm, 6-9:45 pm; Mon, Sat from 6 pm; Sun 5:30-8 pm. Closed major hols. Res required Fri, Sat. French menu. Serv bar. A la carte entrees: lunch $6-$16, dinner $13-$24. Specialties: soufflés, fricassee of lobster, grilled breast of duck. Valet parking. Outdoor dining. French country decor. Cr cds: A, C, D, MC, V.

D

★ ★ ★ **LE VIEUX LOGIS.** *7925 Old Georgetown Rd (20814). 301/652-6816.* Hrs: 5:30-10 pm; Sun 5-9 pm. Closed Jan 1, Dec 25. Res accepted; required Sat. French, Amer menu. Serv bar. Wine list. Semi-a la carte: dinner $15-$21. Specialties: roasted Long Island duckling, grilled Norwegian salmon. Free valet parking. Outdoor dining. Rustic French inn atmosphere. Cr cds: A, C, D, MC, V.

D ♥

✔★ **MATUBA JAPANESE.** *4918 Cordell Ave (20814). 301/652-7449.* Hrs: 11:30 am-2:30 pm, 5-10 pm; Fri to 10:30 pm; Sat noon-3 pm, 5-10:30 pm; Sun 5-10 pm. Japanese menu. Wine, beer. Semi-a la carte: lunch $4.95-$9.95, dinner $6.95-$11.95. Specialties: sushi, chicken teriyaki. Casual decor. Totally nonsmoking. Cr cds: A, MC, V.

D

✔★ ★ **MONTGOMERY'S GRILLE.** *7200 Wisconsin Ave (20814), 4 mi S on I-270 exit Wisconsin Ave, at Bethesda Ave. 301/654-3595.* Hrs: 11:30 am-10 pm; Thurs to 11 pm; Fri, Sat to midnight; Sun from 10 am; Sun brunch to 2 pm. Closed Thanksgiving, Dec 25. Bar to 12:30 am; Fri, Sat to 1:30 am. Semi-a la carte: lunch $5.95-$8.95, dinner $7.95-$14.95. Sun brunch $10.95. Child's meals. Specializes in pasta, fresh grilled seafood, crab cakes. Own baking. Outdoor dining. American pub atmosphere with antique bar, bronze-framed windows, hand-carved woodwork. Totally nonsmoking. Cr cds: A, C, D, DS, MC, V.

D ♥

✔★ ★ **NAM'S OF BETHESDA.** *4928 Cordell Ave (20814). 301/652-2635.* Hrs: 11:30 am-2:30 pm, 5:30-11 pm; Sat 5-11 pm; Sun 5-9:30 pm. Closed Thanksgiving, Dec 25. Res accepted. Vietnamese menu. Bar. Semi-a la carte: lunch $5.50-$8.50, dinner $7.50-$10.50. Specializes in chicken, beef, pork. Contemporary decor. Cr cds: A, MC, V.

D

★ ★ **O'DONNELL'S.** *8301 Wisconsin Ave (20814). 301/656-6200.* Hrs: 11:30 am-10 pm; Sun noon-9 pm. Closed Dec 25. Res accepted. Bar. Semi-a la carte: lunch $5.50-$12.95, dinner $13.95-$21.95. Child's meals. Specializes in seafood. Outdoor dining on patio. Nautical theme. Family-owned. Cr cds: A, C, D, DS, MC, V.

D

★ **ORIGINAL PANCAKE HOUSE.** *7700 Wisconsin Ave (20814). 301/986-0285.* Hrs: 7 am-3 pm. Closed Dec 25. A la carte entrees: bkfst, lunch $3.95-$7.95. Child's meals. Specializes in crepes, waffles, pancakes. Casual dining. Cr cds: A, C, D, MC, V.

D

★ **RAKU.** *7240 Woodmont Ave (20814). 301/718-8681.* Hrs: 11:30 am-10 pm; Fri, Sat to 11 pm. Closed Thanksgiving, Dec 25. Pan-

Asian menu. Serv bar. Semi-a la carte: lunch $2.35-$9.25. A la carte entrees: dinner $2.35-$13.25. Child's meals. Specializes in noodles, wraps, stir fry. Own desserts. Outdoor dining. Casual decor with Oriental flair. Totally nonsmoking. Cr cds: MC, V.

D

★ ★ **RED TOMATO CAFE.** *4910 St Elmo Ave (20814). 301/652-4499.* Hrs: 11:30 am-9:30 pm; Thurs to 10 pm; Fri, Sat to 11 pm; Sun 4:30-9 pm. Closed Jan 1, Thanksgiving, Dec 25. Res accepted Thurs-Sun. Italian, Amer menu. Serv bar. A la carte entrees: lunch $3.95-$15.95, dinner $5.95-$15.95. Specializes in pasta. Valet parking. Colorful, contemporary pizzeria; large mural, wood-burning pizza oven. Totally nonsmoking. Cr cds: A, C, D, DS, MC, V.

D

★ ★ **ROCK BOTTOM BREWERY.** *7900 Norfolk Ave (20814). 301/652-1311.* Hrs: 11-1 am; Fri, Sat to 2 am. Bar. Semi-a la carte: lunch $6.50-$9.95, dinner $8.50-$17.95. Specializes in enchiladas, hamburgers, pizza. Own baking. Musicians Fri, Sat. Valet parking. American brew pub atmosphere with open kitchen, wood-burning pizza oven. Cr cds: A, C, D, MC, V.

D

★ ★ ★ **RUTH'S CHRIS STEAKHOUSE.** *7315 Wisconsin Ave (20814). 301/652-7877.* Hrs: 11:30 am-2 pm, 5-10:30 pm; Sat, Sun from 5 pm. Closed Thanksgiving, Dec 25. Res accepted; required Fri, Sat dinner. Bar to midnight. Extensive wine list. A la carte entrees: lunch $7.95-$29.95, dinner $16.95-$29.95. Specializes in beef, lobster, fresh seafood. Own desserts. Pianist exc Sun. Valet parking. Intimate, club-like atmosphere; artwork. Totally nonsmoking. Cr cds: A, C, D, MC, V.

D

★ ★ ★ **TARA THAI.** *4828 Bethesda Ave (20814). 301/657-0488.* Hrs: 11:30 am-3 pm, 5-10 pm; Fri to 11 pm; Sat noon-3:30 pm, 5-11 pm; Sun noon-3:30 pm, 5-10 pm. Closed July 4, Thanksgiving. Thai menu. Bar. Semi-a la carte: lunch $4.95-$7.95, dinner $6.95-$15.95. Specialties: grilled whole rock fish, crispy whole flounder. Underwater theme. Totally nonsmoking. Cr cds: A, C, D, DS, MC, V.

D

✔★ ★ **TEL-AVIV CAFE.** *4867 Cordell Ave (20814). 301/718-9068.* Hrs: 11:30 am-midnight; Mon to 10 pm; Sat to 1 am; Sun 4:30-10 pm. Closed Yom Kippur, Passover. Mediterranean menu. Bar to 1 am; Fri, Sat to 2 am. Semi-a la carte: lunch $4.95-$6.95, dinner $6.95-$15.95. Specializes in kabobs, vegetarian dishes, kosher dishes. Own breads, desserts. Entertainment Tues, Sat. Outdoor dining. Contemporary Mediterranean decor. Cr cds: A, C, D, DS, MC, V.

D

✔★ **THAI PLACE.** *4828 Cordell Ave (20814). 301/951-0535.* Hrs: 11 am-3 pm, 5-10 pm; Fri, Sat to 10:30 pm; Sun 11 am-10 pm. Thai menu. Serv bar. Semi-a la carte: lunch $5.75-$6.50, dinner $7.50-$12. Specializes in steamed fish, Thai cuisine. Cr cds: A, DS, MC, V.

D

★ ★ **THYME SQUARE.** *4735 Bethesda Ave (20814). 301/657-9077.* Hrs: 11 am-10 pm; Fri, Sat to 11 pm; Sun brunch to 3 pm. Closed Dec 24, 25. Res accepted; required Thurs-Sun dinner. Bar. Semi-a la carte: lunch $5.95-$10.95, dinner $6.95-$18.95. Sun brunch $5.95-$10.95. Specializes in seasonal Amer dishes, vegetarian dishes, fresh seafood. Contemporary decor with extensive murals; open kitchen. Totally nonsmoking. Cr cds: A, MC, V.

D

★ ★ ★ **TRAGARA.** *4935 Cordell Ave (20814). 301/951-4935.* Hrs: 11:30 am-2:30 pm, 5:30-10:30 pm; Sat from 5:30 pm; Sun 5-9 pm. Closed Dec 25. Res accepted; required Fri, Sat. Italian menu. Semi-a la carte: lunch $8.95-$15.95. A la carte: dinner $15.95-$25. Specialties: veal scaloppini, linguine with Maine lobster, lamb chops sauteed with herbs and mustard. Own baking, pastas. Valet parking (dinner). Italian marble, original paintings, chandelier. Cr cds: A, C, D, MC, V.

D

Unrated Dining Spot

BETHESDA CRAB HOUSE. *4958 Bethesda Ave. 301/652-3382.* Hrs: 9 am-midnight. Closed Dec 25. Res accepted. Wine, beer. A la carte entrees: lunch, dinner $10-$30. Serves only spiced shrimp, steamed crab, crabcakes. Outdoor dining. Rustic decor; established 1961. No cr cds accepted.

College Park, MD

Motel

★ ★ ★ **COURTYARD BY MARRIOTT.** *(8330 Corporate Dr, Landover 20785) 1/2 mi W of I-95 exit 19B, on US 50. 301/577-3373; FAX 301/577-1780.* Web www.courtyardlandover.com. 150 rms, 3-4 story. S $86; D $96; suites $105-$115; under 12 free; wkly, wkend rates. Crib free. TV; cable (premium), VCR avail. Indoor pool; whirlpool, lifeguard. Restaurant 6:30-10 am, 5-10 pm; Sat, Sun 7 am-noon, 5-10 pm. Bar. Ck-out noon. Coin Indry. Meeting rms. Business servs avail. In-rm modem link. Valet serv. Exercise equipt; weights, bicycles. Free RR station transportation. Microwaves avail. Many private patios, balconies. Cr cds: A, C, D, DS, MC, V.

D SC

Motor Hotel

★ ★ ★ **COURTYARD BY MARRIOTT.** *(6301 Golden Triangle Dr, Greenbelt 20770) 4 mi NE on I-495, exit 23. 301/441-3311; FAX 301/441-4978.* 152 rms, 4 story, 12 suites. S $95; D $109; each addl $10; suites $124-$134; under 17 free; wkend, wkly rates. Crib free. TV; cable (premium). Complimentary coffee in rms. Restaurant 6:30-10 am, 5-10 pm; wkends 7 am-midnight. Bar 4-11 pm Mon-Thurs. Ck-out noon. Meeting rms. Business servs avail. Bellhops. Valet serv. Sundries. Coin Indry. Exercise equipt; weight machine, bicycle. Indoor pool; whirlpool, lifeguard. Refrigerator in suites; microwaves avail. Some balconies. Cr cds: A, C, D, DS, MC, V.

D SC

Hotels

★ ★ ★ **HOLIDAY INN.** *10000 Baltimore Ave (US 1), I-495/95 exit 25. 301/345-6700; FAX 301/441-4923.* 222 rms in 2 bldgs, 4 story. S, D $119; under 18 free. Crib free. TV; cable (premium), VCR avail. Indoor pool; whirlpool, lifeguard. Coffee in rms. Restaurant 6:30 am-10 pm. Bar 11-2 am. Ck-out noon. Coin Indry. Meeting rms. Business servs avail. In-rm modem link. Gift shop. Exercise equipt; weights, treadmills, sauna. Refrigerators, microwaves avail. Cr cds: A, C, D, DS, ER, JCB, MC, V.

D SC

✔★ ★ ★ **HOLIDAY INN-CALVERTON.** *(4095 Powder Mill Rd, Beltsville 20705) I-95 exit 29B. 301/937-4422; FAX 301/937-4455.* 206 rms, 9 story. S, D $109-$129; each addl $7; suites $165; under 18 free; wkend rates; higher rates Cherry Blossom. Crib free. TV; cable (premium). Pool; lifeguard. Complimentary coffee in rms. Restaurant 6:30 am-10 pm; wkends from 7 am. Bar. Ck-out noon. Coin Indry. Meeting rms. Business servs avail. In-rm modem link. Gift shop. Exercise equipt; bicycle, treadmills. Massage. Game rm. Refrigerator; microwaves avail. Cr cds: A, C, D, DS, JCB, MC, V.

D SC

★ ★ ★ **MARRIOTT GREENBELT.** *(6400 Ivy Lane, Greenbelt 20770) 2 blks N of I-95 exit 23 (Kenilworth Ave N). 301/441-3700; FAX 301/441-3995.* 283 rms, 18 story. S $130-$150; D $134-$160; kit. units (min stay) $99-$136; family, wkend rates. Crib free. TV; cable (premium), VCR avail. 2 pools, 1 indoor; whirlpool, poolside serv, lifeguard. Restaurant 6:30 am-10:30 pm. Bar. Games. Ck-out noon. Coin Indry. Convention facilities. Business center. In-rm modem link. Gift shop. Free Metro transportation. Lighted tennis. Exercise equipt; weights, bicycles, sauna. Refrigerators, microwaves avail. Luxury level. Cr cds: A, C, D, DS, ER, JCB, MC, V.

D SC

Restaurants

✔★ ★ **ALAMO.** *(5508 Kenilworth Ave, Riverdale 20737) S on US 201; 3 mi S of I-95 exit 23. 301/927-8787.* Hrs: 11 am-11 pm. Res accepted. Mexican menu. Bar. Semi-a la carte: lunch $5-$11, dinner $8.30-$12.95. Child's meals. Specializes in tostadas, tacos, enchiladas. Entertainment Fri, Sat. Mexican decor. Cr cds: A, C, D, DS, MC, V.

★ ★ **CALVERT HOUSE INN.** *(6211 Baltimore Ave, Riverdale 20737) 1 mi S on US 1. 301/864-5220.* Hrs: 11 am-10 pm; Sat from 3 pm; Sun 3-9 pm; early-bird dinner 4-6 pm. Closed some major hols. Res accepted; required Fri, Sat dinner. Bar. Semi-a la carte: lunch $4.50-$11.95, dinner $6.95-$19.95. Child's meals. Specializes in fresh seafood, steak, crab cakes. Jazz Fri, Sat. Tavern atmosphere. Cr cds: A, C, D, DS, MC, V.

D

★ ★ ★ **CHEF'S SECRET.** *(5810 Greenbelt Rd, Greenbelt 20770) 301/345-6101.* Hrs: 11:30 am-3 pm, 5-9 pm; Fri, Sat to 10 pm; Sun 4-9 pm; early-bird dinner 5-6 pm. Closed Sun July-Aug; major hols. Res accepted. Continental menu. Serv bar. Semi-a la carte: lunch $7.95-$14.95, dinner $11.95-$17.95. Specializes in seafood, veal, steak. Own desserts. Cr cds: A, C, D, DS, MC, V.

D

✔★ **SANTA FE CAFE.** *4410 Knox Rd, off US 1, on Univ campus. 301/779-1345.* Hrs: 11 am-midnight; Tues, Thurs-Sat to midnight. Closed Sun; Thanksgiving, Dec 25. Res accepted. Southwestern, Amer menu. Bar to 1:30 am. Semi-a la carte: lunch, dinner $3.95-$6.95. Specializes in fajitas, buffalo wings, pizzas. Entertainment Tues, Thurs-Sat. Outdoor dining. Casual Southwestern decor; murals, buffalo heads, Native American rugs. Cr cds: A, DS, MC, V.

Fairfax, VA

Motels

★ ★ ★ **COURTYARD BY MARRIOTT-FAIR OAKS.** *11220 Lee Jackson Hwy (US 50) (22030), I-66, exit 57A. 703/273-6161; FAX 703/273-3505.* Web www.marriott.com/courtyard/va_197.htm. 144 rms, 3 story. S, D $71-$96; suites $89-$109; under 13 free; wkly, wkend rates. Crib free. TV; cable (premium), VCR avail. Indoor pool; whirlpool, lifeguard. Complimentary coffee in rms. Restaurant 6:30-10 am; Sat 7-11 am; Sun 7 am-noon. Bar 4-10 pm. Ck-out noon. Coin Indry. Meeting rms. Business servs avail. In-rm modem link. Valet serv. Sundries. Exercise equipt; weights, bicycles. Health club privileges. Some refrigerators; microwaves avail. Private patios, balconies. Cr cds: A, C, D, DS, JCB, MC, V.

D SC

★ ★ **HAMPTON INN.** *10860 Lee Hwy (22030). 703/385-2600; FAX 703/385-2742.* 86 rms, 5 story. S, D $75-$82; under 18 free. Crib free. TV; cable (premium). Complimentary continental bkfst. Complimentary coffee in rms. Restaurant adj 7 am-11 pm. Ck-out noon. Meeting rms. Business servs avail. In-rm modem link. Exercise equipt; treadmill, stair machine. Health club privileges. Some refrigerators, wet bars; microwaves avail. Cr cds: A, C, D, DS, MC, V.

D SC

Hotels

★ **HOLIDAY INN.** *3535 Chain Bridge Rd (22030). 703/591-5500; FAX 703/591-7483.* 127 rms, 3 story. Mar-Oct: S $79-$99; D $89-$109; each addl $10; suites $99-$129; under 18 free; lower rates rest of yr. Crib free. Pet accepted, some restrictions. TV; cable (premium). Pool. Complimentary coffee in lobby. Restaurant 6:30-10 am, 5-10 pm. Ck-out noon. Meeting rms. Business servs avail. Valet serv. Coin Indry. Health club privileges. Some refrigerators; microwaves avail. Cr cds: A, C, D, DS, JCB, MC, V.

D SC

★ ★ ★ **HOLIDAY INN FAIR OAKS MALL.** *11787 Lee Jackson Hwy (22033), I-66, exit 57B. 703/352-2525; FAX 703/352-4471.* E-mail hifo@erols.com. 312 rms, 6 story. S, D $129-$149; each addl $10; under 19 free; wkend, hol rates. Crib free. Pet accepted. TV; cable (premium), VCR avail. Indoor pool; lifeguard. Complimentary coffee in rms. Restaurant 6:30 am-midnight. Bar; entertainment. Ck-out noon. Coin Indry. Convention facilities. Business center. In-rm modem link. Concierge. Gift shop. Airport transportation. Exercise equipt; weight machine, bicycle, sauna. Health club privileges. Game rm. Microwaves avail. Balconies. Luxury level. Cr cds: A, C, D, DS, ER, JCB, MC, V.

D SC

★ ★ ★ **HYATT FAIR LAKES.** *12777 Fair Lakes Circle (22033), at I-66 exit 55B. 703/818-1234; FAX 703/818-3140.* 316 rms, 14 story. S, D $159-$189; each addl $25; suites $199-$475; under 18 free; wkend rates. Crib free. TV; cable (premium), VCR avail. Indoor pool; whirlpool, lifeguard. Restaurant 6:30 am-11 pm; Fri, Sat to midnight. Bar 11:30-1 am; entertainment. Ck-out noon. Convention facilities. Business center. In-rm modem link. Free airport, RR station transportation. Exercise equipt; weights, bicycles, sauna. Refrigerators avail. Cr cds: A, C, D, DS, ER, JCB, MC, V.

D SC

Inn

★ ★ ★ **BAILIWICK.** *4023 Chain Bridge Rd (VA 123) (22030). 703/691-2266; FAX 703/934-2112; res: 800/366-7666.* E-mail bailiwick@erols.com. 14 rms, some with shower only, 4 story. No elvtr. S, D $130-$299. TV; VCR avail. Complimentary full bkfst. Restaurant (see BAILIWICK INN). Ck-out 11 am, ck-in 2 pm. Health club privileges. Some in-rm whirlpools, fireplaces. Restored private residence (1800); antiques. The first Civil War skirmish occured here in June of 1861. Totally nonsmoking. Cr cds: A, MC, V.

D SC

Restaurants

★ ★ **ARTIE'S.** *3260 Old Lee Hwy (22030). 703/273-7600.* E-mail artiesrest@aol.com. Hrs: 11:30 am-midnight; Fri, Sat to 1 am; Sun 10 am-11 pm; Sun brunch to 3 pm; early-bird dinner Mon-Thurs 5-6 pm. Closed Thanksgiving, Dec 25. Bar. Semi-a la carte: lunch $6.25-$9.75, dinner $6.25-$19.95. Sun brunch $6.25-$9.95. Specializes in steak, seafood, pasta. Parking. Cr cds: A, MC, V.

D

★ ★ **BAILIWICK INN.** *(See Bailiwick Inn) 703/691-2266.* E-mail bailiwick@erols.com. Hrs: noon-2 pm, 6-9 pm; Tues to 2 pm; Sat, Sun from 6 pm. Closed Mon. Res required. French menu. A la carte entrees: lunch $12-$18. Complete meals: dinner $45; Fri, Sat $55. Specializes in chicken, beef, seafood. Parking. Menu changes monthly. Patio dining overlooking English garden. In restored inn (1800). Totally nonsmoking. Cr cds: A, MC, V.

✔★ **BLUE OCEAN.** *9440 Main St (22031). 703/425-7555.* Hrs: 11:30 am-2:30 pm, 5-10 pm; Fri to 10:30 pm; Sat noon-2:30 pm, 5-10:30 pm; Sun from 5 pm. Closed Mon; most major hols. Res accepted. Japanese menu. Serv bar. Semi-a la carte: lunch $7.95-$9.95, dinner $5.50-$17.95. Buffet: lunch $7.95. Specialties: sushi, teriyaki, sukiaki. Salad bar. Authentic Japanese decor; sushi bar. Cr cds: A, C, D, MC, V.

D

★★ **BOMBAY BISTRO.** *3570 Chain Bridge Rd (22030). 703/359-5810.* Hrs: 11:30 am-2:30 pm, 5-10 pm; Fri, Sat to 10:30 pm; Sun brunch noon-3 pm. Closed Thanksgiving. Indian menu. Bar. A la carte entrees: lunch, dinner $5.95-$15.95. Buffet (Mon-Fri) $6.95. Sat, Sun brunch $8.95. Specializes in tandoori, vegetarian dishes. Outdoor dining. Indian decor. Cr cds: A, C, D, DS, MC, V.

D

★★ **CONNAUGHT PLACE.** *10425 North St (22030). 703/352-5959.* Hrs: 11:30 am-2:30 pm, 5-10 pm; Sat noon-3 pm, 5-10 pm; Sun noon-3 pm, 5-9 pm. Closed Thanksgiving, Dec 25. Res accepted. Indian menu. Bar. Semi-a la carte: lunch $5-$11, dinner $6.95-$16.95. Buffet $7.95-$8.95. Sat, Sun brunch $8.95. Specializes in seafood, vegetarian dishes. Middle Eastern decor. Cr cds: A, C, D, MC, V.

D

★★ **HEART-IN-HAND.** *(7145 Main St, Clifton 22024) S on VA 123 to Chapel Rd, then W. 703/830-4111.* Hrs: 11 am-2:30 pm, 6-9:30 pm; Sun 5-8 pm; Sun brunch 11 am-2:30 pm. Closed Jan 1, July 4, Dec 25. Res accepted. Semi-a la carte: lunch $5.95-$12.95, dinner $14.95-$22.95. Sun brunch $6.95-$12.95. Child's meals. Specializes in seafood, beef Wellington, rack of lamb. Own ice cream. Parking. Outdoor dining. Converted general store (ca 1870). Antique decor; original floors, ceiling fans, antique quilts. Totally nonsmoking. Cr cds: A, C, D, DS, MC, V.

★★★ **HERMITAGE INN.** *(7134 Main St, Clifton 22024) W on US 29 to Clifton Rd (VA 645), then S. 703/266-1623.* Hrs: 11:30 am-2:30 pm, 6-10 pm; Sun 11:30 am-2:30 pm, 5-9 pm. Closed Mon. Res accepted. Continental menu. Serv bar. Semi-a la carte: lunch $5.50-$12.75, dinner $13.95-$26.95. Sun brunch $17.95. Specialties: rack of lamb, Long Island duck, châteaubriand. Own pastries. Outdoor dining. Located in 1869 clapboard hotel. Country French decor. Cr cds: A, C, D, DS, MC, V.

D

★★ **J.R.'S STEAK HOUSE.** *9401 Lee Hwy (22030), in Circle Towers office building. 703/591-8447.* Hrs: 5:30-9:30 pm; Fri, Sat to 10:30 pm; Sun 5-9:30 pm. Closed Mon; Thanksgiving, Dec 25. Res accepted. Bar. Semi-a la carte: dinner $12.95-$18.50. Child's meals. Specializes in aged steak, grilled meat and fish. Salad bar. Parking. Patio dining. Cr cds: A, C, D, DS, MC, V.

D

✔★ **P.J. SKIDOO'S.** *9908 Lee Hwy (22030). 703/591-4516.* Hrs: 11-2 am; Sun 10 am-9 pm. Closed Thanksgiving, Dec 25. Bar. Semi-a la carte: lunch, dinner $5.50-$12.95. Sun brunch $8.95. Child's meals. Specializes in prime rib, fresh seafood, chicken. Entertainment Tues, Thurs-Sat. Parking. 1890s saloon atmosphere. Cr cds: A, MC, V.

✔★★ **SILVERADO.** *(7052 Columbia Pike, Annandale 22003) 7 mi SE on VA 244. 703/354-4560.* Hrs: 11:30 am-10:30 pm; Fri to 11:30 pm; Sat noon-11:30 pm; Sun noon-9:30 pm; early-bird dinner Mon-Thurs 5-6 pm. Closed Thanksgiving, Dec 25. Southwestern menu. Bar. Semi-a la carte: lunch $5-$9, dinner $7-$12. Child's meals. Specializes in fajitas, roasted chicken. Own desserts. Southwestern decor; stained glass, Western sculpture and mural. Totally nonsmoking. Cr cds: A, MC, V.

D

✔★★ **TASTE OF THAI.** *9534 Arlington Blvd (22031). 703/352-4494.* Hrs: 11:30 am-10:30 pm; Fri, Sat 11 am-11 pm; Sun 4-9:30 pm. Closed Dec 25. Res accepted; required Fri, Sat dinner. Thai menu. Bar. Semi-a la carte: lunch $5.50-$6.50, dinner $7.95-$11.95. Specialties: duck with basil, garlic shrimp, pad Thai. Thai decor; aquarium along one wall. Cr cds: A, DS, MC, V.

D

Unrated Dining Spot

THE ESPOSITOS/PIZZA 'N PASTA. *9917 Lee Hwy. 703/385-5912.* Hrs: 11 am-11 pm; Fri to midnight; Sat noon-midnight; Sun noon-10 pm. Closed Thanksgiving, Dec 24 evening, Dec 25. Southern Italian menu. Wine, beer. A la carte entrees: lunch, dinner $3.50-$11.50. Semi-a la carte: lunch $5.50-$12.95, dinner $6.25-$13.95. Specialties: pollo cardinale, fettucine alla Romano. Own pasta. Parking. Pizza baked in wood-burning oven imported from Italy. Italian trattoria decor. Cr cds: A, C, D, MC, V.

D

McLean, VA

Restaurants

✔★ **ANGKOR WAT.** *6703 Lowell Ave (22101), at Old Dominion Dr (VA 309), in shopping center. 703/893-6077.* Hrs: 11 am-2:30 pm, 5-9:30 pm; Fri, Sat 5-10 pm; Sun from 5 pm. Closed some major hols; also Sun July-Aug. Res accepted. Cambodian menu. Wine, beer. Semi-a la carte: lunch $5.25-$6.95, dinner $6.95-$9.95. Complete meals: dinner $12.99. Specializes in soup, char-broiled dishes. Cr cds: A, C, D, DS, MC, V.

★★ **CAFE BELLA.** *6710 Old Dominion Rd (22101). 703/448-7787.* Hrs: 11:30 am-2:30 pm, 6-10 pm; Fri to 10:30 pm; Sat 5-10:30 pm; Sun 5-9 pm. Closed some major hols. Res accepted; required Fri, Sat (dinner). French, Italian menu. Serv bar. A la carte entrees: lunch $6.95-$10.95, dinner $10.95-$18.95. Complete meals: lunch $9.95. Specializes in pasta, veal, seafood. Parking. Elegant dining; oil landscapes. Cr cds: A, C, D, DS, MC, V.

D

★★ **CAFE OGGI.** *6671 Old Dominion Dr (22101). 703/442-7360.* Hrs: 11:30 am-2:30 pm, 5:30-10 pm; Sat, Sun from 5:30 pm. Closed major hols. Res accepted; required Fri, Sat dinner. Italian menu. Serv bar. A la carte entrees: lunch $6.95-$9.95, dinner $9.95-$19.95. Specializes in homemade pastas, fresh seafood, veal. Own baking, pasta. Cr cds: A, C, D, DS, MC, V.

★★ **CAFE TAJ.** *1379 Beverly Rd (22101), in Market Place Shopping Ctr. 703/827-0444.* Hrs: 11:30 am-2:30 pm, 5:30-10 pm; Fri, Sat to 10:30 pm. Closed July 4. Res accepted. Indian menu. Bar. Semi-a la carte: lunch $6.95-$8.95, dinner $7.95-$14.95. Lunch buffet (Mon-Fri) $8.99. Specialties: tandoori chicken tikka, prawns masala. Outdoor dining. Modern decor. Cr cds: A, D, DS, MC, V.

D

★ **CHARLEY'S PLACE.** *6930 Old Dominion Dr (22101), jct VA 123 & VA 309/738. 703/893-1034.* Hrs: 11 am-10 pm; Fri to 10:30 pm; Sat noon-10:30 pm; Sun 10:30 am-9 pm; early-bird dinner 4-6 pm; Sun brunch 10:30 am-2 pm. Closed Dec 25. Bar to midnight. Semi-a la carte: lunch $5.99-$8.29, dinner $5.99-$18.49. Child's meals. Specializes in chicken, beef, seafood. Outdoor dining. Parking. Fireplaces. Cr cds: A, C, D, DS, MC, V.

★★★ **DANTE RISTORANTE.** *(1148 Walker Rd, Great Falls 22066) 703/759-3131.* Hrs: 11:30 am-2:30 pm, 5:30-10:30 pm; Sat from

5:30 pm; Sun 4-9 pm. Closed some major hols. Res accepted; required Fri, Sat. Northern Italian menu. Bar. Wine list. A la carte entrees: lunch $9.25-$13.50, dinner $14.25-$22.95. Child's meals. Specialties: grilled Dover sole, grilled veal chops. Own pasta, bread. Parking. Patio dining. Converted country house. Cr cds: A, C, D, DS, MC, V.

D

★ ★ **EVANS FARM INN.** *1696 Chain Bridge Rd (22101). 703/356-8000.* Hrs: 11:30 am-9 pm; Sat to 10 pm; Sun from 11 am, brunch to 2 pm. Closed Dec 25. Res accepted; required Fri-Sun. Semi-a la carte: lunch $7.95-$10.95, dinner $14.95-$24.95. Buffet (Mon-Sat): lunch $11.95. Sun brunch $7.25-$12.95. Child's meals. Specializes in ham, fresh seafood, colonial-era cooking. Own baking. Salad bar. Parking. 18th century-style inn on 21 acres. Family-owned. Cr cds: A, C, D, DS, JCB, MC, V.

D

★ ★ ★ **FALLS LANDING.** *(774 Walker Rd, Great Falls 22066) I-495 exit 13A, 6 mi W in Village Center. 703/759-4650.* Hrs: 11:30 am-2:30 pm, 5:30-10 pm; Fri to 10:30 pm; Sat 5:30-10:30 pm; Sun 4-9 pm; Sun brunch 11:30 am-2:30 pm. Closed Mon; also most major hols. Res accepted. Serv bar. Semi-a la carte: lunch $8.95-$12.95, dinner $16.95-$24.95. Sun brunch $8-$13.95. Child's meals. Specializes in nouvelle cuisine. Outdoor dining. 18th-century colonial-style decor; beamed ceiling, century-old pine paneling. Cr cds: A, C, D, DS, MC, V.

D

★ ★ **KAZAN.** *6813 Redmond Dr (22101). 703/734-1960.* Hrs: 11 am-2:30 pm, 5-10 pm; Sat 5-10:30 pm. Closed Sun. Res accepted. Turkish menu. Serv bar. Semi-a la carte: lunch $6.95-$11.95, dinner $11.95-$18.95. Child's meals. Specializes in seafood, lamb. Middle Eastern decor. Cr cds: A, C, D, MC, V.

D

★ ★ ★ **L'AUBERGE CHEZ FRANCOIS.** *(332 Springvale Rd, Great Falls) 4 mi N of jct VA 7 & 674N. 703/759-3800.* Hrs: 5:30-9:30 pm; Sun 1:30-8 pm. Closed Mon; Jan 1, July 4, Dec 25. Res required. French menu. Serv bar. Wine cellar. Table d'hôte: dinner $32-$41. Prix fixe: dinner $23.50 (Tue-Thur, Sun). Specialties: salmon soufflé de l'Auberge; le sauté gourmandise de l'Auberge; la choucroute royale garnie comme en Alsace. Own baking, ice cream. Outdoor dining. Chef-owned. Jacket. Totally nonsmoking. Cr cds: A, C, D, MC, V.

D

★ ★ ★ **LA BONNE AUBERGE.** *(9835 Georgetown Pike, Great Falls 22066) 6 mi W on VA 193. 703/759-3877.* Hrs: 6-10 pm; Sun 5-8:30 pm. Closed Jan 1, July 4. Res accepted; required Fri, Sat. French menu. Bar. A la carte entrees: dinner $14.95-20.95. Specializes in seafood, rack of lamb. Formal decor. Cr cds: A, C, D, MC, V.

D

★ ★ **PULCINELLA.** *6852 Old Dominion Dr (22101). 703/893-7777.* Hrs: 11:30 am-10:45 pm; Sat, Sun from noon. Closed Thanksgiving, Dec 25. Italian menu. Bar. Semi-a la carte: lunch $4.25-$13.95, dinner $6.50-$16.50. Specializes in pasta, chicken. Italian decor. Cr cds: A, C, D, MC, V.

★ ★ ★ **RISTORANTE IL BORGO.** *1381-A Beverly Rd (22101), in Market Place Shopping Center. 703/893-1400.* Web www.menuson line.com/cities/wash_dc/desc/ilborgoristorante.shtml. Hrs: 11 am-midnight; Fri to 1 am; Sat 5 pm-1 am; Sun 4-10:30 pm. Closed most major hols. Res accepted; required Fri, Sat dinner. Italian menu. Bar. Wine list. Semi-a la carte: lunch $4.75-$9.50, dinner $9-$19.50. Specializes in veal, pasta, seafood. Own pastas, desserts. Cr cds: A, C, D, DS, MC, V.

D

★ ★ ★ **SERBIAN CROWN.** *(1141 Walker Rd, Great Falls 20066) 5 mi W on VA 7, then 1/2 mi N on VA 743. 703/759-4150.* Hrs: 5:30-10 pm; Thurs, Fri noon-2:30 pm; Sun 4-9 pm. Res accepted; required Fri-Sun. Russian, Serbian, French menu. Bar. Wine list. A la carte entrees: lunch $12.50-$19.50, dinner $17.50-$26. Prix fixe: dinner $32, $40. Specialty: kulebiaka. Extensive vodka selection. Piano bar Tue, Fri, Sat. Gypsy music Wed-Sun. Parking. Intimate atmosphere; antique Russian paintings. Enclosed, heated terrace dining. Family-owned. Cr cds: A, C, D, MC, V.

D

★ ★ **SITTING DUCK PUB.** *1696 Chain Bridge Rd (22102), lower level of Evans Farm Inn Restaurant. 703/356-8000.* Hrs: 11:30 am-2 pm, 5-11 pm; Sat 5 pm-midnight; Sun 11 am-2 pm. Closed Dec 25. Res accepted. Continental, Amer menu. Bar. Semi-a la carte: lunch $7.95-$10.95, dinner $14.95-$24.95. Sun brunch $7.25-$12.95. Specializes in beef, seafood. Pianist, guitarist Fri-Sun. Parking. Large stone fireplace. Colonial-era prints. Family-owned. Cr cds: A, C, D, DS, JCB, MC, V.

★ ★ **TACHIBANA.** *6715 Lowell Ave (22101). 703/847-1771.* Hrs: 11:30 am-2 pm, 5-10 pm; Fri to 10:30 pm; Sat 5-10:30 pm. Closed Sun; some major hols. Res accepted Mon-Thurs. Japanese menu. Serv bar. Semi-a la carte: lunch $6.50-$10, dinner $8.95-$20. Complete meals: dinner $16.50-$30. Specialties: sushi, sashimi, soft shell crab tempura (in season). Parking. Circular dining rm. Totally nonsmoking. Cr cds: A, C, D, DS, MC, V.

D

Rockville, MD

Motels

★ ★ ★ **COURTYARD BY MARRIOTT.** *2500 Research Blvd (20850). 301/670-6700; FAX 301/670-9023.* 147 rms, 2 story, 13 suites. S $110; D $120; suites $129-$139; under 12 free; wkly rates. Crib free. TV; cable (premium). Indoor pool; whirlpool, lifeguard. Complimentary coffee. Restaurant 6:30 am-2 pm, 5-10 pm; Sat 7-11 am; Sun 7 am-2 pm. Rm serv 5-10 pm. Bar 5-11 pm. Ck-out 1 pm. Coin Indry. Meeting rms. Business servs avail. In-rm modem link. Valet serv. Sundries. Exercise equipt; weight machine, bicycles. Balconies. Refrigerators avail. Cr cds: A, C, D, DS, MC, V.

D SC

✔★ **DAYS INN.** *16001 Shady Grove Rd (20850). 301/948-4300; FAX 301/947-3235.* 189 rms, 2 story. S, D $45-$70; each addl $5; under 18 free; wkend rates. Crib free. Pet accepted. TV; cable (premium). Pool. Playground. Restaurant 6:30 am-10 pm. Bar 10-12:30 am, Sun from 11 am. Ck-out 11 am. Business servs avail. Cr cds: A, C, D, DS, MC, V.

D SC

Motor Hotels

★ ★ ★ **QUALITY SUITES.** *3 Research Ct (20850), 3 mi N on I-270, exit 8. 301/840-0200; FAX 301/258-0160.* 124 rms, 3 story, 66 kit. suites. S, D $109.95-$119.95; each addl $10; kit. suites $125.95-$139.95; under 18 free; wkend rates. Crib free. TV; cable (premium), VCR avail. Complimentary full bkfst. Complimentary coffee in rms. Restaurant nearby. Ck-out noon. Meeting rms. Business center. Valet serv. Sundries. Gift shop. Coin Indry. Exercise equipt; weight machine, stair machine. Pool; lifeguard. Refrigerators, microwaves, wet bars. Cr cds: A, C, D, DS, MC, V.

D SC

★ ★ ★ **WOODFIN SUITES.** *1380 Piccard Dr (20850), I-270 exit 8. 301/590-9880; FAX 301/590-9614; res: 800/237-8811.* 203 suites, 3 story. S, D $165-$230; each addl $15; 2-bedrm suites $275; under 12 free. Crib free. TV; cable (premium). Pool; whirlpool, lifeguard. Complimentary full bkfst. Restaurant 6-9 am, wkends 7-10 am. Bar 5-10 pm Mon-Thurs. Ck-out noon. Meeting rms. Business center. In-rm modem link. Valet serv. Sundries. Free local transportation. Exercise equipt; weight machine, treadmill. Refrigerators, microwaves. Cr cds: A, C, D, DS, ER, JCB, MC, V.

D SC

Hotel

★ ★ ★ **DOUBLETREE.** *1750 Rockville Pike (20852). 301/468-1100; FAX 301/468-0163.* 315 rms, 8 story. S $149; D $159; each addl $10; suites $195-$325; under 19 free; wkly, wkend rates. Crib free. TV; cable (premium). Indoor/outdoor pool; whirlpool, lifeguard. Coffee in rms. Restaurant 6:30-12:30 am. Bar from 11 am; Fri, Sat to 1 am. Ck-out noon. Convention facilities. Business center. In-rm modem link. Concierge. Gift shop. Beauty shop. Covered valet parking. Exercise equipt: weights, bicycles, sauna. Game rm. Refrigerators, microwaves avail. 8-story atrium; 20-ft waterfall. Gazebo. Luxury level. Cr cds: A, C, D, DS, ER, JCB, MC, V.

D SC

Restaurants

✔ ★ **A & J.** *1319-C Rockville Pike (20852). 301/251-7878.* Hrs: 11:30 am-9 pm; Sat, Sun from 11 am. Chinese menu. A la carte entrees: lunch $4.50-$9, dinner $6.25-$9. Specializes in dim sum. Casual decor. Totally nonsmoking. No cr cds accepted.

D

✔ ★ ★ **ADDIE'S.** *11120 Rockville Pike (20852). 301/881-0081.* Hrs: 11:30 am-2:30 pm, 5:30-9:30 pm; Fri to 10 pm; Sat noon to 3 pm, 5:30-10 pm. Closed Sun; Jan 1, Thanksgiving, Dec 25. Res accepted Mon-Thurs dinner. Regional Amer menu. Bar. Semi-a la carte: lunch $6.50-$10.95, dinner $11.95-$17.50. Child's meals. Specializes in seasonal American dishes. Own pastries. Outdoor dining. Eclectic decor; collection of whimsical clocks; wood-burning grill. Cr cds: A, C, D, MC, V.

D

★ ★ **ANDALUCIA.** *12300 Wilkens Ave (20852). 301/770-1880.* Hrs: 11:30 am-2:30 pm, 5:30-10 pm; Sat 5:30-10:30 pm; Sun 4:30-9:30 pm. Closed Mon; Jan 1. Res accepted; required Fri, Sat dinner. Spanish menu. Serv bar. A la carte entrees: lunch $7.50-$10.95, dinner $12.50-$19.95. Specialties: paella Valenciana, zarzuela costa del sol. Own desserts. Mediterranean decor; many plants. Totally nonsmoking. Cr cds: A, C, D, DS, MC, V.

✔★ ★ **BENJARONG THAI.** *855-C Rockville Pike (20852). 301/424-5533.* Hrs: 11:30 am-9:30 pm; Fri, Sat to 10:30 pm; Sun 5-9:30 pm. Closed most major hols. Res accepted. Thai menu. Bar. Semi-a la carte: lunch $5.95-$7.95, dinner $7.95-$11.95. Specializes in pad thai, chicken satay, seafood. Thai decor. Cr cds: A, C, D, DS, MC, V.

D

✔★ ★ **BOMBAY BISTRO.** *98 W Montgomery Ave (20850). 301/762-8798.* Hrs: 11 am-2:30 pm, 5-9:30 pm; Fri, Sat to 10 pm; Sun noon-3 pm, 5-9:30 pm. Closed Thanksgiving. Indian menu. Wine, beer. A la carte entrees: lunch, dinner $6.95-$15.95. Buffet lunch: $6.95-$8.95. Specializes in vegetarian, tandoori dishes. Casual decor. Cr cds: A, C, D, DS, MC, V.

D

★ ★ **COPELAND'S OF NEW ORLEANS.** *1584 Rockville Pike (20852). 301/230-0968.* E-mail store8@vni.net. Hrs: 11 am-11 pm; Sun, Mon to 10 pm; Fri, Sat to midnight. Closed Thanksgiving, Dec 25. Bar; Semi-a la carte: lunch $6-$13.95, dinner $5.95-$19.95. Child's meals. Specializes in seafood, Creole & Cajun dishes. Art deco decor. Cr cds: A, C, D, DS, MC, V.

D

✔ ★ **FOUR RIVERS.** *184 Rollins Ave (20852). 301/230-2900.* Hrs: 11:30 am-10:30 pm; Fri, Sat to 11 pm; Sun to 10 pm. Res accepted; required Fri, Sat dinner. Chinese menu. Bar. Semi-a la carte: lunch $4.50-$5.95, dinner $6.95-$12.95. Specialties: golden crispy shrimp, sizzling black pepper steak. Casual decor; aquarium in lobby. Totally nonsmoking. Cr cds: DS, MC, V.

D

★ ★ **IL PIZZICO.** *15209 Frederick Rd (20850). 301/309-0610.* Hrs: 11 am-2:30 pm, 5-9:30 pm; Fri to 10 pm; Sat 5-10 pm. Closed Sun; most major hols. Italian menu. Bar. Semi-a la carte: lunch $6.95-$10.95, dinner $8.95-$13.95. Specializes in pasta, seafood. Italian decor. Cr cds: A, MC, V.

D

★ ★ ★ **NORMANDIE FARM.** *(10710 Falls Rd, Potomac 20854) 3½ mi SW on MD 189, I-270 exit 5. 301/983-8838.* Hrs: 11:30 am-2:30 pm, 6-10 pm; Sun 5-9 pm; Sun brunch 11 am-2 pm. Closed Mon. Res accepted. French menu. Bar. Semi-a la carte: lunch $6-$12.50, dinner $12-$23. Sun brunch $16.95. Specializes in seafood, veal. Entertainment Thur-Sat. French provincial decor. Cr cds: A, DS, MC, V.

D

★ ★ ★ **OLD ANGLER'S INN.** *(10801 MacArthur Blvd, Potomac 20854) approx 8 mi S on MD 189, I-270 Exit 5. 301/299-9097.* Hrs: noon-2:30 pm, 6-10:30 pm. Closed Mon. Bar. Wine list. A la carte entrees: lunch $12-$16, dinner $22-$29. Specializes in seafood, rack of lamb. Patio dining overlooking wooded area. Stone inn (1860); fireplace. Family-owned. Cr cds: A, C, D, MC, V.

♥

✔ ★ **RED, HOT & BLUE.** *16811 Crabbs Branch Way (20855), in Grove Shopping Center. 301/948-7333.* Hrs: 11 am-10 pm; Fri to 11 pm; Sat noon-11 pm; Sun from noon. Closed Thanksgiving, Dec 25. Bar. Semi-a la carte: lunch, dinner $5.95-$12.95. Child's meals. Specializes in Memphis pit barbecue, ribs. Outdoor dining. Casual decor; blues memorabilia. Totally nonsmoking. Cr cds: A, MC, V.

D

✔★ **SEVEN SEAS.** *1776 E Jefferson St (20852). 301/770-5020.* Hrs: 11:30-1 am. Closed Thanksgiving. Res accepted. Chinese menu. Bar. Semi-a la carte: lunch $3.95-$6.50, dinner $7.25-$16.95. Specializes in Szechwan, Taiwan, Shanghai. Sushi bar. Chinese artwork. Cr cds: A, DS, MC, V.

D

✔★ **SILVER DINER.** *11806 Rockville Pike (MD 355) (20852), in Mid-Pike Plaza. 301/770-4166.* Hrs: 7-2 am; Fri, Sat to 3 am; early-bird dinner Mon-Fri 4-6 pm. Closed Dec 25. Serv bar. Semi-a la carte: bkfst $3.95-$5.95, lunch $5.45-$7.95, dinner $5.95-$9.99. Child's meals. Specialties: meatloaf, chicken-pot pie, turkey. 1950s-style diner with jukeboxes. Servers dressed in period clothing. Cr cds: A, C, D, DS, MC, V.

D SC ♥

★ ★ **TASTE OF SAIGON.** *410 Hungerford Dr (20850). 301/424-7222.* Hrs: 11 am-10 pm; Fri, Sat to 11 pm; Sun 11 am-9:30 pm. Closed Thanksgiving, Dec 25. Res accepted. Vietnamese menu. Bar. A la carte entrees: lunch $5.95-$14.95, dinner $7.95-$16.95. Specialties: black pepper soft shell crab and shrimp, pepper saigon steak. Outdoor dining. Contemporary decor. Cr cds: A, C, D, DS, MC, V.

D

★ ★ **THAT'S AMORE.** *15201 Shady Grove Rd (20850). 301/670-9666.* Hrs: 11:30 am-10:30 pm; Fri to midnight; Sat 4 pm-midnight; Sun 4-9:30 pm. Closed Labor Day, Thanksgiving, Dec 25. Italian menu. Bar. A la carte entrees: lunch $5.95-$9.95, dinner $15-$38. Specializes in pasta, veal, chicken. Stained-glass windows. Early 20th-century mens club atmosphere. Cr cds: A, C, D, DS, MC, V.

D

✔★ ★ **WÜRZBURG HAUS.** *7236 Muncaster Mill Rd (20855), in Red Mill Shopping Center. 301/330-0402.* Hrs: 11:30 am-9 pm; Fri to 10 pm; Sat noon-10 pm; Sun noon-9 pm. German menu. Wine, beer. A la carte entrees: lunch $8.75-$12.95, dinner $9.95-$14.75. Child's meals. Specializes in schnitzel, wurst. Accordionist Fri, Sat. 2 dining areas. German, Austrian atmosphere; collection of beer steins. Cr cds: A, C, D, DS, MC, V.

D

Unrated Dining Spot

HARD TIMES CAFE. *1117 Nelson St (20850), in Woodley Garden Shopping Center. 301/294-9720.* Hrs: 11:30 am-10 pm; Fri, Sat to 11 pm; Sun noon-9 pm. Closed Thanksgiving, Dec 25. Bar. A la carte entrees: lunch, dinner $4.50-$6. Child's meals. Specializes in chili, vegetarian dishes. Cr cds: A, MC, V.

D

Silver Spring, MD

Motel

★★★ **COURTYARD BY MARRIOTT.** *12521 Prosperity Dr (20904), 6 mi NE on US 29, then E on Cherry Hill Rd to Prosperity Dr. 301/680-8500; FAX 301/680-9232.* 146 units, 3 story. S $99; D $109; suites $131-$141; wkly, wkend rates. Crib free. TV; cable (premium). Indoor pool; whirlpool, lifeguard. Complimentary coffee in rms. Restaurant 6:30-10 am, 5-10 pm; Sat, Sun 7 am-1 pm. Bar 4-10 pm. Ck-out noon. Coin Indry. Meeting rms. Business servs avail. In-rm modem link. Valet serv. Sundries. Exercise equipt; weights, bicycles. Health club privileges. Refrigerators, microwaves avail. Cr cds: A, C, D, DS, ER, JCB, MC, V.

D SC

Restaurants

★★ **BLAIR MANSION INN.** *7711 Eastern Ave (20912). 301/588-1688.* Hrs: 11:30 am-9 pm; Sat from 5 pm; Sun from 2 pm. Res accepted. Continental, Amer menu. Bar. Semi-a la carte: lunch $5.95-$9.95, dinner $9.95-$19.95. Specializes in poultry, beef, crab. Murder mystery dinners Fri, Sat, some Sun. 1890s Victorian mansion; gaslight chandelier, 7 fireplaces. Family-owned. Totally nonsmoking. Cr cds: A, C, D, DS, MC, V.

★★ **CRISFIELD AT LEE PLAZA.** *8606 Colesville Rd (MD 29) (20910), ground floor of high rise building, in Lee Plaza. 301/588-1572.* Hrs: 11:30 am-10 pm; Fri to 11 pm; Sat 4-11 pm; Sun 2:30-9:30 pm. Closed Thanksgiving, Dec 25. Res accepted; required Fri, Sat. Bar. Semi-a la carte: lunch $4.50-$15.95, dinner $14.95-$17.95. Child's meals. Specializes in seafood, baked stuffed shrimp, crab. Art deco decor. Cr cds: A, C, D, MC, V.

D

★★★ **MRS. K'S TOLL HOUSE.** *9201 Colesville Rd (20910). 301/589-3500.* Hrs: 11:30 am-2:30 pm, 5-9 pm; Fri, Sat to 9:30 pm; Sun 11 am-9 pm; Sun brunch to 1 pm. Closed Mon; Dec 25. Serv bar. Complete meals: lunch $11.75, dinner $17.25-$24.95. Sun brunch $15.75. Specializes in regional American cuisine. Century-old tollhouse; antique china, glass. Gardens. Totally nonsmoking. Cr cds: A, C, D, DS, MC, V.

D

★ **VICINO.** *959 Sligo Ave (20910). 301/588-3372.* Hrs: 11:30 am-10:30 pm; Mon to 9:30 pm; Sun 1-9:30 pm. Closed some major hols; also Dec 31. Italian menu. Wine, beer. A la carte entrees: lunch, dinner $6.50-$12. Child's meals. Specializes in pizza, pasta, seafood. Outdoor dining. Casual Italian neighborhood decor. Totally nonsmoking. Cr cds: MC, V.

Tyson's Corner, VA

Motels

★★ **COMFORT INN.** *(1587 Spring Hill Rd, Vienna 22182) 1½ mi W of I-495, exit 10B. 703/448-8020; FAX 703/448-0343.* 250 rms, 3 story. S, D $89-$109; each addl $5; suites $109-$114; under 18 free. Crib free. Pet accepted, some restrictions. TV; cable (premium). Pool; lifeguard. Complimentary continental bkfst. Coffee in rms. Ck-out noon. Coin Indry. Meeting rms. Business servs avail. In-rm modem link. Valet serv. Free airport transportation. Health club privileges. Refrigerators, microwaves avail. Cr cds: A, C, D, DS, ER, JCB, MC, V.

D SC

★★ **RESIDENCE INN BY MARRIOTT.** *(8616 Westwood Center Dr, Vienna 22182) I-495 exit 10B to VA 7, then 2 mi W. 703/893-0120; FAX 703/790-8896.* 96 kit. suites, 2 story. Kit. suites $149-$199; each addl $10; under 18 free; wkend rates. Crib free. Pet accepted; $85 and $5/day. TV; cable (premium), VCR avail (movies). Pool; whirlpool, lifeguard. Complimentary continental bkfst 6:30-9 am; Sat, Sun 7:30-10 am. Restaurant nearby. Ck-out noon. Coin Indry. Meeting rm. Business servs avail. In-rm modem link. Valet serv. Lighted tennis. Health club privileges. Many fireplaces. Picnic tables, grills. Cr cds: A, C, D, DS, MC, V.

D SC

Hotels

★★★ **EMBASSY SUITES.** *(8517 Leesburg Pike, Vienna 22182) I-495 exit 10B to VA 7, then 2 mi W. 703/883-0707; FAX 703/883-0694.* Web www.embassysuites.com. 232 suites, 8 story. S, D $169-$189; each addl $10; under 12 free; wkend rates. Crib free. TV; cable (premium). Indoor pool; whirlpool. Complimentary full bkfst. Restaurant 11:30 am-11 pm. Bar. Ck-out noon. Business servs avail. In-rm modem link. Gift shop. Exercise equipt; bicycles, treadmill, sauna. Refrigerators, microwaves, wet bars. Cr cds: A, C, D, DS, JCB, MC, V.

D SC

✔★★★ **HOLIDAY INN OF TYSONS CORNER.** *(1960 Chain Bridge Rd, McLean 22102) 2 blks W of I-495 exit 11B. 703/893-2100; FAX 703/356-8218.* 316 rms, 9 story. S, D $144-$159; each addl $15; family rates; wkend rates. Crib free. TV; cable (premium). Indoor pool; whirlpool. Restaurant 6:30 am-10 pm. Bar; entertainment. Ck-out 1 pm. Conference facilities. Business center. In-rm modem link. Gift shop. Airport transportation. Exercise equipt; weights, bicycles. Balconies. Cr cds: A, C, D, DS, JCB, MC, V.

D SC

★★★ **MARRIOTT.** *(8028 Leesburg Pike, Vienna 22182) 1 blk W of I-495 exit 10W. 703/734-3200; FAX 703/442-9301.* 390 units, 15 story. S, D $154-$174; suites $250; family rates; wkend packages. Crib free. TV; cable (premium). Indoor pool; whirlpool, poolside serv, lifeguard. Restaurant 6:30 am-11 pm. Bar 4:30 pm-1 am, Fri to 2 am, Sat 7 pm-2 am, closed Sun. Ck-out noon. Convention facilities. Business servs avail. In-rm modem link. Gift shop. Coin Indry. Some covered parking. Exercise equipt; weights, bicycle, sauna. Refrigerators avail. Luxury level. Cr cds: A, C, D, DS, ER, JCB, MC, V.

D SC

★★★ **McLEAN HILTON AT TYSONS CORNER.** *(7920 Jones Branch Dr, McLean 22102-3308) S on VA 123, turn right at Tysons Blvd, right on Galleria Dr/Westpark Dr, then right on Jones Branch Dr. 703/847-5000; FAX 703/761-5100.* E-mail mclean_hilton@hilton.com; web www.hilton.com. 458 units, 9 story. S $150-$210; D $170-$230; each addl $20; suites $375-$1750; wkly, wkend rates. Crib free. TV; cable (premium), VCR avail (free movies). Indoor pool; lifeguard. Restaurant 6:30 am-11 pm. Rm serv 6-2 am. Bar 11-2 am; entertainment. Ck-out noon. Convention facilities. Business center. In-rm modem link. Gift shop. Exercise equipt; weights, bicycles, sauna. Minibars. Atrium lobby; marble floors, fountain. Luxury level. Cr cds: A, C, D, DS, ER, JCB, MC, V.

D SC

★ ★ ★ ★ **THE RITZ-CARLTON, TYSONS CORNER.** *(1700 Tysons Blvd, McLean 22102) N via I-495 exit 11B, adj Tysons II Mall. 703/506-4300; FAX 703/506-4305.* A keynote of this hotel is its superb service. The lobby, furnished with antiques and 18th-century oil paintings, sets a tone of comfort and elegance that is carried through in the generously appointed guest rooms. 399 units, 24 story. S, D $170-$250; suites $375-$1,400; under 16 free; monthly rates; wkend family rates; lower rates some wkends. Crib free. Garage parking $12; valet $4. TV; cable (premium), VCR avail (movies $4). Indoor pool; whirlpool, lifeguard. Supervised child's activities (wkends only). Restaurant (see THE RESTAURANT). Afternoon tea in lounge. Rm serv 24 hrs. Bar 11:30-1 am; entertainment. Ck-out noon. Convention facilities. Business center. In-rm modem link. Concierge. Gift shop. Beauty shop. Tennis privileges. 18-hole golf privileges, greens fee $75, pro, putting green, driving range. Exercise rm; instructor, weight machine, bicycles, sauna. Massage. Bathrm phones, minibars; microwaves avail. Luxury level. Cr cds: A, C, D, DS, JCB, MC, V.

D

★ ★ ★ **SHERATON PREMIERE.** *(8661 Leesburg Pike, Vienna 22182) I-495 exit 10B, then 2½ mi W on VA 7. 703/448-1234; FAX 703/893-8193.* E-mail jkennedy@sptc.com; web www.sptc.com. 437 rms, 24 story. S $155-$170; D $175-$195; each addl $15; suites $375-$2,000; under 17 free; wkly rates. Crib free. TV; cable (premium), VCR avail. 2 pools, 1 indoor; whirlpool, poolside serv, lifeguard. Complimentary coffee in rms. Restaurant 6:30 am-midnight. Rm serv 24 hrs. Bars 11-1 am. Ck-out noon. Convention facilities. Business center. In-rm modem link. Concierge. Gift shop. Drugstore. Free airport transportation. Lighted tennis privileges. 18-hole golf privileges, pro, greens fee. Racquetball. Exercise equipt; weights, bicycles, sauna. Massage. Health club privileges. Bathrm phones; some refrigerators. Cr cds: A, C, D, DS, ER, JCB, MC, V.

D SC

Restaurants

★ ★ **AARATHI INDIAN CUISINE.** *(409 Maple Ave E, Vienna 22180-4722) approx 2 mi S on VA 123, in Danor Plaza. 703/938-0100.* Hrs: 11:30 am-2:30 pm, 5:30-10 pm; Fri, Sat to 10:30 pm. Closed July 4, Dec 25. Res accepted; required Fri, Sat dinner. Indian menu. Serv bar. Semi-a la carte: lunch $4.95-$8.50, dinner $4.95-$12.95. Lunch buffet $6.95. Specializes in curry and vegetarian dishes. Cr cds: A, C, D, DS, MC, V.

D

★ ★ **BONAROTI.** *(428 Maple Ave E, Vienna 22180) 3 mi W on I-495 on VA 123, in Wolf Trappe Shopping Center. 703/281-7550.* Hrs: 11:30 am-3 pm, 5-10:30 pm; Sat 5-11 pm. Closed Sun; some major hols. Res accepted. Italian menu. Bar. Semi-a la carte: lunch $8.95-$13.95, dinner $13.95-$22.95. Child's meals. Specializes in veal, pasta, seafood. Own pastries, pasta. Italian art. Cr cds: A, C, D, MC, V.

✔★ ★ **CLYDE'S.** *(8332 Leesburg Pike, Vienna 22182) 10 blks W of I-495 exit 10B on VA 7, then right. 703/734-1901.* Hrs: 11-2 am; Sun brunch 10 am-4 pm. Res accepted. Bar. A la carte entrees: lunch $4.95-$10.95, dinner $6.50-$15.50. Child's meals. Specializes in pasta, seafood, sandwiches. Entertainment Thurs-Sat. Parking. Original art collection. Cr cds: A, C, D, DS, MC, V.

D SC

★ ★ **DA DOMENICO.** *(1992 Chain Bridge Rd, McLean 22102) 2 blks W of I-495 exit 11B. 703/790-9000.* Hrs: 11:30 am-11 pm; Sat from 5 pm. Closed Sun; major hols. Res accepted; required Fri, Sat. Northern Italian menu. Bar. Semi-a la carte: lunch $7.95-$9.95, dinner $9.95-$23.95. Specializes in veal chop, seafood, fresh pasta. Parking. Italian garden decor. Cr cds: A, C, D, DS, MC, V.

★ ★ **FEDORA CAFE.** *(8521 Leesburg Pike, Vienna 22180) 703/556-0100.* Web fedora@erols.com. Hrs: 11:30 am-10:30 pm; Fri, Sat to 11 pm; Sun 10:30 am-2 pm, 4:30-9:30 pm. Res accepted. Bar to 12:30 am. Semi-a la carte: lunch $6.95-$11.95, dinner $8.95-$22.95. Specializes in rotisserie chicken, spit-roasted duck, fresh fish. Own pasta, desserts. Pianist Wed-Fri, Sun brunch. Valet Wed-Fri. Cr cds: A, C, D, DS, MC, V.

D

★ **HUNAN LION.** *(2070 Chain Bridge Rd, Vienna 22182) S of I-495 on VA 123, I-495 exit 11B, third light on right. 703/734-9828.* Hrs: 11:30 am-10:30 pm; Fri, Sat to 11 pm. Closed Thanksgiving. Res accepted. Chinese menu. Bar. Semi-a la carte: lunch $6-$8, dinner $6-$10.50. Specialties: triple delicacy prawns, orange beef, General Tso's chicken. Parking. Cr cds: A, C, D, DS, MC, V.

D

★ ★ **J.R.'S STOCKYARDS INN.** *(8130 Watson St, McLean 22102) ½ mi W of I-495 exit 10B. 703/893-3390.* E-mail steaks@jrsbeef.com; web www.jrsbeef.com. Hrs: 11:30 am-3 pm, 5-10:30 pm; Fri to 11 pm; Sat 5-11 pm; Sun 5-9 pm. Closed July 4, Thanksgiving, Dec 24, 25. Res accepted; required Fri, Sat. Bar. Semi-a la carte: lunch $4.50-$8.95, dinner $12.95-$19.95. Child's meals. Specializes in marinated sirloin, prime aged beef, fresh seafood. Parking. Western-style chop house. Cr cds: A, C, D, DS, MC, V.

★ ★ ★ **LA PROVENCE.** *(144 W Maple Ave, Vienna 22180) 2½ mi W on VA 123. 703/242-3777.* Hrs: 11:30 am-2:30 pm, 5:30-10 pm. Closed Sun; most major hols. Res accepted; required Fri, Sat dinner. French Provençale menu. Bar. Extensive wine list. Semi-a la carte: lunch $6.95-$12.95, dinner $15.95-$22.95. Specialties: bouillabaisse, duck confit. Own baking. Open bistro atmosphere; large flower murals. Totally nonsmoking. Cr cds: A, C, D, DS, MC, V.

D

★ ★ ★ **LE CANARD.** *(132 Branch Rd, Vienna 22180) VA 123 at Branch Rd, in Danor Shopping Center. 703/281-0070.* E-mail tiger spaw.com/bite/lecanard.htm; web www.erols.com/bitebyte/lecanard.htm. Hrs: 11:30 am-2:30 pm, 5:30-10:30 pm; Fri to 11 pm; Sat 6-11 pm. Res accepted; required Fri, Sat. French menu. Bar to 2 am. Wine list. Semi-a la carte: lunch $4.75-$10, dinner $13.95-$22.95. Specializes in fresh seafood, veal, beef. Own pastries. Piano bar. Cr cds: A, C, D, DS, MC, V.

D

★ ★ **MARCO POLO.** *(245 Maple Ave W, Vienna 22180) 2½ mi N of I-66 exit 62. 703/281-3922.* Hrs: 11:30 am-10:30 pm; Fri, Sat to 11 pm; early-bird dinner Thurs 5:30-7:30 pm. Closed Sun exc Mother's Day. Res accepted. Continental, Northern Italian menu. Serv bar. Semi-a la carte: lunch $6-$9, dinner $11-$18. Buffet: lunch (Tues-Fri) $8.25, dinner (Thurs) $14.50. Child's meals. Specializes in fresh seafood, fresh pasta, veal. Parking. Cr cds: A, C, D, MC, V.

D

✔★ ★ **MASQUERADE.** *(8601 Westwood Center Dr, Vienna 22180) I-495 exit 10B, then 2½ mi W on VA 7. 703/848-9476.* E-mail kabaudan@aol.com. Hrs: 11 am-11 pm; Fri, Sat to 1 am; Sun from 10:30 am; Sun brunch to 2:30 pm. Res accepted. Contemporary American menu. Bar. Semi-a la carte: lunch $6.50-$12.95, dinner $8.95-$16.95. Sun brunch $6.95-$10.95. Child's meals. Specializes in salads, sandwiches, grilled dishes. Parking. Patio dining. Take-out gourmet market. Cr cds: A, C, D, DS, MC, V.

D

★ ★ ★ **MORTON'S OF CHICAGO.** *(8075 Leesburg Pike, Vienna 22182) I-495 exit 10W, then 1/4 mi W on VA 7 (Leesburg Pike) on left. 703/883-0800.* Hrs: 11:30 am-2:30 pm, 5:30-11 pm; Sat from 5:30 pm; Sun 5-10 pm. Closed major hols. Res accepted; required Thurs-Sat. Bar. Wine list. A la carte: lunch $7.95-$18.95, dinner $19.95-$29.95. Specializes in steak, seafood. Valet parking. Jacket. Cr cds: A, C, D, JCB, MC, V.

D

★ ★ ★ **NIZAM'S.** *(523 Maple Ave W, Vienna 22180) In Village Green Shopping Ctr. 703/938-8948.* Hrs: 11 am-3 pm, 5-10 pm; Sat 5-11 pm; Sun 4-9 pm. Closed Jan 1, Thanksgiving, Dec 25. Res accepted, required Fri, Sat. Turkish menu. Serv bar. Semi-a la carte: lunch $5.25-$10.50, dinner $11.95-$17.50. Specializes in beef, lamb, chicken. Turkish artwork. Totally nonsmoking. Cr cds: A, DS, MC, V.

D

✔★ ★ **PANJSHIR II.** *(224 W Maple Ave, Vienna 22180) 3 mi W on I-495, exit 10B; on VA 123. 703/281-4183.* Hrs: 11:30 am-2 pm, 5-10 pm; Sun 5-9 pm. Closed Jan 1, July 4, Thanksgiving. Res accepted. Afghan menu. Bar. Semi-a la carte: lunch $5.95-$7.25, dinner $9.95-$13.25. Specializes in kebabs, saffron rice, vegetarian dishes. Parking. Cr cds: A, C, D, MC, V.

D

★ ★ **PHILLIPS SEAFOOD GRILL.** *(8330 Boone Blvd, Vienna 22182) approx 2 mi S on VA 123, I-495 exit 10A. 703/442-0400.* Hrs: 11:30 am-9:30 pm; wkends to 10 pm; early-bird dinner Mon-Fri 5-6 pm. Closed Dec 25. Res accepted; required Fri, Sat dinner. Bar. Semi-a la carte: lunch $5.95-$9.95, dinner $8.95-$19.95. Child's meals. Specialties: crab cakes, free-range chicken, raw bar. Parking. Outdoor dining. Hickory wood-burning grills. Family-owned. Cr cds: A, C, D, DS, MC, V.

D SC

★ ★ **PIERRE ET MADELEINE.** *(246 E Maple Ave, Vienna 22180) 2 mi N of I-66 exit 62. 703/938-4379.* Hrs: 11:30 am-2 pm, 5:30-10 pm; Fri to 10:30 pm; Sat 5:30-10:30 pm. Closed Sun. Res accepted. French menu. Bar. Semi-a la carte: lunch $4.75-$11.95, dinner $15-$21.95. Complete meals: dinner $34.95. Specialties: fresh Maine lobster with vanilla sauce, ravioli with snails. Parking. Cr cds: A, C, D, MC, V.

★ ★ ★ **PRIMI PIATTI.** *(8045 Leesburg Pike, Vienna 22182) W of I-495 exit 10 W B. 703/893-0300.* Hrs: 11:30 am-2:30 pm, 5:30-10 pm; Fri to 10:30 pm; Sat 5:30-10:30 pm. Closed Sun; most major hols. Res accepted; required Fri, Sat. Italian menu. Bar. Semi-a la carte: lunch $9.95-$14, dinner $11-$18. Specializes in contemporary Italian cuisine. Valet parking. Outdoor dining. Cr cds: A, C, D, MC, V.

D

★ ★ ★ **THE RESTAURANT.** *(See The Ritz-Carlton, Tysons Corner Hotel) 703/506-4300.* Hrs: 6:30 am-10 pm; Sun 6:30-11 am, 5-10 pm; Sun brunch 11 am-2:30 pm. Res accepted. Wine list. Semi-a la carte: lunch $12-$24. Complete meals: dinner $32, $39, $45, $60. Sun brunch $37. Child's meals. Specializes in seafood, lamb chops, prime aged beef. Harpist. Valet parking. Cr cds: A, C, D, DS, JCB, MC, V.

D

★ ★ **TARA THAI.** *(226 Maple Ave W, Vienna 22180) approx 2 mi S on VA 123, 2 mi N I-66 exit 62. 703/255-2467.* Hrs: 11:30 am-3 pm, 5-10 pm; Fri to 11 pm; Sat noon-3:30 pm, 5-11 pm; Sun noon-3:30 pm, 5-10 pm. Closed July 4. Res accepted; required Fri, Sat dinner. Thai menu. Bar. Semi-a la carte: lunch $4.95-$7.95, dinner $6.95-$12.95. Specializes in pad Thai, fresh seafood, grilled fish. Parking. Underwater ocean decor. Cr cds: A, C, D, DS, MC, V.

D

★ **THAT'S AMORE.** *(150 Branch Rd SE, Vienna 22180) approx 2 mi S on VA 123, I-495 exit 11B. 703/281-7777.* Hrs: 11:30 am-10:30 pm; Fri to midnight; Sat 4 pm-midnight; Sun 4-9:30 pm. Closed Labor Day, Thanksgiving, Dec 25. Italian menu. Bar. A la carte: lunch $5.95-$9.95, dinner $15-$38 (dinner entrees serve 2 people). Specializes in pasta, seafood, chicken. Parking. Cr cds: A, C, D, DS, MC, V.

D

✔★ **WU'S GARDEN.** *(418 Maple Ave E, Vienna 22180) 3 mi W off I-495 exit 11A. 703/281-4410.* Hrs: 11:30 am-10 pm; Sat noon-11 pm. Closed Thanksgiving. Res accepted. Chinese menu. Bar. Semi-a la carte: lunch $4-$7, dinner $7.95-$12. Specialties: kung pao chicken, crispy shrimp with walnuts. Parking. Oriental screens and artwork. Cr cds: A, D, DS, MC, V.

D

Houston

Founded: 1836
Pop: 1,630,553
Elev: 55 feet
Time zone: Central
Area codes: 713, 281
Web: www.houston-guide.com

Houston is a big, rich, modern city with an atmosphere of dynamic vitality. From cowboys and cotton to a major seaport and energy technology center, Houston has always been far reaching and prosperous. The space shuttle program has once again brought this city to the forefront of space exploration. All this and a strong commitment to cultural activities makes Houston a city with something for everyone.

From the beginning—when two brothers, in 1836, promoted the sale of 4,429 acres on Buffalo Bayou—Houston has been prosperous. With the discovery of oil in 1901 and again in 1904, Houston plunged headlong into a period of rapid expansion. Even during the Great Depression this city flourished.

The latest census shows Houston to be the fourth most populous city in the the nation. Ongoing development in and around the city, including a new convention center, theater center and visitor center at Johnson Space Center, shows that the same spirit and energy that raised Houston from a small pioneer settlement is still strong today.

Business

Most important to the city of Houston is its seaport—the nation's third largest and the largest in the Southwest. It handles more than 150 steamship lines providing regular service between the Port of Houston and some 250 ports throughout the world. Buffalo Bayou is part of the Houston Ship Channel, a 400-foot-wide, 40-foot-deep, 52-mile-long, man-made waterway that flows into the Gulf of Mexico.

Houston is ranked first in the nation in the manufacturing and distribution of petroleum equipment, first in pipeline transmission and first as a refinery center.

Bordering Houston's city limits is the NASA Lyndon B. Johnson Space Center, which has brought fame and another industry to this city. Space Center Houston, designed by Walt Disney Imagineering, Inc, interprets the past, present and future of American space exploration.

The Texas Medical Center, near downtown, is one of the most renowned modern medical facilities in the world. Some two million patients come here annually from around the globe. Its diversity is seen in more than 40 different medical institutions, the most famous of which specialize in the fields of heart disease and cancer treatment.

Convention Facilities

Houston has three convention centers—the George R. Brown Convention Center, the Summit and Astrodome USA.

The George R. Brown Convention Center, a state-of-the-art facility, has 600,000 square feet of exhibit space, 43 meeting rooms and the largest ballroom in Texas.

The Summit contains 17,000 square feet of space, plus permanent seating for more than 17,000.

Astrodome USA is an all-encompassing, 375-acre area providing year-round entertainment. Astrohall and Astroarena have a total of 750,000 square feet and 300,000 square feet of exhibition and meeting space, respectively, making it the world's largest one-floor exhibition facility. It also has 25 meeting rooms and parking for 25,000 cars.

Sports & Recreation

The world-famous Astrodome, the first all-purpose, air-conditioned, domed stadium, is the home of the Astros (baseball). The Houston Rockets (basketball) play to enthusiastic crowds in the Summit, the city's entertainment/sports complex. Houston's international polo team plays in Memorial Park.

Located across the street from the Astrodome is Six Flags AstroWorld, with its 11 different theme areas offering entertainment for the entire family with 100 rides; Six Flags WaterWorld, a 15-acre water park; live entertainment; and fireworks spectaculars.

Golf courses and tennis courts abound in the Houston area. Horse, dog and car racing are also accessible. The nearby bays and beaches on the Gulf of Mexico provide many opportunities for water sports and fishing.

Entertainment

Houston's cultural events are many and varied, with something to satisfy every taste. Among the nation's oldest permanent resident theaters, the Alley Theatre delights audiences with superb productions. Houston's many other fine repertory, campus and professional companies, including experimental stand-up comedy, Black theater and a local musical production company, round out the city's offerings for theatrical entertainment.

Since its beginning in 1913, the Houston Symphony Orchestra has been inspiring audiences. This professional body of more than 90 musicians performs some 120 concerts each year in Houston, nearby cities, around the country and abroad. During the summer there are concerts at Miller Outdoor Theater in Hermann Park. The Houston Grand Opera, Houston Ballet and many other performing companies add to Houston's cultural flavor.

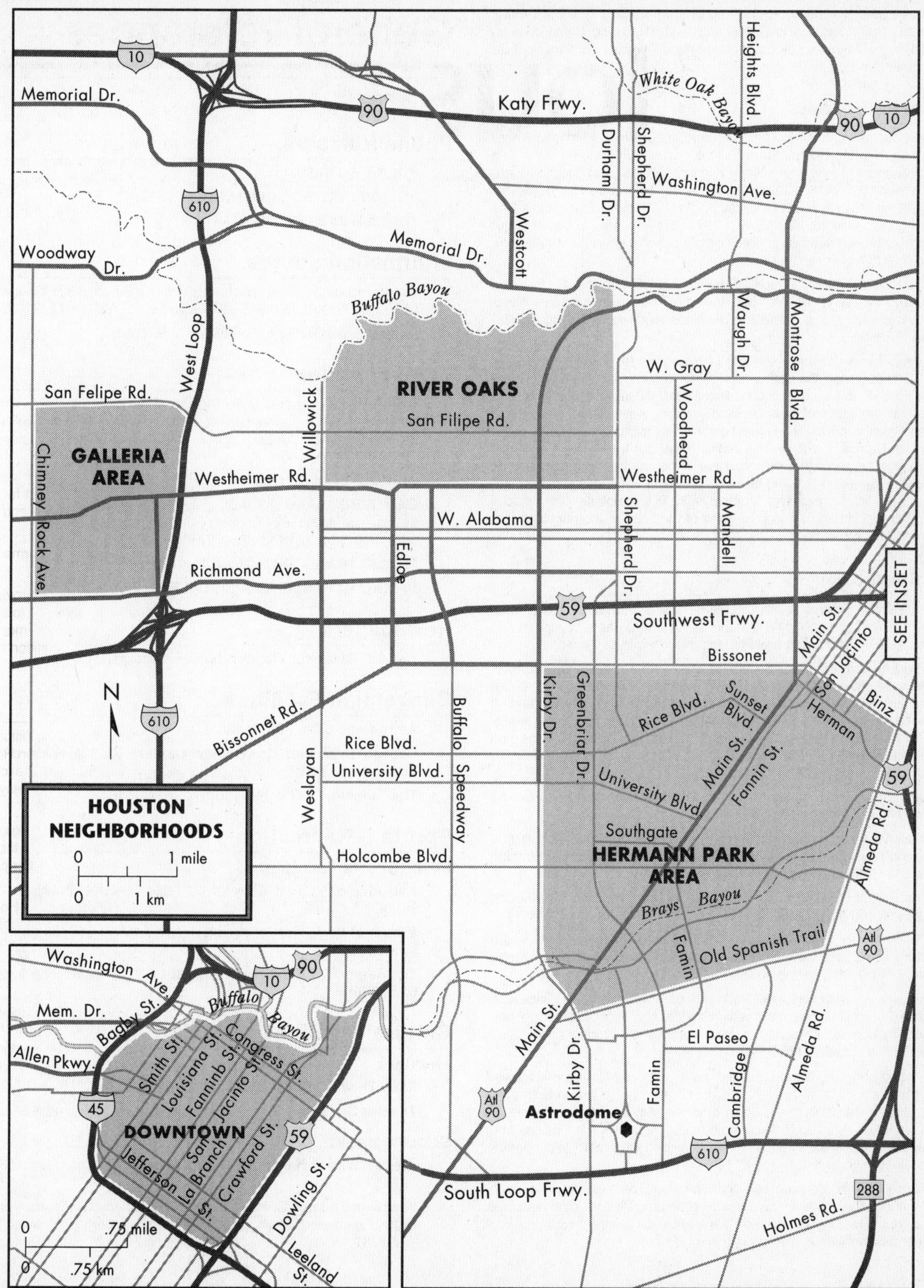

HOUSTON NEIGHBORHOODS
0 1 mile
0 1 km
GALLERIA AREA
RIVER OAKS
HERMANN PARK AREA
DOWNTOWN
Astrodome
Memorial Dr.
Katy Frwy.
White Oak Bayou
Heights Blvd.
Washington Ave.
Durham Dr.
Shepherd Dr.
Westcott
Woodway Dr.
Buffalo Bayou
West Loop
Montrose Blvd.
Waugh Dr.
W. Gray
Woodhead
San Felipe Rd.
San Filipe Rd.
Willowick
Chimney Rock Ave.
Westheimer Rd.
W. Alabama
Mandell
Edloe
Richmond Ave.
Southwest Frwy.
SEE INSET
Main St.
San Jacinto
Bissonet
Bissonnet Rd.
Binz
Herman
Sunset Blvd.
Rice Blvd.
Kirby Dr.
Greenbriar Dr.
Buffalo Speedway
Weslayan
University Blvd.
Fannin St.
Southgate
Holcombe Blvd.
Almeda Rd.
Brays Bayou
Famin
Old Spanish Trail
El Paseo
Cambridge
South Loop Frwy.
Holmes Rd.
Washington Ave.
Mem. Dr.
Bagby St.
Allen Pkwy.
Smith St.
Louisiana St.
Fanninb St.
San Jacinto St.
Congress St.
Crawford St.
Jefferson St.
La Branch
Dowling St.
Leeland St.
0 .75 mile
0 .75 km

Come evening, the choices of nightlife are varied. There are many restaurants that specialize in Gulf seafood. Mexican and Cajun cooking also rank high. Club music includes country and Western, contempory jazz and popular dance.

Historical Areas

San Jacinto Battleground, a 460-acre state park, is the site where Texas won its independence from Mexico. Included in the park is the San Jacinto Museum of Regional History and the 570-foot San Jacinto Monument, one of the world's tallest monumental columns. The battleship *Texas,* presented to the state of Texas by the US Navy on San Jacinto Day in 1948, is also located here. Built in 1914, this ship saw action in major invasions of both World Wars. It is the only remaining dreadnought of its class in the US.

The Christ Church Cathedral, Houston's oldest church, was founded in 1839 and still stands at its original location. The church contains hand-carved woodwork, statuary and stained-glass windows, including two designed by Tiffany.

Allen's Landing Park is the site of Houston's founding in 1836. Old Market Square, once the center of Houston's commerce near the city's original port, is now an interesting dining spot. During the 1800s Market Square was the scene of saloons, food vendors, Native American trading posts and gambling halls. The oldest commercial building in Houston faces Old Market Square; it once was a Native American trading post and also served as a stagecoach inn and slave auction site. Tranquillity Park, downtown, commemorates the historic *Apollo II* moon landing. Its features include a 24-level cascading fountain with five stainless steel stacks resembling rockets and an exact replica of the famous footprint that Neil Armstrong left on the moon.

Sightseeing

A visit to Houston's Zoological Gardens is a memorable experience for both children and adults. Within the zoo is a three-acre children's zoo with separate contact areas representing four regions of the world.

The Museum of Fine Arts presents sculpture, paintings, graphics, decorative arts, outstanding collections of Egyptian handiwork and pre-Columbian art, African and Native American artifacts and an outstanding collection of Remington's Western paintings. The Contemporary Arts Museum has changing exhibits of modern paintings, sculptures, films and multimedia events.

Considered one of the world's most significant private art collections, the Menil Collection is housed in a museum building designed by the renowned Italian architect Renzo Piano.

Displayed in the 24-room former residence of philanthropist Ima Hogg is the Bayou Bend Collection of American decorative arts, spanning the late 17th, 18th and early 19th centuries.

The Port of Houston maintains an observation deck for viewing the turning basin and port in action.

The Houston Arboretum and Nature Center includes a 155-acre arboretum with a large variety of trees and shrubs, as well as a classroom, laboratory, library and greenhouse.

In Sam Houston Historical Park various guided tours are available through restored structures built between 1820 and 1905, including a late 19th-century church, a Texas plantation house and a frontier cabin. Also on premises is a museum gallery.

A good shopping area is located within a 12-block area downtown, making it relatively easy to walk around. There is also an underground tunnel system with boutiques, cafes and specialty shops. Southwest of downtown is the Houston Galleria, a shopping, restaurant, hospitality and entertainment complex. Nearby is The Pavillion on Post Oak, another upscale shopping center.

Space Center Houston is a hands-on facility exploring the past, present and future of America's space program. Visitors can view live pictures from Mission Control and Kennedy Space Center, wear a space helmet or pilot a manned manuvering unit.

General References

Area Codes: 713, 281

Phone Numbers

POLICE & FIRE: 911

POISON CONTROL CENTER: 654-1701

TIME & WEATHER: 529-4444

Information Source

Greater Houston Convention and Visitors Bureau, 801 Congress, 77002; 227-3100, 800/365-7575 (exc TX) or 800/4-HOUSTON.

Department of Parks & Recreation, 845-1000.

Transportation

AIRLINES: Aeromexico; Air France; American; Aviateca; British Airways; Cayman; Continental; Delta; KLM; Lufthansa; SAHSA; Southwest; TACA; United; USAir; VIASA; and other commuter and regional airlines.

AIRPORTS: Intercontinental, 281/230-3100; Hobby, 643-4597.

CAR RENTAL AGENCIES: (See IMPORTANT TOLL-FREE NUMBERS) Avis 443-5800; Budget 449-0145; Dollar 449-0161; Hertz 443-0800; National 443-8850; Thrifty 442-5000.

PUBLIC TRANSPORTATION: Metro Transit 635-4000.

RAILROAD PASSENGER SERVICE: Amtrak 800/872-7245.

Newspapers

Houston Chronicle; Houston Business Journal.

Convention Facilities

Astrodome USA, I-610 & Kirby Dr, 799-9544.

George R. Brown Convention Center, 1001 Avenida de las Americas, 853-8000.

The Summit, 10 Greenway Plaza, 961-9003.

Sports & Recreation

Major Sports Facilities

Astrodome, I-610 at Kirby Dr, 799-9544 (Astros, baseball, 799-9500).

Memorial Park, west of downtown, off I-10 & I-610, on Memorial Loop, 861-3765.

The Summit, 10 Greenway Plaza, 961-9003 (Rockets, basketball, 627-3865).

Cultural Facilities

Theaters

Alley Theatre, 615 Texas Ave, 228-9341.

Theatre Under the Stars, Music Hall, 810 Bagby St, 622-8887.

Concert Halls

Jesse H. Jones Hall for the Performing Arts, 615 Louisiana Ave, 227-2787

Wortham Theater Center (Houston Symphony Orchestra, Ballet, Grand Opera and Society for the Performing Arts), 510 Texas Ave, 227-2787.

Museums & Art Galleries

Bayou Bend Collection, 1 Westcott, 639-7750.

Burke Baker Planetarium, Hermann Park, 639-4600.

Children's Museum of Houston, 1500 Binz, 522-1138.

Contemporary Arts Museum, 5216 Montrose Blvd, 284-8250.

Holocaust Museum Houston, 5401 Caroline, 789-9898.

Houston Museum of Natural Science, 1 Hermann Circle Dr, Hermann Park, 639-4600.

Menil Collection, 1515 Sul Ross, 525-9400.

Museum of Fine Arts, 1001 Bissonnet, 639-7300.

Museum of Health & Medical Science, 1515 Herman Dr, 790-1838.

Rothko Chapel, 3900 Yupon, 524-9839.

San Jacinto Museum of History and Monument, 3800 Park Rd, San Jacinto Battleground, 281/479-2421.

Points of Interest

Historical

Allen's Landing Park, Main St & Buffalo Bayou.

Battleship *Texas,* San Jacinto Battleground, 479-2411.

Christ Church Cathedral, 1117 Texas Ave, 222-2593.

Old Market Square, Congress, Milam, Preston & Travis.

Sam Houston Park, 1100 Bagby, 655-1912.

San Jacinto Battleground, 20 mi E, 479-2421.

Tranquillity Park, 400 Rusk St.

Other Attractions

Arboretum & Nature Center, 4501 Woodway, Memorial Park, 681-8433.

The Orange Show, 2401 Munger, 926-6368.

Port of Houston, Clinton Dr to Port area, 670-2400.

Six Flags AstroWorld & WaterWorld, Kirby Dr at South Loop I-610, 799-1234.

Space Center Houston, 25 mi S on I-45, exit 25, 244-2100.

Zoological Gardens, 1513 N MacGregor, in Hermann Park, 525-3300.

Sightseeing Tours

Gray Line bus tours, 602 Sampson, 223-8800 or 800/334-4441.

Harris County Heritage Society, 1100 Bagby St, in Sam Houston Park, 655-1912.

Annual Events

Houston Livestock Show, Parade & Rodeo, Astrodome. Late Feb-early Mar.

Houston Azalea Trail. 1st 2 wkends Mar.

Houston International Festival. Apr.

Greek Festival. 1st full wkend Oct.

City Neighborhoods

Many of the restaurants, unrated dining establishments and some lodgings listed under Houston include neighborhoods as well as exact street addresses. Geographic descriptions of these areas are given, followed by a table of restaurants arranged by neighborhood.

Downtown: South of Buffalo Bayou, west of US 59, north of I-45 and east of Bagby St. **North of Downtown:** North of Buffalo Bayou. **South of Downtown:** South of I-45 & US 59. **West of Downtown:** West of I-45.

Galleria Area: South of San Felipe, west of Loop 610, north of Richmond Ave and east of Chimney Rock Ave.

Hermann Park Area: South of Bissonnet and Binz Sts, west of Almeda Rd, north of Old Spanish Trail and east of Kirby Dr.

River Oaks: South of Buffalo Bayou, west of S Shepherd Dr, north of Westheimer Rd and east of Willowick Rd.

Lodgings and Food

HOUSTON RESTAURANTS BY NEIGHBORHOOD AREAS
(For full description, see alphabetical listings under Restaurants)

DOWNTOWN
Birraporetti's. 500 Louisiana St
Bistro Lancaster (Lancaster Hotel). 701 Texas Ave
Charley's 517. 517 Louisiana St
Damian's. 3011 Smith St
Deville (Four Seasons Hotel-Houston Center). 1300 Lamar St
Dong Ting. 611 Stuart St
Kim Son. 2001 Jefferson St
Palace Cafe. 401 Louisiana St

NORTH OF DOWNTOWN
Glass Menagerie (Woodlands Resort). 2301 N Millbend St
Kelly's Del Frisco. 14641 Gladebrook
La Tour D'argent. 2011 Ella Blvd

SOUTH OF DOWNTOWN
Baroque. 1700 Sunset Blvd
Benjy's. 2424 Dunstan
Boulevard Bistro. 4319 Montrose Blvd
Brennan's. 3300 Smith St
Goode Co. Texas Bar-B-Q. 5109 Kirby Dr
Khyber. 2510 Richmond Ave
Maxim's. 3755 Richmond Ave

WEST OF DOWNTOWN
Anthony's. 4007 Westheimer Rd
Backstreet Cafe. 1103 S Shepherd
Bistro Vino. 819 W Alabama St
Butera's Fine Foods. 4621 Montrose Blvd
The Cafe (Houstonian Hotel). 111 N Post Oak Lane
Cafe Noche. 2409 Montrose Blvd
Chez Georges. 11920-J Westheimer Rd
Churrasco's. 2055 Westheimer Rd
Confederate House. 2925 Weslayan St
Daily Review Cafe. 3412 W Lamar
The Dining Room (Luxury Collection Hotel). 1919 Briar Oaks Lane
Doneraki. 7705 Westheimer Rd
Empress Of China. 5419A FM 1960 W
Golden Room. 1209 Montrose Blvd
Great Caruso. 10001 Westheimer Rd
Guadalajara. 210 Town & Country Dr
Jags. 5120 Woodway Dr
Joyce's Oyster Resort. 6415 San Felipe
Kaneyama. 9527 Westheimer, Suite D
La Colombe D'or (La Colombe D'or Inn). 3410 Montrose Blvd
La Mora. 912 Lovett
La Reserve (Omni Houston Hotel). 4 Riverway
Las Alamedas. 8615 Katy Frwy
Montesano Ristorante Italiano. 6009 Beverly Hill Lane
Moose Cafe. 1340 W Gray St
Morton's of Chicago. 5000 Westheimer Rd
Nino's. 2817 W Dallas St
Nit Noi. 2462 Bolsover
Ohio Grange Cafe. 1915 Westheimer Rd
Otto's Barbecue. 5502 Memorial Dr
Pappadeaux. 6015 Westheimer Rd
Pappas Bros Steakhouse. 5839 Westheimer Rd
Pappasito's Cantina. 6445 Richmond Ave
Rainbow Lodge. 1 Birdsall St
Redwood Grill. 4611 Montrose Blvd
Rio Ranch. 9999 Westheimer Rd
Rivoli. 5636 Richmond Ave
Rotisserie For Beef And Bird. 2200 Wilcrest Dr
Ruggles Grill. 903 Westheimer Rd
Ruth's Chris Steak House. 6213 Richmond Ave
Sabine. 2606 Sunset Blvd
Sierra. 4704 Montrose Blvd
Svetlana. 80 Woodlake Square
Taste of Texas. 10505 Katy Frwy
Tony Mandola's. 7947 Katy Frwy
Vargo's International Cuisine. 2401 Fondren Rd

GALLERIA AREA
Americas. 1800 S Post Oak Blvd
The Bar and Grill (Luxury Collection Hotel). 1919 Briar Oaks Lane
Cafe Annie. 1728 Post Oak Blvd
Canyon Cafe. 5000 Westheimer Rd
Chianti Cucina Rustica. 1515 S Post Oak Lane
Gugenheim's Delicatessen. 1708 Post Oak Blvd
Hunan. 1800 Post Oak Blvd
Post Oak Grill. 1415 S Post Oak Lane
Rancho Tejas. 4747 San Felipe
Tony's. 1801 Post Oak Blvd

HERMANN PARK AREA
Prego. 2520 Amherst St

RIVER OAKS
Armando's. 2300 Westheimer Rd
Brownstone. 2736 Virginia St
Cafe Japon. 3915 Kirby Dr
Carrabba's. 3115 Kirby Dr
Chuy's Comida Deluxe. 2706 Westheimer Rd
Dacapo's Cafe. 3411 Allen Pkwy
Goode Co. Texas Seafood. 2621 Westpark
Grotto. 3920 Westheimer Rd
Jalapeños. 2702 Kirby Dr
La Griglia. 2002 W Gray St
Mesa Grill. 1971 W Gray St
Ouisie's Table. 3939 San Felipe
P.F. Chang's. 4094 Westheimer Rd
River Oaks Grill. 2630 Westheimer Rd
Sausalito Seafood & Pasta. 3215 Westheimer Rd
Shanghai River. 2407 Westheimer Rd
Tony Mandola's Gulf Coast Kitchen. 1962 W Gray St

Note: When a listing is located in a town that does not have its own city heading, it will appear under the city nearest to its location. In these cases, the address and town appear in parenthesis immediately following the name of the establishment.

Motels

(Rates may be higher for sports & special events in Astrodome.)

✓★ **BEST WESTERN NASA-SPACE CENTER.** *(889 W Bay Area Blvd, Webster 77598) SE on I-45, exit 26. 281/338-6000; FAX 281/338-2834.* 82 rms, 2 story. S, D $53.95-$59.95; each addl $6; under 12 free. Crib free. TV; cable (premium). Complimentary continental bkfst. Restaurant adj open 24 hrs. Ck-out noon. Meeting rms. Business servs avail. Pool. Refrigerators, microwaves. Cr cds: A, D, DS, MC, V.

D SC

★★ **COURTYARD BY MARRIOTT.** *3131 West Loop S (77027), west of downtown. 713/961-1640; FAX 713/439-0989.* 207 rms, 6 story. S, D $49-$99; suites $89-$129; under 18 free; wkend rates. Crib free. TV; cable (premium). Complimentary coffee in rms. Restaurant 6:30 am-2 pm, 5-11 pm. Rm serv from 5 pm. Bar from 5 pm. Ck-out noon. Meeting rms. Business servs avail. In-rm modem link. Valet serv. Coin Indry. Free garage parking. Exercise equipt; treadmill, stair machine. Pool; wading pool, whirlpool. Some refrigerators; microwaves avail. Cr cds: A, C, D, DS, MC, V.

D SC

★★ **DRURY INN.** *1000 N TX 6 (77079), I-10 exit 751, west of downtown. 281/558-7007; FAX 281/558-7007.* 120 rms, 5 story. S $65-

$81; D $75-$91; each addl $10; under 18 free; wkend rates. Crib free. Pet accepted. TV; cable (premium). Indoor pool; whirlpool. Complimentary continental bkfst. Restaurant adj 11 am-10 pm. Ck-out noon. Meeting rm. In-rm modem link. Some refrigerators; microwaves avail. Cr cds: A, C, D, DS, MC, V.

D SC

★ ★ **DRURY INN.** *1615 West Loop 610 S (77027), in Galleria Area. 713/963-0700; FAX 713/963-0700.* 134 rms, 5 story. S $77-$90; D $87-$100; each addl $10; under 12 free; wkend rates. Crib avail. Pet accepted. TV; cable (premium). Heated indoor/outdoor pool; whirlpool. Complimentary continental bkfst. Ck-out noon. Meeting rm. Business servs avail. In-rm modem link. Health club privileges. Some refrigerators; microwaves avail. Cr cds: A, C, D, DS, MC, V.

D SC

✓ ★ **FAIRFIELD INN BY MARRIOTT.** *3131 W Loop S (77027), west of downtown. 713/961-1690; FAX 713/627-8434.* 107 rms, 2 story. S, D $44-$79; under 18 free; wkend rates. Crib free. Pet accepted; $225 ($200 refundable). TV; cable (premium). Complimentary continental bkfst. Restaurant adj 6 am-2 pm, 5-11 pm. Rm serv from 5 pm. Bar from 5 pm. Ck-out noon. Business servs avail. In-rm modem link. Valet serv. Coin Indry. Exercise equipt; weight machine, bicycle. Pool; wading pool, whirlpool. Refrigerators, microwaves avail. Cr cds: A, C, D, DS, MC, V.

D SC

★ **FAIRFIELD INN BY MARRIOTT.** *10155 I-10E (77029), east of downtown. 713/675-2711; FAX 713/674-6853.* 160 rms, 2 story. S $53; D $58; each addl $5; under 16 free. Crib free. Pet accepted, some restrictions. TV; cable (premium). Complimentary continental bkfst. Restaurant adj 6-2 am. Bar from 11 am. Ck-out noon. Meeting rms. Business servs avail. In-rm modem link. Valet serv. Coin Indry. Pool; wading pool. Picnic tables. Cr cds: A, D, DS, MC, V.

D SC

✓★ **HAMPTON INN.** *828 Mercury Dr (I-10 E) (77013), east of downtown. 713/673-4200; FAX 713/674-6913.* 90 rms, 6 story. S $65-$69; D $71-$75; under 18 free; wkend rates. Crib free. Pet accepted; $25 deposit. TV; cable (premium). Pool. Complimentary continental bkfst. Restaurant adj open 24 hrs. Ck-out noon. Coin Indry. Business servs avail. In-rm modem link. Valet serv. Some refrigerators. Cr cds: A, C, D, DS, MC, V.

D SC

✓★ ★ **HAMPTON INN.** *502 N Sam Houston (77060), north of downtown. 281/820-2101; FAX 281/820-9652.* 157 rms, 2 story. S $62-$72; D $71-$78; suites $95-$150; under 18 free. Crib free. TV; cable (premium). Indoor/outdoor pool; whirlpool. Complimentary continental bkfst. Restaurant adj 6:30 am-2 pm, 5-10 pm. Ck-out noon. Meeting rms. Microwaves avail. Business servs avail. Coin Indry. Free airport transportation. Exercise equipt; bicycles, stair machine. Cr cds: A, C, D, DS, MC, V.

D SC

✓★ ★ **HAMPTON INN.** *11333 Katy Frwy (I-10) (77079), west of downtown. 713/935-0022; FAX 713/935-0989.* 120 units, 4 story. S $62-$73; D $70-$81, under 18 free; wknd rates; higher rates special events. Crib free. TV; cable (premium). Pool. Complimentary continental bkfst. Restaurant adj open 24 hrs. Ck-out noon. Meeting rm. Business center. In-rm modem link. Exercise equipt; stair machine, treadmill. Cr cds: A, C, D, DS, MC, V.

D SC

★ ★ **HOLIDAY INN SELECT-INTERNATIONAL AIRPORT.** *15222 JFK Blvd (77032), near Intercontinental Airport, north of downtown. 281/449-2311; FAX 281/449-6726.* 402 rms, 5 story. S, D $89-$135; each addl $10; under 18 free; wkend, wkly rates. Crib $10. Pet accepted; $125 ($100 refundable). TV; cable (premium), VCR avail. Complimentary coffee in lobby. Restaurant 6 am-10:30 pm. Rm serv. Bar from 11 am. Ck-out noon. Convention facilities. Business servs avail. In-rm modem link. Bellhops. Valet serv. Gift shop. Coin Indry. Free airport transportation. Lighted tennis. Exercise equipt; weight machine, bicycle. Pool; wading pool, poolside serv. Lawn games. Some refrigerators; microwaves avail. Cr cds: A, D, DS, JCB, MC, V.

D SC

★ ★ **LA QUINTA-GREENWAY PLAZA.** *4015 SW Frwy (77027), Weslayan Rd exit, south of downtown. 713/623-4750; FAX 713/963-0599.* 131 rms, 2-3 story. S, D $66-$74; each addl $8; suites $82-$90; under 18 free; family units. Crib free. Pet accepted, some restrictions. TV; cable (premium). Pool. Complimentary continental bkfst. Ck-out noon. Coin Indry. Meeting rms. Microwaves avail. Cr cds: A, C, D, DS, MC, V.

D SC

★ ★ **LA QUINTA-WEST.** *11113 Katy Frwy (77079), west of downtown. 713/932-0808; FAX 713/973-2352.* 176 rms, 2 story. S $60-$70; D $68-$78; each addl $8; under 18 free. Crib free. Pet accepted. TV; cable (premium). Pool. Complimentary continental bkfst. Restaurant adj open 24 hrs. Ck-out noon. Coin Indry. Meeting rms. In-rm modem link. Microwaves avail. Cr cds: A, C, D, DS, MC, V.

D SC

✓★ ★ **LEXINGTON HOTEL SUITES.** *16410 I-45N (77090), 25 mi N, north of downtown. 281/821-1000; FAX 281/821-1420.* E-mail lexsvcs@connect.com; web www.lexsvcs.com/hotels.html. 247 kit. suites, 3 story. Suites $55-$99; each addl $6; under 18 free; wkly rates. Crib free. TV; cable (premium). Heated pool. Complimentary continental bkfst. Complimentary coffee in rms. Restaurant adj 6:30 am-10 pm. Ck-out noon. Coin Indry. Meeting rms. Business servs avail. In-rm modem link. Valet serv. Free airport transportation. Health club privileges. Cr cds: A, C, D, DS, MC, V.

D SC

★ **RAMADA LIMITED.** *15350 JFK Blvd (77032), near Intercontinental Airport, north of downtown. 281/442-1830; FAX 281/987-8023.* 126 rms, 3 story. S, D $60-$76; each addl $7; under 15 free; wkend, hol rates. Crib free. TV; cable (premium). Pool; whirlpool. Complimentary continental bkfst. Restaurant adj open 24 hrs. Ck-out noon. Business servs avail. Free airport transportation. Exercise equipt; weights, stair machines. Cr cds: A, C, D, DS, MC, V.

D SC

✓ ★ **RED ROOF INN.** *15701 Park Ten Place (77084), west of downtown. 281/579-7200; FAX 281/579-0732.* 123 rms, 3 story. S $39.99-$59.99; D $52.99-$69.99; under 17 free; wkend rates. Pet accepted. TV; cable (premium). Complimentary coffee in lobby. Restaurant nearby. Meeting rm. Business servs avail. In-rm modem link. Cr cds: A, C, D, DS, MC, V.

D SC

★ ★ **RESIDENCE INN BY MARRIOTT.** *525 Bay Area Blvd (77058), off I-45, south of downtown. 281/486-2424; FAX 281/488-8179.* 110 kit. units, 2 story. S, D $110-$150; under 16 free; wkend rates. Crib free. Pet accepted; $50 and $6/day. TV; cable (premium), VCR avail. Heated pool. Complimentary continental bkfst; evening refreshments. Complimentary coffee in rms. Restaurant adj 11 am-11 pm. Ck-out noon. Coin Indry. Meeting rm. Business servs avail. In-rm modem link. Exercise equipt; weight machine, stair machine. Microwaves. Grills. Cr cds: A, C, D, DS, JCB, MC, V.

D SC

★ ★ **RESIDENCE INN BY MARRIOTT-ASTRODOME.** *7710 S Main St (77030), S edge of medical center, in Hermann Park Area. 713/660-7993; FAX 713/660-8019.* 285 kit. suites. Kit. suites $95-$125; family rates. Crib free. Pet accepted; $25 and $5/day. TV; cable (premium). Heated pool; whirlpool. Complimentary continental bkfst. Bar. Ck-out noon. Meeting rms. Business servs avail. In-rm modem link. Valet serv. Lawn games. Private patios, balconies. Picnic tables, grills. Cr cds: A, C, D, DS, MC, V.

D SC

Motor Hotels

★ ★ ★ **ALLEN PARK INN.** *2121 Allen Parkway (77019), downtown. 713/521-9321; res: 800/231-6310.* 249 rms, 3 story. S, D $88-$98; each addl $8; suites $275; under 10 free; wkly, wkend rates. Crib free. TV; cable (premium). Pool; poolside serv. Restaurant open 24 hrs. Rm serv. Bar 11-2 am; Sun from noon. Ck-out noon. Coin Indry. Meeting rms. Business servs avail. In-rm modem link. Gift shop. Barber, beauty shop. Exercise equipt; weights, bicycles. Bathrm phones; some refrigerators; microwaves avail. Private patios, balconies. Cr cds: A, C, D, DS, MC, V.

D SC

★ ★ **COURTYARD BY MARRIOTT.** *2504 North Loop W (77092), north of downtown. 713/688-7711; FAX 713/688-3561.* 202 rms, 3 story. S, D $84-$104; each addl $10; suite $175; wkend rates. Crib free. TV; cable (premium). Heated pool; whirlpool. Complimentary continental bkfst. Coffee in rms. Restaurant 6:30 am-10 pm. Bar from 11:30 am. Ck-out 1 pm. Coin Indry. Meeting rms. Business servs avail. In-rm modem link. Valet serv. Exercise equipt; weights, bicycles. Some refrigerators, wet bars. Cr cds: A, C, D, DS, MC, V.

D SC

★ ★ **HOLIDAY INN-ASTRODOME.** *8111 Kirby Dr (77054), south of downtown. 713/790-1900; FAX 713/799-8574.* 235 rms, 11 story. S, D $89-$99; each addl $10; suites $125-$325; under 19 free; wkend rates; higher rates Livestock Show & Rodeo. Crib free. TV; cable (premium). Pool; whirlpool. Restaurant 6 am-10 pm. Rm serv. Bar 11-2 am. Ck-out noon. Meeting rms. Business servs avail. In-rm modem link. Bellhops. Valet serv. Sundries. Gift shop. Exercise equipt; weights, bicycles. Some bathrm phones, refrigerators, wet bars; microwaves avail. Cr cds: A, C, D, DS, JCB, MC, V.

D SC

★ ★ **RAMADA HOTEL.** *12801 NW Frwy (77040), north of downtown. 713/462-9977; FAX 713/460-8725.* 296 rms, 10 story. S $85; D $95; each addl $10; suites $119-$148; under 12 free; wkend rates. Pet accepted, some restrictions. TV; cable (premium). Pool; poolside serv. Coffee in rms. Restaurant 6 am-10 pm. Rm serv. Bar 4 pm-2 am. Ck-out noon. Meeting rms. In-rm modem link. Bellhops. Valet serv. Sundries. Gift shop. Free bus depot transportation. Exercise equipt; weights, stair machine, sauna. Health club privileges. Some bathrm phones; refrigerator, wet bar in suites. Balconies. Cr cds: A, C, D, DS, MC, V.

D SC

Hotels

★ ★ ★ **ADAM'S MARK.** *2900 Briar Park (77042), west of downtown. 713/978-7400; FAX 713/735-2727.* Web www.adamsmark.com. 604 rms, 10 story. S, D $79-$164; each addl $15; suites $190-$730; under 18 free; wkend rates. Crib free. TV; cable (premium). Heated indoor/outdoor pool; wading pool, whirlpool, poolside serv. Restaurant 6 am-midnight. Rm serv 24 hrs. Bars 11-2 am; entertainment. Ck-out noon. Meeting rms. Business servs avail. Concierge. Gift shop. Exercise equipt; weights, bicycles, sauna. Game rm. Some refrigerators; microwaves avail. Some balconies. Artwork in lobby. Cr cds: A, C, D, DS, MC, V.

D SC

★ ★ **CROWNE PLAZA-GALLERIA.** *2222 West Loop S (77027), in Galleria Area. 713/961-7272; FAX 713/961-3327.* 477 rms, 23 story. S $89-$139; D $99-$145; each addl $10; suites $150-$250; under 19 free; wkend rates. Valet parking $8; garage free. Crib free. TV; cable (premium). Indoor pool; whirlpool, poolside serv. Complimentary coffee in rms. Restaurants 6 am-10 pm. Bar 11-2 am; entertainment. Ck-out noon. Coin Indry. Convention facilities. Business servs avail. In-rm modem link. Concierge. Gift shop. Exercise equipt; weights, bicycles, sauna. Some refrigerators. Luxury level. Cr cds: A, C, D, DS, JCB, MC, V.

D SC

★ ★ ★ **DOUBLETREE AT ALLEN CENTER.** *400 Dallas St (77002), downtown. 713/759-0202; FAX 713/752-2734.* 341 rms, 20 story. S $145-$185; D $160-$195; each addl $10; suites $225-$675; under 17 free; wkend rates. Crib free. Pet accepted, some restrictions; $75 refundable. TV; cable (premium). Restaurants 6 am-10 pm. Bar 11-2 am; entertainment Mon-Fri. Ck-out noon. Meeting rms. Business center. In-rm modem link. Concierge. Gift shop. Exercise equipt; weights, treadmill. Elegant hanging tapestries. Cr cds: A, C, D, DS, ER, JCB, MC, V.

D SC

★ ★ ★ **DOUBLETREE GUEST SUITES.** *5353 Westheimer Rd (77056), in Galleria Area. 713/961-9000; FAX 713/877-8835.* 335 kit. suites, 26 story. S, D $210; each addl $20; 2-bedrm suites $310; under 18 free; wkend rates. Crib free. Garage $8, valet parking $12. Pet accepted, some restrictions. TV; cable (premium). Pool; whirlpool, poolside serv. Restaurant 6:30 am-2 pm, 5-10 pm; Sat, Sun 6:30 am-1 pm, 5-10 pm. Rm serv 24 hrs. Bar 5 pm-midnight. Ck-out noon. Business servs avail. In-rm modem link. Coin Indry. Tennis privileges. Exercise equipt; weights, bicycles. Health club privileges. Game rm. Refrigerators. Some balconies. Cr cds: A, C, D, DS, MC, V.

D SC

★ ★ ★ **DOUBLETREE-POST OAK.** *2001 Post Oak Blvd (77056), in Galleria Area. 713/961-9300; FAX 713/623-6685.* Web www.doubletreehotels.com. 449 rms, 14 story. S $140-$198; D $160-$218; each addl $20; suites $210-$1,200; under 18 free; wkend rates. Crib free. Valet parking $13; garage $6. TV; cable (premium). Pool; poolside serv. Restaurant 6:30 am-11 pm. Rm serv 24 hrs. Bar 11-1 am; wkends to 2 am; Sun from noon. Ck-out noon. Convention facilities. Business center. In-rm modem link. Concierge. Shopping arcade. Barber, beauty shop. Exercise equipt; weights, stair machine, sauna. Health club privileges. Many bathrm phones; some refrigerators. Balconies. Cr cds: A, C, D, DS, JCB, MC, V.

D SC

★ ★ **EMBASSY SUITES.** *9090 SW Frwy (77074), south of downtown. 713/995-0123; FAX 713/779-0703.* Web www.embassysuites.com. 243 suites, 9 story. Suites $109-$139; each addl $10; under 12 free; wkend rates. Crib free. TV; cable (premium). Indoor pool; whirlpool. Complimentary full bkfst. Complimentary coffee in rms. Restaurant adj 11:30 am-11 pm. Ck-out noon. Meeting rms. Business servs avail. In-rm modem link. Gift shop. Exercise equipt; weights, stair machine, sauna. Game rm. Refrigerators, microwaves, wet bars; some bathrm phones. Balconies. Cr cds: A, C, D, DS, JCB, MC, V.

D SC

★ ★ ★ ★ **FOUR SEASONS HOTEL-HOUSTON CENTER.** *1300 Lamar St (77010), downtown. 713/650-1300; FAX 713/652-6293.* This toney high-rise with etched-glass doors and thick carpeting is all marble, fresh flowers and antiques. Ten of the 30 stories are occupied by apartments that are home to well-to-do Houstonians. 399 rms, 30 story. S $195-$235; D $225-$265; each addl $25; suites $550-$1,200; under 18 free; wkend rates. Crib free. Pet accepted. Valet & covered parking $13/day. TV; cable (premium), VCR avail. Heated pool; whirlpool, poolside serv. Restaurant (see DeVILLE). Rm serv 24 hrs. Bar 11-1 am; entertainment. Ck-out 1 pm. Meeting rms. Business center. In-rm modem link. Concierge. Shopping arcade. Beauty shop. Exercise rm; instructor, bicycles, rowing machine, sauna. Massage. Health club privileges. Bathrm phones, minibars; some refrigerators; microwaves avail. Cr cds: A, C, D, ER, JCB, MC, V.

D

★ **HARVEY SUITES-MEDICAL CENTER.** *6800 Main St (77030), in Hermann Park Area. 713/528-7744; FAX 713/528-6983; res: 800/922-9222.* 285 rms, 12 story, 212 kit. suites. S, D $72-$99; kit. suites $149-$199; under 18 free. Crib free. TV; cable. Pool. Complimentary coffee in rms. Restaurant 6:30 am-11 pm. Rm serv. Bar from 11 am. Ck-out noon. Coin Indry. Business servs avail. In-rm modem link. Bellhops. Concierge. Valet serv. Gift shop. Beauty shop. Exercise equipt; treadmill, stair machine. Game rm. Microwaves avail. Cr cds: A, C, D, DS, MC, V.

D SC

✔★★ **HILTON NASSAU BAY.** *3000 NASA Rd 1 (77058), south of downtown. 281/333-9300; FAX 281/333-3750.* 243 rms, 13 story. S $89-$134; D $99-$134; each addl $10; suites $250-$500; family, wkend rates. Crib avail. TV; cable (premium). Pool; whirlpool, poolside serv. Restaurant 6:30 am-10 pm; Fri 7 am-11 pm. Bar 5 pm-2 am. Ck-out 1 pm. Meeting rms. Business servs avail. In-rm modem link. Beauty shop. Exercise equipt; weights, bicycles. Sailboating, windsurfing, waterskiing. Bathrm phone in suites. Balconies with view of lake, marina. Luxury level. Cr cds: A, C, D, DS, MC, V.

D SC

★★★ **HILTON PLAZA.** *6633 Travis St (77030), adj Medical Center, in Hermann Park Area. 713/313-4000; FAX 713/313-4660.* 181 units, 19 story. S $118-$138; D $128-$148; each addl $10; wkend rates. Crib free. Garage $8 (wkends $4). TV; cable (premium). Heated rooftop pool; whirlpool, poolside serv. Coffee in rms. Restaurant 6:30 am-10 pm. Rm serv 24 hrs. Bar 4 pm-midnight; entertainment. Ck-out noon. Meeting rms. Business servs avail. In-rm modem link. Gift shop. Valet parking. Exercise rm; instructor, weights, bicycles, sauna. Bathrm phones, refrigerators, wet bars. Adj to museums, parks, Rice Univ. Luxury level. Cr cds: A, C, D, DS, MC, V.

D SC

★★★ **HILTON-WESTCHASE.** *9999 Westheimer Rd (77042), west of downtown. 713/974-1000; FAX 713/974-2108.* Web www.hilton.com. 300 rms, 13 story. S, D $159-$189; each addl $10; suites $174-$204; under 18 free; wkend rates. Crib free. TV; cable (premium). Heated pool; whirlpool, poolside serv. Complimentary coffee in rms. Restaurant 6:30 am-10 pm. Rm serv 24 hrs. Bar 11:30 am-midnight. Ck-out 1 pm. Convention facilities. Business center. Concierge. Gift shop. Barber, beauty shop. Exercise equipt; weight machine, stair machine, sauna. Minibars. Luxury level. Cr cds: A, C, D, DS, ER, JCB, MC, V.

D SC

★★ **HOLIDAY INN-HOBBY AIRPORT.** *9100 Gulf Frwy (I-45) (77017), near Hobby Airport, south of downtown. 713/943-7979; FAX 713/943-2160.* 288 rms, 10 story. S $99-$115; D $109-$129; each addl $10; under 12 free; wkend rates. Crib avail. Pet accepted. TV; cable (premium). Indoor pool; whirlpool, poolside serv. Restaurant 5:30 am-10 pm. Bar; pianist. Ck-out noon. Meeting rms. Business servs avail. In-rm modem link. Concierge. Gift shop. Free airport transportation. Exercise equipt; weight machine, stair machine, sauna. Game rm. Luxury level. Cr cds: A, C, D, DS, ER, JCB, MC, V.

D SC

★★ **HOLIDAY INN SELECT.** *2712 SW Frwy (77098), south of downtown. 713/523-8448; FAX 713/526-7948.* 355 rms, 18 story, 36 suites. S $109-$129; D $129; each addl $10; suites $139-$159; under 18 free; wkend rates. Valet parking $8. TV; cable (premium), VCR avail (movies). Complimentary coffee in rms. Restaurant 6 am-11 pm. Bar noon-midnight. Ck-out 1 pm. Convention facilities. Business center. In-rm modem link. Concierge. Gift shop. Coin Indry. Exercise equipt; weight machine, treadmill. Pool; whirlpool, poolside serv. Refrigerator, wet bar in suites; microwaves avail. Cr cds: A, C, D, DS, JCB, MC, V.

D SC

★★ **HOLIDAY INN SELECT-PARK TEN WEST.** *14703 Park Row (77079), west of downtown. 281/558-5580; FAX 281/496-4150.* 349 rms, 19 story. S, D $99-$149; suites $250; under 18 free; wkend rates. TV; cable (premium). Indoor pool; whirlpool, poolside serv. Restaurant 6 am-10 pm. Rm serv. Bar 2 pm-midnight; Fri, Sat to 2 am. Ck-out noon. Convention facilities. Business center. In-rm modem link. Gift shop. Exercise equipt; weights, bicycles. Microwaves avail. Luxury level. Cr cds: A, C, D, DS, MC, V.

D SC

★★★ **HOTEL SOFITEL.** *425 Sam Houston Pkwy E (77060), north of downtown. 281/445-9000; FAX 281/445-9826.* 334 rms, 8 story. S, D $159-$169; each addl $20; suites $299-$400; under 18 free; wkend rates. Crib free. TV; cable (premium). Pool. Restaurant 6 am-11 pm. Rm serv 5:30-1 am. Bar 11-2 am; entertainment. Ck-out noon. Convention facilities. Business center. In-rm modem link. Concierge. Shopping arcade. Airport transportation. Exercise equipt; weight machine, bicycles. Massage. French bakery in lobby. Cr cds: A, C, D, JCB, MC, V.

D SC

★★★ **HOUSTON MEDALLION.** *3000 North Loop W (77092), north of downtown. 713/688-0100; FAX 713/688-9224; res: 800/688-3000.* 382 rms, 10 story. S, D $160-$250; family, wkend rates. Crib free. Pet accepted, some restrictions. TV; cable (premium), VCR avail. Pool; whirlpool, poolside serv. Restaurant 6 am-2 pm, 5 pm-midnight. Rm serv to 1 am. Bar 11 am- midnight. Ck-out 1 pm. Meeting rms. In-rm modem link. Gift shop. Free garage parking. Exercise equipt; weight machine, bicycles, sauna. Refrigerators avail. Luxury level. Cr cds: A, C, D, DS, ER, JCB, MC, V.

D SC

★★★★ **HOUSTONIAN.** *111 N Post Oak Lane (77024), west of downtown. 713/680-2626; FAX 713/680-2992; res: 800/231-2759.* Web www.houstonian.com. In true Texas form, the Houstonian sprawls over 18 acres of heavily wooded land. But don't be put off by its size—the atmosphere is warm and inviting. The real draw is the renowned fitness center, which includes everything from free weights and cardio machines to private TVs and an indoor jogging track. 291 rms, 4 story. S $239; D $249; suites $375-$1,100; under 18 free; wkend, hol rates. Crib free. TV; cable (premium). 3 heated pools; whirlpool. Supervised child's activities; ages 3-16. Restaurant (see THE CAFE). Rm serv 24 hrs. Bar 3 pm-2 am; Sat, Sun from noon. Ck-out noon. Convention facilities. Business center. In-rm modem link. Concierge. Gift shop. Free garage parking; valet $11. Lighted tennis, pro. Exercise rm; instructor, weights, bicycles, sauna. Massage. Game rm. Lawn games. Refrigerators, minibars. Luxury level. Cr cds: A, C, D, DS, MC, V.

D SC

★★★ **HYATT REGENCY.** *1200 Louisiana St (77002), at Polk St, downtown. 713/654-1234; FAX 713/951-0934.* 963 rms, 30 story. S $139-$179; D $155-$204; each addl $25; suites $300-$850; under 18 free; wkend rates. Crib free. Valet parking $15. TV; cable (premium). Heated pool; poolside serv. Restaurant 6 am-11 pm. Bar 11-2 am. Ck-out noon. Convention facilities. Business center. In-rm modem link. Concierge. Beauty shop. Airport transportation. Exercise equipt; weights, treadmill. Health club privileges. Bathrm phones, refrigerators. Built around 30-story atrium; glass-enclosed elvtrs. Covered passage to downtown buildings. Cr cds: A, C, D, DS, ER, JCB, MC, V.

D SC

★★★ **HYATT REGENCY-HOUSTON AIRPORT.** *15747 JFK Blvd (77032), north of downtown. 281/987-1234; FAX 281/590-8461.* Web www.hyatt.com. 309 rms, 7 story. S $119-$149; D $144-$174; each addl $10; under 18 free; package plans; wkend rates. Crib free. Pet accepted; $25. TV; cable (premium). Pool; whirlpool, poolside serv. Restaurant 6 am-2 pm, 5-11 pm. Bar 11 am-midnight. Ck-out noon. Meeting rms. Business servs avail. In-rm modem link. Gift shop. Free airport transportation. Exercise equipt; weight machine, stair machine. Cr cds: A, C, D, DS, ER, JCB, MC, V.

D SC

★★★ **J.W. MARRIOTT-HOUSTON.** *5150 Westheimer Rd (77056), in Galleria Area. 713/961-1500; FAX 713/961-5045.* 502 rms, 23 story. S $139-$189; D $149-$189; suites $175-$600; under 18 free; wkend rates. Crib free. Garage; valet parking $15, self-park $6. TV; cable (premium), VCR avail. Indoor/outdoor pool; whirlpool, poolside serv. Restaurant 6:30 am-2 pm, 5:30-11 pm. Bar 2 pm-midnight. Ck-out noon. Convention facilities. Business servs avail. In-rm modem link. Concierge. Gift shop. Barber, beauty shop. Exercise equipt; weights, stair machine, sauna. Game rm. Bathrm phones; microwaves avail; refrigerator in suites. Lobby furnished with marble, rich paneling and artwork. Luxury level. Cr cds: A, C, D, DS, MC, V.

D SC

★★★★ **LANCASTER.** *701 Texas Ave (77002), downtown. 713/228-9500; FAX 713/223-4528.* Web www.slh.com. In this beautifully refurbished theater-district hotel dating from the 1920s, rich hunter green and deep red draperies provide a backdrop for gleaming antiques. 93 rms, 12 story. S $190-$230; D $200-$250; each addl $25; suites $325-$500; under 16 free; wkend rates. Crib free. Valet parking $13. TV; cable, VCR (movies). Restaurant (see BISTRO LANCASTER). Rm serv 24 hrs. Bars 11 am-midnight. Ck-out 1 pm. Meeting rms. Business center. In-rm modem link. Concierge. Exercise equipt; weights, bicycles. Bathrm phones, refrigerators, minibars; microwaves avail. Cr cds: A, C, D, DS, JCB, MC, V.

D

LUXURY COLLECTION. *(New management, therefore not rated) 1919 Briar Oaks Lane (77027), near Galleria Center, in Galleria Area. 713/840-7600; FAX 713/840-8036; res: 800/241-3333.* 232 rms, 12 story. S, D $190-$260; each addl $30; suites $290-$330; kit. units $550-$800; under 18 free; wkend rates. Valet parking $15.50. Crib free. TV; cable (premium). Heated pool; poolside serv. Continental bkfst. Restaurants (see THE BAR AND GRILL and THE DINING ROOM). Bar; entertainment. Harpist at afternoon tea (3-5 pm). Ck-out noon. Meeting rms. Business center. Concierge. Gift shop. Exercise equipt; treadmill, bicycle. Health club privileges. Bathrm phones; microwaves avail; whirlpool in suites. Luxury level. Cr cds: A, C, D, DS, ER, JCB, MC, V.

D SC

★ ★ ★ **MARRIOTT-AIRPORT.** *18700 JFK Blvd (77032), at Intercontinental Airport, north of downtown. 281/443-2310; FAX 281/443-5294.* 566 rms, 3 & 7 story. S, D $134-$149; suites $250-$350; studio rms $150-$250; under 18 free; wkend rates. Crib free. Pet accepted, some restrictions. Valet parking $16. TV; cable (premium). Pool; poolside serv. Restaurant 6 am-10:30 pm. Bar 11-2 am; Sat from 4 pm; Sun noon-midnight. Ck-out 1 pm. Free Indry facilities. Convention facilities. Business center. In-rm modem link. Shopping arcade. Exercise equipt; weights, stair machine. Some bathrm phones, refrigerators. Some private patios. Luxury level. Cr cds: A, C, D, DS, ER, JCB, MC, V.

D SC

★ ★ ★ **MARRIOTT-MEDICAL CENTER.** *6580 Fannin St (77030), at Texas Medical Center, in Hermann Park Area. 713/796-0080; FAX 713/770-8100.* 386 rms, 26 story. S, D $129-$134; suites $165-$550; under 18 free; wkend rates. Crib free. Garage $7; valet parking $13.75. TV; cable (premium), VCR avail. Indoor pool; whirlpool, poolside serv. Restaurant 6:30 am-11 pm. Ck-out noon. Coin Indry. Convention facilities. Business servs avail. In-rm modem link. Concierge. Shopping arcade. Bus depot transportation. Exercise equipt; bicycles, weights, sauna. Refrigerators; microwaves avail. Connected to Medical Center; covered walks. Luxury level. Cr cds: A, C, D, DS, JCB, MC, V.

D SC

★ ★ ★ **MARRIOTT NORTH AT GREENSPOINT.** *255 N Sam Houston Pkwy E (77060), adj Greenspoint Mall, north of downtown. 281/875-4000; FAX 281/875-6208.* Web www.marriott/marriott/tx181.htm. 391 rms, 12 story. S, D $109-$170; suites $250-$350; under 17 free; wkend rates. Crib free. TV; cable (premium). Indoor/outdoor pool; whirlpool, poolside serv. Restaurant 6:30 am-11 pm. Bar 2 pm-2 am. Ck-out 1 pm. Coin Indry. Convention facilities. Business center. In-rm modem link. Concierge. Gift shop. Free garage parking. Free airport transportation. Exercise equipt; weights, bicycles, sauna. Refrigerators. Luxury level. Cr cds: A, C, D, DS, ER, JCB, MC, V.

D SC

★ ★ ★ **MARRIOTT-WESTSIDE.** *13210 Katy Frwy (77079), west of downtown. 281/558-8338; FAX 281/558-4028.* 400 rms, 5 story. S, D $139-$160; under 18 free; wkend rates. Crib free. Pet accepted; $25. TV; cable (premium). Pool; whirlpool, poolside serv. Restaurant 6 am-3 pm, 5-11 pm. Bar; pianist Mon-Fri. Ck-out noon. Convention facilities. Business center. In-rm modem link. Gift shop. Free garage parking. Lighted tennis. Exercise equipt; weight machine, rowers. Health club privileges. Cr cds: A, C, D, DS, MC, V.

D SC

★ ★ ★ ★ **OMNI HOUSTON HOTEL.** *4 Riverway (77056), west of downtown. 713/871-8181; FAX 713/871-0719; res: 800/843-6664.* This striking, curvilinear, resort-style high-rise has an especially large pool, a dramatic modern lobby and bar with fountains and sculpture. Guest rooms have sitting areas, marble and dark-wood furniture and floor-to-ceiling windows. 381 rms, 11 story. S, D $149-$209; each addl $25; suites $225-$650; under 17 free; wkend rates. Crib free. Garage: valet parking $13, self-park $7. TV; cable (premium), VCR avail. 2 pools, 1 heated; whirlpool, poolside serv. Restaurant (see LA RESERVE). Rm serv 24 hrs. Bar 11:30-2 am; entertainment. Ck-out 1 pm. Meeting rms. Business center. In-rm modem link. Concierge. Tennis. Exercise rm; instructor, weights, bicycles, sauna. Massage. Minibars. Cr cds: A, C, D, DS, ER, JCB, MC, V.

D SC

★ ★ **RED LION.** *2525 West Loop South (77027), in Galleria area. 713/961-3000; FAX 713/961-1490.* 319 rms, 14 story. S $136-$159; D $146-$169; each addl $10; suites $325-$500; under 18 free; wkend rates. Crib free. Pet accepted; $10. Valet parking $9; garage free. TV; cable (premium), VCR avail. Pool; whirlpool, poolside serv. Coffee in rms. Restaurant 6 am-10 pm. Bar 4 pm-midnight. Ck-out 1 pm. Convention facilities. Business center. In-rm modem link. Gift shop. Exercise equipt; weight machine, treadmill, sauna. Microwaves avail. Luxury level. Cr cds: A, C, D, DS, ER, JCB, MC, V.

D SC

★ ★ ★ **RENAISSANCE.** *6 Greenway Plaza E (77046), west of downtown. 713/629-1200; FAX 713/629-4702.* 389 rms, 20 story. S $129-$159; D $139-$169; each addl $10; suites $300-$750; under 18 free; wkend rates. Crib free. Pet accepted, some restrictions. Garage parking; valet $10, self-park free. TV; cable (premium). Heated pool; poolside serv. Complimentary coffee in rms. Restaurant 6 am-10 pm. Rm serv 24 hrs. Bar 11:30-2 am. Ck-out 1 pm. Convention facilities. Business servs avail. In-rm modem link. Tennis privileges. Exercise equipt; weights, bicycles, sauna. Health club privileges. Bathrm phones; some refrigerators. Cr cds: A, C, D, DS, ER, JCB, MC, V.

D SC

★ ★ **SHERATON ASTRODOME.** *8686 Kirby Dr (77054), south of downtown. 713/748-3221; FAX 713/796-9371.* 631 rms, 9 story. S $69-$150; D $69-$165; each addl $10; suites $225-$375; under 18 free. Crib free. Pet accepted, some restrictions. TV; cable (premium). 2 pools; whirlpool. Coffee in rms. Restaurant 6:30 am-10:30 pm. Bar 11-2 am. Ck-out noon. Meeting rms. Business servs avail. In-rm modem link. Valet serv. Gift shop. Exercise equipt; weights, bicycles, sauna. Game rm. Some refrigerators. Cr cds: A, C, D, DS, JCB, MC, V.

D SC

★ **SHERATON CROWN HOTEL & CONFERENCE CENTER.** *15700 JFK Blvd (77032), north of downtown. 281/442-5100; FAX 281/987-9130.* 418 rms, 10 story. S $110-$150; D $120-$160; each addl $10; suites $150-$600; under 18 free; wkend rates. Crib free. TV; cable (premium). 2 pools, 1 indoor; whirlpool. Coffee in rms. Restaurants 6 am-11 pm. Bars 11-1 am. Ck-out noon. Convention facilities. Business center. Gift shop. Free airport transportation. Putting greens. Exercise equipt; treadmill, stair machine. Some refrigerators. Luxury level. Cr cds: A, C, D, DS, ER, JCB, MC, V.

D SC

★ ★ ★ **WYNDHAM GREENSPOINT.** *12400 Greenspoint Dr (77060), adj Greenspoint Mall, north of downtown. 281/875-2222; FAX 281/875-1652.* 472 rms, 16 story. S $139-$179; D $159-$199; each addl $10; suites $185-$500; under 18 free; wkend rates. TV; cable (premium). Pool. Restaurant 6 am-11 pm. Bar 4 pm-2 am; entertainment. Ck-out noon. Coin Indry. Convention facilities. Business center. In-rm modem link. Shopping arcade. Free airport transportation. Exercise equipt; weights, bicycles, sauna. Health club privileges. Some refrigerators; bathrm phone in suites. Distinctive architectural design & decor. Cr cds: A, C, D, DS, JCB, MC, V.

D SC

★ ★ ★ **WYNDHAM WARWICK.** *5701 Main St (77005), near Rice University, in Hermann Park Area. 713/526-1991; FAX 713/639-4545.* 308 rms, 12 story, 46 suites. S, D $135-$185; each addl $20; suites $250-$450; kits. $175-$195; under 18 free; wkend plans. Self-parking $6.50, valet parking $12. TV; cable (premium). Pool; whirlpool, poolside serv. Complimentary coffee in rms. Restaurant 6:30 am-11 pm. Bar 3 pm-1 am. Ck-out noon. Convention facilities. Business servs avail. In-rm modem link. Concierge. Gift shop. Beauty shop. Exercise equipt; weight machine, bicycles, sauna. Bathrm phones; some refrigerators, wet bars; microwaves avail. Balconies. Cr cds: A, C, D, DS, ER, JCB, MC, V.

Inns

★ ★ ★ **LA COLOMBE D'OR.** *3410 Montrose Blvd (77006), west of downtown. 713/524-7999; FAX 713/524-8923.* 6 suites, 3 story. Suites $195-$575. TV; cable (premium), VCR avail. Restaurant (see LA COLOMBE D'OR). Rm serv. Bar. Concierge serv. Ck-out noon, ck-in 3 pm. Whirlpool. Fruit furnished daily. Prairie-style mansion built in 1923 by Walter Fondren, founder of Humble Oil (now Exxon). Cr cds: A, C, D, DS, MC, V.

✔★ ★ ★ **SARA'S BED & BREAKFAST.** *941 Heights Blvd (77008), north of downtown. 713/868-1130; FAX 713/868-1160; res: 800/593-1130.* Web www.virtualcities.com. 14 rms, 2 share bath, 2 story. S, D $55-$110; each addl $10; suites $150; wkly rates. TV; VCR (free movies). Complimentary bkfst. Restaurant nearby. Ck-out noon, ck-in 3 pm. Business servs avail. Antiques, collectibles. Totally nonsmoking. Cr cds: A, C, D, DS, JCB, MC, V.

Resort

★ ★ ★ **WOODLANDS.** *2301 N Millbend St (77380), north of downtown. 713/367-1100; FAX 713/364-6345; res: 800/433-2624 (exc TX), 800/533-3052 (TX).* Web www.weccr.com. 314 rms, 3 story. S $125-$160; D $140-$180; each addl $15; suites $145-$900; kit. units $145-$225; under 12 free; AP avail; wkend rates (seasonal); package plans. TV; cable (premium). 2 pools; wading pool, whirlpool, poolside serv. Restaurants 6 am-11 pm (also see GLASS MENAGERIE). Rm serv. 3 bars 11-2 am; Sun from noon. Ck-out noon, ck-in after 3 pm. Meeting rms. Business center. In-rm modem link. Valet serv. Gift shop. Beauty shop. Airport transportation. Indoor & outdoor lighted tennis, pro. 36-hole golf, greens fee $50-$110, 3 putting greens, 3 driving ranges, pro shop. Hiking, bicycle trails. Bicycle rentals. Game rm. Exercise rm; instructor, weights, bicycles, steam rm, sauna. Massage. Lawn games. Refrigerators; microwaves avail. Private patios, balconies. Some lake views. Outdoor sculpture garden. Cr cds: A, C, D, DS, MC, V.

Restaurants

✔★ ★ **AMERICAS.** *1800 S Post Oak Blvd (77056), in Galleria Area. 713/961-1492.* Hrs: 11:30 am-10 pm; Fri to 11 pm; Sat 5-11 pm. Closed Sun; most major hols. Res accepted. South American menu. Bar. Semi-a la carte: lunch $6-$12, dinner $10-$25. Child's meals. Specialties: roasted quail breast, filet of red snapper with fresh corn, plantain chips. Rain forest, Inca decor. Suspension bridge to second level. Cr cds: A, C, D, DS, MC, V.

★ ★ ★ **ANTHONY'S.** *4007 Westheimer Rd, west of downtown. 713/961-0552.* Hrs: 11:30 am-2 pm, 5:30-10 pm; Tues-Thurs to 11 pm; Fri, Sat to 11:30 pm. Closed Sun; major hols. Res accepted. Bar. Wine list. Semi-a la carte: lunch $8.95-$14.95, dinner $11.95-$26.95. Specializes in osso bucco, lobster and crab ravioli. Own baking. Valet parking. Open hearth cooking. Cr cds: A, D, DS, MC, V.

★ ★ **ARMANDO'S.** *2300 Westheimer Rd, in River Oaks. 713/521-9757.* Hrs: 11 am-2 pm, 5:30-11 pm; Mon-Wed to 10 pm; Sun 11 am-10 pm; Sat, Sun brunch to 2 pm. Closed Thanksgiving, Dec 25. Res accepted. Southwestern, Mexican menu. Bar. Semi-a la carte: lunch $6.95-$16.95, dinner $8.95-$20.95. Sat, Sun brunch $6.95-$10.95. Specializes in fresh grilled seafood, fajitas. Own tortillas. Valet parking. Outdoor dining. Local modern art displays. Cr cds: A, D, DS, MC, V.

★ ★ **BACKSTREET CAFE.** *1103 S Shepherd (77019), 3 mi W on Allen Pkwy, west of downtown. 713/521-2239.* Hrs: 11 am-10 pm; Fri, Sat to 11 pm; Sun brunch to 3 pm. Closed some major hols. Res accepted. Bar. Semi-a la carte: lunch, dinner $8.95-$21.95. Sun brunch $7.95-$8.95. Specialties: smoked corn crab cake, fried green tomato salad, Tandoori chicken sandwich. Own baking. Valet parking. Bi-level outdoor dining. Cr cds: A, MC, V.

THE BAR AND GRILL. *(New management, therefore not rated) (See Luxury Collection Hotel) 713/840-7600.* Specialties: chili-roasted filet, grilled salmon, Felix's mixed grill. Hrs: dinner 6-10:30 pm; lite menu 3-6 pm & 10:30 pm-1:30 am. Res accepted. Bar. Wine cellar. Semi-a la carte: dinner $25-$29. Child's meals. Entertainment exc Sun. Valet parking. Jacket. Cr cds: A, C, D, DS, ER, JCB, MC, V.

★ ★ **BAROQUE.** *1700 Sunset Blvd (77005), south of downtown. 713/523-8881.* Hrs: 11 am-2:30 pm, 5:30-10 pm; Fri to 11 pm; Sat 5:30-11 pm; Sun 5:30-9 pm. Closed Dec 25. Res accepted. Eclectic menu. Bar. Semi-a la carte: lunch $10-$15, dinner $17-$26. Specialties: wild boar, gumbo crab cakes, Tabasco fried oyster salad. Own baking. Valet parking (dinner). 18th-century baroque decor; ornate chandeliers, murals, antiques. Cr cds: A, MC, V.

★ ★ **BENJY'S.** *2424 Dunstan (77005), Rice Univ Village, south of downtown. 713/522-7602.* Hrs: 11 am-2 pm, 6-10 pm; Fri to 11 pm; Sat 6-11 pm; Sun 6-9 pm; Sun brunch 11 am-2:30 pm. Closed Mon; some major hols. Res accepted. Contemporary Amer menu. Bar; Thurs-Sat to 2 am. Semi-a la carte: lunch $6-$10, dinner $8.50-$20. Specialties: polenta lasagna, sesame-crusted tuna, seafood cheesecake. Jazz Thurs. Modern decor. Cr cds: A, C, D, MC, V.

✔★ **BIRRAPORETTI'S.** *500 Louisiana St, adj to Alley Theatre, downtown. 713/224-9494.* Hrs: 11 am-11 pm; Mon to 8 pm; Fri, Sat to midnight. Italian menu. Bar. Semi-a la carte: lunch, dinner $6.95-$17.95. Child's meals. Specialties: lasagne, pollo poretti, chicken alfredo. In Theater District. Cr cds: A, C, D, DS, MC, V.

★ ★ ★ **BISTRO LANCASTER.** *(See Lancaster Hotel) 713/228-9502.* Hrs: 6:30 am-11 pm; Fri, Sat to midnight; Sun from 7:30 am; Sun brunch 11 am-4 pm. Res accepted. Bar. A la carte entrees: bkfst $6-$9.95, lunch $6.50-$17.95, dinner $15.95-$23.95. Sun brunch $17-$25. Specialties: muffuletta quesadillas, pecan & black pepper-crusted venison, crab cakes. Valet parking. Beautifully restored hotel built 1926. Cr cds: A, C, D, JCB, MC, V.

★ ★ **BISTRO VINO.** *819 W Alabama St (77006), west of downtown. 713/526-5500.* Hrs: 11:30 am-11 pm; Fri, Sat to midnight. Closed Sun; most major hols. Res accepted. French, Italian menu. Bar. Semi-a la carte: lunch $6.95-$15, dinner $7.95-$22. Complete meals: dinner $18.95-$26.95. Specialties: veal Milanese, osso bucco, filet au poivre. Entertainment. Valet parking. Outdoor dining. Romantic atmosphere. Cr cds: A, C, D, MC, V.

★ ★ ★ **BOULEVARD BISTRO.** *4319 Montrose Blvd (77006), south of downtown. 713/524-6922.* Hrs: 11 am-3 pm, 5-10 pm; Fri, Sat to 11 pm; Sat, Sun brunch 10 am-3 pm. Closed Mon; most major hols. Res accepted. Semi-a la carte: lunch $6-$8, dinner $9-$19. Sat, Sun brunch $2.50-$9. Child's meals. Specialties: Moroccan lamb shank, pistachio-crusted salmon. Outdoor dining. Parisian bistro decor. Cr cds: A, D, DS, MC, V.

★ ★ ★ **BRENNAN'S.** *3300 Smith St, south of downtown. 713/522-9711.* Hrs: 11:30 am-2 pm, 5:45-10 pm; Sat from 5:45 pm; Sun 5:45-9:30 pm; Sat brunch 11 am-1:30 pm; Sun brunch 10 am-2 pm. Closed Dec 24, 25. Res accepted. Texas Creole menu. Bar. A la carte entrees: lunch $11-$26, dinner $17-$31. Complete meals: lunch $16-$17.50. Sat, Sun brunch $22-$31. Specialties: turtle soup, grilled veal chop with tchoupitoulas sauce, bananas Foster. Own baking. Jazz Sat, Sun brunch. Valet parking. Outdoor dining. Elegant decor in unique building designed by John Staub as headquarters of Junior League. Family-owned. Jacket. Cr cds: A, C, D, DS, MC, V.

D

★ ★ ★ **BROWNSTONE.** *2736 Virginia St, at Westheimer Rd, in River Oaks. 713/520-5666.* Hrs: 11:30 am-2:30 pm, 6-10 pm; Fri, Sat to 10:30 pm. Closed Sun; Dec 25. Res accepted. Continental menu. Bar. Semi-a la carte: lunch $6.95-$13.95, dinner $14.95-$24.95. Prix fixe: lunch $13.95, dinner $38. Specialties: beef Wellington, Jamaican mixed grill, herb-crusted Chilean sea bass. Pianist; harpist Thurs-Sat. Valet parking. Outdoor poolside dining. Elegant; numerous antiques. Cr cds: A, D, DS, MC, V.

D ♥

★ ★ ★ **THE CAFE.** *(See Houstonian Hotel) 713/685-6862.* Hrs: 6:30 am-10 pm; Sat, Sun from 7 am. Res accepted. Southwestern menu. Bar 3 pm-2 am. Wine list. Semi-a la carte: bkfst $6.95-$12.95, lunch $8.95-$15.95, dinner $10.95-$21.95. Specializes in seafood, pasta, beef. European country decor. Cr cds: A, C, D, DS, MC, V.

D ♥

★ ★ ★ **CAFE ANNIE.** *1728 Post Oak Blvd, in Galleria Area. 713/840-1111.* Hrs: 11:30 am-2 pm, 6-10 pm; Fri to 10:30 pm; Sat 6-10:30 pm. Closed Sun; most major hols. Res accepted. Bar. A la carte entrees: lunch $9-$14, dinner $20-$36. Prix fixe: lunch $20. Specialties: poached shrimp with Dallas mozzarella, mesquite-grilled steak, fresh red snapper. Own pastries. Valet parking. Seasonal floral arrangements; harvest mural by local artist. Cr cds: A, D, DS, MC, V.

D

✔ ★ **CAFE JAPON.** *3915 Kirby Dr (77098), in River Oaks. 713/529-1668.* Hrs: 11 am-11 pm; Fri to 2 am; Sat noon-2 am; Sun noon-11 pm. Japanese menu. Wine, beer. Semi-a la carte: lunch $5.25-$9.50, dinner $9-$15. Specializes in sushi, sashimi, teriyaki. Parking. Contemporary Japanese decor. Cr cds: A, C, D, DS, JCB, MC, V.

D

✔ ★ ★ **CAFE NOCHE.** *2409 Montrose Blvd (77006), west of downtown. 713/529-2409.* Hrs: 11 am-11 pm; Fri, Sat to midnight; Sun brunch to 3:30 pm. Closed Jan 1, Thanksgiving, Dec 25. Mexican menu. Bar to 2 am. Semi-a la carte: lunch $6.95-$14.95, dinner $7.95-$14.95. Sun brunch $10.95. Specialties: chicken Acapulco, blackened chicken, cabrito paella. Valet parking. Outdoor dining. Large central fountain. Cr cds: A, D, MC, V.

D

★ ★ **CANYON CAFE.** *5000 Westheimer Rd (77056), in Galleria Area. 713/629-5565.* Hrs: 11 am-11 pm; Sun to 10 pm; Sun brunch to 2 pm. Res accepted. Southwestern menu. Bar. Semi-a la carte: lunch $6.95-$9.95, dinner $8.95-$18.95. Sun brunch $8.95-$10.95. Child's meals. Specialties: chicken-fried tuna, desert fire pasta, barbecue cornhusk salmon. Valet parking. Outdoor dining. Southwestern decor. Cr cds: A, C, D, DS, MC, V.

D

★ ★ **CARRABBA'S.** *3115 Kirby Dr, in River Oaks. 713/522-3131.* Hrs: 11 am-11 pm; Fri to midnight; Sat 11:30 am-midnight; Sun noon-10 pm. Closed Thanksgiving, Dec 25. Italian menu. Bar. Semi-a la carte: lunch, dinner $7.95-$20.95. Specialties: pasta Carrabba, pollo Rosa Maria, Chicken Bryan Texas. Own desserts. Valet parking. Outdoor dining. Modern decor; wood-burning pizza oven. Cr cds: A, C, D, MC, V.

D

★ ★ ★ **CHARLEY'S 517.** *517 Louisiana St, downtown. 713/224-4438.* Hrs: 11:30 am-2 pm, 5:30-10 pm; Thurs, Fri to 11 pm; Sat 5:30-11 pm. Closed Sun; major hols. Res accepted. Bar. Wine cellar. A la carte entrees: lunch $8.50-$16, dinner $23-$36. Specializes in domestic and imported game, seafood. Own pastries. Valet parking. In Theater District. Jacket (dinner). Cr cds: A, C, D, MC, V.

D

★ ★ ★ **CHEZ GEORGES.** *11920-J Westheimer Rd, at Kirkwood, west of downtown. 281/497-1122.* Hrs: 11 am-2 pm, 6-9:30 pm; Fri, Sat to 10 pm; Sun noon-2 pm (brunch), 6-9:30 pm. Closed Dec 25. Res accepted. French menu. Wine, beer. Semi-a la carte: lunch $7.95-$13.95. A la carte entrees: dinner $14-$26. Complete meals: lunch $13.95. Specialties: filet of red snapper with fennel and lime, roasted duck breast with orange brown sauce, sweetbreads with brandy crawfish sauce. Own pastries. Parking. Country French decor. Jacket. Cr cds: A, C, D, MC, V.

D

★ ★ ★ **CHEZ NOUS.** *(217 S Ave G, Humble 77338) approx 22 mi NE on US 59, exit FM 1960. 281/446-6717.* Hrs: 5:30-11 pm. Closed Sun. Res accepted. French menu. Bar. Wine cellar. A la carte entrees: dinner $15.50-$27. Specialties: filet of king salmon, mesquite-grilled rib-eye steak, rack of lamb. Own desserts. Parking. French decor. Former Pentecostal church (1928). Cr cds: A, C, D, MC, V.

✔ ★ ★ **CHIANTI CUCINA RUSTICA.** *1515 S Post Oak Lane, in Galleria Area. 713/840-0303.* Hrs: 11:30 am-2:30 pm, 5:30-10:30 pm; Fri to 11 pm; Sat 5:30-11 pm. Closed Sun; some major hols. Res accepted. Italian menu. Bar. Semi-a la carte: lunch, dinner $4.50-$13. Child's meals. Specialties: antipasti misto, grilled pork chops, tortellini. Bar. Valet parking. Open-hearth cooking. View of garden from dining rm. Cr cds: A, D, MC, V.

D ♥

★ ★ **CHURRASCO'S.** *2055 Westheimer Rd, in Shepherd Square Shopping Center, west of downtown. 713/527-8300.* Hrs: 11 am-10 pm; Fri to 11 pm; Sat 5-11 pm; Closed Sun; most major hols. Res accepted. South American menu. Bar. A la carte entrees: lunch $7-$18, dinner $12-$22. Specialties: churrasco, empanadas, plantain chips. South American estancia atmosphere. Cr cds: A, C, D, DS, MC, V.

D

✔ ★ **CHUY'S COMIDA DELUXE.** *2706 Westheimer Rd (77098), in River Oaks. 713/524-1700.* Hrs: 11 am-11 pm; Fri, Sat to midnight. Closed Thanksgiving, Dec 25. Res accepted. Mexican menu. Bar. Semi-a la carte: lunch, dinner $4.95-$8.25. Specializes in enchilada, fajitas. Parking. Outdoor dining. Cr cds: A, D, DS, MC, V.

D

★ ★ ★ **CONFEDERATE HOUSE.** *2925 Weslayan St, west of downtown. 713/622-1936.* Hrs: 11 am-2:30 pm, 6-10:30 pm; Sat from 6 pm. Closed major hols. Res accepted. Bar. Wine list. Semi-a la carte: lunch $7.50-$17, dinner $12-$26.50. Specialties: grilled red snapper, lamb chops, soft shell crab. Own desserts. Valet parking. Texas colonial decor. Family-owned. Jacket (dinner). Piano bar. Cr cds: A, C, D, DS, MC, V.

✔ ★ ★ **DACAPO'S CAFE.** *3411 Allen Pkwy (77019), in River Oaks. 713/942-9141.* Hrs: 11 am-2 pm, 5-10 pm; Fri to 11 pm; Sat 5-11 pm; Sun 11 am-3 pm (brunch). Closed most major hols. Res accepted. Bar. Semi-a la carte: lunch $6-$15.95, dinner $7.95-$15.95. Child's meals. Specialties: tomato Napoleon, chili-crusted scallops, chipotle-glazed salmon. Valet parking. Cr cds: A, DS, MC, V.

D

✔ ★ ★ **DAILY REVIEW CAFE.** *3412 W Lamar (77019), west of downtown. 713/520-9217.* Hrs: 11:30 am-2 pm, 6-10 pm; Sun 10 am-2 pm. Closed Mon; most major hols. Contemporary Amer menu. Bar. Semi-a la carte: lunch $6-$10, dinner $9-$16. Sun brunch $6-$11. Specialties: baked polenta, chicken pot pie, pork chops. Valet parking. Outdoor dining. Cr cds: A, C, D, MC, V.

D

★ ★ ★ **DAMIAN'S.** *3011 Smith St, downtown. 713/522-0439.* Hrs: 11 am-2 pm, 5:30-10 pm; Fri to 11:30 pm; Sat 5-11:30 pm. Closed Sun; some major hols. Res accepted. Italian menu. Bar. A la carte entrees: lunch, dinner $9.95-$24.95. Specialties: shrimp Damian, involtini di pollo, veal chop Milanese. Valet parking. Terra cotta walls with hand-painted frescoes. Cr cds: A, C, D, MC, V.

D

★ ★ ★ **DeVILLE.** *(See Four Seasons Hotel-Houston Center) 713/652-6250.* Hrs: 6:30 am-1:30 pm, 6-10 pm; wkend hrs vary; Sun brunch 10:30 am-2 pm. Bar. Wine cellar. Complete meals: bkfst $5-$14. A la carte entrees: lunch $9-$17, dinner $16-$32. Sun brunch $33. Child's meals. Specializes in fresh regional American cuisine. Own baking. Entertainment; jazz duo Sun brunch. Valet parking. Cr cds: A, C, D, ER, JCB, MC, V.

D ♥

★ ★ ★ **THE DINING ROOM.** *(See Luxury Collection Hotel) 713/840-7600, ext. 6110.* Hrs: 6:30 am-2:30 pm; Brunch 11 am-2:30 pm. Res accepted. Continental menu. Bar. Wine cellar. A la carte entrees: bkfst $5.50-$15, lunch $8.50-$18. Sun brunch $32. Child's meals. Specialties: tortilla soup, pecanwood smoked salmon. Own baking. Valet parking. Cr cds: A, C, D, DS, ER, JCB, MC, V.

D

✔★ **DONERAKI.** *7705 Westheimer Rd, west of downtown. 713/975-9815.* Hrs: 11 am-midnight; Fri to 4 am; Sat 8-4 am; Sun 8 am-midnight. Res accepted. Mexican menu. Bar. Semi-a la carte: bkfst $3.95-$6.95, lunch, dinner $4.95-$12.95. Child's meals. Specialties: fajitas, shrimp a la Diabla, chicken enchiladas. Mariachis (dinner). Parking. Colorful Mexican decor. Cr cds: A, DS, MC, V.

D

✔★ ★ **DONG TING.** *611 Stuart St, downtown. 713/527-0005.* Hrs: 11:30 am-2 pm, 5:30-10 pm; Fri, Sat to 10:30 pm. Res accepted. Chinese menu. Semi-a la carte: lunch, dinner $7.50-$12. Specialties: lamb dumplings, clay pot pork, jalapeño steak. Valet parking. Heavy wood paneling; hand-painted murals, antiques. Cr cds: A, D, DS, MC, V.

★ ★ **EMPRESS OF CHINA.** *5419A FM 1960 W (77069), 20 mi N on I-45, exit 1960, west of downtown. 713/583-8021.* Hrs: 11 am-2:30 pm, 5-10 pm; Fri, Sat to 10:30 pm. Closed Sun; Jan 1, Thanksgiving, Dec 25. Res accepted. Pacific Rim menu. Wine, beer. Semi-a la carte: lunch $5.50-$15, dinner $8.95-$22.50. Specialties: duck a la empress, Neptune's platter. Parking. Cr cds: A, DS, MC, V.

D

★ ★ **THE FLYING DUTCHMAN.** *(505 2nd St, Kemah 77565) 25 mi SE on US 45, exit NASA Rd 1, then E to Kemah. 281/334-7575.* Hrs: 11 am-10 pm; wkends to 11 pm. Closed Thanksgiving, Dec 25. Res accepted. Bar. Semi-a la carte: dinner $13.95-$18.95. Child's meals. Specializes in Gulf seafood, oyster bar, crawfish. Parking. Outdoor dining with view of boat channel. Cr cds: A, D, DS, MC, V.

★ ★ ★ **GLASS MENAGERIE.** *(See Woodlands Resort) 713/367-1000.* Hrs: 11:30 am-2 pm, 6-10 pm; Sun brunch 11 am-3 pm. Res accepted. Continental menu. Bar. Buffet lunch $11.95. Semi-a la carte: dinner $20-$32. Sun brunch $21.95. Specializes in steak Diane, flambé desserts. Pianist Thurs-Sun. Valet parking. Views of lake. Cr cds: A, C, D, DS, MC, V.

D

✔★ **GOLDEN ROOM.** *1209 Montrose Blvd (77019), west of downtown. 713/524-9614.* Hrs: 11:30 am-2:30 pm, 5:30-9:30 pm; Fri to 10:30 pm; Sat 5:30-10:30 pm. Closed Sun; also Dec 25. Res accepted. Thai menu. Wine, beer. Semi-a la carte: lunch $5.95-$6.50, dinner $9.95-$14.95. Specialties: shrimp Jackson, claypot dishes, spicy mint chicken. Parking. Oriental decor. Cr cds: A, D, DS, MC, V.

★ **GOODE CO. TEXAS SEAFOOD.** *2621 Westpark (77098), in River Oaks. 713/523-7154.* Hrs: 11 am-10 pm; Fri, Sat to 11 pm. Closed Jan 1, Thanksgiving, Dec 25. Bar. Semi-a la carte: lunch, dinner $6-$16.95. Specializes in seafood. Valet parking. Nautical decor. Cr cds: A, C, D, DS, MC, V.

D

★ ★ **GROTTO.** *3920 Westheimer Rd (77027), in River Oaks. 713/622-3663.* Hrs: 11:30 am-11 pm; Fri, Sat to midnight; Sun to 10 pm. Closed major hols. Southern Italian menu. Bar. Semi-a la carte: lunch $6.95-$9.95, dinner $6.95-$17.95. Specialties: grilled red snapper cerretto, linguine alle vongole. Own pizza, pasta. Parking. Outdoor dining. Neapolitan cafe setting; large mural on wall. Cr cds: A, D, DS, MC, V.

D

★ **GUADALAJARA.** *210 Town & Country Dr (77024), at Kimberly Lane, in shopping center, west of downtown. 713/461-5300.* Hrs: 11 am-10 pm; Fri, Sat to 11 pm. Closed Thanksgiving, Dec 25. Mexican menu. Bar. Semi-a la carte: lunch $5.50-$6.95, dinner $5.95-$13.95. Child's meals. Specializes in enchiladas, tortillas, seafood. Strolling musicians wkends. Casual dining; Mexican decor. Outdoor dining. Cr cds: A, DS, MC, V.

D

✔★ ★ **HUNAN.** *1800 Post Oak Blvd (77056), in Galleria Area. 713/965-0808.* Hrs: 11:30 am-10:30 pm; Fri to 11:30 pm; Sat noon-11:30 pm; Sun from noon. Closed Thanksgiving. Res accepted. Chinese, Hunan menu. Bar. Semi-a la carte: lunch $6.85-$8.95, dinner $9.85-$15.50. Specializes in Hunan-style chicken & prawn, Peking duck. Parking. Chinese decor, large Oriental mural. Cr cds: A, C, D, MC, V.

✔★ **JALAPEÑOS.** *2702 Kirby Dr (77098), in River Oaks. 713/524-1668.* Hrs: 11 am-10 pm; Fri, Sat to 11:30 pm; Sun brunch to 2:30 pm. Closed Thanksgiving. Res accepted. Mexican, South Amer menu. Bar. Semi-a la carte: lunch $6-$11, dinner $7-$15. Sun brunch $12.95. Child's meals. Specialties: stuffed jalapeños, spinach enchiladas, mesquite-grilled quail. Own tortillas. Central Mexican decor. Cr cds: A, MC, V.

D

★ **JOYCE'S OYSTER RESORT.** *6415 San Felipe (77058), west of downtown. 713/975-9902.* Hrs: 5:30-10 pm; Sun 4-9 pm. Closed Mon; Jan 1, Thanksgiving, Dec 25. Res accepted. Seafood menu. Bar. Semi-a la carte: dinner $8.95-$18.95. Child's meals. Specializes in oysters, grilled fish, Louisiana gumbo. Nautical decor; marine colors, fish mounted on walls. Cr cds: A, C, D, DS, MC, V.

D

★ **KANEYAMA.** *9527 Westheimer Rd, Suite D (77063), west of downtown. 713/784-5168.* Hrs: 11:30 am-10:30 pm; Fri, Sat to 11 pm. Closed Thanksgiving. Res accepted. Japanese menu. Bar. Semi-a la carte: lunch $5.95-$10, dinner $8.50-$20.45. Specialties: sushi, salmon teriyaki, hamachi kama. Sushi bar. Cr cds: A, C, D, DS, JCB, MC, V.

D

★ ★ **KELLY'S DEL FRISCO.** *14641 Gladebrook (77068), 15 mi N on I-45, exit 1960, north of downtown. 713/893-3339.* Hrs: 4:30 pm-2 am. Closed most hols. Res accepted. Bar. A la carte entrees: dinner $16.95-$22.95. Specializes in steak, beef. Entertainment. Parking. Club atmosphere. Cr cds: A, MC, V.

D ♥

★ **KHYBER.** *2510 Richmond Ave (77098), south of downtown. 713/942-9424.* Hrs: 11 am-2 pm, 5:30-10 pm. Indian menu. Wine, beer. Semi-a la carte: lunch $7.50-$12.50, dinner $11.50-$16. Specialties: grilled lamb leg, mountain-style grilled chicken, homemade bread. Own baking. Outdoor dining. Native American artifacts, decorative rugs on wall; large patio. Cr cds: MC, V.

D

★ **KIM SON.** *2001 Jefferson St, downtown. 713/222-2461.* Hrs: 11 am-11 pm; Fri, Sat to midnight. Vietnamese, Chinese menu. Bar. A la carte entrees: lunch, dinner $6.50-$13.95. Specialties: spring rolls, black pepper crab, Vietnamese fajitas. Parking. Cr cds: A, C, D, DS, MC, V.

D

★ ★ ★ **LA COLOMBE D'OR.** *(See La Colombe D'or Inn) 713/524-7999.* Hrs: 11:30 am-2 pm, 6-10 pm; Fri to 11 pm; Sat, Sun 6-11 pm. Res accepted. French menu. A la carte entrees: lunch $9.50-$15, dinner $22-$29. Specializes in rack of lamb, veal, fish. Own desserts. Valet parking. 21-rm residence decorated with artwork. Cr cds: A, C, D, MC, V.

D

★ ★ ★ **LA GRIGLIA.** *2002 W Gray St, in River Oaks Shopping Center, in River Oaks. 713/526-4700.* Hrs: 11:30 am-2 pm, 5:30-11 pm; Fri to midnight; Sat 5:30 pm-midnight; Sun 5:30-10 pm. Closed Dec 25. Res accepted. Italian menu. Bar. A la carte entrees: lunch $6.95-$14.95, dinner $8.95-$24.95. Specialties: shrimp & crab cheesecake, red snapper La Griglia, linguine pescatore. Valet parking. Outdoor dining. Colorful tilework and murals. Cr cds: A, D, DS, MC, V.

D

★ ★ **LA MORA.** *912 Lovett (77006), west of downtown. 713/522-7412.* Hrs: 11:30 am-2 pm, 5:30-10 pm; Fri, Sat 5:30-11 pm. Closed Sun; most major hols. Res accepted. Northern Italian menu. Bar. Semi-a la carte: lunch, dinner $10.95-$20.95. Specialties: spicy fish soup, cuscinetti, rotisserie-roasted pork loin. Valet parking. Outdoor dining, Italian villa decor. Cr cds: A, C, D, DS, MC, V.

D

★ ★ ★ ★ **LA RESERVE.** *(See Omni Houston Hotel) 713/871-8181.* In this dusty-rose dining room, the many beveled mirrors seem to multiply the eye-catching central flower arrangement. Candlelight and antique accent pieces add intimacy to large contemporary space. Continental menu. Specialties: charred citrus-pepper tuna, grilled double lamb chops, porcini-crusted monkfish. Also dietary menu. Own baking. Menu changes daily. Hrs: 6:30-10:30 pm. Closed Sun. Res accepted. Bar 5 pm-midnight. A la carte entrees: dinner $19-$32. Table d'hôte: dinner $50-$85. Valet parking. Jacket (dinner). Cr cds: A, C, D, DS, ER, JCB, MC, V.

★ ★ ★ **LA TOUR D'ARGENT.** *2011 Ella Blvd, north of downtown. 713/864-9864.* Hrs: 11:30 am-2 pm, 6-11 pm. Closed Sun; major hols. Res accepted; required wkends. French menu. Bar. A la carte entrees: lunch $8.50-$20, dinner $16-$31. Specializes in seafood, pheasant, duck. Own desserts. Valet parking. Antiques. Dining in 1920s hunting lodge, Houston's oldest log cabin. Overlooks bayou. Jacket (dinner). Cr cds: A, C, D, DS, MC, V.

D

★ ★ **LAS ALAMEDAS.** *8615 Katy Frwy (77024), 7 mi W on I-10, exit Bingle/Voss, west of downtown. 713/461-1503.* Hrs: 11 am-3 pm, 6-10 pm; Fri to 11 pm; Sat 6-11 pm; Sun 11 am-3 pm (brunch), 6-9 pm. Closed most major hols. Res accepted. Mexican menu. Bar. Semi-a la carte: lunch, dinner $10-$20. Sun brunch $20. Child's meals. Specialties: enchiladas verdes, grilled red snapper, chile relleno. Own baking. Guitarist Tues-Sat, Sun brunch. Valet parking. Replica of 19th-century Mexican hacienda; entrance arch, stained glass. Cr cds: A, C, D, DS, MC, V.

★ ★ ★ **MAXIM'S.** *3755 Richmond Ave, south of downtown. 713/877-8899.* Hrs: 11:15 am-10:30 pm; Sat 5:30-11 pm. Closed Sun; major hols. Res accepted. French menu. Bar. Wine cellar. Semi-a la carte: lunch $9.75-$12, dinner $15.75-$23.75. Specializes in Gulf seafood. Own baking. Pianist. Valet parking. Family-owned. Jacket. Cr cds: A, C, D, DS, MC, V.

D

✔ ★ **MESA GRILL.** *1971 W Gray St (77019), in River Oaks. 713/520-8900.* Hrs: 11 am-10 pm; Fri, Sat to 11 pm; Sun from 10 am; Sun brunch to 3 pm. Closed Dec 25. Res accepted. Bar; Fri, Sat to 2 am. Semi-a la carte: lunch $5.95-$9.95, dinner $7.95-$14.95. Sun brunch $14.95. Child's meals. Specialties: Adobe pie, southwestern Caesar salad, tortilla soup. Patio dining. Southwestern decor. Cr cds: A, C, D, DS, MC, V.

D

★ ★ **MONTESANO RISTORANTE ITALIANO.** *6009 Beverly Hill Lane, west of downtown. 713/977-4565.* Hrs: 11 am-2:30 pm, 5:30-11 pm; Fri to midnight; Sat 5:30 pm-midnight. Closed Sun; Thanksgiving, Dec 25. Res accepted. Italian menu. Bar. A la carte entrees: lunch $7.95-$13.95, dinner $9:95-$24. Specializes in chicken, veal, seafood. Valet parking. Cr cds: A, D, DS, MC, V.

D

✔ ★ ★ **MOOSE CAFE.** *1340 W Gray St (77019), west of downtown. 713/520-9696.* Hrs: 11 am-11 pm; Fri, Sat to midnight; Sat, Sun brunch 11 am-4 pm. Closed Jan 1, Thanksgiving, Dec 25. Pacific Northwest, Texas barbecue menu. Bar to 2 am. Semi-a la carte: lunch, dinner $6.75-$17.95. Sat, Sun brunch $5.75-$8.75. Specialties: blackened chicken, salmon cake salad, cedar plank salmon. Outdoor dining. Cr cds: A, D, MC, V.

D

★ ★ **MORTON'S OF CHICAGO.** *5000 Westheimer Rd, 5 mi W on Loop 610, exit Westheimer, west of downtown. 713/629-1946.* Hrs: 5-11 pm; Sun to 10 pm. Closed some major hols. Res accepted. Bar. A la carte entrees: $17.95-$29.95. Specializes in steak. Valet parking. Cr cds: A, C, D, JCB, MC, V.

D

★ ★ **NINO'S.** *2817 W Dallas St, west of downtown. 713/522-5120.* Hrs: 11 am-2:30 pm, 5:30-10 pm; Fri to 11 pm; Sat 5:30-11 pm. Closed Sun; major hols. Res accepted. Italian menu. Bar. Semi-a la carte: lunch $8.95-$17.95, dinner $8.95-$21.95. Specializes in veal, seafood, chicken. Parking. Italian decor. Cr cds: A, C, D, MC, V.

D

★ ★ **NIT NOI.** *2462 Bolsover (77005), 2 mi west of downtown. 713/524-8114.* Hrs: 11 am-3 pm, 5-10 pm; Sun 5-9 pm. Closed some major hols. Thai menu. Wine, beer. Semi-a la carte: lunch $5.99-$14.95, dinner $6.95-$14.95. Specialties: spring rolls, chicken basil. Totally nonsmoking. Cr cds: A, D, DS, MC, V.

D

✔ ★ **OHIO GRANGE CAFE.** *1915 Westheimer Rd (77098), west of downtown. 713/529-9500.* Hrs: 11:30 am-2 pm, 5:30-10 pm; Fri to 11 pm; Sat 11:30 am-3 pm, 5:30-11 pm; Sun noon-4 pm, 5:30-10 pm. Closed Thanksgiving, Dec 25. Res accepted. Bar. Semi-a la carte: lunch $5.95-$13.95, dinner $6.95-$15.95. Child's meals. Specialties: meatloaf, grilled mahi mahi, pot pies. Own baking. Valet parking. Outdoor dining. Heartland country decor. Cr cds: A, C, D, DS, MC, V.

D

★ ★ ★ **OUISIE'S TABLE.** *3939 San Felipe (77027), in River Oaks. 713/528-2264.* Hrs: 11 am-10 pm; Fri to 11 pm; Sat 10 am-11 pm; Sun 10 am-9 pm. Sat, Sun brunch 10 am-2:30 pm. Closed Mon. Bar. Semi-a la carte: bkfst $5-$8, lunch $6-$12.50, dinner $11-$23. Sun brunch $5-$12.50. Specialties: Shrimp tacos, chicken curry, crab cakes. Parking. Outdoor dining. Texas ranch-house style. Cr cds: A, C, D, DS, MC, V.

D

✔ ★ ★ **P.F. CHANG'S.** *4094 Westheimer Rd (77027), in River Oaks. 713/627-7220.* Hrs: 11 am-11 pm; Fri, Sat to midnight. Closed Thanksgiving, Dec 25. Res accepted. Chinese menu. Bar. Semi-a la carte:

lunch, dinner $5.95-$12.95. Specialties: dandan noodles, Chang's spicy chicken, Szechwan seafood. Own baking, noodles. Valet parking. Upscale bistro with Oriental mural, bas-relief stone columns. Cr cds: A, MC, V.

D ⚐

★ **PALACE CAFE.** *401 Louisiana St (77002), downtown. 713/222-8900.* Hrs: 8 am-10 pm; Mon to 8 pm; Fri to 11 pm; Sat 11 am-11 pm; Sun 11 am-8 pm; Sun brunch to 3 pm. Closed Thanksgiving, Dec 25. Res accepted. Serv bar. Semi-a la carte: lunch, dinner $7-$10. Sun brunch $8-$10. Specialties: chicken enchilada, tomato basil soup. Valet parking Thurs-Sat (dinner). Restored historic bldg. Cr cds: A, C, D, DS, MC, V.

★ ★ **PAPPADEAUX.** *6015 Westheimer Rd, west of downtown. 713/782-6310.* Hrs: 11 am-11 pm; Fri, Sat to midnight. Closed Thanksgiving, Dec 25. Cajun menu. Bar. Semi-a la carte: lunch $7.45-$9.95, dinner $8.95-$32.95. Specialties: fried alligator, crawfish etouffée, Angus steak. Parking. Cr cds: A, MC, V.

D ⚐

★ ★ ★ **PAPPAS BROS STEAKHOUSE.** *5839 Westheimer Rd (77056), west of downtown. 713/780-7352.* Hrs: 5-10 pm, Fri, Sat to 11 pm. Closed Sun; Jan 1, July 4, Dec 25. Res accepted. Bar. Wine list. A la carte entrees: dinner $16.95-$58.95. Specializes in steak, lobster. Parking. 1930s New York steakhouse atmosphere. Cr cds: A, MC, V.

D ⚐

✔★ **PAPPASITO'S CANTINA.** *6445 Richmond Ave, west of downtown. 713/784-5253.* Hrs: Sun-Thurs 11 am-10 pm; Fri, Sat to midnight. Mexican menu. Bar. A la carte entrees: lunch $5.95-$8.95, dinner $5.95-$17.95. Specializes in seafood, enchiladas, fajitas. Own tortillas, desserts. Mexican decor. Cr cds: A, MC, V.

D ⚐

★ ★ ★ **POST OAK GRILL.** *1415 S Post Oak Lane, in Galleria Area. 713/993-9966.* Hrs: 11 am-midnight; Mon, Tues to 11 pm; Sun 6-10 pm. Closed some major hols. Res accepted. Bar to 2 am. Wine cellar. Semi-a la carte: lunch $6.95-$14.95, dinner $8.25-$21.95. Specialties: tomatoes Manfred, fresh gulf snapper, lemon pepper chicken. Entertainment. Valet parking. Outdoor dining. Festive ambience, colorful Toulouse-Lautrec murals. Cr cds: A, C, D, DS, MC, V.

D ⚐ ♥

★ ★ **PREGO.** *2520 Amherst St, in Hermann Park area. 713/529-2420.* Hrs: 11 am-10 pm; Fri to 11 pm; Sat noon-11 pm; Sun from noon. Closed some major hols. Res accepted. Italian menu. Bar. A la carte entrees: lunch, dinner $5-$20. Child's meals. Specialties: veal alla pego, wild mushroom ravioli, Gulf coast crab cakes. Parking. Bistro-style dining. Cr cds: A, C, MC, V.

D ⚐

★ ★ ★ **RAINBOW LODGE.** *1 Birdsall St, west of downtown. 713/861-8666.* Hrs: 11:30 am-10:30 pm; Sat from 6 pm; Sun from 10:30 am; Sun brunch to 4 pm. Closed Mon; major hols. Res accepted. Bar. Semi-a la carte: lunch $7.25-$28, dinner $16.95-$32. Sun brunch $7.25-$15.95. Specializes in seafood, wild game. Valet parking. Outdoor dining. On Buffalo Bayou; garden, gazebo. Cr cds: A, C, D, DS, MC, V.

D ⚐ ♥

★ ★ **RANCHO TEJAS.** *4747 San Felipe (77056), in Galleria Area. 713/840-0440.* Hrs: 11 am-10 pm; Fri, Sat to 11 pm; Sun brunch 10 am-2 pm. Closed Jan 1, Thanksgiving, Dec 25. Res accepted. Southwestern menu. Bar. Semi-a la carte: lunch $6-$12, dinner $7-$24. Sun brunch $12.95. Child's meals. Specializes in mesquite-grilled steaks, seafood, Mexican dishes. Own baking. Valet parking. Outdoor dining. Ranch-house decor; native Texas limestone, vaulted ceiling. Cr cds: A, C, D, DS, MC, V.

⚐

★ ★ ★ **REDWOOD GRILL.** *4611 Montrose Blvd, west of downtown. 713/523-4611.* Hrs: 11 am-2:30 pm, 6-10:30 pm; Fri to 11 pm; Sat 6-11 pm; Sun 6-9 pm. Closed some major hols. Res accepted, required wkends. Bar. Semi-a la carte: lunch $8.95-$18.95, dinner $10.95-$21.95. Valet parking. Cr cds: A, C, D, DS, MC, V.

D

★ ★ ★ **RIO RANCH.** *9999 Westheimer Rd (77042), west of downtown. 713/952-5000.* Hrs: 6:30 am-10 pm; Fri-Sun to 11 pm; Sun brunch 7 am-2 pm. Semi-a la carte: lunch $5.95-$24.95, dinner $8.95-$24.95. Sun brunch $11.95. Child's meals. Specialties: red snapper with crawfish tails, smoked pork loin with red chili sauce. Cr cds: A, C, D, DS, MC, V.

D SC ⚐

★ ★ **RIVER OAKS GRILL.** *2630 Westheimer Rd, in River Oaks. 713/520-1738.* Hrs: 5:30-10:30 pm; Fri, Sat to 11 pm. Closed Sun; some major hols. Res accepted; required wkends. Bar 4 pm-midnight; Sat from 5 pm. Semi-a la carte: dinner $13.95-$26.95. Specializes in steak, fresh seafood, chops. Pianist Tues-Sat. Valet parking. Club atmosphere; contemporary decor. Cr cds: A, D, DS, MC, V.

D ⚐

★ ★ ★ **RIVOLI.** *5636 Richmond Ave, west of downtown. 713/789-1900.* Hrs: 11:30 am-2 pm, 6-11 pm; Sat from 6 pm. Closed Sun; major hols. Res accepted. Continental menu. Bar. Wine cellar. A la carte entrees: lunch $7.95-$14.95, dinner $16.95-$27. Specialties: Dover sole stuffed with crabmeat and shrimp, rack of lamb Diable, blackened shrimp with mustard sauce. Own pastries. Entertainment Mon-Sat. Valet parking. Jacket. Cr cds: A, D, DS, MC, V.

D ⚐

★ ★ ★ **ROTISSERIE FOR BEEF AND BIRD.** *2200 Wilcrest Dr, west of downtown. 713/977-9524.* Hrs: 11:30 am-2 pm, 6-10 pm; Sat from 6 pm. Closed Sun; Jan 1, Dec 25. Res accepted. Continental menu. Bar. Wine cellar. Semi-a la carte: lunch $9.50-$12.95, dinner $18.95-$35. Specializes in roast duckling, venison, lobster. Valet parking. New England-colonial atmosphere. Jacket (dinner). Cr cds: A, C, D, DS, MC, V.

D ⚐

★ ★ **RUGGLES GRILL.** *903 Westheimer Rd (77006), west of downtown. 713/524-3839.* Hrs: 11:30 am-2 pm, 5:30-11 pm; Fri to midnight; Sat 5:30 pm-midnight; Sun 11 am-2:30 pm, 5:30-10 pm. Closed Mon; July 4, Thanksgiving, Dec 25. Res accepted. Bar. Semi-a la carte: lunch $5.95-$13.95, dinner $9.95-$16.95. Specialties: black pepper pasta, grilled beef filet, Texas goat cheese salad. Valet parking. Contemporary decor. Cr cds: A, D, MC, V.

⚐

★ ★ ★ **RUTH'S CHRIS STEAK HOUSE.** *6213 Richmond Ave, west of downtown. 713/789-2333.* Hrs: 5-11 pm. Closed most major hols. Res accepted. Bar. A la carte entrees: dinner $17-$29. Specializes in steak, lamb chops, lobster. Valet parking. Cr cds: A, C, D, DS, JCB, MC, V.

D ⚐

★ ★ **SABINE.** *2606 Sunset Blvd (77006), Rice Univ Village, west of downtown. 713/662-9041.* Hrs: 11:30 am-2 pm, 5:30-10 pm; Fri to 11 pm; Sat 5:30-11 pm; Sun 11 am-2 pm (brunch), 5:30-9 pm. Closed Mon; most major hols. Res accepted. Regional Amer menu. Bar. Semi-a la carte: lunch $9-$14, dinner $11-$21. Sun brunch $9-$14. Specialties: onion tart with garlic cream sauce, oatmeal-crusted rainbow trout, roast pork tenderloin. Own baking, pasta. Valet parking (dinner). Contemporary decor; paintings by local artists. Cr cds: A, DS, MC, V.

✔★ **SAUSALITO SEAFOOD & PASTA.** *3215 Westheimer Rd (77098), in River Oaks. 713/529-6959.* Hrs: 11 am-10 pm; Fri to 11 pm; Sat from 5 pm; Sun brunch to 3 pm. Closed Jan 1, Dec 25. Res accepted. Italian, Amer menu. Bar. Semi-a la carte: lunch, dinner $6.95-$19.95. Sun brunch $7.50-$10.95. Child's meals. Specializes in veal chops, pasta. Valet parking. Outdoor dining. Contemporary decor. Cr cds: A, C, D, DS, MC, V.

D ⚐

✔★★ **SHANGHAI RIVER.** *2407 Westheimer Rd, in River Oaks. 713/528-5528.* Hrs: 11 am-10 pm; Fri, Sat to 11 pm. Closed Thanksgiving. Res accepted. Chinese menu. Bar. Semi-a la carte: lunch $5.50-$6.95, dinner $5.50-$14.95. Specialties: crispy shrimp, General Tso's chicken, Peking duck. Parking. Chinese porcelains on display. Cr cds: A, C, D, MC, V.

D

★★ **SIERRA.** *4704 Montrose Blvd, west of downtown. 713/942-7757.* Hrs: 11 am-2:30 pm, 5-10:30 pm; Fri to 11:30 pm; Sat 5-11:30 pm; Sun 11 am-10 pm. Closed most major hols. Res accepted. Southwestern menu. Bar. Semi-a la carte: lunch $5.95-$19.95, dinner $7.50-$29.95. Specialties: filet of salmon "campfire style," filet of beef tenderloin. Jazz Sun. Valet parking. Outdoor patio dining. Southwestern decor. Cr cds: A, C, D, DS, MC, V.

D

✔★ **SVETLANA.** *80 Woodlake Square (77063), at Westheimer & Gessner, west of downtown. 713/785-1418.* Hrs: 11:30 am-3 pm, 5:30-11 pm; Mon to 3 pm; Fri to 1 am; Sat 5:30 pm-1 am. Closed Thanksgiving, Dec 25. Res accepted. Russian menu. Bar. Semi-a la carte: lunch $4.95-$10.95, dinner $11.95-$21. Specialties: blintzes with caviar, cabbage rolls, borscht. Entertainment Fri, Sat. Formal setting; lace curtains. Cr cds: A, DS, MC, V.

D

★★★ **TASTE OF TEXAS.** *10505 Katy Frwy (77024), 12 mi W on I-10, exit 756A, west of downtown. 713/932-6901.* Hrs: 11 am-10 pm; Fri to 11 pm; Sat 4-11 pm; Sun from 4 pm. Closed Thanksgiving, Dec 25. Bar. Wine cellar. Semi-a la carte: lunch, dinner $4.95-$29.95. Child's meals. Specializes in steak, prime rib, lobster. Salad bar. Own baking. Historical Texan decor; many local antiques, memorabilia. Family-owned. Cr cds: A, C, D, DS, MC, V.

D

★★ **TONY MANDOLA'S.** *7947 Katy Frwy (77024), 6 mi W on I-10, Wirt exit, west of downtown. 713/680-3333.* Hrs: 11 am-2 pm, 5-10 pm; Sat from 5 pm; Sun 11 am-9 pm. Closed Thanksgiving, Dec 25. Res accepted. Italian menu. Bar. Semi-a la carte: lunch $5-$12, dinner $8-$22. Child's meals. Specialties: blackened snapper in lime butter, calamari ala Mama, baked lasagna. Own baking. Family dining; Italian decor. Cr cds: A, C, D, MC, V.

D

★★ **TONY MANDOLA'S GULF COAST KITCHEN.** *1962 W Gray St, in River Oaks. 713/528-3474.* Hrs: 11 am-10 pm; Fri, Sat to 11 pm; Sun 5-9 pm. Closed some major hols. Res accepted. New Orleans, Cajun menu. Bar. A la carte entrees: lunch, dinner $8.95-$22.95. Child's meals. Specialties: Mama's gumbo, crawfish ravioli, blackened soft-shell crab. Parking. Outdoor dining. New Orleans bistro atmosphere. Cr cds: A, D, MC, V.

D

★★★★ **TONY'S.** *1801 Post Oak Blvd (77056), in Galleria Area. 713/622-6778.* Italian mahogany-lined booths, a large original mural and spot-and-sconce lighting set an elegant tone in this Italian-continental restaurant. Fine china, handblown stemware and fresh flowers grace the tables. Italian, continental menu. Specialties: anatra con lampone, seared red snapper with crabmeat. Hrs: 6-11 pm; Fri, Sat to midnight. Closed Sun; major hols. Res accepted. Bar. Wine list. Semi-a la carte: dinner $19.95-$35. Pianist, vocalist. Valet parking. Family-owned. Cr cds: A, C, D, DS, MC, V.

D

★★ **VARGO'S INTERNATIONAL CUISINE.** *2401 Fondren Rd (77063), west of downtown. 713/782-3888.* Hrs: 11 am-2 pm, 5-11 pm; Sat from 5 pm; Sun 11 am-2:30 pm. Closed Jan 1, Dec 25. Res accepted. Continental menu. Bar 4 pm-midnight. Semi-a la carte: lunch, dinner $21.95-$28.50. Specializes in steaks, fresh seafood. Pianist Thurs-Sun. Valet parking. View of lake and gardens. Cr cds: A, C, D, DS, MC, V.

D

Unrated Dining Spots

BUTERA'S FINE FOODS. *4621 Montrose Blvd, on grounds of Chelsea Market, west of downtown. 713/523-0722.* Hrs: 10:30 am-10 pm; Sun to 8 pm. Closed some major hols. Wine, beer. A la carte entrees: lunch, dinner $6-$8. Specializes in chicken salad, sandwiches, pasta salad. Outdoor dining. Cafeteria-style serv. Cr cds: A, D, DS, MC, V.

D

GOODE CO. TEXAS BAR-B-Q. *5109 Kirby Dr, south of downtown. 713/522-2530.* Hrs: 11 am-10 pm. Closed Jan 1, Thanksgiving, Dec 25. Wine, beer. A la carte entrees: lunch, dinner $4-$9.75. Specializes in barbecued dishes, cheese bread, pecan pie. Entertainment first Fri of month. Parking. Outdoor dining. Relaxed Western atmosphere. Family-owned. Cr cds: A, C, D, DS, MC, V.

D

GREAT CARUSO. *10001 Westheimer Rd, west of downtown. 713/780-4900.* Hrs: 6-10:30 pm; Fri, Sat to 11:30 pm. Closed Mon; Jan 1, Dec 25. Res accepted. Continental menu. Bar to 1 am. A la carte entrees: dinner $12.95-$21.95. Entertainment charge $2.95-$3.95. Specializes in veal, steak, fish. Valet parking. Unique antique decor. Broadway and light operetta performances nightly; singing waiters and dancers. Cr cds: A, C, D, DS, MC, V.

D

GUGENHEIM'S DELICATESSEN. *1708 Post Oak Blvd, in Galleria Area. 713/622-2773.* Hrs: 10 am-9 pm; Fri to 10 pm; Sat 9 am-10 pm; Sun 9 am-9 pm. Closed Jan 1, Thanksgiving, Dec 25. Wine, beer. Semi-a la carte: bkfst $1-$9.95, lunch, dinner $4.95-$9.95. Specializes in deli sandwiches, cheesecake. Own desserts. Parking. Outdoor dining. New York-style deli. Cr cds: A, C, D, DS, MC, V.

D

JAGS. *5120 Woodway Dr, in Decorative Center, west of downtown. 713/621-4766.* Hrs: 11:30 am-2:30 pm. Closed Sat, Sun; Memorial Day, Thanksgiving, Dec 25. Res accepted. Bar. A la carte entrees: lunch $8-$15. Specialties: blini Santa Fe, seared salmon with cucumber salsa. Multi-level dining area surrounded by running stream. Cr cds: A, MC, V.

OTTO'S BARBECUE. *5502 Memorial Dr, west of downtown. 713/864-2573.* Hrs: 11 am-9 pm. Closed Sun; some major hols. Beer. Semi-a la carte: lunch, dinner $4.75-$8.75. Child's meals. Specializes in barbecued meats. Parking. Outdoor dining. Rustic. Western decor; slogan-covered walls. No cr cds accepted.

Indianapolis

Founded: 1820
Pop: 731,327
Elev: 717 feet
Time zone: Eastern
Area code: 317
Web: www.indy.org

Indianapolis, the capital of Indiana, is truly a "city on the move." The changing downtown skyline reflects the progressive drive of this Midwestern city, which was once known only for its annual Indianapolis "500."

Indianapolis became the state capital nearly four years after Indiana was admitted to the Union. Statehood became official on December 11, 1816, at the original capital, Corydon, located in the southern part of the state. The first governor of Indiana, Jonathan Jennings, decided it would be more advantageous to have the capital in the center of the state. By 1832 Indianapolis had its first state fair. The arrival of the railroad in 1847 gave new impetus to the area. Public schools were established in 1853; a university was founded two years later. By the turn of the century, Indianapolis had become the commercial center of the rich agricultural region surrounding it and an important manufacturing center in the Midwest.

Today, Indianapolis is the largest city in the state and 12th largest in the nation. The city also is recognized as one of the nation's amateur sports capitals. It has hosted both the US Olympic Festival, the Pan American Games and multiple NCAA events. The headquarters of several individual sports, including track and field and gymnastics, are located here.

Business

In addition to sports, Indianapolis' economy is boosted by the health industry. Eli Lilly and Company, one of the largest pharmaceutical companies in the world, and the Indiana University Medical Center complex, one of the country's largest, are both in Indianapolis.

The city is one of the nation's leading trucking centers. Dozens of interstate carriers operate out of Indianapolis. American Trans Air, the world's largest charter carrier, is headquartered here. Indianapolis is also one of the leading US grain markets and an important livestock and meat-processing center. Among the products manufactured here are medical supply equipment, aircraft motors, automobile parts, furniture and television sets.

Indianapolis abounds in space for manufacturing, warehousing and distributing. There are virtually no barriers to expansion, since nearly 40 square miles (10 percent of the county's land) have been zoned for industrial use. More than 2,000 acres are in industrial parks, located near the interstate highway system to provide easy access to other cities or downtown Indianapolis.

Office space is plentiful and evenly distributed between downtown and suburban locations. Office space totaling more than 3 million square feet was built during the 1970s. Recently completed construction projects include Victory Field (home of the AAA Indianapolis Indians), Circle Centre mall and the Indianapolis Artsgarden.

Convention Facilities

The Indiana Convention Center and RCA Dome feature 301,500 square feet of column-free exhibit space, including five halls and the stadium floor. Additionally, there are 52 meeting rooms. Meeting space capacity is 127,595 square feet (including ballrooms) in the Convention Center and 60,500 seats in the Dome. Banquets for up to 7,500 can be served in the same room. Indianapolis has more than 16,000 hotel and motel accommodations; 3,000 of those are within walking distance of the Indiana Convention Center and RCA Dome.

Sports & Recreation

The annual 500-mile automobile race at the Indianapolis Motor Speedway has brought international fame to this city. The Indianapolis "500," held each year on the Sunday before Memorial Day, is one of the most important and popular auto competitions in the world. Annual attendance is estimated at more than 350,000 people. The 2.5-mile oval track was built in 1909 as a proving ground for cars. The $7 million Speedway Museum exhibits race cars dating from 1909. The National Hot Rod Association's National Drag Races, held every Labor Day at Indianapolis Raceway Park, is the largest drag racing event of the year, with more than 150,000 fans attending.

Indianapolis has several world-class sports facilities: the Indiana University Natatorium, described by competition swimmers as the fastest pool in the nation; the IU Track and Field Stadium, an eight-lane, all-weather track; the Major Taylor Velodrome, a 333.3-meter banked bicycle track; the Indianapolis Sports Center, a tournament tennis stadium; the 60,500-seat RCA Dome; the 17,000-seat Market Square Arena; and the Pan American Plaza with two indoor skating rinks.

The NFL's Indianapolis Colts provide football excitement at the RCA Dome. For basketball fans, Indianapolis is the home of the Indiana Pacers, who play their home games in the Market Square Arena. Baseball fans can go to Victory Field in White River State Park to see the Indianapolis Indians, and hockey fans can watch the Indianapolis Ice take on opponents at the Market Square Arena.

Thirty golf courses, 12 of which are public, and more than 130 tennis courts are scattered throughout the city. The RCA Championships, held annually in Indianapolis, attract top-name tennis stars from around the world. Parks are abundant in the city and surrounding areas. Garfield Park features sunken gardens, greenhouses and an illuminated fountain; musical programs are presented in the park's amphitheater. Eagle Creek Park, a 3,800-acre park with a 1,300-acre reservoir, is one of the largest metropolitan parks in the country and features one of two US rowing courses sanctioned for international competition.

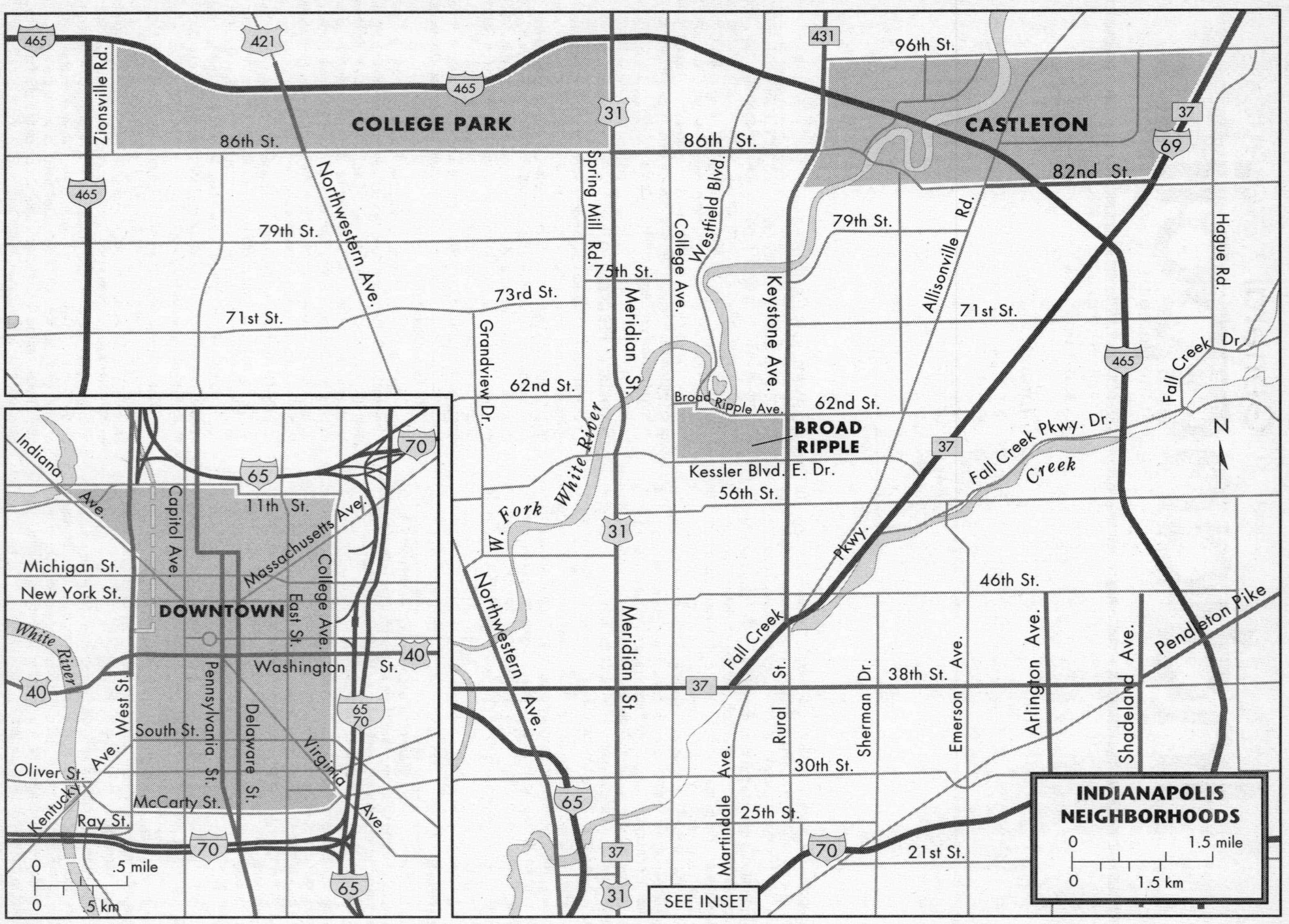
INDIANAPOLIS NEIGHBORHOODS
0 1.5 mile
0 1.5 km
N
COLLEGE PARK
CASTLETON
BROAD RIPPLE
DOWNTOWN
SEE INSET
Zionsville Rd.
86th St.
96th St.
82nd St.
79th St.
75th St.
73rd St.
71st St.
62nd St.
56th St.
46th St.
38th St.
30th St.
25th St.
21st St.
Northwestern Ave.
Spring Mill Rd.
Grandview Dr.
Meridian St.
College Ave.
Westfield Blvd.
Keystone Ave.
Allisonville Rd.
Hague Rd.
Fall Creek Dr.
Broad Ripple Ave.
Kessler Blvd. E. Dr.
Fall Creek Pkwy. Dr.
Fall Creek Pkwy.
Creek
W. Fork White River
Rural St.
Sherman Dr.
Emerson Ave.
Arlington Ave.
Shadeland Ave.
Pendleton Pike
Martindale Ave.
465
421
431
31
37
69
65
70
40
Indiana Ave.
Capitol Ave.
11th St.
Massachusetts Ave.
College Ave.
East St.
Michigan St.
New York St.
White River
Washington St.
West St.
South St.
Pennsylvania St.
Delaware St.
Virginia Ave.
Oliver St.
Kentucky Ave.
McCarty St.
Ray St.
0 .5 mile
0 .5 km

Entertainment

The highly regarded Indianapolis Symphony Orchestra was founded in 1930. Subscription and children's concerts are performed in the ornate Hilbert Circle Theatre (1916), a restored movie palace. In addition, the nationally acclaimed Dance Kaleidoscope Company can be seen at the Indianapolis Civic Theatre. The Indianapolis Opera holds its regular season at Clowes Memorial Hall; the Indianapolis Ballet Theatre performs at Clowes Hall, Murat Theatre and Warren Performing Arts Center.

Butler University's recitals, concerts and other attractions are held in Clowes Hall or in adjacent Lilly Hall. A number of professional and repertory theaters present dramas, comedies, musicals and Broadway shows each year; several community theater groups offer dramatic and diversified programs.

Historical Areas

Outside Indianapolis in Noblesville, William Conner built a cabin and trading post in 1802. It was here, in 1820, that a group of men decided on the site of the new capital. In 1930, Eli Lilly acquired the Conner settlement and restored it. Twenty-five buildings are now included in the Conner Prairie Pioneer Settlement.

The beloved "Hoosier Poet," James Whitcomb Riley, lived in Indianapolis and died here on July 22, 1916. His house, a National Historic Landmark, and his tomb in Crown Hill Cemetery can be visited.

Among several restored houses in Indianapolis are those of Benjamin Harrison, 23rd president of the United States, and Meredith Nicholson, author of many best-sellers. The Morris-Butler House (1862) is now a museum of Victorian decorative arts.

Two churches, St John's, dedicated in 1871, and Christ Church Cathedral, erected in 1857, are of interest.

The state capitol building is an impressive structure of Indiana limestone with a huge copper dome. The Indiana State Museum has exhibits on the natural and cultural history of the state, as well as paintings by Indiana artists.

Sightseeing

In the heart of downtown Indianapolis is the Soldiers' and Sailors' Monument, erected in memory of Civil War soldiers. The monument rises 284 feet and is topped with a 38-foot statue, *Miss Victory.* Completed in 1902, it is on the site originally intended for the governor's mansion.

The Indianapolis Museum of Art consists of the Krannert Pavilion, Lilly Pavilion of Decorative Arts, Mary Fendrich Hulman Pavilion, Clowes Pavilion and the sculpture court with displays of Medieval and Renaissance art and French, English and Italian decorative arts.

The Children's Museum, one of the world's largest, offers history, social culture, science and transportation exhibits. Of particular interest to children are a planetarium, a working carousel, a wood-burning locomotive, a furnished cabin, a giant water clock and a mummy.

The Children's Museum also operates a 312-seat IWERKS Cine-Dome, a large-format theater.

The Indianapolis Zoo in White River State Park features the Whale and Dolphin Pavilion, as well as Indiana's first major aquarium.

The Indiana University Medical Center, at Indiana University-Purdue University at Indianapolis, is one of the foremost medical centers in the world and a primary international center for heart research.

The restored City Market has been a part of the Indianapolis business scene since 1886. In 30 shops and stores, merchants offer a variety of goods from ethnic foods to handcrafted products.

General References

Area code: 317

Phone Numbers

POLICE & FIRE: 911

POISON CONTROL CENTER: 929-2323

TIME & WEATHER: 635-5959

Information Sources

Indianapolis Convention & Visitors Association, 1 RCA Dome, Suite 100, 46225; 639-4282.

Indiana Department of Commerce, 1 N Capitol Ave, Suite 700, 46204; 232-8800.

Indianapolis Chamber of Commerce, 320 N Meridian St, Suite 200, 46204; 464-2200.

Indianapolis City Center, 201 S Capitol Ave, Suite 200, 46225; 237-5200.

Department of Parks & Recreation, 327-0000.

Transportation

AIRLINES: American; American Trans Air; America West; America West Express; American Eagle; Comair; Continental; Delta; Midway Connection; Northwest; Skyway; Southwest; TWA; United; USAir; USAir Express; ValuJet; and other commuter and regional airlines.

AIRPORT: Indianapolis International Airport, 487-9594.

CAR RENTAL AGENCIES: (See IMPORTANT TOLL-FREE NUMBERS) Avis 244-3307; Budget 248-1100; Hertz 243-9321; National 243-1150.

PUBLIC TRANSPORTATION: Metro Transit 635-3344.

RAILROAD PASSENGER SERVICE: Amtrak 800/872-7245.

Newspapers

Indianapolis News; Indianapolis Star; Indianapolis Business Journal.

Convention Facilities

Indiana Convention Center & RCA Dome, 100 S Capitol, 262-3410.

Indiana State Fair Complex, 1202 E 38th St, 923-3431.

Murat Centre, 510 N New Jersey St, 231-0000.

University Conference Center at IUPUI, 850 W Michigan St, 274-2700.

Sports & Recreation

Major Sports Facilities

Indiana State Fairgrounds Pepsi Coliseum, 1202 E 38th St, 927-7622 (ice skating).

Indianapolis Raceway Park, 10267 E US 136, 291-4090.

Indianapolis Motor Speedway, 4400 W 16th St, 241-2500.

Indianapolis Tennis Center, 755 University Blvd, 278-2100

Indiana Track and Field Stadium, 900 W New York, 274-3518.

Indiana University Natatorium, 901 W New York, 274-3518.

Indiana World Skating Academy, 237-5565.

Major Taylor Velodrome, 3649 Cold Spring Rd, 327-8356.

Market Square Arena, 300 E Market St, 639-6411 (Pacers, basketball, 263-2100).

RCA Dome, 100 S Capitol, 262-3389 (Colts, football, 297-2658).

Victory Field, 501 W Maryland, 269-3545.

Cultural Facilities

Theaters

American Cabaret Theater, 401 E Michigan St, 631-0334.

Beef & Boards Dinner Theatre, 9301 N Michigan Rd, 872-9664.

Christian Theological Seminary Repertory Theatre, 1000 W 42nd St, 927-8052.

Indianapolis Civic Theater, 1200 W 38th St, 923-4597.

Indiana Repertory Theatre, 140 W Washington St, 635-5252.

Madame Walker Theater, 617 Indiana Ave, 236-2099.

Phoenix Theater, 749 N Park Ave, 635-PLAY.

Concert Halls

Clowes Memorial Hall, 4600 Sunset Ave, 940-9710 (tickets); 940-9696 (info).

Hilbert Circle Theatre, 45 Monument Circle, 262-1110.

Murat Centre, 510 N New Jersey St, 231-0000.

Museums

The Children's Museum, 3000 N Meridian St, 924-5431.

Hook's Historic Drug Store and Pharmacy Museum, Indiana State Fairgrounds, 1180 E 38th St, 924-1503.

Indianapolis Motor Speedway Hall of Fame Museum, 4790 W 16th St, 484-6747.

Indiana State Museum, 202 N Alabama St, at Ohio St, 232-1637.

Indiana Transportation Museum, 20 mi NW via IN 37, IN 19 in Noblesville, 773-6000 or 773-0300.

Patrick Henry Sullivan Museum, 225 W Hawthorne, 12 mi N off US 421 in Zionsville, 873-4900.

Art Museums

Eiteljorg Museum of American Indians and Western Art, 500 W Washington St, 636-WEST (9378).

Indianapolis Museum of Art, 1200 W 38th St, 923-1331.

Morris-Butler House Museum, 1204 N Park Ave, 636-5409.

Points of Interest

Historical

Carmelite Monastery, 2500 Cold Spring Rd, 926-5654.

Christ Church Cathedral, 125 Monument Circle, 636-4577.

Conner Prairie Pioneer Settlement, 6 mi N via I-465, 13400 Allisonville Rd, Fishers, 776-6000.

Crown Hill Cemetery, 700 W 38th St, 925-8231.

Fort Benjamin Harrison, E 56th St & Post Rd, 546-9211.

James Whitcomb Riley Home, 528 Lockerbie St, 631-5885.

President Benjamin Harrison Memorial Home, 1230 N Delaware St, 631-1898.

Scottish Rite Cathedral, 650 N Meridian St, 262-3100.

Soldiers' and Sailors' Monument, 232-7615.

State Capitol, between Washington & Ohio Sts and Capitol & Senate Aves, 233-5293.

Other Attractions

City Market, 222 E Market St, 634-9266.

Eagle Creek Park, 7840 W 56th St, just W of I-465, 327-7110.

Garfield Park and Conservatory, 2450 S Shelby St at Raymond St & Garfield Dr, 327-7220.

Holcomb Observatory & Planetarium, Butler University campus, W 46th St & Sunset Ave, 283-9333.

Indiana Medical History Museum, 3045 W Vermont St, 635-7329.

Indiana University Medical Center, IUPUI campus, 550 N University Blvd, 274-5000.

Indiana War Memorial Plaza, 431 N Meridian St, 232-7615.

Indianapolis Zoo, 1200 W Washington St, 630-2030.

Lilly Center, 307 E McCarty, 276-2000.

Madame Walker Theatre Center, 617 Indiana Ave, 236-2099.

Union Station, 39 Jackson Place, 267-0700.

Sightseeing Tours

Gray Line bus tours, 9075 N Meridian, 573-0699.

Landmark Tours, 340 W Michigan, 639-4646.

Annual Events

"500" Festival, 636-4556. May.

Indianapolis "500," Indianapolis Motor Speedway, 481-8500. Sun before Memorial Day.

Midsummer Festival, downtown, 637-4574. June.

Strawberry Festival, downtown, 636-4577. June.

Indiana Black Expo, Convention Center, 925-2702. July.

White River Park Games, White River State Park, 634-4567. July.

Indiana State Fair, fairgrounds, 1202 E 38th St, 923-3431 or 927-7500. Aug.

RCA Championships, Indianapolis Tennis Center, 815 W New York St, 632-4100 or 800/622-LOVE. Aug.

National Hot Rod Association US Nationals, Indianapolis Raceway Park, 291-4090. Labor Day.

Penrod Arts Fair, Indianapolis Museum of Art, 923-1331. Sept.

Circle City Classic, RCA Dome, 237-5222. Oct.

International Festival, Indiana State Fairgrounds, 927-7500. Oct.

City Neighborhoods

Many of the restaurants, unrated dining establishments and some lodgings listed under Indianapolis include neighborhoods as well as exact street addresses. Geographic descriptions of these areas are given, followed by a table of restaurants arranged by neighborhood.

Broad Ripple: North of Downtown; south of Broad Ripple Ave, west of Keystone Ave, north of Kessler Blvd and east of College Ave.

Castleton: Northeast area of city south of 96th St, west of IN 37, north of 82nd St and east of Keystone Ave.

College Park: South of I-465, west of Meridian St, north of 86th St and east of Zionsville Rd.

Downtown: South of 11th St, west of College Ave, north of McCarty St and east of West St & Indiana Ave. **North of Downtown:** North of I-65. **South of Downtown:** South of I-70.

Lodgings and Food

INDIANAPOLIS RESTAURANTS BY NEIGHBORHOOD AREAS

(For full description, see alphabetical listings under Restaurants)

BROAD RIPPLE
Aristocrat Pub. 5212 N College Ave
Jazz Cooker. 925 E Westfield Blvd

COLLEGE PARK
Kona Jack's. 9419 N Meridian
Wildcat Brewing Company. 9111 N Michigan Rd

DOWNTOWN
Benvenuti. 1 N Pennsylvania St
The Majestic. 47 S Pennsylvania
Restaurant At The Canterbury (Canterbury Hotel). 123 S Illinois
St Elmo Steak House. 127 S Illinois

NORTH OF DOWNTOWN
Hollyhock Hill. 8110 N College Ave
Iron Skillet. 2489 W 30th St
Peter's. 8505 Keystone Crossing Blvd
Ruth's Chris Steak House. 9445 Threel Rd

Note: When a listing is located in a town that does not have its own city heading, it will appear under the city nearest to its location. In these cases, the address and town appear in parenthesis immediately following the name of the establishment.

Motels

(Rates are usually higher during Indianapolis "500" and state fair; may be 3-day min.)

★ **COMFORT INN.** *5040 S East St (US 31S) (46227), south of downtown. 317/783-6711; FAX 317/787-3065.* 104 rms, 3 story. S $49-$65; D $55-$90; each addl $5; under 18 free. Crib free. Pet accepted, some restrictions. TV; cable (premium). Pool. Complimentary continental bkfst. Restaurant nearby. Ck-out noon. Business servs avail. Refrigerator in suites. Cr cds: A, C, D, DS, JCB, MC, V.

D SC

★ **COUNTRY HEARTH INN.** *3851 Shore Dr (46254), I-465 exit 17, north of downtown. 317/297-1848; FAX 317/297-1848, ext. 125; res: 800/848-5767.* 83 rms, 2 story, 12 suites. S $53-$65; D $59-$71; each addl $6; suites, kits. $74-$86; under 18 free. Crib free. TV; cable (premium). Pool. Complimentary continental bkfst. Restaurant adj 6 am-10 pm. Ck-out noon. Meeting rms. Business servs avail. Health club privileges. Cr cds: A, C, D, DS, MC, V.

D SC

★ ★ **COURTYARD BY MARRIOTT.** *8670 Allisonville Rd (46250), in Castleton. 317/576-9559; FAX 317/576-0695.* 146 rms, 3 story. S, D $92; each addl $10; suites $107-$117; under 18 free; wkend rates. Crib free. TV; cable (premium). Indoor pool; whirlpool. Continental bkfst. Complimentary coffee in rms. Bar. Ck-out noon. Coin Indry. Meeting rms. Business servs avail. In-rm modem link. Valet serv. Sundries. Exercise equipt; weight machine, bicycles. Refrigerators in suites. Balconies. Cr cds: A, C, D, DS, MC, V.

D

★ ★ **COURTYARD BY MARRIOTT.** *10290 N Meridian St (46209), in College Park. 317/571-1110; FAX 317/571-0416.* 149 rms, 4 story. S, D $92-$108; each addl $10; suites $125-$145; under 18 free; higher rates special events. Crib free. TV; cable (premium). Complimentary coffee in rms. Bar 4-11 pm. Ck-out 1 pm. Meeting rms. Business servs avail. In-rm modem link. Sundries. Coin Indry. Exercise equipt; weight machine, stair machine. Indoor pool; whirlpool. Refrigerator in suites. Cr cds: A, C, D, DS, MC, V.

D SC

★ ★ **COURTYARD BY MARRIOTT-AIRPORT.** *5525 Fortune Circle E (46241), at Intl Airport, south of downtown. 317/248-0300; FAX 317/248-1834.* 151 rms, 4 story. S $89; D $99; each addl $10; suites $120; higher rates special events. Crib free. TV; cable (premium), VCR avail. Indoor pool; whirlpool. Continental bkfst. Complimentary coffee in rms. Restaurant nearby. Bar 5-11 pm; closed Sun. Ck-out noon. Meeting rms. Business servs avail. Sundries. Free airport transportation. Exercise equipt; weight machine, bicycles. Balconies. Cr cds: A, C, D, DS, MC, V.

D SC

★ **DRURY INN.** *9320 N Michigan Rd (46268), in College Park. 317/876-9777; FAX 317/876-9777, ext. 473.* 110 rms, 4 story. S $63-$73; D $73-$83; each addl $10; under 18 free; some wkend rates. Crib free. Pet accepted, some restrictions. TV; cable (premium). Pool. Complimentary bkfst. Restaurant nearby. Ck-out noon. Meeting rms. Business servs avail. In-rm modem link. Sundries. Cr cds: A, C, D, DS, MC, V.

D SC

✔★ **FAIRFIELD INN BY MARRIOTT.** *8325 Bash Rd (46250), in Castleton. 317/577-0455.* 132 rms, 3 story. S, D $56-$69; each addl $8; under 18 free. Crib free. TV; cable (premium). Heated pool. Complimentary continental bkfst. Restaurant nearby. Ck-out noon. Business servs avail. In-rm modem link. Cr cds: A, C, D, DS, MC, V.

D SC

★ ★ **HAMPTON INN.** *7220 Woodland Dr (46278), I-465 & 71st St, north of downtown. 317/290-1212; FAX 317/291-1579.* 124 rms, 4 story. S, D $69-$74; under 18 free. Crib free. Pet accepted, some restrictions. TV; cable (premium). Indoor pool; whirlpool. Complimentary continental bkfst. Restaurant adj 24 hrs. Ck-out noon. Meeting rms. Business servs avail. In-rm modem link. Valet serv. Exercise equipt; weight machine, bicycles. Cr cds: A, C, D, DS, MC, V.

D SC

★ ★ **HAMPTON INN-EAST.** *2311 N Shadeland Ave (46219), east of downtown. 317/359-9900; FAX 317/359-1376.* 125 rms, 4 story. S $64-$68; D $68-$76; under 18 free. Crib free. Pet accepted, some restrictions. TV; cable (premium). Indoor pool; whirlpool. Complimentary continental bkfst. Restaurant nearby. Ck-out noon. Meeting rm. Business servs avail. In-rm modem link. Cr cds: A, C, D, DS, MC, V.

D SC

★ ★ **HOMEWOOD SUITES.** *2501 E 86th St (46240), north of downtown. 317/253-1919; FAX 317/255-8223.* 116 suites, 3 story. No elvtr. S, D $94-$104; higher rates special events. Crib free. Pet accepted; $50. TV; cable (premium), VCR. Complimentary continental bkfst. Coffee in rms. Ck-out noon. Meeting rms. Business center. In-rm modem link. Valet serv. Coin Indry. Exercise equipt; weight machine, stair machine, sauna. Heated pool; whirlpool. Refrigerators, microwaves. Cr cds: A, C, D, DS, MC, V.

D SC

★ **LA QUINTA-EAST.** *7304 E 21st St (46219), north of downtown. 317/359-1021; FAX 317/359-0578.* 122 rms, 2 story. S, D $53-$62; each addl $7; under 18 free. Crib free. TV; cable (premium). Heated pool. Continental bkfst. Coffee in rms. Restaurant adj 6 am-11 pm. Ck-out noon. Coin Indry. Valet serv. Cr cds: A, C, D, DS, MC, V.

D SC

★ **RAMADA INN-EAST.** *7701 E 42nd St (46226), north of downtown. 317/897-4000; FAX 317/897-8100.* 192 rms, 2 story. S $64-$66; D $69-$71; each addl $5; suites $110-$150; under 18 free. Crib $10. TV; cable (premium). 2 pools, 1 indoor. Restaurant 6 am-10 pm; Sun to 2 pm. Rm serv. Bars. Ck-out noon. Meeting rms. Business servs avail. Cr cds: A, C, D, DS, MC, V.

SC

★ **RENAISSANCE TOWER.** *230 E 9th St (46204), downtown. 317/261-1652; res: 800/676-7786; FAX 317/262-8648.* 80 kit. units, 6 story. S, D $75; higher rates special events. TV; cable, VCR avail. Complimentary coffee in rms. Ck-out noon. Business servs avail. In-rm modem link. Valet serv. Coin Indry. Microwaves. Cr cds: A, DS, MC, V.

D SC

★ ★ **SIGNATURE INN.** *4402 E Creek View Dr (46237), I-65 & Southport Rd, south of downtown. 317/784-7006.* 101 rms, 2 story. S, D $65-$72; under 18 free; wkend rates Nov-Apr. Crib free. TV; cable (premium). Pool. Complimentary continental bkfst. Restaurant adj 6 am-10 pm. Ck-out noon. Meeting rms. Business servs avail. In-rm modem link. Valet serv. Sundries. Health club privileges. Microwaves avail. Cr cds: A, D, DS, MC, V.

D SC

Motor Hotels

★ ★ **AMERISUITES.** *9104 Keystone Crossing (46240), north of downtown. 317/843-0064; FAX 317/843-1851.* 126 suites, 6 story. S, D $81-$109; each addl $10. Crib free. TV; cable (premium), VCR (movies). Complimentary continental bkfst. Ck-out noon. Meeting rms. Business center. In-rm modem link. Valet serv (Mon-Fri). Coin Indry. Exercise equipt; treadmill, bicycle. Health club privileges. Heated pool. Refrigerators, microwaves, wet bars. Cr cds: A, C, D, DS, MC, V.

D SC

★ ★ **COMFORT INN.** *5855 Rockville Rd (46224), near Intl Airport, west of downtown. 317/487-9800; FAX 317/487-1125.* 94 rms, 4 story, 24 suites. S $79-$180; D $84-$185; each addl $5; suites $91-$185; under 18 free. Crib free. TV; cable. Complimentary continental bkfst. Coffee in rms. Ck-out noon. Meeting rms. Business servs avail. In-rm modem link. Bellhops. Valet serv. Sundries. Coin Indry. Free airport transportation. Exercise equipt; bicycle, stair machine. Indoor pool; whirlpool. Playground. Game rm. Some refrigerators, microwaves, wet bars; in-rm whirlpool in suites. Cr cds: A, C, D, DS, JCB, MC, V.

D SC

★ ★ ★ **DOUBLETREE GUEST SUITES.** *(11355 N Meridian St, Carmel 46032) Approx 15 mi N on Meridian St (US 31). 317/844-7994; FAX 317/844-2118.* 137 suites, 3 story. S, D $85-$129; each addl $15; under 18 free. Crib free. TV; cable. Indoor/outdoor pool; whirlpool, poolside serv. Complimentary coffee in rms. Restaurant 6:30 am-11 pm. Rm serv. Bar from 5 pm. Ck-out noon. Meeting rms. Business servs avail. Exercise equipt; bicycles, stair machine. Refrigerators, microwaves. Private patios. Cr cds: A, C, D, DS, MC, V.

D SC

★ ★ **HAMPTON INN.** *105 S Meridian St (46225), downtown. 317/261-1200; FAX 317/261-1030.* 180 rms, 9 story, 22 suites. S $88-$109; D $99-$109; suites $104-$159; under 18 free; higher rates special events. Crib free. Valet parking $8. TV; cable (premium). Complimentary continental bkfst. Restaurant 11 am-midnight. Rm serv. Bar. Ck-out noon. Meeting rms. Business servs avail. In-rm modem link. Bellhops. Valet serv. Exercise equipt; bicycle, treadmill. Some in-rm whirlpools, refrigerators, wet bars. Cr cds: A, C, D, DS, MC, V.

D SC

★ ★ ★ **HOLIDAY INN SELECT-NORTH.** *3850 De Pauw Blvd (46268), in College Park, at I-465 & US 421 exit 27. 317/872-9790; FAX 317/871-5608.* 349 rms, 5 story. S, D $99-$109; suites $170; under 18 free; wkend rates. Crib free. TV; cable (premium). Heated pool; whirlpool. Coffee in rms. Restaurant 6 am-10 pm. Rm serv. Bar 11-2 am. Ck-out 11 am. Coin Indry. Convention facilities. Business servs avail. In-rm modem link. Bellhops. Valet serv. Gift shop. Sundries. Putting green. Exercise equipt; weight machine, treadmill, sauna. Private patios; balconies. Cr cds: A, C, D, DS, JCB, MC, V.

D SC

★ ★ **HOLIDAY INN-EAST.** *6990 E 21st St (46219), east of downtown. 317/359-5341; FAX 317/351-1666.* 184 rms, 6 story. S, D $89; higher rates special events. Crib free. Pet accepted. TV; cable (premium). Complimentary full bkfst (Mon-Fri). Coffee in rms. Restaurant 6 am-11 pm; Fri-Sun to midnight. Rm serv. Bar. Ck-out noon. Meeting rms. Business center. In-rm modem link. Bellhops. Valet serv. Sundries. Coin Indry. Exercise equipt; treadmill, stair machine. Indoor pool; whirlpool. Game rm. Cr cds: A, C, D, DS, JCB, MC, V.

D SC

★ ★ ★ **MARRIOTT.** *7202 E 21st St (46219), I-70E & I-465, east of downtown. 317/352-1231; FAX 317/352-9775.* 252 rms, 3-5 story. S, D, studio rms $119; each addl $10; suites $300; under 18 free; wkend rates; higher rates Memorial Day wkend. Crib free. Pet accepted, some restrictions. TV; cable, VCR avail. Indoor/outdoor pool; wading pool, whirlpool, poolside serv. Complimentary coffee in lobby. Restaurant 6:30 am-10 pm. Rm serv. Bar 11-1 am, Sun to midnight. Ck-out noon. Coin Indry. Meeting rms. Business center. In-rm modem link. Bellhops. Valet serv. Sundries. Gift shop. Tennis privileges. Putting green. Exercise equipt; weight machine, bicycles. Rec rm. Some private patios. Luxury level. Cr cds: A, C, D, DS, JCB, MC, V.

D SC

★ **RAMADA-AIRPORT.** *2500 S High School Rd (46241), at Intl Airport, south of downtown. 317/244-3361; FAX 317/241-9202.* 288 rms, 6 story. S $119; D $129; each addl $10; suites $195-$275; under 18 free; higher rates special events. Crib $10. TV; cable (premium). Indoor pool. Restaurant 6-11 am, 5-10 pm. Rm serv. Bar 11-1 am. Ck-out noon. Meeting rms. Business servs avail. In-rm modem link. Bellhops. Sundries. Gift shop. Free airport transportation. Cr cds: A, C, D, DS, MC, V.

D SC

★ ★ **ST VINCENT MARTEN HOUSE.** *1801 W 86th St (46260), north of downtown. 317/872-4111; FAX 317/875-7162; res: 800/736-5634.* 176 rms, 2 story. S, D $89-$99; each addl $10; suites $135-$250; under 18 free. Crib free. TV; cable. Indoor pool. Restaurant 6:30 am-2 pm, 5:30-10 pm. Rm serv. Bar 5 pm-midnight. Ck-out noon. Coin Indry. Meeting rms. Business servs avail. In-rm modem link. Bellhops. Valet serv. Exercise equipt; weight machine, treadmill, sauna. Some refrigerators. St Vincent's Hospital adj. Cr cds: A, C, D, DS, MC, V.

D SC

★ ★ ★ **WYNDHAM GARDEN.** *251 E Pennsylvania Pkwy (46280), I-465 & US 31N to 103rd St, north of downtown. 317/574-4600; FAX 317/574-4633.* 171 rms, 6 story. S, D $89-$109; suites $109-$129. Crib free. TV; cable, VCR avail. Indoor pool; whirlpool. Complimentary coffee in rms. Restaurant 6:30 am-10 pm. Rm serv from 5 pm. Bar 11 am-midnight. Ck-out noon. Meeting rms. Business servs avail. Sundries. Exercise equipt; weight machine, bicycles. Cr cds: A, C, D, DS, ER, JCB, MC, V.

D SC

Hotels

★ ★ ★ **CANTERBURY.** *123 S Illinois (46225), downtown. 317/634-3000; FAX 317/685-2519; res: 800/538-8186.* 99 rms, 12 story. S $175-$200; D $200-$225; each addl $25; suites $400-$1,200; lower rates wkends. Crib $25. Garage $12/day. TV; cable, VCR avail. Complimentary continental bkfst. Restaurant (see RESTAURANT AT THE CANTERBURY). Afternoon tea 4-5:30 pm. Ck-out noon. Meeting rms. Business servs avail. In-rm modem link. Concierge. Bathrm phones, minibars. 2-story atrium lobby. Formal decor; 4-poster beds, Chippendale-style furniture. Historic landmark; built 1926. Cr cds: A, C, D, DS, ER, JCB, MC, V.

D

★ ★ ★ **CROWNE PLAZA-UNION STATION.** *123 W Louisiana St (46225), at Union Station, downtown. 317/631-2221; FAX 317/236-7474.* 275 rms, 3 story, 33 suites. S, D $125-$155; suites $185-$250; under 18 free; wkend rates; higher rates Dec 31. Crib free. Valet parking $10. TV; cable. Indoor pool; whirlpool. Restaurant 6 am-midnight. Bar 4 pm-midnight. Ck-out noon. Convention facilities. Business servs avail. In-rm modem link. Concierge. Free airport transportation. Exercise equipt; bicycles, rowers. Rec rm. First US "union" railway depot (1853); Pullman sleeper cars from the 1920s house hotel's suites. Cr cds: A, C, D, DS, MC, V.

D SC

★ ★ ★ **DOUBLETREE-UNIVERSITY PLACE.** *850 W Michigan St (46206), on campus of Indiana University, downtown. 317/269-9000; FAX 317/231-5168; res: 800/627-2700.* 278 rms, 10 story. Mar-May, Sept-Nov: S, D $169; suites $250-$600; lower rates rest of yr. Crib avail. Garage parking $4.75. TV; cable (premium). Coffee in rms. Restaurant 6 am-midnight. Bar from 11 am. Ck-out noon. Convention facilities. Business center. In-rm modem link. Gift shop. Barber. Health club privileges. Refrigerators. Cr cds: A, C, D, DS, MC, V.

D

★ ★ ★ **EMBASSY SUITES.** *110 W Washington St (46204), downtown. 317/236-1800; FAX 317/236-1816.* 360 suites, 18 story. S $139-$179; D $159-$219; under 18 free. Crib free. Parking in/out $5. TV; cable, VCR avail. Indoor pool; whirlpool. Complimentary full bkfst. Complimentary coffee in rms. Restaurant 11 am-10 pm; Sat, Sun from 5 pm. Bar to 1 am. Ck-out noon. Convention facilities. Business servs avail. In-rm modem link. Shopping arcade. Exercise equipt; weights, bicycles. Refrigerators, microwaves. Cr cds: A, C, D, DS, JCB, MC, V.

D SC

★ ★ ★ **EMBASSY SUITES.** *3912 Vincennes Rd (46268-3024), I-465N & US 421, north of downtown. 317/872-7700; FAX 317/872-2974.* 221 suites, 8 story. S, D $109-$189; under 12 free; wkend plan. Crib avail. TV; cable (premium). Indoor pool; whirlpool. Complimentary full bkfst; afternoon refreshments. Complimentary coffee in rms. Restaurant 11 am-2 pm, 5-11 pm. Bar from 4 pm. Ck-out noon. Meeting rms. Business servs avail. In-rm modem link. Gift shop. Exercise equipt; bicycles, treadmill, sauna. Game rm. Refrigerators, microwaves. Cr cds: A, C, D, DS, MC, V.

D SC

★ ★ ★ **HYATT REGENCY.** *One South Capitol (46204), downtown. 317/632-1234; FAX 317/231-7569.* 500 rms, 21 story. S $175; D $200; each addl $25; suites $350-$1,000; parlor $175-$700; under 18 free; some wkend rates. Valet, garage parking $9. Crib free. TV; VCR avail. Indoor pool. Restaurants 6 am-midnight. Bars 11-2 am. Ck-out noon. Convention facilities. Business center. In-rm modem link. Concierge. Barber, beauty shop. Exercise equipt; weight machine, bicycles. Massage. Atrium. Revolving restaurant. Cr cds: A, C, D, DS, ER, JCB, MC, V.

D SC

★ ★ ★ **OMNI-NORTH.** *8181 N Shadeland Ave (46250), I-69 N exit 82nd St, north of downtown. 317/849-6668; FAX 317/849-4936.* 215 rms, 6 story. S, D $89-$149; suites $149-$250; wkend rates. Crib free. TV; cable (premium). Indoor pool. Complimentary coffee in rms. Restaurant 7 am-10 pm; wkend hrs vary. Rm serv to midnight. Bar 11:30 am-midnight. Ck-out noon. Coin Indry. Meeting rms. In-rm modem link. Gift shop. Exercise equipt; bicycles, weight machine; sauna. Game rm. Many refrigerators. Cr cds: A, D, DS, JCB, MC, V.

D SC

★ ★ ★ **OMNI SEVERIN.** *40 W Jackson Place (46225), at Union Station, downtown. 317/634-6664; FAX 317/767-0003.* 423 rms, 13 story. S, D $119-$189; each addl $20; suites $225-$675; under 18 free. Crib free. Garage parking $5. TV; cable, VCR avail. Indoor pool; poolside serv. Coffee in rms. Restaurant 6 am-11 pm. Bar 11-1 am. Ck-out noon. Convention facilities. Business center. In-rm modem link. Concierge. Gift shop. Exercise equipt; weight machine, bicycles. Some refrigerators. Built in 1913. Across from Union Station. Cr cds: A, C, D, DS, MC, V.

D SC

★ ★ ★ **RADISSON.** *8787 Keystone Crossing (46240), at 86th St & Keystone Ave, connected to Fashion Mall, north of downtown. 317/846-2700; FAX 317/846-2700, ext. 402.* 552 units, 2-12 story. S, D $179; each addl $15; suites $199; under 17 free; wkend rates. Crib free. TV; cable (premium), VCR avail (movies). Indoor pool; whirlpool, poolside serv. Restaurants 6:30 am-11 pm. Rm serv to midnight. Bar 5 pm-2 am. Ck-out noon. Guest Indry. Convention facilities. Business center. In-rm modem link. Shopping arcade. Garage parking. Sauna. Health club privileges. Game rm. Refrigerator in suites. Cr cds: A, C, D, DS, ER, JCB, MC, V.

D SC

★ ★ ★ **RADISSON HOTEL CITY CENTER.** *31 W Ohio St (46204), downtown. 317/635-2000; FAX 317/638-0782.* 374 rms, 21 story. S $99-$169; D $99-$184; each addl $15; suites $139-$199; under 18 free. Crib free. Garage $8. TV; cable, VCR avail. Pool; poolside serv. Restaurant 6:30 am-midnight. Bars 11-1 am. Ck-out noon. Convention facilities. Business center. Health club privileges. Luxury level. Cr cds: A, C, D, DS, MC, V.

D SC

★ ★ ★ **THE WESTIN.** *50 S Capitol (46204), downtown. 317/262-8100; FAX 317/231-3928.* 573 rms, 15 story. S $194; D $224; each addl $30; suites $224-$1,000; under 18 free. Crib free. Valet, garage parking $8. TV; cable, VCR avail. Indoor pool; whirlpool. Restaurant 6:30 am-11 pm. Rm serv 24 hrs. Bar 11-2 am, Sun to midnight. Ck-out noon. Convention facilities. Business center. In-rm modem link. Concierge. Exercise equipt; bicycles, treadmill. Health club privileges. Some bathrm phones, minibars. Luxury level. Cr cds: A, C, D, DS, JCB, MC, V.

D SC

Restaurants

✔★ **ARISTOCRAT PUB.** *5212 N College Ave (46220), in Broad Ripple. 317/283-7388.* Hrs: 11 am-11 pm; Wed, Thurs to midnight; Fri, Sat to 1 am; Sun from 10 am; Sun brunch to 3 pm. Closed some major hols. Bar. Semi-a la carte: lunch, dinner $4.95-$14.95. Sun brunch $4.95-$7. Child's meals. Specializes in pasta. Parking. Outdoor dining. Casual atmosphere. Cr cds: A, C, D, DS, MC, V.

D

★ ★ ★ **BENVENUTI.** *1 N Pennsylvania St (46225), downtown. 317/633-4915.* Hrs: 5:30-9 pm; wkends to 9:30 pm. Closed Sun; major hols. Res accepted; required wkends. Italian menu. Bar. Wine list. A la carte entrees: dinner $22-$32.50. Specializes in pasta, fish, veal chops. Elegant atmosphere with European flair. Jacket. Cr cds: A, D, MC, V.

★ ★ **GLASS CHIMNEY.** *(12901 Old Meridian St, Carmel 46032) I-465 NE to Meridian St, 12 mi N to 126th St, E to Old Meridian St. 317/844-0921.* Hrs: 5-10 pm; Fri, Sat to 11 pm. Closed Sun; Thanksgiving, Dec 25. Res accepted. Continental menu. Bar. Semi-a la carte: dinner $15-$38. Specializes in veal, seafood, steak. Outdoor dining. Elegant European decor. Cr cds: A, D, MC, V.

D

★ ★ **HOLLYHOCK HILL.** *8110 N College Ave (46240), north of downtown. 317/251-2294.* Hrs: 5-8 pm; Sun noon-7:30 pm. Closed Mon; July 4, Dec 24 & 25. Res accepted. Serv bar. Complete meals: dinner $12.95-$17.50. Child's meals. Specializes in fried chicken, seafood, steak. Tea room atmosphere. Family-owned. Cr cds: A, MC, V.

D

★ ★ **IRON SKILLET.** *2489 W 30th St (46222), at Cold Spring Rd, north of downtown. 317/923-6353.* Hrs: 5-8:30 pm; Sun noon-7:30 pm. Closed Mon, Tues; Dec 24, 25; also 1st wk July. Res accepted. Serv bar. Complete meals: dinner $11.95-$15.95. Child's meals. Specializes in steak, skillet-fried chicken, fresh fish. Family-style dining. Blackboard menu. Parking. Converted homestead (1870); overlooks golf course. Family-owned. Cr cds: A, C, D, DS, MC, V.

D

✔★ **JAZZ COOKER.** *925 E Westfield Blvd (46220), in Broad Ripple. 317/253-2883.* Hrs: 5-10 pm; Sun to 9 pm. Closed most major hols. Res accepted. Bar. A la carte entrees: dinner $9.25-$15. Specializes in Cajun, Creole dishes. Entertainment Thurs-Sun (summer). Outdoor dining. New Orleans atmosphere. Cr cds: A, C, D, DS, MC, V.

★ ★ **KONA JACK'S.** *9419 N Meridian (46260), in College Park area. 317/843-1609.* Hrs: 11 am-10 pm; Sat 5-11 pm. Closed Sun; major hols. Res accepted. Bar. Semi-a la carte: lunch $4-$8.95, dinner $10.95-$29.95. Specializes in seafood, sushi. Parking. Outdoor dining. Nautical decor. Cr cds: A, D, DS, MC, V.

D

★ ★ **THE MAJESTIC.** *47 S Pennsylvania (46204), downtown. 317/636-5418.* Hrs: 11 am-2 pm, 5-9 pm. Closed Sun; some major hols. Res accepted. Continental menu. Bar. Semi-a la carte: lunch $4.95-$12.95, dinner $12.95-$38.95. Child's meals. Specializes in seafood, steak, chicken. Own pasta, pastries. Old bldg with stained glass, Tiffany fixtures, handcarved bar. Cr cds: A, C, D, DS, MC, V.

D

★ ★ ★ **PETER'S.** *8505 Keystone Crossing Blvd (46240), north of downtown. 317/465-1155.* Hrs: 5-10 pm; Fri, Sat to 10:30 pm. Closed Sun; major hols. Res accepted. Bar. A la carte entrees: dinner $12.95-$23.95. Specializes in Indiana duckling, fresh fish, desserts. Parking. Cr cds: A, C, D, MC, V.

D SC

★ ★ ★ **RESTAURANT AT THE CANTERBURY.** *(See Canterbury Hotel) 317/634-3000.* Hrs: 7-10:30 am, 11:30 am-2 pm, 5:30-10 pm; Fri, Sat to 11 pm; Sun brunch 10:30 am-2 pm. Res accepted. Continental menu. Bar. Wine list. A la carte entrees: bkfst $4.50-$14.95, lunch $6.95-$14.95, dinner $16.50-$29.50. Sun brunch $6.95-$13.95. Specializes in seafood, veal. Own baking. Valet parking. International decor; artwork. Jacket (dinner). Cr cds: A, C, D, DS, ER, JCB, MC, V.

D

★ ★ ★ **RUTH'S CHRIS STEAK HOUSE.** *9445 Threel Rd (46240), at 96th & Keystone, north of downtown. 317/844-1155.* Hrs: 5-11 pm; Sun 4-10 pm. Closed some major hols. Res accepted; required hols. Bar. Extensive wine list. Semi-a la carte: dinner $16-$30. Specializes in steak, pork chop, seafood. Own baking. Parking. English country atmosphere. Cr cds: A, MC, V.

D

★ ★ **ST ELMO STEAK HOUSE.** *127 S Illinois (46204), downtown. 317/637-1811.* Hrs: 4-10:30 pm; Sun 5-9:30 pm. Closed major hols. Res accepted. Bar. Semi-a la carte: dinner $16.95-$34.95. Specializes in steak, fresh seafood. Turn-of-the-century decor, historic photographs. Cr cds: A, C, D, DS, MC, V.

D

★ **WILDCAT BREWING COMPANY.** *9111 N Michigan Rd (46268), in College Park. 317/872-3446.* Hrs: 11 am-11 pm; Sun to 10 pm. Closed Thanksgiving, Dec 25. Res accepted. Bar to 2 am. Semi-a la carte: lunch $5-$11, dinner $7-$19. Specializes in prime rib, Italian dishes, Mexican dishes. Microbrewery can be viewed from two dining areas. Cr cds: A, DS, MC, V.

Kansas City

Settled: 1838
Pop: 435,146
Elev: 800 feet
Time zone: Central
Area codes: 816 (Missouri); 913 (Kansas)
Web: www.experiencekc.com

Kansas City, Missouri, is the most populous city in the state and has a stable position as major distributing point for a vast agricultural region. It also has the distinction of sharing its name and economy with its neighboring city, Kansas City, Kansas.

Until the Civil War, Kansas City's economy was based on supplying and outfitting travelers along the trails to the West. Change was foreshadowed when the first railroad reached the city in 1869. By 1870, Kansas City was a railroad hub, with eight different radiating lines. Within 10 years it became the nation's most important cattle-trading center; it soon became a great grain center as well.

In the 1890s and early 1900s, the city launched a program of civic improvement and beautification. These efforts can still be seen in many wide boulevards and outstanding public buildings. Considerable industrial development followed as a wide variety of new industries, including automobile assembling plants, came to Kansas City.

Business

Traditionally, Kansas City has been regarded as a major transportation, distribution and agribusiness center, but there is much diversification. The city ranks high in marketing and manufacturing. Several national manufacturers have their headquarters here. The federal government maintains many regional headquarters in Kansas City and employs more than 30,000. Eighteen major insurance companies have their home offices here. Some 50 employers maintain payrolls of 1,000 or more. Of *Fortune's* 500 largest industrial firms, almost 200 have operations in greater Kansas City.

The most dynamic growth in Kansas City's economy since 1958 has been in the nonmanufacturing sector. The wholesale and retail trade industries employ the greatest number of people, with the service industry ranking close behind.

Crown Center, developed by Hallmark Cards, Inc, is the largest private urban renewal project in the United States since Rockefeller Center. An 85-acre "city within a city" near the downtown area, Crown Center hosts festivals, fairs and exhibits. A 10-acre outdoor square is the scene of free concerts in spring and summer and provides ice-skating facilities in winter. The complex includes The Westin Hotel, the Hyatt Regency, 80 shops and restaurants, live theater and more than 50 buildings in a model business-residential-entertainment community.

Convention Facilities

Among the top convention cities, Kansas City is host to more than 400,000 annual convention delegates. The H. Roe Bartle Hall and the Municipal Auditorium are located in the heart of the downtown area. By itself the H. Roe Bartle Hall has 388,800 square feet of unobstructed, flexible exhibit space. It is a tri-level facility that offers 26 meeting rooms, seating 35 to 3,000 people, and 73,000 feet of registration area. The H. Roe Bartle Hall is adjacent to the Municipal Auditorium; together they provide 607,800 square feet of exhibit space, 55 meeting rooms (seating from 25 to 20,000), a 600-seat theater, a 2,400-seat music hall, a 10,500-seat arena and registration and dining areas.

The American Royal Center has 627,000 square feet of indoor/outdoor exhibit space, a main arena that seats 5,000 and parking for 3,000 cars. Governors Exhibition Hall offers 96,000 square feet of clear-span, ground-level indoor space.

Sports & Recreation

Kansas City sports lovers enjoy the Royals baseball team and the Chiefs football team, which both play in the Harry S. Truman Sports Complex—side-by-side professional baseball and football stadiums. The Attack indoor soccer team and Blades ice hockey team play in the Kemper Memorial Arena. Two auto racetracks are open from March through September.

Oceans of Fun, 12 miles northeast, offers swimming, surfing, sand and sun that can be enjoyed throughout the 60-acre site.

Entertainment

Jazz survives and prospers in Kansas City. During Prohibition, a whole school of jazz musicians settled here and developed a distinctive style of music. A revival of the Kansas City jam session is again providing a stage for musicians. The spirit of Kansas City jazz is showcased each July, when thousands of devotees come to hear local and national favorites perform during the Kansas City Blues and Jazz Festival. A special service, the Jazz Hotline, is a recording of performances and jam sessions.

The Kansas City Symphony Orchestra gives regular performances from mid-October to mid-May. The Lyric Opera presents operas in English from April through May and mid-September to mid-October; advance tickets are essential. The State Ballet of Missouri has several performances a year.

The Missouri Repertory Theatre presents professional casts in performances from September through May. Starlight Theater, in Swope Park, is one of the nation's finest outdoor theaters, seating nearly 8,000 people. Top stars perform here from early June through August. The Theater League presents Broadway productions at the ornate Midland Theater, and the restored Folly Theater presents musical entertainment and theater productions.

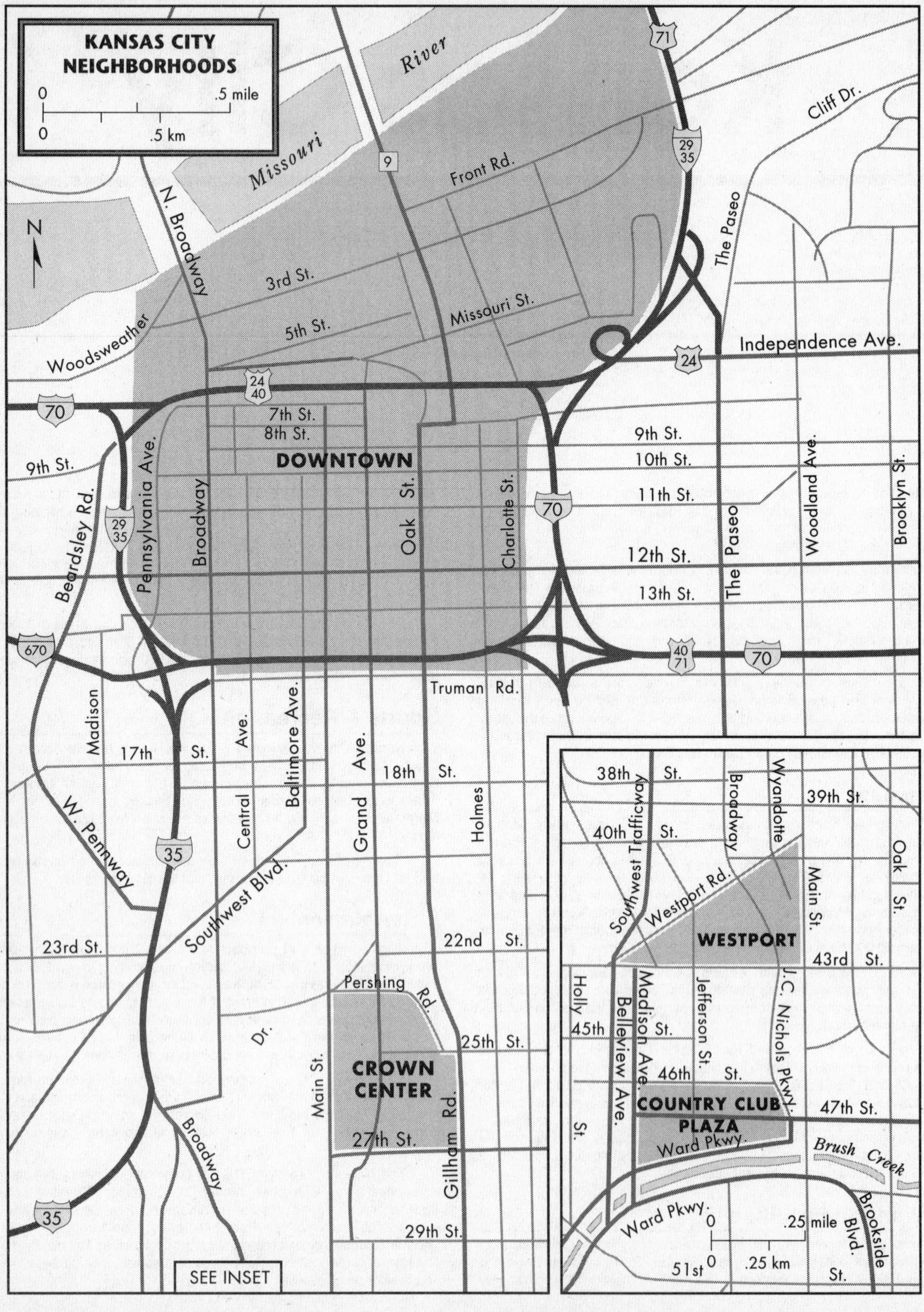
KANSAS CITY NEIGHBORHOODS
0
.5 mile
0
.5 km
N
Missouri River
DOWNTOWN
CROWN CENTER
WESTPORT
COUNTRY CLUB PLAZA
Front Rd.
3rd St.
5th St.
Missouri St.
Woodsweather
N. Broadway
Cliff Dr.
The Paseo
Independence Ave.
7th St.
8th St.
9th St.
10th St.
11th St.
12th St.
13th St.
Truman Rd.
Pennsylvania Ave.
Broadway
Oak St.
Charlotte St.
Woodland Ave.
Brooklyn St.
Beardsley Rd.
Madison
17th St.
18th St.
Central Ave.
Baltimore Ave.
Grand Ave.
Holmes
W. Pennway
Southwest Blvd.
23rd St.
22nd St.
Pershing Rd.
25th St.
Main St.
Dr.
27th St.
Gillham Rd.
29th St.
SEE INSET
38th St.
39th St.
40th St.
Southwest Trafficway
Wyandotte
Westport Rd.
Main St.
Oak St.
43rd St.
Holly St.
Madison Ave.
Belleview Ave.
Jefferson St.
J.C. Nichols Pkwy.
45th St.
46th St.
47th St.
Ward Pkwy.
Brush Creek
Brookside Blvd.
51st St.
.25 mile
.25 km

Historical Areas

Westport, once a prosperous center for outfitting and Native American trade in the 1850s, has become a major restoration area. Kelly's, once a busy dry goods store during the town's heyday and now a tavern, is one of the oldest buildings in the area. Westport Square and Manor Square are the result of the preservation of old facades of other buildings and the restoration of their interiors. They stand as contemporary, yet historic, shopping areas with many shops, art galleries, specialty and jewelry stores and fine dining spots.

Kansas City has a remarkable collection of 19th- and early 20th-century buildings. Efforts made by the city's residents at the turn of the century to improve their city have left a fine architectural legacy.

Sightseeing

Country Club Plaza, south of the downtown area, was developed in the 1920s and is known as the world's first shopping center. This area of open spaces, fountains and art treasures collected from all over the world has the aura of an elegant and venerable European city rather than a booming Midwestern town built on wealth from cattle trading, grain farming and machinery manufacturing.

Only 20 blocks away is the gleaming, ultramodern Crown Center. Its central square is a focal point of activity; various events occur year round under its huge translucent roof. A large ice-skating rink in the square provides a recreation spot during the winter and an area for summer events. Also located in Crown Center are Kaleidoscope, a participatory creative art exhibit for children, and the Hallmark Visitors Center, with exhibits and displays focusing on the history of the firm and the greeting card industry. Crown Center is also a stop on the trolley that links Crown Center to the Plaza, Westport, Town Pavilion and the River Market Area. Crown Center is home to sculptures by noted artists such as Alexander Caulder, Kenneth Snelson and Louise Nevelson.

The Harry S. Truman Library and Museum is in the town of Independence, 10 miles from downtown Kansas City. As many as 30,000 people a month visit the library and Truman gravesite. Covering the lobby wall is a mural entitled *Independence and the Opening of the West,* by Kansas City's own Thomas Hart Benton. Displays of books, documents, pictures and furnishings tell the story of Truman's presidential years; there are also several exhibits relating to other presidents. The Truman residence, an excellent example of late 19th-century Victorian architecture, has been opened to the public by the National Park Service.

A family entertainment theme park is located about 15 minutes northeast of downtown Kansas City. Worlds of Fun, covering 170 acres, is open daily during the summer months, weekends only during the spring and fall. The "worlds" represent America, Europe, Africa, Scandinavia and the Orient. There are live shows and attractions and more than 100 rides, including a giant whitewater raft ride and five roller coasters. Adjacent is a 60-acre water park, Oceans of Fun.

The Kansas City Zoo, located in Swope Park, has a fine feline exhibit, an ape house, an African veldt area and one of the best tropical habitat exhibits in the United States. The zoo also offers pony, camel and miniature train rides.

An annual event that attracts thousands of visitors each fall is the American Royal Livestock, Horse Show and Rodeo in November, the largest combined show of its kind in the country.

General References

Area codes: 816 (Missouri); 913 (Kansas)

Phone Numbers

POLICE, FIRE & AMBULANCE: 911

POISON CONTROL: 234-3434

TIME: 844-4444 **WEATHER:** 531-4444

Information Sources

Convention & Visitors Bureau of Greater Kansas City, City Center Square Bldg, 1100 Main St, Suite 2550, 64105; 221-5242 or 800/767-7700.

The Chamber of Commerce of Greater Kansas City, #2600 Commerce Towers, 911 Main St, 64105; 221-2424.

Kansas City, Kansas Area Convention & Visitors Bureau, PO Box 171517, Kansas City, KS 66117; 913/321-5800.

Department of Parks & Recreation, 871-5600.

Transportation

AIRLINES: Air Canada; American; America West; British Airways; Continental; Delta; KLM Royal Dutch; Lufthansa; Mark Air; Midwest Express; Northwest; Southwest; TWA; United; USAir; and other commuter and regional airlines.

AIRPORT: Kansas City International, 243-5237.

CAR RENTAL AGENCIES: (See IMPORTANT TOLL-FREE NUMBERS) Alamo 464-5151; Avis 243-5760; Budget 243-5756; Dollar 243-5600; Enterprise 842-4700; Hertz 243-5765.

PUBLIC TRANSPORTATION: Area Transit Authority 221-0660.

RAILROAD PASSENGER SERVICE: Amtrak 800/872-7245.

Newspapers

Kansas City Star; Kansas City Business Journal.

Convention Facilities

American Royal Center, Kemper Memorial Arena, 1800 Genessee, 274-1900.

Convention Center/H. Roe Bartle Hall and Municipal Auditorium, 301 W 13th St, 871-3700.

Kansas City Market Center, 1775 N Universal Ave, 241-6200.

Sports & Recreation

Major Sports Facilities

Harry S. Truman Sports Complex, I-435 & I-70, Kauffman Stadium (Royals, baseball, 921-2200); Arrowhead Stadium (Chiefs, football, 924-9300).

American Royal Center, Kemper Memorial Arena, 1800 Genessee (Attack, indoor soccer, 474-2255; Blades, ice hockey, 931-3330).

Racetracks

Kansas City International Raceway, 8201 Noland Rd, 358-6700 (car racing).

Lakeside Speedway, 5615 Wolcott Dr, Kansas City, KS, 913/299-2040 (car racing).

The Woodlands, 99th & Leavenworth Rd, Kansas City, KS, 913/299-9797 (horse & dog racing).

Cultural Facilities

Theaters

American Heartland Theatre, Crown Center, 2450 Grand Ave, 842-9999.

Coterie-Kansas City's Family Theatre, Crown Center, 2450 Grand Ave, 474-6552.

Folly Theater, 12th & Central, 842-5500.

Lyric Theater, 11th & Central (Lyric Opera, 471-7344; Kansas City Symphony Orchestra, 471-0400).

Midland Center for the Performing Arts, 1228 Main St, 471-8600.

Starlight Theater, near 63rd & Swope Pkwy in Swope Park, 363-STAR.

State Ballet of Missouri, 706 W 42nd St, 931-2232.

Concert Halls

Kemper Memorial Arena, 1800 Genessee, 274-1900.

Municipal Auditorium, 1310 Wyandotte St, adj to the Convention Center, 274-2900.

Museums

Arabia Steamboat Museum, 400 Grand Ave, 471-4030.

Civil War Museum, S on MO 291, 10 mi E on US 50, in Lone Jack, 566-2272.

Harry S. Truman Library and Museum, US 24 & Delaware St, Independence, 833-1225.

Jesse James Bank Museum, 15 mi NE on Old Town Square, in Liberty, 781-4458.

Kansas City Museum, 3218 Gladstone Blvd & Town Pavilion Mall, 1111 Main St, 483-8300.

Toy & Miniature Museum, 5235 Oak St at 52nd St, 333-2055.

Art Museums & Galleries

Kansas City Art Institute, 4415 Warwick Blvd, 561-4852.

Kemper Museum of Contemporary Art & Design, 4420 Warwick Blvd, 561-3737.

Nelson-Atkins Museum of Art, 4525 Oak St at 47th St, 751-1ART.

Van Ackeren Gallery, Rockhurst College campus, 5225 Troost Ave, 926-4808.

Points of Interest

Historical

Fort Osage, 14 mi E of Independence on US 24, 3 mi N, in Sibley, 881-4431.

Grinter House, 1420 S 78th St, Kansas City, KS, 913/299-0373.

Harry S. Truman National Historic Site (Truman House), 219 N Delaware St, Independence, 254-9929.

Huron Indian Cemetery, Huron Park, Center City Plaza, between 6th & 7th Sts, Kansas City, KS.

John Wornall House Museum, 146 W 61st Terrace, at Wornall, 444-1858.

Missouri Town 1855, 20 mi SE of Kansas City off US 40, E side of Lake Jacomo, Blue Springs, 881-4431.

Negro League Baseball Museum, 1601 E 18th St, 221-1920.

Thomas Hart Benton Home and Studios State Historic Site, 3616 Belleview, 931-5722.

Union Cemetery, 227 E 28th St Terrace, 221-4373.

Westport Square, Broadway at Westport Rd.

Other Attractions

Agricultural Hall of Fame and National Center, 630 N 126th St, Bonner Springs, KS, 913/721-1075.

Antiques Art and Design Center, 45th & State Line, 531-4414.

Benjamin Ranch, Old Santa Fe Trail, I-435 & E 87th, 761-5055.

Board of Trade, 4800 Main St, 753-7500.

City Market, Main to Grand Sts, 3rd to 5th Sts, 842-1271.

Civic Center, 11th to 13th Sts, Holmes to McGee Sts.

Country Club Plaza, 47th & Main Sts, 753-0100.

Crown Center, Pershing & Grand Ave, 274-8444.

Hallmark Visitors Center, Crown Center, 274-5672.

Kaleidoscope, Crown Center, 274-8300 or 274-8301.

Kansas City Zoo, Swope Park, 871-5700.

Lake Jacomo, Fleming Park, in Blue Springs, 795-8200.

Lakeside Nature Center, 5600 E Gregory, 444-4656.

Lewis & Clark Point, 8th & Jefferson.

Loose Park, 51st St & Wornall Rd.

NCAA Visitors Center, 6201 College Blvd, Overland Park, KS, 913/339-0000.

Oceans of Fun, 10 mi NE of I-435 exit 54, between Parvin Rd & NE 48th St, 454-4545.

Old Shawnee Town, 12 mi SW on I-35 to Johnson Dr, then W to 5th & Cody, Shawnee, KS, 913/268-8772.

Swope Park, Meyer Blvd & Swope Pkwy.

Town Pavilion, 11th & Main Sts, 474-5909.

Worlds of Fun, 10 mi NE via I-435 exit 54, 454-4545.

Sightseeing Tours

Blue Ribbon Tours, 8901 State Line, 361-5111.

Claudette's Theatre on Wheels, 1012 Broadway, 421-1981.

Heart of America Convention Services, 843 South Shore Dr, 741-3410.

Kansas City Trolley, 707 E 19th St, 221-3399.

***Missouri River Queen* Excursion Boat,** 1 River City Dr, Kansas City, KS, 913/281-5300.

Surreys Ltd on the Plaza, PO Box 36294, 531-2673.

Annual Events

Kansas City Pro Rodeo, Benjamin Ranch, 761-5055. Wk of July 4.

Kansas City Blues and Jazz Festival. Late July.

Ethnic Enrichment Festival. 3 days Aug.

Kansas City Spirit Festival. Early Sept.

Plaza Fine Arts Fair. Mid-Sept.

American Royal Livestock, Horse Show and Rodeo, American Royal Center, 1701 American Royal Court, 221-9800. Nov.

Plaza Christmas Lights. Thanksgiving Eve-mid-Jan.

City Neighborhoods

Many of the restaurants, unrated dining establishments and some lodgings listed under Kansas City include neighborhoods as well as exact street addresses. Geographic descriptions of these areas are given, followed by a table of restaurants arranged by neighborhood.

Country Club Plaza: South of Downtown; south of 46th St, west of Nichols Pkwy, north of Ward Pkwy and east of Madison Ave.

Crown Center: South of Pershing Rd, west of Gillham Rd, north of 26th St and east of Main St.

Downtown: South of the Missouri River, west of I-70, north of Truman Rd and east of I-29/I-35. **North of Downtown:** North of Missouri River. **South of Downtown:** South of US 40. **East of Downtown:** East of US 70.

Westport: Area north of Country Club Plaza; south of Westport Rd, west of Main St, north of 43rd St and east of Southwest Trafficway.

Lodgings and Food Kansas City, MO

KANSAS CITY RESTAURANTS BY NEIGHBORHOOD AREAS

(For full description, see alphabetical listings under Restaurants)

COUNTRY CLUB PLAZA
Canyon Cafe. 4626 Broadway
Classic Cup Sidewalk Cafe. 301 W 47th St
Emile's. 302 Nichols Rd
Fedora Cafe & Bar. 210 W 47th St
Figlio. 209 W 46th Terrace
Jules'. 4740 Jefferson St
K.C. Masterpiece. 4747 Wyandotte St
O'Dowd's Little Dublin. 4742 Pennsylvania
Plaza III The Steakhouse. 4749 Pennsylvania
Raphael Dining Room (Raphael Hotel). 325 Ward Pkwy
The Rooftop (The Ritz-Carlton, Kansas City Hotel). 401 Ward Pkwy
Ruth's Chris Steakhouse. 700 W 47th St

CROWN CENTER
The American Restaurant. 25th & Grand Ave
Milano. 2450 Grand Ave

DOWNTOWN
Italian Gardens. 1110 Baltimore
Jennie's. 511 Cherry St
Le Fou Frog. 400 E 5th St
Majestic Steakhouse. 931 Broadway
Savoy Grill (Savoy Bed & Breakfast Hotel). 219 W 9th St

NORTH OF DOWNTOWN
Cascone's. 3733 N Oak
Club 427. 427 Main St
Garozzo's. 526 Harrison
Paradise Grill. 5225 NW 64th St

SOUTH OF DOWNTOWN
André's Confiserie Suisse. 5018 Main St
Berliner Bear. 7815 Wornall
Cafe Allegro. 1815 W 39th St
Cafe Barcelona. 520 Southwest Blvd
Casa De Fajitas. 423 Southwest Blvd
Charlie's Lodge. 7953 State Line Rd
EBT. 1310 Carondelet Dr
Golden Ox. 1600 Genessee
Grand Street Cafe. 4740 Grand Ave
Hereford House. 2 E 20th St
Jasper's. 405 W 75th St
Jess & Jim's Steak House. 517 E 135th St
Macaluso's. 1403 W 39th St
Papagallo. 3535 Broadway
Shiraz. 320 Southwest Blvd
Smoke Stack Bar-B-Q of Martin City. 13441 Holmes St
Stephenson's Apple Farm. 16401 E US 40
Stroud's. 1015 E 85th St
Tasso's. 8411 Wornall
The Velvet Dog. 400 E 31st St

EAST OF DOWNTOWN
Smuggler's. 1650 Universal Plaza Dr

WESTPORT
Californos. 4124 Pennsylvania
Harry's Bar & Tables. 501 Westport Rd
Metropolis American Grill. 303 Westport Rd
Zola. 4113 Pennsylvania Ave

Note: When a listing is located in a town that does not have its own city heading, it will appear under the city nearest to its location. In these cases, the address and town appear in parenthesis immediately following the name of the establishment.

Motels

✔★ ★ **BEST WESTERN COUNTRY INN.** *11900 Plaza Circle (64153), north of downtown. 816/464-2002; FAX 816/464-2002.* 43 rms, 2 story. S $56.95-$62.95; D $58.95-$72.95; each addl $4; under 12 free; higher rates special events. Crib free. TV; VCR avail (movies). Complimentary continental bkfst. Restaurant adj 6 am-11 pm. Ck-out 11 am. Meeting rm. Business servs avail. In-rm modem link. Free airport transportation. Near airport. Cr cds: A, C, D, DS, MC, V.

D SC

★ ★ **BEST WESTERN COUNTRY INN.** *7100 NE Parvin Rd (64117), northeast of downtown. 816/453-3355; FAX 816/453-0242.* Web www.bestwestern.com. 86 rms, 2 story. May-Sept: S $74.95-$79.95; D $79.95-$89.95; each addl $5; under 12 free; lower rates rest of yr. Crib free. TV; cable (premium). Pool. Complimentary continental bkfst. Restaurant nearby. Ck-out 11 am. Business servs avail. In-rm modem link. Microwaves avail. Cr cds: A, C, D, DS, MC, V.

D SC

★ **BEST WESTERN SEVILLE PLAZA.** *4309 Main St (64111), in Country Club Plaza. 816/561-9600.* Web www.bestwestern.com/best.html. 77 rms, 4 story. S, D $79-$109; each addl $5; under 18 free; higher rates: hols, Plaza Lights Festival. Crib free. TV; cable (premium), VCR avail. Complimentary continental bkfst. Coffee in rms. Restaurant nearby. Ck-out noon. Meeting rms. Business servs avail. In-rm modem links. Bellhops. Valet serv. Whirlpool. Health club privileges. Refrigerators. Cr cds: A, C, D, DS, MC, V.

D SC

✔★ **BUDGETEL INN.** *2214 Taney (64116), I-435 exit 55A (US 210 W). 816/221-1200; FAX 816/471-6207.* Web www.budgetel.com. 100 rms, 3 story. S $43.95-$58.95; D $50.95-$70.95; each addl $7; under 18 free. Pet accepted, some restrictions. TV; cable (premium). Complimentary continental bkfst. Restaurant adj 7 am-midnight. Ck-out noon. Business servs avail. In-rm modem link. Sundries. Microwaves avail. Cr cds: A, C, D, DS, MC, V.

D SC

★ **HOLIDAY INN NORTHEAST.** *7333 NE Parvin Rd (64117), I-435 exit 54, north of downtown. 816/455-1060; FAX 816/455-0250.* 167 rms, 3 story. June-Aug: S, D $85-$130; under 18 free; lower rates rest of yr. Crib free. TV; cable (premium). Indoor pool; whirlpool, sauna. Restaurant 6:30-10 am, 6-10 pm. Rm serv. Bar 4 pm-midnight. Ck-out noon. Coin lndry. Meeting rms. Business servs avail. In-rm modem link. Bellhops. Valet serv. Sundries. Free airport transportation. Holidome. Game rm. Near Worlds of Fun. Cr cds: A, C, D, DS, JCB, MC, V.

D SC

★ ★ **RESIDENCE INN BY MARRIOTT.** *9900 NW Prairie View Rd (64153), north of downtown. 816/891-9009; FAX 816/891-8623.* Web www.marriott.com. 110 kit. suites, 2 story. S, D $69-$159; wkly, monthly rates. Crib free. Pet accepted, some restrictions; $100. TV; cable (premium), VCR avail (movies). Heated pool; wading pool, whirlpool. Complimentary continental bkfst. Ck-out noon. Coin lndry. Meeting rms. Business servs avail. In-rm modem link. Valet serv. Sundries. Free airport transportation. Lawn games. Exercise equipt; stair machine, bicycles. Microwaves. Private patios, balconies. Gazebo area with grills. Cr cds: A, C, D, DS, JCB, MC, V.

D SC

Motor Hotels

✔★ **BENJAMIN HOTEL AND SUITES.** *6101 E 87th St (64138), south of downtown, off of I-435. 816/765-4331; FAX 816/765-*

7395. 250 rms, 3-4 story. S $64-$75; D $75-$88; each addl $6; suites $100-$175; studio rms $75; under 18 free; wkend rates. Crib free. TV; cable (premium), VCR avail. Heated pool. Restaurant 6:30 am-2 pm, 5-10 pm; Fri, Sat to 11 pm; Sun 7 am-2 pm, 5-10 pm. Rm serv 7 am-10 pm. Bar 1 pm-1 am, Sun to midnight. Ck-out noon. Convention facilities. Business servs avail. In-rm modem link. Bellhops. Health club privileges. Microwaves. Private patios, balconies. Cr cds: A, C, D, DS, JCB, MC, V.

D SC

✔★ ★ **CLUBHOUSE INN.** *11828 NW Plaza Circle (64153), I-29 exit 13, near Intl Airport, north of downtown. 816/464-2423; FAX 816/464-2560; res: 800/258-2466.* Web www.clubhouseinn.com. 138 rms, 7 story. S, D $79-$89; each addl $10; suites $115-$125; under 10 free. Crib free. TV; cable (premium). Indoor pool; whirlpool. Complimentary bkfst buffet. Ck-out noon. Coin Indry. Meeting rms. Business servs avail. Valet serv. Free airport transportation. Downhill ski 15 mi. Exercise equipt; treadmill, bicycles. Some refrigerators; microwaves avail. Wet bar in suites. Balconies. Cr cds: A, C, D, DS, MC, V.

D SC

★ ★ **HILTON-AIRPORT.** *8801 NW 112th St (64153), near Intl Airport, north of downtown. 816/891-8900; FAX 816/891-8030.* 347 rms, 11 story. S $109-$139; D $119-$149; each addl $10; suites $249-$369; under 18 free; wkend rates. Crib free. Garage parking $5/day. TV; cable (premium). Complimentary coffee in lobby. Restaurant 6 am-10 pm. Rm serv. Bar 11 am-midnight. Ck-out noon. Convention facilities. Business center. In-rm modem link. Bellhops. Concierge. Sundries. Coin Indry. Free airport transportation. Lighted tennis. Exercise equipt; weight machine, treadmill, sauna. Heated indoor/outdoor pool; whirlpool; poolside serv. Some bathrm phones; wet bar in some suites. Cr cds: A, C, D, DS, ER, JCB, MC, V.

D SC

★ ★ ★ **HOLIDAY INN AIRPORT.** *11832 Plaza Circle (64153), I-29 exit 13, near Intl Airport. 816/464-2345; FAX 816/464-2543.* Web www.holidayinn.com. 196 rms, 5 story. S, D $95-$109; family, wkend & hol rates. Crib free. TV; cable (premium), VCR avail. Pool. Restaurant 6 am-11 pm. Rm serv. Bar 1:30 pm-1 am. Ck-out noon. Coin Indry. Meeting rms. Business servs avail. In-rm modem link. Bellhops. Gift shop. Valet serv. Free airport transportation. Exercise equipt; weight machine, bicycles, sauna. Game rm. Lawn games. Some refrigerators. Cr cds: A, C, D, DS, ER, JCB, MC, V.

D SC

★ ★ ★ **HOLIDAY INN-SPORTS COMPLEX.** *4011 Blue Ridge Cutoff (64133), east of downtown. 816/353-5300; FAX 816/353-1199.* Web www.holidayinn.com. 163 rms, 6 story. S $79-$99; D $87-$104; each addl $8; under 18 free. Crib free. TV; cable (premium), VCR avail. Indoor pool; whirlpool. Restaurant 6 am-10 pm. Rm serv. Bar 4 pm-midnight. Ck-out noon. Coin Indry. Meeting rms. Business center. In-rm modem link. Bellhops. Valet serv. Gift shop. Sundries. Underground parking. Exercise equipt; bicycles, treadmill, sauna. Game rm. Microwaves avail. Overlooks Harry S Truman Sports Complex. Cr cds: A, C, D, DS, JCB, MC, V.

D SC

★ ★ ★ **MARRIOTT-AIRPORT.** *775 Brasilia (64153), 15 mi NW on I-29, at Intl Airport, north of downtown. 816/464-2200; FAX 816/464-5915.* Web www.marriott.com. 382 rms, 9 story. S, D, studio rms $69-$150; suites $250-$450; under 18 free; wkend plan. Crib free. Pet accepted. TV; cable (premium). Indoor pool; whirlpool. Restaurant 6 am-11 pm. Rm serv. Bar 11:30-1 am, Sun 12:30 pm-midnight. Ck-out noon. Coin Indry. Meeting rms. Business servs avail. In-rm modem link. Bellhops. Valet serv. Gift shop. Free airport transportation. Downhill ski 15 mi. Excercise equipt; weights, bicycles, sauna. Rec rm. Lawn games. Private patios, picnic tables. On lake. Luxury level. Cr cds: A, C, D, DS, JCB, MC, V.

D SC

★ ★ **QUARTERAGE HOTEL.** *560 Westport Rd (64111), in Westport. 816/931-0001; FAX 816/931-8891; res: 800/942-4233.* Web www.quarterage.hotel. 123 rms, 4 story. S $89-$109; D $99-$119; each addl $10; under 17 free; higher rates special events; wkend rates. Crib free. TV; cable (premium). Complimentary bkfst buffet. Restaurant adj 7 am-10 pm. Ck-out noon. Meeting rms. Business servs avail. Sauna. Whirlpool. Health club privileges. Some bathrm phones, in-rm whirlpools, refrigerators, wet bars. Microwaves avail. Some balconies. Cr cds: A, D, DS, MC, V.

D

Hotels

✔★ ★ ★ **ADAM'S MARK.** *9103 E 39th St (64133), south of downtown. 816/737-0200; FAX 816/737-4713; res: 800/444-2326.* Web www.adamsmark.com. 374 rms, 15 story. S $89-$129; D $89-$139; each addl $10; suites $175-$485; studio rms $150; under 18 free; wkend rates. Crib free. TV; cable. 2 heated pools, 1 indoor; whirlpool. Restaurant 6 am-11 pm. Bars 11-3 am, Sun noon-midnight; entertainment. Ck-out noon. Coin Indry. Convention facilities. Business servs avail. In-rm modem link. Gift shop. Exercise rm; instructor, weights, bicycles, sauna. Rec rm. Some bathrm phones. Adj to Truman Sports Complex. Cr cds: A, C, D, DS, JCB, MC, V.

D SC

★ ★ ★ **CROWNE PLAZA.** *4445 Main St (64111), in Country Club Plaza. 816/531-3000; FAX 816/531-3007.* 296 rms, 19 story. S $129-$159; D $139-$169; each addl $10; suites $350-$550; under 18 free. Crib free. Garage free; valet parking $5. TV; cable. Indoor pool; whirlpool. Restaurant 6:30 am-10 pm. Bar 3 pm-1 am. Ck-out noon. Convention facilities. Business servs avail. In-rm modem link. Gift shop. Concierge. Exercise rm; instructor, weight machines, bicycles. Some refrigerators. Luxury level. Cr cds: A, C, D, DS, JCB, MC, V.

D SC

★ ★ ★ **EMBASSY SUITES.** *7640 NW Tiffany Springs Pkwy (64153), I-29 Tiffany Springs exit, near Intl Airport, north of downtown. 816/891-7788; FAX 816/891-7513.* Web www.embassy.com. 236 suites, 8 story. Suites $92-$144; under 18 free. Crib free. TV; cable (premium), VCR avail. Indoor pool; whirlpool. Complimentary full bkfst. Complimentary coffee in rms. Restaurant 11 am-2 pm, 5-10 pm; wkends from 7 am. Bar 11-1 am, wkends to 3 am; entertainment. Ck-out noon. Coin Indry. Convention facilites. Business servs avail. In-rm modem link. Concierge. Gift shop. Free airport transportation. Exercise equipt; stair machine, bicycles, sauna. Refrigerators, microwaves, wet bars. Cr cds: A, C, D, DS, JCB, MC, V.

D SC

★ ★ **HISTORIC SUITES.** *612 Central (64105), downtown. 816/842-6544; FAX 816/842-0656; res: 800/733-0612.* 100 suites, 5 story. S, D $140-$215; under 18 free; wkly rates; lower rates hol wkends. Crib free. Pet accepted, some restrictions. TV; cable (premium). Pool; whirlpool. Complimentary continental bkfst. Complimentary coffee in rms. Restaurant nearby. No rm serv. Coin Indry. Meeting rms. Business servs avail. In-rm modem link. No bellhops. Garage parking. Exercise equipt; weight machine, bicycles, sauna. Microwaves. Turn-of-the-century design. Cr cds: A, C, D, DS, MC, V.

D SC

★ ★ **HOLIDAY INN.** *1215 Wyandotte (64105), downtown. 816/471-1333; FAX 816/283-0541.* 190 rms, 16 story. S, D $79-$109; each addl $10; suites $99-$125; under 13 free; wkend rates. Crib free. TV; cable (premium). Rm serv. Ck-out noon. Meeting rms. Business servs avail. Covered parking. Exercise equipt; bicycle, treadmill. Health club privileges. Some refrigerators, microwaves. Cr cds: A, C, D, DS, MC, V.

D SC

★ ★ ★ **HYATT REGENCY CROWN CENTER.** *2345 McGee St (64108), in Crown Center. 816/421-1234; FAX 816/435-4190.* Web www.hyatt.com. 731 rms, 42 story. S $109-$165; D $109-$190; each addl $25; suites $215-$800; under 18 free; wkend rates. Crib free. Valet parking $11.50, garage $9. TV; cable (premium), VCR avail. Heated pool; whirlpool, poolside serv. Restaurants 6:30 am-midnight. Bars 11-1 am; entertainment. Ck-out noon. Convention facilities. Business center. In-rm modem link. Concierge. Gift shop. Lighted tennis. Exercise equipt;

weights, bicycles, sauna, steam rm. Minibars. Luxury level. Cr cds: A, C, D, DS, JCB, MC, V.

D SC

★ ★ ★ **MARRIOTT DOWNTOWN.** *200 W 12th St (64105), downtown. 816/421-6800.* 573 rms, 22 story. S $150; D $170; each addl $20; suites $275-$600; wkend rates. Crib free. TV; cable (premium), VCR avail. Indoor pool. Restaurant 6 am-midnight. Bar 11:30-1:30 am; entertainment Wed-Sat. Ck-out noon. Convention facilities. Business center. In-rm modem link. Concierge. Gift shop. Exercise equipt; weights, bicycles. Some refrigerators. Luxury level. Cr cds: A, C, D, DS, MC, V.

D SC

★ ★ ★ **OMNI.** *1301 Wyandotte (64105), downtown. 816/474-6664; FAX 816/474-0424.* 388 rms, 28 story, 99 suites. S, D $149-$179; each addl $10; suites $179-$209; family, wkend, hol rates. Crib free. Valet parking $8, garage $6. TV; cable (premium), VCR avail. Complimentary coffee in rms. Restaurant 6:30 am-10 pm. Bar 5 pm-1 am. Ck-out noon. Convention facilities. Business center. In-rm modem link. Concierge. Gift shop. Exercise equipt; weight machine, bicycle. Pool; whirlpool, poolside serv. Minibars. Refrigerator, microwave, wet bar in suites. Luxury level. Cr cds: A, C, D, DS, MC, V.

D SC

✔★ **PARK PLACE.** *1601 N Universal Ave (64120), I-435 Front St exit, north of downtown. 816/483-9900; FAX 816/231-1418; res: 800/821-8532.* 330 rms, 9 story. S, D $65-$90; each addl $10; suites $89-$129; under 18 free; wkend rates; package plans. Crib free. Pet accepted, some restrictions; $25 deposit. TV; cable (premium). Indoor/outdoor pool. Complimentary coffee in rms. Restaurant 6:30 am-10 pm; Fri, Sat to 11 pm. Bar 11-1:30 am; entertainment exc Sun. Ck-out noon. Meeting rms. Business servs avail. Gift shop. Exercise equipt; weights, bicycles, sauna. Some bathrm phones, refrigerators. Private patios; some balconies. Cr cds: A, C, D, DS, ER, MC, V.

D

★ ★ **RADISSON SUITES.** *106 W 12th St (64105), downtown. 816/221-7000; FAX 816/221-8902.* 240 suites, 20 story, 43 kit. units. S, D $89-$154; each addl $10; kit. units $89-$154; under 18 free; wkend rates. Crib free. TV; cable (premium). Complimentary continental bkfst. Restaurants 6:30 am-11 pm. Bar 10:30 am-midnight; Sat, Sun 11-3 am. Ck-out noon. Guest Indry. Meeting rms. Business center. In-rm modem link. Valet parking. Exercise equipt; weight machines, bicycles. Cr cds: A, C, D, DS, ER, MC, V.

D SC

★ ★ ★ **RAPHAEL.** *325 Ward Pkwy (64112), in Country Club Plaza. 816/756-3800; res: 800/821-5343.* 123 rms, 9 story. S $110-$185; D $130-$185; each addl $20; under 18 free; hol, wkend plans. Crib free. TV; cable (premium). Complimentary continental bkfst in rms. Restaurant (see RAPHAEL DINING ROOM). Rm serv 24 hrs. Bar to 1 am, closed Sun. Ck-out 1 pm. Business servs avail. In-rm modem link. Free garage, valet parking. Health club privileges. Refrigerators, minibars. Cr cds: A, C, D, DS, MC, V.

D SC

★ ★ ★ ★ **THE RITZ-CARLTON, KANSAS CITY.** *401 Ward Pkwy (64112), at Wornall Rd, Country Club Plaza. 816/756-1500; FAX 816/756-1635; res: 800/241-3333.* Web www.ritzcarlton.com. Crystal chandeliers, imported marble and original art create an air of luxury. Some guest rooms have balconies with views of Country Club Plaza. 373 rms, 12 story. S, D $170-$185; suites $235-$1,200; under 17 free; wkend rates; higher rates Thanksgiving. Crib free. Garage: free self-park, valet $9. TV; cable (premium), VCR avail. Heated pool; wading pool, poolside serv. Restaurant 6:30 am-2:30 pm, 5:30-10 pm (also see THE ROOFTOP). Rm serv 24 hrs. Bar 5 pm-midnight; entertainment. Ck-out noon. Convention facilities. Business center. In-rm modem link. Concierge. Airport transportation. Exercise equipt; weights, bicycles, sauna, steam rm. Massage. Bathrm phones, refrigerators, minibars; microwaves avail. Private patios, balconies. Luxury level. Cr cds: A, C, D, DS, ER, JCB, MC, V.

D SC

★ ★ ★ **SAVOY BED & BREAKFAST.** *219 W 9th St (64105), downtown. 816/842-3575.* 100 suites, 6 story. S, D $79-$150; each addl $20; under 16 free. TV; cable (premium). Complimentary full bkfst. Complimentary coffee in rms. Restaurant (see SAVOY GRILL). Bar. Ck-out 1 pm. Coin Indry. Business servs avail. Concierge. Wet bars. Restored 1888 landmark building with original architectural detail; stained & leaded glass, tile floors, tin ceilings. Cr cds: A, C, D, DS, MC, V.

★ ★ ★ **SHERATON SUITES.** *770 W 47th St (64112), in Country Club Plaza. 816/931-4400; FAX 816/516-7330.* Web www.sheraton.com. 258 suites, 18 story. S $140; D $150; each addl $20; under 16 free; wkend rates. Crib free. Valet parking $7.50. TV; cable (premium), VCR avail. Indoor/outdoor pool; whirlpool, poolside serv. Complimentary coffee in rms. Restaurant 6 am-10:30 pm. Bar 11:30 am-midnight. Ck-out noon. Coin Indry. Meeting rms. Business servs avail. In-rm modem link. Exercise equipt; weight machine, rower. Refrigerators; some wet bars. Microwaves avail. Some balconies. Cr cds: A, C, D, DS, ER, JCB, MC, V.

D SC

★ ★ ★ **THE WESTIN CROWN CENTER.** *1 Pershing Rd (64108), at Main St, in Crown Center. 816/474-4400; FAX 816/391-4438; res: 800/228-3000.* Web www.westin.com. 725 rms, 18 story. S $99-$205; D $99-$230; each addl $25; suites $300-$1,000; under 18 free; wkend package. Crib free. Pet accepted. TV; cable, VCR avail. Heated pool; whirlpool, poolside serv. Supervised childs activities (ages 6-12). Restaurants 6 am-midnight. Bars 11:30-1 am; entertainment. Ck-out noon. Convention facilities. Business center. In-rm modem link. Barber. Airport transportation. Lighted tennis. Exercise rm; instructor, weights, bicycles, sauna, steam rm. Rec rm. Lawn games. Refrigerators, wet bars. Private patios, balconies. Indoor tropical waterfall and garden. Luxury level. Cr cds: A, C, D, DS, ER, JCB, MC, V.

D SC

Inns

★ ★ **DOANLEIGH WALLAGH.** *217 E 37th St (64111), south of downtown. 816/753-2667; FAX 816/531-5185.* 5 rms, 3 story. S, D $95-$150; each addl $10. TV; cable (premium), VCR avail (free movies). Whirlpool. Complimentary full bkfst. Restaurant nearby. Ck-out 11 am, ck-in 3 pm. Business servs avail. In-rm modem link. Private parking. Health club privileges. Microwaves avail. Library; grand piano, organ. Built in 1907; many antiques. Totally nonsmoking. Cr cds: A, DS, MC, V.

★ ★ ★ ★ **SOUTHMORELAND.** *116 E 46th St (64112), in Country Club Plaza. 816/531-7979; FAX 816/531-2407.* Accommodations in this 1913 Colonial revival-style mansion honor notable Kansas City citizens. The Thomas Hart Benton Room has the Misson oak furniture favored by the artist, while the Satchel Paige Room resembles a sportsman's lodge. 12 rms, 3 story. S $100-$150; D $120-$170. Adults only. TV in sitting rm; cable (premium), VCR avail. Complimentary full bkfst; afternoon refreshments. Restaurants nearby. Ck-out 11 am, ck-in 4:30 pm. Business servs avail. In-rm modem link. Airport transportation. Health club privileges. Solarium. Totally nonsmoking. Cr cds: A, MC, V.

D

Restaurants

★ ★ ★ ★ **THE AMERICAN RESTAURANT.** *25th & Grand Ave, top floor of Hall's, in Crown Center. 816/426-1133.* Designer pastries are a specialty here. Intricate wood ceilings, a white grand piano and rich burgundy carpeting accent the dining area, which offers broad views of the Kansas City skyline. Specializes in contemporary Amer cuisine with ethnic influences and traditional Amer cuisine. Own baking, ice cream. Hrs: 11:15 am-2 pm, 6-10 pm; Fri, Sat 6-11 pm. Closed Sun; major hols. Res accepted. Bar. Wine cellar. A la carte entrees: lunch $8-$14, dinner $20-$45. Pianist. Free valet parking. Jacket. Cr cds: A, C, D, DS, MC, V.

D

✔★ **BERLINER BEAR.** *7815 Wornall (64114), south of downtown. 816/444-2828.* Hrs: 11 am-9 pm; Fri, Sat to 10 pm. Closed Sun, Mon; major hols. Res accepted. German menu. Bar. Semi-a la carte: lunch, dinner $7.50-$14.95. Specialties: German goulash, cordon bleu, fresh seafood. German decor. Cr cds: DS, MC, V.

D

★ ★ **CAFE ALLEGRO.** *1815 W 39th St (64111), south of downtown. 816/561-3663.* Web www.kcrestaurant.com. Hrs: 11:30 am-2 pm, 6-10 pm. Closed Sun; major hols; also 1 wk Jan; wk of July 4. Res accepted. Continental menu. Bar. Wine list. Semi-a la carte: lunch $6-$11, dinner $16-$25. Specialties: grilled salmon, veal chop with roasted garlic mashed potatoes. Intimate dining rm with original art. Totally nonsmoking. Cr cds: A, D, MC, V.

D ♥

★ ★ ★ **CAFE BARCELONA.** *520 Southwest Blvd (64108), south of downtown. 816/471-4944.* Hrs: 11 am-10 pm; Fri to 11 pm; Sat 4-11 pm. Closed Sun; also major hols. Spanish menu. Bar to 1:30 am. Semi-a la carte: lunch $6.95-$8.95, dinner $9.95-$18.95. Child's meals. Specialties: paella valenciaña, salmon with bernaise sauce. Entertainment Sat. Outdoor dining. Mediterranean decor. Cr cds: A, C, D, DS, MC, V.

D

★ ★ **CALIFORNOS.** *4124 Pennsylvania (64111), in Westport. 816/531-7878.* E-mail californos at juno.com; web www.californos.com. Hrs: 11 am-3 pm, 5-10 pm; Fri, Sat to 11 pm; Sun noon-9 pm. Closed some major hols. Res accepted. Bar to midnight. Semi-a la carte: lunch, dinner $5-$20. Bistro and steakhouse cuisine. Pianist Sat evenings. Valet parking wkends. Outdoor dining. Casual atmosphere. Cr cds: A, MC, V.

D

✔★ ★ **CANYON CAFE.** *4626 Broadway (64112), in Country Club Plaza. 816/561-6111.* Hrs: 11 am-11 pm; Fri, Sat to midnight; Sun to 10 pm; Sun brunch to 3 pm. Closed Dec 25. Res accepted. Southwestern menu. Bar. Semi-a la carte: lunch $3.60-$11.95, dinner $4.25-$16.95. Sun brunch $4.25-$12.95. Child's meals. Specialties: chile-rubbed tuna steak, desert fire pasta, mango chicken. Own baking. Southwestern decor. Cr cds: A, D, DS, MC, V.

D

★ **CASA DE FAJITAS.** *423 Southwest Blvd (64108), south of downtown. 816/471-7788.* Hrs: 11 am-9 pm; Fri & Sat to 11 pm. Closed major hols. Mexican menu. Bar. Semi-a la carte: lunch, dinner $4.95-$11.95. Child's meals. Specializes in fajitas, sampler plates. Casual atmosphere. Cr cds: A, D, DS, MC, V.

D

★ ★ **CASCONE'S.** *3733 N Oak, north of downtown. 816/454-7977.* Hrs: 11 am-10 pm; Fri, Sat to 11 pm; Sun 4-9 pm. Closed July 4, Dec 25. Res accepted. Italian, Amer menu. Bar. Semi-a la carte: lunch $6.50-$9, dinner $12-$24. Child's meals. Specializes in chicken, steak, seafood. Cr cds: A, C, D, DS, MC, V.

D SC

✔★ ★ **CHAPPELL'S.** *(323 Armour Rd, North Kansas City) N on MO 35 to Armour Rd exit. 816/421-0002.* Web www.sky.net/~chappell. Hrs: 11 am-10 pm; Fri, Sat to 11 pm. Closed Sun; most major hols. Bar. Semi-a la carte: lunch $4.95-$7.25, dinner $4.95-$16.95. Child's meals. Specializes in steak, prime rib, hamburgers. Extensive collection of sports memorabilia. Cr cds: A, C, D, DS, MC, V.

D

★ ★ **CHARLIE'S LODGE.** *7953 State Line Rd (64114), south of downtown. 816/333-6363.* Hrs: 11:30 am-10:30 pm; Fri, Sat to 11:30 pm; Sun 10:30 am-9:30 pm; early-bird dinner 4-6 pm. Closed some major hols. Res accepted. Bar. Semi-a la carte: lunch $5-$9, dinner $8-$17. Child's meals. Specializes in steak, fresh seafood. Six dining rooms. Sportsman's lodge atmosphere; hunting and fishing decor. Cr cds: A, DS, MC, V.

D SC

★ ★ ★ **CLASSIC CUP SIDEWALK CAFE.** *301 W 47th St (64112), in Country Club Plaza. 816/753-1840.* E-mail www.classiccu pataol.com; web www.missourirestaurantassociation.com. Hrs: 7 am-midnight; Fri, Sat 8-1 am; Sun brunch 10 am-3:30 pm. Closed most major hols. Res accepted. Bar. Semi-a la carte: lunch $5.95-$8.95, dinner $7.95-$18.95. Sun brunch $8.95. Child's meals. Specialties: Thai chicken pizza, steak medallions. Outdoor dining. Casual dining. Cr cds: A, DS, MC, V.

D

★ ★ **CLUB 427.** *427 Main St (64105), north of downtown. 816/421-2582.* Hrs: 11 am-2:30 pm, 5-10 pm; Fri, Sat to 11 pm. Closed Mon; major hols. Res accepted. Bar to 1 am; Tues, Sat, Sun to 11 pm. Semi-a la carte: lunch $5.95-$11.95, dinner $10.95-$19.95. Specializes in fresh seafood, steak, pasta. Cr cds: A, D, DS, MC, V.

D

★ ★ ★ **EBT.** *1310 Carondelet Dr, in United Missouri Bank Building, south of downtown. 816/942-8870.* Hrs: 11 am-2 pm, 5-9:30 pm; Fri to 10 pm; Sat 5-10 pm. Closed Sun; major hols. Res accepted. Bar. Wine cellar. Semi-a la carte: lunch $6.50-$11.95, dinner $9.95-$21.95. Specializes in seafood, steak, chicken. Own baking. Classical pianist Wed-Sat. Decorated with palm trees, fountain; antiques, gilded iron elevator. Cr cds: A, D, DS, MC, V.

D SC

✔☆ **EMILE'S.** *302 Nichols Rd (64112), in Country Club Plaza. 816/753-2771.* Hrs: 9 am-10 pm; Mon to 5 pm; Fri, Sat to 11 pm; Sun 11 am-5 pm. Closed Jan 1, Dec 25. Res accepted. German, Amer menu. Bar. Semi-a la carte: lunch, dinner $4.95-$15.95. Specialties: beef rouladen, Wienerschnitzel, Kasseler rippchen. Accordionist Fri-Sun. Outdoor dining. Cr cds: A, D, DS, MC, V.

★ ★ **FEDORA CAFE & BAR.** *210 W 47th St (64112), in Country Club Plaza. 816/561-6565.* Hrs: 11:30 am-11 pm; Fri, Sat to midnight; Sun 9 am-10 pm. Res accepted. Bar. A la carte entrees: lunch $3.95-$9.95, dinner $7.95-$24. Specializes in seafood, pasta, steak, salads. Live jazz. European bistro-style cafe; art deco decor. Cr cds: A, C, D, DS, MC, V.

D

★ ★ **FIGLIO.** *209 W 46th Terrace (64112), in Country Club Plaza. 816/561-0505.* Hrs: 11 am-10 pm; Fri, Sat to 11 pm; Sun 10:30 am-10 pm; Sun Brunch to 2:30 pm. Closed Dec 25. Res accepted. Italian, Amer menu. Bar. Semi-a la carte: lunch $5.95-$8.95, dinner $7.95-$16.95. Sun brunch $10.95. Child's meals. Specializes in pasta, gourmet pizza. Accordionist Wed-Sun. Valet parking wkends. Outdoor porch dining. Cr cds: A, C, D, DS, MC, V.

D

★ **GAROZZO'S.** *526 Harrison (64106), north of downtown. 816/221-2455.* Hrs: 11 am-10 pm; Fri to 11 pm; Sat 4-11 pm. Closed Sun; also major hols. Italian menu. Bar. Semi-a la carte: lunch $4.95-$9.95, dinner $7.95-$24.95. Specialties: chicken spidini, stuffed artichoke. Casual decor. Cr cds: A, D, DS, MC, V.

D

★ ★ **GOLDEN OX.** *1600 Genessee (64102), south of downtown. 816/842-2866.* E-mail jratgvi.net; web www.goldenox.com/ox. Hrs: 11:20 am-10 pm; Sat 4-10:30 pm; Sun 4-9 pm. Closed Dec 25. Bar. Semi-a la carte: lunch $4.50-$7.95, dinner $7.50-$19.95. Child's meals. Specializes in steak, prime rib. Western decor with stockyard influence. Family-owned. Cr cds: A, C, D, DS, MC, V.

D

★ ★ **GRAND STREET CAFE.** *4740 Grand Ave (64112), south of downtown. 816/561-8000.* Web www.menusonline.com/cities/kansas_city/desc/grandstcafe.shtml. Hrs: 11 am-10 pm; Fri & Sat to midnight; Sun from 10:30 am; Sun brunch to 3 pm. Closed Dec 25. Res accepted. Bar. Semi-a la carte: lunch $4.95-$10.95, dinner $5.95-$24.95. Sun brunch $4.95-$10.95. Child's meals. Specializes in lamb chops, pork chops, grilled tenderloin, fresh fish. Outdoor dining. Eclectic, contemporary decor. Cr cds: A, C, D, DS, MC, V.

D

✔★ ★ **HARDWARE CAFE.** *(5 E Kansas, Liberty 64068) US 69 N to Liberty, on town square. 816/792-3500.* Hrs: 11 am-9 pm; Mon to 2 pm; Fri, Sat to 10 pm. Closed Sun; major hols. Serv bar. Semi-a la carte: lunch $3.95-$6.95, dinner $3.95-$17.95. Child's meals. Specialties: fried chicken, chicken puff pastries. Own baking. Converted hardware store; old-fashioned soda fountain, many antique farm implements. Gift shop upstairs. Cr cds: DS, MC, V.

D

★ **HARRY'S BAR & TABLES.** *501 Westport Rd (64111), in Westport. 816/561-3950.* Hrs: 11:30 am-midnight; Fri to 2 am; Sat noon-2 am; Sun noon-midnight. Res accepted. Continental menu. Bar. Semi-a la carte: $4-$12.50. Specialties: steak sandwich with garlic mashed potatoes, hand-carved sandwiches. Outdoor dining. Two dining areas. Casual decor. Cr cds: A, D, DS, MC, V.

★ ★ **HEREFORD HOUSE.** *2 E 20th St, at Main St, south of downtown. 816/842-1080.* Web www.herefordhouse.com. Hrs: 11 am-10 pm; Fri to 10:30 pm; Sat 4-10:30 pm; Sun 4-9 pm. Closed major hols. Res accepted. Bar. Semi-a la carte: lunch $5-$15, dinner $12-$30. Child's meals. Specializes in steak, Maine lobster tails. Casual atmosphere. Cr cds: A, C, D, DS, MC, V.

D

✔★ ★ **ITALIAN GARDENS.** *1110 Baltimore, downtown. 816/221-9311.* Hrs: 11 am-9 pm; Fri to 10 pm; Sat noon-10 pm. Closed Sun; major hols. Res accepted. Italian, Amer menu. Bar. Semi-a la carte: lunch $4.50-$6, dinner $7-$15. Child's meals. Specializes in pasta, veal, seafood, chicken, steak. Valet parking. Cr cds: A, C, D, DS, MC, V.

D

★ ★ ★ ★ **JASPER'S.** *405 W 75th St, south of downtown. 816/363-3003.* The three dining rooms in this opulent restaurant are Baroque in style with Venetian crystal chandeliers, gold-leaf trim and red velvet booths. Northern Italian menu. Specialties: Cappeli Angelina, Gambere a la Livornese, Vitello alla Valdostana. Own pastries, pasta. Hrs: 6-10 pm. Closed Sun exc Mother's Day; major hols; also 1st wk July. Res accepted. Bar. Wine cellar. A la carte entrees: dinner $16.95-$25.95. Child's meals. Chef-owned. Jacket. Cr cds: A, C, D, DS, MC, V.

✔★ **JENNIE'S.** *511 Cherry St (64106), downtown. 816/421-3366.* Hrs: 11 am-8 pm; Fri, Sat to 9:30 pm; Sun from noon. Closed most major hols. Res accepted. Italian, Amer menu. Bar. Semi-a la carte: lunch $5.25-$7.95, dinner $7.95-$16.95. Child's meals. Specializes in lasagna, pizza. Family-owned. Cr cds: A, C, MC, V.

D

★ ★ **JESS & JIM'S STEAK HOUSE.** *517 E 135th St (64145), south of downtown. 816/941-9499.* Hrs: 11 am-10 pm; Fri & Sat to 11 pm; Sun noon-9 pm. Closed July 4, Thanksgiving, Dec 25. Bar. Semi-a la carte: lunch $4.95-$6.50, dinner $9.95-$37.50. Child's meals. Specializes in steak, seafood. Casual atmosphere, Western decor. Family-owned since 1938. Cr cds: A, C, D, DS, MC, V.

D

★ ★ ★ **JULES.** *4740 Jefferson St (64112), in Country Club Plaza. 816/561-4004.* Hrs: 11 am-10 pm; Fri, Sat to 11 pm; Sun brunch 10 am-2 pm. Closed Dec 25. Res accepted. Bar 11-1:30 am. Semi-a la carte: lunch $5.95-$8.95, dinner $9.95-$24.95. Sun brunch $13.95. Specializes in seafood. Entertainment Sun-Fri. Named after Jules Verne of *20,000 Leagues Under the Sea.* Upon entering one is on the ocean floor, with waves on the walls, mermaid and palm trees looking down over you. Cr cds: A, C, D, DS, ER, MC, V.

D SC

✔★ ★ **K.C. MASTERPIECE.** *4747 Wyandotte St (64112), in Country Club Plaza. 816/531-3332.* Hrs: 11 am-10 pm; Fri & Sat to 11 pm; Sun to 9:30 pm. Closed Thanksgiving, Dec 25. Bar. Semi-a la carte: lunch $5.99-$14.99, dinner $5.99-$15.99. Child's meals. Specializes in barbecued meats, filet of pork, turkey, brisket. Kansas City memorabilia. Casual atmosphere. Cr cds: A, C, D, DS, MC, V.

D

★ ★ ★ **LE FOU FROG.** *400 E 5th St (64106), downtown. 816/474-6060.* Hrs: 11 am-2 pm, 6-11 pm; Sat from 6 pm; Sun 5:30-10 pm. Closed Mon, Tues; major hols; also last wk Aug-mid-Sept. Res accepted. French menu. Bar to 1 am. Wine cellar. Semi-a la carte: lunch $5-$9.95, dinner $15.95-$23.50. Specialties: salmon tartare with kiwi sauce, steak au poivre, pork chops au Ricard et Panisse. Own desserts. Outdoor dining. French bistro atmosphere; globe lights, antique French posters. Cr cds: A, D, DS, MC, V.

D

★ ★ **MACALUSO'S.** *1403 W 39th St (64111), south of downtown. 816/561-0100.* Hrs: 5:30-10 pm; Fri & Sat to 11 pm. Closed Sun; also major hols. Res accepted. Italian, continental menu. Bar. Semi-a la carte: dinner $12.95-$22.95. Specialties: crab cakes, manicotti, rack of lamb. Casual decor. Cr cds: A, D, DS, MC, V.

D

★ ★ ★ **MAJESTIC STEAKHOUSE.** *931 Broadway (64105), downtown. 816/471-8484.* E-mail majstk@ix.netcom.com; web robro.net com/majestic. Hrs: 11:30 am-10 pm; Fri to 10:30 pm; Sat 5-11pm; Sun 4-9 pm. Closed major hols. Res accepted. Bar. Wine cellar. Semi-a la carte: lunch $3.95-$15, dinner $12.50-$30. Specialties: Kansas City strip steak, prime rib, grilled fresh salmon. Jazz. Valet parking. In former Garment District bldg; turn-of-the-century decor with stained-glass windows, ceiling fans, ornate tin ceiling. Cr cds: A, C, D, DS, JCB, MC, V.

D

★ ★ **METROPOLIS AMERICAN GRILL.** *303 Westport Rd (64111), in Westport. 816/753-1550.* Hrs: 11:30 am-2:30 pm, 5:30-10 pm; wkends to 11 pm. Closed Sun; major hols. Res accepted. Bar. A la carte entrees: lunch $5.95-$11.95, dinner $9.95-$19.95. Specialties: tandoori, sea bass, parmesan lamb chops, wild mushroom strudel. Contemporary decor. Cr cds: A, C, D, DS, MC, V.

★ ★ **MILANO.** *2450 Grand Ave (64108), in Crown Center. 816/426-1130.* Hrs: 11:30 am-9 pm; Fri & Sat to 10 pm; Sun from noon. Closed major hols. Res accepted. Italian menu. Bar. Semi-a la carte: lunch $5-$10.50, dinner $8.95-$19.95. Child's meals. Patio dining. Casual Italian decor. Cr cds: A, D, DS, MC, V.

D

✔★ ★ ★ **O'DOWD'S LITTLE DUBLIN.** *4742 Pennsylvania (64112), in Country Club Plaza. 816/561-2700.* Hrs: 11-1:30 am; Thurs-Sat to 3 am. Closed Dec 25. Irish menu. Bar. Semi-a la carte: lunch $5.95-$8.50, dinner $8.75-$16.95. Specialties: Guiness-braised beef, Dublin fish & chips, corned beef boxty. Own baking. Irish vocalists Wed & Sun evenings. Outdoor dining. Authentic Irish pub decor; entire interior shipped from Ireland. Cr cds: A, D, DS, MC, V.

D

★ ★ **PAPAGALLO.** *3535 Broadway (64111), south of downtown. 816/756-3227.* Hrs: 11 am-11 pm; Sat 5-11 pm; Sun 5-9 pm. Closed Mon; most major hols. Res accepted. Continental menu. Bar. Semi-a la carte: lunch $4.95-$11.95, dinner $11.95-$22. Specializes in beef & chicken kabobs, fresh seafood, pasta. Entertainment Fri, Sat. Valet parking. Original artwork. Contemporary decor. Cr cds: A, C, D, DS, MC, V.

D

✔★ **PARADISE GRILL.** *5225 NW 64th St, north of downtown. 816/587-9888.* Hrs; 11 am-10 pm; Fri, Sat to 11 pm; Sun 10:30 am-9 pm. Closed Thanksgiving, Dec 25. Res accepted. Bar. Semi-a la carte: lunch, dinner $3.99-$18.99. Child's meals. Specializes in chicken, fish. Modern decor. Cr cds: A, D, DS, MC, V.

D

★ ★ ★ **PLAZA III THE STEAKHOUSE.** *4749 Pennsylvania (64112), in Country Club Plaza. 816/753-0000.* Hrs: 11:30 am-2:30 pm, 5:30-10 pm; Fri, Sat to 11 pm; Sun 5-10 pm. Res accepted. Bar 11-1 am; Sun to midnight. Extensive wine list. A la carte entrees: lunch $5.95-$8.95, dinner $14.95-$26.95. Child's meals. Specializes in prime midwestern beef, veal chops, fresh seafood. Entertainment. Valet parking. Cr cds: A, C, D, DS, MC, V.

D

★ ★ ★ **RAPHAEL DINING ROOM.** *(See Raphael Hotel) 816/756-3800.* Hrs: 11 am-3 pm, 5-11 pm. Closed Sun; some major hols. Res accepted. Continental menu. Bar to 1 am. Semi-a la carte: lunch $6.50-$9.50, dinner $11.95-$21.95. Specializes in fresh fish, veal, New Zealand rack of lamb. Entertainment Fri & Sat. Valet parking. Romantic elegance in European-style setting. Cr cds: A, C, D, DS, MC, V.

D

★ ★ ★ **THE ROOFTOP.** *(See The Ritz-Carlton, Kansas City Hotel) 816/756-1500.* Hrs: 5:30-10 pm; Sun brunch 10:30 am-2:30 pm. Res accepted. Bar to 12:30 am; Fri, Sat to 1:30 am; closed Sun, Mon. Wine cellar. Semi-a la carte: dinner $25-$40. Sun brunch $26.95. Child's meals. Specializes in steak, chicken, seafood. Own pastries. Pianist. Rooftop dining rm; panoramic view of plaza. Cr cds: A, C, D, DS, ER, JCB, MC, V.

D ♥

★ ★ ★ **RUTH'S CHRIS STEAKHOUSE.** *700 W 47th St (64112), in Country Club Plaza. 816/531-4800.* Hrs: 5-11 pm; Sun to 10 pm. Closed Thanksgiving, Dec 25. Res accepted. Bar. Wine list. A la carte entrees: $16.25-$29.25. Specializes in porterhouse steak, barbecue shrimp, lobster. Valet parking. Outdoor dining. Upscale atmosphere; large wine display cabinet; ornate artwork. Cr cds: A, D, DS, MC, V.

D

★ ★ ★ **SAVOY GRILL.** *(See Savoy Bed & Breakfast Hotel) 816/842-3890.* Hrs: 11 am-11 pm; Fri, Sat to midnight; Sun 4-10 pm. Closed Dec 25. Res accepted. Bar. Semi-a la carte: lunch $4.50-$12, dinner $14-$27. Specializes in fresh seafood, Maine lobster, prime dry-aged beef. 19th-century hotel dining rm; oak paneling, stained-glass windows, murals of Santa Fe Trail. Ornate back bar. Cr cds: A, C, D, DS, MC, V.

D

★ ★ **SHIRAZ.** *320 Southwest Blvd (64108), south of downtown. 816/472-0015.* Hrs: 11 am-2 pm, 5-10 pm; Fri & Sat to 11 pm. Closed Sun; also most major hols. Res accepted. Continental menu. Bar. Semi-a la carte: lunch $5-$8, dinner $8.95-$20. Specialties: curry chicken, grilled scallops with black bean salsa. Contemporary decor. Cr cds: A, C, D, DS, MC, V.

D

★ ★ ★ **SMOKE STACK BAR-B-Q OF MARTIN CITY.** *13441 Holmes St (64145), south of downtown. 816/942-9141.* Hrs: 11 am-10 pm; Fri, Sat to 10:30 pm. Closed Thanksgiving, Dec 25. Semi-a la carte: lunch $4.75-$10, dinner $6.75-$20. Specializes in barbecue, fresh seafood, steak. Museum-like atmosphere; antiques. Cr cds: A, D, MC, V.

D

★ ★ **SMUGGLER'S.** *1650 Universal Plaza Dr (64120), east of downtown. 816/483-0400.* Hrs: 11 am-10 pm; Sat from 5 pm; Sun 4-9 pm. Closed Jan 1, Thanksgiving, Dec 25. Res accepted. Bar to 1 am. Complete meals: lunch $4.95-$9.95, dinner $10.95-$21.95. Specializes in prime rib, fresh fish. Salad bar. Entertainment Wed-Sat. Casual atmosphere; wood-burning fireplaces. Cr cds: A, C, D, DS, MC, V.

D

★ ★ ★ **STEPHENSON'S APPLE FARM.** *16401 E US 40, jct US 40, Lees Summit Rd, south of downtown. 816/373-5400.* Hrs: 11:30 am-10 pm; Sun 10 am-9 pm; Sun brunch 10 am-2 pm exc hols. Closed Dec 24 & 25. Res accepted. Bar. Semi-a la carte: lunch $6.25-$11.95, dinner $12.95-$18.95. Sun brunch $12.95. Child's meals. Specializes in hickory-smoked meats, apple fritters and dumplings. Own baking. Outdoor dining. Started as a fruit stand (1900). Early Amer decor; farm implements, cider keg in lobby. Country store. Family-owned. Cr cds: A, C, D, DS, MC, V.

D

★ ★ **STROUD'S.** *1015 E 85th St (64131), 85th and Troost, south of downtown. 816/333-2132.* Hrs: 4-10 pm; Fri 11 am-11 pm; Sat 2-11 pm; Sun from 11 am. Closed Thanksgiving, Dec 25. Bar. Semi-a la carte: lunch $5.25-$10.95, dinner $7.95-$16.95. Specializes in pan-fried chicken. Pianist. Cr cds: A, C, D, DS, MC, V.

D

★ ★ **TASSO'S.** *8411 Wornall (64114), south of downtown. 816/363-4776.* E-mail www.tassos1.com; web www.tassos1.com. Hrs: 11 am-3 pm, 5-11 pm; Fri & Sat to midnight. Closed Sun & Mon; also major hols. Res accepted. Greek menu. Bar. Semi-a la carte: lunch $3.75-$6.95, dinner $8.95-$16.95. Child's meals. Specializes in lamb, kabobs. Entertainment. Parking. Outdoor dining. Mediterranean decor. Cr cds: A, MC, V.

D SC

★ **THE VELVET DOG.** *400 E 31st St (64108), south of downtown. 816/753-9990.* E-mail velvet@unicom.not. Hrs: 4 pm-1:30 am; Fri, Sat to 3 am; Sun 6 pm-1:30 am. Closed most major hols. Res accepted. Italian menu. Bar. Semi-a la carte: dinner $8.95-$16.95. Specialties: artichoke heart fritters, lemon butter bowtie pasta. Outdoor dining. Old storefront brick building with wood floors, brick walls, ceiling fans. Cr cds: A, D, DS, MC, V.

D

★ ★ **ZOLA.** *4113 Pennsylvania Ave (64111), in Westport. 816/561-9191.* Hrs: 11:30 am-10 pm; Fri & Sat to midnight; Sun from 5 pm. Continental menu. Bar. Semi-a la carte: $9.50-$18.50. Specialties: pork carnitas, wasabi chicken. Outdoor dining. Contemporary decor. Cr cds: A, C, D, DS, MC, V.

D

Unrated Dining Spot

ANDRÉ'S CONFISERIE SUISSE. *5018 Main St, south of downtown. 816/561-3440.* Hrs: 11 am-2:30 pm. Closed Sun, Mon; major hols. Swiss menu. Complete meal: lunch $7.50. Specializes in quiche, chocolate candy, pastries. Swiss chalet atmosphere. Family-owned since 1955. Totally nonsmoking. Cr cds: A, MC, V.

D

Kansas City, KS

Restaurants

✔★ ★ **MRS. PETER'S CHICKEN DINNERS.** *4960 State Ave (US 24) (66102), 3 blks W of I-635. 913/287-7711.* Hrs: 11 am-2 pm; 5-9 pm; Sat from 5 pm; Sun noon-8 pm. Closed Mon; Jan 1, Dec 25. Complete meals: lunch $6-$6.50, dinner $9.50-$12. Specializes in fried chicken, country-fried steak, pork chops. Child's meals. Gift shop. Antiques. Cr cds: DS, MC, V.

D

★ ★ **PAULO & BILL.** *(16501 Midland Dr, Shawnee 66217) 913/962-9900.* Hrs: 11 am-10 pm; Fri, Sat to midnight; Sun brunch to 2 pm. Closed July 4, Thanksgiving, Dec 25. Res accepted. Italian, Amer menu. Bar. Semi-a la carte: lunch $5.95-$9.95, dinner $8.95-$15.95. Sun brunch $3.95-$8.95. Child's meals. Specialties: osso bucco, lasagna al forno, wood-fired pizza. Outdoor dining. Contemporary decor. Cr cds: A, C, D, DS, MC, V.

D

Overland Park, KS

Motels

★ **CLUBHOUSE INN.** *10610 Marty (66212), I-435, N on Metcalf, W on 107th. 913/648-5555; FAX 913/648-7130.* 143 rms, 3 story, 22 suites. S $75-$89; D $85-$99; each addl $10; suites $89-$109; under 16 free; wkly rates. Crib free. TV; cable (premium). Heated pool; whirlpool. Complimentary full bkfst. Restaurant nearby. Ck-out noon. Coin Indry. Meeting rms. Business servs avail. Valet serv. Exercise equipt; bicycles, treadmill. Microwaves avail. Refrigerator, wet bar in suites. Balconies. Grills. Cr cds: A, C, D, DS, MC, V.

D SC

★ ★ ★ **COURTYARD BY MARRIOTT.** *11301 Metcalf Ave (66210). 913/339-9900; FAX 913/339-6091.* Web www.marriott.com. 149 rms, 3 story. S $119; D $129; each addl $10; suites $129-$149; under 16 free; wkly, wkend rates. Crib free. TV; cable (premium). Indoor pool; whirlpool. Complimentary coffee in rms. Bar 4:30-11 pm. Ck-out 1 pm. Coin Indry. Meeting rms. Business servs avail. In-rm modem link. Valet serv. Sundries. Exercise equipt; weights, bicycles. Microwaves avail. Refrigerator in suites. Balconies. Cr cds: A, C, D, DS, MC, V.

D SC

★ ★ **DRURY INN.** *10951 Metcalf Ave (66210). 913/345-1500.* Web www.Drury-Inn.com. 155 rms, 4 story. S $75-$81; D $85-$91; each addl $10; under 18 free. Crib free. Pet accepted, some restrictions. TV; cable (premium). Pool. Complimentary continental bkfst. Restaurant nearby. Ck-out noon. Meeting rms. Business servs avail. In-rm modem link. Valet serv. Health club privileges. Microwaves avail. Cr cds: A, C, D, DS, MC, V.

D SC

✔★ **FAIRFIELD INN BY MARRIOTT.** *4401 W 107th (66207), I-435 exit 77. 913/381-5700.* 134 rms, 3 story. S $59.95-$69.95; D $61.95-$70.95; under 18 free. Crib free. TV; cable (premium). Pool. Complimentary continental bkfst. Restaurant nearby. Ck-out noon. Business servs avail. In-rm modem link. Valet serv. Sundries. Health club privileges. Cr cds: A, C, D, DS, MC, V.

D SC

★ **HAMPTON INN.** *10591 Metcalf Frontage Rd (66212). 913/341-1551; FAX 913/341-8668.* 134 rms, 5 story. S, D $74-$89; under 18 free. Crib free. TV; cable (premium). Pool; whirlpool. Complimentary continental bkfst. Complimentary coffee in rms. Restaurant nearby. Ck-out noon. Meeting rms. Business servs avail. In-rm modem link. Health club privileges. Cr cds: A, C, D, DS, MC, V.

D SC

★ ★ **RESIDENCE INN BY MARRIOTT.** *6300 W 110th St (66211), I-435, S on Metcalf, E on College, N on Lamar. 913/491-3333; FAX 913/491-1377.* 112 suites, 2 story. S, D $79-$199; under 12 free; wkly, monthly rates. Crib free. Pet accepted, some restrictions. TV; cable (premium). Pool; whirlpool. Complimentary continental bkfst. Ck-out noon. Coin Indry. Meeting rm. Business servs avail. In-rm modem link. Valet serv. Exercise equipt; weights, bicycles, sauna. Sports court. Microwaves; some fireplaces. Private patios, balconies. Picnic tables, grills. Cr cds: A, C, D, DS, JCB, MC, V.

D SC

✔★ ★ **WHITE HAVEN.** *8039 Metcalf Ave (66204). 913/649-8200; res: 800/752-2892.* 79 rms, 1-2 story, 10 kit. units. S $39-$44; D $46-$50; suites, kit. units $70. Crib $2. Pet accepted, some restrictions. TV; cable (premium). Pool. Complimentary coffee. Restaurant nearby. Ck-out noon. Business servs avail. Refrigerators. Microwaves avail. Cr cds: A, C, D, DS, MC, V.

D

★ ★ **WYNDHAM GARDEN.** *7000 W 108th (66211). 913/383-2550; FAX 913/383-2099.* 180 rms, 2 story. S $99-$198; D $109-$218; each addl $10; under 12 free. Crib free. TV; cable (premium). Complimentary coffee in rms. Restaurant 6:30 am-10 pm. Rm serv from 5 pm. Bar 4 pm-midnight. Ck-out noon. Meeting rms. Business center. In-rm modem link. Bellhops. Concierge. Sundries. Coin Indry. Exercise equipt; treadmill, stair machine. Pool. Refrigerators, microwaves avail. Cr cds: A, C, D, DS, ER, JCB, MC, V.

D

Motor Hotels

★ **AMERISUITES.** *6801 W 112th St (66211). 913/451-2553; FAX 913/451-3098.* 126 suites, 6 story. May-Nov: suites $97-$107; under 18 free; wkend rates; lower rates rest of yr. Crib free. Pet accepted, some restrictions. TV; cable (premium), VCR (movies). Complimentary continental bkfst. Complimentary coffee in rms. Restaurant nearby. Ck-out 11 am. Meeting rms. Business center. In-rm modem link. Sundries. Coin Indry. Exercise equipt; weight machine, bicycle. Health club privileges. Pool. Refrigerators, microwaves. Cr cds: A, C, D, DS, MC, V.

D SC

★ ★ **RADISSON.** *8787 Reeder Rd (66214). 913/888-8440; FAX 913/888-3438.* 192 rms, 8 story. S, D $119-$129; each addl $10; suites $100-$120; under 18 free. Crib free. TV; cable (premium). Heated indoor/outdoor pool; whirlpool, sauna. Complimentary coffee in rms. Restaurant 6 am-2 pm, 5-10 pm. Rm serv. Bar; entertainment. Ck-out noon. Meeting rms. Business center. In-rm modem link. Valet serv. Exercise equipt; bicycle, treadmill. Airport transportation. Cr cds: A, C, D, DS, MC, V.

D SC

Hotels

★ ★ ★ **DOUBLETREE.** *10100 College Blvd (66210). 913/451-6100; FAX 913/451-3873.* E-mail mcidt@aol.com; web www.doubletreehotels.com. 357 rms, 18 story. S, D $119-$149; suites $175-$450; under 18 free; wkend rates. Crib free. Pet accepted, some restrictions. TV; cable (premium). Indoor pool; whirlpool, sauna, poolside serv. Coffee in rms. Restaurants 6 am-11 pm (also see ROTISSERIE). Bar 4-1 am, Sun 4 pm-midnight. Ck-out noon. Convention facilities. Business center. In-rm modem link. Gift shop. Airport transportation. Exercise equipt; treadmill, bicycles. Some refrigerators. Cr cds: A, C, D, DS, ER, JCB, MC, V.

D SC

★ ★ ★ **EMBASSY SUITES.** *10601 Metcalf Ave (66212). 913/649-7060; FAX 913/649-9382.* 199 suites, 7 story. Aug: suites $139-$169; under 12 free; lower rates rest of yr. Crib free. TV; cable (premium). Indoor pool; whirlpool, sauna. Complimentary full bkfst. Complimentary coffee in rms. Restaurant 6 am-11 pm. Rm serv from 11 am. Bar 3 pm-midnight. Ck-out noon. Meeting rms. Business servs avail. In-rm modem link. Gift shop. Exercise equipt; bicycle, stair machine. Health club privileges. Game rm. Refrigerators. Microwaves avail. Cr cds: A, C, D, DS, JCB, MC, V.

D SC

★ ★ ★ **MARRIOTT.** *10800 Metcalf (66210). 913/451-8000; FAX 913/451-5914.* Web www.marriott.com. 397 rms, 11 story. S, D $119-$159; suites $225-$400; under 18 free; wkly, wkend rates. Crib free. TV; cable (premium), VCR avail. Indoor/outdoor pool; whirlpool, poolside serv. Complimentary coffee. Restaurant (see NIKKO). Bar 3 pm-1 am. Ck-out noon. Meeting rms. Business servs avail. In-rm modem link. Concierge.

Gift shop. Airport transportation. Exercise equipt; weights, bicycles. Game rm. Luxury level. Cr cds: A, C, D, DS, JCB, MC, V.

D SC

Restaurants

★ ★ **CAFE ITALIA.** *(6524 Martway, Mission 66202) 913/262-9242.* Hrs: 11 am-2 pm, 5-9 pm; Fri, Sat to 10 pm. Closed Sun; major hols. Res accepted. Italian menu. Bar. Semi-a la carte: lunch $5.50-$12, dinner $8-$21. Specializes in veal, lamb, seafood, pasta. Italian decor. Cr cds: A, C, D, DS, MC, V.

D

★ ★ **CHIEN DYNASTY.** *9921 W 87th St (66212). 913/888-3000.* Hrs: 11 am-9:30 pm; Fri & Sat to 10:30 pm; Sun to 9 pm; Sun brunch 11:30 am-2 pm. Closed Thanksgiving, Dec 25. Res accepted. Chinese menu. Bar. Semi-a la carte: lunch $4.50-$5.50, dinner $6.95-$23.75. Lunch buffet $5.45. Sun brunch $6.95. Specializes in Szechuan & Hunan dishes. Three dining areas; Chinese paintings, figurines and vases. Cr cds: A, D, DS, MC, V.

D

★ ★ **COYOTE GRILL.** *(4843 Johnson Dr, Mission) N on US 169, in Mission Shopping Center. 913/362-3333.* Web www.menuson line.comk.c.des/coyotegrill.html. Hrs: 11 am-10 pm; wkends to 11 pm; Sun brunch to 3 pm. Southwestern menu. Bar. Semi-a la carte: lunch $3.50-$12.99, dinner $3.50-$20. Sun brunch $4.50-$10.99. Southwestern art. Cr cds: A, D, DS, MC, V.

D

✔★ **DON CHILITO'S.** *(7017 Johnson Dr, Mission) N on US 169. 913/432-3066.* Hrs: 11 am-9 pm; Fri, Sat to 10 pm; Sun from noon. Closed Thanksgiving, Dec 25. Mexican menu. Beer. Semi-a la carte: lunch, dinner $3-$9.99. Specializes in burritos. Family-owned. Cr cds: DS, MC, V.

D

★ ★ **ELBOW ROOM.** *(7820 Quivira, Lenexa 66216) 913/268-6466.* Hrs: 11 am-10 pm; Fri, Sat to midnight. Closed most major hols. Res accepted. Continental menu. Bar. Semi-a la carte: lunch $4.95-$8.95, dinner $9.95-$16.95. Specialties: saffron shrimp and scallop pasta, New Zealand rack of lamb with demi glaze. Entertainment Mon-Thurs. Original artwork. Cr cds: A, C, D, DS, MC, V.

D SC

★ ★ ★ **HEREFORD HOUSE.** *(5001 Town Center Dr, Leawood 66211) at 119th & Roe, Town Center Plaza. 913/327-0800.* E-mail beef@herefordhouse.com; web www.herefordhouse.com. Hrs: 11 am-10 pm; Fri to 11 pm; Sat noon-11 pm; Sun noon-9 pm. Closed Thanksgiving, Dec 25. Res accepted. Bar. Wine list. Semi-a la carte: lunch $5.95-$12.50, dinner $10.95-$27.95. Child's meals. Specialties: whiskey steak, baseball-cut sirloin, prime rib. Own desserts. Valet parking. Outdoor dining. Western decor; artwork, branding irons, tack, cowboy hats; stone fireplace. Cr cds: A, C, D, DS, MC, V.

D

★ ★ ★ **HOUSTON'S.** *7111 W 95th St (66212), at Metcalf St. 913/642-0630.* Hrs: 11 am-11 pm; Fri, Sat to midnight. Closed Thanksgiving, Dec 25. Bar. Semi-a la carte: lunch, dinner $5.95-$21.95. Child's meals. Specializes in steak, fresh fish. Casual elegance. Cr cds: A, MC, V.

D

✔★ ★ **IL TRULLO.** *9056 Metcalf Ave (66212), in Glenwood Plaza Shopping Center. 913/341-3773.* Web www.trulloatwebtv.com. Hrs: 11 am-2 pm, 5-9 pm; Fri to 10 pm; Sat 5-10 pm; Sun from 5 pm. Closed major hols. Res accepted. Italian menu. Bar. Semi-a la carte: lunch $4.95-$7.95, dinner $5.95-$17.95. Specialties: zuppa di mare, orecchiette con cime di rapa. Cr cds: A, C, D, DS, MC, V.

D

✔★ ★ **INDIA PALACE.** *9918 W 87th St (66212). 913/381-1680.* Hrs: 11:30 am-2:30 pm, 5-10 pm. Closed Thanksgiving, Dec 25. Res accepted. Indian menu. Semi-a la carte: lunch, dinner $5.95-$12.95. Lunch buffet $5.95; wkends $6.95. Specializes in Indian style barbecue. Indian atmosphere. Elegant dining. Totally nonsmoking. Cr cds: A, D, DS, MC, V.

D

★ ★ ★ **J GILBERT'S WOOD-FIRED STEAKS.** *8901 Metcalf Ave (66212), 1 mi N. 913/642-8070.* Hrs: 5-10 pm; Fri, Sat to 10:30 pm; Sun to 9:30 pm. Closed most major hols. Res accepted. Bar from 4:30 pm; Fri, Sat 4-11:30 pm. Semi-a la carte: dinner $9.95-$23.95. Child's meals. Specialties: Louisiana skillet-seared pepper fillet, grilled barbecue salmon. Cr cds: A, C, D, DS, MC, V.

D SC

★ ★ **JOHNNY CASCONE'S.** *6863 W 91st St. 913/381-6837.* Hrs: 11 am-10 pm; Sun 4-9 pm. Closed major hols. Res accepted Sun-Thurs. Italian, Amer menu. Bar. Semi-a la carte: lunch $6-$8, dinner $9-$17. Child's meals. Specializes in lasagne, seafood, steak. Cr cds: A, C, D, DS, MC, V.

D

✔★ **JUN'S.** *(7660 State Line Rd, Shawnee 66208) in Prairie Village. 913/341-4924.* Hrs: 11:30 am-2 pm, 5-10 pm. Closed Sun; most major hols. Res accepted. Japanese menu. Bar. Semi-a la carte: lunch $4.95-$6.95, dinner $9.95-$19.50. Specializes in sushi, teriyaki tempura. Parking. Japanese atmosphere. Cr cds: A, MC, V.

D

★ ★ **K.C. MASTERPIECE.** *10985 Metcalf (66210). 913/345-1199.* Hrs: 11 am-10 pm; Fri, Sat to 11 pm; Sun to 9:30 pm. Closed Thanksgiving, Dec 25. Bar. Semi-a la carte: lunch $6.59-$16.49, dinner $6.59-$17.99. Child's meals. Specializes in baby back ribs, filet of pork, turkey. Authentic 1930s decor; ornamental tile floor. Display of barbecue memorabilia. Cr cds: A, C, D, DS, MC, V.

D

★ ★ ★ **LA MÉDITÉRRANÉE.** *9058-B Metcalf (66210). 913/341-9595.* Hrs: 11:30 am-2 pm, 6-10 pm; Sat from 6 pm. Closed Sun; Jan 1. Res accepted. French menu. Bar. Wine list. Semi-a la carte: lunch $5.95-$9.75, dinner $14.75-$27.50. Specialties: stuffed lamb loin and vegetable tomato sauce, lobster au gratin. Atrium dining. Elegant decor with fireplace and chandeliers. Cr cds: A, D, DS, MC, V.

D

✔★ **LEONA YARBROUGH'S.** *(2800 W 53rd St, Fairway 66205) W on Shawnee Mission Pkwy. 913/722-4800.* Hrs: 7 am-8 pm; Sun to 7 pm. Closed Mon; also Dec 25 and 1 wk following. Semi-a la carte: lunch $3.25-$10.25, dinner $5.25-$10.75. Child's meals. Specializes in fried chicken, liver & onions, roast pork. Full bakery on premises. Family-owned. Cr cds: MC, V.

✔★ **MARTHA'S CAFE.** *(4515 W 90th St, Prairie Village 66207) in Somerset Plaza. 913/385-0354.* Hrs: 11:30 am-10 pm; Sat from noon. Closed Sun; major hols. Res accepted (dinner). Ethiopian menu. Bar. Semi-a la carte: lunch $3.75-$7.25, dinner $5.75-$12.95. Specialties: doro wat (marinated chicken drumstick), gored gored (beef tenderloin tips), tikei gamen (cooked vegetables). Interior decorated with African items, woven baskets, tall plants & trees. Totally nonsmoking. Cr cds: A, D, DS, MC, V.

D

★ ★ ★ **NIKKO.** *(See Marriott Hotel) 913/451-8000.* Hrs: 5-10 pm; Fri, Sat to 11 pm. Closed some major hols. Res accepted. Japanese menu. Bar. Semi-a la carte: dinner $13.95-$24.95. Child's meals. Specializes in swordfish, filet mignon. Japanese decor; teppanyaki table service. Cr cds: A, C, D, DS, MC, V.

D SC

★ ★ ★ **ROTISSERIE.** *(See Doubletree Hotel) 913/451-6100.* Hrs: 6:30 am-10 pm; wkends from 7 am; Sun brunch 10 am-2 pm. Res accepted. Bar 4 pm-1 am. Wine list. Semi-a la carte: bkfst $3.95-$8.95, lunch $5.50-$10, dinner $14.95-$21.95. Buffet: bkfst, lunch $8.95. Sun brunch $16.95. Child's meals. Specializes in prime rib, steak, seafood. Salad bar. Parking. Skylight, waterfall and many plants give the three dining areas a relaxing atmosphere. Cr cds: A, C, D, DS, ER, JCB, MC, V.

D SC

✔ ★ **SUSHI GIN.** *9559 Nall Ave (66207). 913/649-8488.* Hrs: 11:30 am-2 pm, 5:30-9:30 pm; Fri 11:30 am-2:30 pm, 5:30-10 pm; Sat 5-10 pm. Closed Sun; some major hols. Res accepted. Japanese menu. Serv bar. Semi-a la carte: lunch $5.45-$10.95, dinner $9.95-$19.95. Child's meals. Specializes in boat combinations, chicken or beef sukiyaki, tempura. Japanese tapestries. Cr cds: A, D, DS, MC, V.

★ ★ ★ **TATSU'S FRENCH RESTARAUNT.** *(4603 W 90th St, Prairie Village 66207) I-435 to Roe exit, 2 mi N, in Somerset Plaza. 913/383-9801.* E-mail tatsu@primenet.com. Hrs: 11:30 am-2 pm, 5:30-9:30 pm; Fri to 10 pm; Sat 5:30-10 pm. Closed Sun; major hols. Res accepted. French menu. Bar. Semi-a la carte: lunch $6.95-$14.95, dinner $14.95-$23.95. Specialties: Saumon poché au champagne, boeuf à la borguignonne. Small, elegant dining area. Cr cds: A, D, MC, V.

★ ★ **THE WOKS.** *(8615 Hauser Dr, Lenexa 66214) 913/541-1777.* Hrs: 11 am-9:30 pm; Fri, Sat to 10:30 pm; Sun buffet to 2:30 pm. Closed some major hols. Res accepted. Chinese menu. Bar. Semi-a la carte: lunch $4.25-$5.50, dinner $5.75-$10.95. Sun buffet $6.95. Child's meals. Chinese decor. Cr cds: A, DS, MC, V.

D

★ ★ **YIAYIAS EUROBISTRO.** *4701 W 119th St (66209), I-435 to exit Roe. 913/345-1111.* Hrs: 11 am-10 pm; Fri, Sat to midnight; Sun 10:30 am-10 pm, Sun brunch to 2:30 pm. Closed Thanksgiving, Dec 25. Res accepted. Bar to 11 pm; Fri, Sat to 1 am. Wine list. Semi-a la carte: lunch $4.95-$10.95, dinner $8.95-$24.95. Sun brunch $5.95-$12.95. Specializes in steak, fresh seafood, pasta. Outdoor dining. European bistro decor. Cr cds: A, C, D, DS, MC, V.

D

Unrated Dining Spot

GATES BAR-B-QUE. *(2001 W 103rd, Leawood) E on W 103rd St, at state line. 913/383-1752.* Hrs: 10 am-11 pm; Fri, Sat to midnight. Closed Thanksgiving, Dec 25. Beer. A la carte entrees: lunch, dinner $4.50-$14. Specializes in barbecue ribs, beef. No cr cds accepted.

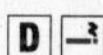

Las Vegas

Settled: 1855
Pop: 258,295
Elev: 2,020 feet
Time zone: Pacific
Area code: 702

Las Vegas is known for exceptional hotels, as well as gambling casinos and nightclubs. Entertainment facilities line its streets, luring travelers to experience all that Las Vegas offers. Nevada's largest city, Las Vegas covers 84 square miles and is centered in a gently sloping valley ringed by mountains. To the west, the Spring Range, capped by 11,918-foot Mt Charleston, dominates the area.

Its green meadows and two natural springs made the Las Vegas valley a favorite camping place for caravans following the old Spanish Trail from Santa Fe to California. Las Vegas was first settled by Americans in 1855, when Brigham Young sent 30 men to build a fort and stockade here. The Mormons tried mining in the area but found that the ore was hard to smelt and that the metal made poor bullets. Later, this "lead" was discovered to be a silver ore.

The Mormons abandoned the settlement in 1857. From 1862 to 1899 it was operated as a ranch. Las Vegas was really born in 1905 with the advent of the railroad. A tent town sprang up, streets were laid out and permanent buildings were soon built. In the years that followed, Las Vegas developed as an agricultural area. The legalization of gambling in Nevada in 1931 paved the way for change, and after World War II a great deal of investment capital was poured into the development of Las Vegas as a resort center.

Business

Tourism is the dominant industry in Las Vegas. The combination of a pleasant year-round climate, legalized gambling and top-name entertainment lures a daily average of nearly 180,000 visitors. Prices for food, hotels and entertainment are comparatively modest, since gambling is the main diversion.

Convention Facilities

Conventions have become the second major industry in Las Vegas. The Las Vegas Convention Center has an impressive total of 1.6 million square feet, 1.3 million of which is meeting and exhibit space. The Cashman Field Center, a convention/sports complex, offers 98,100 square feet of exhibit space, a 10,000-seat stadium and a theater seating 100 to 1,940.

There are more than 101,100 first-class hotel and motel rooms, and restaurants range from very modest to gourmet. Most of the major hotels have convention facilities. The number of conventioneers coming to Las Vegas each year exceeds the permanent population of this desert city.

Sports & Recreation

The city's 31 golf courses (many championship), dotted with lakes and lined with palm trees, make Las Vegas a mecca for the nation's top professional golfers. Hotels and private clubs cater to tennis fans, offering both open play and tournament competition. There are more than 85 tennis courts within a 5-mile radius, and nearly 75 indoor handball and racquetball courts.

Las Vegas attracts a wide variety of national sporting events and top names in tennis, boxing, bowling, golfing and auto racing. Many nationally televised events originate here each year. Frequent horse shows and rodeos are a popular form of entertainment, with the National Finals Rodeo as well as the Elks Helldorado Festival and Rodeo being the best known.

The Thomas and Mack Center at the University of Nevada, Las Vegas campus serves as a center for many of the city's sports, cultural, entertainment and educational events.

In the fall, hunting in this part of the country is excellent, especially for doves, quail, geese and ducks, as well as mule deer and desert bighorn (mountain sheep).

Entertainment

The Strip, Las Vegas Boulevard south of town, and Fremont Street Experience, located on Fremont Street, are the main attractions for most visitors. They glitter with dazzling casinos, whirling roulette wheels, shiny armies of slot machines, luxurious hotels, glamorous chorus lines and brilliant stars of show business.

On a cultural level, the University of Nevada, Las Vegas, houses an art gallery, a concert hall and a theater. The Artemus W. Ham Concert Hall showcases opera, ballet, jazz and popular musical performances. The Judy Bayley Theater presents a variety of shows. The campus also has the Marjorie Barrick Museum of Natural History, with collections of historic and prehistoric Native American artifacts, mining and early pioneer materials and live desert reptiles. The university's Mineral Collection in the Geoscience Building features a display of 1,000 minerals, including specimens from southern Nevada.

Located near the natural springs at Lorenzi Park, the New Nevada State Museum has four galleries tracing the history of southern Nevada through archaeology, anthropology, biology and regional history.

Sightseeing

On a map of the United States, Las Vegas appears to be remote from other centers of population, but today's fine network of highways has placed it within a few hours, by automobile or bus, from some of the most spectacular vacation spots in the West. Mountains, lakes, desert and Utah's red-rock canyons are all there for the curious to see and enjoy.

The Grand Canyon is an ideal two-day, round-trip excursion from Las Vegas. The canyon's vastness, array of colors and beautiful sunsets defy description. The best approach is by way of US 93 and I-40 to Williams, then north on AZ 64 to the South Rim. There are many campsites and several lodges; but the facilities of this park, one of the oldest and most popular in the National Park system, are often filled to capacity, and reservations should be made in advance. Hiking into the canyon is a rugged but worthwhile experience. Other tours are available by air or by mule.

It is possible to go from Las Vegas to Zion National Park (follow I-15) and return in one day, still allowing time to appreciate the geological wonders of the park. The 12-mile Zion Canyon Scenic Drive takes the visitor past constantly changing vistas of multicolored rock formations, which thrust up above the valley floor. Several easy, self-guided nature walks and some more strenuous climbs afford a closer look at the park's natural wonders. Concessionaires provide horses and guided tours. Cabins and a lodge are available for longer stays, but reservations should be made in advance to avoid disappointment.

A little to the north and east of Zion are Cedar Breaks National Monument and Bryce Canyon National Park. Cedar Breaks is a huge natural coliseum made up of pink cliffs averaging more than 10,000 feet in elevation. Bryce Canyon boasts multicolored rock formations suggesting cathedrals, palaces and miniature cities.

Lake Mead National Recreation Area, with nearly two million acres of desert, plateaus, canyons and water playground, is in Las Vegas' backyard. Lake Mead, the country's largest man-made reservoir, was created by the construction of Hoover Dam, 726 feet high, the greatest dam construction of its day and still one of the engineering wonders of the world. Tours descend 528 feet by elevator into the heart of the power plant. The lake attracts more than six million visitors a year for swimming, boating, waterskiing and fishing. Fishing is allowed year-round.

Valley of Fire State Park, just northwest of Lake Mead, is only 55 miles from Las Vegas. Hiking trails lead past petroglyphs, beautiful desert flora, red sandstone canyons and specimens of petrified wood. Camping and picnic areas are available.

In nearby Overton is the Lost City Museum of Archaeology. Displayed here are artifacts and reconstructions of original pit dwellings and pueblos of the Moapa Valley.

Lee Canyon, about 46 miles west of Las Vegas, is southern Nevada's only ski resort. Here, in the Toiyabe National Forest, are towering mountain peaks like Mt Charleston and thick stands of pine.

Half an hour west of Las Vegas, unusual geologic formations of varied colors and shapes make up the unique Red Rock Canyon Recreation Lands. In the canyon is the Spring Mountain Ranch, a 528-acre estate that dates to the early 1900s and at one time was owned by Howard Hughes. A guided tour takes visitors to both restored and original ranch buildings.

Also within the scenic red-rock area and on the site of the Bonnie Springs Ranch is Old Nevada, a complete Old West town that has been re-created. The buildings are designed to duplicate those that stood in many of the famed gold and silver camps. A working replica of the old steam locomotive that served the Comstock takes visitors from the parking lot to the entrance. Many ghost towns also dot the area.

General References

Area code: 702

Phone Numbers

POLICE & FIRE: 911

POISON INFORMATION CENTER: 732-4989

TIME & WEATHER: 248-4800

Information Sources

Las Vegas Convention/Visitors Authority, Convention Center, 3150 Paradise Rd, 89109; 892-0711.

Greater Las Vegas Chamber of Commerce, 711 E Desert Inn Rd, 89109; 735-1616.

Department of Recreation & Leisure Activities, 261-5211.

Transportation

AIRLINES: American; America West; Continental; Delta; Northwest; Southwest; TWA; United; USAir; and other commuter and regional airlines.

AIRPORT: McCarran International, 261-5733.

CAR RENTAL AGENCIES: (See IMPORTANT TOLL-FREE NUMBERS); Avis 261-5595; Brooks 735-3344; Budget 736-1212; Hertz 736-4900; National 261-5391; Thrifty 896-7600; Value 733-8886.

Newspapers

Las Vegas Review Journal; Las Vegas Sun.

Convention Facilities

Cashman Field Center, 850 Las Vegas Blvd N, 386-7100.

Las Vegas Convention Center, 3150 Paradise Rd, 892-0711.

Sports & Recreation

Las Vegas Motor Speedway Motorsports Complex, 7000 Las Vegas Blvd N, 644-4444.

Thomas and Mack Center, University of Nevada, Las Vegas, 895-3900.

Cultural Facilities

Concert Halls

Artemus W. Ham Concert Hall, University of Nevada, Las Vegas, 895-3801.

Cashman Field Center, 850 N Las Vegas Blvd, 386-7100.

Convention Center, 3150 Paradise Rd, 892-0711.

Museums

Las Vegas Art Museum, 9600 W Sahara, 360-8000.

Las Vegas Natural History Museum, 900 Las Vegas Blvd N, 384-3466.

Liberace Museum, 1775 E Tropicana Ave, 798-5595.

Lost City Museum of Archaeology, on NV 169, in Overton, 397-2193.

Marjorie Barrick Museum of Natural History, University of Nevada, Las Vegas, 4505 Maryland Pkwy, 895-3381.

Nevada State Museum and Historical Society, 700 Twin Lakes Dr, in Lorenzi Park, 486-5205.

Points of Interest

Bonnie Springs Old Nevada, 20 mi W via W Charleston Blvd, 875-4191.

Fremont Street Experience, Fremont St.

Hoover Dam, 35 mi SE via US 93, 293-8321 or 293-8367.

Kyle Canyon, 36 mi NW via US 95, NV 39, 872-5486.

Lake Mead, 35 mi SE via US 93, 293-8907.

Lee Canyon, 46 mi NW via US 95, NV 52, 646-0008.

Mount Charleston Recreation Area, Toiyabe National Forest, 15 mi NW on US 95, then 21 mi W on NV 157, 455-8288.

Red Rock Canyon Recreation Lands, 15 mi W on W Charleston Blvd, 363-1921.

Southern Nevada Zoological Park, 1775 N Rancho Dr, 648-5955.

Sightseeing Tours

Gray Line bus tours, 1550 S Industrial Rd, 384-1234.

Scenic Airlines, 2707 Airport Dr, 739-1900.

Annual Events

Las Vegas Senior Classic Golf Tournament. Apr-May.

Helldorado Festival. Late May or early June.

Las Vegas Invitational PGA Golf Tournament. Oct.

National Finals Rodeo. Dec.

Lodgings and Food

Motels

*(**Note on accommodations:** Rates are likely to vary upward in Las Vegas at peak occupancy and sometimes a minimum of three days occupancy is required. In addition, minimum rates quoted are generally available only from Sun through Tues, sometimes on Wed, rarely on holidays. This is not true of all accommodations but is true of many. We urge you to check the rate on any room you occupy and to make certain no other special conditions apply. Show reservations are available at most accommodations.)*

✔★ **ARIZONA CHARLIE'S.** *740 S Decatur Ave (89107), west of the Strip. 702/258-5200; FAX 702/258-5192; res: 800/342-2695.* 257 rms, 7 story. S, D $38-$69; suites $95-$115. Crib free. TV. Pool; lifeguard. Restaurant open 24 hrs. Bar. Ck-out 11 am. Bellhops. Business servs avail. Valet serv. Gift shop. Airport transportation. Casino. Cr cds: A, C, D, DS, MC, V.

D SC

★★ **BEST WESTERN McCARRAN INN.** *4970 Paradise Rd (89119), near McCarran Intl Airport, east of the Strip. 702/798-5530; FAX 702/798-7627.* Web www.bestwestern.com/thisco/bw/29058/29058b.html. 99 rms, 3 story. S, D $49-$70; each addl $7; suites $90-$150; under 12 free; higher rates: national hols, major events. TV. Pool. Complimentary bkfst. Restaurant nearby. Coin Indry. Ck-out noon. Business servs avail. Free airport transportation. Cr cds: A, C, D, DS, ER, JCB, MC, V.

D SC

✔★ **CENTER STRIP INN.** *3688 Las Vegas Blvd S (89109), on the Strip. 702/739-6066; FAX 702/736-2521; res: 800/777-7737.* 156 rms, 5 story, 44 suites. S, D $29.95-$89.95; each addl $10; suites $69-$189; under 18 free. Pet accepted. TV; cable (premium), VCR (movies $3). Pool. Complimentary continental bkfst. Restaurant adj open 24 hrs. Ck-out 11 am. Business servs avail. In-rm modem link. Refrigerators. Whirlpool in suites. Cr cds: A, C, D, DS, JCB, MC, V.

D SC

★ **COMFORT INN.** *211 E Flamingo Rd (89109), east of the Strip. 702/733-7800; FAX 702/733-7353.* 121 rms, 2 story. S, D $55-$125; under 12 free. TV; cable (premium). Pool. Complimentary continental bkfst. Ck-out 11 am. Cr cds: A, C, D, DS, MC, V.

D SC

✔★ **COMFORT INN-AIRPORT.** *5075 Koval Lane (89119), near McCarran Intl Airport, east of the Strip. 702/736-3600; FAX 702/736-0726.* 106 rms, 2 story. S, D $45-$175; under 18 free. Crib free. TV; cable (premium). Pool. Complimentary continental bkfst. Restaurant adj open 24 hrs. Ck-out 11 am. Business servs avail. Cr cds: A, C, D, DS, ER, JCB, MC, V.

D SC

★ **DAYS INN.** *707 E Fremont (89101). 702/388-1400; FAX 702/388-9622.* 147 units, 3 story. Feb-Nov: S $28-$120; D $32-$120; each addl $10; suites $60-$200; under 18 free; lower rates rest of yr. Crib free. TV. Pool. Restaurant 7 am-7 pm. Ck-out noon. Cr cds: A, C, D, DS, JCB, MC, V.

D SC

★★ **FAIRFIELD INN BY MARRIOTT.** *3850 Paradise Rd (89109), near McCarran Intl Airport, east of the Strip. 702/791-0899; FAX 702/791-0899.* 129 rms, 4 story. S, D $62-$150; under 18 free. Crib free. TV; cable (premium). Heated pool; whirlpool. Complimentary continental bkfst. Restaurants nearby. Ck-out noon. Meeting rms. In-rm modem link. Free airport transportation. Cr cds: A, C, D, DS, MC, V.

D SC

★ **LA QUINTA MOTOR INN.** *3782 Las Vegas Blvd S (89109), on the Strip. 702/739-7457; FAX 702/736-1129.* 114 rms, 3 story. S $65-$85; D $65-$119; each addl $10; under 18 free. Crib free. TV; cable. Pool. Restaurant nearby. Ck-out noon. Business servs avail. Free airport transportation. Cr cds: A, C, D, DS, MC, V.

D SC

★★ **RESIDENCE INN BY MARRIOTT.** *3225 Paradise Rd (89109), near McCarran Intl Airport, east of the Strip. 702/796-9300; FAX 702/796-9562.* 192 kit. units, 1-2 story. S, D $95-$219. Crib free. Pet accepted, some restrictions; $7/day. TV; cable (premium), VCR (movies $3.50). Heated pool; whirlpool. Complimentary continental bkfst. Restaurant adj 6:30 am-9 pm. Ck-out noon. Coin Indry. Meeting rms. Business servs avail. Free airport transportation. Balconies. Picnic tables, grills. Cr cds: A, C, D, DS, JCB, MC, V.

D SC

★★★ **ST TROPEZ.** *455 E Harmon Ave (89109), near McCarran Intl Airport, west of the strip. 702/369-5400; FAX 702/369-5400; res: 800/666-5400.* 149 suites, 2 story. Suites $95-$250; family rates. Crib free. TV; VCR. Heated pool; poolside serv. Complimentary coffee in rms. Restaurant adj 11-3 am. Bar. Ck-out noon. Meeting rms. Business servs avail. In-rm modem link. Bellhops. Concierge. Shopping arcade. Airport transportation. Exercise equipt; weight machine, rowers. Refrigerators. Minibars. Cr cds: A, C, D, DS, ER, JCB, MC, V.

D SC

✔★ **TRAVELODGE-DOWNTOWN.** *2028 E Fremont St (89101). 702/384-7540; FAX 702/384-0408.* 58 rms, 2 story. S, D $30-$70; each addl $5; family rates. Crib free. TV; cable. Heated pool. Complimentary coffee in rms. Restaurant nearby. Ck-out noon. Cr cds: A, C, D, DS, ER, JCB, MC, V.

SC

✔★ **TRAVELODGE-LAS VEGAS INN.** *1501 W Sahara Ave (89102), west of the Strip. 702/733-0001; FAX 702/733-1571.* 223 rms, 4 story. S, D $39-$199; under 18 free. TV; cable (premium). Pool. Complimentary continental bkfst. Ck-out noon. Business servs avail. Gift shop. Cr cds: A, C, D, DS, ER, MC, V.

D SC

Motor Hotels

★★ **BOOMTOWN.** *3333 Blue Diamond Rd (89139), S of the Strip. 702/263-7777; FAX 702/896-5635; res: 800/588-7711.* E-mail boomtown@earthlink.net. 300 rms, 4 story. S, D $49-$70; suites $150-$200; under 12 free; higher rates hols. Crib avail. TV; cable (premium). 2 pools; wading pool, whirlpool, poolside serv, lifeguard. Restaurant open 24 hrs. Rm serv. Ck-out noon. Coin Indry. Meeting rms. Business servs avail. In-rm modem link. Shopping arcade. RV park. Cr cds: A, C, D, DS, ER, JCB, MC, V.

D SC

★★ **COURTYARD BY MARRIOTT.** *3275 Paradise Rd (89109), near McCarran Intl Airport, east of the Strip. 702/791-3600; FAX 702/796-7981.* 149 rms, 3 story. S, D $89-$119; higher rates: conventions, hol wkends. Crib free. TV; cable (premium). Heated pool; whirlpool. Complimentary coffee in rms. Restaurant 6:30 am-2 pm; 5-10 pm. Bar 4-11 pm. Ck-out noon. Coin Indry. Meeting rms. Business servs avail. In-rm modem link. Valet serv. Free airport transportation. Exercise equipt; weights, bicycles. Some refrigerators. Balconies. Cr cds: A, C, D, DS, MC, V.

D SC

★★ **HOLIDAY INN.** *325 E Flamingo Rd (89109), near McCarran Intl Airport, east of the Strip. 702/732-9100; FAX 702/731-9784.* 150 units, 3 story, 140 suites. Mid-Sept-May: S, D $69-$175; each addl $15;

suites $99-$165; under 19 free; higher rates: hols, special events; lower rates rest of yr. Crib free. TV; cable (premium), VCR avail. Heated pool; whirlpool, poolside serv. Complimentary coffee in rms. Restaurant 6:30 am-11 pm. Bar noon-2 am. Ck-out noon. Meeting rms. Concierge. Free airport transportation. Exercise equipt; treadmill, stair machine. Refrigerators; wet bars. Cr cds: A, C, D, DS, JCB, MC, V.

D SC

★ ★ **LA QUINTA.** *3970 S Paradise Rd (89109), near McCarran Intl Airport, east of the Strip. 702/796-9000; FAX 702/796-3537.* 228 units, 3 story, 171 kits. S, D $75-$250; under 18 free. Crib free. TV; cable (premium). Pool. Complimentary continental bkfst. Ck-out noon. Coin Indry. Meeting rms. Business servs avail. In-rm modem link. Bellhops. Free airport transportation. In-rm whirlpools; refrigerators. Private patios, balconies. Cr cds: A, C, D, DS, ER, MC, V.

D SC

★ **WESTWARD HO HOTEL & CASINO.** *2900 Las Vegas Blvd S (89109), on the Strip. 702/731-2900; FAX 702/731-6154; res: 800/634-6803 (exc NV).* 777 rms, 2-4 story. S, D $37-$67; each addl $15; 2-bedrm apt $81-$111; package plan. Crib $15. TV. 4 pools, 1 heated; whirlpools. Restaurant open 24 hrs. Rm serv. Bars; entertainment. Ck-out 11 am. Free airport transportation. Some refrigerators; microwaves avail. Casino. Cr cds: A, MC, V.

D

Hotels

★ **ALADDIN.** *3667 Las Vegas Blvd S (89193), near McCarran Intl Airport, on the Strip. 702/736-0111; FAX 702/734-3583; res: 800/634-3424.* 1,100 rms, 22 story. S, D $65-$125; suites $150-$300; under 12 free. Crib free. TV. 2 pools; poolside serv, lifeguard. Supervised child's activities. Restaurants open 24 hrs. Bars. Ck-out noon. Convention facilities. Business servs avail. Concierge. Shopping arcade. Barber, beauty shop. Lighted tennis; pro. Casino. Cr cds: A, D, DS, JCB, MC, V.

D

★ ★ ★ **ALEXIS PARK RESORT.** *375 E Harmon Ave (89109), near McCarran Intl Airport, 1 mi E of the Strip. 702/796-3300; FAX 702/796-4334; res: 800/582-2228 (exc NV).* 500 suites, 2 story. 1-bedrm $85-$500; 2-bedrm $475-$1,150; each addl $15; under 12 free. Crib free. Pet accepted, some restrictions; $60. TV; cable (premium), VCR avail. 3 pools, 1 heated; whirlpool; poolside serv. Restaurant 6 am-3 pm, 6-11 pm (also see PEGASUS). Bar 10-1 am; entertainment. Ck-out noon. Convention facilities. Business center. In-rm modem link. Concierge. Gift shop. Barber, beauty shop. Golf privileges. Putting green. Exercise equipt; weights, bicycles, sauna, steam rm. Refrigerators, minibars; some bathrm phones, in-rm whirlpools. Cr cds: A, C, D, DS, JCB, MC, V.

D

★ ★ ★ **BALLY'S.** *3645 Las Vegas Blvd S (89109), on the Strip. 702/739-4111; FAX 702/739-3848; res: 800/634-3434.* 2,814 rms, 26 story. S, D $99-$169; each addl $15; suites $189-$2,500; under 18 free; package plans. Crib free. TV; cable (premium), VCR avail. Heated pool; whirlpool, poolside serv. Restaurant open 24 hrs. Bars; entertainment. Ck-out 11 am. Convention facilities. Business servs avail. In-rm modem link. Shopping arcade. Barber, beauty shop. Lighted tennis, pro. Exercise equipt; weights, stair machine, sauna. Game rm. Some bathrm phones, refrigerators. Casino, wedding chapel. Cr cds: A, C, D, DS, JCB, MC, V.

D SC

★ ★ **BARBARY COAST.** *3595 Las Vegas Blvd S (89109), on the Strip. 702/737-7111; FAX 702/894-9954; res: 800/634-6755 (exc NV).* 200 rms, 8 story. S, D $50-$125; each addl $10; suites $200-$500; under 12 free. TV; cable (premium). Restaurant open 24 hrs. Bar. Ck-out noon. Gift shop. Free valet, covered parking. Casino. Cr cds: A, C, D, DS, JCB, MC, V.

D

✔★ **BINNION'S HORSESHOE.** *128 Fremont St (89101). 702/382-1600; FAX 702/384-1574; res: 800/622-6468.* 369 rms, 22 story. S, D $40-$60. Crib $8. TV; cable (premium). Pool; lifeguard. Restaurant open 24 hrs. Bar. Ck-out noon. Gift shop. Casino. Cr cds: A, C, D, DS, ER, JCB, MC, V.

D

★ ★ ★ **BOULDER STATION.** *4111 Boulder Hwy (89112), off I-515, east of the Strip. 702/432-7777; FAX 702/432-7744; res: 800/683-7777.* Web www.stationcasinos.com. 300 rms, 16 story. S, D $49-$89; suites $125-$250; under 18 free. Crib free. TV; cable. Pool; poolside serv. Restaurant open 24 hrs. Ck-out noon. Business servs avail. In-rm modem link. Shopping arcade. Victorian-era railroad decor. Cr cds: A, C, D, DS, ER, MC, V.

D

★ **BOURBON STREET.** *120 E Flamingo Ave (89109), W of the Strip. 702/737-7200; FAX 702/794-3490; res: 800/634-6956.* 166 rms, 9 story. S, D $39-$99; under 17 free. TV. Pool privileges. Restaurant open 24 hrs. Ck-out noon. Meeting rms. Concierge. Gift shop. Near airport. Cr cds: A, C, D, DS, MC, V.

D SC

★ ★ ★ ★ **CAESARS PALACE.** *3570 Las Vegas Blvd S (89109), 1 blk E of I-15 Dunes/Flamingo exit, on the Strip. 702/731-7110; FAX 702/731-6636; res: 800/634-6001 (exc NV).* Web www.caesars.com. This opulent casino-hotel with an Ancient Rome accent offers a variety of luxurious accommodations. It often hosts world-class sporting and entertainment events and screens movies in its Omnimax theater. 2,600 rms, 14-32 story. S, D $79-$500; each addl $15; suites $225-$5,000; under 13 free. TV; cable (premium), VCR avail (movies). 4 pools; 2 whirlpools, lifeguard. Restaurant open 24 hrs (also see EMPRESS COURT and PALACE COURT). Bars. Circus Maximus, star entertainment. Ck-out noon. Convention facilities. Business center. In-rm modem link. Concierge. Shopping arcade. Barber, beauty shop. Free parking. Exercise rm; instructor, weight machines, bicycles, sauna, steam rm. Massage. Solarium. Racquetball. Handball. Game rm. Casino. Bathrm phones; many whirlpools; some refrigerators. Many bi-level suites with wet bar. Cr cds: A, C, D, DS, JCB, MC, V.

D

✔★ ★ **CALIFORNIA HOTEL & CASINO.** *1st & Ogden Aves (89125), I-95 Casino Center exit. 702/385-1222; FAX 702/388-2660; res: 800/634-6255.* 781 rms, 9-15 story. S, D $40-$60; each addl $5; under 12 free; package plans. Crib free. TV. Pool. Restaurant open 24 hrs. Bar. Ck-out noon. Gift shop. Refrigerators. Casino. Cr cds: A, D, DS, MC, V.

D

★ ★ **CARRIAGE HOUSE.** *105 E Harmon Ave (89109), east of the Strip. 702/798-1020; res: 800/221-2301.* 154 kit. suites, 9 story. S, D $115-$245; children free; wkly rates; higher rates: special events, hols. Crib free. TV; cable (premium). Heated pool; whirlpool. Complimentary coffee in rms. Restaurant 7-10 am, 5-11 pm. Bar from 5 pm. Ck-out 11 am. Coin Indry. Business servs avail. In-rm modem link. Free airport transportation. Tennis. Microwaves. Cr cds: A, C, D, DS, ER, MC, V.

D SC

✔★ ★ **CIRCUS-CIRCUS HOTEL & CASINO.** *2880 Las Vegas Blvd (89114), S on the Strip. 702/734-0410; FAX 702/734-5897; res: 800/634-3450.* Web www.circuscircus-lasvegas.com. 3,800 rms, 3-29 story. S, D $39-$99; each addl $10; suites $99-$650; under 12 free. Crib $10. TV. 3 pools, 1 heated; poolside serv, lifeguard. Restaurants open 24 hrs (also see THE STEAK HOUSE). Bars; entertainment. Ck-out 11 am. Business servs avail. In-rm modem link. Shopping arcade. Barber, beauty shop. Health club privileges. Casino, performing circus and midway housed together in tent-like structure. Cr cds: A, C, D, DS, MC, V.

D

★ ★ ★ **DESERT INN.** *3145 Las Vegas Blvd S (89109), on the Strip. 702/733-4444; FAX 702/733-4774; res: 800/634-6906.* 715 rms, 7-14 story. S, D $185-$375; each addl $35; suites $350-$10,000. Crib free.

TV; cable (premium), VCR avail (movies). Heated pool; whirlpool, poolside serv, lifeguard. Restaurant (see MONTE CARLO). Rm serv 24 hrs. Bars open 24 hrs; Crystal Room, theater, star entertainment. Ck-out noon. Convention facilities. Business center. In-rm modem link. Concierge. Shopping arcade. Free valet parking. Lighted tennis, pro. 18-hole golf, greens fee, putting green, driving range. Exercise rm; instructor, weights, bicycles, sauna, steam rm. Bathrm phones, refrigerators; wet bar in suites. Private patios, balconies. Casino. Resort hotel on 160 acres. Cr cds: A, C, D, DS, JCB, MC, V.

D

✔★ **EL CORTEZ.** *600 E Fremont St (89125). 702/385-5200; res: 800/634-6703; FAX 702/385-9765.* 293 rms, 15 story. S, D $23-$40; each addl $3. Crib free. TV; cable (premium). Restaurant 4:30-11 pm. Rm serv 7 am-7 pm. Bar open 24 hrs. Ck-out noon. Meeting rms. Shopping arcade. Barber, beauty shop. Free valet parking. Casino. Cr cds: A, C, D, DS, JCB, MC, V.

D

★ ★ **EXCALIBUR.** *3850 Las Vegas Blvd S (89109), on the Strip. 702/597-7777; FAX 702/597-7040; res: 800/937-7777.* Web www.excalibur-casino.com. 4,008 rms, 28 story. S, D $55-$89; each addl $10; suites $275; higher rates: wkends, hols. Crib $10. TV; cable (premium). 2 heated pools; poolside serv, lifeguard. Restaurants open 24 hrs (also see SIR GALLAHAD'S). Dinner theater. Bar open 24 hrs; entertainment. Ck-out 11 am. Business servs avail. In-rm modem link. Health club privileges. Shopping arcade. Barber, beauty shop. Whirlpool in suites. Casino. Castle-like structure with medieval/old English interiors based upon legend of King Arthur and Round Table. Cr cds: A, C, D, DS, MC, V.

D

★ **FIESTA.** *(2400 Rancho Dr, North Las Vegas 89130) 702/631-7000; FAX 702/631-6588; res: 800/731-7333.* 100 rms, 5 story. S, D $49-$129; suites $98-$218; under 16 free. TV; cable. Restaurant open 24 hrs (also see GARDUÑOS). No rm serv. Ck-out noon. Meeting rms. Gift shop. Casino. Near North Las Vegas Airport. Cr cds: A, C, D, DS, ER, MC, V.

D

✔★ ★ **FITZGERALDS.** *301 Fremont St (89101), west of the Strip. 702/388-2400; FAX 702/388-2181; res: 800/274-5825.* 638 rms, 34 story, 14 suites. S, D $40-$90; suites $200-$450; under 18 free. Crib $5. TV. Restaurant open 24 hrs. Rm serv. Bar. Ck-out noon. Coin Indry. Business servs avail. Concierge. Gift shop. Casino. Cr cds: A, C, D, DS, ER, MC, V.

D

★ ★ **FOUR QUEENS.** *202 Fremont St (89125), at Casino Center Blvd. 702/385-4011; FAX 702/387-5122; res: 800/634-6045.* 700 rms, 19 story. S, D $54-$125; each addl $15; suites $99-$125; under 2 free. TV. Restaurant open 24 hrs (also see HUGO'S CELLAR); dining rm 6 pm-midnight. Bar; entertainment. Ck-out noon. Meeting rms. Business servs avail. Garage parking. Wet bar in suites. Casino. Cr cds: A, C, D, DS, MC, V.

D SC

✔★ **FREMONT.** *200 E Fremont St (89125). 702/385-3232; FAX 702/385-6270; res: 800/634-6182.* 452 rms, 14 story. S, D $44-$80; package plan. TV. Restaurant open 24 hrs. Bars. Ck-out noon. Gift shop. Casino. Cr cds: A, C, D, DS, JCB, MC, V.

✔★ ★ **FRONTIER.** *3120 S Las Vegas Blvd (89109). 702/794-8200; res: 800/634-6966; FAX 702/794-8230.* 987 rms, 16 story, 384 suites. S $35-$65; D $55-$95; suites $65-$95; under 12 free; wkends, hols (min stay required); higher rates special events. Crib free. TV. Restaurant open 24 hrs. Bar. Ck-out noon. Meeting rms. Business center. In-rm modem link. Concierge. Shopping arcade. Barber, beauty shop. Lighted tennis. Pool; whirlpool, poolside serv, lifeguard. Some bathrm phones. Cr cds: A, C, D, DS, ER, MC, V.

D

★ ★ **GOLD COAST.** *4000 W Flamingo Rd (89103), at Valley View Blvd, west of the Strip. 702/367-7111; res: 888/402-6278; FAX 702/367-8575.* 711 rms, 10 story. S, D $55-$75; suites $125-$400; family rates; package plan. TV; cable (premium). Pool. Supervised child's activities. Restaurant open 24 hrs. Bars; entertainment. Ck-out noon. Convention facilities. Business servs avail. Barber, beauty shop. Free valet parking. Game rm. Bowling. Some bathrm phones. Casino. Movie theaters. Cr cds: A, C, D, DS, ER, JCB, MC, V.

D SC

✔★ **GOLD SPIKE.** *400 E Ogden Ave (89101). 702/384-8444; res: 800/634-6703.* 109 rms, 7 story. S, D $22; under 12 free. Crib free. TV. Restaurant open 24 hrs. Ck-out noon. Business servs avail. Cr cds: A, C, D, DS, ER, MC, V.

D

★ ★ ★ ★ **GOLDEN NUGGET.** *129 E Fremont St (89125), at Casino Center. 702/385-7111; FAX 702/386-8362; res: 800/634-3454 (exc NV).* Behind the palm-tree-shaded exterior is a lobby filled with gold, white marble and greenery. Guest rooms reflect the same elegance. 1,907 rms, 18-22 story. S, D $59-$129; each addl $20; suites $275-$750. Crib free. TV; cable, VCR avail. Heated pool; whirlpool, poolside serv, lifeguard. Restaurants open 24 hrs (also see LILY LANGTRY'S and STEFANO'S). Bar; entertainment. Ck-out noon. Convention facilities. Business center. In-rm modem link. Gift shop. Barber, beauty shop. Exercise rm; instructor, weight machines, bicycles, sauna, steam rm. Massage. Casino. Some bathrm phones. Cr cds: A, C, D, DS, JCB, MC, V.

D

★ ★ ★ **HARD ROCK.** *4455 Paradise Rd (89109). 702/693-5000; FAX 702/693-5021; res: 800/473-7625.* Web www.hardrock.com. 340 rms, 11 story. S, D $75-$300; suites $250-$500. Crib free. TV; cable (premium). Pool; lifeguard. Restaurants (see MORTONI'S, and see HARD ROCK CAFE, Unrated Dining). Ck-out 3 pm. Concierge. Sundries. Gift shop. Exercise rm; instructor, weights, bicycles. Cr cds: A, C, D, DS, ER, JCB, MC, V.

D

★ ★ ★ **HARRAH'S.** *3475 Las Vegas Blvd S (89109), on the Strip. 702/369-5000; res: 800/427-7247; FAX 702/733-6724.* 2,699 rms, 35 story. S, D $55-$149; each addl $15; suites $395-$800; under 12 free; higher rates special events. Crib free. TV; cable. Pool; whirlpool, poolside serv, lifeguard. Restaurant open 24 hrs. Bar; entertainment exc Sun. Ck-out noon. Coin Indry. Convention facilities. Business servs avail. Shopping arcade. Barber, beauty shop. Valet parking; covered parking free. Exercise equipt; weights, bicycles, sauna. Massage. Game rm. Balconies. Casino. Wedding chapel. Cr cds: A, C, D, DS, JCB, MC, V.

D

★ ★ ★ **HILTON.** *3000 Paradise Rd (89114), east of the Strip. 702/732-5111; FAX 702/794-3611.* Web www.lv/hilton.com. 3,170 rms, 30 story. S, D $95-$275; each addl $20; 1-2 bedrm suites from $320; lanai suites $320-$340. Crib free. TV. Rooftop pool; whirlpool, poolside serv, lifeguard. Restaurant open 24 hrs (also see LE MONTRACHET). Bars; entertainment. Ck-out noon. Convention facilities. Business center. In-rm modem link. Shopping arcade. Barber, beauty shop. Free valet parking. Lighted tennis, pro. Golf privileges, greens fee $80, putting green. Exercise rm; instructor, weights, bicycles, sauna. Massage. Game rm. Some bathrm phones, refrigerators. Private patios, balconies. Casino. Cr cds: A, C, D, DS, JCB, MC, V.

D

★ ★ ★ **HILTON FLAMINGO.** *3555 Las Vegas Blvd S (89109), on the Strip. 702/733-3111; FAX 702/733-3353; res: 800/732-2111 (exc NV).* 3,642 rms, 28 story. S, D $69-$219; each addl $16; suites $250-$580; family rates; package plan. Crib free. TV; cable (premium). 5 pools; whirlpools, poolside serv, lifeguard. Restaurant open 24 hrs. Bar; stage show. Ck-out noon. Convention center. Business center. In-rm modem link. Shopping arcade. Barber, beauty shop. Free valet parking. Tennis privileges. Exercise equipt; weight machines, bicycles, sauna, steam rm.

Some bathrm phones; refrigerators avail. Casino. Cr cds: A, C, D, DS, ER, JCB, MC, V.

D SC

★ ★ **HOLIDAY INN CROWNE PLAZA SUITES.** *4255 Paradise Rd (89109), near McCarran Intl Airport, east of the Strip. 702/369-4400; FAX 702/369-3770.* Web www.crowneplaza.com. 201 suites, 6 story. S, D $105-$250; each addl $20; under 18 free. Crib free. Pet accepted. TV; cable (premium), VCR avail. Heated pool; whirlpool, poolside serv. Complimentary coffee in rms. Restaurant 6 am-2 pm, 5-10 pm. Bar 11 am-midnight. Ck-out noon. Meeting rms. Business center. In-rm modem link. Concierge. Gift shop. Free airport transportation. Exercise equipt; weights, bicycles, sauna. Minibars. Cr cds: A, C, D, DS, ER, JCB, MC, V.

D

★ **IMPERIAL PALACE.** *3535 Las Vegas Blvd S (89109), on the Strip. 702/731-3311; FAX 702/735-8578; res: 800/634-6441 (exc NV), 800/351-7400 (NV).* 2,700 rms, 19 story. S, D $49-$99; each addl $15; suites $159-$499; package plan; higher rates hols. Crib $15. TV; cable (premium). Pool; whirlpool. Restaurant open 24 hrs. Bar; entertainment. Ck-out noon. Convention facilities. Business servs avail. In-rm modem link. Shopping arcade. Barber, beauty shop. Free valet, covered parking. Exercise equipt; weight machines, treadmills. Some bathrm phones, refrigerators. Private balconies. Casino. Antique auto exhibit. Cr cds: A, C, D, DS, JCB, MC, V.

D

★ ★ **LADY LUCK CASINO.** *206 N 3rd St (89101). 702/477-3000; FAX 702/477-7021; res: 800/523-9582.* Web www.ladyluck.com/ladyluck. 792 rms, 17 & 25 story. Feb-Mar & Sept-Oct: S, D $39-$99; suites $49-$100; package plans; lower rates rest of yr. TV. Pool. Restaurant open 24 hrs. Bar. Ck-out noon. Free garage parking. Airport transportation. Refrigerators. Casino. Cr cds: A, C, D, DS, JCB, MC, V.

D

✔ ★ ★ **LAS VEGAS CLUB.** *18 E Fremont St (89101). 702/385-1664; res: 800/634-6532.* 405 rms, 16 story. S, D $40-$55; under 12 free. Higher rates: hols, special events. Crib free. TV; cable. Restaurant open 24 hrs. Ck-out noon. Business servs avail. Shopping arcade. Cr cds: A, C, D, DS, ER, JCB, MC, V.

D

★ ★ ★ **LUXOR.** *3900 Las Vegas Blvd S (89119), near McCarran Intl Airport, on the Strip. 702/262-4000; FAX 702/262-4452; res: 800/288-1000.* Web www.luxor.com. 4,474 rms, 30 story, 473 suites. S, D $59-$359; suites $159-$800; under 12 free. Crib $10. TV; cable (premium), VCR avail. 5 pools, 1 heated; wading pool, poolside serv, lifeguard. Restaurants open 24 hrs (also see SACRED SEA). Bar; entertainment. Ck-out 11 am. Business center. Concierge. Shopping arcade. Barber, beauty shop. Massage. Exercise equipt; weight machine, treadmill, sauna. Casino. Pyramid-shaped hotel with replica of the Great Sphinx of Giza. Extensive lanscaping with Egyptian theme. Cr cds: A, C, D, DS, MC, V.

D

✔ ★ ★ ★ **MAIN STREET STATION.** *200 N Main St (89101). 702/387-1896; res: 800/713-8933; FAX 702/386-4421.* 406 rms, 15 story. S, D $45-$60; under 21 free; higher rates hols. Crib free. TV; cable (premium). Restaurant open 24 hrs. Ck-out noon. Meeting rms. Business center. In-rm modem link. Concierge. Shopping arcade. Cr cds: A, C, D, DS, ER, MC, V.

★ **MAXIM.** *160 E Flamingo Rd (89109), W of the Strip. 702/731-4300; FAX 702/735-3252; res: 800/634-6987.* E-mail maxim@anu.net; web www.maximhotel.com. 798 rms, 17 story. S, D $39-$98; suites $175-$305. Crib $10. TV; VCR avail (movies). Pool; poolside serv, lifeguard. Restaurants. Ck-out noon. Meeting rms. Business servs avail. Gift shop. Barber, beauty shop. Cr cds: A, C, D, DS, ER, JCB, MC, V.

D SC

★ ★ ★ ★ **MGM GRAND.** *3799 Las Vegas Blvd S (89109), near McCarran Intl Airport, on the Strip. 702/891-1111; FAX 702/891-1030; res: 800/929-1111.* Web www.mgmgrand.com. This movieland-styled mega resort is the largest in the world. Outstanding features include a 33-acre theme park, seven-story City of Entertainment, and two showrooms with headline entertainment. 5,005 rms, 30 story, 740 suites. S, D $69-$399; suites $109-$750; under 12 free; higher rates hols. Crib free. TV; cable (premium). Pool; wading pool, poolside serv, lifeguard. Supervised child's activities; ages 3-12. Restaurants open 24 hrs (also see BROWN DERBY, COYOTE CAFE, EMERIL'S NEW ORLEANS, GATSBY'S and WOLFGANG PUCK'S CAFE). Bars; entertainment. Ck-out 11 am. Convention facilities. Business center. In-rm modem link. Concierge. Shopping arcade. Barber, beauty shop. Lighted tennis, pro. Exercise rm; instructor, weight machines, treadmill, steam rm. Spa. Game rm. Cr cds: A, C, D, DS, ER, JCB, MC, V.

D

★ ★ ★ **MIRAGE.** *3400 Las Vegas Blvd S (89109), on the Strip. 702/791-7111; FAX 702/791-7446; res: 800/627-6667.* Web www.mirage.com. 3,044 rms, 30 story. S, D $79-$399; each addl $30; suites $300-$3,000. Crib $30. TV; VCR avail. Pool. Restaurant open 24 hrs (also see BISTRO). Bar; entertainment. Ck-out noon. Convention facilities. Business center. In-rm modem link. Concierge. Shopping arcade. Barber, beauty shop. Valet parking. Exercise rm; instructor, weights, bicycles. Massage. Bathrm phone, refrigerator, wet bar in suites. Casino. Atrium features tropical rain forest; behind front desk is 20,000-gallon aquarium with sharks and tropical fish. On 100 acres with dolphin and white tiger habitats. Cr cds: A, C, D, DS, ER, JCB, MC, V.

D

★ ★ ★ **MONTE CARLO.** *Las Vegas Blvd S (89109), on the Strip. 702/730-7777; res: 800/311-8999; FAX 702/730-7200.* Web www.montecarlo.com. 3,002 rms, 32 story. S, D $59-$159; suites $250-$1,000; under 12 free. Crib free. TV; cable (premium), VCR avail. Pool; poolside serv, lifeguard. Restaurant open 24 hrs. Ck-out 11 am. Gift shop. Concierge. Convention facilities. Business center. In-rm modem link. Tennis. Exercise rm; instructor, bicycles, weights. Some balconies. Cr cds: A, C, D, DS, ER, JCB, MC, V.

D

★ ★ ★ **NEW YORK-NEW YORK.** *3790 Las Vegas Blvd S (89109). 702/740-6969; res: 800/693-6763; FAX 702/740-6510.* 2,034 rms, 47 story. S, D $89-$200; each addl $20; under 12 free; wkends, hols (min stay required). Crib free. TV; cable (premium). Restaurant open 24 hrs (also see MOTOWN CAFE). Bar. Ck-out noon. Convention facilities. Business center. In-rm modem link. Concierge. Shopping arcade. Barber, beauty shop. Free garage parking. Pool; whirlpool, poolside serv, lifeguard. Rec rm. Some bathrm phones. Hotel recreates New York City's famous landmarks and attractions including the Statue of Liberty and the Manhattan Express. Cr cds: A, C, D, DS, MC, V.

D

★ ★ **ORLEANS.** *4500 W Tropicana Ave (89103). 702/365-7111; res: 800/675-3267; FAX 702/365-7499.* 840 rms, 21 story. S, D $49-$1,000; each addl $10; under 12 free; wkends (2-day min); higher rates hols. Crib free. TV; cable (premium). Restaurants open 24 hrs. Bar; entertainment. Ck-out noon. Meeting rms. Business center. Shopping arcade. Barber, beauty shop. Pool; poolside serv. Cr cds: A, C, D, DS, ER, JCB, MC, V.

D SC

★ ★ ★ **PALACE STATION HOTEL & CASINO.** *2411 W Sahara (89102), at I-15, west of the Strip. 702/367-2411; FAX 702/367-2478; res: 800/634-3101 (exc NV).* 1,029 rms, 21 story. S, D $59-$169; each addl $10; suites $250-$1,000; under 12 free. Crib free. TV; cable. 2 pools; whirlpools. Restaurants open 24 hrs. Bars; entertainment. Ck-out noon.

Business servs avail. Gift shop. Garage parking. Game rm. Casino, bingo. Cr cds: A, C, D, DS, ER, MC, V.

D

★ ★ **PLAZA.** *One Main St (89125), east of the Strip. 702/386-2110; FAX 702/382-8281; res: 800/634-6575.* 1,037 rms, 25 story. S, D $30-$75; suites $60-$150; under 12 free. Crib $8. TV; VCR avail. Heated pool; wading pool. Restaurant open 24 hrs. Bar. Ck-out noon. Coin lndry. Convention facilities. Business servs avail. Shopping arcade. Barber. Tennis. Casino. Cr cds: A, C, D, DS, ER, MC, V.

D

★ ★ ★ **RIO SUITE HOTEL & CASINO.** *Box 14160 (89114), I-15 at Flamingo Rd, west of the Strip. 702/252-7777; FAX 702/252-7670; res: 800/752-9746.* Web www.playrio.com. 2,563 suites, 41 story. Suites $95-$149; each addl $15; mid-wk rates. TV; cable (premium). 3 pools; whirlpools. Complimentary coffee in rms. Restaurant open 24 hrs (also see ANTONIO'S and NAPA). Bar; entertainment. Ck-out noon. Convention facilities. Business servs avail. Concierge. Shopping arcade. Barber, beauty shop. Exercise equipt; weights, bicycles. Massage. Refrigerators. Building facade of red and blue glass trimmed in neon. Casino. Cr cds: A, C, D, DS, JCB, MC, V.

D

★ ★ **RIVIERA.** *2901 Las Vegas Blvd S (89109), On the Strip. 702/734-5110; FAX 702/794-9663; res: 800/634-6753 (exc NV).* 2,100 rms, 6-24 story. S, D $59-$99; each addl $20; suites $125-$500; package plan. Crib free. TV; cable (premium). Heated pool; whirlpool, poolside serv, lifeguard. Restaurant open 24 hrs. Bar; Versailles Room, name entertainment. Ck-out 11 am. Convention facilities. Business center. In-rm modem link. Shopping arcade. Barber, beauty shop. Lighted tennis. Exercise equipt; weights, bicycles, sauna, steam rm. Some refrigerators. Bathrm phone in some suites. Some balconies. Casino. Cr cds: A, C, D, DS, MC, V.

D

★ ★ **SAHARA.** *2535 Las Vegas Blvd S (89109), on the Strip. 702/737-2111; FAX 702/791-2027; res: 800/634-6666.* 1,716 rms, 2-27 story. S, D $55-$95; each addl $10; suites $200-$300; under 12 free; package plans. Crib $10. TV; VCR avail. Heated pool; poolside serv, lifeguard. Restaurant open 24 hrs. Bar; Congo Theatre, star entertainment. Ck-out noon. Convention facilities. Business center. In-rm modem link. Shopping arcade. Barber, beauty shop. Free covered parking. Health club privileges. Many bathrm phones. Private patios, balconies. Casino. Cr cds: A, C, D, DS, MC, V.

D SC

★ ★ ★ **SAM'S TOWN.** *Flamingo & Boulder Hwy (89122), E of the Strip. 702/456-7777; FAX 702/454-8107; res: 800/634-6371.* E-mail room res@samstown.boydnet. 648 rms, 9 story. S, D $35-$150; suites $160-$310; under 12 free. Crib free. TV; cable. Heated pool. 10 restaurants (some open 24 hrs). Ck-out noon. Coin lndry. Convention facilities. Business servs avail. In-rm modem link. Concierge. Shopping arcade. Casino, bowling center. Old West decor; atrium. Cr cds: A, C, D, DS, ER, MC, V.

D

★ ★ **SAN REMO.** *115 E Tropicana Ave (89109), near McCarran Intl Airport, east of the Strip. 702/739-9000; FAX 702/736-1120; res: 800/522-7366.* 711 rms, 19 story. S, D $59-$199; each addl $15; suites $125-$500; higher rates: hols, conventions. Crib $15. TV. Heated pool; poolside serv. Restaurant open 24 hrs, dining rm 5-11 pm. Bar; entertainment. Ck-out 11 am. Meeting rms. Business servs avail. In-rm modem link. Gift shop. Free garage parking. Casino. Cr cds: A, C, D, DS, ER, JCB, MC, V.

D

✔★ ★ **SANTA FE HOTEL & CASINO.** *4949 N Rancho Dr (89130). 702/658-4900; FAX 702/658-4919; res: 800/872-6823.* 200 rms, 5 story. S, D $49-$89; each addl $5; under 13 free; higher rates some hols. TV; cable. Supervised child's activities. Restaurant open 24 hrs (also see SUZETTE'S). Bar; entertainment. Ck-out noon. Meeting rm. Business servs avail. Gift shop. Game rm. Bowling lanes. Ice rink. Cr cds: A, D, DS, MC, V.

D

✔★ ★ **SHOWBOAT.** *2800 E Fremont St (89104). 702/385-9123; FAX 702/383-9238; res: 800/826-2800 (exc NV).* 451 rms, 19 story. S, D $39-$89; each addl $10; suites $90-$255; under 12 free. Crib $5. TV. Heated pool; lifeguard. Restaurants open 24 hrs. Bar. Ck-out noon. Meeting rms. Business servs avail. Gift shop. Barber, beauty shop. Free airport transportation. Game rm. Casino; bingo parlor. 106-lane bowling. Cr cds: A, C, D, DS, MC, V.

D

✔★ ★ **STARDUST RESORT & CASINO.** *3000 Las Vegas Blvd S (89109), on the Strip. 702/732-6111; FAX 702/732-6296; res: 800/634-6757.* E-mail roomres@stardust.com; web www.vegas.com. 2,341 rms, 2-32 story. Jan-May, Oct-Nov: S, D $24-$150; suites $150-$500. Crib free. TV. 2 pools; lifeguard, poolside serv. Restaurants open 24 hrs. Bar; entertainment. Ck-out noon. Convention facilities. Business servs avail. In-rm modem link. Shopping arcade. Barber, beauty shop. Health club privileges. Game rm. Some bathrm phones, refrigerators. Some private patios, balconies. Casino. Cr cds: A, C, D, DS, ER, JCB, MC, V.

D

★ ★ **STRATOSPHERE TOWER.** *2000 S Las Vegas Blvd (89104), on the Strip. 702/380-7777; FAX 702/380-7732; res: 800/998-6937.* Web www.grandcasinos.com. 1,500 rms, 24 story. S, D $49-$249; under 12 free. Crib free. TV; cable (premium). Pool; poolside serv, lifeguard. Restaurants open 24 hrs (also see TOP OF THE WORLD). Ck-out 11 am. Concierge. Sundries. Shopping arcade. Tallest free-standing tower in the U.S. which has a roller coaster on the top. Cr cds: A, C, D, DS, ER, JCB, MC, V.

D SC

★ ★ **TEXAS.** *(2101 Texas Star Lane, North Las Vegas 89030) N on Rancho Dr. 702/631-1000; FAX 702/631-8120; res: 800/654-8888.* 200 rms, 6 story. S $49-$189; D $175-$225. Crib free. TV; cable. Pool; poolside serv, lifeguard. Coffee in rms. Restaurants open 24 hrs (also see LAREDO CANTINA). Ck-out noon. Gift shop. Cr cds: A, C, D, DS, ER, JCB, MC, V.

D

★ ★ ★ **TREASURE ISLAND.** *3300 Las Vegas Blvd S (89109), on the Strip. 702/894-7111; FAX 702/894-7414; res: 800/944-7444.* Web www.treasureislandlasvegas.com. 2,679 rms, 36 story. S, D $49-$299; suites $100-$500. Crib $25. TV; cable, VCR avail. 2 heated pools; wading pool, poolside serv, lifeguard. Restaurants open 24 hrs (see BUCCANEER BAY CLUB). Bars; entertainment. Ck-out noon. Convention facilities. Business center. In-rm modem link. Shopping arcade. Barber, beauty shop. Exercise equipt; weights, bicycles. Refrigerators. Casino. Arcade entertainment complex. Buccaneer Bay Village adventure attraction. Cr cds: A, C, D, DS, JCB, MC, V.

D

★ ★ ★ **TROPICANA.** *3801 Las Vegas Blvd S (89109), near McCarran Intl Airport, on the Strip. 702/739-2222; FAX 702/739-2469; res: 800/634-4000 (exc NV).* 1,875 rms, 22 story. S, D $55-$169; each addl $15. TV; cable (premium). Pool; whirlpool, poolside serv, lifeguard. Restaurant open 24 hrs. Bar; Tiffany Theatre, entertainment. Ck-out noon. Convention facilities. Business center. In-rm modem link. Shopping arcade. Barber, beauty shop. Exercise equipt; weights, bicycles, sauna. Some bathrm phones, refrigerators. Private patios, balconies. Casino. Cr cds: A, C, D, DS, JCB, MC, V.

D

Restaurants

★ ★ **ANTONIO'S.** *(See Rio Suite Hotel & Casino) 702/252-7737.* Hrs: 5-11 pm. Res accepted. Italian menu. Bar. Semi-a la carte: dinner $16.95-$35. Specialties: aragosta sardinia, cioppino, scaloppine piccata. Valet parking. Elegant dining; crystal chandeliers, marble columns. Cr cds: A, C, D, DS, ER, JCB, MC, V.

D

★ **BATTISTA'S HOLE IN THE WALL.** *4041 Audrie St, east of the Strip. 702/732-1424.* Hrs: 4:30-11 pm. Closed Thanksgiving, Dec 24 & 25. Res accepted. Italian menu. Bar. Complete meals: dinner $15.95-$29.95. Specializes in fresh pasta. Parking. Casual atmosphere. Family-owned. Cr cds: A, C, D, DS, MC, V.

D

★ ★ **BERTOLINI'S.** *3500 Las Vegas Blvd S (89109). 702/735-4663.* Hrs: 11 am-midnight; Fri, Sat to 1 am. Italian menu. Bar. A la carte entrees: lunch, dinner $5.25-$18.95. Specializes in pasta. Conservative Italian decor. Cr cds: A, D, JCB, MC, V.

D

★ ★ ★ **BISTRO.** *(See Mirage Hotel) 702/791-7111.* Hrs: 5:30-11 pm. Res accepted. French menu. Wine list. Semi-a la carte: dinner $25-$50. Specialties: trio of venison, pecan-crusted rack of lamb. Stained glass dome in center of restaurant. Cr cds: A, C, D, DS, ER, MC, V.

D

★ ★ ★ **BROWN DERBY.** *(See MGM Grand Hotel) 702/891-1111.* Hrs: 5:30-11 pm. Res accepted. Bar. Wine list. Complete meals: dinner $30-$45. Specializes in prime steak. Pianist, vocalist Tues-Sun. Elegant surroundings. Cr cds: A, C, D, DS, ER, MC, V.

D

★ ★ ★ **BUCCANEER BAY CLUB.** *(See Treasure Island Hotel) 702/894-7350.* Hrs: 5-10:30 pm. Res accepted. Continental menu. Bar. Wine list. Semi-a la carte: dinner $15.95-$26.50. Specialties: veal scallopine, duck melba, venison royale. Valet parking. Arched windows with view of pirate ship in front of hotel. Cr cds: A, C, D, DS, ER, MC, V.

D

★ **CAFE MICHELLE WEST.** *2800 W Sahara Ave (89102). 702/873-5400.* Hrs: 11 am-11 pm. Closed Thanksgiving, Dec 25. Res accepted. Eclectic menu. Bar. Semi-a la carte: lunch $7-$16, dinner $11-$28. Specializes in chicken, veal, pasta. Outdoor dining. Contemporary decor. Cr cds: A, C, D, DS, ER, MC, V.

D

★ ★ **CAFE NICOLLE.** *4760 W Sahara Ave (89102). 702/870-7675.* Hrs: 11 am-midnight. Closed major hols. Res accepted. French menu. Bar. Semi-a la carte: lunch $7.50-$12.50, dinner $18-$26.95. Specializes in lamb chops, steak, seafood. Entertainment. Outdoor dining. Casual decor. Cr cds: A, DS, MC, V.

✔★ ★ **CATHAY HOUSE.** *5300 W Spring Mountain Rd (89102). 702/876-3838.* Hrs: 11 am-11 pm. Chinese menu. Bar. Semi-a la carte: lunch $7.50-$12, dinner $10-$15.95. Specialties: strawberry chicken, orange flavored beef. Chinese decor. Cr cds: A, C, D, DS, MC, V.

D

✔★ **CHAPALA.** *2101 S Decatur Blvd, in shopping center. 702/871-7805.* Hrs: 11 am-11 pm; Fri, Sat to midnight. Closed some major hols. Res accepted. Mexican menu. Bar. Semi-a la carte: lunch, dinner $2.50-$10.25. Specialties: fajitas, enchilada ranchero. Cr cds: MC, V.

D

★ ★ ★ **CHIN'S.** *3200 Las Vegas Blvd S, on the Strip. 702/733-8899.* Hrs: 11:30 am-10 pm; Sun from noon. Closed Thanksgiving, Dec 24 & 25. Res accepted. Cantonese menu. Bar. Wine cellar. A la carte entrees: lunch $9.95-$16, dinner $6-$28. Complete meals: lunch $14.50-$15, dinner $29.50-$50. Specialties: Chin's beef, strawberry chicken, shrimp puffs. Pianist. Valet parking. Cr cds: A, MC, V.

D

★ ★ ★ **CIPRIANI.** *2790 E Flamingo Rd. 702/369-6711.* Web www.vegas.com/restaurants/cipriani. Hrs: 11:30 am-2 pm, 5:30-10 pm. Res accepted. Italian menu. Serv bar. Semi-a la carte: lunch $8.95-$15, dinner $15-$26.95. Specialties: scaloppina Monte Bianco, medallion of beef Piemontese, fresh seafood. Accordianist, vocalist. Florentine atmosphere. Cr cds: A, C, D, MC, V.

D

✔★ **COUNTRY INN.** *1401 Rainbow Blvd. 702/254-0520.* Hrs: 7 am-10 pm; wkends to 11 pm. Closed Dec 25. Wine, beer. Semi-a la carte: bkfst $1.95-$6.50, lunch, dinner $5.95-$12.95. Child's meals. Specializes in turkey, fish, steak. Cr cds: A, C, D, DS, MC, V.

D

★ ★ **COYOTE CAFE.** *(See MGM Grand Hotel) 702/891-7349.* Hrs: 8:30 am-11 pm. Res accepted. Southwestern menu. Bar. Semi-a la carte: bkfst $3-$8, lunch $5-$12, dinner $6-$16. Specialties: chicken tostada, beef fajita tostada. Southwestern decor; artwork, cacti. Cr cds: A, C, D, DS, ER, MC, V.

D

✔★ ★ **CREPES PIERETTE.** *4794 S Eastern Ave (89119). 702/434-1234.* Hrs: 8:30 am-10 pm; Sun to 2 pm. Closed Mon; Jan 1, Dec 25. Res required (dinner). French menu. Bar. Semi-a la carte: bkfst $5-$7.50, lunch $7.50-$10, dinner $12-$17. Specializes in crêpes, country French cuisine. Own baking. Outdoor dining. Intimate, country French atmosphere. Cr cds: A, C, D, DS, ER, MC, V.

D

★ ★ **THE DIVE.** *3200 Las Vegas Blvd S (89109), S on I-15 to Spring Mountain Rd exit, W to Las Vegas Blvd. 702/369-2270.* Hrs: 11:30 am-10 pm; Fri, Sat to 11 pm. Res accepted. Bar. Semi-a la carte: lunch $8-$12, dinner $10.95-$16.95. Specialties: bouillabaisse, baby back ribs. Nautical decor; shaped to look like submarine. Cr cds: A, C, D, DS, ER, MC, V.

D

★ ★ ★ **EMERIL'S NEW ORLEANS.** *(See MGM Grand Hotel) 702/891-1111.* Hrs: 11 am-2:30 pm, 5:30-10:30 pm. Res accepted. French menu. Bar. Complete meals: lunch $15-$25, dinner $17-$75. Specializes in seafood. French Quarter decor. Pictures of New Orleans. Cr cds: A, C, D, DS, ER, MC, V.

D

★ ★ ★ **EMPRESS COURT.** *(See Caesars Palace Hotel) 702/731-7110.* Hrs: 6-11 pm. Res accepted. Cantonese menu. Bar. Complete meals: dinner $30-$80. Specializes in shark fin dishes. Valet parking. Elegant dining. Jacket. Cr cds: A, C, D, MC, V.

D

✔★ ★ **FASOLINI'S PIZZA CAFE.** *222 Decatur Blvd (89107). 702/877-0071.* Hrs: noon-10 pm; Sun to 5 pm. Closed Jan 1, Easter, Dec 25. Italian menu. Beer, wine. Semi-a la carte: lunch $5.95-$9.95, dinner $9.95-$12.95. Specialties: chicken cacciatore, spaghetti. Art Deco decor; posters of famous movies. Cr cds: A, C, D, DS, ER, MC, V.

D

★ ★ **FERRARO'S.** *5900 W Flamingo Rd (89103). 702/364-5300.* Hrs: 5:30-11 pm. Closed Dec 25. Res accepted. Italian menu. Bar. Semi-a la carte: dinner $12-$28. Specializes in pasta, seafood, steak. Pianist. Parking. Patio dining. Italian decor. Cr cds: A, C, D, DS, MC, V.

D

★ ★ ★ **FOG CITY DINER.** *325 Hughes Center Dr (89109). 702/737-0200.* Hrs: 11:30 am-10 pm; Fri, Sat to 11 pm. Closed Thanksgiving, Dec 25. Res accepted. Bar. Semi-a la carte: lunch $5.50-$8, dinner $12.50-$22. Child's meals. Specializes in classic diner dishes, seafood. Cr cds: A, C, D, DS, ER, MC, V.

D

✔★ **GARDUÑOS.** *(See Fiesta Hotel) 702/631-7000.* Hrs: 11 am-10 pm; Fri, Sat to 11 pm. Closed Thanksgiving, Dec 25. Mexican menu. Bar.

Semi-a la carte: lunch $5-$10, dinner $10-$15. Specializes in pollo, carnes, fajitas. Old Mexican village decor. Cr cds: A, C, D, DS, ER, MC, V.

D

★ ★ ★ **GATSBY'S.** *(See MGM Grand Hotel) 702/891-1111.* Hrs: 5:30-11 pm. Closed Tues. French menu. Bar. Complete meal: dinner $22.50-$37.95. Specialties: seared breast of duck, Colorado rack of lamb. Formal decor. Cr cds: A, C, D, DS, ER, MC, V.

D

★ **GIO'S CAFE MILANO.** *3900 Paradise Rd. 702/732-2777.* Hrs: 11 am-3 pm, 5-10 pm. Closed Sun. Res accepted. Italian menu. Wine. Semi-a la carte: lunch $5.95-$10.95, dinner $9.50-$27.50. Specializes in chicken, beef, pasta. Parking. Outdoor dining. Cr cds: A, C, D, DS, ER, JCB, MC, V.

D

★ ★ **GOLDEN STEER STEAK HOUSE.** *308 W Sahara Ave, west of the Strip. 702/384-4470.* Hrs: 4:30 pm-midnight. Closed Thanksgiving, Dec 25. Res accepted. Bar. Semi-a la carte: dinner $19.95-$36. Specializes in steak, seafood, Italian specialties. Valet parking. 1890s Western decor. Family-owned. Cr cds: A, C, D, DS, MC, V.

D

★ ★ **HAMADA OF JAPAN.** *598 E Flamingo Rd (89102), 5 mi SE on I-15, E Flamingo exit. 702/733-3005.* Hrs: 5 pm-midnight. Res accepted. Japanese menu. Bar. Semi-a la carte: dinner $6.95-$39. Specializes in traditional Japanese cuisine. Artwork, aquarium. Cr cds: A, C, D, DS, ER, MC, V.

D

★ ★ **HUGO'S CELLAR.** *(See Four Queens Hotel) 702/385-4011.* Hrs: 5:30-11 pm. Res accepted. Bar. Complete meals: dinner $24-$40. Specialties: Australian lobster tails, filet mignon. Intimate dining; original artwork. Jacket. Cr cds: A, C, D, DS, ER, MC, V.

D

✔★ ★ **LANDRY'S.** *2610 W Sahara (89102). 702/251-0101.* Hrs: 11 am-10 pm; Fri, Sat to 11 pm. Closed Dec 25. Res accepted. Bar. Semi-a la carte: lunch $5.95-$8.95, dinner $9.95-$16.95. Specializes in seafood, pasta, beef. Contemporary decor. Cr cds: A, D, DS, MC, V.

D

★ **LAREDO CANTINA.** *(See Texas Hotel) 702/631-1000.* Hrs: 5-11 pm. Closed Tues. Res accepted. Mexican menu. Bar. Semi-a la carte: dinner $8-$20. Specializes in fajitas, burritos, chimichangas. Mexican decor. Cr cds: A, C, D, DS, ER, MC, V.

★ ★ ★ **LAWRY'S THE PRIME RIB.** *4043 Howard Hughes Pkwy (89109), 5 mi SE on I-15 to E Flamingo Rd exit, E on Flamingo Rd, N on Paradise Rd to Howard Hughes Pkwy. 702/893-2223.* Hrs: 5-10 pm; Fri-Sun to 11 pm. Res accepted. Bar. Wine cellar. Semi-a la carte: $20-$40. Specializes in prime rib, lobster. Art Deco decor; red velvet booths, fireplace. Meats carved tableside. Cr cds: A, C, D, DS, ER, MC, V.

D

★ ★ ★ ★ **LE MONTRACHET.** *(See Hilton Hotel) 702/732-5111.* Here's a quiet place away from the chatter of the slot machine. Pastoral scenes of the French countryside on the walls and elaborate table settings mark the luxurious decor. French menu. Specialties: salmon medallions, sauteed lobster tails, roasted breast of Muscovy duck. Hrs: 6-10 pm. Closed Tues. Res accepted. Bar. Wine cellar. A la carte entrees: dinner $23.50-$35. Parking. Cr cds: A, C, D, DS, JCB, MC, V.

D

★ ★ ★ **LILY LANGTRY'S.** *(See Golden Nugget Hotel) 702/385-7111.* Hrs: 5-11 pm. Res accepted. Cantonese menu. Bar. Wine cellar. A la carte entrees: dinner $9-$30. Specialties: lobster Cantonese, Chinese pepper steak, moo goo gai pan. Own baking. Valet parking. Oriental decor. Cr cds: A, C, D, DS, JCB, MC, V.

D

✔★ ★ **MACARONI GRILL.** *2400 W Sahara (89102). 702/248-9500.* Hrs: 11 am-10 pm; Fri, Sat to 11 pm. Closed Thanksgiving, Dec 25. Italian menu. Bar. Semi-a la carte: lunch $7-$9, dinner $6.50-$17.95. Specializes in pizza, pasta, seafood. Italian country decor. Cr cds: A, C, D, DS, ER, JCB, MC, V.

D

★ ★ ★ **MANHATTAN OF LAS VEGAS.** *2600 E Flamingo Rd (89102), E of Las Vegas Blvd. 702/737-5000.* Hrs: 4 pm-1 am. Res accepted. Bar. Wine list. Complete meals: dinner $25-$50. Specializes in beef, veal, lamb. Entertainment. Marble entry leads to intimate dining area with French windows and crystal chandeliers. Cr cds: A, C, D, DS, ER, MC, V.

D

★ ★ **MARRAKECH.** *3900 Paradise Rd. 702/737-5611.* Hrs: 5:30-11 pm. Closed Dec 25. Res accepted. Moroccan menu. Bar. Complete six-course meal: dinner $23.95. Specialties: shish kebab, chicken in light lemon sauce, shrimp scampi. Belly dancers. French Moroccan decor. Cr cds: A, MC, V.

D

★ ★ **MAYFLOWER CUISINIER.** *4950 W Sahara Ave (89102), at Decatur. 702/870-8432.* Hrs: 11 am-3 pm, 5-10 pm; Sat 5-11 pm. Closed Sun; major hols. Res accepted. Chinese menu. Bar. Semi-a la carte: lunch $6.25-$9.95, dinner $8.95-$25.95. Specialties: roast duck, boneless chicken, Thai shrimp. Outdoor dining. Oil paintings. Totally nonsmoking. Cr cds: A, C, D, DS, MC, V.

D

★ ★ ★ **MONTE CARLO.** *(See Desert Inn Hotel) 702/733-4524.* Hrs: 6-11 pm. Closed Tues, Wed. Res accepted. French menu. Serv bar. Wine cellar. Semi-a la carte: dinner $25-$64. Specializes in boneless roast duckling, stuffed veal chop, sea bass Kiev. Own baking. Valet parking. Jacket. Cr cds: A, C, D, DS, JCB, MC, V.

D

★ ★ **MORTONI'S.** *(See Hard Rock Hotel) 702/693-5000.* Web www.hardrock.com. Hrs: 6-11 pm. Res accepted. Italian menu. Bar. Semi-a la carte: dinner $9-$59. Specializes in pasta, seafood, chicken. Outdoor dining. Italian decor. Cr cds: A, C, D, DS, ER, JCB, MC, V.

★ ★ **MOTOWN CAFE.** *(See New York-New York Hotel) 702/740-6969.* Hrs: 7 am-midnight; Sat to 2 am; Sun to 3 am. Bar. Semi-a la carte: bkfst $2.25-$10.25, lunch, dinner $8-$18. Bkfst buffet $7.50. Specializes in waffles, New York-style sandwiches. Entertainment. Outdoor dining. Features Motown music; bronze statues of musical celebrities. Cr cds: A, C, D, DS, ER, MC, V.

D

★ ★ ★ **NAPA.** *(See Rio Suite Hotel & Casino) 702/252-7777.* Hrs: 6-11 pm. Closed Mon, Tues. French menu. Bar. Wine cellar. Semi-a la carte: dinner $22-$34. Specialties: Altlantic salmon, roast rack of veal, duck pithivier. Modern sculpture in center of restaurant highlighted by skylight; oil paintings. Cr cds: A, C, D, DS, ER, JCB, MC, V.

★ ★ ★ **NICKY BLAIR'S.** *3925 Paradise Rd (89109). 702/792-9900.* Hrs: 4-11 pm. Closed Sun; Dec 25. Res required. Northern Italian menu. Bar. Semi-a la carte: dinner $14.25-$28. Specialties: petti di pollo, osso buco, prime filet mignon. Italian decor; extensive wall murals. Cr cds: A, C, D, DS, ER, MC, V.

★ ★ **NORTH BEACH CAFE.** *2605 S Decatur Blvd (89102), I-15 exit Sahara. 702/247-9530.* Hrs: 11:30 am-10 pm. Closed July 4, Dec 25. Res accepted. Italian menu. Bar. Semi-a la carte: lunch $6.25-$8.95, dinner $9.75-$15.75. Specialties: eggplant parmigiana, fettucine salmone, lasagna Bolognese. Pianist Wed-Sun evenings. Outdoor dining. Intimate atmosphere; northern Italian decor, original art. Cr cds: A, C, D, DS, ER, JCB, MC, V.

★★★ **PALACE COURT.** *(See Caesars Palace Hotel) 702/731-7110.* Hrs: 6-11 pm. Res accepted. French, continental menu. Extensive wine list. A la carte entrees: dinner $28-$65. Specializes in French gourmet dishes, lobster, veal. Own baking; own smoked salmon. Pianist 6-11 pm. Valet parking. Jacket. Cr cds: A, C, D, MC, V.

D

★★★ **PALM RESTAURANT.** *3500 Las Vegas Blvd S, Suite A7 (89109), in Forum Shops At Caesars, on the Strip. 702/732-7256.* Hrs: 11:30 am-11 pm. Res accepted. Bar. Wine list. A la carte entrees: lunch $10-$14, dinner $15-$60. Specializes in prime beef, seafood, chops. Valet parking. Counterpart of famous New York restaurant. Caricatures of celebrities on walls. Cr cds: A, C, D, MC, V.

D

★★ **PHILIPS SUPPER HOUSE.** *4545 W Sahara. 702/873-5222.* Hrs: 4:30-11 pm; early-bird dinner 4:30-6:30 pm. Res accepted. Continental menu. Bar. Complete meals: dinner $14.95-$28.95. Specializes in prime aged beef. Parking. Victorian decor. Cr cds: A, C, D, DS, ER, MC, V.

D

✓★★ **RICARDO'S.** *2380 E Tropicana (89119), east of the Strip. 702/798-4515.* Hrs: 11 am-11 pm; Sun noon-10 pm. Closed Jan 1, Thanksgiving, Dec 25. Res accepted. Mexican menu. Bar. Semi-a la carte: lunch, dinner $4.95-$12.95. Buffet lunch $6.75. Specialty: fajitas, chicken Ricardo's. Guitarist, vocalist daily exc Mon. Old Mexican decor. Cr cds: A, C, D, DS, MC, V.

D

★★★ **RUTH'S CHRIS STEAK HOUSE.** *3900 Paradise Rd, suite 121 (89109), east of the Strip. 702/791-7011.* Hrs: 11 am-10:30 pm; Fri, Sat from 4:30 pm. Closed Thanksgiving, Dec 25. Res accepted. Bar. Wine list. A la carte entrees: dinner $18.95-$33. Specializes in steak. 3 dining rms, contemporary decor. Cr cds: A, C, D, DS, ER, MC, V.

D

★★★ **SACRED SEA.** *(See Luxor Hotel) 702/262-4772.* Hrs: 5-11 pm. Res accepted. Bar. Semi-a la carte: dinner $19-$30. Specialties: Alaskan king crab, lobster tail. Own pasta. Valet parking. Egyptian decor, artwork. Cr cds: A, C, D, DS, ER, MC, V.

★ **SAM WOO BBQ.** *4215 Spring Mountain Rd (89102), in Chinatown Mall. 702/368-7628.* Hrs: 10-5 am. Closed Thanksgiving, Dec 25. Chinese menu. Semi-a la carte: lunch $5-$10, dinner $10-$24. Specializes in barbeque, fried rice, seafood. Chinese decor. Cr cds: A, C, D, DS, ER, JCB, MC, V.

D

★★★ **SEASONS.** *(See Bally's Hotel) 702/739-4651.* Hrs: 6-11 pm. Res required. Contemporary Amer menu. Bar. Wine cellar. Semi-a la carte: dinner $24-$50. Specializes in steak, salmon, chicken. Valet parking. Elegant dining; crystal chandeliers, elaborate wall murals. Cr cds: A, C, D, DS, ER, MC, V.

★★ **SFUZZI.** *3200 Las Vegas Blvd S (89109), 5 mi S on I-15 to Spring Mountain Rd exit, W to Las Vegas Blvd. 702/699-5777.* Hrs: 11:30 am-11 pm; Sun from 11 am. Res accepted. Northern Italian menu. Bar. Semi-a la carte: lunch $9-$12, dinner $12-$30. Specialties: skillet-roasted sea bass, osso bucco, grilled Atlantic salmon. Outdoor dining. Exterior features Italian village facade. Cr cds: A, C, D, DS, ER, MC, V.

D

✓★ **SHALIMAR.** *3900 Paradise Rd, in shopping mall, east of the Strip. 702/796-0302.* Hrs: 11:30 am-2 pm, 5:30-10 pm; Sat, Sun from 5:30 pm. Res accepted. Northern Indian menu. Serv bar. Buffet: lunch $6.95. A la carte entrees: dinner $10.50-$15.95. Specialties: chicken tandoori, lamb Shalimar, lamb & seafood curries. Contemporary decor. Cr cds: A, C, D, DS, MC, V.

D

✓★★ **SIR GALLAHAD'S.** *(See Excalibur Hotel) 702/597-7700.* Hrs: 5-10 pm; Fri-Sat to 11 pm. Res accepted. English menu. Bar. Complete meal: dinner $11.95-$17.95. Specialty: prime rib. Medieval decor with suits of armor and cast iron chandeliers. Cr cds: A, C, D, DS, ER, MC, V.

D

★★★ **SPAGO.** *3500 Las Vegas Blvd S (89109), in Forum Shops at Caesars Palace Hotel. 702/369-6300.* Hrs: 11-12:30 am. Res accepted. Varied menu. Bar. Wine cellar. A la carte entrees: lunch $9.50-$18. Complete meals: dinner $17-$30. Specialties: pizza, chicken salad. Jazz pianist Sun. Parking. Modern artwork. Art deco, wrought iron design. Counterpart of famous restaurant in West Hollywood. Cr cds: A, C, D, DS, ER, MC, V.

D

✓★ **STAGE DELI.** *3500 Las Vegas Blvd S (89109), in Forum Shops At Caesars Palace, on the Strip. 702/893-4045.* Hrs: 7:30 am-11 pm. Res accepted. Wine, beer. Semi-a la carte: bkfst $3.75-$7.95, lunch $4.75-$12.95, dinner $9.95-$13.95. Specializes in deli fare. New York deli atmosphere; posters of Broadway shows. Cr cds: A, C, D, DS, ER, MC, V.

D

★★ **THE STEAK HOUSE.** *(See Circus-Circus Hotel & Casino) 702/734-0410.* Hrs: 5-11 pm; Sun brunch 10 am-2 pm. Res accepted. Bar. Semi-a la carte: dinner $15.95-$22.95. Sun brunch $19.95. Specializes in top sirloin, crab legs, halibut. Western decor. Cr cds: A, C, D, DS, ER, JCB, MC, V.

★★★ **STEFANO'S.** *(See Golden Nugget Hotel) 702/385-7111.* Hrs: 6-11 pm; wkends from 5 pm. Italian menu. Bar. Wine cellar. A la carte entrees: dinner $9.95-$27.95. Specializes in northern Italian food. Parking. Singing waiters. Murals of Italy. Cr cds: A, C, D, DS, JCB, MC, V.

D

★★★ **SUZETTE'S.** *(See Santa Fe Hotel & Casino) 702/658-4900.* Hrs: 5-10 pm. Res accepted. French menu. Bar. Wine list. Semi-a la carte: dinner $24-$35. Specialties: chicken breast stuffed with wild mushrooms, medellions of lobster. French decor. Jacket. Totally nonsmoking. Cr cds: A, C, D, DS, MC, V.

D

★★★ **TILLERMAN.** *2245 E Flamingo, east of the Strip. 702/731-4036.* Hrs: 5-11 pm. Closed major hols. Wine list. Semi-a la carte: dinner $14.95-$36.95. Specializes in fresh fish, steak, pasta. Atrium, garden, loft dining areas. Cr cds: A, C, D, DS, MC, V.

D

★★★ **TOP OF THE WORLD.** *(See Stratosphere Tower Hotel) 702/380-7711.* Hrs: 5-11 pm; Sat, Sun to midnight. Res required. Bar. Extensive wine list. Semi-a la carte: dinner $21-$29. Specializes in steak, salmon, lobster. Rotating restaurant from 1,000-ft elevation. Totally nonsmoking. Cr cds: A, C, D, DS, ER, JCB, MC, V.

D

★ **VINEYARD.** *3630 Maryland Pkwy, east of the Strip. 702/731-1606.* Hrs: 11 am-10 pm; Fri, Sat to 11 pm. Closed major hols. Italian, Amer menu. Serv bar. Semi-a la carte: lunch $6.95-$13.95, dinner $8.95-$16.95. Complete meals: dinner for two, $27. Child's meals. Specialties: veal parmigiana, breast of chicken. Salad bar. Italian marketplace decor. Cr cds: A, C, D, MC, V.

SC

★ **VIVA MERCADO'S.** *6182 W Flamingo (89103), 2 mi W of I-15, in shopping center. 702/871-8826.* Hrs: 11 am-10 pm; Fri, Sat to 11 pm. Closed Sun; Thanksgiving, Dec 25. Res accepted (dinner). Mexican menu. Bar. Semi-a la carte: lunch $5.25-$5.75, dinner $11.95-$16.95.

Specialties: orange roughy, camerones rancheros, mariscos vallarta. Mexican decor. Cr cds: A, C, D, DS, MC, V.

D

★ ★ ★ **WOLFGANG PUCK'S CAFE.** *(See MGM Grand Hotel) 702/895-9653.* Hrs: 8 am-11 pm; Fri, Sat to midnight; Sun from 10 am. Bar. A la carte entrees: breakfast, lunch, dinner $4.95-$14.95. Specialties: wood-burning oven pizza, rotisserie chicken. Ultra modern decor. Cr cds: A, C, D, MC, V.

D

★ **XINH-XINH.** *220 W Sahara Ave (89102), W of the Strip. 702/471-1572.* Hrs: 11 am-11 pm. Res accepted. Vietnamese menu. Wine, beer. Semi-a la carte: lunch $5.95-$7.95, dinner $8.95-$16.95. Specializes in Vietnamese cuisine. Cr cds: A, MC, V.

D SC

★ **YOLIE'S CHURRASCARIA.** *3900 Paradise Road, east of the Strip. 702/794-0700.* Hrs: 11 am-11 pm; Sat from 5 pm. Res required. Brazilian menu. Bar. Semi-a la carte: lunch $6.95-$12.95, dinner $14.95-$22.95. Child's meals. Specializes in steak, lamb. Outdoor dining. Cr cds: A, C, D, DS, MC, V.

D

✓★ ★ ★ **Z'TEJAS GRILL.** *3824 Paradise Rd (89109). 702/732-1660.* Hrs: 11 am-11 pm. Closed Thanksgiving, Dec 25. Res accepted. Southwestern menu. Bar. Semi-a la carte: lunch $7.50-$16, dinner $10-$14.95. Specialties: crab-stuffed shrimp, pork roast vera cruz. Southwestern decor. Totally nonsmoking. Cr cds: A, C, D, DS, ER, MC, V.

D

Unrated Dining Spots

HARD ROCK CAFE. *(See Hard Rock Hotel) 702/733-8400.* Hrs: 11 am-11:30 pm. Bar. Semi-a la carte: lunch, dinner $5.50-$13.95. Specializes in chicken, ribs. Valet parking. Rock & Roll memorabilia. Cr cds: A, D, MC, V.

D

PLANET HOLLYWOOD. *3500 Las Vegas Blvd (89109). 702/791-7827.* Hrs: 11 am-midnight; Fri, Sat to 1 am. Bar. A la carte entrees: lunch, dinner $7.95-$17.95. Specializes in California cuisine. Hollywood artifacts and television memorabilia. Cr cds: A, C, D, DS, ER, MC, V.

D

Los Angeles

Founded: 1781
Pop: 3,485,398
Elev: 330 feet
Time zone: Pacific
Area code: 213 (L.A.); 818 (San Fernando Valley); 310 (San Pedro, Santa Monica); 569 (Long Beach)
Web: www.latimes.com/HOME/DESTLA/

Imagine a sprawling formation made up of a thousand pieces from a thousand different jigsaw puzzles, illuminate it with klieg lights and flashing neon signs, garnish it with rhinestones, oranges and oil wells—and you have Los Angeles.

The little Spanish pueblo, begun as "the town of Our Lady the Queen of the Angels of Porciuncula," slumbered until 1846. In the treaty ending the Mexican War, the United States acquired California, and Los Angeles became a vigorous frontier community. Gold was discovered in 1848 in the foothills of the Sierra Nevada, and by 1849, the gold rush was on. For a time lawlessness became so prevalent that the city was referred to as Los Diablos—"the devils." In 1876, a rail line was completed from San Francisco to Los Angeles, and by 1885 the Santa Fe Railroad arrived from Chicago. With the introduction of the railroad, a tidal wave of immigration hit the city. A land boom developed by 1890, and the population reached 50,000. In the half century between 1890 and 1940, Los Angeles grew from 50,395 to 1,504,277—a gain of more than 2,500 percent.

Today, occupying a land area of 464 square miles, Los Angeles has spilled over from the plain into the canyons and foothills. It has spread out and around the surrounding independent cities and towns. Beyond its municipal lines, Los Angeles is hemmed in by almost 100 communities, frequently termed "suburbs in search of a city."

Business

Los Angeles is one of the nation's largest manufacturing and retail trade centers, as well as one of the top oil refining centers. Finance is big business in Los Angeles, and the city is the West Coast's leading financial center. Los Angeles is home to a large number of savings and loan associations and the headquarters for several major banks. Many insurance companies have their headquarters here as well.

A wide variety of products are manufactured here. Los Angeles is a leader in the production of machinery and equipment, electrical machinery, aerospace equipment, instruments and refined petroleum products. Other products manufactured are steel, iron, pottery, glassware, chemicals and trailers. More than 2,000 of the county's 20,000 factories are involved in industry.

Los Angeles has been called the filmmaking capital of the world. Many major movie studios are located in the area, as well as studios for the major television networks.

Convention Facilities

Set within a spacious, beautifully landscaped and lighted plaza, the Los Angeles Convention Center is one of the finest facilities in the world and continues to be expanded.

At plaza level, the main exhibition hall is vast. Within its immense 210,685-square-foot area is one of the largest column-free spaces to be found in any convention center. This area, 557 by 342 feet, can hold three football fields side by side. There are areas of the hall that can accommodate displays up to 25 feet in height. The exhibition hall's capacity is 17,000 persons for a meeting, 13,000 for a banquet or 1,150 exhibit booths. In addition, the room can be divided into two or three sections by the use of sliding, soundproof partitions. The north hall provides an additional 103,500 square feet of exhibition space.

A secondary, column-free hall is also located on the main floor. This room is large enough to accommodate 3,000 people for meetings, 2,000 for banquets or 125 exhibit booths.

The main floor also holds a 124-seat cocktail lounge, 220-seat restaurant, 450-seat cafeteria, four walk-in snack bars and two stand-up snack bars.

The mezzanine has 19 rooms of various sizes that are ideal for meetings, dinners, conferences or small exhibits. The smallest room can seat 12 people for a meeting or 20 for a meal, while the largest can seat 1,600 for a meeting and 800 for a meal.

The center is on a 31-acre site near the downtown hub of the city. Ten access ramps, adjacent to the building, connect with all six major freeways. There is parking for 4,000 cars.

There are more than 93,000 hotel rooms in the Greater Los Angeles area, 4,700 located downtown.

Sports & Recreation

For those interested in major-league sports, Los Angeles is home to the Dodgers baseball team, the Lakers and Clippers basketball teams and Kings hockey team. The Anaheim Angels baseball team and the Mighty Ducks hockey team play in nearby Anaheim.

Because of the moderate year-round temperatures, outdoor recreation is always in vogue. Parks are abundant in the Los Angeles metropolitan area. Thousands of acres of land are set aside for public enjoyment, with plenty of picnic areas, tennis courts, bridle paths, golf courses, swimming pools, nature trails, ball fields and playgrounds.

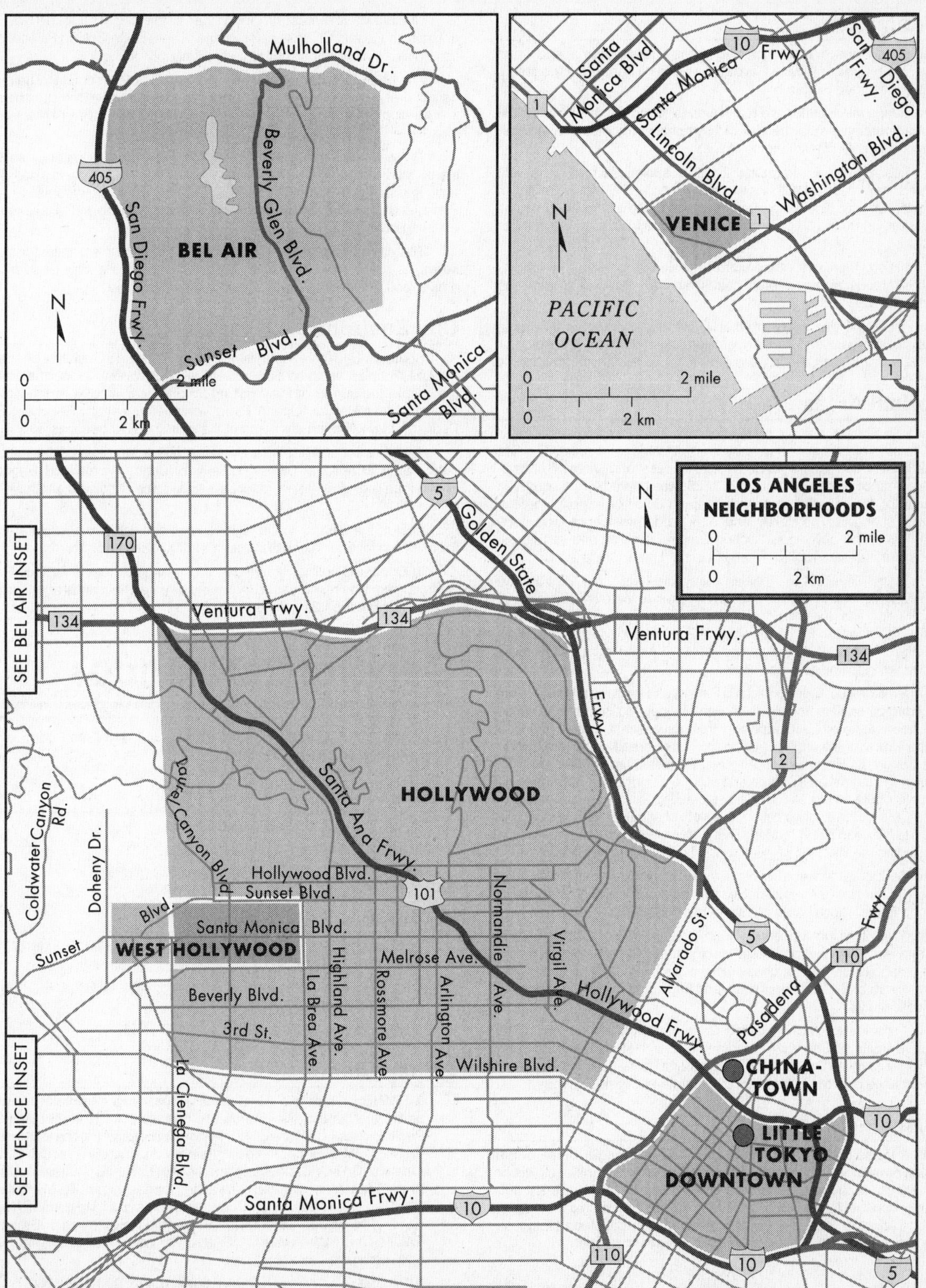

Mulholland Dr.
405
San Diego Frwy.
BEL AIR
Beverly Glen Blvd.
Sunset Blvd.
Santa Monica Blvd.
N
0 2 mile
0 2 km
10
Santa Monica Frwy.
San Diego Frwy.
405
1
Santa Monica Blvd
Lincoln Blvd.
Washington Blvd.
VENICE
PACIFIC OCEAN
0 2 mile
0 2 km
LOS ANGELES NEIGHBORHOODS
0 2 mile
0 2 km
SEE BEL AIR INSET
SEE VENICE INSET
5
Golden State
170
134
Ventura Frwy.
Frwy.
2
HOLLYWOOD
Santa Ana Frwy.
Laurel Canyon Blvd.
Coldwater Canyon Rd.
Doheny Dr.
Hollywood Blvd.
Sunset Blvd.
101
Santa Monica Blvd.
WEST HOLLYWOOD
Sunset Blvd.
Melrose Ave.
Beverly Blvd.
3rd St.
La Brea Ave.
Highland Ave.
Rossmore Ave.
Arlington Ave.
Normandie Ave.
Virgil Ave.
Wilshire Blvd.
Hollywood Frwy.
Alvarado St.
Pasadena Frwy.
110
CHINA-TOWN
LITTLE TOKYO
DOWNTOWN
La Cienega Blvd.
Santa Monica Frwy.
10
110

Entertainment

Performing arts events, including opera, ballet, drama and band concerts, are offered in Griffith Park at the Greek Theatre each season, from mid-June to late September.

Also during the summer, the Hollywood Bowl, one of the world's most beautiful amphitheaters, is the site of "Symphony Under the Stars," an eight-week schedule of outstanding music.

The Los Angeles Philharmonic thrills its audiences each year with superb performances and with visiting musicians at the Music Center of Los Angeles County. The Music Center is also home to the Los Angeles Music Center Opera, which presents performances from early September to June.

In addition, there are numerous professional, repertory, neighborhood and campus theatrical productions, and all forms of drama and comedy are available.

Nightlife in the city ranges from a simple dinner or dinner theater to the most extravagant and lavish nightclub entertainment. Consult *Los Angeles Magazine*, available at newsstands, for up-to-date information.

Historical Areas

Heritage Square, a major restoration site in the Los Angeles area, is a park-like strip of land surrounded by many Victorian buildings. The first two buildings in the square were the Hale house and Valley Knudsen Garden-residence. Hale house, built in 1885, was moved to the square in 1970. Little of the beautiful ornamentation and detail of the original residence was changed. The Valley Knudsen Garden-residence was dedicated in 1971. The building is Second Empire in style, one of the last examples of a mansard-roofed house left in the Los Angeles area.

One of the oldest of Los Angeles' many missions is the Mission San Gabriel Arcángel, built in 1771. Although not open to the public because of earthquake damage, the mission possesses an exceptional collection of relics. The Mission San Fernando Rey de España, founded in 1797, has been restored and contains collections of Native American artifacts, furniture, woodcarvings and gold-leaf altars.

El Pueblo de Los Angeles Historic Park marks the area where the city was founded by settlers from Mission San Gabriel. Much of the area has already been restored, but additional restorations are underway. The Plaza, the center of the original pueblo, has been preserved. Here, too, is Nuestra Señora La Reina de Los Angeles, the first church of Los Angeles, from which the city takes its name and still the center of an active parish. The church contains old statuary and stained-glass windows. Also preserved is Olvera Street, once called "the walk of angels," an authentic and picturesque Mexican street market. There are several annual celebrations here, including the Blessing of Animals held the Saturday before Easter.

The Southwest Museum exhibits early handicrafts and displays on the history of the Native American. Near the museum is Casa de Adobe, a replica of a typical ranch home of 19th-century Spanish California.

The Natural History Museum of Los Angeles County exhibits natural history and early regional and state history; fossil remains of prehistoric animals; ethnological and archeological collections; habitat groups of North American and African mammals and birds; and mineral and marine biology collections.

The Lummis Home and Garden State Historical Monument is the picturesque home of Charles F. Lummis, author, historian, librarian and archaeologist. Just east of the city, in Pasadena, is the Gamble House, a California bungalow-style house built by Henry and Charles Greene.

Sightseeing

Los Angeles is the city of movie and television magic. Some of the most popular movies and television shows were filmed on the back lots or in the confines of the studios located here. Warner Bros, Universal and Paramount conduct tours through their lots, studios and production areas. One of Los Angeles' most famous sites is the forecourt of Mann's Chinese Theatre, where the footprints of movie stars are set in cement.

Chinatown is a must for any visitor to this city. The tourist will find unusual shops and Chinese cafes on the "Street of the Golden Palace" and can enjoy an excellent dinner and a walking tour.

The partially excavated Rancho La Brea Tar Pits contain large numbers of prehistoric remains. Fossils and life-size statues of the giant beasts are on display at the George C. Page Museum of La Brea Discoveries Museum.

There is nothing that cannot be bought or rented in Los Angeles. For specialized shopping there is Little Santa Monica, which is lined with antiques stores, Robertson Boulevard for furniture showrooms, Sunset Plaza, and of course Rodeo Drive, synonymous with opulence, luxury and extravagance.

The city's geographic scope makes a car almost essential for sightseeing in areas other than the downtown section. Parking facilities are ample, and the freeways make travel relatively simple.

City Environs

Southern California's coastline is one long chain of beautiful beaches. No Los Angeles vacation is complete without walking along the shore, romping in the surf or at least gazing from the car window at the ocean. Malibu, Santa Monica, Ocean Park, Venice, Manhattan, Redondo, San Pedro and Long Beach are some of the more popular beaches.

Inland, west of the Sierra Nevadas, lies a montage of the nation's most beautiful national parks—Yosemite, Kings Canyon and Sequoia. Within them are clear lakes, giant sequoias, fields of flowers and towering cliffs.

East of the Sierras, in the high country, one can camp, explore ghost towns or fish for trout in one of the area's 2,000 lakes and streams.

In Coachella Valley, southeast of Los Angeles, is the famous Palm Springs area. The resort has a dry, sunny climate, thousands of swimming pools and more than 20 golf courses.

General References

Area code: 213 (LA); 818 (San Fernando Valley); 310 (San Pedro, Santa Monica); 569 (Long Beach)

Phone Numbers

POLICE, FIRE & AMBULANCE: 911

POISON CONTROL CENTER: 213/222-3212

TIME: 213/853-1212 **WEATHER:** 213/554-1212

Information Sources

Los Angeles Convention and Visitors Bureau, 633 W Fifth St, Ste 6000, 90071; 213/624-7300.

Los Angeles Chamber of Commerce, 404 S Bixel St, 90017; 213/629-0602.

City Recreation & Parks Dept, 213/485-5555.

Transportation

AIRLINES: Aeroflot; Aerolineas Argentinas; Aeromexico; Aeroperu; Air Canada; Air France; Air Jamaica; Air New Zealand; Air Pacific; Alaska; Alitalia; All Nippon Airways; American; America West; AOM French Airlines; Asiana; Avianca; Aviateca; British Airways; CAAC; Canadian; Carnival Air; China; Continental; Delta; El Al; EVA AIR; Garuda; Hawaiian; Iberia; Japan; KLM; Korean; LACSA; Lan Chile; LTU; Lufthansa; Malaysia; Mexicana; Northwest; Philippine; QANTAS; Singapore; Southwest; Swissair; TACA; Thai; TWA; United; USAir; UTA; Varig; and other commuter and regional airlines.

AIRPORT: Los Angeles International (LAX), 310/646-5252.

CAR RENTAL AGENCIES: (See IMPORTANT TOLL-FREE NUMBERS) Avis 310/646-5600; Budget 310/645-4500; Dollar 310/645-9333; Hertz 310/646-4861; National 310/670-4950.

PUBLIC TRANSPORTATION: Metropolitan Transit Authority 213/626-4455.

RAILROAD PASSENGER SERVICE: Amtrak 800/872-7245.

Newspaper

Los Angeles Times.

Convention Facility

Los Angeles Convention Center, 1201 S Figueroa St, 213/741-1151.

Sports & Recreation

Major Sports Facilities

Anaheim Stadium, 2000 Gene Autry Way, Anaheim (Angels, baseball, 714/937-7200).

Arrowhead Pond, 2695 E Katella Blvd, Anaheim (Mighty Ducks, hockey, 714/704-5084).

Dodgers Stadium, 1000 Elysian Park Ave, 213/224-1491 (Dodgers, baseball, 213/224-1500).

The Great Western Forum, 3900 W Manchester Blvd, Inglewood, 310/673-1300 (Kings, hockey, 310/419-3160; Lakers, basketball, 310/419-3100).

Los Angeles Memorial Coliseum & Sports Arena, Exposition Park, 3939 S Figueroa St, 213/747-7111 (Clippers, basketball, 213/745-0400; also collegiate football).

Racetracks

Hollywood Park, Century Blvd & Prairie Ave, Inglewood, 310/419-1500.

Los Alamitos Race Course, 4961 Katella Ave, Los Alamitos, 714/236-4400 or 714/995-1234.

Santa Anita Park, 285 W Huntington Dr, Arcadia, 818/574-7223.

Cultural Facilities

Theaters

Ahmanson Theatre, 135 N Grand Ave, 213/972-7211.

Dorothy Chandler Pavilion, 135 N Grand Ave, 213/972-7211.

Greek Theatre, 2700 N Vermont, Griffith Park, 213/665-5857.

Mark Taper Forum, 135 N Grand Ave, 213/972-7211.

Shubert Theatre, 2020 Avenue of the Stars, 310/201-1500.

Universal Amphitheatre, 100 Universal City Plaza, Universal City, 818/777-3931.

Concert Halls

Hollywood Bowl, 2301 N Highland Ave, Hollywood, 213/850-2000.

Music Center of Los Angeles County, 135 N Grand Ave, at 1st St, 213/972-7211.

Museums

Cabrillo Marine Aquarium, 3720 Stephen White Dr, San Pedro, 310/548-7562.

California Museum of Science and Industry, 700 State Dr, Exposition Park, 213/744-7400.

George C. Page Museum of La Brea Discoveries, 5801 Wilshire Blvd, Hancock Park, 213/857-6311 or 213/936-2230.

Griffith Observatory and Planetarium, Griffith Park, 2800 E Observatory Rd, 818/901-9405 (Laserium) or 213/664-1191 (planetarium).

Hollywood Wax Museum, 6767 Hollywood Blvd, Hollywood, 213/462-8860.

Los Angeles Children's Museum, 310 N Main St, 213/687-8800.

Movieland Wax Museum, 7711 Beach Blvd, Buena Park, 714/522-1155.

Museum of Tolerance, 9786 W Pico Blvd, 310/553-8403.

Natural History Museum of Los Angeles County, 900 Exposition Blvd, Exposition Park, 213/744-3414 or 213/763-3466.

Southwest Museum, 234 Museum Dr, at Marmion Way, 213/221-2163.

Wells Fargo History Museum, 333 S Grand Ave, Plaza Level, 213/253-7166.

Art Museums & Galleries

Armand Hammer Museum of Art and Cultural Center, 10889 Wilshire Blvd, 310/443-7000.

Huntington Library, Art Collection and Botanical Gardens, 1151 Oxford Rd, San Marino, 818/405-2100.

Junior Arts Center, 4814 Hollywood Blvd, in Barnsdall Art Park, 213/485-4474.

Los Angeles County Museum of Art, 5905 Wilshire Blvd, 213/857-6000.

Museum of Contemporary Art (MOCA), 250 S Grand Ave, 213/621-2766.

Norton Simon Museum of Art, 411 W Colorado Blvd, Pasadena, 818/449-6840.

The Getty Center, 1200 Getty Center Dr, 310/440-7300.

Points of Interest

Historical

Avila Adobe, El Pueblo de Los Angeles Historic Park, 213/628-1274.

El Pueblo de Los Angeles Historic Park, 622 N Main, 213/628-1274.

Lummis Home and Garden State Historical Monument, 200 E Ave 43, 213/222-0546.

Mission San Fernando Rey de España, 15151 San Fernando Mission Blvd, San Fernando, 818/361-0186.

Nuestra Señora La Reina de Los Angeles, El Pueblo de Los Angeles Historic Park.

Old Plaza Firehouse, El Pueblo de Los Angeles Historic Park, 213/628-1274.

Olvera Street, El Pueblo de Los Angeles Historic Park, 213/628-1274.

Travel Town, 5200 Zoo Dr, Griffith Park, 213/662-5874.

Will Rogers State Historic Park, 14253 Sunset Blvd, Pacific Palisades, 310/454-8212.

Other Attractions

ARCO Plaza, 505 S Flower St, 213/625-2132.

Catalina Island, approx 22 mi offshore of San Pedro, 310/510-1520.

CBS Television City, 7800 Beverly Blvd, at Fairfax Ave, 213/852-2624.

Chinatown, N Broadway near College St.

City Hall, 200 N Spring St, 213/485-2121.

Crystal Cathedral, 12141 Lewis St, Garden Grove, 714/971-4013.

Descanso Gardens, 1418 Descanso Dr, La Cañada, Flintridge, 818/952-4400.

Disneyland, 26 mi S on Harbor Blvd, off Santa Ana Frwy, Anaheim, 714/999-4565.

Elysian Park, near intersection of Pasadena & Golden State Frwys.

Exposition Park, Figueroa St & Exposition Blvd.

Fisherman's Village, 13755 Fiji Way, Marina del Rey, 310/823-5411.

Griffith Park, N end of Vermont Ave, bordered by Ventura Frwy on N, Golden State Frwy on E, Los Feliz Blvd entrances on S, 213/665-5188.

Hall of Justice, 211 W Temple St.

Knott's Berry Farm, 8039 Beach Blvd, Buena Park, 714/220-5200.

Little Tokyo, 1st St between Main & San Pedro Sts.

Los Angeles Mall, Spring St, across from city hall.

Los Angeles State and County Arboretum, 301 N Baldwin Ave, Arcadia, 818/821-3222.

Los Angeles Zoo, 5333 Zoo Dr, Griffith Park, 213/666-4090.

Mann's Chinese Theatre, 6925 Hollywood Blvd, Hollywood, 213/464-8111.

NBC Studios, 3000 W Alameda Ave, Burbank, 818/840-3537.

Paramount Film and Television Studios, 5555 Melrose Ave, 213/956-1777.

San Antonio Winery, 737 Lamar St, 213/223-1401.

Six Flags Magic Mountain, 26101 Magic Mt Pkwy, Valencia, 805/255-4111.

South Coast Botanic Garden, 26300 Crenshaw Blvd, Palos Verdes Peninsula, 310/544-6815.

Sunset Strip, Sunset Blvd.

UCLA Botanical Garden, Hilgard & Le Conte Aves, 310/825-3620.

Universal Studios Hollywood, 100 Universal City Plaza, Universal City, 818/508-9600.

Watts Towers, 1727 E 107th St, Watts, 213/847-4646.

World Trade Center, 350 S Figueroa St, 213/489-3337.

Sightseeing Tour

Oskar J's, 4334 Woodman Ave, Sherman Oaks 91423; 818/501-2217.

Annual Events

Tournament of Roses Parade and Rose Bowl Game, Pasadena. Jan 1.

Chinese New Year. Feb.

Bunka Sai Japanese Cultural Festival, Torrance Cultural Arts Center. Mid-Apr.

Cinco de Mayo Celebration, El Pueblo de Los Angeles Historic Park. May 5.

Lotus Festival, Echo Park Lake. Mid-July.

Nisei Week, Little Toyko. Mid-Aug.

Los Angeles County Fair, Los Angeles County Fairgrounds, Pomona. Early-late Sept.

City Neighborhoods

Many of the restaurants, unrated dining establishments and some lodgings listed under Los Angeles include neighborhoods as well as exact street addresses. Geographic descriptions of these areas are given, followed by a table of restaurants arranged by neighborhood.

Bel Air: West of Downtown; south of Mulholland Dr, west of Beverly Hills, north of the University of California Los Angeles (UCLA) campus and east of the San Diego Frwy (I-405).

Chinatown: Directly north of Downtown; south of Bernard St, west of N Broadway, north of College St and east of Hill St.

Downtown: South of the Hollywood Frwy (US 101), west of Golden State Frwy (I-5), north of Santa Monica Frwy (I-10) and east of the Pasadena Frwy (CA 110). **North of Downtown:** North of US 101. **South of Downtown:** South of I-10. **West of Downtown:** West of CA 110.

Hollywood: Area northwest of Downtown; south of Mulholland Dr, Universal City and the Ventura Frwy (CA 134), west of the Golden State Frwy (I-5) and Alvarado St (CA 2), north of Wilshire Blvd and east of La Cienega Blvd.

Little Tokyo: Area of Downtown south of 1st St, west of Central Ave, north of 3rd St and east of San Pedro St.

Venice: Oceanfront area south of Santa Monica, west of Lincoln Blvd (CA 1) and north of Washington St.

West Hollywood: Area south and north of Santa Monica Blvd, between Doheny Dr on the west and La Brea Ave on the east.

Lodgings and Food

LOS ANGELES RESTAURANTS BY NEIGHBORHOOD AREAS
(For full description, see alphabetical listings under Restaurants)

BEL AIR
Bel-Air Dining Room (Hotel Bel-Air). 701 Stone Canyon Rd

CHINATOWN
Little Joe's. 900 N Broadway

DOWNTOWN
Bernard's (Regal Biltmore Hotel). 506 S Grand Ave
Cafe Pinot. 700 W 5th St
Checkers (Wyndham Checkers Hotel Los Angeles). 535 S Grand Ave
Ciao Trattoria. 815 W Seventh St
Patinette At Moca. 250 S Grand Ave
Phillipe The Original. 1001 N Alameda St
Seoul Jung (Omni Hotel). 930 Wilshire Blvd
The Tower. 1150 S Olive St

NORTH OF DOWNTOWN
La Golondrina. W-17 Olvera St
Pinot Hollywood. 1448 N Gower St
Taix. 1911 Sunset Blvd
Tam-O-Shanter Inn. 2980 Los Feliz Blvd

WEST OF DOWNTOWN
Al Amir. 5750 Wilshire Blvd
Anna's. 10929 W Pico Blvd
Arnie Morton's of Chicago. 435 S La Cienega Blvd
Campanile. 624 S La Brea Ave
Cassell's. 3266 W 6th St
Cava (Beverly Plaza Hotel). 8384 W Third St
El Cholo. 1121 W Western Ave
Gardens (Four Seasons Hotel). 300 S Doheny Dr
Hard Rock Cafe. 8600 Beverly Blvd
La Cachette. 10506 Little Santa Monica Blvd
Locanda Veneta. 8638 W Third St
Madeo. 8897 Beverly Blvd
Pangaea. (Hotel Nikko At Beverly Hills). 465 S La Cienega Blvd
Park Grill (Park Hyatt Los Angeles Hotel). 2151 Avenue of the Stars
Primi. 10543 W Pico Blvd
Sisley Italian Kitchen. 10800 W Pico Blvd

WEST HOLLYWOOD
Diaghilev (Wyndham Bel Age). 1020 N San Vicente Blvd
Four Oaks. 2181 N Beverly Glen

Note: When a listing is located in a town that does not have its own city heading, it will appear under the city nearest to its location. In these cases, the address and town appear in parenthesis immediately following the name of the establishment.

Motel

★★ **RESIDENCE INN BY MARRIOTT.** *(1700 N Sepulveda Blvd, Manhattan Beach 90266) CA 405 to Rosecrans exit. 310/546-7627; FAX 310/545-1327.* 176 kit. suites, 2 story. S $99-$178; D $150-$198; each addl $10; under 12 free; wkly, monthly rates. Crib free. Pet accepted, some restrictions. TV; cable (premium). Heated pool; whirlpool. Complimentary continental bkfst. Restaurant nearby. Ck-out noon. Meeting rm. Business servs avail. In-rm modem link. Valet serv. Free airport transportation. Microwaves. Balconies. Cr cds: A, C, D, DS, JCB, MC, V.

Motor Hotels

★★ **COURTYARD BY MARRIOTT.** *10320 W Olympic Blvd (90064), Century City, I-405 exit Santa Monica Blvd E. 310/556-2777; FAX 310/203-0563.* Web www.courtyard.com. 134 rms, 4 story. S, D $129-$139; each addl $10; suites $139-$159; wkend rates. TV; cable (premium). Coffee in rms. Restaurant 6-10:30 am. Bar 4:30 pm-midnight. Ck-out noon. Guest lndry. Meeting rm. Business servs avail. In-rm modem link. Bellhops. Valet serv. Free covered parking. Exercise equipt; weights, bicycles, whirlpool. Health club privileges. Minibars; microwaves avail. Balconies. Cr cds: A, C, D, DS, JCB, MC, V.

D SC

✔★★ **HOLIDAY INN DOWNTOWN.** *750 Garland Ave (90017), downtown. 213/628-5242; FAX 213/628-1201.* 205 rms, 6 story. S, D $89-$129; under 18 free. Crib free. TV; cable (premium), VCR avail. Pool. Complimenatry coffee in rms. Restaurant 6 am-2 pm, 5-10 pm. Rm serv. Bar 4:30-midnight. Ck-out noon. Coin lndry. Meeting rms. Business servs avail. In-rm modem link. Gift shop. Bellhops. Valet serv. Airport transportation. Health club privileges. Cr cds: A, C, D, DS, JCB, MC, V.

D SC

✔★ **HOLIDAY INN EXPRESS.** *10330 W Olympic Blvd (90064). 310/553-1000; FAX 310/277-1633.* 47 rms, 3 with shower only, 4 story, 14 suites. S $89; D $99; suites $109; under 18 free. Crib free. Valet parking $7.50, in/out $7.50. TV; cable (premium), VCR (movies). Complimentary continental bkfst. Complimentary coffee in rms. Restaurant nearby. Ck-out noon. Meeting rms. Bellhops. Refrigerators, microwaves. Cr cds: A, C, D, DS, JCB, MC, V.

D SC

Hotels

★★★ **BEVERLY PLAZA.** *8384 W 3rd St (90048), west of downtown. 213/658-6600; FAX 213/653-3464; res: 800/624-6835 (exc CA).* 98 rms, 5 story. S, D $169-$218; under 12 free. TV; cable (premium), VCR avail. Valet parking $11. Heated pool; whirlpool, poolside serv. Restaurant (see CAVA). Rm serv 24 hrs. Bar 11 am-midnight. Ck-out noon. Exercise equipt; weights, bicycles, sauna. Cr cds: A, C, D, MC, V.

D SC

★★ **CHATEAU MARMONT.** *8221 Sunset Blvd (90046), in West Hollywood. 213/656-1010; FAX 213/655-5311.* E-mail chateaula@aol.com. 63 rms, 7 story, 54 kits. S, D $190; suites $240-$1,200; cottages, kits. $260; villas $600; monthly rates. Pet accepted. TV; cable (premium), VCR. Heated pool; poolside serv. Restaurant 6-2 am. Rm serv 24 hrs. Ck-out noon. Meeting rm. Business servs avail. In-rm modem link. Garage, valet parking. Exercise equipt; weight machines, treadmill. Refrigerators, minibars. Private patios, balconies. Neo-Gothic chateau-style building; old Hollywood landmark. Cr cds: A, C, D, MC, V.

D

★★★★ **FOUR SEASONS.** *300 S Doheny Dr (90048), west of downtown. 310/273-2222; FAX 310/859-3824.* This modern high-rise close to downtown has beautifully landscaped grounds with a terrace pool and open-air gym. Guest rooms feature understated decor, and the comfortable lounge bar is a Hollywood hangout. 285 rms, 16 story. S $295-$405; D $325-$405; suites $480-$3,000; family, wkend rates. TV; cable (premium), VCR avail. Pool; whirlpool, poolside serv. Restaurant 6:30 am-11:30 pm (also see GARDENS). Afternoon tea. Rm serv. Bar 11-1 am; pianist. Ck-out 1 pm. Convention facilities. Business center. In-rm modem link. Concierge. Gift shop. Underground parking. Exercise equipt; weights, bicycles. Massage. Bathrm phones, refrigerators. Balconies. Cr cds: A, C, D, ER, JCB, MC, V.

D

✔★★ **HOLIDAY INN BRENTWOOD-BEL AIR.** *170 N Church Lane (90049), I-405 Sunset Blvd exit, west of downtown. 310/476-6411; FAX 310/472-1157.* E-mail hibelair@deltanet.com. 211 rms, 17 story. S, D $109-$149; each addl $10; suites $210; under 12 free; hol, wkend, wkly rates; higher rates special events; some lower rates in winter. Crib free. Pet accepted, some restrictions. TV; cable (premium), VCR avail. Pool; whirlpool. Restaurant 6:30 am-11 pm. Bar 11 am-midnight. Ck-out noon. Coin lndry. Meeting rms. Business servs avail. In-rm modem link. Concierge. Exercise equipt; treadmill, bicycles. Refrigerators avail. Balconies. Cr cds: A, C, D, DS, JCB, MC, V.

D SC

★ ★ **HOLIDAY INN-CITY CENTER.** *1020 S Figueroa St (90015-1392), opp Convention Center, downtown. 213/748-1291; FAX 213/748-6028.* Web www.socalcol.com/la. 195 rms, 9 story. S, D $89-$169; each addl $10; under 18 free. Crib free. Pet accepted, some restrictions. TV; cable (premium), VCR avail. Heated pool. Restaurant 6:30 am-1 pm, 5-10 pm. Bar noon-midnight. Ck-out noon. Coin lndry. Meeting rms. Business servs avail. Gift shop. Exercise equipt; treadmill, stair machine, sauna. Cr cds: A, C, D, DS, JCB, MC, V.

D SC

★ ★ ★ ★ ★ **HOTEL BEL-AIR.** *701 Stone Canyon Rd (90077), I-405 to Sunset Blvd exit, in Bel Air. 310/472-1211; res: 800/648-4097; FAX 310/476-5890.* Set among 12 acres of exotic gardens and a lake, this vintage resort offers serenity, seclusion and a family of resident swans. Unique guest rooms are decorated with peach and earth tones in a Mediterranean style. 92 rms, some kits. S, D $325-$435; suites $525-$2,500. Pet accepted; $250. TV; cable (premium), VCR (movies). Pool; poolside serv. Restaurant (see BEL-AIR DINING ROOM). Rm serv 24 hrs. Bar 10-2 am; entertainment. Ck-out 1 pm. Meeting rms. Business servs avail. In-rm modem link. Concierge. Valet parking. Airport transportation. Exercise equipt; stair machines, treadmills. Massage. Health club privileges. Bathrm phones; some wood-burning fireplaces. Private patios. Cr cds: A, C, D, JCB, MC, V.

D

★ ★ ★ ★ **HOTEL NIKKO AT BEVERLY HILLS.** *465 S La Cienega Blvd (90048), N of Wilshire Blvd, at Burton Way, west of downtown. 310/247-0400; FAX 310/247-0315.* This contemporary hotel, located on Restaurant Row, is marked by bold American architecture and traditional Japanese simplicity. Hotel Nikko offers a state-of-the-art health club and nightly entertainment as well as a wealth of business services. 296 units, 7 story. S $270-$310; D $295-$395; each addl $25; suites $600-$1,800; under 12 free. Crib $25. Pet accepted. Valet parking $16. TV; cable (premium), VCR avail. Pool. Complimentary coffee in rms. Restaurants 6 am-10 pm (also see PANGAEA). Rm serv 24 hrs. Bar 3 pm-1 am; entertainment. Ck-out 1 pm. Business center. In-rm modem link. Concierge. Gift shop. Exercise equipt; weight machine, bicycles. Massage. Bathrm phones, Japanese soaking tubs, minibars. Balconies. Cr cds: A, C, D, DS, JCB, MC, V.

D

★ ★ ★ **HOTEL SOFITEL.** *8555 Beverly Blvd (90048), at La Cienega, west of downtown. 310/278-5444; FAX 310/657-2816; res: 800/521-7772.* E-mail sofitella@aol.com. 311 rms, 10 story. S, D $240-$270; each addl $25; suites $350-$500; under 18 free; wkend rates. Crib free. Valet parking $16.50. TV; cable (premium), VCR avail. Heated pool; poolside serv. Restaurant 6 am-10:30 pm. Rm serv 24 hrs. Bar 11-2 am; entertainment. Ck-out 1 pm. Convention facilities. Business servs avail. In-rm modem link. Concierge. Shopping arcade. Exercise equipt; weight machines, bicycles, sauna. Bathrm phones, refrigerators, minibars, wet bars. Balconies. Contemporary Mediterranean-style hotel features a blend of French and Californian cultures. Cr cds: A, C, D, JCB, MC, V.

D

★ ★ ★ **HYATT REGENCY.** *711 S Hope St (90017), I-110 exit 6th St, downtown. 213/683-1234; FAX 213/629-3230.* 485 rms, 26 story. S $155-$195; D $180-$225; each addl $25; suites $225-$750; under 18 free; wkend rates; package plans. Crib free. Garage parking; valet $15. TV; cable (premium), VCR avail. Restaurants 6 am-11 pm. Bar 11:30-1 am; entertainment. Ck-out noon. Convention facilities. Business center. In-rm modem link. Concierge. Shopping arcade. Barber, beauty shop. Exercise equipt; weights, bicycle, whirlpool. Some minibars. Luxury level. Cr cds: A, C, D, DS, ER, JCB, MC, V.

D SC

MONDRIAN. *(Too new to be rated) 8440 Sunset Blvd, (90069) at La Cienega Blvd, in West Hollywood. 213/650-8999; res: 800/525-8029; FAX 213/650-5215.* 245 rms, 12 story. S, D $150-$300; under 12 free. Covered parking $20. TV; cable (premium), VCR avail. Pool; whirlpool, poolside serv. Restaurant 7 am-11 pm. Rm serv 24 hrs. Bar 11-2 am. Ck-out noon. Business center. In-rm modem link. Concierge. Exercise equipt; weights, bicycles, sauna. Minibars, wet bars. Some balconies. Contemporary decor. Cr cds: A, D, DS, MC, V.

D

★ ★ ★ **NEW OTANI HOTEL & GARDEN.** *120 S Los Angeles St (90012), in Little Tokyo. 213/629-1200; FAX 213/622-0980; res: 800/273-2294 (CA) 800/421-8795 (US).* 434 rms, 21 story. S $155-$275; D $180-$300; each addl $25; suites $450-$1,800; under 12 free. Crib free. Covered parking $13.75/day, valet $18.15/day. TV; cable (premium), VCR avail. Restaurants 6 am-9:30 pm. Bar 10-1 am. Ck-out noon. Meeting rms. Business center. Concierge. Shopping arcade. Barber, beauty shop. Exercise equipt; weights, treadmill. Japanese health spa. Bathrm phones, minibars. Japanese-style decor, garden. Cr cds: A, C, D, DS, ER, JCB, MC, V.

D SC

★ ★ ★ **OMNI.** *930 Wilshire Blvd (90017), downtown. 213/688-7777; FAX 213/612-3987.* 900 rms, 16 story. S $169-$209; D $189-$229; each addl $20; suites $375-$1,200. Crib free. Garage $18. TV; cable (premium). Heated pool; whirlpool, poolside serv. Coffee in rms. Restaurants 6 am-11 pm (also see SEOUL JUNG). Bar 10-2 am; jazz. Ck-out noon. Convention facilities. Business servs avail. In-rm modem link. Concierge. Shopping arcade. Barber, beauty shop. Exercise equipt; weight machines, bicycles. Minibars. Luxury level. Cr cds: A, C, D, DS, ER, JCB, MC, V.

D SC

✔★ ★ **OXFORD PALACE.** *745 S Oxford Ave (90005), I-10 exit Western Ave, 2 mi N, west of downtown. 213/389-8000; FAX 213/389-8500; res: 800/532-7887.* Web www.oxfordhotel.com. 86 rms, 4 story, 9 suites. S $89-$139; D $94-$149; each addl $20; suites $110-$239. TV; cable, VCR (movies $3). Restaurants 7 am-2:30 pm, 5:30-10:30 pm. Bar 9-2 am. Ck-out 11 am. Meeting rms. Business center. Shopping arcade. Garage parking. Health club privileges. Minibars. Some balconies. Cr cds: A, D, MC, V.

D

★ ★ ★ ★ **PARK HYATT LOS ANGELES.** *2151 Ave of the Stars (90067), I-405 exit Santa Monica Blvd to Ave of the Stars, west of downtown. 310/277-1234; FAX 310/785-9240.* Web www.hyatt.com. All elegant guest rooms here offer scenic views; some overlook 20th Century-Fox's back lot. 367 rms, 17 story, 189 suites. S $270-$295; D $284; suites $270-$2,500; under 18 free; wkend rates. Valet parking $17. TV; cable (premium), VCR avail (movies). 2 pools, 1 indoor; whirlpool, poolside serv. Restaurant (see PARK GRILL). Rm serv 24 hrs. Bar 11:30-1:30 am; pianist. Ck-out noon. Meeting rms. Business center. In-rm modem link. Concierge. Shopping arcade. Tennis privileges. Golf privileges. Exercise equipt; weights, bicycles, sauna, steam rm. Massage. Bathrm phones, refrigerators, minibars; microwaves avail. Private patios, balconies. Cr cds: A, C, D, DS, JCB, MC, V.

D SC

★ ★ **RADISSON WILSHIRE PLAZA.** *3515 Wilshire Blvd (90010), west of downtown. 213/381-7411; FAX 213/386-7379.* 380 rms, 12 story. S, D $129-$169; each addl $10; suites $250-$500; under 18 free. Crib free. Valet parking $10. TV; cable (premium). Heated pool; poolside serv. Restaurants 6 am-11 pm. Bar 11-1 am; entertainment Mon-Fri. Ck-out noon. Convention facilities. Business center. In-rm modem link. Concierge. Barber, beauty shop. Exercise equipt; weight machine, treadmill. Minibars. Refrigerator in some suites. Cr cds: A, C, D, DS, ER, JCB, MC, V.

D SC

★ ★ ★ **REGAL BILTMORE.** *506 S Grand Ave (90071), downtown. 213/624-1011; FAX 213/612-1545; res: 800/245-8673.* Web www.regal-hotels.com/losangeles. 683 rms, 12 story. S, D $215-$270; each addl $30; suites $390-$2,000; under 18 free; wkend rates. Valet parking $17.60. Pool; whirlpool. TV; cable (premium), VCR avail. Restaurants 6:30 am-11 pm (also see BERNARD'S). Rm serv 24 hrs. Bars 11-2 am. Ck-out noon. Convention facilities. Business servs avail. In-rm modem link. Shopping arcade. Beauty shop. Exercise rm; instructor, weights, bicycles, sauna. Massage. Health club privileges. Wet bar in most suites; some bathrm phones. Luxury level. Cr cds: A, C, D, DS, ER, JCB, MC, V.

D

★ ★ **SUMMERFIELD SUITES.** *1000 Westmount Dr (90069), I-405 exit Santa Monica Blvd. 310/657-7400; FAX 310/854-6744; res: 800/833-4353.* E-mail sshhollywood@attmail.com. 95 kit. suites, 4 story. S, D $210-$255; under 12 free; monthly rates. Crib free. Pet accepted. Covered parking $9. TV; cable (premium), VCR (movies $5). Pool. Complimentary continental bkfst. Ck-out noon. Coin lndry. Meeting rm. In-rm modem link. Exercise equipt; weight machine, bicycle, sauna. Health club privileges. Refrigerators, microwaves, fireplaces. Balconies. Cr cds: A, C, D, DS, JCB, MC, V.

D

★ ★ **SUMMIT BEL-AIR.** *11461 Sunset Blvd (90049), in Bel Air. 310/476-6571; res: 800/468-3541; FAX 310/471-6310.* 162 rms, 2 story. S $149-$189; D $149-$179; each addl $20; suites $199-$499; under 18 free; wkend rates. TV; cable (premium), VCR avail. Heated pool; poolside serv. Restaurant 6:30 am-11 pm. Bar. Ck-out noon. Meeting rms. Business servs avail. In-rm modem link. Gift shop. Valet parking. Airport transportation. Tennis, pro. Exercise equipt; weight machine, treadmill. Bathrm phones, refrigerators, minibars; microwaves avail. Private patios, balconies. Cr cds: A, C, D, DS, JCB, MC, V.

D SC

★ ★ ★ **SUNSET MARQUIS HOTEL & VILLAS.** *1200 N Alta Loma Rd (90069), 1 blk W of LaCienega Blvd, 1 blk S of Sunset Blvd; west of downtown. 310/657-1333; res: 800/858-9758; FAX 310/652-5300.* E-mail smhsale@aol.com. 114 suites, 10 with kit, 3 story, 12 villas. Suites, kit. units $245-$350; each addl $30; villas $450-$1,200; under 12 free. Crib free. Valet parking $15. TV; cable (premium), VCR avail (movies). 2 heated pools; whirlpool, poolside serv. Restaurant 7 am-10 pm. Rm serv 24 hrs. Bar. Ck-out 1 pm. Meeting rm. Business center. In-rm modem link. Concierge. Butler serv avail. Exercise equipt; weights, bicycles, sauna, steam rm. Massage. Refrigerators; microwaves avail; some in-rm steam baths; wet bar in suites; bathrm phones in villas. Private patios, balconies. Recording studio. Cr cds: A, C, D, DS, MC, V.

D

★ ★ ★ **WESTIN BONAVENTURE.** *404 S Figueroa St (90071), downtown. 213/624-1000; FAX 213/612-4800.* 1,354 rms, 35 story. S $170-$190; D $190-$230; suites $195-$2,500; under 18 free. Crib free. Garage $18.15/day. TV; cable (premium), VCR avail. Heated pool; poolside serv. Restaurants 5:30 am-midnight. Rm serv 24 hrs. Bars 11-2 am. Ck-out noon. Convention facilities. Business center. In-rm modem link. Concierge. Shopping arcade. Barber, beauty shop. Health club privileges. Six-story atrium lobby. Cr cds: A, C, D, DS, ER, JCB, MC, V.

D SC

★ ★ ★ ★ **WESTIN CENTURY PLAZA HOTEL & TOWER.** *2025 Ave of the Stars (90067), in Century City, west of downtown. 310/277-2000; FAX 310/551-3355; res: 800/228-3000.* E-mail westincp@aol.com; web www.centuryplaza.la.com. Sited on some 10 acres landscaped with tropical plants and reflecting pools, this modern high-rise with a 30-story tower offers well-furnished rooms with ocean or city views. 1,072 rms, 19-30 story. S $245; D $270; each addl $25; suites $500-$3,000. Tower: S $295; D $320; suites $750-$5,000; each addl $25; under 18 free. TV; cable (premium), VCR avail. Pool; whirlpool, poolside serv (summer). Restaurant 6 am-11 pm. Rm serv 24 hrs. Bars 11-2 am; entertainment. Ck-out 1 pm. Lndry facilities. Convention facilities. Business center. In-rm modem link. Concierge. Barber, beauty shop. Valet parking. Tennis privileges. Exercise equipt; weight machine, bicycles. Health club privileges. Massage. Bathrm phones. Balconies. Cr cds: A, C, D, DS, ER, JCB, MC, V.

D SC

★ ★ ★ **WYNDHAM BEL AGE.** *1020 N San Vicente Blvd (90069), in West Hollywood. 310/854-1111; FAX 310/854-0926.* 200 suites, 10 story. S, D $205-$510; each addl $25; under 17 free; wkend rates. Valet parking $17. TV; cable (premium), VCR avail. Heated pool; poolside serv. Restaurants 7 am-11 pm (also see DIAGHILEV). Rm serv 24 hrs. Bar 11-2 am; jazz Wed-Sat, Sun brunch. Ck-out 1 pm. Convention facilities. Business servs avail. In-rm modem link. Concierge. Shopping arcade. Barber, beauty shop. Exercise equipt; bicycles, treadmills. Bathrm phones, wet bars; microwaves avail. Private patios, balconies. Cr cds: A, C, D, DS, ER, JCB, MC, V.

D

★ ★ ★ ★ **WYNDHAM CHECKERS HOTEL LOS ANGELES.** *535 S Grand Ave (90071), downtown. 213/624-0000; FAX 213/626-9906.* Having opened in 1927, this residential-style luxury hotel is set in one of this neighborhood's few remaining historical buildings. Guest rooms are furnished with oversize beds, upholstered easy chairs and writing tables, and the lobby features exquisite Oriental and contemporary works of art and antiques. 188 rms, 12 story. S, D $179-$229; each addl $20; suites $380-$950; under 18 free; wkend rates. Crib free. Valet parking $20. TV; cable (premium), VCR avail. Heated pool; whirlpool, poolside serv. Restaurant (see CHECKERS). Rm serv 24 hrs. Bar 11:30 am-11:30 pm. Meeting rms. Business center. In-rm modem link. Concierge. Airport transportation. Exercise equipt; weight machine, bicycles, sauna, steam rm. Massage. Bathrm phones, minibars. Library. Cr cds: A, C, D, DS, ER, JCB, MC, V.

D SC

Restaurants

★ ★ ★ **AL AMIR.** *5750 Wilshire Blvd (90036), in the Wilshire Courtyard Complex, west of downtown. 213/931-8740.* Hrs: 11:30 am-10 pm; Fri to 1 am; Sat 5:30 pm-1 am. Closed Sun; most major hols. Res accepted. Middle Eastern menu. Bar. Semi-a la carte: lunch $8-$12, dinner $11.95-$17.95. Complete meals: dinner $27.95. Specialties: chicken kabob, kafta kabob. Valet parking. Outdoor dining (lunch). Overlooks courtyard with fountains. Cr cds: A, C, D, DS, MC, V.

D

★ **ANNA'S.** *10929 W Pico Blvd (90064), west of downtown. 310/474-0102.* Hrs: 11:30 am-11 pm; Fri to midnight; Sat 4 pm-midnight; Sun from 4 pm. Closed Thanksgiving, Dec 25. Res accepted. Italian menu. Bar. Semi-a la carte: lunch $5.50-$13, dinner $6.95-$22. Specialties: chicken cacciatora, linguine Sorrento. Valet parking. Family-owned. Totally nonsmoking. Cr cds: A, DS, MC, V.

D

★ ★ ★ **ARNIE MORTON'S OF CHICAGO.** *435 S La Cienega Blvd (90048), I-405, E at Santa Monica Blvd exit, west of downtown. 310/246-1501.* Hrs: 5-11 pm; Sun to 10 pm. Closed major hols. Res accepted. Bar. Wine cellar. A la carte entrees: dinner $18-$30. Specializes in steak. Valet parking. Patrons select fresh cuts of meat brought tableside by waitstaff. Cr cds: A, C, D, JCB, MC, V.

D

★ ★ ★ **BEL-AIR DINING ROOM.** *(See Hotel Bel-Air) 310/472-1211.* Hrs: 7-10:30 am, 11:30 am-2:30 pm, 6:30-10:30 pm; Sat, Sun brunch 11 am-2:30 pm. Res accepted. Continental menu. Bar. Complete meals: bkfst $8-$13. A la carte entrees: lunch $15-$26.50, dinner $28-$36. Sun brunch $37.50. Specializes in seasonal dishes. Own pastries. Valet parking. Herb garden. Cr cds: A, C, D, JCB, MC, V.

D

★ ★ ★ **BERNARD'S.** *(See Regal Biltmore Hotel) 213/612-1580.* Hrs: 11:30 am-2:30 pm, 6-10 pm; Fri to 10:30 pm; Sat 6-10:30 pm. Closed Sun; major hols. Res accepted. Continental menu. Wine cellar. A la carte entrees: lunch $13-$21, dinner $17-$30. Specializes in seafood. Own baking. Entertainment. Valet parking. Cr cds: A, C, D, DS, ER, JCB, MC, V.

D

★ ★ ★ **CAFE PINOT.** *700 W 5th St (90071), downtown. 213/239-6500.* Hrs: 11:30 am-2:30 pm, 5:30-9:30 pm; Sat, Sun 5-10 pm. Closed most major hols. Res accepted. Bar. Wine list. Semi-a la carte: lunch $13-$20, dinner $15.75-$19.95. Specialties: rotisserie chicken, suckling pig, Peking duck ravioli. Valet parking (dinner). Outdoor dining. French bistro atmosphere. Totally nonsmoking. Cr cds: A, D, DS, JCB, MC, V.

D

★ ★ **CAMPANILE.** *624 S La Brea Ave, west of downtown. 213/938-1447.* Hrs: 11:30 am-2:30 pm, 6-10 pm; Fri to 11 pm; Sat 8 am-1:30 pm, 5:30-11 pm; Sun 8 am-1:30 pm. Closed Memorial Day, Thanksgiving, Dec 25. Res accepted. California, Italian menu. Bar. Semi-a la carte: bkfst $3-$15, lunch $8-$18, dinner $18-$28. Specialties: focaccia, risotto cake, prime rib. Own baking. Valet parking. Charlie Chaplin's original studio. Mexican tile fountain; skylights. Cr cds: A, C, D, DS, MC, V.

D

★ ★ **CAVA.** *(See Beverly Plaza Hotel) 213/658-8898.* Hrs: 6:30 am-11 pm; Fri, Sat to midnight. Res accepted. Contemporary Spanish menu. Bar. A la carte entrees: bkfst $4.50-$9.75, lunch, dinner $7.50-$17.95. Specialties: pescado Vera Cruz, pollo diablo, paella Valenciana. Jazz Tues, Fri, Sat evenings. Valet parking. Outdoor dining. Contemporary decor. Cr cds: A, C, D, DS, MC, V.

D

★ ★ ★ **CHECKERS.** *(See Wyndham Checkers Hotel Los Angeles) 213/624-0000.* Hrs: 5:30 am-9 pm; Sat, Sun brunch 10 am-2 pm. Res accepted. Bar. Wine list. Semi-a la carte: bkfst $8-$15, lunch $10-$25, dinner $25-$40. Sat, Sun brunch $10-$18. Specializes in fresh seafood dishes. Valet parking. Outdoor dining. Intimate dining in formal setting. Totally nonsmoking. Cr cds: A, C, D, DS, ER, JCB, MC, V.

D

★ ★ ★ **CIAO TRATTORIA.** *815 W Seventh St (90017), at Figueroa, downtown. 213/624-2244.* Hrs: 11 am-10 pm; Sat from 5 pm. Closed Sun; major hols. Res accepted. Italian menu. Bar. A la carte entrees: lunch $9.95-$14.50, dinner $11.50-$17.95. Specialties: chicken cacciatore, farfalle gustose, veal saltimbocca. Valet parking. In historic Fine Arts Bldg. Intimate, European atmosphere. Cr cds: A, D, MC, V.

D

★ ★ ★ **DIAGHILEV.** *(See Wyndham Bel Age Hotel) 310/854-1111.* Hrs: 6-11 pm. Closed Sun, Mon; Jan 1. Res accepted. French, Russian menu. Bar. A la carte entrees: dinner $15-$34. Complete meal: dinner $75. Specialties: braised leg of duck, filet of salmon with sturgeon mousse, braised veal chop. Elegant dining. Jacket. Cr cds: A, C, D, DS, ER, JCB, MC, V.

D

★ ★ **EL CHOLO.** *1121 W Western Ave (90006), west of downtown. 213/734-2773.* Hrs: 11 am-10 pm; Fri, Sat to 11 pm; Sun to 9 pm. Closed July 4, Thanksgiving, Dec 25. Res accepted. Mexican menu. Bar. Semi-a la carte: lunch, dinner $6.45-$13.95. Specialties: fajitas, green corn tamales, margaritas. Valet parking. Family-owned since 1927. Casual dining. Cr cds: A, D, MC, V.

D

★ ★ ★ **FOUR OAKS.** *2181 N Beverly Glen, in West Hollywood. 310/470-2265.* Hrs: 11:30 am-2 pm, 6-10 pm; Sun, Mon from 6 pm; Sun brunch 10:30 am-2 pm. Closed some major hols. Res accepted. Modern French, Amer menu. Bar. A la carte entrees: lunch $15-$22, dinner $22-$27. Sun brunch $29.50. Menu changes seasonally; emphasizes natural ingredients. Own desserts. Valet parking. Patio dining. Mediterranean decor. Built 1890. Cr cds: A, D, MC, V.

D

★ ★ ★ **GARDENS.** *(See Four Seasons Hotel) 310/273-2222.* Hrs: 7 am-11 pm; Sun brunch 10 am-2:30 pm. Res accepted. Mediterranean menu. Bar 11-1 am. Wine cellar. A la carte entrees: bkfst $5.95-$18, lunch $8.95-$18, dinner $18-$35. Sun brunch $41. Child's meals. Specializes in steak, lamb, seafood. Own baking, ice cream. Valet parking. Outdoor dining. Florentine decor. Cr cds: A, C, D, ER, JCB, MC, V.

D ♥

★ ★ ★ **LA CACHETTE.** *10506 Little Santa Monica Blvd (90025), in West LA. 310/470-4992.* Web www.restaurant.pages.com.lacachette. Hrs: 11:30 am-2:30 pm, 6-10 pm; Fri to 10:30 pm; Sat 5:30-10:30 pm; Sun 5:30-9 pm. Closed most major hols. Res accepted. French menu. Bar. A la carte entrees: lunch $12-$18, dinner $15-$26. Specialties: shellfish bouillabaisse, double-roasted muscovy duck, grilled swordfish. Intimate dining. Totally nonsmoking. Cr cds: A, D, MC, V.

D

✔ ★ ★ **LA GOLONDRINA.** *W-17 Olvera St (90012), north of downtown. 213/628-4349.* Hrs: 10 am-9 pm; Fri, Sat to 10 pm; Sun from 9 am. Closed Jan 1, Dec 25. Res accepted. No A/C. Mexican menu. Bar. Semi-a la carte: bkfst $4.25-$8.95, lunch, dinner $4.25-$13.95. Child's meals. Specialties: carnitas, costillas en adobado. Own breads. Mexican guitarists. Outdoor dining. Historical landmark; 1st brick bldg in Los Angeles (1855). Family-owned since 1924. Cr cds: A, C, D, DS, MC, V.

SC

★ ★ **LITTLE JOE'S.** *900 N Broadway, in Chinatown. 213/489-4900.* Hrs: 11 am-9 pm; Sat from 3 pm. Closed Sun; major hols. Res accepted. Italian, Amer menu. Bar. Semi-a la carte: lunch $6.50-$10.75, dinner $7.50-$19.95. Child's meals. Specialties: homemade ravioli, butterflied halibut. Valet parking. Near Dodger Stadium, Civic Center. Family-owned since 1910. Cr cds: A, C, D, DS, JCB, MC, V.

★ ★ **LOCANDA VENETA.** *8638 W Third St, opp Cedars Sinai Hospital, west of downtown. 310/274-1893.* Hrs: 11:30 am-2:30 pm, 5:30-10:30 pm; Fri to 11 pm; Sat 5:30-11 pm. Closed Sun. Res accepted. Northern Italian menu. Beer. Wine list. A la carte entrees: lunch, dinner $10-$25. Specializes in seafood, pasta. Own baking. Valet parking. Patio dining. Windows open to street; open kitchen. Cr cds: A, D, DS, MC, V.

★ ★ **MADEO.** *8897 Beverly Blvd, west of downtown. 310/859-4903.* Hrs: noon-3 pm, 6:30-11 pm; Sat, Sun from 6:30 pm. Closed Dec 25. Res accepted. Italian menu. Bar. Wine cellar. A la carte entrees: lunch $10-$30, dinner $30-$50. Specialties: branzino, leg of veal. Own pastries. Valet parking. Wood-burning oven. Cr cds: A, C, D, MC, V.

D

★ ★ ★ **PANGAEA.** *(See Hotel Nikko at Beverly Hills) 310/247-0400.* Hrs: 6:30 am-2:30 pm, 6-10:30 pm; Sun 11 am-3 pm (brunch), 6-10:30 pm. Res accepted. Continental menu. Bar. Wine cellar. Semi-a la carte: bkfst $8.75-$11.50, lunch $11-$22, dinner $18-$29. Sun brunch $35. Specialties: sushi, sautéed Alaskan halibut. Jazz band Sun brunch. Valet parking. Elegant dining. Totally nonsmoking. Cr cds: A, C, D, DS, JCB, MC, V.

D

★ ★ ★ **PARK GRILL.** *(See Park Hyatt Los Angeles Hotel) 310/277-6600.* Hrs: 6:30 am-10:30 pm; Sat, Sun from 7 am; Sun brunch 10:30 am-2 pm. Res accepted. Continental, California menu. Bar 11:30-1:30 am. Wine cellar. A la carte entrees: bkfst $8-$14.75, lunch $11.95-$18, dinner $13.50-$25. Bkfst buffet $17. Sun brunch $24.95. Seasonal menu; changes monthly. Own baking. Valet parking. Outdoor dining overlooking garden. Cr cds: A, C, D, DS, JCB, MC, V.

D

✔ ★ **PATINETTE AT MOCA.** *250 S Grand Ave, at Museum of Contemporary Art, downtown. 213/626-1178.* Hrs: 11 am-4:30 pm; Thurs to 8 pm. Closed Mon; major hols. A la carte entrees: lunch, dinner $5.95-

$9.25. Specializes in salads, sandwiches, light entrees. Outdoor dining on terrace. Totally nonsmoking. Cr cds: A, C, D, DS, JCB, MC, V.

D

✔★★★ **PINOT HOLLYWOOD.** *1448 N Gower St (90028), north of downtown. 213/461-8800.* Hrs: 11:30 am-10:30 pm; Sat 5:30-11 pm. Closed Sun; most major hols. Res accepted. French menu. Bar to 1:30 am. Extensive wine list. Semi-a la carte: lunch $7.25-$16.50, dinner $14.25-$19.95. Specializes in beef, chicken. Valet parking. Outdoor dining. French bistro decor. Cr cds: A, D, DS, MC, V.

D

★★★ **POSTO.** *(14928 Ventura Blvd, Sherman Oaks 91403) 2 blks E of I-405 at US 101. 818/784-4400.* Hrs: 11:30 am-2:30 pm, 5-10 pm; Sat from 5 pm. Closed Sun; major hols. Res accepted. Italian menu. Bar. Wine cellar. A la carte entrees: lunch, dinner $8-$26. Specialties: veal osso bucco, risotto lobster, filet mignon with onions. Valet parking. Original artwork. Cr cds: A, D, MC, V.

D

★★★ **PRIMI.** *10543 W Pico Blvd, west of downtown. 310/475-9235.* Hrs: 11:30 am-2:30 pm, 5:30-10:30 pm; Sat from 5:30 pm. Closed Sun. Res accepted. Italian menu. Bar. A la carte entrees: lunch $10-$19, dinner $16-$22. Specializes in homemade pasta. Own baking. Valet parking. Outdoor dining. Cr cds: A, C, D, MC, V.

D

★★★ **SEOUL JUNG.** *(See Omni Hotel) 213/688-7880.* Hrs: 11:30 am-2 pm, 5:30-9:30 pm. Res accepted. Korean menu. Bar. Wine list. A la carte entrees: lunch, dinner $12-$25. Specialties: marinated short ribs, noodle casserole. Valet parking. Elegant dining; many Korean artifacts. Totally nonsmoking. Cr cds: A, D, DS, JCB, MC, V.

D

✔★ **SISLEY ITALIAN KITCHEN.** *10800 W Pico Blvd (91355), in Westside Pavilion Shopping Center, west of downtown. 310/446-3030.* Hrs: 11:30 am-10 pm; Fri, Sat to 10:30 pm; Sun to 9 pm. Res accepted. Italian, California menu. Bar. A la carte entrees: lunch $5.95-$10.95, dinner $7.50-$12. Specialty: cioppino. Valet parking. Italian cafe decor. Cr cds: A, MC, V.

D

✔★★★ **TAIX.** *1911 Sunset Blvd (90026), north of downtown. 213/484-1265.* Hrs: 11 am-10 pm; Sun to 9 pm. Closed most major hols. Res accepted. Country French menu. Bar. Extensive wine list. Complete meals: lunch $6.95-$15.95, dinner $6.95-$16.95. Child's meals. Specialty: escargots à la Bourguignonne. Own soups. Valet parking. Family-owned since 1927. Cr cds: A, C, D, DS, MC, V.

D

★★★ **TAM-O-SHANTER INN.** *2980 Los Feliz Blvd (90039), 5 blks E of I-5, north of downtown. 213/664-0228.* Hrs: 11 am-3 pm, 5-10 pm; Fri, Sat to 11 pm; Sun 10:30 am-2:30 pm (brunch), 4-10 pm. Closed July 4, Dec 25. Continental, Amer menu. Bar. A la carte entrees: lunch $8.95-$14.95, dinner $9.95-$19.95. Sun brunch $9.50-$15.95. Child's meals. Specialties: prime rib & Yorkshire pudding, creamed spinach, roast duckling. Valet parking. Scottish motif. Family-owned since 1922. Cr cds: A, D, DS, MC, V.

D SC

★★★ **THE TOWER.** *1150 S Olive St, on top of Trans-America Center, downtown. 213/746-1554.* Hrs: 11:30 am-2 pm, 5:30-10 pm; Fri to 11 pm; Sat 5:30-11 pm; early-bird dinner 5:30-6:30 pm. Closed Sun; major hols. Res accepted. Continental menu. Bar. Wine cellar. A la carte entrees: lunch $15-$20, dinner $23-$29. Specializes in contemporary dishes. Harpist (lunch), pianist (dinner). Valet parking. 360° view of city from 32nd floor. Jacket. Cr cds: A, D, MC, V.

D

Unrated Dining Spots

CASSELL'S. *3266 W 6th St, west of downtown. 213/480-8668.* Hrs: 10:30 am-4 pm. Closed Sun; major hols. A la carte entrees: lunch $4.60-$5.80. Specializes in prime beef hamburgers. Old-style hamburger diner. No cr cds accepted.

D

HARD ROCK CAFE. *8600 Beverly Blvd, in Beverly Shopping Center, west of downtown. 310/276-7605.* Hrs: 11:30-12:30 am. Closed Labor Day, Thanksgiving, Dec 25. Bar. Semi-a la carte: lunch, dinner $5.95-$15. Child's meals. Specialties: lime barbecued chicken, grilled hamburgers. Valet parking. Extensive rock 'n roll memorabilia collection. Cr cds: A, D, MC, V.

D

PHILLIPE THE ORIGINAL. *1001 N Alameda St, downtown. 213/628-3781.* Hrs: 6 am-10 pm. Closed Thanksgiving, Dec 25. Wine, beer. A la carte entrees: bkfst $1-$4.50, lunch, dinner $3.25-$5. Specializes in French dip sandwiches, salads, baked apples. Own cinnamon rolls, muffins, donuts. Parking. Since 1908; old-style dining hall. Totally nonsmoking. No cr cds accepted.

D

UNCLE BILL'S PANCAKE HOUSE. *(1305 Highland Ave, Manhattan Beach) S on Pacific Coast Hwy. 310/545-5177.* Hrs: 6 am-3 pm; wkends, hols from 7 am. Closed Jan 1, Thanksgiving, Dec 25. Semi-a la carte: bkfst $3.25-$5.95, lunch $3.50-$6.50. Specializes in potatoes Stroganoff, strawberry waffles, homemade muffins. Parking. Small, cozy atmosphere. Converted 1908 house. No cr cds accepted.

Los Angeles Intl Airport Area

Motels

✔★★ **HAMPTON INN.** *(10300 La Cienega Blvd, Inglewood 90304) 3/4 mi E on Century Blvd, then S on La Cienega Blvd. 310/337-1000; FAX 310/645-6925.* Web www.hampton-inn.com. 148 rms, 7 story. S, D $66-$86; under 18 free. Crib free. Pet accepted, some restrictions. TV; cable (premium). Complimentary continental bkfst. Restaurant nearby. Ck-out noon. Meeting rms. In-rm modem link. Valet serv. Free airport transportation. Exercise equipt; stair machine, bicycles. Cr cds: A, C, D, DS, MC, V.

D SC

✔★★ **TRAVELODGE-LAX.** *(5547 W Century Blvd, Los Angeles 90045) 1/2 mi W off I-405, at Century Blvd & Aviation Blvd. 310/649-4000; FAX 310/649-0311.* E-mail aci@chms.net; web www.chms.net. 147 rms, 2 story. S $64-$74; D $69-$88; each addl $8; under 18 free. Pet accepted. TV; cable (premium), VCR. Pool. Coffee in rms. Restaurant open 24 hrs. Rm serv 6 am-10 pm. Bar 10-2 am. Ck-out noon. Coin lndry. Bellhops. Valet serv. Gift shop. Free airport transportation. Exercise equipt; bicycle, rower. Some private patios, balconies. Cr cds: A, C, D, DS, ER, JCB, MC, V.

Hotels

★★ **BARNABEY'S.** *(3501 Sepulveda Blvd, Manhattan Beach 90266) S via I-405 exit Rosecrans W. 310/545-8466; FAX 310/545-8621; res: 800/552-5285 (US), 800/851-7678 (CAN).* Web www.barnabeys-hotel.com. 120 rms, 3 story. S $149; D $164-$174; under 12 free; hol, wkend rates. Crib $15. Overnight valet parking $6. TV; cable (premium), VCR avail. Pool. Complimentary full bkfst. Complimentary coffee in rms. Restaurant 6:30 am-10 pm. Bar 11 am-midnight; entertainment. Ck-out noon. Meeting rms. In-rm modem link. Gift shop. Free airport transportation. Health club privileges. Microwaves avail. European-style decor; antiques. Cr cds: A, C, D, DS, MC, V.

D SC

★ ★ ★ **CROWNE PLAZA-L.A. INTERNATIONAL AIRPORT.** *(5985 W Century Blvd, Los Angeles 90045) 1/4 mi E on Century Blvd. 310/642-7500; FAX 310/417-3608.* E-mail laxales@crowneplaza.com; web www.crowneplaza.com. 615 rms, 16 story. S $139-$169; D $154-$185; suites $350-$550; under 12 free; wkend rates. Crib free. Garage $9. TV; cable (premium), VCR avail. Heated pool; whirlpool. Coffee in rms. Restaurant 6 am-11 pm. Bar 11-2 am; entertainment Tues-Thurs. Ck-out noon. Coin Indry. Business servs avail. Concierge. Gift shop. Free airport transportation. Exercise equipt; weights, bicycles, sauna. Luxury level. Cr cds: A, C, D, DS, JCB, MC, V.

D SC

★ ★ **DOUBLETREE CLUB.** *(1985 E Grand Ave, El Segundo 90245) 1 1/2 mi S of airport on Sepulveda Blvd, in business park. 310/322-0999; FAX 310/322-4758.* E-mail dtclax@aol.com. 215 rms, 7 story. S $102; D $112; each addl $10; suites $125; under 18 free. Crib $10. TV; cable (premium). Heated pool; whirlpool, poolside serv. Complimentary full bkfst. Restaurant 6-10 am, 11 am-2 pm, 5-10 pm. Bar. Ck-out 1 pm. Meeting rms. Business servs avail. In-rm modem link. Free airport transportation. Exercise equipt; weight machines, bicycles. Cr cds: A, C, D, DS, JCB, MC, V.

D SC

★ ★ **EMBASSY SUITES.** *(1440 E Imperial Ave, El Segundo 90245) 1/2 mi S on Sepulveda Blvd, then 1 blk W on Imperial Ave. 310/640-3600; FAX 310/322-0954.* Web www.embassy-suites.com. 350 suites, 5 story. S, D $119-$169; each addl $15; under 18 free; wkend rates. Pet accepted, some restrictions. Parking $6. TV; cable (premium), VCR avail. Indoor pool; whirlpool. Complimentary full bkfst. Restaurant 11 am-10 pm. Bar to 2 am. Ck-out noon. Meeting rms. Business center. In-rm modem link. Gift shop. Free airport transportation. Exercise equipt; weight machine, bicycles. Refrigerators, microwaves. Balconies. Sun deck. Spanish mission architecture. Near beach. Cr cds: A, C, D, DS, ER, JCB, MC, V.

D SC

✓★ **FURAMA.** *(8601 Lincoln Blvd, Los Angeles 90045) jct Lincoln Blvd & Manchester Ave, NW edge of Intl Airport. 310/670-8111; res: 800/225-8126; FAX 310/337-1883.* E-mail fhla@furama-hotels.com; web www.furama-hotels.com. 760 rms, 12 story. S, D $69-$125; each addl $10; suites $175-$250; under 18 free. Crib free. TV; cable (premium). Pool. Restaurants 6 am-11 pm. Bar 3 pm-2 am; entertainment. Ck-out noon. Meeting rms. Barber, beauty shop. Free airport transportation. Exercise equipt; weights, bicycle. Some private patios. Garden patio. Golf, tennis opp. Luxury level. Cr cds: A, C, D, DS, ER, JCB, MC, V.

D SC

★ ★ ★ **HILTON & TOWERS-LOS ANGELES AIRPORT.** *(5711 W Century Blvd, Los Angeles 90045) 3/4 mi W of I-405. 310/410-4000; FAX 310/410-6250.* 1,234 rms, 17 story. S $109-$169; each addl $20; suites $150-$900; family, wkend rates. Valet parking $13, garage $9. Pet accepted. TV; cable (premium), VCR avail. Heated pool; whirlpools, poolside serv (seasonal). Restaurants open 24 hrs. Bar 11-2 am. Ck-out noon. Convention facilities. Business center. In-rm modem link. Drugstore. Coin Indry. Free airport transportation. Exercise rm; instructor, weights, bicycles, sauna. Some bathrm phones; refrigerators, microwaves avail. Some private patios. Luxury level. Cr cds: A, C, D, DS, ER, JCB, MC, V.

D SC

★ ★ **MARRIOTT-AIRPORT.** *(5855 W Century Blvd, Los Angeles 90045) I-405 exit Century Blvd W. 310/641-5700; FAX 310/337-5358.* 1,010 rms, 18 story. S, D $135-$160; suites from $189; family, wkend rates. Crib free. Pet accepted, some restrictions. Parking $10, valet $12. TV; cable (premium), VCR avail. Heated pool; whirlpool, poolside serv. Restaurants 6 am-midnight. Rm serv 24 hrs. Bars; entertainment. Ck-out 1 pm. Coin Indry. Convention facilities. Business center. In-rm modem link. Concierge. Shopping arcade. Beauty shop. Free airport transportation. Exercise equipt; weights, bicycles. Some bathrm phones, refrigerators. Balconies. Luxury level. Cr cds: A, C, D, DS, JCB, MC, V.

D SC

✓★ ★ **QUALITY HOTEL-LOS ANGELES AIRPORT.** *(5249 W Century Blvd, Los Angeles 90045) I-405 exit Century Blvd W. 310/645-2200; FAX 310/641-8214.* 278 rms, 10 story. S, D $89-$119; each addl $10; under 18 free; wkend rates. Pet accepted. TV; cable (premium), VCR avail. Pool; poolside serv. Restaurant 6 am-10 pm. Bar 5-11 pm. Ck-out noon. Convention facilities. Business center. Free airport transportation. Exercise equipt; bicycles, treadmill. Cr cds: A, C, D, DS, ER, JCB, MC, V.

D SC

★ ★ ★ **RENAISSANCE.** *(9620 Airport Blvd, Los Angeles 90045) 1 mi N. 310/337-2800; FAX 310/216-6681.* 505 rms, 11 story, 56 suites. S, D $160-$200; each addl $10; suites $225; under 16 free; wkend rates. Valet parking $12, garage $8. TV; cable (premium), VCR avail. Heated pool; whirlpool, poolside serv. Restaurants 6-10:30 am, 11:30 am-2:30 pm, 5-11 pm. Rm serv 24 hrs. Bar. Meeting rms. Business servs avail. In-rm modem link. Concierge. Gift shop. Free airport transportation. Tennis privileges. Golf privileges. Exercise equipt; weights, bicycle, sauna. Massage. Minibars. Cr cds: A, C, D, DS, ER, JCB, MC, V.

D SC

★ ★ ★ **SHERATON GATEWAY.** *(6101 W Century Blvd, Los Angeles 90045) 1/4 mi E on Century Blvd. 310/642-1111; FAX 310/410-1267.* E-mail greg_moon@ittsheraton.com; web www.ittsheraton.com. 804 rms, 15 story. S $145-$185; D $165-$205; each addl $20; suites $180-$500; under 17 free; wkend rates. Crib free. Valet parking $15. TV; cable (premium), VCR avail. Heated pool; whirlpool, poolside serv. Restaurants 6-10:30 pm. Bar 11-2 am; entertainment. Ck-out noon. Convention facilities. Business center. In-rm modem link. Concierge. Gift shop. Free airport transportation. Exercise equipt; weights, bicycles. Minibars; microwaves avail. Luxury level. Cr cds: A, C, D, DS, ER, JCB, MC, V.

D SC

★ ★ ★ **WESTIN-L.A. AIRPORT.** *(5400 W Century Blvd, Los Angeles 90045) 1 mi E on Century Blvd. 310/216-5858; FAX 310/645-8053.* Web www.westin.com. 723 rms, 12 story. S, D $129-$159; each addl $20; suites $275-$1,500; under 18 free; wkend rates. Covered parking $8. Pet accepted. TV; cable (premium). Heated pool; whirlpool. Restaurant (see CHARISMA CAFE). Rm serv 24 hrs. Bar 10-2 am; entertainment. Ck-out noon. Convention facilities. Business center. In-rm modem link. Gift shop. Free airport transportation. Guest Indry. Exercise equipt; weight machine, bicycles, sauna. Minibars; bathrm phones in suites; microwaves avail. Balconies. Luxury level. Cr cds: A, C, D, DS, ER, JCB, MC, V.

D SC

★ ★ **WYNDHAM HOTEL.** *(6225 W Century Blvd, Los Angeles 90045) at entrance to Intl Airport. 310/337-9000; FAX 310/670-8110.* 591 rms, 12 story. S $129-$159; D $139-$179; each addl $20; suites $350-$600; under 18 free; wkend rates. TV; cable (premium), VCR avail. Heated pool; whirlpool, poolside serv. Restaurant 6:30-1:30 am; dining rms 11 am-10:30 pm. Bars 11-2 am, entertainment exc Sun. Ck-out noon. Convention facilities. Business center. In-rm modem link. Concierge. Garage parking. Free airport transportation. Exercise equipt; weights, rower. Bathrm phones; wet bar in suites. Sun deck. Luxury level. Cr cds: A, C, D, DS, ER, JCB, MC, V.

D SC

Beverly Hills

Hotels

★ ★ ★ ★ ★ **BEVERLY HILLS HOTEL AND BUNGALOWS.** *9641 Sunset Blvd (90210), at Rodeo Dr. 310/276-2251; FAX 310/887-2887; res: 800/283-8885.* The legendary Pink Palace is back and better than ever. It sparkles, from its opulent circular lobby and its lovely hallways with the famous palm tree wall covering to its individually decorated guest rooms. Each room has its own CD sound system, private phone and fax number. 203 rms, 37 suites, 22 bungalows with 53 rms, 1-4 story, 12 kits. S, D $275-$350; suites $595-$3,000; 1-4 bdrm kit. bungalows $275-$2,750; under 12 free. Crib free. Valet parking $15. TV; cable (premium), VCR (movies). Pool; whirlpool, poolside serv. Restaurant (see POLO LOUNGE). Rm serv 24 hrs. Ck-out noon. Meeting rms. Business servs avail. In-rm modem link. Concierge. Shopping arcade. Beauty shop. Airport transportation. Lighted tennis, pro. Exercise equipt; weights, treadmill. Cr cds: A, C, D, JCB, MC, V.

D

★ ★ ★ **BEVERLY HILTON.** *9876 Wilshire Blvd (90210). 310/274-7777; FAX 310/285-1313.* 581 rms, 8 story. S, D $285-$315; each addl $20; suites $500-$1,500; family rates. Crib free. Pet accepted. Garage, valet parking $17. TV; cable (premium), VCR avail. Heated pool; wading pool, poolside serv. Restaurant 6:30-10 pm; dining rm 5:30 pm-midnight. Rm serv 24 hrs. Bars 11:30-2 am. Ck-out noon. Meeting rms. Business center. In-rm modem link. Concierge. Shopping arcade. Barber, beauty shop. Complimentary transportation to nearby shopping. Exercise equipt; weight machines, bicycles. Some bathrm phones, refrigerators. Patio, balconies. Lanai rms around pool. Cr cds: A, C, D, DS, ER, JCB, MC, V.

D SC

★ ★ ★ **BEVERLY PRESCOTT.** *(1224 S Beverwil Dr, Los Angeles 90035) at Pico Blvd. 310/277-2800; FAX 310/203-9537; res: 800/421-3212.* 137 rms, 12 story, 21 suites. S, D $170-$205; suites $250-$1,000; family, wkend rates. Crib free. Covered parking $17. TV; cable (premium), VCR. Heated pool; poolside serv. Restaurant 7 am-10 pm. Rm serv 24 hrs. Bar 11-2 am. Ck-out noon. Meeting rms. Business center. In-rm modem link. Concierge. Exercise equipt; weight machine, stair machine. Health club privileges. Minibars. Balconies. Cr cds: A, C, D, DS, ER, JCB, MC, V.

D

★ ★ ★ ★ ★ **THE PENINSULA, BEVERLY HILLS.** *9882 Little Santa Monica Blvd (90212), at Wilshire Blvd. 310/551-2888; FAX 310/788-2319; res: 800/462-7899.* E-mail pbh@peninsula.com; web www.peninsula.com. A semicircular driveway leads to this ultra-luxurious French Renaissance-style hotel set amid gardens and fountains. Guest rooms are distinguished by original art, down-filled duvets and oversize bathrooms in polished marble. 200 units, 4 story, 32 suites, 16 villas (2 story, 1-2 bedrm). S, D $325-$450; each addl $30; suites, villas $600-$3,000; under 12 free; wkend rates. Crib free. Valet parking $17. TV; cable (premium), VCR (movies). Rooftop pool; whirlpool, poolside serv. Complimentary beverages on arrival. Restaurant (see THE BELVEDERE). Rm serv 24 hrs. Bar from 11:30 am; pianist. Ck-out noon. Meeting rms. Business center. In-rm modem link. Concierge. Gift shop. Clothing, jewelry stores. Airport transportation. Tennis privileges. 18-hole golf privileges, pro, putting green, driving range. Exercise equipt; weights, treadmill, sauna. Massage. Bathrm phones, minibars; many wet bars. Balconies. Cr cds: A, C, D, DS, ER, JCB, MC, V.

D

✔★ ★ **PLAZA BEVERLY HILLS.** *10300 Wilshire Blvd (90024). 310/275-5575; FAX 310/275-3257; res: 800/800-1234.* 116 suites, 5 story. S, D $135-$385. Crib avail. Pet accepted. TV; cable (premium), VCR avail. Heated pool; whirlpool, poolside serv. Restaurant 7 am-10 pm. Bar. Ck-out noon. Meeting rm. Business servs avail. In-rm modem link. Gift shop. Exercise equipt; weight machine, treadmill. Refrigerators, minibars. Many balconies. Garden; tropical plants. Cr cds: A, C, D, DS, JCB, MC, V.

SC

★ ★ ★ ★ **REGENT BEVERLY WILSHIRE.** *9500 Wilshire Blvd (90212). 310/275-5200; FAX 310/274-2851; res: 800/545-4000.* Web www.rih.com. Sited at the south end of Rodeo Drive, this hotel is often home to visiting celebrities. 275 rms, 10 & 12 story, 69 suites. S, D $285-$425; suites $450-$4,500; under 16 free. Pet accepted. Covered parking, valet $20. TV; cable (premium), VCR avail (movies). Pool; whirlpool, poolside serv. Restaurant (see THE DINING ROOM). Rm serv 24 hrs. Bar 11-2 am; entertainment. Ck-out noon. Convention facilities. Business center. In-rm modem link. Concierge. Gift shops. Beauty shop. Exercise rm; instructor, weights, bicycles, sauna, steam rm. Massage. Bathrm phones, refrigerators. Some balconies. Cr cds: A, C, D, DS, ER, JCB, MC, V.

D

★ ★ **SUMMIT.** *360 N Rodeo Dr (90049). 310/273-0300; FAX 310/859-8730; res: 800/HOTEL-411.* 86 rms, 3 story. S, D $195-$295; each addl $25; suites $400; under 17 free. Crib free. Valet parking $12, in/out $12. TV; cable. Complimentary coffee in rms. Restaurant 8 am-10:30 pm. Ck-out noon. Airport transportation. Tennis privileges. Health club privileges. Some refrigerators. Cr cds: A, C, D, DS, JCB, MC, V.

D SC

Inn

★ ★ ★ **CARLYLE.** *(1119 S Robertson Blvd, Los Angeles 90035) W on Wilshire Blvd to Robertson Blvd, then S; between Olympic & Pico Blvds. 310/275-4445; FAX 310/859-0496; res: 800/3-CARLYLE.* 32 rms, 5 story. S $110; D $120 each addl $10; suites $180-$200; under 12 free. Crib free. TV; cable, VCR (movies $6). Complimentary full bkfst, afternoon refreshments. Complimentary coffee in rms. Restaurant nearby. Ck-out noon, ck-in 3 pm. Business servs avail. In-rm modem link. Luggage handling. Valet serv. Concierge serv. Airport transportation avail. Exercise equipt; bicycles, treadmill, whirlpool. Rms are on 4 levels of circular terraces overlooking a lush courtyard, terrace and spa. Cr cds: A, C, D, DS, JCB, MC, V.

D SC

Restaurants

★ ★ ★ ★ **THE BELVEDERE.** *(See The Peninsula, Beverly Hills Hotel) 310/788-2306.* E-mail pbh@peninsula.com; web www.peninsula.com. This elegant, formal dining room is decorated in shades of blue, green and yellow. Award-winning chef Bill Bracken works with locally grown ingredients—including herbs from the Belvedere's rooftop garden—and ordinary ingredients to create some of the most extraordinary food in southern California. Specialties: potato-crusted Chilean sea bass, lightly spiced corn chowder with house-smoked shrimp, tenderloin of beef in a merlot reduction. Hrs: 6:30 am-2:30 pm, 6-10:30 pm; Sun brunch 11 am-2:30 pm. Res accepted. Bar. Wine cellar. A la carte entrees: bkfst, lunch $16-$21, dinner $19.50-$26. Brunch $14-$23. Child's meals. Guitarist or harpist Sun brunch. Valet parking. Outdoor dining in partially covered terrace. Totally nonsmoking. Cr cds: A, C, D, DS, ER, JCB, MC, V.

D ♥

★ ★ ★ **CRUSTACEAN.** *9646 Little Santa Monica Blvd (90210). 310/205-8990.* Hrs: 11:30 am-10:30 pm; Fri to 11:30 pm; Sat 4:30-11:30 pm. Closed Sun; major hols. Res required. Asian, French menu. Bar. Wine list. A la carte entrees: lunch $11.95-$19.95, dinner $17.95-$31.95. Specialties: garlic-roasted crab, colossal royal prawns with garlic noodles, whole roasted dungeness crab. Pianist. Valet parking. Outdoor dining. Atmosphere is replica of 1930s French Colonial estate. Overlooks bamboo garden verandas. Cr cds: A, C, D, MC, V.

D

★ ★ **DA PASQUALE.** *9749 Little Santa Monica Blvd (90210). 310/859-3884.* Hrs: 11:30 am-3 pm, 5-10 pm; Fri to 11 pm; Sat 5-11 pm.

Closed Sun; major hols. Res accepted; required wkends. Italian menu. Wine, beer. A la carte entrees: lunch $7-$15, dinner $15-$30. Specializes in pizza, pasta, fish. Patio dining. Italian atmosphere. Totally nonsmoking. Cr cds: A, D, MC, V.

D

★ ★ **DA VINCI.** *9737 Little Santa Monica Blvd (90210). 310/273-0960.* Hrs: 11:30 am-2:30 pm, 5:30-10:30 pm; Sat, Sun from 5:30 pm. Res accepted. Italian menu. Bar. A la carte entrees: lunch $10-$15, dinner $15-$30. Specialty: osso buco Milanese. Own pasta, desserts. Valet parking. Cr cds: A, C, D, JCB, MC, V.

D

★ ★ ★ ★ **THE DINING ROOM.** *(See Regent Beverly Wilshire Hotel) 310/275-5200.* In a famous hotel facing Rodeo Drive and the Hollywood Hills, this superb restaurant with a display kitchen is decorated in grand European style. Continental menu. Specializes in mesquite-grilled meats and fish. Own baking. Seasonal menu with daily specials. Hrs: 6:30 am-2:30 pm, 6-10 pm; Sun from 7 am. Res accepted. Bar 11-2 am; pianist. Wine cellar. A la carte entrees: bkfst $6-$20, lunch $12-$26, dinner $16-$30. Prix fixe: dinner $49. Valet parking. Jacket. Cr cds: A, C, D, DS, ER, JCB, MC, V.

D

★ ★ **THE GRILL.** *9560 Dayton Way (90210). 310/276-0615.* E-mail thegrillonthealley@juno.com. Hrs: 11:30 am-11 pm; Fri, Sat to midnight; Sun 5-9 pm. Closed major hols. Res accepted. Bar. A la carte entrees: lunch $12-$20, dinner $15-$30. Specializes in fresh seafood, steak, chops. Valet parking. Turn-of-the-century decor. Cr cds: A, D, MC, V.

D

★ ★ ★ **IL CIELO.** *9018 Burton Way, I-405 exit Wilshire Blvd E. 310/276-9990.* Hrs: 11:30 am-3 pm, 6-10:30 pm; Fri, Sat to 11 pm. Closed Sun; most major hols. Res accepted. Northern Italian menu. Beer. Wine list. A la carte entrees: lunch $10-$15, dinner $15-$25. Specializes in fresh seafood, homemade pasta, veal. Own pastries. Valet parking. Outdoor dining. Gardens, fountains. Cr cds: A, C, D, DS, JCB, MC, V.

D

✓★ ★ **IL PASTAIO.** *400 N Canon Dr (90210). 310/205-5444.* Hrs: 11 am-11 pm; Sun 5-10 pm. Closed some major hols. Italian menu. Bar. A la carte entrees: lunch $8.50-$12, dinner $9.50-$15. Specializes in pasta. Valet parking. Patio dining. Contemporary decor, artwork. Cr cds: A, D, MC, V.

D

★ ★ ★ **JIMMY'S.** *201 Moreno Dr. 310/552-2394.* Hrs: 11:30 am-3 pm, 5:30 pm-midnight; Sat from 5:30 pm. Closed Sun; major hols. French menu. Bar 11:30-2 am. Wine cellar. A la carte entrees: lunch $12-$18, dinner $21-$25. Specialties: peppered salmon, crème brulée Napoleon, Maryland crab cakes. Own pastries. Elegant French decor with a California touch. Cr cds: A, C, D, MC, V.

D

★ ★ ★ **LAWRY'S THE PRIME RIB.** *100 N La Cienega Blvd, I-465 exit Wilshire Blvd E. 310/652-2827.* Hrs: 5-10 pm; Fri to 11 pm; Sat 4:30-11 pm; Sun 4-10 pm. Closed Dec 25. Res accepted. Bar. Semi-a la carte: dinner $19.95-$26.95. Limited menu. Specialties: prime rib, spinning salad bowl, Yorkshire pudding. Own desserts. Valet parking. Cr cds: A, C, D, DS, JCB, MC, V.

D

★ ★ ★ **MAPLE DRIVE.** *345 N Maple Dr. 310/274-9800.* Web www.restaurant-pages.com/mapledrive. Hrs: 11:30 am-2:30 pm, 6-10 pm; Fri to 11 pm; Sat 6-11 pm. Closed Sun; major hols. Res accepted. Bar. A la carte entrees: lunch $14-$19, dinner $16-$32. Specialties: fried calamari, tuna tartar, grilled swordfish. Pianist. Valet parking (dinner). Terrace dining. Exhibition kitchen. Changing display of artwork. Cr cds: A, C, D, MC, V.

D

★ ★ **MATSUHISA.** *129 N La Cienega Blvd. 310/659-9639.* Hrs: 11:45 am-2:15 pm, 5:45-10:15 pm; Sat, Sun from 5:45 pm. Closed most major hols. Res accepted. Japanese menu. Wine, beer. Semi-a la carte: lunch $15-$25, dinner $40-$60. Omakase dishes from $60. Specializes in gourmet seafood, sushi. Valet parking. Totally nonsmoking. Cr cds: A, D, MC, V.

★ ★ ★ **OBACHINE.** *242 N Beverly Dr (90210). 310/274-4440.* Hrs: 11:30 am-2:30 pm, 5:30-10:30 pm. Res accepted. Asian menu. Bar. A la carte entrees: lunch $8.95-$12, dinner $12.95-$19.95. Complete meals: lunch $22-$32, dinner $32-$55. Specialties: sizzling catfish, Peking duck. Valet parking. Oriental decor. Cr cds: A, D, MC, V.

D

★ ★ ★ **POLO LOUNGE.** *(See Beverly Hills Hotel and Bungalows) 310/276-2251.* Hrs: 7-2 am; Sun brunch 11 am-3 pm. Res required. Bar. Wine cellar. A la carte entrees: bkfst $8-$14, lunch $14-$24, dinner $18-$28. Sun brunch $39. Specializes in California cuisine. Pianist. Valet parking. Outdoor dining. Jacket. Cr cds: A, C, D, JCB, MC, V.

D

★ ★ ★ **PREGO.** *362 N Camden Dr, I-405 exit Wilshire Blvd E. 310/277-7346.* Hrs: 11:30 am-midnight; Sun from 5 pm. Closed Thanksgiving, Dec 25. Res accepted. Northern Italian menu. Bar. A la carte entrees: lunch $8-$18, dinner $15-$28. Specializes in homemade pasta, fresh fish. Valet parking evenings. Oak-burning pizza oven & mesquite grill. Cr cds: A, D, JCB, MC, V.

D

★ **STINKING ROSE.** *55 N La Cienega (90211), I-405 exit Wilshire Blvd E. 310/652-7673.* Hrs: 11 am-11 pm; Fri, Sat to midnight. Res accepted. Italian menu. Bar to 2 am. A la carte entrees: lunch $8-$11, dinner $8-$25. Specialties: Lucifer's garlic steak alla Dante, bagna calda. Valet parking. Casual, eclectic decor. Cr cds: A, D, JCB, MC, V.

D

Unrated Dining Spots

ED DEBEVIC'S. *134 N La Cienega Blvd. 310/659-1952.* Hrs: 11:30 am-10 pm; Fri & Sat to midnight. Closed Thanksgiving, Dec 25. Bar. Semi-a la carte: lunch, dinner $4.50-$7.95. Specializes in: hamburgers, chicken. Own desserts. Valet parking. 1950s-style diner; memorabilia of the era. Staff provides entertainment: singing, dancing. Cr cds: A, MC, V.

D

PLANET HOLLYWOOD. *9560 Wilshire Blvd (90212). 310/275-7828.* Hrs: 11 am-midnight; Fri, Sat to 1 am. Bar. A la carte entrees: lunch, dinner $7.50-$18.95. Child's meals. Specializes in pasta, pizza, salads. Valet parking. Movie posters and memorabilia. Totally nonsmoking. Cr cds: A, C, D, DS, JCB, MC, V.

D

Hollywood

Motel

✓★ ★ **BEST WESTERN HOLLYWOOD HILLS.** *6141 Franklin Ave (90028), US 101 Gower St exit to Franklin Ave, then 1 blk W. 213/464-5181; FAX 213/962-0536.* 86 units, 3-4 story, 47 kits. S $50-$70; D $70-$85; each addl $5; kit. units $10 addl; under 12 free; wkly rates; higher rates Rose Bowl. Crib $5. Pet accepted, some restrictions; $10. Heated pool. TV; cable (premium). Restaurant 7 am-10 pm; Sun, Mon to 4 pm. Rm serv. Ck-out noon. Business servs avail. Sundries. Health club privileges. Refrigerators; microwaves avail. Cr cds: A, C, D, DS, MC, V.

SC

Hotels

★ ★ ★ **THE ARGYLE.** *(8358 Sunset Blvd, Los Angeles 90069) 1 mi W on Sunset Blvd. 213/654-7100; res: 800/225-2637; FAX 213/654-9287.* Web www.slh.com. Mythological creatures, zeppelins and myriad other images comingle above the street entrance and along the building setbacks of this magnificent art-deco restoration. Rooms are custom decorated and equipped with everything from two-line phones to marble baths and jacuzzis. 64 rms, 15 story, 44 suites. S $175; D $225; each addl $25; suites $325-$1,200; wkend rates. Crib free. Valet parking $17. TV; cable (premium), VCR (movies). Pool; poolside serv. Complimentary coffee in lobby. Restaurant (see FENIX). Rm serv 24 hrs. Bar 11-1 am. Ck-out 1 pm. Meeting rms. Business center. In-rm modem link. Concierge. Exercise rm; instructor, weights, bicycle, sauna. Massage. Bathrm phones, refrigerators, minibars; some in-rm whirlpools, wet bars; microwaves avail. Some balconies. Cr cds: A, C, D, JCB, MC, V.

D

★ ★ **CLARION HOLLYWOOD ROOSEVELT.** *7000 Hollywood Blvd (90028), US 101 exit Highland Ave, S to Hollywood Blvd. 213/466-7000; FAX 213/462-8056.* Web www.hotelchoice.com. 320 rms, 2-12 story, 47 suites. S, D $119-$149; each addl $20; suites $249-$1,500; under 18 free. Crib free. Valet parking $9.50. TV; cable (premium), VCR avail. Heated pool; whirlpool, poolside serv. Coffee in rms. Restaurant 6 am-11 pm. Rm serv to 1 am. Bars 11-1 am; entertainment. Convention facilities. Business servs avail. Concierge. Gift shop. Exercise equipt; weight machine, bicycle. Massage. Minibars; some bathrm phones; refrigerators, microwaves avail. Site of first Academy Awards presentation. Cr cds: A, C, D, DS, ER, JCB, MC, V.

D SC

★ ★ **HOLIDAY INN.** *1755 N Highland Ave (90028), US 101 exit Highland Ave, S 1/2 mi. 213/462-7181; FAX 213/466-9072.* Web www.socalcol.com/hollywood. 470 rms, 23 story. S, D $129-$169; each addl $15; suites $159-$199; under 18 free. Self park $6.50. Crib free. TV; cable (premium). Heated pool. Coffee in rms. Restaurant 6 am-10 pm. Bar 11-2 am; entertainment. Ck-out noon. Coin lndry. Convention facilities. Business servs avail. Concierge. Gift shop. Exercise equipt; bicycles, stair machine. Game rm. Refrigerators avail. Cr cds: A, C, D, DS, JCB, MC, V.

D SC

★ ★ ★ **LE MONTROSE SUITE HOTEL DE GRAN LUXE.** *(900 Hammond St, Los Angeles 90069) US 101 exit Sunset Blvd, W 4 mi to Hammond St. 213/855-1115; FAX 213/657-9192; res: 800/776-0666.* Web www.travel2000.com. 128 kit. suites, 5 story. Suites $220-$500; under 12 free. Crib free. Covered parking $14. Pet accepted. TV; cable (premium), VCR avail. Pool; whirlpool, poolside serv. Restaurant 5 am-10:45 pm. Rm serv 24 hrs. Ck-out noon. Meeting rm. Business servs avail. In-rm modem link. Concierge. Lighted tennis, pro. Exercise rm; instructor, weight machine, stair machine, sauna. Massage. Bathrm phones, refrigerators, fireplaces; many wet bars; microwaves avail. Some balconies. Art nouveau decor. Cr cds: A, C, D, ER, JCB, MC, V.

D SC

★ ★ **RAMADA PLAZA-WEST HOLLYWOOD.** *(8585 Santa Monica Blvd, Los Angeles 90069) US 101 exit Santa Monica Blvd W. 213/652-6400; FAX 213/652-2135.* E-mail info@ramada-wh.com; web www.ramada-wh.com. 175 rms, 4 story, 44 suites. S, D $125-$145; each addl $15; suites $159-$279; under 18 free. Crib free. TV; cable (premium), VCR avail. Heated pool. Restaurant 6:30 am-11:30 pm. Bar. Ck-out noon. Coin lndry. Business servs avail. Shopping arcade. Airport transportation. Health club privileges. Bathrm phones; some refrigerators, wetbars; microwaves avail. Some balconies. Cr cds: A, C, D, DS, JCB, MC, V.

D SC

Restaurants

★ ★ **ALTO PALATO TRATTORIA.** *(755 N La Cienega Blvd, Los Angeles 90069) US 101 Santa Monica Blvd exit, W 3 mi to La Cienega Blvd, then S. 310/657-9271.* Hrs: 6-11 pm; Fri, Sat also noon-2:30 pm; Sun 5:30-10:30 pm. Closed Jan 1, Thanksgiving, Dec 25. Res accepted. Italian menu. Bar. A la carte entrees: lunch, dinner $9.50-$28.50. Specialties: wood-fired pizza, pumpkin gnocchi, sautéed breast of chicken. Own pasta, desserts. Valet parking. Outdoor dining. Two-story; Italian cafe atmosphere. Cr cds: A, D, MC, V.

D

✔★ ★ **ANTONIO'S.** *7472 Melrose Ave (90046), US 101 Melrose Ave exit, W 3 mi. 213/655-0480.* Hrs: 11 am-11 pm. Closed Mon; Thanksgiving, Dec 25. Res accepted. Mexican menu. Bar. A la carte entrees: lunch, dinner $8.50-$15.95. Specialties: pollo yucateco, blue corn tamales with spinach. Strolling musicians wkend evenings. Valet parking. Outdoor dining. Colorful Mexican decor. Family-owned. Cr cds: A, MC, V.

D

✔★ ★ **BOOK SOUP BISTRO.** *(8800 Sunset Blvd, Los Angeles 90069) 213/657-1072.* Hrs: noon-10 pm; Fri to 11 pm; Sat 11:30 am-11 pm; Sun from 11:30 am. Closed Thanksgiving, Dec 25, Jan 1. Res accepted. French, Amer menu. Bar. Semi-a la carte: lunch $7.50-$14.50, dinner $7.50-$16.50. Child's meals. Specialties: roasted beet salad, penne with grilled eggplant, sterling silver N.Y. steak. Own desserts. Outdoor dining. Casual dining. Adj large bookstore. Cr cds: A, D, DS, MC, V.

D

★ ★ **CA' BREA.** *346 S La Brea Ave (90036), I-10 La Brea Ave exit, N 2 mi. 213/938-2863.* Web www.ladining.com/cabrea. Hrs: 11:30 am-2:30 pm, 5:30-11 pm; Sat from 5:30 pm. Closed Sun. Res accepted. Northern Italian menu. Bar. A la carte entrees: lunch, dinner $8.95-$22.95. Specializes in authentic Venetian dishes. Own pasta, desserts. Valet parking. Patio dining. Italian cafe decor. Totally nonsmoking. Cr cds: A, C, D, DS, MC, V.

D

✔★ **CAIOTI.** *2100 Laurel Canyon Blvd, N of Sunset Blvd at jct Kirkwood Dr. 213/650-2988.* Hrs: 4:30-11 pm. Closed some major hols. Res accepted. Italian, Amer menu. Wine, beer. Semi-a la carte: dinner $4.75-$14.25. Specializes in pizza, pasta, salad, grilled entrees. Own pizza dough. Outdoor dining. Rural setting. Cr cds: A, MC, V.

★ ★ ★ **CHIANTI RISTORANTE & CUCINA.** *7383 Melrose Ave (90046), US 101 Melrose Ave exit, W 3 mi. 213/653-8333.* Hrs: Cucina 11:30 am-11:30 pm; Fri, Sat to midnight; Sun 4-11 pm. Chianti 5:30-10 pm; Fri, Sat to 11 pm; Sun 5-10:30 pm. Closed Thanksgiving, Dec 25. Res accepted. Northern Italian menu. Bar. A la carte entrees: lunch, dinner $6.75-$19.95. Specializes in fresh seafood, pasta. Own baking. Valet parking. Two distinct dining areas. Cr cds: A, C, D, MC, V.

D

★ ★ ★ **CITRUS.** *6703 Melrose Ave (90038), US 101 Melrose Ave exit, W 2 mi. 213/857-0034.* E-mail citrusinla@aol.com. Hrs: noon-2:30 pm, 6:30-10:30 pm; Fri, Sat 6-11 pm. Closed Sun; major hols. Res accepted. California, French cuisine. Bar. A la carte entrees: lunch $13-$17, dinner $25-$32. Complete meals: dinner $50-$60. Specialties: Whitefish wrapped in caramelized onions, shiitake mushroom and garlic Napoleon. Own pastries. Valet parking. Open kitchen, garden setting. Cr cds: A, D, JCB, MC, V.

D

★ ★ **DAN TANA'S.** *(9071 Santa Monica Blvd, Los Angeles 90069) I-405 exit Santa Monica blvd, E 4 mi. 213/275-9444.* Hrs: 5 pm-1 am; Sun to 12:30 am. Closed Thanksgiving, Dec 25. Res required. Northern Italian menu. Bar. A la carte entrees: dinner $13-$39. Specializes in NY prime steak, whitefish. Valet parking. 2 dining areas. New York-style Italian restaurant with fireplace. Family-owned. Cr cds: A, C, D, DS, MC, V.

★ ★ ★ **DRAI'S.** *(730 N La Cienega Blvd, Los Angeles 90069) US 101 exit Santa Monica Blvd, W 3 mi to La Cienega Blvd, then S. 213/358-*

8585. Hrs: 6:30-10:30 pm. Closed Thanksgiving, Dec 25. Res required. Southern French menu. Bar. Wine cellar. A la carte entrees: dinner $14-$28. Specialties: sashimi of ahi tuna layered on toasted filo; ravioli with fresh Maine lobster; glazed Chilean sea bass with soy sauce, garlic and ginger. Jazz Mon. Valet parking. Three distinct dining areas with modern decor; French doors lead to garden rm; landscape mural, original artwork. Cr cds: A, D, MC, V.

D

★ ★ ★ **ECLIPSE.** *(8800 Melrose Ave, Los Angeles 90069) US 101 exit Melrose Ave, 5 mi W. 213/724-5959.* Hrs: 6-10:30 pm. Closed Sun; Thanksgiving, Dec 25. Res accepted. Bar. Extensive wine list. A la carte entrees: dinner $16-$28. Specialty: whole fish roasted in wood-burning oven. Own desserts. Valet parking. Outdoor dining. Modern artwork. Cr cds: A, C, D, DS, JCB, MC, V.

D

★ ★ ★ **EMI.** *6602 Melrose Ave (90038), US 101 Melrose Ave exit, W 2 mi. 213/935-4922.* Hrs: noon-3 pm, 6-11 pm. Closed Mon; most major hols. Res accepted. Continental menu. Bar. Wine cellar. A la carte entrees: lunch $9-$16, dinner $12-$28. Specialties: sautéed shrimp with a Thai cucumber salad, safran fettuccine with thyme and Santa Barbara mussels, sautéed filet mignon with fresh asparagus sauce. Own baking. Valet parking. Balcony dining. Cr cds: A, ER, MC, V.

D

★ ★ ★ ★ **FENIX.** *(See The Argyle Hotel) 213/848-6677.* Inside the historic building is art-deco decor, while outside on the terrace is a view overlooking the city. French, California menu. Specialties: Alaskan ling cod with Yukon gold risotto, daikon sesame salad, grilled Texas black antelope. Hrs: 6:30-10:30 am, 11:30 am-2:30 pm, 6-10:30 pm. Closed Sun. Res accepted. Bar. Extensive wine list. A la carte entrees: bkfst $7.75-$9.50, lunch $14-$22, dinner $23-$29. Complete meal: dinner $48. Valet parking. Outdoor dining. Cr cds: A, C, D, JCB, MC, V.

D

★ ★ ★ ★ ★ **L'ORANGERIE.** *903 N La Cienega Blvd (90069), US 101 Santa Monica Blvd exit, W 3 mi to La Cienega Blvd then S 2 blks. 310/652-9770.* E-mail loranger@pacbell.net; web www.orangerie.com. The atmosphere is as elegantly French as the cuisine at this fine restaurant, thanks to tall Palladian windows, decor reminiscent of a château and the talent of master chef Ludovic Lefebvre. There is also dining outside on the courtyard terrace and patio. Classic French menu. Specialties: poached lobster tail on asparagus risotto, seabass filet skewered with fennel branches. Hrs: 6:30-11 pm. Closed Mon. Res required. Extensive wine list. Bar. A la carte entrees: dinner $26-$40. Complete meals: dinner $80. Valet parking. Jacket. Cr cds: A, C, D, DS, JCB, MC, V.

D

★ ★ **LA MASIA.** *(9077 Santa Monica Blvd, Los Angeles 90069) US 101 Santa Monica Blvd exit, 3 mi W. 213/273-7066.* Hrs: 6-11 pm; Fri, Sat to 12:30 am; Sun from 5:30 pm. Closed Mon, Tues; Jan 1, July 4, Dec 25. Res accepted. Spanish menu. Bar to 2 am. Semi-a la carte: dinner $14.50-$26.50. Specialties: paella, chuleta de ternera. Salsa, Latin jazz. Valet parking. Intimate dining. Tapas bar. Family-owned. Cr cds: A, C, D, DS, MC, V.

D

★ ★ ★ **LE DOME.** *(8720 Sunset Blvd, Los Angeles 90069) US 101 Sunset Blvd exit, 4 mi W. 213/659-6919.* Hrs: noon-midnight; Sat from 6 pm. Closed Sun; major hols. Res accepted. French, continental menu. Bar. Extensive wine list. A la carte entrees: lunch $11.75-$19.75, dinner $14-$30. Specializes in fresh fish, prime beef. Own desserts. Valet parking. Outdoor dining. Art noveau decor. Cr cds: A, C, D, MC, V.

D

✔★ **LE PETIT FOUR.** *8654 Sunset Blvd (90069), US 101 Sunset Blvd exit, 4 mi W. 310/652-3863.* Hrs: 9 am-12:30 am; Sun brunch to 6 pm. Closed Dec 25. Res accepted. French, Italian menu. Bar. A la carte entrees: bkfst $4.50-$9.95, lunch, dinner $5.50-$16.50. Sun brunch $4.50-$9.95. Specializes in fresh fish, pasta, salad. Own baking, ice cream. Parking. Outdoor dining. Collection of antique mirrors. Sidewalk dining area has bistro atmosphere. Cr cds: A, C, D, MC, V.

✔★ ★ **LOLA'S.** *(945 N Fairfax Ave, Los Angles 90046) US 101 exit Melrose Ave, W 3½ mi to Fairfax Ave, then N. 213/736-5652.* Hrs: 5:30 pm-2 am. Closed Thanksgiving, Dec 24, 25. Res accepted. Bar. Semi-a la carte: dinner $7.50-$16. Specialties: grilled pork chop, baked macaroni & cheese, chocolate kiss cake. Own desserts. Valet parking. Skylights, chandeliers. Cr cds: A, D, MC, V.

D

★ ★ ★ **MORTON'S.** *(8764 Melrose Ave, Los Angeles 90069) at Robertson Ave. 310/276-5205.* Hrs: noon-3 pm, 6-11 pm; Sat from 6 pm. Closed Sun; major hols. Res accepted. Bar to 1 am. Wine cellar. A la carte entrees: lunch $11-$17, dinner $17-$30. Specialties: tuna sashimi, grilled marinated lamb loin, grilled swordfish. Own desserts. Valet parking. Modern decor. Cr cds: A, D, MC, V.

D

★ **MUSSO & FRANK GRILL.** *6667 Hollywood Blvd (90028). 213/467-7788.* Hrs: 11 am-11 pm. Closed Sun, Mon; major hols. Res accepted. Continental menu. Bar. A la carte entrees: lunch, dinner $4.95-$28.50. Specialties: Bouillabaisse Marseillaise, homemade chicken pot pie. Own desserts. Historic restaurant opened 1919. Famed "Round Table" of Saroyan, Thurber, Falkner and Fitzgerald met here. Menu changes daily. Totally nonsmoking. Cr cds: A, C, D, DS, MC, V.

★ ★ **PALM.** *(9001 Santa Monica Blvd, Los Angeles 90069) I-405 exit Santa Monica Blvd, E 3 mi. 213/550-8811.* Hrs: noon-10:30 pm; Sat from 5 pm; Sun 5-9:30 pm. Closed most major hols. Res accepted. Bar. A la carte entrees: lunch $10-$18, dinner $16-$30. Specializes in steak, lobster. Valet parking. Several dining areas. Hollywood celebrity caricatures cover walls. Cr cds: A, C, D, MC, V.

D

★ ★ ★ ★ **PATINA.** *5955 Melrose Ave (90038), US 101 Melrose Ave exit, W 1½ mi. 213/467-1108.* This is an intimate setting, decorated with white walls, pale woods, frosted glass and pigmented metals. Candlelight dances across the white linens of the understated dining room. French, California menu. Specialties: Santa Barbara shrimp, peppered tournedos of tuna. Hrs: 6-9:30 pm; Tues noon-2 pm, 6-9:30 pm; Fri to 10:30 pm; Sat 5:30-10:30 pm. Closed some major hols. Res accepted; required wkends. Bar. Wine cellar. A la carte entrees: lunch $14.50-$21.50, dinner $14.75-$27.50. Complete meals: lunch $32-$38, dinner $55-$69. Valet parking. Cr cds: A, D, DS, MC, V.

D

★ ★ ★ **SONORA CAFE.** *(180 S La Brea Ave, Los Angeles 90036) I-10 to La Brea Ave exit, N 2 mi. 213/857-1800.* Web www.sonoracafe.com. Hrs: 11:30 am-10 pm; Fri to 11 pm; Sat 5:30-11 pm; Sun 5-9 pm. Closed major hols. Res accepted. Southwestern menu. Bar. Extensive wine list. Semi-a la carte: lunch $9.95-$16, dinner $12-$28. Specialties: Prince Edward Island mussels, Texas barbecue pork chops, wood-grilled sea scallops. Own desserts. Valet parking. Outdoor dining. Southwestern decor; original Southwestern and early American artwork; fireplace. Cr cds: A, DS, MC, V.

D

★ ★ ★ **SPAGO.** *(8795 Sunset Blvd, Los Angeles 90069) US 101 Sunset Blvd exit, approx 4 mi W. 213/652-4025.* Hrs: 6-11 pm; Sat from 5:30 pm. Closed Mon; some major hols. Res required. California menu. Bar. A la carte entrees: dinner $11.50-$28.50. Specializes in gourmet pizza, lobster ravioli, fresh fish. Own pasta. Valet parking. View of Sunset Strip, West Hollywood. Cr cds: A, C, D, DS, MC, V.

D

★ ★ ★ **YUJEAN KANG'S.** *(8826 Melrose Ave, Los Angeles 90069) 213/288-0806.* Hrs: noon-2:30 pm, 6-11 pm; Sat, Sun brunch to 2:30 pm. Closed Thanksgiving. Res accepted. Chinese menu. Bar. Wine cellar. Semi-a la carte: lunch $8-$12, dinner $12-$18. Sat, Sun brunch $8-$12. Specialties: Chilean sea bass in spicy sesame sauce, tea-smoked duck, lamb loin. Valet parking. Oriental decor; antiques. Totally nonsmoking. Cr cds: A, C, D, DS, JCB, MC, V.

D

Westwood Village

Motel

★★ **HOTEL DEL CAPRI.** *10587 Wilshire Blvd (90024). 310/474-3511; FAX 310/470-9999; res: 800/44-HOTEL.* 80 units, 2-4 story, 46 kit. suites. S $90; D $100-$110; each addl $10; kit. suites $115-$145. Crib $10. Pet accepted, some restrictions. TV; cable (premium), VCR avail. Heated pool. Complimentary continental bkfst. Restaurants nearby. Ck-out noon. Guest lndry. Business servs avail. Bellhops. Valet serv. Health club privileges. Bathrm phones, refrigerators; many in-rm whirlpools. Cr cds: A, C, D, MC, V.

SC

Hotels

★★★ **DOUBLETREE.** *(10740 Wilshire Blvd, Los Angeles 90024) I-405 exit Wilshire Blvd. 310/475-8711; FAX 310/475-5220.* 295 rms, 19 story. S $119-$160; D $129-$170; each addl $10; suites $200-$230; under 18 free. Crib free. TV; cable (premium), VCR avail. Pool; whirlpool, poolside serv. Restaurant 6:30 am-2 pm; 5-10 pm. Bar 2 pm-midnight. Ck-out noon. Meeting rms. Business center. In-rm modem link. Concierge. Gift shop. Valet parking. Exercise equipt; treadmill, bicycles, sauna. Game rm. Refrigerators. Cr cds: A, C, D, DS, JCB, MC, V.

D SC

★★ **HILGARD HOUSE.** *927 Hilgard Ave (90024), I-405 exit Wilshire Blvd E. 310/208-3945; FAX 310/208-1972; res: 800/826-3934.* E-mail reservations@hilgard-house.com; web www.hilgard-house.com. 47 rms, 4 story. S $99-$109; D $109-$119; each addl $10; under 18 free. Crib free. TV; cable (premium). Complimentary continental bkfst. Ck-out noon. Guest lndry. Free covered parking. Refrigerators avail. Cr cds: A, C, D, DS, JCB, MC, V.

D SC

★★★ **WESTWOOD MARQUIS HOTEL & GARDEN.** *930 Hilgard Ave (90024). 310/208-8765; FAX 310/824-0355; res: 800/421-2317.* E-mail padavis@earthlink.net. 257 suites (1-3 bedrm), 16 story. S, D $235-$650; wkend rates. Crib free. Pet accepted. Garage; valet parking, in/out $18. TV; cable (premium), VCR avail (movies). 2 heated pools. Restaurants 6:30 am-11 pm (also see DYNASTY ROOM). Rm serv 24 hrs. Bar 10-2 am; entertainment Fri-Sun. Ck-out noon. Meeting rms. Business servs avail. In-rm modem link. Concierge. Maid serv 24 hrs. Gift shop. Exercise equipt; weights, bicycles. Massage. Health club privileges. Refrigerators, minibars; microwaves avail. Cr cds: A, C, D, DS, JCB, MC, V.

D

Restaurants

★★★ **DYNASTY ROOM.** *(See Westwood Marquis Hotel & Garden) 310/208-8765.* E-mail padavis@earthlink.net. Hrs: 6-10:30 pm. Res accepted. California menu. Bar 10-1:30 am. A la carte entrees: dinner $18-$28. Specialties: potato pancake with smoked salmon and cavier, rack of lamb. Valet parking. Elegant setting; with exclusive collection of objets d'art from the Tang dynasty. Cr cds: A, C, D, DS, JCB, MC, V.

D

★★ **MONTY'S STEAK HOUSE.** *1100 Glendon Ave, I-405 exit Wilshire Blvd E. 310/208-8787.* Hrs: 11 am-3 pm, 5 pm-1 am; Sat, Sun 5 pm-midnight. Closed Thanksgiving. Res accepted. Bar to 2 am; Sat, Sun from 5 pm. Semi-a la carte: lunch $8-$20, dinner $15-$65. Specializes in steak, seafood. Entertainment. Valet parking. Located on 21st floor of building; panoramic view. Cr cds: A, C, D, MC, V.

D

Louisville

Founded: 1778
Pop: 269,063
Elev: 462 feet
Time zone: Eastern
Area code: 502
Web: www.louisville-visitors.com

To the horse racing enthusiast, Louisville means only one thing—the famed Kentucky Derby, culmination of a two-week festival that has been held here each spring for more than 100 years. But there is more to Louisville than the enjoyment of jockeys and juleps—it is also a major producer of tobacco. And for fans of the great American pastime, the crack of a ball against a Louisville Slugger bat is music to the ears. There is, of course, other music in this diverse city. An opera, orchestra, theaters, ballet and other fine arts organizations are evidence of Louisville's dedication to culture.

The Spanish, French, English, Scots, Irish and Germans all had roles in the exploration and development of the area. George Rogers Clark brought settlers to the region in the winter of 1778-1779. It became an informal military base and played an important role in driving the British and Native Americans out of the Midwest. Located at the falls of the Ohio River, Louisville is a city long nurtured by river traffic. In its early years, before a canal bypassed the falls, Louisville was an important portage point. With the advent of the steamboat on the Ohio in the early 19th century, the city became a vital port, and its growth was rapid.

The social highlight of a very social city is the Derby, a mélange of festival, fashion show, spectacle and celebration of the horse. After the money is lost or won and the last of the mint juleps is swallowed, Louisville returns to normalcy, a city Southern in its manner, Midwestern in its pace.

Business

Louisville is a major distribution point for tobacco. Electrical appliances rank third in a vast array of manufactured products, from candy and clothing to synthetic rubber. Other major industries include lumber milling, meat packing, oil refining, photoengraving and publishing.

Louisville is one of the nation's leading river ports. An enormous amount of coal passes through the locks on the Ohio River each year. Louisville is also an important air and rail center.

Convention Facilities

The Kentucky Fair and Exposition Center is a multipurpose building covering one million square feet of exhibition space under one roof. Freedom Hall, the center's main arena, seats 19,400 people. Meeting rooms can be used individually or in combination to accommodate from 350 to 1,250 people. The ballroom seats up to 850. Newmarket Hall is an air-conditioned amphitheater seating 600. There are 24 buildings in the Exposition Center Complex, with parking for 19,000 cars.

Louisville Gardens has over 36,000 square feet of multiuse space. The main arena has 5,000 permanent seats and room for 2,000 more on the arena floor. The second-floor theater seats 775. Meeting rooms have a capacity of 60 to 700 people. The Grand Arena can accommodate banquets for 2,200. Located in the heart of downtown, it is within easy walking distance of more than 2,200 hotel rooms.

A third exhibit and convention center, Commonwealth Convention Center, is situated on the five-block 4th Avenue Mall. It is ideally suited in size, location and design for intermediate-sized conventions and trade shows. It has 150,000 square feet of exhibit space that can be divided into three halls of 50,000, 30,000 and 20,000 square feet, and 36 meeting rooms holding from 25 to 1,000 people. The center is the heart of a convention complex that includes 600- and 700-car garages and a 388-room hotel. An expansion and renovation project will expand the center to 285,000 square feet.

Historical Areas

Louisville is a city that reveres its past. Two beautiful historic mansions, which are open to the public, are owned and operated by the Historic Homes Foundation. Farmington, located off the intersection of I-264 and US 31E, was built in 1808-1810. The design of this Federal-style mansion was based on a plan by Thomas Jefferson. The original deed to the land, signed by Governor Patrick Henry of Virginia, is displayed on a wall. Locust Grove, the last home of George Rogers Clark, is on Blankenbaker Lane near I-71. Both houses are authentically and beautifully restored and furnished and are complemented by formal gardens.

The Preservation Alliance of Louisville and Jefferson County encourages restoration efforts in the city. The West Main Street Historic District encompasses the founding site of the city and the mercantile district of the late 1800s. Old Victorian warehouses, displaying some of the best remaining cast-iron architecture in the United States, are being converted into performing arts centers and offices.

The Belgravia and St James Courts Historic District was a residential neighborhood developed on the site of the 1883 Southern Exposition. Today the fine late-Victorian houses are being privately preserved and restored.

The 19th-century German community, Butchertown, houses antique shops and the one-time residence of Thomas A. Edison.

Sports & Recreation

Louisville's biggest sporting event is, of course, the Kentucky Derby. But sports in Louisville can also mean college basketball, wrestling, ice skating, hot-air balloon racing, auto racing and Thoroughbred racing.

The Redbirds, minor-league farm team for the St Louis Cardinals, play baseball from April through August in the stadium at the fairgrounds.

Within and surrounding the city are 10,000 acres of park land. There are numerous tennis courts, golf courses and swimming pools, as well as opportunities for fishing, hiking and camping.

Entertainment

The Kentucky Center for the Arts not only houses the Kentucky Opera, Stage One: Children's Theatre, Louisville Ballet and the Louisville Orchestra, it also hosts bluegrass, Broadway, jazz, country & western and film series.

Actors Theatre of Louisville offers major productions, which attract large and enthusiastic audiences.

For a different kind of relaxation, the stern-wheeler steamer *Belle of Louisville,* which has been cruising the Ohio River for half a century, still sets off for pleasant afternoon or evening excursions. Each Derby season it stirs up excitement by challenging Cincinnati's *Delta Queen* to an old-time steamboat race.

Sightseeing

Two famous sights within Louisville are Riverfront Plaza and Churchill Downs. Bus tours of the city begin at First and Liberty streets. A Visitor Information Center is also located here. Other Information Centers are located at Louisville International Airport, I-64W near Simpsonville and in the Galleria shopping mall downtown.

Among the industrial tours of interest is the Louisville Slugger Museum & Bat Factory, where golf clubs and the famous Louisville Slugger baseball bats are manufactured.

The city's major shopping area is Fourth Avenue. On Fourth Avenue is the Galleria Complex, twin 26-story towers with a connecting atrium and enough shops, stores and boutiques to satisfy the most discriminating consumer.

Outside Louisville, temptations for the sightseer include tours of horse farms in the bluegrass region to the east of the city, Fort Knox, Mammoth Cave, Abraham Lincoln's birthplace, Bardstown and a wealth of lovely lakes and mountains.

General References

Area code: 502

Phone Numbers

POLICE & FIRE: 911

POISON CONTROL CENTER: 589-8222

TIME: 585-5961 **WEATHER:** 968-6025

Information Sources

Louisville and Jefferson County Convention & Visitors Bureau, 400 S First St, 40202; 582-3732 or 800/792-5595.

Louisville Chamber of Commerce, 600 W Main St, 40202; 625-0000.

Metropolitan Park and Recreation Board, 456-8100.

Transportation

AIRLINES: American; ASA; Comair; Continental; Delta; Northwest; Southwest; TWA; United; USAir; ValuJet and other commuter and regional airlines.

AIRPORT: Louisville International Airport, 368-6524.

CAR RENTAL AGENCIES: (See IMPORTANT TOLL-FREE NUMBERS) Avis 368-5851; Budget 363-4300; Dollar 366-1600; Hertz 361-0181; National 361-2515; Thrifty 367-2277.

PUBLIC TRANSPORTATION: Transit Authority of River City, 10th & Broadway, 40202; 585-1234. TARC-minibuses and "Toonerville II" Trolley circulate throughout the center city.

Newspaper

The Courier-Journal.

Convention Facilities

Commonwealth Convention Center, 221 S Fourth Ave, 595-4381.

Kentucky Fair & Exposition Center, I-65 at I-264, 367-5000.

Louisville Gardens, 525 W Muhammad Ali Blvd, 587-3800.

Sports & Recreation

Kentucky Fair & Exposition Center, I-65 at I-264, 367-5000 (University of Louisville, basketball).

Racetrack

Churchill Downs, 700 Central Ave, 636-4400.

Cultural Facilities

Theaters

Actors Theatre of Louisville, 316 W Main St, 584-1265.

Bunbury Theatre, 112 S 7th St, 585-5306.

Derby Dinner Playhouse, 525 Marriott Dr, Clarksville, IN, 812/288-8281.

Kentucky Center for the Arts, 5 Riverfront Plaza, 584-7777.

Stage One: Louisville Children's Theatre, 425 W Market St, 589-5946.

Concert Hall

Memorial Auditorium, 970 S 4th St, 584-4911.

Museums

Colonel Harland Sanders Museum, 1441 Gardiner Ln, 456-8353.

Howard Steamboat Museum, 1101 E Market St, Jeffersonville, IN, 812/283-3728.

Kentucky Derby Museum, 704 Central Ave, 637-1111.

Louisville Science Center, 727 W Main St, 561-6100.

Art Museums & Galleries

Allen R. Hite Art Institute, University of Louisville, Belknap Campus, 852-6794.

J.B. Speed Art Museum, 2035 S 3rd St, 636-2893.

Kentucky Art & Craft Gallery, 609 W Main St, 589-0102.

Louisville Visual Art Association, Water Tower, 3005 Upper River Rd, 896-2146.

Points of Interest

Historical

Cave Hill Cemetery, 701 Baxter Ave, 451-5630.

Christ Church Cathedral, 421 S 2nd St, 587-1354.

Farmington, 3033 Bardstown Rd, at jct Watterson Expwy, 452-9920.

Jefferson County Courthouse, Jefferson St, between 5th & 6th Sts, 574-5761.

Locust Grove, 561 Blankenbaker Lane, 897-9845.

Thomas Edison House, 731 E Washington, 585-5247.

Zachary Taylor National Cemetery, 4701 Brownsboro Rd, 893-3852.

Other Attractions

American Printing House for the Blind, 1839 Frankfort Ave, 895-2405.

Hadley Pottery, 1570 Story Ave, 584-2171.

Louisville Falls Fountain, Riverfront Plaza.

Louisville Slugger Museum & Bat Factory, 800 W Main St, 588-7228.

Louisville Zoological Gardens, 1100 Trevilian Way, 459-2181.

Rauch Memorial Planetarium, 2301 S 3rd St, 852-6664.

Sightseeing Tours

Belle of Louisville, 4th St & River Rd, 574-2355.

Gray Line bus tours, 282-7433.

Annual Events

Kentucky Derby Festival, 584-6383. Mid-Apr-early May.

Kentucky Derby, Churchill Downs. 1st Sat May.

Kentucky State Fair, Kentucky Fair & Exposition Center, 367-5000. 10 days late Aug.

Corn Island Storytelling Festival. Late Sept.

St James Court Art Show, Old Louisville, 636-5023. 1st wkend Oct.

City Neighborhoods

Many of the restaurants, unrated dining establishments and some lodgings listed under Louisville include neighborhoods as well as exact street addresses. Geographic descriptions of these areas are given, followed by a table of restaurants arranged by neighborhood.

Downtown: South of the Ohio River, west of Shelby St, north of Oak St and east of 9th St. **South of Downtown:** South of Oak St. **East of Downtown:** East of Shelby St.

Old Louisville: South of Breckenridge St, west of I-65, north of Eastern Pkwy and east of 9th St.

Lodgings and Food

LOUISVILLE RESTAURANTS BY NEIGHBORHOOD AREAS

(For full description, see alphabetical listings under Restaurants)

DOWNTOWN
The English Grill (The Camberley Brown Hotel). 335 W Broadway
Kunz's. 115 S 4th Ave
Old Spaghetti Factory. 235 W Market St
Timothy's. 826 E Broadway
Vincenzo's. 150 S 5th St

SOUTH OF DOWNTOWN
Fifth Quarter. 1241 Durrett Lane
Jessie's. 9609 Dixie Hwy
Masterson's. 1830 S 3rd St
Uptown Cafe. 1624 Bardstown Rd

EAST OF DOWNTOWN
Cafe Metro. 1700 Bardstown Rd
Cafe Mimosa. 1216 Bardstown Rd
Darryl's 1815 Restaurant. 3110 Bardstown Rd
Equestrian Grille. 1582 Bardstown
Ferd Grisanti's. 10212 Taylorsville Rd
Le Relais. Taylorsville Rd
Lilly's. 1147 Bardstown Rd
Mamma Grisanti. 3938 DuPont Circle
Sichuan Garden. 9850 Linn Station Rd

Note: When a listing is located in a town that does not have its own city heading, it will appear under the city nearest to its location. In these cases, the address and town appear in parenthesis immediately following the name of the establishment.

Motels

(Rates are generally much higher during Kentucky Derby; may be 3-day min)

★ ★ **BEST WESTERN REGENCY.** *1301 Kentucky Mills Dr (40299), I-64 exit 17, east of downtown. 502/267-8100.* Web www.bestwestern.com/best.html. 119 rms, 3 story. S $57-$63; D $65-$95; each addl $8; under 18 free. Crib free. TV; cable (premium). Indoor pool; whirlpool, sauna. Complimentary continental bkfst. Restaurant adj 6:30 am-10 pm. Ck-out noon. Coin Indry. Meeting rms. Business serv avail. In-rm modem link. Valet serv. Golf privileges. Some refrigerators; microwaves avail. Cr cds: A, C, D, DS, JCB, MC, V.

D SC

★ ★ **COURTYARD BY MARRIOTT.** *9608 Blairwood Rd (40222), I-64 Hurstbourne Ln exit 15, east of downtown. 502/429-0006; FAX 502/429-5926.* 151 rms, 4 story. S, D $99; suites $115; under 18 free; wkend rates. Crib free. TV; cable (premium). Pool; whirlpool. Complimentary coffee in rms. Bar 5:30-10 pm. Ck-out 1 pm. Coin Indry. Meeting rms. Business servs avail. In-rm modem link. Valet serv. Exercise equipt; weights, bicycles. Health club privileges. Refrigerators, microwaves avail. Cr cds: A, D, DS, MC, V.

D SC

★ ★ **FAIRFIELD INN BY MARRIOTT.** *9400 Blairwood Rd (40222), I-64 exit 15, east of downtown. 502/339-1900.* 105 rms, 3 story. S, D $54.95-$78.95; each addl $10; under 18 free. Crib free. TV; cable (premium). Pool. Continental bkfst. Complimentary coffee in lobby. Restaurant adj 6 am-11 pm. Ck-out noon. Meeting rms. In-rm modem link. Microwaves avail. Cr cds: A, D, DS, MC, V.

D SC

★ ★ **HAMPTON INN.** *1902 Embassy Square Blvd (40299), I-64 Hurstbourne Lane exit 15, east of downtown. 502/491-2577; FAX 502/491-1325.* 119 rms, 2 story. S $64; D $77; under 18 free. Crib free. TV; cable (premium). Pool. Continental bkfst. Restaurant nearby. Ck-out noon. Meeting rm. Business servs avail. In-rm modem link. Microwaves avail. Cr cds: A, C, D, DS, MC, V.

D SC

✔★ **RED ROOF INN.** *9330 Blairwood Rd (40222), 1 blk N of I-64 exit 15, east of downtown. 502/426-7621; FAX 502/426-7933.* 108 rms, 2 story. S $35.99-$69.99; D $43.99-$79.99; each addl $8-$10; under 18 free. Crib free. Pet accepted. TV; cable. Complimentary coffee. Restaurant adj 6 am-11 pm. Ck-out noon. Business servs avail. In-rm modem link. Cr cds: A, C, D, DS, MC, V.

D SC

★ ★ **RESIDENCE INN BY MARRIOTT.** *120 N Hurstbourne Pkwy (40222), east of downtown. 502/425-1821; FAX 502/425-1672.* 96 kit. suites, 2 story. 1-bedrm $86-$106; 2-bedrm $109-$135; family rates; some wkend rates. Crib free. TV; cable (premium). Heated pool; whirlpool, lifeguard. Complimentary continental bkfst. Ck-out noon. Coin Indry. Business servs avail. In-rm modem link. Valet serv. Sport court. Health club privileges. Refrigerators, microwaves, fireplaces. Grills. Cr cds: A, D, DS, MC, V.

D

★ ★ **SIGNATURE INN.** *6515 Signature Dr (40213), I-65 exit 128, south of downtown. 502/968-4100.* 123 rms, 2 story. S $67-$70; D $74-$77; under 18 free; wkend rates Dec-Feb. Crib free. TV; cable (premium). Pool. Complimentary continental bkfst. Restaurant adj 6 am-11 pm. Ck-out noon. Meeting rms. Business center. In-rm modem link. Valet serv. Sundries. Free airport transportation. Health club privileges. Cr cds: A, D, DS, JCB, MC, V.

D SC

✔★ **SUPER 8.** *4800 Preston Hwy (40213), off I-65 exit 130, south of downtown. 502/968-0088; FAX 502/968-0088, ext. 347.* 100 rms, 3 story. S $43.88; D $53.88; each addl $5; under 12 free. Crib free. TV; cable (premium). Complimentary coffee in lobby. Restaurant opp open 24 hrs. Ck-out 11 am. Business servs avail. In-rm modem link. Airport transportation. Cr cds: A, C, D, DS, MC, V.

D SC

Motor Hotels

★ ★ **AMERISUITES.** *701 S Hurstbourne Pkwy (40222), east of downtown. 502/426-0119; FAX 502/426-3013; res: 800/833-1516.* 123 kit. units, 5 story. June-Aug: S, D $84-$118; each addl $10; higher rates special events; lower rates rest of yr. Crib free. TV; cable (premium), VCR (movies). Pool. Complimentary continental bkfst. Complimentary coffee in rms. Restaurant nearby. Ck-out noon. Meeting rms. Business servs avail. Coin Indry. Free airport transportation. Exercise equipt; weight machine, stair machine. Health club privileges. Refrigerators, microwaves. Cr cds: A, C, D, DS, MC, V.

D SC

★ ★ **BRECKINRIDGE INN.** *2800 Breckinridge Lane (40220), I-264 exit 18A, south of downtown. 502/456-5050; FAX 502/451-1577.* 123 rms, 2 story. S, D $65-$95; each addl $7; under 12 free. Crib $7. Pet accepted; $50. TV; cable. 2 pools, 1 indoor; lifeguard. Restaurant 7 am-1:30 pm, 5-9 pm. Rm serv. Bar. Ck-out noon. Meeting rms. Business servs avail. Valet serv. Sundries. Gift shop. Barber shop. Free airport transportation. Lighted tennis. Exercise equipt; weights, bicycle, sauna. Cr cds: A, C, D, DS, MC, V.

SC

★ ★ **COMFORT SUITES.** *1850 Resource Way (40299), east of downtown. 502/266-6509; FAX 502/266-9014.* 70 suites. S $79; D $139. Crib free. TV; cable (premium). Indoor pool; whirlpool. Complimentary continental bkfst. Complimentary coffee in rms. Restaurant nearby. Ck-out

11 am. Business center. Free airport transportation. Refrigerators, microwaves. Cr cds: A, C, D, DS, JCB, MC, V.

D SC

★★★ **EXECUTIVE INN.** *978 Phillips Lane (40213), Watterson Expressway at Fairgrounds, near Standiford Field Airport, south of downtown. 502/367-6161; FAX 502/363-1880; res: 800/626-2706.* 465 rms, 2-6 story. S $84; D $94; each addl $10; suites $188-$282; under 18 free. Crib free. TV; cable, VCR avail. 2 pools, 1 indoor; wading pool, poolside serv, lifeguard. Restaurants 6:30 am-midnight. Rm serv. Bar 11 am-midnight, closed Sun. Ck-out 1 pm. Convention facilities. Business servs avail. Bellhops. Sundries. Gift shop. Barber, beauty shop. Free airport transportation. Exercise rm; instructor, weights, bicycles; sauna. Lawn games. Some private patios, balconies. Tudor-inspired architecture. Cr cds: A, C, D, DS, MC, V.

D SC

★★★ **EXECUTIVE WEST.** *830 Phillips Lane (40209), Freedom Way at Fairgrounds, near Standiford Field Airport, south of downtown. 502/367-2251; FAX 502/363-2087; res: 800/626-2708 (exc KY).* E-mail exwest@iglou.com; web wl.iglou.com/exwest. 611 rms, 8 story. S, D $84-$124; suites $105-$240; under 17 free; wkend rates. Crib free. Pet accepted; $100. TV; cable. Indoor/outdoor pool; poolside serv, lifeguard. Restaurant 6:30 am-11 pm. Rm serv. Bar; entertainment. Ck-out noon. Convention facilities. Business servs avail. In-rm modem link. Bellhops. Gift shop. Barber, beauty shop. Free airport transportation. Health club privileges. Refrigerator in suites. Kentucky Kingdom Amusement Park opp. Cr cds: A, C, D, DS, MC, V.

D SC

✔★★ **HAMPTON INN.** *800 Phillips Lane (40209), near Louisville Intl Airport, south of downtown. 502/366-8100; FAX 502/366-0700.* 130 rms, 4 story. S $69-$74; D $74-$79; under 18 free; wkend rates; higher rates special events. Crib free. TV; cable (premium). Pool; lifeguard. Complimentary continental bkfst. Restaurant nearby. Ck-out noon. Meeting rms. Business servs avail. Free airport transportation. Exercise equipt; weight machines, bicycle. Cr cds: A, C, D, DS, MC, V.

D SC

★★★ **HOLIDAY INN.** *1325 S Hurstbourne Pkwy (40222), at I-64 exit 15, east of downtown. 502/426-2600; FAX 502/423-1605.* 267 rms, 7 story. S, D $85-$105; suites $109-$275; under 18 free. Crib free. TV; cable (premium). Indoor pool; lifeguard. Coffee in rms. Restaurant 6:30 am-10 pm. Rm serv. Bar noon-midnight. Ck-out noon. Meeting rms. Business servs avail. In-rm modem link. Bellhops. Valet serv. Gift shop. Airport transportation. Exercise equipt; bicycles, whirlpool, sauna. Refrigerator in suites. Cr cds: A, C, D, DS, JCB, MC, V.

D SC

★★ **HOLIDAY INN AIRPORT.** *1465 Gardiner Lane (40213). 502/452-6361; FAX 502/451-1541.* 200 rms, 3 story. S, D $92; each addl $7; under 18 free; wkend rates. Crib free. Pet accepted. TV; cable (premium). Pool; poolside serv, lifeguard. Complimentary coffee in rms. Restaurant 11 am-11 pm. Rm serv. Bar to midnight. Ck-out noon. Coin lndry. Meeting rms. Business servs avail. In-rm modem link. Bellhops. Sundries. Valet serv. Free airport transportation. Tennis. Exercise equipt; weight machine, rowers. Game rm. Cr cds: A, C, D, DS, JCB, MC, V.

D SC

✔★ **WILSON INN.** *9802 Bunsen Pkwy (40299), I-64 exit 15, east of downtown. 502/499-0000; res: 800/945-7667.* 108 rms, 5 story, 30 suites, 38 kit. units. S, D $44.95; each addl $5; suites $54.95; kit. units $44.95; under 19 free. Crib free. Pet accepted, some restrictions. TV; cable (premium). Complimentary continental bkfst 6-10 am. Restaurant nearby. Ck-out noon. Meeting rms. Business servs avail. In-rm modem link. Free airport transportation. Refrigerators; microwaves avail. Cr cds: A, D, DS, JCB, MC, V.

D SC

Hotels

★★★★ **THE CAMBERLEY BROWN.** *335 W Broadway (40202), downtown. 502/583-1234; FAX 502/587-7006; res: 800/866-7666.* This elegantly restored 1923 hotel has Old English-style furnishings, artwork, atmosphere and service. 294 rms, 16 story. S, D $175-$215; each addl $15; suites from $425; wkend, family rates. Crib free. Covered parking $10/day; valet $13. TV; cable. Restaurants 6:30 am-11 pm (also see THE ENGLISH GRILL). Rm serv 24 hrs. Bar 11-1 am. Ck-out 11 am. Convention facilities. Business servs avail. In-rm modem link. Shopping arcade. Barber, beauty shop. Airport transportation. Exercise equipt; weights, stair machine. Health club privileges. Refrigerator in suites. Luxury level. Cr cds: A, C, D, DS, ER, JCB, MC, V.

D SC

★★ **GALT HOUSE.** *140 4th St (40202), at River Rd, downtown. 502/589-5200; FAX 502/589-3444; res: 800/626-1814.* 656 rms, 25 story. S $105; D $115; each addl $10; suites $275; under 16 free. Crib free. TV; cable. Pool; lifeguard. Restaurants 6:30 am-midnight; dining rm 5:30-10:30 pm. Bar 11:30-1 am. Ck-out noon. Convention facilities. Business center. Shopping arcade. Garage parking. Refrigerator in suites. Overlooks Ohio River. Cr cds: A, C, D, DS, ER, JCB, MC, V.

D SC

★★★ **GALT HOUSE EAST.** *141 N 4th St (40202), downtown. 502/589-3300; FAX 502/585-4266; res: 800/843-4258.* E-mail info@galthouse.com. 600 suites, 18 story. S $140; D $155; each addl $10; 2-bedrm suites $475; under 16 free. Crib free. TV; cable. Pool privileges adj. Restaurant adj 6:30 am- midnight. Bar from 11 am. Ck-out noon. Business center. Garage parking. Refrigerators, wet bars. Private patios, balconies. Overlooks Ohio River. 18-story atrium. Cr cds: A, C, D, DS, ER, JCB, MC, V.

D SC

★★ **HOLIDAY INN-DOWNTOWN.** *120 W Broadway (40202), downtown. 502/582-2241; FAX 502/584-8591.* 287 rms, 12 story. S $93-$110; D $103-$125; each addl $10; suites $350; under 19 free. Crib free. Pet accepted. TV; cable, VCR avail (movies). Indoor pool; lifeguard. Coffee in rms. Restaurant 6 am-11 pm. Bar 11-2 am. Ck-out noon. Convention facilities. Business servs avail. In-rm modem link. Gift shop. Barber. Free airport transportation. Health club privileges. Some refrigerators, minibars. Some balconies. Luxury level. Cr cds: A, C, D, DS, JCB, MC, V.

D SC

★★★ **HYATT REGENCY.** *320 W Jefferson St (40202), downtown. 502/587-3434; FAX 502/581-0133.* 388 rms, 18 story. S, D $85-$170; each addl $25; suites $250-$650; under 18 free. Crib free. TV; cable (premium), VCR avail (movies). Indoor pool; whirlpool. Restaurants 6:30 am-midnight. Bars 11-2 am; Sun to midnight. Ck-out noon. Convention facilities. Business center. In-rm modem link. Concierge. Gift shop. Tennis. Exercise equipt; weights, treadmill. Access to shopping center via enclosed walkway. Modern design. Luxury level. Cr cds: A, C, D, DS, JCB, MC, V.

D SC

★★ **MARRIOTT EAST.** *1903 Embassy Square Blvd (40299), E of I-264 at jct I-64, Hurstbourne Lane (exit 15), east of downtown. 502/499-6220; FAX 502/499-2480.* 254 rms, 10 story. S, D $109-$139; under 18 free. Crib free. TV; cable (premium). Indoor pool; poolside serv, lifeguard. Restaurant 6:30 am-2 pm, 5-10 pm; Fri, Sat to 11 pm. Bar 2 pm-2 am. Ck-out 11 am. Convention facilities. Business servs avail. In-rm modem link. Concierge. Gift shop. Exercise equipt; weights, bicycles, whirlpool. Balconies. Cr cds: A, C, D, DS, MC, V.

D SC

★★★★ **SEELBACH.** *500 Fourth Ave (40202), downtown. 502/585-3200; FAX 502/585-9239; res: 800/333-3399.* The lobby in this restored hotel, originally opened in 1905, has eight murals by Arthur Thomas depicting Kentucky pioneers and Native Americans. Rooms have four-poster beds, armoires and marble baths. 321 rms, 11 story. S $170-$230; D $180-$230; each addl $10; suites $210-$510; under 18 free; wkend rates. Crib free. Pet accepted; $50 deposit. Parking $10; valet $14. TV; cable, VCR avail. Pool privileges. Restaurants 6:30 am-midnight. Bar 4 pm-2 am; entertainment. Ck-out 1 pm. Convention facilities. Business center. In-rm modem link. Concierge. Shopping arcade. Free airport transportation. Health club privileges. Luxury level. Cr cds: A, C, D, DS, MC, V.

D SC

Inns

★ ★ **THE COLUMBINE.** *1707 S Third St (40208), in Old Louisville. 502/635-5000; res: 800/635-5010.* Web www.bbonline.com/ky/columbine. 5 rms (1 with shower only), 3 story, 1 suite. S $65-$80; D $70-$85; suite $70-$115; wkly, wkend rates. Children over 12 yrs only. TV; cable, VCR (movies). Complimentary full bkfst. Ck-out 11 am, ck-in 3 pm. Business servs avail. In-rm modem link. House built in 1900 with full-length porch. English garden. Cr cds: A, D, MC, V.

★ ★ **OLD LOUISVILLE.** *1359 S 3rd St (40208), in Old Louisville. 502/635-1574; FAX 502/637-5892.* 10 rms, 3 story. No rm phones. D $75-$95; suites $110-$195; under 12 free. Crib free. TV in sitting rm. VCR avail (movies). Complimentary full bkfst. Restaurant nearby. Ck-out noon, ck-in 3 pm. Business servs avail. Exercise equipt; weights, bicycles. Some in-rm whirlpools. Individually decorated rms in Victorian house (1901); antique furnishings. Ceiling murals. Cr cds: MC, V.

★ ★ **WOODHAVEN.** *401 S Hubbards Lane (40207), east of downtown. 502/895-1011; res: 888/895-1011.* 7 rms, 2 story. S, D $65-$85. Crib free. Pet accepted. TV; cable (premium), VCR avail. Complimentary full bkfst. Complimentary coffee in rms. Ck-out 11 am, ck-in 3 pm. Gothic Revival house built in 1853. Totally nonsmoking. Cr cds: MC, V.

Restaurants

★ ★ **CAFE METRO.** *1700 Bardstown Rd, east of downtown. 502/458-4830.* Hrs: 6-10 pm; Fri, Sat to 11 pm. Closed Sun; hols. Res accepted. Continental menu. Bar. A la carte entrees: dinner $18.95. Specialties: grilled swordfish, beef tenderloin with garlic butter, wienerschnitzel. Parking. Collection of pre-WW I German posters. Cr cds: A, D, DS, MC, V.

D

✔★ **CAFE MIMOSA.** *1216 Bardstown Rd (40204), east of downtown. 502/458-2233.* Hrs: 11 am-10 pm; Fri to 11 pm; Sat noon-11 pm; Sun noon-9 pm, brunch to 2 pm. Vietnamese, Chinese menu. Semi-a la carte: lunch, dinner $4.50-$11.95. Sun brunch $6.95. Child's meals. Specializes in chicken, pork, shrimp. Parking. Vietnamese artwork. Cr cds: A, DS, MC, V.

D

✔★ **DARRYL'S 1815 RESTAURANT.** *3110 Bardstown Rd, I-264 exit 16, east of downtown. 502/458-1815.* Hrs: 11 am-11 pm; Fri, Sat to 12:30 am. Bar. Semi-a la carte: lunch $4.99-$9.99, dinner $4.99-$17.99. Child's meals. Specializes in steak, chicken, ribs. Cr cds: A, DS, MC, V.

D

★ ★ ★ **THE ENGLISH GRILL.** *(See The Camberley Brown Hotel) 502/583-1234.* Hrs: 5-11 pm; Sun to 10 pm. Res accepted. Bar. Semi-a la carte: dinner $15.25-$24.95. Specializes in fresh seafood, rack of lamb, steak. Seasonal menus feature regional foods. English motif; leaded and stained-glass windows, artwork featuring English scenes and Thoroughbred horses. Totally nonsmoking. Cr cds: A, C, D, DS, ER, JCB, MC, V.

D

★ ★ ★ **EQUESTRIAN GRILLE.** *1582 Bardstown (40205), at Bonniecastle Rd, east of downtown. 502/454-7455.* Hrs: 5-11 pm; Fri, Sat to midnight. Closed Sun; major hols. Res accepted. Bar. Wine list. A la carte entrees: dinner $11-$26. Complete meals: dinner $25-$100. Specialties: free range chicken, double-cut pork chop, New York strip steak. Own baking. Valet parking. Offers 151 martinis; cigar menu. Upscale atmosphere features original equestrian artwork. Cr cds: A, C, D, MC, V.

D

★ ★ ★ **FERD GRISANTI'S.** *10212 Taylorsville Rd (10212), east of downtown. 502/267-0050.* Hrs: 5-10 pm; Fri, Sat to 11 pm. Closed Sun. Northern Italian menu. Res accepted. Bar. Wine list. Semi-a la carte: dinner $7.25-$17.50. Child's meals. Specializes in veal, pasta. Own baking. Parking. Contemporary Italian decor; artwork. In historic Jeffersontown. Cr cds: A, C, D, DS, MC, V.

D

★ ★ **FIFTH QUARTER.** *1241 Durrett Lane, south of downtown. 502/361-2363.* Hrs: 11 am-2:30 pm, 5-10 pm; Fri to 11 pm; Sat from 4 pm. Closed Dec 25. Bar. Semi-a la carte: lunch $4.59-$7.99, dinner $8.99-$19.99. Specialty: prime rib. Salad bar. Guitarist exc Sun. Parking. Rustic decor. Cr cds: A, C, D, DS, MC, V.

D SC

✔★ **JESSIE'S.** *9609 Dixie Hwy (40272), south of downtown. 502/937-6332.* Hrs: 5:30 am-9 pm; Sun 7 am-3 pm. Closed Thanksgiving, Dec 24, 25; also wk of July 4. A la carte entrees: bkfst $1.95-$4.95, lunch, dinner $1.75-$5.95. Family-owned. No cr cds accepted.

D SC

★ ★ ★ **KUNZ'S.** *115 S 4th Ave, at Market St, downtown. 502/585-5555.* Hrs: 11 am-10:30 pm; Fri, Sat to 11:30 pm; Sun 4-10 pm. Closed Dec 25. Res accepted. Continental menu. Bar. Semi-a la carte: lunch $5.95-$8.95, dinner $10.95-$24.95. Child's meals. Specializes in seafood, steak. Raw bar. Salad bar (lunch). Own breads. Valet. Family-owned. Cr cds: A, C, D, DS, MC, V.

D

★ ★ ★ **LE RELAIS.** *Taylorsville Rd (40205), at Bowman Field, I-264 exit Taylorsville Rd, east of downtown. 502/451-9020.* Hrs: 11:30 am-2:30 pm, 5:30-10 pm; Fri, Sat 5:30-10:30 pm; Sun 5:30-9 pm. Closed Mon, maj hol. Res accepted. French menu. Bar. A la carte: lunch $4.25-$9.50, dinner $14-$22.50. Specializes in fish, crab cakes, lamb chops. Parking. Outdoor dining. Formerly room in airport administration building. View of landing strip. Cr cds: A, D, MC, V.

D

★ ★ ★ ★ **LILLY'S.** *1147 Bardstown Rd (40204), east of downtown. 502/451-0447.* E-mail lillyslp@aol.com. The menu here changes biweekly and is filled with inventive dishes made with fresh, homegrown ingredients. The vaguely art deco-style dining room is decked in shades of green, black and purple. Specialties: pork tenderloin marinated and grilled in an apricot-sage beurre blanc, butterflied leg of lamb with roasted tomato-olive sauce. Hrs: 11 am-3 pm, 5:30-10 pm; Fri, Sat to 11 pm. Closed Sun, Mon; most major hols. Res accepted. Semi-a la carte: lunch $10-$15, dinner $25-$36. Cr cds: A, DS, MC, V.

✔★ ★ **MAMMA GRISANTI.** *3938 DuPont Circle, east of downtown. 502/893-0141.* Hrs: 11:30 am-2 pm, 5-10 pm; Sat 3-11 pm; Sun 11:30 am-9 pm. Res accepted. Italian menu. Bar. Semi-a la carte: lunch $4.95-8.50, dinner $6-$16. Buffet: lunch $5.95. Child's meals. Specialties: lasagne, fettucini Alfredo, veal parmesan. Own pasta. Family-owned. Cr cds: A, D, DS, MC, V.

★ ★ **MASTERSON'S.** *1830 S 3rd St, south of downtown. 502/636-2511.* E-mail sales@mastersons.com. Hrs: 11 am-9 pm; Mon to 4 pm; Sun 11:30 am-4 pm. Closed July 4, Memorial Day, Dec 24, 25. Res accepted. Greek, Amer menu. Bar. Semi-a la carte: lunch $3.25-$9.75, dinner $9.25-$19.75. Lunch buffet $7. Sun brunch $9. Child's meals. Specializes in regional cooking, Greek dishes. Parking. Outdoor dining. Near Univ of Louisville. Family-owned. Cr cds: A, C, D, DS, MC, V.

D SC

✔★ **OLD SPAGHETTI FACTORY.** *235 W Market St, downtown. 502/581-1070.* Hrs: 11:30 am-2 pm, 5-10 pm; Fri to 11 pm; Sat noon-11 pm; Sun 12:30-10 pm. Closed Thanksgiving, Dec 24, 25. Italian menu. Bar. Semi-a la carte: lunch $3.25-$5.45. Complete meals: dinner $4.75-$9.25. Child's meals. Specializes in spaghetti. Cr cds: D, DS, MC, V.

D

✔★ ★ **SICHUAN GARDEN.** *9850 Linn Station Rd, in Plainview Shopping Center, east of downtown. 502/426-6767.* Hrs: 11:30 am-9:30 pm; Fri, Sat to 10:30 pm; Sun brunch noon-2 pm. Closed Thanksgiving, Dec 25. Res accepted. Chinese, Thai menu. Bar. Semi-a la carte: lunch $3.75-$5.95, dinner $5.95-$12.95. Sun brunch $6.95. Specialties: Sichuan orange beef, mandarin seafood-in-a-net, filet mignon. Pianist Fri, Sat evenings. Frosted-glass rm dividers. Cr cds: A, D, DS, MC, V.

D

★ ★ **TIMOTHY'S.** *826 E Broadway, downtown. 502/561-0880.* Hrs: Mon-Thur 11:30 am-11 pm; Fri to midnight; Sat 5:30 pm-midnight. Closed Sun; Easter, Thanksgiving, Dec 25. Res accepted. Italian, Amer menu. Bar. Semi-a la carte: lunch $5.95-$10.95, dinner $7.95-$24.95. Specializes in pasta, fresh seafood, white chili. Parking. Outdoor dining. Contemporary decor; vintage bar. Cr cds: A, D, MC, V.

D

★ ★ **UPTOWN CAFE.** *1624 Bardstown Rd, south of downtown. 502/458-4212.* Hrs: 11:30 am-11 pm; Fri, Sat to midnight. Closed Sun; most major hols. Continental menu. Bar. Semi-a la carte: lunch $5.75-$9.75, dinner $5.75-$17.75. Specialities: duck ravioli, salmon croquettes, veal pockets, vegetarian stir-fry. Parking. Converted store front. Cr cds: A, D, DS, MC, V.

D

★ ★ ★ ★ **VINCENZO'S.** *150 S 5th St, downtown. 502/580-1350.* Highly skilled kitchen and dining room staff and an elegant, relaxed atmosphere are the benchmarks of this Louisville favorite. Diners can choose a simple meal or a multi-course culinary tour of traditional Italian dishes. Eurospa cuisine is available for those who prefer lighter fare. Continental menu. Specialties: crêpes Agostino, veal Gabriele. Own baking. Hrs: 11:30 am-2:30 pm, 5:30-11 pm; Fri, Sat 5:30 pm-midnight. Closed Sun; major hols. Res accepted. Wine list. A la carte entrees: lunch $6.95-$11.95, dinner $15.95-$22.95. Pianist Fri, Sat. Valet parking. Cr cds: A, C, D, DS, MC, V.

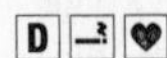

Memphis

Settled: 1819
Pop: 610,337
Elev: 264 feet
Time zone: Central
Area code: 901
Web: www.memphistravel.com

Situated on the high bluffs above the Mississippi River, on its flat, fertile alluvial delta, the city of Memphis was named after the capital of ancient Egypt, whose name meant "place of good abode." Ancient Memphis prospered primarily because of its location on the Nile River Delta, a location similar to the site upon which Andrew Jackson, General James Winchester and John Overton laid out the new Memphis. The site's natural harbor and proximity to the Mississippi promised to make the city as prosperous as its ancient namesake. River traffic rapidly developed Memphis into one of the busiest port cities in America, and the rich native soil, washed up onto the delta by the flow of the Mississippi, made the area a major cotton-producing center as well.

For a short time, Memphis was the Confederate capital of Tennessee, serving as a military supply depot and stronghold for the Southern forces during the Civil War. In 1862, however, an armada of 30 Union ships seized Memphis in a fierce river battle, and the city remained in Union hands for the duration of the war. River trade suffered greatly during the war. Afterward, three separate outbreaks of yellow fever nearly wiped Memphis out entirely. But by 1892, the city had begun to emerge from its slow postwar recovery to become the busiest inland cotton market and hardwood lumber center in the world.

Much has happened in Memphis in the past few decades. A building boom brought many new factories, skyscrapers, expressways and an international airport. Memphis has five times won the Cleanest City in the Nation award and has also received many awards in safety, fire protection and noise abatement.

More than just a commercial city, Memphis has developed a cosmopolitan identity as well, as the home of ballet and opera companies, more than a dozen institutions of higher learning and one of the South's largest medical care and research centers. Still, it seems not to have lost any of its low-key, Southern charm.

Business

While much of the country's cotton crop is bought or sold in Memphis, the city's economy is highly diversified. Other agricultural products of importance are soybeans, rice, livestock and ornamental plants.

A significant percentage of the labor force works in the city's more than 800 manufacturing plants, making chemicals, food products, paper and paper products, electrical equipment, nonelectrical machinery, lumber and wood products. The city is also a large producer of hardwood flooring.

Memphis is a busy inland port on the Mississippi. Major corporations, such as Federal Express and Schering-Plough, have headquarters here. In recent years it has also become notable in the music recording field and is a major convention and distribution center.

The city is an important trade center, with retail sales topping $10 billion a year.

Convention Facilities

The Memphis Cook Convention Center stands on a bluff overlooking the Mississippi in downtown Memphis. The center has a total gross square footage of 1.8 million. Its 20 conference rooms can seat from 75 to 500, and the center can accommodate 25,000 persons attending several major events at the same time. Four halls have a seating capacity of 800 to 4,243; two of them can serve banquets for 800 and 1,200. The main exhibit hall has 220,000 square feet of unobstructed space. A $60-million expansion adding exhibit space and a performing arts center will be completed in 1999.

At the Mid-South Fairgrounds is the 12,000-seat Mid-South Coliseum, with 63,000 square feet of exhibit space. Agricenter International is a 160,000-square-foot exhibition facility. Hotels and motels in Memphis have a total of 14,500 rooms.

Sports & Recreation

The lovely woods and lakes in the Memphis area are favorite spots for hunters and fishermen. Informative pamphlets on hunting and fishing facilities are available from the Visitor Information Center.

Tennessee has an extensive system of state parks; two of them are near Memphis. The T.O. Fuller State Park is the site of the Chucalissa Archaeological Museum. Meeman-Shelby Forest State Park, on the Mississippi, has two lakes and many miles of trails, a museum, nature center, restaurant, pool, horse stable, picnic and camping areas and cabins.

Entertainment

As if to reinforce its connection with its Egyptian namesake, a 32-story steel pyramid, overlooking the Mississippi River, has been built in Memphis. The Pyramid houses a music, sports and entertainment complex.

Memphis enjoys a rich mixture of cultural activities and programs. Several art organizations belong to the Memphis Arts Council, including a ballet company, opera theater, symphony orchestra and repertory theater. A number of local theater groups are active, and more than a dozen colleges provide additional entertainment programs.

Memphis abounds in nightlife. Overton Square offers a variety of restaurants, bars, night spots and shops. Beale Street, birthplace of blues music in America, is another important center for nighttime fun as well as Cooper-Young Entertainment District and The Pinch Historic District.

Historical Areas

In the heart of the city, remnants of 19th-century Memphis have been preserved in an area known as Victorian Village. Occupying the 600 block of Adams and surrounding streets, it contains ten early Memphis houses, from an 1840 neoclassical cottage to grand Victorian mansions. The area was designated a national historic district in 1972. The Fontaine House and the Mallory-Neely House are open to visitors. Beale Street, home of W.C. Handy, father of the blues, and a center of black culture and entertainment, has been restored.

The Magevney House, at 198 Adams, is a picturesque cottage built in 1831 and authentically furnished. The Hunt-Phelan Home on Beale Street is an antebellum mansion built in 1828 that has furniture and artifacts dating back to 1608.

The prehistoric period of Memphis is still evident at Chucalissa Archaeological Museum, on Mitchell Road. This area was a thriving village of 1,000 to 1,500 inhabitants from about A.D. 900 to 1500. Archeological digs and the museum are administered by Memphis State University.

Sightseeing

The Mississippi River is one of Memphis' principal tourist attractions, and river sightseeing tours are an especially enjoyable bonus to a trip here. The Memphis Queen Line has several excursion boats, including the 599-passenger *Memphis Showboat*, the 308-passenger *Memphis Queen II* and the 65-passenger *Belle Carol*. Rides feature sightseeing trips into the river wilderness and short landings on the sandbar banks, with commentary on the sights, history and legends of the area.

Memphis is known throughout the world as the city where the legendary Elvis Presley's career began and where he lived until his death. The destination of thousands of visitors is Graceland, his house and the site of his grave, the Meditation Gardens. Each August, citywide memorial celebrations are held in honor of the "King of Rock and Roll."

General References

Area code: 901

Phone Numbers

POLICE & FIRE: 911

POISON CONTROL CENTER: 528-6048

TIME: 526-5261 **WEATHER:** 522-8888

Information Sources

Memphis Convention & Visitors Bureau, 47 Union Ave, 38103; 543-5300.

Park Commission, 325-5766.

Visitor Information Center, 340 Beale St, 38103; 543-5333.

Transportation

AIRLINES: American; Delta; KLM Royal Dutch Airlines; Northwest; Southwest; TWA Express; United; USAir; ValuJet and other commuter and regional airlines.

AIRPORT: Memphis International, 922-8000.

CAR RENTAL AGENCIES: (See IMPORTANT TOLL-FREE NUMBERS) Avis 345-2847; Budget 398-8888; Hertz 345-5680; National 345-0070; Thrifty 345-0170.

PUBLIC TRANSPORTATION: Memphis Area Transit Authority, 1370 Levee Rd, 274-6282.

RAILROAD PASSENGER SERVICE: Amtrak 800/872-7245.

Newspapers

Daily News; Memphis Business Journal; Memphis Commercial Appeal; The Memphis Flyer; Memphis Times; Tri-State Defender.

Convention Facilities

Agricenter International, 7777 Walnut Grove Rd, 757-7777.

Memphis Cook Convention Center, 255 Main St N, 576-1200.

Mid-South Coliseum, Mid-South Fairgrounds, 996 Early Maxwell Blvd, 274-3982.

Shelby Farms Show Place Arena, 105 Germantown Rd S, Cordova, 756-7433.

Sports & Recreation

Major Sports Facilities

Mid-South Coliseum, Fairgrounds, 996 Early Maxwell Blvd, 274-3982.

Tim McCarver Stadium, Fairgrounds, 800 Home Run Ln, 272-1687.

USA Stadium, 4351 Biloxi St, 872-8326.

Cultural Facilities

Theaters

Children's Theatre, 2635 Avery Ave, 452-3968.

Circuit Playhouse, 1705 Poplar Ave, 726-4656.

Germantown Community Theatre, 3037 Forest-Irene Rd, Germantown, 754-2680.

Opera Memphis, University of Memphis, 678-2706.

Orpheum Theatre, 203 S Main St, 525-7800.

Playhouse on the Square, 51 S Cooper, Overton Square, 726-4656.

Theatre Memphis, 630 Perkins Extd, 682-8601.

Museums

Children's Museum, 2525 Central Ave, 458-2678.

Chucalissa Archaeological Museum, 1987 Indian Village Dr, 785-3160.

Memphis Pink Palace Museum and Planetarium, 3050 Central Ave, 320-6320.

National Civil Rights Museum, 450 Mulberry St, at the Lorraine Motel, 521-9699.

National Ornamental Metal Museum, 374 Metal Museum Dr, at the river, 774-6380.

Art Museums & Galleries

Art Museum, University of Memphis, 678-2224.

Delta Axis Contemporary Arts Center, 639 Marshall Ave, 522-9946.

Dixon Gallery & Gardens, 4339 Park Ave, 761-5250.

Lisa Kurts Gallery, 766 S White Station Rd, 527-2787.

Memphis Brooks Museum of Art, 1934 Poplar Ave, in Overton Park, 722-3500.

Memphis College of Art, 1930 Poplar Ave, 726-4085.

Points of Interest

Historical

Beale Street, downtown, between Riverside Dr & Danny Thomas Blvd.

Hunt-Phelan Home, 533 Beale St, 344-3166.

Magevney House, 198 Adams Ave, 526-4464.

Victorian Village, 600 blk of Adams Ave, 526-1469.

W.C. Handy's Home, 325 Beale St, 522-1556 or 527-3427.

Other Attractions

Graceland (Elvis Presley Mansion), 3734 Elvis Presley Blvd, 332-3322 or 800/238-2000 (outside TN).

Libertyland, Mid-South Fairgrounds, on E Pkwy S, N on Airways off I-240, 274-1776.

Lichterman Nature Center, 1680 Lynnfield, 767-7322.

Meeman-Shelby Forest State Recreation Park, 13 mi N via US 51 near Millington, 876-5215.

***Memphis Belle* B-17 Bomber,** Mud Island, 576-7241.

Memphis Botanic Garden, 750 Cherry Rd, Audubon Park, 685-1566.

Memphis Motorsports Park, N on I-240, at 5500 Taylor Forge Rd, 358-7223.

Memphis Zoo, Overton Park, bounded by N Pkwy, E Pkwy & Poplar Ave, 2000 Galloway, 276-WILD.

Mud Island, riverfront, downtown Memphis at 125 N Front St, 576-7241.

Pyramid Arena, Pinch Historic District, downtown, 1 Auction Ave, 521-9675.

Sun Studio, 706 Union Ave, 521-0664.

T.O. Fuller State Park, 5 mi S on US 61, then 4 mi W on Mitchell Rd, 543-7581.

Wild Water & Wheels, 6880 Whitten Bend Cove, off I-40E, 382-9283.

Sightseeing Tours

Blues City Tours, 164 Union Ave, 522-9229.

Carriage Tours of Memphis, 393 N Main St, 527-7542.

Gray Line bus tours, 3677 Elvis Presley Blvd, 346-8687.

Memphis Queen Line Riverboats, foot of Monroe Ave, 45 Riverside Dr, 527-5694.

Annual Events

Beale St Zydeco Festival, 526-0110. Feb.

Beale St Music Festival, 525-4611. 1st wkend May.

Memphis in May International Festival, 525-4611. May.

Carnival Memphis, Mid-South Fairgrounds, 278-0243. 10 days mid-June.

Elvis Tribute Week, 332-3322. Early-mid-Aug.

Labor Day Fest, 526-0110. Sept.

Mid-South Fair, Fairgrounds, E Parkway S & Southern Ave, 274-8800. Late Sept-early Oct.

Liberty Bowl Football Classic, Liberty Bowl Memorial Stadium, 335 Hollywood S, 274-4600. Dec.

City Neighborhoods

Many of the restaurants, unrated dining establishments and some lodgings listed under Memphis include neighborhoods as well as exact street addresses. Geographic descriptions of these areas are given, followed by a table of restaurants arranged by neighborhood.

Beale Street Area: Downtown area along seven blocks of Beale St from Riverside Dr on the west to Danny Thomas Blvd on the east.

Downtown: South of I-40, west of Danny Thomas Blvd (US 51), north of Calhoun Ave and east of the Mississippi River. **East of Downtown:** East of US 51.

Overton Square: South of Poplar Ave, west of Cooper St, north of Union Ave and east of McLean Blvd.

Lodgings and Food

MEMPHIS RESTAURANTS BY NEIGHBORHOOD AREAS

(For full description, see alphabetical listings under Restaurants)

BEALE STREET AREA
Alfred's. 197 Beale St
Beale Street BBQ. 205 Beale St

DOWNTOWN
Automatic Slim's Tonga Club. 83 S Second St
Butcher Shop. 101 S Front St
Chez Philippe (Peabody Hotel). 149 Union Ave
Dux (Peabody Hotel). 149 Union Ave
Erika's. 52 S Second
The Pier. 100 Wagner Pl
Rendezvous. 52 S 2nd St

EAST OF DOWNTOWN
Aubergine. 5007 Black Rd
Benihana Of Tokyo. 912 Ridge Lake Blvd
Buckley's Fine Filet Grill. 5355 Poplar Ave
Buntyn. 3070 Southern Ave
Ciao Baby Cucina. 735 S Main St
Cooker Bar & Grille. 6120 Poplar Ave
Erling Jensen. 1044 S Yates Rd
Folk's Folly. 551 S Mendenhall Rd
Lulu Grille. 565 Erin Dr
Raji. 712 W Brookhaven Circle
Ronnie Grisanta & Sons. 2855 Poplar Ave
Saigon Le. 51 N Cleveland

OVERTON SQUARE
Anderton's. 1901 N Madison
Ben's. 22 S Cooper
India Palace. 1720 Poplar Ave
La Tourelle. 2146 Monroe Ave
Melos Taverna. 2021 Madison Ave
Paulette's. 2110 Madison Ave
The Public Eye. 17 S Cooper

Note: When a listing is located in a town that does not have its own city heading, it will appear under the city nearest to its location. In these cases, the address and town appear in parenthesis immediately following the name of the establishment.

Motels

★ ★ **COMFORT INN.** *2889 Austin Peay Hwy (38128), north of downtown. 901/386-0033; FAX 901/386-0036.* 83 rms, 20 kit. suites. S, D $49-$67; each addl $5; kit. suites $70-$130; under 16 free. TV; cable (premium). Indoor pool; whirlpool. Complimentary continental bkfst. Restaurant nearby. Ck-out noon. Meeting rms. Business servs avail. Cr cds: A, C, D, DS, ER, MC, V.

D SC

★ ★ **COURTYARD BY MARRIOTT.** *6015 Park Ave (38119), east of downtown. 901/761-0330; FAX 901/682-8422.* 146 units, 3 story. S, D $86-$96; each addl $10; suites $102-$112; under 17 free. Crib free. TV; cable (premium), VCR avail. Heated pool; whirlpool. Complimentary coffee in rms. Restaurant 6:30-10 am. Bar 5-10 pm. Ck-out noon. Coin Indry. Meeting rms. Business servs avail. Valet serv. Sundries. Exercise equipt; weights, bicycles. Health club privileges. Refrigerator; microwaves avail. Cr cds: A, C, D, DS, MC, V.

D SC

✓★ **HAMPTON INN.** *1180 Union Ave (38104), downtown. 901/276-1175; FAX 901/276-4261.* 126 rms, 4 story. S $56-$64; D $64-$70; under 18 free. Crib free. TV; cable (premium), VCR avail. Pool. Complimentary continental bkfst. Restaurant nearby. Ck-out 11 am. Business servs avail. Sundries. Cr cds: A, C, D, DS, MC, V.

D SC

✓★ **RED ROOF INN.** *6055 Shelby Oaks Dr (38134), I-40 exit 12, east of downtown. 901/388-6111; FAX 901/388-6157.* 108 rms, 2 story. S $43.99; D $51.99; each addl $8; under 18 free; higher rates special events. Crib free. Pet accepted, some restrictions. TV; cable (premium). Complimentary coffee in lobby. Restaurant adj open 24 hrs. Ck-out noon. Microwaves avail. Cr cds: A, C, D, DS, MC, V.

D

✓★ **RED ROOF INN SOUTH.** *3875 American Way (38118), east of downtown. 901/363-2335; FAX 901/363-2822.* 109 rms, 3 story. S $38.99-$54.99; D $41.99-$49.99; each addl $8; under 18 free. Pet accepted. TV; cable (premium). Complimentary coffee in lobby. Ck-out noon. Cr cds: A, C, D, DS, MC, V.

D

★ ★ **RESIDENCE INN BY MARRIOTT.** *6141 Poplar Pike (38119), east of downtown. 901/685-9595; FAX 901/685-1636.* 105 kit. suites, 4 story. Kit. suites $109-$154. Crib free. Pet accepted, some restrictions; $100-$200. TV; cable, (premium). Pool; whirlpool. Complimentary continental bkfst. Restaurant nearby. Ck-out noon. Coin Indry. Meeting rms. Business servs avail. Health club privileges. Microwaves. Private patios, balconies. Cr cds: A, C, D, DS, JCB, MC, V.

D SC

Motor Hotels

★ ★ **COMFORT INN-POPLAR EAST.** *5877 Poplar Ave (38119), east of downtown. 901/767-6300; FAX 901/767-0098.* 126 rms, 5 story. S, D $68-$79; each addl $6; under 18 free; higher rates special events. Crib free. Pet accepted, some restrictions, $20. TV; cable (premium). Pool. Complimentary continental bkfst. Rm serv. Ck-out noon. Meeting rms. Bellhops. Sundries. Free airport transportation. Exercise equipt; weight machine, bicycles. Cr cds: A, D, DS, MC, V.

D SC

★ ★ **COUNTRY SUITES BY CARLSON.** *4300 American Way (38118), east of downtown. 901/366-9333; FAX 901/366-7835; res: 800/456-4000.* 120 kit. suites, 3 story. Kit. suites $69-$99; under 16 free. Crib free. Pet accepted; $100. TV; cable (premium). Pool; whirlpool. Complimentary continental bkfst. Complimentary coffee in rms. Restaurant adj open 24 hrs. Ck-out noon. Coin Indry. Meeting rms. Business servs avail. Valet serv. Sundries. Free airport transportation. Health club privileges. Microwaves. Cr cds: A, C, D, DS, MC, V.

D SC

★ ★ **FRENCH QUARTER SUITES.** *2144 Madison Ave (38104), in Overton Square. 901/728-4000; FAX 901/278-1262; res: 800/843-0353 (exc TN).* 105 suites, 4 story. Suites $121-$190. Crib free. TV; cable (premium). Pool. Complimentary continental bkfst. Bar 5-11 pm, Fri & Sat to midnight; entertainment Wed-Sat. Ck-out noon. Meeting rms. Business servs avail. Free airport transportation. Exercise equipt; weight machine, bicycles. Some bathrm phones, refrigerators, in-rm whirlpools; microwave avail. Private patios, balconies. Interior atrium; New Orleans decor. Cr cds: A, C, D, DS, ER, JCB, MC, V.

D SC

★ ★ **RADISSON INN MEMPHIS AIRPORT.** *2411 Winchester Rd (38116), at Intl Airport, south of downtown. 901/332-2370; FAX 901/398-4085.* 211 rms, 3 story. S, D $92-$105; suites $125; under 12 free; wkend rates; higher rates special events. Crib free. TV; cable. Pool. Restaurant 6 am-2 pm, 4:30-10 pm. Rm serv. Bar 4 pm-midnight. Ck-out noon. Meeting rms. Business servs avail. Bellhops. Sundries. Free airport transportation. Exercise equipt; weight machine, bicycles. Lighted tennis. Cr cds: A, C, D, DS, ER, JCB, MC, V.

D SC

★ ★ ★ **THE RIDGEWAY INN.** *5679 Poplar Ave (38119), at I-240, east of downtown. 901/766-4000; FAX 901/763-1857; res: 800/822-3360.* 155 rms, 7 story. S, D $94-$114; each addl $10; suites $195-$295; under 12 free. Crib free. TV; cable (premium). Pool. Restaurant 6:30 am-11 pm; Fri, Sat to 1 am; Sun to 10 pm. Rm serv. Bar from 11 am, Fri, Sat to 1 am, Sun noon-10 pm. Ck-out noon. Meeting rm. Business servs avail. Free airport transportation. Exercise equipt; weight machine, bicycle. Health club privileges. Luxury level. Cr cds: A, C, D, DS, ER, MC, V.

D SC

★ ★ **WILSON WORLD.** *2715 Cherry Rd (38118), east of downtown. 901/366-0000; FAX 901/366-6361; res: 800/872-8366.* 178 rms, 4 story, 90 suites. S, D $79-$85; each addl $6; suites $89-$99; under 18 free. Crib free. TV; cable (premium). Indoor pool. Restaurant 6 am-2 pm, 5:30-10 pm. Rm serv. Bar from 5 pm; pianist exc Sat, Sun. Ck-out noon. Meeting rms. Business servs avail. Bellhops. Gift shop. Barber, beauty shop. Free airport transportation. Refrigerators, wet bars. Balconies. Cr cds: A, D, DS, MC, V.

D SC

Hotels

★ ★ ★ **ADAM'S MARK.** *939 Ridge Lake Blvd (38120), east of downtown. 901/684-6664; FAX 901/762-7411.* 408 rms, 27 story. S, D $119-$165; each addl $10; suites $250-$600; under 18 free; $99 wkend rates. Crib free. TV; cable (premium). Pool. Restaurant 6:30 am-10 pm; Fri, Sat to 11 pm. Bar noon-1 am; Sun to midnight. Entertainment. Ck-out noon. Convention facilities. Business servs avail. Gift shop. Free airport transportation. Exercise equipt; bicycles, stair machine. Wet bar in suites. Cr cds: A, D, DS, MC, V.

D SC

★ ★ ★ **CROWNE PLAZA.** *250 N Main (38103), downtown. 901/527-7300; FAX 901/526-1561.* Web www.crownplaza.com. 402 rms, 18 story. S $125-$155; D $125-$175; each addl $10; suites $250-$400; under 18 free. Crib free. Pet accepted, some restrictions. Valet parking $10, garage $5. TV; cable (premium). Indoor pool; whirlpool, sauna. Restaurant 6 am-11 pm. Bar 11-2 am. Ck-out noon. Convention facilities. Business center. Concierge. Shopping arcade. Exercise equipt; weight machine, bicycles. Some refrigerators. Cr cds: A, C, D, DS, JCB, MC, V.

D SC

★ ★ ★ **EMBASSY SUITES.** *1022 S Shady Grove Rd (38120), east of downtown. 901/684-1777; FAX 901/685-8185.* 220 suites, 5 story. Suites $129-$149; under 12 free; wkend rates. Crib free. TV; cable (premium). Indoor pool; whirlpool. Complimentary full bkfst. Complimentary coffee in rms. Restaurant 11 am-10 pm. Bar to 11 pm. Ck-out noon. Coin lndry. Convention facilities. Business servs avail. In-rm modem link. Gift shop. Free airport transportation. Exercise equipt; weight machine, bicycles, sauna. Game rm. Refrigerators. Cr cds: A, C, D, DS, MC, V.

D SC

★ ★ **FOUR POINTS BY SHERATON.** *2240 Democrat Rd (38132), near Intl Airport, south of downtown. 901/332-1130; FAX 901/398-5206.* 380 rms, 5 story. S $99-$114; D $109; each addl $10; suites $179-$450; under 18 free. Crib free. TV; cable. Pool; poolside serv. Restaurant 6 am-11 pm. Bars 3-11 pm. Fri, Sat to midnight, Sun 3:30-11 pm. Ck-out noon. Convention facilities. Business center. Free airport transportation. 2 lighted tennis courts. Exercise equipt; weights, bicycles, sauna. Wet bar in suites. Indoor courtyard. Cr cds: A, C, D, DS, ER, MC, V.

D SC

★ ★ **HOLIDAY INN MIDTOWN MEDICAL CENTER.** *1837 Union Ave (38104), in Overton Square. 901/278-4100; FAX 901/272-3810.* 173 rms, 8 story. S, D $65-$70; suites $85-$154; under 18 free. Crib free. TV; cable. Pool. Restaurant 6 am-10 pm. Bar 5-11 pm. Ck-out noon. Meeting rms. Business servs avail. Free airport transportation. Health club privileges. Cr cds: A, C, D, DS, ER, JCB, MC, V.

D SC

★ ★ ★ **HOLIDAY INN SELECT.** *160 Union Ave (38103), at 2nd St, downtown. 901/525-5491; FAX 901/525-5491, ext. 2399.* 190 rms, 14 story. S, D $109-$129; each addl $10; suites $199; under 18 free. Crib free. TV; cable (premium). Pool. Restaurant 6 am-midnight. Rm serv. Bar 4 pm-midnight, Sat to 2 am. Ck-out 11 am. Meeting rms. Business center. In-rm modem link. Valet serv. Airport transportation. Exercise equipt; bicycle, treadmill. Wet bar in suites. Refrigerators. Cr cds: A, C, D, DS, ER, JCB, MC, V.

D SC

★ ★ ★ **MARRIOTT.** *2625 Thousand Oaks Blvd (38118), southeast of downtown; I-240, exit 18. 901/362-6200; FAX 901/360-8836.* 320 rms, 12 story. S $79-$146; D $79-$161; suites $200-$350; under 18 free. Crib free. TV; cable (premium). 2 pools, 1 indoor; whirlpool. Restaurant 6:30 am-2 pm, 6-11 pm; wkends from 7 am. Bars 11-midnight. Ck-out noon. Convention facilities. Bellhops. Business servs avail. In-rm modem link. Concierge. Free airport transportation. Exercise equipt; weights, bicycles, sauna. Some bathrm phones, refrigerators. Luxury level. Cr cds: A, C, D, DS, ER, JCB, MC, V.

D SC

★ ★ ★ ★ **PEABODY.** *149 Union Ave (38103), downtown. 901/529-4000; FAX 901/529-3600; res: 800/732-2639.* This Italian Renaissance hostelry, opened in 1869, was rebuilt in 1925 and restored to its former opulence. An ornate travertine marble fountain is home to famed resident ducks, who waddle down from their penthouse apartment each morning and return each evening. 468 rms, 13 story. S $140-$295; D $160-$320; each addl $35; suites $285-$945; under 18 free. Crib free. TV; cable (premium), VCR avail. Heated pool; whirlpool. Restaurants 6:30 am-midnight (also see CHEZ PHILLIPE and DUX). Rm serv 24 hrs. Bar 11-2 am; entertainment. Ck-out 11 am. Convention facilities. Business center. In-rm modem link. Concierge. Shopping arcade. Barber, beauty shop. Extensive exercise rm; instructor, weights, bicycles, sauna, steam rm. Massage. Cr cds: A, C, D, DS, ER, JCB, MC, V.

D SC

★ ★ **RADISSON.** *185 Union Ave (38103), downtown. 901/528-1800; FAX 901/526-3226.* 280 rms, 10 story. S, D $109-$119; each addl $10; suites $125-$245; under 18 free. Crib free. Garage/valet $5. TV; cable (premium). Pool; whirlpool. Restaurant 6 am-11 pm. Bar 11 am-midnight. Ck-out noon. Convention facilities. Business servs avail. Gift shop. Exercise equipt; weight machine, bicycles, sauna. Near Beale St, Mud Island and Pyramid. Cr cds: A, C, D, DS, ER, JCB, MC, V.

D SC

Restaurants

★ **ALFRED'S.** *197 Beale St, in Beale St Area. 901/525-3711.* Hrs: 11-5 am. Bar. Semi-a la carte: lunch $3.95-$4.95, dinner $4.99-$14.99. Specializes in blackened catfish, barbecue ribs. Rock & Roll Wed-Sat; Jazz Sun. Parking. Outdoor dining. Cr cds: A, D, DS, MC, V.

D

★ ★ **ANDERTON'S.** *1901 N Madison (38104), in Overton Square. 914/726-4010.* Hrs: 11 am-10 pm; Sat 4-11 pm. Closed Sun; most major hols. Res accepted. Bar. Semi-a la carte: lunch $5.25-$16, dinner $9.75-$26.95. Child's meals. Specializes in seafood, steak, oyster bar. Parking. Family-owned. Cr cds: A, C, DS, MC, V.

D

★ ★ **AUBERGINE.** *5007 Black Rd (38117), east of downtown. 901/767-7840.* Hrs: 11:30 am-2 pm, 6-9:30 pm; Sat from 6 pm. Closed Sun, Mon; major hols. Res accepted. French menu. Serv bar. A la carte entrees: lunch $10, dinner $20-$25. Specialties: roasted breast of duck a la orange, roasted thigh of chicken with escargot, warm chocolate pyramid cake. Intimate dining. Totally nonsmoking. Cr cds: A, C, D, MC, V.

D

★ **AUTOMATIC SLIM'S TONGA CLUB.** *83 S Second St (38103), downtown. 901/525-7948.* Hrs: 11 am-2:30 pm, 5-10 pm; Fri to 11 pm; Sat 5-11 pm. Closed Sun; Jan 1, July 4, Dec 25. Res accepted. Jamaican menu. Bar. Semi-a la carte: lunch $4.75-$8.95, dinner $12.95-$21.95. Child's meals. Specialties: Argentinian-style churrasco, stacked tenderloin, hauchinango. Jazz Fri. Caribbean decor. Cr cds: A, MC, V.

D

★ **BEALE STREET BBQ.** *205 Beale St, in Beale St Area. 901/526-6113.* Hrs: 11 am-10 pm. Closed Mon, Tues. Bar. Semi-a la carte: bkfst, lunch, dinner $5-$15. Specializes in barbecued ribs, pork. Blues music adjacent. Parking. Cr cds: A, D, DS, MC, V.

D

★ ★ **BEN'S.** *22 S Cooper (37104), in Overton Square. 901/722-8744.* Hrs: 11:30 am-2 pm, 6-10:30 pm; Sat from 6 pm. Closed Sun; most major hols. Res required. French menu. Wine. Semi-a la carte: lunch $13.50, dinner $27.50. Parking. French Provencial decor. Cr cds: A, MC, V.

D

★ ★ **BENIHANA OF TOKYO.** *912 Ridge Lake Blvd, east of downtown. 901/683-7390.* Hrs: 11:30 am-2 pm, 5-10 pm; Fri, Sat to 11 pm; Sun noon-2:30 pm, 5-10 pm; early-bird dinner 5-7 pm. Res accepted. Japanese menu. Bar 4:30-10 pm. Complete meals: lunch $5.75-$13.50, dinner $13-$28. Child's meals. Parking. Cr cds: A, C, D, DS, MC, V.

D

✔★ **BOSCOS PIZZA KITCHEN & BREWERY.** *(7615 W Farmington, Germantown 38138) E on US 72, at Poplar Ave, in Saddle Creek Shopping Plaza. 901/756-7310.* Hrs: 11 am-10:30 pm; Fri & Sat to 12:30 am. Closed Thanksgiving, Dec 25. Bar. Semi-a la carte: lunch $3.95-$8.95, dinner $4.95-$14.95. Specializes in wood-fired oven pizza, pasta. Own beer brewery. Parking. Outdoor dining. Contemporary decor. Cr cds: A, C, D, DS, MC, V.

D SC

★ **BUCKLEY'S FINE FILET GRILL.** *5355 Poplar Ave (38119), at Estate Dr, east of downtown. 901/683-4538.* Hrs: 4-9:30 pm; Fri, Sat to 10:30 pm. Closed Thanksgiving, Dec 24, 25. Bar. Semi-a la carte: dinner $6.99-$17.49. Specializes in filet steak, pasta. Parking. Artwork and hanging plants create a friendly atmosphere in this local favorite. Cr cds: A, D, DS, MC, V.

D

✔★ **BUNTYN.** *3070 Southern Ave (38111), east of downtown. 901/458-8776.* Hrs: 11 am-8 pm. Closed Sat, Sun; major hols. Semi-a la carte: lunch, dinner $3.50-$6.80. Child's meals. Specializes in meatloaf, chicken, beef tips. Own baking. Family-owned since 1920. Cr cds: MC, V.

D

★ ★ ★ **CHEZ PHILIPPE.** *(See Peabody Hotel) 901/529-4188.* Continental menu. Specialties: hushpuppies stuffed with shrimp provençale, roasted lamb rack. Hrs: 6-10 pm. Closed Sun; most major hols. Res accepted. Serv bar. Wine list. A la carte entrees: dinner $20-$30. Jacket. Elegant decor; high ceilings, silk drapes, large murals. Cr cds: A, C, D, DS, ER, JCB, MC, V.

D ♥

★ ★ **CIAO BABY CUCINA.** *(135 S Main St, Memphis 38103) south of downtown. 901/529-0560.* Hrs: 11:30 am-10 pm; Fri to 11 pm; Sat 5-11 pm; Sun 5-9 pm. Closed most major hols. Res accepted. Mediterranean menu. Bar. Semi-a la carte: lunch $7-$11, dinner $11-$20. Lunch buffet $7.95. Child's meals. Specialties: farfalle with chicken and gorgonzola, roma tomato, grilled Atlantic halibut. Mediterranean decor; gourmet coffee shop adj. Cr cds: A, MC, V.

D

✔★ ★ **COOKER BAR & GRILLE.** *6120 Poplar Ave, east of downtown. 901/685-2800.* Hrs: 11 am-10:30 pm; Fri, Sat to 11:30 pm; Sun to 10 pm. Closed Thanksgiving, Dec 25. Bar. Semi-a la carte: lunch $2.95-$7.95, dinner $6.95-$14.95. Child's meals. Specializes in meat loaf, pot roast, pasta. Cr cds: A, D, DS, MC, V.

D ♥

★ ★ ★ **DUX.** *(See Peabody Hotel) 901/529-4199.* Hrs: 6:30-10:30 am, 11:30 am-2:30 pm; 5:30-11 pm; Fri to midnight; Sat noon-2:30 pm, 5:30-midnight; Sun 6:30-11:30 am, 5:30 pm-midnight. Res accepted. Bar. Wine list. Semi-a la carte: bkfst $3.95-$13.95, lunch $6.95-$14.95, dinner $5.95-$28.95. Child's meals. Specializes in mesquite-grilled Black Angus steak and seafood. Own baking. Valet parking. Cr cds: A, C, D, DS, JCB, MC, V.

D ♥

★ **ERIKA'S.** *52 S Second (38103), downtown. 901/526-5522.* Hrs: 11 am-2 pm; Fri, Sat 11 am-2 pm, 5:30-10 pm. Closed Sun; major hols. German menu. Beer. Semi-a la carte: lunch $4.95-$8.95, dinner $5-$11. Cr cds: A, C, D, DS, MC, V.

D

★ ★ ★ **ERLING JENSEN.** *1044 S Yates Rd (38119), east of downtown. 901/763-3700.* Hrs: 5-10 pm; Sun brunch 11:30 am-2 pm. Closed some major hols. Res accepted. French menu. Serv bar. Wine cellar. Semi-a la carte: dinner $21-$27. Sun brunch $20. Specializes in lamb, fresh seafood. Elegant atmosphere. Totally nonsmoking. Cr cds: A, D, MC, V.

D

★ ★ **FOLK'S FOLLY.** *551 S Mendenhall Rd (38117), east of downtown. 901/762-8200.* Web www.memphistravel.com/folksfolly. Hrs: 6-11 pm; Sat from 5 pm; Sun 6-10 pm. Closed most major hols; also Jan 2. Res accepted. Bar. A la carte entrees: dinner $15.50-$36. Specializes in steak, seafood, homemade desserts. Pianist Mon-Sat. Valet parking. Private, intimate dining. Cr cds: A, C, D, MC, V.

D

✔★ **INDIA PALACE.** *1720 Poplar Ave (38104), in Overton Square. 901/278-1199.* Hrs: 11 am-2:30 pm, 5-10 pm; Fri-Sun 11 am-3 pm, 5-10 pm. Closed Thanksgiving, Dec 25. Res accepted. Indian menu. Lunch buffet $5.95. Semi-a la carte: dinner $5.95-$10.95. Specialties: chicken Tikka massala, Palak paneer, Tandoori chicken. Own baking. Elephant and tiger murals; Indian decor. Cr cds: A, D, DS, MC, V.

D

★ ★ ★ **LA TOURELLE.** *2146 Monroe Ave (38104), in Overton Square. 901/726-5771.* Hrs: 6-10 pm; Sun brunch 11:30 am-2 pm. Closed Jan 1, Thanksgiving, Dec 25. Res accepted. French menu. Wine cellar. A la carte entrees: dinner $21-$30. Complete meal: dinner $50. Specialties: rosemary-marinated rack of lamb, ginger-glazed veal chop, balsamic-marinated swordfish. Own baking. Converted 1910 home; intimate dining. Totally nonsmoking. Cr cds: MC, V.

D

★ ★ **LULU GRILLE.** *565 Erin Dr (38117), east of downtown. 901/763-3677.* Hrs: 11 am-10 pm; Fri, Sat to 11 pm. Closed Sun; most major hols. Res accepted. Bar. Semi-a la carte: lunch $5.95-$10.95, dinner $8.50-$22.95. Specializes in fresh seafood, pasta, game. Outdoor dining. Bistro atmosphere. Cr cds: A, C, D, DS, MC, V.

D

★ **MELOS TAVERNA.** *2021 Madison Ave (38104), in Overton Square. 901/725-1863.* Hrs: 4:30-10:30 pm. Closed Sun, Mon; July 4, Thanksgiving, Dec 25. Res accepted. Greek menu. Bar. Semi-a la carte: dinner $8.75-$21. Specializes in lamb, moussaka. Parking. Greek artwork. Cr cds: A, C, D, DS, MC, V.

D

★ ★ **PAULETTE'S.** *2110 Madison Ave, in Overton Square. 901/726-5128.* Hrs: 11 am-10 pm; Fri & Sat to 11:30 pm; Sat, Sun brunch to 4 pm. Closed major hols. Res accepted. Continental menu. Bar. Semi-a la carte: lunch $6.95-$11.95, dinner $9.50-$21.95. Sat, Sun brunch $6.95-$9.95. Child's meals. Specialties: Filet Paulette, grilled salmon, crabcakes. Pianist Fri-Sun. Parking. Cr cds: A, D, DS, MC, V.

D

★ ★ **THE PIER.** *100 Wagner Pl (38103), downtown. 901/526-7381.* Hrs: 5-9:30 pm; Fri, Sat to 10 pm. Closed most major hols; Super Bowl Sun. Res accepted. Semi-a la carte: dinner $11.95-$23.95. Specializes in New England clam chowder, prime rib, fresh fish. On river; nautical decor. Cr cds: A, D, DS, MC, V.

D

★ **THE PUBLIC EYE.** *17 S Cooper (38104), in Overton Square. 901/726-4040.* Hrs: 11 am-10 pm; Fri, Sat to midnight; lunch buffet to 2 pm. Closed Jan 1, Dec 25. Bar. Semi-a la carte: lunch $4-$7, dinner $5-$20. Buffet: lunch $5.95. Child's meals. Specializes in barbecued pork, ribs. Parking. Cr cds: A, C, D, DS, MC, V.

D

★ ★ ★ **RAJI.** *712 W Brookhaven Circle, east of downtown. 901/685-8723.* French, Indian menu. Specialties: tandoori game hens with corn and cumin tomato sauce, grilled scallops and lobster in lentil pastry with ginger-flavored beurre blanc. Hrs: 7-11 pm. Closed Sun, Mon; most major hols. Res required. Bar. Wine list. Semi-a la carte: dinner $40. Several elegant dining rms in former residence. Totally nonsmoking. Cr cds: A, MC, V.

D

★ ★ **RONNIE GRISANTA & SONS.** *2855 Poplar Ave (38111), east of downtown. 901/323-0007.* rs: 5-11 pm. Closed Sun; major hols; also 1st wk July. Italian menu. Bar. Semi-a la carte: dinner $9.95-$25.95. Child's meals. Specialties: grilled porterhouse steak with truffles, grilled tuna in putenesca sauce, frutti di mare. Parking. Italian artwork. Cr cds: A, MC, V.

D

✔ ★ **SAIGON LE.** *51 N Cleveland (38104), east of downtown. 901/276-5326.* Hrs: 11 am-9:30 pm. Closed Sun; Thanksgiving, Dec 25. Res accepted. Chinese, Vietnamese menu. Semi-a la carte: lunch $3.45-$3.95, dinner $6.45-$8.75. Specialties: roasted wheat clute, Saigon egg roll, green shell mussels with French butter. Own baking. Casual dining. Cr cds: A, D, DS, MC, V.

D

Unrated Dining Spots

BUTCHER SHOP. *101 S Front St, downtown. 901/521-0856.* Hrs: 5-10 pm; Fri, Sat to 11 pm. Closed Jan 1, Thanksgiving, Dec 24, 25. Bar. Option to select and cook own steak. Served with salad, potato and bread $15-$21. Child's meals. Salad bar. Grill in dining room; 1907 building. Cr cds: A, D, DS, MC, V.

RENDEZVOUS. *52 S 2nd St, in Gen Washburn Alley, downtown. 901/523-2746.* Hrs: 4:30 pm-midnight; Fri from 11:30 am; Sat from 12:30 pm. Closed Sun, Mon; also 2 wks late July, 2 wks late Dec. Bar (beer). Semi-a la carte: lunch, dinner $3-$10. Specializes in barbecued ribs. In 1890 downtown building; memorabilia, many antiques, collectibles; jukebox. Cr cds: A, C, D, MC, V.

Miami

Settled: 1870
Pop: 358,548
Elev: 5 feet
Time zone: Eastern
Area code: 305
Web: www.miamiandbeaches.com

Although favored by climate and geography, Miami remained a remote tropical village of frame houses until Henry Flagler brought his East Coast Railway here in 1896 and turned his hand to community development. After World War I, Florida tourism began to boom. Two enterprising businessmen, John S. Collins and Carl Fisher, almost single-handedly created Miami Beach out of a mangrove swamp. The big promotion and ballyhoo advertising for Miami Beach and other nearby communities started in 1919. Between 1920 and 1925, the population of Florida's east coast increased by 75 percent.

World War II brought thousands of military personnel to Miami, and many of them returned to the area after the war to live. Since then, the Greater Miami area has reached maturity as a vibrant, exciting major metropolis of two million people.

Business

Although Greater Miami, a conglomerate of 27 separate municipalities, has hundreds of hotels, motels and restaurants catering to a great number of tourists, the city is not as dependent on tourism as many other Florida cities. In addition to tourism, Miami has more than 3,000 manufacturing firms, 170 banks and a $500-million agricultural industry. It is a major gateway to and from Latin America; more than $120 million in customs fees are collected here annually. International banking is important in Miami; there are a dozen banks that engage solely in offshore operations. The Downtown Development Authority, a semiautonomous arm of the city government, works to encourage growth and improvement in the central city. Millions of dollars have been invested in construction of new commercial buildings.

Convention Facilities

The Miami Convention Center is a $139-million conference, convention and hotel complex in the downtown area. It includes the City of Miami-Knight Convention Center, the University of Miami Conference Center and the Hyatt Regency-Miami. The center has a 5,000-seat theater-style convention hall, the 28,000-square-foot James L. Knight Center and Riverfront Exhibit Hall and 37 meeting rooms.

The Miami Beach Convention Center, site of three presidential nominating conventions, has doubled in size to 1.1 million square feet, including more than 500,000 square feet of contiguous exhibit floor space. The center has become one of the 10 largest facilities of its kind in the country. The Coconut Grove Convention Center, overlooking Biscayne Bay, provides a total of 150,000 square feet of contiguous space.

The Greater Miami Convention and Visitors Bureau provides several special convention services free of charge.

Sports & Recreation

The Orange Bowl Football Classic on January 1 is a sports highlight in Miami. The Florida Marlins play major league baseball at Pro Player Stadium during the spring and summer; in the fall, the Miami Dolphins play professional football there. The University of Miami Hurricanes play college football at the Orange Bowl each fall. The Miami Heat play professional basketball and the Florida Panthers play hockey from November through April at the Miami Arena.

Miami offers a long list of activities geared to enjoyment, from deep-sea fishing to watching jai alai; from playing golf to betting on the horses; and from glamorous nightclubbing to tennis, swimming and scuba diving.

Entertainment

Many kinds of cultural events are constantly taking place. The New World Symphony and the Florida Philharmonic Orchestra are orchestras that offer a series of programs. The New World School of the Arts and several youth symphonies give several programs a year. The Concert Association of Florida presents international artists and ensembles.

The Florida Grand Opera, Miami City Ballet, Coconut Grove Playhouse, and more than 70 multicultural theater companies throughout the county all have regular and excellent programs.

Miami evenings offer everything from nightclubs to Latin revues. It is best to consult the local newspapers and magazines for up-to-date entertainment schedules.

Sightseeing

Greater Miami's list of tourist attractions is long and varied; the city has something for everyone. Some of the more popular attractions are Vizcaya Museum and Gardens, Little Havana, Museum of Science and Space Transit Planetarium, Coconut Grove, the Art Deco District, Parrot Jungle and Gardens, Miami Metrozoo, Monkey Jungle and Gulfstream Park.

The spectacular Metro-Dade County Cultural Plaza, a $25-million downtown complex, houses the Historical Museum of Southern Florida, the Center for the Fine Arts (an art museum of traveling exhibits) and the Miami-Dade Public Library.

Biscayne Boulevard is a prime spot for shopping, with the Bayside Marketplace located at 401 Biscayne Blvd. Shopping is also excellent at

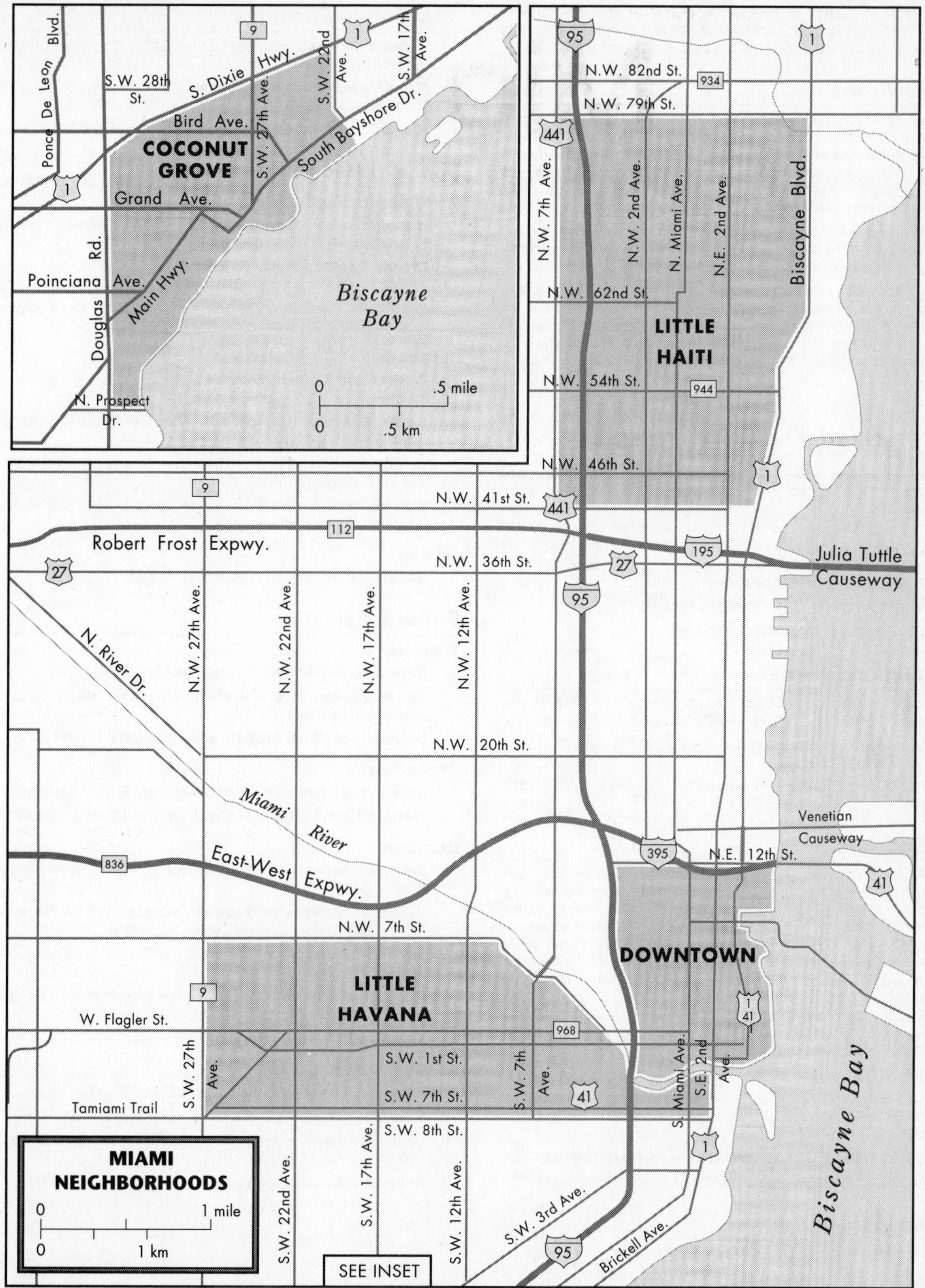
MIAMI NEIGHBORHOODS
COCONUT GROVE
LITTLE HAITI
LITTLE HAVANA
DOWNTOWN
Biscayne Bay
SEE INSET
Robert Frost Expwy.
East-West Expwy.
Julia Tuttle Causeway
Venetian Causeway
Miami River
N. River Dr.
Tamiami Trail
W. Flagler St.
Biscayne Blvd.
Brickell Ave.
S. Dixie Hwy.
South Bayshore Dr.
Main Hwy.
Grand Ave.
Bird Ave.
Poinciana Ave.
Douglas Rd.
Ponce De Leon Blvd.
N. Prospect Dr.

the Cocowalk shopping and entertainment complex and at Mayfair in Coconut Grove, Bal Harbour Shops in Bal Harbour, downtown's Bayside Marketplace and Dadeland Mall and The Falls in southern Miami.

City Environs

A trip into Everglades National Park is a unique sightseeing experience. From Miami, drive south on US 1 or the Florida Turnpike to Florida City. Take W Palm Dr west and follow the signs to the park. It is 38 miles from the Visitor Center to the end of the road, but stop along the way to truly enjoy the park. Various boardwalks lead out over the watery areas; signs and displays identify and describe the flora and fauna.

At Flamingo, there are sightseeing boat trips, and naturalists conduct nature walks along the shore. Talks, films and slide shows are given by Park Service personnel daily during the winter season.

Another beautiful drive can be taken into the Florida Keys—a long stretch of coral and sand with breathtaking views of the Atlantic and the Gulf of Mexico. The Overseas Highway (US 1) stretches from Homestead south to the tip of Key West, crossing several keys and bridges along the way. Charter fishing boats operate from most of the communities in the Keys.

General References

Area code: 305

Phone Numbers

POLICE, FIRE & AMBULANCE: 911

POISON INFORMATION CENTER: 800/282-3171

TIME: 324-8811 **WEATHER:** 229-4530

Information Sources

Greater Miami Convention & Visitors Bureau, 701 Brickell Ave, Suite 2700, 33131; 539-3000 or 800/464-2643.

City of Miami Citizens Response Center, 300 Biscayne Blvd Way, #420, 33131; 579-2457.

Dade County Citizens Information, 140 W Flagler, 33130; 375-5656.

Transportation

AIRLINES: Aeroflot; Aerolineas Argentinas; AeroMexico; Aero Peru; Air Aruba; Air Canada; Air Europa; Air France; Air Jamaica; Alitalia; ALM; American; America West; ATA; Bahamasair; British Airways; BWIA (British West Indian Airways); Canadian Airlines Intl; Carnival; Cayman; Continental; Delta; Ecuatoriana; El Al; Finnair; Guyana; Iberia (Spain); LACSA (Costa Rica); Lan Chile; Lufthansa (Germany); Martinair Holland; Mexicana; Northwest; Qantas; Saeta; South African; Surinam; TACA (El Salvador); TWA; United; USAir; Varig (Brazil); VASP (Brazil); VIASA (Venezuela); Virgin Atlantic (UK); Western Pacific; and other international, regional and commuter airlines.

AIRPORT: Miami International, 876-7000.

CAR RENTAL AGENCIES: (See IMPORTANT TOLL-FREE NUMBERS) Avis 637-4900; Budget 871-3053; Hertz 871-0300; National 638-1026.

PUBLIC TRANSPORTATION: Metro Bus & Rail 638-6700.

RAILROAD PASSENGER SERVICE: Amtrak 800/872-7245.

Newspapers

Miami Herald; Miami Times; Diario Las Americas.

Convention Facilities

Coconut Grove Convention Center, 2700 S Bayshore Dr, Coconut Grove, 579-3310.

Miami Beach Convention Center, 1901 Convention Center Dr, Miami Beach, 673-7311.

Miami Convention Center, 400 SE 2nd Ave, 372-0277.

Sports & Recreation

Major Sports Facilities

Miami Arena, 721 NW First Ave (Heat, basketball, 577-4328; Panthers, hockey, 954/768-1900).

Orange Bowl Stadium, 1501 NW 3rd St, 643-7100 (Hurricanes, college football).

Pro Player Stadium, 2269 NW 199th St, Opa-locka (Dolphins, football, 452-7000; Marlins, baseball, 626-7400).

Racetracks

Calder Race Course, 21001 NW 27th Ave, 625-1311 (horse racing).

Flagler Greyhound Track, NW 37th Ave & 7th St, 649-3000 (greyhound racing).

Gulfstream Park, US 1 & Hallandale Beach Blvd, Hallandale, 454-7000 (horse racing).

Hialeah Park, E 4th Ave between 22nd & 33rd Sts, Hialeah, 885-8000 (Thoroughbred racing).

Jai Alai

Miami Fronton, 3500 NW 37th Ave, 633-6400.

Cultural Facilities

Theaters

Coconut Grove Playhouse, 3500 Main Hwy, 442-4000.

Jackie Gleason Theater of Performing Arts, 1700 Washington Ave, Miami Beach, 673-7300.

University of Miami Ring Theater, 1380 Miller Dr, 284-3355.

Concert Halls

Dade County Auditorium, 2901 W Flagler St, 547-5414.

Gusman Concert Hall, 1314 Miller Dr, Coral Gables, 284-6477.

Museums

American Police Hall of Fame and Museum, 3801 Biscayne Blvd, 573-0070.

Historical Museum of Southern Florida, 101 W Flagler St, Metro-Dade County Cultural Center, 375-1492.

Miami Youth Museum, Miracle Center, 3301 Coral Way, 446-4386.

Museum of Science & Space Transit Planetarium, 3280 S Miami Ave, 854-4247 (museum), 854-2222 (planetarium).

Vizcaya Museum and Gardens, 3251 S Miami Ave, 250-9133.

Art Museums & Galleries

Bacardi Art Gallery, 2100 Biscayne Blvd, 573-8511.

Bass Museum of Art, 21st & Collins Ave, Miami Beach, 673-7533.

Center for the Fine Arts, 101 W Flagler St, Metro-Dade County Cultural Center, 375-1700.

Museum of Contemporary Art, 770 NE 12th St, 893-6211.

Points of Interest

Historical

Art Deco District, from 1st to 23rd Sts, Lenox Court to Ocean Dr, Miami Beach, 672-2014.

Barnacle State Historic Site, 5 mi S, at 3485 Main Hwy, Coconut Grove, 448-9445.

Cape Florida Lighthouse, Bill Baggs Cape Florida State Park, Key Biscayne, 361-5811.

Fort Dallas, Lummus Park, NW North River Dr & NW 3rd St, 416-1313.

Peacock Inn Historic Site, McFarlane Rd at S Bayshore Dr, Coconut Grove.

South Beach. Extends S from vicinity of Dade Blvd, concentrated mainly along Ocean Dr, Miami Beach.

Tequesta Indian Village & Jesuit Mission Site, near mouth of Miami River on the N bank.

Other Attractions

Bayfront Park, NE 5th to SE 2nd Sts, between Biscayne Bay & Biscayne Blvd, 358-7550.

Bayside Marketplace, 401 N Biscayne Blvd, on Biscayne Bay, 577-3344.

Everglades National Park, via US 1, 8 mi SW of jct SW 177th Ave, 247-6211.

Fairchild Tropical Garden, 10901 Old Cutler Rd, Coral Gables, 667-1651.

Gold Coast Railroad Museum, 12450 SW 152nd St, near Metrozoo, 253-0063.

Greynolds Park, 17530 W Dixie Hwy, 945-3425.

Lummus Park, NW N River Dr & NW 3rd St, 673-7730.

Metro-Dade County Cultural Center, 101 W Flagler St.

Metrozoo, 12400 SW 152nd St, 251-0400.

Miami Beach Garden Center and Conservatory, 2000 Convention Center Dr, Miami Beach, 673-7720.

Miccosukee Indian Village and Airboat Tours, 25 mi W on US 41, 223-8380.

Monkey Jungle, 14805 SW 216th St, 235-1611.

New World Center—Bicentennial Park, Biscayne Blvd, MacArthur Causeway & NE 9th St, 575-5240.

Parrot Jungle and Gardens, 11000 SW 57th Ave, 666-7834.

Seaquarium, Rickenbacker Causeway, 6 mi S on Virginia Key, 361-5705.

Watson Island, 40-acre island in Biscayne Bay.

Sightseeing Tours

All Florida Adventure Tours, 8263-B SW 107th Ave, 270-0219.

American Sightseeing Tours, Inc, 11077 NW 36th Ave, 688-7700.

***Island Queen* Bay Cruise,** Bayside Marketplace, 401 Biscayne Blvd, 379-5119.

Annual Events

Orange Bowl Football Classic (preceded by festival beginning mid-Dec). Jan 1.

Art Deco Weekend, Miami Beach. 2nd wkend Jan.

Taste of the Grove, Coconut Grove. Mid-Jan.

Coconut Grove Arts Festival. Mid-Feb.

International Boat Show, Miami Beach Convention Center. Mid-late Feb.

Doral Ryder Open PGA Golf Tournament. Mid-Feb-early Mar.

Carnaval Miami/Calle Ocho Festival. Early Mar.

Italian Renaissance Festival, Vizcaya. Mid-Mar.

South Florida Auto Show, Miami Beach Convention Center. Late Sept-early Oct.

Miccosukee Indian Arts Festival, Miccosukee Indian Village. Late Dec-early Jan.

City Neighborhoods

Many of the restaurants, unrated dining establishments and some lodgings listed under Miami include neighborhoods as well as exact street addresses. Geographic descriptions of these areas are given, followed by a table of restaurants arranged by neighborhood.

Coconut Grove: South of S Dixie Hwy (US 1), west of SW 22nd Ave, north of Biscayne Bay and east of Douglas Rd.

Downtown: South of NE 12th St, west of Biscayne Bay, north of the Miami River and east of NW 27th St. **North of Downtown:** North of I-395. **South of Downtown:** South of US 41. **West of Downtown:** West of I-95.

Little Haiti: South of NW 79th St, west of Biscayne Blvd (US 1), north of NW 41st St and east of NW 7th Ave.

Little Havana: South of NW 7th St, west of the Miami River, north of SW 8th St and east of NW 27th St.

Lodgings and Food

MIAMI RESTAURANTS BY NEIGHBORHOOD AREAS

(For full description, see alphabetical listings under Restaurants)

COCONUT GROVE
Bocca di Rosa. 2833 Bird Ave
Cafe Med. 3015 Grand Ave
Cafe Tu Tu Tango. 3015 Grand Ave
Grand Cafe (Grand Bay Hotel). 2669 S Bayshore Dr
Green Street Cafe. 3468 Main Hwy
Kaleidoscope. 3112 Commodore Plaza
Mambo Cafe. 3105 Commodore Plaza
Marks In The Grove. 4 Grove Isle Dr
Mayfair Grill (Mayfair House Hotel). 3000 Florida Ave
Modern Art Cafe. 2801 Florida Ave
Planet Hollywood. 3390 Mary St
Señor Frog's. 3480 Main Hwy
Trattoria Pampered Chef. 3145 Commodore Plaza
Tuscany Trattoria. 3484 Main Hwy

DOWNTOWN
Capital Grille. 444 Brickell Ave
Las Tapas. 401 Biscayne Blvd
Le Pavillon (Hotel Inter-Continental). 100 Chopin Plaza
Snappers. 401 Biscayne Blvd

NORTH OF DOWNTOWN
Francis On The Bay. 1279 NE 79th St
Il Tulipano. 11052 Biscayne Blvd (US 1)
Mike Gordon. 1201 NE 79th St
Tony Chan's Water Club. 1717 N Bayshore Dr

SOUTH OF DOWNTOWN
Fleming. 8511 SW 136th St
Porcao. 801 S Bayshore Dr
Samurai. 8717 SW 136th St
Thai Orchid. 9565 SW 72nd St
Tropical Chinese. 7991 SW 40th St
Victor's Cafe. 2340 SW 32nd Ave
Wah Shing. 9503 S Dixie Hwy (US 1)

LITTLE HAVANA
Casa Juancho. 2436 SW 8th St

Note: When a listing is located in a town that does not have its own city heading, it will appear under the city nearest to its location. In these cases, the address and town appear in parenthesis immediately following the name of the establishment.

Motels

(Rates are usually higher during football, Bowl games)

★ ★ ★ **COURTYARD BY MARRIOTT.** *3929 NW 79th Ave (33166), west of downtown. 305/477-8118; FAX 305/599-9363.* 145 rms, 4 story. Mid-Jan-mid-Apr: S, D $129; suites $149; under 18 free; lower rates rest of yr. Crib free. TV; cable (premium). Heated pool; whirlpool. Complimentary coffee in rms. Bar 4-10 pm. Ck-out noon. Coin Indry. Meeting rm. Business servs avail. In-rm modem link. Valet serv. Sundries. Free airport transportation. Exercise equipt; weight machine, stair machine. Refrigerator in suites. Balconies. Miami Intl Airport 5 mi SE. Cr cds: A, C, D, DS, MC, V.

D SC

✔★ ★ **FAIRFIELD INN BY MARRIOTT.** *3959 NW 79th Ave (33166), west of downtown. 305/599-5200.* 135 rms, 3 story. Jan-mid-Apr: S $68.95; D $74.95; under 18 free; lower rates rest of yr. Crib free. TV; cable (premium). Heated pool. Complimentary continental bkfst in lobby. Restaurant nearby. Ck-out noon. Business servs avail. In-rm modem link. Free airport transportation. Cr cds: A, C, D, DS, MC, V.

D SC

★ **HAMPTON INN.** *2500 Brickell Ave (33129), I-95 exit 1, south of downtown. 305/854-2070; FAX 305/856-5055.* 69 rms, 3 story. Jan-Apr & Dec: S $82.95-$89.95; D $89.95; under 18 free; lower rates rest of yr. Crib free. Pet accepted. TV; cable. Pool. Complimentary continental bkfst. Bar 3-11 pm. Ck-out noon. Meeting rms. Business servs avail. In-rm modem link. Valet serv. Cr cds: A, C, D, DS, MC, V.

D SC

✔★ ★ **QUALITY INN SOUTH.** *14501 S Dixie Hwy (33176), south of downtown. 305/251-2000; FAX 305/235-2225.* 100 rms, 2 story, 14 kits. Dec-Apr: S $73-$90; D $79-$96; each addl $5; kit. units $96; under 18 free; varied lower rates rest of yr. Crib free. Pet accepted. TV; cable (premium). Heated pool. Restaurant 6:30 am-10 pm; Fri & Sat to 11 pm. Rm serv. Ck-out 11 am. Coin Indry. Cr cds: A, C, D, DS, JCB, MC, V.

SC

★ **WELLESLEY INN AT KENDALL.** *11750 Mills Dr (33183). 305/270-0359; FAX 305/270-1334; res: 800/444-8888.* 106 rms, 4 story. S $79.99-$89.99; D $89.99-$99.99; each addl $10; suites $150; under 12 free. Crib free. TV; cable (premium). Heated pool. Complimentary continental bkfst. Restaurant nearby. Ck-out 11 am. Health club privileges. Cr cds: A, C, D, DS, MC, V.

D SC

✔★ ★ **WELLESLEY INN AT MIAMI LAKES.** *7925 NW 154th St (33016), north of downtown. 305/821-8274; FAX 305/828-2257.* 100 rms, 4 story. Jan-Apr: S $69.99-$79.99; D $79.99-$99.99; under 18 free; higher rates special events; lower rates rest of yr. Crib free. TV; cable (premium). Heated pool. Complimentary continental bkfst. Restaurant adj 7-1 am. Ck-out 11 am. Coin Indry. Meeting rm. Health club privileges. Valet serv. Refrigerator, microwave in suites. Cr cds: A, C, D, DS, MC, V.

D SC

Motor Hotel

★ ★ **AMERISUITES.** *11520 SW 88th St (33176), south of downtown. 305/279-8688; FAX 305/279-7907.* 67 suites, 5 story. Dec-Apr: suites $129-$149; under 16 free; wkend rates; higher rates Boat Show, Grand Prix; lower rates rest of yr. Crib avail. Pet accepted, some restrictions. TV; cable (premium), VCR. Complimentary continental bkfst. Complimentary coffee in rms. Restaurant nearby. Rm serv 11 am-10 pm. Ck-out 11 am. Meeting rms. Business center. In-rm modem link. Bellhops. Valet serv. Concierge. Coin Indry. 18-hole golf privileges, greens fee $30-$50, pro, putting green, driving range. Pool. Refrigerators, microwaves, wet bar. Cr cds: A, C, D, DS, MC, V.

D SC

★ ★ **HOLIDAY INN-CALDER/PRO PLAYER STADIUM.** *21485 NW 27th Ave (33056), NW 27th Ave & County Line Rd, north of downtown. 305/621-5801; FAX 305/624-8202.* 214 rms, 9 story. Jan-Mar: S, D $77-$139; each addl $10; under 19 free; varied lower rates rest of yr. Crib free. TV; cable (premium). Heated pool. Restaurant 6:30 am-2 pm, 5:30-10 pm. Bar 4 pm-midnight; entertainment. Ck-out noon. Coin Indry. Meeting rms. Business servs avail. In-rm modem link. Bellhops. Valet serv. Exercise equipt; bicycle, stair machine. Game rm. Gift shop. Private balconies. Panoramic views of Calder Racetrack and Pro Player Stadium. Cr cds: A, C, D, DS, ER, JCB, MC, V.

D SC

Hotels

★ ★ ★ **CROWNE PLAZA.** *1601 Biscayne Blvd (33132), north of downtown. 305/374-0000; FAX 305/374-0020.* 528 rms, 28 story. Jan-late Mar: S, D $119-$239; each addl $20; suites $250-$2,700; under 17 free;

wkend rates; lower rates rest of yr. Crib free. Parking $10; self-park $8. TV; cable (premium). Heated rooftop pool; poolside serv. Restaurant 6:30 am-11 pm. Bar. Ck-out noon. Convention facilities. Business center. In-rm modem link. Concierge. Golf privileges. Exercise equipt; weights, treadmills. Overlooks bay. 3-level shopping, dining, entertainment complex. Luxury level. Cr cds: A, C, D, DS, ER, JCB, MC, V.

D SC

★ ★ **DOUBLETREE AT COCONUT GROVE.** *2649 S Bayshore Dr (33133), S on US 1 (S Dixie Hwy) S on SW 27th Ave, then N on S Bayshore Dr, in Coconut Grove. 305/858-2500; FAX 305/858-5776.* 192 rms, 20 story. S, D $169-$299; each addl $20; under 18 free. Crib free. Valet parking $9. TV; cable (premium), VCR avail. Heated pool; poolside serv. Restaurant 6:30 am-11 pm. Bars from 11 am. Ck-out noon. Meeting rms. Business center. Lighted tennis. Health club privileges. Microwaves avail. Many balconies with ocean view. Fishing, sailing yachts for charter. Opp Coconut Grove Convention Center. Cr cds: A, C, D, DS, ER, JCB, MC, V.

D SC

★ ★ ★ **DOUBLETREE GRAND HOTEL.** *1717 N Bayshore Dr (33132), north of downtown. 305/372-0313; FAX 305/372-9455.* 227 rms, 42 story, 75 kit. units. Dec-Apr: S, D $129-$149; suites $169-$350; kit. units $175-$375; under 18 free; higher rates Boat Show; lower rates rest of yr. Crib free. TV; cable (premium). Heated pool; whirlpool, poolside serv. Restaurant 7 am-11 pm. Bar. Ck-out noon. Coin Indry. Meeting rms. Business servs avail. Concierge. Gift shop. RR station, bus depot transportation. Exercise rm; instructor, weights, treadmill, sauna. Minibars; microwaves avail. Refrigerator, wet bar in suites. Many balconies. On Biscayne Bay. Skywalk connects to Omni International Mall. Cr cds: A, C, D, DS, JCB, MC, V.

D SC

★ ★ ★ ★ **GRAND BAY.** *2669 S Bayshore Dr (33133), in Coconut Grove. 305/858-9600; FAX 305/858-1532; res: 800/327-2788.* E-mail grandbay@vcn.net; web miami.vcn.net/grandbay. This modern high-rise with a stepped facade resembling a Mayan pyramid features traditional furnishings, original art, attentive service and breathtaking views of Biscayne Bay and downtown Miami. 178 rms, 13 story, 47 suites. S, D $205-$300; each addl $20; suites $350-$1,400; under 15 free; wkend rates. Crib free. TV; cable (premium), VCR (movies avail). Heated pool; whirlpool, poolside serv. Restaurant (see GRAND CAFE). Rm serv 24 hrs. Bar 11:30-2 am; entertainment exc Sun. Ck-out noon. Meeting rms. Business center. In-rm modem link. Concierge. Beauty shop. Exercise rm; instructor, weights, bicycles, sauna. Massage. Bathrm phones, minibars. Private balconies. Cr cds: A, C, D, MC, V.

D

★ ★ ★ **GROVE ISLE CLUB & RESORT.** *4 Grove Isle Dr (33133), in Coconut Grove. 305/858-8300; FAX 305/858-5908; res: 800/88GROVE.* 50 rms, 5 story, 9 suites. Oct-mid-Apr: S $295; D $315; suites $420-$550; under 14 free; lower rates rest of yr. Crib free. Pet accepted, some restrictions. TV; cable (premium), VCR. Pool; whirlpool, poolside serv. Playground. Complimentary coffee in rms. Restaurant 7:30 am-10 pm. Bar. Ck-out noon. Meeting rms. Business servs avail. Concierge. Gift shop. Barber, beauty shop. Lighted tennis, pro. Exercise equipt; weights, bicycles. Refrigerators. Balconies. On Biscayne Bay. Cr cds: A, D, MC, V.

D

★ ★ ★ **HOTEL INTER-CONTINENTAL.** *100 Chopin Plaza (33131), downtown. 305/577-1000; FAX 305/577-0384; res: 800/327-3005.* 644 rms, 34 story. S $199-$259; D $229-$289; each addl $30; suites $325-$2,900; under 14 free; wkly, wkend rates. Garage; valet parking $11. TV; cable (premium). Heated pool; poolside serv. Restaurant 7 am-11 pm (also see LE PAVILLON). Rm serv 24 hrs. Bar 11:30 am-midnight. Ck-out noon. Convention facilities. Business center. In-rm modem link. Concierge. Exercise rm; instructor, weights, bicycles. Minibars. Cr cds: A, C, D, DS, ER, JCB, MC, V.

D

★ ★ **HOWARD JOHNSON.** *1100 Biscayne Blvd (33132). 305/358-3080; FAX 305/358-8631.* 115 rms, 7 story. S, D $89-$99; under 18 free; higher rates special events. Crib free. TV; cable (premium). Pool; poolside serv. Restaurant 7 am-10 pm. Bar 4 pm-midnight. Ck-out noon. Coin Indry. Meeting rms. Business servs avail. Balconies. Cr cds: A, C, D, DS, JCB, MC, V.

D SC

★ ★ ★ **MARRIOTT BISCAYNE BAY HOTEL & MARINA.** *1633 N Bayshore Dr (33132), downtown. 305/374-3900; FAX 305/375-0597.* 605 rms, 31 story. Mid-Dec-Apr: S, D $145; suites $400-$1,100; lower rates rest of yr. Covered parking $7; valet parking $9. TV; cable. Heated pool; poolside serv. Restaurant 6:30 am-11 pm. Bar 11-1 am. Ck-out noon. Coin Indry. Convention facilities. Business servs avail. Shopping arcade. Barber, beauty shop. Exercise equipt; weight machines, treadmill, whirlpool. Game rm. Some bathrm phones. Minibars; refrigerators avail. Balconies. On Biscayne Bay, marina. Luxury level. Cr cds: A, C, D, DS, ER, JCB, MC, V.

D SC

★ ★ ★ **MARRIOTT-DADELAND.** *9090 S Dadeland Blvd (33156), south of downtown. 305/670-1035; FAX 305/670-7540.* 302 rms, 24 story. S, D $164; suites $275-$450; under 18 free. Crib free. Covered parking $9; valet $10. TV; cable (premium). Heated pool; whirlpool, poolside serv. Restaurant 6:30 am-11 pm. Bar 2 pm-midnight; entertainment Mon-Fri. Ck-out 11 am. Meeting rms. Business servs avail. In-rm modem link. Concierge. Free airport, RR station, shopping transportation. Tennis privileges. Golf privileges. Exercise equipt; treadmills, bicycles. Game rm. Luxury level. Cr cds: A, C, D, DS, MC, V.

D SC

★ ★ ★ ★ **MAYFAIR HOUSE.** *3000 Florida Ave (33133), in Coconut Grove. 305/441-0000; FAX 305/441-1647; res: 800/433-4555 (exc FL).* E-mail copyf@bellsouth.net; web www.hotelbook.com. This European-style luxury hotel sits within Mayfair Shops at the Grove, an exclusive open-air shopping mall. Public areas have Tiffany windows, polished mahogany, marble walls and floors, imported crystal and a glassed-in elevator. 183 suites, 5 story. Mid-Dec-Apr: S, D $249-$650; each addl $35; under 12 free; wkend rates; lower rates rest of yr. Crib free. Valet parking $14. TV; cable (premium), VCR (movies avail). Rooftop pool. Restaurant 7 am-11 pm (also see MAYFAIR GRILL). Rm serv 24 hrs. Bars from noon. Ck-out 1 pm. Meeting rms. Business center. Concierge. Shopping arcade. Health club privileges. Massage. Bathrm phones, refrigerators, minibars. Private patios with hot tub. Cr cds: A, C, D, DS, MC, V.

D SC

★ ★ **OCCIDENTAL PLAZA.** *100 SE 4th St (33131), downtown. 305/374-5100; FAX 305/381-9826; res: 800/521-5100 (exc FL).* 134 rms, 16 story, 90 suites. Mid-Dec-Easter: suites $110-$180; under 12 free; lower rates rest of yr. Crib free. TV; cable (premium). Pool. Restaurant 7 am-11 pm. Bar. Ck-out noon. Meeting rms. Business center. Concierge. Exercise equipt; weights, bicycles. Bathrm phones, minibars. On river. Cr cds: A, D, DS, MC, V.

SC

★ ★ ★ **SHERATON BISCAYNE BAY.** *495 Brickell Ave (33131), downtown. 305/373-6000; FAX 305/374-2279.* 598 rms, 18 story. Jan-Mar: S $129-$149; D $139-$169; each addl $20; suites $250 & $350; under 12 free; lower rates rest of yr. Crib free. TV; cable (premium). Heated pool; poolside serv. Restaurant 6:30 am-11:30 pm. Bar 11-2 am; entertainment. Ck-out noon. Meeting rms. Business servs avail. In-rm modem link. Concierge. Covered parking. Exercise equipt; weight machine, treadmill. Microwaves avail. Private patios, balconies. Extensive landscaping; at bayside. Cr cds: A, C, D, DS, ER, MC, V.

D SC

Inn

★ **MIAMI RIVER INN.** *118 SW South River Dr (33130), downtown. 305/325-0045; FAX 305/325-9227; res: 800/468-3589.* 40 rms in 4 bldgs, 2-3 story. S, D $59-$125; higher rates some special events. TV; cable. Pool; whirlpool. Complimentary continental bkfst. Restaurant nearby. Ck-out noon, ck-in 2 pm. Meeting rm. Business servs avail. Lawn games. Opp river. Restored 1908 houses once owned by Miami's founders. Antiques. Cr cds: A, C, D, DS, MC, V.

D SC

Resorts

★ ★ ★ **DON SHULA'S HOTEL & GOLF CLUB.** *(Main St, Miami Lakes 33014) 18 mi NW; N on I-95, W on FL 826 (Palmetto Expy), 1 blk E to Main St. 305/821-1150; FAX 305/820-8190; res: 800/247-4852.* 301 rms, 3 story, 5 kits. Dec-Mar: S, D $199; each addl $10; suites $190-$270; under 12 free; golf package; lower rates rest of yr. Crib $10. TV; cable (premium). 2 pools. Dining rms 6:30 am-11 pm. Snack bars 10 am-7 pm; Fri & Sat from 7 am. Bar 11-2 am. Ck-out noon, ck-in 3 pm. Meeting rms. Business center. Shops. Lighted tennis, pro. Lighted 18-hole golf course, pro, par 3, 2 putting greens, driving range. Exercise rm; instructor, weights, bicycles, whirlpool, steam rm, sauna. Fishing trips. Wet bars; some refrigerators. Private patios, balconies. Luxury level. Cr cds: A, C, D, MC, V.

D SC

★ ★ ★ ★ **DORAL GOLF RESORT AND SPA.** *4400 NW 87th Ave (33178), west of downtown. 305/592-2000; FAX 305/594-4682; res: 800/71-DORAL.* Web www.doralgolf.com. Site of the annual Doral-Ryder Open Tournament, this luxurious resort hotel on 650 elaborately landscaped acres is an inland golf and tennis mecca. Accommodations are in separated three- and four-story lodges nestled beside the golf links. 694 rms in 12 bldgs. Dec-Apr: S, D $225-$370; each addl $40; suites $360-$1,500; under 17 free; lower rates rest of yr. Crib free. TV; cable (premium). Heated pool; wading pool, whirlpool, poolside serv. Playground. Supervised child's activities; ages 3-15. Restaurant 6:30 am-midnight. Rm serv 6-1 am. Snack bar, box lunches. 3 bars 11-1:30 am. Ck-out 11 am, ck-in 4 pm. Convention facilities. Business center. Valet serv. 15 tennis courts, 4 lighted, pro. Four 18-hole golf courses; 9-hole par-3 golf, pro, 4 putting greens, lighted driving range, golf school. Bicycle rentals. Lawn games. Soc dir; entertainment, movies. Game rm. Exercise rm; instructor, weights, bicycles, steam rm. Spa. Bathrm phones, refrigerators, minibars. Private patios, balconies. Cr cds: A, C, D, DS, MC, V.

D

★ ★ ★ **FISHER ISLAND CLUB.** *(1 Fisher Island Dr, Fisher Island 33109) I-95 to MacArthur Causeway, E to ferry terminal. Accesible only by auto ferry, helicopter, boat or seaplane. 305/535-6020; FAX 305/535-6003; res: 800/537-3708.* Web www.fisherisland-florida.com. 60 rms, 1-5 story, 4 kit. cottages. Nov-Apr: S $385-$725; D $385-$1,470; suites, cottages $600-$1,315; under 12 free; golf plan; lower rates rest of yr. Crib free. TV; cable (premium), VCR (movies $3). 4 pools, 1 indoor; whirlpool, poolside serv. Playground. Supervised child's activities; ages 4-10. Complimentary coffee in rms. Dining rm (see VANDERBILT MANSION). Rm serv. Bar 11-2 am; entertainment Wed-Sun. Ck-out noon, ck-in 3 pm. Grocery. Coin Indry. Meeting rms. Business servs avail. In-rm modem link. Bellhops. Valet serv. Concierge. Gift shop. Airport transportation. Sports dir. Lighted tennis; pro. 9-hole golf; greens fee $90, pro, putting green, driving range. Boating. Exercise rm; instructor, weight machine, treadmill, sauna. Spa. Lawn games. Social dir. Minibars; microwaves avail. Balconies. Bird aviary. Swimming beach. Marina; dockage avail. Cottages (ca 1925) on 200 landscaped acres; former William Vanderbilt estate. Cr cds: A, C, D, MC, V.

D

★ ★ ★ ★ **TURNBERRY ISLE RESORT & CLUB.** *(19999 W Country Club Dr, Aventura 33180) Approx 9 mi N via I-95, exit 20 (Ives Dairy Rd), E to US 1 (Biscayne Blvd), to Aventura Blvd. 305/932-6200; FAX 305/933-6560; res: 800/327-7028.* E-mail turnbsale@aol.com; web www.turnberryisle.com. This luxurious, gracious and comfortable resort consists of the European-style Marina hotel, the Yacht Club, the Miznerstyle Country Club Hotel and the new Mediterranean-style annex, all on 300 secluded acres with subtropical gardens. 340 rms in 3 bldgs, 3-7 story. Late Dec-Apr: Country Club: S, D $395-$495; each addl $30; suites $675-$2,100; Yacht Club: S, D $295; each addl $30; Marina Wing: S, D $335; each addl $30; under 12 free; golf, tennis, spa plans; lower rates rest of yr. Crib free. TV; cable, VCR (movies avail). 3 pools; whirlpool, poolside serv. Dining rm 7 am-10 pm. Box lunches, snack bar, picnics. Rm serv 24 hrs. Bars 11-1 am. Ck-out noon, ck-in 4 pm. Grocery, package store 1 blk. Coin Indry. Convention facilities. Business center. In-rm modem link. Lighted tennis, pro. 36-hole golf, greens fee $85 ($55 in summer), pro, putting green. Marina, beach, boats, diving, water sports. Entertainment. Exercise rm; instructor, weights, bicycles, sauna, steam rm. Massage. Refrigerators; many in-rm whirlpools. Cr cds: A, C, D, DS, ER, MC, V.

D

Restaurants

★ ★ **BOCCA DI ROSA.** *2833 Bird Ave (33133). 305/444-4222.* E-mail juditleon@aol.com. Hrs: 6 pm-midnight. Closed July 4, Dec 25. Res required. Italian menu. Bar. A la carte entrees: dinner $9.95-$29.95. Complete meal: dinner $40-$60. Specialties: risotto, tagliata maremana, tuna Marco Polo. Own baking. Valet parking. Outdoor dining. Stained glass; mirrored walls. Cr cds: A, C, D, DS, MC, V.

D

✔ ★ **CAFE MED.** *3015 Grand Ave, in Coconut Grove. 305/443-1770.* Hrs: 10 am-midnight; wkends to 1 am. Italian menu. Bar. A la carte entrees: lunch, dinner $3.95-$16.95. Child's meals. Specializes in brick oven pizza, fresh pasta dishes, Mediterranean salads. Own desserts. Outdoor dining. Cr cds: A, D, DS, MC, V.

D

✔★ ★ **CAFE TU TU TANGO.** *3015 Grand Ave, in Coconut Grove. 305/529-2222.* Hrs: 11:30 am-midnight; Fri, Sat to 2 am. International menu. Bar. A la carte entrees: lunch, dinner $2.75-$7.95. Child's meals. Specialties: Barcelona stir-fry, brick oven pizza. Entertainment. Outdoor dining. On 2nd floor of Cocowalk complex. Artist loft motif; painters at work. Cr cds: A, D, MC, V.

D

★ ★ ★ **CAPITAL GRILLE.** *444 Brickell Ave (33131), downtown. 305/374-4500.* Hrs: 11:30 am-3 pm, 5-10 pm; Fri to 11 pm; Sat 5-11 pm; Sun from 5 pm. Closed July 4, Thanksgiving, Dec 25. Res accepted. Bar. Wine cellar. A la carte entrees: lunch $9-$16, dinner $16-$28. Specializes in dry-aged steak, fresh seafood, chops. Own baking. Valet parking. Meat-aging rm and wine rm in main dining area. Cr cds: A, C, D, DS, MC, V.

D

★ ★ **CASA JUANCHO.** *2436 SW 8th St, in Little Havana. 305/642-2452.* Hrs: noon-midnight; Fri, Sat to 1 am. Res accepted. Spanish menu. Bar. A la carte entrees: lunch $8-$15, dinner $13-$34. Specializes in imported Spanish seafood, tapas. Strolling musicians. Valet parking. Spanish decor. Cr cds: A, C, D, MC, V.

D SC

★ ★ ★ ★ **CHEF ALLEN'S.** *(19088 NE 29th Ave, Aventura 33137) 1 blk E of Biscayne Blvd off of NE 191st St. 954/935-2900.* In this art-deco world of glass block, neon trim, fresh flowers and gallery art, your gaze nevertheless remains riveted on the kitchen. Chef Allen Susser designed it with a picture window 25 feet wide, so you can watch him create new American masterpieces with the help of a wood-burning mesquite grill. Specializes in fresh local seafood, veal chops, dessert soufflés. Own baking. Hrs: 6-10:30 pm. Res accepted. Bar. Wine cellar. A la carte entrees: dinner $24.95-$32.95. Valet parking. Cr cds: A, D, MC, V.

D

✔★ ★ **FLEMING.** *8511 SW 136th St (33156), in shopping center, south of downtown. 305/232-6444.* Hrs: 5:30-10:30 pm. Closed Mon; July 4. Res accepted. Danish, continental menu. Bar. Semi-a la carte: dinner $9.95-$18.95. Specialties: Norwegian salmon, duck Danoise. Patio dining. Scandinavian decor. Cr cds: A, MC, V.

D

★ ★ **FRANCIS ON THE BAY.** *1279 NE 79th St (33138), north of downtown. 305/758-9888.* Hrs: 4:30-10:30 pm; Sun from noon; early-bird dinner to 6 pm; Sun brunch to 4 pm. Res accepted. Continental menu. Bar. A la carte entrees: dinner $7.95-$25.95. Sun brunch $14.95. Child's meals. Specializes in seafood, beef. Band Fri, Sat. Valet parking. Outdoor dining. On bay. Cr cds: A, D, MC, V.

D

★ ★ ★ **GRAND CAFE.** *(See Grand Bay Hotel) 305/858-9600.* Hrs: 7 am-11 pm; Fri, Sat to 11:30 pm. Res accepted. Continental menu. Bar 11:30-1 am; Fri, Sat to 2 am. A la carte entrees: bkfst $7.75-$14, lunch $8.75-$19.50, dinner $21-$32. Sun brunch $29. Specializes in beef, chicken. Own baking. Valet parking. Entertainment. Windows overlook garden area. Cr cds: A, D, MC, V.

D

✔★ ★ **GREEN STREET CAFE.** *3468 Main Hwy, in Coconut Grove. 305/444-0244.* Hrs: 7 am-midnight; Fri, Sat to 1 am. Continental menu. A la carte entrees: bkfst $3-$6, lunch $5-$10, dinner $5-$13. Specializes in pasta, salad, pizza. Outdoor sidewalk cafe on corner lot. Cr cds: A, D, MC, V.

D

★ ★ ★ **GROVE ISLE.** *4 Grove Isle Dr (33133), in Coconut Grove. 305/857-5007.* Hrs: 7:30 am-11 pm; Sun brunch 11 am-2:30 pm. Res accepted. Bar. Wine list. Semi-a la carte: bkfst $3-$12, lunch $6-$15; dinner $9-$26. Sun brunch $6-$18. Child's meals. Specialties: mutton snapper, oak-grilled Chilean salmon, veal tenderloin. Valet parking. Outdoor dining. Modern decor. Waterfront dining. Cr cds: A, D, MC, V.

D

★ ★ ★ **IL TULIPANO.** *11052 Biscayne Blvd (US 1) (33161), north of downtown. 305/893-4811.* Hrs: 6-11 pm; Fri, Sat to midnight. Closed Mon; Dec 24; also Sept. Res accepted. Northern Italian menu. Bar. Wine cellar. A la carte entrees: dinner $14-$32. Specialties: pollo scarpariello, osso bucco, snapper. Own baking. Cr cds: A, D, MC, V.

D

★ ★ **KALEIDOSCOPE.** *3112 Commodore Plaza (33133), in Coconut Grove. 305/446-5010.* Hrs: 11 am-10:30 pm; Fri, Sat to midnight; Sun brunch 11 am-3 pm. Res accepted. Continental menu. Wine, beer. Semi-a la carte: lunch $6.95-$12, dinner $9-$20. Sun brunch $16.95. Specializes in fresh fish, beef. Outdoor dining. Cr cds: A, C, D, MC, V.

★ ★ ★ **LA PALOMA.** *(10999 Biscayne Blvd, North Miami 33161) N on US 1. 305/891-0505.* E-mail m10999@aol.com. Hrs: 11:30 am-3 pm, 5 pm-midnight. Res accepted. Continental menu. Bar. Wine list. A la carte entrees: lunch $6.95-$15, dinner $12.95-$25. Child's meals. Specialties: lamb chops a la diable, Wienerschnitzel, bouillabaise. Piano bar. Valet parking. Elegant, yet informal dining in three areas. Cr cds: A, D, MC, V.

D

★ ★ **LAS TAPAS.** *401 Biscayne Blvd, downtown. 305/372-2737.* Hrs: 11:30 am-midnight; Fri, Sat to 1 am. Spanish menu. Bar. Semi-a la carte: lunch $4.95-$9.95, dinner $9.95-$19.95. Speciaizes in hot & cold tapas, seafood. Strolling minstrels. Outdoor dining. Open kitchen. Spanish contemporary decor. Cr cds: A, C, D, DS, MC, V.

D

★ ★ ★ **LE PAVILLON.** *(See Hotel Inter-Continental) 305/372-4494.* Hrs: noon-2:30 pm, 7-10 pm; Mon to 2:30 pm; Sat from 6 pm. Closed Sun. Res accepted. Continental menu. Bar. Complete meals: lunch $20. Semi-a la carte: dinner $18-$35. Specializes in fresh seafood, steak, salads. Harpist. Valet parking. Cr cds: A, C, D, DS, ER, JCB, MC, V.

D

★ ★ **MAMBO CAFE.** *3105 Commodore Plaza (33133), in Coconut Grove. 305/448-2768.* Hrs: 9-1 am; Sat, Sun brunch 8 am-1 pm. Cuban menu. Semi-a la carte: bkfst $3.50-$7.95, lunch, dinner $4.95-$31.95. Child's meals. Specialties: mariquitas con mojito, zarzuela de mariscos, paella for two. Own baking. Sidewalk dining. Cr cds: A, D, MC, V.

D

★ ★ ★ **MAYFAIR GRILL.** *(See Mayfair House Hotel) 305/441-0000.* Hrs: 7 am-11 pm; Sun brunch 11 am-3 pm. Res accepted. Bar 11 am-11 pm. Wine cellar. A la carte entrees: bkfst $6-$12, lunch $4.95-$13, dinner $16-$26.50. Specializes in seafood, Chilean, Caribbean, European-style foods. Valet parking. Victorian setting with South Florida accents; stained-glass ceiling. Cr cds: A, C, D, DS, ER, JCB, MC, V.

D

✔★ ★ **MIKE GORDON.** *1201 NE 79th St, north of downtown. 305/751-4429.* Hrs: noon-10 pm; early-bird dinner 3:30-6:30 pm. Closed Thanksgiving, Dec 25 from 4 pm. Bar. Semi-a la carte: lunch $5.95-$16.95, dinner $12.95-$22.95. Child's meals. Specializes in fresh seafood. Valet parking; boat docking. Overlooks bay. Family-owned. Cr cds: A, D, DS, MC, V.

D

★ ★ ★ **MODERN ART CAFE.** *2801 Florida Ave (33133), in Coconut Grove. 305/461-1999.* Web www.modernartcafe.com. Hrs: 11:30 am-midnight; Sun brunch to 3 pm. Res accepted. Contemporary Amer menu. Bar. A la carte entrees: lunch $6.95-$14.95, dinner $7.95-$21.95. Sun brunch $4.95-$8.95. Specialties: marinated hanging beef tender, toasted pumpkin seed-crusted baked salmon, roasted duck. Own baking. Valet parking. Art gallery dining area. Cr cds: A, D, DS, MC, V.

D

✔★ ★ **NEWS CAFE.** *2901 Florida Ave (33133), in Coconut Grove. 305/774-6397.* Open 24 hrs. Eclectic menu. Bar 8-5 am. Semi-a la carte: bkfst $3.95-$8.95, lunch $6.95-$11.25, dinner $6.95-$12.95. Specializes in Middle Eastern cuisine. Mediterranean decor. Cr cds: A, C, D, MC, V.

D

★ ★ **PORCAO.** *801 S Bayshore Dr (33131), south of downtown. 305/373-2777.* Web www.auraland.com/porcao. Hrs: noon-midnight. Res accepted, required wkends. Brazilian menu. Bar. Complete meal: lunch $14.95, dinner $18.95-$26.50. Child's meals. Specializes in steaks. Own baking. Entertainment Sat. Valet parking. Brazilian decor. Cr cds: A, D, MC, V.

D

★ ★ **SAMURAI.** *8717 SW 136th St (33176), south of downtown. 305/238-2131.* Hrs: noon-2:30 pm, 5:30-10:30 pm; Fri to 11 pm; Sat to 11:30 pm. Closed Thanksgiving. Res accepted. Japanese menu. Bar. Complete meals: lunch $6.25-$9.95, dinner $12.50-$26. Child's meals. Specializes in steak, chicken, seafood. Parking. Meals prepared in full view of guests. Cr cds: A, C, D, DS, MC, V.

D

✔★ ★ **SEÑOR FROG'S.** *3480 Main Hwy (33133), in Coconut Grove. 305/448-0990.* Hrs: 11:30-1 am; Thurs-Sat to 2 am. Res accepted. Mexican menu. Bar. A la carte entrees: lunch, dinner $7-$15. Specializes in enchiladas, fajitas. Outdoor dining. Mexican cantina decor. Cr cds: A, C, D, MC, V.

D

★ ★ ★ **SHULA'S STEAK HOUSE.** *(7601 NW 154th St, Miami Lakes 33014) N on I-95, W on FL 826, Miami Lakes exit. 305/820-8102.* Hrs: 7-11 am, 11:30 am-2:30 pm, 6-11 pm; Sat 6-11 pm; Sun 6-10 pm. Closed July 4. Res accepted. Bar. Wine list. A la carte entrees: bkfst $5-$10, lunch $7-$16, dinner $15-$58. Child's meals. Specializes in steak, seafood. Valet parking. Overlooks golf course. Family-owned. Cr cds: A, C, D, MC, V.

D

★ **SNAPPERS.** *401 Biscayne Blvd, at Pier #5, complex N111, downtown. 305/379-0605.* Hrs: 7:30 am-midnight. Bar. A la carte entrees: lunch $7.95-$13.95, dinner $9.95-$24.95. Child's meals. Specializes in seafood, pasta. Raw bar. Outdoor dining at bayside. On pier. Cr cds: A, D, MC, V.

D

★ ★ **THAI ORCHID.** *9565 SW 72nd St, south of downtown. 305/279-8583.* Hrs: 11:30 am-3 pm, 5-10:30 pm. Closed Thanksgiving. Thai menu. Wine, beer. A la carte entrees: lunch $4.25-$6.95, dinner $7.25-$16.95. Specializes in macrobiotic vegetables, beef, seafood. Decorated with various types of orchids. Cr cds: A, MC, V.

D

★ ★ ★ **TONY CHAN'S WATER CLUB.** *1717 N Bayshore Dr, north of downtown. 305/374-8888.* Hrs: noon-3 pm, 5-11 pm; Fri to midnight; Sat 5 pm-midnight; Sun 5-11 pm. Closed Thanksgiving. Chinese menu. Bar. A la carte entrees: lunch $6.95-$30, dinner $9-$40. Specialties: Peking duck, honey walnut shrimp, water club sea bass. Valet parking. Main dining rm has view of kitchen and of marina. Cr cds: A, C, D, DS, MC, V.

D

★ ★ **TRATTORIA PAMPERED CHEF.** *3145 Commodore Plaza (33133), in Coconut Grove. 305/567-0104.* Hrs: 11:30 am-11:30 pm; Fri, Sat to 1:30 am; Sun to midnight. Res accepted. Northern Italian menu. Bar. A la carte entrees: lunch $4.95-$7.95, dinner $8.95-$21.95. Child's meals. Specialties: chicken Florentine, veal Marsala, pasta valverde. Sidewalk dining. Cr cds: A, D, DS, MC, V.

D

★ ★ **TROPICAL CHINESE.** *7991 SW 40th St (33155), south of downtown. 305/262-7576.* Hrs: 11 am-11 pm; Fri to midnight; Sat 10:30 am-midnight; Sun from 10:30 am; brunch daily 11 am-3:30 pm. Res accepted. Chinese menu. Bar. Semi-a la carte: lunch $5.25-$8, dinner $6.95-$45. Brunch $2.15-$7.95. Specialties: Peking duck, sizzling black bean, Emperor's prawns. Chinese decor. Cr cds: A, D, MC, V.

D

★ ★ **TUSCANY TRATTORIA.** *3484 Main Hwy, in Coconut Grove. 305/445-0022.* Hrs: 11:30 am-midnight. Res accepted. Italian menu. Bar. A la carte entrees: lunch $5.95-$12.95, dinner $7.95-$19.95. Complete meals: lunch $10-$15, dinner $20-$30. Child's meals. Specialties: osso buco, snapper Livornese. Parking. Outdoor dining. Cr cds: A, C, D, DS, MC, V.

D

★ ★ ★ **VANDERBILT MANSION.** *(See Fisher Island Club Resort) 305/535-6020.* Hrs: 7 pm-midnight. Closed Mon & Tues; also June-Sept. Res required. Continental menu. Bar. Wine cellar. A la carte entrees: dinner $18-$45. Specialties: pan-seared snapper with crabmeat, veal chop, rack of lamb. Harpist & bass player Wed-Sat. Valet parking. Outdoor dining. Elegant dining in mansion built for William K. Vanderbilt. Marble floor, chandeliers. Jacket. Cr cds: A, C, D, MC, V.

D

★ ★ ★ **VICTOR'S CAFE.** *2340 SW 32nd Ave (33145), south of downtown. 305/445-1313.* Hrs: noon-midnight; Fri & Sat to 1 am. Res accepted. Cuban menu. Bar. Wine list. A la carte entrees: lunch $7.95-$16.95, dinner $9.95-$28.95. Child's meals. Specializes in seafood, steak. Entertainment Sat. Valet parking. Original artwork and signed photographs of celebrity guests. Counterpart of NYC restaurant. Cr cds: A, D, MC, V.

D SC

★ ★ **WAH SHING.** *9503 S Dixie Hwy (US 1), in Dadeland Plaza, south of downtown. 305/666-9879.* Hrs: 11:30 am-11 pm. Closed Thanksgiving. Chinese menu. Wine, beer. A la carte entrees: lunch $4.95-$6.95, dinner $7.95-$12.95. Specializes in Cantonese, Mandarin & Szechwan dishes. Oriental decor. Cr cds: A, MC, V.

D

Unrated Dining Spot

PLANET HOLLYWOOD. *3390 Mary St (33133), in Coconut Grove. 305/445-7277.* Hrs: 11-2 am. Bar. Semi-a la carte: lunch, dinner $4.95-$16.95. Child's meals. Specializes in fajitas, pasta, pizza. TV and movie memorabilia. Cr cds: A, D, DS, JCB, MC, V.

D

Miami Intl Airport Area

Motels

✔★ ★ **FAIRFIELD INN BY MARRIOTT-SOUTH.** *(1201 NW LeJeune Rd, Miami 33126) 305/643-0055; FAX 305/649-3997.* 282 rms, 3 story. Dec-Apr: S, D $75; suite $125; lower rates rest of yr. Crib free. TV; cable (premium). Pool; poolside serv wkends. Complimentary continental bkfst. Restaurant 6:30-10:30 am. Rm serv. Bar noon-2 am. Ck-out noon. Coin lndry. Convention facilities. Business center. In-rm modem link. Valet serv. Concierge. Sundries. Gift shop. Barber, beauty shop. Free airport transportation. Lighted tennis, pro. Exercise equipt; weights, bicycle. Cr cds: A, D, DS, MC, V.

D SC

★ ★ **WELLESLEY INN.** *(8436 NW 36th St, Miami 33166) N via LeJeune Rd (NW 42nd Ave) to NW 36th St. 305/592-4799; FAX 305/471-8461.* 106 rms, 4 story, 13 suites. Jan-mid-Apr: S $74.99; D $84.99; under 18 free; lower rates rest of yr. Crib free. TV; cable (premium). Pool. Complimentary continental bkfst. Coffee in rms. Ck-out 11 am. Coin lndry. Meeting rm. Business servs avail. In-rm modem link. Valet serv. Free airport transportation. Refrigerator in suites. Cr cds: A, C, D, DS, MC, V.

D SC

Motor Hotels

★ ★ **AMERISUITES.** *(3655 NW 82nd Ave, Miami 33166) 305/718-8292; FAX 305/718-8295.* 126 suites, 6 story. Jan-Mar: suites $129-$149; under 18 free; wkly, wkend, hol rates; higher rates Grand Prix Doral Ryder; lower rates rest of yr. Crib free. Pet accepted, some restrictions; $10. TV; cable (premium), VCR. Complimentary continental bkfst. Complimentary coffee in rms. Restaurant adj 9 am-midnight. Ck-out 11 am. Meeting rms. Business center. In-rm modem link. Coin lndry. Free airport transportation. Exercise equipt; weight machine, bicycle. Pool. Refrigerators, microwaves. Cr cds: A, C, D, DS, MC, V.

D SC

★ ★ ★ **BEST WESTERN MIAMI AIRPORT INN.** *(1550 NW LeJeune Rd, Miami 33126) 305/871-2345; FAX 305/871-2811.* 208 rms, 6 story. S $79-$99; D $84-$104; each addl $5; suites $195. Crib free. TV; cable (premium). Pool. Restaurant open 24 hrs. Rm serv. Bar 11-3 am. Ck-out 1 pm. Meeting rms. Business servs avail. In-rm modem link. Bellhops. Sundries. Coin lndry. Airport transportation. Exercise equipt; stair machine, bicycle. Game rm. Bathrm phones; some refrigerators. Cr cds: A, C, D, DS, ER, MC, V.

D SC

★ **COMFORT INN EAST.** *(5125 NW 36th St, Miami 33166) 305/887-2153; FAX 305/887-3559.* 110 rms, 6 story. Dec-Apr: S $69.95-$109.95; D $75.95-$115.95; each addl $5; under 18 free; wkend, hol rates; golf plans; higher rates Super Bowl; lower rates rest of yr. Crib free. TV; cable (premium). Complimentary continental bkfst. Restaurant nearby. Ck-out noon. Business servs avail. In-rm modem link. Sundries. Coin lndry.

Free airport transportation. Golf privileges, greens fee $28-$59, pro, putting green, driving range. Pool privileges. Some refrigerators. Cr cds: A, C, D, DS, ER, JCB, MC, V.

D SC

★ ★ **COURTYARD BY MARRIOTT-SOUTH.** *(1201 NW LeJeune Rd, Miami 33126) 305/642-8200.* 123 rms, 5 story. Dec-Apr: S, D $95-$105; suite $150; under 18 free; lower rates rest of yr. Crib free. TV; cable (premium). Heated pool; poolside serv wkends. Complimentary coffee in rms. Restaurant 6:30-10:30 am. Rm serv. Bar noon-2 am. Ck-out noon. Coin Indry. Meeting rms. Business center. Valet serv. Concierge. Sundries. Gift shop. Barber, beauty shop. Free airport transportation. Lighted tennis, pro. Exercise equipt; weights, bicycle, whirlpool. Cr cds: A, D, DS, MC.

D SC

★ ★ **HAMPTON INN.** *(3620 NW 79th Ave, Miami 33166) 305/513-0777; FAX 305/513-9019.* 129 rms, 6 story. Dec-Apr: S $99-$109; D $109-$119; under 18 free; wkend, hol rates; golf plans; higher rates Doral Open, Boat Show; lower rates rest of yr. Crib free. Pet accepted, some restrictions. TV; cable (premium), VCR avail. Complimentary continental bkfst. Restaurant adj 7 am-10 pm. Ck-out 11 am. Meeting rms. Business center. In-rm modem link. Valet serv. Free airport transportation. Pool. Some refrigerators; microwaves avail. Cr cds: A, C, D, DS, MC, V.

D SC

Hotels

✔★ ★ **AIRPORT REGENCY.** *(1000 NW Le Jeune Rd, Miami 33126) 305/441-1600; FAX 305/443-0766; res: 800/367-1039 (exc FL), 800/432-1192 (FL).* 176 rms, 6 story. S $65-$120; D $75-$125; each addl $10; under 12 free. Crib free. TV; cable (premium). Restaurant 6:30 am-11 pm; Fri, Sat to midnight. Bar 11-2 am; Fri, Sat to 4 am; entertainment. Ck-out noon. Meeting rms. Gift shop. Free airport transportation. Balconies. Cr cds: A, C, D, DS, ER, MC, V.

SC

★ ★ **CLARION.** *(5301 NW 36th St, Miami 33166) 305/271-1000; FAX 305/871-4971.* 103 rms, 7 story. Dec-Apr: S, D $110.95-$145.95; each addl $10; suites $145.95-$175.95; under 18 free; wkend, hol rates; golf plans; lower rates rest of yr. Crib free. TV; cable (premium), VCR avail. Complimentary coffee in rms. Restaurant 6 am-11 pm. Bar from 4 pm. Ck-out noon. Meeting rms. Business center. In-rm modem link. Gift shop. Barber, beauty shop. Coin Indry. Tennis privileges. Golf privileges, greens fee $29-$50, pro, putting green, driving range. Exercise equipt; bicycle, weights. Pool. Microwaves avail. Cr cds: A, C, D, DS, MC, V.

D SC

★ ★ **CLUB HOTEL BY DOUBLETREE.** *(1101 NW 57th Ave, Miami 33126) Jct FL 836 & Red Rd exit (57th Ave). 305/266-0000; FAX 305/266-9179.* 266 rms, 10 story. Jan-Mar: S $95-$125; D $105-$135; suites $190-$215; under 18 free; higher rates Boat Show; lower rates rest of yr. Crib free. Pet accepted. TV; cable (premium). Pool; wading pool. Complimentary coffee in rms. Restaurant 6 am-11 pm. Bar 4-11 pm. Ck-out noon. Coin Indry. Meeting rms. Business center. Free airport transportation. Refrigerators avail. Cr cds: A, C, D, DS, JCB, MC, V.

D SC

★ ★ **COMFORT INN AND SUITES.** *(5301 NW 36th St, Miami 33166) 305/871-6000; FAX 305/871-4971.* 165 rms, 11 story, 12 suites. Dec-Apr: S $89.95-$129.95; D $99.95-$139.95; suites $119.95-$129.95; under 18 free; wkend, hol rates; golf plans; lower rates rest of yr. Crib free. TV; cable (premium), VCR avail. Complimentary continental bkfst. Restaurant 6 am-11 pm. Bar 4-11 pm. Ck-out noon. Meeting rms. Business center. In-rm modem link. Gift shop. Barber, beauty shop. Coin Indry. Free airport transportation. Tennis. Golf privileges, greens fee $29-$50, pro, putting green, driving range. Exercise equipt; weights, bicycle. Pool. Microwaves avail. Cr cds: A, C, D, DS, MC, V.

D SC

★ ★ ★ **EMBASSY SUITES.** *(3974 NW South River Dr, Miami Springs 33142) 1/2 mi N on LeJeune Rd (NW 42nd Ave), W on NW South River Dr, just E of airport. 305/634-5000; FAX 305/635-9499.* E-mail orivero@worldnet.att.net; web www.embassysuites.com. 318 suites, 10 story. Oct-mid-Apr: S $139-$199; D $149-$219; each addl $10; under 18 free; lower rates rest of yr. Crib free. TV; cable (premium). Pool; whirlpool. Complimentary full bkfst. Restaurant 11 am-11 pm. Bar to 2 am; entertainment. Ck-out noon. Meeting rms. Business center. In-rm modem link. Airport transportation. Cr cds: A, C, D, DS, ER, MC, V.

D SC

★ ★ ★ **HILTON & TOWERS MIAMI AIRPORT.** *(5101 Blue Lagoon Dr, Miami 33126) S of East-West Expy (Dolphin Expy, FL 836) via Red Rd (FL 959), E on Blue Lagoon Dr. 305/262-1000; FAX 305/261-6769.* E-mail gil_katzman@hilton.com; web www.hilton.com. 500 rms, 14 story, 83 suites. Jan-May: S $140-$220; D $150-$230; each addl $20; suites $190-$525; family rates; wkend plans; lower rates rest of yr. Crib free. TV; cable (premium). Pool; whirlpool, poolside serv. Restaurant 6:30 am-11 pm. Rm serv 24 hrs. Bar 9-2 am, Fri, Sat to 5 am; entertainment. Ck-out noon. Convention facilities. Business center. In-rm modem link. Concierge. Gift shop. Valet parking. Free airport transportation. Lighted tennis. Exercise equipt; weights, bicycles, sauna. Some bathrm phones, refrigerators, minibars; microwaves avail. Private patios, balconies. On lake; marina; sailboats, jet skis; waterskiing, windsurfing. Exotic birds in cages, saltwater tanks with exotic fish. Luxury level. Cr cds: A, C, D, DS, ER, JCB, MC, V.

D SC

★ ★ ★ **HOLIDAY INN-LE JEUNE CENTRE.** *(950 NW LeJeune Rd, Miami 33126) 305/446-9000; FAX 305/441-0725.* 304 rms, 6 story. S, D $110; each addl $10; suites $139; under 19 free; wkend rates. Crib free. TV; cable (premium). Heated pool; poolside serv. Restaurant 6:30 am-2 pm, 5-11 pm. Rm serv 24 hrs. Bar 4 pm-midnight. Ck-out noon. Convention facilities. Business servs avail. Gift shop. Free airport transportation. Exercise equipt; weights, bicycles, whirlpool, sauna. Luxury level. Cr cds: A, C, D, DS, JCB, MC, V.

D SC

★ ★ ★ **MARRIOTT-AIRPORT.** *(1201 NW LeJeune Rd, Miami 33126) SW of FL 836. 305/649-5000; FAX 305/642-3369.* 365 rms, 10 story. Dec-Apr: S, D $139-$169; family, wkend rates; lower rates rest of yr. Crib free. Pet accepted, some restrictions. TV; cable (premium). Pool. Restaurant 6-1 am. Bars 11-2 am. Meeting rms. Business center. In-rm modem link. Gift shop. Barber, beauty shop. Free airport transportation. Lighted tennis, pro. Exercise equipt; weights, bicycles, whirlpool. Rec rm. Private patios. Luxury level. Cr cds: A, C, D, DS, ER, JCB, MC, V.

D SC

★ ★ ★ **MIAMI INTERNATIONAL AIRPORT HOTEL.** *(NW 20th St & LeJeune Rd, Miami 33122) in airport terminal, Concourse E. 305/871-4100; FAX 305/871-0800; res: 800/327-1276.* E-mail miahotelresv@miami-airport.com; web www.miahotel.com. 260 rms, 8 story. S $115-$160; D $130-$185; each addl $15; suites $250-$650; under 12 free. Crib free. TV; cable (premium). Pool; whirlpool. Restaurant 7 am-11 pm. Bar 11-1 am. Ck-out noon. Coin Indry. Meeting rms. Business center. Drugstore. Barber, beauty shop. Free airport transportation. Exercise equipt; weights, bicycles, sauna, steam rm. Cr cds: A, C, D, DS, ER, JCB, MC, V.

D SC

★ ★ ★ **RADISSON MART PLAZA.** *(711 NW 72nd Ave, Miami 33126) Just S of East-West Expy (Dolphin Expy/FL 836) on NW 72nd Ave. 305/261-3800; FAX 305/261-7665.* 334 rms, 12 story. S, D $129-$159; each addl $20; suites $159-$399; under 18 free; wkend package. Crib free. TV; cable (premium). Pool; whirlpool, poolside serv. Restaurant 6 am-11 pm. Bars 11-1 am; entertainment. Ck-out noon. Convention facilities. Business center. In-rm modem link. Shopping arcade. Free airport transportation. Lighted tennis, pro. Exercise rm; instructor, weights, bicycles, steam rm, sauna. Balconies. Luxury level. Cr cds: A, C, D, DS, ER, MC, V.

D SC

★ ★ ★ **SHERATON GATEWAY.** *(3900 NW 21st St, Miami 33142) On NW 21st St, just E of LeJeune Rd (NW 42nd Ave), adj to airport. 305/871-3800; FAX 305/871-0447.* Web www.sheraton.com. 408 rms, 10 story. S, D $95-$180; each addl $15; suites $250-$500; under 13 free. Crib $10. TV; cable (premium). Pool; whirlpool, poolside serv. Restaurant 6 am-11 pm. Rm serv 24 hrs. Bar 11-1 am. Ck-out noon. Convention facilities. Business center. In-rm modem link. Covered parking. Free airport transportation. Lighted tennis. Exercise equipt; weights, bicycles, sauna. Bathrm phone in suites. Golf course adj. On Miami River. Cr cds: A, C, D, DS, ER, JCB, MC, V.

D SC

★ ★ ★ **SOFITEL.** *(5800 Blue Lagoon Dr, Miami 33126) S of East-West Expy (Dolphin Expy, FL 836) via Red Rd (FL 959), W on Blue Lagoon Dr. 305/264-4888; FAX 305/262-9049.* 281 rms, 15 story, 27 suites. S, D $179-$225; each addl $30; suites $219-$599; under 17 free; wkend packages. Crib free. Pet accepted, some restrictions. Valet parking $5. TV; cable (premium). Pool. Restaurant 6 am-11 pm. Bar 11-2 am; entertainment. Ck-out noon. Meeting rms. Business servs avail. In-rm modem link. Concierge. Gift shop. Lighted tennis. Exercise equipt; weights, bicycles. On lagoon. Cr cds: A, C, D, DS, MC, V.

D SC

Milwaukee

Settled: 1822
Pop: 628,088
Elev: 634 feet
Time zone: Central
Area code: 414
Web: www.milwaukee.com

Thriving and progressive, Milwaukee has retained its *gemütlichkeit*—although conviviality is as likely to be expressed at a soccer game or at a symphony concert as at the beer garden. This is not to say that raising beer steins has noticeably declined as a popular local form of exercise. Milwaukee is still the beer capital of the nation. However, Milwaukee's leading single industry is not brewing but the manufacture of X-ray apparatus and tubes.

Milwaukee is on the western shore of Lake Michigan, where the Milwaukee, Menomonee and Kinnickinnic rivers meet. Long before the first settlers came to what eventually would be known as Milwaukee, the Potowatomi had a special name for their land: "Millocki," or, gathering place by the waters. The modern city was founded by Solomon Juneau, who settled on the east side of the Milwaukee River. English settlement began in significant numbers in 1833, followed by an influx of Germans, Scandinavians, Dutch, Bohemians, Irish, Austrians and large numbers of Poles. By 1846, Milwaukee was big and prosperous enough to be incorporated as a city.

By 1850, the population was 20,000, and by 1890 the population had reached 100,000. Milwaukee was a thriving metropolis and a settled community early in the development of metropolitan America. Since World War II, Milwaukee has undergone tremendous development. The skyline changed with new buildings, an expressway system was started, the St Lawrence Seaway opened new markets, new cultural activities were introduced and 44 square miles were added to the city.

Business

A city of 96.5 square miles, Milwaukee is the metropolitan center of four counties. Called the "machine shop of America," Milwaukee has an industrial output of $19.1 billion a year, ranks among the nation's top industrial cities and is a leader in the manufacture of diesel and gasoline engines, outboard motors, motorcycles, X-ray apparatus, mining machinery, padlocks and, of course, beer.

As a result of the opening of the St Lawrence Seaway, Milwaukee has become a major seaport on America's fourth seacoast. Docks and piers accommodate traffic of 15 marine shipping lines.

Metropolitan Milwaukee has more than 100 companies that employ 500 or more people each, producing such goods as electrical motors, electronic components, construction equipment, farming and industrial equipment, auto bodies, gears and couplings, batteries and mining equipment. Advertising and publishing are also important businesses.

Convention Facilities

Located in the heart of downtown Milwaukee is the Midwest Express Center, a modern convention facility. Midwest Express Center is made up of three buildings that cover four city blocks and are connected by a walkway over Kilbourn Ave.

The 132,000-square-foot convention hall can accommodate 750 trade show booths or a banquet for 8,600 people. The center portion of the main floor, the Great Hall, has 66,000 square feet of column-free space with a 45-foot ceiling height.

Flanking the Great Hall are the East and West halls, each containing 33,000 square feet of floor space. These two halls, which may be used either in conjunction with the Great Hall or as separate meeting areas, have ceiling heights of 18 feet.

The second level of the convention hall includes two octagonal meeting rooms, each seating 800 people, that can be divided into two, three or four rooms, and 27 other meeting rooms, seating 50 to 300 persons.

The Milwaukee Arena has a total floor area of 24,550 square feet, and its ceiling is 95 feet high. Its seating capacity is 12,200 people.

The Auditorium, originally constructed in 1909 and restored to its original elegance, will seat 6,000 people for a full stage production in Bruce Hall. In addition, Plankinton Theatre has stage facilities and seats 896 people. Juneau Hall, Kilbourn Hall and Walker Hall are elegant meeting rooms seating 250 to 700 people.

Sports & Recreation

Sports fans can watch the Brewers play baseball at County Stadium; the Green Bay Packers play a portion of their football games here also. The Bucks play basketball, the Admirals play hockey and the Wave play soccer at the Bradley Center.

Jaunt to Juneau Park by the old Coast Guard Station and see bone-crunching rugby played. There are also ample opportunities to view soccer and polo games around town.

Milwaukee winters, not known for their mildness, still fail to keep people indoors. The park department floods more than 50 sites and keeps them clear of snow for ice-skating. Cross-country skiers have numerous parks and frozen rivers from which to choose. Tobogganers will find enough hills, and for those who just enjoy a nice walk, the lakefront, in all its frozen glory, is a good place to start.

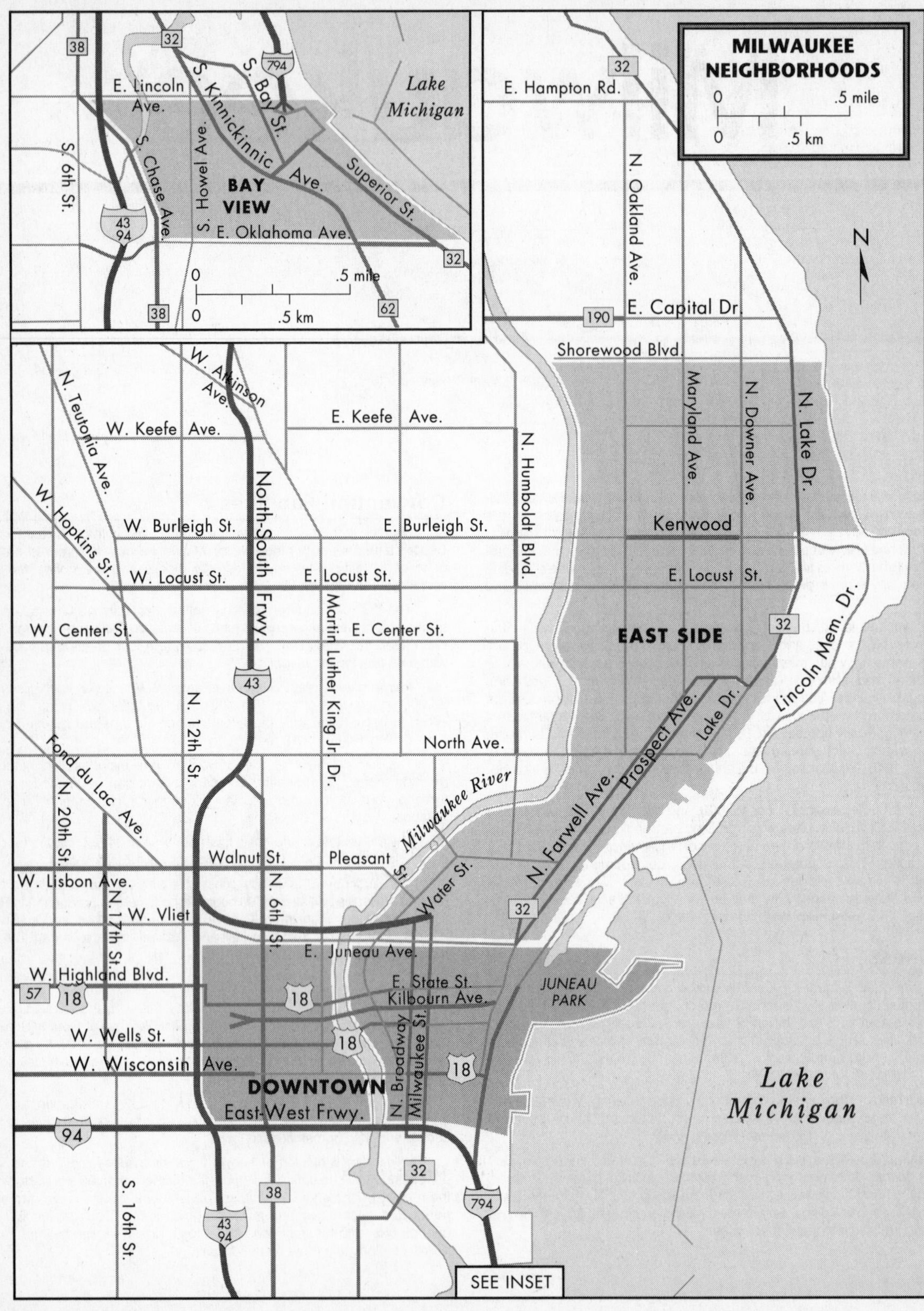
MILWAUKEE NEIGHBORHOODS
0
.5 mile
0
.5 km
BAY VIEW
EAST SIDE
DOWNTOWN
Lake Michigan
Lake Michigan
E. Lincoln Ave.
S. Kinnickinnic Ave.
S. Bay St.
Superior St.
S. 6th St.
S. Chase Ave.
S. Howel Ave.
E. Oklahoma Ave.
E. Hampton Rd.
N. Oakland Ave.
E. Capital Dr.
Shorewood Blvd.
Maryland Ave.
N. Downer Ave.
N. Lake Dr.
Kenwood
E. Locust St.
Lincoln Mem. Dr.
Lake Dr.
Prospect Ave.
N. Farwell Ave.
N. Humboldt Blvd.
W. Atkinson Ave.
N. Teutonia Ave.
W. Keefe Ave.
E. Keefe Ave.
North-South Frwy.
W. Hopkins St.
W. Burleigh St.
E. Burleigh St.
W. Locust St.
E. Locust St.
Martin Luther King Jr. Dr.
W. Center St.
E. Center St.
North Ave.
N. 12th St.
Fond du Lac Ave.
N. 20th St.
Milwaukee River
Walnut St.
Pleasant St.
Water St.
W. Lisbon Ave.
N. 17th St.
W. Vliet
N. 6th St.
E. Juneau Ave.
W. Highland Blvd.
E. State St.
Kilbourn Ave.
JUNEAU PARK
W. Wells St.
W. Wisconsin Ave.
N. Broadway
Milwaukee St.
East-West Frwy.
S. 16th St.
SEE INSET
N

Golf courses and tennis courts abound. Auto racing takes place at the Milwaukee Mile in Wisconsin State Fair Park. And of course there is Lake Michigan, haven for swimmers, sailors and fishing enthusiasts.

Entertainment

Spend an evening listening to the Milwaukee Symphony Orchestra, or pass the time more informally in one of the many neighborhood taverns, drinking the local brew.

From September to June, the Marcus Center for the Performing Arts is host to the Symphony Orchestra. On warm summer afternoons, also on the grounds of the center, are the outdoor Rainbow Summer Concerts. Take in a play or musical at the Milwaukee Repertory Theater, the Broadway Theater Centre or the Pabst Theater. Milwaukee has its own opera and ballet companies as well, the Milwaukee Ballet and Skylight Opera companies.

Historical Areas

The area from South Second to South Fifth and from Florida to Scott streets, known as Walker's Point, has been renovated. Originally settled by New Englanders, Germans and Scandinavians in the 1800s, Walker's Point still has an interesting blend of nationalities. Many buildings survive in nearly original form and are in excellent condition. The area reflects a typical 19th-century working-class, urban neighborhood.

Old World Third Street downtown provides a delightful walking tour for gourmets, historians and lovers of antiques and atmosphere. The tour includes the Milwaukee Journal Company's history of the newspaper. Most establishments along the way are open Monday through Saturday.

The renovated Brady Street offers an eclectic mix of shops and restaurants. It is quickly emerging as a Milwaukee hot spot.

There are also several restored houses in the Milwaukee area, including Lowell Damon house, Kalvelage Schloss, Kilbourntown house and the Captain Frederick Pabst mansion.

Sightseeing

Milwaukee's lakefront is one of the city's scenic highlights. Driving along the shore on Lincoln Memorial Drive, visitors can see many points of interest. The War Memorial Center, designed by Eero Saarinen, houses the expanded Milwaukee Art Museum. Here are spacious galleries with permanent collections of European, American and contemporary art, changing exhibits and a children's gallery.

A popular attraction for families is the Milwaukee County Zoo. The animals, birds and reptiles are arranged in geographical groupings in their native habitats, with only hidden moats separating predator from prey in natural, cageless environments. There are also rides on a miniature train.

The unique Mitchell Park Horticultural Conservatory is a popular attraction. Plants from around the world are displayed in three self-supporting glass domes, each of which simulates a different climate.

The Court of Honor is a three-block area in the city, bounded by Marquette University on the west and the downtown business district on the east. The area is a monument to the Civil War dead and contains several public buildings as well as sculptures of historic figures.

At the Milwaukee Public Museum are dioramas and such exhibits as the Rain Forest, a Trip through Space and Time, Native Americans, Wonders of Life, the Living Ocean, the Third Planet and the Wizard Wing. Another exhibit re-creates old Milwaukee streets.

Milwaukee is well known for its beer production. A trip through one of the city's breweries is worth squeezing into even the busiest schedule. The Pabst, Miller and Sprecher brewing companies offer free tours. At the end of each tour, visitors may sample the brewery's product.

The Milwaukee County Historical Society offers many exhibits of Milwaukee history, including the Panorama Painters, Yesterday's Drug Store, a Cooper's Shop, Children's World of Toys, a mid-Victorian room, Transportation Hall and material from General Douglas MacArthur's family.

Information centers are located at Grand Avenue Shopping Center, Wisconsin St entrance, and at General Mitchell International-Lower Level.

General References

Area code: 414

Phone Numbers

POLICE & FIRE: 911

POISON CONTROL CENTER: 266-2222

TIME: 844-1414 **WEATHER:** 936-1212

Information Sources

The Greater Milwaukee Convention & Visitors Bureau, 510 W Kilbourn Ave, 53203; 800/231-0903.

The Metropolitan Milwaukee Association of Commerce, 756 N Milwaukee St, 4th floor, 53202; 287-4100.

Fun Line, 799-1177 (recording).

Department of Parks, Recreation and Culture, 257-6100.

Transportation

AIRLINES: American; America West; Continental; Delta; Midwest Express; Northwest; TWA; United; USAir; and other commuter and regional airlines.

AIRPORT: General Mitchell International, 747-5300.

CAR RENTAL AGENCIES: (See IMPORTANT TOLL-FREE NUMBERS) Avis 744-2266; Budget 481-2409; Hertz 747-5200; National 483-9800.

PUBLIC TRANSPORTATION: Milwaukee County Transit System, 4212 W Highland Blvd, 53208; 344-6711.

RAILROAD PASSENGER SERVICE: Amtrak 800/872-7245.

Newspaper

Milwaukee Journal Sentinel.

Convention Facilities

Midwest Express Center, 500 W Kilbourn Ave, 271-4000.

Wisconsin State Fair Park, 84th & Greenfield, West Allis, 266-7000.

Sports & Recreation

Bradley Center, 4th & State Sts (Admirals, hockey, 227-0550; Bucks, basketball, 227-0500; Wave, soccer; Marquette University, basketball, 227-0400).

Midwest Express Center, 500 W Kilbourn Ave, 271-2750 (recording of events).

Milwaukee County Stadium, 201 S 46th St (Brewers, baseball, 933-4114; Green Bay Packers, football, 496-5719).

Pettit National Ice Center, 500 S 84th St, 266-0100.

Racetrack

Milwaukee Mile, Wisconsin State Fair Park, 84th & Greenfield, West Allis, 453-8277 (auto racing).

Cultural Facilities

Theaters

Broadway Theater Center, 158 N Broadway, 291-7800.

Milwaukee Repertory Theater, 108 E Wells, 224-1761.

Pabst Theater, 144 E Wells St, 286-3663.

Sunset Playhouse, 800 Elm Grove Rd, Elm Grove, 782-4430.

Concert Hall

Marcus Center for the Performing Arts, 929 N Water St, 273-7206.

Museums

Betty Brinn Children's Museum, 929 E Wisconsin Ave, 291-0888.

Discovery World, The James Lovell Museum of Science, Economics and Technology, 818 W Wisconsin Ave, 765-9966.

Milwaukee County Historical Center, 910 N Old World Third St, Pere Marquette Park, 273-8288.

Milwaukee Public Museum, 800 W Wells St, 278-2700.

Art Museums

Charles Allis Art Museum, 1801 N Prospect Ave & 1630 E Royall Place, 278-8295.

Haggerty Museum of Art, Marquette Univ, 13th & Clybourne Sts, 288-7290.

Milwaukee Art Museum, 750 N Lincoln Memorial Dr, 224-3200.

Villa Terrace Decorative Arts Museum, 2220 N Terrace Ave, 271-3656.

Points of Interest

Historical

Captain Frederick Pabst Mansion, 2000 W Wisconsin Ave, 931-0808.

Kilbourntown House, 5 mi N on I-43, Capitol Dr E exit, in Estabrook Park, 273-8288.

Old World Third Street, W Wells St to Juneau Ave.

St Joan of Arc Chapel, Marquette University, 601 N 14th St, 288-6873.

St John's Cathedral, 802 N Jackson, 276-9814.

St Josaphat Basilica, 2333 S 6th St, 645-5623.

Walker's Point, S 2nd to S 5th Sts & Florida to Scott Sts.

Other Attractions

Annunciation Greek Orthodox Church, 9400 W Congress St, 461-9400.

Boerner Botanical Garden, 5879 S 92nd in Hales Corners, 425-1130.

City Hall, 200 E Wells St, 286-3285.

Civic Center Plaza, N of W Wells St between N 7th & 9th Sts.

Court of Honor, Wisconsin Ave bounded by Marquette University & the downtown business district.

The Grand Avenue, Wisconsin Ave between Plankinton Ave & 5th St.

Marquette University, Wisconsin Ave & 11th-17th Sts, 288-7700.

McKinley Marina, 1750 N Lincoln Memorial Dr, 273-5224.

Miller Brewing Co, 4251 W State St, 931-BEER.

Milwaukee County Zoo, 10001 W Blue Mound Rd, 771-3040.

Mitchell Park Horticultural Conservatory, 524 S Layton Blvd at W Pierce St, 649-9800.

Pabst Brewing Co, 915 W Juneau Ave, 223-3709.

Schlitz Audubon Center, 1111 E Brown Deer Rd, 352-2880.

University of Wisconsin-Milwaukee, 3203 N Downer Ave, 229-1122 or 229-5900.

Sightseeing Tours

Historic Milwaukee, Inc—ArchiTours, 277-7795.

Iroquois Boat Line Tours, boarding at Clybourn St Bridge, 332-4194.

Annual Events

Ethnic Festivals (includes German, Irish, Native American and Polish). Contact Convention & Visitors Bureau. Summer-fall.

Summerfest, Lakefront, 273-FEST. Late June-early July.

Great Circus Parade, downtown. Mid-July.

Wisconsin State Fair, State Fair Park in West Allis, 266-7000. Early Aug.

City Neighborhoods

Many of the restaurants, unrated dining establishments and some lodgings listed under Milwaukee include neighborhoods as well as exact street addresses. Geographic descriptions of these areas are given, followed by a table of restaurants arranged by neighborhood.

Bay View: Area southeast of Downtown; south of E Lincoln Ave, west of Lake Michigan, north of E Oklahoma Ave and east of S Chase Ave.

Downtown: South of Juneau Ave, west of Lake Michigan, north of I-794 and east of the North-South Frwy. **North of Downtown:** North of E Juneau Ave. **South of Downtown:** South of I-794. **West of Downtown:** West of I-43.

East Side: Area northeast of Downtown; south of Shorewood, west of Lake, McKinley and Juneau parks, north of Juneau Ave and east of the Milwaukee River.

Mitchell Street: Area south of Downtown; south of Lapham Ave, west of I-94, north of W Becher St and east of S 16th St.

Yankee Hill: Area of Downtown on and around Cathedral Square; south of E State St, west of N Prospect St, north of E Mason St and east of N Broadway.

Lodgings and Food

MILWAUKEE RESTAURANTS BY NEIGHBORHOOD AREAS

(For full description, see alphabetical listings under Restaurants)

BAY VIEW
Three Brothers. 2414 S St Clair

DOWNTOWN
Au Bon Appétit. 1016 E Brady St
Boulevard Inn. 925 E Wells St
Cafe Knickerbocker. 1030 E Juneau Ave
County Clare. 1234 N Astor St
Eagan's. 1030 N Water St
English Room (Pfister Hotel). 424 E Wisconsin Ave
Grenadier's. 747 N Broadway Ave at Mason
John Ernst's. 600 E Ogden Ave
Karl Ratzsch's. 320 E Mason St
King And I. 823 N 2nd St
Mader's. 1037 N Old World Third St
Mimma's Cafe. 1307 E Brady St
Osteria Del Mondo. 1028 E Juneau Ave
Polaris (Hyatt Regency Hotel). 333 W Kilbourn Ave
Safe House. 779 N Front St
Sanford. 1547 N Jackson St
Weissgerber's Third Street Pier. 1110 N Old World Third St
West Bank Cafe. 732 E Burleigh St

NORTH OF DOWNTOWN
Bavarian Inn. 700 W Lexington Blvd
Dos Bandidos. 5932 N Green Bay Ave
Pandl's In Bayside. 8825 N Lake Dr
Red Rock Cafe. 4022 N Oakland Ave
Yen Ching. 7630 W Good Hope Rd

SOUTH OF DOWNTOWN
Club Tres Hermanos. 1332 W Lincoln Ave
Mike & Anna's. 2000 S Eighth St
Old Town Serbian Gourmet House. 522 W Lincoln Ave
Porterhouse. 800 W Layton Ave
Royal India. 3400 S 27th St

WEST OF DOWNTOWN
Balistreri's Bluemound Inn. 6501 W Bluemound Rd
Pleasant Valley Inn. 9801 W Dakota St
Saz's State House. 5539 W State St

EAST SIDE
Bartolotta's Lake Park Bistro. 3133 E Newberry Blvd
Izumi's. 2178 N Prospect Ave

Note: When a listing is located in a town that does not have its own city heading, it will appear under the city nearest to its location. In these cases, the address and town appear in parenthesis immediately following the name of the establishment.

Motels

(Rates may be higher during state fair)

★ **BUDGETEL INN.** *5442 N Lovers Lane Rd (53225), just E of I-45 Silver Spring Dr exit E, north of downtown. 414/535-1300; FAX 414/535-1724.* 140 rms, 3 story. S $45-$52; D $51-$58; each addl $7; suites $57.95-$67; under 18 free. Pet accepted, some restrictions. TV; cable (premium), VCR avail. Complimentary continental bkfst. Complimentary coffee in rms. Restaurant nearby. Ck-out noon. Meeting rm. Business servs avail. In-rm modem link. Valet serv. Microwaves avail. Cr cds: A, C, D, DS, MC, V.

D SC

★ ★ **CLARION HOTEL & CONFERENCE CENTER.** *5311 S Howell Ave (53207), opp General Mitchell Intl Airport, south of downtown. 414/481-2400; FAX 414/481-4471.* 180 rms, 3 story. S, D $70-$99; suites $89-$150; each addl $5; under 18 free. Crib $7. TV; cable (premium). Indoor pool. Complimentary continental bkfst. Restaurant 7 am-10 pm; Sun 9 am-9 pm. Rm serv. Bar 11 am-11 pm. Ck-out 11 am. Coin lndry. Meeting rms. Business servs avail. Bellhops. Free airport transportation. Exercise equipt; weights, treadmills. Cr cds: A, C, D, DS, ER, JCB, MC, V.

D SC

★ **EXEL INN-NORTHEAST.** *(5485 N Port Washington Rd, Glendale 53217) N on I-43, exit Silver Spring Dr. 414/961-7272; FAX 414/961-1721.* 125 rms, 3 story. S $39.99-$63.99; D $49.99-$76.99; each addl $7; under 17 free; wkend rates; higher rates special events. Crib free. Pet accepted, some restrictions. TV; cable (premium). Complimentary continental bkfst. Restaurant adj open 24 hrs. Ck-out noon. Coin lndry. Business servs avail. In-rm modem link. Sundries. Game rm. Some in-rm whirlpools; microwaves avail. Cr cds: A, C, D, DS, MC, V.

D SC

✔★ **EXEL INN-SOUTH.** *1201 W College Ave (53154), just E of I-94 College Ave exit E, south of downtown. 414/764-1776; FAX 414/762-8009.* 110 rms, 2 story. S $33.99-$59.99; D $34.99-$69.99; each addl $4; under 18 free. Crib free. Pet accepted. TV; cable (premium). Complimentary continental bkfst. Complimentary coffee in lobby. Restaurant opp 6 am-noon. Ck-out noon. Coin lndry. Business servs avail. In-rm modem link. Free airport transportation. Microwaves avail. Cr cds: A, C, D, DS, MC, V.

D SC

★ ★ **HAMPTON INN-NORTHWEST.** *5601 N Lovers Lane Rd (53225), north of downtown. 414/466-8881; FAX 414/466-3840.* 107 rms, 4 story. S, D $69-$99; under 18 free; higher rates: special events, summer wkends. Crib free. TV; cable. Indoor pool; whirlpool. Complimentary continental bkfst. Restaurant adj. Ck-out noon. Meeting rm. Business servs avail. In-rm modem link. Valet serv. Exercise equipt; treadmill, stair machine. Microwaves avail. Cr cds: A, C, D, DS, MC, V.

D SC

✔★ ★ **HOSPITALITY INN.** *4400 S 27th St (53221), just N of I-894 27th St exit N, near General Mitchell Intl Airport, south of downtown. 414/282-8800; FAX 414/282-7713; res: 800/825-8466.* 167 rms in 2 bldgs, 81 suites. S, D $60-$200; each addl $10. TV; cable (premium). 2 indoor pools; whirlpool. Complimentary continental bkfst. Restaurant. Rm serv. Ck-out noon. Meeting rms. Valet serv. Free airport transportation. Exercise equipt; weight machine, stair machine. Many refrigerators; some in-rm whirlpools. Cr cds: A, C, D, DS, MC, V.

D SC

★ ★ **MANCHESTER SUITES-AIRPORT.** *200 W Grange Ave (53207), near General Mitchell Intl Airport, south of downtown. 414/744-3600; FAX 414/744-4188; res: 800/723-8280.* 100 suites, 4 story. S $64-$74; D $72-$82; each addl $8; under 14 free. Crib free. TV; cable (premium). Complimentary full bkfst. Coffee in rms. Ck-out noon. Meeting rm. Business servs avail. In-rm modem link. Valet serv. Sundries. Free airport transportation. Health Club Privileges. Refrigerators, microwaves, wet bars. Cr cds: A, C, D, DS, MC, V.

D SC

✔★ **RED ROOF INN.** *(6360 S 13th St, Oak Creek 53154) At jct College Ave, I-94 exit 319 E. 414/764-3500; FAX 414/764-5138.* 108 rms, 2 story. S $36.99-$58.99; D $41.99-$69.99; under 18 free. Crib free. Pet accepted. TV; cable (premium). Complimentary coffee in lobby. Ck-out noon. Business servs avail. Cr cds: A, C, D, DS, MC, V.

D

Motor Hotels

★ ★ ★ **HOLIDAY INN AIRPORT.** *6331 S 13th St (53221), I-94 exit 319, south of downtown. 414/764-1500; FAX 414/764-6531.* 159 rms, 3 story. S $69-$90; D $79-$110; each addl $10; under 18 free. Crib free. Pet accepted. TV. Indoor pool. Playground. Restaurant 6 am-1 pm, 5-10 pm; Sat, Sun from 7 am. Rm serv. Bar. Ck-out 11 am. Coin Indry. Meeting rms. Business servs avail. Bellhops. Sundries. Free airport transportation. Exercise equipt; weight machine, treadmill, saunas. Game rm. Balconies. Cr cds: A, C, D, DS, JCB, MC, V.

D SC

★ ★ **MANCHESTER SUITES NORTHWEST.** *11777 W Silver Spring Dr (53225), I-45 and Silver Spring, west of downtown. 414/462-3500; FAX 414/462-8166; res: 800/723-8280.* 123 suites, 4 story. Suites $62-$80; under 14 free. Crib free. TV; cable. Complimentary full bkfst. Coffee in rms. Restaurant nearby. Ck-out noon. Meeting rms. Business servs avail. In-rm modem link. Valet serv. Exercise equipt; treadmill, bicycle. Sundries. Refrigerators, microwaves, wet bars. Cr cds: A, C, D, DS, MC, V.

D SC

★ ★ **RAMADA INN DOWNTOWN.** *633 W Michigan St (53203), downtown. 414/272-8410; FAX 414/272-4651.* E-mail ramadadt@execpc.com; web www.execpc.com/ramadadt. 155 rms, 7 story. S $70-$90; D $78-$101; each addl $10; suites $105-$145; under 18 free; wkend rates. Crib free. TV; cable (premium), VCR avail (movies). Heated pool. Restaurant 6 am-10 pm. Rm serv. Bar 11-2 am. Ck-out noon. Meeting rms. Business servs avail. In-rm modem link. Valet serv. Downhill ski 15 mi; x-country ski 7 mi. Exercise equipt; bicycles, treadmill. Cr cds: A, C, D, DS, JCB, MC, V.

D SC

★ ★ **RAMADA INN-WEST.** *201 N Mayfair Rd (53226), just N of I-94 Mayfair Rd (WI 100) exit, west of downtown. 414/771-4400; FAX 414/771-4517.* 230 rms, 3 story. May-Sept: S $84; D $99; under 18 free; lower rates rest of yr. Crib free. Pet accepted, some restrictions. TV; cable (premium). Indoor pool; whirlpool. Playground. Restaurant 6 am-1 pm, 5-9 pm. Rm serv. Bar 3 pm-1 am; Fri, Sat to 2 am. Ck-out noon. Coin Indry. Meeting rms. Business servs avail. Valet serv. Exercise equipt; weights, bicycles, sauna. Picnic tables. Cr cds: A, C, D, DS, ER, JCB, MC, V.

D SC

★ ★ ★ **SHERATON INN-NORTH.** *(8900 N Kildeer Ct, Brown Deer 53209) 10 mi N via I-43 exit 82B Brown Deer Rd W. 414/355-8585; FAX 414/355-3566.* 149 rms, 6 story. S, D $96-$144; each addl $10; suites $141-$225; under 18 free; wkend rates. Crib free. TV; cable (premium), VCR avail. Indoor/outdoor pool; whirlpool, poolside serv. Coffee in rms. Restaurant 6:30 am-10:30 pm. Rm serv. Bar 10-2 am. Ck-out noon. Meeting rms. Business servs avail. In-rm modem link. Bellhops. Valet serv. Barber. Airport transportation. X-country ski 3 mi. Sauna. Health club privileges. Some refrigerators; microwaves avail. Cr cds: A, C, D, DS, JCB, MC, V.

D

Hotels

★ ★ ★ **EMBASSY SUITES-WEST.** *(1200 S Moorland Rd, Brookfield 53008) 10 mi W via I-94, Moorland Rd S exit. 414/782-2900; FAX 414/796-9159.* 203 suites, 5 story. S, D, suites $99-$500; each addl $20; under 12 free; wkend rates; package plans. Crib free. Pet accepted, some restrictions. TV; cable (premium). Indoor pool; whirlpool. Complimentary full bkfst. Complimentary coffee in rms. Restaurant 11 am-11 pm. Bar to 1 am. Ck-out noon. Meeting rms. Business center. In-rm modem link. Concierge. Free airport transportation. Tennis privileges. Golf privileges. Exercise equipt; weight machine, bicycles, sauna, steam rm. Game rm. Refrigerators, microwaves, wet bars. Cr cds: A, C, D, DS, ER, JCB, MC, V.

D SC

★ ★ ★ **THE GRAND MILWAUKEE.** *4747 S Howell Ave (53207), I-94 Airport E exit, near General Mitchell Airport, south of downtown. 414/481-8000; FAX 414/481-8065; res: 800/558-3862.* 510 rms, 6 story. S, D $64-$175; each addl $10; suites $225-$295; under 17 free; package plans. Crib free. TV; cable (premium). 2 heated pools, 1 indoor; whirlpool. Restaurants 6 am-10 pm. Bar 11-2 am. Ck-out noon. Meeting rms. Business center. In-rm modem link. Gift shop. Barber, beauty shop. Free airport transportation. Indoor tennis. Exercise equipt; weight machines, bicycles, sauna. Game rm. Some refrigerators. Cr cds: A, C, D, DS, MC, V.

D SC

★ ★ ★ **HILTON.** *509 W Wisconsin Ave (53203), I-43 Civic Center exit, downtown. 414/271-7250; FAX 414/271-1039.* 500 rms, 25 story. S, D $159-$179; each addl $20; suites $190-$1,000; under 18 free; wkend plan. Crib free. TV; cable (premium). Indoor pool. Restaurant 6:30 am-10 pm. Bar 11-1 am. Ck-out noon. Convention facilities. Business servs avail. In-rm modem link. Concierge. Gift shop. Barber, beauty shop. Exercise equipt; bicycle, treadmill, sauna. Cr cds: A, C, D, DS, MC, V.

D SC

★ ★ **HILTON INN MILWAUKEE RIVER.** *4700 N Port Washington Rd (53212), I-43 exit Hampton Ave E, north of downtown. 414/962-6040; FAX 414/962-6166.* Web www.hilton.com. 163 rms, 5 story. S $97-$111; D $112-$121; each addl $15; suites $180-$370; studio rms $114-$129; family rates. TV; cable (premium). Indoor pool. Coffee in rms. Restaurant 6:30 am-10 pm. Bar 11 am-midnight. Ck-out noon. Meeting rms. Business servs avail. In-rm modem link. Exercise equipt; weight machine, stair machine. Some refrigerators. Overlooks river. Cr cds: A, C, D, DS, ER, JCB, MC, V.

D SC

★ ★ **HOLIDAY INN CITY CENTRE.** *611 W Wisconsin Ave (53203), downtown. 414/273-2950; FAX 414/273-7662.* 245 rms, 10 story. S $66-$119; D $76-$129; each addl $10; suites $119-$199; under 18 free; higher rates special events. Crib free. TV; cable (premium). Pool. Coffee in rms. Restaurant 6 am-10 pm. Rm serv. Bar from 4 pm. Ck-out noon. Meeting rms. Business center. In-rm modem link. Bellhops. Valet serv. Free valet parking. Health club privileges. Microwaves avail. Cr cds: A, C, D, DS, ER, JCB, MC, V.

D SC

★ ★ **HOTEL WISCONSIN.** *720 N Old World 3rd St (53203), downtown. 414/271-4900; FAX 414/271-9998.* 234 rms, 11 story. Mid-June-Sept: S, D $69-$76; each addl $8; suites $85; kit. units $69-$82; under 17 free; lower rates rest of yr. Crib free. Pet accepted. TV; cable (premium), VCR avail. Restaurant 6 am-10 pm. Ck-out 11 am. Meeting rm. Business servs avail. Concierge. Sundries. Valet serv. Coin Indry. Game rm. Health club privileges. Some refrigerators; microwaves avail. Cr cds: A, C, D, DS, ER, JCB, MC, V.

D SC

★ ★ ★ **HYATT REGENCY.** *333 W Kilbourn Ave (53203), downtown. 414/276-1234; FAX 414/276-6338.* 484 rms, 22 story. S $99-$149; D $99-$174; each addl $25; parlor rms $95-$150; suites $175-$750; under 18 free; wkend rates; package plans. TV; cable (premium), VCR avail (movies). Restaurants 6:30 am-midnight (also see POLARIS). Bar from 11 am, Fri, Sat to 2 am. Ck-out noon. Convention facilities. Business center. Concierge. Gift shop. Exercise equipt; weight machine, bicycles. Health club privileges. Microwaves avail. Cr cds: A, C, D, DS, ER, JCB, MC, V.

D SC

★ ★ **PARK EAST.** *916 E State St (53202), downtown. 414/276-8800; FAX 414/765-1919; res: 800/328-7275.* 159 rms, 5 story. S $81-$110; D $91-$120; each addl $10; suites $91-$250; under 18 free; wkend rates; package plans. Crib $5. TV; cable (premium), VCR (movies). Complimentary continental bkfst. Restaurant 6:30-10 am, 4:30-10 pm; wkends to 11 pm. Bar. Ck-out noon. Meeting rms. Business servs avail. In-rm modem link. Health club privileges. Some in-rm whirlpools, refrigerators, wet bars; microwaves avail. Cr cds: A, C, D, DS, MC, V.

D SC

★ ★ ★ **PFISTER.** *424 E Wisconsin Ave (53202), I-794 Van Buren exit, downtown. 414/273-8222; FAX 414/273-5025; res: 800/558-8222.* 307 rms, 23 story. S, D $205-$225; each addl $20; suites $245-$650;

under 18 free; wkend rates. Crib free. Parking $8; valet avail. TV; cable, VCR avail (movies). Indoor pool. Restaurant 6:30 am-11 pm (also see ENGLISH ROOM). Rm serv 24 hrs. Bars 11-2 am; entertainment. Ck-out noon. Convention facilities. Business servs avail. In-rm modem link. Concierge. Gift shop. Barber, beauty shop. Airport transportation. Exercise equipt; weight machine, bicycle. Health club privileges. Bathrm phones. Cr cds: A, C, D, DS, JCB, MC, V.

D SC

★ ★ ★ **WYNDHAM MILWAUKEE CENTER.** *139 E Kilbourn Ave (53202), downtown. 414/276-8686; FAX 414/276-8007.* 221 rms, 10 story, 77 suites. S, D $155-$199; each addl $20; suites $250-$520; under 12 free; wkend rates. Crib free. Garage $9. TV; cable, VCR avail. Complimentary coffee in rms. Restaurant 6:30 am-11 pm. Bar 11-2 am; entertainment Fri-Sat. Ck-out noon. Meeting rms. Business servs avail. Gift shop. Exercise equipt; weight machines, bicycles, sauna, steam rm. Whirlpool. Microwaves avail. Cr cds: A, C, D, DS, ER, JCB, MC, V.

D

Restaurants

✔★ **AU BON APPÉTIT.** *1016 E Brady St (53202), downtown. 414/278-1233.* E-mail 107705,2212@compuserve.com. Hrs: 5-9 pm; Fri, Sat to 10 pm. Closed Sun, Mon; major hols. Res accepted. Mediterranean menu. Wine. Semi-a la carte: dinner $6.95-$11.95. Specializes in Lebanese dishes, hummos, tabouleh. Own baking. Street parking. Casual, intimate restaurant; Mediterranean decor. Cr cds: MC, V.

D

★ **BALISTRERI'S BLUEMOUND INN.** *6501 W Bluemound Rd (53213), west of downtown. 414/258-9881.* Hrs: 11-1 am; Fri to 2 am; Sat 4 pm-2 am; Sun 4 pm-1 am. Closed Thanksgiving, Dec 24, 25. Res accepted. Italian, Amer menu. Bar. Semi-a la carte: lunch, dinner $6-$20. Specialties: veal Balistreri, pollo carcioffi, whitefish Frangelico. Own pasta. Casual, contemporary decor. Cr cds: A, C, D, DS, MC, V.

D

★ ★ **BARTOLOTTA'S LAKE PARK BISTRO.** *3133 E Newberry Blvd (53211), East Side. 414/962-6300.* Hrs: 11:30 am-2 pm, 5:30-9 pm; Fri to 10 pm; Sat 5-10 pm; Sun 10:30 am-2 pm (brunch), 5-8:30 pm. Closed some major hols. Res accepted. French menu. Bar. Semi-a la carte: lunch $7-$15, dinner $12-$22. Sun brunch $18.95. Child's meals. Specializes in New York strip, Atlantic salmon, homemade desserts. Own baking. Former park pavilion; overlooks Lake Michigan. Cr cds: A, D, DS, MC, V.

D

★ ★ **BAVARIAN INN.** *700 W Lexington Blvd, exit I-43 at W Silver Spring Rd, north of downtown. 414/964-0300.* Hrs: 11:30 am-2:30 pm, 5-9 pm; Fri to 10 pm; Sat 5-9 pm; Sun brunch 10:30 am-2 pm. Closed Mon; Jan 1, July 4, Dec 24, 25. Res accepted. German, Amer menu. Bar. Semi-a la carte: lunch $4.95-$9.95, dinner $7.95-$14.95. Sun brunch $12.95. Child's meals. Specializes in schnitzel. Accordionist Fri-Sun. Parking. Chalet-style building; large fireplace, timbered ceilings, stein and alpine bell collections. Cr cds: A, C, D, DS, MC, V.

D

★ ★ ★ **BOULEVARD INN.** *925 E Wells St (53202), in Cudahy Tower, downtown. 414/765-1166.* E-mail blvdin@execpc.com; web www.execpc.com/homepage/~blvdin. Hrs: 11:30 am-9 pm; Fri, Sat to 10 pm; Sun from 10:30 am; Sun brunch to 2 pm. Closed some major hols. Res accepted. Bar. Wine list. Semi-a la carte: lunch $7.50-$11.50, dinner $16.95-$35.95. Sun brunch $10.45. Child's meals. Specializes in fresh fish, veal, German dishes. Own baking. Pianist. Valet parking. Some tableside preparation. Overlooks Lake Michigan. Family-owned. Smoking at bar only. Cr cds: A, C, D, DS, MC, V.

D ♥

★ **CAFE KNICKERBOCKER.** *1030 E Juneau Ave (53202), downtown. 414/272-0011.* Hrs: 6:30 am-10 pm; Fri, Sat to 11 pm; Sun 9 am-10 pm. Sun brunch 9 am-3 pm. Closed Thanksgiving, Dec 25. Res accepted. Bar. Semi-a la carte: bkfst $3.95-$7.95, lunch $3.95-$7.95, dinner $10.95-19.95. Sun brunch $3.95-$7.95. Specializes in seafood, pasta. Outdoor dining. Casual decor. Totally nonsmoking. Cr cds: A, MC, V.

D

✔★ **CLUB TRES HERMANOS.** *1332 W Lincoln Ave (53215), south of downtown. 414/384-9050.* Hrs: 11 am-midnight. Closed Thanksgiving, Dec 25. Res accepted. Mexican menu. Bar. Semi-a la carte: lunch $1.75-$5.99, dinner $1.75-$15. Child's meals. Specializes in seafood, burrito, taco. Salad bar. Entertainment Fri, Sat. Mexican decor. Totally nonsmoking. Cr cds: A, C, MC, V.

D

✔★ **COUNTY CLARE.** *1234 N Astor St (53202), downtown. 888/942-5273.* Hrs: 11:30 am-10 pm; Sun to 9 pm. Closed major hols. Irish menu. Bar to 1 am. Semi-a la carte: lunch $3.50-$9.50, dinner $3.50-$10.95. Specialties: Irish smoked salmon, corned beef and cabbage, Irish root soup. Traditional Irish music Sun. Irish pub decor with cut glass and dark woods. Cr cds: A, C, D, DS, MC, V.

D

✔★ **DOS BANDIDOS.** *5932 N Green Bay Ave (53209), I-43 to Silver Spring exit W, north of downtown. 414/228-1911.* Hrs: 11 am-10:30 pm; Fri to 11:30 pm; Sat noon-11:30 pm; Sun 4-9 pm. Closed major hols. Mexican, Amer menu. Bar. Semi-a la carte: lunch $3.95-$6.50, dinner $7.25-$11.95. Specializes in steak & chicken fajitas, spinach enchiladas, vegetarian dishes. Parking. Patio dining. Mexican cantina decor. Cr cds: A, DS, MC, V.

D

✔★ ★ **EAGAN'S.** *1030 N Water St (53202), downtown. 414/271-6900.* Hrs: 11 am-11 pm; Fri, Sat to 1 am; Sun brunch 11 am-2 pm. Closed most major hols. Bar. Semi-a la carte: lunch, dinner $6.95-$15.95. Sun brunch $6.95-$14.95. Specializes in seafood. Outdoor dining. Contemporary decor. Totally nonsmoking. Cr cds: A, D, DS, MC, V.

D

★ ★ **ELM GROVE INN.** *(13275 Watertown Plank Rd, Elm Grove 53122) W on I-94, N on Moorland Rd to Watertown Plank Rd. 414/782-7090.* Hrs: 11:30 am-2 pm, 5-9:30 pm; Sat from 5 pm. Closed Sun; major hols. Res accepted. Continental menu. Bar to midnight. Semi-a la carte: lunch $7.50-$13, dinner $17-$27. Specializes in fresh fish, veal, beef. Own baking. 1850s bldg has high-backed chairs, stained glass and large fireplace. Cr cds: A, DS, MC, V.

D

★ ★ ★ **ENGLISH ROOM.** *(See Pfister Hotel) 414/390-3832.* Hrs: 11:30 am-2 pm, 5:30-10 pm; Sat 5:30-11 pm; Sun from 5 pm. Res accepted. Bar. Extensive wine list. Semi-a la carte: lunch $7.75-$12. A la carte entrees: dinner $12-$25. Valet parking. Established 1893; past patrons include Teddy Roosevelt, Enrico Caruso. Cr cds: A, C, D, DS, MC, V.

★ ★ ★ ★ **GRENADIER'S.** *747 N Broadway Ave at Mason (53202), just N of I-794 Jackson-Van Buren exit, downtown. 414/276-0747.* Classic yet imaginative European-style cuisine is served on elegantly set tables in four unique and well-appointed dining rooms. French, continental menu. Specialties: Dover sole, lamb curry Calcutta, fresh seared tuna on ocean salad. Own pastries. Hrs: 11:30 am-2:30 pm, 5:30-10:30 pm; Sat from 5:30 pm. Closed Sun; major hols. Res accepted. Bar. Wine cellar. Semi-a la carte: lunch $8.95-$14.95. A la carte entrees: dinner $17.95-$24.95. Dégustation menu: dinner $31.95. Pianist. Valet parking (dinner). Chef-owned. Jacket. Cr cds: A, C, D, DS, MC, V.

D

★ **IZUMI'S.** *2178 N Prospect Ave (53209), on the East Side. 414/271-5278.* Hrs: 11:30 am-2 pm, 5-10 pm; Fri, Sat 5-10:30 pm; Sun 4-9 pm. Closed major hols. Res accepted. Japanese menu. Wine, beer. Semi-a la carte: lunch $4.95-$12.95, dinner $9-$23. Specializes in sushi, sukiyaki, terriyaki dishes. Parking. Contemporary Japanese decor. Cr cds: A, D, MC, V.

★ ★ **JACK PANDL'S WHITEFISH BAY INN.** *(1319 E Henry Clay St, Whitefish Bay 53217) 6 mi N on WI 32, 2 mi NE of I-43 Hampton Ave exit E. 414/964-3800.* Hrs: 11:30 am-2:30 pm, 5-9 pm; Fri, Sat to 10:30 pm; Sun 10:30 am-2:30 pm, 4-8 pm. Res accepted. Bar. Semi-a la carte: lunch $5.95-$9.95, dinner $7.95-$21.95. Child's meals. Specializes in whitefish, German pancakes, Schaum torte. Parking. Established in 1915; antique beer stein collection. Family-owned. Cr cds: A, C, D, DS, MC, V.

★ ★ ★ **JOHN ERNST'S.** *600 E Ogden Ave (53202), at Jackson St, downtown. 414/273-1878.* E-mail jernst@execpc.com; web www.execpc.com/~jernst. Hrs: 11:30 am-10 pm; Sun 11 am-9:30 pm; Sun brunch to 2 pm. Closed Mon. Res accepted. Continental, Amer menu. Bar. Semi-a la carte: lunch $7.50-$10.75, dinner $13.50-$28.95. Child's meals. Specialties: prime steak, Kassler rippchen, jaegerschnitzel. Own pastries. Entertainment. Parking. Old World decor; stained glass, fireplace. Collection of steins. Established in 1878; oldest in city. Family-owned. Cr cds: A, C, D, DS, MC, V.

D

★ **JUDY'S KITCHEN.** *(600 W Brown Deer Rd, Bayside 53217) 12 mi N on I-43. 414/352-9998.* Hrs: 11 am-2 pm, 5-9 pm; Fri to 11 pm; Sat 5-11 pm. Closed Sun; major hols. Bar 3:30 pm-2 am; Sat from 6 pm. Semi-a la carte: lunch $4.50-$10, dinner $8.95-$19.95. Specializes in steak, fresh fish, homemade desserts. Own baking. Outdoor dining. Casual atmosphere; large aquarium at one wall. Totally nonsmoking. Cr cds: A, MC, V.

★ ★ **KARL RATZSCH'S.** *320 E Mason St (53202), I-794 Van Buren St exit, downtown. 414/276-2720.* Hrs: 4-9:30 pm; Sat to 10:30 pm; Sun to 9 pm. Closed major hols. Res accepted. German, Amer menu. Bar. Semi-a la carte: dinner $12.95-$24. Child's meals. Specializes in planked whitefish, roast goose shank, aged prime steak. Pianist evenings. Valet parking. Collection of rare steins, glassware. Old World Austrian atmosphere. Family-owned. Cr cds: A, C, D, DS, MC, V.

★ ★ **KING AND I.** *823 N 2nd St (53203), downtown. 414/276-4181.* Hrs: 11:30 am-10 pm; Sat 5-11 pm; Sun 4-9 pm. Closed major hols. Res accepted. Thai menu. Bar. Semi-a la carte: lunch $5-$8, dinner $9-$18. Specialties: volcano chicken, fresh red snapper, crispy duck. Southeast Asian decor; enameled wood chairs, hand-carved teakwood, native artwork. Cr cds: A, D, DS, MC, V.

D

★ ★ **MADER'S.** *1037 N Old World Third St (53203), downtown. 414/271-3377.* Hrs: 11:30 am-10 pm; Fri, Sat to 11:30 pm; Mon to 9 pm; Sun 10:30 am-9 pm; Sun brunch to 2 pm. Res accepted. German, continental menu. Bar. Semi-a la carte: lunch $4.95-$8.95, dinner $13.95-$23.95. Sun Viennese brunch $14.95. Child's meals. Specialties: Rheinischer sauerbraten, Wienerschnitzel, roast pork shank. Valet parking. Old World German decor; antiques. Gift shop. Family-owned. Cr cds: A, C, D, DS, MC, V.

D

★ ★ ★ **MANIACI'S CAFE SICILIANO.** *(6904 N Santa Monica Blvd, Fox Point 53217) 10 mi N on WI 32. 414/352-5757.* Hrs: 4-10 pm. Closed Sun; major hols; also wk of July 4. Res accepted. Continental menu. Serv bar. Wine cellar. Semi-a la carte: dinner $17.50-$32.95. Child's meals. Specializes in veal, fish, pasta. Own pasta. Sicilian decor with brick columns, tile floors. Family-owned. Cr cds: A, MC, V.

★ ★ **MIKE & ANNA'S.** *2000 S Eighth St (53204), south of downtown. 414/643-0072.* Hrs: 5:30-8:45 pm; Fri, Sat to 9:45 pm. Closed Mon; major hols. Res accepted. Bar. Semi-a la carte: dinner $19-$26.95. Specializes in salmon, rack of lamb. Menu changes daily. Restored corner tavern in residential setting; contemporary atmosphere. Cr cds: A, MC, V.

D

★ ★ ★ **MIMMA'S CAFE.** *1307 E Brady St (53202), downtown. 414/271-7337.* E-mail mimma89@jadetec.com. Hrs: 11:30 am-2:30 pm, 5-10 pm; Fri, Sat to midnight; Sun from 5 pm. Closed major hols. Res accepted. Italian menu. Bar. A la carte entrees: lunch $6-$12, dinner $8-$30. Specializes in pasta, seafood, veal. Contemporary decor. Cr cds: A, C, D, DS, MC, V.

D

★ ★ **NORTH SHORE BISTRO.** *(8649 N Port Washington Rd, Fox Point 53217) 10 mi N on WI 32. 414/351-6100.* Hrs: 11 am-10 pm; Sat to 11 pm; Sun from 4 pm. Closed most major hols. Res accepted. Bar. Semi-a la carte: lunch $6-$9.25, dinner $6-$24.95. Specializes in seafood, steak, pasta. Outdoor dining. Casual bistro atmosphere. Cr cds: A, MC, V.

D

✔★ **OLD TOWN SERBIAN GOURMET HOUSE.** *522 W Lincoln Ave (53207), south of downtown. 414/672-0206; FAX 414/672-0810.* Hrs: 11:30 am-2:30 pm, 5-11 pm; Sat, Sun from 5 pm. Closed Mon; some major hols. Res accepted. Serbian, Amer menu. Bar. Semi-a la carte: lunch $5-$9, dinner $12-$20. Child's meals. Entertainment (wkends). Parking. Family-owned. Cr cds: A, D, DS, MC, V.

D

★ ★ ★ **OSTERIA DEL MONDO.** *1028 E Juneau Ave (53202), downtown. 414/291-3770.* Web www.osteria.com. Hrs: 11 am-2:30 pm, 5-10:30 pm; Sat 5-11 pm; Sun brunch 10 am-3 pm. Closed most major hols. Res accepted. Italian menu. Bar. Semi-a la carte: lunch $5.95-$11.95, dinner $9.95-$24.95. Sun brunch $6.95-$16.95. Specializes in seafood, pasta. Outdoor dining. Italian decor. Totally nonsmoking. Cr cds: A, D, MC, V.

D

★ ★ ★ **PANDL'S IN BAYSIDE.** *8825 N Lake Dr (53217), 10 mi N on WI 32, 1 mi E of I-43 Brown Deer Rd (E) exit, north of downtown. 414/352-7300.* Web www.pandl.com. Hrs: 11:30 am-10 pm; Fri-Sat to 11:30 pm; Sun 10 am-9 pm; Sun brunch to 2 pm. Closed Labor Day, Dec 25. Res accepted. Bar. Semi-a la carte: lunch, dinner $7.50-$19. Sun brunch $18.50. Child's meals. Specializes in fresh fish, prime meats. Salad bar (dinner). Own pastries. Parking. Family-owned. Cr cds: A, C, D, DS, MC, V.

D

★ **PLEASANT VALLEY INN.** *9801 W Dakota St (53227), west of downtown. 414/321-4321.* Hrs: 5-9 pm; Fri, Sat to 10 pm; Sun 4-8 pm. Closed Mon; major hols. Res accepted. Bar. Semi-a la carte: dinner $14-$22. Child's meals. Specializes in steak, seafood. Casual decor. Cr cds: A, DS, MC, V.

D

★ ★ **POLARIS.** *(See Hyatt Regency Hotel) 414/276-1234.* Hrs: 11:30 am-2 pm, 5-11 pm; Sat, Sun from 5 pm. Closed Jan 1, Thanksgiving, Dec 25. Res accepted. Bar. A la carte entrees: lunch $5.95-$8.95, dinner $13.95-$25. Specializes in prime rib au jus, grilled veal chops, chicken tortellini. Parking. Revolving restaurant on 22nd floor. Cr cds: A, C, D, DS, MC, V.

D

★ ★ **PORTERHOUSE.** *800 W Layton Ave (53221), south of downtown. 414/744-1750.* Hrs: 11 am-2:30 pm, 5-10 pm; Fri, Sat to 11 pm; Sun 4-9 pm. Closed Mon. Res accepted. Bar. Semi-a la carte: lunch $6.25-$11.95, dinner $9.95-$49.95. Child's meals. Specializes in charbroiled steak, ribs, seafood. Parking. Cr cds: A, C, D, DS, MC, V.

D

✔★ **RED ROCK CAFE.** *4022 N Oakland Ave (53211), north of downtown. 414/962-4545.* Hrs: 11 am-2 pm, 5-9 pm; Fri, Sat to 10 pm; Sun from 5 pm. Closed Mon; major hols. Bar. Semi-a la carte: lunch $6.95-$11.95, dinner $8.25-$22.50. Child's meals. Specializes in seafood. Nautical decor. Totally nonsmoking. Cr cds: MC, V.

D SC

★ ★ **RIVER LANE INN.** *(4313 W River Lane, Brown Deer 53223) 414/354-1975.* Hrs: 11:30 am-2:30 pm, 5-10 pm. Closed Sun; most major hols. Bar. Semi-a la carte: lunch $6.75-$10.95, dinner $15.95-$20.95. Specializes in seafood. Casual decor. Cr cds: A, MC, V.

D

✔★ **ROYAL INDIA.** *3400 S 27th St (53215), south of downtown. 414/647-2050.* Hrs: 11 am-3 pm, 5-10 pm; Fri, Sat to 10:30 pm. Res accepted. Indian menu. Wine, beer. Buffet: lunch $6.95. Semi-a la carte: dinner $5.95-$11.95. Specializes in tandoori dishes, seafood, lamb. Own baking. Casual Indian decor. Totally nonsmoking. Cr cds: MC, V.

D

★ ★ ★ ★ **SANFORD.** *1547 N Jackson St (53202), downtown. 414/276-9608.* This is an elegant restaurant set in a remodeled grocery store and named for the chef, Sanford D'Amato. The cuisine is a mix of Western and Asian influences and has won national acclaim. Specialties: seared sea scallops; grilled breast of duck; cumin wafers with grilled, marinated tuna. Hrs: 5:30-9 pm; Fri, Sat to 10 pm. Closed Sun; major hols. Res accepted. Serv bar. Wine cellar. Semi-a la carte: dinner $23.95-$29.95. Tasting menu (changes monthly): $35. Valet parking. Totally nonsmoking. Cr cds: A, C, D, DS, MC, V.

D

★ **SAZ'S STATE HOUSE.** *5539 W State St, west of downtown. 414/453-2410.* Hrs: 11 am-midnight; Sun to 10 pm; Sun brunch 10:30 am-2:30 pm. Closed Dec 24, 25. Bar. Semi-a la carte: lunch $4.25-$7.95, dinner $7.50-$19.95. Specializes in barbecued ribs, fresh fish, chicken. Parking. Outdoor dining. 1905 roadhouse. Cr cds: A, MC, V.

D

✔★ ★ **SELENSKY'S GRAND CHAMPION GRILL.** *(4395 S 76th St, Greenfield 53220) 414/327-9100.* Hrs: 3:30-11 pm; Sun 2:30-9 pm. Closed Mon; Jan 1, July 4, Dec 25. Bar. Semi-a la carte: dinner $8.95-$18.95. Child's meals. Specializes in prime rib, steak, fresh seafood. Casual decor. Cr cds: MC, V.

D

✔★ ★ **SINGHA THAI.** *(2237 S 108th St, West Allis 53227) 414/541-1234.* Hrs: 11 am-9 pm; Fri, Sat to 10 pm. Closed most major hols. Res accepted. Thai menu. Semi-a la carte: lunch $5-$10, dinner $6-$15. Specializes in noodle dishes, curry dishes. Casual atmosphere. Cr cds: MC, V.

D

★ ★ ★ **STEVEN WADE'S CAFE.** *(17001 Greenfield Ave, New Berlin 53151) 414/784-0774; FAX 414/784-7311.* Web www.foodspot.com. Hrs: 11:30 am-2 pm, 5:30-10 pm; Mon, Sat from 5:30 pm. Closed Sun; major hols. Res accepted. Contemporary Amer menu. Semi-a la carte: lunch $8-$14, dinner $16-$25. Specializes in wild game, pasta, seafood. Intimate atmosphere. Totally nonsmoking. Cr cds: A, C, D, DS, ER, MC, V.

D SC

✔★ **THREE BROTHERS.** *2414 S St Clair (53207), in Bay View. 414/481-7530.* Hrs: 5-10 pm; Fri, Sat 4-11 pm; Sun 4-10 pm. Closed Mon; some major hols. Res accepted. Serbian menu. Serv bar. Semi-a la carte: dinner $10.95-$14.95. Specialties: burek, roast lamb, gulash. Serbian artwork on display. No cr cds accepted.

★ ★ **WEISSGERBER'S THIRD STREET PIER.** *1110 N Old World Third St (53203), downtown. 414/272-0330.* Hrs: 11:30 am-2 pm, 5-10 pm; Sat from 5 pm; Sun 4-9 pm. Res accepted. Bar 11-1 am. Semi-a la carte: lunch $6-$10, dinner $15.95-$34.95. Child's meals. Specializes in seafood, steak. Own desserts. Pianist Thurs-Sat. Valet parking. Outdoor dining. Lunch, dinner cruises on Lake Michigan avail. In restored landmark building on Milwaukee River. Cr cds: A, DS, MC, V.

D

✔★ ★ **WEST BANK CAFE.** *732 E Burleigh St (53212), downtown. 414/562-5555.* Hrs: 5:30-9:30 pm; Fri, Sat to 10 pm. Closed most major hols. Chinese, Vietnamese menu. Serv bar. Semi-a la carte: dinner $7-$16. Specializes in Vietnamese dishes. Own baking. Street parking. Contemporary Oriental decor. Totally nonsmoking. Cr cds: A, MC, V.

✔★ **YEN CHING.** *7630 W Good Hope Rd (53223), north of downtown. 414/353-6677.* Hrs: 11:30 am-2 pm, 4:30-9:30 pm; Fri, Sat 4:30-10 pm; Sun 11:30 am-2:30 pm, 4:30-9 pm. Mandarin menu. Serv bar. Semi-a la carte: lunch $4.25-$5.50, dinner $6.50-$12. Specializes in beef, chicken, seafood. Parking. Oriental decor. Cr cds: A, C, D, DS, MC, V.

D

Unrated Dining Spots

THE CHOCOLATE SWAN. *(890 Elm Grove Rd, Elm Grove) 2 mi W on Bluemound Rd to N Elm Grove Rd, at Elm Grove Village Court shopping center. 414/784-7926.* Hrs: 11 am-6 pm; Fri to 8:30 pm; Sat from 10 am. Closed Sun; most major hols. Dessert menu only. Desserts $1.75-$5.75. Specialties: Mary's chocolate interlude, yellow strawberry log. Tea room ambiance. Totally nonsmoking. Cr cds: MC, V.

SAFE HOUSE. *779 N Front St, entrance at International Exports, Ltd, downtown. 414/271-2007.* Hrs: 11:30-2 am; Fri, Sat to 2:30 am; Sun 4 pm-midnight. Res accepted. Bar. Semi-a la carte: lunch, dinner $4.25-$12.95. Specializes in sandwiches, specialty drinks. DJ Fri & Sat, magician Sun-Thurs. Spy theme decor. Cr cds: A, MC, V.

Wauwatosa

Motels

✔★ **EXEL INN-WEST.** *115 N Mayfair Rd (US 100) (53226). 414/257-0140; FAX 414/475-7875.* 123 rms, 2 story. S $35.99-$46.99; D $37.99-$56.99; suites $85-$125; each addl (up to 4) $4; under 17 free. Crib free. Pet accepted, some restrictions. TV; cable (premium). Complimentary continental bkfst in lobby. Restaurant adj 6 am-10 pm. Ck-out noon. Business servs avail. Cr cds: A, C, D, DS, MC, V.

D SC

★ **FORTY WINKS INN.** *11017 W Bluemound Rd (53226). 414/774-2800.* 31 rms (12 with shower only), 2 story. June-Aug: S, D $60-$75; each addl $6; kit. units $65-$85; lower rates rest of yr. Crib $5. TV; cable (premium). Complimentary coffee in lobby. Restaurant nearby. Ck-out 11 am. Sundries. X-country ski 1 mi. Some refrigerators. Cr cds: A, DS, MC, V.

D SC

★ ★ **HOLIDAY INN EXPRESS.** *11111 W North Ave (53226), 1 blk E of I-45. 414/778-0333; FAX 414/778-0331.* 122 rms, 3 story. S $65-$79; D $71-$85; each addl $6; suites $85-$95; under 18 free. Crib free. TV; cable (premium), VCR avail. Complimentary continental bkfst. Restaurant adj open 24 hrs. Ck-out noon. Meeting rms. Business servs avail. Valet serv. Heath club privileges. Some refrigerators. Some balconies. Cr cds: A, C, D, DS, ER, JCB, MC, V.

D SC

Motor Hotels

★ ★ **BEST WESTERN MIDWAY HOTEL.** *251 N Mayfair Rd (53226), I-94 exit US 100 N. 414/774-3600; FAX 414/774-5015.* 116 rms, 3 story. S $84-$109; D $94-$119; each addl $10. Crib free. TV; cable (premium). Indoor pool; whirlpool. Complimentary coffee in rms. Restaurant 6 am-10 pm. Rm serv. Bar 11-1:30 am. Ck-out noon. Coin Indry.

Meeting rms. Business servs avail. In-rm modem link. Bellhops. Sundries. Valet serv. Free airport, RR station, bus depot transportation. Exercise equipt; bicycle, stair machine, sauna. Some refrigerators. Cr cds: A, D, DS, MC, V.

D SC

★ ★ ★ **RADISSON.** *2303 N Mayfair Rd (US 100) (53226). 414/257-3400; FAX 414/257-0900.* 150 rms, 8 story. S $79-$128; D $89-$138; each addl $10; under 18 free; lower rates wkends. Crib free. TV; cable (premium). Sauna. Indoor pool. Coffee in rms. Restaurant 6 am-2 pm, 5-10 pm. Rm serv. Bar 11-2 am. Ck-out noon. Meeting rms. Business servs avail. In-rm modem link. Bellhops. Sundries. Free airport transportation. X-country ski 2 mi. Cr cds: A, C, D, DS, MC, V.

D SC

Restaurants

★ ★ **ALIOTO'S.** *3041 N Mayfair Rd (Hwy 100). 414/476-6900.* Hrs: 11:30 am-9 pm; Fri to 10 pm; Sat 4-9:30 pm. Closed Sun (exc hols); also 1st wk July. Res accepted. Italian, Amer menu. Bar. Semi-a la carte: lunch $4.25-$7.95, dinner $7-$18. Child's meals. Specializes in veal, prime rib, breaded Sicilian steak. Family-owned. Cr cds: A, C, D, DS, MC, V.

D SC

★ ★ **JAKE'S.** *6030 W North Ave (53213), at N 61st St. 414/771-0550.* Hrs: 5-10 pm; Sun to 9 pm. Closed some major hols; also Super Bowl Sun. Bar. Semi-a la carte: dinner $10.95-$23.95. Child's meals. Specializes in steak, fresh seafood, roast duck. Family-owned. Totally nonsmoking. Cr cds: A, C, D, MC, V.

D

★ ★ ★ **RISTORANTE BARTOLOTTA.** *7616 W State St (53213). 414/771-7910.* Hrs: 5:30-10 pm; Fri, Sat to 10:30 pm. Closed Sun; major hols. Res accepted. Italian menu. Bar. Semi-a la carte: dinner $12.95-$21.95. Child's meals. Specialties: sautéed veal chop with marsella cream sauce, grilled seafood. Entertainment. Outdoor dining. Italian decor. Totally nonsmoking. Cr cds: A, D, DS, MC, V.

D

Minneapolis

Settled: 1847
Pop: 368,383
Elev: 687-980 feet
Time zone: Central
Area code: 612
Web: www.minneapolis.org

St Paul

Settled: 1840
Pop: 272,235
Elev: 874 feet
Time zone: Central
Area code: 612
Web: www.stpaul.gov

Still harboring traces of frontier vigor, Minneapolis and its twin city, St Paul, form a mighty northern metropolis. In many ways they complement one another. Together they are a center for grain gathering, electronics, transportation, finance and industry. Baseball, football or basketball games at Minneapolis' Hubert H. Humphrey Metrodome and Target Center often rouse the fans of each city into a real competitive spirit.

The Twin Cities are perhaps best known for fine education, excellent cultural facilities and some of the best and most advanced health care in the world. Minneapolis, the largest city in Minnesota, is quite modern with its skyscrapers and skywalks; St Paul, the second-largest city, is rich with the state's heritage and history.

Minneapolis began in the 1800s when two mills were built to cut lumber and grind flour for nearby Fort Snelling. Lumbermen and fur traders from New England and French Canada were its first settlers. St Paul was incorporated as a town in 1849. It was host to the first legislature of the Minnesota Territory and has been the capital ever since. Civic, cultural and industrial development was assisted by railroad magnate James J. Hill, who gave the city a library and the Cathedral of St Paul's.

Business

The Twin Cities area's domination by lumber and grain milling began early. Today, Minneapolis is headquarters for several of the largest milling companies in the world and has a large cash grain market. The Twin Cities area has become a center for major corporations with 3M, Northwest Airlines, Cargill, Honeywell, General Mills, Pillsbury and Control Data headquartered here. Its highly diversified industries include computer manufacturing, electronics, food processing and graphic arts. St Paul is home to the Minnesota World Trade Center, and the area is rated among the top US cities for world trade.

Also important to the local economy is the Twin Cities' placement as gateway to the vast vacationlands—the woods and lakes of northern Minnesota.

Convention Facilities

The Minneapolis Convention Center has three exhibit halls, two with 100,000 square feet of display space and a third with 80,000 square feet of space. The three rooms can be combined to create a 280,000-square-foot exhibit hall. The Convention Center also has a 28,000-square-foot ballroom and 54 smaller meeting rooms, which can accommodate from 70 to 2,000 people.

The newly expanded RiverCentre, located on the banks of the Mississippi River, includes the Roy Wilkins Auditorium and the Convention Center. The complex includes over 250,000 square feet of exhibit space. Audiences of 18,000 can be seated—7,368 in permanent theater seats and 9,800 for banquets. There is a theater with 3,684 seats, a 27,500-square-foot ballroom, 23 meeting rooms for 20 to 175 people and parking for over 2,100 vehicles.

Sports & Recreation

Minnesotans are fiercely proud of their athletes. Baseball's Twins and football's Vikings bring much excitement to the Hubert H. Humphrey Metrodome in Minneapolis. The Minnesota Timberwolves play basketball at Target Center. And Williams Arena, known as "The Barn," is never quiet when the University of Minnesota's Gopher basketball team hits the floor.

Minneapolis and St Paul have all the requisites of a cosmopolitan area with the recreational advantages of the nearby north woods. There is an abundance of lakes, woods, parks, beaches, golf courses and ski areas in the Twin Cities area. Contact the Greater Minneapolis Convention and Visitors Association or St Paul Convention and Visitors Bureau for further information.

Entertainment

Restaurants, theaters, museums and music in the Twin Cities rival the finest in the nation.

The Ordway Music Theatre in downtown St Paul consists of the 1,815-seat theater, which houses opera, concerts, recitals, dance, drama and pop events, and the 317-seat hall, McKnight Theatre, which is used primarily for local music, dance, theater and film presentations.

The Guthrie Theater has a national reputation for presenting fine repertory performances, which draw drama students and theater lovers from throughout the nation.

Minnesota Orchestra Hall has been acclaimed by leading music critics as an outstanding achievement in auditorium architecture. The acoustical engineering allows full appreciation of musical subtleties.

At the Target Center one can enjoy more extravagant events—ice shows and concerts. The University of Minnesota Theatre has summer performances on campus aboard the *Showboat,* moored on the Mississippi River.

Historical Areas

Historic Fort Snelling has been restored to its 1820s appearance. In 1960 it was designated Minnesota's first national historic landmark; the legislature established Fort Snelling State Historical Park in 1963. All 18 buildings of the original fort have been rebuilt, and staff members act as soldiers, cooks, laundresses, blacksmiths and armorers, demonstrating how frontier people lived and worked in the 1820s. The fort is open to the public from May to October.

In the heart of downtown St Paul, the Old Federal Courts Building, renamed the Landmark Center, has been refurbished and opened to the public. Also open is The William L. McKnight/3M Omnitheater in the Science Museum of Minnesota. Unlike a conventional planetarium, the Omnitheater is an amphitheater enclosed in a hemispherical dome. Its highly advanced projection equipment can show the sky from any point in the solar system and actually has the ability to simulate space travel.

The Alexander Ramsey House in St Paul, a 15-room French-Renaissance mansion built in 1872, was the home of Minnesota's first territorial governor. Many of the Victorian furnishings are original pieces. Behind the main house is the reconstructed carriage house, which serves as the visitors' center.

Across from Minnehaha Park in Minneapolis is Minnehaha Depot, an ornate railroad building, dating from the 1890s, which has been restored to its original appearance.

Sightseeing

A stroll in downtown Minneapolis is vastly different from walking about most central cities. A 12-block stretch in the center of the city, the Nicollet Mall is a shopping promenade with a variety of shops, restaurants, museums and nightly entertainment. Private cars are banned, and people can stroll along sidewalks past landscaped plots and fountains. A system of covered skyways weaves across and along the mall at a higher level. About 60 blocks are connected by the skyway system. Crystal Court, made of honeycombed glass and plastic, has an "outdoor" restaurant, 130 feet above ground level, reached by the skyway system. The St Paul skyway connects 25 city blocks and is the largest publicly owned skyway system in the country.

Since the Mississippi River is the reason the Twin Cities came to be, a sightseeing jaunt on or near the river is essential for anyone who wants to know the area. An observation platform at the Upper St Anthony Falls, on Main Street and Central Avenue in Minneapolis, offers a fine view of the river, its traffic, the falls and the Army Corps of Engineers' locks and dams.

For those who would like to cruise the Mississippi on an authentic stern-wheel riverboat, the *Jonathan Padelford, Josiah Snelling* and *Anson Northrop* travel between St Paul and historic Fort Snelling during the summer months.

A drive starting from the Cathedral of St Paul and proceeding west along Summit Avenue passes dozens of beautiful 19th-century mansions, including the official residence of Minnesota's governor. Also in this area are the Alexander Ramsey House and the James J. Hill Mansion. Both are open to the public.

General References Minneapolis

Area code: 612

Phone Numbers

POLICE & FIRE: 911

POISON INFORMATION CENTER: 347-3141

TIME & WEATHER: 375-0830

Information Sources

Greater Minneapolis Convention & Visitors Association, 4000 Multifoods Tower, 33 S 6th St, 55402; 661-4700 or 800/445-7412.

"The Connection," Twin Cities information line, 922-9000.

Park and Recreation Board, 661-4800.

Transportation

AIRLINES: American; America West; Continental; Delta; KLM; Northwest; TWA; United; USAir; and other commuter and regional airlines.

AIRPORT: Minneapolis/St Paul International, 726-5555.

CAR RENTAL AGENCIES: (See IMPORTANT TOLL-FREE NUMBERS) Avis 726-5220; Budget 726-9258; Hertz 726-1600; National 726-5600.

PUBLIC TRANSPORTATION: Metropolitan Transit Commission, 3118 Nicollet, 55408; 349-7000.

RAILROAD PASSENGER SERVICE: Amtrak 800/872-7245.

Newspapers

Star Tribune; Skyway News.

Convention Facility

Minneapolis Convention Center, 1301 S 2nd Ave, 335-6000.

Sports & Recreation

Major Sports Facilities

Hubert H. Humphrey Metrodome, 900 S 5th St, 332-0386 (Twins, baseball, 375-1366; Vikings, football, 828-6500).

Target Center, 600 First Ave N (Timberwolves, basketball, 673-1600).

Racetracks

Canterbury Downs, 1 mi S of MN 101 on County 83, Shakopee 445-0511 (horse racing).

Elko Speedway, 20 mi S via I-35W exit 76, Elko, 461-7223.

Raceway Park, MN 101 between Savage & Shakopee, Shakopee, 445-2257.

Cultural Facilities

Theaters

Children's Theater Co, 2400 3rd Ave S, 874-0400.

Dudley Riggs, 2605 Hennepin Ave, 332-6620.

Guthrie Theater, 725 Vineland Pl, 377-2224.

Historic Orpheum Theater, 910 Hennipen Ave, 339-7007.

Historic State Theater, 805 Hennipen Ave, 339-7007.

Mixed Blood Theatre Co, 1501 S 4th St, 338-0937.

Showboat, University of Minnesota campus on Mississippi River, 625-4001.

Concert Halls

Minneapolis Convention Center, 1301 S 2nd Ave, 335-6000.

Northrop Memorial Auditorium, University of Minnesota, 625-6600.

Orchestra Hall, 1111 Nicollet Mall, 371-5656.

Museums

Bell Museum of Natural History, 17th Ave & University Ave SE, 624-7083.

Hennepin County Historical Society Museum, 2303 3rd Ave S, 870-1329.

Minneapolis Planetarium, 300 Nicollet Mall, at Public Library, 372-6644.

Minnesota Transportation Museum, W 42nd St & Queen Ave S, 228-0263.

Art Museums & Gallery

American Swedish Institute, 2600 Park Ave S, 871-4907.

Minneapolis Institute of Arts, 2400 3rd Ave S, 870-3131.

Walker Art Center, Vineland Pl, 375-7622.

Weisman Art Museum, 333 E River Rd, University of Minnesota, 625-9494.

Points of Interest

Historical

Minnehaha Depot, Minnehaha Ave near 49th St E.

Other Attractions

Buck Hill Ski Area, 14 mi S on I-35W, Burnsville, 435-7174.

Butler Square, 6th St & 1st Ave N.

Eloise Butler Wildflower Garden and Bird Sanctuary, Wirth Park, S of MN 55 (Olsen Memorial Hwy) on Theodore Wirth Pkwy, 348-4448.

Hyland Hills Ski Area, Chalet Rd, 2 mi SW off I-494, 835-4250 or 835-4604.

IDS Tower, 80 S 8th St.

Lyndale Park, off E Lake Harriet Pkwy & Roseway Rd, on NE shore of Lake Harriet.

Minneapolis City Hall, 5th St & 3rd Ave S, 673-2491.

Minneapolis Grain Exchange, 400 S 4th St, 338-6212.

Minneapolis Sculpture Garden, Vineland Pl, opp Walker Art Center.

Minnehaha Park, Minnehaha Pkwy & Hiawatha Ave S, 661-4806.

Minnesota Zoo, 20 mi S via I-35W to MN 77 in Apple Valley, 432-9000.

Mystic Lake Casino, 2400 Mystic Lake Blvd, 445-9000.

St Anthony Falls, Main St SE & Central Ave.

Valleyfair, 20 mi SW on MN 101, Shakopee, 445-6500.

Sightseeing Tours

Gray Line bus tours, 835 Decatur Ave N, 55427; 591-0999.

Minneapolis RiverCity Trolley, 33 S 6th St, 204-0000.

Annual Events

Aquatennial Festival, 377-4621. 10 days July.

Renaissance Festival, Shakopee, 445-7361. 7 wkends beginning mid-Aug.

St Paul

Area code: 612

Phone Numbers

POLICE: 911 or 291-1111; **FIRE:** 911 or 224-7811

POISON TREATMENT CENTER: 221-2113

TIME & WEATHER: 375-0830

Information Sources

St Paul Convention and Visitors Bureau, 102 Norwest Center, 55 E Fifth St, 55101; 297-6985.

"The Connection," Twin Cities information line, 922-9000.

Department of Parks & Recreation, 266-6400.

Transportation

AIRPORT: See Minneapolis.

CAR RENTAL AGENCIES: (See IMPORTANT TOLL-FREE NUMBERS) Avis 726-5220; Budget 726-9258; Hertz 726-1600; National 726-5600.

PUBLIC TRANSPORTATION: Metropolitan Transit Commission, 3118 Nicollet, Minneapolis 55807; 349-7000.

RAILROAD PASSENGER SERVICE: Amtrak 644-1127 or 800/872-7245.

Newspapers

Pioneer Press; Downtowner; Skyway News.

Convention Facility

RiverCentre, 143 W 4th St, 224-7361.

Sports & Recreation

Major Sports Facility

Roy Wilkins Auditorium at RiverCentre, 143 W 4th St, 224-7361.

Racetracks

See Minneapolis.

Cultural Facilities

Theaters

Great American History Theatre, Science Museum of Minnesota, 30 E 10th St, 292-4323.

Ordway Music Theatre, 345 Washington, 224-4222 or 282-3000.

Venetian Playhouse, 2814 Rice St, 484-7215.

Concert Hall

Roy Wilkins Auditorium at RiverCentre, 143 W 4th St, 224-7361.

Museums

Gibbs Farm Museum, 2097 W Larpenteur Ave, Falcon Heights, 646-8629.

Historic Fort Snelling, MN 5 & Post Rd, 725-2390.

Minnesota Children's Museum, 7th St & Wabash, 225-6000.

Minnesota History Center, 345 Kellogg Blvd W, 296-6126.

Science Museum of Minnesota & The William L. McKnight/3M Omnitheater, 30 E 10th St, 221-9444.

Sibley House Museum, 1357 Sibley Memorial Hwy, Mendota, 452-1596.

Art Museum

Minnesota Museum of Art, Landmark Center, 75 W 5th St, 292-4355; Jemne Building, St Peter St & Kellogg Blvd, 292-4355.

Points of Interest

Historical

Alexander Ramsey House, 265 S Exchange St, 296-8760.

Cathedral of St Paul, 239 Selby Ave, 228-1766.

Chapel of St Paul Site, Kellogg Blvd between Cedar & Minnesota Sts.

City Hall and Courthouse, 15 W Kellogg Blvd, 266-8023.

Mounds Park, Earl St & Mounds Blvd in Dayton's Bluff section, 266-6400.

James J. Hill Mansion, 240 Summit Ave, 297-2555.

Landmark Center, 75 W 5th St, 292-3228.

Old Muskego Church, Luther Seminary Campus, 2481 W Como Ave, 641-3456.

Ramsey Mill, MN 291 on Vermillion River, Hastings.

State Capitol, 75 Constitution Ave, 296-2881.

Other Attractions

Afton Alps Ski Area, 11 mi SE on US 10/61, Hastings, 436-5245.

Alexis Bailly Vineyard, 18200 Kirby Ave, Hastings, 437-1413.

Como Park, Midway & Lexington Pkwys, 266-6400.

Norwest Center Skyway, 56 E 6th St, 291-4751.

Town Square Park, 7th & Minnesota Sts, downtown, 266-6400.

Sightseeing Tours

Gray Line bus tours, 21160 Holyoke Ave N, Lakeville 55044; 469-5020.

Boat cruises, Harriet Island Park, W of Wabasha bridge, 227-1100.

Annual Events

Winter Carnival, throughout city, 223-4700. Last wkend Jan-1st wkend Feb.

Festival of Nations, Civic Center, 647-0191. Late Apr.

Macalester College Scottish Country Fair, Macalester College Shaw Field, Snelling & St Clair Aves, 696-6239. 1st Sat May.

Taste of Minnesota, Capitol Mall, 228-0018. Early July.

Minnesota State Fair, fairgrounds, Como & Snelling Aves, 642-2200. Late Aug-early Sept.

City Neighborhoods

Many of the restaurants, unrated dining establishments and some lodgings listed under Minneapolis and St Paul include neighborhoods as well as exact street addresses. Geographic descriptions of these areas are given, followed by a table of restaurants arranged by neighborhood.

Minneapolis

Downtown: South of 3rd St and the Mississippi River, west of I-35W, north of 16th St and east of Spruce Place. **North of Downtown:** North of Mississippi River. **South of Downtown:** South of 16th St.

Nicollet Mall: Downtown area from 16th St, along Nicollet Ave to Washington Ave.

St Paul

Downtown: South of 11th St, west of Jackson St, north of Kellogg Blvd and east of St Peter St. **North of Downtown: North of I-94. West of Downtown: West of St Peter St.**

Summit Hill: Adj to Rice Park; south of I-94, west of Kellogg Blvd, north of Summit Ave and east of Snelling Ave.

Rice Park: Area adj to Downtown; south of 11th St, west of St Peter St and north and east of Kellogg Blvd.

Lodgings and Food Minneapolis

MINNEAPOLIS RESTAURANTS BY NEIGHBORHOOD AREAS

(For full description, see alphabetical listings under Restaurants)

DOWNTOWN
510. 510 Groveland Ave
Backstage at Bravo. 900 Hennepin Ave
Buca Little Italy. 1204 Harmon Place
Cafe Brenda. 300 First Ave N
Cafe Un Deux Trois. 114 S Ninth St
Chez Bananas. 129 N Fourth St
D'Amico Cucina. 100 N Sixth St
Gardens of Salonica. 19 5th St NE
J.D. Hoyt's. 301 Washington Ave N
Linguini & Bob. 100 N Sixth St
Loring Cafe. 1624 Harmon Place
Meadows (Radisson Metrodome Hotel). 615 Washington Ave SE
Murray's. 26 S Sixth St
New French Cafe & Bar. 128 N Fourth St
Origami. 30 N First St
Palomino. 825 Hennepin Ave
Pickled Parrot. 26 N Fifth St
Ruth's Chris Steak House. 920 Second Ave S
Sawatdee. 607 Washington Ave S
Shuang Cheng. 1320 SE Fourth St
Song Thanh. 418 13th Ave SE
Table of Contents. 1310 Hennepin Ave
Whitney Grille (Whitney Hotel). 150 Portland Ave

NORTH OF DOWNTOWN
Emily's Lebanese Deli. 641 University Ave NE
Giorgio. 2451 Hennepin Ave
Jax Cafe. 1928 University Ave NE
Kikugawa. 43 SE Main St
Nye's Polonnaise. 112 E Hennepin Ave
Pracna on Main. 117 Main St
Sidney's Pizza Cafe. 2120 Hennepin Ave
Sophia. 65 SE Main St

SOUTH OF DOWNTOWN
Black Forest Inn. 1 E 26th St
Campiello. 1320 W Lake St
Caravelle. 2529 Nicollet Ave S
Christos. 2632 Nicollet Ave S
Figlio. 3001 Hennepin Ave S
It's Greek to Me. 626 W Lake St
Lowry's. 1934 Hennepin Ave S
Lucia's. 1432 W 31st St
Mud Pie. 2549 Lyndale Ave S
New French Bistrot. 1300 Lagoon Ave

NICOLLET AVE MALL AREA
1313 Nicollet (Regal Minneapolis Hotel). 1313 Nicollet Mall
Goodfellow's. 40 S 7th St
Ichiban Japanese Steak House. 1333 Nicollet Mall Ave
Jerusalem's. 1518 Nicollet Ave
The King & I. 1034 Nicollet Ave
Manny's (Hyatt Regency Hotel). 1300 Nicollet Mall
Market Bar-B-Que. 1414 Nicollet Ave S
Morton's of Chicago. 555 Nicollet Mall
Ping's. 1401 Nicollet Ave S
Pronto (Hyatt Regency Hotel). 1300 Nicollet Mall

Note: When a listing is located in a town that does not have its own city heading, it will appear under the city nearest to its location. In these cases, the address and town appear in parenthesis immediately following the name of the establishment.

Motels

★ **AMERICINN OF ROGERS.** *(Jct 1-94 & MN 101, Rogers 55374) 612/428-4346; res: 800/634-3444.* 35 rms, 2 story. S $39.90-$48.90; D $46.90-$57.90; each addl $5; whirlpool rms $89.90-$109.90; under 12 free. Crib free. Pet accepted. TV; cable (premium), VCR. Complimentary continental bkfst. Restaurant adj open 24 hrs. Ck-out 11 am. Business servs avail. Cr cds: A, C, D, DS, MC, V.

D SC

★ **AQUA CITY.** *5739 Lyndale Ave S (55419), south of downtown. 612/861-6061; res: 800/861-6061.* 37 rms, 1-2 story, 8 kit. units. S $35-$42; D $45-$50; each addl $5; under 5 free. Crib $5. TV; cable (premium). Complimentary coffee. Restaurant nearby. Ck-out 11 am. X-country ski 1/2 mi. Game rm. Cr cds: A, C, D, DS, MC, V.

SC

★ ★ **BEST WESTERN KELLY INN.** *(2705 Annapolis, Plymouth 55441) 612/553-1600; FAX 612/553-9108.* 150 rms, 4 story. S $69-$200; D $75-$200; each addl $8; suites $91-$200; under 13 free. Crib $8. TV; cable. Indoor pool; whirlpool. Complimentary coffee in rms. Restaurant 7 am-midnight. Rm serv. Bar 11-1 am. Ck-out 11 am. Meeting rms. Business servs avail. Downhill ski 20 mi; x-country ski 1 mi. Exercise equipt; bicycles, treadmill, sauna. Some refrigerators. Some balconies. Cr cds: A, C, D, DS, MC, V.

D SC

✔★ **BUDGETEL INN.** *(6415 James Circle, Brooklyn Center 55430) 18 mi N on I-694, change at Shingle Creek Pkwy. 612/561-8400; FAX 612/560-3189.* 99 rms, 3 story. S $43.95-$66.95; D $51.95-$74.95. Crib free. TV; cable (premium). Complimentary continental bkfst. Complimentary coffee in rms. Restaurant nearby. Ck-out noon. Meeting rm. Business servs avail. In-rm modem link. Valet serv. X-country ski 1/2 mi. Cr cds: A, C, D, DS, MC, V.

D SC

★ ★ **CHANHASSEN INN.** *(531 W 79th St, Chanhassen 55317) 3 mi S on MN 101. 612/934-7373; res: 800/242-6466.* 74 rms, 2 story. S $45-$50; D $51-$55; each addl $4; under 17 free. Crib free. TV; cable. Complimentary continental bkfst. Ck-out noon. Business servs avail. In-rm modem link. X-country ski 1 mi. Cr cds: A, C, D, DS, MC, V.

D SC

★ ★ **COMFORT INN.** *(1600 James Circle N, Brooklyn Center 55430) N on US 52. 612/560-7464.* 60 rms, 3 story. June-Sept: S $74.95-$79.95; D $79.95-$84.95; each addl $5; under 19 free; lower rates rest of yr. TV; cable (premium). Complimentary continental bkfst. Restaurant adj 6 am-11 pm. Ck-out 11 am. Meeting rms. Business servs avail. Game rm. Some refrigerators, microwaves. Cr cds: A, C, D, DS, MC, V.

SC

★ **DAYS INN UNIVERSITY.** *2407 University Ave SE (55414), east of downtown. 612/623-3999; FAX 612/331-2152.* 131 rms, 6 story. S $73-$99; D $79-$99; each addl $10; under 18 free. Crib free. TV; cable. Complimentary continental bkfst. Restaurant nearby. Ck-out 11 am. Coin lndry. Meeting rms. Business servs avail. In-rm modem link. Downhill ski 10 mi; x-country ski 1 mi. Some refrigerators. Cr cds: A, C, D, DS, JCB, MC, V.

SC

✔★ **ECONO LODGE.** *2500 University Ave SE (55414), east of downtown. 612/331-6000; FAX 612/331-6821.* 80 rms, 2 story. May-Sept: S $55-$65; D $61-$71; each addl $6; under 18 free; lower rates rest of yr. Crib free. TV; cable (premium). Complimentary coffee in rms. Restaurant nearby. Ck-out 11 am. Business servs avail. In-rm modem link. Pool. Cr cds: A, C, D, DS, JCB, MC, V.

D SC

★ ★ **HAMPTON INN.** *10420 Wayzata Blvd (55343), west of downtown. 612/541-1094; FAX 612/541-1905.* 127 rms, 4 story. S, D $74-$84; under 18 free. Crib free. TV; cable (premium). Complimentary continental bkfst. Restaurant nearby. Ck-out noon. Meeting rms. Business servs avail. In-rm modem link. Downhill ski 25 mi; x-country ski 1 mi. Cr cds: A, C, D, DS, MC, V.

D SC

✓★ **METRO INN.** *5637 Lyndale Ave S (55419), south of downtown. 612/861-6011; FAX 612/869-1041.* 35 rms. Apr-Oct: S $35-$44; D $42-$52; each addl $6; lower rates rest of yr. Crib $4-$5. Pet accepted, some restrictions; $3. TV; cable (premium). Ck-out 11 am. X-country ski 1/2 mi. Cr cds: A, C, D, DS, MC, V.

SC

✓★ ★ **MOUNDS VIEW INN.** *(2149 Program Ave, Mounds View 55112) Jct I-35W & US 10. 612/786-9151; FAX 612/786-2845; res: 800/777-7863.* 70 rms, 2 story. S $35.95-$49.95; D $43.95-$61.95; each addl $5; under 15 free; higher rates special events. Crib $3. TV; cable (premium), VCR (movies). Complimentary continental bkfst. Restaurant adj open 24 hrs. Bar. Ck-out 11 am. Coin Indry. Meeting rms. Business servs avail. Sundries. X-country ski 3 mi. Cr cds: A, C, D, DS, MC, V.

D SC

★ ★ **REGENCY PLAZA-TARGET CENTER.** *41 N 10th St (55403), 3 blks W of Nicollet Mall, downtown. 612/339-9311; FAX 612/339-4765.* 192 rms, 3 story. S, D $59-$109; each addl $6; suites $85-$110; under 18 free; wkend rates. Crib free. TV; cable, VCR avail. Indoor pool; whirlpool, poolside serv. Restaurant 6:30 am-2 pm, 4-11 pm; Sat, Sun from 7:30 am. Rm serv. Bar 4 pm-1 am; entertainment exc Sun. Ck-out noon. Coin Indry. Meeting rms. Business servs avail. In-rm modem link. Bellhops. Sundries. X-country ski 1 mi. Cr cds: A, C, D, DS, MC, V.

SC

✓★ **SUPER 8.** *(6445 James Circle, Brooklyn Center 55430) jct I-94, I-694 & Shingle Creek Pkwy interchange exit 34. 612/566-9810; FAX 612/566-8680.* 102 rms, 2 story. S $51.98; D $56.98-$61.98; each addl $5; under 12 free. Crib free. TV; cable (premium). Complimentary continental bkfst. Restaurant adj. Ck-out 11 am. Business servs avail. Cr cds: A, C, D, DS, MC, V.

D SC

Motor Hotels

★ ★ **BEST WESTERN KELLY INN.** *(5201 Central Ave NE, Fridley 55421) 612/571-9440; FAX 612/571-1720.* 95 rms, 2 story. S, D $64-$72; each addl $8; suites $105-$185; under 18 free. Crib free. Pet accepted. TV; cable (premium). Indoor pool; whirlpool. Restaurant 6 am-9 pm. Rm serv. Ck-out 11 am. Meeting rms. Business servs avail. Exercise equipt; weight machine, bicycles, sauna. Game rm. Some refrigerators. Cr cds: A, D, DS, MC, V.

D SC

✓★ ★ ★ **BEST WESTERN NORMANDY INN.** *405 S Eighth St (55404), downtown. 612/370-1400; FAX 612/370-0351.* 159 rms, 4 story. S $74.50-$104.50; D $82-$108.50; each addl $7.50; under 18 free. Crib free. TV; cable (premium). Indoor pool; whirlpool, poolside serv. Complimentary continental bkfst. Bar 4:30-11 pm. Ck-out noon. Meeting rms. Business servs avail. In-rm modem link. Valet serv. Sundries. Exercise equipt; bicycles, treadmill, sauna. Cr cds: A, C, D, DS, ER, MC, V.

D SC

★ ★ **RAMADA INN.** *2540 N Cleveland Ave (55113). 612/636-4567; FAX 612/636-7110.* 256 rms, 4 story. June-Labor Day: S, D $89; each addl $10; under 19 free; lower rates rest of yr. Crib free. TV; cable. Indoor pool; wading pool, whirlpool. Complimentary coffee in rms. Restaurant 6:30 am-10 pm. Rm serv. Bar 3 pm-1 am. Ck-out noon. Meeting rms. Business servs avail. Valet serv. Coin Indry. Exercise equipt; bicycle, treadmill, sauna. Game rm. Some refrigerators. Cr cds: A, C, D, DS, ER, JCB, MC, V.

D SC

★ ★ ★ **RAMADA PLAZA HOTEL.** *(12201 Ridgedale Dr, Minnetonka 55305) W on Wayzata Blvd, behind Ridgedale Shopping Center. 612/593-0000; FAX 612/544-2090.* 222 rms, 4 story. S $119; D $129; each addl $10; suites $150; under 18 free; wkend rates. Crib free. TV; cable (premium). Indoor pool; poolside serv. Coffee in rms. Restaurant 6:30 am-10 pm. Rm serv 6:30-10 pm. Bar 4 pm-1 am. Ck-out noon. Meeting rms. Business servs avail. In-rm modem link. Gift shop. X-country ski 2 mi. Exercise equipt; bicycles, stair machines. Some private patios, balconies. Cr cds: A, C, D, DS, ER, JCB, MC, V.

D SC

Hotels

★ ★ ★ **DOUBLETREE.** *1101 LaSalle Ave (55403), downtown. 612/332-6800; FAX 612/332-8246.* 230 suites, 12 story. S, D $175; each addl $10; under 17 free; wkend rates. Covered parking $9. Crib free. TV; cable (premium), VCR avail. Restaurant 6:30 am-midnight. Bar 11-1 am. Ck-out 11 am. Meeting rms. Business servs avail. In-rm modem link. Exercise equipt; weights, bicycles, sauna. X-country ski 1 mi. Refrigerators, microwaves. Cr cds: A, C, D, DS, JCB, MC, V.

D SC

★ ★ ★ **EMBASSY SUITES-DOWNTOWN.** *425 S Seventh St (55415), downtown. 612/333-3111; FAX 612/333-7984.* 217 suites, 6 story. S $155-$165; D $165-$185; each addl $10; under 13 free; wkend rates. Crib free. TV; cable (premium). Indoor pool; whirlpool. Complimentary full bkfst. Restaurant 11 am-2:30 pm, 5-10 pm; Fri, Sat 5-11 pm. Bar 11-1 am. Ck-out noon. Meeting rms. Business servs avail. In-rm modem link. X-country ski 1 mi. Exercise equipt; weight machine, bicycles, sauna, steam rm. Refrigerators, microwaves. Cr cds: A, C, D, DS, ER, JCB, MC, V.

D SC

★ ★ ★ **HILTON & TOWERS.** *1001 Marquette Ave S (55403). 612/376-1000; FAX 612/397-4875.* 814 rms, 25 story. S $140-$215; D $160-$235; each addl $20; suites $700-$1,000; under 18 free. Crib avail. Valet parking $15; garage $9.75. TV; cable (premium), VCR avail. Heated pool; whirlpool, poolside serv. Restaurant 6:30 am-11 pm. Bar 11-1 am. Ck-out noon. Convention facilities. Business servs avail. In-rm modem link. Concierge. Sundries. Shopping arcade. X-country ski 1 mi. Exercise equipt; bicycle, treadmill, sauna. Some refrigerators. Cr cds: A, C, D, DS, ER, JCB, MC, V.

D

★ ★ ★ **HOLIDAY INN CROWNE PLAZA NORTHSTAR.** *618 Second Ave S (55402), above 6-story Northstar Parking Ramp, downtown. 612/338-2288; FAX 612/338-2288, ext. 318.* 226 rms, 17 story. June-Sept: S $159.50-$174.50; each addl $15; suites $250-$500; under 17 free; wkend rates; lower rates rest of yr. Crib free. Garage parking $11.50. TV; cable, VCR avail (movies). Restaurants 6:30 am-11:30 pm. Bar 11-1 am. Ck-out 1 pm. Meeting rms. Business servs avail. In-rm modem link. Barber, beauty shop. X-country ski 1 mi. Exercise equipt; bicycles, rowers. Luxury level. Cr cds: A, C, D, DS, MC, V.

D SC

✓★ ★ ★ **HOLIDAY INN-METRODOME.** *1500 Washington Ave S (55454), south of downtown. 612/333-4646; FAX 612/333-7910.* 265 rms, 14 story. S, D $134.50; each addl $10; suites $149.50; under 18 free. Crib free. Garage $8. TV; cable (premium), VCR avail. Indoor pool. Coffee in rms. Restaurant 6:30 am-11 pm. Bar 11-1 am; pianist. Ck-out noon. Meeting rms. Business servs avail. In-rm modem link. Gift shop. Airport transportation. Exercise equipt; weights, bicycles. Cr cds: A, C, D, DS, JCB, MC, V.

D SC

★ ★ ★ **HYATT REGENCY.** *1300 Nicollet Mall (55403), in Nicollet Ave Mall Area. 612/370-1234; FAX 612/370-1463.* 533 rms, 21 suites, 24 story. S $199; D $224; each addl $25; suites $290-$800; under 18 free. Crib free. Parking $9.75. TV; VCR avail (movies). Indoor pool. Restaurants 6:30-1 am; Sun 7 am-11 pm (also see MANNY'S and PRONTO). Bar 11-1 am. Ck-out noon. Convention facilities. Business servs avail. In-rm modem link. Concierge. Shopping arcade. Barber, beauty shop. Airport transportation. Indoor tennis privileges. X-country ski 1 mi. Health club privileges. Luxury level. Cr cds: A, C, D, DS, ER, JCB, MC, V.

D SC

★ ★ ★ **THE MARQUETTE.** *710 Marquette Ave (55402), in IDS Tower, downtown. 612/333-4545; res: 800/328-4782; FAX 612/376-7419.* 278 rms, 19 story. S $228; D $248; each addl $15; suites $349-$810; family rates; wkend packages. Crib free. Garage parking $12; wkends $6. TV; cable (premium), VCR avail. Restaurant 6:30 am-10:30 pm. Bar 11:30-1 am. Ck-out noon. Convention facilities. Business center. In-rm modem link. X-country ski 1 mi. Exercise equipt; weight machines, treadmills. Steam bath in suites. Luxury level. Cr cds: A, C, D, DS, ER, JCB, MC, V.

D

★ ★ ★ **MARRIOTT-CITY CENTER.** *30 S Seventh St (55402), downtown. 612/349-4000; FAX 612/332-7165.* 583 rms, 31 story. S $169; D $189; each addl $10; suites $250-$650; under 18 free; wkend rates. Crib free. Valet parking $17. TV; cable (premium), VCR avail (movies). Restaurants 6:30 am-11 pm. Bar 11-1 am. Ck-out noon. Convention facilities. Business center. In-rm modem link. Shopping arcade. X-country ski 1 mi. Exercise rm; instructor, weights, treadmills, sauna. Massage. Health club privileges. Whirlpool. Some bathrm phones. Luxury level. Cr cds: A, C, D, DS, ER, JCB, MC, V.

D SC

★ ★ ★ **NORTHLAND INN.** *(7025 Northland Dr, Brooklyn Park 55428) 612/536-8300; FAX 612/533-6607; res: 800/441-6422.* 231 rms, 6 story. S, D $125-$195; under 12 free. Crib free. TV; cable (premium), VCR avail. Indoor pool; whirlpool, poolside serv. Restaurant 6:30 am-10 pm. Bar to 1 am. Ck-out noon. Meeting rms. Business servs avail. In-rm modem link. Concierge. Sundries. Gift shop. Valet serv. Downhill ski 20 mi; x-country 1 mi. Exercise equipt; weight machine, bicycles. Game rm. Refrigerators avail. Cr cds: A, C, D, DS, JCB, MC, V.

D

★ ★ ★ **RADISSON HOTEL & CONFERENCE CENTER.** *(3131 Campus Dr, Plymouth 55441) jct I-494, MN 55, on Northwest Business Campus. 612/559-6600; FAX 612/559-1053.* 243 rms, 6 story, 6 suites. S, D $124; each addl $10; suites $159-$249; under 18 free. Crib free. TV; cable (premium), VCR avail. Indoor pool; whirlpool, poolside serv. Restaurant 6:30 am-10 pm. Bar 11-1 am. Ck-out noon. Meeting rms. Business servs avail. In-rm modem link. Gift shop. Lighted tennis. Downhill ski 20 mi; x-country ski 2 mi. Exercise rm; instructor, weight machines, bicycles, sauna. Racquetball. Rec rm. Refrigerators. On wooded site. Cr cds: A, C, D, DS, ER, JCB, MC, V.

D SC

★ ★ ★ **RADISSON-METRODOME.** *615 Washington Ave SE (55414). 612/379-8888; FAX 612/379-8436.* 304 rms, 8 story. S $102; D $112; each addl $10; suites $135-$325; under 18 free. Crib avail. Pet accepted. Valet parking $9.50; garage $6.50. TV; cable, VCR avail. Pool privileges. Complimentary coffee in rms. Restaurants 6:30 am-10:30 pm (also see MEADOWS). Bar to 1 am. Ck-out noon. Meeting rms. Business servs avail. In-rm modem link. Gift shop. Downhill ski 20 mi; x-country ski 1 mi. Exercise equipt; bicycle, weights. Health club privileges. Some refrigerators. Cr cds: A, C, D, DS, ER, JCB, MC, V.

D

★ ★ ★ **RADISSON PLAZA.** *35 S Seventh St (55402), downtown. 612/339-4900; FAX 612/337-9766.* 357 rms, 17 story. S, D $178-$258; each addl $10; suites $310-$410; under 18 free. Crib free. Parking $10. TV; cable (premium), VCR avail. Restaurant 6 am-11 pm. Rm serv 24 hrs. Bar 11-1 am; entertainment. Ck-out noon. Meeting rms. Business servs avail. In-rm modem link. Concierge. Shopping arcade. X-country ski 1 mi. Exercise rm; instructor, weights, bicycles, sauna. Whirlpool. Atrium lobby; fountain, marble columns. Luxury level. Cr cds: A, C, D, DS, ER, JCB, MC, V.

D SC

★ ★ ★ **REGAL MINNEAPOLIS.** *1313 Nicollet Mall (55403), in Nicollet Ave Mall Area. 612/332-6000; FAX 612/359-2160; res: 800/522-8856.* 325 rms, 14 story. S $175; D $195; suites $190-$250. Crib free. Pet accepted. TV; cable (premium). Indoor pool. Restaurant (see 1313 NICOLLET). Bars 11-1 am. Ck-out noon. Coin Indry. Convention facilities. Business servs avail. In-rm modem link. Gift shop. Airport transportation avail. X-country ski 1 mi. Exercise equipt; weight machine, bicycle, sauna. Cr cds: A, C, D, DS, ER, JCB, MC, V.

D SC

★ ★ ★ **SHERATON-METRODOME.** *1330 Industrial Blvd (55413), north of downtown. 612/331-1900; FAX 612/331-6827.* 252 rms, 8 story. S $105-$145; D, studio rms $115-$195; each addl $10; suites $150-$280; wkend packages. Crib free. TV; cable (premium). Indoor pool; whirlpool, poolside serv. Coffee in rms. Restaurant 6:30 am-10:30 pm; Sat, Sun 7:30-11 pm. Bar 11-1 am; entertainment exc Sun. Ck-out 11 am. Meeting rms. Business servs avail. In-rm modem link. Free airport transportation. X-country ski 1 mi. Exercise equipt; bicycles, treadmill, sauna. Luxury level. Cr cds: A, C, D, DS, ER, JCB, MC, V.

D SC

★ ★ ★ **SHERATON-PARK PLACE.** *1500 Park Place Blvd (55416), north of downtown. 612/542-8600; FAX 612/542-8068.* 298 rms, 15 story. S, D $99-$129; each addl $20; suites $129-$169; under 18 free; wkend rates. Crib free. TV; cable (premium), VCR avail. Indoor pool; whirlpool, poolside serv. Restaurant 6:30 am-midnight. Rm serv 24 hrs. Bar 11-1 am. Ck-out noon. Convention facilities. Business servs avail. In-rm modem link. Airport transportation. X-country ski 2 mi. Exercise equipt; weights, bicycles, sauna. Game rm. Cr cds: A, C, D, DS, ER, JCB, MC, V.

D SC

★ ★ ★ **WHITNEY.** *150 Portland Ave (55401), downtown. 612/339-9300; FAX 612/339-1333; res: 800/248-1879.* 97 rms, 8 story, 40 suites. S, D $160-$170; suites 195-$1,600; under 10 free. Crib free. Parking $6. TV; cable (premium), VCR avail. Restaurant (see WHITNEY GRILLE). Rm serv 24 hrs. Bar 11:30-1 am; pianist. Ck-out noon. Meeting rms. Business servs avail. In-rm modem link. Concierge. Airport transportation. Bathrm phones, refrigerators. Bi-level suites with honor bar. Elegantly renovated hotel located on the banks of the Mississippi River; outdoor plaza with fountain. Cr cds: A, C, D, DS, ER, JCB, MC, V.

D

Inns

★ ★ ★ **INN ON THE FARM.** *(6150 Summit Dr N, Brooklyn Center 55430) 612/569-6330; res: 800/428-8382.* 10 rms, 2 story. S, D $100-$130. TV. Complimentary full bkfst; afternoon refreshments. Restaurant nearby. Ck-out 11 am, ck-in 4 pm. Business servs avail. X-country ski 1/2 mi. Built in the 1880s; furnished with antiques. Cr cds: A, C, D, DS, MC, V.

★ ★ **NICOLLET ISLAND INN.** *95 Merriam St (55401), east of downtown. 612/331-1800; FAX 612/331-6528.* 24 rms, 2 story. S, D $115-$254; under 12 free. TV; cable (premium). Complimentary continental bkfst. Restaurant 6 am-10 pm. Rm serv. Ck-out 1 pm, ck-in 3 pm. Business servs avail. In-rm modem link. Downhill ski 20 mi; x-country ski 10 mi. Built in 1893. Cr cds: A, C, D, DS, MC, V.

Restaurants

★ ★ **1313 NICOLLET.** *(See Regal Minneapolis Hotel) 612/332-6000.* Hrs: 6:30 am-2 pm, 5-10 pm. Res accepted. Bar to 1 am. Semi-a la carte: bkfst $6.25-$7.50, lunch $6.25-$8.50, dinner $7.50-$16.95. Child's meals. Specializes in pasta, steak. Contemporary decor. Cr cds: A, C, D, DS, ER, JCB, MC, V.

★ ★ ★ **510.** *510 Groveland Ave, downtown. 612/874-6440.* Hrs: 5:30-10 pm. Closed Sun. Res accepted. French, Amer menu. Wine cellar. Semi-a la carte: dinner $12-$22. Complete meals: dinner $19. Specializes in rack of lamb, seafood. Own baking. Cr cds: A, C, D, DS, MC, V.

D

★ ★ **AUGUST MOON.** *(5340 Watzata Blvd, Golden Valley) Approx 3 mi W on MN 55. 612/544-7017.* Hrs: 11 am-9 pm; Fri to 10 pm; Sat 4-10 pm; Sun 4-9 pm. Closed Dec 25. New Asian menu. Wine, beer. Semi-a la carte: lunch $5-$11.95, dinner $8-$15. Specialties: Cal-Asian crab cakes, tandoori chicken. Parking. Oriental artwork. Cr cds: A, C, D, MC, V.

D

★ ★ **BACKSTAGE AT BRAVO.** *900 Hennepin Ave (55403), downtown. 612/338-0062.* Hrs: 11:30 am-2:30 pm, 5-11:30 pm; Fri to 12:30 am; Sat to midnight. Closed Thanksgiving, Dec 24, 25. Res accepted. Continental menu. Bar. Semi-a la carte: lunch $5.95-$18.50, dinner $12.50-$25. Specializes in fresh oysters, steak. Own pasta. Valet parking (dinner). Outdoor dining. Contemporary decor with rooftop dining. Cr cds: A, C, D, DS, MC, V.

D

✔★ ★ **BLACK FOREST INN.** *1 E 26th St, at Nicollet, south of downtown. 612/872-0812.* Hrs: 11-1 am; Sun noon-midnight. German menu. Semi-a la carte: lunch $3.50-$8, dinner $5.50-$15. Specialties: sauerbraten, Wienerschnitzel, bratwurst. Outdoor dining. German decor. Family-owned. Cr cds: A, C, D, DS, MC, V.

✔★ ★ **BUCA LITTLE ITALY.** *1204 Harmon Place (55403), downtown. 612/638-2225.* Hrs: 5-10 pm; Fri, Sat to 11 pm. Closed Thanksgiving, Dec 24, 25. Italian menu. Bar to midnight. Semi-a la carte: dinner $8.95-$22.95. Specialties: chicken marsala, ravioli with meat sauce. Pictures of Italian celebrities along walls. Cr cds: A, C, D, MC, V.

✔★ ★ **CAFE BRENDA.** *300 First Ave N, downtown. 612/342-9230.* Hrs: 11:30 am-2 pm, 5:30-9 pm; Fri to 10 pm; Sat 5:30-10 pm. Closed Sun; most major hols. Res accepted. Vegetarian, seafood menu. Bar. Semi-a la carte: lunch $6-$10, dinner $9-$16. Specializes in fresh broiled rainbow trout, organic chicken enchiladas. Parking (dinner). Totally nonsmoking. Cr cds: A, C, D, MC, V.

★ ★ **CAFE UN DEUX TROIS.** *114 S Ninth St (55402), downtown. 612/673-0686.* Hrs: 11:30 am-10 pm; Fri, Sat to 11 pm. Closed Sun; most major hols. Res accepted. French bistro menu. Bar. Semi-a la carte: lunch $7.95-$17.50, dinner $12.95-$19.50. Specialties: poulet rôti, roast Long Island duck. Own pasta. Free valet parking (dinner). Eclectic, bistro atmosphere with murals, mirrors on walls. Cr cds: A, C, D, MC, V.

D

★ **CAMPIELLO.** *1320 W Lake St (55408), 5 mi S on Lake St, south of downtown. 612/825-2222.* Hrs: 5-10 pm; Thurs to 10:30 pm; Fri, Sat to 11 pm; Sun 10:30 am-3 pm (brunch), 5-10:30 pm. Closed Dec 25. Res accepted. Italian menu. Bar to midnight. Semi-a la carte: dinner $8.95-$17.95. Sun brunch $8.95-$13.95. Specialties: balsamic-glazed short ribs, wood-oven pizzas. Own pasta. Valet parking. Outdoor dining. Upscale atmosphere with high ceilings, chandeliers. Cr cds: A, C, D, DS, MC, V.

✔★ **CARAVELLE.** *2529 Nicollet Ave S, south of downtown. 612/871-3226.* Hrs: 11 am-9 pm; Sat from noon; Sun noon-7 pm. Closed July 4, Thanksgiving, Dec 25. Res accepted. Chinese menu. Semi-a la carte: lunch, dinner $5.95-$8.95. Buffet: lunch $5.50, dinner $5.95. Specializes in shrimp, scallops. Parking. Outdoor dining. Oriental decor. Cr cds: MC, V.

★ **CHEZ BANANAS.** *129 N Fourth St, downtown. 612/340-0032.* Hrs: 11:30 am-10 pm; Fri to 11 pm; Sat, Sun 5-11 pm. Closed some major hols. Res accepted Sun-Thurs. Caribbean menu. Bar. Semi-a la carte: lunch $4.50-$9, dinner $6.50-$15. Specializes in mustard pepper chicken, Caribbean barbecue. Informal & fun atmosphere; inflatable animals hanging from ceiling, toys at tables. Cr cds: A, MC, V.

✔★ **CHRISTOS.** *2632 Nicollet Ave S, south of downtown. 612/871-2111.* Hrs: 11 am-10 pm; Fri to 10:30 pm; Sat noon-10:30 pm; Sun noon-9 pm. Closed most major hols. Res accepted. Greek menu. Wine, beer. Semi-a la carte: lunch $4.50-$7.50, dinner $7.95-$12.95. Specialties: spanakópita, moussaka, shish kebab. Cr cds: A, C, D, DS, MC, V.

★ ★ ★ **D'AMICO CUCINA.** *100 N Sixth St, downtown. 612/338-2401.* Hrs: 5:30-10 pm; Fri, Sat to 11 pm; Sun 5-9 pm. Closed major hols. Res accepted. Italian menu. Bar. Semi-a la carte: dinner $21-$29.50. Specializes in Modern Italian cuisine. Piano, bass Fri, Sat. Restored warehouse. Cr cds: A, C, D, DS, MC, V.

D

★ **FIGLIO.** *3001 Hennepin Ave S, Calhoun Square, south of downtown. 612/822-1688.* Hrs: 11:30-1 am; Fri, Sat to 2 am. Res accepted. Italian menu. Bar. Semi-a la carte: lunch, dinner $6.50-$16.95. Specializes in pasta, pizza, sandwiches. Outdoor dining. Art-deco decor; neon lighting. Cr cds: A, C, D, DS, MC, V.

✔★ **GARDENS OF SALONICA.** *19 5th St NE (55413), downtown. 612/378-0611.* Hrs: 11 am-9 pm; Fri, Sat to 10 pm. Closed Sun; Thanksgiving, Dec 25. Greek menu. Bar. Semi-a la carte: lunch, dinner $5-$10. Specilizes in boughatsa, lamb dishes. Own pasta. Casual dining; Greek decor. No cr cds accepted.

✔★ ★ **GIORGIO.** *2451 Hennepin Ave (55408), north of downtown. 612/374-5131.* Hrs: 11:30 am-2:30 pm, 5-11 pm; Sun 5-11 pm. Closed Thanksgiving, Dec 24, 25. Res accepted wkdays. Italian menu. Wine, beer. Semi-a la carte: lunch $2.95-$10.95, dinner $2.95-$16.50. Specialties: marinated leg of lamb, calamari steak. Outdoor dining. Italian decor. Cr cds: D, MC, V.

★ ★ ★ **GOODFELLOW'S.** *40 S 7th St, in Nicollet Ave Mall Area. 612/332-4800.* Hrs: 11:30 am-2 pm, 5:30-9 pm; Fri to 10 pm; Sat 5:30-10 pm. Closed Sun; major hols. Res accepted. Bar. Wine list. Semi-a la carte: lunch $6-$13, dinner $20-$31. Specialties: grilled salmon, hickory-grilled Wisconsin veal chop. Beamed ceiling. Cr cds: A, C, D, DS, MC, V.

★ ★ **ICHIBAN JAPANESE STEAK HOUSE.** *1333 Nicollet Mall Ave, in Nicollet Ave Mall Area. 612/339-0540.* Hrs: 4:30-9:30 pm; Fri, Sat to 10 pm. Closed Thanksgiving, Dec 24. Res accepted. Japanese menu. Bar. Semi-a la carte: dinner $13.95-$29.50. Specializes in sushi, tempura. Tableside cooking. Japanese decor. Cr cds: A, C, D, DS, MC, V.

✔★ **IT'S GREEK TO ME.** *626 W Lake St, south of downtown. 612/825-9922.* Hrs: 11 am-11 pm. Closed major hols. Greek menu. Bar. Semi-a la carte: lunch, dinner $7.75-$13.95. Specialties: lamb kebab, pastitsio. Parking. Cr cds: MC, V.

★ ★ **J.D. HOYT'S.** *301 Washington Ave N, downtown. 612/338-1560.* Hrs: 7-1 am; Sat from 7:30 am; Sun 10 am-midnight; Sun brunch 10 am-2 pm. Closed some major hols. Res accepted. Bar. Semi-a la carte: bkfst $1.99-$7, lunch $7.50-$9.95, dinner $8-$27.95. Sun brunch $9.95. Specializes in pork chops, charcoal-grilled steak. Valet parking. Casual dining; roadhouse atmosphere. Cr cds: A, C, D, DS, MC, V.

★ ★ ★ **JAX CAFE.** *1928 University Ave NE, north of downtown. 612/789-7297.* Hrs: 11 am-10:30 pm; Sun to 9 pm; Sun brunch 10 am-1:30 pm. Closed major hols. Res accepted. Wine list. Semi-a la carte: lunch $6.95-$12.95, dinner $14-$25. Sun brunch $14.50. Specializes in prime rib, seafood, rainbow trout (in season). Pianist Thurs-Sun. Parking. Overlooks trout pond; waterwheel. Fireplace. Family-owned. Cr cds: A, C, D, DS, MC, V.

✔★ **JERUSALEM'S.** *1518 Nicollet Ave (55403), in Nicollet Ave Mall Area. 612/871-8883.* Hrs: 11 am-10 pm; Fri to 11 pm; Sat, Sun noon-10 pm. Closed Thanksgiving, Dec 25. Res accepted. Middle Eastern menu. Bar. Semi-a la carte: lunch $4.25-$8.25, dinner $9.95-$15.95. Specializes in vegetarian combination. Middle Eastern tapestries on walls. Cr cds: D, DS, MC, V.

★ ★ **KIKUGAWA.** *43 SE Main St, Riverplace, north of downtown. 612/378-3006.* Hrs: 11:30 am-2 pm, 5-10 pm; Sat noon-2 pm, 5-11 pm; Sun noon-2:30 pm, 4:30-9:30 pm. Closed Jan 1, Thanksgiving, Dec 25. Res accepted. Japanese menu. Bar. Semi-a la carte: lunch $4.95-$10, dinner $9.50-$26.50. Specialties: sukiyaki, sushi bar. Parking. Modern Japanese decor. Overlooks Mississippi River. Cr cds: A, C, D, DS, JCB, MC, V.

✔★ **THE KING & I.** *1034 Nicollet Ave, in Nicollet Ave Mall Area. 612/332-6928.* Hrs: 11 am-10 pm; Sat from 5 pm. Closed Sun. Res accepted. Thai menu. Wine, beer. Semi-a la carte: lunch, dinner $7.25-$17.95. Specialties: pad Thai, king's spring roll, tom yum goong. Informal dining. Cr cds: A, C, D, DS, MC, V.

D

★ ★ **LINGUINI & BOB.** *100 N Sixth St, downtown. 612/332-1600.* Hrs: 5-9:30 pm; Fri, Sat to 11 pm. Closed Sun; most major hols. Res accepted. Italian menu. Bar. Semi-a la carte: dinner $8.95-$17.95. Specializes in spicy shrimp, pasta. 2nd floor overlooks Butler Square. Cr cds: A, C, D, MC, V.

★ ★ ★ **LORD FLETCHER'S OF THE LAKE.** *(3746 Sunset Dr, Spring Park) 18 mi W on US 12, 6 mi S on County 15W, then 1/2 mi N on County 19 to signs, on Lake Minnetonka. 612/471-8513.* Hrs: 11:30 am-2:30 pm, 5-10 pm; Sun 4:30-9:30 pm; Sun brunch 11 am-2 pm. Closed Jan 1, Dec 24 evening-25. Res accepted. English, Amer menu. Bar. Wine list. Semi-a la carte: lunch $6.25-$11.50, dinner $12.95-$22.95. Sun brunch $10.95. Specializes in beef, fish, prime rib. Outdoor dining. Mesquite charcoal grill. Old English decor; fireplaces, wine kegs, antiques. Boat dockage. Cr cds: A, C, D, DS, MC, V.

★ **LOWRY'S.** *1934 Hennepin Ave S, south of downtown. 612/871-0806.* Hrs: 11 am-10 pm; Fri to 11 pm; Sat 10 am-11 pm; Sun 10 am-9 pm; Sun brunch 10 am-2 pm. Closed Thanksgiving, Dec 25. Res accepted. Wine, beer. Semi-a la carte: lunch $5-$9, dinner $7-$18. Sun brunch $6-$12. Specializes in risotto, polenta. Parking. Cr cds: A, MC, V.

★ ★ **LUCIA'S.** *1432 W 31st St, south of downtown. 612/825-1572.* Hrs: 11:30 am-2:30 pm, 5:30-9:30 pm; Fri, Sat to 10 pm; Sun 10 am-2 pm, 5:30-9 pm; Sat, Sun brunch 10 am-2 pm. Closed Mon; most major hols. Res accepted. Contemporary American menu. Bar. Semi-a la carte: lunch $5.50-$8.95, dinner $8.95-$16.95. Sat, Sun brunch $5.95-$8.95. Specialties: polenta, crostini. Parking. Outdoor dining. Menu changes wkly. Cr cds: MC, V.

★ ★ **MANNY'S.** *(See Hyatt Regency Hotel) 612/339-9900.* Hrs: 5:30-10 pm; Sun to 9 pm. Closed major hols. Res accepted. Bar. A la carte entrees: $20-$40. Specializes in steak, lobster. Contemporary decor. Cr cds: A, C, D, DS, MC, V.

✔★ ★ **THE MARSH.** *(15000 Minnetonka Blvd, Minnetonka 55345) 15 mi W on Hwy 5. 612/935-2202.* Hrs: 7 am-9 pm; Sat 8 am-8:30 pm; Sun 8 am-5 pm; Sun brunch 11 am-2 pm. Closed Thanksgiving, Dec 25. Res accepted. Bar. Semi-a la carte: lunch $3.50-$8.50, dinner $8-$15. Sun brunch $8.50. Child's meals. Specialties: portobello mushroom melt, fish of the day. Own baking, pasta. Outdoor dining. Adj large fitness facility; menu changes daily, features healthy choices. Cr cds: A, MC, V.

D

★ ★ ★ **MEADOWS.** *(See Radisson Metrodome Hotel) 612/379-8888.* Hrs: 5:30-10 pm. Closed Sun; most major hols. Res accepted. Continental menu. Bar 4 pm-1 am. Semi-a la carte: dinner $18.95-$30.95. Specializes in wild game, walleye. Own pasta. Pianist Fri, Sat. Valet parking. Elegant, semi-formal atmosphere; brass ceiling fans, high-backed chairs. Cr cds: A, C, D, DS, ER, JCB, MC, V.

D

★ ★ ★ **MORTON'S OF CHICAGO.** *555 Nicollet Mall (55402), in Nicollet Ave Mall Area. 612/673-9700.* Hrs: 11:30 am-2:30 pm, 5:30-11 pm; Sat 5:30-11 pm; Sun 5-10 pm. Closed most major hols. Res accepted. Continental menu. Bar. Semi-a la carte: lunch $9.95-$29.95, dinner $29.95-$59.95. Specializes in steak, lobster. Contemporary decor. Cr cds: A, C, D, JCB, MC, V.

★ ★ ★ **MURRAY'S.** *26 S Sixth St, downtown. 612/339-0909.* Hrs: 11 am-10:30 pm; Fri to 11 pm; Sat 4-11 pm; Sun 4-10 pm. Res accepted. Bar. Wine list. Semi-a la carte: lunch $5.25-$12.25, dinner $19.50-$32.50. Tea time: 2-3:30 pm Mon-Fri. Specialty: silver butter knife steak for 2. Own baking. Entertainment Thurs-Sat. Family-owned. Cr cds: A, C, D, DS, JCB, MC, V.

D

★ ★ **NEW FRENCH BISTROT.** *1300 Lagoon Ave (55408), south of downtown. 612/825-2525.* Hrs: 11 am-10 pm; Fri, Sat to 11 pm; Sun 9 am-2 pm (brunch). Closed Thanksgiving, Dec 25. Res accepted. French menu. Bar. Semi-a la carte: lunch $6.50-$13, dinner $8-$21. Sun brunch $6.50-$13. Specializes in fresh seafood. Outdoor dining. Modern decor; large windows, high ceiling. Cr cds: A, C, D, MC, V.

D

★ ★ **NEW FRENCH CAFE & BAR.** *128 N Fourth St, downtown. 612/338-3790.* Hrs: 7 am-2 pm, 5:30-10 pm; Fri to 11 pm; Sat 5:30-11 pm; Sun 5-9 pm; Sat, Sun brunch 8 am-2 pm. Res accepted. Country & contemporary French menu. Bar 11-1 am, Sun from 6 pm. Semi-a la carte: bkfst $3.95-$7.95, lunch $6.95-$11, dinner $16.95-$23. Prix fixe dinner: $18. Sat, Sun brunch $3.50-$10.75. Specializes in duck, seafood. Outdoor dining (bar). Remodeled building (1900); French bistro theme. Cr cds: A, C, D, MC, V.

✔★ ★ **NYE'S POLONNAISE.** *112 E Hennepin Ave (55414), north of downtown. 612/379-2021.* Hrs: 11 am-11 pm; Sun 5-10 pm. Closed Dec 25. Res accepted. Polish, Amer menu. Bar to 1 am. Semi-a la carte: lunch $4.95-$7.95, dinner $11.95-$17.95. Specializes in prime rib, pierogi. Polka Thurs-Sat. Casual decor. Cr cds: A, C, D, DS, MC, V.

★ **ORIGAMI.** *30 N First St, downtown. 612/333-8430.* Hrs: 11 am-2 pm, 5-9:30 pm; Fri, Sat to 11 pm, Sun 5-9 pm. Closed most major hols. Japanese menu. Bar. Semi-a la carte: lunch $5-$12, dinner $7-$25. Specialties: sushi bar, sashimi. Parking. Outdoor dining. Cr cds: A, C, D, DS, MC, V.

★ ★ ★ **PALOMINO.** *825 Hennepin Ave (55402), downtown. 612/339-3800.* Hrs: 11:15 am-2:30 pm, 5-10 pm; Fri, Sat to 11 pm; Sun 5-10 pm. Closed most major hols. Res accepted. Mediterranean menu. Bar to 1 am. Semi-a la carte: lunch $4.50-$16.95, dinner $6.95-$25.95. Specialties: spit-roasted garlic chicken, hardwood grilled salmon. Contemporary decor. Cr cds: A, C, D, DS, MC, V.

D

✔★ **PICKLED PARROT.** *26 N Fifth St, downtown. 612/332-0673.* Hrs: 11-1 am; Sun 10 am-10 pm; Sun brunch 10 am-2 pm. Closed Jan 1, Dec 24, 25. Res accepted. Bar. Semi-a la carte: lunch $7.95-$13, dinner $12.95-$22.50. Sun brunch $12.95. Specialties: barbecued ribs, pork sandwich, Southern dishes. Colorful decor. Cr cds: A, C, D, DS, MC, V.

✔★ ★ **PING'S.** *1401 Nicollet Ave S, in Nicollet Ave Mall Area. 612/874-9404.* Hrs: 11 am-10 pm; Fri to midnight; Sat noon-midnight; Sun noon-9 pm. Closed Easter, Thanksgiving, Dec 24, 25. Res accepted. Chinese menu. Bar. Lunch buffet $6.95. Semi-a la carte: dinner $9-$14. Specialties: Peking duck, Ping's wings, Szechwan trio. Valet parking. Cr cds: A, C, D, DS, MC, V.

★ **PRACNA ON MAIN.** *117 Main St, under 3rd Ave Bridge on Mississippi River, north of downtown. 612/379-3200.* Hrs: 11:30 am-10 pm. Bar to 1 am. Semi-a la carte: lunch $6-$10, dinner $12-$17.95. Outdoor dining. Warehouse (1890); turn-of-the-century decor. Overlooks Mississippi River. Cr cds: A, C, D, DS, MC, V.

★ ★ **PRONTO.** *(See Hyatt Regency Hotel) 612/333-4414.* Hrs: 11:30 am-2 pm, 5-10 pm; Fri, Sat to 11 pm; Sun 5-9 pm. Closed Thanksgiving, Dec 25. Res accepted. Italian menu. Bar. Semi-a la carte: lunch $10-$15, dinner $20-$30. Specializes in fresh fish, provimi veal. Own pasta. On 2nd floor; large windows overlook Nicollet Ave. Cr cds: A, D, DS, MC, V.

D

★ ★ ★ **RUTH'S CHRIS STEAK HOUSE.** *920 Second Ave S (55402), downtown. 612/672-9000.* Hrs: 5-10:30 pm. Closed Thanksgiving, Dec 25. Res accepted. Bar. Semi-a la carte: dinner $35-$45. Specializes in steak. Elegant decor. Cr cds: A, C, D, JCB, MC, V.

✔★ ★ **SANTORINI.** *(9920 Wayzata Blvd, St Louis Park 55426) 612/546-6722.* Hrs: 11 am-3 pm, 5-10 pm; Fri, Sat to 11 pm. Sun brunch 10:30 am-2:30 pm. Closed Memorial Day, July 4. Res accepted. Mediterranean menu. Bar to 1 am. Semi-a la carte: lunch $4.50-$9.50, dinner $4.50-$13. Sun brunch $15.95. Specialties: saganaki, souvlaki, moussaka. Mediterranean decor. Cr cds: A, C, D, DS, MC, V.

✔★ **SAWATDEE.** *607 Washington Ave S, downtown. 612/338-6451.* Web www.sawatdee.com. Hrs: 11 am-10 pm; Fri, Sat to 11 pm. Res accepted. Thai menu. Bar. A la carte entrees: lunch, dinner $8.25-$14.95. Buffet: lunch $7.95. Specialties: Pad Thai, Bangkok seafood special. Parking. Cr cds: A, C, D, DS, MC, V.

✔★ ★ **SHUANG CHENG.** *1320 SE Fourth St (55414), downtown. 612/378-0208.* Hrs: 10 am-10 pm; Fri, Sat 11 am-11 pm; Sun 4-10 pm. Chinese menu. Semi-a la carte: lunch $3.55-$4.75, dinner $4.50-$10.95. Specializes in seafood, pork, chicken. Casual decor. Cr cds: A, C, D, DS, MC, V.

✔★ **SIDNEY'S PIZZA CAFE.** *2120 Hennepin Ave (55405), north of downtown. 612/870-7000.* Hrs: 7 am-11 pm; Fri to midnight; Sat 10 am-midnight; Sun 10 am-11 pm. Closed Dec 24, 25. Italian, Amer menu. Wine, beer. Semi-a la carte: bkfst $4.95-$9.95, lunch, dinner $4.95-$9.95. Specializes in pizza, pasta. Outdoor dining. Casual decor. Cr cds: A, C, D, DS, MC, V.

★ **SONG THANH.** *418 13th Ave SE (55414), downtown, near Univ of Minnesota campus. 612/379-3121.* Hrs: 11 am-10 pm; Fri, Sat to 11 pm. Res accepted. Vietnamese menu. Semi-a la carte: lunch $3.95-$6.95, dinner $4.95-$24.95. Specialties: flaming game hen, lemon grass chicken. Own noodles. Casual dining in colorful Vietnamese atmosphere. Cr cds: A, C, D, DS, MC, V.

D

★ ★ **SOPHIA.** *65 SE Main St, north of downtown. 612/379-1111.* Hrs: 11 am-3 pm, 5-9:45 pm; Fri, Sat to 11:45 pm; Sun 11 am-3 pm. Closed Jan 1, Dec 25. Res accepted. French, continental menu. Bar. Semi-a la carte: lunch $5.95-$10.95, dinner $11.95-$19.95. Specializes in Norwegian salmon, steaks. Pianist Tues-Sat. Outdoor dining. Many of the ingredients are provided through the restaurant's own ranch. Overlooks river. Cr cds: A, C, D, MC, V.

D

★ **TABLE OF CONTENTS.** *1310 Hennepin Ave (55403), downtown. 612/339-1133.* Hrs: 11:30 am-2 pm, 5-10 pm; Fri, Sat to 11 pm; Sun 10 am-3 pm, 5-9 pm. Closed most major hols. Res accepted. Contemporary Amer menu. Bar. Semi-a la carte: lunch $7.50-$12.50, dinner $12.50-$22.95. Sun brunch $4.95-$11.95. Specializes in grilled fish, grilled beef tenderloin. Contemporary decor. Cr cds: A, C, D, DS, MC, V.

★ ★ ★ **WHITNEY GRILLE.** *(See Whitney Hotel) 612/372-6405.* Hrs: 6:30 am-10:30 pm; Sun 10 am-3 pm. Closed Dec 25. Res accepted. Bar to midnight. Semi-a la carte: bkfst $6-$10, lunch $7-$13, dinner $19-$29. Sun brunch $19.95. Specialty: Minnesota walleye. Entertainment Fri, Sat. Outdoor dining. Formal decor. Totally nonsmoking. Cr cds: A, C, D, DS, ER, JCB, MC, V.

D

Unrated Dining Spots

EMILY'S LEBANESE DELI. *641 University Ave NE, north of downtown. 612/379-4069.* Hrs: 9 am-9 pm; Fri, Sat to 10 pm. Closed Tues; Easter, Thanksgiving, Dec 25. Lebanese menu. Semi-a la carte: lunch, dinner $4.50-$7.50. Specialties: spinach pie, tabooleh salad. Parking. No cr cds accepted.

LINCOLN DEL. *(4100 W Lake St, St Louis Park) Approx 3 mi S on MN 100. 612/927-9738.* Hrs: 7 am-11 pm; Fri, Sat to 1 am; Sun 8 am-11 pm. Closed Dec 25. Semi-a la carte: bkfst $2-$5, lunch $4-$8, dinner $6-$11. Specializes in corned beef. Parking. New York-style deli. Cr cds: A, D, MC, V.

SC

LORING CAFE. *1624 Harmon Place, adj Loring Playhouse Theatre, downtown. 612/332-1617.* Hrs: 11:30 am-3:30 pm, 5:30-11 pm; Fri, Sat 11:30 am-3 pm, 4 pm-midnight; Sun 11:30 am-3 pm, 5:30-11 pm. Closed Dec 24, 25. Res accepted. Bar. Semi-a la carte: lunch $9-$15, dinner $12-$25. Specialties: shrimp with pears, manicotti with lamb & cheese. Entertainment. Outdoor dining. Restored 1918 building. Eclectic decor. Cr cds: MC, V.

MARKET BAR-B-QUE. *1414 Nicollet Ave S, in Nicollet Ave Mall Area. 612/872-1111.* Hrs: 11:30-2:30 am; Sun noon-midnight. Bar. Semi-a la carte: lunch $5-$9, dinner $9-$15.95. Specializes in barbecued chicken, ribs, pork. Valet parking. 1930s cafe atmosphere. Cr cds: A, C, D, DS, MC, V.

D

MUD PIE. *2549 Lyndale Ave S (55405), south of downtown. 612/872-9435.* Hrs: 11 am-10 pm; Sat, Sun from 8 am. Closed major hols. Vegetarian menu. Wine, beer. Semi-a la carte: bkfst $2-$4.50, lunch $4-$12, dinner $7-$15. Outdoor dining. Cr cds: A, D, DS, MC, V.

D

St Paul

ST PAUL RESTAURANTS BY NEIGHBORHOOD AREAS

(For full description, see alphabetical listings under Restaurants)

DOWNTOWN
Gallivan's. 354 Wabasha St
Leeann Chin Chinese Cuisine. 214 E 4th St
Mancini's Char House. 531 W Seventh St

No Wake Cafe. Pier One
The Saint Paul Grill (The Saint Paul Hotel). 350 Market St
Sakura. 34 W 6th St
Sawatdee. 289 E Fifth St

NORTH OF DOWNTOWN
Dakota Bar & Grill. 1021 E Bandana
Muffuletta in the Park. 2260 Como Ave
Toby's on the Lake. 249 Geneva Ave N

WEST OF DOWNTOWN
Buca Little Italy. 2728 Gannon Rd
Caravan Serai. 2175 Ford Pkwy
Cecil's Delicatessen, Bakery & Restaurant. 651 S Cleveland
Forepaugh's. 276 S Exchange St
Old City Cafe. 1571 Grand Ave
Ristorante Luci. 470 Cleveland Ave S
Table of Contents. 1648 Grand Ave
Tulips. 452 Selby Ave
W.A. Frost & Company. 374 Selby Ave

SUMMIT HILL
Ciatti's. 850 Grand Ave
Dixie's. 695 Grand Ave
Green Mill Inn. 57 S Hamline Ave
Lexington. 1096 Grand Ave

Note: When a listing is located in a town that does not have its own city heading, it will appear under the city nearest to its location. In these cases, the address and town appear in parenthesis immediately following the name of the establishment.

Motels

★ ★ **BEST WESTERN DROVER'S INN.** *(701 S Concord St, South St Paul 55075) At jct I-494 & Concord St. 612/455-3600; FAX 612/455-0282.* 85 rms, 4 story. S, D $70-$90; each addl $10; under 19 free. Crib free. TV; cable (premium). VCR avail. Indoor pool; whirlpool. Coffee in rms. Restaurant 6:30 am-2 pm, 5-9 pm; Sun 8 am-1 pm. Rm serv. Bar 2 pm-1 am; closed Sun. Ck-out noon. Meeting rms. Business servs avail. Valet serv. Sundries. Free airport transportation. Microwaves avail. Cr cds: A, C, D, DS, MC, V.

D

★ ★ **BEST WESTERN MAPLEWOOD INN.** *1780 E County Road D (55109), adj to Maplewood Mall, north of downtown. 612/770-2811; FAX 612/770-2811, ext. 184.* 118 rms, 2 story. S $58-$108; D $62-$108; each addl $4; under 18 free. Crib free. Pet accepted; $5 deposit. TV; cable (premium). Indoor pool; whirlpool. Coffee in rms. Restaurant 6:30 am-2 pm, 5-10 pm. Rm serv. Bar 4 pm-1 am; entertainment Fri, Sat. Ck-out noon. Coin Indry. Meeting rms. Business servs avail. In-rm modem link. Valet serv. Sundries. Sauna. Health club privileges. Game rm. Microwaves avail. Cr cds: A, C, D, DS, ER, JCB, MC, V.

D SC

★ ★ **COUNTRY INN BY CARLSON.** *(6003 Hudson Rd, Woodbury 55125) 4 mi E on I-94, exit Century Ave (MN 120). 612/739-7300; FAX 612/731-4007; res: 800/456-4000.* Web www.countryinns-suites .com. 158 rms, 2 story. S, D $81-$99; each addl $8; under 19 free. Crib free. TV; cable (premium). Indoor pool; whirlpool. Complimentary continental bkfst. Complimentary coffee in rms. Restaurant 11 am-10 pm; Fri, Sat to midnight. Rm serv. Bar from 11 am. Ck-out noon. Coin Indry. Meeting rms. Business servs avail. In-rm modem link. Concierge. Valet serv. Downhill ski 12 mi, x-country ski 11 mi. Exercise equipt; weight machine, treadmill, sauna. Game rm. Many refrigerators. Cr cds: A, C, D, DS, MC, V.

D SC

✔★ **EXEL INN.** *1739 Old Hudson Rd (55106). 612/771-5566; FAX 612/771-1262.* 100 rms, 3 story. S $38.99-$53.99; D $43.99-$58.99; each addl $5; under 18 free; ski, wkly plans; higher rates special events. Crib free. Pet accepted. TV; cable (premium). Complimentary continental bkfst. Restaurant adj open 24 hrs. Ck-out noon. Coin Indry. Business servs avail. In-rm modem link. Downhill ski 15 mi; x-country ski 2 mi. Game rm. Refrigerators; microwaves avail. Cr cds: A, C, D, DS, MC, V.

D SC

★ ★ **HAMPTON INN-NORTH.** *(1000 Gramsie Rd, Shoreview 55126) 612/482-0402; FAX 612/482-8917.* 120 rms, 2 story. S, D $69-$89; under 16 free. Crib free. TV; cable (premium). Indoor pool; whirlpool. Complimentary continental bkfst. Restaurant 11 am-11 pm. Rm serv. Bar to 1 am. Ck-out 11 am. Meeting rms. Business servs avail. In-rm modem link. Coin Indry. Exercise equipt; bicycle, stair machine. Cr cds: A, C, D, DS, MC, V.

SC

★ ★ **HOLIDAY INN EXPRESS.** *1010 Bandana Blvd W (55108), north of downtown. 612/647-1637; FAX 612/647-0244.* 109 rms, 2 story. S, D $81-$101; suites $101-$131. Crib free. TV; cable (premium). Indoor pool; wading pool, whirlpool. Complimentary continental bkfst. Ck-out noon. Meeting rms. Business servs avail. In-rm modem link. Valet serv. Downhill ski 15 mi; x-country ski 1 mi. Sauna. Some refrigerators. Motel built within exterior structure of old railroad repair building; old track runs through lobby. Shopping center adj; connected by skywalk. Cr cds: A, C, D, DS, ER, MC, V.

D SC

✔★ **RED ROOF INN.** *(1806 Wooddale Dr, Woodbury 55125) I-494 at Valley Creek Rd. 612/738-7160; FAX 612/738-1869.* 108 rms, 2 story. S $33.99-$58.99; D $46.99-$68.99; each addl $8; under 18 free. Crib free. Pet accepted. TV; cable (premium). Complimentary coffee. Restaurant nearby. Ck-out noon. Business servs avail. In-rm modem link. Downhill ski 15 mi; x-country ski 3 mi. Cr cds: A, C, D, DS, MC, V.

D

★ **SUPER 8.** *(285 N Century Ave, Maplewood 55119) 612/738-1600; FAX 612/738-9405.* 112 rms, 4 story. Late May-early Sept: S $48.88-$55.88; D $55.88-$60.88; each addl $5; under 12 free; lower rates rest of yr. Crib free. Pet accepted; $50. TV; cable (premium). Complimentary continental bkfst. Restaurant adj. Ck-out 11 am. Coin Indry. Business servs avail. In-rm modem link. Sundries. Airport transportation. Downhill ski 15 mi; x-country ski 2 mi. Health club privileges. Microwaves avail. Picnic tables. On lake. Cr cds: A, C, D, DS, MC, V.

D SC

Motor Hotels

★ **BEST WESTERN KELLY INN.** *161 St Anthony Blvd (55103), I-94 exit Marion St, west of downtown. 612/227-8711; FAX 612/227-1698.* 126 rms, 7 story. S $74-$89; D $79-$99; each addl $8; suites $115-$185; under 15 free; higher rates special events. Crib free. Pet accepted. TV; cable. Indoor pool; wading pool, whirlpool. Restaurant 6:30 am-9 pm. Rm serv. Bar 11-1 am; Sat 4 pm-midnight; Sun 4-10 pm. Meeting rms. Business servs avail. In-rm modem link. Sundries. Valet serv. Downhill ski 20 mi; x-country ski 4 mi. Sauna. Game rm. Microwaves in suites. Cr cds: A, C, D, DS, MC, V.

D SC

★ **DAYS INN-CIVIC CENTER.** *175 W Seventh St (55102), at Kellogg, opp St Paul Civic Center, downtown. 612/292-8929; FAX 612/292-1749.* E-mail daysinnmn@aol.com. 203 rms, 8 story. S $60-$75; D $68-$83; each addl $8; suites $115-$155; under 18 free; wkend rates; higher rates state tournament wkends. Crib free. Pet accepted. TV; cable (premium). Restaurant 6 am-midnight. Bar 4 pm-1 am. Ck-out 11 am. Meeting rms. Business servs avail. In-rm modem link. Valet serv. Downhill ski 20 mi; x-country ski 4 mi. Health club privileges. Some refrigerators; microwaves avail. Cr cds: A, C, D, DS, ER, JCB, MC, V.

D SC

★ ★ ★ **HOLIDAY INN.** *1201 W County Rd E (55112). 612/636-4123; FAX 612/636-2526.* Web www.traveler.net/ht10/custom/1910.html. 156 rms, 4 story. S, D $89-$130; each addl $10; suites $99-$149; under 19 free. Crib free. TV; cable (premium). Indoor pool; whirlpool. Complimentary full bkfst. Coffee in rms. Restaurant 6:30 am-10 pm. Bar to 1 am. Ck-out noon. Meeting rms. Business servs avail. Valet serv. Coin Indry. Exercise equipt; bicycles, treadmill. Some refrigerators. Cr cds: A, C, D, DS, MC, V.

D SC

★ ★ ★ **HOLIDAY INN-EAST.** *2201 Burns Ave (55119), I-94 & McKnight Rd, east of downtown. 612/731-2220; FAX 612/731-0243.* 192 rms, 8 story. S, D $86-$96; under 19 free; wkend rates. Crib free. TV; cable (premium). Indoor pool; whirlpool. Restaurant 6 am-2 pm, 5-10 pm; Sat, Sun from 7 am. Rm serv. Bar 4 pm-1 am. Ck-out noon. Coin Indry. Meeting rms. Business servs avail. In-rm modem link. Bellhops. Valet serv. Sundries. Gift shop. Downhill ski 10 mi; x-country ski 1/2 mi. Exercise equipt; weight machine, bicycles, sauna. Game rm. Some bathroom phones. Luxury level. Cr cds: A, C, D, DS, JCB, MC, V.

D SC

★ ★ ★ **SHERATON-MIDWAY.** *400 Hamline Ave N (55104), west of downtown. 612/642-1234; FAX 612/642-1126.* 197 rms, 4 story. S $95-$125; D $102-$125; each addl $10; under 18 free; wkend rates. Crib free. TV; cable (premium). Indoor pool; whirlpool. Complimentary coffee in rms. Restaurant 6:30 am-10:30 pm. Rm serv. Bar 11 am-midnight, Sun from noon. Ck-out noon. Meeting rms. Business servs avail. In-rm modem link. Bellhops. Downhill ski 15 mi; x-country ski 7 mi. Exercise equipt; weights, bicycles. Health club privileges. Cr cds: A, C, D, DS, MC, V.

D SC

Hotels

★ ★ ★ **EMBASSY SUITES.** *175 E 10th St (55101), downtown. 612/224-5400; FAX 612/224-0957.* Web www.embassy-suites.com. 210 suites, 8 story. S $129; D $139; each addl $10; under 12 free; wkend, hol rates. Crib free. TV; cable (premium). Indoor pool; whirlpool. Complimentary full bkfst. Coffee in rms. Restaurant 11 am-10 pm. Bar to 1 am. Ck-out noon. Coin Indry. Meeting rms. Business servs avail. In-rm modem link. Gift shop. Free airport transportation. Exercise equipt; weight machine, bicycles, sauna, steam rm. Refrigerators, microwaves, wet bars. Atrium with pond, waterfalls, fountains, ducks; many plants and trees. Cr cds: A, C, D, DS, ER, JCB, MC, V.

D SC

★ ★ ★ **HOLIDAY INN SELECT-MINNEAPOLIS AIRPORT/EAGAN.** *(2700 Pilot Knob Rd, Eagan 55121) SW on I-494. 612/454-3434; FAX 612/454-4904.* 187 rms, 6 story. S, D $79-$109; suites $129-$149; under 20 free. Crib free. TV; cable (premium). Indoor pool; whirlpool. Coffee in rms. Restaurant 7 am-11 pm. Bar. Ck-out noon. Coin Indry. Meeting rms. Business servs avail. In-rm modem link. Free airport transportation. Exercise equipt; stair machine, bicycles, sauna. Health club privileges. Cr cds: A, C, D, DS, JCB, MC, V.

D SC

★ ★ ★ **RADISSON.** *11 E Kellogg Blvd (55101), downtown. 612/292-1900; FAX 612/224-8999.* Web www.radisson.com. 475 rms, 22 story. S $110; D $140; each addl $10; under 18 free; package plans. Crib free. Pet accepted, some restrictions. Garage parking $11. TV; cable (premium), VCR avail. Indoor pool. Restaurant 6:30 am-10:30 pm; Fri, Sat to 11:30 pm. Bars 11:30-1 am. Ck-out noon. Convention facilities. Business servs avail. In-rm modem link. Concierge. Downhill ski 15 mi; x-country ski 4 mi. Exercise equipt; weight machine, stair machine. Health club privileges. Some refrigerators, microwaves. Indoor skyway to major stores, businesses. Luxury level. Cr cds: A, C, D, DS, ER, MC, V.

D SC

★ ★ ★ ★ **THE SAINT PAUL.** *350 Market St (55102), downtown. 612/292-9292; FAX 612/228-9506; res: 800/292-9292.* This stately, stone hotel overlooks Rice Park and the center of St Paul. Rooms are done in a pleasing, traditional decor. Business services and health club privileges are available; exercise equipment will be delivered to your room on request. 254 rms, 12 story. S, D $149-$164; each addl $15; suites $425-$650; under 19 free; wkend rates; package plans. Crib free. Garage $10.95. TV; cable, VCR avail. Restaurant (see THE SAINT PAUL GRILL). Bar 11-1 am. Ck-out noon. Convention facilities. Business center. In-rm modem link. Concierge. Downhill ski 15 mi; x-country ski 4 mi. Exercise equipt; bicycles, stair machine; equipt delivered to rms on request. Health club privileges. Connected to downtown skyway system. Cr cds: A, C, D, DS, MC, V.

D SC

Restaurants

✔★ **BUCA LITTLE ITALY.** *2728 Gannon Rd (55116), west of downtown. 612/772-4388.* Hrs: 5-10 pm; Fri to 11 pm; Sat 4-11 pm; Sun 4-10 pm. Closed Thanksgiving, Dec 24, 25. Italian menu. Bar. A la carte entrees: dinner $13-$17. Specializes in pasta, seafood. Outdoor dining. Italian decor. Cr cds: A, D, MC, V.

D

✔★ ★ **CARAVAN SERAI.** *2175 Ford Pkwy, west of downtown. 612/690-1935.* Hrs: 11 am-2 pm, 5-9:30 pm; Mon from 5 pm; Fri to 10:30 pm; Sat 5-10:30 pm; Sun 4:30-9:30 pm; early-bird dinner Sun-Thurs 5-6 pm. Closed most major hols. Res accepted. Afghani, Northern Indian menu. Wine, beer. Semi-a la carte: lunch $3.25-$6.25, dinner $8.95-$16.95. Child's meals. Specialties: tandoori chicken, vegetarian combination platter. Guitarist, Egyptian dancers Tues, Thurs-Sat. Hand-crafted tapestries, floor seating. Cr cds: A, C, D, MC, V.

★ ★ **CIATTI'S.** *850 Grand Ave, in Summit Hill. 612/292-9942.* Hrs: 11 am-10 pm; Fri, Sat to 11 pm; Sun from 2:30 pm; Sun brunch 10 am-2 pm. Closed Thanksgiving, Dec 24, 25. Italian menu. Res accepted. Bar to 1 am. Semi-a la carte: lunch $6.95-$9.95, dinner $7.95-$14.95. Sun brunch $6.95-$11.95. Child's meals. Specializes in northern Italian dishes. Own sauces. Cr cds: A, D, DS, MC, V.

D

★ ★ **DAKOTA BAR & GRILL.** *1021 E Bandana, north of downtown. 612/642-1442.* E-mail dakotajazz@aol.com. Hrs: 5:30-10:30 pm; Fri, Sat to 11:30 pm; Sun to 9:30 pm; Sun brunch 11 am-2:30 pm. Closed most major hols. Res accepted. Bar 4 pm-midnight; Fri, Sat to 1 am. Semi-a la carte: dinner $13-$26.95. Sun brunch $9.95-$18.95. Child's meals. Specializes in regional and seasonal dishes. Jazz evenings. Parking. Outdoor dining. Located in restored railroad building in historic Bandana Square. Modern decor. Cr cds: A, C, D, DS, MC, V.

D

★ **DIXIE'S.** *695 Grand Ave (55105), in Summit Hill. 612/222-7345.* E-mail dixies@iaxs.net; web www.iaxs.net/~dixies. Hrs: 11 am-midnight; Sun 2:30-11 pm; Sun brunch 10 am-2 pm. Closed Thanksgiving. Res accepted. Southern, Cajun menu. Bar to 1 am; Sun to midnight. Semi-a la carte: lunch $4.50-$9.95, dinner $4.95-$15.95. Sun brunch $10.95. Specialties; hickory-smoked ribs, Key lime pie. Parking. Informal dining. Cr cds: A, D, DS, MC, V.

D

★ ★ ★ **FOREPAUGH'S.** *276 S Exchange St, west of downtown. 612/224-5606.* Hrs: 11:30 am-2 pm, 5:30-9;30 pm; Sat from 5:30 pm; Sun 5-8:30 pm; Sun brunch 10:30 am-1:30 pm. Closed some hols. Res accepted. French menu. Bar to 1 am; Sun to midnight. Semi-a la carte: lunch $7.50-$9.95, dinner $11.95-$18.75. Sun brunch $12.50. Child's meals. Specialties: shrimp scampi, twin tournedos, veal calvados. Valet parking. Outdoor dining. Restored mansion (1870); 9 dining rms. Cr cds: A, D, MC, V.

D

★ ★ **GALLIVAN'S.** *354 Wabasha St, downtown. 612/227-6688.* Hrs: 11 am-10 pm; Fri, Sat to 11 pm; Sun 4-8 pm. Closed major hols. Res accepted. Bar to 1 am. Semi-a la carte: lunch $3.95-$8.45, dinner $9.95-$21.95. Specializes in steak, prime rib, seafood. Entertainment Fri, Sat. Cr cds: A, C, D, DS, MC, V.

D

★ ★ ★ **KOZLAK'S ROYAL OAK.** *(4785 Hodgson Rd, Shoreview 55126) 3 mi N of I-694 on MN 49. 612/484-8484.* Hrs: 11 am-2:30 pm,

4-9:30 pm; Fri to 10:30 pm; Sat 4-10:30 pm; Sun 10 am-1:30 pm (brunch), 4-8:30 pm; early-bird dinner Sun-Fri to 5:45 pm. Closed most major hols. Res accepted. Bar to midnight; Fri, Sat to 1 am. Semi-a la carte: lunch $5.50-$12, dinner $15.50-$27. Sun brunch $9.95-$16.95. Child's meals. Specialties: steer tenderloin filet, duckling, salmon. Salad bar. Own baking. Strolling jazz musicians Sun brunch. Outdoor dining. Elegant decor with arched windows, etched glass; dining rm overlooks garden that changes seasonally. Family-owned. Cr cds: A, C, D, DS, MC, V.

D

★ ★ ★ **LAKE ELMO INN.** *(3442 Lake Elmo Ave, Lake Elmo 55042) 12 mi E on I-94 to I-694, 2 mi N to MN 5, then 4 mi E. 612/777-8495.* Hrs:11 am-2 pm, 5-10 pm; Sun 10 am-2 pm, 4:30-8:30 pm. Closed some major hols. Res accepted. Continental menu. Bar to midnight. Wine list. Semi-a la carte: lunch $6-$8.95, dinner $14-$18. Sun brunch $13.95. Child's meals. Specializes in rack of lamb, roast duckling. Outdoor dining. Casual elegance in restored inn & stagecoach stop (1881). Cr cds: A, C, D, DS, MC, V.

D

✔★ ★ **LEEANN CHIN CHINESE CUISINE.** *214 E 4th St (55101), downtown. 612/224-8814.* Hrs: 11 am-2:30 pm, 5-9 pm; Fri, Sat to 10 pm. Closed major hols. Res accepted. Chinese menu. Serv bar. Buffet: lunch $7.95, dinner $13.95. Child's meals. Specializes in Cantonese, mandarin and Szechwan dishes. Contemporary decor. Totally nonsmoking. Cr cds: A, D, DS, MC, V.

D

★ ★ ★ **LEXINGTON.** *1096 Grand Ave, at Lexington Pkwy, in Summit Hill. 612/222-5878.* Hrs: 11 am-10 pm; Fri, Sat to 11 pm; Sun 4-9 pm; Sun brunch 10 am-3 pm. Closed Dec 24 evening, 25, July 4. Res accepted. Bar. Semi-a la carte: lunch $6.95-$11.95, dinner $9.95-$27. Sun brunch $4.95-$11.95. Child's meals. Specializes in prime rib, fresh walleye. Parking. French Provincial decor. Cr cds: A, C, D, DS, MC, V.

D

★ **LINDEY'S.** *(3600 Snelling Ave N, Arden Hills 55112) 612/633-9813.* Hrs: 5-10:30 pm; Fri, Sat to 11:30 pm. Closed Sun; major hols. Bar. Semi-a la carte: dinner $13.65-$19.85. Child's meals. Specializes in steak. Rustic, Northwoods lodge atmosphere. No cr cds accepted.

D

★ **MANCINI'S CHAR HOUSE.** *531 W Seventh St, downtown. 612/224-7345.* Hrs: 5-11 pm; Fri, Sat to 12:30 am. Closed major hols. Bar to 1 am. Semi-a la carte: dinner $10-$29. Specializes in steak, lobster. Entertainment Wed-Sat. Parking. Open charcoal hearths; 2 fireplaces. Family-owned. Cr cds: A, C, D, MC, V.

D

★ ★ **MUFFULETTA IN THE PARK.** *2260 Como Ave, north of downtown. 612/644-9116.* Hrs: 11 am-2:30 pm, 5-9:30 pm; Fri, Sat to 10 pm; Sun 10 am-2 pm, 5-8 pm. Closed some major hols. Res accepted. Continental menu. Wine, beer. Semi-a la carte: lunch $5.95-$9.95, dinner $7.95-$15.95. Sun brunch $5.25-$9.95. Specializes in pasta, fresh fish. Own soup, dressings. Parking. Outdoor dining. Cafe decor. Totally nonsmoking. Cr cds: A, D, DS, MC, V.

✔★ ★ **RISTORANTE LUCI.** *470 Cleveland Ave S (55105), west of downtown. 612/699-8258.* Hrs: 5-9:30 pm; Fri, Sat to 10:30 pm; Sun 4:30-9 pm. Closed major hols. Res accepted. Italian menu. Wine, beer. Semi-a la carte: dinner $7.75-$18.95. Child's meals. Specializes in pasta, seafood. Italian decor. Totally nonsmoking. Cr cds: MC, V.

★ ★ ★ **THE SAINT PAUL GRILL.** *(See The Saint Paul Hotel) 612/224-7455.* Hrs: 11:30 am-midnight; Sun brunch 11 am-2 pm. Res accepted. Bar to 1 am; Sun to midnight. Wine list. Semi-a la carte: lunch $6-$12, dinner $9-$26. Sun brunch $9-$15. Child's meals. Specializes in fresh fish, regional cuisine. Valet parking. Elegant dining rm in historic hotel offers panoramic view of Rice Park. Cr cds: A, C, D, DS, MC, V.

D

✔★ **SAKURA.** *34 W 6th St (55102), downtown. 612/224-0185.* Hrs: 11:30 am-2:30 pm, 5-10:30 pm; Fri, Sat to 11 pm; Sun to 9:30 pm. Closed Jan 1, Thanksgiving, Dec 25. Res accepted. Japanese menu. Bar. Semi-a la carte: lunch $6-$10, dinner $10-$15. Specializes in sushi, sashimi, teriyaki. Validated parking. Contemporary Japanese decor; sushi bar. Cr cds: A, D, DS, JCB, MC, V.

D

★ **SAWATDEE.** *289 E Fifth St (55101), downtown. 612/222-5859.* Web www.sawatdee.com. Hrs: 11 am-10 pm; Fri, Sat to 11 pm. Closed most major hols. Res accepted. Thai menu. Bar. Semi-a la carte: lunch, dinner $6-$8. Buffet: lunch $5.95. Specializes in noodle dishes, curry dishes. Thai decor. Cr cds: A, D, DS, MC, V.

★ **TABLE OF CONTENTS.** *1648 Grand Ave (55105), west of downtown. 612/699-6595.* Hrs: 11:30 am-2 pm, 5:30-9:30 pm; Fri, Sat to 10:30 pm; Sun 10 am-2 pm, 5-9 pm. Closed most major hols. Res accepted. Contemporary Amer menu. Wine, beer. Semi-a la carte: lunch $5.95-$11.95, dinner $10.95-$19.95. Sun brunch $5.25-$9.75. Specializes in pasta, seafood. Contemporary decor. Adj bookstore. Cr cds: A, D, DS, MC, V.

D

★ ★ ★ **TOBY'S ON THE LAKE.** *249 Geneva Ave N, on Tanners Lake, north of downtown. 612/739-1600.* Hrs: 11 am-2:30 pm, 5-10 pm; Sat 11 am-11 pm; Sun 11 am-9 pm; Sun brunch to 2 pm. Closed Dec 25. Res accepted. Bar. Semi-a la carte: lunch $5.95-$11.95, dinner $9.95-$19.95. Sun brunch $5.95-$8.50. Child's meals. Specializes in prime rib, fresh seafood. Parking. Outdoor dining. Olde English atmosphere. Overlooks Tanners Lake. Cr cds: A, C, D, DS, MC, V.

D

✔★ **TULIPS.** *452 Selby Ave (55102), Cathedral Hill area, west of downtown. 612/221-1061.* Hrs: 11:30 am-3 pm, 5-10 pm; Fri, Sat to 11 pm; Sun brunch to 2:30 pm. Closed most major hols. Res accepted. French menu. Wine, beer. Semi-a la carte: lunch $6-$12, dinner $10-$20. Sun brunch $6-$15. Specialties: sea scallops, herbed walnut walleye, filet mignon with béarnaise sauce. Outdoor dining. Country French decor; intimate dining. Cr cds: D, MC, V.

D

★ ★ **VENETIAN INN.** *(2814 Rice St, Little Canada) S of I-694 Rice St exit. 612/484-7215.* Hrs: 11 am-10 pm; Fri, Sat to 11 pm. Closed Sun; most major hols. Res accepted. Italian, Amer menu. Bar to 1 am. Semi-a la carte: lunch $6.50-$8.50, dinner $7.95-$17.95. Complete meals: Sicilian dinner (for 2 or more) $22.50. Child's meals. Specializes in steak, barbecued ribs, lasagne. Theatre entertainment Fri, Sat. Parking. Family-owned. Cr cds: A, C, D, DS, MC, V.

D

★ ★ **W.A. FROST & COMPANY.** *374 Selby Ave (55102), west of downtown. 612/224-5715.* E-mail wafrost@popp.ix.netcom.com. Hrs: 11-1 am; Sun 10:30 am-midnight; Sun brunch to 2 pm. Closed some major hols. Res accepted. Bar. Semi-a la carte: lunch $7-$11, dinner $6.95-$22. Sun brunch $5-$10. Child's meals. Specialties: Nantucket chicken, chocolate silk pie. Parking. Outdoor dining in garden area. Three dining rms; Victorian-style decor. Renovated pharmacy (1887). Totally nonsmoking. Cr cds: A, C, D, DS, MC, V.

D

Unrated Dining Spots

CECIL'S DELICATESSEN, BAKERY & RESTAURANT. *651 S Cleveland, west of downtown. 612/698-0334.* Hrs: 9 am-8 pm. Semi-a la carte: bkfst $1.75-$4.50, lunch, dinner $3-$6.50. Specializes in corned beef, pastrami sandwiches, homemade desserts. Own baking, soups. Parking. Family-owned. Cr cds: MC, V.

GREEN MILL INN. *57 S Hamline Ave, in Summit Hill. 612/698-0353.* Hrs: 11 am-11 pm; Fri, Sat to midnight. Closed Dec 24 eve-Dec 25. Italian, Amer menu. Wine, beer. Semi-a la carte: lunch, dinner

$2.95-$10.75. Specializes in deep dish pizza, sandwiches. Own soups, chili. Cr cds: A, D, MC, V.

D

NO WAKE CAFE. *Pier One (55107), Harriet Island, downtown. 612/292-1411.* Hrs: 8 am-2 pm; Thur also 5-9 pm; Fri, Sat also 5-10 pm; Sun 8 am-noon. Closed Mon; most major hols; also Jan-Feb. Wine, beer. Semi-a la carte: bkfst $4-$6, lunch $3.50-$7, dinner $9-$15. Specialties: Tuscan tenderloin, almond crusted walleye. Vintage towboat on Mississippi River. Cr cds: MC, V.

OLD CITY CAFE. *1571 Grand Ave (55105), west of downtown. 612/699-5347.* Hrs: 11 am-9 pm; Fri to 2 pm; Sun from 10 am. Closed Sat; major Jewish hols. Wine, beer. A la carte entrees: bkfst $1.25-$4.95, lunch $1.50-$4.95, dinner $3.50-$8.50. Specializes in kosher deli fare, Middle Eastern salads, falafel. Informal neighborhood deli with Middle Eastern decor. No cr cds accepted.

D SC

Bloomington

Motels

★ ★ ★ **BEST WESTERN THUNDERBIRD.** *2201 E 78th St (55425). 612/854-3411; FAX 612/854-1183.* 263 rms, 2 story. S $85-$110; D $91-$110; each addl $6; suites $135-$370; under 13 free. Crib free. Pet accepted. TV; cable. 2 pools, 1 indoor; whirlpool. Restaurant 6:30 am-10:30 pm. Rm serv to 11 am. Bar 4-11:30 pm; entertainment. Ck-out 11 am. Meeting rms. Business servs avail. Valet serv. Sundries. Gift shop. Free airport transportation. Downhill ski 10 mi; x-country ski 1 mi. Exercise equipt; weights, bicycles, sauna. Game rm. Refrigerators, microwaves avail. Cr cds: A, C, D, DS, ER, JCB, MC, V.

D SC

✔★ **BUDGETEL INN.** *7815 Nicollet Ave S (55420). 612/881-7311; FAX 612/881-0604.* 190 rms, 2 story. S $55.95; D $63.95; under 18 free. Crib free. Pet accepted, some restrictions. TV; cable (premium). Complimentary continental bkfst. Restaurant nearby. Ck-out noon. Meeting rms. Business servs avail. In-rm modem link. Downhill ski 10 mi; x-country ski 1/2 mi. Cr cds: A, C, D, DS, MC, V.

D SC

★ ★ **DAYS INN-AIRPORT.** *1901 Killebrew Dr (55420), near Minneapolis/St Paul Intl Airport. 612/854-8400; FAX 612/854-3615.* 207 rms, 2 story. May-Oct: S $110; D $120-$130; under 17 free; lower rates rest of yr. Crib avail. TV; cable (premium). Heated pool; whirlpool. Complimentary coffee in lobby. Restaurant nearby. Ck-out 11 am. Meeting rms. Free airport transportation. Downhill ski 12 mi; x-country 1 mi. Sauna. Game rm. Some balconies. Cr cds: A, C, D, DS, MC, V.

D

★ **EXEL INN.** *2701 E 78th St (55425), near Minneapolis/St Paul Intl Airport. 612/854-7200; FAX 612/854-8652.* 203 rms, 2 story. S $50-$70; D $60-$75; whirlpool rms $85.99-$125.99; under 18 free. Crib free. TV; cable (premium), VCR avail. Complimentary continental bkfst. Restaurant nearby. Ck-out noon. Business servs avail. In-rm modem link. Sundries. Free airport transportation. Downhill ski 10 mi; x-country ski 2 mi. Exercise equipt; bicycles, treadmill. Microwaves avail. Cr cds: A, C, D, DS, MC, V.

D SC

★ ★ **HAMPTON INN.** *4201 W 80th St (55437), near Minneapolis/St Paul Intl Airport. 612/835-6643; FAX 612/835-7217.* 135 rms, 4 story. S $64-$104; D $74-$114; each addl $10; suites $89-$119; under 18 free. Crib free. TV; cable (premium). Complimentary continental bkfst. Restaurant adj open 24 hrs. Ck-out noon. Meeting rms. Business servs avail. In-rm modem link. Valet serv. Free airport transportation. Downhill/x-country ski 2 mi. Health club privileges. Private balconies. Cr cds: A, C, D, DS, ER, JCB, MC, V.

D SC

★ ★ **HAMPTON INN.** *(7740 Flying Cloud Dr, Eden Prairie 55344) NW on I-494 to exit 11A. 612/942-9000; FAX 612/942-0725.* 122 rms, 3 story. S $69-$79; D $75-$79; under 18 free. Crib free. TV; cable (premium). Complimentary continental bkfst. Restaurant nearby. Ck-out noon. Meeting rms. Business servs avail. In-rm modem link. Downhill ski 6 mi; x-country ski 1 mi. Cr cds: A, C, D, DS, MC, V.

D SC

★ ★ **HOLIDAY INN EXPRESS-AIRPORT.** *814 E 79th St (55420). 612/854-5558; FAX 612/854-4623.* 142 rms, 4 story. S $74-$90; D $79-$95; each addl $10; suites $90; under 18 free. Crib free. TV; cable (premium). Complimentary continental bkfst. Restaurant open 24 hrs. Ck-out noon. Business servs avail. In-rm modem link. Free airport transportation. Downhill ski 15 mi; x-country ski 2 mi. Refrigerator in suites. Cr cds: A, C, D, DS, ER, JCB, MC, V.

D SC

★ ★ **QUALITY INN & SUITES-BURNSVILLE.** *(250 N River Ridge Circle, Burnsville 55337) S on I-35. 612/890-9550; FAX 612/890-5161.* 94 rms, 2 story, 30 suites. May-Oct: S $69; D $79; each addl $8; suites $99-$280; under 18 free; lower rates rest of yr. TV; cable (premium), VCR avail (movies). Indoor/outdoor pool; whirlpool. Bar. Ck-out noon. Meeting rms. Business servs avail. Balconies. Suites decorated in different themes. Cr cds: A, C, D, DS, MC, V.

D SC

★ ★ **RESIDENCE INN BY MARRIOTT.** *(7780 Flying Cloud Dr, Eden Prairie 55344) W on I-494. 612/829-0033; FAX 612/829-1935.* 126 kit. suites, 1-2 story. S, D $129-$195; under 18 free. Pet accepted, some restrictions; $50. TV; cable (premium), VCR (movies $3.50). Heated pool; whirlpool. Complimentary bkfst buffet. Ck-out noon. Coin lndry. Meeting rms. Business servs avail. In-rm modem link. Valet serv. Airport transportation avail. Downhill ski 10 mi; x-country ski 1 mi. Exercise equipt; stair machine, weights. Refrigerators. Private patios, balconies. Cr cds: A, C, D, DS, JCB, MC, V.

D SC

✔★ **SELECT INN.** *7851 Normandale Blvd (55435). 612/835-7400; FAX 612/835-4124; res: 800/641-1000.* 148 rms, 2 story. S $46.90; D $55.90; each addl $4; under 13 free. Crib $3. Pet accepted; $25. TV; cable. Indoor pool. Complimentary continental bkfst. Restaurant nearby. Ck-out 11 am. Coin lndry. Meeting rms. Business servs avail. Free airport transportation. Downhill ski 5 mi. Exercise equipt; weights, treadmill. Cr cds: A, C, D, DS, MC, V.

D SC

✔★ **SUPER 8.** *(11500 W 78th St, Eden Prairie 55344) W on I-494 to US 169. 612/829-0888; FAX 612/829-0854.* 61 rms, 3 story. No elvtr. S $50.88; D $60.88; each addl $6; under 12 free. Crib free. TV; cable (premium). Complimentary continental bkfst. Ck-out 11 am. Coin lndry. Business servs avail. X-country ski. Cr cds: A, C, D, DS, MC, V.

D SC

Motor Hotels

★ ★ **COMFORT INN.** *1321 E 78th St (55425). 612/854-3400; FAX 612/854-2234.* 272 rms, 5 story. S, D $69-$89; each addl $7; suites $145; under 17 free. Crib free. TV; cable (premium). Indoor pool. Coffee in rms. Restaurant 6-11 am, 5-10 pm; Sat 7 am-midnight; Sun 8 am-10 pm. Bar 11-1 am. Ck-out 11 am. Meeting rms. Business servs avail. Valet serv. Sundries. Free airport transportation. Downhill ski 10 mi; x-country ski 1 mi. Exercise equipt; weights, bicycles. Cr cds: A, C, D, DS, ER, JCB, MC, V.

D SC

★ ★ **COUNTRY INN AND SUITES.** *2221 Killebrew Dr (55425). 612/854-5555; FAX 612/854-5564.* 234 rms, 6 story. S $95-$165; D $109-$165; each addl $10; suites $109-$165; under 19 free. Crib free. TV; cable (premium). Indoor pool; whirlpool, poolside serv. Complimentary continental bkfst. Restaurant adj 11 am-midnight. Ck-out noon. Meeting rms. Business servs avail. Free airport transportation. Downhill ski 14 mi; x-country 1 mi. Exercise equipt; weights, treadmills. Some refrigerators; microwaves avail. Cr cds: A, C, D, DS, MC, V.

D SC

★ ★ **FAIRFIELD INN BY MARRIOTT.** *2401 E 80th St (55425). 612/858-8475; FAX 612/858-8475.* 134 rms, 4 story. May-Oct: S, D $79-$140; under 18 free; lower rates rest of yr. Crib avail. Pet accepted. TV; cable (premium). Indoor pool; whirlpool. Complimentary continental bkfst. Restaurant adj 6 am-11 pm. Ck-out noon. Meeting rms. Business servs avail. Downhill ski 15 mi; x-country ski 1 mi. Rec rm. Some refrigerators. Cr cds: A, C, D, DS, JCB, MC, V.

D

✓★ ★ **HOLIDAY INN CENTRAL.** *1201 W 94th St (55431). 612/884-8211; FAX 612/881-5574.* 171 rms, 4 story. S, D $89-$104; under 19 free. Crib avail. TV; cable. Indoor pool; whirlpool, poolside serv. Restaurant 6:30 am-10 pm. Rm serv. Bar. Ck-out 11 am. Coin Indry. Meeting rms. Business servs avail. In-rm modem link. Sundries. Free airport transportation. Downhill ski 6 mi. Exercise equipt; bicycles, treadmill, sauna. Game rm. Refrigerators avail. Cr cds: A, C, D, DS, JCB, MC, V.

D SC

★ ★ ★ **MARRIOTT.** *2020 E 79th St (55425), at jct 24th Ave & I-494, near Minneapolis/St Paul Intl Airport. 612/854-7441; FAX 612/854-7671.* Web www.marriott.com. 478 rms, 2-5 story. S $99-$175; D $109-$170; under 18 free; wkend rates. Crib free. TV; cable (premium), VCR. Indoor pool; whirlpool. Restaurant 6 am-10 pm; Sat, Sun 7 am-11 pm. Rm serv. Bar 11-1 am. Ck-out noon. Meeting rms. Business center. In-rm modem link. Gift shop. Free airport transportation. Exercise equipt; bicycles, stair machine. Game rm. Luxury level. Cr cds: A, C, D, DS, ER, JCB, MC, V.

D SC

★ ★ ★ **SHERATON-AIRPORT.** *2500 E 79th St (55425), near Minneapolis/St Paul Intl Airport. 612/854-1771; FAX 612/854-5898.* 250 rms, 2-4 story. S, D $110-$120; suites $140-$160; each addl $10; under 18 free. Crib free. TV; cable (premium), VCR avail. Indoor pool; whirlpool. Restaurant 6 am-10:30 pm; Sat, Sun from 7 am. Rm serv. Bar 11:30-1 am. Ck-out noon. Meeting rms. Business servs avail. Valet serv. Sundries. Free airport transportation. Downhill ski 10 mi; x-country ski 2 mi. Exercise equipt; weights, bicycles. Microwaves avail. Near Mall of America. Cr cds: A, C, D, DS, ER, JCB, MC, V.

D SC

★ ★ **WYNDHAM GARDEN.** *4460 W 78th St Circle (55435), near Minneapolis/St Paul Intl Airport. 612/831-3131; FAX 612/831-6372.* 209 rms, 8 story. S $79-$125; D $89-$135; each addl $10; suites $99-$145; under 19 free; wkend rates. Crib free. TV; cable (premium). Indoor pool; whirlpool. Coffee in rms. Restaurant 7 am-10 pm. Rm serv from 5 pm. Bar. Ck-out noon. Meeting rms. Business servs avail. In-rm modem link. Valet serv. Sundries. Free airport transportation. Exercise equipt; weights, stair machine. Downhill/x-country ski 2 mi. Wet bar in suites. Cr cds: A, C, D, DS, ER, JCB, MC, V.

D SC

Hotels

✓★ ★ **BEST WESTERN BRADBURY SUITES.** *7770 Johnson Ave (55435). 612/893-9999; FAX 612/893-1316.* 164 rms, 6 story. S $69.95-$79.95; D $90.95; each addl $5; under 16 free. Crib free. TV; cable (premium), VCR. Complimentary bkfst buffet. Restaurant adj. Ck-out noon. Meeting rms. Business servs avail. In-rm modem link. Airport transportation. Downhill/x-country ski 1 mi. Health club privileges. Refrigerators. Cr cds: A, C, D, DS, MC, V.

D SC

✓★ ★ **BEST WESTERN HOTEL SEVILLE.** *8151 Bridge Rd (55437). 612/830-1300; FAX 612/830-1535.* Web www.bestwestern.com. 252 rms, 18 story. S, D $79.95-$89.95; under 16 free; wkend rates. Crib free. TV. Indoor pool; whirlpool. Restaurant 6 am-1:30 pm, 5:30-9:30 pm; wkend hrs vary. Bar. Ck-out 11 am. Convention facilities. Business servs avail. In-rm modem link. Free airport transportation. Downhill ski 5 mi; x-country ski 1 mi. Sauna. Health club privileges. Game rm. Balconies. Cr cds: A, C, D, DS, JCB, MC, V.

D SC

★ ★ ★ **DOUBLETREE GRAND HOTEL-MALL OF AMERICA.** *7901 24th Ave S (55425), just off I-494 exit 24th Ave, opp Mall of America, near Minneapolis/St Paul Intl Airport. 612/854-2244; FAX 612/854-4421.* 321 rms, 15 story. S, D $135-$155; each addl $20; suites $225-$400; wkend rates. TV; cable (premium), VCR. Indoor pool; whirlpool, poolside serv. Restaurant 6 am-10 pm. Rm serv 24 hrs. Bar from 11 am. Ck-out noon. Business center. In-rm modem link. Gift shop. Free airport transportation. Exercise equipt; weights, stair machine, sauna. Some private patios, balconies. Luxury level. Cr cds: A, C, D, DS, ER, MC, V.

D SC

★ ★ ★ **DOUBLETREE GUEST SUITES.** *2800 W 80th (55431), near Minneapolis/St Paul Intl Airport. 612/884-4811; FAX 612/884-8137.* Web www.doubletreehotels.com. 219 rms, 8 story. S, D $110-$179; each addl $10; under 12 free. Crib free. TV; cable (premium). Indoor pool; whirlpool. Restaurant 11:30 am-10 pm. Bar to 1 am. Ck-out noon. Coin Indry. Meeting rms. Business servs avail. In-rm modem link. Free airport transportation. Downhill ski 8 mi; x-country ski 1 mi. Exercise equipt; weights, stair machines, sauna, steam rm. Game rm. Refrigerators, microwaves. Private patios, balconies. Cr cds: A, C, D, DS, JCB, MC, V.

D SC

★ ★ ★ **EMBASSY SUITES-AIRPORT.** *7901 34th Ave S (55425), near Minneapolis/St Paul Intl Airport. 612/854-1000; FAX 612/854-6557.* 310 rms, 10 story. S, D $129-$159; each addl $10; under 18 free. Crib free. TV; cable (premium). Indoor pool; whirlpool. Complimentary full bkfst. Restaurant 11 am-10 pm. Bar to 1 am. Ck-out noon. Meeting rms. Business servs avail. In-rm modem link. Gift shop. Free airport transportation. Downhill ski 15 mi; x-country ski 2 mi. Exercise equipt; weight machine, treadmills, sauna. Microwaves. Private balconies. All rms open to courtyard atrium. Cr cds: A, C, D, DS, ER, JCB, MC, V.

D

★ ★ **HAWTHORN SUITES.** *(3400 Edinborough Way, Edina 55435) 1/2 mi E of jct MN 100 & I-494. 612/893-9300; FAX 612/893-9885.* 141 kit. suites, 7 story. S, D $135-$145; under 18 free; wkend rates. Crib free. TV; cable (premium), VCR (movies $6). Indoor pool. Playground. Complimentary full bkfst. Complimentary coffee in rms. Restaurant nearby. No rm serv. Ck-out noon. Coin Indry. Meeting rms. Business servs avail. In-rm modem link. Sundries. Airport transportation. Downhill ski 7 mi; x-country ski 1 mi. Health club privileges. Microwaves. Cr cds: A, C, D, DS, MC, V.

D SC

★ ★ ★ **HOLIDAY INN SELECT-INTERNATIONAL AIRPORT.** *3 Apple Tree Square (55425), I-494 exit 34th Ave, opp river, near Minneapolis/St Paul Intl Airport. 612/854-9000.* 430 rms, 13 story. S, D $97-$169; each addl $10; suites $103-$250; under 19 free; wkend plans. Crib free. TV; cable (premium), VCR avail. Indoor pool; whirlpool, poolside serv. Restaurant 6 am-11 pm. Bar 11-1 am. Ck-out noon. Convention facilities. Business servs avail. In-rm modem link. Free covered parking. Free airport transportation. Downhill/x-country ski 10 mi. Exercise rm; instructor, weights, bicycles, sauna. Massage. Some refrigerators. Cr cds: A, C, D, DS, ER, JCB, MC, V.

D SC

★ ★ ★ **HOTEL SOFITEL.** *5601 W 78th St (55439), at jct MN 100 & I-494. 612/835-1900; FAX 612/835-2696; res: 800/876-6303 (exc MN).* 282 rms, 6 story. S $149-$167; D $164-$181; each addl $15; suites $185-$275; wkend rates. Crib free. TV; cable (premium), VCR avail. Indoor pool. Restaurants 6:30-1 am (also see LA TERRASSE, Unrated Dining). Bars 11-1 am; Sun 10 am-midnight. Ck-out noon. Convention facilities. Business center. In-rm modem link. Concierge. Valet parking. Airport transportation. Downhill/x-country ski 1 mi. Exercise equipt; weights, bicycles. Massage. Cr cds: A, C, D, MC, V.

D

★ ★ ★ **RADISSON-SOUTH.** *7800 Normandale Blvd (55439), jct I-94 & MN 100. 612/835-7800; FAX 612/893-8419.* Web www.radisson.com. 580 rms, 22 story. S, D $139-$159; each addl $15; suites $250-$450; under 18 free; cabanas $125-$135; wkend rates. Crib free. TV; VCR avail. Indoor pool; whirlpool. Coffee in rms. Restaurant 6:30 am-10 pm. Bar 11-1 am. Ck-out noon. Convention facilities. Business servs avail. In-rm modem link. Shopping arcade. Airport transportation avail. Downhill/x-country ski 2 mi. Exercise equipt; weights, bicycle, sauna. Luxury level. Cr cds: A, C, D, DS, ER, JCB, MC, V.

D SC

Restaurants

✔★ ★ **ASIA GRILLE.** *(549 Prairie Center Dr, Eden Prairie 55344) 612/944-4095.* Hrs: 11 am-10 pm; Fri, Sat to 11 pm. Closed most major hols. Asian menu. Bar. Semi-a la carte: lunch $6.95-$9.95, dinner $6.95-$14.95. Specialties: spit-roasted garlic chicken, Asian pork with mushrooms. Contemporary decor. Cr cds: A, C, D, DS, MC, V.

D

✔★ ★ **ASIA GRILLE.** *(14023 Aldrich Ave S, Burnsville 55337) S on US 35W. 612/898-3303.* Hrs: 11:30 am-10 pm; Fri, Sat to 11 pm; Sun, Mon to 9 pm. Closed Memorial Day, Thanksgiving, Dec 25. Res accepted. Chinese menu. Bar. Semi-a la carte: lunch $5-$7, dinner $7-$12. Specialties: Asian tacos, soy-garlic rotisserie chicken. Own noodles. Outdoor dining. Casual, Asian decor. Cr cds: A, D, DS, MC, V.

D

★ **DAVID FONG'S.** *9392 Lyndale S (55420). 612/888-9294.* Hrs: 11 am-9 pm; Thurs-Sat to 10 pm. Closed Sun; most major hols. Res accepted. Chinese menu. Bar to 1 am. Semi-a la carte: lunch, dinner $10.75-$21.95. Child's meals. Oriental decor. Cr cds: A, C, D, MC, V.

★ ★ ★ **KINCAID'S.** *8400 Normandale Lake Blvd. 612/921-2255.* Hrs: 11 am-2:30 pm, 5-10 pm; Sat 4:30-11 pm; Sun 5-9 pm; Sun brunch 10 am-2 pm. Closed July 4, Thanksgiving, Dec 25. Res accepted. Bar to midnight. Semi-a la carte: lunch $5.95-$14.95, dinner $14.95-$26.95. Sun brunch $8.95-$16.95. Child's meals. Specialties: mesquite-grilled king salmon, rock salt prime rib. Own baking, desserts. Parking. Outdoor dining. In 5-story atrium; overlooks Lake Normandale. Cr cds: A, C, D, DS, MC, V.

✔★ **TEJAS.** *3910 W 50th St (55424). 612/926-0800.* Hrs: 11:30 am-10 pm; Fri, Sat to 10:30 pm; Sun 11 am-9 pm. Res accepted. Southwestern menu. Wine, beer. A la carte entrees: lunch $5.25-$8.50, dinner $7-$17. Specialties: smoked chicken nachos, braised lamb shank. Patio dining in summer. Totally nonsmoking. Cr cds: A, C, D, DS, MC, V.

D

Unrated Dining Spots

DA AFGHAN. *929 W 80th St. 612/888-5824.* Hrs: 4:30-9:30 pm; Thur, Fri 11 am-1:30 pm, 4:30-9:30 pm; Sat 4-9:30 pm; Sun 4-9 pm. Closed July 4. Res accepted. Middle Eastern, Greek menu. Wine, beer. Semi-a la carte: lunch $4.95-$9.95, dinner $8.95-$16. Child's meals. Specializes in lamb, chicken, vegetarian dishes. Parking. Cr cds: A, MC, V.

LA TERRASSE. *(See Hotel Sofitel) 612/835-1900.* Hrs: 11 am-midnight; Fri-Sat to 1 am; Sun 10:30 am-midnight; Sun brunch to 2:30 pm. French menu. Bar to 1 am. Semi-a la carte: lunch, dinner $5.75-$11.50. Sun brunch $8.50. Specializes in onion soup, seasonal French dishes. Valet parking. Outdoor dining. Cr cds: A, C, D, MC, V.

PLANET HOLLYWOOD. *S-402 (55425), Mall of America. 612/854-7827.* Hrs: 11-1 am; Sun to midnight. Closed Thanksgiving, Dec 25. Bar. Semi-a la carte: lunch, dinner $6.50-$17.95. Specialties: chicken tenders, fajitas. Authentic Hollywood memorabilia displayed. Gift shop. Cr cds: A, C, D, DS, JCB, MC, V.

RAINFOREST CAFE. *S-102 (55425), Mall of America. 612/854-7500.* Hrs: 11 am-10 pm; Sat 10 am-11 pm; Sun to 9 pm. Closed Thanksgiving, Dec 25. Bar. Semi-a la carte: lunch, dinner $8.95-$15.95. Child's meals. Specialties: rasta pasta, pita quesadillas. Rainforest atmosphere with flashing lighting, roaring thunder. Cr cds: A, C, D, DS, JCB, MC, V.

Montréal

Founded: 1642
Pop: 3,100,000
Elev: 117 feet
Time zone: Eastern
Area code: 514
Web: www.pagemontreal.qc.ca

Montréal's identity is shaped by its island location, its French-speaking population and its blend of old and new. Situated at the junction of the Ottawa and St Lawrence Rivers, Montréal is Canada's transportation center. While the St Lawrence River leads to the Atlantic Ocean, the St Lawrence Seaway travels inland to the Great Lakes. Railroads converge on Montréal as well, and two major railroad companies are headquartered here.

Montréal has the largest French-speaking population outside of Paris—about two-thirds of Montréal's citizens are of French ancestry—and much of this North American city's unique atmosphere evolved from their influence. Traditionally, French Montréalers have lived in the East End area, but a recent trend shows some movement toward predominantly English-speaking suburbs.

Native Americans thrived in the area of Montréal before the arrival of Europeans. Jacques Cartier, who named the island's mountain Mont Real, came upon the native village of Hochelaga in 1535, followed by Samuel de Champlain in the early 1600s. The first permanent settlement, Ville-Marie, was established in 1642, and as trade prospered, the population increased. By the early 1700s the town's name had changed from Ville-Marie to Montréal. English-speaking settlers began arriving after the 1763 Treaty of Paris ceded Canada to the British. In 1832 Montréal was incorporated as a city, and growth continued into the 20th century. Québec's separatist movement was born here in 1960, but so far voters have chosen to remain Canadian.

Today, the stone buildings and narrow cobblestone streets of Old Montréal, on the site of Ville-Marie, contrast with modern Montréal's skyscrapers, museums, theaters and nightlife. Horse-drawn carriages called calèches meander through the town, while underground are miles of shops, restaurants and galleries. Here, the city blends not only the old and the new, but also the functional and the artistic, as reflected in the subway system: a different architect designed each of the subway's stations in a different style, creating an "underground art gallery."

Sports & Recreation

Montréal's National League baseball team, the Montréal Expos, play at Olympic Stadium, which was also the site of the 1976 summer Olympic Games. Hockey is played at the Molson Centre by the Montréal Canadiens, a National Hockey League team. Football, soccer, bike and auto races are Montréal's other popular spectator sports. Le Tour de l'Ile de Montréal is a 38-mile (70-kilometer) bicycle race through the city's streets. The Canadian Grand Prix, a Formula 1 auto race, is held at Gilles-Villeneuve track, on the Île Notre-Dame.

Each season offers a variety of participant sports. Paths for bicycling, jogging and cross-country skiing are found throughout the city. Water sports include white-water rafting in the Lachine Rapids, swimming in pools or at the beach at Île Notre-Dame, windsurfing and sailing. Tennis and squash courts are available, and so are ice-skating rinks: the city has more than 200 indoor and outdoor rinks.

Montréal's many parks provide both recreation and beauty. Landscape architect Frederick Law Olmsted designed Mount Royal Park, situated in the heart of the city and offering nearly every recreational activity, plus calèche and sleigh rides. La Fontaine Park has examples of both French and English landscape design and provides bicycling and cross-country-skiing trails, ice-skating and hockey rinks, paddleboats and a playground. Parc des Îles comprises two islands in the St Lawrence River: Île Ste-Helene, with three pools, skiing and snowshoeing, and Île Notre-Dame, the site of the Gilles-Villeneuve Grand Prix race track as well as recreational amenities.

Entertainment

Place des Arts, a theater complex, is home to L'Opera de Montréal, the Montréal Symphony Orchestra, Les Grands Ballets Canadiens, and La Compagnie Jean-Duceppe theatrical troupe.

In addition to Les Grands Ballets Canadiens, many dance companies, traditional and modern, are based in Montréal. Ballets Classiques de Montréal, O Vertigo Danse, Montréal Danse and Tangente can often be seen at Place des Arts.

The Molson Centre and Olympic Stadium frequently host rock and pop concerts. The Montréal Jazz Festival, held each summer, draws people from around the world.

Drama is a popular art in Montréal, with French-language productions predominating in venues such as the Théâtre d'Aujourd'hui, Théâtre du Nouveau Monde and Théâtre du Rideau Vert. English-language plays are produced at the Centaur Theatre and Saidye Bronfman Centre, and touring Broadway shows often play here in summer. The open-air Théâtre des Lilas, on Île Notre-Dame, has a variety of shows.

A variety of choices are available for Montréal nightlife, including comedy clubs, bars, discos and folk, jazz and rock clubs.

Historical Areas

Old (Vieux) Montréal—bordered by McGill and Berri Streets on the west and east, and Notre-Dame Street and the St Lawrence River on the north and south—lies within the borders of the original settlement of Ville-Marie. Here is the largest collection of 19th-century buildings in North

America, and several of Ville-Marie's original buildings remain as well. Place d'Armes, the central square of Old Montréal, was a French-Iroquois battle site, and in the center of the square is a statue of the founder of Ville-Marie, Paul de Chomedey, Sieur de Maisonneuve. Lining the square are St Sulpice seminary, the city's oldest building, and the Bank of Montréal, which contains a banking museum.

Churches of note within Old Montréal are the Notre-Dame Basilica, built in 1829, situated across the square from the Bank of Montréal, and Notre-Dame-de-Bonsecours, founded in 1657 and rebuilt in 1772. Notre-Dame-de-Bonsecours is on St Paul Street, the oldest street in Montréal.

Also in Old Montréal is Château Ramezay, a historical museum that was once the governor's home. Southwest of the Château Ramezay is Place Jacques-Cartier, formerly a thriving marketplace and now the site of the oldest monument in the city—the Nelson Column, built in 1809.

Historical areas are preserved outside of Old Montréal as well. Maison St-Gabriel, built in the late 1700s, contains period furnishings and other items. St Joseph's Oratory, with a chapel dating from 1904 and the crypt-church from 1916, is a famous shrine visited by more than 2 million pilgrims annually. And the Westmount area, adjacent to Mount Royal Park, contains homes built in the early 1900s, many with English gardens.

The Old Fort, built from 1820 to 1824, is the oldest remaining fort in Montréal, and in its arsenal is the David M. Stewart Museum, displaying artifacts from Canada's history.

Sightseeing

Montréal's many museums reflect its position as a cultural leader. The nation's oldest art museum, founded in 1860, is the Montréal Museum of Fine Arts (Musee des Beaux-Arts de Montréal). The works exhibited here range from Egyptian statues to 20th-century abstracts. Other art museums are the Byzantine Museum, showing Rosette Mociomitza's works, done in the style of the Byzantine period; the Museum of Decorative Arts, a 1918 mansion housing glass, textile and ceramic art; and the Notre-Dame Basilica Museum, with religious and historical art, furniture, statues and local folklore paintings.

Other museums focus on different aspects of science: The Pointe-à-Callière, the Montréal Museum of Archaeology and History, contains fascinating changing and permanent exhibits on the founding and development of Montréal. The Montréal Planetarium presents sky shows complete with special effects. And the Biodôme de Montréal is an environmental museum combining the features of a botanical garden, aquarium, zoo and nature center.

The Montréal Botanical Garden covers 180 acres (73 hectares) with almost 30,000 species and varieties of plants. On the grounds is the Insectarium de Montréal, with hands-on exhibits on insects and six themed areas. Beautiful flowers can also be seen in Floral Park, on Île Ste-Hélène.

An outdoor destination with family appeal is the Parc Safari, which has 750 animals, a drive-through wild-animal preserve, rides, shows and children's theater. Families also enjoy La Ronde, an amusement park on Île Notre-Dame.

General References

Area code: 514

Phone Numbers

Police & Fire: 911

Poison Control Center: 800/463-5060

Weather: 283-4006

Information Sources

For further information contact Québec Tourism, PO Box 979, Montréal, H3C 2W3, 800/363-7777 or in person at Infotouriste, 1001 rue de Square-Dorchester (between Peel & Metcalf Sts); also office at Old Montréal, Place Jacques-Cartier, 174 Notre-Dame St E; all have helpful information for tourists.

Transportation

AIRLINES: Air Canada, Air France, Air Ontario, American, British Airways, Business Express, Canadian, Cubana, El Al, KLM, Northwest, Olympic, Swissair, USAir, Canada 3000 and other commuter and regional airlines.

AIRPORTS: Dorval Int'l Airport, 633-3105; Mirabel Int'l Airport, 476-3010.

CAR RENTAL AGENCIES: (See IMPORTANT TOLL-FREE NUMBERS) Avis 866-7906; Budget 938-1000; Hertz 842-8537; Thrifty 631-5567; Tilden/National 878-2771.

PUBLIC TRANSPORTATION: Societe deTransport de la Communaute Urbaine de Montréal (STCUM), 288-6287.

RAILROAD PASSENGER SERVICE: Amtrak 800/872-7245.

Newspapers

La Presse; Le Journal de Montréal; Le Devoir; The Gazette.

Convention Facilities

Palais des Congres de Montréal, 201 Viger West, 871-3170.

Sports & Recreation

Major Sports Facilities

Molson Centre, 1260 de la Gauchautière W, 932-2582 (Canadiens, hockey).

Olympic Stadium, 4141 Pierre de Coubertin St, 252-8687 (Expos, baseball, 253-3434).

Gilles-Villeneuve, Île Notre-Dame, 350-0000.

Cultural Facilities

Theater & Concert Halls

Place des Arts, 260 boulevard de Maisonneuve, 842-2112.

Théâtre des Lilas, Île Notre-Dame.

Théâtre d'Aujourd'hui, 3900 rue St-Denis, 282-3900.

Théâtre du Nouveau Monde, 84 rue Ste-Catherine Ouest, 866-8667.

Théâtre du Rideau Vert, 4664 rue St-Denis, 844-1793.

Museums

Biodome de Montréal, 4777 Pierre de Coubertin St, 868-3000.

David M. Steward Museum, St Helen's Island, 861-6701.

Montréal Planetarium, 1000 Saint-Jacques St W, 872-4530.

The Old Fort, St Helen's Island.

Point-à-Callière, the Montréal Museum of Archaeology and History, 350 Place Royale, 872-9150.

Art Museums

Byzantine Museum, 6780 Biarritz Ave, 656-0188.

The Montréal Museum of Fine Arts, 1379-1380 Sherbrooke St W, 285-2000.

Museum of Decorative Arts, 2929 rue Jeanne d'Arc, 259-2575.

Notre-Dame Basilica Museum, 424 Saint Sulpice St, 842-2925.

Points of Interest

Historical

Château Ramezay, 280 Notre-Dame E, 861-3708.

Maison Saint-Gabriel, 2146 Dublin Pl, 935-8136.

Old (Vieux) Montréal, bounded by McGill, Berri, Notre-Dame Sts & the St Lawrence River.

Notre-Dame Basilica, 116 Notre-Dame St W

Notre-Dame-de-Bonsecours Church, Place Jacques-Cartier, Notre-Dame St.

Place d'Armes, St Sulpice & Notre-Dame Sts.

Saint Joseph's Oratory, 3800 Queen Mary Rd, 733-8211.

Saint-Paul St, in Old Montréal.

Other Attractions

Angrignon Park, 3400 des Trinitaires Blvd, 872-3816.

Casino Montréal, 1 Ave du Casino, 392-2746.

Dorchester Square, René-Lévesque Blvd W between Peel and Matcalfe Sts.

Floral Park, Parc des Îles, 872-6093.

Fort Lennox, 10 mi N off Hwy 223, 291-5700.

Insectarium de Montréal, 4101Sherbrooke St E, 872-1400.

La Fontaine Park, Sherbrook St & Papineau Ave, 872-2644.

La Ronde, Parc des Îles, 872-6222.

McGill University, 398-4455.

Montréal Botanical Garden, 4101 Sherbrooke St E, 872-1400.

Mount Royal Park, Côte des Neiges & Remembrance Rds, 872-6559.

Olympic Park, 4141 Pierre de Coubertin St, 252-8687.

Parc Safari, 33 mi S on Hwy 15 to exit 6, 247-2727.

Parc des Îles, two islands in the middle of St Lawrence River, 872-6093.

Université de Montréal, N slope of Mount Royal, 2900 boulevard Edouard Montpetit.

Université du Québec, rues Sanguinet & Berri and boulevards de Maisonneuve & René-Lévesque.

Sightseeing Tours

Calèche tours, Dominion Square, Mount Royal Park or Old Port of Montréal.

Montréal Harbour Cruises, at foot of Berri St, 842-7655.

Gray Line bus tours, 1140 Wellington St, 934-1222.

Annual Events

Canadian Grand Prix, Parc des Îles, 350-0000. June.

Fête Nationale. June 24.

Antiques Bonaventure, East Exhibition Hall, Place Bonaventure, 397-2222. Mid-June.

Montréal Jazz Festival, downtown, 871-1881. Late June-early July.

Just for Laughs, 845-3155. Late July.

World Film Festival, 848-3883. 2 wks late Aug.

Lodgings and Food

Motels

★ ★ **AUBERGES WANDLYN.** *(7200 Sherbrooke St E, Montréal QE H1N 1E7) 514/256-1613; FAX 514/256-5150.* 123 rms, 2 story. June-Oct: S $63-$89.50; D $63-$99.50; each addl $10; suites $99.50-$129.50; under 18 free; lower rates rest of yr. TV; cable. Heated pool; poolside serv; lifeguard. Restaurant 7 am-2 pm. Bar 4 pm-midnight. Ck-out noon. Meeting rms. Business servs avail. Balconies. Cr cds: A, C, D, DS, ER, MC, V.

SC

★ **FRANDY.** *(3520 Hwy 132W, Ville Ste-Catherine QE J0L 1E0) On Hwy 132W, 7 mi W of Champlain Bridge. 514/632-2870.* 18 rms. May-Sept: S $45; D $60-$65; each addl $5; lower rates rest of yr. Crib free. TV; cable. Pool. Restaurant nearby. Ck-out noon. Picnic tables. Refrigerators. Cr cds: A, MC, V.

★ ★ ★ **HOSTELLERIE LES TROIS TILLEULS.** *(290 Richelieu Blvd, St-Marc-sur-Richelieu QE J0L 2E0) 26 mi SE on Hwy 20E, exit 112, then 5 mi N on Hwy 223. 514/584-2231; FAX 514/584-3146; res: 800/263-2230.* 24 rms, 3 story. S $92-$125; D $110-$145; each addl $20; suites $225-$390. Crib free. TV; cable (premium), VCR (free movies). Heated pool. Restaurant (see LES TROIS TILLEULS). Rm serv. Bar 11-2 am. Ck-out noon. Meeting rms. Business center. In-rm modem links. Lighted tennis. X-country ski 10 mi. Hunting trips. Private marina. Boat tours. Some in-rm whirlpools. Balconies. Golf nearby. In 1880 farmhouse. On Richelieu River. Cr cds: A, C, D, ER, MC, V.

★ **HÔTEL LE SAINT-ANDRÉ.** *(1285 rue St-André, Montréal QE H2L 3T1) 514/849-7070; FAX 514/849-8167; res: 800/265-7071.* 61 rms, 4 story. May-Oct: S $64.50; D $69.50; each addl $5; lower rates rest of yr. TV. Complimentary continental bkfst. Restaurant nearby. Ck-out noon. Meeting rm. Business servs avail. Sundries. Small, contemporary hotel. Cr cds: A, D, DS, ER, MC, V.

★ **MOTEL DU FLEUVE.** *(7600 Marie Victorin Blvd, Brossard QE J4W 1B2) 3 mi SW on Hwy 15, exit Rome Blvd. 514/671-2299; FAX 514/671-0066.* 25 rms. May-Oct: S $69; D $75; each addl $8; wkly rates off-season; lower rates rest of yr. Crib free. TV; cable, VCR avail (movies). Complimentary coffee in lobby. Restaurant nearby. Ck-out noon. Business servs avail. Sundries. Cr cds: A, D, ER, MC, V.

SC

Motor Hotels

★ **DAYS INN-MONTRÉAL AIRPORT.** *(4545 Côte-Vertu W, Montréal QE H4S 1C8) 8 mi N on Hwy 40, exit 62W. 514/332-2720; FAX 514/332-4512.* 91 rms, 3 story. S, D $55-$95; wkend rates. Crib free. Pet accepted. TV; VCR avail. Pool; lifeguard. Coffee in rms. Restaurant 7 am-11 pm. Rm serv. Bar 4-11 pm. Ck-out 1 pm. Coin lndry. Meeting rms. Business servs avail. In-rm modem link. Cr cds: A, C, D, DS, ER, JCB, MC, V.

SC

★ ★ ★ **HOSTELLERIE RIVE GAUCHE.** *(1810 Richelieu Blvd, Beloeil QE J3G 4S4) CAN 20E exit 112, at jct Hwy 223. 514/467-4477; FAX 514/467-0525.* 22 rms, 3 story. S $92-$125; D $110-$145; each addl $20; suites $225-$235. Crib free. TV; cable (premium). Pool. Restaurant 7:30 am-10:30 pm. Bar 11-midnight. Ck-out noon. Meeting rms. Business servs avail. Lighted tennis. X-country ski 8 mi. Balconies. View of Richelieu River & Mont St-Hilaire. Cr cds: A, C, D, DS, ER, MC, V.

✔★ **HOTEL LA RÉSIDENCE DU VOYAGEUR.** *(847 Sherbrooke East, Montréal QE H2L 1K6) 514/527-9515; FAX 514/526-1070.* Web wworks.com~resvoyager. 28 units, 4 story. June-mid-Sept: S $50-$90; D $65-$105; each addl $5; under 5 free; wkly rates winter; lower rates rest of yr. TV; cable, VCR avail. Complimentary continental bkfst. Restaurants nearby. Ck-out noon. Business servs avail. Free parking. Airport transportation. Refrigerators, microwaves avail. Cr cds: C, D, ER, MC, V.

SC

★ ★ **QUALITY HOTEL DORVAL.** *(7700 Côte de Liesse, Montréal QE H4T 1E7) near Dorval Intl Airport. 514/731-7821; FAX 514/731-1538.* 159 rms, 4 story, 47 kits. S, D $98-$145; each addl $10; wkend rates. Crib free. TV; cable (premium). Pool; whirlpool, lifeguard, poolside serv. Restaurant 6:30 am-2 pm, 6-11 pm. Rm serv. Bar 5 pm-1 am. Ck-out noon. Coin lndry. Meeting rms. Business servs avail. Concierge. Valet serv. Free airport transportation. Exercise equipt; weights, stair machine, sauna. Massage. Minibars. Cr cds: A, C, D, DS, ER, JCB, MC, V.

D SC

✔★ ★ **QUALITY INN LE BOULEVARD.** *(6680 Taschereau Blvd, Brossard QE J4W 1M8) E on Hwy 10, exit 8E (Taschereau Blvd). 514/671-7213; FAX 514/671-7041.* 100 rms, 3 story. May-Oct: S, D $77-$82; each addl $10; under 18 free; lower rates rest of yr. TV. Pool. Complimentary continental bkfst. Restaurant 11:30 am-10:30 pm. Bar. Ck-out noon. Meeting rms. Business servs avail. Cr cds: A, D, ER, MC, V.

SC

Hotels

★ ★ ★ **BONAVENTURE HILTON.** *(1 Place Bonaventure, Montréal QE H5A 1E4) 514/878-2332; FAX 514/878-3881.* Web www.travelweb.com/hiltnint.html. 395 rms, 3 story. S $135-$244; D $145-$268; each addl $25; suites $360-$1,100; wkend package. Crib free. Pet accepted. TV; cable, VCR avail. Heated pool; poolside serv in summer, lifeguard. Restaurant 6:30 am-11 pm (also see LE CASTILLON). Bar 11:30-1 am. Ck-out noon. Meeting rms. Business center. In-rm modem link. Garage; valet parking. Exercise equipt; bicycles, stair machine. Massage. Minibars. 17th-floor garden courtyard; pheasants, ducks, goldfish ponds. Access to subway via underground mall. Cr cds: A, C, D, DS, ER, JCB, MC, V.

D SC

★ ★ **CHÂTEAU ROYAL HOTEL SUITES.** *(1420 Crescent St, Montréal QE H3G 2B7) 514/848-0999; FAX 514/848-1891; res: 800/363-0335.* 112 kit. suites, 21 story. S, D $89-$169; each addl $15; under 14 free; wkend rates. Crib free. Garage $12. TV; cable (premium). Complimentary coffee in rms. Restaurant 7-1 am. Ck-out noon. Coin lndry. Meeting rms. Business servs avail. Health club privileges. Microwaves avail. Balconies. Apartment-style units. Cr cds: A, C, D, DS, ER, MC, V.

D SC

★ ★ ★ **CHÂTEAU VAUDREUIL.** *(21700 Trans-Canada Hwy, Vaudreuil QE J7V 8P3) W on Trans-Canada Hwy 40, exit 36. 514/455-0955; FAX 514/455-6617; res: 800/363-7896.* 117 rms, 6 story, 103 suites. May-Dec: S, D $125-$165; each addl $20; suites $135-$400; under 16 free; wkend rates; higher rates special events; lower rates rest of yr. Crib free. TV; cable, VCR (movies). Indoor pool; whirlpool, sauna. Complimentary coffee in rms. Restaurant 6:30 am-11 pm. Bar 11-2 am; entertainment Tues-Sun. Ck-out noon. Meeting rms. Business center. In-rm modem link. Concierge. Tennis. Downhill/x-country ski 15 mi . Exercise equipt; weight machine, bicycle. Minibars. Some balconies. On lake. Cr cds: A, D, ER, MC, V.

D SC

★ ★ ★ **CHÂTEAU VERSAILLES.** *(1659 Sherbrooke St W, Montréal QE H3H 1E3) at St-Mathieu. 514/933-3611; FAX 514/933-6867; res: 800/361-7199 (CN); 800 361-3664 (US).* 176 rms, 3-14 story, 35 kits. S $105-$175; D $125-$175; each addl $15; suites $325-$350; under 14 free; wkend packages. Crib free. Heated garage; valet $10.50. TV; cable. Restaurant (see CHAMPS ELYSÉES). Meeting rms. Business center. In-rm modem link. Health club privileges. Some minibars. Comprised of 4 renovated Victorian houses and a 14-story tower. Cr cds: A, D, DS, ER, MC, V.

D SC

★ **DAYS INN-MIDTOWN.** *(1005 Guy St, Montréal QE H3H 2K4) at René Lévesque Blvd W. 514/938-4611; FAX 514/938-8718.* 205 rms, 7 story. May-Oct: S $109; D $119; each addl $10; suites $175-$250; under 18 free; wkend package; lower rates rest of yr. Crib $15. Parking (fee). TV; cable. Heated pool; lifeguard. Restaurant 7 am-10 pm; closed Nov-Apr. Ck-out noon. Meeting rms. Business servs avail. Gift shop. Cr cds: A, D, DS, ER, MC, V.

SC

★ ★ ★ **DELTA.** *(475 President Kennedy, Montréal QE H3A 1V7) 514/286-1986; FAX 514/284-4342; res: 800/268-1133 (CN); 800/877-1133 (US).* 453 rms, 23 story. S, D $195-$210; each addl $15; suites $315-$880; under 18 free; wkend packages. Crib free. Pet accepted. Covered parking $12. TV; cable, VCR avail. 2 pools, 1 indoor; whirlpool. Supervised child's activities; ages 2-17, wkends only. Coffee in rms. Restaurant 7 am-9:30 pm. Rm serv to 1 am. Bar 11:30-1:30 am; entertainment exc Sun. Ck-out noon. Convention facilities. Business center. In-rm modem link. Concierge. Barber, beauty shop. Exercise rm; instructor, weights, bicycles, sauna. Massage. Minibars. Balconies. Cr cds: A, C, D, ER, JCB, MC, V.

D SC

★ ★ **HOLIDAY INN SELECT CENTRE VILLE.** *(99 Viger Ave W, Montréal QE H2Z 1E9) 514/878-9888; FAX 514/878-6341.* 235 rms, 8 story. May-Oct: S $160-$185; D $170-$195; each addl $10; suites $375-$475; family, wkly, wkend rates; lower rates rest of yr. Crib free. Garage fee in/out. TV; cable. Indoor pool; whirlpool. Coffee in rms. Restaurant 6:30 am-11 pm. Bar 11-1 am. Ck-out noon. Meeting rms. Business center. In-rm modem link. Gift shop. Barber, beauty shop. Exercise equipt; weight machine, bicycles, saunas, steam rm. Massage. Some balconies. Pagoda-topped building in Chinatown area. Cr cds: A, C, D, DS, ER, JCB, MC, V.

D SC

★ ★ **HOTEL AUBERGE UNIVERSEL MONTREAL.** *(5000 Sherbrooke St E, Montréal QE H1V 1A1) 514/253-3365; FAX 514/253-9958; res: 800/567-0223.* 231 rms, 7 story. S $97; D $107; each addl $12; suites $175-$225; under 16 free. TV; cable (premium), VCR avail. 2 pools, 1 indoor; whirlpool, sauna. Restaurant 7 am-11 pm. Bar; entertainment Tues-Sat. Ck-out noon. Meeting rms. Business servs avail. Gift shop. Valet serv. Free covered parking. Refrigerator in suites. Microwaves avail. Across from Olympic stadium, biodome, botanical gardens. Cr cds: A, C, D, ER, MC, V.

SC

★ ★ ★ **HÔTEL COMPLEXE DESJARDINS.** *(4 Complexe Desjardins, Montréal QE H5B 1E5) at Jeanne Mance St, opp Place des Arts, downtown. 514/285-1450; res: 800/361-8234; FAX 514/285-1243.* Web www.hoteldesjardins.com. 600 rms, 12 story. S, D $170; each addl $20; suites $340-$950; under 17 free; wkend rates. Crib free. Garage fee. TV; cable (premium), VCR avail. Indoor pool; whirlpool, poolside serv, lifeguard. Restaurant 7 am-midnight (also see LE CAFE FLEURI). Rm serv. Bar 11:30-1 am; entertainment. Ck-out noon. Meeting rms. Business center. In-rm modem link. Concierge. Shopping arcade. Exercise rm; instructor, bicycles, stair machine, sauna. Health club privileges. Massage. Minibars. Cr cds: A, C, D, DS, ER, JCB, MC, V.

D SC

★ ★ ★ **HOTEL DU PARC.** *(3625 Parc Ave, Montréal QE H2X 3P8) 514/288-6666; FAX 514/288-2469.* 449 rms, 16 story. May-Oct: S, D $99-$129; each addl $10; suites $150-$350; under 18 free; wkend rates; lower rates rest of yr. Crib free. Garage (fee). Pet accepted, some restrictions. TV; cable, VCR avail. Free coffee in rms. Restaurant 7 am-10:30 pm. Bar from 4 pm. Ck-out noon. Meeting rms. Business servs avail. Exercise equipt: weights, bicycles. Health club privileges. Shopping arcade. Barber, beauty shop. Luxury level. Cr cds: A, C, D, DS, ER, JCB, MC, V.

D SC

★ **HOTEL LORD BERRI.** *(1199 Berri St, Montréal QE H2L 4C6) 514/845-9236; res: 888/363-0363 (NE US, CAN); FAX 514/849-9855.* 154 rms, 10 story. May-Oct: S, D $89-$99; each addl $10; suites $129.50; lower rates rest of yr. Crib free. Parking $10. TV; cable (premium). Complimentary coffee in rms. Restaurant 7 am-11 pm. Bar. Ck-out noon. Meeting rms. Business servs avail. In-rm modem link. Garage parking. Cr cds: A, C, D, DS, ER, JCB, MC, V.

D SC

★ **HOWARD JOHNSON-PLAZA.** *(475 Sherbrooke St W, Montréal QE H3A 2L9) 514/842-3961; FAX 514/842-0945.* 194 rms, 20 story, 89 suites. May-Oct: S $95-$105; D $110-$120; each addl $15; suites $125-$400; under 12 free; package plans; lower rates rest of yr. Crib $15. Pet accepted. Parking (fee). TV; cable. Restaurant 7 am-10 pm. Bar from 10 am. Ck-out noon. Meeting rms. Business center. In-rm modem link. Concierge. Exercise equipt; weights, bicycles, sauna. Some minibars. Cr cds: A, C, D, ER, MC, V.

SC

★ ★ ★ **INTER-CONTINENTAL.** *(360 rue St-Antoine W, Montréal QE H2Y 3X4) at the World Trade Centre. 514/987-9900; FAX 514/847-8550.* 357 rms, 17 story. May-mid-Oct: S, D $235-$315; each addl $25; suites $360-$2,000; under 14 free; family, wkend rates; lower rates rest of yr. Crib free. Pet accepted. Garage parking $16; valet. TV; cable, VCR avail. Indoor pool. Restaurant 6:30 am-11:30 pm. Rm serv 24 hrs. Bar 11:30-1 am; entertainment. Ck-out 1 pm. Convention facilities. Business center. In-rm modem link. Concierge. Shopping arcade. Barber, beauty shop. Exercise rm; instructor, weight machine, treadmill, saunas, steam rm. Massage. Bathrm phones, minibars. Located on 10th-26th floors of 26-story building. Cr cds: A, C, D, DS, ER, JCB, MC, V.

D SC

★ ★ ★ **LE CENTRE SHERATON.** *(1201 Rene Levesque W, Montréal QE H3B 2L7) 514/878-2000; FAX 514/878-3958; res: 800/325-3535.* 824 rms, 37 story, 40 suites. S, D $199; each addl $25; suites $275-$375; under 17 free; wkend packages. Crib free. Covered, valet parking (fee). TV; cable (premium). Indoor pool; whirlpool, poolside serv (summer only), lifeguard. Complimentary coffee in rms. Restaurant 6:30 am-2 pm, 5:30 pm-midnight. 2 bars 11:30-2 am. Ck-out noon. Convention facilities. Business center. In-rm modem link. Shopping arcade. Barber, beauty shop. Airport transportation. Exercise rm; instructor, weights, bicycles, sauna. Massage. Many minibars. Luxury level. Cr cds: A, C, D, DS, ER, JCB, MC, V.

D SC

★ ★ **LE CHATEAU DE L'AIRPORT MIRABEL.** *(12555 Commerce A-4, Mirabel QE J7N 1E3) At Mirabel Airport. 514/476-1611; FAX 514/476-0873.* 355 rms, 5 story. Dec-Apr: S, D $115; suites $175-$325; under 18 free; lower rates rest of yr. Crib free. TV. Indoor pool; wading pool, whirlpool, sauna, poolside serv. Restaurant 7 am-10:30 pm. Rm serv wkends. Bar 11-2 am. Ck-out noon. Meeting rms. Business servs avail. No bellhops. Exercise equipt; weight machines, bicycles. Some bathrm phones. Some balconies. Cr cds: A, D, ER, MC, V.

D SC

★ ★ **LE NOUVEL HÔTEL.** *(1740 René Levesque Blvd W, Montréal QE H3H 1R3) 514/931-8841; FAX 514/931-3233; res: 800/363-6063.* 126 rms, 32 studios, 8 story. S, D $130-$150; each addl $10; studio $150-$170; under 12 free. Crib free. Indoor parking $9. TV; cable (premium). Pool; whirlpool. Restaurant 7-11 am, noon-2:30 pm, 4:30-10 pm. Bar 4:30-10 pm. Ck-out noon. Meeting rms. Business servs avail. In-rm modem link. Valet serv. Exercise equipt; weights, bicycles. Gift shop. Beauty shop. Game rm. Microwaves avail. Near Molson Centre. Cr cds: A, C, D, DS, ER, MC, V.

D SC

★ ★ ★ **LE WESTIN MONT-ROYAL.** *(1050 Sherbrooke St W, Montréal QE H3A 2R6) at Peel St, downtown. 514/284-1110; FAX 514/845-3025.* 300 rms, 32 story. May-Oct: S $175-$225; D $200-$250; each addl $25; suites $375-$1,180; under 18 free; wkend rates; lower rates rest of yr. Crib free. Pet accepted, some restrictions. Garage (fee). TV; cable, VCR avail (movies). Heated pool; whirlpool, poolside serv, lifeguard. Complimentary continental bkfst. Restaurants (see LE ZEN). Rm serv 24 hrs. Bar noon-1 am; pianist. Ck-out 1 pm. Meeting rms. Business center. In-rm modem link. Concierge. Shopping arcade. Barber, beauty shop.

Exercise rm; instructor, weights, bicycles, sauna, steam rm. Massage. Bathrm phones, minibars. Cr cds: A, C, D, DS, ER, JCB, MC, V.

D

★ ★ ★ ★ **LOEWS HÔTEL VOGUE.** *(1425 rue de la Montagne, Montréal QE H3G 1Z3) 514/285-5555; FAX 514/849-8903.* This small luxury hotel in the heart of Montréal has an elegant facade of polished rose granite, trimmed in aqua, with tall windows. Guest rooms are decorated with satiny duvets on the beds and striped silk. 126 rms, 9 story, 16 suites. Mid-May-mid-Oct: S, D $195-$285; each addl $20; suites $405-$1,260; under 18 free; wkend rates; lower rates rest of yr. Crib free. Pet accepted. Garage; valet parking $15. TV; cable, VCR (movies). Restaurant 7 am-11 pm. Rm serv 24 hrs. Bar 3 pm-1 am. Ck-out 1 pm. Meeting rms. Business servs avail. In-rm modem link. Concierge. Gift shop. Exercise equipt; weights, rower. Massage. Health club privileges. In-rm whirlpools, minibars. Cr cds: A, C, D, ER, JCB, MC, V.

D

★ ★ ★ **MARRIOTT CHÂTEAU CHAMPLAIN.** *(1 Place du Canada, Montréal QE H3B 4C9) 514/878-9000; FAX 514/878-6761.* 611 rms, 36 story. May-Dec: S, D $225; suites $238-$1,350; under 18 free; wkend packages; lower rates rest of yr. Crib free. Parking (fee). TV; cable (premium), VCR avail. Indoor pool; whirlpool, poolside serv, lifeguard. Restaurant 7 am-2:30 pm, 5:30-10:30 pm. Rm serv 6:30 am-11 pm. Bars. Ck-out noon. Meeting rms. Business center. In-rm modem link. Shopping arcade. Barber, beauty shop. Exercise rm; instructor, weights, bicycles, sauna. Massage. Minibars. Luxury level. Cr cds: A, C, D, DS, ER, JCB, MC, V.

D SC

★ ★ ★ **NOVOTEL.** *(1180 rue de la Montagne, Montréal QE H3G 1Z1) 514/861-6000; FAX 514/861-0992; res: 800/221-4542.* 199 rms, 9 story. May-Oct: S, D $160-$170; each addl $15; suites $200; family, wkend & hol rates; higher rates during Grand Prix; lower rates rest of yr. Crib free. Pet accepted, some restrictions. Parking garage $9.75. TV; cable (premium). Restaurant 6:30 am-10:30 pm. Bar noon-midnight. Ck-out 1 pm. Meeting rms. Business servs avail. In-rm modem link. Exercise equipt; weights, bicycles. Health club privileges. Indoor playground. Minibars. Cr cds: A, C, D, DS, ER, MC, V.

D SC

★ ★ ★ **QUEEN ELIZABETH.** *(900 Rene Levesque Blvd W, Montréal QE H3B 4A5) 514/861-3511; FAX 514/954-2256; res: 800/441-1414.* 1,020 rms, 21 story. S, D $120-$220; each addl $30; suites $225-$1,850; under 18 free; wkend rates. Crib free. Garage $14. TV; cable (premium). Indoor pool; whirlpool. Restaurant (see THE BEAVER CLUB). Rm serv 24 hrs. Bars from 11 am. Ck-out noon. Convention facilities. Business center. In-rm modem link. Shopping arcade. Beauty shop. Exercise rm; instructor, bicycles, treadmill. Massage. Minibars. Underground passage to Place Ville Marie. Luxury level. Cr cds: A, C, D, DS, ER, JCB, MC, V.

D SC

★ ★ ★ ★ **THE RITZ-CARLTON, KEMPINSKI MONTRÉAL.** *(1228 Sherbrooke St W, Montréal QE H3G 1H6) at Drummond, downtown. 514/842-4212; FAX 514/842-2268; res: 800/363-0366.* E-mail ritz@citenet.net. Opened in 1912 by a group of local investors who wanted an elegant hotel in which to woo their rich European friends, the Ritz-Carlton Kempinski Montréal has been the backdrop for many noteworthy events ever since. Guest rooms are decorated in Edwardian style; service is impeccable. 230 rms, 9 story. May-Oct: S $190-$205; D $205-$235; each addl $35; suites $385-$760; under 14 free; wkend rates; lower rates rest of yr. Crib free. TV; cable. Restaurants 6:30 am-10 pm (also see CAFÉ DE PARIS). Rm serv 24 hrs. Bar 11:30-2:30 am; pianist. Ck-out noon. Meeting rms. Business servs avail. In-rm modem link. Barber. Valet parking. Exercise equipt; bicycles, treadmill. Massage. Health club privileges. Minibars. Cr cds: A, C, D, ER, JCB, MC, V.

D SC

Inns

★ ★ ★ **AUBERGE DE LA FONTAINE.** *(1301 rue Rachel E, Montréal QE H2J 2K1) 514/597-0166; FAX 514/597-0496; res: 800/597-0597.* 21 rms, 3 story, 3 suites. May-Oct: S $99-$125; D $120-$140; each addl $15; suites $175; under 12 free. TV; cable, VCR avail. Complimentary bkfst buffet 7-10 am. Complimentary coffee in kitchen. Ck-out noon, ck-in 3 pm. Meeting rm. Business servs avail. In-rm modem link. Sun deck. Some in-rm whirlpools. Some balconies. Former residence; quiet setting in urban location; opp La Fontaine Parc. Cr cds: A, C, D, ER, MC, V.

D SC

★ ★ ★ **AUBERGE HANDFIELD.** *(555 Chemin du Prince, St-Marc-sur-Richelieu QE J0L 2E0) 28 mi SE on Hwy 20, exit 112; 6 mi N on Hwy 223. 514/584-2226; FAX 514/584-3650; res: 800/667-1087 (CAN).* 55 rms, 2 story. S $60-$65; D $70-$175; each addl $10; under 4 free; theatre, winter package plans. Crib free. TV; cable (premium), VCR (free movies). Pool; whirlpool, poolside serv. Restaurant (see AUBERGE HANDFIELD). Bar 11 am-midnight. Ck-out noon, ck-in 11 am. Meeting rms. Business servs avail. Golf privileges. Tennis privileges. Horseback riding. Downhill ski 15 mi; x-country ski on site. Exercise equipt; bicycles, stair machines, sauna. Theater-boat (late June-early Sept). Marina. Sugar cabin (late Feb-late Apr). Built in 1880. Cr cds: A, C, D, DS, ER, MC, V.

✔★ **LE BRETON.** *(1609 rue St-Hubert, Montréal QE H2L 3Z1) 514/524-7273; FAX 514/527-7016.* 13 rms, 11 with bath, 3 story. Some rm phones. S $30-$55; D $45-$60; each addl $8. TV; cable. Complimentary continental bkfst. Restaurant nearby. Ck-out noon, ck-in 2 pm. Business servs avail. Street parking. Cr cds: MC, V.

✔★ **MANOIR AMBROSE.** *(3422 Stanley St, Montréal QE H3A 1R8) 514/288-6922; FAX 514/288-5757.* 22 rms, 15 with bath, 6 A/C, 3 story. May-Oct: S $30-$75; D $50-$75; each addl $10; under 12 free; wkly rates; lower rates rest of yr. Crib free. Parking $5. TV; cable. Complimentary continental bkfst. Restaurant nearby. Ck-out noon, ck-in 2:30 pm. Business servs avail. Victorian mansion (1883); large windows, high ceilings. Near Peel metro station. Cr cds: MC, V.

Restaurants

(Reservations are important at most Montréal restaurants)

(There is a 15% tax added to all restaurant checks in the province of Québec.)

★ ★ **AUBERGE HANDFIELD.** *(See Auberge Handfield Inn) 514/584-2226.* Canadian, French menu. Specialties: lapin sauté, petit cochon de lait, ragoût de pattes. Hrs: 8 am-midnight; Sun brunch 10 am-3 pm. Res accepted. Bar. A la carte entrees: lunch, dinner $14-$25. Sun brunch $19.50. Child's meals. Parking. In 1880 building. Indoor terrace with view over Richelieu River. Family-owned. Cr cds: A, C, D, DS, ER, MC, V.

★ ★ ★ ★ ★ **THE BEAVER CLUB.** *(See Queen Elizabeth Hotel) 514/861-3511.* Founded by fur traders during Montréal's colonial days and serving as a social club for the city's elite during the 19th century, the Beaver Club maintains the august atmosphere of a men's club. Classic haute cuisine and an extraordinary wine cellar help make it one of the most unusual and best dining rooms in North America. Continental menu. Specialties: steak Charles, saffroned frog legs, pan-fried duckling foie gras. Hrs: noon-3 pm, 6-11 pm; Sat from 6 pm. Closed Sun & Mon eve; also July. Res accepted. Bar. Wine cellar. A la carte entrees: lunch $16.75-$20.75, dinner $24-$32. Complete meal: lunch $16.75-$29, dinner $32-$38. Child's meals. Valet parking. Jacket. Cr cds: A, C, D, DS, ER, JCB, MC, V.

D

★ ★ ★ **CAFÉ DE PARIS.** *(See The Ritz-Carlton, Kempinski Montréal Hotel) 514/842-4212.* French menu. Specialties: feuilleté de saumon, chicken, scallops. Own pastries. Hrs: 6:30-11:30 am, noon-2:30 pm, 3:30-5 pm, 6-10 pm; Sun brunch 11 am-2:30 pm. Res accepted. Bar. Wine list. A la carte entrees: bkfst $10-$19, dinner $25-$40. Table d'hôte: lunch, dinner $23-$35. Sun brunch $39.50. Child's meals. Entertainment. Valet parking. Cr cds: A, C, D, ER, JCB, MC, V.

D

✔★ **CAFE ST ALEXANDRE.** *(518 Duluth St E, Montréal QE) 514/849-4251.* Greek menu. Specialties: pikilia, shish kebab. Hrs: 11 am-midnight. Res accepted. Setups. A la carte entrees: lunch $7.50-$11, dinner $7.95-$15.95. Table d'hôte: dinner $15.95-$17.95. Child's meals. Outdoor dining. Cr cds: A, MC, V.

D

★ ★ ★ **CHAMPS ELYSÉES.** *(See Château Versailles Hotel) 514/939-1212.* French menu. Specialties: braised salmon, rib steak with fresh onions, crêpes suzette. Hrs: 7-10:30 am, noon-2:30 pm, 6-10 pm; Sat 7:30-11 am, 6-10 pm; Sun 7:30-11 am. Res accepted. Bar. Wine cellar. Complete meal: bkfst $7.25-$9.75, lunch $12.95-$22.50, dinner $19.50-$26.50. Valet parking. Jazz trio Fri, Sat. Elegant French bistro. Cr cds: A, D, DS, ER, MC, V.

D

★ ★ ★ **CHEZ FRÉDÉRIC.** *(1175 A rue Crescent, Montréal QE H3G 2B1) 514/395-8730.* French menu. Specialties: escargot, filet mignon of lamb, sweetbread. Hrs: noon to 3 pm, 5:30-10:30 pm. Closed Sun. Res accepted. Semi-a la carte: lunch $14-$16, dinner $18-$24. Outdoor dining. French bistro decor and atmosphere; oil paintings. Cr cds: A, C, D, ER, MC, V.

★ ★ ★ **CHEZ LA MÈRE MICHEL.** *(1209 Guy St, Montréal QE H3H 2K5) 514/934-0473.* French, nouvelle cuisine. Specialties: suprême de pintade au vinaigre de framboises, homard soufflé. Own pastries. Hrs: noon-2:30 pm, 5:30-10:30 pm; Sat, Mon from 5:30 pm. Closed Sun. Res required. Bar. Wine cellar. Table d'hôte: lunch $14.50-$17.50. A la carte entrees: dinner $22-$30. French provincial decor. Family-owned. Cr cds: A, ER, MC, V.

★ ★ ★ **CHEZ PAUZÉ.** *(1657 rue St Catherine Ouest, Montréal QE H3H 1L9) 514/932-6118.* Continental menu. Specialties: lobster, scampi, smoked salmon. Hrs: 11:30 am-10 pm; Thurs to 10:30 pm; Fri to 11 pm; Sat, Sun 3-11 pm. Res accepted. Bar. Wine list. Complete meals: lunch, dinner $10.95-$39.50. Pianist Fri, Sat. Free indoor parking. Outdoor dining. Montréal theme. Cr cds: A, C, D, DS, ER, MC, V.

D

★ ★ ★ **EXOTIKA.** *(400 Ave Laurier Ouest, Montréal QE H2V 2K7) 514/273-5015.* Eclectic menu. Specialties: alligator, bar rayé Pacifiko, royal praline. Hrs: 7:30 am-midnight. Closed Mon, Sun (formal dining rm only). Res accepted (formal dining rm only). Bar 11:30 am-midnight. Wine list. A la carte entrees: bkfst $2.50-$10, lunch $6.50-$10, dinner $13-$28. Jazz. Multi-sensory adventure with African decor; safari motif. Cr cds: A, D, ER, MC, V.

★ ★ ★ **KATSURA MONTRÉAL.** *(2170 Rue de la Montagne, Montréal QE H3G 1Z7) 514/849-1172.* Japanese menu. Specializes in sushi, steak, teriyaki. Sushi bar. Hrs: 11:30 am-2:30 pm, 5:30-10 pm; Fri, Sat to 10:30 pm; Sun 5:30-9 pm. Closed most major hols. Res accepted. Wine list. A la carte entrees: lunch $8.10-$14.50, dinner $14-$27. Complete meals: dinner $27-$37. Cr cds: A, D, ER, JCB, MC, V.

✔★ ★ **L'EXPRESS.** *(3927 Saint Denis, Montréal QE H2W 2M4) 514/845-5333.* French, continental menu. Specialties: steak tartare, fresh salmon, chicken liver mousse with pistachio. Hrs: 8-2 am; Sat, Sun from 10 am. Closed Dec 25. Res accepted. Bar to 3 am. A la carte entrees: bkfst $2.45-$3.45, lunch, dinner $9.95-$16.50. Cr cds: A, D, ER, MC, V.

D

★ **LA CAVERNE GRECQUE.** *(105 Prince Arthur E, Montréal QE H2X 1B6) 514/844-5114.* Greek menu. Specializes in seafood, steak, chicken brouchettes. Hrs: 11-midnight; Fri, Sat to 1 am. Res accepted. Setups. Complete meals: lunch $5-$10. A la carte entrees: dinner $8.95-$19.95. Child's meals. Cr cds: A, D, ER, MC, V.

★ ★ ★ ★ **LA MARÉE.** *(404 Place Jacques Cartier, Montréal QE H2Y 3B2) in Old Montréal. 514/861-8126.* Housed in an 1808 building, this restaurant has two distinct dining areas: one small and intimate, the other larger and brightly lit. Service is impeccable and formal. French menu. Specialties: homard brunetiere, châteaubriand grille. Own pastries, sherbets. Hrs: noon-3 pm, 6-11 pm; Sat, Sun from 5:30 pm. Closed Jan 1, Dec 25. Res required. Serv bar. Wine cellar. Complete meals: lunch $13.50-$15.50. A la carte entrees: dinner $24-$33. Cr cds: A, C, D, DS, ER, JCB, MC, V.

★ ★ ★ **LA RAPÈIRE.** *(1155 rue Metcalfe, Montréal QE H3B 2V6) 514/871-8920.* French menu. Specialties: foie gras de canard, le confit de canard au vinaigre de framboise, le cassoulet à la Toulousaine. Hrs: noon-3 pm, 5:30-10 pm; Sat from 5:30 pm. Closed Sun; major hols; also mid-July-mid-Aug. Res accepted. Bar. Wine list. A la carte entrees: lunch $17.75-$26.50, dinner $24.25-$27.75. French decor. Jacket. Cr cds: A, C, D, ER, MC, V.

D

★ ★ ★ **LALOUX.** *(250 ave des Pine est, Montréal QE H2W 1P3) 514/287-9127.* French menu. Specialties: caribou mignon, pave royal, fresh fish. Hrs: noon-2:30 pm, 5:30-10:30 pm; Thurs, Fri to 11:30 pm; Sat 5:30-11:30 pm; Sun 5:30-10:30 pm. Closed Jan 1, Dec 24, 25. Res accepted. Bar. Wine list. Complete meal: lunch $7.95-$13.75, dinner $16.95-$24.50. Outdoor dining. Cr cds: A, D, ER, MC, V.

D

★ ★ ★ **LE CAFE FLEURI.** *(See Hotel Complexe Desjardins) 514/285-1450.* Web www.hoteldesjardins.com. French, continental menu. Specialties: marinated Canadian salmon, casserole of scallops, puffed pastry shell stuffed with wild mushrooms. Salad bar. Own pastries. Hrs: 7 am-9:45 pm. Res accepted. Serv bar. Semi-a la carte: bkfst $8.25-$12.50, lunch $7.75-$28.50. Table d'hôte: lunch, dinner $19.50. A la carte entrees: dinner $9.75-$12.50. Sun brunch $24.50. Child's meals. Parking. Terrace. Cr cds: A, C, D, DS, ER, JCB, MC, V.

D

★ ★ ★ **LE CASTILLON.** *(See Bonaventure Hilton Hotel) 514/878-2332.* French menu. Specializes in fresh fish, rack of lamb. Own baking. Hrs: noon-2:30 pm, 6-11 pm; Sat, Sun from 6 pm. Res accepted. Serv bar. Wine cellar. A la carte entrees: lunch $17-$22, dinner $22.25-$44. Table d'hôte: dinner $39.75. Child's meals. Valet parking. Outdoor dining. 17th-century French castle decor. Cr cds: A, C, D, DS, ER, JCB, MC, V.

D

★ ★ ★ **LE CAVEAU.** *(2063 Victoria St, Montréal QE H3A 2A3) between University & McGill Sts. 514/844-1624.* French menu. Specializes in fresh fish. Own pastries. Hrs: 11:30 am-11 pm; Sat, Sun from 5 pm. Res accepted. Bar. Wine cellar. A la carte entrees: lunch, dinner $11.95-$25. Complete meals: lunch $11.95-$25, dinner $14.95-$25. Chef's menu $25. Child's meals. Dinner parking. Family-owned. Cr cds: A, C, D, ER, MC, V.

SC

★ ★ ★ **LE CHRYSANTHÈME.** *(1208 Crescent, Montréal QE H3G 2A9) 514/397-1408.* Chinese, Szechuan menu. Specializes in jumbo shrimp with spicy sauce, beef with orange flavor. Hrs: noon-2:30 pm, 6-10:30 pm; Fri, Sat 6-11:30 pm; Sun from 6 pm; closed Mon; Jan 1, Dec 24, 25. Res accepted. Bar. A la carte entrees: lunch $10-$14. Complete meals: lunch $10-$13, dinner $12-$20. Chinese decor, artifacts. Cr cds: A, D, ER, MC, V.

★ **LE JARDIN DE PANOS.** *(521 Duluth St E, Montréal QE H2L 1A8) 514/521-4206.* Greek, French menu. Specialties: calmars frits, cotelettes d'agneau, brochette de poulet. Hrs: noon-midnight. Res accepted. Complete meals: lunch $7-$15. A la carte entrees: dinner $9-$18. Outdoor dining. Mediterranean decor. Cr cds: A, MC, V.

★ **LE KEG/BRANDY'S.** *(25 St Paul E, Montréal QE H2Y 1G2) 514/871-9093.* Specializes in steak, chicken, seafood. Salad bar. Hrs: 11:30 am-2:30 pm; 5-10 pm; Thurs, Fri to 11 pm; Sat 4 pm-midnight; summer hrs vary. Closed Dec 24, 25. Res accepted. Bar 11:30-3 am. A la carte entrees: lunch $4.29-$14.99, dinner $11.99-$23.79. Child's meals. Cr cds: A, MC, V.

★ ★ ★ **LE MITOYEN.** *(652 Place Publique Ste-Dorothée Laval, Montréal QE H7X 1G1) 514/689-2977.* Nouvelle cuisine. Specialties: medaillons de caribou aux framboises, Magrets de canard. Own pastries, baking. Hrs: 6-11 pm. Closed Mon. Res accepted. Wine list. A la carte entrees: dinner $20.50-$27.50. Complete meals: dinner $28.50 & $55. Child's meals. Parking. Renovated 1870 house. Fireplace. Outdoor terrace. Cr cds: A, D, ER, MC, V.

D

★ ★ **LE PARIS.** *(1812 St Catherine Ouest, Montréal QE H5H 1M1) 514/937-4898.* French menu. Specializes in fish, liver, steak. Hrs: noon-3 pm, 5-10 pm. Closed Sun; Dec 25. Res accepted. A la carte entrees: lunch, dinner $12-$19. Country French atmosphere. Cr cds: A, C, D, ER, MC, V.

★ ★ ★ **LE PASSE-PARTOUT.** *(3857 Boul Décarie, Montréal QE H4A 3J6) 514/487-7750.* French menu. Specialties: smoked salmon, red snapper à la Provencale. Own baking. Hrs: 11:30 am-2 pm; Thurs, Fri 11:30 am-2 pm, 6:30-9:30 pm; Sat 6:30-9:30 pm. Closed Mon, Sun; most major hols. Res accepted. Complete meals: lunch $18.50, dinner $40-$50. Classic French decor. Cr cds: A, D, ER, MC, V.

D

★ ★ ★ **LES CAPRICES DE NICOLAS.** *(2072 rue Drummond, Montréal QE H3G 1W9) 514/282-9790.* Modern French menu. Frequently changing market menu. Hrs: noon-2 pm, 6-10 pm; Sat to 6-11 pm. Closed Sun; most major hols; also June 24. Res accepted. Bar. Wine list. A la carte entrees: lunch $16-$29, dinner $22-$34. Complete meals: lunch $26-$30. Courtyard; atrium. Antique bar. Cr cds: A, D, ER, MC, V.

★ ★ ★ **LES CHENÊTS.** *(2075 Bishop St, Montréal QE H3G 2E8) downtown. 514/844-1842.* French menu. Specialties: délice du Chambord, filet of beef Rossini, pheasant with cream and morel sauce. Own pastries. Hrs: 11:30 am-3 pm, 5:30-11 pm; Sat, Sun from 5:30 pm. Res accepted. Extensive cognac list. Wine cellar. A la carte entrees: lunch $12-$22.95, dinner $22.50-$35. Table d'hôte: lunch $14.50, dinner $35. Chef-owned. Cr cds: A, C, D, ER, MC, V.

★ ★ ★ **LES HALLES.** *(1450 Crescent St, Montréal QE H3G 2B6) 514/844-2328.* French menu. Own pastries. Hrs: 11:45 am-2:30 pm, 6-11 pm; Mon, Sat from 6 pm. Closed Sun. Res accepted. Bar. Wine cellar. Complete meals: lunch $13.50-$23. A la carte entrees: dinner $19.95-$32. Complete meals: dinner $32-$43. Murals. Family-owned. Jacket. Cr cds: A, C, D, DS, ER, JCB, MC, V.

★ ★ ★ **LES TROIS TILLEULS.** *(See Hostellerie Les Trois Tilleuls Motel) 514/584-2231.* French menu. Specialties: ris de veau trois tilleuls, cuisse de canard confite et son aiguillette. Own baking. Hrs: 7:30 am-10 pm. Res accepted. Bar 11-2 am. Wine cellar. Complete meals: lunch $18.50-$22. A la carte entrees: dinner $28-$40. Child's meals. Parking. In 1880 farmhouse with garden, terrace; view of river. Cr cds: A, C, D, DS, ER, MC, V.

★ **MOKUM.** *(5795 rue Sherbrooke Ouest, Montréal QE H4A 1X2) 514/488-4827.* Continental menu. Frequently changing international menu. Hrs: 11:30 am-2:30 pm, 5:30-9:30 pm; Sat from 5:30 pm. Closed Mon, Sun; Jan 1, Dec 25. Res accepted. No A/C.Semi-a la carte: lunch $10.75-$14.50, dinner $19.75-$28.50. Outdoor dining. Casual dining. No cr cds accepted.

D

★ ★ ★ ★ ★ **NUANCES.** *(1 ave de Casino, Montréal QE H3C 4W7) in Casino de Montréal. 514/392-2708.* In a city noted for fine restaurants, this is one of the best. High ceilings, stunning views and exquisite contemporary French cuisine make for memorable dining. French menu. Specialties: roast loin of Québec lamb, duo of lobster and scallops, foie gras of duck. Hrs: 5:30-11 pm; Fri-Sun to 11:30 pm. Res required. Bar. Extensive wine list. Semi-a la carte: dinner $27-$33. Cr cds: A, D, ER, MC, V.

D ♥

★ **PICCADELI.** *(3271 Taschereau Blvd, Greenfield Park QE J4V 2H5) Hwy 10 exit 8E, Tacheran Blvd, N on Hwy 134. 514/462-1166.* Specializes in seafood, steak, lasagna. Hrs: 7:30-2 am. Res accepted. Bar. Complete meal: bkfst $1.95-$2.95, lunch, dinner $4.95-$23.95. Child's meals. Entertainment Wed-Sun. Parking. Family-owned. Cr cds: A, C, D, ER, MC, V.

D

★ ★ **SZECHUAN.** *(400 Notre Dame St W, Montréal QE H2Y 1V3) 514/844-4456.* Chinese menu. Specializes in Szechuan, Hunan dishes. Hrs: 11:30 am-3 pm, 5:30-10:30 pm; Sat 5:30-11 pm. Closed Sun; Jan 1, Dec 24, 25. Res accepted. Bar. Semi-a la carte: lunch $10.95-$15.95, dinner $15-$25. Cr cds: A, D, MC, V.

★ ★ **TOKYO SUKIYAKI.** *(7355 Mountain Sights Ave, Montréal QE H4P 2A7) 514/737-7245.* Japanese menu. Specialties: shabu shabu, sushi, sukiyaki. Hrs: 5:30-11:30 pm. Closed Mon; Jan 1, Dec 25. Res accepted. Japanese whiskey, wine, beer. Complete meals: dinner $26. Parking. Japanese decor; traditional Japanese seating. Family-owned. Cr cds: A, D, ER, MC, V.

★ ★ ★ **TOQUÉ!.** *(3842 rue St-Denis, Montréal QE H2W 2M2) 514/499-2084.* French menu. Specialties: hot foie gras, salmon tartare, manjari chocolat crème brûlée. Hrs: 6-11 pm. Closed most major hols. Res required. Bar. Wine list. A la carte entrees: dinner $22-$26. Art deco decor. Cr cds: A, D, ER, MC, V.

D

★ ★ ★ **ZEN.** *(See Le Westin Mont-Royal Hotel) 514/499-0801.* Chinese menu. Specialties: Szechuan duck, General Tao's chicken, sesame orange beef. Hrs: 11:30 am-2:30 pm, 5:30-10 pm. Closed Dec 25. Res required. A la carte entrees: lunch, dinner $10.50-$20. Complete meal: lunch $12-$25, dinner $27. Modern decor. Cr cds: A, D, ER, MC, V.

D

Unrated Dining Spots

BENS DELICATESSEN. *(990 De Maisonneuve Blvd, Montréal QE) W at Metcalfe. 514/844-1001.* Specializes in pastrami, smoked meat, corned beef. Hrs: 7-4 am; Fri, Sat to 5 am; Dec 24 to 6 pm. Serv bar. Semi-a la carte: bkfst, lunch, dinner $3.60-$10.95. Family-owned. Cr cds: MC, V.

BIDDLE'S JAZZ & RIBS. *(2060 Aylmer, Montréal QE) 514/842-8656.* Specializes in chicken, ribs. Hrs: 11:30-2:30 am; Sun from 5:30 pm. Res accepted. Bar. A la carte entrees: lunch $4.95-$11.95, dinner $5.95-$12.95. Jazz combo. Parking. Cr cds: A, C, D, ER, MC, V.

PIZZA MELLA. *(107 Prince Arthur E, Montréal QE) 514/849-4680.* Italian menu. Specializes in 30 types of pizza. Hrs: 11:30-1 am; wkends to 2 am. Closed Dec 25. Setups. Semi-a la carte: lunch, dinner $5.25-$9.35. Outdoor dining. Cooking on 3 woodburning brick ovens; open kitchen. Cr cds: A, C, D, ER, MC, V.

Nashville

Settled: 1779
Pop: 488,374
Elev: 440 feet
Time zone: Central
Area code: 615
Web: www.nashville.musiccityusa.com/tour

Commercial center and capital city, Nashville is part Andrew Jackson's Hermitage and part Grand Ole Opry. It is often referred to as the "Athens of the South" because of its many colleges and universities, religious publishing houses and churches. Nashville is also known to many as "Music City USA," the home of country music and many of its stars.

Nashville, located in the heart of the rolling Tennessee hills, cherishes a rich history. Although fur traders came on the scene around 1710, the first settlers arrived in 1779, at what was then called French Lick or Big Salt Lick, along the shore of the Cumberland River. By 1796, Tennessee was part of the Union; 50 years later Nashville was named the permanent capital. In the intervening years the town went through a period of rapid growth. River traffic increased, and the city became a trading center, handling many diverse goods. Early industries included cotton mills and foundries. An early advantage in transportation facilities was later enhanced by the beginning of steamboat service in 1819 and railroad service in 1854.

During the Civil War, Nashville escaped heavy physical damage and even prospered from the Union supply activities. After a severe but short carpetbag rule, the city entered into a new era, leading as a commercial, industrial and financial center. Another surge of growth occurred in 1933 when the Tennessee Valley Authority was created.

Business

Nashville's diversified economy includes many different kinds of goods and services. As the state capital, the city employs a great number of people in federal, state and local government. With its colleges, universities and two teaching hospitals, there is also considerable employment in the educational and medical fields.

Important manufacturing operations include automobiles, printing and publishing, production of automobile and architectural glass, clothing and footwear, food products, chemicals, heating, cooling and transportation equipment. The city is the headquarters for one of the largest hospital management companies. Nashville is also a major insurance investment banking center in the South.

And, of course, this is the home of the "Nashville Sound," which has made Nashville the premier recording center in North America. Music and its related businesses continue to play a multibillion-dollar tune for the city's economy.

Convention Facilities

Within Nashville are 12 meeting facilities including two convention centers, with seating capacity ranging from 1,000 to more than 20,000 people and exhibit space ranging from 33,000 square feet to 300,000 square feet. There are 26,000 motel and hotel rooms in the city.

Sports & Recreation

The area's many parks and lakes are paradise for the amateur photographer and for those who simply enjoy the outdoors.

The hills of Tennessee invite nature lovers for leisurely drives and hikes. Within a short driving distance of Nashville are six large lakes and state parks offering many recreational facilities. Old Hickory Lake and J. Percy Priest Reservoir and their recreation areas are ideal spots for fishing, boating or picnicking. More than 5,500 acres of public parks plus numerous playgrounds, golf courses, swimming pools and tennis courts are provided by the city government.

In 1999, the former Houston Oilers NFL team will move into their new stadium in downtown Nashville on the banks of the Cumberland River. The stadium is part of a $292-million redevelopment project along the East Bank.

Entertainment

The city provides a wide range of theatrical and concert performances. Several tourist guide publications, including the *Music City Vacation Guide*, the *Nashville Scene* and special sections in both daily newspapers, give extensive schedules of performances. The 16 area college campuses also host many events that are open to the public. Other outstanding facilities include Circle Theater, Chaffin's Barn Dinner Theater, Cheekwood: Nashville's Home of Arts and Gardens and Nashville Children's Theater. While country music is king here, Nashville is also the home of a symphony orchestra as well as professional opera, ballet and repertory companies.

The Tennessee Performing Arts Center is one of the first such facilities in the country. The center also houses the Tennessee State Museum.

For those with a variety of tastes, The District, a 16-block downtown area encompassing lower Broadway, First through Fifth Avenues North and Printer's Alley, has many clubs and bars featuring live entertainment.

Historical Areas

Andrew Jackson's house, the Hermitage, was built in 1821, on a site chosen by his wife, Rachel. Certified as a national historic landmark, the fine old mansion graces a 660-acre tract of spacious and well-kept grounds near Old Hickory Lake. The grounds include a museum, log cabin, carriage house and formal gardens containing the burial place of Jackson and his wife.

Near the Hermitage is Tulip Grove, the lovely house of Andrew Donelson, who was the private secretary and nephew of President Jackson. It was Donelson who conducted the negotiations for the annexation of Texas. He later became an ambassador to Prussia. The house was built in 1836, during Jackson's presidency.

Travellers' Rest is worth a short side trip, for it was the scene of many political gatherings during the campaign days of Andrew Jackson. The house was built in 1799 by Tennessee's first supreme court judge, John Overton, Jackson's law partner, campaign manager and lifelong friend.

Another lovely mansion, Belle Meade, is also open to the public. This house was one of the most impressive showplaces in the South. Built by General William Giles Harding, it was originally part of a 5,300-acre plantation. Used as headquarters by Confederate General Chalmers during the Battle of Nashville, Belle Meade also was the breeding farm of many Thoroughbred horses, the most famous of which was Iroquois.

Also of interest is the replica of Fort Nashborough, which has been built only blocks from the original site. Within the fort are exhibits of pioneer tools and implements.

Sightseeing

Sightseers in the downtown area can follow the two-mile teal-colored line on the city streets known as the Citywalk. The historical trail begins at Fort Nashborough; brochures are available at the Convention & Visitors Bureau and at the Visitor Information Center inside the glass tower of the Nashville Arena.

The River Taxis at Riverfront Park provide a quick cruise to Opryland. Opryland features rides, shops, restaurants and more than 12 live musical performances, which range from the best of Broadway to the down-home sound of banjos and country music. The rides include a treetop sky trip with a breathtaking view of the Cumberland River, a trip on the old-time Opryland Railroad, a whitewater raft ride and a spin on roller coasters *Wabash Cannonball*, *Chaos* and *Hangman*. *General Jackson,* a 300-foot paddle-wheeler, departs from the Opryland docks year-round for day and evening cruises and includes a stage show.

Music is everywhere in Opryland, with many live musical productions, featured bands, singing groups, strolling musicians and the Grand Ole Opry itself. The park's Grand Ole Opry House is the current broadcast site of the nation's oldest continuous radio show. Started in 1925, the show features big-name entertainers and promising newcomers providing the best in country music. The home of the show from 1943 to 1974 was the Ryman Auditorium in downtown Nashville, which underwent a multi-million dollar renovation in 1994 and is open daily for tours, special concerts and television tapings.

General References

Area code: 615

Phone Numbers

POLICE & FIRE: 911

POISON CONTROL CENTER: 322-6435 or 800/288-9999

TIME: 259-2222 **WEATHER:** 244-9393

Information Sources

Nashville Convention & Visitors Bureau, 161 4th Ave N, 37219, 259-4700.

Visitor Information Center, 501 Broadway, 259-4747.

Department of Parks & Recreation, 862-8400.

Transportation

AIRLINES: Air Canada; American; American Eagle; Comair; Continental; Delta; Delta Express; Midway Connection; Northwest; Skyway; Southwest; Trans States; TWA; United; USAir; USAir Express and other commuter and regional airlines.

AIRPORT: International Airport, 275-1675.

CAR RENTAL AGENCIES: (See IMPORTANT TOLL-FREE NUMBERS) Alamo 275-1050; Avis 361-1212; Budget 366-0800; Dollar 366-5000; Enterprise 872-7722; Hertz 361-3131; National 361-7467; Thrifty 361-6050.

PUBLIC TRANSPORTATION: Metro Transit Authority, 862-5950.

Newspapers

Nashville Banner; Nashville Business Journal; The Tennessean.

Convention Facilities

The Municipal Auditorium, 417 4th Ave N, 862-6392.

Nashville Arena, 501 Broadway, 770-2000.

Nashville Convention Center, 601 Commerce St, 742-2000.

Opryland Hotel & Convention Center, 2800 Opryland Dr, 889-1000.

State Fairgrounds, off I-65 S on Wedgewood, 862-8980.

Sports & Recreation

Centennial Sportsplex, 222 25th Ave N, 862-8480.

Greer Stadium, 534 Chestnut, 242-4371 (Sounds, baseball).

Nashville Arena, 501 Broadway, 770-2000.

Racetrack

Nashville Speedway USA, State Fairgrounds, 726-1818.

Cultural Facilities

Theaters

Chaffin's Barn Dinner Theatre, 8204 TN 100, 646-9977.

Nashville Children's Theater, 724 2nd Ave S, 254-9103.

Concert Halls

Grand Ole Opry House, 2804 Opryland Dr, 6 mi E on I-40, then 4 mi N on Briley Pkwy, 889-6611.

Nashville Municipal Auditorium, 417 4th Ave N, 862-6390.

Starwood Ampitheatre, 3839 Murfreesboro Rd, 641-5800.

Tennessee Performing Arts Center, 505 Deadrick St, 782-4000.

Museums

Country Music Hall of Fame and Museum, 4 Music Square E, 256-1639.

Country Music Wax Museum, 118 16th Ave S, 256-2490.

Cumberland Science Museum, 800 Ft Negley Blvd, 862-5160.

Jim Reeves Museum, 1023 Joyce Ln, off Gallatin Rd, 226-2065.

Museum of Tobacco Art & History, 800 Harrison St, 271-2349.

Nashville Toy Museum, 2613 McGavock Pike, 883-8870.

Tennessee State Museum, James K. Polk State Bldg, 5th Ave between Union and Deaderick Sts, 741-2692.

Points of Interest

Historical

Belle Meade, 5025 Harding Rd, 7 mi SW, 356-0501 or 800/270-3991.

Belmont Mansion, 1900 Belmont Blvd, 460-5459.

Fort Nashborough, 170 1st Ave N.

The Hermitage and Tulip Grove, 12 mi E off I-40, The Hermitage exit, 889-2941.

The Parthenon, Centennial Park, West End Ave & 25th Ave N, 862-8431.

Ryman Auditorium, 116 5th Ave N, 254-1445.

State Capitol, Charlotte Ave between Sixth and Seventh Aves, 741-1621.

Travellers' Rest Historic House, on Farrell Pkwy, 5 mi S off US 31, 832-8197.

The Upper Room, 1908 Grand Ave, 340-7207.

Other Attractions

Car Collectors Hall of Fame, 1534 Demonbreun St, 255-6804.

Cheekwood: Nashville's Home of Art & Gardens, 1200 Forest Park Dr, 356-8000.

Grand Ole Opry, 2804 Opryland Dr, 889-3060 or 889-6611.

J. Percy Priest Lake, 11 mi E off I-40, 889-1975.

Nashville Zoo, 17 mi NW in Joelton, 370-3333.

Opryland USA, 2802 Opryland Dr, 8 mi E on I-40, then 4 mi N on Briley Pkwy, 889-6611.

Sightseeing Tours

Grand Ole Opry Tours, 2810 Opryland Dr, 889-9490.

Gray Line bus tours, 2416 Music Valley Dr, Suite 102, 883-5555 or 800/251-1864.

Nashville Black Heritage Tours, 5188 Almaville Rd, 890-8173.

Annual Events

Tennessee Crafts Fair, Centennial Park, 665-0502. Early May.

Running of the Iroquois Memorial Steeplechase, Old Hickory Blvd, at entrance to Percy Warner Park, 322-7450. 2nd Sat May.

Summer Lights in Music City Festival, 259-0900. Memorial Day wkend.

International Country Music Fan Fair, 889-7503. Mid-June.

Tennessee State Fair, fairgrounds, 862-8980. Sept.

City Neighborhoods

Many of the restaurants, unrated dining establishments and some lodgings listed under Nashville include neighborhoods as well as exact street addresses. Geographic descriptions of these areas are given, followed by a table of restaurants arranged by neighborhood.

Downtown: South of Harrison St, west of I-24/65, north of McGavock St and east of 10th Ave N. **East of Downtown:** East of I-24/I-65. **West of Downtown:** West of I-40.

Music Row: Area includes 16th Ave S from West End Ave to Demonbreun St; Music Square E from South St to Demonbreun St; Music Square W from South St to Division St; and Division and Demonbreun Sts from 18th Ave S to I-40.

Opryland: Area south of McGavock Pike, west of Briley Pkwy (TN 155) and north and east of the Cumberland River.

Lodgings and Food

NASHVILLE RESTAURANTS BY NEIGHBORHOOD AREAS

(For full description, see alphabetical listings under Restaurants)

DOWNTOWN
Arthur's (Union Station Hotel). 1001 Broadway
Capitol Grille (The Hermitage Hotel). 231 6th Ave N
Gerst Haus. 228 Woodland St
Goten 2. 209 10th Ave S
Mère Bulles. 152 2nd Ave N
Mario's. 2005 Broadway
The Merchants. 401 Broadway
Old Spaghetti Factory. 160 2nd Ave N
Pinnacle (Crowne Plaza Hotel). 623 Union St
Prime Cut Steakhouse. 170 2nd Ave N
Royal Thai. 204 Commerce St
Stock-Yard. 901 2nd Ave N
Towne House Tea Room & Restaurant. 165 8th Ave N
The Wild Boar. 2014 Broadway

NORTH OF DOWNTOWN
The Mad Platter. 1239 6th Ave N
Sitar. 116 21st Ave N

SOUTH OF DOWNTOWN
Bluebird Cafe. 4104 Hillsboro Rd
Boscos. 1805 21st Ave S
Boundry. 911 20th Ave S
Loveless Cafe. 8400 TN 100
Santa Fe Steak Co. 902 Murfreesboro Rd
Sunset Grill. 2001 A Belcourt Ave

EAST OF DOWNTOWN
101st Airborne. 1362 A Murfreesboro Rd
New Orleans Manor. 1400 Murfreesboro Rd

WEST OF DOWNTOWN
Belle Meade Brasserie. 101 Page Rd
Cakewalk. 3001 W End Ave
F Scott's. 2210 Crestmoor Rd
Golden Dragon. 94 White Bridge Rd
Green Hills Grille. 2122 Hillsboro Dr
J Alexander's. 73 White Bridge Rd
Jimmy Kelly's. 217 Louise Ave
Sperry's. 5109 Harding Rd
Valentino's. 1907 West End Ave

OPRYLAND AREA
Cock Of The Walk. 2624 Music Valley Dr

Note: When a listing is located in a town that does not have its own city heading, it will appear under the city nearest to its location. In these cases, the address and town appear in parenthesis immediately following the name of the establishment.

Motels

(Rates may be higher during Fan Fair Week)

★ ★ **BUDGETEL INN.** *5612 Lenox Ave (37209), I-40 exit 204, west of downtown. 615/353-0700; FAX 615/352-0361.* 110 rms, 3 story. S $59.95-$71.95; D $59.95-$79.95; each addl $7; under 18 free; higher rates special events. Crib free. TV; cable (premium). Pool. Complimentary continental bkfst. Complimentary coffee in rms. Restaurant adj 6 am-11 pm. Ck-out noon. Meeting rms. Business servs avail. Sundries. Cr cds: A, C, D, DS, MC, V.

✔★ ★ **BUDGETEL INN GOODLETTSVILLE.** *(120 Cartwright Court, Goodlettsville 37072) 14 mi N on I-65, at exit 97. 615/851-1891; FAX 615/851-4513.* 102 rms, 3 story. Apr-Oct: S, D $45.95-$60.95; each addl $6; under 18 free; lower rates rest of yr. Crib free. Pet accepted, some restrictions. TV; cable (premium). Pool. Complimentary continental bkfst. Restaurant adj. 6 am-10 pm. Ck-out noon. Meeting rm. Business servs avail. Valet serv. Sundries. Cr cds: A, C, D, DS, MC, V.

★ ★ **CLUBHOUSE INN.** *2435 Atrium Way (37214), east of downtown. 615/883-0500; FAX 615/889-4827.* 135 rms, 3 story, 17 suites. Apr-Oct: S $79, D $89; each addl $10; suites $98-$108; under 16 free; wkend rates; lower rates rest of yr. TV; cable (premium), VCR avail. Heated pool; whirlpool. Complimentary full bkfst. Ck-out noon. Coin lndry. Meeting rms. Business servs avail. Valet serv. Free airport transportation. Refrigerator. Balconies. Cr cds: A, C, D, DS, MC, V.

★ ★ **COMFORT INN-NORTH.** *2306 Brick Church Pike (37207), I-65 exit 87B, north of downtown. 615/226-9560.* 95 rms, 4 story. S $42.95-$50.95; D $48.95-$56.95; each addl $5; under 16 free; higher rates special events. Crib free. Pet accepted, some restrictions. TV; cable (premium). Pool. Complimentary continental bkfst. Restaurant adj open 24 hrs. Ck-out noon. Business servs avail. Cr cds: A, C, D, DS, MC, V.

★ ★ ★ **COURTYARD BY MARRIOTT-AIRPORT.** *2508 Elm Hill Pike (37214), near International Airport, east of downtown. 615/883-9500; FAX 615/883-0172.* 145 rms, 4 story. S, D $87-$120; wkend rates. Crib free. TV; cable (premium), VCR avail. Pool; whirlpool. Complimentary coffee in rms. Restaurant 6:30-11 am; wkend hrs vary. Bar 5-11 pm. Ck-out noon. Coin lndry. Meeting rms. Business servs avail. Valet serv. Sundries. Free airport transportation. Exercise equipt; weight machines, bicycles. Refrigerator, microwaves avail. Some balconies. Cr cds: A, C, D, DS, MC, V.

✔★ **DAYS INN RIVERGATE.** *(809 Wren Rd, Goodlettsville 37072) 12 mi N on I-65, Rivergate exit 96. 615/859-1771.* 46 rms, 3 story. No elvtr. May-Aug: S,D $39.95-$89.95; each addl $5; under 12 free; higher rates special events; lower rates rest of yr. TV; cable (premium). Complimentary continental bkfst. Restaurant nearby. Ck-out 11 am. Business servs avail. Microwaves avail. Cr cds: A, D, DS, MC, V.

★ ★ **ECONO LODGE OPRYLAND.** *2460 Music Valley Dr (37214), in Opryland Area. 615/889-0090; FAX 615/889-0086.* 86 rms, 3 story. May-Oct: S, D $69.95-$74.95; each addl $10; under 18 free; higher rates special events; lower rates rest of yr. Crib free. Pet accepted, some restrictions. TV; cable (premium). Pool. Complimentary coffee in lobby. Restaurant nearby. Ck-out noon. Gift shop. Cr cds: A, C, D, DS, MC, V.

★ ★ **FAIRFIELD INN BY MARRIOTT.** *211 Music City Circle (37214), in Opryland area. 615/872-8939; FAX 615/872-7230.* 109 rms, 3 story. May-Oct: S, D $83-$93; each addl $10; suites $129; under 18 free; higher rates Fanfare; lower rates rest of yr. Crib free. TV; cable (premium), VCR avail (movies). Complimentary continental bkfst. Restaurant nearby. Ck-out noon. Meeting rm. Business servs avail. Free airport transportation. Exercise equipt; bicycle, treadmill. Indoor pool. Cr cds: A, C, D, DS, MC, V.

✔★ **FIDDLERS INN.** *2410 Music Valley Dr (37214), in Opryland Area. 615/885-1440; FAX 615/883-6477.* 202 rms, 2-3 story. Apr-Oct: S $46-$64, D $52-$72; each addl $5; lower rates rest of yr. Crib $5. TV; cable (premium). Pool. Restaurant adj 6:30 am-10 pm. Ck-out 11 am. Business servs avail. Gift shop. Cr cds: A, DS, MC, V.

✔★★ **HAMPTON INN.** *(202 Northgate Circle, Goodlettsville 37072) 13 mi N on I-65, exit 97. 615/851-2828; FAX 615/851-2830.* Web www.hampton-inn.com. 61 rms, 3 story. June-mid-Sept: S $69-$74; D $74-$79; under 18 free; higher rates Fanfare; lower rates rest of yr. Crib free. TV; cable (premium). Complimentary continental bkfst. Restaurant nearby. Ck-out noon. Meeting rms. Business servs avail. In-rm modem link. Health club privileges. Pool. Bathroom phones; some in-rm whirlpools, refrigerators, microwaves, wet bars. Cr cds: A, C, D, DS, MC, V.

D SC

★★ **HAMPTON INN.** *2350 Elm Hill Pike (37214), east of downtown. 615/871-0222; FAX 615/885-5325.* Web www.hampton.com. 120 rms, 3 story. S, D $67-$85; each addl $10; under 18 free. Crib free. TV; cable (premium). Pool. Complimentary continental bkfst. Restaurant adj open 24 hrs. Ck-out 11 am. Meeting rm. Business servs avail. In-rm modem link. Health club privileges. Near airport. Cr cds: A, C, D, DS, MC, V.

D SC

★ **HAMPTON INN-BRENTWOOD.** *(5630 Franklin Pike Circle, Brentwood 37027) S on I-65, exit 74B. 615/373-2212; FAX 615/370-9832.* 114 air-cooled rms, 5 story. S, D $70-$85; under 18 free. Crib free. TV; cable (premium). Complimentary continental bkfst. Restaurant adj 6 am-midnight. Ck-out noon. Meeting rms. Business servs avail. Some refrigerators. Cr cds: A, C, D, DS, MC, V.

D SC

★★ **HOLIDAY INN EXPRESS.** *(909 Conference Dr, Goodlettsville 37072) 13 mi N on I-65, exit 97. 615/851-6600; FAX 615/851-4723.* 66 rms, 2 story. June-Aug: S, D $56-$120; each addl $5; under 12 free; lower rates rest of yr. Crib free. TV; cable. Complimentary continental bkfst. Restaurant nearby. Ck-out 11 am. Meeting rms. Pool. Some in-rm whirlpools. Cr cds: A, D, DS, JCB, MC, V.

D SC

★★ **HOLIDAY INN EXPRESS.** *981 Murfreesboro Rd (37217), east of downtown. 615/367-9150; FAX 615/361-4865.* 210 rms, 2 story. S, D $65-$85; each addl $6; under 18 free; higher rates special events. Crib free. TV; cable (premium). Pool; whirlpool. Complimentary continental bkfst. Complimentary coffee in rms. Restaurant adj 11 am-11 pm; wkends to midnight. Ck-out noon. Coin lndry. Meeting rms. Business servs avail. Bellhops. Valet serv. Free airport transportation. Cr cds: A, D, DS, MC, V.

D SC

★★ **LA QUINTA.** *2001 Metrocenter Blvd (37228), north of downtown. 615/259-2130; FAX 615/242-2650.* Web www.laquinta.com. 120 rms, 2 story. S, D $63-$70; each addl $7; under 18 free. Crib free. TV; cable (premium). Pool. Complimentary continental bkfst. Restaurant adj 6 am-midnight. Ck-out noon. Business servs avail. Coin lndry. Microwaves avail. Cr cds: A, C, D, DS, MC, V.

D SC

★★ **RAMADA INN AIRPORT.** *709 Spence Lane (37217), southeast of downtown. 615/361-0102; FAX 615/361-4765.* 228 rms, 2 story. S, D $50-$75; each addl $8; under 12 free. Crib $8. TV; cable (premium), VCR avail. Pool. Restaurant 6 am-2 pm, 5-9:30 pm. Rm serv. Bar 4 pm-2 am; entertainment. Ck-out noon. Bellhops. Sundries. Coin lndry. Meeting rms. Business servs avail. In-rm modem link. Airport transportation. Cr cds: A, C, D, DS, JCB, MC, V.

D SC

★★ **RAMADA INN SUITES-SOUTH.** *2425 Atrium Way (37214), near International Airport, east of downtown. 615/883-5201; FAX 615/883-5594.* Web wwwramada.com/ramada.html. 120 suites, 3 story. S, D $75-129; each addl $10; under 18 free. Crib free. Pet accepted, some restrictions. TV; cable (premium), VCR avail. Pool. Complimentary continental bkfst. Coffee in rms. Ck-out noon. Coin lndry. Meeting rms. Business servs avail. Valet serv. Free airport transportation. Health club privileges. Refrigerators; microwaves avail. Cr cds: A, C, D, DS, JCB, MC, V.

D SC

★★ **RAMADA LIMITED.** *(5770 Old Hickory Blvd, Hermitage 37076) 6 mi E on I-40, exit 221. 615/889-8940; FAX 615/871-4444.* Web www.rds2.com/motels/ramadsltd. 100 rms, 3 story. June-Aug: S $35-$55; D $40-$70; each addl $6; under 18 free; lower rates rest of yr. Crib free. Pet accepted, some restrictions; $5. TV; cable. Pool. Complimentary continental bkfst. Restaurant nearby. Ck-out noon. Business servs avail. Microwaves avail. Cr cds: A, C, D, DS, MC, V.

D SC

✔★ **RED ROOF INN.** *510 Claridge St (37214), I-40 exit 216, near International Airport, east of downtown. 615/872-0735; FAX 615/871-4647.* 120 rms, 3 story. Mar-Sept: S $39.99-$49.99; D $45.99-$55.99; each addl $6; under 17 free; higher rates special events; lower rates rest of yr. Crib avail. Pet accepted, some restrictions. TV; cable (premium). Complimentary coffee in lobby. Restaurant nearby. Ck-out 11 am. Free airport transportation. Cr cds: A, C, D, DS, MC, V.

D

✔★ **RED ROOF INN-SOUTH.** *4271 Sidco Dr (37204), at jct I-65 & Harding Pl, south of downtown. 615/832-0093; FAX 615/832-0097.* 85 rms, 3 story. Mar-Sept: S $43.99-$69.99; D $46.99-$69.99; each addl $8; under 18 free; lower rates rest of yr. Crib free. Pet accepted. TV; cable. Complimentary coffee in lobby. Restaurant nearby. Ck-out 11 am. Business servs avail. Cr cds: A, C, D, DS, MC, V.

D

★★★ **RESIDENCE INN BY MARRIOTT.** *2300 Elm Hill Pike (37214), near International Airport, east of downtown. 615/889-8600; FAX 615/871-4970.* Web www.ResidenceInn.com. 168 kit. suites, 2 story. Suites: 1-bedrm studio $89-$129; 2-bedrm penthouse $99-$149. TV; cable. Pool; whirlpool. Complimentary continental bkfst. Ck-out noon. Coin lndry. Meeting rms. Business servs avail. Refrigerators, microwaves; many fireplaces. Balconies. Cr cds: A, C, D, DS, JCB, MC, V.

D SC

★★ **SHONEY'S INN.** *1521 Demonbreun St (37203), in Music Row. 615/255-9977; FAX 615/242-6127; res: 800/222-2222.* 147 rms, 3 story. S $62-$72; D $72-$75; each addl $6; suites $109-$119; under 18 free; higher rates special events. Crib free. TV; cable (premium). Pool. Complimentary coffee in lobby. Restaurant adj 6 am-midnight. Ck-out noon. Meeting rms. Business servs avail. Cr cds: A, C, D, DS, ER, MC, V.

D SC

★★ **SHONEY'S INN NORTH.** *(100 Northcreek Blvd, Goodlettsville 37072) 13 mi N on I-65, exit 97. 615/851-1067; FAX 615/851-6069; res: 800/222-2222.* 111 rms, 3 story. S $55-$65; D $61-$71; each addl $6; under 17 free. Crib free. TV; cable (premium). Pool. Complimentary coffee in lobby. Restaurant adj 6 am-11 pm; Fri, Sat to 1 am. Ck-out noon. Meeting rm. Business servs avail. Microwaves avail. Cr cds: A, D, DS, ER, MC, V.

D SC

★ **SUPER 8.** *412 Robertson Ave (37209), I-40 exit 204, west of downtown. 615/356-0888.* 73 rms, 3 story. June-July: S $50-$57; D $59.88-$69.88; each addl $5; suites $69-$75; under 12 free; higher rates for special events; lower rates rest of yr. Crib free. Pet accepted. TV; cable (premium). Complimentary continental bkfst. Restaurant adj open 24 hrs. Ck-out 11 am. Business servs avail. Cr cds: A, C, D, DS, MC, V.

D SC

✔★ **TRAVELERS REST INN.** *(107 Franklin Rd, Brentwood 37027) 1 blk W of I-65 exits 74B. 615/373-3033; FAX 615/370-5709; res: 800/852-0618.* 35 rms, 1-2 story, 2 kits. S $40-$49; D $50-$57; each addl $4; under 18 free. Crib $2. TV; cable (premium). Pool; wading pool. Complimentary coffee in rms. Restaurant nearby. Ck-out noon. Coin lndry. Business servs avail. Some refrigerators. Picnic table. Cr cds: A, C, D, DS, MC, V.

SC

Motor Hotels

★ ★ **AMERISUITES.** *220 Rudy's Circle (37214), in Opryland Area. 615/872-0422; FAX 615/872-9283.* 125 suites, 5 story. June-mid-Sept: S, D $110-$120; each addl $10; under 18 free; higher rates special events; lower rates rest of yr. Crib free. TV; cable (premium), VCR (movies $6.95). Pool. Complimentary continental bkfst. Complimentary coffee in rms. Restaurant nearby. Ck-out 11 am. Coin Indry. Meeting rms. Business center. Bellhops. Valet serv. Free airport transportation. Exercise equipt; bicycles, treadmills. Refrigerators. Cr cds: A, C, D, DS, ER, MC, V.

D SC

★ ★ **AMERISUITES.** *(202 Summit View Dr, Brentwood 37027) Approx 9 mi S on I-65, exit 74A. 615/661-9477; FAX 615/661-9936.* Web www.travelbase.com/destination/nashville/amerisuites-brentwood. 126 kit. suites, 6 story. Mar-Oct: S, D $80-$150; each addl $10; under 18 free; higher rates special events; lower rates rest of yr. Crib free. Pet accepted, some restrictions; $10. TV; cable (premium), VCR (movies). Heated pool. Complimentary continental bkfst. Complimentary coffee in rms. Restaurant nearby. Ck-out noon. Coin Indry. Meeting rms. Business center. Valet serv. Sundries. Exercise equipt; bicycle, weight machine. Refrigerators. Cr cds: A, C, D, DS, ER, JCB, MC, V.

D SC

★ **GUESTHOUSE INN & SUITES MEDCENTER.** *1909 Hayes St (37203), downtown. 615/329-1000; res: 800/777-4904.* 108 rms, 7 story. Mar-Aug: S, D $64-$91; each addl $7; under 18 free; lower rates rest of yr. Crib free. TV; cable, VCR avail (movies). Complimentary continental bkfst. Restaurant nearby. Ck-out noon. Coin Indry. Meeting rm. Business servs avail. Refrigerators, microwaves, wet bars. Cr cds: A, C, D, DS, MC, V.

D SC

★ ★ **HAMPTON INN AND SUITES.** *583 Donelson Pike (37214), near Nashville Intl Airport, east of downtown. 615/885-4242; FAX 615/885-6726.* 111 rms, 7 story, 31 kit. suites. S, D $84-$129; each addl $10; kit. suites $102-$129; under 18 free; higher rates special events. Crib free. Parking. TV; cable (premium), VCR. Pool. Complimentary continental bkfst. Complimentary coffee in rms. Restaurant nearby. Ck-out noon. Meeting rms. Business servs avail. Gift shop. Free airport transportation. Exercise equipt; bicycle, treadmill. Some refrigerators. Cr cds: A, C, D, DS, MC, V.

D SC

★ ★ **HAMPTON INN-NORTH.** *2407 Brick Church Pike (37207), I-65 exit 87B, north of downtown. 615/226-3300; FAX 615/226-0170.* 125 rms, 5 story. S, D $58-$73; under 18 free; higher rates special events. Crib free. TV; cable (premium). Pool. Restaurant nearby. Ck-out noon. Meeting rms. Business servs avail. Exercise equipt; weights, bicycles. Game rm. Cr cds: A, C, D, DS, MC, V.

D SC

★ ★ ★ **HILTON SUITES-BRENTWOOD.** *(9000 Overlook Blvd, Brentwood 37027) S on I-65, exit 74B. 615/370-0111; FAX 615/370-0272.* Web www.hiltons.com. 203 suites, 4 story. S, D $115-$155; each addl $15; family rates. Crib free. Pet accepted, some restrictions. TV; cable (premium), VCR (movies $2). Indoor pool; whirlpool. Complimentary full bkfst. Coffee in rms. Restaurant 6-9:30 am, 11:30 am-1:30 pm, 5-10 pm; Sat, Sun 7-11 am, 5-10 pm. Rm serv from 5 pm. Bar 4 pm-midnight. Ck-out noon. Free Indry facilities. Meeting rms. Business center. Gift shop. Exercise equipt; weight machine, bicycles. Rec rm. Refrigerators, wet bars. Balconies. Cr cds: A, C, D, DS, ER, JCB, MC, V.

D SC

★ ★ ★ **HOLIDAY INN BRENTWOOD.** *(760 Old Hickory Blvd, Brentwood 37027) I-65 exit 74A. 615/373-2600; FAX 615/377-3893.* 248 rms, 8 story. S, D $69-$139; under 18 free; wkend rates. Crib free. TV; cable (premium). Pool; whirlpool. Complimentary coffee in rms. Restaurant 6:30 am-10 pm. Rm serv. Bar 4 pm-midnight. Ck-out noon. Coin Indry. Meeting rms. In-rm modem link. Bellhops. Valet serv. 18-hole golf privileges. Exercise equipt; weight machine, stair machine, sauna. Cr cds: A, C, D, DS, JCB, MC, V.

D SC

★ ★ **HOLIDAY INN EXPRESS.** *1111 Airport Center Dr (37214), near International Airport, east of downtown. 615/883-1366; FAX 615/889-6867.* 206 rms, 3 story. S, D $89-$99; each addl $8; under 18 free. Crib free. TV; cable (premium). Pool. Complimentary continental bkfst. Restaurant nearby. Ck-out noon. Meeting rms. Business servs avail. Bellhops. Free airport transportation. Some balconies. Cr cds: A, C, D, DS, JCB, MC, V.

D SC

★ ★ **HOLIDAY INN EXPRESS-NORTH.** *2401 Brick Church Pike (37207), I-65 exit 87B, north of downtown. 615/226-4600; FAX 615/228-6412.* 172 rms, 5 story. Apr-Oct: S, D $60-$80; under 18 free; higher rates special events; lower rates rest of yr. Crib free. TV; cable (premium). Pool. Ck-out 11 am. Coin Indry. Meeting rms. Business servs avail. In-rm modem link. Exercise equipt; weights, bicycle, sauna. Cr cds: A, C, D, DS, JCB, MC, V.

D SC

★ ★ **RAMADA INN.** *2401 Music Valley Dr (37214), opp Opryland Area. 615/889-0800; FAX 615/883-1230.* 307 rms, 3 story. June-Oct: S, D $78-$105; each addl $8; suites $130-$160; under 18 free; lower rates rest of yr. TV: cable. Heated pool; wading pool, whirlpool. Restaurant 6 am-10 pm. Rm serv. Bar noon-1 am. Ck-out 11 am. Meeting rms. Business servs avail. Bellhops. Valet serv. Sundries. Gift shop. Free airport transportation. Exercise equipt; weight machine, bicycle, sauna. Game rm. Cr cds: A, C, D, DS, MC, V.

D SC

★ ★ **SHONEY'S INN.** *2420 Music Valley Dr (37214), in Opryland Area. 615/885-4030; FAX 615/391-0632; res: 800/222-2222.* E-mail shoneysnashville@travelbase.com. 185 rms, 5 story. June-Aug: S, D $105-$115; each addl $8; suites $129-$149; under 18 free; higher rates special events; lower rates rest of yr. TV; cable (premium). Indoor pool; whirlpool. Complimentary continental bkfst. Complimentary coffee in rms. Restaurant adj 6-11 am. Bar 4-11 pm. Ck-out 11 am. Meeting rms. Business servs avail. Valet serv. Sundries. Gift shop. Free garage parking. Free airport transportation. Cr cds: A, C, D, DS, MC, V.

D SC

✔★ **WILSON INN.** *600 Ermac Dr (37214), east of downtown. 615/889-4466; res: 800/945-7667; FAX 615/889-0464.* 80 rms, 5 story. S, D $54.95-$76.95; each addl $7; suites $69.95-$86.95; under 19 free; higher rates special events. Crib free. Pet accepted. TV; cable (premium). Complimentary continental bkfst. Restaurant adj open 24 hrs. Ck-out noon. Meeting rms. Business servs avail. Free airport transportation. Refrigerators; wet bar in suites; microwaves avail. Cr cds: A, C, D, DS, JCB, MC, V.

D SC

Hotels

★ ★ **CLUBHOUSE INN CONFERENCE CENTER.** *920 Broadway (37203), downtown. 615/244-0150; FAX 615/244-0445.* Web www.clubhouseinn.com. 285 rms, 8 story. S, D $90-$119; each addl $10; suites $119-$139; under 12 free. Crib free. TV. Pool. Complimentary bkfst buffet. Restaurant 5:30-8:30 pm. Ck-out noon. Convention facilities. Busines servs avail. Gift shop. Exercise equipt; bicycles, stair machine, treadmill. Cr cds: A, C, D, DS, MC, V.

D SC

★ ★ **COURTYARD BY MARRIOTT.** *1901 West End Ave (37203). 615/327-9900; FAX 615/327-8127.* 136 rms, 7 story. S, D $85-$95; suites $125-$135; under 16 free; higher rates special events. Crib free. TV; cable (premium). Complimentary coffee in rms. Restaurant 6:30 am-11 am. Bar 4-11 pm. Ck-out noon. Coin Indry. Meeting rms. Business servs avail. Exercise equipt; bicycle, stair machine, whirlpool. Refrigerator, microwave in suites. Balconies. Cr cds: A, C, D, DS, JCB, MC, V.

D SC

★ ★ ★ **CROWNE PLAZA.** *623 Union St (37219), opp capitol, downtown. 615/259-2000; FAX 615/742-6056.* Web www.com.crowne plaza.com. 473 rms, 28 story. S, D $157-$178; each addl $15; under 18 free; wkend rates. Crib free. Garage $10; valet parking $14. TV; cable (premium), VCR avail. Indoor pool. Restaurant 6 am-midnight (also see PINNACLE). Bars 4 pm-2 am. Ck-out noon. Meeting rms. Business center. Concierge. Gift shop. Airport transportation. Exercise equipt; bicycle, treadmill. Luxury level. Cr cds: A, C, D, DS, ER, JCB, MC, V.

D SC

★ ★ ★ **DOUBLETREE.** *315 Fourth Ave N (37219), downtown. 615/244-8200; FAX 615/747-4894.* 336 rms, 9 story. S, D $119-$159; each addl $10; suites $125-$650; under 18 free; wkend rates. Crib free. Garage $10. TV; cable (premium), VCR avail. Indoor pool. Restaurant 6:30 am-10:30 pm. Rm serv. Bar 4 pm-1 am. Ck-out noon. Convention facilities. Business center. In-rm modem link. Gift shop. Free airport transportation. Exercise equipt; weights, bicycles, sauna. Wet bar in suites. Cr cds: A, C, D, DS, ER, MC, V.

D SC

★ ★ ★ **DOUBLETREE GUEST SUITES.** *2424 Atrium Way (37214), near International Airport, east of downtown. 615/889-8889; FAX 615/883-7779.* 138 suites, 3 story. Mar-Oct: S $170; D $185; each addl $10; under 18 free; lower rates rest of yr. Crib free. TV; cable (premium). Indoor/outdoor pool; poolside serv. Complimentary coffee in rms. Restaurant 6:30 am-10 pm. Bar 4-11 pm. Ck-out noon. Meeting rms. Business servs avail. In-rm modem link. Free airport transportation. Exercise equipt; weights, bicycles. Game rm. Refrigerators; microwaves avail. Some private patios, balconies. Cr cds: A, C, D, DS, MC, V.

D SC

★ ★ ★ **EMBASSY SUITES.** *10 Century Blvd (37214), near International Airport, east of downtown. 615/871-0033; FAX 615/883-9245.* Web www.embassysuites.com. 296 suites, 9 story. Suites $129-$169; each addl $10; under 17 free; wkend plans. Crib free. Pet accepted, some restrictions. TV; cable (premium), VCR avail. Indoor pool; whirlpool. Complimentary full bkfst. Restaurant 6:30-9:30 am, 11 am-2 pm, 5-10 pm; Fri, Sat to 11 pm. Rm serv 11 am-11 pm. Bar 5 pm-midnight. Ck-out noon. Convention facilities. Business servs avail. Concierge. Gift shop. Free airport transportation. Exercise equipt; weights, bicycles, sauna. Game rm. Refrigerators, microwaves, wet bars. Atrium. Cr cds: A, C, D, DS, JCB, MC, V.

D SC

★ ★ ★ **THE HERMITAGE.** *231 6th Ave N (37219), downtown. 615/244-3121; res: 800/251-1908; FAX 615/254-6909.* 120 suites, 9 story. 1-bedrm suites $129-$179; 2-bedrm suites $250; each addl $15; wkend rates. Valet parking $10. TV; cable (premium), VCR avail. Restaurant (see CAPITOL GRILLE). Bars 11 am-midnight. Ck-out noon. Meeting rms. Business servs avail. Health club privileges. Bathrm phones, refrigerators, wet bars; microwaves avail. Hotel built in 1910 as a tribute to Beaux Arts Classicism; fully restored to original elegance. Cr cds: A, D, DS, MC, V.

D

★ ★ **HOWARD JOHNSON AIRPORT PLAZA.** *733 Briley Pkwy (37217), I-40 exit 215, east of downtown. 615/361-5900; FAX 615/367-0339.* 200 rms, 11 story. June-Oct: S $85; D $95; each addl $10; suites $100-$167; under 18 free; lower rates rest of yr. Crib free. TV; cable (premium). Pool. Playground. Restaurant 6 am-10 pm. Bar 4 pm-midnight; entertainment. Ck-out noon. Meeting rms. Business servs avail. Free airport transportation. Cr cds: A, C, D, DS, MC, V.

D SC

★ ★ ★ **LOEWS VANDERBILT PLAZA.** *2100 West End Ave (37203), downtown. 615/320-1700; FAX 615/320-5019.* 340 rms, 12 story. S $159-$209; D $179-$229; each addl $20; suites $400-$750; under 18 free. Crib free. Pet accepted. Garage $8; valet parking $10. TV; cable (premium), VCR avail. Restaurants 6:30 am-10 pm. Rm serv to midnight; Fri-Sat to 1 am. Bars 3 pm-1 am; entertainment exc Sun. Ck-out noon. Convention facilities. Business center. In-rm modem link. Concierge. Shopping arcade. Barber, beauty shop. Exercise equipt; weights, treadmill. Minibars; microwaves avail. Luxury level. Cr cds: A, C, D, DS, JCB, MC, V.

D SC

★ ★ ★ **MARRIOTT.** *600 Marriott Dr (37214), east of downtown. 615/889-9300; FAX 615/889-9315.* 399 rms, 18 story. S $133-$150; D $146-$162; suites $225-$550; under 17 free; wkend plans. TV; cable (premium), VCR avail. Indoor/outdoor pool; whirlpool, poolside serv. Restaurant 6 am-10:30 pm. Bar 11-2 am. Ck-out noon. Lndry facilities. Convention facilities. Business center. In-rm modem link. Free parking. Free airport transportation. Lighted tennis. Exercise equipt; weight machines, bicycles, sauna. Picnic tables, grills. Near Percy Priest Lake. Luxury level. Cr cds: A, C, D, DS, ER, JCB, MC, V.

D SC

★ ★ ★ **OPRYLAND HOTEL.** *2800 Opryland Dr (37214), 5 mi NE of jct I-40 & Briley Pkwy, in Opryland Area. 615/889-1000; FAX 615/871-5728.* 2,882 rms, 6 story. S, D $199-$249; each addl $15; suites $259-$2,500; under 12 free. Crib free. Valet parking $12. TV; cable (premium), VCR avail. Heated pools; wading pools, poolside serv, lifeguard. Restaurants 6:30-1 am. Rm serv 24 hrs. Bars 11-2 am; entertainment. Ck-out 11 am. Convention facilities. Business center. Shopping arcades. Barber, beauty shop. Airport transportation. 18-hole golf, greens fee $60-$80. Exercise equipt; weights, bicycles. Massage. Some refrigerators. Some balconies overlooking garden conservatory, cascades and delta. Showboat cruises avail. Cr cds: A, C, D, DS, MC, V.

D

★ ★ ★ **REGAL MAXWELL HOUSE.** *2025 Metrocenter Blvd (37228), north of downtown. 615/259-4343.* Web www.regal-hotels.com/Nashville. 289 rms, 10 story. S $112-$158; D $127-$178; each addl $15; suites $175-$395; under 17 free; wkend plans. Crib free. TV; cable (premium). Pool; whirlpool. Restaurants 6:30 am-10 pm. Bar 11 am-midnight. Ck-out noon. Meeting rms. Business servs avail. Gift shop. Lighted tennis. Exercise equipt; weight machine, bicycles, sauna, steam rm. Luxury level. Cr cds: A, D, DS, MC, V.

D SC

★ ★ ★ **RENAISSANCE.** *611 Commerce St (37203), downtown. 615/255-8400; FAX 615/255-8163.* Web www.renaissance.com. 673 rms, 25 story. S, D $170-$220; each addl $20; suites $275-$1100; under 18 free; wkend packages. Crib free. Garage $6; valet parking $12. TV; cable (premium), VCR avail. Indoor pool; whirlpool, poolside serv. Restaurant 6 am-10 pm; Fri, Sat to 11 pm. Rm serv 24 hrs. Bar 11-2 am; entertainment. Ck-out noon. Convention facilities. Business center. Shopping arcade. Concierge. Exercise equipt; weights, bicycles, sauna. Some bathrm phones, refrigerators. Luxury level. Cr cds: A, C, D, DS, ER, JCB, MC, V.

D SC

★ ★ ★ **SHERATON-MUSIC CITY.** *777 McGavock Pike (37214), near International Airport, east of downtown. 615/885-2200; FAX 615/231-1134.* Web www.tenn.com/sheraton. 412 rms, 4 story. S, D $148-$168; each addl $15; suites $170-$550; under 17 free; wkend rates. Pet accepted. TV; cable (premium), VCR avail. Indoor/outdoor pools; wading pool, whirlpool, poolside serv. Restaurants 6 am-11 pm. Bar 11-3 am; entertainment. Ck-out noon. Convention facilities. Business center. Concierge. Beauty shop. Gift shop. Free airport transportation. Lighted tennis. Golf privileges. Exercise rm; instructor, weight machine, bicycles, sauna. Bathrm phones; some refrigerators. Private balconies. On 23 landscaped acres on top of hill. Semiformal decor. Cr cds: A, C, D, DS, ER, JCB, MC, V.

D SC

★ ★ ★ **UNION STATION.** *1001 Broadway (37203), downtown. 615/726-1001; res: 800/331-2123; FAX 615/248-3554.* Web www.Grand Heritage.com. 124 rms, 7 story, 12 suites. S, D $129-$215; each addl $10; suites $215-$400; under 13 free; wkend rates. Crib free. Pet accepted. Valet parking $10. TV; cable (premium), VCR avail (movies). Coffee in rms. Restaurant 6:30 am-11 pm (also see ARTHUR'S). Bar 11 am-11 pm.

Ck-out 11 am. Business center. Concierge. Valet parking. Gift shop. Airport transportation. Tennis, 18-hole golf privileges. In renovated historic train station (1897); stained-glass roof. Cr cds: A, C, D, DS, MC, V.

D SC

Restaurants

★ ★ **101ST AIRBORNE.** *1362 A Murfreesboro Rd, east of downtown. 615/361-4212.* Hrs: 11 am-2:30 pm, 4:30-10 pm; Fri, Sat 5-11 pm; Sun 4:30-10 pm; Sun brunch 9:30 am-2:30 pm. Closed Dec 25. Res accepted. Bar from 4 pm. Semi-a la carte: lunch $5.95-$10.95, dinner $9.95-$24.95. Sun brunch $15.95. Child's meals. Specializes in steak, seafood, prime rib. Parking. House dramatizes a headquarters operation for the 101st Airborne Division; World War II memorabilia. Cr cds: A, D, DS, MC, V.

D

★ ★ ★ **ARTHUR'S.** *(See Union Station Hotel) 615/255-1494.* Hrs: 5:30-10:30 pm; Fri, Sat to 11 pm; Sun to 9 pm. Closed major hols. Res accepted. Continental menu. Bar 5 pm-1 am. Wine cellar. Table d'hôte: dinner $55-$70. Specializes in seafood, lamb, flaming desserts. Own baking. Valet parking. Jacket. Menu changes wkly. In an Old World-style hotel converted from an 1897 train station. Cr cds: A, C, D, DS, MC, V.

D ♥

★ ★ **BELLE MEADE BRASSERIE.** *101 Page Rd, west of downtown. 615/356-5450.* E-mail chefrobt@edge.net; web edge.net/~chefrobt. Hrs: 5:30-10 pm; Fri, Sat to 11 pm. Closed Sun; some major hols. Res accepted. Continental menu. Bar. A la carte entrees: dinner $12-$24. Specializes in seafood, pasta, homemade desserts. Parking. Outdoor dining. Contemporary decor; original art. Cr cds: A, D, MC, V.

D

★ **BLUEBIRD CAFE.** *4104 Hillsboro Rd (37215), south of downtown. 615/383-1461.* Hrs: from 5:30 pm; Sun from 6 pm. Closed some major hols. Res accepted. Bar. Semi-a la carte: dinner $4-$9. Specialties: Cajun catfish, chocolate chunk cheesecake. Parking. Popular performance club featuring songwriters and other entertainers. Cr cds: A, D, DS, MC, V.

D

✓ ★ **BOSCOS.** *1805 21st Ave S (37212), south of downtown. 615/385-0050.* Hrs: 11 am-11 pm; Fri, Sat to midnight; Sun brunch to 3 pm; hrs vary in Jan. Closed Thanksgiving, Dec 25. Res accepted. Mediterranean menu. Bar to 1 am; Fri, Sat to 2 am. Semi-a la carte: lunch $3.95-$11.95, dinner $3.95-$15.95. Sun brunch $3.95-$8.95. Child's meals. Specializes in wood-fired oven pizza, pasta, fresh fish. Valet parking. Brewery on site. Cr cds: A, D, MC, V.

D

★ ★ **BOUNDRY.** *911 20th Ave S (37212), south of downtown. 615/321-3043.* E-mail boundry@bellsouth.net. Hrs: 5-10:30 pm; Fri, Sat to 1 am. Closed most major hols. Res accepted. Eclectic menu. Bar 4 pm-2:30 am. Semi-a la carte: dinner $9.95-$23.50. Specialties: planked trout, grilled Tennessee ostrich, lobster BLT pizza. Valet parking. Outdoor dining. Murals, artwork throughout. Cr cds: A, C, D, DS, MC, V.

D

★ ★ **CAKEWALK.** *3001 W End Ave (37203), west of downtown. 615/320-7778.* Hrs: 5:30-10 pm; Fri to 11 pm, Sat 5:30-11 pm; Sun brunch 11 am-3 pm. Closed most major hols. Res accepted. Semi-a la carte: dinner $10.50-$21.95. Sun brunch $6.95-$12. Specializes in fish, poultry, vegetarian entrees. Displays work of local artists. Cr cds: A, DS, MC, V.

D ♥

★ ★ ★ **CAPITOL GRILLE.** *(See The Hermitage Hotel) 615/244-3121.* Hrs: 6:30 am-2 pm, 5:30-10 pm; Sun brunch 11 am-2 pm. Res accepted. Bar 11 am-11 pm; Fri, Sat to midnight. Extensive wine list. Semi-a la carte: bkfst $3.50-$9.95, lunch $5.95-$8.95, dinner $16.50-$24.95. Sun brunch $19.95-$21.95. Specialties: sautéed red snapper, creme brulee Napoleon, soft-shell crawfish. Pianist Sun brunch. Valet parking. Russian paneling; marble columns. Cr cds: A, D, DS, MC, V.

D

✓ ★ **COCK OF THE WALK.** *2624 Music Valley Dr, in Opryland Area. 615/889-1930.* Hrs: 5-9 pm; Fri, Sat to 10 pm. Closed Thanksgiving, Dec 24, 25; also Super Bowl Sun. Res accepted. Bar. Semi-a la carte: dinner $8.95-$12.50. Child's meals. Specializes in catfish, fried dill pickles, flipped cornbread. Parking. Split level dining in rustic atmosphere. Cr cds: A, D, MC, V.

D

★ ★ ★ **F SCOTT'S.** *2210 Crestmoor Rd, west of downtown. 615/269-5861.* Hrs: 11:30 am-2 pm, 5:30-10 pm; Fri to 11 pm; Sat 5:30-11 pm; Sun brunch 11 am-2 pm. Closed most major hols. Res accepted. Bar. Wine list. A la carte entrees: lunch $5-$8.95, dinner $10.95-$19.95. Sun brunch $6.95-$10.95. Child's meals. Specializes in seafood, lamb. Entertainment Tue- Sat. Valet parking. Art deco decor. Cr cds: A, C, D, DS, MC, V.

D

✓ ★ **GERST HAUS.** *228 Woodland St, downtown. 615/256-9760.* Hrs: 11 am-9 pm; Fri, Sat to 10 pm; Sun 4-9 pm. Closed Jan 1, Thanksgiving, Dec 25. Res accepted Mon-Fri. German, Amer menu. Bar. Semi-a la carte: lunch, dinner $6.95-$12.95. Specialties: Wienerschnitzel, pork loin, fresh oyster roll. German band Sat. Beer hall atmosphere. Bavarian decor; antiques. Family-owned. Cr cds: A, D, MC, V.

D

✓ ★ **GOLDEN DRAGON.** *94 White Bridge Rd, west of downtown. 615/356-4558.* Hrs: 11 am-10 pm; Fri, Sat to 11 pm. Chinese menu. Bar. Semi-a la carte: lunch $4.25-$7.50, dinner $6.25-$14.95. Lunch buffet $6.25, dinner buffet $10.95. Child's meals. Specializes in Hunan, Szechwan and Shanghai dishes. Parking. Chinese decor; lanterns. Cr cds: A, D, DS, MC, V.

D

✓ ★ **GOTEN 2.** *209 10th Ave S (37203), downtown. 615/251-4855.* Hrs: 11 am-midnight; Fri to 1 am; Sat 5 pm-1 am; Sun 5-10 pm. Closed Thanksgiving, Dec 25. Res accepted. Japanese menu. Bar. Semi-a la carte: lunch, dinner $4-$12.75. Specialties: sushi, tempura, bento box. Parking. Casual sushi bar in redeveloped historic building. Cr cds: A, D, DS, MC, V.

D

✓ ★ ★ **GREEN HILLS GRILLE.** *2122 Hillsboro Dr (37215), west of downtown. 615/383-6444.* Hrs: 11 am-10 pm; Fri, Sat to 11 pm. Closed Thanksgiving, Dec 25. Continental menu. Bar to 11 pm; Fri, Sat to midnight. Semi-a la carte: lunch, dinner $6.50-$15.45. Child's meals. Specialties: lemon artichoke chicken, roasted chicken, barbecue ribs. Valet parking. Southwestern decor. Cr cds: A, C, D, DS, MC, V.

D

✓ ★ ★ **J ALEXANDER'S.** *73 White Bridge Rd, west of downtown. 615/352-0981.* Hrs: 11 am-10 pm; Fri, Sat to 11 pm. Closed Thanksgiving, Dec 25. Bar. Semi-a la carte: lunch, dinner $4.95-$17.95. Child's meals. Specializes in prime rib, fresh seafood, salads. Parking. Glass window permits diners to observe salad preparation area. Cr cds: A, C, D, DS, MC, V.

D

★ ★ **JIMMY KELLY'S.** *217 Louise Ave, west of downtown. 615/329-4349.* Hrs: 5 pm-midnight. Closed Sun; some major hols. Res accepted. Bar. Semi-a la carte: dinner $11-$24. Child's meals. Specializes in hand-cut aged beef. Valet parking. Outdoor dining. In renovated Victorian mansion (1911). Family-owned. Cr cds: A, C, D, MC, V.

D ♥

✓ ★ **LOVELESS CAFE.** *8400 TN 100 (37221), south of downtown. 615/646-9700.* Hrs: 8 am-2 pm, 5-9 pm; Sat, Sun 8 am-9 pm. Closed Jan 1, Thanksgiving, Dec 25. Res accepted. Semi-a la carte: bkfst $3.95-

$8.95, lunch, dinner $4-$14.95. Child's meals. Specializes in scratch biscuits, fried chicken. Parking. Outdoor dining. Private dining in rms that were previously motel rms. Family-owned. Cr cds: A, MC, V.

D SC

★★ **MÈRE BULLES.** *152 2nd Ave N (37201), downtown. 615/256-1946.* Hrs: 11 am-3 pm, 5:30-10 pm; Fri, Sat to 11 pm; Sun brunch 11 am-3 pm. Closed Jan 1. Res accepted. Bar. Semi-a la carte: lunch $4.95-$12.95, dinner $14.95-$29.95. Sun brunch $23.95. Specializes in pasta, seafood, steak. Entertainment. Local art on display. Cr cds: A, C, D, DS, MC, V.

D

★★ **THE MAD PLATTER.** *1239 6th Ave N (37208), north of downtown. 615/242-2563.* Hrs: 11 am-2 pm, 5:30-11 pm; Mon to 2 pm. Closed Sun; most major hols. Res required. Wine list. Semi-a la carte: lunch $6.25-$11.95, dinner $18.50-$48. Specialties: rack of lamb moutarde, chocolate Elvis. Building more than 100 yrs old. Cr cds: A, DS, MC, V.

D

★★★ **MARIO'S.** *2005 Broadway, downtown. 615/327-3232.* Hrs: 5:30-10:30 pm. Closed Sun; major hols. Res accepted. Northern Italian, continental menu. Bar. Wine cellars. A la carte entrees: dinner $18-$26. Specializes in pastas, fresh seafood, veal. Theater dining rm. Pianist Sat, Sun. Parking. Family-owned. Cr cds: A, C, D, DS, MC, V.

D

★★★ **THE MERCHANTS.** *401 Broadway (37203), downtown. 615/254-1892.* Web www.themerchants.com. Hrs: 11 am-2:30 pm, 5-10 pm; Fri to 11 pm; Sat 5-11 pm; Sun 5-9 pm; Sun brunch 11 am-2 pm. Closed Jan 1. Res accepted. Bar. Wine cellar. A la carte entrees: lunch $3.95-$10.95, dinner $11.95-$23.95; Sun brunch $8.95-$16.95. Specializes in fresh grilled meats and seafood. Own baking. Pianist. Valet parking. Outdoor dining. In historic building; original wood floors; dining on 3 levels. Cr cds: A, C, D, DS, MC, V.

D

★★ **NEW ORLEANS MANOR.** *1400 Murfreesboro Rd (37217), east of downtown. 615/367-2777.* Hrs: 5:30-9 pm. Closed Sun, Mon; Jan 1, Thanksgiving, Dec 24, 25. Res accepted. Serv bar. Dinner buffet $29-$37. Child's meals. Specializes in seafood, lobster, prime rib. Salad bar. Parking. Scenic grounds; colonial-type mansion built in 1930. Cr cds: A, C, D, DS, MC, V.

D

✔★ **OLD SPAGHETTI FACTORY.** *160 2nd Ave N (37201), downtown. 615/254-9010.* Hrs: 11:30 am-2 pm, 5-10 pm; Fri to 11 pm; Sat noon-11 pm; Sun 4-10 pm. Closed Thanksgiving, Dec 24, 25. Bar. Semi-a la carte: lunch $3.25-$5.60. Complete meals: dinner $4.50-$8.50. Child's meals. Specializes in spaghetti with a variety of sauces. In converted 1869 warehouse; doorway arch from the Bank of London; antiques. Cr cds: D, DS, MC, V.

D

★★ **PINNACLE.** *(See Crowne Plaza Hotel) 615/259-2000.* Web www.com.crowneplaza.com. Hrs: 6-11 pm; Sun 5-9 pm. Res accepted. Continental menu. Wine. Semi-a la carte: dinner $19.95-$33.95. Specializes in steak, veal chops, peppered salmon steak. Valet parking. Revolving restaurant of 28th floor of downtown hotel. Cr cds: A, C, D, DS, ER, JCB, MC, V.

D

★★ **PRIME CUT STEAKHOUSE.** *170 2nd Ave N, downtown. 615/242-3083.* Hrs: 5-10 pm; Fri, Sat to 11 pm. Closed Thanksgiving, Dec 25. Res accepted. Bar from 4 pm. Semi-a la carte: dinner $15.95-$19.95. Child's meals. Specializes in steak, marinated chicken, fresh fish. Entertainment Fri, Sat. Outdoor dining. Option of cooking own steak. Cr cds: A, C, D, DS, MC, V.

D

✔★★ **ROYAL THAI.** *204 Commerce St (37201), downtown. 615/255-0821.* Hrs: 11 am-3 pm, 5-10 pm; Fri to 11 pm; Sat 11 am-11 pm; Sun 4-10 pm. Closed Jan 1, Dec 25. Res accepted. Thai menu. Bar. Semi-a la carte: lunch $4.95-$6.95, dinner $6.95-$19.95. Specialties: pad kra pao, pla sam rod, pad Thai. Oriental decor. Family-owned. Cr cds: A, D, DS, MC, V.

D

★ **SANTA FE STEAK CO.** *902 Murfreesboro Rd, south of downtown. 615/367-4448.* Hrs: 11 am-11 pm; Fri, Sat to midnight. Closed Thanksgiving, Dec 25. Bar to 11 pm, Fri, Sat to 1 am. Semi-a la carte: lunch $4.49-$7.99, dinner $6.95-$14.99. Child's meals. Specializes in Southwestern cuisine, steak, chicken. Parking. Outdoor dining. Informal dining in three areas. Cr cds: A, D, DS, MC, V.

D

✔★ **SITAR.** *116 21st Ave N (37203), north of downtown. 615/321-8889.* Hrs: 11 am-2:30 pm, 5-10 pm; Sun noon-3 pm, 5-10 pm. Indian menu. Bar. Semi-a la carte: lunch $6.95-$7.95, dinner $6.95-$14.95. Lunch buffet $5.99. Specialties: chicken tikka masala, lamb pasanda, karahai shrimp. Indian artwork. Cr cds: A, C, D, DS, MC, V.

D

★★★ **SPERRY'S.** *5109 Harding Rd, west of downtown. 615/353-0809.* Hrs: 5-10 pm; Fri, Sat to 11 pm. Closed major hols. Continental menu. Bar to midnight. A la carte entrees: dinner $12.50-$26.95. Specializes in fresh seafood, steak. Salad bar. Own desserts, soups, sauces. Parking. Nautical and hunting decor. Cr cds: A, C, D, MC, V.

D

★★ **STOCK-YARD.** *901 2nd Ave N, downtown. 615/255-6464.* Web www.citysearch.com/stockyard. Hrs: 11 am-2 pm, 5-10 pm; Fri, Sat to 11pm; Sun 5-9 pm. Closed Dec 25. Bars 4:30 pm-2 am. Semi-a la carte: dinner $15-$50. Child's meals. Specializes in charcoal-grilled steak, fresh seafood, grilled chicken breast. Entertainment. Parking. Cr cds: A, D, DS, MC, V.

★★ **SUNSET GRILL.** *2001 A Belcourt Ave (37212), south of downtown. 615/386-3663.* E-mail SunsetGrill@MindSpring.com; web www.SunsetGrill.com. Hrs: 11-1:30 am; Sat from 4:45 pm; Sun 5-11 pm. Closed some major hols. Res accepted. Bar. Semi-a la carte: lunch $5-$10, dinner $6-$24. Child's meals. Specializes in fresh seafood, pasta, lamb. Valet Parking. Five dining areas include a glass-enclosed patio. Original artwork. Cr cds: A, C, D, DS, JCB, MC, V.

D

★★★ **VALENTINO'S.** *1907 West End Ave (37203), west of downtown. 615/327-0148.* Hrs: 11 am-2 pm, 5-10 pm. Closed Sun; major hols. Res accepted. Northern Italian menu. Bar. Semi-a la carte: lunch $5.95-$10.95, dinner $9.95-$22.95. Specializes in chicken, seafood, pasta. Valet parking. Cr cds: A, C, D, DS, MC, V.

D

★★★ **THE WILD BOAR.** *2014 Broadway (37203), downtown. 615/329-1313.* Hrs: 11:30 am-2 pm, 6-10 pm; Fri to 10:30 pm; Sat 6-10:30 pm. Closed Sun; major hols. Res accepted. Contemporary French menu. Bar. Wine cellar. Semi-a la carte: lunch $21.95-$34.95, dinner $55-$135. Specializes in fresh wild game, fresh seafood, souffles. Pianist Fri, Sat. Valet parking. European hunting lodge atmosphere; artwork, antiques. Cr cds: A, C, D, DS, MC, V.

D

Unrated Dining Spot

TOWNE HOUSE TEA ROOM & RESTAURANT. *165 8th Ave N, downtown. 615/254-1277.* Hrs: 8:30 am-2:30 pm; Fri 8:30 am-2:30 pm, 5:30-10 pm; Sat 5:30-10 pm. Closed Sun; major hols. Semi-a la carte: bkfst $3.95-$7.95, lunch $3.45-$7.50, dinner $7.95-$18.95. Buffet: lunch $4.95, dinner $8.95. Salad bar. Own baking, soups. Historic 24-room mansion (1840's); fireplaces, oak floors, antiques, paintings. Cr cds: A, C, D, DS, MC, V.

SC

New Orleans

Founded: 1718
Pop: 496,938
Elev: 5 feet
Time zone: Central
Area code: 504
Web: www.nawlins.com

Few cities can compete with New Orleans' reputation for charm. Worldwide travelers come here to dine in superb restaurants, listen to incomparable jazz, browse in Royal Street's fine antique shops and dance in the streets at Mardi Gras. With top billing in food, entertainment and music, New Orleans has mastered the art of festivity.

The people of New Orleans come from a variety of backgrounds. There are Creoles, descendants of the early French and Spanish immigrants; Acadians or "Cajuns," descendants of refugees from Nova Scotia; and black descendants of the Santo Domingo slaves, who practiced a curious mix of Roman Catholicism and West African ritual known as voodoo.

Named for the Duc d'Orléans, Regent of France, New Orleans was founded by Jean Baptiste Le Moyne in 1718. Over the course of the next 85 years, the Louisiana territory changed hands three times, finally being bought by the US in 1803. The city was laid out along the lines of a late medieval French town, with a central square on the river, now called Jackson Square. The influence of its past owners, France and Spain, can be seen throughout New Orleans.

In the 1790s, great plantations were built when vast fortunes could be made from sugar cane. In 1812 (the year Louisiana became a state) steamboat transportation was begun, stimulating the trade in cotton. Before the Civil War, there was a greater concentration of millionaires in the Louisiana sugar belt than anywhere else in the country.

In the 1800s, New Orleans was known as the Paris of America. Today, it is truly an international city, one of the busiest and most efficient ports in the nation. More than 35 countries maintain consular offices here, and many public places are staffed with multilingual personnel. Foreign trade is a significant part of the city's economy.

Business

Since World War II, New Orleans has experienced enormous growth and change. The construction of new bridges, expressways, public buildings and housing developments, along with important improvements in rail traffic and handling, stimulated industrial and commercial growth.

With sources of petroleum and natural gas nearby, relatively cheap electricity and an abundance of fresh water, manufacturing has become increasingly important. Today, more than 1,000 manufacturing and processing plants employ approximately 45,000 workers.

Convention Facilities

The Ernest N. Morial Convention Center, the city's largest convention center, has 700,000 square feet of exhibit space and approximately 130,000 square feet of meeting rooms. The center is continuing to undergo expansion.

The Louisiana Superdome, located on a 52-acre site only six blocks from the French Quarter, seats up to 77,000 spectators for football and has a total of 252,350 square feet of convention and exhibit space on its four levels. The main exhibit floor has 166,000 square feet of space and can accommodate 22,500 people for meetings or 15,000 for dining. The parking lot holds 5,000 cars and an estimated 14,000 additional parking spaces are within walking distance. There are restaurants, snack bars, cafeterias and lounges throughout the building.

There are more than 25,000 guest rooms in greater New Orleans, and more than half are accessible to the central business district/French Quarter area. Many of the major downtown hotels have extensive facilities for conventions and meetings.

Sports & Recreation

The Louisiana Superdome, New Orleans' busiest sports center, is the home of the city's professional football team, the Saints. Every January, the Sugar Bowl College Football Classic is played. The Tulane University football team also plays here.

Horse racing can be enjoyed at Fair Grounds Racetrack from Thanksgiving to late March.

No trip to New Orleans would be complete without a boat ride on a stern-wheeler. Daily narrated cruises depart from Toulouse Street Wharf at Jackson Square and from Canal Street Wharf. A Saturday night moonlight cruise with dancing is a true delight.

Entertainment

The Louisiana Philharmonic Orchestra, Orpheum Theater, Opera Guild, Opera House Association and Community Concert Association present many classical music performances. There are also several professional theater companies. In addition, the Louisiana Superdome offers visitors a rich program of major concerts and events.

On the upriver side of Canal Street is the area known as Uptown. Much of Uptown is easily accessible by the frequently run St Charles Avenue Streetcar. Numerous restaurants and lounges along St Charles Avenue offer a fascinating alternative to the French Quarter. The management at some of the more elegant restaurants frown on informal attire; be warned that New Orleans is somewhat formal.

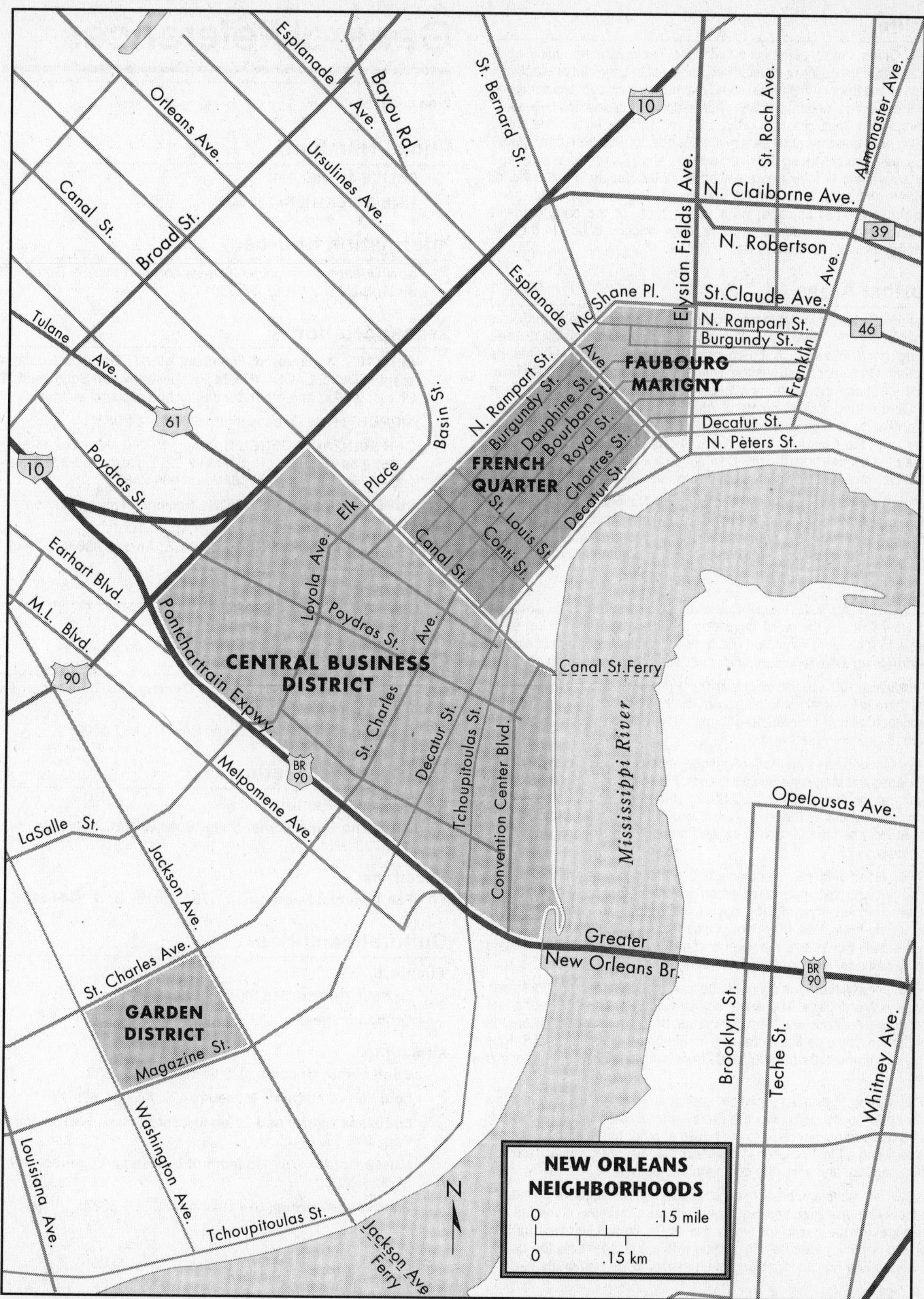
NEW ORLEANS NEIGHBORHOODS
FRENCH QUARTER
FAUBOURG MARIGNY
CENTRAL BUSINESS DISTRICT
GARDEN DISTRICT
Mississippi River
Esplanade Ave.
Bayou Rd.
Orleans Ave.
Ursulines Ave.
St. Bernard St.
Canal St.
Broad St.
Esplanade Ave
McShane Pl.
Elysian Fields Ave.
St. Roch Ave.
Almonaster Ave.
N. Claiborne Ave.
N. Robertson
Franklin Ave.
St.Claude Ave.
N. Rampart St.
Burgundy St.
Decatur St.
N. Peters St.
Tulane Ave.
Basin St.
Dauphine St.
Bourbon St.
Royal St.
Chartres St.
Poydras St.
Elk Place
St. Louis St.
Conti St.
Earhart Blvd.
M.L. Blvd.
Loyola Ave.
Pontchartrain Expwy.
St. Charles Ave.
Decatur St.
Tchoupitoulas St.
Convention Center Blvd.
Canal St.Ferry
Melpomene Ave.
LaSalle St.
Jackson Ave.
Opelousas Ave.
Greater New Orleans Br.
St. Charles Ave.
Magazine St.
Brooklyn St.
Teche St.
Whitney Ave.
Washington Ave.
Louisiana Ave.
Tchoupitoulas St.
Jackson Ave Ferry
N
0 .15 mile
0 .15 km
10
39
46
61
90
BR 90

Nightlife

New Orleans really comes to life at night. The quaint, tranquil French Quarter is transformed into a music-filled center of excitement and activity. People stroll the brightly lit streets, some of which are closed to automobile traffic in the evening, and take rides in horse-drawn buggies and carriages. They sample the exquisite fare offered by restaurants known the world over; sit on park benches and listen to the sounds coming from open doors of bistros; take cruises along the river; window shop for antiques, arts and crafts or souvenirs; or relax and enjoy some of the best jazz in the world. To compete with the large, well-known clubs and concert halls, hotel lounges present small combos; as a result, most of the entertainment throughout the city is far above average. New Orleans is one of the few cities left that is lively 24 hours a day.

Historical Areas

Not only is it impossible, in a few paragraphs, to describe all that New Orleans has to offer, but the visitor also will find it impossible to see everything on a first visit. A brochure published by the New Orleans Metropolitan Convention and Visitors Bureau, located at 1520 Sugar Bowl Drive in the Superdome, contains a map and guide for a walking tour of the French Quarter and lists 36 points of interest, ranging from 18th-century houses and early 19th-century apartments to the stately St Louis Cathedral (1789-94) and the Old Ursuline Convent (1745). Many of New Orleans' most beautiful houses from the pre-Civil War era are located in the Garden District in Uptown. Also see oak-shaded Audubon Park and Zoo.

A few miles from downtown is Chalmette National Historical Park. Here, General Andrew Jackson's army defeated the British in a battle that was actually fought after the peace treaty that ended the War of 1812 was signed. A beautiful plantation house in the park is open to visitors.

Sightseeing

In New Orleans the word *lagniappe* means a little something extra and refers to a small, unexpected gift. It also signifies that there is always a little something extra to experience in and near this captivating city.

There are 100 square blocks in the French Quarter. Hours spent strolling there will reveal something extra for the historian, gourmet, shopper, architecture buff or interested tourist. There is an information desk located at 529 Saint Ann Street.

New Orleans has a plethora of antique shops located on Royal Street in the Quarter and Magazine Street Uptown. For mall shopping, there is the Riverwalk, at the river and Poydras Street; Jackson Brewery, adjacent to Jackson Square; Canal Place, at Canal and N Peters Sts; New Orleans Centre, at Poydras and La Salle Sts; and the Uptown Square, on Broadway, Uptown.

River Road features plantation houses and "Louisiana cottages," which have been lovingly preserved or restored. Boat trips on beautiful Lake Pontchartrain or along the bayou are further enticements. Baton Rouge, a one-hour drive from New Orleans, with its skyscraper capitol building, stately governor's mansion and the impressive Louisiana State University campus, also has special appeal.

New Orleans has a variety of annual celebrations. First and foremost, of course, is Mardi Gras. The entire city strives to make each year's fete better than the previous one. The celebration begins two weeks before the start of Lent, with the parties increasing in number and activity until Shrove Tuesday. Costume balls, parades and street festivities draw everyone into the fun.

The Spring Fiesta Association sponsors what is virtually a New Orleans open house beginning the Friday after Easter. Tours of historic houses and gardens, not open to the public at other times of the year, are conducted, and a Fiesta Queen is crowned. Candlelight courtyard tours, a historical pageant and a parade complete the festivities.

Late in April the emphasis is on jazz, with two consecutive weekends of the New Orleans Jazz and Heritage Festival. Concerts, seminars and parades feature the music for which the city is known, as well as folk, gospel and popular music. In conjunction with the jazz festival, the Louisiana Heritage Fair honors local, and often exotic, foods and crafts.

General References

Area code: 504

Phone Numbers

POLICE & FIRE: 911

TIME & WEATHER: 828-4000

Information Source

New Orleans Metropolitan Convention and Visitors Bureau, 1520 Sugar Bowl Dr, 70112; 566-5011.

Transportation

AIRLINES: Aeromexico; American; AVIATECA (Guatemala); Continental; Delta; LACSA (Costa Rica); Northwest; Southwest; TWA; United; USAir; and other commuter and regional airlines.

AIRPORT: New Orleans International, 464-0831.

CAR RENTAL AGENCIES: (See IMPORTANT TOLL-FREE NUMBERS) Avis 464-9511; Budget 467-2277; Hertz 468-3695; National 466-4335; Thrifty 467-8796; Value 469-2688.

PUBLIC TRANSPORTATION: Regional Transit Authority, 242-2600.

RAILROAD PASSENGER SERVICE: Amtrak 800/872-7245.

Newspaper

Times-Picayune.

Convention Facilities

Ernest N. Morial Convention Center, 900 Convention Center Blvd, 582-3000.

Louisiana Superdome, Sugar Bowl Dr, 587-3808.

Sports & Recreation

Major Sports Facility

Louisiana Superdome, Sugar Bowl Dr, 587-3808 (Saints, football, 733-0255).

Racetrack

Fair Grounds Racecourse, 1751 Gentilly Blvd, 944-5515.

Cultural Facilities

Theaters

Le Petit Theatre, 616 St Peter St, 522-9958.

Orpheum Theatre, 129 University Pl, 524-3285.

Museums

Confederate Museum, 929 Camp St, 523-4522.

Louisiana Children's Museum, 428 Julia St, 523-1357.

Louisiana Nature and Science Center, Reed Blvd, in Joe Brown Park, 246-5672.

Musée Conti—Wax Museum of Louisiana Legends, 917 Conti St, 525-2605.

Pharmacy Museum, 514 Chartres St, 565-8027.

Art Museums

Historic New Orleans Collection, 533 Royal St, 523-4662.

New Orleans Museum of Art, 1 Collins Diboll Circle, City Park, 488-2631.

Points of Interest

Historical

Beauregard-Keyes House, 1113 Chartres St, 523-7257.

Chalmette Natl Historical Park, 6 mi E on LA 46 in Chalmette, 589-4428.

Destrehan Plantation, 17 mi W via I-10 to E 220, Destrehan, 524-5522.

Dueling Oaks, City Park.

The 1850 House, 523 St Ann St, 568-6968.

French Quarter, fronting on the Mississippi River and bounded by Esplanade Ave, N Rampart, Canal and Decatur Sts.

Gallier House Museum, 1118-32 Royal St, 523-6722.

Hermann-Grima Historic House, 820 St Louis St, 525-5661.

Jackson Square, Chartres, St Peter, Decatur & St Ann Sts.

Jean Lafitte Natl Historical Park and Preserve, 916 N Peter St, 589-3719.

Louis Armstrong Park (Beauregard Square), Rampart St at St Peter St.

Old Absinthe House, Bienville & Bourbon Sts, 523-3181.

Old U.S. Mint, Esplanade and Decatur Sts, 568-6968.

Pirate's Alley, off Jackson Square.

Pontalba Bldg, facing Jackson Square, 568-6968.

The Presbytère, 751 Chartres St, 568-6968.

St Louis Cathedral, 615 Pere Antoine Alley, 525-9585.

San Francisco Plantation, approx 45 mi W via I-10, in Garyville, 535-2341.

Other Attractions

Aquarium of the Americas, 1 Canal, along river between Canal & Bienville Sts, 861-2537.

Audubon Park and Zoological Gardens, 6500 Magazine, 861-2537.

French Market, Decatur St, beginning at St Ann St.

Garden District, Magazine St, St Charles, Jackson & Louisiana Aves.

Jackson Brewery, 620 Decatur, 586-8015.

Levee and docks, from foot of Canal St.

Longue Vue House & Gardens, 7 Bamboo Rd, 488-5488.

Riverwalk, Mississippi River at Poydras St, 522-1555.

World Trade Center, in ITM Building, 2 Canal St, 522-9795.

Sightseeing Tours

Cajun Queen, Creole Queen, Poydras St Wharf, 529-4567.

Gay 90s Carriages, Inc, 1824 N Rampart St, 943-8820.

Gray Line bus tours, 1300 World Trade Center, 70130; 587-0861 or 800/535-7786.

St Charles Ave Streetcar, St Charles & Carrollton Aves, 242-2600.

Sternwheeler *Natchez,* 586-8777 or 587-0734.

Annual Events

Nokia Sugar Bowl, Superdome. Jan 2.

Mardi Gras. Feb 11.

Spring Fiesta, 581-1367. Begins 1st Fri after Easter.

French Quarter Festival, 522-5730. Apr 11-13.

Jazz & Heritage Festival, 522-4786. Last wkend Apr-1st wkend May.

Gumbo Festival, 436-4712. 2nd wkend Oct.

City Neighborhoods

Many of the restaurants, unrated dining establishments and some lodgings listed under New Orleans include neighborhoods as well as exact street addresses. Geographic descriptions of these areas are given, followed by a table of restaurants arranged by neighborhood.

Central Business District: Fronting on the Mississippi River and bounded by Canal St, I-10 and US 90 Business. **North of Central Business District:** North of I-10. **West of Central Business District:** West of I-10/US 90 Business.

Faubourg Marigny: Adjacent to the French Quarter across Esplanade Ave; south of McShane Pl, west of Elysian Fields Ave and northeast of Esplanade Ave.

French Quarter (*Vieux Carré*): Fronting on the Mississippi River and bounded by Esplanade Ave, N Rampart, Canal and Decatur Sts.

Garden District: South of St Charles Ave, west of Jackson Ave, north of Magazine St and east of Washington Ave.

Lodgings and Food

NEW ORLEANS RESTAURANTS BY NEIGHBORHOOD AREAS

(For full description, see alphabetical listings under Restaurants)

CENTRAL BUSINESS DISTRICT
Allegro. 1100 Poydras
Bon Ton Cafe. 401 Magazine St
Emeril's. 800 Tchoupitoulas St
Grill Room (Windsor Court Hotel). 300 Gravier St
L'Economie. 325 Girod St
La Gauloise Bistro (Le Meridien Hotel). 614 Canal St
Michaul's. 840 St Charles Ave
Mike's On The Avenue. 628 St Charles Ave
Mother's. 401 Poydras St
Sapphire (Omni Royal Crescent Hotel). 535 Gravier St
Sazerac (Fairmont Hotel). 123 Baronne
Upperline. 1413 Upperline St
The Veranda (Inter-Continental Hotel). 444 St Charles Ave

NORTH OF CENTRAL BUSINESS DISTRICT
Cafe Vôlage. 720 Dublin St
Chez Daniel. 2037 Metairie Rd
Christian's. 3835 Iberville St
Dooky Chase. 2301 Orleans Ave
Gabrielle. 3201 Esplanade Ave
Tavern On The Park. 900 City Park Ave

WEST OF CENTRAL BUSINESS DISTRICT
Bangkok Cuisine. 4137 S Carrollton Ave
Brigtsen's. 723 Dante St
Camellia Grill. 626 S Carrollton Ave
Chez Nous Charcuterie. 5701 Magazine St
Five Happiness. 3605 S Carrollton Ave
Gautreau's. 1728 Soniat St
Martinique. 5908 Magazine St
Mosca's. 4137 US 90W
Vizard's. 5538 Magazine St

FAUBOURG MARIGNY
Feelings Cafe. 2600 Chartres St
Praline Connection. 542 Frenchmen St
Sante Fe. 801 Frenchman
Snug Harbor Jazz Bistro. 626 Frenchmen St

FRENCH QUARTER (VIEUX CARRÉ)
Alex Patout. 221 Royal St
Andrew Jaeger's House Of Seafood. 622 Rue Conti
Antoine's. 713 St Louis St
Arnaud's. 813 Rue Bienville
Bacco (Hotel de la Poste). 310 Chartres St
Bayona. 430 Rue Dauphine
Begue's (Royal Sonesta Hotel). 300 Bourbon St
Bella Luna. 914 N Peter
Bistro (Hotel Maison De Ville Inn). 727 Toulouse St
Brennan's. 417 Royal St
Broussard's. 819 Rue Conti
Cafe Du Monde. 800 Decatur St
Cafe Giovanni. 117 Rue Decatur
Cafe Pontalba. 546 St Peter St
Cafe Rue Bourbon. 241 Rue Bourbon
Central Grocery. 923 Decatur St
Clover Grill. 900 Bourbon St
Court Of Two Sisters. 613 Royal St
Crescent City Brewhouse. 527 Decatur St
Desire Oyster Bar (Royal Sonesta Hotel). 300 Bourbon St
Dominique's (Maison Dupuy Hotel). 1001 Toulouse St
G & E Courtyard Grill. 1113 Decatur St
Galatoire's. 209 Bourbon St
K-Paul's Louisiana Kitchen. 416 Chartres St
La Madeleine. 547 St Ann St
Louis XVI (The Saint Louis Motor Hotel). 730 Rue Bienville
Maximo's Italian Grill. 1117 Decatur
Mike Anderson's. 215 Bourbon St
Mr B's Bistro. 201 Royal St
Napolean House. 500 Charles St
Nola. 534 St Louis St
The Original French Market. 1001 Decatur St
Palace Cafe. 605 Canal St
Pelican Club. 312 Exchange Place
Peristyle. 1041 Dumaine St
Rib Room (Omni Royal Orleans Hotel). 621 St Louis St
Shalimar Indian Cuisine. 535 Wilkinson St
Tony Moran's Pasta E Vino. 240 Bourbon St
Tujague's. 823 Decatur St
Vino Vino. 1119 Decatur St

GARDEN DISTRICT
Caribbean Room (Pontchartrain Hotel). 2031 St Charles Ave
Commander's Palace. 1403 Washington Ave
Kelsey's. 3923 Magazine St

Note: When a listing is located in a town that does not have its own city heading, it will appear under the city nearest to its location. In these cases, the address and town appear in parenthesis immediately following the name of the establishment.

Motels

(Most accommodations increase their rates greatly for the Mardi Gras Festival and the Sugar Bowl Game wkend. Reservations should be made as far ahead as possible and confirmed.)

★ ★ **AMBASSADOR HOTEL.** *535 Tchoupitoulas St (70130), in central business district. 504/527-5271; res: 888/527-5271; FAX 504/527-5270.* E-mail amb@neworleans.com; web www.neworleans.com/ambassador. 71 rms, 4 story. S, D $59-$179; under 16 free; higher rates special events (3, 4-day min). Crib free. Pet accepted; $50 deposit. Valet parking $12. TV; cable. Complimentary coffee in rms. Restaurant 7 am-10 pm. Rm serv noon-2 pm, 7-9 pm. Bar. Ck-out noon. Business servs avail. In-rm modem link. Bellhops. Concierge. Airport transportation. Cr cds: A, C, D, DS, MC, V.

D SC

✔★ **CHATEAU.** *1001 Rue Chartres (70116), in French Quarter. 504/524-9636.* 45 rms, 2 story, 5 suites. S $79-$99; D $99-$109; each addl $10; suites $109-$165; under 18 free; higher rates special events. Crib free. TV; cable (premium). Pool. Restaurant 7 am-3 pm. Rm serv. Bar. Ck-out 1 pm. Business servs avail. Bellhops. Valet serv. Valet parking. Made up of 18th-century bldgs around courtyard. Cr cds: A, C, D, ER, MC, V.

SC

★ **FRENCH QUARTER COURTYARD.** *1101 N Rampart (70116), in French Quarter. 504/522-7333; FAX 504/522-3908; res: 800/290-4233.* E-mail amb@neworleans.com; web www.neworleans.com/ambassador. 51 rms, 2-3 story. S, D $69-$250; under 17 free; higher rates special events. Pet accepted. Valet parking $10. TV; cable. Pool; poolside serv. Complimentary continental bkfst. Restaurant nearby. Bar open 24 hrs. Ck-out noon. Business servs avail. Bellhops. Valet serv. Some balconies. Cr cds: A, C, D, DS, MC, V.

SC

✔★ ★ **HOLIDAY INN EXPRESS.** *10020 I-10 Service Rd at Read Blvd (70127), I-10 exit 244, north of central business district. 504/244-9115; FAX 504/244-9150.* 142 rms, 2 story. S, D $64-$79; each addl $10; suites $100; family rates; higher rates special events. Crib free. TV; cable (premium). Pool. Complimentary continental bkfst. Coffee in rms. Ck-out noon. Business servs avail. In-rm modem link. Refrigerators, microwaves. Cr cds: A, C, D, DS, MC, V.

D SC

★ ★ **PRYTANIA PARK.** *1525 Prytania St (70130), in Garden District. 504/524-0427; FAX 504/522-2977; res: 800/862-1984.* 62 units, 2 story, 49 kits. S $99-$109; D $109-$119; suites $119-$165; each addl $10; under 12 free; summer packages. Crib free. TV; cable. Continental bkfst. Restaurant nearby. Ck-out noon. Business servs avail. Free parking. Refrigerators, some microwaves. Some balconies. Cr cds: A, C, D, DS, MC, V.

D SC

★ ★ **TRAVELODGE.** *(2200 Westbank Expy, Harvey 70058) 504/366-5311; FAX 504/368-2774.* E-mail tlneworlns@aol.com; web www.neworleans.com/travelodge. 212 rms, 2 story. S $64; D $70; under 17 free; wkly rates; higher rates special events (2-,4-day min). Crib free. TV; cable (premium). Complimentary coffee in rms. Restaurant 6 am-10 pm; Sun to 3 pm. Rm serv. Bar from 4 pm. Ck-out noon. Meeting rm. Business servs avail. Bellhops. Coin Indry. 3 pools. Many refrigerators, microwaves. Cr cds: A, C, D, DS, ER, JCB, MC, V.

D SC

Motor Hotels

★ ★ **BIENVILLE HOUSE.** *320 Decatur St (70130), in French Quarter. 504/529-2345; FAX 504/525-6079; res: 800/535-7836.* 83 rms, 4 story. Sept-May: S, D $115-$175; each addl $18; suites $175-$375; under 16 free; lower rates rest of yr. Crib free. Valet parking $11-$15. TV; cable, VCR avail. Pool. Complimentary continental bkfst. Restaurant 11:30 am-2 pm, 5 pm-midnight. Ck-out noon. Meeting rms. Business servs avail. Bellhops. Valet serv. Health club privileges. Balconies. Courtyard surrounds pool. Late 18th century building. Cr cds: A, C, D, DS, MC, V.

★ **CLARION CARRIAGE HOUSE-FRENCH MARKET INN.** *501 Rue Decatur (70130), in French Quarter. 504/561-5621; FAX 504/566-0160; res: 800/548-5148.* E-mail www.hsiweb.com/decatur; web www.hotelchoice.com. 54 units, 4 story. S, D $79-$299; each addl $10; suites $149-$399; higher rates special events. TV; cable (premium). Whirlpool. Complimentary continental bkfst. Restaurant nearby. Bar. Ck-out 11 am. Business servs avail. In-rm modem link. Bellhops. Concierge. Microwave avail. Built in 1753 for the Baron de Pontalba; served as residence for French governor. Cr cds: A, C, D, DS, ER, JCB, MC, V.

D SC

★ ★ **DAUPHINE ORLEANS.** *415 Dauphine St (70112), in French Quarter. 504/586-1800; FAX 504/586-1409; res: 800/521-7111.* Web www.dauphineorleans.com. 111 rms, 2-4 story. S $129-$169; D $149-$189; each add $15; suites $189-$359; under 17 free; higher rates special events. Crib free. Garage $12. TV; cable (premium). Pool; whirlpool. Complimentary continental bkfst; afternoon refreshments. Bar 3:30 pm-midnight; Sat, Sun from noon. Ck-out noon. Meeting rms. Business servs avail. In-rm modem link. Bellhops. Valet parking. Exercise equipt; weights, bicycles. Minibars. Balconies. Also patio courtyard opp with 16 rms; varied styles, sizes. Library. Cr cds: A, C, D, DS, ER, JCB, MC, V.

D SC

★ ★ ★ **HOLIDAY INN-CHATEAU LE MOYNE.** *301 Dauphine St (70112), in French Quarter. 504/581-1303; FAX 504/523-5709.* Web www.holiday.com. 171 rms, 5 story. S $89-195; D $99-$225; each addl $15; suites $205-$450; under 18 free. Crib free. Garage $12. TV; cable (premium). Heated pool; poolside serv. Restaurant 6:30 am-2 pm, 6-10 pm. Rm serv. Bar 7 am-10 pm. Ck-out 11 am. Meeting rms. Business servs avail. In-rm modem link. Bellhops. Valet serv. Concierge. Some bathrm phones in suites. Balconies. Tropical courtyards. Cr cds: A, C, D, DS, JCB, MC, V.

D SC

✓★ ★ **LE RICHELIEU.** *1234 Chartres St (70116), in French Quarter. 504/529-2492; FAX 504/524-8179; res: 800/535-9653.* E-mail nawlinssk@aol.com; web www.travel2000. 86 rms, 4 story. S $85-$140; D $95-$150; each addl $15; suites $170-$475; higher rates special events. Crib free. TV, VCR avail. Pool; poolside serv. Restaurant 7 am-9 pm. Rm serv. Bar to 1 am. Ck-out 1 pm. Business servs avail. Bellhops. Valet serv. Concierge. Free Parking. Health club privileges. Refrigerators. Balconies. Landscaped courtyard. Cr cds: A, C, D, DS, ER, JCB, MC, V.

D

★ ★ **PROVINCIAL.** *1024 Rue Chartres (70116), in French Quarter. 504/581-4995; FAX 504/581-1018; res: 800/535-7922.* 105 rms, 2-4 story. S, D $150-$165; each addl $15; suites from $225; under 17 free; higher rates special events. Crib free. Parking $8. TV; cable (premium), VCR avail. 2 pools; poolside serv. Restaurant 7 am-10 pm. Rm serv. Bar. Ck-out noon. Meeting rm. Business servs avail. In-rm modem link. Valet serv. Microwaves avail. Balconies. Carriageway entrance; antique furnishings. Cr cds: A, C, D, DS, ER, JCB, MC, V.

D SC

✓★ **QUALITY INN-MIDTOWN.** *3900 Tulane Ave, west of central business district. 504/486-5541; FAX 504/488-7440.* 102 rms, 4 story. S, D $99-$138; higher rates special events (2-,4-day min). TV; cable (premium). Complimentary coffee in rms. Restaurant 7 am-2 pm, 5-10:30 pm. Rm serv. Bar 11 am-midnight; Sat, Sun from 4 pm. Ck-out 11 am. Meeting rms. In-rm modem link. Whirlpool. Some refrigerators, microwaves. Cr cds: A, C, D, DS, ER, JCB, MC, V.

D SC

★ ★ **SAINT ANN-MARIE ANTOINETTE.** *717 Rue Conti (70130), in French Quarter. 504/581-1881.* 66 rms, 5 story, 18 suites. S $119-$189; D $139-$219; each addl $15; suites $199-$499; summer rates. Crib free. Valet parking $16. TV; cable (premium). Pool; poolside serv. Restaurant 7-11 am; Sat, Sun to noon. Rm serv. Bar. Ck-out noon. Meeting rms. Business servs avail. Bellhops. Valet serv. Concierge. Bathrm phones; refrigerators avail. Balconies. Cr cds: A, C, D, JCB, MC, V.

D SC

★ ★ ★ **THE SAINT LOUIS.** *730 Rue Bienville (70130), in French Quarter. 504/581-7300; FAX 504/524-8925; res: 800/535-9111.* 72 rms, 5 story, 32 suites. S $139-$199; D $159-$229; each addl $15; suites $239-$649; under 12 free; summer rates. Crib free. Valet parking $16. TV; cable (premium). Swimming privileges. Restaurant (see LOUIS XVI). Rm serv. Bar 5 pm-midnight; entertainment. Ck-out 11 am. Meeting rms. Business servs avail. In-rm modem links. Bellhops. Valet serv. Concierge. Bathrm phones; refrigerators avail; minibar in suites. Some balconies. French antiques. Enclosed courtyard with fountains, tropical patio. Cr cds: A, C, D, JCB, MC, V.

D SC

Hotels

★ ★ ★ **BOURBON ORLEANS.** *717 Orleans St (70116), I-10 exit 235 A. 504/523-2222; FAX 504/525-8166; res: 800/521-5338.* Web www.bourbon-orleans.com. 216 rms, 6 story, 60 suites. Mid-Sept-mid-June: S $129-$189; D $139-$199; each addl $20; suites $165-$360; under 12 free; higher rates special events; lower rates rest of yr. Crib free. Valet parking $12. TV; cable (premium), VCR avail. Pool; poolside serv. Coffee in rms. Restaurant 7 am-10 pm. Rm serv 24 hrs. Bar 11 am-midnight; wkends to 2 am. Ck-out noon. Meeting rms. Business servs avail. In-rm modem link. Health club privileges. Concierge. Bathrm phones, refrigerators, minibars. Some balconies. Cr cds: A, C, D, DS, MC, V.

D SC

★ ★ **CHATEAU DUPRÉ.** *131 Rue Decatur (70130), in French Quarter. 504/569-0600; res: 800/285-0620; FAX 504/569-0606.* 54 rms, 4 story, 10 suites. Sept-May: S, D $79-$249; suites $249-$399; under 13 free; higher rates special events; lower rates rest of yr. Crib free. Valet parking $13.50. TV; cable, VCR. Complimentary continental bkfst. No rm serv. Ck-out 11 am. Business servs avail. Tennis privileges. Refrigerator, microwave in suites. Cr cds: A, C, D, DS, MC, V.

D SC

★ ★ ★ **CHATEAU SONESTA.** *800 Iberville St (70112), in French Quarter. 504/586-0800; res: 800/766-3782; FAX 504/565-4505.* 250 rms, 4 story. S $140-$240; D $175-$275; under 17 free; higher rates special events. Crib free. Valet parking $15. TV; cable. Restaurant 11 am-10 pm. Rm serv 7 am-2 pm. Bar to 2 am; entertainment Thurs-Sat (in season). Ck-out noon. Meeting rms. Business servs avail. In-rm modem link. Concierge. Gift shop. Barber, beauty shop. Exercise equipt; weight machine, bicycle. Pool; poolside serv. Minibars. Cr cds: A, C, D, DS, MC, V.

D SC

★ ★ ★ **CROWNE PLAZA.** *333 Poydras St (70130), in central business district. 504/525-9444; FAX 504/581-7179.* 439 units, 23 story. S, D $115-$295; each addl $15; suites $325-$900; under 12 free; higher rates special events. Crib free. Garage parking $8; valet $12. TV; cable (premium). Pool. Restaurant 6:30 am-10 pm. Coffee in rms. Bar noon-midnight. Ck-out noon. Convention facilites. Business servs avail. In-rm modem link. Concierge. Exercise equipt; weights, bicycles. Refrigerators avail. Luxury level. Cr cds: A, C, D, DS, ER, JCB, MC, V.

D SC

★ ★ **DOUBLETREE.** *300 Canal St (70130), in central business district. 504/581-1300; FAX 504/522-4100.* Web www.dtree.com. 363 rms, 17 story. S, D $99-$215; each addl $20; suites $250-$1,500; under 18 free. Crib free. Valet parking $15. TV; cable (premium). Pool; poolside serv. Coffee in rms. Restaurant 6:30 am-10 pm; Fri, Sat to 11 pm. Rm serv. Bar from 11 am. Ck-out noon. Convention facilities. Business center. Exercise equipt; weights, bicycles. Adj to French Quarter, convention center and Aquarium of the Americas. Cr cds: A, C, D, DS, ER, MC, V.

D SC

★ ★ **EMBASSY SUITES.** *315 Julia St (70130), in central business district. 504/525-1993; FAX 504/525-3437.* 282 suites, 16 story. S, D $189-$209; under 18 free. Crib free. Valet parking $12. TV; cable (premium), VCR avail. Heated pool; whirlpool, poolside serv. Complimentary full bkfst. Complimentary coffee in rms. Restaurant 11:30 am-2 pm, 5-10 pm. Bar noon-midnight. Ck-out noon. Meeting rms. Business servs avail. In-rm modem links. Bellhops. Concierge. Gift shop. Exercise equipt; weights, bicycle. Game rm. Refrigerators, microwaves. Balconies. Cr cds: A, C, D, DS, ER, JCB, MC, V.

D SC

★ ★ ★ **FAIRMONT.** *123 Baronne (70140), 1/2 blk off Canal St between University Place & Baronne, in central business district. 504/529-7111; FAX 504/522-2303.* Web www.fairmont.com. 700 rms, 14 story. S $199-$259; D $229-$289; each addl $25; suites $250-$750; under 12 free; package plans. Crib free. Valet parking $15. TV; cable. Heated pool; poolside serv. Restaurant 6 am-11 pm; Fri, Sat to midnight (also see SAZERAC). Rm serv 24 hrs. Bar. Ck-out 1 pm. Convention facilities. Business servs avail. In-rm modem link. Concierge. Drugstore. Barber, beauty shop. Lighted tennis. Exercise equipt; weight machine, bicycle. Landmark turn-of-the-century hotel. Cr cds: A, C, D, DS, JCB, MC, V.

D SC

★ ★ ★ **HILTON RIVERSIDE.** *Poydras St (70140), at the Mississippi River, in central business district. 504/561-0500; FAX 504/568-1721.* Web www.hilton.com. 1,600 rms, 29 story. S $170-$270; D $195-$295; each addl $25; suites from $395; wkend packages. Crib free. Valet parking $12. TV; cable (premium), VCR avail (movies). 2 heated pools; whirlpool, poolside serv. Restaurant 6-2 am. Rm serv 24 hrs. Ck-out noon. Convention facilities. Business center. In-rm modem link. Concierge. Gift shop. Barber, beauty shop. Indoor, outdoor tennis, pro. Exercise equipt; weights, bicycles, sauna. Minibars; microwaves avail. Connected to riverwalk. Luxury level. Cr cds: A, C, D, DS, ER, JCB, MC, V.

D SC

✔★ ★ **HOLIDAY INN DOWNTOWN-SUPERDOME.** *330 Loyola Ave (70012), in central business district. 504/581-1600; FAX 504/586-0833.* E-mail superdom@sprynet.com; web www.holiday-inn.com/hotels/msydt. 297 rms, 18 story. S $75-$150; D $90-$165; each addl $15; under 19 free. Crib free. Garage parking $11. TV; cable (premium). Heated pool. Restaurant 6 am-10 pm. Bar. Ck-out noon. Meeting rms. Business servs avail. In-rm modem link. Gift shop. Balconies. Luxury level. Cr cds: A, C, D, DS, JCB, MC, V.

D SC

★ ★ **HOTEL DE LA POSTE.** *316 Rue Chartres (70130), in French Quarter. 504/581-1200; FAX 504/523-2910; res: 800/448-4927.* E-mail hoteldelaposte@worldnet.att.net. 100 rms, 5 story. S $125-$140; D $150-$160; each addl $25; suites $165-$200; under 16 free. Crib free. Valet parking $14. TV; cable (premium). Pool; poolside serv. Coffee in lobby. Restaurant 7:30 am-10 pm (also see BACCO). Bar. Ck-out noon. Meeting rm. Business servs avail. In-rm modem link. Built around landscaped courtyard. Cr cds: A, C, D, DS, MC, V.

D SC

★ ★ ★ **HYATT REGENCY.** *Poydras Plaza (70140), at Loyola, adj to Superdome in central business district. 504/561-1234; FAX 504/587-4141.* Web www.travelweb.com/thisco/hyatt/975_b.html. 1,184 rms, 32 story. S, D $114-$185; each addl $25; suites $350-$850; under 18 free; wkend rates. Crib free. Valet parking $15. TV; cable (premium), VCR avail. Heated pool; whirlpool, poolside serv. Restaurant 6 am-midnight; dining rms 10:30 am-2:30 pm, 6-10:30 pm. Bars 11-2 am. Ck-out noon. Convention facilities. Business center. In-rm modem link. Concierge. Barber, beauty shop. Airport transportation; free local transportation. Exercise equipt; weights, treadmill. Connected to Superdome & shopping complex. Luxury level. Cr cds: A, C, D, DS, ER, JCB, MC, V.

D SC

★ ★ ★ ★ **INTER-CONTINENTAL.** *444 St Charles Ave (70130), in central business district. 504/525-5566; FAX 504/523-7310; res: 800/327-0200.* Web www.interconti.com. Pale golden marble and lush landscaping greet guests of this modern high-rise. Most rooms are decorated in contemporary style, but some suites have antiques. 482 units, 15 story. S $210-$250; D $230-$270; each addl $20; suites $400-$2,000; under 14 free; wkend rates. Valet parking $14. TV; cable (premium). Heated pool; poolside serv. Restaurant 6 am-10 pm (also see THE VERANDA). Rm serv 24 hrs. Bars 11-1 am; entertainment. Convention facilities. Business center. In-rm modem link. Concierge. Gift shop. Beauty shop. Airport transportation. Exercise equipt; weight machine, bicycles. Massage. Bathrm phones and TVs; some refrigerators, minibars. Some balconies. Luxury level. Cr cds: A, C, D, DS, ER, JCB, MC, V.

D SC

★ ★ ★ **LAFAYETTE.** *600 St Charles (70130), in central business district. 504/524-4441; FAX 504/523-7327; res: 800/733-4754.* 44 rms, 5 story, 20 suites. S, D $155-$390; suites $275-$650; family rates; higher rates special events, wkends (2-day min) & Jazz Fest. Crib free. Valet parking $10. TV; cable (premium), VCR avail. Coffee in rms. Restaurant 7 am-11 pm. Bar. Ck-out 11 am. Business servs avail. In-rm modem link. Concierge. Airport transportation. Health club privileges. Minibars. Balconies. Renovated hotel first opened 1916. Cr cds: A, C, D, DS, ER, JCB, MC, V.

D SC

★ **LANDMARK.** *920 N Rampart (70116), in French Quarter. 504/524-3333; FAX 504/522-8044.* 100 rms, 3 story. S, D $99-$159; under 18 free; higher rates special events. Crib free. Garage $7. TV; cable. Pool; poolside serv. Restaurant 7-11 am, noon-midnight. Bar. Ck-out noon. Coin lndry. Meeting rm. Business servs avail. Microwaves avail. Cr cds: A, C, D, DS, MC, V.

SC

★ ★ ★ **LE MERIDIEN.** *614 Canal St (70130), in central business district. 504/525-6500; FAX 504/525-8068; res: 800/543-4300.* E-mail meridien@gnofn.org; web www.meridienhotel.com. 494 rms, 30 story. S $185-$245; D $215-$275; each addl $30; suites $600-$1,700; under 16 free. Crib free. Garage $15; valet. TV; cable (premium), VCR avail. Heated pool; whirlpool, poolside serv. Coffee in rms. Restaurant (see LA GAULOISE BISTRO). Rm serv 24 hrs. Bar 4 pm-1 am; entertainment. Ck-out noon. Convention facilities. Business center. In-rm modem link. Concierge.

Shopping arcade. Exercise rm; instructor, weight machines, bicycles, sauna. Bathrm phones, minibars. Adj to French Quarter. Cr cds: A, C, D, DS, ER, JCB, MC, V.

D SC

★ ★ ★ **LE PAVILLON.** *833 Poydras St (70140), in central business district. 504/581-3111; FAX 504/522-5543; res: 800/535-9095.* Web www.lepavillon.com. 226 rms, 10 story. S, D $105-$270; suites $495-$1,495; under 18 free; higher rates special events. Crib free. Valet parking $12. TV; cable (premium). Heated pool; whirlpool, poolside serv. Restaurant 6:30 am-10 pm. Rm serv 24 hrs. Bar 11-1 am. Ck-out noon. Meeting rms. Business servs avail. In-rm modem link. Concierge. Airport transportation avail. Exercise equipt; stair machine, bicycle. Bathrm phones; refrigerators, microwaves avail. 90-yr-old hotel listed on National Register of Historic Places. Original artwork, antiques, chandeliers. Cr cds: A, C, D, DS, ER, JCB, MC, V.

D SC

★ ★ ★ **MAISON DUPUY.** *1001 Toulouse St (70112), at Burgundy, in French Quarter. 504/586-8000; FAX 504/566-7450; res: 800/535-9177.* 198 rms, 5 story. S, D $205-$250; each addl $25; suites $240-$1500; under 17 free. Crib free. Valet parking $12. TV; cable (premium), VCR avail. Heated pool; poolside serv. Restaurant 7 am-2 pm, 5-10 pm. Bar from 11 am. Ck-out 11 am. Valet serv. Meeting rms. Business servs avail. In-rm modem link. Exercise equipt; weights, bicycles. Balconies. Cr cds: A, C, D, DS, MC, V.

D SC

★ ★ ★ **MARRIOTT.** *555 Canal St (70140), at Chartres St, in central business district. 504/581-1000; FAX 504/523-6755.* 1,290 units, 41 story. S, D $199; each addl $20; suites $600-$1,200; under 17 free; wkend rates. Crib free. Valet parking $14. TV; cable (premium), VCR avail. Heated pool; wading pool, poolside serv. Restaurant 6:30 am-11 pm. Rm serv 24 hrs. Bar 10-2 am; entertainment. Ck-out noon. Coin Indry. Convention facilities. Business center. In-rm modem link. Concierge. Gift shop. Exercise equipt; weights, bicycles, sauna. Refrigerators avail. Adj to French Quarter. Luxury level. Cr cds: A, C, D, DS, ER, JCB, MC, V.

D SC

★ ★ **MONTELEONE.** *214 Rue Royale (70140), in French Quarter. 504/523-3341; FAX 504/528-1019; res: 800/535-9595.* E-mail sales@hotelmonteleone.com; web www.hotelmonteleone.com. 600 rms, 28 suites, 17 story. S $115-$165; D $145-$210; each addl $25; suites $250-$680; under 18 free; higher rates special events. Crib free. Valet parking $11. TV; cable (premium). Rooftop heated pool; poolside serv. Complimentary coffee by pool in morning. Restaurant 6:30 am-11 pm. Revolving bar 11-2 am; entertainment. Ck-out noon. Meeting rms. Business center. In-rm modem link. Concierge. Shopping arcade. Barber. Exercise equipt; weights, bicycles. Some bathrm phones. Family-owned since 1886. Cr cds: A, C, D, DS, JCB, MC, V.

D SC

★ ★ ★ **OMNI ROYAL CRESCENT.** *535 Gravier St (70130), in central business district. 504/527-0006; FAX 504/523-0806.* 98 rms, 8 story. S $225; D $235; suites $235-$335; under 18 free; higher rates special events. Valet parking $15. TV; cable (premium), VCR avail (movies). Restaurant (see SAPPHIRE). Rm serv 24 hrs. Ck-out noon. Meeting rms. Business servs avail. In-rm modem link. Concierge. Exercise equipt; bicycle, treadmill, sauna. Pool; whirlpool, poolside serv. Cr cds: A, C, D, DS, MC, V.

D SC

★ ★ ★ ★ **OMNI ROYAL ORLEANS.** *621 St Louis St (70140), in French Quarter. 504/529-5333; FAX 504/529-7089; res: 800/843-6664.* Built in 1960, this property re-creates a grand hotel of the 1800s. Gilt mirrors and Italian marble abound in guest rooms and public areas alike; three magnificent lobby chandeliers were imported from France. 346 rms, 7 story. S, D $139-$329; each addl $20; suites $369-$1,000; under 17 free; package plans. Crib free. Valet parking $14. TV; cable (premium), VCR avail. Rooftop heated pool; poolside serv. Restaurant (see RIB ROOM); La Riviera poolside restaurant 9 am-8 pm (Apr-Oct). Rm serv 24 hrs. Bars 11-2 am; entertainment. Ck-out noon. Meeting rms. Business center. In-rm modem link. Concierge. Barber, beauty shop. Exercise equipt; weight machine, bicycles. Bathrm phones, minibars; some whirlpools. Some balconies. Observation deck. Cr cds: A, C, D, DS, ER, JCB, MC, V.

D SC

✔★ **PALLAS.** *1732 Canal St (70112), in central business district. 504/558-0201.* 370 rms, 17 story, 50 suites. S, D $89-$99; each addl $10; suites $119-$169; under 12 free; higher rates special events. Crib free. Garage $5. TV; cable (premium). Complimentary continental bkfst. Bar. Ck-out noon. Meeting rms. Business servs avail. Microwaves avail. Cr cds: A, D, DS, MC, V.

D SC

★ ★ ★ **PELHAM.** *444 Common St (70130), in central business district. 504/522-4444; res: 888/659-5621.* Web www.hsiweb.com/decatur. 60 air-cooled rms, 4 story. S $144-$325; D $164-$325; each addl $10; suites $185-$350; under 17 free; higher rates special events. Crib $25. Valet parking $13.50. TV; cable (premium), VCR avail. Restaurant 6:30 am-10 pm. Bar. Ck-out 11 am. Meeting rms. Business servs avail. In-rm modem link. Concierge. Tennis privileges. Individually decorated rms; antiques, marble baths. Cr cds: A, MC, V.

D SC

★ ★ ★ **PONTCHARTRAIN.** *2031 St Charles Ave (70140), in Garden District. 504/524-0581; FAX 504/529-1165; res: 800/777-6193.* Web www.grandheritage.comm. 104 rms, 12 story. S, D $130-$185; each addl $25; 1-2 bedrm suites $260-$600; under 12 free. Crib free. Valet parking $13. TV; cable, VCR avail. Restaurants 7 am-2:30 pm, 5:30-10 pm (also see CARIBBEAN ROOM). Rm serv 24 hrs. Bar 11-1 am; entertainment Thurs-Sat. Ck-out 1 pm. Meeting rms. Business center. In-rm modem link. Airport transportation. Health club privileges. Many refrigerators; some wet bars. Landmark of historic neighborhood, rms are individually decorated with an antique motif. Cr cds: A, C, D, DS, MC, V.

D SC

★ ★ **QUEEN & CRESCENT.** *344 Camp St (70130), in central business district. 504/587-9700; res: 800/975-6652; FAX 504/587-9701.* Web www.queenandcrescent.com. 129 rms, 12 story. S, D $109-$179; under 18 free; higher rates special events. Crib free. Valet parking $15. TV; cable (premium), VCR avail. Complimentary continental bkfst. No rm serv. Bar 10 am-11 pm. Ck-out noon. Business servs avail. In-rm modem link. Exercise equipt; bicycle, treadmill. Minibars. Cr cds: A, C, D, DS, MC, V.

D SC

★ ★ **RADISSON.** *1500 Canal St (70112), in central business district. 504/522-4500; FAX 504/525-2644.* Web www.radisson.com. 759 rms, 18 story. S, D $109-$189; each addl $15; suites $150-$350; under 18 free; higher rates special events. Crib free. Valet parking $13.44. TV; cable (premium). Pool; whirlpool, poolside serv. Complimentary coffee in lobby. Restaurant 6 am-2 pm, 5-10 pm. Bar. Ck-out 11 am. Coin Indry. Meeting rms. Business center. Concierge. Gift shop. Exercise equipt; weights, bicycle. Refrigerators in suites. Cr cds: A, D, DS, MC, V.

D

✔★ ★ **RAMADA.** *2203 St Charles Ave (70140), in Garden District. 504/566-1200; FAX 504/581-1352.* 133 units, 9 story. S $99; D $109; each addl $10; suites $139; under 17 free; higher rates special events. Crib free. TV; cable (premium). Restaurant 6:30 am-2 pm, 5-10 pm. Bar 4-11 pm. Ck-out noon. Meeting rms. Business servs avail. In-rm modem link. Valet parking. Health club privileges. Some refrigerators; microwaves avail. Cr cds: A, C, D, DS, ER, JCB, MC, V.

D SC

★ ★ ★ **ROYAL SONESTA.** *300 Bourbon St (70140), in French Quarter. 504/586-0300; FAX 504/586-0335; res: 800/766-3782.* 500 rms, 7 story. S $145-$260; D $165-$290; each addl $40; suites $350-$1,000; studio rms $260; under 17 free; min stay required Mardi Gras, special events. Crib free. Garage $14. TV; cable, VCR avail. Heated pool; poolside serv. Restaurants 6:30 am-11:30 pm (also see DESIRE OYSTER BAR and BEGUE'S). Bars 9-3 am; entertainment. Ck-out noon. Meeting rms. Business center. In-rm modem link. Exercise equipt; weight machine, bicycle. Minibars; microwaves avail. Luxury level. Cr cds: A, C, D, DS, ER, JCB, MC, V.

D SC

★ ★ ★ **SHERATON.** *500 Canal St (70130), adj to French Quarter, in central business district. 504/525-2500; FAX 504/595-5550.* Web www.sheraton.com. 1,102 rms, 49 story. S $130-$215; D $155-$239; each addl $25; suites from $250; under 18 free. Crib free. Valet parking $15. TV; cable (premium), VCR avail (movies). Pool; poolside serv. Complimentary coffee in rms. Restaurants 6:30-11 pm. Rm serv 24 hrs. Bar from 11 am; entertainment. Ck-out noon. Convention facilities. Business center. In-rm modem link. Concierge. Shopping arcade. Exercise equipt; weight machine, bicycles. Microwaves avail. Luxury level. Cr cds: A, C, D, DS, ER, JCB, MC, V.

D SC

★ ★ ★ **THE WESTIN CANAL PLACE.** *100 Rue Iberville (70130), in Canal Place Shopping Ctr, in French Quarter. 504/566-7006; FAX 504/553-5120.* 439 rms, 18 story. S, D $150-$259; each addl $20; suites $329-$3,000; under 19 free; wkend packages. Crib free. Garage $15; valet. TV; cable (premium), VCR avail. Rooftop heated pool; poolside serv. Restaurant 6:30 am-10 pm. Rm serv 24 hrs. Bar 11-2 am; entertainment. Ck-out noon. Convention facilities. Business center. In-rm modem link. Concierge. Shopping arcade. Barber, beauty shop. 18-hole golf privileges, pro, putting green, driving range. Exercise equipt; bicycles, treadmills. Bathrm phones, minibars. Views of Mississippi River. Luxury level. Cr cds: A, C, D, DS, ER, JCB, MC, V.

D SC

★ ★ ★ ★ **WINDSOR COURT.** *300 Gravier St (70140), in central business district. 504/523-6000; FAX 504/596-4513; res: 800/262-2662.* This gracious hotel is full of notable art and antiques (art tours are Saturday at 4 pm), yet features exceptionally friendly service. The famous Grill Room is one of the city's best restaurants, and guest rooms feature a muted, elegant decor, with parquet floors and travertine and marble bathrooms. 324 units, 23 story, 275 suites. S, D $235-$320; suites $310-$990, each addl $25; under 18 free. Crib free. Valet parking $17. TV; cable (premium), VCR avail. Heated pool; whirlpool, poolside serv. Restaurant (see GRILL ROOM). Afternoon tea 2-6 pm. Rm serv 24 hrs. 2 bars from 9 am; entertainment. Ck-out noon. Convention facilities. Business servs avail. In-rm modem link. Concierge. Gift shop. Airport transportation. Indoor tennis privileges adj, pro. 18-hole golf privileges, greens fee $35, pro, putting green, driving range. Exercise rm; instructor, weights, bicycles, sauna, steam rm. Massage. Health club privileges. Bathrm phones, refrigerators, minibars; microwaves avail; wet bar in suites. Balconies. Cr cds: A, C, D, DS, MC, V.

D SC

★ ★ ★ **WYNDHAM RIVERFRONT.** *701 Convention Center Blvd (70130), in central business district. 504/524-8200; FAX 504/524-0600.* 202 rms, 6 story, 26 suites. Sept-June: S $220; D $240; each addl $15; suites $179-$700; under 12 free; wkend, hol rates; lower rates rest of yr. Crib free. Valet parking $14.50, garage parking $6. TV; cable (premium), VCR avail (movies). Pool privileges. Complimentary coffee in rms. Restaurant 6-11 pm. Rm serv 24 hrs. Bar 11-2 am. Ck-out noon. Meeting rms. Business center. In-rm modem link. Concierge. Gift shop. Exercise equipt; weights, bicycle. Health club privileges. Cr cds: A, C, D, DS, ER, JCB, MC, V.

D SC

Inns

★ ★ **CHIMES.** *Constantinople St & Coliseum St (70115), west of central business district. 504/899-2621; res: 800/729-4640.* 5 rms, 3 with full bathrm. Oct-May: S, D $79-$129; wkends (3-day min); higher rates Jazz Fest; lower rates rest of yr. Crib free. Pet accepted, some restrictions. TV; cable (premium). Complimentary continental bkfst. Complimentary coffee in rm. Ck-out, Ck-in hrs vary. Luggage handling. Picnic tables. Totally nonsmoking. Antiques. No cr cds accepted.

D

★ **FRENCH QUARTER GUEST HOUSE.** *623 Ursulines Ave (70116), in French Quarter. 504/529-5489.* 20 rms, 2 suites. Sept-May: S, D $79-$125; each addl $15; under 12 free; higher rates jazz fest; lower rates rest of yr. TV; cable. Complimentary continental bkfst. Ck-out noon, ck-in varies. Public parking $5. Built in early 1800s. Cr cds: A, D, DS, MC, V.

★ **THE FRENCHMEN.** *417 Frenchmen St (70116), in Faubourg Marigny. 504/948-2166; FAX 504/948-2258; res: 800/831-1781.* 27 rms, 2 story. S, D $84-$135; each addl $20; summer rates. TV; cable (premium). Pool; whirlpool. Complimentary continental bkfst. Serv bar 24 hrs. Ck-out 11 am, ck-in 3 pm. Business servs avail. Concierge serv. Balconies. Two town houses built 1860; individually decorated rms; antiques. Rms overlook courtyard, pool & patio. Cr cds: A, MC, V.

D SC

★ ★ **GIROD HOUSE.** *835 Esplanade Ave (70116), in French Quarter. 504/522-5214; FAX 504/522-7208.* 6 suites, 2 story, 5 kit. suites. 1 rm phone. Sept-June: S, D $100-$225; wkends (3-day min); higher rates jazz fest; lower rates rest of yr. Children over 12 yrs only. TV. Complimentary continental bkfst. Complimentary coffee in rms. Restaurant nearby. Ck-out 1 pm, ck-in varies. Business servs avail. In-rm modem link. Luggage handling. Concierge serv. Street parking avail. Refrigerators; some fireplaces. Some balconies. Built in 1833 by 1st mayor of New Orleans. Creole decor; exotic flowers. Cr cds: A, MC, V.

D

★ ★ ★ **HOTEL MAISON DE VILLE.** *727 Toulouse St (70130), in French Quarter. 504/561-5858; FAX 504/528-9939; res: 800/634-1600.* 23 rms, 1-3 story, 7 cottages. S, D $195-$305; each addl $30; suites $295-$315; kit. cottages $475-$555. Children over 12 yrs only. Valet parking $16. TV; cable (premium), VCR. Pool at cottages. Complimentary continental bkfst. Restaurant (see BISTRO). Rm serv. Ck-out noon, ck-in 3 pm. Business servs avail. In-rm modem link. Bellhops. Valet serv. Health club privileges. Private patios, balconies. Overlooks courtyard with fountain and garden. Cr cds: A, C, D, DS, MC, V.

SC

★ **HOTEL ST PIERRE.** *911 Rue Burgundy (70116), in French Quarter. 504/524-4401; FAX 504/524-6800.* 75 rms, 2 story. S $109; D $129; each addl $10; under 12 free; wkends (2-night min); higher rates special events. Crib free. TV. 2 pools. Complimentary continental bkfst. Restaurant nearby. Ck-out 11 am. In-rm modem link. Bellhops. Concierge. Cr cds: A, C, D, DS, MC, V.

D

★ ★ ★ **HOUSE ON BAYOU.** *2275 Bayou Rd (70119), in Faubourg Marigny. 504/945-0992; res: 800/882-2968.* 8 rms, 1 with shower only, 2 story. Oct-May: S $155; D $120-$245; kit. $115-$145; lower rates rest of yr. Children over 12 yrs only. TV; cable, VCR avail. Pool; whirlpool. Complimentary full bkfst; afternoon refreshments. Ck-out noon, ck-in 3 pm. Meeting rm. Business servs avail. Luggage handling. Concierge serv. Health club privileges. Microwaves avail. Indigo plantation house built 1798; antiques. Dining rm overlooks tropical courtyard. Cr cds: A, MC, V.

★ ★ **LAFITTE GUEST HOUSE.** *1003 Bourbon St (70116), in French Quarter. 504/581-2678; res: 800/331-7971 LA.* 14 rms, 4 story. S, D $89-$169; under 5 free; higher rates special events; lower rates rest of yr. TV in common rm. Complimentary continental bkfst. Complimentary coffee. Restaurant nearby. Concierge. Business servs avail. Parking $8.50. Some refrigerators, minibars. Balconies. Totally nonsmoking. Located in French manor building (1849). Period decor. Many antiques. Cr cds: A, D, DS, MC, V.

✔★ ★ **LAMOTHE HOUSE.** *622 Esplanade Ave (70116), in Faubourg Marigny. 504/947-1161; FAX 504/943-6536; res: 800/367-5858.* 20 rms, 3 story. S, D $95-$195; suites $140-$250. Crib free. TV; cable (premium). Complimentary continental bkfst. Restaurant nearby. Ck-out

11 am, ck-in 2 pm. Business servs avail. Restored townhouse built around patio; antique furnishings. Adj to French Quarter. Cr cds: A, MC, V.

D SC

★ ★ ★ **MELROSE MANSION.** *937 Esplanade Ave (70116), in Faubourg Marigny. 504/944-2255.* 8 rms, 2 story, 4 suites. D $225-$250; suites $325-$425. TV; cable, VCR avail. Heated pool. Complimentary full bkfst. Restaurant nearby. Rm serv. Ck-out noon, ck-in 1 pm. Business servs avail. Exercise equipt; weight machine, treadmill. Some in-rm whirlpools in suites. Many refrigerators. Balconies. Antiques. Library. Historic Victorian-Gothic mansion (1884); pillared verandas, tropical patio. Overlooks French Quarter. Cr cds: A, DS, MC, V.

★ ★ **RATHBONE INN.** *1227 Esplanade Ave (70116), near French Quarter. 504/947-2101; res: 800/947-2101.* 9 kit. units, shower only, 3 story, 3 suites. S, D $90-$145; each addl $10; under 12 free; higher rates jazz fest. Pet accepted. TV; cable. Complimentary continental bkfst. Complimentary coffee in rms. Ck-out noon, ck-in 1-2 pm. Business servs avail. Luggage handling. Coin lndry. Street parking. Whirlpool. Refrigerators, microwaves. Built in 1850 as mansion for private family. Antebellum period decor; ornamental cast-iron fence. Cr cds: A, C, D, DS, MC, V.

SC

★ **RUE ROYAL INN.** *1006 Rue Royal (70116), in French Quarter. 504/524-3900; res: 800/776-3901; FAX 504/558-0566.* 17 kit. units, 4 story. Sept-May: S, D $75-$120; each addl $15; suites $145; under 12 free; hols, special events (3-4-day min); higher rates jazz fest; lower rates rest of yr. Pet accepted, some restrictions. TV; cable, VCR avail. Complimentary continental bkfst. Coffee in rms. Ck-out noon, ck-in varies. Luggage handling. Parking $8. Airport, RR station transportation. Refrigerators, microwaves. Built in 1830 as Creole townhouse. Cr cds: A, C, D, DS, JCB, MC, V.

D SC

★ ★ ★ **SONIAT HOUSE.** *1133 Chartres St (70116), in French Quarter. 504/522-0570; FAX 504/522-7208; res: 800/544-8808.* Web www.soniathouse.com. 31 rms, 3 story, 14 suites. S, D $145-$250; each addl $25; suites $250-$590. Children over 12 yrs only. Valet parking $14. TV. Ck-out 1 pm, ck-in 3 pm. Meeting rm. Luggage handling. Concierge. Bathrm phones; whirlpool in suites. 1830s town house with carriage entrance and sweeping stairways. Hand-carved four-poster beds; antiques. Private courtyard with fountain and tropical plants. Cr cds: A, MC, V.

D

★ **ST. PETER GUEST HOUSE.** *1005 St. Peter (70116), in French Quarter. 504/524-9232.* 28 rms, 5 suites. S $79-$89; D $109-$179. TV; cable. Complimentary continental bkfst. Restaurant nearby. Ck-out 11 am, ck-in 3 pm. Balconies. Built in pre-1900's as private residence; antiques. Cr cds: A, MC, V.

SC

Restaurants

★ ★ ★ **ALEX PATOUT.** *221 Royal St (70130), in French Quarter. 504/525-7788.* Hrs: 5:30-10 pm. Closed Dec 25. Res accepted. Contemporary Louisiana menu. Bar. Semi-a la carte: dinner $15-$26. Child's meals. Specialties: Cajun smothered roast duck, paneed smoked salmon. Cr cds: A, C, D, DS, ER, JCB, MC, V.

D

★ ★ **ALLEGRO.** *1100 Poydras (70163), in central business district. 504/582-2350.* Hrs: 11 am-2:30 pm. Closed major hols. Res accepted. Bar. Semi-a la carte: $7-$15.95. Specialties: fettucini allegro, crispy duck with andouille rice. Outdoor dining. Bistro atmosphere. Cr cds: A, C, D, DS, JCB, MC, V.

D

★ ★ **ANDREW JAEGER'S HOUSE OF SEAFOOD.** *622 Rue Conti (70130), in French Quarter. 504/522-4964.* Hrs: 5:30-11 pm. Closed Thanksgiving, Dec 25. Res accepted. Cajun menu. Bar. Semi-a la carte: dinner $9.95-$24.95. Specializes in fresh seafood, veal, pasta. Own baking. New Orleans piano & blues evenings. Outdoor dining. Three distinct levels of dining in 1832 French Quarter Creole cottage. Cr cds: A, C, D, DS, MC, V.

D

★ ★ ★ **ANTOINE'S.** *713 St Louis St, in French Quarter. 504/581-4422.* Web www.antoines.com. Hrs: 11:30 am-2 pm, 5:30-9:30 pm. Closed Sun; Mardi Gras; major hols. Res required. French, Creole menu. Serv bar. Wine cellar. A la carte entrees: lunch $12-$24, dinner $20-$50. Specialties: oysters Rockefeller, pompano en papillote, souffléed potatoes. Many world-famous dishes have been created & served by Antoine's. Established 1840. Family-owned. Jacket (dinner). Cr cds: A, C, D, MC, V.

D

★ ★ ★ **ARNAUD'S.** *813 Rue Bienville, in French Quarter. 504/523-5433.* Hrs: 11:30 am-2:30 pm, 6-10 pm; Fri to 10:30 pm; Sat 6-10:30 pm; Sun from 6 pm; Sun jazz brunch 10 am-2:30 pm. Closed major hols. Res accepted. French, Creole menu. Bars. Wine cellar. A la carte entrees: lunch $10.25-$15.25, dinner $17.50-$40. Complete meals: lunch $10.25-$15.25. Sun brunch $18.50-$26. Specialties: shrimp Arnaud, pompano en croute, filet Charlemond. Own desserts. Built in 1790; opened in 1918 and restored to original design. Jacket (dinner). Cr cds: A, C, D, MC, V.

D

★ ★ **BACCO.** *(See Hotel de la Poste Hotel) 504/522-2426.* Web www.bacco.com. Hrs: 7-10 am, 11:30 am-2:30 pm, 6-10 pm; Sat 8:30-10 am, 11:30 am-2:30 pm, 5:30-10:30 pm; Sun 8:30-10 am, 10:30 am-2:30 pm (brunch), 6-10 pm. Closed Mardi Gras, Dec 24-25. Res accepted. Contemporary Creole cuisine with Italian accent. Bar. Semi-a la carte: bkfst $5-$10, lunch $7.75-$12, dinner $10.50-$27. Sun brunch $7-$15. Specializes in wood-fired pizza, grilled seafood. Parking. Cr cds: A, C, D, MC, V.

D

★ **BANGKOK CUISINE.** *4137 S Carrollton Ave (70119), west of central business district. 504/482-3606.* Hrs: 11 am-3 pm, 5-10 pm; Fri to 11 pm; Sat 5-11 pm; Sun from 5 pm. Closed July 4, Thanksgiving, Dec 25. Res accepted. Thai menu. Semi-a la carte: lunch $4.95-$6.95, dinner $7.95-$16.95. Specializes in seafood. Parking. Candlelight dining. Cr cds: A, D, MC, V.

★ ★ ★ ★ **BAYONA.** *430 Rue Dauphine (70140), in French Quarter. 504/525-4455.* Chef Susan Spicer presents original cuisine in this century-old Creole cottage in the French Quarter. There's outdoor dining in a well-planted courtyard with fountain. The homemade soups and ice cream are worth a trip. Contemporary Amer menu. Specializes in grilled duck, fresh seafood. Hrs: 11:30 am-2 pm, 6-10 pm; Fri to 11 pm; Sat 6-11 pm. Closed Sun; Mardi Gras, Easter, Dec 25; also 1 wk Aug. Res required. Serv bar. Semi-a la carte: lunch $8-$16.75, dinner $11-$22. Cr cds: A, D, DS, JCB, MC, V.

★ ★ ★ **BEGUE'S.** *(See Royal Sonesta Hotel) 504/586-0300.* Hrs: 6:30 am-2 pm, 6-11 pm; Sun brunch 10:30 am-2:30 pm. Res accepted. French, Creole menu. Bar. Semi-a la carte: bkfst $3.50-$12.50, lunch $7-$16; dinner $15-$29. Sun brunch $22.50. Specializes in seafood buffet. Seasonal menus. Pianist Thurs, Fri, Sun brunch. Overlooks courtyard. Cr cds: A, C, D, DS, ER, JCB, MC, V.

D

★ ★ ★ **BELLA LUNA.** *914 N Peter (70116), Decatur at Dumaine, in French Quarter. 504/529-1583.* Hrs: 6-10 pm; Fri, Sat to 10:30 pm; Sun to 9:30 pm. Closed Dec 24, 25; Mardi Gras. Res accepted. Continental menu. Bar. A la carte entrees: dinner $15-$25. Specialties: house-cured pork chop in pecan crust, Maine lobster with calamari fettuccine. Valet parking. Located in French Market; view of Mississippi River. Cr cds: A, D, DS, MC, V.

D

★ ★ ★ **BISTRO.** *(See Hotel Maison De Ville Inn) 504/528-9206.* Hrs: 11:30 am-2 pm, 6-10 pm. Res accepted. Serv bar. Wine list. Semi-a la carte: lunch $10-$13, dinner $17-$25. Specializes in local seafood. Own desserts. Outdoor dining. Bistro setting, in 18th-century house. Cr cds: A, D, MC, V.

★ ★ **BON TON CAFE.** *401 Magazine St, in central business district. 504/524-3386.* Hrs: 11 am-2 pm, 5-9:30 pm. Closed Sat, Sun; major hols. Cajun menu. A la carte entrees: lunch $8.50-$19.50, dinner $17.50-$24.25. Child's meals. Specialties: red fish Bon Ton, crawfish dishes. Wrought iron chandelier, shuttered windows, wildlife prints on exposed brick walls. Cr cds: A, D, MC, V.

D

★ ★ ★ **BRENNAN'S.** *417 Royal St, in French Quarter. 504/525-9711.* Hrs: 8 am-2:30 pm, 6-10 pm. Closed Dec 24 (evening), 25. Res required. French, Creole menu. Bar. Wine cellar. A la carte entrees: bkfst $11.50-$35, dinner $28.50-$35. Complete meals: bkfst $35, dinner $28.50-$35. Specialty: Bananas Foster. Own desserts. Located in 1795 mansion where Andrew Jackson was a frequent guest. Family-owned. Cr cds: A, C, D, DS, MC, V.

D

★ ★ ★ **BRIGTSEN'S.** *723 Dante St, west of central business district. 504/861-7610.* Hrs: 5:30-10 pm. Closed Sun, Mon; most major hols, Dec 24. Res accepted. Cajun, Creole menu. Serv bar. A la carte entrees: dinner $14-$24. Specializes in rabbit, duck, seafood. Parking. In restored 1900s house built from river barge timbers. French-country decor. Menu changes daily. Cr cds: A, D, MC, V.

★ ★ ★ **BROUSSARD'S.** *819 Rue Conti, in French Quarter. 504/581-3866.* Hrs: 5:30-10 pm. Closed Dec 25. Res required. French, Creole menu. Bar. A la carte entrees: dinner $19.75-$32.50. Specialties: veal Broussard, Pompano Napoleon, bananas Foster. Pianist Fri, Sat. Outdoor dining. Courtyard patio. Cr cds: A, C, D, DS, MC, V.

D

★ ★ **CAFE GIOVANNI.** *117 Rue Decatur (70130), in French Quarter. 504/529-2154.* Hrs: 5:30-10 pm; Fri, Sat to 11 pm. Closed major hols; Mardi Gras; Sun in July & Aug. Res accepted. Italian menu. Wine. A la carte entrees: dinner $8.95-$23.95. Specialties: pasta gambino, spicy seared pork filet. Own desserts. Valet parking. Arched brick doorway leads to dining area with mirrored column in center; French doors open to face Quarter. Cr cds: A, C, D, DS, MC, V.

D

★ **CAFE PONTALBA.** *546 St Peter St (70116), in French Quarter. 504/522-1180.* Hrs: 10:30 am-10 pm; wkends 10 am-11 pm. Closed Dec 25. Cajun, Creole menu. Bar. Semi-a la carte: lunch, dinner $5.95-$16.95. Specialties: gumbo, jambalaya, etouffee. Open restaurant overlooking Jackson Square. Family-owned. Cr cds: D, DS, MC, V.

★ ★ **CAFE RUE BOURBON.** *241 Rue Bourbon (70130), in French Quarter. 504/524-0114.* Hrs: 5:30 pm-midnight; early-bird dinner to 7 pm. Res accepted. Cajun menu. Bar. Semi-a la carte: dinner $12.95-$19.95. Child's meals. Specialties: gulf shrimp combo, shrimp & tasso pasta. Own desserts. Outdoor dining. 1831 bldg. Cr cds: A, C, D, MC, V.

★ ★ **CAFE VÔLAGE.** *720 Dublin St (70118), north of central business district. 504/861-4227.* Hrs: 11 am-10 pm; Sun to 9 pm; early-bird dinner Mon-Thurs 4-7 pm; Sun brunch 11 am-3 pm (exc summer). Closed major hols; Mardi Gras. Res accepted. French, Creole menu. Wine. A la carte entrees: lunch $6.25-$8.25. Semi-a la carte: dinner $14.95-$18.95. Sun brunch $13.95. Child's meals. Specializes in veal chop, duck, salmon. Outdoor dining. Two intimate dining areas in 1800s Victorian cottage. Cr cds: A, DS, MC, V.

D

★ ★ ★ **CARIBBEAN ROOM.** *(See Pontchartrain Hotel) 504/524-0581.* Web www.grandheritage.com. Hrs: 6-10 pm. Closed Sun, Mon. Creole menu. Bar. Wine cellar. A la carte entrees: dinner $15.95-$39.95. Child's meals. Specialties: trout Eugene, crab Remick, Creole classic gumbo. Valet parking. Formal dining in romantic setting. Established in 1927. Totally nonsmoking. Cr cds: A, C, D, DS, MC, V.

D

★ ★ **CHEZ DANIEL.** *2037 Metairie Rd (70124), north of central business district. 504/837-6900.* Hrs: 5-9:30 pm; Fri, Sat to 10 pm; early-bird dinner 5-6:15 pm. Closed Sun, Mon; major hols. Res accepted. French menu. Bar. A la carte entrees: dinner $9.75-$19.50. Specializes in seafood, traditional French. Own focaccia. Entertainment Sat. Bistro atmosphere. Cr cds: A, C, MC, V.

D

★ ★ ★ **CHRISTIAN'S.** *3835 Iberville St (70119), north of central business district. 504/482-4924.* Hrs: 11:30 am-2 pm, 5:30-10 pm; Sat from 5:30 pm. Closed Sun & Mon; Dec 25. Res accepted. French, Creole menu. Bar. Wine cellar. Complete meals: lunch $9.75-$17.50. A la carte entrees: dinner $14.25-$24.95. Specialties: oysters Roland, baby veal Christian, bouillabaisse. Own ices, ice cream. Parking. In renovated former church (1914). Cr cds: A, C, D, MC, V.

D

★ ★ ★ ★ **COMMANDER'S PALACE.** *1403 Washington Ave, in Garden District. 504/899-8221.* Web www.commanderspalace.com. Eight separate and uniquely appointed dining rooms offer formal and informal venues in which to sample the best of New Orleans' gastronomic tradition. Delicate murals and garden views reflect the spirit of the city in every room. Haute Creole menu. Specialties: turtle soup, trout with roasted pecans, bread pudding soufflé. Hrs: 11:30 am-2 pm, 6:30-9 pm; Fri, Sat to 10 pm; Sat brunch to 1:30 pm; Sun brunch 10:30 am-1:30 pm. Closed Mardi Gras, Dec 24, 25. Res accepted. Bar. Wine cellar. Semi-a la carte: lunch $13.50-$25, dinner $22-$33. Complete meals: lunch $13.50-$27, dinner $32-$38. Sat, Sun Brunch $20-$26. Dixieland band at brunch. Valet parking. Outdoor dining. Family-owned. Jacket (dinner & brunch). Cr cds: A, C, D, DS, MC, V.

D

★ ★ **COURT OF TWO SISTERS.** *613 Royal St, in French Quarter. 504/522-7261.* Web www.courtoftwosisters.com. Hrs: 5:30-10 pm; brunch 9 am-3 pm. Closed Dec 25. Res accepted. French, Creole menu. Bar. A la carte entrees: dinner $15-$30. Complete meals: dinner $35, brunch $21. Child's meals. Specialties: shrimp Toulouse, lobster étouffée. Jazz trio at brunch. Outdoor dining. Built in 1832; spacious patio; courtyard. Family-owned. Cr cds: A, C, D, DS, MC, V.

D

✓ ★ ★ **CRESCENT CITY BREWHOUSE.** *527 Decatur St (70130), in French Quarter. 504/522-0571.* Hrs: 11 am-10 pm; Fri, Sat to midnight. Closed Thanksgiving, Dec 25. Res accepted. Cajun menu. Bar. Semi-a la carte: lunch, dinner $6.95-$17.95. Child's meals. Specialties: Louisiana bouillabaisse, grilled tuna Orleans. Jazz evenings. Outdoor dining. 1795 bldg is active brewery; balcony dining area offers views of Mississippi River and Natchez Steamboat. Cr cds: A, C, D, DS, MC, V.

D

✓ ★ ★ **DESIRE OYSTER BAR.** *(See Royal Sonesta Hotel) 504/586-0300.* Hrs: 11:30 am-11:30 pm; Fri, Sat to 12:30 am. Bar. Semi-a la carte: lunch, dinner $7-$15.25. Child's meals. Specializes in Creole cuisine. Own baking. Parking. Bistro doors & windows offer view of French Quarter streets. Cr cds: A, C, D, DS, ER, JCB, MC, V.

D

★ ★ ★ **DOMINIQUE'S.** *(See Maison Dupuy Hotel) 504/522-8800.* Hrs: 11:30 am-2 pm, 6-10 pm; Sun brunch 11 am-2 pm; early-bird dinner 6-7 pm. Res accepted. French menu. Bar. Wine list. Semi-a la carte: dinner $20-$28. Specialties: grilled chimayo-crusted swordfish, fire-roasted Louisiana shrimp. Valet parking. Outdoor dining. View of courtyard. Totally nonsmoking. Cr cds: A, C, D, DS, MC, V.

D

★ ★ **DOOKY CHASE.** *2301 Orleans Ave (70119), north of central business district. 504/821-0600.* Hrs: 11:30 am-10 pm; Fri, Sat to 11:30 pm. Closed Dec 25. Res accepted. Creole menu. Bar. Semi-a la carte: lunch $10.95, dinner $15-$25. Complete meal: $25. Specializes in seafood, gumbo. Parking. Collection of African-American artwork. Antique parlor rm for waiting. Family-owned 50 yrs. Cr cds: A, D, MC, V.

D

★ ★ ★ ★ **EMERIL'S.** *800 Tchoupitoulas St (70140), in central business district. 504/528-9393.* This is a large, renovated warehouse, conveniently located near the convention center. It's contemporary in style with brick and glass walls, gleaming wood floors, burnished-aluminum lamps and a huge abstract-expressionist oil painting. Emeril's is considered by many to be the pacesetter for Creole cuisine in the '90s. Creole, Amer menu. Menu changes seasonally. Hrs: 11:30 am-2 pm, 6-10 pm; Sat 6-10:30 pm. Closed Sun; Mardi Gras, most major hols; also 1st 2 wks July. Res required (dinner). Bar. Wine list. A la carte entrees: lunch $15-$20, dinner $19-$30. Cr cds: A, C, D, DS, MC, V.

D

★ ★ **FEELINGS CAFE.** *2600 Chartres St, in Faubourg Marigny. 504/945-2222.* Hrs: 6-10 pm; Fri 11 am-2 pm, 6-11 pm; Sat 6-11 pm; Sun 5-10 pm; Sun brunch 11 am-2 pm. Closed Thanksgiving, Dec 25; also Mardi Gras. Creole menu. Bar. Semi-a la carte: lunch $8.75-$14.75, dinner $11.75-$20.50. Sun brunch $14-$18.50. Specializes in seafood, veal, baked duck with orange glaze. Own desserts. Pianist Fri-Sat. Patio dining wkdays. Located in out-building of 18th-century plantation; antiques, original artwork. Cr cds: A, C, D, DS, MC, V.

D

✔★ ★ **FIVE HAPPINESS.** *3605 S Carrollton Ave, west of central business district. 504/488-6468.* Hrs: 11:30 am-10:30 pm; Fri, Sat to 11:30 pm; Sun noon-10:30 pm. Closed Thanksgiving. Chinese menu. Bar. Semi-a la carte: lunch from $5.75, dinner from $7.50. Specializes in mandarin & Szechwan dishes. Cr cds: A, C, D, DS, MC, V.

D

★ ★ **G & E COURTYARD GRILL.** *1113 Decatur St, in French Quarter. 504/528-9376.* Hrs: 6-10 pm; Fri, Sat 11:30 am-2:30 pm, 6-11 pm; Sun 11:30 am-2:30 pm, 6-10 pm. Closed Thanksgiving, Dec 25. Res accepted. Contemporary creole menu. Bar. A la carte entrees: lunch $10-$15, dinner $13-$27. Specialties: rotisserie roasted pork loin, braised lamb osso bucco. Patio dining in canopied courtyard. European cafe atmosphere. Cr cds: A, C, D, DS, MC, V.

D

★ ★ ★ **GABRIELLE.** *3201 Esplanade Ave (70119), north of central business district. 504/948-6233.* Hrs: 5:30-10 pm; Fri 11:30 am-2 pm, 5:30-10 pm; Oct-May hrs vary. Closed Sun, Mon; major hols; Mardi Gras. Res accepted. Bar. Semi-a la carte: dinner $15.50-$21. Specializes in contemporary Creole cuisine. Own sausage, desserts. Parking. Outdoor dining. Bistro atmosphere. Cr cds: A, C, D, DS, MC, V.

★ ★ ★ **GALATOIRE'S.** *209 Bourbon St, in French Quarter. 504/525-2021.* Hrs: 11:30 am-9 pm; Sun from noon. Closed Mon; major hols; also Mardi Gras. French, Creole menu. Serv bar. A la carte entrees: lunch, dinner $13-$24. Specialties: trout Marguery, oysters en bronchette. Family-owned. Jacket (evening). Cr cds: A, MC, V.

D

★ ★ ★ **GAUTREAU'S.** *1728 Soniat St (70115), west of central business district. 504/899-7397.* Hrs: 11:30 am-2 pm, 6-10 pm. Closed Sun; most major hols. Res accepted. New American, continental cuisine. Wine. A la carte entrees: dinner $11-$21.95. Specializes in seafood, Contemporary Louisiana cooking. Menu changes seasonally. Valet parking. Former drug store from early 1900s; original medicine cabinets, pressed-tin ceiling. Totally non-smoking. Cr cds: A, C, D, DS, MC, V.

★ ★ ★ ★ ★ **GRILL ROOM.** *(See Windsor Court Hotel) 504/522-1992.* Rejuvenated Creole classics are elegantly served on the covered terrace or in the deep-carpeted dining rooms outfitted with British furnishings and paintings spanning several centuries. Continental, regional cuisine. Specialties: mushroom-crusted halibut, Chinese-style smoked lobster, grilled veal rack chop. Own baking. Hrs: 7-10:30 am, 11:30 am-2:30 pm, 6:30-10:30 pm; Sun from 10 am; Sun brunch to 2 pm. Res accepted. Bar 11 am-midnight. Wine cellar. Semi-a la carte entrees: bkfst $8-$13, lunch $9.75-$19.75, dinner $31-$39. Sun brunch $25-$27.50. Jazz Sun brunch. Free valet parking. Jacket. Cr cds: A, C, D, DS, MC, V.

D

★ ★ **K-PAUL'S LOUISIANA KITCHEN.** *416 Chartres St (70130), in French Quarter. 504/524-7394.* Hrs: 11:30 am-2:30 pm, 5:30-10 pm. Closed Sun; Mardi Gras, Dec 25. Res accepted; required upper level. Bar. Semi-a la carte: lunch $9.95-$12.95, dinner $15-$30. Specializes in blackened fish and steak. Menu changes daily. Cr cds: A, C, D, MC, V.

D

★ ★ ★ **KELSEY'S.** *3923 Magazine St (70115), in Garden District. 504/897-6722.* Hrs: 11:30 am-2 pm, 5:30-9:30 pm; Fri to 10 pm; Sat 5:30-10 pm. Closed Sun, Mon; some major hols. Res accepted. Creole menu. Bar from 5 pm. Semi-a la carte: lunch $6.95-$12.95, dinner $12.95-$24.95. Specializes in seafood. Cr cds: A, C, D, DS, MC, V.

D

★ ★ **L'ECONOMIE.** *325 Girod St, in central business district. 504/524-7405.* Hrs: 11:30 am-2 pm, 6-10 pm; Fri-Sat to 11 pm. Closed Sun-Mon; Mardi Gras, major hols. Res accepted. French menu. Bar. A la carte entrees: lunch $6-$13, dinner $12-$24. Specialties: seared ostrich with port wine, poached salmon with mango buerre blanc, pan fried catfish with wasabi buerre blanc. Bistro atmosphere. Cr cds: A, C, D, DS, MC, V.

D

★ ★ **LA GAULOISE BISTRO.** *(See Le Meridien Hotel) 504/527-6712.* E-mail meridien@gnofn.org; web www.meridienhotel.com. Hrs: 6:30 am-10 pm; Sun brunch 11 am-3 pm. Res accepted. French menu. Wine. Semi-a la carte: bkfst $4.50-$12, lunch $4.95-$19.50, dinner $5.95-$24.50. Sun brunch $27.50. Specialties: rack of lamb, shrimp a la provençale. Valet parking. French bistro atmosphere with private balcony; bi-level dining area. Cr cds: A, C, D, DS, ER, JCB, MC, V.

★ ★ ★ **LOUIS XVI.** *(See The Saint Louis Motor Hotel) 504/581-7000.* Hrs: 7-11 pm; Sat, Sun to midnight. Closed July 4, Mardi Gras. Res accepted. French menu. Bar. A la carte entrees: dinner $18-$34. Child's meals. Specializes in lamb chop, seafood. Strolling guitarist; also pianist. Valet parking. Outdoor dining. Elegant decor, formal dining. Family-owned. Jacket. Cr cds: A, D, JCB, MC, V.

✔★ ★ ★ **MARTINIQUE.** *5908 Magazine St (70118), west of central business district. 504/891-8495.* Hrs: 5:30-9:30 pm; Fri, Sat to 10:30 pm. Closed Jan 1, Dec 25. French menu. Semi-a la carte: dinner $11.95-$15.50. Specialty: pork chop with coconut and balsamic vinaigrette. Outdoor dining. View of patio with fountain, greenery. Totally nonsmoking. Cr cds: MC, V.

★ ★ **MAXIMO'S ITALIAN GRILL.** *1117 Decatur (70116), in French Quarter. 504/586-8883.* Hrs: 6-11 pm. Northern Italian menu. Bar. Semi-a la carte: dinner $8.95-$28.95. Specializes in pasta, veal, grilled fish. Own desserts, ice cream. Outdoor balcony dining. Contemporary decor with antique light fixtures, jazz art. Cr cds: A, C, D, DS, MC, V.

D

★ ★ **MICHAUL'S.** *840 St Charles Ave (70130), in central business district. 504/522-5517.* Hrs: 5-11 pm; Sat 6 pm-midnight. Closed Sun; Easter, Thanksgiving, Dec 25; also last 2 wks in Aug. Res accepted. Cajun menu. Bar. Semi-a la carte: dinner $12.25-$18.95. Child's meals. Specialties: alligator sauce picante, blackened shrimp. Cajun, zydeco music. Offers complete Cajun cultural experience; Cajun dance lessons nightly. Cr cds: A, D, DS, MC, V.

D

★ **MIKE ANDERSON'S.** *215 Bourbon St (70130), in French Quarter. 504/524-3884.* Hrs: 11:30 am-10 pm; Fri, Sat to 11 pm. Closed Easter, Thanksgiving, Dec 25. Bar. Semi-a la carte: lunch, dinner $7.95-$15.95. Specializes in broiled seafood, Po-Boys, guitreau. Oyster bar. Nautical decor. Balcony overlooks Bourbon St. Cr cds: A, D, DS, MC, V.

D

★ ★ ★ **MIKE'S ON THE AVENUE.** *628 St Charles Ave, in the Lafayette Hotel, in central business district. 504/523-1709.* Hrs: 11:30 am-2 pm, 6-10 pm; Sat, Sun from 6 pm. Closed some major hols. Res accepted. Bar. Wine list. New American cuisine. Semi-a la carte: lunch $10-$20, dinner $32-$50. Specializes in Chinese dumplings, crawfish cakes, grilled lamb chops. Cr cds: A, C, D, DS, MC, V.

D

★ ★ **MOSCA'S.** *4137 US 90W (70152), 4 1/2 mi W of Huey Long Bridge, west of central business district. 504/436-9942.* Hrs: 5:30-9:30 pm. Closed Sun, Mon; Dec 25; also Aug. Res accepted exc Sat. Italian menu. Bar. A la carte entrees: dinner $25-$28. Specializes in shrimp, chicken, oysters. Own pasta. Parking. Family-owned. No cr cds accepted.

★ ★ ★ **MR B'S BISTRO.** *201 Royal St, in French Quarter. 504/523-2078.* Web www.mrbsbistro.com. Hrs: 11:30 am-3 pm, 5:30-10 pm; Sun jazz brunch 10:30 am-3 pm. Closed Mardi Gras, Dec 24, 25. Res accepted. Continental, Creole menu. Bar. Wine list. Complete meals: lunch $10-$15, dinner $18-$30. Semi-a la carte: lunch $9-$11, dinner $15-$22. Sun brunch $7.50-$12.75. Specializes in hickory-grilled seafood. Entertainment. Bistro decor with mahogany bar, etched-glass walls, white marble-topped tables. Cr cds: A, C, D, DS, MC, V.

D

★ ★ **NAPOLEAN HOUSE.** *500 Charles St (70130), in French Quarter. 504/524-9752.* Hrs: 11 am-midnight; Sun to 7 pm. Closed most major hols; Mardi Gras, Dec 24. Creole menu. Bar. A la carte entrees: lunch $4.50-$10, dinner $13-$18.75. Specialties: muffaletta, grilled breast of duck. Own breads. Outdoor dining. Historic 1797 bldg offers dining in central courtyard. Family-owned. Cr cds: A, C, D, DS, MC, V.

D

★ ★ **NOLA.** *534 St Louis St (70130), in French Quarter. 504/522-6652.* Hrs: 11:30 am-2 pm, 6-10 pm; Fri, Sat to midnight; Sun from 6 pm. Closed Mardi Gras, Thanksgiving, Dec 24, 25. Res accepted. Creole menu. Bar. Semi-a la carte: lunch $12-$19, dinner $16-$22. Specialties: Lafayette Boudin stewed with beer, onions, cane syrup and Creole mustard, cedar plank roasted Gulf fish. In renovated warehouse. Original artwork. Cr cds: A, C, D, DS, MC, V.

D

★ **THE ORIGINAL FRENCH MARKET.** *1001 Decatur St, in French Quarter. 504/581-9855.* Hrs: 11 am-11 pm; Fri to midnight; Sat to 1 am. Closed Thanksgiving, Dec 25. Creole, Cajun menu. Bar. Semi-a la carte: lunch, dinner $6.95-$20. Child's meals. Specializes in fresh seafood. Oyster bar. Balcony dining. Beamed ceiling, gaslight sconces, brick bar. Cr cds: A, D, DS, MC, V.

★ ★ ★ **PALACE CAFE.** *605 Canal St (70130), in French Quarter. 504/523-1661.* Hrs: 11:30 am-2:30 pm, 5:30-10 pm, Sun from 5:30 pm, Sun brunch 10:30 am-2:30 pm. Closed Mardi Gras, Dec 24, 25. Res accepted. Bar. Semi-a la carte: lunch $8-$13, dinner $16-$30. Specialties: Creole bouillabaisse, Ella's whole roasted gulf fish, white chocolate bread pudding. Contemporary bistro decor. Cr cds: A, C, D, MC, V.

D

★ ★ ★ **PELICAN CLUB.** *312 Exchange Place (70130), in French Quarter. 504/523-1504.* Hrs: 5:30-11 pm. Closed most maj hols; also Mardi Gras. Res accepted. Continental menu. Bar. Wine cellar. Semi-a la carte: $5.50-$21.50; prix fixe: dinner $19.50. Specialties: pan seared cajun spiced salmon, pecan-crusted fish with baked Louisiana oysters, Louisiana ciopinno with linguine. Piano bar. Three dining rms in a converted townhouse. Casual elegance. Cr cds: A, D, DS, MC, V.

D

★ ★ ★ **PERISTYLE.** *1041 Dumaine St (70116), in French Quarter. 504/593-9535.* Hrs: 6-10 pm, Fri 11:30 am-2 pm, 6-11 pm, Sat 6-11 pm. Closed Sun, Mon, hols. Res required wkends. Bar. Complete meals: lunch $16. Semi-a la carte: dinner $18-$24. Specialties: pan-seared foie gras, crab salad, pan-roasted lamb loin chops. Free valet parking. Cr cds: D, MC, V.

D

✔★ **PRALINE CONNECTION.** *542 Frenchmen St, in Faubourg Marigny. 504/943-3934.* Hrs: 11 am-10:30 pm; Fri, Sat to midnight. Closed Dec 25. Southern Creole menu. Bar. Semi-a la carte: lunch $4-$7.95, dinner $4.50-$13.95. Child's meals. Specializes in fried chicken, pork chops, bread pudding with praline sauce. Candy room features praline confections. Cr cds: A, C, D, DS, MC, V.

D

★ ★ ★ **RIB ROOM.** *(See Omni Royal Orleans Hotel) 504/529-7045.* Hrs: 6:30 am-3 pm, 6-11 pm; Sat, Sun brunch 11:30 am-3 pm. Res accepted. Bar. Wine cellar. Semi-a la carte: lunch $12-$17, dinner $20-$32. Sat, Sun brunch $8.50-$15.50. Specializes in rotisserie prime rib, seafood, traditional dishes with Creole flair. Own pastries. Parking. Cr cds: A, C, D, DS, MC, V.

D SC

★ ★ **SANTE FE.** *801 Frenchman (70116), in Faubourg Marigny. 504/944-6854.* Hrs: 5-11 pm; Fri-Sat from 3 pm. Closed Sun, Mon; also Dec 24-Jan 1. Gourmet Mexican menu. Bar. A la carte entrees: $6.25-$15.25. Child's meals. Specializes in chicken, seafood. Casual decor. Cr cds: A, MC, V.

D

★ ★ **SAPPHIRE.** *(See Omni Royal Crescent Hotel) 504/571-7500.* Hrs: 6:30-10:30 am, 11:30 am-2 pm, 6:30-10 pm; Fri, Sat to 11 pm. Res accepted. Continental menu. Semi-a la carte: bkfst $8-$13. A la carte entrees: lunch $8-$16, dinner $16-$29. Child's meals. Specialties: laquered duck, tomato & wild mushroom bisque. Own baking. Valet parking. Etched-glass windows face street; chandeliers. Jacket (dinner). Cr cds: A, D, DS, MC, V.

D

★ ★ ★ **SAZERAC.** *(See Fairmont Hotel) 504/529-7111.* Hrs: 11:30 am-2 pm, 6-10 pm. Res accepted. French Creole menu. A la carte entrees: lunch $10-$15, dinner $17-$32. Complete meals: lunch $14.95. Specialties: roast Louisiana duckling, grilled pompano, grilled veal chops. Own pastries, desserts. Pianist 6-10 pm and Sun brunch. Valet parking. Formal decor; original art. Cr cds: A, C, D, DS, JCB, MC, V.

★ ★ **SHALIMAR INDIAN CUISINE.** *535 Wilkinson St (70130), in French Quarter. 504/523-0099.* E-mail akeswani.msn. Hrs: 11:30 am-2:30 pm, 5:30-10:30 pm. Res accepted. Indian menu. Bar. Semi-a la carte: lunch $6.95-$15.95, dinner $6.95-$18.95. Lunch buffet $6.95. Specialties: vindaloo curry, shahi murgh, nargishi ghosht. Indian decor. Cr cds: A, MC, V.

D

★ **SNUG HARBOR JAZZ BISTRO.** *626 Frenchmen St (70116), in Faubourg Marigny. 504/949-0696.* Hrs: 5-11 pm; Fri, Sat to midnight. Closed Dec 25. Bar to 1:30 am. Semi-a la carte: dinner $7-$22. Specializes in regional cuisine, seafood, steak. Modern jazz. Casual dining. Cr cds: A, MC, V.

D

★ ★ **TAVERN ON THE PARK.** *900 City Park Ave (70119), north of central business district. 504/486-3333.* Web www.tavernonpark.com. Hrs: 11:30 am-2:30 pm, 5-10 pm; Sat from 5 pm. Closed Sun, Mon; Thanksgiving, Dec 25; also Mardi Gras. Res accepted. Contemporary New Orleans menu. Bar. Semi-a la carte: lunch $7-$11, dinner $20-$25. Complete meals: lunch $10.95, dinner $24.95. Child's meals. Specialties: porterhouse, stuffed soft shell crab, trout Martha. Parking. Outdoor dining. Overlooks park. Cr cds: A, C, D, DS, JCB, MC, V.

D

★ ★ **TONY MORAN'S PASTA E VINO.** *240 Bourbon St, at Old Absinthe House, in French Quarter. 504/523-3181.* Hrs: 5:30 pm-midnight. Closed Mon; Dec 25. Res accepted. Italian menu. Bar. A la carte entrees: dinner $7-$16. Specializes in Northern Italian cuisine, fresh pasta. Family-owned. 1806 French Quarter Building overlooks small courtyard. Cr cds: A, C, D, MC, V.

D

★ ★ **TUJAGUE'S.** *823 Decatur St (70116), in French Quarter. 504/525-8676.* Hrs: 11 am-3 pm, 5-10:30 pm; Sat to 11 pm. Res accepted. French, Creole menu. Bar 10 am-11 pm. Complete meals: lunch $6.95-$13.95, dinner $24.95-$28.95. Child's meals. Specialties: shrimp Creole, crawfish, crab & spinach bisque. Established in 1856 in old Spanish armory (1750); original tile, authentic beams. Oldest standing bar in city. Cr cds: A, C, D, DS, JCB, MC, V.

D

★ ★ ★ **UPPERLINE.** *1413 Upperline St (70115), in central business district. 504/891-9822.* Hrs: 5:30-9:30 pm; Fri, Sat to 10 pm. Closed Mon, Tues; Mardi Gras; July 4, Thanksgiving, Dec 25. Res accepted. Bar. Wine cellar. A la carte entrees: dinner $13.50-$22.50. Complete meals $27.50. Child's meals. Specialties: roast duck with garlic port, fried green tomatoes with shrimp remoulade sauce. Parking. Famous for the local folk art displayed. French windows offer view of garden. Cr cds: A, D, MC, V.

D

★ ★ ★ **THE VERANDA.** *(See Inter-Continental Hotel) 504/525-5566.* Hrs: 6:30 am-2 pm, 5:30-10 pm; Sun jazz brunch 11 am-2:30 pm. Res accepted. Continental menu. Bar 11-1 am. A la carte entrees: bkfst $8.95-$13, lunch $7-$14, dinner $12-$21. Buffet: bkfst $12.95, lunch $11.95. Sun brunch $25. Specializes in regional American dishes, seafood. Valet parking. Garden-like setting. Cr cds: A, C, D, DS, ER, JCB, MC, V.

D ♥

★ ★ **VINO VINO.** *1119 Decatur St (70116), in French Quarter. 504/529-4553.* Hrs: 5:30-11 pm; June-Aug to 10 pm. Closed Sun, Mon; Jan 1, Dec 25. Res accepted. French menu. Bar. Semi-a la carte: lunch $5.50-$12.50, dinner $7.50-$15. Specializes in seafood, lamb. Wine tasting every Weds 5-7 pm. Bistro atmosphere. Cr cds: A, MC, V.

D

✔ ★ ★ **VIZARD'S.** *5538 Magazine St, west of Central Business District. 504/895-5000.* Hrs: 6-10 pm; Fri, Sat to 11 pm. Closed Sun, Mon; Jan 1, Mardi Gras, Dec 25. Res accepted. Creole menu. Bar. Semi-a la carte: dinner $12.95-$16.25. Specializes in roasted duck, roasted chicken, panéed rabbit. Own pastries. Corner bldg with oval windows. Cr cds: DS, MC, V.

Unrated Dining Spots

CAFE DU MONDE. *800 Decatur St, at St Ann St in French Quarter. 504/525-4544.* Open 24 hrs. Closed Dec 25. Specialties: beignets, New Orleans chicory coffee, cafe au lait. Covered outdoor dining. In French Market. No cr cds accepted.

CAMELLIA GRILL. *626 S Carrollton Ave, west of central business district. 504/866-9573.* Hrs: 9-1 am; Fri to 3 am; Sat 8-3 am; Sun 8-1 am. Closed most hols. Semi-a la carte: bkfst, lunch, dinner $1.50-$7. Specializes in omelettes, gourmet sandwiches, pecan pie. Popular night spot; unique place. Family-owned. No cr cds accepted.

CENTRAL GROCERY. *923 Decatur St, in French Quarter. 504/523-1620.* Hrs: 8 am-5:30 pm; Sun from 9 am. Continental menu. A la carte entrees: bkfst, lunch, dinner $3.75-$6.95. Specialty: muffuletta sandwich. Sandwich bar in Italian grocery. Near Jackson Square. Family-owned. No cr cds accepted.

CHEZ NOUS CHARCUTERIE. *5701 Magazine St, west of central business district. 504/899-7303.* Hrs: 11 am-6:30 pm; Sat to 5 pm. Closed Sun; most major hols. Creole menu. A la carte entrees: lunch $1.65-$6.50. Specialties: grillades, jambalaya. Outdoor dining. Gourmet delicatessen in grocery store. Cr cds: MC, V.

CLOVER GRILL. *900 Bourbon St (70116), in French Quarter. 504/523-0904.* Open 24 hrs. A la carte entrees: bkfst $2-$5, lunch, dinner $3-$7. Specializes in hamburgers, club sandwiches. Open kitchen. No cr cds accepted.

LA MADELEINE. *547 St Ann St, in French Quarter. 504/568-9950.* Hrs: 7 am-9 pm. Closed Dec 25. French menu. Wine, beer. Avg ck: bkfst $5, lunch, dinner $7.50. Specializes in croissants, quiche, pastries. Own baking. Located in one of the famous Pontalba Bldgs (1851) on Jackson Square. Cr cds: A, D, DS, MC, V.

SC

MOTHER'S. *401 Poydras St, in central business district. 504/523-9656.* Hrs: 5 am-10 pm; Sun from 7 am. Creole menu. A la carte entrees: bkfst $4.75-$7.50, lunch, dinner $3.75-$8. Specializes in New Orleans plate lunches, po' boys sandwiches, Mother's ferdi special. Former residence (1830); extensive collection of US Marine memorabilia. Cafeteria-style service. No cr cds accepted.

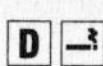

New York City

Settled: 1615
Pop: 7,322,564
Elev: 0-410 feet
Time zone: Eastern
Area codes: 212 (Manhattan); 718 (Bronx, Brooklyn, Queens, Staten Island)
Web: www.TheInsider.com/nyc/

New York is the nation's most populous city and the capital of finance, business, communications and theater. It may not be the center of the universe, but it does occupy a central place in the world's imagination. In one way or another, New York affects the lives of nearly every American. Other cities may attempt to imitate, but nowhere are things done with such style and abundance as the Big Apple.

On April 30, 1789, George Washington took his oath as first president of the United States on the steps of a building on Wall Street, and for a brief time the city was the capital of the new nation. During the 1800s, New York experienced tremendous growth, partially due to the opening of the Erie Canal in 1825. The New York Stock Exchange had its origin when local brokers, who had been selling securities under an old buttonwood tree, made formal agreements to do business in 1792. The NYSE opened in 1825 with most shares in canal and mining companies; no shares in industrial corporations were to appear until 1831.

After the Civil War, hardworking immigrants poured in from abroad, and their efforts produced great wealth. Hundreds of new millionaires built mansions along Fifth Avenue and Riverside Drive. In 1898, the city of New York expanded to almost 3.5 million people. Manhattan was made a borough, and four more boroughs were annexed: Bronx, Brooklyn, Queens and Richmond (now the borough of Staten Island).

The 20th century saw the city expanding upward, with the construction of dozens of skyscrapers, and underground, with the building of the world's most extensive subway system.

Business

As the largest city in the United States, New York City is growing stronger every year. Seven of the ten largest banks in the country as well as most of the nation's leading investment banking firms are located here. All three stock exchanges are headquartered in New York. The World Trade Center, with its landmark twin towers, focuses on international trade and finance.

New York City is in the geographic center of the nation's largest market for goods and services. The metropolitan area tops the list in population, personal income and retail sales. The city itself represents a consumer market totaling over $100 billion in resident buying power.

The overall figures of services offered in this city are overwhelming: over 5,000 law and legal service firms, over 3,500 public relations and management consultant companies, nearly 550 commercial photography businesses, about 1,800 computer companies, many of the nation's largest advertising agencies and so on. New York City is the communications capital of the world. All major radio and television networks, major wire services, dozens of mass circulation and specialty publications and many of the nation's leading book publishers are located here.

New York City is also one of the nation's most popular vacation destinations. Expenditures made by more than 30 million visitors annually (5.8 million from other countries) provide a substantial part of the city's total income.

Convention Facilities

Convention and meeting facilities in New York City are extensive. There are approximately 60,000 hotel rooms located in the city. Many of the large hotels have numerous meeting rooms, banquet facilities and exhibit space. There are auditoriums for large conventions with seating capacities up to 25,000, and stadiums that seat as many as 85,000. The Jacob K. Javits Convention Center boasts 900,000 square feet of exhibit space and more than 100 meeting rooms.

Sports & Recreation

Sports fans have Madison Square Garden, where the Knicks play basketball and the Rangers play hockey; Yankee and Shea stadiums where the Yankees and Mets play baseball; Giants Stadium, East Rutherford, New Jersey, where the Jets and Giants play football; Aqueduct, Roosevelt and Belmont Park racetracks in Queens.

Many parks with ample recreation opportunities are scattered throughout the boroughs; the queen of city parks is, of course, Central Park in Manhattan. Within Central Park's 840 acres are a lake with boat rentals, skating rinks, a zoo, outdoor theater, restaurants, a castle, gardens and miles of jogging paths.

Entertainment

New York City can satisfy every taste. Cultural activities range from the traditional to the avant-garde: plays, ballet, modern dance, street theater, symphony, opera, free concerts in the parks, jazz festivals, Shakespeare in Central Park during summer, folk music, bluegrass, rock and nightclub performers.

The theater districts are known as Broadway, Off-Broadway and Off-Off-Broadway. Tickets for many shows and events are available from Ticketmaster outlets (phone 212/307-7171) or at a discount on the day of performance from the TKTS booths at 2 World Trade Center in Lower Manhattan and 47th Street and Broadway in Midtown.

Times Square, the heart of entertainment is undergoing a rebirth. New theaters, cinemas, skyscrapers and shops have been opened.

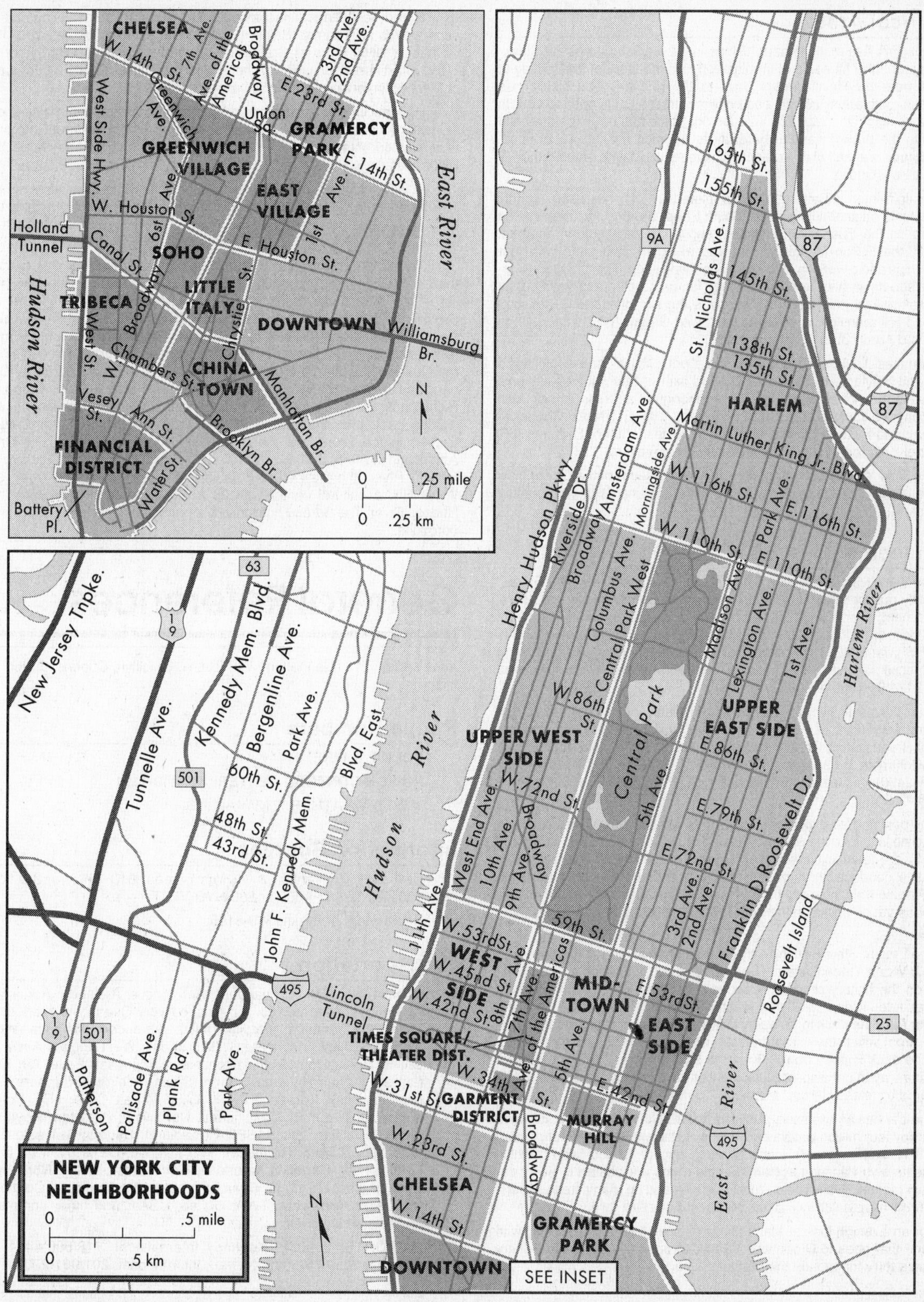
NEW YORK CITY NEIGHBORHOODS
CHELSEA
GREENWICH VILLAGE
GRAMERCY PARK
EAST VILLAGE
SOHO
TRIBECA
LITTLE ITALY
DOWNTOWN
CHINA-TOWN
FINANCIAL DISTRICT
Hudson River
East River
Holland Tunnel
Williamsburg Br.
Manhattan Br.
Brooklyn Br.
Battery Pl.
HARLEM
UPPER WEST SIDE
UPPER EAST SIDE
Central Park
WEST SIDE
MID-TOWN
EAST SIDE
TIMES SQUARE/ THEATER DIST.
GARMENT DISTRICT
MURRAY HILL
Lincoln Tunnel
Roosevelt Island
Harlem River
Henry Hudson Pkwy.
Franklin D. Roosevelt Dr.
New Jersey Tnpke.
SEE INSET

Historical Areas

New York has much to offer historians. Liberty Island has the Statue of Liberty, and the Museum of Immigration tells the story of the settling of America from pre-Revolutionary days to the present. The statue has undergone restoration, including some reconstruction. It is open to visitors every day except December 25. Ellis Island, which has been restored and opened to the public, was the gateway to America for millions of immigrants; nearly one-half of all Americans have relatives who entered the US through Ellis Island.

Castle Clinton in Battery Park, completed in 1811, has been expertly restored to its original appearance. South Street Seaport, the sightseeing attraction on the East River, includes renovated 19th-century landmark buildings, the Fulton Market, a maritime museum, two piers with four historic ships and a working 19th-century printing shop. The Charlton-King-Vandam streets area in Greenwich Village features well-preserved Federal and Greek-revival town houses. Nearby is the site of the long-vanished Richmond Hill mansion, once associated with George Washington, John Adams and Aaron Burr.

Fraunces Tavern Museum has excellent exhibits of the building's history and the famous people associated with it. Federal Hall National Memorial is the site of Washington's first inaugural address and of John Peter Zenger's famous freedom-of-the-press trial. St Paul's Chapel at Broadway and Fulton Street is Manhattan's oldest church. Built in 1766, the chapel is surrounded by a picturesque old graveyard.

The New York Historical Society and the Museum of the City of New York are both rich in art, artifacts and historic documents of 18th-century New York.

Sightseeing

The New York Convention & Visitors Bureau publishes "The Guide," a quarterly publication that includes hotels, restaurants, museums, tours, entertainment, events and other attractions. A multilingual staff can direct foreign visitors to foreign-language tours and to attractions, restaurants and hotels with multilingual personnel. Information is also provided about many special services. The Bureau is located at 810 7th Ave, 3rd floor, 10019; 212/484-1200 or 800/NYC-VISIT.

Free tickets to live TV shows are available on a day-to-day, first come-first served basis. For information on availability of tickets, contact National Broadcasting Co, 30 Rockefeller Plaza, 10112 (phone 212/664-4000); Columbia Broadcasting System, 524 W 57th St, 10019 (phone 212/975-2476); or American Broadcasting Co, 77 W 66th St, 10023 (phone 212/456-7777).

The best and least expensive way to get a panoramic view of the New York skyline is to take the Staten Island Ferry across New York Harbor and back, still the least expensive sea voyage to be found anywhere. The Circle Line conducts three-hour narrated boat tours around Manhattan Island. To see the whole city from above, millions of visitors each year go to the observation decks on the 86th and 102nd floors of the Empire State Building.

The Empire State Building's rival is the observation deck on the 107th floor at 2 World Trade Center. The enclosed deck includes a fascinating exhibit on the history of trade, a souvenir shop and the world's highest escalator ride. When wind and weather permit, visitors may take the escalator from the deck to an open walkway on the roof, a quarter-mile in the sky, from which there is a dramatic and uncluttered view in all directions. The deck is open from 9:30 am to 9:30 pm seven days a week. A high-flying way to get a spectacular view of the city is by helicopter. Tours are offered by Island Helicopter (phone 212/683-4575).

The city has an extensive public transportation system. The subways carry nearly four million people on weekdays and are crowded during rush hours. The system covers every borough except Staten Island, which provides its own transport system. Simple maps are posted in every car and every station. Buses run on most avenues and on many cross streets. Riders must have a subway token, Metrocard or exact fare.

For an evening look at Manhattan's skyline, take a tour (2 hrs) with Gray Line that goes to Greenwich Village, through Chinatown to Battery Park and a ferry trip around the Statue of Liberty.

Greenwich Village, a fashionable art and literary center, is famous for such writers as Thomas Paine, Dylan Thomas, Henry James and Willa Cather. Walking tours of Greenwich Village, two artists' neighborhoods, SoHo and Tribeca, as well as other historic and culturally significant areas of Manhattan, are conducted by various companies.

Harlem Spirituals and Harlem Your Way! provide an interesting look at Harlem. A wide range of other tours, catering to many different interests, is available in New York. Contact the Convention & Visitors Bureau for further details.

A visit to New York City is not complete without an afternoon of window shopping down Fifth or Madison avenues. Absolutely anything can be bought here, for a price. But the store windows themselves are attractions.

To remind visitors and conventioneers that New York City is more than Manhattan, the Convention & Visitors Bureau has compiled this brief list of top attractions in the other four boroughs: in Brooklyn are the Brooklyn Museum, with the Botanic Garden next door, the New York Aquarium and Coney Island; in Queens are the Aqueduct and Belmont racetracks, Shea Stadium and Flushing Meadows Corona Park, containing the Queens Museum, the USTA Tennis Center, Zoo and Botanical Gardens and the American Museum of the Moving Image; in Staten Island are Richmondtown, an ongoing restoration of the borough's architectural and historic past, plus the Staten Island Ferry and Snug Harbor Cultural Center; in the Bronx are the Bronx Zoo, the Hall of Fame for Great Americans at Bronx Community College, which stands on a bluff above the Harlem River, the New York Botanical Garden, Yankee Stadium, and Wave Hill, a cultural center with 28 acres of gardens overlooking the Hudson River. The Bureau has individual pamphlets describing each of the boroughs.

General References

Area codes: 212 (Manhattan); 718 (Bronx, Brooklyn, Queens, Staten Island)

Phone Numbers

POLICE & FIRE: 911

POISON CONTROL CENTER: 212/340-4494

TIME & WEATHER: 212/976-1616

Information Sources

New York Convention & Visitors Bureau, 810 7th Ave, 3rd floor, 10019; 212/484-1200 or 800/NYC-VISIT.

Department of Parks, 360-8196.

Transportation

AIRLINES: *JFK International:* Aer Lingus (Ireland); Aerolineas Argentinas; Aeromexico; Air Afrique (Ivory Coast); Air France; Air India; Air Jamaica; Alitalia (Italy); American; America West; Avensa; British Airways; BWIA (British West Indian Airways); China; Delta; Dominicana (Dominican Republic); Egypt Air; El Al (Israel); Finnair (Finland); Iberia (Spain); Icelandair; Japan; KLM (Netherlands); Korean; Kuwait; LASCA; Lan Chile; LOT Polish; Lufthansa (Germany); Mexicana; Northwest; Pakistan; Royal Air Maroc; Russian Intl; SABENA (Belgium); Saudia; Swissair; TAP (Portugal); Tarom (Romania); TWA; United; USAir. *Newark International:* Air Canada; American; Continental; Delta; Northwest; TWA; United; USAir. *La Guardia:* Air Canada; American; Continental; Delta; Northwest; TWA; United; USAir; and other commuter and regional airlines.

AIRPORTS: John F. Kennedy International, 718/656-4444; La Guardia, 718/476-5000; Newark International, 201/961-2000.

CAR RENTAL AGENCIES: In the New York area call agencies' toll-free numbers (see IMPORTANT TOLL-FREE NUMBERS) to obtain accurate information for each airport.

PUBLIC TRANSPORTATION: Metropolitan Transportation Authority, NYC Transit Authority, 212/878-7000 or 718/330-1234.

RAILROAD PASSENGER SERVICE: Amtrak 800/872-7245.

Newspapers

Amsterdam News; Journal of Commerce; New York Daily News; New York Post; New York Times; Newsday; Village Voice; Wall Street Journal; Women's Wear Daily.

Convention Facility

Jacob K. Javits Convention Center, 34th to 39th Sts, between Eleventh & Twelfth Aves, 212/216-2000.

Sports & Recreation

Major Sports Facilities

Giants Stadium, East Rutherford, NJ, 201/935-3900 (Giants, 201/935-8111, Jets, 516/560-8100, football).

Madison Square Garden, between Seventh & Eighth Aves & W 31st & 33rd Sts (Knicks, basketball, 212/465-6000; Rangers, hockey, 465-6485).

Nassau Veterans Memorial Coliseum, Hempstead, L.I., 516/794-4100 (Islanders, hockey).

Shea Stadium, Flushing, Queens, 718/507-6387 (Mets, baseball).

Yankee Stadium, 161st St & River Ave, Bronx, 718/293-4300 (Yankees, baseball).

Racetracks

Aqueduct Race Track, near Cross Bay Blvd just off Belt Pkwy in Queens, 718/641-4700.

Belmont Park Race Track, Hempstead Tpke, Cross Island Pkwy & Plainfield Ave, L.I., 718/641-4700.

Yonkers Raceway, Yonkers & Central Aves, Yonkers, 914/968-4200.

Cultural Facilities

Theaters

MANHATTAN

Ambassador Theater, 215 W 49th St, 239-6200.

Belasco Theater, 111 W 44th St, 239-6200.

Booth Theatre, 222 W 45th St, 239-6200.

Broadhurst Theatre, 235 W 44th St, 239-6200.

Broadway Theater, 1681 Broadway, at 53rd St, 239-6200.

Brooks Atkinson, 256 W 47th St, 719-4099.

Circle in the Square, 1633 Broadway, 239-6200.

City Center Theater, 130 W 56th St, 581-1212.

Cort Theatre, 138 W 48th St, 239-6200.

Ethel Barrymore Theater, 243 W 47th St, 239-6200.

Eugene O'Neill Theater, 230 W 49th St, 239-6200.

Gershwin Theatre, 222 W 51st St, 586-6510.

Golden Theater, 252 W 45th St, 239-6200.

Helen Hayes Theater, 240 W 44th St, 944-9450.

Imperial Theater, 249 W 45th St, 239-6200.

Juilliard School Theater, Broadway at 144 W 66th St, 799-5000.

Longacre Theater, 220 W 48th St, 239-6200.

Lunt-Fontaine Theatre, 205 W 46th St, 575-9200.

Lyceum Theatre, 149 W 45th St, 239-6200.

Majestic Theater, 245 W 44th St, 239-6200.

Martin Beck Theater, 302 W 45th St, 239-6200.

Minskoff Theatre, Broadway at 45th St, 869-0550.

Music Box, 239 W 45th St, 239-6200.

Nederlander, 208 W 41st St, 921-8000.

Neil Simon Theatre, 250 W 52nd St, 757-8646.

New York Shakespeare Festival, Delacorte Theater in Central Park, 861-PAPP, and Public Theater, at Lafayette St & Astor Place, 260-2400 (425 Lafayette St).

New York State Theater, Broadway at 64th St, 870-5570.

Palace Theater, Broadway at 47th St, 730-8200.

Plymouth Theater, 236 W 45th St, 239-6200.

Richard Rodgers Theater, 226 W 46th St, 221-1211.

Royale Theater, 242 W 45th St, 239-6200.

St James Theater, 246 W 44th St, 239-6200.

Shubert Theater, 225 W 44th St, 239-6200.

Virginia Theater, 245 W 52nd St, 239-6200.

Walter Kerr Theatre, 219 W 48th St, 239-6200.

Winter Garden Theater, 1634 Broadway, 239-6200.

Concert Halls

Brooklyn Academy of Music, 30 Lafayette Ave, 718/636-4100.

Brooklyn Center for the Performing Arts at Brooklyn College, Nostrand Ave & Ave H, 718/951-4500.

Carnegie Hall, 154 W 57th St at Seventh Ave, 212/247-7800.

Lincoln Center for the Performing Arts, 70 Lincoln Center Plaza, 212/875-5350.

Town Hall, 123 W 43rd St, 212/840-2824.

Museums

MANHATTAN

American Museum of Immigration, base of the Statue of Liberty, Liberty Island, 363-3200.

American Museum of Natural History, Central Park W at 81st St, 769-5100.

Bible House, American Bible Society, 1865 Broadway & 61st St, 408-1200.

Ellis Island Immigration Museum, Ellis Island, 363-3200.

Fraunces Tavern Museum, 54 Pearl St, 425-1778.

Hispanic Society of America, Broadway between W 155th & 156th Sts, 926-2234.

Jewish Museum, 1109 Fifth Ave at E 92nd St, 423-3200.

Museum of Television and Radio, 25 W 52nd St, 621-6600.

Museum of the American Indian (The Heye Foundation), Broadway & W 155th St, 283-2420.

Museum of the City of New York, 1220 Fifth Ave, between E 103rd & 104th Sts, 534-1672.

New York Public Library at Lincoln Center—Library & Museum of the Performing Arts, Lincoln Center, Broadway & 65th Sts, 870-1600.

Pierpont Morgan Library, 29 E 36th St, 685-0610.

South Street Seaport Museum, 207 Front St, 748-8600.

BRONX

City Island Historical Nautical Museum, 190 Fordham St, 718/885-1616.

Museum of Bronx History, 3266 Bainbridge Ave, at E 208th St, 718/881-8900.

BROOKLYN

Brooklyn Children's Museum, 145 Brooklyn Ave, 718/735-4400.

Brooklyn's History Museum: The Brooklyn Historical Society, 128 Pierrepont St, 718/624-0890.

New York Transit Museum, Boerum Place & Schermerhorn St, 718/330-3060.

QUEENS

Queens Museum, NYC Building, Flushing Meadows-Corona Park, 718/592-2405.

STATEN ISLAND

Museum of Staten Island, 75 Stuyvesant Place, 718/727-1135.

Staten Island Children's Museum, 1000 Richmond Terrace, at Snug Harbor, 718/273-2060 or 718/448-6557.

Art Museums & Galleries

MANHATTAN

American Craft Museum, 40 W 53rd St, 956-3535.

Asia Society Galleries, 725 Park Ave, at 70th St, 517-NEWS.

The Cloisters, Fort Tryon Park off Henry Hudson Pkwy, 923-3700.

Cooper-Hewitt Museum, 2 E 91st St, 860-6868.

El Museo del Barrio, 1230 Fifth Ave, 831-7272 or 831-7273.

The Frick Collection, 1 E 70th St, at Fifth Ave, 288-0700.

International Center of Photography, 1130 Fifth Ave, at 94th St, 860-1777.

Metropolitan Museum of Art, Fifth Ave at 82nd St, 535-7710.

Museum of Modern Art, 11 W 53rd St, 708-9480.

Solomon R. Guggenheim Museum, 1071 Fifth Ave, 423-3500.

Studio Museum in Harlem, 144 W 125th St, 864-4500.

Whitney Museum of American Art, 945 Madison Ave, 570-3676.

(There are many fine art galleries along 57th St near Fifth Ave, Madison Ave, and in the downtown section known as SoHo; consult local magazines for listings.)

BRONX

Bronx Museum of the Arts, 1040 Grand Concourse, 718/681-6000.

BROOKLYN

Brooklyn Museum, 200 Eastern Pkwy at Washington Ave, 718/638-5000.

QUEENS

American Museum of the Moving Image, 35th Ave at 36th St, Astoria, 718/784-0077.

STATEN ISLAND

Jacques Marchais Center of Tibetan Art, 338 Lighthouse Ave, between New Dorp & Richmondtown, 718/987-3500.

Points of Interest

Historical

MANHATTAN

Bowling Green, Battery Park.

Castle Clinton National Monument, Battery Park, 344-7220.

Cathedral Church of St John the Divine, Amsterdam Ave & 112th St, 316-7540 or 932-7314.

The Church of the Ascension, 10th St & Fifth Ave, 254-8620.

City Hall Park, Broadway between Chambers & Barclay Sts.

Dyckman House Park and Museum, 4881 Broadway, at 204th St, 304-2342.

Ellis Island, 363-3200.

Federal Hall National Memorial, 26 Wall St.

General Grant National Memorial, Riverside Dr & W 122nd St, 666-1640.

Morris-Jumel Mansion, 65 Jumel Terrace at W 160th St, 923-8008.

St Mark's-in-the-Bowery, Second Ave & 10th St, 674-6377.

St Patrick's Cathedral, Fifth Ave & 50th St.

St Paul's Chapel, Fulton St & Broadway.

Theodore Roosevelt Birthplace National Historic Site, 28 E 20th St, 260-1616.

Trinity Church, Broadway & Wall St.

US Custom House, S side of Bowling Green, Battery Park.

BRONX

Bartow-Pell Mansion, Shore Rd in Pelham Bay Park, 718/885-1461.

Hall of Fame for Great Americans, W 181st St & University Ave, 718/289-5162.

Poe Cottage, Grand Concourse & E Kingsbridge Rd, 718/881-8900.

Van Cortlandt Mansion, Van Cortlandt Park, N of Broadway at 246th St, 718/543-3344.

BROOKLYN

Plymouth Church of the Pilgrims, Orange St between Hicks & Henry Sts.

QUEENS

Bowne House, 37-01 Bowne St, Flushing, 718/359-0528.

STATEN ISLAND

Conference House, 7455 Hylan Blvd, Tottenville, 718/984-2086.

Richmondtown Restoration, 441 Clarke Ave, Richmond & Arthur Kill Rds, 718/351-1611.

Snug Harbor Cultural Center, 1000 Richmond Terrace, 718/448-2500.

Other Attractions

MANHATTAN

American Stock Exchange, 86 Trinity Place, 306-1000.

Brooklyn Bridge, across East River to Brooklyn.

Central Park, Fifth Ave-Central Park W (Eighth Ave) & 59th St-110th St.

Chase Manhattan Bank, 1 Chase Manhattan Plaza, Nassau & Pine Sts.

Chinatown, Pell & Mott Sts, E of Bowery.

Citicorp Center, 1 Citicorp Center, 54th St & Lexington Ave.

Cooper Union, between Third & Fourth Aves at 7th St, 353-4195.

Empire State Building, 350 Fifth Ave, at 34th St, 736-3100.

Federal Reserve Bank of New York, 33 Liberty St, 720-6130.

The Garment District, S of 42nd St, W of Sixth Ave, N of 34th St & E of Eighth Ave.

Greenwich Village, from Broadway W to the Hudson River, between 14th St & Houston St.

Macy's, on Herald Square, 34th St & Broadway, 695-4400.

New York Public Library, 42nd St & Fifth Ave, 221-7676.

New York Stock Exchange, 20 Broad St, 656-5167.

One Times Square, 42nd St & Broadway.

Radio City Music Hall, Rockefeller Center, 50th St & Ave of Americas, 247-4777.

Rockefeller Center, Fifth to Sixth Aves & beyond, 47th to 51st Sts.

Schomburg Center for Research in Black Culture, 515 Malcolm X Blvd, at W 135th St, 491-2200.

SoHo, W Broadway, Sixth Ave, Houston & Canal Sts (Friends of Cast Iron Architecture walking tours), 369-6004.

Statue of Liberty, Liberty Island, 363-3200.

Temple Emanu-El, Fifth Ave & 65th St, 744-1400.

Times Square & Theater District, Sixth to Ninth Aves, 41st to 53rd Sts.

United Nations, First Ave from 42nd-48th Sts, 963-7713.

Wall Street, downtown, E from Broadway.

Washington Square, S end of Fifth Ave.

Woolworth Building, 233 Broadway.

World Trade Center, downtown off Church St, 435-4170.

BRONX

Bronx Zoo, Bronx Park, S of Fordham Rd & Bronx River Pkwy, 718/367-1010.

New York Botanical Garden, Bronx Park, entrance on Southern Blvd, 718/817-8705.

Wave Hill, 675 W 252nd St, 549-3200.

BROOKLYN

Brooklyn Botanic Garden, Eastern Pkwy, Washington & Flatbush Aves, 718/622-4433.

Coney Island, Surf Ave, Ocean Pkwy-37th St, 718/266-1234.

New York Aquarium, Boardwalk & W 8th St, Coney Island, 718/265-FISH.

QUEENS

Flushing Meadow-Corona Park, Grand Central Pkwy-Van Wyck Expwy, Union Tpke-Northern Blvd.

Queens Botanical Garden, 43-50 Main St, 718/886-3800.

STATEN ISLAND

Staten Island Ferry, Manhattan to St George, Staten Island, 718/390-5253.

Staten Island Zoo, Barrett Park, between Broadway & Clove Rd, W New Brighton, 718/442-3100.

Verrazano-Narrows Bridge, connects Staten Island & Brooklyn.

Sightseeing Tours

Adventure on a Shoestring, 300 W 53rd St, 10019; 212/265-2663.

Circle Line Sightseeing, Inc., W 43rd St & Hudson River, Pier 83, 212/563-3200.

Gray Line bus tours, 254 W 54th St, 10019; 212/397-2620.

Harlem Spirituals, 1697 Broadway, Suite 203, 212/757-0425.

Shortline, 166 W 46th St, 212/736-4700.

Annual Events

Chinese New Year, in Chinatown. Early-mid-Feb.

USA/Mobil Indoor Track & Field Championships. Usually last Fri Feb.

St Patrick's Day Parade, Fifth Ave. Mar 17.

Easter Parade, Fifth Ave near St Patrick's Cathedral.

Ninth Avenue International Food Festival. Mid-May.

JVC Jazz Festival-New York, 787-2020. Late June-early July.

Harbor Festival. Wkend of July 4.

San Gennaro Festival, Little Italy. Mid-late Sept.

Columbus Day Parade, upper Fifth Ave. Early Oct.

Hispanic Day Parade, Fifth Ave. Mid-Oct.

New York City Marathon. Sun, usually Nov.

Thanksgiving Day Parade, Broadway.

Lighting of Christmas tree at Rockefeller Center. Early Dec.

City Neighborhoods

Many of the restaurants, unrated dining establishments and some lodgings listed under Manhattan include neighborhoods as well as exact street addresses. Geographic descriptions of these areas are given, followed by a table of restaurants arranged by neighborhood.

Chelsea: Area of West Side south of 31st St, west of Sixth Ave, north of 14th St and east of the Hudson River.

Chinatown: Area of Downtown south of Canal St and east and west of Bowery; particularly along Bayard, Pell and Mott Sts east of Bowery.

Downtown: South of 14th St, west of the East River and east of the Hudson River; also refers specifically to the Financial District.

East Side: Area of Midtown south of 59th St, west of the East River, north of 42nd St and east of Lexington Ave.

East Village: Area of Downtown south of 14th St, west of First Ave, north of E Houston St and east of Broadway.

Financial District: Area of Downtown south of Vesey and Ann Sts, west of the East River, north of Water St and Battery Park and east of the Hudson River.

Garment District: Area of Midtown south of 42nd St, west of Sixth Ave, north of 34th St and east of Eighth Ave.

Gramercy Park: Area of Midtown on and around Gramercy Park; south of E 23rd St, west of First Ave, north of 14th St and east of Broadway.

Greenwich Village: Area of Downtown south of 14th St, west of Broadway, north of W Houston St and east of Greenwich Ave.

Harlem: South of 165th St, west of the Harlem River, north of 110th St and east of Morningside Ave and St Nicholas Ave.

Little Italy: Area of Downtown south of Houston St, west of Chrystie St and the Sara Delano Roosevelt Pkwy, north of Canal St and east of Broadway.

Midtown: Between 59th St and 34th St and the East and Hudson rivers; south of 59th St, west of Eighth Ave, north of 34th St and east of Lexington Ave.

Murray Hill: Area of Midtown south of 42nd St, west of Second Ave, north of 32nd St and east of Fifth Ave.

SoHo: Area of Downtown south of Houston St, west of Broadway, north of Canal St and east of Avenue of the Americas (Sixth Ave).

Times Square/Theater District: Area of Midtown south of 53rd St, west of Avenue of the Americas (Sixth Ave), north of 40th St and east of Eighth Ave; intersection of Broadway and Seventh Ave.

Tribeca: Area of Downtown south of Canal St, west of Broadway, north of Chambers St and east of the Hudson River.

Upper East Side: Area south of 110th St, west of the East River, north of 59th St and east of Central Park.

Upper West Side: Area south of 110th St, west of Central Park, north of 59th St and east of the Hudson River.

West Side: Area of Midtown south of 59th St, west of Eighth Ave, north of 34th St and east of the Hudson River.

Lodgings and Food

No city in the United States has as many fine restaurants serving as many different and exciting international dishes as New York. Eating here is an adventure as well as an art. With thousands of restaurants to choose from, it can also be bewildering. The list that follows is organized alphabetically under each neighborhood/area heading.

MANHATTAN RESTAURANTS BY NEIGHBORHOOD AREAS

(For full description, see alphabetical listings under Restaurants)

CHELSEA

Caffe Bondi. 7 W 20th St
Cal's. 55 W 21st St
Campagna. 24 E 21st St
Chelsea Bistro & Bar. 358 W 23rd St
Da Umberto. 107 W 17th St
Empire Diner. 210 Tenth Ave
Follonico. 6 W 24th St
Gascogne. 158 Eighth Ave
Hot Tomato. 676 6th Ave
La Traviata. 461 W 23rd St
Le Madri. 168 W 18th St
Lola. 30 W 22nd St
Periyali. 35 W 20th St
Steak Frites. 9 E 16th St
Trois Canards. 184 Eighth Ave
Zucca. 227 10th Ave

CHINATOWN

20 Mott Street. 20 Mott St
Harmony Palace. 94-98 Mott St
Hunan Garden. 1 Mott St
Saigon House. 89-91 Bayard St

DOWNTOWN

Fraunces Tavern. 54 Pearl St

EAST SIDE

Ambassador Grill (U.N. Plaza-Park Hyatt Hotel). 1 UN Plaza
Dawat. 210 E 58th St
Delegates Dining Room. In United Nations General Assembly Bldg
Felidia. 243 E 58th St
Girafe. 208 E 58th St
Hosteria Fiorella. 1081 Third Ave
Il Nido. 251 E 53rd St
La Mangeoire. 1008 Second Ave
Le Colonial. 149 E 57th St
P.J. Clarke's. 915 Third Ave
Palm. 837 Second Ave
Rosa Mexicano. 1063 First Ave
Shun Lee Palace. 155 E 55th St
Smith & Wollensky. 201 E 49th St
Tatou. 151 E 50th St

EAST VILLAGE

First. 87 First Ave
Hasaki. 210 E 9th St
Japonica. 100 University Place
Riodizio. 417 Lafayette St
Second Ave Deli. 156 Second Ave

FINANCIAL DISTRICT

Edward Moran Bar And Grill. 250 Vesey St
Fulton Street Cafe. 11 Fulton St
The Grill Room. 225 Liberty St
Harbour Lights. Fulton Pier 17
Hudson River Club. 250 Vesey St
Liberty Cafe. 89 South St
Wall Street Kitchen & Bar. 70 Broad St
Windows On The World. 1 World Trade Center
Yankee Clipper. 170 John St

GRAMERCY PARK

Aja. 937 Broadway
Alva. 36 E 22nd St
Angelo and Maxie's Steakhouse. 233 Park Ave S
Bolo. 23 E 22nd St
Da Vittorio. 43 E 20th St
Gramercy Tavern. 42 E 20th St
The Lemon. 230 Park Ave S
Mesa Grill. 102 Fifth Ave
Moreno. 65 Irving Place
Novita. 102 E 22nd St
Patria. 250 Park Ave S
Republic. 37 Union Square W

GREENWICH VILLAGE

Cafe De Bruxelles. 118 Greenwich Ave
Chez Michallet. 90 Bedford St
Cuisine De Saigon. 154 W 13th St
Da Silvano. 260 Sixth Ave
Elephant & Castle. 68 Greenwich Ave
Florent. 69 Gansevoort St
Gotham Bar And Grill. 12 E 12th St
Home. 20 Cornelia St
Indigo. 142 W 10th St
Ithaka. 48 Barrow St
La Metairie. 189 W 10th St
Marylou's. 21 W 9th St
Mi Cocina. 57 Jane St
One If By Land, Two If By Sea. 17 Barrow St
Pó. 31 Cornelia St
Village Grill. 518 LaGuardia Pl

LITTLE ITALY

Grotta Azzurra. 387 Broome St
Il Cortile. 125 Mulberry St
Sal Anthony's Spqr. 133 Mulberry St
Taormina. 147 Mulberry St

MIDTOWN

21 Club. 21 W 52nd St
Adrienne (The Peninsula New York Hotel). 700 Fifth Ave
American Festival. 20 W 50th St
An American Place. 2 Park Ave
Aquavit. 13 W 54th St
Barbetta. 321 W 46th St
Bice. 7 E 54th St
Box Tree (Box Tree Inn). 250 E 49th St
Brooklyn Diner Usa. 212 W 57th St
Bryant Park Grill. 25 W 40th St
Bull & Bear Steakhouse (Waldorf-Astoria Hotel). 301 Park Ave
Cafe Pierre (The Pierre Hotel). 2 E 61st St
Carnegie Deli. 854 Seventh Ave
Castellano. 138 W 55th St
Christer's. 145 W 55th St
Cibo. 767 Second Ave
Cité. 120 W 51st St
Comfort Diner. 214 E 45th St
Domingo. 209 E 49th St
Fantino (Luxury Collection Hotel). 112 Central Park South
Fifty Seven Fifty Seven (Four Seasons Hotel). 57 E 57th St
The Four Seasons. 99 E 52nd St
Harley-Davidson Cafe. 1370 Ave of the Americas
Harry Cipriani. 781 Fifth Ave
Il Toscanaccio. 7 E 59th St
Jean Georges (Trump International Hotel). 1 Central Park W
Jubilee. 347 E 54th St
Judson Grill. 152 W 52nd St
Keens Steakhouse. 72 W 36th St
La Bonne Soupe. 48 W 55th St

La Côte Basque. 60 W 55th St
La Caravelle. 33 W 55th St
La Maison Japonaise. 125 E 39th St
La Reserve. 4 W 49th St
Le Chantilly. 106 E 57th St
Le Cirque 2000 (The New York Palace Hotel). 455 Madison Ave
Le Perigord. 405 E 52nd St
Les Célébrités (Essex House Hotel Nikko). 160 Central Park South
Lespinasse (The St Regis Hotel). 2 E 55th St
Lutèce. 249 E 50th St
Maloney & Porcelli. 37 E 50th St
Manhattan Ocean Club. 57 W 58th St
Med Grill Bistro & Cafe. 725 5th Ave
Michael's. 24 W 55th St
Mickey Mantle's Restaurant & Sports Bar. 42 Central Park South
Monkey Bar. 60 E 54th St
Morton's of Chicago. 551 Fifth Ave
Nadaman Hakubai. 66 Park Ave
Oak Room (The Plaza Hotel). Fifth Ave at 59th St & Central Park South
Oceana. 55 E 54th St
Osterio Del Circo. 120 W 55th St
Otabe. 68 E 56th St
Oyster Bar. At Grand Central Station
Palm Court (The Plaza Hotel). Fifth Ave at 59th St & Central Park South
Patroon. 160 E 46th St
Peacock Alley (Waldorf-Astoria Hotel). 301 Park Ave
Petrossian. 182 W 58th St
Planet Hollywood. 140 W 57th St
Rainbow Room. 30 Rockefeller Plaza
Raphael. 33 W 54th St
Redeye Grill. 890 Seventh Ave
Remi. 145 W 53rd St
The Rotunda (The Pierre Hotel). 2 E 61st St
Ruth's Chris Steak House. 148 W 51st St
San Domenico. 240 Central Park South
San Martin's. 143 E 49th St
San Pietro. 18 E 54th St
Savories. 30 Rockefeller Center
Sea Grill. 19 W 49th St
Shaan. 57 W 48th St
Sparks Steak House. 210 E 46th St
Stage Deli. 834 Seventh Ave
Sushisay. 38 E 51st St
Trattoria Dell'arte. 900 7th Ave
Two Rooms. 313 E 58th St
Typhoon Brewery. 22 E 54th St
Union Square Cafe. 21 E 16th St
Vong. 200 E 54th St
Water Club. 500 E 30th St
Zarela. 953 2nd Ave

MURRAY HILL
Aunt Suzie. 126 E 28 St
Belluno Ristorante. 340 Lexington Ave
I Trulli. 122 E 27th St
La Colombe D'or. 134 E 26th St
Park Bistro. 414 Park Ave S
Sonia Rose. 132 Lexington Ave

SOHO
Alison On Dominick Street. 38 Dominick St
Aquagrill. 210 Spring St
Baluchi's. 193 Spring St
Barolo. 398 W Broadway
Blue Ribbon. 97 Sullivan St
Boom. 152 Spring St
Cascabel. 218 Lafayette St
Cub Room. 131 Sullivan St
Erizo Latino. 422 W Broadway
I Tre Merli. 463 W Broadway
Manhattan Bistro. 129 Spring St
Mezzogiorno. 195 Spring St
Penang Malaysian. 109 Spring St
Provence. 38 MacDougal St
Quilty's. 177 Prince St
Raoul's. 180 Prince St
Sanzin. 180 Spring St
Savore. 200 Spring St
Savoy. 70 Prince St
Zoë. 90 Prince St

TIMES SQUARE/THEATER DISTRICT
Becco. 355 W 46th St
Chez Napoleon. 365 W 50th St
Coco Pazzo Teatro. 235 W 46th St
Firebird. 365 W 46th St
Gallagher's. 228 W 52nd St
Joe Allen. 326 W 46th St
Le Bernardin. 155 W 51st St
Marlowe. 328 W 46th St
Orso. 322 W 46th St
Osteria Al Doge. 142 W 44th St
Palio. 151 W 51st St
Pierre Au Tunnel. 250 W 47th St
René Pujol. 321 W 51st St
Sardi's. 234 W 44th St
Siam Grill. 586 Ninth Ave
Siam Inn. 916 8th Ave
Trionfo. 224 W 51st St
Victor's Cafe 52. 236 W 52nd St
The View (Marriott Marquis Hotel). 1535 Broadway
Virgil's Real Barbecue. 152 W 44th St

TRIBECA
Arqua. 281 Church St
Barocco. 301 Church St
Capsouto Frères. 451 Washington St
Chanterelle. 2 Harrison St
City Wine & Cigar Co. 62 Laight St
Duane Park Cafe. 157 Duane St
El Teddy's. 219 W Broadway
Gigino Trattoria. 323 Greenwich St
Layla. 211 W Broadway
Montrachet. 239 W Broadway
Nobu. 105 Hudson St
Noor's. 94 Chambers
The Odeon. 145 W Broadway
Salaam Bombay. 317 Greenwich St
Screening Room. 54 Varick St
Spartina. 355 Greenwich St
Tribeca Grill. 375 Greenwich St

UPPER EAST SIDE
540 Park (The Regency Hotel). 540 Park Ave
Arcadia. 21 E 62nd St
Arizona 206. 206 E 60th St
Aureole. 34 E 61st St
Bistro Du Nord. 1312 Madison Ave
Boathouse Cafe. In Central Park
Cafe Nosidam. 768 Madison Ave
Cafe Trevi. 1570 First Ave
Carlyle Restaurant (Carlyle Hotel). Madison Ave at E 76th St
Coco Pazzo. 23 E 74th St
Contrapunto. 200 E 60th St
Daniel. 20 E 76th St
Demi. 1316 Madison Ave
Destinée. 134 E 61st St
Erminia. 250 E 83rd St
Gertrude's. 33 E 61st St
Il Monello. 1460 Second Ave
Jackson Hole. 1611 Second Ave
Jim Mcmullen. 1341 Third Ave
Jo Jo. 160 E 64th St
Kings' Carriage House. 251 E 82nd St
Le Boeuf à La Mode. 539 E 81st St
Le Régence (Plaza Athénée Hotel). 37 E 64th St

Le Refuge. 166 E 82nd St
Lenox Room. 1278 Third Ave
Lobster Club. 24 E 80th St
Lumi. 963 Lexington Ave
Lusardi's. 1494 Second Ave
Manhattan Cafe. 1161 First Ave
March. 405 E 58th St
Matthew's. 1030 Third Ave
Mesa City. 1059 Third Ave
Mezzaluna. 1295 Third Ave
Nino's. 1354 1st Ave
Our Place. 1444 Third Ave
Parioli Romanissimo. 24 E 81st St
Park Avenue Cafe. 100 E 63rd St
Pig Heaven. 1540 Second Ave
Polo (Westbury Hotel). 15 E 69th St
Post House. 28 E 63rd St
Primavera. 1578 First Ave
Red Tulip. 439 E 75th St
Savann Est. 181 E 78th St
Serendipity 3. 225 E 60th St
Shabu-Tatsu. 1414 York Ave
Sign Of The Dove. 1110 Third Ave
Table d'Hote. 44 E 92nd St
Willow. 1022 Lexington Ave
Yellowfingers. 200 E 60th St

UPPER WEST SIDE
Ansonia. 329 Columbus Ave
Cafe Des Artistes. 1 W 67th St
Cafe Fiorello. 1900 Broadway
Cafe Luxembourg. 200 W 70th St
Carmine's. 2450 Broadway
Diane's Downtown. 249 Columbus Ave
Gabriel's. 11 W 60th St
Merlot. 44 W 63rd St
Panevino Ristorante/Cafe Vienna. In Avery Fisher Hall
Picholine. 35 W 64th St
Rain. 100 W 82nd St
Sarabeth's. 423 Amsterdam Ave
Shark Bar. 307 Amsterdam Ave
Shun Lee. 43 W 65th St
Tavern On The Green. Central Park at W 67th St
Terrace. 400 W 119th St
Two Two Two. 222 W 79th St
Vince & Eddie's. 70 W 68th St

Hotels

★ ★ **ALGONQUIN.** *59 W 44th St (10036), between Fifth Ave and Avenue of the Americas, Midtown. 212/840-6800; FAX 212/944-1419; res: 800/548-0345.* 165 rms, 12 story. S $255; D $275; each addl $25; suites $375-$550; wkend rates. Crib free. TV; cable (premium). Complimentary continental bkfst. Restaurant 7-1 am; Sun from noon. Bar from 11 am. Ck-out 1 pm. Meeting rms. Business servs avail. Refrigerator in suites. 18th-century English decor; English club atmosphere. Visited by numerous literary and theatrical personalities. Cr cds: A, C, D, DS, ER, JCB, MC, V.

D

★ ★ **BARBIZON.** *140 E 63rd St (10021), between Third & Lexington Aves, Upper East Side. 212/838-5700; FAX 212/888-4271; res: 800/223-1020.* 300 rms, 22 story. S $170-$235; D $190-$255; each addl $20; suites $375-$450; under 12 free; wkend rates. Garage parking $29. TV; cable (premium). Pool; whirlpool. Ck-out noon. Business servs avail. In-rm modem link. Concierge. Exercise rm; instructor, weights, treadmills, sauna. Minibars. Some balconies. Landmark bldg known around the world as the Barbizon Hotel for Women from mid-1920s to mid-1970s. Cr cds: A, C, D, DS, JCB, MC, V.

D SC

✔★ ★ **BEACON.** *2130 Broadway (10023), at W 75th St, Upper West Side. 212/787-1100; res: 800/572-4969; FAX 212/724-0839.* Web www.beaconhotel.com. 200 kit. units, 25 story. S $120-$130; D $140-$150; each addl $15; suites $180-$350; under 17 free. Crib free. Garage parking $15. TV; cable, VCR avail. Complimentary coffee in rms. Restaurant adj open 24 hrs. Ck-out noon. Coin Indry. Meeting rms. Health club privileges. Microwaves avail. Cr cds: A, C, D, DS, MC, V.

D SC

★ ★ **BEDFORD.** *118 E 40th St (10016), between Park & Lexington, Midtown. 212/697-4800; FAX 212/697-1093; res: 800/221-6881.* Web www.bedfordhotel.com. 200 rms, 17 story, 137 suites. S $160-$170; D $170-$180; each addl $10; suites $200-$250; under 13 free; wkend rates. Crib free. Garage $14. TV; cable (premium). Complimentary continental bkfst. Restaurant noon-11 pm. Bar. Ck-out noon. Coin Indry. Business servs avail. Some refrigerators. Cr cds: A, C, D, JCB, MC, V.

SC

★ ★ ★ **BEEKMAN TOWER.** *Three Mitchell Place (10017), at 49th St and First Ave, on the East Side. 212/355-7300; FAX 212/753-9366; res: 800/637-8483.* 175 kit. suites, 26 story. S, studio suites $239; D $259-$299; each addl $20; 2-bedrm suites $499; under 12 free; wkend rates; lower rates June-Aug. Crib free. Garage $23. TV; cable, VCR avail. Complimentary coffee in rms. Restaurant 7 am-10:30 pm. Bar 5 pm-2 am; entertainment Tues-Sat. Ck-out noon. Coin Indry. Meeting rms. Business center. In-rm modem link. Concierge. Exercise equipt; weights, bicycles, sauna. Microwaves. Some private patios, balconies. Restored art-deco landmark completed in 1928. Cr cds: A, C, D, JCB, MC, V.

SC

★ ★ **BEST WESTERN.** *17 W 32nd St (10001), between Fifth Ave & Broadway, Midtown. 212/736-1600; FAX 212/790-2760.* 176 rms, 14 story, 33 suites. S, D $119-$179; each addl $10; suites $149-$259; under 12 free. Crib free. Garage parking $20. TV; cable (premium). Complimentary continental bkfst. Complimentary coffee in rms. Restaurant open 24 hrs. Bar 11-2 am. Ck-out noon. Meeting rms. Business center. Concierge. Gift shop. Barber, beauty shop. Exercise equipt; bicycle, treadmill. Some in-rm whirlpools. Cr cds: A, D, DS, ER, JCB, MC, V.

D SC

★ ★ **BEST WESTERN SEAPORT INN.** *33 Peck Slip (10038), at Front St, Financial District. 212/766-6600; FAX 212/766-6615.* E-mail bwseaportinn@juno.com. 72 rms, 7 story. Memorial Day wkend-Oct: S $140-$175; D $170-$225; each addl $10; under 18 free; wkend rates; higher rates special events; lower rates rest of yr. Crib free. Garage parking $25. TV; VCR (movies $6). Complimentary continental bkfst. Restaurant nearby. No rm serv. Ck-out 11 am. Business servs avail. In-rm modem link. No bellhops. Health club privileges. Refrigerators. Balconies. Located in historic district in restored 19th-century building. Cr cds: A, C, D, DS, MC, V.

D SC

★ ★ **BEST WESTERN WOODWARD.** *210 W 55th St (10019), between Broadway & 7th Ave, Midtown. 212/247-2000; FAX 212/581-2248.* 140 rms, 20 with shower only, 14 story, 40 suites. S, D $170-$200; each addl $20; suites $200-$325; under 12 free; wkend, hol rates. Crib free. Garage parking $24. TV; cable (premium), VCR avail. Complimentary coffee in rms. Restaurant 6:30 am-midnight. Rm serv to 3 am. Ck-out noon. Business servs avail. Concierge. Health club privileges. Cr cds: A, C, D, DS, ER, JCB, MC, V.

SC

★ ★ **BEVERLY.** *125 E 50th St (10022), at Lexington Ave, Midtown. 212/753-2700; FAX 212/759-7300; res: 800/223-0945.* Web www.bevhotel.com. 187 rms, 26 story, 86 suites, 150 kits. S $139; D $149-$169; studio rms $149-$159; suites $189-$220; wkend rates. Crib free. Garage $27. TV; cable (premium), VCR avail. Complimentary continental bkfst. Complimentary coffee in rms. Restaurant 7 am-midnight. Rm serv to 11 pm. Bar 11:30-2 am. Ck-out noon. Meeting rms. Concierge. Drugstore. Barber, beauty shop. Refrigerators. Some balconies. Cr cds: A, C, D, JCB, MC, V.

SC

★★★★★ **CARLYLE.** *Madison Ave at E 76th St (10021), Upper East Side. 212/744-1600; FAX 212/717-4682; res: 800/227-5737.* The fabled Carlyle has hosted world leaders and the very, very rich for years and continues to be a symbol of European graciousness. And it's just steps away from the tony boutiques of Madison Avenue. 196 rms, 35 story. S $300-$450; D $330-$480; suites (1-2 bedrm) $500-$2,000. Pet accepted, some restrictions. Garage $39. TV; cable (premium), VCR (movies). Restaurant (see CARLYLE RESTAURANT). Rm serv 24 hrs. Bar from noon; Café Carlyle from 6 pm; entertainment (cover charge). Ck-out 1 pm. Meeting rms. Business center. In-rm modem link. Concierge. Exercise rm; instructor, weights, bicycles, sauna, steam rm. Massage. Bathrm phones, refrigerators, wet bars, minibars; microwaves avail. Many in-rm whirlpools, serv pantries. Grand piano in many suites. Some terraces. Cr cds: A, C, D, JCB, MC, V.

★★★ **CASABLANCA.** *147 W 43rd St (10036), between Broadway & Sixth, Times Square/Theater District. 212/869-1212; res: 888/922-7225; FAX 212/391-7585.* E-mail casahotel@aol.com; web members.aol.com/casahotel. 48 rms, 8 with shower only, 6 story. S $225-$245; D $245; each addl $20; suites $325; under 12 free; wkend, hol rates. Crib free. Garage parking $24. TV; cable (premium), VCR (movies). Complimentary continental bkfst; afternoon refreshments. Restaurant 11 am-11 pm. Rm serv. Ck-out noon. Meeting rms. Business center. In-rm modem link. Concierge. Health club privileges. Bathrm phones, refrigerators. Cr cds: A, D, JCB, MC, V.

D SC

✔★ **COMFORT INN.** *42 W 35th St (10001), between 5th & 6th Aves, Murray Hill. 212/947-0200; FAX 212/594-3047.* E-mail acw64@aol.com; web www.comfortinn.com. 131 rms, 12 story. S $119-$229; D $129-$229; each addl $12; under 18 free. Crib free. TV; cable (premium). Complimentary continental bkfst. Coffee in rms. Restaurant 7 am-8 pm. Ck-out noon. Business servs avail. In-rm modem link. Some refrigerators, microwaves. Cr cds: A, C, D, DS, MC, V.

SC

★★★ **CROWNE PLAZA.** *1605 Broadway (10019), at 49th St, Midtown. 212/977-4000; FAX 212/333-7393.* 770 rms, 46 story. S, D $179-$299; each addl $20; under 19 free. Crib avail. Garage $34. TV; cable (premium), VCR avail (movies). Indoor pool; lifeguard. Coffee in rms. Restaurant 6:30 am-2 pm, 5 pm-2 am; Sun hrs vary. Rm serv 24 hrs. Bar from 11:30 am. Ck-out noon. Convention facilities. Business center. In-rm modem link. Concierge. Exercise rm; instructor, weight machines, bicycles, sauna, steam rm. Minibars. Refrigerator avail. Luxury level. Cr cds: A, C, D, DS, JCB, MC, V.

D SC

★★★ **CROWNE PLAZA-UNITED NATIONS.** *304 E 42nd St (10017), between 2nd and 1st Aves, Midtown. 212/986-8800; FAX 212/986-1758; res: 800/879-8836.* 300 rms in 2 towers, 17 & 20 story. S $249-$299, D $269-$299; each addl $25; suites $349-$599; under 12 free; wkend rates. Crib free. Garage parking $20-$23. TV; cable (premium), VCR avail. Restaurant 6:30 am-10:30 pm; Sat, Sun 7 am-11 pm. Rm serv 24 hrs. Bar. Ck-out noon. Meeting rms. Business servs avail. In-rm modem link. Concierge. Exercise equipt; weight machines, bicycles; saunas. Massage. Minibars. Some balconies. Cr cds: A, C, D, DS, ER, JCB, MC, V.

D SC

✔★★ **DAYS HOTEL.** *790 Eighth Ave (10019), at 49th St, Times Square/Theater District. 212/581-7000; FAX 212/974-0291.* 367 rms, 15 story. S $130-$165; D $142-$177; each addl $20; suites $240-$365; under 18 free. Crib free. TV. Pool. Restaurant 7 am-midnight. Bar noon-2 am. Ck-out 1 pm. Meeting rm. Business servs avail. Cr cds: A, C, D, DS, JCB, MC, V.

SC

★★ **DELMONICO.** *502 Park Ave (10022), at 59th St, Midtown. 212/355-2500; FAX 212/755-3779; res: 800/821-3842.* 125 kit. suites, 32 story. Suites $295-$550; each addl $30; under 12 free; monthly, wkend rates. Crib free. Valet parking $29. TV; cable (premium), VCR avail. Bar noon-1 am. Ck-out noon. Business servs avail. In-rm modem link. Concierge. Exercise rm; instructor, bicycles, stair machine. Microwaves. Some balconies. Restored 1929 building. Cr cds: A, D, DS, MC, V.

★★★ **DORAL COURT.** *130 E 39th St (10016), between Park & Lexington Aves, Murray Hill. 212/685-1100; FAX 212/889-0287; res: 800/223-6725.* 199 rms, 16 story, 53 kit. suites. S $175-$275; D $195-$295; each addl $20; kit. suites $250-$500; under 12 free; wkend packages. Crib free. Garage $25; wkends $10. TV; cable (premium). Restaurant 7-10 am, noon-2 pm, 5-10 pm. Bar 5 pm-midnight. Ck-out 1 pm. Meeting rms. Business servs avail. Concierge. Health club privileges. Refrigerators. Some balconies. Restored hotel in quiet residential neighborhood. Cr cds: A, C, D, DS, JCB, MC, V.

SC

★★ **DORAL INN.** *541 Lexington Ave (10022), between 49th & 50th Sts, Midtown. 212/755-1200; FAX 212/319-8344; res: 800/223-6725 (NY).* 652 rms, 18 story. S $145-$180; D $155-$190; each addl $15; 1-2 bedrm suites $200-$600. Crib free. Garage parking $26, valet. TV; cable (premium). Ck-out noon. Coin lndry. Business servs avail. Concierge. Exercise rm; instructor, weights, treadmill, sauna. Many refrigerators. Cr cds: A, C, D, ER, JCB, MC, V.

SC

★★★ **DORAL PARK AVENUE.** *70 Park Ave (10016), at E 38th St, Murray Hill. 212/687-7050; FAX 212/808-9029; res: 800/223-6725.* 188 rms, 17 story. S, D $185-$325; each addl $20; suites $400-$1,000; under 12 free; wkend rates. Crib free. Parking $25. TV; cable. Restaurant 7-10:30 am, noon-2 pm, 5-10 pm. Bar noon-midnight. Ck-out noon. Business servs avail. Health club privileges. Minibars. Neo-classical decor. Cr cds: A, C, D, DS, ER, JCB, MC, V.

D SC

★★★ **DORAL TUSCANY.** *120 E 39th St (10016), between Park & Lexington Aves, Murray Hill. 212/686-1600; FAX 212/779-7822; res: 800/22-DORAL.* 121 rms, 17 story. S $185-$285; D $205-$305; each addl $20; suites $400-$850; under 12 free. Crib free. Garage $25. TV; cable (premium). Restaurant 7-10:30 am, noon-2:30 pm, 5 pm-midnight. Rm serv 6 am-10 pm. Bar 5 pm-midnight. Ck-out 1 pm. Business servs avail. Health club privileges. Bathrm phones, refrigerators, minibars. Cr cds: A, C, D, DS, JCB, MC, V.

SC

★★ **DOUBLETREE GUEST SUITES.** *1568 Broadway (10036), at 47th St & 7th Ave, Times Square/Theater District. 212/719-1600; FAX 212/921-5212.* Web www.doubletree.com. 460 suites, 43 story. S $210-$350; D $350-$750; each addl $20; under 12 free; wkend rates; higher rates special events. Crib free. Garage; valet parking $30/day. TV; cable (premium) VCR avail. Complimentary coffee in rms. Restaurant 6:30 am-11 pm. Rm serv. Bar to 1 am. Ck-out noon. Coin lndry. Meeting rms. Business servs avail. In-rm modem link. Concierge. Gift shop. Exercise equipt; weight machine, bicycles. Bathrm phones, refrigerators, minibars, wet bars. Cr cds: A, C, D, DS, JCB, MC, V.

D SC

★★★ **DRAKE SWISSÔTEL.** *440 Park Ave (10022), at E 56th St, Midtown. 212/421-0900; FAX 212/371-4190; res: 800/372-5369.* Web www.travelweb.com/thisco/swiss/9404. 494 units, 98 suites, 21 story. S $295-$315; D $325-$345; one addl $30; 1-, 2-bedrm suites $450-$1,200; under 12 free; wkend plan. Crib free. Garage $30. TV; cable (premium), VCR avail. Restaurant 6:30 am-11 pm. Rm serv 24 hrs. Bar noon-2 am. Ck-out noon. Conference facilities. Business center. In-rm modem link. Concierge. Free morning Wall Street transportation. Exercise rm; instructor, weights, rowers, sauna, steam room. Health club privileges. Bathrm phones, minibars. Wet bar in suites. Cr cds: A, C, D, DS, ER, JCB, MC, V.

D

★★ **DUMONT PLAZA.** *150 E 34th St (10016), near Lexington Ave, Murray Hill. 212/481-7600; FAX 212/889-8856; res: 800/637-8483.* 247 kit. suites, 37 story. S $189-$249; D $209-$484; each addl $20; under 12 free. Crib free. TV; cable, VCR avail. Complimentary coffee in rms. Restaurant 7 am-10 pm. Rm serv 24 hrs. Ck-out noon. Coin lndry. Meeting rms. Business servs avail. In-rm modem link. Exercise equipt; weight machines, bicycles, sauna. Microwaves. Plaza with fountain. Cr cds: A, C, D, DS, ER, JCB, MC, V.

D

★ ★ **EASTGATE TOWER SUITES.** *222 E 39th St (10016), between Lexington and Park Aves, Murray Hill. 212/687-8000; FAX 212/490-2634; res: 800/637-8483 (NY).* 188 kit. suites, 25 story. S $220-$255; D $240-$275; each addl $20; wkly rates. Garage; valet parking $22. TV; cable (premium). Restaurant noon-2 am. Bar. Ck-out noon. Business center. In-rm modem link. Exercise equipt; weight machines, stair machines. Microwaves. Landscaped plaza with gazebo, fountain. Cr cds: A, C, D, ER, JCB, MC, V.

D

✔★ ★ **EDISON.** *228 W 47th St (10036), Times Square/Theater District. 212/840-5000; FAX 212/596-6850; res: 800/637-7070.* Web www.edisonhotelnyc.com. 1,000 rms, 22 story. S $105; D $115; each addl $10; suites $150-$170; family rms $130-$135. Crib free. Garage $17.50. TV; cable (premium). Restaurant 6:15 am-midnight, Sun to 7 pm; dining rm noon-1 am. Bar noon-2 am. Ck-out 1 pm. Meeting rm. Business servs avail. Gift shop. Beauty shop. Airport transportation. Cr cds: A, C, D, DS, JCB, MC, V.

D SC

★ ★ ★ **ELYSEE.** *60 E 54th St (10022), between Park & Madison Aves, Midtown. 212/753-1066; FAX 212/980-9278; res: 800/535-9733.* 99 rms, 15 story. S, D $245-$265; suites $325-$775; under 12 free. Crib free. TV; cable, VCR (free movies). Complimentary continental bkfst; afternoon refreshments. Restaurant noon-midnight. Rm serv 7 am-10:30 pm. Bar noon-2 am. Ck-out 1 pm. Meeting rms. Business servs avail. Health club privileges. Refrigerators, bathrm phones. Microwaves avail. Country French decor, antiques. Cr cds: A, C, D, JCB, MC, V.

D

★ ★ ★ ★ **ESSEX HOUSE HOTEL NIKKO NEW YORK.** *160 Central Park South (10019), between 6th & 7th Aves, Midtown. 212/247-0300; res: 800/645-5687; FAX 212/315-1839.* This New York landmark (1931) overlooks Central Park and exemplifies classic art-deco style. The spacious guest rooms are traditional with marble baths. Many have park views. 597 units, 40 story, 80 suites. S $295-$355; D $320-$380; each addl $25; suites $395-$2,500; under 18 free; wkend rates. Crib free. Garage parking, valet $36. TV; cable (premium), VCR. Restaurants 7 am-11 pm (also see LES CÉLÉBRITÉS). Rm serv 24 hrs. Bar noon-1 am. Ck-out noon. Convention facilities. Business center. In-rm modem link. Concierge. Gift shop. Exercise rm; instructor, weight machine, bicycles, saunas, steam rms. Spa. Minibars. Cr cds: A, C, D, DS, ER, JCB, MC, V.

D

★ ★ ★ **FITZPATRICK MANHATTAN.** *687 Lexington Ave (10022), 57th St on the East Side. 212/355-0100; FAX 212/355-1371; res: 800/367-7701.* E-mail fitzusa@aol.com. 92 rms, 17 story, 52 suites. S $245; D $260; suites $295-$310; each addl in suite $25 wkday, $50 wkend; under 12 free; wkend, hol rates. Crib free. Garage $35. TV; cable (premium), VCR avail. Restaurant 7 am-10:30 pm. Rm serv 24 hrs. Bar noon-2 am. Ck-out noon. Meeting rms. Business servs avail. In-rm modem link. Concierge. Airport transportation. Health club privileges. Many refrigerators, wet bars. Cr cds: A, C, D, DS, MC, V.

SC

★ ★ ★ ★ ★ **FOUR SEASONS.** *57 E 57th St (10022), between Madison & Park Aves, on the East Side. 212/758-5700; res: 800/332-3442; FAX 212/758-5711.* Web www.fshr.com. The elegant, five-year-old, 52-story hotel—New York's tallest—offers large guest rooms, meticulous service and spectacular views of the city skyline and Central Park. The huge, multilevel marble lobby seems almost like an Egyptian monument. 370 rms, 52 story, 61 suites. S $440-$580; D $490-$675; each addl $50; suites $825-$7,000; under 12 free; wkend rates. Crib free. Pet accepted, some restrictions. Garage, valet parking $35. TV; cable (premium), VCR. Restaurant 7 am-10:30 pm (also see FIFTY SEVEN FIFTY SEVEN). Rm serv 24 hrs. Bar 11:30-1 am. Ck-out noon. Convention facilities. Business center. In-rm modem link. Concierge. Extensive exercise rm; instructor, weight machine, bicycles, whirlpool, sauna, steam rm. Massage. Health club privileges. Bathrm phones, minibars. Some terraces. Cr cds: A, C, D, ER, JCB, MC, V.

D

✔★ ★ **THE FRANKLIN.** *164 E 87th St (10128), between Lexington & 3rd Aves, Upper East Side. 212/369-1000; FAX 212/369-8000; res: 800/600-8787.* 50 rms, 9 story. S, D $169-$189. Garage parking free, in/out $10. TV; cable, VCR (free movies). Complimentary continental bkfst. Restaurant nearby. Ck-out 1 pm. Refrigerators avail. Renovated boutique hotel. Cr cds: A, MC, V.

★ ★ **GORHAM NEW YORK.** *136 W 55th St (10019), between 6th & 7th Aves, Midtown. 212/245-1800; FAX 212/582-8332; res: 800/735-0710.* 114 kit. units, 17 story. S, D $180-$320; each addl $20; suites $210-$395; under 16 free. Crib free. Garage adj $20. TV; cable (premium), VCR avail. Ck-out noon. Business servs avail. In-rm modem link. Exercise equipt; bicycle, weight machine. Microwaves. Cr cds: A, C, D, JCB, MC, V.

D SC

★ ★ ★ **GRAND HYATT.** *Park Ave at Grand Central (10017), 42nd St between Lexington & Vanderbilt, Midtown. 212/883-1234; FAX 212/697-3772.* 1,347 rms, 30 story. S $300-$325; D $325-$350; each addl $25; suites $450-$2,000; under 18 free; wkend rates. Crib free. Garage $34. TV; cable (premium). Restaurant 6:30 am-midnight. Rm serv 24 hrs. Bar 11-2 am; entertainment. Ck-out noon. Convention facilities. Business center. Drugstore. Health club privileges. Refrigerator in suites. Luxury level. Cr cds: A, C, D, DS, ER, JCB, MC, V.

D SC

★ ★ **HELMSLEY MIDDLETOWNE.** *148 E 48th St (10017), Midtown. 212/755-3000; FAX 212/832-0261; res: 800/843-2157 (exc NY).* Web hrlmsleyhotels.com. 192 rms, 17 story. S $160-$200; D $170-$210; each addl $10; suites $215-$300; under 12 free; wkend rates. Crib free. Garage; valet parking $27. TV; cable (premium), VCR avail. Complimentary coffee in lobby. Restaurant nearby. Ck-out 1 pm. Business servs avail. In-rm modem link. Health club privileges. Bathrm phones, refrigerators, microwaves, wet bars. Many balconies. Convenient to UN. Cr cds: A, C, D, DS, JCB, MC, V.

D SC

★ ★ ★ **HELMSLEY PARK LANE.** *36 Central Park South (10019), between 5th & 6th Aves, Midtown. 212/371-4000; FAX 212/319-9065; res: 800/221-4982.* E-mail sales@helmsleyparklane.com; web www.helmsleyhotel.com. 640 rms, 46 story. S, D $275-$375; each addl $30; suites $450-$1,800; under 12 free; wkend rates. Crib free. Garage parking $34. TV; VCR avail (movies). Restaurant 7 am-midnight. Rm serv 24 hrs. Bar 11-2 am. Ck-out 1 pm. Business center. In-rm modem link. Barber, beauty shop. Health club privileges. Refrigerators. Cr cds: A, C, D, DS, JCB, MC, V.

D

★ ★ **HELMSLEY WINDSOR.** *100 W 58th St (10019), at Avenue of the Americas, Midtown. 212/265-2100; FAX 212/315-0371.* 245 rms, 15 story. S $160-$195; D $170-$205; each addl $20; suites $250-$500; summer, wkend rates. Crib free. Garage $21. TV; cable (premium). Complimentary continental bkfst. No rm serv. Ck-out 1 pm. Business servs avail. Health club privileges. Serv pantry in suites. Cr cds: A, C, D, DS, JCB, MC, V.

D SC

✔★ **HERALD SQUARE.** *19 W 31st St (10001), between 5th Ave & Broadway, near Macy's, south of Midtown. 212/279-4017; FAX 212/643-9208; res: 800/727-1888.* 114 rms, some share bath, 9 story. S $50-$95; D $95-$125; each addl $5; under 10 free. Crib free. Garage $20-$25. TV; cable. Restaurant nearby. No rm serv. Ck-out noon. No bellhops. Airport transportation. In landmark beaux-arts building (1893) designed by Carrere and Hastings; was once lived in by Charles Dana Gibson, illustrator who created the Gibson girl; was original headquarters of Life magazine. Hotel interior decorated with Life covers & graphics.

Located in shopping area; midway between Midtown & Downtown. Cr cds: A, DS, JCB, MC, V.

★ ★ ★ **HILTON AND TOWERS AT ROCKEFELLER CENTER.** *1335 Avenue of the Americas (10019), between W 53rd & 54th Sts, Midtown. 212/586-7000; FAX 212/315-1374.* Web www.travelweb.com. 2,040 rms, 46 story. S $185-$295; D $215-$325; each addl $30; suites $425-$625; family rates; package plans. Crib free. Pet accepted. Garage $35. TV; cable (premium), VCR avail. Restaurant 6 am-midnight. Bar 11-2 am. Ck-out noon. Convention facilities. Business center. In-rm modem link. Shopping arcade. Barber, beauty shop. Exercise rm; instructor, weights, bicycles, sauna. Minibars. Refrigerators avail. Luxury level. Cr cds: A, C, D, DS, ER, JCB, MC, V.

D

★ ★ **HOLIDAY INN-DOWNTOWN.** *138 Lafayette St (10013), at Howard St, in Chinatown. 212/966-8898; FAX 212/966-3933.* 223 rms, 14 story. S, D $155-$185; each addl $15; suites $175-$205; under 12 free. Crib free. Valet parking $25. TV; cable. Complimentary coffee in rms. Restaurant 6:30 am-11 pm. Bar noon-midnight. Ck-out noon. Meeting rms. Business servs avail. In-rm modem link. Concierge. Health club privileges. Renovated landmark building. Cr cds: A, C, D, DS, JCB, MC, V.

D SC

✔★ ★ **HOWARD JOHNSON PLAZA.** *851 Eighth Ave (10019), between 51st and 52nd Sts, Midtown. 212/581-4100; FAX 212/974-7502.* 300 rms, 11 story. S $130-$202; D $142-$214; each addl $20; suites $281-$325; under 17 free; wkend packages. Crib free. Garage $11. TV; cable. Restaurant 6 am-midnight. Bar 11-2 am. Ck-out 1 pm. Business servs avail. Gift shop. Health club privileges. Cr cds: A, C, D, DS, JCB, MC, V.

SC

★ ★ ★ **INTER-CONTINENTAL.** *111 E 48th St (10017), between Lexington & Park Aves, Midtown. 212/755-5900; FAX 212/644-0079; res: 800/327-0200.* E-mail newyork@interconti.com; web www.interconti.com. 683 rms, 14 story. S, D $250-$369; each addl $40; suites $495-$4,500; under 14 free; wkend package. Crib free. Garage parking $35; valet. TV; cable (premium). Restaurant 7 am-midnight. Bar 11:30-1 am. Ck-out noon. Meeting rms. Business center. In-rm modem link. Concierge. Gift shop. Exercise equipt; bicycles, stair machine, sauna, steam room. Massage. Minibars. Microwaves avail. Cr cds: A, C, D, DS, ER, JCB, MC, V.

D

★ ★ **JOLLY MADISON TOWERS.** *22 E 38th St (10016), at Madison Ave, Midtown. 212/802-0600; FAX 212/447-0747; res: 800/225-4340.* 225 rms, 18 story. S $160-$190, D $170-$200; each addl $30; suites $300; under 12 free. Crib free. TV; cable (premium). Restaurant 6:30 am-11 pm. Bar 10-1 am. Ck-out noon. Business servs avail. In-rm modem link. Concierge. Cr cds: A, C, D, JCB, MC, V.

SC

★ ★ ★ **KIMBERLY.** *145 E 50th St (10022), between Lexington & 3rd Ave, Midtown. 212/755-0400; FAX 212/486-6915; res: 800/683-0400.* 184 suites, 30 story. S, D $235-$415; under 18 free. Crib free. Garage parking $24. TV; cable (premium), VCR avail. Complimentary coffee in rms. Restaurant 7 am-11 pm. Bar noon-midnight; entertainment Thurs-Sat. Ck-out noon. Coin lndry. Business servs avail. Concierge. Health club privileges. Minibars. Terraces. Cr cds: A, C, D, DS, JCB, MC, V.

★ ★ ★ **THE KITANO.** *66 Park Ave (10016), at 38th ST, in Murray Hill. 212/885-7000; res 800/548-2666; FAX 212/885-7100.* 149 rms, 18 story, 18 suites. S, D $285-$395; each addl $25; suites $465-$1,295; under 12 free; wkend rates. Crib free. Valet parking $26-$30. TV; cable (premium), VCR avail. Complimentary green tea in rms. Restaurants 6 am-11 pm. Bar 5 pm-12:30 am; entertainment. Ck-out noon. Meeting rms. Business servs avail. In-rm modem link. Concierge. Gift shop. Health club privileges. Minibars. Cr cds: A, C, D, DS, JCB, MC, V.

D SC

✔★ ★ **LEXINGTON.** *511 Lexington Ave (10017), at E 48th St, Midtown. 212/755-4400; FAX 212/751-4091; res: 800/448-4471.* 700 rms, 27 story. S, D $165-$185; each addl $15; suites $325-$550. Crib free. TV; cable (premium). Restaurant 6:30 am-midnight; entertainment. Bar 4 pm-1 am. Ck-out noon. Meeting rm. Business servs avail. Exercise equipt; bicycle, treadmill. Refrigerators, microwaves. Near Grand Central Station. Cr cds: A, C, D, DS, ER, JCB, MC, V.

SC

★ ★ **LOEWS NEW YORK.** *569 Lexington Ave (10022), at E 51st St, Midtown. 212/752-7000; FAX 212/758-6311.* Web www.loewshotels.com. 722 rms, 20 story. S, D $189-$279; each addl $25; suites $250-$850; under 16 free; wkend rates. Crib free. Pet accepted, some restrictions. Garage $25. TV; cable (premium). Restaurant 7 am-midnight. Bar 11-2 am. Ck-out noon. Meeting rms. Business center. In-rm modem link. Barber. Exercise rm; instructor, weight machines, bicycles, sauna. Bathrm phones, refrigerators; microwaves avail. Luxury level. Cr cds: A, C, D, DS, JCB, MC, V.

D SC

★ ★ ★ **THE LOMBARDY.** *111 E 56th St (10022), between Park & Lexington Aves, Midtown. 212/753-8600; res: 800/223-5254; FAX 212/754-5683.* Web www.primahotels.com. 105 kit. units, 21 story, 60 suites. S, D $230; each addl $20; suites $295; under 12 free; wkend rates (summer). Crib free. Garage parking $18. TV; cable (premium), VCR avail. Restaurant noon-10 pm. Rm serv from 6 am. Bar noon-midnight. Ck-out 1 pm. Meeting rms. Business servs avail. In-rm modem link. Concierge. Exercise equipt; bicycle, stair machine. Refrigerators; many microwaves. Some balconies. Cr cds: A, C, D, DS, JCB, MC, V.

D

★ ★ ★ ★ **LOWELL.** *28 E 63rd St (10021), between Madison & Park Aves, Upper East Side. 212/838-1400; FAX 212/319-4230; res: 800/221-4444.* E-mail lowellhtl@aol.com; web www.preferredhotels.com/preferred.html. Accommodations are elegant, decorated with French and Oriental period furnishings, in this New York institution. 65 rms, 17 story, 56 kit. suites. S, D $315-$415; each addl $20; kit. suites $515-$1,800; under 12 free; wkend rates. Crib free. Valet parking $35. TV; cable (premium), VCR (movies). Restaurants 7 am-11 pm. Afternoon tea 3:30-6:30 pm. Bar noon-midnight. Ck-out 1 pm. Meeting rm. Business servs avail. In-rm modem link. Concierge. Exercise equipt; bicycles, treadmills. Health club privileges. Bathrm phones, refrigerators, minibars; many fireplaces; microwaves avail. Some balconies. Cr cds: A, C, D, DS, ER, JCB, MC, V.

D

LUXURY COLLECTION. *(New management, therefore not rated) 112 Central Park South (10019), near 6th Ave, Midtown. 212/757-1900; FAX 212/757-9620.* 214 rms, 25 story. S, D $199-$529; each addl $30; suites $595-$4,000; under 16 free. Crib free. Garage $35. TV; cable (premium), VCR avail. Restaurant (see FANTINO). Rm serv 24 hrs. Bar noon-1 am. Ck-out noon. Business center. In-rm modem link. Exercise rm; instructor, bicycles, treadmill, sauna. Massage. Health club privileges. Some refrigerators. Cr cds: A, C, D, DS, ER, JCB, MC, V.

D SC

★ ★ **LYDEN GARDENS.** *215 E 64th St (10021), between Second & Third Aves, Upper East Side. 212/355-1230; FAX 212/758-7858; res: 800/637-8483.* 133 kit. suites, 13 story. S $225-$245; D $245-$265; each addl $20; 1-bedrm $269-$289; 2-bedrm $450-$470; under 12 free; wkend rates. Crib free. Garage $18.50. TV; cable (premium). Complimentary coffee in rms. Restaurant nearby. No rm serv. Ck-out noon. Business servs avail. Concierge. Health club privileges. Microwaves. Terraces, gardens. Cr cds: A, C, D, ER, JCB, MC, V.

D

★ ★ **LYDEN HOUSE.** *320 E 53rd St (10022), Midtown, between 1st & 2nd Aves. 212/888-6070; FAX 212/935-7690; res: 800/637-8483.* 81 kit. units, 11 story, 8 suites. S, studio rms $220; D $220-$240; suites $240-$269; under 12 free; wkend rates. Crib free. TV; cable (premium).

Coffee in rms. Ck-out noon. Coin Indry. Health club privileges. Microwaves. Cr cds: A, C, D, DS, ER, JCB, MC, V.

D

★ ★ **THE MANSFIELD.** *12 W 44th St (10036), between 5th & 6th Aves, Midtown. 212/944-6050; FAX 212/764-4477; res: 800/255-5167.* 123 rms, 36 with shower only, 13 story, 24 suites. S, D $195-$245; suites $275; wkend rates. Crib free. TV; cable (premium), VCR (free movies). Complimentary continental bkfst. Ck-out noon. Business servs avail. Concierge. Free garage parking. Health club privileges. Refrigerators. Cr cds: A, MC, V.

★ ★ ★ **THE MARK.** *25 E 77th St (10021), between Madison & 5th Aves, Upper East Side. 212/744-4300; FAX 212/744-2749; res: 800/843-6275.* 120 rms, 16 story, 60 suites. S $355-$405; D $380-$430; each addl $25; suites $550-$2,500; under 15 free; wkend, hol rates. Crib free. Garage $35. TV; cable (premium), VCR (movies). Restaurant 7 am-10:30 pm. Rm serv 24 hrs. Bar 12:30 pm-midnight. Ck-out 1 pm. Meeting rms. Business servs avail. In-rm modem link. Concierge. Exercise equipt; bicycles, treadmill, sauna, steam rm. Bathrm phones. Cr cds: A, C, D, DS, ER, JCB, MC, V.

D

★ ★ ★ **MARRIOTT-EAST SIDE.** *525 Lexington Ave (10017), between E 48th and 49th Sts, Midtown. 212/755-4000; FAX 212/751-3440.* 650 rms, 34 story. S, D $189-$299; suites $600-$900; under 18 free; wkend packages. Crib free. TV; cable (premium). Restaurant 7 am-10 pm. Bar noon-1 am. Ck-out noon. Business center. In-rm modem link. Concierge. Exercise equipt; weight machine, stair machine. Bathrm phones, minibars. Designed by Arthur Loomis Harmon, architect of Empire State Bldg; hotel was subject of Georgia O'Keefe cityscapes. Luxury level. Cr cds: A, C, D, DS, ER, JCB, MC, V.

D SC

★ ★ ★ **MARRIOTT-FINANCIAL CENTER.** *85 West St (10006), at Albany St, Financial District. 212/385-4900; FAX 212/227-8136.* 504 rms, 38 story. S $269; D $289; each addl $25; suites $349-$1,500; under 18 free; wkend rates. Crib free. Garage parking $23. TV; cable (premium), VCR avail (movies). Indoor pool. Restaurant 6:30 am-10 pm. Bar 11:30-2 am. Ck-out 11 am. Convention facilities. Business center. In-rm modem link. Concierge. Gift shop. Exercise rm; instructor, weight machine, bicycles, sauna, steam rm. Massage. Microwaves avail. Walking distance to Wall St, ferry to Statue of Liberty. Cr cds: A, C, D, DS, ER, JCB, MC, V.

D SC

★ ★ ★ **MARRIOTT MARQUIS.** *1535 Broadway (10036), between 45th & 46th Sts, Times Square/Theater District. 212/398-1900; FAX 212/704-8930.* 1,919 rms, 50 story. S $216-$350; D $225-$360; each addl $15; suites $400-$3,500; under 18 free; package plans. Covered parking, valet $35. TV; cable (premium). Restaurants 7 am-midnight (also see THE VIEW). Rm serv 24 hrs. Bars. Ck-out noon. Convention facilities. Business center. In-rm modem link. Concierge. Gift shop. Exercise equipt; weights, bicycles, sauna, steam rm. Whirlpool. Minibars. Luxury level. Cr cds: A, C, D, DS, JCB, MC, V.

D SC

★ ★ ★ **MARRIOTT-WORLD TRADE CENTER.** *3 World Trade Center (10048), main entrance West St at Liberty St, in Financial District. 212/938-9100; FAX 212/444-3444.* Web www.marriott.com. 820 rms, 23 story. S $269; D $289-$319; each addl $25; suites $369-$800; under 12 free; wkend rates. Garage parking $23. TV; cable, VCR avail (movies). Indoor pool; lifeguard. Restaurant 6:30 am-11 pm. Rm serv 24 hrs. Bar noon-1 am. Ck-out 1 pm. Convention facilities. Business center. In-rm modem link. Concierge. Gift shop. Raquetball court. Exercise rm; instructor, weight machine, treadmill, sauna. Massage. Minibars. Cr cds: A, C, D, DS, ER, JCB, MC, V.

D

★ ★ **THE MAYFLOWER.** *15 Central Park West (10023), at 61st St, Upper West Side. 212/265-0060; FAX 212/265-5098; res: 800/223-4164.* 365 rms, 18 story, 200 suites. S $155-$195; D $170-$210; each addl $20; suites $205-$285; under 18 free; wkly, wkend, hol rates; lower rates July, Aug & mid-Dec-Mar 31. Pet accepted. Garage parking, valet $25. TV; cable (premium). Restaurant 7 am-10 pm. Bar 11:30-1 am. Ck-out noon. Meeting rms. Business servs avail. In-rm modem link. Concierge. Exercise equipt; treadmill, stair machine. Many refrigerators. Some terraces. Cr cds: A, C, D, DS, ER, JCB, MC, V.

SC

★ ★ ★ **THE MICHELANGELO.** *152 W 51st St (10019), between 6th & 7th Aves, Times Square/Theater District. 212/765-1900; FAX 212/541-6604; res: 800/237-0990.* 178 rms, 7 story, 52 suites. S, D $275-$325; each addl $30; suites $375-$950; under 16 free; wkend rates. Crib free. Valet parking $28/day. TV; cable (premium), VCR avail (movies $5). Complimentary continental bkfst. Restaurant 7 am-2:30 pm, 5:30-11:30 pm. Rm serv 24 hrs. Bar. Ck-out 1 pm. Meeting rms. Business center. In-rm modem link. Concierge. Exercise equipt; treadmill, weight machine. Health club privileges. Bathrm phones; minibars. Refrigerators avail. Cr cds: A, C, D, DS, ER, JCB, MC, V.

D

★ ★ ★ ★ **MILLENIUM HILTON.** *55 Church St (10007), Dey & Fulton Sts, Financial District. 212/693-2001; res: 800/445-8667; FAX 212/571-2316.* A high-rise hotel with a high-tech look, this property has amenities for both business and pleasure. 561 units, 55 story. S $290-$350; D $320-$370; each addl $25; suites $450-$1,500; under 16 free; wkend rates; package plans. Crib free. Garage; valet parking $35. TV; cable (premium), VCR avail. Indoor pool; lifeguard. Supervised child's activities (wkends). Restaurants 6:30 am-midnight. Rm serv 24 hrs. Bar 11:30-1:30 am; pianist exc Sun. Ck-out noon. Meeting rms. Business center. In-rm modem link. Concierge. Gift shop. Exercise rm; instructor, weight machine, bicycles, sauna. Massage. Bathrm phones, minibars. Cr cds: A, D, DS, ER, JCB, MC, V.

D SC

★ ★ ★ **MILLENNIUM BROADWAY.** *145 W 44th St (10036), between Sixth Ave & Broadway, Times Square/Theater District. 212/768-4400; FAX 212/789-7688; res: 800/622-5569.* Web www.mill.bdwy.com. 627 rms, 52 story. S $250-$300; D $270-$320; suites $495-$3,500; under 18 free; wkend rates. Crib free. Valet parking $30. TV; cable (premium), VCR avail. Restaurant 6:30 am-11 pm. Bar 11-1 am. Ck-out noon. Convention facilities. Business center. In-rm modem link. Concierge. Gift shop. Exercise equipt; weights, bicycles, steam rm. Massage. Health club privileges. Minibars. Bathrm phone in suites. Post-modern skyscraper, with moderne setbacks, deco detailing, incorporates landmark, beaux-arts Hudson Theatre (1903), which has been restored. Cr cds: A, C, D, DS, ER, JCB, MC, V.

D SC

★ ★ ★ **MORGANS.** *237 Madison Ave (10016), between 37th & 38th Sts, Murray Hill. 212/686-0300; FAX 212/779-8352; res: 800/334-3408.* 113 rms, 19 story. S $205-$250; D $230-$275; each addl $30; suites $395-$600; under 12 free; wkend rates. Garage, valet parking $32. TV; cable (premium). Complimentary continental bkfst. Rm serv 24 hrs. Bar 5 pm-4 am; Sun, Mon to 2 am. Ck-out 1 pm. Business servs avail. In-rm modem link. Concierge. Health club privileges. Bathrm phones, refrigerators, minibars. Andree Putman designed interiors; combines high-tech ultra-modern look with 1930s moderne styling. Cr cds: A, C, D, ER, JCB, MC, V.

★ ★ ★ **NEW YORK HELMSLEY.** *212 E 42nd St (10017), between Second and Third Aves, on the East Side. 212/490-8900; FAX 212/986-4792; res: 800/221-4982.* Web www.helmsleyhotels.com. 800 rms, 41 story. S $230-$270; D $255-$295; each addl $30; suites $500-$875; under 12 free; wkend plan. Crib free. Garage $33. TV; cable, VCR avail (movies). Restaurant 7 am-11:30 pm. Bar 11-1 am; entertainment. Ck-out noon. Meeting rms. Business center. In-rm modem link. Gift shop. Health club privileges. Bathrm phones; some refrigerators. 2 blks E of Grand Central Station. Cr cds: A, C, D, DS, JCB, MC, V.

D

★ ★ ★ ★ **THE NEW YORK PALACE.** *455 Madison Ave (10022), at 50th St, Midtown. 212/888-7000; FAX 212/303-6000; res: 800/697-2522.* E-mail hrihotel@haven.ios.com; web www.nypalace.com. Rooms in this centrally located New York institution have it all—from large desks for the business traveler to plush, pillow-covered beds for the vacationer. The dramatically renovated lobby leads out to one of the most famous areas of Manhattan. 900 rms, 53 story, 104 suites. S, D $395-$425; suites $650-$7,500; under 18 free; wkend rates. Crib free. Garage parking $48. TV; cable, VCR avail (movies). Restaurants 6:30 am-10:30 pm (also see LE CIRQUE 2000). Rm serv 24 hrs. Bars 11:30-1 am. Ck-out 1 pm. Meeting rms. Business center. In-rm modem link. Concierge. Exercise rm; instructor, weights, treadmills, steam rm. Massage. Health club privileges. Refrigerator in suites. Cr cds: A, C, D, DS, JCB, MC, V.

D

✔★ ★ **NEW YORK'S HOTEL PENNSYLVANIA.** *401 Seventh Ave (10001), at 33rd St, opp Madison Square Garden, in Garment District. 212/736-5000; FAX 212/502-8712; res: 800/223-8585.* 1,705 rms, 22 story. S, D $149; suites $250-$450; under 16 free. Crib free. Garage $26. TV; VCR avail. Restaurant 6:30-1 am. Bar noon-2 am, entertainment. Ck-out noon. Convention facilities. Business servs avail. Concierge. Shopping arcade. Barber, beauty shop. Health club privileges. Cr cds: A, C, D, DS, ER, JCB, MC, V.

D SC

★ ★ **NOVOTEL.** *226 W 52nd St (10019), at Broadway, Midtown. 212/315-0100; FAX 212/765-5369; res: 800/221-3185.* 474 rms, 33 story. S, D $179-$279; each addl $20; under 16 free. Crib $10. Pet accepted. Parking $12. TV; cable (premium). Complimentary coffee in lobby. Restaurant 6 am-midnight. Bar 3:30 pm-1 am; entertainment exc Sun. Ck-out 1 pm. Meeting rm. Business center. In-rm modem link. Exercise equipt; weights, treadmill. Cr cds: A, C, D, ER, JCB, MC, V.

D SC

★ ★ ★ **OMNI BERKSHIRE PLACE.** *21 E 52nd St (10022), between Madison and 5th Aves, in Midtown. 212/753-5800; FAX 212/754-5020.* E-mail williamd@interport.com; web www.omnihotels.com. 396 rms, 21 story, 64 suites. S, D $355-$395; each addl $30; suites $695-$1,200; under 17 free; wkend rates (2-day min). Valet parking $32. TV; cable (premium), VCR avail. Restaurant 6:30 am-9 pm; wkend hrs vary. Rm serv 24 hrs. Bar 11-1:30 am. Ck-out noon. Meeting rms. Business center. In-rm modem link. Concierge. Gift shop. Exercise equipt; weights, bicycles. Health club privileges. Minibars. Balconies. Cr cds: A, C, D, DS, ER, JCB, MC, V.

D SC

★ ★ ★ **PARAMOUNT.** *235 W 46th St (10036), between Broadway & Eighth Ave, Times Square/Theater District. 212/764-5500; FAX 212/354-5237; res: 800/225-7474.* 600 rms, 20 story. S $160-$250; D $195-$265; each addl $20; suites $395-$495; under 16 free; monthly rates; wkend packages. Crib free. Garage $20. TV; cable (premium), VCR (movies). Restaurant 7-1 am; Fri, Sat to 2 am. Bar 4 pm-4 am; Sun to 3 am. Ck-out noon. Meeting rms. Business center. In-rm modem link. Concierge. Exercise equipt; weight machine, treadmill. Public areas and guest rms designed in a high-tech, futuristic style. Cr cds: A, D, DS, JCB, MC, V.

D

★ ★ ★ **PARKER MERIDIEN.** *118 W 57th St (10019), between 6th & 7th Aves, Midtown. 212/245-5000; FAX 212/708-7477; res: 800/543-4300.* Web www.parkermeridien.com. 700 rms, 42 story. S $300-$340; D $325-$365; each addl $30; suites $325-$2,500; under 12 free; wkend plan. Crib free. Pet accepted. Garage parking, valet $32. TV; VCR avail. Indoor pool; whirlpool. Restaurant 6:30 am-10:45 pm. Rm serv 24 hrs. Bar 3 pm-midnight. Ck-out 1 pm. Business center. In-rm modem link. Exercise rm; instructor, bicycles, stair machine, sauna. Microwaves avail. French ambience; Italian marble flooring, French tapestries. Cr cds: A, C, D, DS, ER, JCB, MC, V.

D

★ ★ ★ ★ **THE PENINSULA NEW YORK.** *700 Fifth Ave (10019), at 55th St, Midtown. 212/247-2200; FAX 212/903-3949; res: 800/262-9467.* E-mail pny@peninsula.com; web www.peninsula.com. The lobby of this 1905 Beaux Arts building features a vast marble staircase and a lavish carved ceiling. 200 rms, 23 story, 42 suites. S, D $365-$475; each addl $20; suites $700-$4,500; under 12 free. Crib free. Parking $31. TV; cable (premium), VCR avail (movies). Indoor pool; whirlpool, poolside serv, lifeguard. Restaurant 7 am-midnight (also see ADRIENNE). Rm serv 24 hrs. Afternoon tea in Gotham Lounge 2:30-5:30 pm. Rooftop bar noon-midnight; closed Sun. Ck-out noon. Meeting rms. Business servs avail. In-rm modem link. Concierge. Extensive exercise rm; instructor, weight machines, bicycles, sauna, steam rm. Spa. Bathrm phones, minibars. Cr cds: A, C, D, DS, ER, JCB, MC, V.

★ ★ ★ ★ **THE PIERRE.** *2 E 61st St (10021), at Fifth Ave, Midtown. 212/838-8000; FAX 212/940-8109; res: 800/743-7734.* Web www.fourseasons.com. Personal service and traditional style are hallmarks of this landmark at Central Park. 202 rms, 42 story. S $425-$625; D $475-$675; suites $695-$1,100. Crib free. Garage $33. TV; cable (premium), VCR avail. Restaurants 7-1 am (also see CAFE PIERRE; and see THE ROTUNDA, Unrated Dining). Rm serv 24 hrs. Bar from 11 am; entertainment from 8 pm. Ck-out noon. Meeting rms. Business servs avail. In-rm modem link. Concierge. Barber, beauty shop. Exercise equipt; bicycles, treadmill. Massage. Health club privileges. Minibars. Serv pantry in suites. Cr cds: A, C, D, DS, ER, JCB, MC, V.

D

★ ★ ★ ★ **PLAZA ATHÉNÉE.** *37 E 64th St (10021), between Madison & Park Aves, Upper East Side. 212/734-9100; FAX 212/772-0958; res: 800/447-8800.* Marble, reproductions of fine antiques, and Oriental rugs add style to this tastefully decorated hotel in the mode of the Paris original. The property is grand, but on an intimate scale. 153 rms, 17 story. S, D $370-$560; each addl $35; suites $690-$2,900. Crib free. Parking $38/day. TV; cable (premium), VCR avail. Restaurant 7 am-9:30 pm (also see LE RÉGENCE). Rm serv 24 hrs. Bar 11 am-midnight. Ck-out 1 pm. Meeting rm. Business servs avail. In-rm modem link. Concierge. Exercise equipt; weights, bicycles. Health club privileges. Refrigerators. Some suites with private dining rm. Some private patios, glassed-in balconies. Cr cds: A, C, D, ER, JCB, MC, V.

D

★ ★ ★ **PLAZA FIFTY.** *155 E 50th St (10022), between Lexington & 3rd Aves, Midtown. 212/751-5710; FAX 212/753-1468; res: 800/ME-SUITE.* 209 rms, 22 story, 135 suites. S $229; D $249; each addl $20; suites $279-$459; under 12 free; wkend rates. Crib free. TV; cable (premium). Coffee in rms. Ck-out noon. Business servs avail. In-rm modem link. Exercise equipt; bicycles, stair machine. Refrigerators, microwaves. Some balconies. Cr cds: A, C, D, ER, JCB, MC, V.

D

★ ★ ★ ★ **THE PLAZA HOTEL.** *Fifth Ave at 59th St & Central Park South (10019), Midtown. 212/759-3000; FAX 212/759-3167; res: 800/759-3000.* E-mail plaza@fairmont.com; web www.fairmont.com. Set on the southwest corner of Central Park West and Fifth Avenue, the world-renowned Plaza occupies one of the most valuable pieces of real estate in Manhattan. Spacious guest rooms are furnished in fine period details, including marble fireplaces and crystal chandeliers. A drink at the Oak Bar or brunch at Palm Court are New York experiences that should not be missed. 805 rms, 18 story. S, D $250-$675; each addl $35; suites $450-$3,500; under 18 free. Crib free. Garage $35. TV; cable (premium), VCR avail. Restaurants (see OAK ROOM and PALM COURT). Rm serv 24 hrs. Bar 11-2 am. Ck-out noon. Business center. In-rm modem link. Concierge. Gift shop. Barber, beauty shop. Exercise equipt; bicycles, treadmills. Health club privileges. Refrigerators, minibars. Cr cds: A, C, D, DS, ER, JCB, MC, V.

D SC

★ **QUALITY HOTEL FIFTH AVENUE.** *3 E 40th St (10016), between Fifth & Madison Aves, Murray Hill. 212/447-1500; FAX 212/213-0972.* 189 rms, 30 story. S $162-$180; D $177-$199; each addl $15; wkend rates; under 18 free. Crib free. Garage parking $18. TV; cable (premium). Complimentary coffee in rms. Restaurant adj. Ck-out noon.

Business servs avail. In-rm modem link. Health club privileges. Cr cds: A, C, D, DS, ER, JCB, MC, V.

D SC

★ ★ **RADISSON EMPIRE.** *44 W 63rd St (10023), at Lincoln Center, Upper West Side. 212/265-7400; FAX 212/315-0349.* 375 rms, 11 story. S, D $155-$245; each addl $20; suites $275-$600; under 17 free. Crib free. Garage $20. TV; cable (premium), VCR (movies). Restaurant 6:30-11 am, 5 pm-midnight. Rm serv 24 hrs. Bar 11 am-midnight. Ck-out noon. Business servs avail. In-rm modem link. Health club privileges. Cr cds: A, C, D, DS, ER, JCB, MC, V.

D SC

✔★ ★ **RAMADA MILFORD PLAZA.** *270 W 45th St (10036), at Eighth Ave, Times Square/Theater District. 212/869-3600; FAX 212/944-8357.* 1,300 rms, 28 story. S $109-$179; D $114-$194; each addl $15; suites $260-$500; under 14 free. Crib free. Garage $11. TV; cable (premium). Restaurant 7 am-11 pm. Bar from noon. Ck-out noon. Convention facilities. Business servs avail. In-rm modem link. Exercise equipt; weight machine, bicycles. Refrigerators avail. Cr cds: A, C, D, DS, ER, JCB, MC, V.

SC

★ ★ ★ ★ **THE REGENCY HOTEL.** *540 Park Ave (10021), at E 61st St, Upper East Side. 212/759-4100; FAX 212/826-5674; res: 800/233-2356.* Web www.loewshotels.com. The graceful guest rooms here are decorated with period furniture, and suites have marble foyers. 362 rms, 21 story, 185 kit. suites. S, D $315-$395; suites $420-$1,800 under 18 free; wkend rates. Crib free. Garage $32. TV; cable (premium), VCR. Restaurant (see 540 PARK). Rm serv 24 hrs. Ck-out 1 pm. Meeting rms. Business center. In-rm modem link. Concierge. Barber, beauty shop. Exercise rm; instructor, weights, bicycles, sauna. Massage. Refrigerators, bathrm TVs. Cr cds: A, C, D, DS, MC, V.

D

★ ★ ★ **RENAISSANCE NEW YORK.** *714 7th Ave (10036), Times Square/Theater District, between 47th & 48th Sts. 212/765-7676; FAX 212/765-1962.* 305 rms, 26 story. S, D $275-$330; each addl $20; suites $425-$450; under 12 free; wkend rates. Crib free. Garage $28. TV; cable (premium), VCR. Complimentary coffee in rms. Restaurant 6:30 am-11 pm. Rm serv 24 hrs. Bar; pianist. Ck-out noon. Meeting rms. Business servs avail. In-rm modem link. Concierge. Masseur avail. Exercise equipt; weight machine, treadmill. Minibars. Cr cds: A, C, D, DS, ER, JCB, MC, V.

D SC

★ ★ ★ **RIHGA ROYAL.** *151 W 54th St (10019), between Sixth and Seventh Aves, Midtown. 212/307-5000; FAX 212/765-6530; res: 800/937-5454.* 496 suites, 54 story. 1-bedrm $350-$500; 2-bedrm $700-$1,000; each addl $25; Crown suites $1,200; Grand Royal suites S, D $2,500-$2,800; family, wkend, hol rates. Crib free. Garage, valet parking $35. TV; cable, VCR. Restaurant 6:30-1 am. Rm serv 24 hrs. Bar 11:30-2 am; entertainment. Ck-out 1 pm. Meeting rms. Business center. In-rm modem link. Concierge. Exercise rm; instructor, weights, bicycles, sauna. Bathrm phones, refrigerators, minibars. Complimentary shoeshine. Architecturally reminiscent of the classic skyscrapers of the 1920s and 1930s. Cr cds: A, C, D, DS, ER, JCB, MC, V.

D

★ ★ **ROGER WILLIAMS.** *131 Madison Ave (10016), in Murray Hill. 212/448-7000; FAX 212/448-7007.* 200 rms, 20 with shower only, 15 story. S, D $165; each addl $20; suites $225; under 12 free. Crib free. Garage parking $25. TV; cable (premium), VCR (movies). Complimentary continental bkfst. Restaurant nearby. No rm serv. Ck-out 1 pm. Business servs avail. In-rm modem link. Concierge. Health club privileges. Bathrm phones. Cr cds: A, D, MC, V.

D

★ ★ ★ **ROYALTON.** *44 W 44th St (10036), between Fifth & Sixth ave, Midtown. 212/869-4400; FAX 212/869-8965; res: 800/635-9013.* 205 rms, some with shower only, 16 story. S $295-$390; D $330-$400; each addl $30; suites $450; wkend rates. Crib $25. Pet accepted, some restrictions. Valet parking $38. TV; cable (premium), VCR (movies). Restaurant 7-1 am. Rm serv 24 hrs. Bar. Ck-out 1 pm. Meeting rm. Business servs avail. In-rm modem link. Concierge. Exercise equipt; bicycles, treadmill. Bathrm phones, refrigerators, minibars; some fireplaces. Some balconies. Ultramodern rm decor. Cr cds: A, C, D, ER, JCB, MC, V.

D

★ ★ **SALISBURY.** *123 W 57th St (10019), between 6th & 7th Aves, Midtown. 212/246-1300; res: 888/223-5757; FAX 212/977-7752.* E-mail nycsalisbury@worldnet.att.net; web www.nycsalisbury.com. 320 rms, 17 story. S $189; D $209; each addl $20; suites $239-$349; under 15 free; wkend rates. Crib free. TV; cable, VCR avail. Complimentary continental bkfst. Ck-out noon. Meeting rms. Business servs avail. In-rm modem link. Concierge. Health club privileges. Many refrigerators. Cr cds: A, C, D, JCB, MC, V.

SC

★ ★ **SAN CARLOS.** *150 E 50th St (10022), Midtown, between Lexington & 3rd. 212/755-1800; FAX 212/688-9778; res: 800/722-2012.* E-mail sancarlos@pobox.com; web www.sancarlos.com. 200 rms, 18 story, 138 kits. S $160-$180; D $170-$190; each addl $10; suites $200-$275; under 14 free; wkend rates. Crib free. TV, cable (premium). Complimentary continental bkfst. Restaurant 6 am-11 pm. Ck-out 11 am. Coin lndry. In-rm modem link. Microwaves. Cr cds: A, C, D, JCB, MC, V.

★ ★ **SEAPORT SUITES.** *129 Front St (10005), between Wall & Pine Sts, at South Street Seaport, in Financial District. 212/742-0003; FAX 212/742-0124; res: 800/77-SUITE.* 49 kit. suites, 8 story. S, D $195-$235; under 12 free; wkend rates. Crib avail. Garage parking $15. TV; cable (premium), VCR (movies $2). Complimentary continental bkfst. Complimentary coffee in rms. Restaurant noon-midnight; closed Sat, Sun. No rm serv. Bar. Ck-out noon. Meeting rm. Business servs avail. In-rm modem link. Concierge. Health club privileges. Microwaves. Cr cds: A, D, MC, V.

★ ★ ★ **SHELBURNE MURRAY HILL.** *303 Lexington Ave (10016), between 37th & 38th Sts, Murray Hill. 212/689-5200; FAX 212/779-7068; res: 800/637-8483.* 258 suites, 16 story. Suites $205-$450; under 12 free; wkend rates. Garage $24; $21 wkends. TV; cable (premium), VCR avail. Restaurant 7 am-11 pm. Bar. Ck-out noon. Coin lndry. Convention facilities. Business servs avail. In-rm modem link. Concierge. Exercise equipt; weights, bicycles, sauna. Microwaves. Private patios, balconies. Cr cds: A, C, D, DS, JCB, MC, V.

D

★ ★ ★ **SHERATON MANHATTAN.** *790 Seventh Ave (10019), between W 51st & 52nd Sts, Midtown. 212/581-3300; FAX 212/262-4410.* 650 rms, 22 story. S, D $210-$275; each addl $30; suites $350-$650; under 17 free; wkend plans. Crib free. Garage $19. TV; cable (premium), VCR avail. Indoor pool; lifeguard. Complimentary continental bkfst. Complimentary coffee in rms. Restaurant 6:30 am-11 pm. Rm serv 24 hrs. Bar 11 am-11 pm. Ck-out noon. Business center. In-rm modem link. Concierge. Gift shop. Exercise rm; instructor, weight machine, bicycles. Minibars. Refrigerators, microwaves avail. Cr cds: A, C, D, DS, ER, JCB, MC, V.

D SC

★ ★ ★ **SHERATON NEW YORK HOTEL & TOWERS.** *811 Seventh Ave (10019), between 52nd & 53rd Sts, Midtown. 212/581-1000; FAX 212/262-4410.* Web www.sheratonhotelsofny.com. 1,750 rms, 50 story. S, D $195-$295; each addl $30; suites $350-$1,000; under 17 free; wkend package plan. Crib free. Garage $29. TV; cable (premium), VCR avail. Pool privileges. Complimentary coffee in rms. Restaurant 6:30 am-midnight. Bars 11:30-4 am; entertainment. Ck-out noon. Convention facilities. Business center. In-rm modem link. Gift shop. Exercise rm; instructor, weight machines, bicycles, sauna. Minibars. Luxury level. Cr cds: A, C, D, DS, ER, JCB, MC, V.

D SC

★ ★ ★ **SHERATON RUSSELL.** *45 Park Ave (10016), in Murray Hill. 212/685-7676; FAX 212/889-3193.* Web sheratonhotelsofny.com/itt sheraton.com. 146 rms, 10 story, 26 suites. S, D $239-$285; each addl

$30; suites $375-$410; under 17 free; wkend rates. Crib free. Valet, garage parking $24. TV; cable (premium), VCR avail. Complimentary continental bkfst. Complimentary coffee in rms. Restaurant 6 am-midnight. Bar from 5 pm. Ck-out by 5 pm. Meeting rm. Business center. In-rm modem link. Concierge. Exercise equipt; weights, treadmills. Health club privileges. Pool privileges. Bathrm phones, minibars; many fireplaces; refrigerators, microwaves avail. Some balconies. Cr cds: A, C, D, DS, ER, JCB, MC, V.

D SC

★ ★ **THE SHOREHAM.** *33 W 55th St (10019), between Fifth & Sixth Aves, Midtown. 212/247-6700; FAX 212/765-9741; res: 800/553-3347.* E-mail shorehotel@aol.com; web www.vacation-inc.com. 84 rms, 11 story, 37 suites. S, D $275; suites $325; wkend, hol rates. Crib free. Valet parking $18. TV; cable (premium), VCR (free movies). Complimentary continental bkfst. Complimentary coffee in rms. Restaurant nearby. Ck-out noon. Business servs avail. In-rm modem link. Concierge. Health club privileges. Refrigerators. Renovated hotel built 1930. Cr cds: A, D, MC, V.

D SC

★ ★ ★ **SOHO GRAND.** *310 W Broadway (10013), between Grand & Canal St, in SoHo. 212/965-3000; res: 800/965-3000; FAX 212/965-3200.* 367 rms, 17 story. S $209-$349; D $229-$369; each addl $20; suites $949-$1149; under 12 free. Crib free. Pet accepted. Garage parking $25. TV; cable (premium), VCR avail. Restaurant 6 am-midnight; Sat, Sun from 7 am. Rm serv 24 hrs. Bar noon-2 am; Sat, Sun from 1 pm. Ck-out noon. Meeting rms. Business center. In-rm modem link. Concierge. Free valet parking. Exercise equipt; rower, stair machines. Massage. Minibars. Cr cds: A, D, DS, JCB, MC, V.

D

★ ★ ★ **SOUTHGATE TOWER SUITE.** *371 Seventh Ave (10001), at 31st St, south of Midtown. 212/563-1800; FAX 212/643-8028; res: 800/637-8483.* 522 kit. suites, 28 story. S $159-$194; D $179-$214; each addl $20; suites $194-$254; wkend, wkly, monthly rates. Crib free. TV; cable (premium). Complimentary coffee. Restaurant 7 am-midnight. Ck-out noon. Coin Indry. Meeting rms. Business servs avail. Concierge. Barber. Exercise equipt; weight machines, bicycles. Some balconies. Cr cds: A, C, D, DS, ER, JCB, MC, V.

D

★ ★ ★ ★ ★ **THE ST REGIS HOTEL.** *2 E 55th St (10022), at Fifth Ave, Midtown. 212/753-4500; FAX 212/787-3447; res: 800/759-7550.* Web www.ITTsheraton.com. Even in big, brash New York in the turbulent '90s, elegant tradition can be maintained. The St Regis, built by John Jacob Astor in 1904, has been restored to its Louis XV style. 313 rms, 20 story, 92 suites. S, D $495-$620; suites $765-$5,000; under 12 free; wkend rates. Crib free. Garage parking, valet, in/out $36. TV; cable (premium), VCR. Restaurant (see LESPINASSE). Afternoon tea in Astor Court 2:30-5:30 pm; harpist. Rm serv 24 hrs. Bar 11-1 am; Fri, Sat 11:30-2 am; Sun noon-midnight. Ck-out 1 pm. Meeting rms. Business center. In-rm modem link. Concierge. Extensive shopping arcade. Barber, beauty shop. Exercise rm; instructor, weight machine, bicycles, sauna. Massage. Health club privileges. Bathrm phones. Cr cds: A, C, D, DS, ER, JCB, MC, V.

D SC

✔★ **STANFORD.** *43 W 32nd St (10001), between Fifth Ave & Broadway, near Macy's, south of Midtown. 212/563-1480; FAX 212/629-0043; res: 800/365-1114.* 121 rms, 12 story, 30 suites. S $85; D $99; each addl $15; suites $130-$180. Crib free. TV; cable. Restaurant 7 am-10 pm. No rm serv. Ck-out noon. Business servs avail. In-rm modem link. Refrigerators. Near Madison Square Garden. Cr cds: A, C, D, JCB, MC, V.

D SC

★ ★ ★ ★ **THE STANHOPE.** *995 Fifth Ave (10028), at 81st St, opp Metropolitan Museum of Art, Upper East Side. 212/288-5800; FAX 212/517-0088; res: 800/828-1123.* This stylish 1926 landmark hotel is across the street from Central Park. Many rooms offer views of the Manhattan skyline. 140 units, 17 story, 48 suites, some with kits. S, D $325; suites $450-$1,325; under 12 free; wkend rates; package plans. Crib free. Garage $38. TV; cable (premium), VCR (movies). Restaurant 7 am-11 pm. Rm serv 24 hrs. Bar noon-1 am. Ck-out 1 pm. Meeting rms. In-rm modem link. Concierge. Exercise equipt; weight machine, bicycles, sauna. Bathrm phones, minibars; some wet bars; microwaves avail. Cr cds: A, C, D, DS, JCB, MC, V.

D

★ ★ ★ **SURREY.** *20 E 76th St (10021), Upper East Side. 212/288-3700; FAX 212/628-1549.* 130 rms, 16 story. S $250-$270; D $270-$290; each addl $20; suites $545-$615; under 12 free; wkly rates; wkend rates. Crib avail. Garage $14. TV; cable (premium), VCR (movies). Restaurant noon-3 pm, 5:30-11 pm. Rm serv. Bar. Ck-out noon. Coin Indry. Meeting rms. Business servs avail. In-rm modem link. Concierge. Exercise equipt; bicycles, treadmill. Refrigerators, microwaves avail. Cr cds: A, C, D, MC, V.

D

TRUMP INTERNATIONAL. *(Too new to be rated) 1 Central Park W (10023), at Columbus Circle, Midtown. 212/299-1000; res: 888/448-7867; FAX 212/299-1150.* 168 kit. units, 52 story, 130 suites. S, D $395-$475; suites $625-$1,325; wkend rates. Crib free. Valet parking $42. TV; cable (premium), VCR (movies). Complimentary coffee in rms. Restaurant (see JEAN GEORGES). Rm serv 24 hrs. Bar. Ck-out noon. Business center. In-rm modem link. Concierge. Exercise rm; instructor, weights, bicycles, sauna, steam rm. Massage. Indoor pool. Bathrm phones, in-rm whirlpools, refrigerators, microwaves, minibars. Cr cds: A, C, D, JCB, MC, V.

D

★ ★ ★ ★ **U.N. PLAZA-PARK HYATT.** *1 UN Plaza (10017), at First Ave & E 44th St, on the East Side. 212/758-1234; res: 800/228-9000; FAX 212/702-5051.* Web www.hyatt.com. Guest rooms in this modern chrome-and-glass tower offer fine views of UN Headquarters and the surrounding area. 427 rms on floors 28-38, 45 suites. S, D $330; each addl $35; suites $500-$1,500; under 18 free; wkend rates. Crib free. Garage; valet parking $26/day. TV; cable (premium), VCR avail. Indoor pool; lifeguard. Complimentary refreshments in rm. Restaurant (see AMBASSADOR GRILL). Bar noon-1 am. Ck-out noon. Meeting rms. Business center. In-rm modem link. Indoor tennis. Exercise rm; instructor, weights, bicycles, sauna, steam rm. Massage. Minibars, bathrm phones; some refrigerators; microwaves avail. Cr cds: A, C, D, DS, ER, JCB, MC, V.

D

★ ★ ★ ★ **WALDORF-ASTORIA.** *301 Park Ave (10022), between E 49th & 50th Sts, Midtown. 212/355-3000; FAX 212/872-7272; res: 800/HILTONS.* This art-deco masterpiece personifies New York at its most lavish and powerful. The richly tinted, hushed lobby serves as an interior centerpoint of city life. 1,219 rms, 42 story. S $300-$370, D $340-$410; each addl $40; suites $400-$1,050; children free; wkend rates. Crib free. Garage $37/day. TV; cable (premium), VCR avail (movies). Restaurant 7 am-11:45 pm (also see BULL & BEAR STEAKHOUSE and PEACOCK ALLEY). Rm serv 24 hrs. Bars 10:30-2:30 am; Sun noon-1 am. Ck-out noon. Convention facilities. Business center. In-rm modem link. Concierge. Barber, beauty shop. Shopping arcade. Extensive exercise rm; instructors, weight machines, bicycles, steam rm. Massage. Refrigerators, minibars. Luxury level. Cr cds: A, C, D, DS, ER, JCB, MC, V.

D SC

★ ★ **WALES.** *1295 Madison Ave (10128), between 92nd & 93rd Sts, Upper East Side. 212/876-6000; FAX 212/860-7000; res: 800/428-5252 (exc NYC).* E-mail hotelwales@aol.com; web www.vacationsinc.com. 92 units, 10 story, 40 suites. S, D $185; each addl $25; suites $245. Crib free. Valet parking $28. TV; cable (premium), VCR (free movies). Complimentary continental bkfst; afternoon refreshments. Restaurant 8 am-11 pm. Harpist 5-6 pm Mon-Fri, chamber music 6-8 pm Sun. Ck-out 1 pm. Business servs avail. Health club privileges. Refrigerators avail. Restored 1902 hotel; original fireplaces. Cr cds: A, MC, V.

★ ★ **WARWICK.** *65 W 54th St (10019), at 6th Ave, Midtown. 212/247-2700; FAX 212/957-8915; res: 800/223-4099.* 425 rms, 33 story. S $215-$265; D $245-$270; each addl $25; suites $400-$1,000; under 12 free; wkend rates. Crib free. Garage $19-$30. TV; cable (premium). Restaurant 6:30 am-11 pm. Bar 11-1 am. Ck-out 1 pm. Meeting rms. Business center. Exercise equipt; bicycles, stair machine. Health club privileges. Microwaves avail. Many terraces. Cr cds: A, C, D, JCB, MC, V.

D

★ ★ ★ **WESTBURY.** *15 E Madison Ave (10021), at 69th St, Upper East Side. 212/535-2000; FAX 212/535-5058; res: 800/321-1569.* 228 rms, 17 story, 52 suites. S $315-$345; D $345-$375; each addl $30; 2, 3-rm suites $525-$1,750; under 12 free; wkend rates. Pet accepted. TV; cable (premium), VCR avail (free movies). Restaurant (see POLO). Rm serv 24 hrs. Bar noon-midnight. Ck-out 1 pm. Business center. In-rm modem link. Exercise equipt; bicycles, treadmill, sauna. Microwaves avail. Bathrm phones. Cr cds: A, C, D, DS, ER, JCB, MC, V.

D

✔★ ★ **WYNDHAM.** *42 W 58th St (10019), off 5th Ave, Midtown. 212/753-3500; FAX 212/754-5638.* 204 rms, 16 story. S $120-$135; D $135-$150; suites $175-$210. Crib free. TV. Restaurant 7:30 am-10:30 pm. Bar from noon. Ck-out 1 pm. Business servs avail. In-rm modem link. Garage adj. Refrigerator, serv pantry in suites. Cr cds: A, C, D, MC, V.

D

Inns

★ ★ **BOX TREE.** *250 E 49th St (10017), at Second Ave, Midtown. 212/758-8320.* 13 suites in 2 town houses, 3 story. MAP (Fri & Sat): suites $290-$330; lower rates (AP) wkdays. TV. Complimentary continental bkfst. Restaurant (see BOX TREE). Dining credit $100 per night included in MAP rates. Limited rm serv 24 hrs. Ck-out 11 am, ck-in 3 pm. Concierge. Bathrm phones, fireplaces. 1840s brownstones; antique furnishings; imported French amenities; rms individually decorated. Cr cds: A, MC, V.

✔★ **BROADWAY INN.** *264 W 46th St (10036). 212/997-9200; FAX 212/768-2807; res: 800/826-6300.* 40 rms, 15 with shower only, 3 story. S $85-$185; D $95-$185; each addl $10; suites $165-$185; under 3 free. Closed Jan-Feb. Crib free. TV; cable. Complimentary continental bkfst. Restaurant noon-4 am. Rm serv 24 hrs. Ck-out 1 pm, ck-in 3 pm. Luggage handling. Some refrigerators, microwaves. Cr cds: A, D, DS, MC, V.

★ ★ ★ **INN AT IRVING PLACE.** *56 Irving Place (10003), between 17th & 18th Sts, in Gramercy Park. 212/533-4600; FAX 212/533-4611; res: 800/685-1447.* E-mail irving56@aol.com; web www.slh.com. 12 rms, 2 with shower only, 4 story. S $275; D $350; each addl $25; monthly rates. Children over 12 yrs only. TV; cable (premium), VCR (movies). Complimentary continental bkfst; afternoon refreshments. Dining rm noon-3 pm, 5-10 pm. Bar. Rm serv 24 hrs. Bar. Ck-out noon, ck-in 3 pm. Luggage handling. Business servs avail. In-rm modem link. Health club privileges. Refrigerators, minibars. Elegant country-style inn with all modern conveniences. Cr cds: A, C, D, MC, V.

Restaurants

✔★ ★ **20 MOTT STREET.** *20 Mott St (10013), between Pell & Bowery Sts, in Chinatown. 212/964-0380.* Chinese menu. Specialties: dim sum, baked conch with curry sauce, filet mignon with black pepper sauce. Hrs: 9 am-11 pm; Sat, Sun from 8:30 am. A la carte entrees: dim sum from $1.90, lunch, dinner $7.95-$20. Fish tank. Cr cds: A, DS, JCB, MC, V.

★ ★ ★ **21 CLUB.** *21 W 52nd St (10019), between Fifth & Sixth Aves, Midtown. 212/582-7200.* Specializes in fresh seafood, steak, "21" burger. Own pastries. Hrs: noon-11 pm. Closed Sun; major hols; also Sat June-Aug. Res accepted. Bar. Wine cellar. A la carte entrees: lunch $21-$39, dinner $24-$39. Prix fixe: lunch $25. Pre-theater dinner $29. Jacket, tie. Cr cds: A, C, D, DS, JCB, MC, V.

★ ★ ★ **540 PARK.** *(See The Regency Hotel) 212/339-4050.* Web www.loewshotels.com. Specialties: cedar planked salmon, seafood pot pie with herb crust, peach melba shortcake. Hrs: 7 am-10 pm; Sat, Sun brunch 11 am-3 pm. Res accepted. Bar noon-1 am. Wine cellar. A la carte entrees: bkfst $8-$20, lunch $13.50-$25, dinner $19-$30. Sun brunch $18-$24. Child's meals. Cr cds: A, C, D, DS, MC, V.

D

★ ★ ★ **ADRIENNE.** *(See The Peninsula New York Hotel) 212/903-3918.* E-mail pny@peninsula.com; web www.peninsula.com. Continental, Amer menu. Specialties: seared tuna in rice paper, crisp sweetwater prawns, trilogy of salmon. Own baking. Hrs: 7-10:30 am, noon-2:30 pm, 6-10 pm; Sun brunch 11:30 am-2:30 pm. Res accepted. Bar. A la carte entrees: bkfst $6-$22, lunch $18-$27, dinner $21-$32. Prix fixe: bkfst $25, lunch $34, dinner $35. Sun brunch $40. Seasonal menu. Pianist Tue-Fri. Valet parking. Jacket. Totally nonsmoking. Cr cds: A, C, D, DS, ER, JCB, MC, V.

D

★ ★ ★ **AJA.** *937 Broadway (10010), at 22nd St, Gramercy Park. 212/473-8388.* American with Asian influence menu. Specialties: steamed lobster with denang curry, sauteed venison with roasted pear, roasted halibut with lobster summer rolls. Hrs: noon-10:30 pm; Fri, Sat to 11:30 pm; Sun 6-10 pm. Closed major hols. Res accepted. Bar 4 pm-2 am. Semi-a la carte: lunch $12-$18, dinner $22-$28. Casual decor. Totally nonsmoking. Cr cds: A, MC, V.

D

★ ★ ★ **ALISON ON DOMINICK STREET.** *38 Dominick St (10013), between Hudson & Varick Sts, in SoHo. 212/727-1188.* Country French menu. Specialties: seared foie gras, roast Long Island duck breast, Maine lobster stew. Hrs: 5:30-10:30 pm; Fri, Sat to 11 pm; Sun to 9:30 pm; pre-theater dinner to 6:15 pm. Closed Labor Day, Dec 25; 1st wk July. Res accepted. Bar. Wine cellar. A la carte entrees: dinner $24-$35. Pre-theater dinner $34. Intimate and romantic dining. Cr cds: A, D, MC, V.

★ ★ ★ **ALVA.** *36 E 22nd St (10010), in Gramercy Park area. 212/228-4399.* Specialties: grilled herb-crusted salmon, pan-seared duck breast, seared tuna. Own desserts. Hrs: noon-3 pm, 5:30-midnight; Sat, Sun from 5:30 pm. Closed last wk Aug. Res accepted. Bar. A la carte entrees: lunch $10-$20, dinner $15-$24. Cr cds: A, D, MC, V.

D

★ ★ ★ **AMBASSADOR GRILL.** *(See U.N. Plaza-Park Hyatt Hotel) 212/702-5014.* Specialties: rotisserie special, seared salmon, grilled rack of lamb. Hrs: 7 am-2:30 pm, 6-10:30 pm; Sat, Sun brunch 11:30 am-3:30 pm. Res accepted. Bar to midnight, Sat to 2 am. Wine list. A la carte entrees: lunch $21-$23, dinner $23-$27. Complete meals: bkfst $19. Sat, Sun brunch $45. Child's meals. Piano bar Thur-Sat. Valet parking. Modern decor. Jacket. Cr cds: A, C, D, DS, ER, JCB, MC, V.

D

★ ★ **AMERICAN FESTIVAL.** *20 W 50th St (10019), between Fifth & Sixth Aves, at Rockefeller Center, Midtown. 212/332-7621.* Web www.restaurantassoc.com. Regional Amer menu. Hrs: 7:30 am-11 pm; Fri to midnight; Sat 9 am-midnight; Sun 9 am-10 pm; Sat, Sun brunch 11 am-2 pm (Nov-Apr). Res accepted. Bar noon-midnight. A la carte entrees: bkfst $4.75-$14, lunch, dinner $12-$27; Sat, Sun brunch $19.97. Prix fixe: dinner $21.95, $24.95. Seasonal dishes. Parking (after 5 pm). Outdoor dining (May-Oct). Overlooks Rockefeller Center's famous Prometheus fountain and sunken pool (summer), skating rink (winter). Cr cds: A, C, D, JCB, MC, V.

D

★ ★ ★ **AN AMERICAN PLACE.** *2 Park Ave (10016), on 32nd St, Midtown. 212/684-2122.* Specializes in seafood, game. Hrs: 11:45 am-3 pm, 5:30-9:30 pm; Sat from 5:30 pm. Closed Sun; major hols. Res accepted. Bar. Wine cellar. A la carte entrees: lunch $15-$22, dinner $25-$32. Art deco dining rm with Prairie School-style furniture. Cr cds: A, D, DS, MC, V.

★ ★ ★ **ANGELO AND MAXIE'S STEAKHOUSE.** *233 Park Ave S (10003), at 19th St, in Gramercy Park. 212/220-9200.* Specialties: Angelo and Maxie's 28-oz ribeye steak, porterhouse steak deluxe for two, grilled veal chop with lemon-parsley butter. Own desserts. Hrs: 11:30 am-4 pm, 5 pm-midnight; Fri to 1 am; Sat 5 pm-1 am; Sun 5-11 pm. Closed Dec 25. Res accepted. Bar. Wine list. A la carte entrees: lunch, dinner $9-$24. Bustling steakhouse; murals of cows in back rm. Cr cds: A, MC, V.

D

★ ★ ★ **ANSONIA.** *329 Columbus Ave (10023), between 75th & 76th Sts, Upper West Side. 212/579-0505.* Contemporary Amer menu. Specialties: foie gras terrine, lavender-glazed muscovy duck, bacon-wrapped monkfish. Own pastries. Hrs: 5:30-11:30 pm; Fri, Sat to midnight. Closed some major hols. Res accepted. Bar. Wine list. A la carte entrees: dinner $18-$27.50. Complete meal: dinner $29.50. Outdoor dining. 1902 bldg now contemporary, two-level dining rm with stainless steel, ornate globe lighting. Cr cds: A, MC, V.

★ ★ ★ **AQUAGRILL.** *210 Spring St (10012), at 6th Ave, in SoHo. 212/274-0505.* Specializes in seafood. Hrs: noon-3 pm, 6-11 pm; Fri to midnight; Sat noon-4 pm, 6 pm-midnight; Sun 6-11 pm; Sat, Sun brunch noon-4 pm. Closed Mon; major hols. Res accepted. Bar. Semi-a la carte: lunch $8-$16.50, dinner $13-$22. Sat, Sun brunch $8-$16. Outdoor dining. Casual decor. Totally nonsmoking. Cr cds: A, MC, V.

★ ★ ★ ★ **AQUAVIT.** *13 W 54th St (10019), between Fifth & Sixth Aves, Midtown. 212/307-7311.* A towering glass-walled atrium and indoor waterfall accent this cooly elegant restaurant set in a townhouse once owned by Nelson Rockefeller. The extensive wine list is accompanied by New York's largest selection of aquavits. Scandinavian menu. Specializes in Scandinavian shrimp, game salmon. Hrs: noon-3 pm, 5:30-10:30 pm; Sat from 5:30 pm; Sun brunch noon-3 pm. Closed major hols. Res accepted. Bar. Wine cellar. A la carte entrees: lunch, dinner $13-$18. Prix fixe: lunch $29, dinner $25-$58. Cr cds: A, D, MC, V.

★ ★ ★ **ARCADIA.** *21 E 62nd St, between Madison & Fifth Aves, Upper East Side. 212/223-2900.* Specialties: chimney-smoked lobster, chocolate bread pudding with brandy custard sauce, corn cakes with caviar and creme fraiche. Own baking. Hrs: noon-2:30 pm, 6-10 pm; Fri, Sat 6-10:30 pm. Closed Sun; Jan 1, July 4, Dec 25. Res accepted. Bar. A la carte entrees: lunch $18-$25. Prix fixe: dinner $58. Cr cds: A, D, MC, V.

D

✔★ ★ **ARIZONA 206.** *206 E 60th St (10022), between 2nd & 3rd Aves, Upper East Side. 212/838-0440.* Southwestern menu. Specialities: cured salmon and potato tostada, smoked venison, tortilla crusted trout. Hrs: Cafe: noon-midnight; Sun to 11 pm; Sun brunch 11:30 am-4 pm. Dining rm: noon-3 pm, 5:30-11 pm; Fri, Sat to 11:30 pm; Sun 5:30-10:30 pm. Closed Dec 25. Res accepted. Bar. A la carte entrees: Cafe: lunch, dinner $10-$16; Sun brunch $9-$15; Dining rm: lunch $14-$18, dinner $22-$30; complete meals: Cafe: lunch $15; Dining rm: lunch $19.98. Adobe pueblo decor; Western art. Outdoor dining. Cr cds: A, D, DS, MC, V.

★ ★ ★ **ARQUA.** *281 Church St (10013), at White St, in Tribeca. 212/334-1888.* Italian menu. Specialties: homemade pastas, Venetian cuisine, desserts. Hrs: noon-3 pm, 5-10 pm; Fri, Sat to 11:30 pm, Sun from 5 pm. Closed major hols; also last 2 wks Aug. Res accepted. Bar. A la carte entrees: lunch, dinner $16-$28. Prix fixe: (Mon-Fri): lunch $19.98, (Sat, Sun) dinner $35. Cr cds: A, D, MC, V.

✔★ **AUNT SUZIE.** *126 E 28 St (10016), in Murray Hill. 212/689-1992.* Italian, Southern menu. Specializes in pasta, chicken, seafood. Hrs: 11:30 am-11 pm; Sat from 5 pm; Sun 5-10 pm. Closed Thanksgiving, Dec 25. Bar. Semi-a la carte: lunch $8.90-$12.90, dinner $8.90-$14.90. Casual decor. Cr cds: A, MC, V.

D

★ ★ ★ ★ **AUREOLE.** *34 E 61st St, between Madison & Park Aves, Upper East Side. 212/319-1660.* Charles Palmer's fashionable restaurant is one of the toughest reservations in town. The elegant townhouse location with lovely outdoor garden offers a lush, romantic setting. French, Amer menu. Specializes in fish, game. Own baking. Hrs: noon-2:30 pm, 5:30-11 pm; Sat from 5:30 pm. Closed Sun; some major hols. Res required. Bar. Wine list. A la carte entrees: lunch $16-$24. Prix fixe: lunch $32, dinner $63. Tasting menu: dinner $85. Jacket, tie. Cr cds: A, C, D, JCB, MC, V.

★ ★ **BALUCHI'S.** *193 Spring St (10012), between Sullivan & Thompson Sts, in SoHo. 212/226-2828.* Indian menu. Specialties: whole leg of lamb marinated, lamb curry in cardamun sauce, vegetable balls in tomato sauce. Hrs: noon-3 pm, 5-11 pm; Sat noon-11:30 pm; Sun noon-11 pm. Res accepted. Bar. Semi-a la carte: lunch, dinner $9.95-$29.95. Indian decor. Totally nonsmoking. Cr cds: A, D, MC, V.

★ ★ ★ ★ **BARBETTA.** *321 W 46th St (10036), between 8th & 9th Aves, Midtown. 212/246-9171.* E-mail barbetta90@aol.com. An 18th-century Venetian harpsichord sets the mood in this venerable establishment, known for classic northern Italian cooking. The property comprises two elegant, antique-furnished townhouses and an enchanting garden with century-old trees, perfumed in season with magnolia, wisteria, jasmine and gardenia. Italian menu. Hrs: noon-2 pm, 5 pm-midnight. Closed Sun. Res accepted. A la carte entrees: lunch $14-$21, dinner (after 8 pm) $22-$29. Cr cds: A, C, D, DS, JCB, MC, V.

★ ★ **BAROCCO.** *301 Church St (10013), between Walker & White Sts, in Tribeca. 212/431-1445.* Regional Italian menu. Specialties: ravioli verdi, calamari fritti, pappardelle noodles with squab. Own gelato. Hrs: noon-3 pm, 6-11 pm; Sat 6-11:30 pm; Sun 6-10:30 pm. Closed major hols. Res accepted. Bar. A la carte entrees: lunch $7-$20, dinner $13-$27. Casual trattoria dining in industrial loft space. Cr cds: A, D, MC, V.

★ ★ ★ **BAROLO.** *398 W Broadway (10012), between Spring & Broome Sts, in SoHo. 212/226-1102.* Northern Italian menu. Specialties: filet with barolo wine sauce, trenette with Genovese pesto, risotto with porcini mushrooms. Antipasto bar. Hrs: noon-midnight; Fri, Sat to 1 am. Res accepted. Bar to 2 am. A la carte entrees: lunch $11.50-$23, dinner $13.50-$26. Garden dining among cherry trees and fountain. Three levels of dining. Contemporary decor. Cr cds: A, D, MC, V.

D

★ ★ ★ **BECCO.** *355 W 46th St (10036), between 8th & 9th Aves, Times Square/Theater District. 212/397-7597.* Italian menu. Specializes in grilled rack of lamb, whole spicy free-range chicken, osso buco. Hrs: noon-3 pm, 5 pm-midnight; Sun noon-10 pm. Closed Dec 25. Res accepted; required pre-theater dinner. Bar. A la carte entrees: lunch $13.95-$25.95, dinner $16.95-$27.95. Pre-theater dinner $19.95. Three dining rms on two levels. Rustic, Northern Italian atmosphere. Totally nonsmoking. Cr cds: A, C, D, DS, MC, V.

✔★ ★ **BELLUNO RISTORANTE.** *340 Lexington Ave (10016), between 39th & 40th Sts, in Murray Hill. 212/953-3282.* Specialties: shrimp martini; risotto with shrimp, scallops and clams; veal with porcini and shallots. Hrs: noon-3 pm, 5-10 pm. Closed Sun; most major hols. Res accepted. Bar to midnight. Semi-a la carte: lunch, dinner $13-$19. Tri-level; contemporary decor. Totally nonsmoking. Cr cds: A, C, MC, V.

D

★ ★ **BICE.** *7 E 54th St (10022), just off Fifth Ave, Midtown. 212/688-1999.* Italian menu. Specialties: lobster salad with raspberry vinaigrette, marinated salmon and swordfish with celery root. Own pasta, desserts. Menu changes daily. Hrs: noon-3 pm, 6 pm-midnight. Closed Dec 25. Res accepted. Bar. A la carte entrees: lunch, dinner $20-$38. Outdoor dining. Branch of original restaurant in Milan. Cr cds: A, C, D, DS, JCB, MC, V.

★ ★ **BISTRO DU NORD.** *1312 Madison Ave (10028), Upper East Side at 93rd St. 212/289-0997.* French menu. Specialties: sautéed calves liver, 3 peppercorn sirloin steak. Hrs: noon-4 pm, 5-11:30 pm; Sat, Sun brunch noon-4 pm. Closed Dec 25. Res accepted. Bar. Semi-a la carte: lunch $8-$14, dinner $18-$24. Complete meal: lunch $10.95. Pre-theater: dinner $11.95-$18.45. Sat, Sun brunch $13.95. French bistro decor. Totally nonsmoking. Cr cds: A, D, MC, V.

✔★ ★ **BLUE RIBBON.** *97 Sullivan St (10012), between Spring and Prince Sts, in SoHo. 212/274-0404.* French, Amer menu. Specialties: paella royale, chocolate bruno. Hrs: 4 pm-4 am. Closed Mon; major hols; also last 2 wk in Aug. Bar. Semi-a la carte: dinner $9.50-$27. Casual decor. Totally nonsmoking. Cr cds: A, D, DS, MC, V.

★ ★ **BOATHOUSE CAFE.** *In Central Park (10028), enter at 72nd St & 5th Ave, at lake, Upper East Side. 212/517-2233.* Specializes in pasta, pan-roasted organic chicken, seafood. Hrs: 11 am-10 pm; Sat, Sun 11 am-4 pm, 5:30-10 pm. Sat, Sun brunch to 4 pm. Closed Nov-mid-Mar. Bar. A la carte entrees: lunch $14-$20, dinner $19-$28. Sat, Sun brunch $11-$20. Child's meals. Outdoor dining overlooking lake. View of Bethesda Fountain. Cr cds: A, MC, V.

★ ★ ★ **BOLO.** *23 E 22nd St (10010), between Broadway & Park Ave S, in Gramercy Park area. 212/228-2200.* Spanish menu. Specialities: individual shellfish paella, baby clams in green onion broth. Hrs: noon-2:30 pm, 5:30 pm-midnight; Sat from 5:30 pm; Sun 5:30-11 pm. Closed Dec 25. Res accepted. A la carte entrees: lunch $11-$17, dinner $22-$28. Eclectic decor. Cr cds: A, D, DS, MC, V.

★ ★ **BOOM.** *152 Spring St (10012), between W Broadway & Wooster, in SoHo. 212/431-3663.* International menu. Specialties: Vietnamese five-spiced grilled quail, pan-seared salmon, Chinese barbeque shrimp. Hrs: noon-1 am; Thurs-Sat to 3:30 am; Sat, Sun brunch noon-1 am. Res accepted. Bar. A la carte entrees: lunch $7-$17, dinner $10-$19. Sat, Sun brunch $6-$12. Old World atmosphere; frescoed walls, hanging sculpture. Cr cds: A.

[nonsmoking symbol]

★ ★ **BOX TREE.** *(See Box Tree Inn) 212/758-8320.* Continental menu. Specializes in lobster, filet of beef, rack of lamb. Own baking. Hrs: noon-3 pm, 5:30-9:30 pm; Sat from 5:30 pm. Res required. Bar. Prix fixe: lunch $42, 5-course dinner $86. Pre-theater menu (5:30-6:45 pm) $65. Jacket. Cr cds: A, V.

✔★ ★ **BROOKLYN DINER USA.** *212 W 57th St (10019), in Midtown. 212/977-1957.* Specializes in chicken pot pie, chicken noodle soup, chinese chicken salad. Own pastries, desserts. Hrs: 8 am-midnight; Fri, Sat to 1 am; Sun to 11 pm. Res accepted. Bar. Semi-a la carte: bkfst $4.50-$12, lunch $9.95-$19.95, dinner $11.95-$19.95. Art-deco style diner. Cr cds: A, D, DS, MC, V.

D

★ ★ **BRYANT PARK GRILL.** *25 W 40th St (10018), in Midtown. 212/840-6500.* Contemporary Amer menu. Specialties: confit of duck burritos, Caesar salad with parmesan toast. Hrs: 11:30 am-3:30 pm, 5 pm-1 am. Res accepted. Bar. A la carte entrees: lunch $12-$20, dinner $12-$23. Outdoor dining. Windows overlook Bryant Park. Totally nonsmoking. Cr cds: A, D, DS, MC, V.

D

★ ★ ★ **BULL & BEAR STEAKHOUSE.** *(See Waldorf-Astoria Hotel) 212/872-4900.* Specializes in Maine lobster, Angus prime beef, grilled fish. Own baking. Hrs: noon-11:30 pm; Sat, Sun from 5 pm. Res accepted. Bar to midnight. A la carte entrees: lunch $17-$25, dinner $23-$42. Child's meals. Open kitchen. Jazz trio Thurs, Fri. Elegant club-like atmosphere. Jacket. Cr cds: A, C, D, DS, ER, JCB, MC, V.

D [nonsmoking symbol]

✔★ ★ **CAFE DE BRUXELLES.** *118 Greenwich Ave (10011), at W 13th St, Greenwich Village. 212/206-1830.* French menu. Specialties: grilled pork chops with apples and mushrooms, seafood casserole, steamed mussels prepared six different ways. Hrs: noon-11:30 pm; Fri, Sat to 12:30 am; Sun noon-10:30 pm; Sun brunch to 3:30 pm. Closed most major hols. Res accepted. Bar. A la carte entrees: lunch $7.50-$12.50, dinner $13.50-$18.50. Sun brunch $7.50-$12.50. Contemporary decor. Cr cds: A, MC, V.

[nonsmoking symbol]

★ ★ ★ **CAFE DES ARTISTES.** *1 W 67th St (10023), Upper West Side. 212/877-3500.* Country French menu. Specializes in cassoulet, grilled smoked salmon. Hrs: noon-3 pm, 5:30 pm-12:30 am; Sun 10 am-3 pm, 5:30 pm-midnight; Sat brunch 11 am-3 pm. Closed Dec 25. Res required. Bar. Wine list. A la carte entrees: lunch $15-$24, dinner $25-$32.50. Prix fixe: lunch $23, dinner $37.50. Romantic, Old World decor; Howard Chandler Christy murals. Near Lincoln Center. Jacket (after 5 pm). Cr cds: A, D, JCB, MC, V.

★ ★ **CAFE FIORELLO.** *1900 Broadway (10023), between W 63rd & 64th Sts, across from Lincoln Center, Upper West Side. 212/595-5330.* Italian menu. Specialties: mixed antipasto, vitello alla parmigiana, grilled filet of tuna. Own pastries. Hrs: 11:30 am-11:30 pm; Fri 11-12:30 am; Sun 11 am-10:30 pm; Sat, Sun brunch 11 am-3 pm. Closed Dec 25. Res accepted. Bar. A la carte entrees: lunch $14.95-$25.75, dinner $15.75-$28.95. Sat, Sun brunch $10.75-$28.95. Child's meals. Outdoor dining. Glass-front Italian trattoria with contemporary art; antipasto bar. Family-owned. Totally nonsmoking. Cr cds: A, C, D, MC, V.

★ ★ **CAFE LUXEMBOURG.** *200 W 70th St (10023), at Amsterdamn Ave, Upper West Side. 212/873-7411.* French, Amer menu. Specialties: country salad, steak frites, fresh fish. Hrs: noon-midnight; Sat brunch noon-3 pm; Sun brunch 11 am-3 pm. Res accepted. Bar. A la carte entrees: lunch $9-$18, dinner $16.50-$28. Prix fixe: lunch $19.98, prix fixe: dinner $26.50, $38.50. Bistro atmosphere; art-deco decor. Near Lincoln Center. Cr cds: A, C, D, MC, V.

★ ★ **CAFE NOSIDAM.** *768 Madison Ave (10021), between 65th & 66th Sts, Upper East Side. 212/717-5633.* Italian, Amer menu. Specializes in pasta, fish, lamb. Hrs: 11:30 am-midnight; Sun to 11 pm; Sun brunch to 3 pm. Res accepted. Bar. A la carte entrees: lunch, dinner $13.95-$28. Complete meals: lunch, dinner $19.95. Sun brunch $19.95. Outdoor dining. Contemporary decor; original art. Cr cds: A, MC, V.

[nonsmoking symbol]

★ ★ ★ **CAFE PIERRE.** *(See The Pierre Hotel) 212/940-8185.* Web www.fourseasons.com. Contemporary, continental menu. Specializes in seasonal offerings. Own pastries. Hrs: 7 am-11 pm; Sun brunch noon-2:30 pm. Res required. Bar 11:30-1 am. Wine list. A la carte entrees: bkfst $9.50-$21, lunch $18-$36, dinner $23-$36. Prix fixe: lunch $30. 4-course tasting menu $60. Pre-theater menu (6-7 pm) $34. Sun brunch $34-$40. Entertainment. Jacket. Cr cds: A, C, D, DS, ER, JCB, MC, V.

D ♥

★ ★ **CAFE TREVI.** *1570 First Ave, between 81st & 82nd Sts, in Yorkville section of Upper East Side. 212/249-0040.* Italian menu. Specializes in veal, pasta, chicken. Hrs: 5:30 pm-midnight. Closed Sun. Res accepted. Northern Bar. A la carte entrees: dinner $14.75-$24.75. Child's meals. Trattoria atmosphere. Cr cds: A, D, MC, V.

D

★ ★ ★ **CAFFE BONDI.** *7 W 20th St (10011), between 5th & 6th Aves, in Chelsea. 212/691-8136.* Sicilian menu. Specialties: pasta con sarde, wild game, seafood. Hrs: 11:30 am-11:30 pm. Sat, Sun brunch noon-5 pm. Bar. A la carte entrees: lunch $12-$21, dinner $14-$24. Complete meal: lunch $19.98, dinner $29. Sat, Sun brunch $6.95-$15. Outdoor dining. Tapestries and changing photographic exhibits add to the casual elegance of this restaurant. Cr cds: A, D, DS, JCB, MC, V.

SC [nonsmoking symbol]

★ ★ **CAL'S.** *55 W 21st St (10010), Chelsea. 212/929-0740.* Mediterranean menu. Specializes in seafood, duck, lamb. Hrs: 11:30 am-midnight; Sat from 5 pm; Sun 5-10:30 pm. Closed Jan 1, July 4, Dec 25. Res accepted. Bar. A la carte entrees: lunch $9.50-$18, dinner $12-$24. Outdoor dining. Former warehouse; casual decor. Cr cds: A, C, D, MC, V.

D [nonsmoking symbol]

★ ★ ★ **CAMPAGNA.** *24 E 21st St (10010), between Broadway and Park Ave South, Chelsea. 212/460-0900.* Italian menu. Specialties: roasted halibut with fennel orange and saffron, tagliolini with lobster and shrimp. Hrs: noon-2:30 pm, 6-11:45 pm; Sat from 6 pm; Sun 5:30-10:45 pm. Closed some major hols. Res required. Bar. Wine cellar. A la carte entrees: lunch $11-$16.50, dinner $15-$29.50. Child's meals. Warm, comfortable atmosphere. Cr cds: A, C, D, MC, V.

D

★ ★ ★ **CAPSOUTO FRÈRES.** *451 Washington St (10013), 1 blk S of Canal St, near Hudson River, in Tribeca. 212/966-4900.* Contemporary French menu. Specializes in poached salmon, roast duckling, filet of beef with Madeira sauce. Own baking. Hrs: noon-3:30 pm, 6-11 pm; Fri to midnight; Sat 6 pm-midnight; Mon 6-11 pm; Sat, Sun brunch noon-3:30 pm. Res accepted. Bar to midnight. Wine cellar. A la carte entrees: lunch $9-$22, dinner $14-$24. Prix fixe: lunch $19.98. Sat, Sun brunch $8.50-$20. Outdoor dining. In converted neo-Flemish, landmark warehouse (1891). Cr cds: A, C, D, MC, V.

★ ★ ★ **CARLYLE RESTAURANT.** *(See Carlyle Hotel) 212/744-1600.* French, continental menu. Seasonal specialties. Own baking. Hrs: 7-10:30 am, noon-2:30 pm, 6 pm-1 am; Sun from 7:30 am; Sun brunch noon & 2 pm. Res accepted. Bar noon-2 am. Wine list. A la carte entrees: bkfst $9.50-$22.50, lunch $19.50-$36.50, dinner $26.50-$38.50. Buffet: bkfst $25, lunch $32.50. Sun brunch $42.50. Valet parking. Cr cds: A, C, D, JCB, MC, V.

♥

★ ★ **CARMINE'S.** *2450 Broadway (10024), between 90th & 91st Sts, Upper West Side. 212/362-2200.* Southern Italian menu. Specialties: country-style rigatoni with sausage, cannellini beans and broccoli; porterhouse steak for four; chicken scarpariello. Hrs: 11:30 am-11 pm; Fri, Sat to midnight; Sun 2-10 pm. Bar. A la carte entrees: dinner $16-$46. Complete dinner $10.95. Single entrees served family-style for 2-4 people. Outdoor dining. Dining rm, originally a hotel ballroom, is re-creation of 1940s neighborhood Italian restaurant. Cr cds: A, MC, V.

★ ★ ★ **CASCABEL.** *218 Lafayette St (10012), between Spring and Broome Sts, in SoHo. 212/431-7300.* Specialties: pan-seared halibut with truffled herb salad, pan-roasted duck breast with honey-braised onions. Hrs: 5:45-10:45 pm. Closed Sun (summer). Res accepted. Bar. A la carte entrees: dinner $18-$28. Complete meals: dinner $42 & $48. Outdoor dining. Contemporary decor; modern artwork. Totally nonsmoking. Cr cds: A, D, MC, V.

D

★ ★ **CASTELLANO.** *138 W 55th St (10019), between 6th & 7th Aves, Midtown. 212/664-1975.* Tuscan, Italian menu. Specialties: grilled calamari, fegato Castellano, risotti. Hrs: noon-3 pm, 5:30-11 pm; Sat, Sun from 5:30 pm. Closed some major hols. Res accepted. Bar. A la carte entrees: lunch, dinner $18-$35. Outdoor terrace dining. 3 dining areas on 2 levels. Tuscan decor. Cr cds: A, C, D, JCB, MC, V.

★ ★ ★ ★ ★ **CHANTERELLE.** *2 Harrison St (10013), in Mercantile Exchange Bldg, at Hudson St, in Tribeca. 212/966-6960.* Web www.newyorkeats.com/chanterelle. A gem of a restaurant tucked away in the formerly grim but gentrified neighborhood of Tribeca, Chanterelle offers top-quality contemporary French cuisine and excellent service, with a painstakingly selected menu that changes monthly. French menu. Specialty: grilled seafood sausage. Hrs: noon-2:30 pm, 5:30-11 pm; Mon from 5:30 pm. Closed Sun; major hols; also 2 wks Aug. Res required. Bar. Wine cellar. A la carte entrees: lunch $18.50-$25. Prix fixe: lunch $35, dinner $75 & $89. Chef-owned. Cr cds: A, C, D, DS, JCB, MC, V.

D

★ ★ ★ **CHELSEA BISTRO & BAR.** *358 W 23rd St, between 8th & 9th Aves, in Chelsea. 212/727-2026.* Specialties: escalope of salmon, Hanger steak, roasted duck two ways. Hrs: 5:30-11 pm; Fri, Sat to midnight; Sun 5-10:30 pm. Res accepted. Bar. A la carte entrees: dinner $17.22-$22. Glass-enclosed garden; casual dining. Cr cds: A, MC, V.

D

★ ★ **CHEZ MICHALLET.** *90 Bedford St (10014), at Grove St, in Greenwich Village. 212/242-8309.* French menu. Specialties: steak au poivre, poulet grille a la marocaine. Hrs: 5:30-11 pm; Sun to 10:30 pm. Closed Jan 1, Dec 25. Res accepted. Wine, beer. A la carte entrees: dinner $17.25-$22. Pre-theater dinner 5:30-6:30 pm. Bistro decor. Totally nonsmoking. Cr cds: A, MC, V.

★ ★ **CHEZ NAPOLEON.** *365 W 50th St (10019), between Eighth & Ninth Aves, in Theater District. 212/265-6980.* French menu. Specialties: bouillabaisse, steak au poivre, duck à l'orange. Hrs: noon-2:30 pm, 5-10 pm; Fri to 11 pm; Sat 5-11 pm. Closed Sun; major hols. Res accepted. Bar. A la carte entrees: lunch $8-$15, dinner $13-$20.50. Small French bistro. Family owned. Cr cds: A, C, D, DS, MC, V.

★ ★ ★ **CHRISTER'S.** *145 W 55th St (10019), between 6th & 7th Aves, Midtown. 212/974-7224.* Scandinavian, Amer menu. Specialties: gravlax with mustard sauce, smoked serrano salmon, baked salmon on oak board. Smorgasbord. Hrs: noon-2:30 pm, 5:30-11 pm; Sat from 5:30 pm. Closed Sun; also major hols. Res accepted. Bar. A la carte entrees: lunch $14.50-$24, dinner $17.50-$29.50. Complete lunch: $19.98. Pre theater menu $27-$34. Rustic fishing camp atmosphere with colorful decor. Cr cds: A, C, D, MC, V.

D

★ ★ ★ **CIBO.** *767 Second Ave (10017), between 41st & 42nd Sts, Midtown. 212/681-1616.* Web www.menusonline.com. Contemporary Amer menu. Specializes in wild game, seafood, pastas. Own baking, pasta. Hrs: 11:30 am-3 pm, 5:30-10 pm; Fri, Sat to 11 pm; Sat, Sun brunch to 3:30 pm. Closed some major hols; also Sun in summer. Res accepted. Bar. Wine list. Semi-a la carte: lunch $12-$25, dinner $14-$25. Complete meal: dinner $24.95. Sat, Sun brunch $7-$19.98. Outdoor dining. In landmark Daily News bldg; contemporary pastel decor. Cr cds: A, C, D, DS, MC, V.

★ ★ ★ **CITÉ.** *120 W 51st St (10020), between Sixth & Seventh Aves, In Time/Life Bldg, Midtown. 212/956-7100.* French, Amer menu. Specialties: spit-roasted chicken, pepper-crusted swordfish, steak. Own baking. Hrs: 11:30 am-midnight. Closed Jan 1, July 4, Dec 25. Res accepted. Bar. Wine list. A la carte entrees: lunch, dinner $19.50-$29.50. Prix fixe: dinner $39.50 & $49.50. Zinc-covered bar. One rm informal bistro. Cr cds: A, C, D, DS, JCB, MC, V.

D

★ ★ ★ **CITY WINE & CIGAR CO.** *62 Laight St (10013), corner of Greenwich St, in Tribeca. 212/334-2274.* E-mail dmon@erols.com; web www.cuisine.com. Southwestern, Amer menu. Specialties: martini salad with bleu cheese-filled olives, guava-glazed tuna, ancho-rubbed chicken. Own pastries. Hrs: 11:30 am-2:30 pm, 5:30-11:30 pm; Thurs-Sat to 1 am; Sat brunch to 3 pm. Closed Sun; Dec 25. Res accepted. Bar 4:30 pm-2 am; Thurs-Sat to 3:30 am. Wine cellar. Semi-a la carte: lunch $12-$23, dinner $14-$27. Sat brunch $12-$23. Outdoor dining. Landmark bldg now contemporary restaurant with copper-topped tables, leather banquettes. Cr cds: A, C, D, MC, V.

D

★ ★ ★ **COCO PAZZO.** *23 E 74th St (10021), between Fifth Ave & Madison Ave, Upper East Side. 212/794-0205.* Italian menu. Specializes in Tuscan Italian cuisine. Hrs: noon-3 pm, 6-11:45 pm; Sat to 3 pm; Sun 11:30 am-3 pm. Closed Sat, Sun lunch in summer; also most major hols. Res required. Bar. Wine cellar. A la carte entrees: lunch $14.50-$25, dinner $15.50-$34.50. Decor features large still-life frescoes in the Morandi style. Jacket. Cr cds: A, D, MC, V.

D

★ ★ ★ **COCO PAZZO TEATRO.** *235 W 46th St (10019), between Broadway & 8th Ave, in Times Square/Theater District. 212/827-4222.* Italian menu. Specialties: florentine steak with Coco Pazzo fries, lobster with saffron pasta, mastro raviolo con aragosta. Own pastries. Hrs: 11:30 am-3 pm, 5:30 pm-midnight; Sun 5-11 pm. Closed major hols. Res accepted; required dinner. Bar to 1 am. Wine list. A la carte entrees: lunch $12.50-$16, dinner $15-$25. Informal Italian decor with marble columns, soft lighting. Cr cds: A, D, MC, V.

D

✔★ **COMFORT DINER.** *214 E 45th St (10017), between 2nd & 3rd Aves, Midtown. 212/867-4555.* Specialties: Mom's meatloaf, wild mushroom potato pancakes, cobb salad sandwich. Own desserts. Hrs:

7:30 am-10 pm; Sat, Sun from 9 am. Closed Dec 25. Semi-a la carte: bkfst $1.99-$9.95, lunch $5.75-$9.95, dinner $5.75-$10.95. Child's meals. 1950s-style diner. Totally nonsmoking. Cr cds: A, D, DS, MC, V.

★★ **CONTRAPUNTO.** *200 E 60th St (10022), at Third Ave, Upper East Side. 212/751-8616.* Italian menu. Specialties: tagliarini "forte" with smoked bacon, papparadelle with mushrooms, roast rack of lamb. Hrs: noon-midnight; Sun 2-11 pm. Closed Thanksgiving, Dec 25. Serv bar. A la carte entrees: lunch $12-$21, dinner $13-$25. Open kitchen. Cr cds: A, D, DS, MC, V.

★★★ **CUB ROOM.** *131 Sullivan St (10012), in SoHo. 212/677-4100.* Specialties: chateaubriand with wild mushrooms, yellowfin tuna on bed of Asian greens. Hrs: noon-midnight. Closed Dec 25. Res accepted. Bar to 2 am. Wine list. Semi-a la carte: lunch, dinner $18-$28. Contemporary decor. Totally nonsmoking. Cr cds: A.

D

★★ **CUISINE DE SAIGON.** *154 W 13th St (10011), between 6th St & 7th Ave, in Greenwich Village. 212/255-6003.* Vietnamese menu. Specialties: shrimp wrapped with sugar cane, Vietnamese spring roll, Saigon famous pasta (steamed wide noodles rolled with minced pork).Hrs: 5-11 pm; Fri, Sat to 11:30 pm; Sun to 10:30 pm. Closed most major hols. Res accepted; required wkends. Bar. A la carte entrees: dinner $7.95-$15.95. Cr cds: A, C, D, MC, V.

★★★ **DA SILVANO.** *260 Sixth Ave (10014), between Houston and Bleecker Sts, in Greenwich Village. 212/982-2343.* Italian menu. Specialties: boneless quails al radicchio, seasonal Florentine dishes, stewed tripes. Hrs: noon-11:30 pm; Fri, Sat to midnight; Sun 2-10:30 pm. Res accepted. Serv bar. A la carte entrees: lunch, dinner $11.50-$27.50. Outdoor dining. Cr cds: A, MC, V.

D

★★ **DA UMBERTO.** *107 W 17th St, between Sixth & Seventh Aves, in Chelsea. 212/989-0303.* Northern Italian menu. Specializes in antipasto buffet, wild game, pasta. Hrs: noon-3 pm, 5-11 pm; Sat from 5:30 pm. Closed Sun; Jan 1, Dec 25; also wk of July 4. Res accepted. Bar. A la carte entrees: lunch $11-$24, dinner $15-$32. Florentine decor. Cr cds: A.

★★ **DA VITTORIO.** *43 E 20th St (10003), Gramercy Park. 212/979-6532.* Italian menu. Specialties: potato gnocchi with gorgonzola and rosemary, risotto del gorno. Hrs: noon-3 pm, 5:30-11 pm; Fri to 11:30 pm; Sat 5:30-11:30 pm. Closed Sun; major hols. Res accepted. Bar. Semi-a la carte: lunch, dinner $15.50-$35. Rustic Italian decor. Cr cds: A.

★★★★★ **DANIEL.** *20 E 76th St (10021), between Fifth & Madison Aves, Upper East Side. 212/288-0033.* E-mail restaurantdaniel@msn.com. Meals at this establishment are served in a French country setting with a changing display of paintings from local galleries. Entrance is through a circular foyer paved with authentic 18th-century clay tiles. French menu. Specialties: black sea bass in a crispy potato shell with red wine sauce; salad of Maine crab with mango, coriander and lime dressing; seasonal cuisine. Hrs: noon-3:30 pm, 5:45-11:30 pm; Mon from 5:45 pm. Closed Sun; most major hols. Res required. Bar. Wine cellar. A la carte entrees: lunch $28-$34, dinner $31-$38. Table d'hôte: lunch $35, dinner $69, $85 & $110. Outdoor sidewalk terrace dining. Chef-owned. Jacket. Cr cds: A, D, MC, V.

★★★ **DAWAT.** *210 E 58th St (10022), between Second & Third Aves, on the East Side. 212/355-7555.* Indian menu. Specializes in curried shrimp, salmon in coriander chutney. Hrs: 11:30 am-3 pm, 5:30-11 pm; Fri, Sat to 11:15 pm; Sun from 5:30 pm. Res required. Bar. A la carte entrees: lunch, dinner $12.95-$22.95. Complete meals: lunch $13.95 & $14.95, dinner $23.95. Parking (dinner). Contemporary East Indian decor. Cr cds: A, C, D, MC, V.

D

★★ **DELEGATES DINING ROOM.** *In United Nations General Assembly Bldg (10017), 4th floor, at First Ave & 46th St, visitors entrance, on the East Side. 212/963-7625.* International menu. Specializes in ethnic food festivals, seasonal salads, fresh seafood. Hrs: 11:30 am-2:30 pm. Closed Sat, Sun; some major hols. Res required. Serv bar. A la carte entrees: lunch $17.50-$25. Buffet: lunch $19.75. Panoramic view of East River. Open to public; identification with photograph required. Jacket. Cr cds: A, C, D, JCB, MC, V.

D

★★ **DEMI.** *1316 Madison Ave (10128), at 93rd St, Upper East Side. 212/534-3475.* Continental menu. Specialties: rack of lamb, American red snapper with braised spinach, grilled shrimp with asparagus and fresh thyme risotto. Hrs: 11:30 am-11 pm; Sun 5-10 pm; Sun brunch 11:30 am-3:30 pm. Closed July 4, Labor Day, Dec 25. Res accepted. Bar. A la carte entrees: lunch $9-$25, dinner $16-$27. Sun brunch $12.75. Terrace dining. Attractive restaurant in townhouse; romantic atmosphere. Cr cds: A, MC, V.

★★★ **DESTINÉE.** *134 E 61st St (10021), Upper East Side. 212/888-1220.* Modern French menu. Specialties: smoked duck liver in oxtail broth, whole steamed lobster with lobster and garlic sauce, roasted herb-crust rack of lamb. Own pastries. Hrs: noon-2:30 pm, 5:30-10:30 pm; Fri, Sat to 11:30 pm. Closed Sun; major hols. Res accepted. Bar. Wine cellar. A la carte entrees: lunch $12-$19. Prix fixe: lunch $28, dinner $42. Contemporary decor with modern art displayed. Totally nonsmoking. Cr cds: A, D, JCB, MC, V.

★★★ **DOMINGO.** *209 E 49th St (10017), between 2nd & 3rd Aves, Midtown. 212/826-8154.* Spanish menu. Specialties: tapas, paella Valenciana, monkfish a la Catalana. Own desserts. Hrs: 11:30 am-3 pm, 5 pm-midnight. Closed Sun. Res accepted. Bar. Wine list. A la carte entrees: lunch, dinner $5.50-$26. Outdoor dining. Spanish Colonial decor; hand-carved woodwork, large skylight, Spanish mural. Cr cds: A, D, MC, V.

★★★ **DUANE PARK CAFE.** *157 Duane St (10013), between Hudson & W Broadway, in Tribeca. 212/732-5555.* Italian, Amer menu. Specialties: seared tuna with savoy cabbage, crispy skate with ponzu, grilled miso marinated duck salad. Hrs: noon-2:30 pm, 5:30-10 pm; Fri to 10:30 pm; Sat 5:30-10:30 pm. Closed Sun; most major hols; also first wk July. Bar. A la carte entrees: lunch $14-$19.98, dinner $16-$22. Prix fixe: lunch $19.98. Intimate atmosphere with Italian accents. Cr cds: A, C, D, DS, JCB, MC, V.

✔★ **EDWARD MORAN BAR AND GRILL.** *250 Vesey St (10281), in Bldg 4 of World Financial Center, in Financial District. 212/945-2255.* Specializes in hamburgers, sandwiches, seafood. Salad bar. Hrs: 11:30 am-midnight. Res accepted. Bar to 1 am. A la carte entrees: lunch, dinner $8.50-$18.50. Outdoor dining. Pub-like atmosphere. Nautical decor. View of Ellis Island and Statue of Liberty. Cr cds: A, C, D, DS, MC, V.

D

✔★★ **EL TEDDY'S.** *219 W Broadway (10013), between Franklin & White Sts, in Tribeca. 212/941-7070.* Contemporary Mexican menu. Specializes in grilled seafood. Hrs: noon-3 pm, 6-11:30 pm; Thurs, Fri to 1 am; Sat 6 pm-1 am; Sun 6-11 pm. Closed Jan 1, Dec 25. Res accepted. Bar. A la carte entrees: lunch $7-$13, dinner $14-$19. Outdoor dining. Wild, eccentric decor spans styles from 1920s to the present. Located in white building with replica of Statue of Liberty's spiked crown on roof. Cr cds: A, D, MC, V.

★★ **ERIZO LATINO.** *422 W Broadway (10012), between Prince & Spring Sts, in SoHo. 212/941-5811.* Latin menu. Specialties: steamed little neck clams, crispy seared Chilean sea bass. Hrs: noon-3 pm, 6 pm-midnight; Fri, Sat to 2 am. Closed major hols. Res accepted. Bar. Semi-a la carte: lunch, dinner $9-$21. Entertainment Thurs, Fri. Outdoor dining. Rustic room with exposed brick and mustard-colored walls. Totally nonsmoking. Cr cds: A, C, D, DS, MC, V.

★★ **ERMINIA.** *250 E 83rd St (10028), Upper East Side. 212/879-4284.* Italian menu. Specialties: artichokes sautéed in olive oil and garlic; skewer of veal stuffed with prosciutto, pecorino cheese, pine nuts. Hrs: 5-11 pm. Closed Sun; major hols; last wk of June-first wk July. Res required. Wine, beer. Semi-a la carte: dinner $16.95-$27.95. Rustic Italian decor. Jacket. Cr cds: A.

★ ★ ★ **FANTINO.** *(See Luxury Collection Hotel) 212/757-1900.* Northern Italian menu. Specialties: veal osso bucco, roasted rack of lamb, black sea bass. Hrs: 7-10:30 am, 5:30-11 pm; Mon 7-10:30 am, noon-2 pm; Sat 7:30-11:30 am, 5:30-11 pm; Sun 7:30 am-2 pm. Res accepted. Bar noon-1 am. A la carte entrees: dinner $24-$30; buffet: breakfast $23.75; complete meal: lunch $23.75. Pre-theater dinner (5:30-7 pm) $32. Sun brunch $33. Traditional European decor; fireplaces. Cr cds: A, C, D, DS, ER, JCB, MC, V.

[D]

★ ★ ★ **FELIDIA.** *243 E 58th St (10022), between Second & Third Aves, on the East Side. 212/758-1479.* Italian menu. Specializes in homemade pasta, veal, seafood. Own baking. Menu changes daily. Hrs: noon-3 pm, 5-11 pm; Sat 5-11:30 pm. Closed Sun; major hols. Res accepted. Bar. Wine cellar. A la carte entrees: lunch $18-$26, dinner $18-$29. Complete meals: lunch $27.50. Hanging tapestry, plants are found throughout the different dining rms. Jacket. Cr cds: A, C, D, DS, MC, V.

★ ★ ★ ★ **FIFTY SEVEN FIFTY SEVEN.** *(See Four Seasons Hotel) 212/758-5700.* Web www.fshr.com. Housed in the Four Seasons Hotel, designed by I.M. Pei, this is a spectacular, open, airy variation on a brasserie, with 22-foot coffered ceilings, bare maple floors with walnut inlays, bronze chandeliers and art-deco touches. Dining is sophisticated, luxurious and comfortable. Specializes in Maryland crab cakes, thyme-seared Atlantic salmon, herb-roasted rack of lamb. Hrs: 7 am-2 pm, 6-10:30 pm. Bar to 1 am; Fri, Sat to 2 am; Sun to midnight. A la carte entrees: bkfst $12.50-$18.50, lunch $19-$29, dinner $24-$31. Child's meals. Pianist Thurs-Sat to 1 am. Valet parking. Jacket. Cr cds: A, C, D, ER, JCB, MC, V.

[D] [♥]

★ ★ ★ **FIREBIRD.** *365 W 46th St (10036), between 8th & 9th Aves, in Times Square/Theater District. 212/586-0244.* Russian menu. Specialties: caviar with sour cream and blini, herring under a blanket, grilled marinated lamb loin. Own baking. Hrs: 11:45 am-2:30 pm, 5-11 pm; Sun, Mon from 5 pm; Fri, Sat to 11:30 pm. Closed major hols. Res accepted. Bar. Wine cellar. Semi-a la carte: lunch $13.75-$16.75, dinner $17.25-$23.75. Complete meal: dinner $19.50. Opulent replica of Czarist mansion (1912); two-level dining with ornate decor, antique furnishings. Totally nonsmoking. Cr cds: A, C, D, DS, JCB, MC, V.

[D]

✔★ ★ ★ **FIRST.** *87 First Ave (10003), between 5th and 6th Sts; in East Village. 212/674-3823.* Specialties: grilled hanger steak, rotisserie free-range chicken. Hrs: 6 pm-2 am; Thurs-Sat to 3 am; Sun 4 pm-1 am; Sun brunch 11 am-3 pm. Closed Dec 25. Res accepted. Bar. A la carte entrees: dinner $18. Sun brunch $11. Entertainment Sun, Tues. Stylish industrial decor. Cr cds: A, MC, V.

★ ★ ★ **FOLLONICO.** *6 W 24th St (10010), between 5th & 6th Aves, in Chelsea. 212/691-6359.* Italian menu. Specialties: wood-roasted calamari, herb-printed fazzoletto over wild mushroom ragout, whole red snapper in rock-salt crust. Hrs: noon-3 pm, 6-10:30 pm; Fri, Sat 6-11 pm. Closed most major hols. Res accepted. Bar. Wine cellar. A la carte entrees: lunch $12-$18, dinner $16-$24. Tuscany farm house decor with wood-burning oven, beamed ceilings and original art. Cr cds: A, D, MC, V.

[D]

★ ★ ★ ★ **THE FOUR SEASONS.** *99 E 52nd St (10022), Seagram Bldg, between Park & Lexington Aves, Midtown. 212/754-9494.* Web www.citysearch/fourseasons.com. Designed by Philip Johnson, this New York favorite is now a designated local landmark. Menu changes with the season. Own baking. Grow own herbs. Hrs: Pool Dining Room: noon-2:30 pm, 5-9:30 pm; Sat to 11:15 pm. Grill Room: noon-2 pm, 5:30-9 pm; Sat 5-10 pm. Closed Sun; major hols. Res accepted. Bar. Wine cellar. A la carte entrees: Pool Dining Room: lunch $29.50-$48, dinner $32.50-$45. Grill Room: a la carte entrees: lunch $25-$38.50, dinner $37-$48. Jacket. Cr cds: A, C, D, DS, JCB, MC, V.

★ ★ **FRAUNCES TAVERN.** *54 Pearl St (10005), at Broad St, downtown. 212/269-0144.* Specializes in fish from Fulton fishmarket. Hrs: 7-10 am, 11:30 am-4 pm, 5-9:30 pm. Closed Sat, Sun; major hols. Res accepted. Bar. Prix fixe: bkfst $14.95. A la carte entrees: lunch, dinner $15-$25. Child's meals. Historic landmark built 1719; George Washington bade farewell to his officers here in 1783. Museum. Family-owned since 1937. Cr cds: A, C, D, MC, V.

✔★ **FULTON STREET CAFE.** *11 Fulton St (10038), at pier, in South Street Seaport, in Financial District. 212/227-2288.* Specializes in seafood. Hrs: 11:30 am-midnight. Bar. A la carte entrees: lunch, dinner $5-$18.95. Outdoor dining. Nautical decor. Cr cds: A, D, MC, V.

[D]

★ ★ ★ **GABRIEL'S.** *11 W 60th St (10023), between Broadway & Columbus Ave, Upper West Side. 212/956-4600.* Italian menu. Specialties: wood pan-roasted snapper in white wine, slow-roasted kid with white wine and rosemary, wood-grilled sturgeon. Hrs: noon-3 pm, 5:30-11 pm; Fri to midnight; Sat 5:30 pm-midnight. Closed Sun; most major hols. Res required. Bar. Wine list. A la carte entrees: lunch $12-$16, dinner $16-$27. Mahogany bar; original art. Cr cds: A, D, MC, V.

[D]

★ ★ **GALLAGHER'S.** *228 W 52nd St (10019), at Broadway, Times Square/Theater District. 212/245-5336.* Specializes in prime beef, sirloin steak, seafood. Hrs: noon-midnight. Res accepted. Bar. A la carte entrees: lunch $12.75-$42, dinner $14.95-$43. Open kitchen. Photographs of sports & theater personalities. Cr cds: A, C, D, DS, JCB, MC, V.

[♿]

✔★ ★ **GASCOGNE.** *158 Eighth Ave (10011), at 18th St, in Chelsea. 212/675-6564.* French menu. Specialties: roasted quail with fresh spicy peaches, cassoulet bean stew with duck confit and sausages, warm fresh foie gras with seasonal fruit. Hrs: noon-3 pm, 6-10:30 pm; Fri, Sat to 11 pm; Sun noon-3 pm, 5-10 pm. Closed some major hols. Res accepted. Bar. A la carte entrees: lunch $8.75-$15, dinner $19-$21. Sun brunch $8.75-$15. Pre-theatre dinner $25. Garden dining. French country-style decor; farmhouse ambiance. Cr cds: A, C, D, MC, V.

★ ★ ★ **GERTRUDE'S.** *33 E 61st St (10021), between Madison and Park Aves, Upper East Side. 212/888-9127.* French country menu. Specialties: ravioli of foie gras, roasted monkfish Basque-style, grilled veal chop. Hrs: noon-3 pm, 6-11 pm. Res accepted. Bar to 1 am. Wine list. A la carte entrees: lunch $19-$24, dinner $22-$29. Outdoor dining. French country decor. Cr cds: A, D, MC, V.

[♿]

★ ★ **GIGINO TRATTORIA.** *323 Greenwich St (10013), between Duane & Reade Sts, in Tribeca. 212/431-1112.* Southern Italian menu. Specialties: grilled portobello mushrooms with herbed polenta, linguini alla Vongole, spaghetti Padrino. Hrs: 11:30 am-11 pm; Fri to midnight; Sat 4 pm-midnight; Sun from 4 pm. Closed Jan 1, Memorial Day, Dec 25. Res accepted. Bar. A la carte entrees: lunch $10-$18, dinner $12-$21. Outdoor dining. Country farmhouse atmosphere. Cr cds: A, C, D, MC, V.

★ ★ ★ **GIRAFE.** *208 E 58th St (10022), between Second & Third Aves, on the East Side. 212/752-3054.* Northern Italian menu. Hrs: noon-3 pm, 5:30-10:30 pm; Sat 5:30-11 pm. Closed Sun; major hols; also 1st wk July. Res accepted. Bar. Wine list. A la carte entrees: lunch $15-$25, dinner $17-$30. Prix fixe: lunch $18.50. Pre-theater dinner $29.75. Wild animal motif. Cr cds: A, C, D, DS, MC, V.

★ ★ ★ ★ **GOTHAM BAR AND GRILL.** *12 E 12th St (10003), between Fifth Ave & University Pl, in Greenwich Village. 212/620-4020.* E-mail gotham@aol.com. Chef Alfred Portale originated the vertical style of food presentation here—each plate is an artful, edible tower. Multi-leveled and post-modern in design, the Gotham was the prototype of the new-style New York restaurant. Specializes in game, seafood, lamb. Own pastries. Menu changes seasonally. Hrs: noon-2 pm, 5:30-10 pm; Fri to 11 pm; Sat 5:30-11 pm; Sun from 5:30 pm. Closed most major hols. Res required. Bar. A la carte entrees: lunch $9.25-$18, dinner $26-$31. Prix fixe: lunch $19.98. Cr cds: A, C, D, MC, V.

★ ★ ★ ★ **GRAMERCY TAVERN.** *42 E 20th St (10003), between Park Ave S & Broadway, in Gramercy Park. 212/477-0777.* A 91-foot-long mural of fruit and vegetables wraps around the bar of this cozy colonial-decor tavern. Elegant dining is available in three rooms; furnishings include a blend of antiques, quilts and modern art. Specialties: salt-baked salmon, roast rabbit with black olives and sherry vinegar, lobster and artichoke salad. Hrs: 5:30-10 pm; Fri, Sat to 11 pm. Closed major hols. Res required. Bar to midnight. Wine cellar. A la carte entrees: lunch $15-$21. Complete meal: lunch $33, dinner $56. Totally nonsmoking. Cr cds: A, D, MC, V.

D

★★★ **THE GRILL ROOM.** *225 Liberty St (10281), at World Financial Center, in Financial District. 212/945-9400.* Specialties: roasted corn & seafood chowder, cowboy prime rib steak, James Beard's traditional fresh berry shortcake. Own baking. Hrs: noon-4 pm, 5:30-8:30 pm. Closed Sat, Sun; July 4, Labor Day, Dec 25. Res accepted. Bar noon-11 pm. Wine cellar. Semi-a la carte: lunch $19.50-$32, dinner $22-$32. Glass-fronted bldg overlooks Hudson River, offers views of Statue of Liberty and marina. Cr cds: A, DS, MC, V.

D

✔★★ **GROTTA AZZURRA.** *387 Broome St (10013), at Mulberry St, in Little Italy. 212/925-8775.* Neapolitan menu. Specialties: spedini alla Romana, linguine with mussels, chicken cacciatore. Own pasta, cheesecake. Hrs: noon-11 pm; Fri to midnight; Sat to 12:30 am. Closed Mon; wk of Dec 25-Jan 1; also July. Wine, beer. A la carte entrees: lunch, dinner $8.95-$19.95. Parking. Open kitchen. Family-style serv. Family-owned. Cr cds: A, MC, V.

★★ **HARBOUR LIGHTS.** *Fulton Pier 17 (10038), South Street Seaport, in Financial District. 212/227-2800.* Continental, Amer menu. Specializes in seafood, steak. Hrs: 11-1 am; Sun brunch to 3:30 pm. Closed Dec 25. Res accepted. Bar. A la carte entrees: lunch $11-$29, dinner $19-$34. Parking. Outdoor dining. Glass greenhouse-style building; large wraparound outdoor terrace. Overlooks East River; view of Brooklyn Bridge. Cr cds: A, D, DS, JCB, MC, V.

D

✔★★ **HARMONY PALACE.** *94 Mott St (10013), between Canal & Hester Sts, in Chinatown. 212/226-6603.* Chinese menu. Specializes in Cantonese banquet dishes. Hrs: 8 am-10:30 pm. Res accepted. A la carte entrees: dim sum $1.95-$6.50, lunch, dinner from $8.50. Original Oriental art and objets d'art. Cr cds: A, MC, V.

★★★ **HARRY CIPRIANI.** *781 Fifth Ave (10022), at 59th St, Midtown. 212/753-5566.* Italian menu. Specialties: risotto alla primavera, calf's liver veneziana, baked green noodles with ham. Hrs: 7-10:30 am, noon-3 pm, 6-10:45 pm. Res accepted. Bar. Wine cellar. A la carte entrees: bkfst $15-$25, lunch $23.95-$42.95, dinner $23.95-$46.95. Complete meals: lunch $25.95-$42.95, dinner $45.95-$64.95. Understated decor; display of photos, posters and lithographs, reminiscent of Hemingway in Harry's Bar in Venice. Family-owned since 1931. Jacket. Cr cds: A, C, D, DS, MC, V.

✔★★ **HASAKI.** *210 E 9th St (10003), between 2nd and 3rd Aves; East Village. 212/473-3327.* Japanese menu. Specialties: sushi, sashimi. Sushi bar. Hrs: 5-11:30 pm. Closed Jan 1, July 4, Dec 25. Wine, beer. A la carte entrees: dinner $15-$20. Rock wall entrance with wooden benches. Totally nonsmoking. Cr cds: A, D, DS, MC, V.

✔★★ **HOME.** *20 Cornelia St (10014), Between Bleeker & 4th Sts in Greenwich Village. 212/243-9579.* Specialties: blue cheese fondue, roasted chicken sautéed greens with ketchup. Hrs: 9 am-3 pm, 6-11 pm; Sun 5:30-10 pm, Sat, Sun brunch 11 am-4 pm. Closed 2 wks in Jan, July. Res accepted. Wine, beer. Semi-a la carte: bkfst $2-$6, lunch $6-$9, dinner $13-$17. Sat, Sun brunch $5-$10. Outdoor dining. Contemporary decor. Totally nonsmoking. Cr cds: A.

★★ **HOSTERIA FIORELLA.** *1081 Third Ave (10021), between 63rd & 64th Sts, East Side. 212/838-7570.* Italian menu. Specializes in mixed antipasto, homemade pizzas, mixed seafood grill. Own pastries. Hrs: 11:30 am-11:30 pm; Sat from 11 am; Sun 11 am-11 pm; Sat, Sun brunch to 3 pm. Closed Thanksgiving. Res accepted. Bar. A la carte entrees: lunch $12-$23, dinner $12-$32. Sat, Sun brunch $10.50-$16. Casual Tuscan decor with nautical theme; two-level dining. Cr cds: A, D, MC, V.

★ **HOT TOMATO.** *676 6th Ave (10010), at W 21st St, in Chelsea. 212/691-3535.* Specialties: free-range bison burger, "best" Yankee meatloaf, "best" macaroni & cheese. Own pastries. Hrs: 11:30-1 am; Thurs to 2 am; Fri to 4 am; Sat 10-4 am; Sun 10 am-10 pm; Sat, Sun brunch to 5 pm. Closed Dec 25. Bar. Semi-a la carte: lunch $6.95-$13.95, dinner $7.95-$18.95. Sat, Sun brunch $5.95-$14.95. Outdoor dining. Casual decor with tomato fixtures. Totally nonsmoking. Cr cds: A, C, D, MC, V.

★★★★ **HUDSON RIVER CLUB.** *250 Vesey St (10281), in building 4 of World Financial Center, lobby level, Financial District. 212/786-1500.* Web hudsonriverclub.com. As its name suggests, this spacious and clubby dining room has river views of New York Harbor and the Statue of Liberty. Rotating art is displayed on walls. Hudson River Valley produce is showcased, and the towering desserts are like edible sculptures. Specialties: foie gras duo, roasted oysters with leeks, Hudson River Valley dishes. Own pastries. Hrs: 11:30 am-2:30 pm, 5-9:30 pm; Fri to 10 pm; Sat 5-10 pm; Sun brunch 11:30 am-2:30 pm. Closed Memorial Day, Labor Day, Dec 25; also Sun July-Aug. Res required. Bar. Wine cellar. A la carte entrees: lunch $24-$29, dinner $28-$36. Menu dégustation: 6-course dinner $60. Sun brunch $32. Child's meals. Jacket. Cr cds: A, C, D, DS, MC, V.

D

✔★ **HUNAN GARDEN.** *1 Mott St (10013), at Bowery St, in Chinatown. 212/732-7270.* Chinese menu. Specialties: Peking duck, Kwi Yong spiced eggplant, Hong Kong stuffed scallops. Hrs: 11 am-11 pm; Fri, Sat to midnight. Bar. A la carte entrees: lunch, dinner $6-$15. Enclosed sidewalk cafe. Cr cds: A, MC, V.

★★★ **I TRE MERLI.** *463 W Broadway (10012), between Prince & Houston Sts, in SoHo. 212/254-8699.* Northern Italian menu. Specialties: herb ravioli with walnut sauce, focaccia sandwiches, sea bass with artichoke. Hrs: noon-1 am; Fri, Sat to 2 am. Res required Fri-Sun dinner. Bar to 4 am. Wine cellar. A la carte entrees: lunch $10-$23, dinner $12-$25. Outdoor dining. Over 1,000 wine bottles line exposed brick walls in converted warehouse bldg. Cr cds: A, D, MC, V.

★★★ **I TRULLI.** *122 E 27th St (10016), in Murray Hill. 212/481-7373.* Italian menu. Specialties: baked oysters, pancetta, grilled baby octopus. Hrs: noon-3 pm, 5:30-11 pm; Fri to midnight; Sat 5:30 pm-midnight. Closed Sun; major hols. Res accepted. Bar. A la carte entrees: lunch $16-$28, dinner $16-$28. Outdoor dining. Wood-burning oven in the shape of a domed stone structure. Cr cds: A, C, D, MC, V.

✔★★ **IL CORTILE.** *125 Mulberry St (10013), between Canal & Hester Sts, in Little Italy. 212/226-6060.* Web www.menusonline.com. Italian menu. Specialties: capellini piselli e prosciutto, rack of veal sautéed in wine sauce, shrimp and seppioline grilled with garlic. Own pasta. Hrs: noon-midnight; Fri, Sat to 1 am. Closed Thanksgiving, Dec 24, 25. Res accepted. Bar. A la carte entrees: lunch, dinner $15-$18. Dining in skylighted garden rm. Cr cds: A, C, D, MC, V.

★★★ **IL MONELLO.** *1460 Second Ave, between 76th & 77th Sts, Upper East Side. 212/535-9310.* Northern Italian menu. Specialties: combination pasta, stuffed veal chop, fish. Own breads. Hrs: noon-3 pm, 5-11 pm; Fri, Sat to midnight. Closed major hols. Res accepted. Bar. Wine cellar. A la carte entrees: lunch $21-$31, dinner $25-$35. Print collection by renowned 20th-century artists. Cr cds: A, C, D, MC, V.

★★★ **IL NIDO.** *251 E 53rd St (10022), between Second & Third Aves, on the East Side. 212/753-8450.* Northern Italian menu. Specializes in seasonal dishes. Own pastries. Hrs: noon-3 pm, 5:30-11 pm. Closed Sun; major hols. Res required. Bar. Wine cellar. A la carte entrees: lunch $21-$30, dinner $21-$38. Jacket. Cr cds: A, C, D, MC, V.

★★ **IL TOSCANACCIO.** *7 E 59th St (10022), between Fifth & Madison Aves, Midtown. 212/935-3535.* Italian menu. Specializes in rustic Tuscan cuisine. Hrs: noon-3 pm, 5:30-11:30 pm. Closed Sat lunch (in summer), Sun; also some major hols. Res accepted. Bar. A la carte entrees: lunch $14-$28, dinner $16-$32. Photographs of Tuscan countryside and marketplace. Outdoor dining. Cr cds: A, D, MC, V.

D

✔★ ★ **INDIGO.** *142 W 10th St (10014), between Greenwich Ave and Waverly Pl in Greenwich Village. 212/691-7757.* Contemporary Amer menu. Specialties: wild mushroom strudel, roast leg of lamb, grilled salmon. Hrs: 6-11 pm; Fri, Sat to 11:30 pm; Sun to 10:30 pm. Closed major hols. Res accepted. Bar. A la carte entrees: dinner $13-$16. Contemporary decor. Cr cds: A.

✔★ ★ **ITHAKA.** *48 Barrow St (10014), between Bleeker St and 7th Ave S, in Greenwich Village. 212/727-8886.* Greek menu. Specializes in baked shrimp, baby lamb, stuffed eggplant. Hrs: noon-midnight; Fri, Sat to 1 am. Res accepted. Bar. A la carte entrees: lunch $7.95-$13.95, dinner $11.95-$18.95. Outdoor dining. Greek taverna decor. Cr cds: A, D, MC, V.

★ ★ **JAPONICA.** *100 University Place (10003), at 12th St, East Village. 212/243-7752.* Japanese menu. Specializes in sushi, tataki, vegetable dumplings. Hrs: noon-10:30 pm; Fri, Sat to 11 pm; summer hrs vary. Closed Jan 1, Dec 25. Wine, beer. A la carte entrees: lunch $9-$23, dinner $14-$26. Japanese decor. Cr cds: A.

JEAN GEORGES. *(Too new to be rated) (See Trump International Hotel) 212/299-3900.* French menu. Specialties: Arctic char baked with wood sorrel, lobster tartine with pumpkin seed and pea shoots, muscovy duck steak with spices. Own baking. Hrs: 7-11 am, noon-3 pm, 5:30-11 pm; Sat, Sun from 8 am; Sun brunch 11 am-3 pm. Res required (lunch, dinner). Bar. Wine list. A la carte entrees: bkfst $12-$28, lunch $18-$30, dinner $29-$35. Sun brunch $12-$28. Outdoor dining. Elegant decor, high ceilings; glass walls surround restaurant and overlook Central Park. Jacket. Cr cds: A, C, D, JCB, MC, V.

D

✔★ ★ **JIM McMULLEN.** *1341 Third Ave (10021), between 76th & 77th Sts, Upper East Side. 212/861-4700.* Specializes in fresh fish, chicken pot pie, steaks. Hrs: 11:30 am-11 pm; Fri, Sat to midnight. Bar. A la carte entrees: lunch $7.50-$14.95, dinner $11.95-$19.95. Pub-like atmosphere. Outdoor dining. Cr cds: A, D, MC, V.

D

★ ★ ★ **JO JO.** *160 E 64th St (10021), between Lexington & 3rd Aves, Upper East Side. 212/223-5656.* French menu. Specialties: codfish sautéed; roasted duck breast & leg baked in crispy spring roll, morel and asparagus; chicken roasted in ginger, olive and coriander. Hrs: noon-2:30 pm, 6-11 pm; Sat 5:30-11 pm. Closed Sun; Jan 1, July 4, Dec 25. Res required. Serv bar. A la carte entrees: lunch, dinner $19-$30. Complete meals: lunch $25, dinner $55. 2-story townhouse; casual French bistro atmosphere. 1 dining area on main floor, 2 dining rms on 2nd floor. Cr cds: A, MC, V.

★ ★ **JOE ALLEN.** *326 W 46th St (10036), between 8th & 9th Aves, in Times Square/Theater District. 212/581-6464.* Web www.joeallenorso.com. Specialties: Caesar salad, sautéed calf's liver, meatloaf with mashed potatoes. Hrs: noon-11:45 pm; Sun, Wed, Sat from 11:30 am; Sun brunch to 4 pm. Closed Thanksgiving, Dec 25. Res accepted; required dinner. Bar. Semi-a la carte: lunch $9-$19.50, dinner $12.50-$19.50. Sun brunch $9-$19.50. Casual, American pub atmosphere; posters of failed Broadway shows line walls. Family-owned. Cr cds: MC, V.

★ ★ **JUBILEE.** *347 E 54th St (10022), between 1st & 2nd Aves, Midtown. 212/888-3569.* French bistro menu. Specialties: broiled snails skewer with garlic and parsley butter, mussels prepared five different ways, grilled shell steak with green peppercorn sauce. Own pastries. Hrs: noon-3 pm, 5:30-11 pm; Sat from 5:30 pm; Sun 5:30-10:30 pm; Sun brunch noon-3 pm. Closed Jan 1, Dec 24, 25. Res accepted; required dinner. Bar. Semi-a la carte: lunch $13-$16.50, dinner $14.50-$23.50. Complete meal: lunch $18. Sun brunch $20.50. Jazz Thurs. Intimate French country bistro in townhouse bldg. Cr cds: A, D, MC, V.

★ ★ ★ **JUDSON GRILL.** *152 W 52nd St (10019), between 6th & 7th Aves, Midtown. 212/582-5252.* Specialties: seared tuna loin, black Angus sirloin, ten spice loin of lamb. Hrs: noon-2:30 pm, 5:30-11 pm; Fri to 11:30 pm; Sat 5:30-11:30 pm. Closed Sun. Closed major hols. Res accepted. Bar. A la carte entrees: lunch $17-$24.50, dinner $17-$29. Vaulted ceiling; all glass 2-story front. Circular mahogany bar. Cr cds: A, D, DS, MC, V.

D

★ ★ **KEENS STEAKHOUSE.** *72 W 36th St (10018), between Fifth & Sixth Aves, Midtown. 212/947-3636.* Specializes in aged Porterhouse steak for 2 or 3, mutton chops. Hrs: 11:45 am-3 pm, 5:30-10 pm; Sat from 5 pm. Closed Sun; some major hols; also Sat, Sun in summer. Res accepted. Bar. A la carte entrees: lunch $7.95-$18, dinner $15-$30. Historic restaurant, established 1885; dark oak paneling, leaded-glass windows, famous clay pipe collection on ceiling. Famous patrons have included Teddy Roosevelt, Albert Einstein and Lillie Langtry, who sued to enter the once all-male premises. Cr cds: A, C, D, MC, V.

★ ★ **KINGS' CARRIAGE HOUSE.** *251 E 82nd St (10028), between 2nd & 3rd Aves, Upper East Side. 212/734-5490.* Irish, English menu. Specialties: grilled loin of lamb, pan-seared wild salmon, grilled filet mignon. Own pastries. Hrs: noon-3 pm, 6-10:30 pm; Sun 2-10 pm; high tea Mon-Fri 3-4 pm. Closed Dec 25. Res required high tea & Fri, Sat dinner. Bar. Prix fixe: lunch $12.95, dinner $39. High tea $14. Turn-of-the-century carriage house; romantic, intimate atmosphere. Totally nonsmoking. Cr cds: A, MC, V.

D

✔★ **LA BONNE SOUPE.** *48 W 55th St (10019), Midtown. 212/586-7650.* French menu. Seasonal specialties. Hrs: 11:30 am-midnight; Sun to 11 pm; Sun brunch 11:30 am-3 pm. Closed Jan 1, July 4, Thanksgiving, Dec 25. Bar. A la carte entrees: lunch, dinner $8.75-$18.95. Sun brunch $12.75. Child's meals. Limited outdoor balcony dining. Open kitchen. French bistro decor. Cr cds: A, MC, V.

★ ★ ★ ★ **LA CARAVELLE.** *33 W 55th St, between 5th & 6th Aves in Midtown. 212/586-4252.* Murals of Parisian scenes decorate the walls, and light peach banquettes provide seating in this spacious and comfortable dining room. Classic and contemporary French menu. Specialties: truffeled pike quenelles in lobster sauce, crispy duck with cranberries, souffles. Own baking. Hrs: noon-2:30 pm, 5:30-10 pm. Closed Sun; major hols; also 1 wk prior to Labor Day. Res required. Bar. Wine cellar. A la carte entrees: lunch from $25, dinner from $40. Prix fixe: 3-course lunch $36, 3-course dinner $62, 5-course tasting menu $75, 7-course tasting menu $90. Child's meals. Cr cds: A, C, D, JCB, MC, V.

D

★ ★ ★ **LA COLOMBE D'OR.** *134 E 26th St, off Lexington Ave, in Murray Hill. 212/689-0666.* French Provençale menu. Specialties: couscous chicken with roasted shallots and truffled mashed potatoes, bouillabaisse, cassoulet. Own baking. Seasonal menu. Hrs: 5:30 pm-midnight. Closed major hols. Res accepted. Wine list. A la carte entrees: dinner $15-$25. Pre theater dinner (5:30-7 pm): $29. Country French atmosphere. Cr cds: A, C, D, MC, V.

★ ★ ★ ★ **LA CÔTE BASQUE.** *60 W 55th St, Midtown. 212/688-6525.* Murals of the Basque coast, dark wooden cross beams and faux windows are just some of the elements that have followed this restaurant to its new home. Dramatic presentation—such as the signature roast duckling carved at tableside, or the glazed pumpkin custard served with a flaming candle inside a pumpkin lantern—adds to the dining experience here. French menu. Own pastries. Hrs: noon-2:30 pm, 5:30-10:30 pm; Fri to 11:30 pm; Sat 5:30-11:30 pm; Sun 5-10 pm. Closed major hols. Res required. Bar. Prix fixe: lunch $33, dinner $59. Chef-owned. Jacket, tie. Cr cds: A, C, D, MC, V.

D

✔★ ★ ★ **LA MAISON JAPONAISE.** *125 E 39th St (10016), at Lexington Ave, Midtown. 212/682-7375.* French, Japanese menu. Specialties: chicken flambé, filet of sole chinoise, filet of tuna "La Maison Japonaise."

Hrs: 11:45 am-2:30 pm, 5:30-10:30 pm; Sat from 5:30 pm. Closed Sun; major hols. Res accepted. Bar. Semi-a la carte: lunch $10.95-$16.75, dinner $10.95-$16.95. Complete meals: lunch $17.95, dinner $19.95. Cr cds: A, C, D, DS, MC, V.

✔★ ★ **LA MANGEOIRE.** *1008 Second Ave (10022), between 53rd and 54th Sts, on the East Side. 212/759-7086.* Southern French menu. Specialties: Mediterranean-style fish soup, roasted rack of lamb, lavender scented crème brûlée. Hrs: noon-2:30 pm, 5:30-10:30 pm; Fri to 11 pm; Sat 5:30-11 pm; Closed major hols. Res accepted. Serv bar. A la carte entrees: lunch $7.50-$21, dinner $14-$25. Prix fixe: lunch $19.98, dinner 5:30-6:45 pm $19.98-$25. Country French inn atmosphere. Cr cds: A, C, D, MC, V.

★ ★ ★ **LA METAIRIE.** *189 W 10th St (10014), west of 7th Ave S, in Greenwich Village. 212/989-0343.* French menu. Specialties: filet mignon, rack of lamb. Hrs: 5-11 pm; Fri, Sat to midnight; Sun to 10 pm; Sat, Sun brunch noon-3 pm. Res required. A la carte entrees: dinner $14-$23. Wkend brunch $9-$18. French country atmosphere. Cr cds: A, D, DS.

D

★ ★ ★ **LA RESERVE.** *4 W 49th St (10019), between Fifth & Sixth Aves, Midtown. 212/247-2993.* French haute cuisine. Specialties: lobster and scallops in basil sauce, sautéed squab in foie gras wine sauce, grilled baby chicken with lemon olive oil and rosemary. Own pastries. Hrs: noon-3 pm, 5:30-10:30 pm; Fri, Sat to 11 pm. Closed Sun; major hols; also 1st wk July. Res required. Bar. Prix fixe: lunch $32, dinner $54. Pre-theater dinner $39.50. Wood paneled dining rm with wildlife murals, Venetian glass sconces, chandeliers. Jacket. Cr cds: A, D, JCB, MC, V.

D

✔★ ★ **LA TRAVIATA.** *461 W 23rd St (10011), Chelsea. 212/243-5497.* Italian menu. Specialties: veal medallions with prosciutto, filet of red snapper, penne with spicy tomato sauce. Hrs: 11:30 am-10:30 pm; Fri to 11 pm; Sat 4:30-11 pm; Sun brunch 1-9 pm. Closed Sun (Memorial Day-Labor Day); July 4. Res accepted. Bar. Semi-a la carte: lunch, dinner $9.50-$20.95. Sun brunch $9.50-$20.95. Entertainment Wed-Sat. Northern Italian decor. Cr cds: A, D, DS, MC, V.

D

★ ★ ★ **LAYLA.** *211 W Broadway (10013), at Franklin St, in Tribeca. 212/431-0700.* Web interactive gourmet www.cuisine.com. Mediterranean menu. Specialties: cumin-spiced swordfish kebob, Moroccan shepard's pie, grilled salmon wrapped in grape leaves. Hrs: noon-2:30 pm, 5:30-10:45 pm; Fri to 11:30 pm; Sat 5:30-11:30 pm; Sun 5:30-9:45 pm. Closed most major hols. Res accepted. Bar to midnight. Semi-a la carte: lunch $12-$18, dinner $19-$27. Prix fixe: lunch $19.98. Outdoor dining. Arabian nights decor. Totally nonsmoking. Cr cds: A, D, MC, V.

★ ★ ★ ★ **LE BERNARDIN.** *155 W 51st St (10019), in Equitable Life Tower, between Sixth & Seventh Aves, Times Square/Theater District. 212/489-1515.* Web www.le-bernardin.com. Huge seascapes fill the paneled walls of this polished, high-ceilinged restaurant, where fish and seafood dinners are as delicious and well prepared as you can get anywhere. French, seafood menu. Specialties: monkfish with cabbage, thyme and pepper rare-seared yellowfin tuna, crispy Chinese-spiced red snapper. Own pastries. Hrs: noon-2:15 pm, 6-10:30 pm; Fri, Sat 5:30-11 pm. Closed Sun; major hols. Res accepted. Bar. Prix fixe: lunch $42, dinner $68. Jacket. Cr cds: A, C, D, JCB, MC, V.

D

★ ★ ★ **LE BOEUF À LA MODE.** *539 E 81st St, near East End Ave, in Yorkville section of Upper East Side. 212/249-1473.* French menu. Specialties: duck á l'orange, rack of lamb, daily fish specials. Hrs: 5:30-11 pm. Closed major hols; also Sun in July & Aug. Res accepted. Bar. A la carte entrees: dinner $18-$28. Prix fixe: dinner $32. Outdoor dining. Intimate dining rm with colorful murals. Cr cds: A, D, MC, V.

★ ★ ★ ★ **LE CHANTILLY.** *106 E 57th St (10022), between Lexington & Park Aves, Midtown. 212/751-2931.* Murals of the château of Chantilly, fresh flowers and comfortable banquettes set a French mood at this New York institution. French menu. Specialties: grilled red snapper, roasted loin of rabbit, composition of Maine lobster with crispy noodle cake. Daily specials. Own baking. Hrs: noon-3 pm, 5:30-10:30 pm; Sat 5:30-11 pm; Sun 5-9:30 pm. Closed major hols. Res required. Bar. Wine list. A la carte entrees: lunch $18-$24. Prix fixe: lunch $20-$30, dinner $55. 7-course tasting menu: dinner $75. Cr cds: A, JCB, MC, V.

D

LE CIRQUE 2000. *(Too new to be rated) (See The New York Palace Hotel) 212/303-7788.* French menu. Specialties: sea bass wrapped in crisp potatoes with barolo sauce, braised veal shank, lobster roasted with young artichokes. Hrs: 11:30 am-3 pm, 5:30-11 pm; Fri, Sat to midnight. Res required. Bar to 1 am. Wine list. A la carte entrees: lunch $26-$32, dinner $27-$35. Complete meals: lunch $35, dinner $90. Jacket, tie. Cr cds: A, C, D, MC, V.

D

★ ★ ★ **LE COLONIAL.** *149 E 57th St (10022), between Third & Lexington Aves, on the East Side. 212/752-0808.* Vietnamese menu. Specialties: whole red snapper with spicy sour sauce, roast duck with tamarind sauce, sautéed jumbo shrimp with curried coconut sauce. Hrs: noon-2:15 pm, 5:30-11:30 pm; Fri to midnight; Sat 5:30 pm-midnight; Sun 5:30-11 pm. Closed July 4, Thanksgiving, Dec 25. Res accepted. Bar 4:30 pm-2 am. A la carte entrees: lunch $10.50-$19.50, dinner $12.50-$19.50. Multi-level dining. Bamboo furniture, bird cages. Cr cds: A, D, MC, V.

D

★ ★ ★ **LE MADRI.** *168 W 18th St, at 7th Ave, in Chelsea. 212/727-8022.* Italian menu. Specializes in regional Italian cuisine, seasonal dishes. Hrs: noon-3 pm, 5:30-11:30 pm; Sat, Sun to 10:30 pm. Closed some major hols. Res accepted. Bar. A la carte entrees: lunch $13-$21, dinner $16-$32. Valet parking. Outdoor dining. Vaulted ceiling supported by columns; colorfully tiled wood-burning pizza oven. Jacket. Cr cds: A, D, MC, V.

★ ★ ★ **LE PERIGORD.** *405 E 52nd St (10022), between First Ave & Sutton Place, Midtown. 212/755-6244.* Modern French cuisine. Specialties: confit of duck, grilled Dover sole, boneless quails stuffed with vegetables. Own desserts. Hrs: noon-3 pm, 5:15-10:30 pm; Sat, Sun 5:15-11 pm. Res accepted. Bar. Wine cellar. Prix fixe: lunch $32, dinner $52. Family-owned. Cr cds: A, C, D, DS, MC, V.

★ ★ ★ **LE REFUGE.** *166 E 82nd St (10021), between Lexington & Third Aves, Upper East Side. 212/861-4505.* French menu. Specialties: roast duck with fresh fruit sauce; poached salmon garnished with diced tomatoes, garlic and olive oil; loin of lamb stuffed with spinach. Own baking. Hrs: noon-3 pm, 5-11 pm; Sun noon-4 pm, 5-9:30 pm; Sat brunch to 3 pm; Sun brunch to 4 pm. Closed major hols. Res accepted. Beer. Wine cellar. A la carte entrees: lunch $12.50-$15.50, dinner $17.50-$24.50. Sat, Sun brunch $17.50. Garden terrace dining (summer). French country inn decor. Cr cds: A.

★ ★ ★ **LE RÉGENCE.** *(See Plaza Athénée Hotel) 212/606-4647.* French menu. Specializes in filet of red snapper, filet mignon of beef, roast rack of lamb. Own pastries. Hrs: 7-10 am, noon-2:30 pm, 6-9:30 pm; Sun brunch noon-2:30 pm. Res accepted. Bar 11 am-midnight. Wine cellar. A la carte entrees: bkfst $9-$16.50, lunch $21-$28, dinner $25.50-$30.50. Prix fixe: bkfst $19, lunch $25.50, dinner $49. Sun brunch $42.50. Child's meals. Elegant decor. Cr cds: A, C, D, ER, JCB, MC, V.

D

✔★ ★ **THE LEMON.** *230 Park Ave S (10003), at 19th St, Gramercy Park. 212/614-1200.* Specialties: crispy duck spring rolls, five spice Chilean sea bass. Hrs: 11:30 am-4 pm, 5:30 pm-midnight; Thur-Sat to 2 am; Sat, Sun brunch 11:30 am-4 pm. Closed Jan 1, Dec 25. Res accepted. Bar to 3 am. Semi-a la carte: lunch $7-$15, dinner $10-$20. Sat, Sun brunch $7-$15. Entertainment Sun. Outdoor dining. Bistro decor. Cr cds: A, C, MC, V.

D

★ ★ ★ **LENOX ROOM.** *1278 Third Ave (10021), Between 73 & 74th Sts, upper East Side. 212/772-0404.* Web www.lenoxroom.com. Specializes in progressive American cuisine, fresh seafood. Hrs: noon-2:30 pm, 6-11 pm. Closed Jan 1. Res accepted. Bar. A la carte entrees:

lunch $12-$17, dinner $19-$32; complete meal: lunch $19.98. Raw bar. Several intimate dining areas. Cr cds: A, C, D, MC, V.

D

★★★★★ **LES CÉLÉBRITÉS.** *(See Essex House Hotel Nikko) 212/484-5113.* Chef Christian Delouvrier and the staff have forged this young restaurant at Central Park into one of New York's finest. The superb French menu is complemented by the elegant surroundings, in which paintings by Hollywood celebrities adorn the walls. French menu. Specialties: grilled turbot with champagne sauce, filet of veal with morels, crispy duck braised in ginger and pineapple. Hrs: 6-10 pm; Sat to 10:30 pm. Closed Sun, Mon; also mid-Aug-mid-Sept. Res required. Bar. Wine cellar. A la carte entrees: dinner $30-$42. Table d'hôte: dinner $75 & $105. Valet parking. Jacket. Cr cds: A, C, D, DS, ER, JCB, MC, V.

D

★★★★★ **LESPINASSE.** *(See The St Regis Hotel) 212/339-6719.* Web www.ITTsheraton.com. A high, gilded ceiling, crystal chandelier, plush rugs, murals and large armchairs characterize this grand and spacious Louis XV dining room. An outstanding continental culinary experience features the best of the season by chef Gray Kunz, often with Asian flavors. French menu. Specialties: turbotin with herb broth, roast lamb chop, braised rib of beef. Hrs: 7-10:30 am, noon-2 pm, 5:30-10 pm; Sun 7-11 am. Res required. Bar 11:30-1 am; Fri, Sat to 2 am. Extensive wine list. A la carte entrees: bkfst $13-$21, dinner $36-$43. Complete meals: lunch $48, dinner $78-$130. Valet parking. Jacket, tie. Cr cds: A, C, D, DS, ER, JCB, MC, V.

D

★ **LIBERTY CAFE.** *89 South St (10038), at Pier 17, South Street Seaport, in Financial District. 212/406-1111.* Specializes in lobster, crab meat & shrimp fettucini, 21-day aged NY sirloin. Hrs: 11:30-2 am; Sun to 1 am. Closed Dec 25. Bar to 3 am. A la carte entrees: lunch $8-$15, dinner $12-$22. Child's meals. Outdoor dining. Overlooks harbor and waterfront; view of downtown skyline and Statue of Liberty. Cr cds: A, C, D, DS, MC, V.

★★ **LOBSTER CLUB.** *24 E 80th St (10021), Upper East Side. 212/249-6500.* Eclectic Amer menu. Specialties: matzo brei with smoked salmon and dill, meatloaf, almond-crusted banana split with malted milk. Hrs: 11:30 am-3 pm, 5:30-10:30 pm; Fri, Sat to 11 pm. Closed major hols. Res accepted. Bar. A la carte entrees: lunch $15-$24.50, dinner $16.50-$29. Bi-level dining room with fireplace. Totally nonsmoking. Cr cds: A, D, MC, V.

★★★ **LOLA.** *30 W 22nd St (10010), between 5th & 6th Aves, in Chelsea. 212/675-6700.* Web www.lola.com. Contemporary Amer menu. Specialties: Lola fried chicken with Cuban black beans, pineapple-glazed salmon with noodle cake, corn and rock shrimp. Own pastries. Hrs: noon-3 pm, 6 pm-12:30 am; Sat from 6 pm; Sun brunch sittings 9:30 am, 11:30 am & 1:45 pm. Closed major hols. Res accepted. Bar noon-1 am. Wine list. Semi-a la carte: lunch $15-$20.50, dinner $22-$32.50. Sun brunch $29.75. Blues Wed-Sat, gospel Sun brunch. Elegant decor; French doors; black and white prints of city. Totally nonsmoking. Cr cds: A, D, MC, V.

★★ **LUMI.** *963 Lexington Ave (10021), at 70th St, Upper East Side. 212/570-2335.* Italian menu. Specialties: veal and ricotta ravioli, osso buco con risotto all' ortolana. Hrs: noon-11 pm. Res accepted. Bar. A la carte entrees: lunch $12.50-$22, dinner $14-$29. Outdoor dining. Contemporary decor. Cr cds: A, D, MC, V.

★★ **LUSARDI'S.** *1494 Second Ave (10021), between 77th & 78th Sts, Upper East Side. 212/249-2020.* Northern Italian menu. Specialties: risotto with truffles or with wild mushrooms. Hrs: noon-3 pm, 5 pm-midnight. Closed most major hols. Res accepted. Bar. A la carte entrees: lunch, dinner $13-$22. Italian-style trattoria. Seasonal menu. Totally nonsmoking. Cr cds: A, C, D, DS, MC, V.

D

★★★★ **LUTÈCE.** *249 E 50th St (10022), between 2nd & 3rd Aves, Midtown. 212/752-2225.* Dining at this New York City culinary favorite is in four different rooms: an airy, high-ceilinged main room in a covered garden, a quiet room decorated with stenciled foliage and two upstairs rooms subtly lighted by crystal chandeliers and hung with original oil paintings. French haute cuisine. Specialties: snails and wild mushroom in phyllo, sauteed turbotin on a black truffle vinaigrette, roast rack of lamb with a mustard honey glaze. Hrs: noon-2 pm, 5:30-10 pm; Mon from 5:30 pm; Fri to 10:30 pm; Sat 5:30-10:30 pm. Closed Sun. Res required. Bar. Wine cellar. Table d'hôte: lunch $38. Prix fixe: dinner $65. Cr cds: A, C, D, DS, MC, V.

★★★ **MALONEY & PORCELLI.** *37 E 50th St (10022), between Madison & Park Aves, Midtown. 212/750-2233.* Specialties: angry lobster, crackling pork shank, drunken donuts. Own desserts. Hrs: 11:30 am-midnight; Sat, Sun 11:30 am-3 pm (brunch), 5 pm-midnight. Closed Jan 1, Dec 25. Res accepted. Bar. Wine list. A la carte entrees: lunch $12.50-$19.50, dinner $19.50-$29.75. Sat, Sun brunch $20-$30. Two-story restaurant with grand staircase, skylights, fireplaces. Cr cds: A, C, D, JCB, MC, V.

✔★★ **MANHATTAN BISTRO.** *129 Spring St (10012), between Wooster & Greene, in SoHo. 212/966-3459.* French menu. Hrs: 11:30 am-midnight; Fri, Sat to 2 am; Sat, Sun brunch 11:30 am-4:30 pm. Closed Memorial Day, Dec 25. Res accepted. Bar from 11:30 am. A la carte entrees: lunch $8.50-$15, dinner $13-$24.95. Complete meals: lunch $13.95, dinner $19.95. Sat, Sun brunch $8.50-$15. Intimate storefront bistro in area of studios, art galleries. Family-owned. Cr cds: A, MC, V.

★★★ **MANHATTAN CAFE.** *1161 First Ave, between 63rd & 64th Sts, Upper East Side. 212/888-6556.* Web www.dinette.com. Specializes in steak, lobster. Hrs: noon-11 pm; Sun brunch 11:30 am-3:30 pm. Closed Thanksgiving, Dec 25. Res accepted. Bar from 4 pm. Prix fixe: lunch, Pre-theater dinner $17.95-$27.95. A la carte entrees: lunch $8.50-$19, dinner $18.75-$35.75. Sun brunch $17.95. Club-like atmosphere; paneling, Oriental rugs, 1920s period lighting. Cr cds: A, C, D, DS, JCB, MC, V.

★★★ **MANHATTAN OCEAN CLUB.** *57 W 58th St (10019), off Sixth Ave, Midtown. 212/371-7777.* Specialties: red snapper with rosemary crust, roasted blackfish, Dover sole. Own pastries. Hrs: noon-11:30 pm; Sat, Sun from 5 pm. Closed Jan 1, Thanksgiving, Dec 25. Res required. Bar. Wine list. A la carte entrees: lunch, dinner $19.50-$29.50. Atmosphere of luxury ocean liner; broad sweeping staircase connects 2 floors. Cr cds: A, C, D, DS, JCB, MC, V.

★★★★ **MARCH.** *405 E 58th St (10022), between First Ave & Sutton Place, Upper East Side. 212/754-6272.* Elegantly understated, the three dining rooms in this romantic townhouse are filled with antiques, a travertine floor and burled wood wainscoting. Service is polished, and there are hints of Asian influences in the cuisine. Specialties: five-spice salmon, grilled Long Island duck, roast rack of lamb with herbed crust. Hrs: 6-10:30 pm. Closed Jan 1, Thanksgiving, Dec 25. Res required. Bar. Complete meals: dinner $63. Tasting menu: dinner $75 & $90. Outdoor dining. Jacket. Cr cds: A, C, D, JCB, MC, V.

★★ **MARLOWE.** *328 W 46th St (10036), between 8th & 9th Aves, Times Square/Theater District. 212/765-3815.* Specialties: spiced seared yellow fin tuna, black Angus sirloin with caramelized shallot confit, grilled leg of lamb with ragout of woodland mushrooms. Hrs: noon-3 pm, 5 pm-midnight; Sun brunch noon-3 pm. Closed Dec 25. Res accepted. Bar. A la carte entrees: lunch $6-$13, dinner $9-$24. Complete meals: lunch $10, dinner $19. Sun brunch $4.95-$12.95. Outdoor dining. French country inn atmosphere. Totally nonsmoking. Cr cds: A, C, D, MC, V.

★★ **MARYLOU'S.** *21 W 9th St (10011), between Fifth & Sixth Aves, in Greenwich Village. 212/533-0012.* Continental menu. Specialties: seafood platter, grilled swordfish steak, linguini pescatore. Hrs: 5:30 pm-midnight; Fri, Sat to 1 am; Sun 5:30-11 pm; Sun brunch noon-4 pm. Closed some major hols. Res accepted. Bar. A la carte entrees: dinner $14.95-$28. Sun brunch $13.95. In 19th-century town house; fireplace, library, changing art exhibits. Cr cds: A, C, D, DS, MC, V.

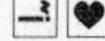

★ ★ ★ **MATTHEW'S.** *1030 Third Ave (10021), at 61st St, on the upper East Side. 212/838-4343.* Specialties: crispy red snapper, Maine crab cakes, lamb shank. Hrs: noon-11 pm; Fri, Sat to midnight. Closed Dec 25. Res accepted. Bar. A la carte entrees: lunch $14-$19, dinner $19-$27. Mediterranean atmosphere; white tented ceilings. Cr cds: A, C, D, MC, V.

D

★ **MED GRILL BISTRO & CAFE.** *(725 5th Ave, New York 10022) between 56th & 57th Sts, in Trump Tower, Midtown. 212/751-3526.* Continental, Italian menu. Specializes in salad, pasta, risotto. Hrs: Cafe 8:30 am-6:30 pm, Bistro 11:30 am-4 pm. Closed some major hols. Res accepted. Bar 11:30 am-4 pm. A la carte entrees: lunch $9.95-$21.23. Contemporary decor with prints & oils on display; overlooks wall with cascading water. Cr cds: A, D, DS, MC, V.

D

★ ★ ★ **MERLOT.** *44 W 63rd St (10023), between Broadway & Columbus Ave, Upper West Side. 212/582-2121.* Web www.iridiumjazz.com. Specialties: beef bourguignon, seared salmon, pasta with jumbo shrimp. Jazz club on lower level. Hrs: 5:30 pm-1 am; Sun to 11 pm; Sun brunch 11:30 am-4 pm. Res accepted. Bar 4 pm-midnight. A la carte entrees: dinner $14-$23; prix fixe gospel brunch $19.95. Eccentric, colorful decor based on question: what would music look like if it could be seen? Unique architectural design emphasizes curves. Cr cds: A, C, D, DS, MC, V.

★ ★ **MESA CITY.** *1059 Third Ave (10021), between 62nd & 63rd Sts, Upper East Side. 212/207-1919.* Southwestern menu. Specialties: blue corn pancake, barbecued chicken, crispy bacon and hash brown quesadilla. Own pastries. Hrs: noon-3 pm, 5:30-11 pm; Fri, Sat to midnight; Sat, Sun brunch 11:30 am-3 pm. Closed Thanksgiving. Res accepted. Bar. A la carte entrees: lunch $12-$17, dinner $12-$22. Sat, Sun brunch $11-$15. Child's meals. Casual atmosphere. Totally nonsmoking. Cr cds: A, C, D, MC, V.

★ ★ ★ **MESA GRILL.** *102 Fifth Ave (10011), between 15th & 16th Sts, in Gramercy Park area. 212/807-7400.* Contemporary Southwestern menu. Specialties: shrimp and roasted garlic corn tamale, blue corn tortilla-crusted red snapper, black Angus steak. Hrs: noon-2:30 pm, 5:30-10:30 pm; Fri to 11 pm; Sat 5:30-11 pm; Sun 5:30-10:30 pm; Sat, Sun brunch 11:30 am-3 pm. Closed some major hols. Res accepted. Bar. A la carte entrees: lunch $12-$16, dinner $17-$26. Industrial designed loft. Cr cds: A, D, DS, MC, V.

D

★ **MEZZALUNA.** *1295 Third Ave (10021), between 74th & 75th Sts, Upper East Side. 212/535-9600.* Italian menu. Specializes in pizza baked in wood-burning oven, light antipasti. Own pasta. Hrs: noon-3:30 pm, 6 pm-12:30 am. Closed Dec 25. Wine, beer. A la carte entrees: lunch $15-$21, dinner $25-$30. Outdoor dining. Trattoria atmosphere. Antique marble top tables and bar. Cr cds: A.

✔★ ★ **MEZZOGIORNO.** *195 Spring St (10012), near Sullivan St, in SoHo. 212/334-2112.* Northern Italian menu. Specializes in brick-oven pizza. Hrs: noon-3 pm, 6 pm-1 am; Sat, Sun noon-1 am. Closed Dec 25. Res accepted. Bar. A la carte entrees: lunch, dinner $13-$16. Outdoor dining. Cr cds: A.

✔★ ★ **MI COCINA.** *57 Jane St (10014), at Hudson St, in Greenwich Village. 212/627-8273.* Mexican menu. Specialties: pechuga con rajas, camarones enchipotlados, enchiladas de mole poblano. Hrs: 5:30-10:30 pm; Fri, Sat to 11:30 pm; Sun 4:30-10 pm; Sun brunch 11:30 am-3 pm. Closed Dec 24, 25; also 2 wks Aug. Res accepted. Bar. A la carte entrees: dinner $9.95-$17.95. Sun brunch $7.95-$13.95. Child's meals. Modern Mexican atmosphere; colorful decor with yellow stucco walls, red tile floors. Outdoor dining. Cr cds: A, C, D, JCB, MC, V.

★ ★ ★ **MICHAEL'S.** *24 W 55th St, between Fifth & Sixth Aves, Midtown. 212/767-0555.* Specialties: chicken with goat cheese, Atlantic swordfish with tomato basil vinaigrette, Canadian salmon with grilled peppers and onions. Own baking. Hrs: 7:30-9:30 am, noon-3 pm, 5:30-10:30 pm; Sat from 5:30 pm. Closed Sun; some major hols. Res accepted. Bar. Wine cellar. A la carte entrees: bkfst $5-$15, lunch, dinner $16-$24.50. Serv charge 15%. Child's meals. Original artwork throughout. Cr cds: A, D, MC, V.

✔★ **MICKEY MANTLE'S RESTAURANT & SPORTS BAR.** *42 Central Park South (10019), between Fifth & Sixth Aves, Midtown. 212/688-7777.* Specializes in chicken-fried steak, seafood, baby back ribs. Hrs: noon-midnight; Sun to 11 pm. Res accepted. Bar to 1 am, Sun to midnight. A la carte entrees: lunch, dinner $10-$20. Child's meals. Outdoor dining. Rotating collection of baseball memorabilia; original sports art. Cr cds: A, C, D, DS, MC, V.

D

★ ★ ★ **MONKEY BAR.** *60 E 54th St (10022), between Park & Madison Aves, Midtown. 212/838-2600.* Specialties: roasted Amish chicken breast, mustard-crusted rack of lamb, roasted cod. Hrs: noon-2:30 pm, 6-11 pm; Fri to 11:30 pm; Sat 5:30-11:30 pm; Sun 6-10 pm. Closed Dec 25. Res accepted. Bar to 2 am; Fri, Sat to 3 am. A la carte entrees: lunch $16-$21, dinner $19-$34. 5-course tasting menu: dinner $65. Pianist. Monkeys hang from lighting; murals of monkeys decorate the bar. Jacket. Cr cds: A, D, MC, V.

✔★ ★ ★ **MONTRACHET.** *239 W Broadway (10013), between Walker & White Sts, in Tribeca. 212/219-2777.* Web www.interactivegourmet.cuisine.com. French menu. Specializes in soufflé, lobster, vegetable terrine. Own pastries. Hrs: 6-11 pm; Fri also noon-2:30 pm. Closed Sun; major hols. Res required. Bar. Wine list. A la carte entrees: lunch $16-$24, dinner $23-$30. Prix fixe: lunch $19.98, dinner $32, $38, tasting $70. Cr cds: A.

D

★ ★ **MORENO.** *65 Irving Place, at E 18th St, in Gramercy Park area. 212/673-3939.* Contemporary Italian menu. Specializes in seafood, pasta. Seasonal menu. Hrs: noon-3 pm, 5:30 pm-midnight; Sat from 5:30 pm; Sun noon-10:30 pm. Res accepted. Bar. A la carte entrees: lunch $15-$20.95, dinner $16.50-$24.95. Prix fixe: Sun $19.95. Child's meals. Outdoor dining. Cr cds: A, D, DS, MC, V.

D

★ ★ ★ **MORTON'S OF CHICAGO.** *551 Fifth Ave (10017), at 45th St, Midtown. 212/972-3315.* Specializes in steak, lobster. Hrs: 11:30 am-2:30 pm, 5 pm-midnight; Sat from 5 pm; Sun 5-11 pm. Closed most major hols. Res accepted. Bar. A la carte entrees: lunch, dinner $19.95-$31.95. Counterpart of famous Chicago steak house. Cr cds: A, D, JCB, MC, V.

★ ★ ★ **NADAMAN HAKUBAI.** *66 Park Ave (10016), in Midtown. 212/885-7111.* Japanese menu. Specializes in traditional Kaiseki dishes. Hrs: 7-9:30 am, 11:45 am-2:30 pm, 6-10 pm. Res accepted. Bar. A la carte entrees: lunch, dinner $12-$24. Complete meals: bkfst $24, lunch $26-$45, dinner $60-$150. Elegant Japanese decor. Totally nonsmoking. Cr cds: A, C, D, DS, JCB, MC, V.

D

★ ★ ★ **NINO'S.** *1354 1st Ave (10021), between 72nd & 73rd Sts, Upper East Side. 212/988-0002.* Northern Italian menu. Specialties: zuppa di pesce, pick-your-own live lobster, rack of veal. Own pastries. Hrs: 5 pm-midnight; Sun 3-11 pm. Closed Jan 1, Memorial Day, Dec 25. Res required. Bar to 2 am. Wine cellar. A la carte entrees: dinner $17.95-$40. Complete meal: dinner $24.95. Tasting menu: dinner $60. Entertainment. Valet parking. Italian decor. Cr cds: A, C, D, DS, MC, V.

★ ★ ★ ★ **NOBU.** *105 Hudson St (10013), at Franklin St, in Tribeca. 212/219-0500.* A curved wall of river-worn black pebbles, bare-wood tables, birch trees and a hand-painted beech floor create a dramatic setting that invites conversation. Sake is the drink of choice; the clientele is as interesting as the menu, which features such tours de force as rock-shrimp tempura and black cod with miso. Japanese menu. Sushi bar. Hrs: 11:45 am-2:15 pm, 5:45-10:15 pm; Sat, Sun from 5:45 pm. Closed some major hols. Res accepted. Serv bar. A la carte entrees: lunch $12-$30, dinner $18-$30. Complete meals: lunch $20. Tasting menu: dinner $60. Cr cds: A, D, MC, V.

✔★ **NOOR'S.** *94 Chambers (10007), between Broadway & Church, in Tribeca. 212/732-5011.* Indian menu. Specializes in chicken tikka masalla, tandoori mixed grill. Hrs: 11 am-11 pm; Sat, Sun from noon. Res accepted. Bar. Semi-a la carte: lunch, dinner $7.95-$21.95. Casual decor. Cr cds: A, D, DS, MC, V.

D

★ ★ ★ **NOVITA.** *102 E 22nd St (10010), Gramercy Park. 212/677-2222.* Italian menu. Specialties: porcini ravioli in black truffle sauce, roasted duck with barolo sauce, tuna carpaccio with capers. Hrs: noon-3 pm, 6-11 pm; Fri, Sat 6 pm-midnight. Closed Sun; major hols. Res accepted. Bar. A la carte entrees: lunch $10-$20, dinner $11-$21. Complete meals: lunch $19.98. Outdoor dining. Casual decor. Totally nonsmoking. Cr cds: A, C, D, MC, V.

★ ★ ★ **OAK ROOM.** *(See The Plaza Hotel) 212/759-3000.* E-mail plaza@fairmont.com; web www.fairmont.com. Traditional European, Amer menu. Specialties: black Angus beef, roasted rack of lamb, surf and turf. Seasonal menu. Own baking. Hrs: 11:30 am-3 pm, 5:30-11:30 pm; Sun 5:30-10:30 pm. Pre theatre 5:30-7:30 pm. Res accepted. Serv bar. Wine list. A la carte entrees: lunch $14-$26, dinner $24-$34. Pre-theater dinner $42, includes free transportation to theaters. Pianist. Valet parking. Historic grand dining rm (1907) with hand-painted murals and 25-ft ceilings. Jacket. Cr cds: A, C, D, DS, ER, JCB, MC, V.

D

★ ★ ★ **OCEANA.** *55 E 54th St (10022), between Park & Madison Aves, Midtown. 212/759-5941.* Hrs: noon-2:30 pm, 5:30-10:30 pm; Sat from 5:30 pm. Closed Sun; most major hols. Res accepted. Wine cellar. Complete meals: lunch $35, dinner $55. Located in 2-story townhouse; spacious, bi-level dining rm. Elegant decor. Jacket. Cr cds: A, C, D, DS, JCB, MC, V.

★ ★ **THE ODEON.** *145 W Broadway (10013), between Thomas & Duane Sts, in Tribeca. 212/233-0507.* E-mail theodeon@aol.com. French, Amer menu. Specializes in seafood, grilled dishes. Hrs: noon-2 am; Fri, Sat to 3 am; Sun brunch 11:30 am-4 pm. Res accepted. Bar to 4 am. Complete meals: lunch $17. A la carte entrees: lunch $8.50-$21.50, dinner $11-$23. Sun brunch $8.50-$21.50. Child's meals. Outdoor dining. Brasserie in 1930s, cafeteria-style art deco. Cr cds: A, D, MC, V.

★ ★ ★ **ONE IF BY LAND, TWO IF BY SEA.** *17 Barrow St (10014), between Seventh Ave S & West Fourth, in Greenwich Village. 212/228-0822.* Continental menu. Specialties: beef Wellington, seafood. Own pastries. Hrs: 5:30 pm-midnight. Closed most major hols. Res required. Bar 4 pm-2 am. Wine cellar. A la carte entrees: dinner $22-$35. Pianist; vocalist Fri-Sat. In restored 18th-century carriage house once owned by Aaron Burr; many framed historical documents; dining rm overlooks courtyard garden. Jacket. Cr cds: A, D, MC, V.

★ ★ ★ **ORSO.** *322 W 46th St (10036), between Eighth and Ninth Aves, Time Square/Theater District. 212/489-7212.* Web www.JoeAllen/OrsoTeaneck.com. Regional Italian menu. Own gelato. Hrs: noon-11:45 pm; Wed & Sat from 11:30 am. Res required (1 wk in advance). Bar. A la carte entrees: lunch, dinner $12-$22. Italian-style trattoria with skylighted, vaulted ceiling; celebrity photo collection. Cr cds: MC, V.

★ ★ **OSTERIA AL DOGE.** *142 W 44th St (10036), between 6th Ave & Broadway, Times Square/Theater District. 212/944-3643.* Italian menu. Specializes in Venetian dishes, seafood, pizza. Hrs: noon-11:30 pm; Fri, Sat to midnight; Sun 4:30-10:30 pm. Closed Jan 1, Dec 25. Res accepted. Bar. A la carte entrees: lunch $10.50-$18.50, dinner $11.50-$19.50; Sat brunch $13.95; prix fixe pre-theater dinner (5-7 pm) $22.95. Child's meals. Cr cds: A, D, DS, MC, V.

★ ★ ★ **OSTERIO DEL CIRCO.** *120 W 55th St (10019), Midtown. 212/265-3636.* E-mail circony@aol.com. Italian menu. Specialties: Tuscan fish soup, spinach ravioli. Hrs: 11:30 am-2:30 pm, 5:30-11 pm; Thurs-Sat to 11:30 pm. Closed major hols. Res accepted. Bar. A la carte entrees: lunch $10-$24.75, dinner $15.50-$27.75. Outdoor dining. Pseudo circus tent made of red and yellow panels of cloth. Cr cds: A, D, MC, V.

D

★ ★ ★ ★ **OTABE.** *68 E 56th St (10022), Midtown. 212/223-7575.* Complete dinners, which change monthly to reflect the seasons, are served in the traditional Japanese dining room. In the Teppan Grill Room, personal chefs prepare steak, fish and other seafood on steel griddles built onto a large semicircular counter and into tables in secluded alcoves. Japanese menu. Specialties: swordfish teriyaki, eel teriyaki, traditional Kaiseki tasting menu including sashimi & tempura. Hrs: Teppan Grill: noon-2:30 pm, 5:30-10:30 pm; Sat, Sun from 5:30 pm. Japanese dining room: noon-10:30 pm; Sat, Sun from 5:30 pm. Res accepted. A la carte entrees: lunch, dinner $15-$25. Complete meal: dinner $50-$70. Cr cds: A, C, D, JCB, MC, V.

D

★ ★ **OUR PLACE.** *1444 Third Ave, at 82nd St, Upper East Side. 212/288-4888.* Chinese menu. Specialties: tangerine beef, Peking duck, Grand Marnier prawns. Hrs: noon-11 pm; early-bird dinner Mon-Sat 5-7 pm. Closed Thanksgiving. Res accepted. Bar. A la carte entrees: lunch $6.95-$8.95, dinner $10.95-$31. Interior designed by protégé of I.M. Pei. Cr cds: A, C, D, MC, V.

D

★ ★ ★ **OYSTER BAR.** *At Grand Central Station (10017), Vanderbilt Ave at 42nd St, Midtown. 212/490-6650.* Extensive variety of fish, shellfish; own smoked salmon. Hrs: 11:30 am-9:30 pm. Closed Sat, Sun; major hols. Res accepted. Bars. Wine list. A la carte entrees: lunch, dinner $8.95-$25.95. In landmark railroad station; Gustivino tiled vaulted ceilings, mahogany paneling. Cr cds: A, C, D, JCB, MC, V.

D

★ ★ ★ **PALIO.** *151 W 51st St (10019), at Equitable Center, Times Square/Theater District. 212/245-4850.* Italian menu. Menu changes daily. Own baking. Hrs: noon-2:30 pm, 5:30-11 pm; Sat from 5:30 pm. Closed Sun; major hols. Res accepted. Bar 11:30 am-midnight; Sat from 4:30 pm. Wine cellar. A la carte entrees: bar lunch $14.50-$20, lunch, dinner $19-$38. Prix fixe: pre-theater dinner $45. Walls are painted with a Chia mural that transports you to Sienna. Cr cds: A, C, D, DS, JCB, MC, V.

D

★ ★ **PALM.** *837 Second Ave (10017), near E 45th St, on the East Side. 212/687-2953.* Specializes in steak, seafood, veal. Hrs: noon-11:30 pm; Sat from 5 pm. Closed Jan 1, Thanksgiving, Dec 25. Res required, 4 or more. Bar. A la carte entrees: lunch, dinner $14-$24. Complete meals: lunch (Mon-Fri) $19.98. Menu recited. Valet parking after 6:30 pm. Original murals; celebrity caricatures. Popular with writers and artists. Family-owned. Cr cds: A, C, D, MC, V.

★ ★ ★ **PALM COURT.** *(See The Plaza Hotel) 212/546-5350.* E-mail plaza@fairmont.com; web www.fairmont.com. Specialties: fresh raspberry Napoleon, scones with Devonshire cream, Brazilian cake. Own baking. Hrs: 6:30 am-midnight. Sun brunch 10 am-2 pm. Res required Sun brunch. Bar from noon. Wine cellar. A la carte entrees: bkfst $12-$16.50, lunch, dinner $18-$25. Sun brunch $49. Pianist, violinist; harpist. Valet parking. Edwardian, columned court off lobby; a New York tradition. Cr cds: A, C, D, DS, ER, JCB, MC, V.

D

★ ★ ★ ★ **PARIOLI ROMANISSIMO.** *24 E 81st St (10028), between Madison & Fifth Aves, Upper East Side. 212/288-2391.* At this townhouse restaurant with neo-Renaissance architecture, seating is inside in an elegant dining room or outside in the striking garden. The clientele is of the money-is-no-object genre. Northern Italian menu. Specializes in fetuccine with white truffles, venison, roasted rack of lamb. Own baking. Hrs: 5:30-11 pm; Fri, Sat to 11:30 pm. Closed Sun; major hols; also 2 wks in Aug. Res required. Bar. Wine cellar. A la carte entrees: dinner $29.50-$35.50. Jacket, tie. Cr cds: A, D, MC, V.

★ ★ ★ **PARK AVENUE CAFE.** *100 E 63rd St, at Park Ave, Upper East Side. 212/644-1900.* Specialties: tuna & salmon tartare with cavier, swordfish chop, Mrs. Ascher's steamed vegetable torte. Hrs: 11:30 am-2:30 pm, 5:30-11 pm; Fri to 11:30 pm; Sat 5:30-11:30 pm; Sun 5-10:30 pm; Sat brunch seatings 11:15 am, 1:15 pm. Closed Jan 1, Dec 25. Res accepted. Bar. A la carte entrees: lunch $19.50-$26, dinner $24.50-$33.50. Complete meals: dinner $52-$67. Authentic American antiques, folk art, mix and match plates. Cr cds: A, C, D, DS, JCB, MC, V.

★ ★ ★ **PARK BISTRO.** *414 Park Ave S (10016), between 28th & 29th Sts, in Murray Hill. 212/689-1360.* French Provençale menu. Specialties: warm potato salad with goat cheese and herbs, fresh codfish with mashed potato and fried leeks in onion sauce, braised lamb shank with dry fruits sauce. Hrs: noon-3 pm, 5:30-11 pm; Sat, Sun from 5:30 pm. Closed major hols. Res accepted. Bar. A la carte entrees: lunch $15.50-$22, dinner $18-$27.50. Casual dining; Parisian bistro decor and atmosphere. Cr cds: A, D, MC, V.

★ ★ ★ ★ **PATRIA.** *250 Park Ave S (10003), at 20th St, in Gramercy Park area. 212/777-6211.* Latin American menu. Specialties: Ecuadorian ceviche, Nicaraguan skirt steak, sugar cane tuna with malanga puree. This trendy, tri-level Caribbean cafe is painted in striking earth tones and decorated in colorful mosaics and Latin American art. The signature dessert is a chocolate-filled cigar with edible matches. Hrs: noon-2:45 pm, 6-11 pm; Fri to midnight; Sat 5:30 pm-midnight; Sun 5:30-10:30 pm. Closed Thanksgiving, Dec 25. Res accepted. Bar to 1 am. A la carte entrees: lunch $9-$16, dinner $17-$28. Cr cds: A, D, MC, V.

★ ★ ★ **PATROON.** *160 E 46th St (10017), between Lexington & 3rd Aves, Midtown. 212/883-7373.* Specialties: lobster and cod cake with snow pea shoots, wood-grilled porterhouse steak for two, spit-fired roasted chicken for two. Own pastries. Hrs: noon-2:30 pm, 5:30-11:30 pm; Sat from 5:30 pm; early-bird dinner to 6 pm. Closed Sun; major hols. Res accepted. Bar noon-11:30 pm. Wine cellar. A la carte entrees: lunch $18-$35, dinner $26-$35. Outdoor dining. Three-level dining rm with rooftop garden; contemporary decor. Jacket. Cr cds: A, D, DS, MC, V.

D

★ ★ ★ ★ **PEACOCK ALLEY.** *(See Waldorf-Astoria Hotel) 212/872-4895.* This very luxurious Waldorf-Astoria salon has always offered professional service, fine china, a comprehensive wine cellar, soothing lighting and cushy seating. Recently, however, it's added an updated classical decor and such interesting culinary offerings as theme dinners, showcasing famous chefs and cuisines from around the world. Continental menu. Specialties: ravioli of foie gras and duck civet, roasted monkfish, fricassee of free-range chicken. Own baking. Hrs: 7-10:30 am, noon-2:30 pm, 5:30-10:30 pm; Sat 7:30-10:30 am, 5:30-10:30 pm; Sun brunch 11 am-2:30 pm. Res accepted. Bar. Wine cellar. A la carte entrees: bkfst $14-$23, lunch $18-$29.50, dinner $23-$39.50. Complete meals: lunch $30, dinner $48, $58, $68. Sun brunch $45. Entertainment Fri, Sat. Cr cds: A, D, MC, V.

D

★ ★ **PENANG MALAYSIAN.** *109 Spring St (10012), between Mercer and Green Sts, in SoHo. 212/274-8883.* Malaysian menu. Specialties: roti canai, sotong goreng, udang halia. Hrs: noon-midnight; Fri, Sat to 1 am. Bar. A la carte entrees: lunch $5.95-$19, dinner $7.95-$19. Exotic plants and a waterfall add to the rain forest atmosphere of this restaurant. Cr cds: A, MC, V.

★ ★ ★ **PERIYALI.** *35 W 20th St, between Fifth & Sixth Aves, in Chelsea. 212/463-7890.* Nouvelle Greek menu. Specializes in charcoal-grilled fish, octopus, lamb chops. Own pastries. Hrs: noon-3 pm, 5:30-11 pm; Sat 5:30-11:30 pm. Closed Sun. Res required. Bar. A la carte entrees: lunch $15-$22, dinner $17-$25. Outdoor dining in garden courtyard. Greek taverna decor. Cr cds: A, C, D, MC, V.

★ ★ ★ **PETROSSIAN.** *182 W 58th St (10019), at 7th Ave, Midtown. 212/245-2214.* French, Amer menu. Specializes in caviar, smoked salmon, foie gras. Own pastries. Menu changes quarterly. Hrs: 11:30 am-3 pm, 5:30 pm-1 am; Sat 11:30 am-3 pm (brunch), 5:30 pm-1 am; Sun 11:30 am-3 pm (brunch), 5:30-10:30 pm. Res accepted. Bar. A la carte entrees: lunch $19, dinner $25-$34. Prix fixe: lunch $22-$39, dinner $35. Sat, Sun brunch $12-$25. Art-deco dining room is decorated with Erté murals and Lalique crystal panels. Jacket. Cr cds: A, C, D, JCB, MC, V.

★ ★ ★ **PICHOLINE.** *35 W 64th St (10023), at Broadway & Central Park West, Upper West Side. 212/724-8585.* French, Mediterranean menu. Specialties: grilled octopus, wild mushroom and duck risotto, Morrocan spiced loin of lamb. Hrs: 11:45 am-2 pm, 5:30-11:45 pm; Mon from 5:30 pm; Sun to 10 pm. Closed major hols. Res accepted. Bar. Wine cellar. A la carte entrees: lunch $12-$20, dinner $23-$35. Complete meal: dinner $58. Fine dining in comfortable Provençale farmhouse atmosphere. Totally nonsmoking. Cr cds: A, D, MC, V.

★ ★ ★ **PIERRE AU TUNNEL.** *250 W 47th St (10036), between Eighth Ave & Broadway, Times Square/Theater District. 212/575-1220.* French menu. Hrs: noon-3 pm, 5:30-11:30 pm; Wed, Sat noon-2:30 pm, 4:30-11:30 pm. Closed Sun; major hols. Res accepted. Bar. A la carte entrees: lunch $10-$17. Complete meals: dinner $30. French-country dining rm decor; fireplace. Family-owned. Cr cds: A, MC, V.

★ ★ **PIG HEAVEN.** *1540 Second Ave, at 80th St, Upper East Side. 212/744-4333.* Chinese menu. Specializes in pork dishes, seafood, poultry. Hrs: noon-midnight; Sat, Sun brunch to 4:30 pm. Res required. Bar. A la carte entrees: lunch $4.95-$6.25, dinner $10.95-$19.95. Cr cds: A, C, D, DS, MC, V.

D

✔★ **P.J. CLARKE'S.** *915 Third Ave (10022), at 55th St, on the East Side. 212/759-1650.* Specializes in hamburgers, steak, veal. Hrs: noon-4 am. Res accepted. Bar. A la carte entrees: lunch, dinner $6.70-$22. Juke box. Traditional, old New York-style pub (1864). Cr cds: A, C, D, MC, V.

✔★ ★ **PÓ.** *31 Cornelia St (10014), between Bleecker & W 4th Sts in Greenwich Village. 212/645-2189.* Italian menu. Specialties: goat cheese truffle, marinated quail. Hrs: 11:30 am-2:30 pm, 5:30-11 pm; Fri, Sat to 11:30 pm; Sun 11:30 am-2:30 pm, 5-10 pm. Closed Mon; major hols; 2 wks in Jan & Sept. Res accepted. Bar. A la carte entrees: lunch $5-$9, dinner $10-$15. Prix fixe: dinner $29. Outdoor dining. Italian decor. Totally nonsmoking. Cr cds: A.

D

★ ★ ★ **POLO.** *(See Westbury Hotel) 212/439-4835.* Seasonal menu. Specialties: grilled Louisiana shrimp, seered spice-crusted tuna, yellowfin tuna sashimi. Hrs: 7-10 am, noon-2:30 pm, 6-10 pm; Sun brunch noon-2:30 pm. Res accepted. Bar noon-midnight. A la carte entrees: bkfst $14.50-$22, lunch $14-$24, dinner $19-$31. Sun brunch $33.50. Elegant English club decor; polo motif. Jacket. Cr cds: A, C, D, DS, ER, JCB, MC, V.

D

★ ★ **POST HOUSE.** *28 E 63rd St, Upper East Side. 212/935-2888.* Specialties: grilled Atlantic salmon, Maryland crab cakes, Cajun rib steak. Hrs: noon-11 pm; Fri to midnight; Sat 5:30 pm-midnight; Sun 5:30-11 pm. Closed Jan 1, Thanksgiving, Dec 25. Res accepted. Bar. Wine list. A la carte entrees: lunch $18.50-$28.50, dinner $22.50-$34. Own pastries. Club atmosphere. Cr cds: A, C, D, DS, JCB, MC, V.

★ ★ ★ **PRIMAVERA.** *1578 First Ave, at 82nd St, Upper East Side. 212/861-8608.* Northern Italian menu. Specialties: baby goat, primavera pasta, risotto ai porcini. Hrs: 5:30 pm-midnight; Sun from 5 pm. Closed major hols. Res required. Bar. Wine cellar. A la carte entrees: dinner $19.75-$32. Tuscan decor. Jacket. Cr cds: A, C, D, MC, V.

✔★ ★ **PROVENCE.** *38 MacDougal St (10012), at Avenue of the Americas (Sixth Ave), in SoHo. 212/475-7500.* Southern French menu. Specializes in seafood, bouillabaisse. Hrs: noon-3 pm, 6-11:30 pm; Fri, Sat to midnight. Closed major hols. Res required. Bar. A la carte entrees: lunch $8.50-$17, dinner $16-$19. Bistro atmosphere. Cr cds: A.

★ ★ ★ **QUILTY'S.** *177 Prince St (10012), between Thompson & Sullivan, in SoHo. 212/254-1260.* Contemporary Amer menu. Specialties: char-grilled baby artichoke skewer, peppered yellowfin tuna steak frites, rack of Colorado lamb brushed with anise. Hrs: noon-11 pm; Mon from 6 pm; Sun 11 am-10 pm; Sun brunch to 3 pm. Closed Jan 1, Thanksgiving, Dec 25. Res required (dinner). Bar to 1 am. Wine list. Semi-a la carte: lunch

$9-$15, dinner $18-$29. Sun brunch $5-$13. Outdoor dining. Simple decor with antique florist rack, plants, wood floors. Cr cds: A, C, D, DS, MC, V.

★ ★ **RAIN.** *100 W 82nd St (10024), between Amsterdam & Columbus; Upper West Side. 212/501-0776.* Thai menu. Specialties: green curry chicken, crispy whole fish, pan-seared coconut shrimp. Hrs: noon-3 pm, 6-11 pm; Fri to midnight; Sat noon-4 pm, 5 pm-midnight; Sun noon-4 pm, 5-10 pm. Closed Dec 25. Res accepted. Bar. A la carte entrees: lunch $6-$14, dinner $11-$22. Thai decor. Cr cds: A, D, DS, MC, V.

★ ★ ★ ★ **RAINBOW ROOM.** *30 Rockefeller Plaza (10112), 65th floor of GE Bldg, Midtown. 212/632-5000.* At the top of a restored landmark skyscraper (1934) is this famous restaurant with a revolving dance floor under a domed ceiling. It boasts views of midtown Manhattan through two-story, floor-to-ceiling windows. Continental menu. Specialties: seafood extravaganza, lobster Thermidor, baked Alaska. Own baking. Hrs: 5 pm-1 am; Sun 6 pm-midnight; Sun brunch 11 am-2 pm. Closed Mon. Res required. Bar. Wine cellar. A la carte entrees: dinner $26-$42. Sun brunch $39.50. Cover charge $20/person (exc pre-theater & brunch). Entertainment. Jacket, tie. Cr cds: A, C, D, MC, V.

D

★ ★ **RAOUL'S.** *180 Prince St (10012), between Sullivan & Thompson St, in SoHo. 212/966-3518.* French menu. Specialty: steak au poivre. Own desserts. Hrs: 5:30 pm-2 am. Res accepted. Bar. Wine list. Semi-a la carte: dinner $15-$28. Casual storefront dining rm; original artwork, objets d'art. Cr cds: A, D, MC, V.

★ ★ ★ **RAPHAEL.** *33 W 54th St (10019), between Fifth & Sixth Aves, Midtown. 212/582-8993.* French menu. Specializes in seafood, filet of lamb, game in winter. Own baking. Hrs: noon-2:30 pm, 6-10 pm; Sat 6-11 pm. Closed Sun; major hols. Res accepted. Bar. A la carte entrees: lunch $20-$24, dinner $23-$36. Complete meals: lunch $30. Tasting menu: dinner $70 & $90. Outdoor dining. In turn-of-the-century town house; fireplace; murals from Provence. Jacket. Cr cds: A, C, D, MC, V.

✔★ ★ **RED TULIP.** *439 E 75th St (10021), between York & First Aves, Upper East Side. 212/734-4893.* Hungarian menu. Specialties: roasted pheasant, venison steak hunter, roasted quail. Hrs: 6 pm-midnight; Sun 5-11 pm. Closed Mon, Tues. Res accepted. Bar. A la carte entrees: dinner $14.50-$23. Strolling violinist; Gypsy music. European folk art; Hungarian antiques. Family-owned. Cr cds: A, D, MC, V.

D

★ ★ ★ **REDEYE GRILL.** *890 Seventh Ave (10019), at 56th St, Midtown. 212/541-9000.* Contemporary Amer menu. Specialties: twelve dancing shrimp, clay pot red gulf snapper, ribeye steak frites with redeye potatoes. Hrs: 11:30-4 am; Sun, Mon to 11:30 pm; Sun brunch to 3 pm. Res accepted. Bar. Wine cellar. Semi-a la carte: lunch $13.50-$26.75, dinner $13.50-$29.95. Jazz Tues-Sat evening, Sun brunch. Outdoor dining. Copper shrimp statues pirouette over raw seafood bar; colorful murals, toy airplanes decorate two separate dining rms. Cr cds: A, C, D, DS, JCB, MC, V.

D

★ ★ ★ **REMI.** *145 W 53rd St (10019), between Sixth & Seventh Aves, Midtown. 212/581-4242.* Venetian menu. Specialties: rack of lamb with pistachio herb crust, seared rare tuna with spinach & shallot sauce, calf's liver in black truffle butter. Hrs: 11:45 am-2:30 pm, 5:30-11:30 pm; Sat from 5:30 pm; Sun 5:30-10 pm. Closed major hols. Res required. Bar. A la carte entrees: lunch $14-$22, dinner $16-$26. Outdoor dining. Venetian-style trattoria with high, vaulted ceiling, Gothic detailing and room-length, fantasy mural of Venice. Cr cds: A, C, D, JCB, MC, V.

D

★ ★ ★ **RENÉ PUJOL.** *321 W 51st St (10019), between 8th & 9th Aves, Times Square/Theater District. 212/246-3023.* French menu. Specialties: onion tart, roasted rack of lamb with herb crust, roasted Atlantic salmon with green lentils. Own pastries. Hrs: noon-3 pm, 5-10:30 pm; Fri, Sat to 11:30 pm. Closed Sun; major hols. Res accepted. Bar. Wine cellar. A la carte entrees: lunch $16-$24, dinner $18-$27. Complete meals: lunch $25, dinner $36. Informal country-French atmosphere. Cr cds: A, C, D, MC, V.

★ ★ ★ **RIODIZIO.** *417 Lafayette St (10003), between Astor Pl and E 4th St; in East Village. 212/529-1313.* Brazilian menu. Specialties: rodizio, Carmen Miranda brazil nut cookie hat. Seafood raw bar. Hrs: 5 pm-midnight; Fri, Sat to 1 am; Sun, Mon to 11 pm. Closed Thanksgiving, Dec 25. Res accepted. Bar. A la carte entrees: dinner $15.95-$24.95. Complete meal: dinner $24.95. Outdoor dining. Brazilian decor. Totally nonsmoking. Cr cds: A, MC, V.

D

★ ★ **ROSA MEXICANO.** *1063 First Ave (10022), at 58th St, on the East Side. 212/753-7407.* Mexican menu. Specialties: enchiladas de mole poblano, crepas camerones. Guacamole prepared tableside. Hrs: 5 pm-midnight. Closed Thanksgiving. Res accepted. Bar. A la carte entrees: dinner $16-$27. Casual dining. Cr cds: A, C, D, MC, V.

★ ★ **RUTH'S CHRIS STEAK HOUSE.** *148 W 51st St (10019), between 6th & 7th Aves, Midtown. 212/245-9600.* Specializes in steak, lobster. Hrs: noon-midnight; Sat from 4 pm; Sun 4-10 pm. Closed Thanksgiving, Dec 25. Res accepted. Bar. A la carte entrees: lunch $10.95-$26, dinner $17.50-$33.95. Men's club decor. Cr cds: A, C, D, MC, V.

✔★ **SAIGON HOUSE.** *89-91 Bayard St (10013), at Mulberry St, in Chinatown. 212/732-8988.* Vietnamese menu. Specialties: spring roll, chicken with lemon grass, Vietnamese hot & sour soup. Hrs: 11 am-10:30 pm; Fri, Sat to 11 pm. Res accepted. Bar. A la carte entrees: lunch, dinner $5.95-$15. Cr cds: A, D, MC, V.

★ ★ **SAL ANTHONY'S SPQR.** *133 Mulberry St (10013), between Hester & Grand Sts, in Little Italy. 212/925-3120.* Italian menu. Specialties: linguini with fresh clams, whole boneless trout, calamari. Hrs: noon-11 pm; Fri, Sat to midnight. Res accepted. Bar. Complete meals: lunch $9, dinner (until 6:30 pm) $16.50. A la carte entrees: dinner $14.75-$17.95. Child's meals. Parking. Outdoor dining. Spacious, elegant dining area. Cr cds: A, C, D, JCB, MC, V.

✔★ ★ **SALAAM BOMBAY.** *317 Greenwich St (10013), between Duane & Reade, in Tribeca. 212/226-9400.* Indian menu. Specialties: rack of lamb marinated with ginger and lemon, chicken cooked with roasted coconut and spices, undhiyu. Hrs: noon-3 pm, 5:30-11 pm. Res accepted. Bar. A la carte entrees: dinner $9.95-$22.95. Complete meal: lunch $10.95. Colorful Indian canopy in middle of room. Totally nonsmoking. Cr cds: A, DS, MC, V.

★ ★ ★ ★ **SAN DOMENICO.** *240 Central Park South (10019), Midtown. 212/265-5959.* E-mail sandomenico@aol.com; web www.food#2go .com. The setting overlooking Central Park is like a private villa, with terra-cotta and Italian marble floors, Florentine stucco walls, sumptuous leather chairs and lots of warm, earthy hues. Italian menu. Specialties: ravioli with truffle butter, Alaskan prawns with beans, roasted veal loin with bacon cream sauce. Hrs: noon-2:30 pm, 5:30-11 pm; Sat from 5:30 pm; Sun 5:30-10 pm. Closed Jan 1, Thanksgiving, Dec 25. Res accepted. Bar. Wine cellar. A la carte entrees: lunch $15.50-$32, dinner $16.50-$42.50. Tasting menu: dinner $65. Jacket. Cr cds: A, C, D, MC, V.

★ ★ **SAN MARTIN'S.** *143 E 49th St (10017), between 3rd & Lexington Aves, Midtown. 212/832-9270.* Continental menu. Specialties: rack of baby lamb, paella Valenciana, roast suckling pig. Hrs: noon-midnight. Res accepted. Bar. A la carte entrees: lunch, dinner $9-$20. Complete meals: lunch $16, dinner $21. Outdoor dining. Cr cds: A, C, D, DS, MC, V.

★ ★ **SAN PIETRO.** *18 E 54th St (10022), between Fifth & Madison Aves, Midtown. 212/753-9015.* Southern Italian menu. Specializes in fish, pasta. Hrs: noon-midnight. Closed Sun; major hols. Res required. Bar. A la carte entrees: lunch, dinner $16-$28. Outdoor dining. 2 large dining areas; massive ceramic scene of Amalfi coast. Jacket. Cr cds: A, D, MC, V.

✔★ ★ **SANZIN.** *180 Spring St (10012), at Thompson, in SoHo. 212/965-0710.* Hrs: 5 pm-midnight; Sat to 1 am; Sun brunch noon-3:30 pm. Res accepted. Bar. A la carte entrees: dinner $16-$25. Sun brunch $12. Outdoor dining. Contemporary decor. Large murals on walls. Cr cds: A, D, DS, MC, V.

★ ★ **SARABETH'S.** *423 Amsterdam Ave (10024), between 80th & 81st Sts, Upper West Side. 212/496-6280.* Specialties: pumpkin waffles, farmer's omelette, warm berry bread pudding. Hrs: 8 am-3:30 pm, 6-10:30 pm; Fri to 11 pm; Sat 6-11 pm; Sun 6-9:30 pm; Sat, Sun brunch 9 am-4 pm. Closed Labor Day, Thanksgiving, Dec 25. Serv bar. A la carte entrees: bkfst $6-$10, lunch $8.50-$12, dinner $15-$25. Sat, Sun brunch $8-$15. New England atmosphere. Totally nonsmoking. Cr cds: A, C, D, DS, JCB, MC, V.

D

★ ★ **SARDI'S.** *234 W 44th St (10036), between Broadway & 8th Ave, Times Square/Theater District. 212/221-8440.* Web www.sardis.com. Specialties: shrimp a la Sardi, canneloni, chicken a la Sardi. Hrs: 11:30-12:30 am; Fri, Sat to 1 am. Res accepted. Bars. Semi-a la carte: lunch $11-$26, dinner $20-$30. Prix fixe: lunch $28, dinner $39. Jazz, Fri. Established 1921. Famous gathering place of theatrical personalities, columnists, publishers, agents; popular for before and after-theater dinner or drinks. Family-owned. Cr cds: A, C, D, MC, V.

★ ★ **SAVANN EST.** *181 E 78th St (10021), between Lexington & 3rd Aves, Upper East Side. 212/396-9300.* Continental menu. Specialties: grilled squid with parsnip horseradish puree, sesame-crusted salmon, grilled leg of lamb Napoleon. Own pastries. Hrs: 6-11 pm; Fri, Sat to midnight. Closed Memorial Day, Labor Day, Dec 25. Res accepted. Beer, wine. A la carte entrees: dinner $13-$18. Minimalist decor with open kitchen; large front windows. Totally nonsmoking. Cr cds: D, MC, V.

★ ★ ★ **SAVORE.** *200 Spring St (10012), at Sullivan St, in SoHo. 212/431-1212.* Italian menu. Specialties: corn mousse with wild boar sauce; salad of beets, zucchini, carrots and potatoes marinated in Balsamic vinegar. Own baking, pasta. Hrs: noon-3 pm, 5:30 pm-midnight; Sat, Sun noon-midnight. Closed Dec 25. Res accepted. Bar. Wine cellar. A la carte entrees: lunch, dinner $12-$26. Outdoor dining. Elegant decor with polished wood, antique furniture, alabaster chandeliers. Totally nonsmoking. Cr cds: A, MC, V.

D

★ ★ **SAVOY.** *70 Prince St (10012), at Crosby St, in SoHo. 212/219-8570.* French, Mediterranean menu. Specializes in seafood, duck, chicken. Hrs: noon-3 pm, 6-10:30 pm; Fri, Sat to 11 pm; Sun to 10 pm. Closed most major hols. Res accepted. Bar. Semi-a la carte: lunch $8-$12, dinner $18-$29. Contemporary decor. Cr cds: A, DS, MC, V.

★ ★ **SCREENING ROOM.** *54 Varick St (10003), jct Varick & Laight, in Tribeca. 212/334-2100.* Specialties: pan-fried artichokes, macaroni with spinach, cedar-planked salmon. Own pastries. Hrs: noon-1 am; Fri to 2:30 am; Sat 6 pm-2:30 am; Sun from 11:30 am; Sun brunch to 3 pm. Res accepted. Bar. Semi-a la carte: lunch $9-$17, dinner $15-$23. Complete meal: dinner $30. Sun brunch $5-$12. Casual decor; movie theater adj. Cr cds: A, D, DS, MC, V.

D

★ ★ ★ **SEA GRILL.** *19 W 49th St (10019), at Rockefeller Plaza, Midtown. 212/332-7610.* Specialties: Maryland crab cakes with stone ground mustard, grilled Artic char with vintage balsamic vinegar, roasted cod with cous cous. Own pastries. Hrs: noon-3 pm, 5-10 pm; Sat from 5 pm. Closed Sun. Res required. Bar. Wine cellar. A la carte entrees: lunch $19-$28, dinner $23-$30. Complete meals: dinner $39. Outdoor dining. Floral, garden displays. Overlooks Prometheus fountain and pool (summer); ice-skating rink (winter). Jacket (dinner). Cr cds: A, C, D, ER, JCB, MC, V.

D

★ ★ **SHAAN.** *57 W 48th St (10020), between 5th & 6th Aves; Midtown. 212/977-8400.* Indian menu. Specialties: chicken makhani, prawns bengali, paneer pasanda. Salad bar. Hrs: noon-3 pm, 5:30-11 pm. Res accepted. Bar. Semi-a la carte: lunch, dinner $10.95-$29.95. Complete meals: lunch $15.95-$18.95, dinner $21.95-$25.95. Lunch buffet $13.95; pre-theatre 5:30-7 pm $21.95; tasting menu 7-11 pm $25.95. Entertainment Fri, Sat. Framed Indian tapestries on walls. Totally nonsmoking. Cr cds: A, D, MC, V.

D

✔★ **SHABU-TATSU.** *1414 York Ave (10021), at 75th St, Upper East Side. 212/472-3322.* Japanese menu. Specializes in shabu-shabu (tabletop cooking), sukiyaki (hot pot with sauce), yakiniku (Japanese barbecue). Hrs: noon-2:30 pm, 5-10:30 pm; Fri to 11:30 pm; Sat noon-11:30 pm; Sun noon-10:30 pm; Sat, Sun brunch to 5 pm. Closed some major hols. Res accepted. Bar. A la carte entrees: lunch $5.95-$11.95, dinner $8-$17. Complete meal: dinner $28-$38. Sat, Sun brunch $7-$12. Cook your own meal; each table surrounds a stovetop. Totally nonsmoking. Cr cds: A, D, DS, JCB, MC, V.

★ ★ **SHARK BAR.** *307 Amsterdam Ave (10023), between 74th & 75th Sts, Upper West Side. 212/874-8500.* Regional Amer menu. Specialties: Louisiana deep-fried crab cakes, Georgia bank farm-bred catfish, honey-dipped southern fried chicken. Own baking. Hrs: noon-3 pm, 5-11:30 pm; Mon, Tues from 5 pm; Wed to midnight; Thurs to 12:30 am; Fri to 1:30 am; Sat 11:30 am-3 pm (brunch), 5 pm-1:30 am; Sun 11:30 am-3 pm (brunch), 5-11:30 pm. Closed Dec 25. Res accepted. Bar. A la carte entrees: lunch $8.95-$10.95, dinner $10.95-$17.95. Sat, Sun brunch $15.95. Harlem Renaissance-era decor; red velvet, extensive woodwork; multi-level dining. Totally nonsmoking. Cr cds: A, D, DS, MC, V.

★ ★ ★ **SHUN LEE.** *43 W 65th St (10023), between Central Park West & Columbus Ave, Upper West Side. 212/595-8895.* Chinese menu. Specialties: jumbo prawns with broccoli in curry sauce, Peking duck, Norwegian salmon (Szechwan or Mandarin style). Hrs: noon-midnight; Sat from 11:30 am; Sun to 10:30 pm. Closed Thanksgiving. Bar. A la carte entrees: lunch $10.25-$17.95, dinner $13.95-$35. Contemporary decor. Jacket. Cr cds: A, C, D, MC, V.

★ ★ ★ **SHUN LEE PALACE.** *155 E 55th St (10022), between Third & Lexington Aves, on the East Side. 212/371-8844.* Chinese menu. Specializes in Cantonese, Hunan and Szechwan dishes. Hrs: noon-11:30 pm; Sun to 11 pm. Closed Thanksgiving. Res required. Bar. Wine cellar. A la carte entrees: lunch $16.50-$24.95, dinner $18.95-$37.95. Complete meals (Mon-Fri): lunch $19.98. Cr cds: A, C, D, MC, V.

D ♥

✔★ **SIAM GRILL.** *586 Ninth Ave (10036), between 42nd & 43rd Sts, in Theater District. 212/307-1363.* Thai menu. Specialties: sautéed chicken with cashew nuts & chili paste sauce, homemade red & green Thai curry, garlic duck. Hrs: 11:30 am-11 pm; Fri to 11:30 pm; Sat 4-11:30 pm; Sun 4-10:30 pm. Closed some major hols. Res accepted. Serv bar. A la carte entrees: lunch, dinner $6.25-$15.95. Complete meal: dinner $8.95. Cr cds: A, MC, V.

★ ★ **SIAM INN.** *916 8th Ave (10019), between W 54th & 55th Sts, Times Square/Theater District. 212/489-5237.* Thai menu. Specialties: deep-fried whole fish, duck with tamarind sauce. Hrs: noon-3 pm, 5-11:30 pm; Sat from 4 pm; Sun 5-11 pm. Closed most major hols. Res accepted Mon-Thurs; required Fri, Sat. Bar. A la carte entrees: lunch $8.25-$15.95, dinner $8.95-$15.95. Thai decor; artifacts displayed, photos of Bangkok, statues, plaques. Cr cds: A, D, MC, V.

★ ★ ★ ★ **SIGN OF THE DOVE.** *1110 Third Ave (10021), at E 65th St, Upper East Side. 212/861-8080.* Skylights, stunning floral arrangements, well-spaced tables, brick arches and 19th-century antiques distinguish the dining rooms here, some of the prettiest in town. There's also outdoor dining, enhancing the garden atmosphere. Specialties: roast loin of venison, crispy sea bass with polenta gnocchi, tian of spring lamb with garlic confit. Own baking. Hrs: noon-2:30 pm, 6-11 pm; Mon from 5:30 pm; Sat 11:30 am-2:30 pm (brunch), 5:30-11 pm; Sun 11:30 am-2:30 pm (brunch), 6-10 pm. Res accepted. Bar. Wine cellar. A la carte entrees: lunch $16-$22. Prix fixe: lunch $20 & $25, dinner $30-$45. Sat, Sun brunch $12-$20. Jazz combo, vocalist. Cr cds: A, C, D, DS, JCB, MC, V.

★ ★ ★ **SMITH & WOLLENSKY.** *201 E 49th St (10022), at Third Ave, on the East Side. 212/753-1530.* Specializes in steak, seafood. Hrs:

noon-midnight; Sat, Sun from 5 pm. Closed Jan 1, Thanksgiving, Dec 25. Res accepted. Bar. Wine cellar. A la carte entrees: lunch $14.50-$27.75, dinner $18-$42. Built 1897; turn-of-the-century decor; old New York steakhouse atmosphere. Also Wollensky's Grill, entrance at 205 E 49th St, open 11:30-2 am. Outdoor dining. Cr cds: A, C, D, DS, JCB, MC, V.

✓★★★ **SONIA ROSE.** *132 Lexington Ave (10016), between 28th and 29th Sts; Murray Hill. 212/545-1777.* French menu. Specialties: warm asparagus puff pastry; tenderloin of beef with chanterelle, black trumpet, and morel sauce. Hrs: noon-2 pm, 6-9:30 pm; Mon from 6 pm; Fri to 10:30 pm; Sat 6-10:30 pm; Sun 5-9 pm. Res accepted. Bar. Complete meals: lunch $23, dinner $38. Contemporary decor. Jacket. Totally nonsmoking. Cr cds: A, D, MC, V.

★★★ **SPARKS STEAK HOUSE.** *210 E 46th St (10017), between 2nd & 3rd Aves; Midtown. 212/687-4855.* Specializes in steak, lobster, seafood. Hrs: noon-3 pm, 5-11 pm; Fri to 11:30 pm; Sat 5-11:30 pm. Closed Sun; major hols. Res required. Bar. Wine list. A la carte entrees: lunch, dinner $19.95-$29.95. Early Amer decor; etched glass, wood paneling. Jacket. Cr cds: A, C, D, MC, V.

✓★★★ **SPARTINA.** *355 Greenwich St (10013), at Harrison St, in Tribeca. 212/274-9310.* Mediterranean menu. Specialties: lamb shank Catalan-style, pepper-crusted tuna, grilled pizza. Hrs: 11:30 am-3 pm, 5:30-11:30 pm; Mon to 11 pm; Fri to midnight; Sat 5:30 pm-midnight. Closed most major hols. Bar. A la carte entrees: lunch $8.50-$16, dinner $12.50-$24. Outdoor dining. Custom-made Mission-style chairs, wood floors, some exposed brick walls. Cr cds: A, D, MC, V.

★★ **STEAK FRITES.** *9 E 16th St (10003), between Fifth Ave & Broadway, in Chelsea. 212/463-7101.* French menu. Specializes in black Angus steak. Hrs: noon-11:30 pm, Fri-Sat to 12:30, Sun to 10 pm; Sun brunch noon-4 pm. Closed Jan 1, Dec 25. Res accepted. Bar. A la carte entrees: lunch $8-$17.50, dinner $12.50-$19. Sun brunch $7-$17.50. Outdoor dining. French bistro-style atmosphere; murals of Paris scenes. Cr cds: A, D, MC, V.

D

★★★ **SUSHISAY.** *38 E 51st St (10022), between Park and Madison Aves in Midtown. 212/755-1780.* Japanese menu. Specializes in sushi, bento. Hrs: noon-2:15 pm, 5:30-10:15 pm; Sat 5-9:15 pm. Closed Sun; also major hols. Res required. Bar. A la carte entrees: lunch $17.50-$33, dinner $19.50-$33. Traditional and serene Japanese decor. Totally nonsmoking. Cr cds: A, D, MC, V.

★★ **TABLE D'HOTE.** *44 E 92nd St (10028), between Madison & Park Aves, Upper East Side. 212/348-8125.* French menu. Specialties: seared tuna with Japanese rice cake, rack of lamb shank with spring pea risotto, bistro-style hanger steak. Hrs: noon-3 pm, 5:30-10:30 pm; Sat 11 am-4 pm; Sun 10:30 am-4 pm. Closed Dec 25. Res accepted. Wine, beer. A la carte entrees: lunch $8.75-$13.50, dinner $18-$24. Sun brunch $8.50-$13.50. Prix fixe: dinner $19.95 (5-7 pm). Small, intimate bistro-style dining rm. Totally nonsmoking. Cr cds: A, D, MC, V.

✓★★ **TAORMINA.** *147 Mulberry St (10013), between Grand & Hester Sts, in Little Italy. 212/219-1007.* Italian menu. Specializes in seafood, pasta, penne al cognac. Hrs: 11 am-11:30 pm; Sat to 1 am; Sun to 11 pm. Closed Thanksgiving, Dec 25, 31. Res required. Bar. A la carte entrees: lunch, dinner $9.90-$18. Valet parking. Modern Italian decor. Cr cds: A, C, D, MC, V.

★★ **TATOU.** *151 E 50th St (10022), between Lexington & 3rd Aves, on the East Side. 212/753-1144.* Specialties: lamb chop Provençal, grilled black Angus sirloin steak, grilled Atlantic salmon. Hrs: noon-3 pm, 5:30-10:30 pm; Sat from 5:30 pm. Closed Sun; some major hols. Res required. Bar. A la carte entrees: lunch $15-$22, dinner $17-$29. Pre-theater dinner (before 7 pm) $19. Entertainment Tues-Sat. Terrace dining. Old theater setting; former nightclub from the 1940s. Jacket. Cr cds: A, D, MC, V.

★★★ **TAVERN ON THE GREEN.** *Central Park at W 67th St (10023), Upper West Side. 212/873-3200.* American menu. Own baking. Hrs: 11:30 am-midnight; Fri, Sat 5 pm-12:45 am; Sun 5-11 pm; Sat, Sun brunch 10 am-3:30 pm. Res accepted. Bar. A la carte entrees: lunch $14-$27, dinner $22-$33. Table d'hôte: lunch $19.98-$26, pre-theater dinner (5-6:30 pm) $22-$28.50. Sat, Sun brunch $14-$27. Entertainment (exc Mon) in Chestnut Room: show times 8 pm, 10 pm; Fri, Sat 8:30, 10:30 pm; $17-$25. Valet parking. Garden terrace. Gift shop. Elaborate decor; in 1874 building within Central Park. Cr cds: A, C, D, JCB, MC, V.

D

★★★ **TERRACE.** *400 W 119th St (10027), between Amsterdam & Morningside Dr, on rooftop of Butler Hall, Columbia University, Upper West Side. 212/666-9490.* French menu. Specializes in seafood, game. Own pastries. Hrs: noon-2:30 pm, 6-10 pm; Sat from 6 pm. Closed Sun & Mon; Dec 25. Res accepted. Bar to 11 pm. Wine cellar. A la carte entrees: lunch $8.50-$24, dinner $24-$32. Prix fixe: lunch $25, dinner $42. Classical harpist evenings. Valet parking (dinner). Outdoor terrace. Panoramic view of Hudson River, George Washington Bridge and Manhattan skyline. Cr cds: A, C, D, DS, MC, V.

★★ **TRATTORIA DELL'ARTE.** *900 7th Ave (10019), at 57th St, Midtown. 212/245-9800.* Italian menu. Specializes in pizza, veal chops, seafood. Own pastas. Hrs: 11:30 am-2:45 pm, 5-11:30 pm; Fri, Sat to 12:30 am; Sun to 10:30 pm; Sat, Sun brunch to 3 pm. Closed Dec 25. Res accepted. Bar. A la carte entrees: lunch, dinner $12-$29. Sat, Sun brunch $16-$17. Authentic Italian antipasto bar. Modern Italian atmosphere. Opp Carnegie Hall; frequented by celebrities. Cr cds: A, D, DS, MC, V.

★★★ **TRIBECA GRILL.** *375 Greenwich St (10013), at Franklin St, in Tribeca. 212/941-3900.* Web www.interactivegourmetsite.cuisine.com. Specializes in fish, ravioli, duck. Hrs: 11:30 am-3 pm, 5:30-11 pm; Fri to 11:30 pm; Sat 5:30-11:30 pm; Sun 5-10 pm; Sun brunch 11:30 am-3 pm. Res accepted. Bar. A la carte entrees: lunch $12-$18, dinner $19-$27. Prix fixe: lunch $19.98. Casual dining in converted warehouse. Cr cds: A, D, MC, V.

D

✓★★ **TRIONFO.** *224 W 51st St (10019), Times Square/Theater District. 212/262-6660.* Italian menu. Specialties: osso buco "Trinofo," beef carpaccio with arugula and parmigiano, lobster-filled ravioli. Hrs: 11:30 am-3:30 pm, 5-11:30 pm; Sat from 5 pm. Closed Sun; major hols. Res accepted. Bar. A la carte entrees: lunch, dinner $12.50-$20.95. Outdoor dining. Italian decor with murals of Chianti. Cr cds: A, C, D, MC, V.

✓★★ **TROIS CANARDS.** *184 Eighth Ave (10011), Chelsea. 212/929-4320.* French menu. Specialties: Dover sole, roast duckling with seasonal fruit sauce, filet mignon with pearl onions and wild mushrooms. Hrs: noon-3 pm, 5-11 pm; Fri to midnight; Sat 5 pm-midnight; Sat, Sun brunch 11 am-4 pm. Res accepted. Bar. A la carte entrees: lunch $6-$8, dinner $13.95-$20.95. Sat, Sun brunch $10.95. Duck motif. Contemporary decor. Totally nonsmoking. Cr cds: A, MC, V.

D

★★ **TWO ROOMS.** *313 E 58th St (10022), between 1st & 2nd Aves, Midtown. 212/223-1886.* Eclectic menu. Specialties: Vietnamese five-spice grilled quail, Capetown vegetable curry, roasted striped bass. Hrs: 6 pm-midnight; Fri, Sat to 1 am; Sun noon-4 pm (brunch). Closed Jan 1. Res accepted. Bar to 4 am. Semi-a la carte: dinner $14-$25. Sun brunch $11-$17. In 1856 bldg; African safari motif. Cr cds: A, D, MC, V.

★★★ **TWO TWO TWO.** *222 W 79th St (10024), between Amsterdam & Broadway, Upper West Side. 212/799-0400.* Continental menu. Specialties: medallions of Canadian salmon, prime rack of Colorado lamb, wood-fired filet mignon. Hrs: 5-11 pm. Res accepted. Bar. Wine list. A la carte entrees: dinner $23-$39. Complete meal: pre-theater dinner $36. Cr cds: A, C, D, DS, MC, V.

★★★ **TYPHOON BREWERY.** *22 E 54th St (10022), between Madison & 5th Aves, Midtown. 212/754-9006.* Thai menu. Specialties: crispy duck with sweet & sour five-spice sauce, grilled rare tuna, pan-seared monkfish. Own baking. Hrs: noon-2:30 pm, 5:30-10:30 pm; Fri to

11:30 pm; Sat 5:30-11:30 pm. Closed Sun; major hols. Res accepted. Bar. Wine list. Semi-a la carte: lunch $12-$18, dinner $13.75-$21. Industrial decor with metal tabletops, brick walls; large beer vats at entrance. Totally nonsmoking. Cr cds: A, D, DS, JCB, MC, V.

D

★ ★ ★ **UNION SQUARE CAFE.** *21 E 16th St (10003), between Fifth Ave & Union Square W, Midtown. 212/243-4020.* French, Italian menu. Specialties: grilled marinated filet of tuna, fried calamari with spicy anchovy mayonnaise, seasonal vegetables. Own pastries. Hrs: noon-2:15 pm, 6-10:15 pm; Fri, Sat to 11:15 pm; Sun 5:30-9:45 pm. Closed major hols. Res required. Bar. Wine list. A la carte entrees: lunch $11-$18, dinner $19-$27. Contemporary American bistro. Cr cds: A, D, MC, V.

★ ★ **VICTOR'S CAFE 52.** *236 W 52nd St (10019), between Broadway and 8th Ave; Times Square/Theater District. 212/586-7714.* Cuban, Caribbean menu. Specialties: paella, stone crab creole, suckling roast pig. Hrs: noon-midnight. Res accepted. Bar. A la carte entrees: lunch $7.95-$18.95, dinner $9-$29. Entertainment. Skylight; garden. Cr cds: A, C, D, MC, V.

★ ★ ★ **THE VIEW.** *(See Marriott Marquis Hotel) 212/704-8900.* Continental menu. Own baking. Hrs: 5:30-11 pm; Fri, Sat 5 pm-midnight; Sun brunch 10:30 am-2 pm. Res required. Bar. Wine cellar. A la carte entrees: dinner $24.95-$33. Prix fixe: pre-theater dinner $39.95, $49.95. Sun brunch $31. Child's menu. Valet parking. Revolving rooftop restaurant, lounge and ballroom. Braille menu. Jacket. Cr cds: A, C, D, DS, ER, JCB, MC, V.

D

✔★ ★ **VILLAGE GRILL.** *518 LaGuardia Pl (10014), at Bleecker St, in Greenwich Village. 212/228-1001.* Contemporary Amer menu. Specialties: seared yellowfin tuna, Phuket-style steamed mussels, barbecued Carolina babyback ribs. Hrs: 11:30-2 am; Fri, Sat to 3 am; Sat, Sun brunch to 4 pm. Closed Thanksgiving, Dec 25. Res accepted. Bar to 4 am. Semi-a la carte: lunch, dinner $7.50-$17.50. Sat, Sun brunch $9-$12.50. Outdoor dining. 1904 bldg with 30-ft-high ceilings, stainless-steel open kitchen; candid photos of Jack Kerouac, Allen Ginsberg and more. Cr cds: A, C, D, MC, V.

✔★ ★ **VINCE & EDDIE'S.** *70 W 68th St (10023), Upper West Side. 212/721-0068.* Regional Amer menu. Specialties: Chesapeake crab cakes, fried calamari with lime juice, pan-roasted chicken. Hrs: noon-midnight. Res accepted. Bar. A la carte entrees: lunch $8.95-$14.95, dinner $17.50-$20.95. Outdoor dining. New England country inn decor. Cr cds: A, C, D, DS, MC, V.

★ **VIRGIL'S REAL BARBECUE.** *152 W 44th St (10036), Between 6th Ave & Broadway, Times Square/Theater District. 212/921-9494.* Specializes in barbecued Memphis pork ribs, pulled pork sandwiches, grilled catfish filet. Hrs: 11:30 am-midnight; Mon to 11 pm; Sun to 10 pm. Closed Dec 25. Res accepted. Bar. A la carte entrees: lunch, dinner $6.50-$24.95. Child's meals. Multi-level Southern-style restaurant. Walls lined with Americana. Totally nonsmoking. Cr cds: A, MC, V.

D

★ ★ ★ **VONG.** *200 E 54th St (10022), between 2nd & 3rd Aves, Midtown. 212/486-9592.* Thai, French menu. Specialties: sautéed foie gras with ginger and mango, black bass with wok-fried Napa cabbage, lobster with Thai herbs. Hrs: noon-2:30 pm, 6-11 pm; Sat 5:30-11:30 pm; Sun 5:30-10 pm. Pre theatre 5:30-6:30 pm. Closed major hols. Res required. Bar. Wine cellar. A la carte entrees: lunch, dinner $19-$32. Prix fixe: lunch $25, pre theatre $35-$65. Outdoor dining. Exotic decor of Southeast Asia; ceiling and walls covered with gold leaf collage; Thai-style seating (sunken seating) in one area of dining rm. Cr cds: A, D, MC, V.

D

✔★ ★ **WALL STREET KITCHEN & BAR.** *70 Broad St (10004), at Beaver St, in Financial District. 212/797-7070.* Specializes in pizza, steak, hamburgers. Hrs: 11:30 am-11:30 pm. Closed Thanksgiving, Dec 25. Bar. Semi-a la carte: lunch, dinner $6.75-$19.50. Restored 1908 bdlg has vaulted ceiling, overhanging balcony, tiered seating. Cr cds: A, D, DS, MC, V.

D

★ ★ ★ **WATER CLUB.** *500 E 30th St (10016), at the East River, Midtown. 212/683-3333.* Specializes in lobster, oysters, swordfish. Hrs: noon-2:30 pm, 5:30-11 pm; Sun 5:45-10 pm; Sun brunch 11:15 am-3 pm. Res required. Bar. A la carte entrees: lunch $15-$18, dinner $22-$32. Prix fixe: lunch $19.98, dinner $28. Sun brunch $29. Piano bar. Free valet parking. Outdoor dining (Memorial Day-Labor Day). Located on barge in the East river. Jacket. Cr cds: A, C, D, JCB, MC, V.

D

★ ★ **WILLOW.** *1022 Lexington Ave (10021), at 73rd St, Upper East Side. 212/717-0703.* French menu. Specialties: seared Atlantic salmon, rack of lamb, warm chocolate cake with Tahitian ice cream. Hrs: noon-3 pm, 5:30-11 pm; Sun brunch 11 am-4 pm. Closed Dec 25. Res accepted. Bar. A la carte entrees: lunch $8.50-$14, dinner $14.50-$25. Sun brunch $8.50-$14. Outdoor dining. French decor. Totally nonsmoking. Cr cds: A, D, MC, V.

★ ★ ★ **WINDOWS ON THE WORLD.** *1 World Trade Center (10048), on 107th floor, in Financial District. 212/524-7011.* Web www.windowsontheworld.com. Specialties: filet of buffalo, porcini-crusted halibut, silver pot of seafood in ginger broth. Hrs: noon-2:30 pm, 5-10:30 pm; Fri to 11:30 pm; Sat noon-3 pm, 5-11:30 pm; Sun 11 am-3 pm, 5-10 pm. Res accepted. Bar noon-1 am; Fri, Sat to 2 am; Sun to 11 pm. Wine cellar. Buffet: lunch $40. A la carte entrees: lunch $16-$24, dinner $26-$35. Prix fixe: 5-course dinner $125. Dance band Wed-Sat. Valet parking. Panoramic views. Jacket. Cr cds: A, C, D, DS, MC, V.

D

★ ★ ★ **YANKEE CLIPPER.** *170 John St (10005), at South St, in Financial District. 212/344-5959.* Specializes in jumbo shrimp, Norwegian salmon, grilled swordfish steak. Hrs: 11:30 am-10 pm; Sun noon-9 pm. Closed Thanksgiving, Dec 25. Res accepted. Bar. A la carte entrees: lunch, dinner $11-$24. Prix fixe: lunch, dinner $23. Three dining areas; main dining rm resembles dining salon on a luxury liner; display of ship models and prints of ships. Cr cds: A, C, D, DS, MC, V.

✔★ **YELLOWFINGERS.** *200 E 60th St (10022), at Third Ave, Upper East Side. 212/751-8615.* Italian, California menu. Specializes in grilled fish and meat, salads, gourmet individual pizza. Own desserts. Hrs: 11:30-1 am; Fri, Sat to 2 am; Sun to 11:45 pm. Bar. A la carte entrees: lunch, dinner $10-$19. Sun brunch $9.50-$19.50. Outdoor dining. Cr cds: A, D, DS, MC, V.

★ ★ **ZARELA.** *953 2nd Ave (10022), between 50th & 51st Sts, Midtown. 212/644-6740.* Mexican menu. Specializes in roasted duck, snapper hash, regional cuisine. Hrs: noon-3 pm, 5-11 pm; Fri to 11:30 pm; Sat 5-11:30 pm; Sun 5-10 pm. Closed major hols. Res accepted. Bar. A la carte entrees: lunch $11-$16, dinner $13-$16.95. Entertainment Tues-Sat. Colorful Mexican decor; paper lanterns, masks, toys, piñatas. Cr cds: A, D.

★ ★ ★ **ZOË.** *90 Prince St (10012), between Broadway and Mercer St, in SoHo. 212/966-6722.* Specialties: roasted Maine day-boat cod, grilled salmon with crisp noodle roll. Hrs: noon-3 pm, 6-10:30 pm; Mon from 6 pm; Fri to 11 pm; Sat 5:30-11:30 pm; Sun 5:30-10 pm; Sat, Sun brunch to 3 pm. Closed July 4, Dec 25. Res accepted. Bar. Wine list. A la carte entrees: lunch $9.50-$14, dinner $16-$25. Sat, Sun brunch $9.50-$14. Eclectic decor. Totally nonsmoking. Cr cds: A, C, D, MC, V.

D

★ ★ **ZUCCA.** *227 10th Ave (10011), between 23rd & 24th Sts, in Chelsea. 212/741-1970.* Mediterranean menu. Specialties: zuppa di Zucca, golden beet salad, Portuguese fish soup. Own pastries. Hrs: 11:30 am-2:30 pm, 5:30-10:30 pm; Mon from 5:30 pm; Fri to midnight; Sat 5:30 pm-midnight; Sun 5:30-9:30 pm. Closed Jan 1, Dec 25. Res accepted (dinner). Bar 5:30 pm-midnight; Fri, Sat to 1 am A la carte entrees: lunch

$8-$12, dinner $16-$24. Casual decor; limestone-topped bar. Cr cds: A, D, MC, V.

Unrated Dining Spots

CARNEGIE DELI. *854 Seventh Ave, off 55th St, Midtown. 212/757-2245.* Kosher deli menu. Specializes in sandwiches, corned beef, cheesecake. Hrs: 6:30-3:45 am. Semi-a la carte: bkfst $5-$7, lunch $7-$12, dinner $8-$15. Traditional Jewish-style New York deli. No cr cds accepted.

DIANE'S DOWNTOWN. *249 Columbus Ave, between 71st & 72nd Sts, Upper West Side. 212/799-6750.* Specializes in hamburgers, sodas, ice cream sundaes. Hrs: Noon-midnight; Fri to 1 am; Sat 11:30-1 am; Sun 11:30 am-midnight. Closed Thanksgiving, Dec 24-25. Wine, beer. A la carte entrees: bkfst, lunch, dinner from $2.50. Totally nonsmoking. No cr cds accepted.

ELEPHANT & CASTLE. *68 Greenwich Ave, Seventh Ave & 11th St, in Greenwich Village. 212/243-1400.* Specializes in salads, hamburgers, Indian puddings. Daily specials. Hrs: 8:30 am-midnight; Fri to 1 am; Sat 10-1 am; Sun 10 am-midnight. Wine, beer, setups. A la carte entrees: bkfst $2.75-$7, lunch, dinner $2.75-$11.50. Village coffee shop. Totally nonsmoking. Cr cds: A, C, D, MC, V.

EMPIRE DINER. *210 Tenth Ave, between 22nd & 23rd Sts, in Chelsea. 212/243-2736.* Specializes in sandwiches, omelettes. Own muffins, scones. Open 24 hrs; Sun brunch noon-4 pm. Bar. A la carte entrees: bkfst $1.50-$8.50, lunch, dinner $4.25-$14.95. Sun brunch $9.50. Pianist. Outdoor dining. Authentic chrome and stainless steel art-deco diner. Cr cds: A, D, DS, MC, V.

FLORENT. *69 Gansevoort St, between Washington & Greenwich Sts, in Greenwich Village. 212/989-5779.* French, Amer menu. Specialties: boudin noir, fresh fish. Open 24 hrs. Closed Dec 25. Res accepted. Bar. A la carte entrees: bkfst $3.50-$10, lunch $3.95-$11, dinner $8.50-$13.50. Chrome- & aluminum-trimmed diner attached to meat market in warehouse area of the Village. No cr cds accepted.

HARLEY-DAVIDSON CAFE. *1370 Ave of the Americas (10019), at 56th St, Midtown. 212/245-6000.* Specializes in seafood, barbecue chicken, Harley Hog sandwich. Hrs: 11:30 am-midnight; Fri, Sat to 1 am. Closed Dec 25. Semi-a la carte: lunch, dinner $7.50-$19.95. Child's meals. Outdoor dining on wrap-around terrace. Extensive Harley-Davidson motorcycle memorabilia; multi-media displays. Cr cds: A, D, MC, V.

JACKSON HOLE. *1611 Second Ave, between 83rd & 84th Sts, Upper East Side. 212/737-8788.* Specializes in sandwiches, hamburgers. Hrs: 10-1 am; Fri, Sat to 4 am; Sat, Sun brunch 10:30 am-3 pm. Closed Thanksgiving, Dec 25. Bar. A la carte entrees: bkfst $4-$6, lunch, dinner $6-$10. Outdoor dining. Chrome and stainless steel art deco diner; juke box. Cr cds: A, MC, V.

D

PANEVINO RISTORANTE/CAFE VIENNA. *In Avery Fisher Hall, Lincoln Center, Broadway & 64th St, Upper West Side. 212/874-7000.* Italian menu at Panevino Ristorante; Viennese dessert & coffee menu at Cafe Vienna. Hrs: Panevino Ristorante 11:30 am-8 pm; Cafe Vienna 11:30 am-11 pm. Bar. A la carte entrees at Panevino: lunch $10-$14, dinner $13-$21. A la carte desserts at Cafe Vienna: $5-$7. Outdoor dining. Cafe is authentic Viennese coffee house. Both establishments overlook Lincoln Center plaza. Cr cds: A, D, MC, V.

PLANET HOLLYWOOD. *140 W 57th St, Midtown. 212/333-7827.* Specializes in pizza, hamburgers, homemade bread pudding with homemade whiskey sauce. Hrs: 11-1 am. Closed Dec 25. Bar to 1:45 am. Semi-a la carte: lunch, dinner $6.95-$16.95. Music videos and movie clips are shown daily. Authentic Hollywood memorabilia displayed. Cr cds: A, C, D, DS, JCB, MC, V.

REPUBLIC. *37 Union Square W (10003), in Gramercy Park. 212/627-7172.* Asian menu. Specialties: salmon sashimi salad, fried wontons. Hrs: noon-midnight. Closed Memorial Day, Dec 25. Bar. Semi-a la carte: lunch, dinner $6-$9. Former warehouse converted to noodle shop. Totally nonsmoking. Cr cds: A, D, MC, V.

THE ROTUNDA. *(See The Pierre Hotel) 212/940-8195.* Web www.fourseasons.com. Hrs: 8 am-midnight, tea 3-5:30 pm. A la carte entrees: bkfst, lunch $6.50-$26. Prix fixe: tea $26. Beaux-arts architecture with marble columns & pilasters. Murals by Edward Melcarth. Cr cds: A, C, D, ER, JCB, MC, V.

SAVORIES. *30 Rockefeller Center, downstairs, Midtown. 212/332-7630.* Specializes in hot and cold pasta, desserts. Hrs: 7 am-6 pm; Sat 9 am-5 pm. Closed Sun May-Nov. Wine, beer. A la carte entrees: bkfst $2.50-$3.95, lunch $5-$13. Outdoor garden dining. Afternoon tea after 3 pm. Parking. Bistro atmosphere. Cr cds: A, C, D, MC, V.

SECOND AVE DELI. *156 Second Ave, at 10th St, in the East Village. 212/677-0606.* Kosher menu. Specializes in pastrami, corned beef, chopped liver. Hrs: 8 am-midnight; Fri, Sat to 2 am. Closed Rosh Hashanah, Yom Kippur, Passover. Semi-a la carte: bkfst, lunch, dinner $7.95-$15. Complete meals: dinner $13.40-$20.45. Kosher deli; full menu served all day. Family-owned. Cr cds: A.

SERENDIPITY 3. *225 E 60th St, Upper East Side. 212/838-3531.* Specializes in burgers, frozen hot chocolate. Hrs: 11:30-12:30 am; Fri to 1 am; Sat to 2 am; Sun to midnight. Closed Dec 25. Res accepted. A la carte entrees: lunch, dinner $4.50-$15. Art nouveau decor; Tiffany lamps; marble-top tables. Famous for ice cream specialties, pies, chocolate blackout cake. Enter restaurant through gift shop. Favorite of celebrities. Cr cds: A, C, D, DS, MC, V.

STAGE DELI. *834 Seventh Ave, at 53rd St, Midtown. 212/245-7850.* Kosher deli menu. Specializes in corned beef, pastrami, brisket. Hrs: 6-2 am. Bar. A la carte entrees: bkfst $2.95-$7.50, lunch $4.50-$13.95, dinner $5.50-$20. Deli counter. Well-known New York deli; pickles own meats. Enclosed sidewalk dining. Celebrity photos. Cr cds: A, MC, V.

Bronx

Inn

★★ **LE REFUGE.** *620 City Island Ave (10464), Rt 95 to City Island, exit 8B. 718/885-2478; FAX 718/885-1519.* 8 rms, 4 share baths, 3 story. 2 suites, 1 cottage. No rm phones. S $65; D $75; each addl $15; suite $125; cottage $175. TV; cable. Playground. Complimentary continental bkfst; afternoon refreshments. Dining rm 6-9 pm. Ck-out, ck-in by arrangement. Luggage handling. Picnic tables. Victorian house (1880) with individually decorated rms featuring many antiques. On Long Island Sound with views of Manhattan. Totally nonsmoking. Cr cds: A.

Restaurants

★★★ **AMERIGO'S.** *3587 E Tremont Ave (10465). 718/792-3600.* Italian menu. Specialties: osso buco with risotto, veal chops, seafood. Hrs: noon-11 pm. Closed Mon; Thanksgiving, Dec 25; also 3 wks July. Res accepted; required wkends. Bar. Wine cellar. A la carte entrees: lunch

$8.95-$15, dinner $8.95-$25.95. Child's meals. Valet parking wkends. Cr cds: A, C, D, DS, MC, V.

D

★ ★ **EMILIA'S.** *2331 Arthur Ave (10458), Between 184th & 186th Sts. 718/367-5915.* Italian menu. Specialties: fettuccine marinara, eggplant parmigiana, chicken Daniella with mushrooms. Hrs: noon-10 pm. Closed Mon, Tues; Thanksgiving, Dec 25. Res accepted. Bar. Semi-a la carte: lunch $9.95-$16.95, dinner $9.95-$25. Family-style restaurant. Cr cds: A, MC, V.

★ ★ **LOBSTER BOX.** *34 City Island Ave (10464), on City Island. 718/885-1952.* Specializes in lobster, shrimp, steamed clams. Hrs: noon-11 pm; Fri, Sat to 1 am. Closed Jan, Feb. Bar. Semi-a la carte: lunch $9.45-$12.95, dinner $12.95-$29.95. Valet parking. Terrace dining overlooks L.I. Sound. Family-owned. Cr cds: A, C, D, DS, MC, V.

★ ★ ★ **MARIO'S.** *2342 Arthur Ave (10458), between 184th & 186th Sts. 718/584-1188.* Italian menu. Specializes in pasta, veal, seafood. Hrs: noon-11 pm; Fri, Sat to 11:30 pm. Closed Mon; Dec 25; also last 2 wks Aug, first wk Sept. Res accepted. Semi-a la carte: lunch, dinner $13-$28. Valet parking. Family-owned. Cr cds: A, C, D, DS, MC, V.

D

★ ★ **SEA SHORE.** *591 City Island Ave (10464), on City Island. 718/885-0300.* Specializes in fresh seafood, jumbo lobster. Hrs: 11 am-midnight; Fri, Sat to 2 am. Res accepted. Bar. A la carte entrees: lunch $9.95-$18.95, dinner $16.95-$38.95. Child's meals. Valet parking. Outdoor dining. Greenhouse dining rm & dock area overlooking L.I. Sound; marina. Family-owned. Cr cds: A, C, D, DS, MC, V.

D

Brooklyn

Restaurants

★ ★ **ABBRACCIAMENTO ON THE PIER.** *2200 Rockaway Pkwy (11236), at Canarsie Pier, in Canarsie area. 718/251-5517.* Northern Italian, Amer menu. Specialties: veal scaloppini with artichoke champagne sauce, chicken breast stuffed with fontina cheese, pasta seafood bianco. Hrs: 11:30 am-midnight; Fri, Sat to 1 am; Sun brunch 11:30 am-3 pm. Closed Jan 1, Dec 25. Res required. Bar. A la carte entrees: lunch $9-$15, dinner $12-$25. Complete meals: dinner $19.95-$22.50. Sun brunch $15.95. Entertainment. Outdoor dining. On Canarsie Pier; overlooks Jamaica Bay; docking facilities. Cr cds: A, C, D, MC, V.

D

★ ★ **CUCINA.** *256 5th Ave (11215), between Carrol & Garfield Place, Park Slope area. 718/230-0711.* Italian menu. Specialties: roast rack of lamb, cappelli vongole, osso buco & pappardelle. Antipasto bar. Hrs: 5:30-10:30 pm; Fri, Sat to 11 pm; Sun 5-10 pm. Closed Thanksgiving, Dec 25. Res accepted. Bar. A la carte entrees: dinner $10-$25. Child's meals. Two dining rms; gold leaf wall montage by New York artist. Cr cds: A, MC, V.

D

★ ★ **EMBERS.** *9519 Third Ave (11209), between 95th & 96th Sts, in Bayridge area. 718/745-3700.* Specializes in pasta, T-bone steak. Hrs: noon-2:45 pm, 5-10:30 pm; Fri to 11:30 pm; Sat noon-1:45 pm, 4:30-11:30 pm; Sun 2-9:30 pm. Closed Thanksgiving, Dec 24, 25. Bar. A la carte entrees: lunch $4.50-$7.95, dinner $10.95-$16.95. Adj to meat market. No cr cds accepted. No cr cds accepted.

D

★ ★ **GIANDO ON THE WATER.** *400 Kent Ave (11211), under Williamsburg Bridge, Kent Ave at Broadway. 718/387-7000.* Italian menu. Specializes in seafood, fish, penne a la vodka. Hrs: noon-11 pm; Sat from 4 pm; Sun 3-9 pm; early-bird dinner 5-7 pm, Sat 4-6 pm, Sun 3-6 pm. Res accepted. Bar. Prix fixe: lunch $19.95, dinner $29.95. A la carte entrees: dinner $12-$27. Pianist Fri, Sat. Valet parking. On East River overlooking Williamsburg & Brooklyn bridges and Manhattan skyline from Empire State Bldg to Statue of Liberty. Cr cds: A, C, D, DS, MC, V.

D

✓★ ★ **GREENHOUSE CAFE.** *7717 Third Ave (11209), between 77th & 78th Sts, in Bayridge area. 718/833-8200.* Specialties: roast Long Island duckling, aged steak, seafood festival platter. Hrs: 11:30 am-11 pm; Fri, Sat to midnight; Sun 4-10 pm; Sun brunch noon-3 pm. Closed Dec 25. Res accepted. Bar. A la carte entrees: lunch $5.25-$13. Semi-a la carte: dinner $10.95-$17.95. Child's meals. Garden atrium. Cr cds: A, C, D, DS, MC, V.

D

★ ★ **PETER LUGER'S.** *178 Broadway (11211), at foot of Williamsburg Bridge. 718/387-7400.* Specializes in steak, lamb chops. Hrs: 11:30 am-9:45 pm; Fri, Sat to 10:45 pm; Sun 1-9:45 pm. Res accepted. Bar. Semi-a la carte: lunch $12.95. A la carte entrees: dinner $28.95-$60. Established in 1887; in 19th-century riverfront building. No cr cds accepted.

D

★ ★ **PONTE VECCHIO.** *8810 Fourth Ave (11209), between 88th & 89th Sts, in Bayridge area. 718/238-6449.* Italian menu. Specializes in pasta, veal, seafood. Hrs: noon-10:30 pm; Fri, Sat to 11:30 pm. Closed July 4, Thanksgiving, Dec 25. Res accepted. Serv bar. A la carte entrees: lunch $14-$22, dinner $27-$32. Valet parking. Cr cds: A, MC, V.

D

★ ★ ★ **RIVER CAFE.** *1 Water St (11201), on East River at foot of Brooklyn Bridge, in Brooklyn Heights area. 718/522-5200.* Specializes in rack of lamb, homemade chocolate desserts. Own baking. Hrs: noon-2:30 pm, 6-11:30 pm; Sun brunch 11:30 am-2:30 pm. Res required. A la carte entrees: lunch $20-$26. Prix fixe: dinner $68, tasting menu $85. Sun brunch $13-$26. Pianist. Valet parking. Jacket. Cr cds: A, C, D, MC, V.

★ ★ **TOMMASO.** *1464 86th St (11228), in Bayridge area. 718/236-9883.* Italian menu. Specializes in regional Italian dishes. Hrs: 4-11 pm; Sat to midnight; Sun 1-10 pm. Closed Dec 25. Res accepted. Bar. A la carte entrees: lunch, dinner $8-$20. Complete meals: lunch $8.95, dinner $19.96. Opera Thurs-Sun evenings. Family-owned. Cr cds: A, C, D, MC, V.

D

Queens (La Guardia & JFK Intl Airport Areas)

Hotels

★ ★ ★ **CROWNE PLAZA LA GUARDIA.** *(104-04 Ditmars Blvd, East Elmhurst 11369) Grand Central Pkwy exit 94th St, near La Guardia Airport. 718/457-6300; FAX 718/899-9768.* 358 rms, 200 with shower only, 7 story. S $175-$195; D $195-$205; each addl $20; suites $199-$600; under 19 free; wkly, wkend & hol rates. Crib free. Garage parking $5. TV; cable (premium), VCR (movies avail). Indoor pool; whirlpool, poolside serv. Complimentary coffee in rms. Restaurant 6 am-midnight. Bar 4 pm-2 am. Ck-out noon. Coin lndry. Convention facilities. Business center. In-rm modem link. Concierge. Gift shop. Free airport transportation. Tennis privileges. Exercise rm; instructor, weight machine, treadmill, sauna. Many refrigerators. Luxury level. Cr cds: A, C, D, DS, JCB, MC, V.

D SC

★ ★ **HILTON JFK AIRPORT.** *138-10 135th Ave (11436), at Kennedy Intl Airport. 718/322-8700; FAX 718/529-0749.* E-mail jfk3@idt.net. 333 rms, 9 story. S $179-$240; D $189-$250; each addl $20; suites $289-$650; under 21 free. Crib free. TV; cable (premium), VCR avail. Restaurant 6 am-11:30 pm. Bar noon-2 am. Ck-out noon. Convention facilities. Business servs avail. In-rm modem link. Free airport transportation. Exercise equipt; weights, bicycles. Luxury level. Cr cds: A, C, D, DS, ER, JCB, MC, V.

D SC

★ ★ **HOLIDAY INN-JFK.** *144-02 135th Ave (11436), near Kennedy Intl Airport. 718/659-0200; FAX 718/322-2533.* 360 rms, 12 story. S, D $189; each addl $15; suites from $239; under 19 free. Crib free. TV; cable, VCR avail (movies). Indoor/outdoor pool; whirlpool, sauna, lifeguard. Restaurant 6 am-10 pm. Bar 3 pm-1 am. Ck-out noon. Convention facilities. Business servs avail. Free airport transportation. Exercise rm; instructor, bicycles, stair machine. Cr cds: A, C, D, DS, JCB, MC, V.

D SC

★ ★ ★ **MARRIOTT LAGUARDIA.** *102-05 Ditmars Blvd (11369), opp La Guardia Airport, in East Elmhurst area. 718/565-8900; FAX 718/898-4995.* Web www.marriot.com/lgaap. 436 rms, 9 story. S $150; D $170; suites $350-$650; under 18 free; wkly rates; wkend plans. Crib free. Pet accepted. Covered parking $5. TV; cable (premium), VCR avail. Indoor pool; whirlpool, lifeguard. Restaurants 6:30 am-11 pm. Bar 11-1 am. Ck-out 1 pm. Convention facilities. Business center. In-rm modem link. Gift shop. Free airport transportation. Exercise equipt; weight machines, bicycles, sauna. Microwaves avail. Luxury level. Cr cds: A, C, D, DS, ER, JCB, MC, V.

D SC

Restaurants

★ ★ **IL TOSCANO.** *(42-05 235th St, Douglaston 11363) in Douglaston area. 718/631-0300.* Italian menu. Specialties: sweetbreads sautéed with fresh thyme, green peppercorn and sherry; grilled brook trout with raspberry lemon. Hrs: 5-10 pm. Closed Sun. Res required. Bar. A la carte entrees: dinner $14-$24. Casual, trattoria atmosphere. Cr cds: A, C, D, MC, V.

★ ★ **MANDUCATIS.** *13-27 Jackson Ave (11101), at 47th Ave, in Long Island City. 718/729-9845.* E-mail 103752.2264@compuserve.com. Italian menu. Specializes in grilled seafood, pappardelle Casertana, eggplant Napoletana. Hrs: noon-3 pm, 5-10 pm; Sat 5-11 pm; Sun 2-8 pm. Closed Sun July-Aug; last 2 wks in Aug; also most major hols. Res accepted. Bar. A la carte entrees: lunch $5-$18, dinner $7-$18.50. Attractive, comfortable neighborhood restaurant. Cr cds: A, C, D, MC, V.

D

★ ★ **MARBELLA.** *220-33 Northern Blvd (11361), 2 blks W of Cross Island Pkwy, in Bayside area. 718/423-0100.* Spanish, continental menu. Specializes in paella, rack of lamb, duckling Valenciana. Hrs: noon-midnight; Sat to 1 am. Res accepted. Bar. A la carte entrees: lunch $6.95-$10.95, dinner $8.95-$17.95. Harpist Fri-Sun. Parking. Spanish artifacts. Family-owned. Cr cds: A, D, MC, V.

D

★ ★ **PARK SIDE.** *107-01 Corona Ave (11368), at 51st St, in Corona area. 718/271-9274.* Italian menu. Specializes in pasta, veal, fish. Hrs: noon-11:30 pm. Res accepted. Bar. A la carte entrees: lunch $10-$18, dinner $10-$21. Valet parking. The five dining areas include a glass-enclosed garden rm. Cr cds: A, C, D, MC, V.

D

★ ★ **PICCOLA VENEZIA.** *42-01 28th Ave (11103), at 42nd St, Astoria area. 718/721-8470.* Northern Italian menu. Specializes in seafood, rack of lamb, pasta. Hrs: noon-11 pm; Sat 4:30-11:30 pm; Sun 2-10:30 pm. Closed Tues; Jan 1, Dec 25, also July 24-Aug 24. Res accepted. A la carte entrees: lunch $15-$35, dinner $15-$40. Complete meals: dinner $38.95-$46.95. Valet parking. Attractive restaurant with exposed brick walls and etched mirrors. Family-owned. Cr cds: A, C, D, MC, V.

D

★ ★ ★ **WATER'S EDGE.** *(44th Drive, Long Island City 11101) at East River. 718/482-0033.* Specializes in seafood, lobster. Own baking. Hrs: noon-3 pm, 5-11 pm; Fri, Sat 5:30-11:30 pm. Closed Sun. Res required. Bar. Wine cellar. A la carte entrees: lunch $10-$16, dinner $22-$31. Pianist. Valet parking. Complimentary river boat transportation to and from Manhattan. Outdoor dining. European decor. On riverfront opp United Nations complex; views of New York City midtown skyline. Cr cds: A, C, D, JCB, MC, V.

D

Newark Intl Airport Area

Motels

★ ★ ★ **COURTYARD BY MARRIOTT.** *(600 US 1/9, Newark 07114) NJ Tpke exit 14, S on US 1/9. 973/643-8500; FAX 973/648-0662.* 146 rms, 3 story. S, D $129-$134; suites $159-$169; under 16 free; wkly, wkend rates. Crib free. TV; cable (premium), VCR avail. Indoor pool; whirlpool. Complimentary coffee in rms. Restaurant 6:30 am-10 pm. Rm serv Mon-Thurs. Bar 5-11 pm. Ck-out noon. Coin lndry. Meeting rms. Business servs avail. In-rm modem link. Valet serv. Sundries. Free airport transportation. Exercise equipt; weight machine, bicycles. Microwave, refrigerator in suites. Some balconies. Cr cds: A, C, D, DS, MC, V.

D SC

✔★ ★ **DAYS INN-NEWARK AIRPORT.** *(450 US 1S, Newark 07114) Off NJ Tpke exit 14, S on US 1/9. 973/242-0900; FAX 973/242-8480.* 191 rms, 8 story. S, D $64.95-$89.95; each addl $5; suites $99-$120; wkend rates. TV; cable (premium). Restaurant 6:30 am-midnight. Bar. Ck-out noon. Coin lndry. Meeting rms. Business servs avail. Free airport transportation. Exercise equipt; weight machine, bicycle. Microwave avail. Cr cds: A, C, D, DS, ER, JCB, MC, V.

D SC

✔★ **HOWARD JOHNSON.** *(50 Port St, Newark 07114) Off NJ Tpke exit 14, Frontage Rd. 973/344-1500; FAX 973/344-3311.* 170 rms, 3 story. S, D $59.99-$89.99; under 18 free; wkend rates. Crib free. TV; cable (premium). Restaurant open 24 hrs; Fri, Sat 6-1 am. Ck-out noon. Coin lndry. Meeting rms. Business servs avail. In-rm modem link. Gift shop. Free airport transportation. Cr cds: A, C, D, DS, MC, V.

D SC

Motor Hotel

★ ★ **HOLIDAY INN INTL AIRPORT-NORTH.** *(160 Frontage Rd, Newark 07114) Off NJ Tpke exit 14, opp N terminal; use Frontage Rd. 973/589-1000; FAX 973/589-2799.* 234 rms, 10 story. S, D $99-$149; under 18 free; wkend rates by res. Crib free. TV; cable (premium). Pool; lifeguard. Restaurant 6 am-midnight. Rm serv. Bar 11-2 am; entertainment. Ck-out noon. Meeting rms. Business servs avail. In-rm modem link. Bellhops. Sundries. Gift shop. Free airport transportation. Exercise equipt; weight machine, treadmills. Cr cds: A, C, D, DS, JCB, MC, V.

D SC

Hotels

★ ★ ★ **HILTON-NEWARK AIRPORT.** *(1170 Spring St, Elizabeth 07201) Off NJ Tpke exit 13 A. 908/351-3900; FAX 908/351-9556.* Web www.hilton.com/hilton. 375 rms, 12 story. S, D $164-$209; each addl $10; suites $295-$650; under 18 free; wkend rates. Crib free. TV; cable (premium), VCR avail. Indoor pool; whirlpool. Coffee in rms. Restaurant 6:30 am-11 pm. Rm serv 24 hrs. Bar 4 pm-2 am. Ck-out noon. Convention facilities. Business center. In-rm modem link. Gift shop. Free airport, RR station transportation. Valet parking. Exercise equipt; weight machines, bicycles, sauna. Cr cds: A, C, D, DS, ER, JCB, MC, V.

D SC

★ ★ **HOLIDAY INN.** *(1000 Spring St, Elizabeth 07201) 3 mi N on NJ Tpke, exit 13-A. 908/355-1700; FAX 908/355-1741.* 392 rms, 10 story. S $121-$145; D $131-$155; each addl $13; suites $175-$350; under 18 free; wkend, hol rates. Pet accepted, some restrictions. TV; cable (premium), VCR avail (movies). Complimentary coffee in lobby. Restaurant 6:30 am-10:30 pm. Bar; entertainment Tues, Fri, Sat. Ck-out noon. Convention facilities. Business servs avail. In-rm modem link. Gift shop. Coin lndry. Free airport, RR station transportation. Exercise equipt; bicycle, treadmill. Indoor pool; lifeguard. Some bathrm phones. Refrigerators avail. Cr cds: A, C, D, DS, JCB, MC, V.

D SC

★ ★ ★ **MARRIOTT-AIRPORT.** *(Newark Intl Airport, Newark 07114) On airport grounds; follow signs for main terminal. 973/623-0006; FAX 973/623-7618.* 590 rms, 10 story. S, D $169-$199; suites $400-$500; under 18 free; wkend rates. Crib free. TV; cable (premium), VCR avail. Indoor/outdoor pool; whirlpool, poolside serv. Restaurants 6 am-11 pm. Rm serv 24 hrs. Bars 11:30-1:30 am. Ck-out noon. Convention facilities. Business center. Concierge. Free airport transportation. Free parking. Exercise equipt; weights, bicycles, sauna. Some refrigerators. Luxury level. Cr cds: A, C, D, DS, ER, JCB, MC, V.

D SC

★ ★ ★ **SHERATON-NEWARK AIRPORT.** *(128 Frontage Rd, Newark 07114) Off NJ Tpke exit 14; use Frontage Rd. 973/690-5500; FAX 973/465-7195.* 502 rms, 12 story. S, D $175; each addl $10; suites $395-$495; under 18 free; wkend rates. Crib free. TV; cable (premium), VCR avail. Indoor pool; whirlpool, poolside serv, lifeguard. Coffee in rms. Restaurants 6:30 am-11 pm. Bar 2 pm-2 am; entertainment Mon-Fri. Ck-out noon. Convention facilities. Business center. In-rm modem link. Concierge. Gift shop. Free airport transportation. Exercise equipt; weights, bicycles. Game rm. Refrigerators avail. Balconies. Atrium. Luxury level. Cr cds: A, C, D, DS, MC, V.

D SC

★ **TRAVELODGE.** *(50 Park Place, Newark 07102) 973/622-1000; FAX 973/622-6410.* 169 rms, 12 story. S $65-$85; D $75-$90; suites $275-$375; under 16 free; wkend rates. Crib avail. TV; cable (premium), VCR avail. Complimentary coffee in rms. Restaurant 7 am-11 pm. No rm serv. Bar 4 pm-midnight; entertainment Thurs. Ck-out noon. Meeting rms. Business servs avail. In-rm modem link. Gift shop. Coin lndry. Free airport, RR station transportation. Exercise equipt; weight machine, bicycles. Game rm. Bathrm phone, in-rm whirlpool, refrigerator, minibar in suites. Cr cds: A, C, D, DS, ER, JCB, MC, V.

SC

Oklahoma City

Founded: 1889
Pop: 444,719
Elev: 1,207 feet
Time zone: Central
Area code: 405
Web: www.okccvb.org

On the morning of April 22, 1889, with the sound of a gunshot, a thunder of hooves and a billowing cloud of dust, what had been a barren prairie became a metropolis of 10,000. Oklahoma City was born in one morning when the federal government opened to settlement land that had previously been granted to five Native American tribes. Today, while continuing its commitment to development, the community is holding on to its heritage, as a wealth of museums and monuments attest.

Oklahoma City was incorporated in 1890. By 1910, the population had grown to more than 64,000, making Oklahoma City the largest city in the state. In December, 1928, oil was discovered here. In fact, the city stands in the middle of an oil field—there are even oil wells on the lawn of the capitol. Oklahoma City now produces large quantities of high-gravity oil and manufactures oil-well equipment as well.

Business

The city's industries produce fabricated iron and steel, furniture, tires, electrical equipment, electronics, aircraft and automobiles. Research into aeronautical development and space medicine also takes place here. Tinker Air Force Base is one of the city's major employers.

Oklahoma City's stockyard and meat-packing plants are the largest in the state; in fact, the city claims to be the nation's leading cattle market. Oklahoma City is also a grain-milling and cotton-processing center.

Convention Facilities

For conventions, sports, meetings, exhibits, entertainment, social gatherings and religious presentations, the Myriad Convention Center provides a variety of accommodations.

The Great Hall has nearly 17,000 square feet of space, which can be divided into halves by electrically operated soundproof walls. There is also an 80-by-40-foot stage with offstage dressing room facilities. When used as an auditorium, the hall's capacity is 2,200; as a dining room, 1,500; as a ballroom, 1,200.

The center's exhibition hall has 140,000 square feet of space and can be divided into as many as eight smaller areas, each with its own utility, light and sound services. A stage area and arena floor are also available.

On the upper concourse level, 24 meeting rooms are designed to accommodate between 50 and 400 people. These rooms are also suited for club luncheons or dinners, parties, convention committee sessions, lectures or seminars.

Sports & Recreation

Oklahoma City offers a wide variety of sporting events to both spectators and players alike. The 89ers, AAA farm team for the Texas Rangers, start swinging their bats here every spring. Throughout the year, Oklahoma City is host to many world class, state and regional horse shows, thus earning the title "horse show capital of the world."

The Myriad Convention Center Arena, with a permanent hockey rink, a basketball floor and a portable indoor track, can host just about any indoor sport, including rodeos. The total seating capacity is 15,600, of which 12,000 are permanent seats. The arena seats 13,800 for basketball and 13,400 for hockey.

Many challenging golf courses, most of which are open year-round, dot the metro area. Tennis players also will find an abundance of both indoor and outdoor courts. Water lovers will be pleased to know that Oklahoma has more man-made shoreline than the entire Atlantic coast of the US; Oklahoma City has a good share of that shoreline. There are several lakes and recreation areas within the metropolitan district that offer facilities for fishermen, sailors, swimmers, horseback riders and campers.

Entertainment

The city's many professional theaters provide audiences with everything from the traditional to the avant-garde. The Lyric Theatre, a professional summer stock company, presents musicals from mid-June through mid-August. Ballet Oklahoma, the city's professional ballet company, dances from October through April.

The Oklahoma City Philharmonic Orchestra performs from September through April. On Friday and Saturday nights, the doors of the Oklahoma Opry swing open for live country and western music. There are also taverns and clubs throughout the city that cater to a variety of musical tastes.

Historical Areas

The Oklahoma Heritage Center is concerned with the preservation of the state's past and the direction of its future. The center is located in the mansion of Judge R.A. Hefner, who in 1970 gave his house to the Oklahoma Heritage Association for its permanent headquarters and for the public's enjoyment.

The Heritage Center includes Oklahoma Hall of Fame Galleries, exhibiting portraits, bronzes and photographs of prominent Oklahomans; Oklahoma Heritage Galleria, exhibiting art and displays pertaining to the state's history; Shepherd Oklahoma Heritage Library, housing 10,000 volumes of Oklahoma-oriented books and periodicals; and the Oklahoma Heritage Archives, containing historical documents, letters and papers. Also included are the Hefner Memorial Chapel and Chapel Garden, Anthony Oklahoma Heritage Gardens and the Robert A. Hefner, Jr. Conservatory.

The National Cowboy Hall of Fame and Western Heritage Center contains statuary and paintings by Remington and Russell and a Rodeo Hall of Fame. This museum, sponsored by 17 Western states, also contains exhibits explaining the development of the West, with sight and sound, and an animated relief map depicting the nation's westward expansion.

Sightseeing

Oklahoma City is the home of several art museums and galleries. Exhibits include modern paintings and sculpture and collections of art and artifacts from Egypt, Mesopotamia, the Orient and pre-Columbian America.

Another sight to see in Oklahoma City is Omniplex, a 10-acre facility that houses the International Photography Hall of Fame and Museum, Red Earth Indian Center, and the Kirkpatrick Science and Air Space Museum, featuring both art and hands-on exhibits. Not to be missed are the Myriad Botanical Gardens, a beautiful landscaped lake retreat in the heart of downtown Oklahoma City.

Also of interest are the neoclassical State Capitol Building, with working oil wells on its grounds; the Oklahoma Historical Society Building, which contains an extensive collection of Native American material, as well as exhibits on the history of the state; the Civic Center, which houses the Music Hall; the National Softball Hall of Fame and Museum; the Oklahoma Firefighters Museum, which displays the state's first fire station and antique firefighting equipment; and the Oklahoma City Zoo, which features a dolphin and sea lion show.

Sightseers who are interested in shopping will find an interesting variety here—from authentic Western wear and Native American art and jewelry at Stockyards City, to designer jeans, dinner jackets and diamonds at the posh 50 Penn Place. Shopping malls, department stores, boutiques and antique shops throughout the city cater to a whole range of needs, wants and whims.

General References

Area code: 405

Phone Numbers

POLICE & FIRE: 911

POISON CONTROL CENTER: 271-5454

TIME: 720-8463 **WEATHER:** 478-3377

Information Sources

Oklahoma City Convention and Visitors Bureau, 189 W Sheridan, 73102; 297-8912 or 800/225-5652.

Oklahoma Tourism and Recreation Department, 15 N Robinson, 73105; 521-2406.

Oklahoma City Chamber of Commerce, 123 Park Ave, 73102; 297-8900.

Department of Parks & Recreation, 297-3882.

Transportation

AIRLINES: American; Continental; Delta; Northwest; Southwest; TWA; United; and other commuter and regional airlines.

AIRPORT: Will Rogers World, 680-3200.

CAR RENTAL AGENCIES: (See IMPORTANT TOLL-FREE NUMBERS) Avis 685-7781; Budget 681-4977; Dollar 681-0151; Hertz 681-2341; National 685-7726; Thrifty 682-5433.

PUBLIC TRANSPORTATION: Central Oklahoma Transportation & Parking Authority, 300 SW 7th St, 235-7433.

Newspapers

Daily Oklahoman; The Journal-Record.

Convention Facilities

Myriad Convention Center, 1 Myriad Gardens, 232-8871.

State Fair Park, Fair Park, 500 Land Rush St, 948-6700.

Sports & Recreation

Major Sports Facilities

All Sports Stadium, state fairgrounds, 946-8989.

Myriad Convention Center Arena, Sheridan & Robinson Aves, 232-8871.

Racetrack

Remington Park, off I-35 at NE 50th St & Martin Luther King, Jr Blvd, 424-9000 or 800/456-9000 (horse racing).

Cultural Facilities

Theaters

Carpenter Square Theatre, 400 W Main St, 232-6500.

Jewel Box Theatre, 3700 N Walker Ave, 521-1786.

Lyric Theatre, 2501 N Blackwelder Ave, 524-7111.

Concert Hall

Civic Center Music Hall, 201 Channing Square, 297-2584.

Museums

Enterprise Square, USA, 2501 E Memorial Rd, 425-5030.

45th Infantry Division Museum, 2145 NE 36th St, 424-5313.

Harn Homestead & 1889er Museum, 313 NE 16th St, 235-4058.

International Photography Hall of Fame & Museum, Omniplex, 424-4055.

Kirkpatrick Science and Air Space Museum, 2100 NE 52nd St, 424-5545.

Museum of Natural History, 1335 Asp Ave, Oklahoma University campus, Norman, 325-4711.

National Cowboy Hall of Fame & Western Heritage Center, 1700 NE 63rd St, 478-2250.

National Softball Hall of Fame and Museum, 2801 NE 50th St, 424-5266.

Oklahoma Firefighters Museum, 2716 NE 50th St, 424-3440.

Oklahoma Heritage Center, 201 NW 14th St, 235-4458.

Red Earth Indian Center, Omniplex, 427-5228.

State Museum of History, 2100 N Lincoln Blvd, 521-2491.

Art Museums & Galleries

Oklahoma City Art Museum, 3113 Pershing Blvd, 946-4477.

Oklahoma Indian Art Gallery, 2335 SW 44th St, 685-6162.

Points of Interest

Historical

Governor's Mansion, 820 NE 23rd St, 521-2342.

Overholser Mansion, 405 NW 15th St, 528-8485.

Other Attractions

Frontier City, 11501 NE Expy (I-35), 478-2412.

Garden Exhibition Building and Horticulture Gardens, 3400 NW 36th St, 943-0827.

Heritage Place (Horse Sale Pavilion), 2829 S MacArthur Blvd, 682-4551.

Kirkpatrick Planetarium, Kirkpatrick Science and Air Space Museum, 424-5545.

Myriad Botanical Gardens, Reno & Robinson Sts, downtown, 297-3995.

Oklahoma City Zoo, 2101 NE 50th St, 424-3344.

Oklahoma National Stockyards, 2501 Exchange Ave, 235-8675.

State Capitol Building, NE 23rd St & Lincoln Blvd, 521-3356.

State Fair Park, NW 10th St & N May Ave, 948-6700.

White Water Bay, 3908 W Reno, 943-9687.

Sightseeing Tour

Territorial Tours, 1636 SW 79th Terrace, 681-6432.

Annual Events

International Finals Rodeo, Myriad Convention Center, 235-6540. Mid-Jan.

Festival of the Arts, downtown. Late Apr.

State Fair of Oklahoma, Fair Park, NW 10th St & N May Ave, 948-6700. Late Sept-early Oct.

World Championship Quarter Horse Show, state fairgrounds, NW 10th St & N May Ave. Early Nov.

(For further information contact the Chamber of Commerce or Department of Parks & Recreation, 297-3882.)

City Neighborhoods

Many of the restaurants, unrated dining establishments and some lodgings listed under Oklahoma City include neighborhoods as well as exact street addresses. Geographic descriptions of Downtown and Bricktown are given, followed by a table of restaurants arranged by neighborhood.

Bricktown: South of Sheridan Ave, west of Oklahoma Ave, east of the railroad tracks and along California St from Oklahoma Ave.

Downtown: South of 10th St, west of Walnut St, north of I-40/US 270 and east of Classen Blvd. **North of Downtown** North of 10th St. **South of Downtown** South of I-40/US 270.

Lodgings and Food

OKLAHOMA CITY RESTAURANTS BY NEIGHBORHOOD AREAS

(For full description, see alphabetical listings under Restaurants)

BRICKTOWN
Bricktown Brewery. 1 N Oklahoma Ave

NORTH OF DOWNTOWN
Bellini's. 63rd & Pennsylvania
Classen Grill. 5124 N Classen Blvd
Coach House. 6437 Avondale Dr
The County Line. 1226 NE 63rd St
Don Serapio's. 11109 N May
Eddy's Of Oklahoma City. 4227 N Meridian Ave
Jamil's. 4910 N Lincoln
La Baguette Bistro. 7408 N May Ave
Nikz At The Top. 5900 Mosteller Dr
Sleepy Hollow. 1101 NE 50th St
The Tower. 1601 Northwest Expy (OK 3)
The Waterford (The Waterford Marriott Hotel). 6300 Waterford Blvd

SOUTH OF DOWNTOWN
Aloha Garden. 2219 SW 74th St
Cattleman's Steakhouse. 1309 S Agnew St

WEST OF DOWNTOWN
Applewoods. 4301 SW 3rd St
JW's Steakhouse (Marriott Hotel). 3233 Northwest Expy
Kona Ranch Steakhouse. 2037 S Meridian
Logan's Roadhouse. 1100 S Meridian
Shorty Small's. 4500 W Reno
Texanna Red's. 4600 W Reno

Note: When a listing is located in a town that does not have its own city heading, it will appear under the city nearest to its location. In these cases, the address and town appear in parenthesis immediately following the name of the establishment.

Motels

★ ★ ★ **BEST WESTERN-SADDLEBACK INN.** *4300 SW 3rd St (73108), 1/2 blk NE of I-40 Meridian Ave exit, west of downtown. 405/947-7000; FAX 405/948-7636.* 220 rms, 2-3 story. S, D $65-$72; each addl $7; suites $79-$86; under 17 free; wkend rates. Crib free. TV; cable (premium), VCR avail. Heated pool; whirlpool, poolside serv. Coffee in rms. Restaurant 6 am-2 pm, 5-10 pm; Sun from 8 am. Rm serv. Bar 4 pm-midnight. Ck-out noon. Coin Indry. Meeting rms. Business servs avail. In-rm modem link. Bellhops. Valet serv. Gift shop. Sundries. Free airport transportation. Exercise equipt; weights, bicycles, sauna. Southwestern decor. Cr cds: A, C, D, DS, MC, V.

D SC

✔★ **COMFORT INN.** *4017 NW 39th Expy (US 66/270) (73112), north of downtown. 405/947-0038; FAX 405/946-7450.* 112 rms, 2 story, 15 kit. units. S, D $51-$62; each addl $6; kit. units $59-$71; under 18 free. Crib free. Pet accepted, some restrictions. TV; cable (premium), VCR avail (movies). Pool. Complimentary continental bkfst. Coffee in rms. Restaurant adj open 24 hrs. Ck-out noon. Coin Indry. Meeting rms. Business servs avail. Valet serv. Health club privileges. Some refrigerators; microwaves avail. Cr cds: A, C, D, DS, ER, JCB, MC, V.

D SC

★ ★ ★ **COURTYARD BY MARRIOTT.** *4301 Highline Blvd (73108), near Will Rogers World Airport, west of downtown. 405/946-6500; FAX 405/946-7638.* 149 rms, 3 story. S $90; D $100; suites $115-$120; under 12 free; wkend rates. TV; cable (premium), VCR avail (movies). Heated pool; whirlpool. Complimentary coffee in rms. Restaurant 6:30-10:30 am; wkends 7-11 am. Bar 4:30-10:30 pm. Ck-out noon. Coin Indry. Meeting rms. Business servs avail. In-rm modem link. Valet serv. Sundries. Free airport transportation. Exercise equipt; weight machine, bicycle. Refrigerator in suites. Balconies. Cr cds: A, C, D, DS, MC, V.

D SC

✔★ **DAYS INN-NORTHWEST.** *2801 NW 39th St (73112), north of downtown. 405/946-0741; FAX 405/942-0181.* E-mail gertysocks@msn.com. 117 rms, 2 story. S $45-$51; D $46-$55; each addl $6; suites $150; under 16 free; wkend rates. Crib free. Pet accepted. TV; cable (premium). Coffee in rms. Pool. Restaurant 6:30 am-1 pm, 5-9 pm. Rm serv. Bar 2 pm-2 am. Ck-out 11 am. Coin Indry. Meeting rms. Business center. Valet serv. Sundries. Free airport transportation. Some bathrm phones, refrigerators. Cr cds: A, C, D, DS, JCB, MC, V.

D SC

★ **GOVERNORS SUITES.** *2308 S Meridian (73108), near Will Rogers World Airport, west of downtown. 405/682-5299; FAX 405/682-3047.* 50 units, 3 story. S, D $65-$95. TV; cable. Pool; whirlpool. Complimentary continental bkfst. Complimentary coffee in rms. Restaurant nearby. Ck-out 11 am. Meeting rm. Business servs avail. Free airport transportation. Exercise equipt; weight machine, treadmill, sauna. Microwaves. Cr cds: A, C, D, DS, MC, V.

D SC

✔★ **HOWARD JOHNSON.** *400 S Meridian (73108), west of downtown. 405/943-9841; FAX 405/942-1869.* 96 rms, 2 story. S $49-$60; D $49-$63; each addl $6; under 17 free. Crib free. Pet accepted, some restrictions. TV; cable (premium). Pool. Complimentary continental bkfst. Complimentary coffee in rms. Restaurant adj 10:30 am-11 pm. Ck-out noon. Coin Indry. Business servs avail. Many refrigerators; microwaves avail. Cr cds: A, C, D, DS, MC, V.

SC

★ ★ **LA QUINTA.** *800 S Meridian Ave (73108), west of downtown. 405/942-0040; FAX 405/942-0638.* 168 rms, 2 story. S $69-$89; D $79-$99; each addl $10; under 18 free. Pet accepted, some restrictions. TV; cable (premium), VCR avail. Pool; wading pool, poolside serv. Complimentary continental bkfst. Restaurant 6:30 am-midnight. Rm serv. Bar from 10 am. Ck-out noon. Meeting rms. Business servs avail. In-rm modem link. Free airport, bus depot transportation. Refrigerators, microwaves avail. Cr cds: A, C, D, DS, MC, V.

D SC

★ ★ **LA QUINTA.** *8315 S I-35 (73149), 7 mi SE on I-35, exit 121A, south of downtown. 405/631-8661; FAX 405/631-1892.* 122 rms, 2 story. S, D $62-$72; each addl $7; under 18 free. Crib free. TV; cable (premium). Pool. Complimentary continental bkfst. Restaurant opp open 24 hrs. Ck-out noon. Business servs avail. Valet serv. Health club privileges. Microwaves avail. Cr cds: A, C, D, DS, MC, V.

D SC

★ ★ **RESIDENCE INN BY MARRIOTT.** *4361 W Reno Ave (73107), 2 blks NE of I-40 Meridian exit, west of downtown. 405/942-4500; FAX 405/942-7777.* 135 kit. suites, 1-2 story. 1-bedrm suites $105; 2-bedrm suites $135. Crib free. Pet accepted, some restrictions. TV; cable (premium), VCR avail (movies). Heated pool; whirlpool. Complimentary continental bkfst. Complimentary coffee in rms. Ck-out noon. Coin Indry. Meeting rms. Business servs avail. In-rm modem link. Valet serv. Airport transportation. Health club privileges. Refrigerators, microwaves, fireplaces. Private patios, balconies. Picnic tables, grills. Cr cds: A, C, D, DS, JCB, MC, V.

D SC

★ ★ **RICHMOND SUITES HOTEL.** *1600 Richmond Square (73118), north of downtown. 405/840-1440; FAX 405/843-4272; res: 800/843-1440.* 51 suites, 2 story. S, D $88-$150; under 18 free; wkend, hol rates. Crib $5. Pet accepted, some restrictions; $50. TV; cable (premium). Pool. Complimentary continental bkfst. Complimentary coffee in rms. Restaurant 11:30 am-2 pm, 6-9:30 pm; Fri, Sat to 10 pm; closed Sun. Rm serv. Bar; closed Sun; pianist. Meeting rms. Business servs avail. In-rm modem link. Free airport transportation. Health club privileges. Refrigerators, microwaves. Cr cds: A, C, D, DS, MC, V.

D SC

★ **TRAVELERS INN.** *504 S Meridan (73108), jct I-40, west of downtown. 405/942-8294; FAX 405/947-3529.* 136 rms, 2 story. S $34.99; D $41.99; each addl $4; suites $47.99-$54.99; under 18 free. Crib free. TV; cable (premium). Heated pool. Complimentary continental bkfst. Restaurant adj 11 am-11 pm. Ck-out 11 am. Coin Indry. Business servs avail. In-rm modem link. Valet serv. Near airport. Cr cds: A, C, D, DS, MC, V.

D SC

Motor Hotels

★ ★ **BEST WESTERN SANTA FE INN.** *6101 N Santa Fe (73118), I-44 exit 127. 405/848-1919; FAX 405/840-1581.* 96 rms, 3 story. S $65-$85; D $73-$95; each addl $10; suites $85-$125; under 12 free. Crib free. TV; cable (premium). Pool; whirlpool. Complimentary full bkfst. Complimentary coffee in rms. Restaurant 6 am-1:30 pm, 5-9 pm; closed Sun evening. Rm serv. Bar 5 pm-midnight. Ck-out 11 am. Meeting rms. Business servs avail. In-rm modem link. Valet serv. Health club privileges. Some refrigerators. Cr cds: A, C, D, DS, MC, V.

D SC

★ **LEXINGTON HOTEL SUITES.** *1200 S Meridian (73108), near Will Rogers World Airport. 405/943-7800; FAX 405/943-8346.* 145 kit. suites, 3 story. S $69-$79; D $69-$109; under 16 free; wkend rates; higher rates special events. Crib free. TV; cable (premium), VCR avail. Complimentary continental bkfst. Complimentary coffee in rms. Restaurant adj 10-2 am. Rm serv 24 hrs. Ck-out noon. Meeting rms. Business servs avail. In-rm modem link. Valet serv. Coin Indry. Free airport transportation. Health club privileges. Heated pool. Refrigerators; many microwaves. Cr cds: A, C, D, DS, MC, V.

D SC

★ ★ **RADISSON.** *401 S Meridian Ave (73108), at I-40, Meridian Ave exit, west of downtown. 405/947-7681; FAX 405/947-4253.* 509 rms, 2 story. S $65-$88; D $75-$91; each addl $10; suites $89-$195; family, wkend rates. Crib free. Pet accepted, some restrictions. TV; cable (premium), VCR avail. 4 pools, 1 indoor; whirlpool, poolside serv. Restaurants 6 am-11 pm. Rm serv. Bars 11:30-2 am; entertainment. Ck-out noon. Meeting rms. Business servs avail. In-rm modem link. Bellhops. Sundries. Gift shop. Barber shop. Free airport transportation. Tennis. Exercise equipt; weights, bicycles, sauna. Rec rm. Bathrm phone, microwave, wet bar in townhouse suites; whirlpool in some suites. Cr cds: A, C, D, DS, ER, JCB, MC, V.

D SC

Hotels

★ ★ ★ **EMBASSY SUITES.** *1815 S Meridian Ave (73108), west of downtown. 405/682-6000; FAX 405/682-9835.* 236 suites, 6 story. S, D $129; each addl $10; under 12 free; wkend rates. Crib free. Pet accepted; some restrictions. TV; cable (premium). Indoor pool; whirlpool. Complimentary bkfst. Complimentary coffee in rms. Restaurant 6 am-10 pm. Bar 4 pm-2 am. Ck-out noon. Meeting rms. Business center. In-rm modem link. Gift shop. Airport transportation. Exercise equipt; weights, bicycles, steam rm, sauna. Refrigerators, microwaves, wet bars. Some balconies. Atrium. Cr cds: A, C, D, DS, MC, V.

D SC

★ ★ **FIFTH SEASON.** *6200 N Robinson Ave (73118), north of downtown. 405/843-5558; FAX 405/840-3410; res: 800/682-0049 (exc OK), 800/522-9458 (OK).* 202 rms, 3 story, 27 suites. S, D $89-$99; each addl $10; suites $95-$105; under 12 free; wkend rates; package plans. Crib free. Pet accepted, some restrictions. TV; cable (premium). Indoor pool; poolside serv. Complimentary full bkfst. Complimentary coffee in rms. Restaurant 6:30 am-2 pm, 5-10 pm. Bar 4 pm-midnight. Ck-out noon. Coin Indry. Meeting rms. Business servs avail. Gift shop. Free airport transportation. Health club privileges. Refrigerator, minibar in suites. Cr cds: A, C, D, DS, JCB, MC, V.

D SC

★ ★ ★ **HILTON-NORTHWEST.** *2945 Northwest Expy (OK 3) (73112), west of downtown. 405/848-4811; FAX 405/843-4829.* 218 rms, 9 story. S $95-$149; D $99-$159; each addl $10; suites $175-$299; under 18 free; wkend rates. Crib free. TV; cable (premium), VCR avail. Heated pool; poolside serv, whirlpool. Complimentary coffee in rms. Restaurant 6 am-2 pm, 5-10 pm. Rm serv. Bar 4 pm-midnight; Fri, Sat to 1 am; Sun to 10 pm. Ck-out noon. Meeting rms. Business servs avail. In-rm modem link. Free airport transportation. Exercise equipt; weights, bicycles. Health club privileges. Refrigerator avail. Cr cds: A, C, D, DS, ER, MC, V.

D SC

★ ★ ★ **MARRIOTT.** *3233 Northwest Expy (OK 3) (73112), west of downtown. 405/842-6633; FAX 405/840-5338.* Web www.marriott.com. 354 rms, 15 story. S, D $139-$149; suites $175-$350; studio rms $99; under 18 free; wkend rates. Crib free. Pet accepted, some restrictions. TV; cable (premium). Indoor/outdoor pool. Restaurant (see JW's STEAKHOUSE). Bar 3 pm-2 am; Sun to midnight; entertainment Sat. Ck-out noon. Coin Indry. Convention facilities. Business servs avail. In-rm modem link. Concierge. Gift shop. Exercise equipt; weights, bicycles. Health club privileges. Some balconies. Luxury level. Cr cds: A, C, D, DS, ER, JCB, MC, V.

D SC

★ ★ ★ **MEDALLION.** *One N Broadway (73102), adj Myriad Convention Center, downtown. 405/235-2780; FAX 405/272-0369; res: 800/285-2780.* 399 rms, 15 story. S $125-$155; D $135-$165; each addl $10; suites $450-$850; wkend rates. Crib free. Garage $4. TV; cable (premium), VCR avail. Pool. Restaurant 6 am-11 pm. Rm serv 24 hrs. Bar 11-2 am. Ck-out noon. Convention facilities. Business servs avail. In-rm modem link. Valet parking. Health club privileges. Luxury level. Cr cds: A, C, D, DS, MC, V.

D SC

★ ★ **RAMADA PLAZA.** *(930 E 2nd St, Edmond 73034) 10 mi N, 1½ mi W of I-35 exit Edmond-2nd St, opp University of Central OK. 405/341-3577; FAX 405/341-9279..* 145 rms, 8 story. S $69-$79; D $79-$89; each addl $10; suites $89-$150; under 18 free; wkend rates. Crib free. TV; cable (premium). Pool; whirlpool. Complimentary full bkfst. Complimentary coffee in rms. Restaurant 6 am-2 pm, 5-10 pm. Rm serv. Bar 5 pm-midnight; Fri, Sat to 1:30 am, Sun 4-10 pm; entertainment Fri, Sat. Ck-out 11 am. Meeting rms. Business servs avail. In-rm modem link. Exercise equipt; treadmills, stair machine. Microwaves avail. Cr cds: A, C, D, DS, JCB, MC, V.

D SC

★ ★ ★ **THE WATERFORD MARRIOTT.** *6300 Waterford Blvd (73118), north of downtown. 405/848-4782; FAX 405/843-9161; res: 800/992-2009.* 197 rms, 9 story. S, D $114-$149; each addl $10; suites $165-$750; under 18 free; package plans. Crib free. TV; cable (premium), VCR avail. Heated pool; whirlpool, poolside serv. Restaurant (see THE WATERFORD). Bar 11-1 am; entertainment. Ck-out noon. Business center. In-rm modem link. Concierge. Barber. Exercise rm; instructor, bicycles, treadmill, sauna. Massage. Squash. Bathrm phones; some refrigerators. Some balconies. Luxury level. Cr cds: A, C, D, DS, JCB, MC, V.

D SC

Restaurants

✔★ **ALOHA GARDEN.** *2219 SW 74th St (73159), in Walnut Square Shopping Center, I-240 exit Pennsylvania Ave S, south of downtown. 405/686-0288.* Hrs: 11 am-9:30 pm; Fri, Sat to 10:30 pm; Sun brunch to 2:30 pm. Closed major hols. Res accepted. Chinese, Amer menu. Bar. Semi-a la carte: lunch $3.95-$5.50, dinner $4.25-$13.95. Sun brunch $6.25. Buffet: lunch $5.25, dinner (Fri, Sat) $7.75. Child's meals. Specializes in seafood combinations, willow beef. Own sauces. Oriental decor. Cr cds: A, C, D, DS, MC, V.

D

★ ★ **APPLEWOODS.** *4301 SW 3rd St (73108), west of downtown. 405/947-8484.* Hrs: 11 am-2 pm, 5-10 pm; Fri to 11 pm; Sat 4-11 pm; Sun 11 am-3 pm, 4:30-10 pm. Closed major hols. Bar. Semi-a la carte: lunch $3.95-$7.95, dinner $9.95-$17. Buffet: lunch (Sun) $6.95. Child's meals. Specializes in pot roast, pork chops, hot apple dumplings. Cr cds: A, DS, MC, V.

D

★ ★ ★ **BELLINI'S.** *63rd & Pennsylvania (73118), in underground parking garage, north of downtown. 405/848-1065.* Hrs: 11 am-10:30 pm; Fri, Sat to 11:30 pm; Sun to 9 pm; Sun brunch to 2:30 pm. Closed major hols. Italian, Amer menu. Bar. Semi-a la carte: lunch $4.80-$12.95, dinner $7.95-$19.95. Sun brunch $4.95-$8.95. Specializes in Angus beef, pasta, pizza. Patio dining, view of park and fountain. Open brick pizza oven. Cr cds: A, C, D, DS, MC, V.

D

✓★ ★ **BRICKTOWN BREWERY.** *1 N Oklahoma Ave (73104), in Bricktown. 405/232-2739.* Web www.bricktownbrewery.com. Hrs: 11 am-midnight; Sun, Mon to 10 pm; Fri, Sat to 2 am. Closed Thanksgiving, Dec 24, 25. Res accepted. Bar. Semi-a la carte: lunch, dinner $4.95-$12.95. Child's meals. Specializes in hearty American cuisine, handcrafted beers. Entertainment Fri, Sat. Renovated building in warehouse district. Cr cds: A, C, D, DS, MC, V.

D

★ ★ **CATTLEMAN'S STEAKHOUSE.** *1309 S Agnew St (73108), south of downtown. 405/236-0416.* Hrs: 6 am-10 pm; Fri, Sat to midnight. Closed Thanksgiving, Dec 25. Serv bar. Semi-a la carte: bkfst $1.40-$6, lunch $2.25-$17.95, dinner $5.95-$17.95. Sat, Sun bkfst buffet $4.95. Specializes in steak, lamb. In historic Stockyards City district, opened in 1910. Cr cds: A, DS, MC, V.

D

★ ★ ★ **COACH HOUSE.** *6437 Avondale Dr (73116), north of downtown. 405/842-1000.* Hrs: 11:30 am-2 pm, 6-10 pm; Sat from 6 pm. Closed Sun; major hols. Res accepted. French, Amer menu. Serv bar. A la carte entrees: lunch $9-$14, dinner $19-$34. Specialties: rack of lamb, Dover sole, Grand Marnier souffle. Formal dining. Cr cds: A, C, D, DS, MC, V.

D

★ **THE COUNTY LINE.** *1226 NE 63rd St (73111), north of downtown. 405/478-4955.* Hrs: 11 am-9 pm; Fri, Sat to 10 pm. Closed some major hols. Bar. Semi-a la carte: lunch $4.95-$10.95, dinner $6.95-$16.95. Child's meals. Specializes in barbecue, prime rib. Nostalgic decor and atmosphere. Cr cds: A, C, D, DS, MC, V.

D

★ **DON SERAPIO'S.** *11109 N May (73120), north of downtown. 405/755-1664.* E-mail jamesm3033@aol.com. Hrs: 11 am-10 pm; Fri, Sat to 11 pm; Sun to 9 pm. Closed Mon; major hols. Res accepted. Mexican menu. Bar. Semi-a la carte: lunch $5.79; dinner $5.45-$15.95. Child's meals. Specialties: fajitas, chile relleno, chile burrito. Own tamales. Mexican cantina-style dining. Cr cds: A, C, D, DS, MC, V.

D SC

★ ★ **EDDY'S OF OKLAHOMA CITY.** *4227 N Meridian Ave (73112), north of downtown. 405/787-2944.* Hrs: 5-10:30 pm; Fri, Sat to 11 pm. Closed Sun; Thanksgiving, Dec 25. Semi-a la carte: dinner $9.95-$18.95. Child's meals. Specializes in Lebanese hors d'oeuvres, steak, seafood. Own pastries. Display of crystal, collectables. Family-owned. Cr cds: A, C, D, DS, MC, V.

D

★ **JAMIL'S.** *4910 N Lincoln (73105), north of downtown. 405/525-8352.* Hrs: 11 am-2 pm, 5-10 pm; Fri to 11 pm; Sat 5-11 pm; Sun from 5 pm. Closed most major hols. Res accepted. Bar. Complete meals: lunch $3.95-$7.95, dinner $9.95-$22.95. Child's meals. Specializes in steak. Antiques from frontier period; Tiffany-style lamps, etched-glass doors. Family-owned. Cr cds: A, DS, MC, V.

D SC

★ ★ ★ **JW'S STEAKHOUSE.** *(See Marriott Hotel) 405/842-6633, ext. 7509.* Hrs: 6-10 pm; Fri, Sat to 11 pm. Closed Sun; Jan 1, Thanksgiving, Dec 25. Res accepted. Bar 3 pm-1:30 am; Sun to midnight. A la carte entrees: dinner $13.95-$27.95. Child's meals. Specializes in seafood, steaks. Valet parking. Cr cds: A, C, D, DS, ER, JCB, MC, V.

D

✓★ ★ **KONA RANCH STEAKHOUSE.** *2037 S Meridian (73108), west of downtown. 405/681-1000.* Hrs: 11 am-10 pm; Fri, Sat to 11 pm. Closed Thanksgiving, Dec. 25. Hawaiian menu. Bar. Semi-a la carte: lunch $5.75-$9.95, dinner $7.65-$17. Child's meals. Specialties: coconut shrimp, smoked prime rib. Unique Hawaiian/cowboy decor. Cr cds: A, C, D, DS, MC, V.

D

★ **LA BAGUETTE BISTRO.** *7408 N May Ave (73116), north of downtown. 405/840-3047.* Hrs: 8 am-10 pm; Mon to 5 pm; Sun 9:30 am-2:30 pm (brunch). Closed some major hols. Res accepted. French menu. Bar. Semi-a la carte: bkfst $2.75-$6.95, lunch $3.50-$10.50, dinner $6.95-$20.95. Sun brunch $4.95-$8.95. Specializes in French cuisine. Bistro atmosphere. Cr cds: A, C, D, DS, MC, V.

D SC

★ **LOGAN'S ROADHOUSE.** *1100 S Meridian (73108), 3 mi S on I-46, exit Meridian, west of downtown. 405/942-1360.* Hrs: 11 am-10 pm; Fri, Sat to 11 pm; Sun from 10:30 am; early-bird dinner 3-5 pm. Closed Thanksgiving, Dec 25. Bar. Semi-a la carte: lunch, dinner $3.95-$16.95. Child's meals. Specializes in steak, fried green tomatoes, roadhouse tea. Own baking. Outdoor dining. Neon lights, murals. Cr cds: A, C, D, DS, MC, V.

D

★ ★ ★ **NIKZ AT THE TOP.** *5900 Mosteller Dr (73112), 20th floor of United Founders Tower, north of downtown. 405/843-7875.* Hrs: 11 am-11 pm; Thurs to midnight; Fri to 2 am; Sat 6 pm-2 am. Closed Sun; Jan 1, Dec 25. Res accepted. Bar. Wine list. Semi-a la carte: lunch $5.95-$8.95, dinner $12.95-$24.95. Specializes in steak, seafood, pasta. Own baking. Musicians Thurs-Sat. Rotating dining area. Cr cds: A, DS, MC, V.

D ♥

✓★ ★ **SHORTY SMALL'S.** *4500 W Reno (73132), west of downtown. 405/947-0779.* E-mail shortys1@theshop.net. Hrs: 11 am-10 pm; Fri, Sat to 11 pm. Closed Thanksgiving, Dec 25. Bar. Semi-a la carte: lunch, dinner $2.99-$15.99. Child's meals. Specializes in St Louis-style ribs, barbecued brisket, steak. Rustic decor. Cr cds: A, C, D, DS, MC, V.

D

★ ★ **SLEEPY HOLLOW.** *1101 NE 50th St (73111), north of downtown. 405/424-1614.* E-mail 6920@aol.com. Hrs: 11 am-10 pm; Sat from 5 pm. Closed most major hols. Res accepted. Bar. Semi-a la carte: lunch $4-$9. Complete meals: dinner $10.95-$19.95. Specializes in pan-fried chicken, steak. Own biscuits. Valet parking. Country decor. Cr cds: A, DS, MC, V.

D

✓★ ★ **TEXANNA RED'S.** *4600 W Reno (73127), west of downtown. 405/947-8665.* Hrs: 11 am-10 pm; Fri, Sat to 11 pm. Closed major hols. Mexican menu. Bar. Semi-a la carte: lunch, dinner $4.95-$17.95. Child's meals. Specializes in fajitas, mesquite-broiled dishes. Southwestern decor. Cr cds: A, C, D, DS, MC, V.

D

★ ★ **THE TOWER** *1601 Northwest Expy (OK 3) (73118), in the Tower, north of downtown. 405/842-5464.* Hrs: 11 am-2 pm, 5:30-11 pm. Closed Sun; most major hols. Res accepted. Bar to 1 am. Semi-a la carte:

lunch $6-$9.95, dinner $7.95-$23.95. Specializes in steak, seafood, veal. Own baking. Pianist evenings. Skylight, Italian chandelier. Cr cds: A, C, D, MC, V.

★ ★ ★ **THE WATERFORD.** *(See The Waterford Marriott Hotel) 405/848-4782.* Hrs: 6-10:30 pm; Fri, Sat to 11 pm. Closed Sun. Res accepted. Continental menu. Bar. Wine list. A la carte entrees: dinner $6.75-$25.95. Specializes in black Angus beef. Own baking, sauces. Valet parking. English country decor. Cr cds: A, C, D, DS, JCB, MC, V.

Unrated Dining Spot

CLASSEN GRILL. *5124 N Classen Blvd, north of downtown. 405/842-0428.* Hrs: 7 am-10 pm; Sat from 8 am; Sun 8 am-2 pm. Closed Mon; some major hols. Bar from 10 am. Semi-a la carte: bkfst $2.50-$5.95, lunch $4-$6, dinner $5-$9. Child's meals. Specializes in chicken-fried steak, fresh seafood. Local artwork. Cr cds: C, D, DS, MC, V.

Orlando/Walt Disney World

Founded: 1837
Pop: 169,675
Elev: 106 feet
Time zone: Eastern
Area code: 407
Web: www.goflorida.com/orlando

Orlando has always enjoyed the advantage of being a city with unusually lush gardens and beautiful scenic areas for walking and biking. Today, as the host to Walt Disney World, it is also a growing metropolitan area with the greater Orlando population reaching more than one million.

It has been said that one of the best things about Orlando is its location: it is within a short day's drive of many of Florida's major attractions and less than 400 miles from either of the two most remote Florida cities—Pensacola and Key West. Orlando is an ideal headquarters for the business traveler or vacationer interested in covering much of the state.

Orlando lies in the heart of the citrus and lake country of central Florida, just north of the cattle-growing region. It is only about 100 miles from the Gulf coast and half that distance from the Atlantic.

Business

As recently as the early 1970s, Orlando was a sleepy little community that depended largely on the citrus industry. Today it is a major transportation hub, as well as a center for high technology industries, film/TV production, manufacturing, warehousing, insurance and support services for tourism. Orlando is also an important service center for the Kennedy Space Center.

More than 850 manufacturers in the area employ in excess of 43,000 workers. The principal industries are the manufacturing of electronic supplies and laser systems, the processing of food and food products and printing and publishing. Orlando is a shipping center for citrus and vegetable crops. Agricultural products include oranges, grapefruit, cabbage, celery, beans, sweet corn, lettuce, spinach, escarole, endive, radishes, beef, dairy products, poultry and ornamental plants.

The opening of Walt Disney World gave an enormous boost to the neighboring economies. Motels, hotels and shopping centers were constructed with unprecedented speed as everyone rushed to accommodate the expected influx of tourists. Overnight, Walt Disney World became one of the most popular tourist attractions in the world and a favorite honeymoon destination.

Convention Facilities

There are more than 84,000 rooms at 363 hotels and motels in the greater Orlando area, with 30 major hotels providing meeting rooms and exhibit space for conventions. There are more than 150 meeting rooms in all, with capacities ranging from 25 to 2,500 people. Exhibit areas range from approximately 300 to more than 733,000 square feet.

The Orange County Convention Center provides 733,000 square feet of exhibit space with seven connecting halls ranging from 45,000 to 108,000 square feet, 138 meeting and breakout rooms and a 2,650-seat auditorium.

Expo Center in downtown Orlando offers 71,000 square feet of convention/exhibition space and seven connecting halls seating up to 2,500.

The Tupperware Convention Center is also available for conferences, meetings, musicals, theatricals, exhibits and seminars. The facility includes a 2,000-seat theater/auditorium, a 2,000-seat dining area and a 23,600-square-foot conference/exhibit hall.

Walt Disney World

Every company produces its own product; the Walt Disney Company manufactures fantasy. From the Magic Kingdom to the *Empress Lilly* riverboat restaurants, everything is run with a touch of make-believe. It takes approximately 35,000 people to keep the "Vacation Kingdom" moving, and every facet of operation is devoted to keeping visitors happy and content. Since its opening in 1971, millions of people have passed through the gates of Walt Disney World, making it one of the most visited tourist attractions in history.

The Magic Kingdom, the first of the theme parks constructed, offers attractions as well as shows, shops, exhibits, refreshment areas and special experiences divided into seven "lands": Adventureland, Frontierland, Liberty Square, Fantasyland, Tomorrowland, Mickey's Starland and Main Street, U.S.A.

While the Magic Kingdom is the heart of Walt Disney World, it takes up only a fraction of the thousands of acres that make up the total vacation complex. Linked to the Kingdom by monorail is Epcot (Experimental Prototype Community of Tomorrow). This park, situated on 260 acres of land, is a sprawling two-part entertainment and educational complex. Future World, sponsored by several American corporations, is a futuristic look at technology and its possible directions. World Showcase is an architectural and cultural appreciation of 11 nations, including the United Kingdom, France, Norway, Canada, Mexico, Italy, Germany, Japan, China, Morocco and the United States. Disney-MGM Studios, southwest of Epcot, houses production and administration facilities of the Walt Disney Company, as well as movie and television-related attractions. A tour of the area includes an animation studio, backlots, TV theaters and sound effects theaters.

In addition to the three major theme parks, the Walt Disney World complex includes several other interesting and imaginative areas. Typhoon Lagoon, a 56-acre water park between Epcot and Disney Village Marketplace, features the world's largest wave pool, nine waterslides, saltwater snorkeling, inner-tube rides, restaurants and picnic sites.

Fort Wilderness Campground has 785 campsites and 407 "wilderness homes" with complete utilities, shopping and recreation facilities, a restaurant featuring Western menus and entertainment and a ranch with trail rides. Within Fort Wilderness are River Country, a water recreation complex with waterfalls, slides and rapids reminiscent of the old swimming hole, and Discovery Island, housing exotic birds and animals, a flower garden and nature trails.

Walt Disney World Village in Lake Buena Vista, five miles east of the Magic Kingdom, is a vacation community of town houses, a European-style shopping center, conference center, major hotels and tennis and boating facilities. Also here is Pleasure Island, a nighttime entertainment center, featuring a ten-screen theater complex, night clubs, restaurant and snack facilities and the *Empress Lilly,* an authentically reconstructed riverboat that boasts three dining salons. The *Empress Lilly* is permanently anchored at Walt Disney World Village. Other types of recreation available in Walt Disney World include horseback riding, fishing, swimming, sailing, motorboating, waterskiing, tennis, steamboat excursions, picnicking and nature hikes. Five championship golf courses are here as well as miles of beaches.

The Disney-owned hotels are a form of entertainment unto themselves, with imaginatively decorated interiors, bars and restaurants and swimming pool fantasies. They include the All-Star Music Resort, All-Star Sports Resort, Disney's Yacht Club and Beach Club resorts, Disney's Boardwalk Resort, Disney's Caribbean Beach Resort, Disney's Contemporary Resort, Disney's Grand Floridian Beach Resort, Disney Institute, Disney's Polynesian Resort, Disney's Port Orleans and Dixie Landings resorts, Disney Vacation Club and Disney's Wilderness Lodge. Other hotels on Disney property but run by private companies include the Walt Disney World Dolphin and Walt Disney World Swan.

A conservation/wilderness area of 7,500 acres is at the southern end of the park. The area retains virgin stands of pine, cypress and bay trees and maintains a buffer zone for ecological protection.

Walt Disney World is open every day of the year, with extended hours during the summer and holiday periods. Various ticket combinations are available. For further information phone 824-4321; for hotel reservations phone W-DISNEY.

Sports & Recreation

Orlando itself has much to offer the visitor. The Orlando Magic play professional basketball at the 17,500-seat Orlando Arena. There are also football games and concerts at the Florida Citrus Bowl, dog racing at the Sanford-Orlando Kennel Club and Seminole Greyhound Park, and jai alai at nearby Orlando-Seminole Jai Alai Fronton.

Entertainment

The Florida Symphony Orchestra performs in Bob Carr Performing Arts Centre from September to May with a series of classical, pops, chamber and outdoor concerts.

Food and entertainment also can be found at Church Street Station in downtown Orlando and at the dinner theaters southeast of town in the Kissimmee/St Cloud area.

Sightseeing

The John F. Kennedy Space Center is located 47 miles east of Orlando. It was from here that Apollo astronauts left earth for man's first voyages to the moon. Today, Kennedy Space Center Visitor Center is the launch and landing site of the Space Shuttle, the world's first reusable, manned space vehicle.

Millions of tourists visit the Space Center each year, coming from across the country and around the world. The visitors center and two-hour bus tours focus on the Apollo, Skylab and Space Shuttle programs based here. Tours of Cape Canaveral Air Force Station, which is near the Space Center, include the launch sites of the Mercury and Gemini missions and the Air Force Space Museum.

Universal Studios Florida, southwest of Orlando, is one of central Florida's major attractions. Universal's 444-acre lot accommodates more than 40 rides, shows and attractions, 35 full-scale movie sets and six working sound stages.

Other attractions less than 100 miles from Orlando include Sea World of Florida, Busch Gardens Tampa, Adventure Island, Cypress Gardens, Silver Springs-Source of the Silver River, Gatorland, Mystery Fun House, Xanadu and Wet 'n Wild.

General References Orlando

Area code: 407

Phone Numbers

POLICE, FIRE & PARAMEDICS: 911

POISON CONTROL CENTER: 813/253-4444

Information Sources

Orlando/Orange County Convention & Visitors Bureau, 6700 Forum Dr, Suite 100, 32821; 363-5800.

Orlando Official Visitor Center, 8723 International Dr, Ste 101, 32819; 363-5872.

Parks & Special Facilities, 246-2283.

Transportation

AIRLINES: Air South; American; Bahamasair; British Airways; Continental; Delta; KLM (Netherlands); Northwest; Sobelair; Southwest; Trans Brasil; TWA; United; USAir; ValuJet; Virgin Atlantic; and other commuter and regional airlines.

AIRPORT: Orlando International Airport, 825-2001.

CAR RENTAL AGENCIES: (See IMPORTANT TOLL-FREE NUMBERS) Avis 825-3700; Budget 850-6749; Hertz 859-8400; Thrifty 380-1002.

PUBLIC TRANSPORTATION: Orlando Transit Authority 841-8240.

RAILROAD PASSENGER SERVICE: Amtrak 800/872-7245.

Newspaper

Orlando Sentinel.

Convention Facilities

Orange County Convention Center, 9800 International Dr, 345-9800.

Orlando Expo Center, 500 W Livingston St, 849-2562.

Tupperware Convention Center, 5 mi S of FL Tpke, 847-1809.

Sports & Recreation

Major Sports Facilities

Florida Citrus Bowl, 1610 W Church St, 423-2476.

Orlando Arena, 600 W Amelia St, 896-2442 or 849-2020 (Orlando Magic, basketball, 649-3200).

Racetracks

Sanford-Orlando Kennel Club, Longwood, 831-1600 (greyhound racing).

Seminole Greyhound Park, 2000 Seminole Blvd, Casselberry, 699-4510 (greyhound racing).

Jai Alai

Orlando-Seminole Jai Alai, 6405 N US 17/92, Fern Park, 339-6221.

Cultural Facilities

Theaters & Concert Halls

Civic Theatre of Central Florida, 1001 E Princeton St, 896-7365.

Mark Two Dinner Theater, 3376 Edgewater Dr, 843-6275.

Tupperware Convention Center, S on US 441, 847-1802.

Museums & Art Museums

Charles Hosmer Morse Museum of American Art, 445 Park Ave N, Winter Park, 645-5311.

Orange County Historical Museum, 812 E Rollins St, Loch Haven Park, 897-6350.

Orlando Museum of Art, 2416 N Mills Ave, Loch Haven Park, 896-4231.

Orlando Science Center, 777 E Princeton St, Loch Haven Park, 514-2000.

Points of Interest

Bok Tower Gardens, off US 27A, 1151 Tower Blvd, Lake Wales, 941/676-1408.

Busch Gardens Tampa, 3000 E Busch Blvd, Tampa, 813/987-5082.

Church Street Station, 129 W Church St, 422-2434.

Cypress Gardens, FL 540 near Winter Haven, 2641 S Lake Summit Dr, 941/324-2111.

Flying Tigers Warbird Air Museum, 231 N Hoagland Blvd, Kissimmee, 933-1942.

Kennedy Space Center, 47 mi E, entrance at Visitor Center; N or S via US 1, I-95 to NASA Pkwy then E, 452-2121.

Harry P. Leu Gardens, 1920 N Forest Ave, 246-2620.

Marineland, on FL A1A, S of St Augustine, 904/471-1111.

Mystery Fun House, 5767 Major Blvd, off Kirkman Rd, 351-3355.

Sea World of Florida, 7007 Sea World Dr, 351-3600.

Silver Springs-Source of the Silver River, on FL 40 near Ocala, 352/236-2121.

Universal Studios Florida, 10 mi SW on I-4, exits 29 & 30B, at jct FL Tpke, 363-8000.

Walt Disney World, 22 mi SW of Orlando via I-4, at FL 535, 824-4321; W-DISNEY (res).

Wet 'n Wild, 6200 International Dr, 10 mi SW via I-4, at FL 435, 351-1800.

Sightseeing Tours

Gray Line bus tours, PO Box 1671, Orlando 32802, 422-0744.

Rivership *Grand Romance,* 15 mi NE on I-4, Sanford, 321-5091 or 800/423-7401.

St Johns River Cruises & Tours, 15 mi NE on US 17/92, 4255 Peninsula Pt, Sanford, 330-1612.

Annual Events

Florida Citrus Bowl. Jan 1.

Central Florida Fair, 295-3247. Late Feb-early Mar.

Walt Disney World Golf Classic, at the "Magic Linkdom." Late Oct.

City Neighborhoods

Many of the restaurants, unrated dining establishments and some lodgings listed under Orlando include neighborhoods as well as exact street addresses. Geographic descriptions of Downtown and the International Drive Area are given, followed by a table of restaurants arranged by neighborhood.

Downtown: South of Colonial Dr (FL 50), west of Magnolia Ave (FL 527), north of Holland East-West Expy and east of Parramore Ave. **North of Downtown:** North of FL 50. **South of Downtown:** South of FL 408. **East of Downtown:** East of Magnolia Ave. **West of Downtown:** West of Parramore Ave.

International Drive Area: On and around International Drive between the FL Turnpike on the north and I-4 (exit 27A) on the south.

Lodgings and Food Orlando

ORLANDO RESTAURANTS BY NEIGHBORHOOD AREAS

(For full description, see alphabetical listings under Restaurants)

DOWNTOWN
Cafe Europa. 55 W Church St
Crackers. 129 W Church St
Le Provence. 50 E Pine St
Lee's Lakeside. 431 E Central Blvd
Lili Marlene's Aviators Restaurant & Pub. 129 W Church St
Manuel's On The 28th. 390 Orange Ave
Vivaldi. 107 Pine St

NORTH OF DOWNTOWN
Del Frisco's. 729 Lee Rd
Straub's Boatyard. 743 Lee Rd

SOUTH OF DOWNTOWN
Charley's Steak House. 6107 S Orange Blossom Trail
Chatham's Place. 7575 Dr Phillips Blvd
Hard Rock Cafe. 5800 Kirkman Rd
Le Coq Au Vin. 4800 S Orange Ave
Ming Court. 9188 International Dr
Sizzling Wok. 1453 Sand Lake Rd

EAST OF DOWNTOWN
4th Fighter Group Restaurant. 494 Rickenbacker Dr
Bacco. 10065 University Blvd
La Normandie. 2021 E Colonial Dr (FL 50)

INTERNATIONAL DRIVE AREA
Bergamo's. 8445 International Dr
Charlie's Lobster House. 8445 International Dr
Dux (Peabody Orlando Hotel). 9801 International Dr
Hanamizuki. 8255 International Dr
King Henry's Feast. 8984 International Dr
La Grille. 8445 International Dr
Passage To India. 5532 International Dr
Siam Orchid. 7575 Republic Dr

Note: When a listing is located in a town that does not have its own city heading, it will appear under the city nearest to its location. In these cases, the address and town appear in parenthesis immediately following the name of the establishment.

Motels

✓★ ★ **COMFORT INN-SOUTH.** *8421 S Orange Blossom Trail (32809), at Florida Mall, south of downtown. 407/855-6060; FAX 407/859-5132.* 204 rms, 2 story. S, D $49-$99; each addl $6; suites $59-$145; under 18 free. TV; cable. Heated pool; poolside serv. Playground. Bkfst buffet 7-11 am. Ck-out 11 am. Coin Indry. Meeting rms. Business servs avail. Sundries. Gift shop. Free transportation to area attractions. Game rm. Microwaves avail. Florida Mall adj. Cr cds: A, C, D, DS, ER, JCB, MC, V.

D SC

★ ★ **COMFORT SUITES.** *9350 Turkey Lake Rd (32819), off I-4 exit 29, south of downtown. 407/351-5050; FAX 407/363-7953.* E-mail info@comfortsuites.com; web www.comfortsuitesorlando.com. 215 rms, 3 story. Dec-mid-Apr, mid-June-Aug: S, D $99-$119; lower rates rest of yr. Crib free. TV; cable. Heated pool; wading pool, whirlpool, poolside serv. Playground. Complimentary continental bkfst. Bar. Ck-out 11 am. Coin Indry. Business servs avail. Sundries. Airport transportation. Refrigerators. Cr cds: A, C, D, DS, ER, JCB, MC, V.

D SC

★ ★ **COUNTRY HEARTH INN.** *9861 International Dr (32819), in International Drive Area. 407/352-0008; FAX 407/352-5449; res: 800/447-1890.* 150 rms, 2 story. Late Dec-early Jan, Feb-Apr; Aug-Nov: S, D $79-$109; each addl $10; under 18 free; lower rates rest of yr. Crib free. TV; cable. Heated pool. Restaurant 6:30-10:30 am, 6-10 pm. Rm serv. Bar. Ck-out noon. Coin Indry. Meeting rms. Business servs avail. Valet serv. Sundries. Refrigerators. Gazebo. Cr cds: A, C, D, DS, ER, MC, V.

D SC

★ ★ ★ **COURTYARD BY MARRIOTT.** *7155 Frontage Rd (32812), near Intl Airport, south of downtown. 407/240-7200; FAX 407/240-8962.* 149 rms, 3 story. S, D $89-$129; suites $109-$139; under 18 free; wkend rates. Crib free. TV; cable (premium). Heated pool; whirlpool, poolside serv. Complimentary coffee in rms. Restaurant 6-11 am. Ck-out noon. Coin Indry. Meeting rms. Business servs avail. In-rm modem link. Free airport transportation. Exercise equipt; weights, bicycles. Some refrigerators. Balconies. Cr cds: A, D, DS, MC, V.

D SC

★ **ECONO LODGE.** *5859 American Way (32819), in International Drive Area. 407/345-8880; FAX 407/363-9366.* 192 rms, 4 story. Mid-Feb-mid-Apr, June-early Sept, late Dec: S, D $59-88; each addl $6; under 18 free; lower rates rest of yr. Crib $6. Pet accepted, some restrictions. TV; cable. Heated pool. Complimentary coffee in lobby. Restaurant adj open 24 hrs. Ck-out 11 am. Coin Indry. Business servs avail. Gift shop. Free transportation to area attractions. Game rm. Cr cds: A, C, D, DS, ER, JCB, MC, V.

SC

★ **ECONO LODGE-CENTRAL.** *3300 W Colonial Dr (32808), west of downtown. 407/293-7221; FAX 407/293-1166.* 103 rms, 1-2 story. Feb-Apr, mid-June-mid-Aug: S $46; D $52; each addl $6; under 18 free; higher rates special events; lower rates rest of yr. Crib free. TV; cable (premium). Pool. Complimentary coffee in lobby. Restaurant adj open 24 hrs. Bar 11-2 am. Ck-out 11 am. Coin Indry. Meeting rm. Business servs avail. Lawn games. Picnic tables. Cr cds: A, C, D, DS, MC, V.

SC

★ **FAIRFIELD INN BY MARRIOTT.** *8342 Jamaican Ct (32819), I-4 exit 29 off International Dr. 407/363-1944; FAX 407/363-1944.* 134 rms, 3 story. Mid-Dec-Aug: S, D $59-$69; under 18 free; lower rates rest of yr. Crib free. TV; cable (premium). Pool. Complimentary continental bkfst. Ck-out noon. Cr cds: A, C, D, DS, MC, V.

D SC

★ ★ **GATEWAY INN.** *7050 Kirkman Rd (32819), east of I-4, in International Drive Area. 407/351-2000; FAX 407/363-1835; res: 800/327-3808.* 354 rms, 2 story. Feb-mid-Apr, early June-early Sept, mid-Dec-early Jan: S, D $74-94; each addl $6; under 18 free; lower rates rest of yr. Crib $3. Pet accepted, some restrictions. TV; cable. 2 pools, heated; wading pool, poolside serv. Playground. Restaurant 7 am-10 pm. Bar 11:30-2 am; entertainment. Ck-out 11 am. Coin Indry. Meeting rm. Business servs avail. Bellhops. Sundries. Gift shop. Free transportation to area attractions. Miniature golf. Game rm. Lawn games. Picnic tables. Cr cds: A, C, D, ER, MC, V.

SC

★ ★ **HAMPTON INN.** *7110 S Kirkman (32819), in International Drive Area. 407/345-1112; FAX 407/352-6591.* 170 rms, 8 story. Feb-late Apr, early June-early Sept & late Dec-early Jan: S $69-$89; D $79-$94; suites $119; under 17 free; lower rates rest of yr. Crib free. TV; cable (premium), VCR avail. Heated pool; wading pool. Complimentary continental bkfst. Restaurant adj open 24 hrs. Ck-out 11 am. Coin Indry. Meeting rms. Business servs avail. In-rm modem link. Gift shop. Exercise equipt; weight machine, stair machine. Game rm. Microwaves avail. Cr cds: A, C, D, DS, MC, V.

D SC

★ ★ **HAWTHORN SUITES.** *6435 Westwood Blvd (32821), in International Drive Area. 407/351-6600; FAX 407/351-1977.* 150 suites, 5 story. 1-2 bedrm: suites $89-$189; under 18 free; Crib free. TV; cable (premium), VCR (movies $5). Heated pool; wading pool, whirlpool, poolside serv. Playground. Complimentary coffee in rms. Restaurant adj 7 am-11 pm. Ck-out 11 am. Coin Indry. Meeting rms. Business servs avail. In-rm modem link. Bellhops. Concierge. Sundries. Exercise equipt; weight machine, stair machine. Game rm. Refrigerators, microwaves, wet bars. Cr cds: A, C, D, DS, ER, JCB, MC, V.

D SC

★ ★ **HOLIDAY INN-MALL AT CENTRAL PARK.** *7900 S Orange Blossom Trail (32809), south of downtown. 407/859-7900; FAX 407/859-7442.* 266 rms, 2 story. S, D $65-$95; each addl $7; under 18 free. Crib free. TV; cable (premium). Pool; wading pool. Restaurant 6:30 am-2 pm, 5:30-10 pm. Rm serv. Bar 5 pm-midnight. Ck-out 11 am. Coin Indry. Meeting rms. Business servs avail. Bellhops. Exercise equipt; weight machine, bicycles. Cr cds: A, C, D, DS, JCB, MC, V.

D SC

✔★ **INNS OF AMERICA.** *8222 Jamaican Ct (32819), I-4 exit 29 off International Dr. 407/345-1172; FAX 407/352-2801.* 121 rms, 4 story. Mid-Jan-mid-Apr: S, D $49.90-$85; lower rates rest of yr. TV; cable (premium). Heated pool. Complimentary continental bkfst. Ck-out 11 am. Coin Indry. Business servs avail. Cr cds: A, MC, V.

D SC

★ **LA SUITE.** *5858 International Dr (32819), International Drive area. 407/351-4410; FAX 407/351-2481.* Web www.lasuite.com. 270 rms, 2-4 story. Mid-June-Sept, Mid-Dec-Apr: S, D $39-$109; higher rates some hols; lower rates rest of yr. Crib free. TV; cable (premium). Heated pool; poolside serv. Complimentary continental bkfst. Restaurant adj open 24 hrs. Bar. Ck-out 11 am. Coin Indry. Meeting rms. Business servs avail. Free airport transportation. Game rm. Some refrigerators, microwaves. Picnic tables. Cr cds: A, C, D, DS, MC, V.

D SC

✔★ **RAMADA LIMITED.** *8296 S Orange Blossom Trail (32809), 10 mi S on FL 441, near Florida Mall, south of downtown. 407/240-0570; FAX 407/856-5507.* 75 rms, 2 story. Mid-Dec-mid-Apr: S $55-$85; D $59-$89; each addl $6; under 9 free; higher rates special events; lower rates rest of yr. Crib $10. TV; cable (premium). Pool. Complimentary continental bkfst. Restaurant nearby. Ck-out noon. Coin Indry. Bellhops. Airport, RR station, bus depot, Walt Disney World transportation. Cr cds: A, C, D, DS, ER, JCB, MC, V.

D SC

★ ★ **RAMADA SUITES AT SEAWORLD.** *6800 Villa DeCosta Dr (32821). 407/239-0707; FAX 407/239-8243.* Web www.ramada.com/ramada.html. 160 kit. suites, 2-3 story. S, D $139-$209; each addl $10; under 18 free; higher rates special events. Crib free. TV; cable (premium). Pool. Playground. Supervised child's activities; ages 3-8. Complimentary continental bkfst. Ck-out noon. Coin Indry. Business center. Sundries. Valet serv. 18-hole golf privileges; greens fee $59-$89. Exercise equipt; weights, stair machine, whirlpool. Game rm. Microwaves. Balconies. Cr cds: A, C, D, DS, ER, JCB, MC, V.

D SC

★ ★ **RESIDENCE INN BY MARRIOT ORLANDO INTL DRIVE.** *7975 Canada Ave (32819), south of downtown. 407/345-0117; FAX 407/352-2689.* E-mail riorlando@bellsouth.net; web marriottresidence inn.com. 176 kit. suites (1-2 bedrm). S, D $104-$199; wkly, monthly rates. Crib free. Pet accepted; some restrictions. Heated pool; whirlpools. Complimentary continental bkfst. Restaurant nearby. Ck-out 11 am. Coin Indry. Meeting rms. Business servs avail. Valet serv. Many fireplaces; microwaves avail. Balconies. Grills. Lighted sports court. Cr cds: A, C, D, DS, JCB, MC, V.

D SC

✔★ **TRAVELODGE CENTROPLEX.** *409 N Magnolia Ave (32081), downtown. 407/423-1671; FAX 407/423-1523.* 75 rms, shower only, 2 story. Feb-Apr, June-Aug: S $55; D $65; under 18 free; higher rates special events; lower rates rest of yr. TV; cable (premium). Pool. Complimentary coffee in rms. Restaurant adj. Ck-out noon. Business servs avail. In-rm modem link. Coin Indry. Cr cds: A, C, D, DS, ER, JCB, MC, V.

SC

✔★ ★ **WYNFIELD INN.** *6263 Westwood Blvd (32821), in International Drive Area. 407/345-8000; FAX 407/345-1508.* 299 rms, 3 story. Feb-late Apr, early June-late Aug: S, D $88-$98; each addl $5; under 18 free; lower rates rest of yr. Crib free. TV. 2 pools, 1 heated; 2 wading pools, poolside serv. Complimentary coffee. Restaurant adj 6:30 am-midnight. Ck-out 11 am. Coin Indry. Business servs avail. Gift shop. Game rm. Cr cds: A, C, D, DS, MC, V.

D SC

Motor Hotels

★ ★ **BEST WESTERN PLAZA INTERNATIONAL.** *8738 International Dr (32819), in International Drive Area. 407/345-8195; FAX 407/352-8196.* 673 rms, 4 story, 176 kits. Mid-Feb-mid-Apr, mid-June-Aug, mid-Dec-early Jan: S, D $95; each addl $10; suites $115; kit. units $105; under 19 free; lower rates rest of yr. Crib free. TV; cable. Heated pool; wading pool, whirlpool, poolside serv. Ck-out 11 am. Coin Indry. In-rm modem link. Bellhops. Gift shop. Free Walt Disney World transportation. Health club privileges. Game rm. Some in-rm whirlpools. Cr cds: A, C, D, DS, MC, V.

D SC

★ ★ **COLONY PLAZA.** *11100 W Colonial Dr (34761), on FL 50, west of downtown. 407/656-3333; FAX 407/656-2232; res: 800/821-0136.* E-mail colony@intelistar.net. 253 kits, 7 story. S, D $65-100; under 18 free; higher rates special events. Crib free. TV; cable (premium). Heated pool; poolside serv. Playground. Restaurant 7 am-3 pm, 5-9 pm. Ck-out 11 am. Coin Indry. Meeting rms. Gift shop. Tennis. Exercise equipt; bicycles, treadmill. Game rm. Cr cds: A, DS, MC, V.

D SC

★ ★ ★ **DELTA ORLANDO RESORT.** *5715 Major Blvd (32819), jct FL 435 & I-4 exit 30B at entrance of Universal Studios, south of downtown. 407/351-3340; FAX 407/351-5117; res: 800/634-4763.* E-mail deltaor@magicnet.net; web www.intpro.com/delta. 800 units, 4 story. Mid-Feb-Apr, mid-June-Aug, late Dec: S, D $118-$158; suites $175-$475; under 18 free; lower rates rest of yr. Crib free. Pet accepted, some restrictions; $25. TV; cable (premium). 3 pools, heated; wading pools, whirlpools, sauna, poolside serv. Playground. Free supervised child's activities; ages 4-12. Restaurants 6:30 am-midnight. Child's meals. Rm serv. Bar 11:30-2 am; entertainment. Ck-out 11 am. Coin Indry. Convention facilities. Business servs avail. Bellhops. Valet serv. Airport transportation. Free transportation to area attractions. Concierge. Sundries. Gift shop. Lighted tennis. Golf privileges. Miniature golf. Game rm. Lawn games. Microwaves avail. Private balconies. Cr cds: A, C, D, DS, ER, JCB, MC, V.

D SC

★ ★ **FLORIDIAN.** *7299 Republic Dr (32819), in International Drive Area. 407/351-5009; FAX 407/363-7807; res: 800/445-7299.* 304 rms, 8 story. Feb-Aug, late Dec: S, D $95-$150; lower rates rest of yr. Crib free. TV; cable, VCR avail (movies). Heated pool; poolside serv. Restaurant 7-11 am, 6-11 pm. Rm serv. Bar 5 pm-2 am. Ck-out 11 am. Coin Indry. Meeting rms. Business servs avail. Bellhops. Valet serv. Concierge. Sundries. Gift shop. Airport transportation. Game rm. Cr cds: A, C, D, DS, MC, V.

D SC

✔★ ★ **HAMPTON INN.** *6101 Sand Lake Rd (32819), in International Drive Area. 407/363-7886; FAX 407/345-0670.* 316 rms, 4 story, 12 suites. Late Dec-Apr, June-mid-Aug: S $59-$74; D $64-$79; each addl $5; suites $109-$149; under 18 free; min stay special events; higher rates Daytona 500, July 4, Dec 31; lower rates rest of yr. Crib free. TV; cable (premium), VCR avail. Complimentary continental bkfst. Restaurant nearby. Ck-out 11 am. Meeting rms. Business servs avail. Valet serv.

Concierge. Sundries. Gift shop. Coin lndry. Exercise equipt; bicycle, treadmill. Pool; wading pool. Game rm. Many refrigerators, microwaves. Totally nonsmoking. Cr cds: A, C, D, DS, ER, MC, V.

D SC

★ ★ **HAMPTON INN.** *5767 T.G. Lee Blvd (32822), near Intl Airport, south of downtown. 407/888-2995; FAX 407/888-2418.* 123 rms, 7 story. Jan-May, Oct-Dec: S $99; D $109; higher rates Race Week, Citrus Bowl; lower rates rest of yr. TV; cable (premium). Complimentary continental bkfst. Complimentary coffee in rms. Restaurant nearby. Ck-out 11 am. Meeting rms. Business servs avail. Gift shop. Coin lndry. Free airport transportation. Exercise equipt; bicycle, treadmill. Pool. Game rm. Cr cds: A, C, D, DS, MC, V.

D SC

✔★ ★ **HAMPTON INN AT UNIVERSAL.** *5621 Windhover Dr (32819), in International Drive Area. 407/351-6716; FAX 407/363-1711.* E-mail mcowh@juno.com. 120 rms, 5 story. Late May-mid-Aug & late Dec-late Mar: S $71; D $79; under 18 free; lower rates rest of yr. Crib free. TV; cable (premium). Heated pool. Complimentary continental bkfst. Restaurant opp 7 am-midnight. Ck-out noon. Meeting rms. Business servs avail. Game rm. Cr cds: A, C, D, DS, MC, V.

D SC

★ ★ **HARLEY COLONIAL PLAZA.** *2801 E Colonial Dr (32803), 2 mi E of I-4 on FL 50. 407/894-2741; FAX 407/896-9858; res: 800/321-2323.* 230 rms, 2 story. S, D $42; each addl $6; suites $75-$125; under 18 free. Crib free. TV; cable (premium); VCR avail. Heated pool; whirlpool. Restaurant 6 am-2:30 pm; wkend hrs vary. Ck-out 11 am. Coin lndry. Meeting rms. Business servs avail. Refrigerators. Cr cds: A, C, D, DS, ER, MC, V.

D

★ ★ **HOLIDAY INN.** *626 Lee Rd (32810), north of downtown. 407/645-5600; FAX 407/740-7912.* 201 rms, 5 story. Jan-mid-Apr: S, D $79-$109; under 18 free; lower rates rest of yr. Crib free. TV; cable (premium), VCR avail. Pool. Restaurant 6 am-2 pm; 5-10 pm. Rm serv. Bar 4 pm-midnight; entertainment Fri-Sat. Ck-out 11 am. Coin lndry. Meeting rms. Business servs avail. Bellhops. Golf privileges, greens fee $18-$30, driving range. Exercise equipt; weight machine, bicycle. Game rm. Microwaves avail. Cr cds: A, C, D, DS, JCB, MC, V.

D SC

★ ★ ★ **HOLIDAY INN-SELECT UNIVERSITY OF CENTRAL FLORIDA.** *12125 High Tech Ave (32817), off University Blvd, east of downtown. 407/275-9000; FAX 407/381-0019.* 250 units, 6 story. S, D $140; suites $175; under 18 free. Crib free. TV; cable (premium), VCR avail (free movies). Pool; whirlpool. Restaurant 6:30 am-2 pm, 5-10 pm. Rm serv. Bar 11 am-midnight. Ck-out 11 am. Meeting rms. Business servs avail. Bellhops. Airport transportation. Tennis privileges. Golf privileges. Exercise equipt; weights, bicycles, sauna. Lawn games. Some refrigerators. On lake. Luxury level. Cr cds: A, C, D, DS, JCB, MC, V.

D SC

★ **HOWARD JOHNSON.** *9956 Hawaiian Court (32819), in International Drive Area. 407/351-5100; FAX 407/352-7188.* 222 rms, 2 story, 49 kit. suites. S, D $65; suites $87; under 18 free. Crib free. TV; cable. Pool; whirlpool. Playground. Complimentary coffee in lobby. Restaurant nearby. Bar 5:30 pm-1 am. Ck-out noon. Meeting rms. Coin lndry. Valet serv. Game rm. Refrigerator in suites. Cr cds: A, C, D, DS, ER, MC, V.

D SC

★ ★ ★ **MARRIOTT.** *8001 International Dr (32819), off I-4 exit 29, in International Drive Area. 407/351-2420; FAX 407/345-5611.* 1,064 units in 16 bldgs, 2 story, 191 kits. S, D $125-$164; suites $210-$450; under 18 free. Crib free. TV; cable (premium). 3 pools, heated; 2 wading pools, whirlpool, poolside serv. Playground. Restaurant 6:30 am-2 pm; 4-11 pm. Rm serv. Bar 11-2 am; entertainment. Ck-out 11 am. Coin lndry. Convention facilities. Business center. Bellhops. Sundries. Gift shop. Lighted tennis. Golf privileges. Exercise equipt; weight machine, rowers. Game rm. Balconies. Cr cds: A, C, D, DS, ER, JCB, MC, V.

D SC

✔★ **QUALITY INN-PLAZA.** *9000 International Dr (32819), in International Drive Area. 407/345-8585; FAX 407/352-6839.* 1,020 rms, 4-10 story. S, D $34-$79. Crib free. Pet accepted, some restrictions; $5. TV; cable. 3 pools, heated. Restaurant 6:30-10:30 am, 5:30-9:30 pm. Bar 4 pm-2 am. Ck-out 11 am. Coin lndry. Business servs avail. Gift shop. Health club privileges. Game rm. Cr cds: A, C, D, DS, ER, JCB, MC, V.

D SC

★ ★ **RADISSON BARCELO.** *8444 International Dr (32819), in International Drive Area. 407/345-0505; FAX 407/352-5894.* E-mail radisson-orlando.com. 299 rms, 5 story. Mid-Dec-Apr: S, D $69-$99; each addl $10; lower rates rest of yr. Crib free. TV; cable (premium), VCR avail. Pool; poolside serv. Restaurant 6:30 am-10 pm. Bar. Ck-out noon. Meeting rms. Business servs avail. In-rm modem link. Gift shop. Lighted tennis. Health club privileges. Game rm. Microwaves avail. Shopping center opp. Cr cds: A, C, D, DS, ER, JCB, MC, V.

D SC

✔★ **RODEWAY INN INTERNATIONAL.** *6327 International Drive (32819), in International Drive Area. 407/351-4444; FAX 407/352-5806.* 315 rms, 4-9 story. Mid Dec-Jan 1, June-Sept: S, D $59.95; lower rates rest of yr. Crib free. Pet accepted, some restrictions. TV; cable, VCR (movies). Heated pool. Restaurant 6:30-10:30 am, 5:30-9 pm. Bar 6 pm-midnight. Ck-out 11 am. Coin lndry. Meeting rm. Valet serv. Sundries. Gift shop. Health club privileges. Game rm. Refrigerators avail. Cr cds: A, C, D, DS, ER, JCB, MC, V.

★ ★ ★ **SHERATON WORLD RESORT.** *10100 International Dr (32821), in International Drive Area. 407/352-1100; FAX 407/352-3679.* 800 units, 2-3 story. S, D $120-$160; each addl $15; suites $275-$575; under 18 free. Crib free. TV; cable (premium). 3 pools, heated; 2 wading pools, whirlpool, poolside serv. Playground. Restaurants 6:30 am-11 pm. Rm serv. Bar; entertainment. Ck-out 11 am. Coin lndry. Meeting rms. Business center. Bellhops. Sundries. Gift shop. Free Walt Disney World transportation. Lighted tennis. Golf privileges. Miniature golf. Exercise equipt; weights, bicycles. Game rm. Cr cds: A, C, D, DS, ER, JCB, MC, V.

D SC

★ ★ ★ **SUMMERFIELD SUITES.** *8480 International Dr (32819), in International Drive Area. 407/352-2400; FAX 407/352-4631; res: 800/833-4353.* E-mail sshorlres@mail.att.net; web www.travelbase.com/. 146 kit. suites, 5 story. Feb-Apr, June-Aug & late Dec: S, D $209-$269; lower rates rest of yr. Crib free. TV; cable (premium), VCR (movies $5). Heated pool; wading pool, whirlpool. Complimentary continental bkfst. Complimentary coffee in rms. Restaurant nearby. Bar 5-11 pm. Ck-out 11 am. Meeting rms. Business servs avail. In-rm modem link. Concierge. Gift shop. Grocery. Valet serv. Coin lndry. Exercise equipt; weight machine, stair machine. Game rm. Refrigerators; microwaves avail. Cr cds: A, C, D, DS, JCB, MC, V.

SC

★ ★ **SUMMERFIELD SUITES.** *8751 Suiteside Dr (32836). 407/238-0777.* 150 suites, 3 story. No elvtr. Mid-June-mid-August: suites $209-$269; higher rates special events; lower rates rest of yr. Crib free. TV; cable (premium), VCR (movies). Complimentary continental bkfst; coffee in rms. Restaurant nearby. Ck-out 11 am. Meeting rms. Bellhops. Valet serv. Concierge. Sundries. Gift shop. Coin lndry. Exercise equipt; bicycle, treadmill. Heated pool; wading pool, whirlpool. Game rm. Refrigerators. Cr cds: A, D, DS, JCB, MC, V.

D

Hotels

★ ★ ★ **ADAM'S MARK.** *1500 Sand Lake Rd (32809), at Florida Mall, south of downtown. 407/859-1500; FAX 407/855-1585.* 496 rms, 11 story. S, D $99-$169; each addl $10; under 18 free; hols (2-day min). Crib free. Valet parking $8. TV; cable (premium). Restaurant 6 am-11 pm. Bar 11 am-midnight. Ck-out noon. Convention facilities. Business center. Concierge. Gift shop. Exercise equipt; weight machine, bicycle. Pool; whirlpool. Bathrm phone, refrigerator in suites. Some balconies. Luxury level. Cr cds: A, C, D, DS, JCB, MC, V.

D

★ ★ ★ **CLARION PLAZA.** *9700 International Dr (32819), in International Drive Area. 407/352-9700; FAX 407/351-9111.* 810 rms, 14 story. S, D $135-$155; suites $225-$680; under 18 free. Crib free. Valet parking $5.50. TV; cable. Heated pool; whirlpool. Restaurant 6:30 am-10:30 pm. Bar 11-2 am; entertainment. Ck-out noon. Coin Indry. Convention facilities. Business center. Shopping arcade. Airport transportation. Golf privileges, pro, putting green, driving range. Game rm. Some refrigerators, bathrm phones. Cr cds: A, C, D, DS, ER, JCB, MC, V.

D SC

✔★ **DOUBLETREE UNIVERSAL TOWER.** *5905 International Dr (32819), at jct FL 435 & I-4, in International Drive Area. 407/351-2100; FAX 407/352-2991.* 302 units, 21 story. Feb-Aug, late Dec-early Jan: S, D $79-$199; under 18 free; lower rates rest of yr. Crib free. TV; cable (premium). Heated pool; wading pool, poolside serv. Restaurant 6:30-11:30 am, 5:30-10 pm. Bar 4:30 pm-2 am; entertainment. Ck-out noon. Coin Indry. Meeting rms. In-rm modem link. Concierge. Gift shop. Barber, beauty shop. Game rm. Rec rm. Refrigerators avail. Cylindrical building. Cr cds: A, C, D, DS, ER, JCB, MC, V.

D SC

★ ★ ★ **EMBASSY SUITES.** *8978 International Dr (32819), in International Drive Area. 407/352-1400; FAX 407/363-1120.* E-mail essouth@aol.com. 244 kit. suites, 8 story. Suites $129-$189; each addl $15; under 17 free. Crib free. TV; cable (premium). 2 pools, 1 indoor; whirlpool. Complimentary full bkfst. Restaurant 11 am-11 pm. Bar. Ck-out noon. Coin Indry. Meeting rms. Business servs avail. In-rm modem link. Gift shop. Valet parking. Free airport, Walt Disney World transportation. Exercise equipt; weight machines, bicycles, treadmills, sauna, steam rm. Game rm. Refrigerators; microwaves avail. Sun deck. Mediterranean-style atrium. Cr cds: A, C, D, DS, MC, V.

D SC

★ ★ ★ **EMBASSY SUITES INTERNATIONAL.** *8250 Jamaican Ct (32819), I-4 exit 29 off International Dr. 407/345-8250; FAX 407/352-1463.* 246 suites, 8 story. Suites $95-$195; under 18 free; package plans. Crib free. TV; cable (premium). Indoor/outdoor pool; whirlpool, poolside serv. Complimentary full bkfst. Bar 5-11 pm. Ck-out noon. Business servs avail. In-rm modem links. Gift shop. Tennis privileges. Golf privileges. Exercise equipt; weights, rower, sauna. Game rm. Refrigerators; microwaves avail. Cr cds: A, C, D, DS, JCB, MC, V.

D SC

★ ★ **THE ENCLAVE.** *6165 Carrier Dr (32819), south of downtown. 407/351-1155; FAX 407/351-2001; res: 800/457-0077.* Web www:www.prov.com. 321 kit. suites, 10 story. Mid-Dec-mid-Apr & mid-June-mid-Aug: studio & 2-bedrm suites $99-$160; golf, Walt Disney World packages; lower rates rest of yr. Crib $5. TV; cable (premium). 3 pools, 2 heated, 1 indoor; wading pool, whirlpool. Complimentary continental bkfst. Ck-out 11 am. Coin Indry. Meeting rm. Business servs avail. Lighted tennis. Exercise equipt; rowers, bicycles. Game rm. Microwaves avail. Private patios, balconies. On lake. Cr cds: A, C, D, DS, MC, V.

D SC

★ ★ **HARLEY.** *151 E Washington St (32801), downtown. 407/841-3220; FAX 407/849-1839.* 281 units, 6 story. S, D $99-$109; 2-bedrm suites $140; under 18 free. Crib free. TV; cable (premium). Heated pool; poolside serv. Restaurant 6:30 am-10:30 pm, Fri-Sat to 11 pm. Bar 3 pm-midnight; entertainment. Ck-out 11 am. Meeting rms. Business servs avail. Garage parking. Airport, Walt Disney World transportation. Exercise equipt; weights, bicycles. Refrigerators avail. Some balconies. Cr cds: A, C, D, DS, MC, V.

D SC

★ ★ **HOLIDAY INN-UNIVERSAL STUDIOS.** *5905 Kirkman Rd (32819), just W of jct FL 435 & I-4 exit 30B, south of downtown. 407/351-3333; FAX 407/351-3577.* 256 units, 10 story. Mid-Feb-mid-Apr, mid-June-mid-Aug, last 2 wks Dec: S, D $89-$139; each addl $10; under 18 free; lower rates rest of yr. Crib free. TV; cable (premium), VCR (movies). Pool; wading pool. Restaurant 7 am-midnight. Rm serv to 10 pm. Bar. Ck-out noon. Coin Indry. Meeting rms. Business servs avail. Gift shop. Health club privileges. Game rm. Private patios, balconies. Near main entrance to Universal Studios Florida. Cr cds: A, C, D, DS, ER, JCB, MC, V.

D SC

★ ★ ★ **HYATT REGENCY-ORLANDO INTL AIRPORT.** *9300 Airport Blvd (32827), atop main terminal of Intl Airport, south of downtown. 407/825-1234; FAX 407/856-1672.* 446 rms, 10 story. S, D $150-$225; suites $225-$500; under 18 free. Crib avail. Garage parking $8; valet parking $11. TV; cable (premium), VCR avail. Heated pool; whirlpool. Restaurant 6:30 am-11 pm. Rm serv 24 hrs. Bar. Ck-out noon. Convention facilities. Business center. In-rm modem link. Concierge. Shopping arcade. Golf privileges. Exercise equipt; weights, bicycles. Bathrm phones; microwaves avail. Balconies. 7-story atrium lobby; airport's main terminal is located 1 level below. Cr cds: A, C, D, DS, ER, JCB, MC, V.

D SC

★ ★ ★ **MARRIOTT-DOWNTOWN.** *400 W Livingston St (32801), at Orlando Centroplex Center, downtown. 407/843-6664; FAX 407/648-5414.* 290 rms, 15 story. S $79-$155; D $114-$155; each addl $15; suites $225-$775; under 18 free; wkend, special package plans. Crib free. Valet parking. TV; cable (premium), VCR avail. Pool; whirlpool, poolside serv. Restaurant 6:30 am-10 pm. Bar. Ck-out noon. Convention facilities. Business center. In-rm modem link. Gift shop. Airport transportation. Exercise equipt; weight machines, bicycles. Bathrm phones. Refrigerators avail. Landscaped garden terrace. Luxury level. Cr cds: A, C, D, DS, ER, MC, V.

D SC

★ ★ ★ **MARRIOTT-ORLANDO AIRPORT.** *7499 Augusta National Dr (32822), near Intl Airport, south of downtown. 407/851-9000; FAX 407/857-6211.* 484 units, 9 story. S, D $79-$209; suites $175-$500; under 18 free; wkend rates. Crib free. TV; cable (premium). Indoor/outdoor pool; wading pool, whirlpool, poolside serv. Restaurant 6 am-11 pm. Bar 11-2 am. Ck-out noon. Convention facilities. Business center. Gift shop. Free airport transportation. Lighted tennis. Exercise equipt; weights, bicycles, steam rm, sauna. Game rm. Rec rm. Luxury level. Cr cds: A, C, D, DS, ER, MC, V.

D SC

★ ★ ★ **OMNI ROSEN.** *9840 International Dr (32819), in International Drive Area. 407/204-7234; FAX 407/248-6869.* Web www.omnirosen.com. 1,334 rms, 24 story, 80 suites. S, D $180-$210; each addl $15; suites $395-$595; under 18 free. Crib free. Valet/garage parking $3. TV; cable, VCR avail (movies). Pool; wading pool, whirlpool, poolside serv. Restaurant 6:30 am-11 pm. Bar 11 am-2 am. Ck-out 11 am. Coin Indry. Convention facilities. Business center. Concierge. Gift shop. Beauty shop. Lighted tennis. Exercise rm; instructor, weights, bicycle. Refrigerator in suites. Cr cds: A, C, D, DS, JCB, MC, V.

D SC

★ ★ ★ ★ **PEABODY ORLANDO.** *9801 International Dr (32819), opp Convention & Civic Center, in International Drive Area. 407/352-4000; FAX 407/351-9177; res: 800/PEABODY.* E-mail peab-orl@interramp; web www.peabody-orlando.com. This is an impressive high-rise with sweeping views and extensive grounds. Famous are the resident ducks who parade to the lobby fountain each morning at 11, splash around in it all day and return to their duck palace with fanfare at 5 pm. 891 units, 27 story. S, D $270-$330; each addl $15; suites $475-$1,400; under 18 free; package plans. Crib free. Valet parking $7. TV; cable (premium). Heated pool; wading pool, whirlpool, poolside serv. Restaurant open 24 hrs (also see DUX). Bar 11-2 am; entertainment exc Sun. Ck-out noon. Convention facilities. Business center. In-rm modem link. Shopping arcade. Beauty shop. Lighted tennis, pro shop. 18-hole golf privileges, greens fee. Exercise rm; instructor, weight machines, bicycles, sauna, steam rm. Massage. Game rm. Refrigerators avail. Luxury level. Cr cds: A, C, D, DS, ER, JCB, MC, V.

D SC

★ ★ ★ **RADISSON PLAZA.** *60 S Ivanhoe Blvd (32804), I-4 exit 42, north of downtown. 407/425-4455; FAX 407/843-0262.* 340 rms, 15 story. S, D $158; each addl $15; under 17 free; wkend rates. TV; cable (premium). Heated pool; whirlpool, poolside serv. Restaurant 6:30 am-10 pm. Bar. Ck-out noon. Meeting rms. Business servs avail. Concierge. Gift shop. Lighted tennis. Exercise equipt; weights, bicycles, sauna. Minibars; some refrigerators. Luxury level. Cr cds: A, C, D, DS, ER, MC, V.

D SC

★ ★ ★ **RADISSON TWIN TOWERS.** *5780 Major Blvd (32819), in International Drive Area. 407/351-1000; FAX 407/363-0106.* 760 rms, 18-19 story. Mid-Feb-mid-Apr: S, D $99-$169; suites $250-$750; under 18 free; lower rates rest of yr. Crib free. TV; cable (premium). Heated pool; wading pool, whirlpool, poolside serv. Playground. Restaurant 6 am-10 pm. Rm serv 24 hrs. Bar 4:30 pm-2 am; entertainment Tues-Sat. Ck-out noon. Coin Indry. Convention facilities. Business center. In-rm modem link. Shopping arcade. Beauty shop. Airport transportation. Exercise equipt; weight machine, rowers, sauna. Game rm. Refrigerator, wet bar in suites. Located directly in front of Universal Studios entrance. Cr cds: A, C, D, DS, ER, JCB, MC, V.

D SC

★ ★ ★ **RENAISSANCE.** *5445 Forbes Place (32812), near Orlando Intl Airport, south of downtown. 407/240-1000; FAX 407/240-1005.* 300 rms, 9 story. S, D $150-$200; each addl $15; suites $350-$500; under 17 free. Crib free. TV; cable. Heated pool; whirlpool, poolside serv. Coffee in rms. Restaurant 6 am-11 pm. Bar. Ck-out 1 pm. Convention facilities. Business center. Concierge. Gift shop. Free airport transportation. 36-hole golf privileges. Exercise equipt; weight machines, bicycles, sauna, steam rm. Bathrm phones, minibars. Luxury level. Cr cds: A, C, D, DS, ER, JCB, MC, V.

D SC

★ ★ ★ **RENAISSANCE ORLANDO RESORT.** *6677 Sea Harbor Dr (32821), in International Drive Area. 407/351-5555; FAX 407/351-9991.* 780 rms, 10 story. Late Dec-mid-May: S, D $189-$299; each addl $10; suites $478-$717; under 18 free; lower rates rest of yr. Crib free. TV; cable (premium). Heated pool; wading pool, whirlpool, poolside serv. Supervised child's activities; ages 6 mo-12 yrs. Restaurant open 24 hrs. Bar; entertainment. Ck-out noon. Convention facilities. Business center. In-rm modem link. Shopping arcade. Barber, beauty shop. Airport, area attractions transportation. Lighted tennis. Golf privileges. Exercise rm; instructor, weights, bicycles, steam rm, sauna. Massage. Game rm. Bathrm phones, minibars. Balconies. Atrium lobby; extensive art collection. Luxury level. Cr cds: A, C, D, DS, ER, JCB, MC, V.

D SC

Inns

★ ★ ★ **COURTYARD AT LAKE LUCERNE.** *211 N Lucerne Circle E (32801), near Church St Station, downtown. 407/648-5188; FAX 407/246-1368; res: 800/444-5289.* Web www.travelbase.com/destinations/orlando. 24 units in 3 bldgs, 2 story. S, D $75-$165; kit. unit $105. Children over 12 yrs only. TV; cable. Complimentary continental bkfst. Restaurant nearby. Ck-out 11 am, ck-in 3 pm. Meeting rm. In-rm modem link. Airport, RR station, bus depot transportation. Consists of 3 houses—Victorian, antebellum and art deco—located in historic downtown neighborhood; Victorian Norment-Parry is city's oldest structure (1883). Each guest rm uniquely designed by different artist; large collection of English and American antiques and objets d'art. Gardens. Cr cds: A, MC, V.

SC

★ ★ ★ **MEADOW MARSH.** *(940 Tildenville School Rd, Winter Garden 34787) Approx 16 mi W on FL 50. 407/656-2064; res: 888/656-2064; FAX 407/654-0656.* 5 rms, 3 story, 2 suites. No rm phones. S, D $95-$125; each addl $25; suites $180-195; higher rates sports events. Children over 12 yrs only. Complimentary full bkfst. Ck-out 11 am, ck-in 3 pm. Business servs avail. Lawn games. Picnic tables. Built in 1877. Victorian farmhouse; antiques. Totally nonsmoking. Cr cds: DS, MC, V.

D

Restaurants

★ ★ **4TH FIGHTER GROUP RESTAURANT.** *494 Rickenbacker Dr, east of downtown. 407/898-4251.* Hrs: 11 am-2:30 pm, 4:30-10 pm; Fri, Sat to 11 pm; early-bird dinner to 6:30 pm; Sun brunch 9:30 am-2:30 pm. Res accepted. Bar. Semi-a la carte: lunch, dinner $14.95-$21.95. Sun brunch $15.95. Child's meals. Specializes in steak, fresh seafood. Parking. Modeled after WWII English farmhouse; many air-force, war artifacts. Dedicated to 4th fighter group vets. Overlooks Orlando Executive Airport. Table-side prep. Cr cds: A, C, D, DS, MC, V.

D

★ ★ ★ **BACCO.** *10065 University Blvd (32817), in Suncrest Village Shopping Center, east of downtown. 407/678-8833.* Hrs: 11:30 am-2 pm, 6-10 pm; Fri, Sat 5-10 pm. Closed Sun, Mon; Easter, Thanksgiving, Dec 25. Res accepted. Italian menu. Bar. A la carte entrees: lunch $12, dinner $10.50-$19.50. Specializes in chicken, beef, fish. Antique furnishings. Cr cds: A, MC, V.

D

★ ★ ★ **BERGAMO'S.** *8445 International Dr (32819), 8 mi S on I-4, exit 29 at Mercado Shopping Village, in International Drive Area. 407/352-3805.* Hrs: 5-10:30 pm. Closed Dec 25. Res accepted. Italian menu. Bar. Wine cellar. A la carte entrees: dinner $15.95-$27. Child's meals. Specializes in veal, steak, pasta. Own pastries. Opera theme with photos and singing servers. Cr cds: A, D, MC, V.

D

✔ ★ ★ **CAFE EUROPA.** *55 W Church St (32801), in Church St Marketplace, downtown. 407/872-3388.* Hrs: 11 am-10 pm; Fri, Sat to 11 pm; Sun from noon. Closed Memorial Day, Thanksgiving, Dec 25. Res accepted Fri-Sun dinner. Continental menu. Semi-a la carte: lunch $5.25-$8.25, dinner $10-$17. Child's meals. Specialties: goulash, chicken Paprikash. Salad bar. European garden atmosphere. Cr cds: A, C, D, DS, MC, V.

★ ★ **CHARLEY'S STEAK HOUSE.** *6107 S Orange Blossom Trail, at Oakridge Rd, south of downtown. 407/851-7130.* Hrs: 4:30-10 pm; Fri, Sat to 11 pm. Closed Thanksgiving, Dec 25. Res accepted. Bar. Semi-a la carte: dinner $12.95-$19.95. Child's meals. Specializes in flame-broiled aged steak, fresh seafood. Salad bar. Parking. Antiques. Cr cds: A, MC, V.

D SC

★ ★ **CHARLIE'S LOBSTER HOUSE.** *8445 International Dr, at Mercado Shopping Village, in International Drive Area. 407/352-6929.* Hrs: 4-10 pm; Fri, Sat to 11 pm. Res accepted. Bar. Semi-a la carte: dinner $12.95-$36.95. Child's meals. Specializes in seafood. Nautical decor with wood and brass fixtures. Cr cds: A, C, D, DS, ER, MC, V.

D

★ ★ **CHATHAM'S PLACE.** *7575 Dr Phillips Blvd, in Phillips Place, south of downtown. 407/345-2992.* Hrs: 11:30 am-2:30 pm, 6-10 pm; Sun brunch 10:30 am-2:30 pm. Closed most major hols. Res accepted. Beer. Semi-a la carte: lunch $7-$12, dinner $20-$40. Specialties: filet mignon, grouper with pecan butter, rack of lamb. Own specialty desserts. Parking. Intricate wrought-iron grillwork on windows. Totally nonsmoking. Cr cds: A, D, DS, MC, V.

D

★★ **CRACKERS.** *129 W Church St, at Church Street Station, downtown. 407/422-2434.* Web www.churchstreetstation.com. Hrs: 11 am-11:30 pm; Fri, Sat to midnight. Bar. Semi-a la carte: lunch $5.50-$7.95, dinner $9.75-$19.95. Child's meals. Specialties: seafood gumbo, clam chowder, live Maine lobster. Turn-of-the-century carved and paneled bar. Cr cds: A, D, DS, MC, V.

D

★★ **DEL FRISCO'S.** *729 Lee Rd (32810), north of downtown. 407/645-4443.* Hrs: 5-10 pm; wkends to 11 pm. Closed Sun; Jan 1, Memorial Day, Thanksgiving, Dec 25. Res accepted. Bar from 4 pm. A la carte entrees: dinner $15.95-$28.95. Specializes in prime beef, lobster tails. Parking. Steak house atmosphere. Cr cds: A, C, D, DS, MC, V.

D

★★★★ **DUX.** *(See Peabody Orlando Hotel) 407/345-4550.* Web www.peabody-orlando.com. Expert service and innovative cuisine are the hallmarks of this hotel dining room. The room itself is warm and comfortable, adorned with flowers and crystal chandeliers; around the perimeter is a mural painted with—what else—ducks. Continental menu. Specializes in wild game, seafood. Hrs: 6-10 pm; Fri, Sat to 11 pm. Closed Sun; also month of Aug. Res accepted. Bar. Wine cellar. Semi-a la carte: dinner $23-$40. Child's meals. Valet parking. Jacket. Totally nonsmoking. Cr cds: A, C, D, DS, ER, JCB, MC, V.

D

★★ **HANAMIZUKI.** *8255 International Dr (32819), in International Drive Area. 407/363-7200.* Hrs: 5-10:30 pm. Res accepted. Japanese menu. A la carte entrees: $10-$35. Specializes in Japanese cuisine. Japanese decor. Cr cds: A, D, JCB, MC, V.

D

★★★ **LA GRILLE.** *8445 International Dr (32819), 8 mi S on I-4, exit 29, at Mercado Shopping Village, in International Drive Area. 407/345-0883.* Hrs: 6-11 pm. Res accepted. French menu. Bar. Wine cellar. Semi-a la carte: dinner $15.95-$23.95. Child's meals. Specialties: rack of lamb, steak frites, tuna Nicoise. Own pastries. Medieval European architecture. Cr cds: A, C, D, DS, JCB, MC, V.

D

★★ **LA NORMANDIE.** *2021 E Colonial Dr (FL 50), east of downtown. 407/896-9976.* Hrs: 11:30 am-2 pm, 5-10 pm; early-bird dinner Mon-Sat to 6:30 pm. Closed Sun; Dec 25. Res accepted. French, continental menu. Bar. Wine list. Semi-a la carte: lunch $7-$11, dinner $11-$21. Specialties: veal fishermen, salmon with lobster sauce, soufflé Grand Marnier. Own baking. Country French decor. Cr cds: A, C, D, DS, ER, MC, V.

D

★★ **LE COQ AU VIN.** *4800 S Orange Ave, south of downtown. 407/851-6980.* Hrs: 11:30 am-2 pm, 5:30-10 pm; Sat from 5:30 pm; Sun 5-9 pm. Closed Mon; Jan 1, Easter, Dec 25. Res accepted. French, Amer menu. Wine, beer. Semi-a la carte: lunch $6.50-$12.50, dinner $13-$19.50. Child's meals. Parking. French decor. Cr cds: A, C, D, MC, V.

D

★★★ **LE PROVENCE.** *50 E Pine St (32801), downtown. 407/843-1320.* Hrs: 11 am-2 pm, 5:30-9:30 pm; Fri, Sat to 10:30 pm. Closed Sun; some major hols. Res accepted. French menu. Bar. Wine cellar. A la carte entrees: lunch $4.25-$9.95, dinner $14.50-$30. Prix fixe: dinner $25.95 & $51.95. Child's meals. Specializes in fresh seafood, rack of lamb, veal. Entertainment; Fri, Sat. In former bank; large mahogany bar. Cr cds: A, C, D, MC, V.

D

★★ **LEE'S LAKESIDE.** *431 E Central Blvd, downtown. 407/841-1565.* Hrs: 11 am-11 pm; Sat from 5 pm; Sun to 9 pm; early-bird dinner 4-6 pm. Res accepted. Continental menu. Bar. Semi-a la carte: lunch $7.95-$10.95, dinner $16.95-$26.95. Child's meals. Specializes in fresh seafood, beef, veal. Entertainment. Parking. View of skyline across Lake Eola. Cr cds: A, D, DS, MC, V.

D SC

★★ **LILI MARLENE'S AVIATORS RESTAURANT & PUB.** *129 W Church St, at Church Street Station, downtown. 407/422-2434.* Web www.churchstreetstation.com. Hrs: 11 am-4 pm, 5:30-11 pm; Fri, Sat to midnight; Sun brunch 10:30 am-3 pm. Bar 11-1 am. Semi-a la carte: lunch $4.95-$9.95. A la carte entrees: dinner $17-$29. Sun brunch $10.95. Child's meals. Specializes in aged beef, fresh grilled Florida seafood. Entertainment. Valet parking. In historic district; antiques, WWI aviation artifacts. Cr cds: A, C, D, DS, MC, V.

D

★★★ **MANUEL'S ON THE 28TH.** *390 Orange Ave (32801), in Barnett Bank Bldg, downtown. 407/246-6580.* Web www.manuels.com. Hrs: 6-10 pm. Closed Sun, Mon; Thanksgiving, Dec 25. Res accepted. Serv bar. Wine list. Semi-a la carte: dinner $26-$32. Specializes in tuna, lamb. Garage parking. View of city. Totally nonsmoking. Cr cds: A, C, D, DS, MC, V.

D

★★★ **MING COURT.** *9188 International Dr, south of downtown. 407/351-9988.* Hrs: 11 am-2:30 pm, 4:30 pm-midnight. Res accepted. Chinese menu. Bar. Semi-a la carte: lunch $5-$9, dinner $10.95-$19.95. Specialties: Peking duck, dim sum. Chinese performers. Parking. Chinese-style architecture with undulating Great Wall enclosing gardens and waterways. Live seafood tanks. Cr cds: A, C, D, DS, JCB, MC, V.

D

✔★★ **PASSAGE TO INDIA.** *5532 International Dr, in International Drive Area. 407/351-3456.* Web www.destinationusa.com/india1.html. Hrs: 2 pm-midnight; wkends from 1pm. Res accepted. Indian menu. Wine, beer. A la carte entrees: dinner $12.95-$19.95. Child's meals. Specializes in clay oven preparations, vegetarian dishes. Parking. Richly carved wooden screens, brass. Cr cds: A, C, D, DS, MC, V.

D SC

★★★ **SIAM ORCHID.** *7575 Republic Dr, in International Drive Area. 407/351-0821.* Hrs: 5-11 pm. Closed July 4, Dec 25. Res accepted. Thai menu. Bar. Semi-a la carte: dinner $10.25-$26.95. Specialty: Siam Orchid roast duck, fresh seafood. Parking. Thai decor and artifacts. On lake. Cr cds: A, D, MC, V.

D

✔★ **SIZZLING WOK.** *1453 Sand Lake Rd (32809), south of downtown. 407/438-8389.* Hrs: 11 am-10 pm; Fri, Sat to 10:30. Res accepted hols. Chinese menu. Semi-a la carte: lunch $4.25-$5.50, dinner $4.95-$8.95. Buffet: lunch $4-$7, dinner $9-$11. Child's meals. Specializes in Chinese cuisine. Salad bar. Parking. Cr cds: A, D, DS, MC, V.

D SC

✔★★ **STRAUB'S BOATYARD.** *743 Lee Rd, north of downtown. 407/628-0067.* Hrs: 11 am-10 pm; Fri, Sat to 11 pm; early-bird dinner 4:30-6 pm. Closed Sun; Thanksgiving, Dec 25. Res accepted (dinner). Bar. Semi-a la carte: lunch $4-$8.95, dinner $11.95-$19.95. Child's meals. Specializes in steak, seafood. Parking. Nautical decor. Cr cds: A, C, D, DS, MC, V.

D

★★★ **VIVALDI.** *107 Pine St, downtown. 407/423-2335.* Hrs: 11 am-11 pm; Sat, Sun from 4 pm. Closed Thanksgiving, Dec 25. Res accepted. Italian menu. Bar. A la carte entrees: lunch $6.95-$9.95, dinner $9.90-$22.95. Specialty: Vivaldi's Pride. Parking. Own bread, pasta. Outdoor dining. Intimate gourmet dining. Cr cds: A, D, DS, MC, V.

D SC

Unrated Dining Spots

HARD ROCK CAFE. *5800 Kirkman Rd, at Universal Studios Florida, south of downtown. 407/351-7625.* Hrs: 11-2 am. Bar. Semi-a la carte: lunch, dinner $6.95-$15.95. Child's meals. Specializes in hamburgers, barbecue dishes. Parking. Outdoor dining. Building shaped like an electric guitar; stained-glass windows depict Elvis Presley, Jerry Lee Lewis and Chuck Berry. Rock & roll and entertainment memorabilia throughout. Cr cds: A, MC, V.

D

KING HENRY'S FEAST. *8984 International Dr (32819), in International Drive Area. 407/351-5151.* Dinner show hrs vary each season. Res required. Bar. Complete meals: adult $34.95; children 3-11 $21.95. Specializes in baked chicken, barbecued ribs. Entertainment includes dueling knights, aerial ballerina, jesters. Parking. Medieval palace decor; costumed servers. Cr cds: A, C, D, DS, ER, JCB, MC, V.

Walt Disney World

Motor Hotels

★ ★ ★ **BUENA VISTA SUITES.** *(14450 International Dr, Lake Buena Vista 32830) at International Dr & FL 535. 407/239-8588; FAX 407/239-1401; res: 800/537-7737.* 280 suites, 7 story. Jan-mid-Apr, June-Aug, hols: suites $129-$169; each addl $10; under 17 free; lower rates rest of yr. Crib free. TV; cable (premium), VCR (movies). Pool; whirlpool, poolside serv. Complimentary full bkfst. Complimentary coffee in rms. Rm serv 11 am-11 pm. Restaurant opp 6 am-11 pm. Ck-out 11 am. Coin Indry. Meeting rms. Business servs avail. In-rm modem link. Bellhops. Concierge. Sundries. Gift shop. Free transportation to Walt Disney World. Lighted tennis. Golf privileges 1.5 mi. Exercise equipt; weights, bicycle. Game rm. Refrigerators, microwaves. Cr cds: A, C, D, DS, ER, JCB, MC, V.

D SC

✔★ **COMFORT INN.** *(8442 Palm Pkwy, Lake Buena Vista 32830) at Vista Ctr. 407/239-7300; FAX 407/239-7740.* 640 rms, 5 story. Feb-mid-Apr, June-Aug: S, D up to 4, $59-$85; family rates; lower rates rest of yr. Crib free. Pet accepted; $6. TV; cable (premium). 2 pools, 1 heated. Restaurant 6:30-10:30 am, 5:30-9 pm. Bar 5:30 pm-2 am. Ck-out 11 am. Coin Indry. Business servs avail. Valet serv. Sundries. Gift shop. Free Walt Disney World transportation. Game rm. Cr cds: A, C, D, DS, ER, JCB, MC, V.

D SC

★ ★ **DAYS INN.** *(12799 Apopka-Vineland Rd, Orlando 32836) I-4 exit 27. 407/239-4441; FAX 407/239-0325.* 203 rms, 8 story. S, D $139; higher rates special events. Crib free. Pet accepted, some restrictions; $10. TV; cable (premium), VCR (movies avail). Restaurant 6-11 am, 5-10 pm. Ck-out noon. Business servs avail. Gift shop. Coin Indry. Pool. Playground. Game rm. Balconies. Cr cds: A, C, D, DS, MC, V.

D SC

★ ★ ★ **HOLIDAY INN LAKE SUN SPREE RESORT.** *(13351 FL 535, Lake Buena Vista 32830) I-4 exit 27, S on FL 535. 407/239-4500; FAX 407/239-7713.* E-mail @/worldnet.att.net; web www.kidsuites.com. 507 rms, 6 story. Mid-Feb-late Apr, mid-June-mid-Aug, late Dec: S, D $106-$140; under 18 free; lower rates rest of yr. Crib free. TV; cable, VCR (movies $6). Heated pool; whirlpools, wading pool, poolside serv. Playground. Supervised child's activities; ages 3-12. Coffee in rms. Restaurant 7 am-10 pm. Rm serv. Bar from 4:30 pm; entertainment. Ck-out 11 am. Coin Indry. Business servs avail. Bellhops. Valet serv. Concierge. Sundries. Free Walt Disney World transportation. Exercise equipt; weight machine, stair machine. Game rm. Refrigerators; microwaves avail. Cr cds: A, C, D, DS, ER, JCB, MC, V.

D SC

★ ★ **HOWARD JOHNSON PARK SQUARE INN AND SUITES.** *(8501 Palm Pkwy, Lake Buena Vista 32830) I-4 exit 27 to FL 535, N to Vista Center. 407/239-6900; FAX 407/239-1287.* Web HoJo @LBV.com. 222 rms, 3 story, 86 suites. Feb-mid-Apr, June-Aug, late Dec: S, D $85-125, each addl $10; suites $95-$150; under 17 free; lower rates rest of yr. Crib free. TV. 2 pools, heated; wading pool, whirlpool. Playground. Restaurant 7-11 am, 5-10 pm. Bar 4:30 pm-midnight. Ck-out 11 am. Coin Indry. Meeting rms. Business servs avail. Bellhops. Sundries. Gift shop. Airport transportation. Free Walt Disney World transportation. Game rm. Lawn games. Refrigerator in suites. Balconies. Landscaped courtyard. Cr cds: A, C, D, DS, ER, JCB, MC, V.

D SC

Hotels

★ ★ ★ **BUENA VISTA PALACE.** *(1900 Buena Vista Dr, Lake Buena Vista 32830) in Walt Disney World Village. 407/827-2727; FAX 407/827-6034; res: 800/327-2990.* E-mail 102167.1170@compuserv.com; web www.bvp-resort.com. 1,013 rms, 27 story, 128 suites. Feb-Apr, late Dec: S, D $169-$240; suites $290-$850; under 18 free; lower rates rest of yr. Crib free. TV; cable, VCR avail. 3 pools, 2 heated; wading pool, whirlpool, poolside serv. Playground. Supervised child's activities; ages 4-12. Restaurant open 24 hrs (also see ARTHUR'S 27). Bar 11-2 am; entertainment. Ck-out 11 am. Coin Indry. Convention facilities. Business center. In-rm modem link. Shopping arcade. Barber, beauty shop. Valet parking. Free Walt Disney World transportation. Lighted tennis. 18-hole golf privileges, pro, putting green, driving range, pro shop. Exercise equipt; weights, bicycles, sauna. Game rm. Minibars; some in-rm whirlpools, refrigerators; microwaves avail. Many balconies. Luxury level. Cr cds: A, C, D, DS, MC, V.

D

★ ★ ★ **CARIBE ROYALE.** *(14300 International Dr, Orlando 32821) 2 mi S on I-4 exit 27. 407/238-8000; res: 800/823-8300; FAX 407/238-8400.* E-mail cariberoyale.com; web www.cariberoyale.com. 1,218 suites, 10 story. Mid-Dec-mid-Apr, mid-June-mid-Aug: suites $179-$209; under 18 free; lower rates rest of yr. Crib free. TV; cable (premium), VCR avail. Complimentary bkfst buffet. Restaurant 6:30-2 am. Ck-out 11 am. Coin Indry. Convention facilities. Business center. In-rm modem link. Concierge. Free Walt Disney World transportation. Lighted tennis. Golf privileges. Exercise equipt; weight machine, bicycle. Heated pool; wading pool, whirlpool, poolside serv, lifeguard. Supervised child's activities. Refrigerators, microwaves, wet bars. Some in-rm whirlpool, minibars. Cr cds: A, C, D, DS, ER, JCB, MC, V.

D SC

✔★ ★ **COURTYARD BY MARRIOTT-WALT DISNEY WORLD VILLAGE.** *(1805 Hotel Plaza Blvd, Lake Buena Vista 32830) In Walt Disney World Village. 407/828-8888; FAX 407/827-4623.* 323 rms, 14 story. S, D $89-$149; suites $250-$395; under 18 free. Crib free. TV; cable (premium). 2 pools; wading pool, whirlpool, poolside serv. Restaurant 6 am-midnight. Rm serv 7 am-10 pm. Bar from 4 pm. Ck-out 11 am. Coin Indry. Convention facilities. Gift shop. Free Walt Disney World transportation. Tennis privileges. Golf privileges. Exercise equipt; weights, bicycles. Game rm. Many private patios, balconies. Cr cds: A, C, D, DS, ER, JCB, MC, V.

D SC

★ ★ ★ **DOUBLETREE GUEST SUITES RESORT.** *(2305 Hotel Plaza Blvd, Lake Buena Vista 32830) In Walt Disney World Village. 407/934-1000; FAX 407/934-1011.* Web dtdisney@earthlink.net. 229 suites (1-2 bedrm), 7 story. Late Dec-Apr: S, D $139-$280; each addl $20; lower rates rest of yr. Crib free. TV; cable (premium). Heated pool; wading pool, whirlpool, poolside serv. Playground. Restaurant 7 am-11 pm. Bar 4-11 pm. Ck-out 11 am. Coin Indry. Meeting rms. Business servs avail. Concierge. Gift shop. Free Walt Disney World transportation. Lighted tennis. 18-hole golf privileges, pro, putting green, driving range. Exercise equipt; weights, bicycles. Game rm. Lawn games. Refrigerators, microwaves. Some private patios. Cr cds: A, C, D, DS, ER, MC, V.

D SC

★ ★ ★ **EMBASSY SUITES RESORT.** *(8100 Lake Ave, Orlando 32836) Near jct I-4 & FL 535. 407/239-1144; FAX 407/239-1718.* 280 suites, 6 story. Feb-Apr & mid-Dec-Jan 1: S, D (up to 4 adults) $135-$250; family rates; golf, Disney plans; lower rates rest of yr. Crib free. TV; cable (premium), VCR (movies). 2 heated pools, 1 indoor; wading pool, whirlpool, poolside serv. Playground. Supervised child's activities; ages 3-13. Complimentary full bkfst. Complimentary coffee in rms. Restaurant 11 am-11 pm. Bar 5 pm-midnight. Ck-out 11:30 am. Coin lndry. Meeting rms. Business servs avail. In-rm modem link. Gift shop. Free scheduled shuttle to all Disney theme parks. Lighted tennis. 18-hole golf privileges, pro, putting green, driving range. Exercise equipt; weight machines, bicycles, sauna. Game rm. Rec rm. Refrigerators, microwaves, minibars. Cr cds: A, C, D, DS, ER, JCB, MC, V.

D SC

★ ★ ★ **GROSVENOR RESORT.** *(1850 Hotel Plaza Blvd, Lake Buena Vista 32830) In Walt Disney World Village. 407/828-4444; FAX 407/828-8192; res: 800/624-4109.* E-mail grovnor@magicnet.net; web ten-io.com/Disney-vha/gros.html. 626 rms, 19 story. Feb-mid Apr: S, D $160-$195; suites $175-$750; under 18 free; lower rates rest of yr. Crib free. TV; cable, VCR (movies $5). 2 heated pools; wading pool, whirlpool, poolside serv. Playground. Coffee, tea in rms. Restaurant open 24 hrs. Bar 11-2 am; entertainment in season. Ck-out 11 am. Coin lndry. Convention facilities. Business servs avail. In-rm modem link. Concierge. Shopping arcade. Free Walt Disney World transportation. Lighted tennis. Golf privileges, pro, putting green, driving range. Exercise equipt: weights, bicycles. Game rm. Lawn games. Activities dir (summer). Sherlock Holmes Museum on grounds. Cr cds: A, C, D, DS, ER, JCB, MC, V.

D SC

★ ★ ★ **HILTON AT WALT DISNEY WORLD VILLAGE.** *(1751 Hotel Plaza Blvd, Lake Buena Vista 32830) In Walt Disney World Village. 407/827-4000; FAX 407/827-6370.* 814 rms, 10 story. Feb-mid-Apr, late Dec: S, D $175-$255; each addl $20; suites $459-$1,500; family rates; lower rates rest of yr. Crib free. TV; cable (premium), 2 heated pools; wading pool, whirlpool, poolside serv. Supervised child's activities; ages 4-11. Restaurant 6:30 am-midnight. Rm serv 24 hrs. Bar 11-2 am. Ck-out 11 am. Coin lndry. Convention facilities. Business center. In-rm modem link. Barber, beauty shop. Valet parking. Free Walt Disney World transportation. Tennis privileges. Golf privileges, pro, putting green, driving range. Exercise equipt; bicycles, treadmills, sauna. Game rm. Minibars; some bathrm phones, refrigerators; microwaves avail. Some private patios, balconies. Luxury level. Cr cds: A, C, D, DS, ER, JCB, MC, V.

D

✔★ ★ **RIU ORLANDO.** *(8688 Palm Pkwy, Lake Buena Vista 32836) I-4 exit 27 to FL 535, N to Vista Center. 407/239-8500; FAX 407/239-8591.* 167 rms, 6 story. S, D $79-$99; each addl $10; under 12 free. Crib free. TV; cable, VCR avail. Heated pool; whirlpool, poolside serv. Restaurant 6:30-11 am, 5-11 pm. Bar to midnight. Ck-out 11 am. Coin lndry. Meeting rms. Business servs avail. In-rm modem link. Concierge. Free Walt Disney World transportation. Exercise equipt; treadmill, stair machine. Game rm. Rec rm. Microwaves; refrigerators avail. Cr cds: A, C, D, DS, ER, JCB, MC, V.

D SC

★ ★ ★ **ROYAL PLAZA.** *(1905 Hotel Plaza Blvd, Lake Buena Vista 32830) In Walt Disney World Village. 407/828-2828; FAX 407/827-6338; res: 800/248-7890.* 396 rms, 2-17 story. Feb-Apr: S, D $129-$189; suites $169-$650; lower rates rest of yr. Crib free. TV; cable, VCR (movies $6). Heated pool; whirlpool, sauna, poolside serv. Restaurant 6:30 am-midnight. Bar 11-2:00 am; entertainment. Ck-out 11 am. Coin lndry. Convention facilities. Business servs avail. Gift shop. Free valet parking. Free Walt Disney World transportation. Lighted tennis. 18-hole golf privileges, driving range. Game rm. Lawn games. Some bathrm phones. Refrigerators avail. Balconies. Cr cds: A, C, D, DS, ER, JCB, MC, V.

D SC

★ ★ ★ **TRAVELODGE.** *(2000 Hotel Plaza Blvd, Lake Buena Vista 32830) In Walt Disney World Village. 407/828-2424; FAX 407/828-8933.* Web www.travelweb.com. 325 rms, 18 story. S, D $109-$169; suites $199-$359. Crib free. TV; cable (premium). Heated pool; wading pool. Playground. Coffee in rms. Restaurant 7-11 am, 5-11 pm. Bar 4 pm-1:30 am. Ck-out 11 am. Coin lndry. Meeting rms. Concierge. Gift shop. Airport transportation. Free Walt Disney World transportation. Lighted tennis privileges, pro. 18-hole golf privileges, pro, putting green, driving range. Game rm. Lawn games. Minibars; some refrigerators. Balconies. On lake. Cr cds: A, C, D, DS, ER, JCB, MC, V.

D SC

Inn

✔★ ★ ★ **PERRI HOUSE BED & BREAKFAST.** *(10417 FL 535, Orlando 32836) N of I-4 exit 27 on FL 535. 407/876-4830; FAX 407/876-0241; res: 800/780-4830.* E-mail perrihse@iag.net; web www.shoppersmart.com/perrihse. 8 rms. S $85-95; D $95-$104; higher rates: special events, major hols. Crib free. TV; cable. Pool. Complimentary continental bkfst. Ck-out 11 am, ck-in 3 pm. On 4 acres; bird sanctuary. Adj Walt Disney World property. Cr cds: A, D, DS, MC, V.

SC

Resorts

★ ★ **ALL-STAR MUSIC RESORT.** *(1801 W Buena Vista Blvd, Lake Buena Vista 32830) 407/939-6000; FAX 407/939-7222.* Web www.disney.com. 1,920 rms, 3 story. Mid Feb-Late Apr, Late Dec: S, D $89; each addl $10; under 18 free; golf plan, lower rates rest of yr. Crib free. TV; cable (premium). Heated pool; wading pool, poolside serv, lifeguard. Playground. Restaurant 6 am-midnight. Ck-out 11 am, ck-in 4 pm. Gift shop. Grocery. Coin lndry. Valet serv. Tennis privileges. 99-hole golf privileges, greens fee $85, putting green, driving green. Health club privileges. Game rm. Some refrigerators. Picnic tables. Buildings have musical instrument theme. Cr cds: A, MC, V.

D

★ ★ **ALL-STAR SPORTS RESORT.** *(1701 W Buena Vista Dr, Lake Buena Vista 32830) 407/939-5000; FAX 407/939-7333.* Web www.disney.com. 1,920 rms, 3 story. Mid Feb-late Apr, late Dec: S, D $89; each addl $10; golf plans, lower rates rest of yr. Crib free. TV; cable (premium). Heated pool; wading pool, poolside serv, lifeguard. Restaurant 6 am-midnight. Ck-out 11 am, ck-in 4 pm. Gift shop. Grocery. Coin lndry. Valet serv. Tennis privileges. 99-hole golf privileges, greens fee $85. Health club privileges. Some refrigerators. Buildings have various sport themes: baseball, football, tennis, etc. Cr cds: A, MC, V.

D

★ ★ ★ **DISNEY'S BEACH CLUB RESORT.** *(1800 Epcot Resorts Blvd, Lake Buena Vista 32830) 407/934-8000; FAX 407/934-3850.* Web www.disneyworld.com. 584 rms, 5 story. Mid-Feb-Apr, mid-June-late Aug: S, D $260-$340; each addl $15; suites $435-$935; under 18 free; Disney packages; higher rates hols; lower rates rest of yr. Crib free. TV; cable (premium), VCR avail. 2 pools; poolside serv. Supervised child's activities; ages 4-12. Dining rm 7 am-10 pm. Rm serv 24 hrs. Bar 11-1 am. Ck-out 11 am, ck-in 3 pm. Coin lndry. Convention facilities. Business center. In-rm modem link. Bellhops. Valet serv. Sundries. Gift shop. Barber, beauty shop. Free valet parking. Free Disney transportation, water transportation to Disney-MGM Studios Theme Park. Lighted tennis. Golf privileges. Mini waterpark; boating, marina. Lawn games. Game rm. Exercise rm; instructor, weight machine, bicycles, sauna, steam rm. Bathrm phones, minibars; microwaves avail. Wet bar in suites. Balconies. Located on the shores of a 25-acre man-made lake. Architect Robert A.M. Stern has re-created a New England Village with a turn-of-the-century theme. DISNEY'S BEACH CLUB RESORT meets with DISNEY'S YACHT CLUB RESORT (see) in a central courtyard and shares a Fantasy Lagoon. Cr cds: A, MC, V.

★ ★ ★ **DISNEY'S BOARDWALK INN.** *(2101 N Epcot Resort Blvd, Lake Buena Vista 32830) in Epcot Resort area. 407/939-5100; FAX 407/939-5155.* Web www.disneyworld.com. 378 rms, 5 story. Mid-Feb-Apr, mid-late Dec: S, D $279-$490; each addl $15; suites $650-$1,200; under 18 free; lower rates rest of yr. Crib free. TV; cable (premium), VCR avail (movies). Restaurant (see FLYING FISH CAFE). Rm serv 24 hrs. Bar 11 am-midnight. Ck-out 11 am. Convention facilities. Business center. In-rm modem link. Concierge. Shopping arcade. Coin Indry. Airport transportation. Lighted tennis, pro. 99-hole golf course privileges, pro, putting green, driving range. Exercise rm; instructor, bicycles, stair machine, sauna. Massage. Pool; wading pool, whirlpool, poolside serv, lifeguard. Supervised child's activities 4 pm-midnight. Game rm. Rec rm. Bathrm phones; some in-rm whirlpools. Balconies. Luxury level. Cr cds: A, MC, V.

D

★ ★ **DISNEY'S CARIBBEAN BEACH RESORT.** *(900 Cayman Way, Lake Buena Vista 32830) off I-4 exit 36B. 407/934-3400; FAX 407/934-3288.* Web WDW.DISNEY.COM\CBR. 2,112 rms in several village groups, 2 story. Mid Feb-late Apr, late Dec: S, D $139-$154; each addl $15; under 18 free, lower rates rest of yr. Crib free. TV; cable. 7 heated pools; wading pool, whirlpool, poolside serv, lifeguard. 4 playgrounds. Coffee in rms. Dining rm 5:30 am-midnight; several dining areas. Bar noon-1:30 am. Ck-out 11 am, ck-in 3 pm. Coin Indry. Business servs avail. Shopping arcade. Tennis privileges. Golf privileges, greens fee. Health club privileges. Marina; boat rentals. Game rm. Minibars. Picnic tables. 1½-acre island-like resort with lake. Each village has a pool and beach area. 1¼-mi promenade around lake; island play area for children in middle of lake. Cr cds: A, MC, V.

D

★ ★ ★ **DISNEY'S CONTEMPORARY RESORT.** *(Box 10000, Lake Buena Vista 32830) Off US 192, I-4 in Walt Disney World. 407/824-1000; FAX 407/824-3539.* Web www.disneyworld.com. 1,041 rms, 14-story tower, 2 3-story bldgs. Mid-Dec-Jan 1, mid-Feb-late Apr, early June-mid-Aug: S, D $244-$299; each addl $15; 1-bedrm suites $325-$940; under 18 free; lower rates rest of yr. Crib free. TV; cable (premium). 2 heated pools; wading pool, lifeguard. Playground. Supervised child's activities; ages 3-12. Restaurant (see CALIFORNIA GRILL). Snack bar 24 hrs. Rm serv 24 hrs. Bars noon-1 am. Ck-out 11 am, ck-in 3 pm. Coin Indry. Convention facilities. Business center. In-rm modem link. Shopping arcade. Barber, beauty shop. Valet parking. Lighted tennis, pro. 99-hole golf privileges. Exercise rm; instructor, weights, bicycles, sauna. Massage. Game rm. Lawn games. Refrigerator in suites. Balconies. Monorail runs through 12-story atrium lobby. On lake. Luxury level. Cr cds: A, MC, V.

D

★ ★ ★ ★ **DISNEY'S GRAND FLORIDIAN BEACH RESORT.** *4401 Floridian Way (32830), in Walt Disney World. 407/824-3000; FAX 407/824-3186.* Web www.disneyworld.com. On the shores of the Seven Seas Lagoon, this looks like a turn-of-the-century summer resort, thanks to a gabled red roof, rambling verandas, cupolas and gingerbread porches and an open-cage elevator. 900 rms: 65 rms in main bldg, 9 suites; 817 rms, 16 suites in 5 lodge bldgs, 4 & 5 story. Mid-Dec-Jan 1, mid-Feb-late Apr, early June-mid-Aug: S, D $314-$515; each addl $25; suites $678-$1,565; under 18 free; special plans; lower rates rest of yr. Crib free. TV; cable (premium), VCR avail (movies). Heated pool; wading pool, whirlpool, poolside serv, lifeguard. Supervised child's activities (June-Aug); ages 3-12. Dining rms 7 am-11 pm (also see VICTORIA & ALBERT'S). Rm serv 24 hrs. Bar 11-1 am. Ck-out 11 am, ck-in 3 pm. Coin Indry. Convention facilities. Business center. In-rm modem link. Valet parking. Barber, beauty shop. Monorail to Magic Kingdom, Epcot Center & Disney/MGM Studios. Tennis, clay courts, pro. 99-hole golf privileges, greens fee, pro. Private beach; waterskiing, sailing, marina, boat rentals. Lawn games. Game rm. Exercise rm; instructor, weight machines, bicycles, steam rm. Massage. Fishing guides. Bathrm phones, minibars; wet bar in suites. Balconies. Kennels avail. On 40 acres. Bldgs #6, #7 and #9 (431 rms) are totally nonsmoking. Luxury level. Cr cds: A, MC, V.

D

★ ★ ★ **DISNEY'S POLYNESIAN RESORT.** *(Box 10000, Lake Buena Vista 32830) Off US 192, I-4 in Walt Disney World. 407/824-2000; FAX 407/824-3174.* Web www.Disney.com. 853 rms, 2-3 story. Mid-Dec-late Dec, early Feb-Apr: S, D $305-$445; each addl $15; suites $420-$1,200; under 18 free; lower rates rest of yr. Crib free. TV; cable, VCR avail. 2 heated pools; wading pool, poolside serv, lifeguard. Playground. Supervised child's activities; ages 3-11. Restaurant open 24 hrs; dining rm 7 am-11 pm (also see 'OHANA). Children's dinner theater. Rm serv 6:30 am-midnight. Bar 1 pm-1:30 am; entertainment. Ck-out 11 am, ck-in 3 pm. In-rm modem link. Coin Indry. Sundries. Shopping arcade. Lighted tennis privileges, pro. 99-hole golf privileges, greens fee, pro. Health club privileges. Fishing (guides avail). Game rm. Balconies. Kennels. On lake; 2 swimming beaches, boat rentals, waterskiing, marina. Monorail access. Luxury level. Cr cds: A, MC, V.

D

★ ★ **DISNEY'S PORT ORLEANS.** *(1662 Old South Rd, Lake Buena Vista 32830) I-4 exit 26B. 407/934-5000; FAX 407/934-5353.* Web www.disney.com. 1,008 rms in 7 bldgs, 3 story. Mid-Feb-late Apr, late Dec: S, D $139-$154; each addl $15; under 18 free, lower rates rest of yr. Crib free. TV; cable (premium), VCR avail. Pool; wading pool, whirlpool, sauna. Restaurants 5-10 pm. Bar 11 am-midnight. Ck-out 11 am, ck-in 3 pm. Grocery. Coin Indry. Business servs avail. Bellhops. Valet serv. Gift shop. Lighted tennis privileges, pro. Golf privileges, pro, putting green, driving range. Health club privileges. Boats. Bicycle rentals. Game rm. Located on a canal, ornate row-house buildings with courtyards and intricate railings are reminiscent of the French Quarter in New Orleans; cobblestone streets, trips by flat-bottom boats down river to shops and showplaces. Cr cds: A, MC, V.

D

★ ★ ★ **DISNEY'S WILDERNESS LODGE.** *(901 Timberline Dr, Lake Buena Vista 32830) in Walt Disney World. 407/824-3200; FAX 407/824-3232.* Web www.disneyworld.com. 728 rms, 7 story. Early Feb-early July, mid-late Dec: S, D $199-$315; each addl $15; suites $280-$665; family, wkend rates; golf plan; lower rates rest of yr. Crib free. TV; cable, VCR avail. Heated pool; wading pool, whirlpool, poolside serv, lifeguard. Supervised child's activities; ages 4-12. Restaurant 7:30 am-10 pm. Rm serv 7 am-noon, 4 pm-midnight. Bar 11 am-midnight. Ck-out noon. In-rm modem link. Bellhops. Valet serv. Shopping arcade. Coin Indry. Lighted tennis privileges. 99-hole golf privileges; greens fee $85, putting green, driving range. Health club privileges. Game rm. Refrigerators, microwaves avail. Some balconies. Picnic tables. Cr cds: A, MC, V.

D

★ ★ ★ ★ **DISNEY'S YACHT CLUB RESORT.** *(1700 Epcot Resort Blvd, Lake Buena Vista 32830) 5 minute walk to Epcot Center. 407/934-7000; FAX 407/934-3450.* Web www.disneyworld.com. This refreshingly unstuffy property designed by noted architect Robert A.M. Stern is just right for families. Set on a 25-acre man-made lake, it has a gray clapboard facade, evergreen landscaping and a lighthouse on its pier, recalling the turn-of-the-century New England seacoast. 635 rms, 5 story. Mid-Feb-mid-Apr, mid-June-late Aug: S, D $260-$340; each addl $15; suites $435-$1,085; under 18 free; Disney plans; higher rates hols; lower rates rest of yr. Crib free. TV; cable (premium), VCR avail. Pool; whirlpool. Supervised child's activities; ages 4-12. Dining rm 7 am-10 pm (also see YACHTSMAN STEAKHOUSE). Rm serv 24 hrs. Bar 11-1 am. Ck-out 11 am, ck-in 3 pm. Coin Indry. Convention facilities. Business center. In-rm modem link. Bellhops. Valet serv. Concierge. Gift shop. Barber, beauty shop. Free Disney transportation, including water taxi, to Disney-MGM Studios Theme Park & Epcot Center. Lighted tennis. Golf privileges. Mini waterpark; boating, marina. Lawn games. Game rm. Exercise rm; instructor, weight machine, bicycles, sauna, steam rm. Massage. Bathrm phones, minibars; microwaves avail; wet bar in suites. DISNEY'S YACHT CLUB RESORT meets with DISNEY'S BEACH CLUB RESORT (see) in a central courtyard with a "quiet pool" and shares a Fantasy Lagoon with poolside serv. Luxury level. Cr cds: A, MC, V.

D

★ ★ ★ **DIXIE LANDINGS.** *(1251 Dixie Dr, Lake Buena Vista 32830) I-4 exit 26B. 407/934-6000; FAX 407/934-5024.* Web www.disney.com. 2,048 units in 15 bldgs, 2-3 story. Mid Feb-late Apr, late Dec: S, D $139-$154; each addl $15; family rates; golf plans, lower rates rest of yr. Crib free. TV; cable (premium), VCR avail. 6 pools; wading pool, whirlpool, poolside serv, lifeguards. Playground. Restaurant 6:30 am-midnight. Bar; entertainment. Ck-out 11 am, ck-in 3 pm. Grocery, package store. Coin lndry. Business servs avail. Bellhops. Gift shop. Lighted tennis, pro. 99-hole golf, greens fee, pro, putting green, driving range. Health club privileges. Boat, bicycle rentals. Game rm. Old South plantation-style project located on the Sassagoula River. Alligator Bayou region is reminiscent of old Cajun country, while Magnolia Bend showcases stately mansions typical of the upriver South. Cr cds: A, MC, V.

D

★ ★ ★ ★ **HYATT REGENCY GRAND CYPRESS.** *(1 Grand Cypress Blvd, Orlando 32836) 2 mi E of I-4 exit 27, Lake Buena Vista exit. 407/239-1234; FAX 407/239-3800.* Web www.hyatt.com. Part of what is perhaps the Orlando area's most spectacular resort, this hotel offers virtually every resort amenity and then some. It rests on 1,500 landscaped acres. 750 units, 18 story, 75 suites. Jan-May: S, D $265-$420; suites $650-$3,000; golf plans; lower rates rest of yr. Crib free. Valet parking $9. TV; cable (premium), VCR avail. Heated pool; whirlpool, poolside serv. Supervised child's activities (Memorial Day-Labor Day); ages 3-17. Restaurants (see HEMINGWAY'S and LA COQUINA). Rm serv 24 hrs. Bar; entertainment. Ck-out noon, ck-in 4 pm. Convention facilities. Business center. Valet serv. Concierge. Shopping arcade. Beauty shop. Airport, Walt Disney World transportation. 12 tennis courts, 6 lighted, pro, instruction avail. 45-hole golf, Academy of Golf, pro, putting green, driving range, pitch & putt. Sailing, canoes, paddleboats; rentals avail. Lake with white sand beach. Nature area, Audubon walk; jogging trails. Bicycle rentals. Lawn games. Game rm. Equestrian center; Western and English trails. Exercise rm; instructor, weights, bicycles, sauna, steam rm. Massage. Minibars; microwaves avail. Bathrm phone, refrigerator in some suites. Some private patios. Balconies. Luxury level. Cr cds: A, C, D, DS, ER, JCB, MC, V.

D SC

★ ★ ★ **MARRIOTT'S ORLANDO WORLD CENTER.** *(8701 World Center Dr, Orlando 32821) I-4 exit 26A, jct FL 536. 407/239-4200; FAX 407/238-8777.* 1,503 rms, 28 story. S, D $159-$239; suites from $350; under 18 free. Crib free. Valet parking $5, overnight $8. TV; cable (premium), VCR avail. 3 heated pools, 1 indoor; wading pool, whirlpool, poolside serv. Playground. Supervised child's activities; ages 4-12. Dining rms 6 am-11 pm (also see TUSCANY'S). Rm serv 24 hrs. Bar; pianist. Ck-out 11 am, ck-in 4 pm. Coin lndry. Convention facilities. Business center. In-rm modem link. Concierge. Shopping arcade. Barber, beauty shop. Airport, area attractions transportation avail. Lighted tennis, pro. 18-hole golf, greens fee $50-$110, pro, putting green, driving range. 5-acre activity court with pools, lagoon, waterfalls, sun deck. Lawn games. Game rm. Exercise equipt; weights, bicycles, sauna. Massage. Some refrigerators, minibars. Private patios, balconies. On 200 landscaped acres; view of many lakes. Cr cds: A, C, D, DS, ER, JCB, MC, V.

D SC

★ ★ **RESIDENCE INN BY MARRIOTT.** *(8800 Meadow Creek Dr, Orlando 32821) 1 mi S, I-4 exit 27. 407/239-7700; FAX 407/239-7605.* 688 kit. villas, 2 story. Mid-Dec-early Jan, mid-Feb-Apr, mid-June-mid-Aug: S, D $179-$219; wkly, monthly rates; lower rates rest of yr. Crib free. Pet accepted, some restrictions. TV; cable (premium), VCR (movies). 3 heated pools; poolside serv. Complimentary coffee in rms. Ck-out 11 am, ck-in 4 pm. Grocery. Coin lndry. Meeting rms. Bellhops. Gift shop. Walt Disney World transportation. Lighted tennis. Golf privileges. Health club privileges. Balconies. Cr cds: A, C, D, DS, JCB, MC, V.

D SC

★ ★ ★ ★ **VILLAS OF GRAND CYPRESS.** *(1 N Jacaranda, Orlando 32836) N on FL 535. 407/239-4700; FAX 407/239-7219; res: 800/835-7377.* E-mail resortinfo@grandcypress.com; web www.grandcypress.com. It's hard to believe that this tranquil, 1,500-acre resort is just minutes from the bustle of Walt Disney World. Spacious villas offer fully equipped kitchens, plush furnishings and private patios overlooking the expansive golf courses. 146 suites, 2 story, 48 kit. units. Late Jan-Apr: S, D, kit. units $350-$1,600; under 18 free; lower rates rest of yr. Crib free. TV; cable (premium), VCR avail (movies). Pool; whirlpool, poolside serv. Complimentary coffee in rms. Restaurant 7 am-10 pm. Rm serv 24 hrs. Box lunches, snacks. Bar from 11 am; entertainment. Ck-out noon, ck-in 4 pm. Grocery. Bellhops. Valet serv. Concierge. Meeting rms. Business center. Lighted tennis, pro. 45-hole golf course, greens fee $90-130, pro, putting green, driving range. Hiking. Bicycles. Health club privileges. Minibars; some refrigerators; microwaves avail. Balconies. Cr cds: A, C, D, DS, JCB, MC, V.

D

★ ★ ★ **WALT DISNEY WORLD DOLPHIN.** *(1500 Epcot Resorts Blvd, Lake Buena Vista 32830) In Walt Disney World Village, adj Epcot Center. 407/934-4000; FAX 407/934-4099; res: 800/227-1500.* E-mail info@swandolphin.com; web www.swandolphin.com. 1,509 rms, 27 story. Mid-Feb-mid-Apr, late Dec: S, D $285-$365; suites from $610; under 18 free; Disney packages; lower rates rest of yr. Crib free. TV; cable (premium). 4 pools, 3 heated; wading pool, whirlpool, poolside serv, lifeguard. Playground. Supervised child's activities; ages 4-12. Dining rm 6 pm-midnight. Rm serv 24 hrs. Bars noon-2 am; pianist. Ck-out 11 am, ck-in 3 pm. Coin lndry. Convention facilities. Business center. Concierge. Shopping arcade. Barber, beauty shop. Free Walt Disney World transportation, by both land and water. Lighted tennis, pro. Golf privileges. Exercise rm; instructor, weight machine, bicycles. Game rm. Rec rm. Minibars; many bathrm phones; microwaves avail. Wet bar in suites. Designed by architect Michael Graves as entertainment architecture; the hotel features a waterfall cascading down the front of the building into a pool supported by two dolphin statues. Luxury level. Cr cds: A, C, D, DS, ER, JCB, MC, V.

D

★ ★ ★ **WALT DISNEY WORLD SWAN.** *(1200 Epcot Resorts Blvd, Lake Buena Vista 32830) In Walt Disney World Village, adj Epcot Center. 407/934-3000; FAX 407/934-4499; res: 800/248-SWAN.* E-mail info@swandolphin.com; web www.swandolphin.com. 758 rms, 12 story. S, D $265-$380; each addl $20; suites $610-$2,850; under 18 free; Disney packages. Crib free. Valet parking $8. TV; cable (premium), VCR avail. 2 pools, 1 rock-sculptured grotto; wading pool, whirlpool, poolside serv, lifeguard (grotto). Playground. Coffee in rms. Dining rm 6:30 am-11 pm. Rm serv 24 hrs. Bar 4 pm-midnight. Ck-out 11 am, ck-in 3 pm. Convention facilities. Business center. Concierge. Gift shop. Airport transportation. Free transportation, including water taxi, to Epcot Center, Disney-MGM Studios Theme Park and other Kingdom areas. 4 lighted tennis courts, pro. Golf privileges. Exercise equipt; weight machine, bicycles, sauna. Game rm. Minibars; many bathrm phones; some wet bars. Balconies. Situated on 150-acre resort site. Dramatic style of entertainment architecture; created by Michael Graves; two 28-ton, 47.3-ft swan statues grace the roofline. Luxury level. Cr cds: A, C, D, DS, ER, JCB, MC, V.

D SC

Restaurants

★ ★ ★ **ARTHUR'S 27.** *(See Buena Vista Palace Hotel) 407/827-3450.* Web www.bvp-resort.com. Hrs: 6-10 pm. Res accepted. International menu. Bar. Wine cellar. A la carte entrees: dinner $26-$29. Complete meals: dinner $49-$60. Specializes in gourmet dishes, some custom-prepared. Pianist. Valet parking. On 27th floor; view of Walt Disney World. Cr cds: A, C, D, DS, MC, V.

D

★ ★ ★ **CALIFORNIA GRILL.** *(See Disney's Contemporary Resort) 407/824-3611.* Web www.disneyworld.com. Hrs: 5:30-10 pm. Res accepted. Bar noon-1:30 am. Wine list. A la carte entrees: dinner $16.75-$24.75. Child's meals. Specializes in chicken, beef, seafood. Valet parking. Rooftop dining; view of the Magic Kingdom. Totally nonsmoking. Cr cds: A, MC, V.

D

★ ★ **CRAB HOUSE.** *(8496 Palm Pkwy, Lake Buena Vista) I-4 exit 27 to FL 535, N to Vista Center. 407/239-1888.* Hrs: 11:30 am-11 pm; Sun from 1 pm. Bar. Semi-a la carte: lunch $4.99-$9.99, dinner $10.99-$19.99. Child's meals. Specializes in beef, fresh seafood, Maryland crab.

Salad bar. Valet parking. Patio dining. Rustic, New England-style decor. Cr cds: A, C, D, DS, MC, V.

D

★ ★ ★ **FLYING FISH CAFE.** *(See Disney's Boardwalk Inn Resort) 407/939-2359.* Hrs: 5:30-10:30 pm; Fri, Sat to 11 pm. Res accepted. Bar. Extensive wine list. A la carte entrees: dinner $18-$25. Child's meals. Specialties: NY strip steak, red snapper, chocolate lava cake. Own baking. Valet parking. Carnival atmosphere resembling 1930s Coney Island. Totally nonsmoking. Cr cds: A, MC, V.

D

★ ★ **FULTON'S CRAB HOUSE.** *1670 Buena Vista Dr (32830), on Express Lilly Boat in Walt Disney World Village. 407/934-2628.* Hrs: 8:30 am & 10 am sittings (character bkfst), 5 pm-2 am. Res required (bkfst). Bar 11:30-2 am. Complete meal: bkfst $12.95. Semi-a la carte: dinner $15-$30. Child's meals. Specializes in fresh fish, crab, oysters. Valet parking. Nautical decor. Cr cds: A, MC, V.

D

★ ★ ★ **HEMINGWAY'S.** *(See Hyatt Regency Grand Cypress Resort) 407/239-1234.* Web www.hyatt.com. Hrs: 11:30 am-2:30 pm, 6-10:30 pm; Sun, Mon from 6 pm. Res accepted. Bar to 1 am. Extensive wine list. A la carte entrees: lunch $7-$15, dinner $19-$30. Child's meals. Specializes in live Maine lobster, steak. Valet parking. Outdoor dining. Atmosphere of old Key West with ceiling fans, wicker furnishings, tropical palms. Perched atop a rock precipice; multi-level dining overlooks lagoon-like pool. Cr cds: A, C, D, DS, ER, JCB, MC, V.

D

★ ★ ★ **LA COQUINA.** *(See Hyatt Regency Grand Cypress Resort) 407/239-1234.* Web www.hyatt.com. Hrs: 6:30-10:30 pm; Sun brunch 10:30 am-2:30 pm. Closed Tues, Wed. Res accepted. Bar. Wine list. A la carte entrees: dinner $27-$35. Sun brunch $38. Child's meals. Specialties: steamed petite lobsters with ricotta gnocchi; rack of lamb in herb crust with spinach and red pepper tomato compote. Pianist. Free valet parking. Dining rm with crystal chandeliers and floral centerpieces overlooks lake and grounds. Cr cds: A, C, D, DS, ER, JCB, MC, V.

D

✔★ ★ ★ **'OHANA.** *(See Disney's Polynesian Resort) 407/824-1334.* Hrs: 7:30-11 am, 5-10 pm. Res accepted. South Pacific menu. Bar. Character bkfst buffet: $14.95. Complete meal: dinner $19.95. Child's meals. Own baking. South Pacific decor; stone carvings, open kitchen called the Fire Pit. Overlooks lagoon. Totally nonsmoking. Cr cds: A, MC, V.

D

★ ★ **PEBBLES.** *(12551 SR 535, Lake Buena Vista 12551) I-4 to FL 535, right to Crossroads Shopping Center. 407/827-1111.* Hrs: 11 am-11 pm; Fri, Sat to midnight. Closed Thanksgiving, Dec 25. Bar. Semi-a la carte: lunch, dinner $5.25-$19.95. Child's meals. Specialties: Mediterranean salad, chicken with avocado and sour orange sauce, daily specials. Parking. Vaulted ceilings. Window alcoves provide semi-private dining with view of lake. Cr cds: A, D, DS, MC, V.

D

★ ★ **PORTOBELLO YACHT CLUB.** *Pleasure Island (32830), in Walt Disney World Village. 407/934-8888.* Hrs: 11:30 am-midnight. Italian menu. Bar. Semi-a la carte: lunch $4.95-$8.95, dinner $12.95-$22.95. Child's meals. Specializes in seafood. Valet parking. Outdoor dining. Nautical theme. Cr cds: A, MC, V.

D

★ **RAINFOREST CAFE.** *(1800 E Buena Vista Dr, Lake Buena Vista 32830) I-4 exit 27. 407/827-8500.* Web www.rainforestcafe.com. Hrs: 10:30 am-11 pm; Fri, Sat to midnight. Bar. Semi-a la carte: lunch, dinner $7.95-$18.95. Child's meals. Specialties: Rasta Pasta, Rumble in the Jungle, Mojo Bones. Outdoor dining. Tropical rainforest theme; unique decor. Cr cds: A, D, DS, MC, V.

D

★ ★ **SPOODLES.** *(2101 N Epcot Resort Blvd, Lake Buena Vista 32830) on Boardwalk. 407/939-2380.* Hrs: 7:30 am-10 pm. Res accepted. Mediterranean menu. Bkfst buffet $10.95. A la carte entrees: lunch $6.95-$10.95, dinner $7-$21. Child's meals. Specializes in tapas, chicken, beef. Mediterranean decor. Cr cds: A, MC, V.

D

★ ★ ★ **TUSCANY'S.** *(See Marriott's Orlando World Center Resort) 407/239-4200.* Hrs: 6-10 pm. Res accepted. Bar. Wine list. Semi-a la carte: dinner $18-$29. Child's meals. Specializes in seafood, pasta combo. Own baking. Valet parking. Elegant dining; European decor. Cr cds: A, C, D, DS, ER, JCB, MC, V.

D

★ ★ ★ **VICTORIA & ALBERT'S.** *(See Disney's Grand Floridian Beach Resort) 407/824-2383.* Web www.disneyworld.com. Sittings: 6 & 9 pm. Res required. Regional Amer menu. Wine cellar. Complete meals: dinner $80-$100. Child's meals. Own baking. Harpist. Valet parking. Gourmet menu changes daily. Victorian decor. Jacket. Totally nonsmoking. Cr cds: A, D, MC, V.

D

★ ★ ★ **YACHTSMAN STEAKHOUSE.** *(See Disney's Yacht Club Resort) 407/934-3356.* Web www.disneyworld.com. Hrs: 5:30-10 pm. Res accepted. Bar 11 am-midnight. Semi-a la carte: dinner $17-$27. Child's meals. Specialties: Kansas City strip steak, porterhouse. Valet parking. Butcher shop in entry for personalized orders. Totally nonsmoking. Cr cds: A, MC, V.

D

Philadelphia

Founded: 1682
Pop: 1,585,577
Elev: 45 feet
Time zone: Eastern
Area codes: 215; 610
Web: www.libertynet.org/phila-visitor

The Quakers, Philadelphia's first settlers, arrived in 1681 and prospered in trade and commerce, making the city the leading port in the colonies. The first and second Continental Congresses convened here, and Philadelphia became the headquarters of the Revolution. The city continued to be, for the most part, the main seat of the new federal government until 1800.

The Cradle of the Nation, as Philadelphia is often called, is now enjoying the advantages of a much-deserved face lift. Restoration of old houses and historic landmarks is matched only by the redevelopment of previously barren areas of the city—all of which has given Philadelphia a rebirth of tourist interest. The city-wide improvement program has brought Philadelphia's historic sites to the forefront. Entire neighborhoods have been restored; vast highway systems have been superimposed on the city; blocks of warehouses that impinged on Independence Hall have been torn down; and Fairmount Park, one of the world's largest municipal parks, has been developed further. By the waterfront, a major redevelopment program has given new life to Penn's Landing, offering maritime lovers a commercial and recreational paradise.

Business

Philadelphia has a prosperous and diversified economy. One important factor that adds to the success of the city's industries is the Port of Philadelphia, with its ample facilities for international shipping.

About 20 percent of the city's work force is engaged in manufacturing such items as communications equipment, electrical and nonelectrical machinery, appliances, automobile and truck bodies, carpets, periodicals, cigars, scientific instruments, food products, chemicals and apparel.

Many small businesses are opening regularly, particularly retail shops, restaurants and entertainment spots. With a number of medical schools, dental schools and a host of research institutions located here, the health care industry continues to expand.

Convention Facilities

The Pennsylvania Convention Center opened in 1993 and is one of the largest and most versatile convention centers in the nation.

The total area of the Center is 1,300,000 square feet. The Main Exhibit Hall features 315,000 continuous square feet of exhibit space on one level and a second 115,300-square-foot exhibit hall for a total of 430,300 square feet of exhibit space. The Center has 42 meeting rooms, offering 116,700 total square feet of meeting space.

The Philadelphia Convention Center incorporates the renovated, century-old historic Reading Train Shed. The historic Reading Terminal Market is an indoor farmer's market located beneath the shed.

The Convention Center is connected to the 1,200-room Philadelphia Marriott, which opened in January 1995. The hotel has 41 meeting rooms and a 33,000-square-foot ballroom. The hotel increases the area of the Convention Center complex by 88,000 square feet.

The Center is accessible by plane, train and highway. The Market Street East rail station, which offers a high-speed rail link to Amtrak's 30th Street Station and the Philadelphia International Airport, is linked to the Convention Center.

Sports & Recreation

For the professional sports fan, the Phillies play baseball and the Eagles play football in Veterans Stadium. The 76ers play basketball and the Flyers play hockey at the CoreStates Center.

There are four major racetracks in the area: Philadelphia Park in nearby Bensalem, Atlantic City and Garden State in New Jersey and Brandywine in Delaware.

Entertainment

Free concerts are performed at Temple University, Community College of Philadelphia, the University of Pennsylvania, the Mann Music Center, and the Free Library. The Philadelphia Orchestra, the Philly Pops, the Opera Company of Philadelphia, and the Pennsylvania Ballet hold their regular seasons at the Academy of Music. Other musical series include All-Star Forum Concerts, Concerto Soloists of Philadelphia, Philadelphia Chamber Music Society and the Philadelphia Folk Festival. For repertory theater, there are the Wilma Theater, the Arden Theatre, the Philadelphia Theater Company (four contemporary American plays per season) and the Walnut Street Theatre. Many performances take place along the Avenue of the Arts, South Broad Street.

Nightlife also thrives in Philadelphia. When the sun sets, entertainment establishments come alive, offering an exciting array of places from which to choose. For those seeking rock or jazz, South Street by the Delaware River is a hot spot. Many of the downtown hotels have live music.

Historical Areas

Few places in the world have as many spots of historic significance concentrated within a small area as does the vicinity of Independence National Historical Park.

Two areas are especially important to see early in any visit to Philadelphia—the Benjamin Franklin Parkway, the city's cultural esplanade, and

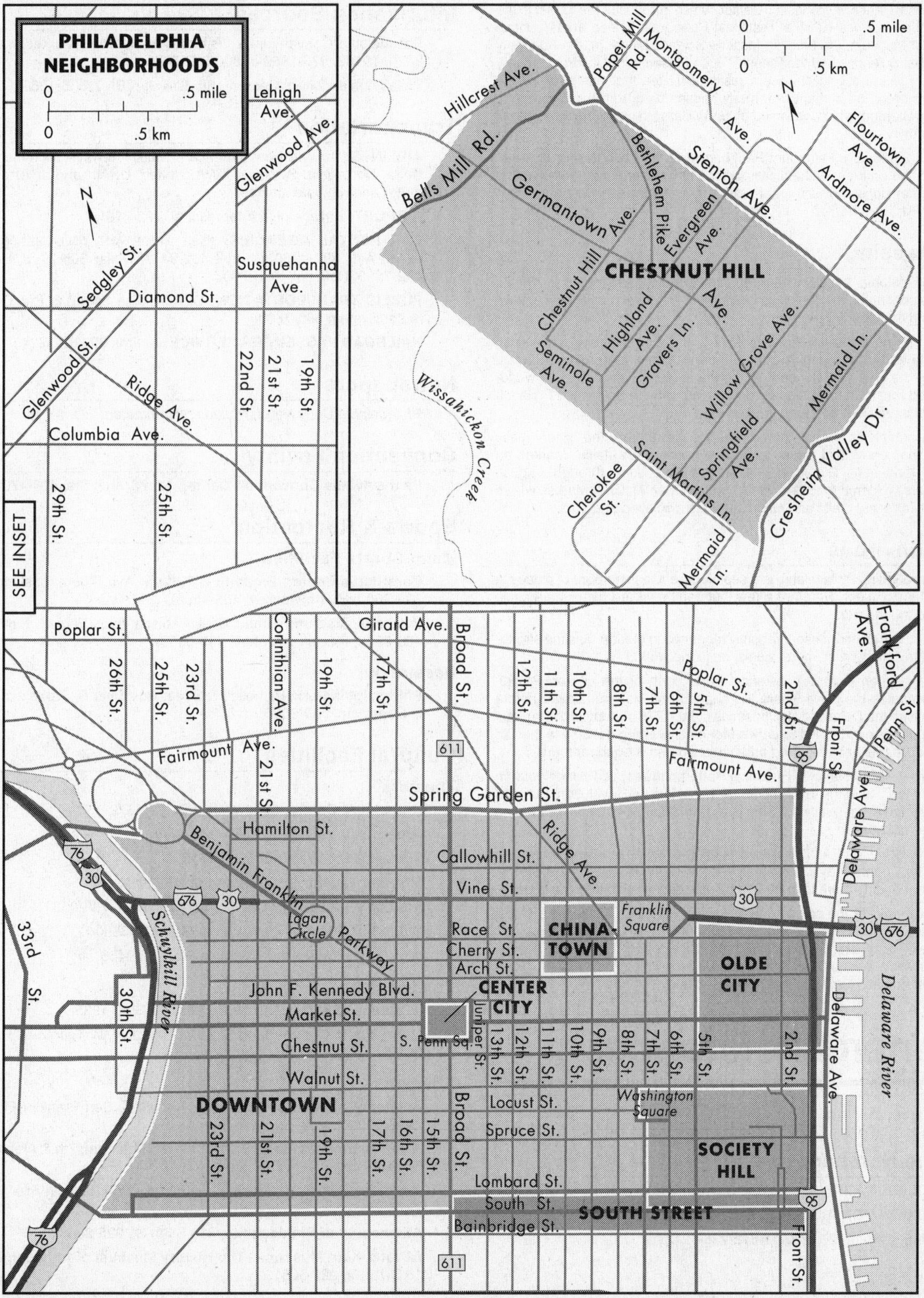
PHILADELPHIA NEIGHBORHOODS
0 .5 mile
0 .5 km
N
SEE INSET
Lehigh Ave.
Glenwood Ave.
Susquehanna Ave.
Sedgley St.
Diamond St.
Glenwood St.
Ridge Ave.
22nd St.
21st St.
19th St.
Columbia Ave.
29th St.
25th St.
Poplar St.
Girard Ave.
26th St.
25th St.
23rd St.
Corinthian Ave.
19th St.
17th St.
Broad St.
12th St.
11th St.
10th St.
8th St.
7th St.
6th St.
5th St.
2nd St.
Front St.
Frankford Ave.
Penn St.
Poplar St.
Fairmount Ave.
21st St.
611
95
Fairmount Ave.
Spring Garden St.
Hamilton St.
Benjamin Franklin Parkway
Ridge Ave.
Callowhill St.
Vine St.
76
30
676
30
30
30
676
Delaware Ave.
Franklin Square
CHINA-TOWN
Race St.
Cherry St.
Arch St.
Logan Circle
33rd St.
Schuylkill River
30th St.
John F. Kennedy Blvd.
CENTER CITY
OLDE CITY
Market St.
S. Penn Sq.
Juniper St.
Chestnut St.
13th St.
12th St.
11th St.
10th St.
9th St.
8th St.
7th St.
6th St.
5th St.
2nd St.
Delaware Ave.
Delaware River
Walnut St.
Locust St.
Washington Square
DOWNTOWN
23rd St.
21st St.
19th St.
17th St.
16th St.
15th St.
Broad St.
Spruce St.
SOCIETY HILL
Lombard St.
South St.
SOUTH STREET
Bainbridge St.
95
76
611
Front St.
0 .5 mile
0 .5 km
N
Paper Mill Rd.
Montgomery Ave.
Hillcrest Ave.
Flourtown Ave.
Bells Mill Rd.
Bethlehem Pike
Stenton Ave.
Ardmore Ave.
Germantown Ave.
Evergreen Ave.
CHESTNUT HILL
Chestnut Hill Ave.
Highland Ave.
Gravers Ln.
Willow Grove Ave.
Mermaid Ln.
Seminole Ave.
Wissahickon Creek
Cresheim Valley Dr.
Springfield Ave.
Saint Martins Ln.
Cherokee St.
Mermaid Ln.

the National Park Service Visitor Center, which introduces the tourist to the entire Independence National Historical Park area. These areas contain the Rodin Museum, the Franklin Institute Science Museum, the Academy of National Sciences and the Please Touch Museum for Children. Nearby is Society Hill, a revolutionary-era residential area that has been extensively restored. In Germantown, many houses date from the Revolution, including Stenton, which was used by Sir William Howe during the battle of Germantown.

The 8,000-acre Fairmount Park begins at the Philadelphia Museum of Art. In the park are authentically preserved and furnished 18th-century colonial mansions and such great cultural institutions as the Museum of Art and the Philadelphia Zoo.

Sightseeing

Philadelphia, the city where the most significant events of 1776 took place, is continuing to develop its history with historical music shows, town criers and the Liberty Tale Tour.

Along the Schuylkill River in May, the nation's leading scholastic, collegiate and club rowing and sculling crews compete in many regattas, including the Dad Vail. Concerts at the Mann Music Center feature world-renowned musicians and singers performing with the acclaimed Philadelphia Orchestra from late June through July.

Philadelphia's shopping areas run the gamut from the glittery glass Gallery mall on Market Street to South Philadelphia's Italian Market, an outdoor food mall. During weekends from late June through August, visitors are welcome to explore Head House Open Air Craft Market, where antiques, arts and crafts and ethnic food are displayed and sold.

City Environs

Surrounding Philadelphia is a seemingly endless number of places to attract the sightseer. Here are a few that can be visited by taking a circle drive around the city:

The Barnes Foundation, recently reopened in Merion, has the strongest private collection of Impressionist art in the world.

Washington Crossing Historical Park, north of the city on PA 32, commemorates the place where the general and his men stayed before they crossed the Delaware on Christmas night, 1776. A copy of the famous painting of this event is in the park's Memorial Building. Nearby is the Old Ferry, which has been restored and furnished and is open for tours.

Valley Forge National Historical Park, northwest of Philadelphia on PA 23, is the site of the turning point of the American Revolution. Bus and auto tape tours are available. This is a dramatically beautiful spot during the dogwood season.

New Hope, on PA 32, is proud of its art galleries, unusual shops and the Bucks County Playhouse. In Doylestown, on US 202, is the Mercer Museum, housing more than 30,000 objects dating back to colonial days.

Southwest of the city, on the Delaware River, is Chester, the oldest settlement in the state. It was established in 1643 by Swedes and Finns. This is where William Penn landed in 1682. The Caleb Pusey House, at Landingford Plantation, west of town near Upland, was built for Penn's agent. It has been restored and furnished with period pieces.

General References

Area codes: 215; 610

Phone Numbers

POLICE & FIRE: 911

POISON CONTROL CENTER: 386-2100

TIME: 846-1212 **WEATHER:** 936-1212

Information Sources

Philadelphia Convention & Visitors Bureau, 1515 Market St, Ste 2020, 19102, 636-1666 or 800/537-7676.

Philadelphia Visitors Center, 16th St & JFK Blvd, 636-1666.

Transportation

AIRLINES: Air Jamaica; American; British Airways; Continental; Delta; Northwest; Swissair; TWA; United; USAir; and other commuter and regional airlines.

AIRPORT: Philadelphia International, 492-3181.

CAR RENTAL AGENCIES: (See IMPORTANT TOLL-FREE NUMBERS) Avis 492-0900; Budget 492-9447; Dollar 365-2700; Hertz 492-7200; National 492-2750.

PUBLIC TRANSPORTATION: SEPTA High Speed & Rail Commuter System 580-7800.

RAILROAD PASSENGER SERVICE: Amtrak 800/872-7245.

Newspapers

Philadelphia Daily News; Philadelphia Inquirer.

Convention Facility

Pennsylvania Convention Center, 12th & Arch Sts, 418-4700.

Sports & Recreation

Major Sports Facilities

CoreStates Center, Broad St & Pattison Ave (76ers, basketball, 339-7600; Flyers, hockey, 465-4500).

Veterans Stadium, Broad St & Pattison Ave (Eagles, football, 463-2500; Phillies, baseball, 463-6000).

Racetrack

Philadelphia Park, Richelieu & Street Rds, near PA Tpke exit 28, in Bensalem, 639-9000.

Cultural Facilities

Theaters

Annenberg Center, 3680 Walnut St, 898-6791.

Arden Theatre, 40 N 2nd St, 922-8900.

Forrest, 1114 Walnut St, 923-1515.

Merriam Theater, 250 S Broad St, 732-5446.

Philadelphia Theater Co, 1714 Delancey St, 735-0631.

Walnut St Theatre, 9th & Walnut Sts, 574-3550.

Wilma Theater, Broad & Spruce Sts, 893-9456.

Concert Halls

Academy of Music, Broad & Locust Sts, 893-1935.

Mann Music Center, 52nd St & Parkside Ave, W Fairmount Park, 567-0707.

Museums

Academy of Natural Sciences, 19th St & Ben Franklin Pkwy, 299-1000.

Afro-American Historical and Cultural Museum, 7th & Arch Sts, 574-0380.

American Swedish Historical Museum, 1900 Pattison Ave, 389-1776.

Athenaeum of Philadelphia, 219 S 6th St, 925-2688.

Atwater Kent Museum—The History Museum of Philadelphia, 15 S 7th St, 922-3031.

Balch Institute for Ethnic Studies, 18 S 7th St, 925-8090.

Civil War Library & Museum, 1805 Pine St, 735-8196.

Fireman's Hall Museum, 149 N 2nd St, 923-1438.

Franklin Institute Science Museum, 20th St & Ben Franklin Pkwy, 448-1200.

Historical Society of Pennsylvania, 1300 Locust St, 732-6201.

Independence Seaport Museum, Delaware Ave & Walnut St, 925-5439.

Mummer's Museum, 2nd St & Washington Ave, 336-3050.

Mütter Museum, 19 S 22nd St, 563-3737.

National Museum of American Jewish History, 55 N 5th St, 923-3811.

New Hall (Marine Corps Memorial Museum), 4th & Chestnut Sts.

Pearl S. Buck's House, Green Hills Farm, 520 Dublin Rd, in Perkasie, 249-0100.

Please Touch Museum for Children, 210 N 21st St, 963-0667.

Port of History Museum, Penn's Landing, Columbus Blvd & Walnut St, 823-7280.

Rosenbach Museum, 2010 DeLancey Pl, 732-1600.

University of Pennsylvania Museum of Archaeology and Anthropology, 33rd & Spruce Sts, 898-4000.

Wagner Free Institute of Science, 17th & Montgomery Sts, 763-6529.

Art Museums & Galleries

Barnes Foundation, 300 N Latch's Lane, 610/667-0290.

Brandywine River Museum, 25 mi SW via US 1 at Brandywine River, Chadd's Ford, 388-7601.

Institute of Contemporary Art, 36th & Sansom Sts, University of Pennsylvania, 898-7108.

Norman Rockwell Museum, 601 Walnut St, 922-4345.

Pennsylvania Academy of the Fine Arts, 118 N Broad St, 972-7600.

Philadelphia Art Alliance, 251 S 18th St, 545-4302.

Philadelphia Museum of Art, 26th St & Ben Franklin Pkwy, 763-8100.

Rodin Museum, 22nd St & Ben Franklin Pkwy, 563-1948.

Points of Interest

Historical

Arch St Friends Meeting House, 4th & Arch Sts, 627-2667.

Bartram's Garden, 54th St & Lindbergh Blvd, 729-5281.

Betsy Ross House, 239 Arch St, 627-5343.

Bishop White House, 309 Walnut St, 597-8974.

Carpenters' Hall, 320 Chestnut St, 925-0167.

Christ Church, 2nd St between Market & Arch Sts, 922-1695.

Christ Church Burial Ground, 5th & Arch Sts, 922-1695.

City Tavern, 2nd & Walnut Sts, 923-6059.

Cliveden, 6401 Germantown Ave (US 422) between Johnson & Cliveden Sts, 848-1777.

Colonial Mansions, Fairmount Park, 684-7922.

Congress Hall, 6th & Chestnut Sts, 597-8974.

Deshler-Morris House, 5442 Germantown Ave, 596-1748.

Edgar Allan Poe National Historic Site, 532 N 7th St, 597-8780.

Elfreth's Alley, off 2nd St between Arch & Race Sts, 574-0560.

First Bank of the United States, 3rd St between Walnut & Chestnut Sts, 597-8974.

Franklin Court, between Market & Chestnut Sts, in blk bounded by 3rd & 4th Sts.

Gloria Dei Church National Historic Site, Columbus Blvd & Christian St, 389-1513.

Hill-Physick-Keith House, 321 S 4th St, 925-7866.

Independence Hall, Chestnut betweeen 5th & 6th Sts, 597-8974.

Independence National Historical Park, visitor center located at 3rd & Chestnut Sts, 597-8974.

Independence Square, Chestnut, Walnut, 5th & 6th Sts.

Jacob Graff House, 701 Market St.

Liberty Bell Pavilion, Market St between 5th & 6th Sts.

Library Hall, 5th & Library Sts.

Longwood Gardens, 30 mi SW via US 1 near Kennett Square, 388-6741.

Memorial Hall, 42nd St & Parkside Ave, Fairmount Park.

Mikveh Israel Cemetery, 8th & Spruce Sts.

New Hall, 4th & Chestnut Sts, in Carpenters' Court.

Old City Hall, Chestnut & 5th Sts.

Old Pine St Presbyterian Church, 412 Pine St, 925-8051.

Old St Mary's Church, 252 S 4th St between Locust & Spruce Sts, 923-7930.

Pennsylvania Hospital, 8th & Spruce Sts.

Powel House, 244 S 3rd St, 627-0364.

St George's United Methodist Church, 235 N 4th St, 925-7788.

St Peter's Church, 3rd & Pine Sts, 925-5968.

Second Bank of the United States, 420 Chestnut St between 4th & 5th Sts.

Society Hill Area, bounded by Front, Walnut, 7th & Lombard Sts.

Stenton House, 18th St & Windrim Ave, 329-7312.

Todd House, 4th & Walnut Sts.

USS *Olympia,* Penn's Landing, Columbus Blvd & Spruce St, 922-1898.

Valley Forge National Historical Park, 22 mi NW via I-76 & PA 23, 783-1077.

Washington Square, Walnut St from 6th St.

Other Attractions

Boat House Row, on E bank of Schuylkill River, 546-9000.

The Bourse, 21 S 5th St, Independence Mall East, 625-0300.

City Hall, Broad & Market Sts.

Fairmount Park, NW on both sides of Wissahickon Creek & Schuylkill River, 685-0000.

Free Library, Logan Sq, 19th & Vine Sts, 686-5322.

Head House Open Air Craft Market, Pine & 2nd, in Society Hill.

Japanese Exhibition House, Horticulture Center, Fairmount Park, 878-5097.

Morris Arboretum, Northwestern & Germantown Aves, in Chestnut Hill, 247-5777.

Pennypack Environmental Center, 8600 Verree Rd, 671-0440.

Philadelphia Zoo, 3400 Girard Ave, Fairmount Park, 243-1100.

Schuylkill Center for Environmental Education, 8480 Hagy's Mill Rd, 482-7300.

Sesame Place, 20 mi NE via I-95, near Bristol, 757-1100.

Tinicum National Environmental Center, 86th St & Lindbergh Blvd, 365-3118 or 610/521-0662.

US Mint, 5th & Arch Sts, 597-7350.

Sightseeing Tours

AudioWalk and Tour, 6th & Sansom Sts, 922-4345.

Centipede Tours, 1315 Walnut St, 735-3123.

Gray Line bus tours, 3101 E Orthodox St, 569-3666 or 800/220-3133.

Philadelphia Carriage Co, 500 N 13th St, 922-6840.

Spirit of Philadelphia, Columbus Blvd & Market St, Pier 3, 923-1419.

Annual Events

Mummers' Parade, Broad St. Jan 1.

Philadelphia Flower Show, Pennsylvania Convention Center, 12th & Arch Sts. Early-mid-Mar.

Penn Relays, Franklin Field. Late Apr.

Devon Horse Show, 20 mi NW via US 30 at Horse Show Grounds, in Devon, 610/964-0550. Nine days beginning Memorial Day wkend.

Elfreth's Alley Fete Days. 1st wkend June.

Freedom Festival. Early July.

Cliveden Battle of Germantown Re-enactment and the Upsala Country Fair, 6401 Germantown Ave. 1st Sat Oct.

Thanksgiving Day Parade.

Army-Navy Football Game, Veterans Stadium. 1st Sat Dec.

Historical Christmas Tours, Fairmount Park, 684-7922. Early Dec.

City Neighborhoods

Many of the restaurants, unrated dining establishments and some lodgings listed under Philadelphia include neighborhoods as well as exact street addresses. Geographic descriptions of these areas are given, followed by a table of restaurants arranged by neighborhood.

Center City: Area of Downtown around city hall; south of Kennedy Blvd, west of Juniper St, north of S Penn Square and east of 15th St.

Chestnut Hill: South of Stenton Ave, west and north of Cresheim Valley Dr and east of Fairmount Park; commercial area along Germantown Ave.

Chinatown: North central area of Downtown; south of Vine St, west of 8th St, north of Arch St and east of 11th St.

Downtown: South of Spring Garden St, west of I-95, north of South St and east of the Schuylkill River. **North of Downtown** North of Spring Garden St. **South of Downtown** South of South St. **West of Downtown** West of Schuylkill River.

Olde City: Area of Downtown south of I-696, west of the Delaware River, north of Chestnut St and east of Independence Mall.

Society Hill: Southeast side of Downtown; south of Walnut St, west of Front St, north of Lombard St and east of 7th St.

South Street: Downtown area of South St between Broad St on the west and the Delaware River on the east; also north to Pine St and south to Bainbridge St.

Lodgings and Food

PHILADELPHIA RESTAURANTS BY NEIGHBORHOOD AREAS

(For full description, see alphabetical listings under Restaurants)

CENTER CITY
Bookbinder's 15th Street Seafood House. 215 S 15th St

CHESTNUT HILL
Flying Fish. 8142 Germantown Ave
Roller's. 8705 Germantown Ave
Under The Blue Moon. 8042 Germantown Ave

CHINATOWN
Ho Sai Gai. 1000 Race St
Rangoon. 112 N 9th St
Vang's Garden. 121 N 11th St

DOWNTOWN
Bistro Bix. 114 S 12th St
Brasserie Perrier. 1619 Walnut St
Cary. 211 S 15th St
Chanterelles. 1312 Spruce St
Ciboulette. 200 S Broad St
Circa. 1518 Walnut St
Cuvee Notredame. 1701 Green St
Deux Cheminées. 1221 Locust St
The Dining Room (The Ritz-Carlton, Philadelphia Hotel). 17th & Chestnut Sts
Dock Street Brewery. 2 Logan Square
The Founders (Park Hyatt Philadelphia At The Bellevue Hotel). Broad & Walnut Sts
Fountain (Four Seasons Hotel Philadelphia). 1 Logan Square
The Garden. 1617 Spruce St
The Grill (The Ritz-Carlton, Philadelphia Hotel). 17th & Chestnut Sts
Harry's Bar & Grill. 22 S 18th St
Italian Bistro. 211 S Broad St
Le Bar Lyonnais. 1523 Walnut St
Le Bar Nostradamus. 1701 Green St
Le Bec-Fin. 1523 Walnut St
Napoleon. 1500 Locust St
Nicholas Nickolas (The Rittenhouse Hotel). 210 W Rittenhouse Square
Nick's (The Rittenhouse Hotel). 210 W Rittenhouse Square
Opus 251. 251 S 18th St
The Palm. 200 S Broad St
Peacock On The Parkway. 1700 Benjamin Franklin Pkwy
Striped Bass. 1500 Walnut St
Susanna Foo. 1512 Walnut St
Swann Cafe (Four Seasons Hotel Philadelphia). 1 Logan Square
Swann Lounge (Four Seasons Hotel Philadelphia). 1 Logan Square
Tony Clark's. 121 S Broad St
Treetops (The Rittenhouse Hotel). 210 W Rittenhouse Square
White Dog Cafe. 3420 Sansom St

NORTH OF DOWNTOWN
Berlengas. 4926 N 5th St
Fisher's Seafood. 7312 Castor Ave
Isabella's. 6516 Castor Ave
Moonstruck. 7955 Oxford Ave
Umbria. 7131 Germantown Ave

SOUTH OF DOWNTOWN
Assaggi Italiani. 935 Ellsworth St
Dmitri's. 795 S 3rd St
Famous 4th St Delicatessen. 700 S 4th St
Felicia's. 1148 S 11th St
Michael's. 824 S 8th St

WEST OF DOWNTOWN
The Marker (Adam's Mark Hotel). City Ave & Monument Rd
The Restaurant School. 4207 Walnut St
Zócalo. 3600 Lancaster Ave

OLDE CITY
Azalea (Omni Hotel At Independence Park). 4th & Chestnut
Dinardo's. 312 Race St
La Famiglia. 8 S Front St
Meiji-En. Pier 19 North
Middle East. 126 Chestnut St
New Mexico Grille. 50 S 2nd St
Ristorante Panorama (Penn's View Hotel). Front & Market Sts
Rococo. 123 Chestnut St
Sassafras. 48 S 2nd St
Serrano. 20 S 2nd St
Spirit Of Philadelphia. Pier 3

SOCIETY HILL
City Tavern. 138 S 2nd St at Walnut
Dickens Inn. Head House Square
Old Original Bookbinder's. 125 Walnut St

SOUTH STREET AREA
Bridget Foy's South Street Grill. 200 South St
Cafe Nola. 603 S 3rd St
Knave Of Hearts. 230 South St
Monte Carlo Living Room. 2nd & South Sts
Moshulu. Pier 34
Overtures. 609 E Passyunk Ave
Pompano Grille. 701 E Passyunk Ave
The Saloon. 750 S 7th St
South Street Diner. 140 South St

Note: When a listing is located in a town that does not have its own city heading, it will appear under the city nearest to its location. In these cases, the address and town appear in parenthesis immediately following the name of the establishment.

Motels

★ ★ **BEST WESTERN HOTEL-NORTHEAST.** *11580 Roosevelt Blvd (19116), north of downtown. 215/464-9500; FAX 215/464-8511.* 100 rms, 2 story. S, D $90-$125; under 18 free; wkly, wkend rates. Crib free. TV; cable (premium). Pool; lifeguard. Playground. Complimentary continental bkfst. Bar from 4 pm. Ck-out 11 am. Coin Indry. Meeting rms. Business servs avail. Exercise equipt; stair machine, bicycles. Lawn games. Some bathrm phones, refrigerators. Many balconies. Picnic tables. Cr cds: A, C, D, DS, MC, V.

D SC

✔★ ★ **COMFORT INN.** *(3660 Street Rd, Bensalem 19020) N on I-95 to Street Rd W exit, 3 mi W. 215/245-0100; FAX 215/245-1851.* 141 units, 3 story. S $75-$109; D $85-$125; each addl $10; suites $125; family rates. Crib free. Pet accepted, some restrictions. TV; cable (premium). Complimentary continental bkfst. Restaurant nearby. Bar 4 pm-2 am; entertainment. Ck-out noon. Meeting rms. Business servs avail. In-rm modem link. Gift shop. Exercise equipt; weights, bicycles. Game rm. Some in-rm whirlpools. Cr cds: A, C, D, DS, ER, JCB, MC, V.

D SC

Motor Hotels

✔★ ★ **BEST WESTERN-CENTER CITY.** *501 N 22nd St (19130), in Center City. 215/568-8300; FAX 215/557-0259.* 183 rms, 3 story. Apr-Oct: S $99-$119.50; D $109-$129; each addl $10; suites $150; under 18 free; family rates. Pet accepted, some restrictions. TV; cable (premium), VCR avail. Complimentary coffee in lobby. Restaurant 6:30 am-10:30 pm. Bar 11-2 am. Ck-out noon. Meeting rms. Business servs avail. In-rm modem link. Bellhops. Valet serv. Gift shop. Exercise equipt; treadmill, stair machine. Pool; lifeguard. Refrigerators, microwaves avail. Cr cds: A, C, D, DS, MC, V.

✔★★ **DAYS INN-AIRPORT.** *4101 Island Ave (19153), near Intl Airport, south of downtown. 215/492-0400; FAX 215/365-6035.* 177 rms, 5 story. S $108; D $118; each addl $15; under 18 free. Crib free. TV; cable (premium), VCR avail. Pool; lifeguard. Coffee in rms. Restaurant 6 am-2 pm, 5 pm-midnight; Sat to noon. Rm serv. Bar 4 pm-midnight. Ck-out noon. Coin lndry. Meeting rms. Business servs avail. Valet serv. Free airport transportation. Refrigerators, microwaves avail. Cr cds: A, C, D, DS, MC, V.

D SC

★★★ **DOUBLETREE CLUB HOTEL.** *9461 Roosevelt Blvd (19114), north of downtown. 215/671-9600; FAX 215/464-7759.* 188 rms, 6 story. S $119; D $129; each addl $10; suites $175; under 17 free; wkend rates. Crib free. TV; cable, VCR avail. Indoor pool. Restaurant 6 am-11 pm. Bar 5 pm-midnight. Ck-out 11 am. Coin lndry. Meeting rms. Business center. In-rm modem link. Valet serv. Sundries. Gift shop. Exercise equipt; weight machine, bicycles. Health club privileges. Some refrigerators; microwaves avail. Cr cds: A, C, D, DS, MC, V.

D SC

★★★ **HILTON-PHILADELPHIA AIRPORT.** *4509 Island Ave (19153), at Intl Airport, south of downtown. 215/365-4150; FAX 215/937-6382.* 330 rms, 9 story. S, D $109-$149; suites $325; studio rms $150; under 18 free; wkend rates. Crib free. Pet accepted, some restrictions. TV; cable (premium). Indoor pool; whirlpool. Restaurant 6 am-11 pm. Rm serv 24 hrs. Bar 11-2 am. Ck-out noon. Meeting rms. Business center. In-rm modem link. Bellhops. Valet serv. Gift shop. Free airport transportation. Exercise equipt; weights, bicycles. Luxury level. Cr cds: A, C, D, DS, ER, MC, V.

D SC

★★ **HOLIDAY INN EXPRESS MIDTOWN.** *1305 Walnut St (19107), downtown. 215/735-9300; FAX 215/732-2682.* E-mail midtown@erols.com. 166 rms, 20 story. S $110-$135; D $120-$145; each addl $10; under 19 free. Crib free. Garage $11.75. TV; cable (premium). Pool. Complimentary continental bkfst. Ck-out 1 pm. Meeting rms. Business servs avail. In-rm modem link. Bellhops. Valet serv. Concierge. Health club privileges. Cr cds: A, C, D, DS, JCB, MC, V.

D SC

★★ **HOLIDAY INN-INDEPENDENCE MALL.** *400 Arch St (19106), downtown. 215/923-8660; FAX 215/923-4633.* 364 rms, 8 story. S, D $95-$169; each addl $10; suites $275-$300; under 19 free; wkend rates. Garage $10. Crib free. TV; cable (premium), VCR avail. Rooftop pool; lifeguard. Restaurant 6:30 am-10:30 pm; dining rm 11:30 am-2 pm, 5:30-10:30 pm. Rm serv. Bar 11-1 am, Sun from noon. Ck-out 11 am. Coin lndry. Meeting rms. Business center. Bellhops. Valet serv. Sundries. Gift shop. Health club privileges. Cr cds: A, C, D, DS, JCB, MC, V.

D SC

Hotels

★★★ **ADAM'S MARK.** *City Ave & Monument Rd (19131), west of downtown. 215/581-5000; FAX 215/581-5069; res: 800/444-2326.* Web www.adamsmark.com. 515 rms, 23 story. S $94-$219; D $94-$235; each addl $15; suites $179-$925; under 18 free; wkend, wkly rates. Crib free. TV; cable, VCR avail. Indoor/outdoor pool; whirlpool, poolside serv. Restaurant 6 am-11 pm. Bars; entertainment. Ck-out noon. Convention facilities. Business center. In-rm modem link. Shopping arcade. Barber, beauty shop. Airport, RR station, bus depot transportation. Exercise rm; instructor, weights, bicycles, sauna, steam rm. Refrigerators. Cr cds: A, C, D, DS, MC, V.

D SC

✔★ **COMFORT INN.** *100 N Christopher Columbus Blvd (19106), downtown. 215/627-7900; FAX 215/238-0809.* 185 rms, 10 story. S, D $99-$129; each addl $10; suites $160; under 18 free; higher rates some hols. Crib free. TV. Complimentary continental bkfst. Coffee in rms. Restaurant nearby. Bar 5 pm-2 am. Ck-out noon. Meeting rms. Business servs avail. In-rm modem link. Airport, RR station, bus depot transportation. Health club privileges. View of Delaware River. Cr cds: A, C, D, DS, ER, JCB, MC, V.

D SC

★★★ **DOUBLETREE.** *Broad St at Locust (19107), downtown. 215/893-1600; FAX 215/893-1663.* Web www.doubletree.com. 427 rms, 26 story. S $160-$175; D $185-$200; each addl $15; suites $250-$500; under 18 free; wkend rates; higher rates New Year's hols. Crib free. Garage $13, valet $17. TV; cable (premium), VCR avail. Indoor pool; whirlpool. Restaurant 6:30 am-11 pm; Fri, Sat to midnight. Bar to 1 am. Ck-out noon. Convention facilities. Business servs avail. In-rm modem link. Concierge. Gift shop. Airport transportation avail. Exercise equipt; weights, bicycles, sauna, steam rm. Luxury level. Cr cds: A, C, D, DS, ER, JCB, MC, V.

D SC

★★★ **DOUBLETREE GUEST SUITES.** *(640 W Germantown Pike, Plymouth Meeting 19462) W on I-76, exit I-476N to Germantown Pike West exit, right on Hickory Rd. 610/834-8300; FAX 610/834-7813.* Web www.doubletreehotels.com. 252 suites, 7 story. S, D $210-$230; family, wkend rates. Crib $10. TV; cable (premium), VCR avail. Indoor pool; whirlpool, wading pool, poolside serv, lifeguard. Restaurant 6:30 am-10 pm. Bar. Ck-out noon. Coin lndry. Meeting rms. Business servs avail. In-rm modem link. Gift shop. Airport, RR station, bus depot transportation. Exercise equipt; weights, bicycles, sauna. Bathrm phones, refrigerators, minibars; microwaves avail. Some private patios, balconies. Cr cds: A, C, D, DS, MC, V.

D SC

★★★★ **FOUR SEASONS HOTEL PHILADELPHIA.** *1 Logan Square (19103), on Logan Circle, downtown. 215/963-1500; FAX 215/963-9506.* Web www.fshr.com. This elegant eight-story hotel has a magnificent setting on Logan Circle, reminiscent of the Place de la Concorde in Paris. Guest rooms are large and uncluttered, and the spacious marble lobby has an indoor garden with a fountain that makes it easy to forget that this is the heart of a large city. 371 rms, 8 story. S $250-$325; D $280-$355; each addl $30; suites $540-$1,290; under 18 free; wkend rates. Pet accepted. Garage $12-$24. TV; cable (premium), VCR avail. Indoor pool; whirlpool, poolside serv, lifeguard. Restaurants 6:30-1 am; Sat, Sun from 7 am (also see FOUNTAIN and SWANN CAFE; and see SWANN LOUNGE, Unrated Dining). Rm serv 24 hrs. Bar 11-2 am; pianist. Ck-out 1 pm. Convention facilities. Business center. In-rm modem link. Concierge. Beauty shop. Exercise rm; instructor, weights, bicycles, sauna. Massage. Minibars; microwaves avail. Some balconies. Cr cds: A, C, D, ER, JCB, MC, V.

D

★★★ **HOLIDAY INN SELECT-CENTER CITY.** *1800 Market St (19103), in Center City. 215/561-7500; FAX 215/561-4484.* Web www.holidayinnselect-phila.com. 445 rms, 25 story. S $175-$215; D $185-$225; each addl $10; suites $450; under 19 free; wkend rates. Crib free. Garage fee. TV; cable (premium), VCR avail. Pool. Restaurant 6 am-2 am. Bar from 11 am. Ck-out noon. Coin lndry. Convention facilities. Business center. In-rm modem link. Gift shop. Airport transportation. Exercise equipt; weights, bicycles. Health club privileges. Microwaves avail. Luxury level. Cr cds: A, C, D, DS, JCB, MC, V.

D SC

✔★★★ **KORMANSUITES.** *2001 Hamilton St (19130), just off the Pkwy, museum area, in Center City. 215/569-7000; FAX 215/496-0138.* 125 suites, 25 story. S $129-$169, D $159-$189; under 18 free; wkend rates. Crib free. TV; cable (premium). Pool; whirlpool, poolside serv, lifeguard. Complimentary coffee. Restaurant 6:30-2 am. Bar; entertainment. Ck-out 11 am. Convention facilities. Business servs avail. In-rm modem link. Gift shop. Barber, beauty shop. Garage parking. Exercise equipt; weight machine, bicycles. Microwaves. Landscaped Japanese sculpture garden. Cr cds: A, C, D, MC, V.

D SC

★★★ **THE LATHAM.** *135 S 17th St (19103), at Walnut St, downtown. 215/563-7474; FAX 215/563-4034; res: 800/LATHAM-1.* 139 rms, 14 story. S, D $185-$235; each addl $20; suites $325 & $425; under 18 free; wkend, hol rates. Crib free. Valet parking $14. TV; cable (premium), VCR avail (movies). Pool privileges. Restaurant 6:30 am-10:30 pm. Bar 11:30-2 am. Ck-out noon. Meeting rms. Business servs avail. In-rm modem link. Concierge. Exercise equipt; treadmills, bicycles. Many minibars. European ambience in intimate, boutique-style hotel. Cr cds: A, C, D, DS, ER, JCB, MC, V.

D SC

★ ★ ★ **MARRIOTT.** *1201 Market St (19107), in Center City. 215/625-2900; FAX 215/625-6000.* E-mail 74161.1366@compuserv.com. 1,200 rms, 23 story, 56 suites. S $159-$208; D $179-$228; suites $350-$1,000; under 12 free; wkend, hol rates. Crib free. Pet accepted. Valet parking $21. TV; cable (premium), VCR avail. Indoor pool; wading pool, whirlpool, poolside serv. Restaurants 6-1:30 am. 24 hr rm serv. Bar 5 pm-2 am. Ck-out 12:30 pm. Coin lndry. Convention facilities. Business center. In-rm modem link. Concierge. Shopping arcade. Beauty shop. Exercise equipt; weight machine, stair machine, sauna. Refrigerator in suites; microwaves avail. Connected to shopping mall. Luxury level. Cr cds: A, C, D, DS, ER, JCB, MC, V.

D SC

★ ★ ★ **MARRIOTT PHILADELPHIA WEST.** *(111 Crawford Ave, West Conshohocken 19428) 11 mi W on I-76, exit 29. 610/941-5600; FAX 610/940-1060.* 288 rms, 17 story. S $159-$169; D $174-$189; each addl $30; suites $375; wkend, hol rates. Crib free. TV; cable (premium), VCR avail. Indoor pool; whirlpool, poolside serv, lifeguard. Restaurant 6 am-11 pm. Bar. Ck-out 1 pm. Convention facilities. Business servs avail. In-rm modem link. Concierge. Gift shop. Airport, RR station transportation. Exercise equipt; bicycles, stair machines, sauna. Microwaves avail. 1 blk from Schuylkill River. Atrium deck. Luxury level. Cr cds: A, C, D, DS, MC, V.

D SC

★ ★ ★ ★ **OMNI HOTEL AT INDEPENDENCE PARK.** *4th & Chestnut Sts (19106), on Independence Park, adj to Independence Hall, in Olde City. 215/925-0000; FAX 215/925-1263.* Imported marble floors, fine fabrics and classical music greet you in the lobby of this elegant Philadelphia establishment. The thoughtfully detailed rooms offer soothing views of Independence Park, a peaceful oasis in the heart of the city. The pool, spa and health club have been renovated for luxury and comfort. 150 rms, 14 story. S $229; D $249; each addl $20; suites from $300; under 18 free; wkend rates. Garage, valet parking (fees). TV; cable (premium), VCR avail. Indoor pool; whirlpool. Restaurant (see AZALEA). Rm serv 24 hrs. Bar 3-11 pm; entertainment Tues-Sat. Ck-out 11 am. Meeting rms. Business center. In-rm modem link. Concierge. Gift shop. Exercise equipt; weight machine, bicycles, sauna. Massage. Bathrm phones, minibars; microwaves avail. Cr cds: A, C, D, DS, ER, JCB, MC, V.

D SC

★ ★ ★ ★ **PARK HYATT PHILADELPHIA AT THE BELLEVUE.** *Broad & Walnut Sts (19102), downtown. 215/893-1776; FAX 215/893-9868; res: 800/221-0833.* Web www.hyatt.com. This classic hotel, located on the Avenue of Arts, occupies the top seven stories of a landmark building. It has lavish public rooms, including the seven-story Conservatory atrium and the stained-glass-domed Barrymore Room in which high tea is served. Guest rooms are spacious and pleasant. 170 rms, 7 story. S $225-$295; D $250-$320; suites $350-$1,800; under 18 free; special plans. Crib free. Garage $14, valet $21. TV; cable (premium), VCR. Indoor pool privileges; whirlpool, sauna, lifeguard. Restaurants 7 am-11 pm (also see THE FOUNDERS). Rm serv 24 hrs. Bar 11-1 am; entertainment. Ck-out 1 pm. In-rm modem link. Concierge. Shopping arcade. Barber, beauty shop. Massage. Health club privileges. Bathrm phones, minibars. Cr cds: A, C, D, DS, ER, JCB, MC, V.

D SC

★ ★ ★ **PENN'S VIEW.** *Front & Market Sts (19106), in Olde City. 215/922-7600; FAX 215/922-7642; res: 800/331-7634.* E-mail 74161.355. compuserve.com. 40 rms, 5 story. S, D $108-$185; under 12 free; wkend rates. Crib free. TV; cable, VCR avail. Complimentary continental bkfst. Dining rm (see RISTORANTE PANORAMA). Ck-out noon, ck-in 4 pm. Meeting rms. Business servs avail. In-rm modem link. Concierge. Airport, RR station, bus depot transportation. Health club privileges. Overlooks Delaware River. Built 1828; Old World elegance. Fireplaces, whirlpools in some rms. Cr cds: A, C, D, ER, JCB, MC, V.

D SC

★ ★ ★ **RADISSON.** *500 Stevens Dr (19113), at Intl Airport (US 291), south of downtown. 610/521-5900; FAX 610/521-4362.* Web www. radisson.com. 353 rms, 12 story. S $135; D $145; each addl $10; suites $165; under 18 free; wkend packages. Crib free. TV; cable. Indoor pool; whirlpool, poolside serv. Restaurant 6:30 am-2 pm, 5-11 pm. Bars 2 pm-midnight. Ck-out noon. Meeting rms. Business center. In-rm modem link. Gift shop. Free airport transportation. Exercise equipt; weight machine, bicycles. Game rm. Microwaves avail. Atrium. Cr cds: A, C, D, DS, ER, MC, V.

D SC

★ ★ ★ **RADISSON-NORTHEAST.** *(2400 Old Lincoln Hwy, Trevose 19053) 16 mi N on I-95, exit 24. 215/638-8300; FAX 215/638-4377.* 282 rms, 6 story. S $119; D $130; each addl $10; suites $199-$299; under 18 free; family rates. TV; cable (premium), VCR avail. Complimentary coffee in rms. Restaurant 6:30 am-10 pm; Sun 7 am-noon, 5-10 pm. Bar noon-2 am; entertainment. Ck-out noon. Convention facilities. Business servs avail. In-rm modem link. Concierge. Gift shop. Barber, beauty shop. Coin lndry. Exercise equipt; bicycle, treadmill. Indoor/outdoor pool; poolside serv, lifeguard. Game rm. Some refrigerators; wet bars. Some balconies. Cr cds: A, C, D, DS, ER, JCB, MC, V.

D SC

✔★ ★ ★ **RADNOR.** *(591 E Lancaster, St Davids 19087) 17 mi W on US 30, 1/4 mi W of Blue Rte (I-476) exit 5. 610/688-5800; FAX 610/341-3299; res: 800/537-3000.* 170 rms, 4 story. S $145-$160; D $155-$170; each addl $10; suites $220; under 16 free. Crib free. TV; cable (premium), VCR avail. Pool; wading pool, lifeguard. Restaurant (see ABBEY GRILL). Rm serv 24 hrs. Bar 11-2 am; entertainment wkends. Ck-out noon. Meeting rms. Business center. In-rm modem link. Airport transportation. Exercise equipt; weight machine, rower. Game rm. Microwaves avail. Luxury level. Cr cds: A, C, D, DS, ER, JCB, MC, V.

D SC

★ ★ ★ ★ **THE RITTENHOUSE.** *210 W Rittenhouse Square (19103), downtown. 215/546-9000; FAX 215/732-3364; res: 800/635-1042.* E-mail hotel@rittenhouse.com. Subdued elegance and superior, intimate service are the hallmarks of the lower floors of a residential building on fashionable Rittenhouse Square, a verdant park in central Philadelphia. The hotel is suitable for business travelers, family vacationers and honeymooners. 133 rms, 9 story. S, D $315-$340; suites $475-$1,200; wkend rates. Crib free. Pet accepted. Garage; valet parking $23. TV; cable (premium), VCR (movies avail). Indoor pool; poolside serv. Restaurants (see NICHOLAS NICKOLAS, NICK'S and TREETOPS). Rm serv 24 hrs. Bar; entertainment. Ck-out 1 pm. Meeting rms. Business center. In-rm modem link. Concierge. Barber, beauty shop. Exercise rm; instructor, weight machine, bicycles, sauna, steam rm. Massage. Bathrm phones, minibars; microwaves avail. Cr cds: A, C, D, DS, MC, V.

D

★ ★ ★ ★ **THE RITZ-CARLTON, PHILADELPHIA.** *17th & Chestnut Sts (19103), at Liberty Place, downtown. 215/563-1600; FAX 215/567-2822.* Web www.ritzcarlton.com. The opulent decor of this contemporary hotel includes Italian mantelpieces, silk wallpaper and an art collection worth one million dollars. The fully appointed guest rooms are furnished in refined colonial style. 290 rms, 15 story. S, D $245-$305; suites $395-$1,250; wkend rates. Crib free. Garage (fee). TV; cable (premium), VCR avail. Restaurants (see THE DINING ROOM and THE GRILL). Rm serv 24 hrs. Bar 11-1 am; pianist. Ck-out noon. Meeting rms. Business center. In-rm modem link. Concierge. Gift shop. Airport, RR station transportation. Exercise equipt; weights, bicycles, sauna. Massage. Health club privileges. Bathrm phones, minibars. Luxury level. Cr cds: A, C, D, DS, ER, JCB, MC, V.

D

★ ★ ★ **SHERATON SOCIETY HILL.** *1 Dock St (19106), in Society Hill. 215/238-6000; FAX 215/922-2709.* Web www.ITTsheraton.com. 365 units, 4 story. S, D $169-$225; suites $375-$3,000; under 17 free; wkend rates. Crib free. Pet accepted. Covered parking (fee). TV; cable (premium), VCR avail. Indoor pool; whirlpool, wading pool, poolside serv. Coffee in rms. Restaurants 6:30 am-2 pm, 5-10 pm. Rm serv 24 hrs. Bar noon-2 am. Ck-out noon. Convention facilities. Business servs avail. In-rm modem link. Concierge. Shopping arcade. Exercise rm; instructor, weights, bicycles, sauna. Massage. Minibars; some refrigerators. Cr cds: A, C, D, DS, ER, JCB, MC, V.

D SC

★ ★ **TRAVELODGE.** *2015 Penrose Ave (19145), in Packer Park subdivision, near Intl Airport, south of downtown. 215/755-6500; FAX 215/465-7517.* 208 rms, 17 story. S $79-$99; D $89-$109; each addl $6; under 18 free; wkly, wkend, hol rates; higher rates special events. Crib free. Pet accepted, some restrictions; $35. TV; cable (premium). Heated pool; wading pool, poolside serv. Complimentary continental bkfst. Complimentary coffee in rms. Restaurant 6:30 am-10 pm. Bar 7-2 am. Ck-out noon. Coin lndry. Meeting rms. Business servs avail. In-rm modem link. Gift shop. Free airport, RR station transportation. Tennis privileges. 18-hole golf privileges. Exercise equipt; weights, bicycle. Some refrigerators; microwaves avail. Cr cds: A, C, D, DS, JCB, MC, V.

D SC

★ ★ ★ **THE WARWICK.** *1701 Locust St (19103), downtown. 215/735-6000; FAX 215/790-7766; res: 800/523-4210 (exc PA).* 180 rms, 20 story, 20 kits. S $165-$185; D $195-$200; each addl $15; suites $185-$390; studio rms $185; apt $195; under 12 free; wkend plans. Crib free. Pet accepted, some restrictions. Garage (fee). TV; cable (premium), VCR avail. Restaurant 6:30 am-midnight. Bar 11-2 am. Ck-out noon. Meeting rms. Business servs avail. In-rm modem link. Concierge. Barber, beauty shop. Health club privileges. Cr cds: A, C, D, MC, V.

D SC

★ ★ ★ **WESTIN SUITES.** *4101 Island Ave (19153), at I-95 Island Ave exit, near Intl Airport, south of downtown. 215/365-6600; FAX 215/492-8471.* 251 suites, 8 story. S, D $170-$180; each addl $15; under 18 free; wkend rates. Crib free. TV; cable (premium), VCR avail. Indoor pool; whirlpool, lifeguard. Coffee in rms. Restaurant 6 am-11 pm. Bar noon-2 am. Ck-out noon. Meeting rms. Business center. In-rm modem link. Gift shop. Free airport transportation. Exercise equipt; weights, bicycles, sauna, steam rm. Bathrm phones, refrigerators, minibars; microwaves avail. Cr cds: A, C, D, DS, JCB, MC, V.

D SC

★ ★ ★ **WYNDHAM FRANKLIN PLAZA.** *2 Franklin Plaza (19103), jct 17th & Race Sts, downtown. 215/448-2000; FAX 215/448-2864.* E-mail franklinplaza@wyndham.com; web www.wyndham.com. 758 rms, 26 story. S $165-$200; D $175-$210; each addl $20; suites $300-$1,000; under 18 free; wkend rates. Crib free. Pet accepted; some restrictions. Garage $15. TV; cable (premium), VCR avail. Indoor pool; whirlpool, poolside serv. Complimentary coffee in rms. Restaurant 6 am-11 pm. Bars 11-1 am. Ck-out noon. Convention facilities. Business center. In-rm modem link. Drugstore. Barber, beauty shop. Tennis. Exercise rm; instructor, weights, bicycles, sauna, steam rm. Massage. Refrigerators; microwaves avail. Cr cds: A, C, D, DS, ER, JCB, MC, V.

D SC

Inns

✓★ **LA RESERVE.** *1804 Pine St (19103), in Center City. 215/735-1137; res: 800/354-8401; FAX 215/735-0582.* 8 rms, 5 share bath, 4 story, 3 suites. No rm phones. S, D $50-$95; suites $95. Crib avail. TV in common rm; cable (premium), VCR avail (movies). Complimentary full bkfst. Restaurant nearby. Ck-out, ck-in times vary. Business servs avail. Luggage handling. Concierge serv. Street parking. Many fireplaces; microwaves avail. Built in 1868. Victorian decor; antiques. Totally nonsmoking. Cr cds: A, MC, V.

✓★ **THOMAS BOND HOUSE.** *129 S 2nd St (19106), in Olde City. 215/923-8523; FAX 215/923-8504; res: 800/845-2663.* Web www.libertynet.org/phila-visitor. 12 rms, 4 story, 2 suites. No elvtr. S, D $90-$160; each addl $15; suites $160. TV. Complimentary continental bkfst; afternoon refreshments. Restaurants nearby. Ck-out noon, ck-in 3-9 pm. Business servs avail. Airport transportation. Health club privileges. Library/sitting rm; antiques. Restored guest house (1769) built by Dr Thomas Bond, founder of the country's first public hospital. Individually decorated rms. Totally nonsmoking. Cr cds: A, D, DS, MC, V.

★ **WALNUT STREET INN.** *1208 Walnut St (19107), in Center City. 215/546-7000; res: 800/887-1776; FAX 215/546-7573.* E-mail murrayorgn@aol.com. 25 rms, 22 with shower only, 7 story, 6 suites. S, D $95; each addl $15; suites $125. Crib free. Parking adj $9. TV; cable. Complimentary continental bkfst; afternoon refreshments. Complimentary coffee in main rm. Restaurant nearby. Ck-out noon, ck-in 3 pm. Luggage handling. Business servs avail. In-rm modem link. Built in 1890s; early American decor. Walking distance from Pennsylvania Convention Center. Cr cds: A, C, D, DS, MC, V.

SC

Restaurants

★ ★ ★ **ABBEY GRILL.** *(See Radnor Hotel) 610/341-3165.* Hrs: 6:30 am-10 pm; wkends to 11 pm; Sun brunch 10 am-2 pm. Res accepted. Bar to 2 am. Wine list. Semi-a la carte: lunch $5.95-$12.95, dinner $12.95-$19.95. Sun brunch $17.95. Child's meals. Specializes in beef, seafood. Salad bar. Entertainment Fri. Parking. Outdoor dining. Cr cds: A, C, D, DS, ER, JCB, MC, V.

D SC

★ ★ **AMERICAN BISTRO.** *(PA 420 & Morton Ave, Morton 19070) I-95, exit 9A, N on PA 420. 610/543-3033.* Hrs: 11:30 am-2:30 pm, 5-9:30 pm; Sat from 5 pm; Sun 4-8 pm. Closed Mon; some major hols. Res accepted. American fusion menu. Semi-a la carte: lunch $5-$10, dinner $18-$28. Prix fixe $28.95. Specializes in fresh seafood. Parking. Cr cds: A, C, D, DS, MC, V.

★ ★ **ARROYO GRILLE.** *(1 Leverington Ave, Manayunk 19127) 6 mi W on I-76, exit 31, right at 1st light, left on Main St, left on Leverington. 215/487-1400.* Hrs: 11-2 am; Sun brunch to 3 pm. Closed Thanksgiving. Res accepted. Southwestern menu. Bar. A la carte entrees: lunch $5-$8, dinner $13-$16. Sun brunch $16.95. Child's meals. Specializes in smokehouse barbecue, margaritas. Own baking, pasta. Musicians Sun. Outdoor dining. Southwestern decor with woodburning fireplace; two-level dining area. Cr cds: A, DS, MC, V.

D

★ **ASSAGGI ITALIANI.** *935 Ellsworth St (19147), south of downtown. 215/339-0700.* Hrs: 5:30-10 pm; Fri, Sat to 11 pm. Closed Sun; most major hols. Res accepted; required Fri, Sat. Italian menu. Bar. A la carte entrees: dinner $7.50-$19. Specializes in pasta, grilled fish, veal dishes. Own baking.Casual Italian atmosphere. Cr cds: A, D, MC, V.

★ ★ ★ **AZALEA.** *(See Omni Hotel At Independence Park) 215/931-4270.* Hrs: 7 am-2:30 pm, 5:30-10 pm; wkends to 11 pm. Sun brunch 11 am-2 pm. Res accepted. Bar. Extensive wine list. A la carte entrees: bkfst $8.95-$17, lunch $8.75-$16.50, dinner $12.50-$19.50. Sun brunch $21.95. Specializes in venison, duck, seafood. Valet parking. Cr cds: A, C, D, DS, ER, JCB, MC, V.

D SC

★ **BERLENGAS.** *4926 N 5th St (19120), north of downtown. 215/324-3240.* Hrs: noon-10 pm. Closed Wed. Res required Fri-Sun dinner. Portuguese menu. Bar 9 am-midnight. A la carte entrees: lunch, dinner $11-$25. Specializes in seafood. Jacket. Intimate atmosphere. Cr cds: MC, V.

★ ★ **BIG FISH.** *(140 Moorehead Ave, Conshohocken 19428) 11 mi W on I-76, exit 29. 610/834-7224.* Hrs: 11:30 am-10 pm; Fri, Sat to 11 pm, Sun noon-9 pm. Res accepted. Bar. Semi-a la carte: lunch $6-$19, dinner $10-$23. Child's meals. Specializes in fresh seafood. Free parking. Nautical decor. Cr cds: A, C, D, DS, MC, V.

D

★ ★ **BISTRO BIX.** *114 S 12th St (19107), downtown. 215/925-5336.* Hrs: 11 am-3 pm, 5-10 pm; Fri, Sat to 11 pm. Closed some major hols. Res accepted. Continental menu. Bar. Semi-a la carte: lunch $7-$16, dinner $14-$22. Specialties: wild stripped bass, 13 oz. veal chops. Cr cds: A, D, MC, V.

★ ★ **BOOKBINDER'S 15TH STREET SEAFOOD HOUSE.** *215 S 15th St (19102), in Center City. 215/545-1137.* Hrs: 11:30 am-10 pm; Sat 4-11 pm; Sun 3-10 pm. Closed Thanksgiving, Dec 25. Res accepted. Bar. Semi-a la carte: lunch $6-$13.50, dinner $15.95-$24.95. Child's meals. Specializes in seafood, steak. Own pastries. Family-owned since 1893. Cr cds: A, C, D, DS, MC, V.

D

★ ★ ★ ★ **BRASSERIE PERRIER.** *1619 Walnut St (19102), downtown. 215/568-3000.* E-mail saugustine@brasserieperrier.com; web www.brasserieperrier.com. Original paintings and sculpture complement the art-deco decor of this elegant restaurant. Contemporary Amer menu. Specializes in pasta, fresh seafood. Hrs: 5:30-11 pm. Closed most major hols. Res required. Bar to 1 am. Wine cellar. Semi-a la carte: dinner $19-$35. Valet parking. Totally nonsmoking. Cr cds: A, DS, MC, V.

D

✔★ ★ **BRIDGET FOY'S SOUTH STREET GRILL.** *200 South St (19147), near Head House Square, in South Street Area. 215/922-1813.* Hrs: 11:30 am-10:30 pm; Fri, Sat to midnight. Closed Thanksgiving, Dec 25. Res accepted. Bar to 2 am. A la carte entrees: lunch $6.95-$12.95, dinner $11.95-$19.95. Specializes in grilled fish, meat. Valet parking on wkends. Outdoor dining. Cr cds: A, C, D, DS, MC, V.

★ ★ **CAFE NOLA.** *603 S 3rd St (19147), in South Street Area. 215/627-2590.* Web www.cafenola.com. Hrs: noon-4 pm, 5-10 pm; Mon from 5 pm; Fri, Sat to 11 pm; Sun brunch 11 am-3 pm. Res required Fri, Sat. Bar to 2 am. A la carte entrees: lunch $8-$14, dinner $15-$26. Sun brunch $19.50. Specializes in Creole, Cajun dishes. Outdoor dining. Colorful New Orleans decor. Cr cds: A, C, D, DS, MC, V.

D

★ ★ **CARY.** *211 S 15th St (19102), downtown. 215/735-9100.* Web www.caryrestaurant.com. Hrs: 11:30 am-11 pm. Res accepted. Contemporary Amer menu. Bar. A la carte entrees: lunch $4.50-$10.50, dinner $12.50-$18. Child's meals. Specializes in fresh seafood, homemade soups, salads. Valet parking. Outdoor dining. Cr cds: A, D, DS, MC, V.

D

★ ★ ★ **CHANTERELLES.** *1312 Spruce St (19107), downtown. 215/735-7551.* Hrs: 5-10:30 pm; Fri, Sat to 11 pm. Closed Sun, most hols. Res accepted. French, Asian menu. Bar. Wine list. A la carte entrees: $22-$28. Complete meals: $29-$55. Child's meals. Specialties: venison cutlets, rack of lamb. French country inn decor. Totally nonsmoking. Cr cds: A, D, MC, V.

★ ★ ★ **CIBOULETTE.** *200 S Broad St (19102), downtown. 215/790-1210.* Hrs: 5:30-9 pm; Fri, Sat to 10:30 pm. Closed Sun; most major hols. Res accepted; required Sat. French Provençal menu. Bar. Wine cellar. A la carte entrees (appetizer portions): $6-$18. Specialties: roasted Maine lobster, black sea bass, loin of veal. Own desserts. Valet parking. French Renaissance-style architecture; display of local artists; original mosaic tile floor; one rm with ceiling mural. Cr cds: A, MC, V.

D

★ ★ ★ **CIRCA.** *1518 Walnut St (19102), downtown. 215/545-6800.* Web circarestaurant.com. Hrs: 11:30 am-2:30 pm, 5-10 pm; Thurs, Sat to 11 pm; Mon from 5 pm; Sun 4:30-9 pm. Closed Jan 1, Dec 25. Res accepted. Bar. Wine list. Semi-a la carte: lunch $8-$13, dinner $11-$20. Child's meals. Specialties: roast Chilean sea bass, fire grilled spice-rubbed filet mignon, crazy E's BBQ pork loin chop. Valet parking. Former bank lobby, cathedral ceilings. Cr cds: A, D, MC, V.

D

★ ★ **CITY TAVERN.** *138 S 2nd St at Walnut (19106), in Society Hill area. 215/413-1443.* Web www.staib.com. Hrs: 11:30 am-10:30 pm; Fri, Sat to 11:30 pm. Res accepted. Bar. Semi-a la carte: lunch $8.95-$16.95, dinner $17.95-$26.95. Child's meals. Specializes in fresh fish, poultry, meats. Entertainment Sat. Outdoor dining. Historic colonial tavern (1773). Cr cds: A, C, D, DS, ER, JCB, MC, V.

D

★ ★ **COYOTE CROSSING.** *(800 Spring Mill Rd, Conshohocken 19428) 15 mi W on I-76, exit Conshohocken. 610/825-3000.* Hrs: 11:30 am-2:30 pm, 4:30-9:30 pm; Fri to 10:30 pm; Sat 4:30-10:30 pm; Sun from 4:30 pm. Closed Jan 1, July 4, Dec 25. Southwestern menu. Bar. A la carte entrees: lunch $5.75-$7.95, dinner $10.95-$18.95. Specialties: homemade stuffed crepes, filet mignon. Own baking. Classical guitarist Thurs, Sat. Modern southwestern decor. Cr cds: A, D, DS, MC, V.

D

★ ★ **CUVEE NOTREDAME.** *1701 Green St (19130), downtown. 215/765-2777.* Hrs: 11:30-2 am; Sun brunch 11:30 am-2:30 pm. Closed Thanksgiving, Dec 25. Res accepted. Belgian menu. Bar. A la carte entrees: lunch $5, dinner $15-$21. Sun brunch $5. Child's meals. Specializes in mussels, duck. Belgian atmosphere. Cr cds: A, DS, MC, V.

D

★ ★ ★ **DEUX CHEMINÉES.** *1221 Locust St (19107), downtown. 215/790-0200.* Hrs: 5:30-8:30 pm; Sat to 9 pm. Closed Sun, Mon; major hols. Res accepted. French menu. Serv bar. Wine cellar. Prix fixe: dinner $68. Specialties: rack of lamb, crab soup. Menu changes daily. Own baking. Chef-owned. Totally nonsmoking. Cr cds: A, C, D, MC, V.

♥

★ ★ ★ **DICKENS INN.** *Head House Square (19147), on 2nd St, in Society Hill. 215/928-9307.* Hrs: 11:30 am-3 pm, 5-10 pm; Sat to 10:30 pm; Sun 4:30-9 pm; Sun brunch 11 am-3 pm. Closed Mon; Jan 1, Dec 25. Res accepted. Continental menu. Bar 11:30-2 am; Mon from 5 pm. A la carte entrees: lunch $4.75-$10.75, dinner $12-$22. Sun brunch $14.75. Child's meals. Specialties: roast beef with Yorkshire pudding, beef Wellington, fish & chips. In historic Harper House (1788); Victorian decor; artwork imported from England. Cr cds: A, D, DS, MC, V.

D

★ ★ ★ **DINARDO'S.** *312 Race St (19106), in Olde City. 215/925-5115.* Web www.menusonline.com. Hrs: 11 am-10 pm; Fri, Sat to 11 pm; Sun 3-9 pm. Closed major hols. Bar. Semi-a la carte: lunch $5-$10, dinner $9-$25. Child's meals. Specializes in seafood. Historic bldg (1740). Cr cds: A, C, D, MC, V.

D SC

★ ★ ★ ★ **THE DINING ROOM.** *(See The Ritz-Carlton, Philadelphia Hotel) 215/563-1600.* Web www.ritzcarlton.com. Hardwood floors, crystal chandeliers and blue cobalt stemware set an elegant stage for a traditional fine-dining experience. Chef Trish Morrissey serves up impressive New American cuisine. But arrive early—the restaurant is only open for breakfast and lunch. Specialties: fresh crab cakes, baby rack of lamb with eggplant. Hrs: 6:30 am-2:30 pm; Sun brunch from 11 am. Res accepted. Bar 11-1 am. Wine list. A la carte entrees: bkfst $7-$18, lunch $15-$30. Sun brunch $35. Child's meals. Pianist. Valet parking. Cr cds: A, C, D, DS, ER, JCB, MC, V.

D

★ **DMITRI'S.** *795 S 3rd St (19047), south of downtown. 215/625-0556.* Hrs: 5:30-11 pm; Sun 5-10 pm. Closed Easter, Thanksgiving, Dec 24, 25. Mediterranean menu. Setups. A la carte entrees: $12-$20. Specializes in seafood, lamb. No cr cds accepted.

✔★ ★ **DOCK STREET BREWERY.** *2 Logan Square (19103), at 18th & Cherry Sts, downtown. 215/496-0413.* Hrs: 11:30 am-midnight; Fri to 2 am; Sat noon-2 am; Sun noon-11 pm. Closed Labor Day, Dec 25. Res accepted. Bar. A la carte entrees: lunch $5.75-$9.95, dinner $7-$17.50. Specializes in freshly brewed beer, homemade breads, grilled meats and fish. Entertainment Fri, Sat. Brewery tanks; beer brewed on premises, tours avail Wed, Sat. Dartboard and billiard tables. Cr cds: A, D, DS, MC, V.

D

★ ★ **FELICIA'S.** *1148 S 11th St (19147), south of downtown. 215/755-9656.* Hrs: 11:30-2 am. Closed Mon; most major hols. Res accepted; required Sat, Sun. Italian menu. Bar. Semi-a la carte: lunch $6.95-$12.50, dinner $11.95-$21.95. Specialties: seafood ravioli, ricotta gnocci, ricotta cheesecake, veal chop. Own desserts. Valet parking. Piano in bar. Cr cds: A, C, D, DS, MC, V.

D

✔★★ **FISHER'S SEAFOOD.** *7312 Castor Ave (19152), north of downtown. 215/725-6201.* Hrs: 11 am-9 pm; Fri, Sat to 10 pm; Sun noon-9 pm. Closed Mon; Labor Day, Thanksgiving, Dec 25. Res accepted. Bar. Semi-a la carte: lunch $3.25-$6.95, dinner $6.25-$12.95. Complete meals: lunch $4.95-$9.20, dinner $7.95-$15.95. Child's meals. Specializes in seafood, stir-fried dishes. Parking. Six large dining areas, individually decorated. Family-owned. Cr cds: DS, MC, V.

D

★★ **FLYING FISH.** *8142 Germantown Ave (19118), in Chestnut Hill. 215/247-0707.* Hrs: 11:30 am-2:30 pm, 5:30-9 pm; Mon from 5:30 pm; Fri, Sat noon-2:30 pm, 5:30-10 pm. Closed Sun; some major hols. Bar. A la carte entrees: lunch $6.50-$8.75, dinner $13-$22. Child's meals. Specializes in seafood, clam bake (summer). Own pasta, pastries, ice cream. Totally nonsmoking. Cr cds: MC, V.

D

★★★ **THE FOUNDERS.** *(See Park Hyatt Philadelphia At The Bellevue Hotel) 215/790-2814.* Web www.hyatt.com. Hrs: 6:30 am-2:30 pm, 5-11 pm; Sun brunch 10:30 am-3 pm; pre-theater dinner $5:30-6:30 pm. Res accepted. French, Asian menu. Bar 11-2 am. Wine cellar. Complete meals: bkfst $9.50-$12.50, dinner $65. A la carte entrees: lunch $9.50-$16.50, dinner $24-$36. Sun brunch $34.50. Specialties: filet de boeuf à la Moëlle, red snapper en papillote. Entertainment. Valet parking. Rotunda with sweeping views of city. Elegant turn-of-the-century decor. Jacket (dinner). Cr cds: A, C, D, DS, ER, JCB, MC, V.

D SC

★★★★ **FOUNTAIN.** *(See Four Seasons Hotel Philadelphia) 215/963-1500.* Web www.fshr.com. This quiet, luxurious restaurant, nestled in the lavish yet dignified lobby of the Four Seasons, maintains the atmosphere of a private club. Breads and pastries are made on site; entrees are predominantly local and American. Continental menu. Specialties: rack of lamb, sautèed snapper, sautéed venison medallion. Own baking, desserts. Hrs: 6:30 am-2:30 pm, 6-10:30 pm; Sun brunch 11 am-2:30 pm. Res accepted. Bar to 2 am. Wine cellar. A la carte entrees: bkfst $12-$17, lunch $22-$27.50, dinner $32-$38. Prix fixe: 4-course dinner $74. Sun brunch $31-$39. Child's meals. Entertainment. Valet parking. Jacket (dinner). Cr cds: A, C, D, DS, MC, V.

D

★★★ **THE GARDEN.** *1617 Spruce St (19103), downtown. 215/546-4455.* Web www.thegardenrestaurant.com. Hrs: 11:30 am-1:30 pm, 5:30-9:30 pm; Mon, Sat from 5:30 pm. Closed Sun; major hols. Res accepted. Continental menu. Bar. Extensive wine list. A la carte entrees: lunch $10.95-$24.95, dinner $16.95-$25.95. Specializes in fresh seafood, aged prime beef. Valet parking. Spacious outdoor dining. City skyline views. Cr cds: A, C, D, MC, V.

★★★ **THE GRILL.** *(See The Ritz-Carlton, Philadelphia Hotel) 215/563-1600.* Web www.ritzcarlton.com. Hrs: 6:30 am-2:30 pm; 5:30-10:30 pm; Sat, Sun from 5:30 pm. Res accepted. Bar. Semi-a la carte: bkfst $7-$18, lunch $12-$28. A la carte entrees: dinner $19-$40. Specializes in grilled beef, seafood. Club atmosphere. Cr cds: A, C, D, DS, ER, JCB, MC, V.

D

★★★ **HARRY'S BAR & GRILL.** *22 S 18th St, downtown. 215/561-5757.* Hrs: 11:30 am-1:45 pm, 5:30-9 pm; Fri to 1:45 pm. Closed Sat, Sun; major hols. Res accepted. Italian, Amer menu. Bar 11:30 am-9 pm. Wine cellar. A la carte entrees: lunch $9.95-$23.95, dinner $14.95-$23.95. Specializes in fresh seafood, homemade pasta, aged prime steak. Own pastries. Parking. English club atmosphere. Cr cds: A, C, D, MC, V.

D

✔★ **HO SAI GAI.** *1000 Race St (19107), in Chinatown. 215/922-5883.* Hrs: 11:30-4 am; Fri, Sat to 5 am. Closed Thanksgiving. Res accepted. Chinese menu. Serv bar. Semi-a la carte: lunch $4.95-$8.95, dinner $9-$15.95. Specializes in Mandarin & Hunan cuisine. Cr cds: A, C, MC, V.

★★ **HUSCH.** *(301 Woodbine Ave, Narberth 19072) 7 mi N on I-76, exit City Line, follow Montgomery Ave to Woodbine Ave. 610/668-6393.* Hrs: 11 am-2:30 pm, 5-10 pm; Fri to 11 pm; Sat 11 am-3 pm (brunch), 5-11 pm; Sun 11 am-3 pm (brunch), 5-10 pm. Closed Dec 25. Res accepted; required Fri, Sat dinner. Continental menu. Bar. A la carte entrees: lunch $6-$9, dinner $12-$25. Sat, Sun brunch $6-$11. Child's meals. Specializes in tuna, rack of lamb, sushi. Own baking. Contemporary atmosphere; blends East and West Coast styles. Cr cds: A, MC, V.

D

★★ **ISABELLA'S.** *6516 Castor Ave (19149), I-95N, exit Cottman Ave, to Castor Ave, north of downtown. 215/533-0356.* Hrs: 5:30-9 pm; Fri, Sat to 9:30 pm; Sun to 8 pm. Closed Mon; Easter, Thanksgiving, Dec 25. Res required. French, Italian menu. Bar. Semi-a la carte: dinner $13.50-$20.50. Child's meals. Specialties: shrimp and crab risotto cakes, potato gnocchi, grilled whole striped bass. Own baking. Intimate atmosphere with modern European decor. Cr cds: A, D, MC, V.

D

★★ **ITALIAN BISTRO.** *211 S Broad St (19107), downtown. 215/731-0700.* Hrs: 11:30 am-11 pm; wkends 12:30 pm-midnight. Closed Dec 25. Res accepted. Bar. Complete meals: lunch $5.50-$6.25. A la carte entrees: dinner $8-$18. Child's meals. Specializes in Northern Italian dishes, brick oven pizza. Own pasta, desserts. Cr cds: A, D, DS, MC, V.

D

★★★ **JAKE'S.** *(4365 Main St, Manayunk 19127) I-76, exit 31. 215/483-0444.* Web www.jakes_restaurant.com. Hrs: 11:30 am-2:30 pm, 5:30-9:30 pm; Sun 10:30 am-2:30 pm, 5-9 pm. Closed Jan 1, Thanksgiving, Dec 25. Res accepted. Contemporary Amer menu. Bar. Extensive wine list. A la carte entrees: lunch $7-$15, dinner $18-$30. Child's meals. Sun brunch $7-$13. Specialties: crab cakes, barbecue salmon, tuna. Valet parking. Cr cds: A, D, MC, V.

★★ **KANSAS CITY PRIME.** *(4417 Main St, Manayunk 19127) off I-76, exit 31. 215/482-3700.* Web www.kansascityprime.com. Hrs: 5:30-11 pm; Sun 5-10 pm. Closed Thanksgiving. Res accepted. Bar to 2 am. A la carte entrees: dinner $17-$31. Specializes in aged prime beef, grilled seafood. Contemporary decor. Cr cds: A, C, D, DS, JCB, MC, V.

D

★ **KNAVE OF HEARTS.** *230 South St (19147), in South Street Area. 215/922-3956.* Hrs: noon-4 pm, 5:30-10:30 pm; Fri, Sat to 11:30 pm; Sun 5-10 pm; Sun brunch 11 am-4 pm. Closed Dec 25. Res accepted. Bar. A la carte entrees: lunch $5-$9, dinner $12-$20. Sun brunch $12.50-$13.50. Specialties: filet mignon, roast duckling. Intimate dining. Cr cds: A, MC, V.

★★★ **LA FAMIGLIA.** *8 S Front St (19106), in Olde City. 215/922-2803.* Hrs: noon-2 pm, 5:30-9:30 pm; Sat 5:30-10 pm; Sun 5-9 pm. Closed Mon; major hols; also last wk Aug. Res required. Italian menu. Bar. Wine cellar. A la carte entrees: lunch $12.95-$19.95, dinner $22-$40. Specializes in veal, fresh fish, pasta. Own desserts. Built in 1878 in one of city's first blocks of buildings. Jacket. Cr cds: A, C, D, MC, V.

★★★ **LE BAR LYONNAIS.** *1523 Walnut St (19102), downstairs at Le Bec Fin, downtown. 215/567-1000.* Web www.lebecfin.com. Hrs: 11:30-1:30 am; Sat 6-9 pm. Closed Sun; major hols. French bistro menu. Bar. A la carte entrees: lunch, dinner $12-$18. Specialties: escargots au champagne, galette de crabe, thon au poivres. Valet parking (dinner). Elegant bistro atmosphere; original art. Cr cds: A, C, D, DS, MC, V.

★ ★ **LE BAR NOSTRADAMUS.** *1701 Green St (19130), downtown. 215/765-3360.* Hrs: 5 pm-2 am. Closed Thanksgiving, Dec 25. Res accepted. Belgian steakhouse menu. Bar. A la carte entrees: dinner $15-$21. Specializes in steaks, chops. Musicians Fri. Casual atmosphere; humorous artwork, brick fireplace. Cr cds: A, D, DS, MC, V.

★ ★ ★ ★ ★ **LE BEC-FIN.** *1523 Walnut St (19102), downtown. 215/567-1000.* Web www.lebecfin.com. There's probably no better French cuisine outside France than at this fine dining room decorated in Louis XVI style with crystal chandeliers, red silk wallpaper and gilt mirrors. The prix-fixe dinner is steep, but it includes six superb courses featuring a broad choice of delicately prepared appetizers, fish, meats and desserts. French menu. Specializes in seasonal dishes. Own baking. Sittings: lunch 11:30 am & 1:30 pm, dinner 6 & 9 pm; Fri & Sat dinner 9:30 pm. Closed Sun; major hols. Res required. Bar to 1 am. Wine cellar. Prix fixe: lunch $36, dinner $102. Valet parking (dinner). Chef-owned. Jacket. Cr cds: A, C, D, DS, MC, V.

D

★ ★ ★ **THE MARKER.** *(See Adam's Mark Hotel) 215/581-5010.* Hrs: 11 am-2:30 pm, 5:30-10 pm; Fri to 11 pm; Sat, Sun 5:30-11 pm; Sun brunch 10:30 am-2:30 pm. Closed some major hols. Res accepted. Contemporary Amer menu. Bar. Wine cellar. Semi-a la carte: lunch $8.95-$13.95, dinner $17.95-$25.95. Sun brunch $22.95. Specialties: lemon mint-cured salmon, wasabi and citrus-crusted tuna mignon, lavender-honey and apple cider-glazed duck. Own baking, pasta. Pianist. Formal French and English decor with stained glass, tapestries, stone fireplace and gold-plated chandelier. Jacket. Cr cds: A, C, D, DS, MC, V.

D

★ ★ ★ **MEIJI-EN.** *Pier 19 North (19106), Columbus Ave at Callowhill St, Delaware River Waterfront, in Olde City. 215/592-7100.* Hrs: 5-9:30 pm; Fri, Sat to 11 pm; Sun brunch 10:30 am-3 pm. Res accepted, required for brunch. Japanese menu. Bar; wkends to 1 am. A la carte entrees: $13-$30. Sun brunch $19.95. Specializes in sushi, tempura, teppanyaki-grilled items. Jazz Fri-Sun brunch. Valet parking. Overlooks Delaware River. Cr cds: A, C, D, DS, MC, V.

D ♥

★ ★ **MICHAEL'S.** *824 S 8th St (19147), south of downtown. 215/922-3986.* Web www.michaelsristorante.com. Hrs: 5-11 pm; Sun 3-10 pm. Closed Mon. Res accepted. Italian menu. Bar. A la carte entrees: dinner $10.95-$23.95. Child's meals. Specialties: veal chop, gnocchi. Valet parking. Exposed brick, stucco walls; statuary in alcoves. Bronze, glass chandeliers. Cr cds: A, C, D, DS, MC, V.

D

★ ★ **MIDDLE EAST.** *126 Chestnut St (19106), in Olde City. 215/922-1003.* Hrs: 5 pm-midnight; Fri, Sat to 2 am; Sun from 3 pm. Closed Thanksgiving, Dec 24, 25. Res accepted. Middle Eastern, Amer menu. Bar. Semi-a la carte: dinner $14.50-$21.50. Specialty: shish kebab. Middle Eastern band Fri-Sat. Middle Eastern decor. Cr cds: A, C, D, DS, MC, V.

D SC

★ ★ ★ **MONTE CARLO LIVING ROOM.** *2nd & South Sts (19147), in South Street Area. 215/925-2220.* Hrs: 6-10:30 pm; Fri, Sat 5:30-11 pm; Sun 5-9 pm. Closed major hols. Res accepted. Northern Italian menu. Bar. Wine cellar. A la carte entrees: dinner $28-$40. Degustation dinner $65. Specializes in fresh fish, veal, beef. Daily menu. Own pastries. Mediterranean decor. Jacket. Cr cds: A, D, MC, V.

✔★ ★ ★ **MOONSTRUCK.** *7955 Oxford Ave (19111), north of downtown. 215/725-6000.* Hrs: 5-9 pm; Fri, Sat to 10 pm; Sun 4:30-8 pm. Closed Jan 1, July 4, Dec 25. Italian menu. Wine cellar. Semi-a la carte: dinner $14-$20. Specializes in homemade pasta, veal dishes, seafood. Own pastries. Parking. Cr cds: A, D, MC, V.

D

★ ★ ★ **MOSHULU.** *Pier 34 (19147), in South Street area. 215/923-2500.* Hrs: 11:30 am-3 pm, 5:30-10 pm; Sun 11 am-2 pm (brunch), 5:30-10 pm. Closed Jan 1, Dec 25. Res accepted. Continental menu. Bar to midnight. Wine cellar. Semi-a la carte: lunch $7-$14, dinner $17-$28. Sun brunch $19.95. Specializes in steak, seafood. Entertainment Wed-Sat. Valet parking. Outdoor dining. Restored 400-ft sailing ship (1904); turn-of-the-century nautical decor with mahogany paneling and brass trim. Jacket. Cr cds: A, D, DS, MC, V.

D

★ **NAIS CUISINE.** *(13-17 W Benedict Ave, Haverstown 19083) I-476, exit 3. 610/789-5983.* Hrs: 5-9 pm, wkends to 10 pm. Res accepted, required Fri, Sat. French menu with Thai influence. A la carte entrees: $13.25-$23.50. Specialties: roast duckling, steamed salmon stuffed with crab meat, snow pea salad. Cr cds: A, MC, V.

★ ★ ★ **NAPOLEON.** *1500 Locust St (19102), downtown. 215/893-9100.* Hrs: 11:30 am-2:30 pm, 5-10 pm; Fri to 11 pm; Sat 5-11 pm; Sun from 5 pm. Closed major hols. Res required. Continental menu. Bar. Extensive wine list. A la carte entrees: lunch $8-$15, dinner $15-$28. Specializes in beef, fish, chicken. Own pasta. Valet parking. Modern decor with old-world charm. Cr cds: A, MC, V.

D

✔★ ★ **NEW MEXICO GRILLE.** *50 S 2nd St (19106), in Olde City. 215/922-7061.* E-mail losamigos@hotmail.com; web www.losamigos.com. Hrs: 11:30 am-10 pm; Fri, Sat to 1:30 am; Sun noon-10 pm. Closed some major hols. Southwestern menu. Bar. Semi-a la carte: lunch $4.95-$11.95, dinner $11.95-$20.95. Specializes in grilled meats, seafood. Cr cds: A, C, D, MC, V.

D

★ ★ ★ **NICHOLAS NICKOLAS.** *(See The Rittenhouse Hotel) 215/546-8440.* Web www.harman-nickolas.com. Hrs: 5:30-10:30 pm; Fri, Sat to 11 pm. Closed Sun. Res accepted. Continental menu. Bar 11:30-2 am; Sat from 5 pm. Wine cellar. A la carte entrees: dinner $19-$46. Specialties: lobster thermidor, cioppino Raymondo, prime cowboy steak. Pianist. Valet parking. Modern decor; view of Rittenhouse Square. Totally nonsmoking. Cr cds: A, C, D, DS, MC, V.

D

✔★ ★ **NICK'S.** *(See The RittenhouseHotel) 215/546-8440.* Web www.harman-nickolas.com. Hrs: 11:30-2 am. Closed Sun. Bar from 5:30 pm. Semi-a la carte: lunch, dinner $13.50-$14.95. Specializes in portabella sandwiches, blue plate special, salads. Pianist. Valet parking. Piano and sports bar; large aquarium. Cr cds: A, C, D, DS, MC, V.

D

★ ★ ★ **OLD ORIGINAL BOOKBINDER'S.** *125 Walnut St (19106), in Society Hill. 215/925-7027.* E-mail johnny@lobsters.com; web www.oldbookbinders.com. Hrs: 11:45 am-10 pm; Sat 4:30-10 pm; Sun 3-9 pm. Closed Thanksgiving, Dec 25. Res accepted. Bars. Wine list. Complete meals: lunch $7.95-$14.95, dinner $16.95-$35. Child's meals. Specializes in lobster, snapper soup, mile high desserts. Own pastries. Valet parking. Established 1865; in historic bldg. Family-owned. Cr cds: A, C, D, DS, MC, V.

D ♥

★ ★ ★ **OPUS 251.** *251 S 18th St (19103), downtown. 215/735-6787.* Web www.nitescene.com/opus251. Hrs: 11 am-2:30 pm, 5-10 pm; Fri, Sat to 11 pm; Sun to 9 pm; Sun brunch to 3 pm. Closed Mon; Memorial Day, Thanksgiving, Dec 25. Res required (dinner). Bar. Wine cellar. Semi-a la carte: lunch $3.75-$10.75, dinner $14-$24.50. Sun brunch $15. Specialties: Cervena venison mignonettes, eggplant pasta pillows, sun-dried tomato-dusted red snapper. Own baking, sausage, ice cream. Valet parking. Outdoor dining. Casually elegant dining in Philadelphia Art Alliance; arched windows, European garden. Cr cds: A, D, MC, V.

D

★ ★ ★ **OVERTURES.** *609 E Passyunk Ave (19147), in South Street area. 215/627-3455.* Hrs: 6-10:30 pm; Sun 5-9:30 pm. Closed Mon, hols. Res accepted. Mediterranean menu. Setups. A la carte entrees: $10-$28. Specialties: sautéed veal sweetbreads in port, roast saddle of lamb. Cr cds: A, C, D, MC, V.

★ ★ **THE PALM.** *200 S Broad St (19102), downtown. 215/546-7256.* Hrs: 11:30 am-11 pm; Sat from 5 pm; Sun 4:30-9 pm. Closed most major hols. Res accepted. Bar. A la carte entrees: lunch $7.50-$18, dinner $16.50-$40. Specializes in fresh seafood, prime aged beef, lamb chops. Valet parking. Counterpart of famous New York restaurant. Caricatures of celebrities. Cr cds: A, C, D, MC, V.

D

✔ ★ ★ **PEACOCK ON THE PARKWAY.** *1700 Benjamin Franklin Pkwy (19103), downtown. 215/569-8888.* Hrs: 11:30 am-3 pm, 5:30-10 pm; Sat from 5:30 pm. Closed Sun. Continental menu. Prix fixe: lunch $10, dinner $15. Semi-a la carte: dinner $11.95-$16.95. Child's meals. Specialties: lobster, shrimp and scallops over portabello mushroom; shish-kebob mix; crispy duck with wild berries. Own baking. Valet parking. Outdoor dining. Three-level dining area overlooks parkway; casual dining. Cr cds: A, C, D, MC, V.

D

★ ★ **POMPANO GRILLE.** *701 E Passyunk Ave (19147), at 5th & Bainbridge, in South Street area. 215/923-7676.* Hrs: 5 pm-2 am. Closed Dec 25. Res accepted. Caribbean fusion menu. Bar. A la carte entrees: dinner $15-$23. Complete meals: dinner $25-$50. Specializes in shrimp, crab cakes. Own baking. Musicians Fri, Sat. Valet parking. Outdoor dining. Converted bank bldg has large windows and three dining levels. Cr cds: A, MC, V.

D

★ ★ **PROVENCE.** *(379 Lancaster Ave, Haverford 19041) 13 mi W on I-76, exit Villa Nova, to US 30E (Lancaster Ave). 610/896-0400.* Hrs: 11:30 am-2:30 pm, 5:30-10 pm; Fri, Sat to 11 pm; Sun to 9 pm; Sun brunch to 2:30 pm. Closed most major hols. Res accepted; required dinner. French Provençale menu. Bar. A la carte entrees: lunch $10-$15, dinner $17-$25. Sun brunch $10-$22. Child's meals. Specialties: marinated venison with figs, seared yellowfin tuna, shrimp and crab Napoleon. Own baking, pasta. Cr cds: A, D, MC, V.

♥

✔ ★ ★ **RANGOON.** *112 N 9th St (19107), in Chinatown. 215/829-8939.* Hrs: 11:30 am-9 pm; Fri to 10 pm; Sat 1-10 pm; Sun from 1 pm. Closed Mon; July 4, Thanksgiving, Dec 25. Res accepted. Burmese menu. Bar. Semi-a la carte: lunch $4.50-$12.50, dinner $8.50-$12.50. Specializes in salads, curry dishes, appetizers. Authentic Burmese atmosphere. Totally nonsmoking. Cr cds: MC, V.

D

★ ★ **RISTORANTE ALBERTO.** *(1415 City Line Ave, Wynnewood 19096) I-76 W to City Line Ave exit. 610/896-0275.* Hrs: 11:30 am-2:30 pm, 5-10 pm; Fri, Sat 5-11 pm; Sun from 4 pm. Closed Jan 1, Thanksgiving, Dec 25. Res accepted; required Fri, Sat. Northern Italian menu. Bar. A la carte entrees: lunch $5.95-$11.95; dinner $12.95-$22.95. Specialties: grilled Dover sole, double veal chop. Own pasta. Valet parking. Display of wine bottles; original art. Cr cds: A, C, D, MC, V.

D

★ ★ ★ **RISTORANTE PANORAMA.** *(See Penn's View Hotel) 215/922-7800.* Hrs: noon-2:30 pm, 5:30-10 pm; Fri, Sat 5:30-11 pm. Closed most major hols. Res accepted, required wkends. Italian menu. Bar. Extensive wine list. A la carte entrees: lunch, dinner $14.50-$22.95. Child's meals. Specializes in veal, seafood. Own pasta. Parking. Cr cds: A, C, D, ER, JCB, MC, V.

D

★ **RIVER CITY DINER.** *(3720 Main St, Manayunk 19127) 6 mi W on I-76, exit 31, at Ridge & Main. 215/483-7500.* E-mail mainstr @axs2000.net; web www.rivercitydiner.com. Hrs: 7-2 am; Fri, Sat to 4 am. Bar. A la carte entrees: bkfst, lunch, dinner $4-$12. Child's meals. Specialties: chicken-in-a-pot, grilled River City Caesar salad, Kansas City meatloaf. Outdoor dining. Dramatic diner decor with stainless steel, glass and granite. Cr cds: A, C, D, DS, MC, V.

D

★ ★ ★ **ROCOCO.** *123 Chestnut St (19106), in Olde City. 215/629-1100.* Hrs: 5-11 pm; Fri, Sat to midnight; Sun to 10 pm. Closed Dec 25. Res accepted. Eclectic menu. Bar to 2 am. Wine cellar. Semi-a la carte: dinner $12-$24. Specializes in seafood, beef, lamb. Valet parking. European decor in converted bank bldg; cathedral ceiling. Cr cds: A, D, MC, V.

D

★ ★ ★ **THE SALOON.** *750 S 7th St (19148), in South Street area. 215/627-1811.* Hrs: 11:30 am-2 pm, 5-10 pm; Sat to midnight. Closed Sun, hols. Res accepted. Italian menu. Bar. Wine list. A la carte entrees: lunch, dinner $18-$28. Specializes in veal, steak, seafood. Pianist Wed-Sat. Parking. Family-owned. Cr cds: A.

✔ ★ ★ **SERRANO.** *20 S 2nd St (19106), in Olde City. 215/928-0770.* Hrs: 5-10:30 pm; Fri, Sat to 11:30 pm; Sun 4-10 pm. Closed major hols. Res accepted. International menu. Bar. A la carte entrees: dinner $8-$18. Specialties: chicken Hungarian, Malaysian pork chops, Korean rolled bulgogi. Own desserts. Entertainment Wed-Sat. Theatrical decor with puppets and tapestries from around the world. Cr cds: A, D, DS, MC, V.

D

★ ★ **SIGGIE'S L'AUBERGE.** *(101 Ford St, West Conshohocken 19428) 15 mi W on I-76, exit 28B. 610/828-6262.* Hrs: 11:30 am-2:30 pm, 5:30-10 pm; Fri to 11 pm; Sat 5:30-11 pm. Closed Sun; major hols. Res required. Continental menu. Bar. A la carte entrees: lunch $8.95-$11.95, dinner $19.95-$24.95. Specialties: crisp shrimp with fruit sauce, jumbo lump crab cakes, sea bass. Valet parking. Rustic French decor. Jacket. Cr cds: A, MC, V.

D

✔ ★ ★ **SONOMA.** *(4411 Main St, Manayunk 19127) 6 mi W on I-76, exit 31, at Main & Gay Sts. 215/483-9400.* Hrs: 11 am-11 pm; Fri, Sat to midnight; early-bird dinner Sun-Thurs 5-6 pm; Sun brunch to 3:30 pm. Continental menu. Bar to 2 am. Semi-a la carte: lunch, dinner $6.50-$14. Sun brunch $6-$12. Child's meals. Specialties: refried risotto, honey-lavender hickory-roasted salmon, garlic-grilled ribeye steak. Own baking, pasta. Valet parking. Outdoor dining. Modern, eclectic decor; revolving art display. Cr cds: A, C, D, DS, MC, V.

D

✔ ★ **SOUTH STREET DINER.** *140 South St (19147), in South Street area. 215/627-5258.* Open 24 hrs. Closed Dec 25. Bar. Semi-a la carte: bkfst $4.50-$7, lunch $5-$7.50, dinner $8.50-$10.50. Child's meals. Specializes in bkfst dishes, Greek dishes, meats. Own pasta. Outdoor dining. Patio and sports bar. Cr cds: A, MC, V.

★ ★ ★ ★ **STRIPED BASS.** *1500 Walnut St (19102), downtown. 215/732-4444.* This stylish, highly popular, fish-and-seafood-only restaurant is in a striking former bank building with marble columns. The creative menu is accompanied by a broad international selection of wines by the bottle and glass. Specializes in fresh seafood, shellfish. Menu changes daily. Hrs: 11:30 am-2:30 pm, 5-11 pm; Fri to 11:30 pm; Sat 5-11:30 pm; Sun 11 am-2:30 pm, 5-10 pm. Closed major hols. Res accepted. Bar. Wine cellar. A la carte entrees: lunch $14-$22, dinner $30-$50. Valet parking. Cr cds: A, D, MC, V.

D

★ ★ ★ ★ **SUSANNA FOO.** *1512 Walnut St (19102), downtown. 215/545-2666.* Fresh ingredients and cooking techniques from around the world come together here in chef Susanna Foo's unique cuisine. Silk lanterns and bouquets of orchids create a romantic setting. Chinese,

French menu. Specialties: crispy duck, soft-shell crabs, hundred corner crab cake. Hrs: 11:30 am-2:30 pm, 5:30-10 pm; Fri, Sat to 11 pm; Sun 5-9 pm. Closed some major hols. Res accepted; required Sat. Bar. Wine cellar. A la carte entrees: lunch $10-$18, dinner $18-$30. Valet parking. Jacket. Cr cds: A, C, D, MC, V.

D

★ ★ ★ **SWANN CAFE.** *(See Four Seasons Hotel Philadelphia) 215/963-1500.* Web www.fshr.com. Hrs: 11:30-1 am; Sun 10 am-midnight; Sun brunch to 3 pm. Res accepted. Continental menu. Bar. Wine cellar. A la carte entrees: lunch, dinner $10-$22. Sun brunch $42. Child's meals. Specialties: minute steak with country potato; osso bucco; shrimp, crab and scallop salad. Own baking, pasta. Entertainment. Valet parking. Outdoor dining. Intimate atmosphere; luxurious decor uses mahogany, silk and large chandeliers. Cr cds: A, C, D, DS, MC, V.

D

★ ★ ★ **TONY CLARK'S.** *121 S Broad St 19107), downtown. 215/772-9238.* Hrs: 11:30 am-2:30 pm, 5:30 pm-1:30 am; Sun from 5:30 pm. Closed major hols. Res accepted. Bar. Wine cellar. A la carte entrees: lunch $13-$17, dinner $21-$29. Child's meals. Specialties: roasted rack of lamb, crisp duck with bean cassoulet, sautéed medallions of beef. Valet parking. Modern, intimate atmosphere. Cr cds: A, D, DS, MC, V.

D

★ ★ ★ **TOSCANA CUCINA RUSTICA.** *(24 N Merion Ave, Bryn Mawr 19010) 15 mi W on I-76, exit City Ave to US 30 (Lancaster Ave) to N Merion Ave. 610/527-7700.* Hrs: 11:30 am-2:30 pm, 5:30-10 pm; Fri to 11 pm; Sat 5:30-11 pm; Sun from 5:30 pm. Closed Thanksgiving, Dec 25. Res accepted. Tuscan Italian menu. Bar. Wine cellar. A la carte entrees: lunch $7-$13, dinner $12.95-$25. Specializes in grilled meats, wafer-thin-crusted brick-oven pizza, homemade pasta. Own baking, pasta. Wine list offers over 550 selections. Totally nonsmoking. Cr cds: A.

D

★ ★ ★ **TREETOPS.** *(See The Rittenhouse Hotel) 215/790-2534.* Hrs: 6:30 am-10:30 pm; Sat, Sun from 7 pm. Res accepted. Regional Amer menu. Bar 11:30-1 am. Wine list. Semi-a la carte: lunch $15-$20, dinner $20-$35. Specializes in seafood, steak, veal. Seasonal menu. Own pastries. Valet parking. Casual decor. Overlooks park. Cr cds: A, C, D, DS, MC, V.

D

★ ★ **UMBRIA.** *7131 Germantown Ave (19119), north of downtown. 215/242-6470.* Hrs: 6-9 pm. Closed Mon; major hols. Res accepted. Eclectic menu. A la carte entrees: dinner $16.95-$24.95. Specialties: filet au poivre, curried lamb, soft shelled crabs in season. Blackboard menu changed daily. Totally nonsmoking. No cr cds accepted.

★ ★ **UNDER THE BLUE MOON.** *8042 Germantown Ave (19118), in Chestnut Hill. 215/247-1100.* Hrs: 6-9 pm; Fri, Sat to 10 pm. Closed Sun, Mon; major hols. Continental menu. Bar. A la carte entrees: dinner $19-$25. Specializes in seafood, chicken, duck. Unique modern decor. Cr cds: MC, V.

✔★ **VANG'S GARDEN.** *121 N 11th St (19107), in Chinatown. 215/923-2438.* Hrs: 10 am-10 pm. Closed Thanksgiving. Vietnamese menu. Semi-a la carte: lunch, dinner $3.75-$7.95. Specialties: lobster salad, barbecued beef on rice noodles, sautéed chicken with lemon grass. Adj to convention center. Cr cds: A, MC, V.

★ **VEGA GRILL.** *(4141 Main St, Manayunk 19127) 9 mi W on I-76, exit 31. 215/487-9600.* Hrs: 5:30 pm-1 am; Fri, Sat to 2 am; Sun, Mon to midnight; Sun brunch 11 am-3:30 pm. Closed some major hols. Contemporary Latin Amer menu. Bar 4:30 pm-2 am. A la carte entrees: dinner $12-$18. Sun brunch $7-$12. Child's meals. Specializes in South American meat and fish. Outdoor dining. Neighborhood tavern atmosphere. Cr cds: A, MC, V.

★ ★ **WHITE DOG CAFE.** *3420 Sansom St (19104), downtown. 215/386-9224.* Hrs: 11:30 am-2:30 pm, 5:30-10 pm; Fri, Sat 5:30-11 pm; Sun 5-10 pm; Sat, Sun brunch 11 am-2:30 pm. Closed Thanksgiving, Dec 25. Res accepted. Bar. A la carte entrees: lunch $7.50-$11, dinner $14-$20. Sat, Sun brunch $7-$11. Child's meals. Specializes in Contemporary Amer cuisine. Own desserts. Entertainment Wed-Sun. Outdoor dining. Former house (ca 1870) of author Madame Blavatsky, founder of the Theosophical Society. Cr cds: A, C, D, DS, MC, V.

D

✔★ ★ **ZÓCALO.** *3600 Lancaster Ave (19104), west of downtown in University City. 215/895-0139.* Hrs: noon-10 pm; Fri to 11 pm; Sat 5:30-11 pm; Sun 5-9:30 pm. Closed major hols. Res accepted. Contemporary Mexican menu. Bar. Semi-a la carte: lunch $6-$12, dinner $10-$18. Prix fixe: dinner $13.95 & $15. Specializes in handmade corn tortillas. Parking. Outdoor dining. Cr cds: A, C, D, DS, MC, V.

Unrated Dining Spots

FAMOUS 4TH ST DELICATESSEN. *700 S 4th St, south of downtown. 215/922-3274.* Hrs: 7 am-6 pm; Sun to 4 pm. Closed Rosh Hashana, Yom Kippur. Delicatessen fare. A la carte: bkfst $2-$6, lunch $3.50-$10. Specializes in chocolate chip cookies, fresh roasted turkey, corned beef. Antique telephones. Family-owned more than 70 yrs. Cr cds: A, D, MC, V.

THE RESTAURANT SCHOOL. *4207 Walnut St (19104), near University of Pennsylvania, west of downtown. 215/222-4200.* Hrs: 5:30-10 pm. Closed Sun, Mon; also during student breaks. Res accepted. Bar. Complete meals: dinner $13.50. Seasonal menu; occasionally an extraordinary and elaborate theme dinner is offered. Own baking. Valet parking. Bakery shop on premises. Unique dining experience in a "restaurant school." Consists of 2 buildings; a restored 1856 mansion is linked by a large atrium dining area to a new building housing the kitchen and classrooms. Cr cds: A, C, D, DS, MC, V.

D

ROLLER'S. *8705 Germantown Ave, in Top-of-the-Hill Plaza, in Chestnut Hill. 215/242-1771.* Hrs: 11:30 am-2:30 pm, 5:30-9 pm; Fri to 10 pm; Sat noon-2:30 pm, 5:30-10 pm; Sun 5-9 pm; Sun brunch 11 am-2:30 pm. Closed Mon; most major hols. Bar. Semi-a la carte: lunch $6-$11, dinner $16-$24. Sun brunch $6-$10. Specializes in fresh fish, veal, duck. Parking. Outdoor dining. Modern cafe atmosphere. Totally nonsmoking. No cr cds accepted.

SASSAFRAS. *48 S 2nd St, in Olde City. 215/925-2317.* Hrs: noon-midnight; Fri, Sat to 1 am, Sun to 9 pm. Closed major hols. Bar. A la carte entrees: dinner $5-$18. Specializes in salads, omelettes, grilled fish. Cr cds: A, D, MC, V.

SPIRIT OF PHILADELPHIA. *Pier 3, on Delaware Ave, in Olde City. 215/923-1419.* Hrs: lunch cruise noon-2 pm, dinner cruise 7-10 pm; Sun brunch cruise 1-3 pm. Closed Dec 25. Res required. Bar. Buffet: lunch $16.95 (adults), $9.50 (children), dinner $28.95-$32.95 (adults), $15.95 (children). Sun brunch $18.95 (adults), $9.50 (children). Musical revue, bands, dancing. Parking. Dining and sightseeing aboard Spirit cruise liner. Cr cds: A, MC, V.

D

SWANN LOUNGE. *(See Four Seasons Hotel Philadelphia) 215/963-1500.* Hrs: 11:30 am-2:30 pm; tea 3-5 pm; Sun brunch 11 am-2:30 pm; Viennese buffet Fri, Sat 9 pm-1 am. Closed Mon. Res accepted. Bar 11:30-1 am; Fri, Sat to 2 am. Buffet: bkfst $9.75-$14, lunch $12-$21. Afternoon tea $12. Sun brunch $24. Viennese buffet $11. Specializes in English tea service with sandwiches & cakes. Valet parking. Outdoor dining (lunch). Elegant atmosphere. Cr cds: A, C, D, DS, ER, JCB, MC, V.

D

Phoenix

Settled: 1864
Pop: 983,403
Elev: 1,090 feet
Time zone: Mountain
Area code: 602
Web: www.arizonaguide.com/phxcvb

The capital of Arizona lies on a flat desert surrounded by mountains and green fields. The climate, with its warm temperatures and low humidity, makes Phoenix one of the most desirable vacation spots in the United States. In the Valley of the Sun there is just enough rainfall to sustain the summer desert plants, which makes Phoenix ideal for sun-loving visitors.

Phoenix's known history began about 300 B.C. when the Hohokam started irrigation farming in the area. When the present city was founded in 1871, the settlers decided to name their city after the mythological phoenix bird. According to legend, the bird lived 500 years, then burned itself alive, and from its ashes came forth another phoenix.

By 1873, the cultivation of cotton had begun. Phoenix was incorporated in 1881. Six years later, the first railroad was brought to the city, and industrial expansion followed. Within two years Phoenix was chosen as the capital of the territory, and when Arizona attained statehood in 1912, Phoenix was named state capital.

The industrial growth of the city was boosted by the two world wars. After World War II, manufacturing became the chief industry in Phoenix, and the city's population began to increase dramatically. Today, the Phoenix-Scottsdale area continues to prosper as a popular resort and retirement center. As a vacation spot, it combines sophistication with informality.

Business

Phoenix relies on manufacturing for its economic stability. Among the products made here are fertilizers, computers, electronic equipment, chemicals, processed foods and weapons for the military. Almost one-fifth of Phoenix's working population is employed in manufacturing. Honeywell Information Systems, Motorola, Sperry Flight Systems and Western Electric are among the city's larger employers.

Tourism is the city's number two industry and contributes greatly to the local economy.

Convention Facilities

The Phoenix Civic Plaza Convention Center provides 375,000 square feet of exhibit space, part of which can be divided into a 72,000-square-foot exhibit area and a 36,000-square-foot assembly area. The center features five exhibit halls and a 28,000-square-foot ballroom.

The lobby contains 18,000 square feet of space. Symphony Hall, adjacent to the Convention Center, has permanent seating for 2,577 people. The center also has five large meeting rooms that can be divided into 43 smaller rooms, accommodating between 25 and 1,500 people.

A cocktail lounge, which seats 90 people, is just off the lobby. The Executive Conference Room, VIP Lounge, press, TV and broadcasting facilities are on the mezzanine level, which overlooks the exhibit floor. There is parking for 4,000 cars.

The Arizona Veterans Memorial Coliseum and Exposition Center features a 25,500-square-foot arena with 14,000 permanent seats and space for 1,000 additional seats. It also has two exhibition halls, each with 20,000 square feet of space.

America West Arena has 25,000-square-feet of exhibition space and parking garages for 2,500 automobiles.

The Phoenix/Scottsdale and Valley of the Sun area has 36,000 hotel and motel rooms.

Recreation & Entertainment

The Phoenix area offers a wide variety of professional and collegiate sports entertainment. For fans of professional basketball, the Phoenix Suns play from October through March at the America West Arena, downtown. The Arizona Cardinals play professional football at Sun Devil Stadium. This stadium also plays host to the nationally televised collegiate Fiesta Bowl football game every New Year's Day. Bank One Ballpark is scheduled to be completed in spring of 1998 and will field the Arizona Diamondbacks. The Phoenix Coyotes NHL team plays at the America West Arena. Major League Baseball's Angels, Cubs, Giants, Mariners, A's and Brewers all have spring training facilities in the Phoenix area.

More than 140 golf courses in Phoenix range from 9-hole "pitch-and-putt" to championship courses. The Phoenix Tennis Center provides 16 lighted courts for tennis buffs; public courts are located throughout the metropolitan area. There are also many places to enjoy horseback riding, swimming, boating and fishing. Horse, dog, boat and auto racing are popular here as well.

Metropolitan Phoenix features a continuous schedule of music and plays. Concert programs, ranging from pop and semi-classical to the works of the masters, are performed by top musicians, including visiting stars of national and international fame. The Phoenix Symphony's season runs from September through June.

Community theater groups and touring companies of Broadway shows are joined by stars of stage, screen and television. The Scottsdale Center for the Arts has a seating capacity of 1,700 people. It is the home of the Scottsdale Symphony Orchestra and offers year-round performances of symphony, pops, chorale and youth orchestra.

Historical Areas

Phoenix has many fine museums with extensive exhibits. The Arizona Museum exhibits include a post office, a flour mill and pioneer and Native American artifacts; the Pueblo Grande Museum includes a Hohokam ruin, thought to have been occupied from 300 B.C. to A.D. 1400; the Arizona History Room has changing exhibits depicting life in early Arizona; the Heard Museum houses fascinating exhibits detailing the culture of the Southwest; and the Phoenix Art Museum features 15th-20th-century paintings, sculpture and decorative arts.

A gem of Victorian architecture, the 1894 Rosson House is part of Heritage Square, a unique area that includes museums, shops, restaurants and an open-air lath house.

Prehistoric Native American ruins can be found in many nearby sections of the state. Casa Grande Ruins National Monument, located between Phoenix and Tucson at the edge of the Gila River Native American Reservation, consists of a four-story, castle-like building of classic Native American construction. There is a museum with exhibits explaining Arizona archaeology and ethnology. Montezuma Castle, north of the city on the highway to Flagstaff, is another "apartment house" in remarkable condition. It is tucked into the side of a cliff and dates back to the 13th century. Tonto National Monument, east of Phoenix near Theodore Roosevelt Lake, preserves prehistoric cliff dwellings built during the 14th century by tribesmen drifting southward from the Little Colorado River valley.

Other excavated ruins are at Tuzigoot National Monument, west of Montezuma Castle; Walnut Canyon and Wupatki national monuments, near Flagstaff; and Canyon de Chelly and Navajo national monuments, on the Navajo Reservation in the northeastern part of the state.

Sightseeing

Various attractions in Phoenix are worth a visit. One such place is the Hall of Flame Firefighting Museum, which houses a collection of antique firefighting equipment. The Phoenix Zoo contains more than 1,300 mammals, birds and reptiles. A safari train tour and a 45-minute trained animal show are popular with visitors.

Parks are plentiful in the Phoenix area, offering an enormous selection of activities on land and water. There are also thousands of acres of wilderness nearby.

No visit to this part of the country would be complete without seeing Scottsdale, a resort town at the foot of Camelback Mountain. This town is famous for its antiques, crafts, jewelry and Western clothing shops. There are numerous art galleries, resorts and golf courses. Many rodeos and horse shows are held at various times of the year.

Scottsdale is the location of Taliesin West, the architectural school and winter residence of Frank Lloyd Wright. On Scottsdale Road, four miles north of Bell Road, is Rawhide 1880s Western Town, a re-creation of an 1880 pioneer village.

The Arizona scenery is tremendously varied—deserts, mountains, canyons, forests—and easily accessible from Phoenix. Two of the nation's most popular and spectacular national parks, Grand Canyon and Petrified Forest, can be reached within a few hours.

General References

Area code: 602

Phone Numbers

POLICE, FIRE & PARAMEDICS: 911

POISON CONTROL CENTER: 253-3334

TIME & WEATHER: 265-5550

Information Sources

Phoenix & Valley of the Sun Convention & Visitors Bureau, 400 E Van Buren St, Suite 600, 85004; 254-6500.

Visitor Information, activities hotline, 252-5588.

Parks and Recreation Department, 262-6861.

Transportation

AIRLINES: Alaska; American; America West; British Airways; Continental; Delta; Frontier; Northwest; Southwest; TWA; United; USAir; Western Pacific and other commuter and regional airlines.

AIRPORT: Sky Harbor International, 273-3300.

CAR RENTAL AGENCIES: (See IMPORTANT TOLL-FREE NUMBERS) Avis 273-3222; Budget 267-4000; Dollar 275-7588; Hertz 944-5225; National 275-4771.

PUBLIC TRANSPORTATION: City of Phoenix Transit System, 253-5000.

Newspaper

The Arizona Republic.

Convention Facilities

America West Arena, 1st & Jefferson, 379-2000.

Arizona Veterans Memorial Coliseum & Exposition Center, 1826 W McDowell Rd, 252-6771.

Phoenix Civic Plaza Convention Center, 225 E Adams, 262-6225.

Sports & Recreation

Major Sports Facilities

America West Arena, 1st and Jefferson, 379-7800 (Suns, basketball, 379-7900; Coyotes, hockey, 379-2800).

Arizona Veterans Memorial Coliseum & Exposition Center, 1826 W McDowell Rd, 258-6711.

Bank One Ballpark (to be completed Apr 1998), 401 E Jefferson, 514-8500 (Arizona Diamondbacks).

Sun Devil Stadium, Arizona State University, Tempe, 965-3933 (Cardinals, football, 379-0101).

Racetracks

Greyhound Park, 40th & E Washington Sts, 273-7181.

Phoenix International Raceway, Baseline Rd & S 115th Ave, access via I-10W, 252-3833 (auto racing).

Turf Paradise, 19th Ave & Bell Rd, 942-1101 (horse racing).

Cultural Facilities

Theaters

Herberger Theater, 222 E Monroe, 254-7399.

Phoenix Little Theater, 25 E Coronado Rd, in Civic Center, 254-2151.

Concert Halls

Grady Gammage Memorial Auditorium, Arizona State University, Tempe, 965-3434.

Scottsdale Center for the Arts, 7383 Scottsdale Mall, Scottsdale, 994-2301.

Symphony Hall, Phoenix Civic Plaza, 225 E Adams St, 262-7272.

Museums

Arizona Historical Society Museum, 1300 N College Ave, Tempe, 929-0292.

Arizona Mining & Mineral Museum, 1502 W Washington St, 255-3791.

Arizona Science Center, 600 E Washington St, 716-2000.

Hall of Flame Firefighting Museum, 6101 E Van Buren, opposite zoo, 275-3473.

Heard Museum, 22 E Monte Vista Rd, 252-8848.

Phoenix Museum of History, Monroe & 6th Sts, 253-2734.

Art Museum

Phoenix Art Museum, 1625 N Central Ave, 257-1222.

Points of Interest

Historical

Heritage Square, Rosson House, 7th St & Monroe, 262-5029.

Pueblo Grande Museum, 4619 E Washington St, 4 mi S off US 60/89, on AZ 143, 495-0900.

State Capitol, 1700 W Washington St, 542-4581 or 542-4675.

Other Attractions

Arcosanti, 65 mi N via I-17 at Cordes Junction, 632-7135.

Big Surf, 1500 N McClintock Dr, Tempe, 947-7873.

Camelback Mountain, Scottsdale.

Canyon de Chelly National Monument, NE corner of state near Chinle, on Navajo Reservation, 674-5436.

Casa Grande Ruins National Monument, near Coolidge, at edge of Gila River Reservation, 723-3172.

Cosanti Foundation, 6433 Doubletree Ranch Rd, Scottsdale, 948-6145.

Desert Botanical Garden, 1201 N Galvin Pkwy, in Papago Park, 941-1217.

Fifth Avenue Shops, from Scottsdale Rd W to Indian School Rd, Scottsdale.

Gila Indian Center, 25 mi S of Phoenix, on I-10, at Casa Blanca exit 175, near Chandler, on Gila River Reservation, 963-3981.

McCormick Railroad Park, 7301 E Indian Bend Rd, Scottsdale, 994-2312.

Montezuma Castle National Monument, 90 mi N via I-17 exit 289, 567-3322.

Mystery Castle, 800 E Mineral Rd at S 7th St at foot of South Mountain, 268-1581.

Navajo National Monument, 20 mi SW of Kayenta on US 160, then 9 mi N on AZ 564, on Navajo Reservation, 672-2366.

Phoenix Zoo, 455 N Galvin Pkwy, in Papago Park, 273-1341.

Rawhide 1880s Western Town, 23023 N Scottsdale Rd, Scottsdale, 563-1880 or 563-5600.

South Mountain Park, 7 mi S at end of Central Ave, 495-0222.

Superstition Mountain & Tonto National Forest, 20 mi NE on AZ 87.

Taliesin West, Frank Lloyd Wright Blvd & Cactus Rd, Scottsdale, 860-2700.

Tonto National Monument, 3 mi E on US 60/89, then 30 mi NE on AZ 88, 467-2241.

Valley Garden Center, 1809 N 15th Ave, 252-2120.

Walnut Canyon National Monument, 9 mi E of Flagstaff, on I-40, 526-3367.

Wupatki National Monument, 15 mi N of Flagstaff on US 89, then 18 mi N on Forest Service Rd 545, 556-7040.

Annual Events

Indian Fair, Heard Museum, 22 E Monte Vista Rd, 252-8848. 1st wkend Mar.

Jaycees Rodeo of Rodeos, America West Arena, 263-8671. Mid-Mar.

Arizona State Fair, state fairgrounds, 252-6771. Late Oct-Nov.

Cowboy Artists of America, Phoenix Art Museum, 257-1880. Late Oct-Nov.

Lodgings and Food

Motels

★ ★ ★ **COURTYARD BY MARRIOTT.** *2101 E Camelback Rd (85016). 602/955-5200; FAX 602/955-1101.* 155 rms, 4 story. Jan-May: S, D $165-$185; suites $195-$210; wkend, wkly, hol rates; lower rates rest of yr. Crib free. TV; cable (premium). Heated pool; whirlpool. Complimentary coffee in rms. Restaurant 6:30-11 am. Rm serv. Bar 4-11 pm. Ck-out noon. Coin Indry. Meeting rms. Business servs avail. In-rm modem link. Valet serv. Exercise equipt; weight machine, stair machine. Refrigerator in suites. Balconies. Cr cds: A, C, D, DS, MC, V.

D SC

★ ★ ★ **COURTYARD BY MARRIOTT.** *9631 N Black Canyon (85021). 602/944-7373; FAX 602/944-0079.* 146 rms, 3 story. Jan-mid-Apr: S, D $98-$130; under 18 free; wkend rates; lower rates rest of yr. Crib free. TV; cable (premium). Heated pool; whirlpool. Complimentary coffee in rms. Restaurant 6:30-10 am, 5-9 pm. Rm serv. Ck-out noon. Coin Indry. Business servs avail. Valet serv. Exercise equipt; weights, stair machine. Some refrigerators; microwaves avail. Balconies. Cr cds: A, C, D, DS, MC, V.

D SC

★ ★ ★ **COURTYARD BY MARRIOTT-PHOENIX AIRPORT.** *2621 S 47th St (85034), near Sky Harbor Intl Airport. 602/966-4300; FAX 602/966-0198.* 145 units, 4 story. Jan-early May: S, D $149-$159; each addl $10; suites $169-$179; wkend, wkly rates; lower rates rest of yr. Crib free. TV; cable (premium). Heated pool; whirlpool. Complimentary coffee in rms. Restaurant 6 am-2 pm, 5-10 pm; wkends 7 am-noon, 5-11 pm. Bar 4-10 pm. Ck-out noon. Coin Indry. Meeting rms. Business servs avail. In-rm modem link. Valet serv. Free airport transportation. Exercise equipt; weight machine, bicycles. Refrigerator in suites. Many balconies. Cr cds: A, C, D, DS, MC, V.

D SC

★ ★ **HAMPTON INN.** *8101 N Black Canyon Hwy (85021), I-17 exit Northern Ave on frontage rd. 602/864-6233; FAX 602/995-7503.* 149 rms, 3 story. Jan-mid-Apr: S, D $100-$110; under 18 free; higher rates special events; lower rates rest of yr. Crib free. Pet accepted, some restrictions. TV; cable (premium). Heated pool; whirlpool. Complimentary continental bkfst. Ck-out noon. Meeting rms. Business servs avail. In-rm modem link. Cr cds: A, C, D, DS, MC, V.

D SC

★ ★ **HOMEWOOD SUITES.** *2001 E Highland Ave (85016). 602/508-0937; FAX 602/508-0854.* 124 kit. suites, 4 story. Jan-Apr: S $169-$179; D $179-$189; each addl $10; under 18 free; wkly, wkend, hol rates; lower rates rest of yr. Crib free. Pet accepted, some restrictions. TV; cable (premium). Complimentary continental bkfst. Complimentary coffee in rms. Restaurant adj 11 am-11 pm. Ck-out noon. Meeting rm. Business center. In-rm modem link. Valet serv. Sundries. Coin Indry. Exercise equipt; weights, bicycle. Health club privileges. Pool. Refrigerators, microwaves; some fireplaces. Grills. Cr cds: A, C, D, DS, MC, V.

D SC

★ ★ **LA QUINTA-COLISEUM WEST.** *2725 N Black Canyon Hwy (85009), I-17 exit Thomas Rd. 602/258-6271; FAX 602/340-9255.* Web www.laquinta.com. 139 rms, 2 story. Jan-Apr: S, D $95-$110; each addl $10; under 18 free; lower rates rest of yr. Crib free. Pet accepted, some restrictions. TV; cable. Heated pool. Complimentary continental bkfst. Coffee in rms. Restaurant adj open 24 hrs. Ck-out noon. Coin Indry. Business servs avail. In-rm modem link. Valet serv. Some refrigerators. Cr cds: A, C, D, DS, MC, V.

D SC

✔★ **PREMIER INN.** *10402 N Black Canyon Hwy (85051), at I-17 Peoria Ave exit. 602/943-2371; FAX 602/943-5847; res: 800/786-6835.* 253 rms, 2 story. Jan-Apr: S, D $59.95-$89.95; suites $129.95; lower rates rest of yr. Crib $3. Pet accepted, some restrictions. TV; cable (premium). 2 pools, 1 heated; wading pool. Ck-out noon. Coin Indry. Meeting rms. Bathrm phone in suites. Some refrigerators. Some private patios. Cr cds: A, C, D, DS, MC, V.

SC

Motor Hotels

★ ★ **BEST WESTERN GRACE INN AHWATUKEE.** *10831 S 51st St (85044), just S of I-10 Elliott Rd exit. 602/893-3000; FAX 602/496-8303.* 160 rms, 6 story. Jan-May: S, D $100-$132; each addl $10; suites $120-$175; under 17 free; lower rates rest of yr. Crib free. TV; cable (premium). Heated pool; poolside serv. Coffee in rms. Restaurant 6 am-10 pm. Rm serv. Bar 11:30-1 am; Sun from noon; entertainment. Ck-out noon. Meeting rms. Business servs avail. Bellhops. Valet serv. Sundries. Free airport transportation. Lighted tennis. Health club privileges. Lawn games. Refrigerators. Microwaves avail. Many balconies. Luxury level. Cr cds: A, C, D, DS, JCB, MC, V.

D SC

★ ★ **BEST WESTERN INNSUITES.** *1615 E Northern Ave (85020). 602/997-6285; FAX 602/943-1407.* E-mail esphoenix@attmail.com; web www.arizonaguide.com/innsuites. 123 rms, 2 story, 4 kits. Jan-mid-Apr: S, D $119-$129; kit. suites $149-$169; under 19 free; lower rates rest of yr. Crib free. Pet accepted, some restrictions; $25 refundable. TV; cable (premium). Heated pool; whirlpool. Complimentary continental bkfst. Complimentary coffee in rms. Ck-out noon. Coin Indry. Meeting rms. Business servs avail. In-rm modem link. Exercise equipt; stair machine, bicycle. Playground. Refrigerators, microwaves. Picnic tables, grills. Cr cds: A, C, D, DS, MC, V.

D SC

★ ★ ★ **EMBASSY SUITES-NORTH.** *2577 W Greenway Rd (85023). 602/375-1777; FAX 602/375-4012.* 314 suites, 2-3 story. Jan-mid-May: S, D $109-$199; under 18 free; lower rates rest of yr. TV; cable (premium). Heated pool; wading pool, whirlpool. Complimentary full bkfst. Coffee in rms. Restaurant 6 am-11 pm. Rm serv. Bar 11-1 am. Ck-out noon. Coin Indry. Meeting rms. Business servs avail. In-rm modem link. Bellhops. Valet serv. Lighted tennis. Exercise equipt; weights, stair machine, sauna. Lawn games. Refrigerators. Stucco and red-tile roofed building reminiscent of traditional resort hotels. Cr cds: A, C, D, DS, ER, JCB, MC, V.

D

★ ★ ★ **HILTON-PHOENIX AIRPORT.** *2435 S 47th St (85034), near Sky Harbor Intl Airport. 602/894-1600; FAX 602/894-0326.* E-mail pahilton@primenet.com; web www.hilton.com. 255 units, 4 story. Jan-Apr: S $149-$299; D $164-$314; each addl $15; suites $299-$425; under 18 free; lower rates rest of yr. Crib avail. TV; cable (premium), VCR avail. Pool; whirlpool, poolside serv. Coffee in rms. Restaurant 6 am-2 pm, 5-10 pm; Sun 5-9 pm. Rm serv to midnight. Bar 11 am-midnight. Ck-out noon. Convention facilities. Business center. In-rm modem link. Bellhops. Valet serv. Concierge. Sundries. Gift shop. Free airport transportation. Exercise equipt; weight machines, bicycles. Minibars. Many balconies. Luxury level. Cr cds: A, C, D, DS, ER, JCB, MC, V.

D

★ **LOS OLIVOS EXECUTIVE HOTEL.** *202 E McDowell Rd (85004). 602/258-6911; FAX 602/258-5279; res: 800/776-5560.* E-mail losolivos@travelbase.com; web www.travelbase.com. 48 rms, 3 story, 15 suites. Jan-Apr: S, D $82; each addl $3; suites $129; under 15 free; lower rates rest of yr. TV; cable (premium), VCR avail. Whirlpool. Complimentary coffee in rms. Restaurant Mon-Fri 6:30 am-2 pm. Ck-out noon. Coin Indry. Meeting rms. Business servs avail. Sundries. Valet serv. Tennis. Health club privileges. Refrigerator in suites. Balconies. Picnic tables. Cr cds: A, C, D, DS, MC, V.

D SC

★ ★ **PHOENIX INN.** *2310 E Highland Ave (85016), adj to Biltomre Fashion Park. 602/956-5221; FAX 602/468-7220; res: 800/956-*

5221. Web mmm.arizonaguide.com/phoenixinn. 120 rms, 4 story. Jan-May: S, D $109-$155; each addl $10; suites $199-$229; under 18 free; wkend rates; lower rates rest of yr. Crib free. TV; cable (premium), VCR avail. Heated pool; whirlpool. Complimentary continental bkfst. Complimentary coffee in rms. Restaurant nearby. Ck-out noon. Meeting rm. Business servs avail. In-rm modem link. Bellhops. Coin Indry. Free airport transportation. Exercise equipt; weight machine, treadmill. Health club privileges. Refrigerators, microwaves. Cr cds: A, C, D, DS, MC, V.

D SC

✔★ **QUALITY INN SOUTH MOUNTAIN.** *5121 E La Puente Ave (85044). 602/893-3900; FAX 602/496-0815.* 193 rms, 4 story. Jan-Apr: S, D $99-$119; suites $135-$155; under 17 free; lower rates rest of yr. Crib free. Pet accepted; $15. TV; cable. Heated pool; whirlpool. Coffee in rm. Restaurant 6:30-11 am, 5-9 pm. Rm serv. Ck-out 11 am. Coin Indry. Meeting rms. Business servs avail. Valet serv. Health club privileges. Some refrigerators. Microwaves avail. Cr cds: A, C, D, DS, ER, JCB, MC, V.

D SC

★ ★ ★ **RADISSON AIRPORT.** *3333 E University Dr (85034), at I-10 & University Dr, near Sky Harbor Intl Airport. 602/437-8400; FAX 602/470-0998.* Web www.radisson.com. 163 rms, 6 story. Jan-Apr: S $159-$209; D $169-$219; each addl $10; under 18 free; hol rates; higher rates special events; lower rates rest of yr. Crib $10. TV; cable (premium). Heated pool; whirlpool, poolside serv. Complimentary coffee in rms. Restaurant 6 am-2 pm, 5:30-10 pm. Rm serv. Bar 11-1 am. Ck-out noon. Meeting rms. Business servs avail. Bellhops. Valet serv. Sundries. Gift shop. Free airport transportation. Exercise equipt; weight machine, bicycle, sauna. Some refrigerators; microwaves avail. Some balconies. Cr cds: A, C, D, DS, ER, JCB, MC, V.

D SC

✔★ **RAMADA PHOENIX, CAMELBACK.** *502 W Camelback Rd (85013). 602/264-9290; FAX 602/264-3068; res: 800/688-2021.* 166 rms, 4 story. Jan-Apr: S $91-$100; D $101-$110; each addl $10; suites $150-$180; lower rates rest of yr. Crib free. TV; cable (premium). Heated pool; whirlpool, poolside serv. Restaurant 6:30 am-2 pm, 5-9:30 pm. Rm serv. Bar 2-10 pm; wkends to 1 am. Ck-out noon. Coin Indry. Meeting rms. Business servs avail. Valet serv. Free airport transportation. Exercise equipt; bicycle, treadmill. Health club privileges. Refrigerators. Cr cds: A, C, D, DS, MC, V.

D SC

★ ★ **RAMADA PLAZA HOTEL METROCENTER.** *12027 N 28th Dr (85029). 602/866-7000; FAX 602/942-7512.* Web www.ramada.com. 172 rms, 4 story. Jan-Apr: S $129; D $139; each addl $10; suites $159-$179; under 18 free; lower rates rest of yr; rates vary special events. Crib free. TV; cable. Heated pool; whirlpool, poolside serv. Complimentary coffee in rms. Restaurant 6 am-10 pm. Rm serv. Bar 4-11 pm. Ck-out noon. Meeting rms. Business servs avail. Some refrigerators, microwaves. Cr cds: A, C, D, DS, ER, JCB, MC, V.

D SC

★ ★ ★ **WYNDHAM GARDEN HOTEL.** *2641 W Union Hills Dr (85027), at I-17 & Union Hills. 602/978-2222; FAX 602/978-9139.* 166 rms, 2 story. Jan-Apr: S $139; D $149; each addl $10; under 18 free; lower rates rest of yr. Pet accepted, some restrictions; $25. TV; cable. Heated pool; whirlpool, poolside serv. Full bkfst. Coffee in rms. Restaurant 6:30 am-10 pm. Rm serv 5-10 pm. Bar 4:30-11 pm. Ck-out noon. Coin Indry. Meeting rms. Business servs avail. Valet serv. Sundries. Some refrigerators. Some private patios. Cr cds: A, C, D, DS, ER, JCB, MC, V.

D SC

★ ★ **WYNDHAM GARDEN HOTEL-AIRPORT.** *427 N 44th St (85008), near Sky Harbor Intl Airport. 602/220-4400; FAX 602/231-8703.* Web www.travelnet.com/wyndham. 210 rms, 7 story, 24 suites. Jan-May: S $179; D $189; each addl $10; suites $199; under 18 free; lower rates rest of yr. Crib free. TV; cable. Heated pool; whirlpool, poolside serv. Coffee in rms. Restaurant 6:30 am-2 pm, 5-10 pm. Rm serv 5-10 pm. Bar 3-11 pm. Ck-out noon. Meeting rms. Business servs avail. Valet serv. Sundries. Free airport transportation. Exercise equipt; stair machine, rowers. Some bathrm phones. Cr cds: A, C, D, DS, ER, JCB, MC, V.

D SC

Hotels

★ ★ ★ **BEST WESTERN EXECUTIVE PARK.** *1100 N Central Ave (85004). 602/252-2100; FAX 602/340-1989.* Web www.bestwestern.com/best.html. 107 rms, 8 story. Jan-Apr: S, D $119-$135; each addl $10; suites $195; under 18 free; wkend rates; lower rates rest of yr. Crib free. TV; cable. Heated pool; whirlpool, poolside serv. Coffee in rms. Restaurant 6:30 am-10 pm. Bar 11 am-11 pm, Sun from noon. Ck-out noon. Meeting rms. Business servs avail. Free airport transportation. Exercise equipt; weight machine, bicycle, sauna. Health club privileges. Some bathrm phones, refrigerators, wet bars. Balconies. Panoramic mountain views. Cr cds: A, C, D, DS, ER, MC, V.

D SC

★ ★ ★ **DOUBLETREE SUITES-PHOENIX GATEWAY CENTER.** *320 N 44th St (85008), near Sky Harbor Intl Airport. 602/225-0500; FAX 602/225-0957.* 242 suites, 6 story. Jan-Apr: S $165-$265, D $175-$275; each addl $10; under 17 free (exc groups); wkend rates; lower rates rest of yr. Crib free. TV; cable (premium), VCR avail. Heated pool; whirlpool, poolside serv. Complimentary coffee in rms. Restaurant 7 am-10 pm. Bar 11-1 am. Ck-out noon. Meeting rms. Business center. Gift shop. Free airport transportation. Exercise equipt; bicycle, stair machine, sauna. Refrigerators, microwaves, minibars. Atrium with 2 banks of glass elevators. Cr cds: A, C, D, DS, MC, V.

D

★ ★ **EMBASSY SUITES-CAMELHEAD.** *1515 N 44th St (85008), near Sky Harbor Intl Airport. 602/244-8800; FAX 602/244-8114, ext. 7534.* E-mail www.embassy-suites.com. 229 suites, 4 story. Jan-Apr: S, D $185-$209; each addl $15; under 12 free; lower rates rest of yr. Crib free. TV; cable (premium). Heated pool; whirlpool, poolside serv. Complimentary full bkfst. Complimentary coffee in rms. Restaurant 11:30 am-10 pm. Bar. Ck-out noon. Coin Indry. Meeting rms. Business servs avail. Gift shop. Free airport transportation. Refrigerators, microwaves. Balconies. Grills. Glass-enclosed elvtr overlooks courtyard. Cr cds: A, C, D, DS, JCB, MC, V.

D SC

★ ★ ★ **EMBASSY SUITES-PHOENIX BILTMORE.** *2630 E Camelback Rd (85016). 602/955-3992; FAX 602/955-6479.* 232 kit. suites, 5 story. Jan-May: S $250-$300; D $265-$325; each addl $15; under 13 free; lower rates rest of yr. Crib free. TV; cable (premium). Heated pool; whirlpool, poolside serv. Complimentary full bkfst; afternoon refreshments. Complimentary coffee in rms. Restaurant 11 am-10 pm. Bar to midnight. Ck-out 1 pm. Meeting rms. Business servs avail. In-rm modem link. Coin Indry. Gift shop. Tennis privileges. Golf privileges. Exercise equipt; weight machines, bicycles. Health club privileges. Refrigerators, microwaves. Private patios, balconies. Atrium with lush garden & fish pond. Cr cds: A, C, D, DS, ER, JCB, MC, V.

D

★ ★ ★ **HILTON SUITES.** *10 E Thomas Rd (85012), corner of Thomas Rd & Central Ave. 602/222-1111; FAX 602/265-4841.* Web www.hilton.com. 226 suites, 11 story. Jan-May: S, D $199-$214; each addl $15; under 18 free; wkend, hol rates; lower rates rest of yr. Crib free. TV; cable (premium), VCR (movies $2). Indoor pool; whirlpool. Complimentary coffee in rms. Complimentary full bkfst. Restaurant 11 am-2 pm, 5:30-10 pm; Sat, Sun from 5:30 pm. Bar 4 pm-midnight. Ck-out noon. Meeting rms. Business center. Concierge. Gift shop. Grocery. Exercise equipt; weight machine, bicycle, sauna. Health club privileges. Refrigerators, microwaves. Balconies. Cr cds: A, C, D, DS, ER, JCB, MC, V.

D SC

★ ★ **HOLIDAY INN-AIRPORT.** *4300 E Washington St (85034), near Sky Harbor Intl Airport. 602/273-7778; FAX 602/275-5616.* E-mail pheax@aol.com; web www.traveler.net/htio/custom/servico/0440.html. 301 rms, 10 story. Jan-mid-May: S $149-$189; D $159-$199; each addl $10;

suites $198-$298; under 18 free; higher rates hols (3-day min), special events, spring training; lower rates rest of yr. Crib $10. TV; cable (premium), VCR avail. Heated pool; whirlpool, poolside serv. Coffee in rms. Restaurant 6 am-11 pm. Bar 11-1 am; entertainment exc Sun. Ck-out noon. Coin Indry. Convention facilities. Business servs avail. In-rm modem link. Valet serv. Gift shop. Garage parking. Free airport transportation. 18-hole golf privileges, greens fee $35-$120, pro. Exercise equipt; weight machine, treadmill. Game rm. Some refrigerators; microwaves avail. Cr cds: A, C, D, DS, JCB, MC, V.

D SC

★ ★ **HOLIDAY INN-WEST.** *1500 N 51st Ave (85043), I-10 exit 139. 602/484-9009; FAX 602/484-0108.* Web www.traveler.net/ht10/custom/servico/0410.html. 144 rms, 4 story. Jan-Apr: S $179; D $184; each addl $10; suites $259; under 18 free; higher rates special events; lower rates rest of yr. Crib free. TV; cable (premium), VCR avail. Covered pool; whirlpool, poolside serv. Coffee in rms. Restaurant 6 am-10 pm; wkend hrs vary. Bar noon-1 am. Ck-out noon. Meeting rms. Business servs avail. In-rm modem link. Gift shop. Golf privileges, pro, putting green, driving range. Exercise equipt; weight machine, bicycle, sauna. Some refrigerators. Balconies. Cr cds: A, C, D, DS, ER, MC, V.

D SC

★ ★ ★ **HYATT REGENCY PHOENIX AT CIVIC PLAZA.** *122 N 2nd St (85004). 602/252-1234; FAX 602/254-9472.* E-mail concierge @hyatt.com; web www.hyatt.com. 712 rms, 24 story. Oct-Apr: S, D $210-$260; suites $350-$1250; under 18 free; wkend rates; lower rates rest of yr. Crib free. Garage $6/day, valet $8. TV; cable (premium), VCR avail. Heated pool; whirlpool, poolside serv. Restaurant 6 am-midnight (also see COMPASS). Bar 11-1 am. Ck-out noon. Meeting rms. Business center. Concierge. Shopping arcade. Tennis privileges. Golf privileges. Exercise equipt; weight machine, stair machine. Health club privileges. Microwaves avail. Wet bar in some suites. Some balconies. Cr cds: A, C, D, DS, ER, JCB, MC, V.

D

★ ★ **LEXINGTON HOTEL & CITY SQUARE SPORTS CLUB.** *100 W Clarendon Ave (85013). 602/279-9811; FAX 602/631-9358.* 180 rms, 3 & 7 story. Jan-May: S, D $149-$169; under 18 free; wkend rates; lower rates rest of yr. Crib free. Pet accepted, some restrictions. TV; cable (premium). Heated pool; whirlpool. Restaurant 6:30 am-10:30 pm; closed Sun. Bar. Ck-out noon. Business servs avail. Barber, beauty shop. Gift shop. Free valet parking. Exercise rm; instructor, weights, bicycles, steam rm, sauna. Aerobics. Basketball. Racquetball. Some microwaves. Some balconies. Cr cds: A, C, D, DS, ER, MC, V.

★ ★ **QUALITY HOTEL & RESORT.** *3600 N Second Ave (85013). 602/248-0222; FAX 602/265-6331.* Web www.getawaylagoon .com. 280 rms, 8 & 10 story, 33 suites. Jan-Apr: S $109; D $119; each addl $10; suites $150-$185; under 18 free; lower rates rest of yr. Crib free. Pet accepted. TV; cable (premium) VCR avail. Complimentary coffee in rms. Restaurant 6 am-10 pm. Bar 4 pm-midnight; entetainment Tues-Sat. Ck-out noon. Meeting rms. Business center. Gift shop. Grocery store. Coin Indry. Free garage parking. Exercise equipt; bicycle, stair machine. Health club privileges. Pool; wading pool, whirlpool, poolside serv. Playground. Game rm. Lawn games. Refrigerators avail. Picnic tables. Cr cds: A, C, D, DS, ER, JCB, MC, V.

D SC

★ ★ **RADISSON-MIDTOWN.** *401 W Clarendon Ave (85013), between Indian School Rd & Osborn Ave. 602/234-2464; FAX 602/277-2602.* 106 rms, 4 story. Sept-May: S, D $99-$130; each addl $10; suites $110-$140; under 18 free; lower rates rest of yr. Crib free. TV; cable (premium). Heated pool; whirlpool, poolside serv. Complimentary continental bkfst. Coffee in rms. Restaurant 6 am-10 pm. Bar 11:30-1 am. Ck-out noon. Meeting rms. Business servs avail. Free airport transportation. Some refrigerators. Courtyard. Cr cds: A, C, D, DS, ER, JCB, MC, V.

SC

★ ★ ★ ★ **THE RITZ-CARLTON, PHOENIX.** *2401 E Camelback Rd (85016), in the Camelback Esplanade. 602/468-0700; FAX 602/468-9883.* 18th- and 19th-century European paintings and china collections decorate the large public rooms of this elegant hotel fronting Biltmore Fashion Square. 281 rms, 11 story. Jan-May: S, D $260-$315; suites $375-$425; under 12 free; lower rates rest of yr. Crib avail. TV; cable (premium), VCR avail. Pool; poolside serv. Restaurant (see BISTRO 24). Rm serv 24 hrs. Bar 5 pm-1 am; Sat, Sun from 11 am; entertainment. Ck-out noon. Convention facilities. Business center. Concierge. Gift shop. Covered parking. Airport, RR station, bus depot transportation. Lighted tennis. Golf privileges. Exercise rm; instructor, weight machines, treadmill, sauna. Massage. Health club privileges. Bicycle rentals. Bathrm phones, minibars; microwaves avail. Luxury level. Cr cds: A, C, D, DS, JCB, MC, V.

D

✔★ **SAN CARLOS.** *202 N Central Ave (85004). 602/253-4121; FAX 602/253-6668; res: 800/528-5446.* 132 rms, 7 story. Jan-Apr: S, D $99-$109; each addl $10; suites $129-$159; under 12 free. Crib free. Pet accepted, some restrictions. TV; cable (premium). Heated pool. Complimentary continental bkfst. Complimentary coffee in rms. Restaurant 11 am-11 pm. Ck-out noon. Meeting rms. In-rm modem link. Valet. Health club privileges. Refrigerators; microwaves avail. Cr cds: A, C, D, DS, MC, V.

SC

★ ★ ★ **SHERATON CRESCENT.** *2620 W Dunlap Ave (85021), at I-17. 602/943-8200; FAX 602/371-2857.* Web www.arizonaguide.com/sheratoncrescent/. 342 rms, 8 story. Early Jan-mid-May: S, D $165-$239; suites $275-$650; some wkend rates; lower rates rest of yr. Crib free. Pet accepted, some restrictions; $100 ($75 refundable). TV; cable (premium), VCR avail. Heated pool; whirlpool, poolside serv. Complimentary coffee in rms. Restaurant 6 am-11 pm. Bar 11-1 am; entertainment. Ck-out noon. Convention facilities. Business center. Gift shop. Free covered parking. Lighted tennis. Exercise rm; instructor, weights, bicycles, sauna, steam rm. Lawn games. Refrigerators, minibars. Balconies. Some fireplaces. Luxury level. Cr cds: A, C, D, DS, ER, JCB, MC, V.

D

★ ★ ★ **WYNDHAM METRO CENTER.** *10220 N Metro Pkwy E (85051), at Metrocenter Shopping Ctr, I-17 Peoria exit. 602/997-5900; FAX 602/943-6156.* Web www.travelweb.com. 284 rms, 5 story. Jan-May: S 149-$238; D $159-$248; each addl $10; suites $269-$349; under 12 free; wkend rates; lower rates rest of yr. Crib free. TV; cable (premium). Heated pool; whirlpool, poolside serv. Complimentary coffee in rms. Restaurant 6:30 am-11 pm. Bar 11-1 am; Sun from 1 pm. Ck-out noon. Business center. Concierge. Shopping arcade. Lighted tennis. Exercise equipt; weights, bicycles, sauna. Heliport. Luxury level. Some refrigerators. Cr cds: A, C, D, DS, ER, JCB, MC, V.

D SC

Inns

★ ★ ★ **LA ESTANCIA BED AND BREAKFAST.** *4979 E Camelback Rd (85018). 602/808-9924; res: 800/410-7655; FAX 602/808-9925.* E-mail mrinc@goodnet.com; web www.bbonline.com/az/laestancia. 5 rms, 2 story. No rm phones. Jan-May: S, D $165-$195; golf plan; lower rates rest of yr. Closed Aug. Children over 8 yrs only. TV in common rm; cable (premium), VCR avail. Complimentary full bkfst; afternoon refreshments. Restaurant nearby. Ck-out 11 am, ck-in noon-4 pm. Business servs avail. Luggage handling. Concierge serv. Free airport transportation. Tennis privileges. Health club privileges. Pool. Lawn games. In-rm whirlpools. Built in 1929. Totally nonsmoking. Cr cds: A, C, D, DS, MC, V.

★ ★ ★ **MARICOPA MANOR.** *15 W Pasadena Ave (85013). 602/274-6302; FAX 602/266-3904; res: 800/292-6403.* E-mail mmanor@getnet.com. 6 rms, 1 kit. Sept-May: S, D, kit. unit $129-$189; each addl $25; lower rates rest of yr. TV; cable (premium). Pool; whirlpool. Complimentary continental bkfst in rms. Restaurant nearby. Ck-out 11 am, ck-in 4-6 pm. Business servs avail. Health club privileges. Many microwaves. Picnic tables. Restored Spanish mission-style mansion (1928); antiques, library/sitting rm. Gardens, fountains. Totally nonsmoking. Cr cds: A, DS, MC, V.

Resorts

★★★★ **ARIZONA BILTMORE.** *24th St & Missouri Ave (85016), northeast of downtown. 602/955-6600; FAX 602/381-7600; res: 800/950-0086.* The Biltmore, designed by Frank Lloyd Wright's colleague Albert Chase McArthur, is set on 250 acres of magnificent gardens with numerous varieties of palms, flowers and cacti. Stained-glass skylights and wrought-iron pilasters grace the lobby; rooms are filled with Wright-inspired furniture and tan and off-white marble baths. 502 rms, 2-4 story. Jan-Apr: S, D $380-$420; each addl $30; suites from $780; AP, MAP avail; golf plan; lower rates rest of yr. Crib avail. TV; cable (premium). Heated pools; wading pool, whirlpool, poolside serv, lifeguard. Supervised child's activities. Restaurants 7 am-midnight. Rm serv. Bar 11-1 am. Ck-out noon, ck-in 4 pm. Concierge. Shopping arcade. Barber, beauty shop. Lighted tennis. 36-hole golf, greens fee $110 (incl cart), putting greens, driving range. Bicycle rentals. Soc dir; entertainment, dancing. Rec rm. Exercise rm; instructor, weight machines, bicycles, sauna. Refrigerators. Sun decks. Some private patios, balconies. Cr cds: A, MC, V.

D

★★★ **POINTE HILTON AT TAPATIO CLIFFS.** *11111 N 7th St (85020). 602/866-7500; FAX 602/993-0276.* E-mail phxrr_cro@hilton.com; web www.hilton.com/hotels/PHXTCPR. 585 rms, 6 story, 58 suites. Mid-Jan-May: S $189-$325; D $204-$340; each addl $15; under 18 free; wkend, hol rates; golf plan; lower rates rest of yr. Crib free. TV; cable (premium), VCR avail. Complimentary coffee in rms. Restaurant (see DIFFERENT POINTE OF VIEW). Box lunches, snack bar, picnics. Bar 10-1 am; entertainment. Ck-out noon, ck-in 4 pm. Grocery 1 mi. Coin Indry. Package store 1 mi. Convention facilities. Business center. Bellhops. Valet serv. Concierge. Shopping arcade. Barber, beauty shop. Sports dir. Lighted tennis, pro. 18-hole golf, greens fee $130, pro, putting green, driving range. Horse stables. Bicycle rentals. Social dir. Game rm. Exercise rm; instructor, weights, treadmill, sauna, steam rm. Spa. Health club privileges. Pool; whirlpool, poolside serv. Supervised child's activities May-Sept; ages 3-12. Refrigerators, minibars, wet bars; some bathrm phones, fireplaces. Balconies. Picnic tables. Luxury level. Cr cds: A, C, D, DS, ER, JCB, MC, V.

D

★★★ **POINTE HILTON ON SOUTH MOUNTAIN.** *7777 South Pointe Pkwy (85044). 602/438-9000; FAX 602/431-6535.* E-mail phxsm_ns@hilton.com; web www.hilton.com. 638 suites, 2-4 story. Jan-mid-May: S, D $249-$319; each addl $15; suites $299-$475; under 18 free; lower rates rest of yr. TV; cable (premium). 6 heated pools; wading pool, whirlpool, poolside serv. Supervised child's activities; ages 5-12. Complimentary coffee in rms. Dining rm (public by res) 6 am-midnight. Rm serv. Bar 11-1 am. Ck-out noon, ck-in 4 pm. Coin Indry. Convention facilities. Business center. Beauty shop. Sports dir. Lighted tennis, pro. 36-hole golf, greens fee $115 (incl cart), pro, putting green. Bicycles. Exercise rm; instructor, weights, bicycles, sauna, steam rm. Massage. Rec rm. Minibars. Private patios, balconies. Cr cds: A, C, D, DS, ER, JCB, MC, V.

D SC

★★★ **ROYAL PALMS HOTEL AND CASITAS.** *5200 E Camelback Rd (85018). 602/840-3610; res: 800/672-6011; FAX 602/840-6927.* 116 rms, 1-2 story. Jan-May: S, D $390-$525; each addl $50; suites $475-$1,200; under 5 free; some wkend rates; lower rates rest of yr. Serv charge $16/day. Crib free. TV; cable (premium). Pool; poolside serv. Restaurant (see T. COOK'S). Bar 4 pm-midnight; Fri, Sat to 1 am. Ck-out noon. Meeting rms. Business center. Valet serv. Airport transportation. Tennis, pro. Exercise equipt; weights, bicycles. Minibars. Some balconies. Spanish architecture; antiques. Cr cds: A, C, D, DS, MC, V.

D

Restaurants

★★ **ARIZONA CAFE & GRILL.** *3113 E Lincoln Ave (85016). 602/957-0777.* E-mail dine@christophers.com; web www.christophers.com. Hrs: 11 am-9:30 pm; Fri-Sat to 11 pm. Closed some major hols. Res accepted. Bar to 1 am. Semi-a la carte: lunch $6.45-$8.95, dinner $6.95-$19.95. Specialties: lightly smoked prime rib, wood-fired pizza. Outdoor dining. Southwestern deocr. Cr cds: A, C, D, DS, MC, V.

D

★★★ **AVANTI'S OF PHOENIX.** *2728 E Thomas Rd. 602/956-0900.* Hrs: 11:30 am-3 pm, 5:30-11 pm; Sat, Sun from 5:30 pm. Closed Dec 25. Res accepted. Continental, Italian menu. Bar. Wine list. Semi-a la carte: lunch $6.75-$15.50, dinner $15.95-$26.50. Specializes in veal, fresh pasta, fresh seafood. Own pastries, pasta. Entertainment Wed-Sat. Valet parking. Patio dining in season. Cr cds: A, C, D, DS, MC, V.

D

★★ **BABY KAY'S CAJUN KITCHEN.** *2119 E Camelback St (85016), in Town and Country Shopping Center. 602/955-0011.* Hrs: 11 am-3 pm, 5-10 pm; Fri, Sat to 11 pm; Sun 11 am-9 pm. Closed major hols. Cajun menu. Bar. Semi-a la carte: lunch $5.95-$13.95, dinner $7.95-$19.95. Specialties: gumbo, crawfish etouffee, red beans and rice. Blues/jazz Tues-Sat. Outdoor dining. Casual dining. Cr cds: A, MC, V.

D

★★★ **BISTRO 24.** *(See The Ritz-Carlton, Phoenix Hotel) 602/952-2424.* Hrs: 6 am-11 pm; Fri, Sat to midnight; Sun brunch 11 am-2:30 pm. Res accepted. Bar. Wine cellar. Semi-a la carte: bkfst $2.50-$7, lunch $6.75-$15, dinner $13.25-$23. Sun brunch $7-$14.50. Child's meals. Specialties: crab cakes, seafood risotto, crispy skin whitefish. Own baking. Entertainment. Valet parking. Outdoor dining on streetside patio. European-inspired bistro. Cr cds: A, C, D, DS, JCB, MC, V.

D

★★★★ **CHRISTOPHER'S.** *2398 E Camelback Rd (85016), in Biltmore Financial Center. 602/957-3214.* E-mail dine@christophers.com; web www.christophers.com. A glass-enclosed wine cellar, one of Arizona's largest, is the focal point of this elegant, cherrywood-trimmed dining room. Contemporary French cuisine. Specialties: crêpe foie gras, house-smoked salmon, chocolate mousse tower. Own baking. Hrs: 6-10 pm; Fri, Sat to 11 pm. Closed some major hols; also Sun-Wed in summer. Res accepted. Bar. Wine cellar. Semi-a la carte: dinner $32. Prix fixe: dinner $85-$125. Valet parking. Chef-owned. Jacket. Totally nonsmoking. Cr cds: A, C, D, DS, MC, V.

D

★★★ **CHRISTOPHER'S BISTRO.** *2398 E Camelback Rd (85016), in Biltmore Financial Center. 602/957-3214.* E-mail dine@christophers.com; web www.christophers.com. Hrs: 11 am-midnight; Sat, Sun from 5 pm. Closed some major hols. Res accepted. Bar. Wine cellar. A la carte entrees: lunch $7-$16, dinner $18-$26. Child's meals. Specializes in seafood, grilled veal chop, rack of lamb. Valet parking. Outdoor dining. Bistro-style dining room. Cr cds: A, C, D, DS, MC, V.

D

★★ **COMPASS.** *(See Hyatt Regency Phoenix At Civic Plaza Hotel) 602/440-3166.* Hrs: 11:30 am-2 pm, 5:30-10 pm; Sun brunch 10 am-2 pm. Res accepted. Continental menu. Bar to midnight. Semi-a la carte: lunch $6.50-$10.50, dinner $17-$23. Sun brunch $23.95. Child's meals. Specializes in prime rib, filet of sole stuffed with crab. Own baking. Valet parking. Revolving dining area on 24th floor; panoramic view of city. Totally nonsmoking. Cr cds: A, C, D, DS, ER, JCB, MC, V.

D

✔★ ★ **COYOTE GRILL.** *3202 E Greenway, Suite 1315 (85032). 602/404-8966.* Hrs: 11:30 am-10 pm; Fri, Sat to 10:30 pm. Closed Thanksgiving, Dec 25. Res accepted. Southwestern menu. Bar. Semi-a la carte: lunch $6.95-$14.95, dinner $6.95-$15.95. Child's meals. Specialties: baby back ribs with maple barbecue, spicy pork loin, grilled stuffed quail. Own desserts. Outdoor dining. Southwestern decor. Cr cds: A, C, D, DS, MC, V.

D

★ ★ ★ **DIFFERENT POINTE OF VIEW.** *(See Pointe Hilton at Tapatio Cliffs Resort) 602/863-0912.* Hrs: 6-10 pm. Closed Sun, Mon (mid-June-Oct). Res accepted. Regional Amer menu. Bar 5 pm-1 am. Wine cellar. A la carte entrees: dinner $19-$32. Prix fixe: dinner (June-Sept) $27.95. Sun brunch (Oct-Father's Day) $24.95. Child's meals. Specializes in steak, seafood, regional dishes. Own baking. Entertainment Tues-Sat. Valet parking. Outdoor dining. On mountaintop, view of surrounding mountain ranges. Cr cds: A, C, D, DS, MC, V.

D

★ ★ ★ **EDDIE'S GRILL.** *4747 N 7th St (85014), S of Camelback. 602/241-1188.* Hrs: 11:30 am-2:30 pm, 5-11 pm; Fri to midnight; Sat 5 pm-midnight; Sun 4-9 pm. Closed Dec 25. Res accepted. Bar. Wine cellar. Semi-a la carte: lunch $9.95-$14.95, dinner $15.95-$21.95. Child's meals. Specialties: ginger cilantro-crusted salmon, seared New York sirloin, baked meatloaf. Outdoor dining. Surrounded by Koi ponds. Totally nonsmoking. Cr cds: A, C, D, DS, MC, V.

D

★ ★ **FISH MARKET.** *1720 E Camelback Rd. 602/277-3474.* Hrs: 11 am-9:30 pm; Fri, Sat to 10 pm; Sun noon-9:30 pm. Closed Thanksgiving, Dec 24 evening, Dec 25. Res accepted. Bar. Semi-a la carte: lunch $8-$20, dinner $9-$33. Child's meals. Specializes in fresh fish, live shellfish, smoked fish. Oyster bar. Outdoor dining. Nautical decor. Retail fish market. Sushi bars. Cr cds: A, D, DS, MC, V.

D

✔★ **GEORGE & DRAGON.** *4240 N Central Ave (85012). 602/241-0018.* Hrs: 11 am-10 pm; Sat, Sun to 11 pm. Res accepted. English menu. Bar to 1 am. Semi-a la carte: lunch $4.95, dinner $8.95. Child's meals. Specialties: fish and chips, shephard's pie, liver and onions. Authentic British pub. Cr cds: A, D, MC, V.

D

★ ★ **GREEKFEST.** *1940 E Camelback Rd. 602/265-2990.* Hrs: 11 am-2:30 pm, 5-10 pm; Fri, Sat to 11 pm; Sun 5-9 pm. Closed some major hols. Res accepted. Greek menu. Bar. Semi-a la carte: lunch $4.95-$12, dinner $6.95-$25. Child's meals. Specialties: lamb exohiko, rack of lamb, souvlaki. Outdoor dining. Greek decor; festive atmosphere. Cr cds: A, D, DS, MC, V.

D

★ ★ ★ **HARRIS'.** *3101 E Camelback Rd (85016). 602/508-8888.* Hrs: 11:30 am-2 pm, 5:30-10 pm. Closed Dec 25. Res accepted. Bar 11 am-10 pm; Sat, Sun 5-10 pm. Wine cellar. Semi-a la carte: lunch $8.95-$10.95, dinner $16-$29. Specializes in beef, lamb chops, Atlantic salmon. Pianist Tues-Sat. Valet parking. Outdoor dining. Southwestern decor. Cr cds: A, C, D, DS, MC, V.

D

★ ★ **HAVANA CAFE.** *4225 E Camelback Rd (85018). 602/952-1991.* Hrs: 11:30 am-10 pm; Sun 4-9 pm. Closed some major hols. Cuban, Spanish menu. Bar. A la carte entrees: lunch $4.50-$11.95, dinner $7.95-$23. Specialties: pollo Cubano, masas de puerco fritas, paella. Patio dining. Totally nonsmoking. Cr cds: A, C, D, DS, MC, V.

D

✔★ ★ **HOPS! BISTRO & BREWERY.** *2584 E Camelback Rd (85016). 602/468-0500.* E-mail alan@cougans.com. Hrs: 11 am-midnight. Closed Thanksgiving, Dec 25. Res accepted. Bar to 1 am Fri, Sat. Semi-a la carte: lunch, dinner $5.95-$14.95. Child's meals. Specialties: oven-roasted chicken, chinese chicken salad, beer croutons. Valet parking. Outdoor dining. High-tech decor. Cr cds: A, C, D, DS, MC, V.

D ♥

✔★ ★ **HOUSTON'S.** *2425 E Camelback Rd, Ste 110 (85016). 602/957-9700.* Hrs: 11 am-11 pm; Fri, Sat to midnight; Sun to 10 pm. Closed Thanksgiving, Dec 25. Bar. Semi-a la carte: lunch, dinner $7-$17 Specializes in ribs, fresh grilled fish. Outdoor dining. Cr cds: A, MC, V.

D

★ ★ ★ **LA FONTANELLA.** *4231 E Indian School Rd. 602/955-1213.* Hrs: 4:30-9:30 pm; Mon-Fri 11 am-2 pm. Closed Dec 25. Res accepted. Italian menu. Bar. Semi-a la carte: lunch $5-$8.50, dinner $8-$21.75. Child's meals. Specialties: rack of lamb, osso buco, pasta with seafood. Own desserts. Cr cds: A, C, D, DS, MC, V.

D

★ ★ **LE RHONE.** *(9401 W Thunderbird Rd, Peoria 85831) US 101 exit Thunderbird Rd. 602/933-0151.* Hrs: 5:30-8:30 pm. Closed Mon; Jan 1. Res accepted. Swiss, continental menu. Bar. Complete meals: dinner $18.90-$27.95. Specialties: châteaubriand, jumbo gulf shrimp provençale, rack of lamb. Pianist. Cr cds: A, C, D, DS, MC, V.

D

✔★ ★ **LOMBARDI'S AT THE ARIZONA CENTER.** *455 N 3rd St (85004), at the Arizona Center. 602/257-8323.* Hrs: 11 am-11 pm; Fri, Sat to midnight; Sun to 10 pm. Closed Thanksgiving, Dec 25. Res accepted. Italian menu. Bar. A la carte entrees: lunch $9-$18.95, dinner $9.50-$21.95. Specialties: cioppino, tiramisu, risotto del giorno. Patio dining. Open kitchen. Cr cds: A, C, D, MC, V.

D

✔★ **MARILYN'S.** *12631 N Tatum Blvd. 602/953-2121.* Hrs: 11 am-10 pm; Sun & Mon to 9 pm; Fri & Sat to 10:30 pm. Closed Thanksgiving, Dec 25. Mexican menu. Bar. Semi-a la carte: lunch $4.50-$7.50, dinner $7-$14.95. Child's meals. Specialties: fajitas, chimichangas, pollo fundido. Southwestern decor; fiesta atmosphere. Cr cds: A, DS, MC, V.

D

★ ★ **MONTI'S.** *12025 N 19th Ave (85029), corner of 19th Ave and Cactus. 602/997-5844.* Hrs: 11 am-10 pm; Fri, Sat to 11 pm; early-bird dinner 3-6:30 pm. Closed Dec 25. Res accepted. Bar. Semi-a la carte: lunch $3.95-$8.65, dinner $5.15-$20.50. Child's meals. Specializes in sirloin. Outdoor dining. Western motif. Family-owned. Cr cds: A, C, D, DS, MC, V.

D

★ ★ **THE OYSTER GRILL.** *455 N 3rd Ave (85004), in Arizona Center. 602/252-6767.* Hrs: 11 am-10 pm. Closed Easter, Thanksgiving, Dec 25. Bar to 1 am. Semi-a la carte: lunch, dinner $6-$25. Child's meals. Specializes in oysters, sushi, grilled fish. Colorful decor. Separate oyster bar area. Cr cds: A, C, D, DS, MC, V.

D

✔★ ★ **PIZZERIA BIANCO.** *623 E Adams St (85004), in Heritage Square. 602/258-8300.* Hrs: 11:30 am-2 pm, 5:30-10 pm. Sat, Sun from 5:30; Sun to 9 pm. Closed Mon, hols. Italian menu. Bar. A la carte entrees: lunch $4.50-$10.50, dinner $7-$10.50. Specializes in wood-fired pizzas, organic salads. Own dough, mozzarella. Totally nonsmoking. Cr cds: MC, V.

D

★ ★ **PRONTO RISTORANTE.** *3950 E Campbell Ave (85018). 602/956-4049.* Hrs: 11:30 am-2:30 pm, 5:30-10 pm; Fri, Sat to 10:30 pm. Closed Sun; Thanksgiving, Dec 25. Res accepted. Regional Italian menu. Bar. Semi-a la carte: lunch $5.95-$9.95, dinner $9.95-$15.95. Specialties: capellini alla pescarese, veal Marsala, gnocchi di patate. 3 dining areas. Dinner theater Fri, Sat. Stained-glass; antique instruments. Cr cds: A, C, D, DS, MC, V.

D

★ ★ **RAFFAELE'S.** *2999 N 44th St. 602/952-0063.* Hrs: 11:30 am-2:30 pm, 5-10 pm; Fri to 11 pm; Sat 5-11 pm; Sun 5-10 pm. Closed Thanksgiving, Dec 25. Res accepted. Italian menu. Bar. Semi-a la carte: lunch $6.50-$12, dinner $11.50-$28. Specialties: osso bucco, vitello saltimbocca. Valet parking (Mon-Sat). Patio dining. Contemporary decor; view of fountain, courtyard. Cr cds: A, D, DS, MC, V.

D

★ ★ ★ **ROXSAND.** *2594 E Camelback Rd, Biltmore Fashion Park. 602/381-0444.* Hrs: 11 am-10 pm; Fri, Sat to 10:30; Sun noon-9:30 pm. Closed most major hols. Res accepted. Bar. Wine list. Semi-a la carte: lunch $8.25-$11.95, dinner $16.95-$29. Specialties: air-dried duck, roasted lamb chops, Chilean sea bass. Valet parking. Outdoor dining. Offers over 25 daily selections of pastries/desserts. Cr cds: A, C, D, MC, V.

D

★ ★ **RUSTLER'S ROOSTE.** *7777 S Pointe Pkwy (85044), in Pointe Hilton on South Mountain. 602/431-6474.* Hrs: 5-10 pm; Fri, Sat to 11 pm. Res accepted. Steakhouse. Bar 4 pm-1 am. Semi-a la carte: dinner $8.95-$21.95. Child's meals. Specializes in steak, chicken, ribs. Entertainment. Valet parking. Outdoor dining. Rustic decor. Cr cds: A, C, D, DS, ER, JCB, MC, V.

D

★ ★ **RUTH'S CHRIS STEAK HOUSE.** *2201 E Camelback Rd (85016). 602/957-9600.* Hrs: 5-10 pm; Fri, Sat to 10:30 pm. Closed Thanksgiving, Dec 25. Res accepted. Bar. Semi-a la carte: dinner $17.95-$37.95. Specializes in steaks. Valet parking. Outdoor dining. Cr cds: A, C, D, MC, V.

★ ★ **STEAMERS GENUINE SEAFOOD.** *2576 E Camelback Rd (85016). 602/956-3631.* E-mail big4@infinet-is.com; web www.infinet is.com/nbig4. Hrs: 11:30 am-11 pm; Sun noon-10 pm; Closed Thanksgiving, Dec 25. Res accepted. Bar to midnight. Semi-a la carte: lunch $5.95-$14.95, dinner $13.95-$24.95. Child's meals. Specialties: fire-and-ice salmon, coriander charred escalar, live Maine lobster. Oyster bar. Valet parking. Outdoor dining. Bright and colorful, spacious dining area. Cr cds: A, C, D, DS, MC, V.

D

★ **SUCH IS LIFE.** *3602 N 24th St (85016). 602/948-1753.* Hrs: 11:30 am-2:30 pm, 5:30-10 pm; Sat, Sun 5-10 pm. Closed most major hols. Res accepted. Mexican menu. Bar. A la carte entrees: lunch $6-$12, dinner $10-$20. Specialties: fish Vera Cruz, pork, shrimp with garlic. Guitarist and singer Mon-Sat. Two dining areas with Mexican flair. Cr cds: A, D, DS, MC, V.

D

★ **T-BONE STEAKHOUSE.** *10037 S 19th Ave, 11 mi S in South Mountain area. 602/276-0945.* Hrs: 5-10 pm; Fri, Sat to 11 pm. Closed Thanksgiving, Dec 24, 25. Bar. Semi-a la carte: dinner $9.95-$21.95. Child's meals. Specializes in steak. Salad bar. Outdoor dining. Rustic, old Western steakhouse in foothills of the mountains; scenic view of valley and downtown Phoenix. All cooking is done over mesquite coals and much of it is done outside. Cr cds: A, D, MC, V.

D

★ ★ ★ **T. COOK'S.** *(See Royal Palms Hotel and Casitas Resort) 602/808-0766.* Hrs: 6 am-2 pm, 6-10 pm; Sun brunch 10 am-2 pm. Res accepted. Mediterranean menu. Bar 4 pm-midnight; Fri, Sat to 1 am. Extensive wine list. Semi-a la carte: bkfst $6-$14, lunch $9-$14, dinner $14-$23. Sun brunch $12-$30. Specialties: oven-baked John Dory; T. Cook's Mediterranean paella; mussels sautéed in Chardonnay thyme broth. Pianist Tues-Sat. Valet parking. Outdoor dining. Mediterranean decor; handpainted walls. Cr cds: A, C, D, DS, MC, V.

D

★ ★ ★ **TARBELL'S.** *3213 E Camelback Rd (85018). 602/955-8100.* E-mail eat@tarbells.com; web www.tarbells.com. Hrs: 5-11 pm; Sun to 10 pm. Closed most major hols. Res accepted. Bar. Wine cellar. Semi-a la carte: lunch, dinner $13.95-$24.50. Child's meals. Specialties: grilled salmon, potato cake, veal chops. Own baking. Open kitchen with wood-burning oven. Cr cds: A, C, D, DS, JCB, MC, V.

D

★ ★ **TIMOTHY'S.** *6335 N 16th St. 602/277-7634.* Hrs: 11 am-3 pm, 5 pm-midnight; Sat, Sun from 5 pm. Closed Labor Day, Thanksgiving, Dec 24, 25. Continental menu. Res accepted. Bar. Semi-a la carte: lunch $4.75-$7.95, dinner $17.95-$29.95. Specializes in chicken, beef, fish. Jazz musicians nightly. Valet parking. Art deco, jazz theme. Cr cds: A, C, D, DS, MC, V.

D

★ ★ **TOMASO'S.** *3225 E Camelback Rd (85016). 602/956-0836.* Hrs: 11:30 am-2:30 pm, 5-10:30 pm; Sat, Sun from 5 pm. Closed Thanksgiving, Dec 25. Res accepted. Italian menu. Bar. A la carte entrees: lunch $7-$13, dinner $10-$23. Child's meals. Specializes in pasta, veal, seafood. Cr cds: A, C, D, DS, MC, V.

D

★ ★ **TOP OF THE MARKET.** *1720 E Camelback Rd (85016), top floor of Fish Market. 602/277-3474.* Hrs: 5-9:30 pm; Fri, Sat to 10 pm. Closed Thanksgiving, Dec 24 & 25. Res accepted. Bar. A la carte entrees: dinner $12.25-$35. Child's meals. Specializes in seafood, pasta, pizza. Nautical decor. Wood-burning pizza oven. View of Squaw Peak Mountain. Cr cds: A, D, DS, MC, V.

D

✓★ **TUCCHETTI.** *2135 E Camelback Rd (85016), in Town & Country Shopping Center. 602/957-0222.* Hrs: 11:15 am-10 pm; Fri to 11 pm; Sat noon-11 pm; Sun 4:30-9 pm. Closed some major hols. Res accepted. Italian menu. Bar. A la carte entrees: lunch, dinner $5.95-$14.95. Child's meals. Specializes in pasta, chicken, pizza. Outdoor dining. Italian atmosphere. Cr cds: A, C, D, DS, MC, V.

D

★ ★ ★ ★ **VINCENT GUERITHAULT ON CAMELBACK.** *3930 E Camelback Rd (85018). 602/224-0225.* One of the handful of Southwestern cuisine's originators, Guerithault is among the West's master chefs. Decor is country French. Southwestern, Amer menu. Specializes in lamb, chicken, seafood. Own baking, ice cream. Hrs: 11:30 am-2:30 pm, 6-10:30 pm; Sat from 5:30 pm. Closed major hols; also Sun June-Sept. Res accepted. Bar. Wine list. A la carte entrees: lunch $5.50-$8.95, dinner $19.75-$23. Valet parking. Open-air market on Sats, mid-Oct-mid-Apr. Cr cds: A, D, MC, V.

D ♥

Unrated Dining Spots

CHOMPIE'S. *3202 E Greenway Rd, Greenway Park Plaza. 602/971-8010.* Hrs: 6 am-9 pm; Mon to 8 pm; Fri to 9:30 pm; Sat 7 am-9 pm; Sun 7 am-8 pm. Kosher style deli menu. Wine, beer. Semi-a la carte: bkfst $2.50-$6, lunch $3.50-$7, dinner $5.95-$10.95. Child's meals. Specializes in beef, chicken, fish. Own baking. Family-owned New York style, kosher deli, bakery & bagel factory. Cr cds: A, MC, V.

D SC

DUCK AND DECANTER. *1651 E Camelback Rd. 602/274-5429.* Hrs: 9 am-7 pm; Thurs, Fri to 9 pm; Sun from 10 am. Closed some major hols. Bar. A la carte entrees: lunch, dinner $2.50-$5.50. Child's meals. Specialty: albacore tuna sandwich. Guitarist Fri-Sun evenings. Outdoor dining. Gourmet, wine shop. Totally nonsmoking. Cr cds: A, DS, MC, V.

D

ED DEBEVIC'S. *2102 E Highland Ave, in Town & Country Shopping Ctr, at 20th St & Camelback. 602/956-2760.* Hrs: 11 am-10 pm. Closed Thanksgiving, Dec 25. Bar. A la carte entrees: lunch, dinner $2.75-$6.95. Child's meals. Specializes in hamburgers, malts, french fries. Nostalgic 50s-style diner; tabletop jukeboxes. Costumed servers improvise routine of songs, dances, skits, irreverent humor. Cr cds: A, D, DS, MC, V.

D

HARD ROCK CAFE. *2621 E Camelback Rd (85016). 602/956-3669.* Hrs: 11 am-midnight. Closed Thanksgiving, Dec 25. Bar to 1 am. Semi-a la carte: lunch, dinner $5.99-$14.99. Child's meals. Specializes in burgers, chicken. Outdoor dining. Rock and Roll memorabilia. Cr cds: A, D, MC, V.

D

PLANET HOLLYWOOD. *2402 E Camelback Rd, Ste 101 (85016), in Biltmore Fashion Park. 602/954-7827.* Hrs: 11 am-midnight. Closed Dec 25. Bar to 1 am. Semi-a la carte: lunch, dinner $5.95-$17.95. Specialties: Captain Crunch chicken, margherita pasta, white chocolate bread pudding. Movie and Hollywood memorabilia; movie and TV screens throughout dining rm. Cr cds: A, D, MC, V.

D

Scottsdale

Motels

✔★★ **BEST WESTERN PAPAGO INN.** *7017 E McDowell Rd (85257). 602/947-7335; FAX 602/994-0692.* Web www.bestwestern.com/best.html. 56 rms, 2 story. Jan-Apr: S, D $108-$135; each addl $5; under 12 free; lower rates rest of yr. Crib $5. TV; cable (premium). Heated pool. Coffee in rms. Restaurant 7 am-1:30 pm, 5-9 pm. Rm serv. Bar 10-1 am. Ck-out noon. Coin Indry. Business servs avail. Valet serv. Free airport transportation. Exercise equipt; weights, bicycles, sauna. Bathrm phones, refrigerators; some microwaves. Shopping mall adj. Environmentally "green" rm avail. Aviary in courtyard. Cr cds: A, C, D, DS, ER, MC, V.

D SC

★★ **COUNTRY INN & SUITES.** *10801 N 89th Pl (85260). 602/314-1200; FAX 602/314-5868.* E-mail cissccts@ix.netcom.com; web www.arizonaguide.com/countryinnscotts. 163 rms, 3 story, 90 suites. Jan-May: S, D $139-$159; each addl $10; suites $159-$189; under 18 free; lower rates rest of yr. Crib free. TV; cable, VCR avail (movies). Complimentary continental bkfst. Complimentary coffee in rms. Restaurant adj 7 am-11 pm. Rm serv. Ck-out noon. Meeting rms. Business servs avail. In-rm modem link. Bellhops. Coin Indry. Exercise equipt; weights, stair machine. Pool; wading pool, whirlpool. Refrigerator, microwave, wet bar in suites. Grills. Cr cds: A, D, DS, MC, V.

D SC

★★★ **COURTYARD BY MARRIOTT.** *13444 E Shea Blvd (85259), near Mayo Clinic. 602/860-4000; FAX 602/860-4308.* 124 rms, 2 story, 11 suites. Jan-mid-May: S, D $149-$169; suites $169-$189; lower rates rest of yr. Crib free. TV; cable (premium). Heated pool; whirlpool. Complimentary coffee in rms. Restaurant 6:30 am-9 pm; Sat, Sun 7 am-2 pm, 5-9 pm. Rm serv. Bar 4-11 pm. Ck-out noon. Coin Indry. Meeting rms. Business servs avail. Valet serv. Exercise equipt; bicycle, stair machine. Refrigerator, microwave in suites. Many balconies. Cr cds: A, C, D, DS, MC, V.

D

★★ **FAIRFIELD INN BY MARRIOTT.** *5101 N Scottsdale Rd (85250). 602/945-4392; FAX 602/947-3044.* 218 rms, 2 story. Jan-Apr: S, D $134; wkends (2-day min); higher rates special events; lower rates rest of yr. Crib free. TV; cable (premium). Complimentary continental bkfst. Restaurant adj 7 am-11 pm. Ck-out noon. Meeting rm. Business servs avail. Bellhops. Valet serv. Sundries. Coin Indry. Health club privileges. Pool; whirlpool. Cr cds: A, C, D, DS, JCB, MC, V.

D SC

✔★★ **FAIRFIELD INN BY MARRIOTT.** *13440 N Scottsdale Rd (85254). 602/483-0042; FAX 602/483-3715.* 133 rms, 3 story. Jan-Apr: S, D $90-$130; under 18 free; lower rates rest of yr. TV; cable (premium), VCR avail. Pool; whirlpool. Complimentary continental bkfst. Restaurant nearby. Ck-out noon. Coin Indry. Business servs avail. Valet serv. Refrigerators avail. Picnic table. Cr cds: A, D, DS, MC, V.

D SC

★★ **HAMPTON INN.** *10101 N Scottsdale Rd (85253). 602/443-3233; FAX 602/443-9149.* 132 rms, 2 story. Jan-mid-Apr: S $105-$160; D $112-$180; under 18 free; higher rates special events; lower rates rest of yr. Crib free. TV; cable (premium). Complimentary continental bkfst. Restaurant nearby. Ck-out noon. Meeting rms. Business servs avail. Coin Indry. Exercise equipt; bicycles, treadmill. Pool; whirlpool. Refrigerators, microwaves. Cr cds: A, C, D, DS, MC, V.

D SC

★★ **HAMPTON INN.** *4415 N Civic Center Plaza (85251). 602/941-9400; FAX 602/675-5240.* 126 rms, 5 story. Jan-Apr: S, D $114-$150; under 18 free; higher rates special events (3-day min); lower rates rest of yr. Crib free. TV; cable (premium). Complimentary continental bkfst. Restaurant adj 6 am-11 pm. Ck-out noon. Meeting rms. Business servs avail. Valet serv. Coin Indry. Health club privileges. Pool. Cr cds: A, C, D, DS, MC, V.

D SC

★★ **HOSPITALITY SUITE RESORT.** *409 N Scottsdale Rd (85257). 602/949-5115; FAX 602/941-8014; res: 800/445-5115.* E-mail reservations@hospitalitysuites.com; web www.hospitalitysuites.com. 210 kit. suites (1-2 rm), 2-3 story. Mid-Jan-mid-Apr: S, D $169-$199; under 18 free; lower rates rest of yr. Crib $10. Pet accepted, some restrictions; $100 refundable. TV; cable (premium). 3 heated pools; whirlpool, poolside serv. Complimentary full bkfst. Coffee in rms. Restaurant 6:30 am-10 pm. Rm serv. Bar 11-1 am; entertainment (seasonal). Ck-out 11 am. Coin Indry. Meeting rms. Business servs avail. Bellhops. Valet serv. Free airport transportation. Lighted tennis. Lawn games. Health club privileges. Refrigerators, microwaves. Picnic tables; grills. Cr cds: A, C, D, DS, ER, MC, V.

D SC

★★ **LA QUINTA INN & SUITES.** *8888 E Shea Blvd (85260). 602/614-5300; FAX 602/614-5333.* 140 rms, 3 story. Jan-Apr: S, D $134-$144; each addl $10; under 17 free; lower rates rest of yr. Crib $10. Pet accepted, some restrictions. TV; cable (premium). Complimentary continental bkfst. Complimentary coffee in rms. Restaurant adj 7 am-11 pm. Ck-out noon. Meeting rms. Business servs avail. Coin Indry. Exercise equipt; weight machine, bicycle. Pool; whirlpool. Some refrigerators, microwaves. Cr cds: A, C, D, DS, MC, V.

D SC

★★ **RESIDENCE INN BY MARRIOTT.** *6040 N Scottsdale Rd (85253). 602/948-8666; FAX 602/443-4869.* E-mail riscottsdale@marri ott.com; web www.travelbase.com/destinationscottsdale/residence-inn/guest.html. 122 kit. suites, 2 story. Jan-Apr: S $140-$195; D $245-$295; wkly, monthly rates; lower rates rest of yr. Crib free. TV; cable (premium), VCR avail. Heated pool; whirlpool. Complimentary continental bkfst. Complimentary coffee in rms. Restaurant opp 6 am-10 pm. Ck-out noon. Coin Indry. Business servs avail. Valet serv. Lighted tennis privileges. 36-hole golf privileges, pro, putting green, driving range. Exercise equipt; bicycle, treadmill. Microwaves. Grills. Cr cds: A, C, D, DS, JCB, MC, V.

D

★ **RODEWAY INN.** *7110 E Indian School Rd (85251). 602/946-3456; FAX 602/946-4248.* 65 rms, 2 story. Jan-mid-Apr: S $93-$113; D $121; each addl $8; suites $150; under 18 free; wkly rates; lower rates rest of yr. Crib $6. TV; cable (premium). Heated pool; whirlpool. Complimentary continental bkfst. Restaurant nearby. Ck-out noon. Business servs avail. Refrigerators, microwaves. Cr cds: A, C, D, DS, ER, JCB, MC, V.

SC

★ **SAFARI RESORT.** *4611 N Scottsdale Rd (85251). 602/945-0721; FAX 602/946-4703; res: 800/845-4356.* 188 rms, 2 story, 64 kits. Jan-mid-Apr: S $92-$150; D $102-$160; each addl $10; kit. units $130-$160; under 18 free; golf plans; lower rates rest of yr. Crib free. Pet accepted; $50 refundable. TV; cable, VCR avail (movies). 2 heated pools; whirlpool. Complimentary continental bkfst. Restaurant 11 am-11 pm. Rm serv. Bar 11-1 am. Ck-out noon. Coin Indry. Meeting rms. Business servs avail. Bellhops. Valet serv. Gift shop. Health club privileges. Lawn games. Many private patios, balconies. Cr cds: A, C, D, DS, MC, V.

D

Motor Hotels

★★ **BEST WESTERN THUNDERBIRD SUITES.** *7515 E Butherus Dr (85260). 602/951-4000; FAX 602/483-9046.* 120 suites, 4 story. Mid-Jan-mid-Apr: S, D $115-$159; under 14 free; golf plans; lower rates rest of yr. Crib free. TV; cable, VCR avail (movies). Heated pool; whirlpool, poolside serv. Continental bkfst. Restaurant 6:30 am-9 pm. Rm serv. Bar 2 pm-midnight. Ck-out noon. Coin Indry. Meeting rms. Business servs avail. Refrigerators. Microwaves avail. Some balconies. Cr cds: A, C, D, DS, MC, V.

D SC

★★★ **DOUBLETREE LA POSADA RESORT.** *4949 E Lincoln Dr (85253). 602/952-0420; FAX 602/840-8576.* 252 rms, 10 suites. Jan-May: S, D $245; each addl $20; suites $375-$750; under 18 free; package plan; lower rates rest of yr. Crib free. Pet accepted, some restrictions. TV; cable (premium). 2 heated pools; whirlpool, poolside serv. Complimentary coffee in rms. Restaurant 6 am-10 pm; Fri, Sat to 11 pm. Rm serv. Bar noon-1 am. Ck-out noon. Convention facilities. Business servs avail. Bellhops. Valet serv. Sundries. Gift shop. Barber, beauty shop. Lighted tennis, pro, pro shop. Golf privileges, 2 putting greens. Exercise equipt; weights, bicycles, sauna. Lawn games. Some refrigerators, minibars. Private patios. Multiple cascading waterfalls; lagoon-like pool. At foot of Camelback Mountain. Cr cds: A, C, D, DS, ER, JCB, MC, V.

D SC

★★★ **DOUBLETREE PARADISE VALLEY RESORT.** *5401 N Scottsdale Rd (85250). 602/947-5400; FAX 602/946-1524.* 375 rms, 2 story, 12 suites. Jan-mid-May: S, D $205-$300; each addl $10; suites $350-$2,000; under 18 free; wkend rates; golf plans; lower rates rest of yr. Crib free. TV; cable (premium). 2 heated pools; whirlpool, poolside serv. Coffee in rms. Restaurants 6:30 am-11 pm. Rm serv. Bar 11-1 am. Ck-out noon. Convention facilities. Business servs avail. Concierge. Gift shop. Barber, beauty shop. 2 lighted tennis courts. Golf privileges. Exercise rm; instructor, weights, bicycles, sauna, steam rm. Massage. Bathrm phones, minibars; microwaves avail. Private patios, balconies. Grill. Extensive grounds elaborately landscaped; patio area overlooks courtyard. Cr cds: A, C, D, DS, ER, JCB, MC, V.

D

★★★ **HILTON RESORT & VILLAS.** *6333 N Scottsdale Rd (85250). 602/948-7750; FAX 602/948-2232.* 187 rms, 2-3 story, 45 villas. Jan-May: S $160-$245; D $170-$265; each addl $10; suites $245-$395; under 18 free; lower rates rest of yr. Crib free. TV; cable (premium). Heated pools; wading pool, whirlpool, poolside serv. Supervised child's activities (June-mid-Sept); ages 5-12. Coffee in rms. Restaurant 6:30 am-10 pm. Rm serv to 11 pm. Bar 11-1 am. Ck-out noon. Meeting rms. Business servs avail. Bellhops. Valet serv. Gift shop. Beauty shop. Lighted tennis, pro, pro shop. Golf privileges. Exercise rm; instructor, weights, bicycles, sauna, steam rm. Refrigerator, fireplace, patio in villas. Cr cds: A, C, D, DS, ER, MC, V.

D

★★ **RESORT SUITES.** *7677 E Princess Blvd (85255). 602/585-1234; FAX 602/585-1457; res: 800/541-5203.* Web www.resort suites.com. 262 suites (1-4 bedrm), 3 story. Jan-Apr: S, D $205-$695; under 16 free; lower rates rest of yr. Crib free. TV; cable. 3 pools, 2 heated; whirlpool, poolside serv. Complimentary coffee in rms. Restaurant 6-1 am. Rm serv. Bar from 10 am. Ck-out 10 am. Coin Indry. Convention facilities. Business center. Bellhops. Concierge. Golf privileges. Exercise equipt; weight machine, bicycles. Microwaves. Balconies. Cr cds: A, C, D, MC, V.

D

Hotels

★★ **EMBASSY SUITES.** *5001 N Scottsdale Rd (85250). 602/949-1414; FAX 602/947-2675.* 311 suites, 4 story. Jan-Apr: S $180; D $190; each addl $10; under 18 free; lower rates rest of yr. Crib free. TV; cable (premium), VCR avail (movies). 2 heated pools; poolside serv. Complimentary full bkfst. Coffee in rms. Restaurants 11 am-2:30 pm, 5-10 pm; Fri, Sat to 11 pm. Bars to 1 am. Ck-out noon. Coin Indry. Meeting rms. Business servs avail. Concierge. Gift shop. Free airport transportation. Lighted tennis, pro. Golf privileges. Exercise equipt; weights, bicycles. Rec rm. Game rm. Refrigerators; some bathrm phones; microwaves avail. Cr cds: A, C, D, DS, MC, V.

D SC

★★★ **MARRIOTT SUITES.** *7325 E 3rd Ave (85251). 602/945-1550; FAX 602/945-2005.* Web www.marriott.com. 251 suites, 8 story. Jan-May: S, D $209-$235; lower rates rest of yr. Crib free. TV; cable (premium). Heated pool; whirlpool, poolside serv. Complimentary coffee in rms. Restaurant 6:30 am-10 pm; Sat, Sun from 7 am. Bar 5-11 pm. Ck-out noon. Coin Indry. Convention facilities. Business center. Valet; covered parking. Tennis privileges. Golf privileges. Exercise equipt; weight machines, bicycles, sauna. Refrigerators; microwaves avail. Many private patios, balconies. Cr cds: A, C, D, DS, ER, JCB, MC, V.

D SC

Inns

★★★ **HERMOSA INN.** *(5532 N Palo Cristi Rd, Paradise Valley 85253) 602/955-8614; FAX 602/955-8299; res: 800/241-1210.* 35 units, 5 suites, 4 houses, 13 kit. units. Mid-Sept-May: S, D $150-$235; each addl $25; suites/houses $345-$475; under 6 free; lower rates rest of yr. Crib $25. TV; cable. Heated pool; whirlpool. Complimentary continental bkfst. Restaurant (see LON'S). Rm serv. Ck-out noon, ck-in 3 pm. Concierge serv. Luggage handling. Tennis, pro. Many fireplaces, wetbars. Cr cds: A, C, D, DS, MC, V.

★★★ **INN AT THE CITADEL.** *8700 E Pinnacle Peak Rd (85255), at Inn at the Citadel Complex. 602/585-6133; FAX 602/585-3436; res: 800/927-8367.* 11 suites. Mid-Jan-May: S, D $295-$335; under 12 free; lower rates rest of yr. Crib free. Pet accepted. TV; cable. Complimentary continental bkfst. Coffee in rms. Dining rm 7 am-10 pm. Rm serv. Ck-out noon, ck-in 3 pm. Business servs avail. Golf privileges. Some balconies, minibars. Each rm individually decorated with antiques, artwork. View of Sonoran Desert, city. Cr cds: A, C, D, DS, MC, V.

D

Resorts

★★ **HOLIDAY INN SUNSPREE.** *7601 E Indian Bend Rd (85250). 602/991-2400; FAX 602/998-2261.* 200 rms, 3 story. Jan-Apr: S, D $145; each addl $10; under 19 free; package plans; lower rates rest of yr. TV; cable (premium), VCR avail. Heated pool; poolside serv. Supervised child's activities (May-Aug). Coffee in rms. Dining rm 6:30 am-10 pm. Box lunches. Rm serv. Bar 11-1 am. Ck-out noon, ck-in 3 pm. Convention facilities. Business servs avail. Valet serv. Gift shop. Tennis, pro. 36-hole golf privileges, pro. Bicycles (rentals). Lawn games. Exercise equipt; weight machine, rower. Refrigerators. Some private patios. Cr cds: A, C, D, DS, ER, JCB, MC, V.

D SC

★★★★ **HYATT REGENCY SCOTTSDALE.** *7500 E Doubletree Ranch Rd (85258), 1/2 mi E of Scottsdale Rd. 602/991-3388; FAX 602/483-5550.* Located on 640-acre Gainey Ranch, this resort features Sonoran desert landscaping—lagoons plied by gondolas, fountains, waterfalls and date palm trees. 486 units in main bldg, 4 story, 7 casitas (1-4-bedrm) on lake. Jan-mid-June: S, D $365-$500; suites $600-$3,000; under 18 free; golf plans; lower rates rest of yr. Crib free. TV; cable (premium), VCR avail. 10 pools; wading pool, poolside serv; clock tower with waterslide, sand beach. Playground. Supervised child's activities; ages 3-12. Restaurants (public by res) 6:30 am-10:30 pm (also see GOLDEN SWAN). Rm serv 24 hrs. Bar noon-1 am. Ck-out noon, ck-in 4 pm. Meeting rms. Business center. In-rm modem link. Concierge. Gift shop. Free valet parking. Rec dir. 8 tennis courts, 4 lighted, pro. 27-hole golf, greens fee $125, pro, putting green, driving range. Bicycles. Exercise rm; instructor, weights, bicycles, sauna, steam rm. Massage. Minibars; microwaves avail. Fireplace, wet bar in casitas. Balconies. Luxury level. Cr cds: A, C, D, DS, ER, JCB, MC, V.

D

★ ★ ★ ★ ★ **MARRIOTT'S CAMELBACK INN RESORT GOLF CLUB & SPA.** *5402 E Lincoln Dr (85253), Paradise Valley, northeast of downtown. 602/948-1700; FAX 602/951-8469; res: 800/24-CAMEL.* Web www.camelbackinn.com. A southwestern-style lobby and large hilltop spa stand out at this vintage desert oasis on 125 beautifully landscaped acres. The spacious guest rooms have scenic views. 454 rms in 1-2-story casitas. Jan-May: S, D $339-$365; suites $600-$2,000; AP addl $64/person; MAP addl $48/person; Camelback plan (bkfst, lunch) addl $29/person; under 18 free; wkend rates; golf, tennis, spa plan; lower rates rest of yr. Crib free. Pet accepted. TV; cable (premium), VCR avail. 3 pools; whirlpool, poolside serv, lifeguards. Supervised child's activities (June-Aug; also some wkends & hols); ages 3-12. Dining rms 6:30 am-10 pm (also see CHAPARRAL DINING ROOM). Rm serv to midnight. Box lunches. Bars 11-1 am. Ck-out noon, ck-in 4 pm. Coin Indry. Business center. In-rm modem link. Valet serv. Concierge. Barber, beauty shop. Gift & sport shops. Lighted tennis, pro. 36-hole golf, greens fee $105 (incl cart), pros, putting greens, driving range, golf school. Bicycle rental. Lawn games. Soc dir; entertainment; movies winter & spring hols. Extensive exercise rm; instructor, weights, treadmills, sauna, steam rm. Spa. Refrigerators, minibars. Wet bar, microwave; fireplace, private pool in some suites. Private patios; many balconies. Cr cds: A, C, D, DS, ER, JCB, MC, V.

D

★ ★ ★ **MARRIOTT'S MOUNTAIN SHADOWS.** *5641 E Lincoln Dr (85253). 602/948-7111; FAX 602/951-5430.* Web www.marriott.com. 318 rms, 19 suites, 1-2 story. Jan-mid-May: S, D $240-$290; suites $365-$765; under 18 free; lower rates rest of yr. Crib free. TV; cable (premium). 3 heated pools; whirlpool. Dining rms 6:30 am-10 pm. Rm serv. Box lunches. Snack bar. Bars 11-1 am. Ck-out noon, ck-in 4 pm. Convention facilities. Business center. Valet serv. Gift shop. Lighted tennis, pro. 54-hole golf, greens fee $60-$70 (incl cart), pro, putting greens, driving range. Lawn games. Playground. Exercise rm; instructor, weights, bicycles, sauna. Minibars; many bathrm phones. Wet bar in suites. Microwave avail. Private patios, balconies. On 70 acres; 3 acres of gardens. Cr cds: A, C, D, DS, ER, JCB, MC, V.

D

★ ★ ★ **ORANGE TREE GOLF & CONFERENCE RESORT.** *10601 N 56th St (85254). 602/948-6100; FAX 602/483-6074; res: 800/228-0386.* Web www.orangetree.com. 160 suites, 2 story. Jan-May: S, D $220-$249; under 18 free; golf plan; lower rates rest of yr. Crib free. TV; cable (premium), VCR (movies). Heated pool; wading pool, whirlpool, poolside serv. Supervised child's activities. Coffee in rms. Dining rm 6 am-10 pm. Box lunches. Snack bar. Picnics. Rm serv. Bar 11-1 am; entertainment. Ck-out 11 am, ck-in 4 pm. Grocery 1 mi. Coin Indry. Package store 1 mi. Meeting rms. Business servs avail. Bellhops. Valet serv. Concierge. Gift shop. Airport transportation. Sports dir. Tennis privileges. 18-hole golf, greens fee $90 (incl cart), pro. Exercise equipt; weight machine, treadmill. Massage. Health club privileges. Bathrm phones, refrigerators, microwaves. Private patios, balconies. Golf resort with country club atmosphere. Cr cds: A, DS, MC, V.

D SC

★ ★ ★ ★ ★ **THE PHOENICIAN.** *6000 E Camelback Rd (85251), at 60th St. 602/941-8200; FAX 602/947-4311; res: 800/888-8234.* Web www.thephoenician.com. This spectacular hotel at the base of Camelback Mountain overlooks 250 acres with elaborately landscaped gardens, interconnected pools, and a lake with ducks. A sophisticated style results from the masterly blend of nature, landscaping, architecture, fine art and handcrafted furnishings. 654 rms: 468 rms in main bldg, 4-6 story, 119 casitas. Sept-mid-June: S, D, casitas $355-$545; each addl $50; suites $1,075-$1,725; villas $2,000-$3,500; under 17 free; golf plans; lower rates rest of yr. Crib free. TV; cable (premium), VCR avail (movies). 7 pools; 2 wading pools, whirlpool, poolside serv. Supervised child's activities; ages 5-12. Dining rms (public by res) 6 am-10 pm (also see MARY ELAINE'S and WINDOWS ON THE GREEN). Rm serv 24 hrs. Bar 11-1 am; entertainment. Ck-out noon, ck-in 4 pm. Convention facilities. Business center. In-rm modem link. Bellhops. Valet serv. Concierge. Shopping arcade. Barber, beauty shop. Airport transportation. Sports dir. 12 lighted tennis courts, pro. 27-hole golf, greens fee $130-$140, pro, putting green, driving range. Hiking. Bicycle rentals. Lawn games. Exercise rm; instructor, weight machines, bicycles, sauna, steam rm. Spa. Bathrm phones, minibars; some refrigerators, wet bars; microwaves avail. Balconies. Picnic tables. Cr cds: A, C, D, DS, JCB, MC, V.

D

★ ★ ★ **RADISSON.** *7171 N Scottsdale Rd (85253). 602/991-3800; FAX 602/948-1381.* E-mail sctt@cci.chg.carlson.com; web www.radisson.com. 318 rms, 2 story, 45 suites (31 bi-level). Jan-mid-May: S, D $195-$230; each addl $20; suites $325-$1,700; under 18 free; lower rates rest of yr. Crib free. TV; cable (premium), VCR avail. 3 heated pools; whirlpool, poolside serv. Supervised child's activities (June-Aug); ages 3-12. Dining rms 6:30 am-10 pm. Rm serv 24 hrs. Snack bar. Bar 11-1 am. Ck-out noon, ck-in 4 pm. Coin Indry. Convention facilities. Business servs avail. Valet serv. Concierge. Gift shop. Barber, beauty shop. Lighted tennis, pro. 36-hole golf privileges. Exercise equipt; weight machine, bicycle, sauna. Lawn games. Many refrigerators, minibars; some wet bars, fireplaces. Private patios, balconies. On 76 acres. Cr cds: A, C, D, DS, ER, JCB, MC, V.

D SC

★ ★ ★ **REGAL McCORMICK RANCH.** *7401 N Scottsdale Rd (85253). 602/948-5050; FAX 602/991-5572; res: 800/243-1332.* E-mail regal@getnet.com; web www.regal-hotels.com/scottsdale. 125 rms, 3 story, 51 kit. villas (2-3 bedrm). Jan-Apr: S, D $175-$325; each addl $10; villas $350-$575; under 18 free; golf, tennis plans; lower rates rest of yr. Crib free. TV; cable. Heated pool; whirlpool, poolside serv. Coffee in rms. Dining rm 6:30 am-10 pm. Rm serv. Bar 11-1 am; entertainment. Ck-out noon, ck-in 3 pm. Convention facilities. Business center. Valet serv. Valet parking. Concierge. Gift shop. Lighted tennis, pro. Golf privileges, pro, putting green, driving range. Dock; sailboats, paddleboats. Health club privileges. Sightseeing, desert trips. Lawn games. Soc dir. Minibars. Wet bar, fireplace in villas. Private patios, balconies. 10 acres on Camelback Lake; view of McDowell Mountains. Cr cds: A, C, D, DS, MC, V.

D SC

★ ★ ★ **RENAISSANCE COTTONWOODS.** *6160 N Scottsdale Rd (85253). 602/991-1414; FAX 602/951-3350.* Web www.renaissancehotels.com. 107 suites, 64 rms. Jan-May: S, D $245-$260; each addl $10; suites $285-$315; kit. units $345-$355; under 18 free; package plans; lower rates rest of yr. Crib free. Pet accepted, some restrictions. TV; cable (premium), VCR avail (movies). 3 heated pools; whirlpools, poolside serv. Complimentary continental bkfst in rms. Restaurant 7 am-10:30 pm. Rm serv 24 hrs. Bar noon-1 am. Ck-out noon. Meeting rms. Business center. Bellhops. Concierge. Valet serv. Airport transportation. Lighted tennis, pro. Golf privileges, putting green. Health club privileges. Lawn games. Bicycle rentals. Refrigerators, minibars; some bathrm phones, fireplaces; microwaves avail. Whirlpool on patios. Adj to Borgata shopping complex. Cr cds: A, C, D, DS, ER, JCB, MC, V.

D SC

★ ★ ★ **SCOTTSDALE PLAZA.** *7200 N Scottsdale Rd (85253). 602/948-5000; FAX 602/998-5971; res: 800/832-2025.* E-mail res@tspr.com; web www.tspr.com. 404 rms, 2 story, 180 suites. Jan-May: S, D $275-$290; each addl $10; suites $300-$3,500; under 17 free; wkend rates; lower rates rest of yr. Crib free. Pet accepted, some restrictions; $100 ($50 refundable). TV; cable (premium), VCR avail. 5 heated pools; poolside serv. Dining rms 6 am-11 pm (also see REMINGTON). Rm serv.

Bar 11-1 am; entertainment. Ck-out noon, ck-in 3 pm. Valet serv. Convention facilities. Business center. Concierge. Sundries. Gift shop. Beauty shop. Lighted tennis, pro. Racquetball. Bike rentals. Lawn games. Exercise equipt; treadmill, bicycle, sauna. Refrigerators, minibars; many wet bars; microwaves avail. Spanish colonial-style buildings on 40 acres; waterfall. Cr cds: A, C, D, DS, ER, JCB, MC, V.

D SC

★ ★ ★ ★ **SCOTTSDALE PRINCESS.** *7575 E Princess Dr (85255), off Scottsdale Rd just N of Bell Rd. 602/585-4848; FAX 602/585-0086; res: 800/223-1818.* Situated on 450 elaborately landscaped acres, with a waterfall in the central courtyard, this large resort offers airy rooms in a Spanish style. The golf course here is the site of the Phoenix Open, a yearly stop on the PGA Tour. 650 rms, 3-4 story, 75 suites, 119 casitas. Jan-May: S, D $350-$430; each addl $30; suites $470-$2,750; casitas $470-$520; under 16 free; golf, tennis, spa, hol plans; lower rates rest of yr. TV; cable, VCR avail. 3 pools; whirlpool, poolside serv. Supervised child's activities (Memorial Day-Labor Day & hols); ages 5-12. Dining rms 6:30 am-11 pm (also see LA HACIENDA and MARQUESA). Rm serv 24 hrs. Bars 11-1 am; entertainment. Ck-out noon, ck-in 4 pm. Convention facilities. Business center. Concierge. Shopping arcade. Barber, beauty shop. Valet parking. Lighted tennis, pro. 36-hole golf, greens fee $55-$155, pro, putting green, driving range. Lawn games. Basketball. Exercise rm; instructor, weight machines, bicycles, sauna, steam rm. Massage. Stocked lagoons; equipt avail for guests. Bathrm phones, refrigerators, minibars; some fireplaces. Private patios, balconies. Cr cds: A, C, D, DS, ER, JCB, MC, V.

D

★ ★ ★ **SUNBURST RESORT.** *4925 N Scottsdale Rd (85251). 602/945-7666; FAX 602/946-4056; res: 800/528-7867.* Web www.nhhr.com. 210 units, 7 with shower only, 2 story. Jan-Apr: S, D $185-$250; each addl $10; suites $425-$675; under 19 free; family, wkend, hol rates; golf plans; lower rates rest of yr. Crib free. TV; cable (premium). 2 heated pools; whirlpool, lifeguard, poolside serv. Complimentary coffee in rms. Restaurant 6 am-10 pm. Rm serv. Box lunches, snacks. Bar 10-1 am. Ck-out noon, ck-in 3 pm. Gift shop. Grocery, coin lndry 1 mi. Bellhops. Concierge. Valet serv. Meeting rms. Business servs avail. In-rm modem link. Tennis privileges, pro. 18-hole golf privileges, greens fee $95, putting green, driving range, pro. Exercise equipt; stair machine, bicycle. Refrigerators, minibars. Balconies. Picnic tables. Cr cds: A, C, D, DS, JCB, MC, V.

D SC

Restaurants

★ ★ **ALDO BALDO.** *7014 E Camelback Rd (85251), in Fashion Square. 602/994-0062.* Hrs: 11 am-10 pm; Fri, Sat to 11 pm; Sun 11:30 am-9 pm. Closed Thanksgiving, Dec 25. Italian menu. Bar. A la carte entrees: lunch $5-$13.95, dinner $8-$19. Child's meals. Specialties: calamari salad, chicken-and-vegetable lasagna, spinach-and-mushroom pizza. Valet parking. Outdoor dining. Open kitchen. Cr cds: A, C, D, DS, MC, V.

D

★ ★ ★ **AVANTI'S OF SCOTTSDALE.** *3102 N Scottsdale Rd. 602/949-8333.* Hrs: 5:30-10:30 pm; Fri, Sat to 11 pm. Res accepted. Northern Italian, continental menu. Bar 5:30 pm-1 am. Wine list. Semi-a la carte: dinner $14.95-$28.95. Specializes in seafood, veal. Own pasta. Pianist Tues-Sat. Valet parking. Outdoor dining. Black & white decor. Cr cds: A, D, DS, MC, V.

D

★ ★ **BANDERA.** *3821 N Scottsdale Rd (85251). 602/994-3524.* Hrs: 5-10 pm; Sun from 4:30 pm; Fri, Sat 4:30-11 pm. Closed Thanksgiving, Dec 25. Bar. Semi-a la carte: dinner $8.50-$18.95. Child's meals. Specialties: wood-fired, spit-roasted chicken; black bean chicken chili; millionaire's club filet. Parking. Totally nonsmoking. Cr cds: A, C, D, MC, V.

D

★ ★ **BRIO.** *7243 E Camelback Rd (85251). 602/947-0795.* Hrs: 11 am-2:30 pm, 5-10 pm; Fri to 11 pm; Sat 5-11 pm; Sun from 5 pm. Closed Thanksgiving, Dec 25. Res accepted. Bar. Semi-a la carte: lunch $6.95-$9.95, dinner $10.95-$21.95. Child's meals. Specialties: sesame catfish, tea-smoked duck, oven-seared salmon. Valet parking Fri, Sat. Outdoor dining. European roadhouse decor. Cr cds: A, C, D, DS, MC, V.

D

★ ★ **BUSTER'S.** *8320 N Hayden (85258). 602/951-5850.* Hrs: 11:30 am-10 pm; early-bird dinner 4-6 pm. Closed most major hols. Res accepted. Bar. Semi-a la carte: lunch $5.95-$10.95, dinner $6.45-$17.95. Child's meals. Specialties: filet mignon, mesquite grilled chicken pasta. Parking. Outdoor dining. Overlooks Lake Marguerite. Cr cds: A, D, MC, V.

D

★ ★ **CAFE TERRA COTTA.** *6166 N Scottsdale Rd (85253). 602/948-8100.* Web www.traveller.com. Hrs: 11 am-10 pm; Fri, Sat to 11 pm. Closed Thanksgiving, Dec 25. Res accepted. Southwestern menu. Bar. Semi-a la carte: lunch $7.95-$13.95, dinner $10.95-$22.95. Specialties: prawns stuffed with goat cheese, Chile rellano platter. Own desserts. Parking. Patio dining overlooking flower garden. Regional artwork displayed. Totally nonsmoking. Cr cds: A, C, D, DS, MC, V.

D

★ ★ ★ **CHAPARRAL DINING ROOM.** *(See Marriott's Camelback Inn Resort Golf Club & Spa Resort) 602/948-1700.* Web www.camelbackinn.com. Hrs: 6-10 pm; Fri, Sat to 11 pm. Res accepted. Continental menu. Bar to midnight. Wine cellar. A la carte entrees: dinner $19-$28. Specialties: lobster bisque, Dover sole, rack of lamb. Own baking. Valet parking. Jacket (in season). Cr cds: A, C, D, DS, ER, JCB, MC, V.

D SC

★ ★ **CHART HOUSE.** *7255 McCormick Pkwy (85258). 602/951-2550.* Hrs: 5-10 pm. Res accepted. Bar. Semi-a la carte: dinner $12.95-$34.95. Child's meals. Specializes in seafood, fresh fish, steak. Salad bar. Parking. Outdoor dining. All dining areas have good view of McCormick Lake. Cr cds: A, D, DS, MC, V.

D

★ **CHOMPIE'S.** *9301 E Shea Blvd (85260), Mercado del Rancho Center. 602/860-0475.* E-mail chompies@juno.com. Hrs: 6 am-9 pm; Fri, Sat to 9:30; Sun 7 am-8 pm. Closed Jewish hols. Kosher deli menu. Wine, beer. Semi-a la carte: bkfst $1.75-$8.50, lunch $4.50-$7.95, dinner $7.50-$11.95. Specialties: Nova Scotia lox, matzo brye, mile-high sandwiches. New York-style decor. Cr cds: A, MC, V.

D

★ ★ **DON & CHARLIE'S AMERICAN RIB & CHOP HOUSE.** *7501 E Camelback Rd (85251). 602/990-0900.* Hrs: 5-10 pm; Fri, Sat to 10:30 pm; Sun 4:30-9 pm. Closed Thanksgiving. Res accepted. Bar. Semi-a la carte: dinner $11.95-$29.95. Child's meals. Specialties: barbecued ribs, prime center cut steak. Own pies, cakes. Parking. Photos of celebrities, sports memorabilia on walls. Totally nonsmoking. Cr cds: A, C, D, DS, MC, V.

D

★ ★ **DRINKWATERS AT PINNACLE PEAK.** *8711 E Pinnacle Peak Rd (85255). 602/998-2222.* Hrs: 5-9:30 pm. Early-bird dinners 5-6 pm. Closed Mon (June-Aug); Dec 25, Jan 1. Res accepted. Bar from 4:30 pm. Semi-a la carte: dinner $12.95-$27.95. Child's meals. Specializes in beef, seafood, pasta. Parking. Outdoor dining. Mexican courtyard architecture with bell tower; antiques, art work. View of desert gardens. Cr cds: A, C, D, DS, MC, V.

D

★ ★ **EL CHORRO LODGE.** *5550 E Lincoln Dr (85253). 602/948-5170.* E-mail jfmiller@aol.com. Hrs: 11 am-3 pm, 5:30-11 pm; Sat, Sun from 9 am. Res accepted. Bar. Semi-a la carte: bkfst (Sat, Sun) $5-$12, lunch $7-$13.95, dinner $9.50-$58. Sun brunch $8-$14.50. Specialties: châteaubriand, rack of lamb, prime beef. Valet parking. Outdoor dining. Western decor, paintings. Fireplaces. Family-owned. Cr cds: A, C, D, DS, MC, V.

D

★ ★ ★ **GOLDEN SWAN.** *(See Hyatt Regency Scottsdale Resort) 602/991-3388.* Hrs: 6-10 pm; Sun brunch 9:30 am-2:30 pm; July, Aug 9:30 am-2 pm. Closed Sun, Mon (July-Aug). Res accepted. Hispaña menu. Bar. Extensive wine list. A la carte entrees: dinner $24.50-$32.50. Sun brunch $30. Child's meals. Specialties: ranch chicken baked in red rock clay; grilled Pacific salmon filet with mesquite honey barbecue sauce; sautéed veal medallions. Own pastries. Valet parking. Formal room with ebony columns; outdoor dining in pavilion beside lagoon with swans. Sunday brunch buffet in kitchen. Braille menu. Totally nonsmoking. Cr cds: A, C, D, DS, ER, JCB, MC, V.

D

★ ★ **HOPS! BISTRO & BREWERY.** *8668 E Shea (85260), in Pima Crossing. 602/998-7777.* Hrs: 11 am-10 pm; Thur, Fri, Sat to 11 pm. Closed Thanksgiving, Dec 25. Res accepted. Bar to midnight; Fri, Sat to 1 am. Semi-a la carte: lunch, dinner $6-$19. Child's meals. Specializes in chicken, pasta. Entertainment Tues-Thurs. Outdoor dining. Upscale bistro, brewery. Cr cds: A, C, D, DS, MC, V.

D

★ ★ **HOUSTON'S.** *6113 N Scottsdale Rd (85250), in Hilton Village. 602/922-7775.* Hrs: 11 am-10 pm; Fri to 11 pm; Sat 11:30 am-11 pm; Sun 11:30 am- 10 pm. Closed Thanksgiving, Dec 25. Bar. Semi-a la carte: lunch, dinner $6.95-$20.95. Child's meals. Specializes in steak, chicken, barbecue ribs. Outdoor dining. Upscale casual dining. Cr cds: A, MC, V.

D

★ ★ **IMPECCABLE PIG.** *7042 E Indian School Rd (85251). 602/941-1141.* Hrs: 11 am-3 pm, 5-9 pm; Mon to 3 pm; Thurs-Sat to 10 pm; early-bird dinner Tues-Sat 5-6:30 pm. Closed Sun; major hols. Res accepted. Serv bar. Semi-a la carte: lunch $6.95-$8.95, dinner $14.95-$19.95. Specializes in chicken, beef. Own soups. Parking. Glass-enclosed patio dining. Blackboard menu, changes daily. Period decor; antiques. Cr cds: A, C, D, DS, MC, V.

D

★ ★ **JEAN CLAUDE'S PETIT CAFE.** *7340 E Shoeman Lane. 602/947-5288.* Hrs: 11:30 am-2 pm, 6-10 pm; Sat from 6 pm. Closed Sun; most major hols. Res accepted. French menu. Bar. A la carte entrees: lunch $5.50-$10.50, dinner $14.95-$21.95. Specialties: duck with raspberry vinegar sauce, fresh grilled salmon with tarragon sauce, raspberry on chocolate soufflé. Contemporary decor. Cr cds: A, C, D, DS, MC, V.

★ **KYOTO.** *7170 Stetson Dr. 602/990-9374.* Hrs: 11 am-2 pm, 5:30-10 pm; Fri, Sat to 11 pm. Closed most major hols. Res accepted. Japanese menu. Bar. Semi-a la carte: lunch $3.50-$5, dinner $11.95-$24.95. Specialties: sushi, teriyaki chicken. Parking. Tableside cooking. Cr cds: A, C, D, DS, MC, V.

D

★ ★ ★ **L'ECOLE.** *8100 E Camelback Rd. 602/990-7639.* E-mail learm@chefs.com; web www.chefs.com/culinary//. Hrs: 11:30 am-1:30 pm, 6:30-8:30 pm. Closed Sat, Sun; major hols. Res required. Continental menu. Bar. Wine list. Complete meals: lunch $7-$11, dinner $15-$20. Specializes in fish, poultry, beef. Own baking. Tableside cooking. Menu changes wkly. Parking. Primarily staffed by students of the Scottsdale Culinary Institute. Cr cds: DS, MC, V.

D

★ ★ ★ ★ **LA HACIENDA.** *(See Scottsdale Princess Resort) 602/585-4848.* Situated in a tile-roofed hacienda and furnished with carved tables and chairs, this semi-formal restaurant offers refined Sonoran cuisine. Mexican menu. Specialties: filete al chipotle (char-broiled beef tenderloin), char-broiled lamb chops crusted with pumpkin seed, suckling pig. Own baking. Hrs: 6-10 pm; Fri, Sat to 11 pm. Res accepted. Bar from 5 pm. Wine list. A la carte entrees: dinner $17.50-$26. Child's meals. Strolling mariachis. Valet parking. Outdoor dining. Cr cds: A, C, D, DS, ER, JCB, MC, V.

D

★ ★ ★ **LA TÂCHE WORLD BISTRO.** *4175 Goldwater Blvd (85251). 602/946-0377.* Web www.latache.com. Hrs: 5-10 pm; Fri, Sat to 11 pm. Closed Jan 1, Thanksgiving, Dec 25. Res accepted. Continental menu. Bar 4 pm-midnight. Extensive wine list. A la carte entrees: dinner $11.75-$21.50. Prix-fixe: dinner $28. Specialties: pepita-crusted crab cakes, pot roast Provencal, whole sizzling fish. Outdoor dining. Contemporary decor; antique-styled French posters. Totally nonsmoking. Cr cds: A, C, D, DS, MC, V.

D

★ **LANDRY'S PACIFIC FISH COMPANY.** *4321 N Scottsdale Rd, between Camelback & Indian School Rds, in multi-level structure at Galleria. 602/941-0602.* Hrs: 11 am-10 pm; Fri, Sat to 11 pm; Sun noon-10 pm. Closed Thanksgiving, Dec 25. Res accepted. Bar. Semi-a la carte: lunch $4.95-$12.95, dinner $11.95-$21.95. Child's meals. Specialty: mesquite-broiled fish in Southwestern sauces. Entertainment wkends. Complimentary valet parking. Outdoor dining. 2 floors of dining; nautical decor, memorabilia; open kitchen. Cr cds: A, D, DS, MC, V.

D

★ ★ ★ **LON'S.** *(See Hermosa Inn) 602/955-7878.* Hrs: 11:30 am-2 pm, 6-9:30 pm; Sat from 6 pm; Sun 10 am-2 pm, 6-9:30 pm. Closed Memorial Day, July 4, Labor Day. Res accepted. Contemporary Amer/Southwestern menu. Bar. Extensive wine list. Semi-a la carte: lunch $8.95-$14.95, dinner $13.95-$24.95. Specialties: seared breast of duck, osso bucco on saffron risotto, seared Ahi tuna. Parking. Outdoor dining. Old Arizona adobe. Totally nonsmoking. Cr cds: A, D, MC, V.

D

✔★ **LOS OLIVOS.** *7328 E 2nd St (85251). 602/946-2256.* Hrs: 11 am-10:30 pm; Fri, Sat to 1 am. Closed most major hols. Res accepted. Mexican menu. Bar. Semi-a la carte: lunch, dinner $6.25-$13.75. Child's meals. Specialties: sour cream enchiladas, chimichanga supreme, fajitas. Entertainment Wed-Sun. Parking. Family-owned. Cr cds: A, C, D, DS, MC, V.

D

★ ★ ★ **MANCUSO'S.** *6166 N Scottsdale Rd, at the Borgata. 602/948-9988.* Hrs: 5-10:30 pm. Closed Thanksgiving, Dec 25. Res accepted. Northern Italian, continental menu. Bar. Complete meals: dinner $13.95-$24.95. Specializes in veal, pasta, seafood. Piano lounge. Valet parking. Ambiance of castle interior. Cr cds: A, C, D, DS, MC, V.

D

★ ★ **MARCO POLO SUPPER CLUB.** *8608 E Shea Blvd (85260). 602/483-1900.* Hrs: 5-10 pm; Fri, Sat to 11 pm. Closed most major hols. Res required. Continental menu. Bar to 1 am. A la carte entrees: dinner $10.95-$23.95. Child's meals. Specialties: gorgonzola New York strip, grilled veal chop, Hong Kong chicken. Musicians. Valet parking. Outdoor dining. Family photographs adorn walls. Cr cds: A, D, MC, V.

D

★ ★ ★ **MARIA'S WHEN IN NAPLES.** *7000 E Shea Blvd. 602/991-6887.* Hrs: 11:30 am-2:30 pm, 5-10 pm; Sat, Sun from 5 pm. Closed early-mid-Aug; most major hols. Res accepted. Italian menu. Bar. Semi-a la carte: lunch $6.95-$10.95, dinner $10.95-$19.95. Specializes in pasta, veal. Own desserts. Parking. Outdoor dining. Open kitchen. Multi-tiered dining. Cr cds: A, C, D, DS, MC, V.

D

★ ★ ★ ★ **MARQUESA.** *(See Scottsdale Princess Resort) 602/585-4848.* Portraits of Spanish royalty decorate this elegant yet casual restaurant specializing in Catalan cuisine. Spanish menu. Specialties: paella Valencia, sautéed John Dory, gambes Marquesa. Hrs: 6-10 pm; Fri, Sat to 11 pm; Sun brunch 10:30 am-2:30 pm. Closed Mon, Tues mid-June-Labor Day. Res accepted. Bar. Wine cellar. A la carte entrees: dinner $26-$35.

Sun brunch $36. Child's meals. Tapas bar. Flamenco guitarist Sun brunch. Valet parking. Outdoor dining. Cr cds: A, C, D, DS, ER, JCB, MC, V.

D ♥

★★★★ **MARY ELAINE'S.** *(See The Phoenician Resort) 602/423-2530.* The round tables in this bilevel dining room on the top floor of the Phoenician's main building offer panoramic views of the Valley of the Sun. Innovative contemporary French cuisine uses fresh organic ingredients. Contemporary French menu. Specializes in fresh seafood from around the world, rack of lamb, veal. Hrs: 6-10 pm; Fri, Sat to 11 pm. Closed Sun; also Mon mid-June-Aug. Res accepted. Bar. Wine cellar. A la carte entrees: dinner $32-$39. Complete meals: dinner $75-$105. Child's meals. Entertainment. Valet parking. Jacket (Sept-mid-June). Cr cds: A, C, D, DS, JCB, MC, V.

D

✔★★ **MR C'S.** *4302 N Scottsdale Rd (85251), opp the Galleria. 602/941-4460.* Hrs: 11 am-2:30 pm, 5-10 pm; Fri, Sat to 11 pm. Closed Thanksgiving, Dec 25. Res accepted. Chinese menu. Bar. Semi-a la carte: lunch $5.95-$7.50, dinner $7.50-$23. Specialties: macadamia chicken, jade lobster, Royal mandarin and Cantonese cooking. Elegant decor; Chinese paintings, ceramics, artwork. Cr cds: A, C, D, DS, MC, V.

D

★★★ **P.F. CHANG'S CHINA BISTRO.** *7014 E Camelback Rd (85253), in Scottsdale Fashion Square. 602/949-2610.* Hrs: 11 am-11 pm; Fri, Sat to midnight. Closed Thanksgiving, Dec 25. Chinese menu. Bar. A la carte entrees: lunch, dinner $5.95-$12.95. Specialties: orange peel shrimp, Paul's catfish, Chang's spicy chicken. Valet parking. Outdoor dining. Cr cds: A, MC, V.

D

★★★ **PALM COURT.** *7700 E McCormick Pkwy (85258), in Scottsdale Conference Resort. 602/596-7700.* Hrs: 7-11 am, 11:30 am-2 pm, 6-10 pm; Sun 10:30 am-2 pm (brunch), 6-10 pm. Res accepted; required dinner. Bar 10:30-1 am. Wine cellar. Semi-a la carte: bkfst $4.50-$10, lunch $6.50-$16.50, dinner $19-$35. Prix fixe: dinner $49. Sun brunch $24.50. Serv charge 18%. Child's meals. Specialties: duckling, lobster Lord Randolph, rack of lamb. Pianist brunch, evenings. Valet parking. Intimate dining; tableside cooking and preparation. Jacket (dinner). Totally nonsmoking. Cr cds: A, C, D, DS, MC, V.

D

★ **PISCHKE'S PARADISE.** *7217 E 1st St. 602/481-0067.* Hrs: 7 am-11 pm; Sun 8 am-10 pm. Closed most major hols. Bar. Semi-a la carte: bkfst $3-$8, lunch $5-$9, dinner $6-$18. Specialties: Cajun Caesar salad, six-egg omelettes. Outdoor dining. Colorful prints, photos above bar. Cr cds: A, DS, MC, V.

D

★★ **THE QUILTED BEAR.** *6316 N Scottsdale Rd (85253). 602/948-7760.* Hrs: 7 am-10 pm; Sun from 8 am. Res accepted. Semi-a la carte: bkfst $1.99-$7.95, lunch $4.95-$8.50, dinner $6.95-$18.95. Child's meals. Specializes in seafood, beef. Salad bar. Own soups. Outdoor dining. Colorful decor; stained-glass windows. Cr cds: A, C, D, DS, MC, V.

D

★★★ **RANCHO PINOT GRILL.** *6208 N Scottsdale Rd (85253). 602/468-9463.* Hrs: 5:30-10 pm. Closed Sun, Mon; major hols; also mid-Aug-mid-Sept. Contemporary Amer menu. Bar. Wine cellar. Semi-a la carte: $17-$22. Specialties: Nonni's Sunday chicken, mesquite grilled seafood, steaks. Own baking, ice cream. Outdoor dining. Totally nonsmoking. Cr cds: DS, MC, V.

D

★★★ **RAZZ'S RESTAURANT & BAR.** *10321 N Scottsdale Rd (85253). 602/905-1308.* Hrs: 5-10 pm. Closed Sun, Mon; last 2 wks in July, August; most maj hols. Res accepted, required Fri, Sat. International, contemporary menu. Bar. Semi-a la carte: dinner $14.95-$21.95. Child's meals. Specialties: duck cakes with nopalito cactus sauce; rack of lamb with tamarind; cashew, coconut and rosemary encrusted salmon filet. Own baking. Parking. Chef-owned. Cr cds: A, C, D, MC, V.

D

★★★ **REMINGTON.** *(See Scottsdale Plaza Resort) 602/951-5101.* Hrs: 11 am-2:30 pm, 5-10 pm; Sat, Sun from 5 pm. Res accepted. Bar 4:30 pm-midnight. Wine cellar. A la carte entrees: lunch $7.25-$16, dinner $18.50-$32. Specializes in seafood, lamb, mesquite-grilled steak. Jazz. Outdoor dining. Elegant Southwestern decor; columns, vaulted dome ceiling with sky mural. Cr cds: A, D, DS, MC, V.

D

★★ **ROLAND'S.** *4515 N Scottsdale Rd. 602/946-7236.* E-mail tetenoie.aol.com. Hrs: 5-10 pm; Closed Sun; some major hols. Res accepted. Continental menu. Bar. A la carte entrees: dinner $12.95-$20.95. Specialities: grilled Escolar over wilted red cabbage slaw; pan-seared calf's liver with caramelized Bermuda onions with roesti potatoes. Cr cds: A, D, DS, JCB, MC, V.

D

★★★ **RUTH'S CHRIS STEAK HOUSE.** *7001 N Scottsdale Rd (85253). 602/991-5988.* Hrs: 5-10 pm; Fri, Sat to 10:30 pm. Closed Thanksgiving, Dec 25. Res accepted. Bar. A la carte entrees: dinner $17.95-$43.50. Specializes in USDA prime-aged, corn-fed Midwestern beef; fresh seafood, live Maine lobster. Outdoor dining. Traditional steakhouse. Cr cds: A, D, MC, V.

D

★★ **SALT CELLAR.** *550 N Hayden Rd. 602/947-1963.* Hrs: 5-11 pm; Fri, Sat to midnight. Closed Dec 25. Res accepted. Bar 4 pm-1 am. Semi-a la carte: dinner $13.95-$27.95. Child's meals. Specializes in seafood, prime steaks. Parking. Restaurant located underground, in former salt cellar. Rustic, nautical decor. Cr cds: A, MC, V.

✔★★ **SUSHI ON SHEA.** *7000 E Shea Blvd (85254). 602/483-7799.* Hrs: 11:30 am-2:30 pm, 5:30-10 pm; Fri, Sat to 11 pm; Sun from 5:30 pm. Closed most major hols. Japanese menu. Bar. Semi-a la carte: lunch $4.50-$10, dinner $8.25-$15. Child's meals. Specializes in chicken, sushi, tempura. Aquarium; sushi bar. Totally nonsmoking. Cr cds: A, C, D, DS, MC, V.

D

★★★ **VOLTAIRE.** *8340 E McDonald Dr (85250). 602/948-1005.* Hrs: 5:30-10 pm. Closed Sun; some major hols; also June-Sept. Res required. French, continental menu. Bar. Wine list. Semi-a la carte: dinner $16.50-$23. Specialties: rack of lamb, sandabs with white grapes, Cr cds: A, D, MC, V.

D

★★★ **WINDOWS ON THE GREEN.** *(See The Phoenician Resort) 602/423-2530.* Hrs: 11 am-10 pm; Sun brunch from 10 am. Closed Mon (Sept-mid-June); Tues, Wed (mid-June-Aug). Res accepted. Contemporary southwestern menu. Bar. Wine cellar. Semi-a la carte: lunch $7-$16, dinner $23-$30. Sun brunch $9-$15.50. Child's meals. Specialties: campfire salmon, tortilla soup. Valet parking. Outdoor dining. View overlooking golf course. Totally nonsmoking. Cr cds: A, C, D, DS, JCB, MC, V.

★★ **Z'TEJAS GRILL.** *7014 E Camelback Rd (85251), in Scottsdale Fashion Square. 602/946-4171.* Hrs: 11 am-10 pm; Fri, Sat to 11 pm; Sat, Sun brunch to 3 pm. Res accepted. Southwestern menu. Bar. Semi-a la carte: lunch $4.95-$10.75, dinner $8.25-$15.95. Sat, Sun brunch $5.50-$6.75. Child's meals. Specialties: VooDoo tuna, stuffed pork tenderloin, wild mushroom enchilada. Valet parking. Outdoor dining. Cr cds: A, C, D, DS, MC, V.

D

★★ **ZINZIBAR.** *3815 N Scottsdale Rd (85251). 602/990-9256.* Hrs: 5-10 pm; Fri, Sat to 11 pm. Closed major hols. Res accepted. Continental menu. Bar from 4 pm; Sat, Sun 5-11 pm. A la carte entrees: dinner $10-$22. Child's meals. Specialties: Moroccan ahi, veal chop, lobster ravioli. Hand-painted murals in Old-World decor. Cr cds: A, C, D, DS, MC, V.

D

Pittsburgh

Settled: 1758
Pop: 369,879
Elev: 760 feet
Time zone: Eastern
Area code: 412
Web: www.pittsburgh-cvb.org

With dazzling modern buildings, clean parks and community pride, Pittsburgh today has had a remarkable renaissance and has achieved one of the most spectacular civic redevelopments in America.

Industry in Pittsburgh grew out of the West's needs for manufactured goods; foundries and rolling mills began producing nails, axes, frying pans and shovels. The Civil War added tremendous impetus to industry, and by the end of the war, Pittsburgh was producing half of the steel and one-third of the glass made in the country.

By the end of World War II, Pittsburgh was financially prosperous from its war effort but aesthetically bankrupt. Financier Richard King Mellon and Mayor Lawrence were the spiritual architects of the revival. A merciless antismoke campaign swept clean the smog-polluted air, and under the spur of a civic group called the Allegheny Conference on Community Development, great new skyscrapers of steel, aluminum and glass arose. Entire areas of the city were erased and rebuilt. Pittsburgh accomplished this $3-billion civic revitalization without surrendering an ounce of its industrial might. On the contrary, many new companies have located in the area since World War II. They deal in everything from atomic energy to plate glass. Within a 30-mile radius of the city more than 150 research and testing laboratories have opened.

Business

Pittsburgh's economy experienced a successful transformation in the 1980s following the decline of the domestic steel industry. Substantial growth in education, health care, high technology and service industries have helped bridge the gap.

Although Pittsburgh is not one of the largest metropolitan areas in the nation, it is the fourth-largest headquarters city for *Fortune 500* corporations. It also ranks near the top in the number of industrial plants, the number of industrial workers and in value added by manufacturing. Research and development is also an important industry, employing more than 15,000 in the four-county metropolitan area, and more than 20,000 technical and support people in the nine-county economic area.

Convention Facilities

The David L. Lawrence Convention Center has 131,000 square feet of exhibition space and 25 meeting rooms accommodating between 50 and 2,100 people. A glass-enclosed walkway spans the exhibition floor. The center is within walking distance of five major hotels.

To the east, in nearby Monroeville, the Greater Pittsburgh Expo Mart caters to retailers in a three-state area. It has two floors of exhibition space, as well as office space. Total exhibition space is 106,000 square feet. Twenty-four meeting rooms hold between 40 and 2,000 people.

Closer to the airport, The Charles L. Sewall Center for Leadership Development in Coraopolis has 40,000 square feet of display and exhibit space, as well as four meeting rooms, which can accommodate between 20 and 300 people.

The Civic Arena and Exhibit Hall is one of the city's unique structures. Its primary feature is a vast, 148-foot-high retractable stainless steel roof. The roof is divided into eight leaves, six of which rotate around a pin at the top as they roll back for performances under the stars.

Sports & Recreation

Any resident will attest to the fact that Pittsburgh is a sports town. The Steelers football team has enough Super Bowl rings to grace the fingers of one hand. The Pirates baseball team also has had their share of winning seasons. Both play at Three Rivers Stadium. The Pittsburgh Penguins hockey team plays at the Civic Arena. There is also harness racing at the Meadows, south of the city, and Thoroughbred racing in nearby Chester, West Virginia.

Golfers and tennis players will find many courses and courts on which to test their skills. For outdoor enthusiasts, western Pennsylvania is a paradise of mountain wilderness, lakes, rivers, parks and resorts. Within a two-hour drive of the city one can find hiking, camping, whitewater rafting, fishing, hunting and skiing.

Entertainment

The internationally acclaimed Pittsburgh Symphony performs at Heinz Hall. At the Benedum Center, the Civic Light Opera presents a series of Broadway musicals during July and August. The Pittsburgh Ballet and Pittsburgh Opera also give performances. Other quality entertainment is available at the Pittsburgh Folk Festival in late May, as well as other theaters in the city that offer professional performances.

Two Pittsburgh neighborhoods—the South Side and the Strip District—have sprouted numerous restaurants, dance clubs and coffee bars in recent years. The South Side recently received a Main Street USA award from the National Trust for Historic Preservation. The Strip District, downtown along Penn Ave, is the wholesale and retail market area, with 24-hour activity.

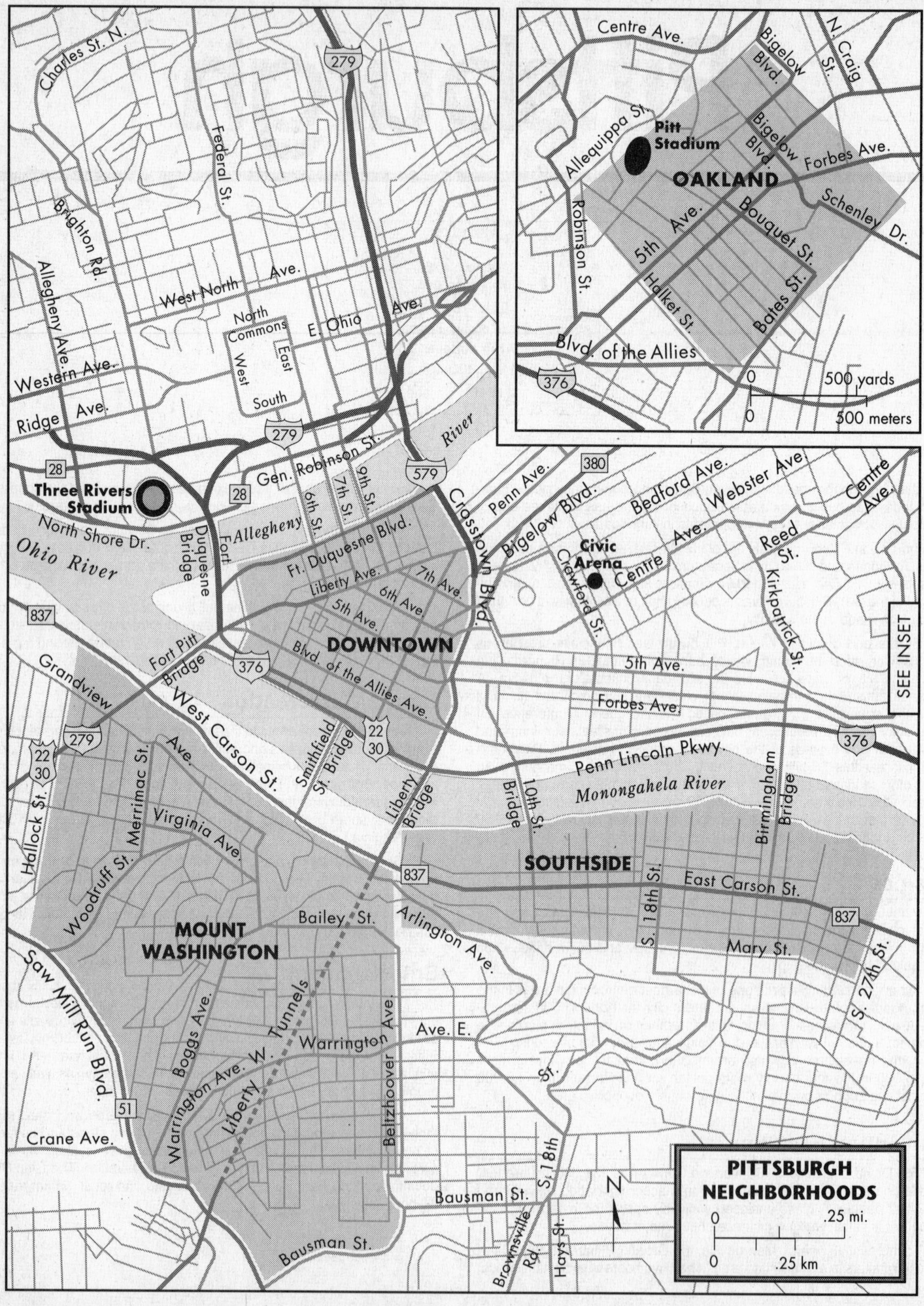
PITTSBURGH NEIGHBORHOODS
DOWNTOWN
OAKLAND
SOUTHSIDE
MOUNT WASHINGTON
Three Rivers Stadium
Pitt Stadium
Civic Arena
Ohio River
Allegheny River
Monongahela River
SEE INSET
Charles St. N.
Federal St.
Brighton Rd.
Allegheny Ave.
West North Ave.
North Commons
East
West
South
E. Ohio Ave.
Western Ave.
Ridge Ave.
Gen. Robinson St.
6th St.
7th St.
9th St.
North Shore Dr.
Duquesne Bridge
Fort
Ft. Duquesne Blvd.
Liberty Ave.
7th Ave.
6th Ave.
5th Ave.
Blvd. of the Allies Ave.
Crosstown Blvd.
Penn Ave.
Bigelow Blvd.
Bedford Ave.
Webster Ave.
Centre Ave.
Reed St.
Crawford St.
Kirkpatrick St.
Forbes Ave.
Penn Lincoln Pkwy
Fort Pitt Bridge
Grandview Ave.
West Carson St.
Smithfield St. Bridge
Liberty Bridge
10th St. Bridge
Birmingham Bridge
Hallock St.
Merrimac St.
Virginia Ave.
Woodruff St.
East Carson St.
S. 18th St.
Mary St.
S. 27th St.
Bailey St.
Arlington Ave.
Saw Mill Run Blvd.
Boggs Ave.
Liberty Tunnels
Warrington Ave. W.
Warrington Ave.
Beltzhoover Ave.
Ave. E.
St.
Crane Ave.
Bausman St.
S. 18th
Brownsville Rd.
Hays St.
N
0
.25 mi.
.25 km
279
579
28
380
837
376
22
30
51
Centre Ave.
Bigelow Blvd.
N. Craig St.
Allequippa St.
Forbes Ave.
Schenley Dr.
Robinson St.
5th Ave.
Bouquet St.
Halket St.
Bates St.
Blvd. of the Allies
500 yards
500 meters

Historical Areas

The Fort Pitt Block House, built in 1764, is the last remaining building of the original fortress. The Fort Pitt Museum, built on part of the original fort, houses exhibits and displays on Native American and frontier life and the military struggles for the Ohio Valley. Also displayed are unusual war artifacts. The museum and blockhouse are located in Point State Park.

On the campus of the University of Pittsburgh is the Stephen Foster Memorial, said to be the most elaborate memorial ever built to a musician. It contains a $250,000 collection of the Pittsburgh-born composer's music and memorabilia.

The Senator John Heinz Regional History Center, a 160,000-square-foot museum and research facility located along the Allegheny River, tells the story of the region up to the present day. This facility houses exhibits on the history of the Western Pennsylvania region, a theater, library and archive and a gift shop.

Sightseeing

For a thrilling and delightful experience, take a ride on the inclines (hill-climbing trolleys). Travelers ascend from the city's South Side to the top of Mount Washington for an excellent view of the Golden Triangle, where two rivers meet to form a third.

Trips aboard the Gateway Clipper Fleet offer the tourist scenic cruises on the three rivers. All the ships have cruises daily year round.

A unique structure on the University of Pittsburgh campus is the Cathedral of Learning, a Gothic skyscraper of classrooms, 42 floors, 542 feet high; an observation point is on the 36th floor. Bordering the three-story Commons Room are 24 rooms, each furnished by a different nationality group.

The Pittsburgh Zoo houses more than 6,000 animals on a 70-acre site. In addition to the Main Habitat Zoo, there is also the Kid's Kingdom, Aqua Zoo and Tropical Forest complex.

Shoppers will find no lack of retail outlets at which to spend their money. The Golden Triangle area has major department stores. Oxford Centre, PPG Place, Fifth Avenue Place and Station Square are unique complexes with shops, restaurants and interesting architectural features. East of the city, in Shadyside and Squirrel Hill, is a variety of boutiques, specialty shops and studios.

General References

Area code: 412

Phone Numbers

POLICE & FIRE: 911

POISON CONTROL CENTER: 681-6669

TIME: 391-9500 **WEATHER:** 936-1212

Information Sources

Greater Pittsburgh Convention & Visitors Bureau, Inc, 4 Gateway Center, 15222; 281-7711, 800/366-0093.

Visitor Information Center, Liberty Ave, adj Gateway Center, 800/366-0093.

24-hour Activities Line, 800/366-0093.

Transportation

AIRLINES: American; British Airways; Continental; Delta; Northwest; TWA; United; USAir; and other commuter and regional airlines.

AIRPORT: Pittsburgh International, 472-3525.

CAR RENTAL AGENCIES: (See IMPORTANT TOLL-FREE NUMBERS) Avis 472-5204; Budget 472-5252; Hertz 472-5955; National 472-5094; Thrifty 264-1775.

PUBLIC TRANSPORTATION: Port Authority of Allegheny County, 442-2000.

RAILROAD PASSENGER SERVICE: Amtrak 800/872-7245.

Newspaper

Pittsburgh Post-Gazette.

Convention Facilities

Charles L. Seawall Center for Leadership Development, Narrows Run Rd, Coraopolis, 262-8436.

David L. Lawrence Convention Center, 1001 Penn Ave, 565-6000.

Expo Mart Radisson, 101-105 Mall Blvd, Monroeville, 800/245-EXPO.

Sports & Recreation

Major Sports Facilities

Three Rivers Stadium, 600 Stadium Circle (Pirates, baseball, 323-5000); 300 Stadium Circle (Steelers, football, 323-0300).

Civic Arena, downtown in Golden Triangle, 642-1800 (Penguins, hockey).

Racetrack

Ladbroke Racing-The Meadows, MeadowLands, I-79 S of exit 8, 225-9300.

Cultural Facilities

Theaters

City Theatre Company, 57 S 13th St, 431-4900.

Pittsburgh Public Theatre, Allegheny Square, 321-9800.

Pittsburgh Playhouse, 222 Craft Ave, Oakland, 621-4445.

Concert Halls

Benedum Center for the Performing Arts, 719 Liberty Ave, 456-6666.

Heinz Hall for the Performing Arts, 600 Penn Ave, 392-4800 or 392-4900.

Museums

The Carnegie Science Center, 1 Allegheny Ave, adj to Three Rivers Stadium, 237-3400.

The Carnegie Museum of Natural History, 4400 Forbes Ave, 622-3360.

Fort Pitt Museum, 101 Commonwealth Pl, Point State Park, 281-9284.

James L. Kelso Bible Lands Museum, Pittsburgh Theological Seminary, 616 N Highland Ave, 362-5610.

Pittsburgh Children's Museum, 10 Children's Way, 322-5058.

Stephen Foster Memorial, Forbes Ave at Bigelow Blvd, University of Pittsburgh, 624-4100.

Art Museums

Andy Warhol Museum, 117 Sandusky St, 237-8300.

The Carnegie Museum of Art, 4400 Forbes Ave, 622-3360.

The Frick Art Museum, 7227 Reynolds St, 371-0600.

Henry Clay Frick Fine Arts Building, Schenley Plaza, University of Pittsburgh, 648-2400.

Pittsburgh Center for the Arts, Mellon Park, 6300 5th Ave, 361-0873.

Points of Interest

Historical

Allegheny County Courthouse, 436 Grant St, 355-5313.

Fort Pitt Block House, Point State Park, 471-0235.

Other Attractions

Alcoa Building, 425 6th Ave, 553-4545.

Allegheny Observatory, 159 Riverview Park Ave, 321-2400.

Cathedral of Learning, 5th Ave & Bigelow Blvd, University of Pittsburgh, 624-6000.

Duquesne Incline, lower station, 1220 Grandview Ave, SW of Fort Pitt Bridge, 381-1665.

Equitable Plaza, Gateway Center.

Fallingwater, approx 60 mi E via PA Tpke to Donegal, then approx 15 mi S on PA 381, near Mill Run, 329-8501.

Frick Park, Beechwood Blvd & English Lane.

One Gateway Center, adj to Point State Park, 392-6000.

Heinz Memorial Chapel, 1212 Cathedral of Learning, University of Pittsburgh, 624-4157.

Kennywood Park, 4800 Kennywood Blvd, in West Mifflin, 461-0500.

Mellon Bank Building, 5th Ave & Grant St.

Mellon Square Park, 6th Ave between Smithfield St & William Penn Place.

Monongahela Incline, W Carson St near Smithfield St Bridge, 442-2000.

National Aviary in Pittsburgh, Allegheny Commons West, 323-7235.

Nationality Classrooms, 157 Cathedral of Learning, 624-6000.

One Oxford Centre, Grant St at 4th Ave, 391-5300.

Phipps Conservatory, One Schenley Pk, 622-6915.

Pittsburgh Zoo, NE on Highland Ave in Highland Park area, 665-3639.

Point State Park, foot of Fort Duquesne & Fort Pitt Blvds, 471-0235.

PPG Place, 1 PPG Place, Market Square.

Rodef Shalom Biblical Botanical Garden, 4905 5th Ave, 621-6566.

Soldiers' and Sailors' Memorial Hall, 4141 Fifth Ave, 621-4253.

Station Square, foot of Smithfield St Bridge, S Side, 471-5808.

Sightseeing Tours

Gray Line bus tours, 110 Lenzer Court, Sewickley 15143; 741-2720.

River Cruises, Gateway Clipper Fleet, 9 Station Square Dock, 355-7980.

Annual Events

Pittsburgh Folk Festival, Expo Mart. Memorial Day wkend.

Three Rivers Arts Festival, Gateway Center Plaza, PPG Place and Point State Park, 481-7040. June.

Fourth of July Celebration, Point State Park.

Three Rivers Regatta, Point State Park. Last wkend July & 1st wkend Aug.

Christmas Tree Display, The Carnegie. Dec.

City Neighborhoods

Many of the restaurants, unrated dining establishments and some lodgings listed under Pittsburgh include neighborhoods as well as exact street addresses. Geographic descriptions of these areas are given, followed by a table of restaurants arranged by neighborhood.

Downtown: South of the Allegheny River, west of I-579, north of the Monongahela River and east of Point State Park. **North of Downtown** North of Allegheny River. **South of Downtown** North of Monongahela River. **East of Downtown** East of US 579.

Mount Washington: Across the Monongahela River south of Downtown; north of Saw Mill Run Blvd, south of West Carson St, east of Hallock and west of Beltzhoover.

Oakland: East of Downtown; centered on and around 5th Ave between Bellefield St on the north and Halket St on the south.

South Side: Across the Monongahela River south of Downtown; Station Square area east and west of the Smithfield St Bridge.

Lodgings and Food

PITTSBURGH RESTAURANTS BY NEIGHBORHOOD AREAS

(For full description, see alphabetical listings under Restaurants)

DOWNTOWN
1902 Landmark Tavern. 24 Market St
British Bicycle Club. 923 Penn Ave
Carlton. 1 Mellon Bank Center
Carmassi's Tuscany Grill. 711 Penn Ave
Common Plea. 308 Ross St
Del Frates. 971 Liberty Ave
Juno Trattoria. One Oxford Center, 3rd floor
Seventh Street Grille. 130 7th St
Terrace Room (Westin William Penn Hotel). 530 Wm Penn Place
Top Of The Triangle. 600 Grant St, 62nd floor

NORTH OF DOWNTOWN
The Church Brew Works. 3525 Liberty Ave
Max's Allegheny Tavern. Middle & Suisman Sts
Penn Brewery. Troy Hill, 800 Vinial St
Rico's. 1 Rico Lane

SOUTH OF DOWNTOWN
Colony. Greentree & Cochran Rds
London Grille. 1500 Washington Rd
Piccolo Mondo. 661 Andersen Dr
Samurai Japanese Steak House. 2100 Greentree Rd
Sushi Two. 2122 E Carson St
Tambellini's. PA 51

EAST OF DOWNTOWN
The Balcony. 5520 Walnut St
Bentley's. 5608 Wilkens Ave
Brandy's Place. 2323 Penn Ave
Cafe At The Frick. 7227 Reynolds St
Casbah. 229 S Highland Ave
China Palace. 5440 Walnut St
D'imperio's. 3412 Wm Penn Hwy
Jimmy Tsang's. 5700 Centre Ave
Kaya. 2000 Smallman St
Max & Erma's. 5533 Walnut St
Nina. 5701 Bryant St
Pasta Piatto. 736 Bellefonte St
Poli. 2607 Murray Ave
Primanti Bros. 46 18th St
Soba Lounge. 5847 Ellsworth Ave
Tessaro's. 4601 Liberty Ave
Thai Place. 809 Bellefonte St
Vermont Flatbread Co. 2701 Penn Ave

MOUNT WASHINGTON
Cliffside. 1208 Grandview Ave
Georgetowne Inn. 1230 Grandview Ave
Le Mont. 1114 Grandview Ave
Tin Angel. 1200 Gandview Ave

OAKLAND
Dave And Andy's Ice Cream Parlor. 207 Atwood St
India Garden. 328 Atwood St

SOUTH SIDE
Cafe Allegro. 51 S 12th St
Grand Concourse. 1 Station Square
Le Pommier. 2104 E Carson St
Station Square Cheese Cellar. #25 Freight House Shops

Note: When a listing is located in a town that does not have its own city heading, it will appear under the city nearest to its location. In these cases, the address and town appear in parentheses immediately following the name of the establishment.

Motels

★ ★ **CLUBHOUSE INN.** *5311 Campbells Run Rd (15205), jct I-279 & PA 60, west of downtown, exit Moon Run Rd. 412/788-8400; FAX 412/788-2577; res: 800/258-2466.* Web www.clubhouseinn.com. 152 rms, 3 story, 26 suites. S $85; D $95; each addl $10; suites $100; under 16 free; lower rates Fri, Sat. Crib free. TV; cable (premium). Heated pool; whirlpool. Complimentary buffet bkfst. Restaurant adj 11 am-11 pm. Ck-out noon. Coin Indry. Meeting rms. Business servs avail. In-rm modem link. Free airport transportation. Exercise equipt; treadmill, stair machine. Some microwaves; refrigerator in suites. Cr cds: A, D, DS, MC, V.

D SC

✔★ ★ **HAMPTON INN.** *555 Trumbull Dr (15205), across river, west of downtown. 412/922-0100; FAX 412/921-7631.* 135 rms, 6 story. June-Nov: S $69-$75; D $79; under 18 free; wkend rates; lower rates rest of yr. Crib free. Pet accepted. TV; cable (premium). Complimentary continental bkfst. Restaurant nearby. Ck-out noon. Meeting rms. Business servs avail. In-rm modem link. Valet serv. Free airport transportation. Health club privileges. Picnic tables. Cr cds: A, C, D, DS, MC, V.

D SC

✔★ ★ **HAMPTON INN-WEST MIFFLIN.** *1550 Lebanon Church Rd (15236), S on US 51, south of downtown. 412/650-1000; FAX 412/650-1001.* 70 rms, 3 story. S $79-$94; D $84-$99; under 18 free; higher rates: hols, football games. Crib free. TV; cable (premium), VCR avail (movies). Restaurant nearby. Ck-out noon. Meeting rms. Business servs avail. In-rm modem link. Valet serv. Concierge. Heated pool; lifeguard. Some in-rm whirlpools, refrigerators, microwaves. Cr cds: A, C, D, DS, JCB, MC, V.

D SC

★ ★ **HAWTHORN SUITES.** *700 Mansfield Ave (15205), at Noblestown Rd, or I-279 exit 4, south of downtown. 412/279-6300; FAX 412/279-4993.* E-mail tn009665@psinet.com; web www.hawthorn.com. 151 suites, 2 story. S $89-$119; D $119-$149; wkly, monthly rates. Crib free. Pet accepted, some restrictions; $50 and $6/day. TV; cable (premium). Pool; whirlpool, lifeguard. Complimentary full bkfst. Ck-out noon. Meeting rms. Business servs avail. Airport, RR station, bus depot transportation. Health club privileges. Refrigerators, microwaves, fireplaces. Private patios, balconies. Picnic tables, grills. Chalet-style buildings. Cr cds: A, C, D, DS, JCB, MC, V.

D SC

★ ★ ★ **HOLIDAY INN GREENTREE-CENTRAL.** *401 Holiday Dr (15220), west of downtown. 412/922-8100; FAX 412/922-6511.* 200 rms, 4 story. S, D $104-$148; each addl $10; under 18 free. Crib free. Pet accepted. TV; cable, VCR avail. Heated pool; poolside serv, lifeguard. Restaurant 6:30 am-10 pm; Fri, Sat to 11 pm. Rm serv. Bar 11-2 am, Sun from 1 pm; entertainment. Ck-out noon. Meeting rms. Business servs avail. In-rm modem link. Valet serv. Sundries. Free airport transportation. Tennis privileges. Golf privileges. Health club privileges. Exercise equipt; weight machine, bicycles. Private patios. Cr cds: A, C, D, DS, JCB, MC, V.

D SC

★ ★ **HOLIDAY INN-ALLEGHENY VALLEY.** *180 Gamma Dr (15238), PA 28 exit 10, north of downtown. 412/963-0600; FAX 412/963-7852.* 223 rms, 2 story. S $90; D $100; each addl $10; suites $120-$150; under 18 free. TV; cable (premium). Heated pool; pooside serv, lifeguard. Restaurant 6 am-10 pm; Sat, Sun from 7 am. Rm serv. Bar 11-2 am; Sun 1 pm-1 am. Ck-out 11 am. Meeting rms. Business servs avail. In-rm modem link. Bellhops. Valet serv. Airport transportation. Exercise equipt; stair machine, bicycles. Refrigerator in suites; microwaves avail. Cr cds: A, C, D, DS, JCB, MC, V.

D SC

★ ★ **HOWARD JOHNSON-SOUTH.** *5300 Clairton Blvd (PA 51) (15236), south of downtown. 412/884-6000; FAX 412/884-6009.* 95 rms, 3 story. No elvtr. S $69-$79; D $79-$89; each addl $10; under 18 free. Crib free. TV; cable (premium). Pool; lifeguard. Complimentary full bkfst; Sat, Sun continental. Restaurant nearby. Ck-out noon. Meeting rms. Business servs avail. In-rm modem link. Valet serv. Exercise equipt; weight machine, bicycles. Microwaves avail. Near Allegheny County Airport. Cr cds: A, C, D, DS, ER, MC, V.

D SC

✔★ **RED ROOF INN.** *6404 Steubenville Pike (PA 60) (15205), south of downtown. 412/787-7870; FAX 412/787-8392.* 120 rms, 2 story. S, D $53.99-$59.99; under 18 free. Crib free. Pet accepted, some restrictions. TV; cable (premium). Complimentary morning coffee. Restaurant adj open 24 hrs. Ck-out noon. Business servs avail. Cr cds: A, C, D, DS, MC, V.

D

Motor Hotels

✔★ ★ ★ **BEST WESTERN-PARKWAY CENTER INN.** *875 Greentree Rd (15220), adj Parkway Center Mall, west of downtown. 412/922-7070; FAX 412/922-4949.* 138 rms, 6 story, 44 kits. S $87-$97; D $96-$106; each addl $9; kit. units $96-$106; under 12 free; wkend rates. Crib free. TV; cable (premium). Indoor pool; lifeguard. Complimentary bkfst. Ck-out noon. Coin lndry. Meeting rms. Business servs avail. In-rm modem link. Bellhops. Valet serv. Sundries. Free airport transportation. Exercise equipt; weight machine, bicycles, sauna. Rec rm. Microwaves avail. Cr cds: A, C, D, DS, ER, MC, V.

D SC

★ ★ ★ **HARLEY.** *699 Rodi Rd (15235), at jct PA 791 & I-376, east of downtown. 412/244-1600; FAX 412/829-2334; res: 800/321-2323.* 152 rms, 3 story. No elvtr. S $112-$122; D $122-$132; each addl $10; under 18 free; wkend plan. Crib free. TV; cable, VCR avail. 2 heated pools, 1 indoor; whirlpool, sauna, poolside serv, lifeguard. Restaurant 6:30 am-2 pm, 5:30-10 pm; Fri, Sat 5:30-11 pm. Rm serv 7 am-11 pm. Bar 4:30 pm-midnight, Fri to 1 am, Sat noon-1 am, Sun 4:30-11 pm; entertainment Fri, Sat. Ck-out 11 am. Meeting rms. Business servs avail. In-rm modem link. Bellhops. Valet serv. Sundries. Airport transportation. Lighted tennis. Private patios, balconies. Cr cds: A, C, D, DS, JCB, MC, V.

D SC

★ ★ ★ **HOLIDAY INN.** *4859 McKnight Rd (15237), 5 mi N on I-279, exit 18, north of downtown. 412/366-5200; FAX 412/366-5682.* 147 rms, 7 story, 19 suites. S, D $99-$109; each addl $10; suites $109-$139; under 18 free. Crib free. Pet accepted. TV; cable (premium). Heated pool; poolside serv, lifeguard. Complimentary coffee in rms. Restaurant 6:30 am-10 pm; Sun from 7 am. Rm serv. Bar 11 am-11 pm; entertainment Fri, Sat. Ck-out noon. Coin lndry. Meeting rms. Business servs avail. In-rm modem link. Valet serv. Sundries. Health club privileges. Refrigerator in suites; microwaves avail. Cr cds: A, C, D, DS, MC, V.

D SC

★ ★ ★ **HOLIDAY INN.** *164 Fort Couch Rd (15241), south of downtown. 412/833-5300; FAX 412/831-8539.* 210 rms, 8 story. S, D $75; each addl $10; suites $120-$130; under 18 free; wkend rates. Crib free. Pet accepted, some restrictions. TV; cable (premium), VCR avail. Pool; poolside serv, lifeguard. Restaurant 6:30 am-11 pm; Sat, Sun from 7 am. Rm serv. Bar 11-2 am; entertainment Tues-Sat. Ck-out noon. Meeting rms. Business servs avail. In-rm modem link. Bellhops. Valet serv. Shopping arcade. Airport transportation. Health club privileges. Game rm. Gift shop. Microwaves avail. Balconies. Cr cds: A, C, D, DS, ER, JCB, MC, V.

D SC

★ ★ **HOLIDAY INN-MONROEVILLE.** *(2750 Mosside Blvd, Monroeville 15146) approx 7 mi E on I-376, exit 16A, at PA 48 & US 22 Business. 412/372-1022; FAX 412/373-4065.* 189 rms, 4 story. S, D $79-$119; each addl $10; under 19 free; wkly, monthly, wkend rates. Crib free. Pet accepted. TV; cable (premium). Pool. Complimentary coffee in rms. Restaurant 6:30 am-2 pm, 5-10 pm. Rm serv. Bar 11-2 am; entertainment Wed-Sun. Ck-out noon. Coin lndry. Meeting rms. Business servs avail. In-rm modem link. Valet serv. Sundries. Exercise equipt; weight machine, stair machines. Health club privileges. Microwaves avail. Cr cds: A, C, D, DS, ER, MC, V.

D SC

★ ★ ★ **HOLIDAY INN-PARKWAY EAST.** *915 Brinton Rd (15221), east of downtown. 412/247-2700; FAX 412/371-9619.* 180 rms, 11 story. Apr-Oct: S, D $99-$119; suites $150; under 18 free; wkend, hol rates; lower rates rest of yr. Crib free. Pet accepted. TV; cable (premium). Indoor pool; lifeguard. Coffee in rms. Restaurant 6:30 am-10 pm. Rm serv. Bar 11-1 am; entertainment Fri, Sat. Ck-out noon. Coin lndry. Meeting rms. Business servs avail. Bellhops. Valet serv. Health club privileges. Some refrigerators, microwaves avail. Cr cds: A, D, DS, ER, JCB, MC, V.

D SC

★ ★ ★ **MARRIOTT GREENTREE.** *101 Marriott Dr (15205), across river, west of downtown. 412/922-8400; FAX 412/922-8981.* Web www.marriott.com. 467 rms, 7 story. S $99-$164; D $114-$179; each addl $15; suites $200-$375; under 18 free; wkend rates; package plans. Crib free. Pet accepted. TV; cable (premium), VCR avail. 3 pools, 1 indoor; whirlpool, poolside serv, lifeguard. Restaurant 6:30 am-midnight. Rm serv. Bar 11-2 am; entertainment. Ck-out noon. Meeting rms. Business servs avail. In-rm modem link. Bellhops. Valet serv. Sundries. Gift shop. Barber, beauty shop. Free airport transportation. Indoor tennis privileges. Exercise equipt; weight machines, bicycles, sauna, steam rm. Health club privileges. Rec rm. Many minibars. Luxury level. Cr cds: A, C, D, DS, ER, MC, V.

D SC

Hotels

★ ★ ★ **DOUBLETREE.** *1000 Penn Ave (15222), downtown. 412/281-3700; FAX 412/227-4500.* 616 rms, 26 story. S $125-$180; D $145-$215; each addl $20; suites $255-$1,550; family rates; wkend rates. Crib free. Pet accepted. TV; cable (premium). Indoor pool; whirlpool. Coffee in rms. Restaurants 6:30 am-10:30 pm. Rm serv 24 hrs. Bar 11-2 am. Ck-out noon. Convention facilities. Business center. In-rm modem link. Concierge. Shopping arcade. Courtesy limo downtown. Exercise rm; instructor, weights, bicycles, sauna, steam rm. Refrigerators; many bathrm phones. Cr cds: A, C, D, DS, ER, JCB, MC, V.

D SC

★ ★ ★ **HILTON.** *Gateway Center (15222), at Point State Park, downtown. 412/391-4600; FAX 412/594-5161.* 711 rms, 24 story. S $139-$196; D $159-$206; each addl $20; suites $325; studio rms $109; children free; wkend plans. Crib free. Pet accepted, some restrictions. TV; cable (premium), VCR avail. Coffee in rms. Restaurant 6:30 am-11:30 pm. 2 bars 11-2 am; entertainment. Ck-out noon. Meeting rms. Business center. In-rm modem link. Concierge. Drugstore. Barber, beauty shop. Garage avail; valet parking. Airport transportation. Exercise equipt; weights, treadmill. Minibars; some bathrm phones, refrigerators. Luxury level. Cr cds: A, C, D, DS, ER, JCB, MC, V.

D SC

★ ★ ★ **SHERATON.** *7 Station Square (15219), on South Side. 412/261-2000; FAX 412/261-2932.* 292 rms, 15 story. S $149-$170; D $164-$185; each addl $15; suites $225-$600; under 18 free; wkend rates. Crib free. TV; cable (premium), VCR avail. Indoor pool; whirlpool, lifeguard. Coffee in rms. Restaurant 6 am-midnight. Bar 11-2 am; entertainment. Ck-out noon. Meeting rms. Business center. In-rm modem link. Shopping arcade. RR station, bus depot transportation. Exercise equipt; weights, bicycles. Health club privileges. Game rm. On riverfront. Luxury level. Cr cds: A, C, D, DS, ER, JCB, MC, V.

D SC

★ ★ ★ **WESTIN WILLIAM PENN.** *530 Wm Penn Place (15219), on Mellon Square, downtown. 412/281-7100; FAX 412/553-5252.* 595 rms, 24 story. S, D $179-$189; each addl $20; suites $398-$1,200; under 18 free; wkend rates. Crib free. Pet accepted. Valet parking $19.50. TV; cable (premium), VCR avail. Restaurant 6:30 am-11 pm (also see TERRACE ROOM, Unrated Dining). Rm serv 24 hrs. Bar 11-2 am; entertainment. Ck-out 1 pm. Convention facilities. Business center. Gift shop. Barber shop. Airport, RR station, bus depot transportation. Exercise equipt; bicycles, treadmill. Health club privileges. Historic, landmark hotel. Cr cds: A, C, D, DS, ER, JCB, MC, V.

D SC

★ ★ ★ **WYNDHAM GARDEN HOTEL.** *1 Wyndham Circle (15273-1000), off PA 60, exit Montour Run Rd, west of downtown. 412/695-0002; FAX 412/695-7262.* Web www.hyatt.com/travelweb. 140 rms, 4 story. S $104; D $114; each addl $10; suites $104-$114; under 18 free; wkend, hol rates. Crib free. TV; cable (premium). Pool; wading pool, lifeguard. Complimentary full bkfst. Complimentary coffee in rms. Restaurant 6:30 am-2 pm, 5-10 pm. Bar 4 pm-midnight. Ck-out noon. Meeting rms. Business center. In-rm modem link. Free airport transportation. Exercise equipt; stair machine, treadmill. Some refrigerators; microwaves avail. Cr cds: A, C, D, DS, ER, JCB, MC, V.

D SC

Inns

★ ★ ★ **THE APPLETREE.** *703 S Negley Ave (15232), east of downtown. 412/661-0631; FAX 412/661-8151.* Web www.appletreeb-b.com. 4 rms, 2 story, suite. MAP: S, D $99-$130; each addl $10; suite $120; wkend plans; hols (2-3 day min); children over 12 yrs only. TV in common rm; VCR. Complimentary full bkfst. Ck-out 11 am, ck-in 3-6 pm. Concierge serv. Luggage handling. Business servs avail. In-rm modem link. Health club privileges. Totally nonsmoking. Historic building (1884). Cr cds: A, DS, MC, V.

SC

★ ★ ★ **INN AT OAKMONT.** *(Oakmont 15139) 15 mi NE on PA 28, adj to golf course. 412/828-0410; FAX 412/828-1358.* Web www.bnb.lm.com. 8 rms, 1 with shower only, 2 story. S $100-$120; D $130-$140; each addl $10. TV; VCR avail. Complimentary full bkfst. Coffee in library. Restaurant nearby. Ck-out 11 am, ck-in 2 pm. Concierge serv. Business servs avail. 18-hole golf privileges. Exercise equipt; weight machine, treadmill. Balconies. Many antiques. Totally nonsmoking. Cr cds: A, DS, MC, V.

D

★ ★ ★ **THE PRIORY.** *614 Pressley St (15212), north of downtown. 412/231-3338; FAX 412/231-4838.* 24 rms, 3 story. S $65-$100; D $103-$120; each addl $10; suites $110-$143; under 7 free; lower rates wkends. TV; cable. Complimentary continental bkfst; evening refreshments. Ck-out 11 am, wkends noon, ck-in 3 pm. Meeting rms. Business servs avail. Health club privileges. Previously a haven for Benedictine monks (1888); European-style inn with fountain and floral arrangements in courtyard. Cr cds: A, C, D, DS, MC, V.

D SC

★ ★ ★ **SHADYSIDE.** *5516 Maple Heights Rd (15232), east of downtown; I-279 exit 13. 412/683-6501; FAX 412/683-7228.* Web www.bnb.lm.com. 7 rms, 2 share bath, 3 story. No elvtr. No rm phones. MAP: S, D $100-$140. TV in sitting rm; cable (premium), VCR, (movies avail). Complimentary continental bkfst. Restaurant nearby. Ck-out noon, ck-in 3 pm. Concierge serv. Luggage handling. Health club privileges. Microwaves avail. Billiard rm, library. Cr cds: A, DS, MC, V.

Restaurants

★ ★ **1902 LANDMARK TAVERN.** *24 Market St (15222), downtown. 412/471-1902.* Hrs: 11:30 am-11 pm; Fri & Sat to midnight. Closed Sun; major hols. Res accepted. Italian-American menu. Bar to 2 am. Semi-a la carte: lunch $5.95-$11.50, dinner $10.95-$22. Specializes in steaks, fresh seafood, oyster bar. Restored tavern (1902); ornate tin ceiling, original tiles. Cr cds: A, D, DS, MC, V.

✔★ ★ **THE BALCONY.** *5520 Walnut St (15232), in Theatre Bldg, Shadyside, east of downtown. 412/687-0110.* Hrs: 11:30 am-midnight; Sun brunch 10:30 am-2:30 pm. Closed most hols. Res accepted. Bar. Semi-a la carte: lunch $5.95-$9.95, dinner $10.95-$15.95. Sun brunch $9.95. Specializes in fresh seafood, vegetarian pasta, focaccia sandwiches. Entertainment Mon-Sat. Cr cds: A, DS, MC, V.

✔★ ★ **BENTLEY'S.** *5608 Wilkens Ave, east of downtown. 412/421-4880.* Hrs: 11:30 am-10 pm; Fri, Sat to 11 pm; extended hrs summer; early-bird dinner Mon-Sat 4-6 pm. Closed Thanksgiving, Dec 25. Res accepted. Continental menu. Bar. Complete meals: lunch $5.95-$6.95, dinner $8.95-$14.95. Child's meals. Specializes in seafood, veal, pasta. Parking. Outdoor dining. Cr cds: A, D, DS, MC, V.

★ ★ **BRANDY'S PLACE.** *2323 Penn Ave (15222), at 24th St, in Strip District, east of downtown. 412/566-1000.* Hrs: 11 am-10 pm. Closed Thanksgiving, Dec 25. Res accepted. Bar to 1 am. Semi-a la carte: lunch $3.95-$7.95, dinner $12.95-$22.95. Child's meals. Specialties: crab cakes, grilled lamb chops, veal parmigiana. Outdoor dining. Restored turn-of-the-century restaurant. Cr cds: A, C, D, DS, MC, V.

✔★ **BRITISH BICYCLE CLUB.** *923 Penn Ave, downtown. 412/391-9623.* Hrs: 10 am-10 pm. Closed Sat, Sun; major hols. Res accepted. Bar. Semi-a la carte: lunch $4.75-$8.75, dinner $4.75-$15.95. Specializes in prime rib, steak salad, steaks. English pub atmosphere. Cr cds: A, C, D, DS, MC, V.

★ ★ ★ **CAFE ALLEGRO.** *51 S 12th St (15203), on South Side. 412/481-7788.* Hrs: 5-11 pm. Closed major hols. Res accepted. Italian menu. Bar. Wine list. Semi-a la carte: dinner $17-$23. Child's meals. Specialties: pasta del sole, seafood arrabbiata, grilled veal medallions. Valet parking. Ambience of Riviera cafe; artwork. Cr cds: A, D, MC, V.

D

★ ★ **CAFE AT THE FRICK.** *7227 Reynolds St (15208), at the Frick Art and Historical Center, east of downtown. 412/371-0600.* Hrs: 11 am-5:30 pm; Sun noon-6 pm; high tea from 3 pm. Closed Mon; most major hols; also Mon-Fri in Jan. Semi-a la carte: lunch $7.95-$10. High tea $9.95. Specializes in grilled chicken, desserts. Outdoor dining. View of garden and Frick estate. Totally nonsmoking. Cr cds: DS, MC, V.

D

★ ★ ★ **CARLTON.** *1 Mellon Bank Center, on grounds of Mellon Bank Center Commercial Bldg, at Grant St, downtown. 412/391-4099.* Hrs: 11:30 am-2:30 pm, 5-10 pm; Fri to 11 pm; Sat 5-11 pm. Closed Sun; major hols. Res accepted. Continental menu. Bar. Extensive wine list. Semi-a la carte: lunch $9.95-$14.95, dinner $19.95-$25.95. Child's meals. Specializes in charcoal-grilled seafood, prime steak, veal. Own pastries. Parking. Cr cds: A, C, D, DS, MC, V.

D

★ ★ ★ **CARMASSI'S TUSCANY GRILL.** *711 Penn Ave (15222), downtown. 412/281-6644.* Hrs: 11 am-10 pm; Sat, Sun 4:30-8 pm. Closed hols. Res accepted. Northern Italian menu. Bar. Semi-a la carte: lunch $9-$12, dinner $17-$25. Child's meals. Specialties: veal a'la lucca, penne arrabiatta. Italian art on display. Cr cds: A, C, D, DS, MC, V.

D

★ ★ ★ **CASBAH.** *229 S Highland Ave (15206), in Shadyside, east of downtown. 412/661-5656.* Hrs: 11:30 am-2:30 pm; 5-11 pm; Sun-Tues 5-10 pm. Closed most major hols. Res accepted. Mediterranean menu. Bar. Semi-a la carte: lunch $5.50-$12, dinner $12-$22. Child's meals. Specialties: lamb mixed grill, roasted vegetable tagine, Mahi Mahi and grape leaves. Cr cds: A, D, DS, MC, V.

D

✔★ ★ **CHINA PALACE.** *5440 Walnut St (15232), in Shadyside, east of downtown. 412/687-7423.* Hrs: 11:30 am-10 pm; Fri, Sat to 11 pm; Sun 2-9 pm. Closed July 4, Labor Day, Thanksgiving. Chinese menu. Bar.

Semi-a la carte: lunch $4.95-$5.50, dinner $6.95-$16.95. Specialties: crispy walnut shrimp, orange beef, lemon chicken. Cr cds: A, D, DS, MC, V.

✓★★ **THE CHURCH BREW WORKS.** *3525 Liberty Ave (15201), north of downtown. 412/688-8200.* E-mail churchbrew@juno.com; web www.churchbrew.com. Hrs: 11:30 am-midnight; Fri, Sat to 1 am; Sun noon-10 pm. Closed Jan 1, Thanksgiving, Dec 25. Regional Amer menu. Bar. Semi-a la carte: lunch $5.75-$7.95, dinner $13.95-$19.95. Specialties: buffalo steak, wood-fired oven pizza, Pittsburgh pierogie. Own pasta. Outdoor dining. Brew-pub in 1902 church; vaulted ceiling, stained-glass windows. Cr cds: A, D, DS, MC, V.

D

★★★ **CLIFFSIDE.** *1208 Grandview Ave, on Mount Washington. 412/431-6996.* Hrs: 5-10 pm; Fri, Sat to 11 pm. Closed major hols. Res accepted. Continental menu. Bar. Semi-a la carte: dinner $16-$22.50. Child's meals. Specializes in fresh seafood, chicken, veal. Pianist. Valet parking. Contemporary decor in older building (1897). Cr cds: A, D, DS, JCB, MC, V.

★★★ **COLONY.** *Greentree & Cochran Rds, south of downtown. 412/561-2060.* Hrs: 5-10:30 pm; Sun 4-9 pm. Res accepted. Continental menu. Bar 4 pm-1 am. Extensive wine list. Complete meals: dinner $21-$42. Specializes in fresh seafood, tournedos of veal, prime Angus steaks. Own baking. Pianist, vocalist Fri, Sat. Valet parking. Family-owned. Jacket. Cr cds: A, C, D, DS, JCB, MC, V.

★★★ **COMMON PLEA.** *308 Ross St, downtown. 412/281-5140.* Hrs: 11:30 am-2:30 pm, 5-10 pm; Sat 5-10 pm. Closed Sun; major hols. Res accepted. Bar. Complete meals: lunch $6.95-$10.75, dinner $18.25-$28. Specializes in seafood, veal, chicken. Own baking. Valet parking (dinner). Courtroom decor. Family-owned. Cr cds: A, D, MC, V.

★★★ **D'IMPERIO'S.** *3412 Wm Penn Hwy (15235), east of downtown. 412/823-4800.* Hrs: 11:30 am-3 pm, 5-11 pm; Mon, Sat from 5 pm. Closed Sun; most major hols. Res accepted; required wkends. Italian, Amer menu. Bar. Semi-a la carte: dinner $13.50-$28. Child's meals. Specialties: shrimp Sorrento, lobster sausage, veal Genovese. Own bread. Pianist. Parking. Different displays of artwork in each dining rm. Cr cds: A, C, D, DS, MC, V.

D

★ **DEL FRATES.** *971 Liberty Ave (15222), downtown. 412/391-2294.* Hrs: 11 am-9 pm; Sat to 10 pm. Closed Sun, hols. Res accepted. Italian, Amer menu. Bar to 2 am; Sat 10 am-10 pm. Semi-a la carte: lunch $5-$8, dinner $7-$14. Specializes in pasta, steak, veal. Cr cds: A, C, D, DS, MC, V.

D

★★ **GEORGETOWNE INN.** *1230 Grandview Ave (15211), on Mount Washington. 412/481-4424.* Hrs: 11 am-3 pm, 5 pm-midnight; Fri, Sat to 1 am; Sun 4-10 pm. Closed most hols. Res accepted. Bar. Semi-a la carte: lunch $5.50-$15.95, dinner $15.95-$31.95. Specializes in steak, fresh seafood. Panoramic view of city. Cr cds: A, D, DS, MC, V.

D

★★★ **GRAND CONCOURSE.** *1 Station Square, jct Carson & Smithfield Sts, on South Side. 412/261-1717.* Hrs: 11:30 am-2:30 pm, 4:30-10 pm; Sat 4:30-11 pm; Sun 4:30-10 pm; early-bird dinner 4:30-6 pm; Sun brunch 10 am-2:30 pm. Closed Dec 25. Res accepted. Continental menu. Bar 11:30-2 am; Sun 11 am-10 pm. Extensive wine list. Semi-a la carte: lunch $6-$12, dinner $10-$30. Sun brunch $16.95. Child's meals. Specializes in seafood, steak, pasta. Own baking, pasta. Pianist. Converted railroad station. Braille menu. Outdoor dining. Cr cds: A, C, D, DS, MC, V.

D SC

★★ **INDIA GARDEN.** *328 Atwood St (15213), in Oakland. 412/682-3000.* Hrs: 11:30 am-2:30 pm, 5-10 pm. Res accepted. Northern Indian menu. Setups. A la carte entrees: $6.95-$13.95. Lunch buffet $6.95. Specialties: tandoori chicken, chicken tekka masala, vegetable korma. Indian decor, chairs. Cr cds: A, DS, MC, V.

✓★★ **JIMMY TSANG'S.** *5700 Centre Ave, at Negley, in Kennilworth Bldg, east of downtown. 412/661-4226.* Hrs: 11:30 am-10 pm; Fri, Sat to 11 pm; Sun 3:30-9 pm; early-bird dinner Mon-Sat 3-6 pm. Closed July 4, Thanksgiving. Chinese menu. Bar. A la carte: lunch $4.95-$5.75, dinner $7.95-$9.95. Specialties: Peking duck, honey chicken, Mongolian beef. Oriental decor, artwork. Cr cds: A, C, D, MC, V.

D

★★ **JUNO TRATTORIA.** *One Oxford Center, 3rd floor (15282), downtown. 412/392-0225.* Hrs: 11 am-2:30 pm, 5-10 pm; Fri, Sat to 11 pm. Closed Sun, most major hols. Regional Italian, Amer menu. Bar. Semi-a la carte: lunch $6-$12, dinner $10-$16. Specializes in pastas, pizza. Cr cds: A, DS, MC, V.

★★ **KAYA.** *2000 Smallman St (15222), in Strip District, east of downtown. 412/261-6565.* Hrs: 11:30 am-11 pm; Fri, Sat to midnight; Sun to 9 pm. Closed some major hols. Carribean menu. Bar. Semi-a la carte: lunch $6.25-$8.95, dinner $6.25-$16.95. Specialties: Jamaican jerk chicken wings, grilled alligator. Outdoor dining. Cr cds: A, C, D, DS, MC, V.

★★★ **LE MONT.** *1114 Grandview Ave, on Mount Washington. 412/431-3100.* E-mail info@le-mont.com; web www.le-mont.com. Hrs: 5-11:30 pm; Sun 4-10 pm. Closed major hols. Res accepted. Contemporary Amer menu. Bar to midnight. Wine list. A la carte entrees: dinner $18.95-$46. Specialties: rack of lamb Persille, variety of wild game dishes, flaming desserts. Own baking. Pianist Fri, Sat. Valet parking. Atop Mt Washington; panoramic view of city. Cr cds: A, C, D, DS, JCB, MC, V.

D

★★★ **LE POMMIER.** *2104 E Carson St, on South Side. 412/431-1901.* E-mail lepommier@lepommier.com; web www.lepommier.com. Hrs: 5:30-9:30 pm; Fri, Sat to 10:30 pm. Closed Mon, Sun; some major hols. Res accepted. French menu. Bar. Wine cellar. A la carte entrees: dinner $14-$28. Specializes in seasonal French country fare. Own baking. Valet parking Fri, Sat. Located in oldest storefront in area (1863). Outdoor dining in season. Country French decor. Cr cds: A, C, D, DS, MC, V.

D

★★★ **LONDON GRILLE.** *(1500 Washington Rd, Mount Lebanon 15228) US 19 S, in Galleria Mall, south of downtown. 412/563-3400.* Hrs: 11:30 am-10 pm; Fri, Sat to 11:30 pm; Sun noon-9 pm. Closed Dec 25. British menu. Bar. Wine list. Semi-a la carte: lunch $7.95-$11.95; dinner $17.95-$25.95. Specialties: prime rib, beef wellington. Valet parking. Patio dining. 4 dining rooms. Cr cds: A, C, D, DS, MC, V.

D

✓★ **MAX & ERMA'S.** *5533 Walnut St (15232), in Shadyside, east of downtown. 412/681-5775.* Hrs: 11:30 am-11 pm; Fri, Sat to midnight; Sun to 10 pm. Closed Thanksgiving, Dec 25. Bar. Semi-a la carte: lunch $6-$10, dinner $8-$14. Specializes in steak, ribs, pasta. Cr cds: A, D, DS, MC, V.

D SC

✓★★ **MAX'S ALLEGHENY TAVERN.** *Middle & Suisman Sts, north of downtown. 412/231-1899.* Hrs: 11 am-midnight; Sun to 10 pm. Closed most major hols. German menu. Bar. A la carte entrees: lunch $4.25-$7.95, dinner $5.95-$13.95. Specialties: jägerschnitzel, käse spätzle, sauerbraten. Tavern with German memorabilia and collection of photographs. Cr cds: A, D, DS, MC, V.

★ ★ ★ **NINA.** *5701 Bryant St (15206), east of downtown. 412/665-9000.* Hrs: 5:30-10 pm; Fri, Sat to 11 pm. Closed Sun, Mon; major hols. Res accepted. Continental menu. Bar. A la carte entrees: dinner $15.50-$23. Complete meal: 3 course dinner $19.97, 5 course dinner $49.97. Specializes in tuna, lamb, quail. Own baking, pasta. Former Highland Park Manor converted to casual yet elegant dining rm; open staircase leads to second dining level. Cr cds: A, D, MC, V.

★ ★ **PASTA PIATTO.** *736 Bellefonte St, in Shadyside, east of downtown. 412/621-5547.* Hrs: 11:30 am-3 pm, 4:30-10 pm; Wed, Thurs to 10:30 pm; Fri, Sat to 11 pm; Sun 4-9 pm. Closed major hols. Northern Italian menu. Bar. Semi-a la carte: lunch $5-$10, dinner $10.95-$22.95. Child's meals. Specializes in homemade pasta, veal, seafood. Cr cds: A, MC, V.

✔★ ★ **PENN BREWERY.** *Troy Hill, 800 Vinial St (15212), north of downtown. 412/237-9402.* Hrs: 11 am-midnight. Closed Sun, hols. German menu. Bar. Semi-a la carte: lunch $4.50-$8.50, dinner $8.50-$15.95. Child's meals. Specialties: weiner schnitzel, sauerbrauten, chicken berlin. Entertainment Tues-Sat. Outdoor dining. Restored 19th-century brewery, German beer hall-style communal dining. Cr cds: A, DS, MC, V.

★ ★ ★ **PICCOLO MONDO.** *661 Andersen Dr, Bldg 7, Foster Plaza, Green Tree, south of downtown. 412/922-0920.* Hrs: 11:30 am-10 pm; Sat to 4-11 pm. Closed Sun exc Mother's Day; some hols. Res accepted. Northern Italian menu. Bar. Wine list. Semi-a la carte: lunch $7.50-$13, dinner $14-$24. Child's meals. Specializes in fresh fish, veal. Own desserts. Parking. Jacket. Cr cds: A, C, D, DS, MC, V.

D

★ ★ ★ **POLI.** *2607 Murray Ave (15217), east of downtown. 412/521-6400.* Hrs: 11:30 am-11 pm; Sun 11 am-9:30 pm; early-bird dinner Tues-Fri 3-5:30 pm. Closed Mon; Thanksgiving, Dec 25. Bar. Semi-a la carte: lunch $6.95-$10.50, dinner $15-$25. Child's meals. Specializes in fresh seafood, veal, pasta. Own baking. Valet parking. Family-owned. Cr cds: A, C, D, MC, V.

D

✔★ **PRIMANTI BROS.** *46 18th St (15222), in Strip District, east of downtown. 412/263-2142.* Hrs: open 24 hrs. Closed Dec 25. Italian, Amer menu. Wine, beer. Semi-a la carte: $3.50-$4.25. Specializes in deli sandwiches with fries and cole slaw inside, soups. Family-owned. No cr cds accepted.

★ ★ ★ **RICO'S.** *1 Rico Lane, off of Evergreen Rd in North Hills, north of downtown. 412/931-1989.* Hrs: 11:30 am-3 pm, 4-10:30 pm; Fri, Sat 4-11:30 pm. Closed Sun; most major hols. Italian, Amer menu. Bar to midnight. Wine cellar. Semi-a la carte: lunch $7.50-$12.50, dinner $15.50-$28. Specializes in fresh seafood, veal. Valet parking. Old World atmosphere; Italian lithographs. Jacket. Cr cds: A, D, DS, MC, V.

D

★ ★ **SAMURAI JAPANESE STEAK HOUSE.** *2100 Greentree Rd, south of downtown. 412/276-2100.* Hrs: 11:30 am-2 pm, 5:30-10 pm; Fri to 11 pm; Sat 5-11:30 pm; Sun 4:30-9 pm. Closed July 4, Thanksgiving, Dec 25. Res accepted. Japanese menu. Bar. Semi-a la carte: lunch $6.25-$9.95, dinner $12.95-$32. Child's meals. Specializes in steak, seafood. Japanese garden. Cr cds: A, C, D, DS, MC, V.

D

✔★ ★ **SEVENTH STREET GRILLE.** *130 7th St (15222), downtown. 412/338-0303.* Hrs: 11:30 am-10 pm. Closed most major hols. Res accepted. Continental menu. Bar. Semi-a la carte: lunch, dinner $5.95-$16.95. Specializes in grilled seafood, prime rib, specialty beers. Cr cds: A, D, DS, MC, V.

D ♥

★ ★ **SOBA LOUNGE.** *5847 Ellsworth Ave (15232), east of downtown. 412/362-5656.* Hrs: 5 pm-midnight; Sun-Tues to 11 pm; Sat, Sun also 11:30 am-4 pm. Closed Thanksgiving. Res accepted. Pan-Asian menu. Bars. Semi-a la carte: lunch $7-$12, dinner $12-$30. Specialties: pork and vegetarian dumplings, wok-seared salmon, zaru soba noodles. Own noodles. Musicians exc Sun. Outdoor dining. Three dining levels, each with its own bar; eclectic decor with original artwork. Cr cds: A, D, DS, MC, V.

D

✔★ ★ **STATION SQUARE CHEESE CELLAR.** *#25 Freight House Shops, Station Square (Smithfield & Carson Sts), on South Side. 412/471-3355.* Hrs: 11:30 am-midnight; Fri & Sat to 1 am; Sun 10:30 am-11 pm. Closed Thanksgiving, Dec 25. Res accepted Sun-Thurs. Continental menu. Bar to 2 am. Semi-a la carte: Sun bkfst $5.95-$6.50, lunch, dinner $4.95-$12.95. Child's meals. Specialty: cheese and chocolate fondue. Outdoor dining. Rustic decor. Cr cds: A, C, D, DS, MC, V.

D ♥

✔★ ★ **SUSHI TWO.** *2122 E Carson St (15203), south of downtown. 412/431-7874.* Hrs: 11:30 am-3 pm, 5-10 pm; Fri to 11:30 pm; Sat 11:30 am-11 pm; Sun 1-9 pm. Closed Labor Day. Res accepted. Japanese menu. Bar. Semi-a la carte: lunch $5.50-$10.95, dinner $9.95-$18.95. Specializes in traditional Japanese dishes. Own baking, noodles. Valet parking Fri, Sat. Contemporary Japanese decor. Cr cds: A, C, D, DS, MC, V.

D

★ ★ ★ **TAMBELLINI'S.** *PA 51 (15226), south of downtown. 412/481-1118.* Hrs: 11:30 am-10 pm. Closed Sun; Jan 1, Thanksgiving, Dec 25. Res accepted. Continental menu. Bar. Semi-a la carte: lunch $7.95-$8.50, dinner $12.95-$27.50. Complete meals: dinner $21.95. Child's meals. Specializes in seafood, pasta, steak. Valet parking. Modern decor. Cr cds: A, D, MC, V.

D

✔★ ★ **TESSARO'S.** *4601 Liberty Ave (15224), at Taylor St, east of downtown. 412/682-6809.* Hrs: 11 am-midnight. Closed Sun; Jan 1, Thanksgiving, Dec 25. Mexican, Amer menu. Bar. Semi-a la carte: lunch $5-$10, dinner $12-$15. Specializes in hamburgers, fresh seafood, filet mignon. Own pasta. Casual decor has pressed tin ceiling (ca early 1900s), paddle ceiling fans, fireplaces. Cr cds: A, D, DS, MC, V.

✔★ ★ **THAI PLACE.** *809 Bellefonte St, in Shadyside, east of downtown. 412/687-8586.* Hrs: 11:30 am-10 pm; Fri to 10:30 pm; Sat noon-11 pm; Sun noon-9:30 pm; Mon from 4:30 pm. Thai menu. Bar. A la carte entrees: lunch $5.50-$7.50, dinner $7.50-$17.95. Specializes in authentic Thai cuisine. Outdoor dining. Asian art. Cr cds: A, D, DS, MC, V.

★ ★ ★ **TIN ANGEL.** *1200 Gandview Ave (15221), on Mount Washington. 412/381-1919.* Hrs: 5-10 pm. Closed Sun, hols. Res accepted. Bar. Wine list. Complete meals: $26.95-$46.95. Specialties: sole baretone, black forest filet. Panoramic view of city. Jacket. Family-owned. Cr cds: A, D, MC, V.

★ ★ ★ **TOP OF THE TRIANGLE.** *600 Grant St, 62nd floor (15219), on 62nd floor of USX Tower, downtown. 412/471-4100.* Hrs: 11:30 am-3 pm, 5:30-10 pm; Sat noon-3 pm, 5:30-11 pm; Sun 4-9 pm. Closed most major hols. Res accepted. Bar to 1 am. Wine list. Semi-a la carte: lunch $6.95-$14.95, dinner $18.95-$29.95. Child's meals. Specialties: grilled molasses glazed fresh swordfish, Colorado lamb chops. Pianist Fri, Sat. Parking (fee). Panoramic view of city. Cr cds: A, D, DS, MC, V.

D

✔★ **VERMONT FLATBREAD CO.** *2701 Penn Ave (15222), east of downtown. 412/434-1220.* Hrs: 11 am-10 pm; Fri, Sat to 11 pm. Closed Sun. Bar. Semi-a la carte: lunch $5.95-$7.50, dinner $5.95-$8.25. Child's meals. Specialties: maple-sugar flatbread, Italian grilled sandwich, sweet stuffed peppers with chorizo sausage. Own baking, pasta. Street parking. Rustic Vermont decor with skylights. Cr cds: D, DS, MC, V.

D

Unrated Dining Spots

DAVE AND ANDY'S ICE CREAM PARLOR. *207 Atwood St, in Oakland. 412/681-9906.* Hrs: 11:30 am-10 pm; Sat & Sun from noon. Closed major hols. Specialties: homemade ice cream (fresh daily), homemade cones. 1930s look; some counters. No cr cds accepted.

PIZZERIA UNO. *(333 Penn Center Blvd, Monroeville 15146) 15 mi E on US 376, Penn Center Blvd exit. 412/824-8667.* Hrs: 11 am-11 pm; Fri & Sat to 12:30 am; Sun noon-10 pm. Closed Thanksgiving, Dec 25. Italian, Amer menu. Bar. Semi-a la carte: lunch $3.95-$8.95, dinner $4.95-$10.95. Specialties: deep-dish pizza. Parking. Casual dining. Cr cds: A, DS, MC, V.

D

TERRACE ROOM. *(See Westin William Penn Hotel) 412/281-7100.* Hrs: tea time 3-6 pm. English custom tea serv. Bar. A la carte items also avail. Specializes in tea, finger sandwiches, pastries. Pianist. Parking avail opp Lobby room; Georgian decor; elaborate floral arrangements. Cr cds: A, C, D, DS, ER, JCB, MC, V.

D

Pittsburgh Intl Airport Area

Motels

★ **HAMPTON INN-NORTHWEST.** *(1420 Beers School Rd, Coraopolis 15108) N on PA Business 60. 412/264-0020; FAX 412/264-3220.* 129 rms, 5 story. S $64; D $74; under 18 free. Crib free. Pet accepted. TV; cable (premium). Complimentary continental bkfst. Restaurant adj 6 am-10 pm. Ck-out noon. Meeting rms. Business servs avail. Valet serv. Free airport transportation. Health club privileges. Cr cds: A, C, D, DS, ER, MC, V.

D SC

★ ★ **LA QUINTA.** *(1433 Beers School Rd, Coraopolis 15108) N on Business PA 60. 412/269-0400; FAX 412/269-9258.* 127 rms, 3 story. S $64-$78; D $71-$85; under 19 free. Crib free. Pet accepted. TV; cable. Heated pool; lifeguard. Complimentary continental bkfst. Coffee in rms. Restaurant adj 6 am-11 pm. Ck-out noon. Coin Indry. Meeting rms. Business servs avail. In-rm modem link. Valet serv. Sundries. Free airport transportation. Exercise equipt; treadmill, rower. Cr cds: A, D, DS, MC, V.

D SC

✔★ ★ **PITTSBURGH PLAZA.** *(1500 Beers School Rd, Coraopolis 15108) I-79 Bus 60 exit to Beers School Rd. 412/264-7900; FAX 412/262-3229; res: 800/542-8111.* 193 rms, 2 story. S, D $49.99-$59.99; under 18 free. Pet accepted; $50 refundable. TV; cable (premium), VCR avail. Complimentary continental bkfst 5-9 am in lobby. Restaurant adj open 24 hrs. Ck-out noon. Meeting rms. Business servs avail. In-rm modem link. Valet serv. Sundries. Free airport transportation. Exercise equipt; weights, bicycles, sauna. Some refrigerators. Some balconies. Cr cds: A, C, D, DS, MC, V.

SC

✔★ **RED ROOF INN.** *(1454 Beers School Rd, Coraopolis 15108) N on Bus PA 60. 412/264-5678; FAX 412/264-8034.* 119 rms, 3 story. S $47.99-$58.99; D $61.99-$66.99; each addl $6; under 18 free. Crib free. Pet accepted. TV; cable (premium). Coffee in lobby 6-10 am. Restaurant opp 6 am-10 pm. Ck-out noon. Coin Indry. Meeting rm. Business servs avail. Valet serv. Free airport transportation. Cr cds: A, C, D, DS, MC, V.

D

Hotels

★ ★ ★ **CLARION-ROYCE.** *(1160 Thorn Run Rd Extension, Coraopolis 15108) N on Bus Rte 60, exit Thorn Run Rd. 412/262-2400; FAX 412/264-9373.* 193 rms, 9 story. S $69-$119; D $69-$129; each addl $10; suites $109-$139; under 18 free; wkend rates. Crib free. Pet accepted. TV; cable (premium). Pool; lifeguard. Restaurant 6 am-2 pm, 5-11 pm; Sat, Sun 7 am-11 pm. Bar 11-2 am; entertainment. Ck-out noon. Meeting rms. Business center. In-rm modem link. Concierge. Airport transportation. Exercise equipt; weight machines, bicycles. Luxury Level. Cr cds: A, C, D, DS, MC, V.

D SC

★ ★ ★ **MARRIOTT.** *(100 Aten Rd, Coraopolis 15108) S on PA 60, exit Montour Run Rd. 412/788-8800; FAX 412/788-6299.* 314 rms, 14 story. S, D $69-$169; each addl $15; suites $175-$425; family, wkly rates. Crib free. Pet accepted. TV; cable (premium). 2 pools, 1 indoor; whirlpool, poolside serv, lifeguard. Restaurant 6:30 am-11 pm. Bar 11-1 am; pianist Wed-Sat. Ck-out noon. Convention facilities. Business center. In-rm modem link. Concierge. Shopping arcade. Free airport, bus depot transportation. Exercise equipt; weights, bicycles, sauna. Some refrigerators. Luxury level. Cr cds: A, C, D, DS, ER, JCB, MC, V.

D SC

Restaurant

★ ★ ★ **HYEHOLDE.** *(190 Hyeholde Dr, Coraopolis 15108) PA Bus N 60 to Beers School Rd, right on Beaver Grade Rd, left on Coraopolis Heights Rd. 412/264-3116.* Hrs: 11:30 am-2 pm, 5-10 pm; Sat from 5 pm. Closed Sun exc Mother's Day; major hols. Res accepted. Continental menu. Serv bar. Wine list. Complete meals: lunch $9.50-$13, dinner $18.50-$36. Specializes in rack of lamb, roasted elk. Own baking. Valet parking. Patio dining. Herb garden. Country French decor; fireplaces; estate grounds. Cr cds: A, C, D, DS, MC, V.

D

Portland

Founded: 1851
Pop: 437,319
Elev: 77 feet
Time zone: Pacific
Area code: 503
Web: www@pova.com

Portland, Oregon's largest city, sprawls across both banks of the northward-flowing Willamette River, just south of its confluence with the Columbia. The lush and fertile Willamette Valley brings the city both beauty and riches. Through its leadership in rose culture, Portland has earned the title "city of roses." The International Rose Test Garden is a showpiece with 8,000 bushes and more than 500 varieties, and the Portland Rose Festival is the biggest event of the year.

Portland was established in 1843, named after Portland, Maine, the hometown of one of its early settlers. In 1851, Portland was incorporated as a town. The city grew steadily during its first 10 years, with the major growth taking place on the west side of the Willamette River. Eventually, small towns and cities were incorporated on the east side as well. A devastating fire burned 22 blocks of the west side of Portland in 1873, but the city was rebuilt and continued to grow. In 1889, the world's first long-distance transmission of electricity brought light to the streets of Portland. The electricity's power came from a plant on the Willamette Falls at Oregon City, southeast of Portland.

During the Depression, Portland's population declined; however, during World War II the population began to increase when people from all parts of the country came to Portland looking for work. Since that time there has been a steady influx of people.

Business

Portland's economy is not dominated by any one firm or industry, but tourism and high-tech timber industries are important economic forces. There are many small and medium-sized firms representing diverse industries. This diversity has resulted in stable economic growth. Some of the items produced here are oscilloscopes, electronic equipment, silicon wafers, pulp, paper, ships, boats, barges, plywood, trucks, railroad cars, power tools, aircraft parts, furniture, lumber, alloy steel, glass containers, sportswear, footwear, canned fruits and vegetables and chocolate candy.

Portland's harbor strengthens the area's economic base. It is one of the more active harbors in the United States; more than 2,500 ships call on the city annually.

The distribution of commodities and merchandise to the Pacific Northwest is another major factor in Portland's economy.

Convention Facilities

The Oregon Convention Center, a state-of-the-art facility, has 150,000 square feet of column-free exhibition space that can accommodate 830 exhibit booths. Theater-style seating is available for up to 13,000. In addition, there are 28 meeting rooms and a 25,000-square-foot ballroom. The convention facility also features a fully staffed visitor center.

The Memorial Coliseum is a fully equipped convention center able to accommodate most functions. The complex itself has a total exhibit area of 108,000 square feet. The arena is equipped with 9,231 permanent theater seats; portable seating can be arranged to increase the capacity to 14,000. There is also a large movable stage and an 85-by-185-foot ice floor.

The exhibit hall has 55,800 square feet of space that can accommodate up to 320 exhibit booths. The convention hall provides an additional 25,200 square feet of exhibit space. The assembly hall, which covers 19,800 square feet, can be used as a single large area or divided into six smaller meeting rooms. In addition to the major rooms, there are five meeting rooms with seating for 30 to 300 persons.

The Portland Metropolitan Exposition Center is also available for most functions. The center has a total exhibit space of 220,400 square feet. The exhibit hall has 84,000 square feet, which can be divided into two sections. The exhibit hall has a seating capacity for 60,000. The arena floor has 23,067 square feet for exhibits. In addition, the west hall can seat 250 individuals within a 12,000-square-foot room.

Sports & Recreation

Portland's professional basketball team, the Trail Blazers, provides exciting sports enjoyment. Both the Trail Blazers and the city's hockey team, the Winter Hawks, play at the Rose Garden. The Rockies, Portland's minor league baseball team, play at the Civic Stadium.

Portland has more than 36 challenging golf courses, all located within 45 minutes of the downtown area. There are approximately 115 tennis courts in the city operated by the Portland Park Bureau and more than 100 additional courts in the suburbs.

In the western hills of Portland, overlooking downtown, is Washington Park, which forms part of a 5,000-acre nature preserve. Within the park are the International Rose Test Garden, the Japanese Gardens and the Metro Washington Park Zoo.

Within 30 miles of the city are seven state parks, including Crown Point, with a view of the Columbia River Gorge National Scenic Area and its 2,000-foot-high rock walls.

Approximately 50 miles east of Portland is Mt Hood National Forest, with one of the best slopes in the Northwest for skiing. The surrounding area is used for camping, climbing, fishing, tobogganing and horseback riding.

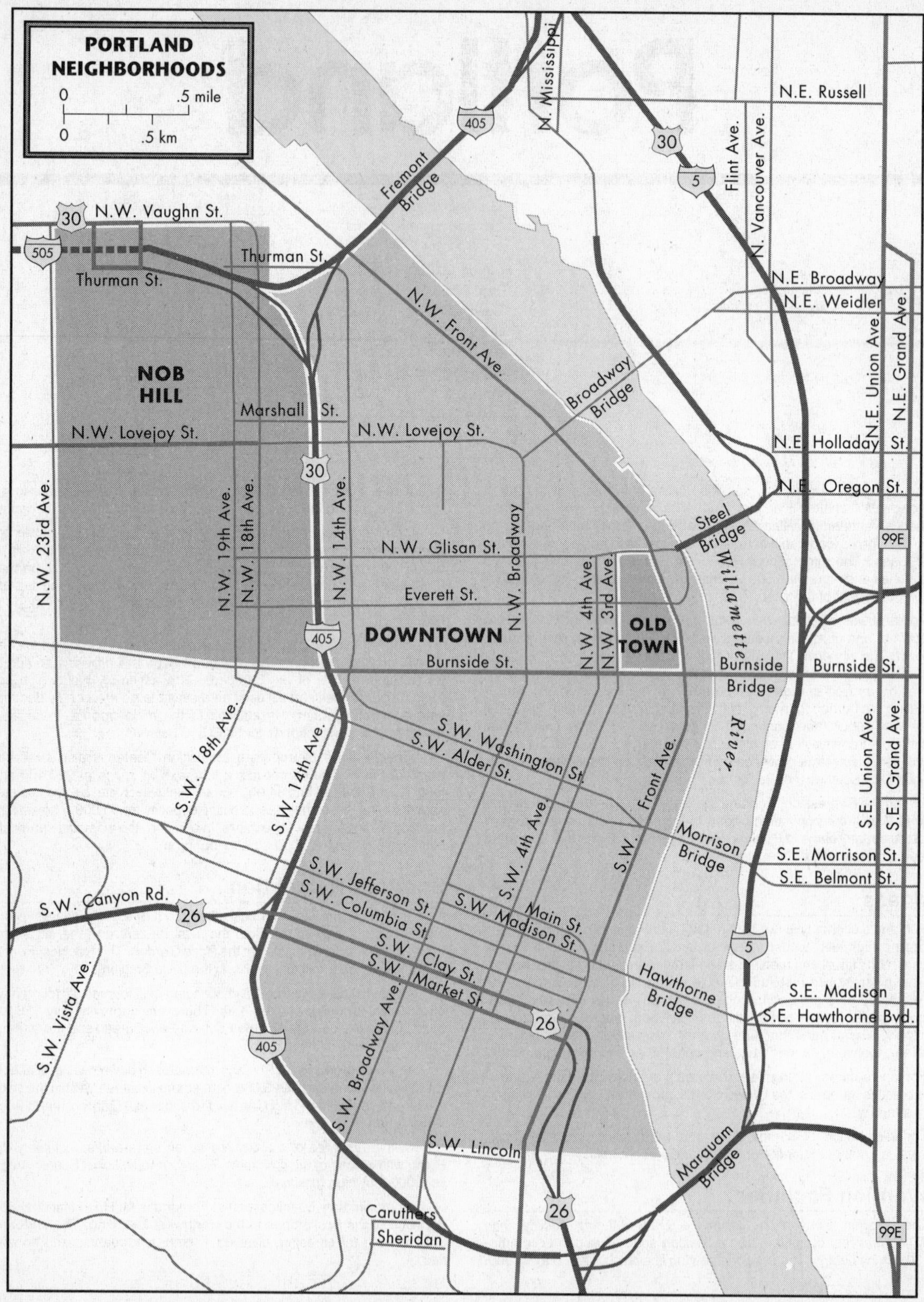
PORTLAND NEIGHBORHOODS
0 .5 mile
0 .5 km
NOB HILL
DOWNTOWN
OLD TOWN
N.W. Vaughn St.
Thurman St.
Thurman St.
Fremont Bridge
N. Mississippi
N.E. Russell
Flint Ave.
N. Vancouver Ave.
N.E. Broadway
N.E. Weidler
N.W. Front Ave.
Broadway Bridge
Marshall St.
N.W. Lovejoy St.
N.W. Lovejoy St.
N.E. Holladay St.
N.E. Union Ave.
N.E. Grand Ave.
N.E. Oregon St.
Steel Bridge
N.W. 23rd Ave.
N.W. 19th Ave.
N.W. 18th Ave.
N.W. 14th Ave.
N.W. Broadway
N.W. Glisan St.
Everett St.
N.W. 4th Ave.
N.W. 3rd Ave.
Willamette River
Burnside St.
Burnside Bridge
Burnside St.
S.W. 18th Ave.
S.W. 14th Ave.
S.W. Washington St.
S.W. Alder St.
S.W. Front Ave.
S.W. 4th Ave.
S.E. Union Ave.
S.E. Grand Ave.
Morrison Bridge
S.E. Morrison St.
S.E. Belmont St.
S.W. Canyon Rd.
S.W. Jefferson St.
S.W. Columbia St.
S.W. Madison St.
Main St.
S.W. Clay St.
S.W. Market St.
Hawthorne Bridge
S.E. Madison
S.E. Hawthorne Bvd.
S.W. Vista Ave.
S.W. Broadway Ave.
S.W. Lincoln
Marquam Bridge
Caruthers
Sheridan
30
505
405
5
26
99E

Entertainment

Touring Broadway companies present performances at the Portland Civic Auditorium. This is also the stage for each season's presentations by the Oregon Ballet Theatre, the Portland Opera Association and other local and traveling artists. Portland has a Youth Philharmonic Orchestra, a Pops Symphony, Symphonic Choir, an active civic theater and numerous small theater groups. During the summer, Washington Park is the scene of outdoor entertainment, including folk dancing, opera, free concerts and theater.

The Portland Center for the Performing Arts houses the 2,750-seat Arlene Schnitzer Concert Hall, the home of the Oregon Symphony Orchestra. Also in the center are the Intermediate Theater and the Winningstad Theater.

Historical Areas

Johns Landing, a major urban development project begun in 1969, has carefully preserved the rambling charm of an old factory. The Water Tower was the first portion of Johns Landing to open. Today, the building houses some 40 apparel, art, gift and import shops, delis, cafes and restaurants.

The Oregon History Center contains a record of the Northwest with permanent and special exhibits and a regional reference library.

Pittock Mansion, a restored French-Renaissance structure, is surrounded by 46 forested and landscaped acres with a view of mountains, rivers and the city.

The Bybee House, built in 1858, has also been restored. The dwelling is located in the Howell Territorial Park, a 120-acre park with an agricultural museum on the grounds.

Sightseeing

St Johns Bridge is an architectural masterpiece, with a beautiful scenic setting in the city. The structural steel is planned for beauty of lines, proportion, light and shadows.

Within the city itself, there is a 22-block transit mall consisting of 11 blocks on both SW Fifth and SW Sixth avenues downtown. Broad red-brick sidewalks with flower-bedecked planters, trees, fountains, statuary and kiosks have transformed once ordinary streets into a park-like setting.

Old Town, located between SW Fifth and Front avenues on both sides of W Burnside Street, has many excellent examples of early Portland architecture. Here, visitors can find ethnic restaurants and many unusual shops. The Tri-Met buses and MAX light rail provide free service within Fareless Square, a 300-block area in Downtown Portland which includes Old Town. A small Chinatown is also located here.

Spectacular *Portlandia* is a hammered-copper statue throned above 5th Avenue on the Portland Building, a structure by Michael Graves that triggered the post-modern movement in American architecture.

Every weekend between early March and Christmas, an open air market is held beneath the west end of the Burnside Bridge between SW First and Front avenues. Crafts, gourmet foods, locally grown produce and many forms of live entertainment abound at Portland Saturday Market.

The Yamhill Historic District has a marketplace housing a small produce market, restaurants and retail shops.

One of the most scenic routes east of Portland is a drive on I-84. Waterfalls, parks, forests and a breathtaking view of the Columbia River Gorge lie along the road.

Spectacular, 620-foot Multnomah Falls, about 30 miles east of the city, is one of 11 waterfalls that adorn this stretch of highway.

Across the Columbia River, in Washington, is Beacon Rock, which has been called the world's second-largest monolith. Trails lead to the top of the rock.

Camping and picnic areas are numerous along the entire drive to The Dalles, a busy city that was a Native American trading area during the time of Lewis and Clark. Located in town is the site of Old Fort Dalles, built around 1850. Only one of the fort's original buildings remains; it is now a historical museum.

Lost Lake, with Mount Hood in the background, is one of the most exquisite sights in Oregon. It lies southwest of Hood River in an area reached by county and forest roads.

General References

Area code: 503

Phone Numbers

POLICE & FIRE: 911

POISON CONTROL CENTER: 279-8968

TIME & WEATHER: 243-7575

Information Sources

Portland Oregon Visitors Association, 26 SW Salmon St, 97204-3299; 222-2223 or 800/606-6363.

Portland Event Line, 225-5555, code 3608.

Portland Parks & Recreation, 823-2223.

Transportation

AIRLINES: Alaska; American; America West; Continental; Delta; Horizon Air; Northwest; Southwest; TWA; United; Western Pacific and other commuter and regional airlines.

AIRPORT: Portland International, 460-4234.

CAR RENTAL AGENCIES: (See IMPORTANT TOLL-FREE NUMBERS) Budget 249-4556; Dollar 249-4792; Hertz 249-8216; National 249-4900; Thrifty 254-6565.

PUBLIC TRANSPORTATION: Tri-County Metropolitan Transportation District (Tri-Met), 701 SW 6th Ave, 238-RIDE.

RAILROAD PASSENGER SERVICE: Amtrak 800/872-7245.

Newspapers

The Oregonian; Daily Journal of Commerce.

Convention Facilities

Memorial Coliseum, 1401 N Wheeler Ave, 234-9291.

Oregon Convention Center, 777 NE Martin Luther King Blvd, 235-7575.

Portland Exposition Center, 2060 N Marine Dr, 285-7756.

Rose Garden, 1 Center Court, 234-9291.

Sports & Recreation

Major Sports Facilities

Civic Stadium, 1844 SW Morrison, 248-4345 (Rockies, baseball).

Memorial Coliseum, 1401 N Wheeler Ave, 235-8771.

Portland Exposition Center, 2060 N Marine Dr, 285-7756.

Rose Garden, 1 Center Court (Trail Blazers, basketball, 234-9291; Winter Hawks, hockey).

Racetracks

Multnomah Greyhound Park, NE 223rd Ave, between NE Halsey & Glisan Sts, 667-7700 (dog racing).

Portland International Raceway, Delta Park, 1940 N Victory Blvd, 285-6635 (auto racing).

Portland Meadows, 1001 N Schmeer Rd, 285-9144 (Thoroughbred and quarter horse racing).

Portland Speedway, 9727 N Union Ave, 285-2883 (auto racing).

Cultural Facilities

Theaters

Firehouse Theatre, 1436 SW Montgomery St, 274-1717.

Ladybug Theater, Oaks Park, SE Spokane St at Sellwood Bridge, 232-2346.

Lakewood Theatre Company, 368 S State St, Lakewood Center for the Arts, Lake Oswego, 635-3901.

Portland Repertory Theatre, 25 SW Salmon, 224-4491.

Concert Halls

Arlene Schnitzer Concert Hall, 1057 SW Broadway, 248-4335.

Memorial Coliseum, 1401 N Wheeler, 235-8771.

Portland Center for the Performing Arts, 1111 SW Broadway, 248-4335.

Portland Civic Auditorium, 222 SW Clay St, 248-4335.

Museums

American Advertising Museum, 50 SW 2nd Ave, 226-0000.

Children's Museum, 3037 SW 2nd Ave, 823-2227.

Oregon History Center, 1200 SW Park Ave, 222-1741.

Oregon Museum of Science and Industry, 1945 SE Water Ave, 797-4000.

Police Historical Museum, 1111 SW 2nd Ave, 823-0019.

World Forestry Center, 4033 SW Canyon Rd, 228-1367.

Art Museums

Oregon Society of Artists, 2185 SW Park Pl, 228-0706.

Portland Art Musuem, 1219 SW Park Ave, 226-2811.

Points of Interest

Historical

Howell Territorial Park and The Bybee House, 12 mi N via US 30, on Howell Park Rd, Sauvie Island, 621-3344 or 222-1741.

Old Church, 1422 SW 11th Ave, 222-2031.

Pittock Mansion, 3229 NW Pittock Dr, 823-3624.

Other Attractions

Council Crest Park, S on SW Greenway Ave, 823-2223.

Crown Point State Park, 25 mi E off I-84 on US 30 Scenic Rte, 695-2230.

Crystal Springs Rhododendron Garden, SE 28th Ave, N of SE Woodstock Blvd, 823-2223.

Forest Park, off US 30, NW of Fremont Bridge, 823-2223.

Grotto—The National Sanctuary of Our Sorrowful Mother, NE 85th Ave at Sandy Blvd, 254-7371.

Hoyt Arboretum, 4000 SW Fairview Blvd, 228-8733.

International Rose Test Garden, Washington Park, 823-2223.

Jantzen Beach Center, I-5 at Jantzen Beach on Hayden Island, 289-5555.

Japanese Garden, Washington Park, 223-1321.

Johns Landing, 5331 SW Macadam Ave, 228-9431.

Leach Botanical Gardens, S of Foster on SE 122nd St, 761-9503.

Lloyd Center, NE 9th Ave & NE Multnomah, 282-2511.

Metro Washington Park Zoo, 4001 SW Canyon Ct, 226-1561.

Mt Hood National Forest, SE on US 26.

Multnomah Falls, 32 mi E on I-84.

Oaks Amusement Park and Roller-Skating Rink, SE Oaks Park Way, E end of Sellwood Bridge, 233-5777.

Pioneer Courthouse Square, 701 SW 6th Ave, 223-1613.

Shakespeare Garden, Washington Park, 823-2223.

Washington Park, accessible via W Burnside St or Canyon Rd, 823-2223.

Washington Square, off OR 217 near Scholls Ferry & Greenburg Rds, 639-8860.

Willamette Stone State Park, at W Burnside & Skyline Blvd.

Sightseeing Tours

Gray Line bus tours, 4320 N Suttle Rd, 285-9845 or 800/442-7042.

Hillsboro Helicopters, Inc, 3565 NE Cornell, Hillsboro 97124; 648-2831.

Sternwheeler *Columbia Gorge,* 1200 NW Front Ave, Suite 110, 223-3928.

Annual Events

Portland Rose Festival, 227-2681. Late May-June.

Portland Scottish Highland Games, Mt Hood Community College, Gresham, 293-8501. Mid-July.

Multnomah County Fair. Late July.

Mt Hood Festival of Jazz, Gresham, 666-3810. 1st wkend Aug.

Portland Marathon, 226-1111. Early Oct.

Holiday Parade of Christmas Ships, along Willamette & Columbia rivers. Early-mid-Dec.

City Neighborhoods

Many of the restaurants, unrated dining establishments and some lodgings listed under Portland include neighborhoods as well as exact street addresses. Geographic descriptions of these areas are given, followed by a table of restaurants arranged by neighborhood.

Downtown: Southeast of I-405, west of the Willamette River, north of SW Lincoln and east of I-30. **East of Downtown** East of Willamette River. **West of Downtown** West of I-30.

Nob Hill: West of Downtown; south of Vaughn St, west of I-405, north of Burnside St and east of NW 23rd St.

Old Town: Area of Downtown south of Glisan St, west of Front St and the river, north of Burnside St and east of NW 3rd St.

Lodgings and Food

PORTLAND RESTAURANTS BY NEIGHBORHOOD AREAS

(For full description, see alphabetical listings under Restaurants)

DOWNTOWN
Al-Amir. 223 SW Stark
Alessandro's. 301 SW Morrison
Atwater's. 111 SW 5th Ave
Bush Garden. 900 SW Morrison
Esplanade At Riverplace (Riverplace Hotel). 1510 SW Harbor Way
Heathman (Heathman Hotel). 1009 SW Broadway
Higgins. 1239 SW Broadway
Huber's. 411 SW 3rd Ave
Jake's Famous Crawfish. 401 SW 12th Ave
Jake's Grill (The Governor Hotel). 611 SW 10th St
London Grill (The Benson Hotel). 309 SW Broadway
Mandarin Cove. 111 SW Columbia
Pazzo Ristorante (Vintage Plaza Hotel). 422 SW Broadway
Red Star. 503 SW Alder
Widmer Gasthaus. 929 N Russell St

EAST OF DOWNTOWN
28 East. 40 NE 28th Ave
Caprial's. 7015 SE Milwaukie Ave
Esparza's Tex Mex Cafe. 2725 SE Ankeny St
Genoa. 2832 SE Belmont St
Ivy House. 1605 SE Bybee
Papa Haydn. 5829 SE Milwaukie
Perry's On Fremont. 2401 NE Fremont
Poor Richard's. 3907 NE Broadway
Rheinlander. 5035 NE Sandy Blvd
Ringside East. 14021 NE Glisan
Salty's On The Columbia. 3839 NE Marine Dr
Sayler's Old Country Kitchen. 10519 SE Stark
Sylvia's. 5115 NE Sandy Blvd
Winterborne. 3520 NE 42nd

WEST OF DOWNTOWN
Avalon Grill & Cafe. 4630 SW Macadam Ave
The Brewhouse. 2730 NW 31st Ave
Cafe Des Amis. 1987 NW Kearney
Chart House. 5700 SW Terwilliger Blvd
Couvron. 1126 SW 18th Ave
Delfina's. 2112 NW Kearney St
L'Auberge. 2601 NW Vaughn
Mazzi's Italian Sicilian Food. 5833 SW Macadam Ave
Old Spaghetti Factory. 0715 SW Bancroft
Original Pancake House. 8601 SW 24th Ave
Paley's Place. 1204 NW 21st Ave
Plainfield's Mayur. 852 SW 21st Ave
Ringside. 2165 W Burnside St
Typhoon! 2310 NW Everett St

NOB HILL
Il Fornaio. 115 NW 22nd Ave
Tribeca. 704 NW 21st St
Wildwood. 1221 NW 21st Ave
Zefiro. 500 NW 21st Ave

OLD TOWN
Alexis. 215 W Burnside
Couch Street Fish House. 105 NW 3rd Ave
Dan & Louis Oyster Bar. 208 SW Ankeny St

Note: When a listing is located in a town that does not have its own city heading, it will appear under the city nearest to its location. In these cases, the address and town appear in parenthesis immediately following the name of the establishment.

Motels

★ ★ ★ **BEST WESTERN PONY SOLDIER.** *9901 NE Sandy Blvd (97220), near Intl Airport, east of downtown. 503/256-1504; FAX 503/256-5928.* 104 rms, 2 story, 15 suites. S $78.50-$84.50; D $78.50-$99.50; each addl $5; suites, kit. units $114.50-$123.50; under 13 free. Crib $3. TV; cable (premium). Heated pool; whirlpool. Complimentary continental bkfst. Restaurant adj 6 am-10 pm. Ck-out noon. Free lndry facilities. Meeting rms. Business servs avail. Valet serv. Sundries. Free airport transportation. Exercise equipt; weight machine, bicycle, sauna. Refrigerators. Balconies. Cr cds: A, C, D, DS, ER, MC, V.

D SC

✔★ **CARAVAN.** *2401 SW 4th Ave (97201), south of downtown. 503/226-1121; FAX 503/274-2681; res: 800/248-0506.* 40 rms in 2 buildings, 2 story. S, D $55-$125; each addl $7. Crib $7. TV; cable (premium). Heated pool. Complimentary coffee in lobby. Restaurant 7 am-10 pm. Bar 11-2 am. Ck-out noon. Business servs avail. Some refrigerators. Balconies. Cr cds: A, C, D, DS, JCB, MC, V.

SC

✔★ **CHESTNUT TREE INN.** *9699 SE Stark St (97216), east of downtown. 503/255-4444.* 58 rms, 2 story. S $39; D $43; each addl $2. Crib free. TV; cable (premium). Complimentary coffee. Restaurant adj 6 am-11 pm. Ck-out noon. Business servs avail. Refrigerators. Cr cds: A, C, D, MC, V.

D

★ **DAYS INN.** *(9717 SE Sunnyside Rd, Clackamas 97015) I-205 Sunnyside exit. 503/654-1699; FAX 503/659-2702.* 110 rms, 3 story. S $55-$95; D $62-$102; each addl $7; studio rms $65-$130; under 12 free. Crib free. TV; cable (premium). Heated pool; whirlpool. Sauna. Complimentary continental bkfst. Ck-out noon. Business servs avail. Some refrigerators. Cr cds: A, C, D, DS, JCB, MC, V.

D SC

✔★ ★ **FAIRFIELD INN BY MARRIOTT.** *11929 NE Airport Way (97220), east of downtown. 503/253-1400; FAX 503/253-3889.* 106 rms, 4 story. Apr-Sept: S, D $65; each addl $10; under 12 free; lower rates rest of yr. Crib free. TV; cable (premium). Heated pool; whirlpool. Complimentary continental bkfst. Restaurant nearby. Ck-out noon. Business servs avail. Sundries. Free airport transportation. Exercise equipt; bicycle, weight machine. Cr cds: A, D, DS, MC, V.

D SC

★ ★ **HOLIDAY INN EXPRESS.** *(2323 NE 181st Ave, Gresham 97230) I-84 exit 13. 503/492-4000; FAX 503/492-3271.* 71 rms, 3 story, 23 suites. May-Sept: S $70; D $77; each addl $7; suites $80-$120; under 18 free; lower rates rest of yr. Crib free. Pet accepted, some restrictions. TV; cable (premium), VCR avail (movies). Indoor pool; whirlpool. Complimentary continental bkfst. Coffee in rms. Restaurant adj 7 am-10 pm. Ck-out 1 pm. Coin lndry. Meeting rms. Business servs avail. Sundries. Valet serv. Exercise equipt; rower, stair machine, sauna. Some refrigerators. Cr cds: A, D, DS, JCB, MC, V.

D SC

★ ★ **McMENAMINS EDGEFIELD.** *(2126 SW Halsey St, Troutdale 97060) E on I-84, Wood Village exit 16A. 503/669-8610; FAX 503/492-7750; res: 800/669-8610.* E-mail edge@mcmenamins.com; web www.mcmenamins.com. 103 rms, 100 share bath, 3 story. No rm phones. S, D $45-$180; each addl $15; under 6 free. Crib free. Complimentary full bkfst. Restaurant (see BLACK RABBIT). Bar 11-1 am. Ck-out 11 am. Business servs avail. Massage. Built 1911 as county poor farm; was converted to nursing home in 1960s. Renovated in style of European village complete with theater, winery and brewery. Herb gardens. Totally nonsmoking. Cr cds: A, DS, MC, V.

D SC

★ ★ **PHOENIX INN.** *(14905 SW Bangy Rd, Lake Oswego 97034) S on I-5, exit 292, at OR 217. 503/624-7400; FAX 503/624-7405; res: 800/824-9992.* 62 rms, 4 story. June-Sept: S, D $89; each addl $5;

suites $119-$129; under 18 free; lower rates rest of yr. Crib free. TV; cable (premium). Indoor pool; whirlpool. Complimentary continental bkfst. Coffee in rms. Restaurant adj 11 am-10 pm. Bar 11 am-10 pm. Ck-out noon. Coin Indry. Meeting rms. Business servs avail. In-rm modem link. Bellhops. Valet serv. Sundries. Airport transportation avail. Exercise equipt; bicycle, treadmill. Refrigerators, minibars. Cr cds: A, C, D, DS, MC, V.

D SC

★ ★ **PHOENIX INN.** *(477 NW Phoenix Dr, Troutdale 97060) 503/669-6500; FAX 503/669-3500; res: 800/824-6824.* 73 rms, 3 story. Mid-May-Sept: S $65-$75; D $79-$85; each addl $7; suites $115; under 17 free; lower rates rest of yr. Crib free. Pet accepted; $10. TV; cable (premium). Indoor pool; whirlpool. Complimentary continental bkfst. Restaurant adj open 24 hrs. Bar 11-2 am. Ck-out noon. Meeting rms. Business servs avail. Free airport transportation. Exercise equipt; bicycle, stair machine. Cr cds: A, D, DS, MC, V.

D SC

★ ★ **RAMADA INN-AIRPORT.** *6221 NE 82nd Ave (97220), east of downtown. 503/255-6511; FAX 503/255-8417.* 202 rms, 2 story. S, D $85-$120; each addl $10; suites $95-$250; under 18 free; wkend rates. Crib free. TV; cable (premium), VCR avail. Heated pool; whirlpool. Coffee in rms. Restaurant 6:30 am-11 pm. Rm serv. Bar. Ck-out noon. Coin Indry. Meeting rms. Business center. Bellhops. Valet serv. Free airport transportation. Exercise equipt; weights, stair machine, sauna. Some private patios, balconies. Cr cds: A, C, D, DS, ER, JCB, MC, V.

D SC

★ ★ **RESIDENCE INN BY MARRIOTT-SOUTH.** *(15200 SW Bangy Rd, Lake Oswego 97035) S on I-5, exit 292. 503/684-2603; FAX 503/620-6712.* 112 kit. units, 2 story. 1 & 2-bedrm suites $120-$175. Crib $5. Pet accepted; $10/day. TV; cable (premium), VCR avail (movies free). Heated pool; whirlpool. Complimentary continental bkfst. Restaurant adj. Ck-out noon. Coin Indry. Business servs avail. Valet serv. Health club privileges. Fireplace in suites. Private patios, balconies. Picnic tables, grills. Cr cds: A, C, D, DS, JCB, MC, V.

D SC

★ ★ **SHILO INN-WASHINGTON SQUARE.** *(10830 SW Greenburg Rd, Tigard 97223) S on OR 217, Greenburg Rd exit. 503/620-4320; FAX 503/620-8277.* 77 rms, 4 story, 6 kits. S, D $59-$89; each addl $10; kit. units $85; under 12 free; wkly, monthly rates. Crib free. Pet accepted; $7/day. TV; cable (premium), VCR avail (movies). Complimentary continental bkfst. Restaurant nearby. Ck-out noon. Coin Indry. Meeting rm. Business servs avail. Valet serv. Free airport transportation. Exercise equipt; weight machines, bicycles, sauna, steam rm. Cr cds: A, C, D, DS, ER, JCB, MC, V.

D SC

✔★ **SUPER 8.** *(25438 SW Parkway Ave, Wilsonville 97070) I-5 exit 286. 503/682-2088; FAX 503/682-0453.* 72 rms, 4 story. S $48.88; D $57.88-$65.88; each addl $4. Crib free. Pet accepted; $25 refundable. TV; cable (premium). Complimentary coffee in lobby. Restaurant opp open 24 hrs. Ck-out noon. Coin Indry. Meeting rm. Business servs avail. Cr cds: A, C, D, DS, MC, V.

D

✔★ ★ **WAYSIDE MOTOR INN.** *(11460 SW Pacific Hwy, Tigard 97223) S on I-5, exit 294. 503/245-6421; FAX 503/245-6425; res: 800/547-8828.* 117 rms, 4 story. S $51-$60; D $57-$70; each addl $6. Crib $5. TV; cable, VCR avail (movies free). Heated pool. Sauna. Complimentary continental bkfst. Restaurant adj open 24 hrs. Ck-out 11 am. Meeting rms. Business servs avail. Valet serv. Cr cds: A, C, D, DS, MC, V.

D SC

Motor Hotels

★ **BEST WESTERN-ROSE GARDEN HOTEL.** *10 N Weidler (97227), east of downtown. 503/287-9900; FAX 503/287-3500.* 181 rms, 5 story. S $70-$75; D $75-$85; each addl $5; suites $140; under 12 free. TV; cable (premium). Indoor pool. Restaurant 6:30 am-9:30 pm. Rm serv. Bar 11-2 am. Ck-out noon. Meeting rms. Business servs avail. Covered parking. Free RR station, bus depot transportation. Cr cds: A, C, D, DS, MC, V.

D SC

★ **DAYS INN.** *1414 SW 6th Ave (97201), at Columbia, downtown. 503/221-1611; FAX 503/226-0447; res: 800/899-0248.* 173 rms, 5 story. S $99-$109; D $104-$114; each addl $5; under 12 free. Crib free. TV; cable (premium). Heated pool. Restaurant 6:30 am-10 pm; Sat, Sun from 7 am. Rm serv. Bar 11 am-midnight. Ck-out noon. Meeting rms. Business servs avail. In-rm modem link. Valet serv. Cr cds: A, C, D, DS, MC, V.

D SC

✔★ **DELTA INN.** *9930 N Whitaker Rd (97217), I-5 exit 306B, north of downtown. 503/289-1800; FAX 503/289-3778; res: 800/833-1800.* 212 rms, 4 story. S, D $55-$65; each addl $5; under 12 free; wkly rates. Crib free. Pet accepted; $10/day. TV; cable (premium). Complimentary coffee. Restaurant adj 6 am-11 pm. Ck-out noon. Coin Indry. Meeting rm. Business servs avail. In-rm modem link. Sundries. Free airport, RR station, bus depot transportation. Park adj. Cr cds: A, C, D, DS, MC, V.

D

★ ★ ★ **DOUBLETREE-COLUMBIA RIVER.** *1401 N Hayden Island Dr (97217), just W of I-5, Jantzen Beach exit, north of downtown. 503/283-2111; FAX 503/283-4718.* 351 rms, 3 story. S, D $150; each addl $15; suites $225-$350; under 18 free. Crib free. Pet accepted; $15. TV; cable, VCR avail. Heated pool. Restaurants 6 am-10 pm. Rm serv. Bars 11-2 am; entertainment. Ck-out noon. Convention facilities. Business servs avail. In-rm modem link. Bellhops. Valet serv. Gift shop. Barber, beauty shop. Free airport, RR station, bus depot transportation. Tennis adj. Putting green. Some refrigerators, bathrm phones. Whirlpool in some suites. Private patios, balconies. On Columbia River. Cr cds: A, C, D, DS, ER, JCB, MC, V.

D

★ ★ ★ **DOUBLETREE-JANTZEN BEACH.** *909 N Hayden Island Dr (97217), just E of I-5 exit Jantzen Beach, north of downtown. 503/283-4466; FAX 503/283-4743.* 320 rms, 4 story. S, D $99-$109; each addl $15; suites $195-$350; under 18 free; package plans; wkend rates. Crib free. Pet accepted; $20. TV; cable, VCR avail. Heated pool; whirlpool. Coffee in rms. Restaurant 6 am-10 pm. Rm serv. Bar 10-2:30 am; entertainment. Ck-out noon. Convention facilities. Business servs avail. Bellhops. Valet serv. Sundries. Free airport transportation. Lighted tennis. Exercise equipt; weights, stair machine. Some bathrm phones, in-rm whirlpools. Private patios, balconies. On river; boat dock. Cr cds: A, C, D, DS, ER, JCB, MC, V.

D SC

★ ★ **HOLIDAY INN-AIRPORT.** *8439 NE Columbia Blvd (97220), 2 1/2 mi N of I-84, on I-205, exit 23B/Columbia Blvd, near Intl Airport, east of downtown. 503/256-5000; FAX 503/257-4742.* 286 rms, 8 story. S, D $108; each addl $8; suites $175-$275. Crib free. TV; cable (premium), VCR avail. Indoor pool; whirlpool. Restaurant 6 am-10 pm. Rm serv. Bar. Ck-out noon. Coin Indry. Convention facilities. Business servs avail. Bellhops. Valet serv Mon-Fri. Gift shop. Free airport transportation. Exercise equipt; weight machine, stair machine, sauna. Game rm. Cr cds: A, C, D, DS, ER, JCB, MC, V.

D SC

★ ★ **RIVERSIDE INN.** *50 SW Morrison St (97204), downtown. 503/221-0711; FAX 503/274-0312; res: 800/899-0247.* 140 rms, 5 story. S $130-$145; D $140-$155; each addl $10; under 17 free. Crib free. Pet accepted, some restrictions; $10/day. TV. Coffee in rms. Restaurant 6:30-10 am, 4-11 pm; Sat, Sun 7 am-noon, 4-11 pm. Rm serv 5 pm-1 am. Bar 4 pm-2 am. Ck-out noon. Meeting rm. Business servs avail. Health club privileges. Balconies. Cr cds: A, C, D, DS, ER, MC, V.

D

★ ★ **SHILO INN.** *9900 SW Canyon Rd (97225), west of downtown. 503/297-2551; FAX 503/297-7708; res: 800/222-2244.* 142 rms, 2-3 story. S, D $79-$99; each addl $10; suites $99-$189; under 12 free. Crib free. TV; cable (premium), VCR avail (movies). Heated pool. Complimentary bkfst buffet. Restaurant 6 am-10 pm. Rm serv. Bar 11-2 am; entertainment exc Sun. Ck-out noon. Meeting rms. Business servs avail. Valet serv. Sundries. Free airport transportation. Exercise equipt; weight machine, bicycles. Refrigerators. Private patios, balconies. Cr cds: A, C, D, DS, ER, JCB, MC, V.

D SC

★ ★ **SWEETBRIER INN.** *(7125 SW Nyberg, Tualatin 97062) approx 10 mi S on I-5, exit 289. 503/692-5800; FAX 503/691-2894; res: 800/551-9167.* 100 rms, 32 suites. S $63-$83; D $73-$93; suites $90-$165; under 18 free; wkend rates. Crib free. Pet accepted; $100 refundable. TV; cable (premium). Heated pool. Playground. Complimentary coffee in rms. Restaurant 6:30 am-10 pm. Rm serv. Bar; entertainment Wed-Sat. Ck-out noon. Meeting rms. Business servs avail. In-rm modem link. Sundries. Valet serv. Refrigerator in suites. Some balconies, patios. Picnic tables. Cr cds: A, C, D, DS, JCB, MC, V.

D SC

Hotels

★ ★ ★ ★ **5TH AVENUE SUITES.** *506 SW Washington (97205), downtown. 503/222-0001; FAX 503/222-0004; res: 800/711-2971.* Built in 1912, this former department store has been completely renovated and redecorated in turn-of-the-century, American country-home style. Rooms are comfortable, light and airy. There are on-site business and fitness centers and the Red Star Tavern is open daily for breakfast, lunch and dinner. 221 rms, 10 story, 139 suites. S $150-$165; D $165-$180; each addl $15; suites $160-$225; under 18 free; wkend, hol rates. Crib free. Pet accepted, some restrictions. Garage/valet parking $13. TV; cable (premium), VCR avail (movies). Pool privileges. Complimentary continental bkfst. Restaurant 6:30 am-10 pm. Rm serv 24 hrs. Bar 11-1 am. Ck-out noon. Meeting rms. Business center. In-rm modem link. Concierge. Exercise equipt; weights, treadmill. Refrigerators. Cr cds: A, C, D, DS, JCB, MC, V.

D

★ ★ ★ **THE BENSON.** *309 SW Broadway (97205), at Oak St, downtown. 503/228-2000; FAX 503/226-4603; res: 800/426-0670.* 286 units, 13 story, 44 suites. S $145-$190; D $185-$210; each addl $25; suites $180-$600; under 18 free; wkend rates. Crib $25. Pet accepted; $50. Garage, valet $12/day. TV; cable, VCR avail. Restaurant (see LONDON GRILL). Rm serv 24 hrs. Bar 11-1 am; entertainment. Ck-out noon. Convention facilities. Business center. In-rm modem link. Concierge. Gift shop. Airport transportation. Exercise equipt; weights, treadmills. Minibars. Bathrm phone in suites. Cr cds: A, C, D, DS, ER, JCB, MC, V.

D

★ ★ **COURTYARD BY MARRIOTT-AIRPORT.** *11550 NE Airport Way (97220), near Intl Airport, east of downtown. 503/252-3200; FAX 503/252-8921.* 150 rms, 6 story. June-Aug: S, D $79-$89; suites $110-$120; under 18 free; wkly rates; lower rates rest of yr. Crib free. TV; cable (premium), some VCRs. Heated pool; whirlpool, poolside serv. Coffee in rms. Restaurant 6 am-11 pm. Rm serv 5-10 pm. Bar 4-11 pm. Ck-out 1 pm. Coin Indry. Business servs avail. Exercise equipt; bicycles, stair machine. Free airport transportation. Refrigerator, wet bar in suites. Cr cds: A, C, D, DS, MC, V.

D SC

★ ★ ★ **CROWNE PLAZA.** *(14811 SW Kruse Oaks Blvd, Lake Oswego 97035) 503/624-8400; FAX 503/684-8324.* 161 rms, 6 story. June-Aug: S $134; D $149; suites $150-$265; under 18 free; lower rates rest of yr. Crib free. Pet accepted. Valet parking $5. TV; cable (premium). Indoor/outdoor pool; whirlpool, sauna. Complimentary coffee in rms. Restaurant 6 am-2 pm, 5-10 pm. Rm serv to midnight. Bar 2 pm-midnight. Ck-out noon. Meeting rms. Business servs avail. Sundries. Gift shop. Valet serv. Free RR transportation. Tennis privileges. Exercise equipt; bicycle, treadmill. Cr cds: A, D, DS, ER, JCB, MC, V.

D SC

★ ★ ★ **DOUBLETREE-LLOYD CENTER.** *1000 NE Multnomah St (97232), I-84 exit 1 (Lloyd Blvd), east of downtown. 503/281-6111; FAX 503/284-8553.* 476 rms, 15 story. S, D $99-$149; each addl $15; suites $269-$575; under 18 free. Crib free. Pet accepted. TV; cable, VCR avail. Pool; poolside serv. Coffee in rms. Restaurant 6 am-midnight. Bar; entertainment. Ck-out noon. Convention facilities. Business center. Valet parking. Free airport transportation. Exercise equipt; weights, bicycles. Some bathrm phones, in-rm whirlpools, refrigerators. Many private patios, balconies. Cr cds: A, C, D, DS, ER, JCB, MC, V.

D

★ ★ ★ **THE GOVERNOR.** *611 SW 10th (97205), at SW Alder Ave, downtown. 503/224-3400; FAX 503/241-2122; res: 800/554-3456.* 100 rms, 6 story, 32 suites. S $160-$185; D $185-$200; each addl $20; suites $195-$500; under 12 free; wkend rates. Crib free. Garage parking $13-$15. TV; cable, VCR avail. Indoor pool; whirlpool. Restaurant 6:30 am-11 pm (also see JAKE'S GRILL). Rm serv 24 hrs. Bar 11 am-midnight. Ck-out noon. Meeting rms. Business center. Concierge. Barber, beauty shop. Exercise rm; instructor, weights, treadmill, sauna. Refrigerators, minibars. Some in-rm whirlpools, fireplaces. Some balconies. Cr cds: A, C, D, DS, JCB, MC, V.

D

★ ★ ★ **HEATHMAN.** *1001 SW Broadway (97205), downtown. 503/241-4100; FAX 503/790-7110; res: 800/551-0011.* 150 rms, 10 story. S $155-$180; D $175-$200; each addl $20; suites $250-$575; under 6 free; wkend rates. Crib $7. Garage in/out $12. TV; cable (premium), VCR avail (movies). Restaurant (see HEATHMAN). Rm serv 24 hrs. Afternoon tea. Bars 11-2 am; entertainment. Ck-out 1 pm. Meeting rms. Business servs avail. In-rm modem link. Concierge. Gift shop. Exercise equipt; bicycles, rowers. Health club privileges. Minibars. Cr cds: A, C, D, DS, ER, JCB, MC, V.

D

★ ★ ★ **HILTON.** *921 SW 6th Ave (97204), downtown. 503/226-1611; FAX 503/220-2565.* 455 rms, 23 story. S $155; D $175; each addl $30; suites $400-$950; family, wkend rates. Garage in/out $14; valet $3 addl. Crib free. TV; cable (premium). Indoor pool; poolside serv. Restaurant 6:30 am-11:30 pm. Bar 11-1 am; entertainment Tues-Sat. Ck-out noon. Convention facilities. Business center. In-rm modem link. Gift shop. Barber, beauty shop. Exercise equipt; weights, treadmills, steam rm, sauna. Cr cds: A, C, D, DS, ER, JCB, MC, V.

D

★ ★ **IMPERIAL.** *400 SW Broadway (97205), at Stark St, downtown. 503/228-7221; FAX 503/223-4551; res: 800/452-2323.* 136 rms, 9 story. S $75-$90; D $80-$100; each addl $5; under 12 free. Crib free. TV; cable (premium). Pet accepted; $10. Restaurants 6:30 am-9 pm. Bar 11-1 am, Sat & Sun 1-9 pm. Ck-out 2 pm. Meeting rms. Business servs avail. In-rm modem link. Valet parking. Cr cds: A, C, D, DS, MC, V.

D

✔★ **MALLORY.** *729 SW 15th Ave (97205), just W of I-405, downtown. 503/223-6311; FAX 503/223-0522; res: 800/228-8657.* 143 rms, 8 story. S $65-$100; D $70-$110; each addl $5; suites $110-$120. Crib free. Pet accepted; $10. TV; cable (premium), VCR avail. Restaurant 6:30 am-9 pm; Sun from 7 am. Bar 11:30-1 am, Sun 1-9 pm. Ck-out 2 pm. Business servs avail. Some refrigerators. Cr cds: A, C, D, DS, MC, V.

D

★ **MARK SPENCER.** *409 SW 11th Ave (97205), downtown. 503/224-3293; FAX 503/223-7848; res: 800/548-3934.* 101 kit. units, 6 story. S, D $69-$105; each addl $10; suites $95-$110; studio rms $69; under 12 free; monthly rates. Crib free. Pet accepted; $200 refundable. Parking lot 1 blk $7. TV; cable, VCR avail. Complimentary coffee in lobby. Complimentary continental bkfst. Restaurant nearby. Ck-out noon. Coin Indry. Business servs avail. Health club privileges. Refrigerators. Rooftop garden. Cr cds: A, C, D, DS, MC, V.

SC

★ ★ ★ **MARRIOTT.** *1401 SW Front Ave (97201), downtown. 503/226-7600; FAX 503/221-1789.* 503 rms, 15 story. S $170-$190; D $180-$200; suites $350-$500; under 18 free. Crib free. Pet accepted. Valet parking in/out $14/day. TV; cable (premium), VCR avail. Indoor pool;

whirlpool, poolside serv. Restaurant 6 am-11 pm; Fri, Sat to midnight. Bar 11:30-2 am; entertainment. Ck-out noon. Coin lndry. Convention facilities. Business center. Concierge. Gift shop. Barber, beauty shop. Exercise equipt; bicycles, rower, sauna. Massage. Game rm. Some bathrm phones, refrigerators; wet bar in suites. Some private patios, balconies. Japanese garden at entrance. Luxury level. Cr cds: A, C, D, DS, ER, JCB, MC, V.

D SC

★ ★ **RAMADA PLAZA.** *1441 NE Second Ave (97232), east of downtown. 503/233-2401; FAX 503/238-7016.* 240 rms, 10 story. S $96; D $106; under 18 free. Crib free. TV; cable (premium). Pool. Complimentary coffee in rms. Restaurant 6:30 am-2 pm, 5:30-10 pm. Bar. Ck-out noon. Meeting rms. Business servs avail. Free airport transportation. Exercise equipt; weights, stair machine. Cr cds: A, C, D, DS, ER, MC, V.

D

★ ★ ★ **RIVERPLACE.** *1510 SW Harbor Way (97201), downtown. 503/228-3233; FAX 503/295-6161; res: 800/227-1333.* 84 rms, 4 story. S, D $185-$245; condos $375-$475; suites $205-$700; under 18 free. Valet, garage parking in/out $15. Crib free. Pet accepted, some restrictions; $100. TV; cable (premium), VCR avail. Complimentary continental bkfst. Restaurant (see ESPLANADE AT RIVERPLACE). Rm serv 24 hrs. Bar 11-1 am; entertainment Wed-Sun evenings. Ck-out 1 pm. Meeting rms. Business servs avail. In-rm modem link. Concierge. Shopping arcade. Whirlpool, sauna. Health club privileges. Minibars; some bathrm phones. Some refrigerators, fireplaces in suites. Balconies. On river. Skyline, marina views. Cr cds: A, C, D, DS, ER, JCB, MC, V.

D

★ ★ ★ **SHERATON-PORTLAND AIRPORT.** *8235 NE Airport Way (97220), near Intl Airport, east of downtown. 503/281-2500; FAX 503/249-7602.* 215 rms, 5 story. S $115; D $127; each addl $10; suites $150-$395; under 18 free; wkend rates. Crib $5. TV; cable (premium). Indoor pool; whirlpool. Coffee in rms. Restaurant 5 am-10:30 pm; Sat, Sun 6 am-10 pm. Rm serv 24 hrs. Bars. Ck-out noon. Meeting rms. Business center. Concierge. Free airport transportation. Exercise equipt; weights, treadmill, sauna. Minibars. Cr cds: A, C, D, DS, JCB, MC, V.

D

★ ★ ★ **SHILO INN SUITES-AIRPORT.** *11707 NE Airport Way (97220), near Intl Airport, east of downtown. 503/252-7500; FAX 503/254-0794.* 200 suites, 4 story. S, D $121-$157; each addl $15; under 13 free; higher rates Rose Festival. Crib free. TV; cable (premium), VCR (movies $3.50). Indoor pool; whirlpool. Complimentary bkfst; afternoon refreshments. Restaurant 6 am-11 pm. Rm serv to 10 pm. Bar 8-2 am; entertainment. Ck-out noon. Coin lndry. Meeting rms. Business center. In-rm modem link. Concierge. Free airport, RR station, bus depot transportation. Exercise equipt; weight machine, bicycles, sauna. Bathrm phones, refrigerators, wet bars. Cr cds: A, C, D, DS, ER, JCB, MC, V.

D SC

★ ★ **SILVER CLOUD INN.** *2426 NW Vaughn St (97210). 503/242-2400; FAX 503/242-1770; res: 800/551-7207.* 81 rms, 4 story. S $79; D $82; each addl $8; suites $91; under 14 free. Crib free. TV; cable (premium). Complimentary continental bkfst. Restaurant nearby. Ck-out noon. Meeting rms. Business servs avail. In-rm modem link. Free lndry. Exercise equipt; treadmill, weight machine. Whirlpool. Some refrigerators. Cr cds: A, D, DS, MC, V.

D

★ ★ ★ ★ **VINTAGE PLAZA.** *422 SW Broadway (97205), downtown. 503/228-1212; FAX 503/228-3598; res: 800/243-0555.* This historic building's dramatic decor was inspired by Oregon vineyards; there's a winery theme throughout. 107 rms, 10 story, 23 suites. S $160-$175; D $175-$190; each addl $15; suites $195-$250; under 18 free; wkend rates. Crib free. Valet parking $13. TV; cable, VCR avail. Restaurant (see PAZZO RISTORANTE). Rm serv 24 hrs. Bar 11-1 am. Ck-out noon. Meeting rms. Business center. In-rm modem link. Concierge. Gift shop. Exercise equipt; bicycles, rowers. Minibars. Cr cds: A, C, D, DS, JCB, MC, V.

D

Inns

★ ★ **GENERAL HOOKER'S.** *125 SW Hooker St (97201). 503/222-4435; FAX 503/295-6410; res: 800/745-4135.* 4 rms, 2 share baths, 1 shower only, 3 story. No elvtr. S $55-$115; D $70-$125; 2-day min. Children over 10 only. TV; cable (premium), VCR (movies). Complimentary continental bkfst; afternoon refreshments. Restaurant nearby. Ck-out 11 am, ck-in 3-5 pm. Health club privileges. Victorian house built in 1888. Totally nonsmoking. Cr cds: A, MC, V.

★ ★ **HERON HAUS.** *2545 NW Westover Rd (97210), in Nob Hill. 503/274-1846; FAX 503/243-1075.* 6 rms, 3 story. S $85; D $125-$250; each addl $65. TV; cable (premium), VCR avail (movies). Pool. Complimentary continental bkfst. Restaurant nearby. Ck-out noon, ck-in 4-6 pm. Business servs avail. In-rm modem link. Restored house (1904) in NW hills overlooking city; library, morning rm. Totally nonsmoking. Cr cds: MC, V.

★ ★ **JOHN PALMER HOUSE.** *4314 N Mississippi Ave (97217), north of downtown. 503/284-5893; FAX 503/284-1239; res: 800/518-5893.* 7 rms, 2 story, 2 suites. May-Oct: S $65-$90; D, suites $70-$100; each addl $15; wkly rates; lower rates rest of yr. Children by appt. Crib free. Complimentary full bkfst. Ck-out 11 am, ck-in 3 pm. Business servs avail. RR station, bus depot transportation. Whirlpool. Picnic tables. Built in 1890; completely furnished with antiques. Totally nonsmoking. Cr cds: A, DS, MC, V.

★ ★ ★ **PORTLAND'S WHITE HOUSE.** *1914 NE 22nd Ave (97212), east of downtown. 503/287-7131.* 6 rms, 2 story. S $93-$111; D $102-$120; each addl $20; under 6 free. Crib free. TV avail. Complimentary full bkfst; afternoon refreshments. Complimentary coffee in rms. Restaurant nearby. Rm serv (bkfst). Ck-out 11 am, ck-in 2 pm. Business servs avail. Luggage handling. Street parking. Free airport, RR station, bus depot transportation. Game rm. Some balconies. White southern colonial mansion with Greek columns and fountain at entrance. Ballroom; antique stained-glass windows. Totally nonsmoking. Cr cds: MC, V.

Restaurants

★ **28 EAST.** *40 NE 28th Ave (97232), east of downtown. 503/235-9060.* Hrs: 11:30 am-3:30 pm, 5-10:30 pm; Fri to 11 pm; Sat 5-11 pm; Sun brunch 10 am-3 pm, also 5-9 pm. Closed Mon; most major hols. Res accepted. Northwestern cuisine. Bar. Semi-a la carte: lunch $5-$9; dinner $7-$18. Sun brunch $4-$8. Specialties: Asian marinated pork chops, pan-roasted rainbow trout. Outdoor dining. Open kitchen. Totally nonsmoking. Cr cds: A, MC, V.

D

★ ★ **AL-AMIR.** *223 SW Stark (97204), downtown. 503/274-0010.* Hrs: 11 am-10 pm; Fri to 1 am; Sat 4 pm-1 am; Sun 4-9 pm. Closed Jan 1, Thanksgiving, Dec 25. Res required Fri, Sat. Lebanese menu. Bar. Semi-a la carte: lunch $3.75-$7.50, dinner $7.50-$15.50. Child's meals. Specialties: maza al-amir, kebab. Entertainment Fri, Sat. Lebanese decor. Totally nonsmoking. Cr cds: A, D, DS, MC, V.

D

★ **ALESSANDRO'S.** *301 SW Morrison (97204), downtown. 503/222-3900.* Hrs: 11:30 am-10 pm; Sat to 11 pm; Sun 2-10 pm. Closed major hols. Res required. Italian menu. Bar. Semi-a la carte: lunch $5.75-$11, dinner $10.50-$19.95. Complete meals: dinner $27.50. Specializes in Roman-style Italian seafood, poultry, veal. Parking. Totally nonsmoking. Cr cds: A, D, MC, V.

D

✔★ ★ **ALEXIS.** *215 W Burnside (97209), in Old Town. 503/224-8577.* Hrs: 11:30 am-2 pm, 5-10 pm; Fri to 11 pm; Sat 5-11 pm; Sun 4:30-9 pm. Closed major hols. Greek menu. Bar. Semi-a la carte: lunch $5.95-$8.95, dinner $8.95-$13.95. Specialties: deep fried squid, eggplant casserole, grape leaves stuffed with ground lamb. Belly dancer Fri, Sat. Greek decor. Cr cds: A, D, DS, MC, V.

D

★ ★ ★ **ATWATER'S.** *111 SW 5th Ave (97204), downtown. 503/275-3622.* Hrs: 5:30-9:30 pm; Fri, Sat to 10 pm; Sun 5-9 pm. Closed most major hols. Res accepted. Contemporary Amer menu. Bar to 1:30 am. Wine list. Semi-a la carte: dinner $15-$24. Child's meals. Specializes in salmon, lamb, duck. Entertainment Wed-Sat. Contemporary decor. Totally nonsmoking. Cr cds: A, C, D, DS, JCB, MC, V.

D

★ ★ ★ **AVALON GRILL & CAFE.** *4630 SW Macadam Ave (97201), west of downtown. 503/227-4630.* Hrs: 11:30 am-2 pm, 5:30-9:30 pm; Fri to 10 pm; Sat 11:30 am-10 pm; Sun brunch 10 am-2 pm, also 5:30-9:30 pm. Closed July 4, Dec 25. Res accepted. Bar. Wine list. Semi-a la carte: lunch $8-$12, dinner $17-$25. Sun brunch $15.95. Child's meals. Specializes in seafood, lamb. Entertainment. Outdoor dining. Views of the river. Totally nonsmoking. Cr cds: A, MC, V.

D

★ ★ **BLACK RABBIT.** *(See McMenamins Edgefield Motel) 503/492-3086.* E-mail edge@mcmenamins.com; web www.mcmenamins.com. Hrs: 7 am-10 pm. Res accepted. Bar 11-1 am. Semi-a la carte: bkfst $5.25-$9.25, lunch $6.25-$12.50, dinner $13.50-$21. Child's meals. Specializes in fresh Northwestern cuisine. Parking. Outdoor dining. Totally nonsmoking. Cr cds: A, DS, MC, V.

D

✔★ **THE BREWHOUSE.** *2730 NW 31st Ave (97210), west of downtown. 503/226-7623.* Hrs: 11 am-11 pm; Mon to 9:30 pm; Fri to 11:30 pm; Sat noon-11:30 pm; Sun noon-9:30 pm. Closed most major hols. Northwestern cuisine. Bar. Semi-a la carte: lunch $4.75-$9.95, dinner $5.50-$12.95. Child's meals. Specialties: MacTarnahan's fish & chips, haystack back ribs. Outdoor dining. Copper beer-making equipment at entrance. Totally nonsmoking. Cr cds: A, MC, V.

D

★ ★ **BUSH GARDEN.** *900 SW Morrison (97205), downtown. 503/226-7181.* Hrs: 11:30 am-1:45 pm, 5-9:45 pm; Sat 5-9:45 pm; Sun 5-8:45 pm. Closed most major hols. Res accepted. Japanese menu. Bar to 12:45 am; Fri, Sat to l:45 am. Semi-a la carte: lunch $5.75-$11.95, dinner $10.50-$24.95. Specializes in sashimi, sukiyaki. Sushi bar. Karaoke singing. Parking. Dining in tatami rms. Cr cds: A, D, DS, JCB, MC, V.

D

★ ★ ★ **CAFE DES AMIS.** *1987 NW Kearney (97209), west of downtown. 503/295-6487.* Hrs: 5:30-10 pm. Closed Sun; major hols. Res accepted. Country French menu. Serv bar. Semi-a la carte: dinner $12.50-$22. Specializes in filet of beef with garlic & port sauce, fresh fish. Own baking. Parking. Country French decor. Totally nonsmoking. Cr cds: A, MC, V.

D

✔★ **CAPRIAL'S.** *7015 SE Milwaukie Ave (97202), east of downtown. 503/236-6457.* Hrs: 11:30 am-3:30 pm, 5-8:30 pm; Fri to 9 pm; Sat noon-3:30 pm, 5-9 pm. Closed Sun, Mon; major hols. Res required. Eclectic menu. Wine, beer. Semi-a la carte: lunch $1.95-$8.25, dinner $14-$19. Specializes in pasta, seafood. Casual decor. Totally nonsmoking. Cr cds: MC, V.

D

★ ★ **CHART HOUSE.** *5700 SW Terwilliger Blvd (97206), west of downtown. 503/246-6963.* Hrs: 11:30 am-2 pm, 5-10 pm; Sat from 5 pm; Sun 5-9 pm. Res accepted. Bar to midnight. Semi-a la carte: lunch $6-$13, dinner $15-$25. Child's meals. Specializes in prime rib, steak, fresh seafood. Valet parking. Fireplace. 1,000 ft above Willamette River; panoramic view of Portland, Mt Hood and Mt St Helens. Totally nonsmoking. Cr cds: A, C, D, DS, MC, V.

D

★ ★ ★ **COUCH STREET FISH HOUSE.** *105 NW 3rd Ave, just N of OR 30, in Old Town. 503/223-6173.* Hrs: 5-10 pm; Fri, Sat to 11 pm; early-bird dinner 5-6:30 pm. Closed Sun; some major hols. Res accepted. Bar. Wine list. Semi-a la carte: dinner $16.95-$28.95. Specializes in Chinook salmon, live Maine lobster, Dungeness crab. Valet parking. Old San Francisco decor. Totally nonsmoking. Cr cds: A, C, D, DS, MC, V.

D

★ ★ **COUVRON.** *1126 SW 18th Ave (97205), west of downtown. 503/225-1844.* Hrs: 5:30-9 pm; Fri, Sat to 10 pm. Closed Sun, Mon; major hols. Res accepted. Continental, French menu. Wine list. Semi-a la carte: dinner $22-$32. 6-course menu $55. Specialties: foie gras, rack of lamb, salmon. Country French decor. Totally nonsmoking. Cr cds: A, DS, MC, V.

D

✔★ **DAN & LOUIS OYSTER BAR.** *208 SW Ankeny St (97204), in Old Town. 503/227-5906.* Hrs: 11 am-10 pm; Fri, Sat to 11 pm. Closed some major hols. Semi-a la carte: lunch $2.75-$6.50, dinner $5.95-$16.95. Child's meals. Specializes in stewed, broiled, fried, pan-fried & raw oysters. Antique seafaring decor. Ship models. 19th-century bldg (1907). Family-owned. Cr cds: A, D, DS, JCB, MC, V.

D SC

★ **DELFINA'S.** *2112 NW Kearney St (97210), west of downtown. 503/221-1195.* Hrs: 11:30 am-2:30 pm, 5-11 pm; Sat, Sun from 5 pm. Closed July 4, Thanksgiving, Dec 25. Res accepted. Italian menu. Bar 11:30-1 am; Sat, Sun from 5 pm. Semi-a la carte: lunch $6-$12, dinner $12-$20. Specializes in seafood, pasta. Valet parking. Outdoor dining. Original artwork. Cr cds: A, D, DS, MC, V.

D

✔★ **ESPARZA'S TEX MEX CAFE.** *2725 SE Ankeny St (97214), east of downtown. 503/234-7909.* Hrs: 11:30 am-10 pm. Closed Sun, Mon; most major hols. Tex-Mex menu. Bar. Semi-a la carte: lunch $4.75-$9.95; dinner $5.75-$11.50. Child's meals. Specialties: stuffed pork-loin with buffalo spicy cactus, carne asada rib-eye steak. Western decor. Totally nonsmoking. Cr cds: A, MC, V.

★ ★ ★ **ESPLANADE AT RIVERPLACE.** *(See Riverplace Hotel) 503/228-3233.* Hrs: 6:30 am-2 pm; 5-10 pm; Sat 6:30-11 am, 5-9 pm; Sun 6:30 am-2 pm, 5-9 pm; Sun brunch 11 am-2 pm. Res accepted. Continental menu. Bar 11-1 am. Wine cellar. Semi-a la carte: bkfst $3.50-$10.50, lunch $6.95-$15, dinner $13.50-$28. Sun brunch $9-$13. Child's meals. Specializes in Northwestern regional cuisine. Own desserts. Outdoor dining. Split-level dining; view of Willamette River & marina. Totally nonsmoking. Cr cds: A, C, D, DS, JCB, MC, V.

D ♥

★ ★ ★ ★ **GENOA.** *2832 SE Belmont St, east of downtown. 503/238-1464.* Don't let the nondescript exterior of this storefront restaurant fool you—inside awaits an exquisite meal delivered with flawless service. The interior features antique sideboards and a 200-year-old Persian tapestry. Northern Italian menu. Specializes in authentic regional Italian dishes. Own baking. Hrs: 5:30-9:30 pm. Closed Sun; major hols. Res accepted. Prix fixe: 7-course dinner $50, 4-course dinner (Mon-Thurs) $40. Menu changes every two wks. Totally nonsmoking. Cr cds: A, C, D, DS, MC, V.

★ ★ ★ **HEATHMAN.** *(See Heathman Hotel) 503/790-7752.* Hrs: 6:30 am-11 pm. Res accepted. French, Amer menu. Bar 11-2 am. Wine cellar. Semi-a la carte: bkfst $4-$14, lunch $8-$18, dinner $13-$35. Specializes in Chinook salmon, halibut confit, Oregon lamb. Own baking. Entertainment. Valet parking. Outdoor dining. Built 1927. Formal decor. Cr cds: A, C, D, DS, ER, JCB, MC, V.

D

★★ **HIGGINS.** *1239 SW Broadway (97205), downtown. 503/222-9070.* Hrs: 11:30 am-2 pm, 5-10:30 pm. Closed most major hols. Res accepted. Northwestern regional menu. Bar to 2 am. Semi-a la carte: lunch $6.75-$11.75; dinner $13.75-$19.75. Child's meals. Specializes in seafood, hamburger. Contemporary decor. Totally nonsmoking. Cr cds: A, C, D, DS, MC, V.

D

★ **HUBER'S.** *411 SW 3rd Ave (97204), downtown. 503/228-5686.* Hrs: 11 am-midnight; Fri to 1 am; Sat noon-1 am. Closed Sun; major hols. Res accepted exc Fri evenings. Bar. Semi-a la carte: lunch $4.95-$9, dinner $6.50-$15. Specialties: roast turkey, flaming Spanish coffees. Originally a saloon established in 1879 that became a restaurant during Prohibition. Arched stained-glass skylight, mahogany paneling and terrazzo floor. Cr cds: A, D, DS, MC, V.

D

★★ **IL FORNAIO.** *115 NW 22nd Ave (97210), in Nob Hill. 503/248-9400.* Hrs: 11 am-11 pm; Fri to midnight; Sat 10 am-midnight; Sun 10 am-10 pm. Closed Thanksgiving, Dec 25. Res accepted. Italian menu. Bar. Semi-a la carte: lunch $4-$15, dinner $4-$19. Child's meals. Specialties: pizza con la luganega, pollo toscano, grigliata di vitello. Parking. Show kitchen; wood-burning pizza oven & rotisserie. Totally nonsmoking dining rm. Cr cds: A, DS, MC, V.

D

★★★ **JAKE'S FAMOUS CRAWFISH.** *401 SW 12th Ave (97205), downtown. 503/226-1419.* Hrs: 11:30 am-11 pm; Fri to midnight; Sat 5 pm-midnight; Sun 5-10 pm. Closed July 4, Thanksgiving, Dec 25. Res accepted. Bar. Wine list. A la carte entrees: lunch $4.95-$10, dinner $8.95-$28.95. Specializes in fresh regional seafood. Own baking. Turn-of-the-century decor. Cr cds: A, C, D, DS, MC, V.

D

★★★ **JAKE'S GRILL.** *(See The Governor Hotel) 503/220-1850.* Hrs: 6:30 am-midnight; Fri to 1 am; Sat 7:30-1 am; Sun 7:30 am-11 pm. Res accepted. Bar. Semi-a la carte: bkfst $2.50-$11.95, lunch $4.95-$18.50, dinner $4.95-$9.95. Child's meals. Specializes in steak, salmon. Outdoor dining. Casual decor. Cr cds: A, D, DS, MC, V.

D

★★★ **L'AUBERGE.** *2601 NW Vaughn (97210), west of downtown. 503/223-3302.* Hrs: 5 pm-midnight; Fri, Sat to 1 am. Closed most major hols. Res accepted. French menu. Bar. Wine list. Complete meals: dinner $9.75-$36. Prix fixe: dinner $42, $60. Specializes in seafood, steak, lamb. Own baking. Parking. Outdoor dining. Tri-level dining; wall hangings, 2 fireplaces. Family-owned. Cr cds: A, C, D, DS, MC, V.

★★★ **LONDON GRILL.** *(See The Benson Hotel) 503/295-4110.* Hrs: 6:30 am-2 pm, 5-10 pm; Fri, Sat to 11 pm; Sun brunch from 9:30 am. Res accepted. Continental menu. Bar 11-2 am. Wine cellar. Semi-a la carte: bkfst $4.95-$9.95, lunch $9-$13, dinner $19.95-$25. Sun brunch $17.50. Child's meals. Specializes in Northwest salmon, Caesar salad, ostrich. Harpist Wed-Sat. Valet parking. Elegant dining in historic hotel. Jacket (dinner). Cr cds: A, C, D, DS, ER, JCB, MC, V.

D

★★ **MANDARIN COVE.** *111 SW Columbia, downtown. 503/222-0006.* Hrs: 11 am-2 pm, 4:30-10 pm; Sat noon-11 pm; Sun 4-10 pm. Res accepted. Mandarin, Chinese menu. Bar. Semi-a la carte: lunch $4.95-$6.50, dinner $6.50-$25.50. Specializes in Hunan and Szechwan meats and seafood. Valet parking. Cr cds: A, D, MC, V.

D

✔★ **MAZZI'S ITALIAN-SICILIAN FOOD.** *5833 SW Macadam Ave (97201), west of downtown. 503/227-3382.* Hrs: 11:30 am-11 pm; Fri to midnight; Sat 5 pm-midnight; Sun 5-11 pm. Closed Thanksgiving, Dec 24, 25. Italian menu. Bar. Semi-a la carte: lunch $3.25-$7.95, dinner $5.50-$14.50. Specializes in fresh seafood, calzone, homemade pasta. Salad bar (lunch). Parking. Mediterranean decor; fireplaces. Totally nonsmoking. Cr cds: A, MC, V.

D

✔★ **OLD SPAGHETTI FACTORY.** *0715 SW Bancroft (97201), west of downtown. 503/222-5375.* Hrs: 11:30 am-2 pm, 5-10 pm; Fri to 11 pm; Sat 1-11 pm; Sun noon-10 pm. Closed Thanksgiving, Dec 24-25. Italian menu. Bar. Semi-a la carte: lunch $3.25-$5.45, dinner $4.50-$8.25. Child's meals. Specializes in pasta. Own sauces. Parking. 1890s decor; dining in trolley car. Family-owned. Cr cds: D, DS, MC, V.

D

✔★★ **PALEY'S PLACE.** *1204 NW 21st Ave (97209), west of downtown. 503/243-2403.* Hrs: 5:30-10 pm; Fri, Sat to 11 pm. Closed Sun, Mon; major hols. Res accepted. Southern French menu. Serv bar. Wine list. Semi-a la carte: dinner $13-$19. Child's meals. Specializes in sweetbreads, seafood. Outdoor dining. Contemporary decor. Totally nonsmoking. Cr cds: A, MC, V.

★★★ **PAZZO RISTORANTE.** *(See Vintage Plaza Hotel) 503/228-1515.* Hrs: 7 am-10 pm; Fri to 11 pm; Sat 8 am-11 pm; Sun from 8 am. Closed some major hols. Res accepted. Italian menu. Bar 11:30 am-midnight; Fri & Sat to 1 am. A la carte entrees: bkfst $3.50-$6.25, lunch $8-$15, dinner $8-$18. Specializes in hardwood-grilled seafood, meat, fowl. Own bread, pasta. Outdoor dining. Italian marble floors, mahogany bar; also dining in wine cellar. Cr cds: A, C, D, DS, MC, V.

D

★★★ **PLAINFIELD'S MAYUR.** *852 SW 21st Ave (97205), west of downtown. 503/223-2995.* Hrs: 5:30-10 pm. Closed Thanksgiving, Dec 25. Res accepted. East Indian menu. Serv bar. A la carte entrees: dinner $7.95-$15.95. Specialties: spiced lamb, lobster & spices, Tandoori chicken. Own baking. Parking. Patio dining. In 1901, shingle-style mansion; centerpiece of dining room is functioning Indian clay oven (tandoor). Cr cds: A, C, D, DS, MC, V.

D

★ **POOR RICHARD'S.** *3907 NE Broadway (97232), at Sandy Blvd, east of downtown. 503/288-5285.* Hrs: 11:30 am-11 pm; Sat 4-11 pm; Sun noon-9 pm. Closed most major hols. Res accepted. Bar. Semi-a la carte: lunch $4.75-$7.50, dinner $6-$14.95. Child's meals. Specializes in steak, seafood. Parking. Colonial decor; fireplace. Family-owned. Cr cds: A, DS, MC, V.

D

✔★★★ **RED STAR.** *503 SW Alder (97205), downtown. 503/222-0005.* Hrs: 7 am-2:30 pm, 5-10 pm; Fri to 11 pm; Sat 8 am-2:30 pm, 5-11 pm; Sun 8 am-10 pm. Closed most major hols. Res accepted. Bar. Semi-a la carte: bkfst $5.50-$8.25, lunch $4.25-$12.95, dinner $5.75-$16.95. Child's meals. Specialties: sage-roasted chicken with buttermilk mashed potatoes, rotisserie pork loin with sweet potato hash and roasted pear-onion jam. Wood-burning oven. Contemporary decor. Totally nonsmoking. Cr cds: A, C, D, DS, JCB, MC, V.

D

★★ **RHEINLANDER.** *5035 NE Sandy Blvd (97213), east of downtown. 503/288-5503.* Hrs: 11 am-10 pm; Sat to midnight; early-bird dinner 4:30-6 pm; Sat from 4 pm; Sun from 3:30 pm. Closed Labor Day, Dec 24, 25. Res accepted. German menu. Bar. Semi-a la carte: dinner $3.95-$16.95. Child's meals. Specialties: hasenpfeffer, homemade sausage, rotisserie chicken. Strolling accordionist; group singing. Parking. Family-owned. Cr cds: A, MC, V.

D

★★ **RINGSIDE.** *2165 W Burnside St (97210), west of downtown. 503/223-1513.* Hrs: 5 pm-midnight; Sun 4-11 pm. Closed some major hols. Res accepted. Bar. Semi-a la carte: dinner $12.50-$38. Specializes in steak, prime rib, seafood. Valet parking. Fireplace. Prizefight pictures; sports decor. Family-owned. Cr cds: A, D, DS, MC, V.

D

★ ★ **RINGSIDE EAST.** *14021 NE Glisan (97230), east of downtown. 503/255-0750.* Hrs: 11:30 am-2:30 pm, 5 pm-midnight; Sat from 5 pm, Sun from 4 pm. Closed most major hols. Res accepted. Bar. Semi-a la carte: lunch $4.50-$10.95, dinner $10.50-$36.75. Specializes in prime rib, steak, seafood. Parking. Cr cds: A, C, D, DS, MC, V.

D

★ ★ **SALTY'S ON THE COLUMBIA.** *3839 NE Marine Dr (97211), east of downtown. 503/288-4444.* Web www.saltys.com. Hrs: 11:30 am-11 pm; Sun 2-10 pm; June-Sept to midnight; Sun brunch 9:30 am-2 pm. Closed Dec 25. Res accepted. Bar. Semi-a la carte: lunch $7.25-$18.95, dinner $14-$51. Sun brunch buffet $7.95-$15.95. Child's meals. Specializes in seafood, halibut supreme, blackened salmon. Free valet parking. Outdoor dining. Overlooks Columbia River. Cr cds: A, C, D, DS, MC, V.

D

★ **SAYLER'S OLD COUNTRY KITCHEN.** *10519 SE Stark (97216), just E of I-205 Washington exit, east of downtown. 503/252-4171.* Hrs: 4-11 pm; Fri to midnight; Sat 3 pm-midnight; Sun noon-11 pm. Closed some major hols. Bar. Complete meals: dinner $8.95-$35. Child's meals. Specializes in steak, seafood, chicken. Parking. Family-owned. Cr cds: A, DS, MC, V.

D SC ♥

✔★ **SYLVIA'S.** *5115 NE Sandy Blvd (97213), east of downtown. 503/288-6828.* Hrs: 4-10 pm; Fri, Sat to 11 pm; early-bird dinner 4-6 pm. Closed Thanksgiving, Dec 24, 25. Res accepted; required for theater. Italian menu. Bar. Semi-a la carte: dinner $7.75-$15.50. Child's meals. Specializes in lasagne, fettucine Alfredo. Parking. Dinner theater adj. Family-owned. Cr cds: A, DS, MC, V.

D ♥

★ ★ **TRIBECA.** *704 NW 21st St (97209), on Nob Hill. 503/226-6126.* Hrs: 4:30-10 pm; Thur-Sat to 11 pm. Closed Jan 1, July 4, Dec 25. Res accepted. Northwestern cuisine. Bar. Semi-a la carte: dinner $9-$20. Specializes in crab cakes, mushroom strudel, salmon. Outdoor dining. Casual decor. Totally nonsmoking. Cr cds: A, MC, V.

D

✔★ ★ **TYPHOON!** *2310 NW Everett St (97201), west of downtown. 503/243-7557.* Hrs: 11:30 am-2:30 pm, 5-10 pm. Closed Sun; most major hols. Res accepted. Thai menu. Wine, beer. Semi-a la carte: lunch $5.95-$7.95, dinner $6.95-$17.95. Specialties: miang kum, drunken noodles. Outdoor dining. Thai decor. Cr cds: A, C, D, DS, MC, V.

D

★ **WIDMER GASTHAUS.** *929 N Russell St (97227), downtown. 503/281-3333.* Hrs: 11 am-11 pm; Fri, Sat to 1 am; Sun to 10 pm. Closed Jan 1, Thanksgiving, Dec 25. Res accepted. German menu. Bar. Semi-a la carte: lunch $5.95-$7.95, dinner $5.95-$13.95. Specializes in schnitzel, sauerbraten. Outdoor dining. Contemporary decor. Totally nonsmoking. Cr cds: A, DS, MC, V.

D

★ ★ ★ **WILDWOOD.** *1221 NW 21st Ave (97209), in Nob Hill. 503/248-9663.* Pacific Northwest menu. Specializes in mussels, breast of duck, salmon. Hrs: 11:30 am-2:30 pm, 5:30-10 pm; Fri, Sat to 10:30 pm; Sun 10 am-2 pm (brunch), 5-8:30 pm. Closed Jan 1, Thanksgiving, Dec 25. Res accepted. Bar. Wine cellar. Semi-a la carte: lunch $8-$13, dinner $16-$24. Sun brunch $5.50-$12. Outdoor dining. Art Deco decor, with blond wood, lofty ceilings, and an open-counter kitchen. Cr cds: A, MC, V.

D

★ ★ **WINTERBORNE.** *3520 NE 42nd (97213), east of downtown. 503/249-8486.* Hrs: 5:30-9:30 pm. Closed Sun-Tue; most major hols. Res accepted. French menu. Serv bar. Semi-a la carte: dinner $13.50-$19. Child's meals. Specializes in seafood. Contemporary decor. Totally nonsmoking. Cr cds: A, DS, MC, V.

D

★ ★ ★ **ZEFIRO.** *500 NW 21st Ave (97209), on Nob Hill. 503/226-3394.* Hrs: 11:30 am-2:30 pm, 6-10:30 pm; Fri, Sat to 11 pm. Closed Sun; major hols. Res accepted. Mediterranean menu. Bar to midnight. Wine list. Semi-a la carte: lunch $4.50-$11, dinner $14-$20. Specializes in caesar salad, oysters. Outdoor dining. Contemporary decor. Totally nonsmoking. Cr cds: A, C, D, MC, V.

D

Unrated Dining Spots

IVY HOUSE. *1605 SE Bybee, east of downtown. 503/231-9528.* Hrs: 11 am-11 pm; Sat 9 am-11 pm; Sun 9 am-10 pm; Sat, Sun brunch 9 am-4 pm. Closed Tues, Wed; Thanksgiving, Dec 24, 25. Res accepted. Continental menu. Wine, beer. A la carte entrees: lunch $3.65-$6.50. Semi-a la carte: dinner $7.95-$18.95. Sat, Sun brunch $3.25-$9.95. Specializes in European pastries, creamed soups, sandwiches. Parking. Outdoor dining. Cr cds: A, MC, V.

ORIGINAL PANCAKE HOUSE. *8601 SW 24th Ave, west of downtown. 503/246-9007.* Hrs: 7 am-3 pm. Closed Mon, Tues. Semi-a la carte: bkfst, lunch $5-$10. Specializes in omelettes, apple pancakes, cherry crêpes. Parking. Colonial decor. No cr cds accepted.

PAPA HAYDN. *5829 SE Milwaukie, east of downtown. 503/232-9440.* Hrs: 11:30 am-11 pm; Fri, Sat to midnight. Closed Sun, Mon; major hols. Continental menu. Wine, beer. Semi-a la carte: lunch $4.95-$6.95, dinner $6.95-$13.95. Specializes in European pastries, desserts. Outdoor dining. Cr cds: A, MC, V.

D

PERRY'S ON FREMONT. *2401 NE Fremont, east of downtown. 503/287-3655.* Hrs: 11 am-9 pm; Fri, Sat to 10 pm; Sun from noon. Closed most major hols. Beer. Semi-a la carte: lunch, dinner $4.50-$7.50. Child's meals. Specializes in desserts, fish & chips, soups. Outdoor dining. Murals. Totally nonsmoking. Cr cds: A, MC, V.

D

St Louis

Settled: 1764
Pop: 396,685
Elev: 470 feet
Time zone: Central
Area code: 314
Web: www.st-louis-cvc.com

One of the oldest settlements in the Mississippi Valley, St Louis was founded as a fur-trading post and named for Louis IX of France. In 1804, the United States annexed the area as part of the Louisiana Purchase, and in 1820, Missouri's first constitutional convention was held in the city.

St Louis played an important role in the westward expansion of the United States. Lewis and Clark set off on their expeditions from this area, and many traders, adventurers, scouts and pioneers passed through on their way west. Steamboats docked here on their way up and down the Mississippi; railroads helped to stimulate trade between the Southwest and the East. The arrival of many German immigrants swelled the population, which had reached more than 160,000 by 1860. During the Civil War, though its residents were divided in sympathy, the city was a base of Union operations. Growth continued after the war, and by 1870 the city was the third-largest in the nation.

For more than 200 years, St Louis has been the dominant city in the state. It is distinguished by wealth, grace and culture, as well as solid and diversified industry. The huge, gleaming stainless-steel Gateway Arch, the symbol of the westward expansion, today casts its shadow over St Louis and provides a landmark for this Midwestern metropolis.

Business

Some 2,000 plants in St Louis produce more than $4 billion worth of goods annually. Approximately half of the area's labor force is employed in industry.

St Louis is one of the world's largest markets for wool, lumber and pharmaceuticals and is an important producer of beer, chemicals and transportation equipment. Other major products of the area include food and food products, aircraft, barges and towboats. Anheuser-Busch, one of the world's largest beer producers, has its headquarters here, as do Ralston Purina, Monsanto and other major companies. McDonnell Douglas, one of the area's largest employers, continues to play an important role in the city's economy.

A principal grain and hog center, St Louis is also the only industrial area in the country producing six basic metals: iron, lead, zinc, copper, aluminum and magnesium. The city is the financial center of the central Mississippi Valley, and its location has helped it become prominent as a railroad and trucking transportation center.

Convention Facilities

The America's Center covers 32 acres in the heart of the downtown area. The exhibit area contains 502,000 square feet of space, which includes the 70,000-seat Trans World Dome. The center is within walking distance of 5,500 hotel rooms. Lambert-St Louis International Airport is 13 miles away, and four interstate highways leading into St Louis are just blocks from the center.

Sports & Recreation

St Louis's Busch Stadium, home of the Cardinals, seats 54,000 for baseball. The Kiel Center hosts the Blues hockey team as well as Ambush home soccer games and college basketball games. The TransWorld Dome hosts the Rams' football games.

Six Flags Over Mid-America, southwest of the city, is a 200-acre entertainment park with more than 100 different rides, shows and attractions, including the Screamin' Eagle roller coaster and Batman, the ride.

Grant's Farm, operated by Anheuser-Busch Company, preserves a 281-acre tract once owned by Ulysses S. Grant. A section of the farm is an open range where buffalo, deer and elk roam. A train carries visitors through the game preserve to the miniature zoo and bird show. Also on the property is the cabin where Ulysses S. Grant, the 18th president, once lived.

Entertainment

The St Louis Symphony Orchestra is the second-oldest symphony in the nation. Its regular season runs from mid-September to June; in the summer, the symphony performs pop concerts at Queeny Park.

Also during the summer months, The Muny performs Broadway musical revivals nightly in a 12,000-seat outdoor theater in Forest Park.

Broadway plays are presented frequently at the Fox Theatre and the Westport Playhouse, and first-rate productions can be seen on local college campuses. The Repertory Theatre of St Louis and the St Louis Black Repertory Theatre present dramas and musicals.

Bars and bistros along St Louis's riverfront and the Soulard neighborhood are alive with the sound of authentic Dixieland jazz, blues and R&B.

Historical Areas

The Old Courthouse at Fourth and Market streets contains exhibits on the Louisiana Purchase and St Louis. This 19th-century building was the scene of slave auctions and of the historic Dred Scott trial. Murals on St Louis history decorate the walls and interior of the cast-iron dome. The Old Cathedral at Second and Walnut streets, St Louis' earliest church, was completed in 1834.

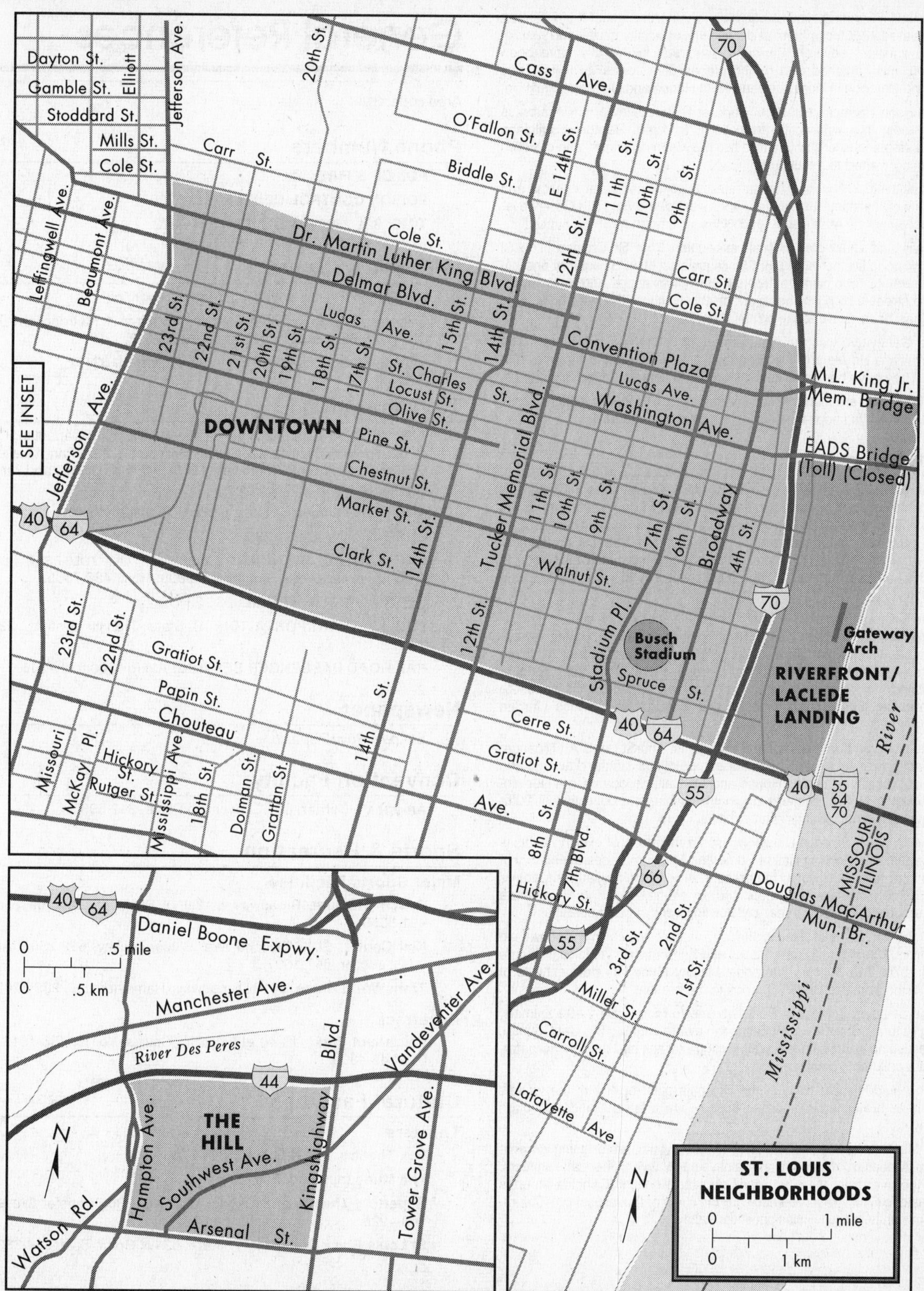

ST. LOUIS NEIGHBORHOODS
DOWNTOWN
RIVERFRONT/ LACLEDE LANDING
THE HILL
SEE INSET
Busch Stadium
Gateway Arch
M.L. King Jr. Mem. Bridge
EADS Bridge (Toll) (Closed)
Douglas MacArthur Mun. Br.
Mississippi River
MISSOURI
ILLINOIS
Dayton St.
Gamble St.
Stoddard St.
Mills St.
Cole St.
Elliott
Jefferson Ave.
20th St.
Cass Ave.
O'Fallon St.
Carr St.
Biddle St.
Cole St.
Dr. Martin Luther King Blvd.
Delmar Blvd.
Convention Plaza
Lucas Ave.
St. Charles St.
Locust St.
Olive St.
Washington Ave.
Pine St.
Chestnut St.
Market St.
Clark St.
Walnut St.
Spruce St.
Stadium Pl.
Tucker Memorial Blvd.
Broadway
Leffingwell Ave.
Beaumont Ave.
Gratiot St.
Papin St.
Chouteau Ave.
Cerre St.
Hickory St.
Rutger St.
Missouri Pl.
McKay
Mississippi Ave.
Dolman St.
Grattan St.
7th Blvd.
Miller St.
Carroll St.
Lafayette Ave.
Daniel Boone Expwy.
Manchester Ave.
River Des Peres
Vandeventer Ave.
Kingshighway Blvd.
Tower Grove Ave.
Hampton Ave.
Southwest Ave.
Arsenal St.
Watson Rd.
0 .5 mile
0 .5 km
0 1 mile
0 1 km
N

Laclede's Landing, nine blocks along the north edge of the riverfront, is a renovated 1850s commercial district with specialty shops and restaurants. In addition, several 19th-century houses in the city have been preserved and furnished with period pieces or historical exhibits. They include the Campbell House, Eugene Field House and De Menil Mansion.

Jefferson Barracks Historical Park, at S Broadway and Kingston, is an army post that was active from 1826 to 1946. Restored buildings include a stable laborer's house and two powder magazines, one of which has been converted to a museum.

Three historic Missouri towns nearby are of particular interest and definitely worth visiting: St Charles, northwest of the city, Ste Genevieve, southeast along the Mississippi, and Florissant, north near the airport.

Lewis and Clark started their expedition from St Charles. The St Charles Historic District is an eight-block area on Main Street that encompasses many historic points of interest as well as shops and restaurants. An entire street, which has been put on the National Register of Historic Places, has been converted to a mall.

Ste Genevieve was the first permanent settlement in Missouri. The Guibourd-Valle House and the Bolduc House were built in the late 18th century. They have been carefully restored and contain period furnishings.

In Florissant are many restored Victorian buildings, as well as antique and arts and crafts shops housed in 19th-century structures.

Sightseeing

The Gateway Arch (Jefferson National Expansion Memorial), a stainless-steel structure that soars 630 feet above the St Louis riverfront, is the city's most recognized landmark. The Arch honors westward expansion, and the museum located beneath the Arch illustrates St Louis's role in the movement to the West. Excursion boats on the Mississippi, which operate during the summer months, provide a pleasant way to view St Louis and its environs.

The Missouri Botanical Garden contains more than 75 acres of nature trails and botanical exhibits. The Climatron, a two-level, transparent, geodesic dome, was the first geodesic greenhouse in the country. Complete climate control allows a great number of tropical and subtropical plants to be exhibited. The garden's Japanese Garden, "Seiwa-En," is complete with teahouse, lake, islands, bridges and waterfall. A Chinese Garden opened in 1996.

The city also boasts many fine museums. The St Louis Art Museum has collections of American and European paintings, prints, drawings and decorative arts. The Cupples House and Art Gallery, located in a Romanesque building (1890), contains original furnishings, a collection of 20th-century graphics and changing art exhibits.

The St Louis Science Center houses a multitude of exciting exhibits and displays. The Bowling Hall of Fame and Museum traces the history of bowling from ancient Egypt to the present. Among the museum's features are memorabilia of bowling greats and an old-time bowling alley where visitors are invited to roll 90-year-old bowling balls at hand-set pins.

At the Museum of Transportation, visitors may climb aboard old locomotives, streetcars, buses, trucks and horse-drawn vehicles that date back to 1870. The Soldiers' Memorial Military Museum offers exhibits of military items from pre-Civil War times to the present.

The St Louis Zoological Park is home to more than 3,400 animals, many in naturalistic exhibits, including the award-winning Big Cat Country. There is also an aquatic house, walk-through aviary, bird garden, herpetarium and a children's petting zoo.

Free guided tours through the St Louis plant of one of the world's largest beer breweries—Anheuser-Busch—are offered Monday through Saturday.

At Mastodon State Historic Site, 20 miles south, are ongoing excavations of American mastodon remains and Native American artifacts. Across the river from the city, near Cahokia, Illinois, is Cahokia Mounds State Historic Site. Preserved here are the ruins of the largest pre-Columbian community in the Mississippi River valley.

General References

Area code: 314

Phone Numbers

POLICE & FIRE: 911

POISON CONTROL CENTER: 772-5200

TIME: 321-2522 **WEATHER:** 321-2222

Information Sources

Fun Phone Events Hotline, 421-2100 (recording).

St Louis Convention & Visitors Commission, 1 Metropolitan Sq, Ste 1100, 63102; 421-1023 or 800/325-7962.

St Louis Visitors Center, 7th at Washington St, 63102.

Transportation

AIRLINES: Air Canada; America West; American; Canadian; Casino Express; Continental; Delta; Frontier; Lone Star; Midwest Express; Northwest; Southwest; TWA; United; USAir; and other commuter and regional airlines.

AIRPORT: Lambert-St Louis International, 426-8000.

BUS TERMINAL: 231-7800.

CAR RENTAL AGENCIES: (See IMPORTANT TOLL-FREE NUMBERS) Avis 426-7766; Budget 423-3000; Hertz 426-7555.

METRO LINK LIGHT RAIL: 231-2345.

PUBLIC TRANSPORTATION: Bi-State Transit System, 231-2345.

RAILROAD PASSENGER SERVICE: Amtrak 800/872-7245.

Newspaper

St Louis Post-Dispatch.

Convention Facility

America's Center, 801 Convention Plaza, 342-5036.

Sports & Recreation

Major Sports Facilities

Busch Stadium, Broadway & Walnut Sts (Cardinals, baseball, 421-3060).

Kiel Center, 5700 Oakland Ave (Blues, hockey, 622-2500; Ambush, soccer, 647-1001).

TransWorld Dome, 901 N Broadway (Rams, football, 982-7267).

Racetrack

Fairmount Park, US 40 at jct I-255, Collinsville, IL, 436-1516 or 618/345-4300.

Cultural Facilities

Theaters

Fox Theatre, 527 N Grand, 534-1678.

The Muny (outdoor), Forest Park, 361-1900.

Repertory Theatre of St Louis, 130 Edgar Rd, Webster Groves, 968-4925.

St Louis Black Repertory Theatre, 634 N Grand Blvd, 534-3807.

Westport Playhouse, Westport Plaza, Page Ave & I-270, 878-3322.

Concert Hall

Powell Symphony Hall, 718 N Grand Blvd, 534-1700 (box office).

Museums

Bowling Hall of Fame, 111 Stadium Plaza, 231-6340.

History Museum-Missouri Historical Society, Forest Park, Lindell Blvd & DeBaliviere Ave, 746-4599.

The Magic House, 516 S Kirkwood Rd, Kirkwood, 822-8900.

Museum of Transportation, 16 mi SW via I-44, N on I-270 to Big Bend & Dougherty Ferry Rd exits, 965-7998.

Museum of Westward Expansion, Gateway Arch, 982-1410.

St Louis Science Center, 5050 Oakland Ave, 289-4400.

Soldiers Memorial Military Museum, 1315 Chestnut St, 622-4550.

Art Museum & Galleries

Cupples House and Art Gallery, St Louis University, 977-3025.

Gallery of Art, Steinberg Hall, Washington University, 935-5490.

St Louis Art Museum, Forest Park, 721-0072.

Points of Interest

Historical

American Institute of Architects, 911 Washington, 621-3484.

Campbell House Museum, 1508 Locust St, 421-0325.

Cathedral of St Louis, 4431 Lindell Blvd at Newstead Ave, 533-2824.

Christ Church Cathedral, 1210 Locust St, 231-3454.

De Menil Mansion and Museum, 3352 De Menil Pl, 771-5828.

Eads Bridge, foot of Washington Ave.

Eugene Field House and Toy Museum, 634 S Broadway, 421-4689.

Grant's Farm, 10501 Gravois Rd, 843-1700.

Jefferson Barracks Historical Park, S Broadway at Kingston, 10 mi S on I-55, 544-5714.

Laclede's Landing, N edge of Riverfront.

Lafayette Square, bounded by Jefferson, I-44, 18th St & Couteau.

Mastadon State Historic Site, 20 mi S off US 67, near US 67 Imperial exit, 464-2976.

Old Cathedral, 209 Walnut St at Memorial Dr, 231-3250.

Old Courthouse, 11 N 4th St at Market St, 425-4465.

Tower Grove House, Missouri Botanical Garden, 577-5150.

Union Station, 1820 Market St, 421-6655 or 421-4314.

Other Attractions

Aloe Plaza, Market St between 18th & 20th Sts.

Anheuser-Busch, 13th & Lynch, 577-2626.

Cahokia Mounds State Historic Site, E on Collinsville Rd, in Collinsville, IL, 618/346-5160.

Forest Park, Skinker & Kingshighway Blvds & Oakland Ave, 535-0100.

Gateway Arch, 11 N 4th St, 982-1410.

Jewel Box Floral Conservatory, Wells & McKinley Drs, Forest Park.

Laumeier Sculpture Garden, Geyer Rd & Rott St, 821-1209.

Missouri Botanical Garden, 4344 Shaw Blvd, 577-9400.

President Casino on the Admiral, at Gateway Arch, 622-3000.

Purina Farms, 35 mi W via I-44, Grays Summit exit to County MM, 982-3232.

St Louis St Louis, Busch Stadium, 100 Stadium Plaza, 421-3263.

St Louis Zoological Park, Forest Park, 781-0900.

Six Flags St Louis, 30 mi SW off I-44, Allenton Rd exit, Eureka, 938-4800.

Sightseeing Tours

Excursion boats *Huck Finn, Tom Sawyer* and *Becky Thatcher*, dock below Gateway Arch, 621-4040.

Gray Line bus tours, 421-4753 or 800/542-4287.

Annual Events

Fair St Louis, On Riverfront. July 4 wkend.

Japanese Festival, Missouri Botanical Garden. Labor Day wkend.

Great Forest Park Balloon Race, Forest Park. Sept.

City Neighborhoods

Many of the restaurants, unrated dining establishments and some lodgings listed under St Louis include neighborhoods as well as exact street addresses. Geographic descriptions of these areas are given, followed by a table of restaurants arranged by neighborhood.

Downtown: South of Martin Luther King Blvd, west of I-70, north of I-64 (US 40) and east of Jefferson Ave. **North of Downtown:** North of Martin Luther King Blvd. **West of Downtown:** West of Jefferson Ave.

The Hill: South of I-44, west of Kingshighway Blvd, north of Arsenal St and east of Hampton Ave.

Riverfront/Laclede Landing: On Mississippi River south of Eads Bridge, east of I-70 and north of I-40; Laclede Landing on riverfront directly north of Eads Bridge and south of M.L. King Jr Memorial Bridge.

Lodgings and Food

ST LOUIS RESTAURANTS BY NEIGHBORHOOD AREAS

(For full description, see alphabetical listings under Restaurants)

DOWNTOWN
Cafe De France. 410 Olive St
Charlie Gitto's. 207 N 6th St
Faust's (Adam's Mark Hotel). 4th & Chestnut
Hannegan's. 719 N Second St
J.F. Sanfilippo's. 705 N Broadway
Joseph's Italian Cafe. 107 N 6th St
Kemoll's. 1 Metropolitan Square
La Sala. 513 Olive
Mike Shannon's. 100 N 7th St
Piccolo's. 211 N Broadway
Premio. 7th & Market Sts
Tony's. 410 Market St

NORTH OF DOWNTOWN
Al's 1200 N Main St
Crown Candy Kitchen. 1401 St Louis Ave
Mandarin House. 9150 Overland Plaza

SOUTH OF DOWNTOWN
Bevo Mill. 4749 Gravois Ave
Giuseppe's. 4141 S Grand Blvd
John D. McGurk's. 1200 Russell Blvd
Lynch Street Bistro. 1031 Lynch St
Patty Long's 9th Street Abbey. 1808 S 9th St
Sidney Street Cafe. 2000 Sidney St

WEST OF DOWNTOWN
Balaban's. 405 N Euclid Ave
Bar Italia. 4656 Maryland Ave
Blueberry Hill. 6504 Delmar Blvd
Cardwell's. 94 Plaza Frontenac
Charcoal House. 9855 Manchester Rd
Cheshire Inn. (Cheshire Inn & Lodge Motor Hotel). 6300 Clayton Rd
Chuy Arzola's. 6405 Clayton Ave
Dierdorf & Hart's. 323 West Port Plaza
Divi (Hilton-Frontenac Motor Hotel). 1335 S Lindbergh Blvd
Harry's. 2144 Market St
House Of India. 8501 Delmar Blvd
Lombardo's Trattoria (Drury Inn Union Station Hotel). 201 S 20th St
Mandarin House. 194 Union Station
Marciano's. 333 West Port Plaza
Museum Cafe. 1 Fine Arts Dr
Patrick's. 342 Westport Plaza
Robata Of Japan. 111 West Port Plaza
Saleem's. 6501 Delmar Blvd
St Louis Brewery & Tap Room. 2100 Locust St
Sunflower Cafe. 5513 Pershing Ave
Sunshine Inn. 8½ S Euclid Ave
Thai Cafe. 6170 Delmar Blvd

THE HILL
Blue Water Grill. 2607 Hampton Ave
Bruno's Little Italy. 5901 Southwest Ave
Cunetto House Of Pasta. 5453 Magnolia Ave
Dominic's. 5101 Wilson Ave
Gian Peppe's. 2126 Marconi Ave
Gino's. 4502 Hampton Ave
Giovanni's. 5201 Shaw Ave
Lorusso's Cucina. 3121 Watson Rd
Mama Campisi's. 2132 Edwards St
O'Connells Pub. 4652 Shaw Ave
Once Upon A Vine. 3559 Arsenal St
Trattoria Marcella. 3600 Watson Rd
Zia's. 5256 Wilson Ave

Note: When a listing is located in a town that does not have its own city heading, it will appear under the city nearest to its location. In these cases, the address and town appear in parenthesis immediately following the name of the establishment.

Motels

★ ★ **COURTYARD BY MARRIOTT.** *2340 Market St (63103), near Union Station, west of downtown. 314/241-9111; FAX 314/241-8113.* 151 units, 4 story, 12 suites. S, D $98-$114; suites $129-$159; under 18 free; wkly rates. Crib free. TV; cable (premium). Indoor pool; whirlpool. Complimentary coffee in rms. Bar. Ck-out noon. Business servs avail. In-rm modem link. Valet serv. Exercise equipt: weight machines, bicycles. Health club privileges. Some balconies. Cr cds: A, C, D, DS, MC, V.

D SC

★ ★ **RESIDENCE INN BY MARRIOTT.** *1881 Craigshire Rd (63146), I-270, Page Ave E exit, west of downtown. 314/469-0060; FAX 314/469-3751.* 128 kit. suites, 2 story. Suites $79-$139; wkly, monthly rates; wkend plans. Crib free. Pet accepted, some restrictions; $25. TV; cable (premium), VCR (movies). Heated pool; whirlpool. Complimentary continental bkfst. Restaurant nearby. Ck-out noon. Coin Indry. Meeting rm. Business servs avail. In-rm modem link. Airport transportation. Health club privileges. Refrigerators, microwaves; many fireplaces. Private patios, balconies. Picnic tables, grills. Cr cds: A, C, D, DS, MC, V.

D SC

★ ★ **SUMMERFIELD SUITES.** *1855 Craigshire Rd (63146), I-270, Page Ave exit E to Craigshire Rd, north of downtown. 314/878-1555; FAX 314/878-9203; res: 800/833-4353.* 106 kit. suites, 2 story. 1-bedrm $139; 2-bedrm $159; wkend rates. Crib free. Pet accepted, some restrictions; $75. TV; cable (premium), VCR (movies). Heated pool; whirlpool. Complimentary continental bkfst. Complimentary coffee in rms. Restaurant nearby. Ck-out noon. Coin Indry. Meeting rms. Business servs avail. In-rm modem link. Valet serv. Sundries. Free airport transportation. Exercise equipt; weight machine, bicycles. Microwaves. Picnic tables, grills. Cr cds: A, C, D, DS, MC, V.

D SC

Motor Hotels

★ ★ **CHESHIRE INN & LODGE.** *6300 Clayton Rd, (63117), west of downtown. 314/647-7300; FAX 314/647-0442; res: 800/325-7378.* Web www.cheshirelodge.com. 106 rms, 4 story. S $105-$115; D $115-$125; each addl $6; suites $130-$200; under 12 free; wkend rates. Crib free. TV; cable (premium), VCR avail. Indoor/outdoor pool; poolside serv. Complimentary continental bkfst Mon-Fri. Restaurant (see CHESHIRE INN). Rm serv. Bar 11-1:30 am; entertainment exc Sun. Ck-out 2 pm. Meeting rms. Business servs avail. In-rm modem link. Bellhops. Valet serv Mon-Fri. Sundries. Free garage. Some refrigerators. Elegant Tudor decor. English garden. Cr cds: A, C, D, DS, MC, V.

D SC

★ ★ ★ **HILTON-FRONTENAC.** *1335 S Lindbergh Blvd, St. Louis (63131), W via I-64 (US 40), at S Lindbergh Blvd, west of downtown. 314/993-1100; FAX 314/993-8546.* Web www.hilton.com. 266 rms, 3 story. S, D $99-$235; each addl $10; suites $130-$500; under 18 free; wkend, wkly rates. Crib free. TV; cable (premium), VCR avail. Pool; poolside serv. Restaurant (see DIVI). Rm serv. Bar 11-1 am; entertainment Thurs-Sat. Ck-out noon. Convention facilities. Business center. In-rm modem link. Bellhops. Valet serv. Sundries. Gift shop. Barber shop. Free airport transportation. Exercise equipt; weights, bicycles, sauna. Microwaves avail. Luxury level. Cr cds: A, C, D, DS, ER, MC, V.

D SC

★ **HOLIDAY INN-FOREST PARK.** *5915 Wilson Ave (63110), I-44 W, exit Hampton Ave, S 1 mi. 314/645-0700.* 120 rms, 7 story. S $69-$99; D $69-$115; each addl $10; under 12 free; family rates. Crib free.

Pet accepted. TV; VCR avail. Complimentary coffee in rms. Restaurant 5:30 am-10 pm. Rm serv. Bar 4 pm-midnight; Sun to 10 pm. Ck-out noon. Meeting rms. Business center. In-rm modem link. Heated pool. Refrigerators, microwaves avail. Balconies. Cr cds: A, C, D, DS, JCB, MC, V.

D SC

✔★ ★ ★ **HOLIDAY INN-SOUTHWEST.** *10709 Watson Rd (63127), SW via I-44 exit 277B, Lindbergh Blvd to Watson Rd, south of downtown. 314/821-6600; FAX 314/821-4673.* 212 rms, 4 story. May-Sept: S $84-$109; D $87-$109; each addl $10; suites $109-$130; under 18 free; lower rates rest of yr. Crib free. TV; cable (premium). 2 pools, 1 indoor. Complimentary coffee in rms. Restaurant 6:30 am-2 pm, 5-10 pm. Rm serv. Bar 11-1 am; entertainment. Ck-out noon. Meeting rms. Business servs avail. In-rm modem link. Bellhops. Valet serv. Airport transportation. Exercise equipt; stair machine, treadmill. Game rm. Some bathrm phones, refrigerators. Cr cds: A, C, D, DS, ER, JCB, MC, V.

D SC

Hotels

★ ★ ★ **ADAM'S MARK.** *4th & Chestnut (63102), opp Gateway Arch, downtown. 314/241-7400; FAX 314/241-6618; res: 800/444-2326.* Web ww.adamsmark.com. 910 rms, 18 story. S $155-$195; D $175-$210; each addl $15; suites $185-$1,200; under 18 free; wkend packages. Crib free. Garage parking $4/hr, in/out $12 unlimited; valet $5. TV; cable, VCR avail. 2 heated pools, 1 indoor; whirlpool, poolside serv. Afternoon tea. Restaurant 6 am-midnight (also see FAUST'S). Rm serv 24 hrs. Bar 11-2 am; entertainment exc Sun. Ck-out noon. Convention facilities. Business center. In-rm modem link. Concierge. Shopping arcade. Barber, beauty shop. Exercise rm; instructor, weight machines, bicycles, sauna. Bathrm phones; some refrigerators. Three-story atrium lobby decorated with bronze equestrian sculpture by De Luigi. View of Gateway Arch & riverfront from many rms; near Laclede's Landing & riverfront showboats. Luxury level. Cr cds: A, C, D, DS, MC, V.

D SC

★ ★ ★ **CROWNE PLAZA-MAJESTIC.** *1019 Pine St (63101), downtown. 314/436-2355; FAX 314/436-0223.* 91 units, 9 story. S, D $165; each addl $15; suites $290-$350; under 12 free; wkend rates. Crib free. Valet, in/out parking $8. TV; cable (premium), VCR avail. Coffee in rms. Restaurant 6 am-10 pm. Bar 11-1 am. Ck-out noon. Meeting rms. Business servs avail. In-rm modem link. Concierge. Airport transportation. Exercise equipt; bicycles, treadmill. Health club privileges. Bathrm phones. European elegance in 1914 building; marble floors, Oriental rugs. Cr cds: A, C, D, DS, ER, JCB, MC, V.

D SC

★ ★ ★ **DOUBLETREE HOTEL & CONFERENCE CENTER.** *(16625 Swingley Ridge Rd, Chesterfield 63017) Approx 20 mi W on I-64 (US 40), exit 19A, N to Swingley Ridge Rd. 314/532-5000; FAX 314/532-9984.* 223 rms, 12 story. S, D $150; under 18 free; wkend rates. Crib free. TV; cable (premium), VCR avail. 2 pools, 1 indoor; wading pool, whirlpool, poolside serv, lifeguard. Supervised child's activities; ages 1-13. Coffee in rms. Restaurant 6:30-10 pm. Bar 11-1 am. Ck-out noon. Meeting rms. Business center. In-rm modem link. Airport, local transportation. Lighted tennis. Exercise rm; instructor, weights, bicycles, steam rm, sauna. Rec rm. Refrigerators, microwaves avail. Luxury level. Cr cds: A, C, D, DS, ER, JCB, MC, V.

D SC

★ ★ **DRURY INN UNION STATION.** *201 S 20th St (63103), west of downtown. 314/231-3900; FAX 314/231-3900.* 176 rms, 7 story. Apr-Oct: S $98-$113; D $108-$123; each addl $10; suites $150; under 18 free; hol rates; lower rates rest of yr. Crib avail. Pet accepted, some restrictions. TV; cable (premium), VCR avail. Indoor pool; whirlpool, lifeguard. Complimentary continental bkfst. Restaurant (see LOMBARDO'S). Bar. Ck-out noon. Coin Indry. Meeting rms. In-rm modem link. No bellhops. Exercise equipt; bicycle, treadmill. Health club privileges. Some refrigerators. Restored 1907 railroad hotel. Cr cds: A, C, D, DS, JCB, MC, V.

D SC

★ ★ **DRURY INN-CONVENTION CENTER.** *711 N Broadway (63102), in Union Market Building, downtown. 314/231-8100; FAX 314/621-6568.* Web www.drury-inn.com. 178 rms, 2 flrs in 6 story bldg. May-Sept: S $96-$112; D $106-$122; each addl $10; under 18 free; wkend rates; higher rates July 4th; lower rates rest of yr. Crib free. Pet accepted, some restrictions. TV; cable (premium). Indoor pool; whirlpool, poolside serv, lifeguard. Complimentary continental bkfst. Restaurant adj 11 am-2 pm, 4:30-11 pm; wkend hrs vary. Ck-out noon. Meeting rms. Business servs avail. In-rm modem link. No bellhops. Some refrigerators. Microwaves avail. Cr cds: A, C, D, DS, MC, V.

D SC

★ ★ **EMBASSY SUITES.** *901 N 1st St (63102), downtown. 314/241-4200; FAX 314/241-6513.* 297 suites, 8 story. S, D $140-$200; each addl $15; under 13 free; wkend rates. Crib free. TV; cable (premium). Indoor pool; wading pool, whirlpool, lifeguard. Complimentary bkfst served in atrium. Restaurant 11 am-11 pm. Bar to 1 am; wkends to 3 am. Ck-out noon. Lndry facilities. Meeting rms. Business servs avail. In-rm modem link. Exercise equipt; treadmill, bicycles. Game rm. Refrigerators, wet bars, microwaves avail. Balconies. 8-story atrium courtyard. Cr cds: A, C, D, DS, JCB, MC, V.

D SC

★ ★ **HAMPTON INN.** *2211 Market St (63103), opp Union Station, west of downtown. 314/241-3200; FAX 314/241-9351.* 239 rms, 11 story, 14 suites. S $84-$125; D $95-$125; suites $110-$135; under 18 free; wkend rates. Crib free. Pet accepted, some restrictions. TV; cable (premium). Indoor pool; whirlpool. Complimentary continental bkfst. Restaurant 11-3 am. Bar. Ck-out noon. Coin Indry. Business servs avail. In-rm modem link. No bellhops. Free garage parking. Exercise equipt; treadmills, bicycles. Refrigerators avail. Cr cds: A, C, D, DS, MC, V.

D SC

✔★ ★ **HOLIDAY INN-DOWNTOWN RIVERFRONT.** *200 N 4th St (63102), downtown. 314/621-8200; FAX 314/621-8073.* 454 rms, 29 story, 282 kits. S $109-$129; D $119-$139; each addl $10; suites $150-$200; under 17 free; wkend rates; higher rates: July 4th. Crib free. TV; VCR avail. Pool; lifeguard. Restaurant 6:30 am-10 pm. Bar 11-3 am; Sun 1 pm-midnight. Ck-out noon. Meeting rms. Business servs avail. In-rm modem link. Gift shop. Exercise equipt; bicycles, rower. Game rm. Microwaves avail. Some balconies. Cr cds: A, C, D, DS, ER, MC, V.

D SC

★ ★ ★ **HYATT REGENCY AT UNION STATION.** *One St. Louis Union Station (63103), west of downtown. 314/231-1234; FAX 314/923-3970.* 538 rms, 6 story. S, D $170-$195; each addl $25; under 18 free; wkend rates. Crib free. Valet parking $13. TV; cable (premium). Outdoor pool; lifeguard. Restaurant 6:30 am-10:30 pm. Bar 11-1:30 am. Ck-out noon. Convention facilities. Business servs avail. In-rm modem link. Shopping arcade. Exercise equipt; weight machine, stair machine. Refrigerators avail. Bathrm phones. In renovated Union Station railroad terminal (1894); main lobby and lounge occupy Grand Hall. Luxury level. Cr cds: A, C, D, DS, ER, JCB, MC, V.

D SC

★ ★ ★ **MARRIOTT PAVILION.** *1 Broadway (63102), downtown. 314/421-1776; FAX 314/331-9029.* Web www.marriott.com/marriott/mo-121.htm. 672 rms, 22-25 story. S $154; D $169; under 18 free; wkend rates. Garage, in/out $11, valet $14. TV; cable (premium). Pool; whirlpool, poolside serv, lifeguard. Coffee in rms. Restaurant 6:30 am-11 pm. Bar 11-1 am. Ck-out noon. Coin Indry. Convention facilities. Business center. In-rm modem link. Concierge. Gift shop. Exercise equipt; weights, bicycles, sauna. Some bathrm phones, refrigerators. Luxury level. Cr cds: A, C, D, DS, ER, JCB, MC, V.

D SC

★ ★ **MAYFAIR.** *806 St Charles St (63101), downtown. 314/421-2500; res: 800/757-8483; FAX 314/421-0770.* Web www.grandheritage.com. 167 rms, 18 story. S, D $95-$175; each addl $10; under 12 free. Crib free. Pet accepted; $50 deposit. TV; cable (premium). Complimentary coffee in rms. Restaurant 6:30 am-2 pm, 5-10:30 pm. Bar 11:30 am-midnight. Ck-out noon. Meeting rms. Business center. In-rm modem link. Concierge. Exercise equipt; weights, stair machine. Bathrm phones, refrigerators, minibars. Luxury level. Cr cds: A, C, D, DS, MC, V.

D SC

★ ★ ★ **REGAL RIVERFRONT.** *200 S 4th St (63102), downtown. 314/241-9500; FAX 314/421-3555; res: 800/325-7353.* E-mail regalstl @accessus.net. 780 rms, 28 story. S $140-$170; D $185-$205; each addl $20; suites $350-$1,000; under 17 free; weekly, wkend rates; higher rates: baseball games, some hols. Crib free. Garage parking $12.50. TV; cable (premium), VCR avail. 2 pools, 1 indoor; wading pool, poolside serv, lifeguard. Restaurant 6:30 am-midnight. Bar. Ck-out noon. Coin Indry. Convention facilities. Business center. In-rm modem link. Gift shop. Exercise equipt; weight machine, bicycles. Game rm. Microwaves avail. Renovated hotel near river. Luxury level. Cr cds: A, C, D, DS, ER, JCB, MC, V.

D SC

★ ★ ★ ★ **THE RITZ-CARLTON, ST LOUIS.** *(100 Carondelet Plaza, Clayton 63105) 7 mi W on I-64, Hanley exit. 314/863-6300; FAX 314/863-3524; res: 800/241-3333.* Fine oil paintings and 18th- and 19th-century antiques decorate public areas throughout the hotel. Some guest rooms on the top floors offer views of the skyline. 301 rms, 18 story, 34 suites. S, D $175-$350; suites $295-$1,500; under 12 free; wkend rates; package plans. Crib free. Garage, valet parking in/out $15/day. TV; cable (premium), VCR avail. Indoor pool; whirlpool, poolside serv. Restaurant (see THE GRILL). Rm serv 24 hrs. Bar 11-1 am; entertainment. Ck-out noon. Convention facilities. Business center. In-rm modem link. Concierge. Gift shop. Exercise rm; instructor, weight machine, bicycles, sauna, steam rm. Massage. Bathrm phones, refrigerators, minibars; microwaves avail. Cr cds: A, C, D, DS, ER, JCB, MC, V.

D

★ ★ ★ **SHERATON PLAZA.** *900 West Port Plaza (63146), W via I-64 (US 40), N on I-270 to Page Ave East exit, west of downtown. 314/434-5010; FAX 314/434-0140.* 209 rms, 12 story. S $145; D $145-$155; each addl $10; suites $179-$477; under 18 free; wkend rates. Crib free. TV; cable (premium), VCR avail (movies). Indoor pool; whirlpool, sauna. Complimentary coffee in rms. Restaurant 6:30 am-10:30 pm. Bar 11-1 am. Ck-out 1 pm. Meeting rms. Business servs avail. In-rm modem link. Concierge. Free covered parking. Free airport transportation. Tennis privileges. Health club privileges. Some refrigerators. Cr cds: A, C, D, DS, JCB, MC, V.

D SC

★ ★ ★ **SHERATON-WEST PORT INN.** *191 West Port Plaza (63146), W via I-64 (US 40), N on I-270 to Page Ave exit, west of downtown. 314/878-1500; FAX 314/878-2837.* 300 rms, 4-6 story. S, D $145-$155; suites $175-$340; under 18 free; wkend rates. TV; cable (premium), VCR avail. Pool; poolside serv, lifeguard. Complimentary coffee in rms. Restaurant 6:30 am-10:30 pm. Bar 11-1 am; pianist Tues-Sat. Ck-out 1 pm. Convention facilities. Business servs avail. In-rm modem link. Concierge. Free covered parking. Free airport transportation. Health club privileges. Some refrigerators. Some balconies. In shopping plaza. Cr cds: A, C, D, DS, JCB, MC, V.

D SC

Restaurants

★ ★ ★ **AL'S.** *1200 N Main St (63102), north of downtown. 314/421-6399.* Hrs: 5-11 pm. Closed Sun; hols; 1st 2 wks July. Res accepted. Italian menu. Bar. Extensive wine list. Semi-a la carte: dinner $20-$45. Child's meals. Specializes in steak, seafood, veal. Valet parking. Classic Italian menu recited by waitstaff; historic building. Family-owned since 1925. Jacket. Cr cds: A, C, D, DS, ER, JCB, MC, V.

D

✔★ ★ **BALABAN'S.** *405 N Euclid Ave (63108), west of downtown. 314/361-8085.* Hrs: 11 am-3 pm, 6-10:30 pm; Fri, Sat 11 am-3 pm, 5:30-11:30 pm; Sun 10 am-3 pm (brunch), 5-10:30 pm. Closed major hols. Res accepted. Continental menu. Bar. Semi-a la carte: lunch $5.95-$11.95, dinner $9.95-$21.95. Sun brunch $10. Child's meals. Specialties: beef Wellington, barbecued spiced salmon, half roast duckling. Own baking, pasta. Musicians Sun. Valet parking. Two dining areas—one formal, one more casual—feature artwork, chandeliers. Family-owned. Cr cds: A, D, DS, MC, V.

D

✔★ **BAR ITALIA.** *4656 Maryland Ave (63108), west of downtown. 314/361-7010.* Hrs: 11:30 am-9:30 pm; Fri, Sat to 10 pm; Sat to 8:30 pm. Closed Mon; Thanksgiving, Dec 25. Res accepted. Italian menu. Bar. Semi-a la carte: lunch $4.50-$8.95, dinner $4.50-$16.95. Child's meals. Specializes in pasta, seafood, chicken. Own baking. Outdoor dining. European cafe atmosphere. Cr cds: A, D, DS, MC, V.

D

★ ★ **BEVO MILL.** *4749 Gravois Ave (63116), south of downtown. 314/481-2626.* Hrs: 11 am-9 pm; Fri, Sat to 10 pm; early-bird dinner Mon-Fri 3-6 pm; Sun brunch 9:30 am-2 pm. Closed Dec 25. Res accepted. German menu. Bar. Semi-a la carte: lunch $5.95-$9.50, dinner $10.95-$17.95. Sun brunch $9.95. Child's meals. Specializes in sauerbraten, Wienerschnitzel, fresh seafood. Own baking. Large stone fireplace. Bavarian exterior; operable windmill. Cr cds: A, C, D, MC, V.

D

✔★ ★ **BIG SKY CAFE.** *(47 S Old Orchard, Webster Groves 63119) 8 mi W on I-44, Shrewsbury West exit, S on Big Bend. 314/962-5757.* Hrs: 5:30-10 pm; Fri, Sat to 11 pm; Sun 4:30-9:30 pm. Closed some major hols. Res accepted. Bar. A la carte entrees: dinner $7.50-$14.50. Specialities: Rosemary grilled chicken breast, barbecued salmon, roasted garlic mashed potatoes. Outdoor dining. Eclectic decor. Cr cds: A, MC, V.

D

✔★ **BLUE WATER GRILL.** *2607 Hampton Ave (63139), on The Hill. 314/645-0707.* Hrs: 11:30 am-2 pm, 5:30-10 pm; Fri, Sat to 11 pm. Closed Sun; major hols. Res accepted. Seafood menu. Bar. Semi-a la carte: lunch $3.75-$7.95, dinner $8.95-$16.95. Specialties: snapper asada, Mexican bouillabaisse, pine nut-encrusted salmon. Own desserts. Outdoor dining. Totally nonsmoking. Cr cds: A, C, D, MC, V.

D

★ ★ **BRISTOL BAR & GRILL.** *(11801 Olive Blvd, Creve Coeur 63141) 14 mi W on I-64 to I-270, N to Olive Blvd, turn E. 314/567-0272.* Hrs: 11:30 am-2:30 pm, 5:30-10 pm; Fri, Sat 5-10:30 pm; Sun 10 am-2 pm, 5-9 pm. Closed Memorial Day, July 4, Labor Day, Dec 25. Res accepted. Bar to 11:30 pm. Semi-a la carte: lunch $5.95-$12.95, dinner $9.95-$20.95. Sun brunch $13.95. Child's meals. Specializes in mesquite-grilled seafood, steak, fresh fish. Own pastries. Stained-glass windows. Cr cds: A, C, D, DS, MC, V.

D SC

★ ★ **BRUNO'S LITTLE ITALY.** *5901 Southwest Ave (63139), on The Hill. 314/781-5988.* Hrs: 5-11 pm. Closed Sun, Mon; major hols. Res accepted Fri-Sun. Italian menu. Bar. Wine cellar. Semi-a la carte: dinner $11-$19. Specialties: papardelle alla Genovese, veal Vesuvio, fresh salmon. Own pastries. Located in old Italian neighborhood. Antiques, stained glass, original art. Cr cds: A, C, D, DS, MC, V.

D

★ ★ **BUSCH'S GROVE.** *(9160 Clayton Rd, Ladue 63124) US 40W, exit Clayton Rd. 314/993-0011.* Hrs: 11:30 am-10 pm; Fri, Sat to 11 pm. Closed Sun, Mon; most major hols. Res accepted. Bar. Semi-a la carte: lunch $6.50-$9.95, dinner $7.99-$23.95. Child's meals. Specializes in seafood, steak. Outdoor dining. Built in 1860. Fireplaces. Original art. Family-owned 106 yrs. Cr cds: A, D, MC, V.

D

★ ★ ★ **CAFE DE FRANCE.** *410 Olive St, downtown. 314/231-2204.* Hrs: 5:30-10:30 pm; Fri, Sat to 11:30 pm. Closed Sun; most major hols. Res accepted. French menu. Bar. Wine cellar. A la carte entrees: dinner $20.75-$36. Complete meals: dinner (3, 4, 5 courses) $20.75, $25.50, $36. Specializes in fresh seafood, breast of duck, game. Own baking. Valet parking. European ambience. Jacket. Cr cds: A, C, D, DS, ER, MC, V.

D ⟶

★★ **CANDICCI'S.** *(12513 Olive St, Creve Couer 63141) 8 mi W on MO 340. 314/878-5858.* Hrs: 11 am-11 pm; Fri, Sat to midnight; Sun noon-9:30 pm. Closed major hols. Res accepted. Italian menu. Bar. Semi-a la carte: lunch $4.95-$8, dinner $8.95-$19.95. Child's meals. Specialties: langusto suprimo, pasta ala lilly, beef spedini. Outdoor dining. Casual Italian decor. Cr cds: A, C, D, DS, MC, V.

D ⟶

★★ **CARDWELL'S.** *94 Plaza Frontenac (63131), west of downtown. 314/997-8885.* Hrs: 11 am-10 pm; Fri & Sat to 11 pm; Sun noon-9 pm. Closed Easter, Thanksgiving, Dec 25. Res accepted. Eclectic menu. Bar. Semi-a la carte: lunch $7.50-$15.75, dinner $10.95-$18.95. Child's meals. Specialties: spicy Vietnamese chicken, Chinese barbecued chicken salad, grilled smoked shrimp. Euro-bistro style. Cr cds: A, MC, V.

D

★ **CHARCOAL HOUSE.** *9855 Manchester Rd (63119), west of downtown. 314/968-4842.* Hrs: 11:30 am-2:30 pm, 5-10:30 pm. Closed Sun; most major hols. Res accepted Mon-Thurs. Bar. Semi-a la carte: lunch $5.50-$10; dinner $12.45-$32.95. Child's meals. Specializes in steak, fresh seafood. Cr cds: A, MC, V.

✔★ **CHARLIE GITTO'S.** *207 N 6th St (63101), downtown. 314/436-2828.* Hrs: 11 am-10:30 pm, Fri, Sat to 11:30 pm. Closed Sun; most major hols. Italian, Amer menu. Bar. A la carte entrees: lunch $5-$8, dinner $7.95-$15.15. Child's meals. Specializes in veal, seafood, pasta. Sports bar atmosphere. Cr cds: A, D, DS, MC, V.

D ⟶

★★ **CHESHIRE INN.** *(See Cheshire Inn & Lodge Motor Hotel) 314/647-7300.* Hrs: 7-10 am, 11 am-2 pm, 5-10 pm; Thurs-Sun to midnight; Sat brunch 7-10 am; Sun brunch 9 am-2 pm. Res accepted. Bar 11-3 am. Semi-a la carte: lunch $5.95-$8.95, dinner $14.95-$25.95. Sat brunch $7.95. Sun brunch $12.95. Child's meals. Specializes in prime rib, steak, fresh seafood. Pianist. Valet parking. Spit roasting in view. Old English architecture, decor. Carriage ride with dinner Fri, Sat (weather permitting; res one wk in advance suggested; fee). Cr cds: A, C, D, DS, MC, V.

D ⟶

✔★ **CHINA ROYAL.** *(5911 N Lindbergh, Hazelwood 63042) S on I-270, exit Lindbergh. 314/731-1313.* Hrs: 11 am-9:30 pm; Fri, Sat to 10:30 pm; Sun brunch to 3:30 pm. Closed some major hols. Res accepted. Chinese menu. Bar. Semi-a la carte: lunch $4.75-$5.45, dinner $5.20-$12.25. Sun brunch $1.25-$3.50. Specialties: sizzling three musketeers, chicken pot Szchuan style, crispy shrimp Hunan style. Own baking. Cr cds: A, C, D, DS, MC, V.

D ⟶

★ **CHUY ARZOLA'S.** *6405 Clayton Ave (63139), I-64, exit Hampton S, W on Clayton Ave, west of downtown. 314/644-4430.* Hrs: 11 am-10 pm; Fri, Sat to 11 pm; Sun 4-9 pm. Closed most major hols. Mexican menu. Bar. Semi-a la carte: lunch, dinner $4.50-$9.95. Specializes in fajitas, burritos, Lone Star quesadilla. Casual neighborhood establishment. Cr cds: DS, MC, V.

D ⟶

✔★ **CICERO'S.** *(6691 Delmar Blvd, University City 63130) W on US 64. 314/862-0009.* Hrs: 11-1 am; Sun to midnight. Closed Thanksgiving, Dec 25. Italian menu. Bar. Semi-a la carte: lunch, dinner $4.95-$14.90. Child's meals. Specializes in pizza, pasta, desserts. Musicians. Outdoor dining. Over 150 different beers avail; modern decor. Family-owned. Cr cds: A, MC, V.

D SC ⟶

★ **CRAVINGS.** *(8149 Big Bend, Webster Groves 63119) W on I-44 Shrewsburg exit, west of downtown. 314/961-3534.* Hrs: 10:30 am-6 pm; Fri, Sat 9 am-midnight. Closed Mon; Thanksgiving, Dec 25. Res accepted. Wine, beer. Semi-a la carte: lunch $5.75-$11.50, dinner $7-$20. Specializes in seasonal dishes. Own breads. Some original art. Totally nonsmoking. Cr cds: MC, V.

D

✔★★ **CUNETTO HOUSE OF PASTA.** *5453 Magnolia Ave (63139), on The Hill. 314/781-1135.* Hrs: 11 am-2 pm, 5-10:30 pm; Fri to 11:30 pm; Sat 5-11:30 pm. Closed Sun; major hols. Italian menu. Bar 11 am-11:30 pm. Semi-a la carte: lunch $4.50-$6, dinner $7-$14. Child's meals. Specialties: linguine tutto mare, veal with crabmeat, Sicilian steak. In old Italian neighborhood. Cr cds: A, C, D, MC, V.

D ⟶

★★ **DIERDORF & HART'S.** *323 West Port Plaza (63146), W via I-64 (US 40) to I-270, N on I-270 to Page Ave exit, west of downtown. 314/878-1801.* Hrs: 11 am-10 pm; Fri to 11 pm; Sat 4:30-11 pm; Sun 4:30-10 pm. Closed July 4, Thanksgiving. Res accepted. Bar to 12:30 am; Fri, Sat to 1:30 am. Semi-a la carte: lunch $5.95-$11.95, dinner $14.75-$37.50. Specializes in steak, broiled seafood. Pianist Wed-Sat. 1940s steakhouse atmosphere. Cr cds: A, D, DS, MC, V.

⟶

★★ **DIVI.** *(See Hilton-Frontenac Motor Hotel) 314/993-1100.* Hrs: 6:30 am-10 pm; Sun brunch 10 am-2 pm. Res accepted. Eclectic menu. Bar 11-1:30 am; Sun to 11:30 pm. Semi-a la carte: bkfst $5.25-$9.75, lunch $5.75-$11.25, dinner $13-$19. Sun brunch $19.95. Child's meals. Specialties: seafood fettucine, Chilean sea bass, crusted lamb chops. Cr cds: A, D, DS, MC, V.

D SC ⟶

★★★ **DOMINIC'S.** *5101 Wilson Ave (63110), on The Hill. 314/771-1632.* Hrs: 5-11 pm; Fri, Sat to midnight. Closed Sun; major hols. Res accepted. Italian menu. Bar. Wine cellar. Semi-a la carte: dinner $14.50-$23. Specialties: osso buco, shrimp elegante, artichoke stuffed with shrimp. Own pastries, pasta. Tableside service. Valet parking. Family-owned. Jacket. Cr cds: A, C, D, DS, ER, MC, V.

⟶ ♥

★★★ **FAUST'S.** *(See Adam's Mark Hotel) 314/342-4690.* Hrs: 11:30 am-2 pm, 5:30-10 pm; Fri to 10:30 pm; Sat 5:30-10:30 pm; Sun from 5:30 pm. Res accepted. Bar. Extensive wine list. A la carte entrees: lunch $9-$17, dinner $20-$35. Child's meals. Specializes in rack of lamb, halibut Chardonnay, crispy duck. Own baking. Valet parking. Two-tiered dining rm with beamed ceilings; upper tier with view of Gateway Arch. Jacket (dinner). Cr cds: A, C, D, DS, MC, V.

D ⟶

★ **FRANK PAPA'S.** *(2241 S Brentwood Blvd, Brentwood 63144) 1/2 mi S of I-64. 314/961-3344.* Hrs: 11 am-2 pm, 5-10 pm; Sat 5-11 pm. Closed Sun; major hols. Res accepted. Italian menu. Wine, beer. Semi-a la carte: lunch $6.95-$12.95, dinner $14.95-$21.95. Specialties: penne amatriciana, carpaccio, vitello alla Diana. Own baking. Storefront restaurant. Cr cds: A, C, D, DS, MC, V.

D ⟶

★★★ **G P AGOSTINO'S.** *(15846 Manchester Rd, Ellisville 63011) 22 mi W on I-64 (US 40) to Clarkson Rd, 4 mi S to Manchester Rd. 314/391-5480.* Hrs: 11 am-2:30 pm, 5 pm-midnight. Closed Jan 1, Thanksgiving, Dec 25. Res accepted. Italian menu. Bar. Wine cellar. Semi-a la carte: lunch $3.95-$9.95, dinner $8.95-$19.95. Sun brunch $11.95 Specialties: veal salto in bocca Romano, ossobuco Milanese, salmon con pappardelle. Chef-owned. Jacket (dinner). Cr cds: A, C, D, DS, ER, JCB, MC, V.

D ⟶

★★ **GIAN PEPPE'S.** *2126 Marconi Ave (63110), on The Hill. 314/772-3303.* Hrs: 11 am-2 pm, 5-11 pm; Sat from 5 pm. Closed Sun; major hols; also Mon Oct-Jan. Res accepted. Italian menu. Bar. Wine list. Semi-a la carte: lunch $6.25-$15.99, dinner $12.50-$26.50. Specializes in veal, fresh seafood. Own pastries. Valet parking. Jacket. Cr cds: A, C, D, MC, V.

D ⟶

✔★ **GINO'S.** *4502 Hampton Ave (63109), on The Hill. 314/351-4187.* Hrs: 11 am-2 pm, 5-10 pm; Fri to 11 pm; Sat 5-11 pm; Sun 5-9 pm. Closed Mon; major hols. Italian menu. Bar. Semi-a la carte: lunch $5.99-$10.95, dinner $6.95-$19.95. Child's meals. Specialties: veal Spedine, linguine Pescatore, veal chops. Cafe atmosphere. Cr cds: A, MC, V.

D

★★★ **GIOVANNI'S.** *5201 Shaw Ave (63110), on The Hill. 314/772-5958.* Hrs: 5-11 pm; Fri & Sat to midnight. Closed Sun; major hols. Res accepted. Italian menu. Wine cellar. A la carte entrees: dinner $14.50-$29.95. Specialties: tuna San Martino, maltagliati al funchetto, ossobucco originale, involtini di pesce spada. Own pastries. Valet parking. Cr cds: A, C, D, DS, ER, MC, V.

★★★ **GIOVANNI'S LITTLE PLACE.** *(14560 Manchester Rd, Ballwin 63011) 14 mi W on I-64 (US 40) to I-270, S on I-270 to Manchester Rd, in Winchester Plaza Center. 314/227-7230.* Hrs: 5-10 pm. Closed hols. Res accepted. Italian menu. Bar. Wine cellar. Semi-a la carte: dinner $10.95-$24. Specialties: fusilli ai quattro formaggi, involtini di vitello alla villa Igea, vitello alla Maria. Own pastries. Cr cds: A, C, D, DS, ER, MC, V.

D

★★ **GIUSEPPE'S.** *4141 S Grand Blvd (63118), south of downtown. 314/832-3779.* Hrs: 11 am-10 pm; Sat 4-10:30 pm; Sun 4-9 pm. Closed Mon; major hols; July 1. Res accepted. Italian menu. Bar. Semi-a la carte: lunch $4.50-$6.75, dinner $6.50-$17.95. Child's meals. Specialties: breaded speidini, breaded veal cutlet, linguini with clam sauce. Mahogany woodwork; ornately-framed artwork. Family-owned. Cr cds: A, C, D, MC, V.

D

★★★ **THE GRILL.** *(See The Ritz-Carlton, St Louis Hotel) 314/863-6300.* Hrs: 5-11 pm. Res accepted. Bar. Wine cellar. A la carte entrees: dinner $22-$48. Child's meals. Specialties: Dover sole, Aquanor salmon, venison. Own baking. Valet parking. Marble fireplace in main rm; English pub atmosphere. Cr cds: A, C, D, DS, ER, JCB, MC, V.

D

✔★★ **HACIENDA.** *(9748 Manchester Rd, Rock Hill 63119) W of downtown via Manchester Rd (MO 100). 314/962-7100.* Hrs: 11 am-10 pm; Fri, Sat to midnight; Sun noon-9 pm. Closed some major hols. Res accepted. Mexican menu. Bar. Semi-a la carte: lunch, dinner $4.95-$10.95. Specialties: chicken mole, fajitas. Parking. Outside dining. Built as residence for steamboat captain (1861). Cr cds: A, C, D, DS, MC, V.

D

★ **HANNEGAN'S.** *719 N Second St (63102), downtown. 314/241-8877.* Hrs: 11 am-10 pm; Fri, Sat to 11 pm. Closed Thanksgiving, Dec 25. Bar. Semi-a la carte: lunch $5-$8, dinner $10-$17. Child's meals. Specializes in fresh seafood, steak. Oyster bar in season. Jazz Fri, Sat. Outdoor dining. Replica of US Senate dining rm; political memorabilia. Cr cds: A, C, D, DS, MC, V.

D

★★ **HARRY'S.** *2144 Market St (63103), west of downtown. 314/421-6969.* Hrs: 11 am-3 pm, 5-11 pm; Sun 5-10 pm. Closed some major hols. Res accepted. Bar. Semi-a la carte: lunch $5-$16, dinner $8-$25. Specializes in smoked meats, fish. Entertainment Wed, Fri, Sat. Valet parking. Patio dining with view of Union Station and skyline. Cr cds: A, D, DS, MC, V.

D

★ **HOUSE OF INDIA.** *8501 Delmar Blvd (63124), west of downtown. 314/567-6850.* Hrs: 11:30 am-2:30 pm, 5-10 pm. Res accepted. Indian menu. Serv bar. Buffet lunch $5.95. Semi-a la carte: dinner $6.95-$13.95. Child's meals. Specialty: yogi thali. Indian art. Totally nonsmoking. Cr cds: A, D, DS, MC, V.

D

★★ **HUNTER'S HOLLOW.** *(Washington & Front Sts, Labadie 63055) 40 mi W on I-44, on Hwy T. 314/742-2279.* Hrs: 11 am-3 pm, 5:30-9 pm; Sun 11 am-8 pm. Closed Mon; Dec 25. Res accepted. Bar. Semi-a la carte: lunch $10-$12, dinner $16-$25. Child's meals. Specializes in quail, pheasant, duck. Outdoor dining. Country decor with hunting theme. Cr cds: A, DS, MC, V.

★★ **J.F. SANFILIPPO'S.** *705 N Broadway (63102), downtown. 314/621-7213.* Hrs: 11 am-2 pm, 4:30-11 pm; Sat from 4:30 pm. Closed Sun (exc football season); some major hols. Res accepted. Italian menu. Bar. Semi-a la carte: lunch $4.50-$10.25, dinner $4.75-$18.50. Child's meals. Specializes in pasta, fresh seafood, veal. Garage parking. Low slatted ceiling of metal and wood. Casual, trattoria atmosphere. Cr cds: A, C, D, DS, MC, V.

D

✔★ **JOHN D. McGURK'S.** *1200 Russell Blvd (63104), 1 mi SW on Broadway to Russell, south of downtown. 314/776-8309.* E-mail mcgurks@swbell.net. Hrs: 11-1:30 am; Sat from 11:30 am; Sun 4 pm-midnight. Closed major hols. Res accepted. Irish, Amer menu. Bar. Semi-a la carte: lunch $4.95-$8.95, dinner $4.95-$15.95. Child's meals. Specialties: Irish soda bread, corned beef and cabbage, Irish stew. Traditional Irish music. Street parking. Housed in 1861 bldg. Family-owned. Cr cds: A, C, D, DS, MC, V.

D SC

★★★ **JOHN MINEO'S.** *(13490 Clayton Rd, Town & Country 63131) 15 mi W of downtown via I-64 (US 40), exit Mason Rd, 1 mi S to Clayton Rd. 314/434-5244.* Hrs: 5 pm-midnight. Closed Sun. Res accepted. Italian menu. Bar. Wine list. A la carte entrees: dinner $9.95-$18.95. Specialties: veal alla panna, Dover sole, fresh fish. Chef-owned. Jacket. Cr cds: A, C, D, DS, MC, V.

D

★★ **JOSEPH'S ITALIAN CAFE.** *107 N 6th St (63101), downtown. 314/421-6366.* Hrs: 11 am-2 pm, 5:30-9:30 pm; Sat 5-10 pm. Closed Sun. Res accepted. Italian menu. Bar. Semi-a la carte: lunch $3.95-$10.95, dinner $8.99-$25.99. Child's meals. Specializes in pasta. Pianist. Outdoor dining. Contemporary decor. Totally nonsmoking. Cr cds: A, C, D, DS, MC, V.

D

★★★ **KEMOLL'S.** *1 Metropolitan Square, downtown. 314/421-0555.* Hrs: 11 am-2 pm, 5-9 pm; Fri to 10 pm; Sat 5-10 pm; early-bird dinner 5-6:30 pm. Closed Sun; major hols. Res accepted. Italian menu. Bar. Semi-a la carte: dinner $15-$32. Specializes in fresh seafood, veal Francesco, carciofi fritti. 3 dining rms. Family-owned. Cr cds: A, C, D, DS, MC, V.

D

★★★ **KREIS'S.** *(535 S Lindbergh, Ladue 63131) approx 7 mi W on I-64. 314/993-0735.* Hrs: 5-10:30 pm; Sat to 11 pm; Sun 4:30-9:30 pm. Closed some major hols. Res accepted. Bar. Semi-a la carte: dinner $11.95-$38. Child's meals. Specializes in prime rib, steak, fresh fish. Valet parking. In renovated 1930s brick house with beamed ceilings. Cr cds: A, D, MC, V.

D

✔★ **LA SALA.** *513 Olive (63101), at N 6th St, near stadium, downtown. 314/231-5620.* Hrs: 11 am-9 pm; Fri to 11 pm. Closed Sat, Sun; major hols. Mexican menu. Bar. Semi-a la carte: lunch, dinner $4.95-$9.25. Parking nearby. Mexican decor; casual atmosphere. Family-owned. Cr cds: A, C, D, DS, MC, V.

D

★★★ **LOMBARDO'S TRATTORIA.** *(See Drury Inn Union Station Hotel) 314/621-0666.* Hrs: 11 am-10 pm; Fri to 11:30 pm; Sat 4-11:30 pm. Closed Sun; most major hols. Res accepted. Italian menu. Bar. Wine list. Semi-a la carte: lunch $4.75-$8.95, dinner $7.50-$22. Child's meals.

Specialties: ravioli, calzoni. Jazz Fri, Sat. Valet parking (dinner). Several dining areas on lower level of historic hotel. Cr cds: A, C, D, MC, V.

D

★★ **LORUSSO'S CUCINA.** *3121 Watson Rd (63139), on The Hill. 314/647-6222.* Hrs: 11:30 am-2 pm, 5-10 pm; Fri, Sat 5-11 pm. Closed Mon, Sun; major hols. Italian menu. Bar 11 am-11 pm. Semi-a la carte: lunch $6.25-$10.95, dinner $8.50-$18.95. Child's meals. Specialties: risotto, vitello, tenderloin Mudega. Entertainment Fri, Sat. Cr cds: A, C, D, DS, MC, V.

D

★★ **LYNCH STREET BISTRO.** *1031 Lynch St (63118), south of downtown. 314/772-5777.* Hrs: 11 am-3 pm, 5-10 pm; Fri, Sat to 11 pm. Closed Sun; major hols. Res accepted. Eclectic menu. Bar. Wine list. Semi-a la carte: lunch $7.95-$9.95. A la carte entrees: dinner $13.95-$18.95. Child's meals. Specialties: cajun fusilli, barbecue crusted salmon, grilled pork tenderloin. Live entertainment. Outdoor dining. Original paintings, art and posters. Cr cds: A, D, MC, V.

D

✓★★★ **MAI LEE.** *(8440 Delmar Blvd, University City 63124) W on MO 340. 314/993-3754.* Hrs: 11 am-9 pm; Fri-Sun to 10 pm. Closed Mon; Dec 25. Res accepted. Vietnamese, Chinese menu. Bar. Semi-a la carte: lunch $1.95-$4.25, dinner $1.95-$8.95. Specialties: sausage shrimp with garlic, seafood with baby bok choy, Vietnamese chicken salad. Cr cds: DS, MC, V.

D

★★★ **MALMAISON.** *(St Albans Rd, St Albans 63055) 30 mi W on Hwy T, off MO 100. 314/458-0131.* Hrs: 5-10 pm; Sat, Sun 11:30 am-3:30 pm, 5-10 pm. Closed Mon, Tues. Res accepted. French menu. Bar. Wine list. A la carte entrees: lunch $8.95-$14.95, dinner $13.95-$22.95. Specializes in wild game, duckling. Outdoor dining. French country decor. Jacket. Cr cds: A, MC, V.

D

★★ **MAMA CAMPISI'S.** *2132 Edwards St (63110), on The Hill. 314/771-1797.* E-mail camp1911@aol.com; web www.intellipages.com/3147711797/index.html. Hrs: 11 am-3 pm, 5-10 pm; Sat to 10:30 pm; Sun 11:30 am-8:30 pm. Closed Mon; most major hols. Res accepted. Italian menu. Bar. Semi-a la carte: lunch $5.95-$7.95, dinner $7.25-$16.95. Specialties: petto de polo picante, vitello alla parmigiano, lasagna al forno. Casual, family atmosphere. Cr cds: A, C, D, DS, MC, V.

D

★ **MANDARIN HOUSE.** *194 Union Station (63103), in Union Station, west of downtown. 314/621-6888.* Hrs: 10 am-10 pm. Res accepted. Chinese menu. Bar. Semi-a la carte: lunch, dinner $6.25-$14. Lunch buffet $5.65. Specializes in Szechuan, Peking dishes. Chinese decor. Inside shopping mall at Union Station. Cr cds: A, C, D, DS, ER, JCB, MC, V.

D

★ **MANDARIN HOUSE.** *9150 Overland Plaza (63114), north of downtown. 314/427-8070.* Hrs: 11:30 am-2 pm, 5-9:30 pm; Fri to 10:30 pm; Sat 5-10:30 pm. Closed Labor Day, Thanksgiving. Res accepted. Chinese menu. Bar. Semi-a la carte: lunch $5.25-$6.55, dinner $5.55-$15.95. Sun brunch $8.95. Chinese decor featuring tapestry of Great Wall; fish pond. Cr cds: A, C, D, DS, MC, V.

D

★ **MARCIANO'S.** *333 West Port Plaza (63146), I-270 W, exit Page E, west of downtown. 314/878-8180.* Hrs: 11 am-10:30 pm; Fri, Sat to midnight; Sun from 3 pm. Closed Easter, Thanksgiving, Dec 25. Res accepted. Italian menu. Bar. Semi-a la carte: lunch $5.95-$7.50. A la carte entrees: dinner $6.95-$15.95. Child's meals. Specializes in pasta, desserts. Outdoor dining. Multi-level dining; Italian posters. Cr cds: A, DS, MC, V.

D

★★ **MIKE SHANNON'S.** *100 N 7th St (63101), at Chestnut, downtown. 314/421-1540.* Web www.bitestl.com/shannons. Hrs: 11 am-11 pm; Sat, Sun 5-10 pm. Closed Easter, Thanksgiving, Dec 25. Res accepted. Bar. Semi-a la carte: lunch $5.25-$10.95, dinner $11.95-$35.95. Specializes in prime rib, steak, seafood. Sports memorabilia. Cr cds: A, D, DS, MC, V.

D

★★ **MOLINA'S WISHING WELL.** *(12949 Olive Blvd, Creve Coeur 63141) 14 mi W on US 40 to I-270, N to Olive Blvd. 314/205-2299.* Hrs: 4:30 pm-midnight. Closed Sun; Dec 25. Res accepted. Continental menu. Bar. Semi-a la carte: dinner $9.95-$19.95. Child's meals. Specialties: stuffed cornish hen, crab-stuffed filet mignon, homard fritt. Own baking. Contemporary Italian decor. Cr cds: A, C, D, DS, MC, V.

D

✓★ **MUSEUM CAFE.** *1 Fine Arts Dr (63110), in St Louis Art Museum, west of downtown. 314/721-5325.* Hrs: 11 am-2 pm, 3:30-8:30; Tues 11 am-2 pm, 5-8:30 pm; Sun 10 am-3:30 pm; Sun Brunch to 2 pm. Closed Mon; Dec 25. Res accepted. Continental menu. Wine, beer. Semi-a la carte: lunch $5.50-$8.50, dinner $6.50-$8.95. Child's meals. Specializes in salads, fresh fish. Menu items reflect current museum exhibits. Cr cds: C, D, DS, MC, V.

D

✓★ **ONCE UPON A VINE.** *3559 Arsenal St (63118), at Grand, on The Hill. 314/776-2828.* Web bitestl.com/once. Hrs: 10:30 am-9 pm; Fri, Sat to 10:30 pm. Closed Sun; major hols. Res accepted. Bar. Semi-a la carte: lunch, dinner $4.95-$12.95. Child's meals. Specialties: chicken salad, smoked pork chops, penne with wild mushrooms and chicken. Outdoor dining. Storefront restaurant; casual dining. Totally nonsmoking. Cr cds: A, D, MC, V.

D

✓★ **PASTA HOUSE COMPANY.** *(295 Plaza Frontenac, Frontenac 63131) 10 mi on I-64 W exit Lindbergh S into Frontier Plaza. 314/569-3040.* Hrs: 11 am-9:30 pm; Fri, Sat to 10 pm; Sun noon-8 pm. Closed Thanksgiving, Easter, Dec 25. Italian menu. Bar. Semi-a la carte: lunch $4.99-$9.50, dinner $6-$15.99. Specializes in pasta. Contemporary decor, casual atmosphere. Cr cds: A, DS, MC, V.

D SC

★★ **PATRICK'S.** *342 Westport Plaza (63146), west of downtown. 314/878-6767.* Hrs: 11 am-11 pm; Fri, Sat to midnight; Sun 9:30 am-2 pm, 4-11 pm. Closed most major hols. Res accepted. Bar. Semi-a la carte: lunch $4.95-$8.95, dinner $8.95-$26.95. Child's meals. Specialties: fresh seafood, prime rib, pasta. Entertainment. Outdoor dining. Casual decor. Cr cds: A, C, D, DS, MC, V.

D

★★ **PATTY LONG'S 9TH STREET ABBEY.** *1808 S 9th St (63104), south of downtown. 314/621-9598.* Hrs: 11 am-2 pm, 5-10 pm; Tues 11 am-2 pm; Sat 5-10 pm; Sun brunch 10 am-2 pm. Closed Sat, Mon; some major hols. Res accepted. Continental menu. Bar. Semi-a la carte: lunch $7.95-$9.95, dinner $9.95-$15.95. Sun brunch $10.95-$13.95. Specialties: almond chicken salad, grilled beef tenderloin, fish of the day. Valet parking. Patio dining. In former church (ca 1895); stained-glass windows and paneling. Cr cds: A, D, MC, V.

D

✓★ **PICCOLO'S.** *211 N Broadway (63102), in Metropolitan Square Bldg, downtown. 314/231-7510.* Hrs: 11 am-2 pm, 5-9 pm; Sat from 5 pm. Closed Sun; major hols; also 1st wk Jan, 1st wk July. Res accepted. Continental menu. Bar. Semi-a la carte: lunch $3.50-$8, dinner $3.50-$15. Child's meals. Specializes in pasta, pizza, tapas. Own baking, pasta. Free valet parking. Casual atmosphere. Cr cds: A, C, DS, ER, JCB, MC, V.

D

★★ **PREMIO.** *7th & Market Sts (63101), downtown. 314/231-0911.* Hrs: 11 am-10 pm; Fri to 11 pm; Sat 5-11 pm. Closed Sun; major hols. Res accepted. Italian menu. Bar. Semi-a la carte: lunch $6.25-$12.95, dinner $7.95-$21. Specializes in fresh seafood, veal, creative pasta. Garage parking; valet Fri, Sat. Outdoor dining. Modern decor. Cr cds: A, C, D, DS, MC, V.

D

★ **RIDDLE PENULTIMATE.** *(6307 Delmar Blvd, University City 63130) W on MO 340, downtown. 314/725-6985.* Hrs: 11-1 am; Sat from 11:30 am; Sun 5 pm-midnight. Closed Mon; July 4, Thanksgiving, Dec 25. Res accepted. Eclectic menu. Bar. Semi-a la carte: lunch $4.25-$8.75, dinner $7.50-$18. Specializes in pastas, veal. Blues, jazz, bluegrass. Street parking. Outdoor dining. Known for extensive wine list—over 350 varieties. Cr cds: A, C, D, MC, V.

★ **ROBATA OF JAPAN.** *111 West Port Plaza (63146), on 12th fl of office bldg, west of downtown. 314/434-1007.* Hrs: 11:30 am-1:30 pm, 5:30-9 pm; wkend hrs vary. Closed Thanksgiving. Res accepted. Japanese menu. Bar. Semi-a la carte: lunch $5-$11, dinner $11-$22. Child's meals. Specializes in steak, seafood, chicken. Japanese decor; teppanyaki cooking. Cr cds: A, D, DS, MC, V.

★ **SALEEM'S.** *6501 Delmar Blvd (63130), west of downtown. 314/721-7947.* Hrs: 5-10 pm; Fri, Sat to 11:30 pm. Closed Sun; Thanksgiving, Dec 25. Middle Eastern menu. Serv bar. Semi-a la carte: dinner $10.95-$14.95. Specializes in vegetarian, chicken, lamb. Middle Eastern decor. Cr cds: DS, MC, V.

D

★ ★ ★ **SCHNEITHORST'S HOFAMBERG INN.** *(1600 S Lindbergh Blvd, Ladue 63131), via I-64 (US 40), exit Lindbergh Blvd, S to Clayton Rd. 314/993-5600.* Web www.schneithorst.com. Hrs: 11 am-9 pm; Fri, Sat to 11 pm; Sun 10 am-8 pm; early-bird dinner Mon-Fri 4-6:30 pm (exc hols); Sun brunch to 1:30 pm. Closed Dec 25. Res accepted. German, Amer menu. Bar. Semi-a la carte: lunch $5.95-$16.95, dinner $10.95-$23.95. Sun brunch $11.95. Child's meals. Specializes in steak, prime rib, fresh seafood. Outdoor dining. Antique clocks, stein display. Cr cds: A, C, D, DS, MC, V.

D

★ ★ ★ **SEVENTH INN.** *(100 Seven Trails, Ballwin 63011) 15 mi W on MO 100. 314/227-6686.* Hrs: 5 pm-1:30 am. Closed Sun, Mon; Easter, Thanksgiving, Dec 25. Res accepted. Continental menu. Bar. Wine list. Semi-a la carte: $19.95-$29.95. Child's meals. Specializes in fresh seafood, prime aged beef. Entertainment Fri & Sat. Elegant European decor. Cr cds: A, C, D, DS, JCB, MC, V.

D

★ ★ **SIDNEY STREET CAFE.** *2000 Sidney St (63104), south of downtown. 314/771-5777.* Hrs: 5-9:30 pm; Fri & Sat 5-9:30 pm. Closed Sun & Mon. Res accepted. Continental menu. Bar. Semi-a la carte: dinner $16-$23. Specializes in grilled seafood, lamb, steak au poivre. In restored building (ca 1885); antiques. Dinner menu recited. Cr cds: A, C, D, DS, MC, V.

D

★ ★ **ST LOUIS BREWERY & TAP ROOM.** *2100 Locust St (63101), west of downtown. 314/241-2337.* Hrs: 11 am-10 pm; Fri, Sat to midnight; Sun noon-9 pm. Closed Jan 1, Easter, Dec 25. Bar. Semi-a la carte: lunch, dinner $6-$12. Specialties: sticky toffee pudding, beer cheese soup, goat cheese Rarebit. English brew pub atmosphere. Cr cds: A, C, D, DS, MC, V.

D

✔★ **SUNFLOWER CAFE.** *5513 Pershing Ave (63112), west of downtown. 314/367-6800.* Hrs: 11 am-2:30 pm, 5-10 pm; Fri, Sat to 11 pm. Closed Sun; most major hols. Italian, Amer menu. Bar. Semi-a la carte: lunch, dinner $4-$14.25. Child's meals. Specializes in pizza, pasta. Street parking. Outdoor dining. Totally nonsmoking. Cr cds: A, C, D, DS, MC, V.

D

★ **SUNSHINE INN.** *8½ S Euclid Ave (63108), west of downtown. 314/367-1413.* Hrs: 11:30 am-9 pm; Fri, Sat to 10 pm; Sun 10 am-2:30 pm (brunch), 5-9 pm. Closed Mon. Res accepted. Bar. Semi-a la carte: lunch $6-$9, dinner $9-$12. Sun brunch $2.50-$7.95. Specializes in vegetarian, all natural dishes. Outdoor dining. Storefront cafe. Totally nonsmoking. Cr cds: A, D, DS, MC, V.

D

✔★ ★ **THAI CAFE.** *6170 Delmar Blvd (63112), west of downtown. 314/862-6868.* Hrs: 11:30 am-2:30 pm, 5-10 pm; Fri, Sat to 10:30 pm. Closed Sun; Dec 25. Res accepted. Thai menu. Serv bar. Semi-a la carte: lunch, dinner $3.90-$10.95. Specialties: Thai satay, pad Thai, red curry. Valet parking. Thai artwork; one rm has only traditional Thai seating (no chairs). Totally nonsmoking. Cr cds: A, C, D, DS, MC, V.

★ ★ ★ ★ **TONY'S.** *410 Market St (63102), downtown. 314/231-7007.* A St Louis favorite ornamented by classical statues, this restaurant has been operated by the Bommarito family for three generations. Italian menu. Specializes in prime veal and beef, fresh seafood, homemade pasta. Own baking. Hrs: 5-11 pm; Fri, Sat to 11:30 pm. Closed Sun; major hols; also 1st wk Jan, 1st wk July. Res accepted. Bar. Wine cellar. Semi-a la carte: dinner $18.75-$29.75. Valet parking. Family-owned. Jacket. Cr cds: A, C, D, DS, ER, JCB, MC, V.

D

✔★ ★ **TRATTORIA MARCELLA.** *3600 Watson Rd (63109), on The Hill. 314/352-7706.* Hrs: 5-10 pm; Fri, Sat to 11 pm. Closed Sun, Mon; major hols. Res accepted. Italian menu. Bar. Semi-a la carte: dinner $8.95-$15.95. Specialties: frito misto of calamari and spinach, risotto with lobster and wild mushrooms. Own baking, pasta. Outdoor dining. Authentic Italian decor; mirrored walls. Family-owned since 1911. Cr cds: A, C, D, MC, V.

★ **ZIA'S.** *5256 Wilson Ave (63110), on The Hill. 314/776-0020.* Hrs: 11 am-10:30 pm. Closed Sun; Memorial Day, July 4. Italian menu. Bar. Semi-a la carte: lunch $5-$8, dinner $7.50-$16.25. Specializes in veal, pasta, chicken. Informal, modern corner restaurant. Outdoor dining. Cr cds: A, D, DS, MC, V.

★ ★ **ZINNIA.** *(7491 Big Bend Blvd, Webster Groves 63119) I-44 W to Big Bend Blvd. 314/962-0572.* Hrs: 11 am-2 pm, 5:30-9:30 pm; Fri to 10:30 pm; Sat 5:30-10:30 pm; Sun 4:30-9 pm. Closed Mon; major hols. Res accepted. Bar. Semi-a la carte: lunch $6-$9.50, dinner $13.50-$19.50. Specialties: sautéed veal sweetbreads, trout Zinnia. Own pasta. Outdoor dining. Upscale dining; wall murals, many flower boxes. Cr cds: DS, MC, V.

D

Unrated Dining Spots

BARN DELI. *(180 Dunn Rd, Florissant) N on I-70 to I-270. 314/838-3670.* Hrs: 11 am-4 pm. Closed Sun; major hols. Wine, beer. Semi-a la carte: lunch $3.50-$4.95. Specializes in deli sandwiches, salads. Own soups, desserts. In late 1800s barn. Cr cds: MC, V.

D

BLUEBERRY HILL. *6504 Delmar Blvd, west of downtown. 314/727-0880.* Hrs: 11 am-midnight; Sun to 11 pm. Closed Jan 1. Res accepted Sun-Thurs. Bar to 1:30 am; Sun to midnight. Semi-a la carte: lunch, dinner $3.25-$7. Specializes in hamburgers, vegetarian platters, soups, salads. Entertainment Fri & Sat evenings. Large displays of pop culture memorabilia including Chuck Berry and Elvis. Vintage jukeboxes. Sidewalk has "Walk of Fame" stars for celebrities from St Louis. Cr cds: A, C, D, DS, MC, V.

CROWN CANDY KITCHEN. *1401 St Louis Ave, north of downtown. 314/621-9650.* Hrs: 10:30 am-10 pm; Sun from noon. Closed some major hols. Specialty: ice cream. Also sandwiches, chili $2-$4. Homemade candy. Old neighborhood building (1889) with old-fashioned soda fountain (1930s), antique juke box and Coca-Cola memorabilia. No cr cds accepted.

O'CONNELLS PUB. *4652 Shaw Ave, on The Hill. 314/773-6600.* Hrs: 11 am-midnight, Sun noon-10 pm. Closed major hols. Bar. Semi-a la carte: lunch, dinner $3.50-$6.50. Specializes in hamburgers, roast beef sandwiches, soup. Pub atmosphere; antique bar, blackboard menu. Cr cds: A, D, DS, MC, V.

St Louis Lambert Airport Area

Motels

✓★ ★ **BEST WESTERN AIRPORT INN.** *(10232 Natural Bridge Rd, Woodson Terrace 63134) I-70 exit 236. 314/427-5955; FAX 314/427-3079.* 138 rms, 2 story. May-Sept: S $59-$70; D $65-$80; under 12 free; lower rates rest of yr. Crib free. TV; cable (premium). Pool. Restaurant adj. Ck-out noon. Coin Indry. Meeting rms. Business servs avail. In-rm modem link. Free airport transportation. Cr cds: A, C, D, DS, ER, JCB, MC, V.

D SC

★ ★ **DRURY INN.** *(10490 Natural Bridge Rd, St Louis 63134) W via I-70, 1 blk N of exit 236. 314/423-7700.* Web www.drury-inn.com. 172 rms, 6 story. S $79.95-$85.95; D $89.95-$99.95; suites $103-$123; under 18 free; some wkend rates. Crib free. Pet accepted, some restrictions. TV; cable (premium), VCR avail. Heated pool. Complimentary continental bkfst. Restaurant adj noon-10 pm. Ck-out noon. Meeting rms. Business servs avail. In-rm modem link. Free airport transportation. Cr cds: A, C, D, DS, MC, V.

D SC

✓★ **FAIRFIELD INN BY MARRIOTT.** *(9079 Dunn Rd, Hazelwood 63042) I-270, exit 25. 314/731-7700.* 135 rms, 3 story. May-Sept: S, D $49-$75; each addl $5; under 12 free; wkend rates; higher rates VP Fair. Crib free. TV; cable (premium). Pool. Complimentary continental bkfst. Restaurant adj 7 am-10 pm. Ck-out noon. Business servs avail. In-rm modem link. Cr cds: A, D, DS, MC, V.

D SC

★ ★ **HOLIDAY INN-AIRPORT WEST.** *(3551 Pennridge Dr, Bridgeton 63044) 1-270 to St Charles Rock Rd, W to Boenker. 314/291-5100.* 327 rms, 4 story. S, D $92-$97; each addl $10; under 18 free. Crib free. Pet accepted. TV; cable (premium), VCR avail. Complimentary coffee in rms. Restaurant 6-10 am. Rm serv. Bar 4 pm-1 am. Ck-out noon. Convention facilities. Business center. In-rm modem link. Bellhops. Valet serv. Coin Indry. Free airport transportation. Exercise equipt; weights, treadmill, sauna. Indoor pool; whirlpool. Game rm. Rec rm. Some refrigerators. Luxury level. Cr cds: A, C, D, DS, MC, V.

D SC

Motor Hotels

✓★ ★ **HENRY VIII.** *(4690 N Lindbergh, St Louis 63044) W via I-70 N Lindbergh exit. 314/731-3040; FAX 314/731-4210; res: 800/325-1588.* 386 units, 2-5 story, 190 suites, 35 kit. units. S $69-$128; D $79-$128; suites $89-$128; under 18 free; wkly, monthly rates. Crib free. TV; cable (premium). 2 pools, 1 indoor; whirlpool. Restaurant 6:30 am-midnight; Sun to 11 pm. Rm serv. Bar from 11 am. Ck-out 11 am. Coin Indry. Convention facilities. Business servs avail. Bellhops. Gift shop. Free airport transportation. Exercise equipt; weights, weight machine, sauna. Game rm. Refrigerators, wet bars; some bathrm phones; microwaves avail. Some balconies. Some English Tudor architecture. Cr cds: A, D, DS, MC, V.

D SC

★ ★ ★ **HOLIDAY INN AIRPORT OAKLAND PARK.** *(4505 Woodson Rd, St. Louis 63134) I-70 exit 236, E on Natural Bridge Rd to Woodson Rd, S on Woodson. 314/427-4700; FAX 314/427-6086.* E-mail stlop@aol.com. 156 rms, 5 story, 13 suites. S $104.50; D $109.50; each addl $10; suites $125-$230; under 19 free; wkend rates. Crib free. TV; cable (premium). Pool; whirlpool. Restaurant 6:30 am-2 pm, 5-10 pm. Rm serv. Bar 4:30 pm-midnight. Ck-out 1 pm. Coin Indry. Meeting rms. Business servs avail. In-rm modem link. Bellhops. Valet serv. Free airport transportation. Exercise equipt; bicycles, weight machine, sauna. Cr cds: A, C, D, DS, JCB, MC, V.

D SC

★ **HOLIDAY INN-AIRPORT NORTH.** *(4545 N Lindbergh Blvd, St Louis 63044) 314/731-2100; FAX 314/731-4970.* 392 rms, 4 story. May-Dec: $94-$114; D $104-$124; under 18 free; family, wkly, wkend, hol rates; lower rates rest of yr. Crib $10. TV; cable (premium). Complimentary coffee in rms. Restaurant 6 am-11 pm. Rm serv. Bar 4 pm-midnight. Ck-out noon. Convention facilities. Business center. In-rm modem link. Bellhops. Valet serv. Concierge. Gift shop. Coin Indry. Free airport transportation. Exercise equipt; weight machine, bicycle. Indoor pool; wading pool, whirlpool, poolside serv. Game rm. Many balconies. Luxury level. Cr cds: A, C, D, DS, MC, V.

D SC

Hotels

★ ★ ★ **EMBASSY SUITES.** *(11237 Lone Eagle Dr, Bridgeton 63044) I-70 exit Lindbergh S (237 A). 314/739-8929; FAX 314/739-6355.* Web www.embassy-suites.com. 159 suites, 6 story. S, D $99-$139; wkend rates; higher rates special events. Crib avail. TV; cable (premium). Indoor pool; whirlpool. Complimentary continental bkfst. Complimentary coffee in rms. Restaurant 11 am-11 pm. Bar 4 pm-midnight. Ck-out noon. Coin Indry. Meeting rms. Business servs avail. In-rm modem link. Gift shop. Free airport transportation. Exercise equipt; weights, treadmill, sauna. Game rm. Refrigerators, microwaves. Cr cds: A, C, D, DS, JCB, MC, V.

D SC

★ ★ ★ **HILTON.** *(10330 Natural Bridge Rd, Woodson Terrace 63134) I-70 exit 236, E on Natural Bridge Rd. 314/426-5500; FAX 314/426-3429.* Web www.hilton.com/hotels/stlhihf/index.html. 220 rms, 9 story. S, D $99-$150; each addl $10; suites $200-$350; under 18 free; wkend package plan. Crib free. TV; cable, VCR avail. Indoor pool; whirlpool, poolside serv. Complimentary coffee in rms. Restaurant 6 am-10 pm; wkends to 11 pm. Bars 11-1:30 am, Sun to midnight. Coin Indry. Ck-out 1 pm. Meeting rms. Business servs avail. In-rm modem link. Gift shop. Free airport transportation. Exercise equipt; weights, bicycles, sauna. Game rm. Some refrigerators; microwaves avail. Luxury level. Cr cds: A, C, D, DS, ER, MC, V.

D SC

★ ★ ★ **MARRIOTT.** *(I-70 at Lambert St Louis Intl Airport, St Louis 63134) I-70 exit 236. 314/423-9700; FAX 314/423-0213.* Web www.marriott.com. 601 rms, 9 story. S, D $99-$134; suites $200-$375. Crib free. Pet accepted. TV; cable (premium), VCR avail. 2 pools, 1 indoor/outdoor; poolside serv, whirlpool. Restaurant 6 am-midnight. Bars 11:30-1 am. Ck-out 1 pm. Coin Indry. Convention facilities. Business center. In-rm modem link. Gift shop. Free airport transportation. 2 lighted tennis courts. Exercise equipt; weights, sauna. Luxury level. Cr cds: A, C, D, DS, ER, JCB, MC, V.

D SC

★ ★ **RADISSON ST LOUIS AIRPORT.** *(11228 Lone Eagle Dr, Bridgeton 63044) I-70 exit 235A, S on Lindberg Dr. 314/291-6700; FAX 314/770-1205.* 353 rms, 8 story. S $109-$119; D $119-$129; each addl $10; suites $379; under 17 free; wkend rates. Crib $10. TV. Indoor pool; whirlpool. Restaurant 6:30 am-midnight. Bar from 11 am. Ck-out noon. Convention facilities. Business servs avail. In-rm modem link. Gift shop.

Free airport transportation. Exercise equipt; weight machine, bicycles. Game rm. Wet bar in suites. Some balconies. Atrium with waterfall. Cr cds: A, C, D, DS, ER, JCB, MC, V.

D SC

✔★ **RAMADA.** *(9600 Natural Bridge Rd, Berkeley 63134) 2 mi E on Natural Bridge Rd. 314/427-7600; FAX 314/427-1614.* 197 rms, 7 story. S, D $79-$89; each addl $7; under 18 free; wkend rates. Crib free. Pet accepted, some restrictions; $50 deposit. TV; cable. Pool; whirlpool. Bar 5:30 pm-1:30 am. Ck-out noon. Meeting rms. Business servs avail. In-rm modem link. Free airport transportation. Exercise equipt; weight machine, stair machine, sauna. Some bathrm phones, refrigerators, minibars. Balconies. Cr cds: A, C, D, DS, MC, V.

SC

★★★ **RENAISSANCE AIRPORT.** *(9801 Natural Bridge Rd, St Louis 63134) I-70 exit 237, 1 mi E on Natural Bridge Rd, adj to airport. 314/429-1100; FAX 314/429-3625.* E-mail renhtl@primary.net. 394 rms, 12 story. S $135-$180; D $150-$185; each addl $15; suites $195-$800; under 18 free; wkend rates. Crib free. TV; cable (premium), VCR avail. 2 pools, 1 indoor; whirlpool, poolside serv. Coffee in rms. Restaurant 6:30 am-11 pm. Rm serv until 1 am. Bar 3 pm-1 am. Ck-out 1 pm. Convention facilities. Business center. In-rm modem link. Gift shop. Concierge. Free airport transportation. Exercise equipt; weights, bicycles, sauna. Bathrm phones, minibars; microwaves avail. Luxury level. Cr cds: A, C, D, DS, ER, JCB, MC, V.

D SC

Restaurants

★★ **LOMBARDO'S.** *(10488 Natural Bridge Rd, St Louis 63134) 314/429-5151.* Hrs: 11 am-10 pm; Sat from 5 pm. Closed Sun; most major hols. Res accepted. Italian menu. Bar. Semi-a la carte: lunch $4.95-$12.75, dinner $9-$24. Specializes in fresh seafood, steak, pasta. Original art; sculptures. Family-owned since 1934. Cr cds: A, C, D, MC, V.

D

★★★ **TORNATORE'S.** *(12315 Natural Bridge Rd, Bridgeton 63044) 1-270 on Natural Bridge Rd exit. 314/739-6644.* Hrs: 11 am-3 pm, 5-10 pm; Sat from 5 pm; early-bird dinner Mon-Fri 5-6:30 pm. Closed Sun; major hols. Res accepted. Continental Italian menu. Bar. Extensive wine list. Semi-a la carte: lunch $7.95-$15.95, dinner $14.95-$30.95. Specializes in fresh seafood, Sicilian veal chops. Own pastries. Modern art; etched glass-paneled room divider. Cr cds: A, D, DS, MC, V.

D SC

Clayton

Hotels

★★★ **DANIELE.** *216 N Meramac, I-64 W to I-170 N, to Ladue Rd, E to Meramac. 314/721-0101; res: 800/325-8302; FAX 314/721-0609.* 82 rms, 4 story. S, D $129; suites $200-$500; under 18 free; wkend rates. Pet accepted. TV; cable (premium), VCR avail. Pool. Restaurant (see DANIELE). Bar. Ck-out noon. Meeting rms. Business servs avail. In-rm modem link. Free covered parking. Free airport transportation. Health club privileges. Some refrigerators, wet bars. Cr cds: A, C, D, DS, MC, V.

SC

★★★ **RADISSON.** *7750 Carondelet Ave, I-64 to Hanley Exit. 314/726-5400; FAX 314/719-1126.* 194 rms, 2-8 story. S $125-$139; D $135-$149; each addl $10; suites $129-$200; under 18 free; wkly rates, wkend package plan. Crib free. TV; cable. Indoor/outdoor pool; whirlpool. Complimentary continental bkfst. Coffee in rms. Restaurant 6 am-11 pm. Bar 11-1 am. Ck-out noon. Meeting rms. Business center. In-rm modem link. Barber. Free garage parking; valet. Airport transportation. Exercise rm; instructor, weights, bicycles. Game rm. Refrigerators; some wet bars; microwaves avail. Cr cds: A, C, D, DS, ER, JCB, MC, V.

D SC

Inns

★ **DAS GAST HAUS NADLER.** *(125 Defiance Rd, Defiance 63341) I-70 to MO 94W. 314/987-2200.* 4 rms, all share bath. No rm phones. S, D $65-$85; under 12 free. Complimentary full bkfst. Restaurant 9 am-9 pm. Ck-out 11 am, ck-in 4 pm. Whirlpool. Game rm. Built in 1907. Cr cds: MC, V.

SC

★★★ **SEVEN GABLES.** *26 N Meramec. 314/863-8400; res: 800/433-6590; FAX 314/863-8846.* E-mail gm@sevengablesinn.com; web www.sevengablesinn.com. 32 rms, 3 story. No elvtr. S, D $115-$215; suites $159-$260; wkend rates. Valet parking $8.50. TV; cable (premium). Restaurant 6:30 am-11 pm. Rm serv. Bar 11-12:30 am. Ck-out 1 pm, ck-in 3 pm. Meeting rm. Bellhops. Valet serv. Health club privileges. Designed in early 1900s; inspired by sketches in Hawthorne's novel House of Seven Gables. Renovated inn; European country-style furnishings. Cr cds: A, C, D, DS, MC, V.

SC

Restaurants

★★ **ANNIE GUNN'S.** *(16806 Chesterfield Airport Rd, Chesterfield 63005) W on I-64 (US 40), exit 19. 314/532-7684.* Hrs: 11 am-10:30 pm; Fri, Sat to 11:30 pm; Sun to 8 pm. Closed Mon; some major hols. Res accepted. Bar. Semi-a la carte: lunch $5.95-$10.95, dinner $5.95-$23.95. Specializes in steak, seafood. Outdoor dining; view of gardens. Originally built in 1935 as a meat market and smokehouse. Cr cds: A, D, MC, V.

D

★★★ **BENEDETTO'S.** *(10411 Clayton Rd, Frontenac 63131) 6 mi W on I-64, in Le Chateau Village. 314/432-8585.* Hrs: 11:30 am-2 pm, 5-11 pm; Sun 4:30-9 pm. Closed some major hols. Res accepted. Italian menu. Bar. Wine cellars. A la carte entrees: lunch $5.50-$9.95, dinner $13.95-$18.95. Specializes in Italian gourmet, veal, fresh fish, beef. Formal dining in elegant surroundings. Tableside preparation. Cr cds: A, D, DS, MC, V.

D

★★ **CAFE PROVENCAL.** *40 N Central. 314/725-2755.* Hrs: 6-10 pm. Closed Sun, Mon; also Easter, Thanksgiving, Dec 25. Res accepted. French menu. Bar. Semi-a la carte: dinner $20-$24. Specializes in southern french cuisine. Entertainment Wed, Thurs. French country decor. Cr cds: A, C, D, MC, V.

D

★ **CAFE ZOË.** *12 N Meramec Ave. 314/725-5554.* Hrs: 11:30 am-2 pm, 5-9 pm; Fri to 10 pm; Sat 5-10 pm. Closed Sun; major hols. Res accepted. Italian, Amer menu. Bar. Semi-a la carte: lunch $7.95-$10.95, dinner $12.95-$17.95. Specialties: risotto, beef filet, linguine with seafood. Own baking. Outdoor dining. Cr cds: A, D, MC, V.

★ **CANDICCI'S.** *7910 Bonhomme. 314/725-3350.* Hrs: 11:30 am-11 pm; Fri, Sat to midnight; Sun 4:30-9:30 pm. Closed major hols. Res accepted. Italian menu. Bar. Semi-a la carte: lunch $4-$8, dinner $7.95-$18.50. Specialty: Langusto supremo. Outdoor dining. In restored apartment building. Cr cds: A, C, D, DS, ER, MC, V.

D

★★★ **CARDWELL'S.** *8100 Maryland. 314/726-5055.* Hrs: 11:30 am-3 pm, 5:45-10 pm; Fri, Sat to 11 pm. Closed Sun; also major hols. Res accepted. Bar to 1:30 am. Semi-a la carte: lunch $5.95-$12.95, dinner

$14.95-$23.95. Child's meals. Specializes in seafood, steak, poultry. Outdoor dining. Contemporary decor. Cr cds: A, D, MC, V.

D

★ **CRAZY FISH FRESH GRILL.** *15 N Meramec Ave. 314/726-2111.* Hrs: 11:30 am-11 pm; Fri, Sat to midnight; Sun 10 am-10 pm. Closed Thanksgiving, Dec 25. Res accepted. Continental menu. Bar. Semi-a la carte: lunch $5.95-$10.95, dinner $11.95-$21.95. Child's meals. Specialties: bison meatloaf, shrimp voodoo pasta, potato crusted grouper. Outdoor dining. Modern decor. Cr cds: A, C, D, DS, MC, V.

D

★ ★ **DANIELE.** *(See Daniele Hotel) 314/721-0101.* Hrs: 6 am-10 pm; Sun to 2 pm. Closed most major hols. Res accepted. Continental menu. Bar. Semi-a la carte: bkfst $4.95-$7.95, lunch $6.95-$10.95, dinner $10.95-$12.95. Complete meals: dinner $16.95. Sun brunch $14.95. Specializes in steak, veal, prime rib. Valet parking. Elegant dining. No smoking at dinner. Cr cds: A, C, D, DS, MC, V.

D

★ ★ ★ **FIO'S LA FOURCHETTE.** *7515 Forsyth Ave. 314/863-6866.* Hrs: 6-9 pm. Closed Sun, Mon; major hols; also 2 wks in summer. Res accepted. French menu. Bar. Extensive wine list. Semi-a la carte: dinner $7-$24.50. Complete meal: dinner $48.75. Specializes in souffles, mussels, wild game. Own baking. Valet parking. Intimate dining. Cr cds: A, D, MC, V.

D ♥

★ ★ ★ **NANTUCKET COVE.** *101 S Hanley St, at Carondolet Ave. 314/726-4900.* Hrs: 11 am-2 pm, 5-10 pm; Fri to 11 pm; Sat 5-11 pm; Sun 5-9:30 pm. Closed Jan 1, Dec 25. Res accepted. Bar. Wine list. Semi-a la carte: lunch $4-$14, dinner $11.95-$24.95. Specializes in fresh seafood, lobster. Outdoor dining. Cr cds: A, D, DS, MC, V.

D

★ ★ **PORTABELLA.** *15 N Central Ave. 314/725-6588.* Hrs: 11 am-3 pm, 5:30-10:30 pm; Fri to 11 pm; Sat 5:30-11 pm. Closed Sun; major hols. Res accepted. Continental menu. Bar to 1:30 am. Semi-a la carte: lunch $6.50-$10.95, dinner $11.50-$18.95. Specialties: porcini-encrusted sea bass, grilled beef tenderloin with white truffle oil, roasted halibut with lemon garlic. Own baking. Valet parking. Modern art. Cr cds: A, D, DS, MC, V.

D

★ ★ **REMY'S KITCHEN & WINE BAR.** *222 S Bemiston, I-64 to Brentwood Blvd exit. 314/726-5757.* Hrs: 11:30 am-2:30 pm, 5:30-10 pm; Fri, Sat 5:30-11:30 pm. Closed Sun; also most major hols. Res accepted. Continental menu. Bar. Semi-a la carte: lunch $5.95-$7.95, dinner $19-$22. Specialties: bronzed snapper filet, brayed lamb shank and hummus. Outdoor dining. Modern decor. Totally nonsmoking. Cr cds: A, D, MC, V.

D

Unrated Dining Spot

ANDRÉ'S SWISS CONFISERIE. *(1026 S Brentwood Blvd, Richmond Heights) S on Brentwood Blvd. 314/727-9928.* Hrs: 7:30 am-5:30 pm; Fri to 9 pm. Closed Sun & Mon; major hols. Res accepted. Swiss menu. Wine, beer. Semi-a la carte: bkfst $2.95-$5.25, lunch, dinner $6-$12.50. Specialties: cheese fondue, vol au vent, quiche Lorraine. Tea rm/candy/pastry shop. Swiss decor. Family-owned. Cr cds: MC, V.

D

Salt Lake City

Founded: 1847
Pop: 159,936
Elev: 4,330 feet
Time zone: Mountain
Area code: 801
Web: www.saltlake.org

Salt Lake City has been called a living monument to the invincibility of the human spirit. Once a desert wilderness, it was built by settlers who sought refuge from religious persecution. Neither the barrenness of the land, drought, a plague of crickets nor the surge of empire to the west that passed through and engulfed their Zion swerved the Mormons from their purpose.

Brigham Young brought the first group of Mormons over the Wasatch Mountains to central Utah in 1847. The city these people built was planned and laid out on a spacious scale, with 132-foot-wide streets and 10-acre blocks. Trees were planted, and despite many obstacles, these industrious and dedicated people succeeded in making their dream come true. In 1869, the completion of the transcontinental railroad helped boost the economy of the Salt Lake City area. During the late 1800s and early 1900s, copper, lead and silver mining in several nearby canyons created great wealth for the city. Between 1900 and 1930 the population of Salt Lake City almost tripled, growing from 53,531 to 140,267. World War II intensified the importance of mining and refining.

In the 1960s, to help counteract the movement away from the city to the suburbs, the Mormon Church invested $40 million in the development of a downtown shopping mall—the ZCMI (Zion's Cooperative Mercantile Institution) Shopping Center. Encouraged by the success of ZCMI, the downtown area expanded rapidly. New business, several shopping malls, the renovation of historic buildings and city-wide beautification projects revitalized the downtown community.

Business

More than 480,000 persons are employed in Salt Lake County. The service industry is the largest sector, followed by trade, government jobs and manufacturing.

Approximately 3,000 manufacturing plants employ some 55,000 people in the production of chemicals, electronics, food and metal products, petroleum and steel.

Salt Lake City is the major banking center for the surrounding geographic area.

An important natural resource is the nearby mountains, where ski areas, an important part of the tourism industry, have been developed.

Convention Facilities

The Salt Palace has 256,000 square feet of exhibit space and banquet facilities. It can seat 10,000 people for meetings, and it is within walking distance of more than 5,000 hotel rooms.

The ballroom, with 36,000 square feet of floor space, has a seating capacity of 4,000 or a dining capacity of 3,500. There are five flexible meeting areas that can be arranged to accommodate from 30 to 1,800 people.

Sports & Recreation

Sports fans can watch professional IHL hockey (Utah Grizzlies) and professional basketball (Utah Jazz) in the Delta Center, downtown, as well as college football and basketball.

The area around Salt Lake City offers unlimited opportunities for the sports activist—superb hunting and fishing, camping, picnicking and hiking in nearby mountains and canyons.

Some skiers call the snow that covers the Wasatch Mountains "the greatest snow on Earth." It is deep and powdery and lasts from November to May. In winter this scenery forms a breathtaking backdrop for unparalleled skiing. Within a 30-mile drive east and southeast of Salt Lake City are seven major ski resorts; Park City, Wolf Mountain and Deer Valley up Parley's Canyon, Solitude and Brighton up Big Cottonwood Canyon and Snowbird and Alta ski resorts in Little Cottonwood Canyon are destinations for thousands of skiers each year.

The Great Salt Lake, which is five times as salty as any ocean, is 16 miles west of the city and offers sailing and swimming. Its white beaches, marshes and bays are inhabited by countless species of waterfowl and upland game birds.

Entertainment

Music has been an important element in Utah life since the first Mormon settlers arrived, bringing their musical instruments with them. The Utah Symphony Orchestra, which has made lengthy and successful tours of Europe and Latin America, regularly performs from September to April in Symphony Hall. The orchestra tours the western states annually.

The Mormon Tabernacle Choir, one of the best-known choral groups in the world, admits the public free of charge to its Sunday morning radio performances and Thursday evening rehearsals. Both the Salt Lake Oratorio Society and the Utah Opera Company present additional concerts.

Ballet West and the Utah Repertory Dance Theatre (RDT), made up of artists-in-residence at the University of Utah, both present dance performances at the restored Capitol Theatre (1913). The University of Utah is one of the nation's few institutions of higher learning to grant a degree in ballet. The Ririe-Woodbury Dance Company, a nationally acclaimed modern dance group that weds multimedia with the choreographic arts, is also showcased in the Capitol Theatre.

Historical Areas

Trolley Square, a registered state historic site, is a renovation of the site used for a territorial fairgrounds at the turn of the century, and later for trolley barns and repair shops. More than 100 shops, markets, restaurants and entertainment spots are busily operating in the remodeled trolley barn. The square is complete with converted trolleys, brick-paved streets, wrought-iron balconies, and stained-glass and ornamental staircases rescued from old Salt Lake mansions.

Another restoration area is Arrow Press Square, where three vintage buildings—the Arrow Press Building (1890), the Upland Hotel (1910) and the Midwest Office Building (1910)—have been gutted, stripped, scrubbed and reshaped into a complex of retail establishments.

For an introduction to the history of the Mormons, the Visitor Centers on Temple Square have information and exhibits. Free daily guided tours of Temple Square are conducted every 15 minutes. The Temple, built in 1867, is open only to Mormons, but other buildings and sites on the square are open to the public. The famous Tabernacle, completed in 1867, has an elongated dome roof with a simple exterior design; its great organ is fitted with 11,000 pipes. The 1882 Assembly Hall and the Lion House and Beehive House are included in the tour. The two houses were residences and offices for Brigham Young, 19 of his wives and 56 children. Also on the square is the Sea Gull Monument, erected in 1913 to commemorate the saving of crops in 1848 from a plague of crickets.

Sightseeing

Few cities can rival Salt Lake City for surrounding natural beauty and variety. The Salt Lake Convention and Visitors Bureau provides many pamphlets and brochures that introduce visitors to the city and the state. Information may also be obtained at Visitor Information Centers, located in Trolley Square, the Delta Terminal building at Salt Lake International Airport, the Utah Travel Council in Council Hall (Old City Hall) and the Salt Palace.

Within the city proper are Hansen Planetarium, with its space science library; Hogle Zoological Garden, with wildlife exhibits; the "This is the Place" monument, opposite the zoo; University of Utah's Red Butte Arboretum, Museum of Natural History and Museum of Fine Arts; and Salt Lake Art Center, with changing exhibitions of Utah art. Pioneer history is memorialized at the state capitol and the Pioneer Memorial Museum.

The Great Salt Lake is 48 miles wide and 92 miles long. Between the lake and the Nevada border are the Bonneville Salt Flats, an incomparable expanse covering more than 200 square miles. The flats were formed when the ancient and gigantic Lake Bonneville receded to the present Great Salt Lake, leaving behind salt beds in its lowest area. Early in this century racers discovered the salt flats to be an ideal place to race automobiles. From late August through September, races between world-speed-record jet cars are held on 12- to 14-mile tracks. During the Bonneville National Speed Trials, the tracks are used by hot rods, motorcycles, drag racers and all types of powerful automobiles attempting to set new records in their class.

Six canyons slice through the Wasatch range of the Rocky Mountains, which rims the city limits. In addition to providing unparalleled skiing, the canyons promenade some of the most spectacular scenery in the West. Aerial trams and gondolas offer summertime rides to the 11,000-foot Hidden Peak, providing riders with a view of mountain peaks including Timpanogos, Lone Peak and the Pfeifferhorn.

Many of Utah's national parks and monuments are located in the southern portion of the state and are approximately a day's drive from Salt Lake City. Timpanogos Cave National Monument, perhaps the most colorful and least developed area, is the closest to the city. Timpanogos is approximately 35 miles southeast, between Salt Lake City and Provo. The national parks include Arches, approximately 235 miles southeast, near Moab; Canyonlands, approximately 245 miles southeast, near Moab; Capitol Reef, approximately 230 miles south, near Loa; Bryce Canyon, about 270 miles south, near Panguitch; and Zion, approximately 320 miles south, near St George.

Utah's national monuments include Dinosaur, approximately 195 miles east, near Vernal; Hovenweep, approximately 350 miles southeast, near Blanding; Cedar Breaks, roughly 260 miles south, near Cedar City; Natural Bridges, approximately 330 miles southeast, near Blanding; and Rainbow Bridge, about 435 miles southeast, near Page, Arizona. The national parks and monuments are filled with natural stone arches, columnns, bridges, spires and precipices.

The national recreation areas in Utah are Flaming Gorge, approximately 220 miles east, on the Utah-Wyoming border, and Glen Canyon, approximately 430 miles southeast, at the Utah-Arizona border. Flaming Gorge forms a 91-mile lake surrounded by vertical cliffs, forested mountains and clear streams.

General References

Area code: 801

Phone Numbers

POLICE & FIRE: 911

POISON CONTROL CENTER: 581-2151

TIME & WEATHER: 486-8463

Information Sources

Salt Lake Convention & Visitors Bureau, 90 S West Temple St, 84101-1406; 534-4973 or 534-4901.

Utah Travel Council and Visitor Information Center, Council Hall, 300 N State St, 84114; 538-1467.

Visitor Information Center, Terminal 2, Salt Lake City International Airport, 84116; 575-2400 or -2401.

Parks Department, 972-7800.

Transportation

AIRLINES: Alaska Air; Alpine Air; American; America West; Continental; Delta; Horizon; Northwest; TWA; United; and other commuter and regional airlines.

AIRPORT: Salt Lake City International, 575-2400.

CAR RENTAL AGENCIES: (See IMPORTANT TOLL-FREE NUMBERS) Agency 534-1622; Alamo 575-2211; Avis 575-2847; Budget 363-1500; Dollar 575-2580; Hertz 575-2683; National 575-2277.

PUBLIC TRANSPORTATION: Utah Transit Authority 287-4636.

RAILROAD PASSENGER SERVICE: Amtrak 800/872-7245.

Newspapers

Salt Lake City Deseret News; Salt Lake City Tribune.

Convention Facility

Salt Palace, 100 S West Temple, 534-4777.

Sports & Recreation

Major Sports Facility

Delta Center, 301 S West Temple, 325-SEAT (Utah Jazz, basketball, 325-2500; Utah Grizzlies, hockey, 325-PUCK).

Cultural Facilities

Theaters

Capitol Theatre, 50 W 200 South St, 355-2787.

Hale Center Theatre, 2801 S Main St, 484-9257.

Kingsbury Hall, University of Utah, 581-7100.

Pioneer Memorial Theatre, 300 South St at University, 581-6961.

Promised Valley Playhouse, 132 S State St, 364-5696.

Salt Lake Acting Company, 168 W 500 North St, 363-7522.

Concert Hall

Maurice Abravanel Hall, 123 W South Temple St, 533-6407.

Museums

Fort Douglas Military Museum, 3 mi NE, Bldg 32, Potter St, 588-5188.

Hansen Planetarium, 15 S State St, 538-2098.

Museum of Church History and Art, 45 N West Temple St, 240-3310.

Pioneer Memorial Museum, 300 N Main St, 538-1050.

Utah Museum of Natural History, University of Utah, 581-4303.

Art Museums

Salt Lake Art Center, 20 S West Temple St, 328-4201.

Utah Museum of Fine Arts, University of Utah, 581-7332.

Points of Interest

Historical

Assembly Hall, SW corner of Temple Square.

Brigham Young Monument, Main & South Temple Sts.

Council Hall, Capitol Hill, 538-1030.

Governor's Mansion, 603 E South Temple St, 538-1005.

Lion House & Beehive House, 67 & 63 E South Temple Sts, 363-5466 (Lion) or 240-2671 (Beehive).

Tabernacle, Temple Square.

Temple Square, bounded by North, South & West Temple Sts & Main St, 240-2534.

Other Attractions

Hogle Zoological Garden, 2600 Sunnyside Ave, 582-1631.

Kennecott Bingham Canyon Mine, 25 mi SW on UT 48, 322-7300.

Lagoon Amusement Park, Pioneer Village and Water Park, 17 mi N on I-15, 451-8000.

Marriott Library, University of Utah, 581-8558.

Old Deseret Pioneer Village, Pioneer Trail State Park, 584-8392.

This Is The Place State Park, 2601 Sunnyside Ave, 584-8392.

Seagull Monument, Temple Square.

State Capitol, 300 N State St, 538-3000.

Timpanogos Cave National Monument, 26 mi S on I-15, then 10 mi E on UT 92, 756-5238 or 756-5239.

Trolley Square, bounded by 500 & 600 South Sts and 600 & 700 East Sts, 521-9877.

Wasatch-Cache National Forest, E & N of city, 524-5030.

ZCMI (Zion's Cooperative Mercantile Institution) Shopping Center, Main & South Temple Sts, 321-8743.

Sightseeing Tours

Gray Line bus tours, 553 W 100 South St, 84101; 521-7060.

Scenic West Tours, PO Box 369, Draper 84020; 572-2717 or 800/723-6429.

Annual Events

Utah Arts Festival, downtown. Last wk June.

"Days of '47" Celebration. Mid-July.

Utah State Fair, State Fairgrounds. Sept 3-13.

Temple Square Christmas, 240-2534. Early Dec.

City Neighborhoods

Many of the restaurants, unrated dining establishments and some lodgings listed under Salt Lake City include neighborhoods as well as exact street addresses. Geographic descriptions of Downtown and Trolley Square are given, followed by a table of restaurants arranged by neighborhood.

Downtown: South of 9th Ave, west of A St and 300 East St, north of 700 South St and east of 400 West St. **East of Downtown:** East of 300 East St.

Trolley Square: South of 500 South St, west of 700 East St, north of 600 South St and east of 600 East St.

Lodgings and Food

SALT LAKE CITY RESTAURANTS BY NEIGHBORHOOD AREAS

(For full description, see alphabetical listings under Restaurants)

DOWNTOWN
Baba Afghan. 55 E 400 S
Baci Trattoria. 134 W Pierpont Ave
Benihana Of Tokyo. 165 S West Temple St
Buffalo Joe's Smokehouse. 5927 S State St
Cafe Bacchus. 358 S West Temple
Cafe Dell àrte. 22 E 100 S
Desert Edge Brewery. 273 Trolley Sq
Litza's For Pizza. 716 E 400 South St
Market Street Grill. 48 Market St
Mikado. 67 West 100 South St
The New Yorker. 60 W Market St
Piña. 327 W 200 South
Pierpont Cantina. 122 W Pierpont Ave
Pomodoro. 2440 E Ft Union Blvd
Rio Grande Cafe. 270 S Rio Grande St
Ristorante Della Fontana. 336 S 400 East St
Salt Lake Brewing Co. 367 W 200 S
Tucci's. 4835 S Highland Dr

EAST OF DOWNTOWN
Cowboy Grub. 2350 1/2 Foothill Blvd
Helen's. 6055 S 900 East
Hungry I. 1440 S Foothill Blvd
Log Haven. 6451 E 3800 S
Market Street Broiler. 258 South 1300 East
Old Salt City Jail. 460 South 1000 East
Redbones. 2207 S 700 East St
Rino's Italian Ristorante. 2302 Parleys Way
Tuscany. 2832 E 6200 S

Note: When a listing is located in a town that does not have its own city heading, it will appear under the city nearest to its location. In these cases, the address and town appear in parenthesis immediately following the name of the establishment.

Motels

(Rates may be higher during state fair)

★ ★ **BEST WESTERN EXECUTIVE INN.** *(280 West 7200 South, Midvale 84047) 8 mi S on I-15, exit 301. 801/566-4141; FAX 801/566-5142.* Web www.travelweb.com/thisco/bw/45063/45063_. 92 rms, 2 story. Late Dec-Mar: S $69-$79; D $79-$89; each addl $5; suites $79-$149; under 18 free; lower rates rest of yr. Crib $6. TV; cable. Heated pool; whirlpool. Complimentary coffee in lobby. Restaurant adj 6 am-midnight. Ck-out noon. Meeting rms. Business servs avail. In-rm modem link. Downhill ski 15 mi; x-country ski 20 mi. Health club privileges. Many refrigerators; microwaves avail. Balconies. Cr cds: A, C, D, DS, ER, JCB, MC, V.

SC

★ **BRIGHTON LODGE.** *(Big Cottonwood Canyon, Brighton 84121) Approx 15 mi W via UT 190. 801/532-4731; FAX 801/649-1787; res: 800/873-5512, ext. 236 (exc UT).* 22 rms, 2 story. Mid-Nov-mid-Apr: S, D $50-$120; lower rates rest of yr. TV rm. Heated pool; whirlpool. Restaurant adj 8 am-10 pm; Sun to 4:30 pm. Bar. Ck-out 11 am. Shopping arcade. Downhill/x-country ski on site. Refrigerators. Picnic tables, grills. On creek. Cr cds: A, DS, MC, V.

SC

★ ★ **COMFORT INN.** *(8955 South 255 West, Sandy 84070) south of downtown. 801/255-4919; FAX 801/255-4998.* 98 rms, 2 story. S,D $60-$135; each addl $5; under 18 free. Crib free. TV; cable (premium), VCR (movies $4). Indoor pool; whirlpool. Complimentary continental bkfst. Ck-out noon. Meeting rm. Business servs avail. In-rm modem links. Game rm. Cr cds: A, C, D, DS, JCB, MC, V.

SC

★ ★ **COURTYARD BY MARRIOTT.** *(10701 Holiday Park Dr, Sandy 84070) 15 mi S on I-15, exit 297. 801/571-3600; FAX 801/572-1383.* Web /www.courtyard.com. 124 rms, 4 story. S $79-$95; D $89-$105; each addl $10; suites $135-$145; under 18 free; ski plan; wkend, hol rates. Crib free. TV; cable (premium). Indoor pool; whirlpool. Complimentary coffee in rms. Restaurant 6:30-10:30 am, 5-10 pm. Rm serv. Bar 5-10 pm. Ck-out noon. Coin Indry. Meeting rms. Business servs avail. Downhill/x-country ski 12 mi. Exercise equipt; weight machine, treadmill. Microwaves avail. Some balconies. Cr cds: A, C, D, DS, MC, V.

D SC

✔★ **DAYS INN AIRPORT.** *1900 W North Temple St (84116), west of downtown. 801/539-8538.* 110 rms, 2 story. S, D $58-$105; each addl $7; suites $98-$125; under 12 free. Crib free. Pet accepted. TV; cable (premium). Complimentary continental bkfst. Restaurant nearby. Ck-out 11 am. Business servs avail. In-rm modem link. Valet serv. Free airport, RR station, bus depot transportation. Health club privileges. Microwaves avail. Cr cds: A, C, D, DS, JCB, MC, V.

D SC

★ ★ **HAMPTON INN.** *(2393 S 800 W, Woods Cross 84087) 801/296-1211; FAX 801/296-1222.* 60 rms, 3 story. S, D $71-$79; suites $125-$160; under 18 free. Crib free. Pet accepted. TV; cable (premium). Indoor pool; whirlpool. Complimentary continental bkfst. Restaurant nearby. Ck-out noon. Meeting rms. Business servs avail. In-rm modem link. Coin Indry. Free airport transportation. Health club privileges. Microwaves avail. Cr cds: A, C, D, DS, MC, V.

D SC

★ ★ **HAMPTON INN.** *(10690 S Holiday Park Dr, Sandy 84070) S via I-15, exit 10600 South St, then 1/2 blk E. 801/571-0800.* Web www.hamptoninn.com. 131 rms, 4 story. S,D $78-$88; under 18 free; wkly rates, ski plans. Crib free. TV; cable (premium). Indoor pool; whirlpool. Complimentary continental bkfst. Restaurant adj 6 am-11 pm. Ck-out noon. Coin Indry. Meeting rms. Business servs avail. In-rm modem links. Sundries. Free bus depot transportation. Downhill ski 14 mi. Health club privileges. Microwaves avail. Shopping center opp. Cr cds: A, D, DS, MC, V.

D SC

✔★ ★ **LA QUINTA.** *(530 Catalpa Rd, Midvale 84047) 8 mi S on I-15, 72nd South St exit, E to Catalpa Rd. 801/566-3291; FAX 801/562-5943.* 122 rms, 2 story. S $75; D $83; each addl $8; under 18 free. Crib free. Pet accepted. TV; cable (premium). Heated pool. Continental bkfst. Complimentary coffee in lobby. Restaurant adj open 24 hrs. Ck-out noon. Coin Indry. Business servs avail. In-rm modem link. Downhill ski 15 mi; x-country ski 20 mi. Health club privileges. Microwaves avail. Cr cds: A, C, D, DS, MC, V.

D SC

★ ★ **QUALITY INN-MIDVALLEY.** *4465 Century Dr (84123), south of downtown. 801/268-2533; FAX 801/266-6206.* 132 rms, 2 story. Feb-Mar, July-Sept: S $69-$89; D $79-$109; under 18 free; ski plan; lower rates rest of yr. Crib free. TV; cable (premium). Pool; whirlpool. Complimentary continental bkfst. Restaurant adj open 24 hrs. Ck-out noon. Coin Indry. Business servs avail. In-rm modem link. Airport transportation. Balconies. Cr cds: A, C, D, DS, ER, JCB, MC, V.

D SC

★ **RAMADA INN-DOWNTOWN.** *230 West 600 South (84102), downtown. 801/364-5200; FAX 801/364-0974.* Web www.accommidations.com. 160 rms, 2 story. S, D $59-$79; each addl $10; under 19 free. Crib free. Pet accepted; some restrictions; $10 deposit. TV; cable. Indoor pool; whirlpool. Restaurant 6:00 am-10 pm; Sun 6:30 am-9 pm. Rm serv. Private club from 5 pm. Ck-out noon. Coin Indry. Meeting rms. Business servs avail. In-rm modem links. Valet serv. Free airport, RR station, bus depot transportation. Exercise equipt; weight machine, bicycles, sauna. Game rm. Rec rm. Microwaves avail. Cr cds: A, C, D, DS, MC, V.

D SC

★★ **RESIDENCE INN BY MARRIOTT.** *765 East 400 South (84102), east of downtown. 801/532-5511; FAX 801/531-0416.* 128 kit. suites (1-2-bedrm), 2 story. Suites $159-$199; wkly, monthly rates; ski packages. Pet accepted. TV; cable (premium), VCR avail (movies). Heated pool. Complimentary continental bkfst. Ck-out noon. Coin Indry. Business servs avail. In-rm modem link. Bellhops. Valet serv. Free airport, RR station, bus depot transportation. Exercise equipt; weights, stair machine. Microwaves; many fireplaces. Sport court. Cr cds: A, C, D, DS, JCB, MC, V.

D SC

★ **SLEEP INN.** *(10676 South 300 West, South Jordan 84095) S on I-15, exit 10600 South, then 1/2 blk W. 801/572-2020; FAX 801/572-2459; res: 800/221-2222.* E-mail sleep-saltlake@travelbase.com. 68 rms, shower only, 2 story. S $59-$69; D $65-$75; each addl $5; family rates. Crib free. TV; cable (premium), VCR (movies). Indoor pool. Complimentary continental bkfst. Coffee in lobby. Restaurant nearby. Ck-out noon. Coin Indry. Business servs avail. In-rm modem link. Downhill ski 20 mi. Cr cds: A, C, D, DS, ER, JCB, MC, V.

D SC

★ **TRAVELODGE CITY CENTER.** *524 S West Temple (84101). 801/531-7100; FAX 801/359-3814.* 60 rms, 3 story. S $50-72; D $58-$75; each addl $6; under 18 free; ski plan. Crib free. Pet accepted; deposit. TV; cable (premium). Heated pool; whirlpool. Complimentary coffee in rms. Restaurant nearby. Ck-out noon. Business servs avail. Cr cds: A, C, D, DS, MC, V.

SC

Motor Hotels

★★ **BEST WESTERN-SALT LAKE PLAZA.** *122 W South Temple St (84101), downtown. 801/521-0130; FAX 801/322-5057; res: 800/366-3684.* E-mail sales@plaza-hotel.com; web www.plaza-hotel.com. 226 rms, 13 story. S $89-$129; D $99-$149; each addl $10; suites $265; under 18 free. Crib free. Pet accepted; $10. TV; cable (premium), VCR avail. Heated pool; whirlpool. Restaurant 6 am-11 pm. Rm serv. Ck-out 11 am. Lndry facilities. Meeting rms. Business servs avail. In-rm modem link. Bellhops. Gift shop. Free airport, RR station, bus depot transportation. Exercise equipt; bicycles, stair machine. Some refrigerators. Cr cds: A, C, D, DS, ER, JCB, MC, V.

D SC

★★ **COMFORT INN.** *200 N Admiral Byrd Rd (84116), in Salt Lake Intl Center, near Intl Airport, west of downtown. 801/537-7444; FAX 801/532-4721.* 154 rms, 4 story. S, D $69-$129; each addl $10; under 18 free. Crib free. Pet accepted; $25 deposit. TV. Heated pool; whirlpool. Restaurant 6 am-midnight. Rm serv. Ck-out 11 am. Meeting rms. Business servs avail. Valet serv. Free airport transportation. Some refrigerators; microwaves avail. Balconies. Cr cds: A, DS, MC, V.

D SC

★★ **CRYSTAL INN.** *230 W 500 South (84101). 801/328-4466; FAX 801/328-4072; res: 800/366-4466.* 175 rms, 4 story. S, D $100-$150; each addl $10; under 16 free; ski plan. Crib free. TV; cable. Indoor pool; whirlpool. Complimentary full bkfst. Restaurant adj open 24 hrs. Ck-out noon. Coin Indry. Meeting rms. Business servs avail. In-rm modem link. Sundries. Valet serv. Free airport transportation. Exercise equipt; treadmill, stair machine, sauna. Refrigerators, microwaves. Cr cds: A, C, D, DS, JCB, MC, V.

D SC

★★★ **HOLIDAY INN-DOWNTOWN.** *999 S Main St (84111), south of downtown. 801/359-8600; FAX 801/359-7186.* 292 rms, 3 story, 14 suites. S, D $98-$179; each addl $10; under 18 free; ski plans. Crib free. TV; cable. Indoor/outdoor pool; whirlpool. Playground. Restaurants 6 am-2 pm, 5-10 pm. Rm serv. Bar. Ck-out noon. Coin Indry. Convention facilities. Business center. Bellhops. Gift shop. Free airport, RR station, bus depot transportation. Tennis. Putting green. Exercise equipt; weight machine, bicycle, sauna. Lawn games. Some refrigerators; wet bar in suites. Cr cds: A, C, D, DS, JCB, MC, V.

D SC

★★★ **RADISSON AIRPORT.** *2177 W N Temple St (84116), near Intl Airport, west of downtown. 801/364-5800; FAX 801/364-5823.* E-mail said@radisson.com; web www.radisson.com. 127 rms, 3 story, 46 suites. S $79-$159; D $89-$169; each addl $10; suites $109-$159; under 18 free; ski, golf plans. Crib free. TV; cable (premium). Heated pool. Complimentary continental bkfst. Complimentary coffee in rms. Restaurant 6:30-10 am, 11:30 am-2 pm, 5-10 pm; Sat, Sun 6:30-11 am. Rm serv. Ck-out noon. Meeting rms. Business servs avail. Bellhops. Free garage parking. Free airport, RR station, bus depot transportation. Exercise equipt; bicycles, stair machine. Bathrm phones, refrigerators, wet bars; some fireplaces; microwaves avail. Balconies. Cr cds: A, C, D, DS, ER, JCB, MC, V.

D SC

Hotels

★★ **BEST WESTERN OLYMPUS.** *161 West 600 South (84101), downtown. 801/521-7373; FAX 801/524-0354.* 393 rms, 13 story. S, D $109-$160; suites $250; under 18 free; wkend rates; ski plan. Crib free. TV; cable. Pool; whirlpool. Restaurant 6 am-midnight. Ck-out noon. Convention facilities. Business servs avail. Barber. Free airport transportation. Exercise equipt; bicycles, stair machine. Some refrigerators; microwaves avail. Balconies. Cr cds: A, C, D, DS, ER, JCB, MC, V.

D SC

★★★ **DOUBLETREE.** *255 S West Temple St (84101), downtown. 801/328-2000; FAX 801/532-1953.* 500 rms, 18 story. S, D $129-$160; each addl $20; suites $200-$500; under 18 free; wkend rates; ski package. Crib free. TV; VCR avail. Indoor pool; whirlpool, poolside serv. Complimentary coffee in rms. Restaurant 6 am-11 pm. Private club; entertainment. Ck-out noon. Convention facilities. Business center. In-rm modem link. Concierge. Gift shop. Covered parking; valet. Free airport, RR station, bus depot transportation. Exercise equipt; weights, bicycles, sauna. Some refrigerators. Luxury level. Cr cds: A, C, D, DS, ER, JCB, MC, V.

D SC

★★★ **EMBASSY SUITES.** *110 West 600 South (84101), downtown. 801/359-7800; FAX 801/359-3753.* 241 suites, 9 story. S $139-$149; D $151-$161; each addl $15; under 12 free; wkend, ski rates. Crib free. TV; cable (premium). Indoor pool; whirlpool. Complimentary full bkfst. Complimentary coffee in rms. Restaurant 11 am-11 pm. Private club to 1 am. Ck-out noon. Coin Indry. Meeting rms. Business center. In-rm modem link. Gift shop. Covered parking. Free airport, RR station, bus depot transportation. Exercise equipt; bicycles, stair machine, sauna. Refrigerators, wet bars, microwaves. Atrium lobby. Cr cds: A, C, D, DS, ER, JCB, MC, V.

D SC

★★★ **HILTON.** *150 W 500 South St (84101), downtown. 801/532-3344; FAX 801/531-0705.* 351 rms, 10 story. S, D $119-$189; each addl $20; suites $159-$350; family rates; ski plans. Crib free. Pet accepted, some restrictions; $50 deposit. TV; cable (premium), VCR avail. Pool; whirlpool, poolside serv. Restaurant 6 am-11:30 pm. Private club 11:30 am-midnight, Sun 5-10 pm; entertainment. Ck-out noon. Convention facilities. Business center. In-rm modem link. Barber, beauty shop. Free airport transportation. Exercise equipt; weight machine, bicycles, sauna. Health club privileges. Ski rentals avail. Balconies. Luxury level. Cr cds: A, C, D, DS, ER, JCB, MC, V.

D SC

✔★★★ **LITTLE AMERICA.** *500 S Main St (84101), downtown. 801/363-6781; FAX 801/596-5911; res: 800/453-9450 (exc UT), 800/662-5888 (UT).* E-mail lahinfo@lamerica.com; web www.lamerica.com. 850 rms, 17 story. S $75-$144; D $85-$154; suites $650; under 13 free. Crib free. TV; cable (premium). 2 pools, 1 indoo.; wading pool, whirlpool. Restaurant 5 am-midnight; dining rm 7-10 am, 11 am-2 pm, 5-11 pm. Bar noon-midnight; entertainment. Ck-out 1 pm. Convention facilities. Business servs avail. Barber, beauty shop. Free covered parking. Free airport, RR station, bus depot transportation. Exercise rm; instructor, weight machine, bicycles, sauna. Many bathrm phones, refrigerators. Garden setting on 10 acres. Cr cds: A, C, D, DS, MC, V.

D

★ ★ ★ **MARRIOTT.** *75 S West Temple St (84101), downtown. 801/531-0800; FAX 801/532-4127.* 515 rms, 15 story. S, D $129-$189; suites $250-$850; family rates; wkend, honeymoon, ski plans. Crib free. TV; cable (premium), VCR avail. Heated indoor/outdoor pool; whirlpool, poolside serv. Complimentary coffee in lobby. Restaurant 6:30 am-11 pm; Fri, Sat to midnight. Private club; entertainment. Ck-out noon. Coin lndry. Convention facilities. Business center. In-rm modem link. Concierge. Covered valet parking. Free airport, RR station, bus depot transportation. Exercise equipt; weights, bicycles, sauna. Balconies. Inside access to shopping mall. Luxury level. Cr cds: A, C, D, DS, ER, JCB, MC, V.

D SC

✔★ ★ **PEERY.** *110 West 300 South (84101), downtown. 801/521-4300; FAX 801/575-5014; res: 800/331-0073.* Web www.citysearchslc.peery. 77 rms, 3 story. S, D $89-$149; under 16 free; wkend rates. Crib free. TV; cable (premium). Whirlpool. Complimentary continental bkfst. Restaurant (see PEERY WASATCH PUB & BISTRO). Bar. Ck-out 11 am. Meeting rms. Business center. Concierge. Gift shop. Free airport transportation. Exercise equipt; weight machine, bicycles. Historic building (1910). Cr cds: A, C, D, DS, MC, V.

SC

★ ★ ★ **SHILO INN.** *206 S West Temple St (84101), downtown. 801/521-9500; FAX 801/359-6527.* 200 rms, 12 story. S, D $105-$129; each addl $12; suites $209-$400; under 12 free. Crib free. TV; cable (premium), VCR (movies $3). Heated pool; whirlpool. Complimentary full bkfst. Restaurant 6 am-10 pm. Ck-out noon. Coin lndry. Meeting rms. Business servs avail. Shopping arcade. Free airport transportation. Exercise equipt; weights, bicycle, sauna. Wet bars, refrigerators, microwaves; some bathrm phones. Cr cds: A, C, D, DS, MC, V.

D SC

★ ★ ★ **UNIVERSITY PARK & SUITES.** *480 Wakara Way (84108), east of downtown. 801/581-1000; FAX 801/583-7641; res: 800/637-4390.* Web www.uparkhotel.com. 220 rms, 7 story, 29 suites. S, D $125-$170; suites $145-$190; under 12 free. Crib free. TV; cable (premium). Indoor pool; whirlpool. Restaurant 6:30 am-10 pm. Bar 11 am-midnight. Ck-out noon. Meeting rms. Business center. Gift shop. Free airport, RR station, bus depot transportation. Downhill/x-country ski 15 mi. Exercise equipt; weight machine, stair machines. Rec rm. Refrigerators, wet bar; microwaves in suites. Cr cds: A, C, D, DS, MC, V.

D SC

★ ★ ★ **WYNDHAM.** *215 W South Temple St (84101), downtown. 801/531-7500; FAX 801/328-1289.* Web www.travelweb.com. 381 rms, 15 story. S, D $79-$179; each addl $10; suites $179-$550; under 18 free; wkend, hol rates; ski packages. TV; cable (premium). Indoor pool. Coffee in rms. Restaurant 6 am-10:30 pm. Bar 11 am-midnight. Ck-out noon; whirlpool. Coin lndry. Convention facilities. Business center. In-rm modem link. Concierge. Gift shop. Free airport, RR station transportation. Exercise equipt; stair machines, bicycles, sauna. Health club privileges. Microwaves avail. Adj to Delta Center. Cr cds: A, C, D, DS, ER, JCB, MC, V.

D SC

Inns

★ ★ ★ **ARMSTRONG MANSION.** *667 E 100 S (84102). 801/531-1333; FAX 801/531-0282; res: 800/708-1333.* E-mail armstrong@vii.mail.com; web www.armstrong-bb.com. 14 rms, 4 with shower only, 3 story. S, D $89-$209; suites $169-$229. TV; cable (premium); VCR. Complimentary full bkfst. Restaurant nearby. Ck-out 11 am, ck-in 3 pm. Luggage handling. Downhill/x-country ski 20 mi. Built in 1893; furnished with antiques. Totally nonsmoking. Cr cds: A, D, DS, MC, V.

SC

★ ★ ★ ★ **BRIGHAM STREET INN.** *1135 E South Temple St (84102), 2 mi E of Main St, east of downtown. 801/364-4461; res: 800/417-4461; FAX 801/521-3201.* Rooms are individually decorated in this restored Victorian mansion. 9 rms, 3 story. S, D $85-$185; each addl $10. Crib free. TV; cable, VCR avail. Complimentary continental bkfst. Setups. Ck-out 11 am, ck-in 3 pm. Business servs avail. X-country ski 15 mi. Fireplace in 5 rms. Cr cds: A, MC, V.

★ ★ ★ **INN AT TEMPLE SQUARE.** *71 W S Temple St (84101), downtown. 801/531-1000; FAX 801/536-7272; res: 800/843-4668.* Web www.theinn.com. 90 rms, 7 story, 10 suites. S, D $125-$145; each addl $10; suites $165-$240; under 18 free. Crib free. TV; cable, VCR avail. Pool privileges. Complimentary continental bkfst. Dining rm 6:30-9:30 am, 11:30 am-2:30 pm, 5-10 pm. Rm serv. Ck-out noon, ck-in 3 pm. Business servs avail. Bellhops. Valet serv. Concierge. Free airport, RR station, bus depot transportation. Health club privileges. Bathrm phones, refrigerators. Elegant inn built in 1929; antiques from old Hotel Utah. Opp Temple Square. Totally nonsmoking. Cr cds: A, C, D, DS, MC, V.

D SC

★ ★ ★ **SALTAIR BED & BREAKFAST.** *164 S 900 E (84102), east of downtown. 801/533-8184; res: 800/733-8184; FAX 801/595-0332.* E-mail saltair@travelbase.com; web travelbase.com/destinations/salt-lake-city/saltair/. 8 rms, 3 shared baths, 2 with shower only, 2 story, 3 suites. Some rm phones. S $55-$60; D $75-$105; each addl $15; suites $129-$225. Children over 12 yrs only. TV in some rms; cable (premium), VCR avail (movies). Complimentary full bkfst; afternoon refreshments. Restaurant nearby. Ck-out 11 am, ck-in 3:30 pm. X-country ski 15 mi. Health club privileges. Whirlpool. Some refrigerators, microwaves, fireplaces. Built in 1870; antiques. Totally nonsmoking. Cr cds: A, DS, MC, V.

SC

✔★ ★ **SPRUCES INN.** *6151 South 900 East (84121), south of downtown. 801/268-8762; res: 800/820-8762.* 4 rms, 1 air-cooled, 2 story, 2 kit. units. S, D $65-$175; under 12 free. TV. Complimentary full bkfst. Restaurant nearby. Ck-out 11 am, ck-in 2 pm. Business servs avail. Downhill/x-country ski 15 mi. Balconies. Picnic tables. Surrounded by spruce trees. Built in 1902 by a Norwegian carpenter; folk art and Southwestern decor. Totally nonsmoking. Cr cds: A, DS, MC, V.

SC

★ ★ **WILDFLOWERS BED & BREAKFAST.** *936 E 1700 S (84105). 801/466-0600; res: 800/569-0009; FAX 801/466-4728.* E-mail lark2spur@aol.com. 5 rms, 3 story. No elvtr. S $80-$97; D $85-$107; kit. unit $130-$160; under 12 free. Crib free. Complimentary continental bkfst. Restaurant nearby. Ck-out 11 am, ck-in 4 pm. Built in 1891; furnished with antiques. Totally nonsmoking. Cr cds: A, DS, MC, V.

SC

Restaurants

✔★ ★ **BABA AFGHAN.** *55 E 400 S (84111), downtown. 801/596-0786.* Hrs: 11:30 am-2:30 pm, 5-9:30 pm; Mon to 2:30 pm; Sat, Sun from 5 pm. Closed some hols. Res accepted (dinner). Afghan menu. Lunch buffet $6.50. Semi-a la carte: dinner $7.95-$14.95. Specializes in lamb, beef, chicken. Own baking. Street parking. Afgahni clothing display. Totally nonsmoking. Cr cds: A, D, DS, MC, V.

D

★ ★ **BACI TRATTORIA.** *134 W Pierpont Ave, downtown. 801/328-1500.* Web www.gastronomy.com. Hrs: 11:30 am-3 pm, 5-10 pm; Fri, Sat to 11 pm; Sun 5-10 pm. Closed major hols; also July 24. Italian menu. Bar. A la carte entrees: lunch $6.99-$16.99, dinner $7.99-$26.99. Specializes in fresh pasta, fresh seafood. Outdoor dining (summer). Large stained-glass partitions. Wood-burning pizza oven. Cr cds: A, D, DS, MC, V.

D

★★ **BENIHANA OF TOKYO.** *165 S West Temple St, Salt Lake Convention Center, on Arrow Press Sq, downtown. 801/322-2421.* Hrs: 11:30 am-2 pm, 5-9:30 pm; Fri, Sat 5-10:30 pm; Sun, hols to 9 pm. Res accepted. Japanese menu. Bar. Semi-a la carte: lunch $5.50-$14, dinner $12.50-$27. Child's meals. Specializes in seafood, steak, chicken. Tableside cooking. Japanese decor. Cr cds: A, C, D, DS, MC, V.

D

✔★ **BUFFALO JOE'S SMOKEHOUSE.** *5927 S State St (84107), downtown. 801/261-3537.* Hrs: 11 am-10 pm; Sat to 10:30 pm; Sun noon-9:30 pm; early-bird dinner 4-6 pm. Closed Thanksgiving, Dec 25. Bar. Semi-a la carte: lunch $5-$8, dinner $8-$16. Child's meals. Specializes in steak, ribs, chicken. Outdoor dining. Casual, Texas-barbecue atmosphere. Totally nonsmoking. Cr cds: A, DS, MC, V.

★★ **CAFE BACCHUS.** *358 S West Temple (84101), downtown. 801/532-1055.* E-mail Garry-7@msn.com. Hrs: 11 am-10 pm; Sat 5:30-10 pm. Closed Sun, major hols. Res accepted. Bar. Semi-a la carte: lunch $5-$9, dinner $9-$18. Specializes in Chilean sea bass, rack of lamb, pasta. Parking. Local art. Totally nonsmoking. Cr cds: A, D, DS, MC, V.

D

★★ **CAFE DELL ÀRTE.** *22 E 100 S (84111), downtown. 801/363-2218.* Hrs: 7 am-10 pm; Mon, Tues to 3 pm. Closed Sun; some major hols. Res accepted. Contemporary Amer menu. Bar. Semi-a la carte: bkfst $3.50-$5.50, lunch $4-$7, dinner $9-$18. Specializes in homemade bkfst breads, pasta, Asian dishes. Own baking, pasta. 100-yr-old brownstone bldg with picture window overlooking downtown. Totally nonsmoking. Cr cds: A, C, D, DS, MC, V.

D

✔★ **COWBOY GRUB.** *2350½ Foothill Blvd (84109), I-80 to Foothill Dr, exit N, east of downtown. 801/466-8334.* E-mail summi@ix.netcom.com. Hrs: 11 am-10 pm; Fri, Sat to 11 pm. Closed Sun; major hols & July 24. Res accepted. Semi-a la carte: lunch, dinner $5-$15. Child's meals. Specializes in pot roast, Mexican dishes. Salad bar. Western decor. Cr cds: A, D, DS, MC, V.

D

★★ **CREEKSIDE.** *(12000 Big Cottonwood Canyon, Solitude 84121-0350) 20 mi E at Creekside Condominiums. 801/536-5787.* Hrs: 8 am-10 pm; Sat, Sun brunch 9 am-2 pm. Closed Mon & Tues in summer. Res accepted (dinner). No A/C. Continental menu. Bar. Semi-a la carte: bkfst $2-$10, lunch, dinner $4-$18. Sat, Sun brunch $5-$12. Child's meals. Specializes in fresh seafood, pasta, wood-burning dishes. Own pasta. Jazz Fri. Outdoor dining. Mediterranean decor; windows overlook pond, ski slopes. Totally nonsmoking. Cr cds: A, C, D, DS, MC, V.

D

✔★★ **DESERT EDGE BREWERY.** *273 Trolley Square (84102), downtown. 801/521-8917.* Hrs: 11 am-midnight; Thurs-Sat to 1 am; Sun noon-10 pm. Closed Dec 25. Contemporary Amer menu. Bar. Semi-a la carte: lunch, $2.25-$7.95, dinner $2.25-$10.95. Specializes in pastas, sandwiches, salads. Own pastas, beer. Outdoor dining. Informal, casual atmosphere; microbrewery. Cr cds: A, DS, MC, V.

★★ **HELEN'S.** *6055 S 900 East (84121), east of downtown. 801/265-0205.* Hrs: 11:30 am-10 pm; Sun 10 am-9 pm. Sun brunch to 2:30 pm. Res accepted. Continental menu. Wine, beer. Semi-a la carte: lunch $7-$9, dinner $8-$18. Sun brunch $6-$9. Specialties: potato-crusted salmon, blackberry brandy chicken, Viennese breaded pork. Outdoor dining. Country home atmosphere. Totally nonsmoking. Cr cds: A, D, DS, MC, V.

★★ **HUNGRY i.** *1440 S Foothill Blvd (84108), east of downtown. 801/582-8600.* Hrs: 11 am-3 pm, 5-10 pm; Sat noon-11 pm; Sun 9 am-9 pm; Sun brunch 10 am-3 pm. Closed Thanksgiving, Dec 25. Res accepted (dinner). Greek menu. Bar. Semi-a la carte: bkfst $4.95-$10.95, lunch $6.95-$11.95, dinner $11.95-$31.95. Lunch buffet $7.95. Sun brunch $11.99. Child's meals. Specialties: filet mignon, halibut, mousaka. Jazz pianist Fri, Sat. Valet parking. Outdoor dining. Cr cds: A, C, D, DS, ER, JCB, MC, V.

D

★★★ **LOG HAVEN.** *6451 E 3800 S (84109), 15 mi SE on I-215S, exit 3900 S to Millcreek Canyon, east of downtown. 801/272-8255.* Hrs: 5:30-9 pm; Sun 4-8 pm. Closed Jan 1, July 4, Dec 25. Res accepted. Continental menu. Bar. Extensive wine list. Semi-a la carte: dinner $14-$30. Child's meals. Specialties: seared rare ahi tuna, grilled black Angus filet mignon, sugar-cured Sonoma duck. Own baking. Valet parking. Outdoor dining. Renovated 1920 log mansion nestled among pine trees; views of waterfall, natural surroundings. Cr cds: A, C, D, DS, MC, V.

D

★★ **MARKET STREET BROILER.** *258 South 1300 East, east of downtown. 801/583-8808.* Web www.gastronomy.com. Hrs: 11 am-10 pm; Sun 4-9 pm; early-bird dinner 4-6 pm. Bar from noon. Semi-a la carte: lunch $4.99-$16.99, dinner $7.99-$29.99. Child's meals. Specializes in fresh fish, barbecued ribs. Outdoor dining. Modern decor in historic former fire station. Cr cds: A, C, D, DS, MC, V.

D

★★ **MARKET STREET GRILL.** *48 Market St (84101), downtown. 801/322-4668.* Hrs: 6:30 am-3 pm, 4-11 pm; Sat 7 am-3 pm; Fri, Sat to midnight; Sun 4-9:30 pm; early-bird dinner 5-7 pm; Sun brunch 9:30 am-3 pm. Closed Labor Day, Thanksgiving, Dec 25. Bar noon-11:30 pm. Semi-a la carte: bkfst $3.99-$7.99, lunch $5.99-$12.99, dinner $11.99-$29.99. Sun brunch $5.99-$12.99. Child's meals. Specializes in steak, seafood. In renovated 1906 hotel. Cr cds: A, C, D, DS, MC, V.

★★ **MIKADO.** *67 West 100 South St (84101), downtown. 801/328-0929.* Hrs: 5:30-9:30 pm; Fri, Sat to 10 pm; summer: 6-9:30 pm; Sun to 9 pm; Closed major hols. Res accepted. Japanese menu. Semi-a la carte: dinner $11-$21. Child's meals. Specialties: shrimp tempura, chicken teriyaki, beef sukiyaki. Sushi bar. Zashiki rms. Cr cds: A, C, D, DS, JCB, MC, V.

D

★★★ **THE NEW YORKER.** *60 W Market St (84101), between Main St & W Temple at 350 S, downtown. 801/363-0166.* Hrs: 11:30 am-11 pm; Fri to 11:30 pm; Sat 5-11:30 pm. Closed Sun; major hols; July 24. Res accepted. Continental menu. Bar. wine cellar. Semi-a la carte: lunch $6.95-$15.95, dinner $8.95-$25.95. Specializes in fresh seafood, beef, veal. Own desserts. Valet parking. Intimate dining club with metropolitan decor; three dining areas include cafe, formal dining rm. Cr cds: A, C, D, DS, MC, V.

★★ **OLD SALT CITY JAIL.** *460 South 1000 East (84102), east of downtown. 801/355-2422.* Hrs: 5-10 pm; Fri 4:30-11 pm; Sat 4-11 pm; Sun 4-9 pm; early-bird dinner 4:30-6 pm. Res accepted. Bar. Semi-a la carte: dinner $9.95-$18.95. Child's meals. Specializes in prime rib, steak, seafood. Salad bar. Entertainment Thurs-Sat. Early brewery re-created as an old country jail. Totally nonsmoking. Cr cds: A, C, D, DS, MC, V.

D

★★ **PEERY WASATCH PUB & BISTRO.** *(See Peery Hotel) 801/521-5037.* Hrs: 11:30 am-11 pm; Sun 5-10 pm. Closed Easter, Dec 25. Res accepted. Continental menu. Bar. Semi-a la carte: lunch $4.95-$9.95, dinner $9.95-$21.95. Specializes in pasta, seafood, beef. Casual decor. Totally nonsmoking. Cr cds: A, C, D, DS, MC, V.

D

✔★★★ **PIÑA.** *327 W 200 South (84101), downtown. 801/355-7462.* Web www.citysearch.com/sic/pina. Hrs: 11 am-10 pm; Fri to 11 pm; Sat 4:30-11 pm; Sun 10:30 am-2:30 pm (brunch), 4:30-9 pm. Closed July 4. Res accepted. Continental menu. Bar. Wine list. Semi-a la carte: lunch, dinner $5.95-$16.95. Sun brunch $4.95-$8.95. Child's meals. Specialties: mahi mahi, jerk chicken, cheesecake chimichanga.

Valet parking. Carribean-style atmosphere. Totally nonsmoking. Cr cds: A, C, D, DS, MC, V.

D

★ ★ **PIERPONT CANTINA.** *122 W Pierpont Ave (84101), downtown. 801/364-1222.* Hrs: 11:30 am-10 pm; Sat 3-10 pm, Sun 10 am-10 pm. Closed Jan 1, Thanksgiving, Dec 25. Res accepted. Mexican menu. Bar. Semi-a la carte: lunch $6.99-$14.99, dinner $7.99-$19. Buffet: $7.99-$9.99. Child's meals. Specializes in carnitas, seafood. Outdoor dining. Mexican decor. Totally nonsmoking. Cr cds: A, C, D, DS, MC, V.

D

★ ★ **POMODORO.** *2440 E Ft Union Blvd (84121), downtown. 801/944-1895.* Hrs: 5:30-10 pm; Fri, Sat 5-11 pm. Closed Mon; most major hols. Res accepted. Italian menu. Bar. Semi-a la carte: dinner $10.50-$21.50. Specializes in seafood, pasta, garlic mashed potatoes. Own pastas, desserts. Cozy atmosphere; fireplace. Totally nonsmoking. Cr cds: A, D, DS, MC, V.

D

✔ ★ **QUILA'S.** *(935 E Fort Union Blvd, Midvale 84047) 9 mi S on I-15. 801/566-9313.* Hrs: 11 am-10 pm; Fri, Sat to 11 pm; Sun from 10 am; Sun brunch to 2:30 pm. Closed Dec 24, 25. Res accepted. Mexican menu. Bar. Lunch buffet: $6.95. Semi-a la carte: lunch $4.99-$7.99, dinner $6.99-$10.99. Sun brunch $10.95. Child's meals. Specialties: fajitas with homemade tortillas, shrimp & fish tacos. Own baking. Guitarist Fri, Sat, Sun brunch. 1940s Mexican roadhouse decor. Totally nonsmoking. Cr cds: A, C, D, DS, MC, V.

D

✔ ★ **RAFAEL'S.** *(889 East 9400 South, Sandy 84094) S on I-15, exit 9000 South St, then 2 mi E, in Aspen Plaza. 801/561-4545.* Hrs: 11:30 am-9 pm; Fri, Sat to 10 pm. Closed Sun; some major hols. Mexican menu. Semi-a la carte: lunch, dinner $4.50-$9.50. Specializes in enchiladas, fajitas. Mexican, Indian and Aztec artwork. Cr cds: DS, MC, V.

D

✔ ★ **REDBONES.** *2207 S 700 East St (84106), east of downtown. 801/463-4800.* Web www.redbones.com. Hrs: 11:30 am-9:30 pm; Fri, Sat to 10 pm; Sun noon-8 pm. Closed most major hols; July 24. Barbecue menu. Beer. Semi-a la carte: lunch, dinner $4.95-$14.95. Specializes in spare ribs, pulled pork, chicken. Outdoor dining. Features architecture of Southern Utah. Separate motorcycle parking; motorcycle on display indoors. Totally nonsmoking. Cr cds: A, C, D, DS, MC, V.

D

★ ★ **RINO'S ITALIAN RISTORANTE.** *2302 Parleys Way (84109), east of downtown. 801/484-0901.* Hrs: 6-10 pm; Fri, Sat 5:30-10:30 pm; Sun 5-9 pm. Closed major hols. Res accepted. Italian, continental menu. Serv bar. Semi-a la carte: dinner $8.99-$21.99. Patio dining. Bistro-style cafe. Cr cds: A, MC, V.

D

✔ ★ ★ **RIO GRANDE CAFE.** *270 S Rio Grande St (84101), downtown. 801/364-3302.* Hrs: 11 am-2:30 pm, 5-10 pm; Fri to 10:30 pm; Sat 11:30 am-2:30 pm, 5-10:30 pm; Sun 4-9 pm. Closed major hols. Mexican menu. Bar. Semi-a la carte: lunch, dinner $5-$9. Child's meals. Specializes in carnitas, traditional Mexican dishes. Outdoor dining. In historic Rio Grande Depot also housing RR museum and displays. Totally nonsmoking. Cr cds: A, DS, MC, V.

D

★ ★ **RISTORANTE DELLA FONTANA.** *336 S 400 East St (84111), downtown. 801/328-4243.* Hrs: 11 am-10 pm. Closed Sun; some major hols; also July 24th. Res accepted. Italian, Amer menu. Semi-a la carte: lunch $6.95-$14.25, dinner $10.95-$17.95. Child's meals. Specializes in pasta, veal, Cordon Bleu. Historic converted church, stained-glass windows, antique chandeliers. Waterfall in dining rm. Cr cds: A, C, D, DS, MC, V.

♥

✔ ★ **SALT LAKE BREWING CO.** *367 W 200 S (84101), downtown. 801/363-7000.* E-mail callen@squatters.com; web www.squatters.com. Hrs: 11:30 am-midnight; Fri, Sat to 1 am. Closed Thanksgiving, Dec 25. Res accepted. Bar. Semi-a la carte: lunch, dinner $3.99-$13.99. Child's meals. Specializes in smoked meats, roasted chicken. Own baking, pasta. Guitarist Wed-Sat evening. Turn-of-the-century bldg; microbrewery. Totally nonsmoking. Cr cds: A, D, DS, MC, V.

D

★ ★ **TUCCI'S.** *4835 S Highland Dr (84117), downtown. 801/277-8338.* Hrs: 11:30 am-10 pm; Fri, Sat to 11 pm; Sun noon-9 pm. Closed Thanksgiving, Dec 25. Italian menu. Bar. Semi-a la carte: lunch $5.95-$9.95, dinner $5.95-$18.95. Child's meals. Specialties: pizza tradizionale, farfalle con sugo blanco, picatta. Outdoor dining. Colorful decor; large display of stuffed animals. Totally nonsmoking. Cr cds: A, D, DS, MC, V.

D

★ ★ ★ **TUSCANY.** *2832 E 6200 S (84121), I-215 to Holladay, east of downtown. 801/277-9919.* Hrs: 11:30 am-10 pm; Mon from 5 pm; Fri to 10:30 pm; Sat 5-10:30 pm; Sun 5-9 pm. Closed most major hols. Res accepted. Italian menu. Bar. Wine list. Semi-a la carte: lunch $7-$13, dinner $11-$23. Child's meals. Specialties: linguini with clams, pesto-crusted salmon, double-cut pork chop. Own baking, pasta. Valet parking. Outdoor dining. Italian villa decor with several unique dining rms; landscaped, wooded grounds near Big Cottonwood Canyon. Cr cds: A, C, D, MC, V.

D

Unrated Dining Spot

LITZA'S FOR PIZZA. *716 E 400 South St, downtown. 801/359-5352.* Hrs: 11 am-11 pm; Fri, Sat to 12:30 am. Closed Sun; Thanksgiving, Dec 25. Italian menu. Semi-a la carte: lunch $5.15-$11, dinner $8-$15. Specializes in pizza. No cr cds accepted.

San Antonio

Founded: 1718
Pop: 935,933
Elev: 701 feet
Time zone: Central
Area code: 210
Web: www.SanAntonioCVB.com

San Antonio has a charm and grace common to many Texas cities. Part of this charm stems from its Spanish beginnings, signs of which can still be found almost everywhere. In the course of its history, San Antonio has been under six flags: France, Spain, Mexico, Republic of Texas, Confederate States of America and United States of America. Although the Spanish influence predominates, traces of each remain today.

The Mission San Antonio de Valero (the Alamo) was founded by Friar Antonio de San Buenaventura Olivares in May 1718, near the San Antonio River. Four more missions were built along the river during the next 13 years, and all continued to operate until about 1794. It was at the Alamo that, from February 23 to March 6, 1836, Davy Crockett, Colonel James Bowie, Colonel William B. Travis and 186 other Texans unsuccessfully resisted Santa Anna and his force of 5,000 troops. Every defender died, their bravery giving rise to the battle cry "Remember the Alamo!" Three months after the tragedy, the city was almost deserted, but within a few years it became a great Western outpost.

The arrival of adventurers and cowboys in the 1870s earned San Antonio a reputation as a tough, hard-drinking, hard-fighting gambling town. Now the state's third largest city, and one of the largest in the country, San Antonio has become a prosperous, modern city that still retains much of the flavor of its colorful past.

Business

About 25 percent of the working population of San Antonio is employed in the retail and wholesale industry. Manufacturing firms in the city employ roughly eight percent of the work force. San Antonio's five military installations also employ more than 66,000 civilians. San Antonio is one of the southwest's leading science centers, particularly in the field of medical research.

Some of the products manufactured in San Antonio are petroleum products, clothing, airplane parts, food products, medical supplies, bowling balls and eyewear.

Convention Facilities

The San Antonio Henry B. Gonzalez Convention Center is a multipurpose facility available for business meetings, conventions, entertainment, trade shows and other events. The Center is undergoing a $187-million expansion project until the year 2001. Convention business will continue during the project.

The Alamodome provides 160,000 gross square feet of exhibit space and 30,000 square feet of conference space and can be configured to host various sports events, major concerts, conventions and trade shows, with seating for up to 77,000.

The San Antonio Municipal Auditorium seats 4,904 people in the main hall, with 23,000 square feet of meeting and exhibit space on the lower level. The Joe and Harry Freeman Coliseum has 155,964 square feet of exhibit space, meeting rooms and parking for 10,000 cars.

Recreation & Entertainment

The almost subtropical climate of San Antonio (average annual temperature of 71°F) allows year-round recreation. Championship golf courses with beautiful greens and tree-lined fairways offer a challenge to golfers. San Antonio has more than 30 public, private and military courses and driving ranges. The city also has numerous public tennis facilities. There is sailing, fishing, waterskiing, sail boarding, canoeing and whitewater rafting within a half-hour drive from the city.

Six Flags Fiesta Texas is a 200-acre amusement park featuring rides and entertainment in four themed areas. Featured are the Roadrunner Express roller coaster and the Crazy Buffalo Saloon Dinner Theater.

Sea World of Texas, located on a 250-acre site in northwest San Antonio, is the world's largest marine-life park and now features The Great White, an inverted steel roller coaster.

San Antonio is the home of the San Antonio Spurs (National Basketball Association), the San Antonio Missions (Texas Baseball League), and the San Antonio Dragons (International Hockey League).

The city has many fine repertory and neighborhood theaters offering diverse entertainment, as well as art galleries and museums.

Historical Areas

The most famous of all historic sites in the city is the Alamo, built in 1718. The Long Barrack, once the mission rectory, has been restored and contains a museum of fascinating Texas relics.

Within walking distance of the Alamo are many historic areas. The Spanish Governor's Palace, completed in 1749, was the residence and office of Spanish administrators. The José Antonio Navarro Residence, home of a Texas patriot, is a complex of three adobe houses built about 1850. The Articles of Capitulation were signed in Cos House by General Perfecto de Cos on December 10, 1835, after Texans had taken the town. The Menger Hotel is a famous hostelry in which Robert E. Lee, Theodore Roosevelt and William Jennings Bryan stayed. Located in the hotel is a bar, still in use, where Roosevelt recruited "Rough Riders."

Dating to 1840, the Market Square area has continued a town market concept with vendors and mariachis in the plaza. The present day market is centered around El Mercado, a large indoor shopping area patterned after an authentic Mexican market.

La Villita, one of the original civil settlement areas, is a neighborhood of old adobe buildings, vine-covered stone walls, flagstone walks and fountains. The area is the setting for various traditional fiestas during the year.

There are several restored missions in the San Antonio area, which, like the Alamo, were founded in the early 1700s by Franciscan friars. Mission Concepción, established in 1731 and constructed of porous limestone, is the oldest unrestored mission in Texas. The San José Mission (1720), one of the most successful missions in the Southwest, includes a restored church, Native American quarters, granary and old mill. Built of limestone and tufa, the church is famous for its carvings, including Pedro Huizar's sacristy window, sometimes referred to as "Rosa's window." Begin at the visitor center at Mission San José for an overview and historical orientation. These missions plus San Juan Capistrano, San Francisco de la Espada and the Espada Dam and Aqueduct form the San Antonio Missions National Historical Park. The missions are active Roman Catholic parishes and are open for public touring and worship. Sunday Mariachi Mass at Mission San José is memorable.

Sightseeing

The heart of San Antonio is the Paseo del Rio or River Walk. Only a few steps away from the business activities of the city is a tranquil, landscaped path reached from the street level by winding stone stairways. Along its route are sidewalk restaurants and cafes, botanical gardens, shops and an outdoor theater. It is a place to relax, to enjoy a glass of wine or a Mexican beer, a Texas steak or a plate heaped with tacos, enchiladas and refried beans. It is ideal for an evening stroll along the cobblestone walkways or a riverboat ride along the 45-minute, round-trip course.

Several great modern buildings were built for the city's HemisFair '68. One of the most interesting is the Institute of Texan Cultures, which honors the contribution to Texas history of 26 ethnic and cultural groups through an unusual audiovisual program and various exhibits. From the imposing 750-foot Tower of the Americas, the city and surrounding hills are spread before the visitor.

San Antonio has a variety of parks to enjoy. Brackenridge Park, covering 340 acres, houses the Pioneer Memorial Hall, Zoological Gardens and Aquarium, the Japanese Tea Gardens, a golf course and the Brackenridge *Eagle* miniature train.

Just north of downtown is the San Antonio Museum of Art, located in a restored Lone Star brewery. Its collection is built around the art of the Americas—Spanish colonial, Mexican folk, contemporary and modern Native American.

North of San Antonio is the Texans' beloved "hill country," a land of gentle hills and rushing rivers; waterfalls, caverns and springs; wild growths of mesquite and neat ranches. Lyndon Johnson was born and grew up here, and it is the location of the LBJ State Park.

The city of New Braunfels attracts more than 100,000 visitors each fall to its 10-day Wurstfest. North of New Braunfels is San Marcos, where a beautiful subtropical resort and park, Aquarena Springs, presents a lush contrast to the rugged country to the west.

General References

Area code: 210

Phone Numbers

POLICE & FIRE: 911

POISON CONTROL CENTER: 911

TIME: 226-3232 **WEATHER:** 737-1400

Information Sources

San Antonio Convention & Visitors Bureau, 121 Alamo Plaza, PO Box 2277, 78298; 270-8700 or 800/447-3372.

Visitor Information Center, 317 Alamo Plaza, 78205; 270-8748.

Transportation

AIRLINES: Aerolitoral; Aeromar; America West; American; Conquest; Continental; Delta; Mexicana; Northwest; Southwest; TWA; United; USAir; and other commuter and regional airlines.

AIRPORT: San Antonio International, 207-3411.

CAR RENTAL AGENCIES: (See IMPORTANT TOLL-FREE NUMBERS) Alamo 828-7967; Avis 826-6332; Budget 828-5693; Enterprise 283-3811; Hertz 841-8800; National 824-7544.

PUBLIC TRANSPORTATION: VIA Metropolitan Transit Service 227-2020.

RAILROAD PASSENGER SERVICE: Amtrak 800/872-7245.

Newspaper

San Antonio Express-News.

Convention Facilities

Alamodome, 100 Montana, 223-3663.

Convention Center, HemisFair Park, 200 E Market St, 207-8500.

Municipal Auditorium and Conference Center, 100 Auditorium Circle, 207-8511.

Sports & Recreation

Alamodome, 100 Montana, 207-3652 (Spurs, basketball, 554-7000).

Cultural Facilities

Concert Halls

Joe & Harry Freeman Coliseum, 3201 E Houston St, 226-1177.

Laurie Auditorium, Trinity University, 736-8117.

Majestic Theatre, 224 E Houston St, 226-3333.

Museums

Buckhorn Hall of Horns and Texas Hall of History, 600 Lone Star Blvd, 226-8301

Fort Sam Houston Museum, off I-35, N New Braunfels Ave exit, 221-1886.

Hertzberg Circus Museum, 210 W Market St, 207-7810.

Institute of Texan Cultures, 801 S Bowie St, 458-2300.

McNay Art Museum, 6000 N New Braunfels Ave at US 81, 824-5368.

Pioneer Memorial Hall, Brackenridge Park, 3805 Broadway, 822-9011.

San Antonio Children's Museum, 305 E Houston St, 212-4453.

San Antonio Museum of Art, 200 W Jones Ave, 978-8100.

Points of Interest

Historical

The Alamo, 300 Alamo Plaza, 225-1391.

Cos House, 418 La Villita, 207-8610.

El Mercado, 514 W Commerce, 207-8600.

José Antonio Navarro State Historical Park, 228 S Laredo St, 226-4801.

La Villita, S of Paseo de la Villita, W at S Alamo St, 207-8610.

Menger Hotel, 204 Alamo Plaza, 223-4361.

Mission Concepción, 807 Mission Rd, 534-1540.

Mission San Francisco de la Espada, 10040 Espada Rd, 627-2021.

Mission San Juan Capistrano, 9102 Graf Rd, 534-0749.

The Quadrangle, Fort Sam Houston, Grayson St, 221-1886.

San Antonio Missions National Historic Park, 534-8833.

San Fernando Cathedral, 115 Main Plaza, 227-1297.

San José Mission, 6539 San Jose Dr, 932-1001.

Spanish Governor's Palace, 105 Military Plaza, 224-0601.

Steves Homestead, 509 King William St, 225-5924.

Other Attractions

Cascade Caverns Park, 14 mi NW on I-10, exit 543, W to Boerne, 755-8080.

HemisFair Park, 200 S Alamo, 207-8579.

Paseo del Rio, 21-blk River Walk along the San Antonio River.

Botanical Gardens, 555 Funston Pl, 821-5115.

Sea World of Texas, 10500 Sea World Dr, 16 mi NW on TX 151, 523-3611.

Six Flags Fiesta Texas, 17000 I-10W, 697-5050.

Splashtown, I-35 exit 160, 227-1100.

Tower of the Americas, HemisFair Park, 207-8615.

Zoological Gardens and Aquarium, 3903 N St Mary's St, 734-7183.

Sightseeing Tours

Gray Line bus tours, 1430 E Houston St, 78202; 226-1706.

Lone Star Trolley & Tours, 301 Alamo Plaza, 222-9090.

Texas Trolley, 217 Alamo Plaza, Suite 400, 228-9776.

Annual Events

San Antonio Livestock Show and Rodeo, Joe and Harry Freeman Coliseum, 3201 E Houston St, 225-5851. Feb 7-22.

Fiesta San Antonio, 227-5191. Apr 17-26.

Texas Folklife Festival, 458-2390. Aug 6-9.

Fiestas Navidenas, Market Square, 207-8600. Mid-Dec.

Las Posadas, 224-6163. Dec.

City Neighborhoods

Many of the restaurants, unrated dining establishments and some lodgings listed under San Antonio include neighborhoods as well as exact street addresses. Geographic descriptions of these areas are given, followed by a table of restaurants arranged by neighborhood.

Downtown: South of I-35, west of I-35/37, north of Durango St and east of I-10. **North of Downtown:** North of I-35. **South of Downtown:** South of Durango St. **West of Downtown:** West of I-10.

La Villita: Downtown area south of Paseo de la Villita, west of S Alamo St, north of Nueva St and east of S Presa St.

River Walk (*Paseo Del Rio*): Downtown area along San Antonio River and along canal extending east from the river between E Commerce and Market Sts.

Lodgings and Food

SAN ANTONIO RESTAURANTS BY NEIGHBORHOOD AREAS

(For full description, see alphabetical listings under Restaurants)

DOWNTOWN

Aldaco's. 1141 E Commerce
Guenther House. 205 E Guenther St
Liberty Bar. 328 E Josephine
Mi Tierra. 218 Produce Row
Morton's of Chicago. 300 Crockett
Paesano's. 555 E Basse Rd
Rosario's. 1014 S Alamo St
Star Anise. 152 Pecan St
Tower of the Americas. 222 HemisFair Plaza

NORTH OF DOWNTOWN

5050 Diner. 5050 Broadway St
Aldino Cucina Italiana. 622 NW Loop 410
Aldo's Ristorante. 8539 Fredericksburg Rd
Antlers Lodge (Hyatt Regency Hill Country Resort). 9800 Hyatt Resort Dr
Barcelona's. 4901 Broadway
Biga. 206 E Locust St
Bistro Time. 5137 Fredericksburg Rd
Brazier at Los Patios. 2015 NE Loop I-410
Cappy's. 5011 Broadway St
Cascabel (Doubletree Hotel). 37 NE Loop 410
Chez Ardid. 1919 San Pedro Ave
Crumpet's. 3920 Harry Wurzbach
El Jarro de Arturo. 13421 San Pedro Ave
Ernesto's. 2559 Jackson Keller
Formosa Gardens. 1011 NE Loop 410
French Quarter Grill. 4903 NW Loop 410
Gazebo at Los Patios. 2015 NE Loop I-410
Grey Moss Inn. 19010 Scenic Loop Rd
La Calesa. 2103 E Hildebrand Ave
La Fogata. 2427 Vance Jackson Rd
Los Barrios. 4223 Blanco Rd
Mencius' Gourmet Hunan. 7959 Fredericksburg Rd
Mesteña. 7959 Broadway
Old San Francisco Steak House. 10223 Sahara St
Romano's Macaroni Grill. 24116 I-10 West
Ruth's Chris Steak House. 7720 Jones Maltsberger Rd

SOUTH OF DOWNTOWN

Carranza Meat Market. 701 Austin St
El Mirador. 722 S St Mary's St

WEST OF DOWNTOWN

La Margarita. 120 Produce Row
Pico de Gallo. 111 S Leona Ave

LA VILLITA

Anaqua Grill (Marriott Plaza Hotel). 555 S Alamo St
Fig Tree. 515 Villita St
Little Rhein Steak House. 231 S Alamo St
Polo's At The Fairmount (Fairmount Hotel). 401 S Alamo St

RIVERWALK

The Bayous. 517 N Presa St
Boudro's, A Texas Bistro. 421 E Commerce St
Casa Rio. 430 E Commerce St
Dick's Last Resort. 406 Navarro St
Las Canarias (La Mansion Del Rio Hotel). 112 College St
Lone Star. 237 Losoya
Michelino's. 521 Riverwalk
Pieca d'Italia. 502 Riverwalk
Rio Rio Cantina. 421 E Commerce St
Zuni Grill. 223 Losoya

Note: When a listing is located in a town that does not have its own city heading, it will appear under the city nearest to its location. In these cases, the address and town appear in parenthesis immediately following the name of the establishment.

Motels

✔★★★ **BEST WESTERN CONTINENTAL INN.** *9735 I-35N (78233), north of downtown. 210/655-3510; FAX 210/655-0778.* 161 rms, 2 story. S $50-$58; D $64-$68; each addl $4. Crib free. TV; cable (premium). Pool; wading pool, whirlpools. Playground. Complimentary full bkfst. Restaurant 6 am-10 pm. Rm serv. Bar. Ck-out noon. Coin lndry. Meeting rms. Business servs avail. In-rm modem link. Sundries. Some refrigerators. Cr cds: A, C, D, DS, MC, V.

D SC

★★ **COURTYARD BY MARRIOTT.** *8585 Marriott Dr (78229), at Fredericksburg Rd, north of downtown. 210/614-7100; FAX 210/614-7110.* 146 rms, 3 story. S, D $73-$89; wkend rates. Crib avail. TV; cable (premium). Pool; whirlpool. Complimentary coffee in rms. Restaurant 6:30-10:30 am; Sat, Sun 7 am-noon. Bar 5-10 pm. Ck-out noon. Coin lndry. Meeting rms. Business servs avail. In-rm modem link. Valet serv. Exercise equipt; weights, bicycles. Microwaves avail; refrigerator in suites. Balconies. Cr cds: A, C, D, DS, MC, V.

D SC

★ **ECONO LODGE.** *218 S.W.W. White Rd (78219), I-10E, exit 580, east of downtown. 210/333-3346; FAX 210/333-7564.* 40 rms, 2 story. S $28-$89; D $29-$119; each addl $5; under 12 free; wkend rates. TV; cable (premium). Complimentary continental bkfst. Complimentary coffee in rms. Restaurant nearby. Ck-out noon. Meeting rms. Business servs avail. Valet serv. Coin lndry. Pool. Some refrigerators, microwaves. Cr cds: A, D, DS, MC, V.

D SC

★★ **HAMPTON INN.** *414 Bowie St (78205), downtown. 210/225-8500; FAX 210/225-8526.* 169 rms, 6 story. Feb-Oct: S $85-$105; D $95-$115; each addl $10; under 18 free; golf plans; higher rates special events; lower rates rest of yr. Crib free. TV; cable (premium). Complimentary continental bkfst. Restaurant nearby. Ck-out 11 am. Meeting rms. Business servs avail. In-rm modem link. Valet serv. Coin lndry. Pool. Cr cds: A, D, DS, MC, V.

D SC

★★ **HAWTHORN SUITES.** *4041 Bluemel Rd (78240), at I-10, Huebner exit. 210/561-9660; FAX 210/561-9663.* 128 kit. suites, 2 story. S, D $89-$138; under 12 free; wkly, wkend rates. Crib free. Pet accepted, some restrictions; $50. TV; cable (premium). Heated pool; whirlpool. Complimentary bkfst; evening refreshments. Ck-out noon. Coin lndry. Meeting rm. Business servs avail. In-rm modem link. Valet serv. Health club privileges. Microwaves; fireplace in most suites. Private patios, balconies. Picnic table. Cr cds: A, C, D, DS, MC, V.

D SC

★ **HOLIDAY INN EXPRESS-SEA WORLD.** *7043 Culebra Rd (78238), west of downtown. 210/521-1485; FAX 210/520-5924.* 72 rms, 2 story. S $59-$99; D $64-$104; each addl $5; under 18 free. Crib free. TV; cable (premium). Pool. Complimentary continental bkfst. Restaurant adj open 24 hrs. Ck-out noon. Meeting rm. Business servs avail. In-rm modem link. Coin lndry. Health club privileges. Refrigerators; microwaves avail. Cr cds: A, C, D, DS, JCB, MC, V.

D SC

★★ **LA QUINTA-INGRAM PARK.** *7134 NW Loop I-410 (78238). 210/680-8883; FAX 210/681-3877.* Web www.laquinta.com. 195 rms, 3 story. S $59-$76; D $69-$76; suites $80-$122; under 18 free. Crib free. Pet accepted, some restrictions. TV; cable (premium). Pool. Complimentary continental bkfst. Restaurant adj open 24 hrs. Ck-out noon.

Meeting rms. In-rm modem link. Refrigerator, microwave in suites. Cr cds: A, C, D, DS, MC, V.

D SC

★★ **LA QUINTA-MARKET SQUARE.** *900 Dolorosa St (78207), downtown. 210/271-0001; FAX 210/228-0663.* 124 rms, 2 story. S, D $84-$91; each addl $10; suites $126; under 18 free; higher rates Fiesta wk. Crib free. Pet accepted, some restrictions. TV; cable (premium). Pool. Continental bkfst. Complimentary coffee. Restaurant opp open 24 hrs. Ck-out noon. Business servs avail. In-rm modem link. Valet serv. Cr cds: A, C, D, DS, MC, V.

D SC

★★ **SIERRA ROYALE HOTEL.** *6300 Rue Marielyne (78238), loop 410 exit Bandera. 210/647-0041; FAX 210/647-4442; res: 800/289-2444.* 88 kit. suites, 1-2 story. May-Sept: S, D $99; each addl $10; monthly rates; lower rates rest of yr. Crib free. TV; cable (premium). Pool; whirlpool. Complimentary continental bkfst. Complimentary coffee in rms. Restaurant nearby. Bar 5:30-7:30 pm. Ck-out noon. Lndry facilities. Meeting rm. Business servs avail. Valet serv. Health club privileges. Microwaves. Balconies. Picnic tables. Cr cds: A, C, D, DS, MC, V.

D SC

★ **TRAVELODGE-ALAMO.** *405 Broadway (78205). 210/222-1000.* 81 rms, 3 story. S, D $60-$120; each addl $5; under 17 free. Crib free. TV; cable (premium), VCR avail (movies). Pool. Restaurant 6 am-4 pm. Ck-out noon. Coin lndry. Game rm. Microwaves avail. Cr cds: A, C, D, DS, MC, V.

D SC

✔★ **TRAVELODGE SUITES.** *4934 NW Loop 410 (78229). 210/680-3351; FAX 210/680-5182.* Web www.dcci.com/travelodge. 201 kit. suites, 3 story. S $49-$69; D $59-$89; each addl $5; under 18 free; wkly rates. Crib free. TV; cable (premium). Pool. Complimentary continental bkfst. Coffee in rms. Restaurant adj 10 am-10 pm. Ck-out noon. Meeting rms. Business servs avail. Coin lndry. Free airport transportation. Health club privileges. Microwaves. Cr cds: A, C, D, DS, MC, V.

D SC

Motor Hotels

✔★ **COMFORT INN AIRPORT.** *2635 NE Loop 410 (78217), near Intl Airport, north of downtown. 210/653-9110; FAX 210/653-8615.* 203 rms, 6 story. S, D $47-$85. Crib free. Pet accepted; fee. TV; cable (premium). Pool. Complimentary continental bkfst. Restaurant adj open 24 hrs. Ck-out noon. Meeting rms. Business servs avail. In-rm modem link. Free airport transportation. Health club privileges. Microwaves avail. Cr cds: A, C, D, DS, ER, MC, V.

SC

★★ **DRURY INN AND SUITES.** *8811 Jones Maltsberger Rd (78216), near Intl Airport, north of downtown. 210/366-4300; FAX 210/308-8100.* E-mail mail@druryinns.com; web www.drury-inns.com. 139 rms, 6 story. S $60-$77; D $67-$87; each addl $10; under 18 free. Crib free. Pet accepted, some restrictions. TV; cable (premium). Pool; whirlpool. Complimentary continental bkfst. Restaurant opp 6 am-midnight. Ck-out noon. Meeting rm. Business servs avail. In-rm modem link. Free airport transportation. Refrigerators, microwaves. Picnic tables. Cr cds: A, C, D, DS, MC, V.

D SC

★★ **EXECUTIVE GUESTHOUSE.** *12828 US 281N (78216), 12 mi N on US 281, exit Bitters, north of downtown. 210/494-7600; FAX 210/545-4314; res: 800/362-8700.* 124 rms, 4 story. S $99-$170; D $109-$180; each addl $10; under 12 free; wkend rates. Crib free. Pet accepted, some restrictions; $100 ($50 refundable). TV; cable (premium). Indoor pool. Complimentary full bkfst; evening refreshments. Complimentary coffee in rms. Ck-out noon. Meeting rms. In-rm modem link. Valet serv. Free airport transportation. Exercise equipt; weight machine, bicycle, sauna. Bathrm phones, refrigerators, microwaves; some in-rm whirlpools. Atrium. Cr cds: A, C, D, DS, MC, V.

D SC

★★ **FOUR POINTS BY SHERATON.** *110 Lexington Ave (78205), downtown. 210/223-9461; FAX 210/223-9267.* 324 rms, 9 story. S, D $79-$139; suites $150-$450; under 18 free. Crib free. Parking: self $5, valet $7. Pool. TV; cable (premium). Restaurant 6:30 am-2 pm, 5-10 pm. Rm serv. Bar 2 pm-midnight. Ck-out noon. Coin lndry. Meeting rms. Business servs avail. Bellhops. Gift shop. Exercise equipt; weights, bicycle. Health club privileges. Game rm. Microwaves avail; refrigerators in suites. Balconies. On river. Cr cds: A, C, D, DS, JCB, MC, V.

D SC

✔★★ **HAMPTON INN.** *11010 I-10W (78230), I-10 Huebner exit, north of downtown. 210/561-9058; FAX 210/690-5566.* 122 rms, 6 story. S $57-$85; D $67-$95; each addl $10; suites $89-$129; under 18 free. Crib free. TV; cable (premium). Pool. Complimentary continental bkfst. Restaurant adj open 24 hrs. Ck-out noon. Meeting rms. Business servs avail. In-rm modem link. Valet serv. Health club privileges. Many refrigerators; microwaves avail. Cr cds: A, C, D, DS, MC, V.

D SC

★★ **HOLIDAY INN EXPRESS-AIRPORT.** *91 NE Loop I-410 (78216), near Intl Airport, north of downtown. 210/308-6700.* 154 rms, 10 story. S $75-$85; D $85-$99; under 19 free. Crib free. Pet accepted, some restrictions. TV; cable (premium). Pool. Complimentary continental bkfst. Restaurant adj 11 am-midnight. Ck-out noon. Meeting rms. Business servs avail. In-rm modem link. Coin lndry. Free airport transportation. Microwaves avail. Cr cds: A, C, D, DS, MC, V.

D SC

★★ **HOMEWOOD SUITES.** *4323 Spectrum One (78230), north of downtown. 210/696-5400; FAX 210/696-8899.* Web www.homewood suites.com. 123 kit. units, 4 story. S $99-$119; D $119-$129; under 12 free; monthly rates. Crib free. TV; cable (premium), VCR (movies). Complimentary continental bkfst. Complimentary coffee in rms. Restaurant nearby. Ck-out noon. Meeting rms. Business center. In-rm modem link. Valet serv. Sundries. Grocery store. Coin lndry. Exercise equipt; bicycle, treadmill. Pool. Lawn games. Refrigerators, microwaves. Cr cds: A, D, DS, MC, V.

D SC

★★ **PEAR TREE INN.** *143 NE Loop 410 (78216), at I-410 & Airport Blvd, near Intl Airport, north of downtown. 210/366-9300.* 125 rms, 4 story. S $49.95-$56.95; D $57.95-$64.95; each addl $8; under 18 free. Crib free. Pet accepted, some restrictions. TV; cable (premium). Pool. Complimentary bkfst. Restaurant adj 6 am-midnight. Serv bar. Ck-out noon. Coin lndry. Meeting rms. Business servs avail. In-rm modem link. Free airport transportation. Some refrigerators; microwaves avail. Cr cds: A, C, D, DS, MC, V.

D SC

✔★ **RED ROOF INN.** *333 Wolfe Rd (78216), near Intl Airport, north of downtown. 210/340-4055.* 135 rms, 3 story. S, D $39.95-$99; each addl $5; under 18 free. Crib free. Pet accepted. TV; cable (premium). Complimentary continental bkfst. Restaurant nearby. Ck-out noon. Meeting rms. Business servs avail. In-rm modem link. Free airport transportation. Cr cds: A, C, D, DS, MC, V.

D SC

Hotels

★★★ **CAMBERLEY GUNTER.** *205 E Houston St (78205), downtown. 210/227-3241; FAX 210/227-3299.* 322 rms, 12 story. S, D $135-$150; each addl $10; suites $195-$750; under 18 free. Crib free. Garage $10. TV; cable (premium). Heated pool; whirlpool. Coffee in rms. Restaurant 6 am-10 pm; Fri, Sat to 11 pm. Bar 4 pm-2 am; Fri, Sat noon-2 am; Sun to midnight. Ck-out noon. Convention facilities. Business servs avail.

In-rm modem link. Barber. Exercise equipt; weights, bicycles. Refrigerators, microwaves avail. Built 1909. Cr cds: A, C, D, DS, ER, JCB, MC, V.

D SC

★ ★ ★ **CROWNE PLAZA ST ANTHONY.** *300 E Travis St (78205), downtown. 210/227-4392; FAX 210/227-0915; res: 800/355-5153.* Web www.crowneplaza.com. 350 rms, 9 story, 42 suites. S, D $135-$190; each addl $15; suites $300-$550; under 12 free; wkend rates. Crib free. Garage parking $8, valet $11. TV; cable (premium). Heated pool; poolside serv. Coffee in rms. Restaurant 6 am-10 pm. Bar 11-2 am. Ck-out noon. Convention facilities. Business center. In-rm modem link. Gift shop. Exercise equipt; weight machine, treadmills. Game rm. Refrigerators avail. This landmark property, built in 1909, is famous for its elegant lobby. Cr cds: A, C, D, DS, ER, JCB, MC, V.

D SC

★ ★ ★ **DOUBLETREE.** *37 NE Loop 410 (78216), near Intl Airport, north of downtown. 210/366-2424; FAX 210/341-0410.* Web www.doubletreehotels.com. 292 rms, 5 story. S $130-$140; D $140-$150; each addl $15; suites $240-$320; under 17 free; wkend rates. Crib free. TV; cable (premium). Pool; whirlpool. Coffee in rms. Restaurants (see CASCABEL). Bar 11-2 am; pianist Mon-Fri. Ck-out noon. Convention facilities. Business servs avail. In-rm modem link. Free airport transportation. Exercise equipt; weight machine, bicycles, sauna. Some refrigerators. Private patios, balconies. Luxury level. Cr cds: A, C, D, DS, ER, JCB, MC, V.

D SC

★ ★ ★ **EMBASSY SUITES.** *10110 US 281N (78216), near Intl Airport, north of downtown. 210/525-9999; FAX 210/525-0626.* 261 suites, 9 story. S $99-$139; D $109-$159; each addl $20; under 18 free; wkend rates. Crib free. TV; cable (premium). Indoor pool; whirlpool. Complimentary full bkfst. Restaurant 11:30 am-2:30 pm, 5-10 pm; Fri, Sat to 11 pm. Bar 2-midnight. Ck-out 1 pm. Coin Indry. Meeting rms. Business center. In-rm modem link. Gift shop. Free airport transportation. Exercise equipt; weights, treadmill, sauna. Game rm. Refrigerators, microwaves. Cr cds: A, C, D, DS, MC, V.

D SC

★ ★ ★ **FAIRMOUNT.** *401 S Alamo St (78205), at La Villita. 210/224-8800; FAX 210/224-2767; res: 800/642-3363.* 37 rms, 3 story, 17 suites. S $200-$230; D $210-$230; suites $230-$550; under 12 free. Crib free. Valet parking $12. TV; cable (premium), VCR (free movies). Restaurant (see POLO'S AT THE FAIRMOUNT). Bar 11:30-1 am; entertainment Wed-Sat. Ck-out noon. Meeting rms. Business servs avail. In-rm modem link. Concierge. Exercise equipt; weight machine, bicycle. Bathrm phones. Balconies. Garden courtyard. Near the Riverwalk. Cr cds: A, C, D, DS, MC, V.

D SC

★ ★ ★ **HILTON PALACIO DEL RIO.** *200 S Alamo St (78205), on Riverwalk. 210/222-1400; FAX 210/270-0761.* 481 rms, 22 story. S $155-$205; D $175-$225; each addl $20; suites $425-$650; package plans. Crib free. Pet accepted, some restrictions. Garage $8, valet $18. TV; cable (premium), VCR avail. Pool; whirlpool, poolside serv. Complimentary coffee in rms. Restaurant 6:30-1 am. Bars 11:30-1:30 am; wkends to 2 am; entertainment. Ck-out 11 am. Convention facilities. Business servs avail. In-rm modem link. Concierge. Gift shop. Tennis privileges. Golf privileges. Exercise equipt; weights, bicycles. Some bathrm phones, refrigerators; microwaves avail. Balconies. Luxury level. Cr cds: A, C, D, DS, ER, JCB, MC, V.

D SC

★ ★ **HOLIDAY INN-RIVERWALK.** *217 N St Mary's St (78205), on Riverwalk. 210/224-2500; FAX 210/223-1302.* 313 rms, 23 story. S, D $119-$159; suites $179-$350; under 18 free. Crib free. Pet accepted, some restrictions. Valet parking $8; in/out $6. TV; cable (premium). Heated pool; whirlpool, poolside serv. Restaurant 6:30 am-2 pm, 5:30-10 pm. Rm serv 6 am-midnight. Bar noon-12:30 am; Fri, Sat to 2 am; entertainment exc Sun & Mon. Ck-out noon. Convention facilities. Business servs avail. In-rm modem link. Exercise equipt; bicycles, treadmill. Refrigerator in suites. Balconies. View of river. Cr cds: A, C, D, DS, JCB, MC, V.

D SC

★ ★ **HOWARD JOHNSON-RIVERWALK PLAZA.** *100 Villita St (78205), near La Villita. 210/226-2271; FAX 210/226-9453.* Web www.tourtexas.com. 133 rms, 6 story. S $89-$109; D $99-$129; each addl $10; under 18 free; higher rates: Fiesta Wk, special events. Crib free. Garage parking $4.75 in/out. TV; cable (premium). Pool. Complimentary coffee in rms. Restaurant 6:30 am-2 pm, 4-11 pm. Bar 4-11 pm. Ck-out 11 am. Meeting rms. Business center. In-rm modem link. Gift shop. Exercise equipt: weights, stair machine. Microwaves avail. Some balconies. Overlooks river. Cr cds: A, C, D, DS, MC, V.

D SC

★ ★ ★ **HYATT REGENCY.** *123 Losoya St (78205), on Riverwalk. 210/222-1234; FAX 210/227-4925.* 631 rms, 11 story. S $110-$230; D $135-$275; each addl $25; suites $200-$665; under 18 free; wkend rates. Garage parking $9, valet $13. TV; cable (premium), VCR avail. Pool; whirlpool, poolside serv. Restaurants 6:30 am-11 pm. Bar 11-2 am; entertainment. Meeting rms. Business center. In-rm modem link. Concierge. Shopping arcade. Exercise equipt; weights, bicycles. Minibars; some refrigerators. Balconies. River flows through lobby; waterfalls, atrium. Cr cds: A, C, D, DS, JCB, MC, V.

D SC

★ ★ ★ **LA MANSION DEL RIO.** *112 College St (78205), on River Walk. 210/225-2581; FAX 210/226-0389; res: 800/323-7500.* Web www.lamansion.com. 337 rms, 7 story. S $185-$280; D $210-$305; each addl $25; suites $475-$1,900; under 18 free; wkend rates; special packages. Crib free. Pet accepted. Valet parking $12. TV; cable, VCR avail. Pool; poolside serv. Restaurants (see LAS CANARIAS). Rm serv 24 hrs. Bar 11-2 am; entertainment. Ck-out noon. Convention facilities. Business servs avail. In-rm modem link. Concierge. Gift shop. Airport transportation. Minibars. Private patios, balconies. Overlooks San Antonio River, courtyard. Cr cds: A, C, D, DS, JCB, MC, V.

D SC

★ ★ ★ **MARRIOTT PLAZA.** *555 S Alamo St (78205), in La Villita. 210/229-1000; FAX 210/229-1418.* Web www .plazasa.com. 252 rms, 5-7 story. S $205-$220; D $225-$240; each addl $20; suites $340-$725; under 18 free; wkend rates. Crib free. Pet accepted, some restrictions. Valet parking $11. TV; cable (premium), VCR avail. Pool; whirlpool, poolside serv. Restaurant (see ANAQUA GRILL). Rm serv 24 hrs. Bar noon-1 am; entertainment Thurs-Sat. Ck-out noon. Meeting rms. Business center. In-rm modem link. Concierge. Lighted tennis. Golf privileges. Exercise equipt; weights, bicycles, sauna. Massage. Complimentary bicycles. Microwaves avail. Private patios. Balconies. Cr cds: A, C, D, DS, ER, MC, V.

D SC

★ ★ ★ **MARRIOTT RIVERCENTER.** *101 Bowie St (78205), opp convention Center, on Riverwalk. 210/223-1000; FAX 210/223-6239.* 1,000 units, 38 story. S $185; D $205; each addl $20; suites $325-$1,200; under 18 free. Crib free. Pet accepted. Garage $9, valet $11. TV; cable (premium), VCR avail. Indoor/outdoor pool; whirlpool, poolside serv. Coffee in rms. Restaurant 6 am-midnight. Rm serv 24 hrs. Bar. Ck-out noon. Free Indry facilities. Convention facilities. Business center. In-rm modem link. Concierge. Shopping arcade. Barber, beauty shop. 18-hole golf privileges, greens fee $65-$85, pro, putting green, driving range. Exercise equipt; weight machine, bicycles, sauna. Some refrigerators, wet bars. Balconies. Located on the banks of the San Antonio River and adj Rivercenter shopping complex. Luxury level. Cr cds: A, C, D, DS, MC, V.

D SC

★ ★ ★ **MARRIOTT RIVERWALK.** *711 E River Walk (78205), on Riverwalk. 210/224-4555; FAX 210/224-2754.* 500 rms, 30 story. S $134-$219; D $144-$229; each addl $20; suites $550; under 17 free; wkend rates. Crib free. Pet accepted. Garage parking $9, valet $12. TV; cable (premium), VCR avail. Indoor/outdoor pool; whirlpool. Restaurant 6:30 am-11 pm. Rm serv 24 hrs. Bar 11:30-2 am; entertainment Tues-Sat. Ck-out noon. Meeting rms. Business center. In-rm modem link. Gift shop. Golf privileges. Exercise equipt; weights, bicycles, sauna. Some bathrm phones, refrigerators. Balconies. Many rms overlook San Antonio River. Luxury level. Cr cds: A, C, D, DS, ER, JCB, MC, V.

D SC

★ ★ ★ **MENGER.** *204 Alamo Plaza (78205), downtown. 210/223-4361; FAX 210/228-0022; res: 800/345-9285.* Web www.mengerhotel.com. 350 rms, 5 story. S $118; D $138; each addl $10; suites $182-$364; under 18 free; package plans. Crib free. Garage $6.95, valet $11. TV; cable (premium), VCR avail. Pool; whirlpool. Restaurant 6:30 am-10 pm; wkends to 11 pm. Rm serv 24 hrs. Bar 11 am-midnight; piano bar. Ck-out noon. Convention facilities. Business servs avail. In-rm modem link. Concierge. Shopping arcade. Exercise equipt; bicycle, stair machine, sauna. Massage. Balconies. Historic atmosphere. Alamo opp. Cr cds: A, C, D, DS, ER, JCB, MC, V.

D SC

★ ★ ★ **OMNI.** *9821 Colonnade Blvd (78230), I-10 Wurzbach exit. 210/691-8888; FAX 210/691-1128.* 326 rms, 20 story. S $129-$160; D $134-$170; each addl $10; suites $275-$535; under 18 free; wkend rates. Crib free. Valet parking $5. TV; cable. 2 pools, 1 indoor; whirlpools, poolside serv. Complimentary coffee in rms. Restaurant 6:30 am-10 pm. Bar 3 pm-1 am; Sun noon-1 am; entertainment. Ck-out noon. Meeting rms. Business center. In-rm modem link. Gift shop. Free airport transportation. Exercise equipt; weights, bicycles, sauna. Health club privileges. Some refrigerators. Garden with fountain. Crystal chandelier, marble in lobby. Cr cds: A, C, D, DS, ER, JCB, MC, V.

D SC

★ ★ **RADISSON DOWNTOWN MARKET SQUARE.** *502 W Durango (78207), downtown. 210/224-7155; FAX 210/224-9130.* E-mail zip@txdirect.net. 250 rms, 6 story. S $69-$119; D $79-$129; each addl $10; suites $135-$195; under 12 free. Crib free. Pet accepted; $50 deposit. TV; cable (premium). Pool; whirlpool. Restaurant 6:30 am-10 pm. Bar noon-midnight. Ck-out noon. Coin lndry. Meeting rms. Business servs avail. Free garage parking. Gift shop. Exercise equipt; weights, stair machine. Game rm. Refrigerator in suites. Balconies. Cr cds: A, C, D, DS, MC, V.

D SC

★ **RAMADA EMILY MORGAN.** *705 E Houston St (78205), adj to the Alamo, downtown. 210/225-8486; FAX 210/225-7227.* 177 rms, 14 story. S $89-$149; D $94-$159; each addl $10; package plans. Crib free. Parking $8. TV; cable (premium). Pool; whirlpool. Complimentary coffee in rms. Restaurant 6:30 am-2 pm, 5-11 pm. Bar 4-11 pm. Ck-out noon. Meeting rms. Business center. In-rm modem link. Exercise equipt; weights, bicycles, sauna. In-rm whirlpools; many refrigerators; microwaves avail. Former medical arts bldg (1925); renovated; contemporary decor. Located adj historic Alamo. Cr cds: A, C, D, DS, ER, JCB, MC, V.

D SC

★ ★ **RESIDENCE INN BY MARRIOTT.** *425 Bonham (78205), downtown. 210/212-5555; FAX 210/212-5554.* 220 kit. suites, 13 story. Kit. suites $159; wkend, wkly, hol rates. Crib free. Pet accepted; $6/day. Garage parking $7. TV; cable (premium). Complimentary continental bkfst. Complimentary coffee in rms. Restaurant nearby. No rm serv. Ck-out noon. Meeting rms. Business servs avail. In-rm modem link. Coin lndry. Exercise equipt; weight machine, bicycle, sauna. Pool; whirlpool. Refrigerators, microwaves. Grills. Cr cds: A, C, D, DS, JCB, MC, V.

D SC

Inns

★ ★ **A YELLOW ROSE.** *229 Madison (78204). 210/229-9903; res: 800/950-9903; FAX 210/229-1691.* 5 rms, 2 story. S $95-$130; D $100-$135; wkly rates. Children over 12 yrs only. TV; cable (premium). Complimentary full bkfst. Restaurant nearby. Ck-out 11 am, ck-in 2 pm. Luggage handling. Game rm. Balconies. Built in 1878; antiques. Totally nonsmoking. Cr cds: A, DS, MC, V.

★ **B & B ON THE RIVER.** *129 Woodward Place (78204), Riverwalk. 210/225-6333; FAX 210/271-3992; res: 800/730-0019.* Web www.hotx.com\sa\bb. 12 rms, 4 with shower only, 3 story. S, D $99-$139; suite $129-$175; each addl $20; under 12 free. TV. Complimentary full bkfst. Ck-out 11 am, ck-in 2 pm. Business servs avail. In-rm modem link. Balconies. Victorian decor; antiques. Totally nonsmoking. Cr cds: A, DS, MC, V.

★ ★ **BEAUREGARD HOUSE.** *215 Beauregard St (78204), downtown. 210/222-1198; res: 800/841-9377.* 4 rms, 1 with shower only, 2 story, 1 suite. S $85; D $89; each addl $11; suite: $109; under 8 free; package plans. Crib avail. TV in sitting rm; cable. Complimentary full bkfst. Restaurant nearby. Ck-out 11 am, ck-in 1 pm. In-rm modem link. Lndry facilities. Restored Victorian house (1902) in King William District; Riverwalk 1 blk. Totally nonsmoking. Cr cds: MC, V.

SC

★ ★ **BECKMANN.** *222 E Guenther St (78204), downtown. 210/229-1449; FAX 210/229-1061; res: 800/945-1449.* Web saweb.com/beckbb. 5 rms, 4 with shower only, 2 story, 2 suites. S, D $90-$115; suites $115-$130. Children over 12 yrs only. TV; cable. Complimentary full bkfst. Restaurant opp 7 am-3 pm. Ck-out 11 am, ck-in 4-5 pm. Luggage handling. Refrigerators. Victorian house (1886) with wrap-around porch. Many antiques. Totally nonsmoking. Cr cds: A, D, DS, MC, V.

SC

★ ★ **BRACKENRIDGE HOUSE.** *230 Madison (78204). 210/271-3442; FAX 210/271-3442; res: 800/221-1412.* 6 rms, 2 with shower only, 2 story. S, D $89-$119; suite $109. Children over 12 yrs only. TV; cable (premium). Complimentary full bkfst. Ck-out 11:30 am, ck-in 3 pm. Individually decorated rms. Totally nonsmoking. Cr cds: A, D, DS, MC, V.

✓★ **BULLIS HOUSE INN.** *621 Pierce (78208). 210/223-9426; FAX 210/299-1479.* 7 rms, 4 share bath, 3 story. Some rm phones. S $45-$65; D $49-$69; each addl $10; under 17 free. Crib free. TV; cable (premium). Pool. Complimentary continental bkfst. Ck-out noon, ck-in 2 pm. Refrigerators. Greek Revival mansion; antiques. Cr cds: A, DS, MC, V.

SC

★ ★ **COLUMNS ON ALAMO.** *1037 S Alamo (78210), downtown. 210/271-3245; res: 800/233-3364.* Web www.travelbase.com/destinations/sanantonio/columns. 11 rms, 1 with shower only, 1 guest house. S, D, guest house $79-$148; each addl $15; hol rates; wkends (2-day min); package plans. Children over 12 yrs only. TV; cable. Complimentary full bkfst. Restaurant opp 10:30 am-10 pm. Ck-out 11 am, ck-in 3 pm. Business servs avail. In-rm modem link. Built in 1892; Greek Revival architecture; Victorian antiques. Totally nonsmoking. Cr cds: A, C, D, DS, MC, V.

SC

★ ★ **HAVANA RIVERWALK INN.** *1015 Navarro (78205), downtown. 210/222-2008; res: 888/224-2008; FAX 210/222-2717.* Web www.havana.com. 27 rms, 3 story, 10 suites. S $150-$170; D $150-$180; suites $200. Children over 14 yrs only. TV; cable (premium), VCR avail. Complimentary continental bkfst. Rm serv. Ck-out noon, ck-in 3 pm. Business servs avail. In-rm modem link. Luggage handling. Valet serv. Concierge serv. Microwaves avail. Many balconies. On river. Boutique hotel built 1914. Eclectic, international decor, antiques. Totally nonsmoking. Cr cds: A, C, D, DS, MC, V.

D SC

★ ★ ★ **JACKSON HOUSE.** *107 Madison St (78204), downtown. 210/225-4045; res: 800/221-4045; FAX 210/227-0877.* E-mail nobleinns@aol.com. 6 rms, 1 with shower only, 2 story. S, D $90-$135; wkends (2-day min); higher rates Fiesta. Children over 14 yrs only. TV; cable (premium). Complimentary full bkfst; afternoon refreshments. Restaurant nearby. Ck-out 11 am, ck-in 3 pm. Business servs avail. In-rm modem link. Luggage handling. Valet serv. Concierge serv. Indoor pool. Fireplaces; some in-rm whirlpools. Built in 1894; Victorian setting. Totally nonsmoking. Cr cds: A, DS, MC, V.

★★★ **OGE HOUSE.** *209 Washington (78204), Riverwalk. 210/223-2353; FAX 210/226-5812; res: 800/242-2770.* Web ogeinn.com. 9 rms, 1 with shower only, 3 story. S, D $135-$195. Children over 16 yrs only. TV; cable. Complimentary full bkfst. Ck-out 11 am, ck-in 3 pm. Business servs avail. In-rm modem link. Luggage handling. Refrigerators; many fireplaces. Mansion built 1857 for prominent rancher; antiques. Cr cds: A, C, D, DS, MC, V.

★ **RIVERWALK.** *329 Old Guilbeau (78204), on Riverwalk. 210/212-8300; FAX 210/229-9422; res: 800/254-4440.* 11 rms, shower only, 2 story. S, D $99-$155; higher rates hols (2-3-day min). TV; cable. Complimentary continental bkfst. Complimentary coffee in rms. Ck-out 11 am, ck-in 3 pm. Business servs avail. In-rm modem link. Refrigerators; many fireplaces. Two authentic log cabins moved here from Tennessee. Totally nonsmoking. Cr cds: A, DS, MC, V.

D

★ **ROYAL SWAN GUEST HOUSE.** *236 Madison (78204), downtown. 210/223-3776; res: 800/368-3073.* E-mail theswan@onr.com. 5 rms, 1 with shower only, 1 suite. S, D $80-$115; suite $115; wkends, hols (2-day min). Children over 12 yrs only. TV; cable, VCR avail. Complimentary full bkfst. Complimentary coffee in rms. Restaurant nearby. Ck-out noon, ck-in 3 pm. Business servs avail. In-rm modem link. Some fireplaces. Built in 1892; stained glass, original woodwork. Totally nonsmoking. Cr cds: A, DS, MC, V.

Resort

★★★ **HYATT REGENCY HILL COUNTRY.** *9800 Hyatt Resort Dr (78251), north of downtown. 210/647-1234; FAX 210/681-9681.* 500 units, 4 story. Mid-Mar-Nov: S, D $240-$315; each addl $25; suites $425-$2,250; under 18 free; hol, golf plans; lower rates rest of yr. Valet parking $8. TV; cable (premium). 2 heated pools; whirlpool, poolside serv. Playground. Supervised child's activities; ages 3-12. Restaurants (see ANTLERS LODGE). Rm serv 6 am-midnight. Bar 4 pm-2 am; entertainment Thurs-Sat. Ck-out noon, ck-in 4 pm. Coin lndry. Convention facilities. Business center. In-rm modem link. Bellhops. Valet serv. Concierge. Shopping arcade. Beauty shop. Lighted tennis, pro. 18-hole golf, greens fee $90-$100, pro. Bicycle rentals. Hiking trail. Exercise rm; instructor, weights, treadmill, sauna. Massage. Lawn games. Rec rm. Game rm. Refrigerators; microwaves avail. Balconies. Ranch-style property on 200 landscaped acres; man-made river. Luxury level. Cr cds: A, C, D, DS, JCB, MC, V.

D SC

Restaurants

✔★ **ALDACO'S.** *1141 E Commerce (78205), St Paul's Square, downtown. 210/222-0561.* Hrs: 10:30 am-10 pm; Mon to 8 pm; Tues to 9 pm; Sat from 8 am. Closed Sun; most major hols. Res accepted. Mexican menu. Bar. Semi-a la carte: bkfst $1-$5, lunch $5-$8, dinner $5-$15. Child's meals. Specialties: chili rellenos, brocheta alcarbon. Entertainment Fri, Sat. Parking. Outdoor dining. Local artwork on display. Cr cds: A, DS, MC, V.

✔★★ **ALDINO CUCINA ITALIANA.** *622 NW Loop 410 (78216), north of downtown. 210/340-0000.* Hrs: 11 am-11 pm. Closed Thanksgiving. Italian menu. Beer, wine. Semi-a la carte: lunch $5-$15, dinner $7-$18. Child's meals. Specialties: fettuccine primavera, rotisserie chicken, duck Aldino. Pompeiian decor with broken columns. Cr cds: A, DS, MC, V.

D

★★ **ALDO'S RISTORANTE.** *8539 Fredericksburg Rd (78229), north of downtown. 210/696-2536.* Hrs: 11 am-10 pm; Fri to 11 pm; Sat 5-11 pm; Sun from 5 pm. Closed most major hols. Res accepted. Italian menu. Bar. Semi-a la carte: lunch $6.50-$9.95, dinner $9.55-$23. Specialty: salmone alla Pavarotti. Outdoor dining. Intimate dining in early 1900s house. Cr cds: A, C, D, DS, MC, V.

★★★ **ANAQUA GRILL.** *(See Marriott Plaza Hotel) 210/229-1000.* Hrs: 7 am-2 pm, 6-10 pm; Fri, Sat to 11 pm; Sun brunch 10 am-2 pm. Res accepted. Bar. A la carte entrees: bkfst $4.25-$9.25, dinner $7.95-$17.95. Semi-a la carte: lunch $7.50-$12. Tapas $3.50-$9.95. Sun brunch $17.95. Child's meals. Specializes in fresh seafood, Southwestern and Eurasian cuisine. Own baking. Valet parking. Outdoor dining. View of garden, courtyard, fountains. Cr cds: A, C, D, DS, ER, MC, V.

D

★★★ **ANTLERS LODGE.** *(See Hyatt Regency Hill Country Resort) 210/520-4001.* Hrs: 5:30-10 pm. Closed Mon. Res accepted. Bar. Wine list. Semi-a la carte: dinner $18-$28. Specialties: mesquite smoked prime rib, chili dusted Ahi tuna steak. Valet parking. Southwestern decor. Cr cds: A, C, D, DS, JCB, MC, V.

D

✔★★ **BARCELONA'S.** *4901 Broadway (78209), in Alamo Heights, north of downtown. 210/822-6129.* Hrs: 11 am-11 pm; Sat, Sun brunch to 3 pm. Closed Thanksgiving, Dec 25. Mediterranean menu. Bar. Semi-a la carte: lunch $6-$13, dinner $8-$16. Sat, Sun brunch $7-$16. Child's meals. Specialties: seafood paella, Spanish shrimp, steak provençe. Flamenco band Sat. Patio dining. Colorful Spanish decor. Cr cds: A, C, D, DS, MC, V.

★ **THE BAYOUS.** *517 N Presa St (78205), on Riverwalk. 210/223-6403.* Hrs: 11:30 am-11 pm; Fri, Sat to midnight; Sun brunch 11:30 am-3 pm. Res accepted. Cajun, Amer menu. Bar. Semi-a la carte: lunch $3.95-$12.95, dinner $7.95-$19.95. Sun brunch $12.95. Child's meals. Specialties: red snapper Valerie, shrimp Barataria, marinated crab claws. Oyster bar. Entertainment. Parking. Outdoor dining. Dining rm overlooks river. Cr cds: A, C, D, DS, MC, V.

D

★★★ **BIGA.** *206 E Locust St, north of downtown. 210/225-0722.* Hrs: 5:30-10:30 pm; Fri, Sat to 11 pm. Closed Sun; some major hols. Extensive wine list. Semi-a la carte: dinner $11-$25. Entertainment Thurs. Specializes in Gulf seafood, breads, wild game. Parking. In converted old mansion. Cr cds: A, C, D, DS, MC, V.

★★★ **BISTRO TIME.** *5137 Fredericksburg Rd (78229), north of downtown. 210/344-6626.* Hrs: 5-9 pm; Fri, Sat to 10 pm; early-bird dinner Mon-Thurs to 6 pm. Closed Sun; July 4, Thanksgiving, Dec 25. Res accepted. Continental menu. Wine, beer. Semi-a la carte: dinner $9-$24. Specialties: lump crab cakes, steak Diane. Cr cds: A, C, D, MC, V.

★★ **BOUDRO'S, A TEXAS BISTRO.** *421 E Commerce St (78205), on Riverwalk. 210/224-8484.* E-mail restaurant@boudros.com; web www.boudros.com. Hrs: 11 am-11 pm; Fri, Sat to midnight. Res accepted. Southwestern menu. A la carte entrees: lunch $4-$9, dinner $12-$22. Specialties: blackened prime rib, smoked shrimp enchiladas, fresh Gulf red fish. Outdoor dining. Historic building; pictographs on walls, original artwork. Cr cds: A, C, D, DS, JCB, MC, V.

D

★★ **CAPPY'S.** *5011 Broadway St, north of downtown. 210/828-9669.* Hrs: 11 am-3 pm, 5-10 pm; Fri, Sat to 11 pm; Sun from 10:30 am; Sat, Sun brunch to 3 pm. Closed July 4, Thanksgiving, Dec 25. Res accepted. Bar. Semi-a la carte: lunch $6.95-$8.95, dinner $11.50-$22. Sat, Sun brunch $8.95-$11.95. Child's meals. Specializes in chicken, swordfish. Parking. Outdoor dining. Local artwork on display. Totally nonsmoking. Cr cds: A, D, MC, V.

D

★ **CARRANZA MEAT MARKET.** *701 Austin St (78215), south of downtown. 210/223-0903.* Hrs: 11 am-2 pm, 5-10 pm; Fri to 11 pm; Sat 5-11 pm. Closed Sun; major hols. Wine, beer. Semi-a la carte: lunch, dinner $6.95-$28.50. Specializes in steak, seafood, barbecue. Parking. Originally a saloon and nightclub (1870). Family-owned. Cr cds: A.

[♿]

✓★ **CASA RIO.** *430 E Commerce St, on Riverwalk. 210/225-6718.* Hrs: 11 am-11 pm. Closed Jan 1, Dec 25. Mexican menu. Serv bar. Semi-a la carte: lunch, dinner $3.95-$8.95. Child's meals. Specialties: green chicken enchiladas, fajitas, pollo asado. Parking. Outdoor dining. Riverboat dining by res. On San Antonio River. Family-owned. Cr cds: A, C, D, DS, MC, V.

[D] [♿]

★★ **CASCABEL.** *(See Doubletree Hotel) 210/321-4860.* Hrs: 6:30 am-10 pm; Fri, Sat to 11 pm. Res accepted. Southwestern menu. Bar. Semi-a la carte: bkfst $4.95-$7.95, lunch $5-$7.95, dinner $14-$22. Specialties: pecan-crusted salmon, grilled Texas ribeye steak, potato-crusted crab cakes. Parking. Cr cds: A, C, D, DS, MC, V.

[D] [♿]

★★★ **CHEZ ARDID.** *1919 San Pedro Ave (78212), north of downtown. 210/732-3203.* Hrs: 6-10:30 pm. Closed Sun; Jan 1, Thanksgiving, Dec 25. Res accepted. French menu. Bar. Wine cellar. Semi-a la carte: dinner $16-$25. Prix fixe: dinner $25-$35. Specialties: grilled quail salad, crab meat Chez Ardid, poached lobster. Chef-owned. Cr cds: A, C, D, MC, V.

[D] [♿]

★★ **CRUMPET'S.** *3920 Harry Wurzbach (78209), north of downtown. 210/821-5454.* Hrs: 11 am-2:30 pm, 5:30-10 pm; Fri to 11 pm; Sat 11 am-3 pm, 5:30-11 pm; Sun 11 am-3 pm, 5-9 pm. Closed Jan 1, Dec 25. Res accepted. Bar. Wine list. Complete meals: lunch $6.95-$7.95, dinner $8.95-$19.50. Brunch $14.95. Specializes in beef, pasta, seafood. Own pasta, pastries. Outdoor dining. Classical musicians. Cr cds: A, C, D, DS, MC, V.

[D] [SC] [♿] [♥]

✓★ **EL JARRO DE ARTURO.** *13421 San Pedro Ave (78216), TX 281N, exit Bitters Rd, north of downtown. 210/494-5084.* Hrs: 11 am-10 pm; Fri, Sat to 12:30 am. Closed Thanksgiving, Dec 25. Res accepted. Mexican menu. Bar. Semi-a la carte: lunch $4.95-$6.50, dinner $6.25-$15.95. Child's meals. Specialties: green enchiladas, chili ancho chicken, black bean nachos. Own baking. Musicians Fri, Sat. Mexican decor. Family-owned. Cr cds: A, C, D, DS, MC, V.

[D]

★★ **ERNESTO'S.** *2559 Jackson Keller, 7 mi W on Loop 410 W, north of downtown. 210/344-1248.* Hrs: 11:30 am-2 pm, 5:30-10 pm; Fri, Sat to 10:30 pm. Closed Sun; Jan 1, Dec 25. Mexican menu. Bar. Semi-a la carte: lunch $5.95-$12.95, dinner $9.75-$17.95. Specialties: green cerviche, snapper Veracruz. Storefront setting. Cr cds: A, C, D, MC, V.

★★★ **FIG TREE.** *515 Villita St (78205), in La Villita. 210/224-1976.* E-mail figtreerestaurant@worldnet.att.net. Hrs: 6-10 pm. Closed most major hols. Res accepted. Continental menu. Serv bar. Semi-a la carte: dinner $18.25-$29.75. Specializes in seafood, châteaubriand, rack of lamb. Outdoor dining. Elegant decor. Overlooks Riverwalk. Cr cds: A, C, D, DS, MC, V.

[D] [♿]

★ **FORMOSA GARDENS.** *1011 NE Loop 410 (78209), north of downtown. 210/828-9988.* Hrs: 11 am-2:30 pm, 5-10 pm; early-bird dinner 5-6:30 pm. Closed Thanksgiving, Dec 25. Res accepted. Chinese menu. Bar. Semi-a la carte: lunch $4.75-$5.25, dinner $6.25-$25. Specializes in Hunan, Szechuan dishes. Valet parking. Outdoor dining. Dining rm divided into small sections. Cr cds: A, C, D, DS, MC, V.

[D] [♿]

✓★ **FRENCH QUARTER GRILL.** *4903 NW Loop 410 (78229), 12 mi NW on Loop 410, Summit Pkwy exit, north of downtown. 210/509-8900.* Hrs: 11:15 am-9:45 pm; Fri, Sat to 10:45 pm; Sun brunch to 3 pm. Closed Thanksgiving, Dec 25. Cajun menu. Bar. Semi-a la carte: lunch $4.95-$11.95, dinner $5.95-$17.95. Sun brunch $14.95. Child's meals. Specializes in seafood, steak. Own baking. Pianist Sun. Patio dining. Hand-painted murals. Cr cds: A, C, D, DS, MC, V.

[D] [♿]

★★ **GREY MOSS INN.** *19010 Scenic Loop Rd (78023), north of downtown. 210/695-8301.* Hrs: 5-10 pm. Closed Jan 1, Dec 25. Res accepted; required Fri, Sat. Serv bar. A la carte entrees: dinner $19.25-$40. Child's meals. Specializes in grilled steaks, seafood, chicken. Own baking. Outdoor dining on patio of historic inn. Cr cds: A, DS, MC, V.

✓★ **LA CALESA.** *2103 E Hildebrand Ave (78209), at Broadway St, north of downtown. 210/822-4475.* Hrs: 11 am-9:30 pm; Fri to 10:30 pm; Sat 9 am-11:30 pm; Sun 11:30 am-9 pm. Closed Easter, Thanksgiving, Dec 25. Mexican menu. Serv bar. Semi-a la carte: lunch, dinner $4.15-$11.95. Child's meals. Specialties: cochinita pibil, pollo en Escabeche. Parking. Outdoor dining. Totally nonsmoking. Cr cds: A, C, D, DS, MC, V.

[D]

✓★ **LA FOGATA.** *2427 Vance Jackson Rd, 6 mi N on I-10, Vance Jackson exit, north of downtown. 210/340-1337.* Hrs: 11 am-11 pm; Fri to midnight; Sat, Sun 9 am-midnight. Closed Jan 1, Dec 25. Mexican menu. Bar. Semi-a la carte: bkfst $3.25-$4.50, lunch, dinner $5.25-$14.95. Child's meals. Specializes in enchilada verdes, chile relleno, Mexican bkfst. Own tortillas. Parking. Outdoor dining. Mexican decor. Cr cds: A, C, D, DS, MC, V.

[D] [♿]

✓★ **LA MARGARITA.** *120 Produce Row, west of downtown. 210/227-7140.* Hrs: 11 am-10 pm; Fri, Sat to midnight. Mexican menu. Bar. Semi-a la carte: lunch, dinner $5.25-$10.50. Child's meals. Specializes in fajitas, shrimp cocktail, oyster cocktail. Entertainment. Parking. Outdoor dining. Restored farmers market building (1910). Cr cds: A, C, D, DS, MC, V.

[D] [♿]

★★★ **LAS CANARIAS.** *(See La Mansion Del Rio Hotel) 210/272-1063.* Hrs: 6:30 am-11 pm; Sun brunch 10:30 am-2:30 pm. Res accepted. Bar to midnight. Wine list. Semi-a la carte: lunch $7.50-$12.50, dinner $22-$35. Sun brunch $24.95. Child's meals. Specialties: seven-spiced tuna steak, grilled swordfish fillet. Entertainment. Overlooks Riverwalk. Cr cds: A, C, D, DS, JCB, MC, V.

[D] [♿]

★ **LIBERTY BAR.** *328 E Josephine (78215), downtown. 210/227-1187.* Hrs: 11:30 am-10:30 pm; Fri, Sat to midnight. Res accepted. French, Mexican menu. Bar to 2 am Fri, Sat. Semi-a la carte: lunch $8-$10, dinner $10-$20. Specialties: lamb sausage, mushroom sandwiches, chicken breast with hoja santa. Parking. Oldest bar in Texas in continuous operation. Cr cds: A, MC, V.

[D] [♿]

★★ **LITTLE RHEIN STEAK HOUSE.** *231 S Alamo St (78205), in La Villita. 210/225-2111.* E-mail little@worldnet.att.net. Hrs: 5-10 pm. Closed most major hols. Res accepted. Bar. A la carte entrees: dinner $16.95-$29.95. Child's meals. Specializes in steak, seafood, lamb chops. Terrace dining. Overlooks San Antonio River and outdoor theater. First 2-story structure in San Antonio (1847). Cr cds: A, C, D, DS, MC, V.

[D] [♿]

★ **LONE STAR.** *237 Losoya (78205), on Riverwalk. 210/223-9374.* Hrs: 11 am-10:30 pm; Fri, Sat to midnight. Closed Thanksgiving, Dec 24, 25. Bar. Semi-a la carte: dinner $7.95-$19.95. Child's meals. Specializes in steak. Outdoor dining. Cr cds: A, DS, MC, V.

[D] [♿]

✓★ **LOS BARRIOS.** *4223 Blanco Rd (78212), north of downtown. 210/732-6017.* Hrs: 10 am-10 pm; Fri, Sat to midnight; Sun from 9 am. Closed Easter, Thanksgiving, Dec 25. Mexican menu. Bar. Semi-a la carte: lunch, dinner $5-$14. Child's meals. Specialties: enchilada verdes, cabrito, churrasco. Entertainment Fri-Sun. Parking. Traditional Mexican dining. Family owned. Cr cds: A, C, D, DS, MC, V.

★ ★ **MENCIUS' GOURMET HUNAN.** *7959 Fredericksburg Rd (78229), north of downtown. 210/615-1288.* Hrs: 11 am-2:15 pm, 5-10 pm; Sun-Tues to 9:30 pm. Closed Jan 1, Thanksgiving, Dec 25. Res accepted. Chinese menu. Bar. Semi-a la carte: lunch $4.75-$5.25, dinner $5.95-$14.95. Specialties: Mencius beef, shrimp & scallops, General Tso's chicken. Parking. Cr cds: A, C, D, DS, MC, V.

D

★ ★ **MESTEÑA.** *7959 Broadway (78209), in Alamo Heights, north of downtown. 210/822-7733.* Hrs: 11:30 am-10 pm; Fri, Sat to 10:30 pm; early-bird dinner Mon-Thurs 5:30-7 pm. Closed Sun; Easter, Thanksgiving, Dec 25. Res accepted. Southwestern menu. Bar. Semi-a la carte: lunch $6-$10, dinner $13-$26. Child's meals. Specialties: red chile pecan-crusted rack of lamb, seared Achiote salmon, aged grilled strip sirloin. Patio dining. Brick arches, stucco walls. Cr cds: A, D, DS, MC, V.

D

✔★ **MI TIERRA.** *218 Produce Row, at Market Square, downtown. 210/225-1262.* Open 24 hrs. Mexican menu. Bar noon-2 am; Sat, Sun from 10 am. Semi-a la carte: bkfst $2.50-$6.75, lunch, dinner $3.45-$9.95. Specializes in fajitas, cabrito, Mexican dinner combinations. Entertainment. Outdoor dining. Located in old farmers market building; built 1910. Family-owned. Cr cds: A, C, D, DS, MC, V.

D

★ **MICHELINO'S.** *521 Riverwalk (78205), on Riverwalk. 210/223-2939.* Hrs: 11 am-11 pm; Fri, Sat to midnight. Northern Italian menu. Bar. Semi-a la carte: lunch $5.25-$13, dinner $7.95-$15.95. Child's meals. Specialties: fettucine verde, chicken Florentine, pizza. Outdoor dining. Cr cds: A, DS, MC, V.

★ ★ ★ **MORTON'S OF CHICAGO.** *300 Crockett (78205), downtown. 210/228-0700.* Hrs: 5:30-11 pm; Sun 5-10 pm. Closed most major hols. Res accepted. Semi-a la carte: dinner $16.95-$29.95. Specializes in steak, fresh seafood. Valet parking. Elegant, contemporary decor. Cr cds: A, C, D, JCB, MC, V.

D

★ ★ **OLD SAN FRANCISCO STEAK HOUSE.** *10223 Sahara St (10223), north of downtown. 210/342-2321.* Hrs: 5-10 pm; Fri, Sat to 11 pm; Sun 4 pm-10 pm. Res accepted. Bar. Complete meals: dinner $8.95-$24.95. Child's meals. Specializes in steak, poultry, prime rib. Pianist. Free valet parking. Victorian decor. Cr cds: A, C, D, DS, MC, V.

D

★ ★ **PAESANO'S.** *555 E Basse Rd (78209), downtown. 210/828-5191.* Hrs: 11 am-11 pm. Closed Thanksgiving, Dec. 25. Northern Italian menu. Bar. A la carte entrees: lunch $6.95-$9.95, dinner $6.95-$26.95. Specialties: shrimp Paesano, penne all'arrabbiata, veal Christina. Parking. Cr cds: A, C, D, MC, V.

D

★ **PICO DE GALLO.** *111 S Leona Ave (78201), west of downtown. 210/225-6060.* Hrs: 8 am-10 pm; Fri, Sat to 2 am. Closed Thanksgiving. Mexican menu. Bar. Semi-a la carte: bkfst $3.95-$5.95, lunch, dinner $4.75-$8.95. Child's meals. Specializes in fajitas. Entertainment Wed-Sun. Mexican artifacts. Family-owned. Cr cds: A, C, D, DS, MC, V.

★ **PIECA D'ITALIA.** *502 Riverwalk (78205), on Riverwalk. 210/227-5511.* Hrs: 10:30 am-10:30 pm; Fri, Sat to midnight. Closed Thanksgiving, Dec 25. Res accepted. Italian menu. Wine, beer. Semi-a la carte: lunch, dinner $4.89-$16.99. Specializes in fresh pasta, pizza, orange roughy. Patio dining overlooking river, many tables under Crockett St Bridge. Cr cds: A, C, D, DS, MC, V.

D SC

★ ★ ★ **POLO'S AT THE FAIRMOUNT.** *(See Fairmount Hotel) 210/224-8800.* Hrs: 7-10:30 am, 11:30 am-2 pm, 6-10 pm; Fri to 10:30 pm; Sat 7-10:30 am, 6-10:30 pm; Sun 7 am-noon. Res accepted. Continental menu. Bar 11:30-1 am. A la carte entrees: bkfst $5-$8, lunch $10-$15, dinner $23-$40. Child's meals. Specialties: stuffed quail, Colorado trout, French bean salad. Valet parking. Outdoor dining. Cr cds: A, C, D, DS, MC, V.

D

★ ★ **RAZMIKO'S RISTORANTE ITALIANO.** *(8055 West Ave, Selma 78213) at Lockhill. 210/366-0416.* Hrs: 11 am-10 pm; Fri, Sat to 11 pm; Sun noon-9 pm. Closed Jan 1, Thanksgiving, Dec 25. Res accepted. Italian menu. Bar. Semi-a la carte: lunch $6.95-$9.95, dinner $9.95-$26.95. Specialties: grilled veal chop, trota Milanese, shrimp Razmiko. Parking. Outdoor dining. Cr cds: A, C, D, DS, MC, V.

D

✔★ **RIO RIO CANTINA.** *421 E Commerce St, on Riverwalk. 210/226-8462.* Hrs: 11 am-11 pm; Fri, Sat to midnight. California, Tex-Mex menu. Bar. Semi-a la carte: lunch $4.95-$10, dinner $6.95-$15. Child's meals. Specialties: botano grande, camarones al mojo de ajo, enchiladas Rio Rio. Outdoor riverside dining. Cr cds: A, C, D, DS, MC, V.

D

★ ★ **ROMANO'S MACARONI GRILL.** *24116 I-10 West (78257), 13 N on I-10W at Leon Springs exit, north of downtown. 210/698-0003.* Hrs: 11 am-10 pm; Fri, Sat to 11 pm. Closed Thanksgiving, Dec 25. Italian menu. Wine, beer. Semi-a la carte: lunch $5.95-$8.95, dinner $6.95-$16.50. Specializes in pasta, calamari fritti. Parking. Cr cds: A, D, MC, V.

D

✔★ **ROSARIO'S.** *1014 S Alamo St (78210), downtown. 210/223-1806.* Hrs: 10:45 am-10 pm; Mon to 3 pm; Fri to midnight; Sat to 11 pm. Closed Sun; Jan 1, Thanksgiving, Dec 25. Mexican menu. Bar. Semi-a la carte: lunch $4.95-$6.95, dinner $5.95-$9.95. Specialties: shrimp fajitas, pollo maria. Entertainment Fri, Sat. Outdoor dining. Contemporary decor. Cr cds: A, C, D, DS, MC, V.

D

★ ★ ★ **RUTH'S CHRIS STEAK HOUSE.** *7720 Jones Maltsberger Rd, at Concord Plaza, north of downtown. 210/821-5051.* Hrs: 5-11 pm; Sun 4-10 pm. Closed Dec 25. Res accepted. Bar. A la carte entrees: dinner $17.95-$29.95. Specializes in steak, live Maine lobster, lamb. Parking. Upscale Southwestern decor. Cr cds: A, C, D, MC, V.

D

★ ★ **STAR ANISE.** *152 Pecan St (78205), downtown. 210/271-0543.* Hrs: 5:30-10:30 pm. Closed Thanksgiving, Dec 24. Res accepted. Pacific Rim menu. Bar. Semi-a la carte: dinner $15-$20. Child's meals. Specialties: Star Anise crab and shrimp cakes, East Indian spiced bass, roasted Asian-style chicken. Free valet parking. Outdoor dining. Mediterranean decor. Cr cds: A, DS, MC, V.

D

★ **TOWER OF THE AMERICAS.** *222 HemisFair Plaza, downtown. 210/223-3101.* Hrs: 11 am-2 pm, 5-10 pm; Fri to 10:30 pm; Sat 11 am-2:30 pm, 5-10:30 pm; Sun 11 am-2:30 pm. Closed Dec 25. Res accepted. Bar 4:30-11 pm; Fri, Sat 11-12:30 am; Sun from 11 am. Complete meals: lunch $7-$15, dinner $12-$35. Child's meals. Specializes in lobster, steak, prime rib. Parking. Revolving tower; view of city. Elvtr fee is added to bill. Cr cds: A, C, D, DS, JCB, MC, V.

D SC

★ **ZUNI GRILL.** *223 Losoya (78205), on Riverwalk. 210/227-0864.* Hrs: 8 am-11 pm; Fri, Sat to midnight. Closed Dec 25. Southwestern menu. Serv bar. Semi-a la carte: bkfst, lunch $4.95-$7.95, dinner $10.95-

$21.95. Child's meals. Specialties: pork loin with adobe sauce, shrimp with Chipotle chile, tortilla lasagna. Outdoor dining. Overlooks river. Cr cds: A, C, D, DS, MC, V.

Unrated Dining Spots

5050 DINER. *5050 Broadway St, north of downtown. 210/828-4386.* Hrs: 11-2 am. Res accepted. Mexican, Amer menu. Bar. Semi-a la carte: lunch, dinner $3.50-$7.50. Child's meals. Specialties: chicken-fried steak, Tex-Mex dishes. Parking. Neighborhood bistro atmosphere; art-deco decor. Cr cds: A, D, DS, MC, V.

BRAZIER AT LOS PATIOS. *2015 NE Loop I-410, Starcrest exit, north of downtown. 210/655-9270.* Hrs: 11:30 am-10 pm. Closed Mon; also Jan-Feb. Southwestern menu. Bar. Semi-a la carte: lunch, dinner $6.95-$17.95. Specializes in mesquite-grilled steak, fish, chicken. Salad bar. Parking. Outdoor dining. On Salado Creek. Cr cds: A, D, DS, MC, V.

DICK'S LAST RESORT. *406 Navarro St, on Riverwalk. 210/224-0026.* Hrs: 11-2 am. Bar. Semi-a la carte: lunch $3.75-$8.95, dinner $8.95-$16.95. Specializes in barbecued ribs, fried catfish, honey-roasted chicken. Entertainment. Outdoor dining. Honky-tonk decor. Cr cds: A, C, D, DS, MC, V.

EL MIRADOR. *722 S St Mary's St, south of downtown. 210/225-9444.* Hrs: 6:30 am-3 pm; Wed-Sat also 5:30-10 pm; Sun 9 am-3 pm. Closed some major hols. Mexican menu. Wine, beer. Semi-a la carte: bkfst $1.50-$4, lunch $2.50-$5.50, dinner $5.95-$11. Specialties: xochitl soup, Azteca soup. Parking. Cr cds: MC, V.

GAZEBO AT LOS PATIOS. *2015 NE Loop I-410, Starcrest exit, north of downtown. 210/655-6190.* Hrs: 11:30 am-2:30 pm; Sun 11 am-3 pm. Closed Jan 1, Thanksgiving, Dec 25. Continental, Mexican menu. Bar 11:30 am-2:30 pm. Semi-a la carte: lunch $7.50-$9.95. Sun brunch $13.95. Specializes in crepes, chicken, quiche. Parking. Outdoor dining. Cr cds: A, DS, MC, V.

GUENTHER HOUSE. *205 E Guenther St (78204), downtown. 210/227-1061.* Hrs: 7 am-3 pm; Sun 8 am-2 pm. Closed Jan 1, Thanksgiving, Dec 25. Semi-a la carte: bkfst $2.95-$6.25, lunch $4.50-$6.75. Specializes in Belgian waffles, chicken salad, pastries. Parking. Outdoor dining. House built by founder of Pioneer Flour Mills (1860). Museum and gift shop on grounds. Cr cds: A, DS, MC, V.

San Diego

Founded: 1769
Pop: 1,110,549
Elev: 42 feet
Time zone: Pacific
Area code: 619
Web: www.sandiego.org

The southernmost city in California, San Diego has a distinct Mexican flavor because of its proximity to Mexico's border city of Tijuana. San Diego is built around the water, with 70 miles of beaches at its western edge. Extending from the Pacific Ocean eastward over rolling hills of 1,591 feet, San Diego is a warm city where the sun almost always shines, summer and winter. This balmy year-round climate encourages outdoor living. Within San Diego County are mountains as high as 6,500 feet, a desert area, resorts, flowers, palm trees and a flourishing cultural program.

San Diego was "the place where California began" when explorer Juan Rodriguez Cabrillo, hired by Spain, landed here in 1542. In 1769, the Franciscan priest Fray Junipero Serra built his first mission here, San Diego de Alcala. In 1821, control of San Diego passed from Spain to the new Mexican government. By 1841, however, enough Americans had settled in the area to warrant interest by the United States in what was undoubtedly good real estate. The Mexican government's loose control over California, combined with the United States' new-found theory of Manifest Destiny, led to the acquisition of San Diego by the United States after the short-lived Mexican War.

For many years San Diego has been an important naval base. Its natural harbor is home to several Coast Guard, Marine Corps and Navy installations, including the largest naval air station on the West Coast. Today, San Diego is a growing oceanography center as well.

Business

Nearly one-third of San Diego County's work force is employed by government agencies; the majority of these workers are employed at the various military bases. Half of these people are in some way involved in the manufacture of aircraft products. Second in importance to government is the production of aerospace equipment and missiles.

There are approximately 3,000 manufacturing firms in San Diego County, employing nearly 15 percent of the work force. Biomedical research and manufacturing, as well as other high-technology fields, are becoming increasingly important to the city's economy. Tourism is the third largest industry.

San Diego County is the world's largest avocado producer and one of the leading agricultural counties in the United States.

Convention Facilities

The San Diego Convention Center, located on San Diego Bay, has 254,000 square feet of space in the main exhibit hall and 100,000 square feet of column-free space in the upper-level special events pavilion. The facility also includes 100,000 square feet of meeting space on the upper and mezzanine levels, 32 meeting rooms and a 40,000-square-foot ballroom. The center is less than 10 minutes away from the airport and has underground parking available for 2,000 vehicles.

The San Diego Concourse is a self-contained complex with facilities for theatrical performances, conventions, conferences, meetings, trade shows, workshops, exhibits, banquets, dances, luncheons, recitals, ceremonies, lectures and receptions. There are 64,000 square feet of exhibit space and 25 meeting rooms with capacities ranging from 35 to 4,300 persons. Parking for 1,100 cars is available.

The Civic Theatre, the showplace of the concourse, incorporates the most modern architectural techniques. Its seating capacity is 2,992.

Golden Hall is the most versatile of the halls in the convention complex. It can be used for conventions, trade shows, exhibits, theatrical presentations, concerts and sport shows. Seating capacity is 4,337.

The Plaza Hall, the Copper Room, the Silver Room and the Terrace Room can accommodate many types of events. The Silver and Terrace rooms have dividers that can be used to reduce or enlarge room size.

Sports & Recreation

Day or night, something is going on in San Diego. The city provides a tremendous variety of spectator and participant sports. Major league sports events include football (Chargers), baseball (Padres), ice hockey (Gulls) and indoor soccer (Sockers). Racing enthusiasts can enjoy Thoroughbred racing at Del Mar Thoroughbred Club in Del Mar.

There are more than 80 municipal and public golf courses and more than 1,200 tennis courts. In addition, visitors can choose hiking, biking, horseback riding, boating in San Diego's protected bays and lagoons, waterskiing, surfing, windsurfing, swimming or sunbathing. A favorite diving spot is San Diego's La Jolla Cove, which has the clearest waters on the California coast. The offshore waters are famous for exceptional, year-round ocean fishing.

Entertainment

At night the city offers an array of nightclub entertainment as well as Broadway theater productions and performances by local professional and repertory theater groups. The 581-seat Old Globe Theatre, a locally treasured landmark, is one of three different theaters of the Simon Edison Centre for the Performing Arts. The others are the 225-seat Cassius Carter Centre Stage and the 612-seat outdoor Lowell Davies Festival Theater.

The San Diego Concourse's Civic Theatre is home to the opera and two ballet companies and also hosts popular performers throughout the

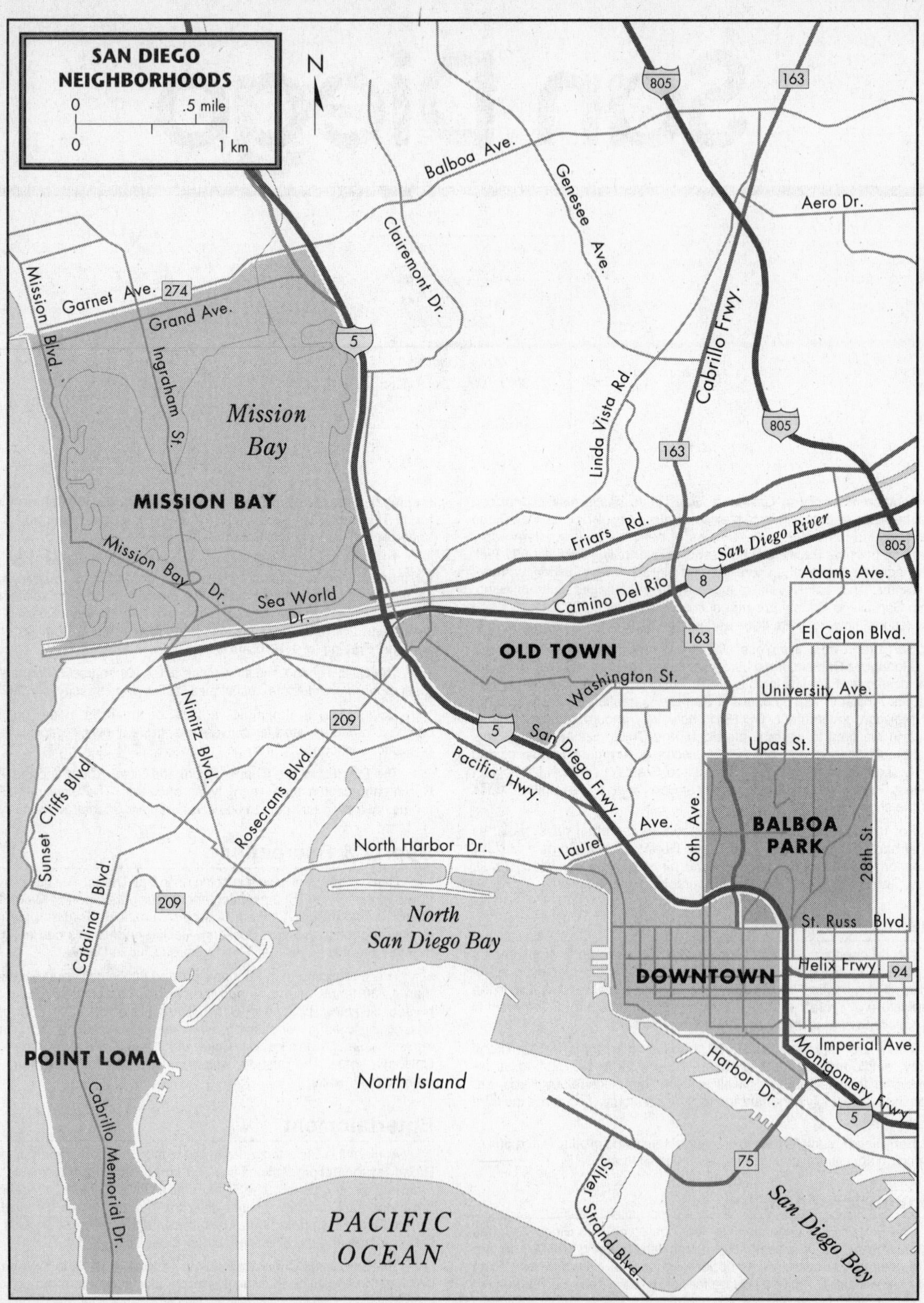
SAN DIEGO NEIGHBORHOODS
0 .5 mile
0 1 km
N
MISSION BAY
Mission Bay
OLD TOWN
BALBOA PARK
DOWNTOWN
POINT LOMA
North San Diego Bay
North Island
PACIFIC OCEAN
San Diego Bay
San Diego River
Balboa Ave.
Genesee Ave.
Aero Dr.
Clairemont Dr.
Cabrillo Frwy.
Mission Blvd.
Garnet Ave.
Grand Ave.
Ingraham St.
Linda Vista Rd.
Friars Rd.
Mission Bay Dr.
Sea World Dr.
Camino Del Rio
Adams Ave.
El Cajon Blvd.
Washington St.
University Ave.
Upas St.
Nimitz Blvd.
Rosecrans Blvd.
Sunset Cliffs Blvd.
Pacific Hwy.
San Diego Frwy.
Laurel Ave.
6th Ave.
28th St.
North Harbor Dr.
Catalina Blvd.
St. Russ Blvd.
Helix Frwy.
Imperial Ave.
Harbor Dr.
Montgomery Frwy.
Cabrillo Memorial Dr.
Silver Strand Blvd.
805
163
274
5
8
209
94
75

year. During the summer, outdoor concerts are staged in picturesque settings overlooking San Diego Bay.

Historical Areas

San Diego's Spanish heritage is nowhere more firmly rooted than in its dramatically beautiful missions. Of the 21-mission chain that began here and stretched northward through California, two missions and two *asistencias* are within the county.

Mission San Diego de Alcala, California's first mission, was founded in 1769 on Presidio Hill and was relocated to its present site along the San Diego River in 1774. Services are held daily in the mission chapel. Cassette tape players allow visitors to take self-conducted tours. A museum contains some of the mission's original records, as well as many liturgical robes, books and relics.

Mission San Luis Rey, largest of all the California missions, was founded in 1798 by Father Fermin Lasuen, near the city of Oceanside. Named for King Louis IX of France, it is often referred to as "king of the missions." Also worth visiting are Asistencia de San Antonio (1816), better known as Mission San Antonio de Pala, and Santa Ysabel Asistencia (1818).

Old Town, site of the first European settlement in California, is one of the most popular attractions for visitors. This historic section of the city has many restored and reconstructed buildings, old adobe structures, museums, quaint shops and restaurants. Guided walking tours are offered daily by the state park and the Old Town Historical Society. Also, a green line painted on the street directs visitors to the many interesting landmarks.

Other points of interest include the Villa Montezuma, a fine example of Victorian Byzantine-style architecture, housing displays of local history; the *Star of India*, a century-old windjammer, which is the oldest iron sailing vessel still afloat and is part of the Maritime Museum; and the famous Hotel del Coronado (1888), located in Coronado, across the bay from downtown San Diego.

Sightseeing

Beautiful Balboa Park, a 1,200-acre site in the center of the city, has art galleries, museums, theaters, restaurants and many recreational facilities in addition to garden walks, subtropical plants and ponds. Most of the park's activities take place in buildings of Spanish-Moorish architecture left from the Panama-California Exposition of 1915 and the California Pacific International Exposition of 1936. This oasis in the middle of the city is best experienced on foot.

The San Diego Zoo, one of the largest and most famous zoos in the world, has some of the rarest specimens in captivity in its vast collection of animals. Exhibits replicate the animals' natural environments. The Skyfari aerial tramway gives zoo-goers a panoramic view of the zoo. In addition, a 40-minute guided tour on double-deck buses takes visitors through miles of winding roads as driver/guides point out interesting sights.

Sea World, the 150-acre oceanarium on Mission Bay's south shore, is one of California's most popular attractions. Featured are aquariums, marine exhibits and shows with performing animals, such as "Baby Shamu" in a killer whale show. Pilot and beluga whales, sea lions, playful dolphins and walruses are included in the shows.

Seaport Village, an elaborate $14 million shopping and dining complex on San Diego Bay, re-creates the atmosphere of 19th-century California with authentic architectural styles and furnishings, including a turn-of-the-century carousel. Just south of downtown San Diego, the sights and sounds of a bustling California waterfront town of the 1890s may be experienced in the Gaslamp Quarter. The most fully renovated street in this 16-block area is Fifth Avenue, with its gas lamps, brick sidewalks and spectacular examples of Victorian architecture. Fifth Avenue formed the city's business center at the turn of the century. Just west of the Gaslamp Quarter is Horton Plaza, a 7-block retail and entertainment district in the heart of downtown; the 11½ acre complex includes 3 major department stores, 150 small shops and restaurants and a 14-screen theater.

Whale-watching cruises are available during the migration season (mid-December-mid-February), when herds of gray whales make their way from Alaska's Bering Sea to the warm bays and lagoons of Baja. A whale-watching station at Cabrillo National Monument on Point Loma has a glassed-in observatory from which to spot the whales.

A ride along San Diego's 59-mile scenic drive gives a quick lesson in the city's fascinating history, scenery, people and places. The drive takes about three hours, but a week could be spent enjoying the sights along the way. The route is marked about every quarter-mile with blue and yellow highway signs illustrated with a white seagull.

A few miles south of San Diego and directly across the border is Tijuana, a popular tourist destination and a short trip by car, bus or the San Diego Trolley. Contact the International Visitor Information Center for border-crossing regulations.

General References

Area code: 619

Phone Numbers

POLICE, FIRE & PARAMEDICS: 911

POISON CONTROL CENTER: 543-6000

TIME: 853-1212 **WEATHER:** 289-1212

Information Sources

San Diego Convention and Visitors Bureau, 401 B St, Suite 1400, 92101; 232-3101.

San Diego Chamber of Commerce, 402 W Broadway, Suite 1000, 92101; 232-0124.

International Visitor Information Center, 11 Horton Plaza, 92101; 236-1212.

Balboa Park Information Center, 239-0512.

Transportation

AIRLINES: Aeromexico; Alaska; American; America West; British Airways; Continental; Delta; Frontier; Midwest Express; Northwest; Southwest; TWA; United; USAir; and other commuter and regional airlines.

AIRPORTS: San Diego International Lindbergh Field, 231-2100.

CAR RENTAL AGENCIES: (See IMPORTANT TOLL-FREE NUMBERS) Alamo 297-0311; Avis 231-7171; Budget 235-8313; Hertz 220-5222; National 231-7100.

PUBLIC TRANSPORTATION: San Diego Transit, San Diego-Tijuana Trolley 231-1466.

RAILROAD PASSENGER SERVICE: Amtrak 800/872-7245.

Newspaper

San Diego Union-Tribune.

Convention Facilities

San Diego Concourse, 202 C St, 236-6500 or 236-6510.

San Diego Convention Center, 111 W Harbor Dr, at 5th Ave, 525-5000.

Sports & Recreation

Major Sports Facilities

Qualcomm Stadium, 9449 Friars Rd (Padres, baseball, 881-6500; Chargers, football, 874-4500).

San Diego Sports Arena, 3942 Hancock St (Sockers, indoor soccer, 224-4625; Gulls, ice hockey, 224-4625).

Racetrack

Del Mar Thoroughbred Club, County Fairgrounds, Del Mar, 755-1141.

Jai Alai

Fronton Palacio, Revolucion Ave & 7th St, Tijuana, Mexico, 231-1910.

Cultural Facilities

Theaters

Cassius Carter Centre Stage, Balboa Park, 234-5623.

Coronado Playhouse, 1775 Strand Way, Coronado, 435-4856.

Hahn Cosmopolitan Theatre, 444 4th Ave, 234-9583.

La Jolla Playhouse, University of California at San Diego, Mandell Weiss Center, La Jolla Village Dr, La Jolla, 550-1010.

Lawrence Welk Resort Theatre-Museum, 8860 Lawrence Welk Dr, Escondido, 749-3448 or 749-3000.

Old Globe Theatre, Balboa Park, 239-2255.

Old Town Theatre, 4040 Twiggs St, 688-2494.

San Diego Repertory Theatre, Lyceum Theatre, 79 Horton Plaza, 231-3586.

Spreckels Theatre, 121 Broadway, 234-8397.

Concert Halls

Civic Theatre, San Diego Concourse, 202 C St, 236-6510.

Museums

International Aerospace Museum Hall of Fame, Aerospace Historical Center, Balboa Park, 232-8322.

Junipero Serra Museum, Presidio Park, 2727 Presidio Dr, 297-3258.

Maritime Museum Association, 1306 N Harbor Dr, 234-9153.

Mingei International Museum of World Folk Art, 1439 El Prado, in Central Plaza of Balboa Park, 239-0003.

Museum of Man, Balboa Park, 239-2001.

Natural History Museum, Balboa Park, 232-3821.

Reuben H. Fleet Space Theater and Science Center, 1875 El Prado, Balboa Park, 238-1168 or 238-1233.

San Diego Aerospace Museum, Aerospace Historical Center, Balboa Park, 234-8291.

San Diego Hall of Champions, 1649 El Prado, Balboa Park, 234-2544.

Stephen Birch Aquarium-Museum, 2300 Expedition Way (entrance on N Torrey Pines), at Scripps Institution of Oceanography, University of California at San Diego, La Jolla, 534-6933, 534-3474 or 534-4109.

Villa Montezuma/Jesse Shepard House, 1925 K St, 239-2211.

Art Museums & Galleries

Museum of Art, Balboa Park, 232-7931.

Museum of Contemporary Art, San Diego, 1001 Kettner Blvd, 234-1001.

Museum of Photographic Arts, 1649 El Prado, Casa de Balboa, 239-5262.

Spanish Village Arts and Crafts Center, 1770 Village Place, Balboa Park, 233-9050.

Timken Museum of Art, 1500 El Prado, Balboa Park, 239-5548.

Points of Interest

Historical

Cabrillo National Monument, 10 mi W of I-8 on Catalina Blvd (CA 209), at tip of Point Loma, 557-5450.

Gaslamp Quarter, bordered by 4th, 6th & Broadway Aves & K St, 233-5227.

Heritage Park, Juan & Harney Sts, near Old Town.

Hotel del Coronado, 1500 Orange Ave, Coronado, 435-6611.

Mission Basilica San Diego De Alcala, 10818 San Diego Mission Rd, 281-8449 or 283-7319.

Mission San Antonio de Pala, 44 mi N via I-15, then 7 mi E on CA 76 in Pala, 742-3317.

Mission San Luis Rey de Francia, N on I-5 to Oceanside, then 4½ mi E on CA 76, 757-3651.

Old Town, around the plaza at Mason St & San Diego Ave.

Presidio Park, Presidio Dr off Taylor St, in Old Town.

Star of India, Maritime Museum Association, 234-9153.

Other Attractions

Balboa Park, center of city; visitor center 239-0512.

House of Pacific Relations, Balboa Park, 234-0739.

Mission Bay Park, N of San Diego River via I-5, 276-8200.

Navy Installation, Broadway Pier, 532-1430 or 532-1431.

San Diego Trolley, Santa Fe Depot, at Kettner Blvd & C St, 595-4949.

San Diego Wild Animal Park, 30 mi NE via I-15 (US 395/CA 163) to Via Rancho Pkwy exit, follow signs, 234-6541.

San Diego Zoo and Children's Zoo, Balboa Park, 234-3153.

Seaport Village, W Harbor Drive at Kettner Blvd, 235-4014.

Sea World, Mission Bay Park, Sea World Dr, exit W off I-5, 226-3901, 800/325-3150 (CA) or 800/SEA-WRLD (exc CA).

Spreckels Outdoor Organ Pavilion, Balboa Park.

Sightseeing Tours

Gray Line bus tours, 3855 Rosencrans St, 491-0011.

Old Town Trolley Tours, 298-8687.

San Diego Harbor Excursion, 1050 Harbor Dr, 234-4111.

Whale-Watching Trips

Fisherman's Landing, 2838 Garrison St, 222-0391.

H & M Landing, 2803 Emerson St, 222-1144.

Horn Blower Invader, 1066 N Harbor Dr, 234-8687.

San Diego Natural History Museum, Balboa Park, 232-3821.

Annual Events

Cinco de Mayo, Old Town San Diego State Historic Park, 237-6770. Wkend closest to May 5.

Corpus Christi Fiesta, Mission San Antonio de Pala. 1st Sun June.

Del Mar Fair, Del Mar Fairgrounds, 755-1161 or 793-5555. 16 days late June-early July.

Festival of Bells, Mission Basilica San Diego de Alcala, 283-7319. Wkend mid-July.

Admission Day, phone 297-1183. Early Sept.

Cabrillo Festival, Cabrillo National Monument. Last wkend Sept-early Oct.

Christmas on the Prado, Spreckles Outdoor Organ Pavilion, Balboa Park. First wkend Dec.

Christmas-Light Boat Parade, San Diego Harbor, Shelter Island Yacht Basin and Mission Bay, 222-4081. Mid-Dec.

City Neighborhoods

Many of the restaurants, unrated dining establishments and some lodgings listed under San Diego include neighborhoods as well as exact street addresses. Geographic descriptions of these areas are given, followed by a table of restaurants arranged by neighborhood.

Balboa Park: Northeast of Downtown; south of Upas St, west of 28th St, north of St Russ Blvd and east of 6th Ave.

Downtown: South and west of I-5 and north and east of the San Diego Bay. **North of Downtown:** North of US 5.

Mission Bay: South of Garnet Ave, west of I-5, north of I-8 and Mission Bay Channel and east of the Pacific Ocean.

Old Town: South of I-8, west of CA 163, north of I-5 and Washington St and east of I-5.

Point Loma: Peninsula west of San Diego Bay and east of the Pacific Ocean.

Lodgings and Food

SAN DIEGO RESTAURANTS BY NEIGHBORHOOD AREAS

(For full description, see alphabetical listings under Restaurants)

BALBOA PARK
Hob Nob Hill. 2271 1st Ave

DOWNTOWN
Anthony's Star Of The Sea Room. 1360 Harbor Dr
Athens Market Taverna. 109 W F Street
Bayou Bar & Grill. 329 Market St
Bella Luna. 748 Fifth Ave
Blue Point. 565 Fifth Ave
Corvette Diner Bar & Grill. 3946 5th Ave
Croce's. 802 Fifth Ave
Dakota. 901 Fifth Ave
Dick's Last Resort. 345 5th Ave
Dobson's. 956 Broadway Circle
Fio's. 801 5th Ave
Harbor House. 831 W Harbor Dr
Karl Strauss' Brewery & Grill. 1157 Columbia St
Kenny's Steak Pub. 939 Fourth Ave
Laurel. 505 Laurel St
Le Fontainebleau (The Westgate Hotel). 1055 Second Ave
Nick's At The Beach. 809 Thomas Ave
Osteria Panevino. 722 Fifth Ave
Panda Inn. 506 Horton Plaza
Rainwater's. 1202 Kettner Blvd
Ruth's Chris Steak House. 1355 N Harbor Dr
Sally's (Hyatt Regency Hotel). One Market Place
Salvatore's. 750 Front St
San Diego Pier Cafe. 885 W Harbor Dr
Top Of The Market. 750 N Harbor Dr
Trattoria Fantastica. 1735 India St
Trattoria La Strada. 702 5th Ave

NORTH OF DOWNTOWN
Aesop's Tables. 8650 Genesee Ave
Afghanistan Khyber Pass. 4647 Convoy St
Anthony's Fish Grotto. 11666 Avena Place
Benihana Of Tokyo. 477 Camino del Rio South
Bernard'o. 12457 Rancho Bernardo Rd
Busalacchi's. 3683 5th Ave
California Cuisine. 1027 University Ave
Celadon. 3628 5th Ave
Chieu-Anh. 16769 Bernardo Center Dr
City Delicatessen. 535 University Ave
D.Z. Akin's. 6930 Alvarado Rd
El Bizcocho (Rancho Bernardo Inn Resort). 17550 Bernardo Oaks Dr
El Indio Shop. 3695 India St
El Tecolote. 6110 Friars Rd
Greek Corner. 5841 El Cajon Blvd
Hob Nob Hill. 2271 1st Ave.
Imperial House. 505 Kalmia St
Jasmine. 4609 Convoy St
Kelly's. 500 Hotel Circle N
La Vache & Co. 420 Robinson St
Lorna's Italian Kitchen. 3945 Governor Dr
Mister A's. 2550 5th Ave
Montana's American Grill. 1421 University Ave
Nati's. 1852 Bacon St
Saffron. 3731-B India St
Taka. 555 Fifth Ave
Thee Bungalow. 4996 W Point Loma Blvd
Tom Ham's Lighthouse. 2150 Harbor Island Dr
Winesellar & Brasserie. 9550 Waples St

MISSION BAY
Baci Ristorante. 1955 W Morena Blvd
Belgian Lion. 2265 Bacon St

OLD TOWN
Cafe Coyote. 2461 San Diego Ave
Cafe Pacifica. 2414 San Diego Ave
Casa De Bandini. 2754 Calhoun St
Jack & Guilio. 2391 San Diego Ave
Lino's. 2754 Calhoun St
Old Town Mexican Cafe & Cantina. 2489 San Diego Ave

POINT LOMA
Fairouz. 3166 Midway Dr

Note: When a listing is located in a town that does not have its own city heading, it will appear under the city nearest to its location. In these cases, the address and town appear in parenthesis immediately following the name of the establishment.

Motels

★ ★ ★ **BALBOA PARK INN.** *3402 Park Blvd (92103), adj to Balboa Park. 619/298-0823; FAX 619/294-8070; res: 800/938-8181.* 26 rms, 2 story, 17 kit. suites. S, D $80; kit. suites $95-$200; under 12 free. Crib $5. TV; cable (premium). Complimentary continental bkfst. Complimentary coffee in rms. Ck-out noon. Free guest lndry. Refrigerators; some in-rm whirlpools, microwaves. Many patios, balconies. Sun deck. Each rm has a distinctly different "theme" and decor. Cr cds: A, C, D, DS, MC, V.

★ ★ **BEST WESTERN ISLAND PALMS HOTEL & MARINA.** *2051 Shelter Island Dr (92106), in Point Loma. 619/222-0561; FAX 619/222-9760.* 97 rms, 80 with shower only, 2 story, 29 kit. units. June-Oct: S, D $109-$149; each addl $10; kits. $149-$199; under 18 free; wkly rates; lower rates rest of yr. Crib free. TV; cable (premium). Pool; whirlpool, poolside serv. Complimentary coffee in rms. Restaurant 6 am-10 pm. Bar 11-midnight; Fri, Sat to 2 am. Ck-out noon. Coin lndry. Meeting rms. Business servs avail. In-rm modem link. Valet serv. Exercise equipt; weight machines, bicycles. Microwaves, refrigerators avail. Many balconies. On bay. Near airport. Cr cds: A, C, D, DS, MC, V.

D SC

✔★ ★ **BEST WESTERN SEVEN SEAS LODGE.** *411 Hotel Circle S (92108), in Old Town. 619/291-1300; FAX 619/291-6933.* 307 rms, 2 story, 9 kit. units. S, D $59-$129; kit. units $69-$139; under 12 free. Crib free. TV; cable (premium). Heated pool; whirlpool, poolside serv. Playground. Complimentary coffee in rms. Restaurant 6 am-10:30 pm. Rm serv. Bar 10-2 am. Ck-out noon. Coin lndry. Meeting rms. In-rm modem link. Bellhops. Valet serv. Free airport, RR station, bus depot transportation. Some refrigerators; microwaves avail. Some balconies. Cr cds: A, C, D, DS, ER, JCB, MC, V.

D SC

★ ★ **COMFORT INN & SUITES-ZOO/SEA WORLD AREA.** *2485 Hotel Circle Place (92108), north of downtown. 619/291-7700; FAX 619/297-6179.* 200 rms, 4 story. July-early Sept: S, D $79-$99; suites $89-$119; under 18 free; lower rates rest of yr. Crib free. TV; cable (premium). Heated pool; whirlpool. Complimentary continental bkfst. Restaurant nearby. Ck-out noon. Coin lndry. Business servs avail. In-rm modem link. Free covered parking. Free airport transportation. Exercise equipt; weight machines, bicycle. Some refrigerators, in-rm whirlpools; microwaves avail. Cr cds: A, C, D, DS, MC, V.

D SC

★ ★ **DANA INN & MARINA.** *1710 W Mission Bay Dr (92109), in Mission Bay. 619/222-6440; FAX 619/222-5916; res: 800/345-9995.* 196 rms, 2 story. S, D $84-$139; each addl $10; under 18 free. Crib free. TV; cable (premium). Heated pool; whirlpool, poolside serv. Coffee in rms. Restaurant 7 am-10 pm. Rm serv. Bar. Ck-out noon. Coin lndry. Business servs avail. Bellhops. Valet serv. Free airport, RR station, bus depot, Sea

World transportation. Tennis. Marina. Boat launch adj. Cr cds: A, C, D, DS, MC, V.

SC

✓★ ★ **DAYS INN-HOTEL CIRCLE.** *543 Hotel Circle S (92108), in Old Town. 619/297-8800; FAX 619/298-6029.* Web www.bartellhotels.com. 280 rms, 3 story, 49 kit. units. S, D $65-$109; each addl $10; kit. units $79-$89; under 18 free; wkly rates; higher rates wkends, special events. Crib free. TV; cable (premium). Heated pool; whirlpool. Coffee in rms. Restaurant 6:30 am-10 pm. Ck-out noon. Coin Indry. Business servs avail. Bellhops. Valet serv. Sundries. Barber, beauty shop. Health club privileges. Free airport, RR station, bus depot transportation. Refrigerators; microwaves avail. Cr cds: A, C, D, DS, JCB, MC, V.

D SC

✓★ **GOOD NITE INN.** *4545 Waring Rd (92120), NE of downtown. 619/286-7000; FAX 619/286-8403; res: 800/648-3466.* Web www.good-nite.com. 94 rms, 2 story. S, D $35-$45; each addl $6; under 18 free. Crib free. Pet accepted. TV; cable (premium). Heated pool. Restaurant adj 10 am-9 pm; Fri-Sun from 7 am. Ck-out 11 am. Coin Indry. Meeting rm. Refrigerator, microwaves avail. Private patios, balconies. Cr cds: A, D, DS, MC, V.

D SC

★ ★ **HAMPTON INN.** *5434 Kearny Mesa Rd (92111), north of downtown. 619/292-1482; FAX 619/292-4410.* Web www.hampton-inn.com. 150 rms, 5 story. June-Aug: S, D $84-$99; under 18 free; lower rates rest of yr. Crib free. TV; cable (premium). Heated pool. Coffee in rms. Complimentary continental bkfst. Restaurant adj 7 am-11 pm. Ck-out 11 am. Coin Indry. Meeting rms. Business servs avail. In-rm modem link. Valet serv. Free local transportation. Health club privileges. Some refrigerators; microwaves avail. Cr cds: A, C, D, DS, MC, V.

D SC

★ ★ ★ **HUMPHREY'S HALF MOON INN & SUITES.** *2303 Shelter Island Dr (92106), in Point Loma. 619/224-3411; FAX 619/224-3478; res: 800/542-7400.* 182 rms, 2 story, 30 kit. units. Late May-early Sept: S $110-$179; D $115-$189; each addl $10; kit. suites $129-$265; under 18 free; lower rates rest of yr. Crib free. TV; cable (premium), VCR avail. Heated pool; whirlpool, poolside serv. Complimentary coffee in rms. Restaurant 6:30 am-10 pm. Rm serv. Bar 11-2 am; entertainment. Ck-out noon. Coin Indry. Meeting rms. Business servs avail. In-rm modem link. Bellhops. Sundries. Free airport, RR station transportation. Bicycles. Health club privileges. Lawn games. Refrigerators. Many private patios, balconies. South Sea island decor. Gardens. Cr cds: A, C, D, DS, MC, V.

D SC

★ ★ **LA QUINTA.** *10185 Paseo Montril (92129), north of downtown. 619/484-8800; FAX 619/538-0476.* 120 rms, 4 story. S, D $58-$66; each addl $6; under 18 free. Crib free. Pet accepted. TV; cable (premium). Heated pool. Complimentary continental bkfst. Restaurant adj 6 am-midnight. Ck-out noon. Cr cds: A, C, D, DS, MC, V.

D SC

★ **OLD TOWN INN.** *4444 Pacific Hwy (92110), near Lindbergh Field Intl Airport, north of downtown. 619/260-8024; FAX 619/296-0524; res: 800/643-3025.* 84 rms (41 with shower only), 1-3 story, 69 with A/C. June-Sept: S, D $36-$58; each addl $5; suites $92-$109; kit units $56-$72; under 12 free; wkly rates; higher rates hols (3-day min); lower rates rest of yr. Crib $5. Pet accepted; $5. TV; cable (premium). Complimentary continental bkfst. Restaurant nearby. Ck-out 11 am. Coin Indry. Refrigerators avail. Cr cds: A, C, D, DS, MC, V.

D SC

★ ★ **TRAVELODGE.** *16929 W Bernardo Dr (92127), north of downtown. 619/487-0445; FAX 619/673-2062.* 49 rms, 2 story. Mid-May-mid-Sept: S, D $55-$75; each addl $5; under 12 free; hols (3-day min); lower rates rest of yr. Crib free. TV; cable (premium). Complimentary continental bkfst. Complimentary coffee in rms. Restaurant nearby. Ck-out 11 am. Pool. Refrigerators, microwaves avail. Cr cds: A, C, D, DS, MC, V.

SC

★ **TRAVELODGE-MISSION VALLEY.** *1201 Hotel Circle S (92108), north of downtown. 619/297-2271; FAX 619/542-1510.* 101 rms, 2 story. June-Sept: S $49-$89; D $59-$99; each addl $10; under 16 free; higher rates special events; lower rates rest of yr. Crib free. TV; cable (premium), VCR avail (movies). Complimentary coffee in rms. Restaurant 6:30-2 am. Ck-out noon. Business servs avail. In-rm modem link. Valet serv. Health club privileges. Pool. Cr cds: A, C, D, DS, MC, V.

D SC

✓★ **VAGABOND INN.** *625 Hotel Circle S (92108), north of downtown. 619/297-1691; FAX 619/692-9009.* 88 rms, 2 story. Mid-May-mid-Sept: S, D $63-$90; each addl $5; under 18 free; lower rates rest of yr. Crib free. Pet accepted; $10. TV; cable (premium). 2 heated pools; whirlpool. Complimentary continental bkfst. Restaurant adj open 24 hrs. Ck-out noon. Business servs avail. In-rm modem link. Cr cds: A, C, D, DS, MC, V.

SC

Motor Hotels

★ ★ ★ **BAY CLUB HOTEL & MARINA.** *2131 Shelter Island Dr (92106), in Point Loma. 619/224-8888; FAX 619/225-1604; res: 800/672-0800.* Web www.bayclubhotel.com. 105 rms, 2 story. S $100-$159; D $110-$179; each addl $10; suites $195-$295; under 12 free; package plans. Crib $10. TV; cable (premium), VCR avail. Heated pool; whirlpool, poolside serv. Complimentary bkfst. Coffee in rms. Restaurant 6:30 am-10 pm. Rm serv. Bar 10 am-midnight. Ck-out noon. Meeting rms. Business servs avail. Bellhops. Valet serv. Concierge. Sundries. Covered parking. Free airport, RR station, bus depot transportation. Exercise equipt; weight machine, bicycles. Refrigerators; microwaves avail. Private patios, balconies. On bay; marina. Fishing from nearby pier. Cr cds: A, C, D, DS, ER, JCB, MC, V.

D SC

★ ★ ★ **BEST WESTERN HACIENDA HOTEL.** *4041 Harney St (92110), in Old Town. 619/298-4707; FAX 619/298-4771.* 169 suites, 2-3 story. June-Aug: S, D $115-$135; each addl $10; under 16 free; lower rates rest of yr. Crib free. TV; cable, VCR (movies). Heated pool; whirlpool, poolside serv. Complimentary coffee in rms. Restaurants 6:30 am-10 pm. Rm serv. Bar 11 am-midnight. Ck-out noon. Meeting rms. Business servs avail. Bellhops. Valet serv. Concierge. Covered parking. Free airport, RR station, bus depot transportation. Exercise equipt; weights, bicycles. Refrigerators, microwaves. Some private patios, balconies. Grills. Spanish architecture. Cr cds: A, C, D, DS, JCB, MC, V.

D SC

★ ★ **DOUBLETREE-RANCHO BERNARDO.** *11611 Bernardo Plaza Court (92128), north of downtown. 619/485-9250; FAX 619/451-7948.* 209 rms, 4 story. S, D $183-$203; each addl $10; suites $400; under 10 free; wkend rates. Crib free. TV; cable. Heated pool; whirlpool. Restaurant 6-9 am, 5-10 pm; Sat, Sun from 7 am. Rm serv. Bar from 5 pm. Ck-out 1 pm. Meeting rms. Business servs avail. In-rm modem link. Exercise equipt; weight machine, bicycles. Microwaves avail. Cr cds: A, C, D, DS, ER, JCB, MC, V.

D SC

★ ★ ★ **HANDLERY HOTEL & RESORT.** *950 Hotel Circle N (92108), I-8 Hotel Circle exit, north of downtown. 619/298-0511; FAX 619/298-9793; res: 800/676-6567.* E-mail sales@handlery.com; web www.handerly.com. 217 rms, 2 story. S, D $99-$129; each addl $10; suites $200; under 14 free. Crib free. TV; cable. 3 pools (1 lap pool); whirlpool, poolside serv. Coffee in rms. Restaurant 6:30 am-10 pm. Rm serv 7 am-9 pm. Bars 11-2 am. Ck-out noon. Lndry facilities. Meeting rms. Business servs avail. In-rm modem link. Bellhops. Valet serv. Sundries. Gift shop. Barber, beauty shop. Tennis, pro. Exercise rm; instructor, treadmilll. Massage. Some balconies. Cr cds: A, C, D, DS, ER, JCB, MC, V.

D SC

★ ★ ★ **HOLIDAY INN RANCHO BERNARDO.** *17065 W Bernardo Dr (92127), north of downtown. 619/485-6530; FAX 619/485-6530, ext. 324.* 178 rms, 2-3 story, 16 kits. S, D $89-$99; each addl $10; suites $109-$169; under 19 free. Crib free. TV; cable (premium). Heated pool;

whirlpool. Complimentary full bkfst. Coffee in rms. Restaurant opp 11 am-midnight. Ck-out noon. Coin Indry. Meeting rms. Business servs avail. In-rm modem link. Some covered parking. Exercise equipt; weights, bicycles, sauna. Health club privileges. Some refrigerators, in-rm whirlpools. Microwaves avail. Many private patios, balconies. Cr cds: A, C, D, DS, JCB, MC, V.

D SC

✓★ ★ **HOLIDAY INN-BAYSIDE.** *4875 N Harbor Dr (92106), near Lindbergh Field Intl Airport, north of downtown. 619/224-3621; FAX 619/224-3629.* Web www.bartellhotels.com/holinnbayside. 237 rms, 2-5 story. S, D $99-$139; each addl $10; suites $169-$209; under 18 free. Crib free. TV; cable (premium). Heated pool. Complimentary coffee in rms. Restaurant adj 6 am-10 pm. Bar 2 pm-2 am. Ck-out noon. Coin Indry. Meeting rms. Business center. In-rm modem link. Bellhops. Valet serv. Sundries. Free airport, RR station, bus depot transportation. Exercise equipt; weights, bicycles. Putting green. Lawn games. Refrigerators. Some private patios, balconies. Opp marina. Cr cds: A, C, D, DS, JCB, MC, V.

D SC

★ ★ **HOLIDAY INN-MISSION VALLEY/STADIUM.** *3805 Murphy Canyon Rd (92123), north of downtown. 619/277-1199; FAX 619/277-3442.* 173 rms, 4 story, 18 suites. S, D $95-$125; each addl $10; suites $100-$120; under 12 free. Crib free. TV; cable (premium). Pool; whirlpool. Coffee in rms. Restaurant 6:30 am-10 pm. Rm serv. Bar. Ck-out noon. Coin Indry. Meeting rms. Business servs avail. Free garage parking. Exercise equipt; weight machine, bicycles. Free airport transportation. Refrigerators; microwaves avail. Wet bar in suites. Most suites with balcony. Cr cds: A, C, D, DS, MC, V.

D SC

★ ★ **QUALITY RESORT.** *875 Hotel Circle S (92108). 619/298-8282; FAX 619/295-5610.* 202 rms, 2 story. June-Aug: S, D $85-$99; suites $119-$149; under 18 free; lower rates rest of yr. Crib free. TV; cable. Pool; poolside serv. Restaurant adj open 24 hrs. Bar 11 am-11 pm. Ck-out noon. Meeting rms. Beauty shop. Valet serv. Coin Indry. Lighted tennis, pro. Exercise equipt; weights, bicycles, sauna. Massage. Lawn games. Microwave in suites. Some balconies. Cr cds: A, C, D, DS, MC, V.

D SC

★ ★ **QUALITY SUITES.** *9880 Mira Mesa Blvd (92131), at jct I-15, north of downtown. 619/530-2000.* 130 suites, 4 story. Early June-mid-Sept: suites $99-$199; each addl $10; under 18 free; lower rates rest of yr. Crib free. TV; cable (premium), VCR. Heated pool. Complimentary continental bkfst. Coffee in rms. Ck-out noon. Meeting rms. Business servs avail. In-rm modem link. Health club privileges. Microwaves. Cr cds: A, C, D, DS, JCB, MC, V.

D SC

✓★ ★ **RAMADA PLAZA-SEA WORLD AREA.** *2151 Hotel Circle S (92108), north of downtown. 619/291-6500; FAX 619/294-7531.* 182 rms, 4 story. S $69-$124; D $74-$134; each addl $5; under 18 free. Crib free. TV; cable (premium). Heated pool; whirlpool. Complimentary coffee in rms. Restaurant 6:30 am-2:30 pm, 5-10 pm. Rm serv. Bar 5-11 pm. Ck-out noon. Coin Indry. Meeting rms. Business servs avail. In-rm modem link. Bellhops. Valet serv. Some covered parking. Free airport, RR station, bus depot transportation. Exercise equipt; weight machine, bicycle. Health club privileges. Game rm. Refrigerators avail. Cr cds: A, C, D, DS, ER, JCB, MC, V.

D SC

✓★ ★ **RODEWAY INN.** *833 Ash St (92101), downtown. 619/239-2285; FAX 619/235-6951.* 45 rms, 4 story. S $59-$89; D $64-$89; each addl $5; under 18 free. Crib free. TV; cable (premium). Complimentary continental bkfst. Restaurant opp open 6 am-3 pm. Ck-out noon. Coin Indry. Business servs avail. In-rm modem link. Valet serv. Health club privileges. Whirlpool, saunas. Some refrigerators; microwaves avail. Some balconies. Cr cds: A, C, D, DS, ER, JCB, MC, V.

D SC

★ ★ **VACATION INN.** *3900 Old Town Ave (92110), in Old Town. 619/299-7400; FAX 619/299-1619; res: 800/451-9846.* 125 rms, 3 story. Mid-May-mid-Sept: S, D $89-$109; each addl $10; suites $105-$160; under 17 free; lower rates rest of yr. Crib free. TV; cable (premium). Heated pool; whirlpool. Complimentary continental bkfst. Complimentary coffee in rms. Restaurant opp 11 am-10 pm. Ck-out noon. Coin Indry. Meeting rms. Business servs avail. In-rm modem link. Covered parking. Free airport, RR station transportation. Refrigerators, microwaves; some wet bars. Some balconies. Cr cds: A, C, D, DS, JCB, MC, V.

D SC

Hotels

★ ★ **BEST WESTERN BAYSIDE INN.** *555 W Ash St (92101), near Lindbergh Field Intl Airport, downtown. 619/233-7500; FAX 619/239-8060.* 122 rms, 14 story. July-early Sept: S, D $89-$119; each addl $10; under 12 free; 2-day min hols; lower rates rest of yrs. Crib $6. TV; cable (premium). Pool; whirlpool. Complimentary continental bkfst. Restaurant adj 6 am-2 pm, 5-9 pm. Ck-out noon. Business servs avail. In-rm modem link. Free airport, RR station tranportation. Health club privileges. Cr cds: A, C, D, DS, ER, JCB, MC, V.

D SC

★ ★ **BEST WESTERN HANALEI.** *2270 Hotel Circle N (92108), downtown. 619/297-1101; FAX 619/297-6049.* 416 rms, 8 story. June-Sept: S, D $79-$169; suite $175-$350; under 18 free; 2-day min hols; lower rates rest of yr. Crib free. Pet accepted, some restrictions; $50 deposit. TV; cable (premium). Pool; whirlpool, poolside serv. Restaurant 6:30 am-10 pm; Sat, Sun to 11 pm. Bar. Ck-out noon. Coin Indry. Meeting rms. Business servs avail. In-rm modem link. Concierge. Tennis privileges. Health club privileges. Lawn games. Some refrigerators. Balconies. Cr cds: A, C, D, DS, JCB, MC, V.

D SC

★ ★ ★ **CLARION BAYVIEW.** *660 K Street (92101), downtown. 619/696-0234; FAX 619/231-8199.* 312 rms, 21 story, 48 suites. Late May-early Sept: S $109-$169; D $119-$129; each addl $15; suites $159-$189; under 18 free; lower rates rest of yr. Crib free. Covered parking $8/day. TV; cable, VCR avail. Coffee in rms. Restaurant 6:30 am-10 pm. Bar 11-2 am; entertainment Fri, Sat. Ck-out noon. Coin Indry. Meeting rms. Business servs avail. In-rm modem link. Gift shop. Exercise equipt; weight machine, bicycles, whirlpool, sauna. Massage. Game rm. Some bathrm phones. Balconies. View of San Diego Bay. Cr cds: A, C, D, DS, JCB, MC, V.

D SC

★ ★ ★ **DOUBLETREE MISSION VALLEY.** *7450 Hazard Center Dr (92108), Mission Valley. 619/297-5466; FAX 619/297-5499.* 300 rms, 11 story. S, D $210; each addl $15; under 18 free. Crib free. Pet accepted. TV; cable. 2 pools, 1 indoor; whirlpool, poolside serv. Complimentary coffee in rms. Restaurant 6 am-11 pm. Bar 5 pm-2 am; entertainment. Ck-out noon. Convention facilities. Business servs avail. In-rm modem link. Gift shop. Garage parking; valet. Free airport, RR station, bus depot transportation. Lighted tennis. Exercise equipt; weight machine, stair machine, sauna. Health club privileges. Minibars. Microwaves avail. Some bathrm phones, wet bars in suites. Some balconies. Luxury level. Cr cds: A, C, D, DS, JCB, MC, V.

D SC

★ ★ ★ **EMBASSY SUITES.** *601 Pacific Hwy (92101), near Seaport Village, west of downtown. 619/239-2400; FAX 619/239-1520.* E-mail es_sdb@ix.netcom.com. 337 suites, 12 story. Mid-June-mid-Sept: suites $155-$240; under 18 free; lower rates rest of yr. Crib free. Covered parking $8. TV; cable (premium). Indoor pool; whirlpool. Complimentary full bkfst. Coffee in rms. Restaurant 11 am-midnight. Bar to midnight. Ck-out noon. Coin Indry. Meeting rms. Business center. In-rm modem link. Concierge. Gift shop. Barber, beauty shop. Free airport transportation. Exercise equipt; weight machine, bicycles, sauna. Refrigerators, microwaves. Some balconies. San Diego Bay 1 blk. Cr cds: A, C, D, DS, JCB, MC, V.

D

★ ★ ★ **HILTON BEACH AND TENNIS RESORT.** *1775 E Mission Bay Dr (92109), in Mission Bay. 619/276-4010; FAX 619/275-8944.* E-mail contact@hiltonsandiego.com. 357 rms, 8 story. S $155-$260; D $175-$280; each addl $20; suites $400-$650; family, wkend rates. Crib free. Pet accepted; $50. TV; cable (premium), VCR avail. Heated pool; wading pool, whirlpool, poolside serv. Playground. Supervised child's activities; ages 6-12. Complimentary coffee in rms. Restaurant 6:30 am-10 pm. Bar 10:30-1 am; entertainment. Ck-out noon. Coin lndry. Convention facilities. Business center. In-rm modem link. Gift shop. Beauty shop. Valet parking. Lighted tennis, pro. Putting greens. Exercise rm; instructor, weights, bicycles, sauna. Massage. Rec rm. Lawn games. Many bathrm phones, refrigerators, minibars; microwaves avail. Private patios, balconies. Dock; boats. On beach. Cr cds: A, C, D, DS, ER, JCB, MC, V.

D SC

★ ★ ★ **HILTON-MISSION VALLEY.** *901 Camino del Rio S (92108), off I-8 Mission Center Rd exit. 619/543-9000; FAX 619/543-9358.* Web www.hilton.com. 350 rms, 14 story. S $179-$189; D $189; each addl $10; suites $200-$400; under 18 free. Crib free. Pet accepted, some restrictions; $25. TV; cable (premium). Heated pool; whirlpool, poolside serv. Coffee in rms. Restaurant 6:30 am-10:30 pm. Bar 11-1 am. Ck-out noon. Convention facilities. In-rm modem link. Some covered parking. Exercise equipt; weight machine, bicycles, sauna. Health club privileges. Refrigerators. Large entrance foyer. Cr cds: A, C, D, DS, MC, V.

D SC

★ ★ **HOLIDAY INN ON THE BAY.** *1355 N Harbor Dr (92101), downtown. 619/232-3861; FAX 619/232-4924.* 600 rms, 14 story. S, D $169.95-$189.95; each addl $10; suites $250-$800; under 19 free. Crib free. Pet accepted, some restrictions. Parking $10/day. TV; cable (premium). Heated pool. Coffee in rms. Restaurant 6:30 am-11 pm. Bar 11-2 am. Ck-out noon. Convention facilities. Business servs avail. In-rm modem link. Shopping arcade. Free airport transportation. Exercise equipt; bicycle, treadmill. Some bathrm phones, refrigerators. Balconies. Many bay view rms. Outside glass-enclosed elvtr. Cruise ship terminal opp. Cr cds: A, C, D, DS, JCB, MC, V.

D SC

★ ★ ★ **THE HORTON GRAND.** *311 Island Ave (92101), downtown. 619/544-1886; FAX 619/544-0058; res: 800/542-1886.* 132 rms, 4 story. S, D $119-$189; each addl $20; suites $189-$259; under 12 free. Crib free. Some covered parking, valet $8. TV; cable, VCR avail. Restaurant 7 am-10 pm. Tea 2:30-5:30 pm. Bar 4 pm-midnight. Ck-out noon. Meeting rms. Business servs avail. Free airport transportation. Health club privileges. Fireplaces; refrigerator in suites. Microwaves avail. Some balconies. Victorian building; built 1886. Antiques, oak staircase. Chinese Museum & Tea Room. Skylight in lobby; bird cages. Oldest building in San Diego. Cr cds: A, D, MC, V.

D SC

★ ★ ★ **HYATT ISLANDIA.** *1441 Quivira Rd (92109), on Mission Bay. 619/224-1234; FAX 619/224-0348.* Web www.hyatt.com. 422 rms, 17 story. S, D $119-$215; suites $215-$2,500; under 18 free. Crib free. TV; cable (premium). Heated pool; whirlpool, poolside serv. Supervised child's activities (June-Sept). Restaurant 6 am-10 pm; Fri-Sun to 11 pm. Bar 11:30-2 am; entertainment Thurs-Sat. Ck-out noon. Convention facilities. Business center. In-rm modem link. Concierge. Exercise equipt; bicycles, treadmills. Some refrigerators. Many private patios, balconies. Bicycle rentals. Marina; sport fishing; sailboat charters. Whale watching (Dec-Mar). Cr cds: A, C, D, DS, ER, JCB, MC, V.

D SC

★ ★ ★ **HYATT REGENCY.** *One Market Place (92101), adj to Convention Center and Seaport Village, downtown. 619/232-1234; FAX 619/233-6464.* 875 units, 40 story, 56 suites. S, D $169-$260; under 18 free. Crib free. Garage parking $9-$13. TV; cable (premium), VCR avail. Pool; whirlpool, poolside serv. Restaurants 6 am-10 pm (also see SALLY'S). Rm serv 24 hrs. Bar noon-1:30 am. Ck-out noon. Convention facilities. Business center. In-rm modem link. Concierge. Shopping arcade. 4 tennis courts. Exercise equipt; weight machine, bicycles, sauna, steam rm. Massage. Some refrigerators, minibars. Microwaves avail. Located on San Diego Bay; panoramic view of harbor and marina. Luxury level. Cr cds: A, C, D, DS, ER, JCB, MC, V.

D SC

★ **J STREET INN.** *222 J St (92101), downtown. 619/696-6922; FAX 619/696-1295.* 221 rms, 4 story. Rm phones avail. S, D $34.95-$60; under 10 free. Parking $5. TV; cable. Complimentary coffee in rms. Restaurant nearby. Ck-out 1 pm. Exercise equipt; weight machine, bicycles. Refrigerators, microwaves. Balconies. Near bay, airport. Cr cds: A, D, DS, MC, V.

D

★ ★ ★ **MARRIOTT HOTEL & MARINA.** *333 W Harbor Dr (92101), adj to Seaport Village & Convention Center, downtown. 619/234-1500; FAX 619/234-8678.* Web www.sdmarriott.com. 1,355 rms, 26 story. S, D $255-$275; each addl $20; suites from $400; under 18 free. Crib free. Pet accepted. TV; cable (premium). Pool; whirlpool, poolside serv. Restaurant 6:30 am-11 pm. Rm serv 24 hrs. Bar 11-2 am; entertainment. Ck-out noon. Coin lndry. Meeting rms. Business center. In-rm modem link. Concierge. Shopping arcade. Barber, beauty shops. 6 lighted tennis courts, pro. Exercise equipt; weight machines, treadmill, sauna. Game rm. Bathrm phones, minibars; some refrigerators. Some balconies. Luxurious; large chandeliers in lobby. Bayside; marina. Luxury level. Cr cds: A, C, D, DS, ER, JCB, MC, V.

D SC

★ ★ ★ **MARRIOTT SUITES-DOWNTOWN.** *701 A Street (92101), downtown. 619/696-9800; FAX 619/696-1555.* 264 suites, 27 story. S, D $199-$209; under 18 free. Crib free. Pet accepted, some restrictions; $50. Garage $10, valet parking $15. TV; cable (premium). Indoor pool; whirlpool. Coffee in rms. Restaurant 6:30 am-10 pm. Bar 11:30 am-midnight. Ck-out noon. Meeting rms. In-rm modem link. Gift shop. Exercise equipt; weight machine, bicycles, sauna. Health club privileges. Refrigerators, minibars; microwaves avail. Cr cds: A, C, D, DS, ER, JCB, MC, V.

D SC

★ ★ ★ **RADISSON.** *1433 Camino del Rio S (92108), Mission Valley. 619/260-0111; FAX 619/260-0853.* E-mail sand@radisson.com; web www.radisson.com. 260 rms, 13 story. S, D $155; each addl $15; under 17 free; wkend rates. Crib free. TV; cable, VCR avail. Heated pool. Restaurant 6:30 am-10 pm. Bar 2 pm-1:30 am. Ck-out noon. Convention facilities. Business servs avail. In-rm modem link. Free airport transportation. Exercise equipt; bicycles, treadmill. Health club privileges. Microwaves avail. Some balconies. Luxury level. Cr cds: A, C, D, DS, ER, JCB, MC, V.

D SC

★ ★ ★ **RADISSON SUITE.** *11520 W Bernardo Court (92127), north of downtown. 619/451-6600; FAX 619/592-0253.* 174 suites, 3 story. S, D $79-$170; each addl $10; under 12 free; golf plans. Crib free. Pet accepted, some restrictions. TV; cable (premium), VCR (movies). Heated pool; whirlpool. Complimentary full bkfst. Complimentary coffee in rms. Restaurant 6-9:30 am, 5-11 pm. Bar 5-11 pm. Ck-out noon. Coin lndry. Meeting rms. Business servs avail. In-rm modem link. Tennis privileges. Golf privileges. Exercise equipt; weight machine, bicycles. Minibars, microwaves. Cr cds: A, C, D, DS, ER, JCB, MC, V.

D SC

★ ★ ★ ★ **SHERATON MARINA.** *1380 Harbor Island Dr (92101), near Lindbergh Field Intl Airport, north of downtown. 619/291-2900; FAX 619/692-2337.* This hotel, set at the edge of San Diego Bay, offers extensive business facilities, health and recreation services and easy access to the treasures of the Bay area. Rooms are warm and casual; all have water views. 1,048 rms, 12 story. S, D $270-$300; each addl $20; suites $375-$1,100; under 18 free. Crib free. TV; cable (premium). 3 pools; whirlpool, 2 wading pools, poolside serv. Complimentary coffee in rms. Restaurant 6 am-10 pm. Rm serv 24 hrs. Bar 11-1 am. Ck-out noon. Coin lndry. Convention facilities. Business center. In-rm modem link. Concierge. Shopping arcade. Free airport transportation. Lighted tennis, pro. Boat dock; beach. Exercise rm; instructor, weights, bicycles, sauna. Massage.

Bicycle rentals. Minibars; microwaves avail. Bathrm phone in suites. Balconies. Cr cds: A, C, D, DS, ER, JCB, MC, V.

D SC

★ ★ ★ **TOWN & COUNTRY.** *500 Hotel Circle N (92108), north of downtown. 619/291-7131; FAX 619/291-3584; res: 800/854-2608.* E-mail consales@towncountry.com; web www.towncountry.com. 964 rms, 1-10 story. S $95-$175; D $110-$190; each addl $15; suites $300-$625; under 18 free. Crib free. Parking $6. TV; cable (premium). 4 pools, 1 heated; whirlpool, poolside serv. Restaurant 6-1 am. Bar 11-2 am; entertainment. Ck-out noon. Convention facilities. Business center. In-rm modem link. Barber. Lighted tennis privileges, pro. Golf privileges; driving range adj. Health club privileges. Some refrigerators; microwaves avail. Some private patios, balconies. On 32 acres. Cr cds: A, C, D, DS, MC, V.

D SC

✔★ ★ **TRAVELODGE HOTEL-HARBOR ISLAND.** *1960 Harbor Island Dr (92101), near Lindbergh Field Intl Airport, north of downtown. 619/291-6700; FAX 619/293-0694.* 207 rms, 9 story. S, D $119-$139; each addl $10; suites $225-$375; under 17 free. Crib free. TV; cable (premium). Heated pool; whirlpool. Complimentary coffee in rms. Restaurant 6:30 am-2 pm, 5:30-10 pm. Bar 11-1 am. Ck-out noon. Meeting rms. Business servs avail. In-rm modem link. Concierge. Gift shop. Free airport transportation. Exercise equipt; weights, bicycles, sauna. Some refrigerators. Balconies. Cr cds: A, C, D, DS, ER, JCB, MC, V.

D SC

★ ★ ★ **U. S. GRANT.** *326 Broadway (92101), downtown. 619/232-3121; FAX 619/232-3626; res: 800/237-5029.* 280 rms, 11 story, 60 suites. S, D $155-$195; each addl $20; suites $275-$1,500. Crib free. Pet accepted. Valet parking $11. TV; cable (premium), VCR avail. Cafe 6:30-10:30 pm. Bar 11-2 am; entertainment Fri, Sat. Ck-out noon. Business center. Concierge. Gift shop. Free airport transportation. Exercise equipt; weights, bicycles. Massage. Bathrm phones, minibars. Antiques, artwork, period chandeliers and fixtures. 1910 landmark has been restored to its original elegance. Luxury level. Cr cds: A, C, D, DS, MC, V.

D SC

★ ★ ★ ★ **THE WESTGATE HOTEL.** *1055 Second Ave (92101), downtown. 619/238-1818; FAX 619/557-3737; res: 800/221-3802.* This opulent hotel in a modern tower features guest rooms furnished with antiques; views are breathtaking from the seventh floor up. 223 units, 19 story, some kits. S, D from $164; each addl $10; suites from $400; under 18 free; wkend rates. Valet parking $10/day. Crib free. TV; cable (premium), VCR avail. Complimentary coffee in lobby. Restaurants 6:30 am-11 pm (also see LE FONTAINEBLEAU). Rm serv 24 hrs. Bar 11-1 am; entertainment. Ck-out noon. Meeting rms. Business servs avail. In-rm modem link. Concierge. Free airport, RR station, bus depot transportation. Exercise equipt; weight machine, bicycles. Bathrm phones, minibars; microwaves avail. Cr cds: A, C, D, DS, MC, V.

★ ★ ★ **WESTIN-HORTON PLAZA.** *910 Broadway Circle (92101), downtown. 619/239-2200; FAX 619/239-0509.* 450 rms, 16 story. S, D $99-$199; each addl $15; suites $250-$975; under 18 free; wkend, wkday packages. Crib free. Covered parking $12; valet $15. TV; cable (premium), VCR avail. Heated pool; whirlpool, poolside serv. Restaurant 6:30 am-11 pm. Rm serv 24 hrs. Bar to 2 am. Ck-out noon. Convention facilities. Business center. In-rm modem link. Concierge. Lighted tennis. Exercise rm; instructor, weight machines, bicycles, sauna. Bathrm phones, refrigerators, minibars; microwaves avail. Some balconies. Connected to Horton Plaza. Luxury level. Cr cds: A, C, D, DS, JCB, MC, V.

D SC

★ ★ ★ **WYNDHAM EMERALD PLAZA.** *400 W Broadway (92101), downtown. 619/239-4500; FAX 619/239-3274.* 436 rms, 25 story. S, D $189-$239; each addl $15; suites $300-$2,000; under 16 free. Crib free. Garage $11. TV; cable (premium), VCR avail. Heated pool; whirlpool, poolside serv. Restaurant 6 am-10 pm. Bar 11-1 am; entertainment Fri, Sat. Ck-out noon. Convention facilities. Business center. In-rm modem link. Concierge. Shopping arcade. Free airport transportation. Exercise rm; instructor, weight machine, bicycle, steam rm, sauna. Massage. Bathrm phones, minibars. Microwaves avail. Cr cds: A, C, D, DS, ER, JCB, MC, V.

D

Inns

★ ★ **ELSBREE HOUSE.** *5058 Narragansett Ave (92107), north of downtown. 619/226-4133.* E-mail ktelsbree@aol.com; web www.oceanbeach-online.com/elsbree/b&b. 6 rms, 1 condo, 2 story. No A/C. No rm phones. June-Sept: S, D $85-$95; condo $215; wkly rates; lower rates rest of yr. TV in sitting rm. Complimentary continental bkfst. Restaurant nearby. Ck-out 11 am, ck-in 3 pm. Balconies. Cape Cod-style house near ocean. Totally nonsmoking. Cr cds: MC, V.

★ ★ ★ **HERITAGE PARK.** *2470 Heritage Park Row (92110), in Old Town. 619/299-6832; FAX 619/995-9465; res: 800/995-2470.* E-mail Innkeeper@HeritageParkInn. 10 rms, 6 with shower only, 2 story, 1 suite. No A/C. S, D $90-$150; each addl $20; suite $225; under 12 free; 2-day min wkends & hols. TV; VCR (movies avail). Complimentary full bkfst; afternoon refreshments. Restaurant nearby. Ck-out 11 am, ck-in 3 pm. In-rm modem link. Free airport transportation. Victorian house (1889) moved to this site. Many antiques. Totally nonsmoking. Cr cds: A, DS, MC, V.

D SC

★ ★ **JULIAN WHITE HOUSE.** *(3014 Blue Jay Dr, Julian 92036) I-8 E to I-79, N to Julian. 760/765-1764; res: 800/948-4687; FAX 760/765-2624.* Web www.julian-whitehouse-bnb.com. 4 rms, shower only, 1 suite. No rm phones. S, D $90-$125; each addl $25; suite $135; under 5 free; wkends, hols (2-day min). Closed Dec 24, 25. Crib free. Complimentary full bkfst. Ck-out noon, ck-in 4 pm. Business servs avail. In-rm modem link. Totally nonsmoking. Cr cds: MC, V.

SC

★ ★ ★ ★ **ORCHARD HILL COUNTRY INN.** *(2502 Washington St, Julian 92036-0425) E on I-8, 15 mi N on CA 79. 760/765-1700; res: 800/716-7242; FAX 760/765-0290.* This inn is a collection of eight structures set amid the pine- and oak-covered hills of San Diego's backcountry. Grounds are peppered with hammocks, chink walls, secluded reading benches and gardens. Rooms are individually decorated in country American style. 22 rms, 2 with shower only, 12 suites. Rm phones in suites. S, D $120-$165; each addl $25; suites $140-$205; wkday rates; 2-day min wkends. Crib $10. TV; cable, VCR (movies). Complimentary full bkfst; afternoon refreshments. Complimentary coffee in rms. Ck-out noon, ck-in 3 pm. Business servs avail. Gift shop. Free lndry facilities. Some in-rm whirlpools; refrigerator, wet bar, fireplace in suites. Balconies on suites. Totally nonsmoking. Cr cds: A, MC, V.

D SC

Resorts

★ ★ ★ **DOUBLETREE CARMEL HIGHLAND GOLF & TENNIS RESORT.** *14455 Penasquitos Dr (92129), north of downtown. 619/672-9100; FAX 619/672-9187.* E-mail carmel@highland.doubletreehotels.com; web www.highlanddoubletreehotels.com. 172 rms, 3 story, 6 suites. S, D $119-$179; each addl $10; suites $179; under 12 free; golf, tennis, fitness plans. Crib free. Pet accepted, some restrictions; $150. TV; cable (premium). 2 pools; whirlpool, poolside serv, lifeguard (summer). Supervised child's activities (June-early Sept); ages 6-12. Complimentary coffee in rms. Dining rms 6:30 am-10 pm. Rm serv. Bar 11-1 am. Ck-out noon, ck-in 3 pm. Convention facilities. Business servs avail. Bellhops. Beauty salon. 5 lighted tennis courts, pro. 18-hole golf, greens fee $45-$58, pro, putting green. Exercise rm; instructor, weights, bicycles, saunas, steam rm. Microwaves avail. Private patios, balconies. On 130 acres. Cr cds: A, C, D, DS, JCB, MC, V.

D SC

★ ★ ★ ★ **RANCHO BERNARDO INN.** *17550 Bernardo Oaks Dr (92128), north of downtown. 619/487-1611; FAX 619/675-8501; res:*

800/542-6096. This inn, featuring great golf and fine restaurants, offers an ambience rich with tradition. Large bouquets, plush easy chairs and tile baths distinguish the spacious rooms at this Mission-style golf and tennis resort. 285 rms, 3 story. Mid-Sept-mid-May: S, D $215-$260; suites $300-$900; under 12 free; golf, tennis plans; lower rates rest of yr. TV; cable (premium), VCR avail. 2 pools; 7 whirlpools, poolside serv. Supervised child's activities (Aug & major hols); ages 5-15. Complimentary afternoon refreshments Wed & Sat. Dining rms 6 am-10 pm (also see EL BIZCOCHO). Snack bar. Rm serv to midnight. Bars 11-1 am. Ck-out 1 pm, ck-in 4 pm. Convention facilities. Business center. In-rm modem link. Concierge. Sundries. Gift shop. Airport transportation. Lighted tennis, pro. Three 18-hole, one 27-hole golf courses, pro, putting green, driving range. Volleyball. Bicycles. Exercise rm; instructor, weight machine, bicycles, sauna, steam rm. Massage. Many minibars; some bathrm phones; microwaves avail. Private patios, balconies. Cr cds: A, C, D, DS, MC, V.

D SC

★ ★ ★ **SAN DIEGO PRINCESS.** *1404 W Vacation Rd (92109), on island in Mission Bay. 619/274-4630; FAX 619/581-5929; res: 800/542-6275.* Web www.princessresort.com/princess. 462 cottage rms, 153 kits. May-Aug: S, D $180-$230; each addl $15; suites $245-$375; kit. units $190-$220; lower rates rest of yr. Crib free. Pet accepted. TV; cable (premium). 5 pools, 2 heated; wading pool, whirlpool, poolside serv. Supervised child's activities (June-Aug); ages 3-18. Complimentary coffee in rms. Dining rms 7 am-11 pm. Rm serv. Bars 11-2 am; entertainment Tues-Sun. Ck-out noon, ck-in 4 pm. Coin lndry. Convention facilities. Business servs avail. In-rm modem link. Valet serv. Concierge. Gift shop. Lighted tennis, pro. Putting green. Exercise rm; instructor, weights, stair machine, sauna, steam rm. Bicycles. Game rm. Lawn games. Boats. Some bathrm phones, refrigerators; microwaves avail. Private patios. On beach. Botanical walk. Cr cds: A, DS, ER, MC, V.

D SC

Restaurants

✔★ ★ **AFGHANISTAN KHYBER PASS.** *4647 Convoy St, north of downtown. 619/571-3749.* Hrs: 11 am-2:30 pm, 5-10 pm; Sun from 5 pm. Res accepted. Afghan menu. Wine, beer. Semi-a la carte: lunch $5.95-$10.95, dinner $10.95-$14.95. Specializes in shish kebab, curries. Interior designed as an Afghan cave. Cr cds: A, DS, MC, V.

★ ★ **ANTHONY'S FISH GROTTO.** *11666 Avena Place, off Bernardo Center Dr in Rancho Bernardo, north of downtown. 619/451-2070.* Hrs: 11:30 am-8:30 pm. Closed major hols. Res accepted. Bar. Semi-a la carte: lunch $4.50-$7.95, dinner $7.50-$26. Child's meals. Specializes in fresh seafood. Parking. Outdoor dining. Overlooks Webb Lake Park. Family-owned. Cr cds: A, C, D, DS, MC, V.

D ♥

★ ★ ★ **ANTHONY'S STAR OF THE SEA ROOM.** *1360 Harbor Dr, downtown. 619/232-7408.* Web www.gofishanthonys.com. Hrs: 5:30-10:30 pm. Closed major hols. A la carte entrees: dinner $25-$49. Specialties: Pacific Abalone Piccata, swordfish "New Rossini". Valet parking. Harbor view. Family-owned. Cr cds: A, D, DS, MC, V.

D

★ ★ **ATHENS MARKET TAVERNA.** *109 W F Street (92101), downtown. 619/234-1955.* Hrs: 11:30 am-10 pm; Sat, Sun from 5 pm; early-bird dinner 4:30-6:30 pm. Closed some major hols. Res accepted. Greek menu. Bar to midnight. Semi-a la carte: lunch $5.25-$13.30, dinner $10.75-$22.75. Specializes in lamb, fish, vegetarian specials. Cr cds: A, C, D, DS, MC, V.

★ ★ ★ **BACI RISTORANTE.** *1955 W Morena Blvd, Mission Bay. 619/275-2094.* Hrs: 11:30 am-2:30 pm, 5:30-10 pm; Sat from 5:30 pm. Closed Sun; major hols. Res required Fri, Sat. Northern Italian menu. Bar. Wine list. A la carte entrees: lunch $8.95-$15.95, dinner $10.95-$17.95. Specializes in seafood, veal, pasta. Own baking, pasta. Intimate atmosphere; many art pieces, prints. Cr cds: A, C, D, DS, MC, V.

D

★ ★ **BAYOU BAR & GRILL.** *329 Market St (92101), downtown. 619/696-8747.* Hrs: 11:30 am-3 pm, 5-10 pm; Fri, Sat to 11 pm; Sun brunch 11:30 am-3 pm. Closed Jan 1, Thanksgiving, Dec 25. Res accepted. Cajun, Creole menu. Bar. Semi-a la carte: lunch $5.95-$8.95, dinner $11.95-$16.95. Sun brunch $12.95. Outdoor dining. Casual dining in New Orleans atmosphere. Cr cds: A, C, D, DS, MC, V.

D

★ ★ ★ **BELGIAN LION.** *2265 Bacon St, Mission Bay. 619/223-2700.* Hrs: 5-10 pm. Closed Sun-Wed; major hols. Res accepted. French, Belgian menu. Beer. Wine list. A la carte entrees: dinner $17.50-$22.50. Specialties: fresh fish, classic duck confit. Own pastries. Parking. Outdoor dining. Country Belgian decor. Cr cds: A, C, D, DS, MC, V.

★ ★ **BELLA LUNA.** *748 Fifth Ave (92101), downtown. 619/239-3222.* Hrs: 11:30 am-2:30 pm, 5-11 pm; Fri & Sat to midnight. Closed Jan 1, Thanksgiving, Dec 25. Res accepted. Italian menu. Bar. Semi-a la carte: lunch $4.95-$10.95, dinner $4.95-$16.95. Specializes in pasta, seafood. Valet parking. Patio dining. Original artwork with moon motif; ceiling painted to look like sky. Cr cds: A, D, MC, V.

D

★ ★ **BENIHANA OF TOKYO.** *477 Camino del Rio South, north of downtown. 619/298-4666.* Hrs: 11:30 am-2 pm, 5-10 pm; Fri to 11 pm; Sat 5-11 pm; Sun 1-10 pm. Res accepted. Japanese menu. Bar. Semi-a la carte: lunch $6.50-$15.50, dinner $13.50-$35. Child's meals. Specializes in Japanese steak & seafood. Sushi bar. Valet parking. Japanese village settings. Cr cds: A, C, D, DS, JCB, MC, V.

D

★ ★ ★ **BERNARD'O.** *12457 Rancho Bernardo Rd (92128), north of downtown. 619/487-7171.* Hrs: 11:30 am-2 pm, 5:30-9 pm; Sun 5-8:30 pm. Closed Mon; Thanksgiving, Dec 25. Res accepted. French menu. Wine, beer. Semi-a la carte: lunch $8-$14, dinner $10-$21. Specialties: confit of moscovy duck, homemade fresh pasta. Harpist Sun. Outdoor dining. Contemporary decor. Cr cds: A, D, DS, MC, V.

D

★ ★ ★ **BLUE POINT.** *565 Fifth Ave (92101), downtown. 619/233-6623.* Hrs: 5-10 pm; Fri, Sat to 11 pm; Sun to 9 pm. Closed Dec 25. Res accepted. Bar. Extensive wine list. Semi-a la carte: dinner $13.95-$23.95. Specialties: sesame crusted salmon, fresh Maine lobster with macadamia nut butter, grilled Hawaiian ahi. Valet parking. Outdoor dining. Oil paintings; oyster bar. Cr cds: A, D, DS, MC, V.

D

★ ★ ★ **BUSALACCHI'S.** *3683 5th Ave, north of downtown. 619/298-0119.* Hrs: 11:30 am-2:15 pm, 5-10 pm; Fri & Sat to 11 pm. Closed most major hols. Res accepted. Italian menu. Bar. A la carte entrees: lunch $7.25-$16.95, dinner $8.95-$23.95. Specializes in Sicilian dishes. Valet parking. Outdoor dining. Victorian-style house. Cr cds: A, C, D, DS, MC, V.

✔★ **CAFE COYOTE.** *2461 San Diego Ave, in Old Town Esplanade, in Old Town. 619/291-4695.* Hrs: 7 am-10 pm; Fri & Sat to 11 pm. Closed Dec 25. Res accepted. Mexican, Amer menu. Bar. Semi-a la carte: bkfst $2.95-$6.95, lunch, dinner $3.95-$9.95. Child's meals. Specialties: blue corn pancakes, carnitas, carne asada. Own tortillas. Entertainment Fri-Sun on patio. Parking. Outdoor dining. Pictures, statues of Southwestern wildlife. Cr cds: A, C, D, DS, MC, V.

D

★ ★ ★ **CAFE PACIFICA.** *2414 San Diego Ave, in Old Town. 619/291-6666.* Hrs: 5:30-10 pm; Sun from 5 pm; early-bird dinner 5:30-6:30 pm. Res accepted. Bar. Semi-a la carte: dinner $12-$18. Specializes in fresh fish. Near Old Spanish Cemetery. Cr cds: A, C, D, DS, JCB, MC, V.

D

★ ★ ★ **CALIFORNIA CUISINE.** *1027 University Ave, north of downtown. 619/543-0790.* Hrs: 11 am-10 pm; Sat, Sun from 5 pm. Closed Mon; Jan 1, Thanksgiving, Dec 25. Res accepted. California menu. Wine, beer. Semi-a la carte: lunch $6.50-$13, dinner $10-$19. Specializes in fresh seafood, pasta, salad. Outdoor dining. Menu changes daily. Original paintings. Cr cds: A, D, DS, MC, V.

★ ★ **CASA DE BANDINI.** *2754 Calhoun St, in Old Town. 619/297-8211.* Hrs: 11 am-10 pm; Sun from 10 am; winter to 9 pm. Closed Thanksgiving, Dec 25. Mexican menu. Bar. Semi-a la carte: lunch, dinner $5.50-$15.50. Child's meals. Specializes in seafood. Mariachi band. Parking. Outdoor dining. Early California atmosphere, garden patio with fountain. Adobe bldg (1829) once served as headquarters for Commodore Stockton. Cr cds: A, C, D, DS, MC, V.

★ ★ **CELADON.** *3628 5th Ave, north of downtown. 619/295-8800.* Hrs: 11:30 am-2 pm, 5-10 pm. Closed Sun; Jan 1, July 4, Thanksgiving, Dec 25. Res accepted. Thai menu. Wine, beer. A la carte entrees: lunch $6.25-$10, dinner $8.25-$15. Specializes in shrimp, chicken, beef, vegetables. Cr cds: A, MC, V.

D

✔★ ★ **CHIEU-ANH.** *16769 Bernardo Center Dr (92128), north of downtown. 619/485-1231.* Hrs: 11 am-2 pm, 5-9:30 pm; Sat, Sun from 5 pm. Closed Dec 25. Res accepted. Vietnamese menu. Wine, beer. Semi-a la carte: lunch $4.95-$6.95, dinner $9-$14. Specializes in rice noodles, clay pot dishes. Contemporary decor. Cr cds: A, C, D, MC, V.

D

★ ★ **CROCE'S.** *802 Fifth Ave (92101), downtown. 619/233-4355.* Web www.croce.com. Hrs: 5 pm-midnight. Closed Thanksgiving, Dec 25. Res accepted. Contemporary Amer menu. Bar to 2 am. Semi-a la carte: dinner $12.95-$19.95. Specializes in seafood. Live jazz. Valet parking. Outdoor dining. Tribute to famous singer, composer Jim Croce. Cr cds: A, C, D, DS, MC, V.

D

✔★ ★ ★ **DAKOTA.** *901 Fifth Ave (92101), downtown. 619/234-5554.* Hrs: 11:30 am-2:30 pm, 5-10 pm; Fri, Sat to 11 pm, Sun 5-9 pm. Closed July 4, Dec 25. Res accepted. Bar. Semi-a la carte: lunch $5.95-$10.95, dinner $10.95-$19.95. Specializes in barbecue ribs, mesquite-broiled meat, seafood. Pianist Wed-Sat. Valet parking. Balcony, patio dining. Original artwork. Cr cds: A, D, DS, MC, V.

D

★ ★ ★ **DOBSON'S.** *956 Broadway Circle, downtown. 619/231-6771.* Hrs: 11:30 am-3 pm, 5:30-10 pm; Thur, Fri to 11 pm; Sat 5:30-11 pm. Closed major hols. Res accepted. Continental menu. Bar to 1:30 am. Semi-a la carte: lunch $5.50-$12.50, dinner $13-$25. Prix fixe: dinner $21.95. Specializes in fresh seafood, veal. Own sourdough bread. Covered parking. Cr cds: A, MC, V.

★ ★ ★ **EL BIZCOCHO.** *(See Rancho Bernardo Inn Resort) 619/675-8500.* Hrs: 6-10 pm; Fri, Sat to 10:30 pm; Sun brunch 10 am-2 pm. Res accepted. French menu. Bar. Extensive wine list. A la carte entrees: dinner $23-$40. Sun brunch $22. Specializes in seasonal cuisine. Pianist. Valet parking. Jacket (exc brunch). Views of grounds with waterfalls. Cr cds: A, C, D, DS, MC, V.

✔★ **EL TECOLOTE.** *6110 Friars Rd, north of downtown. 619/295-2087.* Hrs: 11 am-10 pm; Sun 4-9 pm. Mexican menu. Bar. Semi-a la carte: lunch $2.40-$10.55, dinner $7.35-$11.50. Child's meals. Specialties: cheese-filled zucchinis, mole poblano. Parking. Outdoor dining. Mexican artifacts, photographs, original art. Totally nonsmoking. Cr cds: A, D, DS, MC, V.

D

✔★ **FAIROUZ.** *3166 Midway Dr (92110), in Point Loma. 619/225-0308.* Hrs 11 am-9 pm; Fri, Sat to 10 pm. Closed Jan 1. Res required Fri & Sat. Mediterranean menu. Bar. Semi-a la carte: lunch $3.95-$12.95, dinner $5-$13.95. Buffet: lunch $5.25, dinner $10.95. Specialties: hommos taboleh, kabobs. Parking. Paintings, prints available for purchase. Cr cds: A, D, DS, MC, V.

D

★ ★ ★ **FIO'S.** *801 5th Ave, downtown. 619/234-3467.* Web www.sdtech.com/fios. Hrs: 11:30 am-3 pm, 5-11 pm; Fri, Sat 5 pm-midnight; Sun 5-10 pm. Closed Dec 25. Res accepted. Italian menu. Bar. Wine cellar. Semi-a la carte: lunch, dinner $4.95-$22.50. Specializes in pasta. Outdoor dining. European decor; original artwork depicting Palio of Siena. Cr cds: A, C, D, DS, MC, V.

D

✔★ ★ **FRENCH MARKET GRILLE.** *(15717 Bernardo Heights Pkwy, Rancho Bernardo 92128) 619/485-8055.* Hrs: 11 am-10 pm; Sun 9 am-9 pm. Res accepted. French, Amer menu. Semi-a la carte: lunch $7-$9, dinner $12-$16. Specialties: cog au vin, beef bourguignon, lamb shank on artichoke ravioli and white beans. Opera Tues. Outdoor dining. Intimate dining. Totally nonsmoking. Cr cds: A, D, MC, V.

D

★ ★ **HARBOR HOUSE.** *831 W Harbor Dr, in Seaport Village, downtown. 619/232-1141.* Hrs: 11 am-11 pm. Res accepted. Bar from 11 am. A la carte entrees: lunch $9.95-$19.95, dinner $14.95-$22.95. Child's meals. Specializes in fresh seafood. Oyster bar. Parking. View of harbor, boat docks, Coronado Bay Bridge. Cr cds: A, DS, MC, V.

D

✔★ ★ **HOB NOB HILL.** *2271 1st Ave, adj to Balboa Park, north of downtown. 619/239-8176.* Hrs: 7 am-9 pm. Closed Dec 25. Res accepted. Wine, beer. Semi-a la carte: bkfst $2.35-$10.95. Complete meals: lunch $5.65-$7.75, dinner $5.65-$13.45. Child's meals. Specializes in eastern fried scallops, lamb shanks, roast turkey. Family-owned. Cr cds: A, D, DS, MC, V.

D

★ ★ **IMPERIAL HOUSE.** *505 Kalmia St, north of downtown. 619/234-3525.* Hrs: 11 am-4 pm, 5-9 pm; Mon to 2 pm; Fri, Sat to 11 pm; early-bird dinner Tues-Fri 5-6:30 pm. Closed Sun; most major hols. Res accepted. Continental menu. Bar to 11 pm; Fri, Sat to 12:30 am. A la carte entrees: lunch $6.50-$11, dinner $10-$20. Specializes in rack of lamb, pepper steak, seafood. Pianist Wed-Sat. Valet parking. Old-world decor. Family-owned. Cr cds: A, C, D, MC, V.

✔★ **JACK & GUILIO.** *2391 San Diego Ave (92110), in Old Town. 619/294-2074.* Hrs: 11:30 am-2 pm, 4:30-9:30 pm; Fri, Sat to 10:30 pm. Closed Easter, Thanksgiving, Dec 25. Italian menu. Wine, beer. Semi-a la carte: lunch, dinner $5.95-15.50. Child's meals. Specialties: scampi guilio, tortelloni verdi. Outdoor dining. Italian bistro atmosphere. Cr cds: A, DS, MC, V.

D

★ ★ **JASMINE.** *4609 Convoy St (92111), north of downtown. 619/268-0888.* Hrs: 10 am-11 pm. Res accepted. Chinese menu. Bar. Semi-a la carte: lunch $5.95-$18, dinner $8-$25. Specializes in dim sum, live seafood. Parking. Large dining rm with movable walls. Cr cds: A, MC, V.

✔★ **KARL STRAUSS' BREWERY & GRILL.** *1157 Columbia St, downtown. 619/234-2739.* Web www.karlstrauss.com. Hrs: 11:30 am-10 pm; Thur-Sat to 1 am. Closed most major hols. Res accepted. Bar. Semi-a la carte: lunch $6-$11, dinner $7-$15. Specialties: hamburgers, fresh fish, German-style sausage. Brew own beer; some seasonal varieties. View of microbrewery from restaurant. Cr cds: MC, V.

D

★ ★ **KELLY'S.** *500 Hotel Circle N, north of downtown. 619/291-7131.* Hrs: 11 am-11 pm; Sat, Sun & hols from 4 pm; early-bird dinner 4-6 pm. Closed Easter, Thanksgiving, Dec 25. Bar to 2 am; Sat, Sun from 4 pm. Semi-a la carte: lunch $6.25-$9.95, dinner $8.95-$21.95. Specializes in barbecued ribs, steak. Entertainment. Parking. Waterfalls. Cr cds: A, C, D, DS, MC, V.

★ ★ **KENNY'S STEAK PUB.** *939 Fourth Ave (92101), downtown. 619/231-8500.* Hrs: 11:30 am-9:30 pm; Fri to 10:30 pm; Sat 5-10:30 pm. Closed Sun; Memorial Day, Thanksgiving, Dec 25. Res accepted. Bar. Semi-a la carte: lunch $4.50-$12.95, dinner $9.50-$24.95. Specializes in prime steak. Pianist Fri, Sat. Classic steakhouse atmosphere. Memorabilia from John Wayne movie "The Quiet Man" on display. Cr cds: A, DS, JCB, MC, V.

D

✔★★ **LA VACHE & CO.** *420 Robinson St (92103), north of downtown. 619/295-0214.* Hrs: 11:30 am-2:30 pm, 5-11 pm; Sat, Sun brunch 10 am-3 pm. Closed Easter, Thanksgiving, Dec 25. Res accepted. Country French menu. Wine, beer. Semi-a la carte: lunch $5-$9, dinner $5-$18.50. Outdoor dining. Casual European decor. Totally nonsmoking. Cr cds: A, C, D, DS, MC, V.

D

★★★ **LAUREL.** *505 Laurel St (92101), downtown. 619/239-2222.* E-mail Laurelrb@aol.com; web www.winesellar.com. Hrs: 5-10 pm; Fri, Sat to 11 pm; Sun 4:30-10 pm. Res accepted. French menu. Bar. A la carte entrees: dinner $12-$25. Specializes in seafood, game. Entertainment. Valet parking. Contemporary decor. Cr cds: A, C, D, DS, MC, V.

D

★★★ **LE FONTAINEBLEAU.** *(See The Westgate Hotel) 619/238-1818.* Hrs: 6-10 pm; Sun brunch 10 am-2 pm. Res accepted. Continental menu. Bar. Wine cellar. Semi-a la carte: dinner $15-$24. Sun brunch $28.95. Child's meals. Specializes in seafood, veal. Pianist. Valet parking. Lavish French period setting; antiques. Cr cds: A, C, D, DS, MC, V.

D

✔★★ **LINO'S.** *2754 Calhoun St, in Old Town. 619/299-7124.* Hrs: 11 am-9 pm; Fri & Sat to 10 pm. Closed Jan 1, Thanksgiving, Dec 25. Res accepted. Italian menu. Bar. Semi-a la carte: lunch $4.95-$8.25, dinner $6.95-$14.95. Specializes in veal, chicken, shrimp. Own pasta. Parking. Outdoor dining. Cr cds: A, C, D, DS, ER, JCB, MC, V.

♥

★★★ **MISTER A'S.** *2550 5th Ave, on 12th floor of Financial Center, north of downtown. 619/239-1377.* Hrs: 11 am-2:30 pm; 5:30-10:30 pm; Sat, Sun from 5:30 pm. Closed some major hols. Res accepted. Continental menu. Bar 11-2 am; Sat, Sun from 5 pm. Wine list. Semi-a la carte: lunch $6.95-$12.95, dinner $16.95-$35.95. Prix fixe: dinner $21.95. Specialties: beef Wellington, rack of lamb, fresh fish. Entertainment Fri-Sat. Valet parking. Rococo decor; oil paintings. Rooftop dining; panoramic view. Family-owned. Jacket (dinner). Cr cds: A, C, D, DS, JCB, MC, V.

D

✔★★ **MONTANA'S AMERICAN GRILL.** *1421 University Ave (92103), north of downtown. 619/297-0722.* Hrs: 11:30 am-10 pm; Fri to 11 pm; Sat 5-11 pm; Sun 5-9 pm. Closed most major hols. Res accepted. Bar. Semi-a la carte: lunch $7.95-$10.95, dinner $7.95-$17.95. Specializes in BBQ ribs, skirt steak. Valet parking. Contemporary decor. Totally nonsmoking. Cr cds: A, D, MC, V.

D

✔★ **NATI'S.** *1852 Bacon St, north of downtown. 619/224-3369.* Hrs: 11 am-9 pm; Sun to 8 pm; winter to 8 pm. Closed some major hols. Mexican menu. Bar. Semi-a la carte: bkfst $3-$6.50, lunch, dinner $4.35-$8.50. Specializes in chiles rellenos, sour cream tostadas, carne asada. Parking. Outdoor dining. Cr cds: MC, V.

★★ **NICK'S AT THE BEACH.** *809 Thomas Ave (92106), downtown. 619/270-1730.* Hrs: 11-2 am; Sun brunch 10 am-2 pm. Closed Dec 25. Bar. Semi-a la carte: lunch, dinner $5.95-$14.95. Sun brunch $4.95-$9.95. Child's meals. Specializes in fresh seafood. Casual atmosphere. Totally nonsmoking. Cr cds: A, C, D, DS, MC, V.

D

✔★ **OLD TOWN MEXICAN CAFE & CANTINA.** *2489 San Diego Ave (92110), in Old Town. 619/297-4330.* Hrs: 7 am-11 pm. Closed Thanksgiving, Dec 25. Mexican menu. Bar to 2 am. A la carte entrees: bkfst $2.95-$7.25, lunch, dinner $2.75-$12. Specialties: carnitas, Old Town pollo, Mexican-style ribs, homemade tortillas. Child's meals. Parking. Patio dining. Cr cds: A, DS, MC, V.

D

✔★★ **OSTERIA PANEVINO.** *722 Fifth Ave (92101), downtown. 619/595-7959.* Hrs: 11:30 am-2:30 pm, 5 pm-midnight. Closed Thanksgiving, Dec 25. Res accepted. Italian menu. Bar. Semi-a la carte: lunch $8-$13, dinner $12-$18. Specializes in wood-burning pizza, wild game. Valet parking. Outdoor dining. Mural of Florence on walls. Cr cds: A, C, D, DS, MC, V.

D

★★ **PANDA INN.** *506 Horton Plaza, on top floor, downtown. 619/233-7800.* Hrs: 11 am-10 pm; Fri, Sat to 10:30 pm. Closed Thanksgiving. Res accepted. Mandarin menu. Bar. Semi-a la carte: lunch $6-$9, dinner $8-$12. Specialties: sweet & pungent shrimp, orange-flavored beef. Parking. Outdoor dining. Several dining areas, all with Chinese art pieces, 1 with entire ceiling skylight; pandas depicted in stained-glass windows. Cr cds: A, D, DS, JCB, MC, V.

D

★★★ **RAINWATER'S.** *1202 Kettner Blvd, near train depot, downtown. 619/233-5757.* Hrs: 11:30 am-midnight; Sat 5 pm-midnight; Sun 5-11 pm. Closed Thanksgiving, Dec 25. Res accepted. Bar. Wine list. Semi-a la carte: lunch $7-$15, dinner $19-$40. Specializes in fresh seafood, prime steaks. Own pastries. Valet parking. Outdoor dining. Cr cds: A, C, D, MC, V.

D

★★★ **RUTH'S CHRIS STEAK HOUSE.** *1355 N Harbor Dr (92101), downtown. 619/233-1422.* Hrs: 5-10 pm; Fri, Sat to 10:30 pm. Closed Thanksgiving, Dec 25. Res accepted. Bar. A la carte entrees: dinner $17.95-$29.95. Specializes in steak, lobster. Contemporary decor. Cr cds: A, D, DS, MC, V.

D

★★★ **SALLY'S.** *(See Hyatt Regency Hotel) 619/687-6080.* Hrs: 11:30 am-11 pm. Closed Dec 25. Res accepted. Mediterranean menu. Bar. Semi-a la carte: lunch $8-$14, dinner $17-$28. Specializes in seafood. Outdoor dining. Contemporary decor. Cr cds: A, C, D, DS, ER, JCB, MC, V.

D

★★★ **SALVATORE'S.** *750 Front St (92101), downtown. 619/544-1865.* Hrs: 5-10 pm. Res accepted. Italian menu. Bar. Wine list. A la carte entrees: dinner $11-$23. Specializes in Northern Italian dishes. Parking. Original artwork. Cr cds: A, D, MC, V.

D

★★ **SAN DIEGO PIER CAFE.** *885 W Harbor Dr, in Seaport Village, downtown. 619/239-3968.* Hrs: 7 am-10 pm; Fri & Sat to 11 pm. Serv bar. Semi-a la carte: bkfst $4-$9.95, lunch $5.50-$13.95, dinner $18.95-$19.95. Child's meals. Specializes in fresh fish broiled. Outdoor dining. On harbor pier. Cr cds: A, DS, MC, V.

★★ **TAKA.** *555 Fifth Ave (92101), north of downtown. 619/338-0555.* Hrs: 5:30-10 pm; Fri, Sat to 11:30 pm. Closed Jan 1, Dec 25. Res accepted. Japanese menu. Bar. Semi-a la carte: dinner $6-$24. Specializes in seafood, sushi. Valet parking. Outdoor dining. Japanese decor. Totally nonsmoking. Cr cds: A, C, MC, V.

D

★★★ **THEE BUNGALOW.** *4996 W Point Loma Blvd, north of downtown. 619/224-2884.* Hrs: 5:30-9:30 pm; Fri & Sat 5-10 pm; Sun 5-9 pm. Closed July 4. Res accepted. Extensive wine list. Continental menu. Semi-a la carte: dinner $9.95-$22. Specializes in roast duck, rack of lamb, fresh seafood. Parking. In converted house. Many special wine dinners planned throughout the year. Cr cds: A, C, D, DS, MC, V.

★★ **TOM HAM'S LIGHTHOUSE.** *2150 Harbor Island Dr, north of downtown. 619/291-9110.* E-mail tomhams@juno.com; web www.adpark.com/tomhams. Hrs: 11:15 am-3:30 pm, 5-10:30 pm; Sat 4:30-11 pm;

Sun 4-10 pm; early-bird dinner Mon-Fri 5-6 pm, Sun 4-6 pm; Sun brunch 10 am-2 pm. Closed Dec 25. Res accepted. Bar 11-2 am. Semi-a la carte: lunch $5.95-$13.95, dinner $9.95-$32.95. Sun brunch $11.95. Child's meals. Specializes in steak, seafood. Salad bar (lunch). Entertainment Wed-Sat. Parking. Early California, Spanish decor. View of bay, San Diego skyline. Official Coast Guard No. 9 beacon. Family-owned. Cr cds: A, C, D, DS, MC, V.

SC

★★ **TOP OF THE MARKET.** *750 N Harbor Dr, downtown. 619/234-4867.* Web www.thefishmarket.com. Hrs: 11 am-10 pm; Sun brunch 10 am-2 pm. Closed Thanksgiving, Dec 25. Res accepted. Bar to 10 pm. Semi-a la carte: lunch $9.50-$46.75, dinner $13-$46.75. Sun brunch $16.50. Child's meals. Specializes in seafood. Oyster, sushi bar. Parking. Outdoor dining. Pictures of turn-of-the-century fishing scenes. Retail fish market lower floor. Cr cds: A, C, D, DS, MC, V.

D

★★ **TRATTORIA FANTASTICA.** *1735 India St (92101), downtown. 619/234-1734.* Hrs: 11:30 am-2 pm, 5-11 pm; wkends to midnight. Closed some major hols. Res accepted. Italian menu. Wine, beer. Semi-a la carte: lunch $6-$10, dinner $8-$15. Specializes in family-style cooking. Patio dining. Casual atmosphere. Italian decor. Cr cds: A, D, DS, MC, V.

D

★★ **TRATTORIA LA STRADA.** *702 5th Ave (92101), downtown. 619/239-3400.* Hrs: 11 am-11 pm. Res accepted. Italian menu. Bar. Semi-a la carte: lunch $7.95-$18.95, dinner $8.95-$19.50. Specialties: osso buco alla milanese, salmone ai carciofi e basilico. Outdoor dining. Italian bistro atmosphere. Cr cds: A, C, D, DS, MC, V.

D

★★★ **WINESELLAR & BRASSERIE.** *9550 Waples St, north of downtown. 619/450-9576.* E-mail winesellar@aol.com; web www.winesellar.com. Hrs: 5:30-10 pm; Sun to 9 pm. Closed Mon; also most major hols. Res accepted; required Fri-Sun. Contemporary French menu. Extensive wine list. A la carte entrees: dinner $18-$33. Menu changes seasonally. Intimate, formal dining. Cr cds: A, C, D, DS, MC, V.

Unrated Dining Spots

AESOP'S TABLES. *8650 Genesee Ave, in Costa Verde Center, north of downtown. 619/455-1535.* Hrs: 11 am-10 pm; Sun from 4 pm. Closed major hols. Greek, Middle Eastern menu. Bar. Semi-a la carte: lunch $4-$9.95, dinner $5-$12.95. Patio dining. Cr cds: A, C, D, DS, MC, V.

D

CITY DELICATESSEN. *535 University Ave, north of downtown. 619/295-2747.* Hrs: 7 am-midnight; Fri, Sat to 2 am. Closed Dec 25; Yom Kippur. Jewish-style delicatessen. Wine, beer. A la carte entrees: bkfst, lunch $4.50-$8.50, dinner $4.50-$9.95. Child's meals. Own baking. Delicatessen and bakery. Cr cds: A, D, DS, MC, V.

CORVETTE DINER BAR & GRILL. *3946 5th Ave, downtown. 619/542-1001.* Hrs: 11 am-midnight. Closed Jan 1, Dec 24 eve, 25. Bar. Semi-a la carte: lunch $4.85-$7.95, dinner $5.50-$9.95. Specializes in hamburgers, chicken-fried steak. DJ. 1950s-style diner with soda fountains. Corvette in center of room. Cr cds: A, DS, JCB, MC, V.

D.Z. AKIN'S. *6930 Alvarado Rd, north of downtown. 619/265-0218.* Hrs: 7 am-9 pm; Fri, Sat to 11 pm. Closed July 4, Thanksgiving, Dec 25; some Jewish hols. Semi-a la carte: bkfst $3.50-$6, lunch $6-$8, dinner $8-$12. Specializes in delicatessen items. Own pastries. Parking. Cr cds: MC, V.

DICK'S LAST RESORT. *345 5th Ave (92101), downtown. 619/231-9100.* Hrs: 11-1 am. Closed Dec 25. Res accepted. Bar to 2 am. Semi-a la carte: lunch $3.25-$8.95, dinner $6.95-$14.95. Child's meals. Specialties: beef & pork ribs, crab, chicken. Entertainment. Valet parking Fri & Sat. Outdoor dining. Large warehouse setting. Casual dining. Cr cds: A, C, D, DS, MC, V.

D

EL INDIO SHOP. *3695 India St (92103), north of downtown. 619/299-0333.* Hrs: 7 am-9 pm. Mexican menu. Semi-a la carte: bkfst $3-$4, lunch, dinner $5-$7. Outdoor dining. Cafeteria-style. Tortilla factory in kitchen. Family-owned. Cr cds: DS, MC, V.

D SC

GREEK CORNER. *5841 El Cajon Blvd, north of downtown. 619/287-3303.* Hrs: 11 am-9:30 pm. Greek, Middle Eastern menu. Wine, beer. Semi-a la carte: lunch, dinner $4-$10. Specializes in Greek dishes, Middle Eastern vegetarian dishes. Parking. Outdoor dining. Greek cafe-style dining. Cr cds: MC, V.

LORNA'S ITALIAN KITCHEN. *3945 Governor Dr (92122), north of downtown. 619/452-0661.* Hrs: 11 am-9:30 pm; Fri to 10:30 pm; Sat 4-10:30 pm; Sun 4-9 pm. Closed most major hols. Italian menu. Wine, beer. Semi-a la carte: lunch $4.50-$8.50, dinner $6.50-$14.50. Child's meals. Specializes in pasta, salad. Italian bistro decor. Totally nonsmoking. Cr cds: C, D, DS, MC, V.

SAFFRON. *3731-B India St, north of downtown. 619/574-0177.* Hrs: 11 am-9 pm. Closed Sun; Jan 1, Thanksgiving, Dec 25. Thai menu. A la carte entrees: lunch, dinner $3.75-$12. Specializes in Thai grilled chicken. Picnic baskets avail. Cr cds: MC, V.

San Francisco

Founded: 1776
Pop: 723,959
Elev: 63 feet
Time zone: Pacific
Area code: 415
Web: www.sanfranciscoonline.com

When the fog rolls in off the Pacific and the foghorns bellow from the bay, when the city's lights are muted and the cable cars clatter up and down the hills, San Francisco's many charms become evident. The city's setting is part of its allure. Houses of infinite variety and imagination are perched on hills overlooking the San Francisco Bay, the Golden Gate Bridge and the Pacific Ocean. The town's many cultures coexist peacefully, yet each retains its identity and adds to the city's character. It is an international city—ships from all parts of the world come and go. Even San Francisco's sinful past is an asset, titillating the visitor with reminders of its Barbary Coast beginnings.

San Francisco's lusty story began with early Portuguese, English and Spanish explorers who sailed into the bay in the 1700s. In 1848, gold was discovered in California, and as the news spread around the world, a torrent of people and ships descended on the city. By the next year, San Francisco was a wild boom town of 20,000 transients living in tents. Farsighted businessmen realized that fortunes could be made in San Francisco as well as in the gold camps. Mercantile establishments, small industries and the shipping of goods to the Orient prospered.

On April 18, 1906, the great earthquake and fire struck San Francisco. Raging unchecked for three days, the fire destroyed the entire business area and burned 514 blocks in the heart of the city. Although losses amounted to some 3,000 lives and $500 million, rebuilding started before the ashes cooled, and San Francisco was soon well on its way to becoming the city it is today.

Business

Tourism is the most important industry in San Francisco, but the economy has many other strong bases. San Francisco is a leading seaport, and many people are employed in occupations related directly or indirectly to shipping. Exports, many of which are sent to the Far East and Latin America, include cotton, lumber, machinery, paper and food products. This is a world communications center—most telephone calls and cables that cross the Pacific are relayed through San Francisco.

Healthcare, bioscience, multimedia and arts and culture are major industries here. San Francisco is also a leader in insurance, banking and investment. Government and education are important sectors of employment.

Convention Facilities

The Moscone Center is situated on an 11-acre site at 4th and Howard streets. The main exhibit hall contains 442,000 square feet of exhibit space, seats 20,000 people and can be divided into three sections. The hall is wired for closed-circuit TV and simultaneous translation. There are also 69 additional meeting rooms, with seating capacities from 12 to 5,300, and a 5,300-seat ballroom with 43,000 square feet of space. Parking for 4,000 cars is adjacent.

The Civic Auditorium has theater seating for 7,000; two adjoining halls seat 825 each. The main arena can accommodate 186 exhibit booths, each 10 by 10 feet. The auditorium occupies the entire south side of Civic Center Plaza. Adjoining it is Brooks Hall, where 478 exhibit booths, each 10 by 10 feet, can be set up. An underground garage accommodates 840 cars.

The Nob Hill Masonic Center has theater seating for 3,165 and a 16,500-square-foot exhibit hall. A completely equipped catering kitchen can serve banquets of 1,200 people.

The Cow Palace, on the southern edge of the city, is divided into four exhibit areas; two with 49,000 square feet of space and two with 62,380 square feet of space. The main arena has 30,000 square feet of floor space, seating for 14,700, three restaurants, 12 food stands, four cocktail bars and catering service. There are six meeting rooms for 50 to 600 persons. A lighted parking area accommodates 4,000 cars.

Sports & Recreation

Sports fans can choose from such teams as baseball's San Francisco Giants or football's 49ers; both play in 3COM Park. The Bay Area also hosts baseball's Oakland Athletics, basketball's Golden State Warriors, football's Oakland Raiders, hockey's San Jose Sharks and amateur soccer competitions.

Riding the cable cars, a national historic landmark and a vital part of the city's public transportation system, is a form of recreation unique to San Francisco.

Federally protected Golden Gate National Recreation Area takes in much of San Francisco's shoreline, as well as the bay islands of Angel and Alcatraz and a good portion of the Marin County coast. The area boasts numerous beaches, historic fortifications, hiking trails, a bridle path and much more. The Golden Gate Promenade, a 3 1/2 mile footpath, provides access to previously restricted areas of the Presidio and Fort Mason. Park headquarters is at Fort Mason.

Entertainment

The performing arts are represented by the San Francisco Symphony, the San Francisco Opera, American Conservatory Theatre and the San Francisco Ballet. Various touring concert artists, orchestras and dance

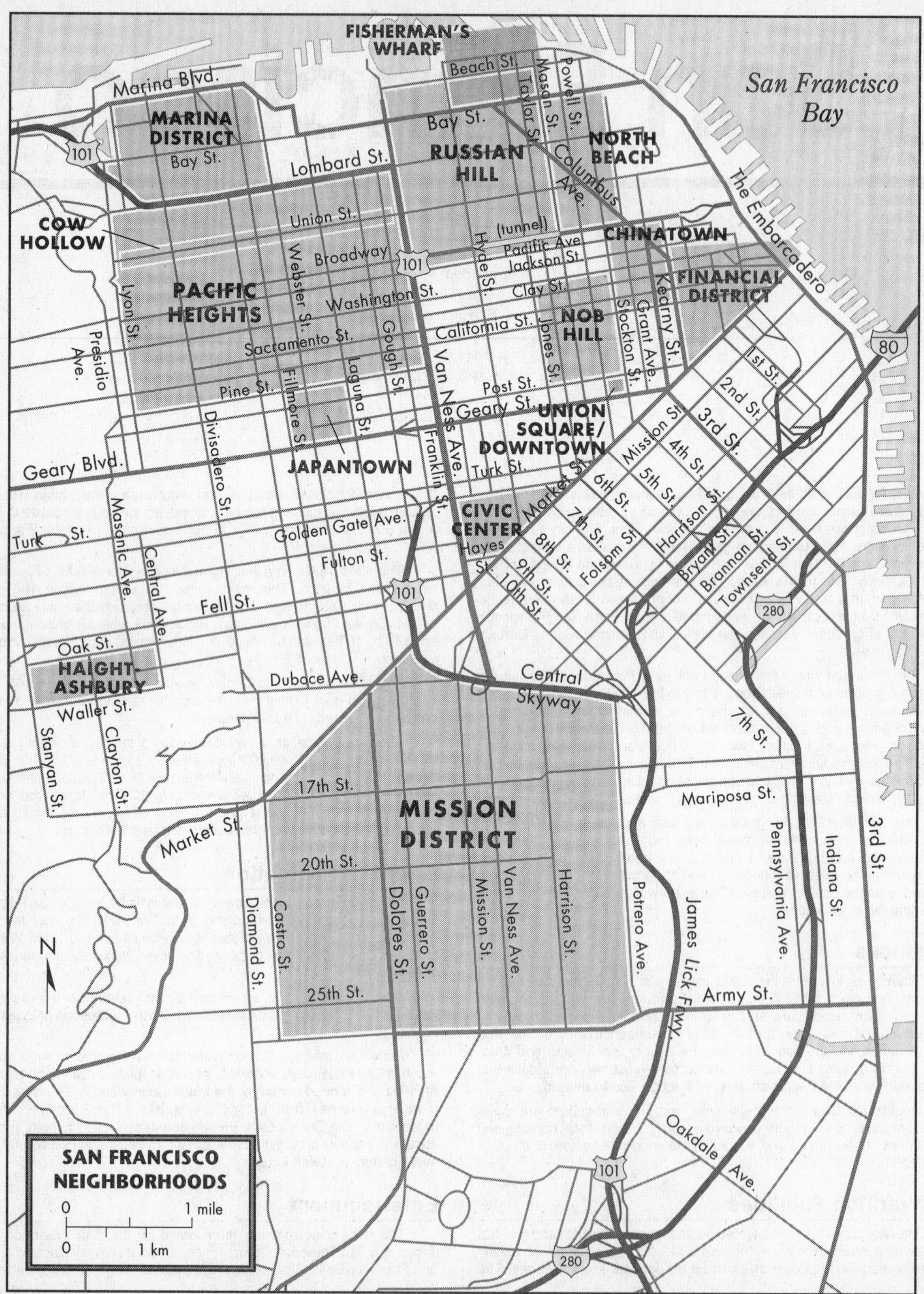
FISHERMAN'S WHARF
San Francisco Bay
MARINA DISTRICT
RUSSIAN HILL
NORTH BEACH
COW HOLLOW
CHINATOWN
FINANCIAL DISTRICT
PACIFIC HEIGHTS
NOB HILL
UNION SQUARE/ DOWNTOWN
JAPANTOWN
CIVIC CENTER
HAIGHT-ASHBURY
MISSION DISTRICT
Marina Blvd.
Beach St.
Bay St.
Lombard St.
Union St.
Broadway
Pacific Ave.
Jackson St.
Washington St.
Clay St.
California St.
Sacramento St.
Pine St.
Post St.
Geary St.
Geary Blvd.
Turk St.
Golden Gate Ave.
Fulton St.
Hayes St.
Fell St.
Oak St.
Waller St.
Duboce Ave.
Central Skyway
17th St.
20th St.
25th St.
Mariposa St.
Army St.
Oakdale Ave.
Market St.
Mission St.
1st St.
2nd St.
3rd St.
4th St.
5th St.
6th St.
7th St.
8th St.
9th St.
10th St.
Folsom St.
Harrison St.
Bryant St.
Brannan St.
Townsend St.
The Embarcadero
Columbus Ave.
Mason St.
Taylor St.
Powell St.
Hyde St.
(tunnel)
Jones St.
Stockton St.
Grant Ave.
Kearny St.
Van Ness Ave.
Franklin St.
Gough St.
Laguna St.
Fillmore St.
Webster St.
Divisadero St.
Lyon St.
Presidio Ave.
Masonic Ave.
Central Ave.
Stanyan St.
Clayton St.
Castro St.
Diamond St.
Dolores St.
Guerrero St.
Mission St.
Van Ness Ave.
Harrison St.
Potrero Ave.
James Lick Fwy.
Pennsylvania Ave.
Indiana St.
3rd St.
7th St.
101
80
280
N
SAN FRANCISCO NEIGHBORHOODS
0
1 mile
0
1 km

companies perform at the War Memorial/Opera House, Louise M. Davies Symphony Hall and the Center for the Arts at Yerba Buena Gardens.

Numerous small theaters, nonequity companies, cabaret theater and university groups present dramatic performances. The San Francisco International Film Festival is held each spring.

Nightlife

Nightlife in San Francisco varies from posh clubs in the best hotels to cozy comedy clubs to bars featuring various entertainers. Most popular are the small, elegant piano bars, where prices are comparatively moderate. One of the most famous cocktail lounges in the world is "The Top of the Mark" in the Mark Hopkins Inter-Continental Hotel. The principal club areas are North Beach, Union Street and south of Market Street (also known as SoMa).

The gold of the mining camps attracted some of the finest chefs in the world to San Francisco. This heritage remains today. More than 3,300 restaurants feature exquisite cuisines with international flair and flavor.

Historical Areas

Alcatraz, the old fortification in San Francisco Bay, used as a penitentiary from 1934 to 1963, is now part of the Golden Gate National Recreation Area. Alcatraz is accessible only by boat; public boats depart frequently from docks, and reservations can be made for a combined boat trip and walking tour of the island.

Jackson Square is a landmark area with many buildings of the past now filled with antique galleries. It is the home of San Francisco's oldest remaining commercial buildings. Mission Dolores, originally the Mission San Francisco de Asis, was the fountainhead from which the city grew. Cornerstone of the present building was laid in 1782. Many pioneers are buried in the ancient cemetery beside the church.

The Presidio, a wooded tract of 1,450 acres, has been fortified since 1776 and is now a part of the Golden Gate National Recreation Area. The Golden Gate Promenade allows visitors to see points of interest in the Presidio indicated by markers.

Union Street, known as Cow Hollow, is an area of restored or renovated turn-of-the-century dwellings, cow barns and carriage houses that now house restaurants, boutiques, shops and art galleries.

Sightseeing

Strolling almost anywhere in San Francisco is a delight, as are drives throughout the Bay Area and beyond. In this city of precipitous hills, Lombard Street at Hyde Street offers a real challenge. Known as "the crookedest street in the world," Lombard Street makes eight hairpin turns in a single block. Coit Memorial Tower, a 210-foot monument to volunteer firemen of the 1850s and 1860s, is located at the top of Telegraph Hill and offers a panoramic view of San Francisco Bay.

One of the most popular destinations for visitors is the famous Fisherman's Wharf, center of a multimillion-dollar commercial fishing industry and location of many seafood restaurants. Other sightseeing areas include the Cannery, a complex of shops, restaurants and markets housed in an old fruit-processing factory; Ghirardelli Square, a shopping-restaurant complex on the site of the Ghirardelli Chocolate Factory; Chinatown, which is believed to be the largest Oriental community outside of Asia; and PIER 39 on the northern waterfront, which has boutiques, entertainment and a marina. Be sure to walk amid the 6,000 different shrubs and plants in the 1,017-acre Golden Gate Park.

More than 475 wineries are located in the Bay Area, many of which conduct tours and are within easy driving distance of San Francisco. The Wine Institute is located in the city.

San Francisco also has a scenic 49-mile drive marked with blue and white seagull signs. The drive begins at City Hall in the Civic Center, then twists around the entire city and leads to the most scenic and historic points. A map of the drive may be obtained from the San Francisco Visitor Information Center.

General References

Area code: 415

Phone Numbers

POLICE & FIRE: 911

POISON CONTROL CENTER: 800/523-2222

WEATHER: 936-1212

Information Sources

San Francisco Convention & Visitors Bureau, PO Box 429097, 94102-9097; 391-2000.

San Francisco Chamber of Commerce, 465 California St, 94104; 392-4511.

Daily Events (recorded), 391-2001.

Visitor Information Center, Hallidie Plaza, Powell and Market Sts, lower plaza level.

Parks Department, 666-7107.

Tix Bay Area Box Office, Union Square, 433-7827.

Transportation

AIRLINES: Aeroflot; Air Canada; Air France; Alaska; American; America West; Asiana; British Airways; CAAC (China); Canadian; China (Taiwan); Continental; Delta; Finnair; Hawaiian; Japan; KLM; Lufthansa; Midwest Express; Mexicana; Northwest; Philippine; Qantas; Singapore; Southwest; TACA; TWA; United; USAir; VASP; and other commuter and regional airlines.

AIRPORT: San Francisco International, 761-0800.

CAR RENTAL AGENCIES: (See IMPORTANT TOLL-FREE NUMBERS) Avis 855-5011; Budget 896-6124; Hertz 771-2200; National 474-5300.

PUBLIC TRANSPORTATION: AC Transit, 817-1717; Bay Area Rapid Transit (BART), 992-2278; Golden Gate Transit, 332-6600; Municipal Railway (MUNI), 673-6864; Samtrans, 508-6200.

RAILROAD PASSENGER SERVICE: Amtrak 800/872-7245.

FERRY SERVICE: Golden Gate Transit 332-6600.

Newspapers

San Francisco Chronicle; San Francisco Examiner; San Francisco Business Times; Wall Street Journal (San Francisco edition).

Convention Facilities

Bill Graham Civic Auditorium & Brooks Hall, 99 Grove St, 974-4060.

Cow Palace, 2600 Geneva Ave, W off Bayshore Blvd, 469-6000.

Fort Mason Center, Marina Blvd & Bucanan St, 441-3400.

Moscone Center, 747 Howard St, 974-4000.

Nob Hill Masonic Center, 1111 California St, 776-4702.

Sports & Recreation

Major Sports Facilities

3COM Park, Gilman Ave, E of Bayshore Frwy (Giants, baseball, 468-3700; 49ers, football, 562-4949).

Oakland Coliseum, 7000 Coliseum Way, 510/467-8000 (Golden State Warriors, basketball, 510/986-2200; Raiders, football, 510/864-5000; Athletics, baseball, 510/638-4900).

San Jose Arena, 525 W Santa Clara St, 408/999-5721 (Sharks, hockey, 408/287-7070).

Racetracks

Bay Meadows Racecourse, Bayshore Frwy (US 101) & Hillsdale Blvd, SE of CA 92, San Mateo, 574-7223.

Golden Gate Fields, 1100 Eastshore Hwy, Albany, 510/526-3020.

Cultural Facilities

Theaters

American Conservatory Theatre, Geary Theatre, 415 Geary St, at Mason St, 834-3200.

Center for the Arts at Yerba Buena Gardens, 701 Mission St, 978-2787.

Curran, 445 Geary St, at Mason St, 551-2000.

Golden Gate Theatre, Golden Gate, Taylor & Market Sts, 551-2000.

Marines' Memorial, 749-2228.

Orpheum Theatre, 1192 Market St at 8th St, 551-2000.

Theatre On The Square, 450 Post St, 2nd floor, 433-9500.

Concert Halls

The Fillmore, Fillmore & Geary St, 281-9239.

Herbst Theatre, 401 Van Ness Ave, 621-6600 or 392-4400.

Louise M. Davies Symphony Hall, Van Ness Ave & Grove St, Civic Center, 431-5400 (symphony, concerts).

Palace of Fine Arts, 3301 Lyon St, 563-6504.

War Memorial Opera House, Van Ness Ave & Grove St, Civic Center, 864-3330 (opera), 621-3838 (ballet).

Museums

California Academy of Sciences, Natural History Museum & Aquarium, Golden Gate Park, 750-7145.

Chinese Culture Center, 750 Kearny St, 3rd floor, 986-1822.

Exploratorium, Palace of Fine Arts, 3601 Lyon St, 561-0360.

The Mexican Museum, Fort Mason Center, Bldg D, Laguna St & Marina Blvd, 441-0445.

National Maritime Museum, foot of Polk St, 556-3002.

Presidio Army Museum, Lincoln Blvd & Funston, the Presidio, 561-3660.

Randall Museum, 199 Museum Way, 554-9600.

Ripley's Believe It or Not Museum, 175 Jefferson St, at Fisherman's Wharf, 771-6188.

San Francisco African-American Historical and Cultural Society, Bldg C, Fort Mason Center, Laguna St & Marina Blvd, 441-0640.

Treasure Island Museum, Bldg #1 on Treasure Island, 395-5067.

Wells Fargo Bank History Museum, 420 Montgomery St, 396-2619.

Art Museums

Asian Art Museum, M.H. deYoung Memorial Museum, Golden Gate Park, 668-8921.

M.H. deYoung Memorial Museum, Golden Gate Park, 863-3330.

San Francisco Museum of Modern Art, 151 3rd St, 357-4000.

Points of Interest

Historical

The *Balclutha*, Hyde St Pier, Aquatic Park, 556-3002.

Fort Point National Historic Site, Long Ave & Marine Dr, the Presidio, 556-1693.

Haas-Lilienthal House, 2007 Franklin St, 441-3004.

Hyde St Pier Historic Ships, Aquatic Park, 556-3002.

Mission Dolores, 16th & Dolores Sts, 621-8203.

The Presidio, Richardson Ave & Lombard St, NW corner of city, 561-3660 or 561-3843.

USS *Jeremiah O'Brien*, Pier 32, 441-3101.

USS *Pampanito*, Pier 45, Fisherman's Wharf, 441-5819.

Other Attractions

Acres of Orchids (Rod McLellan Co), 1450 El Camino Real (CA 82), South San Francisco, 871-5655.

Alcatraz Island, San Francisco Bay, 1 1/4 mi from shore; tours from Pier 41, Fisherman's Wharf, 546-2805 or 392-7469 (Ticketron).

Aquatic Park, foot of Polk St at Beach St.

"A World of Oil" (Chevron USA), 555 Market St, 894-4086.

The Cannery, 2801 Leavenworth St, at Beach St.

Chinatown, Grant Ave, gateway at Bush St.

Civic Center, bounded by Franklin, Hyde, Golden Gate & Hayes Sts.

Coit Tower (Telegraph Hill), Lombard St & Telegraph Blvd.

The Embarcadero, China Basin to Fisherman's Wharf.

Embarcadero Center, between Montgomery St & the Ferry Bldg.

Fisherman's Wharf, foot of Taylor St.

Fort Mason Center, Buchanan St & Marina Blvd, 441-5706.

Ghirardelli Square, North Point, Beach & Larkin Sts, 775-5500.

Golden Gate Bridge, N on CA 1/101.

Golden Gate National Recreation Area, headquarters at Fort Mason, Bldg 201, 556-0560.

Golden Gate Park, bounded by Lincoln Way, Stanyan & Fulton Sts & Great Hwy.

Jackson Square, Washington, Jackson & Pacific Sts from Montgomery St to Battery St.

Japan Center, Post & Geary Sts, between Fillmore & Laguna Sts, 922-6776.

Japanese Tea Garden, Golden Gate Park.

Marine World Africa USA, Marine World Pkwy, jct I-80 & CA 37, Vallejo, 707/643-ORCA.

Muir Woods National Monument, 17 mi N, off CA 1 in Marin County, 388-2595.

Performing Arts Center, Van Ness Ave & Grove St, Civic Center.

PIER 39, 2 blks E of Fisherman's Wharf, 981-7437.

San Francisco Maritime National Historical Park, in Golden Gate National Recreation Area.

San Francisco-Oakland Bay Bridge, E on CA 80.

San Francisco Public Library, Larkin & Grove Sts, 557-4400.

San Francisco Zoo, Sloat Blvd at 45th Ave, 753-7083 or 753-7080.

Sigmund Stern Memorial Grove, Sloat Blvd & 19th Ave.

Twin Peaks, near center of city.

Sightseeing Tours

Blue & Gold Fleet, PIER 39, adj to Fisherman's Wharf, 705-5444.

Gray Line bus tours, 350 8th St, 558-9400.

Hornblower Dining Yachts, Pier 33, along Embarcadero, 394-8900, ext 7 or 788-8866, ext 7.

Annual Events

Chinese New Year Festival, Chinatown. Late Jan-mid-Feb.

Cherry Blossom Festival, Japan Center. 2 wkends Apr.

Carnaval, Mission District. Memorial Day wkend.

Grand National Rodeo, Horse & Stock Show, Cow Palace. Late Oct-early Nov.

City Neighborhoods

Many of the restaurants, unrated dining establishments and some lodgings listed under San Francisco include neighborhoods as well as exact street addresses. Geographic descriptions of these areas are given, followed by a table of restaurants arranged by neighborhood.

Chinatown: South of Broadway, west of Kearny St, north of California St and east of Stockton St; along Grant Ave.

Civic Center: South of Golden Gate Ave, west of 7th St, north of Hayes St and east of Franklin St.

Cow Hollow: Area along Union St between Van Ness Ave on the east and Lyon St on the west.

Downtown: Area on and around Union Square; south of Post St, west of Stockton St, north of Geary St and east of Powell St.

Financial District: South of Jackson St, west of San Francisco Bay, north of Market St and east of Chinatown (Kearny St).

Fisherman's Wharf: On San Francisco Bay, west of Powell St, north of Bay St and east of Hyde St; at foot of Taylor St.

Haight-Ashbury: Between University of San Francisco and University of California San Francisco; south of Oak St (Panhandle of Golden Gate Park), west of Buena Vista Park, north of Waller St and east of Golden Gate Park.

Japantown: South of Pine St, west of Laguna St, north of Geary Blvd and east of Fillmore St.

Marina District: South of Marina Blvd, west of Webster St, north of Lombard St and east of the Palace of Fine Arts and Lyon St.

Mission District: Area around Mission Dolores; south of Market St and I-101, west of Potrero Ave, north of Army St and east of Castro St.

Nob Hill: Area on and around crest at Sacramento and Jones Sts.

North Beach: South of Fisherman's Wharf, west of Telegraph Hill, north of Chinatown and east of Russian Hill.

Pacific Heights: South of Lombard St, east of Van Ness Ave, north of Pine St and west of Lyon St.

Russian Hill: South of Jefferson St, west of Mason St, north of Pacific Ave and west of Van Ness Ave.

Union Square: South of Post St, west of Stockton St, north of Geary St and east of Powell St. **North of Union Square:** North of Post St. **South of Union Square:** South of Geary St. **West of Union Square:** West of Powell St.

Lodgings and Food

SAN FRANCISCO RESTAURANTS BY NEIGHBORHOOD AREAS

(For full description, see alphabetical listings under Restaurants)

CHINATOWN
Empress Of China. 838 Grant Ave
The Pot Sticker. 150 Waverly Place
Yamato. 717 California St

CIVIC CENTER
Eleven. 374 11th St
Hayes Street Grill. 320 Hayes St
Millennium (Abigail Hotel). 246 McAllister
Stars. 555 Golden Gate
Stars Cafe. 500 Van Ness Ave
Zuni Cafe. 1658 Market St

COW HOLLOW
Baker Street Bistro. 2953 Baker St
Betelnut Pejiu Wu. 2030 Union St
Bontà. 2223 Union St
Panne E Vino. 3011 Steiner St
Prego Ristorante. 2000 Union St
Yoshida-Ya. 2909 Webster St

FINANCIAL DISTRICT
Aqua. 252 California St
Bix. 56 Gold St
Cafe Bastille. 22 Belden Place
Cafe Tiramisu. 28 Belden Place
Carnelian Room. 555 California St
Ciao. 230 Jackson St
Cypress Club. 500 Jackson St
Faz. 161 Sutter St
Fog City Diner. 1300 Battery St
Gabbianos. 1 Ferry Plaza
Harbor Village. 4 Embarcadero Center
Harry Denton's. 161 Steuart St
Hunan. 924 Sansome St
Just Desserts. 3 Embarcadero Center
Mac Arthur Park. 607 Front St
Palio D'asti. 640 Sacramento St
Park Grill (Park Hyatt Hotel). 333 Battery St
Pastis. 1015 Battery St
Perry's Downtown. 185 Sutter St
Plouf. 40 Belden Pl
Roti. 155 Stewart St
Rubicon. 558 Sacramento
Sam's Grill. 374 Bush St
Schroeder's. 240 Front St
Silks (Mandarin Oriental Hotel). 222 Sansome
Splendido. Embarcadero Center Four
Tadich Grill. 240 California St
Tommy Toy's. 655 Montgomery St
Vertigo. 600 Montgomery St
Waterfront. Pier 7
Yank Sing. 427 Battery St

FISHERMAN'S WHARF
A. Sabella's. 2766 Taylor St
Bobby Rubino's. 245 Jefferson St
Cafe Pescatore. 2455 Mason St
Chic's Seafood. Pier 39
Franciscan. Pier 43 1/2
Gaylord India. 900 North Point St
Ghirardelli Chocolate Manufactory. 900 North Point St
Lolli's Castagnola. 286 Jefferson St
Mandarin. 900 North Point St
McCormick & Kuleto's. 900 North Point St
Scoma's. Pier 47
Swiss Louis. Pier 39

HAIGHT-ASHBURY
Cha Cha Cha. 1801 Haight St
EOS. 901 Cole St

JAPANTOWN
Isobune. 1737 Post St
Mifune. 1737 Post St
Yoyo (Radisson Miyako Hotel). 1625 Post St

MARINA DISTRICT
Ace Wasabi's Rock & Roll Sushi. 3339 Steiner St
Alegria's Foods From Spain. 2018 Lombard St
Balboa Cafe. 3199 Fillmore St
Cafe Marimba. 2317 Chestnut St
Greens. Building A at Fort Mason
Lhasa Moon. 2420 Lombard St
North India. 3131 Webster St
Plumpjack Cafe. 3127 Fillmore St
Rosti. 2060 Chestnut St
Saji Japanese Cuisine. 3232 Scott St
Scott's Seafood Grill And Bar. 2400 Lombard St

MISSION DISTRICT
The Courtyard Cafe. 1361 Church St
Dame. 1815 Market St
Firefly. 4288 24th St
Mecca. 2029 Market St
Slanted Door. 584 Valencia
Universal Cafe. 2814 19th St

NOB HILL
The Big 4 (Huntington Hotel). 1075 California St
Charles Nob Hill. 1250 Jones St
The Dining Room (The Ritz-Carlton, San Francisco Hotel). 600 Stockton St
Fournou's Ovens (Renaissance Stanford Court Hotel). Nob Hill
Nob Hill (Mark Hopkins Inter-Continental Hotel). 1 Nob Hill
Rue Lepic. 900 Pine St

NORTH BEACH
Albona. 545 Francisco St
Basta Pasta. 1268 Grant St
Enrico's Sidewalk Cafe. 504 Broadway
Figaro. 414 Columbus Ave
Fior D'italia. 601 Union St
Helmand. 430 Broadway
The House. 1230 Grant Ave
Julius Castle. 1541 Montgomery St
La Bodega. 1337 Grant Ave
Mo's Gourmet Hamburgers. 1322 Grant Ave
Moose's. 1652 Stockton St
North Beach. 1512 Stockton St
O'Reilly's. 622 Green St
Ristorante Ideale. 1309 Grant Ave
Rose Pistola. 532 Columbus Ave
Zax. 2330 Taylor St

PACIFIC HEIGHTS
Cafe Kati. 1963 Sutter St
Harris'. 2100 Van Ness Ave
The Meeting House. 1701 Octavia St
Oritalia. 1915 Fillmore
Trio Cafe. 1870 Fillmore St
Tuba Garden. 3634 Sacramento Ave

RICHMOND DISTRICT
Alain Rondelli. 126 Clement
Blue Point. 2415 Clement St

Cafe Riggio. 4112 Geary Blvd
Flower Lounge. 5322 Geary Blvd
Fountain Court. 354 Clement St
Jasmine House. 2301 Clement St
Kabuto Sushi. 5116 Geary Blvd
Katia's. 600 5th Ave
Khan Toke Thai House. 5937 Geary Blvd
La Vie. 5830 Geary Blvd
Laghi. 1801 Clement St

RUSSIAN HILL
Acquerello. 1722 Sacramento St
Antica Trattoria. 2400 Polk St
Chez Michel. 804 North Point St
Coconut Grove. 1415 Van Ness Ave
Frascati. 1901 Hyde St
Golden Turtle. 2211 Van Ness Ave
House Of Prime Rib. 1906 Van Ness Ave
I Fratelli. 1896 Hyde St
Julie Ring's Heart & Soul. 1695 Polk St
Matterhorn Swiss. 2323 Van Ness
Rocco's Seafood Grill. 2080 Van Ness Ave
Ruth's Chris Steak House. 1601 Van Ness Ave
Yabbies. 2237 Polk St
Zarzuela. 2000 Hyde St

UNION SQUARE
Cafe Akimbo. 116 Maiden Lane
Campton Place (Campton Place Hotel). 340 Stockton St
Morton's of Chicago. 400 Post St
Rumpus. 1 Tillman Place
Sears Fine Foods. 439 Powell St

NORTH OF UNION SQUARE
Anjou. 44 Campton Pl
Café Latté. 100 Bush St
Fleur De Lys. 777 Sutter St
Masa's (Vintage Court Hotel). 648 Bush St
Scala's Bistro (Sir Francis Drake Hotel). 432 Powell St

SOUTH OF UNION SQUARE
42 Degrees. 235 16th St
Annabelle's. 54 Fourth St
Bizou. 598 Fourth St
Boulevard. 1 Mission St
El Toreador. 50 W Portal
Eliza's. 1457 18th St
Fino. 1 Cosmo Place
The Fly Trap. 606 Folsom St
Fringale. 570 Fourth St
Garden Court (Palace Hotel). 2 New Montgomery
Hawthorne Lane. 22 Hawthorne St
Infusion. 555 Second St
Kuleto's. 221 Powell St
Lulu. 816 Folsom St
M. Point (Hotel Milano). 55 5th St
Marrakech Moroccan. 419 O'Farrell St
Moxie. 2742 17th St
Puccini & Pinetti. 129 Ellis St

WEST OF UNION SQUARE
Biscuits & Blues. 401 Mason St
Cafe Titanic. 817 Sutter St
David's. 474 Geary St
Dottie's True Blue Cafe. 522 Jones St
French Room (The Clift Hotel). 495 Geary St
Grand Cafe (Monaco Hotel). 501 Geary St
Lehr Brothers Bistro And Grill (Best Western Canterbury Motor Hotel). 750 Sutter
New Joe's. 347 Geary St
Pacific (Pan Pacific Hotel). 500 Post St
Postrio (The Prescott Hotel Inn). 545 Post St
Salmagundi. 442 Geary St
Zingari (The Donatello Hotel). 501 Post St

Note: When a listing is located in a town that does not have its own city heading, it will appear under the city nearest to its location. In these cases, the address and town appear in parenthesis immediately following the name of the establishment.

Motels

★ **BEST WESTERN CIVIC CENTER.** *364 Ninth St (94103), in Civic Center area. 415/621-2826; FAX 415/621-0833.* 57 rms, 2 story. No A/C. May-Oct: S, D $89-$99; each addl $10; under 18 free; lower rates rest of yr. Crib free. TV; cable. Heated pool. Complimentary coffee in rms. Restaurant 7 am-2 pm. Ck-out noon. Coin Indry. Business servs avail. In-rm modem link. Refrigerators; microwaves avail. Cr cds: A, C, D, DS, ER, JCB, MC, V.

SC

★ ★ **BUENA VISTA MOTOR INN.** *1599 Lombard St (94123), at Gough, in Cow Hollow. 415/923-9600; FAX 415/441-4775; res: 800/835-4980.* 50 rms, 3 story. Mid-Apr-mid-Oct: S, D $97; under 12 free; suite $165; lower rates rest of yr. Crib free. TV. Complimentary coffee in rms. Ck-out noon. Business servs avail. Cr cds: A, C, D, DS, MC, V.

D SC

★ **CHELSEA MOTOR INN.** *2095 Lombard St (94123), at Fillmore St, in Marina District. 415/563-5600; FAX 415/567-6475.* 60 rms, 3 story, no ground floor rms. S $78-$88; D $88-$108; each addl $10; under 5 free. Crib free. TV; cable. Complimentary coffee in rms. Restaurant nearby. Ck-out noon. Free covered parking. Health club privileges. Cr cds: A, C, D, MC, V.

D

★ **COLUMBUS MOTOR INN.** *1075 Columbus Ave (94133), in North Beach. 415/885-1492; FAX 415/928-2174.* 45 rms, 5 story. S, D $102-$122; each addl $10. Crib free. TV; cable. Complimentary coffee in rms. Restaurant nearby. Ck-out noon. Business servs avail. Free covered parking. Fisherman's Wharf 4 blks. Cr cds: A, C, D, MC, V.

★ **COVENTRY MOTOR INN.** *1901 Lombard St (94123), in Marina District. 415/567-1200; FAX 415/921-8745.* 69 rms, 3 story. S $84-$96; D $88-$116; each addl $7; under 6 free. Crib free. TV; cable. Complimentary coffee in rms. Restaurant nearby. Ck-out noon. Business servs avail. Free covered parking. Cr cds: A, C, D, MC, V.

D

★ **COW HOLLOW MOTOR INN.** *2190 Lombard St (94123), in Marina District. 415/921-5800; FAX 415/922-8515.* 117 rms, 2-4 story, 12 suites. S $84; D $88-116; each addl $10; suites $185-$265; under 5 free. Crib free. TV; cable. Coffee in rms. Restaurant adj 7 am-2:30 pm. Ck-out noon. Business servs avail. Free covered parking. Health club privileges. Cr cds: A, C, D, MC, V.

D

★ **DAYS INN.** *2600 Sloat Blvd (94116), south of Union Square, opp zoo. 415/665-9000; FAX 415/665-5440.* 33 rms, 2 story. July-mid-Sept: S $70-$90; D $85-$95; suites $95-$130; under 12 free; lower rates rest of yr. Crib free. TV; cable. Complimentary continental bkfst. Restaurant nearby. Ck-out 11 am. Business servs avail. Health club privileges. Refrigerators, microwaves. Cr cds: A, C, D, DS, JCB, MC, V.

D SC

✔ ★ **FRANCISCO BAY.** *1501 Lombard St (94123), in Marina District. 415/474-3030; res: 800/410-7007; FAX 415/567-7082.* 39 rms, 4 story. June-mid-Sept: S $65-$70; D $65-$90; each addl $10; lower rates rest of yr. TV; cable, VCR avail. Complimentary continental bkfst. Complimentary coffee in rms. Restaurant nearby. Ck-out 11 am. Some refrigerators, microwaves. Cr cds: A, C, D, DS, ER, JCB, MC, V.

★ **LOMBARD MOTOR INN.** *1475 Lombard St (94123), at Franklin, in Cow Hollow. 415/441-6000; FAX 415/441-4291; res: 800/835-3639.* Web www.citysearch7.com. 48 rms, 3 story. May-Sept: S $84-$88; D $88-$108; each addl $5; under 5 free; lower rates rest of yr. Crib free. TV. Complimentary coffee in rms. Ck-out noon. Business servs avail. Cr cds: A, C, D, MC, V.

✔★ **NOB HILL.** *1630 Pacific Ave (94109), in Pacific Heights. 415/775-8160; res: 800/343-6900; FAX 415/673-8842.* 29 rms, 12 with shower only, 2 story. Mid-May-Oct: S $75-$85; D $85-$105; each addl $10; suites $160-$185; hols (2-3-day min); higher rates: hols, special events; lower rates rest of yr. TV; cable, VCR avail. Complimentary continental bkfst. Restaurant adj 5-10:30 pm. Ck-out 11 am. Concierge. Free garage parking. Refrigerators; some microwaves. Cr cds: A, C, D, DS, MC, V.

SC

★★ **PACIFIC HEIGHTS INN.** *1555 Union St (94123), in Marina District. 415/776-3310; FAX 415/776-8176; res: 800/523-1801.* 40 rms, 2 story, 17 kits. No A/C. S, D $65-$95; suites $95-$150; family rates. Crib free. TV; cable. Complimentary continental bkfst. Complimentary coffee in rms. Restaurant opp open 24 hrs. Ck-out noon. Business servs avail. In-rm modem link. Bellhops. Refrigerators; some in-rm steam and whirlpool baths. Microwaves avail. Cr cds: A, C, D, DS, MC, V.

SC

★★ **PHOENIX.** *601 Eddy St (94109), at Larkin St, in Civic Center area. 415/776-1380; FAX 415/885-3109; res: 800/248-9466.* Web www.sftups.com. 44 rms, 2 story. No A/C. May-Oct: S, D $109; suites $139-$149; under 12 free. Crib free. TV; cable, VCR avail (free movies). Heated pool; poolside serv. Complimentary continental bkfst. Restaurant 5 pm-midnight. Bar to 2 am. Ck-out noon. Meeting rms. Business servs avail. Concierge. Sundries. Free parking. Health club privileges. Some refrigerators. Private patios, balconies. Cr cds: A, C, D, DS, MC, V.

★★ **RAMADA LIMITED.** *247 7th St (94103), south of Union Square. 415/861-6469; FAX 415/626-4041.* 68 rms, 18 with shower only, two 3 story bldgs. Late May-Oct: S $72-$99; D $79-$109; each addl $10; suites $189-$289; under 12 free; wkend rates; higher rates special events; lower rates rest of yr. Crib free. TV; cable (premium). Complimentary continental bkfst. Restaurant nearby. Ck-out noon. Coin Indry. Meeting rms. Business servs avail. In-rm modem link. Valet serv. Health club privileges. Microwaves avail. Cr cds: A, C, D, DS, JCB, MC, V.

SC

✔★ **ROYAL PACIFIC.** *661 Broadway (94133), in Chinatown. 415/781-6661; FAX 415/781-6688; res: 800/545-5574.* 74 rms, 12 A/C, 5 story. Apr-Nov: S, D $75-$93; each addl $5; suites $85-$105; lower rates rest of yr. Crib $10. TV. Complimentary coffee in rms. Restaurant nearby. Ck-out noon. Coin Indry. Business servs avail. Sauna. Refrigerators avail. Some balconies. Cr cds: A, C, D, MC, V.

✔★ **THRIFTLODGE.** *2011 Bayshore Blvd (94134), south of Union Square. 415/467-8811; res: 800/525-9055 (exc CA), 800/468-1021 (CA); FAX 415/468-3097.* 103 rms, 27 with shower only, 2 story. No A/C. S $59; D $70-$98; each addl $8; under 5 free. TV; cable. Complimentary coffee in lobby. Restaurant open 24 hrs. Ck-out 11:30 am. Meeting rms. Business servs avail. Coin Indry. Indoor/outdoor pool; sauna. Some balconies. Cr cds: A, D, JCB, MC, V.

SC

★ **VAGABOND INN-MIDTOWN.** *2550 Van Ness Ave (94109), in Russian Hill. 415/776-7500; FAX 415/776-5689.* 132 rms, 5 story. No A/C. S, D $99-$149; each addl $5; suites, kit. units $109-$175; under 19 free; higher rates special events. Crib free. TV; cable (premium). Heated pool. Complimentary continental bkfst. Complimentary coffee in rms. Ck-out noon. Meeting rm. Business servs avail. In-rm modem link. Valet serv. Some refrigerators. Some balconies. Cr cds: A, C, D, DS, MC, V.

D SC

★★ **WHARF.** *2601 Mason St (94133), at Fisherman's Wharf. 415/673-7411; FAX 415/776-2181; res: 800/548-9918.* 51 rms, 3-4 story. No A/C. June-Oct: S, D $108-$143; kit. suite $250-$350; lower rates rest of yr. Crib free. TV; cable (premium). Complimentary coffee in lobby. Restaurant nearby. Ck-out 11 am. Concierge. Some balconies. Cr cds: A, C, D, DS, MC, V.

SC

Motor Hotels

★★ **BEST WESTERN AMERICANIA.** *121 Seventh St (94103), in Civic Center area. 415/626-0200; FAX 415/626-3974.* 143 rms, 4 story, 24 suites. No A/C. June-Sept: S $99-$119; D $109-$129; each addl $10; suites $129-$229; under 12 free; lower rates rest of yr. Crib free. TV; cable (premium). Heated pool. Coffee in rms. Restaurant 6:30 am-10 pm. Rm serv. Bar 11 am-midnight. Ck-out noon. Coin Indry. Meeting rms. Business servs avail. In-rm modem link. Valet serv. Exercise equipt; weight machine, stair machine, sauna. Some refrigerators; microwaves avail. Cr cds: A, C, D, DS, ER, JCB, MC, V.

SC

★★ **BEST WESTERN CANTERBURY.** *750 Sutter St (94109), near Taylor St, west of Union Square. 415/474-6464; FAX 415/474-5856.* 250 rms in 2 bldgs, 4 & 10 story. S, D $99-$155; each addl $15; suites $150-$195; under 18 free; wkend, honeymoon plans. Garage parking $15. TV; cable (premium). Pool privileges. Complimentary coffee in rms. Restaurant (see LEHR BROTHERS BISTRO AND GRILL). Rm serv. Bar. Ck-out noon. Meeting rms. Business servs avail. In-rm modem link. Gift shop. Health club privileges. Many refrigerators. Cr cds: A, C, D, DS, JCB, MC, V.

D SC

★★ **BEST WESTERN MIYAKO INN.** *1800 Sutter St (94115), in Japantown. 415/921-4000; FAX 415/923-1064.* E-mail miyakoin@ix.net com.com. 125 rms, 8 story. S $87-$103; D $97-$105; each addl $10; suites $175-$275; under 18 free. Crib free. Garage parking $7.50. TV. Restaurant 7 am-10 pm. Bar to midnight. Ck-out noon. Business servs avail. Bellhops. Valet serv. Gift shop. Health club privileges. Balconies. Cr cds: A, C, D, DS, JCB, MC, V.

SC

★★ **HOLIDAY INN-FISHERMAN'S WHARF.** *1300 Columbus Ave (94133), at Fisherman's Wharf. 415/771-9000; FAX 415/771-7006.* Web www.holiday_inn.com. 584 rms, 2-5 story. June-Nov: S, D $169-$199; each addl $15; suites $300-$400; under 19 free; lower rates rest of yr. Crib free. Parking $12. TV; cable (premium), VCR avail. Heated pool; poolside serv. Restaurants 24 hrs. Bar 4-11:30 pm. Rm serv. Ck-out noon. Coin Indry. Meeting rms. Business center. In-rm modem link. Bellhops. Valet serv. Sundries. Some refrigerators. Cr cds: A, C, D, DS, JCB, MC, V.

D SC

★★ **HOWARD JOHNSON.** *580 Beach St (94133), at Fisherman's Wharf. 415/775-3800; FAX 415/441-7307.* 128 rms, 4 story. S $89-$134; D $99-$144; suites $140-$185; under 18 free. Crib free. Covered parking $5/day. TV; cable (premium), VCR avail. Restaurant 7-11 am. Ck-out noon. Coin Indry. Business servs avail. Bellhops. Valet serv. Health club privileges. Minibars. Cr cds: A, C, D, DS, ER, JCB, MC, V.

D SC

★★ **RAMADA PLAZA AT FISHERMAN'S WHARF.** *590 Bay St (94133), at Fisherman's Wharf. 415/885-4700; FAX 415/771-8945.* 232 rms, 4 story. May-Oct: S $170-$205; D $190-$225; each addl $15; suites $250-$500; under 18 free; lower rates rest of yr. Crib free. Garage in/out $8. TV; cable, VCR avail. Restaurant 6:30 am noon, 5-10 pm. Rm serv. Bar 5 pm-midnight. Ck-out noon. Meeting rms. Business servs avail. In-rm modem link. Valet serv. Sundries. Gift shop. Refrigerator in suites. Cr cds: A, C, D, DS, ER, JCB, MC, V.

D SC

★ ★ ★ **SHERATON AT FISHERMAN'S WHARF.** *2500 Mason St (94133), at Fisherman's Wharf. 415/362-5500; FAX 415/956-5275.* Web www.ittsheraton.com. 524 rms, 4 story. S, D $145-$250; each addl $20; suites from $400-$600; under 17 free; package plans. Crib free. Garage $15. TV; cable (premium), VCR avail. Heated pool. Restaurant 6:30 am-10 pm; Fri, Sat to 11 pm. Rm serv 6:30-1 am. Bar; entertainment Thurs-Sat. Ck-out noon. Convention facilities. Business center. In-rm modem link. Valet serv. Concierge. Gift shop. Barber, beauty shop. Health club privileges. Luxury level. Cr cds: A, C, D, DS, ER, JCB, MC, V.

D SC

★ ★ **SUITES AT FISHERMAN'S WHARF.** *2655 Hyde St (94109), at Fisherman's Wharf. 415/771-0200; FAX 415/346-8058; res: 800/227-3608.* 24 kit. suites, 3 story. No A/C. S $195-$235, D $275; each addl $10; under 12 free. Garage in/out $15. TV; cable, VCR avail. Complimentary continental bkfst. Ck-out noon. Coin lndry. Business servs avail. Concierge. Refrigerators, microwaves avail. Private rooftop patio; some balconies. Ghirardelli Square 1 blk. Totally nonsmoking. Cr cds: A, C, D, DS, JCB, MC, V.

D SC

★ ★ **TRAVELODGE.** *250 Beach St (94133), at Fisherman's Wharf. 415/392-6700.* Web www.travelodge.com. 250 rms, most with shower only, 4 story, 3 suites. May-Oct: S, D $135-$165; each addl $10; suites $225; under 18 free; lower rates rest of yr. Crib free. TV; VCR avail. Heated pool. Complimentary coffee in rms. Restaurant adj. Ck-out noon. Meeting rm. Business servs avail. Health club privileges. Gift shop. Parking in/out $6. Balconies. Opp bay. Cr cds: A, C, D, DS, JCB, MC, V.

D SC

Hotels

✔★ **ABIGAIL.** *246 McAllister St (94102), in Civic Center area. 415/861-9728; FAX 415/861-5848.* E-mail abigailhotel@worldnet.att.net; web www.sftrips.com. 56 rms, 6 with shower only, 6 story. S, D $89-$94; suites $149. Crib free. Parking $10. TV. Complimentary continental bkfst. Restaurant. Ck-out noon. Concierge. Health club privileges. Some refrigerators. Cr cds: A, D, MC, V.

SC

★ ★ ★ **ANA.** *50 Third St (94103), south of Union Square. 415/974-6400; FAX 415/543-8268; res: 800/ANA-HOTE.* Web www.ananet.or.ip/anahotels/e/. 667 rms, 36 story. S, D $230-$285; each addl $25; suites $380-$1,500; under 12 free. Crib free. Valet, garage parking $27. TV; VCR avail. Coffee in rms. Restaurant 6:30 am-10 pm; Fri, Sat to 10:30 pm. Bar 11-1:30 am. Ck-out noon. Convention facilities. Business center. In-rm modem link. Concierge. Gift shop. Tennis privileges. Exercise equipt; weight machine, bicycles, sauna. Health club privileges. Massage. Bathrm phones, minibars; microwaves avail. Cr cds: A, C, D, DS, ER, JCB, MC, V.

D SC

✔★ ★ **ATHERTON.** *685 Ellis St (94109), at Larkin St, west of Union Square. 415/474-5720; FAX 415/474-8256; res: 800/474-5720.* 74 rms, 6 story. No A/C. S, D $69-$119; each addl $10; under 12 free. Crib free. TV; VCR avail. Restaurant 7 am-11 pm. Bar 5 pm-2 am. Ck-out noon. Meeting rm. Business servs avail. Airport, RR station, bus depot transportation. Cr cds: A, C, D, DS, ER, JCB, MC, V.

★ **BERESFORD.** *635 Sutter St (94102), north of Union Square. 415/673-9900; FAX 415/474-0449; res: 800/533-6533.* E-mail beresfordsfo@delphi.com; web www.beresford.com. 114 rms, 7 story. No A/C. S $99; D $109; each addl $10; family units $119-$129; under 12 free. Crib free. Pet accepted, some restrictions. Garage parking $15 in/out. TV; cable, VCR avail. Complimentary continental bkfst. Restaurant 7 am-2 pm, 5:30-10 pm; Sun, Mon to 2 pm. No rm serv. Bar 7-1 am, Sun to 2 pm. Ck-out noon. Business servs avail. In-rm modem link. Health club privileges. Refrigerators, minibars. Cr cds: A, C, D, DS, JCB, MC, V.

SC

★ ★ **BERESFORD ARMS.** *701 Post St (94109), west of Union Square. 415/673-2600; FAX 415/533-5349; res: 800/533-6533.* E-mail beresfordsfo@delphi.com; web www.beresford.com. 96 rms, 8 story, 40 kit. units. No A/C. S, D $99-$109; each addl $10; suites $125-$160, under 12 free. Crib free. Pet accepted, some restrictions. Valet parking $15 in/out. TV; cable, VCR (movies $5). Complimentary continental bkfst. Ck-out noon. Business servs avail. In-rm modem link. No rm serv. Health club privileges. Refrigerators; some bathrm phones, in-rm whirlpools, minibars; microwaves avail. Cr cds: A, C, D, DS, JCB, MC, V.

D SC

✔★ **BIJOU.** *111 Mason St (94102), south of Union Square. 415/771-1200; res: 800/771-1022; FAX 415/346-3196.* 65 rms, 6 story. No A/C. S $79-$99; D $89-$109; each addl $10; under 18 free; hol rates. Crib free. Garage in/out parking $14. TV. Complimentary coffee in lobby. Restaurant opp open 24 hrs. No rm serv. Ck-out noon. Concierge. Cr cds: A, C, D, DS, JCB, MC, V.

D

✔★ **BRITTON.** *112 7th St (94103), near Civic Center area. 415/621-7001; FAX 415/626-3974; res: 800/444-5819.* 79 rms, 5 story. June-Sept: S $79-$109; D $89-$119; each addl $10; suites $79-$119; lower rates rest of yr. Crib free. TV; cable (premium). Coffee in rms. Restaurant 6 am-10 pm. Ck-out noon. Coin lndry. Business servs avail. In-rm modem link. Union Square/Civic Center transportation. Valet. Microwaves avail. Convention Center 3 blks. Cr cds: A, C, D, DS, ER, JCB, MC, V.

D SC

★ ★ ★ ★ **CAMPTON PLACE.** *340 Stockton St (94108), on Union Square. 415/781-5555; FAX 415/955-5536; res: 800/235-4300.* E-mail reserve@campton.com. Uniformed doormen greet you outside a simple brownstone facade with a white awning, but inside the small luxury hotel is lavish decor punctuated with antiques and artwork. Rooms are done with Asian touches in subtle tones of gold and brown. 117 rms, 7-17 story. S, D $230-$355; suites $450-$1,000; under 18 free. Pet accepted, some restrictions; $25. Valet parking $25. TV; cable, VCR avail (movies). Restaurant (see CAMPTON PLACE). Rm serv 24 hrs. Bar 10 am-11 pm; Fri, Sat to midnight. Ck-out noon. Meeting rms. Business servs avail. In-rm modem link. Concierge. Butler serv. Health club privileges. Massage. Bathrm phones, minibars; microwaves avail. Rooftop garden. Cr cds: A, C, D, JCB, MC, V.

D

★ **CARLTON.** *1075 Sutter St (94109), west of Union Square at Larkin. 415/673-0242; FAX 415/673-4904; res: 800/227-4496.* E-mail carlton@carltonhotel.com; web www.carlton.com. 165 rms, 9 story. No A/C. S, D $145; each addl $20; under 12 free. Crib free. TV; cable. Complimentary afternoon refreshments. Coffee in rms. Restaurant 7-11 am, 5-9 pm. Ck-out 1 pm. Meeting rm. Business servs avail. Airport, RR station, bus depot transportation; free Financial District and civic center transportation. Health club privileges. Minibars. Cr cds: A, C, D, DS, JCB, MC, V.

SC

★ **CARTWRIGHT.** *524 Sutter St (94102), at Powell St, north of Union Square. 415/421-2865; res: 800/227-3844.* 114 rms, 34 A/C, 8 story. S, D $129-$169; suites $189-$229; under 3 free. Crib free. Valet parking in/out $21. TV; cable, VCR avail. Complimentary afternoon refreshments. Ck-out noon. Meeting rm. Business servs avail. In-rm modem link. Health club privileges. Game rm/library. Many refrigerators. Antiques. Originally opened 1915. Cr cds: A, C, D, DS, ER, JCB, MC, V.

★ ★ **CATHEDRAL HILL.** *1101 Van Ness Ave (94109), at Geary Blvd, west of Union Square. 415/776-8200; FAX 415/441-2841.* 400 rms, 8 story. S $105-$149; D $125-$200; each addl $20; suites $200-$400;

under 18 free; wkend package. Crib free. Garage parking $13 in/out. TV; cable, VCR avail. Heated pool. Restaurant 6:30 am-10 pm. Bar 11-1 am. Ck-out noon. Convention facilities. In-rm modem link. Concierge. Shopping arcade. Barber, beauty shop. Health club privileges. Bathrm phones; some refrigerators. Balconies; some private patios. Cr cds: A, C, D, DS, JCB, MC, V.

D SC

★ ★ **CHANCELLOR.** *433 Powell St (94102), north of Union Square. 415/362-2004; FAX 415/362-1403; res: 800/428-4748.* 137 rms, 16 story. No A/C. S $120; D $135; each addl $20; suites $230. Crib free. Garage 1/2 blk $18. TV; cable (premium), VCR avail. Restaurant 7 am-3 pm, 5-9:30 pm. Bar 11-1 am. Ck-out noon. Meeting rm. Business servs avail. In-rm modem link. Health club privileges. Gift shop. Tallest building in the city when constructed (1914) after the San Francisco earthquake in 1906. Cr cds: A, C, D, DS, ER, JCB, MC, V.

SC

★ ★ **CLARION BEDFORD.** *761 Post St (94109), west of Union Square. 415/673-6040; FAX 415/563-6739.* E-mail bedfordhotel@compuserv.com. 144 rms, 17 story. No A/C. S, D $129; each addl $10; 2-bedrm family unit $175; under 18 free. Crib free. Valet parking $18. TV; cable. Coffee in rms. Restaurant 6 am-midnight. Bar. Ck-out noon. Meeting rms. Business servs avail. In-rm modem link. Health club privileges. Refrigerators, mini bars. Cr cds: A, C, D, DS, ER, JCB, MC, V.

SC

★ ★ ★ **THE CLIFT.** *495 Geary St (94102), at Taylor St, west of Union Square. 415/775-4700; FAX 415/441-4621.* 329 rms, 17 story. S $245-$400; D $250-$450; each addl $30; suites $395-$700; under 18 free; wkend rates. Crib free. Pet accepted. Valet parking $25. TV; cable (premium), VCR avail. Restaurant (see FRENCH ROOM). Rm serv 24 hrs. Bar 11-2 am; pianist 5:30 pm-1:30 am. Ck-out 1 pm. Valet serv 24 hrs. Concierge. Business center. In-rm modem link. Exercise equipt; bicycles, treadmill. Bathrm phones, refrigerators, minibars; microwaves avail. Cr cds: A, C, D, DS, JCB, MC, V.

D

✔★ ★ **COMFORT INN-BY THE BAY.** *2775 Van Ness Ave (94109), north of Union Square. 415/928-5000; FAX 415/441-3990.* Web www.hotelchoice.com. 138 rms, 11 story. Mid-June-Oct: S, D $119-$189; each addl $10; under 19 free; lower rates rest of yr. Crib free. Garage parking in/out $12. TV; cable. Complimentary continental bkfst. Ck-out noon. Business servs avail. In-rm modem link. Microwaves avail. Cr cds: A, C, D, DS, ER, JCB, MC, V.

D SC

★ **COMMODORE INTERNATIONAL.** *825 Sutter St (94109), west of Union Square. 415/923-6800; res: 800/338-6848.* E-mail commodorehotel@worldnet.att.net. 113 rms, 6 story. No A/C. July-Oct: S, D $89-$119; each addl $10; under 12 free; hols (2-day min); lower rates rest of yr. Crib free. Garage, in/out parking $14. TV; cable, VCR avail. Restaurant 7 am-2 pm. No rm serv. Bar 5 pm-2 am. Ck-out noon. Meeting rm. Business servs avail. In-rm modem link. Concierge. Health club privileges. Some refrigerators. Cr cds: A, C, D, DS, JCB, MC, V.

SC

★ ★ **DIVA.** *440 Geary St (94102), west of Union Square. 415/885-0200; FAX 415/346-6613; res: 800/553-1900.* 111 rms, 7 story. S, D $135; each addl $10; suites $155-$300; under 12 free. Crib free. Valet parking, in/out $17. TV; cable (premium), VCR (movies). Complimentary continental bkfst. Restaurant 11:30 am-10 pm; Fri, Sat to 11 pm; Sun 1-9 pm. Rm serv 7 am-10 pm. Ck-out noon. Meeting rm. Business center. Concierge. Exercise equipt; weight machines, bicycles. Bathrm phones, refrigerators, minibars. Cr cds: A, C, D, DS, ER, JCB, MC, V.

D SC

★ ★ ★ **THE DONATELLO.** *501 Post St (94102), west of Union Square. 415/441-7100; FAX 415/885-8842; res: 800/227-3184.* E-mail sfdntlo@aol.com. 94 rms, 14 story. S, D $175-$225; each addl $25; suites $325-$525; under 12 free; wkend rates. Crib free. Garage, in/out $22. TV; cable (premium), VCR avail (movies $2). Restaurant 6:30 am-11 pm (also see ZINGARI). Bar 11 am-midnight. Ck-out noon. Meeting rms. Business center. In-rm modem link. Concierge. Exercise equipt; weights, bicycles, whirlpool, sauna. Bathrm phones; some refrigerators. Italian Renaissance decor; antiques; classic elegance. Cr cds: A, C, D, DS, JCB, MC, V.

D

✔★ ★ **ESSEX.** *684 Ellis St (94109), at Larkin St, west of Union Square. 415/474-4664; FAX 415/441-1800; res: 800/453-7739 (exc CA), 800/443-7739 (CA).* 96 rms, 7 story. No A/C. S $69; D $79; each addl $10; suites $99; under 12 free. TV. Complimentary coffee in lobby. Ck-out noon. Some balconies. Civic Center 3 blks. Cr cds: A, MC, V.

★ ★ ★ **FAIRMONT HOTEL & TOWER.** *California & Mason Sts (94106), on Nob Hill. 415/772-5000; FAX 415/781-4027.* Web www.fairmont.com. 600 rms, 8 & 24 story. S, D $199-$349; each addl $30; suites $350-$8,000; under 13 free; wkend rates. Crib free. Garage, in/out $27/day, valet. TV; cable, VCR (movies). Restaurant 6 am-11 pm. Rm serv 24 hrs. Bars; entertainment. Ck-out 1 pm. Convention facilities. Business center. In-rm modem link. Concierge. Shopping arcade. Barber, beauty shop. Free financial district transportation. Exercise rm; instructor, weight machine, weights, whirlpool, sauna. Bathrm phones, minibars; microwaves avail. Some suites with private patio. Outside glass-enclosed elvtr to Fairmont Crown Room. Panoramic view of city; rooftop garden. Cr cds: A, C, D, DS, JCB, MC, V.

D

★ ★ ★ **GALLERIA PARK.** *191 Sutter St (94104), in Financial District. 415/781-3060; FAX 415/433-4409; res: 800/792-9639.* E-mail galleria@sirius.com. 177 rms, 8 story. S, D $210-$250; suites $250-$450; family, wkend rates. Garage in/out $23. TV; cable (premium). Restaurant 7 am-11 pm. Bar. Ck-out noon. Meeting rms. Business center. In-rm modem link. Concierge. Shopping arcade. Exercise equipt; stair machines, treadmill. Refrigerators, mini bars. Atrium lobby with unique sculptured fireplace. Cr cds: A, C, D, DS, ER, JCB, MC, V.

D SC

★ ★ ★ **GRAND HYATT SAN FRANCISCO.** *345 Stockton St (94108), on Union Square. 415/398-1234; FAX 415/392-2536.* Web www.gohyatt.com. 687 rms, 36 story, 33 suites. S, D $195-$260; each addl $25; suites $450-$1,550; under 18 free; package plans. Crib free. Valet parking, garage in/out $24. TV; cable (premium), VCR avail. Restaurant 6:30 am-10 pm. Bar 11-2 am; entertainment. Ck-out noon. Convention facilities. Business center. In-rm modem link. Concierge. Shopping arcade. Barber, beauty shop. Exercise equipt; weight machine, bicycles. Masseuse. Refrigerators, minibars, bathrm phones; some wet bars; microwaves avail. Luxury level. Cr cds: A, C, D, DS, ER, JCB, MC, V.

D SC

✔★ **GRANT PLAZA.** *465 Grant St (94108), in Chinatown. 415/434-3883; FAX 415/434-3886; res: 800/472-6899.* E-mail grantplaza@worldnet.att.net; web www.smarttraveler.com/grantplaza.htm. 72 rms, 6 story. S $49-$55; D $59-$67; each addl $10; under 10 free. Crib $10. Garage $11.50. TV; cable (premium), VCR avail. Restaurant adj open 24 hrs. No rm serv. Ck-out noon. Business servs avail. Microwaves avail. Cr cds: A, C, D, JCB, MC, V.

★ ★ ★ **HANDLERY UNION SQUARE.** *351 Geary St (94102), west of Union Square. 415/781-7800; FAX 415/781-0269; res: 800/843-4343.* E-mail hushres@handlery.com. 377 rms, 8 story. S, D $140-$175; each addl $10; suites $155-$350; under 14 free. Crib free. Garage in/out $19. TV; cable, VCR avail. Heated pool, sauna. Coffee in rms. Restaurant 7 am-11 pm. Rm serv 7-10:30 am, 5-10 pm. Bar 10 am-11:30 pm. Ck-out noon. Meeting rms. Business servs avail. In-rm modem link. Concierge. Gift shop. Barber, beauty shop. Luxury level. Cr cds: A, C, D, DS, ER, JCB, MC, V.

D SC

★ ★ **HARBOR COURT.** *165 Steuart St (94105), in Financial District. 415/882-1300; FAX 415/882-1313; res: 800/346-0555.* 131 rms, 5 story. Apr-mid-Nov: S, D $135-$225. Crib free. Parking in/out $25. TV; cable (premium). Indoor pool; lifeguard. Complimentary coffee. Restaurant 7 am-11 pm. Bar to 2 am; entertainment. Ck-out noon. Meeting rm. Business center. In-rm modem link. Concierge. Free Financial District transportation Mon-Fri. Exercise rm; instructor, weights, bicycles, whirlpool, sauna. Refrigerators, minibars. Victorian decor. On waterfront. Cr cds: A, C, D, DS, ER, JCB, MC, V.

D SC

★ ★ ★ **HILTON & TOWERS.** *333 O'Farrell St, south of Union Square. 415/771-1400; FAX 415/771-6807.* 1,891 rms, 19, 23 & 46 story. S $215-$265; D $225-$275; each addl $20; suites from $300-$2,500; wkend rates. Garage, in/out $27. TV; cable (premium), VCR avail. Pool on 16th floor in garden court. Supervised child's activities. Restaurants 6-1 am. Bars 10:30-1:30 am. Ck-out noon. Convention facilities. Business center. In-rm modem link. Shopping arcade. Barber, beauty shop. Exercise rm; instructor, weights, bicycle, sauna. Health club privileges. Masseuse. Balconies. Some penthouse suites with solarium. 16th floor lanai rms. 46-story tower with distinctive rms and rooftop dining. Luxury level. Cr cds: A, C, D, DS, JCB, MC, V.

D

★ ★ ★ **HOLIDAY INN SELECT-UNION SQUARE.** *480 Sutter St (94108), north of Union Square. 415/398-8900; FAX 415/989-8823.* 400 rms, 30 story. S $179-$239; D $195-$255; each addl $15; suites $200-$750; under 19 free; wkend rates. Crib free. Parking in/out $21. TV; cable (premium), VCR avail. Restaurant 6:30-11:30 am, 5-11 pm. Bar. Ck-out noon. Convention facilities. Business center. Bellhops. Valet serv. Gift shop. Exercise equipt; treadmill, bicycle. Refrigerator in suites. Cr cds: A, C, D, DS, JCB, MC, V.

D SC

★ **HOLIDAY INN-CIVIC CENTER.** *50 8th St (94103), at Market St, in Civic Center area. 415/626-6103; FAX 415/552-0184.* 394 rms, 14 story. S $109-$159; D $119-$169; each addl $15; suites $250-$350; under 19 free; wkend rates. Crib free. TV; cable (premium). Heated pool. Restaurant 6-11 am, 5-10 pm. Bar 5 pm-midnight. Ck-out noon. Coin Indry. Meeting rms. Business servs avail. In-rm modem link. Gift shop. Health club privileges. Balconies. Cr cds: A, C, D, DS, JCB, MC, V.

D SC

★ ★ **HOLIDAY INN-GOLDEN GATEWAY.** *1500 Van Ness Ave (94109), at California St, in Russian Hill. 415/441-4000; FAX 415/776-7155.* Web www.holiday-inn/holiday.html. 499 rms, 26 story. May-Oct: S, D $115-$220; each addl $15; suites $185-$460; under 19 free; lower rates rest of yr. Crib free. Parking in/out $16. TV; cable. Heated pool. Restaurant 6 am-10:30 pm. Bar. Ck-out noon. Convention facilities. Business servs avail. In-rm modem link. Gift shop. Exercise equipt; bicycles, stair machine. Some refrigerators. On cable car line. Cr cds: A, C, D, DS, JCB, MC, V.

D SC

★ ★ **HOTEL GRIFFIN.** *155 Stewart St (94105), south of Union Square. 415/495-2100; FAX 415/495-3522; res: 800/321-2201.* 62 rms, 5 story. S, D $185-$285; suites $285; under 18 free. Crib free. Garage parking $15. TV; cable, VCR avail. Indoor pool; whirlpool, sauna. Complimentary continental bkfst. Restaurant 11:30 am-10 pm; Sat, Sun from 5:30 pm. Ck-out noon. Meeting rms. Business servs avail. Concierge. Exercise rm; instructor, weights, stair machine. Cr cds: A, C, D, DS, ER, JCB, MC, V.

D

★ ★ ★ **HOTEL MILANO.** *55 5th St (94103), south of Union Square. 415/543-8555; FAX 415/543-5843.* 108 rms, 8 story. S $129-$189; D $149-$189; each addl $20; under 12 free; wkend, hol rates. Crib free. Parking $19. TV; cable (premium), VCR avail. Restaurant (see M POINT). Bar 5-11 pm. Ck-out noon. Meeting rms. Business servs avail. Concierge. Exercise equipt; treadmill, stair machine. Minibars. Cr cds: A, C, D, DS, JCB, MC, V.

D SC

★ ★ ★ **HOTEL NIKKO.** *222 Mason St (94102), west of Union Square. 415/394-1111; FAX 415/394-1106.* 523 rms, 25 story, 33 suites. S $215-$285; D $245-$315; each addl $30; suites $425-$1,700; under 18 free; wkend rates. Crib free. Covered parking, in/out $25; valet. TV; cable, VCR avail. Indoor pool; whirlpool, poolside serv. Complimentary bkfst, refreshments. Restaurant 6:30 am-10 pm. Rm serv 24 hrs. Bar 11-2 am. Ck-out noon. Convention facilities. Business center. Concierge. Sundries. Barber, beauty shop. Exercise rm; instructor, weight machines, bicycles, steam rm, sauna. Minibars. 2-story marble staircase in lobby frames cascading waterfall. Luxury level. Cr cds: A, C, D, DS, ER, JCB, MC, V.

D SC

★ ★ ★ **HOTEL REX.** *562 Sutter St (94102), north of Union Square. 415/433-4434; FAX 415/433-3695; res: 800/433-4434.* E-mail hotelrex@pop.sfo.com. 94 rms, some A/C, 7 story. S, D $145-$225; each addl $20; suites $450. Crib free. Valet $24 in/out. TV; cable. Complimentary coffee in lobby. Restaurant 7-10 am; Sat, Sun to 11 am. Bar 5-10 pm. Ck-out noon. Business servs avail. In-rm modem link. Concierge. Health club privileges. Minibars. Microwaves avail. Renovated hotel with 1920's atmosphere. Cr cds: A, C, D, DS, JCB, MC, V.

D SC

★ ★ ★ **HOTEL TRITON.** *342 Grant Ave (94108), east of Union Square. 415/394-0500; FAX 415/394-0555; res: 800/433-6611.* Web www.tritonsf.com. 140 rms, 7 story. S, D $139-$229; suites $245-$295; under 16 free. Crib free. Valet, in/out parking $22. Pet accepted; $15. TV; cable, VCR avail. Complimentary morning, afternoon refreshments. Restaurants 6:30 am-10 pm. Bar from 11 am. Ck-out noon. Meeting rm. Business servs avail. Concierge. Exercise equipt: stair machine, bicycle. Health club privileges. Minibars. Whimsical sophisticated design; showcase for local artists. Cr cds: A, C, D, DS, ER, JCB, MC, V.

D SC

★ ★ **HOTEL UNION SQUARE.** *114 Powell St (94102), west of Union Square. 415/397-3000; FAX 415/399-1874; res: 800/553-1900.* 131 rms, 6 story. S, D $102-$139; each addl $10; suites $129-$280; under 12 free. Garage in/out $17. TV. Complimentary continental bkfst. Restaurant adj 11 am-11 pm. Bar 11 am-9 pm. Ck-out noon. Business servs avail. Airport transportation. Health club privileges. Penthouse suites with refrigerator, deck. Cr cds: A, C, D, DS, ER, JCB, MC, V.

SC

★ ★ ★ ★ **HUNTINGTON.** *1075 California St (94108), top of Nob Hill. 415/474-5400; FAX 415/474-6227; res: 800/227-4683 (exc CA), 800/652-1539 (CA).* Atop Nob Hill, the Huntington Hotel is gracious and formal, yet comfortable and accommodating. Rooms are individually decorated with a meticulous attention to detail, and the service is conscientious and personal. 100 rms, 12 story, 40 suites. S $190-$240; D $210-$260; suites $315-$885; under 6 free. Crib free. Garage, in/out $19.50. TV; cable, VCR avail (free movies). Restaurant (see THE BIG 4). Rm serv 6 am-11:30 pm. Bar 11:30-12:30 am; pianist. Ck-out noon. Meeting rms. Business servs avail. Concierge. Health club privileges. Minibars; many wet bars; microwaves avail. Cr cds: A, C, D, DS, JCB, MC, V.

★ ★ ★ **HYATT AT FISHERMAN'S WHARF.** *555 North Point St (94133), at Fisherman's Wharf. 415/563-1234; FAX 415/749-6122.* 313 rms, 5 story. S $175-$205; D $185-$230; suites $295-$595; under 18 free. Crib free. Garage $17 in/out. TV; cable (premium), VCR avail. Heated pool; whirlpool. Restaurant 6:30 am-11 pm; Fri, Sat to 2 am. Rm serv. Bar noon-11 pm, Fri, Sat to 2 am. Ck-out noon. Coin Indry. Meeting rms. Business center. In-rm modem link. Concierge. Gift shop. Exercise equipt; weights, bicycles, sauna. Some bathrm phones. Cable car line opp. Cr cds: A, C, D, DS, ER, JCB, MC, V.

D

★ ★ ★ **HYATT REGENCY.** *5 Embarcadero Center (94111), Market & Drumm Sts, in Financial District. 415/788-1234; FAX 415/398-2567.* 805 rms, 15 story. S $179-$300; D $204-$325; each addl $25; suites $425-$1,400; under 18 free. Crib free. Covered parking, valet $25. TV; cable (premium), VCR avail. Coffee in rms. Restaurant 6-10 pm; wkends to 10:30 pm. Rm serv 6 am-midnight. Bars; entertainment; revolving rooftop restaurant/bar. Ck-out noon. Convention facilities. Business center. In-rm modem link. Concierge. Shopping arcade. Exercise equipt; bicycles, stair machine. Health club privileges. Refrigerators; microwaves avail. Balconies. Spacious 17-story atrium in lobby. Luxury level. Cr cds: A, C, D, DS, JCB, MC, V.

D

★ ★ ★ **INN AT THE OPERA.** *333 Fulton St (94102), in Civic Center area. 415/863-8400; FAX 415/861-0821; res: 800/325-2708 (exc CA), 800/423-9610 (CA).* 30 rms, 7 story, 18 suites. No A/C. S $125-$175; D $140-$190; suites $215-$265. Crib free. Parking $19. TV; cable (premium), VCR avail. Complimentary bkfst. Restaurant 5:30-10 pm. Bar 5:30-10 pm, Fri, Sat to 1 am; entertainment Tues-Sat. Ck-out noon. Business servs avail. In-rm modem link. Concierge. Refrigerators, microwaves, minibars. Elegant European decor. In Performing Arts District. Cr cds: A, D, DS, MC, V.

D

★ ★ **JULIANA.** *590 Bush St (94108), north of Union Square. 415/392-2540; FAX 415/391-8447; res: 800/328-3880.* 106 rms, 9 story. S, D $125-$185; suites $165-$245; monthly rates. Crib free. TV; cable (premium), VCR avail. Complimentary coffee in lobby; afternoon refreshments. Ck-out noon. Business servs avail. In-rm modem link. Free Financial District transportation. Health club privileges. Refrigerators, honor bars. Cr cds: A, C, D, DS, ER, JCB, MC, V.

D SC

★ ★ **KENSINGTON PARK.** *450 Post St (94102), west of Union Square. 415/788-6400; FAX 415/399-9484; res: 800/553-1900.* 87 rms, 12 story. S, D $109-$125; each addl $10; suites $160-$350; under 13 free. Crib free. Valet parking $17. TV; VCR avail. Complimentary continental bkfst; afternoon refreshments. Piano Fri 4-7 pm. Ck-out noon. Meeting rms. Business servs avail. In-rm modem link. Exercise equipt; bicycles, stair machine. Bathrm phones; some refrigerators. Renovated 1924 hotel, guest rms on floors 5-12. Grand piano in lobby. Traditional English decor. Theater in building. Cr cds: A, D, DS, JCB, MC, V.

D SC

★ ★ **KING GEORGE.** *334 Mason St (94102), west of Union Square. 415/781-5050; FAX 415/391-6976; res: 800/288-6005.* Web www.kinggeorge.com. 143 rms, 9 story. No A/C. S $139; D $149; each addl $10; suites $200; under 12 free; 2-night packages. Crib free. Garage, in/out $12.50-$16.50. TV; cable. Continental bkfst. Restaurant 7-10 am, 3-6:30 pm. Rm serv 24 hrs. Bar; entertainment. Ck-out noon. Meeting rms. Business servs avail. In-rm modem link. Concierge. Airport, RR station, bus depot transportation. Health club privileges. Union Square 1 blk. Cr cds: A, C, D, DS, ER, JCB, MC, V.

SC

★ ★ ★ **MAJESTIC.** *1500 Sutter St (94109), at Gough St, in Pacific Heights. 415/441-1100; FAX 415/673-7331; res: 800/869-8966.* Web www.expedia.msn.com. 57 rms, 5 story. S, D $125-$190; each addl $15; suites $295-$395. Covered parking $16; valet parking. TV; VCR avail. Restaurant 7-10:30 am, 5:30-10:30 pm; Sun brunch 7 am-2 pm. Rm serv 24 hrs. Bar 11 am-midnight; pianist. Ck-out noon. Lndry serv. Meeting rms. Business servs avail. Concierge. Health club privileges. Many fireplaces; some refrigerators; microwaves avail. Each rm individually decorated with antiques, custom furnishings. Restored Edwardian hotel (1902); antique tapestries. Cr cds: A, D, DS, JCB, MC, V.

D

★ ★ ★ ★ **MANDARIN ORIENTAL.** *222 Sansome (94104), between Pine & California Sts, in Financial District. 415/885-0999; FAX 415/433-0289; res: 800/622-0404.* E-mail mandarinsfo@mosfo.com; web www.mandarin-oriental.com. Rooms are appealing and have spectacular views thanks to the hotel's location in one of the city's tallest buildings. 158 rms, 11 story; on floors 38-48 of the twin towers in the First Interstate Center. S, D $305-$495; suites $775-$1,600; under 12 free; wkend rates. Crib free. Covered parking $24. TV; cable (premium), VCR avail. Restaurant (see SILKS). Rm serv 24 hrs. Bar 11 am-11 pm; entertainment exc Sun. Ck-out noon. Meeting rms. Business center. In-rm modem link. Concierge. Exercise equipt; weights, bicycles. Health club privileges. Bathrm phones, refrigerators, minibars. Cr cds: A, C, D, DS, JCB, MC, V.

D

★ ★ ★ ★ **MARK HOPKINS INTER-CONTINENTAL.** *1 Nob Hill (94108), on Nob Hill. 415/392-3434; FAX 415/421-3302; res: 800/327-0200.* This landmark hotel on the site of the old Mark Hopkins mansion offers well-maintained guest rooms decorated in a neoclassical style. The noted Top of the Mark lounge features panoramic views. 390 rms, 19 story. S, D $220-$300; each addl $30; suites $375-$2,000; under 14 free; wkend rates. Crib free. Garage, in/out $23/day. TV; cable, VCR avail. Restaurant 6:30 am-11 pm (also see NOB HILL). Bars noon-2 am. Ck-out 1 pm. Convention facilities. Business center. Concierge. Exercise equipt; bicycles, treadmill. Health club privileges. Minibars. Some balconies. Luxury level. Cr cds: A, C, D, DS, ER, JCB, MC, V.

D

★ ★ ★ **MARRIOTT.** *55 4th St (94103), opp Moscone Convention Center, south of Union Square. 415/896-1600; FAX 415/896-6175.* Web www.marriott.com/sfodt. 1,500 rms, 39 story, 133 suites. S, D $189-$285; each addl $20; suites $280-$2,400; under 18 free. Crib free. Garage $25, in/out 24 hrs. TV; cable (premium), VCR avail. Indoor pool; poolside serv. Restaurant 6:30 am-11 pm; Fri, Sat to midnight. Bar 10:30-2 am. Ck-out noon. Convention facilities. Business center. In-rm modem link. Concierge. Gift shop. Sundries. Airport transportation. Exercise equipt; weight machine, bicycles, whirlpool, sauna, steam rm. Minibars; some bathrm phones. Refrigerator, wet bar in suites. Some balconies. Six-story atrium lobby. Luxury level. Cr cds: A, C, D, DS, ER, JCB, MC, V.

D SC

★ ★ ★ **MARRIOTT FISHERMAN'S WHARF.** *1250 Columbus Ave (94133), at Fisherman's Wharf. 415/775-7555; FAX 415/474-2099.* 285 rms, 5 story. S, D $129-$280; suites $300-$750; under 18 free; wkend rates. Crib free. Valet parking in/out $17. TV; cable (premium), VCR avail. Restaurant 6 am-10 pm. Bar 11-1 am. Ck-out noon. Meeting rms. Business center. In-rm modem link. Gift shop. Free morning Financial District transportation (Mon-Fri). Exercise equipt; weight machine, bicycles, sauna. Bathrm phones. Marble floor in lobby. Cr cds: A, C, D, DS, ER, JCB, MC, V.

D SC

★ ★ **MAXWELL.** *386 Geary St (94102), west of Union Square. 415/986-2000; res: 888/574-6299; FAX 415/397-2447.* Web www.joiedevivre-sf.com. 153 rms, 12 story. Apr-mid-Nov: S, D $130-$195; each addl $10; family rates; wkends, hols (2-day min); lower rates rest of yr. Crib free. Garage, in/out parking $17. TV; cable. Restaurant 7-1 am. Bar. Entertainment Fri, Sat. Ck-out noon. Meeting rms. Business servs avail. In-rm modem link. Concierge. Health club privileges. Bathrm phones. Refrigerators avail. Cr cds: A, C, D, DS, MC, V.

SC

★ ★ ★ ★ **MONACO.** *501 Geary St (94102), west of Union Square. 415/292-0100; FAX 415/292-0111; res: 800/214-4220.* Whimsical, eclectic decor gives this French-inspired hotel a romantic atmosphere. 201 rms, 7 story, 34 suites. S, D $165-$245; suites $250-$375; under 16 free; hol rates. Crib free. Valet parking; in/out $24. TV; cable (premium), VCR avail. Restaurant (see GRAND CAFE). Bar 11:30-1:30 am. Ck-out noon. Meeting rms. Business servs avail. In-rm modem link. Concierge. Exercise rm; instructor, weight machine, treadmill. Massage. Minibars. Cr cds: A, C, D, DS, ER, JCB, MC, V.

D SC

★ ★ ★ **MONTICELLO INN.** *127 Ellis St (94102), south of Union Square. 415/392-8800; FAX 415/398-2650; res: 800/669-7777.* E-mail montinn@aol.com; web www.monticelloinn.com. 91 rms, 5 story, 33 suites. S, D $109-$169; suites $159-$229. Crib free. Valet parking $18. TV; cable (premium). Complimentary continental bkfst. Restaurant 11:30 am-10 pm. Ck-out noon. Business servs avail. In-rm modem link. Concierge. Health club privileges. Mini bars. 18th-century decor. Renovated hotel built 1906. Cr cds: A, C, D, DS, ER, JCB, MC, V.

D SC

★ ★ **NOB HILL LAMBOURNE.** *725 Pine St (94108), on Nob Hill. 415/433-2287; FAX 415/433-0975; res: 800/274-8466.* E-mail nobhill lambourne@att.net. 20 kit. units, 3 story, 6 suites. No A/C. S, D $175-$195; suites $275; family, monthly rates. Crib avail. Garage; valet, in/out $22. TV; cable, VCR (free movies). Complimentary continental bkfst. Complimentary coffee in rms. Restaurant nearby. Ck-out noon. Business center. In-rm modem link. Concierge. Exercise equipt; bicycles, treadmill. Health club privileges. Microwaves, wet bars. Balconies. Totally nonsmoking. Cr cds: A, C, D, DS, JCB, MC, V.

SC

★ ★ ★ **PALACE.** *2 New Montgomery St (94105), at Market St, south of Union Square. 415/392-8600; FAX 415/543-0671.* Web www.sheraton.com. 550 rms, 8 story. S $310-$380; D $330-$400; each addl $20; suites $700-$2,900; family, wkend rates. Crib free. Valet parking $20. TV; cable (premium), VCR avail (movies). Indoor pool; whirlpool, poolside serv. Restaurant (see GARDEN COURT). Rm serv 24 hrs. Bar from 11 am; entertainment. Ck-out noon. Convention facilities. Business center. In-rm modem link. Concierge. Shopping arcade. Exercise rm; instructor, weights, treadmill, sauna. Health club privileges. Bathrm phones, refrigerators. Cr cds: A, C, D, DS, ER, JCB, MC, V.

D SC

★ ★ ★ ★ **PAN PACIFIC.** *500 Post St (94102), west of Union Square. 415/771-8600; FAX 415/398-0267; res: 800/533-6465.* E-mail vulrich @sfo.pan-pacific.com; web www.panpac.com. This centrally located hotel features a third-floor atrium lobby, decorated mostly in marble (with commissioned sculpture) and highlighted by a spectacular 17-story skylight. 330 units, 21 story. S, D $280-$390; suites $550-$1,700; under 18 free; wkend rates. Crib free. Garage, in/out $25; valet parking. Pet accepted, some restrictions. TV; cable (premium), VCR avail. Restaurant 6:30 am-10:30 pm (also see PACIFIC). Rm serv 24 hrs. Bar 11 am-11:30 pm; pianist. Ck-out noon. Meeting rms. Business center. In-rm modem link. Personal valet serv. Concierge. Exercise equipt; weight machines, bicycles. Health club privileges. Minibars, bathrm phones. Cr cds: A, C, D, DS, JCB, MC, V.

D

★ ★ ★ **PARC FIFTY-FIVE.** *55 Cyril Magnin St (94102), Market at 5th St, south of Union Square. 415/392-8000; FAX 415/392-4734.* 1,009 rms, 32 story. S, D $155-$195; each addl $15; suites $340-$1,200; under 19 free. Crib free. Garage $25. TV; cable (premium), VCR avail. Restaurants 6:30 am-10 pm. Bar 11-1 am; pianist. Ck-out noon. Convention facilities. Business center. In-rm modem link. Concierge. Drugstore. Exercise equipt; weights, bicycles, sauna. Health club privileges. Massage. Bathrm phones. Luxury level. Cr cds: A, C, D, DS, ER, JCB, MC, V.

D SC

★ ★ ★ ★ **PARK HYATT.** *333 Battery St (94111), at Clay St, in Financial District. 415/392-1234; FAX 415/421-2433.* Situated in Embarcadero Center, this hotel is designed with neoclassical formality. 360 rms, 24 story, 37 suites. S, D $265-$320; each addl $25; suites $350-$2,500; under 18 free; wkend rates. Crib free. Pet accepted, some restrictions. Covered valet parking, in/out $24. TV; cable (premium), VCR avail (movies). Afternoon refreshments. Restaurant (see PARK GRILL). Rm serv 24 hrs. Bar 11-1 am; entertainment. Ck-out noon. Meeting rms. Business center. Concierge. Exercise equipt for in-rm use. Health club privileges. Bathrm phones, minibars; microwaves avail. Some balconies. Reference library with national and international publications. Cr cds: A, C, D, DS, ER, JCB, MC, V.

D SC

★ ★ ★ **RADISSON MIYAKO.** *1625 Post St (94115), in Japantown. 415/922-3200; FAX 415/921-0417.* E-mail miyakosf@slip.net; web www.mim.com/miyako/. 218 rms, 5 & 16 story. S $139-$179; D $159-$199; each addl $20; suites $179-$299; under 18 free. Crib free. Garage in/out $10. Valet $15. TV; cable, VCR avail. Restaurant (see YOYO). Bar 10-1 am. Ck-out 1 pm. Meeting rms. Business center. In-rm modem link. Concierge. Exercise equipt; weight machine, stair machine. Health club privileges. Refrigerator, sauna in suites. Balconies. Shiatsu massage avail. Japanese decor; authentic Japanese furnishings in some rms. Cr cds: A, C, D, DS, ER, JCB, MC, V.

D SC

★ ★ ★ ★ **RENAISSANCE STANFORD COURT.** *Nob Hill (94108). 415/989-3500; FAX 415/391-0513; res: 800/227-4736 (exc CA), 800/622-0957 (CA).* Web www.renaissancehotels.com. This Italianate villa has a circular driveway lit by a domed glass roof and a stained-glass panel at the hotel entrance. Styling throughout evokes the Italian Renaissance, courtesy of antiques, vivid colors, statuary in the lobby area and rooms done in contrasting decors. 402 rms, 8 story. S $255-$400; D $275-$420; each addl $30; 1-bedrm suites $500-$750; 2-bedrm suites $900-$4,500; under 18 free. Crib free. Valet parking, in/out $24/day. TV; cable (premium), VCR avail. Restaurant (see FOURNOU'S OVENS). Afternoon tea in lobby. Rm serv 24 hrs. Bars 11-1 am. Ck-out noon. Meeting rms. Business center. In-rm modem link. Concierge. Shopping arcade. Exercise equipt; weight machine, treadmills. Health club privileges. Marble bathrms with phone. Microwaves avail. Cr cds: A, C, D, DS, JCB, MC, V.

★ ★ ★ ★ ★ **THE RITZ-CARLTON, SAN FRANCISCO.** *600 Stockton St (94108), at California St, on Nob Hill. 415/296-7465; FAX 415/296-8559.* Sited at a cable car stop on Nob Hill, this elegant hotel occupies a neoclassical villa that was designated a city landmark in 1984. Crystal chandeliers, antiques and 18th-century oils grace the lobby, lending a European ambiance; guest rooms have reproduction Louis XVI furniture, jewel-color brocades and marble bathrooms. 336 rms, 9 story, 44 suites. S, D $325-$400; suites $625-$3,500; under 18 free; wkend packages. Crib avail. Garage; valet, in/out $30. TV; cable (premium), VCR avail. Indoor pool; whirlpool. Supervised child's activities; under 13 yrs. Restaurants 6:30 am-11 pm (also see THE DINING ROOM). Rm serv 24 hrs. Bar; entertainment. Ck-out noon. Convention facilities. Business servs avail. In-rm modem link. Concierge. Gift shop. Exercise rm; instructor, weight machine, stair machine, sauna. Spa. Bathrm phones, minibars; some wet bars. Luxury level. Cr cds: A, C, D, DS, ER, JCB, MC, V.

D SC

✔★ **SHEEHAN.** *620 Sutter St (94102), west of Union Square. 415/775-6500; FAX 415/775-3271; res: 800/848-1529.* E-mail sheehot @aol.com; web www.citysearch.com/sfo/sheehanhotel. 68 rms, 58 with bath, 6 story. No A/C. S $49-$80; D $59-$119; each addl $10; under 12 free. Crib free. Garage $15. TV; cable. Indoor pool; lifeguard. Complimentary continental bkfst. Tea rm 7 am-9 pm. No rm serv. Ck-out 11 am. Meeting rms. Business servs avail. Beauty shop. Exercise equipt; weight machines, rowers. Microwaves avail. Cr cds: A, C, D, DS, JCB, MC, V.

D SC

★ ★ ★ **SIR FRANCIS DRAKE.** *450 Powell St (94102), north of Union Square. 415/392-7755; FAX 415/391-8719; res: 800/227-5480.* E-mail sfdsf@aol.com; web www.citysearch.com/sfo/sirfrancisdrake. 417 rms, 21 story. S, D $149-$209; each addl $20; suites $350-$600; under 18 free; package plans. Crib free. Valet parking in/out $24. TV; cable (premium), VCR avail. Restaurant (see SCALA'S BISTRO). Bar 11:30-1 am. Ck-out noon. Meeting rms. Business servs avail. In-rm modem link. Concierge. Shopping arcade. Exercise equipt; weight machine, bicycles. Cr cds: A, C, D, DS, JCB, MC, V.

D SC

★ **SUPER 8.** *1015 Geary St (94109), at Polk St, west of Union Square. 415/673-5232; FAX 415/885-2802; res: 800/777-3210.* Web www.superhotel.com. 101 rms, 6 story. No A/C. S, D $99.88; each addl $10; under 12 free. Crib free. Valet parking in/out $13/day. TV; cable (premium). Complimentary coffee. Restaurant 7-11 am. Ck-out noon. Meeting rm. Business servs avail. Game rm. Some refrigerators. Cr cds: A, C, D, DS, ER, JCB, MC, V.

SC

★ ★ ★ **TUSCAN INN AT FISHERMAN'S WHARF.** *425 North Point St (94133), at Fisherman's Wharf. 415/561-1100; FAX 415/561-1199; res: 800/648-4626.* 221 rms, 4 story, 12 suites. S, D $168-$198; each addl $10; suites $218-$238; under 16 free; package plans avail. Crib free. Garage $15/day. TV; cable, VCR avail. Complimentary coffee. Restaurant 7 am-10 pm. Bar. Ck-out 11 am. Meeting rms. Business servs avail. Concierge. Free Financial District transportation Mon-Fri. Health club privileges. Minibars. European-style "boutique hotel" following the tradition of a classic inn. 3 blks from Pier 39. Cr cds: A, C, D, DS, JCB, MC, V.

D SC

★ ★ **VILLA FLORENCE.** *225 Powell St (94102), south of Union Square. 415/397-7700; FAX 415/397-1006; res: 800/553-4411.* E-mail villaflo@aol.com; web www.citysearch.com/sfo/villaflorence. 180 rms, 7 story, 36 suites. S, D $135-$185; suites $175-$250; under 16 free. Crib free. Valet parking, $23. TV; cable, VCR avail. Coffee in rms. Restaurant 7 am-11 pm. Bar. Ck-out noon. Meeting rms. Business servs avail. In-rm modem link. Concierge. Health club privileges. Refrigerators, minibars. Cr cds: A, C, D, DS, ER, JCB, MC, V.

D SC

★ ★ **VINTAGE COURT.** *650 Bush St (94108), north of Union Square. 415/392-4666; FAX 415/433-4065; res: 800/654-1100.* Web www.vintagecourt.com. 106 rms, 65 A/C, 8 story. S, D $129-$179; each addl $15; under 12 free. Crib free. Valet parking in/out $21. TV; cable (premium), VCR avail. Complimentary coffee in lobby; afternoon refreshments. Restaurant (see MASA'S). Bar 6-10 pm. Ck-out noon. Meeting rm. Business servs avail. In-rm modem link. Health club privileges. Refrigerators. Sitting area most floors. Built 1912. Cr cds: A, C, D, DS, JCB, MC, V.

D SC

★ ★ ★ **WARWICK REGIS.** *490 Geary St (94102), west of Union Square. 415/928-7900; FAX 415/441-8788; res: 800/827-3447.* 80 rms, 8 story. S, D $99-$225; each addl $10; suites $150-$225; under 10 free. Crib free. Valet parking in/out $23. TV; cable (premium), VCR avail. Restaurants 7-10 am, 6-10 pm. Bar 11-2 am. Ck-out 1 pm. Meeting rms. Business center. In-rm modem link. Health club privileges. Refrigerators; some fireplaces. Balconies. Louis XVI decor. Built 1911. Cr cds: A, C, D, DS, ER, JCB, MC, V.

D SC

★ ★ ★ ★ **THE WESTIN ST FRANCIS.** *335 Powell St (94102), on Union Square. 415/397-7000; FAX 415/774-0124.* Web www.westin.com. An impeccably restored, 93-year-old hotel, the Westin St Francis offers luxury and elegance in the heart of downtown San Francisco. The opulent lobby is appointed with gold and crystal chandeliers, lush Oriental carpets and elaborate gold-leafed ceilings. Extensive crown moldings and 19th-century sleigh beds decorate rooms in the main building. 1,192 rms in hotel & tower, 12 & 32 story. S $199-$355; D $209-$385; each addl $30; suites $295-$2,100; under 18 free. Crib free. Pet accepted, some restrictions. Garage in/out, valet parking $24. TV; cable, VCR avail. Restaurants 6 am-midnight. Rm serv 24 hrs. Bars 11-2 am; entertainment. Ck-out 1 pm. Convention facilities. Business center. In-rm modem link. Concierge. Shopping arcade. Barber, Beauty shop. Exercise equipt; weight machines, bicycles. Refrigerators, minibars; microwaves avail; bathrm phone in suites. Cable car stop. Cr cds: A, C, D, DS, JCB, MC, V.

D SC

★ ★ **YORK.** *940 Sutter St (94109), on Nob Hill. 415/885-6800; FAX 415/885-2115; res: 800/808-9675.* 96 rms, 7 story. S, D $95-$137; each addl $10; suites $210; under 12 free; lower rates Nov-mid-Apr. Parking $14-$25. TV; cable. Complimentary continental bkfst. Complimentary coffee in rms. Ck-out noon. Meeting rm. Business servs avail. In-rm modem link. Exercise equipt; weights, bicycles. Health club privileges. Minibars; some refrigerators. Renovated 1922 hotel; marble floors, ceiling fans. Hitchcock's Vertigo filmed here. Cr cds: A, C, D, DS, ER, JCB, MC, V.

SC

Inns

★ ★ **ALAMO SQUARE.** *719 Scott St (94117), west of Union Square. 415/922-2055; FAX 415/931-1304; res: 800/345-9888.* E-mail wcorn@alamoinn.com; web www.alamoinn.com. 14 rms in 2 bldgs, 10 with shower only, 3 story. No A/C. S, D $85-$195; each addl $25; suites $195-$295; wkly rates; wkends (2-day min). Crib free. TV in some rms; VCR avail. Complimentary full bkfst; afternoon refreshments. Restaurant nearby. Ck-out noon, ck-in 2-6 pm. Business servs avail. Concierge. Health club privileges. Some balconies. Picnic tables. Inn complex includes two restored Victorian mansions, 1895 Queen Anne and 1896 Tudor Revival, located in historic district. Antique furnishings, some wood-burning fireplaces; stained-glass skylight. Garden. Overlooks Alamo Square; panoramic view of city skyline. Totally nonsmoking. Cr cds: A, C, JCB, MC, V.

✔★ **ALBION HOUSE.** *135 Gough St (94102), W of Union Square. 415/621-0896.* 8 rms, 2 story. S, D $95-$155; suite $195-$235. TV. Complimentary full bkfst; afternoon refreshments. Ck-out noon, ck-in 4 pm. Business servs avail. Built 1906; individually decorated rms, antiques; piano in parlor. Cr cds: A, D, DS, MC, V.

SC

✔★ ★ **AMSTERDAM.** *749 Taylor St (94108), west of Union Square, between Sutter & Bush. 415/673-3277; FAX 415/673-0453; res: 800/637-3444.* 34 rms, 3 story. No elvtr. S $69-$79; D $79-$129; each addl $10; under 11 free. Crib free. Garage $13 in/out. TV; cable. Complimentary continental bkfst. Restaurant nearby. Ck-out 11 am, ck-in noon. Business servs avail. Garden/patio for guests. Cr cds: A, MC, V.

★ ★ **ANDREWS HOTEL.** *624 Post St (94109), west of Union Square. 415/563-6877; FAX 415/928-6919; res: 800/926-3739.* E-mail andrews-hotel@mcimail.com; web www.joiedevivre-sf.com. 48 rms, 7 story. No A/C. S, D $89-$119; each addl $10; suites $129. Parking adj, $15 in/out. TV. Complimentary continental bkfst. Dining rm 5:30-10 pm. Ck-out noon, ck-in 3 pm. Business servs avail. European decor; impressionist prints. Former Turkish bathhouse built 1905. Cr cds: A, D, JCB, MC, V.

★ ★ ★ **ARCHBISHOPS MANSION.** *1000 Fulton St (94117), at Steiner St, south of Union Square. 415/563-7872; FAX 415/885-3193; res: 800/543-5820.* Web www.joiedevivre.com. 15 rms, 3 story. S, D $129-$199; each addl $20; suites $215-$385. TV; cable, VCR (free movies). Complimentary continental bkfst; afternoon refreshments. Restaurant nearby. Ck-out 11:30 am, ck-in 3 pm. Business servs avail. Concierge serv. Health club privileges. Stained-glass skylight over stairwell. Built 1904; antiques. Individually decorated rms. Cr cds: A, C, D, MC, V.

★ ★ **HOTEL BOHÉME.** *444 Columbus Ave (94133), in North Beach. 415/433-9111; FAX 415/362-6292.* E-mail BA@hotelboheme.com; web www.hotelboheme.com. 15 rms, 2-3 story. S, D $115-$140; each addl $10; under 2 free. TV; cable. Restaurant adj 7-1 am. Ck-out noon, ck-in 2 pm. Concierge. Business servs avail. In-rm modem link. Health club privileges. Cr cds: A, C, D, DS, JCB, MC, V.

★ ★ ★ **INN AT UNION SQUARE.** *440 Post St (94102), west of Union Square. 415/397-3510; FAX 415/989-0529; res: 800/288-4346.* E-mail inn@unionsquare.com; web www.unionsquare.com. 30 rms, 6 story. No A/C. S, D $145-$205; each addl $15; suites $200-$350. Crib free. Valet parking in/out $20. TV; cable, VCR avail. Pool privileges. Complimentary afternoon refreshments. Rm serv 5-10 pm. Bar. Ck-out noon, ck-in 2 pm. Business servs avail. In-rm modem link. Luggage handling. Concierge serv. Health club privileges. Sitting area, fireplace most floors; antiques. Robes in all rms. Penthouse suite with fireplace, bar, whirlpool, sauna. Totally nonsmoking. Cr cds: A, D, DS, JCB, MC, V.

D SC

★ ★ ★ **THE INN SAN FRANCISCO.** *943 S Van Ness Ave (94110), in Mission District. 415/641-0188; FAX 415/641-1701; res: 800/359-0913.* 21 rms, 18 baths, 3 story. No A/C. S, D $85-$225; each addl $20; suites $175-$225. Limited parking avail; $10. TV. Complimentary full bkfst. Restaurant nearby. Ck-out noon, ck-in 2 pm. Business servs avail. Health club privileges. Whirlpool. Refrigerators. Balconies. Library. Italianate mansion (1872) near Mission Dolores; ornate woodwork, fireplaces; antique furnishings; garden with redwood hot tub, gazebo; view of city, bay from rooftop sun deck. Cr cds: A, C, D, DS, MC, V.

★ ★ **JACKSON COURT.** *2198 Jackson St (94115), in Pacific Heights. 415/929-7670; FAX 415/929-1405.* 10 rms, shower only, 3 story. No A/C. S, D $139-$195; each addl $25; under 12 free; wkends (2-day min). TV; cable (premium). Complimentary continental bkfst; afternoon refreshments. Restaurant nearby. Ck-out 11 am, ck-in 2 pm. Concierge serv. Street parking. Some fireplaces; microwaves avail. Brownstone mansion built in 1900. Totally nonsmoking. Cr cds: A, MC, V.

★ ★ **MANSIONS HOTEL.** *2220 Sacramento St (94115), in Pacific Heights. 415/929-9444; FAX 415/567-9391; res: 800/826-9398.* 21 rms, 3 story. No A/C. S, D $129-$350; suites $189-$350. Pet accepted. Complimentary full bkfst. Dining rm (res required) dinner only. Rm serv 7:30 am-midnight. Ck-out noon, ck-in 3 pm. Business servs avail. Luggage handling. Airport transportation. Game rm. Music rm. Evening magic concerts. Some balconies. Built in 1887; Victorian memorabilia, antiques, art. Presidential letter collection. Jack London's typewriter used to write "Call of the Wild." Cr cds: A, C, D, DS, MC, V.

✔★ ★ **MARINA.** *3110 Octavia St (94123), at Lombard St, north of Union Square. 415/928-1000; FAX 415/928-5909; res: 800/274-1420.* 40 rms, 4 story. S, D $65-$115; each addl $10. TV; cable. Complimentary continental bkfst; afternoon refreshments. Ck-out noon, ck-in 2 pm. Business servs avail. Luggage handling. Barber, beauty shop. Restored 1928 bldg; English country ambiance. Cr cds: A, MC, V.

D

★ ★ ★ **PETITE AUBERGE.** *863 Bush St (94108), north of Union Square. 415/928-6000; FAX 415/775-5717.* 26 rms, 5 story. No A/C. S, D $110-$160; each addl $15; suite $220. Crib free. Valet parking in/out $19. TV; cable. Complimentary full bkfst; afternoon refreshments. Ck-out noon, ck-in 2 pm. Business servs avail. In-rm modem link. Luggage handling. Some fireplaces, microwaves avail. French country inn ambiance. Cr cds: A, D, MC, V.

★ ★ ★ **THE PRESCOTT HOTEL.** *545 Post St (94102), west of Union Square. 415/563-0303; FAX 415/563-6831; res: 800/283-7322.* 166 rms, 7 story. S, D $185; each addl $10; suites $235-$1,200; hol rates. Crib free. Covered valet parking, in/out $23. TV; cable, VCR avail. Pool privileges. Dining rm (see POSTRIO). Complimentary coffee; afternoon refreshments. Rm serv 6 am-midnight. Bar 11-2 am. Ck-out noon, ck-in 3 pm. Business servs avail. In-rm modem link. Concierge serv. Health club privileges. Exercise equipt; bicycles, rowers; equipt delivered to rms. Minibars; some wet bars. Union Square shopping 1 blk. Luxury level. Cr cds: A, C, D, DS, ER, JCB, MC, V.

D SC

★ ★ **QUEEN ANNE.** *1590 Sutter St (94109), west of Union Square. 415/441-2828; FAX 415/775-5212; res: 800/227-3970.* E-mail queenanne@sfo.com; web www.queenanne.com. 48 rms, 4 story. No A/C. S, D $110-$175; each addl $10; suites $175-$275; under 12 free. Parking in/out $12. TV; cable (premium), VCR avail. Crib free. Complimentary continental bkfst; afternoon refreshments. Ck-out noon, ck-in 3 pm. Meeting rm. Business servs avail. In-rm modem link. Luggage handling. Health club privileges. Bathrm phones; some wet bars, fireplaces. Restored boarding school for young girls (1890); stained glass, many antiques, carved staircase. Cr cds: A, C, D, DS, JCB, MC, V.

D

✔★ **SAN REMO.** *2237 Mason St (94133), in North Beach. 415/776-8688; FAX 415/776-2811; res: 800/352-7366.* E-mail info@sanremohotel.com. 62 rms, shared baths, 2 story. No rm phones. S $45-$60; D $55-$70. Bar. Parking $8. Ck-out 11 am, ck-in 2 pm. Business servs avail. Lndry facilities. Italianate Victorian bldg; antiques, art. Cr cds: A, C, D, JCB, MC, V.

★ ★ ★ **SHERMAN HOUSE.** *2160 Green St (94123), in Pacific Heights, north of Union Square. 415/563-3600; FAX 415/563-1882; res: 800/424-5777.* 14 rms, 4 story. No elvtr. S, D $325-$425; suites $625-$825; under 18 free. Garage $16. TV; cable (premium), VCR (movies). Dining rm (by res) 7 am-2 pm, 5:30-9 pm. Rm serv 24 hrs. Ck-out noon, ck-in 4 pm. Business servs avail. In-rm modem link. Concierge serv. Butler serv. Health club privileges. Bathrm phones; many wet bars. Roman tub, whirlpool in some rms. Private patios, balconies. In 1876 mansion; individually designed rms feature antiques, marble fireplaces and four-poster beds. Cr cds: A, D, MC, V.

★ ★ ★ **SPENCER HOUSE.** *1080 Haight St (94117), at Baker St, Haight-Asbury. 415/626-9205; FAX 415/626-9230.* Web www.spencerhouse.com. 8 rms, 7 with shower only, 2 story. No A/C. S, D $115-$165; 2-day min wkends. Complimentary full bkfst. Restaurant nearby. Ck-out noon. Business servs avail. Victorian house built in 1887; original light fixtures, many antiques. Totally nonsmoking. Cr cds: A, MC, V.

★ ★ **STANYAN PARK.** *750 Stanyan St (94117), in Haight-Ashbury. 415/751-1000; FAX 415/668-5454.* E-mail info@stanyanpark.com; web www.stanyanpark.com. 36 rms, 3 story, 6 kits. No A/C. S, D $95-$135; suites $159-$199. Municipal parking $5. TV, cable; VCR avail. Complimentary continental bkfst; afternoon refreshments. Ck-out noon. Business servs avail. In-rm modem link. Bellhops. Refrigerator in suites. Restored Victorian hotel. Cr cds: A, C, D, DS, MC, V.

D

★ ★ **VICTORIAN INN ON THE PARK.** *301 Lyon St (94117), in Haight-Ashbury. 415/931-1830; FAX 415/931-1830; res: 800/435-1967.* E-mail vicinn@aol.com; web www.citysearch.com/sfo/victorianinn. 12 rms, 4 story. No A/C. No elvtr. S, D $109-$169; each addl $20; suites $169-$325. Parking $11. TV in lounge, rm TV avail. Complimentary continental bkfst; afternoon refreshments. Ck-out 11:30 am, ck-in 2 pm. Business servs avail. In-rm modem link. Health club privileges. Some fireplaces; microwaves avail. Historic building (1897); Victorian decor. Cr cds: A, D, DS, JCB, MC, V.

★ ★ **WASHINGTON SQUARE.** *1660 Stockton St (94133), in North Beach. 415/981-4220; FAX 415/397-7242; res: 800/388-0220.* 15 rms, 2 story. No A/C. S, D $120-$185; each addl $15. Valet parking $20. TV; cable, VCR avail. Complimentary continental bkfst; afternoon refreshments. Bkfst rm serv on request. Ck-out noon, ck-in 2 pm. Business servs avail. In-rm modem link. Luggage handling. Concierge serv. Health club privileges. Individually decorated rms with English & French country antiques. Opp historic Washington Square. Totally nonsmoking. Cr cds: A, D, DS, JCB, MC, V.

★ ★ ★ **WHITE SWAN.** *845 Bush St (94108), north of Union Square. 415/775-1755; FAX 415/775-5717.* 26 rms, 5 story. S, D $145-$160; each addl $15; suites $195-$250. Crib free. Valet parking in/out $19. TV; cable, VCR avail. Complimentary full bkfst; evening refreshments. Restaurant nearby. Ck-out noon, ck-in 2 pm. Business servs avail. Refrigerators, microwaves avail. Country English theme; antiques, fireplaces. Each rm individually decorated. Gardens. Totally nonsmoking. Cr cds: A, D, MC, V.

Restaurants

★ ★ **42 DEGREES.** *235 16th St (94107), south of Union Square. 415/777-5558.* Hrs: 11:30 am-3 pm, 6:30-11:30 pm; Mon, Tues to 3 pm. Closed Sun; major hols. Res accepted. Mediterranean menu. Bar. Semi-a la carte: lunch $5-$11, dinner $5-$20. Specialties: pan seared sea bass, Iberian sausage, slow roasted lamb shank. Entertainment Wed-Sat. Outdoor dining. Casual decor. Totally nonsmoking. Cr cds: MC, V.

D

★ ★ ★ **A. SABELLA'S.** *2766 Taylor St (94133), at Fisherman's Wharf. 415/771-6775.* E-mail fresh_fish@compuserv.com; web www.asabella.com. Hrs: 11 am-10:30 pm; Sat to 11 pm. Closed Dec 25. Res accepted. Bar. Wine list. A la carte entrees: lunch $7.75-$14.75, dinner $11.25-$46.75. Child's meals. Specializes in fresh local seafood. Own cakes, cheesecake. Pianist evenings. Dinner theater Fri & Sat (7:30 pm). 1,000 gal crab, abalone, and lobster tanks. Overlooks wharf, bay. Family-owned. Cr cds: A, C, D, DS, JCB, MC, V.

D

✔★ ★ **ACE WASABI'S ROCK & ROLL SUSHI.** *3339 Steiner St (94123), in Marina District. 415/567-4903.* Web www.citysearch.com/sfo/acewasabis. Hrs: 5:30-10:30 pm; Fri, Sat to 11 pm; Sun 5-10 pm. Closed Jan 1, Dec 25. Japanese menu. Bar. Semi-a la carte: dinner $4.95-$9.50. Specialties: Ahi and Hamachi pot stickers, flying kamikaze roll. Modern Japanese decor. Totally nonsmoking. Cr cds: A, D, MC, V.

D

★ ★ **ACQUERELLO.** *1722 Sacramento St, in Russian Hill. 415/567-5432.* Web www.acquerello.com. Hrs: 5:30-10:30 pm. Closed Sun, Mon; most major hols. Res accepted. Northern Italian menu. Wine, beer. A la carte entrees: dinner $20-$26. Specializes in pasta, seafood. Menu changes seasonally. Intimate dining in restored chapel (ca 1930); high-beamed ceiling decorated with gold foil. Local artwork on display. Totally nonsmoking. Cr cds: A, C, D, DS, MC, V.

D

★ ★ ★ **ALAIN RONDELLI.** *126 Clement (94118), in Richmond District. 415/387-0408.* Hrs: 5:30-10 pm; Fri, Sat to 10:30 pm. Closed Mon; July 4; also 2 wks in Jan. Res accepted. Comptemporary French menu. Bar. A la carte entrees: dinner $19-$23. Specialties: foie gras with black mission figs, roasted pear with roquefort, champagne vinegar, black pepper gastric. Sophisticated French atmosphere. Cr cds: MC, V.

★ ★ **ALBONA.** *545 Francisco St (94133), in North Beach. 415/441-1040.* Hrs: 5-10 pm. Closed Sun, Mon; Thanksgiving, Dec 25. Res accepted. Northern Italian menu. Wine, beer. A la carte entrees: dinner $12.50-$16.75. Specializes in Italian cuisine with Austrian-Hungarian influence. Free valet parking. Intimate dining. Chef-owned. Totally nonsmoking. Cr cds: A, C, D, DS, MC, V.

★ **ALEGRIA'S FOODS FROM SPAIN.** *2018 Lombard St (94123), in Marina District. 415/929-8888.* Hrs: 5:30-11 pm; Fri-Sun also 11:30 am-2:30 pm. Res accepted. Spanish menu. Bar. A la carte entrees: lunch, dinner $12.50-$14.95. Specialties: zarzuela de mariscos, tapas, paella. Entertainment Thur-Sun. Spanish decor. Totally nonsmoking. Cr cds: A, C, D, JCB, MC, V.

D

★ ★ **ANJOU.** *44 Campton Pl, off Stockton St, north of Union Square. 415/392-5373.* Web www.citysearch7.com/arjou. Hrs: 11:30 am-2:30 pm, 5:30-10 pm. Closed Sun, Mon. Res accepted. French menu. Bar. A la carte entrees: lunch $8-$17, dinner $12-$18. Prix fixe: lunch $12. Specialties: Chilean sea bass, confit of duck leg, honey-roasted chicken. Bi-level dining area, high ceiling. Cr cds: A, D, DS, JCB, MC, V.

★ **ANNABELLE'S.** *54 Fourth St (94103), south of Union Square. 415/777-1200.* Hrs: 7 am-10:30 pm. Closed Dec 25. Res accepted. No A/C. Bar. Semi-a la carte: bkfst $5-$10.50, lunch, dinner $5-$17.95. Specializes in rotisserie cooking. Streetfront cafe was once a bank; teller cages from 1900s. Totally nonsmoking. Cr cds: A, MC, V.

D

★ **ANTICA TRATTORIA.** *2400 Polk St (94109), on Russian Hill. 415/928-5797.* Hrs: 5:30-10 pm; Fri, Sat to 10:30 pm. Closed Mon; most major hols. Res accepted. No A/C. Italian menu. Wine, beer. A la carte entrees: dinner $8-$15. Child's meals. Valet parking. Casual corner cafe. Totally nonsmoking. Cr cds: C, D, MC, V.

D

★ ★ ★ **AQUA.** *252 California St, in Financial District. 415/956-9662.* Specialties: medallions of ahi tuna (rare) with foie gras in wine sauce, Dungeness crab cakes. Hrs: 11:30 am-2:30 pm, 5:30-10:30 pm; Fri, Sat to 11 pm. Closed Sun; most major hols. Res accepted. Bar. A la carte entrees: lunch $14-$19, dinner $28-$39. Complete meals: lunch $35, dinner $50-$65. Valet parking (dinner). Mediterranean atmosphere; sophisticated dining. Cr cds: A, D, MC, V.

D

✔★ **BAKER STREET BISTRO.** *2953 Baker St (94117), between Lombard & Greenwich, in Cow Hollow. 415/931-1475.* Hrs: 11 am-2 pm, 5:30-10:30 pm; Sat from 5:30 pm; Sun 5-9:30 pm; Sat, Sun brunch 10 am- 2 pm. Closed Mon; most major hols. Res aacepted. No A/C. Country French menu. Wine. Semi-a la carte: lunch $4.75-$6.25, dinner $8.75-$13.50. Prix fixe: dinner $14.50. Sat, Sun brunch $4.75-$8.50. Specializes in rabbit, duck, escargot. Street parking. Outdoor dining. Bistro atmosphere; trompe l'oeil painting on front of building. Cr cds: MC, V.

D

✔★ ★ **BALBOA CAFE.** *3199 Fillmore St, in Marina District. 415/921-3944.* Hrs: 11 am-10 pm; Sun brunch 10:30 am-4 pm. Bar to 2 am. A la carte entrees: lunch, dinner $8-$16. Sun brunch $7-$14. Built 1897. Cr cds: A, C, D, MC, V.

D

✔★ ★ **BASTA PASTA.** *1268 Grant St, at Vallejo St, in North Beach. 415/434-2248.* Hrs: 11:30-1:45 am. Closed some major hols. Res accepted. Italian menu. Bar. Semi-a la carte: lunch $6.95-$14.25. A la carte entrees: dinner $7-$15.25. Specializes in pizza baked in wood-burning oven, pasta, veal, chicken. Valet parking. Outdoor (rooftop) dining. Main dining rm on 2nd floor. Cr cds: A, C, D, DS, JCB, MC, V.

D

★ ★ **BETELNUT PEJIU WU.** *2030 Union St (94123), in Cow Hollow. 415/929-8855.* Web ww.citysearch.com. Hrs: 11:30 am-11 pm; Fri, Sat to midnight. Closed Thanksgiving, Dec 25. Res accepted. Southeastern Asian menu. Bar. A la carte entrees: lunch $8-$13, dinner $14-$20. Specializes in multi-regional Pacific Rim cuisine. Outdoor dining. Asian decor. Totally nonsmoking. Cr cds: C, D, DS, MC, V.

D

★ ★ ★ **THE BIG 4.** *(See Huntington Hotel) 415/771-1140.* Hrs: 7-10 am, 11:30 am-3 pm, 5:30-10:30 pm; Sat & Sun 7-11 am, 5:30-10:30 pm. Res accepted. Bar 11:30-midnight. Wine cellar. Contemporary American cuisine. A la carte entrees: bkfst $5-$12.95, lunch $9-$16, dinner $8.50-$28.50. Complete meal: bkfst $15. Specialties: seasonal wild game dishes, lamb sausage with black pepper papardelle noodles. Pianist evenings. Valet parking. Traditional San Francisco club atmosphere. Cr cds: A, C, D, DS, JCB, MC, V.

★ **BISCUITS & BLUES.** *401 Mason St (94102), west of Union Sqaure. 415/292-2583.* Hrs: 5 pm-1 am. Southern, New Orleans cuisine. Bar. A la carte entrees: dinner $9.95. Specializes in biscuits, catfish, jambalaya. Entertainment. Casual decor. Cr cds: A, MC, V.

D

★ ★ **BIX.** *56 Gold St (94133), in Financial District. 415/433-6300.* Hrs: 11:30 am-11 pm; Fri to midnight; Sat 5:30 pm-midnight; Sun 6-10 pm. Closed major hols. Res accepted. Bar to 1:30 am. A la carte entrees: lunch $10-$15, dinner $15-$26. Specializes in classic American dishes with California influence. Jazz nightly. Valet parking (dinner). Modernized 40's supper club with grand piano. Cr cds: A, C, D, DS, JCB, MC, V.

D

✔★ ★ **BIZOU.** *598 Fourth St (94107), at Brannan, south of Union Square. 415/543-2222.* Hrs: 11:30 am-2:30 pm, 5:30-10 pm; Fri to 10:30 pm; Sat 5:30-10:30 pm. Closed Sun; most major hols. Res accepted. No

A/C. French, Italian menu. Bar. Semi-a la carte: lunch $5.50-$14.50, dinner $11.50-$19. Specialties: batter-fried green beans, beef cheek, bittersweet chocolate and coffee vacherin. Street parking. Warm, sunny atmosphere. Totally nonsmoking. Cr cds: A, MC, V.

D

★ ★ **BLUE POINT.** *2415 Clement St (94121), in Richmond District. 415/379-9726.* Hrs: 5-10 pm. Closed Tues; Dec 25. Res accepted. Wine, beer. A la carte entrees: dinner $7.95-$11.75. Specializes in cioppino, salmon cakes. Contemporary decor. Totally nonsmoking. Cr cds: MC, V.

D

★ **BOBBY RUBINO'S.** *245 Jefferson St (94133), at Fisherman's Wharf. 415/673-2266.* Hrs: 11:30 am-11 pm. Res accepted. No A/C. Bar. A la carte entrees: lunch $4.95-$12.95, dinner $6.95-$17.95. Child's meals. Specializes in steak, baby back ribs, fresh seafood. Casual, family dining, on two levels. View of fishing fleet. Cr cds: A, D, DS, JCB, MC, V.

✔★ ★ **BONTÀ.** *2223 Union St (94123), in Cow Hollow. 415/929-0407.* Hrs: 5:30-10:30 pm; Fri, Sat to 11 pm; Sun 5-10 pm. Closed Mon; some major hols. Res accepted. No A/C. Italian menu. Wine, beer. A la carte entrees: dinner $9.75-$18.75. Child's meals. Large vegetarian selection. Storefront dining rm. Totally nonsmoking. Cr cds: MC, V.

D

★ ★ ★ **BOULEVARD.** *1 Mission St (94105), south of Union Square at Embarcadero. 415/543-6084.* E-mail kking@kuleto.com; web www.kuleto.com/boulevard. Hrs: 11:30 am-2:15 pm, 5:30-10 pm; Thurs-Sat to 10:30 pm. Closed major hols. Res accepted. Bar. Semi-a la carte: lunch $20-$30, dinner $40-$50. Specialties: roasted chicken breast, pork loin, pan roasted halibut. Contemporary decor. Totally nonsmoking. Cr cds: A, D, DS, MC, V.

D

✔★ ★ **CAFE AKIMBO.** *116 Maiden Lane (94108), in Union Square. 415/433-2288.* Hrs: 11:30 am-3 pm, 5:30-9 pm; Fri, Sat to 10 pm. Closed Sun; most major hols. Res accepted. Contemporary menu. Wine, beer. Semi-a la carte: lunch $8.95-$12.95, dinner $9.95-$15.95. Specialties: akimbo roll, sauteed prawns with pine nuts. Contemporary decor. Totally nonsmoking. Cr cds: A, DS, JCB, MC, V.

✔★ ★ **CAFE BASTILLE.** *22 Belden Place (94104), in Financial District. 415/986-5673.* Web www.cafebastille.com. Hrs: 11 am-11 pm. Closed Sun; also most major hols. Res accepted. French menu. Bar. Semi-a la carte: lunch, dinner $8-$13. Child's meals. Specializes in crepes, mussels. Entertainment Tue-Sat. Outdoor dining. French bistro decor. Totally nonsmoking. Cr cds: A, D, MC, V.

D

✔★ **CAFE KATI.** *1963 Sutter St (94115), in Pacific Heights. 415/775-7313.* Hrs: 5:30-10 pm. Closed Mon; some major hols. Res accepted. Eclectic menu. Wine, beer. Semi-a la carte: dinner $15-$19. Specialties: vegetarian risotto, grilled sirloin of spring lamb, cider-marinated tenderloin of pork. Valet parking Fri, Sat. Contemporary Asian decor. Totally nonsmoking. Cr cds: MC, V.

★ **CAFE MARIMBA.** *2317 Chestnut St (94123), in Marina District. 415/776-1506.* Hrs: 11:30 am-10 pm; Mon from 5:30 pm; Fri, Sat to 11 pm; Sat, Sun brunch 10:30 am-2 pm. Closed Thanksgiving, Dec 25. Res accepted. Mexican menu. Bar. A la carte entrees: lunch, dinner $4.75-$11.95. Sun brunch $5.75-$7.50. Child's meals. Specialties: chicken breast with mole sauce, Veracruz-style fresh fish, margaritas. Brightly colored restaurant with papier maché figures and Mexican folk art. Cr cds: A, MC, V.

D

★ **CAFE PESCATORE.** *2455 Mason St (94133), at Fisherman's Wharf. 415/561-1111.* Hrs: 7 am-10 pm; Fri & Sat to 11 pm. Closed Dec 25. Res accepted. Italian, Amer menu. Bar. A la carte entrees: bkfst $5.95-$9.95, lunch $6.95-$15.95, dinner $8.75-$15.95. Child's meals. Specializes in fresh seafood, oak burning pizza. Outdoor dining. Trattoria-style dining with maritime memorabilia. Cr cds: A, D, DS, JCB, MC, V.

D

✔★ ★ **CAFE RIGGIO.** *4112 Geary Blvd (94118), in Richmond District. 415/221-2114.* Hrs: 5-10 pm; Fri & Sat to 11 pm; Sun from 4:30 pm. Closed some major hols. Italian menu. Bar. A la carte entrees: dinner $7.95-$14.50. Child's meals. Specializes in veal, fish, pasta. Casual atmosphere. Cr cds: MC, V.

D

★ ★ **CAFE TIRAMISU.** *28 Belden Place (94104), in Financial District. 415/421-7044.* Hrs: 11:30 am-2:30 pm, 5-10 pm; Sat from 5 pm. Closed Sun; some major hols. Res accepted. Italian menu. Wine, beer. Semi-a la carte: lunch, dinner $8.50-$18.50. Specialties: rack of lamb, risotto. Outdoor dining. Italian decor. Totally nonsmoking. Cr cds: A, D, MC, V.

★ ★ ★ **CAMPTON PLACE.** *(See Campton Place Hotel) 415/955-5555.* E-mail reserve@campton.com. Hrs: 7-10:30 am, 11:30 am-2 pm, 6-10 pm; Fri to 10:30 pm; Sat 8-11 am, noon-2 pm, 5:30-10:30 pm; Sun 8 am-2 pm, 6-9:30 pm. Res accepted. Contemporary American cuisine with regional emphasis. Bar 10 am-11 pm; Fri, Sat to midnight. Extensive wine list. A la carte entrees: bkfst $9-$16, lunch $9.50-$16.50, dinner $23-$30. Prix fixe: lunch $19.50, dinner $29-$62. Sun brunch $9-$14.50. Child's meals. Own baking. Menu changes frequently. Valet parking. Brass wall sconces; Oriental antiques. Cr cds: A, C, D, JCB, MC, V.

D

★ ★ ★ **CARNELIAN ROOM.** *555 California St (94104), in Financial District. 415/433-7500.* Hrs: 6-10 pm; Sun brunch 10 am-2 pm. Closed some major hols. Res accepted. Bar from 3 pm; Sun from 10 am. Wine cellar. A la carte entrees: dinner $21-$38. Prix fixe: dinner $35. Sun brunch $24.50. Child's meals. Vintage 18th-century decor; antiques. 11 dining rms. Panoramic view of city. Jacket. Cr cds: A, C, D, DS, JCB, MC, V.

D

★ **CHA CHA CHA.** *1801 Haight St (94117), in Haight-Ashbury. 415/386-5758.* Hrs: 11:30 am-4 pm, 5-11 pm; wkends to 11:30 pm. Closed Dec 25. Caribbean, Cuban menu. Wine, beer. A la carte entrees: lunch $4.75-$7, dinner $5.25-$12.75. Specializes in tapas. Casual dining in colorful atmosphere. Totally nonsmoking. Cr cds: MC, V.

D

★ ★ ★ **CHARLES NOB HILL.** *1250 Jones St (94109), at Clay, on Nob Hill. 415/771-5400.* Hrs: 5:30-10 pm; Fri, Sat to 10:30 pm. Closed Mon. Res accepted. French menu. Bar. Semi-a la carte: dinner $19-$32. Complete meals: dinner $65. Specialties: ahi tuna and lobster parfait, tempura Maryland soft shell crabs. Formal decor. Cr cds: A, MC, V.

D

★ ★ ★ **CHEZ MICHEL.** *804 North Point St (94109), in Russian Hill. 415/775-7036.* Hrs: 5:30-10:30 pm. Closed Mon; some major hols. Res accepted. French menu. Bar. A la carte entrees: dinner $13-$23. Specialties: duck confit, monkfish, lamb. Intimate and sophisticated atmosphere. Totally nonsmoking. Cr cds: MC, V.

D

★ ★ **CHIC'S SEAFOOD.** *Pier 39, at Fisherman's Wharf. 415/421-2442.* Web www.citysearch.com/sfo/chicsseafood. Hrs: 9 am-11 pm. Res accepted. Bar. Semi-a la carte: bkfst $4.50-$7.25, lunch $5.95-$10.95. A la carte entrees: dinner $9.95-$19.95. Specializes in seafood. Own desserts. Parking (Pier 39 garage). View of bay, Alcatraz, Golden Gate Bridge. Cr cds: A, C, D, DS, JCB, MC, V.

D

★ ★ **CIAO.** *230 Jackson St, at Front St, in Financial District. 415/982-9500.* Hrs: 11:30 am-10 pm; Fri, Sat to 11 pm; Sun 4-10 pm. Closed Thanksgiving, Dec 25. Res accepted. No A/C. Italian menu. Bar. A la carte entrees: lunch, dinner $8-$16.95. Specializes in mesquite-grilled fresh fish and meats. Own pastas, desserts. Cr cds: A, D, MC, V.

D

★ ★ ★ **COCONUT GROVE.** *1415 Van Ness Ave (94109), in Russian Hill. 415/776-1616.* Hrs: 5:30-11 pm; Fri, Sat to 2 am. Closed Sun, Mon. Res accepted. Continental menu. Bar. Wine list. A la carte entrees: dinner $10.95-$20. Specialties: whole Thai snapper, wild mushroom bread pudding. Valet parking. Intimate supper club with 40s atmosphere. Jacket. Cr cds: A, C, D, DS, JCB, MC, V.

D

✔★ **THE COURTYARD CAFE.** *1361 Church St (94114), in Mission District. 415/641-0678.* Hrs: 10:30 am-3:30 pm, 5:30-10 pm. Res accepted. Mediterranian menu. Wine, beer. A la carte entrees: bkfst $4.50-$8.95, lunch $4.50-$9.95, dinner $7.95-$13.95. Sat, Sun brunch $4.50-$8.95. Specialties: sesame chicken pasta, cheese blintzes. Patio dining. Built 1903; changing art display monthly. Totally nonsmoking. Cr cds: C, D, DS, MC, V.

★ ★ ★ **CYPRESS CLUB.** *500 Jackson St, in Financial District. 415/296-8555.* Hrs: 5:30-10 pm; Fri & Sat to 11 pm. Closed major hols. Res accepted. Contemporary Amer menu. Bar 4:30 pm-2 am. Wine list. A la carte entrees: dinner $20-$29. Menu changes daily. Jazz nightly. Whimsical, 1940s-style design. Cr cds: A, D, MC, V.

D

✔★ **DAME.** *1815 Market St (94103), in Mission District. 415/255-8818.* E-mail kjdame@earthlink.net; web www.citysearch ch7.com/damerestaurant. Hrs: 11:30 am-2 pm, 5-9:30 pm; Fri to 10:30 pm; Sat 5-10:30 pm; Sun 10 am-2 pm, 5-9:30 pm. Closed Mon; July 4, Thanksgiving, Dec 25. Res accepted. Non-traditional Italian menu. Wine, beer. Semi-a la carte: lunch $6.50-$9, dinner $9.75-$13.50. Sun brunch $6.50-$9.50. Specialties: polenta crusted chicken breast, fettucine with sun- dried tomatoes and grilled chicken. Contemporary decor. Totally nonsmoking. Cr cds: A, D, MC, V.

D

★ ★ ★ ★ **THE DINING ROOM.** *(See The Ritz-Carlton, San Francisco Hotel) 415/296-7465.* Replete with antiques, crystal chandeliers and 18th-century oils, the atmospherically lit, flower-bedecked Dining Room offers menus by the number of courses ordered. Specializes in French, Mediterranean cuisine. Hrs: 6-10 pm. Closed Sun. Res accepted. Bar. Wine cellar. Prix fixe: dinner $59-$73. Child's meals. Entertainment. Valet parking. Totally nonsmoking. Cr cds: A, C, D, DS, ER, JCB, MC, V.

D

★ **EL TOREADOR.** *50 W Portal (94127), south of Union Square. 415/566-8104.* Hrs: 11 am-9 pm; Fri, Sat to 10 pm. Closed Mon; Easter, Dec 25. No A/C. Mexican menu. Wine, beer. Semi-a la carte: lunch, dinner $7.25-$12.95. Child's meals. Specialties: mole poblano, mole de cacahuate, el pipian de pollo. Eclectic, brightly colored decor. Totally nonsmoking. Cr cds: A, MC, V.

D SC

✔★ ★ **ELEVEN.** *374 11th St, at Harrison St, in Civic Center area. 415/431-3337.* Web www.sfstation.com/live/eleven.htm. Hrs: 11 am-5 pm, 5:30-11 pm; Fri & Sat to midnight. Closed Sun; major hols. Res accepted. Italian menu. Bar. A la carte entrees: lunch $6-$7, dinner $10-$19. Specializes in pasta, pizza, fresh seafood. Live Jazz from 7 pm. Rustic Italian courtyard atmosphere; faux stone walls, trompe l'oeil grapevines, antique wrought-iron gates. Cr cds: A, D, MC, V.

D

✔★ **ELIZA'S.** *1457 18th St (94107), south of Union Square. 415/648-9999.* Hrs: 11 am-3 pm, 5-10 pm; Sat 11 am-10 pm; Sun noon-10 pm. Closed Thanksgiving, Dec 25. Res accepted. Chinese menu. Bar. Semi-a la carte: dinner $5.25-$10.15. Specialties: lotus root with prawns, Mongolian beef, Hunan salmon. Modern Chinese decor. Cr cds: MC, V.

D

★ ★ ★ **EMPRESS OF CHINA.** *838 Grant Ave, Top floor of China Trade Center Bldg, in Chinatown. 415/434-1345.* Hrs: 11:30 am-3 pm, 5-11 pm. Chinese menu. Res accepted. Bar. A la carte entrees: lunch $7.50-$10.50, dinner $12.50-$29. Complete meals (for 2 or more persons): lunch $9.50-$16.95, dinner $16.95-$33.95. Specialties: regional delicacies of China. Oriental decor; ancient art objects. View of city, Telegraph Hill. Jacket (dinner). Cr cds: A, D, JCB, MC, V.

D

✔★ **ENRICO'S SIDEWALK CAFE.** *504 Broadway (94133), in North Beach. 415/982-6223.* Hrs: noon-11 pm; Fri, Sat to midnight. Closed Jan 1, Dec 25. Res accepted. No A/C. Mediterranean menu. Bar. A la carte entrees: lunch $8-$10, dinner $8-$15. Live jazz. Outdoor dining. Bistro with glass wall, large terrace. Local artwork. Cr cds: A, MC, V.

D

★ ★ **EOS.** *901 Cole St (94117), in Haight-Ashbury. 415/566-3063.* Hrs: 5:30-11 pm; Sun from 5 pm. Closed major hols. Res accepted. No A/C. Eclectic, Asian menu. Bar. Semi-a la carte: dinner $14.95-$27.95. Specialties: shiitake mushroom dumplings, tea-smoked Peking duck breast. Street parking. Corner cafe. Cr cds: A, MC, V.

D

★ ★ **FAZ.** *161 Sutter St, in Financial District. 415/362-0404.* Hrs: 11:30 am-3 pm, 5-10 pm. Closed Sat, Sun; most major hols. Res accepted. Italian, Mediterranean menu. Bar. A la carte entrees: lunch, dinner $8.95-$19.95. Specializes in fresh pasta. Jazz Mon-Fri 5-9 pm. Outdoor dining. Elegant fine dining. Cr cds: A, C, D, MC, V.

D

✔★ **FIGARO.** *414 Columbus Ave, in North Beach. 415/398-1300.* Hrs: 10 am-midnight. Closed Dec 25. Res accepted. Italian menu. Bar. A la carte entrees: bkfst $4.50-$8.25, lunch, dinner $5.25-$15. Specializes in pizza, pasta, oversize salads. Outdoor dining. Murals on ceiling. Cr cds: A, MC, V.

★ ★ **FINO.** *1 Cosmo Place (94109), south of Union Square. 415/928-2080.* Web www.jocedevivre.com. Hrs: 5:30-10 pm. Closed major hols. Res accepted. Italian menu. Bar. Semi-a la carte: dinner $8.95-$16.95. Specializes in fresh seafood, fresh pasta. Descending staircase leads to dining area; marble fireplace. Totally nonsmoking. Cr cds: A, D, MC, V.

★ ★ **FIOR D'ITALIA.** *601 Union St, in North Beach. 415/986-1886.* Web www.Fior.com. Hrs: 11:30 am-10:30 pm. Res accepted. Northern Italian menu. Bar. A la carte entrees: lunch, dinner $11-$22. Specializes in veal, risotto, homemade pasta. Valet parking. On Washington Square Park; Tony Bennett memorabilia. Family-owned. Totally nonsmoking. Cr cds: A, C, D, DS, JCB, MC, V.

D

★ **FIREFLY.** *4288 24th St (94114), in Mission District. 415/821-7652.* Hrs: 5:30-9:30 pm; Fri, Sat to 10 pm. Res accepted. Contemporary menu. Bar. Semi-a la carte: dinner $11.50-$16. Specializes in seafood, organic produce and meats. Contemporary decor. Totally nonsmoking. Cr cds: A, MC, V.

D

★ ★ ★ ★ **FLEUR DE LYS.** *777 Sutter St (94109), north of Union Square. 415/673-7779.* This intimate French provincial dining room has an unusual tapestry ceiling. French menu. Specialties: salmon baked in tender corn pancake topped with caviar, oven-roasted rack of lamb in black olive juice, chocolate creme brulée. Hrs: 6-10 pm; Fri, Sat 5:30-10:30 pm. Closed Sun; some major hols. Res required. Bar. Wine list. A la carte entrees: dinner $30-$35. Prix fixe: dinner $68, vegetarian $55. Valet parking. Jacket. Totally nonsmoking. Cr cds: A, C, D, MC, V.

D

★ **FLOWER LOUNGE.** *5322 Geary Blvd (94121), at 17th Ave, in Richmond District. 415/668-8998.* Hrs: 11 am-2:30 pm, 5-9:30 pm; Sat, Sun from 10 am. Res accepted. Chinese menu. Bar. A la carte entrees: lunch $8-$10, dinner $15-$25. Complete meals: dinner (for 4) $88. Oriental decor. Cr cds: A, D, MC, V.

D

★ ★ **THE FLY TRAP.** *606 Folsom St (94107), between 2nd & 3rd, south of Union Square. 415/243-0580.* Hrs: 11:30 am-10 pm; Fri to 10:30 pm; Sat, Sun 5:30-10:30 pm. Closed major hols. Res accepted. No A/C. Continental menu. Bar. A la carte entrees: lunch, dinner $8-$18. Specialties: chicken coq au vin, oysters Rockefeller, celery Victor. Own pasta, desserts. Jazz Sun. Valet parking. Courtyard entrance; named after 1898 restaurant. Totally nonsmoking. Cr cds: A, D, MC, V.

D

★ ★ **FOG CITY DINER.** *1300 Battery St (94111), in Financial District. 415/982-2000.* E-mail 103422.3235@compuserve.com. Hrs: 11:30 am-11 pm; Fri & Sat to midnight. Closed Thanksgiving, Dec 25. Res accepted. No A/C. Bar. A la carte entrees: lunch, dinner $9-$20. Specializes in cocktails, seafood. Oyster bar. Railroad dining car atmosphere. Cr cds: C, D, DS, MC, V.

D

✔★ **FOUNTAIN COURT.** *354 Clement St (94118), in Richmond District. 415/668-1100.* Hrs: 11 am-3 pm, 5-10 pm. Closed Thanksgiving. Res accepted. Chinese menu. Wine, beer. A la carte entrees: lunch $4-$4.50, dinner $5.50-$9.50. Specializes in Shanghai cuisine, braised catfish, vegetarian chicken. Modern decor. Cr cds: A, D, MC, V.

D

★ ★ ★ **FOURNOU'S OVENS.** *(See Renaissance Stanford Court Hotel) 415/989-1910.* Web www.renaissancehotels.com. Hrs: 6:30 am-2:30 pm, 5:30-10 pm; Fri & Sat to 10:30 pm; Sun brunch 10 am-2:30 pm. Res accepted; required hols. Mediterranean cuisine. Bar. Extensive wine cellar. A la carte entrees: bkfst, lunch $7.50-$13.50, dinner $9-$28. Table d'hôte: dinner $25-$45. Sun brunch $12-$18.50. Child's meals. Specializes in rack of lamb, farm-raised meats, nightly poultry, fish selections. Own pasta. Valet parking. Cr cds: A, C, D, DS, JCB, MC, V.

D

★ ★ ★ **FRANCISCAN.** *Pier 43½ (94113), at Fisherman's Wharf. 415/362-7733.* Hrs: 11 am-10 pm; Fri & Sat to 10:30 pm. Closed Thanksgiving, Dec 25. Res accepted. Bar. A la carte entrees: lunch, dinner $6.95-$35. Child's meals. Specializes in California contemporary cuisine. Own desserts. View of bay, city, Alcatraz, Golden Gate Bridge. Cr cds: A, C, D, MC, V.

D

★ **FRASCATI.** *1901 Hyde St, in Russian Hill. 415/928-1406.* Hrs: 5:30-10 pm; Fri, Sat to 10:30 pm. Closed Mon; Dec 25. Res accepted. No A/C. Contemporary American menu. Wine list. A la carte entrees: dinner $12-$15. Monthly menus of new American cuisine. Valet. Outdoor dining. Storefront location; bistro atmosphere. Cr cds: MC, V.

★ ★ ★ **FRENCH ROOM.** *(See The Clift Hotel) 415/775-4700.* Hrs: 6:30-10:30 am, 5:30-10 pm; Mon to 10:30 am; Sat, Sun 7-11 am, 5:30-10 pm; Sun brunch 10 am-2 pm. Res accepted. California continental menu. Bar. Wine list. A la carte entrees: bkfst $9-$17, dinner $19-$34. Prix fixe: 5-course dinner $65. Sun brunch $40. Child's meals. Specializes in beef, veal, lamb, fresh seafood specials. Pianist. Valet parking. Classic decor. Jacket. Cr cds: A, C, D, DS, ER, JCB, MC, V.

D

✔★ ★ ★ **FRINGALE.** *570 Fourth St, south of Union Square. 415/543-0573.* E-mail beastro@aol.com. Hrs: 11:30 am-3 pm, 5:30-10:30 pm; Sat from 5:30 pm. Closed Sun; some major hols. Res accepted. No A/C. French menu. Bar. A la carte entrees: lunch $7.50-$14, dinner $11-$17. Upscale bistro fare. Atmosphere of European country cafe. Totally nonsmoking. Cr cds: A, MC, V.

D

★ ★ **GABBIANOS.** *1 Ferry Plaza (94111), at foot of Market St, in Financial District. 415/391-8403.* E-mail gabbiano@hooked.net; web www.hooked.net/~gabbiano. Hrs: 11 am-10 pm; Sun brunch 10:30 am-2 pm. Res accepted. Italian, Amer menu. Bar. A la carte entrees: lunch $7.50-$15.25, dinner $9.75-$19.50. Sun brunch $21.95. Specializes in fresh seafood, pasta. Valet parking. Patio dining. Waterfront with views of Alcatraz, Oakland and Mt Tamalpais. Cr cds: A, C, D, DS, JCB, MC, V.

D

★ ★ ★ **GARDEN COURT.** *(See Palace Hotel) 415/546-5011.* Web www.sheraton.com. Hrs: 6:30 am-2 pm, 6-10 pm; Sun 6:30-10 am, 11:30 am-3:30 pm; Mon to 2 pm. Res accepted. French, Amer menu. Bar. Semi-a la carte: bkfst $9.25-$17.75, lunch $12.50-$18.25, dinner $18-$28. Complete meals: lunch $15, dinner $39. Entertainment Fri. Formal decor. Totally nonsmoking. Cr cds: A, C, D, DS, JCB, MC, V.

D

★ ★ **GAYLORD INDIA.** *900 North Point St (94109), in Ghirardelli Square, at Fisherman's Wharf. 415/771-8822.* Web www.gaylords.com. Hrs: 11:45 am-1:45 pm, 5-10:45 pm; Sun brunch noon-2:45 pm. Closed Thanksgiving, Dec 25. Res accepted. Indian menu. Bar. Semi-a la carte: lunch $9.75-$13.25, dinner $9.95-$21. Complete meals: dinner $22.70-$28.75. Specializes in tandoori dishes, Indian desserts. Parking. View of bay. Totally nonsmoking. Cr cds: A, C, D, DS, JCB, MC, V.

★ ★ **GOLDEN TURTLE.** *2211 Van Ness Ave (94109), at Broadway, in Russian Hill. 415/441-4419.* Hrs: 5-10:30 pm. Closed Mon. Res accepted. Vietnamese menu. Wine, beer. A la carte entrees: dinner $8.95-$18.95. Specialties: imperial beef, spicy calamari sauté, chili chicken, lemon-grass beef & pork, pan-fried Dungeness crab. Carved wooden panels depict scenes of Vietnamese culture. Cr cds: A, D, MC, V.

D

★ ★ **GRAND CAFE.** *(See Monaco Hotel) 415/292-0100.* Hrs: 7 am-10:30 pm; wkends to 11:30 pm; Sat, Sun brunch 9 am-2 pm. Closed July 4, Thanksgiving, Dec 25. Res accepted. Continental menu. Bar 11:30-1:30 am. A la carte entrees: bkfst $7.95-$9.95, lunch $8.95-$16.50, dinner $11.95-$22.95. Sat, Sun brunch $7.95-$12.95. Specializes in pasta, chicken, beef. Valet parking. Chandeliers and bronze sculpture add elegance to this hotel dining rm. Totally nonsmoking. Cr cds: A, C, D, DS, ER, JCB, MC, V.

D

✔★ ★ **GREENS.** *Building A at Fort Mason (94123), in Marina District. 415/771-6222.* Hrs: 11:30 am-2 pm, 5:30-9:30 pm; Mon from 5:30 pm; Sat 11:30 am-2:30 pm, 6-9:30 pm; Sun brunch 10 am-2 pm; Wed-Sat 9:30-11 pm (dessert only). Closed most major hols. Res accepted. Vegetarian menu. Wine, beer. A la carte entrees: lunch $7-$12, dinner $10-$14. Prix fixe: dinner (Sat) $38. Sun brunch $7-$11. Parking. View of bay. Totally nonsmoking. Cr cds: DS, MC, V.

D

★ ★ **HARBOR VILLAGE.** *4 Embarcadero Center (94111), in Financial District. 415/781-8833.* Hrs: 11 am-2:30 pm, 5:30-9:30 pm; Sat from 10:30 am; Sun, hols from 10 am. Res accepted. Chinese menu. Bar. Wine list. A la carte entrees: lunch $2.50-$26, dinner $10-$26. Specializes in Hong Kong-style seafood. Parking. Formal Chinese decor. Cr cds: A, C, D, JCB, MC, V.

D

★ ★ **HARRIS'.** *2100 Van Ness Ave (94109), in Pacific Heights. 415/673-1888.* Hrs: from 6 pm; Sat, Sun from 5 pm. Closed Jan 1, Dec 25. Res accepted. A la carte entrees: dinner $17.95-$54. Specializes in beef, fresh seafood, Maine lobster. Jazz Thur-Sat. Valet parking. Cr cds: A, D, DS, JCB, MC, V.

D

★ ★ **HARRY DENTON'S.** *161 Steuart St (94105), in Financial District. 415/882-1333.* Hrs: 7-10 am, 11:30 am-2:30 pm, 5:30-10 pm. Sat, Sun brunch 8 am-3 pm. Cover charge Wed-Sat $3-$10. Closed most major hols. Res accepted. Bar. A la carte entrees: bkfst $2.75-$9, lunch $7.25-$15.95, dinner $7.95-$25. Sat, Sun brunch $5.75-$10.95. Specializes in steaks, chops, fresh seafood, pasta. Entertainment. Valet parking (dinner). Jazz club atmosphere. Cr cds: A, C, D, DS, MC, V.

D

★★★ **HAWTHORNE LANE.** *22 Hawthorne St (94105), south of Union Square. 415/777-9779.* Web www.hawthornelane.com. Hrs: 11:30 am-2 pm, 5:30-10 pm; Fri, Sat to 10:30 pm. Closed some major hols. Res accepted. Continental menu. Bar to midnight. A la carte entrees: lunch $8.50-$14, dinner $16-$24. Child's meals. Specialties: Dungeness crab and sweet pea soup, tempura-fried lobster salad, glazed quail. Valet parking. Modern decor. Cr cds: C, D, DS, JCB, MC, V.

D

★★ **HAYES STREET GRILL.** *320 Hayes St (94102), in Civic Center area. 415/863-5545.* Hrs: 11:30 am-2 pm, 5-9 pm; Fri to 10:30 pm; Sat 5:30-10:30 pm; Sun 5-8:30 pm. Closed major hols. Res accepted. Bar. A la carte entrees: lunch $9.50-$17, dinner $13-$25. Specializes in fresh seafood, salads, charcoal-grilled fish. Cr cds: A, D, DS, MC, V.

D

✔★★ **HELMAND.** *430 Broadway (94133), in North Beach. 415/362-0641.* Hrs: 5:30-10 pm; Fri, Sat to 11 pm. Res accepted. Afghanistan menu. Wine, beer. Semi-a la carte: dinner $8.95-$14.95. Specialties: seekh kabab, mantwo, rack of lamb. Paintings and photos of Afghani scenes. Cr cds: A, MC, V.

D

✔★★ **THE HOUSE.** *1230 Grant Ave (94133), in North Beach. 415/986-8612.* Hrs: 11:30 am-3 pm, 5:30-10 pm; Sat from 5:30 pm. Closed Sun, Mon. Continental menu. Wine, beer. Semi-a la carte: lunch $5.95-$12.95, dinner $8.95-$15.95. Specializes in fish, rack of lamb, chicken. Contemporary decor. Totally nonsmoking. Cr cds: A, MC, V.

★★ **HOUSE OF PRIME RIB.** *1906 Van Ness Ave, at Washington St, in Russian Hill. 415/885-4605.* Hrs: 5:30-10 pm; Fri, Sat from 4:30 pm; Sun from 4 pm; hols vary. Res accepted. Bar. Wine list. A la carte entrees: dinner $19.65. Semi-a la carte: dinner $19.75-$23.95. Child's meals. Specializes in corn-fed, 21-day aged prime rib of beef, seafood. Prime rib carved at table. Valet parking. English decor. Cr cds: A, D, MC, V.

D

✔★ **HUNAN.** *924 Sansome St, in Financial District. 415/956-7727.* Hrs: 11:30 am-9:30 pm. Closed July 4, Thanksgiving, Dec 25. Res accepted. No A/C. Hunan menu. Bar. A la carte entrees: lunch, dinner $5-$9.95. Specializes in smoked Hunan dishes. Chinese decor. Cr cds: A, C, D, DS, JCB, MC, V.

D

★★ **I FRATELLI.** *1896 Hyde St, at Green, in Russian Hill. 415/474-8603.* Hrs: 5:30-10 pm. Closed major hols. Italian menu. Bar. A la carte entrees: dinner $9-$15. Child's meals. Specializes in homemade pasta. Cafe atmosphere; photos of Italian street scenes. Cr cds: A, MC, V.

D

✔★ **INFUSION.** *555 Second St (94107), south of Union Square. 415/543-2282.* E-mail infusn@aol.com; web www.citysearch.com/sfo/infusion. Hrs: 11:30-2 am; Sat, Sun from 5 pm. Closed most major hols. Res accepted. No A/C. Bar. Semi-a la carte: lunch $5-$13, dinner $10-$18. Specialties: peppered filet mignon, fresh fruit-infused vodkas. Musicians Thurs-Sat. Street parking. Modern lighting, artwork. Totaly nonsmoking. Cr cds: A, D, MC, V.

D

★ **JASMINE HOUSE.** *2301 Clement St (94121), in Richmond District. 415/668-3382.* Hrs: 11 am-10 pm; Mon from 5 pm; Fri, Sat to 11 pm. Res accepted. Vietnamese menu. Wine, beer. Semi-a la carte: lunch $3.95-$6.50, dinner $5.95-$23.95. Specializes in seafood, beef, chicken. Casual decor. Totally nonsmoking. Cr cds: MC, V.

D

★★ **JULIE RING'S HEART & SOUL.** *1695 Polk St (94109), in Russian Hill. 415/673-7100.* E-mail sfswing@aol.com. Hrs: 5 pm-2 am. Closed Sun, Mon; also Easter, Thanksgiving, Dec 25. Res accepted. Bar. A la carte entrees: dinner $10-$15. Specializes in grilled seafood, roast pork chops. Entertainment. Contemporary decor. Cr cds: A, MC, V.

D

★★ **JULIUS CASTLE.** *1541 Montgomery St, on Telegraph Hill, in North Beach. 415/362-3042.* E-mail jcastle@ix.netcom.com. Hrs: 5-10 pm. Res accepted. No A/C. Italian menu. Bar. A la carte entrees: dinner $20-$30. Specializes in veal, rack of lamb, seafood. Own pastries, pasta, ice cream. Valet parking. Turreted castle overlooking San Francisco Bay. Historic landmark (1922). Totally nonsmoking. Cr cds: A, C, D, DS, MC, V.

★ **KABUTO SUSHI.** *5116 Geary Blvd (94118), in Richmond District. 415/752-5652.* Hrs: 5:30-11 pm. Closed Sun, Mon; some major hols. Res accepted. Japanese menu. Semi-a la carte: dinner $9-$18. Specializes in sushi. Street parking. Fish tanks. Cr cds: MC, V.

★ **KATIA'S.** *600 5th Ave (94118), in Richmond District. 415/668-9292.* Web www.citysearch.com/sfo/katias. Hrs: 11:30 am-2:30 pm, 5-9 pm; Fri, Sat to 10 pm; Sun from 5 pm. Closed Mon; most major hols. Res accepted. No A/C. Russian menu. Wine, beer. Semi-a la carte: lunch, dinner $6-$14. Child's meals. Specializes in Russian pastries. Accordianist, guitarist nightly. Intimate corner cafe. Totally nonsmoking. Cr cds: A, C, D, DS, JCB, MC, V.

D

★★ **KHAN TOKE THAI HOUSE.** *5937 Geary Blvd (94121), in Richmond District. 415/668-6654.* Hrs: 5-11 pm. Closed Labor Day, Thanksgiving, Dec 25. Res accepted. Thai menu. Wine, beer. A la carte entrees: dinner $4.95-$10.95. Complete meal: dinner $16.95. Specialties: pong pang (seafood), choo chee goong (prawn in coconut milk curry). Thai classical dancing performance Sun (8:30 pm). Thai decor and furnishings. Family-owned. Totally nonsmoking. Cr cds: MC, V.

D

★★ **KULETO'S.** *221 Powell St (94102), south of Union Square. 415/397-7720.* E-mail kuletos96@aol.com. Hrs: 7-10:30 am, 11:30 am-11 pm; Sat, Sun from 8 am. Closed Labor Day, Thanksgiving, Dec 25. Res accepted. Northern Italian menu. Bar 11 am-midnight. Complete meals: bkfst $4.50-$8.95. A la carte entrees: lunch, dinner $8.25-$17.50. Specializes in grilled fish, chicken, pasta. Italian decor. Cr cds: A, C, D, DS, ER, JCB, MC, V.

D

★ **LA VIE.** *5830 Geary Blvd (94121), in Richmond District. 415/668-8080.* Hrs: 11 am-10 pm; Fri, Sat to 10:30 pm. Res accepted. Vietnamese menu. Wine, beer. A la carte entrees: lunch $4.65-$5.25, dinner $5.25-$9.95. Street parking. Family-style dining. Totally nonsmoking. Cr cds: MC, V.

★ **LAGHI.** *1801 Clement St (94121), in Richmond District. 415/386-6266.* Hrs: 5-9:30 pm. Closed Mon; most major hols. Res accepted. Northern Italian menu. Bar. A la carte entrees: dinner $10.75-$19.50. Specializes in pasta. Own baking, pasta. Street parking. Totally nonsmoking. Cr cds: MC, V.

D

★★ **LEHR BROTHERS BISTRO AND GRILL.** *(See Best Western Canterbury Motor Hotel) 415/474-6478.* Hrs: 6:30 am-10:30 pm. Res accepted. Bar. Semi-a la carte: bkfst $8.95, lunch $7.50-$13.95, dinner $13.95-$29.95. Child's meals. Specializes in steak. Jazz, swing dancing Wed-Sat. Garage parking. Outdoor dining. Tropical decor. Totally nonsmoking. Family-owned. Cr cds: A, C, D, DS, JCB, MC, V.

D SC

✔★ **LHASA MOON.** *2420 Lombard St (94123), in Marina District. 415/674-9898.* Hrs: 5-10 pm; Thurs 11:30 am-2:30 pm, 5-10 pm; Fri, Sat to 10:30 pm; Sun 4:30-9:30 pm. Closed Mon; Dec 25. Tibetan menu.

Bar. Semi-a la carte: lunch, dinner $7.50-$12.50. Specializes in curries, steamed pie. Tibetan decor. Totally nonsmoking. Cr cds: A, MC, V.

D

★ ★ **LOLLI'S CASTAGNOLA.** *286 Jefferson St, at Fisherman's Wharf. 415/776-5015.* Hrs: 9 am-11 pm. Closed Dec 25. Bar. Semi-a la carte: bkfst $3.95-$9.95, lunch, dinner $7-$26.45. Child's meals. Specializes in seafood. Valet parking. Outdoor dining. View of fishing fleet. Cr cds: A, C, D, DS, JCB, MC, V.

D

★ ★ **LULU.** *816 Folsom St (94107), south of Union Square. 415/495-5775.* Web www.citysearch.com/sfo/lulu. Hrs: 11:30 am-2:30 pm, 5:30-10:30 pm; Fri, Sat to 11:30 pm. Res accepted. French, Italian menu. Bar. Semi-a la carte: lunch $6:50-$14, dinner $9-$16. Cr cds: A, D, MC, V.

D

★ ★ **M. POINT.** *(See Hotel Milano) 415/543-7600.* Hrs: 7-10:30 am, 11:30 am-2:30 pm, 5-10 pm; Sun brunch 9 am-2 pm. Res accepted. Continental menu. Bar. A la carte entrees: bkfst $5.50-$7.50, lunch $11.25-$13.50, dinner $18-$26. Sun brunch $6-$13.50. Specializes in sushi. Valet parking. Mural stretching full length of restaurant. Totally nonsmoking. Cr cds: A, DS, JCB, MC, V.

D

★ ★ **MAC ARTHUR PARK.** *607 Front St (94111), in Financial District. 415/398-5700.* Hrs: 11:30 am-3:30 pm, 5-10 pm; Fri to 11 pm; Sat 5-11 pm; Sun 4:30-10 pm. Closed Thanksgiving, Dec 25. Res accepted. Bar. A la carte entrees: lunch, dinner $7.95-$18.95. Specializes in barbecued ribs, mesquite-grilled fish. Valet parking. Outdoor dining. Cr cds: A, C, D, MC, V.

D

★ ★ **MANDARIN.** *900 North Point St (94109), in Ghirardelli Square, at Fisherman's Wharf. 415/673-8812.* Web www.themandarin .com. Hrs: 11:30 am-11 pm. Closed Thanksgiving, Dec 25. Res accepted. Northern Chinese, mandarin menu. Bar. Semi-a la carte: lunch $8.95-$13, dinner $13-$35. Complete meals: dinner $16-$38. Mandarin banquet for 8 or more, $25-$58 each. Specialties: minced squab, beggar's chicken (1-day notice), Peking duck (1-day notice). Parking. Chinese decor; beautifully tiled floor, artifacts. 19th-century structure. View of bay. Cr cds: A, C, D, DS, JCB, MC, V.

D

★ ★ **MARRAKECH MOROCCAN.** *419 O'Farrell St (94102), south of Union Square. 415/776-6717.* Hrs: 6-10 pm. Res accepted. Moroccan menu. Bar. Prix fixe: dinner $22.95-$27.95. Specialties: chicken with lemon, lamb with honey, couscous fassi, b'stila. Belly dancing. Valet parking. Seating on floor pillows or low couches. Moroccan decor. Cr cds: A, D, DS, MC, V.

★ ★ ★ ★ **MASA'S.** *(See Vintage Court Hotel) 415/989-7154.* The artistry of the presentation is as important as the cuisine in this understated, elegant, flower-filled dining spot. French menu. Specialties: foie gras sauté with Madeira truffle sauce, lobster salad with crispy leeks and truffle vinaigrette, sauteéd medallions of New Zealand venison. Hrs: 6-9:30 pm. Closed Sun, Mon; also 2 wks in Jan & 1 wk in July. Res accepted. Bar. Wine cellar. Prix fixe: dinner $70 & $75. Valet parking. Cr cds: A, C, D, DS, JCB, MC, V.

D

✔ ★ ★ **MATTERHORN SWISS.** *2323 Van Ness (94109), in Russian Hill. 415/885-6116.* E-mail mathorn@aol.com. Hrs: 5-10 pm. Closed Mon. Res accepted. Swiss menu. Bar. Semi-a la carte: dinner $12-$21. Specialties: fondue, wienerschnitzel, veal cordon bleu. Valet parking. Casual dining; hand-carved woodwork. Cr cds: A, C, D, DS, MC, V.

D

★ ★ **McCORMICK & KULETO'S.** *900 North Point St (94109), on Ghirardelli Square, in Fisherman's Wharf. 415/929-1730.* Hrs: 11:30 am-11 pm; Sun from 10:30 am. Res accepted. Bar. A la carte entrees: lunch, dinner $5-$20. Child's meals. Specializes in fresh seafood. Parking. Crab Cake Lounge has open kitchen. View of bay. Cr cds: A, D, DS, JCB, MC, V.

D

★ ★ **MECCA.** *2029 Market St (94114), in Mission District. 415/621-7000.* Web www.sfmecca.com. Hrs: 6-11 pm; Thurs-Sat to midnight. Closed Thanksgiving, Dec 25. Res accepted; required Fri, Sat. Mediterranean, Amer menu. Bar. Semi-a la carte: dinner $9.75-$19.50. Own baking. Jazz Sun-Thurs. Valet parking. Ultra-modern ambience. Totally nonsmoking. Cr cds: A, D, MC, V.

D

✔ ★ ★ **THE MEETING HOUSE.** *1701 Octavia St (94109), in Pacific Heights. 415/922-6733.* Web www.citysearch.com. Hrs: 5:30-9:30 pm. Closed Mon, Tues; July 4, Dec 25. Res accepted. Wine, beer. A la carte entree: dinner $13-$19. Specialties: hominy crusted catfish, rock shrimp and scallion johnnycakes. Totally nonsmoking. Cr cds: A, MC, V.

★ ★ **MILLENNIUM.** *(See Abigail Hotel) 415/487-9800.* E-mail millennm@earthlink.net; web www.citysearch.com/sfo/millenium. Hrs: 5-9:30 pm. Closed Dec 25. Res accepted. Organic vegetarian/vegan menu. Wine, beer. A la carte entrees: dinner $10-$16. Child's meals. Specialties: low fat, no cholesterol entrees, plantain torte, Moroccan treasure chest. Relaxing decor and ambiance. Staff nutritionist. Totally nonsmoking. Cr cds: MC, V.

D ♥

★ ★ ★ **MOOSE'S.** *1652 Stockton St, between Union & Filbert Sts, in North Beach. 415/989-7800.* E-mail Dolly@mooses.com. Hrs: 11:30 am-2:30 pm, 5:30-10 pm; Mon from 5:30 pm; Fri & Sat to 11 pm; Sun brunch 9:30 am-2:30 pm. Closed some major hols. Res accepted. Bar. Wine cellar. A la carte entrees: lunch $4.75-$13.75, dinner $4.75-$24. Sun brunch $2.95-$12.95. Child's meals. Jazz evenings. Valet parking. Exhibition kitchen. Dining rm accented with terrazzo tile and ceramics; expansive views of Washington Square Park. Large bronze "moose" near entry. Cr cds: A, D, MC, V.

D

★ ★ **MORTON'S OF CHICAGO.** *400 Post St (94102), in Union Square. 415/986-5830.* Hrs: 5-11 pm; Sun to 10 pm. Closed most major hols. Res accepted. Bar. A la carte entrees: dinner $19.95-$29.95. Specializes in steak. Club atmosphere. Totally nonsmoking. Cr cds: A, C, D, JCB, MC, V.

D

★ **MOXIE.** *2742 17th St (94110), south of Union Square. 415/863-4177.* Hrs: 11:30 am-2:30 pm, 6-10 pm; Fri to midnight; Sat 10 am-3 pm, 6 pm-midnight; Sun 10 am-3 pm, 6-10 pm. Closed Mon; Dec 25. Res accepted (dinner). Eastern European, Mediterranean menu. Bar. A la carte entrees: bkfst $5-$9, lunch $5.50-$8, dinner $10.25-$15.50. Specialties: pan-roasted halibut, beef brisket. Street parking. Totally nonsmoking. Cr cds: MC, V.

D

★ ★ **NEW JOE'S.** *347 Geary St (94102), west of Union Square. 415/397-9999.* Hrs: 7 am-11 pm. Res accepted. Contemporary Italian menu. Bar. A la carte entrees: bkfst $5-$8.75, lunch $6-$14, dinner $9-$16. Child's meals. Specialties: linguine Portofino, chicken Luciano, pizza margharita. Mahogany paneling and moldings. Mural of city. Cr cds: A, C, D, DS, JCB, MC, V.

D

★ ★ ★ **NOB HILL.** *(See Mark Hopkins Inter-Continental Hotel) 415/616-6944.* Hrs: 11:30 am-11 pm. Res accepted. Bar. A la carte entrees: lunch $7.50-$19, dinner $18-$26.50. Child's meals. Specialties: steamed or grilled salmon, sautéed duck foie gras, grilled lamb. Pianist. Valet parking. Contemporary garden atrium w/leaded glass domed ceiling. Cr cds: A, C, D, DS, ER, JCB, MC, V.

D ♥

★ ★ ★ **NORTH BEACH.** *1512 Stockton St, at Columbus, in North Beach. 415/392-1700.* Hrs: 11:30-1 am. Closed some major hols. Res accepted. Northern Italian menu. Wine cellar. A la carte entrees: lunch $8.50-$24, dinner $11.75-$19.75. Complete meals: lunch, dinner from $22.95. Specializes in fresh fish, veal, pasta. Valet parking. Cr cds: A, C, D, DS, JCB, MC, V.

D

★ ★ **NORTH INDIA.** *3131 Webster St, at Lombard St, in Marina District. 415/931-1556.* Web www.citysearch7.com. Hrs: 11:30 am-2:30 pm, 5-10:30 pm; Sat from 5 pm; Sun 5-10 pm. Res accepted. Northern Indian menu. Bar. Semi-a la carte: lunch $7.95-$11.95, dinner $12.95-$24.50. Prix fixe: $12.95. Child's meals. Specializes in tandoori seafood, lamb, poultry, fresh vegetables. Own desserts. Paintings of Moghul and Bengal lancers. Kitchen tours. Cr cds: A, C, D, DS, MC, V.

D

✔★ ★ **O'REILLY'S.** *622 Green St (94133), in North Beach. 415/989-6222.* Hrs: 11-2 am; Sat, Sun from 10 am. Res accepted. Irish menu. Bar. Semi-a la carte: lunch, dinner $5.95-$14. Specializes in corned beef & cabbage, cottage pie. Outdoor dining. Photos and memorabilia from Ireland. Cr cds: MC, V.

D

★ ★ **ORITALIA.** *1915 Fillmore (94115), in Pacific Heights. 415/346-1333.* Hrs: 5-10 pm; Fri, Sat to 11 pm. Closed Thanksgiving, Dec 25. Res accepted. Asian, European menu. Bar. A la carte entrees: dinner $8.75-$19. Specialties: grilled flat iron steak, sesame crusted ahi tuna. Open kitchen; modern art. Cr cds: A, D, MC, V.

D

★ ★ ★ **PACIFIC.** *(See Pan Pacific Hotel) 415/771-8600.* E-mail vulrich@sfo.pan-pacific.com; web www.panpac.com. Hrs: 6:30 am-10 pm; Sun brunch 11 am-2 pm. Res accepted. Bar 11 am-11:30 pm. Wine list. A la carte entrees: bkfst $5-$9.75, lunch $7.25-$12.50, dinner $17-$24. Sun brunch $10-$15. Child's meals. Specializes in Pacific Rim cuisine with French accent. Pianist. Valet parking. Modern decor; atrium setting in lobby of hotel. Cr cds: A, C, D, DS, JCB, MC, V.

D

★ ★ **PALIO D'ASTI.** *640 Sacramento St (94111), at Montgomery St, in Financial District. 415/395-9800.* Hrs: 11:30 am-2:30 pm. Closed Sat, Sun; major hols. Res accepted. Italian menu. Bar. A la carte entrees: lunch $15-$20. Specializes in risotto, seafood, mezzelune alla monferrina. Exhibition pasta-making and pizza-making kitchens; wood-burning ovens. Cr cds: A, C, D, DS, MC, V.

D

★ ★ **PANNE E VINO.** *3011 Steiner St (94123), in Cow Hollow. 415/346-2111.* Hrs: 11:30 am-2:30 pm, 5-10 pm; Fri, Sat to 10:30 pm. Closed major hols. Res accepted. Italian menu. A la carte entrees: lunch, dinner $7.50-$19.95. Specialties: osso buco, branzino. Italian decor. Totally nonsmoking. Cr cds: A, MC, V.

D

★ ★ **PARK GRILL.** *(See Park Hyatt Hotel) 415/296-2933.* Hrs: 6:30 am-9:30 pm; Sun brunch 10 am-2:30 pm. Res accepted. Bar 11 am-9:30 pm. Wine list. A la carte entrees: bkfst $9.75-$17.50, lunch $9.75-$19, dinner $17-$23. Sun brunch $22.50. Child's meals. Specializes in mixed grills. Own baking. Pianist. Valet parking. Outdoor dining. Club rm atmosphere; original art. Cr cds: A, C, D, DS, ER, JCB, MC, V.

D

★ ★ **PASTIS.** *1015 Battery St (94111), in Financial District. 415/391-2555.* Hrs: 11:30 am-3 pm, 5:30-10:30 pm. Closed Sun; most major hols. Res accepted. French menu. Bar. A la carte entrees: lunch $5-$12, dinner $5-$17. Specialties: oxtail rouelle with gribiche, filet of salmon provençale, warm banana and chocolate pannequet. Street parking. Outdoor dining. Original artwork. Cr cds: A, MC, V.

★ **PERRY'S DOWNTOWN.** *185 Sutter St (94104), in Financial District. 415/989-6895.* Hrs: 11 am-9:30 pm. Closed Sun; major hols. Res accepted. Bar to midnight. A la carte entrees: lunch, dinner $5.50-$17.95. Specializes in lobster, pasta. Casual decor. Cr cds: A, D, DS, MC, V.

D

✔★ **PLOUF.** *40 Belden Pl (94104), in Financial District. 415/986-6491.* Hrs: 11:30 am-2:30 pm, 5:30-10 pm; Sat from 5:30 pm. Closed Sun; major hols. Res accepted. No A/C. French menu. Bar. Semi-a la carte: lunch $12-$15, dinner $12-$17. Specializes in seafood. Outdoor dining. Totally nonsmoking. Cr cds: A, D, MC, V.

D

✔★ ★ **PLUMPJACK CAFE.** *3127 Fillmore St (94123), in Marina District. 415/563-4755.* Hrs: 11:30 am-2 pm, 5:30-10 pm; Sat from 5:30 pm. Closed Sun; most major hols. Res accepted; required dinner. Extensive wine list. Semi-a la carte: lunch $8-$15, dinner $15-$20. Specializes in duck, vegetable dishes. Street parking. Henry VIII decor; intimate dining. Totally nonsmoking. Cr cds: A, MC, V.

D

★ ★ ★ ★ **POSTRIO.** *(See The Prescott Hotel) 415/776-7825.* Web postrio.com. Lighting is courtesy of custom Oriental fixtures and a skylight, but the cuisine is courtesy of Wolfgang Puck at this stunning multilevel dining area with open kitchen. California menu with Asian and Mediterranean influences. Specialties: Chinese duck, roasted salmon. Own baking. Hrs: 7-10 am, 11:30 am-2 pm, 5:30-10 pm; Sat, Sun from 5:30 pm; Sat, Sun brunch 9 am-2 pm. Closed July 4, Thanksgiving, Dec 25. Res required. Bar 11:30-2 am. Wine list. A la carte entrees: bkfst $5-$15, lunch $10-$15, dinner $20-$28. Sat, Sun brunch $6-$14. Valet parking. Totally nonsmoking. Cr cds: A, C, D, MC, V.

D

★ **THE POT STICKER.** *150 Waverly Place, in Chinatown. 415/397-9985.* Hrs: 10:30 am-10 pm. Res accepted. No A/C. Hunan/Mandarin/Sechuan menu. A la carte entrees: lunch, dinner $5.25-$18. Complete meals: lunch $4.50-$5, dinner $6.50-$9.95. Specialties: pot stickers, Szechwan crispy fish, orange spareribs. Cr cds: A, DS, MC, V.

★ ★ **PREGO RISTORANTE.** *2000 Union St (94123), in Cow Hollow. 415/563-3305.* Hrs: 11:30 am-midnight. Closed Thanksgiving, Dec 25. Res accepted. Northern Italian menu. Bar to midnight. A la carte entrees: lunch, dinner $6.95-$17.95. Specialties: carpaccio, agnolotti d'aragosta, pizza baked in wood-burning oven. Outside dining. Cr cds: A, D, MC, V.

D

✔★ ★ **PUCCINI & PINETTI.** *129 Ellis St (94102), south of Union Square. 415/392-5500.* Hrs: 11:30 am-10 pm; Fri, Sat to 11 pm; Sun 5-10 pm. Closed July 4, Thanksgiving, Dec 25. Res accepted. Italian menu. Bar. A la carte entrees: lunch $4.95-$10.95, dinner $6.95-$14.95. Specializes in spaghetti putanesca, wood-fired pizza. Open kitchen with wood burning oven. Totally nonsmoking. Cr cds: A, C, D, DS, MC, V.

D

✔★ ★ **RISTORANTE IDEALE.** *1309 Grant Ave (94133), in North Beach. 415/391-4129.* Hrs: 5:30-10:30 pm; Fri, Sat to 11 pm; Sun 5-10 pm. Closed Mon; Easter, Dec 25. Res accepted. Italian menu. Bar. Semi-a la carte: dinner $9-$17.50. Child's meals. Specialties: fettuccine alla Norcina, Saltimbocca alla Romana. Contemporary decor. Cr cds: DS, JCB, MC, V.

D

★ ★ **ROCCO'S SEAFOOD GRILL.** *2080 Van Ness Ave (94109), on Russian Hill. 415/567-7600.* Hrs: 5-10 pm; Fri, Sat to 11 pm. Closed Jan 1, Dec 25. Res accepted. Bar to midnight. A la carte entrees: dinner $13-$19.50. Child's meals. Specializes in seafood, oyster bar. Valet parking. Contemporary decor. Cr cds: A, C, D, DS, MC, V.

D

★ ★ ★ **ROSE PISTOLA.** *532 Columbus Ave (94133), in North Beach. 415/399-0499.* Hrs: 11:30 am-10:30 pm; Fri, Sat to 1 am. Closed July 4, Thanksgiving, Dec 25. Res accepted. Northern Italian menu. Bar. A la carte entrees: lunch, dinner $2.50-$17.50. Child's meals. Specialties:

cioppino, zucchini chips, gnocci. Entertainment. Outdoor dining. Contemporary decor. Totally nonsmoking. Cr cds: A, MC, V.

D

✔★ **ROSTI.** *2060 Chestnut St (94123), in Marina District. 415/929-9300.* Hrs: 11:30 am-10 pm; Sat, Sun to 10:30 pm. Closed Thanksgiving, Dec 25. Italian menu. Wine, beer. Semi-a la carte: lunch, dinner $4.50-$12.95. Child's meals. Specialties: pollo al mattone, rollati, tiramisu. Street parking. Imported Italian tile flooring; Tuscan decor. Totally nonsmoking. Cr cds: DS, MC, V.

D

★★ **ROTI.** *155 Stewart St (94105), in Hotel Griffon, in Financial District. 415/495-6500.* Web www.citysearch7.com. Hrs: 11:30 am-10 pm; Fri, Sat 5:30-11 pm. Closed Memorial Day, Labor Day, Dec 25. Res accepted. Bar. A la carte entrees: lunch, dinner $10.95-$23.95. Specialties: spit-roasted chicken, spit-roasted duck, fresh fish. Valet parking (dinner). Rustic atmosphere, American rotisserie grill. Totally nonsmoking. Cr cds: A, C, D, DS, MC, V.

D

★★★ **RUBICON.** *558 Sacramento, in Financial District. 415/434-4100.* E-mail interactivegourmet@cuisine.com; web www.cuisine.com. Hrs: 11:30 am-2:30 pm, 5:30-10 pm; Sat from 5:30 pm. Closed Sun. Res accepted. Bar. Semi-a la carte: lunch $12.50-$14, dinner $19-$25. Prix fixe: $29-$59. Specialty: muscovy duck breast with baby turnips. Totally nonsmoking. Cr cds: A, D, MC, V.

D

★ **RUE LEPIC.** *900 Pine St, at Mason St, on Nob Hill. 415/474-6070.* Hrs: 11:30 am-2:30 pm, 5:30-10 pm; Sat, Sun from 5:30 pm. Closed most major hols. Res accepted; required wkends. French menu. A la carte entrees: lunch $6-$17, dinner $17-$21. Complete meals: dinner $32-$39. Specialties: roast medallion of veal with mushroom sauce, lobster tail, roasted rack of lamb with garlic. Totally nonsmoking. Cr cds: A, MC, V.

✔★★ **RUMPUS.** *1 Tillman Place (94108), in Union Square. 415/421-2300.* Hrs: 11:30 am-2:30 pm, 5:30-10 pm; Fri, Sat to 11 pm; Sun from 5:30 pm. Closed most major hols. Res accepted. Contemporary menu. Bar. Semi-a la carte: lunch $6-$16, dinner $10-$19. Specialties: pan roasted chicken, risotto. Outdoor dining. Open kitchen; modern art. Totally nonsmoking. Cr cds: A, D, JCB, MC, V.

D

★★ **RUTH'S CHRIS STEAK HOUSE.** *1601 Van Ness Ave (94109), on Russian Hill. 415/673-0557.* Hrs: 5-10:30 pm; Sun to 10 pm. Closed Thanksgiving, Dec 25. Res accepted. Bar. A la carte entrees: dinner $17.95-$29.95. Specializes in steak. Club atmosphere. Totally nonsmoking. Cr cds: A, JCB, MC, V.

D

✔★ **SAJI JAPANESE CUISINE.** *3232 Scott St (94123), in Marina District. 415/931-0563.* Hrs: 5:30-10:30 pm; Fri, Sat to midnight; Sun to 10 pm. Closed Jan 1-2, Thanksgiving, Dec 25. Res accepted. Japanese menu. Complete meals: dinner $9-$14. Specializes in sushi. Japanese decor. Totally nonsmoking. Cr cds: A, D, DS, JCB, MC, V.

D

★ **SAM'S GRILL.** *374 Bush St (94104), in Financial District. 415/421-0594.* Hrs: 11 am-9 pm. Closed Sat, Sun; major hols. Res accepted. Seafood menu. Bar. A la carte entrees: lunch, dinner $7-$25. Specializes in fresh fish. Outdoor dining (lunch). 1867 building with original wooden booths. Family-owned. Cr cds: A, D, MC, V.

★★ **SCALA'S BISTRO.** *(See Sir Francis Drake Hotel) 415/392-7755.* Hrs: 7-10:30 am, 11:30 am-midnight; Fri, Sat from 8 am. Closed most major hols. Res accepted. Italian menu. Bar. Semi-a la carte: bkfst $7-$12; lunch, dinner $8.95-$19.95. Specialties: porcini tagliatelle, seared salmon. Own bread, desserts. Contemporary decor. Cr cds: A, C, D, DS, JCB, MC, V.

D

★ **SCHROEDER'S.** *240 Front St, in Financial District. 415/421-4778.* Hrs: 11 am-9 pm; Fri, Sat to 9:30 pm. Closed Sun; major hols. Res accepted. German, Amer menu. Bar. Semi-a la carte: lunch $7.50-$14, dinner $9.50-$16.50. Child's meals. Specializes in baked chicken & noodles, sauerbraten, Wienerschnitzel. German decor, murals. Established 1893. Family-owned. Cr cds: A, C, D, DS, JCB, MC, V.

D SC

★★ **SCOMA'S.** *Pier 47 (94133), at Fisherman's Wharf. 415/771-4383.* Web www.scomas.com. Hrs: 11:30 am-10:30 pm; Fri, Sat to 11 pm. Closed Thanksgiving, Dec 24, 25. Italian, seafood menu. Bars. A la carte entrees: lunch, dinner $14.95-$54.95. Child's meals. Specialties: calamari, cioppino, sauteed shellfish. Complimentary valet parking. View of fishing fleet. Originally fisherman's shack. Family-owned. Cr cds: A, C, D, DS, JCB, MC, V.

D

★★ **SCOTT'S SEAFOOD GRILL AND BAR.** *2400 Lombard St, in Marina District. 415/563-8988.* Hrs: 11:30 am-10 pm; Sun brunch 11:30 am-3 pm. Closed Thanksgiving, Dec 25. Res accepted. Bar. A la carte entrees: lunch $7.50-$15.50, dinner $8.50-$18.50; prix fixe: dinner $20. Sun brunch $6.50-$16.50. Specializes in fresh seafood. Cr cds: A, D, DS, MC, V.

D

★★★ **SILKS.** *(See Mandarin Oriental Hotel) 415/986-2020.* E-mail mandarinsfo@mosfo.com; web www.mandarin-oriental.com. Hrs: 6:30-10 am, 11:30 am-2 pm, 6-10 pm. Res accepted. Bar 11 am-11 pm. Wine list. A la carte entrees: bkfst $10.95-$16, lunch $15.25-$23, dinner $19-$27. Prix fixe: lunch $32-$46.50, dinner $55-$75. Specializes in contemporary American cuisine. Own pastries. Valet parking. Cr cds: A, C, D, DS, JCB, MC, V.

D

★★ **SLANTED DOOR.** *584 Valencia (94110), between 16th & 17th Sts, in Mission District. 415/861-8032.* E-mail eat@slanteddoor.com; web www.slanteddoor.com. Hrs: 11:30 am-3 pm, 5:30-10 pm; Fri, Sat to 10:30 pm. Closed Mon; most major hols. Res accepted. No A/C. Vietnamese menu. Bar. A la carte entrees: lunch $5.50-$7, dinner $8.50-$18.50. Specialties: Shaking beef, steamed sea bass, spring rolls. Street parking. Modern Asian decor. Totally nonsmoking. Cr cds: MC, V.

D

★★★ **SPLENDIDO.** *Embarcadero Center Four, promenade level, in Financial District. 415/986-3222.* Hrs: 11:30 am-2:30 pm, 5:30-10 pm. Closed major hols. Res accepted. Contemporary Italian menu. Bar. A la carte entrees: lunch $8.95-$18, dinner $8.95-$25. Specializes in fresh seafood, game, baked goods. Own baking, ice cream. Outdoor dining. Cr cds: A, D, DS, MC, V.

D

★★★ **STARS.** *555 Golden Gate, at Van Ness Ave, in Civic Center area. 415/861-7827.* Hrs: 11:30 am-2 pm, 6-10 pm; Fri, Sat from 5:30 pm. Closed Dec 25. Res accepted. Bar from 11 am; wkends from 4 pm. A la carte entrees: lunch $8-$15, dinner $19-$30. Pianist. Changing menu. Bistro decor. Cr cds: A, D, MC, V.

D

★★ **STARS CAFE.** *500 Van Ness Ave (94102), in Civic Center area. 415/861-4344.* Hrs: 11:30 am-10 pm; Sat & Sun brunch to 2 pm. Closed Dec 25. Res accepted. Bar. A la carte entrees: lunch $10-$14, dinner $14-$18. Sat, Sun brunch $10-$16. Specialties: grilled fish, wood oven roasted chicken, wood oven fired pizza. Modern, American bistro atmosphere. Totally nonsmoking. Cr cds: A, MC, V.

D

★★ **SWISS LOUIS.** *Pier 39, at Fisherman's Wharf. 415/421-2913.* Hrs 11:30 am-10 pm; Sat & Sun brunch 10:30 am-4 pm. Closed Dec 25. Res accepted. No A/C. Italian menu. Bar. Semi-a la carte: lunch $9.50-$15, dinner $11.50-$25. Sat & Sun brunch $10.50. Child's meals.

Specializes in veal dishes, seafood. Own desserts. View of bay, Golden Gate Bridge. Cr cds: A, C, D, DS, JCB, MC, V.

D

★ **TADICH GRILL.** *240 California St, in Financial District. 415/391-1849.* Hrs: 11 am-9:30 pm; Sat from 11:30 am. Closed Sun; major hols. Bar. A la carte entrees: lunch, dinner $12-$25. Child's meals. Specializes in fresh seafood. Also counter serv. Turn-of-the-century decor. Established in 1849; family-owned since 1928. Cr cds: MC, V.

D

★ ★ ★ **TOMMY TOY'S.** *655 Montgomery St (94111), in Financial District. 415/397-4888.* Hrs: 11:30 am-3 pm, 6-10 pm; Sat, Sun from 6 pm. Closed Jan 1, Dec 25. Res required. Chinese menu. Bar. A la carte entrees: lunch $11.95-$18.50, dinner $14-$17.95. Table d'hôte: lunch $11.95. Prix fixe: dinner $39.50-$49.50. Specializes in seafood, Peking duck. Valet parking (dinner). Jacket. Cr cds: A, C, D, DS, JCB, MC, V.

D

✔★ ★ **TUBA GARDEN.** *3634 Sacramento Ave (94118), in Pacific Heights. 415/921-8822.* Hrs: 11 am-2:30 pm; Sat, Sun from 10 am. Closed Dec 25. Res accepted. Continental menu. Wine, beer. Semi-a la carte: lunch $8-$12. Child's meals. Specializes in chicken salad Hawaii, cheese blintzes, Belgian waffles. Own desserts. Outdoor dining. Victorian house with original art. Cr cds: A, C, D, DS, MC, V.

✔★ **UNIVERSAL CAFE.** *2814 19th St (94110), in Mission District. 415/821-4608.* Hrs: 7:30 am-10 pm; Sat from 9 am; Sun 9 am-9:30 pm. Closed Mon; some major hols. Res accepted (dinner). Wine, beer. Semi-a la carte: bkfst $5-$8.50, lunch $4-$11.25, dinner $5-$20. Outdoor dining. Contemporary decor. Totally nonsmoking. Cr cds: A, D, MC, V.

★ ★ ★ **VERTIGO.** *600 Montgomery St (94111), in Trans America Pyramid, in Financial District. 415/433-7250.* Hrs: 11:30 am-2:30 pm, 5:30-10 pm; Fri, Sat to 10:30 pm. Closed Sun; Memorial Day, July 4, Dec 25. Res accepted. California menu. Bar to 12:30 am. Wine list. A la carte entrees: lunch $12-$15, dinner $16-$24. Prix fixe: lunch $20, dinner $45. Specializes in fish. Valet parking (dinner). Outdoor dining. Multi-level dining, avant-garde decor. Cr cds: A, D, MC, V.

D

★ ★ **WATERFRONT.** *Pier 7, the Embarcadero at Broadway, in Financial District. 415/391-2696.* Hrs: 11:30 am-10:30 pm; Sun brunch 10 am-3 pm. Closed July 4, Dec 25. Res accepted. No A/C. Bar. A la carte entrees: lunch $9-$22, dinner $9-$28. Sun brunch $8.50-$13. Specializes in seafood from around the world. Valet parking. View of bay. Cr cds: A, C, D, DS, MC, V.

D

✔★ ★ **YABBIES.** *2237 Polk St (94109), in Russian Hill. 415/474-4088.* Hrs: 6-10 pm; Fri, Sat to 10:30 pm. Closed most major hols. Res accepted. No A/C. Seafood menu. Bar. Complete meals: dinner $14-$18.50. Specialties: tuna pokee, oyster bar feast, Maine crab and mango cocktail. Contemporary decor. Totally nonsmoking. Cr cds: MC, V.

D

★ ★ **YAMATO.** *717 California St, in Chinatown. 415/397-3456.* Hrs: 11:45 am-2 pm, 5-10 pm; Sat & Sun from 5 pm. Closed Mon; Jan 1, Thanksgiving, Dec 25. Res accepted. Japanese menu. Bar. A la carte entrees: lunch, dinner $7.75-$23. Complete meals: lunch $7.75-$11.75, dinner $10.50-$23. Specializes in sukiyaki, tempura, chicken or steak teriyaki. Sushi bar. Traditional Japanese decor. Indoor gardens. Some rms with floor & well seating. Family-owned. Cr cds: A, C, D, JCB, MC, V.

✔★ ★ **YANK SING.** *427 Battery St (94111), in Financial District. 415/781-1111.* Web www.yanksing.com. Hrs: 11 am-3 pm; Sat & Sun 10 am-4 pm. Res accepted. Bar. Semi-a la carte: lunch $12-$15. Specialties: dim sum cuisine. Tableside carts in addition to menu. Cr cds: A, D, MC, V.

D

★ ★ **YOSHIDA-YA.** *2909 Webster St, in Cow Hollow. 415/346-3431.* Web www.citysearch.com. Hrs: 11:30 am-2 pm, 5-10:30 pm; Fri to 11 pm; Sat 5-11 pm; Sun 5-10:30 pm. Closed Jan 15, July 4, Thanksgiving Day, Dec 24-25. Japanese menu. Bar. Complete meals: dinner $20-$25. Specialties: sushi, yakitori. Oriental decor; traditional dining upstairs. Totally nonsmoking. Cr cds: A, C, D, DS, JCB, MC, V.

D

★ ★ ★ **YOYO.** *(See Radisson Miyako Hotel) 415/922-7788.* E-mail miyakosf@slip.net; web www.mim.com/miyako/. Hrs: 6:30 am-10 pm. Res accepted. Franco-Japanese menu. Bar. Wine cellar. Prix fixe: bkfst: $18. A la carte entrees: lunch $7-$10, dinner $12-$20; buffet: bkfst $12.50. Mix of modern American and Asian decor. Cr cds: A, C, D, DS, JCB, MC, V.

D

✔★ **ZARZUELA.** *2000 Hyde St (94109), on Russian Hill. 415/346-0800.* Hrs: 12:30 am-10:30 pm; Fri, Sat to 11 pm. Closed Sun; Jan 1. Spanish menu. Wine, beer. Semi-a la carte: lunch, dinner $8.95-$13.95. Specialties: zarzuela, tapas, paella. Spanish decor. Totally nonsmoking. Cr cds: MC, V.

D

✔★ ★ **ZAX.** *2330 Taylor St (94133), in North Beach. 415/563-6266.* Hrs: 5:30-10 pm. Closed Sun, Mon; wk of July 4, Thanksgiving, Dec 25. Res accepted. Mediterranean menu. Bar. Semi-a la carte: dinner $13-$17.50. Specialties: goat cheese souffle. Contemporary decor. Totally nonsmoking. Cr cds: MC, V.

D

★ ★ **ZINGARI.** *(See The Donatello Hotel) 415/885-8850.* Hrs: 6:30-10:30 am, 5:30-10:30 pm; Fri, Sat to 11 pm. Res accepted. Italian menu. Wine, beer. Semi-a la carte: bkfst $8-$13.95, dinner $11.50-$21.95. Specialties: veal loin stuffed with truffles and fontina, marinated lamb chop. Italian decor. Totally nonsmoking. Cr cds: A, C, D, DS, JCB, MC, V.

D

★ ★ **ZUNI CAFE.** *1658 Market St (94102), in Civic Center area. 415/552-2522.* Hrs: 11:30 am-midnight; Sun to 11 pm; Sun brunch 11 am-3 pm. Closed Mon; some hols. Res accepted. Bar. A la carte entrees: lunch $8-$16, dinner $10-$22.50. Sun brunch $7.50-$16. Own desserts. Pianist Fri, Sat. Outdoor dining. Changing art displays. Cr cds: A, MC, V.

D

Unrated Dining Spots

CAFÉ LATTÉ. *100 Bush St, 2nd fl, north of Union Square. 415/989-2233.* Hrs: 7-9:30 am, 11:30 am-3 pm. Closed Sat, Sun; major hols. No A/C. Nouvelle California/northern Italian menu. Wine, beer. Avg ck: bkfst $3.50, lunch $7. Specializes in fresh fish, fresh pasta, salads. Stylish cafeteria in landmark art deco skyscraper; mirrored deco interior with marble counters, tray ledges, floors. Cr cds: A, C, D, MC, V.

CAFE TITANIC. *817 Sutter St (94109), west of Union Square. 415/928-8870.* Hrs: 7:30 am-2:30 pm. Semi-a la carte: bkfst, lunch $3.50-$6. Specializes in omelets, applewood smoked bacon. Casual decor. No cr cds accepted.

D

DAVID'S. *474 Geary St, west of Union Square. 415/771-1600.* Hrs: 7-1 am; Sat, Sun from 8 am. Closed Jewish high hols. Jewish deli menu. Beer, wine. Semi-a la carte: bkfst $3.35-$9.75, lunch $4.95-$9.95, dinner from $6.95. Complete meal: dinner $16.95. Specializes in chopped chicken liver, stuffed cabbage, cheese blintzes. Cr cds: A, C, D, JCB, MC, V.

DOTTIE'S TRUE BLUE CAFE. *522 Jones St, west of Union Square. 415/885-2767.* Hrs: 7:30 am-2 pm. No A/C. Wine, beer. Semi-a la carte: bkfst $3-$7.50, lunch $3.50-$7.50. Specializes in all-American bkfst. Own breads. Cr cds: DS, MC, V.

GHIRARDELLI CHOCOLATE MANUFACTORY. *900 North Point St, on grounds of Ghirardelli Square, at Fisherman's Wharf. 415/771-4903.* Hrs: 10 am-midnight; winter to 11 pm; Fri, Sat to midnight. Closed Thanksgiving, Dec 25. Soda fountain & chocolate shop. Specializes in ice cream sundaes, premium chocolates. Own candy making, ice cream toppings. Parking. Located in former chocolate factory; built in late 1890s. Totally nonsmoking. Cr cds: JCB, MC, V.

D

ISOBUNE. *1737 Post St, in Japantown. 415/563-1030.* Hrs: 11:30 am-10 pm. Closed Jan 1-3, Thanksgiving, Dec 25. Japanese sushi menu. Wine, beer. A la carte entrees: lunch $5-$8, dinner $10-$12. Specializes in sashimi. Dining at counter; selections pass in front of diners on small boats. Cr cds: MC, V.

JUST DESSERTS. *3 Embarcadero Center, in lobby, in Financial District. 415/421-1609.* Hrs: 7 am-6 pm; Sat 9 am-5 pm. Closed Sun; most major hols. A la carte entrees: pastries, cakes, muffins $2.50-$4. Specializes in cheesecake. Own baking. Outdoor dining. Modern cafe atmosphere. Cr cds: MC, V.

D SC

LA BODEGA. *1337 Grant Ave (94133), in North Beach. 415/433-0439.* Hrs: 5 pm-midnight. Res accepted. Spanish menu. Bar. Semi-a la carte: dinner $4-$9. Specialties: tapas, paella. Entertainment. Spanish decor. Totally nonsmoking. Cr cds: A, DS, MC, V.

D

MIFUNE. *1737 Post St, in Japantown. 415/922-0337.* Hrs: 11 am-9:30 pm. Closed Jan 1-3, Thanksgiving, Dec 25. Japanese menu. A la carte entrees: lunch, dinner $3.50-$13. Specializes in noodle dishes. Own noodles. Validated parking. Cr cds: A, C, D, DS, MC, V.

MO'S GOURMET HAMBURGERS. *1322 Grant Ave (94133), in North Beach. 415/788-3779.* Hrs: 11:30 am-10:30 pm; Fri, Sat to 11:30 pm. Closed Dec 25. Wine, beer. Semi-a la carte: lunch, dinner $4.75-$7.75. Specializes in grilled or charbroiled hamburgers. Casual dining with art deco design. Kitchen with rotating grill over lava rocks at front window. Cr cds: MC, V.

D

SALMAGUNDI. *442 Geary St, west of Union Square. 415/441-0894.* Hrs: 11 am-11 pm; Sun & Mon 11 am-9 pm. Closed Thanksgiving, Dec 25. Wine, beer. Soup, salad, roll $3-$7; dessert extra; pasta torte. Specialty: oven-baked onion soup. Own soups. Cr cds: A, MC, V.

D SC

SEARS FINE FOODS. *439 Powell St (94102), in Union Square. 415/986-1160.* Hrs: 6:30 am-3:30 pm. Closed Jan 1, Thanksgiving, Dec 25. Semi-a la carte: bkfst, lunch $7-$15. Child's meals. Specialties: 18 Swedish pancakes, sourdough French toast. Casual decor. Totally nonsmoking. No cr cds accepted.

D

TRIO CAFE. *1870 Fillmore St, in Pacific Heights. 415/563-2248.* Hrs: 8 am-6 pm; Sun 10 am-4 pm. Closed Mon; Easter, Thanksgiving; also Dec 24-Jan 2. Eclectic menu. Bar. A la carte entrees: bkfst, lunch $4-$6. Outdoor dining in cafe setting. Store front entrance. Totally nonsmoking. No cr cds accepted.

San Francisco Airport Area

Motels

★ **COMFORT SUITES.** *(121 E Grand Ave, South San Francisco 94080) 2 mi N on US 101, E Grand Ave exit. 650/589-7766; FAX 650/588-2231.* 166 suites, 3 story. S $69-$79; D $75-$85; each addl $10; under 18 free. TV; cable (premium), VCR (movies). Complimentary continental bkfst. Coffee in rms. Ck-out noon. Business servs avail. In-rm modem link. Valet serv. Free airport, RR station transportation. Whirlpool. Health club privileges. Refrigerators. Grill. Cr cds: A, C, D, DS, ER, JCB, MC, V.

D SC

★ ★ ★ **COURTYARD BY MARRIOTT.** *(1050 Bayhill Dr, San Bruno 94066) 1 1/2 mi N on US 101 to jct I-380 W, then 1 mi W to El Camino Real South (CA 82), then 1 blk S to Bayhill Dr. 650/952-3333; FAX 650/952-4707.* 147 rms, 2-3 story. S, D $105-$115; each addl (after 4th person) $10; suites $120-$130; under 13 free; lower rates wkends. Crib free. TV; cable (premium). Indoor pool. Complimentary coffee in rms. Restaurant 6:30-10:30 am, 3-11 pm. Ck-out 1 pm. Coin lndry. Meeting rms. Business servs avail. Valet serv. Sundries. Free airport transportation. Exercise equipt; weight, stair machines, bicycle, whirlpool. Some balconies. Cr cds: A, C, D, DS, MC, V.

D SC

✔★ ★ **MILLWOOD INN.** *(1375 El Camino Real, Millbrae 94030) 1 mi SE on US 101, then 1/2 mi W on Millbrae Ave to El Camino Real (CA 82), then 1 mi NW. 650/583-3935; FAX 650/875-4354; res: 800/345-1375.* 34 rms, 2 story. S $57-$85; D $62-$95; suites $65-$105. Crib $4. TV; cable (premium), VCR. Complimentary continental bkfst. Coffee in rms. Restaurant nearby. Ck-out 11 am. Coin lndry. Business servs avail. In-rm modem link. Exercise equipt; stair machines, bicycle. Bathrm phones, refrigerators. Cr cds: A, C, D, DS, ER, JCB, MC, V.

D SC

★ ★ **RAMADA HOTEL AIRPORT NORTH.** *(245 S Airport Blvd, South San Francisco 94080) 2 mi N on US 101, off S Airport Blvd exit. 650/589-7200; FAX 650/588-5007.* 175 rms, 2 story. S $80-$110; D $85-$115; each addl $10; under 18 free; wkend rates. Crib free. Pet accepted, some restrictions. TV; cable (premium). Pool. Restaurant 6:30 am-1:30 pm, 5-10 pm. Rm serv. Bar 4-midnight; Sat, Sun 11-1 am. Ck-out noon. Coin lndry. Meeting rms. Business servs avail. Bellhops. Gift shop. Barber shop. Free airport transportation. Health club privileges. Cr cds: A, C, D, DS, ER, JCB, MC, V.

SC

★ **TRAVELODGE.** *(326 S Airport Blvd, South San Francisco 94080) 2 mi N on US 101, exit S Airport Blvd. 650/583-9600; FAX 650/873-9392.* 197 rms, 100 with shower only, 2 story. June-Aug: S $72; D $79; each addl $7; under 17 free; lower rates rest of yr. Crib free. TV; cable (premium). Heated pool. Complimentary coffee in rms. Restaurant open 24 hrs. Ck-out 1 pm. Meeting rms. Business servs avail. Valet serv. Sundries. Free airport transportation. Health club privileges. Picnic tables. Cr cds: A, C, D, DS, JCB, MC, V.

D SC

Motor Hotels

★ ★ **BEST WESTERN EL RANCHO INN.** *(1100 El Camino Real, Millbrae 94030) 1 mi SE on US 101, then 1/2 mi W on Millbrae Ave to El Camino Real (CA 82), then 1 mi NW. 650/588-8500; FAX 650/871-7150.* 300 rms, most A/C, 1-3 story. S $94-$104; D $99-$109; each addl $10; kit. units, suites $135-$160; under 18 free. Crib free. Pet accepted, some restrictions. TV; cable (premium), VCR avail. Heated pool. Coffee in rms. Restaurant 6:30 am-10 pm. Rm serv. Bar. Ck-out 1 pm. Coin lndry. Meeting rms. Business servs avail. In-rm modem link. Bellhops. Valet serv. Free airport transportation. Exercise equipt; weights, bicycles, whirlpool. Some refrigerators. Cr cds: A, C, D, DS, ER, JCB, MC, V.

D SC

★ ★ **BEST WESTERN GROSVENOR.** *(380 S Airport Blvd, South San Francisco 94080) 2 mi N on US 101, exit S Airport Blvd. 650/873-3200; FAX 650/589-3495.* 205 rms, 9 story. June-mid-Sept: S, D $89-$109; each addl $10; suites $175-$275; under 18 free; lower rates rest of yr. Crib free. TV; cable (premium). Heated pool; poolside serv. Complimentary continental bkfst. Complimentary coffee in rms. Restaurant 6 am-2 pm, 5-10 pm. Rm serv. Bar 4 pm-midnight. Ck-out noon. Meeting rms. Business servs avail. Bellhops. Valet serv. Sundries. Free airport transportation. Health club privileges. Some refrigerators. Cr cds: A, C, D, DS, ER, JCB, MC, V.

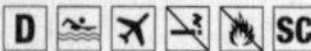

Hotels

★ ★ ★ **CROWNE PLAZA.** *(600 Airport Blvd, Burlingame 94010) $1\frac{1}{2}$ mi S on US 101 to Broadway exit, then E to Airport Blvd, then 1 mi along bay. 650/340-8500; FAX 650/343-1546.* 405 rms, 15 story. S, D $155; each addl $10; suites $350-$450; under 18 free; wkend rates. Crib free. TV; cable (premium). Indoor pool. Restaurant 6 am-midnight. Bar 11-1:30 am; entertainment. Ck-out noon. Meeting rms. Business servs avail. Gift shop. Free covered parking. Free airport transportation. Exercise equipt; weights, bicycles, whirlpool, sauna. Refrigerators avail. Luxury level. Cr cds: A, C, D, DS, JCB, MC, V.

D SC

★ ★ **DOUBLETREE.** *(835 Airport Blvd, Burlingame 94010) 2 mi S on US 101. 650/344-5500; FAX 650/340-8851.* 292 rms, 8 story. S $99-$129; D $109-$139; each addl $10; suites $169-$300; under 17 free. Crib free. Pet accepted, some restrictions; $20. TV; cable, VCR avail. Coffee in rms. Restaurant 6:30 am-10 pm. 24 hr rm serv. Bar 11 am-11:30 pm. Ck-out noon. Meeting rms. Business center. In-rm modem link. Gift shop. Free airport transportation. Exercise equipt; weight machine, bicycles. Refrigerator, wet bar in suites. Cr cds: A, C, D, DS, ER, JCB, MC, V.

D SC

★ ★ ★ **EMBASSY SUITES-AIRPORT NORTH.** *(250 Gateway Blvd, South San Francisco 94080) 2 mi N on US 101, E Grand Ave exit, then N on Gateway Blvd. 650/589-3400; FAX 650/876-0305.* 312 suites, 10 story. S, D $139-$189; each addl $10; under 12 free; wkend rates. Crib free. TV; cable (premium), VCR avail. Indoor pool; whirlpool, sauna. Complimentary full bkfst. Complimentary coffee in rms. Restaurant 11 am-11 pm. Bar 11-1 am; entertainment. Ck-out 1 pm. Coin Indry. Meeting rms. Business servs avail. Gift shop. Free airport transportation. Health club privileges. Refrigerators. Balconies. Atrium courtyard. Cr cds: A, C, D, DS, ER, JCB, MC, V.

D SC

★ ★ ★ **HILTON-SAN FRANCISCO AIRPORT.** *San Francisco Intl Airport (94128). 650/589-0770; FAX 650/589-4696.* 527 rms, 3 story. S $159-$179; D $179-$199; each addl $20; suites $275-$500; family, wkend rates. Crib free. TV; cable (premium), VCR avail. Heated pool; whirlpool, poolside serv. Restaurant 6 am-11 pm. Bar; entertainment. Ck-out noon. Convention facilities. Business center. Concierge. Free airport transportation. Exercise equipt; weights, bicycles. Minibars; bathrm phone in suites. Balconies. Cr cds: A, C, D, DS, ER, JCB, MC, V.

D SC

★ ★ ★ **HYATT REGENCY-SAN FRANCISCO AIRPORT.** *(1333 Bayshore Hwy, Burlingame 94010) Off US 101 Broadway exit. 650/347-1234; FAX 650/696-2669.* 793 rms, 9 story. S $175-$200; D $200-$225; each addl $25; suites $200-$720; under 18 free; wkend rates. Crib free. Valet parking $11. TV; cable (premium). Heated pool; whirlpool. Restaurant 6:30 am-11 pm. Rm serv 24 hrs. Bar 11-1 am. Ck-out noon. Convention facilities. Business center. Concierge. Gift shop. Free airport transportation. Exercise equipt; stair machines, treadmill, sauna. Some bathrm phones, wet bars; refrigerators avail. Atrium. Luxury level. Cr cds: A, C, D, DS, ER, JCB, MC, V.

D SC

★ ★ ★ **MARRIOTT-AIRPORT.** *(1800 Old Bayshore Hwy, Burlingame 94010) 1 mi SE on US 101, then E on Millbrae Ave to Old Bayshore Hwy, then SE on San Francisco Bay. 650/692-9100; FAX 650/692-8016.* 684 rms, 11 story. S, D $179; suites $450-$600; under 18 free; wkend, wkly rates. Crib free. Pet accepted, some restrictions. Valet parking $10. TV; cable (premium), VCR avail. Indoor pool; whirlpool, poolside serv. Restautant 6 am-11 pm. Rm serv 24 hrs. Piano bar. Ck-out noon. Coin Indry. Convention facilities. Business servs avail. In-rm modem link. Concierge. Gift shop. Free airport transportation. Exercise equipt; treadmills, stair machines, sauna. Some bathrm phones, refrigerators. Luxury level. Cr cds: A, C, D, DS, ER, JCB, MC, V.

D SC

★ ★ **PARK PLAZA.** *(1177 Airport Blvd, Burlingame 94010) $1\frac{1}{2}$ mi S on US 101 to Broadway exit, then E to Airport Blvd. 650/342-9200; FAX 650/342-1655; res: 800/411-7275.* 301 rms, 10 story. S, D $150-$195; each addl $10; suites $195-$350; under 18 free; wkend rates. Crib free. Pet accepted. TV; cable (premium), VCR avail. Indoor/outdoor pool; whirlpool. Restaurant 6 am-11 pm. Bar; entertainment. Ck-out 1 pm. Coin Indry. Convention facilities. In-rm modem link. Gift shop. Barber, beauty shop. Free airport transportation. Free covered parking. Exercise equipt; weights, bicycles. Cr cds: A, C, D, DS, ER, MC, V.

D SC

★ ★ ★ **THE WESTIN-SAN FRANCISCO AIRPORT.** *(1 Old Bayshore Hwy, Millbrae 94030) 1 mi SE on US 101, then E on Millbrae Ave to Old Bayshore Hwy. 650/692-3500; FAX 650/872-8111.* 390 rms, 7 story. S, D $175-$195; each addl $20; suites $340-$390; under 18 free; wkend rates. Crib free. Pet accepted, some restrictions. Valet parking $8. TV; cable (premium), VCR avail. Indoor pool; whirlpool, poolside serv. Restaurant 6 am-10 pm. Rm serv 24 hrs. Bar noon-1 am; entertainment. Ck-out 1 pm. Convention facilities. Business center. Concierge. Gift shop. Free airport transportation. Exercise equipt; stair machines, treadmilll. Refrigerators, minibars. Luxury level. Cr cds: A, C, D, DS, ER, JCB, MC, V.

D

Restaurants

★ ★ **EMPRESS COURT.** *(433 Airport Blvd, Burlingame 94010) $1\frac{1}{2}$ mi SE on US 101 to Broadway exit, then NE to Airport Blvd, then 1 mi E along bay. 650/348-1122.* Hrs: 11 am-2:30 pm, 5-9:30 pm; June-Oct to 10 pm; Sat, Sun from 10:30 am. Res accepted. Chinese menu. Bar. Complete meals (4 or more): lunch from $4.95, dinner $14.25-$32. A la carte entrees: dinner from $6.95. Specialties: barbecued baby quail and minced squab, Szechwan spice beef, lemon chicken. Lavish Sung dynasty decor; aviary, pond. View of bay. Cr cds: A, MC, V.

D

★ ★ **IL FORNAIO.** *(327 Lorton Ave, Burlingame 94010) 650/375-8000.* Hrs: 11:30 am-11 pm; Fri to midnight; Sat 10 am-midnight; Sun 10 am-10 pm; Sun brunch to 2:30 pm. Closed Thanksgiving, Dec 25. Res accepted. Italian menu. Bar. Semi-a la carte: lunch, dinner $7.95-$17.95. Sun brunch $4.50-$8.25. Child's meals. Specializes in pasta, pizza. Large exhibition kitchen. Totally nonsmoking. Cr cds: A, D, MC, V.

D

✔★ **STACKS'.** *(361 California Dr, Burlingame 94010) 650/579-1384.* Hrs: 7 am-2:30 pm. Closed Thanksgiving, Dec 25. Complete meals: bkfst $2.95-$7.95, lunch $4.95-$8.25. Specializes in pancakes, skillet breakfast. Casual decor. Totally nonsmoking. Cr cds: MC, V.

D

Seattle

Founded: 1852
Pop: 516,259
Elev: 125 feet
Time zone: Pacific
Area code: 206
Web: www.seeseattle.org

Seattle is among the youngest of the world's major cities. Nestled between Puget Sound and Lake Washington, the city grew up along the shores of Elliott Bay, a natural harbor that today welcomes more than 2,000 commercial deep-sea vessels a year.

Named for a friendly Native American chief, Seattle offered a great harbor and seemingly unlimited stands of timber. Soon a sawmill and a salmon-canning plant were in operation. Isolated at the fringe of the continent, Seattle had great resources but few women, an obvious threat to the growth of the community. Asa Mercer, a civic leader and first president of the territorial university, went east and persuaded 11 proper young women from New England to sail back with him to take husbands among the pioneers; the idea proved so successful that Mercer repeated the trip, this time recruiting 100 Civil War widows. Today, many of Seattle's old families proudly trace their lines to the "Mercer girls."

When a ship arrived from Alaska in 1897 carrying a "ton of gold," the great Yukon Gold Rush was on, converting Seattle into a boomtown. Seattle has remained the natural gateway to Alaska because of the protected Inland Passage. The commercial interests of the two have remained tightly interwoven. The 1915 opening of the Panama Canal nearly halved the passage time between the East and West coasts, creating a tremendous stimulant to Seattle's economy.

Seattle has prospered from the products of its surrounding forests, farms and waterways. It continues to serve as a provisioner to Alaska and the Orient. In recent years, it has acquired a new dimension from the manufacture of jet aircraft, missiles and space vehicles, which are among the city's most important products along with the booming software industry.

Business

There are more than 2,200 industrial firms located in the city, but industry represents only about one-fourth of the city's economy. The Boeing Company, still the largest manufacturer of commercial aircraft in the world, employs the greatest number of people.

About 15 million tons of cargo are handled each year in the Port of Seattle. The city has become a major container port for the Pacific Rim.

Convention Facilities

Bell Harbor International Conference Center is a 47,000-square-foot facility in a waterfront setting at Pier 66. This center has an auditorium, conference rooms, full-service kitchen and dining room.

Seattle Center is a network of buildings where any convention, meeting or banquet can be accommodated.

The Arena is a spectator event facility seating as many as 6,100 people. The exhibit area has 15,600 square feet of space. Banquets for as many as 1,500 people can be arranged.

The Key Arena, with a capacity of 13,000-17,000 is used for sporting events, exhibitions, conventions and trade shows.

The Exhibition Hall has 40,000 square feet for display; for dining, the seating capacity is 1,700 persons. This hall can also be used as a ballroom.

The Opera House is a beautifully constructed, modern theater seating 3,000 people; in addition there are seven separate conference areas of various sizes.

The playhouse, a smaller theater with a seating capacity of 450, provides an artistic setting for imaginative convention utilization. The Bagley Wright Theater has a seating capacity of 850. Throughout the complex, there are a number of meeting rooms, with seating capacities of up to 750 persons. They can be used either singly or in combination with any major Seattle Center structure.

The 204,000-square-foot Washington State Convention and Trade Center accommodates more than 10,000 people. It also boasts a 50,000-square-foot convertible exhibition space on its upper level.

The Seattle International Trade Center, near Pier 70, has trade show and banquet facilities. Its 55,000-square-foot area is divided into booths of varying sizes surrounding an atrium.

The multipurpose Kingdome is located across town from the Seattle Center. In addition to a 65,000-seat stadium, it has 153,000 square feet of floor space, making it the largest exhibit hall in the Pacific Northwest.

Sports & Recreation

Seattle's spectator sports are centered in the all-weather Kingdome. Playing their home games here are the NFL Seattle Seahawks and the American League Seattle Mariners. The NBA Seattle SuperSonics play in the Key Arena at the Seattle Center.

Seattle offers superb outdoor opportunities and spectacular scenery. The freshwater lakes and inlets of Puget Sound are ideal for waterskiing and freshwater and saltwater fishing, and the nearby mountain ranges offer hunting, backpacking and skiing.

Entertainment

Seattle has an international reputation for its fine arts organizations. Among them are the Seattle Symphony Orchestra and the Seattle Opera,

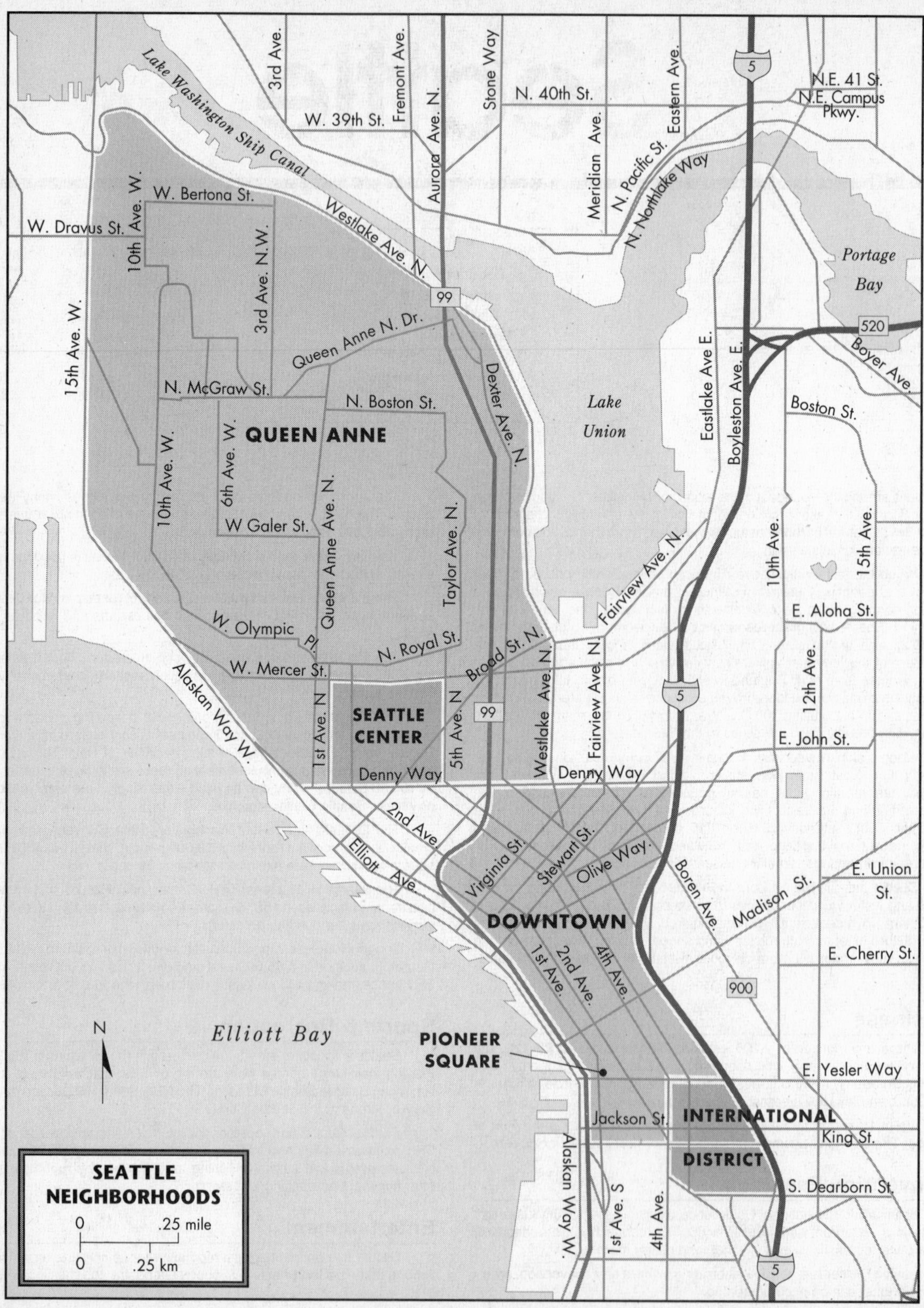
Lake Washington Ship Canal
3rd Ave.
Fremont Ave.
W. 39th St.
Aurora Ave. N.
Stone Way
N. 40th St.
Meridian Ave.
Eastern Ave.
N. Pacific St.
N. Northlake Way
5
N.E. 41 St.
N.E. Campus Pkwy.
W. Bertona St.
W. Dravus St.
10th Ave. W.
3rd Ave. N.W.
Westlake Ave. N.
99
Portage Bay
520
Boyer Ave.
15th Ave. W.
Queen Anne N. Dr.
N. McGraw St.
N. Boston St.
Dexter Ave. N.
Lake Union
Eastlake Ave E.
Boyleston Ave. E.
Boston St.
QUEEN ANNE
10th Ave. W.
6th Ave. W.
W Galer St.
Queen Anne Ave. N.
Taylor Ave. N.
Fairview Ave. N.
10th Ave.
15th Ave.
E. Aloha St.
W. Olympic Pl.
N. Royal St.
Broad St. N.
Westlake Ave. N.
Fairview Ave. N.
W. Mercer St.
Alaskan Way W.
12th Ave.
SEATTLE CENTER
1st Ave. N
5th Ave. N
E. John St.
Denny Way
2nd Ave.
Elliott Ave.
Virginia St.
Stewart St.
Olive Way
Boren Ave.
Madison St.
E. Union St.
DOWNTOWN
1st Ave.
2nd Ave.
4th Ave.
E. Cherry St.
900
Elliott Bay
N
PIONEER SQUARE
E. Yesler Way
Jackson St.
INTERNATIONAL DISTRICT
King St.
Alaskan Way W.
S. Dearborn St.
1st Ave. S
4th Ave.
SEATTLE NEIGHBORHOODS
0
.25 mile
0
.25 km

both of which perform at the Opera House. The Pacific Northwest Ballet presents a mixed repertoire in the Opera House. Performing at the Bagley Wright Theater is the Seattle Repertory Theatre. A Contemporary Theatre (ACT) presents innovative pieces in a contemporary downtown setting connected to the Convention Center.

Historical Areas

Pioneer Square is Seattle's most historic neighborhood. In the middle and late 1800s this was an area of prosperity. After the Klondike Gold Rush in 1897 and 1898, the entire section became known as "skid row," a term that originated in Seattle for an area once used to skid logs. The term later came to describe streets peopled with derelicts. In 1954, a group of interested citizens began restoring the Pioneer Square area. By 1970, the city recognized the district as Seattle's birthplace and a historic site that had to be preserved. This area of Old Seattle is thriving again as the Pioneer Square Historic District.

Pioneer Square is a mélange of art galleries, antique stores, bookshops, saloons, cafes and restaurants. The Klondike Gold Rush Museum details the history of the gold rush and its effect on Seattle.

The Museum of History and Industry tells the story of the city's first hundred years. Exhibits include an old-time fashion gallery, mementos of the Alaskan Gold Rush and souvenirs of the Alaska-Yukon-Pacific Exposition of 1909. The museum also displays old cable cars, Native American canoes, early vehicles and firefighting equipment.

Pike Place Market is a seven-acre maze of craft tables, fish, meat and produce stalls, musicians and painters. It is the oldest continually operating farmers market in the country.

Sightseeing

Because of its hill-and-water geography, Seattle is an exciting town to explore. The city's park system offers many recreational areas. Freeway Park is a five-acre oasis built over a downtown freeway. Discovery Park contains more than 391 acres of urban wilderness and is home for the Daybreak Star Arts & Cultural Center, which features Native American history and culture. Stroll through the International District for authentic Asian food, goods and celebrations. Take the waterfront streetcar under Alaskan Way along Elliott Bay to see ships of all nations in port.

Southeast of Seattle is Mount Rainier National Park. Majestic Mount Rainier towers 14,410 feet above sea level and is part of the 378-square-mile park, which contains 34 waterfalls, 62 lakes, about 40 glaciers, centuries-old trees and hundreds of subalpine meadows lush with wildflowers. The park offers mountain climbing—for expert mountaineers only—and 300 miles of hiking trails, which lead to primitive wilderness sections.

Olympic National Park, within a half day's drive, occupies 1,400 square miles of wilderness on the Olympic Peninsula. The west side of the park receives excessive rainfall, creating a moss-covered rain forest of Sitka spruce, western hemlock, Douglas fir and western red cedar. Glacier-capped mountains contrast with miles of unspoiled beaches.

Lying between the northwest corner of Washington and Vancouver Island, British Columbia, are 172 islands called the San Juan Islands, famous for their history as well as for their beauty. Ferries from Anacortes make stops at the four largest islands.

General References

Area code: 206

Phone Numbers

POLICE & FIRE: 911

POISON CONTROL CENTER: 526-2121

TIME: 361-8463 **WEATHER:** 526-6087

Information Sources

Seattle-King County Convention and Visitors Bureau, 520 Pike St, Suite 1325, 98101; 461-5840.

Visitor Info Center at the Washington State Convention & Trade Center, 800 Convention Place, 461-5840.

Parks & Recreation Department, 684-4075.

Transportation

AIRLINES: Aeroflot; Air Canada; Alaska; America West; American; Asiana; British Airways; Canadian; China Eastern; Continental; Delta; Eva; Frontier; Hawaiian; Northwest; Reno Air; SAS; Southwest; Swissair; TWA; United; USAir; Western Pacific; and other commuter and regional airlines.

AIRPORT: Sea-Tac International, 433-4645.

CAR RENTAL AGENCIES: (See IMPORTANT TOLL-FREE NUMBERS) Avis 433-5238; Budget 243-2400; Dollar 433-6766; Hertz 682-5050; Thrifty 246-7565.

PUBLIC TRANSPORTATION: Metro Transit System, 553-3000.

RAILROAD PASSENGER SERVICE: Amtrak 800/872-7245.

Newspapers

Seattle Daily Journal of Commerce; Seattle Post-Intelligencer; Seattle Times.

Convention Facilities

Bell Harbor International Conference Center, Pier 66, 441-6666.

Kingdome, 201 S King St, 296-3128.

Seattle Center, 305 Harrison St, 684-7200.

Seattle International Trade Center, 2601 Elliott Ave, 441-3000.

Washington State Convention & Trade Center, 800 Convention Place, E of 7th & Union, 447-5000.

Sports & Recreation

Major Sports Facilities

Seattle Center, 684-7200 (SuperSonics, basketball, 281-5000).

Kingdome, 201 S King St, 296-3128 (Seahawks, football, 827-9777; Mariners, baseball, 628-3555).

Cultural Facilities

Theaters

A Contemporary Theatre (ACT), 700 Union St, 285-3220.

5th Avenue Theater, 1308 5th Ave, 625-1900.

Seattle Children's Theatre, Seattle Center, 441-3322.

Seattle Repertory Theater, Seattle Center, 443-2222.

University of Washington theaters, 543-4880.

Concert Halls

Key Arena, Seattle Center, 684-7200.

Meany Hall, Univ of Washington, 543-4880.

Opera House, Seattle Center (Opera & Symphony), 684-7200.

Paramount Theatre, 907 Pine St, 682-1414.

Museums

Burke Memorial-Washington State Museum, Univ of Washington, 17th Ave NE & NE 45th St, 543-5590.

Coast Guard Museum, Pier 36, 1519 Alaskan Way S, 217-6993.

Museum of Flight, 9404 E Marginal Way S, 764-5720.

Museum of History and Industry, 2700 24th Ave E, N side of WA 520, 324-1125.

Nordic Heritage Museum, 3014 NW 67th St, 789-5707.

Pacific Science Center, Seattle Center, 200 2nd Ave N, 443-2001.

Puget Sound & Snoqualmie Valley Railroad, Snoqualmie Falls, 746-4025.

Seattle Children's Museum, Seattle Center, 441-1768.

Art Museums & Galleries

Bellevue Art Museum, NE 8th & Bellevue Way, Bellevue, 454-3322.

Charles and Emma Frye Art Museum, 704 Terry Ave, 622-9250.

Davidson Galleries, 313 Occidental Ave S, 624-7684.

Northwest Craft Center and Gallery, Seattle Center, 728-1555.

Seattle Art Museum, 100 University St, 654-3100.

Seattle Asian Art Museum, Volunteer Park, 654-3100.

William Traver Gallery, 110 Union St, 587-6501.

Woodside & Braseth Galleries, 1533 9th Ave, at Pine St, 622-7243.

Points of Interest

Historical

Klondike Gold Rush National Historical Park, 117 S Main St, 553-7220.

Pioneer Square, S edge of downtown area, bounded by 1st Ave, James St & Yesler Way.

Other Attractions

Alki Beach Park, Alki Ave SW & 59th Ave SW.

Center House, Seattle Center, 305 Harrison St, 684-7200.

Chateau Ste Michelle Winery, 15 mi NE, via WA 405, at 14111 NE 145th St in Woodinville, 488-1133.

Daybreak Star Arts & Cultural Center, Discovery Park, 285-4425.

Discovery Park, 3801 W Government Way, 386-4236.

Evergreen Floating Bridge, on WA 520, near Montlake Pl.

Fisherman's Terminal, seen from Ballard Bridge.

Freeway Park, 6th & Seneca.

Fun Forest Amusement Park, 305 Harrison St, in Seattle Center, 728-1585.

Golden Gardens Park, N end of Seaview Ave NW.

Green Lake and Park, Aurora Ave (WA 99), between N 65th & 72nd Sts, 684-4960.

Hiram H. Chittenden Locks, NW 54th St, Ballard.

International District, 4th Ave to I-5 & Yesler Way to S Dearborn St.

International Fountain, Seattle Center.

Lake Washington Floating Bridge, seen from Lake Washington Blvd & from Lakeside Ave.

Monorail, Seattle Center, runs between Center House and Westlake Center, 684-7200.

Mount Baker-Snoqualmie National Forest, E & S of city, reached via I-90, 220-7450.

Mt Rainier National Park, S via I-5.

Myrtle Edwards/Elliott Bay Parks, N of Pier 70.

Pike Place Market, 1st Ave & Pike St, 682-7453.

Seattle Aquarium, Pier 59, Waterfront Park, 386-4320.

Seattle Center, 305 Harrison St, 684-7200.

Shilshole Bay Marina, 7001 Seaview Ave NW, 728-3385.

Smith Cove, seen from Elliott Ave & W Garfield St.

Snoqualmie Falls, 30 mi E via I-90.

Space Needle, Seattle Center, 443-2111 or 800/937-9582.

Tillicum Village, Blake Island State Park, 443-1244.

University of Washington, 17th Ave NE & NE 45th St, 543-9198.

Warren G. Magnuson Park, NE 65th & Sand Point Way NE.

Washington Park Arboretum & Japanese Garden, both sides of Lake Washington Blvd between E Madison & Montlake, 543-8800.

Waterfront Drive, Alaskan Way along Elliott Bay.

Waterfront Park, Alaskan Way, Pier 57 to Pier 59.

Woodland Park Zoo, Phinney Ave N between N 50th & N 59th Sts, 684-4800.

Sightseeing Tours

Argosy Harbor Tours, from Pier 55, foot of Seneca St, 623-1445.

Bill Speidel's Underground Tour, 610 1st Ave, 682-4646.

Ferry Trips, Seattle Ferry Terminal, Colman Dock, foot of Madison St, 464-6400 or 800/843-3779 (WA).

Gallant Lady Cruises, Lake Union, 463-2073.

Gray Line bus tours, 720 S Forest, 624-5077 or 800/426-7532.

Annual Events

Cherry Blossom & Japanese Cultural Festival. Apr.

Folklife Festival, Seattle Center. Memorial Day wkend.

Pacific Northwest Arts & Crafts Fair, 4 mi E in Bellevue. Late July.

Seattle Seafair, events throughout the city. Late July-early Aug.

Bumbershoot, Seattle Center. Labor Day wkend.

City Neighborhoods

Many of the restaurants, unrated dining establishments and some lodgings listed under Seattle include neighborhoods as well as exact street addresses. Geographic descriptions of these areas are given, followed by a table of restaurants arranged by neighborhood.

Downtown: South of Denny Way, west of I-5, north of S King St and east of Alaskan Way and Elliot Bay. **North of Downtown:** North of E Denny Way. **South of Downtown:** South of Dearborn St. **East of Downtown:** East of I-5.

International District: Southeast of Downtown; south of Yesler St, west of I-5, north of S Dearborn St and east of 4th Ave S.

Pioneer Square: Downtown area on and around Pioneer Square, bounded by 1st and James Sts, Yesler Way and 1st Ave S.

Queen Anne: South of W Nickerson St and Washington Ship Canal, west of Aurora Ave N, north of Denny Way and east of Elliott Ave W and 15th St W.

Seattle Center: South of Mercer St, west of 5th Ave N, north of Denny Way and east of 1st Ave N.

Lodgings and Food

SEATTLE RESTAURANTS BY NEIGHBORHOOD AREAS

(For full description, see alphabetical listings under Restaurants)

INTERNATIONAL DISTRICT
Four Seas. 714 S King St
Linyen. 424 Seventh Ave S

DOWNTOWN
Andaluca. 407 Olive Way
Assaggio Ristorante. 2010 Fourth Ave
Bombore. 89 University St
Brooklyn House. 1212 Second Ave
Buca Di Beppo. 701 Ninth Ave N
Cafe Campagne. 1600 Post Alley
Cafe Sophie. 1921 First Ave
Campagne. 86 Pine St
Chez Shea. 94 Pike St
Dahlia Lounge. 1904 Fourth Ave
El Gaucho. 2505 First Ave
Elliott's Oyster House. 1203 Alaskan Way
Etta's Seafood. 2020 Western Ave
Flying Fish. 2234 First Ave
Fullers (Sheraton Hotel). 1400 6th Ave
Georgian Room (Four Seasons Olympic Hotel). 411 University St
Hunt Club (Sorrento Hotel). 900 Madison St
Il Bistro. 93A Pike St
Ivar's Acres Of Clams. Pier 54
Labuznik. 1924 First Ave
Lampreia. 2400 First Ave
Las Margaritas. 1122 Post Ave
Marco's. 2510 First Ave
Maximilien-In-The-Market. 81A Pike Place
McCormick & Schmick's. 1103 First Ave
McCormick's Fish House. 722 Fourth Ave
Metropolitan Grill. 820 Second Ave
Obachine. 1518 Sixth Ave
Painted Table (Alexis Hotel). 1007 First Ave
Palace Kitchen. 2030 Fifth Ave
Palomino. 1420 Fifth Ave
Pink Door. 1919 Post Alley
Place Pigalle. 81 Pike St
Prego (Renaissance Madison Hotel). 515 Madison St
Queen City Grill. 2201 1st Ave
Reiner's. 1106 Eighth Ave
Roy's (The Westin Hotel). 1900 5th Ave
Ruth's Chris Steak House. 800 Fifth Ave
Sazerac (Hotel Monaco). 1101 4th Ave
Shiro's. 2401 Second Ave
Theoz. 1523 Sixth Ave
Tulio (Hotel Vintage Park). 1100 Fifth Ave
Union Square Grill. 621 Union St
Vina. 2207 First Ave
Virazon. 1329 First Ave
Wild Ginger. 1400 Western Ave

NORTH OF DOWNTOWN
Arnie's Northshore. 1900 N Northlake Way
Asia Grille. 2820 NE University Village
Bandoleone. 2241 Eastlake Ave E
Burrito Loco. 9211 Holman Rd NW
Cafe Lago. 2305 24th Ave E
Carmelita. 7314 Greenwood Ave N
Chinook's. 1900 W Nickerson
Cucina! Cucina!. 901 Fairview Ave N
Doong Kong Lau. 9710 Aurora Ave N
Franco's Hidden Harbor. 1500 Westlake Ave N
Ivar's Indian Salmon House. 401 NE Northlake Way
Jitterbug. 2114 N 45th St
Latitude 47°. 1232 Westlake N
Le Gourmand. 425 NW Market St
Pescatore. 5300 34th St NW
Piatti. 2800 NE University Village
Portage Bay Cafe (University Inn Motor Hotel). 4140 Roosevelt Way NE
Ray's Boathouse. 6049 Seaview Ave NW
Saleh Al Lago. 6804 E Greenlake Way
Serafina. 2043 Eastlake Ave E
Simpatico. 4430 Wallingford Ave
Stella's Trattoria. 4500 Ninth Ave
Surrogate Hostess. 746 19th Ave E
Szmania's. 3321 W McGraw
Union Bay Cafe. 3515 NE 45th St

EAST OF DOWNTOWN
Cactus. 4220 E Madison
Cafe Flora. 2901 E Madison
Dulces Latin Bistro. 1430 34th Ave
Kitto Japanese Noodle House. 614 Broadway E
Madison Park Cafe. 1807 42nd Ave E
Nishino. 3130 E Madison
Rover's. 2808 E Madison St
Z Ritz. 720 E Pike

PIONEER SQUARE
Al Boccalino. 1 Yesler Way
F.X. McRory's Steak, Chop & Oyster House. 419 Occidental Ave S
Il Terrazzo Carmine. 411 First Ave S
La Buca. 102 Cherry St
Trattoria Mitchelli. 84 Yesler Way

QUEEN ANNE
Adriatica. 1107 Dexter N
Canlis. 2576 Aurora Ave N
Chutney's. 519 First Ave N
Kaspar's. 19 W Harrison St
Paragon. 2125 Queen Anne Ave N
Pirosmani. 2220 Queen Anne Ave N
Ponti. 3014 Third Ave N

SEATTLE CENTER
Space Needle. 219 Fourth Ave N

Note: When a listing is located in a town that does not have its own city heading, it will appear under the city nearest to its location. In these cases, the address and town appear in parenthesis immediately following the name of the establishment.

Motels

★ ★ **BEST WESTERN LOYAL INN.** *2301 Eighth Ave (98121), at Denny Way, downtown. 206/682-0200; FAX 206/467-8984.* 91 rms, 4 story. July-Sept: S $88; D $106; each addl $6; suites $200; under 12 free; lower rates rest of yr. Crib $3. TV; cable. Complimentary continental bkfst. Restaurant opp open 24 hrs. Ck-out noon. Coin Indry. Business servs avail. In-rm modem link. Sauna. Whirlpool. Some refrigerators, wet bars; microwaves avail. Cr cds: A, C, D, DS, MC, V.

D

★ **QUALITY INN CITY CENTER.** *2224 8th Ave (98121), downtown. 206/624-6820; FAX 206/467-6926.* 72 rms, 7 story. May-Oct: S $105-$115; D $115-$125; each addl $10; suites $145-$185; under 18 free; lower rates rest of yr. Crib free. Pet accepted. TV; cable (premium), VCR avail (movies). Continental bkfst. Coffee in rms. Ck-out 1 pm. Meeting rms. Business servs avail. In-rm modem link. Valet serv. Sundries. Exercise equipt; weight machine, treadmill, sauna. Whirlpool. Some refrigerators; microwaves avail for suites. Balconies. Cr cds: A, C, D, DS, ER, JCB, MC, V.

D SC

✔★ **TRAVELERS INN.** *(4710 Lake Washington Blvd NE, Renton 98056) S on I-405 exit 7. 253/228-2858; FAX 253/228-3055; res: 800/633-8300.* 116 rms, 2-3 story. No elvtr. S $42.99; D $49.99; each addl $4; suites $63.99-$79.99; under 18 free. Crib free. TV; cable (premium). Heated pool. Complimentary coffee in lobby. Restaurant adj open 24 hrs. Bar 11-2 am. Ck-out 11 am. Coin lndry. Business servs avail. Cr cds: A, D, DS, MC, V.

D SC

Motor Hotels

★ ★ **BEST WESTERN EXECUTIVE INN.** *200 Taylor Ave N (98109), at Seattle Center. 206/448-9444; FAX 206/441-7929.* E-mail executive.inn@juno.com. 123 rms, 5 story. July-Sept: S, D $100-$143; each addl $15; under 18 free; lower rates rest of yr. Crib free. TV; cable (premium), VCR avail. Complimentary coffee in rms Mon-Fri. Restaurant 6:30 am-10 pm; wkends from 7 am. Rm serv. Bar 11-2 am. Ck-out noon. Guest lndry. Meeting rms. Business servs avail. In-rm modem link. Bellhops. Valet serv. Sundries. Exercise equipt; weight machine, stair machine. Whirlpool. Some refrigerators. Cr cds: A, C, D, DS, JCB, MC, V.

D SC

★ ★ **BEST WESTERN-PIONEER SQUARE HOTEL.** *77 Yesler Way (98104), in Pioneer Square. 206/340-1234; FAX 206/467-0707.* Web www.pioneersquare.com. 75 rms, 4 story. S, D $109-$139; each addl $10; under 12 free. Crib free. Valet parking $13. TV; cable, VCR avail. Complimentary continental bkfst. Restaurant opp 7-4 am. Ck-out 11 am. Meeting rms. Business servs avail. In-rm modem link. Bellhops. Valet serv. Health club privileges. In restored building (1914). Cr cds: A, D, DS, JCB, MC, V.

D SC

★ ★ ★ **EDGEWATER INN.** *2411 Alaskan Way (98121), Pier 67, west of downtown. 206/728-7000; FAX 206/441-4119; res: 800/624-0670.* 237 rms, 4 story. S $129-$170; D $129-$240; each addl $15; suites $350-$1,000; under 18 free. Crib free. Valet parking (fee). TV; cable (premium). Coffee in rms. Restaurant 6 am-11 pm. Rm serv. Bar 11-1:30 am; entertainment Tues-Sat. Ck-out noon. Meeting rms. Business center. In-rm modem link. Bellhops. Valet serv. Gift shop. Exercise equipt; bicycles, rower. Guest bicycles. Minibars. Some balconies. Built entirely over water; adj to ferry terminal. Cr cds: A, C, D, DS, ER, JCB, MC, V.

D SC

✔★ ★ **SIXTH AVENUE INN.** *2000 Sixth Ave (98121), downtown. 206/441-8300; FAX 206/441-9903; res: 800/648-6440.* 166 rms, 5 story, no ground floor rms. Mid-May-mid-Oct: S $81-$109; D $93-$121; each addl $12; suites $150; under 17 free. Crib free. TV; cable (premium). Restaurant 6:30 am-10 pm. Rm serv 7 am-9 pm. Bar 11 am-midnight. Ck-out noon. Meeting rms. Business servs avail. In-rm modem link. Bellhops. Valet serv. Sundries. Cr cds: A, C, D, MC, V.

SC

★ ★ **UNIVERSITY INN.** *4140 Roosevelt Way NE (98105), north of downtown. 206/632-5055; FAX 206/547-4937; res: 800/733-3855.* E-mail Univinn@aol.com; web www.travelweb.com. 102 rms, 4 story. May-Oct: S, D $92-$112; suites $122-$132; each addl $10; under 18 free; wkly rates. Crib free. TV; cable (premium). Heated pool. Complimentary continental bkfst. Restaurant 6:30 am-3 pm. Ck-out noon. Coin lndry. Meeting rms. Business center. In-rm modem link. Valet serv. Exercise equipt; weight machine, bicycles. Cr cds: A, D, DS, MC, V.

D SC

Hotels

★ ★ ★ ★ **ALEXIS HOTEL.** *1007 1st Ave (98104), downtown. 206/624-4844; FAX 206/621-9009; res: 800/426-7033.* Web www.alexishotel.com. A charming small hotel, the Alexis is in an artfully restored 1901 building near the waterfront, the Public Market and the Seattle Art Museum. Each room is individually decorated. 109 rms, 6 story. S, D $210-$235; suites $245-$550; under 12 free; some wkend rates. Crib free. Pet accepted. Covered valet parking $18/day. TV; cable (premium), VCR avail. Restaurant 6:30 am-3 pm (also see PAINTED TABLE). Rm serv 24 hrs. Bar 11 am-midnight. Ck-out 1 pm. Meeting rms. Business servs avail. In-rm modem link. Concierge. Shopping arcade. Exercise equipt; treadmill, stair machine, steam rm. Massage. Refrigerators; some bathrm phones; microwaves avail. Wet bar, minibar, beverages, whirlpool in suites. Eight wood-burning fireplaces. Some balconies. Cr cds: A, C, D, DS, MC, V.

D

★ **CAMLIN.** *1619 Ninth Ave (98101), at Pine St, downtown. 206/682-0100; FAX 206/682-7415; res: 800/426-0670.* 136 rms, 36 A/C, 4-10 story. S, D $83-$114; each addl $10; suites $175; under 18 free. Crib free. TV; cable (premium). Pool. Restaurant 6-10:30 am, 11:30 am-2 pm, 6-10 pm; Sat 6:30-11 am, 5:30-10:30 pm; Sun 6:30-11 am, 5-9 pm. Bar; entertainment Tues-Sat. Ck-out noon. Business servs avail. Some balconies. Motor entrance on 8th Ave. Cr cds: A, C, D, DS, JCB, MC, V.

SC

★ ★ ★ **CROWNE PLAZA.** *1113 Sixth Ave (98101), at Seneca St, downtown. 206/464-1980; FAX 206/340-1617.* E-mail cplaza@wolfenet.com; web www.crownwplaza.com. 415 rms, 34 story. June-Oct S, D $240; each addl $20; suites $260-$525; under 18 free; wkend rates; lower rates rest of yr. Crib free. Covered valet parking $18. TV; cable (premium), VCR avail. Coffee in rms. Restaurant 6 am-10 pm. Bar 11-2 am. Ck-out noon. Meeting rms. Business servs avail. In-rm modem link. Concierge. Exercise equipt; weight machine, stair machine, sauna. Whirlpool. Refrigerators avail. Luxury level. Cr cds: A, C, D, DS, JCB, MC, V.

D SC

★ ★ ★ **DOUBLETREE GUEST SUITES.** *16500 Southcenter Pkwy (98188), I-5 Southcenter exit, south of downtown. 206/575-8220; FAX 206/575-4743.* Web www.doubletreehotels.com. 221 suites, 8 story. S, D $119-$238; each addl $15; under 18 free; wkend, seasonal rates. Crib free. TV; cable (premium), VCR avail. Indoor pool; outdoor pool privileges in summer; whirlpool. Coffee in rms. Restaurant 6 am-10 pm; wkends 7 am-11 pm. Bar 11-2 am; entertainment. Ck-out noon. Meeting rms. Business servs avail. Gift shop. Free airport transportation. Exercise equipt; weight machine, bicycles, sauna. Racquetball. Refrigerators; microwaves avail. Atrium lobby. Cr cds: A, C, D, DS, ER, JCB, MC, V.

D SC

★ ★ ★ ★ ★ **FOUR SEASONS OLYMPIC HOTEL.** *411 University St (98101), downtown. 206/621-1700; FAX 206/682-9633.* This elegant Italian Renaissance-style landmark hotel occupies a central position in Seattle's social scene. Known for its opulent decor—oak paneling, antiques and Italian marble—its attentive service and the elegant Georgian Room and Garden Court restaurants, the hotel is a convenient tour base, since it's a short stroll from Pike Place Market and the Seattle Art Museum. 450 rms, 13 story. S $225-$255; D $265-$295; each addl $20; suites $330-$1,250; under 18 free; wkend rates. Crib free. Valet parking $21. TV; cable (premium), VCR avail (movies). Indoor pool; whirlpool, poolside serv. Restaurant (see GEORGIAN ROOM). Rm serv 24 hrs. Bar 11-1 am. Ck-out 1 pm. Convention facilities. Business center. In-rm modem link. Concierge. Shopping arcade. Barber, beauty shop. Airport transportation. Exercise equipt; weight machine, bicycles, sauna. Massage. Bathrm phones, minibars; some refrigerators. Cr cds: A, C, D, ER, JCB, MC, V.

D

★ ★ ★ **HILTON.** *1301 Sixth Ave (98101), W of I-5 Seneca-Union exit, downtown. 206/624-0500; FAX 206/682-9029.* 237 rms, 28 story. S $165-$210; D $185-$230; each addl $15; suites $310-$475; under 18 free; some wkend rates. Crib free. Garage $13. TV; cable (premium). Complimentary coffee in rms. Restaurants 6 am-10 pm. Rm serv 24 hrs. Bar 11-2 am; pianist. Ck-out 1 pm. Meeting rms. Business servs avail. Concierge. Gift shop. Exercise equipt; weight machines, bicycles. Refrigerators, minibars. View of Puget Sound. Cr cds: A, C, D, DS, ER, JCB, MC, V.

D

HOTEL MONACO. *(Too new to be rated) 1101 Fourth Ave (98101), downtown. 206/621-1770; res: 800/945-2240; FAX 206/621-7779.* Web www.monaco-seattle.com. 189 rms, 11 story, 45 suites. May-Sept: S $195; D $210; suites $240-$900; under 18 free; wkly, hol plans;

lower rates rest of yr. Crib free. Pet accepted. Valet parking $18. TV; cable (premium), VCR. Complimentary coffee in rms. Restaurant (see SAZERAC). Rm serv 24 hrs. Bar 11:30 am-midnight. Ck-out noon. Meeting rms. Business center. In-rm modem link. Valet serv. Concierge. Gift shop. Exercise equipt; weights, treadmill. Massage. Health club privileges. Bathrm phones, refrigerators, minibars; some in-rm whirlpools; microwaves avail. Luxury level. Whimsical yet elegant decor with vibrant color scheme throughout. Cr cds: A, D, DS, MC, V.

D SC

★ ★ ★ ★ **HOTEL VINTAGE PARK.** *1100 Fifth Ave (98101), at Spring St, downtown. 206/624-8000; FAX 206/623-0568; res: 800/624-4433.* Web www.hotelvintagepark.com. Built in 1922, this European-style lodging combines the luxury of an upscale hotel with the personality of a bed-and-breakfast. Guest rooms are named for Washington wineries and decorated in rich vineyard shades of dark green, plum and gold. 126 rms, 11 story. S $185-$205; D $200-$220; suites $215-$375; under 12 free; wkend rates; package plans. Crib free. Valet parking $16. TV; cable, VCR avail. Complimentary coffee in rms. Restaurant (see TULIO). Rm serv 24 hrs. Ck-out noon. Meeting rms. Business servs avail. In-rm modem link. Concierge. Exercise equipt delivered to rms. Health club privileges. Bathrm phones, minibars. Wine tasting (Washington wines) in lobby Mon-Sat. Cr cds: A, C, D, DS, ER, JCB, MC, V.

D

★ ★ ★ ★ **INN AT THE MARKET.** *86 Pine St (98101), downtown. 206/443-3600; FAX 206/448-0631; res: 800/446-4484.* Web usa.nia.com/innmarket. Adjacent to the Pike Place Market, this small, deluxe hotel emphasizes the informality of the Pacific Northwest rather than the amenities of a big hotel. Rooms are spacious, have contemporary furnishings and ceramic sculptures, and look out on the city, the market, the hotel courtyard or Elliott Bay. 69 rms, 4-8 story, 10 suites. May-mid-Oct: S, D $145-$210; each addl $15; suites $250-$350; under 16 free; some wkend rates; lower rates rest of yr. Crib free. Parking $15; valet. TV; cable (premium), VCR avail. Complimentary coffee in rms. Ck-out noon. Meeting rm. Business servs avail. Shopping arcade. Beauty shop. Health club privileges. Bathrm phones, refrigerators; microwaves avail. Cr cds: A, C, D, DS, JCB, MC, V.

D SC

★ ★ **INN AT VIRGINIA MASON.** *1006 Spring St (98104), east of downtown. 206/583-6453; FAX 206/223-7545; res: 800/283-6453.* 79 air-cooled rms, 9 story. S, D $98-$155; suites $155-$215. TV; cable (premium), VCR (movies). Restaurant 7-10 am, 11:30 am-3 pm, 5-9 pm. Ck-out noon. Business servs avail. In-rm modem link. Concierge. Microwaves avail. English country-style apartment house (1928); Queen Anne-style furnishings. Totally nonsmoking. Cr cds: A, D, DS, JCB, MC, V.

D SC

★ ★ ★ **MAYFLOWER PARK.** *405 Olive Way (98101), downtown. 206/623-8700; FAX 206/382-6997; res: 800/426-5100.* 172 rms, 12 story. S $135-$155; D $150-$170; each addl $15; suites $175-$350; mini-suites $175-$190; under 18 free. Crib free. Covered valet parking $9. TV; cable (premium). Restaurant 6:30 am-10 pm. Rm serv 24 hrs. Bar 11:30-2 am. Ck-out noon. Meeting rms. Business servs avail. In-rm modem link. Exercise equipt; weights, stair machine. Health club privileges. Cr cds: A, C, D, DS, MC, V.

D SC

✔★ ★ ★ **MEANY TOWER.** *4507 Brooklyn Ave NE (98105), E of I-5 exit 45th St, north of downtown. 206/634-2000; FAX 206/547-6029; res: 800/899-0251.* E-mail meanytwr@aol.com. 155 rms, 15 story. June-Sept: S $145-$165; D $160-$180; each addl $15; under 14 free; lower rates rest of yr. Crib free. TV; cable. Restaurant 6 am-9:30 pm; Sat to 9 pm; Sun to 8:30 pm. Bar 11 am-11 pm; Fri, Sat to midnight. Ck-out noon. Meeting rms. Business servs avail. In-rm modem link. Exercise equipt; rower, weight machine. Game rm. View of mountains, lakes, city. 2 blks from Univ of WA campus. Cr cds: A, C, D, MC, V.

D SC

★ **PACIFIC PLAZA.** *400 Spring St (98104), downtown. 206/623-3900; FAX 206/623-2059; res: 800/426-1165.* E-mail pph400@aol.com. 160 rms, 8 story. S, D $95-$125; under 18 free; wkend rates. Crib free. Garage parking $12 in/out. TV; cable. Complimentary continental bkfst. Ck-out 11 am. Business servs avail. Cr cds: A, D, DS, JCB, MC, V.

SC

★ ★ ★ **PLAZA PARK SUITES.** *1011 Pike St (98101), downtown. 206/682-8282; FAX 206/682-5315; res: 800/426-0670 (exc WA).* 193 suites, 9 story. Studios $125-$190; 1 bedrm $190-$220; 2 bedrm $290-$330; under 18 free. Crib free. Valet parking $13. TV; cable (premium), VCR avail. Heated pool; whirlpool. Complimentary continental bkfst. Complimentary coffee in rms. Restaurant. Ck-out noon. Coin lndry. Meeting rms. Business servs avail. In-rm modem link. Gift shop. Exercise equipt; weight machine, stair machine. Refrigerators, microwaves; many in-rm whirlpools, fireplaces. Balconies. Picnic tables. Cr cds: A, C, D, DS, ER, JCB, MC, V.

D SC

★ ★ ★ **RENAISSANCE MADISON.** *515 Madison St (98104), I-5 S Madison St exit, downtown. 206/583-0300; FAX 206/622-8635.* 553 rms, 28 story. S, D $159-$179; suites $199-$800; wkend rates. Crib free. Covered parking $14. TV; cable, VCR avail. Indoor pool; whirlpool. Complimentary coffee in rms. Restaurant 6:30 am-10 pm; Fri, Sat to 11 pm (also see PREGO). Rm serv 24 hrs. Bars 11-2 am. Ck-out 1 pm. Convention facilities. Business center. In-rm modem link. Concierge. Barber, beauty shop. Gift shop. Exercise equipt; stair machine, weight machine. Health club privileges. Free local transportation. Refrigerators, minibars. Luxury level. Cr cds: A, C, D, DS, ER, JCB, MC, V.

D SC

★ ★ ★ **SHERATON.** *1400 6th Ave (98101), downtown. 206/621-9000; FAX 206/621-8441.* Web www.ITTsheraton.com. 840 units, 35 story. S $200, D $220; suites $275-$600; under 17 free; wkend rates. Crib free. Pet accepted, some restrictions. Valet parking $18. TV; cable (premium), VCR avail. Indoor pool; whirlpool. Complimentary coffee in rms. Restaurant 6 am-midnight (also see FULLER'S). Rm serv 24 hrs. Bar 11-2 am; entertainment. Ck-out noon. Convention facilities. Business center. In-rm modem link. Concierge. Drugstore. Barber. Exercise rm: instructor, weight machine, stair machine, sauna. Minibars; some bathrm phones. Rms with original Northwest art. Luxury level. Cr cds: A, C, D, DS, ER, JCB, MC, V.

D SC

★ ★ **SILVER CLOUD INN.** *5036 25th Ave NE (98105), north of downtown. 206/526-5200; FAX 206/522-1450; res: 800/205-6940.* E-mail heather@scinns.com; web scinns.com. 144 rms, 4 story. July-Oct: S $91-$103; D $103-$115; each addl $10; suites $117-$142; under 12 free; lower rates rest of yr. Crib free. TV; cable (premium). Indoor pool; whirlpool. Complimentary continental bkfst. Restaurant nearby. Ck-out noon. Meeting rms. Business servs avail. In-rm modem link. Guest lndry avail. Exercise equipt; bicycle, stair machine. Refrigerators, microwaves avail. Cr cds: A, C, D, DS, ER, MC, V.

D SC

★ ★ ★ ★ **SORRENTO.** *900 Madison St (98104), I-5 N James, S Madison exits, downtown. 206/622-6400; FAX 206/343-6155; res: 800/426-1265 (exc WA).* Web usa.nia.com/sorrento. Designed in 1909 to resemble an Italian villa, this deluxe hotel offers wonderful views of downtown and the waterfront. Standard rooms are quiet and comfortable; spacious corner suites have antiques and oversize baths. 76 rms, 6 story, 42 suites. S, D $180-$240; each addl $15; suites $220-$1,200; under 16 free. Crib free. Pet accepted. Covered parking; valet $17. TV; cable (premium), VCR avail. Restaurant (see HUNT CLUB). Bar 11:30-2 am. Ck-out noon. Meeting rms. Business servs avail. In-rm modem link. Concierge. Airport transportation. Exercise equipt; weight machines, treadmill. Massage. Refrigerators; many bathrm phones; microwaves avail. Cr cds: A, C, D, DS, JCB, MC, V.

D

★ ★ ★ **WARWICK.** *401 Lenora St (98121), at 4th Ave, downtown. 206/443-4300; FAX 206/448-1662; res: 800/426-9280.* 229 units, 19 story. May-Oct; S $190; D $210; each addl $10; suites $275-$500; under 18 free; lower rates rest of yr. Crib free. Covered valet parking $12. TV; cable, VCR avail. Indoor pool; whirlpool. Restaurant 6:30 am-2 pm, 5:30-10 pm. Rm serv 24 hrs. Bar 11-2 am; pianist Wed-Sat. Ck-out noon. Meeting rms. Business servs avail. In-rm modem link. Exercise equipt: weight machine, treadmill, sauna. Bathrm phones; many refrigerators, wet bars. In-rm whirlpool in suites. Balconies. Fireplace in lobby. Cr cds: A, C, D, DS, ER, JCB, MC, V.

D SC

★ ★ ★ **THE WESTIN.** *1900 5th Ave (98101), at Westlake, downtown. 206/728-1000; FAX 206/728-2259.* 865 rms, 40-47 story. S $135-$240; D $155-$260; each addl $25; suites $295-$1,200; under 18 free; wkend rates. Crib free. Garage $18. TV; cable (premium), VCR avail. Heated pool; whirlpool. Restaurants 6 am-10 pm; Thurs-Sun to 10:30 pm. Rm serv 24 hrs. Bar; entertainment exc Sun. Ck-out noon. Convention facilities. Business center. In-rm modem link. Concierge. Gift shop. Barber, beauty shop. Exercise equipt; weight machines, bicycles, sauna. Refrigerators, minibars. Sun deck. Tower rms with panoramic view. Cr cds: A, C, D, DS, ER, JCB, MC, V.

D

Inns

✔★ ★ **BEECH TREE MANOR.** *1405 Queen Anne Ave N (98109), in Queen Anne. 206/281-7037; FAX 206/284-2350.* 7 rms, 2 share bath, 2 story. No A/C. No rm phones. Mid-May-mid-Oct: S $64-$94; D $74-$94; suite $110; each addl $10; wkly rates; lower rates rest of yr. Pet accepted. TV in sitting rm; cable (premium), VCR. Complimentary full bkfst. Restaurant nearby. Ck-out 11 am, ck-in 4-7 pm. Business servs avail. Street parking. Turn-of-the-century mansion (1903) furnished with many antiques. Totally nonsmoking. Cr cds: MC, V.

★ ★ **CHAMBERED NAUTILUS.** *5005 22nd Ave NE (98105), north of downtown. 206/522-2536.* E-mail chamberednautilus@msn.com. 6 rms, 3 story. No A/C. Rm phones avail. S $74-$105; D $79-$109; each addl $15. Complimentary full bkfst; afternoon refreshments. Restaurant nearby. Ck-out 11 am, ck-in 4-6 pm. Business servs avail. Street parking. Sundeck. Georgian colonial house (1915); library/sitting rm with fireplace. Cr cds: A, MC, V.

★ ★ **CHELSEA STATION ON THE PARK.** *4915 Linden Ave N (98103), north of downtown. 206/547-6077; FAX 206/632-5107; res: 800/400-6077.* 8 rms, 2 story, 6 suites. No A/C. June-Sept: S $84; D $89; each addl $10; suites $119; lower rates rest of yr. Children over 12 yrs only. Complimentary full bkfst; afternoon refreshments. Restaurants nearby. Ck-out 11 am, ck-in 3 pm. Business servs avail. In-rm modem link. Street parking. Microwaves avail. Colonial-style brick house (1929); antiques. Near Woodland Park Zoo. Totally nonsmoking. Cr cds: A, D, DS, MC, V.

✔★ ★ ★ **GASLIGHT.** *1727-1733 15th Ave (98122), east of downtown. 206/325-3654; FAX 206/328-4803.* Web www.gaslight-inn.com. 16 rms, 4 with shower only, 3 share bath, 3 story, 7 suites. No A/C. Some rm phones. S, D $68-$108; suites $128-$148; some wkly rates. TV; cable. Heated pool; poolside serv. Complimentary continental bkfst; afternoon refreshments. Restaurant nearby. Ck-out 11 am, ck-in 3-6 pm. Business servs avail. In-rm modem link. Luggage handling. Refrigerators. Picnic tables. Two buildings; one built 1906. Antiques. Cr cds: A, MC, V.

★ ★ **HILL HOUSE BED & BREAKFAST.** *1113 E John St (98102), east of downtown. 206/720-7161; res: 800/720-7161; FAX 206/323-0772.* E-mail hillhouse@uspan.com; web uspan.com/hillhouse. 5 rms, 2 share bath, 2 suites. No A/C. Some rm phones. Mid-May-mid-Nov: S, D $70-$90; suites $115; wkly rates; wkends, hols (2-4 day min); lower rates rest of yr. Children over 12 yrs only. TV in suites; cable (premium). Complimentary full bkfst. Restaurant nearby. Ck-out 11 am, ck-in (by appt). In-rm modem link. Restored 1903 Victorian inn. Cr cds: A, DS, MC, V.

★ ★ ★ **INN AT HARBOR STEPS.** *1221 First Ave (98101), downtown. 206/748-0973; res: 888/728-8910; FAX 206/682-6045.* Web www.harborsteps.com. 20 rms, 2 story. S, D $150-$200; each addl $15; hol rates. Crib $15. TV; cable, VCR avail. Complimentary full bkfst; afternoon refreshments. Complimentary coffee in rms. Restaurant 8 am-10 pm. Ck-out noon, ck-in 2 pm. Business servs avail. In-rm modem link. Luggage handling. Exercise equipt; weight machine, bicycle. Indoor pool; whirlpool. In-rm whirlpools, refrigerators, fireplaces. Balconies. Ocean and garden views. Cr cds: A, C, D, JCB, MC, V.

D

★ **PRINCE OF WALES.** *133 13th Ave E (98102), east of downtown. 206/325-9692; FAX 206/322-6402; res: 800/327-9692.* E-mail cnorton949@aol.com; web uspan.com/sbba. 4 rms, 2 with shower only, 3 story. Apr-Oct: S, D $99-$125; lower rates rest of yr. Children over 3 yrs only. Complimentary full bkfst; afternoon refreshments. Restaurant nearby. Ck-out 11 am, ck-in 4-6 pm. Business servs avail. Microwaves avail. Built in 1903; furnished with antiques. Totally nonsmoking. Cr cds: DS, MC, V.

★ ★ **ROBERTA'S BED & BREAKFAST.** *1147 16th Ave E (98112), east of downtown. 206/329-3326; FAX 206/324-2149.* E-mail robertsbb@aol.com; web www.robertasbb.com. 5 rms, 3 story. S $82-$105; D $90-$125; each addl $20. Complimentary full bkfst. Complimentary coffee in rms. Ck-out 11 am. Business servs avail. Built 1903; many antiques. Extensive library. Totally nonsmoking. Cr cds: MC, V.

★ ★ ★ **SALISBURY HOUSE.** *750 16th Ave E (98112), east of downtown. 206/328-8682; FAX 206/720-1019.* E-mail cathy@salisburyhouse.com; web www.salisburyhouse.com. 4 rms, 3 with shower only, 2 story. No A/C. No rm phones. May-Oct: S $75-$115; D $85-$125; each addl $15; lower rates rest of yr. Children over 12 yrs only. Complimentary full bkfst. Restaurants nearby. Ck-out 11 am, ck-in 4-6 pm. Business servs avail. In-rm modem link. Built 1904; wraparound porch. Many antiques. Totally nonsmoking. Cr cds: A, D, MC, V.

Restaurants

★ ★ ★ **ADRIATICA.** *1107 Dexter N (98109), in Queen Anne. 206/285-5000.* Hrs: 5-11 pm; Fri, Sat to midnight. Closed some hols. Res accepted. Southern Mediterranean menu. Bar. Wine list. Semi-a la carte: dinner $10.50-$26. Specializes in lamb, pasta, seafood. Own pastries. Parking. Outdoor dining. Built 1922. European villa decor. Overlooks garden, Lake Union. Cr cds: A, D, MC, V.

★ ★ ★ **AL BOCCALINO.** *1 Yesler Way (98104), in Pioneer Square. 206/622-7688.* Hrs: 11:30 am-2 pm, 5-10 pm; Mon from 5 pm; Fri to 10:30 pm; Sat 5-10:30 pm; Sun 5-9:30 pm. Closed major hols. Res accepted. No A/C. Italian menu. Semi-a la carte: lunch $8-$12.50, dinner $11-$21. Specializes in fresh seafood, rissotto, veal chop. Bistro atmosphere. Cr cds: A, D, JCB, MC, V.

D

★ ★ ★ **ANDALUCA.** *407 Olive Way (98101), downtown. 206/382-6999.* Hrs: 6:30 am-2:30 pm, 5-10 pm; Fri, Sat to 11 pm; Sun 7 am-noon. Res required. Bar 11:30 am-closing. Semi-a la carte: bkfst $4.50-$8.25, lunch $7.50-$12.50, dinner $14.50-$23. Specializes in Northwestern cuisine with Mediterranean influence. Cr cds: A, C, D, DS, MC, V.

D

★ ★ **ARNIE'S NORTHSHORE.** *1900 N Northlake Way (98103), opp Gas Works Park, north of downtown. 206/547-3242.* Hrs: 11:30 am-9 pm; Sat 5-10 pm; Sun 10 am-9 pm; early-bird dinner Sun-Thurs 5-6 pm; Sun brunch to 2 pm. Closed Dec 25; also lunch Memorial Day, July 4,

Labor Day. Res accepted. Bar to 2 am. Semi-a la carte: lunch $5.95-$10.95, dinner $10.95-$23.95. Sun brunch $5.95-$10.95. Specializes in Northwest seafood. Own sauces. Parking. Contemporary decor. Panoramic view of Lake Union, Seattle skyline. Cr cds: A, MC, V.

D

★ ★ **ASIA GRILLE.** *2820 NE University Village (98105), 3 mi N on I-5, exit NE 45th, north of downtown. 206/517-5985.* Hrs: 11:30 am-10 pm; Sun to 9 pm. Closed Thanksgiving, Dec 25. Res accepted (dinner). Asian menu. Bar. A la carte entrees: lunch $7.95-$10.95, dinner $7.95-$15.95. Child's meals. Specialties: spit-roasted garlic chicken, szechuan tuna. Outdoor dining. Bright, colorful Chinese decor. Cr cds: A, C, D, DS, MC, V.

D ♥

★ ★ **ASSAGGIO RISTORANTE.** *2010 Fourth Ave (98121), downtown. 206/441-1399.* E-mail assaggiori@aol.com. Hrs: 11:30 am-2:30 pm, 5-10:30 pm; Fri to 11 pm; Sat 5-11 pm. Closed Sun; most major hols. Res accepted. Italian menu. Serv bar. Semi-a la carte: lunch $8.95-$14.95, dinner $9.95-$20.95. Specializes in seafood, risotto. Outdoor dining. Italian decor. Totally nonsmoking. Cr cds: A, D, DS, MC, V.

D

✔★ ★ **BANDOLEONE.** *2241 Eastlake Ave E (98102), north of downtown. 206/329-7559.* Hrs: 5-11 pm; Fri, Sat to 11:30 pm; Sat, Sun brunch 9 am-2:30 pm. Closed Thanksgiving, Dec 24, 25. Res accepted. Latin Amer menu. Bar to 2 am. Semi-a la carte: dinner $8.50-$15.95. Sat, Sun brunch $4.50-$6.95. Child's meals. Specialties: ancho chile-marinated chicken, Jamaican jerk rack of lamb, pistachio-crusted Chilean sea bass. Own pastries. Latino music Sun. Validated parking. Outdoor dining. Casual, eclectic decor with original artwork. Cr cds: MC, V.

D

✔★ ★ **BOMBORE.** *89 University St (98101), downtown. 206/624-8233.* Web www.diningnw.com/bombore/. Hrs: 11:30 am-2:30 pm, 5-10 pm. Closed Sun; most major hols. Res accepted. Continental menu. Semi-a la carte: lunch $6.50-$13.95, dinner $8.50-$17.75. Specializes in pasta, seafood. Outdoor dining. Eclectic decor. Totally nonsmoking. Cr cds: A, DS, MC, V.

D

★ ★ **BROOKLYN HOUSE.** *1212 Second Ave (98101), downtown. 206/224-7000.* Hrs: 11 am-10 pm; Sat 4:30-10:30 pm; Sun 4:30-10 pm. Closed Dec 25. Res accepted. Bar. A la carte entrees: lunch $7-$14, dinner $12-$33. Child's meals. Specializes in seafood, steak. Oyster bar. Valet parking (dinner). Patio/courtyard dining. In 1890s building; artwork. Cr cds: A, D, DS, MC, V.

D

★ **BUCA DI BEPPO.** *701 Ninth Ave N (98109), downtown. 206/244-2288.* Hrs: 5-10 pm; Fri to 11 pm; Sat 4:30-11 pm; Sun from 4 pm. Closed Thanksgiving, Dec 24, 25. Res accepted Sun-Thurs. Italian menu. Bar. A la carte entrees: dinner $7.95-$19.95. Specialties: chicken cacciatore, tiramisu. Outdoor dining. Eclectic decor; mural on dome ceiling; some seating in kitchen. Totally nonsmoking. Cr cds: A, D, MC, V.

D

✔★ **BURRITO LOCO.** *9211 Holman Rd NW (98117), north of downtown. 206/783-0719.* Hrs: 11 am-10 pm. Closed some major hols. Mexican menu. Wine, beer. Semi-a la carte: lunch $3.25-$4.75, dinner $7.50-$8.95. Child's meals. Specialties: chile relleno, chicken en mole, tacos de carnitas. Outdoor dining. Colorful Mexican decor. Totally nonsmoking. Cr cds: MC, V.

D

✔★ ★ **CACTUS.** *4220 E Madison (98112), east of downtown. 206/324-4140.* Hrs: 11:30 am-2:30 pm, 5-10 pm; Sun 5-9:30 pm. Closed some major hols. Hispanic menu. Serv bar. Semi-a la carte: lunch $5.95-$9.95, dinner $7.95-$13.95. Child's meals. Specializes in flan, tapas, fresh fish. Outdoor dining. Southwestern atmosphere. Cr cds: DS, MC, V.

D

✔★ ★ ★ **CAFE CAMPAGNE.** *1600 Post Alley (98101), downtown. 206/728-2233.* Hrs: 8 am-10 pm; Fri, Sat to 11 pm; Sun brunch 8 am-3 pm. Closed some major hols. Res accepted. French menu. Bar. Semi-a la carte: bkfst $6.95-$11.95, lunch $5.95-$14.95, dinner $8.95-$14.95. Sun brunch $6.95-$12.95. Specialties: traditional cassoulet, house-made sausages, rotisserie meats. Outdoor dining. French bistro decor. Cr cds: A, C, D, MC, V.

D

✔★ ★ **CAFE FLORA.** *2901 E Madison (98112), east of downtown. 206/325-9100.* Hrs: 11:30 am-2:30 pm, 5:30-10 pm; Sat from 5 pm; Sun 5-9 pm; Sat, Sun brunch 9 am-2 pm. Closed Mon; some hols. Vegetarian menu. Wine, beer. Semi-a la carte: lunch $6.95-$9.95, dinner $9.95-$14.95. Sat, Sun brunch $5.95-$9.95. Child's meals. Specialties: Oaxca tacos, portabello Wellington, wheatberry burgers. Two large rms, one with stone fountain, decorated with original works of art. Totally nonsmoking. Cr cds: MC, V.

D

★ ★ ★ **CAFE LAGO.** *2305 24th Ave E (98112), north of downtown. 206/329-8005.* Hrs: 5-9:30 pm; Fri, Sat to 10 pm. Closed major hols; also 4th wk in Aug. Italian menu. Wine. A la carte entrees: dinner $10-$20. Specializes in pasta, wood-fired pizza, grilled fish. Trattoria atmosphere. Totally nonsmoking. Cr cds: DS, MC, V.

D

★ ★ **CAFE SOPHIE.** *1921 First Ave (98101-1010), downtown. 206/441-6139.* Hrs: 5-9 pm; Fri, Sat to 10 pm. Closed Sun; major hols. Res accepted. No A/C. Continental menu. Bar. A la carte entrees: dinner $14-$21. Child's meals. Specializes in European cuisine. Jazz Fri, Sat. Outdoor dining. Two dining areas: one with a romantic, intimate setting, the other with a library motif. Cr cds: A, C, D, DS, MC, V.

D

★ ★ ★ **CAMPAGNE.** *86 Pine St (98101), downtown. 206/728-2800.* Hrs: 5:30-10 pm. Closed some major hols. Res accepted. French menu. Bar to 2 am. A la carte entrees: dinner $20-$29. Complete meals: $25-$55. Specializes in fresh seafood, rack of lamb. Valet parking. Outdoor dining. View of Elliott Bay. Cr cds: A, C, D, MC, V.

D

★ ★ ★ **CANLIS.** *2576 Aurora Ave N (98109), in Queen Anne. 206/283-3313.* E-mail 74132.2463@compuserve.com; web www.canlis.com. Hrs: 5:30-10:30 pm. Closed Sun; major hols. Res accepted. Bar 5 pm-midnight. Extensive wine list. Semi-a la carte: dinner $20-$34. Specializes in seafood, steak. Own sauces. Piano bar from 7 pm. Valet parking. Fireplace. Open-hearth grill. Panoramic view of Lake Union, Cascade Mountains. Formal dining. Family-owned. Jacket. Cr cds: A, C, D, DS, JCB, MC, V.

D

★ ★ **CARMELITA.** *7314 Greenwood Ave N (98103), in Phinney Ridge area, north of downtown. 206/706-7703.* Hrs: 5-10 pm; Fri, Sat to 10:45 pm; Sat, Sun brunch 9 am-1:30 pm. Closed Mon; Jan 1, Dec 24, 25. No A/C. Vegetarian menu. Bar. Semi-a la carte: dinner $8.50-$13.95. Sat, Sun brunch $8.95. Child's meals. Specializes in vegetarian and vegan fare with Mediterranean influences. Own baking, pasta. Outdoor dining. Eclectic furnishings decorate this large dining area with high ceilings. Totally nonsmoking. Cr cds: MC, V.

D

✔★ ★ ★ **CHEZ SHEA.** *94 Pike St (98101), in Pike Place Market, downtown. 206/467-9990.* E-mail shea101@aol.com; web www.wct.net/chezshea. Hrs: 4:30 pm-midnight. Closed Mon; most major hols. Res accepted. Contemporary Amer menu. Bar. A la carte entrees: dinner $6-$12. Complete meals: 4-course dinner $39. Child's meals. Specializes in seafood. Contemporary decor. Totally nonsmoking. Cr cds: A, MC, V.

✔★ ★ **CHINOOK'S.** *1900 W Nickerson (98119), in Fisherman's Terminal, north of downtown. 206/283-4665.* Hrs: 11 am-10 pm; Fri to 11 pm; Sat 7:30 am-11 pm; Sun 7:30 am-10 pm. Closed Thanksgiving, Dec 25. Bar to midnight. Complete meals: bkfst $4.95-$9.95. Semi-a la carte:

lunch $4.95-$11.95, dinner $5.95-$16.95. Child's meals. Specializes in Northwest seafood, salmon, halibut. Parking. Outdoor dining. On Fisherman's Wharf. Nautical decor. Cr cds: A, C, D, DS, MC, V.

D

★ ★ **CHUTNEY'S.** *519 First Ave N (98109), in Queen Anne. 206/284-6799.* Hrs: 11:30 am-2:30 pm, 5-10 pm; Fri, Sat to 10:30 pm; Sun from 5 pm. Closed Dec 25. Res accepted. Indian menu. Bar. Semi-a la carte: lunch, dinner $8.95-$13.95. Specialties: tandoori items, tikka masala, curried mussels. Own baking. Indian prints and carved deities decorate walls. Totally nonsmoking. Cr cds: A, C, D, DS, JCB, MC, V.

D

✔★ ★ **CUCINA! CUCINA!.** *901 Fairview Ave N (98109), north of downtown. 206/447-2782.* Hrs: 11:30-2 am. Closed Thanksgiving, Dec 25. Res accepted (lunch). Italian menu. Bar. A la carte entrees: lunch $4.95-$10.95, dinner $4.95-$14.95. Child's meals. Specializes in pizza, pasta, salads. Valet parking. Outdoor dining. Bicycles hang from ceiling in lounge. Cr cds: A, D, DS, JCB, MC, V.

D

★ ★ ★ **DAHLIA LOUNGE.** *1904 Fourth Ave (98101), downtown. 206/682-4142.* E-mail maureen@tomdouglas.com; web www.tomdouglas.com. Hrs: 11:30 am-2:30 pm, 5:30-10 pm; Fri to 11 pm; Sat 5:30-11 pm; Sun 5-9 pm. Closed major hols. Res accepted. Semi-a la carte: lunch $6.50-$12, dinner $9.95-$22. Child's meals. Specializes in crab cakes, salmon, duck. Eclectic decor. Cr cds: A, C, D, DS, JCB, MC, V.

D

★ **DOONG KONG LAU.** *9710 Aurora Ave N (98103), north of downtown. 206/526-8828.* Hrs: 11 am-10 pm. Res accepted. Chinese menu. Semi-a la carte: lunch $3.95-$5.95, dinner $5.95-$10.95. Specializes in northern Hakka cuisine. Parking. Chinese prints, fish tanks. Cr cds: A, D, DS, MC, V.

D

★ ★ **DULCES LATIN BISTRO.** *1430 34th Ave (98122), east of downtown. 206/322-5453.* Hrs: 5-10 pm; Sun to 9 pm. Closed Mon; some major hols. Res accepted. Continental menu. Bar. Semi-a la carte: dinner $14.25-$18.50. Complete meal: dinner $25. Specialties: chiles rellenos, roasted red pepper ravioli, paella Valenciana. Own pasta, pastries. Classical guitarist Wed, Thurs, Sun. Bistro decor with deep gold and bronze accents; completely separate cigar rm. Cr cds: MC, V.

D

★ ★ ★ **EL GAUCHO.** *2505 First Ave (98121), downtown. 206/728-1337.* Hrs: 5 pm-1 am; Sun to 11 pm. Closed most major hols. Res accepted. Continental menu. Bar to 2 am. Wine cellar. A la carte entrees: dinner $13-$30. Specialties: flaming shish kabob, chateaubriand, Angus steak. Own pastries. Pianist. Valet parking. Former union hall for merchent seamen; formal, elegant dining. Cr cds: A, C, D, JCB, MC, V.

D

★ ★ ★ **ELLIOTT'S OYSTER HOUSE.** *1203 Alaskan Way (98101), Pier 56, downtown. 206/623-4340.* Hrs: 11 am-11 pm; Fri, Sat to midnight; winter hrs: 11 am-10 pm; Fri, Sat to 11 pm. Res accepted. Bar. Semi-a la carte: lunch $5.95-$15.95, dinner $10.95-$29.95. Child's meals. Specializes in Pacific salmon, fresh Dungeness crab, fresh oysters. Outdoor dining. View of bay. Cr cds: A, D, DS, JCB, MC, V.

D

★ ★ ★ **ETTA'S SEAFOOD.** *2020 Western Ave (98121), downtown. 206/443-6000.* E-mail maureen@tomdouglas.com; web www.tomdouglas.com. Hrs: 11:30 am-10 pm; Fri to 11 pm; Sat 9 am-11 pm; Sun 9 am-10 pm. Closed major hols. Res accepted. Bar to 1 am. Semi-a la carte: lunch $5-$28, dinner $8-$30. Child's meals. Specializes in Northwestern seafood. Two dining rms. Totally nonsmoking. Cr cds: A, D, DS, JCB, MC, V.

D

★ ★ **F.X. McRORY'S STEAK, CHOP & OYSTER HOUSE.** *419 Occidental Ave S (98104), opp Kingdome, in Pioneer Square. 206/623-4800.* Hrs: 11:30 am-2 pm, 5-10 pm; Sat noon-11 pm; Sun from 3 pm. Closed some major hols. Res accepted. Bar. Semi-a la carte: lunch $6-$12, dinner $10-$25. Child's meals. Specializes in steak, oysters, prime rib. Oyster bar. Outdoor dining. 1920s atmosphere. Cr cds: A, C, D, DS, MC, V.

D

✔★ ★ ★ **FLYING FISH.** *2234 First Ave (98121), downtown. 206/728-8595.* Hrs: 5 pm-1 am. Closed most major hols. Res accepted. Bar to 2 am. Semi-a la carte: dinner $9-$16.95. Specialties: Thai crab cakes, whole fried snapper in lemon grass marinade. Outdoor dining. Eclectic decor. Totally nonsmoking. Cr cds: A, C, D, MC, V.

D SC

✔★ **FOUR SEAS.** *714 S King St (98104), in International District. 206/682-4900.* Hrs: 10 am-midnight; Fri, Sat to 2 am. Res accepted. Cantonese, Mandarin menu. Bar. Semi-a la carte: lunch $5.75-$8.35, dinner $5.25-$15.95. Specialties: Hong Kong-style dim sum, garlic spareribs, moo goo gai pan. Parking. Hand-carved Oriental screens. Cr cds: A, D, DS, MC, V.

D

★ ★ **FRANCO'S HIDDEN HARBOR.** *1500 Westlake Ave N (98109), north of downtown. 206/282-0501.* Hrs: 11 am-9 pm; Fri, Sat to 10 pm; Sun 4-10 pm. Closed Dec 25. Res accepted. Northwestern menu. Bar to 1 am; Sun 1-10 pm. Semi-a la carte: lunch $6-$11, dinner $9.95-$29.95. Child's meals. Specializes in prime rib, fresh seafood. Valet parking. Outdoor dining. Waterfront dining overlooking yacht harbor. Cr cds: A, D, DS, MC, V.

D

★ ★ ★ ★ **FULLERS.** *(See Sheraton Hotel) 206/447-5544.* Original works by Northwest artists are found on permanent display throughout the restaurant. A marble pool and fountain decorate the center of the dining area. Specializes in Northwest seafood, fowl, Ellensberg lamb. Own baking, pastas. Hrs: 11:30 am-2 pm, 5:30-10 pm; Sat from 5:30 pm. Closed Sun; some major hols. Res accepted. Bar. Wine list. A la carte entrees: lunch $10-$17, dinner $18-$30. Child's meals. Totally nonsmoking. Cr cds: A, C, D, DS, ER, JCB, MC, V.

D

★ ★ ★ **GEORGIAN ROOM.** *(See Four Seasons Olympic Hotel) 206/621-7889.* Hrs: 6:30 am-2 pm, 5:30-10 pm; Fri, Sat to 11 pm; Sat 6:30 am-noon; Sun 6:30 am-1:30 pm; Sun brunch in Garden Court 11:30 am-2 pm. Res accepted. Bar. Wine cellar. A la carte entrees: bkfst $4.50-$19.50, lunch $7.75-$19, dinner $14.50-$33. Sun brunch $14.50-$29. Specializes in Pacific Northwest seafood, rack of lamb. Own baking. Pastry chef. Jacket (dinner). Elegant dining in room of Italian Renaissance decor. Cr cds: A, C, D, JCB, MC, V.

D

★ ★ ★ **HUNT CLUB.** *(See Sorrento Hotel) 206/343-6156.* Web www.usa.nia.com.sorrento. Hrs: 7 am-2:30 pm, 5:30-10 pm; Fri, Sat to 11 pm. Res accepted. Bar from 11:30 am. A la carte entrees: bkfst $6-$10, lunch $9-$18, dinner $18-$30. Specializes in seafood of the Northwest, game. Free valet parking. English hunt motif. Cr cds: A, C, D, DS, JCB, MC, V.

D

★ ★ ★ **IL BISTRO.** *93A Pike St (98101), downtown. 206/682-3049.* Hrs: 5:30-10 pm; Fri, Sat to 11 pm. Closed some major hols. Res accepted. Italian menu. Bar to 2 am. A la carte entrees: dinner $11.95-$29.95. Specializes in fresh seafood, pasta, rack of lamb. Valet parking Thurs-Sat. Outdoor dining. Original art. Cr cds: A, C, D, MC, V.

D

★ ★ ★ **IL TERRAZZO CARMINE.** *411 First Ave S (98104), in Pioneer Square. 206/467-7797.* Hrs: 11:30 am-2:30 pm, 5:30-10 pm; Fri, Sat to 10:30 pm. Closed Sun; most major hols. Res accepted. Italian menu. Bar. Semi-a la carte: lunch $8-$13, dinner $9.50-$28. Specializes in osso buco, venison ravioli. Outdoor dining. Elegant decor. Totally nonsmoking. Cr cds: A, C, D, DS, MC, V.

D

★ ★ **IVAR'S ACRES OF CLAMS.** *Pier 54 (98104), downtown. 206/624-6852.* Hrs: 11 am-10 pm; Fri, Sat to 11 pm. Closed Thanksgiving, Dec 25. Res accepted. Bar. Semi-a la carte: lunch $6.95-$13.95, dinner $10.95-$19.95. Child's meals. Specializes in Northwestern king salmon, oven-roasted seafood brochettes, dungeness crab-topped prawns. On pier with windows overlooking waterfront; collection of old photos of the area. Cr cds: A, MC, V.

D

★ ★ **IVAR'S INDIAN SALMON HOUSE.** *401 NE Northlake Way (98105), on N shore of Lake Union, north of downtown. 206/632-0767.* Hrs: 11:30 am-2:30 pm, 4:30-10 pm; Fri to 11 pm; Sat noon-3:30 pm, 4-11 pm; Sun 3:30-10 pm; Sun brunch 10 am-2 pm. Closed Thanksgiving, Dec 25. Res accepted. Bar. Semi-a la carte: lunch $7-$15, dinner $13-$25. Sun brunch $14.95. Child's meals. Specializes in smoked salmon. Parking. Outdoor dining. Indian long house decor. View of lake. Family-owned. Cr cds: A, JCB, MC, V.

D SC

✔★ **JITTERBUG.** *2114 N 45th St (98103), north of downtown. 206/547-6313.* Hrs: 8 am-10 pm; Fri, Sat to 11 pm; June-Aug to 11 pm. Closed some major hols. Bar. Semi-a la carte: bkfst $2-$8.25, lunch $4-$8.25, dinner $8.25-$15.75. Child's meals. Specialties: Italian farmhouse egg rumble, charmoula chicken sandwich, transcontinental tango. Own pasta, pastries. Lively atmosphere; counter service. Cr cds: MC, V.

D

★ ★ ★ **KASPAR'S.** *19 W Harrison St (98119), in Queen Anne. 206/298-0123.* E-mail kaspars@aol.com; web www.uspan.com. Hrs: 5-10 pm; Fri, Sat to 11 pm. Closed Sun, Mon; Jan 1, July 4. Res accepted. Bar. A la carte entrees: dinner $13-$21. Child's meals. Specializes in Northwestern cuisine, vegetarian dishes, smoked salmon. Own ice cream & sorbets. Valet parking. 2 levels. Totally nonsmoking. Cr cds: A, MC, V.

D

✔★ **KITTO JAPANESE NOODLE HOUSE.** *614 Broadway E (98102), east of downtown. 206/325-8486.* Hrs: 11:30 am-10 pm; Fri, Sat to 11 pm. Closed Thanksgiving, Dec 25. Res accepted. Japanese menu. Wine, beer. Semi-a la carte: lunch $4.95-$12.95, dinner $5.75-$12.95. Specializes in tempura, noodles. Oriental decor. Totally nonsmoking. Cr cds: MC, V.

D

★ ★ **LA BUCA.** *102 Cherry St (98104), in Pioneer Square. 206/343-9517.* Hrs: 11:30 am-2:30 pm, 5-10 pm. Closed Jan 1, Thanksgiving, Dec 25. Res accepted. Italian menu. Serv bar. A la carte entrees: lunch $6.95-$10, dinner $8.95-$16. Child's meals. Specializes in classic Italian dishes. Own pastries. Rustic Italian trattoria with separate dining areas underground; one dates to 1890. Cr cds: A, C, D, DS, JCB, MC, V.

★ ★ ★ **LABUZNIK.** *1924 First Ave (98101), downtown. 206/441-8899.* Hrs: 4:30 pm-midnight. Closed Sun, Mon; major hols; also spring break, 3 wks July. Res accepted. Continental menu. Bar. Semi-a la carte: dinner $12.50-$29. Child's meals. Specializes in veal, pork, roast duck. Dining on 2 levels; sliding doors open to street. Original art. Cr cds: A, D, DS, MC, V.

D

★ ★ ★ **LAMPREIA.** *2400 First Ave (98121), downtown. 206/443-3301.* Hrs: 5-11 pm. Closed Sun, Mon; Thanksgiving. Res accepted. Italian, Mediterranean menu. Bar. Wine cellar. Semi-a la carte: dinner $9-$25. Tasting menu: dinner $40. Specializes in seasonal dishes. Own baking, pasta. Wine display at entrance changes frequently. Totally nonsmoking. Cr cds: A, MC, V.

D

✔★ **LAS MARGARITAS.** *1122 Post Ave (98101), downtown. 206/623-7203.* Hrs: 11 am-11 pm; Sun to 9 pm. Closed Dec 25. Res accepted. Mexican menu. Bar. Semi-a la carte: lunch $5.75-$7.95, dinner $2.75-$10.95. Child's meals. Specializes in regional cuisine, carnitas, fajitas. Cr cds: A, D, DS, MC, V.

D

★ ★ ★ **LATITUDE 47°.** *1232 Westlake N (98109), north of downtown. 206/284-1047.* Hrs: 11:30 am-2:30 pm, 5-9:30 pm; Fri, Sat from 5 pm; Sun 3-9 pm; Sun brunch 10 am-2 pm. Closed Dec 25. Res accepted. Bar to 2 am. Wine list. Semi-a la carte: lunch $5.95-$14.50, dinner $10-$18.50. Sun brunch $14.95. Child's meals. Specializes in seafood, steak, pasta. Valet parking. Entertainment. Outdoor dining. Enclosed patio overlooks Lake Union; moorage. Cr cds: A, D, DS, MC, V.

D

★ ★ ★ **LE GOURMAND.** *425 NW Market St (98107), at 6th Ave, north of downtown. 206/784-3463.* Hrs: 5:30-11 pm. Closed Sun-Tues; Easter, Thanksgiving, Dec 24, 25. Res accepted. French, Amer menu. Wine, beer. Complete meals: dinner $18-$30. Specialties: poached salmon with gooseberry & dill sauce, roast duckling with black currant sauce. Original artwork. Totally nonsmoking. Cr cds: A, MC, V.

D

✔★ **LINYEN.** *424 Seventh Ave S (98104), in International District. 206/622-8181.* Hrs: 11-2 am. Res accepted. Chinese menu. Bar. Semi-a la carte: lunch $2.80-$6, dinner $5.95-$15.25. Specializes in fresh Northwest fish and vegetables, lemon chicken, Hong Kong-style dim sum. Valet parking. Cr cds: A, D, DS, MC, V.

D

✔★ ★ **MADISON PARK CAFE.** *1807 42nd Ave E (98112), east of downtown. 206/324-2626.* Hrs: 8 am-2:30 pm; Sun to 2 pm; Fri, Sat also 5:30-10 pm. Closed Mon; some major hols. Res accepted. No A/C. Continental menu. Wine, beer. Semi-a la carte: bkfst $2.50-$7.25, lunch $2.50-$8.50, dinner $12.95-$16.95. Child's meals. Specializes in fresh seasonal pastas and seafoods, homemade bkfst pastries. Own pasta, pastries. Outdoor dining. French bistro atmosphere in converted house; brick courtyard. Totally nonsmoking. Cr cds: A, MC, V.

✔★ ★ **MARCO'S.** *2510 First Ave (98121), downtown. 206/441-7801.* Hrs: 11:30 am-2 pm, 5:30-11 pm; Fri, Sat to midnight; Sun from 5:30 pm. Closed most major hols. Res accepted. Continental menu. Bar. Semi-a la carte: lunch $6.95-$10.95, dinner $10.95-$15.95. Child's meals. Specializes in jerk chicken, fried sage leaves. Outdoor dining. Eclectic decor. Cr cds: A, MC, V.

D

★ ★ **MAXIMILIEN-IN-THE-MARKET.** *81A Pike Place (98101), Pike Place Market, downtown. 206/682-7270.* Hrs: 7:30 am-10 pm; Sun brunch 9:30 am-4 pm. Closed Jan 1, Thanksgiving, Dec 25. Res accepted. French menu. Bar. Semi-a la carte: bkfst $3-$7.25, lunch $5.50-$13, dinner $8.25-$24. French family supper Mon-Fri: $13.25-$24. Sun brunch $1.75-$8.50. Specializes in French-style Northwest seafood. French marketplace decor; antiques. View of bay, mountains. Cr cds: A, D, MC, V.

D

★ ★ **McCORMICK & SCHMICK'S.** *1103 First Ave (98101), downtown. 206/623-5500.* Hrs: 11:30 am-11 pm; Sat 4:30-11 pm; Sun 5-10 pm; summer hrs vary. Closed Thanksgiving, Dec 25. Res accepted. Bar to 12:30 am; Fri, Sat to 1:30 am; Sun to 11:30 pm. Semi-a la carte: lunch $4.95-$12.75, dinner $6.75-$20. Specializes in fresh seafood. Beamed ceilings, Irish bar. Original art. Cr cds: A, C, D, DS, JCB, MC, V.

D

★ ★ **McCORMICK'S FISH HOUSE.** *722 Fourth Ave (98104), downtown. 206/682-3900.* Hrs: 11:30 am-11 pm; Fri to midnight; Sat 4:30 pm-midnight; Sun from 4:30 pm. Closed Memorial Day, Thanksgiving, Dec 25. Res accepted. Bar. Semi-a la carte: lunch $5.95-$11.95, dinner $5.95-

$19.95. Specializes in fresh seafood. Oyster bar. Outdoor dining. Vintage 1920s and 30s atmosphere; tin ceilings. Cr cds: A, C, D, DS, MC, V.

D

★ ★ ★ **METROPOLITAN GRILL.** *820 Second Ave (98104), at Marion St, downtown. 206/624-3287.* Hrs: 11 am-3:30 pm, 5-11 pm; Sat from 4:30 pm; Sun 4:30-10 pm. Closed Thanksgiving. Res accepted. Bar. Wine list. Semi-a la carte: lunch $6.95-$15.95, dinner $10.95-$27.95. Child's meals. Specialties: 28-day aged prime steak, Northwest seafood dishes. Cr cds: A, C, D, DS, JCB, MC, V.

D

★ ★ **NISHINO.** *3130 E Madison (98112), east of downtown. 206/322-5800.* Hrs: 5:30-10:30 pm; Sun to 9:30 pm. Closed some major hols. Res accepted. Japanese menu. Serv bar. Semi-a la carte: dinner $4-$16. Complete meal: dinner $45-$60. Specializes in omakase, sushi. Outdoor dining. Subdued Japanese decor; rooftop dining. Totally nonsmoking. Cr cds: A, MC, V.

D

★ ★ ★ **OBACHINE.** *1518 Sixth Ave (98101), downtown. 206/749-9653.* Hrs: 11:30 am-4:30 pm, 5:30-10 pm. Closed July 4, Thanksgiving, Dec 25. Res accepted. Pan-Asian menu. Bar 11:30 am-midnight. Wine list. A la carte entrees: lunch $5.95-$13.95, dinner $8.95-$18.95. Child's meals. Own pastries. Two-level dining areas feature dramatic colors, Asian artwork. Totally nonsmoking. Cr cds: A, D, MC, V.

D

★ ★ ★ **PAINTED TABLE.** *(See Alexis Hotel) 206/624-3646.* Hrs: 6:30-10 am, 11:30 am-2 pm, 5:30-10 pm; Sat, Sun 7:30 am-noon, 5:30-10 pm. Res accepted. Bar. Wine list. A la carte entrees: bkfst $3.50-$9.50, lunch $6.95-$14.95, dinner $7.95-$24.95. Specializes in Northwest regional produce and seafood. Own baking, sauces. Valet parking. In historic building (1901). Totally nonsmoking. Cr cds: A, C, D, DS, MC, V.

D

★ ★ ★ **PALACE KITCHEN.** *2030 Fifth Ave (98121), downtown. 206/448-2001.* E-mail maureen@www.tomdouglas.com; web www.tomdouglas.com. Hrs: 5 pm-1 am. Closed most major hols. Res accepted. Bar. Wine list. Semi-a la carte: dinner $14-$19. Child's meals. Specializes in applewood-grilled rotisserie dishes. Own baking, pasta. Central kitchen and bar dominate dining rm. Cr cds: A, D, DS, MC, V.

D

★ ★ **PALOMINO.** *1420 Fifth Ave (98101), on 3rd floor of Pacific First Center, downtown. 206/623-1300.* Hrs: 11:15 am-10:30 pm; Tues, Thurs to 11:30 pm; Fri to 12:30 am; Sat 11-12:30 am; Sun 4-10 pm. Closed some major hols. Res accepted. Mediterranean menu. Semi-a la carte: lunch $6.95-$15.95, dinner $7.95-$19.95. Specializes in grilled salmon, spit-roasted chicken, wood oven-roasted prawns. Parking. Original art, exotic African wood. Overlooking atrium. Cr cds: A, D, DS, MC, V.

D

★ ★ **PARAGON.** *2125 Queen Anne Ave N (98109), in Queen Anne. 206/283-4548.* Hrs: 5-11 pm. Closed Dec 25. Res accepted. Contemporary Amer menu. Bar 4 pm-2 am. Semi-a la carte: dinner $9-$18. Specializes in risotto, seafood. Bistro decor. Totally nonsmoking. Cr cds: A, MC, V.

D

★ ★ ★ **PESCATORE.** *5300 34th St NW (98107), north of downtown. 206/784-1733.* Hrs: 11 am-closing; Sat from 4 pm; Sun from 5 pm; Sun brunch 9 am-2:30 pm. Res accepted. Bar to 11:30 pm; Fri-Sun to 12:30 am. Semi-a la carte: lunch $5.95-$11.95, dinner $9.95-$19.95. Sun brunch $10.95-$19.95. Child's meals. Specializes in Italian seafood, pizza, and lasagne. Parking. Outdoor dining. Overlooks Chittendon Locks. Family-owned. Cr cds: A, C, D, DS, JCB, MC, V.

D SC

✔★ ★ **PIATTI.** *2800 NE University Village (98105), north of downtown. 206/524-9088.* Hrs: 11:30 am-10 pm; Fri, Sat to 11 pm. Closed Dec 25. Res accepted. Italian menu. Bar. Semi-a la carte: lunch, dinner $6.95-$19.95. Child's meals. Specializes in regional Italian cuisine. Outdoor dining. Casual decor. Totally nonsmoking. Cr cds: A, D, MC, V.

D

★ ★ **PINK DOOR.** *1919 Post Alley (98101), Pike Place Market, downtown. 206/443-3241.* Hrs: 11:30 am-2:30 pm, 5:30-10 pm. Closed Sun, Mon; some major hols. Res accepted. No A/C. Italian menu. Bar to 11:30 pm; Fri, Sat to 1 am. Semi-a la carte: lunch $6.95-$11.50, dinner $6.95-$17.95. Child's meals. Specializes in rustic Italian dishes. Own baking, pasta. Entertainment. Outdoor dining. Eclectic decor with cherubs, mirrors and a swing; patio offers water view. Totally nonsmoking. Cr cds: A, MC, V.

★ ★ ★ **PIROSMANI.** *2220 Queen Anne Ave N (98109), in Queen Anne. 206/285-3360.* Hrs: 5:30-10 pm. Closed Sun, Mon; Easter, Thanksgiving, Dec 25. Res accepted. No A/C. Mediterranean, Georgian menu. Wine, beer. Semi-a la carte: dinner $16-$22. Seasonal menu. Outdoor dining. Original art and Georgian artifacts are displayed in the dining rms of this 1906 house. Totally nonsmoking. Cr cds: A, D, DS, MC, V.

★ ★ ★ **PLACE PIGALLE.** *81 Pike St (98101), in Pike Place Market, downtown. 206/624-1756.* Hrs: 11:30 am-3 pm, 5:30-10 pm; Fri to 11 pm; Sat 11:30 am-3:30 pm, 6-10:30 pm. Closed Sun; most major hols. Res accepted. Northwest regional menu. Bar. Semi-a la carte: lunch $8-$14, dinner $15-$23. Specialties: rabbit reminiscence, seafood in tamarind broth, duck bijoux. Overlooks Elliott Bay. Casual decor. Cr cds: A, MC, V.

★ ★ ★ **PONTI.** *3014 Third Ave N (98109), in Queen Anne. 206/284-3000.* Hrs: 11:30 am-2:30 pm, 5-10 pm; Fri, Sat to 11 pm; Sun from 10 am; early bird dinner 5-6 pm. Closed Jan 1, July 4, Dec 25. Res accepted. Eclectic menu. A la carte entrees: lunch $8.95-$12.95, dinner $11.95-$19.95. Child's meals. Specializes in Pacific rim seafood. Valet parking. Patio dining. Formal dining in attractive surroundings. View of Lake Washington Canal. Cr cds: A, D, MC, V.

D

✔★ **PORTAGE BAY CAFE.** *(See University Inn Motor Hotel) 206/632-5055.* Hrs: 6 am-3 pm; Sat, Sun from 7 am. Closed Jan 1, Dec 25. Res accepted. Semi-a la carte: bkfst $2-$7.95, lunch $4-$8.25. Child's meals. Specialties: cafe linguine, blackened salmon. Outdoor dining. Bright, contemporary decor with floor-to-ceiling windows. Totally nonsmoking. Cr cds: A, D, DS, MC, V.

D

★ ★ ★ **PREGO.** *(See Renaissance Madison Hotel) 206/583-0300.* Hrs: 11:30 am-1:30 pm, 5:30-10 pm. Closed Dec 25. Res accepted. Italian menu. Bar. Semi-a la carte: lunch $6-$13, dinner $11-$25. Specializes in seafood, pasta. Original Matisse art. Views of skyline, Puget Sound. Cr cds: A, C, D, DS, ER, JCB, MC, V.

D

★ ★ ★ **QUEEN CITY GRILL.** *2201 1st Ave (98121), downtown. 206/443-0975.* Web www.queencitygrill.com. Hrs: 11:30 am-11 pm; Fri, Sat to midnight. Closed some major hols. Res accepted. Bar. Wine cellar. A la carte entrees: lunch $7.95-$13.95, dinner $8.95-$19.50. Child's meals. Specialties: grilled Chilean sea bass with chili-lime butter, grilled ahi tuna, aged Colorado Angus steak. Own pastries, pasta. Exposed brick walls, original artwork and mahogany woodwork accent this dining rm. Cr cds: A, C, D, DS, MC, V.

D

★ ★ ★ **RAY'S BOATHOUSE.** *6049 Seaview Ave NW (98107), north of downtown. 206/789-3770.* E-mail rays@rays.com; web www.rays.com. Hrs: 11:30 am-2 pm, 5-10 pm. Closed Jan 1, Dec 25. Res accepted. Bar to midnight. Wine cellar. Semi-a la carte: lunch $5.95-$9.95, dinner $10.95-$25. Child's meals. Specializes in Northwest seafood. Valet parking. Outdoor dining. View of Olympic Mts. Cr cds: A, D, DS, MC, V.

D

★ ★ ★ **REINER'S.** *1106 Eighth Ave (98101), downtown. 206/624-2222.* Hrs: 5-10 pm. Closed Sun, Mon; some major hols. Res accepted. Continental menu. Serv bar. Wine list. A la carte entrees: dinner $14.50-

$24. Specializes in rack of lamb, crab cakes, calf's liver. Outdoor dining. Intimate dining in European atmosphere. Totally nonsmoking. Cr cds: A, MC, V.

D

★ ★ ★ **RELAIS.** *(17121 Bothell Way NE, Bothell 98011) I-5 N exit 177 E to WA 522 N. 206/485-7600.* Hrs: 5-9 pm; Sun brunch 11 am-3 pm. Closed Mon. Res accepted. No A/C. French menu. Bar. Wine list. Semi-a la carte: dinner $21-$30. Complete meals: dinner $55. Sun brunch $19.95. Specializes in lamb, seafood. Own desserts. Parking. Outdoor dining. Turn-of-the-century French decor. Original artwork, antiques. Cr cds: A, MC, V.

D

★ ★ ★ ★ **ROVER'S.** *2808 E Madison St (98112), east of downtown. 206/325-7442.* Chef Thierry Rautureau's cozy white cottage with country-French decor is an intimate theater for his contemporary regional cuisine with French influences. Only the freshest ingredients—including white asparagus from France, rabbit from Oregon and herbs and flowers from the restaurant's garden—make their way into the award-winning dishes here. Northwest contemporary menu with French accent. Specializes in seafood, Northwest game, vegetarian dishes. Hrs: from 5:30 pm. Closed Sun, Mon; most major hols. Res accepted. Extensive wine list. A la carte entrees: dinner $23-$39.50. Complete meals: dinner $49.50, $59.50 & $89.50. Outdoor dining. Totally nonsmoking. Cr cds: A, D, DS, MC, V.

D

★ ★ ★ **ROY'S.** *(See The Westin Hotel) 206/256-7697.* Hrs: 6 am-10 pm. Res accepted. Continental menu. Bar from 5 pm. Wine cellar. Complete meal: bkfst $8.75-$15.75. Semi-a la carte: bkfst $3.75-$9.75, lunch $4.25-$14, dinner $14.95-$23.95. Child's meals. Specializes in fresh seafood with Pacific Rim influence. Own desserts. Multi-leveled, semi-circular dining rm with nautical theme. Totally nonsmoking. Cr cds: A, C, D, DS, MC, V.

D

★ ★ ★ **RUTH'S CHRIS STEAK HOUSE.** *800 Fifth Ave (98104), downtown. 206/624-8524.* Hrs: 5-10 pm. Closed some major hols. Res accepted. Bar. A la carte entrees: dinner $16-$29.95. Specializes in steak, seafood. Valet parking. Cr cds: A, D, MC, V.

D

★ ★ ★ ★ **SALEH AL LAGO.** *6804 E Greenlake Way (98115), north of downtown. 206/524-4044.* E-mail salehj@msn.com. Dining is offered on two levels in this elegant atmosphere with faux-marble pillars and pale pink trim, mauve and lilac fabrics and carpet, and recessed lighting. The fine china and crystal is replaced annually. Italian menu. Specializes in central Italian cooking. Own pasta. Hrs: 11:30 am-1:30 pm, 5:30-9:30 pm. Closed Sun; major hols. Res accepted. Bar. A la carte entrees: lunch $9-$13, dinner $13-$18. Child's meals. Parking. Patio dining. Cr cds: A, D, MC, V.

D

★ ★ ★ **SAZERAC.** *(See Hotel Monaco) 206/621-1770.* Web www.monaco-seattle.com. Hrs: 6:30 am-10 pm. Res accepted. Bar. Wine list. Semi-a la carte: bkfst $5.95-$12.95, lunch $8.95-$15.95, dinner $14.95-$28.95. Child's meals. Specialties: spit-roasted whole fish with lemon-chili broth, molasses sweet-potato pasta cigars with sausage and sage-butter. Own baking, pasta. Valet parking. Outdoor dining. Contemporary decor with high ceiling, multi-level dining and open, elevated kitchen. Totally nonsmoking. Cr cds: A, D, DS, MC, V.

D

✓★ ★ **SERAFINA.** *2043 Eastlake Ave E (98102), north of downtown. 206/323-0807.* Hrs: 11:30 am-2 pm, 5:30-10 pm; Fri to 11 pm; Sat 5:30-11 pm; Sun 5:30-10 pm. Closed some major hols. Res accepted. Italian menu. Bar. A la carte entrees: lunch $2.95-$8.95, dinner $7.95-$17.95. Specializes in rustic Italian dishes. Entertainment. Outdoor dining in European courtyard. Murals. Cr cds: MC, V.

D

★ ★ **SHIRO'S.** *2401 Second Ave (98121), downtown. 206/443-9844.* Hrs: 11:30 am-1:45 pm, 5:30-10 pm; Sat from 5:30 pm. Closed Sun; major hols. Res accepted. Japanese menu. Wine, beer. Semi-a la carte: lunch $6.95-$14.50, dinner $16-$19.50. Specializes in sushi, full Japanese dinners. Casual decor with large windows, sushi bar. Totally nonsmoking. Cr cds: A, JCB, MC, V.

D

★ ★ **SIMPATICO.** *4430 Wallingford Ave (98103), north of downtown. 206/632-1000.* Hrs: 5-10 pm; Fri, Sat to 11 pm. Closed major hols. Italian menu. Bar. Semi-a la carte: dinner $10.95-$17.95. Child's meals. Specializes in traditional Italian cuisine with Northwestern flair. Parking. Live jazz wkends. Outdoor dining. Intimate dining in converted school building that also houses shops. Cr cds: A, MC, V.

D

★ ★ **SPACE NEEDLE.** *219 Fourth Ave N (98109), in Seattle Center. 206/443-2100.* Web www.spaceneedle.com. Hrs: 8 am-11 pm; Sun brunch to 3 pm. Res accepted. Bar 11 am-midnight. Semi-a la carte: bkfst $9.95-$14.95, lunch $14.95-$19.95, dinner $20.95-$31.95. Sun brunch $17.95-$21.95. Child's meals. Specializes in regional dishes. Valet parking. Revolving dining rm. Family-owned. Totally nonsmoking. Cr cds: A, D, DS, ER, JCB, MC, V.

D ♥

✓★ **STELLA'S TRATTORIA.** *4500 Ninth Ave (98105), northeast of downtown. 206/633-1100.* Open 24 hrs. Sun brunch 4 am-3 pm. Closed Thanksgiving, Dec 25. Italian, Amer menu. Semi-a la carte: bkfst $2.95-$6, lunch $6-$8.50, dinner $7-$13. Sun brunch $2.95-$8. Child's meals. Outdoor dining. Lively atmosphere. Totally nonsmoking. Cr cds: A, DS, MC, V.

D

★ ★ ★ **SZMANIA'S.** *3321 W McGraw (98199), north of downtown. 206/284-7305.* Hrs: 5-9:30 pm; Fri, Sat to 10 pm; Sun 4:30-9 pm. Closed Mon; most major hols. Res accepted. Continental menu. Bar. Wine list. Semi-a la carte: dinner $9-$20. Child's meals. Specialties: German dishes, seasonal Pacific Northwest regional dishes. Parking. Fireplace; open kitchen. Totally nonsmoking. Cr cds: A, D, MC, V.

D

★ ★ ★ **THEOZ.** *1523 Sixth Ave (98101), downtown. 206/749-9660.* Hrs: 11:30 am-2:30 pm, 5-10:30 pm; Fri to 11 pm; Sat 5-11 pm; Sun from 5 pm; early-bird dinner to 6 pm; Sat, Sun brunch 11 am-3 pm. Closed most major hols. Res accepted. Bar to 1 am; Fri to 2 am; Sat 4 pm-2 am. Wine list. Semi-a la carte: lunch $7.50-$9, dinner $12.50-$30. Sat, Sun brunch $9.50-$11. Specializes in northwestern American dishes with Latin American and Indonesian influences. Own baking. Sophisticated decor with Tandoori oven, partially open kitchen. Totally nonsmoking. Cr cds: A, MC, V.

D

✓★ **TRATTORIA MITCHELLI.** *84 Yesler Way (98104), in Pioneer Square. 206/623-3883.* Hrs: 7-4 am; Mon to 11 pm; Sat from 8 am; Sun 8 am-11 pm. Closed Dec 25. Res accepted Sun-Thurs. Italian menu. Bar 11-2 am. Semi-a la carte: bkfst $2.75-$8.75, lunch $4.95-$9.95, dinner $6.75-$14.50. Complete meals: lunch (Mon-Fri) $4.95. Child's meals. Specializes in pizza, pasta, chicken. Outdoor dining. Antique furnishings. Cr cds: A, DS, MC, V.

D

★ ★ ★ **TULIO.** *(See Hotel Vintage Park) 206/624-5500.* Hrs: 7-10 am, 11:30 am-2:30 pm, 5-10 pm; wkend hrs vary. Closed some major hols. Res accepted. Italian menu. Bar. Wine cellar. A la carte entrees: bkfst $5-$9, lunch $9-$15, dinner $9-$21. Child's meals. Specializes in regional Italian cuisine. Valet parking. Outdoor dining. Open view of wood-burning pizza oven. Cr cds: A, C, D, DS, ER, JCB, MC, V.

D

★ ★ ★ **UNION BAY CAFE.** *3515 NE 45th St (98105), north of downtown. 206/527-8364.* Hrs: 5-10 pm; Sun 4:30-9 pm. Closed Mon;

some major hols. Res accepted. Wine list. A la carte entrees: dinner $11.50-$18.75. Child's meals. Specializes in fresh seafood, organic produce, free-range chicken. Own pastries. Outdoor dining. Intimate dining in two dining rms with orginal artwork, wine and flower displays. Totally nonsmoking. Cr cds: A, C, D, DS, MC, V.

D

★ ★ ★ **UNION SQUARE GRILL.** *621 Union St (98101), downtown. 206/224-4321.* Hrs: 11 am-3 pm, 5-10 pm; Fri, Sat to midnight. Closed some major hols. Res accepted. Bar. Wine list. Semi-a la carte: lunch $6.95-$15.95, dinner $15.95-$29.95. Specializes in steaks, chops, Northwestern seafood. Valet parking. Several dining areas; mahogany furnishings, dividers. Cr cds: A, C, D, DS, JCB, MC, V.

D

✔★ ★ ★ **VINA.** *2207 First Ave (98121), downtown. 206/443-1465.* Hrs: 5-10 pm; Fri, Sat to 11 pm. Closed most major hols. Res accepted. Mediterranean menu. Bar to midnight. Semi-a la carte: dinner $10.95-$14.95. Specialties: smoked roasted chicken, Spanish paella. Elegent decor. Totally nonsmoking. Cr cds: MC, V.

D

★ ★ ★ **VIRAZON.** *1329 First Ave (98101), at Union St, downtown. 206/233-0123.* Hrs: 11:30 am-2:30 pm, 5:30-9:30 pm; Mon to 2 pm; Fri, Sat 11:30 am-2:30 pm, 6-10 pm. Closed Sun; major hols. Res accepted. French menu. Beer. Wine list. A la carte entrees: lunch $5-$12, dinner $16-$29. Tasting menu: dinner $49. Child's meals. Specializes in seafood, 5-course tasting menu. Validated parking. Outdoor dining. The menu changes daily in this bright, European-style restaurant. Totally nonsmoking. Cr cds: A, D, JCB, MC, V.

D

★ ★ ★ **WILD GINGER.** *1400 Western Ave (98101), downtown. 206/623-4450.* Hrs: 11:30 am-3 pm, 5-11 pm; Fri 5 pm-midnight; Sat to midnight; Sun 4:30-11 pm. Closed Thanksgiving, Dec 25. Res accepted. Southeast Asian, Chinese menu. Bar. Semi-a la carte: lunch $6.95-$12.95, dinner $9.95-$19.95. Specializes in fresh seafood, curry. Satay bar. Near Pike Place Market. Cr cds: A, C, D, DS, MC, V.

D

★ ★ **Z RITZ.** *720 E Pike (98122), east of downtown. 206/329-6448.* Hrs: 11:30 am-3 pm, 5:30-9:30 pm; Sat to 10:30 pm; Sun 5-9 pm; Sat, Sun brunch 9:30 am-2:30 pm. Closed some major hols. Res accepted. Mediterranean menu. Wine, beer. A la carte entrees: lunch $3.95-$8.95, dinner $8.95-$15.95. Sat, Sun brunch $5.95-$8.95. Child's meals. Specialties: couscous maison, lamb, veal. Own pastries. Outdoor dining. Cozy, intimate bistro atmosphere with private booths. Cr cds: MC, V.

D

Unrated Dining Spot

SURROGATE HOSTESS. *746 19th Ave E, north of downtown. 206/324-1944.* Hrs: 6 am-9 pm. Closed Jan 1, Dec 25. No A/C. Northwest country cooking. Wine, beer. Avg ck: bkfst $3-$7, lunch $4-$7, dinner $4-$11. Specializes in seafood, salads, desserts. Parking. Outdoor dining. Totally nonsmoking. No cr cds accepted.

D

Seattle-Tacoma Intl Airport Area

Motels

★ ★ **BEST WESTERN AIRPORT EXECUTEL.** *(20717 Pacific Hwy S, Seattle 98198) 1 mi S on WA 99, at S 207th St. 206/878-3300; FAX 206/824-9000.* 138 rms, 3 story. June-Sept: S $101-$121; D $107-$135; each addl $6; suites $213-$325; under 18 free; lower rates rest of yr. Crib free. TV; cable (premium). Indoor pool; whirlpool. Complimentary continental bkfst. Complimentary coffee in rms. Restaurant 6 am-10 pm. Bar 3 pm-2 am. Ck-out noon. Meeting rms. Business servs avail. In-rm modem link. Bellhops. Valet serv. Free airport transportation. Exercise equipt; stair machine, bicycle, sauna. Cr cds: A, C, D, DS, JCB, MC, V.

D SC

★ ★ **COMFORT INN.** *(19333 International Blvd, Seattle 98188) 1 mi S on WA 99, at S 193rd St. 206/878-1100; FAX 206/878-8678.* 119 rms, 4 story. S, D $75-$150; each addl $10; suites $135-$175; under 18 free. Crib free. TV; cable (premium), VCR avail. Complimentary continental bkfst. Restaurant adj open 24 hrs. Ck-out noon. Meeting rms. In-rm modem link. Bellhops. Sundries. Free covered parking. Free airport transportation. Exercise equipt; weight machine, bicycles. Whirlpool. Refrigerator in suites. Cr cds: A, C, D, DS, ER, JCB, MC, V.

D SC

✔★ ★ **LA QUINTA.** *(2824 S 188th St, Seattle 98188) 1 mi S on WA 99. 206/241-5211; FAX 206/246-5596.* 142 rms, 6 story. Late May-Sept: S $74; D $82; each addl $8; lower rates rest of yr; under 18 free. Crib free. Pet accepted, some restrictions. TV; cable (premium). Pool; whirlpool. Complimentary continental bkfst. Restaurant opp. Ck-out noon. Coin Indry. Meeting rm. Business servs avail. In-rm modem link. Sundries. Free airport transportation. Exercise equipt; weights, stair machine. Luxury level. Cr cds: A, D, DS, MC, V.

D SC

★ ★ **RAMADA INN-SEATAC EAST.** *(16838 International Blvd, Seattle 98188) 1/4 mi S on WA 99, at S 168th St. 206/248-0901; FAX 206/242-3170; res: 800/845-2968.* 150 rms, 3 story. June-Sept: S, D $78-$87; each addl $10; suites $80; under 12 free; lower rates rest of yr. Crib free. Pet accepted. TV; cable (premium). Restaurant 7 am-10 pm. Ck-out noon. Meeting rm. Business servs avail. In-rm modem link. Sundries. Free airport transportation. Exercise equipt; weight machine, rower. Balconies. Cr cds: A, C, D, DS, ER, JCB, MC, V.

D SC

✔★ **TRAVELODGE.** *(2900 S 192nd St, Seattle 98188) 206/241-9292; FAX 206/242-0681.* 106 rms, 3 story. July-Sept: S, D $65-$90; each addl $6; under 18 free; lower rates rest of yr. Crib free. TV; cable (premium). Complimentary coffee in rms. Restaurant adj open 24 hrs. Ck-out noon. Coin Indry. Business servs avail. In-rm modem link. Free airport transportation. Sauna. Cr cds: A, C, D, DS, ER, JCB, MC, V.

D SC

Motor Hotels

★ ★ **BEST WESTERN EXECUTEL.** *(31611 20th Ave S, Federal Way 98003) I-5 exit 143 S. 253/941-6000; FAX 253/941-9500.* E-mail execute1@ricochet.net. 112 rms, 3 story. Mid-June-mid-Sept: S, D $99-$129; each addl $10; under 18 free; lower rates rest of yr. Crib free. Pet accepted; $20. TV; cable (premium). Heated pool; whirlpool. Restaurant 6 am-11 pm. Rm serv. Bar. Ck-out noon. Meeting rms. Business center. In-rm modem link. Bellhops. Valet serv. Free airport transportation. Health club privileges. Cr cds: A, C, D, DS, JCB, MC, V.

D SC

★ ★ **CLARION.** *(3000 S 176th, Seattle 98188) 206/242-0200; FAX 206/242-1998.* 211 rms, 3 story. June-Oct: S $60-$89; D $70-$99; each addl $10; under 19 free; higher rates Sea Fair; lower rates rest of yr. Crib free. TV; cable (premium), VCR avail. Complimentary coffee in rms. Restaurant 6 am-2 pm, 5-10 pm. Rm serv. Bar from 4 pm. Ck-out noon. Meeting rms. Business center. In-rm modem link. Coin Indry. Free airport transportation. Exercise equipt; treadmill, rowers, sauna. Massage. Indoor pool; whirlpool. Game rm. Some refrigerators, microwaves. Cr cds: A, C, D, DS, JCB, MC, V.

D SC

★ ★ **DOUBLETREE INN.** *(205 Strander Blvd, Seattle 98188) I-5, I-405 Southcenter exit, south of downtown. 206/246-8220; FAX 206/575-4749.* Web www.doubletreehotels.com. 198 rms, 2 story. S, D $99-$178; each addl $10; suites $136-$142; under 18 free; wkend, seasonal rates. Crib free. TV; cable (premium), VCR avail. Heated pool; poolside serv. Playground. Restaurant 6 am-10 pm. Rm serv. Bar 11-2 am. Ck-out noon. Meeting rms. Business servs avail. Bellhops. Valet serv. Health club privileges. Microwaves avail. Some private patios. Cr cds: A, C, D, DS, ER, JCB, MC, V.

D SC

★ ★ ★ **DOUBLETREE-SEATTLE AIRPORT.** *(18740 Pacific Hwy S, Seattle 98188) 206/246-8600; FAX 206/431-8687.* 850 rms, 14 story. S, D, suites $295-$550; under 18 free; wkend rates; lower rates rest of yr. Crib free. TV; cable, VCR avail. Heated pool; poolside serv. Coffee in rms. Restaurant (see MAXI'S). Rm serv 24 hrs. Bars 11:30-2 am; entertainment. Ck-out noon. Convention facilities. Business center. In-rm modem link. Bellhops. Valet serv. Concierge. Sundries. Gift shop. Barber, beauty shop. Free airport transportation 24 hrs. Exercise equipt; weight machines, stair machine. Many bathrm phones. Private patios, balconies. Many rms with view of lake, mountains. Outdoor glass-enclosed elvtrs. On 28 acres. Cr cds: A, C, D, DS, ER, JCB, MC, V.

D

★ ★ ★ **HILTON SEATTLE AIRPORT.** *(17620 International Blvd, Seattle 98188) at S 176th St. 206/244-4800; FAX 206/248-4495.* E-mail debra_noonan@hilton.com; web www.hilton.com. 178 rms, 2-3 story. S, D $109-$159; suites $275-$350; under 18 free; wkend rates. Crib free. Pet accepted. TV; cable (premium), VCR avail. Heated pool; whirlpool, poolside serv. Complimentary coffee in rms. Restaurant 6 am-11 pm. Rm serv 24 hrs. Bar 11 am-midnight. Ck-out 1 pm. Meeting rms. Business center. In-rm modem link. Bellhops. Valet serv. Sundries. Free airport transportation. Exercise equipt; weight machine, bicycles. Private patios. Garden setting. Cr cds: A, C, D, DS, ER, JCB, MC, V.

D SC

★ ★ ★ **HOLIDAY INN.** *(17338 International Blvd, Seattle 98188) at S 173rd St. 206/248-1000; FAX 206/242-7089.* 260 rms, 12 story. S, D $134-$144; suites $200-$250; each addl $10; family, wkend rates. Crib free. TV; cable (premium). Indoor pool; whirlpool. Restaurant 6 am-10 pm; Fri to 10:30 pm; Sat 7 am-10:30 pm; Sun from 7 am. Rm serv. Bars 11 am-11 pm. Ck-out noon. Coin Indry. Meeting rms. Business servs avail. In-rm modem link. Bellhops. Sundries. Gift shop. Free airport transportation. Exercise equipt; weight machine, bicycle. Microwaves avail. Revolving rooftop dining rm. Cr cds: A, C, D, DS, JCB, MC, V.

D SC

★ ★ ★ **MARRIOTT SEA-TAC.** *(3201 S 176th St, Seattle 98188) International Blvd (WA 99) to S 176th St. 206/241-2000; FAX 206/248-0789.* 459 rms. S, D $111-$132; suites $200-$450; under 18 free; wkly, wkend rates. Crib free. Pet accepted. TV; cable (premium), VCR avail. Indoor pool; whirlpool, poolside serv. Restaurant 6 am-11 pm. Rm serv. Bar 11-2 am. Ck-out 1 pm. Convention facilities. Business center. In-rm modem link. Bellhops. Valet serv. Shopping arcade. Free airport transportation. Exercise equipt; weight machines, bicycles, sauna. Game rm. Microwaves avail. 21,000-sq ft atrium with trees, plants, totem poles, waterfall. Luxury level. Cr cds: A, C, D, DS, ER, JCB, MC, V.

D SC

★ ★ **QUALITY INN.** *17101 Pacific Hwy S (98188). 206/246-7000; FAX 206/246-1715.* 138 rms, 3 story. June-Aug: S $79-$115; D $89-$125; each addl $10; suites $145; under 18 free; lower rates rest of yr. Crib free. TV; cable (premium). Heated pool. Complimentary continental bkfst. Coffee in rms. Restaurnt adj 6 am-11 pm. Ck-out noon. Meeting rms. Business servs avail. In-rm modem link. Bellhops. Beauty shop. Free airport transportation. Exercise equipt; treadmills, stair machine. Cr cds: A, C, D, DS, ER, JCB, MC, V.

D SC

★ ★ ★ **RADISSON SEATTLE AIRPORT.** *(17001 International Blvd (Pacific Hwy), Seattle 98188) N on International Blvd (WA 99) at 170th St. 206/244-6000; FAX 206/246-6835.* 170 rms, 2 story. S $119-$159; D $129-$169; each addl $10; under 18 free; wkend rates. Crib free. TV; cable. Heated pool; poolside serv. Coffee in rms. Restaurant 6 am-10 pm. Rm serv. Bar 4 pm-1 am. Ck-out noon. Convention facilities. Business servs avail. In-rm modem link. Bellhops. Sundries. Gift shop. Free airport transportation. Exercise equipt; stair machines, bicycles, sauna. Luxury level. Cr cds: A, C, D, DS, ER, JCB, MC, V.

D SC

★ ★ **WESTCOAST SEA-TAC HOTEL.** *(18220 International Blvd, Seattle 98188) at 182nd St. 206/246-5535; FAX 206/246-9733; res: 800/426-0670.* 146 rms, 5 story. S $95-$105; D $105-$115; each addl $10; suites $150; under 18 free; some wkend rates. Crib free. TV; cable (premium), VCR avail. Heated pool; whirlpool, poolside serv. Restaurant 6 am-10 pm. Rm serv. Bar 11:30-2 am. Ck-out noon. Meeting rms. Business servs avail. Bellhops. Valet serv. Free valet parking. Free airport transportation. Exercise equipt; treadmill, stair machine, sauna. Cr cds: A, C, D, DS, ER, JCB, MC, V.

D SC

Restaurant

★ ★ ★ **MAXI'S.** *(See Doubletree Motor Hotel) 206/246-8600.* Hrs: 5-10 pm; Sun 9 am-2 pm (brunch). Closed Dec 25. Res accepted. Continental menu. Bar to 2 am. Semi-a la carte: dinner $17.95-$39.95. Sun brunch $17.95. Child's meals. Specialties: tableside Caesar salad, tableside steak Diane. Valet parking. Elegant, multi-level dining areas offer views of mountains or airport. Family-owned. Cr cds: A, C, D, DS, MC, V.

D SC

Bellevue

Motels

★ ★ **BEST WESTERN BELLEVUE INN.** *11211 Main St (98004), just W of I-405 exit 12. 425/455-5240; FAX 425/455-0654.* 180 rms, 2 story. S $120; D $130; under 18 free; wkend rates. Crib free. Pet accepted; $30. TV; cable (premium), VCR avail. Heated pool; poolside serv. Coffee in rms. Restaurant 6:30 am-2 pm, 5-10 pm. Rm serv. Bar; entertainment Thurs-Sat. Ck-out noon. Meeting rms. Business servs avail. In-rm modem link. Bellhops. Valet serv. Sundries. Exercise equipt; treadmil, bicycle. Refrigerators; microwaves avail. Balconies. Cr cds: A, C, D, DS, ER, JCB, MC, V.

D SC

★ ★ ★ **RESIDENCE INN BY MARRIOTT.** *14455 NE 29th Place (98007), off WA 520 148th Ave N exit. 425/882-1222; FAX 425/885-9260.* 120 suites, 2 story. S, D $160-$240. Crib $5. Pet accepted; $10/day. TV; cable (premium), VCR avail (free movies). Heated pool. Complimentary continental bkfst. Complimentary coffee in rms. Ck-out noon. Coin Indry. Meeting rms. Business servs avail. In-rm modem link. Valet serv. Lawn games. Refrigerators, microwaves. Private patios, balconies. Picnic tables, grills. Cr cds: A, C, D, DS, JCB, MC, V.

D

★ ★ **SILVER CLOUD INN.** *(12202 NE 124th St, Kirkland 98034) N on I-405, exit 20-B, E on NE 124 St. 425/821-8300; res: 800/205-6933; FAX 425/823-1218.* 99 rms, 3 story. June-Sept: S $69-$97; D $77-$105; suites $98-$145; under 12 free; lower rates rest of yr. Crib free. TV; cable (premium). Complimentary continental bkfst. Restaurant adj open 24 hrs. Rm serv. Ck-out noon. Meeting rms. Business servs avail. In-rm modem link. Concierge. Sundries. Guest Indry. Exercise equipt; weight machine, bicycle. Heated pool; whirlpool. Refrigerators. Microwaves avail. Cr cds: A, C, D, DS, ER, MC, V.

D SC

Motor Hotels

★ ★ **WESTCOAST BELLEVUE HOTEL.** *625 116th Ave NE (98004), E of I-405, NE 8th St exit. 425/455-9444; FAX 425/455-2154; res: 800/426-0670.* 176 rms, 6 story. S $75-$85; D $85-$95; each addl $10; suites $100-$110; under 18 free. Crib free. TV; cable (premium). Heated pool; poolside serv. Complimentary coffee in rms. Restaurant 6 am-10 pm; Sat, Sun from 7 am. Rm serv. Bar 4-11 pm; closed Sun. Ck-out noon. Meeting rms. Business servs avail. In-rm modem link. Sundries. Exercise equipt; stair machine, bicycles. Cr cds: A, D, DS, MC, V.

D SC

Hotels

★ ★ ★ ★ **BELLEVUE CLUB.** *11200 SE 6th (98004). 425/454-4424; FAX 425/688-3101; res: 800/579-1110.* Web www.bellevueclub.com. This four-story, neo-classical structure with Beaux Arts and Palladian influences is matched with interior spaces enveloped in beechwood paneling with French limestone floors and suspended, curved ceilings. The overall effect is clean, contemporary and inviting. The health-club facilities are outstanding, with everything from indoor tennis courts and two fully equipped weight-lifting and aerobic centers, to an Olympic-size swimming pool and running track. 67 rms, 2 with shower only, 4 story. S, D $190-$230; suites $370-$945; under 18 free; wkend rates. Crib free. Valet parking $5. TV; cable (premium), VCR avail. Indoor pool; whirlpool, poolside serv, lifeguard. Supervised child's activities; ages 1-12. Complimentary coffee in lobby. Restaurant (see POLARIS). Rm serv 24 hrs. Bar 11 am-midnight; entertainment Thurs-Sat. Ck-out 1 pm. Guest Indry. Meeting rms. Business center. In-rm modem link. Concierge. Gift shop. Indoor tennis, pro. Extensive exercise rm; instructor, weights, bicycles, sauna, steam rm. Massage. Minibars; microwaves avail. Balconies. Cr cds: A, C, D, MC, V.

D

★ ★ ★ **DOUBLETREE.** *300 112th Ave SE (98004), just W of I-405 exit 12. 425/455-1300; FAX 425/455-0466.* 353 rms, 10 story. S, D $180-$225; each addl $15; suites $250-$495; under 18 free; wkend rates. Crib free. TV; cable (premium), VCR avail. Heated pool; whirlpool, poolside serv. Complimentary coffee in rms. Restaurant 6 am-11 pm. Bar 11-2 am; closed Sun, Mon. Ck-out noon. Convention facilities. Business servs avail. In-rm modem link. Concierge. Gift shop. Barber, beauty shop. Exercise equipt; weight machine, bicycles. Some bathrm phones. Balconies. Glass-enclosed elvtrs in lobby; multi-story glass canopy at entrance. Luxury level. Cr cds: A, C, D, DS, ER, JCB, MC, V.

D SC

★ ★ ★ **HILTON.** *100 112th Ave NE (98004), just off I-405 NE 4th St exit. 425/455-3330; FAX 425/451-2473.* 180 rms, 7 story. May-Oct: S $131-$181; D $141-$191; suites $209-$289; each addl $10; family, wkend rates; lower rates rest of yr. Crib free. TV; cable (premium), VCR avail. Indoor pool; whirlpool. Complimentary coffee in rms. Restaurants 5:30 am-10 pm. Bar 10-2 am. Ck-out noon. Meeting rms. Business center. In-rm modem link. Concierge. Exercise equipt; weight machine, bicycle, sauna. Cr cds: A, C, D, DS, ER, MC, V.

D SC

★ ★ ★ **HYATT REGENCY BELLEVUE.** *900 Bellevue Way NE (98004), at Bellevue Place. 425/462-1234; FAX 425/646-7567; res: 800/233-1234.* 382 rms, 24 story, 29 suites. S $190-$215; D $215-$240; suites $250-$1,000; under 18 free. Crib free. Garage $7; valet parking $11. TV; cable (premium), VCR avail. Coffee in rms. Restaurant 6 am-10:30 pm. Bar 11-2 am. Ck-out noon. Convention facilities. Business center. In-rm modem link. Concierge. Shopping arcade. Barber, beauty shop. Some bathrm phones, refrigerators. Hotel connected to office/retail complex. Luxury level. Cr cds: A, C, D, DS, JCB, MC, V.

D SC

★ ★ **SILVER CLOUD INN.** *10621 NE 12th (98004). 425/637-7000; FAX 425/455-0531; res: 800/205-6937.* 97 rms, 12 with shower only, 4 story. Mar-Sept: S $85; D $95-$135; each addl $8; suites $135; under 12 free; lower rates rest of yr. Crib free. TV; cable (premium). Heated pool; whirlpool. Complimentary continental bkfst. Restaurant nearby. Ck-out noon. Meeting rms. Business servs avail. In-rm modem link. No bellhops. Guest Indry. Exercise equipt; bicycles, weight machine. Refrigerators; microwaves avail. Cr cds: A, C, D, DS, ER, MC, V.

D SC

★ ★ ★ ★ **WOODMARK HOTEL ON LAKE WASHINGTON.** *(1200 Carillon Point, Kirkland 98033) N on Bellevue Way, continue onto Lake Washington Blvd NE. 425/822-3700; FAX 425/822-3699; res: 800/822-3700.* E-mail woodmarkhotel@compuserve.com; web thewoodmark.com. Stroll along a shoreline promenade or lie on the beach and soak in the panoramic views at this contemporary-style resort hotel, the only lodging on the shores of Lake Washington. 100 units, 4 story, 21 suites. S $165-$215; D $180-$230; suites $260-$1,200; under 18 free. Crib free. Overnight parking $9; valet. TV; cable. Complimentary evening refreshments. Complimentary coffee in rms. Restaurant 6:30 am-10 pm; Sat, Sun from 7 am. Bar 11 am-midnight. Ck-out noon. Meeting rms. Business servs avail. In-rm modem link. Concierge. Health club privileges. Refrigerators, minibars. Balconies. Marina; 3 lakeside parks. Cr cds: A, D, MC, V.

D SC

Inn

✔★ ★ ★ **SHUMWAY MANSION.** *(11410 99th Place NE, Kirkland 98033) I-405N, exit 20A, then 1½ mi W. 425/823-2303; FAX 425/822-0421.* 8 rms, 2 story. No A/C. Rm phone avail. S, D $70-$95; each addl $12; suite $105. Children over 12 yrs only. TV avail. Complimentary full bkfst; evening refreshments. Restaurant nearby. Ck-out 11 am, ck-in 3 pm. Business servs avail. In-rm modem link. Health club privileges. A 24-rm historic mansion (1909), restored and moved to present site in 1985. Overlooks Juanita Bay. Totally nonsmoking. Cr cds: A, MC, V.

Restaurants

★ ★ ★ **BISTRO PROVENÇAL.** *(212 Central Way, Kirkland 98033) I-405 Kirkland exit 18. 425/827-3300.* Hrs: 5:30-10:30 pm; Sun 5-9:30 pm. Closed major hols. Res accepted. French menu. Serv bar. Semi-a la carte: dinner $13-$21. Complete meals: dinner $23-$45. Specializes in seafood, rack of lamb. Own baking. French country inn decor. Casual elegance. Fireplace. Cr cds: A, C, D, MC, V.

★ ★ ★ **CAFE JUANITA.** *(9702 120th Pl NE, Kirkland 98034-4206) N on I-405, exit 20A, then approx 1½ mi W. 425/823-6533.* Hrs: 5:30-9:45 pm. Closed some major hols. Res accepted. Italian menu. Serv bar. Wine cellar. A la carte entrees: dinner $14-$22.50. Child's meals. Specialties: pollo pistacchi, venison shank, coniglio con funghi. Own baking, pasta, ice cream. Outdoor dining. Casual dining in converted private home; open kitchen; wine-bottle accents. Family-owned. Totally nonsmoking. Cr cds: MC, V.

D

★ ★ **JAKE O'SHAUGHNESSEY'S.** *401 Bellevue Sq (98004), in Bellevue Sq Mall. 425/455-5559.* Hrs: 11:30 am-3 pm, 5-9 pm; Fri to 10 pm; Sun noon-3 pm, 4:30-9 pm. Closed Easter, Thanksgiving, Dec 25. Res accepted. Bar 11 am-midnight. Semi-a la carte: lunch $3.95-$9.95, dinner $9.95-$19.95. Child's meals. Specializes in fresh salmon, prime rib, Caesar salad. Outdoor dining. Club atmosphere with aquatic decor; several dining areas; open kitchen. Totally nonsmoking. Cr cds: A, D, DS, MC, V.

D

✔★ ★ ★ **POLARIS.** *(See Bellevue Club Hotel) 425/455-1616.* Web www.bellevue.com. Hrs: 7-10 am, 11:30 am-1:30 pm, 6-9 pm; Fri, Sat to 10 pm. Res accepted. Continental menu. Bar to midnight. Semi-a la carte: bkfst $3-$9.25, lunch $5.50-$11.95, dinner $11.50-$20.95. Child's meals. Specializes in pasta, seafood, lamb. Outdoor dining. Contemporary decor. Totally nonsmoking. Cr cds: A, MC, V.

D

✔★ ★ **SPAZZO MEDITERRANEAN GRILL.** *10655 NE Fourth St (98004), on 9th floor of Key Bank Bldg. 425/454-8255.* Hrs: 11:30 am-10 pm; Fri to 11 pm; Sat 4-11 pm; Sun 4-10 pm. Closed Dec 25. Res accepted. Mediterranean menu. Bar. Semi-a la carte: lunch $6.95-$15.95, dinner $8.95-$23.95. Child's meals. Specializes in Italian, Greek and Spanish dishes. View of Lake Washington and downtown. Cr cds: A, D, DS, JCB, MC, V.

D

★ ★ ★ **THIRD FLOOR FISH CAFE.** *(205 Lake St S, Kirkland 98033) I-405 N to Kirkland. 425/822-3553.* Hrs: 5-9:30 pm; Fri, Sat to 10 pm; Sun 4:30-9 pm. Closed Jan 1, Thanksgiving, Dec 25. Res accepted. Bar 4 pm-midnight; Sun to 10 pm. Wine list. A la carte entrees: dinner $17-$35. Specialties: spice-crusted Pacific halibut, pan-seared sturgeon, lamb shank. Own pastries. Jazz Wed, Sat. Three window-walls overlook Lake Washington and marina; dark woods create intimate atmosphere. Totally nonsmoking. Cr cds: A, MC, V.

D

Tampa

Settled: 1824
Pop: 281,837
Elev: 57 feet
Time zone: Eastern
Area code: 813
Web: www.thcva.com

St Petersburg

Founded: 1876
Pop: 238,629
Elev: 44 feet
Time zone: Eastern
Area code: 813
Web: www.stpete-clearwater.com

Third-largest city in Florida and home to a Spanish, Cuban and Italian enclave of 30,000, Tampa, meaning "sticks of fire," is indeed a hot spot on the west Florida coast. More than any other major city in the state, Tampa retains the Latin color and flavor that attest to its Spanish origins.

The fourth-largest city in the state and second only to Miami as a winter resort, St Petersburg is host to a half million visitors each year. St Petersburg wears a fringe of beaches, parks and yacht basins along Tampa Bay and a string of resort-occupied islands on the Gulf of Mexico, connected to the mainland by causeways. These islands form the St Petersburg Beach area.

Tampa and St Petersburg are the gateway cities to Florida's southwest Gulf Coast area. Together, the two cities, along with seven other nearby coastal communities, comprise the Suncoast, a popular vacation destination area.

Business

While tourism is an important factor in the economy of the Tampa-St Petersburg metropolitan area, there is considerable industry as well. The Port of Tampa, the eleventh-largest in the nation, handles more than 52 million tons of shipping a year. The city is a major manufacturing center for cigars; two citrus-processing plants and a variety of other industries are also here. Some 800 small-to-medium-sized manufacturers operate in Tampa.

Hillsborough County is one of Florida's most diverse agricultural counties, with citrus fruit, beef cattle, dairy products, vegetables and ornamental horticulture the main commodities. Some 2,600 Hillsborough County farms produce more than $400 million worth of farm goods each year. In the Greater Tampa area are a large number of feed, fertilizer and insecticide manufacturers, paper and metal container fabricating plants and food processing plants. Some of the world's largest phosphate mines are nearby. The county is the second-largest egg producer in the state and is also second in milk production. Some 350 vegetable farmers cultivate more than 15,000 acres of vegetables and strawberries.

Tampa is the transportation center for the west coast of Florida, as well as a center of banking, insurance and investment. The city is also growing as a medical and high technology center.

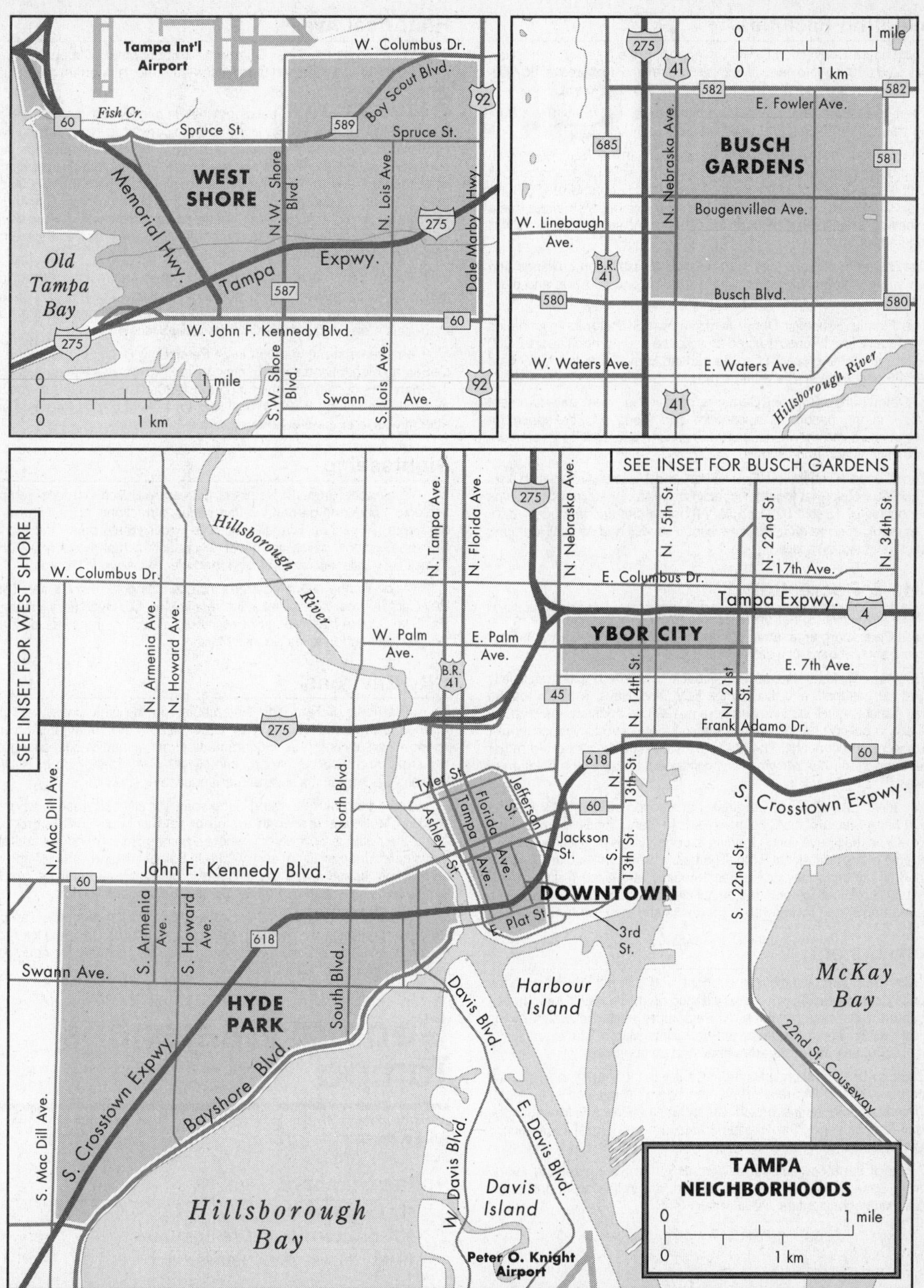

Tampa Int'l Airport
W. Columbus Dr.
Boy Scout Blvd.
Fish Cr.
Spruce St.
WEST SHORE
Memorial Hwy.
N.W. Shore Blvd.
N. Lois Ave.
Dale Marby Hwy.
Old Tampa Bay
Tampa Expwy.
W. John F. Kennedy Blvd.
S.W. Shore Blvd.
S. Lois Ave.
Swann Ave.
0 1 mile
0 1 km
E. Fowler Ave.
BUSCH GARDENS
N. Nebraska Ave.
Bougenvillea Ave.
W. Linebaugh Ave.
Busch Blvd.
W. Waters Ave.
E. Waters Ave.
Hillsborough River
SEE INSET FOR BUSCH GARDENS
SEE INSET FOR WEST SHORE
Hillsborough River
W. Columbus Dr.
N. Armenia Ave.
N. Howard Ave.
N. Tampa Ave.
N. Florida Ave.
N. Nebraska Ave.
N. 15th St.
N. 22nd St.
N. 34th St.
E. Columbus Dr.
17th Ave.
Tampa Expwy.
YBOR CITY
W. Palm Ave.
E. Palm Ave.
E. 7th Ave.
N. 14th St.
N. 21st St.
Frank Adamo Dr.
N. Mac Dill Ave.
North Blvd.
Tyler St.
Ashley St.
Tampa Ave.
Florida Ave.
Jefferson St.
Jackson St.
N. 13th St.
S. 13th St.
S. 22nd St.
S. Crosstown Expwy.
John F. Kennedy Blvd.
DOWNTOWN
E. Plat St.
3rd St.
S. Armenia Ave.
S. Howard Ave.
South Blvd.
Swann Ave.
HYDE PARK
Harbour Island
Davis Blvd.
McKay Bay
22nd St. Causeway
S. Crosstown Expwy.
Bayshore Blvd.
S. Mac Dill Ave.
W. Davis Blvd.
E. Davis Blvd.
Davis Island
Hillsborough Bay
Peter O. Knight Airport
TAMPA NEIGHBORHOODS
0 1 mile
0 1 km

Convention Facilities

The Tampa Convention Center, overlooking the Hillsborough River, includes 200,000 square feet of exhibit space and features a 36,000-square-foot ballroom and 27,000 square feet of meeting rooms.

There are 22 meeting rooms with seating capacities from 40 to 1,000. Parking space for 460 cars is located adjacent to the building.

The Florida State Fairgrounds, located six miles from downtown Tampa, provides versatile facilities for year-round use. The exposition hall has 93,000 square feet of floor space, with a seating capacity of 12,500 or space for 322 exhibits or concessions. The air-conditioned structure has a 45-foot ceiling, enabling it to be used for circuses and sports events as well as trade shows.

The 325-acre complex has numerous other exhibition buildings and entertainment centers, campsites with rest rooms and showers and parking for 16,500 cars with room for expansion.

The Florida Suncoast Dome in downtown St Petersburg contains 152,000 square feet of unobstructed floor space and an additional 22,000 square feet of meeting space. On-site parking is available for 7,500 cars with 32,500 spaces available within a mile.

St Petersburg's Bayfront Center is one of the finest entertainment complexes in the nation. Its auditorium and arena provide space for Broadway shows, ice shows, circuses and concerts, as well as for conventions, exhibitions and trade shows.

The Tampa/Hillsborough Convention and Visitors Association lists more than 50 hotels that together contain more than 210 meeting rooms with capacities of 15 to 1,820 people. All hotels can accommodate banquets for medium-sized groups; all have food service and cocktail lounges; and most have exhibit space.

Sports & Recreation

All of the activities that draw tourists to Florida are available in the Tampa/St Petersburg area; among them are golf, boating, tennis, fishing, swimming, shuffleboard, playgrounds and parks.

Tropicana Field, a stadium with capacity of 43,000, was specifically designed for baseball, and the Tampa Bay Devil Rays, a major league baseball franchise, will start playing here in 1998. In addition, the stadium plays host to college basketball, ice shows, motor sports, indoor tennis, indoor soccer and concerts. The stadium's roof is cable-supported rather than air-supported, thus allowing "self-contained" areas of the stadium to be moved.

In addition, the St Louis Cardinals have spring training in St Petersburg's Al Lang Stadium; the Cincinnati Reds in Plant City Stadium and the New York Yankees have spring training in Legends Field. The Tampa Bay Buccaneers play professional football games in Houlihan Stadium, and the Tampa Bay Lightning play professional hockey at the Ice Palace arena downtown. There is also horse racing, jai alai, college sports, auto racing, golf tournaments, dog racing, various festivals and the Florida State Fair.

Entertainment

Each year Tampa enjoys the bright and colorful tradition of the Gasparilla pirate invasion, when a fully rigged pirate ship sails into the bay and "captures" the city. In March, St Petersburg hosts an ocean racing event called Mid-Winter Regatta, and from late March to mid-April, the Festival of States features parades and band competitions.

Close to St Petersburg's Bayfront Center is the Pier. The revitalized area contains shops and restaurants and offers fishing and other water sports. Nearby are a marina, beach, yacht club, the Fine Arts Museum, the Salvador Dali Museum, the Historical Museum and Great Explorations Museum.

Some of the most famous restaurants in the South, serving everything from Spanish cuisine to fresh seafood, are in this area, and many clubs and nightspots feature live entertainment.

Historical Areas

Ybor City is the Latin Quarter of Tampa where Cuban immigrants established residences and businesses—the most important of which was the cigar industry.

A complex of brick buildings that once housed the largest cigar factory in the world, Ybor Square has been converted into a thriving center containing a nostalgic marketplace, restaurants, old-fashioned ice cream parlor and a variety of shops and boutiques. The original factory was built by Vincente Martinez Ybor in 1886 and employed more than 4,000 cigar makers for five decades. This was the original center of Ybor City and was not only a place of employment, but an educational center for the workers as well. The facades of the buildings are being restored to their original 19th-century appearance.

Today, Ybor City is still a thoroughly Cuban community, with wrought-iron balconies, multicolumned buildings, plazas, arcades and sidewalk coffee shops. New nightclubs, restaurants, stores and art galleries have made this area popular for visitors as well as locals.

An interesting restoration in St Petersburg Beach is that of the Don CeSar, an elegant and striking "pink palace," which was a favorite resort of the members of café society during the 1920s. The Don CeSar was used as a hospital during World War II and for federal offices for some years after. It was later restored and reopened as a resort.

Sightseeing

Within the Tampa/St Petersburg area are Busch Gardens Tampa, a zoological park and garden featuring rides, attractions, animal shows and big game; Adventure Island, a 36-acre water theme park; and Florida's Sunken Gardens, which are especially beautiful in early spring when the camellias, gardenias, azaleas and rhododendrons are in bloom.

Major Tampa shopping areas include Brandon TownCenter, Tampa Bay Center, West Shore Plaza, University Mall, Old Hyde Park Village and Eastlake Square Mall. Major St Petersburg shopping areas include Tyrone Square Mall and Pinellas Square Mall.

City Environs

Just north of Tampa/St Petersburg, on the Gulf Coast, is Tarpon Springs, a town settled largely by Greek fishermen. Today, this area is a sponge market center. Spongeorama features an audiovisual sponge-diving show and displays. Approximately 30 miles farther north is Weeki Wachee Spring with its spectacular underwater show.

South from St Petersburg is the sparkling city of Sarasota, where the Ringling Museums are worth a stop of several hours. Still farther south along the coast is Fort Myers, where Thomas Edison and several of his industrialist friends lived and worked; Sanibel Island, one of the less commercial beach areas to be found in the state; and Naples, home of Jungle Larry's Zoological Park at Caribbean Gardens.

To the east and northeast, within driving distance of the Tampa/St Petersburg area, are Cypress Gardens in Winter Haven, Bok Tower Gardens in Lake Wales, Sea World near Orlando and, of course, the vacation kingdom of Walt Disney World.

General References Tampa

Area code: 813

Phone Numbers

POLICE & FIRE: 911

POISON CONTROL CENTER: 253-4444

TIME: 976-1111 **WEATHER:** 976-1111

Information Sources

Tampa/Hillsborough Convention & Visitors Association, 111 Madison St, Suite 1010, 33602; 223-1111, ext 44, or 800/44-TAMPA.

Greater Tampa Chamber of Commerce, 801 E Kennedy Blvd, PO Box 420, 33601; 228-7777.

Transportation

AIRLINES: Air Aruba; Air Canada; American; America West; British Airways; Canadian Airlines; Cayman; Continental; Delta; Kiwi International; LTU; Northwest; Southwest; TWA; United; USAir; ValuJet; and other commuter and regional airlines.

AIRPORT: Tampa International, 870-8700.

CAR RENTAL AGENCIES: (See IMPORTANT TOLL-FREE NUMBERS) Avis 396-3525; Budget 878-2451; Dollar 396-3640; Hertz 874-3232; National 396-3782.

PUBLIC TRANSPORTATION: HART 254-4278.

RAILROAD PASSENGER SERVICE: Amtrak 800/872-7245.

Newspaper

Tampa Tribune.

Convention Facilities

Florida State Fairgrounds, 4800 US 301, 621-7821.

Tampa Convention Center, 333 S Franklin St, 223-8511.

Sports & Recreation

Major Sports Facilities

Houlihan Stadium, 4201 N Dale Mabry Hwy, 879-2827 (Tampa Bay Buccaneers, football, 870-2700).

Ice Palace, Channel District, downtown, 229-2658 (Tampa Bay Lightning, hockey).

Legends Field, Dale Mabry Hwy & Dr. Martin Luther King, Jr. Blvd, 875-7753 (New York Yankees, baseball, spring training).

Plant City Stadium, Park Rd, 2 mi S of I-4 on Park Rd, 752-1878 (Cincinnati Reds, baseball, spring training).

Tropicana Field, 204 16th St S, 825-3100 (Tampa Bay Devil Rays, baseball, 825-3250).

Racetracks

Tampa Bay Downs, 11 mi NW on FL 580, then 1 mi N on Race Track Rd, Oldsmar, 855-4401 (horse racing).

Tampa Greyhound Track, 8300 Nebraska Ave, 932-4313 (greyhound racing).

Jai Alai

Tampa Jai-Alai Fronton, 5125 S Dale Mabry Hwy at Gandy Blvd, 831-1411.

Cultural Facilities

Theaters & Concert Halls

Tampa Bay Performing Arts Center, 1010 N MacInnes Place, 229-7827.

Tampa Theatre, 711 N Franklin, 223-8981.

Museums

Children's Museum of Tampa at Lowry Park, 7550 N Boulevard, 935-8441.

Henry B. Plant Museum, 401 W Kennedy Blvd, Univ of Tampa, 254-1891.

Museum of African-American Art, 1308 N Marion St, 272-2466.

MOSI Science Center, 4801 E Fowler Ave, 987-6300.

Tampa Bay History Center, 225 S Franklin St, 228-0097.

Tampa Museum of Art, 600 N Ashley Dr, 274-8130.

Ybor City State Museum, 1818 E 9th Ave, 247-6323.

Points of Interest

Adventure Island, 4545 Bougainvillea Ave, 987-5660.

Bok Tower Gardens, 50 mi E, just N of Lake Wales, 676-1408.

Busch Gardens Tampa, 3000 Busch Blvd, entrance on 40th St, 987-5082.

Cypress Gardens, 2 mi SW of Winter Haven on FL 540, 324-2111.

Hillsborough River State Park, 30 mi NE via US 301, in Zephyrhills, 987-6771.

Lowry Park Zoo, 7530 N Boulevard, 932-0245.

Municipal Beach, Courtney Campbell Causeway, FL 60.

University of Tampa, Kennedy Blvd at Hillsborough River, 253-6220.

Waterfront, from Davis Island, Water St or 13th St.

Ybor City, between I-4, 5th Ave, Nebraska Ave & 22nd St.

Ybor Square, 1901 N 13th St, 247-4497.

Sightseeing Tours

Around the Town, 3450 Buschwood Park Dr, Suite 115, 932-7803.

Tampa Tours, 5805 N 50th St, 621-6667.

Annual Events

Gasparilla Festival of Tampa Bay, waterfront. Early Feb.

Florida State Fair, Florida State Fairgrounds and Expo Park. Feb 5-16.

Florida Strawberry Festival, Plant City. Early Mar.

(For further information contact the Tampa/Hillsborough Convention & Visitors Association.)

St Petersburg

Area code: 813

Phone Numbers

POLICE & FIRE: 911

POISON CONTROL CENTER: 253-4444

TIME: 976-1111

Information Sources

St Petersburg-Clearwater Area Convention & Visitors Bureau, 14450 46th St N, Ste 108, Clearwater 34622; 464-7200 or 800/951-1111.

St Petersburg Area Chamber of Commerce, 100 2nd Ave N, PO Box 1371, 33731; 821-4715.

Suncoast Welcome Center, 2001 Ulmerton Rd, 576-1449.

Dept of Leisure Services, 893-7207.

The Pier, 800 2nd Ave NE, 821-6164.

Transportation

AIRPORTS: St Petersburg/Clearwater International, 535-7600 or 531-1451; Tampa International, 870-8700.

AIRLINES: American Trans Air; Canadian Intl; Southwest; and other commuter and regional airlines.

CAR RENTAL AGENCIES: (See IMPORTANT TOLL-FREE NUMBERS) Avis 530-1406; Budget 576-4011; Hertz 531-3774; National 530-5491.

PUBLIC TRANSPORTATION: Pinellas Suncoast Transit Authority 530-9911.

RAILROAD PASSENGER SERVICE: Amtrak 800/872-7245.

Newspaper

St Petersburg Times.

Convention Facility

Bayfront Center, 400 1st St S, 892-5767.

Sports & Recreation

Major Sports Facility

Al Lang Stadium, 1st St S & 2nd Ave S, 822-3384 (St Louis Cardinals, baseball, spring training).

Racetracks

Derby Lane-St Petersburg Kennel Club, 10490 Gandy Blvd NE, 576-1361 (greyhound racing).

Sunshine Speedway, 9 mi N on I-275, then 3 mi W on FL 688, in Pinellas Park, 573-4598 (auto racing).

Tampa Bay Downs, N on US 19, E on FL 580, then 1 mi N on Race Track Rd, Oldsmar, 855-4401 (horse racing).

Cultural Facilities

Theater & Concert Hall

Bayfront Center Theater, 400 1st St S, 892-5767 (Florida Orchestra).

Museums

Great Explorations, 1120 4th St S, 821-8885.

St Petersburg Museum of History, 335 2nd Ave NE, 894-1052.

Florida International Museum, 102 2nd St N, 821-1448.

Art Museums

Museum of Fine Arts, 255 Beach Dr NE, 896-2667.

Salvador Dali Museum, 1000 3rd St S, 823-3767.

Points of Interest

Historical

Coliseum Ballroom, 535 4th Ave N, 892-5202.

Don CeSar Hotel, 3400 Gulf Blvd, St Petersburg Beach, 360-1881.

Other Attractions

De Soto National Memorial, S on US 41 to Bradenton, then 2 mi N off FL 64, on Tampa Bay, 941/792-0458.

Florida's Sunken Gardens, 1825 4th St N, 896-3186.

Fort De Soto Park, Mullet Key, 866-2484.

Lake Maggiore Park, 9th St S.

Planetarium, St Petersburg Jr College, 6605 5th Ave N, 341-4320.

The Pier, 800 2nd Ave NE, 821-6164.

Ringling Museums, 25 mi S via US 10, 41, Sarasota, 941/355-5101.

Science Center of Pinellas County, 7701 22nd Ave N, 384-0027.

Spongeorama, 510 Dodecanese Blvd, Tarpon Springs, 943-9509.

Suncoast Seabird Sanctuary, 18328 Gulf Blvd, Indian Shores, 391-6211.

Weeki Wachee Spring, 30 mi N via US 19, at jct FL 50, 352/596-2062.

Sightseeing Tours

Gray Line bus tours, 6890 142nd Ave N, Largo 33771; 535-0208.

Annual Events

International Folk Fair. Mar.

Renaissance Festival. 6 wkends, early Mar-mid-Apr.

Sunshine Festival of States. Late Mar.

St Anthony's Tampa Bay Triathlon. Late Apr.

Artworks Festival. May.

City Neighborhoods

Many of the restaurants, unrated dining establishments and some lodgings listed under Tampa include neighborhoods as well as exact street addresses. Geographic descriptions of these neighborhoods are given, followed by a table of restaurants arranged by neighborhood.

Tampa

Busch Gardens: West of Busch Gardens amusement park; south of Fowler Ave, north of Busch Blvd and east of I-275.

Downtown: South of Tyler St, west of Jefferson St, north of Water St and Harbour Island and east of Ashley St. **North of Downtown:** North of US 275. **South of Downtown:** South of FL 618. **West of Downtown:** West of Hillsborough River.

Hyde Park: South of Kennedy Blvd, west and north of Bayshore Blvd and east of S MacDill Ave.

West Shore: On Old Tampa Bay south of Courtney Campbell Pkwy and Tampa Intl Airport, west of Dale Mabry Hwy and north of Kennedy Blvd.

Ybor City: South of I-4, west of 22nd St, north of 7th Ave and east of Nebraska Ave.

Lodgings and Food
Tampa

TAMPA RESTAURANTS BY NEIGHBORHOOD AREAS
(For full description, see alphabetical listings under Restaurants)

DOWNTOWN
Harbour View (Wyndham Harbour Island Hotel). 725 S Harbour Island Blvd
Italianissimo (Hyatt Regency Hotel). 2 Tampa City Center

NORTH OF DOWNTOWN
A.J. Catfish. 8751 N Himes Ave
Rumpelmayers. 4812 E Busch Blvd
Sukhothai. 8201 A North Dale Mabry Hwy
Taj. 2734-B Fowler Ave

WEST OF DOWNTOWN
Capdevila's At La Teresita. 3248 W Columbus Dr
Donatello. 232 N Dale Mabry Hwy
Malios. 301 S Dale Mabry Hwy

HYDE PARK
Bern's Steak House. 1208 S Howard Ave
Colonnade. 3401 Bayshore Blvd
Jimmy Mac's. 113 S Armenia Ave
Miguel's. 3035 W Kennedy
Mise En Place. 442 W Kennedy Blvd

WEST SHORE
Armani's (Hyatt Regency Westshore Hotel). 6200 Courtney Campbell Causeway
CK's (Marriott Airport Hotel). Tampa Intl Airport
Landry's Seafood House. 7616 Courtney Campbell Causeway
Ruth's Chris Steak House. 1700 N Westshore Blvd
Shula's Steak House (Sheraton Grand Hotel). 4860 W Kennedy Blvd

YBOR CITY
Columbia. 2117 E 7th Ave

Note: When a listing is located in a town that does not have its own city heading, it will appear under the city nearest to its location. In these cases, the address and town appear in parenthesis immediately following the name of the establishment.

Motels

(Rates may be higher during state fair, Gasparilla Festival)

✓★ **BUDGETEL INN.** *9202 N 30th St (33612), north of downtown. 813/930-6900; FAX 813/930-0563.* 150 rms, 3 story. Jan-mid-Apr, late June-early Sept: S, D $69.95-$77.95; each addl $7; suites $90.95-$97.95; under 18 free; wkly rates; lower rates rest of yr. Crib free. Pet accepted, some restrictions; $10 deposit. TV; cable (premium). Complimentary continental bkfst. Complimentary coffee in rms. Restaurant opp noon-midnight. Ck-out noon. Business servs avail. Shopping arcade. Coin Indry. Pool. Some refrigerators, microwaves. Cr cds: A, C, D, DS, MC, V.

D SC

★★ **COURTYARD BY MARRIOTT.** *3805 W Cypress St (33607), I-275, exit 23B, near Intl Airport, in West Shore. 813/874-0555; FAX 813/870-0685.* 145 rms, 4 story. Jan-Apr: S, D $124-$134; suites $145; under 18 free; lower rates rest of yr. Crib free. TV; cable (premium). Pool; whirlpool. Complimentary bkfst. Complimentary coffee in rms. Rm serv. Ck-out noon. Coin Indry. Meeting rms. Business servs avail. In-rm modem link. Free airport transportation. Exercise equipt; weight machines. Refrigerator in suites. Some balconies. Cr cds: A, C, D, DS, MC, V.

D SC

✓★ **DAYS INN-BUSCH GARDENS NORTH.** *701 E Fletcher Ave (33612), near Busch Gardens. 813/977-1550; FAX 813/977-6556.* 235 rms, 3 story. Jan-Apr: S $42-$62; D $48-$85; each addl $6; wkly, monthly rates; lower rates rest of yr. Crib free. Pet accepted, some restrictions. TV; cable (premium). Pool. Complimentary full bkfst. Restaurant 6-10 am; Sat, Sun 7-11 am. Ck-out noon. Coin Indry. Meeting rms. Business servs avail. Gift shop. Cr cds: A, D, DS, MC, V.

SC

★ **DAYS INN-FAIRGROUNDS.** *9942 Adamo Dr (FL 60) (33619), east of downtown, exit 51 off I 75, west on FL 60. 813/623-5121; FAX 813/628-4989.* 100 rms, 2 story. Jan-Apr: S $64-$69; D $74-$79; each addl $5; under 12 free; lower rates rest of yr. Crib free. TV; cable (premium). Pool. Complimentary continental bkfst. Coffee in rms. Restaurant adj 6 am-10 pm. Ck-out noon. Coin Indry. Meeting rm. Some refrigerators, microwaves. Cr cds: A, C, D, DS, MC, V.

D SC

✓★ **ECONOMY INNS OF AMERICA.** *6606 E Dr Martin Luther King Blvd (33619), I-4 exit 4, east of downtown. 813/623-6667; FAX 813/623-1495.* 128 rms, 2 story. Jan-mid-Apr: S $54.90; D $59.90; lower rates rest of yr. Pet accepted. TV; cable (premium). Heated pool. Complimentary coffee in lobby. Restaurant nearby. Ck-out 11 am. Coin Indry. Cr cds: A, MC, V.

D SC

★★ **HAMPTON INN AIRPORT-WESTSHORE.** *4817 W Laurel St (33607), I-275S exit Westshore (21), N to Laurel. 813/287-0778; FAX 813/287-0882.* 134 rms, 6 story. Jan-Apr: S, D $75-$89; under 19 free; higher rates special events; lower rates rest of yr. TV; cable (premium). Pool. Complimentary continental bkfst. Ck-out noon. Business servs avail. In-rm modem link. Bellhops. Free airport transportation. Cr cds: A, C, D, DS, MC, V.

D SC

★★ **HOLIDAY INN BUSCH GARDENS.** *2701 E Fowler Ave (33612), I-275 exit 34. 813/971-4710; FAX 813/977-0155.* 400 rms, 2 story. Jan-Apr: S, D $89-$99; each addl $10; under 18 free; lower rates rest of yr. Crib free. Pet accepted, some restrictions. TV; cable (premium). Pool; poolside serv. Restaurant 6:30-1 am. Bar 11-2 am. Ck-out noon. Coin Indry. Meeting rms. Business servs avail. In-rm modem link. Bellhops. Free Busch Gardens transportation. Tropical garden. Opp shopping mall. Sundries. Cr cds: A, C, D, DS, JCB, MC, V.

D SC

★★ **HOLIDAY INN EXPRESS-STADIUM.** *4732 N Dale Mabry Hwy (33614), north of downtown. 813/877-6061; FAX 813/876-1531.* 235 rms, 1-2 story, 35 suites. Late Dec-early Apr: S, D $79-$84; each addl $10; suites $95-$125; under 18 free; lower rates rest of yr. Pet accepted; $20. TV; cable (premium). Pool. Complimentary continental bkfst. Restaurant 11 am-11 pm. Ck-out noon. Meeting rms. Business center. In-rm modem link. Bellhops. Valet serv. Free airport transportation. Exercise equipt; treadmills, stair machine. Game rm. Microwaves avail. Cr cds: A, C, D, DS, JCB, MC, V.

D SC

✓★★ **LA QUINTA INN.** *2904 Melbourne Blvd (33605), I-4 exit 3, east of downtown. 813/623-3591; FAX 813/620-1375.* Web www.travelweb.com/laquinta.html. 128 rms, 3 story. S $44-$64; D $51-$71; each addl $7; suites $78-$100; under 18 free. Crib free. Pet accepted, some restrictions. TV; cable (premium). Pool. Complimentary continental bkfst. Ck-out noon. Guest Indry. Meeting rms. In-rm modem link. Sundries. Cr cds: A, C, D, DS, MC, V.

D

★ **RED ROOF INN.** *5001 N US 301 (33610), near I-4 exit 6A, east of downtown. 813/623-5245; FAX 813/623-5240.* 108 rms, 2 story. Jan-Apr: S, D $69.99-$95.99; under 18 free; lower rates rest of yr. Pet accepted, some restrictions. TV; cable (premium). Complimentary coffee. Restaurant adj open 24 hrs. Ck-out noon. Cr cds: A, C, D, DS, MC, V.

D

★ ★ **RESIDENCE INN BY MARRIOTT.** *3075 N Rocky Point Dr (33607), near Intl Airport, west of downtown, off FL 60. 813/281-5677; FAX 813/281-5677.* E-mail notinshow@aol.com; web www.marriott.com. 176 kit. units, 1-2 story. Jan-Apr: S, D $125-$200; family rates; lower rates rest of yr. Crib free. Pet accepted; $100 and $6/day. TV; cable (premium). Pool; whirlpool. Complimentary continental bkfst. Ck-out noon. Coin Indry. Meeting rms. Business servs avail. In-rm modem link. Bellhops. Valet serv Mon-Fri. Free airport transportation. Golf nearby. Health club privileges. Microwaves. Some balconies. Dock; watersports, para-sailing, fishing. On Tampa Bay. Cr cds: A, C, D, DS, MC, V.

D SC

★ ★ **SAILPORT RESORT.** *2506 Rocky Point Dr (33607), west of downtown. 813/281-9599; FAX 813/281-9510; res: 800/255-9599.* 212 kit. suites (1-2 bedrm), 4 story. S, D $109-$169; under 12 free; wkly, monthly rates. Crib $5; TV; cable (premium). Heated pool. Complimentary continental bkfst. Ck-out 11 am. Coin Indry. Meeting rms. Business servs avail. In-rm modem link. Valet serv. Covered parking. Lighted tennis. Health club privileges. Microwaves. Private patios, balconies. Some grills. On bay; dock; all waterfront rms. Cr cds: A, D, MC, V.

SC

✓★ ★ **TAHITIAN INN.** *601 S Dale Mabry Hwy (33609), West Shore. 813/877-6721; FAX 813/877-6218; res: 800/876-1397.* 79 rms, 18 with shower only, 2 story. Mid-Jan-mid-Apr: S $46-$52; D $46-$61; each addl $5; suites $65-$75; under 12 free; higher rates football games; lower rates rest of yr. Crib $5. Pet accepted; $25. TV; cable (premium). Heated pool. Restaurant 7 am-2:30 pm; Tues-Thur also 5-8:30 pm; Sat, Sun 8 am-1:30 pm. Rm serv. Ck-out noon. Meeting rm. Business servs avail. In-rm modem link. Bellhops. Sundries. Microwaves avail. Balconies. Cr cds: A, C, D, DS, MC, V.

D

Motor Hotels

★ ★ **AMERISUITES.** *11408 N 30th St (33612), north of downtown. 813/979-1922; FAX 813/979-1926.* 128 suites, 6 story. Jan-Apr: S $119; D $129; under 17 free; wkend rates; lower rates rest of yr. Crib free. Pet accepted, some restrictions; $50/day. TV; cable (premium), VCR. Complimentary continental bkfst, coffee in rms. Restaurant nearby. Ck-out 11 am. Business center. In-rm modem link. Valet serv. Coin Indry. Exercise rm; instructor, weight machine, treadmill. Pool. Refrigerators, microwaves, wet bars. Picnic table. Cr cds: A, C, D, DS, JCB, MC, V.

D SC

★ ★ **BEST WESTERN RESORT AT BUSCH GARDENS.** *820 E Busch Blvd (33612), jct I-275 & Busch Blvd. 813/933-4011; FAX 813/932-1784; res: 800/288-4011.* 261 rms, 2-4 story. Jan-Apr: S $82.95-$92.95; D $92.95-$102.95; suites $159.95; under 12 free; wkly, wkend rates; higher rates special events; lower rates rest of yr. Crib free. TV; cable (premium). 2 heated pools, 1 indoor; whirlpool. Coffee in rms. Restaurant 6:30 am-2 pm, 5-10 pm. Rm serv. Bar 5-11 pm. Ck-out 11 am. Coin Indry. Convention facilities. Business center. Bellhops. Valet serv. Sundries. Gift shop. Free Busch Gardens transportation. Lighted tennis. Exercise equipt; weight machine, bicycles, sauna. Game rm. Microwaves avail. Cr cds: A, C, D, DS, MC, V.

D SC

★ ★ **QUALITY SUITES.** *3001 University Center Dr (33612), near Busch Gardens. 813/971-8930; FAX 813/971-8935.* 150 suites, 3 story. Suites $99-$159; each addl $7; under 18 free. Crib free. TV; cable (premium), VCR (movies avail). Heated pool; whirlpool. Complimentary full bkfst. Complimentary coffee in rms. Restaurant 6-10 am; wkends 7-11 am, 4-7 pm. Ck-out noon. Coin Indry. Meeting rms. Business servs avail. In-rm modem link. Bellhops. Valet serv. Sundries. Gift shop. Microwaves. Balconies. Cr cds: A, C, D, DS, ER, JCB, MC, V.

D SC

Hotels

★ ★ **AMERISUITES.** *4811 W Main St (33607), near Intl Airport. 813/282-1037; FAX 813/282-1148.* Web www. travelbase.com/destinations/tampa/amerisuites-airport. 126 suites, 6 story. Jan-Apr: S, D $99-$139; each addl $10; family, wkly, monthly rates; 3-day min hols; lower rates rest of yr. Crib free. Pet accepted, some restrictions. TV; cable (premium), VCR. Heated pool. Complimentary continental bkfst. Complimentary coffee in rms. Restaurant adj 5-11 pm. Bar. Ck-out 11 am. Coin Indry. Meeting rms. Business center. Free airport transportation. Exercise equipt; weight machine, bicycle. Refrigerators, microwaves. Picnic tables. Cr cds: A, D, DS, JCB, MC, V.

D SC

★ ★ ★ **CAMBERLEY PLAZA.** *10221 Princess Palm Ave (33610), I-75 exit 52; 1 mi S of I-4. 813/623-6363; FAX 813/621-7224; res: 800/555-8000.* 265 rms, 5 story, 41 suites. Mid-Jan-mid-Apr: S, D $155-$205; suites $170-$500; under 18 free; wkend rates; higher rates special events; lower rates rest of yr. Crib free. TV; cable (premium). Heated pool; wading pool, whirlpool. Restaurant 6:30 am-11 pm. Bar 11-2 am. Ck-out noon. Convention facilities. Business center. In-rm modem link. Concierge. Gift shop. Barber, beauty shop. Free airport transportation. Lighted tennis. Exercise equipt; stair machine, bicycles. Refrigerator in suites. Private patios, balconies. Bldg with distinctive curved structure located on 9 acres; 3-story atrium lobby with waterfall. Luxury level. Cr cds: A, C, D, DS, JCB, MC, V.

D SC

★ ★ ★ **CROWNE PLAZA TAMPA-WESTSHORE.** *700 N Westshore Blvd (33609), exit 21 off I-275, near Intl Airport, in West Shore. 813/289-8200; FAX 813/289-9166.* 272 rms, 11 story. Jan-Apr: S, D $159-$189; each addl $15; under 18 free; wkend rates; lower rates rest of yr. Crib free. TV; cable (premium). Heated pool; whirlpool. Coffee in rms. Restaurant 6:30 am-11 pm. Bar 11 am-midnight. Ck-out noon. Convention facilities. Business servs avail. In-rm modem link. Valet parking. Free airport transportation. Gift shop. Exercise equipt; weights, bicycles, sauna. Microwaves avail. Luxury level. Cr cds: A, C, D, DS, MC, V.

D SC

★ ★ ★ **DOUBLETREE GUEST SUITES ON TAMPA BAY.** *3050 N Rocky Point Dr W (33607), at Courtney Campbell Causeway, near Intl Airport, west of downtown. 813/888-8800; FAX 813/888-8743.* 203 suites, 7 story. Oct-Apr: S $159; D $179; each addl $20; under 13 free; wkend rates; lower rates rest of yr. Crib free. TV; cable (premium). Heated pool; whirlpool. Restaurant 6:30 am-10 pm. Bar 11 am-midnight. Ck-out noon. Coin Indry. Meeting rms. In-rm modem link. Gift shop. Free airport transportation. Exercise equipt; stair machine, weights, sauna. Refrigerators. Microwaves avail. Sun deck. On Tampa Bay. Cr cds: A, C, D, DS, MC, V.

D SC

★ ★ ★ **EMBASSY SUITES-TAMPA AIRPORT/WESTSHORE.** *555 N Westshore Blvd (33609), near Intl Airport, in West Shore. 813/875-1555; FAX 813/287-3664.* 221 kit. suites, 16 story. Jan-Apr: S, D $159-$179; under 18 free; wkly, monthly, wkend rates; lower rates rest of yr. Crib free. Pet accepted, some restrictions; $15/day. TV; cable (premium). Heated pool; whirlpool, poolside serv. Complimentary full bkfst. Coffee in rms. Restaurant 6:30 am-2 pm, 5-10 pm. Rm serv 6 am-11 pm. Bar noon-midnight. Ck-out noon. Coin Indry. Meeting rms. Business servs avail. In-rm modem link. Gift shop. Free covered parking; valet. Free airport transportation. Exercise equipt; bicycles, stair machine, sauna. Microwaves avail. Balconies. Cr cds: A, C, D, DS, ER, JCB, MC, V.

D SC

★ ★ ★ **FOUR POINTS BY SHERATON.** *7401 E Hillsborough Ave (33610), I-4 exit 5, east of downtown. 813/626-0999; FAX 813/622-7893.* 276 rms, 6 story. Jan-Apr: S, D $139-$149; each addl $10; suites $189-$400; under 17 free; wkend rates; lower rates rest of yr. Crib free. Pet accepted; $35. TV; cable (premium), VCR avail (movies). Pool; whirlpool. Restaurant 6:30 am-10:30 pm. Bar 11-2 am. Ck-out noon. Convention facilities. Business center. In-rm modem link. Gift shop. Airport transportation. Exercise equipt; weights, bicycles. Microwaves avail. Private patios, balconies. Cr cds: A, C, D, DS, JCB, MC, V.

D SC

★ ★ ★ **HILTON AT METROCENTER.** *2225 N Lois Ave (33607), near Intl Airport, in West Shore. 813/877-6688; FAX 813/879-3264.* 238 rms, 12 story. Jan-Apr: S $130-$170; D $130-$180; each addl $10; suites $200-$350; family, wkend rates; lower rates rest of yr. Crib free. TV; cable (premium). Pool; whirlpool, poolside serv. Complimentary coffee in rms. Restaurant 6:30 am-11 pm. Rm serv 24 hrs. Bar noon-midnight. Ck-out noon. Meeting rms. Business servs avail. In-rm modem link. Gift shop. Free airport transportation. Lighted tennis. Exercise equipt; bicycle, stair machine, treadmill. Cr cds: A, C, D, DS, ER, JCB, MC, V.

D SC

★ ★ **HOLIDAY INN SELECT DOWNTOWN.** *111 W Fortune St (33602), adj to Performing Arts Center, downtown. 813/223-1351; FAX 813/221-2000.* 312 rms, 14 story. Jan-Apr: S, D $130-$150; each addl $10; suites $219; under 19 free; lower rates rest of yr. Crib free. TV; cable (premium). Pool; whirlpool. Coffee in rms. Restaurant 6:30 am-11 pm. Bar 4 pm-1 am. Ck-out 11 am. Convention facilities. Business center. In-rm modem link. Gift shop. Free airport transportation. Exercise equipt; weights, bicycles. Some refrigerators, microwaves. Luxury level. Cr cds: A, C, D, DS, ER, JCB, MC, V.

D SC

★ ★ ★ **HYATT REGENCY.** *2 Tampa City Center (33602), off I-275 Ashley exit, bear left onto Tampa St to Jackson St, downtown. 813/225-1234; FAX 813/273-0234.* 518 rms, 17 story. Jan-Apr: S, D $175-$195; each addl $25; 1-bedrm suites $200-$490; 2-bedrm suites $280-$590; under 18 free; wkend rates; lower rates rest of yr. Crib free. TV; cable (premium), VCR avail. Heated pool; whirlpool. Restaurant (see ITALIANISSIMO). Rm serv 24 hrs. Bar. Entertainment Tues-Sat. Ck-out noon. Lndry facilities. Convention facilities. Business center. In-rm modem link. Concierge. Garage, valet parking. Free airport transportation. Exercise equipt; weights, bicycles. Massage. Some refrigerators. Luxury level. Cr cds: A, C, D, DS, ER, JCB, MC, V.

D SC

★ ★ ★ ★ **HYATT REGENCY WESTSHORE.** *6200 Courtney Campbell Causeway (33607), near Intl Airport. 813/874-1234; FAX 813/281-9168.* Web www.hyatt.com. This large, business-oriented luxury hotel is well placed, nestled next to a 35-acre nature preserve on Tampa Bay. A courtyard with fountains highlights the elaborate landscaping. 400 rms in main bldg, 14 story, 45 casita villas. Jan-May: S $179-$215; D $204-$230; each addl $25; suites $330-$730; casita villas (1-3 bedrm): $179-$730; under 18 free; wkend rates; lower rates rest of yr. Crib free. Covered parking; valet parking $8/night. TV; cable (premium), VCR avail. 2 heated pools; whirlpool, poolside serv. Coffee in rms. Restaurant 6:30 am-11 pm (also see ARMANI'S and OYSTERCATCHERS). Rm serv to midnight. Bar noon-1 am; pianist. Ck-out noon. Convention facilities. Business center. In-rm modem link. Concierge. Gift shop. Free airport transportation. Tennis. Exercise equipt; weights, bicycles, sauna. Massage. Lawn games. Some refrigerators, minibars. Boat dock. Luxury level. Cr cds: A, C, D, DS, ER, JCB, MC, V.

D SC

★ ★ ★ **MARRIOTT AIRPORT.** *At Tampa Intl Airport (33607), 1 1/2 mi N of jct FL 60 & I-275, near Intl Airport, in West Shore. 813/879-5151; FAX 813/873-0945.* Web www.marriot.com. 300 rms, 6 story. Jan-Apr: S, D $170-$185; suites $275-$550; under 18 free; wkend rates; lower rates rest of yr. Crib free. TV; cable (premium). Pool; poolside serv. Restaurant (see CK'S). Bar 11-1 am. Ck-out 1 pm. Meeting rms. Business center. In-rm modem link. Gift shop. Free airport transportation. Exercise equipt; weights, bicycle. Refrigerator in some suites. Luxury level. Cr cds: A, C, D, DS, ER, JCB, MC, V.

D SC

★ ★ ★ **MARRIOTT WESTSHORE.** *1001 N Westshore Blvd (33607), near Intl Airport, on West Shore, off I-275 2 blks. 813/287-2555; FAX 813/289-5464.* 311 rms, 14 story. Jan-May: S, D $165-189; suites $400; under 18 free; wkend, hol rates; lower rates rest of yr. Crib free. TV; cable (premium). 2 pools, 1 indoor. Restaurant 6:30 am-midnight. Bar 11:30-2 am. Ck-out 1 pm. Convention facilities. Business servs avail. In-rm modem link. Gift shop. Free airport transportation. Exercise equipt; weights, bicycles. Balconies. Cr cds: A, C, D, DS, ER, JCB, MC, V.

D

★ ★ ★ **RADISSON BAY HARBOR INN.** *7700 Courtney Campbell Causeway (33607), west of downtown. 813/281-8900; FAX 813/281-0189.* 257 rms, 6 story. Jan-Apr: S, D $105-$165; each addl $10; suites $175-$525; under 18 free; lower rates rest of yr. Crib free. TV; cable (premium). Heated pool; poolside serv. Restaurant 6:30 am-midnight. Bar 11 am-midnight, Sun from 1 pm. Ck-out noon. Meeting rms. In-rm modem link. Gift shop. Valet parking. Free airport transportation. Lighted tennis. Exercise equipt; weight machine, treadmills. Game rm. Private patios, balconies. On Tampa Bay. Cr cds: A, C, D, DS, MC, V.

D SC

★ ★ ★ **SHERATON GRAND HOTEL.** *4860 W Kennedy Blvd (33609), jct Kennedy & West Shore Blvds, near Intl Airport, in West Shore. 813/286-4400; FAX 813/286-4053.* Web www.sheraton-grand.com. 324 rms, 11 story. Jan-Apr: S, D $159-$195; each addl $15; suites $195-$550; under 18 free; wkend rates; lower rates rest of yr. Crib free. TV; cable (premium). Heated pool; poolside serv. Coffee in rms. Restaurants 6 am-11 pm (also see SHULA'S STEAK HOUSE). Rm serv 24 hrs. Bar 11-2 am; entertainment. Ck-out noon. Convention facilities. Business center. In-rm modem link. Concierge. Shopping arcade. Free airport transportation. Exercise equipt; bicycles, stair machines. Some bathrm phones, refrigerators. Luxury level. Cr cds: A, C, D, DS, ER, MC, V.

D SC

★ ★ ★ **WYNDHAM HARBOUR ISLAND.** *725 S Harbour Island Blvd (33602), I-275 exit 25, south of downtown. 813/229-5000; FAX 813/229-5322.* Web www.travelweb.com. 300 rms, 12 story. Jan-May: S $189-$225; D $209-$245; each addl $20; suites $375-$875; under 18 free; wkend rates; lower rates rest of yr. Crib free. TV; cable. Heated pool; poolside serv. Coffee in rms. Restaurant (see HARBOUR VIEW). Rm serv to 2 am. Bar. Ck-out noon. Convention facilities. Business servs avail. In-rm modem link. Concierge. Free airport transportation. Tennis privileges. Exercise equipt; treadmill, stair machine. Health club privileges. Minibars, wet bars; some bathrm phones; microwaves avail; refrigerator in suites. Cr cds: A, C, D, DS, ER, JCB, MC, V.

D SC

Inn

✔★ ★ **BEHIND THE FENCE.** *(1400 Viola Dr, Brandon 33511) E on I-4, S on I-75, exit 49, S on US 301 to Bloomingdale Ave, left on Countryside to Viola. 813/685-8201.* 5 rms, 3 share bath, 2 story, 2 suites. 3 rm phones. Labor Day-Memorial Day: S, D $59-$72; each addl $10; suites $69-$72; under 10 free; lower rates rest of yr. TV; cable, VCR avail. Pool. Complimentary continental bkfst; afternoon refreshments. Restaurant nearby. Ck-out noon, ck-in 3 pm. Refrigerators; microwaves avail. House design is New England "Salt Box." Totally nonsmoking. No cr cds accepted.

SC

Resort

★ ★ ★ ★ **SADDLEBROOK RESORT.** *(5700 Saddlebrook Way, Wesley Chapel 33543) 25 mi N of Tampa Airport on I-75, exit 58 then 1 mi E on FL 54. 813/973-1111; FAX 813/973-4504; res: 800/729-8383.* Web www.saddlebrookresort.com. One of Florida's premier tennis and golf resorts, it rests on 480 secluded acres of woodlands, lakes and rolling hills. 542 units, 2 story, 411 with kits., 131 hotel rms, 163 1-bedrm condos,

248 2-bedrm condos. Mid-Jan-Apr: S, D $215-$360; each addl $20; under 13 free; lower rates rest of yr. TV; cable. 4 pools, 2 heated; whirlpool, poolside serv. Playground. Free supervised child's activities; ages 3-12. Dining rm (public by res) 6:30 am-10:30 pm (see CYPRESS RESTAURANT AND TERRACE ON THE GREEN). Rm serv to 1 am. Bar 11-1 am; entertainment. Ck-out noon, ck-in 3 pm. Convention facilities. Business center. In-rm modem link. Concierge. Grocery 1 mi. Package store. Gift shop. Barber, beauty shop. Valet parking. Airport transportation. Sports dir. Tennis, 45 courts, 5 lighted, pro. Home of Harry Hopman Tennis Academy. 36-hole golf course designed by Arnold Palmer & Dean Refram, pro, putting green, driving range. Home of Arnold Palmer Golf Academy. Nature walks. Bicycle rentals. Game rm. Extensive exercise rm; instructor, weight machines, bicycles, sauna, steam rm. Massage. Minibars; many refrigerators. Private patios, balconies. Cr cds: A, C, D, DS, MC, V.

Restaurants

★ **A.J. CATFISH.** *8751 N Himes Ave (33614), north of downtown. 813/932-3474.* Hrs: 11:30 am-10 pm; Fri, Sat 5-11 pm; Sun from 5 pm. Closed Mon; most major hols. Semi-a la carte: lunch $3.95-$7.95, dinner $7.95-$14.95. Child's meals. Specializes in steak, seafood, pasta. Outdoor dining. Cypress wood interior, 2nd floor balcony. Cr cds: A, MC, V.

D

★★★ **ARMANI'S.** *(See Hyatt Regency Westshore Hotel) 813/281-9165.* Web www.hyatt.com. Hrs: 6-10 pm; Fri, Sat to 11 pm. Closed Sun; some major hols. Res accepted. Northern Italian menu. Bar 5-11 pm; Fri, Sat to midnight. Semi-a la carte: dinner $25-$40. Child's meals. Specialties: veal Armani, lobster ammiraglia. Antipasta bar. Own baking, desserts. Pianist. Valet parking. Outdoor terrace overlooks bay; on rooftop. Jacket. Cr cds: A, C, D, DS, ER, JCB, MC, V.

D

★★★ **BERN'S STEAK HOUSE.** *1208 S Howard Ave (33606), 4 blks N of Bayshore Blvd, in Hyde Park. 813/251-2421.* Hrs: 5-11 pm. Closed Dec 25. Res accepted. Bar. Wine cellars. Semi-a la carte: dinner $15-$45 (serv charge). Specializes in own organically grown vegetables, aged prime beef, variety of roasted and blended coffees. Own baking, ice cream, sherbet, onion soup. Pianist/accordionist. Valet parking. Chef-owned. Antiques, paintings, statuary. Cr cds: A, C, D, DS, MC, V.

D

✔★★ **CAPDEVILA'S AT LA TERESITA.** *3248 W Columbus Dr (33607), 1 mi NE on I-275, exit Dale Mabry, E on Columbus Dr, at Lincoln, west of downtown. 813/875-2007.* Hrs: 8 am-10 pm; Fri, Sat to 11 pm. Closed Dec 25. Res accepted. Cuban menu. Bar. Semi-a la carte: bkfst $0.90-$3.95, lunch $1.25-$6.50, dinner $1.50-$6.50. Child's meals. Specializes in chicken, beef, pork. Pianist wkends. Valet parking. Spanish/Cuban decor. Family-owned 21 yrs. Cr cds: A, D, DS, MC, V.

D

★★★ **CK'S.** *(See Marriott Airport Hotel) 813/878-6500.* Hrs: 5-10 pm; Fri, Sat to 11 pm; Sun brunch 10:30 am-2:30 pm. Res accepted. Bar from 4 pm. Wine list. A la carte entrees: dinner $10.95-$24.95. Sun brunch $17.95. Child's meals. Specialties: rack of lamb, twin filet of beef, veal and lobster lemuel. Valet parking. Revolving rooftop restaurant on 10th floor. Cr cds: A, C, D, DS, ER, JCB, MC, V.

D

✔★★ **COLONNADE.** *3401 Bayshore Blvd (33629), in Hyde Park. 813/839-7558.* Hrs: 11 am-10 pm; Fri, Sat to 11 pm. Closed Thanksgiving, Dec 25. Bar. Semi-a la carte: lunch $4.99-$7.99, dinner $7.99-$15.99. Child's meals. Specializes in fresh seafood, steak, prime rib, desserts. Nautical decor. Overlooks Tampa Bay. Family-owned since 1935. Cr cds: A, C, D, DS, MC, V.

D

★★★ **COLUMBIA.** *2117 E 7th Ave (33605), in Ybor City. 813/248-4961.* Hrs: 11 am-10 pm; Fri, Sat to 11 pm; Sun noon-9 pm. Res accepted. Spanish menu. Bar. Wine cellars. Semi-a la carte: lunch $4.95-$7.95, dinner $10.95-$18.95. Cover charge $6 (in dining room with show). Child's meals. Specialties: paella a la Valenciana, snapper alicante, filet mignon Columbia. Flamenco dancers (dinner) exc Sun. Valet parking. Built 1905; building decorated with hand-painted Spanish tiles. Balcony surrounds interior courtyard. Many dining areas; all have antique Spanish-style furnishings. Family-owned. Cr cds: A, C, D, DS, MC, V.

D

★★★ **CYPRESS RESTAURANT AND TERRACE ON THE GREEN.** *(See Saddlebrook Resort) 813/973-1111.* Web www.saddlebrookresort.com. Hrs: 6:30 am-3 pm, 6-10 pm; Fri 6-11 pm; hrs may vary seasonally. Res accepted. Mediterranean menu. Bar 11-1 am. Semi-a la carte: bkfst $5-$10.50, lunch $8-$14, dinner $19-$26.50. Serv charge 18%. Child's meals. Specializes in steak, veal, seafood buffet. Pastry shop. Entertainment. Valet parking. Creative food presentation. Contemporary decor. Lakeside terrace dining overlooking golf course. Cr cds: A, C, D, DS, MC, V.

★★★ **DONATELLO.** *232 N Dale Mabry Hwy (33609), west of downtown. 813/875-6660.* E-mail /ldonatelo.com; web www.tampabaydining.com. Hrs: 11:30 am-2:30 pm, 6-11 pm; Sat, Sun from 6 pm. Closed Jan 1, Memorial Day, July 4, Dec 25; also Super Bowl Sun. Res accepted. Northern Italian menu. Bar. Wine list. A la carte entrees: lunch $5.95-$12.95, dinner $15.95-$31.95. Specializes in hand-rolled pasta, veal chops, fresh seafood. Own baking. Valet parking. Pianist Thurs-Sat. Some tableside cooking. Cr cds: A, C, D, DS, MC, V.

D

★★★ **HARBOUR VIEW.** *(See Wyndham Harbour Island Hotel) 813/229-5001.* Hrs: 6:30 am-2 pm, 6-11 pm; Sun brunch 10:30 am-2 pm. Res accepted. Serv bar. A la carte entrees: bkfst $6.25-$10.95, lunch $7-$13.95, dinner $16.50-$24.95. Sun brunch $22.95. Pasta bar (Mon-Fri) $9.75. Child's meals. Specializes in contemporary regional cuisine. Own baking. Valet parking. Private dining rm avail. Waterfront view. Cr cds: A, C, D, DS, ER, JCB, MC, V.

D

★★ **ITALIANISSIMO.** *(See Hyatt Regency Hotel) 813/222-4928.* Hrs: 6 am-3 pm, 5-11 pm; Sun brunch 11 am-2 pm. Res accepted. Italian menu. Serv bar. A la carte entrees: bkfst $7-$9, lunch $8-$11, dinner $11-$30. Sun brunch $16.95. Child's meals. Specializes in beef, lamb, seafood. Entertainment Wed-Sun. Valet parking. Outdoor dining. Elegant dining. Cr cds: A, C, D, DS, ER, JCB, MC, V.

D SC

★ **JIMMY MAC'S.** *113 S Armenia Ave (33609), in Hyde Park. 813/879-0591.* Hrs: 11:30-2 am; Sat from noon; Sun noon-11 pm. Closed most major hols. Res accepted. Bar 11:30-3 am. Semi-a la carte: lunch $4.95-$7.75, dinner $6.50-$17. Child's menu. Specializes in grilled seasonal seafood, hamburgers, steaks. Entertainment. Parking. Located in 2 restored houses; eclectic decor. Cr cds: A, D, DS, MC, V.

★★ **LANDRY'S SEAFOOD HOUSE.** *7616 Courtney Campbell Causeway (33607), in West Shore. 813/289-7773.* Hrs: 11 am-10 pm; Fri, Sat to 11:15 pm. Closed Dec 25. Bar. Semi-a la carte: lunch $3.99-$10.99, dinner $9.99-$21. Child's meals. Specialties: Pontchartrain red snapper, grouper Mellisa. Entertainment Fri, Sat. Valet parking Fri, Sat. Outdoor dining. 1950s riverwalk atmosphere with New Orleans theme. Cr cds: A, C, D, DS, MC, V.

D

★ ★ **MALIOS.** *301 S Dale Mabry Hwy (33609), west of downtown. 813/879-3233.* Hrs: 11:30 am-2:30 pm, 5-10:30 pm; Fri, Sat 5-11 pm. Closed Sun; most major hols. Res accepted. Bar 11:30-2:30 am. A la carte entrees: lunch $4.95-$7.95, dinner $9.95-$29.95. Specializes in steak, seafood, pasta. Valet parking. Large central lounge with entertainment. Cr cds: A, C, D, DS, MC, V.

D

★ **MIGUEL'S.** *3035 W Kennedy (33609), in Hyde Park. 813/876-2587.* Hrs: 11 am-10 pm; Fri to 11 pm; Sat noon-11 pm; Sun noon-9 pm.Closed Thanksgiving, Dec 25. Res accepted. Mexican, Amer menu. Bar. Semi-a la carte: lunch $1.70-$7, dinner $5.75-$13.25. Child's meals. Specialties: stuffed jalapeños, quesadillas, tamales. Mexican decor. Cr cds: DS, MC, V.

D

★ ★ **MISE EN PLACE.** *442 W Kennedy Blvd (33609), in Hyde Park. 813/254-5373.* Hrs: 11 am-3 pm, 5:30-10 pm; Mon to 3 pm; Fri to 11 pm; Sat 5:30-11 pm. Closed Sun; major hols. Bar 5:30 pm-2 am Wed-Fri. Wine list. A la carte entrees: lunch $4.95-$7.95, dinner $11.95-$21.95. Specializes in lamb, grouper, salmon. Valet parking. Contemporary decor. Cr cds: A, C, D, DS, MC, V.

D

★ ★ **OYSTERCATCHERS.** *(See Hyatt Regency Westshore Hotel) 813/281-9116.* Hrs: 11:30 am-2:30 pm, 6-10 pm; Fri, Sat 6-11 pm; Sun from 6 pm; Sun brunch 10:30 am-3 pm. Closed Dec 25. Res accepted. Bar. A la carte entrees: lunch $15-$22, dinner $16-$28. Sun brunch $26. Child's meals. Specializes in fresh seafood, stuffed swordfish. Entertainment Mon-Fri. Valet parking. Overlooks Tampa Bay. Cr cds: A, C, D, DS, ER, JCB, MC, V.

D

★ ★ **RUMPELMAYERS.** *4812 E Busch Blvd (33617), in Ambassador Square Shopping Center, north of downtown. 813/989-9563.* Hrs: 4-10 pm. Res accepted. German menu. Complete meal: dinner $8.95-$17.95. Child's meals. Specialties: wienerschnitzel, sauerbraten, Black Forest cake. Accordionist. Extensive German beer and wine selection. Servers in traditional Bavarian outfits. Cr cds: A, C, D, DS, JCB, MC, V.

D

★ ★ ★ **RUTH'S CHRIS STEAK HOUSE.** *1700 N Westshore Blvd (33607), in West Shore. 813/282-1118.* Hrs: 5-10 pm; Fri, Sat to 11 pm. Closed Thanksgiving, Dec 25. Res accepted. Bar. Wine list. A la carte entrees: dinner $15.95-$29.95. Child's meals. Specializes in beef, steak, lamb chops. Valet parking. Elegant decor with antique fixtures. Cr cds: A, D, JCB, MC, V.

D

★ ★ ★ **SHULA'S STEAK HOUSE.** *(See Sheraton Grand Hotel) 813/286-4366.* Hrs: 11:30 am-2:30 pm, 5:30-10:30 pm; Sat, Sun 5:30-11 pm. Res accepted. Bar. Wine list. A la carte entrees: lunch $8.50-$19, dinner $25-$59. Child's meals. Specialties: lamb chops, lobster, filet mignon. Valet parking. Cr cds: A, C, D, DS, ER, MC, V.

D

★ ★ **SUKHOTHAI.** *8201-A N Dale Mabry Hwy (33614), north of downtown. 813/933-7990.* Hrs: 11 am-11 pm; Sat, Sun from 5 pm. Closed Labor Day, Thanksgiving, Dec 25. Res accepted. Thai menu. Wine, beer. Semi-a la carte: lunch $4.95-$6.95, dinner $8.95-$19.95. Specializes in seafood. Original Thai tables, pillows. Parking. Cr cds: A, C, D, DS, MC, V.

D

✔★ ★ **TAJ.** *2734-B Fowler Ave (33612), north of downtown. 813/971-8483.* Hrs: 11:30 am-2:30 pm, 5-10 pm; Sat, Sun 11:30 am-3 pm, 5-10 pm. Closed Mon; Jan 1, Thanksgiving. Res accepted, required Fri-Sun. Indian menu. Wine, beer. Lunch buffet $6.95-$8.95. Semi-a la carte: dinner $7.50-$16.95. Specializes in Tandoori and Bhuna dishes. Own baking. Authentic Indian decor; Tandoori clay oven. Totally nonsmoking. Cr cds: A, MC, V.

D

St Petersburg

Motels

✔★ ★ **COMFORT INN CENTRAL.** *1400 34th St N (33713), I-275, exit 12. 813/323-3100; FAX 813/327-5792.* 76 rms, 3 story. Jan-Apr: S $63-$83; D $68-$88; family, wkly rates; lower rates rest of yr. TV; cable (premium). Heated pool; whirlpool. Complimentary continental bkfst. Restaurant 6:30-9:30 am. Ck-out 11 am. Coin Indry. Meeting rms. Business servs avail. In-rm modem link. Cr cds: A, C, D, DS, MC, V.

D SC

★ ★ **DAYS INN.** *2595 54th Ave N (33714), I-275, exit 14. 813/522-3191.* 155 rms, 2 story. Feb-mid-Apr: S $45-$55; D $49-$65; each addl $5; under 12 free; lower rates rest of yr. Crib free. Pet accepted; $8 per day. TV; cable (premium). Pool; wading pool. Restaurant 6 am-10 pm; Sun 6 am-8:30 pm. Ck-out 11 am. Coin Indry. Meeting rm. Business servs avail. In-rm modem link. Lawn games. Microwaves avail. Picnic tables. Cr cds: A, C, D, DS, JCB, MC, V.

D SC

★ ★ ★ **HOLIDAY INN SUNSPREE RESORT-MARINA COVE.** *6800 Sunshine Skyway Lane (33711), I-275 exit 3. 813/867-1151; FAX 813/864-4494.* E-mail qzbq76a@prodigy.com; web www.traveldays.com/destinations/st-pete/marina-cove. 157 rms, 2 story, 20 kits. Feb-mid-Apr: S, D $79-$149; each addl $10; suites, townhouses $139-$209; under 19 free; lower rates rest of yr. TV; cable (premium). 2 pools; whirlpool, poolside serv. Playground. Seasonal supervised child's activities; ages 4-11. Coffee in rms. Restaurant 7-11:30 am, 5-10 pm. Bar; entertainment Thurs-Sat. Ck-out 11 am. Coin Indry. Meeting rms. Business servs avail. Sundries. Gift shop. Lighted tennis. Exercise equipt; weights, treadmill. Game rm. Lawn games. Refrigerators, bathrm phone in suites. Microwaves avail. Private patios, balconies. On bay; water sports, private beach. Marina sailing school, boat charter, deep sea fishing. Attraction tours. Cr cds: A, C, D, DS, ER, JCB, MC, V.

D SC

★ **LA MARK CHARLES.** *(6200 34th St N, Pinellas Park 33781) I-275, exit 15. 813/527-7334; FAX 813/526-9294; res: 800/448-6781.* 93 rms, 1-2 story, 35 kits. Feb-Apr: S, D $60; each addl $5; suites $65-$70; kit. units $65-$75; under 12 free; lower rates rest of yr. Crib $3. Pet accepted; $35 ($25 refundable). TV. Heated pool; whirlpool. Restaurant 7-10 am. Ck-out 11 am. Meeting rm. Business servs avail. Coin Indry. Sundries. Cr cds: A, DS, MC, V.

SC

★ ★ **LA QUINTA INN.** *4999 34th St N (33714), I-275, exit 14. 813/527-8421; FAX 813/527-8851.* 120 rms, 2 story. Mid-Jan-Apr: S $79; D $89; each addl $10; lower rates rest of yr. Pet accepted, some restrictions. TV; cable (premium). Heated pool. Complimentary continental bkfst. Ck-out 11 am. Coin Indry. Meeting rm. Business servs avail. In-rm modem link. Exercise equipt; weights, bicycles, stair machine. Cr cds: A, C, D, DS, MC, V.

SC

✔★ **VALLEY FORGE.** *6825 Central Ave (33710). 813/345-0135; FAX 813/384-1671.* 27 rms, 8 kits. Mid-Jan-mid-Apr: S, D $45-$65; lower rates rest of yr. Crib $5. Pet accepted; $3-$5. TV; cable (premium), VCR avail. Pool. Restaurant nearby. Ck-out 11 am. Business servs avail. Lawn games. Refrigerators; microwaves avail. Private patios. Cr cds: A, DS, MC, V.

Hotel

★ ★ ★ **HILTON.** *333 1st St S (33701). 813/894-5000; FAX 813/894-7655.* Web www.hilton.com. 333 units, 15 story, 31 suites. S $99-$189; D $109-$199; each addl $10; suites $139-$449; under 18 free. Crib free. TV; cable (premium), VCR avail. Heated pool; whirlpool, poolside serv. Restaurant 6:30 am-10:30 pm. Bar. Ck-out noon. Convention facilities. Business servs avail. In-rm modem link. Exercise rm; instructor, weights, stair machine. Game rm. Refrigerators avail. Overlooks St. Petersburg marina. Cr cds: A, C, D, DS, JCB, MC, V.

D

Inn

★ ★ **BAY GABLES.** *136 4th Ave NE (33701), downtown, jct 4th Ave NE & Rowland Court NE. 813/822-8855; res: 800/822-8803; FAX 813/824-7223.* 9 rms, 1 with shower only, 3 story, 4 kit. suites. MAP: S, D $85; kit. suites $110-$135; under 18 free; wkly rates. TV. Complimentary continental bkfst, tea. Restaurant adj 11 am-2 pm. Ck-out 11 am, ck-in 2 pm. Business servs avail. Refrigerators. 1 blk to Tampa Bay. Restored Victorian house (1910). In historic district. Totally nonsmoking. Cr cds: MC, V.

D SC

Resort

★ ★ ★ ★ **RENAISSANCE VINOY RESORT.** *501 Fifth Ave NE (33701), off I-275 onto I-375, then 4th Ave N to Beach Dr, left one block, bayfront. 813/894-1000; FAX 813/822-2785.* This 1925 landmark on the National Register of Historic Places has been restored, combining 1920s style with updated amenities and services for '90s lifestyles. Its 14 acres include a 74-slip marina and tropical gardens. 360 units, 7 story. Mid-Jan-May: S, D $265-$325; suites $550-$1,800; under 18 free; wkend rates; golf, tennis plans; lower rates rest of yr. Crib free. Garage, overnight; valet parking $10, self-park $7. TV; cable (premium), VCR avail. 2 heated pools; whirlpool, poolside serv. Supervised child's activities (June-Aug); ages 4-12. Complimentary coffee in rms. Restaurants 6 am-11 pm (also see TERRACE ROOM/MARCHAND'S GRILL). Rm serv 24 hrs. Bar 10-2 am; Sun 1 pm-midnight; entertainment. Ck-out noon. Lndry facilities. Convention facilities. Business center. In-rm modem link. Concierge. Gift shops. Beauty shop. 12 lighted clay tennis courts. 18-hole golf, greens fee $95 (incl cart), pro, putting green, driving range. Exercise rm; instructor, weight machine, bicycles, sauna, steam rm. Spa. Minibars. Wet bar in suites. Cr cds: A, C, D, DS, ER, JCB, MC, V.

D SC

Restaurants

★ ★ ★ **BASTA'S.** *1625 4th St S (33701). 813/894-7880.* Hrs: 5-10 pm; Fri, Sat to 11 pm. Closed some major hols. Res accepted. Northern Italian menu. Bar. A la carte entrees: dinner $13-$24. Specializes in fresh seafood, veal, pasta. Pianist. Italian atmosphere; artwork, mural. Hand-painted ceiling in main dining area. Cr cds: A, D, DS, MC, V.

D

★ **THE GARDEN.** *217 Central Ave (33701). 813/896-3800.* Hrs: 11 am-10:30 pm; Fri, Sat to midnight. Closed Thanksgiving, Dec 25. Res accepted. Mediterranean menu. Bar to 2 am. A la carte entrees: lunch $2.95-$6, dinner $4.50-$14.50. Specialties: tajine, North African couscous, grilled salmis of chicken. Jazz in garden Fri, Sat. Outdoor dining. Mediterranean decor, original artwork. Cr cds: A, MC, V.

D

★ ★ **THE KEYSTONE CLUB.** *320 4th St N (33701). 813/822-6600.* Hrs: 11 am-2:30 pm, 5-10 pm; Sat from 4 pm; Sun 4-9 pm. Closed major hols. Res accepted. Bar. Semi-a la carte: lunch $4.50-$8.50, dinner $10.95-$19.95. Child's meals. Specializes in beef, pork chops, fresh seafood. Parking. Club-like atmosphere. Cr cds: A, D, DS, MC, V.

D

✔★ ★ **NATIVE SEAFOOD & TRADING COMPANY.** *5901 Sun Blvd (33715), 1½mi E of FL 699, on FL 682. 813/866-8772.* Hrs: 5-10 pm; Fri to 11 pm. Closed Jan 1, Dec 25. Bar 4 pm-midnight. Semi-a la carte: dinner $9.95-$16.95. Child's meals. Specializes in seafood. Outdoor dining. Tropical island atmosphere. Cr cds: A, D, DS, MC, V.

★ ★ ★ **PEPIN.** *4125 4th St N (33701). 813/821-3773.* Hrs: 11 am-11 pm; Sat, Sun from 5 pm. Closed some major hols. Res accepted. Spanish menu. Bar. Semi-a la carte: lunch $7-$12, dinner $15-$25. Child's meals. Specialties: paella, filet mignon, pork chops. Salad bar. Pianist. Valet parking Fri, Sat. Elegant decor; Spanish tile, tapestry and artwork. Cr cds: A, C, D, DS, MC, V.

D

★ **SAFFRON'S.** *1700 Park St N (33710), 5 mi W on I-275, exit 12. 813/345-6400.* Hrs: 11 am-10 pm; Sun brunch to 3 pm. Closed Memorial Day, Labor Day. Res accepted. Caribbean menu. Bar. A la carte entrees: lunch $4.95-$9.50, dinner $7.50-$18. Sun brunch $13.95. Child's meals. Specialties: jerk chicken, appleton steak, fish negril. Caribbean band Mon, Tues, Fri-Sun. Outdoor dining. Casual dining; island art. Cr cds: A, C, D, DS, MC, V.

D

✔★ **SMOKEY'S TEXAS BAR-B-QUE.** *(8180 49th St N, Pinellas Park 34665) N via 49th St to 82nd Ave. 813/546-3600.* Hrs: 7 am-10 pm. Bar. Semi-a la carte: bkfst $2-$5, lunch, dinner $3.50-$12. Specializes in hickory-smoked ribs, chicken, steak. Southwestern decor. Cr cds: A, MC, V.

D

★ ★ ★ **TERRACE ROOM/MARCHAND'S GRILL.** *(See Renaissance Vinoy Resort) 813/894-1000.* Hrs: 6 am-3 pm, 5:30-11 pm; early-bird dinner Sun-Thurs 5:30-6:30 pm; Sun brunch 9:30 am-3 pm. Res accepted. Mediterranean menu. Bar 11 am-midnight; Fri-Sat to 1 am; Sun 1-11 pm. Wine list. A la carte entrees: bkfst $5-$11.50, lunch $7.25-$15, dinner $12.50-$21.50. Sun brunch $29. Child's meals. Specialties: 4 cheese tortellini, bouillabaisse, macadamia nut-crusted grouper. Contemporary jazz band Tues-Sat, pianist Mon-Fri. Valet parking. In historic building; flower and griffin designs on high ceiling and just above column were hand-painted as part of an extensive restoration process. Windows are replicas of original 1920s leaded-glass windows. Cr cds: A, C, D, DS, ER, JCB, MC, V.

D

Toronto

Founded: 1793
Pop: 3,400,000 (metro)
Elev: 569 feet
Time zone: Eastern
Area code: 416
Web: www.toronto.com

Situated on the northern shore of Lake Ontario, Toronto is Ontario's thriving cosmopolitan capital and Canada's leader in manufacturing, finance, communications and culture. Despite its growth and modernism, the city has not sacrificed its architectural past, its history or its citizens' comfort and safety: Toronto remains a city of stable neighborhoods with low crime rates and good schools.

Once homogeneously Anglo-Saxon, Toronto experienced post-World War II immigration that made it one of the world's most ethnically diverse cities. Today, more than 70 ethnic groups—including Italians, Chinese, Portuguese, Jews, Muslims, East and West Indians, Ukrainians, South Americans, Vietnamese and others—speak more than 100 languages, yet the city remains free of the tensions existing in large cities elsewhere. This diversity has served only to strengthen the city's cultural offerings.

The rivers here were transportation routes for Native Americans, who named the area between the Humber and Don Rivers Toronto, or "meeting place." In the early 1600s, Etienne Brule, a French explorer, became the first European to visit Toronto. The French later established a trading post and, in 1749, Fort Rouille, which was burned in 1759 to prevent its being taken by the British in the Seven Years' War. In 1763 the Treaty of Paris gave all of Canada to the British, and 30 years later the area became the town of York, capital of Upper Canada Colony and subsequently known as Muddy York because of its unpaved roads and swampy terrain. In the 1800s, immigration from Britain increased, transportation and manufacturing prospered, and the Family Compact, an elite, wealthy group with strong connections to Britain, dominated the government. In 1834 the city was renamed Toronto, and three years later William Mackenzie, Toronto's first mayor, led a rebellion against the British government.

Industry continued to expand into the 20th century, especially during the two world wars. Toronto has not experienced the exodus to the suburbs common in many large cities, and the greatest problem facing Toronto today is a shortage of affordable housing.

Sports & Recreation

Spectator sports are popular in Toronto, and most professional sporting events are sold out months in advance, although scalpers are always available as a last resort. In addition to attending the games, sports fans can visit Canada's Sports Hall of Fame on the north side of Exhibition Stadium—three floors of exhibits on Canadian sports heroes.

Hockey is played in Maple Leaf Gardens by the Maple Leafs, a National Hockey League team. Canada's hockey enthusiasm led to the Hockey Hall of Fame and Museum in downtown Toronto.

The SkyDome, a retractable-roof stadium with restaurants and other amenities, is the site of Blue Jays baseball, an American League team, and Argonauts football, members of the Canadian Football League. Toronto's newest team, the NBA's Raptors, also play at the SkyDome.

Toronto's other spectator sports include Thoroughbred racing at Woodbine Racetrack, the Molson Indy auto race in mid-July, a canoeing and rowing regatta on Toronto Island's Long Pond in July and the Player's International Canadian Open tennis championship each summer.

Opportunities for participant sports and recreation abound in every season, from bicycle trails and water sports to tobogganing and cross-country skiing. Toronto's extensive park system includes ice-skating rinks, tennis courts, swimming pools and playing fields. The Kortright Centre for Conservation has trails, naturalist-guided hikes, cross-country skiing and other activities.

Entertainment

Toronto's many music, drama and dance events uphold its reputation as English-speaking Canada's cultural center. The Toronto Symphony Orchestra, often accompanied by the Mendelssohn Choir, performs in Roy Thomson Hall and, in summer, at Ontario Place. The Canadian Opera Company can be seen at the Hummingbird Centre for the Performing Arts. Other musical groups include the Elmer Isler Singers, the Orford String Quartet and Tafelmusik. Rock, pop and jazz concerts are held in various places, including the moderately priced Molson Amphitheatre.

The National Ballet of Canada performs at the Hummingbird Centre. The Harbourfront Centre's Premiere Dance Theatre hosts the contemporary Toronto Dance Theatre and Dancemakers.

Live theater is found throughout Toronto, including the Hummingbird Centre, the St Lawrence Centre for the Arts and the Elgin and Winter Garden Theatres. The Young People's Theatre stages productions for the family. In summer, Shakespeare is performed at High Park's Dream Site outdoor theater.

Many films have been made in Toronto, and each fall the city hosts the Toronto International Film Festival.

Toronto's nightlife includes music, comedy clubs and dancing.

Historical Areas

Because of Toronto's careful blending of old and new, many historic buildings survive. The St Lawrence area, from Harbourfront Centre to the CN Tower, once the site of the 1793 town of York, embodies this blending. Among examples of the old are St Lawrence Market, the first city hall, built

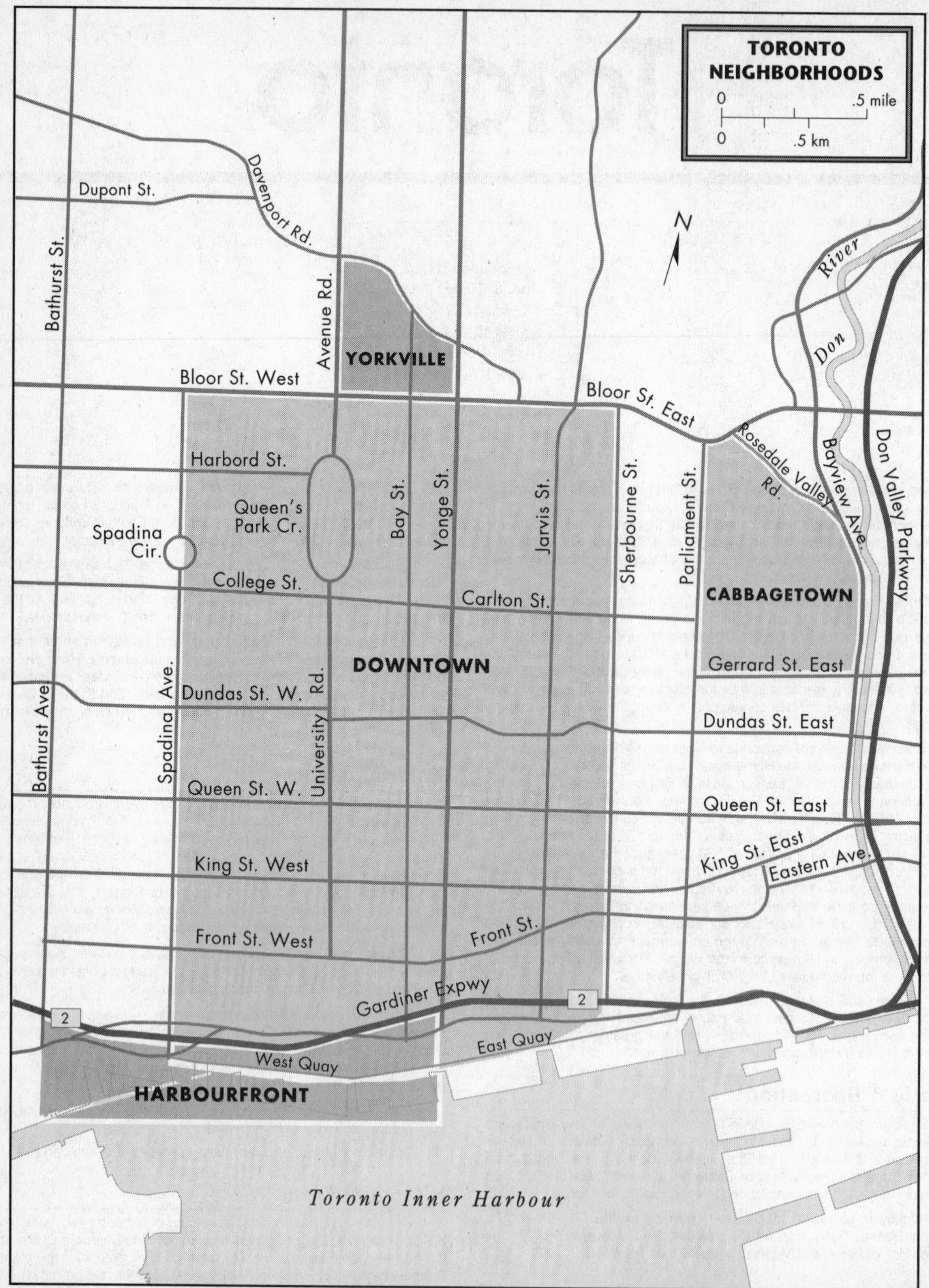
TORONTO
NEIGHBORHOODS
0
.5 mile
0
.5 km
N
Dupont St.
Davenport Rd.
Bathurst St.
Avenue Rd.
YORKVILLE
Bloor St. West
Bloor St. East
River
Don
Rosedale Valley
Rd.
Bayview Ave.
Don Valley Parkway
Harbord St.
Queen's
Park Cr.
Spadina
Cir.
Bay St.
Yonge St.
Jarvis St.
Sherbourne St.
Parliament St.
College St.
Carlton St.
CABBAGETOWN
DOWNTOWN
Gerrard St. East
Bathurst Ave.
Spadina Ave.
Dundas St. W.
University Rd.
Dundas St. East
Queen St. W.
Queen St. East
King St. West
King St. East
Eastern Ave.
Front St. West
Front St.
Gardiner Expwy
2
2
East Quay
West Quay
HARBOURFRONT
Toronto Inner Harbour

in 1844, and St Lawrence Hall, the second city hall, built in 1850. Enoch Turner Schoolhouse is a public school, built in 1848.

Historic Fort York was burned by the Americans during the War of 1812 and rebuilt by the Canadians three years later. The original buildings remain, and a costumed staff gives military demonstrations.

The city's many historic homes include the Grange, an 1817 home restored as a gentleman's house of the mid-1830s; Gibson House, restored and furnished as in the 1850s; Colborne Lodge, a regency-style home built in 1837 by an architect and restored to 1870 style; Mackenzie House, the 19th-century home of the first mayor of Toronto, including an 1840s print shop; and Spadina, an 1865 home done in Victorian and Edwardian style, with fine art and a restored garden.

A unique residence is the medieval-style castle Casa Loma, built by Henry Pellatt, a soldier and financier, between 1911 and 1914, with furnished rooms, secret passages, an underground tunnel, stables and a restored garden.

Some of the city's oldest buildings, built by English settlers and restored on their original sites, are found at Todmorden Mills Heritage Museum & Arts Centre. At Black Creek Pioneer Village, more than 35 buildings show mid-19th-century rural Canadian life.

Sightseeing

Walking tours of Toronto's many distinct neighborhoods give the visitor a feel for the city's ethnic and architectural variety. For a more structured look at the city, the Gray Line bus tours and Toronto Tours Ltd has boat tours.

Near the center of the downtown business district is Toronto's modern City Hall, completed in 1965, with twin towers that support the elevated council chambers. Other government buildings include the Ontario Parliament buildings and the Toronto Stock Exchange.

The Canadian National (CN) Tower is a concrete-and-steel, 1,815-foot, free-standing structure. Three observation decks, a revolving restaurant and a nightclub provide spectacular views.

Toronto's many museums promote topics as varied as shoes, cars, telephones, the police, sugar and the sea. Art museums include the Art Gallery of Ontario, exhibiting paintings, drawings, sculpture and graphics spanning the 14th through the 20th centuries; the Colborne Lodge art gallery, with changing exhibits; and the George R. Gardiner Museum of Ceramic Art, displaying Italian majolica, delftware and porcelain. Toronto is home to many commerical art galleries as well.

Art, archaeology and science are the focus of the Royal Ontario Museum, the largest museum in Canada. Dinosaur skeletons, the hands-on Discovery Gallery, the Roman Gallery, a bat cave and the Ancient Egypt Gallery are some of the museum's exhibits. Science is also promoted at the Ontario Science Centre, with its many amazing exhibits on space, technology and communications.

Family entertainment is found throughout the city. Paramount Canada's Wonderland is a theme park featuring Yogi Bear and Fred Flintstone among others, with more than 160 attractions, water rides, entertainment and special events. The Canadian National Exhibition is the world's largest annual fair. Parades, exhibits, entertainment, rides and sports events are featured, and more than three million people attend each summer.

Ontario Place is a waterfront complex that includes a six-story movie screen, a World War II destroyer, live entertainment and Children's Village, a creative playground.

The Metro Toronto Zoo comprises about 710 acres, with animals and plants of six geographic regions.

General References

Area code: 416

Phone Numbers

POLICE & FIRE: 911

POISON CONTROL CENTER: 813-5900

TIME & WEATHER: 661-0123

Information Source

Tourism Toronto, Queens Quay Terminal at Harbourfront, 207 Queens Quay W, M5J 1A7; 203-2500 or 800/363-1990 (US & Canada).

Transportation

AIRLINES: Air Canada, Air China, Air France, Air Jamaica, Air Ontario, Alitalia, American, British Airways, Business Express, BWIA, Canadian, Comair, Cubana, El Al, KLM, Korean, Lufthansa, National Air, Northwest, Olympic, Pakistan, Sabena, SAS, Swissair, Thai Airways, United, USAir, Varig, VIASA, Canada 3000; and other commuter and regional airlines.

AIRPORT: Pearson International Airport, 676-3506.

CAR RENTAL AGENCIES: (See IMPORTANT TOLL-FREE NUMBERS) Avis 777-2847; Budget; Dollar; Hertz 620-9620; Thrifty; Tilden/National 925-2072.

PUBLIC TRANSPORTATION: Toronto Transit Commission (TTC), 393-4636.

RAILROAD PASSENGER SERVICE: Amtrak 800/872-7245; ViaRail 366-8411.

Newspapers

The Toronto Star; The Toronto Sun; The Globe & Mail.

Convention Facilities

Metro Toronto Convention Centre, 255 Front St W, 585-8000

Exhibition Place, Lakeshore Blvd, 393-6000.

International Centre, 6900 Airport Rd, 674-8425.

Sports & Recreation

Major Sports Facilities

SkyDome, 1 Blue Jay Way, 341-2770 (Blue Jays, baseball, 341-1000; Raptors, basketball, 214-2255).

Maple Leaf Gardens, 60 Carlton St, 977-1641 (Maple Leafs, hockey).

Racetracks

Woodbine Racetrack, 15 mi N via Hwy 427, in Etobicoke, 675-RACE.

Cultural Facilities

Theater & Concert Halls

Elgin Theatre, 189 Yonge St, downstairs, 872-5555.

Ford Centre for the Performing Arts, 5040 Yonge St, 733-9388.

Harbourfront Centre, 235 Queens Quay W, 973-3000.

Hummingbird Centre for the Performing Arts, 1 Front St E, 393-7469.

Roy Thomson Hall, 60 Simcoe St, 593-4828

St Lawrence Centre for the Arts, 27 Front St E, 366-7723.

Toronto Symphony, 60 Simcoe St, 593-4828.

Winter Garden Theatre, 189 Yonge St, upstairs, 872-5555.

Young People's Theatre, 165 Front St E, 862-2222.

Museums

Hockey Hall of Fame and Museum, 30 Yonge St, 360-7765.

Royal Ontario Museum (ROM), 100 Queen's Park, 586-5549.

Art Museums

Art Gallery of Ontario, 317 Dundas St W, 977-0414.

Colborne Lodge, Colborne Lodge Dr & The Queensway in High Park, 392-6916.

George R. Gardiner Museum of Ceramic Art, 111 Queen's Park, 586-8080.

Points of Interest

Historical

Black Creek Pioneer Village, 1000 Murray Ross Pkwy, 736-1733.

Casa Loma, One Austin Terrace, 923-1171.

Colborne Lodge, Colborne Lodge Dr & The Queensway in High Park, 392-6916.

Enoch Turner Schoolhouse, 106 Trinity St, 863-0010.

Gibson House, 5172 Yonge St, in North York, 395-7432.

Historic Fort York, Garrison Rd, 392-6907.

Huronia Historical Parks, 63 mi N via Hwy 400, then 34 mi N to Midland on Hwy 93, 705/526-7838.

Mackenzie House, 82 Bond St, 392-6915.

Spadina, 285 Spadina Rd, 392-6910.

The Grange, behind Art Gallery of Toronto, 317 Dundas St W.

The Market Gallery, 95 Front St E, 392-7604.

Todmorden Mills Heritage Museum & ArtCentre, 67 Pottery Rd, in East York, 396-2819.

Other Attractions

Canadian National (CN) Tower, 301 Front St W, just W of University Ave, 360-8500 (information) or 362-5411 (dining reservations).

City Hall, 100 Queen St W, 392-7341.

High Park, between Bloor St W & the Queensway at Parkside Dr, near lakeshore.

Kortright Centre for Conservation, 9550 Pine Valley Dr, 12 mi (19.3 km) NW via Hwy 400, Major MacKenzie Dr exit, then 2 mi (3 km) W, then S on Pine Valley Dr, at Klienberg, 905/832-2289.

Metro Toronto Zoo, 10 mi (16 km) E of Don Valley Pkwy on Hwy 401, then N on Meadowvale Rd, in Scarborough, 392-5900.

Ontario Parliament Buildings, Queen's Park, 325-7500.

Ontario Place, 955 Lakeshore Blvd W, 314-9900 (recording) or 314-9811.

Ontario Science Centre, 770 Don Mills Rd, 429-4100.

Paramount Canada's Wonderland, 9580 Jane St, 18 mi (29 km) N on Hwy 400, 905/832-7000.

St Lawrence Market and Hall, Front St and Jarvis St, 392-7219.

Toronto Stock Exchange, Exchange Tower, 2 First Canadian Pl (King & York Sts), 947-4676 or 947-4700.

Sightseeing Tours

Gray Line bus tours, 180 Dundas St W, Suite 1100, 594-3310 or 800/243-8453.

Toronto Tours Ltd, 869-1372.

Annual Events

du Maurier International Canadian Open Tennis Championship, York University campus, near Finch Ave and Keele St, 665-9777 (for tickets) or 872-1212 (Ticketron). Summer.

International Caravan, 977-0466. 3rd wk June.

Canoeing and Rowing Regatta, Long Pond, Toronto Island, 426-7170. July 1.

Chin International Picnic, 531-9991. 1st wkend July.

Molson Indy, Canadian National Exhibition, 975-8000. 3 days mid-July.

Outdoor Art Show, Nathan Phillips Sq, 408-2754. Mid-July.

Caribana, 465-3811. Late July-early Aug.

Canadian National Exhibition, 393-6000. Mid-Aug-Labour Day.

Toronto International Film Festival, 967-7371. Early Sept.

Canadian International, Woodbine Racetrack. Mid-Oct.

Royal Agricultural Winter Fair, Coliseum Bldg, 872-7777. Early-mid-Nov.

Lodging and Food Toronto

TORONTO RESTAURANTS BY NEIGHBORHOOD AREAS

(For full description, see alphabetical listings under Restaurants)

CABBAGETOWN
Provence. 12 Amelia St

DOWNTOWN
360 Revolving Restaurant. 301 Front St W
Accents (Sutton Place Grande Hotel). 955 Bay St
Avalon. 270 Adelaide St W
Bangkok Garden. 18 Elm St
Barootes. 220 King St W
Bistro 990. 990 Bay St
Bumpkins. 21 Gloucester St
Cafe Victoria (King Edward Hotel). 37 King St E
Canoe. 66 Wellington St W
Carman's Club. 26 Alexander St
Chanterelles (Crowne Plaza Toronto Centre Hotel). 225 Front St W
Chez Max. 166 Wellington St W
Chiaro's (King Edward Hotel). 37 King St E
Ed's Warehouse. 270 King St W
La Fenice. 319 King St W
Lai Wah Heen (Metropolitan Hotel). 108 Chestnut St
Le Papillion. 16 Church St
Lichee Garden. 595 Bay St
Matienon. 51 Ste Nicholas St
Mövenpick Of Switzerland. 165 York St
Old Spaghetti Factory. 54 The Esplanade
Pawnbrokers Daughter. 1115 Bay St
Rivoli Cafe. 332 Queen St W
Senator. 253 Victoria St
Shopsy's Delicatessen. 33 Yonge St
Splendido. 88 Harbord St
Sushi Bistro. 204 Queen St W
Tiger Lily's Noodle House. 257 Queen St W
Truffles (Four Seasons Hotel). 21 Avenue Rd at Bloor St
Wayne Gretzky's. 99 Blue Jays Way
Xango. 106 John St
Yamase. 317 King St W

NORTH OF DOWNTOWN
Arlequin. 134 Avenue Rd
Centro Grill. 2472 Yonge St
Dimaggio's. 1423 Yonge St
Grano. 2035 Yonge St
Grazie. 2373 Yonge St
Harvest Cafe (Inn On The Park Hotel). 1100 Eglinton Ave E
Jerusalem. 955 Eglinton Ave W
Kally's. 430 Nugget Ave
North 44 Degrees. 2537 Yonge St
Pronto. 692 Mount Pleasant Rd
Scaramouche. 1 Benvenuto Place
Thai Flavour. 1554 Avenue Rd
United Bakers Dairy Restaurant. 506 Lawrence Ave W
Vanipha Lanna. 471 Eglinton Ave W
Zucca Trattoria. 2150 Yonge St

EAST OF DOWNTOWN
Ellas. 702 Pape Ave
Rosewater Supper Club. 19 Toronto St

WEST OF DOWNTOWN
Chiado. 864 College St
Old Mill. 21 Old Mill Rd
Oxford Steak House & Tavern. 1130 Martin Grove Rd
Ukrainian Caravan. 5245 Dundas St W
Villa Borghese. 2995 Bloor St W
Zachary's (Wyndham Bristol Place Hotel). 950 Dixon Rd

HARBOURFRONT
Pier 4 Storehouse. 245 Queen's Quay W

YORKVILLE
Boba. 90 Avenue Rd
Chicqry. 14 Prince Arthur Ave
Corner House. 501 Davenport Rd
Il Posto. 148 Yorkville Ave
Joso's. 202 Davenport Rd
Lovelock's. 838 Yonge St
Marketta. 138 Avenue Rd
Opus. 37 Prince Arthur Ave
Patachou. 1095 Yonge St

Note: When a listing is located in a town that does not have its own city heading, it will appear under the city nearest to its location. In these cases, the address and town appear in parenthesis immediately following the name of the establishment.

Motel

(Rates will be higher during Canadian National Exhibition)

✔★ **SEA HORSE INN.** *(2095 Lakeshore Blvd W (ON 2), Toronto ON M8V 1A1) jct QEW, west of downtown. 416/255-4433; FAX 416/251-5121; res: 800/663-1123.* 74 rms, 1-3 story. S $57-$67; D $57-$85; each addl $5; suites $75-$170; under 18 free. TV; cable (premium). Pool; whirlpool. Playground. Complimentary continental bkfst. Ck-out 11 am. Meeting rms. Lighted tennis. Sauna. Refrigerators. Picnic tables, grills. On Lake Ontario. Cr cds: A, C, D, DS, ER, MC, V.

SC

Motor Hotels

✔★ ★ **HOLIDAY INN EXPRESS.** *(50 Estates Dr, Scarborough ON M1H 2Z1) at jct Hwys 48 & 401. 416/439-9666; FAX 416/439-4295.* 136 rms, 2-3 story. No elvtrs. S $56-$79; D $62-$79; each addl $10; under 19 free; wkend rates. Crib free. TV; cable (premium). Complimentary continental bkfst. Restaurant adj 11:30-1 am, Sat, Sun from 4:30 pm. Ck-out 11 am. Meeting rms. Business servs avail. Health club privileges. Cr cds: A, C, D, DS, ER, JCB, MC, V.

D SC

★ ★ **HOWARD JOHNSON-EAST.** *(940 Progress Ave, Scarborough ON M1G 3T5) 416/439-6200; FAX 416/439-5689.* 186 rms, 6 story. S $99; D $109; each addl $10; under 18 free; wkend package plan. Crib free. Pet accepted. TV; cable (premium). Heated pool; whirlpool. Restaurant 6:30 am-2 pm, 5-10 pm. Rm serv. Bar 4:30 pm-1 am. Ck-out noon. Coin lndry. Meeting rms. Business servs avail. Valet serv. Sundries. Gift shop. Exercise equipt; weight machine, bicycle, sauna. Health club privileges. Microwaves avail. Cr cds: A, C, D, DS, ER, JCB, MC, V.

D SC

✔★ **INN ON THE LAKE.** *(1926 Lakeshore Blvd W, Toronto ON M6S 1A1) west of downtown. 416/766-4392; res: 800/463-9926; FAX 416/766-1278.* 110 rms, 4 story. June-early Sept: S $79-$110; D $79-$125; each addl $10; under 12 free; wkly rates; lower rates rest of yr. Crib free. TV; cable (premium). Restaurant nearby. Ck-out 11 am. Meeting rms. Sundries. Many balconies. Opp park; pool, beach. Cr cds: A, MC, V.

D SC

★ ★ **RAMADA HOTEL-TORONTO AIRPORT.** *(2 Holiday Dr, Etobicoke ON M9C 2Z7) near Lester B Pearson Intl Airport. 416/621-2121; FAX 416/621-9840.* 179 rms, 2-6 story. June-Aug: S, D $140-$150; each addl $10; suites $250-$350; under 19 free; wkly, wkend rates; lower rates rest of yr. Crib free. Pet accepted. TV; cable (premium). Indoor/outdoor pool; whirlpool, lifeguard. Complimentary coffee in rms. Restaurant 6 am-11 pm. Rm serv. Bar 11:30-1 am. Ck-out noon. Business servs avail.

In-rm modem link. Bellhops. Valet serv. Free airport transportation. Exercise equipt; weights, sauna. Some minibars; microwaves avail. Cr cds: A, C, D, DS, ER, JCB, MC, V.

D SC

★ ★ **TRAVELODGE-NORTH.** *(50 Norfinch Dr, North York ON M3N 1X1) N on Hwy 400 to Finch Ave, then E to Norfinch Dr. 416/663-9500; FAX 416/663-8480.* Web www.travelodge.com. 184 rms, 6 story. S $76; D $84; each addl $8; under 17 free. Crib free. Pet accepted, some restrictions. TV; cable (premium). Indoor pool; whirlpool. Coffee in rms. Restaurant 7-1 am. Rm serv. Bar. Ck-out 11 am. Meeting rms. Business servs avail. Sundries. Cr cds: A, D, DS, ER, MC, V.

D SC

★ **TRAVELODGE-TORONTO EAST.** *(20 Milner Business Ct, Scarborough ON M1B 3C6) 416/299-9500; FAX 416/299-6172.* Web www.travelodge.com. 156 rms, 6 story. S, D $66-$76; each addl $6; suites $75-$81; under 17 free. Pet accepted. TV; cable (premium), VCR. Indoor pool; whirlpool. Complimentary coffee in rms. Restaurant 11-2 am. Rm serv noon-11 pm. Ck-out 11 am. Meeting rms. Business servs avail. Sundries. Health club privileges. Microwaves avail. Cr cds: A, D, DS, ER, JCB, MC, V.

D SC

★ ★ ★ **VALHALLA INN.** *(1 Valhalla Inn Rd, Etobicoke ON M9B 1S9) 416/239-2391; FAX 416/239-8764; res: 800/268-2500.* 236 rms, 2-12 story. S $140; D $150; each addl $10; suites $189-230; under 18 free; AP avail; wkend packages. Crib free. Pet accepted. TV; cable (premium). Heated pool. Coffee in rms. Restaurant 6 am-11 pm; dining rm noon-2:30 pm, 5:30-10 pm. Rm serv 6 am-11 pm. Bars 11-1 am; entertainment. Ck-out 1 pm. Meeting rms. Business servs avail. In-rm modem link. Bellhops. Valet serv. Sundries. Free airport transportation. Health club privileges. Some bathrm phones. Private patios, balconies. Grills. Cr cds: A, C, D, DS, ER, MC, V.

SC

★ **VENTURE INN-YORKVILLE.** *(89 Avenue Rd, Toronto ON M5R 2G3) downtown. 416/964-1220; FAX 416/964-8692; res: 800/387-3933.* 71 rms, 8 story. S $124; D $134; each addl $10; under 19 free; wkend rates off-season. Crib free. Pet accepted, some restrictions. Parking $6.50/day. TV; cable (premium), VCR avail. Complimentary continental bkfst. Ck-out 1 pm. Meeting rms. Business servs avail. Health club privileges. Cr cds: A, D, DS, ER, MC, V.

SC

Hotels

★ ★ ★ **BEST WESTERN CARLTON PLACE.** *(33 Carlson Court, Etobicoke ON M9W 6H5) near Lester B. Pearson Intl Airport. 416/675-1234; FAX 416/675-3436.* 524 rms, 12 story. S $160-175; D $175-$190; each addl $15; suites $250-$350; under 18 free; wkend, mid-wk rates. Crib free. Parking in/out $4/day. Pet accepted. TV; cable (premium). Indoor pool; whirlpool. Complimentary coffee in rms. Restaurant 6:30-1 am. Rm serv 24 hrs. Bar 11-1 am. Ck-out 1 pm. Meeting rms. Business center. Gift shop. Airport transportation. Exercise equipt; bicycles, treadmill, sauna. Health club privileges. Minibars. Cr cds: A, D, DS, ER, JCB, MC, V.

D SC

★ ★ **BEST WESTERN PRIMROSE.** *(111 Carlton St, Toronto ON M5B 2G3) at Jarvis St, downtown. 416/977-8000; FAX 416/977-6323.* 338 rms, 23 story. S, D $149; each addl $10; suites $275; under 18 free. Crib free. Garage $12.50. TV; cable. Pool; sauna. Complimentary coffee in rms. Restaurant 6:30 am-10 pm. Bar 11-1 am. Ck-out 11 am. Meeting rms. Business servs avail. Exercise equipt: treadmill, bicycle. Cr cds: A, C, D, DS, ER, JCB, MC, V.

D SC

★ **BOND PLACE.** *(65 Dundas St E, Toronto ON M5B 2G8) east of downtown. 416/362-6061; FAX 416/360-6406; res: 800/268-9390.* 286 rms, 18 story, 51 suites. May-Oct: S, D $89-$109; each addl $15; suites $104-$134; under 15 free; lower rates rest of yr. Crib free. Parking, in/out $11. TV; cable (premium), VCR avail. Restaurant 7 am-11 pm. Rm serv 11 am-10 pm. Bar 11-1 am. Ck-out 11 am. Meeting rms. Business servs avail. Cr cds: A, C, D, DS, ER, MC, V.

D SC

★ ★ ★ **THE CAMBERLEY CLUB HOTEL.** *(40 King St W, Toronto ON M5H 3Y2) at Bay St, in the Scotia Plaza Bldg, downtown. 416/947-9025; FAX 416/947-0622; res: 800/555-8000.* 54 suites on 28th & 29th floors of 68-story bldg. Suites $210-$300; under 16 free; monthly rates. Crib free. Garage parking $20 in/out. TV; cable (premium), VCR (free movies). Complimentary continental bkfst. Restaurant 6:30-1 am. Rm serv 24 hrs. Bar from 11 am. Ck-out noon. Meeting rms. Business center. In-rm modem link. Concierge. Shopping arcade. Barber, beauty shop. Health club privileges. Bathrm phones, in-rm whirlpools. Cr cds: A, D, ER, MC, V.

D

★ ★ ★ **CLARION ESSEX PARK.** *(300 Jarvis St, Toronto ON M5B 2C5) downtown. 416/977-4823; FAX 416/977-4830.* E-mail clarion@net.com.ca; web www.hotelchoice.com. 102 rms, 10 story, 44 suites. S $140; D $155; each addl $15; suites $170-$250; under 18 free. Crib free. Garage parking $15. TV; cable (premium). Indoor pool; whirlpool. Complimentary coffee in lobby. Restaurant 7 am-2 pm, 5-9 pm. Bar from 11 am. Ck-out 11 am. Meeting rms. Business servs avail. Concierge. Downhill/x-country ski 10 mi. Exercise equipt; weights, bicycle, sauna. Rec rm. Refrigerators. Cr cds: A, C, D, DS, ER, JCB, MC, V.

SC

✔★ ★ **COMFORT HOTEL-DOWNTOWN.** *(15 Charles St E, Toronto ON M4Y 1S1) downtown. 416/924-1222; FAX 416/927-1369.* 108 rms, 10 story. S $89; D $99; each addl $10; suites $109-$119; under 18 free; wkend rates. Crib $10. Parking $9. TV; cable (premium), VCR avail. Restaurant noon-10 pm. Piano bar. Ck-out 11 am. Meeting rms. Business servs avail. Health club privileges. Refrigerators; microwaves avail. Cr cds: A, C, D, DS, ER, MC, V.

SC

★ ★ ★ **CROWNE PLAZA-TORONTO CENTRE.** *(225 Front St W, Toronto ON M5V 2X3) downtown. 416/597-1400; FAX 416/597-8128.* Web crowneplaza.com. 587 rms, 25 story. S, D $219-$234; each addl $15; suites $335-$435; under 18 free; wkend rates. Crib free. TV; cable (premium), VCR avail. Indoor pool; wading pool, whirlpool, poolside serv. Coffee in rms. Restaurant 6-2 am (also see CHANTERELLES). Bar 11:30-2 am; entertainment. Ck-out noon. Meeting rms. Business center. In-rm modem link. Concierge. Valet parking. Exercise rm; instructor, weights, bicycles, sauna. Massage. Minibars; microwaves avail. Formal decor. Cr cds: A, C, D, DS, ER, JCB, MC, V.

D SC

★ **DAYS INN-DOWNTOWN.** *(30 Carlton St, Toronto ON M5B 2E9) adj to Maple Leaf Gardens, between Yonge & Church Sts, downtown. 416/977-6655; FAX 416/977-0502.* Web www.daysinn.com/daysinn.html. 536 rms, 23 story. S, D $89-$129; each addl $15; under 16 free. Crib free. Pet accepted, some restrictions. Covered parking $13/day. TV; cable. Indoor pool; sauna. Restaurant 7 am-10 pm. Bar 11:30-2 am. Ck-out 11 am. Coin Indry. Meeting rms. Business servs avail. Sundries. Barber, beauty shop. Some refrigerators. Sun deck. Cr cds: A, D, DS, ER, JCB, MC, V.

SC

★ ★ ★ **DELTA CHELSEA INN.** *(33 Gerrard St W, Toronto ON M5G 1Z4) between Bay & Yonge Sts, downtown. 416/595-1975; FAX 416/585-4362; res: 800/268-1133.* E-mail reservations@deltachelsea.com; web www.deltahotels.com. 1,594 rms, 26 story. S $225-$235; D $240-$250; each addl $15; suites, kit. units $240-$345; under 18 free; wkend rates. Crib free. Pet accepted, some restrictions. Valet parking $21 in/out. TV; cable, VCR avail. 2 heated pools; whirlpool. Supervised child's activities; ages 2-13. Restaurant 6:30-1 am. Rm serv 24 hrs. Bar 11-1 am; entertainment. Ck-out 11 am. Convention facilities. Business center. Gift shop. Exercise equipt; weights, bicycles, sauna. Health club privileges.

Game rm. Refrigerator in some suites. Microwaves avail. Many balconies. Cr cds: A, C, D, DS, ER, JCB, MC, V.

D SC

★ ★ ★ **DELTA-TORONTO AIRPORT.** *(801 Dixon Rd, Etobicoke ON M9W 1J5) near Lester B. Pearson Intl Airport. 416/675-6100; FAX 416/675-4022; res: 800/668-1444.* E-mail delta@nbnet.nb.ca; web www.deltahotels.com. 251 rms, 8 story. S, D $105-$155; each addl $15; suites $155-$205; under 18 free; wkend package plan. Crib free. Pet accepted, some restrictions. TV; cable (premium). Indoor pool; sauna. Supervised child's activities (June-Aug). Restaurant 6 am-11 pm. Rm serv 24 hrs. Bar 11:30-2 am. Ck-out 1 pm. Convention facilities. Business center. Bellhops. Valet serv. Gift shops. Exercise equipt; bicycles, treadmill. Health club privileges. Minibars. Microwave avail. Cr cds: A, C, D, DS, ER, JCB, MC, V.

D SC

★ ★ ★ **EMBASSY SUITES.** *(8500 Warden Ave, Markham ON L6G 1A5) 905/470-8500; FAX 905/477-8611.* 332 suites, 10 story. S, D $152-$172; each addl $20; wkend packages; under 18 free. Crib free. Valet parking $3. TV; cable (premium). Indoor pool; whirlpool. Complimentary full bkfst. Coffee in rms. Restaurant 6:30 am-midnight. Bar 11-2 am. Ck-out noon. Convention facilities. Business center. Shopping arcade. Barber, beauty shop. Exercise rm; instructor, weights, bicycles, sauna, steam rm. Minibars; microwaves avail. Extensive grounds; elaborate landscaping. Elegant atmosphere. Cr cds: A, C, D, ER, MC, V.

D SC

★ ★ ★ ★ **FOUR SEASONS.** *(21 Avenue Rd at Bloor St, Toronto ON M5R 2G1) downtown. 416/964-0411; FAX 416/964-2302; res: 800/268-6282 (CAN & NY).* Web www.fshr.com. This fashionable, elegant hotel has a prime location in Toronto. 380 rms, 32 story. S $250-$280; D $280-$315; each addl $25; suites $375-$2,400; under 18 free; wkend rates. Crib free. Pet accepted. Garage $18.75/day. TV; cable (premium), VCR avail (movies). Indoor/outdoor pool; whirlpool, poolside serv, lifeguard. Restaurants 6:30 am-11 pm (also see TRUFFLES). Rm serv 24 hrs. Bar 11:30-2 am; entertainment exc Sun. Ck-out 1 pm. Convention facilities. Business center. In-rm modem link. Concierge. Barber, beauty shop. Valet parking. Exercise rm; instructor, weights, bicycles, sauna. Massage. Bathrm phones, minibars; microwaves avail. Some balconies. Cr cds: A, C, D, ER, JCB, MC, V.

D SC

★ ★ ★ **HILTON.** *(145 Richmond St W, Toronto ON M5H 2L2) at University Ave, downtown. 416/869-3456; FAX 416/869-1478.* Web www.hilton.com. 601 rms, 32 story. Apr-Nov: S, D $239-$259; each addl $20; suites $249-$1,600; family rates; wkend package plans; lower rates rest of yr. Crib free. Garage $17.50. TV; cable (premium). Indoor/outdoor pool; whirlpool, poolside serv in summer. Restaurant 6:30 am-11 pm. Rm serv 24 hrs. Bar 11:30-2 am. Ck-out noon. Convention facilities. Business center. Exercise equipt; weights, bicycles, sauna. Massage. Minibars. Luxury level. Cr cds: A, C, D, DS, ER, JCB, MC, V.

D

★ ★ ★ **HOLIDAY INN.** *(1100 Eglinton Ave E, Toronto ON M3C 1H8) north of downtown. 416/446-3700; FAX 416/446-3701.* 298 rms, 14 story. S $75-$115; D $85-$125; each addl $10; suites $175-$325; family, wkend, wkly rates. Crib free. Pet accepted, some restrictions. TV; cable (premium), VCR avail (movies). Complimentary coffee in lobby. Restaurant 6:30 am-11 pm. Rm serv from 5 pm. Bar 11:30-1 am; entertainment Thurs-Sat. Ck-out noon. Convention facilities. Business servs avail. In-rm modem link. Concierge. Shopping arcade. Barber, beauty shop. Free valet parking. Airport, RR station transportation. Indoor tennis, pro. X-country ski 1/4 mi. Exercise equipt; weights, stair machine, sauna. Indoor/outdoor pool; whirlpool, poolside serv, lifeguard. Playground. Supervised child's activities (May-Sept); ages 5-12. Game rm. Lawn games. Bathrm phones, refrigerators. Many balconies. Cr cds: A, C, D, DS, ER, JCB, MC, V.

D SC

★ ★ **HOLIDAY INN.** *(970 Dixon Rd, Etobicoke ON M9W 1J9) near Lester B. Pearson Intl Airport. 416/675-7611; FAX 416/674-4364.* 444 rms, 12 story. S, D $160-$175; suites $230-$430; wkend rates. Crib free. Pet accepted. TV; cable (premium). 2 heated pools, 1 indoor; whirlpool. Playground. Coffee in rms. Restaurant 6 am-10:30 pm. Rm serv to 1 am. Bar 11-2 am; Sun noon-11 pm. Ck-out 1 pm. Meeting rms. Business center. Concierge. Barber, beauty shop. Free airport transportation. Exercise equipt; weights, bicycles, sauna. Rec rm. Minibars. Cr cds: A, C, D, DS, ER, JCB, MC, V.

D SC

★ ★ ★ **HOLIDAY INN ON KING.** *(370 King St W, Toronto ON M5V 1J9) downtown. 416/599-4000; FAX 416/599-7394.* E-mail 104664.3505@compuserve.com; web www.hick.com. 425 rms, 20 story. S $169; D $189; each addl $15; suites $209-$239; family, monthly rates. Crib free. Garage $16. TV; cable, VCR avail. Heated rooftop pool; poolside serv, lifeguard. Complimentary coffee in rms. Restaurant 6:30-2 am. Bar from 11 am. Ck-out noon. Convention facilities. Business center. Concierge. Gift shop. Exercise equipt; weight machine, treadmill, sauna. Massage. Wet bars. Cr cds: A, C, D, DS, ER, JCB, MC, V.

D SC

★ ★ **HOLIDAY INN-YORKDALE.** *(3450 Dufferin St, Toronto ON M6A 2V1) 1 blk S of ON 401 Dufferin St exit, north of downtown. 416/789-5161; FAX 416/785-6845.* 365 rms, 12 story. S $134.95; D $149.95; each addl $15; suites $299.95-$499.95; under 19 free; wkend rates. Crib free. TV; cable (premium). Heated pool; whirlpool. Supervised child's activities. Complimentary coffee in rms. Restaurant 6 am-11 pm. Bar 11-1 am. Ck-out noon. Meeting rms. Business center. Exercise equipt; weights, bicycles, sauna. Rec rm. Minibars. Some balconies. Cr cds: A, C, D, DS, ER, JCB, MC, V.

D SC

★ ★ **HOWARD JOHNSON PLAZA.** *(600 Dixon Rd, Etobicoke ON M9W 1J1) 416/240-7511; FAX 416/240-7519.* 172 rms, 2-5 story. S, D $89-$109; each addl $10; suites $129-$149; under 18 free. Crib free. TV; cable, VCR avail. Heated pool; wading pool, poolside serv. Coffee in rms. Restaurant 24 hrs. Ck-out 1 pm. Meeting rms. Business servs avail. Exercise equipt: stair machine, weights. Cr cds: A, C, D, DS, ER, MC, V.

D SC

★ ★ ★ **HOWARD JOHNSON PLAZA.** *(2737 Keele St, North York ON M3M 2E9) N on Hwy 401, exit Keele St, then 1 blk N. 416/636-4656; FAX 416/633-5637.* Web www.hojo.com. 367 rms, most A/C, 10 story, 27 suites. S, D $129-$179; each addl $10; suites $175-$375; family, wkly, wkend, hol rates. Crib free. Pet accepted. TV; cable (premium), VCR avail. Indoor pool. Supervised child's activities (June-Sept); ages 4-12. Complimentary coffee in rms. Restaurant 6:30 am-11 pm, Sun to 10 pm. Bar 11-1 am; entertainment. Ck-out 1 pm. Meeting rms. Business servs avail. Free garage parking. Downhill/x-country ski 10 mi. Exercise equipt; weight machine, treadmill, sauna. Game rm. Rec rm. Some minibars; microwaves avail. Cr cds: A, C, D, DS, ER, JCB, MC, V.

D SC

★ ★ ★ ★ **INN ON THE PARK.** *(1100 Eglinton Ave E, Toronto ON M3C 1H8) at Leslie St, north of downtown. 416/444-2561; FAX 416/446-3308; res: 800/268-6282 (CAN).* This hotel is set in a 600-acre park just 15 minutes from downtown Toronto. Guest rooms are bright and inviting, with all the amenities for relaxation or business. 270 rms, 23 story. S $120-$175; D $135-$195; each addl $20; suites $225-$750; under 18 free; wkend rates. Crib free. TV; cable (premium), VCR avail. 2 heated pools, 1 indoor; whirlpool, lifeguards. Free supervised child's activities (May-Sept); ages 5-12. Restaurants 6:30 am-midnight (also see HARVEST CAFE). Bar 11:30-1 am; vocalist exc Sun. Ck-out noon. Business servs avail. In-rm modem link. Concierge. Barber, beauty shop. Valet parking. Lighted tennis, pro. X-country ski 1/4 mi. Exercise equipt; weights, bicycles, sauna, steam rm. Rec rm. Lawn games. Some minibars. Some private patios, balconies. Cr cds: A, C, D, ER, JCB, MC, V.

D SC

★ ★ ★ ★ **INTER-CONTINENTAL.** *(220 Bloor St W, Toronto ON M5S 1T8) downtown. 416/960-5200; FAX 416/960-8269.* Web www.interconti.com. Edwardian and art-deco touches embellish public spaces and guest rooms of this post-modern structure. 209 rms, 8 story. S $235-$315;

D $255-$335; suites $400-$1,400. Crib free. Valet parking $21.40. TV; cable (premium), VCR avail (movies). Indoor pool. Restaurants 7 am-11 pm. Rm serv 24 hrs. Bar noon-1 am. Ck-out 1 pm. Meeting rms. Business center. In-rm modem link. Concierge. Gift shop. Exercise equipt; weights, treadmill, sauna. Massage. Bathrm phones, minibars. Cr cds: A, C, D, ER, JCB, MC, V.

D SC

★ ★ ★ **INTERNATIONAL PLAZA.** *(655 Dixon Rd, Toronto ON M9W 1J4) near Lester B. Pearson Intl Airport, west of downtown. 416/244-1711; FAX 416/244-8031; res: 800/668-3656.* 415 rms, 12 story. S, D $150; each addl $10; suites $250-$450; under 18 free; wkly, wkend, hol rates. Crib free. Pet accepted. Valet parking $6. TV; cable (premium). Indoor pool; wading pool, poolside serv, lifeguard. Supervised child's activities; ages 3-12. Restaurant 6:30 am-11 pm. Rm serv 24 hrs. Bar 11-2 am. Ck-out noon. Convention facilities. Business center. Concierge. Gift shop. Beauty, barber shop. Exercise equipt; weight machine, treadmill, sauna. Massages. Game rm. Refrigerators. Minibars in suites. Cr cds: A, D, DS, ER, MC, V.

D

★ ★ ★ ★ **KING EDWARD.** *(37 King St E, Toronto ON M5C 1E9) downtown. 416/863-9700; FAX 416/367-5515; res: 800/225-5843.* E-mail 104665.3516@compuserve.com. Built in 1903 and remodelled in the early 1980s, this stately and attractive hotel has a vaulted ceiling, marble pillars and palm trees in its lobby. 299 rms, 9 & 16 story. S $229-$289; D $249-$309; suites $300-$500; under 17 free; wkend rates. Crib free. Covered parking, valet $24. TV; cable (premium), VCR avail. Restaurants 6:30 am-2:30 pm, 5-11 pm (see CHIARO'S, also see CAFE VICTORIA, Unrated Dining). Rm serv 24 hrs. Bars noon-1 am. Ck-out noon. Convention facilities. Business center. In-rm modem link. Concierge. Shopping arcade. Beauty shop. Exercise equipt; weights, bicycles, whirlpools, sauna. Massage. Health club privileges. Bathrm phones, minibars; microwaves avail. Cr cds: A, C, D, ER, JCB, MC, V.

D SC

★ ★ ★ **MARRIOTT-EATON CENTRE.** *(525 Bay St, Toronto ON M5G 2L2) downtown. 416/597-9200; FAX 416/597-9211.* 459 rms, 18 story. May-Oct: S, D $250; suites $600-$1800; family rates; wkly, wkend, hol rates; higher rates special events; lower rates rest of yr. Crib free. Garage parking $14, valet $18. TV; cable (premium), VCR avail. Indoor pool; whirlpool, poolside serv. Restaurant 6:30 am-10 pm. Rm serv 24 hrs. Bar 11-1 am. Ck-out noon. Convention facilities. Business center. Concierge. Shopping arcade. Drug store. Barber, beauty shop. Exercise equipt; weight machine, stair machines, sauna. Cr cds: A, D, JCB, MC, V.

D SC

★ ★ ★ **MARRIOTT-AIRPORT.** *(901 Dixon Rd, Etobicoke ON M9W 1J5) near Lester B. Pearson Intl Airport. 416/674-9400; FAX 416/674-8292.* 424 rms, 9 story. S, D $240; suites $300-$1,000; under 18 free; wkend rates. Crib free. TV; cable (premium). Indoor pool; whirlpool. Restaurants 6 am-11 pm. Bar noon-2 am. Ck-out noon. Convention facilities. Business center. Gift shop. Covered parking. Free airport transportation. Exercise rm; instructor, weights, bicycles, sauna. Luxury level. Cr cds: A, C, D, ER, JCB, MC, V.

D SC

★ ★ ★ **METROPOLITAN.** *(108 Chestnut St, Toronto ON M5G 1R3) downtown. 416/977-5000; res: 800/668-6600; FAX 416/977-9513.* E-mail reservations@metropolitan.com; web www.metropolitan.com. 480 rms, 26 story. S $160; D $180; each addl $20; suites $195-$850; wkend rates. Crib free. Parking, in/out $15.87. Pet accepted, some restrictions. TV; cable (premium), VCR avail (free movies). Indoor pool; whirlpool. Restaurant 6:30 am-midnight (see also LAI WAH HEEN). Rm serv 24 hrs. Bar 11-1 am. Ck-out noon. Meeting rms. Business center. In-rm modem link. Concierge. Gift shop. Exercise equipt; treadmill, bicycles, sauna. Bathrm phones, minibars. Adj to City Hall. Eatons Centre 2 blks. Cr cds: A, C, D, DS, ER, JCB, MC, V.

D SC

★ ★ **NOVOTEL-AIRPORT.** *(135 Carlingview Dr, Etobicoke ON M9W 5E7) near Lester B. Pearson Intl Airport. 416/798-9800; FAX 416/798-1237; res: 800/668-6835.* E-mail tairmail@aol.com. 192 rms, 7 story. S $165; D $175; suites $175; family, wkly, wkend rates. Crib free. Pet accepted. TV; cable (premium), VCR avail. Indoor pool; whirlpool. Restaurant 6 am-11 pm. Bar 11-1 am. Ck-out 1 pm. Meeting rms. Business center. In-rm modem link. Gift shop. Free garage parking. Free airport transportation. Downhill/x-country ski 20 mi. Exercise equipt; weights, treadmill, sauna. Minibars. Cr cds: A, D, DS, ER, JCB, MC, V.

D SC

★ ★ ★ **NOVOTEL-TORONTO CENTRE.** *(45 The Esplanade, Toronto ON M5E 1W2) downtown. 416/367-8900; FAX 416/360-8285; res: 800/668-6835.* Web novotel-northamerica.com/welcome. 262 rms, 9 story. S, D $135-$185; each addl $15; suites $215; under 16 free; wkend rates. Crib free. Pet accepted. Garage (fee). TV; cable (premium). Indoor pool; whirlpool. Restaurant 6 am-midnight. Bar 11-1 am. Ck-out 1 pm. Meeting rms. Business servs avail. Exercise equipt; weights, rowers, sauna. Minibars. Cr cds: A, D, DS, ER, JCB, MC, V.

D SC

★ ★ ★ **PARK PLAZA.** *(4 Avenue Rd, Toronto ON M5R 2E8) at Bloor St, downtown. 416/924-5471; FAX 416/924-6693; res: 800/977-4197.* 261 rms, 12-18 story; 40 suites. S, D $225-$260; each addl $15; suites $350-$750; family, wkend rates. Crib free. Pet accepted. Garage in/out $18. TV; cable (premium), VCR avail. Restaurant 7 am-10:30 pm. Bar 11:30-2 am. Ck-out noon. Meeting rms. Business center. Concierge. Health club privileges. Minibars. Many antique furnishings in public areas. Royal Ontario Museum opp. Cr cds: A, C, D, DS, ER, JCB, MC, V.

D SC

★ **QUALITY.** *(111 Lombard St, Toronto ON M5C 2T9) downtown. 416/367-5555; FAX 416/367-3470; res: 800/228-5151.* 196 rms, 16 story. S $129; D $139; each addl $10; under 18 free. Crib free. Pet accepted. Garage $11.75/day. TV; cable. Ck-out 11 am. Business servs avail. Health club privileges. Cr cds: A, D, DS, JCB, MC, V.

D SC

★ **QUALITY.** *(280 Bloor St W, Toronto ON M5S 1V8) downtown. 416/968-0010; FAX 416/968-7765.* 210 rms, 14 story. Mid-Mar-Oct: S $115-$130; D $127-$152; under 18 free; wkend rates; higher rates special events; lower rates rest of yr. Crib free. Pet accepted, some restrictions. Garage in/out $11.50. TV; cable. Restaurant 7 am-11 pm. Bar 11 am-11 pm. Ck-out 11 am. Meeting rms. Business servs avail. No bellhops. Health club privileges. Cr cds: A, D, DS, JCB, MC, V.

D SC

✔★ **QUALITY SUITES.** *(262 Carlingview Dr, Etobicoke ON M9W 5G1) near Lester B. Pearson Intl Airport. 416/674-8442; FAX 416/674-3088.* Web hotelchoice.com. 254 suites, 12 story. S, D $120-$145; each addl $5; under 18 free; wkend, hol rates. Crib free. Pet accepted. TV; cable (premium), VCR avail (movies). Complimentary coffee in rms. Restaurant 6:30-1 am. Bar. Ck-out 11 am. Meeting rms. Business servs avail. No bellhops. Gift shop. Downhill/x-country ski 15 mi. Exercise equipt; bicycles, stair machine. Health club privileges. Game rm. Minibars; microwaves avail. Cr cds: A, D, DS, ER, JCB, MC, V.

D SC

★ **QUALITY-AIRPORT EAST.** *(2180 Islington Ave, Toronto ON M9T 3P1) west of downtown. 416/240-9090; FAX 416/240-9944.* Web www.qualityinn.com. 214 rms, 12 story. S, D $85-135; each addl $5; under 18 free; wkly, wkend rates; higher rates special events. Crib free. Pet accepted. TV; cable (premium). Restaurant 7 am-10 pm. Bar from 11 am. Ck-out 11 am. Meeting rms. In-rm modem link. Microwaves avail. Near airport. Cr cds: A, D, DS, ER, JCB, MC, V.

D SC

★ ★ ★ **RADISSON.** *(50 E Valhalla Dr, Markham ON L3R 0A3) N on Hwy 404, at jct Hwy 7. 905/477-2010; FAX 905/477-2026.* Web www.radisson.com/toronto/markham. 202 rms, 15 story, 26 suites. S, D $210; each addl $15; suites $250; under 19 free; wkly, wkend rates; golf plans; higher rates Dec 31. Crib free. Indoor pool; whirlpool. Complimentary continental bkfst. Complimentary coffee in rms. Restaurant 6:30 am-11 pm. Bar 11-2 am. Ck-out noon. Meeting rms. Business servs avail. Gift shop. Tennis privileges. 18-hole golf privileges. Downhill/x-country ski 12 mi. Exercise equipt; weights, bicycle, sauna. Rec rm. Minibars; microwaves avail. Picnic tables. Cr cds: A, C, D, DS, ER, JCB, MC, V.

D SC

★ ★ ★ **RADISSON PLAZA.** *(90 Bloor St E, Toronto ON M4W 1A7) at Yonge St, downtown. 416/961-8000; FAX 416/961-4635; res: 800/267-6116.* Web www.radisson.com. 256 rms, 6 story. S $225; D $240; each addl $15; under 18 free. Crib $15. Garage parking, valet $18.50. TV; cable (premium), VCR avail. Coffee in rms. Restaurant 6:30 am-11:30 pm. Bar 11:30-1 am. Ck-out 1 pm. Meeting rms. Business center. Health club privileges. Minibars; bathrm phone in suites, microwaves avail. Luxury level. Cr cds: A, C, D, DS, ER, JCB, MC, V.

D SC

★ ★ ★ **RADISSON PLAZA-HOTEL ADMIRAL.** *(249 Queens Quay W, Toronto ON M5J 2N5) downtown. 416/203-3333; FAX 416/203-3100.* 157 air-cooled rms, 8 story, 17 suites. Early-May-mid-Nov: S, D $205-$255; each addl $20; suites from $450; family, wkend rates. Crib free. Parking $15/day. TV; cable (premium). Heated pool; whirlpool, poolside serv. Restaurant 7 am-11 pm. Rm serv 24 hrs. Bar 11:30-1 am. Ck-out noon. Meeting rms. Business servs avail. Concierge. Gift shop. Health club privileges. Bathrm phones, minibars. On waterfront; nautical theme throughout. View of Harbour. Cr cds: A, C, D, DS, ER, JCB, MC, V.

D SC

★ ★ ★ **RADISSON SUITE-TORONTO AIRPORT.** *(640 Dixon Rd, Etobicoke ON M9W 1J1) near Lester B. Pearson Intl Airport. 416/242-7400; FAX 416/242-9888.* Web www.radisson.com. 215 suites, 14 story. S, D $204-216; under 18 free. Crib free. Pet accepted, some restrictions. TV; cable, VCR avail. Complimentary continental bkfst. Restaurant 6:30 am-11 pm. Bar 11-1 am. Ck-out noon. Meeting rms. Business center. In-rm modem link. Concierge. Gift shop. Free valet parking. Exercise equipt; weights, bicycles. Minibars, microwaves avail. Cr cds: A, C, D, DS, ER, JCB, MC, V.

D SC

★ ★ **RAMADA-DON VALLEY.** *(185 Yorkland Blvd, Toronto ON M2J 4R2) at jct ON 401, Don Valley Pkwy. 416/493-9000; FAX 416/493-5729.* 281 rms, 10 story. S, D $105-$165; each addl $15; suites $175-$300; under 18 free; wkend rates. Crib free. TV; cable (premium), VCR avail (movies). Indoor pool; sauna. Coffee in rms. Restaurant 6:30 am-10:30 pm; Sat from 7 am. Bar 11-2 am; Sun to 11 pm. Ck-out noon. Meeting rms. Business servs avail. In-rm modem link. Exercise equipt; bicycles, weight machine. Health club privileges. Game rm. Rec rm. Some in-rm whirlpools. Luxury level. Cr cds: A, C, D, DS, ER, JCB, MC, V.

D SC

★ ★ ★ **REGAL CONSTELLATION.** *(900 Dixon Rd, Etobicoke ON M9W 1J7) near Lester B. Pearson Intl Airport. 416/675-1500; FAX 416/675-1737; res: 800/268-4838.* Web www.dms-destination.com/regal/regal.htm. 710 rms, 8-16 story. S, D $95-$165; each addl $15; suites from $275; under 18 free; wkend package plan. Crib free. Pet accepted, some restrictions. Valet parking $7.50/day. TV; cable (premium), VCR avail. 2 heated pools, 1 indoor/outdoor; whirlpool, poolside serv in season. Restaurant 6:30 am-11 pm; dining rm 11 am-2 pm, 5:30-10 pm. Rm serv 24 hrs. Bar 11-2 am; entertainment Thurs-Sat. Ck-out noon. Concierge. Convention facilities. Business center. Gift shop. Barber, beauty shop. Airport transportation. Exercise equipt; weights, bicycles, sauna. Some balconies. Cr cds: A, C, D, DS, ER, MC, V.

D SC

★ ★ ★ **ROYAL YORK.** *(100 Front St W, Toronto ON M5J 1E3) opp Union Station, downtown. 416/368-2511; FAX 416/368-2884; res: 800/828-7447 (US).* E-mail reserve@ryh.mhs.compuserve.com; web www.cphotels.ca. 1,365 rms, 22 story. S, D $189-$289; each addl $20; suites $295-$1,750; under 18 free; wkend packages. Crib free. Pet accepted. Garage (fee). TV; cable. Pool; wading pool, whirlpool. Restaurant 6:30 am-10:30 pm. Rm serv 24 hrs. Bars noon-2 am; entertainment. Ck-out noon. Convention facilities. Business center. Concierge. Shopping arcade. Barber, beauty shop. Exercise rm; instructor, weight machines, rower, sauna. Massage. Health club privileges. Minibars; refrigerators, microwaves avail. Luxury level. Cr cds: A, C, D, DS, ER, JCB, MC, V.

D SC

★ ★ ★ **SHERATON CENTRE.** *(123 Queen St W, Toronto ON M5H 2M9) opp City Hall, downtown. 416/361-1000; FAX 416/947-4854.* Web www.sheratonctr.toronto.on.ca. 1,382 rms, 43 story. Late June-Dec: S $250; D $285; each addl $20; suites $405-$780; under 18 free; wkend rates; lower rates rest of yr. Covered parking, valet $22/day. TV; cable (premium), VCR avail. Indoor/outdoor pool; whirlpool, sauna, poolside serv (summer), lifeguard. Supervised child's activities (daily July-mid-Sept; wkends rest of yr). Complimentary coffee in rms. Restaurant 6 am-11 pm. Rm serv 24 hrs. Bars. Ck-out noon. Convention facilities. Business center. Concierge. Shopping arcade. Barber, beauty shop. Exercise equipt; weights, treadmills. Massage. Health club privileges. Rec rm. Minibars; microwaves avail. Private patios, balconies. Waterfall in lobby; pond with live ducks. Cr cds: A, C, D, DS, ER, JCB, MC, V.

D SC

★ ★ ★ **SHERATON GATEWAY.** *(PO Box 3000, Toronto ON L5P 1C4) at Lester B. Pearson Intl Airport, west of downtown. 905/672-7000; FAX 905/672-7100.* 474 rms, 8 story. S, D $180-$210; each addl $15; suites $270-$695; under 18 free; wkly, wkend rates. Crib free. Pet accepted. Garage parking $8; valet $18. TV; cable (premium), VCR avail. Indoor pool; whirlpool. Restaurant 6 am-11 pm. Rm serv 24 hrs. Bar 11-1 am. Ck-out noon. Convention facilities. Business center. Concierge. Shopping arcade. Barber, beauty shop. Free airport transportation. Exercise equipt; weights, rowers, sauna. Massage. Minibars. Modern facility connected by climate-controlled walkway to Terminal 3. Cr cds: A, C, D, DS, ER, JCB, MC, V.

D SC

★ ★ ★ **SHERATON-TORONTO EAST.** *(2035 Kennedy Rd, Scarborough ON M1T 3G2) 416/299-1500; FAX 416/299-8959.* E-mail sheraton@maple.net; web www.sheraton.com/toronto. 371 rms, 13 story. S, D $198; each addl $15; suites $350-$595; under 18 free; wkend rates. Crib free. Pet accepted. TV; cable. Indoor pool; wading pool; whirlpool. Free supervised child's activities (mid-Mar & mid-June-Aug, daily; rest of yr, Sat, Sun & hols); ages 3-15. Restaurants 6:30-2 am. Rm serv 24 hrs. Bar 11-2 am. Ck-out noon. Convention facilities. Business servs avail. In-rm modem link. Concierge. Gift shop. Barber, beauty shop. Covered valet parking. Putting green. Exercise rm; instructor, weights, bicycles, sauna. Game rm. Microwaves avail. Luxury level. Cr cds: A, C, D, DS, ER, JCB, MC, V.

D SC

★ ★ ★ **SKYDOME.** *(1 Blue Jays Way, Toronto ON M5V 1J4) adj CN Tower, downtown. 416/341-7100; FAX 416/341-5090; res: 800/441-1414.* E-mail mgeorge@sky.mhs.compuserv.com; web www.cphotels.ca. 346 rms, 11 story, 70 suites. Apr-Oct: S, D $139-$179; each addl $30; suites from $300; under 18 free; wkend rates; package plans. Crib avail. Pet accepted. Garage parking $16; valet $22. TV; cable, VCR avail. Indoor pool. Complimentary coffee in rms. Supervised child's activities (June-Sept). Restaurant 7-1 am. Rm serv 24 hrs. Bar. Ck-out 9:30 am-noon. Convention facilities. Business center. Concierge. Gift shop. Health club privileges. Massage. Minibars. Modern facility within SkyDome complex; lobby and some rms overlook playing field. Cr cds: A, C, D, DS, ER, JCB, MC, V.

D SC

★ ★ ★ **SUTTON PLACE GRANDE.** *(955 Bay St, Toronto ON M5S 2A2) downtown. 416/924-9221; res: 800/268-3790; FAX 416/924-1778.* E-mail gm@tor.suttonplace.com; web www.travelweb.com/sutton.html. 292 rms, 33 story, 62 suites. S $260; D $280; each addl $20; suites $380-$1,500; under 18 free; wkend rates. Crib free. Garage parking $17, valet $19. TV; cable (premium), VCR avail (movies). Indoor pool; poolside serv. Restaurant (see ACCENTS). Rm serv 24 hrs. Bar 11-2 am; entertainment. Ck-out noon. Convention facilities. Business center. Concierge. Gift shop. Barber, beauty shop. Exercise equipt; weight machine, treadmill, sauna. Massage. Minibars. Cr cds: A, C, D, DS, ER, MC, V.

D SC

★ ★ **TOWN INN.** *(620 Church St, Toronto ON M4Y 2G2) downtown. 416/964-3311; FAX 416/924-9466; res: 800/387-2755.* E-mail mitch@towninn.com; web towninn.com/. 200 kit. units (1-2 bedrm), 26 story. June-Dec: S $95-$125; D $110-$135; each addl $15; under 12 free; monthly rates; lower rates rest of yr. Crib free. Pet accepted. Garage $13. TV; cable (premium). Heated pool; saunas. Complimentary continental bkfst. Restaurant 7-10 am. Ck-out noon. Meeting rms. Business servs avail. Tennis. Exercise equipt; bicycles. Health club privileges. Refrigerators, microwaves. Balconies. Cr cds: A, C, D, ER, MC, V.

D SC

✔★ ★ **TRAVELODGE.** *(55 Hallcrown Pl, North York ON M2J 4R1) ON 401 exit 376, then N on Victoria Park Ave, off Consumer Rd. 416/493-7000; FAX 416/493-6577.* 228 rms, 9 story. S, D $95-$100; each addl $10; suites $150-$225; under 17 free; wkend rates. Crib free. TV; cable (premium), VCR avail. Indoor pool; whirlpool. Complimentary coffee in rms. Restaurant 7 am-10 pm. Bar. Ck-out noon. Meeting rms. Business servs avail. Sauna. Cr cds: A, C, D, DS, ER, JCB, MC, V.

D SC

★ **VENTURE INN-AIRPORT.** *(925 Dixon Rd, Etobicoke ON M9W 1J8) near Lester B. Pearson Intl Airport. 416/674-2222; FAX 416/674-5757; res: 888/4-VENTURE.* Web www.jwg.com/ventureinns/. 283 rms, 17 story. S $95; D $105; each addl $10; suites $140-$275; under 19 free; wkend rates. Crib free. Pet accepted. TV, cable (premium). Indoor pool; whirlpool. Complimentary continental bkfst. Restaurant 11-2 am. Bar. Ck-out 1 pm. Convention facilities. Business servs avail. In-rm modem link. Airport transportation. Sauna. Health club privileges. Gift shop. Cr cds: A, D, DS, ER, MC, V.

D SC

★ ★ ★ **WESTIN PRINCE.** *(900 York Mills Rd, North York ON M3B 3H2) N on Don Valley Pkwy, W on York Mills Rd. 416/444-2511; FAX 416/444-9597.* E-mail toprince@idirect.com; web www.princehotels.co.jp. 381 rms, 22 story. S $190-$225; D $210-$245; each addl $20; suites $340-$1,800; under 18 free; wkend rates. Crib free. TV; cable (premium), VCR avail (movies). Pool; whirlpool, poolside serv. Playground. Restaurant 6:30 am-10 pm. Rm serv 24 hrs. Bar 11:30-2 am; entertainment Mon-Sat. Ck-out 1 pm. Convention facilities. Business center. In-rm modem link. Concierge. Shopping arcade. Barber, beauty shop. Tennis. 18-hole golf privileges. Exercise equipt; weights, bicycle, sauna. Game rm. Refrigerators. Balconies. Cr cds: A, C, D, DS, ER, JCB, MC, V.

D

★ ★ ★ ★ **WYNDHAM BRISTOL PLACE HOTEL.** *(950 Dixon Rd, Etobicoke ON M9W 5N4) near Lester B. Pearson Intl Airport. 416/675-9444; FAX 416/675-4426; res: 800/268-4927.* E-mail bristol@interlog.com. This traditional hotel has a small waterfall in the main lobby, and guest rooms are individually decorated. 287 rms, 15 story. S, D $189-$225; each addl $15; suites from $275; under 18 free; wkend rates; package plans. Crib free. TV; cable (premium). Indoor/outdoor pool; poolside serv. Playground. Supervised child's activities; ages 2-16. Restaurant 7 am-midnight (also see ZACHARY'S). Rm serv 24 hrs. Bars 11-2 am; entertainment. Ck-out 1 pm. Convention facilities. Business center. In-rm modem link. Concierge. Valet parking. Free airport transportation. Exercise equipt; weight machine, bicycle, sauna. Minibars; bathrm phone, whirlpool in some suites; microwaves avail. Some private patios. Cr cds: A, C, D, DS, ER, JCB, MC, V.

D SC

Inns

✔★ ★ **GUILD.** *(201 Guildwood Pkwy, Scarborough ON M1E 1P6) 416/261-3331; FAX 416/261-5675.* 95 rms, 3-6 story. Apr-Dec: S, D $75; each addl $10; suites $125; under 18 free; AP, MAP; wkly rates; lower rates rest of yr. Crib free. TV; cable (premium); VCR (movies). Pool. Restaurant (see GUILD INN). Ck-out noon, ck-in 3 pm. Business servs avail. Tennis. Exercise equipt; weight machine, bicycles. Balconies. Opened in 1923 as art community. On 90-acres overlooking Lake Ontario. Log cabin (1805) on grounds. Cr cds: A, C, D, DS, ER, MC, V.

D SC

★ ★ ★ **MILLCROFT.** *(55 John St, Alton ON L0N 1A0) Hwy 10 to Hwy 24, W to Hwy 136, then N to John St. 519/941-8111; FAX 519/941-9192; res: 800/383-3976 (ON only).* E-mail wstich@auracom.com. 52 rms, 2 story, 20 chalets. S, D $175-$225. Crib free. Heated pool; whirlpool, poolside serv. Complimentary continental bkfst. Restaurant (see MILLCROFT INN). Bar. Ck-out noon, ck-in 4 pm. Guest lndry. Meeting rm. Business servs avail. Valet serv. Tennis. Golf privileges. X-country ski on site. Exercise equipt; weights, bicycles, sauna. Volleyball. Game rm. Some private patios. 100 acres on Credit River. Former knitting mill (1881). Cr cds: A, D, ER, MC, V.

D

Restaurants

★ ★ ★ **360 REVOLVING RESTAURANT.** *(301 Front St W, Toronto ON M5V 2T6) in CN Tower, downtown. 416/362-5411.* Web www.cntower.ca. Continental menu. Specializes in fresh rack of lamb, prime rib, corn-fed free-range chicken. Own baking. Hrs: 10:30 am-2:30 pm, 4:30-9:30 pm; Sat, Sun 10:30 am-2:30 pm, 4:30-10:30 pm; July, Aug hrs vary. Res accepted. Bar. Wine cellar. A la carte entrees: lunch $22-$34, dinner $25-$36. Sun brunch from $25. Revolving restaurant; view of harbor and city. Cr cds: A, D, ER, MC, V.

D

★ ★ ★ **ACCENTS.** *(See Sutton Place Grande Hotel) 416/324-5633.* Continental menu. Specializes in market fresh cuisine. Hrs: 6:30 am-11:30 pm. Res accepted. Bar. Wine cellar. A la carte entrees: bkfst $2.95-$10.50, lunch $8.50-$14.50, dinner $14.50-$32. Pianist Thurs-Sat. Parking. Continental atmosphere. Cr cds: A, C, D, DS, ER, JCB, MC, V.

D

★ ★ **ARKADIA HOUSE.** *(2007 Eglinton Ave E, Scarborough ON M1L 2M9) Approx 10 mi E on Hwy 2. 416/752-5685.* Greek menu. Specializes in roast lamb, fresh fish, souvlaki. Hrs: 11:30 am-3 pm, 4 pm-midnight. Closed Dec 24. Res accepted. Bar. Wine list. A la carte entrees: lunch $5.95-$11.95, dinner $10.95-$19.95. Child's meals. Parking. Garden cafe atmosphere. Cr cds: A, D, ER, MC, V.

★ **ARLEQUIN.** *(134 Avenue Rd, Toronto ON M5R 2H6) north of downtown. 416/928-9521.* French, Mediterranean menu. Hrs: 8:30 am-10 pm; Fri, Sat to 11 pm. Closed most major hols. Res accepted. Bar. A la carte entrees: lunch $7.95-$10, dinner $12.95-$18.95. Complete meals (Mon-Thurs): dinner $22.95. Small bistro with harlequin motif. Cr cds: A, D, ER, MC, V.

★ ★ ★ **AVALON.** *(270 Adelaide St W, Toronto ON M5H 1X6) downtown. 416/979-9918.* Specialties: wood-roasted cornish hen, yellow fin tuna steak, grilled dry-aged rib steak. Hrs: noon-2:30 pm, 5:30-10 pm; Mon, Tues from 5:30 pm; Fri to 11 pm; Sat 5:30-11 pm. Closed Sun; most major hols. Res accepted. Bar. Wine list. A la carte entrees: lunch $13-$22, dinner $20-$30. Artwork by local artists. Cr cds: A, D, ER, MC, V.

★ ★ ★ **BANGKOK GARDEN.** *(18 Elm St, Toronto ON M5G 1G7) downtown. 416/977-6748.* Thai menu. Specializes in lemon shrimp soup, curry dishes, seafood. Hrs: 11:30 am-2 pm, 5-10 pm; Sat, Sun from 5 pm. Res accepted. Bar. A la carte entrees: lunch $7.95-$14.95, dinner $14.95-$19.25. Complete meals: dinner $25.95-$39.95. Buffet (Mon, Fri): lunch $9.95. Child's meals. Thai decor; indoor garden. Cr cds: A, C, D, ER, MC, V.

✔★ ★ **BAROOTES.** *(220 King St W, Toronto ON M5H 1K4) downtown. 416/979-7717.* International menu. Specialties: fresh stir-fry, Thai satay combination, grilled marinated lamb tenderloin. Hrs: 11:30 am-2:30 pm, 5-11 pm. Closed Sun; Jan 1, Dec 25. Res accepted. Bar. A la carte entrees: lunch $8.95-$21.95, dinner $11.50-$24.95. Traditional dining rm; fine wood paneling throughout. Cr cds: A, D, ER, MC, V.

★ ★ **BISTRO 990.** *(990 Bay St, Toronto ON M5S 2A5) downtown. 416/921-9990.* Specializes in lamb, fresh fish. Hrs: noon-10:30 pm; Sat from 5:30 pm. Closed Sun. Res accepted. Bar. A la carte entrees: lunch $14-$19, dinner $13.50-$29.50. Prix fixe: lunch, dinner $19.90. Outdoor dining. French bistro decor. Cr cds: A, D, ER, MC, V.

D

★ ★ ★ **BOBA.** *(90 Avenue Rd, Toronto ON M5R 2H2) in Yorkville. 416/961-2622.* Specializes in vegetarian dishes, desserts. Hrs: 5:30-10 pm. Closed Sun; Jan 1, Dec 25, 26. Res required. Bar. A la carte entrees: dinner $19.50-$26.95. Patio dining. Intimate dining rm; bistro atmosphere. Totally nonsmoking. Cr cds: A, D, ER, MC, V.

D

★ ★ **BOY ON A DOLPHIN.** *(1911 Eglinton Ave E, Scarborough ON M1L 2L6) 416/759-4448.* Specializes in steak, seafood. Salad bar. Hrs: 11 am-midnight; Sat from 4 pm; Sun 4-10 pm; Sun brunch 11 am-2:30 pm. Res accepted. Bar to 1 am. Semi-a la carte: lunch $7.95-$12.95, dinner $14.95-$29.95. Sun brunch $9.95. Child's meals. Parking. Mediterranean decor. Cr cds: A, D, ER, MC, V.

D

★ ★ **BUMPKINS.** *(21 Gloucester St, Toronto ON M4Y 1L8) between Church & Yonge Sts, downtown. 416/922-8655.* Web www.wheremags.com. French, Amer menu. Specialty: shrimp Bumpkins. Hrs: noon-2:30 pm, 5-11 pm; Sat from 5 pm. Closed Sun. A la carte entrees: lunch $3.95-$8.50, dinner $8.75-$22.95. Child's meals. Outdoor dining. Cr cds: A, ER, MC, V.

★ ★ ★ **CANOE.** *(66 Wellington St W, Toronto ON M5K 1H6) downtown. 416/364-0054.* Specialties: Québec foie gras, Yukon caribou, roast sea scallops. Hrs: 11:30 am-2:30 pm, 5-10:30 pm. Closed Sat, Sun; major hols. Res accepted. Bar to 2 am. Wine cellar. Semi-a la carte: lunch $17-$24, dinner $21-$32. View of harbor and islands. Totally nonsmoking. Cr cds: A, D, ER, MC, V.

D

★ ★ ★ **CARMAN'S CLUB.** *(26 Alexander St, Toronto ON) downtown. 416/924-8558.* Web www.dine.net/visit/carmans. Specializes in steak, rack of lamb, Dover sole. Own pastries. Hrs: 5:30 pm-midnight. Closed Good Friday, Dec 25. Res accepted. Serv bar. Wine cellar. Complete meals: dinner $31.95-$35.95. Child's meals. In pre-1900 house; fireplaces. Family-owned. Cr cds: A, MC, V.

★ ★ ★ ★ **CENTRO GRILL.** *(2472 Yonge St, Toronto ON M4P 2H5) north of downtown. 416/483-2211.* The facade of etched glass, granite and marble may seem hard-edged, but the interior is as warm as the folksy town of Asolo. Massive columns that seem to hold up a bright blue ceiling and salmon-colored walls lined with comfortable banquettes help to create an intimate setting. Italian, Amer menu. Specialty: rack of lamb with tomato, garlic, Spanish capers, eggplant and salsa. Own baking. Hrs: 5 pm-1 am. Closed Sun. Res accepted. Bar. A la carte entrees: dinner $18.50-$30.95. Pianist. Cr cds: A, D, ER, MC, V.

★ ★ ★ **CHANTERELLES.** *(See Crowne Plaza Toronto Centre Hotel) 416/597-1400.* Web crowneplaza.com. Continental menu. Specialty: aiguilettes of duck. Own baking. Hrs: 11:45 am-2 pm, 5:45-10 pm; Sat, Sun from 6 pm. Res accepted. Bar to 1 am. Semi a la carte: lunch $11.95-$21.95, dinner $15.50-$26. Table d'hôte: lunch $21.95-$28. Valet parking. Cr cds: A, C, D, DS, ER, JCB, MC, V.

D

★ ★ ★ **CHEZ MAX.** *(166 Wellington St W, Toronto ON) downtown. 416/599-9633.* French menu. Specialties: filet mignon with red wine sauce, shrimp with pink peppercorn and vegetables. Hrs: noon-2:30 pm, 5:30-10 pm; Sat from 5:30 pm. Closed Sun; Jan 1, Dec 25. Res accepted. Bar. A la carte entrees: lunch $8.95-$17.25, dinner $16.50-$28.95. Patio dining. Modern decor. Jacket. Cr cds: A, D, ER, MC, V.

★ ★ ★ **CHIADO.** *(864 College St, Toronto ON M6H 1A3) west of downtown. 416/538-1910.* Portuguese menu. Specializes in Portuguese classical cuisine. Hrs: noon-midnight; early-bird dinner 5-7 pm. Closed Sun; Dec 24-26. Res accepted. Wine cellar. A la carte entrees: lunch $9.50-$14, dinner $16-$27. Child's meals. Oil paintings. Cr cds: A, C, D, ER, MC, V.

★ ★ ★ ★ **CHIARO'S.** *(See King Edward) 416/863-9700.* Web toprestaurants.com/toronto/chiaros.htm. Located in the opulent King Edward Hotel, this softly lit, plush dining room in shades of gray serves superior French-and-other-inspired cuisine. Continental menu. Specializes in rack of lamb, Dover sole, New York steak. Hrs: 6-10 pm. Closed Sun. Res accepted. Bar to 1 am. Wine cellar. Semi-a la carte: dinner $23-$38. Child's meals. Valet parking. Cr cds: A, C, D, ER, JCB, MC, V.

D

★ ★ ★ **CHICQRY.** *(14 Prince Arthur Ave, Toronto ON M5R 1A6) in Yorkville. 416/922-2988.* Hrs: 11 am-11 pm. Closed Sun; Dec 25. Res accepted. Mediterranean menu. Wine cellar. A la carte entrees: lunch $7.50-$9.95, dinner $14.95-$20.95. Specializes in pasta, seafood, beef. Outdoor dining. Glassed cathedral entrance. Cr cds: A, D, DS, ER, MC, V.

★ ★ **CORNER HOUSE.** *(501 Davenport Rd, Toronto ON M4V 1B8) in Yorkville. 416/923-2604.* French menu. Specializes in rack of lamb, poached salmon. Hrs: 6-10 pm. Closed Sun; major hols, also 1st Mon Aug. Res accepted; required lunch. Bar. Prix fixe: dinner $23.75. Four intimate dining rms in old house. Family-owned. Cr cds: A, D, ER, MC, V.

★ ★ ★ **DAVID DUNCAN HOUSE.** *(125 Moatfield Dr, North York ON) 1 mi S of ON 401, Leslie St exit. 416/391-1424.* Specializes in steak, seafood, rack of lamb. Hrs: 11:30 am-3 pm, 5-11 pm; Sat, Sun from 5 pm. Res accepted. Bar. Wine list. Semi-a la carte entrees: lunch $8.95-$13.95, dinner $16.95-$41.95. Valet parking. In restored, Gothic-revival house (1865) with elaborate gingerbread & millwork, antiques, stained-glass skylight. Jacket. Cr cds: A, D, ER, MC, V.

D

★ ★ ★ **DIMAGGIO'S.** *(1423 Yonge St, Toronto ON M4T 1Y7) north of downtown. 416/924-3288.* Mediterranean menu. Specialties: honey pecan rack of lamb, maple-marinated salmon. Hrs: 11:30 am-3 pm, 5-10 pm; Fri to 11 pm; Sat 5-11 pm. Closed Sun; most major hols. Res accepted. Bar. Wine cellar. A la carte entrees: lunch $8.95-$14.95, dinner $15.95-$21.95. Original artwork throughout restaurant, including on the tables. Cr cds: A, D, ER, MC, V.

D

★ ★ ★ **THE DOCTOR'S HOUSE.** *(21 Nashville Rd, Kleinberg ON L0J 1C0) 20 mi N on Hwy 27/427 to Kleinburg, turn right on Nashville Rd to top of hill. 905/893-1615.* Continental menu. Hrs: 11-1 am; Sun brunch 10:30 am-3 pm. Res accepted; required Sun brunch. Bar. Semi-a la carte: lunch $12-$16; dinner $16-$34. Sun brunch $28.50. Child's meals. Pianist Fri, Sat. Parking. Outdoor dining. Early Canadian atmosphere; antique cabinets with artifacts. Cr cds: A, MC, V.

D

★ ★ ★ **ED'S WAREHOUSE.** *(270 King St W, Toronto ON M5V 1H8) downtown. 416/593-6676.* English, Amer menu. Specializes in roast beef, steak. Own baking. Hrs: 4:30-8 pm; Sat to 9 pm. Closed Dec 24, 25. Serv bar. Wine list. A la carte entrees: dinner $10.95-$16.95. Unusual theatrical decor; many French antiques & statues, Tiffany lamps. Family-owned. Cr cds: A, D, MC, V.

★ ★ ★ **ELLAS.** *(702 Pape Ave, Toronto ON) east of downtown. 416/463-0334.* E-mail eria@ellas.com; web www.ellas.com. Greek menu. Specializes in lamb, shish kebab, seafood. Own pastries. Hrs: 11-1 am; Sun to 11 pm. Closed Dec 25. Res accepted. Bar. Semi-a la carte: lunch

$7.95-$9.95, dinner $10.95-$32.95. Ancient Athenian decor; sculptures. Family-owned. Cr cds: A, D, ER, MC, V.

✔★★ **GRANO.** *(2035 Yonge St, Toronto ON M4S 2A2) north of downtown. 416/440-1986.* Italian menu. Specializes in pasta. Hrs: 10 am-11 pm. Closed Sun; major hols. Res accepted. Bar. Semi-a la carte: lunch $7.95-$13.95, dinner $8.95-$18.95. Outdoor dining. Italian street cafe ambience. Cr cds: A, D, ER, MC, V.

★★ **GRAZIE.** *(2373 Yonge St, Toronto ON M4P 2C8) north of downtown. 416/488-0822.* Italian menu. Specializes in pizza, pasta. Hrs: noon-11 pm; Fri, Sat to midnight. Closed some major hols. Res accepted. Bar. A la carte entrees: lunch, dinner $9-$14. Child's meals. Bistro atmosphere. Cr cds: A, MC, V.

D

★★★ **GUILD INN.** *(See Guild Inn) 416/261-3331.* Continental menu. Specialties: smoked Atlantic salmon, prime rib. Salad bar. Own baking. Hrs: 7 am-10 pm; Sun brunch 10:30 am-2:30 pm. Res accepted. Bar. Wine list. Semi-a la carte: bkfst $2.75-$8.50, lunch $6.50-$15.95, dinner $14-$29.50. Sun brunch $17.95. Child's meals. Garden setting in former artist colony. Cr cds: A, C, D, DS, ER, MC, V.

★★★ **HARVEST CAFE.** *(See Inn On The Park Hotel) 416/444-2561.* Continental menu. Own baking. Hrs: 6:30 am-11:30 pm. Res accepted. Wine list. A la carte entrees: bkfst $3.95-$11.95, lunch, dinner $8.50-$18.95. Child's meals. Valet parking. Cr cds: A, C, D, DS, ER, JCB, MC, V.

D

★★ **IL POSTO.** *(148 Yorkville Ave, Toronto ON M5R 1C2) in Yorkville. 416/968-0469.* Northern Italian menu. Specializes in liver & veal chops, pasta with lobster, carpaccio. Hrs: noon-2:30 pm, 6-10:30 pm. Closed Sun; hols. Res accepted. A la carte entrees: $11.75-$16, dinner $13.50-$29. Outdoor dining. Cr cds: A, D, ER, MC, V.

★★ **JERUSALEM.** *(955 Eglinton Ave W, Toronto ON M6C 2C4) north of downtown. 416/783-6494.* Middle Eastern menu. Specialties: shish tawoo, siniyeh bitaheena, falafel plate. Hrs: 11:30 am-10:30 pm; Fri to 11:30 pm; Sat noon-11:30 pm; Sun noon-10 pm. Closed Jan 1, Dec 25. Res accepted. A la carte entrees: lunch $5.95-$6.50, dinner $8.95-$13.95. Child's meals. Outdoor dining. Old-world decor. Family-owned. Cr cds: A, MC, V.

★★★ **JOSO'S.** *(202 Davenport Rd, Toronto ON M5R 1J2) in Yorkville. 416/925-1903.* Mediterranean menu. Specializes in Italian dishes, seafood. Hrs: 11:30 am-2:30 pm, 5:30-11 pm; Sat from 5:30 pm. Closed Sun; some major hols. Res accepted. A la carte entrees: lunch $7-$19, dinner $9-$27. Child's meals. Outdoor dining. Wine cellar. Cr cds: A, D, ER, MC, V.

D

★★ **KALLY'S.** *(430 Nugget Ave, Toronto ON M1S 4A4) north of downtown. 416/293-9292.* Specializes in steak, ribs. Salad bar. Hrs: 11:30 am-10 pm; Sun 4-9 pm. Closed hols; also 1st Mon in Aug. Serv bar. A la carte entrees: lunch $4.45-$11.95, dinner $6.95-$13.45. Child's meals. Parking. Pyramid-shaped skylights. Cr cds: A, MC, V.

D

★★★ **LA FENICE.** *(319 King St W, Toronto ON M5V 1J5) downtown. 416/585-2377.* Italian menu. Specializes in fresh seafood, pasta. Hrs: 11:30 am-2:30 pm, 5:30-10:30 pm; Sat from 5:30 pm. Closed Sun; major hols. Res accepted. Bar to 1 am. Wine list. A la carte entrees: lunch $10.50-$24, dinner $14.50-$26. Sleek Milan-style trattoria. Near theater district. Cr cds: A, D, ER, JCB, MC, V.

★★★ **LAI WAH HEEN.** *(See Metropolitan Hotel) 416/977-9899.* E-mail lwh@metropolitan.com. Specializes in Cantonese dishes. Hrs: 11:30 am-3 pm, 5-11:30 pm. Res accepted. Wine cellar. A la carte entrees: lunch $12-$25, dinner $18-$48. Complete meal: lunch $16-$32, dinner $58. Chinese decor. Cr cds: A, D, DS, ER, JCB, MC, V.

D

✔★★ **LE PAPILLION.** *(16 Church St, Toronto ON M5E 1M1) downtown. 416/363-0838.* French menu. Specialties: crêpes Bretonne, French onion soup. Hrs: noon-2:30 pm, 5-10 pm; Fri, Sat to midnight; Sun brunch to 3 pm. Closed Mon. Res accepted. Bar. Semi-a la carte: lunch, dinner $7.75-$18.95. Sun brunch $16.95. Child's meals. Parking. Patio dining. French country kitchen decor. Braille menu. Cr cds: A, D, ER, MC, V.

D

★★★ **LICHEE GARDEN.** *(595 Bay St, Toronto ON M5G 2C2) opp Eaton's Centre, downtown. 416/977-3481.* Cantonese, Szechwan menu. Specialties: Peking duck, steak kew, kung po chicken. Own pastries. Hrs: 11:30 am-midnight; Fri, Sat to 1 am; Sun to 11 pm. Closed Dec 25. Res accepted. Bar. A la carte entrees: lunch $4-$10.50, dinner $9.95-$17.50. Entertainment exc Sun. Parking. Oriental decor. Cr cds: A, D, ER, MC, V.

D

✔★ **LOVELOCK'S.** *(838 Yonge St, Toronto ON M4W 2H1) in Yorkville. 416/968-0063.* Continental menu. Specialties: grilled calamari, rack of lamb. Hrs: 11:30 am-10 pm; Thurs-Sat to 11 pm. Closed Sun; Jan 1, Dec 25. Res accepted. Bar to 2 am. Wine list. A la carte entrees: lunch $6.95-$10.50, dinner $10.95-$19.95. Outdoor dining. French bistro atmosphere. Cr cds: A, MC, V.

★★ **MARKETTA.** *(138 Avenue Rd, Toronto ON M5R 2H7) in Yorkville. 416/924-4447.* Mediterranean menu. Specialties: grilled sirloin burger, brick-grilled chicken. Hrs: 11:30 am-3 pm, 5-10:30 pm; Thurs-Sat to 11 pm; Sun 11 am-3 pm (brunch), 5-10 pm. Closed Mon; most major hols. Res accepted. Bar. A la carte entrees: lunch $9.95-$16.95, dinner $10.95-$16.95. Sun brunch $9.95-$16.95. French bistro ambience. Cr cds: A, D, ER, MC, V.

D

★★ **MATIENON.** *(51 Ste Nicholas St, Toronto ON M4Y 1W6) downtown. 416/921-9226.* Specializes in rack of lamb, duck breast, la darne de saumon aux câpres. Hrs: 11:30 am-2:30 pm, 5-10 pm. Res accepted. Bar. A la carte entrees: lunch $8.95-$15.95, dinner $13.50-$17.95. French atmosphere. Cr cds: A, D, ER, MC, V.

★★★ **MILLCROFT INN.** *(See Millcroft Inn) 519/941-8111.* Continental menu. Specializes in game meat. Hrs: 7:30-10 am, noon-2 pm, 6-9 pm; Sat, Sun 8-10:30 am; Sun brunch 11:30 am-2 pm. Res accepted. Bar from 11 am. A la carte entrees: bkfst $6.95-$9.95, lunch $16-$18.95, dinner $26-$35.98. Sun brunch $26.95. Valet parking. Restored knitting mill (1881) on the Credit River. Cr cds: A, D, ER, MC, V.

✔★ **MILLER'S COUNTRY FARE.** *(5140 Dundas St W, Etobicoke ON M9A 1C2) 416/234-5050.* Specializes in ribs, chicken, beef stew. Hrs: 11 am-10 pm; Fri to 11 pm; Sat 10 am-11 pm; Sat, Sun brunch to 2:30 pm. Closed Dec 25. Bar from 11 am. Semi-a la carte: lunch, dinner $6.25-$13.95. Sat, Sun brunch $3.95-$10.95. Child's meals. Parking. Country decor. Cr cds: A, D, ER, MC, V.

D

★★ **MÖVENPICK OF SWITZERLAND.** *(165 York St, Toronto ON M5H 3R8) downtown. 416/366-5234.* Continental menu. Specializes in Swiss dishes. Salad bar. Hrs: 7:30 am-midnight; Fri to 1 am; Sat 9-1 am; Sun 9 am-midnight. Res accepted. Bar. Semi-a la carte: bkfst $2.50-$13.80, lunch $6.50-$16.90, dinner $9.25-$16.80. Buffet: dinner (exc Sun)

$16.80-$27.50. Sun brunch $21.80. Child's meals. Parking. Outdoor dining. European decor. Cr cds: A, D, ER, MC, V.

D

★ ★ ★ ★ **NORTH 44 DEGREES.** *(2537 Yonge St, Toronto ON M4P 2H9) north of downtown. 416/487-4897.* North 44, Toronto's latitude, is the restaurant's logo and an oft-repeated visual refrain. The trendy atmosphere is fostered by a metallic, modern look, but chef Mark McEwan's dishes more than hold their own in this singular decor. Specializes in mixed appetizer platters, angel hair pasta, rack of lamb. Hrs: 5 pm-1 am. Closed Sun; some major hols. Res accepted. Bar. A la carte entrees: dinner $12.95-$31.95. Child's meals. Entertainment Wed-Sat. Cr cds: A, D, ER, MC, V.

D

★ ★ ★ **OLD MILL.** *(21 Old Mill Rd, Toronto ON M8X 1G5) west of downtown. 416/236-2641.* Continental menu. Specializes in roast beef, roast duck. Own baking. Hrs: noon-2:30 pm, 3-5 pm (afternoon tea), 5:30-10 pm; Sat 5:30-11 pm; Sun 5:30-9 pm; Sun brunch 10:30 am-2 pm. Closed Dec 24. Res accepted. Bar. A la carte entrees: lunch $10.95-$16.95, dinner $24.50-$33. Buffet: lunch (Mon-Fri) $19.95, dinner (Sun) $24.95. Sun brunch $22.95. Cover charge (Fri, Sat from 8 pm) $3.50. Child's meals. Parking. Old English castle motif. Jacket (dinner). Cr cds: A, D, ER, MC, V.

D

✔★ **OLD SPAGHETTI FACTORY.** *(54 The Esplanade, Toronto ON M5E 1A6) downtown. 416/864-9761.* Italian menu. Specialties: fettucine with seafood, chicken parmigiana.Hrs: 11:30 am-11 pm; Fri, Sat to midnight. Closed Dec 24. Bar. Semi-a la carte: lunch $3.95-$7.50, dinner $6.99-$14.25. Child's meals. Outdoor dining. Bright decor; carousel effect. Family-owned. Cr cds: A, D, DS, ER, MC, V.

D

★ ★ ★ **OPUS.** *(37 Prince Arthur Ave, Toronto ON) in Yorkville. 416/921-3105.* Web www.cook-book.com\opus. Continental menu. Hrs: 5:30-11:30 pm. Res accepted. Bar to 2 am. Wine list. Semi-a la carte: dinner $12.95-$29.95. Cr cds: A, ER, MC, V.

★ **OXFORD STEAK HOUSE & TAVERN.** *(1130 Martin Grove Rd, Etobicoke ON M9N 4W1) 416/249-1516.* Specializes in steak, pasta. Hrs: 7-1 am. Closed Good Friday, Dec 25; other hols for dinner. Bar from 11 am. Semi-a la carte: bkfst $2.50-$7.95, lunch $3.95-$12.95 dinner $7-$15.95. Child's meals. Entertainment Wed-Sat. Parking. English-style dining rm; prints. Cr cds: A, D, ER, MC, V.

★ **PAWNBROKERS DAUGHTER.** *(1115 Bay St, Toronto ON M5S 2B3) downtown. 416/920-9078.* Hrs: 11-2 am. Res accepted. Bar. A la carte entrees: lunch, dinner $4-$14.95. Pub atmosphere; pool table, video games. Cr cds: A, MC, V.

★ ★ **PIER 4 STOREHOUSE.** *(245 Queen's Quay W, Toronto ON M5J 2K9) Harbourfront. 416/203-1440.* Specialties: pepper steak Peru, red snapper. Pasta bar. Hrs: noon-2:30 pm; 4:30 pm-midnight; Sun 11:30 am-2:30 pm, 4:30-10 pm. Closed Dec 25. Res accepted. Bar. Semi-a la carte: lunch $7-$11, dinner $12.75-$34.95. Child's meals. Patio dining. Located at water end of a quay on Toronto Bay. Cr cds: A, D, DS, ER, JCB, MC, V.

D

★ ★ **PREGO.** *(15474 Yonge St, Aurora ON L4G 1P2) approx 30 mi (48 km) N of downtown Toronto. 905/727-5100.* Italian menu. Specializes in baked rack of lamb, pasta. Hrs: 11:30 am-2:30 pm, 5:30-10:30 pm; Sat from 5:30 pm; Sun 5-9:30 pm. Closed Mon; Jan 1, Good Friday, Dec 25, 26. Res accepted. Bar. A la carte entrees: lunch $7.95-$11.95, dinner $8.95-$19. Parking. Casual atmosphere. Cr cds: A, D, ER, MC, V.

D

★ ★ ★ **PRONTO.** *(692 Mount Pleasant Rd, Toronto ON) north of downtown. 416/486-1111.* Italian, continental menu. Hrs: 5-11:30 pm; Sun to 10:30 pm. Closed Jan 1, Dec 24, 25. Res accepted. Bar. A la carte entrees: dinner $12.95-$28.95. Valet parking. Elegant modern decor; local artwork. Cr cds: A, C, D, ER, MC, V.

✔★ ★ **PROVENCE.** *(12 Amelia St, Toronto ON M4X 1A1) in Cabbagetown. 416/924-9901.* French menu. Specialties: rack of lamb, duck confit, steak. Hrs: 11:30-1 am; Sat, Sun brunch 11:30 am-3 pm. Closed Dec 25. Res accepted. Bar to 1 am. Semi-a la carte: lunch, dinner $14.95-$21. Sat, Sun brunch $12.95. French country cottage decor; original artwork. Cr cds: A, MC, V.

✔★ **RIVOLI CAFE.** *(332 Queen St W, Toronto ON M5V 2A2) downtown. 416/596-1908.* Web home.1star.cia/~rivoli. Asian, Caribbean menu. Specialties: Sri Malay Bombay, Laotian spring rolls. Hrs: 11:30-2 am. Closed most major hols. Bar. A la carte entrees: lunch $5.95-$9.50, dinner $7.50-$12.95. Patio dining. Adj club offers comedy/variety shows evenings. Totally nonsmoking. Cr cds: A, MC, V.

★ ★ ★ **ROSEWATER SUPPER CLUB.** *(19 Toronto St, Toronto ON M5C 2R1), east of downtown. 416/214-5888.* Continental menu. Own baking. Hrs: noon-2:30 pm, 5:30-11 pm; Sat from 5:30 pm. Closed Sun; major hols; July 1, Dec 26. Res required. Bar 11:30-2 am. Wine cellar. A la carte entrees: lunch $13-$19, dinner $19-$31. Pianist evenings. Early 20th-century atmosphere; elaborate Victorian crown moldings and cathedral-style windows. Totally nonsmoking. Cr cds: A, D, ER, MC, V.

★ ★ ★ ★ **SCARAMOUCHE.** *(1 Benvenuto Place, Toronto ON M4V 2L1) north of downtown. 416/961-8011.* This is Toronto's most luxurious French restaurant. Superb service and delicious food are served up in an atmosphere of understated elegance. Continental, French menu. Specialties: grilled Atlantic salmon, roasted rack of lamb. Own baking. Hrs: 6-10 pm; Sat to 11 pm. Closed Sun; major hols. Res accepted. Bar to midnight. A la carte entrees: dinner $24.75-$29.75. Pasta bar $13.75-$22.75. Valet parking. Cr cds: A, D, ER, MC, V.

D

★ **SEA SHACK.** *(2130 Lawrence Ave E, Scarborough ON M1R 3A6) 416/288-1866.* Continental menu. Specializes in seafood, steak. Hrs: 11 am-11 pm; Sat 4-11 pm; Sun noon-10 pm. Closed Jan 1, Dec 25. Res accepted. Bar. Semi-a la carte: lunch $5.50-$9.95, dinner $7.95-$26.95. Child's meals. Parking. Nautical theme. Cr cds: A, MC, V.

★ ★ **SENATOR.** *(253 Victoria St, Toronto ON M5B 1T8) downtown. 416/364-7517.* Specializes in steak, seafood. Hrs: 11:30 am-2:30 pm, 5 pm-midnight. Closed Mon; some major hols. Res accepted. Bar. A la carte entrees: lunch $9.95-$14.95, dinner $19.95-$33.95. Parking. 1920s decor; in heart of theatre district. Cr cds: A, D, ER, JCB, MC, V.

D

★ ★ ★ **SPLENDIDO.** *(88 Harbord St, Toronto ON M5S 1G5) downtown. 416/929-7788.* Continental menu. Specialties: rack of veal with grilled tomatoes, grilled peppered beef tenderloin with crispy fries. Hrs: 5-11 pm. Closed Sun. Res accepted. Bar. Semi-a la carte: dinner $19.95-$28.95. Valet parking. Fashionable trattoria with inviting atmosphere. Cr cds: A, D, ER, MC, V.

D

✔★ **SUSHI BISTRO.** *(204 Queen St W, Toronto ON M5V 1Z2) downtown. 416/971-5315.* Japanese menu. Specialties: shrimp and mushrooms, sushi rolls, sashimi. Hrs: noon-2:45 pm, 5-10 pm; Fri, Sat noon-midnight. Closed Sun; major hols. Res accepted. Bar. A la carte entrees: lunch $7-$11, dinner $8.50-$18. Child's meals. Traditional Japanese food in modern setting. Cr cds: A, D, JCB, MC, V.

D

★ **THAI FLAVOUR.** *(1554 Avenue Rd, Toronto ON M5M 3X5) north of downtown. 416/782-3288.* Thai menu. Specialties: cashew nut chicken, pad Thai, basil shrimp. Hrs: 11 am-3 pm, 5-11 pm; Sun 5-10 pm. Closed Jan 1, Dec 25. Res accepted. Serv bar. A la carte entrees: lunch, dinner $7.45-$9.50. Cr cds: A, MC, V.

★ ★ **TIGER LILY'S NOODLE HOUSE.** *(257 Queen St W, Toronto ON M5V 1Z4) downtown. 416/977-5499.* Pan-Asian menu. Specializes in home-style egg roll. Hrs: 11:30 am-9 pm; Wed to 10 pm; Thurs-Sat to 11 pm. Closed most major hols. A la carte entrees: lunch, dinner $5.95-$10.95. Totally nonsmoking. Cr cds: A, MC, V.

★ ★ **TRAPPER'S.** *(3479 Yonge St, North York ON M4N 2N3) 416/482-6211.* Web www.yongestreet.com. Continental menu. Specializes in fresh fish, steak, pasta. Hrs: 11:30 am-2:30 pm, 5-10:30 pm; Sat from 5 pm; Sun 5-9:30 pm. Closed Dec 25. Res accepted. Bar. A la carte entrees: lunch $8.50-$11.95, dinner $12.95-$25.95. Child's meals. Casual dining. Cr cds: A, D, ER, MC, V.

★ ★ ★ ★ **TRUFFLES.** *(See Four Seasons Hotel) 416/964-0411.* The wine list offers rare European and North American vintages in this formal, contemporary restaurant with bay windows and a high ceiling. Murals and ceramics by local artists decorate the room. Provençale cuisine. Specialties: Québec duck, rack of lamb with mustard seed sauce. Own pastries. Hrs: 6-11 pm. Res accepted. Wine cellar. Semi-a la carte: dinner $26-$39. Table d'hôte: dinner $75. Child's meals. Valet parking. Jacket. Cr cds: A, C, D, ER, JCB, MC, V.

D

★ **UKRAINIAN CARAVAN.** *(5245 Dundas St W, Toronto ON M9B 1A5) west of downtown. 416/231-7447.* Ukrainian, Amer menu. Specializes in pierogies, meat-on-a-stick. Own coffees. Hrs: 11-2 am; Sun 10 am-10 pm. Res accepted. Bar. Semi-a la carte: lunch $3.99-$11.95, dinner Mon-Fri (nonshow nights) $10-$20, Sat (show nights) $21.95-$30.95. Cossack cabaret Sat. Cr cds: A, D, ER, MC, V.

SC

★ ★ **UNIONVILLE HOUSE.** *(187 Main St, Unionville ON L3R 2G8) N on Don Valley Pkwy, E on Hwy 7 to Kennedy Rd, then N. 905/477-4866.* Continental menu. Specializes in pasta, fish. Hrs: 11:30 am-2:30 pm, 5:30-10 pm; Sun to 9 pm. Res accepted. Semi-a la carte: lunch $6.95-$8.95, dinner $9.95-$23.95. Outdoor dining. Authentic pioneer-style cottage (1840); antique furnishings, decor. Cr cds: A, D, ER, MC, V.

★ ★ **VANIPHA LANNA.** *(471 Eglinton Ave W, Toronto ON M5N 1A7) north of downtown. 416/484-0895.* Thai menu. Specializes in northern Thai dishes. Hrs: noon-11 pm; Sat to midnight. Closed Sun; most major hols. Res accepted Fri, Sat. A la carte entrees: lunch $6.25-$9.95; dinner $8.25-$12.50. Thai decor. Totally nonsmoking. Cr cds: A, MC, V.

D

★ ★ **VILLA BORGHESE.** *(2995 Bloor St W, Etobicoke ON M8X 1C1) 416/239-1286.* Italian menu. Specializes in fresh fish, veal, pepper steak. Own pasta. Hrs: noon-midnight; Sat, Sun from 4 pm. Closed Mon; Easter, Dec 25. Res accepted. Bar. Semi-a la carte: lunch $8-$15, dinner $12.95-$23.95. Entertainment. Italian villa decor. Cr cds: A, D, MC, V.

✔★ **WAYNE GRETZKY'S.** *(99 Blue Jays Way, Toronto ON M5V 9G9) downtown. 416/979-7825.* Specializes in pasta, grilled meats. Hrs: 11:30-1 am. Closed Dec 25. Res accepted. Bar. Semi-a la carte: lunch, dinner $6.99-$24.99. Rooftop patio dining. Display of Gretzky memorabilia. Cr cds: A, D, ER, MC, V.

D

★ ★ **XANGO.** *(106 John St, Toronto ON M5V 2E1) downtown. 416/593-4407.* South Amer menu. Specialty: raw fish marinated in lime juice. Hrs: 5 pm-2 am. Closed Dec 24-26. Res accepted. Bar. A la carte entrees: dinner $21-$28. Complete meal: dinner $18-$48. Outdoor dining. Converted house with veranda. Cr cds: A, D, MC, V.

★ **YAMASE.** *(317 King St W, Toronto ON M5V 1J5) downtown. 416/598-1562.* Japanese menu. Specializes in sushi, teriyaki, tempura dishes. Hrs: noon-2:30 pm, 5:30-11 pm; Sat from 5 pm. Sun 5-10 pm. Closed Jan 1. Res accepted. Bar. A la carte entrees: lunch $5.50-$14.50, dinner $7.50-$24.50. Complete meals: dinner $15-$50. Intimate atmosphere; Japanese decor, artwork. Cr cds: A, D, ER, MC, V.

★ ★ ★ **ZACHARY'S.** *(See Wyndham Bristol Place Hotel) 416/675-9444.* E-mail bristol@interlog.com. Continental menu. Specialty: rack of lamb. Own baking. Hrs: noon-2:30 pm, 6-10 pm; Sat from 6 pm; Sun brunch 11 am-2:30 pm. Res accepted. Bar 11-1 am. Wine list. A la carte entrees: lunch $13.25-$18.50, dinner $22.50-$32.50. Complete meals: lunch $19.75, dinner $29.50. Sun brunch $23.50. Valet parking. Modern decor with Chinese prints. Cr cds: A, C, D, DS, ER, JCB, MC, V.

SC

✔★ ★ **ZUCCA TRATTORIA.** *(2150 Yonge St, Toronto ON M4S 2A8) north of downtown. 416/488-5774.* Web www.yongestreet.com/food/zucca. Italian menu. Specializes in whole grilled fish, pasta. Hrs: noon-2:30 pm, 6-10:30 pm. Closed Sun; major hols. Res accepted. Bar. A la carte entrees: lunch $7.50-$12.95, dinner $11-$17. Totally non smoking. Cr cds: A, MC, V.

Unrated Dining Spots

CAFE VICTORIA. *(See King Edward Hotel) 416/863-9700.* Continental menu. Specializes in scones, pastries, sandwiches. Own baking. Hrs: 6:30 am-2:30 pm, 5-9 pm; Fri to 11 pm; Sat, Sun 7:30 am-2:30 pm, 5-11 pm. Traditional English tea service $13.95. Valet parking. Cr cds: A, D, MC, V.

D

PATACHOU. *(1095 Yonge St, Toronto ON) in Yorkville. 416/927-1105.* French menu. Specialties: cafe au lait, croque Monsieur. Own baking. Hrs: 8:30 am-6 pm; Sun from 10:30 am. Closed statutory hols. Pastries, croissants, desserts, sandwiches, quiche $5-$10. Patio dining. No cr cds accepted.

SHOPSY'S DELICATESSEN. *(33 Yonge St, Toronto ON) downtown. 416/365-3333.* Delicatessen, all-day bkfst menu. Hrs: 7-1 am. Bar 11-1 am. A la carte entrees: bkfst $2.10-$6.75, lunch $3.95-$8.95, dinner $3.75-$11.75. Outdoor dining. Cr cds: A, MC, V.

D

UNITED BAKERS DAIRY RESTAURANT. *(506 Lawrence Ave W, Toronto ON) in the Lawrence Plaza, north of downtown. 416/789-0519.* Jewish menu. Specializes in cheese blintzes, soups, gefilte fish. Hrs: 7 am-10 pm; Fri to 8 pm; Sat, Sun to 9 pm. A la carte entrees: lunch $5-$10, dinner to $12. Parking. Bakery on premises. Family-owned. Cr cds: MC, V.

Notes

Mobil Travel Guide

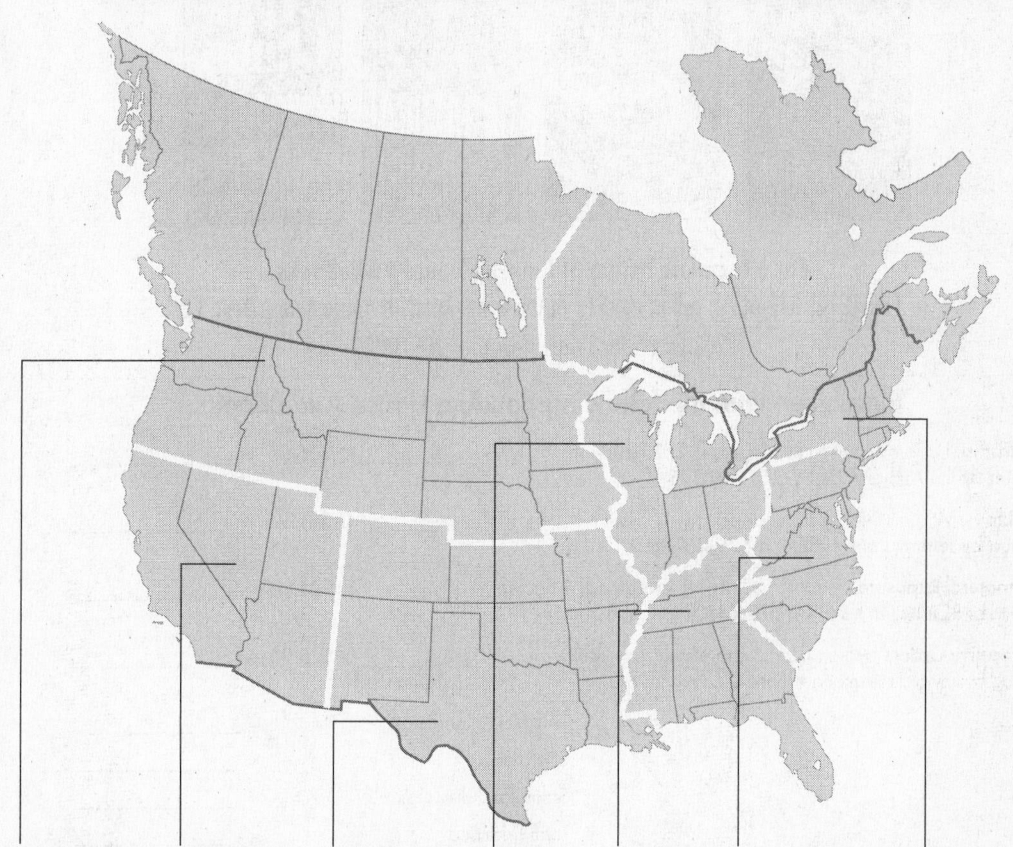

Northwest & Great Plains
Idaho
Iowa
Minnesota
Montana
Nebraska
North Dakota
Oregon
South Dakota
Washington
Wyoming
Canada:
Alberta
British Columbia
Manitoba

California & the West
Arizona
California
Nevada
Utah

Southwest & South Central
Arkansas
Colorado
Kansas
Louisiana
Missouri
New Mexico
Oklahoma
Texas

Great Lakes
Illinois
Indiana
Michigan
Ohio
Wisconsin
Canada:
Ontario

Southeast
Alabama
Florida
Georgia
Kentucky
Mississippi
Tennessee

Mid-Atlantic
Delaware
District of Columbia
Maryland
New Jersey
North Carolina
Pennsylvania
South Carolina
Virginia
West Virginia

Northeast
Connecticut
Maine
Massachusetts
New Hampshire
New York
Rhode Island
Vermont
Canada:
New Brunswick
Nova Scotia
Ontario
Prince Edward Island
Quebec

HELP US GET TO KNOW YOU AND RECEIVE A FREE KEY CHAIN!

Please complete and return this postage paid card to Mobil Travel Guide. The information on you and your travel habits will help us improve the Guide to better serve you in the future. The first 500 respondents who successfully complete and return this questionnaire will receive a free Mobil key chain with our thanks and appreciation. The information supplied herein will be treated in confidence; names and addresses will not be released to mailing list houses or any other associations or organizations.

Please circle the appropriate letter or number, or fill in the blank, as necessary.

1. 1.__Mr. 2.__Mrs. 3.__Ms. 4.__Miss

____
First Name Initial Last Name

____
Street Apt. No.

____
City State Zip Code

2. Date of Purchase: Month___ Date___ Year___

3. How many round trips of 200 miles or more via any method of transportation have you taken in the last year?
a) How many of these were for leisure/pleasure? _________
b) How many of these were for business? _________

4. What is the duration of your average trip?
a) Leisure/pleasure travel? _______________
b) Business travel? _______________

5. How many of these trips were by car?
a) Leisure/pleasure travel? _______________
b) Business travel? _______________

6. Do you use the Mobil Travel Guide in your car?
a) Yes b) No

7. What cities/towns/states or regions were your destinations for your last three (3) leisure/pleasure trips?
____________ ____________ ____________

8. What cities/towns/states or regions were your destinations for your last three (3) business trips?
____________ ____________ ____________

9. What kinds of activities do you prefer when you travel for leisure/pleasure? Circle all that apply.
a) Sightseeing-Historical
b) Sightseeing-Scenic
c) Camping/hiking
d) Sports and recreation
e) Shopping
f) Rest and relaxation
g) Visiting museums/galleries
h) Fine dining
i) Going to the beach

10. How much do you typically spend (on a per-night basis) for your accommodations when you travel for leisure/pleasure?
$_________ per night

11. How much do you typically spend (on a per-night basis) for your accommodations when you travel for business?
$_________ per night

12. What are your restaurant preferences when you travel for leisure/pleasure?
a) 4 or 5 Star c) Family
b) Moderately priced d) Fast food chain

13. What are your restaurant preferences when you travel for business?
a) 4 or 5 Star c) Family
b) Moderately priced d) Fast food chain

14. What kind of resources are used to plan your trips?
a) Leisure/pleasure travel?
i) Travel books/guides
ii) Magazines
iii) Internet
iv) Friends/family recommendations
v) Travel agent
vi) Other _______________
b) Business travel?
i) Travel books/guides
ii) Magazines
iii) Internet
iv) Friends/family recommendations
v) Travel agent
vi) Other _______________

15. If your vacation/business travel requires you to rent an automobile, how likely would you be to buy a travel guide of the area if offered (1: Not likely 5: Very likely)
1 2 3 4 5

16. Did you purchase the Mobil Travel Guide primarily for (choose one)?
a) Leisure/pleasure travel
b) Business travel
c) Maps
d) Coupons
e) Other _______________

17. How did you hear about the Mobil Travel Guide?
a) Advertisement
b) Friends and family
c) Colleague
d) Point of sale (bookstore, service station)
e) Other _______________

18. Where did you purchase the Mobil Travel Guide?
a) Furnished by employer
b) It was a gift
c) Chain bookstore Which? _______________
d) Independent bookstore Which? _______________
e) Travel store Which? _______________
f) Department store
g) Drug store
h) Gift shop
i) Newsstand
j) Service station
k) Other _______________

19. When was the last time you purchased a Mobil Travel Guide?
a) Never d) Three to five years ago
b) Last year e) More than five years ago
c) Two years ago

20. Why did you choose the Mobil Travel Guide in lieu of other options (choose three)?
a) Price
b) Quality ratings of accommodations
c) Quality ratings of restaurants
d) Factual information on accommodations
e) Factual information on restaurants
f) Information on things to see and do in the area
g) Maps
h) Discount coupons
i) Background information on states, cities and towns
j) Other _______________

003

CUT ALONG DOTTED LINE

FOLD AND TAPE (OR SEAL) FOR MAILING—PLEASE DO NOT STAPLE

21. What three (3) features would you like to see more of?
a) Accommodation choices
b) Details/comments on accommodations
c) Restaurant choices
d) Details/comments on restaurants
e) Things to see and do in the area
f) State/city background information
g) Maps
h) Icons/Easy-to-use symbols
i) Discount Coupons
j) Other__________________

22. In your opinion, does the Mobil Travel Guide improve Mobil Corporation's image?
a) Yes c) Not sure
b) No

23. You are:
a) Female b) Male

24. Your age is:
a) 18–24 d) 45–54
b) 25–34 e) 55–64
c) 35–44 f) 65+

25. You are:
a) Single/never married c) Separated/divorced
b) Married d) Widowed

26. The ethnic group that best describes you is:
a) African-American d) Caucasian/White
b) Asian e) Hispanic
c) Other__________________

27. Highest level of education:
a) Some High School
b) High School Graduate
c) Some College
d) Technical Certification
e) College Degree (2- or 4-Year)
f) Some Post College Study
g) Advanced Degree

28. Your occupation is:
a) Professional
b) Executive, Managerial, Administrative
c) Military
d) Clerical, Sales, Technical
e) Precision, Crafts, Repair
f) Retired
g) Other__________________

29. Your spouse/significant other's occupation is:
a) Professional
b) Executive, Managerial, Administrative
c) Military
d) Clerical, Sales, Technical
e) Precision, Crafts, Repair
f) Retired
g) Other

30. How many children do you have living at home in the following age groups?
a) None f) 10–11 Years
b) < 1 Year g) 12–14 Years
c) 1–2 Years h) 15–18 Years
d) 3–5 Years i) Over 18
e) 6–9 Years

31. Which choice best describes your household income level?
a) Under $10,000
b) $10,000–$19,999 g) $60,000–$69,999
c) $20,000–$29,999 h) $70,000–$79,999
d) $30,000–$39,999 i) $80,000–$89,999
e) $40,000–$49,999 j) $90,000–$99,999
f) $50,000–$59,999 k) >$100,000

32. Which types of credit cards do you use most for travel?
a) American Express, Diners Club, Discover, Carte Blanche
b) Bank Card (Mastercard, Visa)
c) Gas, Department Store
d) None of the Above

33. What type of vehicle do you drive on your trips?
a) Luxury d) Mini Van
b) Mid Size e) Sport Utility
c) Compact f) RV

34. Do you belong to an automobile club?
a) Yes Which? __________________
b) No

35. What other products/services do you purchase specifically for travel?
a) Tire/Auto Service
b) Luggage
c) Travel Store Items
d) Maps
e) Other__________________

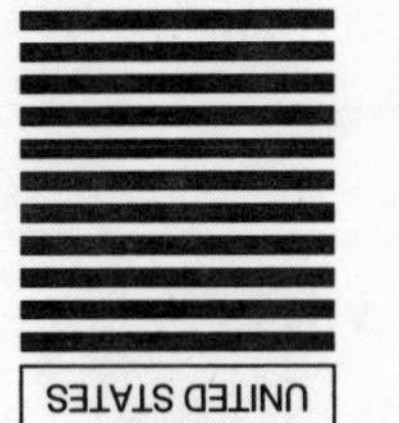

NO POSTAGE NECESSARY IF MAILED IN THE UNITED STATES

BUSINESS REPLY MAIL
FIRST CLASS PERMIT NO. 253 SKOKIE, IL

POSTAGE WILL BE PAID BY ADDRESSEE

Mobil Travel Guide
4709 W. GOLF RD.
SUITE 803
SKOKIE, IL 60076

CUT ALONG DOTTED LINE

YOU CAN HELP MAKE THE *MOBIL TRAVEL GUIDE* MORE ACCURATE AND USEFUL

ALL INFORMATION WILL BE KEPT CONFIDENTIAL

Your Name ______________ (Please Print)	Were children with you on trip? ☐ Yes ☐ No
Street ______________	Number of people in your party ______
City, State, Zip ______________	Your occupation ______________

1. Establishment name ______________ Hotel ☐ Resort ☐ Other ☐ Motel ☐ Inn ☐ Restaurant ☐

Street ______________ City ______________ State ______

Do you agree with our description? ☐ Yes ☐ No; if not, give reason ______________

Please give us your opinion of the following:

DECOR	CLEANLINESS	SERVICE	FOOD
☐ Excellent	☐ Spotless	☐ Excellent	☐ Excellent
☐ Good	☐ Clean	☐ Good	☐ Good
☐ Fair	☐ Unclean	☐ Fair	☐ Fair
☐ Poor	☐ Dirty	☐ Poor	☐ Poor

1998 *GUIDE* RATING ______ *

CHECK YOUR SUGGESTED RATING BELOW:

☐ * good, satisfactory ☐ **** outstanding
☐ ** very good ☐ ***** one of best in country
☐ *** excellent
☐ ✓unusually good value

Comments: ______________

Date of visit ______________ First visit? ☐ Yes ☐ No

2. Establishment name ______________ Hotel ☐ Resort ☐ Other ☐ Motel ☐ Inn ☐ Restaurant ☐

Street ______________ City ______________ State ______

Do you agree with our description? ☐ Yes ☐ No; if not, give reason ______________

Please give us your opinion of the following:

DECOR	CLEANLINESS	SERVICE	FOOD
☐ Excellent	☐ Spotless	☐ Excellent	☐ Excellent
☐ Good	☐ Clean	☐ Good	☐ Good
☐ Fair	☐ Unclean	☐ Fair	☐ Fair
☐ Poor	☐ Dirty	☐ Poor	☐ Poor

1998 *GUIDE* RATING ______ *

CHECK YOUR SUGGESTED RATING BELOW:

☐ * good, satisfactory ☐ **** outstanding
☐ ** very good ☐ ***** one of best in country
☐ *** excellent
☐ ✓unusually good value

Comments: ______________

Date of visit ______________ First visit? ☐ Yes ☐ No

3. Establishment name ______________ Hotel ☐ Resort ☐ Other ☐ Motel ☐ Inn ☐ Restaurant ☐

Street ______________ City ______________ State ______

Do you agree with our description? ☐ Yes ☐ No; if not, give reason ______________

Please give us your opinion of the following:

DECOR	CLEANLINESS	SERVICE	FOOD
☐ Excellent	☐ Spotless	☐ Excellent	☐ Excellent
☐ Good	☐ Clean	☐ Good	☐ Good
☐ Fair	☐ Unclean	☐ Fair	☐ Fair
☐ Poor	☐ Dirty	☐ Poor	☐ Poor

1998 *GUIDE* RATING ______ *

CHECK YOUR SUGGESTED RATING BELOW:

☐ * good, satisfactory ☐ **** outstanding
☐ ** very good ☐ ***** one of best in country
☐ *** excellent
☐ ✓unusually good value

Comments: ______________

Date of visit ______________ First visit? ☐ Yes ☐ No

FOLD AND TAPE (OR SEAL) FOR MAILING—PLEASE DO NOT STAPLE

98

BUSINESS REPLY MAIL
FIRST CLASS PERMIT NO. 253 SKOKIE, IL

POSTAGE WILL BE PAID BY ADDRESSEE

Mobil Travel Guide
4709 W. GOLF RD.
SUITE 803
SKOKIE, IL 60076

Revised editions are now being prepared for publication next year:

California and the West: Arizona, California, Nevada, Utah.

Northeast: Connecticut, Maine, Massachusetts, New Hampshire, New York, Rhode Island, Vermont; Eastern Canada.

Mid-Atlantic: Delaware, District of Columbia, Maryland, New Jersey, North Carolina, Pennsylvania, South Carolina, Virginia, West Virginia.

Southeast: Alabama, Florida, Georgia, Kentucky, Mississippi, Tennessee.

Great Lakes: Illinois, Indiana, Michigan, Ohio, Wisconsin; Ontario, Canada.

Northwest and Great Plains: Idaho, Iowa, Minnesota, Montana, Nebraska, North Dakota, Oregon, South Dakota, Washington, Wyoming; Western Canada.

Southwest and South Central: Arkansas, Colorado, Kansas, Louisiana, Missouri, New Mexico, Oklahoma, Texas.

Major Cities: Detailed coverage of 45 Major Cities.

The Mobil Travel Guide is available at Mobil Service Stations, bookstores, or by mail from the Mobil Travel Guide, Random House, 400 Hahn Rd., Westminster, MD 21157, or call toll-free, 24 hours a day, 1-800/533-6478.

HOW CAN WE IMPROVE *THE MOBIL TRAVEL GUIDE*?

Mobil Travel Guides are constantly being revised and improved. All attractions are updated and all listings are revised and evaluated annually. You can contribute to the accuracy and usefulness of the guides by sending us your reactions to the places you have visited. Your suggestions for improving the guides are also welcome. Just complete this prepaid mailing form or address letters to: *Mobil Travel Guide,* 4709 W. Golf Rd., Suite 803, Skokie, IL 60076. The editors appreciate your comments.

Have you sent us one of these forms before? ☐ Yes ☐ No

Please make any general comment here. Thanks! ________________________________

____

____

____

Please note: All offers may not be available in Canada. Call **(410) 825-3463** if you are unable to use an 800 number listed on the coupon.

National Car Rental.

TERMS AND CONDITIONS:
Valid for car classes indicated on front at participating National locations in the U.S. (Not valid in Manhattan, NY.) • Subject to availability and blackout dates. • Rate and time parameters, local rental and minimum rental day requirements apply. • Cannot be used in multiples or with any other certificate, special discount or promotion. • Standard rental qualifications apply. • Minimum rental age at most locations is 25.

In addition to rental charges, where applicable, renter is responsible for: Optional loss Damage Waiver, up to $15.99 per day; a per mile charge in excess of mileage allowance; taxes; surcharges; additional charges if car is not returned within a prescribed rental period; drop charge and additional driver fee; optional refueling charge; optional insurance benefits.

RENTAL AGENT INSTRUCTIONS: **1.** Rental Screen 1: • Key Promo Coup # from the front side. **2.** Rental Screen 3: • Key Discount # from the front side in "RATE RECAP #" field. • Key applicable rate in "RATE RECAP #" field. • Change rate for one car class lower than class of car actually rented. **3.** Write RA# and rental date below. **4.** Retain certificate at rental. Send certificate to Headquarters, Attn: Travel Industry Billing. RA#________________ Rental Date ___/___/___

TASTE PUBLICATIONS INTERNATIONAL

Las Vegas TRAVEL

Advance reservations required. For show, wedding, or casino information call 900-RESORT CITY. Valid Sunday thru Thursday only, except holidays and during city-wide conventions. May not be used in conjunction with any other discount or promotion.

800-449-4697 – One Toll-Free Call Gives You All These:
Luxor • Monte Carlo • Tropicana • Circus Circus • Caesar's Palace New York-New York • Bally's • The Orleans • Rio Suite Hotel • Plaza Stardust • Stratosphere • Boomtown • Sahara • Westward Ho Holiday Inn Board • Excalibur • Flamingo Hilton • Las Vegas Hilton Lucky Lady • The Plaza • San Remo • And so many more.

TASTE PUBLICATIONS INTERNATIONAL

ONE HOUR MOTOPHOTO®

TASTE PUBLICATIONS INTERNATIONAL

Not valid with other discount offers or on holidays.
Valid Monday-Friday in season.

TASTE PUBLICATIONS INTERNATIONAL

SUPER 8 MOTEL

SUPER 8 MOTELS

Not valid in conjunction with other discounts or promotions.
Each Super 8 Motel is independently owned and operated.

TASTE PUBLICATIONS INTERNATIONAL

Alamo

TERMS AND CONDITIONS:
- Upgrade is subject to availability at time of rental, as certain car categories may be sold out. Valid on self-drive rentals only.
- Only one certificate per rental; not to be used in conjunction with any other discounted or promotional rate. Cannot be used with any Alamo Express Plus(SM) or a Quicksilver(SM) rental.
- Please make your reservations at least 24 hours before arrival. Travel agents please include /SI-C-UM5B in the car sell. Valid only on Association Rate Codes.
- You must present this certificate at the Alamo counter on arrival. It is void once redeemed.
- Certificate has no cash value and does not include taxes (including in California, VLF taxes ranging up to $1.89 per day), registration fee/tax reimbursements, airport concession recoupment charges, fuel, other optional items, or airport access fees, if any.
- Any used portion is non-refundable.
- Reproductions will not be accepted and expired or lost certificates cannot be replaced.
- Offer valid through March 1, 1998 through June 15, 1999. The following blackout dates apply: In the United States and Canada: 4/09-4/11/98, 5/21-5/23/98, 7/02-7/04/98, 7/16-8/15/98, 9/03-09/05/98, 10/08-10/10/98, 11/25-11/27/98, 12/17-12/31/98, 2/11-2/13/99 and 4/1-4/3/99.
  In the United Kingdom, Germany, Belgium, The Netherlands and Switzerland: 6/15-7/31/98 and 12/20-12/31/98.
  In Ireland, Greece, Portugal, the Czech Republic, and Malta: 7/15-9/30/98 and 12/20-12/31/98.
  In Mexico: 7/15-8/31/98 and 12/15/98-1/31/99.
- Offer is valid at airport and airport serving locations and at participating European or Mexican locations operating under the name of Alamo.
- Coupon not valid on plan code A1.

TASTE PUBLICATIONS INTERNATIONAL

Offer not available in conjunction with other discount offers or promotional rates. Excludes other rental charges, deposits, sales tax, and fuels. Normal rental conditions and customer qualification procedures apply. Members must reserve vehicle through Central Reservations only, at least one week in advance of pick up and mention membership affiliation at time of reservation.

TASTE PUBLICATIONS INTERNATIONAL

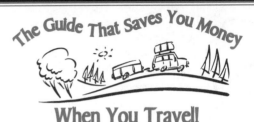

TASTE PUBLICATIONS INTERNATIONAL • 1031 CROMWELL BRIDGE ROAD • BALTIMORE, MD 21286

Budget
All The Difference In The World.

TERMS AND CONDITIONS

Be sure to mention BCD# T445311 when reserving an economy through full-size car and present this certificate at participating U.S. Budget locations (except in the New York metro area) to receive your member savings discount. This offer requires a one-day advance reservation, and is subject to vehicle availability. Vehicle must be returned to the original renting location except where intra-inter metro area drop-offs are permitted. Local age and rental requirements apply. Locations that rent to drivers under 25 may impose an age surcharge. Offer is not available with CorpRate, government or tour/wholesale rates, or with any other promotion. Refueling services, taxes, surcharges, and optional items are extra. Blackout dates may apply. Limit one certificate per rental.

TASTE PUBLICATIONS INTERNATIONAL

Audio Diversions

Good Books are for listening too!

More than 2,600 titles carefully drawn from among the best in travelbooks, adventure, biographies, business, children's, classics, education, how to's, foreign language, inspirational, literature, motivational, mystery, and self help books, Audio Diversions is sure to have what you need. Rentals are 10% off plus come with addressed and stamped packages for easy return.
10 % off everything.

TASTE PUBLICATIONS INTERNATIONAL

Available at participating properties. This coupon cannot be combined with any other special discount offer. Limit one coupon per room, per stay. Not valid during blackout periods or special events. Void where prohibited. No reproductions accepted.

TASTE PUBLICATIONS INTERNATIONAL

Built in 1931, this 1,454 foot high skyscraper was climbed by King Kong in the movie classic. View Manhattan from the 86th floor observatory with outdoor promenade. Also enjoy the enclosed 102nd floor and exhibits of the eight wonders of the world.

TASTE PUBLICATIONS INTERNATIONAL

Present this coupon when purchasing your ticket at any Busch Gardens Williamsburg or Water Country USA General admission price. Children two and under are admitted FREE. Admission price includes all regularly scheduled rides, shows and attractions. This coupon has no cash value and cannot be used in conjunction with any other discount. Prices and schedule subject to change without notice. Busch Gardens Williamsburg and Water Country USA have a "no solicitation" policy. Limit six tickets per coupon.

1 2 3 4 5 6

PLU #R364 C365

Please circle number of admissions.

TASTE PUBLICATIONS INTERNATIONAL

KOA has over 550 locations throughout the U.S. and Canada. Cruise America and Cruise Canada have over 100 rental centers.

TASTE PUBLICATIONS INTERNATIONAL

AVIS We try harder.

TERMS AND CONDITIONS (*Save up to $20.00 on a Weekend Rental*)
Offer valid on an Intermediate (Group C) through a Full Size 4-door (Group E) car for a 2-day minimum rental. Coupon must be surrendered at time of rental; one per rental. Coupon valid at Avis corporate and participating licensee locations in the continental U.S. Weekend rental period begins Thursday noon, and car must be returned by Monday 11:59 p.m. or a higher rate will apply. Offer not available during holiday and other blackout periods. Offer may not be available on all rates at all times. An advance reservation is required. Cars subject to availability. Taxes, local government surcharges and optional items, such as LDW, additional driver fee and refueling, are extra. Renter must meet Avis age, driver and credit requirements. Minimum age is 25. Offer expires June 30, 1999.

RENTAL SALES AGENT INSTRUCTION AT CHECKOUT: **1.** In AWD, enter A291814. **2.** For a 2 day rental, enter MUGD717 in CPN. **3.** For a 3 day rental, enter MUGD718 in CPN. **4.** For a 4 day rental, enter MUGD719 in CPN. **5.** Complete this information:
RA#____________________ Rental Date ___/___/___ **6.** Attach to COUPON tape.

TASTE PUBLICATIONS INTERNATIONAL

Mobil Travel Guide®

When You Travel!

FREE FANNY PACK

YOURS FREE WHEN YOU JOIN NPCA NOW!

Join NPCA and save our national treasures! We are offering a special one-year introductory membership for only $15.00! Enjoy the many benefits of a NPCA membership and receive: a free National Parks and Conservation Association Fanny Pack, a free PARK-PAK, travel information kit, an annual subscription to the award-winning National Parks magazine, the NPCA discount photo service, car rental discounts and more.

See reverse for order form. MTG98

OFFER EXPIRES JUNE 30, 1999

Ripley's Believe It or Not!®

BUY ONE GET ONE FREE!*

(Limit 6 people)

***Receive one complimentary admission with purchase of an equal value ticket.**

Not valid with any other offers. Not for resale.
Valid only at locations listed. Coupon non-relinquishable.
Ripley's and Believe It or Not! are registered trademarks of Ripley Entertainment Inc.

PLU-MOBIL

OFFER EXPIRES JUNE 30, 1999

$7.00 OFF

SAVE $7.00 OFF EACH REGULAR ADMISSION (UP TO 6 PEOPLE) WHEN YOU PRESENT THIS COUPON AT ANY ADVENTURE WORLD TICKET WINDOW.

One (1) coupon good for up to six people and cannot be combined with any other discount, sold, or be redistributed, and not valid with Junior or Senior admission. Valid 1998/1999 season. Call for details **301-249-1500**, for dates and time.

Code: 1017

OFFER EXPIRES JUNE 30, 1999

10% OFF

ENJOY A 10% DISCOUNT AT PARTICIPATING COMFORT, QUALITY, CLARION, SLEEP, ECONO LODGE AND RODEWAY INN HOTELS AND SUITES.

The next time you're traveling call **800-4-CHOICE** and request Mobil discount #00052333. Advance reservations required. Kids 18 and under stay free and 1,400 hotels will provide free continental breakfast.

OFFER EXPIRES JUNE 30, 1999

Travel Discounters

UP TO $100.00 OFF

RECEIVE UP TO $100.00 OFF WHEN YOU BUY AN AIRLINE TICKET FROM TRAVEL DISCOUNTERS. CALL 800-355-1065 AND MENTION CODE MTG IN ORDER TO RECEIVE THE DISCOUNT.

Savings are subject to certain restrictions and availability. Valid for flights on most major airlines. See reverse for discount chart.

OFFER EXPIRES JUNE 30, 1999

LOEWS THEATRES
SONY THEATRES

UNITED ARTISTS

THEATER DISCOUNT

Valid at all participating theatres.

Please send me:

_______ Sony/Loews at $4.50 each = _______
_______ United Artists at $4.50 each = _______
_______ General Cinema at $5.00 each = _______

Add $1.00 for handling. Allow 2-3 weeks for delivery. Orders over $75.00 will be sent via certified mail and may require additional processing time. Limit 20 tickets per order.

OFFER EXPIRES JUNE 30, 1999

COMPANY STORE

SAVE 20% OFF

SHOPPING SPREE!

20% off selected merchandise when you visit any American Tourister or Samsonite Company Store. All stores carry first quality luggage, accessories and gifts to fit all your travel needs at 35%-50% off comparable prices.

Call 1-800-547-BAGS for a location nearest you.

OFFER EXPIRES JUNE 30, 1999

Read each coupon carefully before using. Discounts only apply to the items and terms specified in the offer at participating locations. Remove the coupon you wish to use.

Ripley's Believe It or Not!®

Atlantic City, NJ	Myrtle Beach, SC
Branson, MO	Newport, OR
Buena Park, CA	Niagara Falls, Canada
Cavendish, P.E.I.	Orlando, FL
Grand Prairie, TX	San Antonio, TX
Hollywood, CA	San Francisco, CA
Jackson Hole, WY	St. Augustine, FL
Key West, FL	Wisconsin Dells, WI

TASTE PUBLICATIONS INTERNATIONAL

❑ YES! I want to preserve and protect our National Parks by becoming a National Parks and Conservation Association Member.

❑ I have enclosed a check in the amount of $15.00 for my one-year membership.

❑ Charge my annual dues to my ❑ Visa ❑ MasterCard ❑ Amex

Acct. #: ______ Exp. Date: ______

Signature: ______

Name: ______

Address: ______

City: ______ State: ______ Zip: ______

Phone: ______

Please allow 6-8 weeks for delivery of your fanny pack and first issue of National Parks Magazine.

Make checks payable and mail to: NPCA, 1776 Massachusetts Ave. NW, Washington, DC 20036-1904

TASTE PUBLICATIONS INTERNATIONAL

CHOICE HOTELS INTERNATIONAL

Discount is limited to availability at participating hotels and cannot be used with any other discount. Kids stay free in same room as parents. Advance reservations through **1-800-4-CHOICE** required.

TASTE PUBLICATIONS INTERNATIONAL

13710 Central Ave. · Largo, MD
301-249-1500

From Washington, DC metro area,
take I-495/I-95 to exit 15A (Rt. 214 east, Central Ave.).
Adventure World located 5 miles on left.

From Baltimore metro area,
take I-695 to I-97 south to Exit 7, Rt. 3/301 south, to Rt. 214/Central Ave. west.
Adventure World located 3 miles on right.

TASTE PUBLICATIONS INTERNATIONAL

General Cinema  

Prices are subject to change. A self-addressed stamped envelope must be enclosed to process your order. No refunds or exchanges. Mail order only, not redeemable at box office. Passes have expiration dates, generally one year from purchase. In some cases, tickets cannot be used during the first two weeks of a first-run movie.

Name: ______

Address: ______

City: ______ State: ______ Zip: ______

Make check payable to:
Taste Publications International, 1031 Cromwell Bridge Road, Baltimore, MD 21286.

TASTE PUBLICATIONS INTERNATIONAL

Travel Discounters

Minimum ticket price	*Save*
$200.00	$25.00
$250.00	$50.00
$350.00	$75.00
$450.00	$100.00

TASTE PUBLICATIONS INTERNATIONAL

COMPANY STORE

20% Off Selected Merchandise.

SHOPPING SPREE!

Call 1-800-547-BAGS

Not valid with any other promotional offer. Not valid on sale or previously purchased merchandise. Not valid on Kodak, Hasbro, Safety 1st or Ex Officio Products.

TASTE PUBLICATIONS INTERNATIONAL

Mobil Travel Guide®

UP TO $24.00 OFF

Save up to $24.00 on admission to Six Flags Theme Parks.

$4.00 savings per ticket, up to six (6) admissions.

NLU 758000T 7580 1C

OFFER EXPIRES DECEMBER 31, 1998

Because it's from you.™
1-800-225-3232

SAVE 20%

Receive a 20% discount on all floral and gift purchases from FLOWERS USA. Whether you are traveling or at home, celebrate birthdays, anniversaries, holidays and more with fresh cut flowers, floral arrangements, plants, gourmet food baskets, chocolates, fruits and balloons. To receive your savings, call **1-800-225-3232** and ask for referral code E59.

OFFER EXPIRES JUNE 30, 1999

National Audubon Society

FREE BACKPACK

Sign me up for a 1-year membership at the special low rate of $20.00 and send me my Free Backpack upon receiving my payment. Member benefits include Six bi-monthly issues of AUDUBON magazine, savings on select Audubon nature products and discounts on exciting trips and tours, automatic membership in your local chapter (if there's one in your area), invitations to Audubon sanctuaries and Nature centers located around the country, and your official Audubon welcome pack, and more!

See reverse for order form.

OFFER EXPIRES JUNE 30, 1999

The One Accessory Every RV Needs

$5.00 OFF

With the world's largest selection of RV accessories and supplies, the Camping World catalog is a must for every RV. It's like having a store next door. Shop 24 hours a day, 7 days a week. Call today for a FREE catalog and receive $5 off your first order of $25 or more.

Call 1-800-845-7875 CAMPING WORLD.

Mention Code **MT**

OFFER EXPIRES JUNE 30, 1999

10% OFF

Howard Johnson Makes You Feel at Home.

You're invited to stay at one of nearly 600 Howard Johnson Plazas, Hotels, Inns, and Express Inns throughout the United States, Canada and Mexico. And, if you present this certificate upon check-in, we'll take 10% off the regular room rate for your stay up to 7 nights. So make your reservation today! Call **1-800-I-GO-HOJO®** and ask for the TravelDeal discount.

1-800-I-GO-HOJO®

OFFER EXPIRES JUNE 30, 1999

NYI

SAVE $5.00

Great Photos With Any Camera

How to take great vacation pictures with your Point-and-Shoot camera. Learn to take better vacation pictures with this fun and easy video program! Whether you use a point-and-shoot, a "cardboard" camera, or an SLR, you'll be taking better pictures in just a few hours after watching this tape …or your money back. Guaranteed! From New York Institute of Photography - World's Largest Photography School. Founded 1910.

Regularly: $19.95 –Your Price: **ONLY $14.95.**

To order, call **1-800-453-3686**, Dept. TG.

Add $4.95 shipping and handling.

OFFER EXPIRES JUNE 30, 1999

FREE UPGRADE

Free One Car Class Upgrade Certificate

For worldwide reservations, call your professional travel agent or:

1-800-800-4000, Reference ID# PC3007

www.dollarcar.com.

OFFER EXPIRES JUNE 30, 1999

Coupons may not be used in conjunction with any other promotion or discount offers. **Example:** special promotional pricing. If in doubt, please check with the establishment.

Present this coupon at any Six Flags Theme Park main gate ticket booth on any regular operating day through December 31, 1998 and save $4.00 off a one-day full-price adult admission. Valid for up to six (6) tickets. Coupon must be presented at time of purchase and tickets must be used the same day. Not valid on Six Flags Wild Safari Animal Park, Six Flags Hurricane Harbor, Six Flags WaterWorld or Wet 'n Wild individual park tickets. Cannot be combined with any other discount admission offer including Child, Sr. Citizen, Two-day and After 4pm tickets. Coupon cannot be resold or redeemed for cash and is void if reproduced. Call parks for operating schedule.

Six Flags Over Texas Arlington, TX 817-640-8900	Six Flags AstroWorld Houston, TX 713-799-8404	Six Flags Fiesta Texas San Antonia, TX 210-697-5050	Six Flags Over Georgia Atlanta, GA 770-948-9290
Six Flags St. Louis St. Louis, MO 314-938-5300	Six Flags Great America Chicago, IL 847-249-2133	Six Flags Magic Mountain Los Angeles, CA 805-255-4100	Six Flags Great Adventure Jackson, NJ 908-928-2000

TASTE PUBLICATIONS INTERNATIONAL

Because it's from you.™
1-800-225-3232

Offer does not apply to service charge and applicable tax. Discount cannot be combined with any other offers. Void where prohibited.

TASTE PUBLICATIONS INTERNATIONAL

RV Accessories and Supplies

Call 1-800-845-7875

for a FREE Catalog

Code **MT**

TASTE PUBLICATIONS INTERNATIONAL

National Audubon Society

Mail this coupon to:
National Audubon Society, Membership Data Center
P.O. Box 52529, Boulder, CO 80322-2529

Yes! Please enroll me as a 1-year member for $20.00 to the National Audubon Society.
Check one: ___ Payment enclosed. ___ Bill me later.

Name: ______________________________

Address: ______________________________

City: ____________ State: _____ Zip: __________

5MB96

TASTE PUBLICATIONS INTERNATIONAL

SAVE $5.00 — Great Photos With Any Camera
How To Take Great Vacation Photos

GUARANTEED: You'll take better photos after just watching this video...or your money back. Regularly: $19.95 – Your Price: **ONLY $14.95**. To order, call **1-800-453-3686**, Dept. TG. Or write to: NYI, 211 East 43rd St., New York, N.Y. 10017 Dept T

Add $4.95 shipping and handling.

TASTE PUBLICATIONS INTERNATIONAL

Call 1-800-I-GO-HOJO® and ask for the 10% TravelDeal discount.

Children under 18 always stay free in their parent's room★. Advance reservations required. Original certificate must be presented at check-in.

★ Children 17 and under stay free in their parent's room with existing bedding.

TASTE PUBLICATIONS INTERNATIONAL

This coupon entitles you to a one-class upgrade to the next higher car group at no extra charge. Simply make a reservation for a compact or intermediate class car, then present this certificate to any *Dollar*® rental agent when you arrive. You'll receive an upgrade to the next car class at no additional charge. Upgrade subject to vehicle availability. This certificate must be surrendered at time of rental, may not be used in conjunction with any other certificate or promotion, has no cash value, and expires 6/30/99. Upgrade certificate valid at participating locations only. Renter must meet age and credit requirements. FASTLANE℠ Instructions: Proceed to special documents window, use document code UPG.